LONDON

A-Z ®

Geographers' A-Z Map Company Ltd.

D0115014

Geographers' A-Z Map Company Ltd.

Fairfield Road, Borough Green, Sevenoaks, Kent TN15 8PP
Telephone : 01732 781000 (Enquiries & Trade Sales)
           01732 783422 (Retail Sales)

www.a-zmaps.co.uk

Edition 7 2007
© Copyright of Geographers' A-Z Map Company Limited

The publishers are deeply grateful for the ready co-operation and valuable help
given to them in the production of this atlas. They would like to record their
obligation to: The Engineers and Surveyors Departments and Planning Offices
of all the Local Authorities covered in this atlas, The Department for Transport,
Highways Agency, Transport for London, The Post Office, Police Authorities,
Fire Brigades, Taxi Drivers, Members of the Public.

Printed and bound in the United Kingdom by Polestar Wheatons Ltd., Exeter.

An AtoZ Publication

CONTENTS

Key to Map Pages	2-3	Index to Hospitals & Hospices	419-422
Super Scale Map Pages @ 5¾" to 1 mile	4-19	Index to Stations	423-425
Map Pages @ approx. 3" to 1 mile	20-173	Railway Connections Map	426-427
West End Cinemas & Theatres Maps	174-175	Underground Railway Map	428-429
Index to Streets, Areas & selected Places of Interest	176-418	Congestion Charging Overview and Information	430 Inside Back Cover

REFERENCE

Motorway	**M1**	House Numbers A & B Roads only 51 22 19 48	
A Road	**A2**	Airport	✈
Under Construction		Car Park Selected	**P**
Proposed		Church or Chapel	†
B Road	**B408**	Fire Station	■
Dual Carriageway		Hospital	**H**
One-way Traffic flow on A Roads is indicated by a heavy line on the driver's left.	→	Information Centre	**i**
Junction Name	**MARBLE ARCH**	Park & Ride	Bromley **P+**
Restricted Access		Police Station	▲
Pedestrianized Road		Post Office	★
Track & Footpath		River Bus Stop	**R**
Residential Walkway		Toilet	▽
Congestion Charging Zone		with facilities for the Disabled	▽
Railway	Tunnel / Level Crossing	Disabled facilities only	▽
Stations:		Educational Establishment	◥
National Rail Network		Hospital or Hospice etc.	◥
Docklands Light Railway	**DLR**	Industrial Building	◥
Underground Station ● ⊖ is the registered trade mark of Transport for London		Leisure or Recreational Facility	◥
Croydon Tramlink Tunnel Stop The boarding of Tramlink trams at stops may be limited to a single direction, indicated by the arrow.		Place of Interest	◥
		Public Building	◥
Map Continuation **62** Large Scale Map Pages **12**		Shopping Centre or Market	◥
National Grid Reference	530	Other Selected Buildings	◺
Built-up Area	BANK STREET		

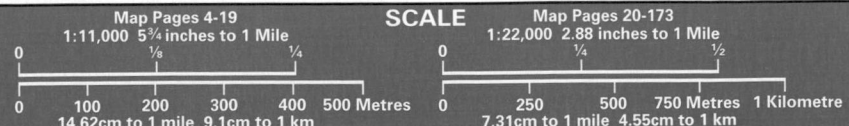

SCALE

Map Pages 4-19
1:11,000 5¾ inches to 1 Mile

Map Pages 20-173
1:22,000 2.88 inches to 1 Mile

14.62cm to 1 mile 9.1cm to 1 km

7.31cm to 1 mile 4.55cm to 1 km

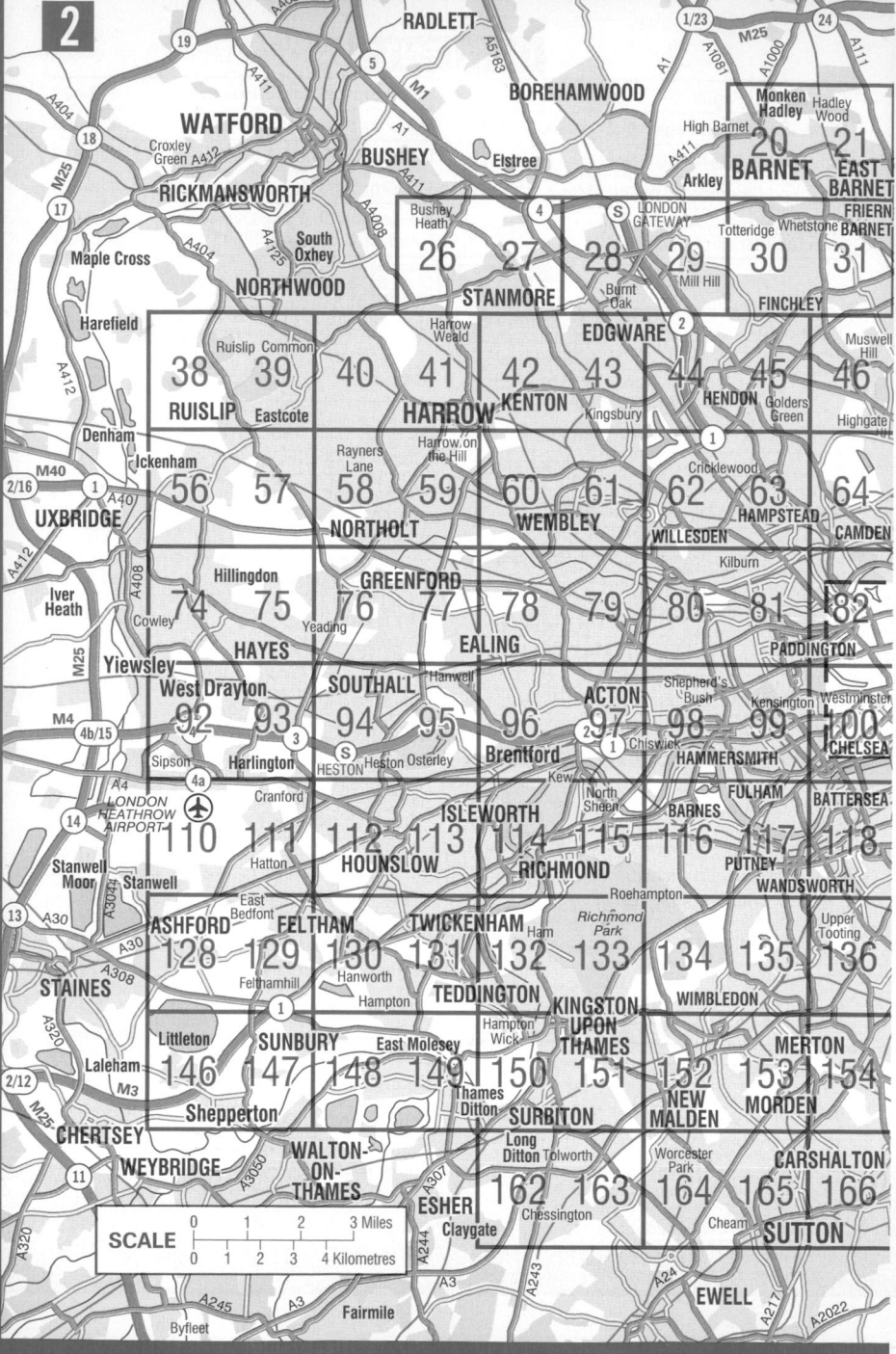
2
RADLETT
BOREHAMWOOD
WATFORD
Croxley Green
BUSHEY
Elstree
RICKMANSWORTH
Monken Hadley
Hadley Wood
High Barnet
20
21
BARNET
EAST BARNET
Arkley
Bushey Heath
LONDON GATEWAY
FRIERN BARNET
Totteridge
Whetstone
Maple Cross
South Oxhey
26
27
28
29
30
31
Mill Hill
Burnt Oak
NORTHWOOD
STANMORE
FINCHLEY
Harefield
Harrow Weald
EDGWARE
Muswell Hill
Ruislip Common
38
39
40
41
42
43
44
45
46
RUISLIP
Eastcote
HARROW
KENTON
Kingsbury
HENDON
Golders Green
Highgate
Denham
Rayners Lane
Harrow on the Hill
Cricklewood
Ickenham
56
57
58
59
60
61
62
63
64
UXBRIDGE
NORTHOLT
WEMBLEY
HAMPSTEAD
WILLESDEN
CAMDEN
Kilburn
Hillingdon
GREENFORD
Iver Heath
74
75
76
77
78
79
80
81
82
Cowley
Yeading
HAYES
EALING
PADDINGTON
Yiewsley
Hanwell
West Drayton
SOUTHALL
ACTON
Shepherd's Bush
Kensington
Westminster
92
93
94
95
96
97
98
99
100
Chiswick
HAMMERSMITH
CHELSEA
Sipson
Harlington
HESTON
Heston
Osterley
Brentford
Kew
North Sheen
FULHAM
BATTERSEA
LONDON HEATHROW AIRPORT
Cranford
ISLEWORTH
BARNES
110
111
112
113
114
115
116
117
118
Hatton
HOUNSLOW
RICHMOND
PUTNEY
Stanwell Moor
Stanwell
WANDSWORTH
Roehampton
East Bedfont
Richmond Park
Upper Tooting
ASHFORD
FELTHAM
TWICKENHAM
Ham
128
129
130
131
132
133
134
135
136
Hanworth
Felthamhill
STAINES
Hampton
TEDDINGTON
KINGSTON UPON THAMES
WIMBLEDON
Littleton
SUNBURY
East Molesey
Hampton Wick
MERTON
Laleham
146
147
148
149
150
151
152
153
154
Thames Ditton
NEW MALDEN
MORDEN
Shepperton
SURBITON
CHERTSEY
Long Ditton
Tolworth
Worcester Park
CARSHALTON
WEYBRIDGE
WALTON-ON-THAMES
162
163
164
165
166
ESHER
Chessington
Cheam
SUTTON
Claygate
SCALE
0 1 2 3 Miles
0 1 2 3 4 Kilometres
EWELL
Fairmile
Byfleet
M25
M1
M40
M4
M3
A1
A405
A5183
A1081
A1000
A111
A411
A404
A412
A4008
A4125
A40
A408
A4
A30
A3044
A308
A320
A3050
A307
A244
A243
A3
A245
A24
A217
A2022

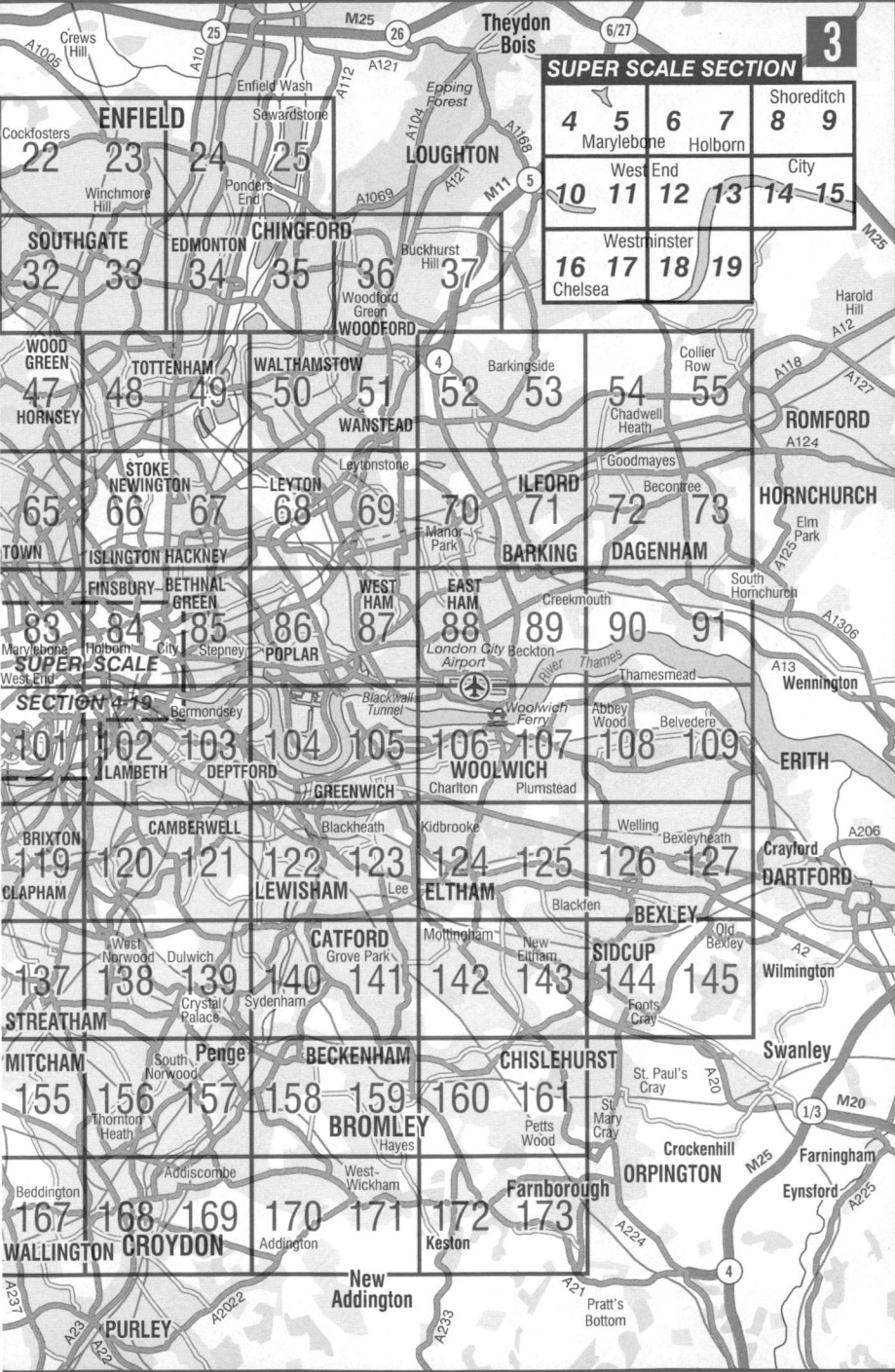
SUPER SCALE SECTION
4 5 Marylebone
6 7 Holborn
Shoreditch 8 9
West End 10 11 12 13
City 14 15
Westminster 16 17 18 19
Chelsea
Crews Hill
A1005
25
A10
M25
26
Theydon Bois
6/27
A121
A112
Epping Forest
Enfield Wash
Sewardstone
ENFIELD
Cockfosters
22 23 24 25
Winchmore Hill
Ponders End
A104
A1168
LOUGHTON
A121
A1069
M11
5
M25
SOUTHGATE
EDMONTON
CHINGFORD
32 33 34 35 36 37
Buckhurst Hill
Woodford Green
WOODFORD
Harold Hill
A12
WOOD GREEN
TOTTENHAM
WALTHAMSTOW
4
Barkingside
Collier Row
A118
A127
47 48 49 50 51 52 53 54 55
HORNSEY
WANSTEAD
Chadwell Heath
ROMFORD
A124
STOKE NEWINGTON
Leytonstone
LEYTON
ILFORD
Goodmayes
Becontree
HORNCHURCH
65 66 67 68 69 70 71 72 73
Manor Park
Elm Park
TOWN
ISLINGTON
HACKNEY
BARKING
DAGENHAM
A125
FINSBURY
BETHNAL GREEN
WEST HAM
EAST HAM
Creekmouth
South Hornchurch
83 84 85 86 87 88 89 90 91
A1306
Marylebone
Holborn
City
Stepney
POPLAR
London City Airport
Beckton
River Thames
SUPER SCALE
West End
SECTION 4-19
Thamesmead
A13
Wennington
Blackwall Tunnel
Woolwich Ferry
Bermondsey
Abbey Wood
Belvedere
101 102 103 104 105 106 107 108 109
ERITH
LAMBETH
DEPTFORD
WOOLWICH
GREENWICH
Charlton
Plumstead
CAMBERWELL
Blackheath
Kidbrooke
Welling
Bexleyheath
A206
BRIXTON
Crayford
119 120 121 122 123 124 125 126 127
DARTFORD
CLAPHAM
LEWISHAM
Lee
ELTHAM
Blackfen
BEXLEY
CATFORD
Mottingham
New Eltham
Old Bexley
West Norwood
Dulwich
Grove Park
SIDCUP
A2
137 138 139 140 141 142 143 144 145
Wilmington
Crystal Palace
Sydenham
Foots Cray
STREATHAM
Penge
BECKENHAM
CHISLEHURST
Swanley
MITCHAM
South Norwood
St. Paul's Cray
A20
155 156 157 158 159 160 161
M20
1/3
Thornton Heath
BROMLEY
Petts Wood
St. Mary Cray
Hayes
Crockenhill
Farningham
Addiscombe
West-Wickham
M25
ORPINGTON
Farnborough
Eynsford
Beddington
A225
167 168 169 170 171 172 173
WALLINGTON
CROYDON
Addington
Keston
A224
4
New Addington
A21
A237
Pratt's Bottom
A2022
A233
A23
PURLEY
A22

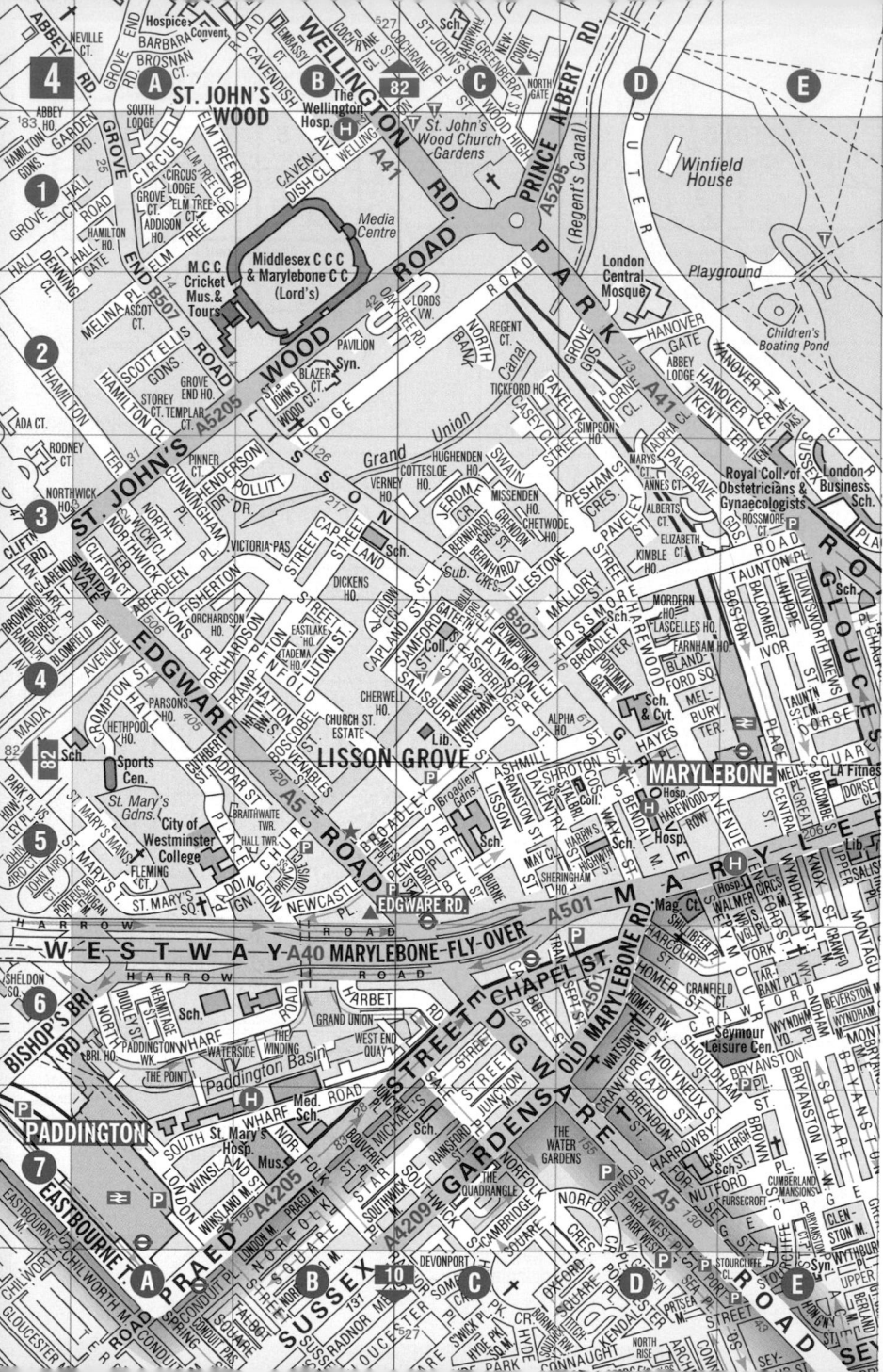

4
82
10
A
B
C
D
E
1
2
3
4
5
6
7
ST. JOHN'S WOOD
ABBEY RD.
NEVILLE CT.
Hospice
Convent
BARBARA
BROSNAN CT.
GROVE END RD.
CAVENDISH
EMBASSY
WELLINGTON
COCHRANE ST.
ST. JOHN'S WOOD HIGH ST.
BARRWILL
GREENBERRY ST.
NEWCOURT ST.
NORTH GATE
PRINCE ALBERT RD.
ABBEY HO.
SOUTH LODGE
HAMILTON GDNS.
GARDEN RD.
The Wellington Hosp.
St. John's Wood Church Gardens
A41
Winfield House
CIRCUS RD.
ELM TREE RD.
CIRCUS LODGE
GROVE CT.
ELM TREE CL.
ADDISON HO.
CAVENDISH CL.
Media Centre
A5205
(Regent's Canal)
OUTER CIRCLE
GROVE HALL CT.
HAMILTON HO.
HALL GATE
DENNING CL.
M C C Cricket Mus.& Tours
Middlesex C C C & Marylebone C C (Lord's)
ROAD
PARK
London Central Mosque
Playground
Children's Boating Pond
LORDS VW.
OAK TREE RD.
MELINA PL.
ASCOT CT.
B507
NORTH BANK
REGENT CT.
PAVILION
Syn.
BLAZER CT.
ST. JOHN'S WOOD CT.
GROVE GDNS.
HANOVER GATE
ABBEY LODGE
HANOVER TER.
HANOVER TER. M.
KENT TER.
SCOTT ELLIS GDNS.
HAMILTON
GROVE END HO.
STOREY CT.
TEMPLAR CT.
LODGE
Canal
TICKFORD HO.
PAVELEY
LORNE CL.
ALPHA CL.
SUSSEX
ADA CT.
RODNEY CT.
NORTHWICK HO.
Grand Union
HUGHENDEN HO.
SWAIN
SIMPSON HO.
MARYS CT.
ANNES CT.
PALGRAVE GDNS.
Royal Coll. of Obstetricians & Gynaecologists
London Business Sch.
PINNER CT.
HENDERSON DR.
POLLITT DR.
CUNNINGHAM PL.
VERNEY HO.
COTTESLOE HO.
JEROME CR.
MISSENDEN HO.
RESHAM ST.
ALBERTS CT.
ROSSMORE CT.
LISSON
CAPLAND ST.
Sch.
BERNHARDT CRES.
GRENDON ST.
CHETWODE HO.
ELIZABETH CT.
KIMBLE HO.
ROAD
GLOUCESTER
ST. JOHN'S
NORTHWICK TER.
CLIFTON CT.
MAIDA VALE
CLIFTON RD.
CLARENDON CL.
LANARK PL.
VICTORIA PAS.
ABERDEEN PL.
LYONS PL.
FISHERTON
DICKENS HO.
BLEDLOW CL.
LILESTONE
MALLORY ST.
ROSSMORE
TAUNTON PL.
BALCOMBE
LINHOPE
HUNTSWORTH MEWS
BOSTON
IVOR
BROWNING CL.
RANDOLPH
ROBERT CL.
BLOMFIELD RD.
ORCHARDSON HO.
ORCHARDSON
EASTLAKE HO.
TADEMA HO.
LUTON ST.
PENFOLD
FRAMPTON
SAMFORD
GATEFORTH ST.
PLYMPTON PL.
ASHBRIDGE ST.
BROADLEY TER.
MORDERN HO.
LASCELLES HO.
FARNHAM HO.
BLANDFORD SQ.
PORTMAN GATE
HAREWOOD
MELBURY TER.
TAUNTON M.
DORSET SQUARE
Coll.
Sch. & Cvt.
EDGWARE
AVENUE
MAIDA
CROMPTON ST.
HALL
PARSONS HO.
HETHPOOL HO.
HATTON
CHERWELL HO.
SALISBURY
MULROY
WHITEHAVEN
CHURCH ST. ESTATE
ALPHA HO.
HAYES PL.
BOSCOBEL
VENABLES
LISSON GROVE
Lib.
MARYLEBONE
MELCOMBE PL.
LA Fitness
DORSET CL.
Sports Cen.
St. Mary's Gdns.
CUTHBERT
PADPAR ST.
ASHMILL
SHROTON ST.
DAVENTRY
STALBRIDGE
Coll.
COSWAY
BENDALL M.
Hosp.
HAREWOOD ROW
CENTRAL
GREAT
PARK PL. VS.
HOWLEY PL.
BRAITHWAITE TWR.
HALL TWR.
City of Westminster College
A5
CHURCH
PLACE
Broadley Gdns.
LISSON
TRANSEPT ST.
MAY CL.
SHERINGHAM HO.
HIGHWITH ST.
Sch.
JOHN AIRD CT.
ST. MARY'S MANS.
FLEMING CT.
ST. MARY'S
PORTEUS RD.
HOGAN M.
ST. MARY'S SQ.
PADDINGTON GN.
PADDINGTON
NEWCASTLE PL.
PENFOLD
BURNE
EDGWARE RD.
A501
MARYLEBONE
Hosp.
WALMER PL.
CIRCUS M.
WYNDHAM ST.
KNOX
UPPER
Lib.
MONTAGU
HARROW ROAD
WESTWAY
A40 MARYLEBONE FLY-OVER
Mag. Ct.
SHILLIBEER PL.
HARCOURT ST.
SEYMOUR
YORK
CRAWFORD
SHELDON SQ.
BISHOP'S BRI. RD
HARBET
CHAPEL ST.
CABBELL ST.
OLD MARYLEBONE RD.
HOMER
CRANFIELD CT.
TARRANT PL.
BEVERSTON M.
WYNDHAM
NORTH WHARF
DUDLEY ST.
HERMITAGE ST.
Sch.
GRAND UNION
WEST END QUAY
STREET
EDGWARE
HOMER RW.
WATSON'S M.
CRAWFORD PL.
MOLYNEUX ST.
SHOULDHAM
Seymour Leisure Cen.
BRYANSTON
BRI. HO.
PADDINGTON WK.
WHARF
WATERSIDE
THE WINDING
Paddington Basin
THE POINT
JUNCTION M.
SALE PL.
CATO ST.
BRENDON ST.
BROWN ST.
PADDINGTON
Med. Sch.
ROAD
SOUTH WHARF
St. Mary's Hosp.
Mus.
NORFOLK
BOUVERIE
ST. MICHAEL'S
RAINSFORD
GARDENS
THE WATER GARDENS
HARROWBY ST.
CASTLEREAGH
Sch.
EASTBOURNE T.
LONDON
WINSLAND ST.
WINSLAND M.
A4205
PRAED M.
STAR
SOUTHWICK
THE QUADRANGLE
NORFOLK
BURWOOD PL.
PARK WEST PL.
A5
NUTFORD
FURSECROFT
CUMBERLAND MANSIONS
CLENSTON M.
Syn.
WYTHBURN
EASTBOURNE M.
CHILWORTH ST.
CHILWORTH M.
PRAED
CONDUIT PL.
NORFOLK SQUARE
A4209
CAMBRIDGE SQUARE
NORFOLK CRES.
OXFORD SQUARE
SOUTHWICK PL.
DEVONPORT
PORTSEA PL.
STOURCLIFFE CL.
ROAD
UPPER
BERLAND
GLOUCESTER
ROAD
CONDUIT
SPRING
CONDUIT PAS.
TALBOT SQUARE
SUSSEX
RADNOR M.
GLOUCESTER
HYDE PK. SQ. M.
HYDE PARK CR.
SOUTHWICK
KENDAL
CONNAUGHT
NORTH RISE
ARCHERY
SEYMOUR

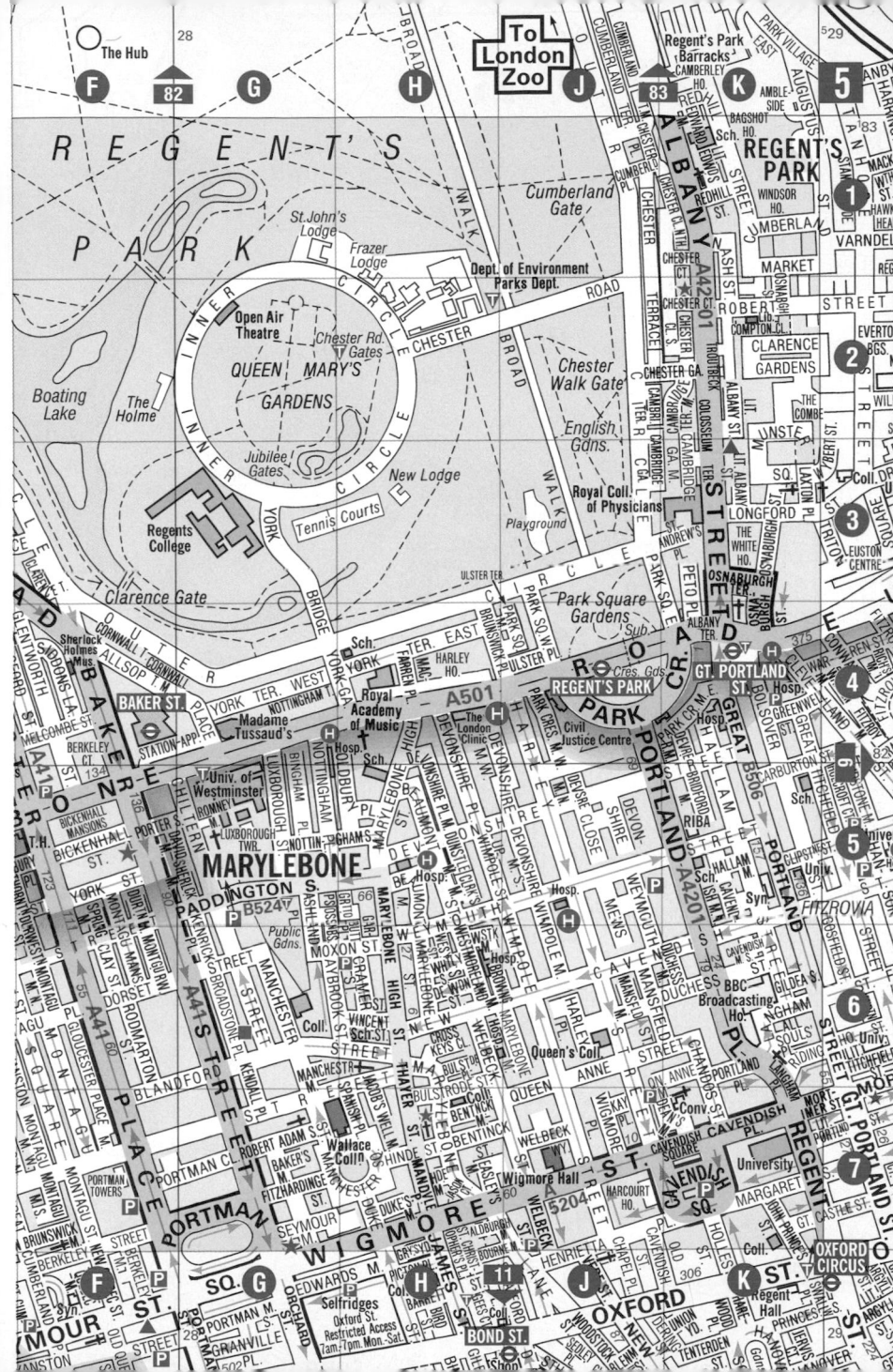

To London Zoo
The Hub
Regent's Park Barracks
REGENT'S PARK
Cumberland Gate
St.John's Lodge
Frazer Lodge
Dept. of Environment Parks Dept.
Open Air Theatre
Chester Rd. Gates
QUEEN MARY'S GARDENS
INNER CIRCLE
CHESTER ROAD
Boating Lake
The Holme
Jubilee Gates
New Lodge
Chester Walk Gate
English Gdns.
Royal Coll. of Physicians
Regents College
Tennis Courts
Playground
Clarence Gate
Park Square Gardens
OUTER CIRCLE
Sherlock Holmes Mus.
BAKER ST.
Madame Tussaud's
Royal Academy of Music
The London Clinic
REGENT'S PARK
GT. PORTLAND ST.
PARK CRESCENT
Civil Justice Centre
Univ. of Westminster
MARYLEBONE
MARYLEBONE ROAD
A501
ALBANY STREET
A4201
GREAT PORTLAND STREET
FITZROVIA
BBC Broadcasting Ho.
Queen's Coll.
Wallace Colln
Wigmore Hall
CAVENDISH SQ.
University
OXFORD CIRCUS
Regent Hall
Selfridges Oxford St. Restricted Access 7am.-7pm. Mon.-Sat.
BOND ST.
PORTMAN SQ.
WIGMORE ST.
OXFORD ST.
BAKER STREET
GLOUCESTER PLACE
MONTAGU SQUARE
MANCHESTER SQ.
HARLEY ST.
WIMPOLE ST.
PORTLAND PL.
REGENT ST.

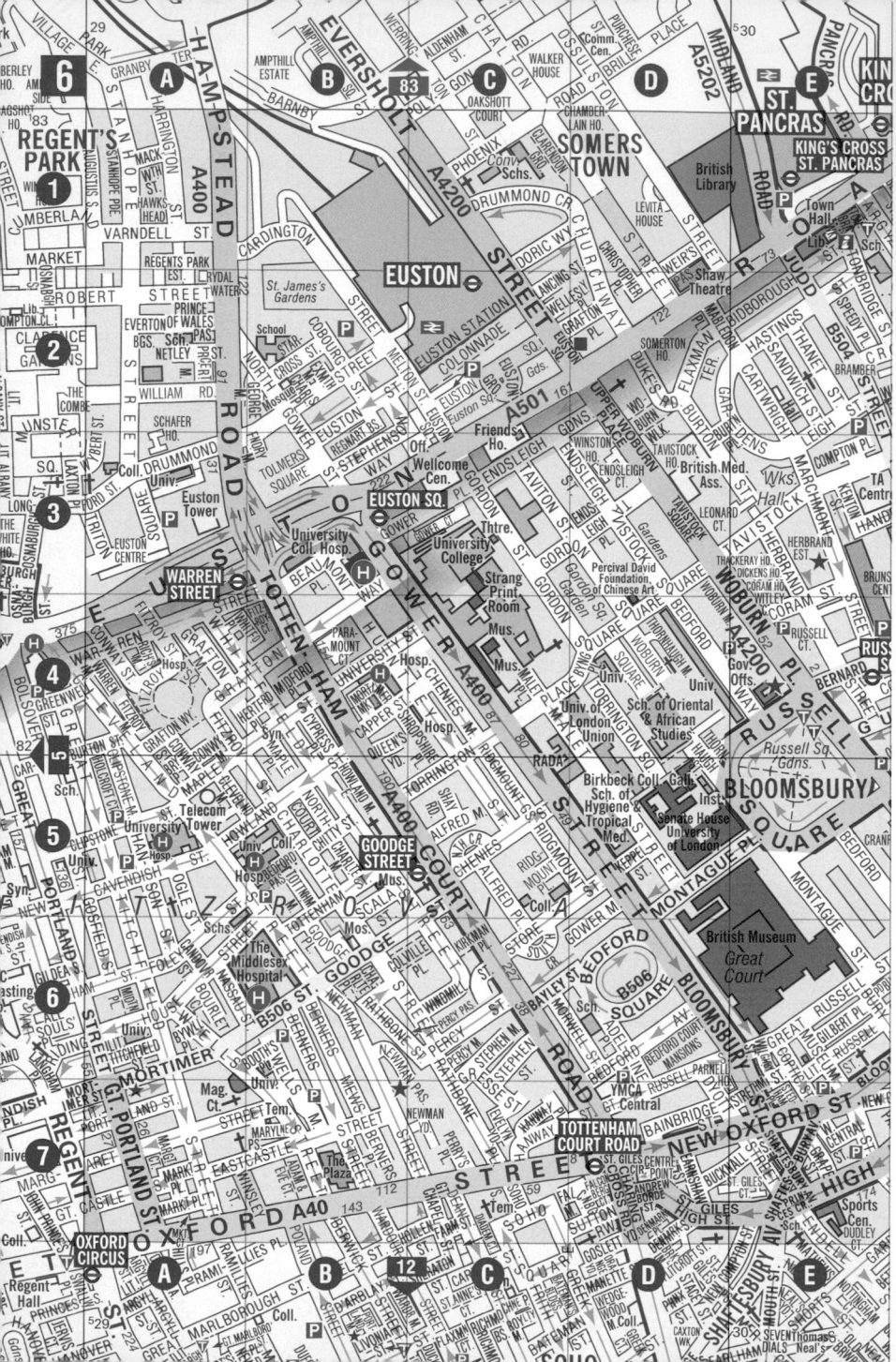
6
83
REGENT'S PARK
HAMPSTEAD ROAD
A400
EVERSHOLT
AMPTHILL ESTATE
SOMERS TOWN
A5202
MIDLAND
ST. PANCRAS
KING'S CROSS ST. PANCRAS
British Library
EUSTON
EUSTON STATION
EUSTON SQ.
A4200
A501
EUSTON ROAD
St. James's Gardens
DRUMMOND CR.
CARDINGTON
Shaw Theatre
Town Hall
CUMBERLAND MARKET
VARNDELL ST.
ROBERT STREET
Euston Tower
EUSTON CENTRE
WARREN STREET
University Coll. Hosp.
University College
Strang Print Room
Wellcome Cen.
Friends Ho.
TAVISTOCK SQUARE
Percival David Foundation of Chinese Art
Gordon Sq. Garden
WOBURN PL.
RUSSELL SQUARE
Russell Sq. Gdns.
BLOOMSBURY
British Med. Ass.
Univ. of London Union
Sch. of Oriental & African Studies
Birkbeck Coll.
Sch. of Hygiene & Tropical Med.
Senate House University of London
British Museum
Great Court
RADA
GOWER STREET
A400
TOTTENHAM COURT ROAD
GOODGE STREET
FITZROVIA
FITZROY SQ.
Telecom Tower
The Middlesex Hospital
GOODGE ST.
BEDFORD SQUARE
B506
TOTTENHAM COURT ROAD
NEW OXFORD ST.
OXFORD STREET
A40
OXFORD CIRCUS
REGENT ST.
GT. PORTLAND ST.
MORTIMER
The Plaza
YMCA Central
ST. GILES CIRCUS
CENTRE POINT
SHAFTESBURY AV.
HIGH HOLBORN
Sports Cen.
SOHO SQUARE
SEVEN DIALS
12
5

83
84
7
8
13
KING'S CROSS THAMESLINK
ST. PANCRAS
CLERKENWELL
HOLBORN
CHANCERY LA.
Lincoln's Inn Fields
Post Office Mount Pleasant
The Angel Centre
Sadler's Wells
Coram's Fields
The Foundling Museum
Great Ormond Street Hosp. for Children
Westminster Kingsway Coll.
The Eastman Dental Hosp. & Institute
Dickens' Ho.
Gray's Inn
Lincoln's Inn Hall
Royal Coll. of Surgeons
Land Registry Off.
King's College Library
Royal Courts of Justice
Freemasons' Hall
London Metropolitan Archives
Family Records Cen.
Spa Fields Open Space
Islamic Cen.
PENTONVILLE ROAD
KING'S CROSS ROAD
FARRINGDON ROAD
ROSEBERY AVENUE
GRAY'S INN ROAD
THEOBALD'S ROAD
CLERKENWELL ROAD
HOLBORN
HIGH HOLBORN
KINGSWAY
SOUTHAMPTON ROW
ST. JOHN ST.
F G H J K
1 2 3 4 5 6 7

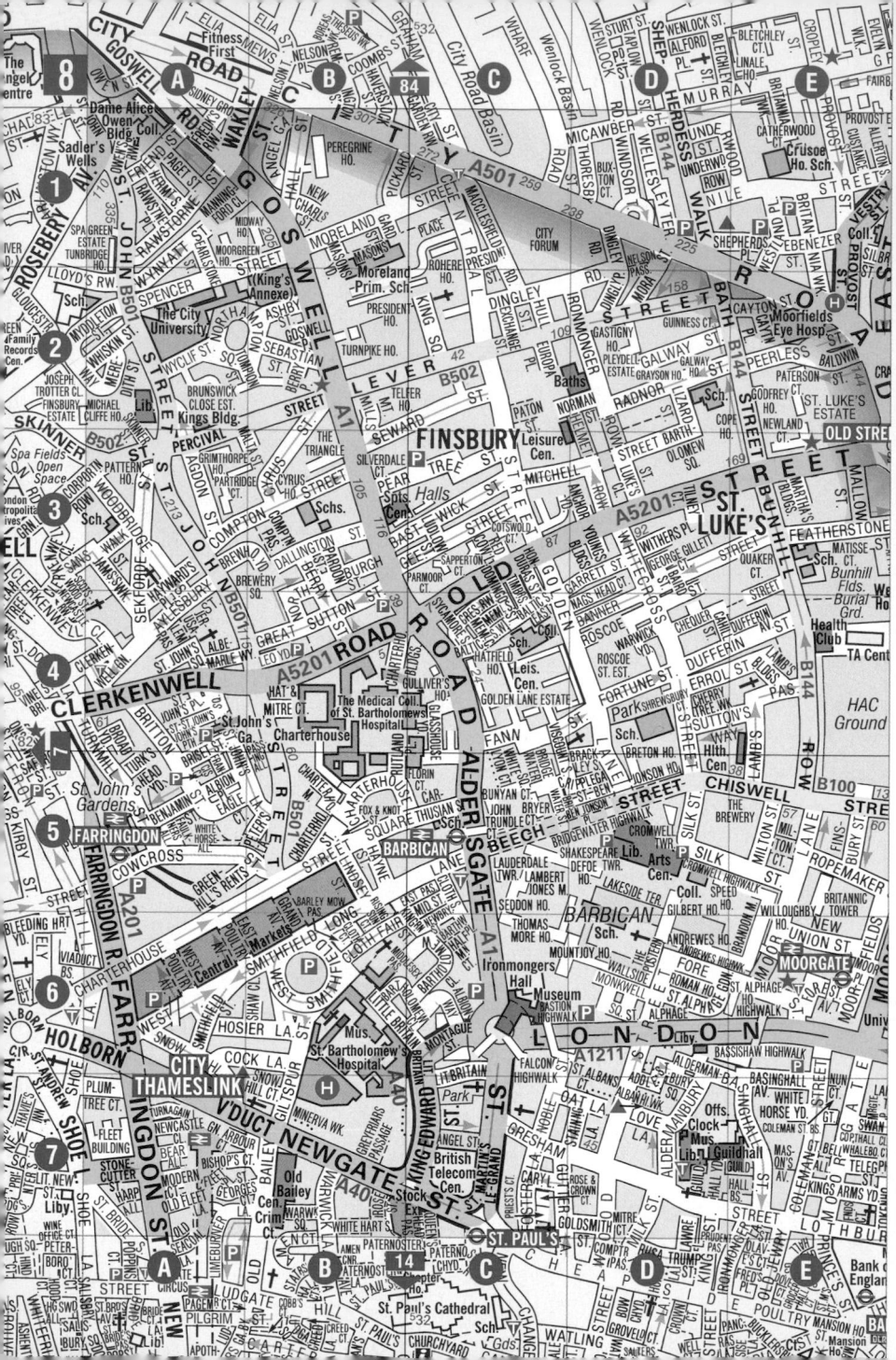

8
A
B
C
D
E
1
2
3
4
5
6
7
84
14
7
CITY ROAD
GOSWELL ROAD
City Road Basin
Wenlock Basin
A501
A1
A5201
B501
B502
B144
B100
A201
A40
A1211
The Angel Centre
Sadler's Wells
Dame Alice Owen Bldg.
Fitness First
Peregrine Ho.
City Forum
Crusoe Ho. Sch.
Moorfields Eye Hosp.
Moreland Prim. Sch.
The City University
King's Annexe
Family Records Cen.
FINSBURY
Baths
Leisure Cen.
ST. LUKE'S
OLD STREET
Spa Fields Open Space
CLERKENWELL ROAD
OLD STREET
St. Luke's Estate
Bunhill Flds. Burial Grd.
Health Club
HAC Ground
TA Cent
Golden Lane Estate
Leis. Cen.
The Medical Coll. of St. Bartholomew's Hospital
Charterhouse
St John's Ga.
St. John's Gardens
FARRINGDON
BARBICAN
MOORGATE
CHISWELL STREET
The Brewery
Lib.
Arts Cen.
BARBICAN
Ironmongers Hall
Museum
LONDON WALL
Central Markets
SMITHFIELD
Mus.
St. Bartholomew's Hospital
CITY THAMESLINK
HOLBORN
HOLBORN CIR.
FARRINGDON ST.
NEWGATE ST.
KING EDWARD ST.
ST. MARTIN'S LE-GRAND
ALDERSGATE
Old Bailey
Cen. Crim. Ct.
British Telecom Cen.
Stock Exch.
ST. PAUL'S
St. Paul's Cathedral
CHEAPSIDE
POULTRY
LOTHBURY
Guildhall
Clock Mus.
Bank of England

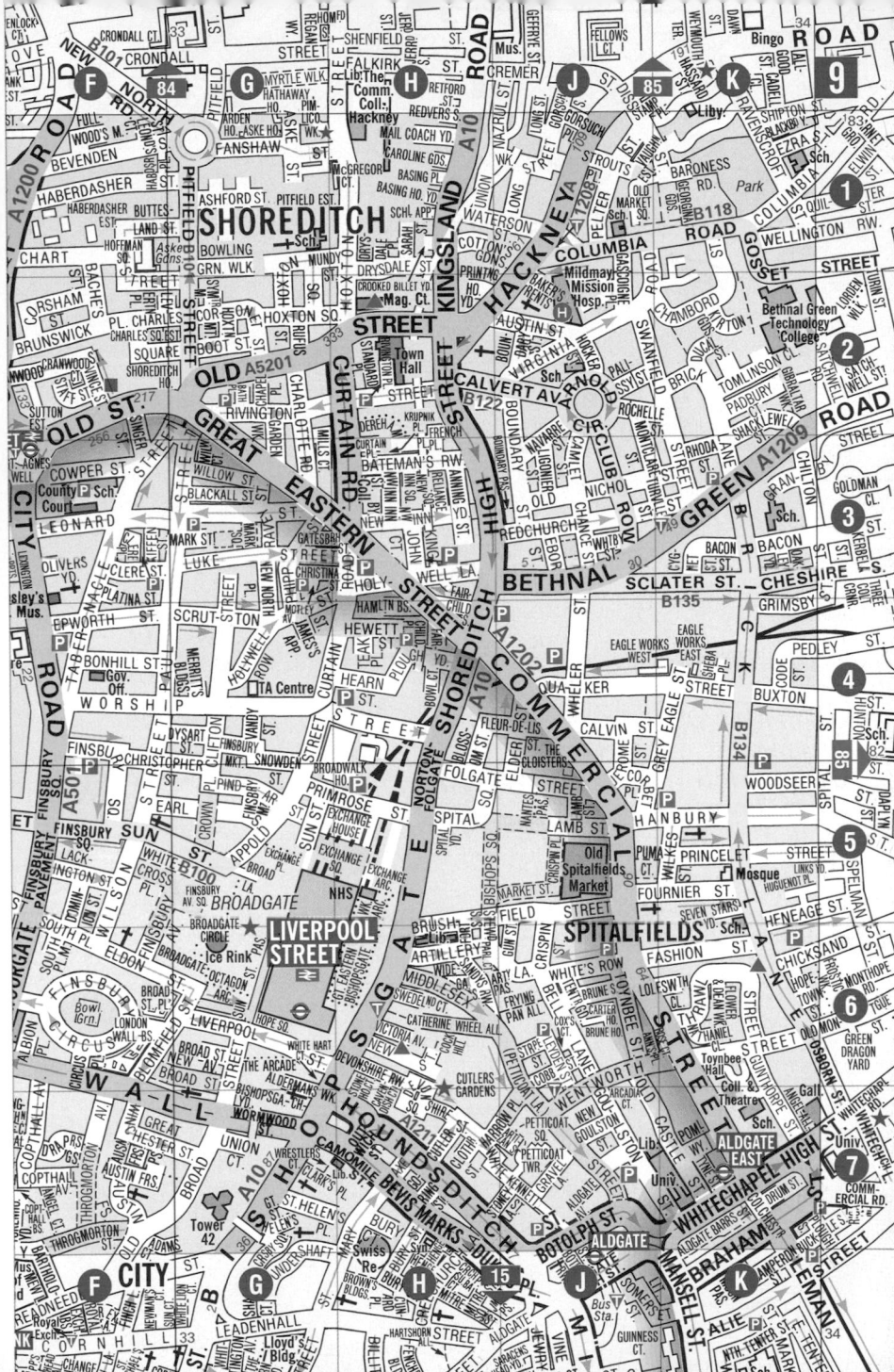

84
85
9
F
G
H
J
K
1
2
3
4
5
6
7
15
SHOREDITCH
SPITALFIELDS
BROADGATE
CITY
LIVERPOOL STREET
ALDGATE
ALDGATE EAST
CRONDALL CT.
CRONDALL
NEW NORTH RD.
B101
SHENFIELD ST.
FALKIRK STREET
Lib. The Comm. Coll.: Hackney
RETFORD ST.
REDVERS S.
CREMER
Mus.
GEFFRYE ST.
FELLOWS CT.
WEYMOUTH TER.
HASSARD ST.
Bingo
ROAD
Liby.
RAVENSCROFT
SHIPTON ST.
EZRA ST.
Sch.
FULLWOOD'S M.
BEVENDEN
FANSHAW
MYRTLE WLK.
HATHAWAY HO.
ARDEN HO.
ASKE HO.
PIMLICO WK.
MAIL COACH YD.
CAROLINE GDS.
BASING PL.
BASING HO. YD.
McGREGOR CT.
A10
KINGSLAND ROAD
GORSUCH PL.
STROUTS
BARONESS RD.
Park
COLUMBIA ROAD
B118
OLD MARKET SQ.
WELLINGTON RW.
A1200
HABERDASHER
HABERDASHER EST.
BUTTESLAND ST.
ASHFORD ST.
PITFIELD EST.
PITFIELD STREET
B101
HOFFMAN SQ.
Aske Gdns.
BOWLING GRN. WLK.
CHART
BACHE'S
WATERSON
COTTON'S GDNS.
PRINTING HO. YD.
HACKNEY ROAD
A1208
Mildmay Mission Hosp.
BAKER'S RENTS
GASCOIGNE
SWANFIELD
CHAMBORD
GOSSET STREET
TURIN ST.
Bethnal Green Technology College
CORSHAM ST.
BRUNSWICK
CHARLES SQUARE
CHARLES SQ. EST.
HOXTON SQ.
RUFUS
SHOREDITCH HO.
BOOT ST.
DRYSDALE ST.
CROOKED BILLET YD.
Mag. Ct.
STREET
Town Hall
AUSTIN ST.
VIRGINIA
HOCKER
ARNOLD CIR.
CALVERT AV.
Sch.
PALISSY ST.
BRICK
TOMLINSON CL.
PADBURY CT.
GIBRALTAR WK.
SHACKLEWELL ST.
SATCHWELL RD.
OLD ST.
A5201
CURTAIN RD.
CRANWOOD ST.
SUTTON EST.
GREAT EASTERN STREET
RIVINGTON
CHARLOTTE RD.
KRUPNIK PL.
FRENCH PL.
BATEMAN'S RW.
B122
BOUNDARY
ROCHELLE ST.
MONTCLARE ST.
RHODA ST.
ROAD
A1209
CHILTON
GOLDMAN CL.
COWPER ST.
County Court
WILLOW ST.
BLACKALL ST.
MILLS CT.
NEW INN YD.
RELIANCE SQ.
HIGH STREET
NICHOL ST.
OLD
CLUB ROW
BETHNAL GREEN
LEONARD
MARK ST.
LUKE
GATESBOROUGH ST.
CHRISTINA
HOLYWELL LA.
REDCHURCH
CHANCE ST.
BACON ST.
BACON
KERBELA ST.
SCLATER ST.
CHESHIRE S.
B135
GRIMSBY
OLIVERS YD.
CLERE ST.
PLATINA ST.
EPWORTH ST.
SCRUTTON
NEW NORTH PL.
HAMLIN BS.
HEWETT ST.
FAIRCHILD ST.
SHOREDITCH
A1202
COMMERCIAL
EAGLE WORKS WEST
EAGLE WORKS EAST
PEDLEY ST.
TABERNACLE
BONHILL ST.
Gov. Off.
HOLYWELL ROW
MERRITT'S BLDGS.
TA Centre
HEARN ST.
QUAKER STREET
WHEELER
BUXTON
WORSHIP
CURTAIN
BOWL CT.
FLEUR-DE-LIS
CALVIN ST.
GREY EAGLE ST.
B134
DYSART ST.
FINSBURY MKT.
VANDY
SNOWDEN
CHRISTOPHER
FINSBURY
CITY ROAD
A501
BROADWALK HO.
NORTON FOLGATE
ELDER ST.
THE CLOISTERS
FOLGATE STREET
WOODSEER
CORBET PL.
SPITAL ST.
EARL
PRIMROSE ST.
EXCHANGE HOUSE
SPITAL SQ.
LAMB ST.
HANBURY
BISHOPSGATE
FINSBURY SQ.
SUN ST.
APPOLD ST.
WHITE CROSS PL.
B100
EXCHANGE PL.
EXCHANGE SQ.
EXCHANGE ARC.
Old Spitalfields Market
PUMA CT.
WILKES
PRINCELET STREET
Mosque
LINKS YD.
HUGUENOT PL.
SPELMAN
FINSBURY PAVEMENT
FINSBURY AV. SQ.
NHS
MARKET ST.
BISHOPS SQ.
FOURNIER ST.
FIELD STREET
HENEAGE ST.
SEVEN STARS YD.
Sch.
BROADGATE CIRCLE
Ice Rink
BRUSHFIELD
ARTILLERY
CRISPIN
FASHION ST.
CHICKSAND
SOUTH PL.
ELDON
BROADGATE
OCTAGON ARC.
MIDDLESEX
WHITE'S ROW
FRYING PAN ALL.
BRUNE'S
CARTER HO.
BRUNE HO.
LOLESWORTH CL.
THRAWL
FLOWER & DEAN WK.
HOPE TOWN
MONTHOPE RD.
FINSBURY CIRCUS
Bowl. Grn.
BROAD ST. PL.
LONDON WALL BS.
LIVERPOOL
HOPE SQ.
GT. EASTERN
SWEDELAND CT.
CATHERINE WHEEL ALL.
TOYNBEE ST.
CHANEL ST.
OSBORN ST.
GREEN DRAGON YARD
WHITE HART CT.
VICTORIA AV.
NEW ST.
COCK HILL
PETTICOAT LA.
COBB
WENTWORTH
ARCADIA CT.
Toynbee Hall
GUNTHORPE
Coll. & Theatre
ALBION
CIRCUS PL.
BROAD ST. AV.
NEW BROAD ST.
THE ARCADE
DEVONSHIRE RW.
CUTLERS GARDENS
OLD CASTLE ST.
Gall.
WHITECHAPEL
WALL
ALDERMANS WK.
BISHOPSGATE CH. YD.
WORMWOOD ST.
PETTICOAT SQ.
PETTICOAT TWR.
NEW GOULSTON ST.
GOULSTON
Lib.
POMELL WY.
Univ.
WHITECHAPEL HIGH ST.
COMMERCIAL RD.
COPTHALL AV.
GREAT WINCHESTER ST.
AUSTIN FRS.
UNION CT.
HOUNDSDITCH
A1211
CAMOMILE
WRESTLERS CT.
CLARK'S PL.
BEVIS MARKS
WHITE KENNETT
GRAVEL LA.
STONEY LA.
BOTOLPH ST.
ALDGATE AV.
DRUM ST.
COLCHESTER
THROGMORTON AV.
COPTHALL BS.
THROGMORTON
OLD BROAD
Tower 42
ST. HELEN'S PL.
BURY ST.
Swiss Re
UNDERSHAFT
ST. MARY AXE
DUKE'S PL.
MANSELL ST.
BRAHAM
ALDGATE BARRS
LEMAN STREET
ADAMS CT.
CITY
BROWN'S BLDGS.
MITRE ST.
Bus Sta.
SOMERSET
ALIE
THREADNEEDLE
Royal Exch.
CORNHILL
LEADENHALL
Lloyd's Bldg.
HARTSHORN ALL.
STREET
ALDGATE
SARACENS HEAD YD.
JEWRY
VINE
GUINNESS CT.
NTH. TENTER ST.
MARK
34
33
36

10
PADDINGTON
A
B
C
D
E
1
2
3
4
5
6
7
82
100
4
16
EAST-BOURNE TER.
PRAED ST.
WINSLAND ST.
WINSLAND M.
LONDON ST.
NORFOLK SQUARE
NORFOLK SQ. M.
LONDON M.
CONDUIT PL.
CONDUIT PAS.
CONDUIT M.
SPRING ST.
TALBOT SQUARE
SUSSEX GDNS.
SUSSEX SQ.
SUSSEX PLACE
A4209
RADNOR MEWS
RADNOR PL.
GLOUCESTER SQUARE
SOUTHWICK ST.
SOUTHWICK PL.
SOUTHWICK M.
STAR ST.
CAMBRIDGE SQUARE
THE QUADRANGLE
NORFOLK CRES.
HYDE PK. CR.
HYDE PK. SQ. M.
OXFORD SQUARE
SOMERS CR.
DEVONPORT
BURWOOD PL.
PORCHESTER PL.
EDGWARE ROAD
A5
NUTFORD PL.
CASTLEREAGH ST.
FURSECROFT
CUMBERLAND MANSIONS
CLENSTON M.
WYTHBURN
STOURCLIFFE CL.
STOURCLIFFE ST.
UPPER BERKELEY ST.
BERKELEY M.
SEYMOUR PL.
SEYMOUR ST.
SEYMOUR ROAD
WATER GARDENS
Hosp.
Mus.
Sch.
Syn.
CHILWORTH ST.
CHILWORTH M.
WESTBOURNE TERRACE
GLOUCESTER M.
CRAVEN TERRACE
CRAVEN RD.
B410
BROOK M.
BROOK ST.
WESTBOURNE CR.
WESTBOURNE ST.
WESTBOURNE GATE
LANCASTER TER.
LANCASTER GATE
LANCASTER M.
BARRIE EST.
ELMS M.
BATHURST MEWS
BATHURST ST.
CLIFTON PL.
STANHOPE TER.
STRATHEARN PL.
HYDE PARK SQUARE
HYDE PARK GDNS.
HYDE PK. GDNS. M.
HYDE PARK ST.
CLARENDON PL.
CLARENDON CL.
CONNAUGHT ST.
CONNAUGHT SQ.
ALBION ST.
ALBION M.
ALBION GATE
HYDE PARK PL.
NORTH RISE
ST. GEORGE'S FLDS
KENDAL STEPS
HANOVER STEPS
WEST RISE
PARK STEPS
ARCHERY STEPS
SOUTH RISE
FREDERICK CL.
STANHOPE PL.
CONNAUGHT PL.
ARCHERY CL.
KENDAL ST.
PORTSEA PL.
A402
BAYSWATER ROAD
Stanhope Place Gate
Albion Gate
Clarendon Gate
(NORTH CARRIAGE DR.)
Victoria Gate
Westbourne Gate
Marlborough Gate
THE RING
THE NORTH RIDE
BUCK HILL WALK
NORTH FLOWER WALK
LANCASTER WALK
BUDGE'S WALK
The Fountains
THE LONG WATER
Speke's Monument
Peter Pan
KENSINGTON GARDENS
Temple Lodge
(W. CARRIAGE DR.)
(Closed midnight - 5am)
Nursery
HYDE PARK
MAGAZINE GATE
Rangers Lodge
SERPENTINE RD.
Serpentine Bridge
Boat Houses
THE SERPENTINE
Boating Lake
Serpentine Gallery
Cafeteria
Fishermans Keep
Princess of Wales Memorial Fountain
(WEST CARRIAGE DR.)
ROTTEN ROW
Bowling Greens
FLOWER WALK
Albert Memorial
Alexandra Gate
Prince of Wales Gate
Rutland Gate
SOUTH CARRIAGE DR.
NEW
Hyde Park Barracks
EDINBURGH GA.
A315
KENSINGTON ROAD
KENSINGTON GORE
KNIGHTSBRIDGE
R.G.S.
Royal Coll. of Art
Royal Albert Hall
Imperial Coll.
ALBERT HALL MNS.
ALBERT CT.
EXHIBITION ROAD
MONTROSE CT.
PRINCE'S GATE
PRINCE'S GA.
PRINCE CONSORT ROAD
PRINCE'S GDNS.
BOLNEY GA.
ENNISMORE GDNS.
ENNISMORE M.
ENNISMORE ST.
MONCORVO CL.
RUTLAND GATE
RUTLAND GA. M.
RUTLAND GDNS.
RUTLAND GDNS. M.
RUTLAND CT.
RUTLAND M. W.
TREVOR SQUARE
TREVOR PL.
TREVOR ST.
KENT YD.
MONTPELIER PL.
MONTPELIER SQ.
MONTPELIER ST.
MONTPELIER WK.
MONTPELIER M.
RELTON M.
LANCELOT PL.
RAPHAEL ST.
KNIGHTSBRIDGE GRN.
A4
BROMPTON RD.
KNIGHTSBRIDGE
HANS CR.
HANS ST.
HANS CT.
BASIL ST.
Harrods
QUEEN'S GATE
JAY M.
BREMNER RD.
CALLENDAR RD.
Royal College of Music
AYRTON ROAD
Imperial Coll. of
Univ.
BOWIE ST.

Wallace Colln
Wigmore Hall
University
Oxford Circus
11
Portman Square
Wigmore St.
Selfridges
Oxford St. Restricted Access 7am.-7pm. Mon.-Sat.
Bond St.
Oxford St. A40
Marble Arch
Speakers' Corner
Park Lane
Roosevelt Memorial
American Embassy
Grosvenor Square
Brook St.
Mayfair
Berkeley Square
Hay's M.
Curzon St.
Piccadilly
Green Park
Regent Hall
Faraday Mus.
Achilles Statue
Wellington Mus.
Apsley Ho.
Hyde Park Corner
Hyde Pk. Cnr.
Wellington Arch
Wellington Mon.
Commonwealth Memorial Gates
Constitution Hill (Closed to traffic on Sundays)
Green Park
Bandstand
Nannies Lawn
The Dell
The Holocaust Memorial Gdns.
Rose Garden
Queen Elizabeth Gate
Knightsbridge
Sloane St.
Belgrave Sq.
Grosvenor Place
Grosvenor Cr.
Wilton Crescent
Buckingham Palace Gardens
Buckingham Palace
The Quadrangle
Queen Victoria M.
Ambassadors Ct.
Queens Gallery
The Royal Mews
Royal Mews
Buckingham Gate
Dept. for Transport
Lwr. Grosvenor Pl.
12
17
5

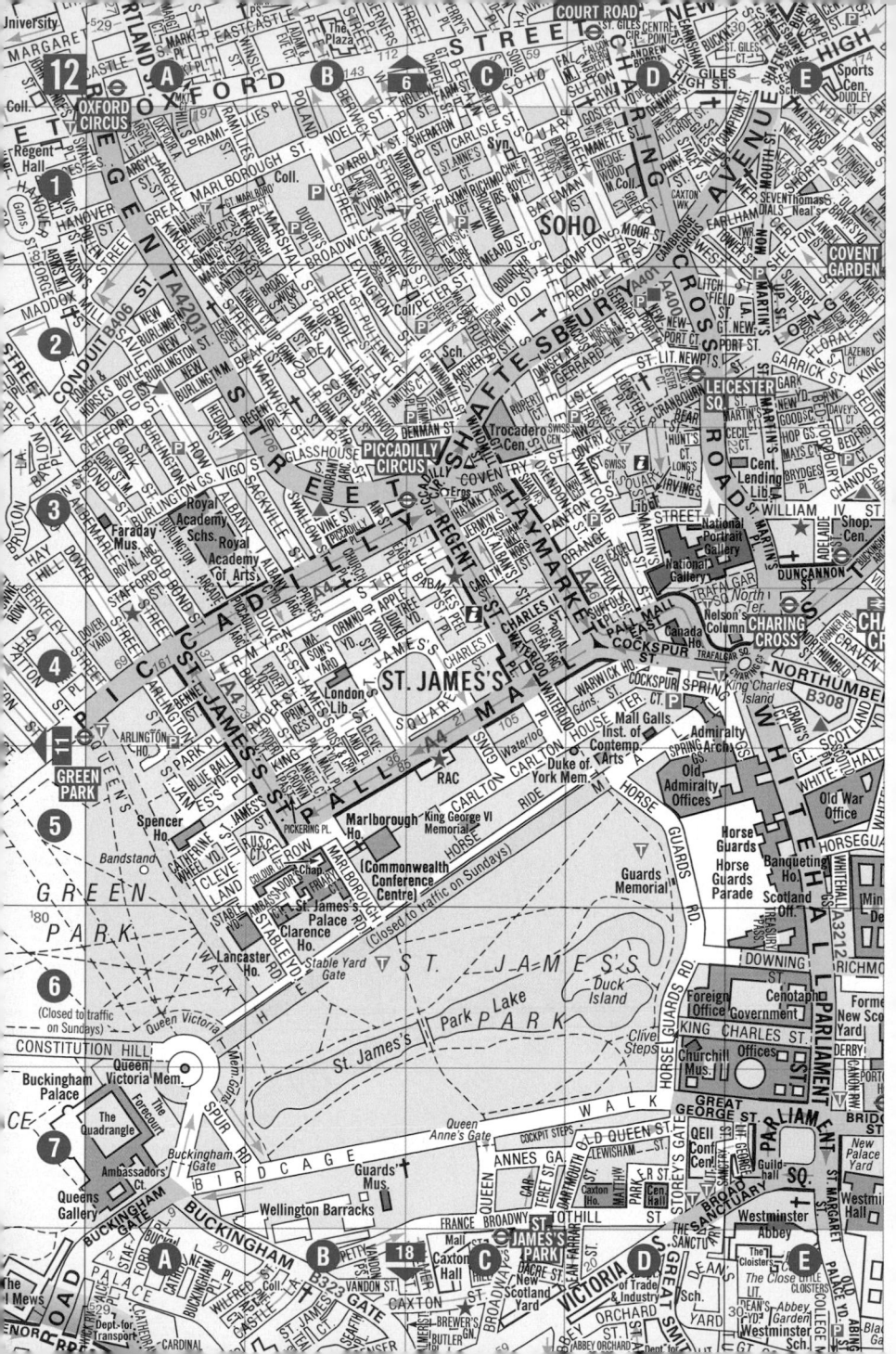

12
A
B
C
D
E
6
1
2
3
4
5
6
7
11
18
OXFORD CIRCUS
OXFORD ST.
REGENT STREET
COURT ROAD
ST. GILES CIR.
CENTRE POINT
CHARING CROSS ROAD
SHAFTESBURY AVENUE
HIGH ST.
SOHO
SOHO SQUARE
GREAT MARLBOROUGH ST.
BROADWICK ST.
WARDOUR ST.
DEAN ST.
FRITH ST.
GREEK ST.
OLD COMPTON ST.
CAMBRIDGE CIRCUS
SEVEN DIALS
COVENT GARDEN
LONG ACRE
GARRICK ST.
LEICESTER SQ.
GERRARD ST.
LISLE ST.
CRANBOURN ST.
Trocadero Cen.
PICCADILLY CIRCUS
GLASSHOUSE ST.
COVENTRY ST.
HAYMARKET
JERMYN ST.
PICCADILLY
Royal Academy Schs.
Royal Academy of Arts
Faraday Mus.
ALBEMARLE ST.
DOVER ST.
OLD BOND ST.
NEW BOND ST.
CONDUIT ST.
SAVILE ROW
MADDOX ST.
HANOVER SQ.
Regent Hall
ST. JAMES'S SQUARE
London Lib.
ST. JAMES'S ST.
PALL MALL
National Gallery
National Portrait Gallery
TRAFALGAR SQ.
Nelson's Column
Canada Ho.
COCKSPUR ST.
CHARING CROSS
WILLIAM IV ST.
DUNCANNON ST.
NORTHUMBERLAND
Admiralty Arch
Old Admiralty Offices
Horse Guards
Horse Guards Parade
Banqueting Ho.
Scotland Off.
Old War Office
WHITEHALL
DOWNING ST.
Cenotaph
Foreign Office
Government Offices
KING CHARLES ST.
Churchill Mus.
PARLIAMENT ST.
PARLIAMENT SQ.
GREAT GEORGE ST.
QEII Conf. Cen.
Guild hall
New Palace Yard
Westminster Abbey
Westminster Hall
THE SANCTUARY
BROAD SANCTUARY
Mall Galls.
Inst. of Contemp. Arts
Duke of York Mem.
CARLTON HOUSE TER.
RAC
Marlborough Ho.
King George VI Memorial
(Commonwealth Conference Centre)
St. James's Palace
Clarence Ho.
Lancaster Ho.
Spencer Ho.
Bandstand
GREEN PARK
(Closed to traffic on Sundays)
CONSTITUTION HILL
Queen Victoria Mem.
Buckingham Palace
The Forecourt
The Quadrangle
Ambassadors' Ct.
Queens Gallery
BIRDCAGE WALK
Guards' Mus.
Wellington Barracks
BUCKINGHAM GATE
ST. JAMES'S PARK
St. James's Park Lake
Duck Island
Guards Memorial
HORSE GUARDS RD.
Clive Steps
Queen Anne's Gate
OLD QUEEN ST.
TOTHILL ST.
BROADWAY
Caxton Hall
New Scotland Yard
VICTORIA ST.
Dept. of Trade & Industry
GREAT SMITH ST.
Dean's Yard
The Cloisters
Westminster Sch.
Abbey Garden
Dept. for Transport
PALACE ST.
The Mews

HOLBORN
Lincoln's Inn Fields
Lincoln's Inn Hall
Land Regy. Off.
Royal Coll. of Surgeons
King's College Library
Royal Courts of Justice
FLEET ST.
FETTER LA.
CHANCERY LA.
13
7
F
G
H
J
K
1
2
3
4
5
6
7
Freemasons Hall
KINGSWAY
ALDWYCH
STRAND
A4
Temple Bar
COVENT GARDEN
Royal Opera House
The Market
Jubilee Hall
London Transport Mus.
Lyceum
Bush Ho.
LA Fitness
Courtauld Inst. & Galls.
Somerset House
King's Coll.
TEMPLE
Inner Temple
Inner Temple Gardens
Mid. Temple
TEMPLE CHAMBERS
BLACKFRIARS UNDERPASS
EMBANKMENT
Blackfriars Millennium Pier
HMS President
HQS Wellington
St. Katharine
Temple Pier
Lifeboat Station
THAMES
A3211
A301
WATERLOO BRIDGE
Queen Mary
Savoy Pier
Cleopatra's Needle
Embankment Pier
EMBANKMENT
Bandstand
Victoria Embankment Gardens
Stamford Wharf
THE QUEEN'S WALK
Oxo Tower Wharf
Reach
Festival Pier
Kings
South Bank
The London Television Centre
The National Film Theatre
National Theatre
Queen Elizabeth Hall
South Bank
Royal Festival Hall
Hayward Gallery
Hungerford Bridge
HUNGERFORD LA.
NORTHUMBERLAND AV.
Hispaniola
PS Tattershall Castle
The Bernie Spain Gdns.
MULBERRY HOUSING CO-OPERATIVE
The London Nautical Sch.
STAMFORD ST.
A3200
King's College
Univ.
UPPER GROUND
PEABODY ESTATE
14
IMAX
TENISON WAY
CONCERT HALL APP.
Whitehall Stairs
Waterloo Millennium Pier
Jubilee Gardens
London Eye
Dali Universe
London Aquarium
County Hall (Former)
COUNTY HALL APARTMENTS
WATERLOO INTERNATIONAL
WATERLOO
WATERLOO EAST
The Young Vic Theatre
Southwark Coll.
The Old Vic Th.
YORK ROAD
WATERLOO ROAD
RIVER
VICTORIA
Westminster Millennium Pier
WESTMINSTER
WESTMINSTER BRI.
WESTMINSTER BRIDGE RD.
A302
Big Ben
Houses of Parliament
Museum
St. Thomas' Hosp.
A3036
PALACE RD.
A23
LAMBETH NORTH
LAMBETH
Evelina Children's Hosp.
19
Kagyu Samye Dzong London
St. George's Cathedral
BAYLIS
LOWER MARSH
Teacher Training Cen.
MATHESON LANG HO.
SANTLEY HO.
DAUNCEY HO.
MAWDLEY HO.
PEABODY SQ.

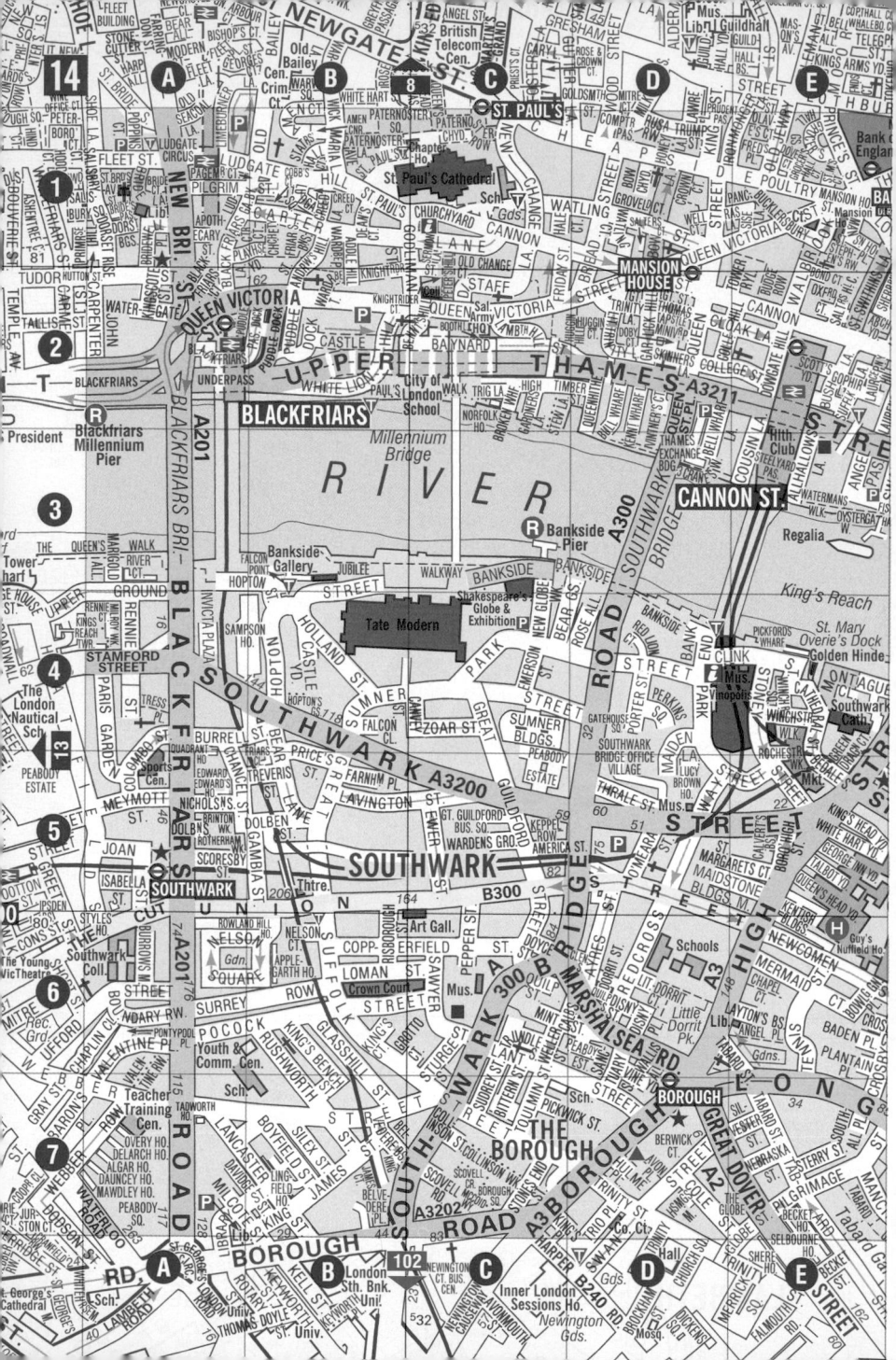

14
A
B
C
D
E
1
2
3
4
5
6
7
8
13
102
NEWGATE ST.
Old Bailey
Cen. Crim. Ct.
British Telecom Cen.
ST. PAUL'S
St. Paul's Cathedral
Chapter Ho.
Bank of England
LUDGATE CIRCUS
LUDGATE HILL
FLEET ST.
NEW BRI. ST.
QUEEN VICTORIA ST.
CHEAPSIDE
POULTRY
MANSION HOUSE
CANNON ST.
UPPER THAMES ST.
A3211
BLACKFRIARS
BLACKFRIARS UNDERPASS
Blackfriars Millennium Pier
President
City of London School
Millennium Bridge
RIVER
Bankside Pier
CANNON ST.
Regalia
King's Reach
St. Mary Overie's Dock
Golden Hinde
Southwark Cath.
Bankside Gallery
Shakespeare's Globe & Exhibition
Tate Modern
BANKSIDE
HOPTON STREET
SOUTHWARK BRIDGE
A300
SOUTHWARK BRIDGE ROAD
BLACKFRIARS BRI.
BLACKFRIARS ROAD
A201
STAMFORD STREET
SOUTHWARK STREET A3200
The London Nautical Sch.
PEABODY ESTATE
Sports Cen.
SOUTHWARK
SOUTHWARK ST.
UNION ST.
B300
Art Gall.
Crown Court
THE CUT
The Young Vic Theatre
Southwark Coll.
NELSON SQUARE
SURREY ROW
Youth & Comm. Cen.
Teacher Training Cen.
SOUTHWARK BRIDGE ROAD
MARSHALSEA RD.
Little Dorrit Pk.
Schools
BOROUGH HIGH ST.
A3
Guy's Nuffield Ho.
LONG LANE
BOROUGH
THE BOROUGH
BOROUGH ROAD
A3202
A3 BOROUGH
GREAT DOVER ST.
A2
PILGRIMAGE
Mus. Vinopolis
CLINK STREET
London Sth. Bnk. Uni.
Inner London Sessions Ho.
Newington Gds.
St. George's Cathedral
LAMBETH ROAD
WATERLOO ROAD
Tabard Gdns.

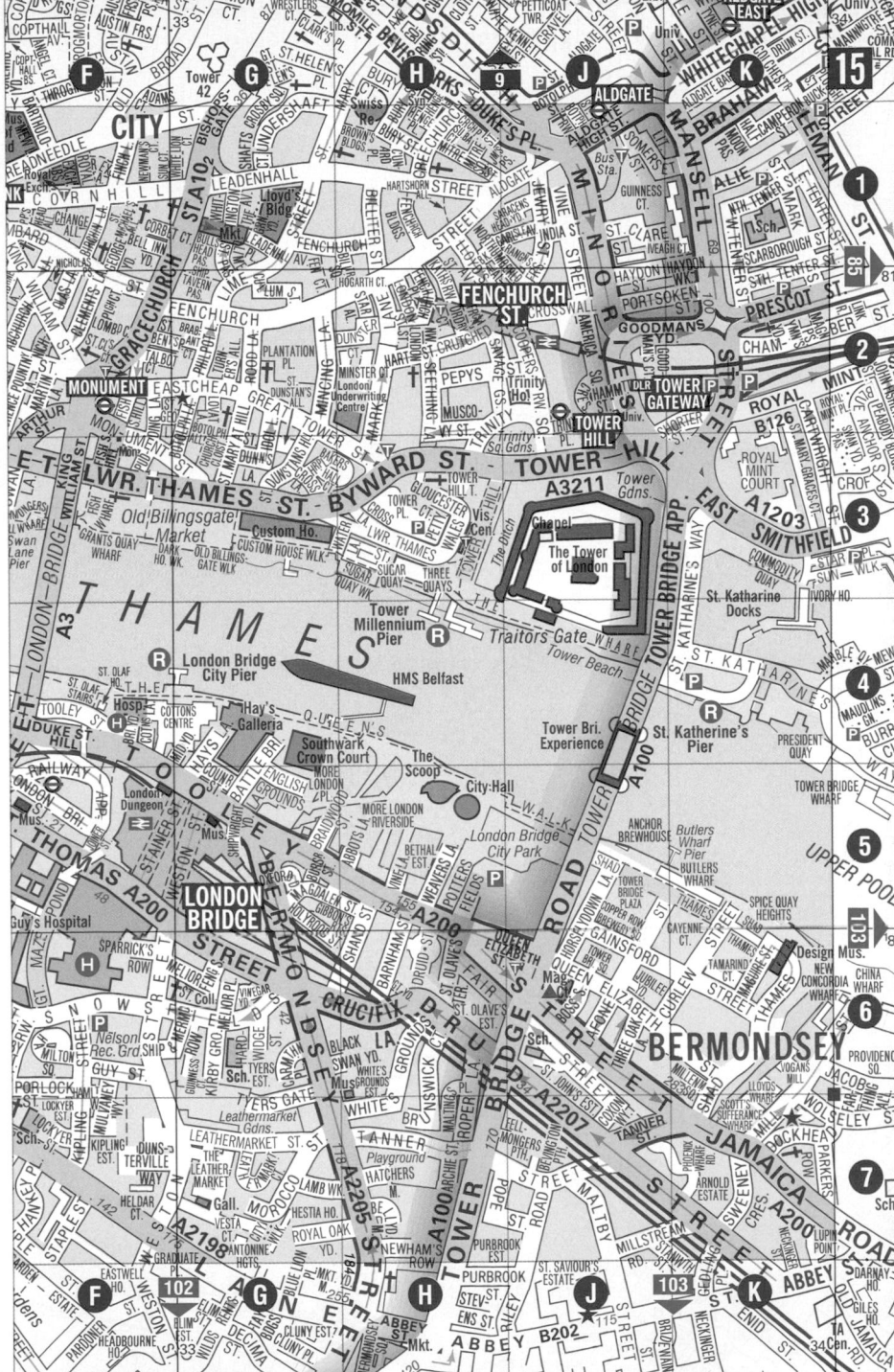

15
F
G
H
J
K
1
2
3
4
5
6
7
CITY
Tower 42
Swiss Re
Lloyd's Bldg
ALDGATE
ALDGATE EAST
WHITECHAPEL HIGH
MANSELL
MINORIES
LEMAN STREET
PRESCOT ST.
ROYAL MINT COURT
EAST SMITHFIELD
A1203
FENCHURCH ST.
MONUMENT
TOWER GATEWAY
TOWER HILL
BYWARD ST.
LWR. THAMES ST.
GRACECHURCH
LEADENHALL
CORNHILL
EASTCHEAP
GREAT TOWER ST.
Old Billingsgate Market
Custom Ho.
A3211
The Tower of London
Chapel
Traitors Gate
Tower Beach
Tower Millennium Pier
London Bridge City Pier
HMS Belfast
T H A M E S
St. Katharine Docks
St. Katharine's Pier
Tower Bri. Experience
TOWER BRIDGE APP.
TOWER BRIDGE ROAD
A100
Hay's Galleria
Southwark Crown Court
City Hall
The Scoop
More London Riverside
London Bridge City Park
London Dungeon
LONDON BRIDGE
TOOLEY ST.
ST. THOMAS ST.
A200
Guy's Hospital
BERMONDSEY ST.
BERMONDSEY
Butlers Wharf Pier
UPPER POOL
Design Mus.
JAMAICA ROAD
A2207
DRUID ST.
CRUCIFIX LA.
Leathermarket Gdns.
LEATHERMARKET ST.
A2205
A2198
LONG LANE
ABBEY ST.
B202
85
103
102
9

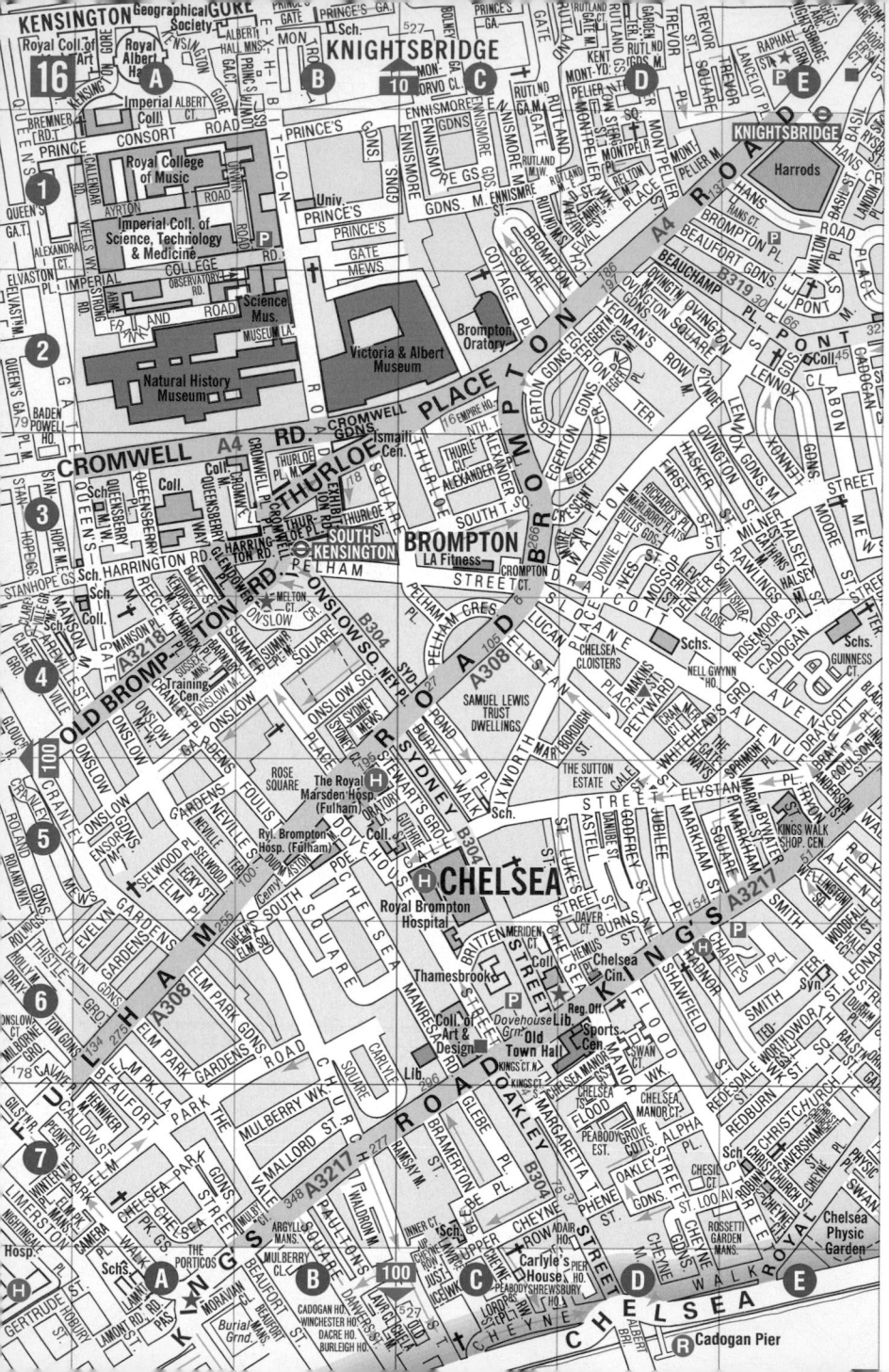
16
KENSINGTON
KNIGHTSBRIDGE
10
Royal Coll. of Art
Royal Albert Hall
Geographical Society
Imperial Coll.
Royal College of Music
Imperial Coll. of Science, Technology & Medicine
Science Mus.
Natural History Museum
Victoria & Albert Museum
Brompton Oratory
Harrods
PRINCE CONSORT ROAD
CROMWELL RD.
A4
CROMWELL PLACE
THURLOE PLACE
BROMPTON ROAD
SOUTH KENSINGTON
BROMPTON
LA Fitness
PELHAM STREET
HARRINGTON RD.
OLD BROMPTON RD.
A3218
ONSLOW SQ.
B304
FULHAM ROAD
A308
The Royal Marsden Hosp. (Fulham)
Ryl. Brompton Hosp. (Fulham)
SAMUEL LEWIS TRUST DWELLINGS
THE SUTTON ESTATE
CHELSEA CLOISTERS
SLOANE AVENUE
CHELSEA
Royal Brompton Hospital
KINGS ROAD
A3217
Chelsea Cin.
Old Town Hall
Sports Cen.
Coll. of Art & Design
Thamesbrook
KINGS WALK SHOP. CEN.
Carlyle's House
Chelsea Physic Garden
CHEYNE WALK
CHELSEA EMBANKMENT
Cadogan Pier
100
1
2
3
4
5
6
7
A
B
C
D
E

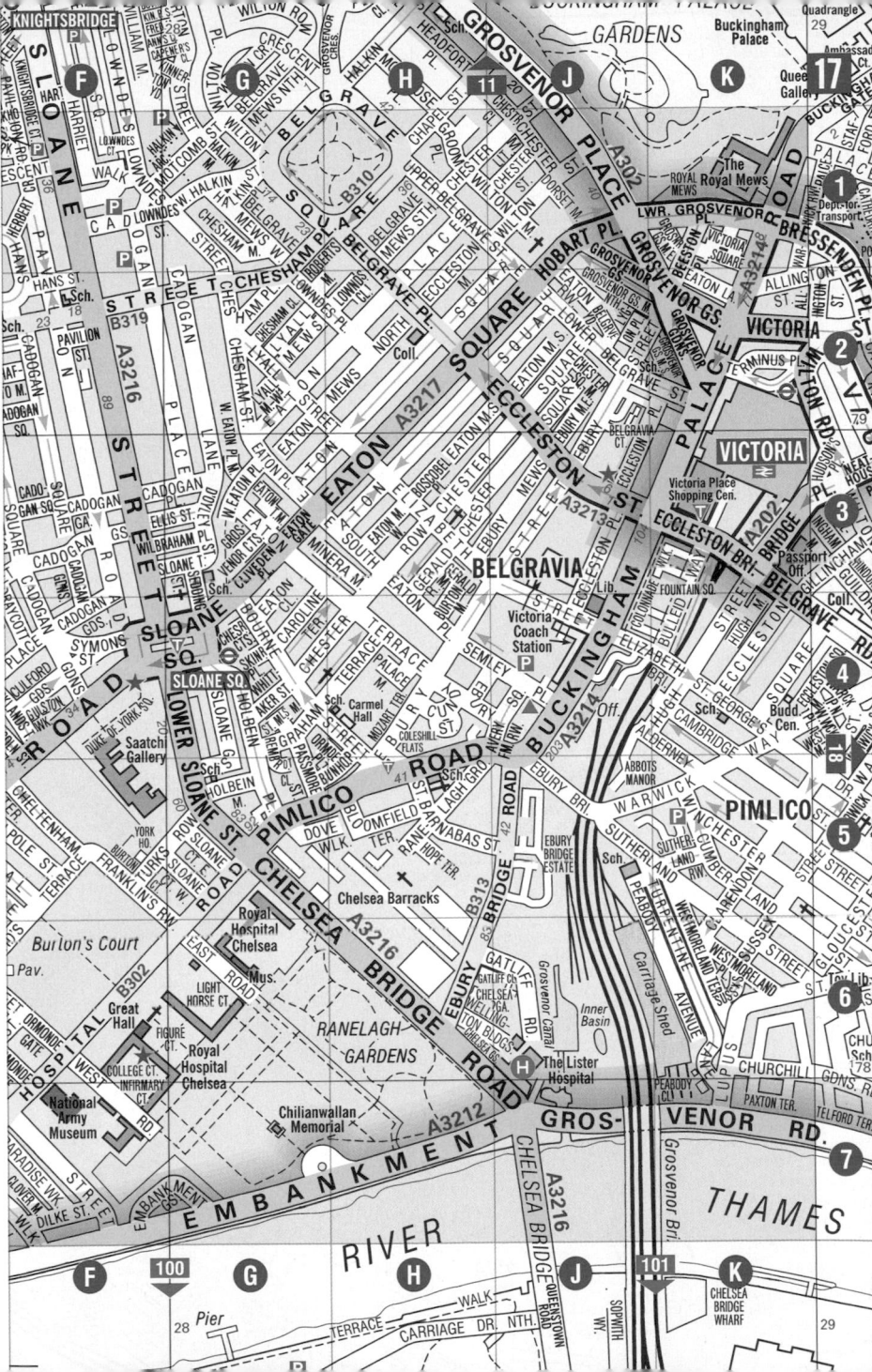

KNIGHTSBRIDGE
BUCKINGHAM PALACE GARDENS
Buckingham Palace
17
11
GROSVENOR PLACE
BELGRAVE SQUARE
VICTORIA
BELGRAVIA
EATON SQUARE
SLOANE SQ.
Victoria Coach Station
PIMLICO
PIMLICO ROAD
CHELSEA BRIDGE ROAD
Chelsea Barracks
Royal Hospital Chelsea
RANELAGH GARDENS
Saatchi Gallery
National Army Museum
Burton's Court
The Lister Hospital
Chilianwallan Memorial
GROSVENOR RD.
EMBANKMENT
RIVER THAMES
18
100
101

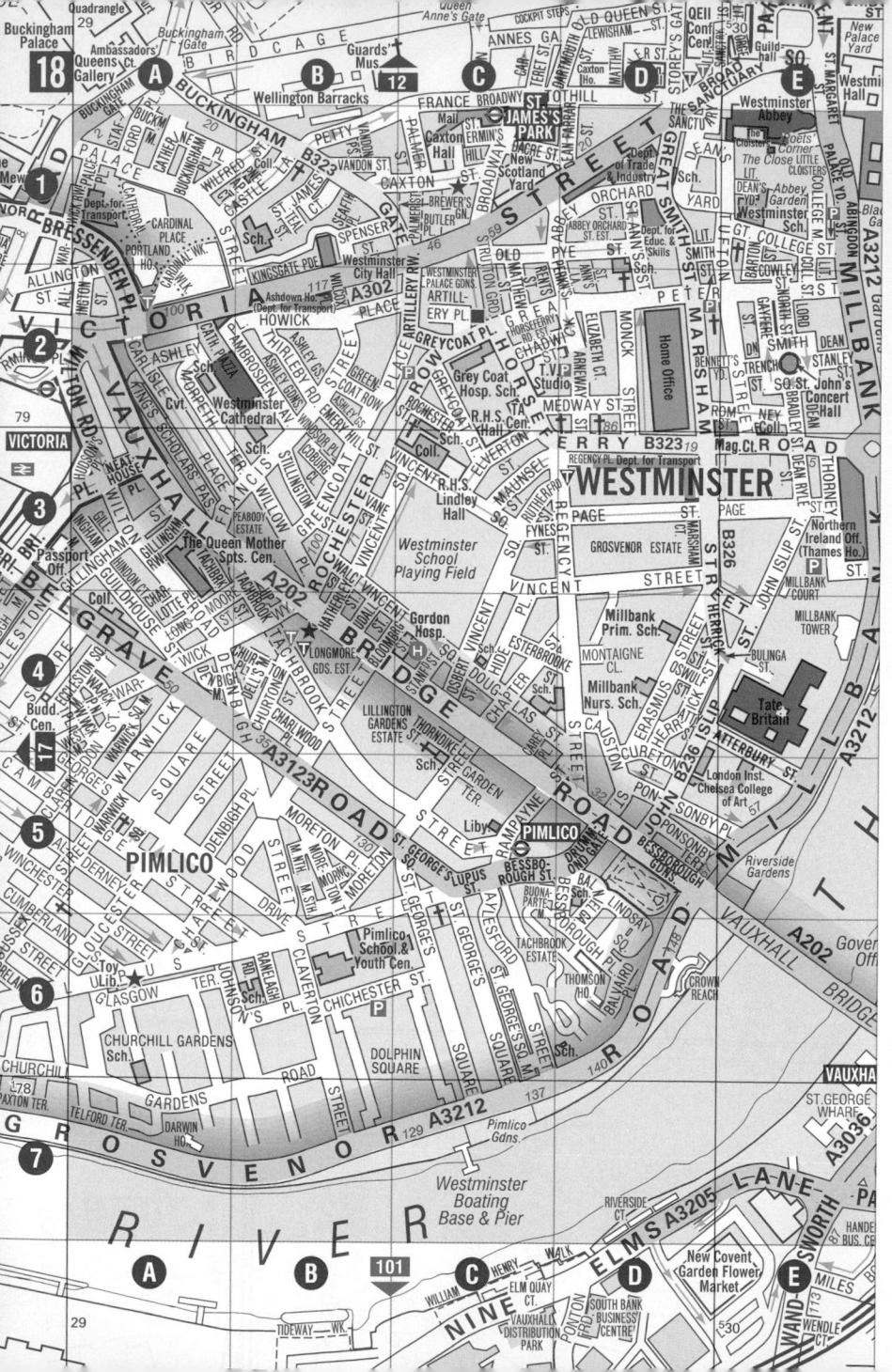

18
Buckingham Palace
Queens Gallery
Quadrangle
Ambassadors' Ct.
Birdcage Walk
Guards' Mus.
12
Wellington Barracks
Queen Anne's Gate
Cockpit Steps
Old Queen St.
Lewisham St.
QEII Conf. Cen.
Guild-hall
New Palace Yard
Parliament Sq.
Westminster Hall
St. Margaret St.
Broad Sanctuary
The Sanctuary
Westminster Abbey
The Cloisters
Poets' Corner
The Close
Little Cloisters
Dean's Yd.
Abbey Garden
Westminster Sch.
Gt. College St.
Cowley St.
Lord North St.
Barton St.
Great Peter St.
Dean Trench St.
Smith Sq.
St. John's Concert Hall
Dean Stanley St.
Millbank
A3212
Horseferry Road
B323
Thorney St.
Dean Ryle St.
Northern Ireland Off. (Thames Ho.)
Millbank Court
Millbank Tower
John Islip St.
Bulinga St.
Tate Britain
Atterbury St.
London Inst. Chelsea College of Art
Ponsonby Pl.
Ponsonby Ter.
Bessborough Gdns.
Riverside Gardens
Vauxhall Bridge
A202
Government Off.
Vauxhall
St. George Wharf
A3036
Buckingham Gate
Buckingham St.
Palace St.
Stafford Pl.
Catherine Pl.
Wilfred St.
Castle La.
Petty France
Broadway
Tothill St.
St. James's Park
Caxton Hall
Caxton St.
St. Ermin's Hill
New Scotland Yard
Dacre St.
Dean Farrar St.
Dept. of Trade & Industry
Abbey Orchard St.
Dept. for Educ. & Skills
Great Smith St.
Old Pye St.
Victoria Street
Dept. for Transport
Cardinal Place
Portland Ho.
Bressenden Pl.
Allington St.
Victoria
Kingsgate Pde.
Westminster City Hall
Ashdown Ho. (Dept. for Transport)
A302
Howick Place
Artillery Row
Artillery Pl.
Westminster Palace Gdns.
Greycoat Pl.
Grey Coat Hosp. Sch.
Horseferry Rd. Est.
Chadwick St.
Elizabeth Ct.
Monck Street
Home Office
Marsham Street
T.V. Studio
Medway St.
R.H.S. Hall
T.A. Cen.
Ashley Pl.
Carlisle Pl.
Cathedral Piazza
Westminster Cathedral
Ambrosden Av.
Thirleby Rd.
Morpeth Ter.
Francis St.
Vauxhall Bridge Road
Emery Hill St.
Stillington St.
Greencoat Pl.
Rochester Row
Vincent Sq.
R.H.S. Lindley Hall
Westminster School Playing Field
Regency St.
Regency Pl.
Westminster
Page St.
Grosvenor Estate
Vincent Street
Fynes St.
Maunsel St.
Elverton St.
Neathouse Pl.
Wilton Rd.
Hudson's Pl.
Gillingham St.
Peabody Estate
The Queen Mother Spts. Cen.
Passport Off.
Belgrave Road
Eccleston Sq.
Warwick Way
Warwick Sq.
Tachbrook St.
Longmore Gds. Est.
Gordon Hosp.
Bloomburg St.
Osbert St.
Vincent St.
Hide Pl.
Esterbrooke St.
Montaigne Cl.
Millbank Prim. Sch.
Millbank Nurs. Sch.
Erasmus St.
Herrick St.
Cureton St.
Causton St.
John Islip St.
Lillington Gardens Estate
Thorndike St.
Garden Ter.
Chapter St.
Douglas St.
Carey Pl.
Pimlico
Rampayne St.
Drummond Gate
Bessborough St.
Lupus St.
St. George's Sq.
Moreton St.
Moreton Pl.
Denbigh Pl.
Denbigh St.
Charlwood St.
Churton St.
A3123
Liby.
Budd. Cen.
17
Cambridge St.
Winchester St.
Cumberland St.
Sussex St.
Gloucester St.
Clarendon St.
Alderney St.
St. George's Dr.
Warwick Way
Toy Lib.
Glasgow Ter.
Johnson's Pl.
Ranelagh Rd.
Claverton Street
Pimlico School & Youth Cen.
Chichester St.
Aylesford St.
St. George's Square
Bessborough Pl.
Tachbrook Estate
Thomson Ho.
Balvaird Pl.
Lindsay Sq.
Bonaparte M.
Crown Reach
Churchill Gardens
Dolphin Square
Paxton Ter.
Telford Ter.
Darwin Ho.
Grosvenor Road
A3212
Pimlico Gdns.
Westminster Boating Base & Pier
River Thames
Riverside Ct.
Nine Elms Lane
A3205
Henry Walk
William
Elm Quay Ct.
Vauxhall Distribution Park
Ponton Rd.
South Bank Business Centre
New Covent Garden Flower Market
Wandsworth Rd.
Miles St.
Wendle Ct.
Tideway Wk.
101
A B C D E
1 2 3 4 5 6 7

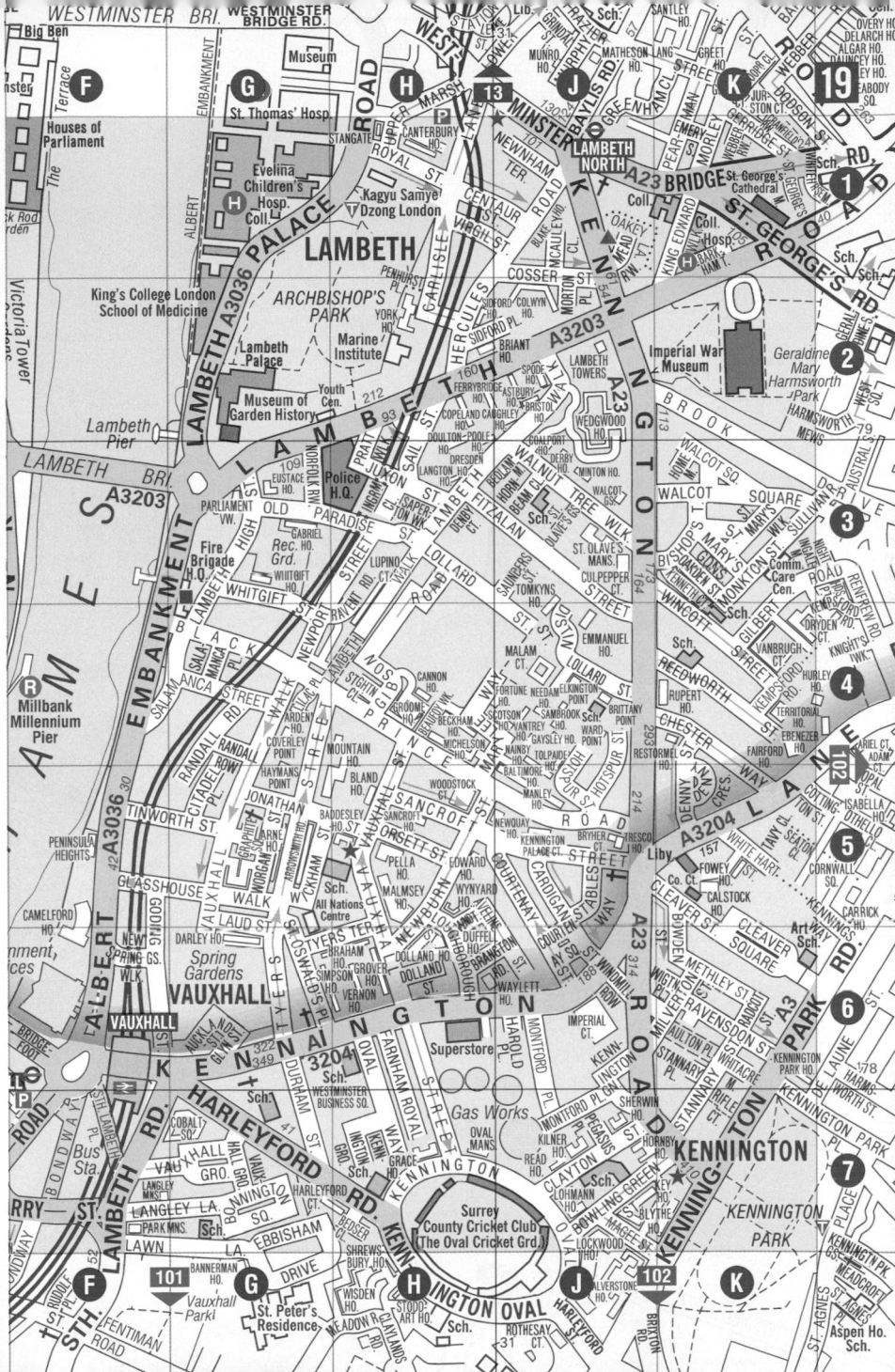

19
LAMBETH
ARCHBISHOP'S PARK
Houses of Parliament
Big Ben
St. Thomas' Hosp.
Evelina Children's Hosp.
Museum
King's College London School of Medicine
Lambeth Palace
Museum of Garden History
Marine Institute
Kagyu Samye Dzong London
Lambeth Pier
LAMBETH BRI.
WESTMINSTER BRIDGE RD.
LAMBETH PALACE ROAD
LAMBETH ROAD
A3203
A3036
ALBERT EMBANKMENT
Victoria Tower Gardens
LAMBETH NORTH
ST. GEORGE'S RD.
St. George's Cathedral
Imperial War Museum
Geraldine Mary Harmsworth Park
KENNINGTON ROAD
A23
Police H.Q.
Fire Brigade H.Q.
Millbank Millennium Pier
Peninsula Heights
Spring Gardens
VAUXHALL
KENNINGTON LANE
A3204
KENNINGTON
KENNINGTON PARK
KENNINGTON OVAL
Surrey County Cricket Club (The Oval Cricket Grd.)
Gas Works
Superstore
HARLEYFORD RD.
St. Peter's Residence
Vauxhall Park
All Nations Centre
Bus Sta.
101
102
13
F G H J K
1 2 3 4 5 6 7

20
A
B
C
D
E
1
2
3
4
5
6
7
24
525
98
97
195
ST. ALBANS ROAD
A1081
GT. NORTH RD.
A1000
HIGHSTONE
(HADLEY HIGHSTONE)
KITTS END ROAD
WARWICK GDNS.
BEAUMONT PL.
LANGLEY ROW
OLD FOLD MANOR GOLF COURSE
BRIDGEDOWN GOLF COURSE
Club House
Club Ho.
Rectory Farm
St. Martha's Convent RC School
Monken Hadley C of E Prim. Sch.
CAMLET WAY
VALE GDS.
BROADGATES AV.
Bournwell Hill
MONKEN HADLEY COMMON
HADLEY ROAD
MONKEN HADLEY
WILBRAHAMS ALMSHOUSES
SYDNEY CHAPMAN WY.
HADLEY GREEN
Hadley Green
BOUNDARY CL.
DURY RD
Electricity Transformer Sta.
Playing Field
Burial Ground
HIGH BARNET
Play. Fld.
Christ Church C of E Prim. Sch.
SUNSET VW.
Priddeon's Hill
COMMON
BAKERS
THE CRESCENT
THE SPINNEY
HADLEY
LATIMER
WOODVILLE
ROAD
CLIFFORD
TUDOR
NORFOLK
BOSWORTH ROAD
SHAKESPEARE CT.
SANDFORD CT.
ORCHARD CT.
SLADE CT.
BARNET
BARNET TRADING ESTATE
QUEEN ELIZABETH CT.
King George's Field
HADLEY
WYBURN AV.
HYDE CL.
SOUTH CL.
STREET
MOON
Queen Elizabeth Girls Sch.
Sports Cen.
GORDON WY.
High Barnet
MEADWAY
KINGSMEAD
HILLARY RISE
EDWARD
WARWICK ROAD
POTTER'S
BULWER
CRABTREE CT.
HEXHAM RD.
HOCKINGTON
WINDERMERE HO.
VALE CT.
THE SPIRES SHOP CEN.
BARRACKS LA.
CHURCH PAS.
STAPYLTON
SALISBURY
CARNARVON RD.
STRAFFORD RD.
ALSTON ROAD
WENTWORTH
CALVERT RD.
SEBRIGHT
QUEENS
ELIZABETH CL.
Queen Elizabeth's School
MARRIOTT RD.
THE AVENUE
THE BRADDON DRIVE
THORNTON RD.
HART LODGE
UNION ST.
RAVENSCROFT PK.
Ravenscroft Gdns.
BLENHEIM ROAD
GRANVILLE RD.
ARGYLE
KINGS RD.
JENNINGS WAY
OLD FOLD VW.
CAVENDISH RD.
WOOD STREET
A411
Whalebone Park
WEST END LA.
BARNET HOSP.
Psychiatric Unit
Cemy.
WELLHOUSE
WELLSIDE CL.
LEXINGTON WAY
DUNSTER
SUTTON CRESCENT
CHIPPING BARNET
LEECROFT RD.
MANORSIDE
CHARTWELL CT.
WILLOW DR.
CEDAR LAWN AV.
Rec. Grd.
Bowl. Grns.
Ten. Cts.
Mus.
ORCHARD
NEWLYN RD.
NORMANDY
ELLESMERE GRO.
BEDFORD
MILTON
WOODFALL
ELTON AV.
VALE AV.
VICTORIA
Mag. Ct.
BARNET HILL
GREAT NORTH ROAD
STATION
A110
Sch.
UNDERHILL
WESTCOMBE DR.
PRIORY
FAIRFIELD WAY
PROSPECT
Highlands Gds.
ABBOTTS RD.
LEICESTER
Res.
POTTERS LA.
GLOUCESTER
Barnet Vale
GREENHILL
Odeon Cin.
WESTERN
RAYDEAN
Barnet FC (Underhill Stadium)
Underhill Playing Fields
The Rainbow Cen.
Pav.
VALLEY
THE RIDGE
HOME FIELD
GARROWSFIELD
MILL BRIDGE
DOLLIS VALLEY WY.
MEADOW
CROCUS
FIELD
School
MAYHILL
LITTLE LARKINS
VALLEY VIEW
NORTHBROOK RD
ROSSITER FLDS.
NEW FIELDWAYS
HAMMOND CL.
LEESIDE
FITZJOHN
GARDENS
KENERNE DR.
DARLANDS
SAMPSON AV.
JARVIS CL.
GOLDA CL.
ALAN DR.
CONNAUGHT RD.
WINDSOR RD.
BROOKSIDE CL.
DOLLIS BROOK WK.
Ducks Island Recreation Ground
RIDGEVIEW
SOUTHFIELD
BISHOPS CL.
STANHOPE
NITON CL.
DEXTER
CHESTERFIELD
PALMER GS.
DORMER CL.
EDWYN CL.
WHITINGS
Whitings Hill Prim. Sch.
PEPYS CRES
SPRING CL.
STEPHEN'S RD.
RIVERSIDE WLK.
KING GEORGE PLAYING FIELDS
Dollis Brook
Grasvenor Avenue Inf. Sch.
GRASVENOR AVENUE
SHERRARDS
THE LINKWAY
WESTERN WY.
Wyatts Farm Open Space
Recreation Ground
COUNTY GATE
CHERRY HILL
HILLIER CL.
DALE CL.
FAIRWAY
Pav.
Grange Playing Fields
East Barnet Old Grammarians Playing Field
Grange Avenue Open Space
Totteridge Park Open Space
Tennis Courts
Ravenscroft School
Playing Field
Sports Centre
OAKLANDS RD.
PRIORY CL.
WHITE ORCHARDS
BARNET LANE
SOUTH HERTS GOLF COURSE
Pavilion
Brook Farm Open Space
Sports Ground
Club House
GRANGE AVENUE
Hall
BADGERS CROFT
30
TOTTERIDGE VILLAGE
WYKEHAM RISE
TOTTERIDGE
TOTTERIDGE A5109 COMMON
Redings
Hillsdown
Montebello
Fairlight Cottage
Hillsborough Cottage
Totteridge Park
BELMONT
ROWBEN CL.
WEST HILL
CLIFFE DRIVE
BARNWOOD CL.

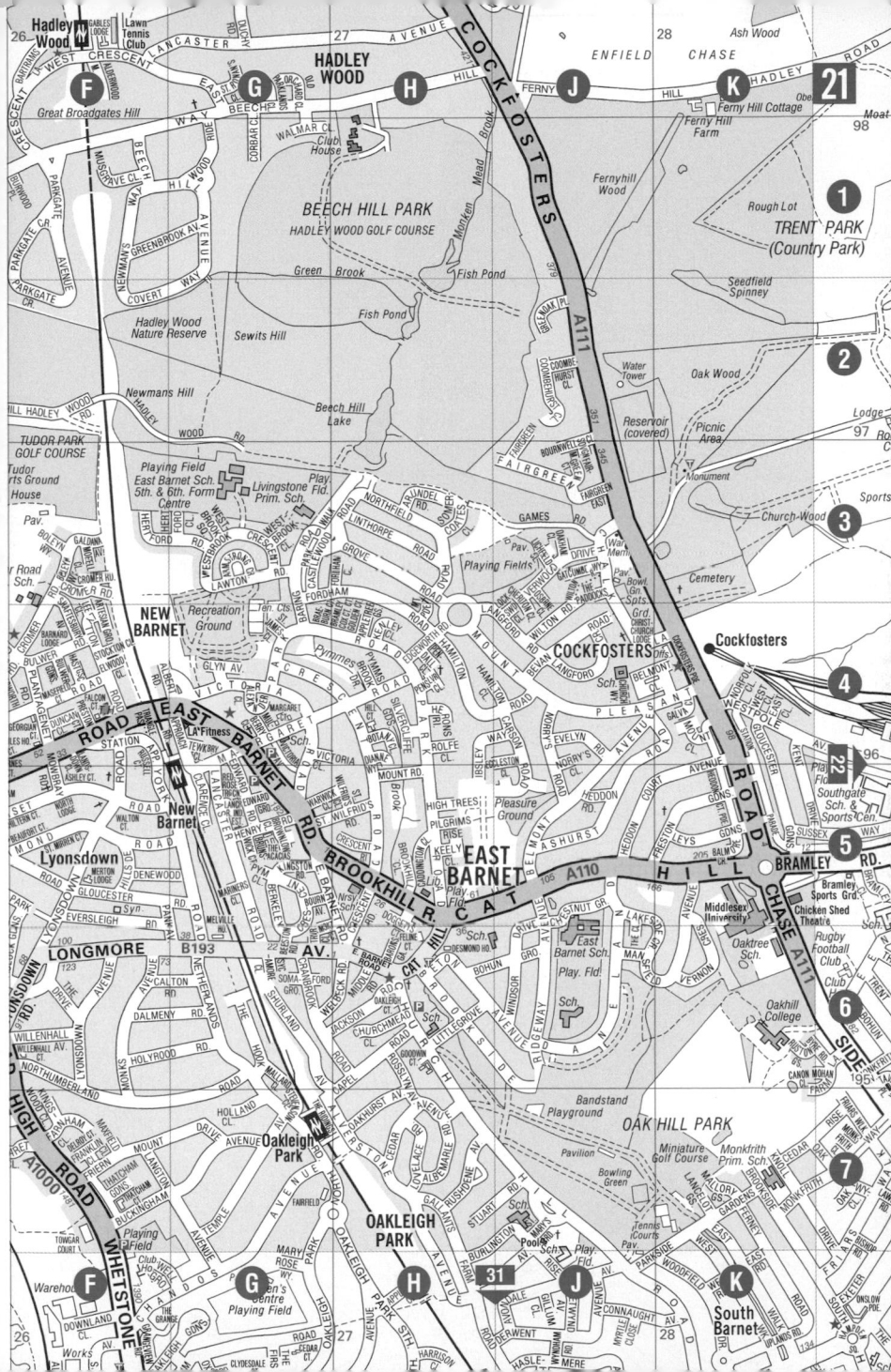

Hadley Wood
HADLEY WOOD
COCKFOSTERS
ENFIELD CHASE
Ash Wood
21
Ferny Hill Cottage
Ferny Hill Farm
BEECH HILL PARK
HADLEY WOOD GOLF COURSE
Fernyhill Wood
Rough Lot
TRENT PARK (Country Park)
Seedfield Spinney
Green Brook
Fish Pond
Hadley Wood Nature Reserve
Sewits Hill
Oak Wood
Water Tower
Newmans Hill
Beech Hill Lake
Reservoir (covered)
Picnic Area
TUDOR PARK GOLF COURSE
Playing Field East Barnet Sch. 5th. & 6th. Form Centre
Livingstone Prim. Sch.
Monument
Church Wood
Playing Fields
Cemetery
NEW BARNET
Recreation Ground
Cockfosters
Lyonsdown
New Barnet
Pleasure Ground
EAST BARNET
Southgate Sch. & Sports Cen.
22
Bramley Sports Grd.
Middlesex University
Chicken Shed Theatre
Oaktree Sch.
Rugby Football Club
East Barnet Sch.
Oakhill College
Bandstand Playground
OAK HILL PARK
Oakleigh Park
Miniature Golf Course
Monkfrith Prim. Sch.
Bowling Green
OAKLEIGH PARK
Playing Field
Queen's Centre Playing Field
31
South Barnet

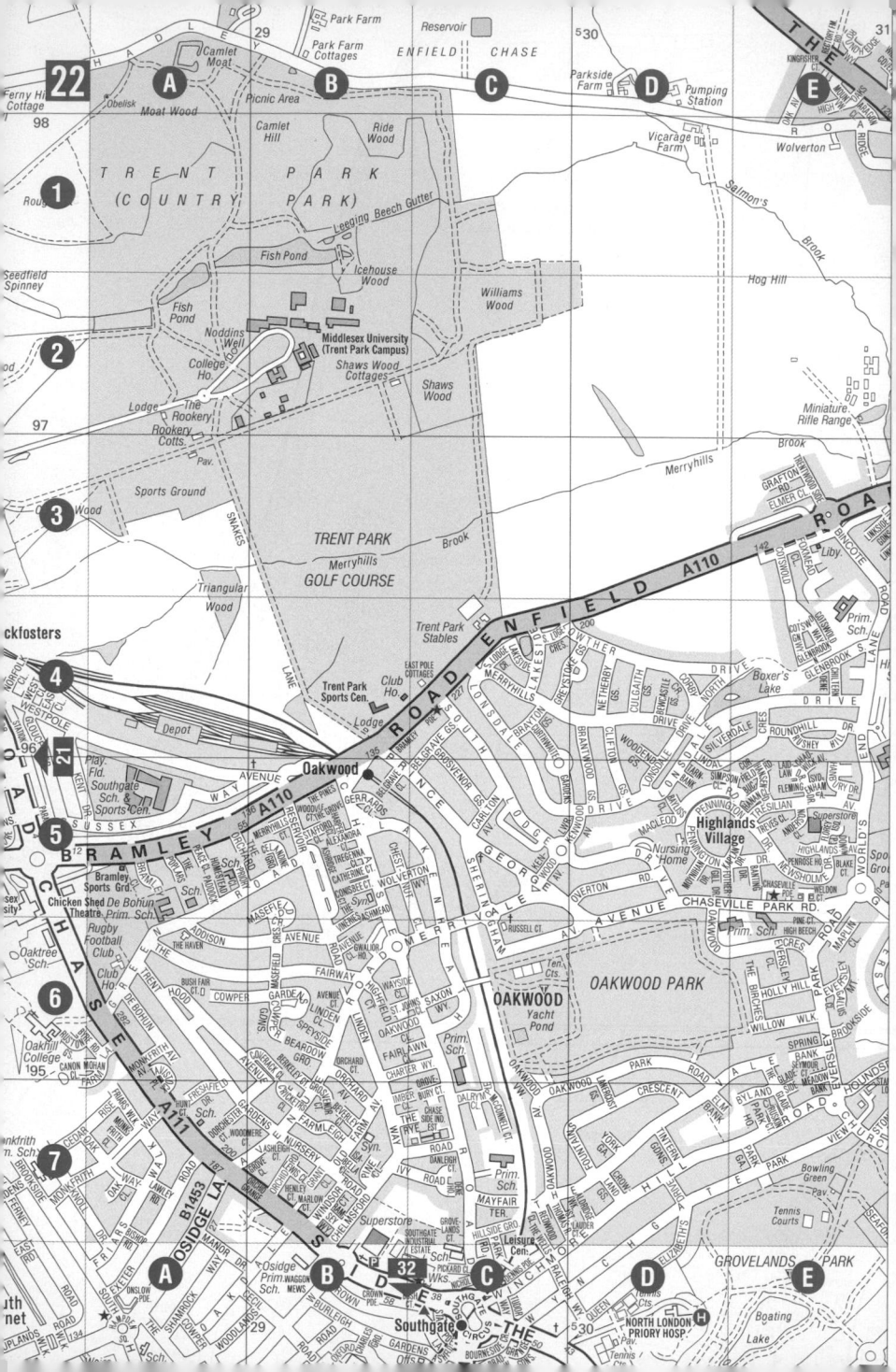
22
TRENT PARK (COUNTRY PARK)
ENFIELD CHASE
Camlet Moat
Moat Wood
Obelisk
Ferny Hill Cottage
Picnic Area
Camlet Hill
Ride Wood
Park Farm
Park Farm Cottages
Reservoir
Parkside Farm
Pumping Station
Vicarage Farm
Wolverton
Salmon's Brook
Hog Hill
Leeging Beech Gutter
Fish Pond
Icehouse Wood
Williams Wood
Seedfield Spinney
Noddins Well
Middlesex University (Trent Park Campus)
College Ho.
Shaws Wood Cottages
Shaws Wood
Lodge
The Rookery
Rookery Cotts.
Miniature Rifle Range
Merryhills Brook
Sports Ground
TRENT PARK GOLF COURSE
Triangular Wood
SNAKES LANE
Trent Park Stables
Trent Park Sports Cen.
Club Ho.
Depot
Oakwood
ENFIELD ROAD A110
BRAMLEY ROAD A110
Southgate Sch. & Sports Cen.
Bramley Sports Grd.
Chicken Shed Theatre
De Bohun Prim. Sch.
Rugby Football Club
Oaktree Sch.
Oakhill College
CHASE SIDE A111
Highlands Village
Nursing Home
Boxer's Lake
Prim. Sch.
Superstore
OAKWOOD PARK
OAKWOOD
Yacht Pond
GROVELANDS PARK
Boating Lake
Tennis Courts
Bowling Green
NORTH LONDON PRIORY HOSP.
Southgate
Leisure Cen.
Southgate Industrial Estate
Osidge Prim. Sch.
OSIDGE LA. B1453
HIGH STREET
CHASEVILLE PARK RD.
MERRIVALE
LONSDALE DRIVE
WORLD'S END LANE
32
21

23
FORTY HILL
KING'S OAK BMI HOSP.
CHASE FARM HOSPITAL
CEMETERY
Gordon Hill
Chase Side
St. Michael's Cen.
Chace Com. Sch. & Spts. Cen.
Enfield Grammar School (Lower)
ENFIELD TOWN
ENFIELD
Civic Cen.
Enfield Chase
Enfield Town
World's End
Moat
Club House
ENFIELD GOLF COURSE
Playing Fields
Playing Field
Grange Park Prim. Sch.
GRANGE PARK
Grange Park
Town Park
Tennis Courts
New River (old course)
BUSH HILL PARK GOLF COURSE
Bush Hill
BUSH HILL PARK
Bush Hill Park
WINCHMORE HILL
Winchmore Hill
The Paulin Ground
Bury Lodge Park
Sports Ground
A1005
A110
A105
A10
B154
RIDGEWAY
SLADES HILL
WINDMILL HILL
CHURCH ST.
SOUTHBURY ROAD
CECIL ROAD
LONDON ROAD
PARK AV.
VILLAGE RD.
RIDGE AV.
GREEN LANES
CHURCH ST.
GT. CAMBRIDGE RD.
LANCASTER RD.
GORDON HILL
CHASE SIDE
PARSONAGE LA.
BAKER ST.
CHURCHBURY LA.
WILLOW RD.
LAVENDER HILL
BYCULLAH RD.
OLD PARK RIDINGS
BUSH HILL
WADES HILL
24
33
1
2
3
4
5
6
7
F
G
H
J
K

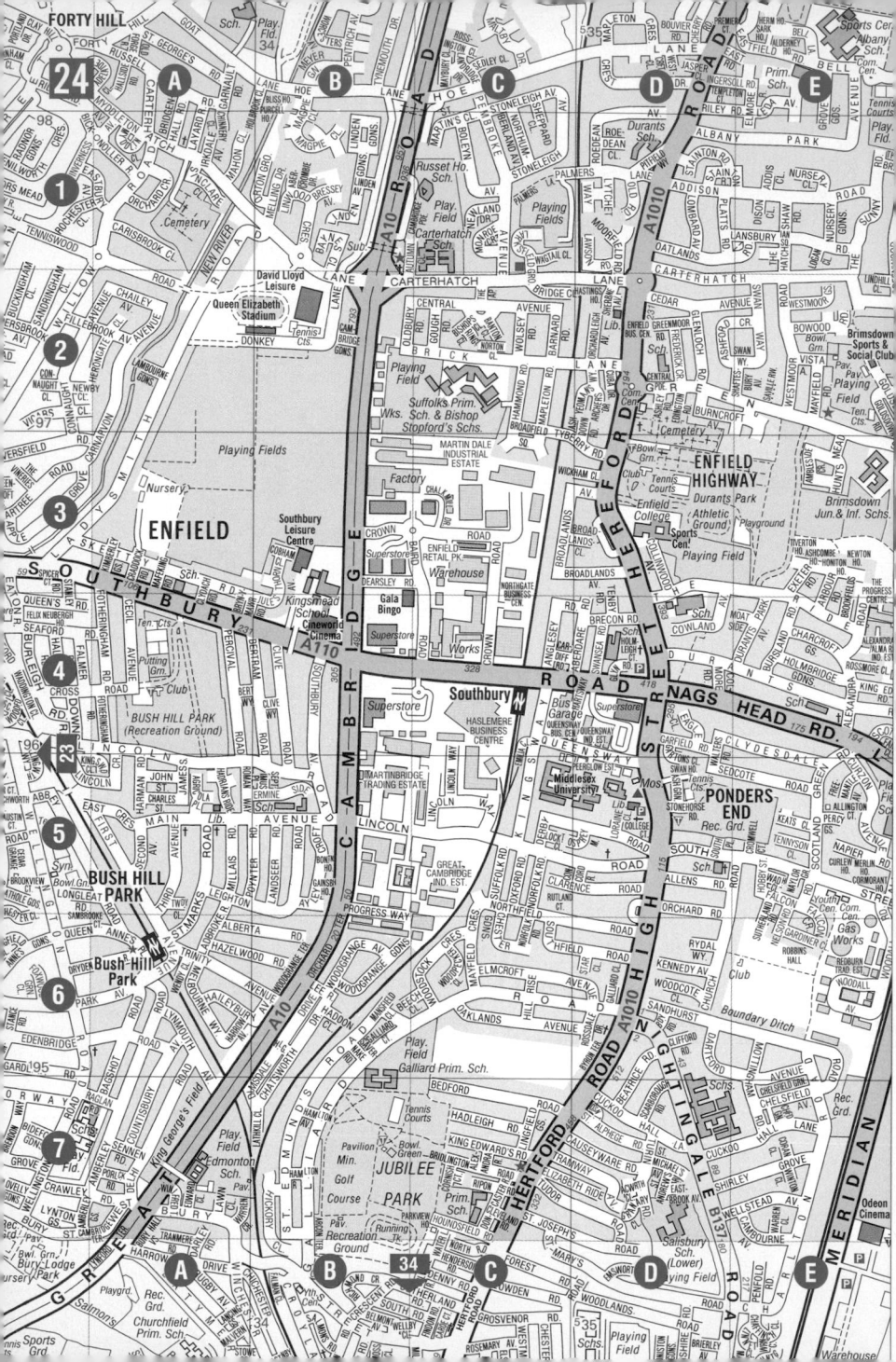

FORTY HILL
24
A
B
C
D
E
1
2
3
4
5
6
7
23
34
ENFIELD
ENFIELD HIGHWAY
PONDERS END
BUSH HILL PARK
Bush Hill Park
JUBILEE PARK
Queen Elizabeth Stadium
David Lloyd Leisure
Southbury Leisure Centre
Kingsmead School
Cineworld Cinema
Gala Bingo
Southbury
Middlesex University
Enfield College
Durants Park
Athletic Ground
Brimsdown Jun.& Inf. Schs.
Brimsdown Sports & Social Club
Suffolks Prim. Sch. & Bishop Stopford's Schs.
Russet Ho. Sch.
Carterhatch Sch.
Durants Sch.
Galliard Prim. Sch.
Salisbury Sch. (Lower)
Churchfield Prim. Sch.
Edmonton Sch.
Bury Lodge Park
Odeon Cinema
MARTIN DALE INDUSTRIAL ESTATE
ENFIELD RETAIL PK.
HASLEMERE BUSINESS CENTRE
MARTINBRIDGE TRADING ESTATE
GREAT CAMBRIDGE IND. EST.
NORTHGATE BUSINESS CEN.
BUSH HILL PARK (Recreation Ground)
Playing Fields
Cemetery
Min. Golf Course
Recreation Ground
Boundary Ditch
King George's Field
CARTERHATCH LANE
SOUTHBURY ROAD
A110
A10
A1010
B137
GREAT CAMBRIDGE ROAD
HERTFORD ROAD
HIGH STREET
NAGS HEAD RD.
MERIDIAN
NIGHTINGALE ROAD
GREEN STREET
LADYSMITH ROAD
NEW RIVER
CARTERHATCH ROAD
DONKEY LANE
BRICK LANE
LINCOLN ROAD
MAIN AVENUE
QUEENSWAY
CROWN ROAD
SOUTH STREET
DURANTS ROAD
ALBANY PARK AV.
HOE LANE
BELL LANE
ST. EDMUND'S ROAD
GALLIARD ROAD
PROGRESS WAY
OAKLANDS AVENUE
COWLAND AV.
CUCKOO HALL LANE
BEDFORD ROAD
HADLEIGH RD.

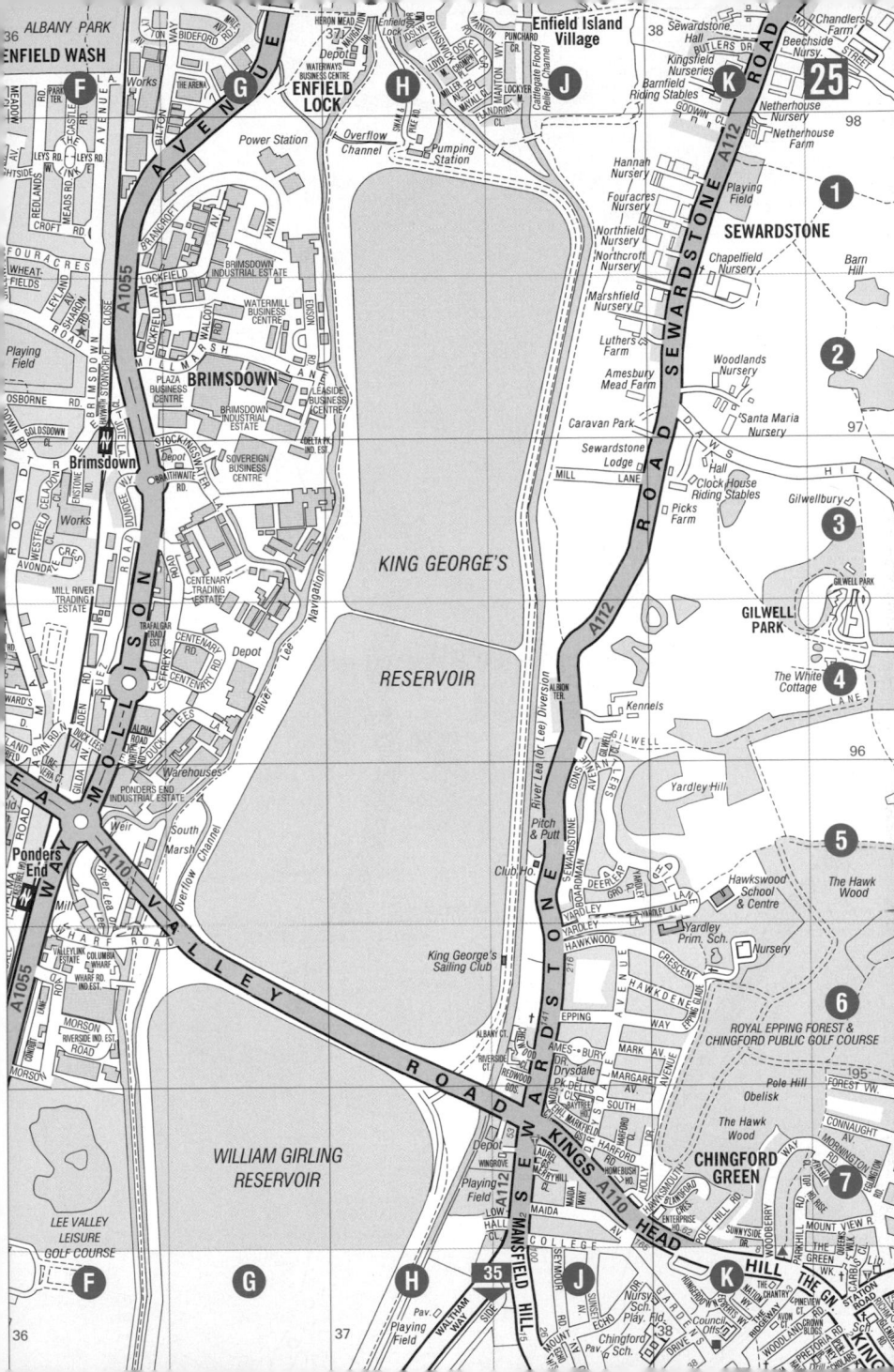

25
ALBANY PARK
ENFIELD WASH
Enfield Island Village
ENFIELD LOCK
Enfield Lock
Sewardstone Hall
Chandlers Farm
Beechside Nursy.
Kingsfield Nurseries
Barnfield Riding Stables
Netherhouse Nursery
Netherhouse Farm
Power Station
Overflow Channel
Pumping Station
Cattlegate Flood Relief Channel
Hannah Nursery
Fouracres Nursery
Northfield Nursery
Northcroft Nursery
Marshfield Nursery
Playing Field
SEWARDSTONE
Chapelfield Nursery
Barn Hill
BRIMSDOWN INDUSTRIAL ESTATE
WATERMILL BUSINESS CENTRE
PLAZA BUSINESS CENTRE
BRIMSDOWN
LEASIDE BUSINESS CENTRE
DELTA PK. IND. EST.
SOVEREIGN BUSINESS CENTRE
Brimsdown
Luthers Farm
Amesbury Mead Farm
Woodlands Nursery
Caravan Park
Santa Maria Nursery
Sewardstone Lodge
Hall
Clock House Riding Stables
Picks Farm
Gilwellbury
Works
KING GEORGE'S RESERVOIR
River Lee Navigation
MILL RIVER TRADING ESTATE
CENTENARY TRADING ESTATE
TRAFALGAR TRAD. EST.
Depot
GILWELL PARK
The White Cottage
Kennels
River Lea (or Lee) Diversion
Yardley Hill
Warehouses
PONDERS END INDUSTRIAL ESTATE
Weir
South Marsh
Overflow Channel
Ponders End
Pitch & Putt
Club Ho.
Hawkswood School & Centre
The Hawk Wood
Yardley Prim. Sch.
Nursery
VALLEYLINK ESTATE
COLUMBIA WHARF
WHARF RD. IND. EST.
RIVERSIDE IND. EST.
King George's Sailing Club
ROYAL EPPING FOREST & CHINGFORD PUBLIC GOLF COURSE
Pole Hill
Obelisk
The Hawk Wood
CHINGFORD GREEN
WILLIAM GIRLING RESERVOIR
LEE VALLEY LEISURE GOLF COURSE
Playing Field
Depot
ENTERPRISE HO.
Nursy. Sch.
Play. Fld.
Council Offs.
Chingford Sch.
Pav.
A1055
A110
A112
MOLLISON AVENUE
LEA VALLEY ROAD
SEWARDSTONE ROAD
KINGS HEAD HILL
MANSFIELD HILL
35
36
37
38
98
97
96
95
F
G
H
J
K
1
2
3
4
5
6
7

26
41
Bushey Golf Course
Swim. Pool
Tennis Courts
Play. Fld.
Ashfield Jun. Sch.
St. Margaret's School
Merry Hill Fm.
Sports Hall
Merry Hill
BUSHEY
Sparrows Herne
Heath Ho.
Caldecote Hill
BUSHEY HOSP. (BUPA)
Works
BUSHEY HEATH
Belswood Cottage
STANMORE COMMON
SPARROWS HERNE
ELSTREE ROAD
HIGH ROAD
A411
A4140
A409
HEATHBOURNE ROAD
THE COMMON
COMMON
BROOKSHILL
OXHEY LANE
A4008
UXBRIDGE ROAD
A410
A409
HIGH ROAD
Hartsbourne Prim. Sch.
Hartsbourne Country Club (Club House)
Tennis Courts
Kestrel Grove (Offices)
Peterborough & St. Margaret's School
The Cedars
Bentley Priory (RAF)
Lodge
HARTSBOURNE GOLF & COUNTRY CLUB
Levels Wood
HARROW WEALD COMMON
The Princess Alexandra Home
Tennis Court
Deer Park
Grim's Ditch
Grim's Dyke
Grimsdyke Open Space
Harrow Weald Common
Nurseries
The Old Barn
Heriot's Wood
GRIM'S DYKE GOLF COURSE
Weald Wood
The City
Lodge
Scout Hall
Priory House
REDDING
Club House
The City
Harrow Weald Common
Hertfordshire & Middlesex Country Club
Copse Farm
Lower Priory Farm
Nursery
Bentley Wood High Sch. for Girls
Tennis Courts
Stony Wood
Grimswood Lodge
Grimswood House
Highcroft
Hermitage Cottages
Hermitage Gate
Woodland Hall
The Lodge
Harrow Weald Cemetery
Saddlers Mead
Harrow Coll. (Harrow Weald Campus)
Brockhurst Cnr.
The Roger Bannister Sports Centre
Playing Fields
Play. Fld.
Grave Yard
Playing Fields
The Cedars
Harrow Arts Cen.
Superstore
Liby.
Swim. Pool
Hatch End Play. Flds.
HATCH END
Schs.
Hatch End High Sch.
Cedars Schs.
HARROW WEALD
Bus Depot
Superstore
Recreation Ground
Tennis Cts.
Weald Schs.
Football Ground
Bedford Coll. Sports Grd.
First & Mid. Sch.
Pav.
194
93
92
91
15
A
B
C
D
E
1
2
3
4
5
6
7

27
28
42
Junction 4
M1
M1-MOTORWAY
WATFORD A41 BY-PASS
A41 (WATFORD BY-PASS)
A5183
EDGWARE
BROCKLEY HILL
A5 (WATLING STREET)
Elstree Open Space
Norwegian Barn
Penniwells Fm.
Brockley Hill Farm
Brockley Grange
Sports Ground
ROYAL NATIONAL ORTHOPAEDIC HOSP.
Brockley Hill Ho.
ASPIRE
Pear Wood Cottages
Pear Wood
Wood Farm
Fish Pond
Limes House
Works
Lodge
THE GROVE
Cricket Ground
Grove Field
Pavilion
Islamic Centre
Tennis Cts.
Cloisters Wood
Stanmore Hall
Driving Range
Club House
Brockley Hill Golf Course
Newlands
Edgwarebury Golf Course
Club Ho.
Playing Field
WAY
A410 SPUR RD.
Stonegrove
The London Academy
CANONS CORNER
STONEGROVE
Stanmore
LONDON ROAD
STANMORE HILL
A4140
A410
CHURCH RD.
THE BROADWAY
MARSH LANE
A4140
Aylward First & Mid. Sch.
Playing Field
Tennis Courts
North London Collegiate School
Lake Grove Rec. Grd.
The Lake
King George V Memorial Gdns.
CANONS PARK
Canons Park
STANMORE
Stanmore College
St. John's First & Mid. Schs.
Stanmore Rec. Grd.
Bowling Green
Lib.
Temple Pond
Boot Pond
Club House
STANMORE GOLF COURSE
Gas Works
Stanmore Marsh
Whitchurch First & Mid. Schs.
Sports Ground
Bowling Green
Stanburn Schs.
WHITCHURCH LANE
B461
Offices
HONEYPOT LANE
Works
Sports Ground
LITTLE STANMORE
Little Stanmore First & Middle Sch.
Prince Edward Playing Field
Tennis Courts Pav.
Bowls
Tennis Courts
Playing Field
HONEYPOT BUS. CEN.
F
G
H
J
K
1
2
3
4
5
6
7
16
17
18
194
93
92
91

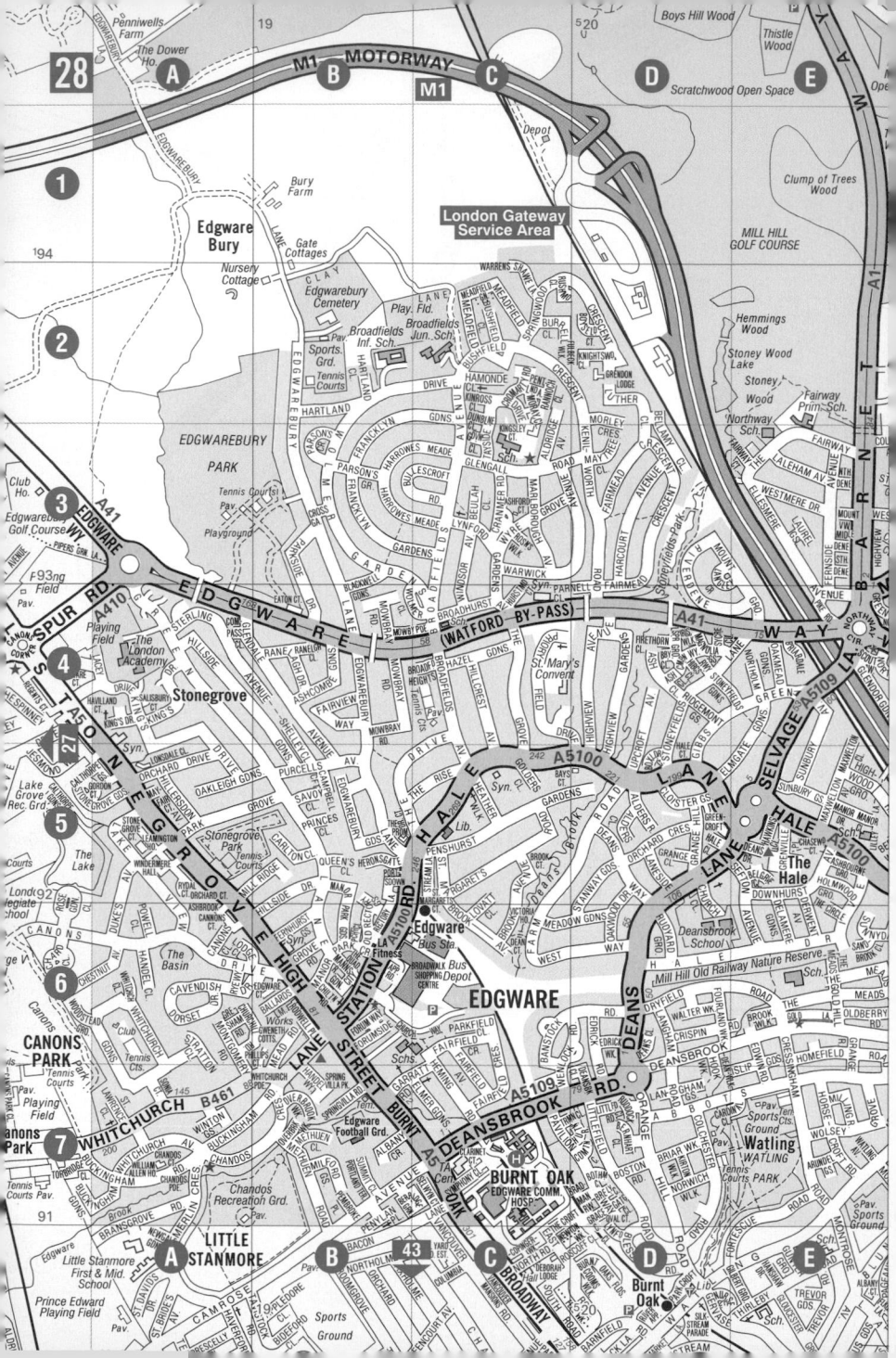
M1 MOTORWAY
M1
Penniwells Farm
The Dower Ho.
Boys Hill Wood
Thistle Wood
Scratchwood Open Space
Depot
Bury Farm
London Gateway Service Area
Clump of Trees Wood
MILL HILL GOLF COURSE
Edgware Bury
Gate Cottages
Nursery Cottage
Edgwarebury Cemetery
Play. Fld.
Broadfields Jun. Sch.
Broadfields Inf. Sch.
Sports Grd.
Tennis Courts
Hemmings Wood
Stoney Wood Lake
Stoney Wood
Fairway Prim. Sch.
Northway Sch.
EDGWAREBURY PARK
Tennis Courts
Playground
Club Ho.
Edgwarebury Golf Course
Playing Field
The London Academy
Stonegrove
EDGWARE WAY (WATFORD BY-PASS)
A41
SPUR RD.
A410
St. Mary's Convent
Stoneyfields Park
NORTHWAY CIR.
SELVAGE LA.
A5109
HALE LANE
A5100
The Hale
Lake Grove Rec. Grd.
The Lake
Stonegrove Park
STONEGROVE
HIGH STREET
STATION RD.
Edgware
Bus Sta.
LA Fitness
BROADWALK SHOPPING CENTRE
Bus Depot
EDGWARE
DEANS LANE
Deansbrook School
Mill Hill Old Railway Nature Reserve
The Basin
CANONS PARK
Canons Park
Tennis Courts
Playing Field
WHITCHURCH LANE
B461
Edgware Football Grd.
DEANSBROOK RD.
BURNT OAK
EDGWARE COMM. HOSP.
Chandos Recreation Grd.
Watling
WATLING PARK
Sports Ground
LITTLE STANMORE
Little Stanmore First & Mid. School
Prince Edward Playing Field
Sports Ground
BROADWAY
Burnt Oak
SILK STREAM PARADE
A5
27
43
A B C D E
1 2 3 4 5 6 7

29
30
44
Junction 2
M1
F
G
H
J
K
1
2
3
4
5
6
7
Hyver Manor
Gravel Pit Wood
Tanglewood
Barnet Gate Wood
HENDON WOOD LANE
B552
BARNET GATE LANE
MAYS LA.
Allendale
Brent Lodge Farm
Dollis Brook
Open Space
Hendon Wood Lane Open Space
Sports Ground
MOAT MOUNT OPEN SPACE
The Shrubbery
Moat Mount Camp Site
Leg of Mutton Pond
Mote End Farm
Mote Mount
Nut Wood
White Lodge
Fairlight Cottage
Totteridge Park
Abattoir
St. Edward's College
TOTTERIDGE COMMON
A5109
Oak Lodge
Boundary House
Farmleigh
Totteridge Common
Ellern Mede Nursing Home
Ellern Mede Farm
The Lynch House
Fairlawn
Monte
Burnhams
The Wa
Hendon Park
CROWN CL.
CLARK'S LANE
Highwood Park
The Barn
Beech Wood
Highwood Ho.
Highwood
Highwood Hill
HIGHWOOD HILL
MARSH LANE
Tennis Courts
Mill Hill High Sch.
Club House
Playing Field
Sch.
HANKINS RD.
BEDFORD RD.
RAMILLIES
WORCESTER
NORBURY GRO.
GLENWOOD RD.
CRESCENT
Highwood Hill Cottage
Holcombe Dale
Folly Brook
Holcombe Hill
THE LINCOLNS
ABBEY VIEW
LAWRENCE GDS.
HOLCOMBE HILL
Pool
Playing Field
Riding School
Folly Farm
Sports Ground
Cricket Club
Pav.
Burtonhole Farm
BRABOURNE HGTS.
AUSTELL GDS.
HORNBEAM
THE REDDINGS
REDDINGS CL.
SUNNYFIELD
UPHILL RD.
RETAWN PK.
TRETAWN
LAWRENCE
GARDENS
Belmont Sch.
Belmont Farm
St. Mary's Abbey
The Mill Field
Lawrence Green
MILLERS CL.
Cemetery
Sports Ground
Nursery
Tennis Courts
DRAPERS' COTTAGE HOMES
CHALET ESTATE
APEX CORNER
WATFORD WAY
A1
GREENDALE
St. Paul's C of E Prim. Sch.
Burtonhole Farm
St. Joseph's RC College
Leisure Cen.
Spts. Grd.
LANE
RIDGEWAY
KINGSHEAD HO.
St. Vincent's School
St. Vincent's Convent
Medical Research Laboratory
Works
SHAKESPEARE RD.
B1461
MARSHALE ESTATE
Mill Hill School
HIGH ST.
THE B552 RIDGEWAY
BURTONHOLE LA.
Oakfield House
MILTON RD.
TAYLORSMEAD
TENNYSON RD.
HAMMERS
MILL HILL
Playing Field
Ten. Cts.
St. Vincent's RC Prim. Sch.
Wentworth Hall
Drivers Hill
Play. Fld.
The Mount Sch.
VINERIES BANK
HOLLIES END
MILESPIT HILL
WEYMOUTH AV.
RUSSELL GRO.
NEWCOMBE
Hall
VICTORIA RD.
ALBERT RD.
MILL HILL CIRCUS
DAWS LANE
BIRKBECK ROAD
BYRON RD.
MARION RD.
Tennis Court
Ridgeway Ho.
Pavilion
WILLS GRO.
Burton Bank
School Park
Arrandene Open Space
Watch Tower House
BITTACY PARK
BITTACY RISE
THE BROADWAY
M1-MOTORWAY
GOODWYN
MONTEREY PL.
SHOPPING CEN.
Lib.
HARTLEY AV.
FLOWER LANE
Garden Centre
WINTER STOKE GS.
WISE LANE
Featherstone Hill
Playground
Mill Hill Cemetery
RUSHDENE
WOODCOTE
MELDEX CL.
Univ.
SYLVAN AV.
WISTERIA CL.
COURTGATE CL.
PARKMEAD GDS.
WOODLAND WAY
Pav.
Cricket Ground
Tennis Courts
MILL HILL PARK
(BARNET BY-PASS)
Mill Hill Broadway
GRANARD BUS. CEN.
Lyndhurst Park
Sub.
LANE WISE
Ten. Cts.
HOLMDENE AV.
GLENMERE AV.
PARKSIDE
BROOKFIELD AV.
BROOKFIELD CRES.
MOORLANDS AV.
FEATHERSTONE RD.
Bittacy Hill Park
Ten. Cts.
ENGEL PARK
BITTACY
SANDERS LANE
SALCOMBE
MORETON CL.
HARTLEY
LYNDHURST AV.
ROAD
WOODCROFT AVENUE
Woodcroft Park
MILL HILL IND. EST.
BUNNS LANE
DOVE
THE RISE
HILLSIDE GRO.
COPTHALL GDNS.
TUDOR CL.
HOLLAND CT.
Playing Field
Copthall Sch. & Sports Cen.
PAGE MDW.
GRENFELL CT.
Dollis Jun. & Inf. Schs.
GRANTS CL.
TAVISTOCK AV.
WOODBERRY WAY
Sports Ground
Pavilion
GRAHAME PARK
PENTAVIA RETAIL PK.
PURSLEY RD.
Chase Lodge Playing Fields
Chase Lodge
Powerleague Soccer Cen.
Club House
ASHLEY LANE
ABERDARE GDNS.
Tennis Courts
ROWLANDS CL.
COLENSO DR.
LADYSMITH CL.
SANDWICK CL.
BAMPTON DR.
MARDALE DR.
MOSTYN RD.
MAPLE GDNS.
STORKSMEAD RD.
WARDELL CL.
FIELD MEAD
CLAYTON FIELD
LONG FIELD
VANGUARD
SOPWITH
SLATTER
CORNER MEAD
PARK
BIRCH GRN.
WILLOW GN.
BROOKLEA CL.
LARCH GN.
Play. Fld.
Tennis Cts.
Barnet Coll.
LONGFIELD AVENUE
Copthall Swimming Pool
Barnet Copthall Stadium
Rugby Club
CHAMPIONS WAY
GREENLANDS
HENDON GOLF COURSE
SATCHELL MEAD
SASSOON
WITHERS MEAD
ORDE
OSPREY
THE WLK.
WAY
PAGE ST.
Hendon High Sch.
PARKLEA CL.
SOUTH GN.
Grahame Park
NIGHTHAWK
THE CONCOURSE
MOORHOUSE
MARTYNSIDE
LONG MEAD
SOUTH MEAD
LYSANDER
MEAD
Sub.
BARNET COPTHALL SPORTS CENTRE
Pavilion
CHADBURY CT.
WALLIAT
GRAHAME PARK
HEMSWELL
JULBECK DR.
DISHFORTH
AVENUE
HEYWOOD
ALCONBURY
DRAYCOT
Hendon Crematorium
HENDON

TOTTERIDGE COMMON
A5109
TOTTERIDGE
TOTTERIDGE VILLAGE
SOUTH HERTS GOLF COURSE
Club House
Brook Farm Open Space
Recreation Ground
Playing Field
Sports Centre
OAKLANDS RD.
20
Hillsborough Cottage
Fairlight Cottage
Redings
Hillsdown
Montebello
Burnhams
Chestnut Cottages
The Warren
Ellern Mede Nursing Home
Copped Hall
Waverley
Windyridge
Lyenells
The Croft
Darland Lake Nature Reserve
Laurel Farm
Woodridge Prim. Sch.
Cricket Ground
Folly Farm
Burtonhole Lane Farm Estate
Sports Ground
Nursery
Burtonhole Farm
Works
Oakfield House
Wentworth Hall
Mill Hill Sub. Sta.
London Equestrian Centre
Frith Manor Ho.
Partingdale Manor
Frith Manor Prim. Sch.
FINCHLEY GOLF COURSE
Watch Tower House
Inglis Barracks
Bittacy Hill Park
Depot
BITTACY BUSINESS CENTRE
Nether Court (Club House)
Mill Hill East
Woodside Park Club
Woodside Park
West Finchley
North London Hospice
Jun. & Inf. Schs.
Hendon Crematorium
HENDON CEMETERY
HENDON GOLF COURSE
CHURCH END
FINCHLEY
Finchley Central
Victoria Rec. Grd.
B552
B1462
A598
DOLLIS ROAD
NETHER ST.
BALLARDS LANE
29
45

31
21
32
46
OAKLEIGH PARK
Totteridge and Whetstone
WHETSTONE
NORTH MIDDLESEX GOLF COURSE
South Barnet
BRUNSWICK PARK
NEW SOUTHGATE CEMETERY
FRIERN BARNET
Friary Park
Bethune Park Recreation Ground
NORTH FINCHLEY
COLNEY HATCH
Coppetts Wood
Glebelands Local Nature Reserve
Fallow Corner
FINCHLEY MEM. HOSP.
Finchley Lido
GREAT NORTH LEISURE PARK
ST. PANCRAS & ISLINGTON CEMETERY
Islington Crematorium
Owen's Centre Playing Field
Swan Lane Open Space
Sports Ground
Glebe Land Open Space
Wingate & Finchley Rugby FC Grd. Football Ground
Cricket & Football Grounds
Compton Sports Cen.
Refuse Destructor
Powerleague Soccer Cen
Esporta Hlth. & Fitness
Curtis Family Centre
Tally Ho Corner
Woodhouse College
David Lloyd Leisure
Cinema
HIGH ROAD A1000
WHETSTONE HIGH ROAD
OAKLEIGH LANE
OAKLEIGH ROAD
RUSSELL ROAD A109
OAKLEIGH ROAD NORTH A109
FRIERN BARNET ROAD B550
FRIERN BARNET ROAD A1003
WOODHOUSE ROAD A1003
COLNEY HATCH LANE B550
NORTH CIRCULAR ROAD A406
PINKHAM WAY
BOBBY MOORE WAY
OSIDGE LANE
BRUNSWICK PARK ROAD
FRIERN BARNET LANE
BALLARDS LANE
FINCHLEY
Barnet Tunnel

32
A
B
C
D
E
22
47
31
1
2
3
4
5
6
7
CHASE
LANE
A111
SIDE
Southgate
SOUTHGATE CIRCUS
THE BOURNE
A111 BOURNE
GROVELANDS PARK
Boating Lake
NORTH LONDON PRIORY HOSPITAL
Pitch & Putt Course
Club Ho.
Sports Grd.
Leisure Cen.
Works
Super-store
SOUTHGATE INDUSTRIAL ESTATE
Osidge Prim. Sch.
WAGGON MEWS
OSIDGE
Weirs
Club
Brunswick Park Prim. Sch.
HAMPDEN
WATERFALL
Pymme's Brook
NEW SOUTHGATE CEMETERY
New Southgate Crematorium
War Mem.
Recreation
Cricket Ground
SOUTHGATE
Ashmole Sch. & Sports Cen.
Southgate Coll.
Tennis Courts
Playing Fields
HIGH STREET
A1004
Southgate Cricket Club Ground
Cemetery
A1003 ROAD
THE GREEN
CANNON HILL
ALDERMANS
A1004 HILL
Palmers Green
THE MALL
Bowling Greens
Tennis Courts
The Avenue
Broomfield Park
Sports Ground
ARNOS PARK
Putting Green
Playground
Arnos Grove
BOWES
A1110
Swim. Pool
WILMER WY.
B1452
POWYS LA.
A406
ROAD
CLOCKHOUSE JUNCTION
Factory
OAKLEIGH RD.
A109
Curtis Family Centre
FRIERN BARNET
STATION RD.
New Southgate
NEW SOUTHGATE
FRIERN BRIDGE RETAIL PARK
Esporta Hlth. & Fitness
Superstore
Depot
TELFORD RD.
BOUNDS
WAY
PINKHAM
Hollickwood Park
MUSWELL HILL
GOLF
COURSE
Bounds Green
BROWNLOW RD.
B106
Bowes Park
GREEN
A109
DURNSFORD
B106
Scout Park
Bowls & Tennis Club
WHITTINGTON
A105
HIGH RD.
Durnsford Spts. Cen.
Club House
ALBERT RD.
Rec. Grd.
Depot
29
530

33
23
34
48
WINCHMORE HILL
Winchmore Hill
PALMERS GREEN
TOTTENHAM
White Hart Lane
GREEN LANES
RIDGE AV.
A105
A10
A111
A406
A1080
B154
GREAT CAMBRIDGE ROAD
NORTH CIRCULAR ROAD
SILVER STREET
STIRLING WAY
HEDGE LANE
HERTFORD ROAD
CHURCH STREET
BURY STREET
FIRS LANE
WHITE HART LANE
LORDSHIP LANE
THE ROUNDWAY
GREAT CAMBRIDGE JUNCTION
Edmonton Cemetery
Firs Farm Playing Fields
Firs Farm Prim. Sch.
The Paulin Ground
Highfield Sch.
Winchmore Sch.
City Amenity Site
Clowes Sports Grd.
Recreation Ground
Playing Field Latymer School
West Lea Sch.
Hazelbury Jun. & Inf. Schs.
Tatem Rec. Grd.
Hollywood Gardens
Aylward Sch.
Bury Lodge Park
Salmon's Brook
Pymme's Brook
New River
THE NORTH MIDDLESEX HOSP.
Wilbury Prim. Sch.
Sports Ground
Playing Fields
Football Ground
Miniature Golf Course
New River Sports Centre
White Hart Lane Sch.
The Selby Cen.
Middlesex University
Garden of Peace
TOTTENHAM CEMETERY
Bruce Castle Park
Bruce Castle & Haringey Mus.
Superstore
F
G
H
J
K
1
2
3
4
5
6
7
31
32
33
44
91
92
93
94

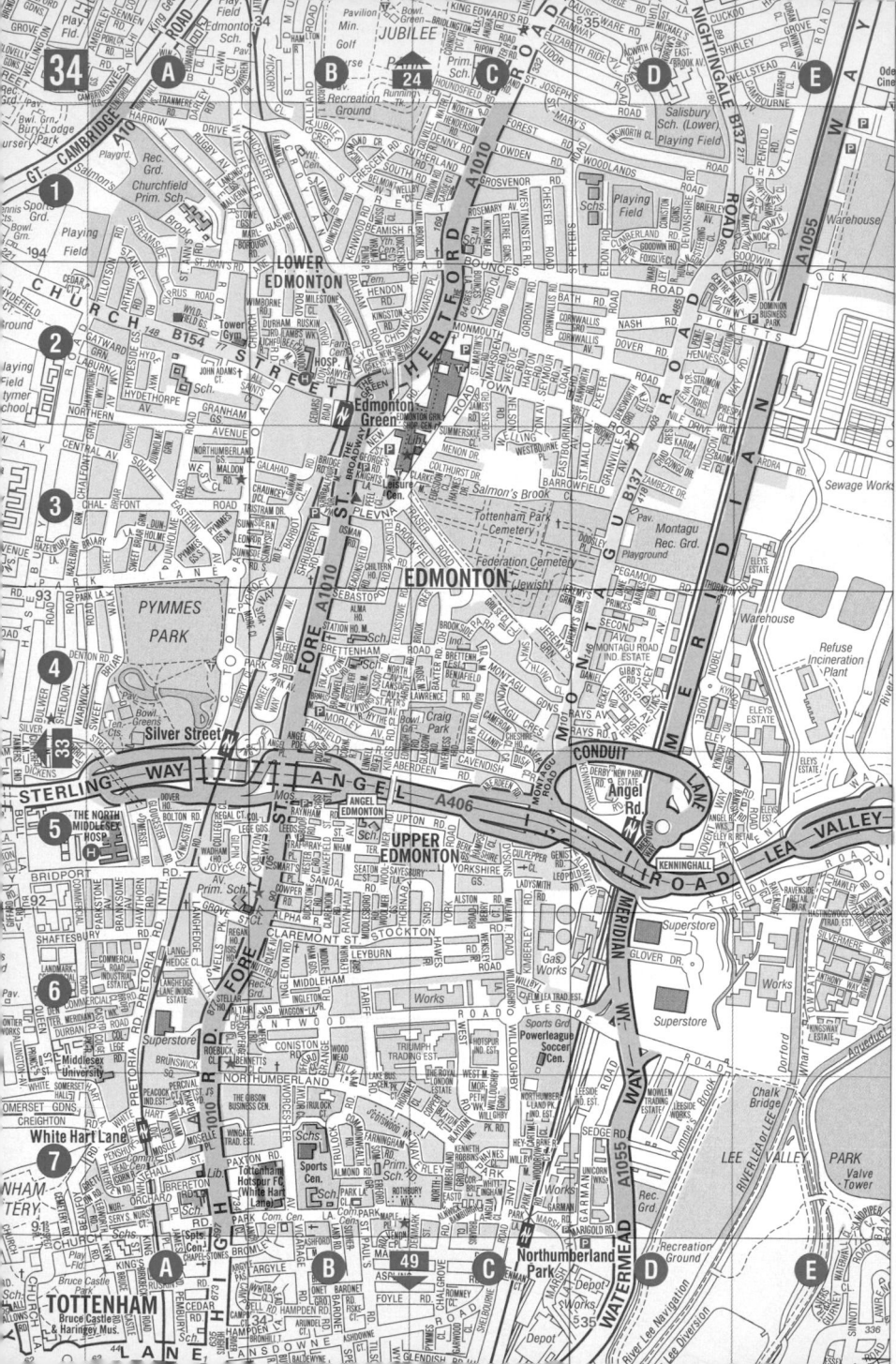

34
A
B
C
D
E
24
JUBILEE
Pavilion
Golf
Recreation Ground
Running Tk.
Edmonton Sch.
GT. CAMBRIDGE
A10
Bury Lodge Park
Rec. Grd.
Churchfield Prim. Sch.
Salmon's Brook
Sports Grd.
Playing Field
1
194
CHURCH
STREET
B154
Tower Gym
LOWER EDMONTON
HERTFORD
ROAD
A1010
Salisbury Sch. (Lower) Playing Field
NIGHTINGALE
B137
FOREST
LOWDEN
WOODLANDS
GROSVENOR RD.
Playing Field
Warehouse
A1055
BOUNCES
2
GATWARD GRN.
HOSP.
Edmonton Green
Edmonton Grn. Shop. Cen.
Leisure Cen.
THE BROADWAY
PICKETTS
LOCK
DOMINION BUSINESS PARK
MERIDIAN WAY
3
Salmon's Brook
Tottenham Park Cemetery
Federation Cemetery (Jewish)
EDMONTON
Montagu Rec. Grd.
Playground
MONTAGU
Sewage Works
ELEYS ESTATE
93
PYMMES PARK
FORE ST.
Warehouse
Refuse Incineration Plant
4
Craig Park
MONTAGU ROAD IND. ESTATE
Silver Street
33
STERLING WAY
ANGEL
A406
CONDUIT LANE
Angel Rd.
ANGEL EDMONTON
5
THE NORTH MIDDLESEX HOSP.
UPPER EDMONTON
KENNINGHALL
ROAD
LEA VALLEY
92
Prim. Sch.
Superstore
Gas Works
GLOVER DR.
6
COMMERCIAL ROAD INDUSTRIAL ESTATE
LANGHEDGE LANE INDUS. ESTATE
Superstore
Works
Superstore
Sports Grd.
Powerleague Soccer Cen.
TRIUMPH TRADING EST.
HOTSPUR IND. EST.
THE ROYAL LONDON ESTATE
Middlesex University
THE GIBSON BUSINESS CEN.
Aqueduct
Chalk Bridge
MOWLEM TRADING ESTATE
White Hart Lane
7
Tottenham Hotspur FC (White Hart Lane)
Sports Cen.
Schs.
Pymme's Brook
LEE VALLEY PARK
Valve Tower
WATERMEAD WAY
A1055
91
Rec. Grd.
Northumberland Park
Recreation Ground
RIVER LEA or LEE
49
Bruce Castle Park
TOTTENHAM
Bruce Castle & Haringey Mus.
HIGH RD.
Depot
Works
River Lee Navigation
Lee Diversion
535
LANE

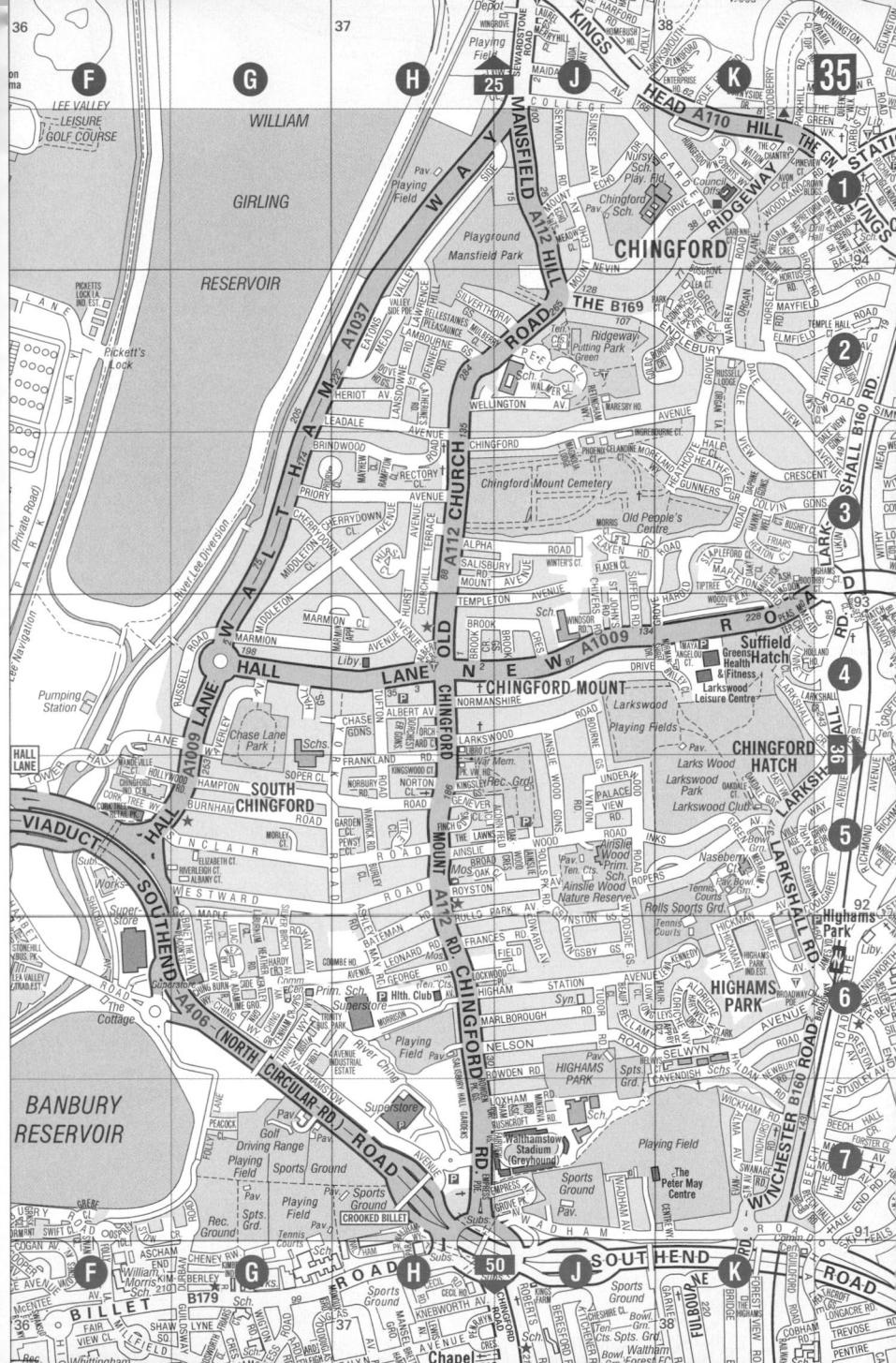

35
36
37
38
F
G
H
J
K
1
2
3
4
5
6
7
25
50
36
WILLIAM
GIRLING
RESERVOIR
LEE VALLEY LEISURE GOLF COURSE
Pickett's Lock
Pumping Station
River Lee Diversion
Lee Navigation
HALL LANE
VIADUCT
BANBURY RESERVOIR
CHINGFORD
SOUTH CHINGFORD
CHINGFORD MOUNT
CHINGFORD HATCH
HIGHAMS PARK
Mansfield Park
Playground
Playing Field
Ridgeway Putting Park Green
Chingford Mount Cemetery
Old People's Centre
Chase Lane Park
Larkswood Playing Fields
Larks Wood
Larkswood Park
Larkswood Club
Larkswood Leisure Centre
Greens Health & Fitness
Suffield Hatch
Ainslie Wood Prim. Sch.
Ainslie Wood Nature Reserve
Rolls Sports Grd.
Walthamstow Stadium (Greyhound)
The Peter May Centre
Golf Driving Range
Sports Ground
CROOKED BILLET
River Ching
WALTHAM WAY
A1037
MANSFIELD HILL
A112
OLD CHURCH RD.
CHINGFORD MOUNT RD.
HALL LANE
NEW ROAD
A1009
THE RIDGEWAY
KINGS HEAD HILL
A110
LARKSHALL RD.
B160
SOUTHEND ROAD
A406 (NORTH CIRCULAR RD.)
BILLET ROAD
B179
B169

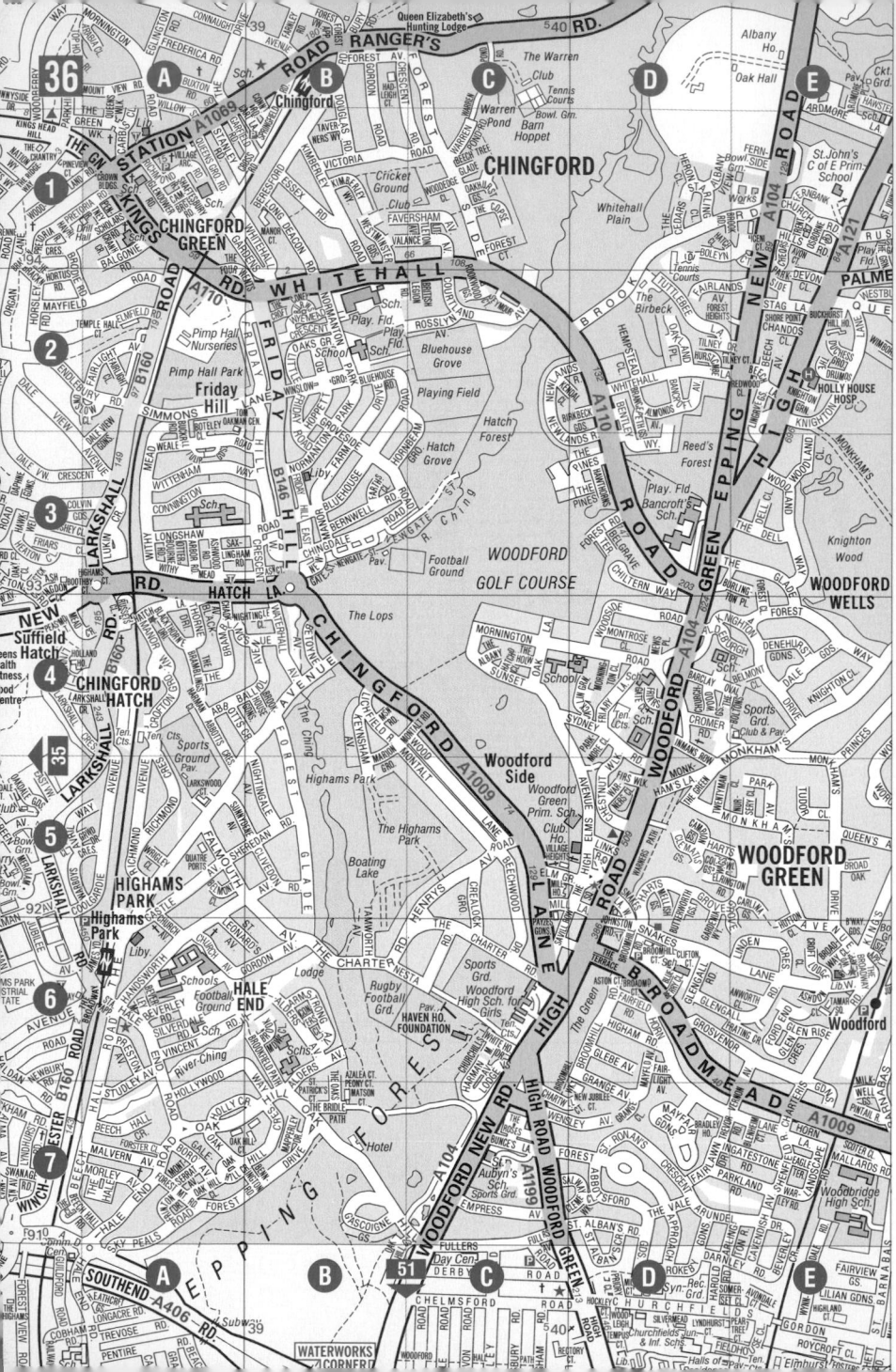

36
A
B
C
D
E
1
2
3
4
5
6
7
35
51
Queen Elizabeth's Hunting Lodge
RANGER'S ROAD
Chingford
STATION ROAD
A1069
CHINGFORD
CHINGFORD GREEN
KINGS HEAD HILL
THE GN
The Warren
Club
Tennis Courts
Bowl. Grn.
Warren Pond
Barn Hoppet
Albany Ho.
Oak Hall
Cricket Ground
Club
Whitehall Plain
WHITEHALL RD.
A110
Pimp Hall Nurseries
Pimp Hall Park
Friday Hill
FRIDAY HILL
B146
Bluehouse Grove
Playing Field
Hatch Forest
Hatch Grove
R. Ching
Football Ground
WOODFORD
GOLF COURSE
The Birbeck
Tennis Courts
Reed's Forest
Bancroft's Sch.
St.John's C of E Prim. School
HOLLY HOUSE HOSP.
NEW ROAD
A104
EPPING
HIGH
A121
Knighton Wood
WOODFORD WELLS
LARKSHALL RD.
B160
NEW RD.
Suffield Hatch
CHINGFORD HATCH
HATCH LA.
CHINGFORD ROAD
A1009
The Lops
The Ching
Highams Park
The Highams Park
Boating Lake
Sports Ground
Woodford Side
Woodford Green Prim. Sch.
WOODFORD GREEN
HIGHAMS PARK
Highams Park
HALE END
Lodge
Rugby Football Grd.
HAVEN HO. FOUNDATION
Sports Grd.
Woodford High Sch. for Girls
River Ching
EPPING FOREST
Hotel
HIGH ROAD WOODFORD GREEN
A1199
WOODFORD NEW RD.
St. Aubyn's Sch.
BROADMEAD ROAD
The Green
Woodford
Woodbridge High Sch.
SOUTHEND RD.
A406
WATERWORKS CORNER
CHELMSFORD ROAD
DERBY ROAD
Day Cen.
Churchfields Jun. & Inf. Schs.
Halls of

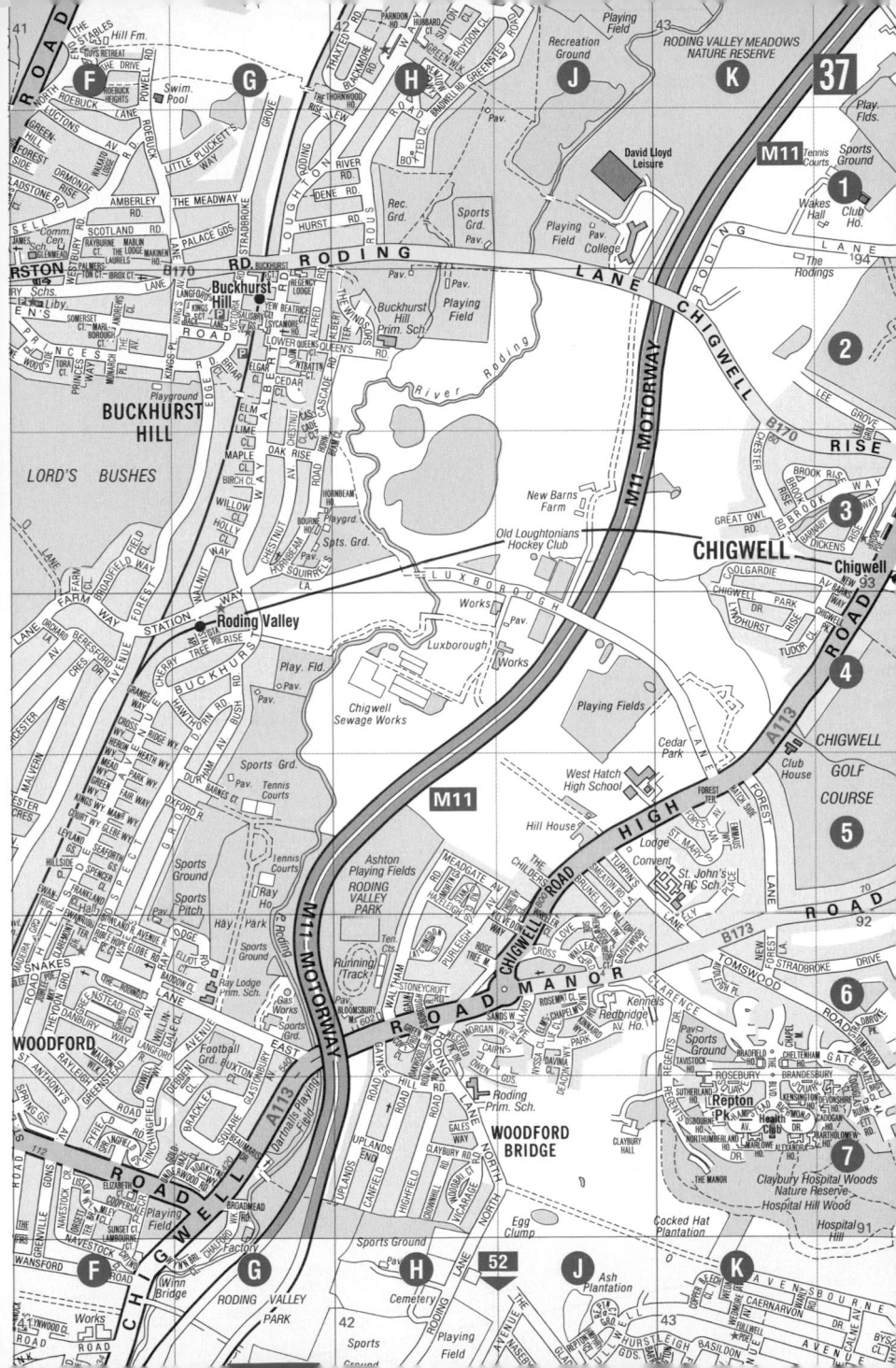
37
41
42
43
F
G
H
J
K
1
2
3
4
5
6
7
52
94
93
92
91
70
Playing Field
Recreation Ground
RODING VALLEY MEADOWS
NATURE RESERVE
Hill Fm.
Swim. Pool
David Lloyd Leisure
M11
Tennis Courts
Sports Ground
Play. Flds.
Wakes Hall
Club Ho.
The Rodings
RODING LANE
CHIGWELL LANE
LEE GROVE
RISE
B170
BROOK RISE
BROOK WAY
GREAT OWL RD.
DICKENS RISE
CHIGWELL
Chigwell
COOLGARDIE AV.
CHIGWELL PARK DR.
LYNDHURST RISE
TUDOR CL.
ROAD
A113
CHIGWELL GOLF COURSE
Club House
HIGH ROAD
West Hatch High School
Cedar Park
Playing Fields
Hill House
Lodge
Convent
St. John's RC Sch.
ROAD
B173
TOMSWOOD ROAD
STRADBROKE DRIVE
CLARENCE AV.
Redbridge Ho.
Kennels
Sports Ground
Repton Pk
Health Club
ROSEBURY SQUARE
BRANDESBURY SQUARE
CLAYBURY HALL
THE MANOR
Claybury Hospital Woods
Nature Reserve
Hospital Hill Wood
Hospital Hill
Cocked Hat Plantation
Egg Clump
Ash Plantation
WOODFORD BRIDGE
Roding Prim. Sch.
MANOR ROAD
CHIGWELL ROAD
M11 MOTORWAY
Ashton Playing Fields
RODING VALLEY PARK
Running Track
Ten. Cts.
Chigwell Sewage Works
Luxborough
Works
LUXBOROUGH LANE
Old Loughtonians Hockey Club
New Barns Farm
River Roding
Buckhurst Hill Prim. Sch.
Playing Field
Pav.
Sports Grd.
Rec. Grd.
College
Playing Field
RODING RD.
B170
Buckhurst Hill
BUCKHURST HILL
LORD'S BUSHES
Playground
QUEEN'S RD.
PRINCES WAY
Roding Valley
STATION WAY
FOREST WAY
FARM WAY
BUCKHURST WAY
Play. Fld.
Sports Grd.
Tennis Courts
Sports Ground
Sports Pitch
Ray Ho.
Ray Park
Ray Lodge Prim. Sch.
Gas Works
Football Grd.
Dartnalls Playing Field
WOODFORD
SNAKES LANE
CHIGWELL ROAD
A113
ROAD
Playing Field
Factory
Winn Bridge
RODING VALLEY PARK
Works
Sports Ground
Cemetery
Playing Field
Sports
AVENUE
CAERNARVON DR.
AVENUE
Liby.
Comm. Cen.
Schs.

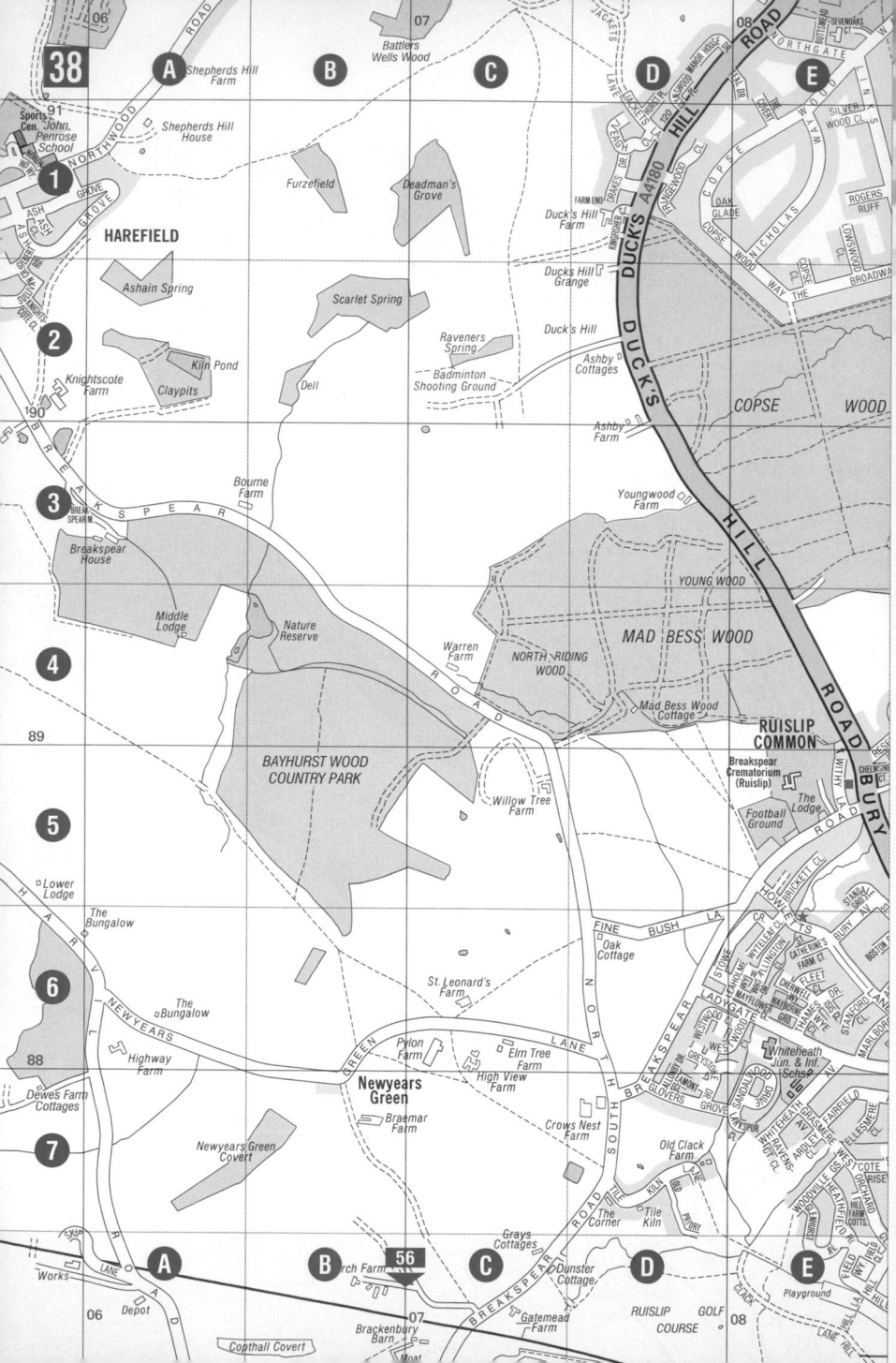
38
56
A
B
C
D
E
1
2
3
4
5
6
7
06
07
08
91
90
89
88
HAREFIELD
Shepherds Hill Farm
Battlers Wells Wood
Shepherds Hill House
Sports Cen.
John Penrose School
NORTHWOOD ROAD
ASH GROVE
ASH CL.
Furzefield
Deadman's Grove
Ashain Spring
Scarlet Spring
Kiln Pond
Claypits
Knightscote Farm
Raveners Spring
Badminton Shooting Ground
Dell
Duck's Hill Farm
Ducks Hill Grange
Duck's Hill
Ashby Cottages
Ashby Farm
DUCK'S HILL ROAD
A4180
COPSE WOOD
NORTHGATE
SEVENOAKS CT.
SILVER WOOD CL.
ROGERS RUFF
OAK GLADE
COPSE WOOD WAY
NICHOLAS
LOWSWOOD CL.
THE BROADWAY
IRVINGEWOOD CL.
DRAKES DR.
FARM END
KINGFISHER
JACKETS LANE
HURST PL.
Bourne Farm
BREAKSPEAR ROAD
Breakspear House
Middle Lodge
Nature Reserve
Youngwood Farm
YOUNG WOOD
MAD BESS WOOD
Warren Farm
NORTH RIDING WOOD
Mad Bess Wood Cottage
RUISLIP COMMON
Breakspear Crematorium (Ruislip)
The Lodge
Football Ground
WITHY LA.
BAYHURST WOOD COUNTRY PARK
Willow Tree Farm
Lower Lodge
The Bungalow
HAREFIELD ROAD
FINE BUSH LA.
Oak Cottage
St. Leonard's Farm
NEWYEARS GREEN LANE
Pylon Farm
Elm Tree Farm
Highway Farm
High View Farm
Newyears Green
Braemar Farm
Dewes Farm Cottages
Crows Nest Farm
Newyears Green Covert
NORTH SOUTH ROAD
BREAKSPEAR ROAD NORTH
Old Clack Farm
TILE KILN LANE
Tile Kiln
The Corner
Grays Cottages
Dunster Cottage
Gatemead Farm
Brackenbury Barn
Copthall Covert
Works
Depot
RUISLIP GOLF COURSE
Playground
HOWLETTS
BRICKETT CL.
LADYGATE
WESTWOOD CL.
Whiteheath Jun. & Inf. Schs.
GLOVERS GROVE
SANDALWOOD DRIVE
WHITEHEATH AV.
GRASMERE AV.
FAIRFIELD
ELLESMERE
ARDLEY CL.
WEST COTE RISE
ORCHARD
WOODVILLE GS.
HEATHFIELD RI.
HILL FARM COTTS.
FIELD WY.
CLACK LANE
HILL LA.

39
NORTHWOOD
NORTHWOOD HILLS
Northwood Hills
HASTE HILL GOLF COURSE
NORTHWOOD GOLF COURSE
RUISLIP LIDO
PARK WOOD
EASTCOTE VILLAGE
EASTCOTE
RUISLIP
Ruislip Manor
PINNER ROAD
RICKMANSWORTH ROAD
JOEL STREET
HIGH ROAD
EASTCOTE B466
40
57
F G H J K
1 2 3 4 5 6 7

40
A
B
C
D
E
1
2
3
4
5
6
7
39
58
11
12
13
91
190
89
88
Pinner Hill Golf Course
Pinnerwood Park
Pinner Green
Hatch End
Rugby Football Ground
Pinner Park
Pinner Park Farm
Uxbridge Road
A404
A410
St. Thomas' Dr.
George V Avenue
Rickmansworth Road
Cuckoo Hill
B466
High Rd.
Eastcote
Eastcote Road
Cuckoo Hill
Montesole Play. Flds.
Little Common
Paine's Br.
Cemetery
Innellan Ho. Sch.
Pinner Village Hall
Pinner Memorial Park
West Lodge Schs.
Superstore
Pinner
PINNER
Reddiford Sch.
Nower Hill
Pinner New Cemetery
Nower Hill High Sch.
Woodlands Open Space
North Harrow
Pinner Village Gardens (Rec. Grd.)
Yeading Brook Open Space
The Croft
Play. Fld.
Cannon Lane First & Mid. Schs.
Heathfield Sch.
Streamside Rec. Grd.
Longfield Schs.
Roxborough Rough
Roxbourne Park
Playground
Rayners Lane
RAYNERS LANE
Alexandra Av.
Imperial
A4090
Rayners La. Junc.
Sports Ground
Cavendish Recreation Ground
Eastcote Ind. Est.
River Pinn
Pinn

41
42
26
59
F
G
H
J
K
1
2
3
4
5
6
7
14
16
91
90
89
88
HARROW WEALD
Harrow Weald Rec. Ground
Hatch End Play. Flds.
Hatch End High Sch.
Cedars Schs.
First & Mid. Sch.
Headstone Lane
Headstone Lane Sports Grd.
Pinner Pk. Schs.
Play Fld.
Bowling Grn.
Tennis Courts
Sports Ground
Open Air Theatre
Headstone Manor
Harrow Museum & Heritage Cen.
Headstone Manor Recreation Ground
Yeading Brook
Salvatorian Coll.
Works
WORKS
The Cliveden Cen.
Waverley Industrial Est.
Tudor Enterprise Park
Harrow Crown Court
Harrow & Wealdstone
WEALDSTONE
Recreation Ground
Harrow Driving Cycling and Road Safety Centre
Harrow Leisure Centre
Belmont First & Mid. Schs.
Civic Centre
Ind. Est.
Phoenix Ind. Est.
Hawthorn Centre
HEADSTONE
Sports Grd.
Mosque
Bowl Alley
Harrow Recreation Ground
Harrow Cemetery
Rec. Grd.
Playgrd
GREENHILL
Superstore
Cin. Gala Bingo
Troy Ind. Est.
Middlesex Ct.
Sports Cen.
St. George's Shop. & Leis. Cen.
St. Ann's Shopping Cen.
Harrow-on-the-Hill
Bus Sta.
Harrow Hill Golf Course
HARROW
The Grove Open Space
Miniature Rifle Range
Playing Fields
Music Sch.
Harrow School Playing Fields
HARROW ON THE HILL
Harrow Sch.
Parad Grd.
Cricket Ground
Ckt. Grd.
Pavilion Lodge
NORTH HARROW
West Harrow
WEST HARROW
Vaughan Schs.
Putting Grn.
Whitmore High Sch.
Whitmore Sports Cen.
Grange Schs
Com. Cen.
Harrovian Bus. Village
A409
A404
A4005
A312
B457
HIGH ROAD
ST. GEORGE GANGE WAY
STATION ROAD
GREENHILL ROAD
LOWLANDS RD.
KENTON RD.
SHEEPCOTE RD.
BESSBOROUGH RD.
LWR. RD.
HIGH ST.
PETERBOROUGH RD.
WATFORD RD.
PINNER RD.
HEADSTONE GS.
HEADSTONE DR.
HEADSTONE LANE
LONG ELMES
COLLEGE AV.
HARROW VIEW
PINNER VIEW
PINNER PARK AV.
PARKFIELD AV.
CARMELITE AV.
WHITMORE RD.
RIDGEWAY
VAUGHAN RD.
COLLEGE ROAD
HINDES RD.
WELLESLEY RD.
MARLBOROUGH HILL
CANTERBURY RD.
CUMBERLAND RD.
KINGSFIELD AV.
KINGSWAY
PARKSIDE WAY
DURHAM RD.
SUSSEX RD.
ELMGROVE RD.
BONNERSFIELD LA.
NORTHWICK PK. RD.
GAYTON RD.
MANOR RD.
PALMERSTON RD.
MASONS AV.
CHRISTCHURCH AVENUE
BELMONT RD.
GRANT ROAD
LOCKET RD.
CHURCH AV.
MOUNTSIDE

42
27
41
60
A
B
C
D
E
1
2
3
4
5
6
7
16
17
18
STANMORE GOLF COURSE
Canons Park
WHITCHURCH
B461
Whitchurch First & Mid. Schs.
Sports Ground
Bowling Green
Stanburn Schs.
Offices
Works
Little Stanmore First
Prince Edward Playing Field
HONEYPOT LANE
A4140
BELMONT
Belmont First & Mid. Schs.
Kenton Lane Farm
Play. Field Schs.
Priestmead Rec. Grd.
Centenary Park
Park High Sch.
Pitch & Putt
Putting Green
Sports Ground
WEALDSTONE
Byron Recreation Ground
Cemetery
Harrow Driving, Cycling and Road Safety Centre
Harrow Leisure Centre
Schs. Comm. Cen.
Glebe Schs.
Liby.
Hall
Elmgrove First & Middle Schools
Kenton Recreation Ground
KENTON
Bowling Green
Tennis Courts
Ind. Est.
Hindu Tem.
Hospice
KENTON ROAD
A4006
Wealdstone Brook
WOODCOCK PARK
School
Play. Fld.
Super-store
Kenton
Sports Cen.
Mt. Stewart Jun. & Inf. Sch.
University of Westminster (Harrow Campus)
Univ. of Westminster Sports Centre
Northwick Park
NORTHWICK PARK HOSPITAL
ST. MARK'S HOSP.
HARROW HILL GOLF COURSE
HARROW
WATFORD ROAD
A404
John Billam Playing Fields
Sports Grd.
PRESTON
Preston Road
Playing Fields
NORTHWICK PARK
Harrow School Playing Fields
Rugby Football Grounds
Playground
KENTON RD.
SHEEPCOTE RD.

43
F
G
H
J
K
1
2
3
4
5
6
7
19
20
21
88
89
28
44
61
BURNT OAK
EDGWARE COMM. HOSP.
Edgware Football Grd.
Watling
WATLING
Tennis Courts PARK
LITTLE STANMORE
Chandos Recreation Grd.
Stanmore & Mid. School
Sports Ground
Burnt Oak
Canons High Sch.
School
QUEENSBURY
Queensbury
Depot
Mecca Burnt Oak
EUROPEAN BUSINESS CENTRE
COLINDALE BUSINESS PARK
Montrose Recreation Ground
COLINDALE HOSPITAL
Colindale
COLINDALE
Superstore
ORIENTAL CITY
Sikh Tem.
Roe Green
Spts. Grd.
Works
Eton Grove Open Space
Queensbury Park
Rec. Grd.
KINGSBURY COMM. HOSP.
Schools
Kingsbury High Sch.
Roe Grn. Jun. & Inf. Sch.
Play. Fld.
Kingsbury Manor
Roe Green Park
Kingsbury Manor Studio
Playground
Buddhist Cen.
Kingsbury
TA Centre
Sports Ground
Recreation Ground
Kingsbury Grn. Prim. Sch.
St. Robert Southwell Sch.
JFS School
Kingsbury Green
Rec. Grd.
Silver Jubilee Park
Kingsbury Town FC Grd.
KINGSBURY
FRYENT COUNTRY PARK
Barn Hill Open Space
Barn Hill
Field Study Centre
Woodfield Sch.
Welsh Harp
BROADWAY
EDGWARE
A5
A4140
A4006
KINGSBURY ROAD
FRYENT WAY
B454
CHURCH LANE

44
A
B
C
D
E
1
2
3
4
5
6
7
29
43
62
Grahame Park
THE CONCOURSE
GRAHAME PARK ESTATE
Colindale
COLINDALE
COLINDALE HOSPITAL
Montrose Recreation Ground
Colindale Park
Newspaper Library
COLINDEEP LANE
EDGWARE ROAD
Superstore
THE HYDE
WATLING AV.
KINGSBURY RD.
A4006
A5
A5150
M1
M1 MOTORWAY
WATFORD WAY
A1
A41
A504
A502
A406 NORTH CIRCULAR
Junction 2
FIVEWAYS CORNER
Junc. 1
GREAT NORTH WAY
(BARNET BY-PASS)
Hasmonean High Sch.
BARNET COPTHALL SPORTS CENTRE
Barnet Copthall Stadium
Copthall Swimming Pool
Rugby Club
Powerleague Soccer Cen.
Chase Lodge Playing Fields
HENDON GOLF COURSE
SUNNY HILL PARK
RAF Museum Hendon
Battle of Britain Hall
Peel Centre (Metropolitan Police Training Establishment)
Sports Ground
Rushgrove Park
Barnet Coll.
High Sch.
THE GARDEN BMI HOSP
St. Mary's C of E High Sch.
The Burroughs Club
Middlesex University
HENDON
Hendon Central
QUEENS ROAD
B551
B552
PARSON STREET
BRENT ST.
FINCHLEY
CHURCH RD.
THE BURROUGHS
HENDON PARK
Hendon
STATION ROAD
Malcolm Park
BROADWAY
WEST HENDON
WEST HENDON PLAYING FIELDS
Silver Jubilee Park
Kingsbury Town FC Grd.
Cool Oak Bridge
COOL OAK LANE
Youth Sailing Base
York Park
BRENT RESERVOIR
Welsh Harp Nature Reserve
WOODFIELD PARK
Rifle Range
BRENT CROSS INTERCHANGE
BRENT CROSS SHOPPING CENTRE
Brent Cross
STAPLES CORNER
CLAREMONT WAY INDUSTRIAL ESTATE
GARRICK INDUSTRIAL ESTATE
JVC BUSINESS PARK
LONDON GROUP BUS. PK.
21
22
23
88
89
90
91

FINCHLEY
CHURCH END
Finchley Central
Holders Hill
HENDON CEMETERY
Hendon Crematorium
HENDON GOLF COURSE
Windsor Open Space
College Farm
Avenue House Grounds
Sports Ground
St. Marylebone Crematorium
ST. MARYLEBONE CEMETERY
Christ's College
HENLYS CORNER
Temple Fortune
Princes Park
Big Wood
Little Wood
Willifred Green
Jewish Cemetery
Golders Green Crematorium
GOLDERS GREEN
Golders Green
Brent Cross
BRENT CROSS FLY-OVER
HAMPSTEAD HEATH
Bunkers Hill
Victoria Rec. Grd.
Pentland Centre
Superstores
Sports Cen.
Clitterhouse Recreation
NORTH CIRCULAR ROAD
A406
A504
A598
A1
A41
A502
A598
B552
B1462
REGENTS PARK ROAD
FINCHLEY ROAD
HENDON LANE
HENDON WAY
BALLARDS LANE
EAST END ROAD
FALLODEN WAY
GOLDERS GREEN RD.
NORTH END RD.
DOLLIS ROAD
NETHER ST.
HOLDERS HILL ROAD
A1 WAY
F
G
H
J
K
1
2
3
4
5
6
7
24
25
26
30
46
63

46
26
27
28
A
B
C
D
E
1
2
3
4
5
6
7
31
45
64
FINCHLEY
Fallow Corner
FINCHLEY MEM. HOSP.
Finchley Lido
Glebe Open Space
Powerleague Soccer Cen.
FC Grd. Football Ground
Cricket & Football Grounds
NORTH CIRCULAR ROAD
A406
BOBBY MOORE WAY
COLNEY HATCH LANE
HIGH RD. NTH. FINCHLEY
A1000
HIGH ROAD
EAST FINCHLEY
EAST END ROAD
A504
FORTIS GREEN
FORTIS GREEN ROAD
Islington Crematorium
ST. PANCRAS & ISLINGTON CEM.
Muswell Hill Spts. Grd.
COLDFALL WOOD
Coldfall Prim. Sch.
Recreation Ground
Martin Jun. & Inf. School
Fortismere Sch.
Our Lady of Muswell RC Prim. Sch.
ST. MARYLEBONE CEMETERY
St. Marylebone Crem.
Oak Lodge Sch.
ABBOTS GARDENS
East Finchley
Cherry Tree Wood
FORTIS GREEN
ST. LUKE'S WOODSIDE HOSP.
HIGHGATE WOOD
Sports Ground
Stormont Lawn Tennis & Squash Club
St. James CE Prim. Sch.
LYTTELTON ROAD
A1
AYLMER ROAD
GREAT NORTH RD.
ARCHWAY ROAD
HAMPSTEAD GARDEN SUBURB
Playing Fields
HIGHGATE GOLF COURSE
Club House
HIGHGATE
HIGHGATE HOSPITAL
NORTH HILL
B519
Mallinson Sports Centre
Highgate School Playing Field
HAMPSTEAD GOLF COURSE
Bunkers Hill
HAMPSTEAD HEATH
Turners Wood
HAMPSTEAD LANE
North Wood
Kenwood House
Ken Wood Towers Farm
The Spaniards
SOUTHWOOD LANE
B550
MUSWELL HILL
HIGHGATE
Open Air Stage
Bowling Green

47
32
48
65
29
30
31
F
G
H
J
K
1
2
3
4
5
6
7
MUSWELL HILL GOLF COURSE
Club House
Durnsford Spts. Cen.
Rec. Grd.
Tennis Courts
Pool
DURNSFORD RD.
ALBERT RD.
BIDWELL
CRESCENT RISE
CLIFTON RD.
VICTORIA ROAD
ALEXANDRA PARK RD.
B106
ALEXANDRA PARK ROAD
PALACE GATES RD.
Alexandra Palace
WOOD GREEN
BOUNDS GREEN RD.
A109
A105
HIGH ROAD
Civic Cen.
Wood Green
Nightingale Gdns.
Avenue Gds.
STATION RD.
MAYES RD.
Wood Gn. Common
Middlesex Univ. (Quicksilver Pl. Campus)
Reservoir
Filter Beds
Gas Works
OLYMPIA IND. EST.
SHOPPING CITY
PARK RD.
HORNSEY PARK RD.
B138
The Lake
Ice Rink
Alexandra Palace
Miniature Golf Course
ALEXANDRA PARK
Cricket Ground
Playing Field
Playing Field
MUSWELL HILL
The Grove
Muswell Hill Prim. Sch.
MUSWELL HILL
MUSWELL HILL BROADWAY
A504
PRIORY RD.
HIGH STREET
A504
TURNPIKE LA.
Hornsey
HORNSEY
PRIORY PARK
Academy
CHURCH LA.
TOTTENHAM LA.
A103
A1201
PARK ROAD
Cranley Gardens
CRANLEY GARDENS
Cricket Ground
QUEEN'S WOOD
B550
Play. Flds.
Sports Cen.
Swim. Pool
Ckt. Grd.
The Hornsey Club
Sports Gd.
Shepherd's Hill Gds.
Stationers Park
HORNSEY VALE
Town Hall
THE BROADWAY
TOTTENHAM LA.
Highgate
SHEPHERD'S HILL
Sports Field
CROUCH END
Play. Fd.
Parkland Walk
CROUCH END HILL
CROUCH HILL
A1201
Crouch Hill Rec. Cen.
Reservoirs (covered)
STROUD GREEN
Crouch Hill
HORNSEY LANE
HORNSEY RISE
HORNSEY ROAD
B540
A1
ARCHWAY RD.
HIGH ST.
HIGHGATE HILL
Lauderdale House
Tennis Courts
WATERLOW
STROUD GRN. RD.

48
TOTTENHAM
TOTTENHAM CEMETERY
White Ha
WOOD GREEN
Wood Green
NOEL PARK
LORDSHIP RECREATION GROUND
Playing Field
Open Air Theatre
The Moselle
BROADWATER FARM ESTATE
Belmont Rec. Grd.
DOWNHILLS PARK
WEST GREEN
Park View Academy Spts. Cen.
HORNSEY
Hornsey
Turnpike La.
HARRINGAY
Harringay
Harringay Green Lanes
Chestnuts Rec. Ground
ST. ANN'S HOSPITAL
SOUTH TOTTENHAM
Stamford Hill
STROUD GREEN
FINSBURY PARK
Sports Arena
Manor House
MANOR HO.
EAST RESERVOIR
WEST RESERVOIR
Sir Thomas Abney Prim. Sch.
Stationers Park
Railway Flds. Nature Pk.
Cricket Ground
American Gds.
Reservoir (covered)
Bruce Castle
Bruce Castle & Haringey Mus.
Garden of Peace
LORDSHIP LANE
A109
THE ROUNDWAY
A10
A1080
WESTBURY AVENUE
DOWNHILLS WAY
B155
WEST GREEN ROAD
A504
PHILIP LANE
WIGHTMAN ROAD
GREEN LANES
GRAND PARADE
A105
ST. ANN'S ROAD
B152
SEVEN SISTERS ROAD
A503
AMHURST
A107
B138
B150
B153
33
47
66
A B C D E
1 2 3 4 5 6 7

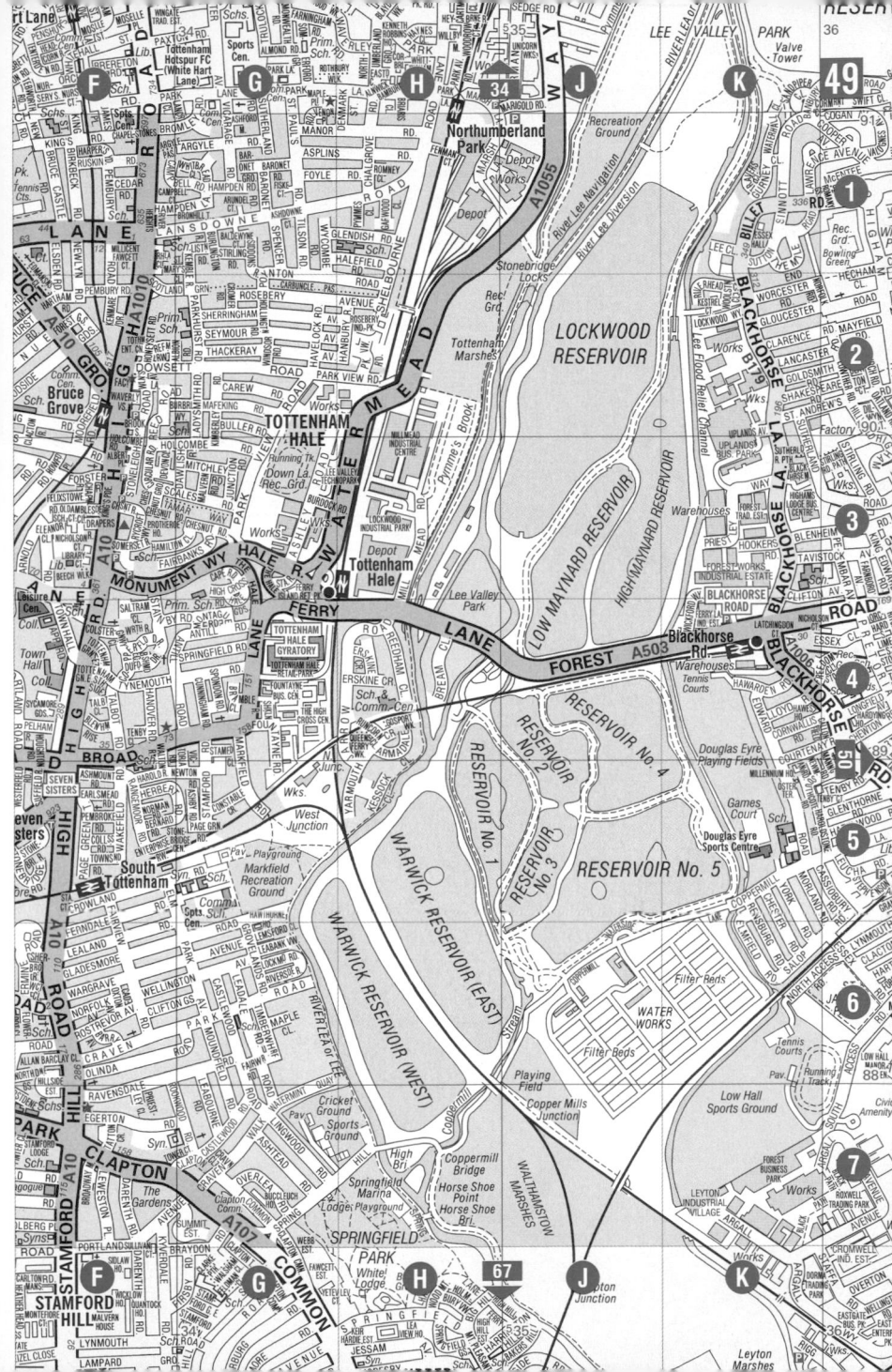

36
49
50
34
67
F
G
H
J
K
1
2
3
4
5
6
7
LEE VALLEY PARK
Valve Tower
Northumberland Park
Recreation Ground
Depot
Works
River Lee Navigation
River Lee Diversion
Stonebridge Locks
Rec. Grd.
Tottenham Marshes
LOCKWOOD RESERVOIR
Lee Flood Relief Channel
LOW MAYNARD RESERVOIR
HIGH MAYNARD RESERVOIR
Pymme's Brook
MILLMEAD INDUSTRIAL CENTRE
LOCKWOOD INDUSTRIAL PARK
Tottenham Hale
TOTTENHAM HALE
TOTTENHAM HALE GYRATORY
TOTTENHAM HALE RETAIL PARK
Lee Valley Park
FERRY LANE
FOREST ROAD
A503
Blackhorse Rd.
BLACKHORSE LANE
BLACKHORSE ROAD
B179
A1006
A1055
WATERMEAD WAY
MONUMENT WY
HALE RD.
HIGH RD.
A10
A1010
BROAD LANE
Bruce Grove
Seven Sisters
South Tottenham
Tottenham Hotspur FC (White Hart Lane)
Sports Cen.
Leisure Cen.
Town Hall
Warehouses
Tennis Courts
FOREST WORKS INDUSTRIAL ESTATE
UPLANDS BUS. PARK
HIGHAMS LODGE BUS. CENTRE
Douglas Eyre Playing Fields
Games Court
Douglas Eyre Sports Centre
RESERVOIR No. 1
RESERVOIR No. 2
RESERVOIR No. 3
RESERVOIR No. 4
RESERVOIR No. 5
WARWICK RESERVOIR (EAST)
WARWICK RESERVOIR (WEST)
West Junction
Markfield Recreation Ground
Playground
Filter Beds
WATER WORKS
Low Hall Sports Ground
Running Track
Playing Field
Copper Mills Junction
Coppermill Bridge
Horse Shoe Point
Horse Shoe Bri.
WALTHAMSTOW MARSHES
Cricket Ground
Sports Ground
Springfield Marina
SPRINGFIELD PARK
White Lodge
High Bri.
FOREST BUSINESS PARK
LEYTON INDUSTRIAL VILLAGE
ROXWELL TRADING PARK
Clapton Junction
Leyton Marshes
STAMFORD HILL
STAMFORD HILL
CLAPTON COMMON
A107
The Gardens
Civic Amenity Site

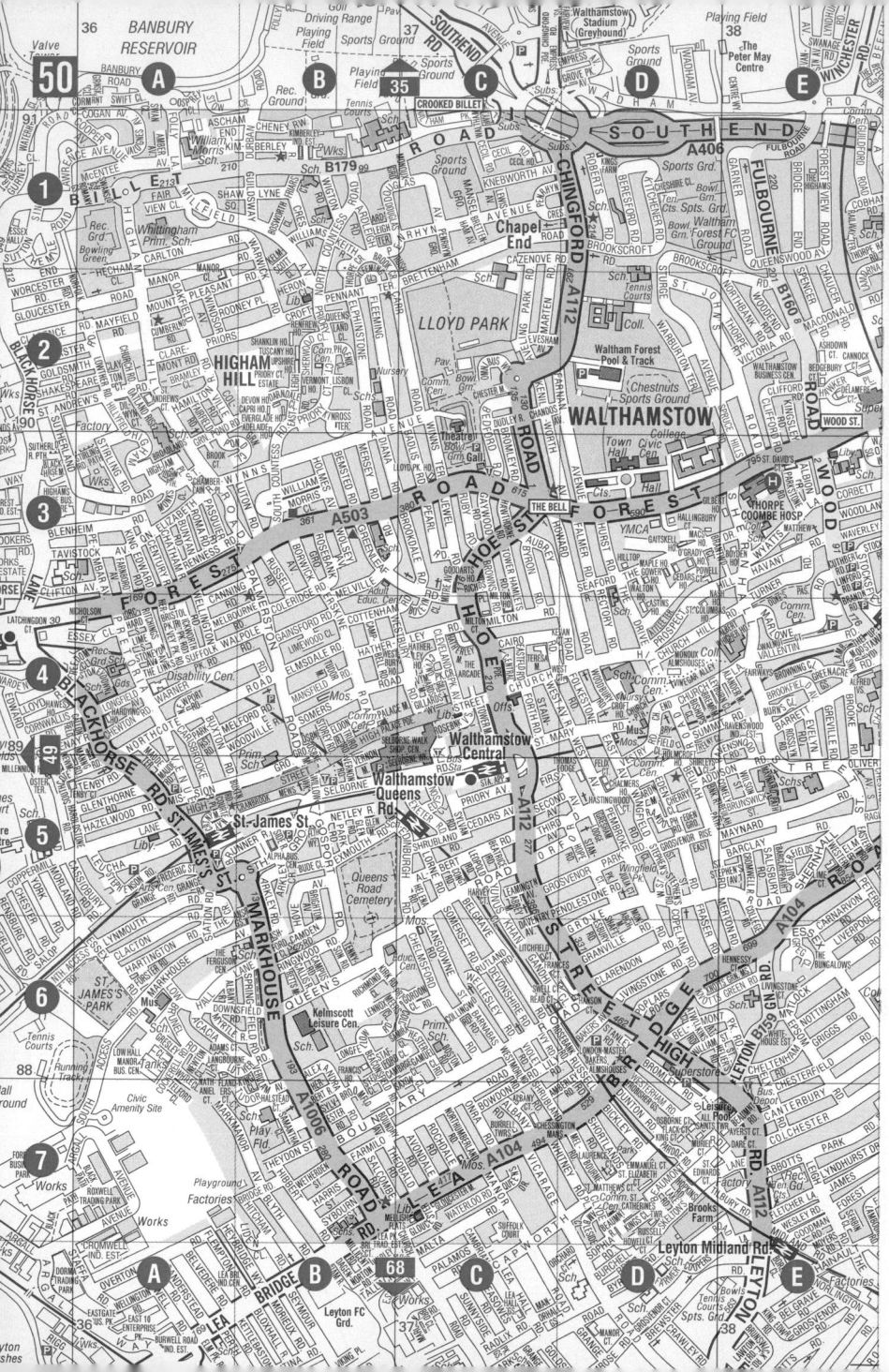

50
BANBURY RESERVOIR
Valve Tower
36
37
38
A
B
C
D
E
1
2
3
4
5
6
7
35
68
49
Golf Driving Range
Playing Field
Sports Ground
SOUTHEND RD.
Walthamstow Stadium (Greyhound)
Playing Field
The Peter May Centre
WINCHESTER
Rec. Ground
Tennis Courts
CROOKED BILLET
SOUTHEND
A406
BILLET ROAD
B179
William Morris Sch.
HIGHAM HILL
Whittingham Prim. Sch.
Sports Ground
Chapel End
CHINGFORD ROAD
A112
Sports Grd.
Bowl. Grn.
Ten. Cts.
Spts. Grd.
Waltham Forest FC Ground
FULBOURNE ROAD
B160
LLOYD PARK
Waltham Forest Pool & Track
Chestnuts Sports Ground
WALTHAMSTOW
Town Hall
Civic Cen.
College
WOOD ST.
THE BELL
FOREST ROAD
A503
THORPE COOMBE HOSP.
YMCA
HOE ST.
BLACKHORSE LANE
BLACKHORSE RD.
Disability Cen.
Walthamstow Central
Walthamstow Queens Rd.
St. James St
ST. JAMES'S ST.
HIGH STREET
SELBORNE WALK SHOP. CEN.
Queens Road Cemetery
MARKHOUSE ROAD
A1006
ST. JAMES'S PARK
Kelmscott Leisure Cen.
Tennis Courts
Running Track
Civic Amenity Site
A112
HOE STREET
BRIDGE
HIGH
A104
LEA BRIDGE ROAD
Superstore
Leisure Pool
Bus Depot
LEYTON RD.
Playground
Factories
Works
ROXWELL TRADING PARK
CROMWELL IND. EST.
Brooks Farm
Leyton Midland Rd.
LEYTON
Leyton FC Grd.
Sch.
Tennis Courts
Spts. Grd.
Factories

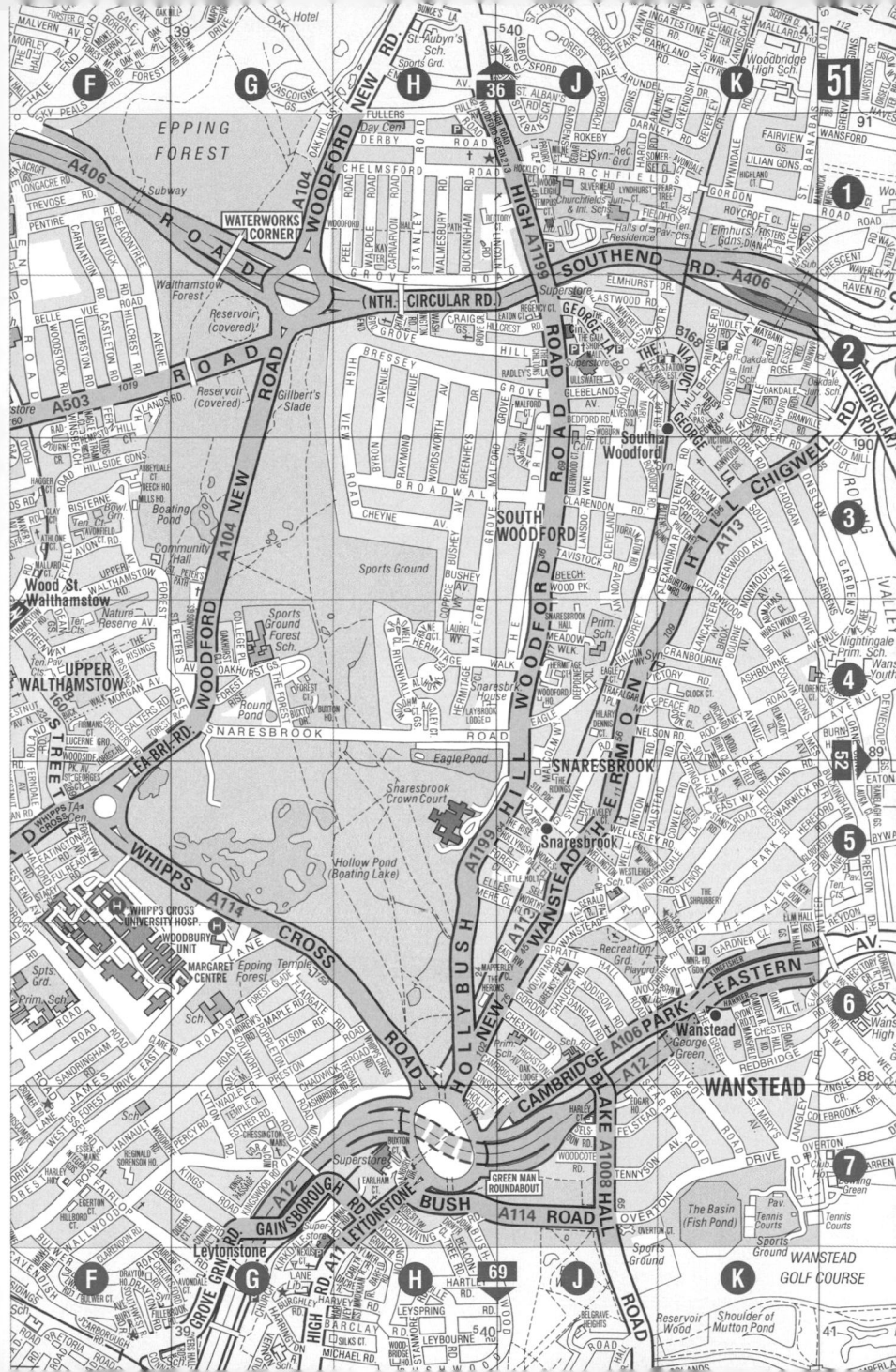

51
36
52
69
F
G
H
J
K
1
2
3
4
5
6
7
EPPING FOREST
A406
ROAD
WATERWORKS CORNER
Walthamstow Forest
Reservoir (covered)
Reservoir (Covered)
A503
ROAD
Gilbert's Slade
NEW ROAD
A104
WOODFORD NEW ROAD
A104 NEW ROAD
WOODFORD
Boating Pond
Community Hall
Wood St. Walthamstow
UPPER WALTHAMSTOW
Nature Reserve AV.
Sports Ground Forest Sch.
Round Pond
SNARESBROOK ROAD
Eagle Pond
Snaresbrook Crown Court
Hollow Pond (Boating Lake)
LEA-BRI. RD.
WHIPPS CROSS
WHIPPS A114 CROSS ROAD
WHIPPS CROSS UNIVERSITY HOSP.
WOODBURY UNIT
MARGARET CENTRE
Epping Forest
Temple
Sports Ground
SOUTH WOODFORD
South Woodford
HIGH A1199
WOODFORD ROAD
SOUTHEND RD. A406
(NTH. CIRCULAR RD.)
N. CIRCULAR RD.
Superstore
GEORGE LA.
B168
CHIGWELL HILL A113
Churchfields Jun. & Inf. Schs.
Halls of Residence
Elmhurst Gdns.
Oakdale Inf. Sch.
Oakdale Jun. Sch.
Woodbridge High Sch.
St. Aubyn's Sch.
Sports Grd.
Hotel
CHURCHFIELDS
SNARESBROOK
Snaresbrook
Snaresbrk. House
HOLLYBUSH HILL
A1199
WANSTEAD HIGH ST.
HERMON HILL
A113
Nightingale Prim. Sch.
Recreation Grd.
CAMBRIDGE PARK A106
EASTERN AV.
A12
Wanstead
George Green
WANSTEAD
GREEN MAN ROUNDABOUT
BUSH A114 ROAD
BLAKE HALL ROAD A1008
The Basin (Fish Pond)
Tennis Courts
Sports Ground
WANSTEAD GOLF COURSE
Reservoir Wood
Shoulder of Mutton Pond
Leytonstone
GAINSBOROUGH RD.
HIGH RD. A11 LEYTONSTONE
A12
Superstore
JAMES LANE
WEST ESSEX FOREST DRIVE EAST
GROVE GRN. RD.
Bowling Green

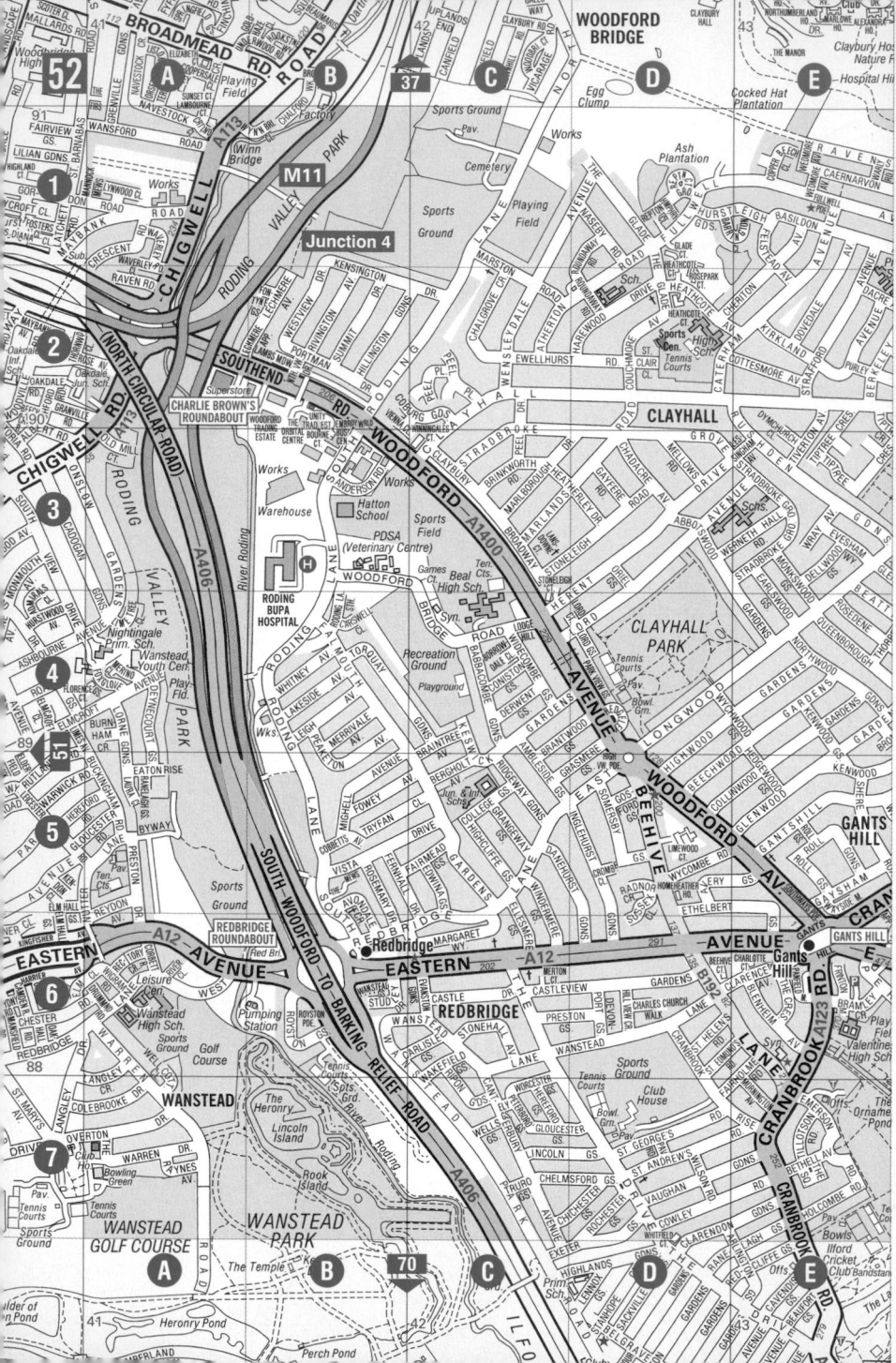

52
37
70
51
A
B
C
D
E
1
2
3
4
5
6
7
41
42
43
91
90
89
88
BROADMEAD RD.
ROAD
WOODFORD BRIDGE
Egg Clump
Cocked Hat Plantation
Hospital Hill
Claybury Hospital Nature Reserve
THE MANOR
Playing Field
Factory
Sports Ground
Pav.
Works
Ash Plantation
Cemetery
Winn Bridge
M11
Junction 4
CHIGWELL
RODING VALLEY PARK
A113
FAIRVIEW GS.
LILIAN GDNS.
WANSFORD ROAD
NAVESTOCK CR.
MAYBANK
CRESCENT
WAVERLEY RD.
RAVEN RD.
KENSINGTON DR.
WESTVIEW DR.
RIVINGTON AV.
SUMMIT DR.
HILLINGTON GDNS.
PORTMAN DR.
MARSTON
CHALGROVE CR.
WENSLEYDALE AV.
ATHERTON RD.
HAREWOOD DR.
ROUNDAWAY RD.
NASEBY RD.
THE GLADE
FULLWELL AV.
HURSTLEIGH GDNS.
HEATHCOTE
Sports Cen.
High Sch.
Tennis Courts
ST. CLAIR CL.
EWELLHURST RD.
COUCHMORE AV.
CATERHAM AV.
CHERITON
COTTESMORE AV.
KIRKLAND
DOVEDALE
DACRE
STRAFFORD
PURLEY
BERKELEY
BASILDON
FELSTEAD AV.
CAERNARVON
RAVENSBOURNE
SOUTHEND RD.
Superstore
CHARLIE BROWN'S ROUNDABOUT
WOODFORD TRADING ESTATE
THE ORBITAL CENTRE
(NORTH CIRCULAR ROAD)
CHIGWELL RD.
OAKDALE
Oakdale Inf. Sch.
Oakdale Jun. Sch.
GRANVILLE RD.
CLAYHALL AV.
CLAYHALL
STRADBROKE GROVE
PEEL DR.
BRINKWORTH RD.
MARLBOROUGH
HEATHERLEY DR.
MARLANDS
GAYFERE RD.
CHADACRE AV.
MELLOWS RD.
ABBOTSWOOD
DRIVE
RUSHDEN
TIVERTON AV.
TIPTREE
WERNETH HALL RD.
EVESHAM
WRAY AV.
DELLWOOD
MONKSWOOD
EARLSWOOD
GARDENS
WOODFORD
A1400
BROADWAY
STONELEIGH
CLAYBURY
Works
Warehouse
Hatton School
Sports Field
PDSA (Veterinary Centre)
Beal High Sch.
RODING BUPA HOSPITAL
River Roding
A406
RODING
VALLEY
ONSLOW
CADOGAN
Nightingale Prim. Sch.
Wanstead Youth Cen.
Play. Fld.
PARK
ASHBOURNE
HURSTWOOD
BURNHAM CR.
LORNE GDNS.
DEYNECOURT
EATON RISE
BYWAY
BUCKINGHAM
WARWICK RD.
GLOUCESTER RD.
HEREFORD
PRESTON
REYDON AV.
Recreation Ground
Playground
TORQUAY
WHITNEY
LAKESIDE AV.
MERRIVALE AV.
PEAKETON AV.
BRAINTREE
FOWEY AV.
TRYFAN CL.
DRIVE
VISTA
ROSEMARY DR.
FERNHALL DR.
FAIRMEAD
EDWINA GS.
GARDENS
BERGHOLT
Jun. & Inf. Schs.
RIDGEWAY GDNS.
COLLEGE GS.
GRANGEWAY
HIGHCLIFFE GS.
ELLESMERE GS.
WINDERMERE
DANEHURST
INGLEHURST GDNS.
SOMERSBY
AMBLESIDE
GRASMERE
BRANTWOOD
CONISTON
DERWENT
CLAYHALL PARK
Tennis Courts
Pav.
Bowl. Grn.
LONGWOOD GARDENS
AVENUE
HIGH VW. PDE.
BEEHIVE LANE
WOODFORD AV.
HIGHWOOD
BEECHWOOD
HEDGEWOOD
COLLINWOOD
GLENWOOD
GANTSHILL
GANTS HILL
ROLL GDNS.
GAYSHAM
NORTHWOOD
KENWOOD
QUEENBOROUGH
ROSEDENE
LIMEWOOD CT.
WYCOMBE RD.
ETHELBERT
SOUTH REDBRIDGE
MARGARET WY.
Redbridge
EASTERN AVENUE
A12
REDBRIDGE ROUNDABOUT
Red Bri.
Sports Ground
SOUTH WOODFORD TO BARKING RELIEF ROAD
Leisure Cen.
Wanstead High Sch.
Sports Ground
Golf Course
Pumping Station
CASTLE DR.
REDBRIDGE
CASTLEVIEW
MERTON CT.
PRESTON GS.
CHARLES CHURCH WALK
GARDENS
CLARENCE AV.
BLENHEIM
Gants Hill
B192
A123
CRANBROOK RD.
CRANBROOK
LANE
WANSTEAD LANE
STONEHALL AV.
CARLISLE GS.
WAKEFIELD GS.
Sports Ground
Club House
Tennis Courts
Bowl. Grn.
Pav.
ST. GEORGE'S RD.
GLOUCESTER
LINCOLN GS.
CHELMSFORD GS.
CHICHESTER GS.
ROCHESTER GS.
VAUGHAN
ST. ANDREW'S
WILSON RD.
COWLEY
CLARENDON
EXETER
HIGHLANDS
LENNOX
Prim. Sch.
SACKVILLE GDNS.
STANHOPE
BELGRAVE
HOLCOMBE RD.
BETHELL AV.
TILLOTSON RD.
EMERSON
Ilford Cricket Club
Bowls
Bandstand
Valentines High Sch.
The Ornamental Pond
Offs.
WANSTEAD
WANSTEAD GOLF COURSE
WANSTEAD PARK
The Temple
The Heronry
Lincoln Island
River Roding
Rook Island
Heronry Pond
Perch Pond
WARREN DR.
LANGLEY
COLEBROOKE DR.
OVERTON DRIVE
Club Ho.
Bowling Green
Tennis Courts
Sports Ground
RAYNES AV.
ST. MARY'S AV.
REDBRIDGE
CHESTER
EASTERN
WEST
ILFORD

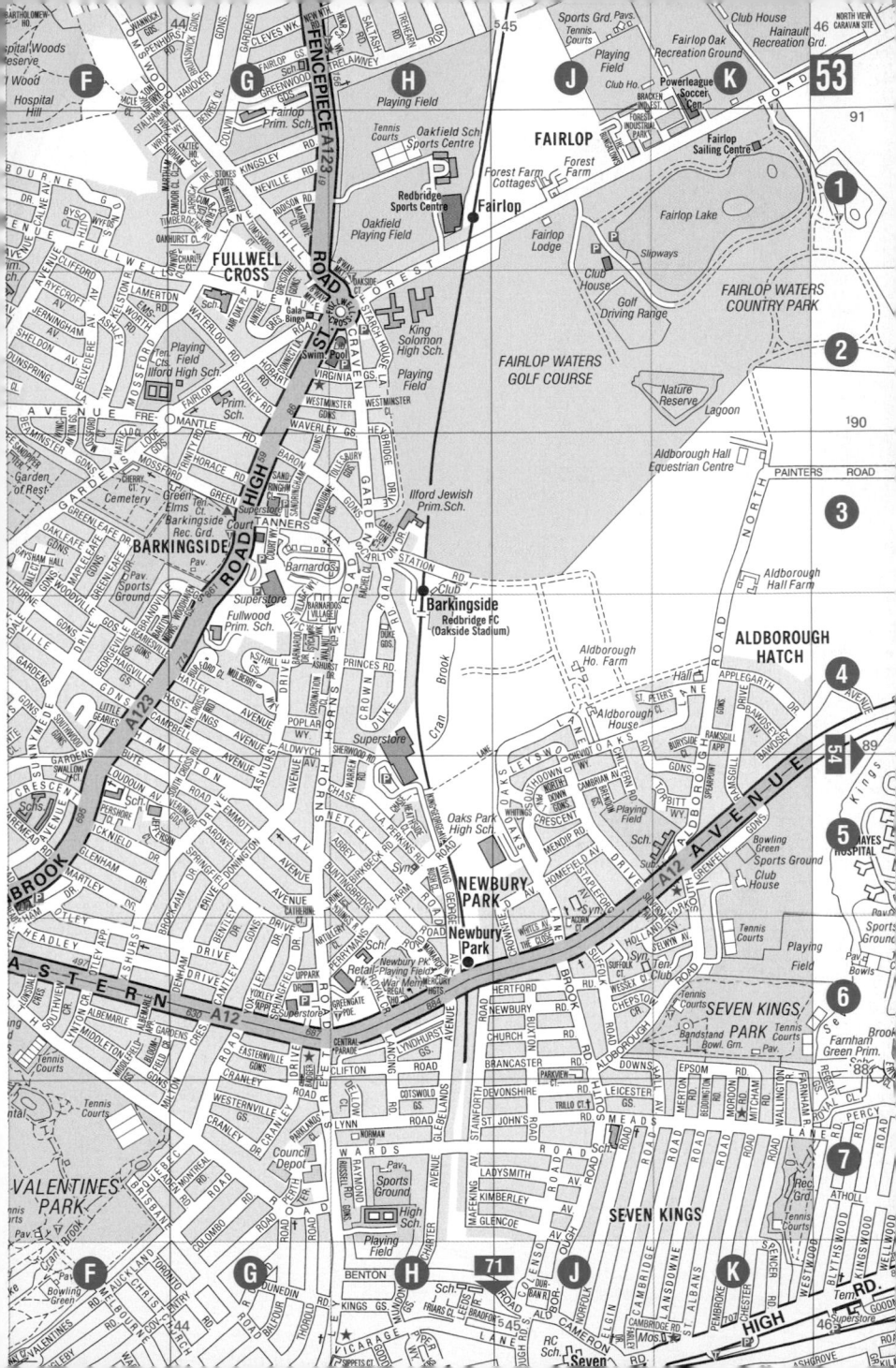
53
54
71
FULLWELL CROSS
BARKINGSIDE
FAIRLOP
NEWBURY PARK
ALDBOROUGH HATCH
SEVEN KINGS
FAIRLOP WATERS COUNTRY PARK
FAIRLOP WATERS GOLF COURSE
Fairlop Lake
VALENTINES PARK
SEVEN KINGS PARK
Hainault Recreation Grd.
Fairlop Oak Recreation Ground
Fairlop Sailing Centre
Redbridge Sports Centre
King Solomon High Sch.
Oakfield Playing Field
Ilford Jewish Prim.Sch.
Barkingside
Redbridge FC (Oakside Stadium)
Oaks Park High Sch.
Newbury Park
Aldborough Hall Equestrian Centre
Aldborough Hall Farm
Aldborough Ho. Farm
Aldborough House
Fullwood Prim. Sch.
Fairlop Prim. Sch.
Ilford High Sch.
Barkingside Rec. Grd.
Council Depot
Cran Brook
EASTERN AVENUE A12
HIGH ROAD A123
FENCEPIECE ROAD A123
FOREST ROAD
HORNS ROAD
ALDBOROUGH ROAD NORTH
PAINTERS ROAD
HIGH RD.

54
53
72
A
B
C
D
E
1
2
3
4
5
6
7
46
47
48
91
90
89
88
Hainault Rec. Grd.
NORTH VIEW CARAVAN SITE
FOREST ROAD
HAINAULT ROAD
Kings Water
WHALEBONE LANE
A1112
Fairlop Sailing Centre
Hainault Works
Farm Cottages
Hainault Farm
FAIRLOP WATERS COUNTRY PARK
FAIRLOP WATERS
Seven Kings Water
Marks Gate
Furze Cottage
Furze House Farm
PAINTERS ROAD
NORTH ROAD
Aldborough Hall Farm
ALDBOROUGH HATCH
Red House Farm
Hainault House
BILLET ROAD
Willow Farm
Playing Field
Little Heath Sch.
Sports Ground
ROSE LANE
Chadwell Heath Cemetery
Jun. Sch.
Comm. Cen.
Infant Sch.
EASTERN AVENUE
A12
AVENUE EAST
KING GEORGE HOSPITAL
North Residence
South Residence
Nursery
Redbridge College
Ethel Davis Sch.
Grove Prim. Sch.
LITTLE HEATH
GOODMAYES HOSPITAL
Sports Ground
Club House
Tennis Courts
Playing Field
Bowls
SEVEN KINGS PARK
Farnham Green Prim. Sch.
Brookside
B177
CHADWELL HEATH
ST. CHAD'S PARK
Playground
Playgrd.
WHALEBONE LA. NORTH
A118
HIGH ROAD
Mecca Bingo
GROVE FARM RETAIL PK.
Chadwell Heath
Works
Warehouse
MIRRAVALE TRADING EST.
CHADWELL HEATH INDUSTRIAL PARK
Goodmayes
GOODMAYES RETAIL PARK
Superstore
Play. Field
Mayfield Sc. Coll.
Prim. Sch.
Play. Fld.
Rec. Grd.
Playing Field

55
Cold Blow Farm
HOG HILL RD.
COLLIER ROW B174 RD.
CHASE CROSS RD.
B1459
COLLIER ROW
Lawns Rec. Grd.
Rise Park Jun. & Inf. Schs.
RISE PARK
Gobions Farm
Works
Football Grd.
NORTHGATE INDUSTRIAL PARK
City Limits
Whites Farm
Nursery
Crownfield Jun. & Inf. Schs.
Mill Farm
Mawney
MAWNEY ROAD
HAINAULT ROAD
HAVERING ROAD
LANE
Warehouse
King Georges Field
River Rom
MAWNEY PARK
EASTERN AVENUE
A12
WEST
NORTH ST.
A125
Bus Depot
Prim. Schs.
Moat
Warren Farm
A12 AVENUE
MOBY DICK
Warren Park Golf Course
Club House
Rec. Ground
Warren Sports Centre
Warren Jun. Sch.
Playing Field
Sports Ground
Crown Farm
Crown Cottages
ROMFORD
Cottons Rec. Grd.
MARKS ROAD
ST. EDWARDS WAY
WATERLOO RD.
THE BREWERY
Esporta Bowl. Alley
LONDON ROAD
A118
Pavilion
St. Edward's C of E Comp. School
Westlands Playing Field
Romford Stadium (Greyhound)
Sports Ground
Tennis Courts
Crowlands
Works
Jutsums Rec. Grd.
Gas Works
OLDCHURCH RD.
ROMFORD NEW HOSPITAL
Oldchurch Park
Helipad
CROW LANE
Romford Cemetery
Crowlands Sports Ground
RUSH GREEN
WHALEBONE LA. STH.
A1112
Whalebone Bri.
Depot
CROWLANDS HEATH GOLF COURSE
Playing Field
BEACONTREE HEATH
All Saints RC Comp. Sch. & Tech.
Robert Clack Sch.
Club House
Football Ground
Fords Sports Ground
Wood Lane Sports Centre
Aqua Driving Range
RUSH GREEN ROAD
A124 ROAD
73
F
G
H
J
K
1
2
3
4
5
6
7

38
74
Newyears Green Covert
Old Clack Farm
Research Farm
Grays Cottages
Dunster Cottage
Gatemead Farm
The Corner
Brackenbury Barn
Moat
Copthall Covert
Works
Depot
RUISLIP GOLF COURSE
WEST RUISLIP
Golf Driving Range
Club Ho.
West Ruislip
Playground
Playing Field
Cricket Ground
Club House
Harvil Farm
Copthall Farm
UXBRIDGE GOLF COURSE
Harefield Place
Weatherlys Covert
ICKENHAM
Ickenham
Compass Theatre & Arts Cen.
Lib.
Tennis Courts
Bowling Green
Swakeleys
Sports Ground
The Clump
River Pinn
SWAKELEYS ROUNDABOUT
Common Plantation
Vyners School
The Doway Martyrs Sch.
Park Wood
Ickenham Manor
Play. Flds.
Long Lane Farm
Fray's Farm
Clare House
Sports Ground
Hillingdon Ski Centre
Ski Slope
Uxbridge Athletic Track
Uxbridge Common
Cricket Ground
Hillingdon House Farm Showground
Uxbridge College
UXBRIDGE
Superstore
Prim. Sch.
TA Centre
RAF Uxbridge Track
Playing Field
Hillingdon
HILLINGDON CIRCUS
Motel
Freezeland Covert
Rec. Grd.
HILLINGDON COURT PARK
ACS Hillingdon International Sch.
RAF STATION
Convent
WESTERN AVENUE
A40
B467
B466
B483
A437
LONG LANE
HIGH ROAD
SWAKELEYS ROAD
HAREFIELD RD.

RUISLIP
RUISLIP MANOR
RUISLIP GARDENS
NORTH HILLINGDON
RAF NORTHOLT AERODROME
57
39
58
75
F
G
H
J
K
1
2
3
4
5
6
7
Ruislip
Ruislip Manor
Ruislip Gardens
South Ruislip
HIGH STREET
WEST END ROAD
A4180
A40
AVENUE
B466
EASTCOTE ROAD
BURY ST.
KINGSEND
WOOD LANE
PEMBROKE ROAD
PARK WAY
VICTORIA ROAD
ELM AVENUE
WEST WAY
MIDCROFT
MANOR RD.
TORCROSS ROAD
WHITBY ROAD
VICTORIA ROAD
HERLWYN AVENUE
SEATON GDNS.
SIDMOUTH
BESSINGBY ROAD
BRIDGWATER
TRENCHARD AVENUE
STATION APPROACH
SHARVEL LANE
Bishop Ramsey Sch.
Warrender Prim. Sch.
Ten. Cts. Warrender Park
Sports Grd.
Ruislip Manor Sports & Social Club
Ruislip Rugby Club
Sacred Heart RC Primary School
Works
Playing Field
Recreation Ground
Ruislip Gardens Primary School
Cavendish Recreation Ground
Bessingby Playing Fields
Depot
ODYSSEY BUSINESS PARK
Glebe Primary School
Ickenham Marsh
Yeading Brook
Cutthroat Wood
Gutteridge Wood
POLISH WAR MEMORIAL
C & L Golf & Country Club
Sports Ground
Priors Pk.
Glebe Farm
War Mem.
Ten Acres
The Gorse
Ryefield Primary Sch.
Club House
Moat
Towne Barns Fm.

58
40
57
76
12
13
A
B
C
D
E
1
2
3
4
5
6
7
Eastcote
Rayners Lane
RAYNERS LANE
SOUTH RUISLIP
South Ruislip
NORTHOLT
Northolt
Roxborough
Roxbourne Park
Cavendish Recreation Ground
Bessingby Playing Fields
Pine Gdns.
Bowling Green
Miniature Railway
Roxbourne First & Mid. Schs.
Recreation Ground
Field End Jun. & Inf. Schs.
Newton Farm First & Mid. Sch.
Newton Park West
Newton Ecology Park
Alexandra Sch.
High Sch.
Deane Park
Learning Cen.
Deanesfield Prim. Sch.
Queensmead Sch.
Queensmead Sports Centre
Playing Fields
Superstore
Warehouses
Victoria Retail Park
Waste Transfer Station
Earlsmead Sch.
Harrow Borough FC
Northolt Park
Play Centre
Northolt High Sch.
Lord Halsbury Memorial Playing Flds.
Willow Tree Prim. Sch.
Bourne Primary School
Sports Ground
POLISH WAR MEMORIAL
Priors Fm.
Glebe Farm
War Mem.
C & L Country Club
LONDON GOLF COURSE
Northolt Prim. Sch.
John Chilton Sch.
West London Academy
TARGET ROUNDABOUT
Islip Manor Park
Northolt Swimarama
Belvue Park
Health Club
Driving Range
Golf Club
Towne Barns Fm.
Club House
Moat
WESTERN AVENUE
A40
A4180
A4090
A312
ALEXANDRA AVENUE
MANDEVILLE ROAD
WEST END RD.
CHURCH ROAD
EASTCOTE LANE
FIELD END ROAD
VICTORIA RD.
LONG DR.
EASTCOTE ROAD
WHITBY ROAD

59
WEST HARROW
HARROW
ROXETH
SOUTH HARROW
HARROW ON THE HILL
South Harrow
Northolt Pk.
Sudbury Hill Harrow
Sudbury Hill
Wood End
Greenford Green
Greenford
BERKELEY FIELDS
Nature Reserve
Horsenden Hill Rec. Grd.
Perivale Wood Local Nature Reserve
THE CLEMENTINE CHURCHILL BMI HOSPITAL
ST. ANDREW'S AT HARROW
Harrow School
Harrow School Playing Fields
Playing Fields
School Lake
Cricket Ground
Harrow Ckt. Club
Toll Gate
Orley Farm Sch.
Whitmore High Sch.
Whitmore Sports Cen.
Grange Schs.
Welldon Park First Sch.
David Lloyd Leisure
Ealing Northern Sports Centre
Horsenden Primary Sch.
GRAND UNION CANAL
(PADDINGTON BRANCH)
GREENFORD INDUSTRIAL ESTATE
KELVIN IND. EST.
Warehouses
Factory
Works
ALEXANDRA PARK
Cemetery
LOWER RD.
ROXETH HILL
LONDON RD.
SUDBURY HILL
WHITTON AVENUE
WEST WHITTON AV.
EAST
NORTHOLT ROAD
PETT'S HILL
GREENFORD ROAD
A312
A4090
A4127
A4005
B457
41
60
77
1
2
3
4
5
6
7
F
G
H
J
K

HARROW
60
42
59
78
A
B
C
D
E
1
2
3
4
5
6
7
16
17
18
87
86
185
84
Northwick Park Hospital
St. Mark's Hosp.
Sports Centre
Golf Course
Playing Fields
NORTHWICK PARK
Harrow School Playing Fields
Rugby Football Grounds
Harrow School Farm
WATFORD ROAD
A404
A4127
SUDBURY COURT DRIVE
Clementine Churchill Hospital
NORTH WEMBLEY
Byron Ct. Prim. Sch.
South Kenton
Preston Road
PRESTON
Preston Park Recreation Ground
Tennis Courts
John Billam Playing Fields
Sports Ground
WOODCOCK HILL
WINDERMERE AV.
Play. Fld. Wembley High Tech. Coll.
North Wembley
EAST LANE
A4088
Vale Farm Sports Ground
East Lane Pavilion Rugby Football Grd.
Vale Farm Sports Centre
Wembley FC (Vale Farm)
East La. Theatre Club
Wembley Commercial Centre
Train. Cen.
East Lane Business Park
Sports Grd.
Wembley Manor Jun. & Inf. Sch.
KING EDWARD VII PARK
HARROW ROAD
A4005
Harrow
Sudbury Hill Play. Flds.
Elmwood Pk.
SUDBURY
Maybank Open Space
Sudbury & Harrow Road
BARHAM PARK
Library
HARROW RD.
HIGH RD.
Wembley Central
WEMBLEY (MATS) HOSP.
WHITTON AVENUE
A4090
EAST
Sudbury Town
BRIDGEWATER RD.
EALING ROAD
A4089
Horsenden Wood
Club House
HORSENDEN HILL GOLF COURSE
Horsenden Hill
SUDBURY GOLF COURSE
Horsenden Farm
GRAND UNION CANAL (PADDINGTON BRANCH)
Alperton Cemetery
One Tree Hill Rec. Grd.
Hindu Tem.
Alperton Sch.
Spts. Cen.
Alperton
Bus Garage
PERIVALE
Comm. Centre
Perivale Wood Local Nature Reserve
Govt. Training Cen.
Phoenix Trad. Est.
Abercorn Commercial Cen.
Warehouse

61
43
62
79
FRYENT COUNTRY PARK
Barn Hill
Open Space
WEMBLEY PARK
Wembley Park
Wembley Arena
Wembley Stadium
Wembley Stadium
Market
Works
Depot
Railway Works
Neasden Depot
NEASDEN JUNCTION
BRENT RESERVOIR
Welsh Harp Nature Reserve
Field Study Centre
Sailing Club
Nursery
Sports Ground
Youth Comm. Cen.
Kingsbury Bridge Comm. Cen.
Sports Ground
Play. Fld.
St. Margaret Clitherow RC Prim. Sch.
Chalkhill Prim. Sch.
Town Hall
Liby.
Superstore
Superstores
Stadium Business Centre
Wembley Park Business Centre
Wembley Retail Park
Cannon Trading Estate
Hallmark Trad. Cen.
Pop-In Commercial Centre
Adams Bri. Bus. Cen.
Drury Way Industrial Estate
Vernon Ho. Sch.
Sherrans Farm Open Space
Comm. Cen.
Oakington Mnr. Prim. Sch.
Bowling Grn.
Recreation Ground
TOKYNGTON
WEMBLEY
Playing Fld.
Youth & Comm. Cen.
Elsley Prim. Sch.
Schools
Wembley Brook
Depot
Carriage Shed
Stonebridge Park
STONEBRIDGE PARK
Brent Junction
Bridge Park
Gibbons Recreation Ground
Hindu Temple
Power Station
CHURCH END
School
ALPERTON
Sports Ground
Open Space
NORTHFIELDS INDUSTRIAL ESTATE
STONEBRIDGE
PREMIER PARK
Stanmore Junction
Wealdstone Brook
FORTY AVENUE
FORTY LANE
A4088
SALMON STREET
FRYENT WAY
A4140
BLACKBIRD HILL
NEASDEN LA.
CHURCH LANE
B454
WEMBLEY PARK DR.
A4089
EMPIRE WAY
B4565
BRIDGE RD
GREAT CENTRAL WAY
B4557
SOUTH WAY
DRURY WAY
HARROW ROAD
A404
NORTH CIRCULAR ROAD
A406
HILLSIDE
BRENTFIELD
WEMBLEY HILL RD.
CRAVEN PK.
Brent Trading Centre
F
G
H
J
K
1
2
3
4
5
6
7
19
20
21
87
86
85
84

62
A
B
C
D
E
44
WEST HENDON
80
61
21
22
23
87
86
85
84
1
2
3
4
5
6
7
Cool Oak Bridge
Youth Sailing Base
Sailing Club
Field Study Cen.
Woodfield Sch.
Sports Ground
Rifle Range
Nursery
WOODFIELD PARK
Welsh Harp Nature Reserve
BRENT RESERVOIR
Old Welsh Harp
Brent Bridge
M1 MOTORWAY
THE BROADWAY
NORTH CIRCULAR ROAD
EDGWARE ROAD
STAPLES CORNER
Junc. 1
Cineworld Cinema
CLAREMONT WAY INDUSTRIAL ESTATE
Brent Sidings
Depot
Neasden Recreation Ground
Playground
Youth & Comm. Cen.
Sports Grd.
Braintcroft Prim. Sch.
Technology Colleges
NEASDEN
NEASDEN JUNCTION
Neasden Depot
Railway Wks.
Mus.
DUDDEN HILL LANE
Arts Centre
Dollis Hill House
Tennis Courts
Putting Green
GLADSTONE PARK
DOLLIS HILL
Water Works
Dudding Hill Junction
Reservoir
Bus Garage
Superstores
Neasden
Dollis Hill
DUDDEN HILL
Willesden Green
CHURCH END
Roundwood Park
Recreation Ground
Power Station
WILLESDEN
WILLESDEN NEW CEMETERY
Jewish Cemy.
Sports Ground
Summer Theatre
ROUNDWOOD PARK
Willesden Cen. for Health & Care
BELVEDERE DAY HOSP.
Capital City Academy
Willesden Sports Stadium
Willesden Sports Cen.
King Edward VII Recreation Ground
WILLESDEN GREEN
Cannns Hlth. Club
HIGH ROAD
A407
A406
A4088
B453
B4557
CHURCH RD.
CRAVEN PK.
HARLESDEN
Day Nursery

63
45
64
81
F
G
H
J
K
1
2
3
4
5
6
7
GOLDERS GREEN
Golders Green
HAMPSTEAD
HEATH
GOLDERS HILL PARK
Leg of Mutton Pond
West Heath
Jack Straws Castle
CHILD'S HILL
Clitterhouse Recreation Ground
Hendon FC
Tennis Courts
Basing Hill Park
Childs Hill Park
Synagogue
CRICKLEWOOD
Cricklewood
Sports Ground
Hampstead Cemetery
Hampstead School
Fortune Green
WEST HAMPSTEAD
West Hampstead Thameslink
West Hampstead
Finchley Rd. & Frognal
Camden Arts Cen.
SOUTH HAMPSTEAD
Kilburn
Brondesbury
BRONDESBURY
Brondesbury Park
BRONDESBURY PARK
Hindu Temple
Willesden Lane Cemetery
Kilburn Grange Park
The Hope Cen.
Mosque
Superstore
Bingo Hall
Works
BELSIZE
HENDON WAY
A41
A407
A5
A502
A598
B510
B520
B509
A4003
FINCHLEY ROAD
NORTH END ROAD
CRICKLEWOOD LANE
CRICKLEWOOD BROADWAY
SHOOT UP HILL
KILBURN HIGH RD.
WEST END LANE
FORTUNE GREEN RD.
WILLESDEN LANE
IVERSON RD.
ABBEY RD.
WEST HEATH ROAD
PLATT'S LANE
GOLDERS GREEN ROAD
MILL LANE
CHICHELE RD.

64
HAMPSTEAD HEATH
HAMPSTEAD
HIGHGATE
PARLIAMENT HILL
GOSPEL OAK
SOUTH HAMPSTEAD
PRIMROSE HILL
VALE OF HEALTH
North End
Kenwood House
KEN WOOD
Highgate Ponds
Hampstead Ponds
Ladies Bathing Pond
Parliament Hill Fields
Parliament Hill Fields Athletics Track
William Ellis School
Parliament Hill School
Highgate School
HIGHGATE CEMETERY
West Heath
Sandy Heath
East Heath
North Wood
Turners Wood
Jack Straws Castle
THE ROYAL FREE HOSPITAL
Swiss Cottage
Chalk Farm
Belsize Pk.
Finchley Rd. & Frognal
Finchley Rd.
South Hampstead
Hampstead Heath
Hampstead
Gospel Oak
Camden Arts Cen.
Sigmund Freud Statue
Keats Ho.
Burgh Ho.
Reservoir (covered)
NORTH END RD.
SPANIARDS ROAD
HAMPSTEAD LANE
MILLFIELD LA.
HAVERSTOCK HILL
ROSSLYN HILL
FITZJOHN'S AV.
FINCHLEY ROAD
CHALK FARM ROAD
MALDEN ROAD
MANSFIELD ROAD
FLEET ROAD
AGINCOURT RD.
POND ST.
BELSIZE RD.
ADELAIDE RD.
ETON AVENUE
BELSIZE AVENUE
A502
A41
B519
B518
B511
B509
B517
46
63
82
A B C D E
1 2 3 4 5 6 7

65
47
83
F
G
H
J
K
1
2
3
4
5
6
7
DARTMOUTH PARK
UPPER HOLLOWAY
TUFNELL PARK
KENTISH TOWN
LOWER HOLLOWAY
CAMDEN TOWN
BARNSBURY
HIGHGATE CEMETERY
WATERLOW PARK
Lauderdale House
Highgate Mental Health Centre
WHITTINGTON HOSPITAL
Middlesex Uni.
Archway
Upper Holloway
Tufnell Pk.
Kentish Town
Kentish Town W.
Camden Rd.
Camden Town
Caledonian Rd.
Caledonian Rd. and Barnsbury
Holloway Rd.
Crouch Hill
Elthorne Park
Whittington Park
HMP HOLLOWAY
HMP PENTONVILLE
Islington Ten. Cen.
Odeon Cinema
NAG'S HEAD
NAGS HEAD SHOPPING CENTRE
Sobell Leisure Cen.
HOLLOWAY ROAD
JUNCTION RD.
KENTISH TOWN ROAD
CAMDEN ROAD
CALEDONIAN RD.
YORK WAY
HORNSEY RISE
HORNSEY RD.
SEVEN SISTERS RD.
STROUD GREEN RD.
CROUCH HILL
HIGHGATE HILL
DARTMOUTH PARK HILL
TOLLINGTON PARK
BRECKNOCK RD.
PARKHURST RD.
HILLMARTON RD.
CAMDEN PARK RD.
ST. PANCRAS WAY
AGAR GROVE
ARCHWAY RD.
FORTESS ROAD
A1
A103
A400
A503
A5200
A5203
A1201
B540
B519
A5202
B514

66
48
84
65
A
B
C
D
E
1
2
3
4
5
6
7
FINSBURY PARK
Manor House
MANOR HO.
Reservoir (covered)
Sports Arena
FINSBURY PARK
Finsbury Park
Rowans Complex
WEST RESERVOIR
West Reservoir Centre
The Castle Climbing Cen.
WEST RESERVOIR
Sir Thomas Abney Prim. Sch.
STOKE NEWINGTON
ABNEY PARK CEMETERY
BROWNSWOOD PARK
CLISSOLD PARK
Council Offices
Clissold Ho.
Paddling Pool
Clissold Leisure Cen.
Tennis Courts
Old Peoples Home
BIRCHMORE HALL
Isledon Village
Gillespie Local Park
Arsenal
Highbury Stadium
Arsenal FC (Emirates Stadium)
ASHBURTON TRIANGLE
Drayton Park
Sobell Leisure Cen.
Holloway Rd.
University
HIGHBURY
HIGHBURY FIELDS
Highbury Pool
Highbury & Islington
HIGHBURY CNR.
Canonbury
CANONBURY
Dalston Kingsland
KINGSLAND
BARNSBURY
ISLINGTON
Essex Rd.
DE BEAUVOIR TOWN
City Farm
Paradise Park
SEVEN SISTERS RD.
GREEN LANES
BLACKSTOCK RD.
HIGHBURY PARK
HIGHBURY GROVE
ST. PAUL'S ROAD
BALLS POND RD.
NEWINGTON GRN. RD.
ALBION RD.
STOKE NEWINGTON CHURCH ST.
LORDSHIP PARK
MANOR RD.
HOLLOWAY RD.
LIVERPOOL RD.
UPPER ST.
CANONBURY RD.
NEW NTH. RD.
ESSEX RD.
HORNSEY RD.
TOLLINGTON RD.
ISLEDON RD.
STROUD GREEN RD.
A105
A503
A1201
A1199
A104
A1
A103
A1200
A10
B105
B104
B515

67
49
85
68
CLAPTON
STAMFORD HILL
Stoke Newington
UPPER CLAPTON
SPRINGFIELD PARK
WALTHAMSTOW
Clapton Junction
MARSHES
RIVER LEA or LEE
Leyton Marshes
Lea Bridge Riding Sch.
Playing Field
LEYTON INDUSTRIAL VILLAGE
FOREST BUSINESS PARK
Lee Valley Ice Centre
Filter Beds
NORTH MILLFIELDS Recreation Ground
LEA BRIDGE
Middlesex Filter Beds Nature Reserve
SOUTH MILL FIELDS
South Millfields Rec. Grd.
Clapton
LEA BRIDGE ROAD
A104
UPPER CLAPTON ROAD
A107
LOWER CLAPTON ROAD
NORTHWOLD RD.
Rectory Road
STOKE NEWINGTON HIGH ST.
STOKE NEWINGTON RD.
A10
SHACKLEWELL
LOWER CLAPTON
HACKNEY DOWNS
Stormont House Sch.
Mossbourne Community Academy
Petchey Academy
Arcola Thtre.
HOMERTON
HOMERTON UNIVERSITY HOSPITAL
HOMERTON HIGH ST.
A102
Homerton
Hackney Downs
Hackney Cen.
DALSTON LA.
AMHURST RD.
GRAHAM ROAD
A1207
MORNING LANE
B113
WICK RD.
KINGSLAND HIGH S.
DALSTON
QUEENSBRIDGE RD.
B108
HACKNEY
London Fields
LONDON FIELDS
MARE STREET
WELL STREET
ST. CASSLAND RD.
A106
SOUTH HACKNEY
WELL STREET COMMON
VICTORIA PARK
Victoria Fountain
Royal Gate East
Bandstand
Regent's Canal
Acton's Lock
St. Agnes Gate
Hospice
F
G
H
J
K
1
2
3
4
5
6
7
34
35
36

68
A
B
C
D
E
1
2
3
4
5
6
7
36
37
38
50
67
86
84
85
86
87
FOREST BUSINESS PARK
ROXWELL TRADING PARK
CROMWELL IND. EST.
Playground
Factories
Brooks Farm
Leyton Midland Rd.
Leyton FC Grd.
LEA BRIDGE
A104
ORIENT WAY
A1006
Tennis Courts
Gas Works
The Lammas Sec. Sch.
Playing Fields
MARSH LANE
FAIRWAYS BUSINESS PARK
Manor Lodge
Marsh Lane Cottage
Playing Fields
Running Track
Dagenham Brook
Play. Fld.
LEYTON
Valley Pitch & Putt Golf Course
RIVER LEA or LEE
Middlesex Filter Beds Nature Reserve
Cow Bridge
Changing Rooms
HACKNEY MARSH
RECREATION GROUND
Recreation Ground
Changing Rooms
Dressing Rooms
MARKET PAVILION
NEW SPITALFIELDS MARKET
Leyton Orient FC
Superstore
Leyton
A112
HIGH ROAD
LEYTON
A12
RUCKHOLT ROAD
A106
Temple Mills
Play. Flds.
Cricket Ground
Lee Valley Spts. Cen.
Temple Mills Bri.
B112
Marshgate Bri.
LEA INTERCHANGE
EAST CROSS ROUTE
Wick Field Recreation Ground
Lee Valley Cycle Circuit
Lee Valley Park
Camp Site
Football Ground
Container Terminal
STRATFORD NEW TOWN
CLAPTON PARK
Prim. Sch.
Rec. Grd.
HOMERTON
HOMERTON HIGH ST.
MARSH HILL
Recreation Ground
Football Ground
Mabley Green
A102
KENWORTHY RD.
Homerton
HACKNEY WICK
Kingsway International Christian Centre
Arena Field Rec. Grd.
Warehouse
Channelsea River
Depot
Cold Stores
Stratford International
(Due Open April 2007)
EAST CROSS CENTRE
WICK RD.
B113
Hackney Wick
CARPENTER'S ROAD
A115
KINGS YARD
CHAPMAN R.
A12 EAST CROSS ROUTE
CADOGAN
Cadogan Gate
VICTORIA PARK
A106
Tennis Courts
Playground
Bowling Green
Victoria Park Athletics Arena
Mitford Bri.
Bandstand
Victoria Fountain
Royal Gate East
Three Colt Bridge
OLD FORD
ROAD
CARPENTERS BUS. PK.
BOW INDUSTRIAL PARK
Stratford Marsh
Sun Wharf
Works
MARSHGATE TRADING EST.
MARSHGATE SIDINGS (BOW DEPOT)
City Mill River
Waterworks River
Stratford (Low Level)
STRATFORD
Youth Cen.
WELL STREET COMMON

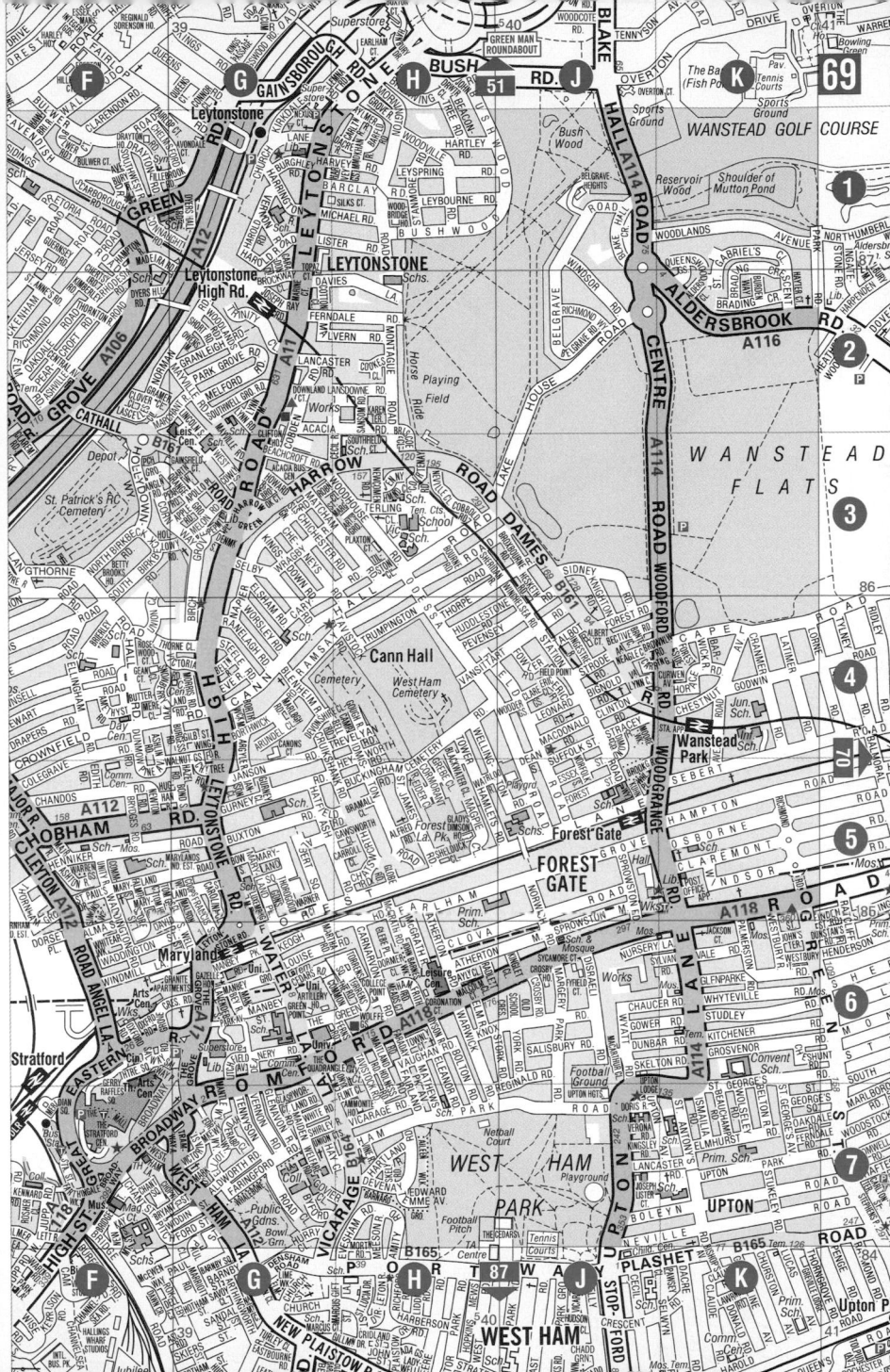

69
70
51
87
F
G
H
J
K
1
2
3
4
5
6
7
GREEN MAN ROUNDABOUT
BUSH RD.
BLAKE HALL ROAD
A114
WANSTEAD GOLF COURSE
Shoulder of Mutton Pond
Reservoir Wood
Bush Wood
Sports Ground
OVERTON
The Basin (Fish Pond)
Tennis Courts
Bowling Green
WOODLANDS AVENUE
ALDERSBROOK RD.
A116
Leytonstone
LEYTONSTONE
Leytonstone High Rd.
GAINSBOROUGH RD.
LEYTONSTONE HIGH ROAD
A11
A12
A106
GREEN
GROVE
CATHALL
HARROW ROAD
B161
St. Patrick's RC Cemetery
Depot
Playing Field
Horse Ride
LAKE HOUSE ROAD
WANSTEAD FLATS
CENTRE ROAD
WOODFORD RD.
WOODGRANGE RD.
DAMES ROAD
CAPEL ROAD
Cann Hall
West Ham Cemetery
Cemetery
Wanstead Park
Forest Gate
FOREST GATE
CHOBHAM RD.
A112
LEYTON ROAD
ANGEL LA.
Maryland
Stratford
ROMFORD ROAD
A118
GREEN STREET
UPTON LANE
WEST HAM PARK
Football Ground
Playground
Netball Court
Football Pitch
Tennis Courts
PORTWAY
B165
PLASHET
UPTON
WEST HAM
VICARAGE LA.
B164
BROADWAY
WEST HAM LA.
HIGH ST.
GREAT EASTERN RD.
NEW PLAISTOW RD.
Upton Park

70
52
69
88
A
B
C
D
E
1
2
3
4
5
6
7
41
42
43
86
85
84
WANSTEAD PARK
WANSTEAD GOLF COURSE
The Temple
Keepers Lodge
Heronry Pond
Perch Pond
Rook Island
Sewage Works
Aldersbrook Prim. Sch.
ALDERSBROOK
ALDERSBROOK ROAD
A116
WANSTEAD FLATS
CITY OF LONDON CEMETERY
City of London Crematorium
GOLF COURSE
River Roding
Alders Brook
SOUTH WOODFORD TO BARKING RELIEF ROAD
ILFORD
CRANBROOK
Cranbrook Coll.
NHS Walk-In Cen.
Ilford Cricket Club
A123
A406
NORTH CIRCULAR ROAD
ROMFORD ROAD
A118
FOREST DRIVE
A117
MANOR PARK
Manor Park
THE MANOR PARK CEMETERY
Manor Park Crem.
CITY OF LONDON CEMETERY
LITTLE ILFORD
Little Ilford Park
LITTLE ILFORD LA.
CHURCH RD.
BROWNING ROAD
B165
Woodgrange Park
Woodgrange Park Cemetery
HIGH STREET NORTH
PLASHET
Jewish Cemetery
PLASHET PARK
KATHERINE ROAD
B109
GREEN STREET
B167
PLASHET RD.
PLASHET GROVE
East Ham
WALLEND
Sports Ground
Gasholder
Running Track
Playing Field
Depot
Upton Park
UPTON PARK
RON LEIGHTON WY.
BARKING RD.
SOUTH WOODFORD TO BARKING RELIEF ROAD

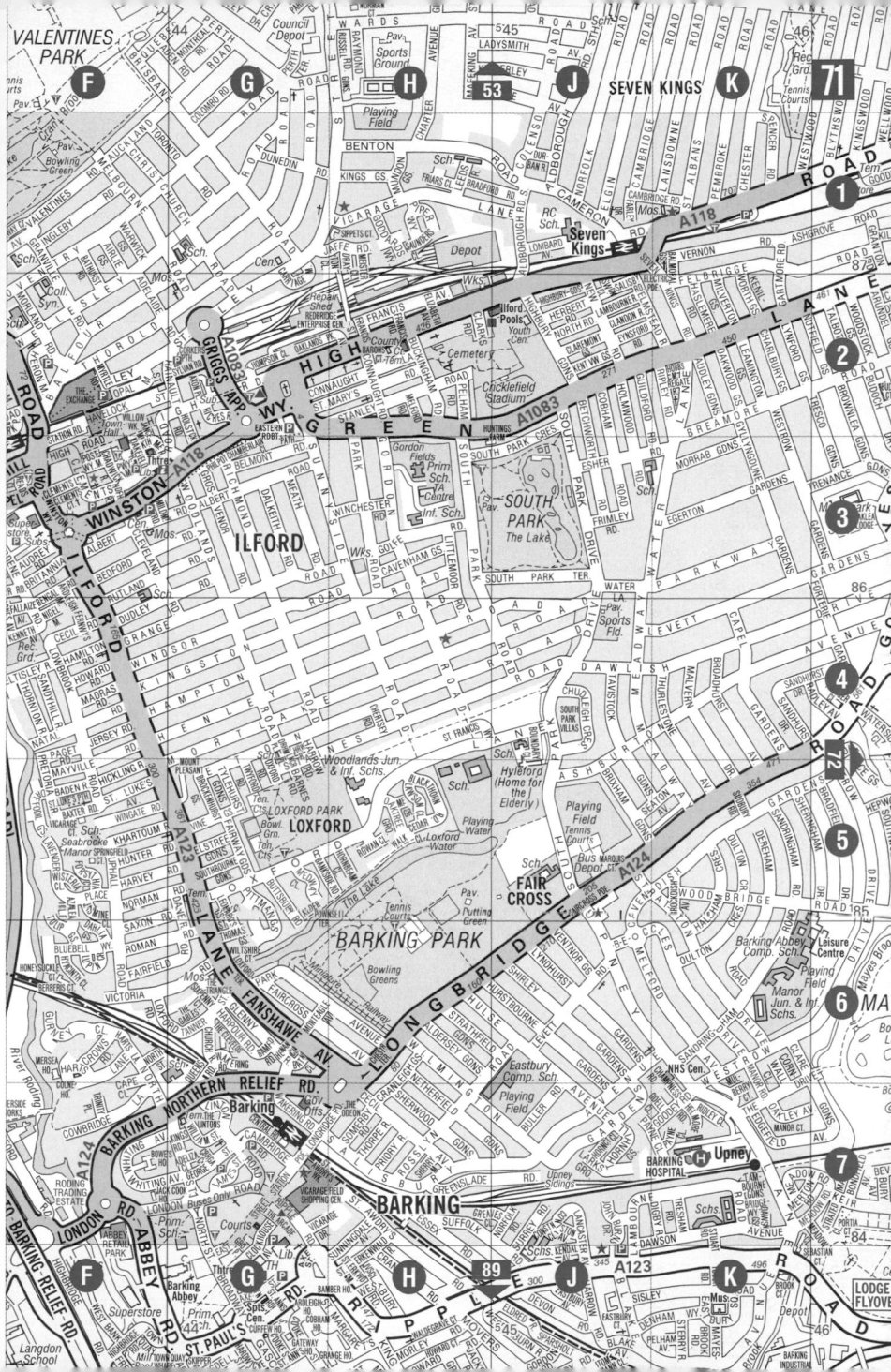

VALENTINES PARK
SEVEN KINGS
71
53
72
89
F
G
H
J
K
1
2
3
4
5
6
7
44
45
46
84
85
86
87
Council Depot
Sports Ground
Playing Field
Seven Kings
Depot
Ilford Pools
Youth Cen.
Cemetery
Cricklefield Stadium
HIGH ROAD
A118
A1083
HIGH LANE
GREEN LANE
GRIGGS APP.
WINSTON WY.
EASTERN RDBT.
THE EXCHANGE
Town Hall
ILFORD
ILFORD LANE
A123
SOUTH PARK
The Lake
SOUTH PARK DRIVE
PARKWAY
Sports Fld.
Gordon Fields
Prim. Sch.
TA Centre
Inf. Sch.
LOXFORD
LOXFORD PARK
Woodlands Jun. & Inf. Schs.
Hyleford (Home for the Elderly)
Playing Field
Tennis Courts
Bus Depot
FAIR CROSS
A124
LONGBRIDGE ROAD
BARKING PARK
Bowling Greens
Miniature Railway
FANSHAWE AV.
BARKING NORTHERN RELIEF RD.
Barking
Gov. Offs.
THE ODEON
Eastbury Comp. Sch.
Barking Abbey Comp. Sch.
Leisure Centre
Manor Jun. & Inf. Schs.
NHS Cen.
Upney
BARKING HOSPITAL
Upney Sidings
BARKING
VICARAGE FIELD SHOPPING CEN.
RODING TRADING ESTATE
LONDON RD.
ABBEY RD.
BARKING RELIEF RD.
ABBEY RETAIL PARK
Courts
Barking Abbey
Superstore
Langdon School
RIPPLE RD.
A123
ST. PAUL'S RD.
River Roding
LODGE FLYOVER
Mus.
Depot

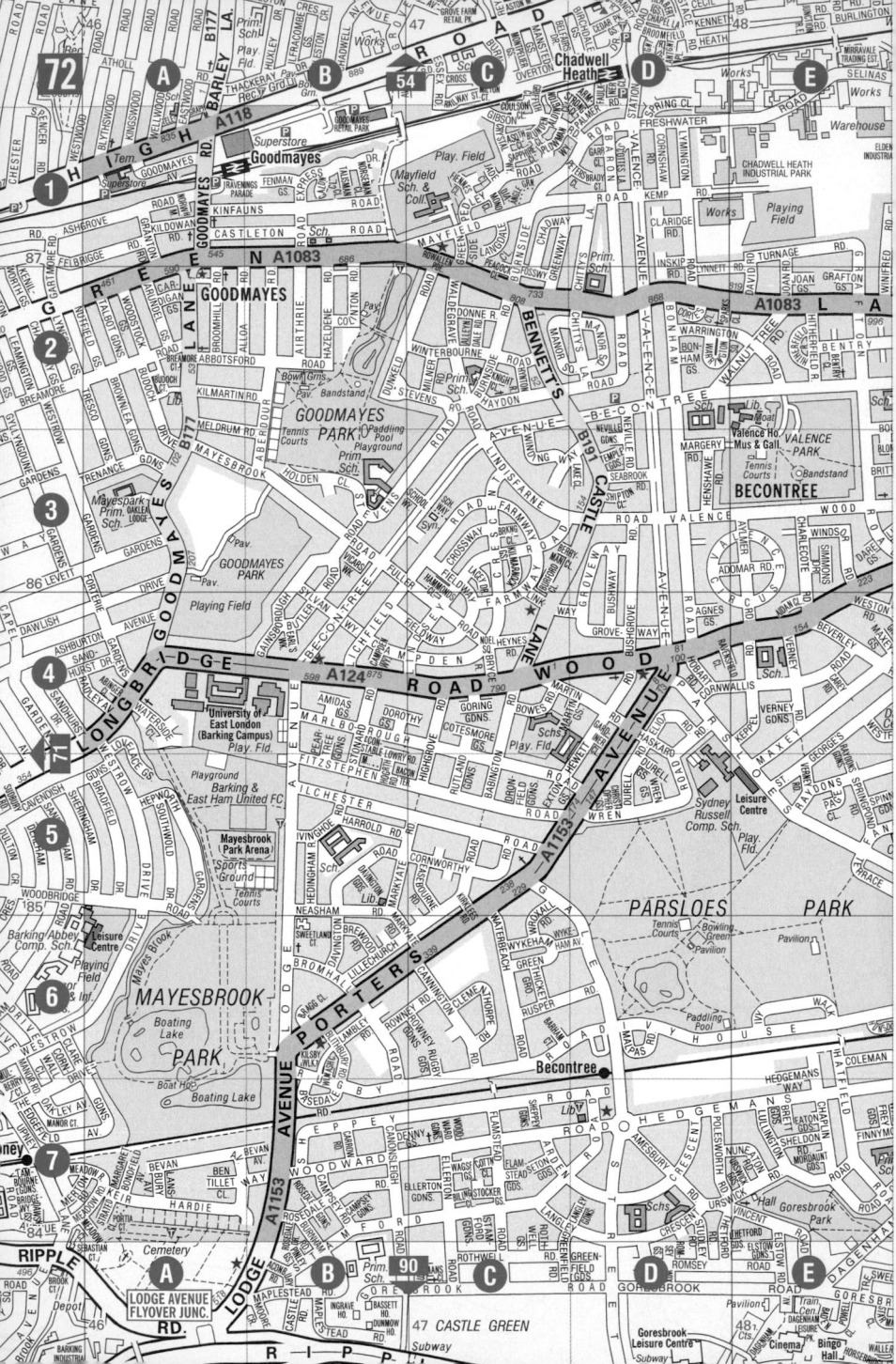

72
54
71
90
46
47
48
87
86
85
84
A
B
C
D
E
1
2
3
4
5
6
7
Chadwell Heath
Goodmayes
GOODMAYES
GOODMAYES PARK
BECONTREE
Becontree
VALENCE PARK
Valence Ho. Mus & Gall.
PARSLOES PARK
MAYESBROOK PARK
Mayesbrook Park Arena
Sports Ground
Boating Lake
University of East London (Barking Campus)
Barking & East Ham United FC
Barking Abbey Comp. Sch.
Sydney Russell Comp. Sch.
Mayfield Sch. & Coll.
Mayespark Prim. Sch.
CHADWELL HEATH INDUSTRIAL PARK
Goresbrook Park
Goresbrook Leisure Centre
Cemetery
LODGE AVENUE FLYOVER JUNC.
47 CASTLE GREEN
HIGH ROAD A118
GREEN LANE A1083
LONGBRIDGE ROAD A124
WOOD LANE
BECONTREE AVENUE
PORTERS AVENUE A1153
LODGE AVENUE A1153
GOODMAYES LANE B177
BARLEY LA. B177
BENNETT'S CASTLE LANE B191
VALENCE AVENUE
RIPPLE RD.
GORESBROOK ROAD
HEDGEMANS ROAD
IVYHOUSE ROAD
GOODMAYES RETAIL PARK
GROVE FARM RETAIL PK.
MIRRAVALE TRADING EST.

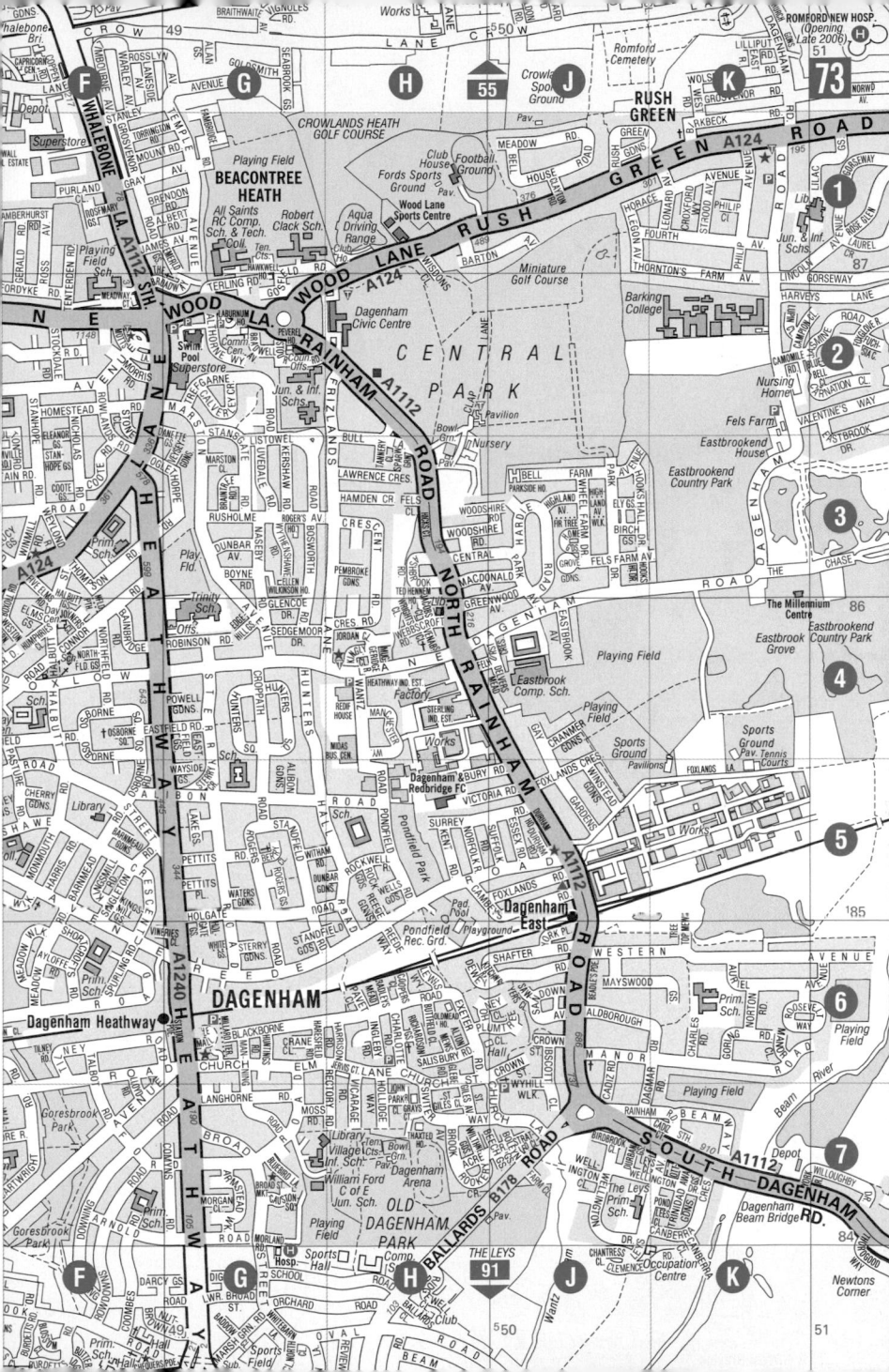

ROMFORD NEW HOSP. (Opening Late 2006)
Romford Cemetery
RUSH GREEN
55
CROW LANE
Crowlands Sports Ground
CROWLANDS HEATH GOLF COURSE
BEACONTREE HEATH
Playing Field
All Saints RC Comp. Sch. & Tech. Coll.
Robert Clack Sch.
Fords Sports Ground
Club House
Football Ground
Aqua Driving Range
Wood Lane Sports Centre
WOOD LANE
RUSH GREEN ROAD
A124
WHALEBONE LA. STH.
A1112
Superstore
Miniature Golf Course
Barking College
Dagenham Civic Centre
CENTRAL PARK
Pavilion
Nursery
RAINHAM ROAD NORTH
Swim. Pool
Superstore
Jun. & Inf. Schs.
Nursing Home
Fels Farm
Eastbrookend House
Eastbrookend Country Park
The Millennium Centre
Eastbrook Grove
Eastbrook Comp. Sch.
Playing Field
Sports Ground
Pavilions
Tennis Courts
Trinity Sch.
Works
Dagenham & Redbridge FC
Library
Pondfield Park
Pondfield Rec. Grd.
Dagenham East
DAGENHAM
Dagenham Heathway
HEATHWAY
A1240
Prim. Sch.
Goresbrook Park
Playing Field
OLD DAGENHAM PARK
Dagenham Arena
Village Inf. Sch.
William Ford C of E Jun. Sch.
BALLARDS ROAD
B178
THE LEYS
91
The Leys Prim. Sch.
Occupation Centre
SOUTH DAGENHAM RD.
Dagenham Beam Bridge
Beam River
Depot
Newtons Corner
F
G
H
J
K
1
2
3
4
5
6
7
49
50
51
84
85
86
87

74
56
92
A
B
C
D
E
1
2
3
4
5
6
7
UXBRIDGE
RAF STATION
HILLINGDON
HILLINGDON HEATH
COWLEY
COWLEY PEACHEY
PIELD HEATH
COLHAM GREEN
YIEWSLEY
West Drayton
Goulds Green
Stockley Park
HILLINGDON COURT PARK (Recreation Ground)
HILLINGDON GOLF COURSE
STOCKLEY COUNTRY PARK
STOCKLEY PARK GOLF COURSE
ACS Hillingdon International Sch.
Brunel University
University Halls
Hillingdon Cem.
Uxbridge Cem.
Bishopshalt School
The Grove Nature Reserve
HILLINGDON HOSPITAL
Meadow High Sch.
Moorcroft School
Moorcroft Children's Home
Stockley Academy
Colham Manor Sch.
Swakeleys School
Abbotsfield School
Uxbridge High Sch.
Pield Heath House Sch.
Rabbsfarm Prim. Sch.
Yiewsley Swim. Pool
Uxbridge FC
Virgin Active
Mellow Lane Farm
HILLINGDON ROAD
HILLINGDON HILL
A4020
UXBRIDGE ROAD
LONG LANE
A437
HARLINGTON ROAD
FALLING LANE
A408
STOCKLEY ROAD
WEST DRAYTON ROAD
B465
DAWLEY ROAD
PIELD HEATH ROAD
ROYAL LANE
COLHAM GREEN ROAD
KINGSTON LANE
PARK VIEW ROAD
HORTON ROAD

Yeading Brook
Cutthroat Wood
Gutteridge Wood
F
G
H
57
J
K
75
MEMORIAL
C & L Golf & Country Club
Club Ho.
WEST END RD.
NORTH HILLINGDON
Playing Field
Ryefield Primary Sch.
Ten Acres
The Gorse
Recreation Ground
Rugby Ground
Hare Plantation
Westways Fm.
Lane Covert
SHARVEL LANE
Club House
Moat
Barns Fm.
1
RUISLIP
West London Shooting Grounds
Children's Cen.
Comm. Cen.
Charville Prim. Sch.
Canal Feeder
Grosvenor Playing Field
2
Hedgewood School
LANSBURY
GROSVENOR
BOURNE
MEAD AV.
RUSHDENE
HARTFIELD AV.
TITHE
DOWN WAY
CRESCENT
83
Prim. Sch.
GURNEY
ROAD
ATTLEE
AVENUE
OWEN
3
KINGSHILL CL.
Comm. Cen.
Belmore Prim. Sch.
Barnhill High Sch.
Playing Fields
Hayes Shrub
Hayes Park
KINGSHILL DRIVE
Home Farm
HAYES END
The Paddocks Fm.
Sch.
Play. Fld.
FREDORA AV.
Grange Park Jun. & Inf. Schs.
4
Hostel
Nursery
WESTCOMBE LODGE DRIVE
Library
YEADING
76
82
Belmore Playing Fields
5
UXBRIDGE ROAD
A4020
Rec. Grd
Rosedale Park
WOOD END GREEN
Pav.
Bowl. Gn.
County Ct.
Nurs. Home
Norman Leddy Mem. Gds.
Day Cen.
The Beck Theatre
WOOD END
Cricket Grd.
Tom.
Yeading Schs.
Warren Park
Lib
Hayes Manor Spts. Cen.
The Hayes Manor Sch. Playing Fld.
Hayes Stadium & Sports Cen.
Barra Hall
Open Air Theatre
Town Hall Park
Play. Fld.
Prim. Sch.
Mecca Bingo
6
PARKWAY
81
OSSIE GARVIN ROUNDABOUT
HEATH LANE
Ten. Cts.
Uxbridge Coll. (Hayes Campus)
LOMBARDY RETAIL PARK
HAYES
Hayes FC
Bell Ho. Fld.
Convent
Bowl. Grn.
7
UXBRIDGE RETAIL P.
ELYSTAN BUS. CENTRE
HAYES METRO CENTRE
Hillingdon Cycling Circuit
A437
Works
BMX Track
Lake Farm Country Park
93
Comm. Cen.
Minet Jun. & Inf. Schs.
THE A312
Spts. Grd.
Subway
F
G
H
J
K
ROAD
09
10
11
Tennis

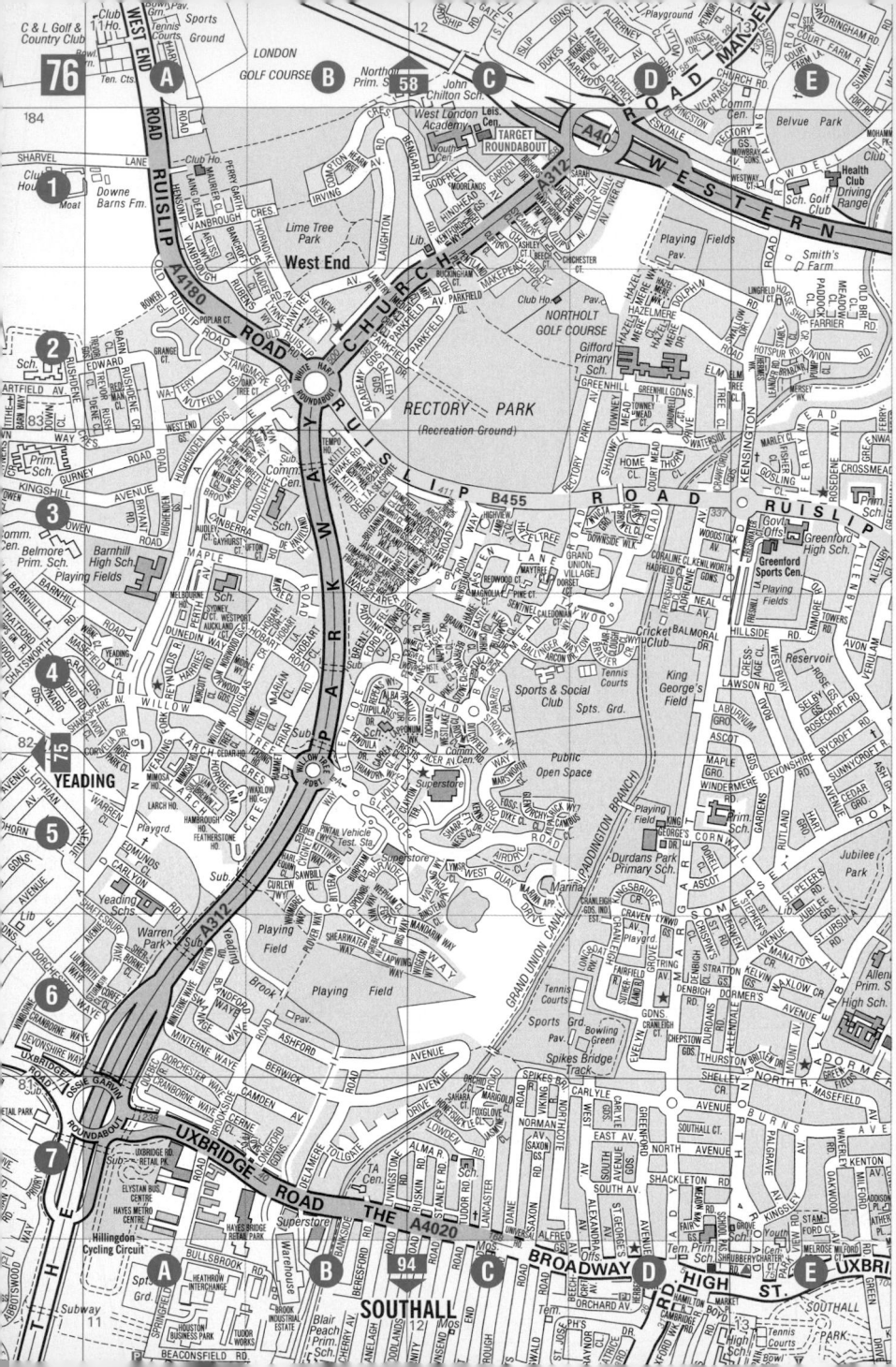
76
58
94
75
YEADING
SOUTHALL
West End
C & L Golf & Country Club
LONDON GOLF COURSE
NORTHOLT GOLF COURSE
RECTORY PARK
(Recreation Ground)
Lime Tree Park
Belvue Park
Downe Barns Fm.
Barnhill High Sch.
Belmore Prim. Sch.
Gifford Primary Sch.
Greenford High Sch.
Greenford Sports Cen.
Durdans Park Primary Sch.
King George's Field
Sports & Social Club
Public Open Space
Jubilee Park
Reservoir
Marina
GRAND UNION CANAL (PADDINGTON BRANCH)
West London Academy
John Chilton Sch.
TARGET ROUNDABOUT
WHITE HART ROUNDABOUT
WILLOW TREE RDBT.
OSSIE GARVIN ROUNDABOUT
WESTERN AV.
A40
A312
A4180
A4020
B455
RUISLIP ROAD
CHURCH ROAD
PARKWAY
WEST END ROAD
UXBRIDGE ROAD
THE BROADWAY
HIGH ST.
LADY MARGARET ROAD
SOMERSET ROAD
ALLENBY ROAD
KENSINGTON ROAD
YEADING LANE
WILLOW TREE LANE
GLENCOE ROAD
Warren Park
Yeading Brook
Playing Field
Spikes Bridge Track
Hillingdon Cycling Circuit
UXBRIDGE RD. RETAIL PK.
HAYES BRIDGE RETAIL PARK
HEATHROW INTERCHANGE
HOUSTON BUSINESS PARK
BROOK INDUSTRIAL ESTATE
Warehouse
Superstore
Smith's Farm
Health Club
Driving Range
Blair Peach Prim. Sch.
Yeading Schs.
A B C D E
1 2 3 4 5 6 7
184
12
13
11
83
82
81

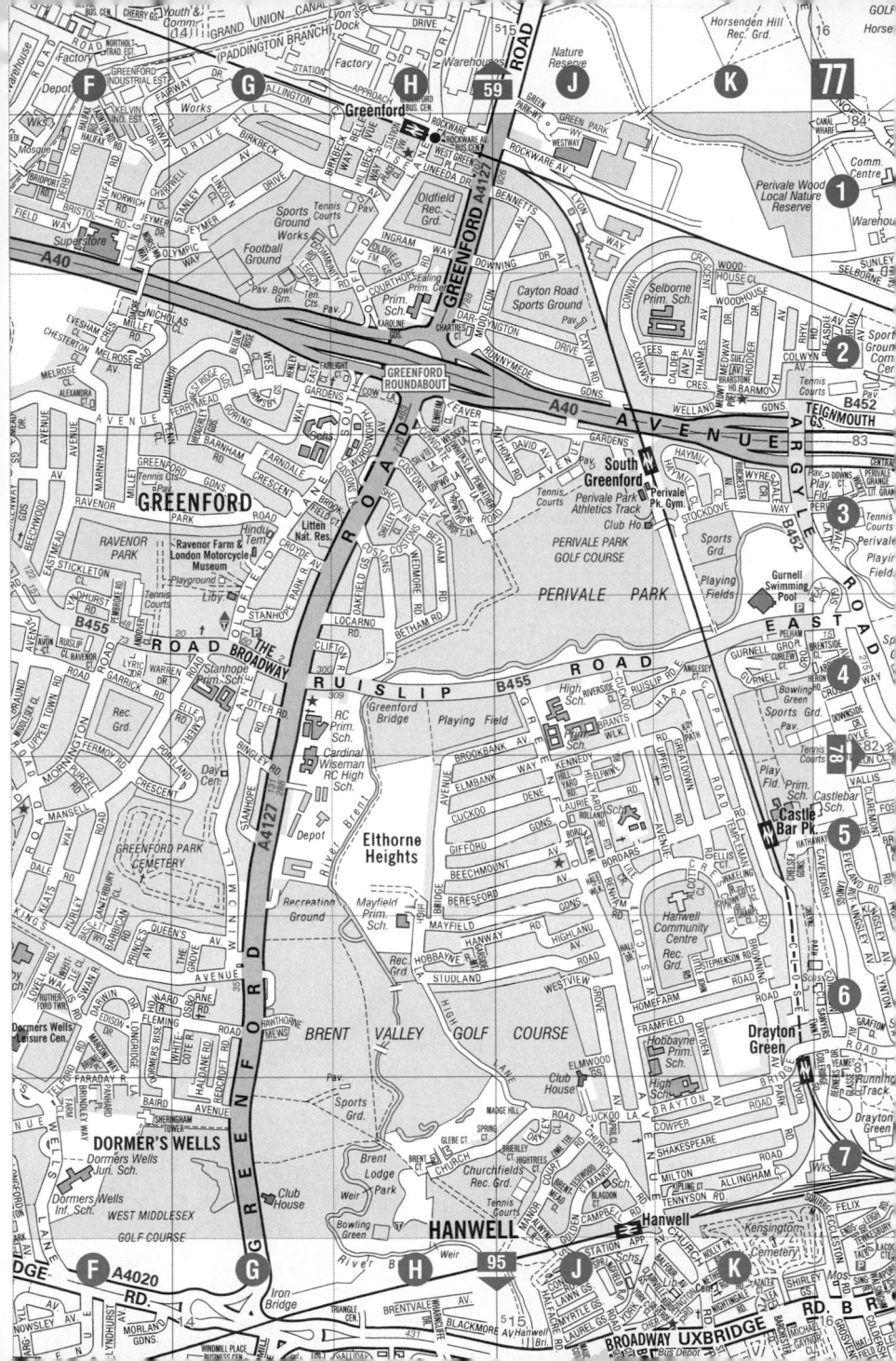

GRAND UNION CANAL
(PADDINGTON BRANCH)
Lyon's Dock
Horsenden Hill Rec. Grd.
Nature Reserve
Warehouses
Factory
GREENFORD INDUSTRIAL EST.
KELVIN IND. EST.
NORTHOLT TRAD. EST.
Works
Greenford
GREENFORD BUS. CEN.
ROCKWARE AV.
GREEN PARK WY.
WESTWAY
CANAL WHARF
Comm. Centre
Perivale Wood Local Nature Reserve
Warehouse
Mosque
Superstore
A40
Sports Ground Works
Tennis Courts
Oldfield Rec. Grd.
Football Ground
Ealing Prim. Cen.
Prim. Sch.
Cayton Road Sports Ground
Selborne Prim. Sch.
GREENFORD ROUNDABOUT
A40 AVENUE
WESTERN AVENUE
GREENFORD ROAD
A4127
B452
ARGYLE ROAD
TEIGNMOUTH GDNS.
South Greenford
Perivale Park Athletics Track
Perivale Pk. Gym.
Club Ho.
PERIVALE PARK GOLF COURSE
PERIVALE PARK
Sports Grd.
Playing Fields
Gurnell Swimming Pool
EAST
GREENFORD
RAVENOR PARK
Ravenor Farm & London Motorcycle Museum
Hindu Tem.
Litten Nat. Res.
Playground
Liby.
Tennis Courts
B455
RUISLIP ROAD
THE BROADWAY
Stanhope Prim. Sch.
Rec. Grd.
RC Prim. Sch.
Cardinal Wiseman RC High Sch.
Greenford Bridge
Playing Field
High Sch.
Prim. Sch.
Bowling Green
Sports Grd.
Castlebar Sch.
Castle Bar Pk.
Day Cen.
Depot
Elthorne Heights
River Brent
GREENFORD PARK CEMETERY
Recreation Ground
Mayfield Prim. Sch.
Hanwell Community Centre
Rec. Grd.
BRENT VALLEY GOLF COURSE
Drayton Green
Dormers Wells Leisure Cen.
HAWTHORNE MEWS
Club House
Hobbayne Prim. Sch.
High Sch.
Running Track
Sports Grd.
DORMER'S WELLS
Dormers Wells Jun. Sch.
Dormers Wells Inf. Sch.
WEST MIDDLESEX GOLF COURSE
Club House
Brent Lodge Park
Weir
Bowling Green
Churchfields Rec. Grd.
Tennis Courts
HANWELL
Hanwell
Kensington Cemetery
A4020
UXBRIDGE RD.
BROADWAY UXBRIDGE
Iron Bridge
Bus Depot
F
G
H
J
K
77
78
59
95
1
2
3
4
5
6
7

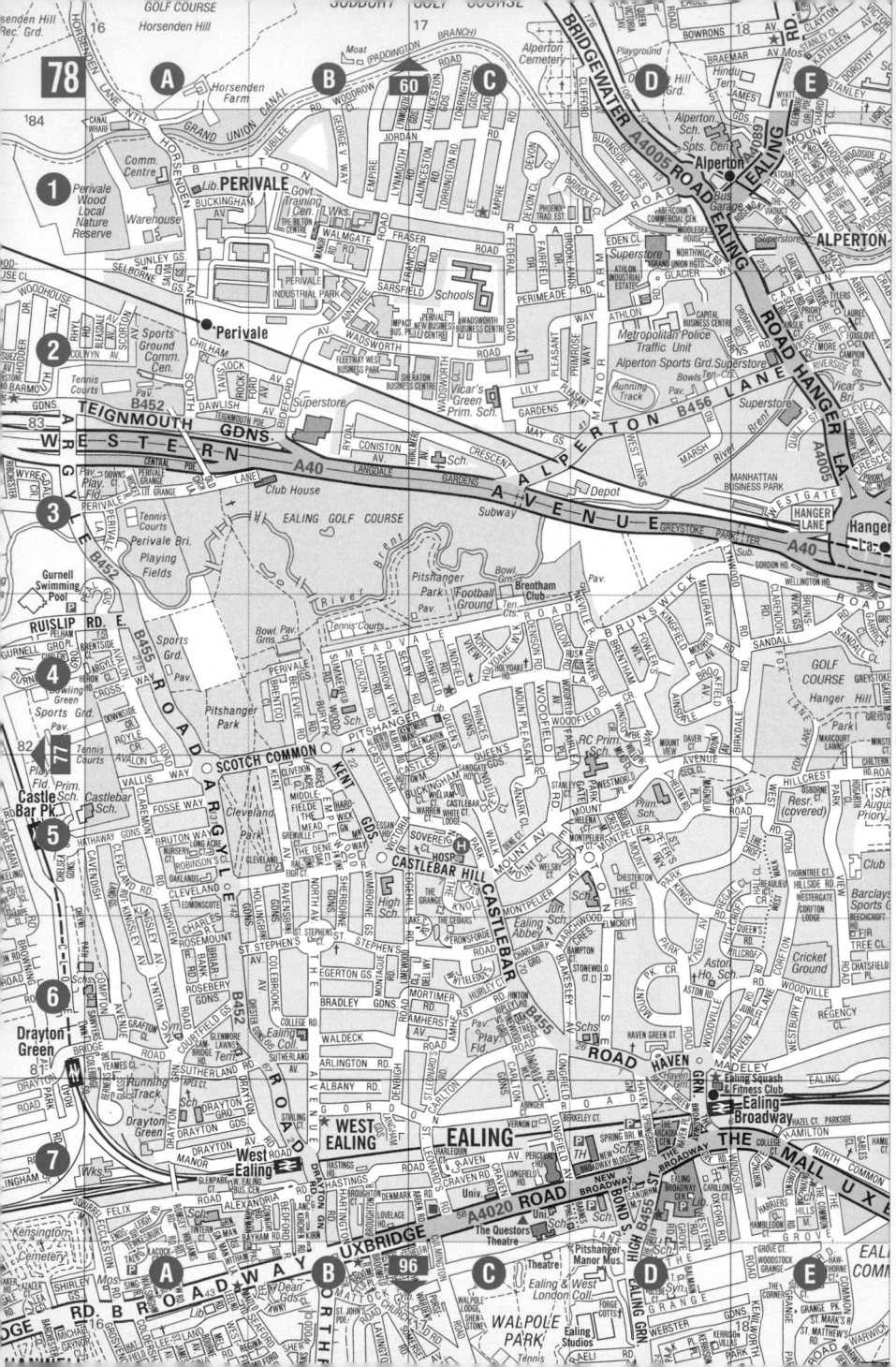

78
GOLF COURSE
Horsenden Hill
A
B
C
D
E
60
96
77
1
2
3
4
5
6
7
16
17
18
84
83
82
81
Horsenden Farm
GRAND UNION CANAL
(PADDINGTON BRANCH)
Moat
Alperton Cemetery
BRIDGEWATER
A4005
ROAD
Alperton
Alperton Sch.
Spts. Cen.
A4089
EALING
Playground
Hindu Tem.
PERIVALE
Perivale Wood Local Nature Reserve
Comm. Centre
Warehouse
Lib.
Govt. Training Cen.
THE BILTON CENTRE
Wks.
PERIVALE INDUSTRIAL PARK
Schools
Superstore
ALPERTON
Metropolitan Police Traffic Unit
Alperton Sports Grd.
Running Track
Perivale
Sports Ground Comm. Cen.
Tennis Courts
TEIGNMOUTH GDNS.
WESTERN
A40
AVENUE
ALPERTON
B456
LANE
HANGER LANE
Hanger La.
MANHATTAN BUSINESS PARK
WESTGATE
Club House
EALING GOLF COURSE
Tennis Courts
Perivale Bri. Playing Fields
Gurnell Swimming Pool
RUISLIP RD. E.
Pitshanger Park
Football Ground
Brentham Club
River Brent
Subway
Depot
Vicar's Green Prim. Sch.
GOLF COURSE
Hanger Hill
Sports Grd.
Pitshanger Park
SCOTCH COMMON
Castlebar Sch.
Castle Bar Pk.
Cleveland Park
ARGYLE
ROAD
B455
PITSHANGER
KENT
CASTLEBAR HILL
CASTLEBAR
High Sch.
HOSP.
RC Prim. Sch.
Prim. Sch.
Ealing Abbey
Jun. Sch.
Aston Ho. Sch.
Cricket Ground
Barclays Sports Grd.
Club
Resr. (covered)
Drayton Green
Running Track
Ealing Coll.
WEST EALING
West Ealing
EALING
HAVEN GRN.
Ealing Squash & Fitness Club
Ealing Broadway
THE MALL
A4020
UXBRIDGE
ROAD
BROADWAY
The Questors Theatre
Univ.
Theatre
Pitshanger Manor Mus.
Ealing & West London Coll.
WALPOLE PARK
Ealing Studios
Kensington Cemetery
Dean Gdns.
HIGH ST.
B455
EALING GRN.

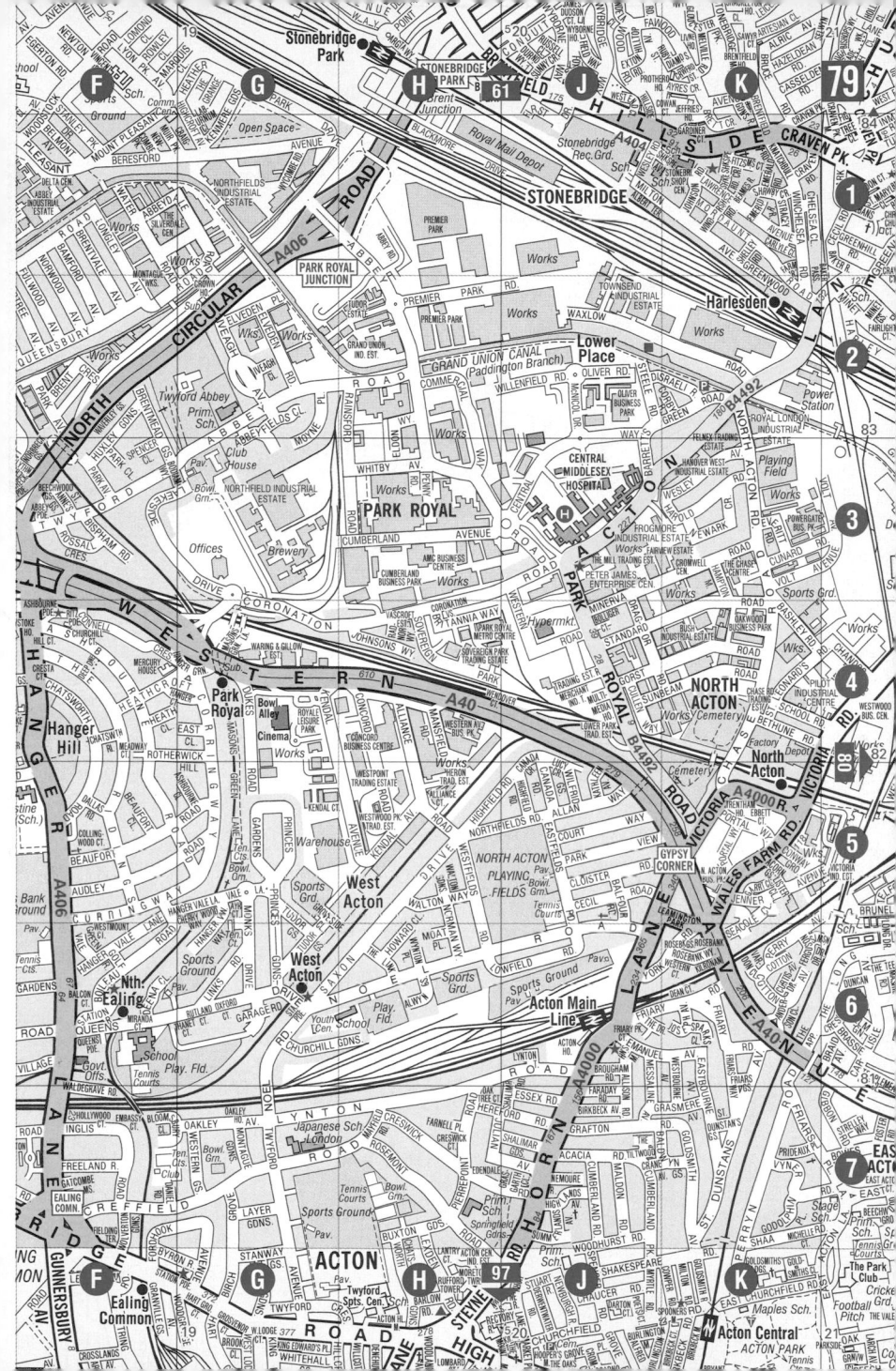

79
80
82
83
84
61
97
F
G
H
J
K
1
2
3
4
5
6
7
19
20
21
Stonebridge Park
STONEBRIDGE PARK
Brent Junction
Royal Mail Depot
STONEBRIDGE
Stonebridge Rec. Grd.
HILLSIDE
CRAVEN PK.
A404
Harlesden
Sports Ground
Open Space
NORTHFIELDS INDUSTRIAL ESTATE
PREMIER PARK
PARK ROYAL JUNCTION
NORTH CIRCULAR
A406
ABBEY RD.
PREMIER PARK RD.
TOWNSEND INDUSTRIAL ESTATE
Works
WAXLOW
Lower Place
GRAND UNION CANAL (Paddington Branch)
OLIVER BUSINESS PARK
Power Station
ROYAL LONDON INDUSTRIAL ESTATE
B4492
Twyford Abbey
Club House
NORTHFIELD INDUSTRIAL ESTATE
PARK ROYAL
CENTRAL MIDDLESEX HOSPITAL
ACTON
FROGMORE INDUSTRIAL ESTATE
Playing Field
NORTH ACTON RD.
CUMBERLAND AVENUE
Offices
Brewery
AMC BUSINESS CENTRE
CUMBERLAND BUSINESS PARK
Sports Grd.
Hypermkt.
WESTERN
CORONATION
A40
Park Royal
Hanger Hill
Bowl. Alley
Cinema
ROYALE LEISURE PARK
CONCORD BUSINESS CENTRE
WESTPOINT TRADING ESTATE
NORTH ACTON
Cemetery
North Acton
VICTORIA RD.
A4000
GYPSY CORNER
WALES FARM RD.
PARK ROYAL ROAD
Warehouse
West Acton
NORTH ACTON PLAYING FIELDS
HANGER LANE
Nth. Ealing
Sports Ground
Acton Main Line
School
Play. Fld.
HORN LANE
Japanese Sch. London
Sports Ground
ACTON
Twyford Spts. Cen.
Ealing Common
GUNNERSBURY AV.
UXBRIDGE
STEYNE RD.
HIGH
Acton Central
ACTON PARK
Maples Sch.
The Park Club
Football Pitch
EAST ACTON

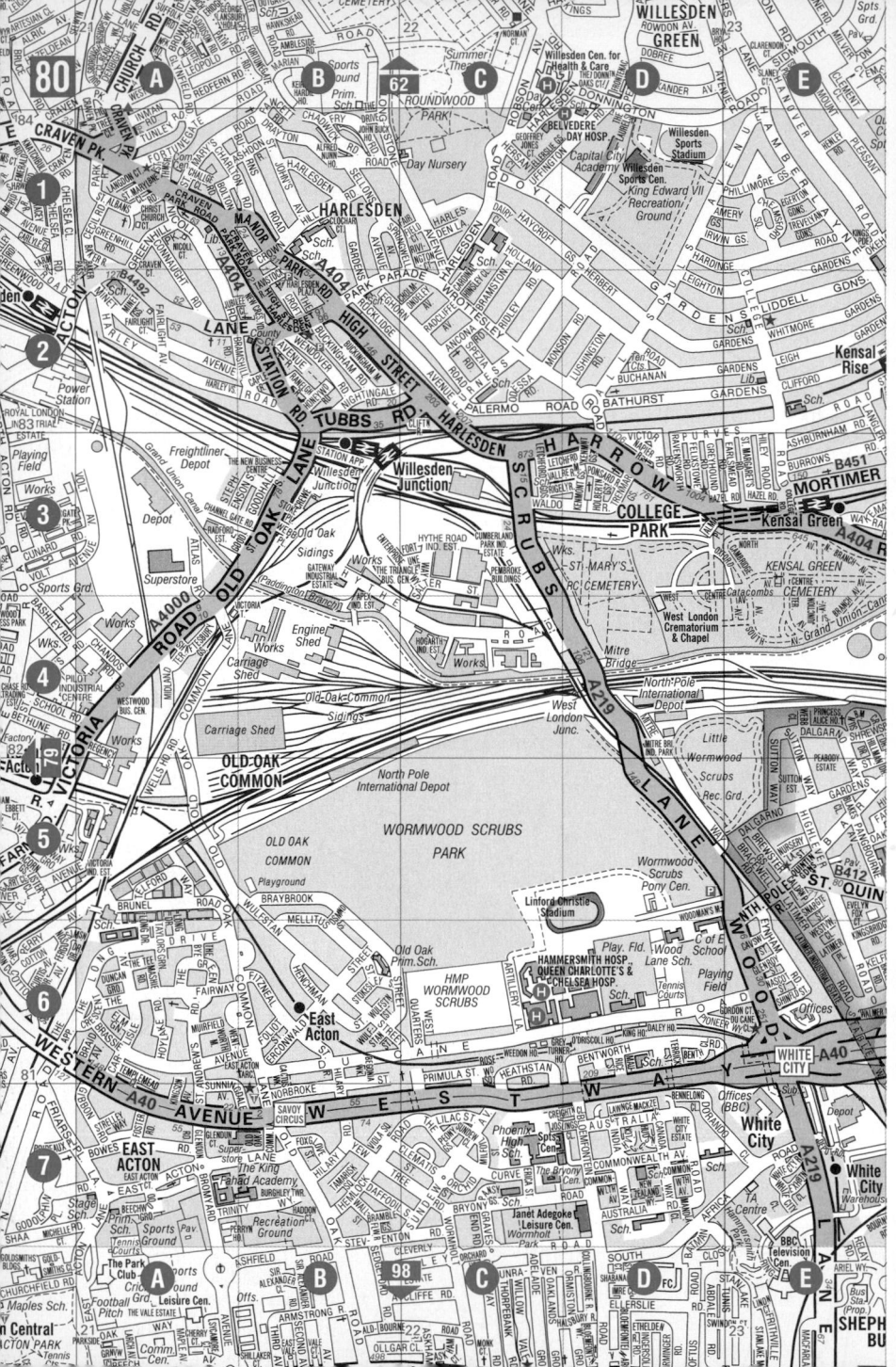

80
62
98
79
WILLESDEN GREEN
HARLESDEN
Willesden Junction
COLLEGE PARK
Kensal Green
Kensal Rise
KENSAL GREEN CEMETERY
ST. MARY'S RC CEMETERY
West London Crematorium & Chapel
Willesden Sports Stadium
Willesden Sports Cen.
King Edward VII Recreation Ground
Capital City Academy
ROUNDWOOD PARK
Willesden Cen. for Health & Care
BELVEDERE DAY HOSP.
OLD OAK COMMON
Old Oak Common Sidings
North Pole International Depot
WORMWOOD SCRUBS PARK
Little Wormwood Scrubs Rec. Grd.
Wormwood Scrubs Pony Cen.
Linford Christie Stadium
HMP WORMWOOD SCRUBS
HAMMERSMITH HOSP., QUEEN CHARLOTTE'S & CHELSEA HOSP.
EAST ACTON
East Acton
White City
BBC Television Cen.
Phoenix High Sch.
Janet Adegoke Leisure Cen.
The King Fahad Academy
Recreation Ground
Old Oak Prim. Sch.
Power Station
Freightliner Depot
Grand Union Canal
Carriage Shed
Engine Shed
Superstore
Depot
Works
West London Junc.
Mitre Bridge
WESTERN AVENUE
WESTWAY
A40
A404
A4000
A219
B451
B412
B4492
OLD OAK ROAD
OLD OAK LANE
VICTORIA ROAD
SCRUBS LANE
HARROW ROAD
HARLESDEN HIGH STREET
MANOR PARK RD.
CRAVEN PK.
TUBBS RD.
STATION RD.
ACTON LANE
WOOD LANE
DU CANE RD.
MORTIMER
ST. QUINTIN
SAVOY CIRCUS
WHITE CITY
SHEPH BU
Central
ACTON PARK

BRONDESBURY
WILLESDEN
KILBURN
63
ABBEY ROAD
BELSIZE ROAD
BRONDESBURY PARK
Brondesbury Park
Willesden Lane Cemetery
QUEENS PARK
KILBURN
Kilburn High Road
Kilburn Park
MAIDA VALE
KENSAL RISE
Queens Park
HARVIST ROAD
CARLTON VALE
KENSAL GREEN
WEST KILBURN
Paddington Rec. Grd.
Maida Vale
SHIRLAND ROAD
MAIDA VALE
HARROW ROAD
KENSAL TOWN
MAIDA HILL
Paddington Bowl. & Spts. Club
BBC Studios
WARWICK AVENUE
ELGIN AVENUE
ST. CHARLES HOSPITAL
WESTBOURNE GREEN
Westbourne Park
Royal Oak
NORTH KENSINGTON
WESTWAY
A40
82
WESTBOURNE PARK ROAD
CAMBRIDGE GDNS.
Ladbroke Gro.
CHEPSTOW RD
BAYSWATER
BISHOP'S BRI. RD.
WESTBOURNE GRO.
Latimer Rd.
NOTTING HILL
KENSINGTON PARK RD
PEMBROKE
Bayswater
QUEENSWAY
Queensway
BAYSWATER RD A402
Notting Hill Gate
KENSINGTON GARDENS
WEST CROSS ROUTE
99
Holland Park
LADBROKE GROVE
PORTOBELLO RD
WESTBOURNE GROVE
Ladbroke Square Gardens
1
2
3
4
5
6
7
F
G
H
J
K

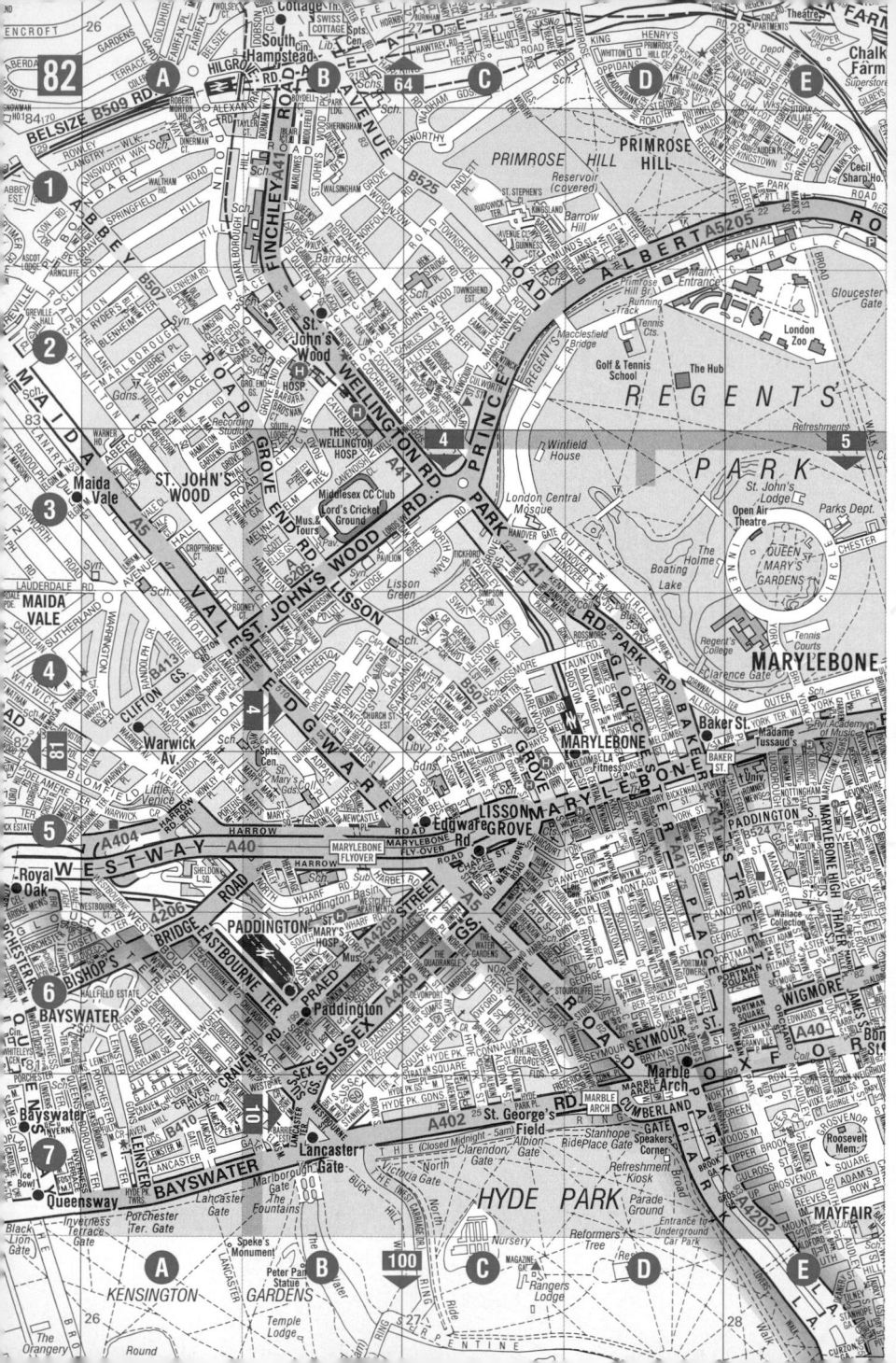

82
A
B
C
D
E
1
2
3
4
5
6
7
64
81
100
4
5
10
PRIMROSE HILL
Reservoir (covered)
Barrow Hill
Primrose Hill Br.
Running Track
Tennis Cts.
Macclesfield Bridge
Golf & Tennis School
The Hub
London Zoo
Gloucester Gate
Main Entrance
CANAL
ALBERT
A5205
PRINCE
REGENTS
PARK
Refreshments
Winfield House
London Central Mosque
Hanover Gate
St. John's Lodge
Parks Dept.
Open Air Theatre
The Holme
Boating Lake
QUEEN MARY'S GARDENS
Regent's College
Tennis Courts
Clarence Gate
MARYLEBONE
Baker St.
Madame Tussaud's
Ryl. Academy of Music
Chalk Farm
Superstore
Cecil Sharp Ho.
PRIMROSE HILL
South Hampstead
Swiss Cottage
BELSIZE
B509
FINCHLEY ROAD
A41
AVENUE
B525
ABBEY ROAD
B507
St. John's Wood
WELLINGTON RD.
THE WELLINGTON HOSP
Middlesex CC Club
Lord's Cricket Ground
Mus.& Tours
ST. JOHN'S WOOD RD.
A5205
LISSON
Lisson Green
GROVE END RD.
ST. JOHN'S WOOD
MAIDA VALE
Maida Vale
A5
CLIFTON GS.
B413
Warwick Av.
Little Venice
EDGWARE
HARROW
A404
WESTWAY
A40
MARYLEBONE FLYOVER
Edgware Rd.
LISSON GROVE
MARYLEBONE
Paddington Basin
PADDINGTON
ST. MARY'S HOSP
Paddington
PRAED
A4205
A4209
SUSSEX
BISHOP'S
BRIDGE
EASTBOURNE TER.
A4206
Royal Oak
BAYSWATER
Bayswater
Queensway
B410
LEINSTER
Lancaster Gate
THE WATER GARDENS
GLOUCESTER PLACE
BAKER STREET
A41
B524
PADDINGTON ST.
MARYLEBONE HIGH
Wallace Collection
WIGMORE
PORTMAN SQUARE
SEYMOUR ST.
Marble Arch
MARBLE ARCH
OXFORD
CUMBERLAND GATE
A402
St. George's Field
Albion Gate
Stanhope Place Gate
Speakers' Corner
Clarendon Gate
Victoria Gate
Marlborough Gate
The Fountains
HYDE PARK
Refreshment Kiosk
Parade Ground
Reformers Tree
Entrance to Underground Car Park
Nursery
Magazine
Rangers Lodge
PARK LANE
A4202
Roosevelt Mem.
GROSVENOR
MAYFAIR
Lancaster Gate
Porchester Ter. Gate
Inverness Terrace Gate
Black Lion Gate
Speke's Monument
Peter Pan Statue
Temple Lodge
KENSINGTON GARDENS
The Orangery
Round
SERPENTINE
(Closed Midnight - 5am)
Ice Bowl
HYDE PK. TWRS.

CAMDEN TOWN
Camden Town
Camden Rd.
and Barnsbury
BRITANNIA JUNC.
65
F
G
H
J
K
1
2
3
4
5
6
7
REGENT'S PARK
Mornington Cres.
SOMERS TOWN
EUSTON
Euston Sq.
EUSTON UNDERPASS
Warren St.
Regent's Park
Gt. Portland St.
KING'S CROSS
King's Cross
King's Cross (Thameslink)
ST. PANCRAS
British Library
PENTONVILLE
PENTONVILLE ROAD
CLERKENWELL
ST. PANCRAS
6
7
84
The Raceway (Go-Kart Track)
Driving Range
London Wildlife Trust
ST. PANCRAS HOSPITAL
Ryl. Veterinary Coll.
University College
Petrie Mus.
Russell Sq.
BLOOMSBURY
Univ. of London
British Museum
Goodge St.
Tottenham Ct. R.
Oxford Circus
SOHO
Holborn
HOLBORN
Covent Gdn.
Leicester Sq.
Piccadilly Circus
Eros
National Gallery
Nelson's Col.
Charing Cross
CHARING CROSS
Embankment
Embankment Pier
Savoy Pier
Cleopatra's Needle
Somerset Ho.
Law Courts
Temple
Temple Pier
RIVER THAMES
South Bank
National Theatre
Royal Festival Hall
The London Television Centre
Green Park
Admiralty Arch
101
Hungerford Bri.
Lincoln's Inn
PICCADILLY
REGENT ST.
SHAFTESBURY AV.
CHARING CROSS RD.
STRAND
ALDWYCH
KINGSWAY
EMBANKMENT
WATERLOO BRI.
EUSTON RD.
GOWER ST.
TOTTENHAM COURT RD.
HAMPSTEAD RD.
EVERSHOLT ST.
PANCRAS WAY
CALEDONIAN RD.
YORK WAY
GRAY'S INN RD.
KING'S CROSS RD.
FARRINGDON RD.
THEOBALDS RD.
SOUTHAMPTON ROW
NEW OXFORD ST.
OXFORD ST.
NEW BOND ST.
PORTLAND PL.
ALBANY ST.
PARKWAY
CAMDEN HIGH ST.
DELANCEY ST.
CROWNDALE RD.
MIDLAND RD.
PALL MALL
HAYMARKET
WOBURN PL.
MONTAGUE PL.
BEDFORD SQ.
CONDUIT ST.

84
A
B
C
D
E
66
Essex Rd.
ISLINGTON
DE BEAUVOIR TOWN
1
2
3
4
5
6
7
Barnard Park
Angel
PENTONVILLE RD.
A501
7
8
9
FINSBURY
SHOREDITCH
HOXTON
CLERKENWELL
Old Street
ST. LUKE'S
Charterhouse
Farringdon
Barbican
Moorgate
LIVERPOOL ST.
83
HOLBORN
City Thameslink
St. Paul's
CITY
Bank
Mansion Ho.
Monument
Temple
VICTORIA EMB.
BLACKFRIARS
SOUTHWARK
CANNON STREET
RIVER
THAMES
102
LONDON BRIDGE HOSP
FENCHURCH ST.
LONDON WALL
CHEAPSIDE
FLEET ST.
STRAND
Blackfriars Millennium Pier
Bankside Pier
London Bri. City Pier
Tower Millennium Pier

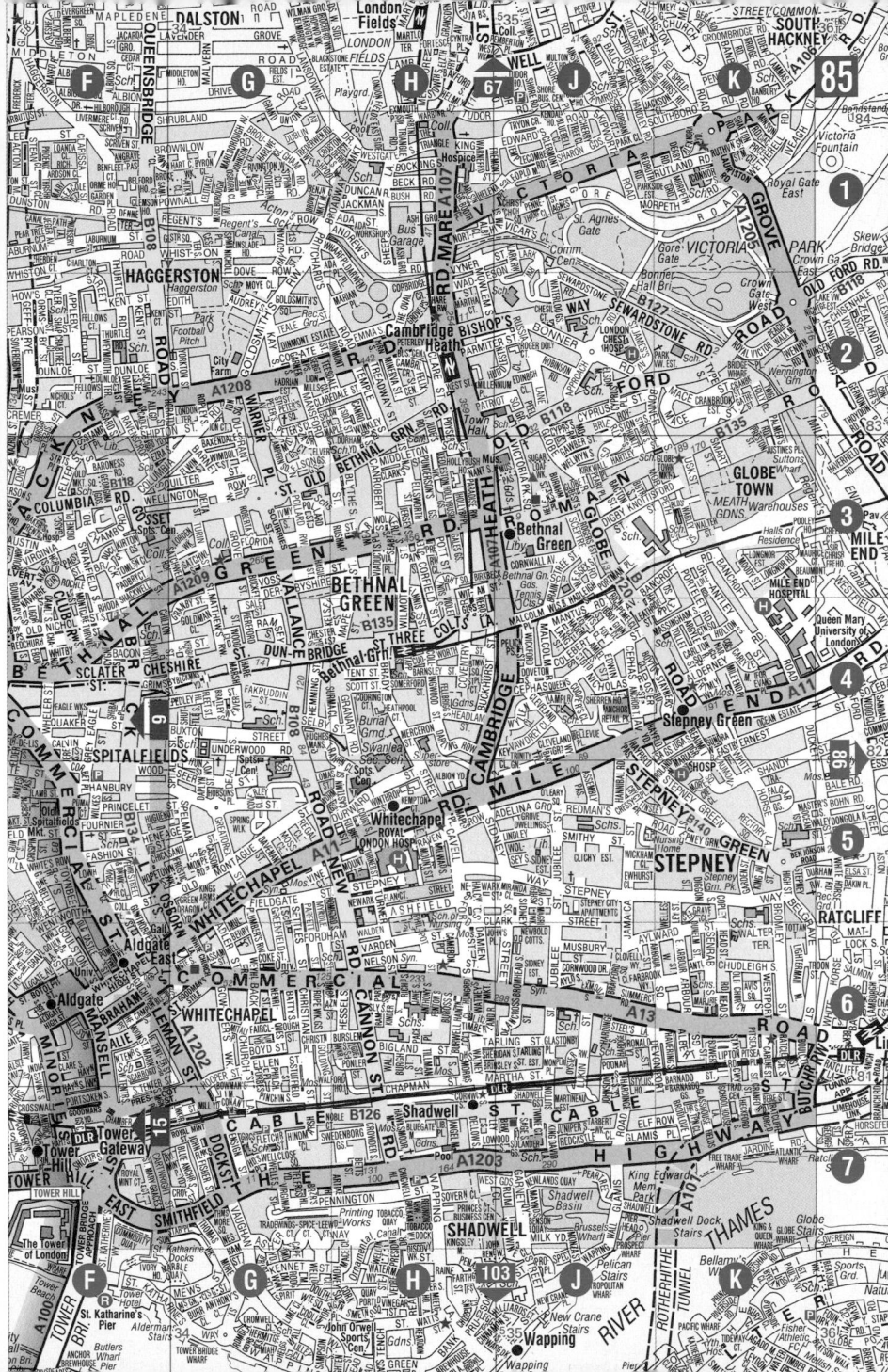

85
67
DALSTON
London Fields
SOUTH HACKNEY
HAGGERSTON
Haggerston
Cambridge Heath
VICTORIA PARK
Victoria Fountain
Royal Gate East
St. Agnes Gate
Gore Gate
Bonner Hall Bri.
Crown Gate West
Skew Bridge
Crown Ga. East
OLD FORD RD.
VICTORIA
GROVE ROAD
SEWARDSTONE RD.
MARE ST.
A107
A1205
B127
B118
B135
A1208
A1209
A11
A13
A1202
A1203
B126
B108
B134
B140
A101
A100
BISHOP'S WAY
BETHNAL GREEN
Bethnal Green
GREEN RD.
HACKNEY RD.
CAMBRIDGE HEATH
OLD FORD RD.
ROMAN RD.
GLOBE RD.
GLOBE TOWN
MILE END
Mile End Hospital
Queen Mary University of London
MILE END RD.
Stepney Green
STEPNEY
STEPNEY GREEN
RATCLIFF
SPITALFIELDS
Old Spitalfields Mkt.
COMMERCIAL ST.
COLUMBIA RD.
WHITECHAPEL RD.
Whitechapel
ROYAL LONDON HOSP.
WHITECHAPEL
COMMERCIAL RD.
NEW RD.
CANNON ST. RD.
Aldgate East
Aldgate
MINORIES
MANSELL
LEMAN ST.
BRAHAM
Tower Gateway
Tower Hill
TOWER HILL
The Tower of London
TOWER BRIDGE APPROACH
TOWER BRI.
St. Katharine's Pier
St. Katharine Docks
EAST SMITHFIELD
THE HIGHWAY
CABLE ST.
Shadwell
SHADWELL
Shadwell Basin
King Edward Mem. Park
ROTHERHITHE TUNNEL
RIVER THAMES
Wapping
New Crane Stairs
Pelican Stairs
Brussels Wharf
Globe Stairs
Limehouse
LIMEHOUSE LINK
103
9
15
86
F
G
H
J
K
1
2
3
4
5
6
7

86
68
85
104
A
B
C
D
E
1
2
3
4
5
6
7
SOUTH HACKNEY
STRATFORD
Stratford Marsh
VICTORIA PARK
OLD FORD
Victoria Park Athletics Arena
Victoria Fountain
Three Colt Bridge
Skew Bridge
Crown Gate East
Crown Gate West
GROVE ROAD
ROMAN ROAD
OLD FORD ROAD
PARNELL ROAD
EAST CROSS ROUTE
FAIRFIELD RD.
BLACKWALL
A12
Pudding Mill Lane
BOW INTERCHANGE
THE BOW QUARTER
BOW
Bow Church
Bow Rd.
BOW ROAD
HIGH ST.
GLOBE TOWN
MILE END
MILE END HOSPITAL
Mile End
Queen Mary University of London
ST. CLEMENT'S HOSPITAL
TOWER HAMLETS CEMETERY
MILE END ROAD
BURDETT ROAD
A1205
BROMLEY
Bromley-by-Bow
ST. ANDREW'S HOSP.
DEVAS ST.
Devons Rd.
DEVONS ROAD
BOW COMMON
NORTHERN APPROACH
BLACKWALL TUNNEL
Three Mills Green
Three Mills
TV & Film Studios
Mile End Park Leisure Centre
Mile End Stadium
Ragged Sch. Mus.
Gas Works
BEN JONSON RD.
ST. PAULS WAY
DEVONS WAY
RATCLIFF
LIMEHOUSE
Limehouse
Limehouse Basin
COMMERCIAL ROAD
EAST INDIA DOCK ROAD
A13
All Saints
POPLAR
Poplar
Langdon Park
Bartlett Park
Westferry
West India Quay
Canary Wharf
Canary Wharf Pier
Billingsgate Fish Market
WEST INDIA DOCKS
ASPEN WAY
A1261
LIMEHOUSE LINK
WESTFERRY RD.
RIVER THAMES
LIMEHOUSE REACH
Ratcliff Cross Stairs
Globe Stairs
Pageant Stairs
ROTHERHITHE
SALTER RD.
Hilton Docklands Pier
Westferry Circus
Museum in Docklands
BLACKWALL BASIN
PRESTON'S RD.
COTTON ST.
Depot
Works

87
88
69
105
F
G
H
J
K
1
2
3
4
5
6
7
WEST HAM
PARK
UPTON
Upton Park
WEST HAM
PLAISTOW
CANNING TOWN
Mill Meads
Prescott Channel
Pumping Station
Jubilee Line Depot
Bridge Rd. Depot
Gas Depot
West Ham
Plaistow
East London Crematorium
EAST LONDON CEMETERY
Memorial Recreation Ground
Recreation Ground
Sorting Office
Depot
Gas Works
Star Park
BOW CREEK
Warehouse
Depots
Wharves
Canning Town
CANNING TOWN
STH. BROMLEY
East India
LEAMOUTH
Virginia Quay
Blackwall Pier
Blackwall
Blackwall Point
RIVER THAMES
BLACKWALL TUNNEL
The O2 (Millennium Dome)
London City Airport Pier
Brewery
Works
Royal Victoria
Custom House for ExCeL
ExCeL
Prince Regent
Tidal Basin
Watersports Centre
ROYAL VICTORIA DOCK
Millennium Mill
Pontoon Dock
PORTWAY
PLASHET
UPTON LA.
STOPFORD RD.
NEW PLAISTOW RD.
PLAISTOW RD.
HIGH ST.
GREENGATE ST.
PRINCE REGENT LA.
MANOR RD.
MANOR ROAD
STEPHENSON STREET
BARKING RD.
NEWHAM WAY
BALAAM ST.
SILVERTOWN WAY
LOWER LEA CROSSING
SILVERTOWN VIADUCT
NORTH WOOLWICH RD.
VICTORIA DOCK ROAD
ABBEY RD.
CORPORATION ST.
A112
A114
A1011
A124
A13
A1020
B164
B165
B166
B125

88
70
87
106
A
B
C
D
E
1
2
3
4
5
6
7
PLASHET RD.
PLASHET GRO.
GREEN ST.
Upton Park
UPTON PARK
KATHERINE
B109
ROAD
East Ham
HIGH ST. NTH.
RON LEIGHTON WY.
A117
WALLEND
BARKING RD.
A124
A13
B167
STREET
CENTRAL PARK RD.
EAST HAM
CENTRAL PARK
RANCLIFFE RD.
HIGH STREET SOUTH
A117
West Ham Utd. FC (Upton Pk.)
Gala Bingo
Leisure Cen.
Comm. Cen.
Flanders Playing Fields
Brampton Prim. Sch.
Brampton Park
East Ham Synagogue
Jewish Cemetery
NHS Walk-In Cen.
NEWHAM GENERAL HOSPITAL
Cumberland Sch. Specialist Sports College
Terence McMillan Stadium
Newham Leisure Centre
Brampton Youth Centre
Playing Field
East Ham Nature Reserve
Superstore
The Docklands Equestrian Centre
BECKTON ALPS
ALPINE BUSINESS CENTRE
BECKTON RETAIL PK.
NEWHAM WAY
PRINCE REGENT LANE
A112
North Beckton
TOLLGATE RD.
BECKTON
Beckton
CUSTOM HOUSE
King George V Park
Newham City Farm
West Beckton
Mid Beckton
Globe & Lib.
EAST BECKTON DISTRICT CEN.
MANOR A117
WOOLWICH MANOR WAY
Beckton Park
New Beckton Park
The Stroud Pavilion
Hospice
Stables
Pavilion
VICTORIA DOCK RD.
ROYAL ALBERT WAY
Beckton Park
A1020
Cyprus
CYPRUS
University
UNIVERSITY
Custom Ho. for ExCeL
ExCeL
Prince Regent
Royal Albert
London Regatta Centre
ROYAL ALBERT DOCK
LONDON CITY AIRPORT
ROYAL VICTORIA DOCK
CONNAUGHT A1020 BRIDGE
Go-kart Circuit
Millennium Mill
Pontoon Dock
D Silo
Depot
London City Airport
KING GEORGE V DOCK
King George V
DLR
NTH. WOOLWICH
ROAD

89
BARKING
Upney
BARKING HOSPITAL
Upney Sidings
GREENSLADE RD.
71
VICARAGE FIELD SHOPPING CEN.
RODING TRADING ESTATE
LONDON ROAD
ABBEY RETAIL PARK
Buses Only
Courts
Prim. Sch.
Lib.
Thtre
Barking Abbey
Superstore
Spts. Cen.
ST. PAUL'S RD.
ABBEY RD.
CIRCULAR ROAD
RIPPLE ROAD
A123
SUFFOLK RD.
ESSEX RD.
LAMBOURNE RD.
DAWSON AVENUE
Mus.
Depot
BARKING INDUSTRIAL PARK
Langdon School
Ten. Cts.
Works
Adult Training Cen.
ABBEY PARK IND. EST.
THE SHAFTESBURYS
NEW ENGLAND INDUSTRIAL ESTATE
Greatfields Park
Playground
EAST-HAM-&-BARKING-BY-PASS
A13
Subway
WAYSIDE COMMERCIAL CEN.
ALFREDS WAY INDUSTRIAL ESTATE
Library
Hlth. Cen.
Youth Centre
Thames View Jun. Sch.
Thames View Inf. Sch.
MOVERS LANE
LYON BUSINESS PARK
Hand Trough Creek
Cuckold's Haven
Refuse & Sewage Works
JENKINS LANE
ALFREDS WAY
A406
ABBEY WHARF IND. ESTATE
KINGSBRIDGE WHARF
River Roding
Showcase Cinema
Hollywood Bowl Barking
Powerleague Soccer Centre
Refuse Transfer Station
CLARKE LANE
Long Mark
KATELLA TRAD. EST.
CROMWELL TRAD. CEN.
RIVER ROAD BUSINESS PARK
THAMES ROAD
BARKING BUS. PK.
BANKSIDE PARK
Warehouses
Long Reach
Wharf
Barking Creek
CREEKMOUTH IND. PARK
LONG REACH RD.
TRAFALGAR BUSINESS CEN.
Beckton Sewage Treatment Works
Thameside Nature
CREEKMOUTH
ANGLIAN INDUS. EST.
90
82
BECKTON TRIANGLE RETAIL PK.
GATEWAY RETAIL PARK
Greenway
Factory
THE LONDON INDUSTRIAL PARK
ROYAL DOCKS ROAD
A1020
(Proposed)
Superstore
GALLIONS REACH SHOPPING PARK
Sewage Treatment Works
Tanks
Warpools Reach
BALMORAL TRADING EST.
BUZZARD CREEK IND. EST.
Barking Creek Flood Barrier
Jetty
Pier
ARMADA WAY
Gas Works
Winsor Park
Docklands Light Railway Depot
Engine Shed
THAMES
RIVER
Margaret or Tripcock Ness
Gallions Reach
DLR
GALLIONS ROUNDABOUT
Pump. Sta.
THAMES GATEWAY BRIDGE (Proposed)
Gallions Reach
Works
ALBERT BASIN
Gallions Point Marina
Thames House
Newham Coll. of Further Education (Royal Docks Campus)
WOOLWICH MANOR WAY
A117
Drawbridge
Custom House
107
Twin Tumps
CANNON RETAIL PK.
THAMESMEAD CENTRAL
CENTRAL WAY
Tor
Play. Fld.
F G H J K
1 2 3 4 5 6 7
44 45 46 81 83 84

90
72
68
108
A
B
C
D
E
1
2
3
4
5
6
7
46
47
48
81
82
83
84
LODGE AVENUE FLYOVER JUNC.
Cemetery
RIPPLE A123 ROAD
LODGE AV.
A1153
A13
RIPPLE ROAD
ALFREDS WY.
CASTLE GREEN
Goresbrook Leisure Centre
Cinema
Bingo Hall
Pavilion
GORESBROOK ROAD
ROTHWELL RD.
MAPLESTEAD RD.
Prim. Sch.
Subway
Rippleside
Depot
Warehouse
BARKING INDUSTRIAL PARK
RIPPLESIDE COMMERCIAL ESTATE
PORTLAND COMMERCIAL ESTATE
MAYBELLS COMMERCIAL ESTATE
RENWICK INDUSTRIAL ESTATE
DAVENPORT CENTRE
ALFREDS WAY INDUSTRIAL ESTATE
WAYSIDE COMMERCIAL CEN.
THE INVICTA CEN.
Ripple Lane Sidings
Channel Tunnel Rail Link
Scrattons Farm Eco-Park
Factory
Warehouses
SCRATTONS TERRACE
Newlands Park
Library
WIVENHOE RD.
ROXWELL RD.
CHELMER CRES.
CROUCH AV.
CHOATS ROAD
ALDERMAN AV.
Thames View Jun. Sch.
Youth Centre
Thames View Inf. Sch.
Works
RIVERSIDE INDUSTRIAL ESTATE
BARKING BUS. PK.
THAMES ROAD
Thameside Park City Fm.
The Ripple Nature Reserve
Barking Riverside
Oil Storage Depot
Depot
RENWICK ROAD
Power Station (disused)
Thameside Community Nature Reserve
Horse Shoe Corner
CREEKMOUTH
TRAFALGAR BUSINESS CEN.
ANGLIAN IND. EST.
BALMORAL TRADING EST.
BUZZARD CREEK IND. EST.
RIVER RD.
Jetty
Pier
Barking or False Point
RIVER
BARKING REACH
Abbey Sluice
Cross Ness
Thamesmead North
THAMESMEAD
Castilion Prim. Sch.
Driving Range
RIVERSIDE GOLF COURSE
Pumping Station
THAMESIDE
Library & Comm. Hall
Thamesmere Leisure Cen.
Superstore
CANNON RETAIL PK.
A2041
CARLYLE WAY
THAMESMEAD CENTRAL
Bishop John Robinson Prim. Sch.
Ecumenical Cen.
Youth Club
Butts Wood
Woolwich Poly. Sch.
Football Ground
Playing Field
A2016
EASTERN WAY
BELVEDERE
Lakeside
CENTRAL WAY

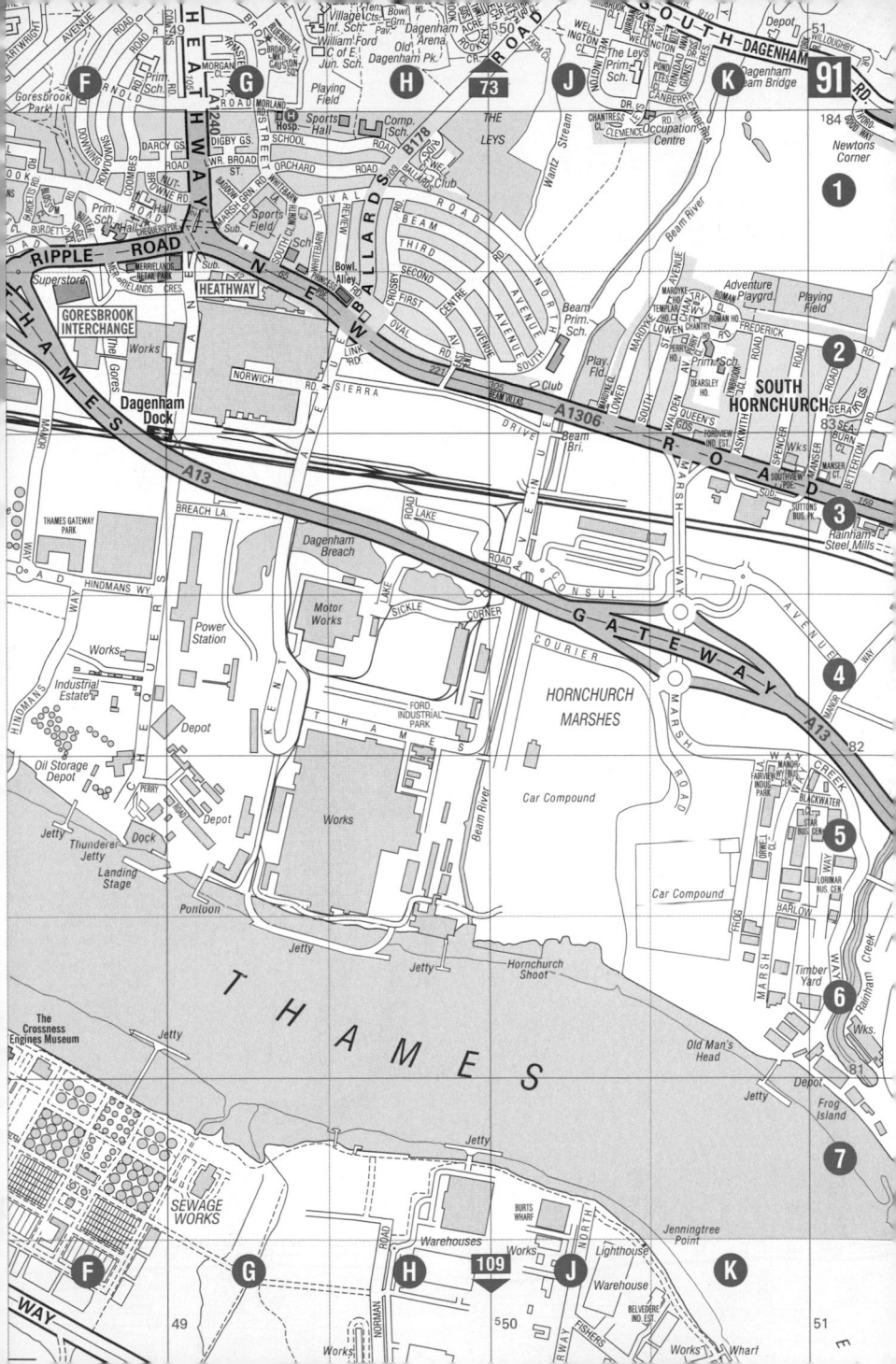

91
73
109
F
G
H
J
K
1
2
3
4
5
6
7
49
50
51
184
83
82
81
SOUTH DAGENHAM
Depot
Dagenham Beam Bridge
Newtons Corner
Goresbrook Park
Prim. Sch.
Playing Field
Old Dagenham Pk.
Dagenham Arena
William Ford C of E. Jun. Sch.
Village Inf. Sch.
The Leys Prim. Sch.
Comp. Sch.
Sports Hall
Hosp.
THE LEYS
Occupation Centre
Wantz Stream
Beam River
Club
Sports Field
Bowl. Alley
RIPPLE ROAD
Superstore
GORESBROOK INTERCHANGE
HEATHWAY
NEW ROAD
BALLARDS ROAD
OVAL ROAD
BEAM AVENUE
A1240
A1306
B178
Works
Dagenham Dock
Beam Prim. Sch.
Play. Fld.
Adventure Playgrd.
Playing Field
SOUTH HORNCHURCH
Rainham Steel Mills
THAMES AVENUE
A13
THAMES GATEWAY PARK
BREACH LA.
Dagenham Breach
Motor Works
Power Station
Works
Industrial Estate
Depot
Oil Storage Depot
Jetty
Thunderer Jetty
Landing Stage
Pontoon
Dock
FORD INDUSTRIAL PARK
HORNCHURCH MARSHES
Car Compound
Car Compound
GATEWAY
MARSH WAY
FRIARS WAY
FRIARS CREEK
Timber Yard
Rainham Creek
Wks.
Old Man's Head
Depot
Frog Island
Jetty
Hornchurch Shoot
THAMES
The Crossness Engines Museum
SEWAGE WORKS
BURTS WHARF
Warehouses
Works
Lighthouse
Warehouse
Jenningtree Point
BELVEDERE IND. EST.
Works
Wharf
NORMAN ROAD
FISHERS WAY
WAY

92
74
110
A
B
C
D
E
1
2
3
4
5
6
7
06
07
08
80
79
78
77
STOCKLEY COUNTRY PARK
STOCKLEY PARK GOLF COURSE
Stockley Park
Club House
The Arena
Virgin Active
Uxbridge FC
Recreation Ground
Yiewsley Swim. Pool
Library
Bowls
RAINBOW IND. EST.
Comm. Cen.
WHITETHORN AV.
FAIRFIELD RD.
HORTON ROAD
West Drayton
Colham Bri.
Horton Bridge
INDEPENDENT IND. EST.
HORTON RD. IND. EST.
HORTON IND. PK.
Warehouses
Wks.
IRON BRIDGE RD.
STOCKLEY ROAD
A408
BENNETS FIELD RD.
LONGWALK
ROUNDWOOD AV.
FURZEGROUND WAY
Stockley Bridge
RIGBY
Works
Depot
Government Offices
STORMOUNT DR.
DENBIGH DR.
SNOWDON CR.
BOURNE AV.
GLAMIS
Bourne Farm Playing Field
Tennis Cts.
PINKWELL PARK
PINKWELL
Pinkwell Prim. Sch.
Frogs Ditch Farm
Burial Ground
Frogs Ditch
WARWICK ROAD
STATION RD.
Fray's River
SWAN RD.
DRAYTON GDNS.
BELLCLOSE RD.
FURZEHAM RD.
West Drayton Prim. Sch.
Play. Fld.
Lib.
CHURCH RD.
WEST DRAYTON ROAD
Spts. Grd.
RAF Station
PORTERS WAY
THORNTON AV.
SIPSON ROAD
Drayton Hall
Comm. Cen.
Youth Cen.
Tennis Courts
Playgrd.
The Closes Rec. Grd.
The Avenue
St. Georges Meadow
WEST DRAYTON
Cemetery
The Dell
LAVENDER RISE
Recreation Ground
Works
HEATHPARK GOLF COURSE
Club Ho.
Hotel
CHERRY LANE
Cherry Lane Roundabout
SHEPISTON
Cherry La. Prim. Sch.
Longmead Prim. Sch.
LAUREL LANE
BERBERIS WK.
GREAT BRAMBLES
M4 MOTORWAY
M4
Junction 4
Subway
A3044
HARMONDSWORTH LANE
HOLLOWAY
Nursery
Heathrow Primary School
SIPSON LANE
SIPSON
Wall Garden Farm
Little Harlington Field
Sports Ground
Burial Ground
Tennis Courts
Pavilion
William Byrd Prim. Sch.
Pav.
HARMONDSWORTH
HARLINGTON
Pheasant Nursery
CANDOVER CL.
ZEALAND AV.
SKYPORT DR.
Summit Cen.
PINGLESTONE CL.
POLAR PARK
THE NORMAN HAY TRADING ESTATE
HEATHROW BLVRD.
AIRPORT GATE
Recreation Ground
Junction 4a
Tennis Cts.
Playgrd.
Hotel
BLUNTS AV.
DORTON VILLAS
Excelsior Hotel
DOGHURST AV.
EGERTON WY.
MONDIAL WAY
The Edwardian International Hotel
BATH ROAD
A4
NEWBURY RD.
NORTHOLT RD.
NORTHROOD RD.
NELSON RD.
NORTHERN PERIMETER ROAD (WEST)
Statue
NENE ROAD ROUNDABOUT
Customs Ho.
The Renaissance Hotel
Heathrow Visitors Cen.
NEWALL

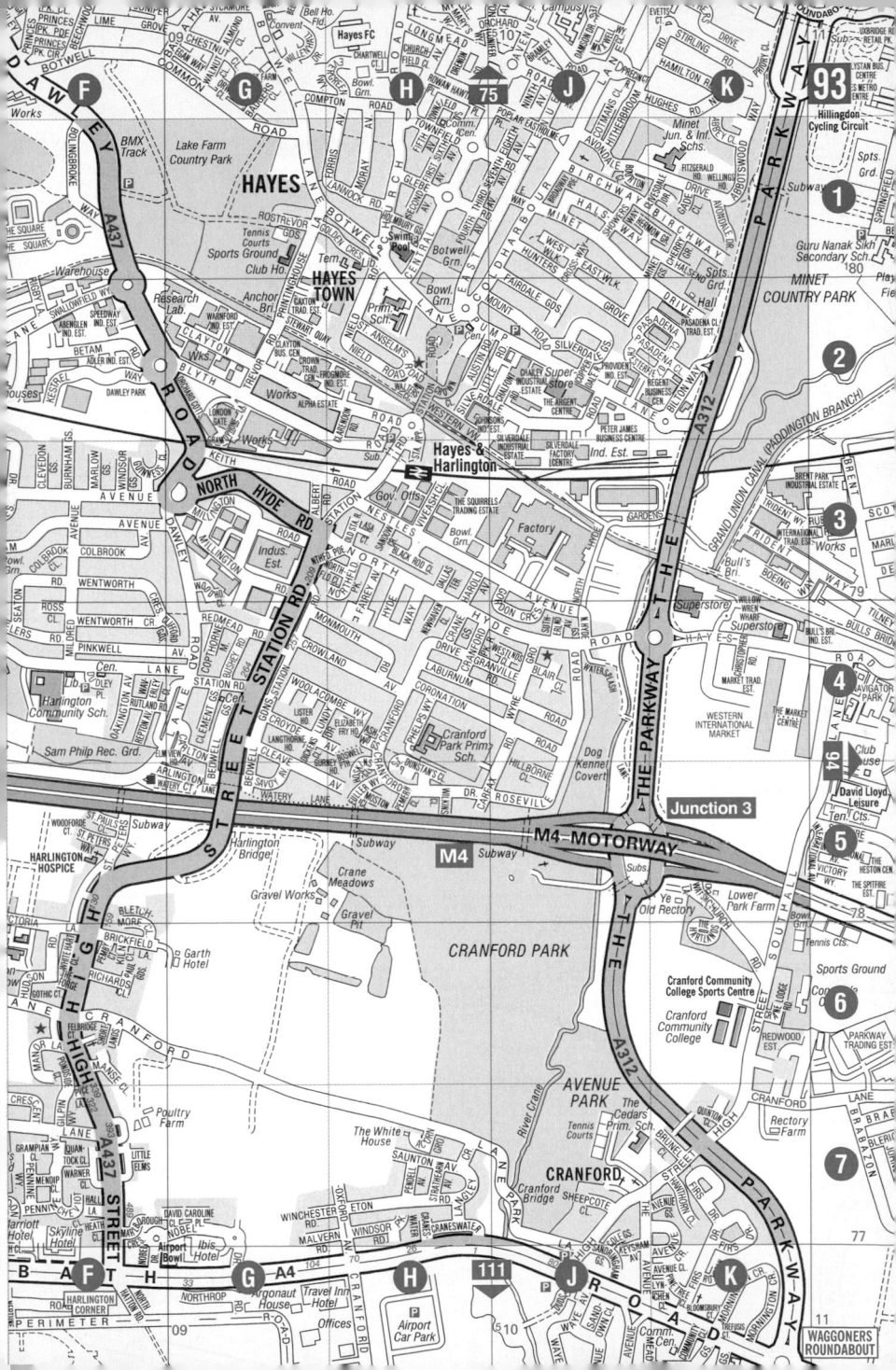

93
75
94
111
F
G
H
J
K
1
2
3
4
5
6
7
HAYES
HAYES TOWN
CRANFORD
Hayes FC
Lake Farm Country Park
BMX Track
Hillingdon Cycling Circuit
MINET COUNTRY PARK
Minet Jun. & Inf. Schs.
Guru Nanak Sikh Secondary Sch.
Tennis Courts
Sports Ground
Club Ho.
Research Lab.
Anchor Bri.
Swim Pool
Botwell Grn.
Prim. Sch.
DAWLEY PARK
Works
Warehouse
Hayes & Harlington
Superstore
THE ARGENT CENTRE
PETER JAMES BUSINESS CENTRE
Ind. Est.
Factory
THE SQUIRRELS TRADING ESTATE
Indus. Est.
Gov. Offs.
GRAND UNION CANAL (PADDINGTON BRANCH)
BRENT PARK INDUSTRIAL ESTATE
INTERNATIONAL TRAD. EST.
Bull's Bri.
WILLOW WREN WHARF
BULL'S BRI. IND. EST.
WESTERN INTERNATIONAL MARKET
THE MARKET CENTRE
MARKET TRAD. EST.
NAVIGATOR PARK
Club House
David Lloyd Leisure
Ten. Cts.
THE HESTON CEN.
THE SPITFIRE EST.
Junction 3
M4 MOTORWAY
M4
Subway
Subs.
Harlington Community Sch.
Sam Philp Rec. Grd.
Cranford Park Prim. Sch.
Dog Kennel Covert
HARLINGTON HOSPICE
Harlington Bridge
Crane Meadows
Gravel Works
Gravel Pit
CRANFORD PARK
Garth Hotel
Poultry Farm
Ye Old Rectory
Lower Park Farm
Tennis Cts.
Sports Ground
Cranford Community College Sports Centre
Cranford Community College
REDWOOD EST.
PARKWAY TRADING EST.
Rectory Farm
AVENUE PARK
The Cedars Prim. Sch.
Tennis Courts
River Crane
Cranford Bridge
The White House
Skyline Hotel
Airport Bowl
Ibis Hotel
HARLINGTON CORNER
Argonaut House
Travel Inn Hotel
Offices
Airport Car Park
Comm. Cen.
WAGGONERS ROUNDABOUT
A437
A312
A4
THE PARKWAY
DAWLEY ROAD
NORTH HYDE RD.
STATION RD.
HIGH STREET
BATH ROAD
PERIMETER ROAD
BOTWELL COMMON ROAD
BOTWELL LANE
COLDHARBOUR LANE
PUMP LANE
BIRCHWAY
MINET DRIVE
SILVERDALE ROAD
CLAYTON ROAD
BLYTH ROAD
KEITH ROAD
NESTLES AVENUE
NORTH HYDE GARDENS
HAYES ROAD
SOUTHALL LANE
CRANFORD LANE
WATERY LANE
STATION ROAD
PINKWELL AV.
WENTWORTH CRES.
COLBROOK AV.
MONMOUTH RD.
CROWLAND RD.
CORONATION ROAD
WYRE ROAD
ROSEVILLE AV.
SAUNTON AV.
WINCHESTER RD.
MALVERN RD.
CRANESWATER
CRANFORD LANE
09
10
11
77
78
79
180

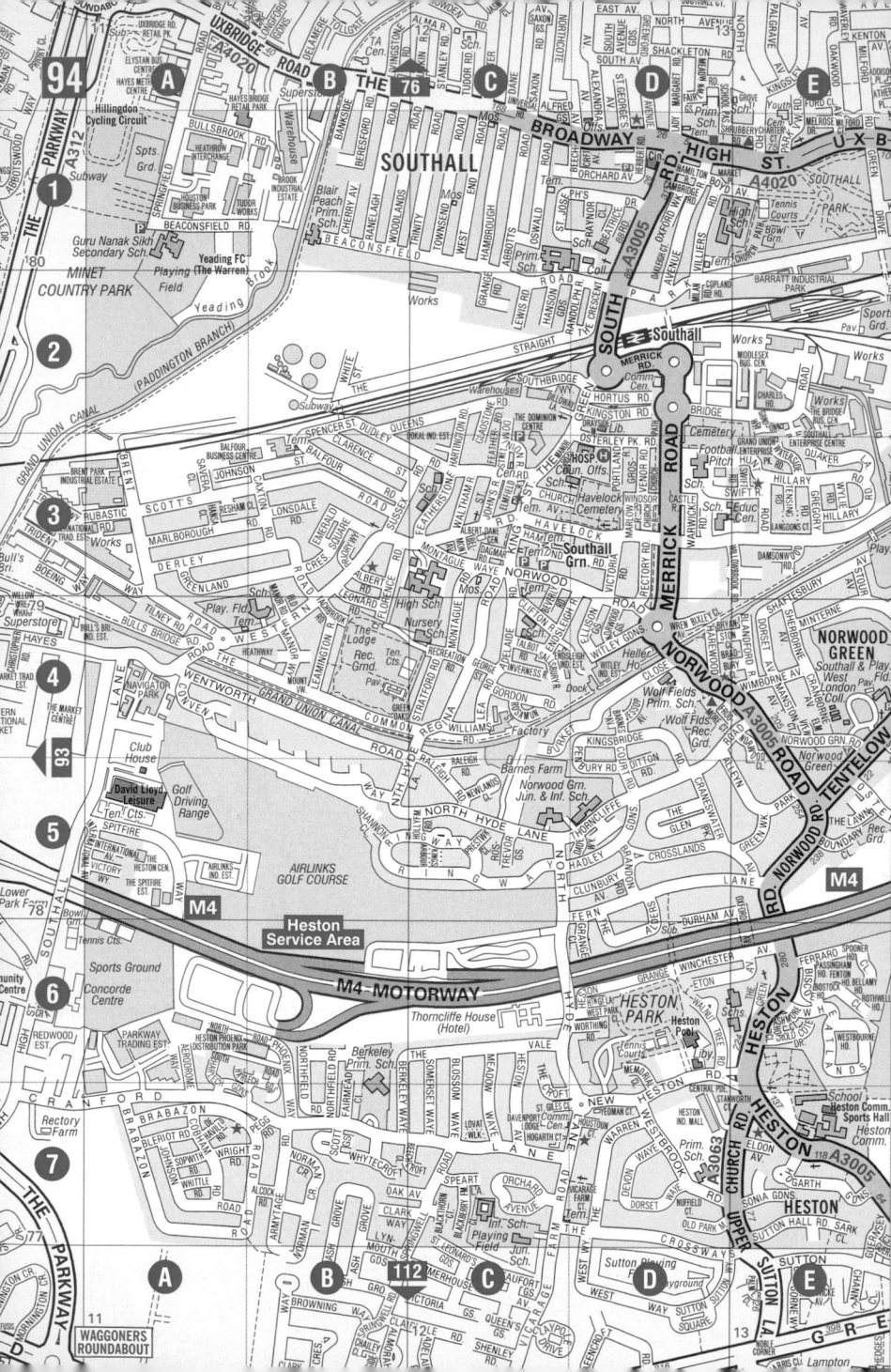

94
76
93
112
A
B
C
D
E
1
2
3
4
5
6
7
11
12
13
UXBRIDGE ROAD
A4020
THE BROADWAY
HIGH ST.
SOUTHALL
SOUTHALL PARK
THE PARKWAY
A312
Hillingdon Cycling Circuit
Spts. Grd.
HEATHROW INTERCHANGE
HOUSTON BUSINESS PARK
TUDOR WORKS
BROOK INDUSTRIAL ESTATE
HAYES BRIDGE RETAIL PARK
UXBRIDGE RD. RETAIL PK.
ELYSTAN BUS. CENTRE
HAYES METRO CENTRE
Warehouse
Superstore
BEACONSFIELD RD.
Guru Nanak Sikh Secondary Sch.
Yeading FC (The Warren)
Playing Field
MINET COUNTRY PARK
Yeading Brook
(PADDINGTON BRANCH)
GRAND UNION CANAL
Blair Peach Prim. Sch.
BEACONSFIELD
Works
THE STRAIGHT
Southall
SOUTH RD.
A3005
MERRICK RD.
MERRICK ROAD
Comm. Cen.
HORTUS RD.
KINGSTON RD.
BRIDGE
Lib.
Cemetery
THE DOMINION CENTRE
OSTERLEY PK. RD.
HOSP.
Coun. Offs.
Havelock Cemetery
HAVELOCK RD.
Southall Grn.
NORWOOD RD.
BARRATT INDUSTRIAL PARK
MIDDLESEX BUS. CEN.
THE BRIDGE BUS. CEN.
SOUTHALL ENTERPRISE CENTRE
GRAND UNION ENTERPRISE PK.
Football Pitch
Educ. Cen.
BALFOUR BUSINESS CENTRE
BRENT PARK INDUSTRIAL ESTATE
INTERNATIONAL TRAD. EST.
Works
SCOTT'S RD.
MARLBOROUGH RD.
DERLEY RD.
GREENLAND CRES.
WESTERN RD.
BULLS BRIDGE RD.
Bull's Bri.
Superstore
BULL'S BRI. IND. EST.
HAYES RD.
THE MARKET CENTRE
NAVIGATOR PARK
THE WENTWORTH
GRAND UNION CANAL
The Lodge
Rec. Grnd.
High Sch.
Nursery Sch.
Heller Ho.
Wolf Fields Prim. Sch.
Wolf Flds. Rec. Grd.
NORWOOD ROAD
NORWOOD GREEN
Southall & Play. Flds.
West London Coll.
Norwood Green
TENTELOW
THE LAWN
Rec. Grd.
Barnes Farm
Norwood Grn. Jun. & Inf. Sch.
NORTH HYDE LANE
Club House
David Lloyd Leisure
Golf Driving Range
AIRLINKS GOLF COURSE
AIRLINKS IND. EST.
THE HESTON CEN.
THE SPITFIRE EST.
M4
Heston Service Area
M4 MOTORWAY
Thorncliffe House (Hotel)
Lower Park Farm
Tennis Cts.
Sports Ground
Concorde Centre
REDWOOD EST.
PARKWAY TRADING EST.
HESTON PHOENIX DISTRIBUTION PARK
CRANFORD
Rectory Farm
Berkeley Prim. Sch.
HESTON PARK
Heston Pool
Liby.
NEW HESTON RD.
HESTON IND. MALL
Prim. Sch.
A3063
HESTON RD.
Heston Comm. Sports Hall
HESTON
SUTTON HALL RD.
Sutton Playing Fields
Playground
Inf. Sch.
Playing Field
Jun. Sch.
SUTTON LA.
WAGGONERS ROUNDABOUT
Lampton

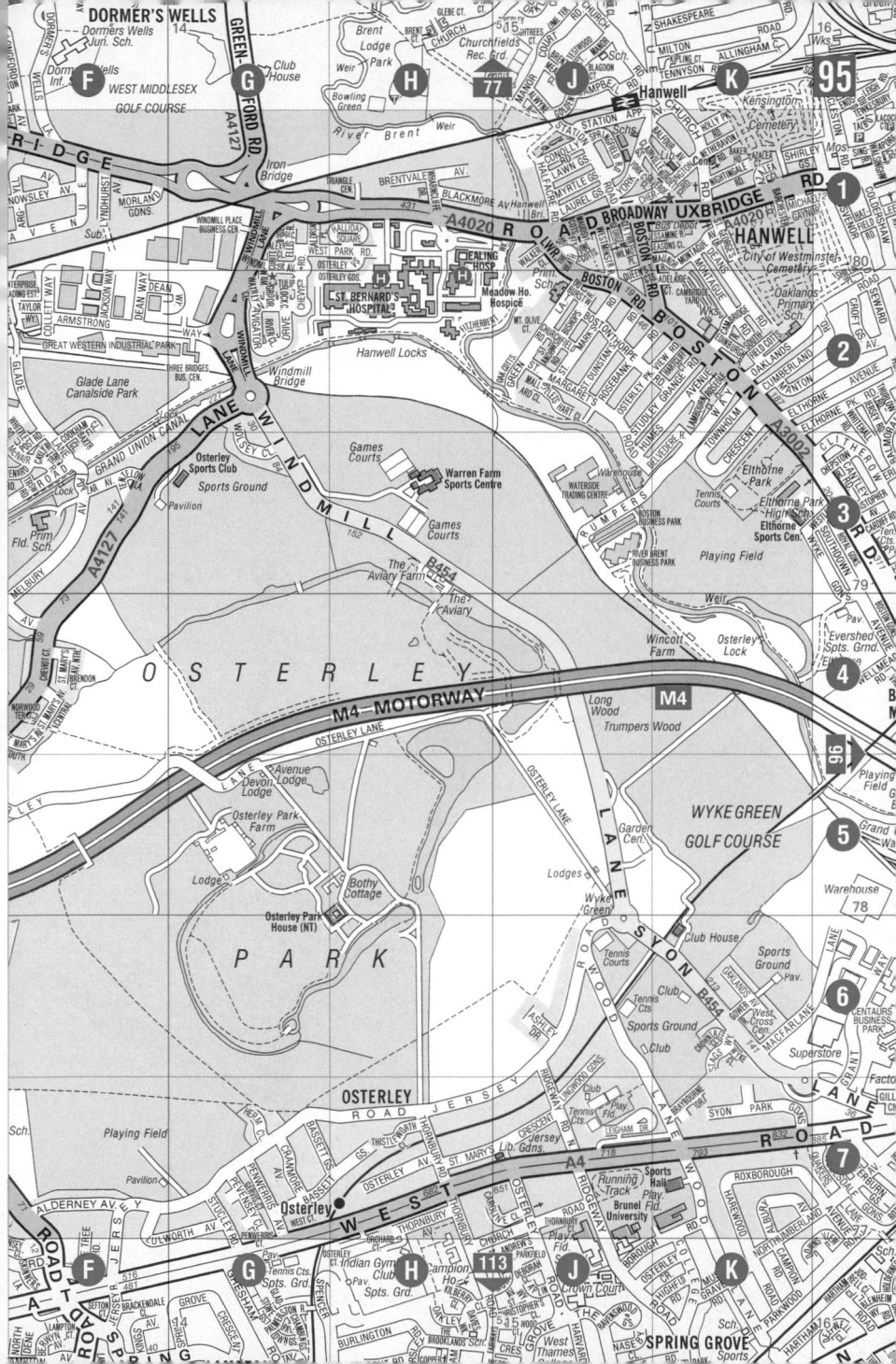
DORMER'S WELLS
Dormers Wells Jun. Sch.
WEST MIDDLESEX GOLF COURSE
GREENFORD RD.
A4127
Club House
Brent Lodge Park
Bowling Green
River Brent
Weir
Churchfields Rec. Grd.
77
Hanwell
95
Kensington Cemetery
Iron Bridge
BRENTVALE AV.
BLACKMORE AV.
UXBRIDGE ROAD
BROADWAY
A4020
HANWELL
City of Westminster Cemetery
Oaklands Primary Sch.
WINDMILL PLACE BUSINESS CEN.
WINDMILL LANE
HALLIDAY SQUARE
WEST PARK RD.
EALING HOSP.
ST. BERNARD'S HOSPITAL
Meadow Ho. Hospice
BOSTON RD.
A3002
GREAT WESTERN INDUSTRIAL PARK
THREE BRIDGES BUS. CEN.
Glade Lane Canalside Park
Windmill Bridge
Hanwell Locks
GRAND UNION CANAL
Osterley Sports Club
Sports Ground
Pavilion
Games Courts
Warren Farm Sports Centre
B454
The Aviary Farm
The Aviary
WATERSIDE TRADING CENTRE
BOSTON BUSINESS PARK
RIVER BRENT BUSINESS PARK
TRUMPERS WAY
Elthorne Park
Elthorne Park High Sch.
Elthorne Sports Cen.
Playing Field
Wincott Farm
Osterley Lock
Evershed Spts. Grnd.
OSTERLEY
M4 MOTORWAY
M4
Long Wood
Trumpers Wood
OSTERLEY LANE
96
Avenue Lodge
Devon Lodge
Osterley Park Farm
WYKE GREEN GOLF COURSE
Lodges
Garden Cen.
Bothy Cottage
Osterley Park House (NT)
PARK
Wyke Green
SYON LANE
WOOD LANE
Club House
Warehouse
78
Tennis Courts
Sports Ground
CENTAURS BUSINESS PARK
Superstore
MACFARLANE LANE
JERSEY ROAD
RIDGEWAY RD.
Playing Field
Pavilion
A4
GREAT WEST ROAD
SYON PARK GDNS.
Osterley
Running Track
Sports Hall
Brunel University
113
Indian Gym Club
Crown Court
SPRING GROVE
West Thames
ALDERNEY AV.
ULWORTH AV.
THORNBURY RD.
NORTHUMBERLAND AVENUE
1
2
3
4
5
6
7
F
G
H
J
K

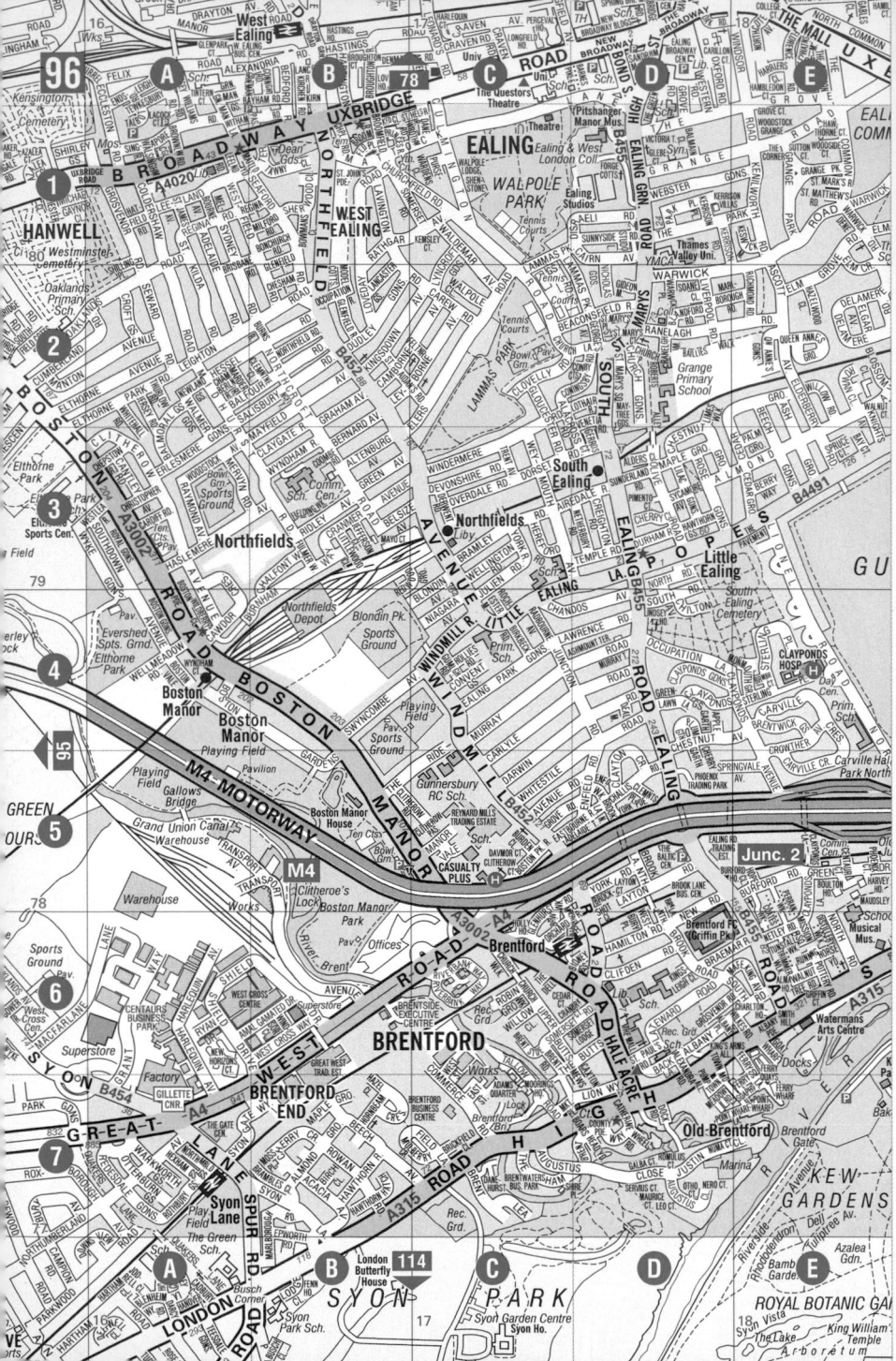
96
A
B
C
D
E
1
2
3
4
5
6
7
16
17
18
80
79
78
77
78
95
114
West Ealing
The Questors Theatre
Pitshanger Manor Mus.
Theatre
EALING
Ealing & West London Coll.
WALPOLE PARK
Ealing Studios
Tennis Courts
Thames Valley Uni.
YMCA
UXBRIDGE ROAD
BROADWAY
A4020
NEW BROADWAY
HIGH ST.
THE BROADWAY
THE MALL
UXBRIDGE ROAD
THE GROVE
EALING GRN.
B455
HANWELL
Kensington Cemetery
Westminster Cemetery
Oaklands Primary Sch.
WEST EALING
NORTHFIELD
B452
Grange Primary School
LAMMAS PARK
SOUTH EALING ROAD
ST. MARYS ROAD
South Ealing
Northfields
Liby
Little Ealing
POPES LA.
B4491
South Ealing Cemetery
CLAYPONDS HOSP.
BOSTON ROAD
A3002
Elthorne Park
Elthorne Park High Sch.
Elthorne Sports Cen.
Northfields Depot
Blondin Pk. Sports Ground
Evershed Spts. Grnd.
Elthorne Park
Boston Manor
Boston Manor Playing Field
Pavilion
Playing Field
Gallows Bridge
Grand Union Canal
Warehouse
M4 MOTORWAY
M4
Junc. 2
Boston Manor House
Gunnersbury RC Sch.
REYNARD MILLS TRADING ESTATE
CASUALTY PLUS
Clitheroe's Lock
Boston Manor Park
River Brent
Offices
Brentford
Brentford FC (Griffin Pk.)
Musical Mus.
Watermans Arts Centre
Docks
BRENTFORD
BRENTSIDE EXECUTIVE CENTRE
WEST CROSS CENTRE
CENTAURS BUSINESS PARK
Superstore
Factory
GILLETTE CNR.
GREAT WEST ROAD
A4
SYON LANE
B454
BRENTFORD END
GREAT WEST TRAD. EST.
BRENTFORD BUSINESS CENTRE
Brentford Bri.
HIGH ST.
A315
LONDON ROAD
HALF ACRE
Old Brentford
Marina
KEW GARDENS
Brentford Gate
Riverside Avenue
Rhododendron Dell
Tuliptree Av.
Azalea Gdn.
Bamboo Garden
ROYAL BOTANIC GARDENS
Syon Vista
The Lake
King William's Temple
Arboretum
Syon Lane
Play Field
The Green Sch.
Busch Corner
Syon Park Sch.
London Butterfly House
SYON PARK
Syon Garden Centre
Syon Ho.
Sports Ground
West Cross Cen.
Rec. Grd.
ROAD
GREEN

97
79
98
115
EAST ACTON
ACTON
Ealing Common
Acton Central
ACTON PARK
SOUTH ACTON
Acton Town
South Acton
SOUTHFIELD
BEDFORD PARK
ACTON GREEN
Chiswick Pk.
GUNNERSBURY
GUNNERSBURY PARK
Gunnersbury
TURNHAM GREEN
CHISWICK
Chiswick
Chiswick House
Kew Bridge
KEW
KEW GREEN
Kew Gds.
Strand on the Green
Oliver's Island
The National Archives
GROVE PARK
Grove Park Sports Ground
Chiswick Cemetery
Kensington Cemetery
Kew East Junc.
Gunnersby Junc.
Junc.1
M4 MOTORWAY
M4
A4
A406
A4020
A4000
A315
A3000
A205
A307
A316
B491
B490
B409
GUNNERSBURY LANE
GUNNERSBURY AVENUE
HIGH ST.
THE VALE
CHISWICK HIGH RD.
HEATHFIELD TER.
CEDARS RD.
ELLESMERE RD.
GT. WEST RD.
SOUTH PARADE
THE AVENUE
ACTON LANE
KEW BRI. RD.
KEW RD.
MORTLAKE RD.
GREAT CHERTSEY RD.
ALEXANDRA AV.
BURLINGTON LANE
WELLESLEY
Popefield Playing Flds.
Sports Grnd.
Boating Lake
Museum
Nurseries
Bowling Green
Miniature Golf Course
Refreshment Pavilion
Potomac (Fish Pond)
Tennis Courts
Works
Acton Sports Club
Esporta Health & Fitness
Nature Res.
Super store
Brentford Fountain Leis. Cen.
Stoam Mus.
Kew Pier
Brentford Ait
Botanical Library
Kew Green
Main Gate
Kew Gardens Gallery
Orangery
Princess of Wales Conservatory
Seven Sisters
Plants & People Exhibition
Palm House
The Pond
Rose Garden
Visitor Cen.
Temple of Bellona
Berberis Dell
Cricket Ground
Temple
Sports Hall
Riverside Lands
Stadium
Yacht Basin
Southfields Rec. Grd.
Acton Grn. Comn.
Chiswick Common
Twyford Spts. Cen.
Reynolds Sports Cen.
Acton High Sch.
Acton & W. London Coll.
Depot
Care Home
The Park Club
Maples Sch.
F
G
H
J
K
1
2
3
4
5
6
7

98
80
97
116
A
B
C
D
E
1
2
3
4
5
6
7
EAST ACTON
White City
SHEPHERDS BUSH
Shepherd's Bush
BBC Television Centre
QPR FC
Janet Adegoke Leisure Cen.
Wormholt Park
The Park Club
Cricket Ground
Football Pitch
Leisure Cen.
THE VALE ESTATE
ACTON PARK
ACTON PARK ESTATE
Maples Sch.
THE VALE
UXBRIDGE ROAD
A4020
A219
Shepherd's Bush Mkt.
Goldhawk Rd.
GOLDHAWK ROAD
A402
B408
Wendell Park
Cathnor Park
Adventure Playground
Ravenscourt Park
RAVENSCOURT PARK HOSP.
BEDFORD PARK
SOUTHFIELD RD.
THE AVENUE
B491
BATH RD.
B409
STH. PDE.
Turnham Green
TURNHAM GREEN
Chiswick Common
Stamford Brook
Ravenscourt Park
Hammersmith
GLENTHORNE ROAD
KING ST.
Lyric Theatre
Riverside Studios
CHISWICK HIGH RD.
A315
A316
CHISWICK LA.
GREAT WEST ROAD
A4
HAMMERSMITH FLYOVER
HOGARTH LA.
HOGARTH RBT.
Homefield Recreation Ground
Hammersmith Pier
Chiswick Eyot
RIVER THAMES
St. Pauls School
Playing Field
Brewery
Swedish Sch.
Church Wharf
Corney Reach
CHISWICK
Chiswick House
BURLINGTON LA.
ALEXANDRA AV.
Riverside Recreation Ground
Sports Ground
Chiswick Pier
Nature Reserve
The Harrodian Sch.
LONSDALE ROAD
B350
CASTELNAU
A306
HAMMERSMITH BRI.
Castelnau
LONDON WETLAND CENTRE
Peter Scott Visitor Centre
Barn Elms
Blakes Wharves
Small Profits
Bandstand
Pavilion

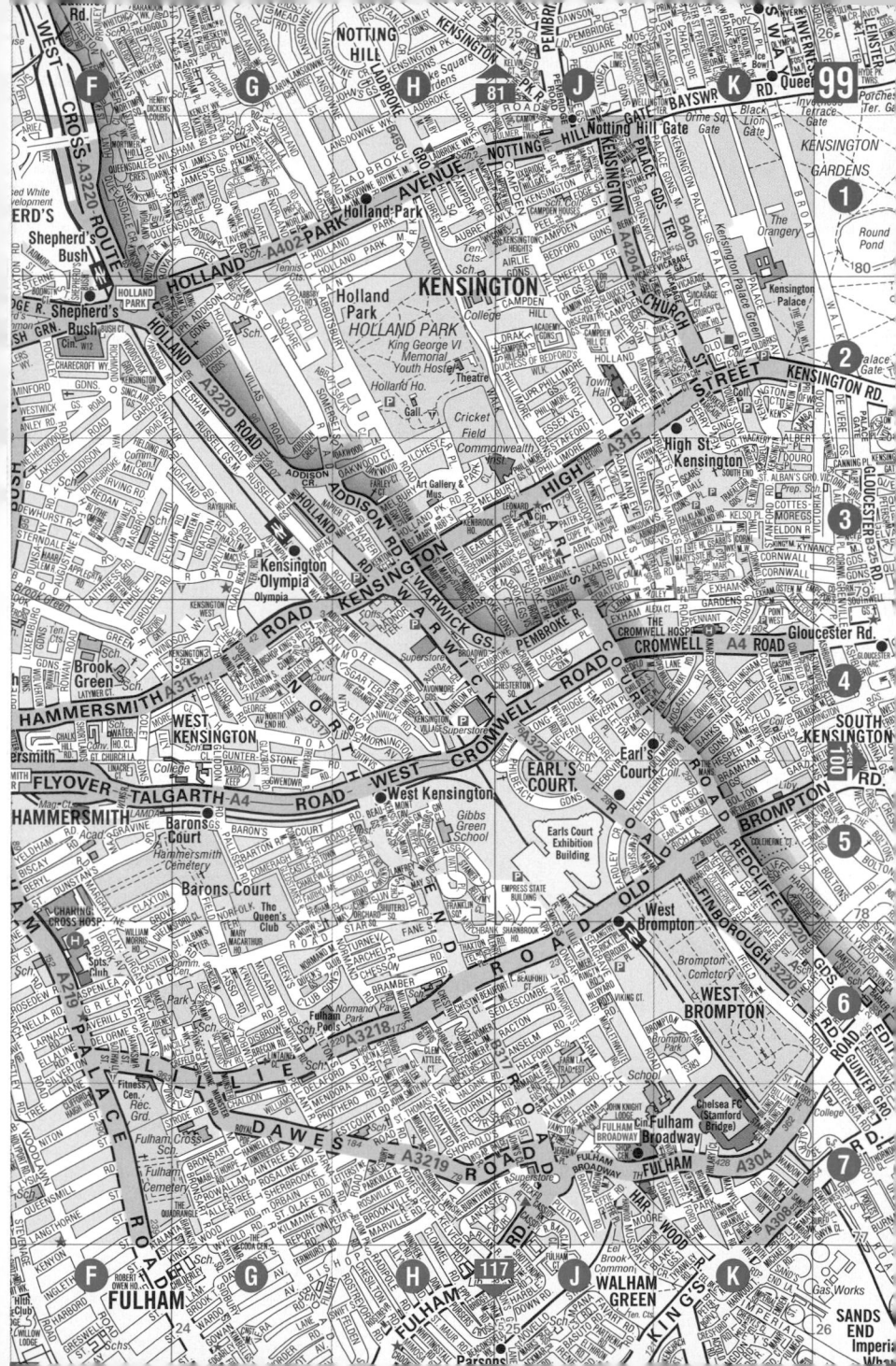

99
81
100
117
F
G
H
J
K
1
2
3
4
5
6
7
24
25
26
NOTTING HILL
Notting Hill Gate
KENSINGTON GARDENS
The Orangery
Round Pond
Kensington Palace
Holland Park
HOLLAND PARK
KENSINGTON
Shepherd's Bush
King George VI Memorial Youth Hostel
Holland Ho.
Theatre
Cricket Field
Commonwealth Inst.
Art Gallery & Mus.
High St. Kensington
Kensington Olympia
Olympia
Brook Green
HAMMERSMITH
WEST KENSINGTON
West Kensington
EARL'S COURT
Earl's Court
Earls Court Exhibition Building
Gloucester Rd.
SOUTH KENSINGTON
Barons Court
Hammersmith Cemetery
The Queen's Club
Gibbs Green School
CHARING CROSS HOSP.
West Brompton
Brompton Cemetery
WEST BROMPTON
Fulham Pools
Chelsea FC (Stamford Bridge)
Fulham Broadway
Fulham Cemetery
FULHAM
WALHAM GREEN
Eel Brook Common
SANDS END
Gas Works
HOLLAND PARK AVENUE
HOLLAND ROAD
KENSINGTON HIGH STREET
KENSINGTON ROAD
CROMWELL ROAD
WEST CROMWELL ROAD
TALGARTH ROAD
HAMMERSMITH ROAD
NORTH END ROAD
WARWICK ROAD
EARL'S COURT ROAD
OLD BROMPTON ROAD
LILLIE ROAD
DAWES ROAD
FULHAM PALACE ROAD
FULHAM ROAD
KING'S ROAD
REDCLIFFE GDS.
FINBOROUGH ROAD
BROMPTON RD.
FLYOVER
A4
A315
A402
A3220
A3218
A3219
A219
A304
A308
A4204
B317
B405

100
A
B
C
D
E
82
Lancaster Gate
BAYSWATER RD.
Marlborough Gate
Lancaster Gate
The Fountains
Victoria Gate
Clarendon Gate
Albion Gate
Stanhope Place Gate
Speakers' Corner
Refreshment Kiosk
Roosevelt Mem.
MAYFAIR
Porchester Ter. Gate
Inverness Terrace Gate
Black Lion Gate
Speke's Monument
Peter Pan Statue
The Long Water
Nursery
Reformers Tree
Entrance to Underground Car Park
HYDE PARK
Rangers Lodge
KENSINGTON GARDENS
Temple Lodge
Round Pond
The Orangery
THE SERPENTINE
Fishermans Keep
Nannies Lawn
The Holocaust Mem. Gdn.
Rose Garden
Queen Elizabeth Gate
10
Serpentine Gallery
Princess of Wales Memorial Fountain
Cafeteria
Bandstand
Kensington Palace
ROTTEN ROW
Albert Memorial
Flower Walk
(Closed Midnight - 5am) New Ride
Prince of Wales Gate
SOUTH CARRIAGE
Alexandra Gate
Queen's Gate
Palace Gate
SCOTCH HOUSE
Hyde Park Corner
KENSINGTON ROAD
KENSINGTON GORE
A315
KNIGHTSBRIDGE
Knightsbridge
Royal Albert Hall
Rytl. Coll. of Music
Imperial Coll.
KNIGHTSBRIDGE
Science Museum
Natural History Mus.
Victoria & Albert Museum
Brompton Oratory
Harrods
BELGRAVE SQ.
BROMPTON RD.
A4
CROMWELL RD.
Gloucester Rd.
THURLOE PL.
Sth. Kensington
BROMPTON
PONT ST.
SLOANE ST.
EATON SQ.
SOUTH KENSINGTON
16
99
A3218 BROMPTON RD.
FULHAM RD.
SYDNEY ST.
The Royal Marsden Hosp.
Royal Brompton Hosp.
Sloane Square
Saatchi Gallery
KING'S RD.
PIMLICO RD.
CHELSEA
Burton's Court
ROYAL HOSPITAL RD.
Royal Hospital Chelsea
Ranelagh Gardens
Chelsea Barracks
CHELSEA BRIDGE RD.
Chelsea & Westminster Hosp.
WEST BROMPTON
REDCLIFFE GDNS.
EDITH GRO.
A3217
CHEYNE WALK
CHELSEA EMBANKMENT
17
THAMES
RIVER
Cadogan Pier
CHELSEA REACH
Peace Pagoda
Children's Zoo
British Genius Site
Tennis Courts
Millennium Arena
A3212
Cremorne Gardens
Chelsea Wharf
Cremorne Wharf
Chelsea Creek
A3220
BATTERSEA BRI.
ALBERT BRIDGE ROAD
A3031
BATTERSEA PARK
The Pump Ho. Gallery
Boating Lake
CENTRAL AVENUE
BATTERSEA BRI. RD.
118
Gas Works
SANDS END
Imperial Wharf
Wharves
BATTERSEA

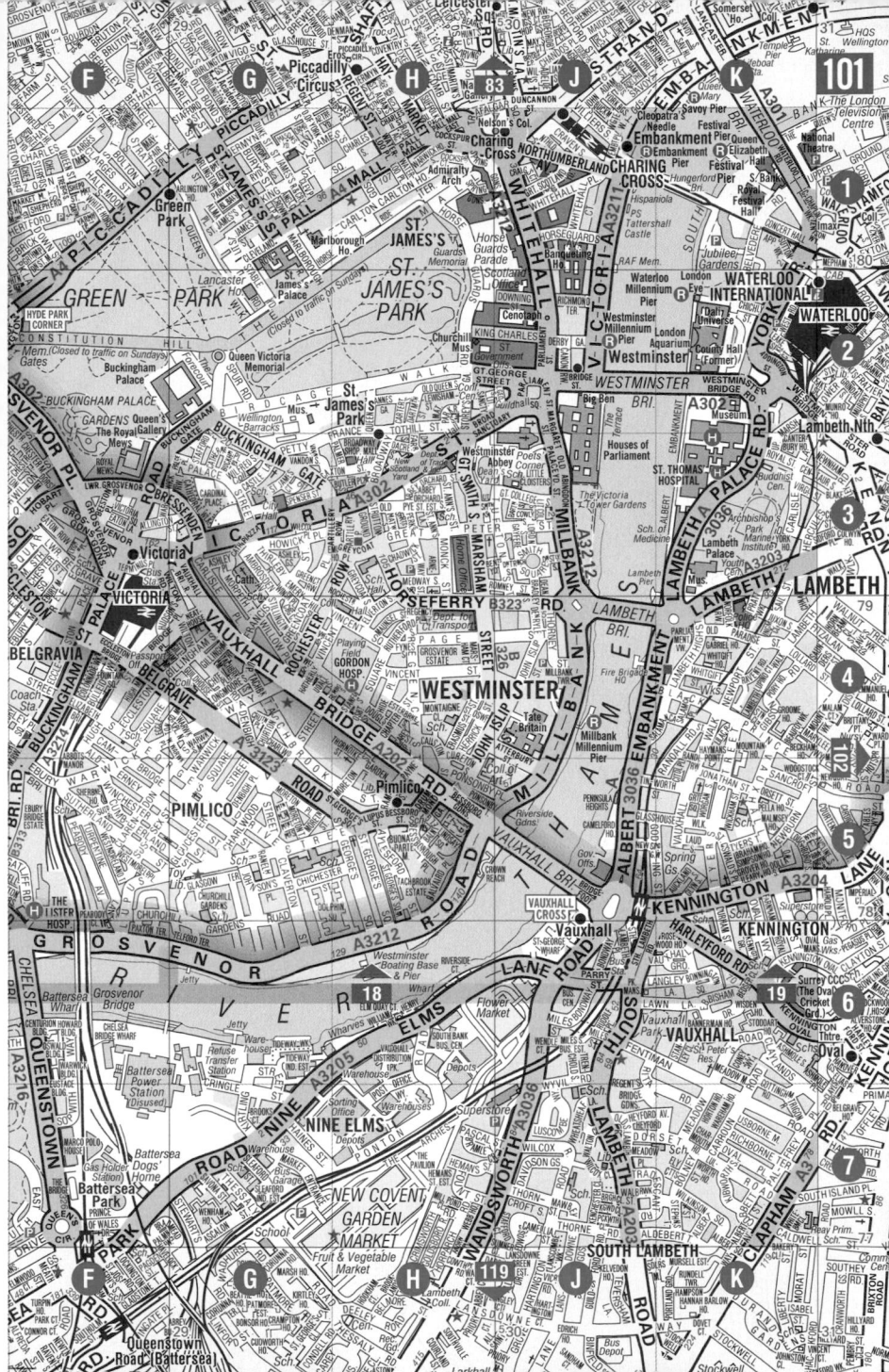

101
F
G
H
J
K
83
Piccadilly Circus
Eros
Leicester Sq.
STRAND
EMBANKMENT
Somerset Ho.
Charing Cross
Nelson's Col.
Admiralty Arch
NORTHUMBERLAND AV.
CHARING CROSS
Embankment
Embankment Pier
Festival Pier
Queen Elizabeth Hall
Royal Festival Hall
National Theatre
The London Television Centre
WATERLOO
Imax
1
PICCADILLY
A4
Green Park
ST. JAMES'S ST.
PALL MALL
A4 MALL
Marlborough Ho.
St. James's Palace
ST. JAMES'S
Horse Guards Parade
Scotland Office
WHITEHALL
A3212
VICTORIA
A3211
Banqueting Ho.
Hispaniola
PS Tattershall Castle
RAF Mem.
Jubilee Gardens
Waterloo Millennium Pier
London Eye
WATERLOO INTERNATIONAL
GREEN PARK
ST. JAMES'S PARK
HYDE PARK CORNER
CONSTITUTION HILL
(Closed to traffic on Sundays)
Lancaster Ho.
Cenotaph
DOWNING ST.
KING CHARLES ST.
Churchill Mus.
Westminster Millennium Pier
London Aquarium
Dali Universe
County Hall (Former)
Westminster
YORK RD.
2
Queen Victoria Memorial
Buckingham Palace
BUCKINGHAM PALACE GARDENS
Queen's Gallery
The Royal Mews
A302
BIRDCAGE WALK
St. James's Park
Wellington Barracks
BUCKINGHAM GATE
WESTMINSTER BRIDGE
Big Ben
Houses of Parliament
The Terrace
Museum
ST. THOMAS' HOSPITAL
Lambeth Nth.
Westminster Abbey
Poets' Corner
New Scotland Yard
Dept. of Trade & Industry
VICTORIA ST.
GROSVENOR PL.
BRESSENDEN PL.
Victoria
VICTORIA
Cath.
Home Office
MILLBANK
The Victoria Tower Gardens
Sch. of Medicine
LAMBETH PALACE RD.
Archbishop's Park
Lambeth Palace
3
LAMBETH
HORSEFERRY RD.
Dept. for Transport
LAMBETH BRI.
BELGRAVIA
VAUXHALL BRIDGE RD.
ROCHESTER ROW
GORDON HOSP.
WESTMINSTER
Tate Britain
Millbank Millennium Pier
Fire Brigade HQ
ALBERT EMBANKMENT
A3036
4
102
BELGRAVE RD.
A3123
Pimlico
PIMLICO
A202
THAMES
Riverside Gdns.
5
Vauxhall
VAUXHALL CROSS
KENNINGTON
A3204
KENNINGTON LANE
THE LISTER HOSP.
GROSVENOR ROAD
A3212
RIVER
18
Westminster Boating Base & Pier
Grosvenor Bridge
19
Surrey CCC (The Oval Cricket Grd.)
6
Oval
VAUXHALL
Vauxhall Park
NINE ELMS LANE
A3205
Flower Market
Battersea Power Station (Disused)
Refuse Transfer Station
NINE ELMS
QUEENSTOWN RD.
A3216
Battersea Dogs' Home
Battersea Park
NINE ELMS ROAD
NEW COVENT GARDEN MARKET
Fruit & Vegetable Market
WANDSWORTH RD.
A3036
SOUTH LAMBETH RD.
A203
CLAPHAM RD.
7
SOUTH LAMBETH
119
Lambeth Coll.
Queenstown Road (Battersea)
Bus Depot
STOCKWELL

102
A
B
C
D
E
1
2
3
4
5
6
7
84
14
15
19
101
120
EMBANKMENT
RIVER THAMES
BLACKFRIARS
Blackfriars Millennium Pier
Millennium Bridge
Bankside Pier
CANNON STREET
Tate Modern
SOUTHWARK
London Bridge City Pier
HMS Belfast
Tower Millennium Pier
LONDON BRIDGE HOSP
National Theatre
Royal Festival Hall
STAMFORD ST.
SOUTHWARK ST.
LONDON BRIDGE
THE BOROUGH
GUY'S HOSP.
TOOLEY ST.
WATERLOO
WATERLOO INTERNATIONAL
Waterloo East
THE CUT
UNION ST.
BLACKFRIARS RD.
SOUTHWARK BRIDGE RD.
BOROUGH HIGH ST.
Borough
LONG LA.
BERMONDSEY ST.
TOWER BRIDGE RD.
Lambeth Nth.
WESTMINSTER BRI. RD.
ST. GEORGE'S CIRCUS
BOROUGH RD.
LONDON RD.
NEWINGTON CAUSEWAY
GREAT DOVER ST.
Imperial War Mus.
Geraldine Mary Harmsworth Park
ST. GEORGE'S RD.
LAMBETH RD.
NEWINGTON
Elephant & Castle
ELEPHANT & CASTLE
NEW KENT RD.
BRICKLAYER'S ARMS
LAMBETH
KENNINGTON RD.
WALWORTH RD.
WALWORTH
KENNINGTON LANE
Kennington
KENNINGTON PARK RD.
KENNINGTON
Surrey CCC (The Oval Cricket Grd.)
Oval
KENNINGTON OVAL
Kennington Park
CAMBERWELL NEW RD.
CAMBERWELL RD.
ALBANY RD.
BURGESS PARK
Burgess Park
SOUTHAMPTON WAY
CAMBERWELL GREEN
BRIXTON RD.
CLAPHAM RD.
PECKHAM

103
85
15
121
104
F
G
H
J
K
1
2
3
4
5
6
7
Tower Hill
Gateway
TOWER HILL
EAST SMITHFIELD
The Tower of London
SHADWELL
King Edward Mem. Park
THAMES
Shadwell Dock Stairs
Shadwell Basin
PENNINGTON
St. Katharine's Pier
St. Katharine Docks
Tower Hotel
Butlers Wharf Pier
Aldermans Stairs
UPPER POOL
THE POOL
WAPPING
Wapping
Wapping Dock Stairs
RIVER
New Crane Stairs
Pelican Stairs
Wapping Old Stairs
Wapping New Stairs
LOWER POOL
Cherry Garden Pier
King's Stairs
Cumberland Wharf
John Orwell Sports Cen.
A100
TOWER BRI. ROAD
A101
ROTHERHITHE TUNNEL
BERMONDSEY
Bermondsey
JAMAICA ROAD
A200
BRUNEL RD.
TUNNEL APP.
Rotherhithe
SALTER RD.
Canada Water
ROTHERHITHE
Superstores
Surrey Quays Shopping Centre
Surrey Quays
REDRIFF RD.
GREENLAND DOCK
Watersports
PLOUGH WY.
Printing Works
Bowl. Alley & Gala Bingo
Odeon Cinema
Sports Cen.
Ecological Park
Russia Dock Woodland
Stave
LOWER ROAD
SOUTHWARK PARK
Southwark Pk. Sports Cen. Track
Sports Complex
Cafe Gallery
Leisure Cen.
SOUTHWARK PARK RD.
RAYMOUTH RD.
A2206
A2208
ROTHERHITHE NEW ROAD
ABBEY ST.
B202
Mun. Offices
Bermondsey Spa
SPA RD.
DRUMMOND RD.
B203
DUNTON RD.
ROLLS RD.
B204
Superstore
OLD KENT ROAD
A2
South Bermondsey
Lewisham Lions Cen.
Millwall FC (The Den)
Waste Transfer Station
SURREY CANAL ROAD
TRUNDLEYS RD.
B207
EVELYN ST.
South Eastern Gas Works
CANAL BRIDGE
Burgess Pk.
TRAFALGAR AV.
B215
PECKHAM PARK RD.
B216
PECKHAM HILL ST.
ASYLUM RD.
Brimmington Pk.
NEW CROSS RD.
New Cross Gate
NEW CROSS GATE
Bus Garage
QUEEN'S ROAD
PECKHAM HIGH ST.
A202
Queens Rd (Peckham)
Leisure Cen.
POMEROY ST.
KENDER ST.
Eckington Gdns.
DEPTFORD PARK
Sports Grd.
Folkestone

104
A
B
C
D
E
86
1
2
3
4
5
6
7
103
122
POPLAR
Poplar
West India Quay
Canary Wharf
WEST INDIA
DOCKS
Heron Quays
South Quay
ISLE OF DOGS
MILLWALL
CUBITT TOWN
MUDCHUTE PARK
Mudchute
Island Gds.
Crossharbour & London Arena
MILLWALL OUTER DOCK
Printing Works
Docklands Sailing Cen.
Masthouse Terrace Pier
Canary Wharf Pier
Hilton Docklands Pier
Greenland Pier
RIVER THAMES
LIMEHOUSE REACH
GREENWICH REACH
CONVOY'S WHARF
DEPTFORD
Cutty Sark for Maritime Greenwich
Greenwich Pier
Greenwich Foot Tunnel
Greenwich
Deptford
Deptford Bri.
New Cross
New Cross Gate
NEW CROSS
NEW CROSS GATE
Goldsmiths' College
DEPTFORD PARK
Pepys Park
SALTER ROAD
REDRIFF ROAD
PLOUGH WAY
EVELYN STREET
DEPTFORD CHURCH ST.
CREEK ROAD
NEW CROSS RD.
BLACKHEATH RD.
BLACKHEATH HILL
GREENWICH HIGH RD.
ROYAL HILL
WESTFERRY RD.
MANCHESTER ROAD
PRESTON'S ROAD
GREENLAND DOCK
SOUTH DOCK
Ecological Park
Stave Hill
A1261
A1206
A2202
A200
A206
A2
B205
B206
B207
B208
B209

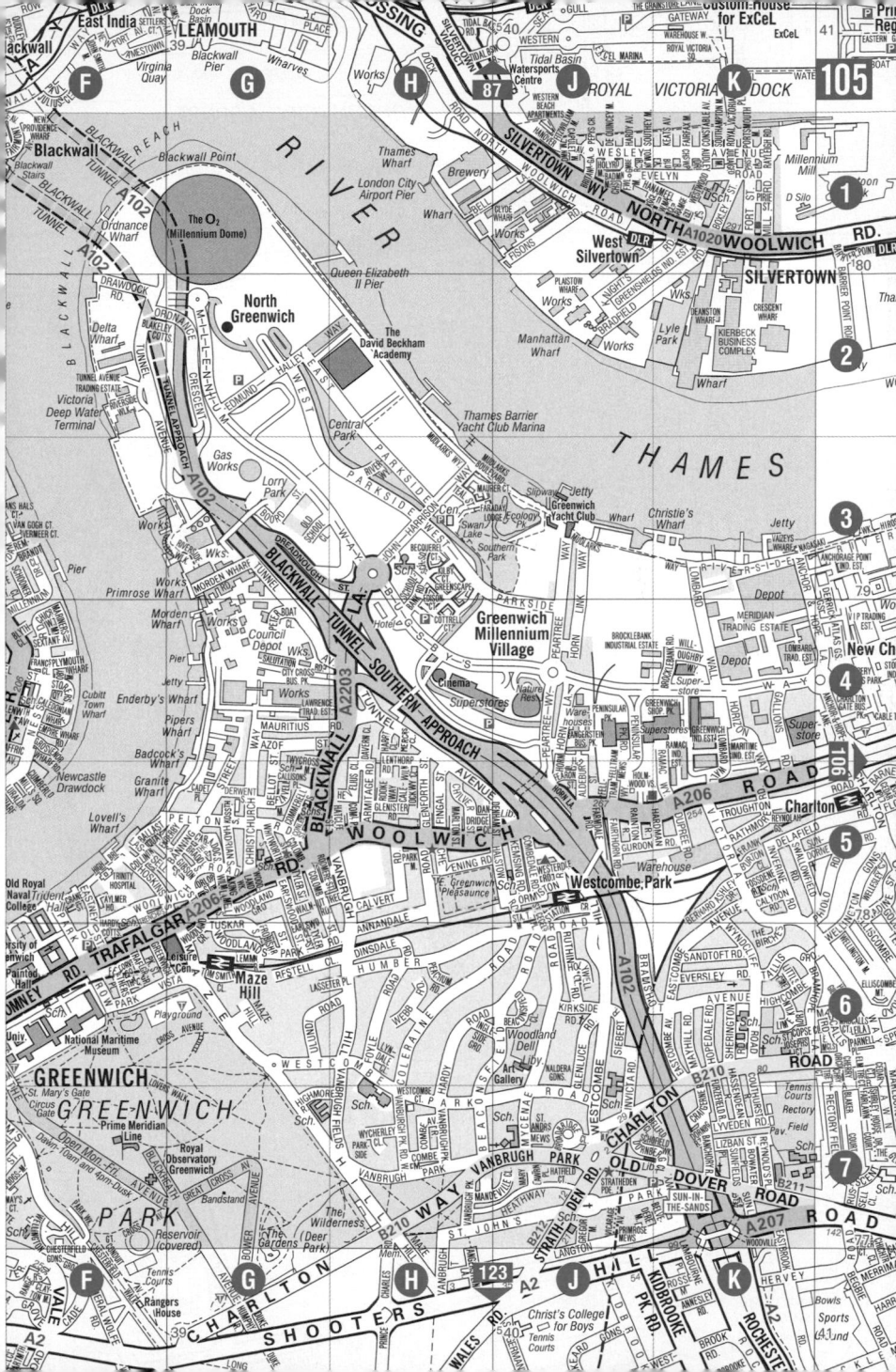

105
106
87
123
F
G
H
J
K
1
2
3
4
5
6
7
East India
LEAMOUTH
Blackwall
Virginia Quay
Blackwall Pier
Wharves
Works
Tidal Basin
Watersports Centre
ROYAL VICTORIA DOCK
Custom House for ExCeL
ExCeL
Millennium Mill
SILVERTOWN WY.
NORTH WOOLWICH RD.
West Silvertown
SILVERTOWN
Brewery
Thames Wharf
London City Airport Pier
RIVER
THAMES
Blackwall Point
BLACKWALL REACH
BLACKWALL TUNNEL
The O2 (Millennium Dome)
Ordnance Wharf
Queen Elizabeth II Pier
North Greenwich
The David Beckham Academy
Delta Wharf
Victoria Deep Water Terminal
Manhattan Wharf
Lyle Park
KIERBECK BUSINESS COMPLEX
Thames Barrier Yacht Club Marina
Central Park
Gas Works
Lorry Park
TUNNEL APPROACH
BLACKWALL TUNNEL SOUTHERN APPROACH
Greenwich Yacht Club
Christie's Wharf
Ecology Pk.
Southern Park
Greenwich Millennium Village
MERIDIAN TRADING ESTATE
Depot
Cinema
Superstores
Primrose Wharf
Morden Wharf
Council Depot
Enderby's Wharf
Cubitt Town Wharf
Pipers Wharf
Badcock's Wharf
Granite Wharf
Lovell's Wharf
Newcastle Drawdock
WOOLWICH ROAD
A206 ROAD
Charlton
Westcombe Park
Maze Hill
TRAFALGAR RD.
Old Royal Naval College
National Maritime Museum
GREENWICH
GREENWICH PARK
Prime Meridian Line
Royal Observatory Greenwich
Open Mon.-Fri. Dawn-10am and 4pm-Dusk
The Wilderness (Deer Park)
The Gardens
Reservoir (covered)
Rangers House
Woodland Dell
Art Gallery
WESTCOMBE PARK ROAD
VANBRUGH PARK
CHARLTON ROAD
SHOOTERS HILL
OLD DOVER ROAD
Christ's College for Boys
KIDBROOKE PK. RD.
ROCHESTER WAY
New Charlton

106
88
105
124
A
B
C
D
E
1
2
3
4
5
6
7
41
42
43
ExCeL
Prince Regent
Beckton Park
Cyprus
University
Royal Albert
London Regatta Centre
ROYAL VICTORIA DOCK
ROYAL ALBERT DOCK
LONDON CITY AIRPORT
Terminal Building
London City Airport
KING GEORGE V DOCK
King George V
Go-kart Circuit
Millennium Mill
Pontoon Dock
CONNAUGHT BRIDGE
A1020
NORTH WOOLWICH RD.
Pontoon Dock
SILVERTOWN
Thames Barrier Park
Silvertown
THAMESIDE INDUSTRIAL ESTATE
Sugar Refinery
ALBERT ROAD
A112
STANDARD INDUSTRIAL ESTATE
North Woolwich
NORTH WOOLWICH
PIER RD.
A117
North Woolwich Pier
Victoria
WOOLWICH REACH
THAMES FLOOD BARRIER
RIVER
WOOLWICH FREE FERRY
Barrier Gardens Pier
Thames Barrier Visitors Cen.
Waterfront Leisure Cen.
Gala Bingo
WOOLWICH CHURCH ST.
WOOLWICH HIGH ST.
Woolwich Dockyard
WOOLWICH
JOHN WILSON ST.
WOOLWICH ROAD
A206
New Charlton
STONE LAKE RETAIL PK.
Superstore
Charlton
Charlton Athletic FC (The Valley)
MARYON WILSON PARK
Maryon Park
Tennis Courts
LITTLE HEATH
HILL REACH
ARTILLERY PL.
WELLINGTON
B210
Royal Artillery Barracks
Gun Park
Playground
Rifle Range
Repository Woods
Barrack Field
Blue Gate
White Gate
GRAND DEPOT RD.
A205
WOOLWICH COMMON
CHARLTON PARK RD.
CHARLTON
Charlton House
Library
CHARLTON CEMETERY
Charlton School
CHARLTON PARK
Cricket Ground
HA HA
QUEEN ELIZABETH HOSPITAL
Sports Ground
Hornfair Park
Charlton Lido
Bowling Green
CHARLTON ROAD
CANBERRA ROAD
SHOOTERS HILL ROAD
A207
ACADEMY ROAD
Old Royal Military Academy
Playing Field
Eaglesfield School
Reservoir (covered)
Recreation Ground
Bowls
Sports Ground
ROCHESTER WAY

F
G
H
J
K
89
107
125
108
1
2
3
4
5
6
7
44
45
46
77
78
79
80
THAMESMEAD CENTRAL
THAMESMEAD
THAMESMEAD WEST
Thamesmead South West
(Proposed)
Twin Tumps
CANNON RETAIL PK.
GALLIONS ROUNDABOUT
ALBERT
BASIN
Gallions Point Marina
Thames House
Newham Coll. of Further Education (Royal Docks Campus)
Drawbridge
Custom House
MANOR WAY
A117
WOOLWICH
THAMES
REACH
Gallions Point
GALLIONS
WICH REACH
Gallions Reach
Hoba Wharf
Royal Arsenal Woolwich Pier
Firepower (The Royal Artillery Mus.)
Greenwich Heritage Cen.
Royal Arsenal West
Royal Brass Foundry
British Liby.
BERESFORD ST.
PLUMSTEAD
A206
RD.
PETTMAN
CRES.
WESTERN WAY
A2016
Plumstead
Woolwich Arsenal
Bus Depot
WOOLWICH TRADE PK.
Works
WEST THAMESMEAD BUSINESS PARK
WEST THAMESMEAD BUSINESS PK.
HMP BELMARSH
Crown Ct. & Magistrates Ct.
PLUMSTEAD MARSHES
Gallions Park
Gallions Lake
Broadwater
Broadwater Green
Tor
Southern Outflow Sewers
Comm. Cen.
Recreation Ground
Bowling Green
Sports Pav. Ground
CENTRAL WAY
HIGH STREET
PLUMSTEAD HIGH ST.
Plumstead Gdns.
Leisure Cen.
Lib.
St. Nicholas Gdns.
WICKHAM A209
WICKHAM LA.
PLUMSTEAD
PLUMSTEAD COMMON
WINN'S COMMON
Bleak Hill
BLEAK HILL LANE
KING'S HIGHWAY
Super-store
Woolwich Cemetery
Rockliffe Gds.
The William Barefoot Gdn.
Playing Field
Tennis Courts
Play. Field
Plumstead Common
SHREWSBURY PARK
SHOOTERS HILL GOLF COURSE
Clothworkers Wood
Woodlands Abattoir
Lowood Club Ho.
Tennis Courts
Rec. Grd.
Bowl. Grn.
Willow Dene School
East Wickham Open Space
SHOOTERS HILL

108
90
107
126
A
B
C
D
E
1
2
3
4
5
6
7
46
47
48
180
79
78
77
THAMESMEAD CENTRAL
THAMESMEAD
THAMESMEAD SOUTH
ERITH
ABBEY WOOD
PLUMSTEAD
WEST HEATH
EAST WICKHAM
LESNES ABBEY
BOSTALL WOODS
BOSTALL HEATH
EASTERN WAY
A2016
A2041
A2041 RD.
A206
A209
B213
HARROW MANOR WAY
KNEE HILL
McLEOD RD.
ABBEY WOOD RD.
BOSTALL HILL
WOOLWICH RD.
PLUMSTEAD HIGH ST.
WICKHAM LANE
UPPER WICKHAM LANE
CARLYLE RD.
Twin Tumps
Woolwich Poly. Sch.
Birchmere
Birchmere Park
Lakeside Centre
Southmere Lake
The Business Academy, Bexley
Abbey Wood Pk.
Abbey Wood Park
Abbey Wood
Lesnes Abbey
Lesnes Abbey Pk.
Cooperative Woods
BELVEDERE PRIVATE CLINIC
Hospice
Bostall Ho.
Clam Field Recreation Ground
HEATHVIEW DAY CENTRE
Bowling Green
Turpins Cave
Playing Field
Plumstead Cemetery
Woolwich Cemetery
The William Barefoot Gdn.
Hill Grove
East Wickham Open Space
Stevens Park
Bedonwell Jun. & Inf. Schs.
Bleak Hill
Rockliffe Gds.
St. Margaret Clitherow RC Prim. Sch.
Tump 53 Natural Park
Football Ground
Sports Ground
Recreation Ground
WEST THAMESMEAD BUSINESS PK.
BIRCHMERE BUSINESS PARK
Superstore
THISTLEBROOK IND. EST.
LYNDEAN IND. EST.
ABBEY WOOD CAMPING & CARAVAN SITE

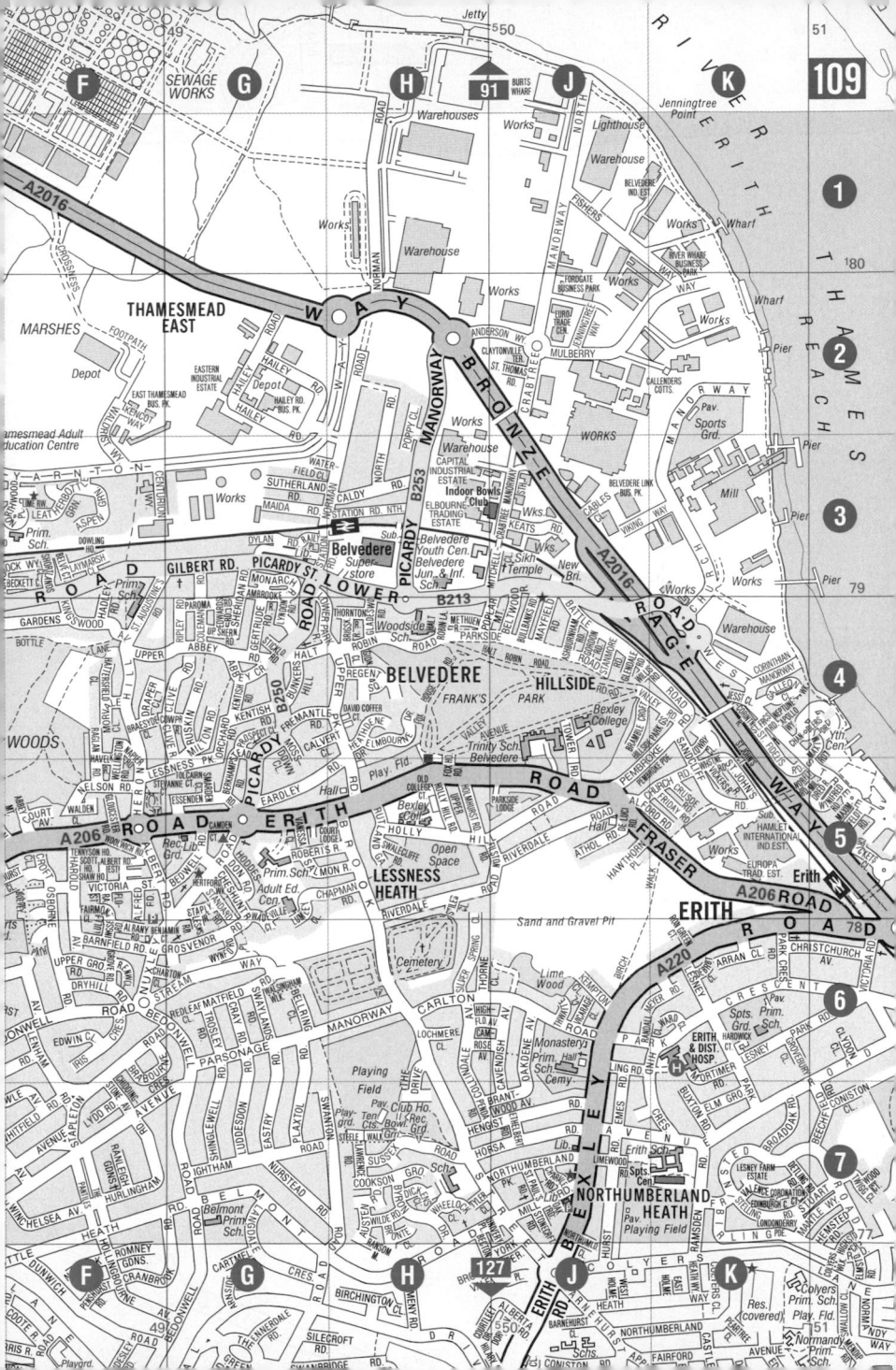

109
RIVER THAMES
ERITH REACH
Jenningtree Point
SEWAGE WORKS
THAMESMEAD EAST
MARSHES
BELVEDERE
HILLSIDE
LESSNESS HEATH
ERITH
NORTHUMBERLAND HEATH
FRANK'S PARK
Sand and Gravel Pit
Cemetery
Open Space
Playing Field
Lime Wood
WOODS
Belvedere
Erith
A2016
A206
A220
B253
B213
B250
WAY
BRONZE
ROAD
ERITH
FRASER
YARNTON
MANORWAY
PICARDY
LOWER
BEXLEY
THAMESMEAD ADULT EDUCATION CENTRE
EASTERN INDUSTRIAL ESTATE
EAST THAMESMEAD BUS. PK.
HAILEY RD. BUS. PK.
BELVEDERE IND. EST.
RIVER WHARF BUSINESS PARK
FORDGATE BUSINESS PARK
EURO TRADE CEN.
CAPITAL INDUSTRIAL ESTATE
ELBOURNE TRADING ESTATE
BELVEDERE LINK BUS. PK.
HAMLET INTERNATIONAL IND. EST.
EUROPA TRAD. EST.
Indoor Bowls Club
Belvedere Youth Cen.
Belvedere Jun. & Inf. Sch.
Sikh Temple
Bexley College
Trinity Sch. Belvedere
ERITH & DIST. HOSP.
Monastery Prim. Sch.
Erith Sch.
Belmont Prim. Sch.
Colyers Prim. Sch.
Normandy Prim. Sch.
Warehouses
Warehouse
Works
Lighthouse
Mill
Wharf
Pier
Jetty
BURTS WHARF
Depot
91
127
F
G
H
J
K
1
2
3
4
5
6
7
49
50
51
80
79
78
77

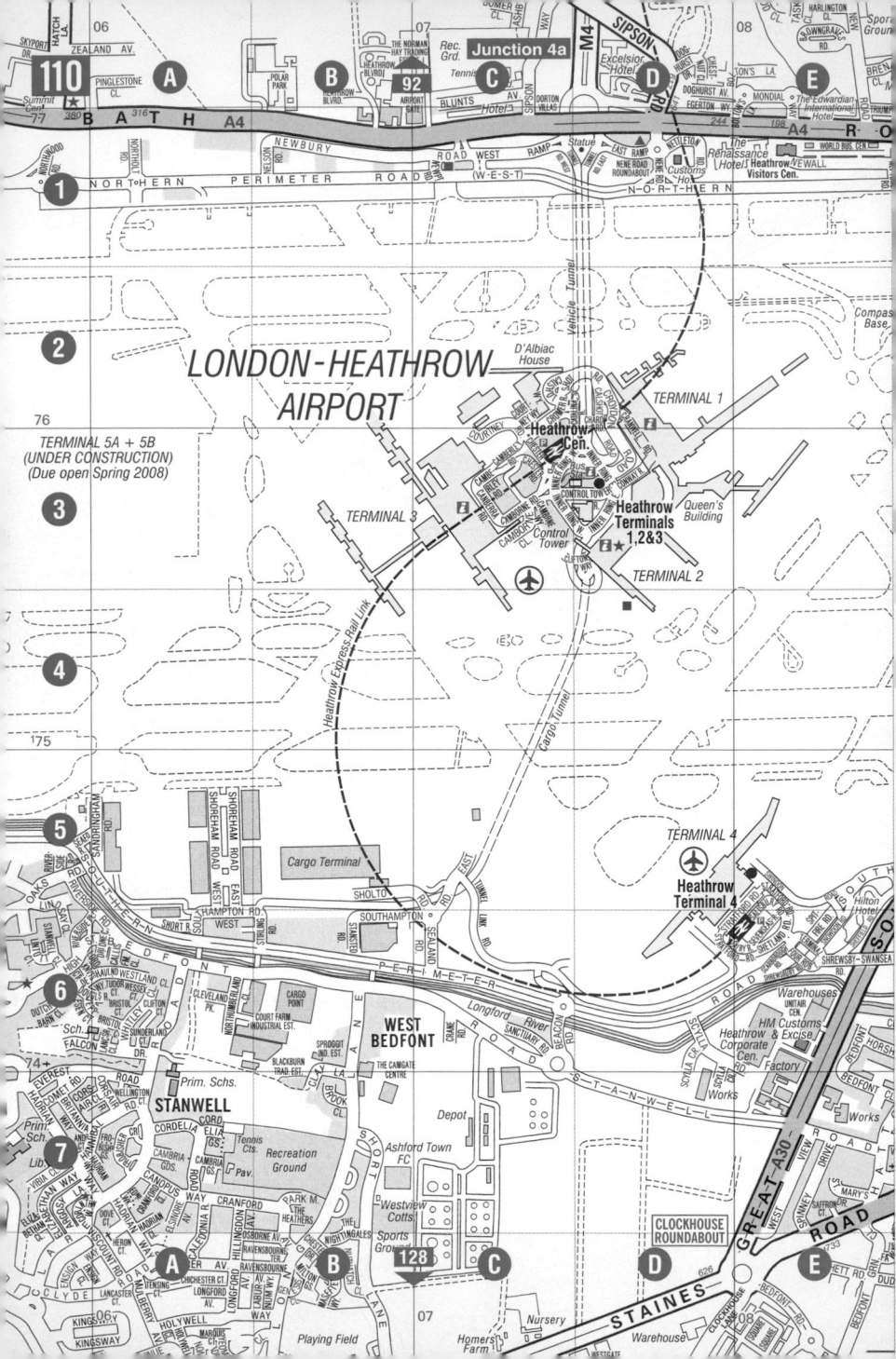

110
A
B
C
D
E
1
2
3
4
5
6
7
06
07
08
76
175
74
Junction 4a
92
128
BATH ROAD A4
M4
SIPSON RD.
NORTHERN PERIMETER ROAD
LONDON-HEATHROW AIRPORT
TERMINAL 5A + 5B (UNDER CONSTRUCTION) (Due open Spring 2008)
TERMINAL 1
TERMINAL 2
TERMINAL 3
TERMINAL 4
Heathrow Cen.
Heathrow Terminals 1,2&3
Heathrow Terminal 4
D'Albiac House
Queen's Building
Control Tower
Vehicle Tunnel
Cargo Tunnel
Heathrow Express Rail Link
Cargo Terminal
Compass Base
Excelsior Hotel
The Renaissance Hotel
Heathrow Visitors Cen.
The Edwardian International Hotel
Customs Ho.
Hilton Hotel
SOUTHERN PERIMETER ROAD
WEST BEDFONT
STANWELL
Recreation Ground
Ashford Town FC
Westview Cotts.
Sports Ground
Depot
Warehouses
HM Customs & Excise
Heathrow Corporate Cen.
Factory
Works
Longford River
CLOCKHOUSE ROUNDABOUT
STAINES ROAD
GREAT SOUTH WEST ROAD A30
Playing Field
Nursery
Homers Farm
Warehouse

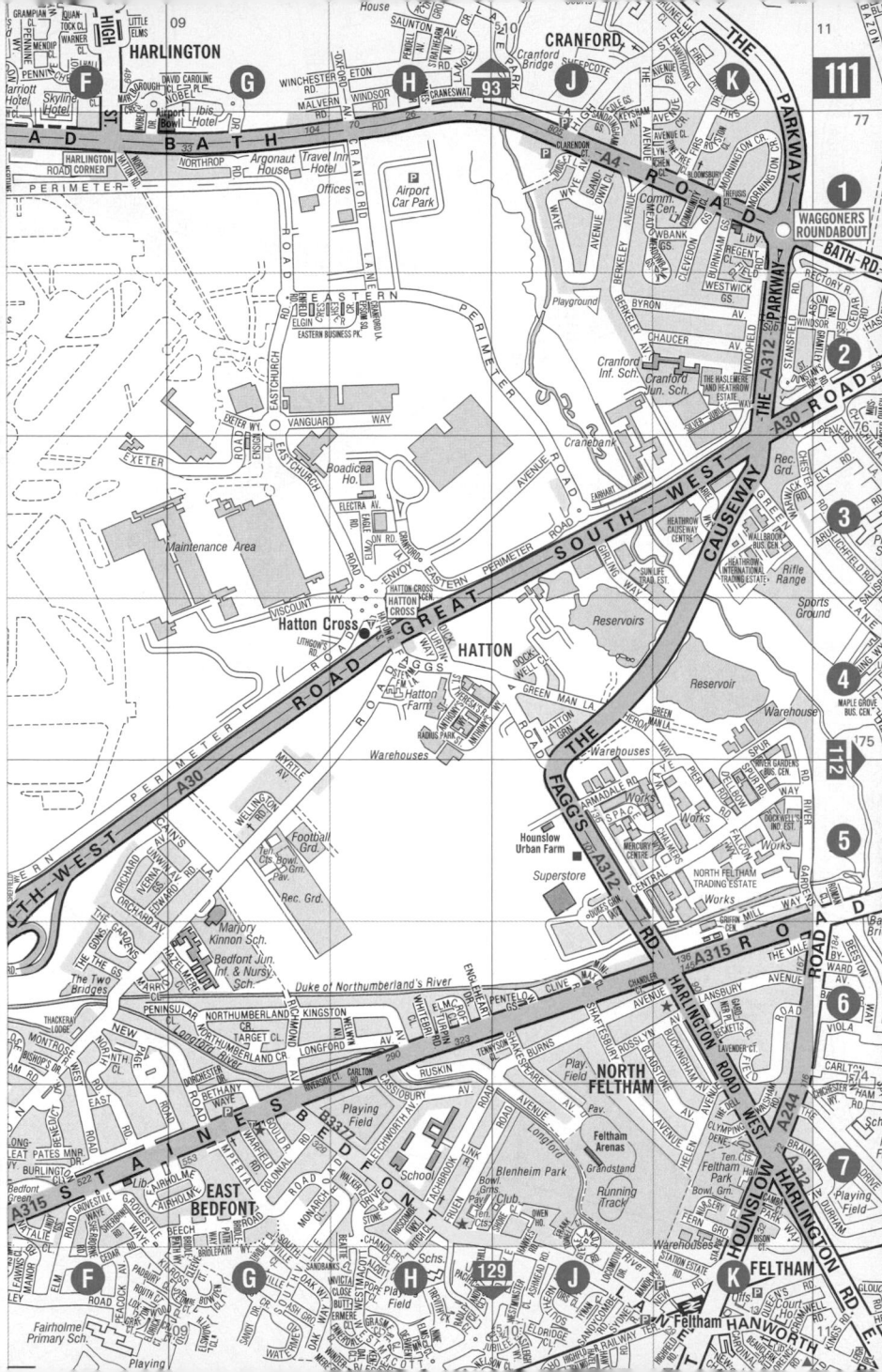

111
HARLINGTON
CRANFORD
Cranford Bridge
HATTON
NORTH FELTHAM
EAST BEDFONT
FELTHAM
HANWORTH
BATH ROAD
A4 ROAD
GREAT SOUTH WEST ROAD
A30
A30 ROAD
THE PARKWAY
A312
THE CAUSEWAY
FAGG'S RD.
A315
STAINES RD.
B3377
BEDFONT
HARLINGTON ROAD WEST
HOUNSLOW RD.
A244
HARLINGTON RD. E.
WAGGONERS ROUNDABOUT
PERIMETER
EASTERN PERIMETER ROAD
SOUTH PERIMETER ROAD
NORTHROP
CRANFORD LANE
EASTCHURCH ROAD
VANGUARD WAY
EXETER ROAD
VISCOUNT WY.
ENVOY
FAGGS ROAD
GREEN MAN LA.
HARLINGTON CORNER
Marriott Hotel
Skyline Hotel
Airport Bowl
Ibis Hotel
Argonaut House
Travel Inn Hotel
Offices
Airport Car Park
EASTERN BUSINESS PK.
Boadicea Ho.
Maintenance Area
Hatton Cross
HATTON CROSS CEN.
Hatton Farm
RADIUS PARK
Warehouses
Reservoirs
Reservoir
Warehouse
MAPLE GROVE BUS. CEN.
RIVER GARDENS BUS. CEN.
DOCKWELL'S IND. EST.
NORTH FELTHAM TRADING ESTATE
Works
MERCURY CENTRE
Hounslow Urban Farm
Superstore
GRIFFIN CEN.
HEATHROW CAUSEWAY CENTRE
WALLBROOK BUS. CEN.
HEATHROW INTERNATIONAL TRADING ESTATE
SUN LIFE TRAD. EST.
Rifle Range
Sports Ground
Rec. Grd.
Cranebank
Playground
Cranford Inf. Sch.
Cranford Jun. Sch.
THE HASLEMERE AND HEATHROW ESTATE
Comm. Cen.
Liby.
Football Grd.
Marjory Kinnon Sch.
Bedfont Jun. Inf. & Nursy. Sch.
The Two Bridges
Duke of Northumberland's River
Longford River
Playing Field
School
Blenheim Park
Feltham Arenas
Grandstand
Running Track
Feltham Park
Bowl. Grn.
Fairholme Primary Sch.
Bedfont Green
Lib.
Schs.
Feltham
Court Ho.
93
112
129
09
10
11
77
175

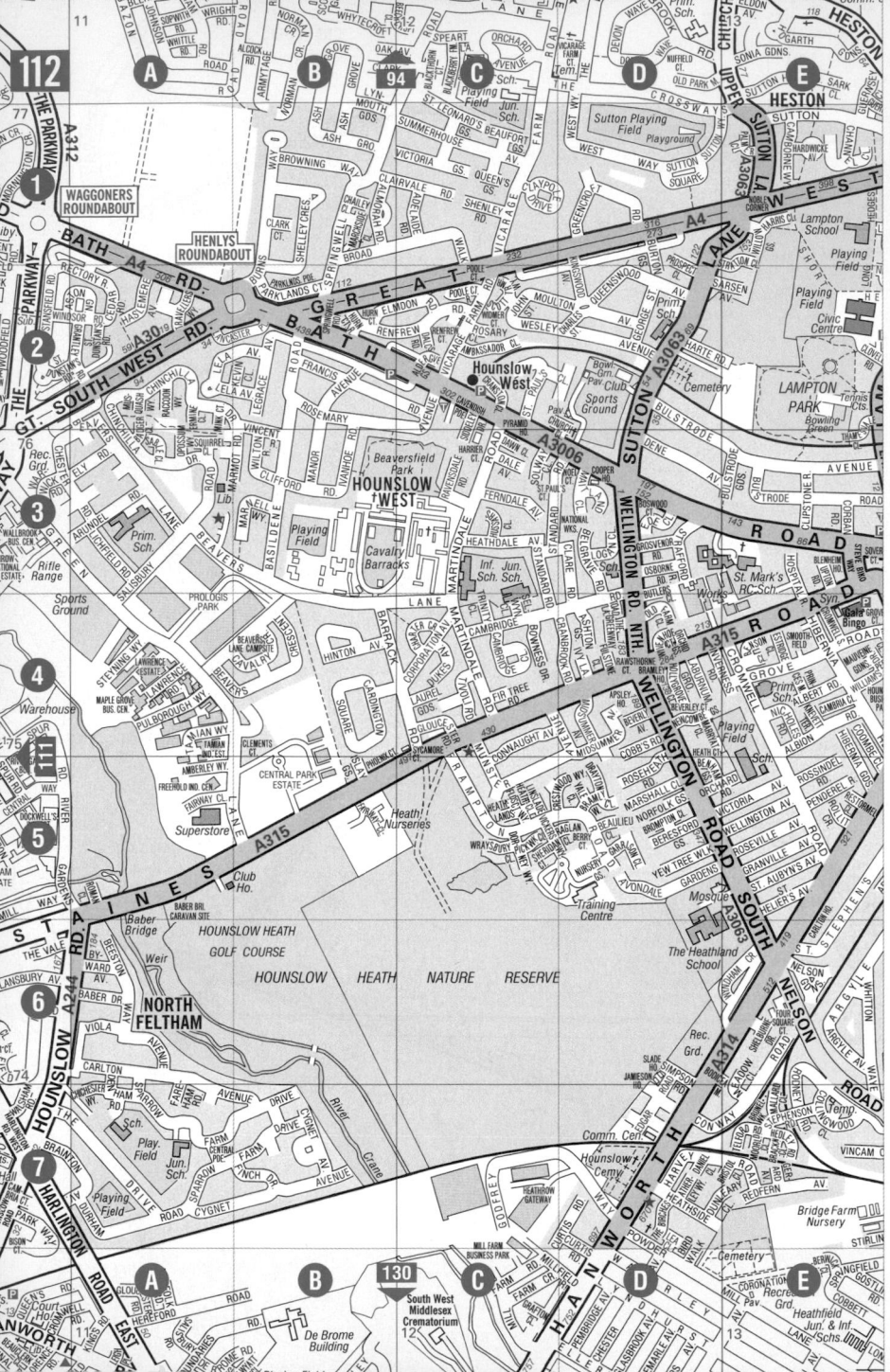

94
111
130
WAGGONERS ROUNDABOUT
HENLYS ROUNDABOUT
THE PARKWAY
A312
BATH RD.
A4
GT. SOUTH WEST RD.
A30
GREAT WEST ROAD
A3006
A3063
SUTTON LA.
SUTTON LANE
HESTON
Sutton Playing Field
Playground
Lampton School
Playing Field
Civic Centre
LAMPTON PARK
Tennis Cts.
Bowling Green
Hounslow West
HOUNSLOW WEST
Beaversfield Park
Cavalry Barracks
Playing Field
Sports Ground
Cemetery
BULSTRODE AVENUE
WELLINGTON RD. NTH.
WELLINGTON ROAD SOUTH
A315
STAINES RD.
St. Mark's RC Sch.
Gala Bingo
PROLOGIS PARK
BEAVERS LANE
CENTRAL PARK ESTATE
Superstore
Heath Nurseries
Club Ho.
Baber Bridge
Weir
HOUNSLOW HEATH GOLF COURSE
HOUNSLOW HEATH NATURE RESERVE
NORTH FELTHAM
HOUNSLOW RD.
A244
Training Centre
Mosque
The Heathland School
Rec. Grd.
A314
HANWORTH ROAD
NELSON ROAD
Comm. Cen.
Hounslow Cemy.
HEATHROW GATEWAY
MILL FARM BUSINESS PARK
River Crane
Sports Ground
Rifle Range
Warehouse
Play. Field
Playing Field
HARLINGTON ROAD EAST
South West Middlesex Crematorium
De Brome Building
Bridge Farm Nursery
Cemetery
Recreation Grd.
Heathfield Jun. & Inf. Schs.
HANWORTH

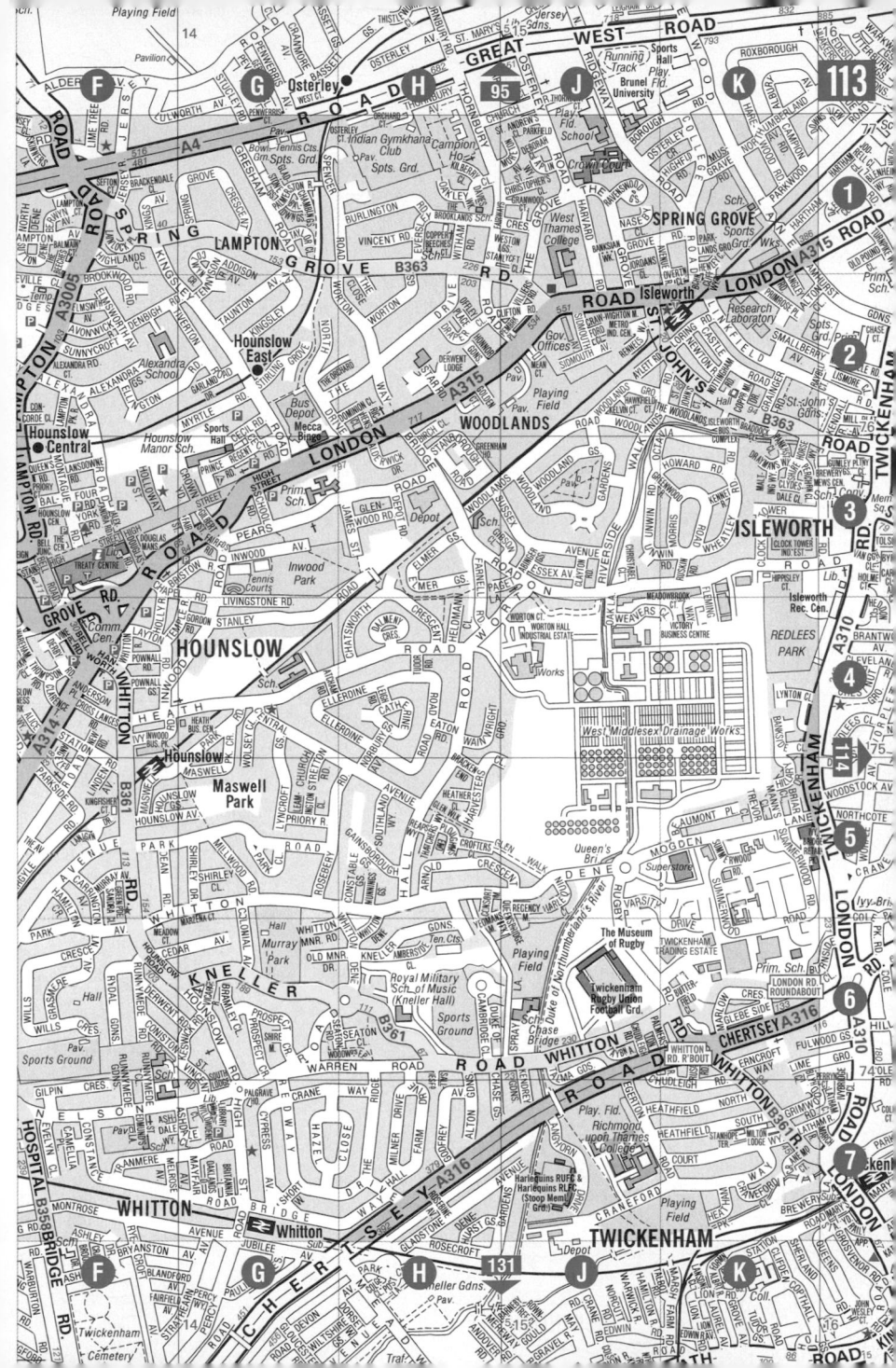

GREAT WEST ROAD
Osterley
Brunel University
Crown Court
SPRING GROVE
LAMPTON
West Thames College
LONDON ROAD
A315
Isleworth
Hounslow East
Hounslow Central
WOODLANDS
ISLEWORTH
Inwood Park
HOUNSLOW
Redlees Park
West Middlesex Drainage Works
Hounslow
Maswell Park
The Museum of Rugby
Twickenham Rugby Union Football Grd.
Royal Military Sch. of Music (Kneller Hall)
KNELLER
WHITTON ROAD
CHERTSEY ROAD
A316
WHITTON
Whitton
Richmond upon Thames College
Harlequins RUFC & Harlequins RLFC (Stoop Meml. Grd.)
TWICKENHAM
Twickenham Cemetery
TWICKENHAM ROAD
LONDON ROAD
A310
B361
B363
B358
A3005
A314
A4
95
114
131

114
A
B
C
D
E
96
1
2
3
4
5
6
7
113
132
Syon Lane
Old Brentford
Brentford Gate
Marina
LONDON ROAD
TWICKENHAM ROAD
A315
A310
B454
SPUR RD.
Busch Corner
London Butterfly House
SYON PARK
Syon Garden Centre
Syon House
Syon Park Sch.
DUKE OF NORTHUMBERLAND ESTATE
RIVER THAMES
Syon Reach
Isleworth Ferry Gate (Closed)
Water Lily Pond
Conservation Area
Queen Charlotte's Cottage
King's Steps Gate
ROYAL BOTANIC GARDENS
KEW
Bamboo Garden
Azalea Gdn.
Rhododendron
Syon Vista
The Lake
King William's Temple
Arboretum
Evolution House
Temperate House
Cedar Vista
Pavilion Restaurant
Japanese Gateway & Landscape
Pagoda
London Welsh RUFC
WEST MIDDLESEX UNIVERSITY HOSP.
Cemetery
OLD DEER PARK
ROYAL MID-SURREY GOLF COURSE
King's Observatory
Royal Mid-Surrey Golf Club
Richmond Athletic Ground
Rugby Grd.
Grand Stand
Tennis Courts
Pools on the Park
Obelisk
Old Deer Park Recreation Ground
Old Isleworth
Isleworth Ait
Nazareth Ho.
Brunel Univ.
Richmond Lock
ISLEWORTH
REDLEES PARK
SOUTH ST.
RICHMOND RD.
A3004
ST. MARGARETS RD.
ST. MARGARETS
Pleasure Gdns.
TWICKENHAM RD.
A316
THE AVENUE
RICHMOND
Richmond
Richmond Green
RICHMOND CIRCUS
LOWER RICHMOND ROAD
KEW RD.
SHEEN RD.
PARADISE RD.
GEORGE ST.
Asgill Ho.
Corporation Island
RICHMOND BRIDGE
RICHMOND ROAD
A305
PETERSHAM RD.
A307
RICHMOND HILL
B321
FRIARS STILE RD.
Terrace Gardens
Terrace Fld.
Royal Star & Garter Home
Richmond Univ.
Petersham Common
STAR & GARTER HILL
Buccleugh Gdns.
Glover's Island
Petersham Meadows
Petersham Farm
PETERSHAM ROAD
MARBLE HILL PARK
Marble Hill House
Orleans Ho. Gallery
Orleans Gdns.
Foot Ferry
WARREN
RIVER THAMES
TWICKENHAM
Twickenham
St. Margarets
Cole Park
Moor Mead Bridge
LONDON RD. ROUNDABOUT
ST. MARGARETS R'BOUT
CHERTSEY RD.
CROWN RD.
A316 ROAD
Playing Field
Tennis Courts
Sports Grd.
The German Sch., London
Theatre
Baths
KING ST.
YORK ST.
PETERSHAM

115
KEW
Princess of Wales Conservatory
Seven Sisters
Palm House
The Pond
Rose Garden
Visitor Centre
Temple of Bellona
Berberis Dell
Pagoda Vista
Marianne North Gallery
Lion Gate
The National Archives
Kew Riverside Park
Kew Retail Pk.
Kew Gds.
97
Chiswick
Burlington
Sports Hall
Cemetery
Tennis Courts
GROVE PARK
University of Westminster Sports Ground
Thames Village
Yacht Basin
Stadium
Sports Ground
Westminster Boathouse
Riverside Lands
Playing Fields
DUKE'S MEADOWS
Sports Ground
Driving Range
Tennis Courts
Pavilion
Boat Houses
Tennis Cts.
RIVER
THAMES
Refuse Dpt.
Mortlake Crematorium
Hammersmith Cemetery
FULHAM (NORTH SHEEN) CEMETERY
CHALKER'S CORNER
NORTH SHEEN
Playing Field
Rec. Ground
Rec. Grd.
Brewery
MORTLAKE
A3003
MORTLAKE HIGH ST
The Green
Mortlake
Sports Ground
A316
A205
A307
B353
A305
B351
B322
GREAT CHERTSEY ROAD
CHISWICK BRI.
CLIFFORD AV.
RICHMOND ROAD
LOWER RICHMOND RD.
UPPER RICHMOND RD.
MORTLAKE RD.
SANDYCOMBE ROAD
KEW ROAD
MANOR ROAD
KINGS ROAD
QUEEN'S ROAD
SHEEN LANE
North Sheen
Super-store
Depot
Holy Trinity C of E Prim. Sch.
Hickey's Almshouses
WEST
EAST SHEEN
Sheen Mt Prim. Sch.
Day Cen.
Shene Sch.
116
Pale Well
Pitch and Putt Course
Palewell Common
Palewell Fields
Playing Fields
Pesthouse Common
Christ's Sch.
Play. Fld.
East Sheen Cemetery
King's House Sch.
Richmond Cemetery
SHEEN COMMON
Football Ground
Bowling Green
Tennis Courts
Ranger's Gdn.
Teck Plantation
Sheen Wood
East Sheen Gate
Adam's Pond
Horse Ride
Bog Gate
The Bog
Riding Ring
RICHMOND PARK
Roehampton Gate
(Open during daylight hours only)
Sheen Cross Wood
Polo Field
Playing Field
Cambrian Gate
Bishop's Pond
Conduit Wood
Holly Lodge
Barn Wood Pond
Richmond Gate
SAWYER'S HILL
Saw Pit Plantation
Kidney Wood
Jubilee Plantation
Queen's Ride
133
Duchess' Wood
Deer Pen
White Lodge Plantation
Queen Mothers Copse
SIDMOUTH WOOD
King Henry VIII Mound
Pen Ponds
White Lodge (The Royal Ballet School)
Victory Plantation
F G H J K
1 2 3 4 5 6 7
19 20 21
74 75 76 77

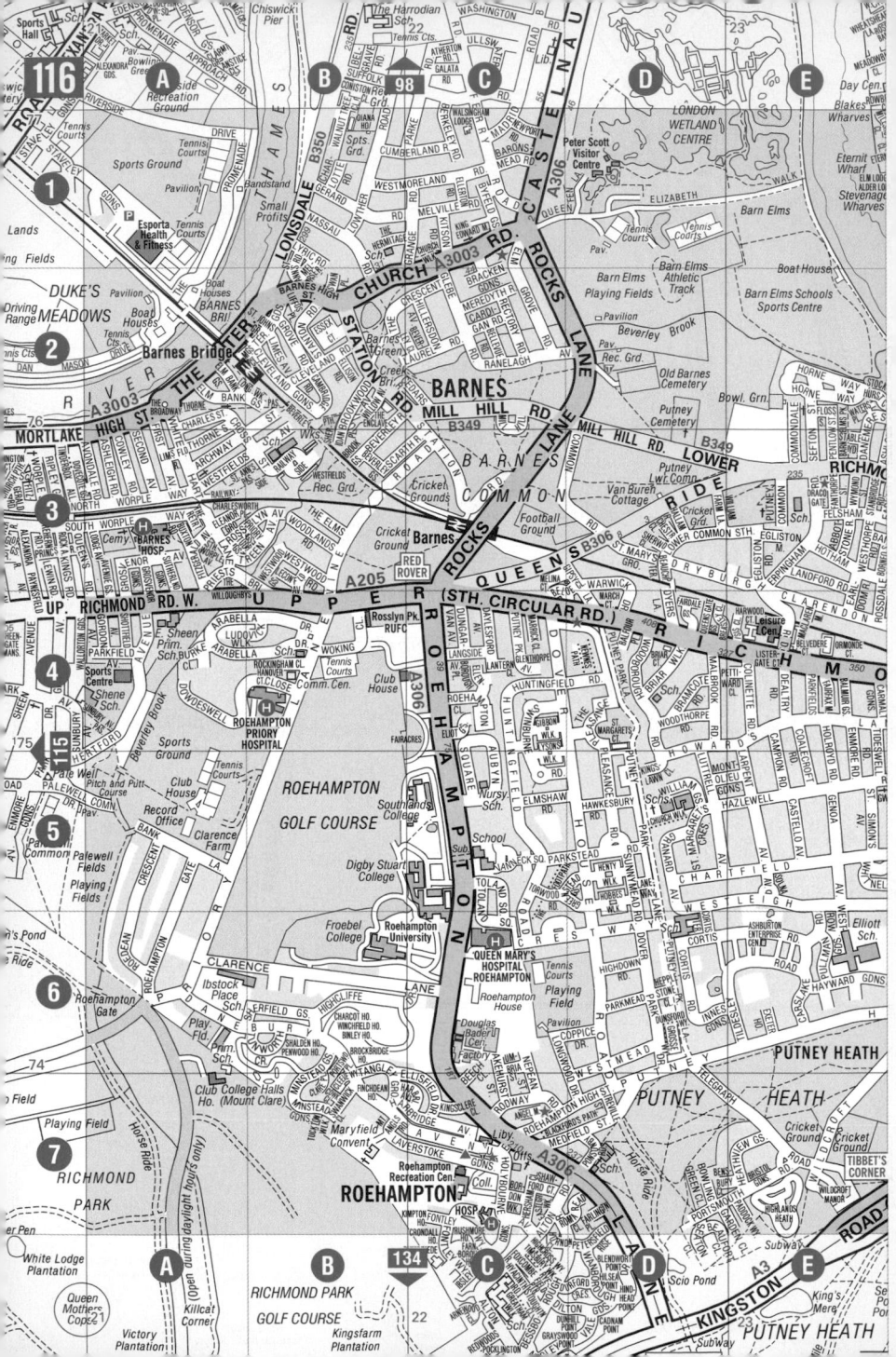

116
98
115
134
A
B
C
D
E
1
2
3
4
5
6
7
Chiswick Pier
The Harrodian Sch.
WASHINGTON RD.
LONDON WETLAND CENTRE
Peter Scott Visitor Centre
Day Cen.
Blakes Wharves
Eternit Wharf
Stevenage Wharves
Sports Hall
Riverside Recreation Ground
Sports Ground
Pavilion
Esporta Health & Fitness
Tennis Courts
Bandstand
Small Profits
THAMES
LONSDALE RD.
B350
CASTELNAU
A306
Barn Elms
Barn Elms Athletic Track
Barn Elms Playing Fields
Boat House
Barn Elms Schools Sports Centre
Beverley Brook
Old Barnes Cemetery
Putney Cemetery
Bowl. Grn.
DUKE'S MEADOWS
Driving Range
Boat Houses
BARNES BRI.
Barnes Bridge
RIVER
CHURCH RD.
A3003
BARNES HIGH ST.
STATION RD.
ROCKS LANE
BARNES
MILL HILL RD.
B349
LOWER RICHMOND
MORTLAKE
MORTLAKE HIGH ST.
THE TERRACE
BARNES COMMON
Cricket Grounds
Van Buren Cottage
Football Ground
QUEENS RIDE
B306
Cricket Ground
Barnes
RED ROVER
A205
BARNES HOSP.
UP. RICHMOND RD. W.
UPPER RICHMOND RD.
(STH. CIRCULAR RD.)
Rosslyn Pk. RUFC
Leisure Cen.
Sports Centre
Shene Sch.
E. Sheen Prim. Sch.
ROEHAMPTON PRIORY HOSPITAL
Sports Ground
Club House
Record Office
Clarence Farm
ROEHAMPTON GOLF COURSE
Southlands College
Digby Stuart College
Froebel College
Roehampton University
QUEEN MARY'S HOSPITAL ROEHAMPTON
Roehampton House
Playing Field
Pale Well
Pitch and Putt Course
Palewell Common
Palewell Fields
Playing Fields
Roehampton Gate
Ibstock Place Sch.
Club College Halls Ho. (Mount Clare)
Maryfield Convent
Roehampton Recreation Cen.
ROEHAMPTON
PUTNEY HEATH
Cricket Ground
TIBBET'S CORNER
KINGSTON ROAD
A3
Scio Pond
King's Mere
RICHMOND PARK
Horse Ride
(Open during daylight hours only)
White Lodge Plantation
Queen Mothers Copse
Killcat Corner
Victory Plantation
RICHMOND PARK GOLF COURSE
Kingsfarm Plantation
ROEHAMPTON LANE
ROEHAMPTON HIGH ST.
DANEBURY AV.
CLARENCE LANE
PRIORY LANE
ELIZABETH WALK
QUEEN ELIZABETH
CLARENDON
HOWARDS LANE
CHARTFIELD AV.
WESTLEIGH AV.
CRESTWAY
DOVER HOUSE ROAD
PUTNEY PARK LA.
HAWKESBURY RD.
WESTMEAD

FULHAM
Fulham Cemetery
Fulham FC (Craven Cottage)
FULHAM PALACE RD.
Moat Garden
The Warren Playground
Fulham Palace
BISHOP'S PARK
RIVER
Putney Pier
PARSONS GRN
Parsons Grn.
WALHAM GREEN
Eel Brook Common
SANDS END
Gas Works
FULHAM RD.
NEW KINGS RD.
WANDSWORTH BRIDGE RD.
SOUTH PARK
HURLINGHAM PARK
Hurlingham Stadium
Running Track
Hurlingham
The Hurlingham Club
Swim. Pool
Ckt. Grd.
CARNWATH RD.
Hurlingham Wharf
Trinidad Wharf
THAMES
Putney Bri.
PUTNEY BRIDGE
FULHAM HIGH STREET
PUTNEY HIGH ST.
WANDSWORTH PARK
PUTNEY BRIDGE RD.
A3209
Solid Waste Transfer Station
Fitness Club
Wandsworth Town
WANDSWORTH GYRATORY
WANDSWORTH
PUTNEY
Putney
East Putney
WEST HILL
WANDSWORTH HIGH ST.
ARMOURY WAY
SWANDON WAY
GARRATT LA.
BUCKHOLD RD.
MERTON RD.
King George's Park
Rec. Cen.
ROYAL HOSP FOR NEURO-DISABILITY
Playing Fld.
Mosque
Play. Fld.
WEST HILL
PUTNEY HILL
TIBBET'S RIDE
WIMBLEDON PARK SIDE
Saint Cecilia's
SOUTHFIELDS
Southfields
Play. Fields
Southfields Comm. Coll.
Sports Grd.
Mecca Bingo
Earlsfield
EARLSFIELD
F
G
H
J
K
1
2
3
4
5
6
7
99
118
135
24
25
26

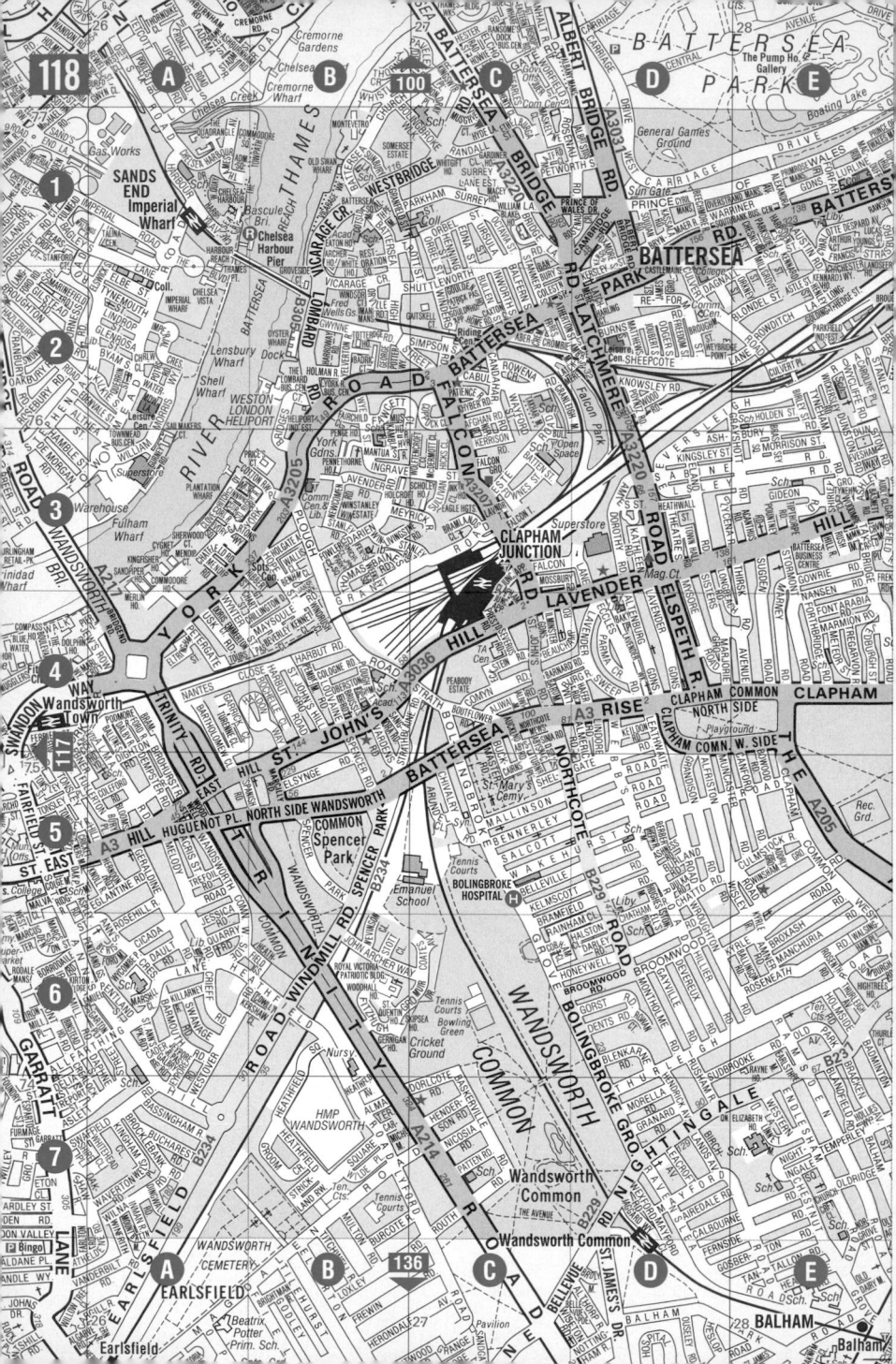

A
B
C
D
E
1
2
3
4
5
6
7
100
117
136
BATTERSEA PARK
The Pump Ho. Gallery
Boating Lake
General Games Ground
CARRIAGE DRIVE
Cremorne Gardens
Cremorne Wharf
Chelsea Creek
Gas Works
SANDS END
Imperial Wharf
Bascule Bri.
Chelsea Harbour Pier
RIVER THAMES
Lensbury Wharf
Shell Wharf
WESTON LONDON HELIPORT
Fulham Wharf
Warehouse
Superstore
Leisure Cen.
ALBERT BRIDGE RD.
BATTERSEA BRIDGE RD.
A3220
A3031
PRINCE OF WALES DR.
BATTERSEA
BATTERSEA PARK RD.
LATCHMERE RD.
Falcon Park
Open Space
CLAPHAM JUNCTION
Superstore
LAVENDER HILL
ELSPETH R.
CLAPHAM COMMON NORTH SIDE
CLAPHAM COMN. W. SIDE
THE CHASE
Playground
Rec. Grd.
A205
YORK RD.
A3205
A3036
A3207
FALCON RD.
WESTBRIDGE RD.
VICARAGE CR.
LOMBARD RD.
B305
York Gdns.
BATTERSEA RISE
A3
ST. JOHN'S HILL
EAST HILL
WANDSWORTH BRI.
A217
WANDSWORTH
Wandsworth Town
SWANDON WAY
TRINITY RD.
NORTH SIDE WANDSWORTH COMMON
HUGUENOT PL.
Spencer Park
Emanuel School
St. Mary's Cemy.
BOLINGBROKE HOSPITAL
Tennis Courts
Bowling Green
Cricket Ground
NORTHCOTE ROAD
B229
WANDSWORTH COMMON
Wandsworth Common
WINDMILL RD.
SPENCER PARK
B234
HMP WANDSWORTH
A214
GARRATT LANE
EARLSFIELD
Earlsfield
WANDSWORTH CEMETERY
Beatrix Potter Prim. Sch.
NIGHTINGALE LA.
BALHAM
Balham
B231
BOLINGBROKE GRO.
Pavilion

119
101
120
137
F
G
H
J
K
1
2
3
4
5
6
7
29
30
31
Battersea Park
Queenstown Road (Battersea)
NEW COVENT GARDEN MARKET
Fruit & Vegetable Market
SOUTH LAMBETH
Lambeth Coll.
Larkhall Park
Heathbrook Park
Works
Viaducts
Stockwell
STOCKWELL
Angell Town
Stockwell Park Sch.
Bus Depot
Wandsworth Rd.
WANDSWORTH ROAD
A3036
CLAPHAM
Clapham High St.
Clapham North
LAMBETH HOSPITAL
CLAPHAM COMMON
Clapham Comm.
BRIXTON
Superstore
COLDHARBOUR
CLAPHAM PARK
HMP BRIXTON
Sports Ground
Windmill Gdns.
Sorting Office
Clapham Sth.
Mount Pond
Eagle Pond
Long Pond
Bandstand
Basketball Courts
Tennis Courts
Hospice
Liby
Cin.
Leis. Cen.
Spts. Cen.
Sch.
Mos.
Lib.
Prim. Sch.
Res. (covered)
Bus Depot
STREATHAM
QUEENSTOWN RD.
SILVERTHORNE RD.
CEDARS RD.
A3216
COMMON NORTH SIDE
LONG RD.
A3
CLAPHAM COMMON SOUTH SIDE
A24
AVENUE
CLAPHAM PARK RD.
ACRE LANE
A2217
BEDFORD RD.
STOCKWELL RD.
SOUTH LAMBETH RD.
A203
CLAPHAM RD.
BRIXTON HILL
A23
BRIXTON RD.
A205
POYNDERS RD.
CAVENDISH RD.
KINGS AVENUE
B221
STREATHAM PL.
ATKINS RD.
CHRISTCHURCH RD.
BALHAM HIGH ROAD
OLD TOWN
THE PAVEMENT
B303
B224
A3205
LARKHALL LA.
LANDOR RD.
FERNDALE RD.
TULSE HILL
BRIXTON WATER LA.
ELM PARK
UPPER TULSE HILL

120
102
119
138
A
B
C
D
E
1
2
3
4
5
6
7
CAMBERWELL
CAMBERWELL GREEN
CAMBERWELL RD.
CAMBERWELL CHURCH STREET
CAMBERWELL STATION RD.
NEW MEDLAR ST.
SOUTHAMPTON
PECKHAM
Angell Town
STOCKWELL
STOCKWELL PK. CR.
STOCKWELL RD.
BRIXTON RD.
BRIXTON
Brixton
BRIXTON HILL
BRIXTON WATER LA.
BRIXTON STATION ROAD
COLDHARBOUR LANE
A2217
A23
A215
A2216
A2214
A2199
A204H
A202
B222
B223
LOUGHBOROUGH RD.
Loughborough Junc.
LOUGHBOROUGH ESTATE
MYATTS FIELDS
St. Gabriel's Manor
Mostyn Gardens
Max Roach Pk.
CAMBERWELL TRADING EST.
Camberwell Leisure Cen.
Bus Depot
DENMARK HILL
Denmark Hill
THE MAUDSLEY HOSP.
KINGS'COLLEGE HOSPITAL
The Rayne Inst.
Dental Institute
CHAMPION PK.
CHAMPION HILL
Wm. Booth Meml. Coll.
RUSKIN PARK
RUSKIN PARK HOUSE
Tennis Courts
Playground
HERNE HILL
Herne Hill
MILKWOOD ROAD
RAILTON ROAD
EFFRA RD.
MORVAL RD.
DULWICH ROAD
HALF MOON LA.
VILLAGE WAY
NORWOOD ROAD
CROXTED ROAD
BROCKWELL PARK
Brockwell Park Lido
Bowling Green
Tennis Courts
The Mansion
New Lodge
BROCKWELL PARK GDS.
TULSE HILL
TULSE HILL EST.
Knight's Hill
Herne Hill Stadium
Sports Ground
Graveyard
DULWICH VILLAGE
Dulwich Old College
Dulwich Picture Gallery
Old College Gate
Belair Park
Playing Fields
Boating Lake
North Dulwich
The Charter School
James Allen's Girls Sch.
EAST DULWICH GROVE
East Dulwich
Dulwich Hamlet FC
Superstore
DULWICH COMMUNITY HOSP.
DOG KENNEL HILL
GROVE LA.
Lettsom Gds.
Lucas Gds.
Alleyn's Sch.
Running Track
TURNEY ROAD
GALLERY ROAD
COLLEGE ROAD
Leisure Cen.
Brunswick Park
Gala Bingo

121
103
122
139
F
G
H
J
K
1
2
3
4
5
6
7
34
35
36
PECKHAM
PECKHAM HIGH ST.
QUEEN'S ROAD
A202
Queens Rd. (Peckham)
NEW CROSS GATE
NEW CROSS RD.
Peckham Rye
RYE LANE
A2215
HANOVER PK.
Telegraph Hill Park
Nunhead
EVELINA RD.
A2214
NUNHEAD
NUNHEAD CEMETERY
BROCKLEY
B2142
NUNHEAD LA.
EAST DULWICH ROAD
EAST DULWICH
PECKHAM RYE COMMON
PECKHAM RYE PARK
PECKHAM ROAD
B219
B238
Reservoirs (covered)
Waverley School
AQUARIUS GOLF COURSE
Playing Field
Newlands
Honor Oak Crematorium
Camberwell New Cemetery
Recreation Ground
ONE TREE HILL
HONOR OAK
HONOR OAK RD.
Honor Oak Park
Camberwell Old Cemetery
FOREST HILL
LORDSHIP LANE
A2216
GROVE VALE
DULWICH PARK
DULWICH COMMON
THE GROVE
Horniman Gardens
Horniman Museum
STANSTEAD
BROCKLEY RISE
STONDON PK.

122
104
121
140
A
B
C
D
E
1
2
3
4
5
6
7
NEW CROSS ROAD
New Cross Gate
New Cross
NEW CROSS
NEW CROSS GATE
Goldsmiths College
Deptford Bri.
BROOKMILL ROAD
GREENWICH HIGH RD.
BLACKHEATH RD.
BLACKHEATH HILL
LEWISHAM WAY
LEWISHAM RD.
ST. JOHNS
St. Johns
Elverson Rd.
LOAMPIT HILL
LOAMPIT VALE
THURSTON RD.
Lewisham
LEWISHAM
Lewisham College
DRAKEFELL RD.
Telegraph Hill Park
Brockley
BROCKLEY
BROCKLEY ROAD
HILLY FIELDS
Prendergast School
Brockley Cemetery
Ladywell Cemetery
Crofton Park
ADELAIDE AV.
LADYWELL RD.
Ladywell
LADYWELL
LEWISHAM UNIVERSITY HOSPITAL
Lewisham Park
LEWISHAM HIGH STREET
Crofton Pk.
Honor Oak Crematorium
Honor Oak Pk.
HONOR OAK PARK
HONOR OAK PK.
STONDON PARK
Blythe Hill
Blythe Hill Fields
Crofton Leisure Centre
Ladywell Arena/ (Running Track)
Ladywell Fields
Catford Bridge
Catford
CATFORD
CATFORD GYRATORY
BROWNHILL RD.
RUSHEY GREEN
STANSTEAD ROAD
CATFORD RD.
Powerleague Soccer Centre
Private Banks Sports Ground
36
37
38
74
75
76

123
124
105
141
F
G
H
J
K
1
2
3
4
5
6
7
GREENWICH PARK
Royal Observatory Greenwich
Bandstand
Reservoir (covered)
The Wilderness
The Gardens (Deer Park)
Rangers House
CHARLTON
HILL
ROAD
A2
B210
SHOOTERS
BLACK HEATH
PRINCE OF WALES RD.
B212
PRINCE CHARLES ROAD
OLD DOVER ROAD
SUN-IN-THE-SANDS
Christ's College for Boys
Tennis Courts
Morden College (Almshouses)
KIDBROOKE PARK ROAD
A2213
ROCHESTER WAY RELIEF ROAD
Blackheath Vale
BLACKHEATH
Blackheath
Concert Halls
LEE TERRACE
Hollyhedge Ho.
College
Playing Field
Kidbrooke Nature Reserve
Kidbrooke
Thomas Tallis Sch.
Depot
Sports Grd.
Sports Ground
BLACKHEATH PARK
LEE
B220
A20
HIGH ROAD
ELTHAM ROAD
Manor House Gdns
Manor Park
Sports Grounds
David Lloyd Leis.
Golf Driving Range
Quaggy River
SUTCLIFFE PARK
Sutcliffe Pk. Athletics Track
Harrow Meadow
Roan School Playing Fields
BURNT ASH HILL
A2212
Brindishe Prim. Sch.
Hither Green
HITHER GREEN
Lee
Horn Park
Colfes Sch.
Playing Field
CHILTONIAN IND. EST.
WESTHORNE AVENUE
A205
SIDCUP ROAD
ST. MILDREDS ROAD
BARING ROAD
Horn Park Prim. Sch.
Warehouse
Hadlow Coll. (Mottingham Centre)
MOTTINGHAM LA.

124
106
123
142
A
B
C
D
E
1
2
3
4
5
6
7
41
42
43
SHOOTERS HILL ROAD
A207
NIGERIA RD.
CHARLTON
CRESCENT
GRENADA
INDUS
KENYA RD.
DENE
PRINCE HENRY
GREENBAY RD.
Hornfair Park
Bowling Green
Tennis Courts
Playing Fields
WOOLWICH COMMON
Reservoir
Old Royal Military Academy
Eaglesfield School
ACADEMY ROAD
A205
HERBERT
IMPERIAL
BROMPTON TER.
Reservoir (covered)
ACADEMY
PLACE
LION
CONSTITUTION RISE
SHOOTERS
ELTHAM COMMON
MEMORIAL HOSPITAL
Severndroog Castle
CASTLE WOOD
Rose Cottage
JACK WOOD
CROOKSTON
DAIRSIE
DUMBRECK
ELTHAM PARK
ROCHESTER
WESTMOUNT
ELIBANK
ROAD
GREENVALE
ELTHAM PARK
RELIEF
DUNVEGAN
GLENLEA
GLENLYON
GLENSHIEL
Prim. Sch.
ROCHESTER WAY
RELIEF ROAD
ROCHESTER WAY
Sports Ground
Bowls
HARRADEN RD.
WICKLEMARSH
WEYMAN
MERRIMAN
Recreation Ground
FARJEON
HOLBURNE
HOLBURNE GDNS
WHETSTONE
DURSLEY ROAD
KELLAWAY
Kidbrooke School
Playing Fields
KIDBROOKE
Sam Montague Boys Club
Sports Ground
Tennis Courts
MAYDAY GARDENS
CEMETERY
WESTMOUNT
CASTLEWOOD
HEATHERBANK
GRANBY
ARSENAL
DUNBLANE
ALLENSWOOD
ARBROATH
WELL HALL
ROAD
Rec. Grd.
ROYAL HERBERT PAVILIONS
KENDALL RD.
BARLOW
CROSIER
HOWERD
Kidbrooke Grn Nature Res.
Thomas Tallis Sch.
Superstore
Kidbrooke
PARK
KIDBROOKE ESTATE
Nature Res.
TILBROOK RD.
MEERBROOK RD.
RIDGEBROOK
PURNEYS
CROOKS
GARDENS
BRISET
WENDOVER
HENWICK RD.
WINCHCOMB GARDENS
APPLETON RD.
ROSS WAY
PHINEAS PETT RD.
DOWNMAN RD.
DICKSON RD.
SANDBY GRN.
Support Cen.
KINGSHOLM GDS.
RANCLIFFE GARDENS
AVENUE
WELL HALL ROUNDABOUT
KIDBROOKE LA.
Sports Ground
Tennis Courts
Tudor Barn
Bowling Green
Eltham
A208
ELTHAM
MEADOWSIDE
EDGEWORTH
FARNABY
EALDHAM SQ.
JEKEN RD.
MESSENT
Meadowside Leis. Cen.
TUDWAY RD.
ROMERO SQ.
CAMBERT WAY
David Lloyd Leis.
KIDBROOKE
SUTCLIFFE PARK
Harrow Meadow
Football Ground
Sutcliffe Park Athletics Track
ELTHAM ROAD
A210
WESTHORNE AVENUE
ELTHAM
KATHERINE GDS.
KNOCKHOLT RD.
PHILIPPA GDNS.
SHAWBROOKE
FROISSART RD.
KEYNSHAM
MAYERNE
BASKET GS.
TATTERSALL CL.
SHERARD RD.
EVEREST
LASSA
JOHN RD.
LILBURNE RD.
SOWERBY
Swim. Pool
ELTHAM HILL
YORKSHIRE GREY
Eltham Green Sch.
Playing Field
Moatbridge Sch.
ELTHAM
Coll.
Queenscroft Park
Eltham Hill Sch.
QUEENSCROFT
ELTHAM HIGH STREET
DOBELL
ORANGERY LA.
STRONGBOW
ARCHERY
BEECHILL
GLENHOUSE
GOUROCK
Liby.
Supermarket
ST. MARY'S PATH
MESSETER PL.
WOODINGTON CL.
Horn Park
SCOTSDALE
STRATHAVEN
ABERGELDIE
CRATHIE
SIDCUP
WESTHORNE
ELTHAM PALACE RD.
Sports Ground
Bowling Grn.
Sports Ground
River Quaggy
Spts. Grd.
MIDDLE PARK AV.
CHURCHBURY
GLASBROOK RD.
GREGORY CR.
CAMPFIELD
Sch.
KING JOHN'S WALK
Community Centre
Eltham Palace
Institute of Army Education
COURT ROAD
NORTH PARK
Comp. Sch.
Superstore
SCRAY
Club House
ROYAL BLACKHEATH GOLF COURSE
Sports Grd.
Tennis Cts.
Bird Sanctuary
The Tarn
Mottingham
AVENUE
SHRUBSALL CL.
A20
ROAD
MOTTINGHAM ROAD
MOTTINGHAM LA.
Hadlow Coll. (Mottingham Centre)
Mottingham Farm
SIBTHORPE
Comm. Cen.
PASTON
HORSA RD.
Horn Park Prim. Sch.
GAVESTONE
Horn Park
ALNWICK
ASHDALE RD.

F
G
H
J
K
107
SHREWSBURY PARK
Clothworkers Wood
Willow Dene School
Playing Field
Woolwich Cemetery
Barefoot Gdn.
East Wickham Open Space
Woodlands Abattoir
Lowood Club Ho.
SHOOTERS HILL
Eaglesfield Rec. Grd.
SHOOTERS HILL GOLF COURSE
Woodlands Farm
Garden Centre
Council Offices
A207
SHOOTERS HILL
BELLEGROVE
ROAD
Welling
Jackwood Ho.
Oxleas Meadows
OXLEAS WOOD
Eastcote Prim. Sch.
WELLING WAY
Falconwood Field
Falconwood
SHEPHERDLEAS WOOD
ELTHAM PARK NORTH
FALCONWOOD
A2
ROAD
ROCHESTER WAY
EAST ROCHESTER WAY
Eltham Cemetery
Eltham Crematorium
ELTHAM PARK SOUTH
ELTHAM WARREN GOLF COURSE
Club House
Crown Woods School
Nature Study Centre
Playing Field
BEXLEY ROAD
BLACKFEN ROAD
A210
University of Greenwich (Avery Hill Campus)
AVERY HILL
AVERY HILL PARK
AVERY HILL RD.
B2214
(Halls of Residence)
Alderwood Prim. Sch.
Parish Wood
BLACKFEN
Hollyoak Wood Park
Days Lane Prim. Sch.
Sports Ground
Sparrow's Farm Leisure Cen.
HALFWAY STREET
A211
126
143
1
2
3
4
5
6
7
Willersley Pk.
Marlborough Sch.
Comm. Cen.
Lamorbey
44
45
46

126
A
B
C
D
E
1
2
3
4
5
6
7
108
125
144
Plumstead Cemetery
Woolwich Cemetery
Barefoot Gdn.
Hill Grove
East Wickham Open Space
EAST WICKHAM
Stevens Park
WELLING
Welling
Welling Corner
Welling Sch.
Playing Field
Warehouse
BELLEGROVE RD.
WELLING HIGH ST.
PARK VIEW RD.
A207
CROOK LOG
Bexleyheath
Bexleyheath Station
UPPER WICKHAM LANE
A209
Brampton Prim. Sch.
Hook La. Prim. Sch.
Westbrooke Sch.
The Danson Cen.
Crook Lodge Spts. Cen.
Crook Log Prim. Sch.
Welling United FC
Bexleyheath Sports Club
Tennis Courts
Pitch & Putt
Playground
Danson Ho.
Bexley Grammar Sch.
Playing Field
Danson Water Sports Centre
DANSON PARK
THE LAKE
DANSON ROAD
A221
Upton
Upton Centre
Red House
Club Ho.
BEXLEYHEATH GOLF COURSE
EAST ROCHESTER WAY
A2
DANSON INTERCHANGE
DANSON UNDERPASS
ROCHESTER WAY
BLACKFEN
BLACKFEN ROAD
A210
Blackfen Sch. for Girls
Sherwood Park Prim. Sch.
Days Lane Prim. Sch.
PENHILL PARK
PENHILL RD.
Blendon
BLENDON RD.
B2210
BRIDGEN RD.
Bridgen
Bexley Park Wood
Hollyoak Wood Park
Willersley Pk.
Marlborough Park
Marlborough Sch.
SIDCUP GOLF COURSE
River Shuttle
Hurst Prim. Sch.
Rec. Grd.
Playing Fld.
Hurstmere Sch.
Chatsworth Inf. Sch.
Lamorbey Park
Lamorbey
The Barn
HURST ROAD

127
109
145
F
G
H
J
K
1
2
3
4
5
6
7
49
50
51
74
75
76
NORTHUMBERLAND HEATH
BARNEHURST
BEXLEYHEATH
BEXLEY
OLD BEXLEY
CRAYFORD
Barnehurst
Bexley
BARNEHURST GOLF COURSE
Mayplace (Club Ho.)
Crayford Manor House (Adult Ed. Cen.)
Bursted Wood Prim. Sch.
Bursted Wood
Russell Park
Martens Grove Park
Martens Grove
Mayplace Prim. Sch.
Bexleyheath School
St. Thomas More RC Prim. Sch.
Gravel Hill Prim. Sch.
St. Catherine's Sch. for Girls
St. Columba's RC Boys Sch.
Grammar Sch.
Hall Place & Visitors Centre
Hall Place Gardens
BLACK PRINCE INTERCHANGE
SPORTS FIELD
Pumping Station
The Old Orchard
Churchfield Wood
Old Bexley C of E Prim. Sch.
Cricket Ground
Colyers Prim. Sch.
Normandy Prim. Sch.
Bigs Hill Wood
SHENSTONE PARK
Gas Works
Youth Cen.
Civic Offices
Gala Bingo
Mega-bowl
Football Cen.
Cemetery
Bus Depot
THE BROADWAY SHOP. CEN.
THE MALL
A220
A221
A207
A2
A223
A222
A2000
B2210
BROADWAY
WATLING ST.
LONDON RD.
ROCHESTER WAY
DARTFORD-BY-PASS
GRAVEL HILL
BOURNE ROAD
MAYPLACE RD.
ALBION ROAD
ARNSBERG WAY
BEXLEY HIGH ST.
PARKHILL ROAD
COLYERS LA.
NORTHUMBERLAND AVENUE
LONG LANE
BELMONT ROAD
MEREWOOD ROAD
NORTHALL ROAD
WOOLWICH ROAD
VICARAGE ROAD
Riverside Walk
River Shuttle
Subway
River Cray
Weir
Works
Factory

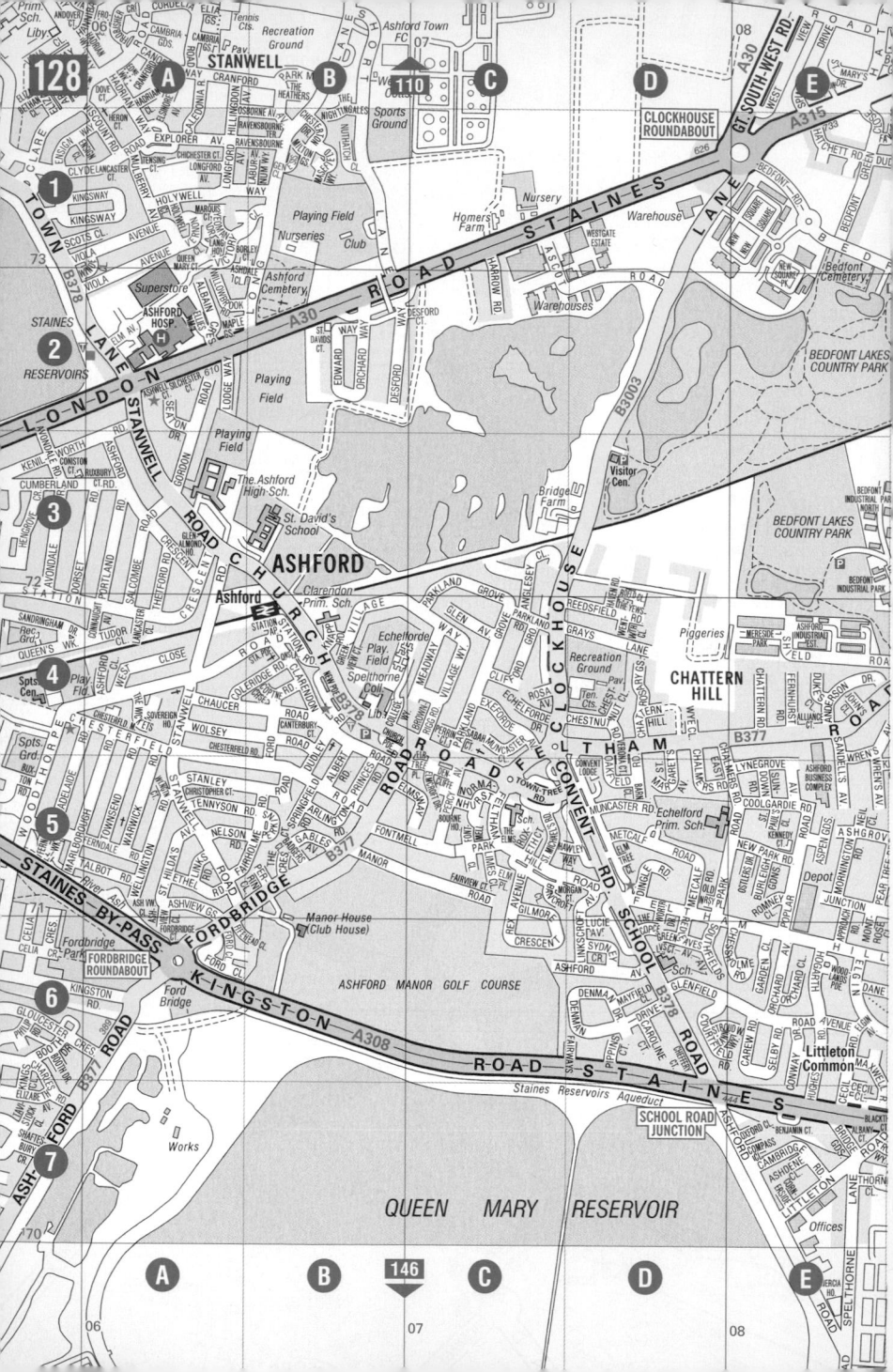

128
110
146
A
B
C
D
E
1
2
3
4
5
6
7
06
07
08
73
72
71
170
STANWELL
ASHFORD
CHATTERN HILL
Littleton Common
CLOCKHOUSE ROUNDABOUT
FORDBRIDGE ROUNDABOUT
SCHOOL ROAD JUNCTION
LONDON ROAD
STAINES ROAD
KINGSTON ROAD
STAINES-BY-PASS
GT. SOUTH-WEST RD.
FELTHAM ROAD
CHURCH ROAD
CLOCKHOUSE LANE
STANWELL ROAD
SCHOOL ROAD
CONVENT RD.
FORDBRIDGE
A30
A315
A308
B377
B378
B3003
STAINES RESERVOIRS
QUEEN MARY RESERVOIR
Staines Reservoirs Aqueduct
ASHFORD MANOR GOLF COURSE
BEDFONT LAKES COUNTRY PARK
Bedfont Cemetery
Ashford Cemetery
ASHFORD HOSP.
Superstore
Recreation Ground
Playing Field
Sports Ground
Ashford Town FC
Nurseries
Nursery
Homers Farm
Warehouse
Warehouses
WESTGATE ESTATE
The Ashford High Sch.
St. David's School
Clarendon Prim. Sch.
Echelforde Play. Field
Spelthorne Coll.
Echelford Prim. Sch.
Visitor Cen.
Bridge Farm
Piggeries
ASHFORD INDUSTRIAL EST.
MERESIDE PARK
ASHFORD BUSINESS COMPLEX
BEDFONT INDUSTRIAL PARK
BEDFONT INDUSTRIAL PARK NORTH
Manor House (Club House)
Fordbridge Park
Ford Bridge
Works
Offices
Depot
Ashford

129
111
130
147
F
G
H
J
K
1
2
3
4
5
6
7
EAST BEDFONT
Fairholme Primary Sch.
Playing Field
Feltham Arenas
Grandstand
Running Track
Blenheim Pk.
School
Schs.
Playing Field
Feltham Park
Warehouses
Feltham
HANWORTH RD.
B3377
A312
HARLINGTON ROAD
HOUNSLOW ROAD
BEDFONT LANE
Industrial Est.
Edward Pauling Prim. Sch.
Vineyard Nurseries
Playing Field
Grosvenor Park
Gala Bingo
Bowl. Alley
Cineworld
Sports Centre
FELTHAM
Ordnance Depot
Sports Ground
Works
HM Young Offenders Institution Feltham
LOWER FELTHAM
Feltham Hill Jun. & Inf. Schs.
HIGH STREET
A244
ASHFORD ROAD
B377
Cemetery
Rec. Grd.
Croft Farm
Hall Grange Mews
Garden Centre
Moat
SNAKEY LANE
Works
Club Ho.
Rugby Football Ground
CHERTSEY ROAD
Sports Ground
Sports Ground
FELTHAMHILL
Playing Field
Laboratories
Club
King George's Fld.
Kenyngton Manor Prim. Sch.
Dairy
Works
Filter Beds
Spelthorne Jun. & Inf. Schs.
Offices
Staines Reservoir
Hall
ASHFORD COMMON
SUNBURY COMMON
COUNTRY WAY
HANWORTH RD.
Warehouse
Junc.1
A316
ROAD A308
WEST
Club Ho.
Sports Ground
Library
M3 MOTORWAY
SUNBURY CROSS
STAINES A308 ROAD
Depot
Stables
Kempton Park
KEMPTON PARK RACECOURSE
Grandstand
Pumping Station
Filter Beds
Superstore
Sunbury
Adult Edu. Cen.
Sports Grd.
Playing Field
Sunbury Manor Sch.
St. Paul's
M3
WINDMILL RD.
CADBURY RD.

130
112
148
129
A
B
C
D
E
1
2
3
4
5
6
7
FELTHAM
HANWORTH
Hounslow Cemy.
HEATHROW GATEWAY
MILL FARM BUSINESS PARK
South West Middlesex Crematorium
De Brome Building
Playing Field
Cemetery
Recreation Grd.
Heathfield Jun. & Inf. Schs.
Gala Bingo
Bowl. Alley
LEISURE WEST
Cineworld
Sports Centre
Feltham Community College
FELTHAM BUSINESS COMPLEX
Works
Pav. Sports Ground
Tennis Courts
Feltham Airparcs Leisure Centre
Mount Corner
Hanworth Park House
HANWORTH PARK
Nature Reserve
School
HAMPTON FARM IND. ESTATE
HANWORTH TRAD. EST.
APEX RETAIL PK.
APEX CORNER
The Racquets & Fitness Spa
Club Ho.
TWICKENHAM GOLF COURSE
Superstore
Longford River
Hounslow College
Rectory Meadow
Rec. Grd.
Moat
Dairy
Filter Beds
The Lindon Bennett Sch.
Play. Fld.
Reservoir
Staines Reservoirs Aqueduct
Football Ground
Hatherop Park
Half Moon Covert
Stables
Grandstand
KEMPTON PARK RACECOURSE
Portlane Bridge
Hydes Field
Oldfield Works
Hampton Comm. Coll.
Hampton Spts. Cen.
Hampton School
Richmond Ho.
Hospice
Sports Hall
Comm. Cen.
Inf. Sch.
Cemy.
UXBRIDGE ROAD
A312
HANWORTH ROAD
A314
HOUNSLOW ROAD
HAMPTON RD. WEST
HAMPTON RD. EAST
GREAT CHERTSEY ROAD
TWICKENHAM RD.
A305
COUNTRY WAY
A316
HARLINGTON ROAD EAST
STAINES RD. EAST
BUCKINGHAM ROAD
OLD FARM ROAD
PERCY ROAD
PRIORY ROAD
OLDFIELD ROAD

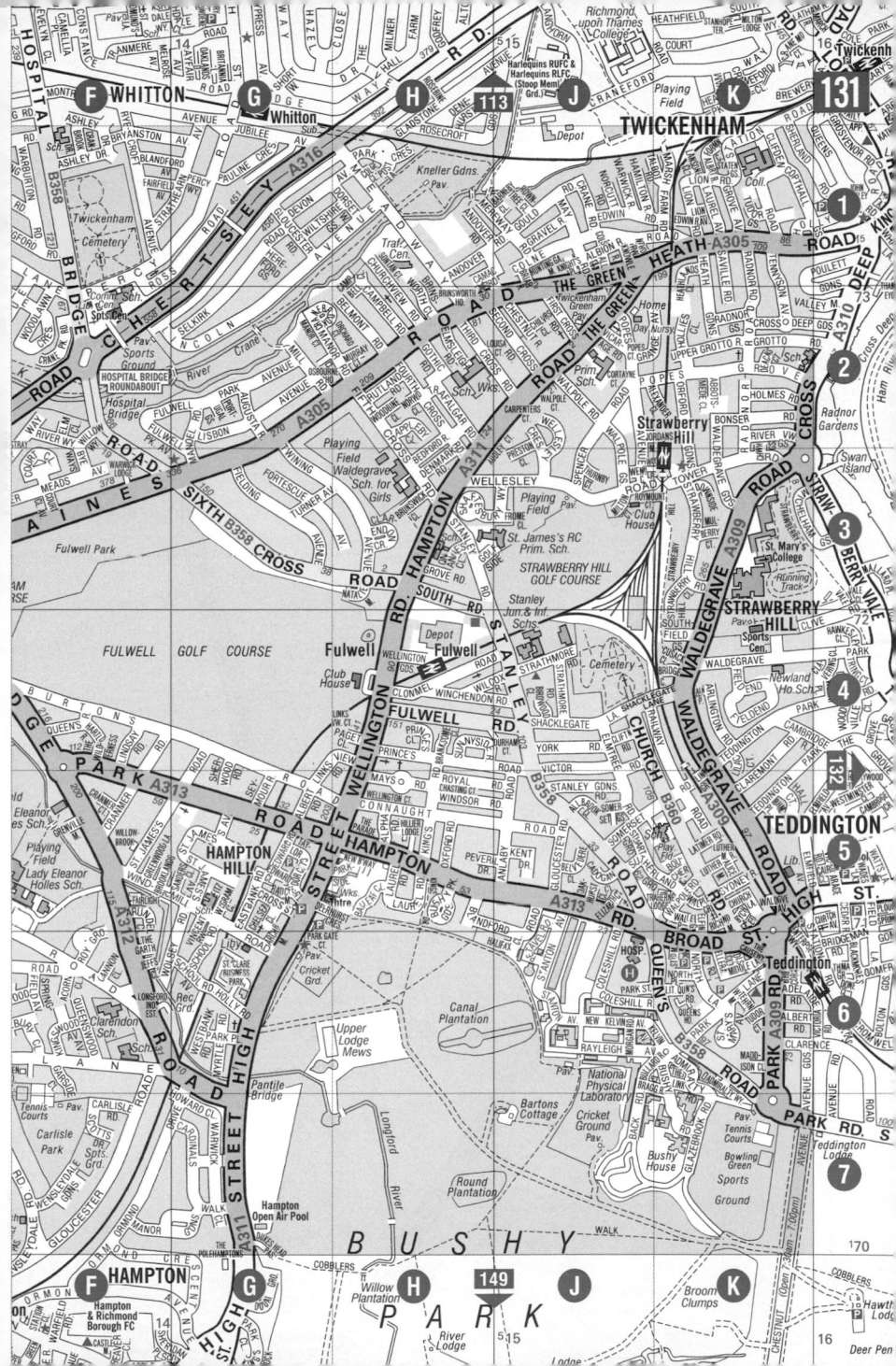

132
114
131
150
Twickenham
TWICKENHAM
MARBLE HILL PARK
Marble Hill House
Orleans Ho. Gallery
Orleans Gdns.
Glover's Island
Petersham Meadows
Petersham Farm
Royal Star & Garter Home
Petersham Common
STAR & GARTER HILL
B353
RIVER THAMES
Foot Ferry
WARREN FOOTPATH
Eel Pie Island
Theatre
Baths
Ham House
Playing Field
Tennis Cts.
Club
Miniature Rifle Range
Polo Ground
The German Sch. London
The Russell Prim. Sch.
Strathmore Sch.
The Copse
PETERSHAM
PETERSHAM PARK
SUDBROOK PARK
Sudbrook Park (Club Ho.)
The Wilderness
RICHMOND GOLF COURSE
Ham Riverside Lands
Nature Reserve
Radnor Gardens
Swan Island
Cross Deep
CROSS DEEP
HEATH RD.
KING ST.
YORK ST.
RICHMOND RD.
A305
A310
A307
A313
B352
B358
STRAWBERRY VALE
STRAWBERRY HILL
St. Mary's College
Running Track
Sports Cen.
Ham Fields
Thames Young Mariners Base
Grey Court School
Ham Green
C of E Prim. Sch.
HAM
Meadlands Prim. Sch.
HAM COMMON
HAM GATE AV.
THE CASSEL HOSP.
Convent
UPPER HAM RD.
PETERSHAM RD.
RICHMOND RD.
SANDY LANE
RIVERSIDE DRIVE
DUKES AV.
LOCK RD.
Ham Riverside Lands
Teddington Locks
Teddington Weir
Rec. Gd.
Teddington Studios
Sports Ground
Lensbury Club
Trowlock Island
YMCA Sports Grd.
St. George's Industrial Estate
The Tiffin Girls' Sch.
Fern Hill Prim. Sch.
TEDDINGTON
Teddington
Pool
Arts Cen.
Udney Hall Gdns.
HIGH STREET
KINGSTON RD.
TWICKENHAM RD.
MANOR RD.
BROOM ROAD
Athletic Ground
Collis Prim. Sch.
Teddington Sch. & Sports Cen.
Recreation Ground
Steven's Eyot
Canbury Gdns.
The Avenue Centre (Coll.)
KINGSTON UPON THAMES
HAMPTON WICK
Hampton Wick
Fitness Club
Superstore
Mosque
BUSHY PARK
SANDY LANE
PARK RD.
Teddington Lodge
Warren Plantation
Hawthorn Lodge
Half Moon Plantation
Deer Pen
Leg-of-Mutton
Thatched Cottage
COBBLERS WALK
Open 7.30am - 7.00pm
UP. TEDDINGTON RD.
LOWER HAM RD.
CHURCH RD.
TUDOR AV.
CARDINAL AV.
LATCHMERE RD.
KING'S RD.
A B C D E
1 2 3 4 5 6 7
16 17 18

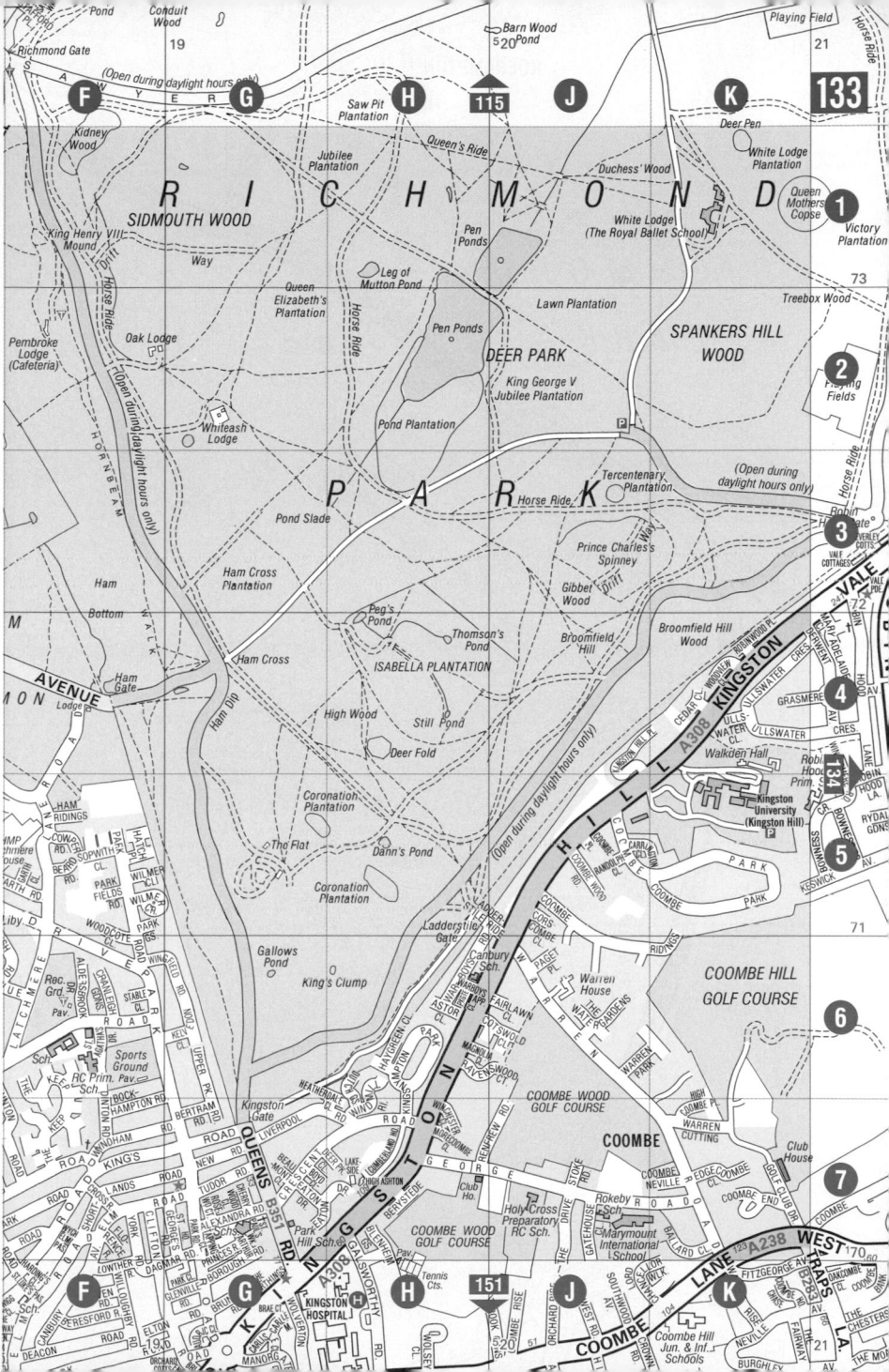
RICHMOND PARK
Richmond Gate
Sawyer's Hill (Open during daylight hours only)
Conduit Wood
Pond
Barn Wood Pond
Playing Field
Horse Ride
Kidney Wood
Saw Pit Plantation
Queen's Ride
Jubilee Plantation
Deer Pen
White Lodge Plantation
Duchess' Wood
Queen Mothers Copse
Victory Plantation
SIDMOUTH WOOD
King Henry VIII Mound
White Lodge (The Royal Ballet School)
Pen Ponds
Leg of Mutton Pond
Queen Elizabeth's Plantation
Lawn Plantation
Treebox Wood
Drift Way
Oak Lodge
Pembroke Lodge (Cafeteria)
DEER PARK
SPANKERS HILL WOOD
King George V Jubilee Plantation
Playing Fields
Pond Plantation
Whiteash Lodge
HORNBEAM WALK
(Open during daylight hours only)
Tercentenary Plantation
(Open during daylight hours only)
Robin Hood Gate
Beverley Cotts.
Vale Cottages
Pond Slade
Horse Ride
Prince Charles's Spinney
Ham Cross Plantation
Ham
Gibbet Wood
Ham Bottom
Peg's Pond
Thomson's Pond
Broomfield Hill
Broomfield Hill Wood
Ham Cross
ISABELLA PLANTATION
Ham Gate
HAM GATE AVENUE
Lodge
Ham Dip
High Wood
Still Pond
Deer Fold
KINGSTON HILL A308
KINGSTON VALE
Walkden Hall
Kingston University (Kingston Hill)
Robin Hood Prim. Sch.
Coronation Plantation
The Flat
Dann's Pond
Coronation Plantation
COOMBE PARK
Ladderstile Gate
Ladderstile Ride
Gallows Pond
King's Clump
Canbury Sch.
Warren House
The Water Gardens
COOMBE HILL GOLF COURSE
Warren Park
Sports Ground
RC Prim. Sch.
Kingston Gate
COOMBE WOOD GOLF COURSE
COOMBE
Club House
Warren Cutting
QUEENS RD. B351
George Road
Club Ho.
Holy Cross Preparatory RC Sch.
Rokeby Sch.
Marymount International School
Park Hill Sch.
COOMBE WOOD GOLF COURSE
Tennis Cts.
KINGSTON HOSPITAL
COOMBE LANE WEST A238
TRAPS LA. B283
Coombe Hill Jun. & Inf. Schools
115
151
134
19
20
21
73
72
71
170

134
116
133
152
ROEHAMPTON
RICHMOND PARK
RICHMOND PARK GOLF COURSE
PUTNEY HEATH
PUTNEY VALE
KINGSTON VALE
WIMBLEDON COMMON
WIMBLEDON COMMON & LONDON SCOTTISH GOLF COURSE
ROYAL WIMBLEDON GOLF COURSE
COOMBE HILL GOLF COURSE
COPSE HILL
KINGSTON VALE
ROEHAMPTON VALE
KINGSTON ROAD
ROBIN HOOD WAY
A3 (KINGSTON BY-PASS)
COOMBE LANE WEST
ROEHAMPTON LANE
WINDMILL ROAD
STAG LANE
ROBIN HOOD
COOMBE LANE
TIBBET'S CORNER
Putney Vale Crematorium
PUTNEY VALE CEMETERY
Wimbledon Windmill Museum
Kingston University (Roehampton Vale Centre)
Kingston University (Kingston Hill)
Hall School Wimbledon
The Wolfson Rehabilitation Cen.
NEW VICTORIA HOSPITAL
Caesar's Camp
Cannizaro Park
Queen's Mere
King's Mere
Scio Pond
Beverley Brook
Robin Hood Gate
Horse Ride
Playing Fields

WIMBLEDON
WIMBLEDON PARK
Wimbledon Park
Wimbledon
SOUTH WIMBLEDON
South Wimbledon
MERTON
SOUTHFIELDS
Southfields
SUMMERSTOWN
Earlsfield
Haydons Road
Dundonald Rd.
Merton Park
PARKSIDE HOSP.
Wimbledon All England Lawn Tennis & Croquet Club
Museum
Indoor Ten. Cts.
Aorangi Park
Tennis Courts
Buddhist Temple
Wimbledon Park Athletics Track
Bowling Greens
Putting Green
Cricket Ground
Club House
WIMBLEDON PARK GOLF COURSE
Wimbledon Cemetery
Bishop Gilpin C of E First Sch.
The Priory C of E Sch.
Wimbledon High Sch.
Wimbledon Coll.
Ursuline Prep. Sch.
Dundonald Prim. Sch.
Recreation Ground
South Park Gardens
King George's Park
Southfields Comm. Coll.
Play. Fields
Westfield House Sports Grd.
Carriage Cleaning Shed
Superstore
Depot
Works
Football Grd.
Caravan Site
River Wandle
Garratt Park
Saint Cecilia's
Rushmere Pond
King's Coll. Sch.
Esporta
Leisure Cen.
YMCA
Theatre-rites
THE BROADWAY
WIMBLEDON HILL RD.
WIMBLEDON PARK SIDE
PARKSIDE
MERTON RD.
DURNSFORD RD.
HAYDONS ROAD
ALEXANDRA ROAD
HARTFIELD ROAD
KINGSTON ROAD
GAP ROAD
PLOUGH LANE
GARRATT LANE
MERTON HIGH ST.
MERANTUN WAY
HIGH ST.
ARTHUR ROAD
HOME PARK ROAD
CHURCH ROAD
QUEENS ROAD
WORPLE ROAD
A219
A218
A217
A238
B235
B285
117
136
153
F
G
H
J
K
1
2
3
4
5
6
7

136
118
135
154
A
B
C
D
E
1
2
3
4
5
6
7
EARLSFIELD
Earlsfield
WANDSWORTH CEMETERY
Wandsworth Common
BALHAM
Beatrix Potter Prim. Sch.
Sports Ground
THE CENTRAL LONDON GOLF COURSE
The Joan Bicknell Centre
SPRINGFIELD UNIVERSITY HOSPITAL
Cottage Day Hospital
Burntwood School
Garratt Green
Garratt Park
STREATHAM CEMETERY
UPPER TOOTING
Playing Field
Tooting Bec
SUMMERSTOWN
Wimbledon Stadium (Greyhound & Speedway)
Lambeth Crematorium
LAMBETH CEMETERY
River Wandle
Haydons Road
Tooting Leisure Cen.
Tooting Gardens
ST. GEORGE'S HOSPITAL
Tooting Broadway
TOOTING
TOOTING GRAVENEY
Gala Bingo
Professional Centre
Wandle Meadow Nature Park
Garfield Prim. Sch.
Wandle Park
Colliers Wood
COLLIER'S WOOD
Tooting
MERTON
Superstore
Cemetery
Lavender Park
Edenvale Open Space
Mecca Bingo
Theatre-rites
BURNTWOOD LANE
TRINITY ROAD
BALHAM HIGH ROAD
UPPER TOOTING ROAD
TOOTING BEC ROAD
GARRATT LANE
SUMMERSTOWN
PLOUGH LANE
HAYDONS ROAD
MITCHAM ROAD
TOOTING HIGH ST.
COLLIERS WOOD
HIGH STREET
MERTON HIGH STREET
LONDON ROAD
STREATHAM ROAD
MERANTUN WAY
RECTORY LANE
LONGLEY
Tamworth Rec. Grd.
FIGGE'S MARSH

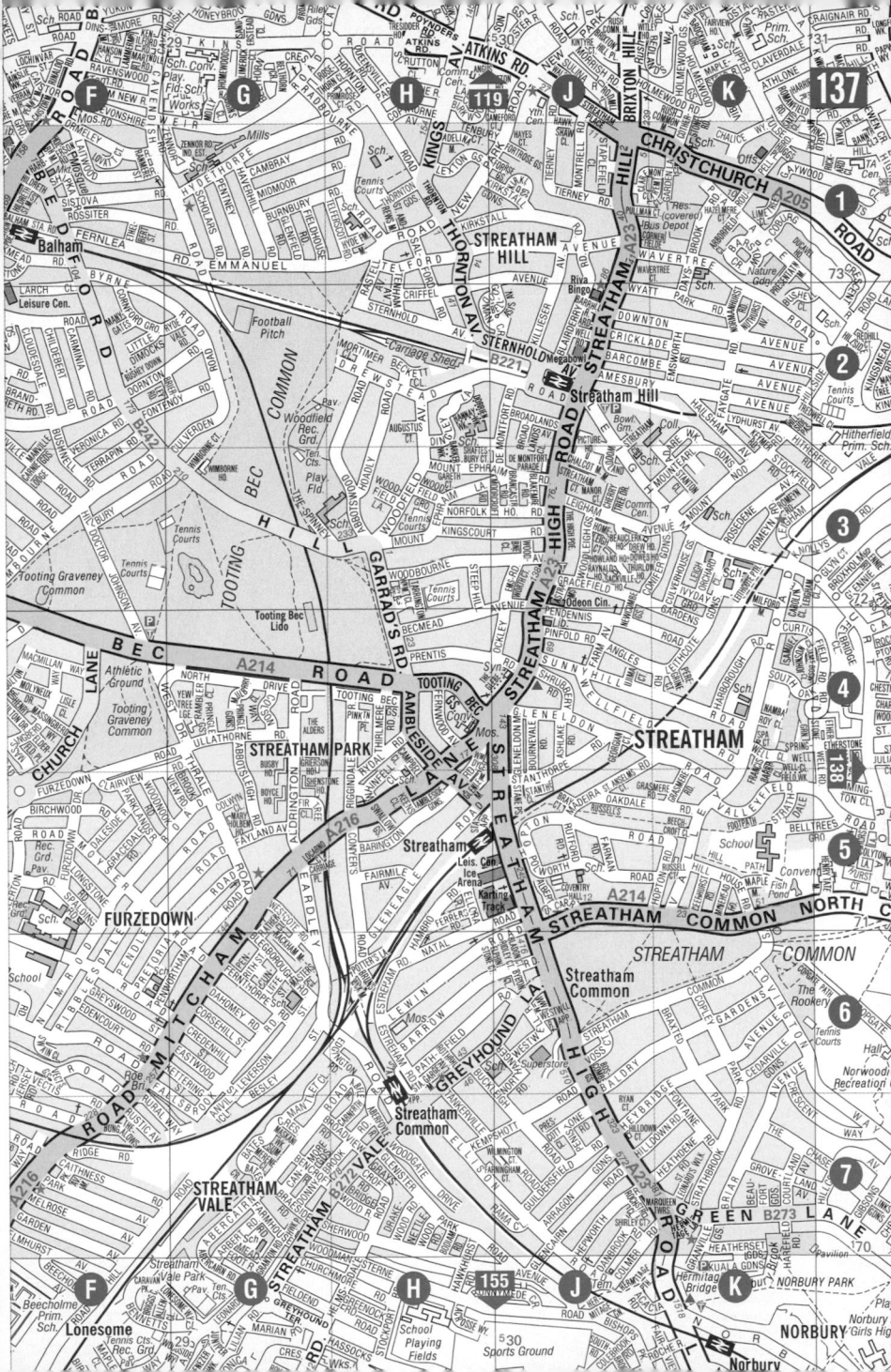

137
119
138
155
F
G
H
J
K
1
2
3
4
5
6
7
Balham
STREATHAM HILL
Streatham Hill
TOOTING BEC COMMON
Tooting Graveney Common
Tooting Bec Lido
STREATHAM PARK
STREATHAM
Streatham
FURZEDOWN
STREATHAM COMMON
Streatham Common
STREATHAM VALE
Streatham Vale Park
Lonesome
NORBURY
Norbury
Norbury Park
CHRISTCHURCH ROAD
A205
BRIXTON HILL
STREATHAM HIGH ROAD
A23
BEC ROAD
A214
STREATHAM COMMON NORTH
MITCHAM ROAD
A216
MITCHAM LANE
THORNTON AV.
KINGS AV.
ATKINS RD.
BEDFORD ROAD
B242
STERNHOLD AV.
B221
GARRAD'S RD.
GREYHOUND LA.
GREEN LANE
B273
B272
School Playing Fields
Sports Ground

138
120
137
156
A
B
C
D
E
1
2
3
4
5
6
7
BROCKWELL PARK
DULWICH VILLAGE
Dulwich Picture Gallery
Dulwich Old College
Belair Park
Dulwich College
TULSE HILL
Tulse Hill
Knight's Hill
CHRISTCHURCH RD.
A205
A204
A215
A2199
A214
A212
B232
B273
NORWOOD ROAD
THURLOW PARK
DULWICH ROAD
CROXTED ROAD
SOUTH CROXTED ROAD
West Dulwich
WEST DULWICH
West Norwood
WEST NORWOOD
West Norwood Crematorium
Cemetery
NORWOOD HIGH ST.
KNIGHTS HILL
ELDER RD.
GIPSY RD.
Gipsy Hill
NORWOOD PARK
Kingswood Prim. Sch.
KINGSWOOD ESTATE
STREATHAM COMN. NTH.
STREATHAM COMMON
CROWN LA.
CROWN DALE
CENTRAL HILL
BEULAH HILL
NORWOOD NEW TOWN
Rockmount Prim. Sch.
Norwood Grove Recreation Ground
Playing Fields
Recreation Ground
Biggin Wood
Downsview Prim. Sch.
Westwood Language Coll. for Girls
NORWOOD
Westow Park
CHURCH RD.
UPPER NORWOOD
The Lawns
NORBURY PARK
NORBURY
Norbury Manor Girls High Sch.
NORBURY LANE
GREEN LANE
Hitherfield Prim. Sch.
St. Joseph's College
St. Joseph's RC Jun. & Inf. Schs.
Convent Wood
Elm Wood Prim. Sch.
The Michael Tippett Sch.

139
140
121
157
F
G
H
J
K
1
2
3
4
5
6
7
34
35
36
DULWICH PARK
Aviary
Court La. Gate
Horse Ride
Queen Mary's Gate
Sports Ground
Sports Grounds
Rosebery Lodge Ga.
COMMON
LORDSHIP LA. A205
LONDON ROAD
A205
THE GROVE
Grove House
Horniman Gardens
Horniman Museum
DULWICH & SYDENHAM HILL GOLF COURSE
The Grange
Club House
DULWICH
Toll Gate
Beechgrove
Dulwich Wood
PECKARMANS WOOD
LOW CROSS WOOD LA.
Sydenham Hill
UPPER SYDENHAM
Sydenham Wells Park
FOREST HILL
Forest Hill
DARTMOUTH RD. A2216
KIRKDALE
WALDRAM PK. RD.
STANSTEAD RD.
DEVONSHIRE RD.
PERRY VALE
B227
Swim. Pool
FOREST HILL IND. EST.
LOWER SYDENHAM
Mayow Park
SYDENHAM
Sydenham
SYDENHAM ROAD A212
A212 HILL
WESTWOOD HILL
CRYSTAL PALACE PARK RD.
A234
Rockhills Entrance Camping Site
TV Transmitter
Fisherman's Gate
Intermediate Lake
CRYSTAL PALACE PARK
The Maze
Sydenham Entrance
Crystal Palace National Sports Centre
Site of Crystal Palace
Tennis Courts
CRYSTAL PALACE
Crystal Palace Museum
Crystal Palace Athletics Stadium
Penge Entrance
Lower Lake
Anerley Entrance
Crystal Palace
COLLEGE RD.
A2199
CRYSTAL PALACE PDE.
A212
ANERLEY HILL
ANERLEY RD.
A214
CHURCH RD.
Bingo
St. Christopher's Hospice
The Haven
Penge East
Penge West
HIGH ST.
A234
NEWLANDS PARK A213
PARISH LANE
Alexandra Rec. Grd.
Alexandra Jun. Sch.
Playing Field
PENGE
Anerley
CROYDON ROAD A213
Superstore
Play Fld
The Kentwood Cen.
Depot
Kent House
BECKENHAM
City Technology Coll.
Leis. Cen.
Orchard Lodge (Remand Centre)
James Dixon Prim. Sch.
Games Court
Bowls
Civic Halls
Nature Reserves
Rec. Grd.

140
A
B
C
D
E
1
2
3
4
5
6
7
122
139
158
36
37
38
Blythe Hill
Catford Bridge
Catford
CATFORD
BROWNHILL
STANSTEAD ROAD
A205
CATFORD ROAD
CATFORD HILL
A212
PERRY HILL
PERRY RISE
PERRY VALE
B227
B218
BROCKLEY RISE
BROMLEY RD.
A21
Powerleague Soccer Centre
Private Banks Sports Ground
CATFORD TRADING ESTATE
Bellingham
BELLINGHAM
BROADMEAD
Playing Fields
Gasholder Station
BELL GREEN
Superstore
SOUTHEND LANE
A2218
STANTON WAY
LWR. SYDENHAM
SYDENHAM RD.
Lwr. Sydenham
Southend Park
Beckenham Hill
BECKENHAM HILL ROAD
Secondary School
Stumpshill Wood
Ash Plantation
Recreation Gr
BECKENHAM PLACE PARK
GOLF COURSE
Beckenham Place Club House
Summerhouse Wood
NEW BECKENHAM
New Beckenham
CATOR PARK
SOUTHEND ROAD
A2015
Kent House
Beckenham Road
Beckenham Junc.
BECKENHAM
Sports Ground
Athletic Ground
Playing Field
Alexandra Jun. Sch.
Home Park
Cricket Grd.
Worsley Bri.
Bank Cottage
The Cottage
St. Mary's RC Prim. School
Westgate Lodge

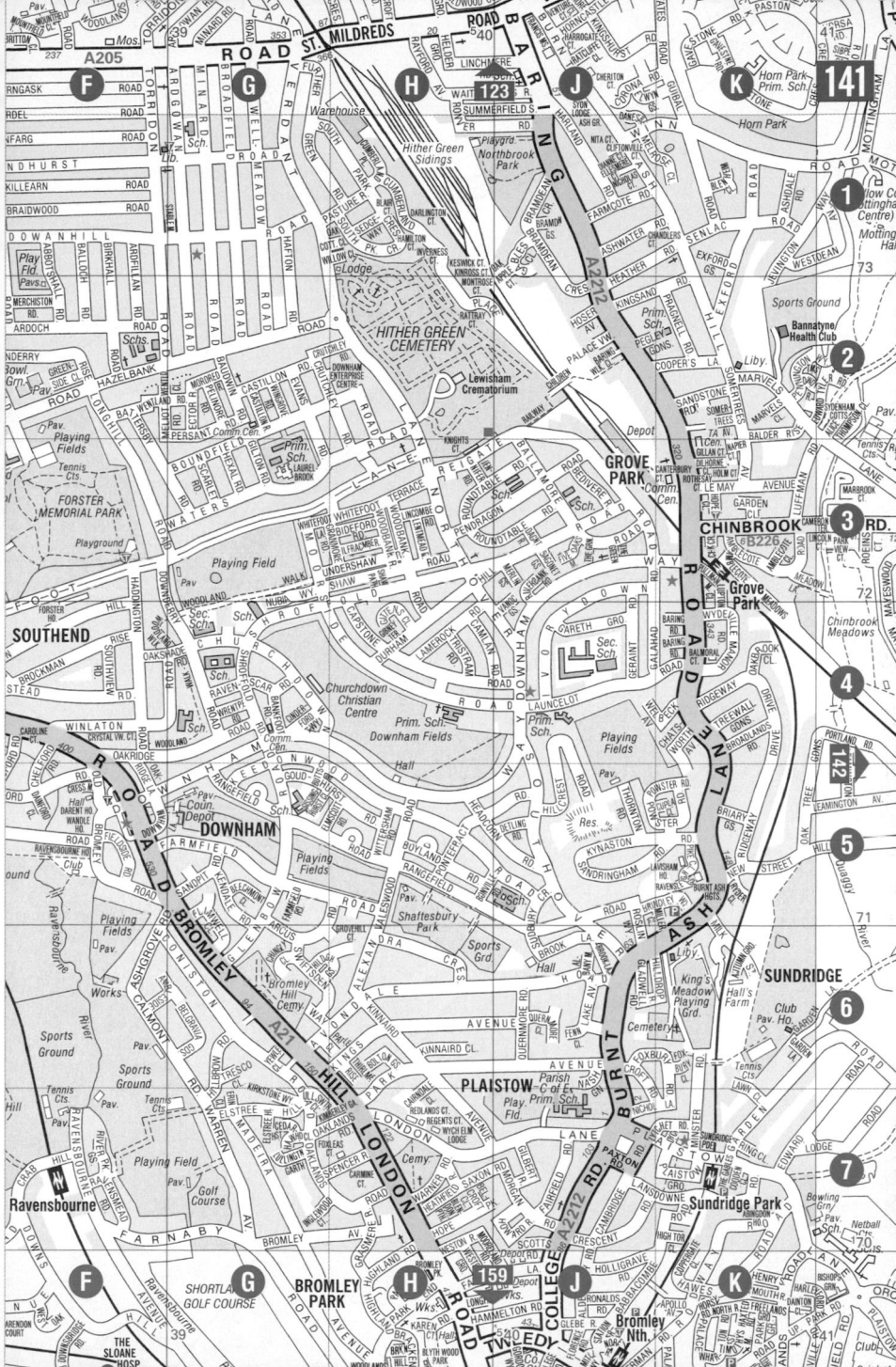

141
123
142
159
F
G
H
J
K
1
2
3
4
5
6
7
ST. MILDREDS ROAD
A205
BARING ROAD
A2212
BURNT ASH LANE
BURNT ASH HILL
COLLEGE RD.
A21
BROMLEY ROAD
LONDON ROAD
HILL
CHINBROOK RD.
B226
Horn Park
Horn Park Prim. Sch.
Hither Green Sidings
Northbrook Park
HITHER GREEN CEMETERY
Lewisham Crematorium
GROVE PARK
Grove Park
Chinbrook Meadows
Sports Ground
Bannatyne Health Club
FORSTER MEMORIAL PARK
Playing Fields
Playing Field
SOUTHEND
Churchdown Christian Centre
Downham Fields
DOWNHAM
Shaftesbury Park
Bromley Hill Cemy.
SUNDRIDGE
King's Meadow Playing Grd.
Hall's Farm
PLAISTOW
Sundridge Park
Ravensbourne
Golf Course
SHORTLANDS GOLF COURSE
BROMLEY PARK
Bromley Nth.
THE SLOANE HOSP
River Ravensbourne
Quaggy River

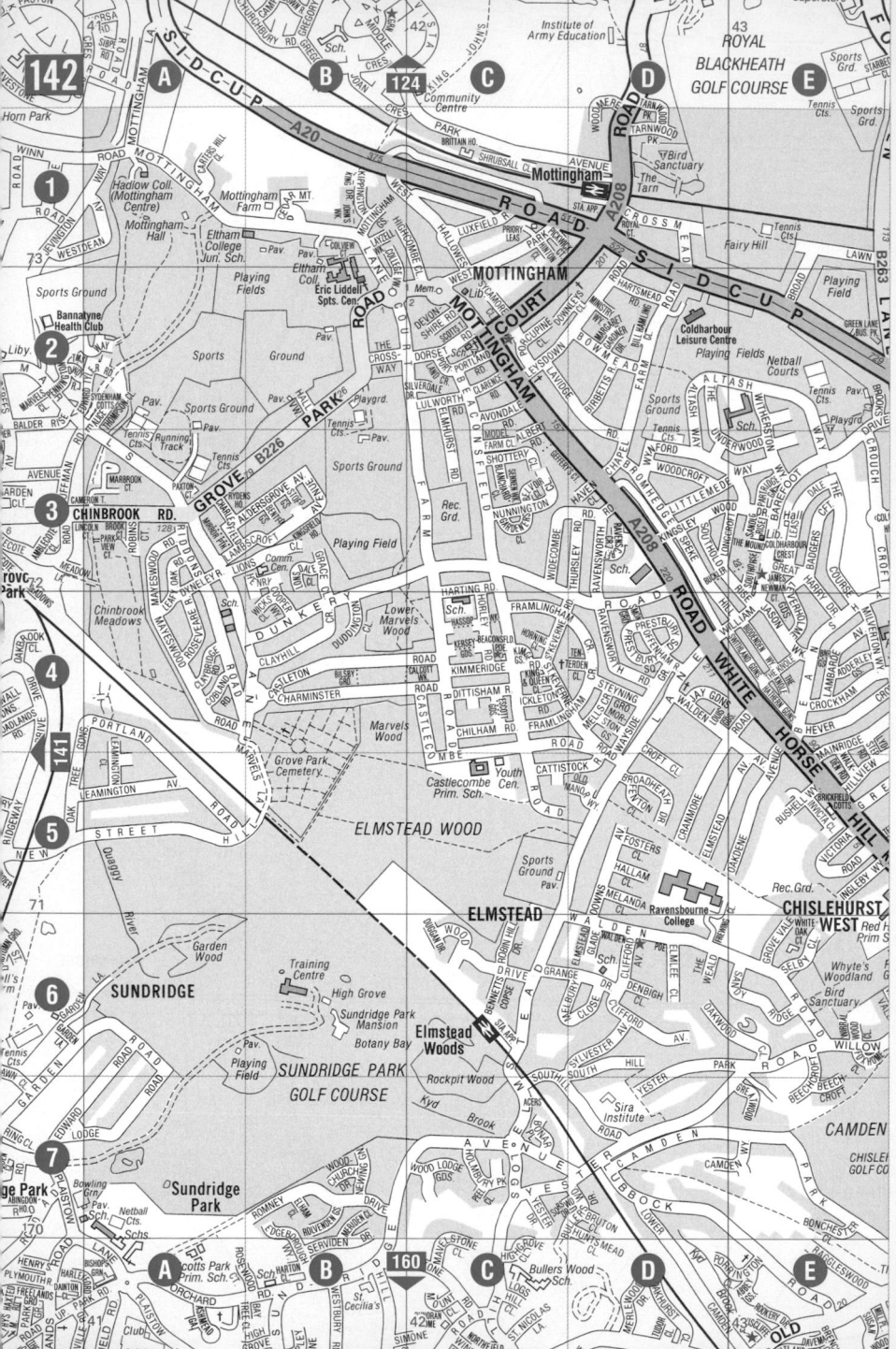

142
124
141
160
A
B
C
D
E
1
2
3
4
5
6
7
SIDCUP ROAD
A20
A208
B226
B263
MOTTINGHAM
Mottingham
ROYAL BLACKHEATH GOLF COURSE
Institute of Army Education
Community Centre
Bird Sanctuary
The Tarn
Fairy Hill
Hadlow Coll. (Mottingham Centre)
Mottingham Farm
Mottingham Hall
Eltham College Jun. Sch.
Eltham Coll.
Eric Liddell Spts. Cen.
Playing Fields
Sports Ground
Bannatyne Health Club
Coldharbour Leisure Centre
Netball Courts
Running Track
MOTTINGHAM LANE
MOTTINGHAM ROAD
WEST PARK
COURT ROAD
GROVE PARK ROAD
CHINBROOK RD.
Chinbrook Meadows
Grove Park
DUNKERY RD.
Lower Marvels Wood
Marvels Wood
Grove Park Cemetery
Castlecombe Prim. Sch.
Youth Cen.
ELMSTEAD WOOD
Rec. Grd.
Playing Field
BEACONSFIELD RD.
FRAMLINGHAM RD.
RAVENSWORTH RD.
KIMMERIDGE RD.
WHITE HORSE HILL
CHISLEHURST WEST
Ravensbourne College
ELMSTEAD
ELMSTEAD LANE
Elmstead Woods
Training Centre
High Grove
Sundridge Park Mansion
Botany Bay
SUNDRIDGE
SUNDRIDGE PARK GOLF COURSE
Rockpit Wood
Kyd Brook
Garden Wood
Quaggy River
Sundridge Park
Whyte's Woodland
Bird Sanctuary
Sira Institute
CAMDEN
LOGS HILL
Bullers Wood Sch.
St. Cecilia's
Scotts Park Prim. Sch.
Bowling Grn.
PLAISTOW LANE
WIDMORE ROAD
SOUTHILL ROAD
CAMDEN PARK ROAD
NEW STREET HILL
SIDCUP ROAD

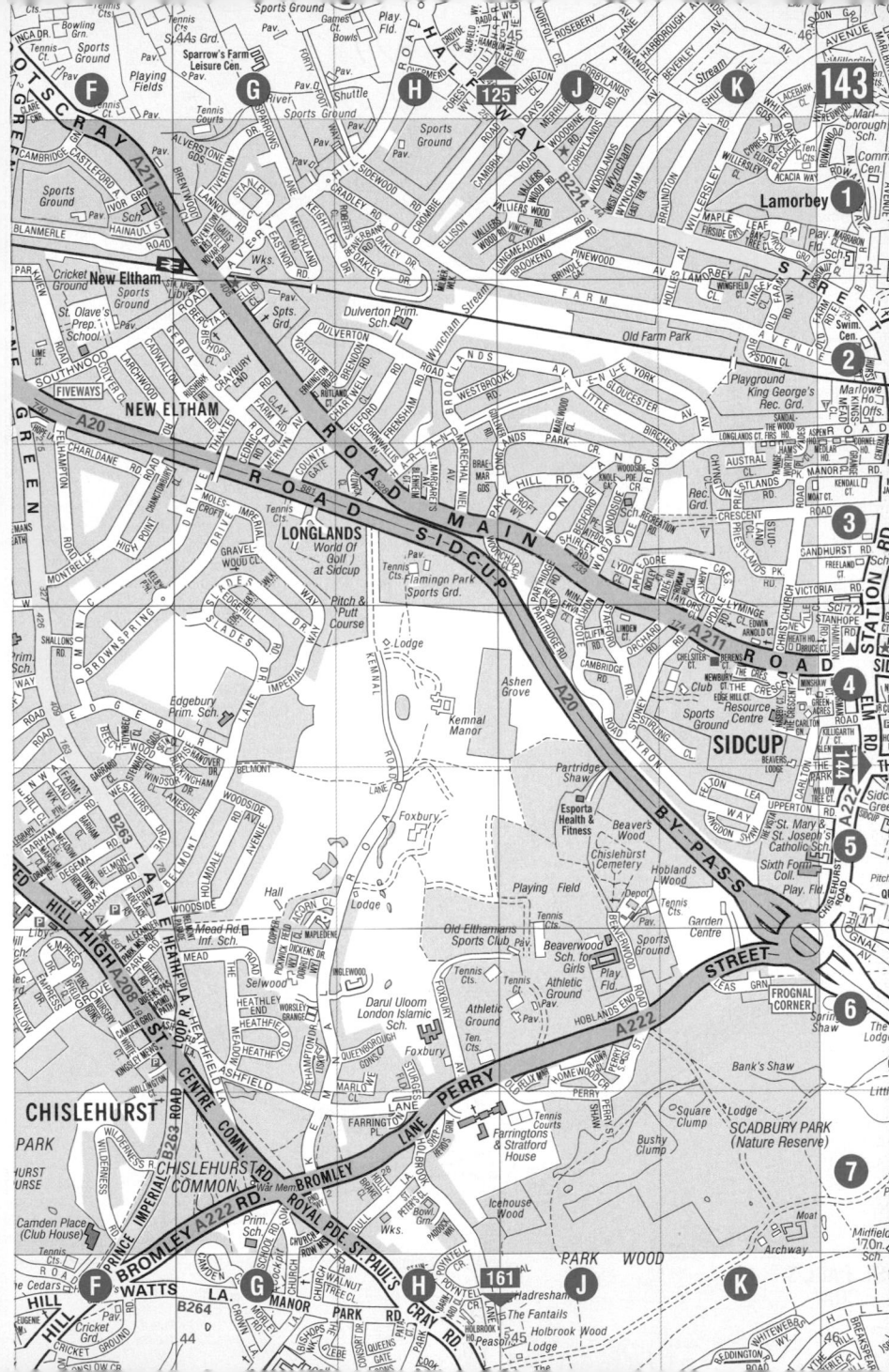

143
125
144
161
F
G
H
J
K
1
2
3
4
5
6
7
Sports Ground
Play. Fld.
Bowling Grn.
Sparrow's Farm Leisure Cen.
Playing Fields
Tennis Courts
River Shuttle
HALFWAY
ROAD
NORFOLK CR.
ROSEBERY AV.
HARBOROUGH AV.
ANNANDALE RD.
BEVERLEY AV.
Stream
AVENUE
Lamorbey
Marlborough Sch.
Comm. Cen.
ACACIA WAY
WILLERSLEY AV.
MAPLE LEAF DR.
FIRSIDE GRO.
Swim. Cen.
Old Farm Park
BURSDON CL.
Playground
King George's Rec. Grd.
Marlowe Ho.
Offs.
STREET
FARM AV.
LAMORBEY CL.
WINGFIELD CT.
HOLLIES AV.
PINEWOOD
BRINDLE GA.
BROOKEND RD.
LONGMEADOW RD.
Wyncham Stream
Dulverton Prim. Sch.
DULVERTON RD.
WYNCHAM AV.
WOODLANDS AV.
BRAUNDTON AV.
CORBYLANDS RD.
B2214
CAMBRIA CL.
ELLISON
CROMBIE
SIDEWOOD RD.
CRADLEY RD.
OLD FARM RD.
Sports Ground
KEIGHTLEY DR.
OAKLEY DR.
AVERY HILL RD.
EASTNOR RD.
MERCHLAND RD.
Wks.
New Eltham
Sports Ground
Cricket Ground
St. Olave's Prep. School
Spts. Grd.
BLANMERLE ROAD
HAINAULT ST.
CAMBRIDGE GN.
CASTLEFORD AV.
Sports Ground
IVOR GRO.
Sch.
POTSCRAY ROAD
A211
SOUTHWOOD RD.
FIVEWAYS
NEW ELTHAM
A20
MAIN ROAD
SIDCUP ROAD
BY-PASS
CRAYBURY END
BISHOP'S CL.
LARCHWOOD RD.
CADWALLON RD.
GERDA RD.
THAXTED RD.
CEDRIC RD.
MERVYN AV.
CLAY FARM RD.
TELFORD RD.
FRENSHAM RD.
CHARTWELL RD.
BRENDON RD.
COUNTY GATE
BROOKLANDS AV.
WESTBROOKE RD.
YORK AV.
GLOUCESTER AV.
LITTLE BIRCHES
MARECHAL NIEL AV.
LONGLANDS PARK CR.
PARK HILL RD.
BRAEMAR GDS.
LONGLANDS
World Of Golf (at Sidcup)
Flamingo Park Sports Grd.
Pitch & Putt Course
Tennis Cts.
FELHAMPTON RD.
CHARLDANE RD.
CHANCTONBURY WAY
HIGH POINT
MONTBELLE RD.
DOMONIC DR.
BROWNSPRING DR.
SHALLONS RD.
IMPERIAL DR.
MOLESCROFT WAY
GRAVELWOOD CL.
SLADES DR.
EDGEHILL CL.
GREEN
Prim. Sch.
Lodge
KEMNAL ROAD
Kemnal Manor
Ashen Grove
Partridge Shaw
Esporta Health & Fitness
Beaver's Wood
Chislehurst Cemetery
Hoblands Wood
Depot
Garden Centre
Playing Field
Foxbury
Hall
Lodge
Edgebury Prim. Sch.
EDGEBURY
IMPERIAL WAY
BELMONT LANE
WESTHURST DR.
WOODSIDE AV.
HOLMDALE RD.
BUCKINGHAM RD.
WINDSOR DR.
B263
LANE
CROFT WY.
PARTRIDGE RD.
WOODSIDE RD.
BEDFORD RD.
CAMBRIDGE RD.
ORCHARD
STAFFORD CL.
SYDNEY RD.
STIRLING CL.
TYRON WAY
SIDCUP
Club
Resource Centre
Sports Ground
THE CRESCENT
A211 ROAD
STATION RD.
ELM RD.
A222
FELTON LEA
UPPERTON RD.
LANGDON SHAW
St. Mary & St. Joseph's Catholic Sch.
Sixth Form Coll.
Play. Fld.
CHRISTCHURCH RD.
VICTORIA RD.
SANDHURST RD.
CRESCENT
PRIESTLANDS PK. RD.
STANHOPE RD.
MANOR RD.
Rec. Grd.
LYMINGE CL.
UPDALE RD.
APPLEDORE CRES.
AUSTRAL CL.
LONGLANDS CT.
STREET
LEAS GRN.
FROGNAL CORNER
FROGNAL AV.
Spring Shaw
The Lodge
Bank's Shaw
Square Clump
Lodge
SCADBURY PARK (Nature Reserve)
Bushy Clump
Icehouse Wood
Moat
Archway
PARK WOOD
Farringtons & Stratford House
Tennis Courts
PERRY LANE
A222
HOBLANDS END
HOMEWOOD CR.
PERRY ST.
Beaverwood Sch. for Girls
Athletic Ground
Sports Ground
BEAVERWOOD ROAD
Old Elthamians Sports Club
Play Fld.
Darul Uloom London Islamic Sch.
Foxbury
FOXBURY AV.
Tennis Cts.
Athletic Ground
Selwood
Mead Rd. Inf. Sch.
ACORN CL.
HEATHFIELD LA.
HEATHLEY END
ASHFIELD LA.
QUEENBOROUGH GDNS.
MARLOWE CL.
FARRINGTON PL.
KEMNAL ROAD
HIGH ST.
A208
HILL
CHISLEHURST
PARK
Camden Place (Club House)
PRINCE IMPERIAL RD.
B263 ROAD
CHISLEHURST COMMON
CENTRE COMN. RD.
BROMLEY LANE
BROMLEY RD.
A222
War Mem.
ROYAL PDE.
ST. PAUL'S CRAY RD.
Prim. Sch.
SCHOOL RD.
CHURCH ROW
Wks.
HOLBROOK LA.
WATTS LA.
B264
MANOR PARK RD.
Cricket Grd.
CRICKET GROUND
The Cedars
Pav.
Hadresham
The Fantails
Holbrook Wood
Lodge
BEDDINGTON RD.
WHITEWEBB WY.
BREAKSPEAR

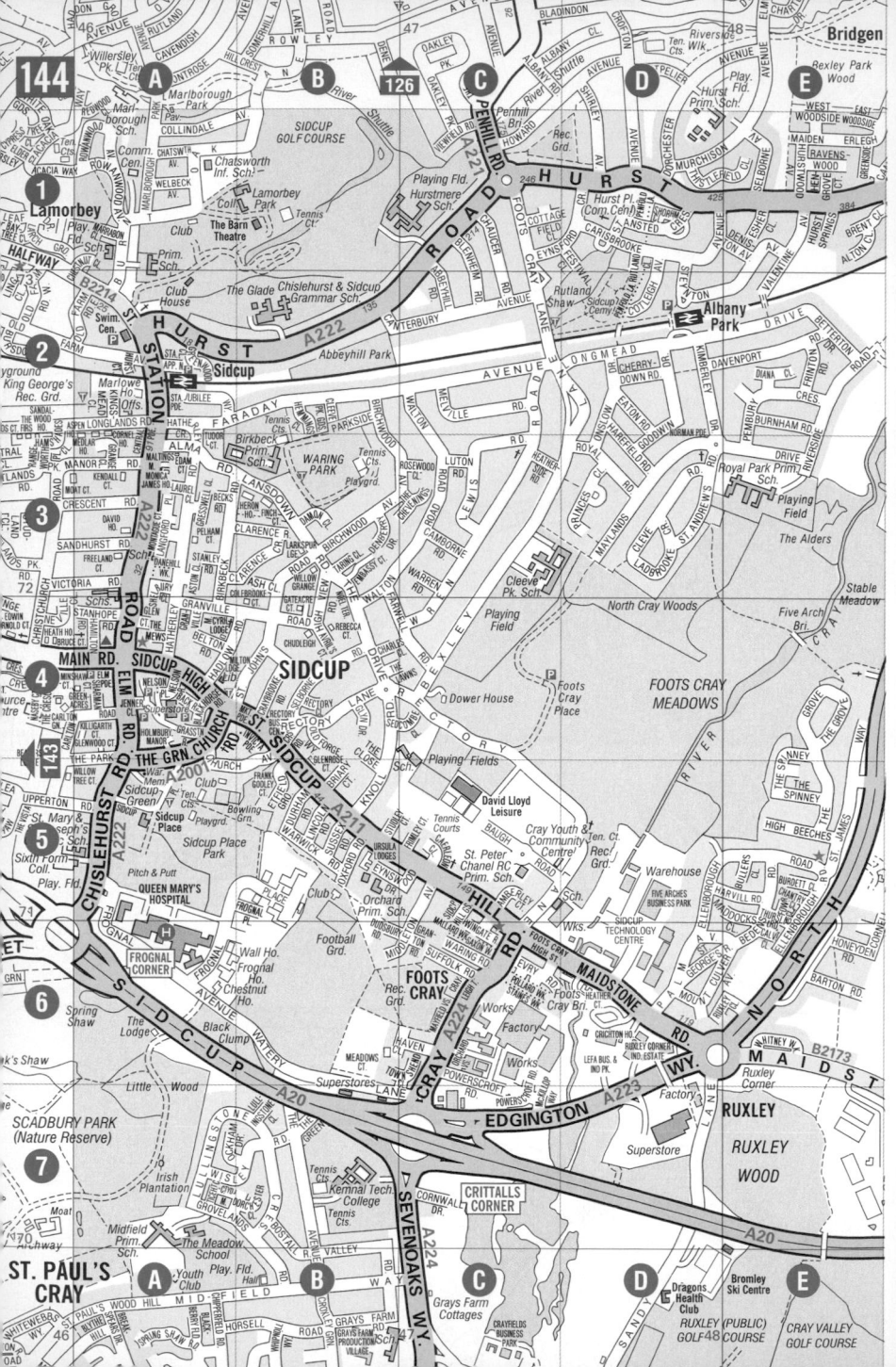
144
126
143
A
B
C
D
E
1
2
3
4
5
6
7
46
47
48
72
71
70
Bridgen
Bexley Park Wood
Willersley Pk.
Marlborough Park
Marlborough Sch.
Lamorbey
Halfway
SIDCUP GOLF COURSE
River Shuttle
Chatsworth Inf. Sch.
Lamorbey Park
Coll.
The Barn Theatre
Club
Club House
Prim. Sch.
Comm. Cen.
The Glade
Chislehurst & Sidcup Grammar Sch.
Playing Fld.
Hurstmere Sch.
Penhill Bri.
Rec. Grd.
Play. Fld.
Hurst Prim. Sch.
Hurst Pl. (Com. Cen.)
Rutland Shaw
Sidcup Cemy.
Albany Park
Abbeyhill Park
Sidcup
Swim. Cen.
King George's Rec. Grd.
Marlowe Ho. Offs.
HURST ROAD
PENHILL RD.
A221
A222
B2214
ROWLEY
AVENUE
LONGMEAD
FARADAY
BIRCHWOOD
WARING PARK
Birkbeck Prim. Sch.
Royal Park Prim. Sch.
Playing Field
The Alders
Cleeve Pk. Sch.
North Cray Woods
Stable Meadow
Five Arch Bri.
SIDCUP
STATION ROAD
SIDCUP HIGH ST.
MAIN RD.
ELM RD.
THE GRN.
CHURCH RD.
A2001
CHISLEHURST RD.
BEXLEY LANE
RECTORY LANE
Dower House
Foots Cray Place
FOOTS CRAY MEADOWS
RIVER CRAY
Playing Fields
David Lloyd Leisure
Cray Youth & Community Centre
Ten. Ct.
Rec. Grd.
St. Peter Chanel RC Prim. Sch.
Warehouse
FIVE ARCHES BUSINESS PARK
SIDCUP TECHNOLOGY CENTRE
Sidcup Green
War. Mem.
Sidcup Place
Sidcup Place Park
St. Mary & St. Joseph's Sch.
Sixth Form Coll.
Play. Fld.
Pitch & Putt
QUEEN MARY'S HOSPITAL
FROGNAL CORNER
Wall Ho.
Frognal Ho.
Chestnut Ho.
Orchard Prim. Sch.
Football Grd.
Club
A211
HILL RD.
MAIDSTONE RD.
FOOTS CRAY
Rec. Grd.
Works
Factory
Foots Cray Bri.
A224
NORTH CRAY RD.
B2173
MAIDSTONE RD.
Ruxley Corner
RUXLEY CORNER IND. ESTATE
LEFA BUS. & IND PK.
EDGINGTON WY.
A223
RUXLEY
RUXLEY WOOD
Superstore
Superstores
SIDCUP BY-PASS
A20
Spring Shaw
The Lodge
Black Clump
Little Wood
SCADBURY PARK (Nature Reserve)
Irish Plantation
Moat
Archway
Midfield Prim. Sch.
The Meadow School
Play. Fld.
Youth Club
ST. PAUL'S CRAY
Tennis Cts.
Kemnal Tech. College
CRITTALLS CORNER
SEVENOAKS WY.
Grays Farm Cottages
CRAYFIELDS BUSINESS PARK
GRAYS FARM PRODUCTION VILLAGE
Dragons Health Club
Bromley Ski Centre
RUXLEY (PUBLIC) GOLF COURSE
CRAY VALLEY GOLF COURSE
MIDFIELD WAY
SANDY LANE

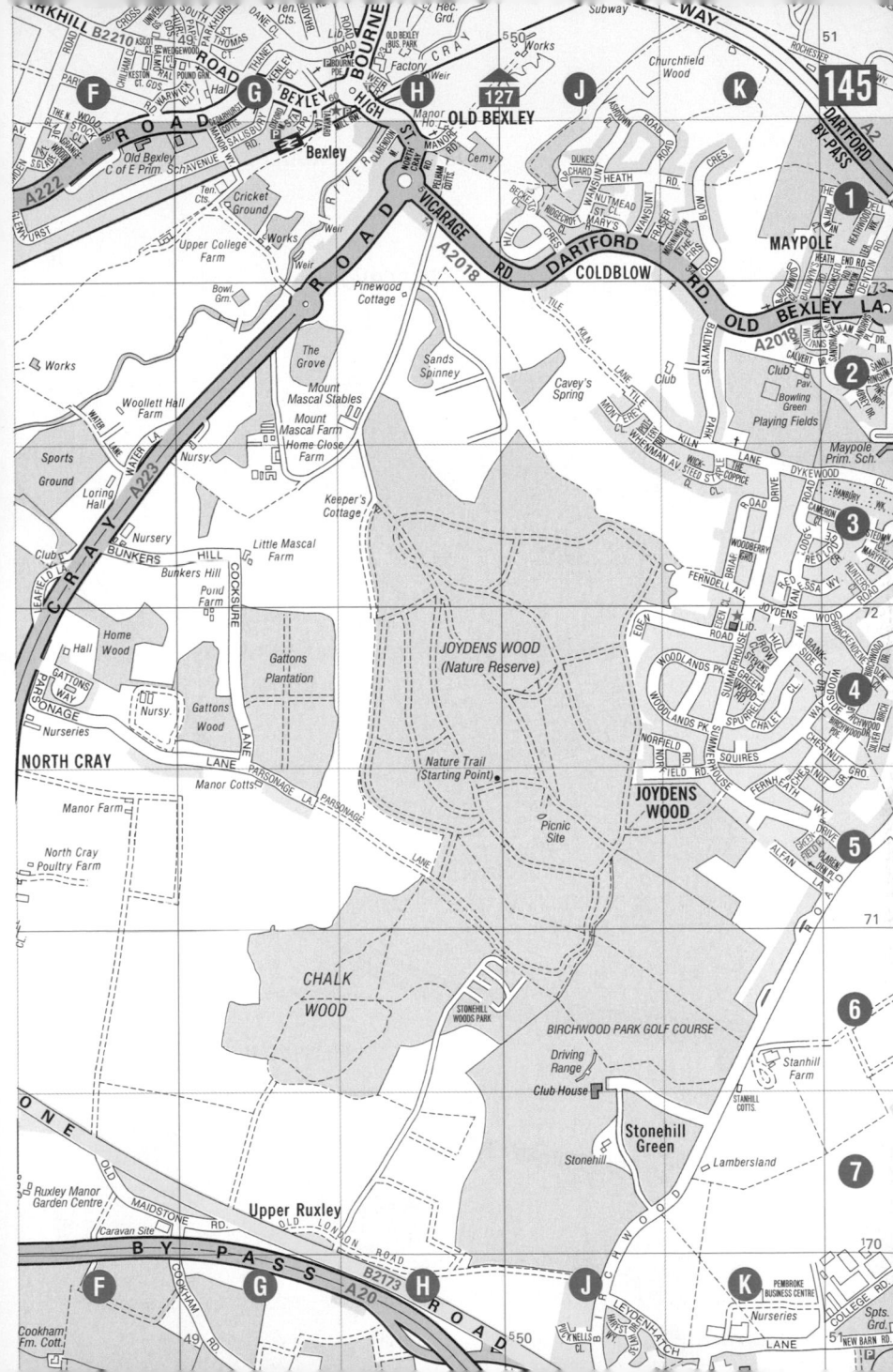

145
127
OLD BEXLEY
Bexley
BEXLEY
HIGH ST.
BOURNE
CRAY
Factory
Weir
Works
Subway
WAY
ROCHESTER
DARTFORD BY-PASS
A2
Churchfield Wood
Old Bexley C of E Prim. Sch.
A222
ROAD
AVENUE
SALISBURY RD.
MANOR WY.
Cricket Ground
Ten. Cts.
Upper College Farm
Bowl. Grn.
RIVER
Weir
CLARENDON
NORTH CRAY RD.
PELHAM COTTS.
MANOR RD
Cemy.
VICARAGE RD.
A2018
DARTFORD RD.
COLDBLOW
OLD BEXLEY LA.
MAYPOLE
HEATH RD.
WANSUNT
ORCHARD
DUKES
NUTMEAD CL.
ST. MARY'S CL.
RIDGECROFT CL.
BECKETS CL.
HILL CRES.
FRASER CL.
MORNINGTON
THE FIRS
BLOW
COLD
CRES.
ASHDOWN
ROAD
Pinewood Cottage
Sands Spinney
The Grove
Mount Mascal Stables
Mount Mascal Farm
Home Close Farm
Keeper's Cottage
Cavey's Spring
TILE KILN LANE
Club
BALDWYN'S PARK
Playing Fields
Bowling Green
Pav.
Maypole Prim. Sch.
DYKEWOOD CL.
KILN LANE
WHENMAN AV.
WICKSTEED CL.
STAPLE CL.
THE COPPICE
MONTEREY CL.
Works
Woollett Hall Farm
WATER LA.
Sports Ground
Loring Hall
Nursy.
Nursery
CRAY ROAD
A223
BUNKERS HILL
Bunkers Hill
Little Mascal Farm
Pond Farm
COCKSURE LANE
LEAFIELD LA.
Home Wood
Hall
GATTONS WAY
PARSONAGE
Nurseries
Gattons Plantation
Gattons Wood
Nursy.
NORTH CRAY
LANE
PARSONAGE LA.
Manor Cotts
Manor Farm
North Cray Poultry Farm
JOYDENS WOOD (Nature Reserve)
Nature Trail (Starting Point)
Picnic Site
JOYDENS WOOD
FERNDELL AV.
BRIAR ROAD
DRIVE
WOODBERRY GRO.
VANESSA WY.
JOYDENS WOOD
EDEN ROAD
Lib.
WOODLANDS PK
SUMMERHOUSE
SPURRELL
CHALET CL.
NORFIELD RD.
SQUIRES
CHESTNUT GRO.
FERNHEATH WY.
ALFAN LA
DRIVE
CHALK WOOD
STONEHILL WOODS PARK
BIRCHWOOD PARK GOLF COURSE
Driving Range
Club House
Stonehill Green
Stonehill
Lambersland
STANHILL COTTS.
Stanhill Farm
BIRCHWOOD
ROAD
Ruxley Manor Garden Centre
MAIDSTONE RD.
Caravan Site
Upper Ruxley
OLD LONDON ROAD
BY PASS
A20
B2173
ROAD
COOKHAM RD.
Cookham Fm. Cott.
LEYDENHATCH LANE
Nurseries
PEMBROKE BUSINESS CENTRE
COLLEGE RD.
Spts. Grd.
NEW BARN RD.
F
G
H
J
K
1
2
3
4
5
6
7
73
72
71
170
49
550
51

128
A
B
C
D
E
1
2
3
4
5
6
7
06
07
08
70
69
68
67
QUEEN
MARY
RESERVOIR
Works
Pumping Station
Round Copse
Ponds
River Ash
Laleham Nurseries
Nurseries
Squire's Bridge
Shepperton Film Studios
The Green
LITTLETON
Littleton Fm.
Play. Fld.
SHEPPERTON GREEN
CHARLTON
Manor Farm
Driving Range
SUNBURY GOLF
Rec. Grd.
Staines Road Farm
Nurseries
Saxon Prim. Sch.
Gravel Pit
Pool End
Playing Field
Shepperton
SHEPPERTON
Prim. Sch.
Lib.
M3 MOTORWAY
M3
SHEPPERTON RD.
B376
LALEHAM ROAD
LITTLETON LANE
CHERTSEY BRI. RD.
CHERTSEY ROAD
RENFREE WAY
B375
Riversleigh Farm
Mead Farm
The Range
DUMSEY EYOT
RIVER THAMES
DOCKETT EDDY LANE
TOWPATH
DOCKETT MOORINGS
DOCKETT EDDY
Chertsey Meads
Halliford Mere Lake
Cemetery
War Close
Cricket Ground
Las Palmas Estate
Lords Bri.
Pav.
Desborough Sailing Club
DESBOROUGH ISLAND
Works
FERRY LANE
CHURCH ROAD
CHURCH SQ.
ST. NICHOLAS DRIVE
HIGH ST.
RUSSELL ROAD
GREEN
SANDHILLS MDW.
Play. Fld.
Halliford Sch.
MANYGATE LANE
GLEBELAND GS.
BROADLANDS AV.
GROVE RD.
KILMISTON AV.
STATION RD.
STATION APP.
SHEPPERTON BUSINESS PK.
CRESCENT
LINDEN WY.
CHARLTON ROAD
CHARLTON LANE
NEW ROAD
QUEEN MARY RD.
SPELTHORNE LANE
WALNUT TREE CL.
ASHFORD ROAD
MERCIA HO.
STUDIOS ROAD
HITCHCOCK CL.
KORDA CL.
OBERON WY.
SQUIRE'S BRIDGE ROAD
MAGDALENE ROAD
RECTORY CL.
OLD MANOR HO. M.
GLEN CL.
ELLIOTT GS.
STEWART AV.
ASH ROAD
FRANCIS CL.
GRANGE CT.
HARVEST CT.
WATERSPLASH
PETTS LA.
HORNE RD.
SQUIRE'S RD.
WOOD ROAD
FORD CL.
CRANWELL GRO.
WINCHSTONE CL.
MILTON DR.
ASHURST DRIVE
BRAVINGTON CL.
FAIRVIEW DR.
ROSEWOOD
BRIAR ROAD
BUSH ROAD
ROSE ACRE CL.
WRIGHT GS.
MANDEVILLE RD.
SHEEP WALK
SHEEP WK.
POOL END CL.
ACACIA AV.
PRESTON RD.
PENTLAND AV.
JOHN KAYE CT.
JESSIMAN TER.
GREENO CR.
HARRISON WY.
VINTER CT.
TANGLYN AV.
B376
VILLAGE GATE
MARION AV.
MANOR FARM AV.
SHEPHERDS CL.
BARTON CL.
CLAREMONT DR.
GRANT CL.
THURLESTNE CL.
GOVETT AVENUE
ARUNDEL DR.
BARBARA CL.
LOIS DRIVE
SCHOOL LANE
WADHAM MEWS
DUNBOE PL.
MERVIN RD.
CHURCHFIELD PL.
CEMETERY LA.
DESBOROUGH CL.
MANOR HO. CT.
FARM CL.
RANGE WAY

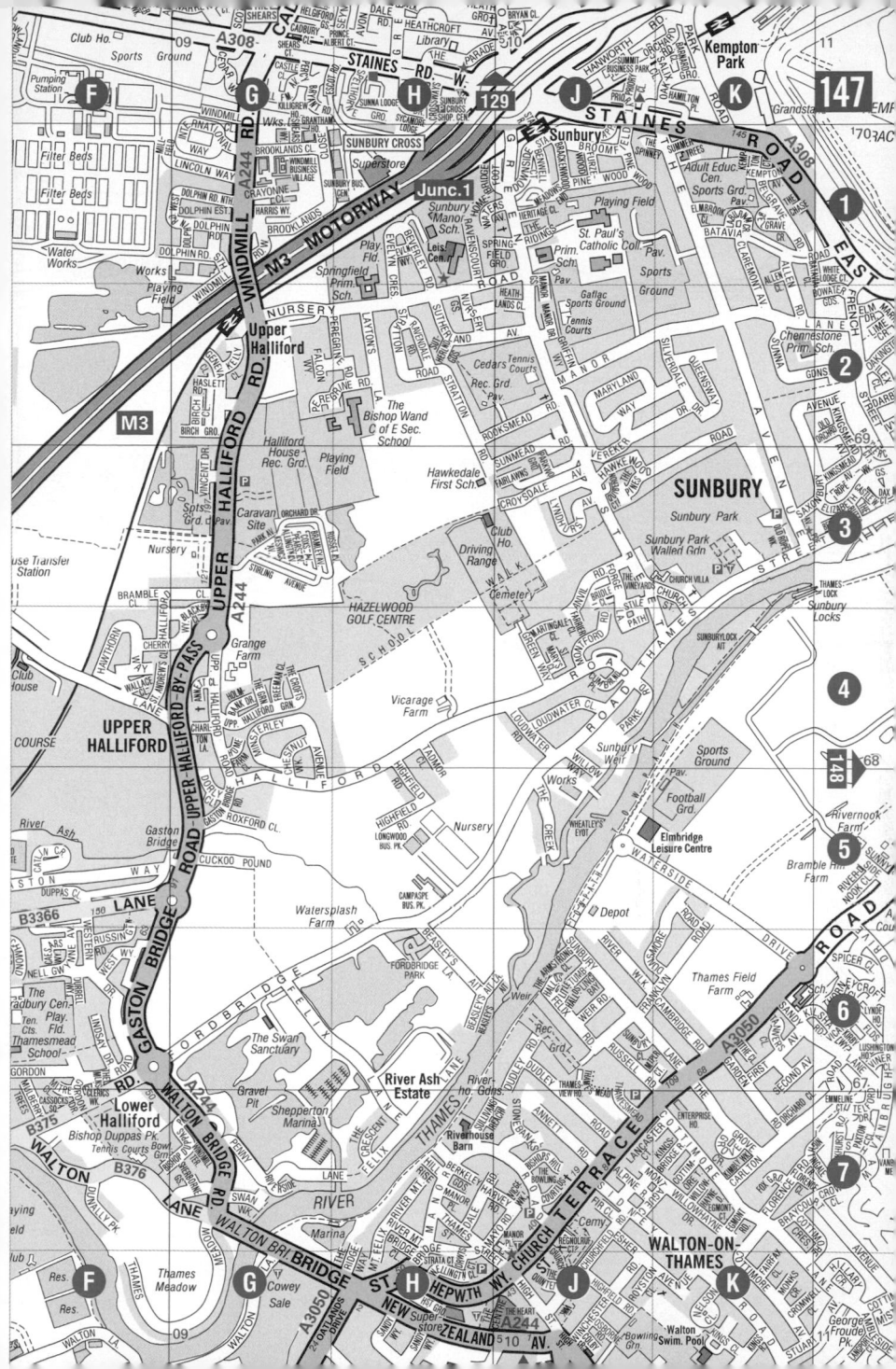
147
129
148
Junc.1
M3 MOTORWAY
M3
A308
A244
A3050
B3366
B375
B376
F
G
H
J
K
1
2
3
4
5
6
7
09
10
11
68
69
67
70
SUNBURY
UPPER HALLIFORD
Upper Halliford
Lower Halliford
WALTON-ON-THAMES
Kempton Park
Sunbury
SUNBURY CROSS
STAINES RD. W.
STAINES ROAD
ROAD EAST
WINDMILL RD.
UPPER HALLIFORD RD.
UPPER HALLIFORD BY-PASS
UPPER-HALLIFORD-BY-PASS ROAD
GASTON BRIDGE RD.
WALTON BRIDGE RD.
WALTON BRI. BRIDGE ST.
NEW ZEALAND AV.
CHURCH TERRACE
THAMES ST.
FRENCH STREET
HALLIFORD RD.
SCHOOL WALK
THAMES ROAD
NURSERY RD.
MANOR LANE
FORDBRIDGE RD.
WALTON LANE
CHENNESTONE LANE
ROOKSMEAD RD.
VEREKER RD.
SPRINGFIELD ROAD
STRATTON ROAD
WATERSIDE DRIVE
CUCKOO POUND
LADY RIVER
Club Ho.
Sports Ground
Pumping Station
Filter Beds
Water Works
Works
Playing Field
Superstore
Library
Sunbury Manor Sch.
Springfield Prim. Sch.
Leis. Cen.
St. Paul's Catholic Coll.
Prim. Sch.
Sports Ground
Gaflac Sports Ground
Tennis Courts
Adult Educ. Cen. Sports Grd.
Chennestone Prim. Sch.
Cedars Rec. Grd.
The Bishop Wand C of E Sec. School
Halliford House Rec. Grd.
Hawkedale First Sch.
Caravan Site
Sunbury Park
Sunbury Park Walled Gdn
Driving Range
Cemetery
HAZELWOOD GOLF CENTRE
Grange Farm
Vicarage Farm
Sunbury Locks
Sunbury Weir
Sports Ground
Football Grd.
Elmbridge Leisure Centre
Riverook Farm
Bramble Hill Farm
Nursery
Watersplash Farm
Depot
Thames Field Farm
FORDBRIDGE PARK
The Swan Sanctuary
Gravel Pit
Shepperton Marina
River Ash Estate
Riverhouse Barn
Thamesmead School
Bishop Duppas Pk.
Tennis Courts
Thames Meadow
Cowey Sale
Marina
Res.
Walton Swim. Pool
George Froude Pk.
Gaston Bridge
COURSE
Transfer Station

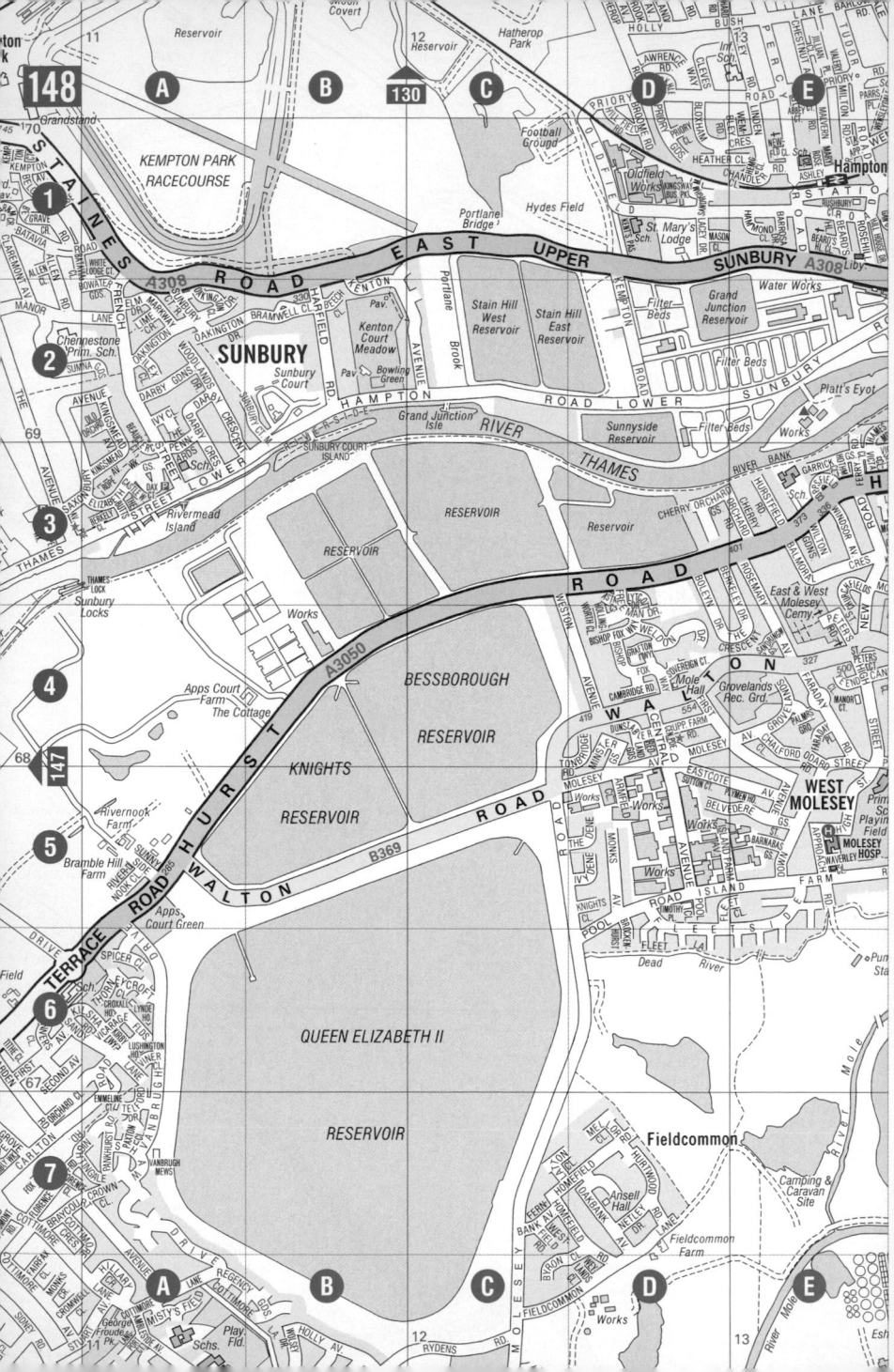

148
130
147
A
B
C
D
E
1
2
3
4
5
6
7
11
12
13
170
69
68
67
Reservoir
Hatherop Park
Grandstand
KEMPTON PARK RACECOURSE
Football Ground
Hydes Field
Portlane Bridge
Oldfield Works
St. Mary's Lodge
Hampton
STAINES ROAD
EAST UPPER SUNBURY ROAD
A308
Water Works
Grand Junction Reservoir
Filter Beds
Stain Hill West Reservoir
Stain Hill East Reservoir
Portlane Brook
Kenton Court Meadow
Bowling Green
SUNBURY
Sunbury Court
Chennestone Prim. Sch.
HAMPTON ROAD
LOWER SUNBURY ROAD
Platt's Eyot
Grand Junction Isle
RIVER THAMES
Sunnyside Reservoir
Works
SUNBURY COURT ISLAND
RESERVOIR
Reservoir
Rivermead Island
THAMES LOCK
Sunbury Locks
ROAD
A3050
HURST ROAD
BESSBOROUGH RESERVOIR
KNIGHTS RESERVOIR
Apps Court Farm
The Cottage
Rivernook Farm
Bramble Hill Farm
Apps Court Green
WALTON ROAD
B369
TERRACE ROAD
East & West Molesey Cemy.
Mole Hall
Grovelands Rec. Grd.
WEST MOLESEY
MOLESEY HOSP.
Dead River
QUEEN ELIZABETH II RESERVOIR
Fieldcommon
Ansell Hall
Fieldcommon Farm
Camping & Caravan Site
River Mole
George Froude Pk.
Play. Fld.
Schs.

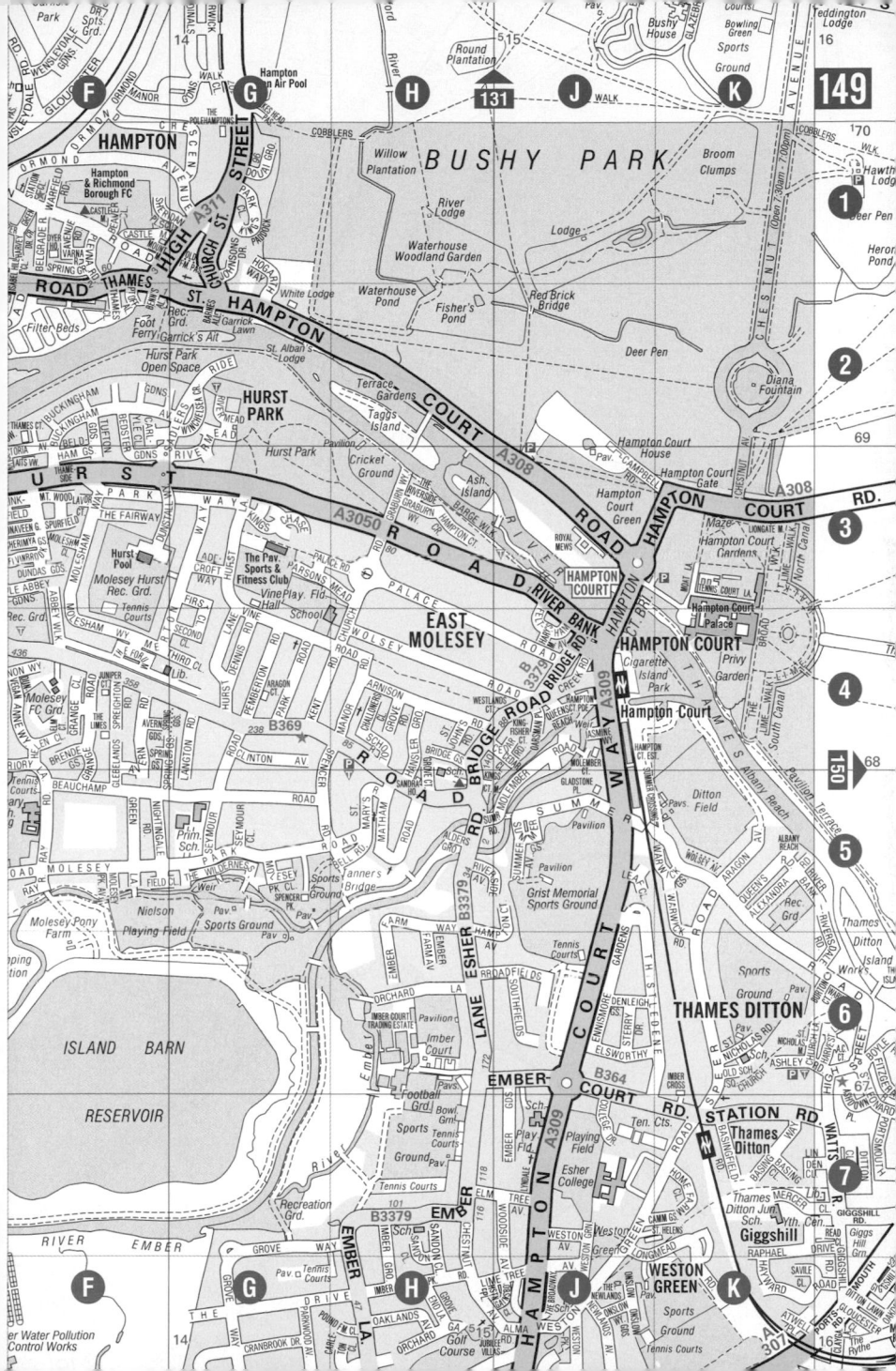

149
131
150
F
G
H
J
K
1
2
3
4
5
6
7
HAMPTON
Hampton & Richmond Borough FC
Hampton Open Air Pool
BUSHY PARK
Bushy House
Sports Ground
Teddington Lodge
Round Plantation
Willow Plantation
River Lodge
Waterhouse Woodland Garden
Waterhouse Pond
Fisher's Pond
Red Brick Bridge
White Lodge
Lodge
Deer Pen
Broom Clumps
Diana Fountain
Heron Pond
CHESTNUT AVENUE
HIGH STREET
A311
THAMES ST.
HAMPTON COURT ROAD
A308
Filter Beds
Garrick's Ait
Garrick Lawn
Foot Ferry
St. Alban's Lodge
Hurst Park Open Space
HURST PARK
Hurst Park
Terrace Gardens
Taggs Island
Cricket Ground
Ash Island
Hampton Court House
Hampton Court Gate
Hampton Court Green
Maze
Hampton Court Gardens
Hampton Court Palace
HAMPTON COURT
Privy Garden
Cigarette Island Park
Hampton Court
North Canal
South Canal
Albany Reach
Pavilion Terrace
HURST ROAD
A3050
Hurst Pool
Molesey Hurst Rec. Grd.
Tennis Courts
The Pav. Sports & Fitness Club
Vine Hall
Play. Fld.
School
EAST MOLESEY
PALACE ROAD
WOLSEY ROAD
B3379
BRIDGE ROAD
B369
A309
HAMPTON COURT WAY
Molesey FC Grd.
Prim. Sch.
Lib.
Ditton Field
Pavilion
Grist Memorial Sports Ground
Tanners Bridge
Sports Ground
Nielson Playing Field
Molesey Pony Farm
ISLAND BARN RESERVOIR
RIVER EMBER
Imber Court Trading Estate
Imber Court
Football Grd.
Tennis Courts
Recreation Grd.
ESHER LANE
EMBER LA.
EMBER COURT RD.
B364
Esher College
Playing Field
THAMES DITTON
Thames Ditton
STATION RD.
Thames Ditton Jun. Sch.
Giggshill
Thames Ditton Island
Works
WESTON GREEN
Weston Green
Golf Course
Sewer Water Pollution Control Works

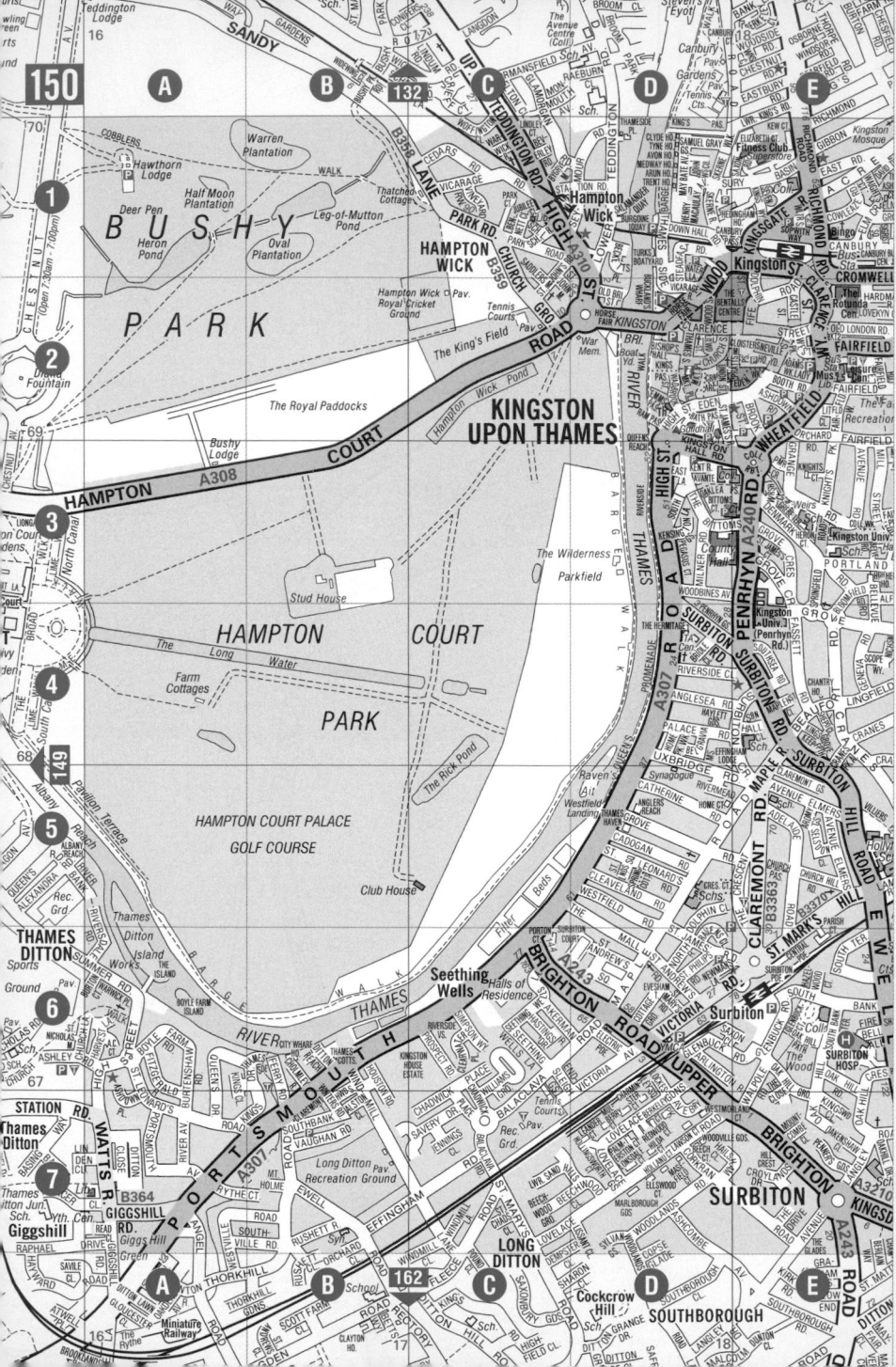
150
A
B
C
D
E
1
2
3
4
5
6
7
132
149
162
BUSHY PARK
Warren Plantation
Hawthorn Lodge
Half Moon Plantation
Deer Pen
Heron Pond
Leg-of-Mutton Pond
Oval Plantation
Thatched Cottage
Diana Fountain
CHESTNUT AV.
(Open 7:30am - 7:00pm)
The Royal Paddocks
Bushy Lodge
HAMPTON COURT ROAD
A308
HAMPTON WICK
Hampton Wick
Hampton Wick Royal Cricket Ground
The King's Field
Hampton Wick Pond
Tennis Courts
War Mem.
KINGSTON UPON THAMES
Kingston
Stud House
HAMPTON COURT PARK
The Long Water
Farm Cottages
The Rick Pond
HAMPTON COURT PALACE GOLF COURSE
Club House
The Wilderness
Parkfield
RIVER THAMES
BARGE WALK
QUEEN'S PROMENADE
Raven's Ait
Westfield Landing
Filter Beds
Seething Wells
Halls of Residence
THAMES DITTON
Thames Ditton
Sports Ground
Thames Ditton Island
Boyle Farm Island
Albany Reach
Pavilion Terrace
PORTSMOUTH ROAD
A307
Long Ditton Recreation Ground
Kingston House Estate
LONG DITTON
Giggshill
Giggs Hill Green
Miniature Railway
Cockcrow Hill
SOUTHBOROUGH
SURBITON
Surbiton
BRIGHTON ROAD
A243
UPPER BRIGHTON ROAD
VICTORIA RD.
CLAREMONT RD.
B3363
ST. MARK'S HILL
B3370
SURBITON HILL ROAD
SURBITON RD.
PENRHYN RD.
A240
County Hall
Kingston Univ.
HIGH ST.
TEDDINGTON RD.
A310
HIGH ST.
RICHMOND ROAD
CLARENCE ST.
WHEATFIELD WAY
Fitness Club Superstore
Kingston Mosque
The Rotunda
SURBITON HOSP.
Surbiton Jun. Sch.
The Wood
STATION RD.
WATTS R.
B364
B358
B359
KINGSTON BRI.
The Avenue Centre (Coll)
Canbury Gardens
Steven's Eyot

151
152
133
163
F
G
H
J
K
1
2
3
4
5
6
7
19
20
21
67
68
69
70
COOMBE
COOMBE WOOD GOLF COURSE
Holy Cross Preparatory RC Sch.
Rokeby Sch.
Marymount International School
Club House
Park Hill Sch.
KINGSTON HOSPITAL
KINGSTON HILL
QUEENS RD.
A308
COOMBE LANE WEST
TRAPS LANE
B283
A238
COOMBE ROAD
COOMBE LANE
Coombe Hill Jun. & Inf. Schools
Coombe Girls' Sch.
Norbiton
NORBITON
LONDON RD.
CAMBRIDGE RD.
Tiffin Sch.
Islamic Cen.
CLARENCE AVENUE
Rec. Grd.
Corpus Christi RC Prim. Sch.
Retail Park
Kingston Cemetery
Kingston upon Thames Crematorium
Athletics Centre
Kingstonian FC (Kingsmeadow)
Recreation Ground
Sludge Beds
Hogsmill River
Waste Disposal Centre
Sewage Works
KINGSTON ROAD
A2043
Surbiton Cemetery
Berrylands
BERRYLANDS
SURBITON HILL PARK
ELMBRIDGE AVENUE
Recreation Ground
Pavilion
Sports Ground
Tennis Courts
Bowling Green
Club House
MALDEN WAY
A3 (KINGSTON BY-PASS)
Grand Avenue Prim. Sch.
Alexandria Millennium Grn.
Recreation Ground
Richard Challoner School
Sports Field
Malden Manor Prim. Sch.
Malden Manor
A240
B3364
EWELL ROAD
TOLWORTH
WARREN DRIVE NORTH
ALEXANDRA DRIVE
HOLLYFIELD RD.

152
A
B
C
D
E
1
2
3
4
5
6
7
COOMBE LA. WEST
COPSE HILL
The Wolfson Rehabilitation Cen.
Rowans Sch.
Playing Field
COOMBE LANE
134
COOMBE FLYOVER
NEW VICTORIA HOSPITAL
BEVERLEY WAY
COOMBE
A238
St. Matthew's C of E Sch.
Wimbledon College Playing Fields
COTTENHAM PARK
Cottenham Park
DURHAM ROAD
B281
WORPLE RD.
Raynes Park
MALDEN GOLF COURSE
Coombe Brook
Coombe Girls' Sch.
Club House
Sports Ground
COOMBE LANE
B283
TRAPS LANE
Civil Service Sports Ground
Raynes Park Sports Ground
Tennis Courts
Bowling Green
A3
(KINGSTON BY-PASS)
Beverley Brook
A298
BUSHEY ROAD
Alliance Sports Ground
New Malden
HIGH ST.
B283
BEVERLEY PARK
Golf Driving Range
Emanuel School Playing Field
Blagdon House
Sports Cen.
Raynes Pk. High Sch.
Superstore
WEST BARNES
WEST BARNES LANE
B282
RAYNES PARK
Spts. Grd.
B279
NEW MALDEN
Com. Cen. Sch.
The Malden Cen.
BURLINGTON RD.
KINGSTON RD.
SHANNON CORNER
151
FOUNTAIN ROUNDABOUT
MALDEN RD.
A2043
Beverley Sch.
MALDEN JUNC.
The Study Sch.
MALDEN (KINGSTON BY-PASS)
University of London Athletic Ground
Running Track
Motspur Park
King's Coll. Sch. Sports Grd.
St. John Fisher RC Prim. Sch.
Old Blues Rugby Football Grd.
North East Surrey Crematorium
The Sir Joseph Hood Memorial Playing Fields
MORDEN CEMETERY
BBC Sports Ground
MOTSPUR PARK
Gas Works
Playing Fields
Green Lane Prim. Sch.
Merton & Sutton Joint Cemetery
ASM Ten. Cen.
MANOR PARK
Bowling Green
Malden Manor Prim. Sch.
Malden Manor
OLD MALDEN
B284
CHURCH RD.
164
Malden Green
Worcester Park
Mayflower Park
Refuse Destructor

153
135
154
165
68
69
F
G
H
J
K
1
2
3
4
5
6
7
24
25
26
MERTON
MERTON PARK
MORDEN
MORDEN PARK
BUSHEY MEAD
ROSEHILL
Wimbledon Chase
South Merton
Merton Park
Sth. Wimbledon
Morden
Morden Rd.
Morden South
St. Helier
KINGSTON ROAD
MARTIN WAY
LONDON ROAD
MORDEN ROAD
MERTON HIGH ST.
MERANTUN WY.
JUBILEE WAY
DORSET ROAD
CENTRAL ROAD
EPSOM ROAD
STONECOT HILL
SUTTON COMMON ROAD
TUDOR DRIVE
CANNON HILL LANE
LOWER MORDEN LA.
GREEN LANE
ST. HELIER AVENUE
ROSE HILL
REIGATE AV.
MORDEN HALL RD.
ABERCONWAY RD.
HARTFIELD ROAD
A24
A238
A239
A219
A217
A297
B285
B286
B279
B278
B235
B2230
Wimbledon Coll.
College
High Sch.
Dundonald Rd.
Dundonald Prim. Sch.
Recreation Ground
Sports Ground
Schs. Play. Fld.
NELSON HOSP.
John Innes Park
Rec. Grd.
Rutlish Sch.
Playing Field
David Lloyd Leisure & Lloyds Lanes Raynes Park
Messines Playing Field
Joseph Hood Recreation Ground
Bowling Green
Tennis Courts
CANNON HILL COMMON (Recreation Ground)
Pavilion
Cannon Hill
Raynes Park Playing Fields
Cherry Wood
Morden Park School Sports Centre
School Playing Fields
Sports Centre
Merton College
Bandstand
Morden Park Pool
Hatfeild First Sch.
Liby.
Nursery
Aragon Prim. Sch.
King George's Field
THE WOODSTOCK
Recreation Ground
Mostyn Gardens
Poplar Prim. Sch.
Liby. Civic Cen.
Mosque
Depot
Play. Fld.
Prim. Sch.
Scout Hall
Risley Sports Ground
Merton Coll. 6th Form Cen.
Playing Fields
Rosehill Nurs. Sch.
ROSE HILL ROUNDABOUT
Abbey Prim. Sch.
TA Cen.
Morden Hall
River Wandle
NELSON TRADING ESTATE
MERTON IND. EST.
SAXON BUSINESS CENTRE
LOMBARD BUSINESS PARK
WORKS
Works
Kendor Gardens
Glenthorne

154
136
166
153
A
B
C
D
E
1
2
3
4
5
6
7
COLLIER'S WOOD
Colliers Wood
MERTON
MERANTUN WAY
A24
Colour Ho. Th.
Superstore
TANDEM CENTRE
WESTERN ROAD
A236
Lavender Park
Deen City Farm
Morden Rd.
MORDEN HALL PARK
Phipps Bridge
Morden Hall
Morden Cottage
Morden Lodge
River Wandle
MORDEN HALL RD.
A297
MORDEN ROAD
A239
Ravensbury Park
Belgrave Wlk.
Melrose Sch.
Cricket Green
The Canons Leisure Centre & Lib.
Sports Ground
MITCHAM
Mitcham
CRICKET GRN.
MADEIRA RD.
CRANMER RD.
COMMONSIDE WEST
LONDON ROAD
A217
STREATHAM ROAD
A216
Gas Works
Watermeads
Tooting & Mitcham United FC (Imperial Fields)
Poulter Park
Bishopsford House
Bishopsford Comm. Sch.
BISHOPSFORD ROAD
ST. HELIER AVENUE
ST. HELIER
Open Space
Playing Fields
Sutton Arena Leisure Centre
St. Helier Open Space
ROSEHILL
ROSE HILL ROUNDABOUT
ST. HELIER HOSPITAL
BEDDINGTON CORNER
Nature Reserves
Mitcham Junction
MITCHAM GOLF C
CARSHALTON ROAD
A237
LONDON ROAD
Cemetery
Beehive Bridge
Blue Houses Bridge
Cranmer Bri.
Willow Lane Bri.
Mill Green

155
137
156
167
STREATHAM VALE
Streatham Vale Park
Lonesome
Beecholme Prim. Sch.
Lonesome Prim. Sch.
Mitcham Vale High School
South London Crematorium
Jewish Cemetery
Streatham Park Cemetery
Sports Ground
Playing Field
School Playing Fields
Sports Ground
Powerleague Soccer Centre
Stanford Prim. Sch.
NORBURY
Norbury
NORBURY PARK
Hermitage Bridge
NORBURY TRADING ESTATE
Norbury Hall Sports Grd.
Cannons Health Club
Tamworth Manor High Sch.
Recreation Ground
William Morris Primary Sch.
Garden Prim. Sch.
Donnelly Green
Sherwood Park Sch.
MITCHAM
COMMON
Mitcham Common
Playing Fields
Mill House
Gonville Prim. Sch.
Croydon Athletic FC Grd.
Croydon Crematorium
CROYDON CEMETERY
The Archbishop Lanfranc Sch.
Beddington Lane
Hundred Acre Bridge
Irrigation Bridge
Beddington Sewage Treatment Works
Therapia Lane
LOMBARD ROUNDABOUT
Ampere Way
PIONEERS INDUSTRIAL PARK
PROLOGIS PARK
BEDDINGTON CROSS
LONDON ROAD
A23
A236
B272
B273
MITCHAM ROAD
WINDMILL RD.
BEDDINGTON LANE
ROWAN RD.
MANOR RD.
NORTHBOROUGH ROAD
THORNTON ROAD
PURLEY WAY
F
G
H
J
K
1
2
3
4
5
6
7
29
30
31

156
A
B
C
D
E
1
2
3
4
5
6
7
138
155
168
NORBURY
Norbury
NORBURY PARK
Norbury Manor Girls High Sch.
Kensington Avenue Jun. & inf. Schs.
Biggin Wood
Downsview Prim. Sch.
UPPER NORWOOD
The Lawns
David Livingstone Prim. Sch.
Westwood Language Coll. for Girls'
Beaulieu Heights
Cypress Inf. Sch.
Spurgeon's College
Coun. Offs.
Grangewood Park
Norbury Hall
Sports Grd.
Cannons Health Club
Sports Ground
Comm. Cen.
RC Prim. Sch.
Rec. Ground
Thornton Heath
Sport Croydon
THORNTON HEATH
Crystal Palace FC (Selhurst Park)
Gala Bingo
THORNTON HEATH POND
Bensham Manor Sch.
Ecclesbourne Jun. & Inf. Schs.
Queen's Rd. Cemy.
MAYDAY UNIVERSITY HOSP.
St. Chad's RC Prim. Sch.
Heavers Farm Centre
Selhurst
SELHURST
Playing Field
Works
Lupin Bri.
Gloucester Rd. Junc.
Cottage Bri.
Cottage Junc.
BROAD GREEN
Lib. Canterbury Rec. Grd.
West Croydon
CROYDON
Gym
Super store
GREEN LANE
LONDON ROAD
PARCHMORE ROAD
BRIGSTOCK ROAD
HIGH ROAD
WHITEHORSE ROAD
ST. JAMES'S RD.
WINDMILL RD.
MITCHAM ROAD
PURLEY WAY
SUMNER ROAD
LOWER ADDISCOMBE ROAD
SELHURST ROAD
SOUTH NORWOOD HILL
BEULAH HILL
CHURCH ROAD
GRANGE ROAD
NORTHCOTE RD.
QUEEN'S ROAD
PAWSONS ROAD
MELFORT AVENUE
CRESCENT AVENUE
A23
A235
A212
A213
A215
A222
A236
B266
B273

F
G
H
J
K
139
Anerley
PENGE
Kent House
1
2
3
4
5
6
7
Harris City Technology Coll.
Leis. Cen.
Anerley Sch.
Civic Halls
Orchard Lodge (Remand Centre)
Games Court
James Dixon Prim. Sch.
Tennis Courts
Nursing Home
Orchard School Sports Centre
Playing Field
Bowling Green
Tennis Courts
South Norwood Lake
Athletic Grounds
Betts Park
ANERLEY
Bowls
Superstore
Play. Fld.
The Kentwood Cen.
Depot
ANERLEY ROAD
CROYDON ROAD
ELMERS END ROAD
HIGH ST.
BECKENHAM RD.
A214
A213
A234
Pool River
Avenue Road
Depots
Prim. Sch.
Playing Field
Bromley Junction
Birkbeck
Beckenham Crematorium
SOUTH NORWOOD
High Sch.
Stanley Hall
Harrington Rd.
Blind Corner
Pitch & Putt Course
SOUTH NORWOOD COUNTRY PARK
ELMERS END
Elmers End
Play. Fld.
Superstore
CHAFFINCH BUSINESS PARK
CROYDON ROAD IND. EST.
Rec. Grd.
Playgrd.
Primary School
158
NORWOOD HIGH ROAD
PORTLAND ROAD
Works
Norwood Junc.
Priory Sch.
Tennis Courts
Recreation Ground
Beavers Farm Prim. Sch.
Meadow
South Norwood Country Park Visitors Cen.
Play. Fld.
Playground
Croydon Sports Arena
Croydon FC Grd.
Ryelands Prim. Sch.
Arena
Swim. Pools
Temple
A215
Croydon Golf Driving Range
Long Lane Wood
Bird Sanctuary
Monks Orchard Prim. Sch.
Chaffinch Brook
WOODSIDE
Brickfields Mdw.
Prim. Sch.
Play. Fld.
LONG LANE
A222
SPRING LANE
WOODSIDE GREEN
Woodside
Tennis Courts
Ashburton Park
Library
Training Cen.
Davidson Primary Sch.
WOODSIDE ROAD
B243
Blackhorse La.
Sch.
Play. Fld.
Playground
Ashburton Playing Fields
Glade Wood
Hall
SHIRLEY OAKS BMI HOSPITAL
Ashburton High Sch.
Tennis Courts
Playing Fields
ADDISCOMBE
SHIRLEY ROAD
169
Addiscombe
LOWER ADDISCOMBE ROAD
Shirley Oaks
Playing Field
34
35
36
67
68
69
70

158
140
157
170
36
37
38
A
B
C
D
E
1
2
3
4
5
6
7
CATOR PARK
Kent House
Beckenham Road
Clock Ho.
BECKENHAM ROAD
A234
Beckenham Junc.
A2015
RECTORY ROAD
HIGH STREET
A222
SOUTHEND ROAD
ALBEMARLE ROAD
MANOR RD.
BROMLEY RD.
WICKHAM ROAD
Odeon Cinema
BECKENHAM HOSPITAL
Recreation Ground
BECKENHAM
Kelsey Park
Elgood Playing Field
Kelsey Park Sch.
Crease Park
CROYDON ROAD
UPPER ELMERS END ROAD
ELMERS END
Amida Leisure Cen.
EDEN PARK
HAYES
PARK LANGLEY
Langley Court (Research Labs)
Unicorn Prim. Sch.
Langley Park Schools
Sports Centre
LANGLEY PARK GOLF COURSE
LANGLEY
The Rookery
UPPER ELMERS END
Crouch Oak Wood
MONKS ORCHARD
High Broom Wood
THE BETHLEM ROYAL HOSPITAL
Edenham High Sch.
Oak Lodge Prim. Sch.
Blake Recreation Ground
West Wickham
WEST WICKHAM
West Wickham Pools
Nurses' Home
Caravan Park
Parkfields Recreation Ground
SOUTH EDEN PARK RD.
B230
A214
LINKS WAY
BECKENHAM RD.

159
141
160
171
Ravensbourne
Sundridge Park
Bromley Nth.
Shortlands
Bromley South
Hayes
F
G
H
J
K
1
2
3
4
5
6
7
BROMLEY PARK
SHORTLANDS GOLF COURSE
THE SLOANE HOSP.
BROMLEY
SHORTLANDS
HAYES
NORMAN PARK
Norman Park Athletics Track
Bromley Civic Centre
Churchill Theatre
Leisure Cen.
THE GLADES SHOPPING CENTRE
Queens Gdn.
Cannons Health Club
Bromley FC Ground
Fishers Wood
Cricket Ground
Bowling Green
Recreation Ground
Cupola Wood
Pickhurst Jun. & Inf. Schs.
Pickhurst Green
Brook Wood
Hayes Street Farm
Hayes Prim. Sch.
Sports Grounds
Tennis Courts
Golf Course
Playing Field
Martin's Hill
Rec. Grd. Queen's Mead
Bishop Challoner Sch.
The Ravensbourne Sch.
Ravensbourne Sch.
Hayesford
Weir
Moat
Hostel
Bromley (Oct. to Jan.)
BECKENHAM LANE
WIDMORE RD.
KENTISH WAY
MASONS HILL
TWEEDY RD.
LONDON RD.
HIGH ST.
COLLEGE RD.
HAYES ROAD
HAYES LANE
WESTMORELAND ROAD
PICKHURST LANE
WEST WICKHAM
FARNABY RD.
ROCHESTER AVENUE
MEADOW WAY
A21
A222
A2212
B228
B2212
B251
B265

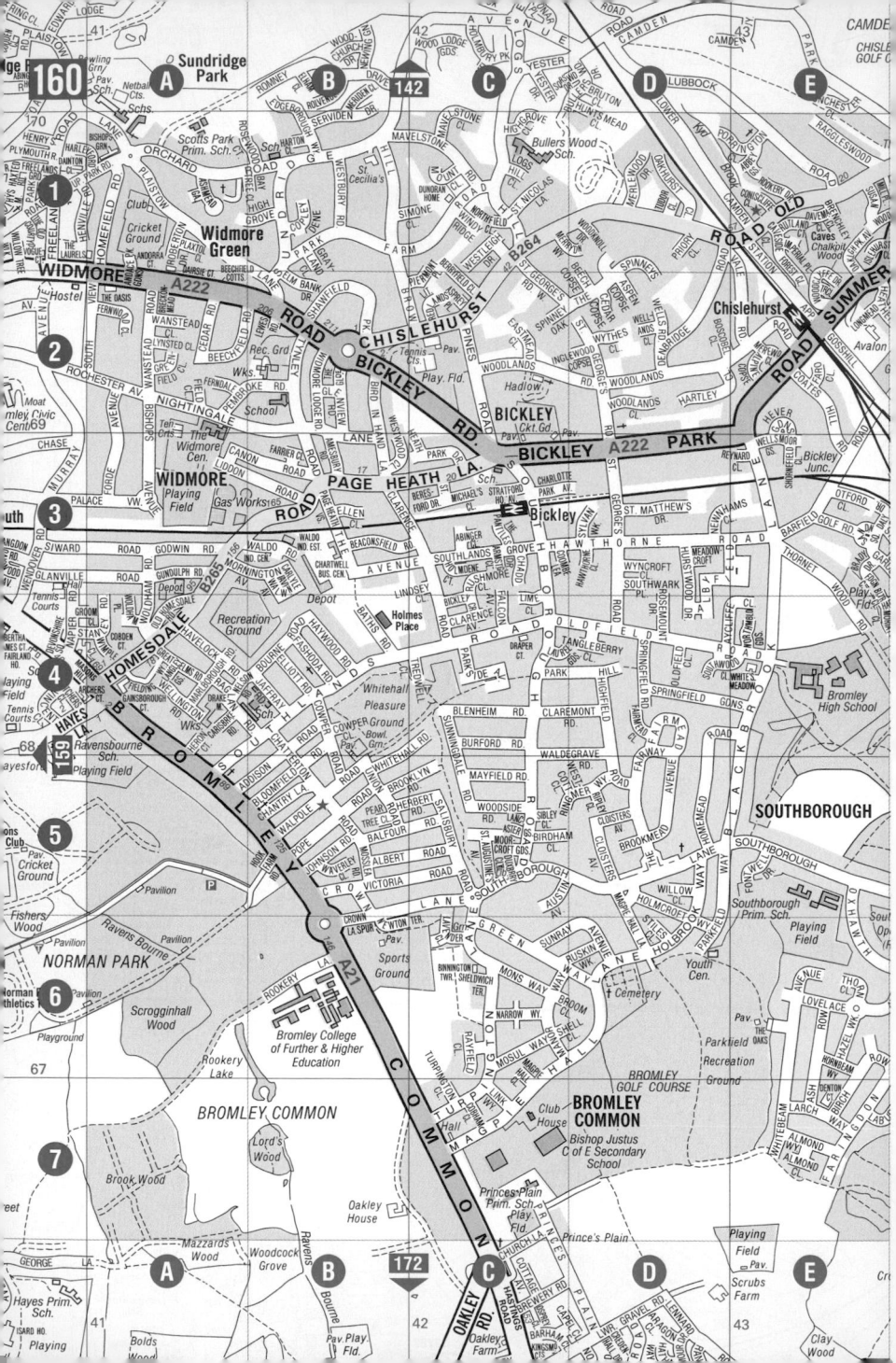

160
Sundridge Park
A
B
C
D
E
142
172
159
1
2
3
4
5
6
7
41
42
43
67
68
69
170
Widmore Green
WIDMORE
A222
ROAD
CHISLEHURST
BICKLEY
RD.
BICKLEY
A222
PARK
B264
B265
A21
Chislehurst
Bickley
BICKLEY
Ckt.Gd.
Hadlow
Bullers Wood Sch.
Scotts Park Prim. Sch.
St. Cecilia's
Cricket Ground
Club
Hostel
Rec. Grd.
Tennis Cts.
Pav.
Play. Fld.
School
Wks.
The Widmore Cen.
WIDMORE
Playing Field
Gas Works
PAGE HEATH LA.
ROAD
Recreation Ground
Depot
Holmes Place
Whitehall Pleasure Ground
Bowl. Grn.
Ravensbourne Sch.
Playing Field
HOMESDALE
BROMLEY
COMMON
NORMAN PARK
Scrogginhall Wood
Playground
Rookery Lake
BROMLEY COMMON
Bromley College of Further & Higher Education
Sports Ground
Cemetery
Youth Cen.
Parkfield Recreation Ground
BROMLEY GOLF COURSE
BROMLEY COMMON
Club House
Bishop Justus C of E Secondary School
Princes Plain Prim. Sch.
Play. Fld.
Prince's Plain
Oakley House
Lord's Wood
Brook Wood
Mazzards Wood
Woodcock Grove
Ravens Bourne
Hayes Prim. Sch.
Bolds Wood
Oakley Farm
OAKLEY RD.
Playing Field
Scrubs Farm
Clay Wood
SOUTHBOROUGH
Southborough Prim. Sch.
Playing Field
Bromley High School
Bickley Junc.
Avalon
Caves
Chalkpit Wood
Pavilion
Fishers Wood
Cricket Ground
Tennis Courts
Moat
Bromley Civic Centre

161
143
173
F
G
H
J
K
1
2
3
4
5
6
7
44
45
46
CHISLEHURST COMMON
BROMLEY RD.
BROMLEY LA.
ROYAL PDE.
PRINCE IMPERIAL RD.
B263
War Mem.
Camden Place (Club House)
Tennis Cts.
The Cedars
Hangman's Cnr.
HILL
A222
WATTS LA.
B264
MANOR PARK RD.
CAMDEN CL.
SCHOOL RD.
Cockpit
CHURCH ROW
CHURCH LA.
Hall
WALNUT TREE CL.
Wks.
ST. PAUL'S CRAY ROAD
A208
SCADBURY PARK (Nature Reserve)
Moat
Archway
Sch.
PARK WOOD
Drive
CARDINAL CL.
Hadresham
The Fantails
Holbrook Wood
Peasons
Lodge
The Larches
Pav.
Cricket Grd.
CRICKET GROUND
ONSLOW CR.
PAGET GS.
CRES.
Bansome Wood
THE OLD LAUNDRY
Coll.
Tennis Cts.
Marjorie McClure School
Playing Field
BISHOPS WK.
THE GLEBE
CONSORT DR.
QUEENS GATE GDNS.
COOKHAM DENE CL.
RIVERWOOD LA.
MANOR PL.
MANOR PK.
WALSINGHAM PK.
Play Fld.
The Gorse Children's Home
St. Peter & St. Paul RC Prim. Sch.
Playing Field
Hoblingwell Wood
Brackenwood
Playgrd.
ST. PAUL'S CRAY
Pav.
Rec. Grd.
BEDDINGTON RD.
WHITEWEBB WY.
MICKLEHAM
THORNDON RD.
CHORLEYWOOD CRES.
LEESON'S WAY
PETERSHAM DRIVE
HIGHFIELD
MANORFIELDS CL.
SOUTHFIELD RD.
AVENUE
LEESONS HILL
CLARENDON WAY
BERENS WAY
RAVENSBURY ROAD
WIMBORNE AV.
KEVINGTON DRIVE
MARLINGS PARK AV.
Butts
Rifle Range
Birch Wood
Hawkwood Nursery
Pond Wood
Hawkwood Estate
BOTANY BAY LANE
Hawkwood Farm
Tongs Farm
Walk Wood
Mem.
St. Paul's Cray Common
PETTS WOOD
Edlmann Memorial Wood
Meml.
Willett Memorial Wood
ORPINGTON RD.
Chislehurst Junction
Great Thrift
St. Mary Cray Junction
LITTLE THRIFT
HAZELMERE WAY
Blackbrook Wood
JUBILEE COUNTRY PARK
Petts Wood Junction
Thornet Wood
Sydney Shaw
GREAT THRIFT
SILVERDALE ROAD
WOODLAND
MANOR
CRESCENT ROAD
BIRCHWOOD ROAD
CROSSWAY
Bowl. Grn.
Pav.
Rec. Grd.
Tennis Courts
TOWNCOURT
KINGSWAY
WOOD RIDE
PETTS WOOD
PETTS WOOD ROAD
CHISLEHURST RD.
SEFTON CL.
AMHERST
TILLINGBOURNE GRN.
SHERBORNE ROAD
POVEREST
POVEREST ROAD
Prim. Sch.
CRAY VALLEY RD.
Hall
MERTON GDNS.
CREST VIEW DR.
PEGLA
Liby.
St. James' RC Prim. Sch.
MAYBURY CL.
FRANKS WOOD AV.
LANE
LAKESWOOD
Lakeswood Hall
QUEENSWAY
Petts Wood
STATION SQ.
WESTWAY
FAIRWAY
MAPLE CL.
ACACIA
ASH
HAWTHORN CL.
GREENCOURT ROAD
PRINCES AVENUE
LADYWOOD AV.
THE CHENIES
GROSVENOR ROAD
ELYSIAN AV.
SUTHERLAND AVENUE
KEDLESTON
OAKDENE
LOCKESLEY
DRIVE
FOREST WY.
FRIAR RD.
ARCHER RD.
Covet Wood
Hall
Recreation Ground
Tennis Court
Bowling Green
Playground
Perry Hall Prim. Sch.
PERRY HALL RD.
CRESCENT
AVENUE
CHESHAM AVENUE
ROLLESTON
PRESCOTT AVENUE
FELTON CL.
HOLLINGWORTH RD.
WOODHURST
NIGHTINGALE
SHEPPERTON
TRANSMERE RD.
KENILWORTH RD.
ADDISON CL.
TUDOR WAY
TOWNCOURT
ST. JOHN'S RD.
ST. GEORGE'S RD.
DUNSTAN GLADE
EASTBURY RD.
FIELDWAY
BEAUMONT ROAD
WILLETT CL.
OAKLANDS CL.
THE CLOSE
DENVER CL.
COVERT
FAIRFIELD RD.
APPLEBY CL.
BUCKINGHAM
HOMESDALE RD.
BERKELEY CL.
ROAD
AYLESHAM
COWDEN RD.
CHISLEHURST ROAD
CAMBRAY RD.
NURSERY CL.
SANDY LA.
CRESCENT
DIAMETER RD.
AVENUE
EMBER CL.
FAIROAK CL.
Pav.
Tennis Courts
Petts Wood Recreation Ground
Sparrow Wood
KYDBROOK CL.
BUSHEY AV.
Crofton Jun. Sch.
Crofton Inf. Sch.
CROFTON LANE
DERWENT
GREENFIELD GS.
DRIVE
BECKFORD DR.
BROADCROFT RD.
HEATHSIDE
CLAY WOOD CL.
RED CEDARS RD.
DALE WOOD ROAD
DOWNEY
MELBOURNE CL.
BRICKNOR RD.
BROOKSIDE
IRVINE WY.
WESTHOLME
BROOM HILL
Knoll Lawn Tennis Club
NOVAR CL.
SEQUOIA GS.
KESWICK RD.
CYRIL RD.
Gds.
ST. KILDA RD.
STANLEY RD.
ORPINGTON
OATFIELD RD.
LUCERNE RD.
MAYFIELD AVENUE
BANCROFT GS.
GROVE
KNOLL
Sparrow Common
Roundabout Wood
Crofton Heath
BRAMLEY CL.
LANSDOWNE
SPARROW DRIVE
CROFTON
ABBOTS
ST. THOMAS
FERNDOWN AV.
DRIVE
HILL VIEW
PEPYS RI.
ROBERTS M.
VINSON CL.

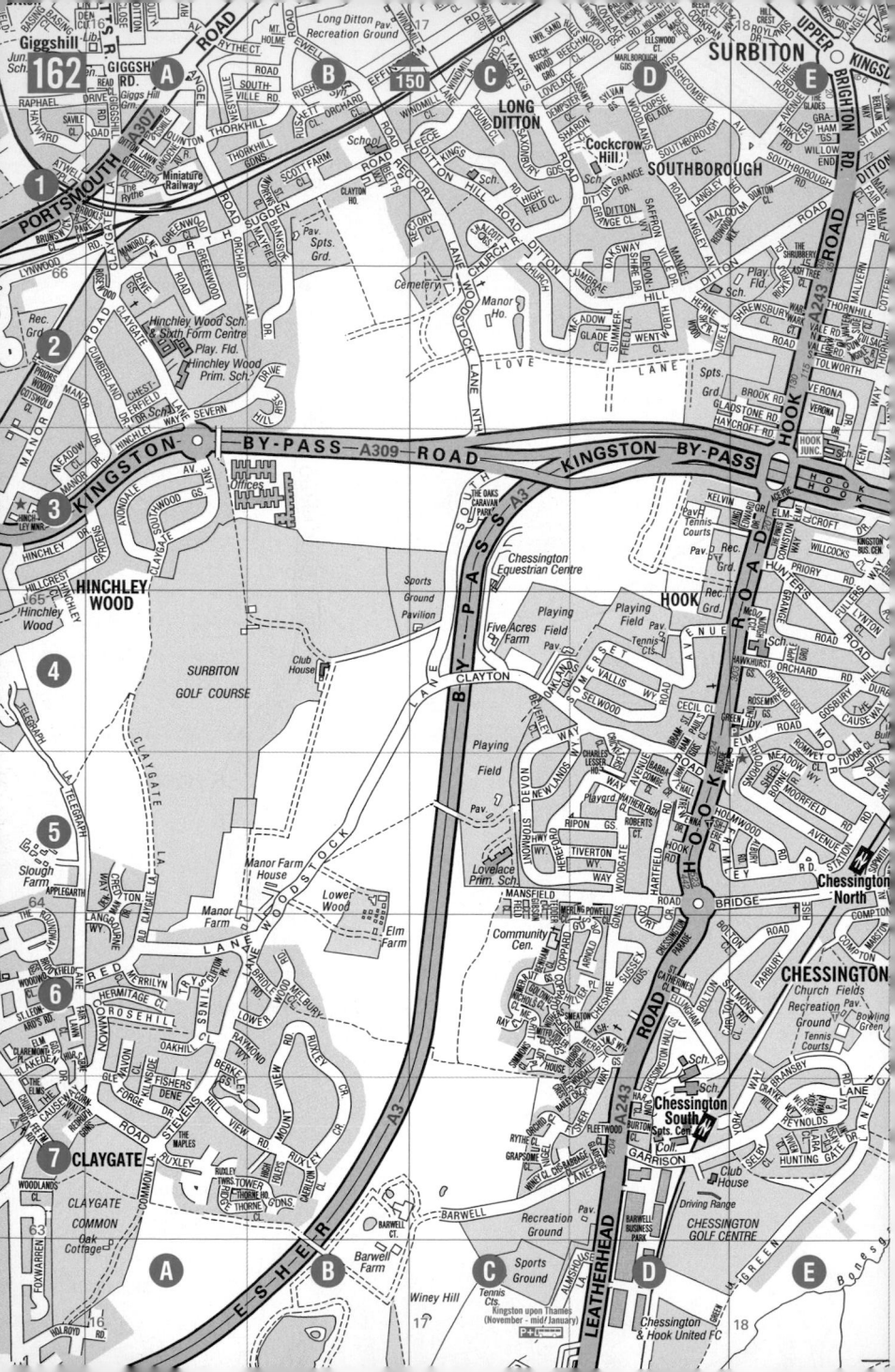162
150
A
B
C
D
E
1
2
3
4
5
6
7
16
17
18
66
65
64
63
Giggshill
Jun. Sch.
GIGGSHILL RD.
Giggs Hill Grn.
PORTSMOUTH ROAD
A307
Long Ditton Pav.
Recreation Ground
SURBITON
LONG DITTON
Cockcrow Hill
SOUTHBOROUGH
Miniature Railway
The Rythe
Scott Farm Cl.
School
Pav. Spts. Grd.
Cemetery
Manor Ho.
LOVE LANE
NORTH SUGDEN ROAD
DITTON HILL ROAD
Rec. Grd.
Hinchley Wood Sch. & Sixth Form Centre
Play. Fld.
Hinchley Wood Prim. Sch.
KINGSTON BY-PASS
A309
ROAD
A3
A243
HOOK ROAD
HOOK JUNC.
Offices
HINCHLEY WOOD
Hinchley Wood
SURBITON GOLF COURSE
Club House
Sports Ground Pavilion
THE OAKS CARAVAN PARK
Chessington Equestrian Centre
Five Acres Farm
Playing Field
HOOK
Rec. Grd.
Tennis Courts
CLAYTON ROAD
Playing Field
Lovelace Prim. Sch.
Manor Farm House
Manor Farm
Lower Wood
Elm Farm
WOODSTOCK LANE
CLAYGATE LA.
TELEGRAPH LA.
Slough Farm
Community Cen.
Chessington North
BRIDGE RD.
CHESSINGTON
Church Fields Recreation Ground
Tennis Courts
Bowling Green
Chessington South
Spts. Cen.
Coll.
Club House
Driving Range
CHESSINGTON GOLF CENTRE
CLAYGATE
CLAYGATE COMMON
Oak Cottage
ESHER BY-PASS
BARWELL LANE
Barwell Farm
Winey Hill
Recreation Ground
Sports Ground
BARWELL BUSINESS PARK
LEATHERHEAD ROAD
Kingston upon Thames (November - mid/ January)
Chessington & Hook United FC
GARRISON LANE
HOLROYD RD.
FOXWARREN
WOODLANDS CL.

163
151
164
F
G
H
J
K
1
2
3
4
5
6
7
19
20
21
TOLWORTH
Tolworth Hosp.
TOLWORTH JUNCTION
Tolworth
A240
ROAD
A3
KINGSTON BY-PASS
KINGSTON ROAD
B3364 ROAD
ALEXANDRA
Alexandria Millennium Grn.
Recreation Ground
Tennis Cts.
WARREN DRIVE NORTH
WARREN DRIVE SOUTH
ELMDENE DR.
KNOLLMEAD
ALPINE AV.
Malden Manor
Richard Challoner School
Playing Field
Tennis Courts
Nursery
Maori Sports Ground
RIVERHILL MOBILE HOME PARK
Riverhill
Cricket Ground
Sports Ground
Community Centre
Knollmead Prim. Sch.
Bowl. Alley
Government Offices
King George's Field Playing Field
Corinthian Casuals FC Grd.
King George's Field
Works
JUBILEE WAY
Tolworth Court Bridge
WORCESTER PARK RD.
B284
OLD MALDEN LANE
CHURCH RD.
Linden Bridge S & Spring Cen.
Tolworth Rec. Cen.
Red Lion Bus. Park
Swallow Park Caravan Site
Hook Rise South Ind. Park
King George's Trading Est.
Chessington Trade Pk.
Chessington Park
Four Oaks Centre
Buckland Inf. Sch.
Moor Lane Jun. Sch.
Playing Field
DAVIS ROAD
Hogsmill River
Youth Cen.
Comm. Cen.
Riverview C of E Prim. Sch.
Dragons Hlth. Club
Sports Ground
West Ewell Inf. Sch.
Epsom & Ewell High Sch.
RUXLEY LANE
CHESSINGTON ROAD
B2200
Butcher's Grove
Castle Hill
HORTON COUNTRY PARK
HORTON PARK GOLF & COUNTRY CLUB
Club Ho.
Driving Range
Hook Arena
HOOK ROAD
North Farm Cottage
Gt. Wood
Sports Grd.
Cemetery
St. Ebba's Farm Cottage
ST. EBBA'S
Playing Field
Tennis Cts. Playing Field Jun. Sch.
King George's Field
Running Track
Pack Horse Br.
WEST EWELL
Hogsmill
Rec. Grd.

164
152
163
A
B
C
D
E
1
2
3
4
5
6
7
21
22
23
66
165
64
63
Malden Manor
OLD MALDEN
Malden Green
Worcester Park
WORCESTER PARK
STONELEIGH
Stoneleigh
WEST EWELL
Ewell West
EWELL
NONSUCH PARK
BEGGAR'S HILL
ORGAN CROSSROADS
MALDEN ROAD
CENTRAL ROAD
A2043
CHEAM ROAD
COMMON RD.
LONDON ROAD
A24
KINGSTON ROAD
A240
EWELL BY-PASS
OLD MALDEN LANE
CHURCH ROAD
B284
SALISBURY ROAD
CHESSINGTON RD.
B2200
HIGH ST.
LONDON RD.
MANOR DRIVE
HIGHDOWN
STONELEIGH PARK ROAD
STONELEIGH AVENUE
Linden Bridge Sch. & Spring Cen.
Wandgas Athletic Ground
Dancer Dick Wood
Cuddington Prim. Sch.
King George's Field
Auriol Park
Shadbolt Park
Cuddington Recreation Ground
Beverley Brook
Tennis Courts
Sports Ground
Superstore
Cemy.
Dorchester Prim. Sch.
Mayflower Park
Refuse Destructor
Oak Plantation
London Road Plantation
Mansion House
Hogsmill River
Chamber Mead
Playing Fields
Playing Field
Bourne Hall Museum
Glyn Ho.
Ewell Castle Sch.
Schools
Prim. Sch.
Hall
Nursery
Manor Park
Bowling Green
THE AVENUE

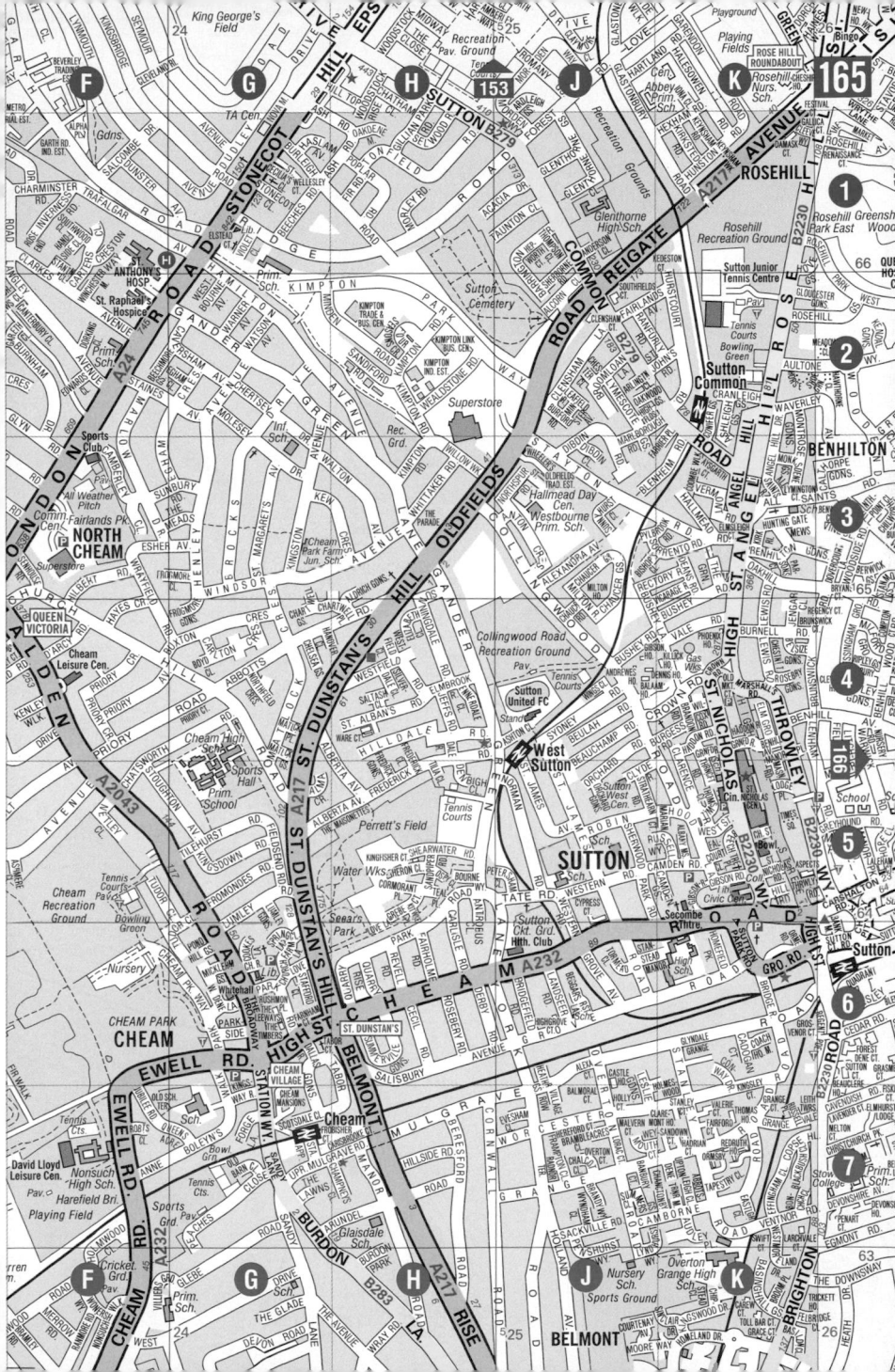
165
153
166
F
G
H
J
K
1
2
3
4
5
6
7
24
25
26
King George's Field
Recreation Pav. Ground
Playground
Playing Fields
ROSE HILL ROUNDABOUT
Rosehill Nurs. Sch.
Abbey Prim. Sch.
TA Cen.
SUTTON B279
STONECOT HILL
STONECOT
ROSEHILL
A217 AVENUE
Rosehill Recreation Ground
Rosehill Park East
Greenshaw Wood
Recreation Grounds
Glenthorne High Sch.
COMMON
REIGATE
ROAD
Sutton Cemetery
Sutton Junior Tennis Centre
Tennis Courts
Bowling Green
Sutton Common
KIMPTON PARK WAY
KIMPTON TRADE & BUS. CEN.
KIMPTON LINK BUS. CEN.
KIMPTON IND. EST.
Superstore
ST. ANTHONY'S HOSP.
St. Raphael's Hospice
LONDON ROAD A24
GANDER GREEN LANE
Inf. Sch.
Rec. Grd.
Hallmead Day Cen.
Westbourne Prim. Sch.
OLDFIELDS TRAD. EST.
BENHILTON
ANGEL HILL
ST. DUNSTAN'S HILL
OLDFIELDS
Sports Club
All Weather Pitch
Comm. Cen.
Fairlands Pk.
NORTH CHEAM
Superstore
QUEEN VICTORIA
Cheam Leisure Cen.
Cheam Park Farm Jun. Sch.
Collingwood Road Recreation Ground
Sutton United FC
Tennis Courts
Gas Wks.
HIGH ST.
ST. NICHOLAS
THROWLEY
West Sutton
Cheam High Sch.
Sports Hall
Prim. School
A2043
A217 ST. DUNSTAN'S
Perrett's Field
Water Wks.
Tennis Courts
Sutton West Cen.
ST. NICHOLAS CEN.
Bowl.
SUTTON
Sch.
Civic Cen.
Sutton Park Ctr.
Secombe Thtre.
High Sch.
Cheam Recreation Ground
Bowling Green
Nursery
Seears Park
Sutton Ckt. Grd.
Hlth. Club
CHEAM A232
Whitehall
BROADWAY
CHEAM PARK
CHEAM
HIGH ST.
ST. DUNSTAN'S
CHEAM VILLAGE
BELMONT
EWELL RD.
STATION WY.
Cheam
Sch.
David Lloyd Leisure Cen.
Nonsuch High Sch.
Harefield Bri.
Playing Field
Tennis Cts.
Sports Grd.
Bowl Grn.
MULGRAVE
Glaisdale Sch.
BURDON
Cricket Grd.
Prim. Sch.
A232
CHEAM RD.
B283
A217 RISE
Overton Grange High Sch.
Nursery Sch.
Sports Ground
BELMONT
BRIGHTON ROAD
B2230
Carshalton Rd.
Stowe College
THE DOWNSWAY
Sutton
School
A
B
C

166
154
165
BEDDINGTON CORNER
HACKBRIDGE
ROSEHILL
BENHILTON
THE WRYTHE
CARSHALTON
SUTTON
CARSHALTON BEECHES
CARSHALTON ON THE HILL
A
B
C
D
E
1
2
3
4
5
6
7
26
27
28
Sutton Arena Leisure Centre
St. Helier Open Space
Rosehill Park East
Greenshaw Wood
ST. HELIER HOSPITAL
QUEEN MARY'S HOSPITAL FOR CHILDREN
Running Track
Comm. Hall
Nature Reserves
Limes Grn.
Sports Cen.
Muschamp Prim. Sch.
Rushy Meadow Prim. Sch.
Royston Park
Wrythe Rec. Grd.
Carshalton Athletic FC
Playing Field
Benhill Rec. Grd.
Carshalton Coll.
Wilderness Island
Wandle Bri.
Westcroft Leisure Cen.
The Grove
Council Offices
Studio Thtre.
Heritage Cen.
St. Philomena's School
The Frying Pan
CARSHALTON PARK
CARSHALTON WAR MEMORIAL HOSP.
Manor Park
Super-store
Rec. Grd.
Carshalton
Sutton
Carshalton Beeches
Little Holland Ho.
Stanley Pk. Rec. Grd.
Stowford College
Resrs (covered)
Tennis Cts.
FELNEX TRADING ESTATE
WRYTHE
GREEN
WRYTHE LANE
NORTH STREET
NIGHTINGALE RD.
HACKBRIDGE RD.
LONDON RD.
CARSHALTON ROAD
HIGH ST.
RUSKIN ROAD
PARK LA.
BEECHES AV.
BANSTEAD RD.
STANLEY PARK ROAD
BRIGHTON ROAD
THROWLEY WAY
ROSE HILL
BENHILL
WESTMEAD
ERSKINE ROAD
A232
B278
B277
B271
B2230
A2232

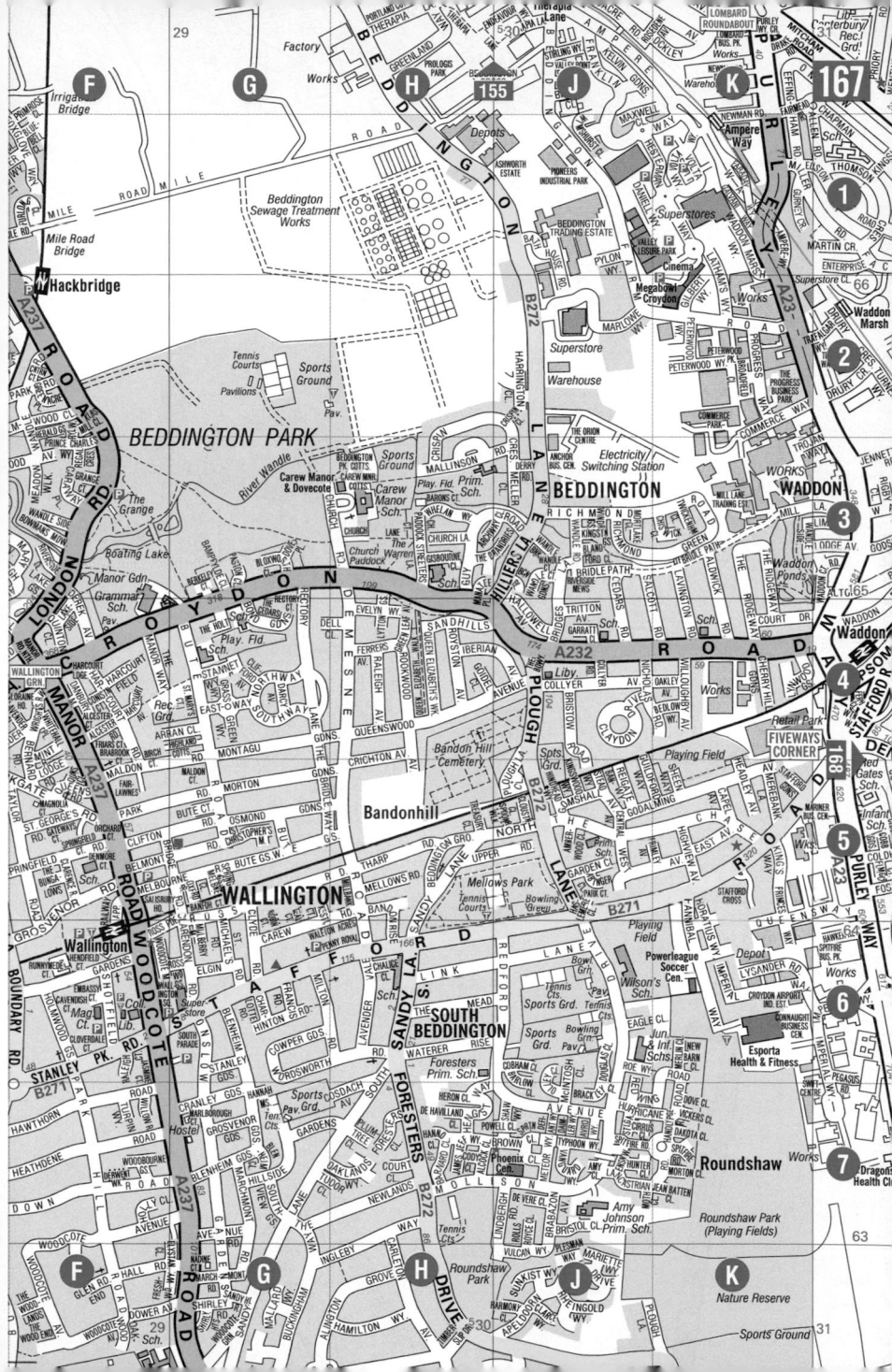

167
155
168
29
30
31
F
G
H
J
K
1
2
3
4
5
6
7
63
64
65
66
Factory
Works
Irrigation Bridge
Therapia Lane
LOMBARD ROUNDABOUT
MITCHAM ROAD
PROLOGIS PARK
Depots
ASHWORTH ESTATE
PIONEERS INDUSTRIAL PARK
Ampere Way
ROAD MILE
MILE ROAD
Mile Road Bridge
Hackbridge
Beddington Sewage Treatment Works
BEDDINGTON LANE
BEDDINGTON TRADING ESTATE
VALLEY LEISURE PARK
Superstores
Cinema
Megabowl Croydon
Superstore
Warehouse
Waddon Marsh
THE PROGRESS BUSINESS PARK
COMMERCE PARK
COMMERCE WAY
Tennis Courts
Sports Ground
Pavilions
Pav.
BEDDINGTON PARK
River Wandle
The Grange
Boating Lake
Manor Gdn.
Grammar Sch.
Carew Manor & Dovecote
Carew Manor Sch.
Prim. Sch.
Sports Ground
Play. Fld.
Church Paddock
The Warren
THE ORION CENTRE
ANCHOR BUS. CEN.
Electricity Switching Station
BEDDINGTON
WADDON
MILL LANE TRADING EST.
Waddon Ponds
RICHMOND ROAD
BRIDLE PATH
LONDON ROAD
CROYDON ROAD
A232
A237
A23
B272
B271
PURLEY WAY
Waddon
WALLINGTON GRN.
MANOR ROAD
Rec. Grd.
Bandon Hill Cemetery
Bandonhill
Spts. Grd.
Playing Field
Retail Park
FIVEWAYS CORNER
Red Gates Sch.
Infant Sch.
STAFFORD CROSS
WALLINGTON
Wallington
Mellows Park
Tennis Courts
Bowling Green
STAFFORD ROAD
SANDY LANE
Powerleague Soccer Cen.
Wilson's Sch.
Depot
Works
CROYDON AIRPORT IND. EST.
CONNAUGHT BUSINESS CEN.
Esporta Health & Fitness
SOUTH BEDDINGTON
Sports Grd.
Foresters Prim. Sch.
Jun. & Inf. Schs.
Phoenix Cen.
Roundshaw
WOODCOTE ROAD
STANLEY PARK RD.
Hostel
FORESTERS DRIVE
MOLLISON
Amy Johnson Prim. Sch.
Roundshaw Park (Playing Fields)
Roundshaw Park
Nature Reserve
Sports Ground
PLOUGH LANE
ROUNDSHAW AVENUE

168
156
167
A
B
C
D
E
1
2
3
4
5
6
7
CROYDON
West Croydon
East Croydon
South Croydon
Sanderstead
Waddon
WADDON
Waddon Marsh
WANDLE PARK
Wandle Park
SOUTH CROYDON
FIVEWAYS CORNER
Reeves Cnr.
Church St.
George St.
Wellesley Rd.
Lebanon Rd.
Centrale
FLYOVER
Duppas Hill
Recreation Ground
Sports Ground
Retail Park
Roundshaw Park (Playing Fields)
Nature Reserve
PURLEY WAY PLAYING FIELDS
Whitgift Sch.
HALING PARK Play. Flds.
HALING GROVE
Croydon Rec. Grd.
Russell Hill Resr. (covered)
Fairfield Halls
Croydon Coll.
Coombe Cliff (Educ. Cen)
Esporta Health & Fitness
Dragons Health Club
Living Well Health Club
Haling Manor High Sch.
Regina Coeli RC Prim. Sch.
St. Giles Sch.
Cumnor House Sch.
Capital Business Centre
Twin Bridges Business Park
Sports Club
Council Offices
Warehouses
Superstore
A23
A232
A235
A236
A212
A222
A213
B243
B275
B271
B269
B274
PURLEY WAY
DUPPAS HILL RD.
BRIGHTON ROAD
SOUTH END
WELLESLEY ROAD
ROMAN WAY
OLD TOWN
COOMBE RD.
PARK LANE
LOWER ADDISCOMBE ROAD
WADDON WAY
DENNING AV.
WARHAM ROAD

169
157
170
F
G
H
J
K
1
2
3
4
5
6
7
ADDISCOMBE
Addiscombe
ADDISCOMBE ROAD
A222
A232
A215
A212
A2022
SHIRLEY ROAD
WICKHAM ROAD
SHIRLEY
Shirley Oaks
SHIRLEY OAKS BMI HOSPITAL
Ashburton Playing Fields
Ashburton Sch.
Library
Playing Fields
Playing Field
PRIMROSE
SHIRLEY AVENUE
SHIRLEY OAKS ROAD
Syn. Hall
Recreation Grd.
Ten. Cts.
MULBERRY LA.
CARLYLE RD.
ASHBURTON AV.
ASHBURTON CL.
ASHBURTON GDNS.
HAVELOCK RD.
CLYDE RD.
NICHOLSON RD.
GRANT PL.
EAST INDIA WY.
ACADEMY GS.
HAMILTON CT.
BINGHAM RD.
SEFTON RD.
COMPTON RD.
CRAVEN RD.
CRAIGEN AV.
ASHBURTON AVENUE
GREENCOURT AV.
SELWOOD RD.
WHITETHORN GDNS.
BIRCH TREE WAY
ASHURST WLK.
FRYSTON AV.
NORTHAMPTON RD.
CHEYNE WK.
ANNANDALE RD.
HARRIET GS.
ASHBURTON RD.
OUTRAM RD.
Sandilands
Sandilands Junc.
LYNDEN HYRST
WOODBURY CL.
SAVILE GS.
BISHOPS CT.
GARDEN CT.
SANDILANDS
FITZJAMES AVENUE
UPFIELD
MAPLEDALE AV.
HARLAND AV.
HARDING CL.
DIGBY PL.
DEEPDENE AV.
ROWAN GS.
DANECOURT GS.
Trinity School Playing Field
Pav.
Tennis Courts
Sports Ground
GRIMWADE AVENUE
RANMORE AV.
Bowling Green
SHIRLEY PARK GOLF COURSE
Club House
SHIRLEY PARK
Trinity Sch.
Sports Cen.
BARNFIELD AVENUE
ELDON AV.
VALLEY WLK.
UPPER SHIRLEY ROAD
Nursery
NURSERY CL.
BARMOUTH RD.
SPRING PARK AV.
THE VALE
THE GLEN
Prim. Sch.
Play. Fld.
Hall Grange
SHIRLEY CHURCH ROAD
Coloma Convent RC Sch.
Shirley High Sch.
Rec. Grd.
Tennis Courts
HARTLAND WAY
PINEWOOD CL.
Pinewoods
Shirley Windmill
Shirley Court
POSTMILL CLOSE
TANGLEWOOD CL.
Lacrosse Pitch
THE DENE
SANDPITS RD.
BIRKDALE GDNS.
SPRUCEDALE GDNS.
BADGERS HOLE
FARRER'S PL.
COOMBE
Weir
Oaks Farm
OAKS LANE
Coombe Farm
COOMBE PARK
Winwood
LLOYD PARK
Lloyd Park
Bowling Green
Ten. Cts.
Pavilion
LARCOMBE CL.
LLOYD PK. AV.
WEAVER CL.
RUSHMEAD CL.
UPPER SHIRLEY
PINE COOMBE
BIRCH HILL
SHIRLEY HILLS RD.
Addington Hills
ADDINGTON GOLF COURSE
Geoffrey Harris House
Pav.
OAKS ROAD
COOMBE ROAD
COOMBE LANE
Coombe Lodge
Coombe Lodge Nurseries
Pavilion
Playing Field
Meadow View
Coombe Wood
CONDUIT LANE
Reservoir (covered)
Coombe Lane
SUNKEN RD.
BISHOPS WALK
64
ADDINGTON
GRAVEL HILL
BINFIELD RD.
BALLATER RD.
CASTLEMAINE AV.
PARK AVENUE
BLOSSOM CL.
MELVILLE AV.
PHOENIX CT.
Sch.
BENCHFIELD
Sports Ground
Ballards Plantation
Royal Russell Sch.
Royal Russell Preparatory Sch.
Bandy Mount
Sports Grd.
Ten. Cts.
Swim. Pool
Tennis Courts
Cottage in the Woods
Playing Field
Old Ballards Cottage
Lodge
Heathfield (Train. Cen.)
Heathfield Farm
RIESCO DR.
BALLARDS WAY
CROHAM ROAD
BALLARDS FARM ROAD
BALLARDS RISE
HOLLINGSWORTH RD.
BALLARDS FM. RD.
BALLARDS RISE
WINCHELSEY RISE
MANOR GDNS.
BANKSIDE
Club House
CROHAM HURST GOLF COURSE
CROHAM HURST
Breakneck Hill
CROHAM HURST GOLF COURSE
Thrift Wood
FARLEY RD.
LITTLEHEATH
CREST RD.
RUFFETTS CL.
HOFFMANN GDS.
THE RUFFETTS
THE CHESTNUT
The Ruffett
GALLOP
GROVE
VIEW ROAD
CHAPEL VIEW
Bramley Bank Nature Reserve
Playing Field
Gilbert Scott Jun. & Inf. Schs.
Monks Hill Sports Centre
High Sch.
BROADCOOMBE
WARREN
SHEPHERDS WAY
MOSS GDS.
FREELANDS AV.
HEATHER WY.
HEATHFIELD
FARNBOROUGH AV.
COPSE VIEW
EDGECOOMBE
Water Tower
Queenhill Shaw
Rec. Grd.
LITTLEHEATH WOOD
SELSDON
Selsdon Prim. Sch.
Play. Fld.
FOXEARTH SPUR
INGHAM RD.
ADDINGTON RD.
SELSDON PK. RD.
SELSDON RD.
BRENT RD.
UPPER SELSDON RD.
WISBOROUGH RD.
EWHURST AV.
BRIDLE ROAD
34
35
36
63
65
66
LANE
Lodge

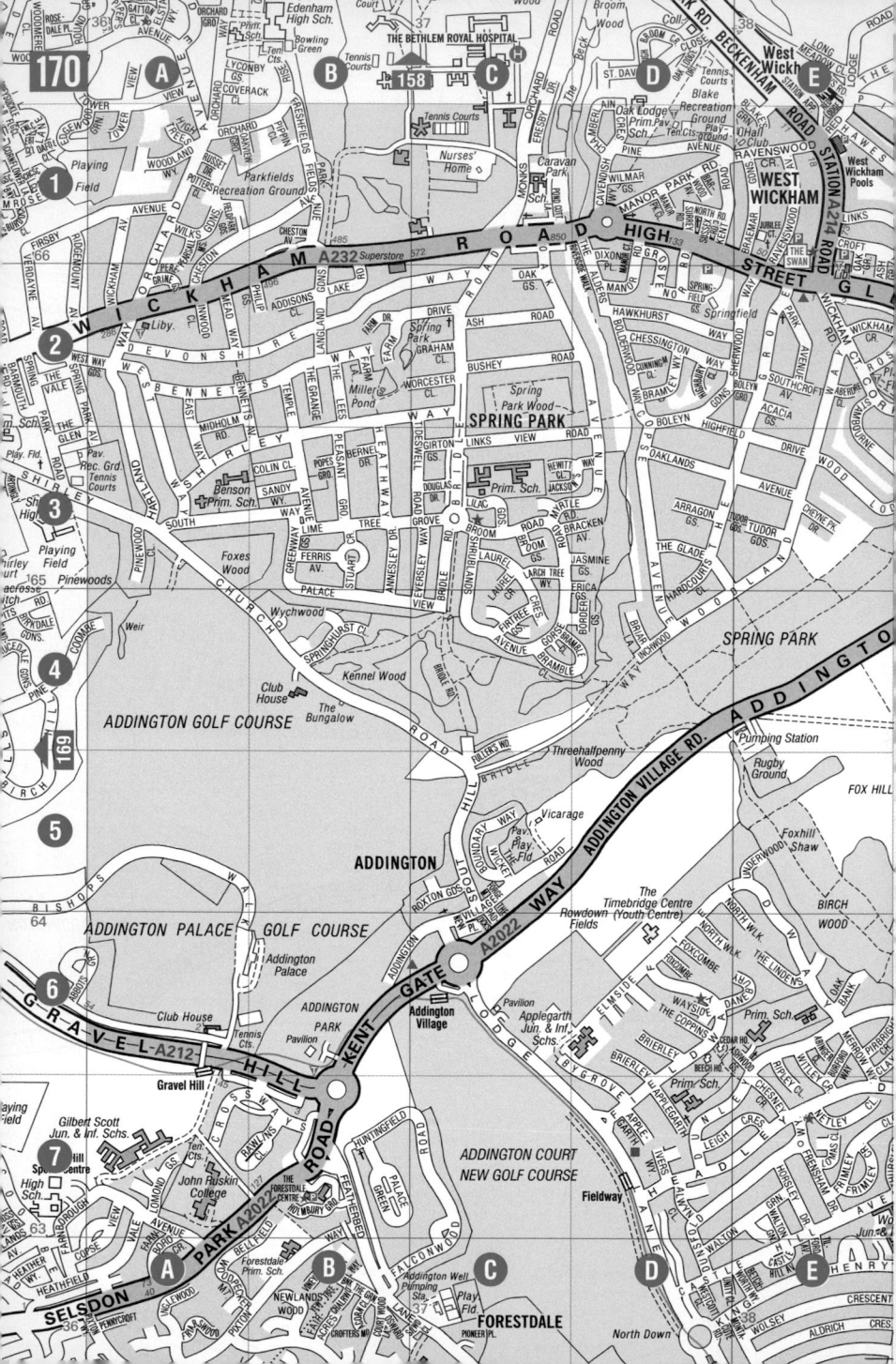

170
158
169
A
B
C
D
E
1
2
3
4
5
6
7
Edenham High Sch.
Bowling Green
THE BETHLEM ROYAL HOSPITAL
Tennis Courts
Nurses' Home
Broom Wood
The Beck
Blake Recreation Ground
Oak Lodge Prim. Sch.
West Wickham
WEST WICKHAM
West Wickham Pools
STATION ROAD A214
BECKENHAM RD.
LONG MEADOW CL.
RAVENSWOOD CR.
Caravan Park
Playing Field
Parkfields Recreation Ground
WICKHAM ROAD A232
HIGH STREET
Superstore
Liby.
DEVONSHIRE WAY
BENNETTS WAY
SHIRLEY WAY
SPRING PARK
Spring Park Wood
Miller's Pond
Spring Park
Benson Prim. Sch.
Prim. Sch.
LINKS VIEW ROAD
BUSHEY ROAD
ASH ROAD
OAK GS.
HAWKHURST WAY
CHESSINGTON WAY
BOLEYN GDNS.
HIGHFIELD DRIVE
OAKLANDS
WOOD LODGE LA.
TUDOR GDS.
THE GLADE
WOODLAND WAY
Foxes Wood
Pinewoods
Weir
Wychwood
Kennel Wood
Club House
The Bungalow
ADDINGTON GOLF COURSE
CHURCH ROAD
SPRING PARK
Threehalfpenny Wood
Pumping Station
Rugby Ground
FOX HILL
Foxhill Shaw
BIRCH WOOD
Vicarage
ADDINGTON
ADDINGTON VILLAGE RD.
ADDINGTON WAY A2022
KENT GATE WAY
The Timebridge Centre (Youth Centre)
Rowdown Fields
BISHOPS WALK
ADDINGTON PALACE GOLF COURSE
Addington Palace
Club House
Tennis Cts.
ADDINGTON PARK
Pavilion
Addington Village
GRAVEL HILL A212
Gravel Hill
Applegarth Jun. & Inf. Schs.
Prim. Sch.
LODGE LANE
Gilbert Scott Jun. & Inf. Schs.
John Ruskin College
PARK ROAD A2022
THE FORESTDALE CENTRE
ADDINGTON COURT NEW GOLF COURSE
Fieldway
Forestdale Prim. Sch.
Addington Well Pumping Sta.
Play. Fld.
FORESTDALE
NEWLANDS WOOD
SELSDON PARK
North Down
KING HENRY'S DR.
CRESCENT

171
159
172
HAYES
Hayes Farm
Brook Wood
Bolds Wood
Hayes Prim. Sch.
Playing Field
Hall
Liby.
Baston Pre - Jun. School
Play. Fld.
Tennis Court
Hayes Sch.
Spts. Grd.
Pav.
THE HAYES GROVE PRIORY HOSP.
Hayes Court
HAYES COMMON
Five Elms
Gorsewood
Tennis Courts
Club
Baston Manor
Hast Hill
Keston Court Riding School
Miry Grove
Rouse Farm
Arlington Orchard
Elm Farm
Nash
NASH
Nash Farm
Fox Hill Nursery
Milchden
James's Wood
Fuller's Wood
North Pole Farm
Five Oaks
Baldwin Shaw
Broomfieldbank Shaw
Metropolitan Police Dog Training Establishment
Rushfield Shaw
Bradmanshill Wood
Waytes
Cooper's Wood
Long Shaw
Well Wood
Electricity Sub Station
NEW ADDINGTON
ROWDOWN WOOD
Castlehill Ruffs
The Bungalows
The Cottages
Wickham Court Farm
Wickham Court
Emmaus Conference Centre
St. John Rigby RC College
Tower
Lodge
Coney Hall Rec. Grd.
CONEY HALL
Recreation Ground
Bowling Green
Sparrow's Den Playing Fields
West Wickham Common
Sports Ground
The Warren Bowl. Grn.
Nash Ho.
Sch.
School
Playing Field
Hayes
Play Fld.
Hawes Down Jun.& Inf. Schs.
Youth Cen.
Glebe Sch.
Sports Grounds
Sports Ground
Tennis Courts
Bowling Green
Club
Sports Ground
War Mem.
Rec. Grd.
CROYDON ROAD
A232
A2022
B251
B265
HAYES LANE
BASTON ROAD
BASTON MANOR RD.
FIVE ELMS ROAD
FOX LANE
JACKASS LANE
NASH LANE
NORTH POLE LANE
HAST HILL
SYLVAN WAY
HAMS LANE
GATES GREEN ROAD
KINGSWAY
CONEY HILL RD.
ADDINGTON RD.
PICKHURST LANE
RIDGEWAY
WARREN ROAD
PRESTONS ROAD
HARVEST BANK ROAD
COURTFIELD RISE
SILVERDALE
F
G
H
J
K
1
2
3
4
5
6
7
39
40
41
63
64
65
66

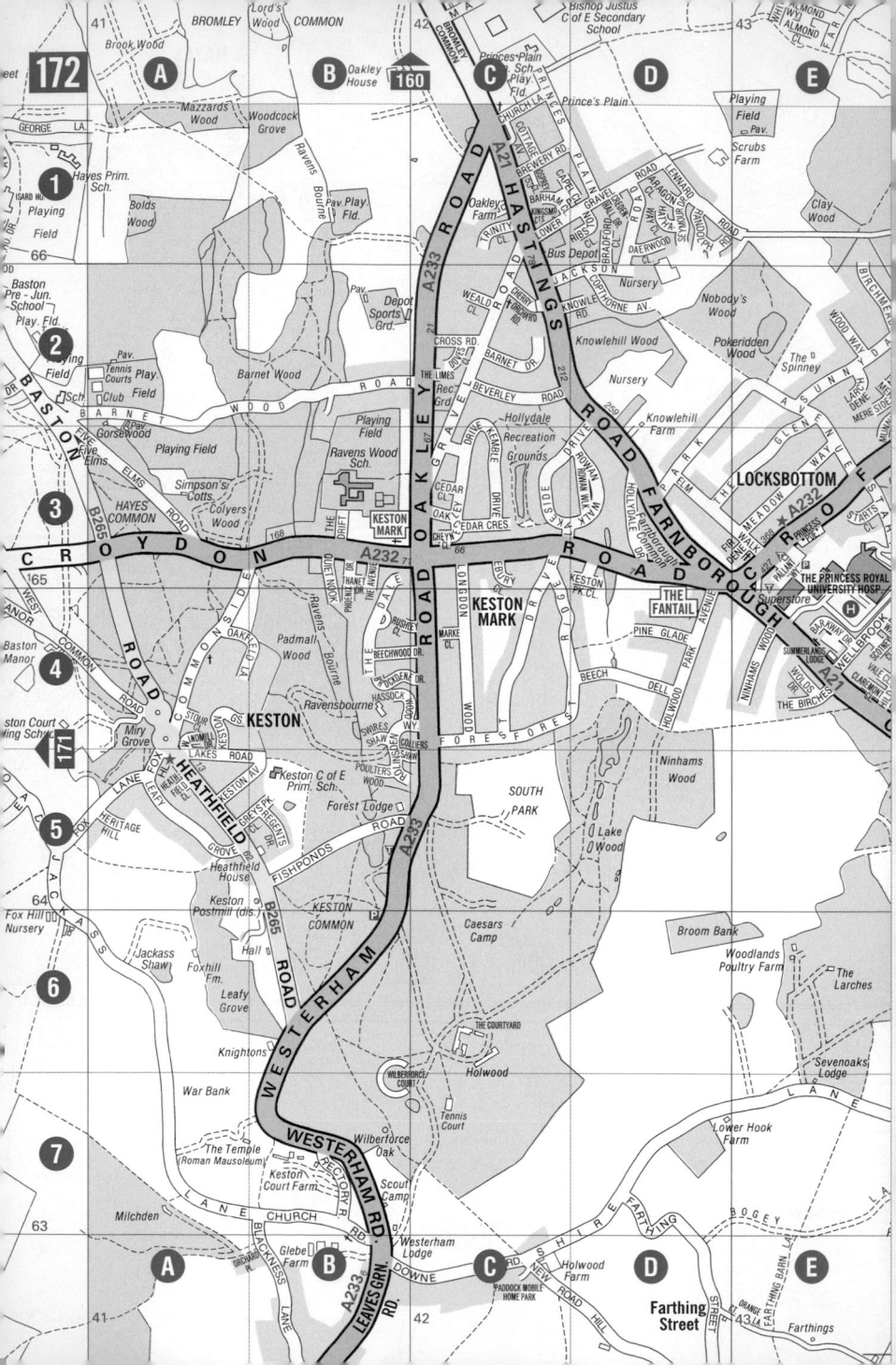

BROMLEY COMMON
Lord's Wood
Brook Wood
Oakley House
160
Bishop Justus C of E Secondary School
Princes Plain
Prince's Plain
Mazzards Wood
Woodcock Grove
GEORGE LA.
Hayes Prim. Sch.
Playing Field
Bolds Wood
Ravens Bourne
Pav. Play. Fld.
Oakley Farm
Scrubs Farm
Clay Wood
Baston Pre - Jun. School
Play. Fld.
Depot Sports Grd.
Bus Depot
Nursery
Nobody's Wood
Pokeridden Wood
Knowlehill Wood
The Spinney
Barnet Wood
BARNET WOOD ROAD
Tennis Courts
Play. Field
Club
Gorsewood
Playing Field
Ravens Wood Sch.
Hollydale Recreation Grounds
Knowlehill Farm
LOCKSBOTTOM
Simpson's Cotts.
Colyers Wood
HAYES COMMON
KESTON MARK
CROYDON ROAD
A232
A21
A233
B265
OAKLEY ROAD
HASTINGS ROAD
FARNBOROUGH COMMON
THE FANTAIL
KESTON MARK
THE PRINCESS ROYAL UNIVERSITY HOSP.
Superstore
Baston Manor
Padmall Wood
Ravensbourne
KESTON
Miry Grove
171
HEATHFIELD
Keston C of E Prim. Sch.
Forest Lodge
FISHPONDS ROAD
SOUTH PARK
Ninhams Wood
Lake Wood
Heathfield House
Keston Postmill (dis.)
KESTON COMMON
Caesars Camp
Fox Hill Nursery
Broom Bank
Woodlands Poultry Farm
The Larches
Jackass Shaw
Foxhill Fm.
Hall
Leafy Grove
WESTERHAM ROAD
THE COURTYARD
Knightons
Holwood
WILBERFORCE COURT
Sevenoaks Lodge
War Bank
Tennis Court
Lower Hook Farm
The Temple (Roman Mausoleum)
Wilberforce Oak
Keston Court Farm
Scout Camp
Milchden
CHURCH LANE
Westerham Lodge
Glebe Farm
DOWNE RD.
Holwood Farm
PADDOCK MOBILE HOME PARK
SHIRE LANE
FARTHING STREET
BOGEY LANE
Farthing Street
Farthings
LEAVES GRN. RD.

173
161
F
G
H
J
K
1
2
3
4
5
6
7
Sparrow Wood
Petts Wood Recreation Ground
Crofton Jun. Sch.
Crofton Inf. Sch.
Sparrow Common
Roundabout Wood
Crofton Heath
BROOM HILL
Knoll Lawn Tennis Club
ORPINGTON
Orpington
Civic Halls
CROFTON
A232
ROAD
STATION ROAD
Gumping Common
Hall
Darrick Wood Pool
Darrick Wood Sec. Sch.
Sports Centre
Darrick Wood
Darrick Wood Jun. & Inf. Schs.
Tennis Courts
Farnborough Pav.
Recreation Ground
Newstead Wood
Play. Fld.
Newstead Wood Sch. for Girls
Playing Field
Tubbenden Jun. & Inf. Schools
Rec. Grd.
Prim. Sch.
Ontario Centre
Hospice
ORPINGTON HOSPITAL
Play. Fld.
A223
SEVENOAKS
SEVENOAKS RD.
FARNBOROUGH COMMON
A21
HIGH STREET FARNBOROUGH
B2158
Scouts Hall
Club Sports Ground
Pav.
FARNBOROUGH
Farnborough Prim. Sch.
The Manse
The Green
Bassetts Cen.
Mill Hill
Church Field Plantation
Glentrammon Rec. Grd.
Ramus Wood
GREEN STREET GREEN
Cocksett Plantation
Cocksett Hill
The Lodge
High Elms Nature Cen.
Woodpiece
Chelsfield Hall
North End Farm
North End Farm Cotts
HIGH ELMS COUNTRY PARK
Whitelands Wood
Club House
Playgrd.
Rounds Wood
Blacklands
High Elms Clockhouse
The Rookery
HIGH ELMS GOLF COURSE
Rec. Grd.
HIGH ST.
WAY
HILL
SHIRE LANE
NORTH END LANE
HIGH ELMS ROAD
OLD LANE
CUDHAM LANE
44
545
46
63
64
65
66

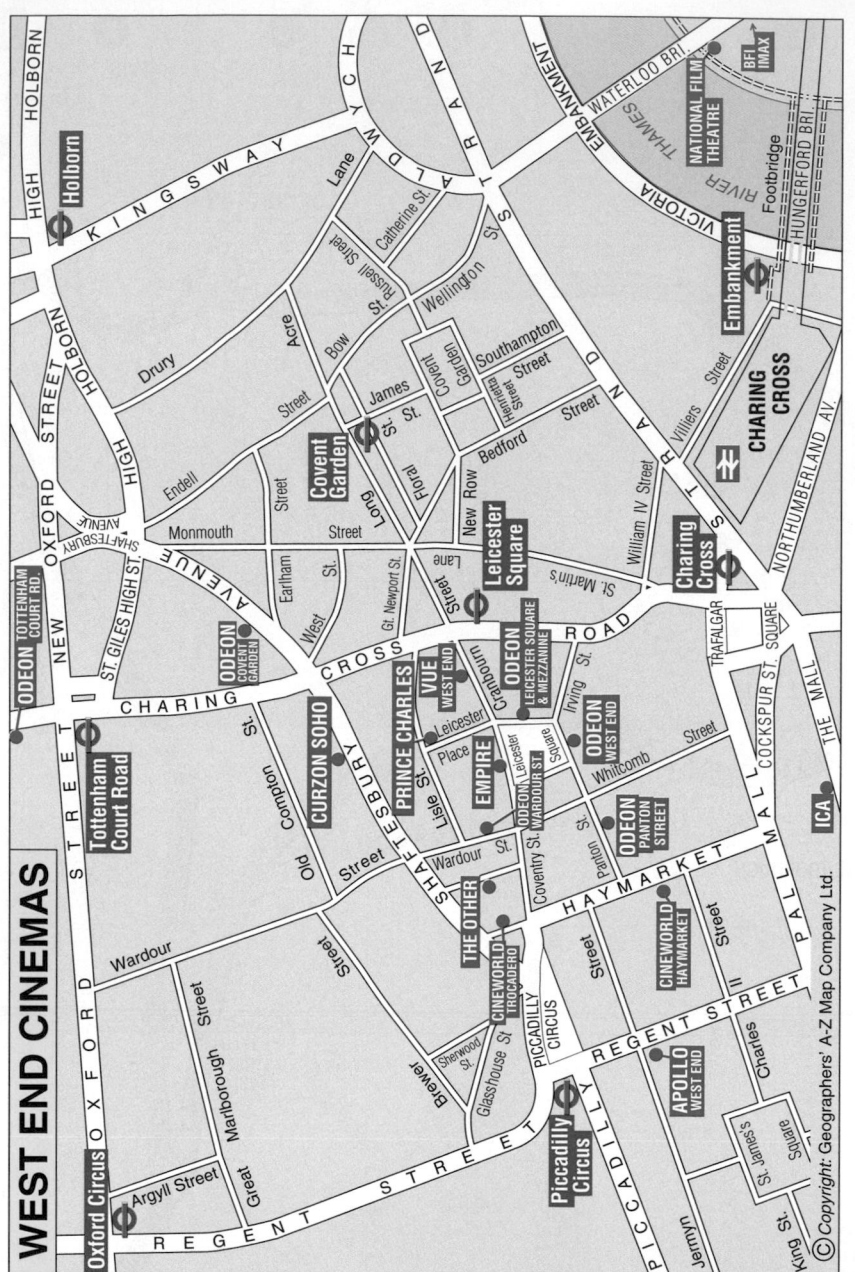

WEST END CINEMAS
ODEON TOTTENHAM COURT RD.
ODEON COVENT GARDEN
CURZON SOHO
PRINCE CHARLES
VUE WEST END
ODEON LEICESTER SQUARE & MEZZANINE
EMPIRE
ODEON WARDOUR ST.
ODEON WEST END
ODEON PANTON STREET
THE OTHER
CINEWORLD TROCADERO
CINEWORLD HAYMARKET
APOLLO WEST END
ICA
NATIONAL FILM THEATRE
BFI IMAX
Oxford Circus
Tottenham Court Road
Holborn
Covent Garden
Leicester Square
Charing Cross
Embankment
Piccadilly Circus
CHARING CROSS
OXFORD STREET
NEW OXFORD STREET
HIGH HOLBORN
KINGSWAY
ALDWYCH
STRAND
VICTORIA EMBANKMENT
WATERLOO BRI.
HUNGERFORD BRI.
Footbridge
RIVER THAMES
SHAFTESBURY AVENUE
CHARING CROSS ROAD
REGENT STREET
PICCADILLY
PICCADILLY CIRCUS
HAYMARKET
PALL MALL
COCKSPUR ST.
TRAFALGAR SQUARE
THE MALL
NORTHUMBERLAND AV.
ST. GILES HIGH ST.
Monmouth Street
Endell Street
Drury Lane
Long Acre
Bow St.
Russell Street
Catherine St.
Wellington St.
Southampton Street
Henrietta Street
Covent Garden
James St.
Floral St.
Bedford Street
New Row
William IV Street
Villiers Street
St. Martin's Lane
Earlham Street
West St.
Gt. Newport St.
Cranbourn St.
Leicester Place
Lisle St.
Leicester Square
Irving St.
Whitcomb Street
Wardour St.
Coventry St.
Panton St.
Old Compton Street
Wardour Street
Great Marlborough Street
Argyll Street
Brewer Street
Sherwood St.
Glasshouse St
Jermyn Street
Charles II Street
St. James's Square
King St.
© Copyright: Geographers' A-Z Map Company Ltd.

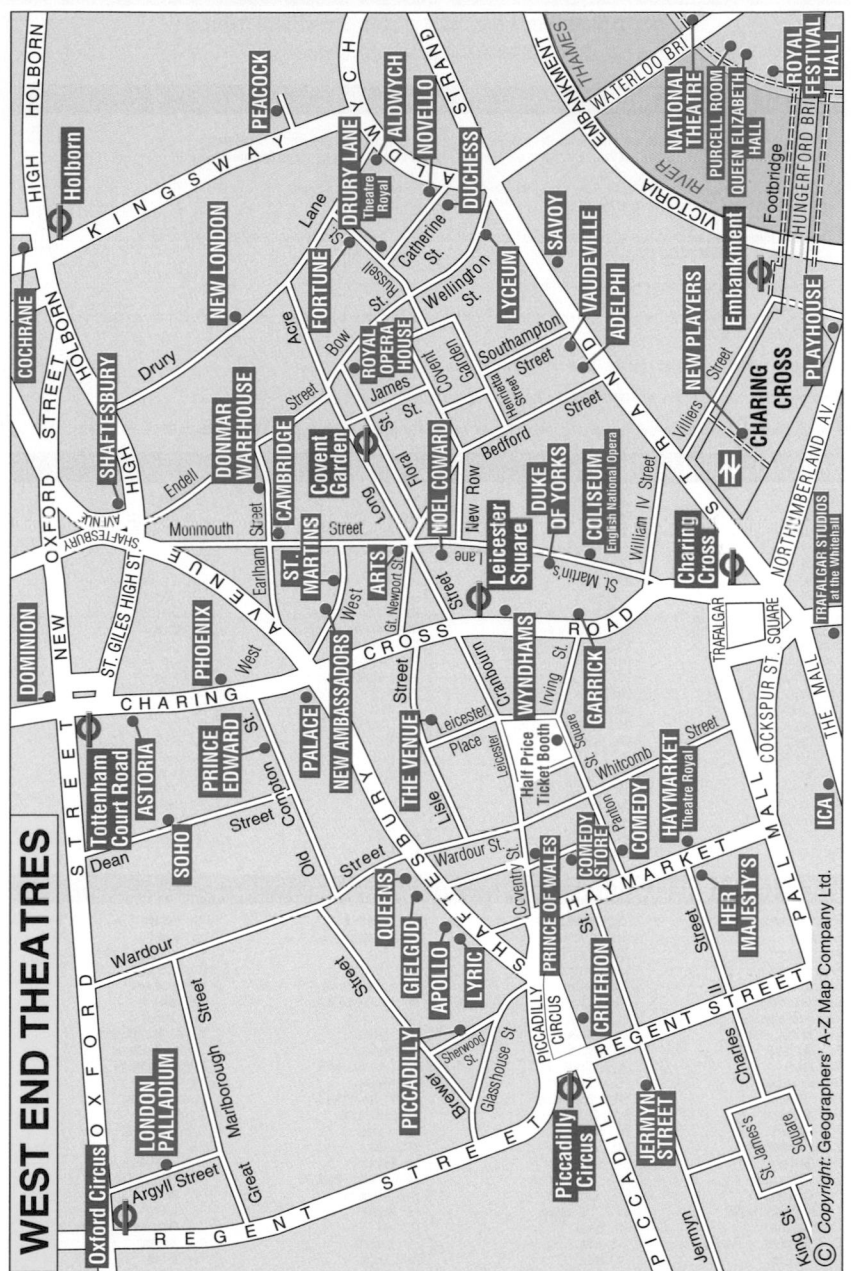

WEST END THEATRES
DOMINION
COCHRANE
Holborn
Oxford Circus
Tottenham Court Road
ASTORIA
LONDON PALLADIUM
SOHO
PRINCE EDWARD
PHOENIX
SHAFTESBURY
NEW LONDON
PEACOCK
DONMAR WAREHOUSE
CAMBRIDGE
ST. MARTINS
PALACE
NEW AMBASSADORS
Covent Garden
FORTUNE
DRURY LANE Theatre Royal
ALDWYCH
NOVELLO
DUCHESS
ROYAL OPERA HOUSE
ARTS
QUEENS
PICCADILLY
GIELGUD
APOLLO
LYRIC
THE VENUE
NOEL COWARD
LYCEUM
Leicester Square
WYNDHAMS
Half Price Ticket Booth
DUKE OF YORKS
SAVOY
PRINCE OF WALES
Piccadilly Circus
CRITERION
COMEDY STORE
GARRICK
COLISEUM English National Opera
VAUDEVILLE
ADELPHI
COMEDY
JERMYN STREET
HAYMARKET Theatre Royal
Charing Cross
NEW PLAYERS
NATIONAL THEATRE
PURCELL ROOM
Embankment
QUEEN ELIZABETH HALL
HER MAJESTY'S
CHARING CROSS
ROYAL FESTIVAL HALL
PLAYHOUSE
ICA
TRAFALGAR STUDIOS at the Whitehall
OXFORD STREET
NEW OXFORD STREET
HIGH HOLBORN
ST. GILES HIGH ST.
SHAFTESBURY AVENUE
KINGSWAY
ALDWYCH
STRAND
CHARING CROSS ROAD
REGENT STREET
PICCADILLY
PICCADILLY CIRCUS
HAYMARKET
PALL MALL
COCKSPUR ST.
TRAFALGAR SQUARE
NORTHUMBERLAND AV.
THE MALL
VICTORIA EMBANKMENT
RIVER THAMES
WATERLOO BRI
HUNGERFORD BRI
Footbridge
Argyll Street
Great Marlborough Street
Wardour Street
Dean Street
Old Compton Street
Greek St.
West Street
Earlham Street
Monmouth Street
Endell Street
Drury Lane
Long Acre
Bow St.
Russell St.
Floral St.
James St.
Catherine St.
Wellington St.
Covent Garden
Southampton Street
Henrietta Street
Bedford Street
New Row
St. Martin's Lane
Gt. Newport St.
Cranbourn Street
Lisle Street
Leicester Place
Leicester Square
Irving St.
Wardour St.
Coventry St.
Brewer Street
Sherwood St.
Glasshouse St
Panton St.
Whitcomb Street
William IV Street
Villiers Street
Jermyn
Charles II Street
St. James's Square
King St.
© Copyright: Geographers' A-Z Map Company Ltd.

INDEX

Including Streets, Places & Areas, Industrial Estates, Selected Flats & Walkways,
Junction Names and Selected Places of Interest.

HOW TO USE THIS INDEX

1. Each street name is followed by its Postcode District (or, if outside the London Postcodes, by its Locality Abbreviation(s)), and then by its map reference;
e.g. **Abbeville Rd.** SW4 . . . .6G **119** is in the SW4 Postcode District and is to be found in square 6G on page **119**. The page number being shown in bold type.

2. A strict alphabetical order is followed in which Av., Rd., St., etc. (though abbreviated) are read in full and as part of the street name;
e.g. **Ash Cl.** appears after **Ashchurch Ter.** but before **Ashcombe Av.**

3. Streets and a selection of flats and walkways too small to be shown on the maps, appear in the index with the thoroughfare to which it is connected shown in brackets;
e.g. **Abady Ho.** SW1 . . . .3D **18** (off Page St.)

4. Addresses that are in more than one part are referred to as not continuous.

5. Places and areas are shown in the index in BLUE TYPE and the map reference is to the actual map square in which the town centre or area is located and not to the place name shown on the map;
e.g. **ABBEY WOOD** 4C **108**

6. An example of a selected place of interest is **Alexander Fleming Labratory Mus.** 7B **4**

7. Junction names are shown in the index in BOLD CAPITAL TYPE; e.g. **ALDGATE** 6F **85**

8. Map references for entries that appear on large scale pages **4-19** are shown first, with small scale map references shown in brackets; e.g. **Abbey Orchard St.** SW1 . . . .1C **18** (3H **101**)

GENERAL ABBREVIATIONS

All. : Alley	**Cott.** : Cottage	**Ind.** : Industrial	**Pct.** : Precinct
App. : Approach	**Cotts.** : Cottages	**Info.** : Information	**Prom.** : Promenade
Arc. : Arcade	**Ct.** : Court	**Intl.** : International	**Quad.** : Quadrant
Av. : Avenue	**Cres.** : Crescent	**Junc.** : Junction	**Ri.** : Rise
Bk. : Back	**Cft.** : Croft	**La.** : Lane	**Rd.** : Road
Blvd. : Boulevard	**Dpt.** : Depot	**Lit.** : Little	**Rdbt.** : Roundabout
Bri. : Bridge	**Dr.** : Drive	**Lwr.** : Lower	**Shop.** : Shopping
B'way. : Broadway	**E.** : East	**Mnr.** : Manor	**Sth.** : South
Bldg. : Building	**Emb.** : Embankment	**Mans.** : Mansions	**Sq.** : Square
Bldgs. : Buildings	**Ent.** : Enterprise	**Mkt.** : Market	**Sta.** : Station
Bungs. : Bungalows	**Est.** : Estate	**Mdw.** : Meadow	**St.** : Street
Bus. : Business	**Fld.** : Field	**Mdws.** : Meadows	**Ter.** : Terrace
Cvn. : Caravan	**Flds.** : Fields	**M.** : Mews	**Twr.** : Tower
C'way. : Causeway	**Gdn.** : Garden	**Mt.** : Mount	**Trad.** : Trading
Cen. : Centre	**Gdns.** : Gardens	**Mus.** : Museum	**Up.** : Upper
Chu. : Church	**Gth.** : Garth	**Nth.** : North	**Va.** : Vale
Chyd. : Churchyard	**Ga.** : Gate	**No.** : Number	**Vw.** : View
Circ. : Circle	**Gt.** : Great	**Pal.** : Palace	**Vs.** : Villas
Cir. : Circus	**Grn.** : Green	**Pde.** : Parade	**Vis.** : Visitors
Cl. : Close	**Gro.** : Grove	**Pk.** : Park	**Wlk.** : Walk
Coll. : College	**Hgts.** : Heights	**Pas.** : Passage	**W.** : West
Comn. : Common	**Ho.** : House	**Pav.** : Pavilion	**Yd.** : Yard
Cnr. : Corner	**Ho's.** : Houses	**Pl.** : Place	

LOCALITY ABBREVIATIONS

Addtn : **Addington**	Clay : **Claygate**	G'frd : **Greenford**	Lale : **Laleham**
Ark : **Arkley**	Cockf : **Cockfosters**	Had W : **Hadley Wood**	Lon : **London**
Ashf : **Ashford**	Col R : **Collier Row**	Ham : **Ham**	H'row A : **London Heathrow Airport**
Bark : **Barking**	Cowl : **Cowley**	Hamp : **Hampton**	Lough : **Loughton**
Barn : **Barnet**	Cran : **Cranford**	Ham H : **Hampton Hill**	Mawney : **Mawney**
Beck : **Beckenham**	Cray : **Crayford**	Ham W : **Hampton Wick**	Mitc : **Mitcham**
Bedd : **Beddington**	Croy : **Croydon**	Hanw : **Hanworth**	Mord : **Morden**
Bedf : **Bedfont**	Dag : **Dagenham**	Hare : **Harefield**	New Ad : **New Addington**
Belv : **Belvedere**	Dart : **Dartford**	Harl : **Harlington**	New Bar : **New Barnet**
Bexl : **Bexley**	Downe : **Downe**	Harm : **Harmondsworth**	N Mald : **New Malden**
Bex : **Bexleyheath**	E Barn : **East Barnet**	Harr : **Harrow**	N'olt : **Northolt**
Bford : **Brentford**	E Mos : **East Molesey**	Hrw W : **Harrow Weald**	Nwood : **Northwood**
Brim : **Brimsdown**	Eastc : **Eastcote**	H End : **Hatch End**	Orp : **Orpington**
Brom : **Bromley**	Edg : **Edgware**	Hayes : **Hayes**	Pet W : **Petts Wood**
Buck H : **Buckhurst Hill**	Els : **Elstree**	Hest : **Heston**	Pinn : **Pinner**
Bush : **Bushey**	Enf : **Enfield**	Hil : **Hillingdon**	Pond E : **Ponders End**
Bushy : **Bushy Heath**	Enf H : **Enfield Highway**	Hin W : **Hinchley Wood**	Prat B : **Pratts Bottom**
Cars : **Carshalton**	Enf L : **Enfield Lock**	Houn : **Hounslow**	Purl : **Purley**
Chad H : **Chadwell Heath**	Enf W : **Enfield Wash**	Ick : **Ickenham**	Rain : **Rainham**
Cheam : **Cheam**	Eps : **Epsom**	Ilf : **Ilford**	Rich : **Richmond**
Chels : **Chelsfield**	Erith : **Erith**	Isle : **Isleworth**	Rom : **Romford**
Chert : **Chertsey**	Esh : **Esher**	Kent : **Kenton**	Ruis : **Ruislip**
Chess : **Chessington**	Ewe : **Ewell**	Kes : **Keston**	Rush G : **Rush Green**
Chig : **Chigwell**	Farnb : **Farnborough**	Kew : **Kew**	St M Cry : **St Mary Cray**
Chst : **Chislehurst**	Felt : **Feltham**	King T : **Kingston Upon Thames**	St P : **St Pauls Cray**

Sand : **Sanderstead**
Sels : **Selsdon**
Shep : **Shepperton**
Sidc : **Sidcup**
Sip : **Sipson**
S'hall : **Southall**
S Croy : **South Croydon**
Staines : **Staines**
Stan : **Stanmore**
Stanw : **Stanwell**
Stock P : **Stockley Park**
Sun : **Sunbury**
Surb : **Surbiton**
Sutt : **Sutton**
Swan : **Swanley**
Tedd : **Teddington**
T Ditt : **Thames Ditton**
Thor H : **Thornton Heath**
Twick : **Twickenham**
Uxb : **Uxbridge**
Wadd : **Waddon**
Wall : **Wallington**
Walt T : **Walton-on-Thames**
W'stone : **Wealdstone**
Well : **Welling**
Wemb : **Wembley**
W Dray : **West Drayton**
W Mole : **West Molesey**
W W'ck : **West Wickham**
Weyb : **Weybridge**
Whit : **Whitton**
Wfd G : **Woodford Green**
Wor Pk : **Worcester Park**
Yead : **Yeading**
Yiew : **Yiewsley**

198 Gallery *6B* ***120***
(off Railton Rd.)

A

Aaron Hill Rd. E6 . . . . 5E **88**
Abady Ho. *SW1* *3D* ***18***
(off Page St.)
Abberley M. SW4 . . . . 3F **119**
Abbess Cl. E6 . . . . 5C **88**
SW2 . . . . 1B **138**
Abbeville M. SW4 . . . . 4H **119**
Abbeville Rd. N8 . . . . 5H **47**
SW4 . . . . 6G **119**
Abbey Av. HA0: Wemb 2E **78**
Abbey Bus. Cen. SW8 . . . . 1G **119**
Abbey Cl. E5 . . . . 4G **67**
HA5: Pinn 3K **39**
SW8 . . . . 1H **119**
UB3: Hayes 1K **93**
UB5: N'olt 3D **76**
Abbey Ct. *NW8* *2A* ***82***
(off Abbey Rd.)
SE17 . . . . *5C* ***102***
(off Macleod St.)
TW12: Hamp 7E **130**
Abbey Cres. DA17: Belv 4G **109**
Abbeydale Ct. E17 . . . . 3F **51**
Abbeydale Rd. HA0: Wemb 1F **79**
Abbey Dr. DA2: Bexl 2K **145**
SW17 . . . . 5E **136**
Abbey Est. NW8 . . . . 1K **81**
Abbeyfield Cl. CR4: Mitc 2C **154**
Abbeyfield Est. SE16 . . . . 4J **103**
Abbeyfield Rd. SE16 . . . . 4J **103**
(not continuous)
Abbeyfields Cl. NW10 . . . . 2G **79**
Abbey Gdns. BR7: Chst 1E **160**
NW8 . . . . 2A **82**
SE16 . . . . 4G **103**
W6 . . . . 6G **99**
Abbey Gro. SE2 . . . . 4B **108**
Abbeyhill Rd. DA15: Sidc 2C **144**
Abbey Ho. *E15* *2G* ***87***
(off Baker's Row)
NW8 . . . . 1A **4**
Abbey Ind. Est. CR4: Mitc 5D **154**
HA0: Wemb 1F **79**
Abbey La. BR3: Beck 7C **140**
E15 . . . . 2E **86**
Abbey La. Commercial Est. E15 . . . . . 2G **87**
Abbey Life Ct. E16 . . . . 5K **87**
Abbey Lodge NW8 . . . . 2D **4**
Abbey M. E17 . . . . 5C **50**
TW7: Isle 1B **114**
Abbey Mt. DA17: Belv 5F **109**
Abbey Orchard St. SW1 . . . . . 1C **18** (3H **101**)
Abbey Orchard St. Est.
SW1 . . . . 1D **18** (3H **101**)
(not continuous)
Abbey Pde. *SW19* *7A* ***136***
(off Merton High St.)
W5 . . . . 3F **79**
Abbey Pk. BR3: Beck 7C **140**
Abbey Pk. Ind. Est. IG11: Bark 2G **89**
Abbey Retail Pk. IG11: Bark 7F **71**
Abbey Rd. CR0: Croy 3B **168**
DA7: Bex 4E **126**
DA17: Belv 4D **108**
E15 . . . . 2F **87**
EN1: Enf 5K **23**
IG2: Ilf 5H **53**
IG11: Bark 1F **89**
NW6 . . . . 7K **63**
NW8 . . . . 1A **4** (7K **63**)
NW10 . . . . 1H **79**
SE2 . . . . 4D **108**
SW19 . . . . 7A **136**
Abbey Sports Cen. 1G **89**
Abbey St. E13 . . . . 4J **87**
SE1 . . . . 7H **15** (3F **103**)
Abbey Ter. SE2 . . . . 4C **108**
Abbey Trad. Est. SE26 . . . . 5B **140**
Abbey Vw. NW7 . . . . 3G **29**
Abbey Wlk. KT8: W Mole 3F **149**
Abbey Wharf Ind. Est.
IG11: Bark 3H **89**
ABBEY WOOD 4C **108**
Abbey Wood Camping & Cvn. Site
SE2 . . . . 4C **108**
Abbey Wood Rd. SE2 . . . . 4B **108**
Abbot Cl. HA4: Ruis 3B **58**
Abbot Ct. *SW8* *7J* ***101***
(off Hartington Rd.)
Abbot Ho. *E14* *7D* ***86***
(off Smythe St.)
Abbotsbury *NW1* *7H* ***65***
(off Camley St.)
Abbotsbury Cl. E15 . . . . 2E **86**
W14 . . . . 2G **99**
Abbotsbury Gdns. HA5: Eastc 7A **40**
Abbotsbury Ho. W14 . . . . 2G **99**
Abbotsbury M. SE15 . . . . 3J **121**
Abbotsbury Rd. BR2: Hayes 2H **171**
SM4: Mord 5K **153**
W14 . . . . 2G **99**
Abbots Cl. BR5: Farnb 1G **173**
Abbots Ct. *W8* *2K* ***99***
(off Thackeray St.)
Abbots Dr. HA2: Harr 2E **58**
Abbotsford Av. N15 . . . . 4C **48**
Abbotsford Gdns. IG8: Wfd G 7D **36**
Abbotsford Rd. IG3: Ilf 2A **72**
Abbots Gdns. N2 . . . . 4B **46**
Abbots Grn. CR0: Addtn 6K **169**
Abbotshade Rd. SE16 . . . . 1K **103**
Abbotshall Av. N14 . . . . 3B **32**
Abbotshall Rd. SE6 . . . . 1F **141**
Abbot's Ho. *W14* *3H* ***99***
(off St Mary Abbots Ter.)
Abbots La. SE1 . . . . 5H **15** (1E **102**)
Abbotsleigh Cl. SM2: Sutt 7K **165**
Abbotsleigh Rd. SW16 . . . . 4G **137**
Abbots Mnr. SW1 . . . . . . 5J **17** (4F **101**)
Abbots Mead TW10: Ham 4D **132**
Abbotsmede Cl. TW1: Twick 2K **131**
Abbots Pk. SW2 . . . . 1A **138**
Abbot's Pl. NW6 . . . . 1K **81**
Abbots Rd. E6 . . . . 1B **88**
HA8: Edg 7D **28**
Abbots Ter. N8 . . . . 6J **47**
Abbotstone Rd. SW15 . . . . 3E **116**
Abbot St. E8 . . . . 6F **67**
Abbots Wlk. W8 . . . . 3K **99**
Abbots Way BR3: Beck 5A **158**
Abbotswell Rd. SE4 . . . . 5B **122**
Abbotswood Cl. DA17: Belv 3E **108**
Abbotswood Gdns. IG5: Ilf 3D **52**
Abbotswood Rd. SE22 . . . . 4E **120**
SW16 . . . . 3H **137**
Abbotswood Way UB3: Hayes 1K **93**
Abbott Av. SW20 . . . . 1F **153**
Abbott Cl. TW12: Hamp 6C **130**
UB5: N'olt 6D **58**
Abbott Rd. E14 . . . . 5E **86**
(not continuous)
Abbotts Cl. N1 . . . . 6C **66**
RM7: Mawney 3H **55**
SE28 . . . . 7C **90**
UB8: Cowl 5A **74**
Abbotts Cres. E4 . . . . 4A **36**
EN2: Enf 2G **23**
Abbotts Dr. HA0: Wemb 2B **60**
Abbotts Ho. *SW1* *6C* ***18***
(off Aylesford St.)
Abbotts Pk. Rd. E10 . . . . 7E **50**
Abbotts Rd. CR4: Mitc 4G **155**
(not continuous)
EN5: New Bar 4E **20**
SM3: Cheam 4G **165**
UB1: S'hall 1C **94**
Abbott's Wlk. DA7: Bex 7D **108**
Abbott's Wharf *E14* *6C* ***86***
(off Stainsby Pl.)
Abchor Ho. *SW1* *5J* ***17***
(off Warwick Way)
Abchurch La. EC4 . . . . . . 2F **15** (7D **84**)
(not continuous)
Abchurch Yd. EC4 . . . . . . 2E **14** (7D **84**)
Abdale Rd. W12 . . . . 1D **98**
Abel Ho. *SE11* *7K* ***19***
(off Kennington Rd.)
Abenglen Ind. Est. UB3: Hayes 2F **93**
Aberavon Rd. E3 . . . . 3A **86**
Abercairn Rd. SW16 . . . . 7G **137**
Aberconway Rd. SM4: Mord 4K **153**
Abercorn Cl. NW7 . . . . 7B **30**
NW8 . . . . 3A **82**
Abercorn Commercial Cen.
HA0: Wemb 1D **78**
Abercorn Cotts. *NW8* *3A* ***82***
(off Abercorn Wlk.)
Abercorn Cres. HA2: Harr 1F **59**
Abercorn Gdns. HA3: Kent 7D **42**
RM6: Chad H 6B **54**
Abercorn Gro. HA4: Ruis 4F **39**
Abercorn Ho. *SE10* *7D* ***104***
(off Tarves Way)
Abercorn Mans. *NW8* *2A* ***82***
(off Abercorn Pl.)
Abercorn M. TW10: Rich 4F **115**
Abercorn Pl. NW8 . . . . 3A **82**
Abercorn Rd. HA7: Stan 7H **27**
NW7 . . . . 7B **30**
Abercorn Wlk. NW8 . . . . 3A **82**
Abercorn Way SE1 . . . . 5G **103**
Abercrombie Dr. EN1: Enf 1B **24**
Abercrombie St. SW11 . . . . 2C **118**
Aberdale Ct. *SE16* *2K* ***103***
(off Garter Way)
Aberdare Cl. BR4: W W'ck 2E **170**
Aberdare Gdns. NW6 . . . . 7K **63**
NW7 . . . . 7A **30**
Aberdare Rd. EN3: Pond E 4D **24**
Aberdeen Cotts. HA7: Stan 7H **27**
Aberdeen Ct. *W9* *4A* ***4***
(off Maida Va.)
Aberdeen La. N5 . . . . 5C **66**
Aberdeen Mans. *WC1* *3E* ***6***
(off Kenton St.)
Aberdeen Pde. *N18* *5C* ***34***
(off Aberdeen Rd.)
N18 . . . . *5C* ***34***
(off Montagu Rd.)
Aberdeen Pk. N5 . . . . 5C **66**
Aberdeen Pl. NW8 . . . . 4A **4** (4B **82**)
Aberdeen Rd. CR0: Croy 4C **168**
HA3: W'stone 2K **41**
N5 . . . . 4C **66**
N18 . . . . 5B **34**
(not continuous)
NW10 . . . . 5B **62**
Aberdeen Sq. E14 . . . . 1B **104**
Aberdeen Ter. SE3 . . . . 2F **123**
Aberdeen Wharf *E1* *1H* ***103***
(off Wapping High St.)
Aberdour Rd. IG3: Ilf 3B **72**
Aberdour St. SE1 . . . . 4E **102**
Aberfeldy Ho. SE5 . . . . 7B **102**
(not continuous)
Aberfeldy St. E14 . . . . 5E **86**
(not continuous)
Aberford Gdns. SE18 . . . . 1C **124**
Aberfoyle Rd. SW16 . . . . 6H **137**
(not continuous)
Abergeldie Rd. SE12 . . . . 6K **123**
Abernethy Rd. SE13 . . . . 4G **123**
Abersham Rd. E8 . . . . 5F **67**
Abery St. SE18 . . . . 4J **107**
Ability Towers *EC1* *1C* ***8***
(off Macclesfield Rd.)
Abingdon *W14* *4H* ***99***
(off Kensington Village)
Abingdon Cl. NW1 . . . . 6H **65**
SE1 . . . . *4F* ***103***
(off Bushwood Dr.)
SW19 . . . . 6A **136**
UB10: Hil 1B **74**
Abingdon Ct. *W8* *3J* ***99***
(off Abingdon Vs.)
Abingdon Gdns. W8 . . . . 3J **99**
Abingdon Ho. BR1: Brom 7K **141**
E2 . . . . *3J* ***9***
(off Boundary St.)
Abingdon Lodge *BR2: Brom* *2H* ***159***
(off Beckenham La.)
W8 . . . . 3J **99**
Abingdon Mans. *W8* *3J* ***99***
(off Pater St.)
Abingdon Rd. N3 . . . . 2A **46**
SW16 . . . . 2J **155**
W8 . . . . 3J **99**
Abingdon St. SW1 . . . . . . 1E **18** (3J **101**)
Abingdon Vs. W8 . . . . 3J **99**
Abinger Cl. BR1: Brom 3C **160**
CR0: New Ad 6E **170**
IG11: Bark 4A **72**
SM6: Wall 5J **167**
Abinger Ct. *SM6: Wall* *5J* ***167***
(off Abinger Cl.)
W5 . . . . 7C **78**
Abinger Gdns. TW7: Isle 3J **113**
Abinger Gro. SE8 . . . . 6B **104**
Abinger Ho. *SE1* *7E* ***14***
(off Gt. Dover St.)
Abinger M. W9 . . . . 4J **81**
Abinger Rd. W4 . . . . 3A **98**
Ablett St. SE16 . . . . 5J **103**
Abney Gdns. N16 . . . . 2F **67**

Abney Pk. Ter. *N16* 2F 67
(off Cazenov Rd.)
Aborfield NW5 5G 65
Aboyne Dr. SW20 2C 152
Aboyne Rd. NW10 3A 62
SW17 3B 136
Abraham Fisher Ho. E12 5E 70
Abridge Way IG11: Bark 2B 90
Abyssinia Cl. SW11 4C 118
Abyssinia Ct. N8 5K 47
Abyssinia Rd. SW11 4C 118
Acacia Av. HA4: Ruis 1J 57
HA9: Wemb 5E 60
N17 7J 33
TW8: Bford 7B 96
TW17: Shep 5C 146
UB3: Hayes 6H 75
UB7: Yiew 7B 74
Acacia Bus. Cen. E11 3G 69
Acacia Cl. BR5: Pet W 5H 161
HA7: Stan 6D 26
SE8 4A 104
SE20 2G 157
Acacia Ct. HA1: Harr 5F 41
Acacia Dr. SM3: Sutt 1H 165
Acacia Gdns. BR4: W W'ck 2E 170
NW8 2B 82
Acacia Gro. KT3: N Mald 3K 151
SE21 2D 138
Acacia Ho. *N22* 1A 48
(off Douglas Rd.)
Acacia M. UB7: Harm 6A 92
Acacia Pl. NW8 2B 82
Acacia Rd. BR3: Beck 3B 158
CR4: Mitc 2E 154
E11 2G 69
E17 6A 50
EN2: Enf 1J 23
N22 1A 48
NW8 2B 82
SW16 1J 155
TW12: Hamp 6E 130
W3 7J 79
Acacias, The EN4: E Barn 5G 21
Acacia Wlk. *SW10* 7A 100
(off Tadema Rd.)
Acacia Way DA15: Sidc 1K 143
Academy Apartments *E8* 5H 67
(off Dalston La.)
E8 5H 67
(off Institute Pl.)
Academy Bldgs. *N1* 1G 9
(off Fanshaw St.)
Academy Ct. *E2* 3J 85
(off Kirkwall Pl.)
Academy Gdns. CR0: Croy 1F 169
UB5: N'olt 2B 76
W8 2J 99
Academy Ho. *E3* 5D 86
(off Violet Rd.)
Academy Pl. SE18 1D 124
Academy Rd. SE18 1D 124
Acanthus Dr. SE1 5G 103
Acanthus Rd. SW11 3E 118
Accommodation Rd. KT17: Ewe 5C 164
NW11 1H 63
AC Court KT7: T Ditt 6A 150
Ace Pde. KT9: Chess 3E 162
Acer Av. UB4: Yead 5C 76
Acers BR7: Chst 7C 142
Acfold Rd. SW6 1K 117
Achilles Cl. SE1 5G 103
Achilles Ho. *E2* 2H 85
(off Old Bethnal Grn. Rd.)
Achilles Rd. NW6 5J 63
Achilles Statue 5H 11 (1E 100)
Achilles St. SE14 7A 104
Achilles Way W1 5H 11 (1E 100)
Acklam Rd. W10 5G 81
(not continuous)
Acklington Dr. NW9 1A 44
Ackmar Rd. SW6 1J 117
Ackroyd Dr. E3 5B 86
Ackroyd Rd. SE23 7K 121
Acland Cl. SE18 7H 107
Acland Cres. SE5 3D 120
Acland Ho. SW9 1K 119
Acland Rd. NW2 6D 62
Acle Cl. IG6: Ilf 1F 53
Acme Ho. E14 5E 86
Acock Gro. UB5: N'olt 4F 59
Acol Ct. NW6 7J 63
Acol Cres. HA4: Ruis 5K 57
Acol Rd. NW6 7J 63
Aconbury Rd. RM9: Dag 1B 90
Acorn Cl. BR7: Chst 5G 143
E4 5J 35
EN2: Enf 1G 23
HA7: Stan 7G 27
TW12: Hamp 6F 131
Acorn Ct. E6 7C 70
IG2: Ilf 6J 53
Acorn Gdns. SE19 1F 157
W3 5K 79
Acorn Gro. HA4: Ruis 4H 57
UB3: Harl 7H 93
Acorn Pde. SE15 7H 103
Acorn Production Cen. N7 7J 65
Acorn Wlk. SE16 1A 104
Acorn Way BR3: Beck 5E 158
BR6: Farnb 4F 173
SE23 3K 139
Acqua Ho. TW9: Kew 7H 97
Acre Dr. SE22 4G 121
Acrefield Ho. *NW4* 4F 45
(off Belle Vue Est.)
Acre La. SM5: Cars 4E 166
SM6: Wall 4F 167
SW2 4J 119
Acre Path *UB5: N'olt* 6C 58
(off Arnold Rd.)
Acre Rd. KT2: King T 1E 150
RM10: Dag 7H 73
SW19 6B 136
Acre Way HA6: Nwood 1H 39
Acris St. SW18 5A 118
Acropolis Ho. *KT1: King T* 3F 151
(off Winery La.)
ACTON 1J 97
Acton Central Ind. Est. W3 1H 97
Acton Cl. N9 2B 34
ACTON GREEN 3J 97
Acton Hill M. W3 1H 97
Acton Ho. *E8* 1F 85
(off Lee St.)
W3 6J 79
Acton La. NW10 3J 79
W3 2J 97
Acton M. E8 1F 85
Acton Pk. Est. W3 2K 97
Acton Pk. Royal Vue 4G 79
Acton Sports Club 4G 97
Acton St. WC1 2G 7 (3K 83)
Acton Swimming Baths 1J 97
Acton Va. Ind. Pk. W3 2B 98
Acuba Rd. SW18 2K 135
Acworth Cl. N9 7D 24
Acworth Ho. *SE18* 6F 107
(off Barnfield Rd.)
Ada Cl. N11 3J 31
Ada Ct. *N1* 1C 84
(off Packington St.)
W9 2A 4 (3A 82)
Ada Gdns. E14 6F 87
E15 1H 87
Ada Ho. *E2* 1G 85
(off Ada Pl.)
Adair Cl. SE25 3H 157
Adair Ho. *SW3* 6C 100
(off Oakley St.)
Adair Rd. W10 4G 81
Adair Twr. *W10* 4G 81
(off Appleford Rd.)
Ada Kennedy Ct. *SE10* 7E 104
(off Greenwich Sth. St.)
Ada Lewis Ho. HA9: Wemb 4F 61
Adam & Eve Ct. W1 7B 6
Adam & Eve M. W8 3J 99
Adam Cl. SE6 4B 140
Adam Ct. SE11 4K 19
SW7 4A 100
(off Gloucester Rd.)
Adam Rd. E4 6G 35
Adams Bri. Bus. Cen.
HA9: Wemb 5H 61
Adams Cl. KT5: Surb 6F 151
N3 7D 30
NW9 2H 61
Adams Ct. E17 6A 50
EC2 7F 9 (6E 84)
Adams End TW8: Bford 7C 96
Adams Gdns. Est. SE16 2J 103
Adams Ho. *E14* 6F 87
(off Aberfeldy St.)
Adams M. N22 7E 32
SW17 2D 136
Adamson Ct. N2 3C 46
Adamson Rd. E16 6J 87
NW3 7B 64
Adamson Way BR3: Beck 5E 158
Adams Pl. *E14* 1D 104
(off The Nth. Colonnade)
N7 5K 65
Adamsrill Cl. EN1: Enf 6J 23
Adamsrill Rd. SE26 4K 139
Adams Rd. BR3: Beck 5A 158
N17 2D 48
Adam's Row W1 3H 11 (7E 82)
Adams Sq. DA6: Bex 3E 126
Adam St. WC2 3F 13 (7J 83)
Adams Wlk. KT1: King T 2E 150
Adams Way CR0: Croy 6F 157
SE25 5H 157
Adam Wlk. SW6 7E 98
Ada Pl. E2 1G 85
Adare Wlk. SW16 3K 137
Ada Rd. HA0: Wemb 3D 60
SE5 7E 102
Adastral Ho. *WC1* 5G 7
(off New Nth. St.)
Ada St. E8 1H 85
Ada Workshops E8 1H 85
Adcock Wlk. BR6: Orp 4K 173
Adderley Gdns. SE9 4E 142
Adderley Gro. SW11 5E 118
Adderley Rd. HA3: W'stone 1K 41
Adderley St. E14 6E 86
Addey Ho. SE8 7B 104
ADDINGTON 5C 170
Addington Ct. SW14 3K 115
Addington Dr. N12 6G 31
Addington Gro. SE26 4A 140
Addington Ho. *SW9* 2K 119
(off Stockwell Rd.)
Addington Rd. BR4: W W'ck 4E 170
CR0: Croy 1A 168
CR2: Sand, Sels 7K 169
E3 3C 86
E16 4G 87
N4 6A 48
Addington Sq. SE5 6D 102
(not continuous)
Addington St. SE1 7H 13 (2K 101)
Addington Village Rd. CR0: Addtn 6B 170
(not continuous)
Addis Cl. EN3: Enf H 1E 24
ADDISCOMBE 1G 169
Addiscombe Av. CR0: Croy 1G 169
Addiscombe Cl. HA3: Kent 5C 42
Addiscombe Ct. Rd. CR0: Croy 1E 168
Addiscombe Gro. CR0: Croy 2E 168
Addiscombe Rd. CR0: Croy 2E 168
Addis Ho. *E1* 5J 85
(off Lindley St.)
Addisland Ct. *W14* 2G 99
(off Holland Vs. Rd.)
Addison Av. N14 6A 22
TW3: Houn 1G 113
W11 1G 99
Addison Bri. Pl. W14 4H 99
Addison Cl. BR5: Pet W 6G 161
HA6: Nwood 1J 39
Addison Ct. *NW6* 1J 81
(off Brondesbury Rd.)
Addison Cres. W14 3G 99
(not continuous)
Addison Dr. SE12 5K 123
Addison Gdns. KT5: Surb 4F 151
W14 3F 99
Addison Gro. W4 3A 98
Addison Ho. NW8 1A 4
Addison Pk. Mans. *W14* 3F 99
(off Richmond Way)
Addison Pl. SE25 4G 157
UB1: S'hall 7E 76
W11 1G 99
Addison Rd. BR2: Brom 5A 160
E11 6J 51
E17 5D 50
EN3: Enf H 1D 24
IG6: Ilf 1G 53
SE25 4G 157
TW11: Tedd 6B 132
W14 2G 99
Addisons Cl. CR0: Croy 2B 170
Addison Ter. *W4* 4J 97
(off Chiswick Rd.)
Addison Way HA6: Nwood 1H 39
NW11 4H 45
UB3: Hayes 6J 75
Addle Hill EC4 1B 14 (6B 84)
Addlestone Ho. *W10* 5E 80
(off Sutton Way)
Addle St. EC2 7D 8 (6C 84)
Addy Ho. SE16 4J 103
Adecroft Way KT8: W Mole 3G 149
Adela Av. KT3: N Mald 5D 152
Adela Ho. *W6* 5E 98
(off Queen Caroline St.)
Adelaide Av. SE4 4B 122
Adelaide Cl. EN1: Enf 1K 23
HA7: Stan 4F 27
SW9 4A 120
Adelaide Ct. BR3: Beck 7B 140
NW8 2A 82
(off Abbey Rd.)
W7 2K 95
Adelaide Gdns. RM6: Chad H 5E 54
Adelaide Gro. W12 1C 98
Adelaide Ho. E15 2H 87
E17 2B 50
SE5 2E 120
W11 6H 81
(off Portobello Rd.)
Adelaide Rd. BR7: Chst 5F 143
E10 3D 68
IG1: Ilf 2F 71
KT6: Surb 5E 150
NW3 7B 64
SW18 5J 117
TW5: Hest 1C 112
TW9: Rich 4F 115
TW11: Tedd 6K 131
TW15: Ashf 5A 128
UB2: S'hall 4C 94
W13 1A 96
Adelaide St. WC2 3E 12 (7J 83)
Adelaide Ter. TW8: Bford 5D 96
Adela St. W10 4G 81
Adelina Gro. E1 5J 85
Adelina M. SW12 1H 137
Adelina Yd. *E1* 5J 85
(off Adelina Gro.)
Adeline Pl. WC1 6D 6 (5H 83)
Adeliza Cl. IG11: Bark 7G 71
Adelphi Ct. *E8* 7F 67
(off Celandine Dr.)
SE16 2K 103
(off Garter Way)
W4 6K 97
Adelphi Cres. UB4: Hayes 3G 75
Adelphi Ter. WC2 3F 13 (7J 83)

Adelphi Theatre *3F 13*
(off Strand)
Adelphi Way UB4: Hayes 3H 75
Adeney Cl. W6 . . . . .6F 99
Aden Gro. N16 . . . . .4D 66
Aden Ho. *E1* *5K 85*
(off Duckett St.)
Ademmore Rd. SE6 . . . . .7C 122
Aden Rd. EN3: Brim 4F 25
IG1: Ilf 7G 53
Aden Ter. N16 . . . . .4D 66
Adeyfield Ho. *EC1* *2F 9*
(off Cranwood St.)
Adie Rd. W6 . . . . .3E 98
Adine Rd. E13 . . . . .4K 87
Adler Ind. Est. UB3: Hayes 2F 93
Adler St. E1 . . . . .6G 85
Adley St. E5 . . . . .5A 68
Adlington Cl. N18 . . . . .5J 33
Admaston Rd. SE18 . . . . .7G 107
Admiral Cl. IG11: Bark 2B 90
SM5: Cars 1C 166
SW10 . . . .*1A 118*
(off Admiral Sq.)
W1 . . . .*6G 5*
(off Blandford St.)
Admiral Ho. *SW1* *3B 18*
(off Willow Pl.)
TW11: Tedd 4A 132
Admiral Hyson Ind. Est.
SE16 . . . . .5H 103
Admiral M. W10 . . . . .4F 81
Admiral Pl. SE16 . . . . .1A 104
Admirals Cl. E10 . . . . .4K 51
Admirals Ct. *E6* *6F 89*
(off Trader Rd.)
SE1 . . . .*5J 15*
(off Horselydown La.)
Admiral Seymour Rd. SE9 . . . . . . .4D 124
Admiral's Ga. SE10 . . . . .1D 122
Admiral Sq. SW10 . . . . .1A 118
Admiral St. SE8 . . . . .2C 122
Admirals Wlk. NW3 . . . . .3A 64
Admirals Way E14 . . . . .2C 104
Admiralty Arch 4D 12 (1H 101)
Admiralty Cl. SE8 . . . . .7C 104
UB7: W Dray 2A 92
Admiralty Rd. TW11: Tedd 6K 131
Admiralty Way TW11: Tedd 6K 131
Admiral Wlk. W9 . . . . .5J 81
Adolf St. SE6 . . . . .4D 140
Adolphus Rd. N4 . . . . .2B 66
Adolphus St. SE8 . . . . .7B 104
Adomar Rd. RM8: Dag 3D 72
Adpar St. W2 . . . . .5A 4 (5B 82)
Adrian Av. NW2 . . . . .1D 62
Adrian Boult Ho. *E2* *3H 85*
(off Mansford St.)
Adrian Cl. EN5: Barn 6A 20
Adrian Ho. *N1* *1K 83*
(off Barnsbury Est.)
SW8 . . . .*7J 101*
(off Wyvil Rd.)
Adrian M. SW10 . . . . .6K 99
Adriatic Bldg. *E14* *7A 86*
(off Horseferry Rd.)
Adriatic Ho. *E1* *4K 85*
(off Ernest St.)
Adrienne Av. UB1: S'hall 4D 76
Adron Ho. *SE16* *4J 103*
(off Millender Wlk.)
Adstock Ho. *N1* *7B 66*
(off The Sutton Est.)
Advance Rd. SE27 . . . . .4C 138
Adventurers Ct. *E14* *7F 87*
(off Newport Av.)
Advent Way N18 . . . . .5D 34
Adys Lawn NW2 . . . . .6D 62
Ady's Rd. SE15 . . . . .3F 121
Aegean Apartments *E16* *7J 87*
(off Western Gateway)
Aegon Ho. *E14* *3D 104*
(off Lanark Sq.)

Aerodrome Rd. NW4 . . . . .2B 44
NW9 . . . . .2B 44
Aerodrome Way TW5: Hest 6A 94
Aeroville NW9 . . . . .2A 44
Affleck St. N1 . . . . .1G 7 (2K 83)
Afghan Rd. SW11 . . . . .2C 118
Afsil Ho. *EC1* *6K 7*
(off Viaduct Bldgs.)
Aftab Ter. *E1* *4H 85*
(off Tent St.)
Agamemnon Rd. NW6 . . . . .4H 63
Agar Cl. KT6: Surb 2F 163
Agar Gro. NW1 . . . . .7G 65
Agar Gro. Est. NW1 . . . . .7H 65
Agar Ho. *KT1: King T* *3E 150*
(off Denmark Rd.)
Agar Pl. NW1 . . . . .7G 65
Agar St. WC2 . . . . .3E 12 (7J 83)
Agate Cl. E16 . . . . .6B 88
Agate Rd. W6 . . . . .3E 98
Agatha Cl. E1 . . . . .1H 103
Agaton Rd. SE9 . . . . .2G 143
Agave Rd. NW2 . . . . .4E 62
Agdon St. EC1 . . . . .3A 8 (4B 84)
Agincourt Rd. NW3 . . . . .4D 64
Agnes Av. IG1: Ilf 4E 70
Agnes Cl. E6 . . . . .7E 88
Agnesfield Cl. N12 . . . . .6H 31
Agnes Gdns. RM8: Dag 4D 72
Agnes Ho. W11 . . . .*7F 81*
(off St Ann's Rd.)
Agnes Rd. W3 . . . . .1B 98
Agnes St. E14 . . . . .6B 86
Agnew Rd. SE23 . . . . .7K 121
Agricola Pl. EN1: Enf 5A 24
Aidan Cl. RM8: Dag 4E 72
Aigburth Mans. *SW9* *7A 102*
(off Mowll St.)
Aileen Wlk. E15 . . . . .7H 69
Ailsa Av. TW1: Twick 5A 114
Ailsa Ho. *E16* *7E 88*
(off University Way)
Ailsa Rd. TW1: Twick 5B 114
Ailsa St. E14 . . . . .5E 86
Ailsa Wlk. *E14* *2C 104*
(off Cassilis Rd.)
Ainger M. *NW3* *7D 64*
(off Ainger Rd., not continuous)
Ainger Rd. NW3 . . . . .7D 64
Ainsdale NW1 . . . .*1A 6*
(off Harrington St.)
Ainsdale Cl. BR6: Orp 1H 173
Ainsdale Cres. HA5: Pinn 3E 40
Ainsdale Dr. SE1 . . . . .5G 103
Ainsdale Rd. W5 . . . . .4D 78
Ainsley Av. RM7: Rom 6H 55
Ainsley Cl. N9 . . . . .1K 33
Ainsley St. E2 . . . . .3H 85
Ainslie Rd. HA0: Wemb 2E 78
Ainslie Wlk. SW12 . . . . .7F 119
Ainslie Wood Cres. E4 . . . . .5J 35
Ainslie Wood Gdns. E4 . . . . .4J 35
Ainslie Wood Nature Reserve 5J 35
Ainslie Wood Rd. E4 . . . . .5H 35
Ainsty St. SE16 . . . . .2K 103
Ainsty St. SE16 . . . . .2J 103
Ainsworth Cl. NW2 . . . . .3C 62
SE15 . . . . .2E 120
Ainsworth Ho. *NW8* *1K 81*
(off Ainsworth Way)
W10 . . . .*3G 81*
(off Kilburn La.)
Ainsworth Rd.
CR0: Croy 1B 168
E9 . . . . .7J 67
Ainsworth Way NW8 . . . . .1A 82
Aintree Av. E6 . . . . .1C 88
Aintree Cl. UB8: Hil 6D 74
Aintree Cres. IG6: Ilf 2G 53
Aintree Est. SW6 . . . . .7G 99
(off Aintree St.)
Aintree Rd. UB6: G'frd 2B 78
Aintree St. SW6 . . . . .7G 99

Airbourne Ho. *SM6: Wall* *4G 167*
(off Maldon Rd.)
Air Call Bus. Cen. NW9 . . . . .3K 43
Aird Ho. *SE1* *3C 102*
(off Rockingham St.)
Airdrie Cl. N1 . . . . .7K 65
UB4: Yead 5C 76
Airedale Av. W4 . . . . .4B 98
Airedale Av. Sth. W4 . . . . .5B 98
Airedale Rd. SW12 . . . . .7D 118
W5 . . . . .3C 96
Airlie Gdns. IG1: Ilf 1F 71
W8 . . . . .1J 99
Air Links Ind. Est.
TW13: Hanw 3C 130
Airlinks Ind. Est. TW5: Cran 5A 94
Air Pk. Way TW13: Felt 2K 129
Airport Bowl 1G 111
Airport Ga. UB7: Sip 7B 92
Air St. W1 . . . . .3B 12 (7G 83)
Airthrie Rd. IG3: Ilf 2B 72
Aisgill Av. W14 . . . . .5H 99
(not continuous)
Aisher Rd. SE28 . . . . .7C 90
Aislibie Rd. SE12 . . . . .4G 123
Aiten Pl. W6 . . . . .4C 98
Aithan Ho. *E14* *6B 86*
(off Copenhagen Pl.)
Aitken Cl. CR4: Mitc 7D 154
E8 . . . . .1G 85
Aitken Rd. SE6 . . . . .2D 140
Aits Vw. KT8: W Mole 3F 149
Ajax Av. NW9 . . . . .3A 44
Ajax Ho. *E2* *2H 85*
(off Old Bethnal Grn. Rd.)
Ajax Rd. NW6 . . . . .4H 63
Akabusi Cl. CR0: Croy 6G 157
Akbar Ho. *E14* *4D 104*
(off Cahir St.)
Akehurst St. SW15 . . . . .6C 116
Akenside Rd. NW3 . . . . .5B 64
Akerman Rd. KT6: Surb 6C 150
SW9 . . . . .2B 120
Akintaro Ho. *SE8* *6B 104*
(off Alverton St.)
Alabama St. SE18 . . . . .7H 107
Alacross Rd. W5 . . . . .2C 96
Alamaro Lodge SE10 . . . . .3H 105
Alandale Dr. HA5: Pinn 1K 39
Aland Cl. SE16 . . . . .3A 104
Alander M. E17 . . . . .4E 50
Alan Dr. EN5: Barn 6B 20
Alan Gdns. RM7: Rush G 7G 55
Alan Hocken Way E15 . . . . .2G 87
Alan Preece Cl. NW6 . . . . .7F 63
Alan Rd. SW19 . . . . .5G 135
Alanthus Cl. SE12 . . . . .6J 123
Alaska Bldg. *SE8* *1D 122*
(off Deal's Gateway)
Alaska Bldgs. SE1 . . . . .4E 102
Alaska St. SE1 . . . . . . .5J 13 (1A 102)
Alastor Ho. *E14* *3E 104*
(off Strattondale Ho.)
Alba Cl. UB4: Yead 4B 76
Albacore Cres. SE13 . . . . .6D 122
Alba Gdns. NW11 . . . . .6G 45
Albain Cres. TW15: Ashf 2A 128
Alba M. SW18 . . . . .2J 135
Alban Highwalk EC2 . . . . .7D 8
(not continuous)
Albany N12 . . . . .6E 30
W1 . . . . .3A 12 (7G 83)
Albany, The IG8: Wfd G 4C 36
Albany Cl. DA5: Bexl 7C 126
N15 . . . . .4B 48
SW14 . . . . .4H 115
UB10: Ick 5C 56
Albany Ct. E4 . . . . .5G 35
E4: Pond E 6H 25
E10 . . . . .7C 50
HA8: Edg 1K 43
NW8 . . . .*1A 4*
(off Abbey Rd.)

Albany Ct. *NW10* *3D 80*
(off Trenmar Gdns.)
TW15: Ashf 7E 128
Albany Courtyard W1 . . . .3B 12 (7G 83)
Albany Cres. HA8: Edg 7B 28
Albany Mans. SW11 . . . . .7C 100
Albany M. BR1: Brom 6J 141
KT2: King T 6D 132
N1 . . . . .7A 66
SE5 . . . . .6C 102
SM1: Sutt 5K 165
Albany Pde. TW8: Bford 6E 96
Albany Pk. Av. EN3: Enf W 1D 24
Albany Pk. Rd. KT2: King T 6D 132
Albany Pas. TW10: Rich 5E 114
TW8: Bford 6D 96
Albany Reach KT7: T Ditt 5K 149
Albany Rd. BR7: Chst 5F 143
DA5: Bexl 7C 126
DA17: Belv 6F 109
E10 . . . . .7C 50
E12 . . . . .4B 70
E17 . . . . .6A 50
KT3: N Mald 4K 151
N4 . . . . .6A 48
N18 . . . . .5D 34
RM6: Chad H 6F 55
SE5 . . . . .6D 102
SW9 . . . . .5K 135
SW19 . . . . .6D 96
TW8: Bford 6D 96
TW10: Rich 5F 115
W13 . . . . .7B 78
NW11 . . . . .1K 5 (2F 83)
Albany Ter. NW1 . . . . .4K 5
TW10: Rich 5F 115
(off Albany Pas.)
Albany Vw. IG9: Buck H 1D 36
Alba Pl. W11 . . . . .6H 81
Albatross NW9 . . . . .2B 44
Albatross Cl. E6 . . . . .5D 88
Albatross St. SE18 . . . . .7J 107
Albatross Way SE16 . . . . .2K 103
Albemarle SW19 . . . . .2F 135
Albemarle App. IG2: Ilf 6F 53
Albemarle Av. TW2: Whit 1D 130
Albemarle Gdns. IG2: Ilf 6F 53
KT3: N Mald 4K 151
Albemarle Ho. *SE8* *4B 104*
(off Foreshore)
SW9 . . . . .3A 120
Albemarle Pk. BR3: Beck 1D 158
HA7: Stan 5H 27
Albemarle Rd. BR3: Beck 1D 158
EN4: E Barn 7H 21
Albemarle St. W1 . . . . . .3K 11 (7F 83)
Albemarle Way EC1 . . . . .4A 8 (4B 84)
Alberon Gdns. NW11 . . . . .4H 45
Alberta Av. SM1: Sutt 4G 165
Alberta Est. SE17 . . . . .5B 102
(off Alberta St.)
Alberta Ho. *E14* *1E 104*
(off Gaselee St.)
Alberta Rd. DA8: Erith 1J 127
EN1: Enf 6A 24
Alberta St. SE17 . . . . .5B 102
Albert Av. E4 . . . . .4H 35
SW8 . . . . .7K 101
Albert Barnes Ho. *SE1* *3C 102*
(off New Kent Rd.)
Albert Basin Way E16 . . . . .7G 89
Albert Bigg Point *E15* *2E 86*
(off Godfrey St.)
Albert Bri. SW3 . . . . .7D 16 (7C 100)
Albert Bri. Rd. SW11 . . . . .7C 100
Albert Carr Gdns.
SW16 . . . . .5J 137
Albert Cl. E9 . . . . .1H 85
N22 . . . . .1H 47
Albert Cotts. *E1* *5G 85*
(off Deal St.)
Albert Ct. E7 . . . . .4J 69
SW7 . . . . .7A 10 (3B 100)

Albert Ct. Ga.—Aldwych Ct.

Albert Ct. Ga. SW1 ... 7E 10
(off Knightsbridge)
Albert Cres. E4 ... 4H 35
Albert Dane Cen.
UB2: S'hall ... 3C 94
Albert Dr. SW19 ... 2G 135
Albert Emb. SE1 ... 1G 19 (3K 101)
(Lambeth Pal. Rd.)
SE1 ... 6F 19 (5J 101)
(Vauxhall Bri.)
Albert Gdns. E1 ... 6K 85
Albert Ga. SW1 ... 6F 11 (2D 100)
Albert Gray Ho. SW10 ... 7B 100
(off Worlds End Est.)
Albert Gro. SW20 ... 1F 153
Albert Hall Mans. SW7 ... 7A 10 (2B 100)
(not continuous)
Albert Ho. E18 ... 3K 51
(off Albert Rd.)
SE18 ... 3G 107
Albert Mans. CR0: Croy ... 1D 168
(off Lansdowne Rd.)
Albert Memorial ... 7A 10 (2B 100)
Albert M. E14 ... 7A 86
(off Northey St.)
N4 ... 1K 65
SE4 ... 4A 122
W8 ... 3A 100
Albert Pal. Mans. SW11 ... 1F 119
(off Lurline Gdns.)
Albert Pl. N3 ... 1J 45
N17 ... 3F 49
W8 ... 3K 99
Albert Rd. BR2: Brom ... 5B 160
CR4: Mitc ... 3D 154
DA5: Bexl ... 6G 127
DA17: Belv ... 5F 109
E10 ... 2E 68
E16 ... 1C 106
E17 ... 5C 50
E18 ... 3K 51
EN4: E Barn ... 4F 21
HA2: Harr ... 3G 41
IG1: Ilf ... 3F 71
IG9: Buck H ... 2G 37
KT1: King T ... 2F 151
KT3: N Mald ... 4B 152
N4 ... 1K 65
N15 ... 6E 48
N22 ... 1G 47
NW4 ... 4F 45
NW6 ... 2H 81
NW7 ... 5G 29
RM8: Dag ... 1G 73
SE9 ... 3C 142
SE20 ... 6K 139
SE25 ... 4G 157
SM1: Sutt ... 5B 166
TW1: Twick ... 1K 131
TW3: Houn ... 4E 112
TW10: Rich ... 5E 114
TW11: Tedd ... 6K 131
TW12: Ham H ... 5G 131
TW15: Ashf ... 5B 128
UB2: S'hall ... 3B 94
UB3: Hayes ... 3G 93
UB7: Yiew ... 1A 92
W5 ... 4B 78
Albert Rd. Est. DA17: Belv ... 5F 109
Alberts Ct. NW1 ... 3D 4
Albert Sleet Ct. N9 ... 3C 34
(off Colthurst Dr.)
Albert Sq. E15 ... 5G 69
SW8 ... 7K 101
Albert Starr Ho. SE8 ... 4K 103
(off Bush Rd.)
Albert St. N12 ... 5F 31
NW1 ... 1F 83
Albert Studios SW11 ... 1D 118
Albert Ter. IG9: Buck H ... 2H 37
NW1 ... 1E 82
NW10 ... 1J 79
W5 ... 4B 78
Albert Ter. W6 ... 5C 98
(off Beavor La.)
Albert Ter. M. NW1 ... 1E 82
Albert Victoria Ho. N22 ... 1A 48
Albert Wlk. E16 ... 2E 106
Albert Way SE15 ... 7H 103
Albert Westcott Ho. SE17 ... 5B 102
Albert Whicher Ho. E17 ... 4E 50
Albert Yd. SE19 ... 6E 138
Albery Ct. E8 ... 7F 67
(off Middleton Rd.)
Albery Theatre ... 2E 12
(off St Martin's La.)
Albion Av. N10 ... 1E 46
SW8 ... 2H 119
Albion Bldgs. N1 ... 2J 83
(off Albion Yd.)
Albion Cl. RM7: Rom ... 6K 55
W2 ... 2D 10 (7C 82)
Albion Ct. SM2: Sutt ... 7B 166
W6 ... 4D 98
(off Albion Pl.)
Albion Dr. E8 ... 7F 67
Albion Est. SE16 ... 2K 103
Albion Gdns. W6 ... 4D 98
Albion Ga. W2 ... 2D 10
(not continuous)
Albion Gro. N16 ... 4E 66
Albion Ho. E16 ... 1F 107
(off Church St.)
SE8 ... 7C 104
(off Watsons St.)
Albion M. N1 ... 1A 84
NW6 ... 7H 63
W2 ... 2D 10 (7C 82)
W6 ... 4D 98
Albion Pde. N16 ... 4D 66
Albion Pl. EC1 ... 5A 8 (5B 84)
EC2 ... 6F 9 (5D 84)
SE25 ... 3G 157
W6 ... 4D 98
Albion Riverside Bldg. SW11 ... 7C 100
Albion Rd. DA6: Bex ... 4F 127
E17 ... 3E 50
KT2: King T ... 1J 151
N16 ... 4D 66
N17 ... 2G 49
SM2: Sutt ... 6B 166
TW2: Twick ... 1J 131
TW3: Houn ... 4E 112
UB3: Hayes ... 6G 75
Albion Sq. E8 ... 7F 67
(not continuous)
Albion St. CR0: Croy ... 1B 168
SE16 ... 2J 103
W2 ... 1D 10 (6C 82)
Albion Ter. E4 ... 4J 25
E8 ... 7F 67
Albion Vs. Rd. SE26 ... 3J 139
Albion Wlk. N1 ... 1F 7
(off York Way)
Albion Way EC1 ... 6C 8 (5C 84)
HA9: Wemb ... 3G 61
SE13 ... 4E 122
Albion Yd. E1 ... 5H 85
N1 ... 2J 83
Albon Ho. SW18 ... 6K 117
(off Neville Gill Cl.)
Albrighton Rd. SE22 ... 3E 120
Albuhera Cl. EN2: Enf ... 1F 23
Albury Av. DA7: Bex ... 2E 126
TW7: Isle ... 7K 95
Albury Cl. TW12: Hamp ... 6F 131
Albury Ct. CR2: S Croy ... 4C 168
(off Tanfield Rd.)
CR4: Mitc ... 2B 154
SM1: Sutt ... 4A 166
UB5: Yead ... 3A 76
(off Canberra Dr.)
Albury Dr. HA5: Pinn ... 1A 40 & 1C 40
Albury Ho. SE1 ... 7B 14
(off Boyfield St.)
Albury M. E12 ... 2A 70
Albury Rd. KT9: Chess ... 5E 162
Albury St. SE8 ... 6C 104
Albyfield BR1: Brom ... 4D 160
Albyn Rd. SE8 ... 1C 122
Alcester Ct. SM6: Wall ... 4F 167
Alcester Cres. E5 ... 2H 67
Alcester Rd. SM6: Wall ... 4F 167
Alcock Cl. SM6: Wall ... 7H 167
Alcock Rd. TW5: Hest ... 7B 94
Alconbury DA6: Bex ... 5H 127
Alconbury Rd. E5 ... 2G 67
Alcorn Cl. SM3: Sutt ... 2J 165
Alcott Cl. TW14: Felt ... 1H 129
W7 ... 5K 77
Alcuin Ct. HA7: Stan ... 7H 27
Aldam Pl. N16 ... 2F 67
Aldborough Ct. IG2: Ilf ... 5K 53
(off Aldborough Rd. Nth.)
ALDBOROUGH HATCH ... 4K 53
Aldborough Rd. RM10: Dag ... 6J 73
Aldborough Rd. Nth. IG2: Ilf ... 5K 53
Aldborough Rd. Sth. IG3: Ilf ... 1J 71
Aldbourne Rd. W12 ... 1B 98
(not continuous)
Aldbridge St. SE17 ... 5E 102
Aldburgh M. W1 ... 7H 5 (6E 82)
(not continuous)
Aldbury Av. HA9: Wemb ... 7H 61
Aldbury Ho. SW3 ... 5C 16
(off Marlborough St.)
Aldbury M. N9 ... 7J 23
Aldebert Ter. SW8 ... 7J 101
Aldeburgh Cl. E5 ... 2H 67
Aldeburgh Pl. IG8: Wfd G ... 4D 36
SE10 ... 4J 105
(off Aldeburgh St.)
Aldeburgh St. SE10 ... 5J 105
Alden Av. E15 ... 3H 87
Alden Ct. CR0: Croy ... 3E 168
Aldenham Dr. UB8: Hil ... 4D 74
Aldenham Ho. NW1 ... 1B 6
(off Aldenham St.)
Aldenham St. NW1 ... 1C 6 (2G 83)
Alden Ho. E8 ... 1H 85
(off Duncan Rd.)
Aldensley Rd. W6 ... 3D 98
Alderbrook Rd. SW12 ... 6F 119
Alderbury Rd. SW13 ... 6C 98
Alder Cl. SE15 ... 6F 103
Alder Gro. NW2 ... 2C 62
Aldergrove Gdns. TW3: Houn ... 2C 112
Alder Ho. NW3 ... 6D 64
SE4 ... 3C 122
SE15 ... 6F 103
(off Cator St.)
Alder Lodge SW6 ... 1E 116
Alderman Av. IG11: Bark ... 3A 90
Aldermanbury EC2 ... 7D 8 (6C 84)
Aldermanbury Sq. EC2 ... 6D 8 (5C 84)
Alderman Judge Mall KT1: King T ... 2E 150
(off Eden St.)
Aldermans Hill N13 ... 4D 32
Aldermans Wlk. EC2 ... 6G 9 (5E 84)
Aldermary Rd. BR1: Brom ... 1J 159
Alder M. N19 ... 2G 65
Aldermoor Rd. SE6 ... 3B 140
Alderney Av. TW5: Hest, Isle ... 7F 95
Alderney Gdns. UB5: N'olt ... 7D 58
Alderney Ho. EN3: Enf W ... 1E 24
N1 ... 6C 66
(off Arran Wlk.)
Alderney Rd. E1 ... 4K 85
Alderney St. SW1 ... 4K 17 (4F 101)
Alder Rd. DA14: Sidc ... 3K 143
SW14 ... 3K 115
Alders, The BR4: W W'ck ... 1D 170
N21 ... 6F 23
SW16 ... 4G 137
TW5: Hest ... 6D 94
TW13: Hanw ... 4C 130
Alders Av. IG8: Wfd G ... 6B 36
ALDERSBROOK ... 2K 69
Aldersbrook Av. EN1: Enf ... 2K 23
Aldersbrook Dr. KT2: King T ... 6F 133
Aldersbrook La. E12 ... 3D 70
Aldersbrook Rd. E11 ... 2K 69
E12 ... 2K 69
Alders Cl. E11 ... 2K 69
HA8: Edg ... 5D 28
W5 ... 3D 96
Aldersey Gdns. IG11: Bark ... 6H 71
Aldersford Cl. SE4 ... 5K 121
Aldersgate St. EC1 ... 5C 8 (5C 84)
Alders Gro. KT8: E Mos ... 5H 149
Aldersgrove Av. SE9 ... 3B 142
Aldershot Rd. NW6 ... 1H 81
Aldershot Ter. SE18 ... 7E 106
Aldersmead Av. CR0: Croy ... 6K 157
Aldersmead Rd. BR3: Beck ... 7A 140
Alderson Pl. UB2: S'hall ... 1G 95
Alderson St. W10 ... 4G 81
Alders Rd. HA8: Edg ... 5D 28
Alderton Cl. NW10 ... 3K 61
Alderton Ct. KT8: W Mole ... 4D 148
(off Walton Rd.)
Alderton Cres. NW4 ... 5D 44
Alderton Rd. CR0: Croy ... 7F 157
SE24 ... 3C 120
Alderton Way NW4 ... 5D 44
Alderville Rd. SW6 ... 2H 117
Alder Wlk. IG1: Ilf ... 5G 71
Alderwick Ct. N7 ... 6K 65
(off Cornelia St.)
Alderwick Dr. TW3: Houn ... 3H 113
Alderwood M. EN4: Had W ... 1F 21
Alderwood Rd. SE9 ... 6H 125
Aldford Ho. W1 ... 4G 11
(off Park St.)
Aldford St. W1 ... 4H 11 (1E 100)
ALDGATE ... 6F 85
Aldgate E1 ... 7J 9
(off Whitechapel High St.)
EC3 ... 1H 15 (6E 84)
Aldgate Av. E1 ... 7J 9 (6F 85)
Aldgate Barrs E1 ... 7K 9
Aldgate High St. EC3 ... 1J 15 (6F 85)
Aldgate Triangle E1 ... 6G 85
(off Coke St.)
Aldham Ho. SE14 ... 2B 122
(off Malpas Rd.)
Aldine Ct. W12 ... 2E 98
(off Aldine St.)
Aldine Pl. W12 ... 2E 98
Aldine St. W12 ... 2E 98
Aldington Cl. RM8: Dag ... 1C 72
Aldington Ct. E8 ... 7G 67
(off London Flds. W. Side)
Aldington Rd. SE18 ... 3B 106
Aldis M. SW17 ... 5C 136
Aldis St. SW17 ... 5C 136
Aldred Rd. NW6 ... 5J 63
Aldren Rd. SW17 ... 3A 136
Aldrich Cres. CR0: New Ad ... 7E 170
Aldriche Way E4 ... 6K 35
Aldrich Gdns. SM3: Cheam ... 3H 165
Aldrich Ter. SW18 ... 2A 136
Aldrick Ho. N1 ... 1K 83
(off Barnsbury Est.)
Aldridge Av. HA4: Ruis ... 5K 39
HA7: Stan ... 1E 42
HA8: Edg ... 3C 28
Aldridge Ct. W11 ... 5H 81
(off Aldridge Rd. Vs.)
Aldridge Ri. KT3: N Mald ... 7A 152
Aldridge Rd. Vs. W11 ... 5H 81
Aldridge Wlk. N14 ... 7D 22
Aldrington Rd. SW16 ... 5G 137
Aldsworth Cl. W9 ... 4K 81
Aldwick Cl. SE9 ... 3H 143
Aldwick Rd. CR0: Bedd ... 3K 167
Aldworth Gro. SE13 ... 6E 122
Aldworth Rd. E15 ... 7G 69
Aldwych WC2 ... 2G 13 (6K 83)
Aldwych Av. IG6: Ilf ... 4G 53
Aldwych Ct. E8 ... 7F 67
(off Middleton Rd.)

180 A-Z London

Aldwych Theatre 1G 13
  (off Aldwych)
Aldwyn Ho. SW8 . . . . .7J 101
  (off Davidson Gdns.)
Alers Rd. DA6: Bex 5D 126
Alesia Cl. N22 . . . . .7D 32
Alestan Beck Rd. E16 . . . . .6B 88
Alexa Ct. SM2: Sutt 6J 165
  W8 .4J 99
Alexander Av. NW10 . . . . .7D 62
Alexander Cl. BR2: Hayes 1J 171
  DA15: Sidc 5J 125
  EN4: E Barn 4G 21
  TW2: Twick 2J 131
  UB2: S'hall 1G 95
Alexander Ct. BR3: Beck 1F 159
  HA7: Stan 3F 43
Alexander Evans M. SE23 . . . . .2K 139
Alexander Fleming Laboratory Mus. . .7B 4
Alexander Ho. E14 . . . . .3C 104
  (off Tiller Rd.)
  KT2: King T 1E 150
  (off Seven Kings Way)
Alexander M. W2 . . . . .6K 81
Alexander Pl. SW7 . . . . . . .3C 16 (4C 100)
Alexander Rd. BR7: Chst 6F 143
  DA7: Bex 2D 126
  N19 . . . . .3J 65
Alexander Sq. SW3 . . . . . . .3C 16 (4C 100)
Alexander St. W2 . . . . .6J 81
Alexander Studios SW11 . . . . .4B 118
  (off Haydon Way)
Alexander Ter. SE2 . . . . .5B 108
Alexandra Av. HA2: Harr 1D 58
  N22 . . . . .1H 47
  SM1: Sutt 3J 165
  SW11 . . . . .1E 118
  UB1: S'hall 7D 76
  W4 .7K 97
Alexandra Cl. HA2: Harr 3E 58
  SE8 .6B 104
  TW15: Ashf 7F 129
Alexandra Cotts. SE14 . . . . .1B 122
Alexandra Ct. HA9: Wemb 4F 61
  N14 . . . . .5B 22
  SW7 . . . . .1A 16
  TW3: Houn 2F 113
  TW15: Ashf 6F 129
  UB6: G'frd 2F 77
  W2 .7K 81
  (off Moscow Rd.)
  W9 .4A 82
  (off Maida Va.)
Alexandra Cres. BR1: Brom 6H 141
Alexandra Dr. KT5: Surb 7G 151
  SE19 . . . . .5E 138
Alexandra Gdns. N10 . . . . .4F 47
  SM5: Cars 7E 166
  TW3: Houn 2F 113
  W4 .7A 98
Alexandra Gro. N4 . . . . .1B 66
  N12 . . . . .5E 30
Alexandra Ho. E16 . . . . .1K 105
  (off Wesley Av.)
  IG8: Ilf 7K 37
  W6 .5E 98
  (off Queen Caroline St.)
Alexandra Mans. SW3 . . . . .7A 16
  (off King's Rd.)
Alexandra M. N2 . . . . .3D 46
  SW19 . . . . .6H 135
Alexandra National Ho. N4 . . . . .1B 66
Alexandra Palace 2H 47
Alexandra Pal. Way N22 . . . . .4G 47
Alexandra Pde. HA2: Harr 4F 59
Alexandra Pk. Rd. N10 . . . . .2F 47
  N22 . . . . .1G 47
Alexandra Pl. CR0: Croy 1E 168
  NW8 . . . . .1A 82
  SE25 . . . . .5D 156
Alexandra Rd. CR0: Croy 1E 168
  CR4: Mitc 7C 136
  E6 .3E 88

Alexandra Rd. E10 . . . . .3E 68
  E17 . . . . .6B 50
  E18 . . . . .3K 51
  EN3: Pond E 4E 24
  KT2: King T 7G 133
  KT7: T Ditt 5K 149
  N8 .3A 48
  N9 .7C 24
  N10 . . . . .7A 32
  N15 . . . . .5D 48
  NW4 . . . . .4F 45
  NW8 . . . . .1A 82
  RM6: Chad H 6E 54
  SE26 . . . . .6K 139
  SW14 . . . . .3K 115
  SW19 . . . . .6H 135
  TW1: Twick 6C 114
  TW3: Houn 2F 113
  TW8: Bford 6D 96
  TW9: Kew 2F 115
  TW15: Ashf 7F 129
  W4 .2K 97
Alexandra Rd. Ind. Est.
  EN3: Pond E 4E 24
Alexandra Sq. SM4: Mord 5J 153
Alexandra St. E16 . . . . .5J 87
  SE14 . . . . .7A 104
Alexandra Ter. E14 . . . . .5D 104
  (off Westferry Rd.)
Alexandra Wlk. SE19 . . . . .5E 138
Alexandra Yd. E9 . . . . .1K 85
Alexandria Apartments SE17 . . . . . . .4E 102
  (off Townsend St.)
Alexandria Rd. W13 . . . . .7A 78
Alexis St. SE16 . . . . .4G 103
Alfan La. DA2: Dart 5K 145
Alfearn Rd. E5 . . . . .4J 67
Alford Cl. W4 . . . . .4K 97
Alfred Dickens Ho. E16 . . . . .6H 87
  (off Hallsville Rd.)
Alfred Finlay Ho. N22 . . . . .2B 48
Alfred Gdns. UB1: S'hall 7C 76
Alfred Ho. E9 . . . . .5A 68
  (off Homerton Rd.)
  E12 . . . . .7C 70
  (off Tennyson Av.)
Alfred M. W1 . . . . .5C 6 (5H 83)
Alfred Nunn Ho. NW10 . . . . .1B 80
Alfred Pl. WC1 . . . . .5C 6 (5H 83)
Alfred Prior Ho. E12 . . . . .4E 70
Alfred Rd. DA17: Belv 5F 109
  E15 . . . . .5H 69
  IG9: Buck H 2G 37
  KT1: King T 3E 150
  SE25 . . . . .5G 157
  SM1: Sutt 5A 166
  TW13: Felt 2A 130
  W2 .5J 81
  W3 .1J 97
Alfred's Gdns. IG11: Bark 2J 89
Alfred St. E3 . . . . .3B 86
Alfreds Way IG11: Bark 3F 89
Alfreds Way Ind. Est. IG11: Bark 1A 90
Alfred Vs. E17 . . . . .4E 50
Alfreton Cl. SW19 . . . . .3F 135
Alfriston Av. CR0: Croy 7J 155
  HA2: Harr 6E 40
Alfriston Cl. KT5: Surb 5F 151
Alfriston Rd. SW11 . . . . .5D 118
Algar Cl. HA7: Stan 5E 26
  TW7: Isle 3A 114
Algar Ho. SE1 . . . . .7A 14
Algar Rd. TW7: Isle 3A 114
Algarve Rd. SW18 . . . . .1K 135

Algernon Rd. NW4 . . . . .6C 44
  NW6 . . . . .1J 81
  SE13 . . . . .4D 122
Algiers Rd. SE13 . . . . .4C 122
Alibon Gdns. RM10: Dag 5G 73
Alibon Rd. RM9: Dag 5F 73
  RM10: Dag 5G 73
Alice Cl. EN5: New Bar 4F 21
  (off Station App.)
Alice Gilliatt Ct. W14 . . . . .6H 99
  (off Star Rd.)
Alice La. E3 . . . . .1B 86
Alice M. TW11: Tedd 5K 131
Alice Owen Technology Cen.
  EC1 . . . . .1A 8
  (off Goswell Rd.)
Alice Shepherd Ho. E14 . . . . .2E 104
  (off Manchester Rd.)
Alice St. SE1 . . . . .3E 102
  (not continuous)
Alice Thompson Cl. SE12 . . . . .2A 142
Alice Walker Cl. SE24 . . . . .4B 120
Alicia Av. HA3: Kent 4B 42
Alicia Cl. HA3: Kent 4C 42
Alicia Gdns. HA3: Kent 4B 42
Alicia Ho. DA16: Well 1B 126
Alie St. E1 . . . . .1K 15 (6F 85)
Alington Cres. NW9 . . . . .7J 43
Alington Gro. SM6: Wall 7G 167
Alison Cl. CR0: Croy 1K 169
  E6 .6E 88
Alison Ct. SE1 . . . . .5G 103
Aliwal M. SW11 . . . . .4C 118
Aliwal Rd. SW11 . . . . .4C 118
Alkerden Rd. W4 . . . . .5A 98
Alkham Rd. N16 . . . . .2F 67
Allan Barclay Cl. N15 . . . . .6F 49
Allan Cl. KT3: N Mald 5K 151
Allandale Av. N3 . . . . .3G 45
Allanson Ct. E10 . . . . .2C 68
  (off Leyton Grange Est.)
Allan Way W3 . . . . .5J 79
Allard Cres. WD23: Bushy 1B 26
Allard Gdns. SW4 . . . . .5H 119
Allardyce St. SW4 . . . . .4K 119
Allbrook Cl. TW11: Tedd 5J 131
Allcott Ho. W12 . . . . .7D 80
  (off Du Cane Rd.)
Allcroft Rd. NW5 . . . . .5E 64
Allder Way CR2: S Croy 7B 168
Allenby Cl. UB6: G'frd 3E 76
Allenby Rd. SE23 . . . . .3A 140
  SE28 . . . . .3G 107
  UB1: S'hall 3E 76
Allen Cl. CR4: Mitc 1F 155
  TW16: Sun 1K 147
Allen Ct. E17 . . . . .6C 50
  (off Yunus Khan Cl.)
  UB6: G'frd 5K 59
Allendale Av. UB1: S'hall 6E 76
Allendale Cl. SE5 . . . . .2D 120
  SE26 . . . . .5K 139
Allendale Rd. UB6: G'frd 6B 60
Allen Edwards Dr. SW8 . . . . .1J 119
Allenford Ho. SW15 . . . . .6B 116
  (off Tunworth Cres.)
Allen Ho. W8 . . . . .3J 99
Allenswood SW19 . . . . .1G 135
Allenswood Rd. SE9 . . . . .3C 124
Allerford Ct. HA2: Harr 5G 41
Allerford Rd. SE6 . . . . .3D 140

Allerton Ho. N1 . . . . .1E 8
  (off Fairbank Est.)
Allerton Rd. N16 . . . . .2C 66
Allerton St. N1 . . . . .1E 8 (3D 84)
Allerton Wlk. N7 . . . . .2K 65
Allestree Rd. SW6 . . . . .7G 99
Alleyn Cres. SE21 . . . . .2D 138
Alleyndale Rd. RM8: Dag 2C 72
Alleyn Ho. SE1 . . . . .3D 102
  (off Burbage Cl.)
Alleyn Pk. SE21 . . . . .2D 138
  UB2: S'hall 5E 94
Alleyn Rd. SE21 . . . . .3D 138
Allfarthing La. SW18 . . . . .6K 117
Allgood Cl. SM4: Mord 6F 153
Allgood St. E2 . . . . .1K 9 (2F 85)
Allhallows La. EC4 . . . . . . .3E 14 (7D 84)
All Hallows Rd. N17 . . . . .1E 48
Allhallows Rd. E6 . . . . .5C 88
Alliance Cl. HA0: Wemb 4D 60
Alliance Ct. TW15: Ashf 4E 128
  W3 .5H 79
Alliance Rd. E13 . . . . .5A 88
  SE18 . . . . .6A 108
  W3 .4H 79
Allied Ind. Est. W3 . . . . .2A 98
Allied Way W3 . . . . .2A 98
Allingham Cl. W7 . . . . .7K 77
Allingham M. N1 . . . . .2C 84
  (off Allingham St.)
Allingham St. N1 . . . . .2C 84
Allington Av. N17 . . . . .6K 33
  TW17: Shep 3G 147
Allington Cl. SW19 . . . . .5F 135
  UB6: G'frd 7G 59
Allington Ct. EN3: Pond E 5E 24
  (not continuous)
  SW1 . . . . .2K 17
  (off Allington St.)
  SW8 . . . . .2G 119
Allington Rd. BR6: Orp 2H 173
  HA2: Harr 5G 41
  NW4 . . . . .5D 44
  W10 . . . . .3G 81
Allington St. SW1 . . . . .2K 17 (3F 101)
Allison Cl. SE10 . . . . .1E 122
Allison Gro. SE21 . . . . .1E 138
Allison Rd. N8 . . . . .5A 48
  W3 .6J 79
Alliston Ho. E2 . . . . .2K 9
  (off Gibraltar Wlk.)
Allitsen Rd. NW8 . . . . .2C 82
All Nations Ho. E8 . . . . .7H 67
  (off Martello St.)
Allnutt Way SW4 . . . . .5H 119
Alloa Rd. IG3: Ilf 2A 72
  SE8 .5K 103
Allom Ho. W11 . . . . .7G 81
  (off Clarendon Rd.)
Allonby Dr. HA4: Ruis 7D 38
Allonby Gdns. HA9: Wemb 1C 60
Allonby Ho. E14 . . . . .5A 86
  (off Aston St.)
Alloway Rd. E3 . . . . .3A 86
Allport Ho. SE5 . . . . .3D 120
  (off Denmark Hill)
Allport M. E1 . . . . .4J 85
  (off Hayfield Pas.)
All Saints Cl. N9 . . . . .2B 34
  SW8 . . . . .1J 119
All Saints Ct. E1 . . . . .7J 85
  (off Johnson St.)
  SW11 . . . . .7F 101
  (off Prince of Wales Dr.)
  TW5: Hest 1B 112
All Saints Dr. SE3 . . . . .2G 123
  (not continuous)
All Saints Ho. W11 . . . . .5H 81
  (off All Saints Rd.)
All Saints M. HA3: Hrw W 6D 26

All Saints Pas. SW18 5J 117
All Saints Rd. SM1: Sutt 3K 165
SW19 7A 136
(not continuous)
W3 3J 97
W11 5H 81
All Saints St. N1 2K 83
All Saints Twr. E10 7D 50
Allsop Pl. NW1 4F 5 (4D 82)
All Souls Av. NW10 2D 80
All Souls' Pl. W1 6K 5 (5F 83)
Allum Way N20 1F 31
Alluvium Ct. *SE1* *7G 15*
(off Long La.)
Allwood Cl. SE26 4K 139
Alma Av. E4 7K 35
Alma Birk Ho. NW6 7G 63
Almack Rd. E5 4J 67
Alma Cl. N10 1F 47
Alma Ct. HA2: Harr 2H 59
Alma Cres. SM1: Sutt 5G 165
Alma Gro. SE1 4F 103
Alma Ho. N9 4B 34
TW8: Bford 6E 96
Alma Pl. CR7: Thor H 5A 156
NW10 3D 80
SE19 7F 139
Alma Rd. DA14: Sidc 3A 144
EN3: Pond E 5F 25
KT10: Esh 7J 149
N10 7A 32
SM5: Cars 5C 166
SW18 4A 118
UB1: S'hall 7C 76
Alma Rd. Ind. Est.
EN3: Pond E 4E 24
Alma Row HA3: Hrw W 1H 41
Alma Sq. NW8 2A 82
Alma St. E15 6F 69
NW5 6F 65
Alma Ter. *E3* *1B 86*
(off Beale Rd.)
SW18 7B 118
W8 3J 99
Almeida St. N1 1B 84
Almeida Theatre *1B 84*
(off Almeida St.)
Almeric Rd. SW11 4D 118
Almer Rd. SW20 7C 134
Almington St. N4 1K 65
Almond Av. SM5: Cars 2D 166
UB7: W Dray 3C 92
UB10: Ick 3D 56
W5 3D 96
Almond Cl. BR2: Brom 7E 160
HA4: Ruis 3H 57
SE15 2G 121
TW13: Felt 1J 129
TW17: Shep 2E 146
UB3: Hayes 7G 75
Almond Gro. TW8: Bford 7B 96
Almond Rd. N17 7B 34
SE16 4H 103
Almonds Av. IG9: Buck H 2D 36
Almond Way BR2: Brom 7E 160
CR4: Mitc 5H 155
HA2: Harr 2F 41
Almorah Rd. N1 7D 66
TW5: Hest 1B 112
Almshouse La. KT9: Chess 7C 162
Alnmouth Ct. *UB1: S'hall* *6G 77*
(off Fleming Rd.)
Alnwick N17 7C 34
Alnwick Gro. SM4: Mord 4K 153
Alnwick Rd. E16 6A 88
SE12 6K 123
ALPERTON 2E 78
Alperton Community School Sports Cen. 1D 78
Alperton La. HA0: Wemb 3C 78
UB6: G'frd 3C 78
Alperton St. W10 4H 81
Alphabet Gdns. SM5: Cars 6B 154
Alphabet Sq. E3 5C 86
Alpha Bus. Cen. E17 5B 50
Alpha Cl. NW1 3D 4 (4C 82)
Alpha Est. UB3: Hayes 2G 93
Alpha Gro. E14 2C 104
Alpha Ho. NW6 2J 81
NW8 4C 4
SW4 4K 119
Alpha Pl. NW6 2J 81
SM4: Mord 1F 165
SW3 7D 16 (6C 100)
Alpha Rd. CR0: Croy 1E 168
E4 3H 35
EN3: Pond E 4F 25
KT5: Surb 6F 151
N18 6B 34
SE14 1B 122
TW11: Tedd 5H 131
UB10: Hil 4D 74
Alpha St. SE15 2G 121
Alphea Cl. SW19 7C 136
Alpine Av. KT5: Surb 2J 163
Alpine Bus. Cen. E6 5E 88
Alpine Cl. CR0: Croy 3E 168
Alpine Copse BR1: Brom 2E 160
Alpine Gro. E9 7J 67
Alpine Rd. E10 2D 68
KT12: Walt T 7J 147
SE16 4J 103
Alpine Vw. SM5: Cars 5C 166
Alpine Wlk. HA7: Stan 2D 26
Alpine Way E6 5E 88
Alric Av. KT3: N Mald 3A 152
NW10 7K 61
Alroy Rd. N4 7A 48
Alsace Rd. SE17 5E 102
Alscot Rd. SE1 4F 103
(not continuous)
Alscot Rd. Ind. Est. SE1 3F 103
Alscot Way SE1 4F 103
Alsike Rd. DA18: Erith 3D 108
SE2 3D 108
Alsom Av. KT4: Wor Pk 4C 164
Alston Cl. KT6: Surb 7B 150
Alston Rd. EN5: Barn 3B 20
N18 5C 34
SW17 4B 136
Altair Cl. N17 6A 34
Altash Way SE9 2D 142
Altenburg Av. W13 3B 96
Altenburg Gdns. SW11 4D 118
Alt Gro. SW19 7H 135
Altham Ct. HA2: Harr 1F 41
Altham Rd. HA5: Pinn 1C 40
Althea St. SW6 2K 117
Althorne Gdns. E18 4H 51
Althorne Way RM10: Dag 2G 73
Althorp Cl. EN5: Ark 1H 29
Althorpe M. SW11 1B 118
Althorpe Rd. HA1: Harr 5G 41
Althorp Rd. SW17 1D 136
Altima Ct. SE22 4G 121
Altior Ct. N6 6G 47
Altmore Av. E6 7D 70
Alton Av. HA7: Stan 7E 26
Alton Cl. DA5: Bexl 1E 144
TW7: Isle 2K 113
Alton Gdns. BR3: Beck 7C 140
TW2: Whit 7H 113
Alton Rd. CR0: Wadd 3A 168
N17 3D 48
SW15 1C 134
TW9: Rich 4E 114
Alton St. E14 5D 86
Altyre Cl. BR3: Beck 5B 158
Altyre Rd. CR0: Croy 2D 168
Altyre Way BR3: Beck 5B 158
Aluna Ct. SE15 3J 121
Alvanley Gdns. NW6 5K 63
Alverstone Av. EN4: E Barn 7H 21
SW19 2J 135
Alverstone Gdns. SE9 1G 143
Alverstone Ho. SE11 7J 19 (6A 102)
Alverstone Rd. E12 4E 70
HA9: Wemb 1F 61
KT3: N Mald 4B 152
NW2 7E 62
Alverston Gdns. SE25 5E 156
Alverton St. SE8 5B 104
(not continuous)
Alveston Av. HA3: Kent 3B 42
Alveston Sq. E18 2J 51
Alvey St. SE17 5E 102
Alvia Gdns. SM1: Sutt 4A 166
Alvington Cres. E8 5F 67
Alway Av. KT19: Ewe 5K 163
Alwold Cres. SE12 6K 123
Alwyn Av. W4 5K 97
Alwyn Cl. CR0: New Ad 7D 170
Alwyne La. N1 7B 66
Alwyne Pl. N1 6C 66
Alwyne Rd. N1 7C 66
SW19 6H 135
W7 7J 77
Alwyne Sq. N1 6C 66
Alwyne Vs. N1 7B 66
Alwyn Gdns. NW4 4C 44
W3 6H 79
Alyth Gdns. NW11 6J 45
Alzette Ho. *E2* *2K 85*
(off Mace St.)
Amadeus Ho. *BR1: Brom* *3K 159*
(off Elmfield Rd.)
Amalgamated Dr.
TW8: Bford 6B 96
Amanda Ct. *TW15: Ashf* *2B 128*
(off Edward Way)
Amanda M. RM7: Rom 5J 55
Amar Ct. SE18 4K 107
Amar Deep Ct. SE18 5K 107
Amazon Bldg. N8 4K 47
Amazon St. E1 6G 85
Ambassador Cl. TW3: Houn 2C 112
Ambassador Gdns. E6 5D 88
Ambassadors Ct. *E8* *7F 67*
(off Holly St.)
SW1 5B 12
Ambassador Sq. E14 4D 104
Ambassadors Theatre *2D 12*
(off West St.)
Amber Av. E17 1A 50
Amber Ct. CR0: Croy 1E 168
KT5: Surb 7F 151
Amberden Av. N3 3J 45
Ambergate St. SE17 5B 102
Amber Gro. NW2 1F 63
Amberley Cl. BR6: Chels 5K 173
HA5: Pinn 3D 40
Amberley Ct. BR3: Beck 7B 140
DA14: Sidc 5C 144
Amberley Gdns. EN1: Enf 7K 23
KT19: Ewe 4B 164
Amberley Gro. CR0: Croy 7F 157
SE26 5H 139
Amberley Rd. E10 7C 50
EN1: Enf 7A 24
IG9: Buck H 1F 37
N13 2E 32
SE2 6D 108
W9 5J 81
Amberley Way
RM7: Mawney 4H 55
SM4: Mord 7H 153
TW4: Houn 5A 112
UB10: Uxb 2A 74
Amber M. *N22* *3A 48*
(off High Rd.)
Amberside Cl. TW7: Isle 6H 113
Amber Wharf *E2* *1F 85*
(off Nursery La.)
Amberwood Cl. SM6: Wall 5J 167
Amberwood Ri. KT3: N Mald 6A 152
Amblecote Cl. SE12 3K 141
Amblecote Mdws. SE12 3K 141
Amblecote Rd. SE12 3K 141
Ambler Rd. N4 3B 66
Ambleside BR1: Brom 6F 141
NW1 1K 5
SW19 1G 135
Ambleside Av. BR3: Beck 5A 158
KT12: Walt T 7A 148
SW16 4H 137
Ambleside Cl. E9 5J 67
E10 7D 50
N17 3F 49
Ambleside Cres. EN3: Enf H 3E 24
Ambleside Dr. TW14: Felt 1H 129
Ambleside Gdns. HA9: Wemb 1D 60
IG4: Ilf 4C 52
SM2: Sutt 6A 166
SW16 5H 137
Ambleside Point *SE15* *7J 103*
(off Tustin Est.)
Ambleside Rd. DA7: Bex 2G 127
NW10 7B 62
Ambleside Wlk. *UB8: Uxb* *1A 74*
(off Cumbrian Way)
Ambrooke Rd. DA17: Belv 3G 109
Ambrosden Av. SW1 2B 18 (3G 101)
Ambrose Av. NW11 7G 45
Ambrose Cl. BR6: Orp 3K 173
E6 5D 88
Ambrose Ho. *E14* *5C 86*
(off Selsey St.)
Ambrose M. SW11 2D 118
Ambrose St. SE16 4H 103
Ambrose Wlk. E3 2C 86
AMC Bus. Cen. NW10 3H 79
Amelia Cl. W3 1H 97
Amelia Ho. *W6* *5E 98*
(off Queen Caroline St.)
Amelia St. SE17 5C 102
Amen Cnr. EC4 1B 14 (6B 84)
SW17 6D 136
Amen Ct. EC4 1B 14 (6B 84)
Amenity Way SM4: Mord 7E 152
American International University of
London, The *7E 114*
(in Richmond University)
America Sq. EC3 2J 15 (7F 85)
America St. SE1 5C 14 (1C 102)
Amerland Rd. SW18 5H 117
Amersham Av. N18 6J 33
Amersham Gro. SE14 7B 104
Amersham Rd. CR0: Croy 6C 156
SE14 1B 122
Amersham Va. SE14 7B 104
Amery Gdns. NW10 1E 80
Amery Ho. *SE17* *5E 102*
(off Kinglake St.)
Amery Rd. HA1: Harr 2A 60
Amesbury Av. SW2 2J 137
Amesbury Cl. KT4: Wor Pk 1E 164
Amesbury Ct. EN2: Enf 2F 23
Amesbury Dr. E4 6J 25
Amesbury Rd. BR1: Brom 3B 160
RM9: Dag 7D 72
TW13: Felt 2B 130
Amesbury Twr. SW8 2G 119
Ames Cotts. *E14* *5A 86*
(off Maroon St.)
Ames Ho. *E2* *2K 85*
(off Mace St.)
Amethyst Cl. N11 7C 32
Amethyst Ct. *BR6: Chels* *5J 173*
(off Farnborough Hill)
Amethyst Rd. E15 4F 69
AMF Bowling
Lewisham 3E 122
Amherst Av. W13 6C 78
Amherst Dr. BR5: St M Cry 4K 161
Amherst Gdns. *W13* *6C 78*
(off Amherst Rd.)
Amherst Ho. *SE16* *2K 103*
(off Wolfe Cres.)
Amherst Rd. W13 6C 78
Amhurst Gdns. TW7: Isle 2A 114
Amhurst Pde. *N16* *7F 49*
(off Amhurst Pk.)

Amhurst Pk. N16 7D 48
Amhurst Pas. E8 4G 67
Amhurst Rd. E8 5H 67
N16 4F 67
Amhurst Ter. E8 4G 67
Amhurst Wlk. SE28 1A 108
Amias Ho. *EC1* *3C 8*
(off Central St.)
Amida Leisure Cen. 5B 158
Amidas Gdns. RM8: Dag 4B 72
Amiel St. E1 4J 85
Amies St. SW11 3D 118
Amigo Ho. *SE1* *1K 19*
(off Morley St.)
Amina Way SE16 3G 103
Amis Av. KT19: Ewe 6H 163
Amity Gro. SW20 1D 152
Amity Rd. E15 7H 69
Ammanford Grn. NW9 6A 44
Ammonite Ho. E15 7H 69
Amner Rd. SW11 6E 118
Amor Rd. W6 3E 98
Amory Ho. *N1* *1K 83*
(off Barnsbury Est.)
Amott Rd. SE15 3G 121
Amoy Pl. E14 7C 86
(not continuous)
Ampere Way CR0: Wadd 7J 155
Ampleforth Rd. SE2 2B 108
Ampthill Est. NW1 1B 6 (2G 83)
Ampthill Sq. NW1 1B 6 (2G 83)
Ampton Pl. WC1 2G 7 (3K 83)
Ampton St. WC1 2G 7 (3K 83)
Amroth Cl. SE23 1H 139
Amroth Grn. NW9 6A 44
Amstel Ct. *SE15* *7F 103*
Amsterdam Rd. E14 3E 104
Amundsen Ct. *E14* *5C 104*
(off Napier Av.)
Amunsden Ho. *NW10* *7K 61*
(off Stonebridge Pk.)
Amwell Cl. EN2: Enf 5J 23
Amwell Ct. Est. N4 2C 66
Amwell St. EC1 1J 7 (3A 84)
Amyand Cotts. TW1: Twick 6B 114
Amyand La. TW1: Twick 7B 114
Amyand Pk. Gdns. TW1: Twick 7B 114
Amyand Pk. Rd. TW1: Twick 7A 114
Amy Cl. SM6: Wall 7J 167
Amy Johnson Ct. HA8: Edg 2H 43
Amyruth Rd. SE4 5C 122
Amy Warne Cl. E6 4C 88
Anatola Rd. N19 2G 65
Ancaster Cres. KT3: N Mald 6C 152
Ancaster M. BR3: Beck 3K 157
Ancaster Rd. BR3: Beck 3K 157
Ancaster St. SE18 7J 107
Anchor SW18 4K 117
Anchorage Cl. SW19 5J 135
Anchorage Ho. *E14* *7F 87*
(off Clove Cres.)
Anchorage Point *E14* *2B 104*
(off Cuba St.)
Anchorage Point Ind. Est. SE7 3A 106
Anchor & Hope La. SE7 3K 105
Anchor Brewhouse SE1 5J 15 (1F 103)
Anchor Bus. Cen. CR0: Bedd 3J 167
Anchor Cl. IG11: Bark 3B 90
Anchor Ct. EN1: Enf 5K 23
SW1 *4C 18*
(off Vauxhall Bri. Rd.)
Anchor Ho. *E16* *5H 87*
(off Barking Rd.)
E16 *6A 88*
(off Prince Regent La.)
EC1 *3C 8*
(off Old St.)
SW10 *6B 100*
(off Moravian Pl.)
Anchor M. SW12 6F 119
Anchor Retail Pk. E1 4J 85
Anchor Rd. E12 2B 70
Anchor St. SE16 4H 103
Anchor Ter. E1 4J 85
Anchor Wharf *E3* *5D 86*
(off Yeo St.)
Anchor Yd. EC1 3D 8 (4C 84)
Ancill Cl. W6 6G 99
Ancona Rd. NW10 2C 80
SE18 5H 107
Andace Pk. Gdns. BR1: Brom 2A 160
Andalus Rd. SW9 3J 119
Andaman Ho. *E1* *5A 86*
(off Duckett St.)
Ander Cl. HA0: Wemb 4D 60
Anderson Cl. N21 5E 22
SM3: Sutt 1J 165
W3 6K 79
Anderson Ct. NW2 1E 62
Anderson Dr. TW15: Ashf 4E 128
Anderson Hgts. SW16 2K 155
Anderson Ho. *E14* *7E 86*
(off Woolmore St.)
IG11: Bark 1H 89
SW17 5B 136
W12 *6D 80*
(off Du Cane Rd.)
Anderson Pl. TW3: Houn 4F 113
Anderson Rd. E9 6K 67
IG8: Wfd G 3B 52
Anderson Sq. *N1* *1B 84*
(off Gaskin St.)
Anderson St. SW3 5E 16 (5D 100)
Anderson Way DA17: Belv 2H 109
Anderton Cl. SE5 3D 120
Anderton Ct. N22 2H 47
Andorra Ct. BR1: Brom 1A 160
Andover Av. E16 6B 88
Andover Cl. TW14: Felt 1H 129
UB6: G'frd 4F 77
Andover Ct. TW19: Stanw 7A 110
Andover Pl. NW6 2K 81
Andover Rd. BR6: Orp 1H 173
N7 2K 65
TW2: Twick 1H 131
Andoversford Ct. *SE15* *6E 102*
(off Bibury Cl.)
Andreck Ct. *BR3: Beck* *2E 158*
(off Crescent Rd.)
Andre St. E8 5G 67
Andrew Borde St. WC2 7D 6 (6H 83)
Andrew Cl. DA1: Cray 5K 127
Andrew Ct. SE23 2K 139
Andrewes Gdns. E6 6C 88
Andrewes Highwalk EC2 6D 8
Andrewes Ho. EC2 6D 8
SM1: Sutt 4J 165
Andrew Pl. SW8 7H 101
Andrew Reed Ho. *SW18* *7G 117*
(off Linstead Way)
Andrews Cl. HA1: Harr 7H 41
IG9: Buck H 2F 37
KT4: Wor Pk 2E 164
Andrews Crosse WC2 1J 13
Andrews Ho. CR2: S Croy 6C 168
NW3 *7D 64*
(off Fellows Rd.)
Andrews Pl. DA2: Bexl 2K 145
SE9 6F 125
Andrew's Rd. E8 1H 85
Andrew St. E14 6E 86
Andrews Wlk. SE17 6B 102
Andringham Lodge *BR1: Brom* *1K 159*
(off Palace Gro.)
Andrula Ct. N22 1B 48
Andwell Cl. SE2 2B 108
ANERLEY 2H 157
Anerley Gro. SE19 7F 139
Anerley Hill SE19 6F 139
Anerley Pk. SE20 7G 139
Anerley Pk. Rd. SE20 7H 139
Anerley Rd. SE19 7G 139
SE20 7G 139
Anerley Sta. Rd. SE20 1H 157
Anerley Va. SE19 7F 139
Aneurin Bevan Ct. NW2 2D 62
Aneurin Bevan Ho. N11 7C 32
Anfield Cl. SW12 7G 119
ANGEL 2A 84
Angela Davies Ind. Est. SE24 4B 120
Angel All. E1 7K 9
Angel Cen., The N1 1K 7
Angel Cl. N18 5A 34
Angel Cnr. Pde. N18 4B 34
Angel Ct. EC2 7F 9 (6D 84)
SW1 5B 12 (1G 101)
ANGEL EDMONTON JUNC. 5B 34
Angelfield TW3: Houn 4F 113
Angel Ga. EC1 1B 8 (3B 84)
(not continuous)
Angel Hill SM1: Sutt 3K 165
(not continuous)
Angel Hill Dr. SM1: Sutt 3K 165
Angelica Cl. UB7: Yiew 6A 74
Angelica Dr. E6 5E 88
Angelica Gdns. CR0: Croy 1K 169
Angelina Ho. *SE15* *1G 121*
(off Goldsmith Rd.)
Angelis Apartments *N1* *1B 8*
(off Graham St.)
Angel La. E15 6F 69
UB3: Hayes 5F 75
Angell Pk. Gdns. SW9 3A 120
Angell Rd. SW9 3A 120
ANGELL TOWN 1A 120
Angell Town Est. SW9 2A 120
Angel M. E1 7H 85
N1 2A 84
SW15 7C 116
Angel Pas. EC4 3E 14 (7D 84)
Angel Pl. N18 4B 34
SE1 6E 14 (2D 102)
Angel Rd. HA1: Harr 6J 41
KT7: T Ditt 7A 150
N18 5B 34
Angel Rd. Works N18 5D 34
Angel Sq. EC1 2B 84
Angel St. EC1 7C 8 (6C 84)
Angel Wlk. W6 4E 98
Angel Way RM1: Rom 5K 55
Angel Yd. N6 1E 64
Angerstein Bus. Pk. SE10 4J 105
Angerstein La. SE3 1H 123
Anglebury *W2* *6J 81*
(off Talbot Rd.)
Angle Cl. UB10: Hil 1C 74
Angle Grn. RM8: Dag 1C 72
Anglers, The *KT1: King T* *3D 150*
(off High St.)
Anglers Cl. TW10: Ham 4C 132
Angler's La. NW5 6F 65
Anglers Reach KT6: Surb 5D 150
Anglesea Av. SE18 4F 107
Anglesea Ho. *KT1: King T* *4D 150*
(off Anglesea Rd.)
Anglesea M. SE18 4F 107
Anglesea Rd. KT1: King T 4D 150
SE18 4F 107
Anglesea Ter. W6 3D 98
Anglesey Cl. TW15: Ashf 3C 128
Anglesey Ct. W7 4K 77
Anglesey Ct. Rd. SM5: Cars 6E 166
Anglesey Gdns. SM5: Cars 6E 166
Anglesey Ho. *E14* *6C 86*
(off Lindfield St.)
Anglesey Rd. EN3: Pond E 4C 24
Anglesmede Cres. HA5: Pinn 3E 40
Anglesmede Way HA5: Pinn 3E 40
Angles Rd. SW16 4J 137
Anglia Cl. N17 7C 34
Anglia Ct. *RM8: Dag* *1D 72*
(off Spring Cl.)
Anglia Ho. *E14* *6A 86*
(off Salmon La.)
Anglian Ind. Est. IG11: Bark 4K 89
Anglian Rd. E11 3F 69
Anglia Wlk. *E6* *1E 88*
(off Napier Rd.)
Anglo Rd. E3 2B 86
Angrave Ct. *E8* *1F 85*
(off Scriven St.)
Angrave Pas. E8 1F 85
Angus Cl. KT9: Chess 5G 163
Angus Dr. HA4: Ruis 4A 58
Angus Gdns. NW9 1K 43
Angus Ho. SW2 7H 119
Angus Rd. E13 3A 88
Angus St. SE14 7A 104
Anhalt Rd. SW11 7C 100
Ankerdine Cres. SE18 7F 107
Anlaby Rd. TW11: Tedd 5J 131
Anley Rd. W14 2F 99
Anmersh Gro. HA7: Stan 1D 42
Annabel Cl. E14 6D 86
Anna Cl. E8 1F 85
Annandale Gro. UB10: Ick 3E 56
Annandale Rd. CR0: Croy 2G 169
DA15: Sidc 7J 125
SE10 6H 105
W4 5A 98
Anna Neagle Cl. E7 4J 69
Annan Way RM1: Rom 1K 55
Anne Boleyn Ct. SE9 6G 125
Anne Boleyn's Wlk. KT2: King T 5E 132
SM3: Cheam 7F 165
Anne Case M. KT3: N Mald 3K 151
Anne Compton M. SE12 7H 123
Anne Goodman Ho. *E1* *6J 85*
(off Jubilee St.)
Anne of Cleeves Ct. SE9 6H 125
Annes Ct. NW1 3D 4
Annesley Av. NW9 3K 43
Annesley Cl. NW10 3A 62
Annesley Dr. CR0: Croy 3B 170
Annesley Ho. SW9 1A 120
Annesley Rd. SE3 1K 123
Annesley Wlk. N19 2G 65
Anne St. E13 4J 87
Anne Sutherland Ho. BR3: Beck 7A 140
Annett Cl. TW17: Shep 4G 147
Annette Cl. HA3: W'stone 2J 41
Annette Cres. N1 7C 66
Annette Rd. N7 3K 65
(not continuous)
Annett Rd. KT12: Walt T 7J 147
Anne Way KT8: W Mole 4F 149
Annie Besant Cl. E3 1B 86
Annie Taylor Ho. *E12* *4E 70*
(off Walton Rd.)
Anning St. EC2 3H 9 (4E 84)
Annington Rd. N2 3D 46
Annis Rd. E9 6A 68
Ann La. SW10 6B 100
Ann Moss Way SE16 3J 103
Ann's Cl. SW1 7F 11
Ann's Pl. E1 6J 9
Ann St. SE18 5G 107
(not continuous)
Ann Stroud Ct. SE12 5J 123
Annsworthy Av. CR7: Thor H 3D 156
Annsworthy Cres. SE25 2D 156
Ansar Gdns. E17 5B 50
Ansdell Rd. SE15 2J 121
Ansdell St. W8 3K 99
Ansdell Ter. W8 3K 99
Ansell Gro. SM5: Cars 1E 166
Ansell Ho. *E1* *5J 85*
(off Mile End Rd.)
Ansell Rd. SW17 3C 136
Anselm Cl. CR0: Croy 3F 169
Anselm Rd. HA5: H End 1D 40
SW6 6J 99
Ansford Rd. BR1: Brom 5E 140
Ansleigh Pl. W11 7F 81
Anson Cl. RM7: Mawney 2H 55
Anson Ho. *E1* *4A 86*
(off Shandy St.)
SW1 *7A 18*
(off Churchill Gdns.)
Anson Pl. SE28 2H 107
Anson Rd. N7 4G 65
NW2 4D 62

Anson Ter. UB5: N'olt 6F 59
Anstey Ct. W3 .2H 97
Anstey Ho. E9 . . . . .1J 85
    (off Templecombe Rd.)
Anstey Rd. SE15 . . . . .3G 121
Anstey Wlk. N15 . . . . .4B 48
Anstice Cl. W4 . . . . .7A 98
Anstridge Path SE9 . . . . .6H 125
Anstridge Rd. SE9 . . . . .6H 125
Antelope Rd. SE18 . . . . .3D 106
Antenor Ho. E2 . . . . .2H 85
    (off Old Bethnal Grn. Rd.)
Anthony Cl. NW7 . . . . .4F 29
Anthony Cope Ct. N1 . . . . .1F 9
    (off Chart St.)
Anthony Ho. NW8 . . . . .4C 4
    (off Ashbridge St.)
Anthony Rd. DA16: Well 1A 126
SE25 . . . . .6G 157
UB6: G'frd 3J 77
Anthony St. E1 . . . . .6H 85
Anthony Way N18 . . . . .6E 34
Antigua Wlk. SE19 . . . . .5D 138
Antilles Bay E14 . . . . .2E 104
Antill Rd. E3 .3A 86
N15 . . . . .4G 49
Antill Ter. E1 .6K 85
Antlers Hill E4 . . . . .5J 25
Anton Cres. SM1: Sutt 3J 165
Antoneys Cl. HA5: Pinn 2B 40
Antonine Hgts. SE1 . . . . .7G 15
Anton Pl. HA9: Wemb 3H 61
Anton St. E8 .5G 67
Antony Ho. SE14 . . . . .7K 103
    (off Barlborough St.)
SE16 . . . . .4J 103
    (off Raymouth Rd.)
Antrim Gro. NW3 . . . . .6D 64
Antrim Ho. E3 . . . . .1B 86
    (off Birdsfield La.)
Antrim Rd. NW3 . . . . .6D 64
Antrobus Cl. SM1: Sutt 5H 165
Antrobus Rd. W4 . . . . .4J 97
Anvil Cl. SW16 . . . . .7G 137
Anvil Rd. TW16: Sun 3J 147
Anworth Cl. IG8: Wfd G 6E 36
Apeldoorn Dr. SM6: Wall 7J 167
Apex Cl. BR3: Beck 1D 158
APEX CORNER
    Feltham 3D 130
    Mill Hill 4F 29
Apex Ct. W13 . . . . .7A 78
Apex Ind. Est. NW10 . . . . .4B 80
Apex Pde. NW7 . . . . .4E 28
    (off Selvage La.)
Apex Retail Pk.
    TW13: Hanw 3D 130
Aphrodite Ct. E14 . . . . .4C 104
    (off Homer Dr.)
Aplin Way TW7: Isle 1J 113
Apollo Av. BR1: Brom 1K 159
Apollo Bldg. E14 . . . . .4C 104
Apollo Bus. Cen. SE8 . . . . .5K 103
Apollo Ct. E1 .7G 85
    (off Thomas More St.)
SW9 . . . . .1A 120
    (off Southey Rd.)
Apollo Ho. E2 . . . . .2H 85
    (off St Jude's Rd.)
N6 . . . . .7D 46
SW10 .7B 100
    (off Milman's St.)
Apollo Pl. E11 . . . . .3G 69
SW10 .7B 100
Apollo Theatre
    Soho 2C 12
    (off Shaftesbury Av.)
    Victoria 2A 18
    (off Wilton Rd.)
Apollo Way DA8: Erith 4K 109
SE28 . . . . .3H 107
Apollo West End Cinema 3C 12
    (off Regent St.)

Apostle Way CR7: Thor H 2B 156
Apothecary St. EC4 . . . . . . .1A 14 (6B 84)
Appach Rd. SW2 . . . . .5A 120
Apple Blossom Ct. SW8 . . . . .7H 101
    (off Pascal St.)
Appleby Cl. BR5: Pet W 7J 161
E4 . . . . .6K 35
N15 . . . . .5D 48
TW2: Twick 2H 131
Appleby Ct. W3 . . . . .2J 97
    (off Newport Rd.)
Appleby Gdns. TW14: Felt 1H 129
Appleby Rd. E8 . . . . .7G 67
E16 . . . . .6H 87
Appleby St. E2 . . . . .2F 85
Appledore Av. DA7: Bex 1J 127
HA4: Ruis 3K 57
Appledore Cl. BR2: Brom 5H 159
HA8: Edg 1G 43
SW17 .2D 136
Appledore Cres. DA14: Sidc 3J 143
Appledore Way NW7 . . . . .7A 30
Appleford Ho. W10 . . . . .4G 81
    (off Bosworth Rd.)
Appleford Rd. W10 . . . . .4G 81
Apple Gth. TW8: Bford 4D 96
Applegarth CR0: New Ad 7D 170
    (not continuous)
KT10: Clay 5A 162
Applegarth Dr. IG2: Ilf 4K 53
Applegarth Ho. SE1 . . . . .6B 14
SE15 . . . . .7G 103
    (off Bird in Bush Rd.)
Applegarth Rd. SE28 . . . . .1B 108
W14 . . . . .3F 99
Apple Gro. EN1: Enf 3K 23
KT9: Chess 4E 162
Apple Mkt. KT1: King T 2D 150
    (off Market Pl.)
Apple Rd. E11 . . . . .3G 69
Appleshaw Ho. SE5 . . . . .3E 120
Appleton Cl. DA7: Bex 2J 127
Appleton Gdns. KT3: N Mald 6C 152
Appleton Rd. SE9 . . . . .3C 124
Appleton Sq. CR4: Mitc 1C 154
Apple Tree Av. UB8: Hil 5B 74
Appletree Cl. SE20 . . . . .1H 157
Appletree Gdns. EN4: E Barn 4H 21
Apple Tree Rdbt. UB7: Yiew 7B 74
Apple Tree Yd. SW1 . . . . . .4B 12 (1G 101)
Applewood Cl. N20 . . . . .1H 31
NW2 . . . . .3D 62
UB10: Ick 4A 56
Applewood Dr. E13 . . . . .4K 87
Appold St. EC2 . . . . .5G 9 (5E 84)
Apprentice Way E5 . . . . .4H 67
Approach, The BR6: Orp 2K 173
EN1: Enf 2C 24
NW4 . . . . .5F 45
W3 . . . . .6K 79
Approach Cl. N16 . . . . .4E 66
Approach Rd. E2 . . . . .2J 85
EN4: E Barn 4G 21
HA8: Edg 6B 28
KT8: W Mole 5E 148
SW20 .2E 152
TW15: Ashf 6E 128
Aprey Gdns. NW4 . . . . .4E 44
April Cl. BR6: Chels 5K 173
TW13: Felt 3J 129
W7 . . . . .7J 77
April Ct. E2 . . . . .2G 85
    (off Teale St.)
April Glen SE23 . . . . .3K 139
April St. E8 . . . . .4F 67
Apsley Cen., The NW2 . . . . .2C 62
Apsley Cl. HA2: Harr 5G 41
Apsley House 6H 11
Apsley Ho. E1 . . . . .5J 85
    (off Stepney Way)
NW8 . . . . .2B 82
    (off Finchley Rd.)
TW4: Houn 4D 112

Apsley Rd. KT3: N Mald 3J 151
SE25 . . . . .4H 157
Apsley Way NW2 . . . . .2C 62
W1 . . . . .6H 11 (2E 100)
    (not continuous)
Aquarius TW1: Twick 1B 132
Aquarius Bus. Pk. NW2 . . . . .1C 62
    (off Priestley Way)
Aquila St. NW8 . . . . .2B 82
Aquinas St. SE1 . . . . .5K 13 (1A 102)
Arabella Dr. SW15 . . . . .4A 116
Arabia Cl. E4 .7K 25
Arabian Ho. E1 . . . . .4A 86
    (off Ernest St.)
Arabin Rd. SE4 . . . . .4A 122
Aragon Av. KT7: T Ditt 5K 149
Aragon Cl. BR2: Brom 1D 172
EN2: Enf 1E 22
TW16: Sun 6H 129
Aragon Dr. HA4: Ruis 1B 58
Aragon Ho. E16 . . . . .1J 105
    (off Capulet M.)
Aragon Rd. KT2: King T 5E 132
SM4: Mord 6F 153
Aragon Twr. SE8 . . . . .4B 104
Aral Ho. E1 . . . . .4K 85
    (off Ernest St.)
Arandora Cres. RM6: Chad H 7B 54
Aran Dr. HA7: Stan 4H 27
Arapiles Ho. E14 . . . . .6F 87
    (off Blair St.)
Arbery Rd. E3 . . . . .3A 86
Arbon Ct. N1 .1C 84
    (off Linton St.)
Arbor Cl. BR3: Beck 2D 158
Arbor Ct. N16 . . . . .2D 66
Arboretum Ct. N1 . . . . .6D 66
    (off Dove Rd.)
Arborfield Cl. SW2 . . . . .1K 137
Arborfield Ho. E14 . . . . .7C 86
    (off E. India Dock Rd.)
Arbor Rd. E4 .3A 36
Arbour Ct. N16 . . . . .6K 85
    (off Arbour Sq.)
Arbour Rd. EN3: Pond E 3E 24
Arbour Sq. E1 . . . . .6K 85
Arbroath Rd. SE9 . . . . .3C 124
Arbury Ter. SE26 . . . . .3G 139
Arbuthnot La. DA5: Bexl 6E 126
Arbuthnot Rd. SE14 . . . . .2K 121
Arbutus St. E8 . . . . .1F 85
Arcade CR0: Croy 2C 168
Arcade, The CR0: Croy 3C 168
    (off High St.)
E17 . . . . .4C 50
EC2 . . . . .6G 9
IG11: Bark 7G 71
N7 . . . . .4J 65
    (off Macready Pl.)
SE9 . . . . .6E 124
    (off High St.)
Arcade Chambers SE9 . . . . .6E 124
Arcade Pde. KT9: Chess 5D 162
Arcadia Av. N3 . . . . .2J 45
Arcadia Cen., The W5 . . . . .7D 78
Arcadia Cl. SM5: Cars 4E 166
Arcadia Ct. E1 . . . . .7J 9
Arcadian Av. DA5: Bexl 6E 126
Arcadian Cl. DA5: Bexl 6E 126
Arcadian Gdns. N22 . . . . .7E 32
Arcadian Rd. DA5: Bexl 6E 126
Arcadia St. E14 . . . . .6C 86
Archangel St. SE16 . . . . .2K 103
Archbishop Lanfranc School Sports Cen.
    . . . . .6J 155
Archbishop's Pl. SW2 . . . . .7K 119
Archdale Bus. Cen. HA2: Harr 2G 59
Archdale Cl. W12 . . . . .1D 98
Archdale Ho. SE1 . . . . .7G 15
    (off Long La.)
Archdale Pl. KT3: N Mald 3H 151
Archdale Rd. SE22 . . . . .5F 121

Archel Rd. W14 . . . . .6H 99
Archer Apartments N1 . . . . .2E 84
    (off Fern Cl.)
Archer Cl. KT2: King T 7E 132
Archer Ho. N1 .1E 84
    (off Whitmore Est.)
SE14 . . . . .1A 122
SW11 .1B 118
W11 . . . . .7H 81
    (off Westbourne Gro.)
W13 . . . . .1B 96
    (off Sherwood Cl.)
Archer M. TW12: Ham H 6G 131
Archer Rd. BR5: St M Cry 5K 161
SE25 . . . . .4H 157
Archers Cl. BR2: Brom 4K 159
CR2: S Croy 5C 168
    (off Nottingham Rd.)
Archers Dr. EN3: Enf H 2D 24
Archers Lodge SE16 . . . . .5G 103
    (off Culloden Cl.)
Archer Sq. SE14 . . . . .6A 104
Archer St. W1 . . . . .2C 12 (7H 83)
Archer Ter. UB7: Yiew 7A 74
Archery Cl. HA3: W'stone 3K 41
W2 . . . . .1D 10 (6C 82)
Archery Rd. SE9 . . . . .5D 124
Archery Steps W2 . . . . .2D 10
Arches, The HA2: Harr 2F 59
NW1 . . . . .7F 65
SW8 . . . . .7H 101
WC2 . . . . .4F 13
    (off Villiers St.)
Arches Bus. Cen., The UB2: S'hall 2D 94
    (off Merrick Rd.)
Arches Leisure Cen. 6G 105
Archgate Bus. Cen. N12 . . . . .5F 31
Archibald M. N1 . . . . .3J 11 (7E 82)
Archibald Rd. N7 . . . . .4H 65
Archibald St. E3 . . . . .3C 86
Archie Cl. SE1 . . . . .7H 15 (2E 102)
Arch St. SE1 .3C 102
ARCHWAY 2G 65
Archway Bus. Cen. N19 . . . . .3H 65
Archway Cl. N19 . . . . .2G 65
SM6: Bedd 3H 167
SW19 .3K 135
W10 . . . . .5F 81
Archway Leisure Cen. 2G 65
Archway Mall N19 . . . . .2G 65
Archway M. SW15 . . . . .4G 117
    (off Putney Bri. Rd.)
Archway Rd. N6 . . . . .6E 46
N19 . . . . .6E 46
Archway St. SW13 . . . . .3A 116
Arcola St. E8 .5F 67
Arcola Theatre 4F 67
Arcon Dr. UB5: Yead 4C 76
Arctic St. NW5 . . . . .5F 65
Arcus Rd. BR1: Brom 6G 141
Ardbeg Rd. SE24 . . . . .5D 120
Arden Cl. HA1: Harr 3H 59
SE28 . . . . .6D 90
Arden Ct. Gdns. N2 . . . . .6B 46
Arden Cres. E14 . . . . .4C 104
RM9: Dag 7C 72
Arden Est. N1 .2E 84
Arden Grange N12 . . . . .4F 31
Arden Gro. BR6: Farnb 4F 173
Arden Ho. N1 . . . . .1G 9
SE11 . . . . .4G 19
SW9 . . . . .2J 119
    (off Grantham Rd.)
Arden M. E17 .5D 50
Arden Mhor HA5: Eastc 4K 39
Arden Rd. N3 .3H 45
W13 . . . . .7C 78
Ardent Cl. SE25 . . . . .3E 156
Ardent Ho. E3 .2A 86
    (off Roman Rd.)
Ardfern Av. SW16 . . . . .3A 156
Ardfillan Rd. SE6 . . . . .1F 141

Ardgowan Rd. SE6 ....7G **123**
Ardilaun Rd. N5 ....4C **66**
Ardingly Cl. CR0: Croy 3K **169**
Ardleigh Gdns. SM3: Sutt 7J **153**
Ardleigh Ho. IG11: Bark 1G **89**
Ardleigh M. IG1: Ilf 3F **71**
Ardleigh Rd. E17 ....1B **50**
N1 ....6E **66**
Ardleigh Ter. E17 ....1B **50**
Ardley Cl. HA4: Ruis 7E **38**
NW10 ....3A **62**
SE6 ....3A **140**
Ardlui Rd. SE27 ....2C **138**
Ardmay Gdns. KT6: Surb 5E **150**
Ardmere Rd. SE13 ....6F **123**
Ardmore La. IG9: Buck H 1E **36**
Ardmore Pl. IG9: Buck H 1E **36**
Ardoch Rd. SE6 ....2F **141**
Ardra Rd. N9 ....3E **34**
Ardrossan Gdns. KT4: Wor Pk ...3C **164**
Ardshiel Cl. SW15 ....3F **117**
Ardwell Av. IG6: Ilf 5G **53**
Ardwell Rd. SW2 ....2J **137**
Ardwick Rd. NW2 ....4J **63**
Arena, The EN3: Enf L 1G **25**
Arena Bus. Cen. N4 ....6C **48**
Arena Ind. Est. N4 ....6B **48**
Arena Shopping Pk. N4 ....6C **48**
Ares Ct. E14 ....4C **104**
(off Homer Dr.)
Arethusa Ho. E14 ....4C **104**
(off Cahir St.)
Argali Ho. DA18: Erith 3E **108**
(off Kale Rd.)
Argall Av. E10 ....7K **49**
Argall Way E10 ....1K **67**
Argenta Way HA9: Wemb 6G **61**
NW10 ....7H **61**
Argent Cen., The
UB3: Hayes 2J **93**
Argent Ct. KT6: Chess 3G **163**
Argo Bus. Cen. NW6 ....3J **81**
(off Kilburn Pk. Rd.)
Argon M. SW6 ....7J **99**
Argon Rd. N18 ....5D **34**
Argos Ct. SW9 ....1A **120**
(off Caldwell St.)
Argos Ho. E2 ....2H **85**
(off Old Bethnal Grn. Rd.)
Argosy Ho. SE8 ....4A **104**
Argosy La. TW19: Stanw 7A **110**
Argus Cl. RM7: Mawney 1H **55**
Argus Way UB5: N'olt 3C **76**
Argyle Av. TW3: Houn 6E **112**
(not continuous)
Argyle Cl. W13 ....4A **78**
Argyle Ho. E14 ....3E **104**
Argyle Pas. N17 ....1F **49**
Argyle Pl. W6 ....4D **98**
Argyle Rd. E1 ....4K **85**
E15 ....4G **69**
E16 ....6K **87**
EN5: Barn 4A **20**
HA2: Harr 6F **41**
IG1: Ilf 2E **70**
N12 ....5C **30**
N17 ....1G **49**
N18 ....4B **34**
TW3: Houn 5F **113**
UB6: G'frd 3K **77**
W13 ....5A **78**
Argyle Sq. WC1 ....1F 7 (3J **83**)
Argyle St. WC1 ....1E 6 (3J **83**)
Argyle Wlk. WC1 ....2F 7 (3J **83**)
Argyle Way SE16 ....5G **103**
Argyll Av. UB1: S'hall 1F **95**
Argyll Cl. SW9 ....3K **119**
Argyll Gdns. HA8: Edg 2H **43**
Argyll Mans. SW3 .....7B **16** (6B **100**)
W14 ....4G **99**
(off Hammersmith Rd.)
Argyll Rd. SE18 ....3G **107**
W8 ....2J **99**

Argyll St. W1 ....1A **12** (6G **83**)
Arica Ho. SE16 ....3H **103**
(off Slippers Pl.)
Arica Rd. SE4 ....4A **122**
Ariel Ct. SE11 ....4K **19** (4B **102**)
Ariel Rd. NW6 ....6J **63**
Ariel Way TW4: Houn 3K **111**
W12 ....1E **98**
Aristotle Rd. SW4 ....3H **119**
Arizona Bldg. SE8 ....1D **122**
(off Deal's Gateway)
Ark, The W6 ....5F **99**
(off Talgarth Rd.)
Arkell Gro. SE19 ....7B **138**
Arkindale Rd. SE6 ....3E **140**
Arklay Cl. UB8: Hil 4B **74**
Arkley Cres. E17 ....5B **50**
Arkley Rd. E17 ....5B **50**
Arklow Ho. SE17 ....6D **102**
Arklow M. KT6: Surb 2E **162**
Arklow Rd. SE14 ....6B **104**
Arklow Rd. Trad. Est. SE14 ....6A **104**
Arkwright Ho. SW2 ....7J **119**
(off Streatham Pl.)
Arkwright Rd. CR2: Sand 7F **169**
NW3 ....5A **64**
Arlesey Cl. SW15 ....5G **117**
Arlesford Rd. SW9 ....3J **119**
Arlidge Ho. EC1 ....5K **7**
(off Kirby St.)
Arlingford Rd. SW2 ....5A **120**
Arlington N12 ....3D **30**
Arlington Av. N1 ....1C **84**
(not continuous)
Arlington Cl. DA15: Sidc 7J **125**
SE13 ....5F **123**
SM1: Sutt 2J **165**
TW1: Twick 6C **114**
Arlington Ct. UB3: Harl 5G **93**
W3 ....2H **97**
(off Mill Hill Rd.)
Arlington Dr. HA4: Ruis 6F **39**
SM5: Cars 2D **166**
Arlington Gdns. IG1: Ilf 1E **70**
W4 ....5J **97**
Arlington Grn. NW7 ....7A **30**
Arlington Ho. EC1 ....1K **7**
(off Arlington Way)
SE8 ....6B **104**
(off Evelyn St.)
SW1 ....4A **12** (1G **101**)
TW9: Kew 7H **97**
W12 ....1D **98**
(off Tunis Rd.)
Arlington Lodge SW2 ....4K **119**
Arlington M. TW1: Twick 6B **114**
Arlington Pk. Mans. W4 ....5J **97**
(off Sutton La. Nth.)
Arlington Pas. TW11: Tedd 4K **131**
Arlington Pl. SE10 ....7E **104**
Arlington Rd. IG8: Wfd G 1J **51**
KT6: Surb 6D **150**
N14 ....2A **32**
NW1 ....1F **83**
TW1: Twick 6C **114**
TW10: Ham 2D **132**
TW11: Tedd 4K **131**
TW15: Ashf 5B **128**
W13 ....6B **78**
Arlington Sq. N1 ....1C **84**
Arlington St. SW1 ....4A **12** (1G **101**)
Arlington Way EC1 ....1K **7** (3A **84**)
Arliss Ho. HA1: Harr 5K **41**
Arliss Way UB5: N'olt 1A **76**
Arlow Rd. N21 ....1F **33**
Armada Ct. SE8 ....6C **104**
Armadale Cl. N17 ....4H **49**
Armadale Rd. SW6 ....7J **99**
TW14: Felt 5J **111**
Armada St. SE8 ....6C **104**
(off McMillan St.)
Armada Way E6 ....5F **89**
(Gallions Reach Shop. Pk.)

Armada Way E6 ....7F **89**
(Woolwich Mnr. Way)
Armagh Rd. E3 ....1B **86**
Armfield Cl. KT8: W Mole 5D **148**
Armfield Cres. CR4: Mitc 2D **154**
Armfield Rd. EN2: Enf 1J **23**
Arminger Rd. W12 ....1D **98**
Armistice Gdns. SE25 ....3G **157**
Armitage Ho. NW1 ....5D **4**
(off Cosway St.)
Armitage Rd. NW11 ....1G **63**
SE10 ....5H **105**
Armour Cl. N7 ....6K **65**
Armoury Rd. SE8 ....2D **122**
Armoury Way SW18 ....5J **117**
Armsby Ho. E1 ....5J **85**
(off Stepney Way)
Armstead Wlk. RM10: Dag 7G **73**
Armstrong Av. IG8: Wfd G 6B **36**
Armstrong Cl. BR1: Brom 3C **160**
E6 ....6D **88**
HA5: Eastc 6J **39**
KT12: Walt T 6J **147**
RM8: Dag 7D **54**
Armstrong Cres. EN4: Cockf ...3G **21**
Armstrong Rd. SE18 ....3G **107**
SW7 ....2A **16** (3B **100**)
TW13: Hanw 5C **130**
W3 ....1B **98**
Armstrong Way
UB2: S'hall 2F **95**
Armytage Rd. TW5: Hest 7B **94**
Arnal Cres. SW18 ....7G **117**
Arncliffe NW6 ....2K **81**
Arncliffe Cl. N11 ....6K **31**
Arncroft Ct. IG11: Bark 3B **90**
Arndale Wlk. SW18 ....5K **117**
Arne Gro. BR6: Orp 3K **173**
Arne Ho. SE11 ....5G **19**
Arne St. WC2 ....1F 13 (6J **83**)
Arnett Sq. E4 ....6G **35**
Arne Wlk. SE3 ....4H **123**
Arneways Av. RM6: Chad H 3D **54**
Arneway St. SW1 ......2D **18** (3H **101**)
Arnewood Cl. SW15 ....1C **134**
Arneys La. CR4: Mitc 6E **154**
Arngask Rd. SE6 ....7F **123**
Arnham Pl. E14 ....3C **104**
Arnham Way SE22 ....5E **120**
Arnhem Wharf E14 ....3B **104**
Arnison Rd. KT8: E Mos 4H **149**
Arnold Bennett Way N8 ....3A **48**
Arnold Cir. E2 ....2J 9 (3F **85**)
Arnold Cl. HA3: Kent 7F **43**
Arnold Cres. TW7: Isle 5H **113**
Arnold Dr. KT9: Chess 6D **162**
Arnold Est. SE1 ....7K **15** (2F **103**)
(not continuous)
Arnold Gdns. N13 ....5G **33**
Arnold Ho. SE3 ....7A **106**
(off Shooters Hill Rd.)
SE17 ....5B **102**
(off Doddington Gro.)
Arnold Mans. W14 ....6H **99**
(off Queen's Club Gdns.)
Arnold Rd. E3 ....3C **86**
N15 ....3F **49**
RM9: Dag 7F **73**
SW17 ....7D **136**
UB5: N'olt 6C **58**
Arnold Ter. HA7: Stan 5E **26**
ARNOS GROVE 4B **32**
Arnos Gro. N14 ....4C **32**
Arnos Gro. Ct. N11 ....5B **32**
(off Palmer's Rd.)
Arnos Rd. N11 ....5B **32**
Arnos Swimming Pool 5C **32**
Arnot Ho. SE5 ....7C **102**
(off Comber Gro.)
Arnott Cl. SE28 ....1C **108**
W4 ....4K **97**
Arnould Av. SE5 ....4D **120**

Arnsberg Way DA6: Bex 4F **127**
DA7: Bex 4F **127**
Arnside Gdns. HA9: Wemb 1D **60**
Arnside Ho. SE17 ....6D **102**
(off Merrow St.)
Arnside Rd. DA7: Bex 1G **127**
Arnside St. SE17 ....6D **102**
Arnulf St. SE6 ....4D **140**
Arnulls Rd. SW16 ....6B **138**
Arodene Rd. SW2 ....5K **119**
Arosa Rd. TW1: Twick 6D **114**
(not continuous)
Arpley Sq. SE20 ....1J **139**
(off High St.)
Arragon Gdns. BR4: W W'ck ...3D **170**
SW16 ....7J **137**
Arragon Rd. E6 ....1B **88**
SW18 ....1J **135**
TW1: Twick 7A **114**
Arran Cl. DA8: Erith 6K **109**
SM6: Wall 4F **167**
Arran Ct. NW9 ....2B **44**
NW10 ....3K **61**
Arran Dr. E12 ....1B **70**
Arran Ho. E14 ....1E **104**
(off Raleana Rd.)
Arran M. W5 ....1F **97**
Arran Rd. SE6 ....2D **140**
Arran Wlk. N1 ....7C **66**
Arras Av. SM4: Mord 5A **154**
Arrol Ho. SE1 ....3C **102**
Arrol Rd. BR3: Beck 3J **157**
Arrow Ct. SW5 ....4J **99**
(off W. Cromwell Rd.)
Arrow Ho. N1 ....1E **84**
(off Wilmer Gdns.)
Arrow Rd. E3 ....3D **86**
Arrowscout Wlk. UB5: N'olt 3C **76**
(off Argus Way)
Arrows Ho. SE15 ....7J **103**
(off Clifton Way)
Arrowsmith Ho. SE11 ....5G **19**
Arsenal FC 4A **66**
Arsenal Rd. SE9 ....2D **124**
Arsenal Way SE18 ....3G **107**
Arta Ho. E1 ....6J **85**
(off Devonport St.)
Artemis Ct. E14 ....4C **104**
(off Homer Dr.)
Arterberry Rd. SW20 ....7E **134**
Artesian Cl. NW10 ....7K **61**
Artesian Gro. EN5: New Bar ...4F **21**
Artesian Rd. W2 ....6J **81**
Artesian Wlk. E11 ....3G **69**
Arthingworth St. E15 ....1G **87**
Arthur Ct. CR0: Croy 3E **168**
(off Fairfield Path)
SW11 ....1E **118**
W2 ....6K **81**
(off Queensway)
W10 ....6F **81**
(off Silchester Rd.)
Arthur Deakin Ho. E1 ....5K **9**
(off Hunton St.)
Arthurdon Rd. SE4 ....5C **122**
Arthur Gro. SE18 ....4G **107**
Arthur Henderson Ho. SW6 ....2H **117**
(off Fulham Rd.)
Arthur Horsley Wlk. E7 ....5H **69**
(off Twr. Hamlets Rd.)
Arthur Ho. N1 ....1E **84**
(off New Era Est.)
Arthur Rd. E6 ....2D **88**
KT2: King T 7G **133**
KT3: N Mald 5D **152**
N7 ....4K **65**
N9 ....2A **34**
RM6: Chad H 6C **54**
SW19 ....5H **135**
Arthur St. EC4 ....2F **15** (7D **84**)
Artichoke Hill E1 ....7H **85**
Artichoke M. SE5 ....1D **120**
(off Artichoke Pl.)

Artichoke Pl. SE5 1D 120
Artillery Cl. IG2: Ilf 6G 53
Artillery Ho. E15 6G 69
SE18 *5E 106*
(off Connaught M.)
Artillery La. E1 6H 9 (5E 84)
W12 6C 80
Artillery Pas. E1 6J 9
Artillery Pl. HA3: Hrw W 7B 26
SE18 5D 106
SW1 2C 18 (3H 101)
Artillery Row SW1 2C 18 (3G 101)
Artillery Sq. *SE18* *3F 107*
(off No 1 St.)
Artington Cl. BR6: Farnb 4G 173
Artisan Cl. E6 6F 89
Artisan Ct. E8 6G 67
Artisan M. *NW10* *3F 81*
(off Warfield Rd.)
Artisan Quarter *NW10* *3F 81*
(off Wellington Rd.)
Artizan St. E1 7J 9
Arts Theatre *2E 12*
(off St Martin's St.)
Arun Ct. SE25 5G 157
Arundale *KT1: King T* *4D 150*
(off Anglesea Rd.)
Arundel Av. SM4: Mord 4H 153
Arundel Bldgs. *SE1* *3E 102*
(off Swan Mead)
Arundel Cl. CR0: Wadd 3B 168
DA5: Bexl 6F 127
E15 4G 69
SW11 5C 118
TW12: Ham H 5F 131
Arundel Ct. BR2: Brom 2G 159
HA2: Harr 4E 58
N12 6H 31
N17 1G 49
SE16 *5H 103*
(off Varcoe Rd.)
SW3 *5D 16*
(off Jubilee Pl.)
SW13 *6D 98*
(off Arundel Ter.)
Arundel Dr. HA2: Harr 4D 58
IG8: Wfd G 7D 36
Arundel Gdns.
HA8: Edg 7E 28
IG3: Ilf 2A 72
N21 1F 33
W11 7H 81
Arundel Gt. Ct. WC2 2H 13 (7K 83)
Arundel Gro. N16 5E 66
Arundel Ho. *CR0: Croy* *5D 168*
(off Heathfield Rd.)
W3 *2H 97*
(off Park Rd. Nth.)
Arundel Mans. *SW6* *1H 117*
(off Kelvedon Rd.)
Arundel Pl. N1 6A 66
Arundel Rd. CR0: Croy 6D 156
EN4: Cockf 3H 21
KT1: King T 2H 151
SM2: Cheam, Sutt 7H 165
TW4: Houn 3A 112
Arundel Sq. N7 6A 66
Arundel St. WC2 2H 13 (7K 83)
Arundel Ter. SW13 6D 98
Arun Ho. KT2: King T 1D 150
Arvon Rd. N5 5A 66
(not continuous)
Asa Ct. UB3: Harl 3H 93
Asbridge Ct. *W6* *3D 98*
(off Dalling Rd.)
Ascalon Ho. *SW8* *7G 101*
(off Thessaly Rd.)
Ascalon St. SW8 7G 101
Ascham Dr. E4 7J 35
Ascham End E17 1A 50
Ascham St. NW5 5G 65
Aschurch Rd. CR0: Croy 7F 157
Ascot Cl. UB5: N'olt 5E 58
Ascot Ct. DA5: Bexl 7F 127
NW8 2A 4
Ascot Gdns. UB1: S'hall 4D 76
Ascot Ho. NW1 1K 5
W9 *4J 81*
(off Harrow Rd.)
Ascot Lodge NW6 1K 81
Ascot Pl. HA7: Stan 5H 27
Ascot Rd. BR5: St M Cry 4K 161
E6 3D 88
N15 5D 48
N18 4B 34
SW17 6E 136
TW14: Bedf 1C 128
Ascott Av. W5 2E 96
Ascott Cl. HA5: Eastc 4J 39
Ashanti M. E8 5J 67
Ashbee Ho. *E2* *3J 85*
(off Portman Pl.)
Ashbourne Av. DA7: Bex 7E 108
E18 4K 51
HA2: Harr 2H 59
N20 2J 31
NW11 5H 45
Ashbourne Cl. N12 4E 30
W5 5G 79
Ashbourne Ct. E5 4A 68
N12 *4E 30*
(off Ashbourne Cl.)
Ashbourne Gro. NW7 5E 28
SE22 4F 121
W4 5A 98
Ashbourne Pde. NW11 4H 45
W5 4F 79
Ashbourne Ri. BR6: Orp 4J 173
Ashbourne Rd. CR4: Mitc 7E 136
W5 4F 79
Ashbourne Ter. SW19 7H 135
Ashbourne Way NW11 4H 45
Ashbridge Rd. E11 7G 51
Ashbridge St. NW8 4C 4 (4C 82)
Ashbrook HA8: Edg 6A 28
Ashbrook Rd. N19 1H 65
RM10: Dag 3H 73
Ashburn Gdns. SW7 4A 100
Ashburnham Av. HA1: Harr 6K 41
Ashburnham Cl. N2 3B 46
Ashburnham Ct. BR3: Beck 2E 158
Ashburnham Gdns. HA1: Harr 6K 41
Ashburnham Gro. SE10 7D 104
Ashburnham Mans. *SW10* *7A 100*
(off Ashburnham Rd.)
Ashburnham Pl. SE10 7D 104
Ashburnham Retreat SE10 7D 104
Ashburnham Rd. DA17: Belv 4J 109
NW10 3E 80
SW10 7A 100
TW10: Ham 3B 132
Ashburnham Twr. *SW10* *7B 100*
(off Worlds End Est.)
Ashburn Pl. SW7 4A 100
Ashburton Av. CR0: Croy 1H 169
IG3: Ilf 5J 71
Ashburton Cl. CR0: Croy 1G 169
Ashburton Ent. Cen. SW15 6E 116
Ashburton Gdns. CR0: Croy 2G 169
Ashburton Gro. N7 4A 66
Ashburton Ho. *W9* *4H 81*
(off Fernhead Rd.)
Ashburton Memorial Homes
CR0: Croy 7H 157
Ashburton Rd. CR0: Croy 2G 169
E16 6J 87
HA4: Ruis 2J 57
Ashburton Ter. E13 2J 87
Ashburton Triangle N7 4A 66
Ashbury Dr. UB10: Ick 3D 56
Ashbury Gdns. RM6: Chad H 5D 54
Ashbury Pl. SW19 6A 136
Ashbury Rd. SW11 3D 118
Ashby Av. KT9: Chess 6G 163
Ashby Ct. *NW8* *3B 4*
(off Pollitt Dr.)
Ashby Gro. N1 7C 66
(not continuous)
Ashby Ho. *N1* *7C 66*
(off Essex Rd.)
SW9 2B 120
Ashby M. SE4 2B 122
SW2 *5J 119*
(off Prague Pl.)
Ashby Rd. N15 5G 49
SE4 2B 122
Ashby St. EC1 2B 8 (3B 84)
Ashby Wlk. CR0: Croy 6C 156
Ashby Way UB7: Sip 7C 92
Ashchurch Gro. W12 3C 98
Ashchurch Pk. Vs. W12 3C 98
Ashchurch Ter. W12 3C 98
Ash Cl. BR5: Pet W 5H 161
DA14: Sidc 3B 144
HA7: Stan 6F 27
HA8: Edg 4D 28
KT3: N Mald 2K 151
RM5: Col R 1H 55
SE20 2J 157
SM5: Cars 2D 166
UB9: Hare 1A 38
Ashcombe Av. KT6: Surb 7D 150
Ashcombe Gdns. HA8: Edg 4B 28
Ashcombe Ho. EN3: Pond E 3E 24
Ashcombe Pk. NW2 3A 62
Ashcombe Rd. SM5: Cars 6E 166
SW19 5J 135
Ashcombe Sq. KT3: N Mald 3J 151
Ashcombe St. SW6 2K 117
Ash Ct. KT19: Ewe 4J 163
SW19 7G 135
Ash Cft. HA5: H End 6A 26
Ashcroft N14 2C 32
Ashcroft Av. DA15: Sidc 6A 126
Ashcroft Ct. N20 2G 31
Ashcroft Cres. DA15: Sidc 6A 126
Ashcroft Ho. *SW8* *1G 119*
(off Wadhurst Rd.)
Ashcroft Rd. KT9: Chess 3F 163
Ashcroft Sq. W6 4E 98
Ashcroft Theatre *3D 168*
(in Fairfield Halls)
Ashdale Cl. TW2: Whit 7G 113
TW19: Stanw 2A 128
Ashdale Gro. HA7: Stan 6E 26
Ashdale Ho. N4 7D 48
Ashdale Rd. SE12 1K 141
Ashdale Way TW2: Whit 7F 113
Ashdene HA5: Pinn 3A 40
SE15 7H 103
Ashdene Cl. TW15: Ashf 7E 128
Ashdon Cl. IG8: Wfd G 6E 36
Ashdon Rd. NW10 1B 80
Ashdown *W13* *5B 78*
(off Clivedon Ct.)
Ashdown Cl. BR3: Beck 2D 158
DA5: Bexl 7J 127
Ashdown Ct. E17 2E 50
SM2: Sutt 6A 166
Ashdown Cres. NW5 5E 64
Ashdowne Ct. N17 1G 49
Ashdown Ho. SW1 2B 18
Ashdown Pl. KT7: T Ditt 7A 150
KT17: Ewe 7B 164
Ashdown Rd. EN3: Enf H 2D 24
KT1: King T 2E 150
UB10: Hil 2C 74
Ashdown Wlk. *E14* *4C 104*
(off Copeland Dr.)
RM7: Mawney 1H 55
Ashdown Way SW17 2E 136
Ashe Ho. TW1: Twick 6D 114
Ashen E6 6E 88
Ashenden *SE17* *4C 102*
(off Deacon Way)
Ashenden Rd. E5 5A 68
Ashen Gro. SW19 3J 135
Ashentree Ct. EC4 1K 13
Asher Loftus Way N11 6J 31
Asher Way E1 7G 85
Ashfield Av. TW13: Felt 1K 129
WD23: Bush 1B 26
Ashfield Cl. BR3: Beck 7C 140
TW10: Ham 1E 132
Ashfield Ct. *SW9* *2J 119*
(off Clapham Rd.)
Ashfield Ho. *W14* *5H 99*
(off W. Cromwell Rd.)
Ashfield La. BR7: Chst 6F 143
(not continuous)
Ashfield Pde. N14 1C 32
Ashfield Rd. N4 6C 48
N14 3B 32
W3 1B 98
Ashfield St. E1 5H 85
Ashfield Yd. E1 5J 85
ASHFORD 4B 128
Ashford Av. N8 4J 47
TW15: Ashf 6D 128
UB4: Yead 6B 76
Ashford Bus. Complex TW15: Ashf 5E 128
Ashford Cl. E17 6B 50
TW15: Ashf 4A 128
ASHFORD COMMON 7F 129
Ashford Ct. HA8: Edg 3C 28
NW2 4F 63
Ashford Cres. EN3: Enf H 2D 24
TW15: Ashf 3A 128
Ashford Ho. SE8 6B 104
SW9 4B 120
Ashford Ind. Est. TW15: Ashf 4E 128
Ashford M. N17 1G 49
Ashford Pas. NW2 4F 63
Ashford Rd. E6 7E 70
E18 2K 51
NW2 4F 63
TW13: Felt 4F 129
TW15: Ashf 7E 128
TW18: Lale, Staines 7A 128
Ashford Sports Cen. 4A 128
Ashford St. N1 1G 9 (3E 84)
Ash Gro. BR4: W W'ck 2E 170
E8 1H 85
(not continuous)
EN1: Enf 7K 23
HA0: Wemb 4A 60
N10 4F 47
N13 3H 33
NW2 4F 63
SE12 1J 141
SE20 2J 157
TW5: Hest 1B 112
TW14: Felt 1G 129
UB1: S'hall 5E 76
UB3: Hayes 7F 75
UB7: Yiew 7B 74
UB9: Hare 1A 38
W5 2E 96
Ashgrove Ct. *W9* *5J 81*
(off Elmfield Way)
Ashgrove Ho. *SW1* *5D 18*
(off Lindsay Sq.)
Ashgrove Rd. BR1: Brom 6F 141
IG3: Ilf 1K 71
TW15: Ashf 5E 128
Ash Hill Cl. WD23: Bush 1A 26
Ash Hill Dr. HA5: Pinn 3A 40
Ash Ho. *E14* *2E 104*
(off E. Ferry Rd.)
SE1 *4F 103*
(off Longfield Est.)
W10 *4G 81*
(off Heather Wlk.)
Ashingdon Cl. E4 3K 35
Ashington Ho. *E1* *4H 85*
(off Barnsley St.)
Ashington Rd. SW6 2H 117
Ashlake Rd. SW16 4J 137
Ashland Pl. W1 5G 5 (5E 82)
Ashlar Pl. SE18 4F 107
Ashleigh Commercial Est.
SE7 3A 106

Ashleigh Ct. N14 7B **22**
W5 *4D* ***96***
(off Murray Rd.)
Ashleigh Gdns. SM1: Sutt 2K **165**
Ashleigh Point SE23 3K **139**
Ashleigh Rd. SE20 3H **157**
SW14 3A **116**
Ashley Av. IG6: Ilf 2F **53**
SM4: Mord 5J **153**
Ashley Cl. HA5: Pinn 2K **39**
NW4 2E **44**
Ashley Ct. EN5: New Bar 5F **21**
NW4 2E **44**
NW9 *2B* ***44***
(off Guilfoyle)
SW1 *2A* ***18***
(off Morpeth Ter.)
UB5: N'olt 1C **76**
Ashley Cres. N22 2A **48**
SW11 3E **118**
Ashley Dr. TW2: Whit 7F **113**
TW7: Isle 6J **95**
Ashley Gdns. BR6: Orp 5J **173**
HA9: Wemb 2E **60**
N13 4H **33**
SW1 2B **18** (3G **101**)
(not continuous)
TW10: Ham 2D **132**
Ashley La. CR0: Wadd 4B **168**
NW4 7K **29**
Ashley Pl. SW1 2A **18** (3G **101**)
(not continuous)
Ashley Rd. CR7: Thor H 4K **155**
E4 6H **35**
E7 7A **70**
EN3: Enf H 2D **24**
KT7: T Ditt 6K **149**
N17 3G **49**
N19 1J **65**
SW19 6K **135**
TW9: Rich 3E **114**
TW12: Hamp 1E **148**
Ashley Wlk. NW7 7A **30**
Ashling Rd. CR0: Croy 1G **169**
Ashlin Rd. E15 4F **69**
Ash Lodge *TW16: Sun* *7H* ***129***
(off Forest Dr.)
Ashlone Rd. SW15 3E **116**
Ashlyns Way KT9: Chess 6D **162**
Ashmead N14 5B **22**
Ashmead Bus. Cen.
E16 4F **87**
Ashmead Ga. BR1: Brom 1A **160**
Ashmead Ho. *E9* *5A* ***68***
(off Homerton Rd.)
Ashmead M. SE8 2C **122**
Ashmead Rd. SE8 2C **122**
TW14: Felt 1J **129**
Ashmere Av. BR3: Beck 2F **159**
Ashmere Cl. SM3: Cheam 5F **165**
Ashmere Gro. SW2 4J **119**
Ash M. NW5 5G **65**
Ashmill St. NW1 5C **4** (5C **82**)
Ashmole Pl. SW8 6K **101**
(not continuous)
Ashmole St. SW8 6K **101**
Ashmore *NW1* *7H* ***65***
(off Agar Gro.)
Ashmore Cl. SE15 7F **103**
Ashmore Ct. N11 6J **31**
TW5: Hest 6E **94**
Ashmore Gro. DA16: Well 3H **125**
Ashmore Ho. *W14* *3G* ***99***
(off Russell Rd.)
Ashmore Rd. W9 2H **81**
Ashmount Est. N19 7H **47**
Ashmount Rd. N15 5F **49**
N19 7G **47**
Ashmount Ter. W5 4D **96**
Ashmour Gdns. RM1: Rom 2K **55**
Ashneal Gdns. HA1: Harr 3H **59**
Ashness Gdns. UB6: G'frd 6B **60**
Ashness Rd. SW11 5D **118**
Ashpark Ho. *E14* *6B* ***86***
(off Norbiton Rd.)
Ashridge Cl. HA3: Kent 6C **42**
Ashridge Ct. N14 5B **22**
UB1: S'hall *6G* ***77***
(off Redcroft Rd.)
Ashridge Cres. SE18 7G **107**
Ashridge Gdns. HA5: Pinn 4C **40**
N13 5C **32**
Ashridge Way SM4: Mord 3H **153**
TW16: Sun 6J **129**
Ash Rd. BR6: Chels 7K **173**
CR0: Croy 2C **170**
E15 5G **69**
SM3: Sutt 7G **153**
TW17: Shep 4C **146**
Ash Row BR2: Brom 7E **160**
Ashtead Rd. E5 7G **49**
Ashton Cl. SM1: Sutt 4J **165**
Ashton Ct. E4 3B **36**
HA1: Harr 3K **59**
Ashton Gdns. RM6: Chad H 6E **54**
TW4: Houn 4D **112**
Ashton Hgts. SE23 1J **139**
Ashton Ho. SW9 7A **102**
Ashton Rd. E15 5F **69**
Ashton St. E14 7E **86**
Ashtree Av. CR4: Mitc 2B **154**
Ash Tree Cl. CR0: Croy 6A **158**
KT6: Surb 2E **162**
Ashtree Cl. BR6: Farnb 4F **173**
Ash Tree Ct. *TW15: Ashf* *5D* ***128***
(off Feltham Hill Rd.)
Ash Tree Dell NW9 5J **43**
Ash Tree Ho. *SE5* *7C* ***102***
(off Pitman St.)
Ash Tree Way CR0: Croy 5K **157**
Ashurst Cl. SE20 1H **157**
Ashurst Dr. IG2: Ilf 6F **53**
IG6: Ilf 5G **53**
(Hamilton Av.)
IG6: Ilf 4G **53**
(Horns Rd.)
TW17: Shep 5A **146**
Ashurst Gdns. SW2 1A **138**
Ashurst Rd. EN4: Cockf 5J **21**
N12 5H **31**
Ashurst Wlk. CR0: Croy 2H **169**
Ashvale Rd. SW17 5D **136**
Ash Vw. Cl. TW15: Ashf 6A **128**
Ashview Gdns. TW15: Ashf 5A **128**
Ashville Rd. E11 2F **69**
Ash Wlk. HA0: Wemb 4C **60**
Ashwater Rd. SE12 1J **141**
Ashway Cen., The KT2: King T 1E **150**
Ashwell Cl. E6 6C **88**
Ashwell Ct. TW15: Ashf 2A **128**
Ashwin St. E8 6F **67**
Ashwood Av. UB8: Hil 6C **74**
Ashwood Gdns. CR0: New Ad 6E **170**
UB3: Harl 4H **93**
Ashwood Ho. *NW4* *4E* ***44***
(off Harmony Way)
Ashwood Rd. E4 3A **36**
Ashworth Cl. SE5 2D **120**
Ashworth Est. CR0: Bedd 1J **167**
Ashworth Mans. *W9* *3K* ***81***
(off Elgin Av.)
Ashworth Rd. W9 3K **81**
Aske Ho. N1 1G **9**
(not continuous)
Asker Ho. N7 4J **65**
Askern Cl. DA6: Bex 4D **126**
Aske St. N1 1G **9** (3E **84**)
Askew Cres. W12 2B **98**
Askew Est. *W12* *1B* ***98***
(off Uxbridge Rd.)
Askew Rd. W12 2B **98**
Askham Ct. W12 1C **98**
Askham Rd. W12 1C **98**
Askill Dr. SW15 5G **117**
Askwith Rd. RM13: Rain 3K **91**
Asland Rd. E15 1G **87**
Aslett St. SW18 7K **117**
Asmara Rd. NW2 5G **63**
Asmuns Hill NW11 5J **45**
Asmuns Pl. NW11 5H **45**
Asolando Dr. SE17 4C **102**
Aspect Ct. *E14* *2E* ***104***
(off Manchester Rd.)
Aspects SM1: Sutt 5K **165**
Aspen Cl. N19 2G **65**
UB7: Yiew 1B **92**
W5 2F **97**
Aspen Copse BR1: Brom 2D **160**
Aspen Dr. HA0: Wemb 3A **60**
Aspen Gdns. CR4: Mitc 5E **154**
TW15: Ashf 5E **128**
W6 5D **98**
Aspen Grn. DA18: Erith 3F **109**
Aspen Gro. HA5: Eastc 3H **39**
Aspen Ho. DA15: Sidc 2A **144**
SE15 *6J* ***103***
(off Sharratt St.)
Aspen La. UB5: N'olt 3C **76**
Aspenlea Rd. W6 6F **99**
Aspen Lodge *W8* *3K* ***99***
(off Abbots Wlk.)
Aspen Way E14 7D **86**
TW13: Felt 3K **129**
Aspern Gro. NW3 5C **64**
Aspinall Rd. SE4 3K **121**
(not continuous)
Aspinden Rd. SE16 4H **103**
Aspire National Training Cen. 2G **27**
Aspley Rd. SW18 5K **117**
Asplins Rd. N17 1G **49**
Asprey M. BR3: Beck 5B **158**
Asprey Pl. BR1: Brom 2C **160**
Asquith Cl. RM8: Dag 1C **72**
Assam St. *E1* *6G* ***85***
(off White Church La.)
Assata M. N1 6B **66**
Assembly Pas. E1 5J **85**
Assembly Wlk. SM5: Cars 7C **154**
Ass Ho. La. HA3: Hrw W 4A **26**
Association Gallery, The *3G* ***9***
(off Leonard St.)
Astall Cl. HA3: Hrw W 1J **41**
Astbury Bus. Pk. SE15 1J **121**
Astbury Ho. SE11 2J **19**
Astbury Rd. SE15 1J **121**
Astell Ho. *SW3* *5D* ***16***
(off Astell St.)
Astell St. SW3 5D **16** (5C **100**)
Aste St. E14 2E **104**
Astey's Row N1 7C **66**
Asthall Gdns. IG6: Ilf 4G **53**
Astins Ho. E17 4D **50**
Astleham Rd. TW17: Shep 3A **146**
Astle St. SW11 2E **118**
Astley Av. NW2 5E **62**
Astley Ho. *SE1* *5F* ***103***
(off Rowcross St.)
SW13 *6D* ***98***
(off Wyatt Dr.)
W2 *5J* ***81***
(off Alfred Rd.)
Aston Av. HA3: Kent 7C **42**
Aston Cl. DA14: Sidc 3A **144**
Aston Ct. IG8: Wfd G 6D **36**
Aston Grn. TW4: Cran 2A **112**
Aston Ho. SW8 1H **119**
W11 *7H* ***81***
(off Westbourne Gro.)
Aston M. RM6: Chad H 7C **54**
Aston Pl. SW16 6B **138**
Aston Rd. SW20 2E **152**
W5 6D **78**
Aston St. E14 5A **86**
Aston Ter. SW12 6F **119**
Astonville St. SW18 1J **135**
Aston Webb Ho. *SE1* *5G* ***15***
(off Braidwood St.)
Astor Av. RM7: Rom 6J **55**
Astor Cl. KT2: King T 6H **133**
Astor Ct. *E16* *6A* ***88***
(off Ripley Rd.)
SW6 *7A* ***100***
(off Maynard Cl.)
Astoria, The *7D* ***6***
(off Falconberg M.)
Astoria Ct. *E8* *7F* ***67***
(off Queensbridge Rd.)
Astoria Mans. SW16 3J **137**
Astoria Wlk. SW9 3A **120**
Astra Ho. *SE14* *6B* ***104***
(off Arklow Rd.)
Astrid Ho. TW13: Felt 2A **130**
Astrop M. W6 3E **98**
Astrop Ter. W6 2E **98**
Astwood M. SW7 4A **100**
Asylum Rd. SE15 7H **103**
Atalanta St. SW6 7F **99**
Atbara Rd. TW11: Tedd 6B **132**
Atcham Rd. TW3: Houn 4G **113**
Atcost Rd. IG11: Bark 5A **90**
Atcraft Cen. HA0: Wemb 1E **78**
Atheldene Rd. SW18 1K **135**
Athelney St. SE6 3C **140**
Athelstane Gro. E3 2B **86**
Athelstane M. N4 1A **66**
Athelstan Gdns. NW6 7G **63**
Athelstan Ho. *KT1: King T* *4F* ***151***
(off Athelstan Rd.)
Athelstan Rd. KT1: King T 4F **151**
Athelstone Rd. HA3: W'stone 2H **41**
Athena Cl. HA2: Harr 2H **59**
KT1: King T 3F **151**
Athenaeum Ct. N5 4C **66**
Athenaeum Pl. N10 3F **47**
Athenaeum Rd. N20 1F **31**
Athena Pl. HA6: Nwood 1H **39**
Athene Pl. *EC4* *7K* ***7***
(off St Andrew St.)
Athenia Ho. *E14* *6F* ***87***
(off Blair St.)
Athenlay Rd. SE15 5K **121**
Athens Gdns. *W9* *4J* ***81***
(off Harrow Rd.)
Atherden Rd. E5 4J **67**
Atherfold Rd. SW9 3J **119**
Atherley Way TW4: Houn 7D **112**
Atherstone Ct. *W2* *5K* ***81***
(off Delamere Ter.)
Atherstone M. SW7 4A **100**
Atherton Dr. SW19 4F **135**
Atherton Hgts. HA0: Wemb 7C **60**
Atherton Leisure Cen. 6H **69**
Atherton M. E7 6H **69**
Atherton Pl. HA2: Harr 3H **41**
UB1: S'hall 7E **76**
Atherton Rd. E7 6H **69**
IG5: Ilf 2C **52**
SW13 7C **98**
Atherton St. SW11 2C **118**
Athlone Cl. E5 5H **67**
Athlone Ct. E17 3F **51**
Athlone Ho. *E1* *6J* ***85***
(off Sidney St.)
Athlone Rd. SW2 7K **119**
Athlone St. NW5 6E **64**
Athlon Ind. Est. HA0: Wemb 1D **78**
Athlon Rd. HA0: Wemb 2D **78**
Athol Cl. HA5: Pinn 1K **39**
Athole Gdns. EN1: Enf 5K **23**
Athol Gdns. HA5: Pinn 1K **39**
Atholl Ho. *W9* *3A* ***82***
(off Maida Va.)
Atholl Rd. IG3: Ilf 7A **54**
Athol Rd. DA8: Erith 5J **109**
Athol Sq. E14 6E **86**
Athol Way UB10: Hil 3C **74**
Atkin Bldg. *WC1* *5H* ***7***
(off Raymond Bldgs.)
Atkins Dr. BR4: W W'ck 2F **171**
Atkinson Cl. BR6: Chels 5K **173**
Atkinson Ct. *E10* *7D* ***50***
(off Kings Cl.)

Atkinson Ho. E2 ....2G 85
  (off Pritchards Rd.)
 E13 ....4H 87
  (off Sutton Rd.)
 SE17 ....4D 102
  (off Catesby St.)
Atkinson Rd. E16 ....5A 88
Atkins Rd. E10 ....6D 50
 SW12 ....7G 119
Atlanta Bldg. SE10 ....1D 122
  (off Deal's Gateway)
Atlanta Ho. SE16 ....3A 104
  (off Brunswick Quay)
Atlantic Ct. E14 ....7F 87
  (off Jamestown Way)
Atlantic Ho. E1 ....5A 86
  (off Harford St.)
Atlantic Rd. SW9 ....4A 120
Atlantic Wharf E1 ....7K 85
Atlantis Cl. IG11: Bark 3B 90
Atlas Bus. Cen. NW2 ....1D 62
Atlas Gdns. SE7 ....4A 106
Atlas M. E8 ....6F 67
 N7 ....6K 65
Atlas Rd. E13 ....2J 87
 HA9: Wemb 4J 61
 N11 ....7K 31
 NW10 ....3A 80
Atlas Wharf E9 ....6C 68
Atley Rd. E3 ....1C 86
Atlip Rd. HA0: Wemb 1E 78
Atney Rd. SW15 ....4G 117
Atrium Apartments N1 ....1D 84
  (off Felton St.)
Atterbury Rd. N4 ....6A 48
Atterbury St. SW1 ......4D 18 (4J 101)
Attewood Av. NW10 ....3A 62
Attewood Rd. UB5: N'olt 6C 58
Attfield Cl. N20 ....2G 31
Attfield Ct. KT1: King T 2F 151
  (off Albert Rd.)
Attilburgh Ho. SE1 ....7J 15
  (off Abbey St.)
Attleborough Ct. SE23 ....2G 139
Attle Cl. UB10: Hil 2C 74
Attlee Cl. CR7: Thor H 5C 156
 UB4: Yead 3K 75
Attlee Rd. SE28 ....7B 90
 UB4: Yead 3J 75
Attlee Ter. E17 ....4D 50
Attneave St. WC1 ....2J 7 (3A 84)
Atunbi Ct. NW1 ....7G 65
  (off Farrier St.)
Atwater Cl. SW2 ....1A 138
Atwell Cl. E10 ....6D 50
Atwell Pl. KT7: T Ditt 7K 149
Atwell Rd. SE15 ....2G 121
Atwood Av. TW9: Kew 2G 115
Atwood Ho. W14 ....4H 99
  (off Beckford Cl.)
Atwood Rd. W6 ....4D 98
Atwoods All. TW9: Kew 1G 115
Aubert Cl. N5 ....4B 66
Aubert Pk. N5 ....4B 66
Aubert Rd. N5 ....4B 66
Aubrey Beardsley Ho. SW1 ......4B 18
  (off Vauxhall Bri. Rd.)
Aubrey Mans. NW1 ....5C 4
  (off Lisson St.)
Aubrey Moore Point E15 ....2E 86
  (off Abbey La.)
Aubrey Pl. NW8 ....2A 82
Aubrey Rd. E17 ....3C 50
 N8 ....5J 47
 W8 ....1H 99
Aubrey Wlk. W8 ....1H 99
Auburn Cl. SE14 ....7A 104
Aubyn Hill SE27 ....4C 138
Aubyn Sq. SW15 ....5C 116
Auckland Cl. SE19 ....1F 157
Auckland Ct. UB4: Yead 4A 76
Auckland Gdns. SE19 ....1E 156
Auckland Hill SE27 ....4C 138

Auckland Ho. W12 ....7D 80
  (off White City Est.)
Auckland Ri. SE19 ....1E 156
Auckland Rd. E10 ....3D 68
 IG1: Ilf 1F 71
 KT1: King T 4F 151
 SE19 ....1F 157
 SW11 ....4C 118
Auckland St. SE11 ......6G 19 (5K 101)
Audax NW9 ....2B 44
Auden Pl. NW1 ....1E 82
  (not continuous)
 SM3: Cheam 4E 164
Audleigh Pl. IG7: Chig 6K 37
Audley Cl. N10 ....7A 32
 SW11 ....3E 118
Audley Ct. E18 ....4H 51
 HA5: Pinn 2A 40
 TW2: Twick 3H 131
 UB5: Yead 3A 76
Audley Dr. E16 ....1K 105
Audley Gdns. IG3: Ilf 2K 71
Audley Pl. SM2: Sutt 7K 165
Audley Rd. EN2: Enf 2G 23
 NW4 ....5C 44
 TW10: Rich 5F 115
 W5 ....5F 79
Audley Sq. W1 ....4H 11 (1E 100)
Audrey Cl. BR3: Beck 6D 158
Audrey Gdns. HA0: Wemb 2B 60
Audrey Rd. IG1: Ilf 3F 71
Audrey St. E2 ....2G 85
Audric Cl. KT2: King T 1G 151
Augurs La. E13 ....3K 87
Augusta Cl. KT8: W Mole 3D 148
Augusta Rd. TW2: Twick 2G 131
Augusta St. E14 ....6D 86
Augustine Rd. HA3: Hrw W 1F 41
 W14 ....3F 99
Augustus Cl. TW8: Bford 7C 96
 W12 ....2D 98
Augustus Ct. SE1 ....4E 102
  (off Old Kent Rd.)
 SW16 ....2H 137
 TW13: Hanw 4D 130
Augustus Ho. NW1 ....1A 6
  (off Augustus St.)
Augustus La. BR6: Orp 2K 173
Augustus Rd. SW19 ....1F 135
Augustus St. NW1 ......1K 5 (2F 83)
Aultone Way SM1: Sutt 2K 165
 SM5: Cars 3D 166
Aultone Yd. Ind. Est.
 SM5: Cars 3D 166
Aulton Pl. SE11 ....6K 19 (5A 102)
Aura Ct. SE15 ....4H 121
Aura Ho. TW9: Kew 1H 115
Aurelia Gdns. CR0: Croy 5K 155
Aurelia Rd. CR0: Croy 6J 155
Auriel Av. RM10: Dag 6K 73
Auriga M. N1 ....5D 66
Auriol Cl. KT4: Wor Pk 3A 164
Auriol Dr. UB6: G'frd 7H 59
 UB10: Hil 6C 56
Auriol Ho. W12 ....1D 98
  (off Ellerslie Rd.)
Auriol Mans. W14 ....4G 99
  (off Edith Rd.)
Auriol Pk. Rd. KT4: Wor Pk 3A 164
Auriol Rd. W14 ....4G 99
Aurora Bldg. E14 ....1E 104
  (off Blackwall Way)
Aurora Ho. E14 ....6D 86
  (off Kerbey St.)
Austell Gdns. NW7 ....3F 29
Austell Hgts. NW7 ....3F 29
  (off Austell Gdns.)
Austen Cl. SE28 ....1B 108
Austen Ho. NW6 ....3J 81
  (off Cambridge Rd.)
Austen Rd. DA8: Erith 7H 109
 HA2: Harr 2F 59
Austin Av. BR2: Brom 5C 160

Austin Cl. SE23 ....7A 122
 TW1: Twick 5C 114
Austin Ct. E6 ....1A 88
 EN1: Enf 5K 23
 SE15 ....3G 121
  (off Philip Wlk.)
Austin Friars EC2 ......7F 9 (6D 84)
  (not continuous)
Austin Friars Pas. EC2 ....7F 9
Austin Friars Sq. EC2 ....7F 9
Austin Ho. SE14 ....7B 104
  (off Achilles St.)
Austin Rd. SW11 ....1E 118
 UB3: Hayes 2H 93
Austin's La. HA4: Ruis 4F 57
 UB10: Ick 3E 56
Austin St. E2 ....2J 9 (3F 85)
Austin Ter. SE1 ....1K 19
  (off Morley St.)
Austral Cl. DA15: Sidc 3K 143
Australian War Memorial 6H 11
  (off Duke of Wellington Pl.)
Australia Rd. W12 ....7D 80
 Austral St. SE11 ......3K 19 (4B 102)
Austyn Gdns. KT5: Surb 1H 163
Austyns Pl. KT17: Ewe 7C 164
Autumn Cl. EN1: Enf 1B 24
 SW19 ....6A 136
Autumn Gro. BR1: Brom 6K 141
Autumn Lodge CR0: Croy 4E 168
  (off South Pk. Hill Rd.)
Autumn St. E3 ....1C 86
Avalon Cl. EN2: Enf 2F 23
 SW20 ....2G 153
 W13 ....5A 78
Avalon Rd. SW6 ....1K 117
 W13 ....4A 78
Avante KT1: King T 3D 150
Avard Gdns. BR6: Farnb 4G 173
Avarn Rd. SW17 ....6D 136
Avebury Ct. N1 ....1D 84
  (off Imber St.)
Avebury Pk. KT6: Surb 7D 150
Avebury Rd. BR6: Orp 3H 173
 E11 ....1F 69
 SW19 ....1H 153
Avebury St. N1 ....1D 84
Aveley Mans. IG11: Bark 7F 71
  (off Whiting Av.)
Aveley Rd. RM1: Rom 4K 55
Aveline St. SE11 ......5H 19 (5A 102)
Aveling Pk. Rd. E17 ....2C 50
Ave Maria La. EC4 ......1B 14 (6B 84)
Avenell Mans. N5 ....4B 66
Avenell Rd. N5 ....3B 66
Avenfield Ho. W1 ....2F 11
  (off Park La.)
Avening Rd. SW18 ....7J 117
Avening Ter. SW18 ....7J 117
Avenons Rd. E13 ....4J 87
Avenue, The BR1: Brom 3B 160
 BR2: Kes 4B 172
 BR3: Beck 1D 158
  (not continuous)
 BR4: W W'ck 7E 158
 BR5: St P 7B 144
 BR6: Orp 2K 173
 CR0: Croy 3E 168
 DA5: Bexl 7D 126
 E4 ....6A 36
 E11 ....6K 51
 EN5: Barn 3B 20
 HA3: Hrw W 1K 41
 HA5: Pinn 6D 40
 HA9: Wemb 1E 60
 IG9: Buck H 2F 37
 KT4: Wor Pk 2B 164
 KT5: Surb 6F 151
 KT17: Ewe 7D 164
 N3 ....2J 45
 N8 ....3A 48
 N10 ....2G 47
 N11 ....5A 32

Avenue, The N17 ....3D 48
 NW6 ....1F 81
 RM1: Rom 4K 55
 SE10 ....7F 105
 SM2: Cheam 7G 165
 SM3: Cheam 7E 164
 SM5: Cars 7E 166
 SW4 ....5E 118
 SW18 ....7C 118
 TW1: Twick 5B 114
 TW3: Houn 5F 113
 TW5: Cran 7J 93
 TW9: Kew 2F 115
 TW12: Hamp 6D 130
 TW16: Sun 1K 147
 UB10: Ick 4C 56
 W4 ....3A 98
 W13 ....6B 78
Avenue Cl. N14 ....6B 22
 NW8 ....1C 82
 TW5: Cran 1K 111
 UB7: W Dray 3A 92
Avenue Ct. N14 ....6B 22
 NW2 ....3H 63
 SW3 ....4E 16
  (off Draycott Av.)
Avenue Cres. TW5: Cran 1K 111
 W3 ....2H 97
Avenue Elmers KT6: Surb 5E 150
Avenue Gdns. SE25 ....2G 157
 SW14 ....3A 116
 TW5: Cran 7K 93
 TW11: Tedd 7K 131
 W3 ....2H 97
Avenue Ho. NW8 ....2C 82
  (off Allitsen Rd.)
 NW10 ....2D 80
  (off All Souls Av.)
Avenue Ind. Est. E4 ....6G 35
Avenue Lodge NW8 ....7B 64
  (off Avenue Rd.)
Avenue Mans. NW3 ....5K 63
  (off Finchley Rd.)
Avenue M. N10 ....3F 47
Avenue Pde. N21 ....7J 23
 TW16: Sun 3K 147
Avenue Pk. Rd. SE27 ....2B 138
Avenue Rd. BR3: Beck 2K 157
 DA7: Bex 3E 126
 DA8: Erith 7J 109
 DA17: Belv, Erith 4J 109
 E7 ....4K 69
 HA5: Pinn 3C 40
 IG8: Wfd G 6F 37
 KT1: King T 3E 150
 KT3: N Mald 4A 152
 N6 ....7G 47
 N12 ....4F 31
 N14 ....7B 22
 N15 ....5D 48
 NW3 ....7B 64
 NW8 ....7B 64
 NW10 ....2B 80
 RM6: Chad H 7B 54
 SE20 ....1J 157
 SE25 ....2F 157
 SM6: Wall 7G 167
 SW16 ....2H 155
 SW20 ....2D 152
 TW7: Isle 1K 113
 TW8: Bford 5C 96
 TW11: Tedd 7A 132
 TW12: Hamp 1F 149
 TW13: Felt 3H 129
 UB1: S'hall 1D 94
 W3 ....2H 97
Avenue Sth. KT5: Surb 7G 151
Avenue Ter. KT3: N Mald 3U 151
Averil Gro. SW16 ....6B 138
Averill St. W6 ....6F 99
Avern Gdns. KT8: W Mole 4F 149
Avern Rd. KT8: W Mole 4F 149
Avery Farm Row SW1 .....4J 17 (4E 100)

Avery Gdns. IG2: Ilf 5D **52**
AVERY HILL 6H **125**
Avery Hill Rd. SE9 6H **125**
Avery Row W1 2J **11** (7F **83**)
Aviary Cl. E16 5H **87**
Aviemore Cl. BR3: Beck 5B **158**
Aviemore Way BR3: Beck 5A **158**
Avignon Rd. SE4 3K **121**
Avingdor Ct. *W3* *1J* ***97*** *(off Horn La.)*
Avington Ct. *SE1* *4E* ***102*** *(off Old Kent Rd.)*
Avington Gro. SE20 7J **139**
Avion Cres. NW9 1C **44**
Avis Sq. E1 6K **85**
Avoca Rd. SW17 4E **136**
Avocet Cl. SE1 5G **103**
Avocet M. SE28 3H **107**
Avon Cl. KT4: Wor Pk 2C **164**
SM1: Sutt 4A **166**
UB4: Yead 4A **76**
Avon Ct. E4 1K **35**
IG9: Buck H 1E **36**
N12 5E **30**
SW15 5G **117**
UB6: G'frd 4F **77**
W9 *5J* ***81*** *(off Elmfield Way)*
Avondale Av. EN4: E Barn 1J **31**
KT4: Wor Pk 1B **164**
KT10: Hin W 3A **162**
N12 5E **30**
NW2 3A **62**
Avondale Ct. E11 1G **69**
E16 5G **87**
E18 1K **51**
SM2: Sutt *7A* ***166*** *(off Brighton Rd.)*
Avondale Cres. EN3: Enf H 3F **25**
IG4: Ilf 5B **52**
Avondale Dr. UB3: Hayes 1J **93**
Avondale Gdns. TW4: Houn 5D **112**
Avondale Ho. *SE1* *5G* ***103*** *(off Avondale Sq.)*
Avondale Pk. Gdns. W11 7G **81**
Avondale Pk. Rd. W11 7G **81**
Avondale Pavement SE1 5G **103**
Avondale Ri. SE15 3F **121**
Avondale Rd. BR1: Brom 6G **141**
CR2: S Croy 6C **168**
DA16: Well 2C **126**
E16 5G **87**
E17 7C **50**
HA3: W'stone 3K **41**
N3 1A **46**
N13 2F **33**
N15 5B **48**
SE9 2C **142**
SW14 3A **116**
SW19 5K **135**
TW15: Ashf 3A **128**
Avondale Sq. SE1 5G **103**
Avonfield Ct. E17 3F **51**
Avon Ho. KT2: King T 1D **150**
W8 *3J* ***99*** *(off Allen St.)*
W14 *4H* ***99*** *(off Kensington Village)*
Avonhurst Ho. NW2 7G **63**
Avonley Rd. SE14 7J **103**
Avon M. HA5: H End 1D **40**
Avonmore Gdns. W14 4H **99**
Avonmore Pl. W14 4G **99**
Avonmore Rd. W14 4G **99**
Avonmouth St. SE1 7C **14** (3C **102**)
Avon Path CR2: S Croy 6C **168**
Avon Pl. SE1 7D **14** (2C **102**)
Avon Rd. E17 3F **51**
SE4 3C **122**
TW16: Sun 7H **129**
UB6: G'frd 4E **76**
Avonstowe Cl. BR6: Farnb 3G **173**
Avon Way E18 3J **51**
Avonwick Rd. TW3: Houn 2F **113**
Avril Way E4 5K **35**
Avro Ho. *SW8* *7F* ***101*** *(off Havelock Ter.)*
Avro Way SM6: Wall 7J **167**
Awlfield Av. N17 1D **48**
Awliscombe Rd. DA16: Well 2K **125**
Axe St. IG11: Bark 1G **89** (not continuous)
Axholme Av. HA8: Edg 1G **43**
Axiom Apartments *BR2: Brom* *4K* ***159*** *(off Masons Hill)*
Axis Ct. *SE10* *6G* ***105*** *(off Woodland Cres.)*
SE16 *2G* ***103*** *(off Nth. Flock St.)*
Axminster Cres. DA16: Well 1C **126**
Axminster Rd. N7 3J **65**
Axon Pl. IG1: Ilf 2G **71**
Aybrook St. W1 6G **5** (5E **82**)
Aycliffe Cl. BR1: Brom 4D **160**
Aycliffe Ho. *SE17* *6D* ***102*** *(off Portland St.)*
Aycliffe Rd. W12 1C **98**
Ayerst Ct. E10 7E **50**
Aylands Cl. HA9: Wemb 2E **60**
Aylesbury Cl. E7 6H **69**
Aylesbury Ct. SM1: Sutt 3A **166**
Aylesbury Ho. *SE15* *6G* ***103*** *(off Friary Est.)*
Aylesbury Rd. BR2: Brom 3J **159**
SE17 5D **102**
Aylesbury St. EC1 4A **8** (4B **84**)
NW10 3K **61**
Aylesford Av. BR3: Beck 5A **158**
Aylesford Ho. *SE1* *7F* ***15*** *(off Long La.)*
Aylesford St. SW1 5C **18** (5H **101**)
Aylesham Cen., The SE15 1G **121**
Aylesham Cl. NW7 7H **29**
Aylesham Rd. BR6: Orp 7K **161**
Ayles Rd. UB4: Yead 3K **75**
Aylestone Av. NW6 7F **63**
Aylett Rd. SE25 4H **157**
TW7: Isle 2J **113**
Ayley Cft. EN1: Enf 5B **24**
Ayliffe Cl. KT1: King T 2G **151**
Aylmer Cl. HA7: Stan 4F **27**
Aylmer Ct. N2 5D **46**
Aylmer Dr. HA7: Stan 4F **27**
Aylmer Ho. SE10 5F **105**
Aylmer Pde. N2 5D **46**
Aylmer Rd. E11 1H **69**
N2 5C **46**
RM8: Dag 3E **72**
W12 2B **98**
Ayloffe Rd. RM9: Dag 6F **73**
Aylsham Dr. UB10: Ick 2E **56**
Aylton Est. SE16 2J **103**
Aylward Rd. SE23 2K **139**
SW20 2H **153**
Aylward School Sports Cen. 4J **33**
Aylwards Ri. HA7: Stan 4F **27**
Aylward St. E1 6J **85** (Jamaica St.)
E1 6J **85** (Jubilee St.)
Aylwin Est. SE1 3E **102**
Aynhoe Mans. *W14* *4F* ***99*** *(off Aynhoe Rd.)*
Aynhoe Rd. W14 4F **99**
Aynscombe Path SW14 2J **115**
Ayr Ct. W3 5G **79**
Ayres Cl. E13 3J **87**
Ayres Cres. NW10 7K **61**
Ayres St. SE1 6D **14** (2C **102**)
Ayr Grn. RM1: Rom 1K **55**
Ayrsome Rd. N16 3E **66**
Ayrton Gould Ho. *E2* *3K* ***85*** *(off Roman Rd.)*
Ayrton Rd. SW7 1A **16** (3B **100**)
Ayr Way RM1: Rom 1K **55**
Aysgarth Ct. SM1: Sutt 3K **165**
Aysgarth Rd. SE21 7E **120**
Ayshford Ho. *E2* *3H* ***85*** *(off Viaduct St.)*
Ayston Ho. *SE16* *4K* ***103*** *(off Plough Way)*
Ayton Ho. *SE5* *7D* ***102*** *(off Edmund St.)*
Aytoun Pl. SW9 2K **119**
Aytoun Rd. SW9 2K **119**
Azalea Cl. IG1: Ilf 5F **71**
W7 1K **95**
Azalea Ct. IG8: Wfd G 6B **36**
W7 1K **95**
Azalea Ho. *SE14* *7B* ***104*** *(off Achilles St.)*
Azalea Wlk. HA5: Eastc 5K **39**
Azania M. NW5 6F **65**
Azenby Rd. SE15 2F **121**
Azof St. SE10 4G **105**
Azov Ho. *E1* *4A* ***86*** *(off Commodore St.)*
Aztec Ho. IG6: Ilf 1G **53**
Azure Ho. *E2* *3G* ***85*** *(off Buckfast St.)*

B

Baalbec Rd. N5 5B **66**
Babbacombe Cl. KT9: Chess 5D **162**
Babbacombe Gdns. IG4: Ilf 4C **52**
Babbacombe Rd. BR1: Brom 1J **159**
Baber Bri. Cvn. Site TW14: Felt 5A **112**
Baber Dr. TW14: Felt 6A **112**
Babington Ct. WC1 5G **7**
Babington Ho. *SE1* *6D* ***14*** *(off Disney St.)*
Babington Ri. HA9: Wemb 6G **61**
Babington Rd. NW4 4D **44**
RM8: Dag 5C **72**
SW16 5H **137**
Babmaes St. SW1 3C **12** (7H **83**)
Bacchus Wlk. *N1* *2E* ***84*** *(off Regan Way)*
Bache's St. N1 1F **9** (3D **84**)
Back All. EC3 1H **15**
Bk. Church La. E1 6G **85**
Back Hill EC1 4K **7** (4A **84**)
Backhouse Pl. SE17 4E **102**
Back La. DA5: Bexl 7G **127**
HA8: Edg 1J **43**
IG9: Buck H 2G **37**
N8 5J **47**
NW3 4A **64**
RM6: Chad H 7D **54**
TW8: Bford 6D **96**
TW10: Ham 3C **132**
Backley Gdns. SE25 6G **157**
Bk. Passage *EC1* *5B* ***8*** *(off Long La.)*
Back Rd. DA14: Sidc 4A **144**
TW11: Tedd 7J **131**
Bacon Gro. SE1 3F **103**
Bacon La. HA8: Edg 1G **43**
NW9 4H **43** (not continuous)
Bacon's College Sports Cen. 1A **104**
Bacons La. N6 1E **64**
Bacon St. E1 3K **9** (4F **85**)
E2 3K **9** (4F **85**)
Bacon Ter. RM8: Dag 5B **72**
Bacton NW5 5E **64**
Bacton St. E2 3J **85**
Baddeley Ho. *KT8: W Mole* *5E* ***148*** *(off Down St.)*
Baddesley Ho. SE11 5H **19**
Baddow Cl. IG8: Wfd G 6F **37**
RM10: Dag 1G **91**
Baddow Wlk. *N1* *1C* ***84*** *(off New Nth. Rd.)*
Baden Pl. SE1 6E **14** (2D **102**)
Baden Powell Cl. KT6: Surb 2F **163**
RM9: Dag 1E **90**
Baden Powell Ho. *DA17: Belv* *3G* ***109*** *(off Ambrooke Rd.)*
SW7 2A **16**
Baden Rd. IG1: Ilf 5F **71**
N8 4H **47**
Badger Cl. IG2: Ilf 6G **53**
TW4: Houn 3A **112**
TW13: Felt 3K **129**
Badger Ct. NW2 3E **62**
Badgers Cl. EN2: Enf 3G **23**
HA1: Harr 6H **41**
TW15: Ashf 5B **128**
UB3: Hayes 7G **75**
Badgers Copse BR6: Orp 2K **173**
KT4: Wor Pk 2B **164**
Badgers Cft. N20 7B **20**
SE9 3E **142**
Badgers Hole CR0: Croy 4K **169**
Badgers Wlk. KT3: N Mald 2A **152**
Badlis Rd. E17 3C **50**
Badma Cl. N9 3D **34**
Badminton Cl. HA1: Harr 4J **41**
UB5: N'olt 6E **58**
Badminton M. E16 1J **105**
Badminton Rd. SW12 6E **118**
Badric Ct. SW11 2B **118**
Badsworth Rd. SE5 1C **120**
Baffin Way E14 1E **104**
Bafton Ga. BR2: Hayes 1K **171**
Bagley Cl. UB7: W Dray 2A **92**
Bagley's La. SW6 1K **117**
Bagleys Spring RM6: Chad H 4E **54**
Bagnigge Ho. *WC1* *2J* ***7*** *(off Margery St.)*
Bagshot Ct. SE18 1E **124**
Bagshot Ho. NW1 1K **5**
Bagshot Rd. EN1: Enf 7A **24**
Bagshot St. SE17 5E **102**
Baildon *E2* *2J* ***85*** *(off Cyprus St.)*
Baildon St. SE8 7B **104**
Bailey Cl. E4 4K **35**
N11 7C **32**
SE28 1J **107**
Bailey Cotts. *E14* *5A* ***86*** *(off Maroon St.)*
Bailey Cres. KT9: Chess 7C **162**
Bailey Ho. *SW10* *7K* ***99*** *(off Coleridge Gdns.)*
Bailey M. SW2 5A **120**
W4 *6H* ***97*** *(off Hervert Gdns.)*
Bailey Pl. SE26 6K **139**
Baillies Wlk. W5 2D **96**
Bainbridge Cl. TW10: Ham 5E **132**
Bainbridge Rd. RM9: Dag 4F **73**
Bainbridge St. WC1 7D **6** (6H **83**)
Baines Cl. CR2: S Croy 5D **168**
Baird Av. UB1: S'hall 7F **77**
Baird Cl. E10 1C **68**
NW9 6J **43**
Baird Gdns. SE19 4E **138**
Baird Ho. *W12* *7D* ***80*** *(off White City Est.)*
Baird Memorial Cotts. *N14* *2C* ***32*** *(off Balaams La.)*
Baird Rd. EN1: Enf 3C **24**
Baird St. EC1 3D **8** (4C **84**)
Bairny Wood App. IG8: Wfd G 6E **36**
Baizdon Rd. SE3 2G **123**
Baker Beal Ct. DA7: Bex 3H **127**
Baker Ho. W7 1K **95**
WC1 *4F* ***7*** *(off Colonnade)*
Baker La. CR4: Mitc 2E **154**
Baker Pas. NW10 1A **80**
Baker Rd. NW10 1A **80**
SE18 7C **106**
Bakers Av. E17 6D **50**
Bakers Ct. SE25 3E **156**
Bakers End SW20 2G **153**
Baker's Fld. N7 4J **65**
Bakers Gdns. SM5: Cars 2C **166**

Bakers Hall Ct. EC3 ....3G 15
Bakers Hill E5 ....1J 67
  EN5: New Bar 2E 20
Bakers Ho. W5 ....7D 78
  (off The Grove)
Bakers La. N6 ....6D 46
Bakers M. BR6: Chels 6K 173
  W1 ....7G 5 (6E 82)
Bakers Pas. NW3 ....4A 64
  (off Heath St.)
Baker's Rents E2 ....2J 9 (3F 85)
Baker's Row E15 ....2G 87
  EC1 ....4J 7 (4A 84)
BAKER STREET 5D 82
Baker St. EN1: Enf 3J 23
  NW1 ....4F 5 (4D 82)
  W1 ....5F 5 (4D 82)
Baker's Yd. EC1 ....4J 7
Bakery Cl. SW9 ....7K 101
Bakery M. KT6: Surb 1G 163
Bakery Path HA8: Edg 6C 28
  (off St Margaret's Rd.)
Bakery Pl. SW11 ....4D 118
Bakewell Way KT3: N Mald 2A 152
Balaam Ho. SM1: Sutt 4J 165
Balaam Leisure Cen. 4J 87
Balaams La. N14 ....2C 32
Balaam St. E13 ....4J 87
Balaclava Rd. KT6: Surb 7C 150
  SE1 ....4F 103
Bala Grn. NW9 ....6A 44
  (off Ruthin Cl.)
Balcaskie Rd. SE9 ....5D 124
Balchen Rd. SE3 ....2B 124
Balchier Rd. SE22 ....6H 121
Balcombe Cl. DA6: Bex 4D 126
Balcombe Ho. NW1 ....3E 4
  (off Taunton Pl.)
Balcombe St. NW1 ....3E 4 (4D 82)
Balcon Cl. W5 ....6F 79
Balcorne St. E9 ....7J 67
Balder Ri. SE12 ....2K 141
Balderton Flats W1 ....1H 11
  (off Balderton St.)
Balderton St. W1 ......1H 11 (6E 82)
Baldewyne Ct. N17 ....1G 49
Baldock St. E3 ....2D 86
Baldrey Ho. SE10 ....5H 105
  (off Blackwall La.)
Baldry Gdns. SW16 ....6J 137
Baldwin Cres. SE5 ....1C 120
Baldwin Gdns. TW3: Houn 1G 113
Baldwin Ho. SW2 ....1A 138
Baldwins Gdns. EC1 ....5J 7 (5A 84)
Baldwin St. EC1 ....2E 8 (3D 84)
Baldwin Ter. N1 ....2C 84
Baldwyn Gdns. W3 ....7K 79
Baldwyn's Pk. DA5: Bexl 2K 145
Baldwyn's Rd. DA5: Bexl 2K 145
Balearic Apartments E16 ....7J 87
  (off Western Gateway)
Bale Rd. E1 ....5A 86
Bales Ter. N9 ....3A 34
Balfern Gro. W4 ....5A 98
Balfern St. SW11 ....2C 118
Balfe St. N1 ....2J 83
Balfour Av. W7 ....1K 95
Balfour Bus. Cen. UB2: S'hall ...3A 94
Balfour Gro. N20 ....3J 31
Balfour Ho. W10 ....5F 81
  (off St Charles Sq.)
Balfour M. N9 ....3B 34
  W1 ....4H 11 (1E 100)
Balfour Pl. SW15 ....4D 116
  W1 ....3H 11 (7E 82)
Balfour Rd. BR2: Brom 5B 160
  HA1: Harr 5H 41
  IG1: Ilf 2F 71
  N5 ....4C 66
  SE25 ....5G 157
  SM5: Cars 7D 166
  SW19 ....7K 135
  TW3: Houn 3F 113

Balfour Rd. UB2: S'hall 3B 94
  W3 ....5J 79
  W13 ....2A 96
Balfour St. SE17 ....4D 102
Balfour Ter. N3 ....2K 45
Balfron Twr. E14 ....6E 86
Balgonie Rd. E4 ....1A 36
Balgowan Cl. KT3: N Mald 5A 152
Balgowan Rd. BR3: Beck 3A 158
Balgowan St. SE18 ....4K 107
BALHAM 1E 136
Balham Continental Mkt. SW12 ..1F 137
  (off Shipka Rd.)
Balham Gro. SW12 ....7E 118
Balham High Rd. SW12 ....3E 136
  SW17 ....3E 136
Balham Hill SW12 ....7F 119
Balham Leisure Cen. 2F 137
Balham New Rd. SW12 ....7F 119
Balham Pk. Rd. SW12 ....1D 136
Balham Rd. N9 ....2B 34
Balham Sta. Rd. SW12 ....1F 137
Balin Ho. SE1 ....6E 14
  (off Long La.)
Balkan Wlk. E1 ....7H 85
Balladier Wlk. E14 ....5D 86
Ballamore Rd. BR1: Brom 3J 141
Ballance Rd. E9 ....6K 67
Ballantine St. SW18 ....4A 118
Ballantrae Ho. NW2 ....4H 63
Ballard Cl. KT2: King T 7K 133
Ballard Ho. SE10 ....6D 104
  (off Thames St.)
Ballards Cl. RM10: Dag 1H 91
Ballards Farm Rd. CR0: Croy ..6G 169
  CR2: S Croy 6G 169
Ballards La. N3 ....1J 45
  N12 ....1J 45
Ballards M. HA8: Edg 6B 28
Ballards Ri. CR2: Sels 6G 169
Ballards Rd. NW2 ....2C 62
  RM10: Dag 2H 91
Ballards Way CR0: Croy 6G 169
  CR2: Sels 6G 169
Ballast Quay SE10 ....5F 105
Ballater Rd. CR2: S Croy 5F 169
  SW2 ....4J 119
Ball Ct. EC3 ....1F 15
  (off Cornhill)
Ballina St. SE23 ....7K 121
Ballin Ct. E14 ....2E 104
  (off Stewart St.)
Ballingdon Rd. SW11 ....6E 118
Ballinger Way UB5: Yead 4C 76
Balliol Av. E4 ....4B 36
Balliol Rd. DA16: Well 2B 126
  N17 ....1E 48
  W10 ....6E 80
Balloch Rd. SE6 ....1F 141
Ballogie Av. NW10 ....4A 62
Ballow Cl. SE5 ....7E 102
Balmain Cl. W5 ....1D 96
Balmain Ct. TW3: Houn 1F 113
Balmain Lodge KT5: Surb 4E 150
  (off Cranes Pk. Av.)
Balman Ho. SE16 ....4K 103
  (off Rotherhithe New Rd.)
Balmer Rd. E3 ....2B 86
Balmes Rd. N1 ....1D 84
Balmoral Apartments W2 ....6C 4
  (off Praed St.)
Balmoral Av. BR3: Beck 4A 158
  N11 ....6K 31
Balmoral Cl. SW15 ....6F 117
Balmoral Ct. BR3: Beck 1E 158
  (off The Avenue)
  HA9: Wemb 3F 61
  KT4: Wor Pk 2D 164
  SE12 ....4K 141
  SE16 ....1K 103
  (off King & Queen Wharf)

Balmoral Ct. SE17 ....5D 102
  (off Lytham St.)
  SE27 ....4C 138
  SM2: Sutt 7J 165
Balmoral Cres. KT8: W Mole ...3E 148
Balmoral Dr. UB1: S'hall 4D 76
  UB4: Hayes 4G 75
Balmoral Gdns. DA5: Bexl 7F 127
  IG3: Ilf 1K 71
  W13 ....3A 96
Balmoral Gro. N7 ....6K 65
Balmoral Ho. E14 ....3D 104
  (off Lanark Sq.)
  E16 ....1K 105
  (off Keats Av.)
  W14 ....4G 99
  (off Windsor Way)
Balmoral M. W12 ....3B 98
Balmoral Rd. E7 ....4A 70
  E10 ....2D 68
  HA2: Harr 4E 58
  KT1: King T 4F 151
  KT4: Wor Pk 3D 164
  NW2 ....6D 62
Balmoral Trad. Est. IG11: Bark ..5K 89
Balmore Cl. E14 ....6E 86
Balmore Cres. EN4: Cockf 5K 21
Balmore St. N19 ....2F 65
Balmuir Gdns. SW15 ....4E 116
Balnacraig Av. NW10 ....4A 62
Balniel Ga. SW1 ......5D 18 (5H 101)
Balnie Ho. E14 ....7D 86
  (off E. India Dock Rd.)
Baltic Apartments E16 ....7J 87
  (off Western Gateway)
Baltic Cen., The TW8: Bford ..5D 96
Baltic Cl. SW19 ....7B 136
Baltic Ct. SE16 ....2K 103
Baltic Ho. SE5 ....2C 120
Baltic Pl. N1 ....1E 84
Baltic St. E. EC1 ......4C 8 (4C 84)
Baltic St. W. EC1 .....4C 8 (4C 84)
Baltimore Ct. SW1 ....4C 18
  (off Chapter St.)
Baltimore Ho. SE11 ....5J 19
Baltimore Pl. DA16: Well 2K 125
Balvaird Pl. SW1 .....6D 18 (5H 101)
Balvernie Gro. SW18 ....7H 117
Balvernie M. SW18 ....7J 117
Bamber Ho. IG11: Bark 1H 89
Bamber Rd. SE15 ....1F 121
Bamborough Gdns. W12 ....2E 98
Bamford Av. HA0: Wemb 1F 79
Bamford Ct. E15 ....5D 68
  (off Clays La.)
Bamford Rd. BR1: Brom 5E 140
  IG11: Bark 6G 71
Bampfylde Cl. SM6: Wall 3G 167
Bampton Cl. W5 ....6D 78
Bampton Dr. NW7 ....7H 29
Bampton Rd. SE23 ....3K 139
Banavie Gdns. BR3: Beck 1E 158
Banbury Cl. EN2: Enf 1G 23
Banbury Ct. SM2: Sutt 7J 165
  WC2 ....2E 12
Banbury Ho. E9 ....7K 67
Banbury Rd. E9 ....7K 67
  E17 ....7E 34
Banbury St. SW11 ....2C 118
Banbury Wlk. UB5: N'olt 2E 76
  (off Brabazon Rd.)
Banchory Rd. SE3 ....7K 105
Bancroft Av. IG9: Buck H 2D 36
  N2 ....5C 46
Bancroft Ct. TW15: Ashf 5C 128
Bancroft Ct. SW8 ....7J 101
  (off Allen Edwards Dr.)
  UB5: N'olt 1A 76
Bancroft Gdns. BR6: Orp 1K 173
  HA3: Hrw W 1G 41
Bancroft Ho. E1 ....(off Cephas St.)

Bancroft Rd. E1 ....3J 85
  HA3: Hrw W 2G 41
Bandon Cl. UB10: Uxb 2B 74
BANDONHILL 5H 167
Bandon Ri. SM6: Wall 5H 167
Banfield Rd. SE15 ....3H 121
Banfor Ct. SM6: Wall 5G 167
Bangalore St. SW15 ....3E 116
Bangor Cl. UB5: N'olt 5F 59
Banim St. W6 ....4D 98
Banister Ho. E9 ....5K 67
  SW8 ....1G 119
  (off Wadhurst Rd.)
  W10 ....3G 81
  (off Bruckner St.)
Banister M. NW6 ....7K 63
Banister Rd. W10 ....3F 81
Bank, The N6 ....1F 65
Bank Av. CR4: Mitc 2B 154
Bank Bldgs. E4 ....6A 36
  (off The Avenue)
Bank End SE1 ....4D 14 (1C 102)
Bankfoot Rd. BR1: Brom 4G 141
Bankhurst Rd. SE6 ....7B 122
Bank La. KT2: King T 7E 132
  SW15 ....5A 116
Bank M. SM1: Sutt 6A 166
Bank of England 1E 14 (6D 84)
Bank of England Mus. 1F 15
Banks Ho. SE1 ....3C 102
  (off Rockingham St.)
Banksian Wlk. TW7: Isle 1J 113
Banksia Rd. N18 ....5E 34
Bankside CR2: S Croy 6C 169
  EN2: Enf 1G 23
  SE1 ....3C 14 (7C 84)
  (not continuous)
  UB1: S'hall 1B 94
Bankside Art Gallery 3B 14 (7B 84)
Bankside Av. UB5: Yead 2J 75
Bankside Cl. DA5: Bexl 4K 145
  IG1: Ilf 5G 71
  SM5: Cars 6C 166
  TW7: Isle 1K 113
Bankside Dr. KT7: T Ditt 1B 162
Bankside Ho. IG11: Bark 3A 90
Bankside Rd. IG1: Ilf 5G 71
Bankside Way SE19 ....6E 138
Banks La. DA6: Bex 4F 127
Bank St. E14 ....1D 104
Banks Way E12 ....4E 70
Bankton Rd. SW2 ....4A 120
Bankwell Rd. SE13 ....4G 123
Bannatyne's Health Club
  Chingford 6H 35
  Grove Park 2K 141
Banner Ct. SE16 ....4J 103
  (off Rotherhithe New Rd.)
Bannerman Ho. SW8 ......7G 19 (6K 101)
Banner St. EC1 ....4D 8 (4C 84)
Banning St. SE10 ....5G 105
Bannister Cl. SW2 ....1A 138
  UB6: G'frd 5H 59
Bannister Ho. SE14 ....6K 103
  (off John Williams Cl.)
Bannockburn Rd. SE18 ....4J 107
Bannow Cl. KT19: Ewe 4A 164
Banqueting House 5E 12 (1J 101)
Banstead Gdns. N9 ....3K 33
Banstead Rd. SM5: Cars 7B 166
Banstead Rd. Sth. SM2: Sutt ..7B 166
Banstead St. SE15 ....3J 121
Banstead Way SM6: Wall 5J 167
Banstock Rd. HA8: Edg 6C 28
Banting Dr. N21 ....5E 22
Banting Ho. NW2 ....3C 62
Bantock Ho. W10 ....3G 81
  (off Third Av.)
Banton Cl. EN1: Enf 2C 24
Bantry Ho. E1 ....4K 85
  (off Ernest St.)
Bantry St. SE5 ....7D 102
Banwell Rd. DA5: Bexl 6D 126
Banyard Rd. SE16 ....3H 103

Baptist Gdns. NW5 ....6E 64
Barandon Rd. W11 ....7F 81
(off Grenfell Rd.)
Barandon Wlk. W11 ....7F 81
Barbanel Ho. E1 ....4J 85
(off Cephas St.)
Barbara Brosnan Ct. NW8 ....1A 4 (2B 82)
Barbara Castle Cl. SW6 ....6H 99
(off Coomer Pl.)
Barbara Cl. TW17: Shep 5D 146
Barbara Hucklesby Cl.
  N22 ....2B 48
Barbauld Rd. N16 ....3E 66
Barber Beaumont Ho.
  E1 ....3K 85
(off Bancroft Rd.)
Barber Cl. N21 ....7F 23
Barbers All. E13 ....3K 87
Barbers Rd. E15 ....2D 86
Barbican Arts Cen. 5D 8 (5C 84)
Barbican Cinema 5D 8
(in Arts Cen.)
Barbican Rd. UB6: G'frd 6F 77
Barbican Theatre 5D 8
(off Silk St.)
Barbican Trade Cen. EC1 ....5D 8
(off Beech St.)
Barb M. W6 ....3E 98
Barbon All. EC2 ....7H 9
(off Houndsditch)
Barbon Cl. WC1 ....5F 7 (5K 83)
Barbot Cl. N9 ....3B 34
Barchard St. SW18 ....5K 117
Barchester Cl. W7 ....1K 95
Barchester Rd. HA3: Hrw W 2H 41
Barclay Cl. SW6 ....7J 99
Barclay Ho. E9 ....7J 67
(off Well St.)
Barclay Oval IG8: Wfd G 4D 36
Barclay Path E17 ....5E 50
Barclay Rd. CR0: Croy 3D 168
  E11 ....1H 69
(not continuous)
  E13 ....4A 88
  E17 ....5E 50
  N18 ....6J 33
  SW6 ....7J 99
Barcombe Av. SW2 ....2J 137
Barcombe Cl. BR5: St P 3K 161
Bardell Ho. SE1 ....7K 15
(off Parkers Row)
Barden St. SE18 ....7J 107
Bardfield Av. RM6: Chad H 3D 54
Bardney Rd. SM4: Mord 4K 153
Bardolph Rd. N7 ....4J 65
  TW9: Rich 3F 115
Bard Rd. W10 ....7F 81
Bardsey Pl. E1 ....4J 85
(off Mile End Rd.)
Bardsey Wlk. N1 ....6C 66
(off Douglas Rd. Nth.)
Bardsley Cl. CR0: Croy 3F 169
Bardsley Ho. SE10 ....6E 104
(off Bardsley La.)
Bardsley La. SE10 ....6E 104
Barents Ho. E1 ....4K 85
(off White Horse La.)
Barfett St. W10 ....4H 81
Barfield Av. N20 ....2J 31
Barfield Rd. BR1: Brom 3E 160
  E11 ....1H 69
Barfleur La. SE8 ....4B 104
Barford Cl. NW4 ....2C 44
Barford St. N1 ....1A 84
Barforth Rd. SE15 ....3H 121
Barfreston Way SE20 ....1H 157
Bargate Cl. KT3: N Mald 7C 152
  SE18 ....5K 107
Barge Ho. Rd. E16 ....2F 107
Barge Ho. St. SE1 ....4K 13 (1A 102)
Barge La. E3 ....1A 86
Bargery Rd. SE6 ....1D 140

Barge Wlk. KT1: Ham W 3D 150
  KT8: E Mos 3H 149
(Hampton Court)
  KT8: E Mos 6A 150
(Thames Ditton)
Bargrove Cl. SE20 ....7G 139
Bargrove Cres. SE6 ....2B 140
Barham Cl. BR2: Brom 1C 172
  BR7: Chst 5F 143
  HA0: Wemb 6R 60
  RM7: Mawney 2H 55
Barham Ct. CR2: S Croy 4C 168
(off Barham Rd.)
Barham Ho. SE17 ....5E 102
(off Kinglake St.)
Barham Rd. BR7: Chst 5F 143
  CR2: S Croy 4C 168
  SW20 ....7C 134
Baring Cl. SE12 ....2J 141
Baring Ct. N1 ....1D 84
(off Baring St.)
Baring Ho. E14 ....6C 86
(off Canton St.)
Baring Rd. CR0: Croy 1G 169
  EN4: Cockf 4G 21
  SE12 ....7J 123
Baring St. N1 ....1D 84
Barker Cl. HA6: Nwood 1H 39
  KT3: N Mald 4H 151
  TW9: Rich 2H 115
Barker Dr. NW1 ....7G 65
Barker M. SW4 ....4F 119
Barkers Arc. W8 ....2K 99
Barker Rd. SW10 ....6A 100
Barker Wlk. SW16 ....3H 137
Barkham Rd. N17 ....7J 33
Barkham Ter. SE1 ....1K 19
BARKING 7G 71
Barking Abbey 1G 89
Barking Abbey School Leisure Cen.
  ....6A 72
Barking Bus. Pk. IG11: Bark 3A 90
Barking Ind. Pk. IG11: Bark 1K 89
Barking Northern Relief Rd.
  IG11: Bark 7F 71
BARKING RIVERSIDE 3C 90
Barking Rd. E6 ....2A 88
  E13 ....5H 87
  E16 ....5H 87
BARKINGSIDE 3G 53
Bark Pl. W2 ....7K 81
Barkston Gdns. SW5 ....4K 99
Barkway Ct. N4 ....2C 66
(off Queen's Dr.)
Barkway Dr. BR6: Farnb 4E 172
Barkwith Ho. SE14 ....6K 103
(off Cold Blow La.)
Barkworth Cl. RM7: Rom 5J 55
Barkworth Rd. SE16 ....5H 103
Barlborough St. SE14 ....7K 103
Barlby Gdns. W10 ....4F 81
Barlby Rd. W10 ....5E 80
Barley Cl. HA0: Wemb 4D 60
Barleycorn Way E14 ....7B 86
Barleyfields Cl. RM6: Chad H ...6B 54
Barley La. IG3: Ilf 7A 54
  RM6: Chad H 4B 54
Barley Mow Pas. EC1 ....5B 8
  W4 ....5K 97
Barleymow Way TW17: Shep ...4C 146
Barley Shotts Bus. Pk. W10 .....5H 81
Barling NW1 ....6F 65
(off Castlehaven Rd.)
Barlings Ho. SE4 ....4K 121
(off Frendsbury Rd.)
Barlow Cl. SM6: Wall 6J 167
Barlow Dr. SE18 ....1C 124
Barlow Ho. N1 ....1E 8
(off Fairbank Est.)
  SE16 ....4H 103
(off Rennie Est.)
  W11 ....7G 81
(off Walmer Rd.)

Barlow Pl. W1 ....3K 11 (7F 83)
Barlow Rd. NW6 ....6H 63
  TW12: Hamp 7E 130
  W3 ....1H 97
Barlow St. SE17 ....4D 102
Barlow Way RM13: Rain 5K 91
Barmeston Rd. SE6 ....2D 140
Barmor Cl. HA2: Harr 2F 41
Barmouth Av. UB6: G'frd 2K 77
Barmouth Rd. CR0: Croy 2K 169
  SW18 ....6A 118
Barnabas Cl. EN2 ....4F 23
Barnabas Rd. E9 ....5K 67
Barnaby Cl. HA2: Harr 2G 59
Barnaby Ct. NW9 ....3A 44
  SE16 ....2G 103
(off Scott Lidgett Cres.)
Barnaby Way IG7: Chig 3K 37
Barnard Cl. BR7: Chst 1H 161
  SE18 ....4E 106
  SM6: Wall 7H 167
  TW16: Sun 7A 129
Barnard Gdns. KT3: N Mald 4C 152
  UB4: Yead 4K 75
Barnard Gro. E15 ....7H 69
Barnard Hill N10 ....1F 47
Barnard Ho. E2 ....3H 85
(off Ellsworth St.)
Barnard Lodge EN5: New Bar 4F 21
  W9 ....5J 81
(off Admiral Wlk.)
Barnard M. SW11 ....4C 118
Barnardo Dr. IG6: Ilf 4G 53
Barnardo Gdns. E1 ....7K 85
Barnardo St. E1 ....6K 85
Barnardos Village IG6: Ilf 4G 53
Barnard Rd. CR4: Mitc 3E 154
  EN1: Enf 2C 24
  SW11 ....4C 118
Barnards Ho. SE16 ....2B 104
(off Wyatt Cl.)
Barnard's Inn EC1 ....6J 7
Barnbrough NW1 ....1G 83
(off Camden St.)
Barnby Sq. E15 ....1G 87
Barnby St. E15 ....1G 87
  NW1 ....1B 6 (2G 83)
Barn Cl. NW5 ....5H 65
(off Torriano Av.)
  TW15: Ashf 5D 128
  UB5: Yead 2A 76
Barn Cres. HA7: Stan 6H 27
Barncroft Cl. UB8: Hil 5D 74
Barncroft Rd. TW2: Twick 1J 131
BARNEHURST 3J 127
Barnehurst Av. DA7: Bex 1J 127
  DA8: Erith 1J 127
Barnehurst Cl. DA8: Erith 1J 127
Barnehurst Rd. DA7: Bex 2J 127
Barn Elms Athletic Track 1D 116
Barn Elms Pk. SW15 ....3E 116
BARNES 2B 116
Barnes All. TW12: Hamp 2G 149
Barnes Av. SW13 ....7C 98
  UB2: S'hall 4D 94
Barnes Cl. E12 ....4B 70
Barnes Ct. E16 ....5A 88
  EN5: New Bar 4E 20
  IG8: Buck H, Wfd G 5G 37
  N1 ....7A 66
Barnes End KT3: N Mald 5C 152
Barnes High St. SW13 ....2B 116
Barnes Ho. E2 ....2J 85
  EN5: New Bar 4E 20
  IG11: Bark 1H 89
  SE14 ....6K 103
(off John Williams Cl.)
Barnes Pikle W5 ....7D 78
Barnes Rd. IG1: Ilf 5G 71
  N18 ....4D 34
Barnes St. E14 ....6A 86
Barnes Ter. SE8 ....5B 104

Barnes Wallis Ct. HA9: Wemb 3J 61
BARNET 3B 20
Barnet Bus. Cen. EN5: Barn 3B 20
Barnet By-Pass NW7 ....6G 29
Barnet Copthall Stadium 7K 29
Barnet Dr. BR2: Brom 2C 172
Barnet FC 5D 20
Barnet Ga. La. EN5: Ark 1H 29
Barnet Gro. E2 ....1K 9 (3G 85)
Barnet Hill EN5: Barn 4C 20
Barnet Ho. N20 ....2F 31
Barnet La. EN5: Barn 1C 30
  N20 ....1C 30
Barnet Mus. 4B 20
Barnet Trad. Est. EN5: Barn 3C 20
Barnetts Ct. HA2: Harr 3F 59
Barnett St. E1 ....6H 85
BARNET VALE 5E 20
Barnet Way NW7 ....3E 28
Barnet Wood Rd.
  BR2: Brom 2A 172
Barney Cl. SE7 ....5A 106
Barn Fld. NW3 ....5D 64
Barnfield Av. CR0: Croy 2J 169
  CR4: Mitc 4F 155
  KT2: King T 4D 132
Barnfield Cl. N4 ....7J 47
  SW17 ....3B 136
Barnfield Gdns. KT2: King T 4E 132
  SE18 ....6F 107
Barnfield Pl. E14 ....4C 104
Barnfield Rd. CR2: Sand 7C 168
  DA17: Belv 6F 109
  HA8: Edg 1J 43
  SE18 ....6F 107
(not continuous)
  W5 ....4C 78
Barnfield Wood Cl. BR3: Beck ...6F 159
Barnfield Wood Rd. BR3: Beck ...6F 159
Barnham Dr. SE28 ....1K 107
(not continuous)
Barnham Rd. UB6: G'frd 3G 77
Barnham St. SE1 ....6H 15 (2E 102)
Barnhill HA5: Eastc 5A 40
Barnhill Av. BR2: Brom 5H 159
Barnhill La. UB4: Yead 3K 75
Barnhill Rd. HA9: Wemb 3J 61
  UB4: Yead 6K 43
Barningham Way NW9 ....6K 43
Barnlea Cl. TW13: Hanw 2C 130
Barnmead Gdns. RM9: Dag 5F 73
Barnmead Rd. BR3: Beck 1K 157
  RM9: Dag 5F 73
Barn M. HA2: Harr 3E 58
Barn Ri. HA9: Wemb 1G 61
BARNSBURY 7K 65
Barnsbury Cl. KT3: N Mald 4J 151
Barnsbury Cres. KT5: Surb 1J 163
Barnsbury Est. N1 ....1K 83
(not continuous)
Barnsbury Gro. N7 ....7K 65
Barnsbury Ho. SW4 ....6H 119
Barnsbury La. KT5: Surb 2H 163
Barnsbury Pk. N1 ....7A 66
Barnsbury Rd. N1 ....2A 84
Barnsbury Sq. N1 ....7A 66
Barnsbury St. N1 ....7A 66
Barnsbury Ter. N1 ....7K 65
Barnscroft SW20 ....3D 152
Barnsdale Av. E14 ....4D 104
Barnsdale Rd. W9 ....4H 81
Barnsley St. E1 ....4H 85
Barnstable La. SE13 ....4E 122
Barnstaple Ho. SE10 ....7D 104
(off Devonshire Dr.)
  SE12 ....5K 123
(off Taunton Rd.)
Barnstaple Rd. HA4: Ruis 3A 58
Barnston Wlk. N1 ....1C 84
(off Popham St.)
Barn St. N16 ....2E 66

Barn Theatre, The—Bathurst Rd.

Barn Theatre, The
Bexley 1A 144
Barn Way HA9: Wemb 1G 61
Barnwell Ho. *SE5* 1E 120
(off St Giles Rd.)
Barnwell Rd. SW2 5A 120
Barnwood Cl. HA4: Ruis 2F 57
N20 1C 30
W9 4K 81
Baron Cl. N11 5K 31
Baroness Rd. E2 1K 9 (3F 85)
Baronet Gro. N17 1G 49
Baronet Rd. N17 1G 49
Baron Gdns. IG6: Ilf 3G 53
Baron Gro. CR4: Mitc 4C 154
Baron Ho. SW19 1B 154
Baron Rd. RM8: Dag 1D 72
Barons, The TW1: Twick 6B 114
Baronsclere Ct. N6 7G 47
BARONS COURT 5G 99
Barons Ct. IG1: Ilf 2H 71
NW9 6K 43
SM6: Bedd 3H 167
Baron's Ct. Rd. W14 5G 99
Barons Court Theatre 5G 99
(off Comeragh Rd.)
Baronsfield Rd. TW1: Twick 6B 114
Barons Ga. EN4: E Barn 6H 21
W4 3J 97
Barons Keep W14 5G 99
Barons Mead HA1: Harr 4J 41
Baronsmead Rd. SW13 1C 116
Baronsmede W5 2F 97
Baronsmere Ct. EN5: Barn 4B 20
Baronsmere Rd. N2 4C 46
Baron's Pl. SE1 7K 13 (2A 102)
Baron St. N1 2A 84
Baron's Wlk. CR0: Croy 6A 158
Baron Wlk. CR4: Mitc 4C 154
E16 5H 87
Barque M. SE8 6C 104
Barrack Rd. TW4: Houn 4B 112
Barracks La. EN5: Barn 3B 20
Barra Hall Cir. UB3: Hayes 7G 75
Barra Hall Rd. UB3: Hayes 7G 75
Barratt Av. N22 2K 47
Barratt Ho. *N1* 7B 66
(off Sable St.)
Barratt Ind. Pk. E3 4E 86
UB1: S'hall 2E 94
Barratt Way HA3: W'stone 2H 41
Barrenger Rd. N10 1D 46
Barret Ho. NW6 1J 81
SW9 3K 119
(off Benedict Rd.)
Barrett Ho. *SE17* 5C 102
(off Browning St.)
Barrett Rd. E17 4E 50
Barrett's Grn. Rd. NW10 3J 79
Barrett's Gro. N16 5E 66
Barrett St. W1 1H 11 (6E 82)
Barrhill Rd. SW2 2J 137
Barrie Ct. *EN5: New Bar* 5F 21
(off Lyonsdown Rd.)
Barriedale SE14 2A 122
Barrie Est. W2 2A 10 (7B 82)
Barrie Ho. *W2* 7A 82
(off Lancaster Ga.)
Barrier App. SE7 3B 106
Barrier Point Rd. E16 1A 106
Barringers Ct. HA4: Ruis 7F 39
Barringer Sq. SW17 4E 136
Barrington Cl. IG5: Ilf 1D 52
NW5 5E 64
Barrington Ct. N10 2E 46
SW4 2J 119
W3 2H 97
(off Cheltenham Pl.)
Barrington Rd. DA7: Bex 2D 126
E12 6E 70
N8 5H 47
SM3: Sutt 2J 165
SW9 3B 120
Barrington Vs. SE18 1E 124
Barrington Wlk. SE19 6E 138
Barrosa Dr. TW12: Hamp 1E 148
Barrow Av. SM5: Cars 7D 166
Barrow Cl. N21 3G 33
Barrow Ct. *SE6* 1H 141
(off Cumberland Pl.)
Barrowdene Cl. HA5: Pinn 2C 40
Barrowell Grn. N21 2G 33
Barrowfield Cl. N9 3C 34
Barrowgate Rd. W4 5J 97
Barrow Hedges Cl. SM5: Cars 7C 166
Barrow Hedges Way SM5: Cars 7C 166
Barrow Hill KT4: Wor Pk 2A 164
Barrow Hill Cl. KT4: Wor Pk 2A 164
Barrow Hill Est. *NW8* 2C 82
(off Barrow Hill Rd.)
Barrow Hill Rd. NW8 1C 4 (2C 82)
Barrow Point Av. HA5: Pinn 2C 40
Barrow Point La. HA5: Pinn 2C 40
Barrow Rd. CR0: Wadd 5A 168
SW16 6H 137
Barrow Store Ct. *SE1* 7G 15
(off Decima St.)
Barrow Wlk. TW8: Bford 6C 96
Barrs Rd. NW10 7K 61
Barry Av. DA7: Bex 7E 108
N15 6F 49
Barry Cl. BR6: Orp 3J 173
Barrydene N20 1G 31
Barry Ho. *SE16* 4H 103
(off Rennie Est.)
Barry Rd. E6 6C 88
NW10 7J 61
SE22 6G 121
Barset Rd. SE15 3J 121
(not continuous)
Barson Cl. SE20 7J 139
Barston Rd. SE27 3C 138
Barstow Cres. SW2 1K 137
Barter St. WC1 6F 7 (5J 83)
Barters Wlk. HA5: Pinn 3C 40
Barth M. SE18 4J 107
Bartholomew Cl. EC1 6B 8 (5C 84)
(not continuous)
SW18 4A 118
Bartholomew Ct. *E14* 7F 87
(off Newport Av.)
EC1 3D 8
(off Old St.)
HA8: Edg 7J 27
Bartholomew Ho. IG8: Ilf 7K 37
Bartholomew La. EC2 1F 15 (6D 84)
Bartholomew Pl. EC1 6C 8
Bartholomew Rd. NW5 6G 65
Bartholomew Sq. E1 4H 85
EC1 3D 8 (4C 84)
Bartholomew St. SE1 3D 102
Bartholomew Vs. NW5 6G 65
Barth Rd. SE18 4J 107
(not continuous)
Bartle Av. E6 2C 88
Bartle Rd. W11 6G 81
Bartlett Cl. E14 6C 86
Bartlett Ct. EC4 7K 7 (6A 84)
Bartlett Ho's. *RM10: Dag* 7H 73
(off Vicarage Rd.)
Bartletts Pas. *EC4* 7K 7
(off Fetter La.)
Bartlett St. CR2: S Croy 5D 168
Bartlow Gdns. RM5: Col R 1K 55
Bartok Ho. *W11* 1H 99
(off Lansdowne Wlk.)
Barton Av. RM7: Rush G 1H 73
Barton Cl. DA6: Bex 5E 126
E6 6D 88
E9 5J 67
NW4 5C 44
SE15 3H 121
TW17: Shep 6D 146
Barton Ct. *W14* 5G 99
(off Baron's Ct. Rd.)
Barton Grn. KT3: N Mald 2K 151
Barton Green Theatre 2K 151
Barton Ho. *N1* 7B 66
(off Sable St.)
SW6 3K 117
(off Wandsworth Bri. Rd.)
Barton Mdws. IG6: Ilf 4F 53
Barton Rd. DA14: Sidc 6E 144
W14 5G 99
Barton St. SW1 1E 18 (3J 101)
Bartonway *NW8* 1B 82
(off Queen's Ter.)
Bartram Cl. UB8: Hil 4D 74
Bartram Rd. SE4 5A 122
Bartrams La. EN4: Had W 1F 21
Bartrip St. E9 6B 68
Barts Cl. BR3: Beck 5C 158
Barville Cl. SE4 4A 122
Barwell Bus. Pk. KT9: Chess 7D 162
Barwell Ct. KT9: Chess 7B 162
Barwell Ho. *E2* 4G 85
(off Menotti St.)
Barwell La. KT9: Chess 7C 162
Barwick Dr. UB8: Hil 5D 74
Barwick Ho. *W3* 2J 97
(off Strafford Rd.)
Barwick Rd. E7 4K 69
Barwood Av. BR4: W W'ck 1D 170
Bascombe Gro. DA1: Bexl, Cray 7K 127
Bascombe St. SW2 6A 120
Basden Gro. TW13: Hanw 2E 130
Basden Ho. TW13: Hanw 2E 130
Basedale Rd. RM9: Dag 7B 72
Baseing Cl. E6 7E 88
Baseline Bus. Studios *W11* 7F 81
(off Barandon Wlk.)
Basevi Way SE8 6D 104
Bashley Rd. NW10 4K 79
Basil Av. E6 3C 88
Basildene Rd. TW4: Houn 3B 112
Basildon Av. IG5: Ilf 1E 52
Basildon Cl. SM2: Sutt 7K 165
Basildon Ct. *W1* 5H 5
(off Devonshire Rd.)
Basildon Rd. SE2 5A 108
Basil Gdns. CR0: Croy 1K 169
SE27 5C 138
Basil Ho. *SW8* 7J 101
(off Wyvil Rd.)
Basil Mans. *SW3* 7E 10
(off Basil St.)
Basilon Rd. DA7: Bex 2E 126
Basil Spence Ho. N22 1K 47
Basil St. SW3 1E 16 (3D 100)
Basin App. E14 6A 86
E16 7F 89
Basing Cl. KT7: T Ditt 7K 149
Basing Ct. SE15 1F 121
Basingdon Way SE5 4D 120
Basing Dr. DA5: Bexl 6F 127
Basingfield Rd. KT7: T Ditt 7K 149
Basinghall Av. EC2 7E 8 (6D 84)
Basinghall Gdns. SM2: Sutt 7K 165
Basinghall St. EC2 7E 8 (6D 84)
Basing Hill HA9: Wemb 2F 61
NW11 1H 63
Basing Ho. *IG11: Bark* 1H 89
(off St Margarets)
Basing Ho. Yd. E2 1H 9 (3E 84)
Basing Pl. E2 1H 9 (3E 84)
Basing St. W11 6H 81
Basing Way KT7: T Ditt 7K 149
N3 3J 45
Basire St. N1 1C 84
Baskerville Gdns. NW10 4A 62
Baskerville Rd. SW18 7C 118
Basket Gdns. SE9 5C 124
Baslow Cl. HA3: Hrw W 1H 41
Baslow Wlk. E5 4K 67
Basnett Rd. SW11 3E 118
Basque Ct. *SE16* 2K 103
(off Garter Way)
Bassano St. SE22 5F 121
Bassant Rd. SE18 6K 107
Bassein Pk. Rd. W12 2B 98
Bassett Gdns. TW7: Isle 7G 95
Bassett Ho. RM9: Dag 1B 90
Bassett Rd. E7 4B 70
W10 6F 81
Bassett's Cl. BR6: Farnb 4F 173
Bassett St. NW5 6E 64
Bassett's Way BR6: Farnb 4F 173
Bassett Way UB6: G'frd 6F 77
Bassingbourn Ho. *N1* 7A 66
(off The Sutton Est.)
Bassingham Rd. HA0: Wemb 6D 60
SW18 7A 118
Bassishaw Highwalk EC2 6D 8
Basswood Cl. SE15 3H 121
Bastable Av. IG11: Bark 2J 89
Basterfield Ho. *EC1* 4C 8
(off Golden La. Est.)
Bastion Highwalk EC2 6C 8
Bastion Ho. *EC2* 6D 8
(off London Wall)
Bastion Rd. SE2 5A 108
Baston Mnr. Rd. BR2: Hayes, Kes 3K 171
Baston Rd. BR2: Hayes 2K 171
Bastwick St. EC1 3C 8 (4C 84)
Basuto Rd. SW6 1J 117
Batavia Cl. TW16: Sun 1K 147
Batavia Ho. *SE14* 7A 104
(off Batavia Rd.)
Batavia M. SE14 7A 104
Batavia Rd. SE14 7A 104
TW16: Sun 1K 147
Batchelor St. N1 1A 84
Bateman Cl. IG11: Bark 6G 71
Bateman Ho. *SE17* 6B 102
(off Otto St.)
Bateman Rd. E4 6H 35
Bateman's Bldgs. W1 1C 12
Bateman's Row EC2 3H 9 (4E 84)
Bateman St. W1 1C 12 (6H 83)
Bates Cres. CR0: Wadd 5A 168
SW16 7G 137
Bateson St. SE18 4J 107
Bates Point *E13* 1J 87
(off Pelly Rd.)
Bate St. E14 7B 86
Bath Cl. SE15 7H 103
Bath Ct. EC1 4J 7
SE26 3G 139
(off Droitwich Cl.)
Bathgate Rd. SW19 3F 135
Bath Gro. *E2* 2G 85
(off Horatio St.)
Bath Ho. *E2* 4G 85
(off Ramsey St.)
SE1 3C 102
(off Bath Ter.)
Bath Ho. Rd. CR0: Bedd 1J 167
Bath Pas. KT1: King T 2D 150
Bath Pl. EC2 2G 9 (3E 84)
EN5: Barn 3C 20
W6 5E 98
(off Peabody Est.)
Bath Rd. E7 6B 70
N9 2C 34
RM6: Chad H 6E 54
TW3: Houn 2B 112
TW4: Houn 2B 112
TW5: Cran 1G 111
TW6: H'row A 1G 111
UB3: Harl 1G 111
UB7: Harm, Sip 1A 110
W4 4A 98
Baths App. SW6 7H 99
Baths Rd. BR2: Brom 4B 160
Bath St. EC1 2D 8 (3C 84)
Bath Ter. SE1 3C 102
Bathurst Av. SW19 1K 153
Bathurst Gdns. NW10 2D 80
Bathurst Ho. *W12* 7D 80
(off White City Est.)
Bathurst M. W2 2B 10 (6B 82)
Bathurst Rd. IG1: Ilf 1F 71

192 A-Z London

Bathurst St. W2 2B 10 (7B 82)
Bathway SE18 4E 106
Batley Cl. CR4: Mitc 7D 154
Batley Pl. N16 3F 67
Batley Rd. EN2: Enf 1H 23
N16 3F 67
Batman Cl. W12 1D 98
Batoum Gdns. W6 3E 98
Batson Ho. *E1* 6G 85
(off Fairclough St.)
Batson St. W12 2C 98
Batsworth Rd. CR4: Mitc 3B 154
Battenberg Wlk. SE19 6E 138
Batten Cl. E6 6D 88
Batten Cotts. *E14* 5A 86
(off Maroon St.)
Batten Ho. SW4 5G 119
W10 3G 81
(off Third Av.)
Batten St. SW11 3C 118
Battersby Rd. SE6 2F 141
BATTERSEA 1E 118
Battersea Bri. SW11 7B 100
Battersea Bri. Rd. SW11 7C 100
Battersea Bus. Cen. SW11 3E 118
Battersea Church Rd.
SW11 1B 118
Battersea High St. SW11 1B 118
(not continuous)
Battersea Pk. 7D 100
Battersea Pk. Children's Zoo 7E 100
Battersea Pk. Equestrian Cen. 2C 118
Battersea Pk. Rd. SW8 1E 118
SW11 2C 118
Battersea Ri. SW11 5C 118
Battersea Sports Cen. 3B 118
Battersea Sq. SW11 1B 118
Battery Rd. SE28 2J 107
Battishill St. N1 7B 66
Battlebridge Ct. *N1* 2J 83
(off Wharfdale Rd.)
Battle Bri. La. SE1 5G 15 (1E 102)
Battle Bri. Rd. NW1 2J 83
Battle Cl. SW19 6A 136
Battledean Rd. N5 5B 66
Battle Ho. *SE15* 6G 103
(off Haymerle Rd.)
Battle Rd. DA8: Erith 4J 109
DA17: Belv, Erith 4J 109
Batty St. E1 6G 85
Baudwin Rd. SE6 2G 141
Baugh Rd. DA14: Sidc 5C 144
Baulk, The SW18 7J 117
Bavant Rd. SW16 2J 155
Bavaria Rd. N19 2J 65
(not continuous)
Bavdene M. *NW4* 4D 44
(off The Burroughs)
Bavent Rd. SE5 2C 120
Bawdale Rd. SE22 5F 121
Bawdsey Av. IG2: Ilf 4K 53
Bawtree Rd. SE14 7A 104
Bawtry Rd. N20 3J 31
Baxendale N20 2F 31
Baxendale St. E2 3G 85
Baxter Cl. BR1: Brom 3F 161
UB2: S'hall 3F 95
UB10: Hil 3D 74
Baxter Rd. E16 6A 88
IG1: Ilf 5F 71
N1 6D 66
N18 4C 34
Bayard Ct. DA6: Bex 4H 127
Bay Ct. *E1* 4K 85
(off Frimley Way)
W5 3E 96
Baycroft Cl. HA5: Eastc 3A 40
Baydon Ct. BR2: Brom 3H 159
Bayer Ho. *EC1* 4C 8
(off Golden La. Est.)
Bayes Cl. SE26 5J 139
Bayes Ct. *NW3* 7D 64
(off Primrose Hill Rd.)
Bayfield Ho. *SE4* 4K 121
(off Coston Wlk.)
Bayfield Rd. SE9 4B 124
Bayford M. *E8* 7H 67
(off Bayford St.)
Bayford Rd. NW10 3F 81
Bayford St. E8 7H 67
Bayford St. Bus. Cen. *E8* 7H 67
(off Sidworth St.)
Baygrove M. KT1: Ham W 1C 150
Bayham Pl. NW1 1G 83
Bayham Rd. SM4: Mord 4K 153
W4 3K 97
W13 7B 78
Bayham St. NW1 1G 83
Bayhurst Wood Country Pk. 5B 38
Bayleaf Cl. TW12: Ham H 5H 131
Bayley St. WC1 6C 6 (5H 83)
Bayley Wlk. SE2 6E 108
Baylis M. TW1: Twick 7A 114
Baylis Rd. SE1 7J 13 (2A 102)
Bayliss Av. SE28 7D 90
Bayliss Cl. N21 5D 22
Bayne Cl. E6 6D 88
Baynes Cl. EN1: Enf 1B 24
Baynes M. NW3 6B 64
Baynes St. NW1 7G 65
Baynham Cl. DA5: Bexl 6F 127
Bayonne Rd. W6 6G 99
Bays Ct. HA8: Edg 5C 28
Bayshill Ri. UB5: N'olt 6F 59
Bayston Rd. N16 3F 67
BAYSWATER 7A 82
Bayswater Rd. W2 3A 10 (7K 81)
Baythorne St. E3 5B 86
Bayton Ct. *E8* 7G 67
(off Lansdowne Dr.)
Bay Tree Cl. BR1: Brom 1B 160
Baytree Cl. DA15: Sidc 1K 143
Baytree Ct. SW2 4K 119
Baytree Ho. E4 7J 25
Baytree Rd. SW2 4K 119
Bazalgette Cl. KT3: N Mald 5K 151
Bazalgette Gdns. KT3: N Mald 5K 151
Bazalgette Ho. *NW8* 3B 4
(off Orchardson St.)
Bazeley Ho. *SE1* 7A 14
(off Library St.)
Bazely St. E14 7E 86
Bazile Rd. N21 6F 23
BBC Broadcasting House 6K 5 (5F 83)
BBC Television Cen. 7E 80
BBC Worldwide 6E 80
(off Wood La.)
Beacham Cl. SE7 5B 106
Beachborough Rd. BR1: Brom 4E 140
Beachcroft Rd. E11 3G 69
Beachcroft Way N19 1H 65
Beach Gro. TW13: Hanw 2E 130
Beach Ho. *SW5* 5J 99
(off Philbeach Gdns.)
TW13: Hanw 2E 130
Beachy Rd. E3 7C 68
Beacon Bingo Hall 4F 63
Beacon Cl. UB8: Uxb 5A 56
Beacon Ga. SE14 3K 121
Beacon Gro. SM5: Cars 4E 166
Beacon Hill N7 5J 65
Beacon Ho. *E14* 5D 104
(off Burrells Wharf Sq.)
SE5 7E 102
(off Southampton Way)
Beacon Pl. CR0: Bedd 3J 167
Beacon Rd. SE13 6F 123
TW6: H'row A 6C 110
Beacons Cl. E6 5C 88
Beaconsfield Cl. N11 5K 31
SE3 6J 105
W4 5J 97
Beaconsfield Pde. SE9 4C 142
Beaconsfield Rd. BR1: Brom 3B 160
CR0: Croy 6D 156
DA5: Bexl 2K 145
Beaconsfield Rd. E10 2E 68
E16 4H 87
E17 6B 50
KT3: N Mald 2K 151
KT5: Surb 7F 151
N9 3B 34
N11 3K 31
N15 4E 48
NW10 6B 62
SE3 7H 105
SE9 2C 142
SE17 5D 102
TW1: Twick 6B 114
UB1: S'hall 1B 94
UB4: Yead 1A 94
W4 3K 97
W5 2C 96
Beaconsfield Ter. RM6: Chad H 6D 54
Beaconsfield Ter. Rd. W14 3G 99
Beaconsfield Wlk. E6 6E 88
SW6 1H 117
Beacontree Av. E17 1F 51
BEACONTREE HEATH 1G 73
Beacontree Rd. E11 1H 69
Beadle's Pde. RM10: Dag 6J 73
Beadlow Cl. SM5: Cars 6B 154
Beadman Pl. SE27 4B 138
Beadman St. SE27 4B 138
Beadnell Rd. SE23 1K 139
Beadon Rd. BR2: Brom 4J 159
W6 4E 98
Beaford Gro. SW20 3G 153
Beagle Cl. TW13: Felt 4K 129
Beak St. W1 2B 12 (7G 83)
Beal Cl. DA16: Well 1A 126
Beale Cl. N13 5G 33
Beale Pl. E3 2B 86
Beale Rd. E3 1B 86
Beal Rd. IG1: Ilf 2E 70
Beam Av. RM10: Dag 1H 91
Beames Rd. NW10 1K 79
Beaminster Gdns. IG6: Ilf 2F 53
Beaminster Ho. *SW8* 7K 101
(off Dorset Rd.)
Beamish Dr. WD23: Bushy 1B 26
Beamish Ho. *SE16* 4H 103
(off Rennie Est.)
Beamish Rd. N9 1B 34
Beam Vs. RM9: Dag 2J 91
Beamway RM10: Dag 7K 73
Beanacre Cl. E9 6B 68
Bean Rd. DA6: Bex 4D 126
Beanshaw SE9 4E 142
Beansland Gro. RM6: Chad H 2E 54
Bear All. EC4 7A 8 (6B 84)
Bear Cl. RM7: Rom 6H 55
Beardell St. SE19 6F 139
Beardow Gro. N14 6B 22
Beard Rd. KT2: King T 5F 133
Beardsfield E13 2J 87
Beard's Hill TW12: Hamp 1E 148
Beard's Hill Cl. TW12: Hamp 1E 148
Beardsley Ter. *RM8: Dag* 5B 72
(off Fitzstephen Rd.)
Beardsley Way W3 2K 97
Beard's Rd. TW15: Ashf 6G 129
Bearfield Rd. KT2: King T 7E 132
Bear Gdns. SE1 4C 14 (1C 102)
Bear La. SE1 4B 14 (1B 102)
Bear Rd. TW13: Hanw 4B 130
Bearstead Ri. SE4 5B 122
Bearsted Ter. BR3: Beck 1C 158
Bear St. WC2 2D 12 (7H 83)
Beasley's Ait TW16: Sun 6H 147
Beasley's Ait La. TW16: Sun 6H 147
Beaton Cl. SE15 1F 121
Beatrice Av. HA9: Wemb 5E 60
SW16 3K 155
Beatrice Cl. E13 4J 87
HA5: Eastc 4J 39
Beatrice Ct. IG9: Buck H 2G 37
Beatrice Ho. *W6* 5E 98
(off Queen Caroline St.)
Beatrice Pl. W8 3K 99
Beatrice Rd. E17 5C 50
N4 7A 48
N9 7D 24
SE1 4G 103
TW10: Rich 5F 115
UB1: S'hall 1D 94
Beatrix Ho. *SW5* 5K 99
(off Old Brompton Rd.)
Beatson Wlk. SE16 1A 104
(not continuous)
Beattie Cl. TW14: Felt 7H 111
Beattie Ho. SW8 1G 119
Beattock Ri. N10 4F 47
Beatty Ho. *E14* 2C 104
(off Admirals Way)
NW1 3A 6
(off Drummond St.)
SW1 6B 18
(off Dolphin Sq.)
Beatty Rd. HA7: Stan 6H 27
N16 4E 66
Beatty St. NW1 2G 83
Beattyville Gdns. IG6: Ilf 4E 52
Beauchamp Cl. W4 3J 97
Beauchamp Ct. *EN5: Barn* 4C 20
(off Victors Way)
HA7: Stan 5H 27
Beauchamp Pl. SW3 1D 16 (3C 100)
Beauchamp Rd. E7 7K 69
KT8: W Mole, E Mos 5F 149
SE19 1D 156
SM1: Sutt 4J 165
SW11 4C 118
TW1: Twick 7A 114
Beauchamp St. EC1 6J 7 (5A 84)
Beauchamp Ter. SW15 3D 116
Beauclerc Ct. TW16: Sun 2A 148
Beauclerc Rd. W6 3D 98
Beauclere Ho. SM2: Sutt 6A 166
Beauclerk Cl. TW13: Felt 1K 129
Beauclerk Ho. SW16 3J 137
Beaudesert M.
UB7: W Dray 2A 92
Beaufort E6 5E 88
Beaufort Av. HA3: Kent 4A 42
Beaufort Cl. E4 6J 35
RM7: Mawney 4J 55
SW15 7D 116
W5 5F 79
Beaufort Ct. *E14* 2C 104
(off Admirals Way)
EN5: New Bar 5F 21
N11 5A 32
(off The Limes Av.)
SW6 6J 99
TW10: Ham 4C 132
Beaufort Dr. NW11 4J 45
Beaufort Gdns. IG1: Ilf 1E 70
NW4 6E 44
SW3 1D 16 (3C 100)
SW16 7K 137
TW5: Hest 1C 112
Beaufort Ho. *E16* 1K 105
(off Fairfax M.)
SW1 6C 18
(off Aylesford St.)
SW1 5K 17
(off Sutherland Row)
SW3 7B 16
(off Beaufort St.)
Beaufort Mans. SW10 7B 16 (6B 100)
Beaufort M. SW6 6H 99
Beaufort Pk. NW11 4J 45
Beaufort Rd. HA4: Ruis 2F 57
KT1: King T 4E 150
TW1: Twick 7C 114
TW10: Ham 4C 132
W5 5F 79
Beaufort St. SW3 7A 16 (6B 100)
Beaufort Ter. *E14* 5E 104
(off Ferry St.)
Beaufort Way KT17: Ewe 7C 164

Beaufoy Ho.—Beech Ct.

Beaufoy Ho. SE27 3B **138**
SW8 *7K* ***101***
(off Rita Rd.)
Beaufoy Rd. N17 7K **33**
Beaufoy Wlk. SE11 4H **19** (4K **101**)
Beaulieu Av. E16 1K **105**
SE26 4H **139**
Beaulieu Cl. CR4: Mitc 1E **154**
NW9 4A **44**
SE5 3D **120**
TW1: Twick 6D **114**
TW4: Houn 5D **112**
Beaulieu Ct. W5 5E **78**
Beaulieu Dr. HA5: Pinn 6B **40**
Beaulieu Gdns. N21 7H **23**
Beaulieu Lodge *E14* *3F* ***105***
(off Schooner Cl.)
Beaulieu Pl. W4 3J **97**
Beaumanor Gdns. SE9 4E **142**
Beaumanor Mans. *W2* *7K* ***81***
(off Queensway)
Beaumaris Dr. IG8: Wfd G 7G **37**
Beaumaris Grn. NW9 6A **44**
Beaumaris Twr. *W3* *2H* ***97***
(off Park Rd. Nth.)
Beaumont *W14* *4H* ***99***
(off Kensington Village)
Beaumont Av. HA0: Wemb 5C **60**
HA2: Harr 6F **41**
TW9: Rich 3F **115**
W14 5H **99**
Beaumont Bldgs. *WC2* *1F* ***13***
(off Martlett Ct.)
Beaumont Cl. KT2: King T 7G **133**
Beaumont Ct. E1 3A **86**
E5 3H **67**
HA0: Wemb 5C **60**
NW1 1H **83**
NW9 *2B* ***44***
(off Cherry Cl.)
W1 *5H* ***5***
(off Beaumont St.)
W4 5J **97**
Beaumont Cres. W14 5H **99**
Beaumont Dr. KT4: Wor Pk 7D **152**
TW15: Ashf 5F **129**
Beaumont Gdns. NW3 3J **63**
Beaumont Gro. E1 4K **85**
Beaumont Ho. *E10* *7D* ***50***
(off Skelton's La.)
E15 *1H* ***87***
(off John St.)
W9 *3H* ***81***
(off Denholme Rd.)
Beaumont Lodge *E8* *6G* ***67***
(off Greenwood Rd.)
Beaumont M. HA5: Pinn 3C **40**
W1 5H **5** (5E **82**)
Beaumont Pl. EN5: Barn 1C **20**
TW7: Isle 5K **113**
W1 3B **6** (4G **83**)
Beaumont Ri. N19 1H **65**
Beaumont Rd. BR5: Pet W 6H **161**
E10 7D **50**
(not continuous)
E13 3K **87**
SE19 6C **138**
SW19 7G **117**
W4 3J **97**
Beaumont Sq. E1 5K **85**
Beaumont St. W1 5H **5** (5E **82**)
Beaumont Ter. *SE13* *7G* ***123***
(off Wellmeadow Rd.)
Beaumont Wlk. NW3 7D **64**
Beauvais Ter. UB5: Yead 3B **76**
Beauvale *NW1* *7E* ***64***
(off Ferdinand St.)
Beauval Rd. SE22 6F **121**
Beaux Arts Bldg., The N7 3J **65**
Beaverbank Rd. SE9 1H **143**
Beaver Cl. SE20 7G **139**
SM4: Mord 7E **152**
TW12: Hamp 1F **149**
Beaver Ct. BR3: Beck 7D **140**
Beaver Gro. UB5: N'olt 3C **76**
Beavers Cres. TW4: Houn 4A **112**
Beavers La. TW4: Houn 2A **112**
(not continuous)
Beavers La. Campsite TW4: Houn 4B **112**
Beavers Lodge DA14: Sidc 4K **143**
Beaverwood Rd. BR7: Chst 5J **143**
Beavor Gro. *W6* *5C* ***98***
(off Beavor La.)
Beavor La. W6 5C **98**
Bebbington Rd. SE18 4J **107**
Beblets Cl. BR6: Chels 5K **173**
Beccles Dr. IG11: Bark 6J **71**
Beccles St. E14 6B **86**
Bec Cl. HA4: Ruis 3B **58**
Bechervaise Ct. *E10* *1D* ***68***
(off Leyton Grange Est.)
Bechtel Ho. *W6* *4F* ***99***
(off Hammersmith Rd.)
Beck Cl. SE13 1D **122**
Beck Ct. BR3: Beck 3K **157**
BECKENHAM 1C **158**
Beckenham Bus. Cen. BR3: Beck 6A **140**
Beckenham Crematorium
BR3: Beck 3J **157**
Beckenham Gdns. N9 3K **33**
Beckenham Gro. BR2: Brom 2F **159**
Beckenham Hill Est. BR3: Beck 5D **140**
Beckenham Hill Rd. BR3: Beck 6D **140**
SE6 6D **140**
Beckenham La. BR2: Brom 2G **159**
Beckenham Pl. Pk. BR3: Beck 7D **140**
Beckenham Rd. BR3: Beck 1K **157**
BR4: W W'ck 7D **158**
Beckenham Theatre Cen., The 2D **158**
Beckers, The N16 4G **67**
Becket Av. E6 3E **88**
Becket Cl. SE25 6G **157**
SW19 *1K* ***153***
(off High Path)
Becket Fold HA1: Harr 5K **41**
Becket Ho. *E16* *1K* ***105***
(off Constable Av.)
SE1 7E **14**
Becket Rd. N18 4D **34**
Becket St. SE1 7E **14** (3D **102**)
Beckett Cl. DA17: Belv 3F **109**
NW10 6A **62**
SW16 2H **137**
Beckett Ho. *E1* *5J* ***85***
(off Jubilee St.)
SW9 2J **119**
Becketts Cl. BR6: Orp 3K **173**
DA5: Bexl 1J **145**
TW14: Felt 6K **111**
Becketts Ho. IG1: Ilf 3E **70**
Becketts Pl. KT1: Ham W 1D **150**
Beckett Wlk. BR3: Beck 6A **140**
Beckfoot *NW1* *1B* ***6***
(off Ampthill Est.)
Beckford Cl. W14 4H **99**
Beckford Dr. BR5: Orp 7H **161**
Beckford Ho. N16 5E **66**
Beckford Pl. SE17 5C **102**
Beckford Rd. CR0: Croy 6F **157**
Beckham Ho. SE11 4H **19** (4K **101**)
Beck Ho. *N18* *5C* ***34***
(off Upton Rd.)
Beck La. BR3: Beck 3K **157**
Becklow Gdns. *W12* *2C* ***98***
(off Becklow Rd.)
Becklow M. *W12* *2C* ***98***
(off Becklow Rd.)
Becklow Rd. W12 2B **98**
(not continuous)
Beck River Pk. BR3: Beck 1C **158**
Beck Rd. CR4: Mitc 6D **154**
E8 1H **85**
Becks Rd. DA14: Sidc 3A **144**
Beck Theatre, The 6H **75**
BECKTON 5E **88**
BECKTON ALPS 4D **88**
BECKTON PARK 6D **88**
Beckton Retail Pk. E6 5E **88**
Beckton Rd. E16 5H **87**
Beckton Triangle Retail Pk. E6 4F **89**
Beck Way BR3: Beck 3B **158**
Beckway Rd. SW16 2H **155**
Beckway St. SE17 4E **102**
(not continuous)
Beckwith Ho. *E2* *2H* ***85***
(off Wadeson St.)
Beckwith Rd. SE24 5D **120**
Beclands Rd. SW17 6E **136**
Becmead Av. HA3: Kent 5B **42**
SW16 4H **137**
Becondale Rd. SE19 5E **138**
BECONTREE 4D **72**
Becontree Av. RM8: Dag 4B **72**
Becquerel Ct. SE10 3H **105**
Bective Pl. SW15 4H **117**
Bective Rd. E7 4J **69**
SW15 4H **117**
Becton Pl. DA8: Erith 7H **109**
Bedale Rd. EN2: Enf 1H **23**
Bedale St. SE1 5E **14** (1D **102**)
Beddalls Farm Ct. E6 5B **88**
BEDDINGTON 4J **167**
BEDDINGTON CORNER 7E **154**
Beddington Cross CR0: Bedd 7H **155**
Beddington Farm Rd. CR0: Bedd 7J **155**
Beddington Gdns. SM5: Cars 6E **166**
SM6: Wall 6E **166**
Beddington Grn. BR5: St P 1K **161**
Beddington Gro. SM6: Wall 5H **167**
Beddington La. CR0: Croy 5G **155**
Beddington Pk. 2F **167**
Beddington Pk. Cotts. SM6: Bedd 3H **167**
Beddington Path BR5: St P 1K **161**
Beddington Rd. BR5: St P 2J **161**
IG3: Ilf 7K **53**
Beddington Ter. CR0: Croy 7K **155**
Beddington Trad. Est. CR0: Bedd 1J **167**
Bede Cl. HA5: Pinn 1B **40**
Bedefield WC1 2F **7** (3J **83**)
Bede Ho. *SE4* *1B* ***122***
(off Clare Rd.)
Bedens Rd. DA14: Sidc 6E **144**
Bede Rd. RM6: Chad H 6C **54**
Bedfont Cl. CR4: Mitc 2E **154**
TW14: Bedf 6E **110**
Bedfont Grn. Cl. TW14: Bedf 1E **128**
Bedfont Ind. Pk. TW15: Ashf 3E **128**
Bedfont Ind. Pk. Nth. TW15: Ashf 3E **128**
Bedfont Lakes Country Pk. 2E **128**
Bedfont Lakes Country Pk. Vis. Cen.
3D **128**
Bedfont La. TW13: Felt 7G **111**
TW14: Felt 7G **111**
Bedfont Rd. TW13: Felt 1E **128**
TW14: Bedf 1E **128**
TW19: Stanw 6A **110**
Bedford Av. EN5: Barn 5C **20**
UB4: Yead 6K **75**
WC1 6D **6** (5H **83**)
Bedfordbury WC2 2E **12** (7J **83**)
Bedford Cl. N10 7K **31**
W4 6A **98**
Bedford Cnr. *W4* *4A* ***98***
(off South Pde.)
Bedford Ct. *CR0: Croy* *1C* ***168***
(off Tavistock Rd.)
WC2 3E **12** (7J **83**)
(not continuous)
Bedford Ct. Mans. WC1 6D **6**
Bedford Gdns. W8 1J **99**
Bedford Gdns. Ho. *W8* *1J* ***99***
(off Bedford Gdns.)
Bedford Hill SW12 1F **137**
SW16 1F **137**
Bedford Ho. *SW4* *4J* ***119***
(off Solon New Rd. Est.)
Bedford M. N2 3C **46**
SE6 2D **140**
BEDFORD PARK 3K **97**
Bedford Pk. CR0: Croy 1C **168**
Bedford Pk. Cnr. W4 4A **98**
Bedford Pk. Mans. W4 4K **97**
Bedford Pas. *SW6* *7G* ***99***
(off Dawes Rd.)
W1 5B **6** (5G **83**)
Bedford Pl. CR0: Croy 1D **168**
WC1 5E **6** (5J **83**)
Bedford Rd. DA15: Sidc 3J **143**
E6 1E **88**
E17 2C **50**
E18 2J **51**
HA1: Harr 6G **41**
HA4: Ruis 4H **57**
IG1: Ilf 3F **71**
KT4: Wor Pk 2E **164**
N2 3C **46**
N8 6H **47**
N9 7C **24**
N15 4E **48**
N22 2J **47**
NW7 2F **29**
SW4 4J **119**
TW2: Twick 3H **131**
W4 3K **97**
W13 7B **78**
Bedford Row WC1 5H **7** (5K **83**)
Bedford Sq. WC1 6D **6** (5H **83**)
Bedford St. WC2 2E **12** (7J **83**)
Bedford Ter. SM2: Sutt 6A **166**
SW2 5J **119**
Bedford Way WC1 4D **6** (4H **83**)
Bedgebury Ct. E17 2E **50**
Bedgebury Gdns. SW19 2G **135**
Bedgebury Rd. SE9 4B **124**
Bedivere Rd. BR1: Brom 3J **141**
Bedlam M. SE11 3J **19**
Bedlow Way CR0: Bedd 4K **167**
Bedmond Ho. *SW3* *5C* ***16***
(off Ixworth Pl.)
Bedonwell Rd.
DA7: Belv, Bex, Erith 6F **109**
DA17: Belv 6E **108**
SE2 6E **108**
Bedser Cl. CR7: Thor H 3C **156**
SE11 7H **19** (6K **101**)
Bedser Dr. UB6: G'frd 5H **59**
Bedster Gdns. KT8: W Mole 2F **149**
Bedwardine Rd. SE19 7E **138**
Bedwell Ct. *RM6: Chad H* *7D* ***54***
(off Broomfield Rd.)
Bedwell Gdns. UB3: Harl 5G **93**
(not continuous)
Bedwell Ho. SW9 2A **120**
Bedwell Rd. DA17: Belv 5G **109**
N17 1E **48**
Beeby Rd. E16 5K **87**
Beech Av. DA15: Sidc 7A **126**
HA4: Ruis 1K **57**
IG9: Buck H 2E **36**
N20 1H **31**
TW8: Bford 7B **96**
W3 1A **98**
Beech Cl. N9 6B **24**
SE8 6C **104**
SM5: Cars 2D **166**
SW15 7C **116**
SW19 6E **134**
TW15: Ashf 5F **129**
TW16: Sun 2B **148**
UB7: W Dray 3C **92**
Beech Copse BR1: Brom 1D **160**
CR2: S Croy 5E **168**
Beech Ct. *BR1: Brom* *1H* ***159***
(off Blyth Rd.)
BR3: Beck 7B **140**
HA6: Nwood 1G **39**
IG1: Ilf *3E* ***70***
(off Riverdene Rd.)
KT6: Surb 7D **150**
UB5: N'olt 1C **76**
W9 *5J* ***81***
(off Elmfield Way)

Beech Cres. Ct. N5 4B 66
Beechcroft BR7: Chst 7E 142
Beechcroft Av. DA7: Bex 1K 127
HA2: Harr 7E 40
KT3: N Mald 1J 151
NW11 7H 45
UB1: S'hall 1D 94
Beechcroft Cl. BR6: Orp 4H 173
SW16 5K 137
TW5: Hest 7C 94
Beechcroft Ct. N12 4E 30
NW11 7H 45
(off Beechcroft Av.)
Beechcroft Gdns. HA9: Wemb 3F 61
Beechcroft Ho. W5 5E 78
Beechcroft Lodge SM2: Sutt 7A 166
Beechcroft Rd. BR6: Orp 4H 173
E18 2K 51
KT9: Chess 3F 163
SW14 3J 115
SW17 2C 136
Beechdale N21 2E 32
Beechdale Rd. SW2 6K 119
Beech Dell BR2: Kes 4D 172
Beechdene *SE15* 1H 121
(off Carlton Gro.)
Beech Dr. N2 2D 46
Beechen Cliff Way TW7: Isle 2K 113
Beechen Gro. HA5: Pinn 3D 40
Beechen Pl. SE23 2K 139
Beeches, The *CR2: S Croy* 5D 168
(off Blunt Rd.)
E12 7C 70
TW3: Houn 1F 113
Beeches Av. SM5: Cars 7C 166
Beeches Cl. SE20 1J 157
Beeches Rd. SM3: Sutt 1G 165
SW17 3C 136
Beeches Wlk. SM5: Cars 7B 166
Beechey Ho. *E1* 1H 103
(off Watts St.)
Beechfield Cotts. BR1: Brom 1A 160
Beechfield Ct. *CR2: S Croy* 4C 168
(off Bramley Hill)
Beechfield Gdns. RM7: Rush G 7J 55
Beechfield Rd. BR1: Brom 2A 160
DA8: Erith 7K 109
N4 6C 48
SE6 1B 140
Beech Gdns. *EC2* 5C 8
(off Beech St.)
RM10: Dag 7J 73
W5 2E 96
Beech Gro. CR4: Mitc 5H 155
(not continuous)
KT3: N Mald 3K 151
Beech Hall Cres. E4 7A 36
Beech Hall Rd. E4 7K 35
Beech Haven Ct. *DA1: Cray* 5K 127
(off London Rd.)
Beech Hill EN4: Had W 1G 21
Beech Hill Av. EN4: Had W 1F 21
Beechhill Rd. SE9 5E 124
Beech Ho. CR0: New Ad 6D 170
E17 3F 51
SE16 2J 103
(off Ainsty Est.)
Beech Ho. Rd. CR0: Croy 3D 168
Beech La. IG9: Buck H 2E 36
Beech Lawns N12 5G 31
Beechmont Cl. BR1: Brom 5G 141
Beechmore Gdns. SM3: Cheam 2F 165
Beechmore Rd. SW11 1D 118
Beechmount Av. W7 5H 77
Beecholme N12 5E 30
Beecholme Av. CR4: Mitc 1F 155
Beecholme Est. E5 3H 67
Beech Rd. N11 6D 32
SW16 2J 155
TW14: Bedf 7G 111
Beechrow TW10: Ham 4E 132
Beech St. EC2 5C 8 (5C 84)
RM7: Rom 4J 55
Beech Tree Cl. HA7: Stan 5H 27
N1 7A 66
Beech Tree Glade E4 1C 36
Beech Tree Pl. SM1: Sutt 5K 165
Beechvale Cl. N12 5H 31
Beech Wlk. N17 3F 49
NW7 6F 29
Beech Way NW10 7K 61
TW2: Twick 3E 130
Beechway DA5: Bexl 6D 126
Beechwood Av. BR6: Chels 5J 173
CR7: Thor H 4B 156
HA2: Harr 3F 59
HA4: Ruis 2H 57
N3 3H 45
TW9: Kew 1G 115
TW16: Sun 6J 129
UB3: Hayes 7F 75
UB6: G'frd 3F 77
UB8: Hil 6C 74
Beechwood Circ. HA2: Harr 3F 59
Beechwood Cl. KT6: Surb 7C 150
N2 4D 46
(off Western Rd.)
NW7 5F 29
Beechwood Ct. SM5: Cars 4D 166
TW16: Sun 6J 129
W4 6K 97
Beechwood Cres. DA7: Bex 3D 126
Beechwood Dr. BR2: Kes 4B 172
IG8: Wfd G 5C 36
Beechwood Gdns. HA2: Harr 3F 59
IG5: Ilf 5D 52
NW10 3F 79
Beechwood Gro. KT6: Surb 7C 150
W3 7A 80
Beechwood Hall N3 3H 45
Beechwood Ho. *E2* 2G 85
(off Teale St.)
Beechwood M. N9 2B 34
Beechwood Pk. E18 3J 51
Beechwood Ri. BR7: Chst 4F 143
Beechwood Rd. CR2: Sand 7E 168
E8 6F 67
N8 4H 47
Beechwoods Ct. SE19 5F 139
Beechworth NW6 7G 63
Beechworth Cl. NW3 2J 63
Beecroft La. SE4 5A 122
Beecroft M. SE4 5A 122
Beecroft Rd. SE4 5A 122
Beehive Cl. E8 7F 67
UB10: Uxb 7B 56
Beehive Ct. IG1: Ilf 6D 52
Beehive La. IG1: Ilf 5D 52
IG4: Ilf 5D 52
Beehive Pl. SW9 3A 120
Beeken Dene BR6: Farnb 4G 173
Beeleigh Rd. SM4: Mord 4K 153
Beemans Row SW18 2A 136
Bee Pas. *EC3* 1G 15
(off Lime St.)
Beeston Cl. E8 5G 67
Beeston Ho. *SE1* 3D 102
(off Burbage Cl.)
Beeston Pl. SW1 1K 17 (3F 101)
Beeston Rd. EN4: E Barn 6G 21
Beeston Way TW14: Felt 6A 112
Beethoven St. W10 3G 81
Beeton Cl. HA5: H End 1E 40
Begbie Rd. SE3 1A 124
BEGGAR'S HILL 6B 164
Beggar's Hill KT17: Ewe 7B 164
Beggars Roost La. SM1: Sutt 6J 165
Begonia Cl. E6 5D 88
Begonia Pl. TW12: Hamp 6E 130
Begonia Wlk. W12 6B 80
Beira St. SW12 7F 119
Bekesbourne St. E14 6A 86
Belcroft Cl. BR1: Brom 7H 141
Beldanes Lodge NW10 7C 62
Beldham Gdns. KT8: W Mole 2F 149
Belfairs Dr. RM6: Chad H 7C 54
Belfast Rd. N16 2F 67
SE25 4H 157
Belfield Rd. KT19: Ewe 7K 163
Belfont Wlk. N7 4J 65
(not continuous)
Belford Gro. SE18 4E 106
Belford Ho. E8 1F 85
Belfort Rd. SE15 2J 121
Belfry Cl. BR1: Brom 4F 161
SE16 5H 103
Belfry Rd. E12 2B 70
Belgrade Rd. N16 4E 66
TW12: Hamp 1F 149
Belgrave Cl. N14 5B 22
NW7 5E 28
W3 2H 97
Belgrave Ct. *E2* 2H 85
(off Temple St.)
E13 4A 88
E14 7B 86
(off Westferry Cir.)
SW8 7G 101
(off Ascalon St.)
W4 5J 97
Belgrave Cres. TW16: Sun 1K 147
Belgrave Gdns. HA7: Stan 5H 27
N14 5C 22
NW8 1K 81
Belgrave Hgts. E11 1J 69
Belgrave Ho. SW9 7A 102
Belgrave Mans. *NW8* 1K 81
(off Belgrave Gdns.)
Belgrave M. Nth. SW1 7G 11 (2E 100)
Belgrave M. Sth. SW1 1H 17 (3E 100)
Belgrave M. W. SW1 1G 17 (3F 100)
Belgrave Pl. SW1 1H 17 (3E 100)
Belgrave Rd. CR4: Mitc 3B 154
E10 1E 68
E11 2J 69
E13 4A 88
E17 5C 50
IG1: Ilf 1D 70
SE25 4F 157
SW1 4K 17 (4F 101)
SW13 7B 98
TW4: Houn 3D 112
TW16: Sun 1K 147
Belgrave Sq. SW1 1G 17 (3E 100)
Belgrave St. E1 5K 85
Belgrave Ter. IG8: Wfd G 3D 36
Belgrave Wlk. CR4: Mitc 3B 154
Belgrave Yd. SW1 2J 17
BELGRAVIA 2H 17 (3E 100)
Belgravia Cl. EN5: Barn 3C 20
Belgravia Ct. SW1 2J 17
Belgravia Gdns. BR1: Brom 6G 141
Belgravia Ho. *SW1* 1G 17
(off Halkin Pl.)
SW4 6H 119
Belgravia M. KT1: King T 4D 150
Belgravia Workshops *N19* 2J 65
(off Marlborough Rd.)
Belgrove St. WC1 1F 7 (3J 83)
Belham Wlk. SE5 1D 120
Belinda Rd. SW9 3B 120
Belitha Vs. N1 7K 65
BELL, THE 3C 50
Bella Best Ho. *SW1* 5K 17
(off Westmoreland Ter.)
Bellamy Cl. E14 2C 104
HA8: Edg 2D 28
UB10: Ick 3C 56
W14 5H 99
Bellamy Ct. HA7: Stan 1B 42
Bellamy Dr. HA7: Stan 1B 42
Bellamy Ho. SW17 4B 136
TW5: Hest 6E 94
Bellamy Rd. E4 6J 35
EN2: Enf 2J 23
Bellamy's Ct. *SE16* 1K 103
(off Abbotshade Rd.)
Bellamy St. SW12 7F 119
Bel La. TW13: Hanw 3C 130
Bellasis Av. SW2 2J 137
Bell Av. UB7: W Dray 4B 92
Bell Cl. HA4: Ruis 3H 57
HA5: Pinn 2A 40
Bellclose Rd. UB7: W Dray 2A 92
Bell Ct. NW4 4E 44
Bell Dr. SW18 7G 117
Bellefields Rd. SW9 3K 119
Bellegrove Cl. DA16: Well 2K 125
Bellegrove Pde. DA16: Well 3K 125
Bellegrove Rd. DA16: Well 2H 125
Bellenden Rd. SE15 1F 121
Bellermine Cl. SE28 1K 107
Bellestaines Pleasaunce E4 2H 35
Belleville Rd. SW11 5C 118
Belle Vue UB6: G'frd 1H 77
Belle Vue Est. NW4 4F 45
Bellevue La. WD23: Bushy 1C 26
Bellevue M. N11 5K 31
Bellevue Pde. SW17 1D 136
Bellevue Pk. CR7: Thor H 3C 156
Bellevue Pl. E1 4J 85
Belle Vue Rd. E17 2F 51
NW4 4E 44
Bellevue Rd. DA6: Bex 5F 127
KT1: King T 3E 150
(not continuous)
N11 4K 31
SW13 2C 116
SW17 1C 136
W13 4B 78
Bellew St. SW17 3A 136
Bell Farm Av. RM10: Dag 3J 73
Bellfield CR0: Sels 7A 170
Bellfield Av. HA3: Hrw W 6C 26
Bellfield Cl. SE3 7J 105
Bellflower Cl. E6 5C 88
Bell Gdns. *E10* 1C 68
(off Church Rd.)
Bellgate M. NW5 4F 65
BELL GREEN 4A 140
Bell Grn. SE26 4B 140
Bell Grn. La. SE26 5B 140
Bell Hill CR0: Croy 2C 168
Bell Ho. HA9: Wemb 3E 60
SE10 6E 104
(off Haddo St.)
Bellhouse Cotts. UB3: Hayes 7G 75
Bell Ho. Rd. RM7: Rush G 1J 73
Bellina M. NW5 4F 65
Bell Ind. Est. W4 4J 97
BELLINGHAM 3C 140
Bellingham *N17* 7C 34
(off Park La.)
Bellingham Ct. IG11: Bark 3B 90
Bellingham Grn. SE6 3C 140
Bellingham Rd. SE6 3D 140
Bellingham Trad. Est. SE6 3D 140
Bell Inn Yd. EC3 1F 15 (6D 84)
Bell Junc. TW3: Houn 3F 113
Bell La. E1 6J 9 (5F 85)
E16 1H 105
EN3: Enf H, Enf W 1E 24
HA9: Wemb 2D 60
NW4 4F 45
TW1: Twick 1A 132
Bellmaker Ct. E3 5C 86
Bell Mdw. SE19 5E 138
Bell Moor *NW3* 3A 64
(off E. Heath Rd.)
Bello Cl. SE24 7B 120
Bellot Gdns. *SE10* 5G 105
(off Bellot St.)
Bellot St. SE10 5G 105
Bellring Cl. DA17: Belv 6G 109
Bell Rd. EN1: Enf 1J 23
KT8: E Mos 5H 149
TW3: Houn 3F 113
Bells All. SW6 2J 117
Bells Hill EN5: Barn 5A 20
Bellsize Ct. NW3 5B 64
Bell St. NW1 5C 4 (5C 82)
SE18 1C 124

Belltrees Gro. SW16 . . . . . 5K **137**
Bell Vw. Mnr. HA4: Ruis 7F **39**
Bell Water Ga. SE18 . . . . . 3E **106**
Bell Wharf La. EC4 . . . . . 3D **14** (7C **84**)
Bellwood Rd. SE15 . . . . . 4K **121**
Bell Yd. WC2 . . . . . 1J **13** (6A **84**)
Bell Yd. M. SE1 . . . . . 7H **15** (2E **102**)
Belmarsh Rd. SE28 . . . . . 2J **107**
BELMONT
Harrow **2A 42**
Sutton **7J 165**
Belmont Av. DA16: Well 2J **125**
EN4: Cockf 5J **21**
HA0: Wemb 1F **79**
KT3: N Mald 5C **152**
N9 . . . . . 1B **34**
N13 . . . . . 5E **32**
N17 . . . . . 3C **48**
UB2: S'hall 3C **94**
Belmont Circ. HA3: Kent 1B **42**
Belmont Cl. E4 . . . . . 5A **36**
EN4: Cockf 4J **21**
IG8: Wfd G 4E **36**
N20 . . . . . 1E **30**
SW4 . . . . . 3G **119**
UB8: Uxb 6A **56**
Belmont Ct. N5 . . . . . 4C **66**
NW11 . . . . . 5H **45**
Belmont Gro. SE13 . . . . . 3F **123**
W4 . . . . . 4K **97**
Belmont Hall Ct. SE13 . . . . . 3F **123**
Belmont Hill SE13 . . . . . 3E **122**
Belmont La. BR7: Chst 5G **143**
(not continuous)
HA7: Stan 1C **42**
Belmont Lodge HA3: Hrw W 7C **26**
Belmont M. SW19 . . . . . 2F **135**
Belmont Pde. BR7: Chst 5G **143**
NW11 . . . . . 5H **45**
Belmont Pk. SE13 . . . . . 4F **123**
Belmont Pk. Cl. SE13 . . . . . 4G **123**
Belmont Pk. Rd. E10 . . . . . 6D **50**
Belmont Ri. SM2: Sutt 6H **165**
Belmont Rd. BR3: Beck 2A **158**
BR7: Chst 5F **143**
DA8: Erith 7G **109**
HA3: W'stone 3K **41**
IG1: Ilf 3G **71**
N15 . . . . . 4C **48**
N17 . . . . . 4C **48**
SE25 . . . . . 5H **157**
SM6: Wall 5F **167**
SW4 . . . . . 3G **119**
TW2: Twick 2H **131**
UB8: Uxb 7A **56**
W4 . . . . . 4K **97**
Belmont St. NW1 . . . . . 7E **64**
Belmont Ter. W4 . . . . . 4K **97**
Belmore Av. UB4: Hayes 6J **75**
Belmore Ho. N7 . . . . . 5H **65**
Belmore La. N7 . . . . . 5H **65**
Belmore St. SW8 . . . . . 1H **119**
Beloe Cl. SW15 . . . . . 4C **116**
Belsham St. E9 . . . . . 6J **67**
Belsize Av. N13 . . . . . 6E **32**
NW3 . . . . . 6B **64**
W13 . . . . . 3B **96**
Belsize Ct. Garages *NW3* *5B **64***
(off Belsize La.)
Belsize Cres. NW3 . . . . . 5B **64**
Belsize Gdns. SM1: Sutt 4K **165**
Belsize Gro. NW3 . . . . . 6C **64**
Belsize La. NW3 . . . . . 6B **64**
Belsize M. NW3 . . . . . 6B **64**
Belsize Pk. NW3 . . . . . 6B **64**
Belsize Pk. Gdns. NW3 . . . . . 6B **64**
Belsize Pk. M. NW3 . . . . . 6B **64**
Belsize Pl. NW3 . . . . . 5B **64**
Belsize Rd. HA3: Hrw W 7C **26**
NW6 . . . . . 1K **81**
Belsize Sq. NW3 . . . . . 6B **64**
Belsize Ter. NW3 . . . . . 6B **64**
Belson Rd. SE18 . . . . . 4D **106**
Beltane Dr. SW19 . . . . . 3F **135**
Belthorn Cres. SW12 . . . . . 7G **119**
Belton Rd. DA14: Sidc 4A **144**
E7 . . . . . 7K **69**
E11 . . . . . 4G **69**
N17 . . . . . 3E **48**
NW2 . . . . . 6C **62**
Belton Way E3 . . . . . 5C **86**
Beltran Rd. SW6 . . . . . 2K **117**
Beltwood Rd. DA17: Belv 4J **109**
BELVEDERE **3G 109**
Belvedere, The *SW10* *1A **118***
(off Chelsea Harbour)
Belvedere Av. IG5: Ilf 2F **53**
SW19 . . . . . 5G **135**
Belvedere Bldgs. SE1 . . . . . 7B **14** (2B **102**)
Belvedere Cl. TW11: Tedd 5J **131**
Belvedere Ct. DA17: Belv 3F **109**
N1 . . . . . *1E **84***
(off De Beauvoir Cres.)
N2 . . . . . 5B **46**
NW2 . . . . . *6F **63***
(off Willesden La.)
SW15 . . . . . 4E **116**
Belvedere Dr. SW19 . . . . . 5G **135**
Belvedere Gdns. KT8: W Mole 5D **148**
Belvedere Gro. SW19 . . . . . 5G **135**
Belvedere Ind. Est. DA17: Belv 1J **109**
Belvedere Link Bus. Pk.
DA8: Erith 3J **109**
Belvedere M. SE3 . . . . . 7K **105**
SE15 . . . . . 3J **121**
Belvedere Pl. SE1 . . . . . 7B **14** (2B **102**)
SW2 . . . . . 4K **119**
Belvedere Rd. DA7: Bex 3F **127**
E10 . . . . . 1A **68**
SE1 . . . . . 6H **13** (1K **101**)
SE2 . . . . . 1C **108**
SE19 . . . . . 7F **139**
W7 . . . . . 3K **95**
Belvedere Sq. SW19 . . . . . 5G **135**
Belvedere Strand NW9 . . . . . 2B **44**
Belvedere Way HA3: Kent 6E **42**
Belvoir Cl. SE9 . . . . . 3C **142**
Belvoir Rd. SE22 . . . . . 7G **121**
Belvue Bus. Cen. UB5: N'olt 7F **59**
Belvue Cl. UB5: N'olt 7E **58**
Belvue Rd. UB5: N'olt 7E **58**
Bembridge Cl. NW6 . . . . . 7G **63**
Bembridge Gdns. HA4: Ruis 2F **57**
Bembridge Ho. *KT2: King T* *2G **151***
(off Coombe Rd.)
SE8 . . . . . *4B **104***
(off Longshore)
SW18 . . . . . *6K **117***
(off Iron Mill Rd.)
Bemersyde Point *E13* *3K **87***
(off Dongola Rd. W.)
Bemerton Est. N1 . . . . . 7J **65**
Bemerton St. N1 . . . . . 1K **83**
Bemish Rd. SW15 . . . . . 3F **117**
Bempton Dr. HA4: Ruis 2K **57**
Bemsted Rd. E17 . . . . . 3B **50**
Benares Rd. SE18 . . . . . 4K **107**
Benbow Ct. *W6* *3E **98***
(off Benbow Rd.)
Benbow Ho. *SE8* *6C **104***
(off Benbow St.)
Benbow Rd. W6 . . . . . 3D **98**
Benbow St. SE8 . . . . . 6C **104**
Benbury Cl. BR1: Brom 5E **140**
Bence Ho. *SE8* *4A **104***
(off Rainsborough Av.)
Bench, The TW10: Ham 3C **132**
Bench Fld. CR2: S Croy 6F **169**
Bencroft Rd. SW16 . . . . . 7G **137**
Bencurtis Pk. BR4: W W'ck 3F **171**
Bendall Ho. *NW1* *5D **4***
(off Bell St.)
Bendall M. NW1 . . . . . 5D **4**
Bendemeer Rd. SW15 . . . . . 3F **117**
Benden Ho. *SE13* *5E **122***
(off Monument Gdns.)
Bendish Point SE28 . . . . . 2G **107**
Bendish Rd. E6 . . . . . 7C **70**
Bendmore Av. SE2 . . . . . 5A **108**
Bendon Valley SW18 . . . . . 7K **117**
Benedict Cl. BR6: Orp 3J **173**
DA17: Belv 3E **108**
Benedict Ct. RM6: Chad H 6F **55**
Benedict Dr. TW14: Bedf 7F **111**
Benedict Rd. CR4: Mitc 3B **154**
SW9 . . . . . 3K **119**
Benedict Way N2 . . . . . 3A **46**
Benedict Wharf CR4: Mitc 3C **154**
Benenden Grn. BR2: Brom 5J **159**
Benenden Ho. *SE17* *5E **102***
(off Mina Rd.)
Benett Gdns. SW16 . . . . . 2J **155**
Ben Ezra Ct. *SE17* *4C **102***
(off Asolando Dr.)
Benfleet Cl. SM1: Sutt 3A **166**
Benfleet Ct. E8 . . . . . 1F **85**
Benfleet Way N11 . . . . . 2K **31**
Bengal Ct. *EC3* *1F **15***
(off Birchin La.)
Bengal Ho. *E1* *5K **85***
(off Duckett St.)
Bengal Rd. IG1: Ilf 4F **71**
Bengarth Dr. HA3: Hrw W 2H **41**
Bengarth Rd. UB5: N'olt 1C **76**
Bengeo Gdns. RM6: Chad H 6C **54**
Bengeworth Rd. HA1: Harr 2A **60**
SE5 . . . . . 3C **120**
Ben Hale Cl. HA7: Stan 5G **27**
Benham Cl. KT9: Chess 6C **162**
SW11 . . . . . 3B **118**
Benham Gdns. TW4: Houn 5D **112**
Benham Ho. *SW10* *7K **99***
(off Coleridge Gdns.)
Benham Rd. W7 . . . . . 5J **77**
Benham's Pl. NW3 . . . . . 4A **64**
Benhill Av. SM1: Sutt 4K **165**
(not continuous)
Benhill Rd. SE5 . . . . . 7D **102**
SM1: Sutt 3A **166**
Benhill Wood Rd. SM1: Sutt 3A **166**
BENHILTON **2K 165**
Benhilton Gdns. SM1: Sutt 3K **165**
Benhurst Ct. SW16 . . . . . 5A **138**
Benhurst La. SW16 . . . . . 5A **138**
Benin St. SE13 . . . . . 7F **123**
Benjafield Cl. N18 . . . . . 4C **34**
Benjamin Cl. E8 . . . . . 1G **85**
Benjamin Ct. DA17: Belv 6F **109**
TW15: Ashf 7E **128**
Benjamin Franklin House *4E **12***
(off Craven St.)
Benjamin St. EC1 . . . . . 5A **8** (5B **84**)
Ben Jonson Ct. N1 . . . . . 2E **84**
Ben Jonson Ho. EC2 . . . . . 5D **8**
Ben Jonson Pl. EC2 . . . . . 5D **8**
Ben Jonson Rd. E1 . . . . . 5K **85**
Benledi St. E14 . . . . . 6F **87**
Benlow Works *UB3: Hayes* *2H **93***
(off Silverdale Rd.)
Bennelong Cl. W12 . . . . . 7D **80**
Bennerley Rd. SW11 . . . . . 5C **118**
Bennets Fld. Rd. UB11: Stock P 1D **92**
Bennet's Hill EC4 . . . . . 2B **14** (7C **84**)
Bennet St. SW1 . . . . . 4A **12** (1G **101**)
Bennett Cl. DA16: Well 2A **126**
HA6: Nwood 1H **39**
KT1: Ham W 1C **150**
Bennett Ct. N7 . . . . . 3K **65**
Bennett Gro. SE13 . . . . . 1D **122**
Bennett Ho. *SW1* *3D **18***
(off Page St.)
Bennett Pk. SE3 . . . . . 3H **123**
Bennett Rd. E13 . . . . . 4A **88**
N16 . . . . . 4E **66**
RM6: Chad H 6E **54**
SW9 . . . . . 2A **120**
Bennetts Av. CR0: Croy 2A **170**
UB6: G'frd 1J **77**
Bennett's Castle La. RM8: Dag 2C **72**
Bennetts Cl. CR4: Mitc 1F **155**
N17 . . . . . 6A **34**
Bennetts Copse BR7: Chst 6C **142**
Bennetts Courtyard SW19 . . . . . 1A **154**
Bennett St. W4 . . . . . 6A **98**
Bennetts Way CR0: Croy 2A **170**
Bennett's Yd. SW1 . . . . . 2D **18** (3H **101**)
Benningholme Rd. HA8: Edg 6F **29**
Bennington Rd. IG8: Wfd G 7B **36**
N17 . . . . . 1E **48**
Benn's All. TW12: Hamp 2F **149**
Benn St. E9 . . . . . 6A **68**
Benns Wlk. *TW9: Rich* *4E **114***
(off Michelsdale Dr.)
Benrek Cl. IG6: Ilf 1G **53**
Bensbury Cl. SW15 . . . . . 7D **116**
Bensham Cl. CR7: Thor H 4C **156**
Bensham Gro. CR7: Thor H 2C **156**
Bensham La. CR0: Croy 7B **156**
CR7: Thor H 5B **156**
Bensham Mnr. Rd.
CR7: Thor H 4C **156**
Bensham Mnr. Rd. Pas.
CR7: Thor H 4C **156**
Bensley Cl. N11 . . . . . 5J **31**
Ben Smith Way SE16 . . . . . 3G **103**
Benson Av. E6 . . . . . 2A **88**
Benson Cl. TW3: Houn 4E **112**
UB8: Hil 5A **74**
Benson Ho. *E2* *3J **9***
(off Ligonier St.)
SE1 . . . . . *5K **13***
(off Hatfields)
Benson Quay E1 . . . . . 7J **85**
Benson Rd. CR0: Wadd 3A **168**
SE23 . . . . . 1J **139**
Bentalls Cen., The KT1: King T 2D **150**
Bentfield Gdns. SE9 . . . . . 3B **142**
Benthal Rd. N16 . . . . . 2G **67**
Bentham Ct. *N1* *7C **66***
(off Ecclesbourne Rd.)
Bentham Ho. *SE1* *3D **102***
(off Falmouth Rd.)
Bentham Rd. E9 . . . . . 6K **67**
SE28 . . . . . 7B **90**
Bentham Wlk. NW10 . . . . . 5J **61**
Ben Tillet Cl. E16 . . . . . 1D **106**
IG11: Bark 7A **72**
Ben Tillet Ho. N15 . . . . . 3B **48**
Bentinck Cl. NW8 . . . . . 2C **82**
Bentinck Ho. *W12* *7D **80***
(off White City Est.)
Bentinck Mans. *W1* *7H **5***
(off Bentinck St.)
Bentinck M. W1 . . . . . 7H **5** (6E **82**)
Bentinck Rd. UB7: Yiew 1A **92**
Bentinck St. W1 . . . . . 7H **5** (6E **82**)
Bentley Cl. SW19 . . . . . 3J **135**
Bentley Ct. *SE13* *4E **122***
(off Whitburn Rd.)
Bentley Dr. IG2: Ilf 6G **53**
NW2 . . . . . 3H **63**
Bentley Ho. *SE5* *1E **120***
(off Peckham Rd.)
Bentley M. EN1: Enf 6J **23**
Bentley Rd. N1 . . . . . 6E **66**
Bentley Way HA7: Stan 5F **27**
IG8: Buck H, Wfd G 2D **36**
Benton Rd. IG1: Ilf 1H **71**
Bentons La. SE27 . . . . . 4C **138**
Benton's Ri. SE27 . . . . . 5D **138**
Bentry Cl. RM8: Dag 2E **72**
Bentry Rd. RM8: Dag 2E **72**
Bentworth Ct. *E2* *3K **9***
(off Granby St.)
Bentworth Rd. W12 . . . . . 6D **80**
Benville Ho. *SW8* *7K **101***
(off Oval Pl.)
Benwell Ct. TW16: Sun 1J **147**
Benwell Rd. N7 . . . . . 4A **66**
Benwick Cl. SE16 . . . . . 4H **103**
Benwood Ct. SM1: Sutt 3A **166**
Benworth St. E3 . . . . . 3B **86**

Benyon Ct.—Betty May Gray Ho.

Benyon Ct. *N1* . . . 1E 84
(off De Beauvoir Est.)
Benyon Ho. *EC1* . . . 1K 7
(off Myddelton Pas.)
Benyon Rd. N1 . . . 1D 84
Benyon Wharf *N1* . . . 1E 84
(off Kingsland Rd.)
Berberis Ct. IG1: Ilf . . . 6F 71
Berberis Ho. *E3* . . . 5C 86
(off Gale St.)
Berberis Wlk. UB7: W Dray . . . 4A 92
Berber Pl. E14 . . . 7C 86
Berber Rd. SW11 . . . 5D 118
Berberry Cl. HA8: Edg . . . 4D 28
Bercta Rd. SE9 . . . 2G 143
Berenger Twr. *SW10* . . . 7B 100
(off Worlds End Est.)
Berenger Wlk. *SW10* . . . 7B 100
(off Worlds End Est.)
Berens Ct. DA14: Sidc . . . 4K 143
Berens Rd. NW10 . . . 3F 81
Berens Way BR7: Chst . . . 3K 161
Beresford Av. HA0: Wemb . . . 1F 79
KT5: Surb . . . 1H 163
N20 . . . 2J 31
TW1: Twick . . . 6C 114
W7 . . . 5H 77
Beresford Dr. BR1: Brom . . . 3C 160
IG8: Wfd G . . . 4F 37
Beresford Gdns. EN1: Enf . . . 4K 23
RM6: Chad H . . . 5E 54
TW4: Houn . . . 5D 112
Beresford Rd. E4 . . . 1B 36
E17 . . . 1D 50
HA1: Harr . . . 5H 41
KT2: King T . . . 1F 151
KT3: N Mald . . . 4J 151
N2 . . . 3C 46
N5 . . . 5D 66
N8 . . . 5A 48
SM2: Sutt . . . 7H 165
UB1: S'hall . . . 1B 94
Beresford Sq. SE18 . . . 4F 107
Beresford St. SE18 . . . 3F 107
Beresford Ter. N5 . . . 5C 66
Berestede Rd. W6 . . . 5B 98
Bere St. E1 . . . 7K 85
Bergen Ho. *SE5* . . . 2C 120
(off Carew St.)
Bergen Sq. SE16 . . . 3A 104
Berger Cl. BR5: Pet W . . . 6H 161
Berger Rd. E9 . . . 6K 67
Berghem M. W14 . . . 3F 99
Bergholt Av. IG4: Ilf . . . 5C 52
Bergholt Cres. N16 . . . 7E 48
Bergholt M. NW1 . . . 7H 65
Berglen Ct. E14 . . . 6A 86
Bering Sq. E14 . . . 5C 104
Bering Wlk. E16 . . . 6B 88
Berisford M. SW18 . . . 6A 118
Berkeley Av. DA7: Bex . . . 1D 126
IG5: Ilf . . . 2E 52
RM5: Col R . . . 1J 55
TW4: Cran . . . 2J 111
UB6: G'frd . . . 6H 59
(not continuous)
Berkeley Cl. BR5: Pet W . . . 7J 161
HA4: Ruis . . . 3J 57
KT2: King T . . . 7E 132
Berkeley Ct. *CR0: Croy* . . . 4D 168
(off Coombe Rd.)
KT6: Surb . . . 7D 150
N3 . . . 1K 45
N14 . . . 6B 22
NW1 . . . 4F 5
NW10 . . . 4A 62
NW11 . . . 7H 45
(off Ravenscroft Av.)
SM6: Wall . . . 3G 167
W5 . . . 7C 78
(off Gordon Rd.)
Berkeley Cres. EN4: E Barn . . . 5G 21
Berkeley Dr. KT8: W Mole . . . 3D 148
Berkeley Gdns. KT10: Clay . . . 6A 162
KT12: Walt T . . . 7H 147
N21 . . . 7J 23
W8 . . . 1J 99
Berkeley Ho. *SE8* . . . 5B 104
(off Grove St.)
TW8: Bford . . . 6D 96
(off Albany Rd.)
Berkeley M. W1 . . . 1F 11 (6D 82)
Berkeley Pl. SW19 . . . 6F 135
Berkeley Rd. E12 . . . 5C 70
N8 . . . 5H 47
N15 . . . 6D 48
NW9 . . . 4G 43
SW13 . . . 1C 116
UB10: Hil . . . 7E 56
Berkeley Sq. W1 . . . 3K 11 (7F 83)
Berkeley St. W1 . . . 3K 11 (7F 83)
Berkeley Twr. *E14* . . . 1B 104
(off Westferry Cir.)
Berkeley Wlk. *N7* . . . 2K 65
(off Durham Rd.)
Berkeley Waye TW5: Hest . . . 6B 94
Berkely Cl. TW16: Sun . . . 3A 148
Berkhampstead Rd. DA17: Belv . . . 5G 109
Berkhamsted Av. HA9: Wemb . . . 6F 61
Berkley Cl. *TW2: Twick* . . . 3J 131
(off Wellesley Rd.)
Berkley Gro. NW1 . . . 7E 64
Berkley Rd. NW1 . . . 7D 64
Berkshire Ct. *W7* . . . 4K 77
(off Copley Cl.)
Berkshire Gdns. N13 . . . 6F 33
N18 . . . 5C 34
Berkshire Ho. SE6 . . . 4C 140
Berkshire Rd. E9 . . . 6B 68
Berkshire Sq. CR4: Mitc . . . 4J 155
Berkshire Way CR4: Mitc . . . 4J 155
Bermans Way NW10 . . . 4A 62
BERMONDSEY . . . 7K 15 (2G 103)
Bermondsey Sq. SE1 . . . 7H 15 (3E 102)
Bermondsey St. SE1 . . . 5G 15 (1E 102)
Bermondsey Trad. Est. SE16 . . . 5J 103
Bermondsey Wall E. SE16 . . . 2G 103
Bermondsey Wall W. SE16 . . . 2G 103
Bernal Cl. SE28 . . . 7D 90
Bernard Angell Ho. *SE10* . . . 6F 105
(off Trafalgar Rd.)
Bernard Ashley Dr. SE7 . . . 5K 105
Bernard Av. W13 . . . 3B 96
Bernard Cassidy St. E16 . . . 5H 87
Bernard Gdns. SW19 . . . 5H 135
Bernard Hegarty Lodge *E8* . . . 7G 67
(off Lansdowne Dr.)
Bernard Mans. *WC1* . . . 4E 6
(off Bernard St.)
Bernard Rd. N15 . . . 5F 49
RM7: Rush G . . . 7J 55
SM6: Wall . . . 4F 167
Bernard Shaw Ct. *NW1* . . . 7G 65
(off St Pancras Way)
Bernard Shaw Ho. *NW10* . . . 1K 79
(off Knatchbull Rd.)
Bernard St. WC1 . . . 4E 6 (4J 83)
Bernard Sunley Ho. *SW9* . . . 7A 102
(off Sth. Island Pl.)
Bernays Cl. HA7: Stan . . . 6H 27
Bernays Gro. SW9 . . . 4K 119
Bernel Dr. CR0: Croy . . . 3B 170
Berne Rd. CR7: Thor H . . . 5C 156
Berners Dr. W13 . . . 7A 78
Berners Ho. *N1* . . . 2A 84
(off Barnsbury Est.)
Berners M. W1 . . . 6B 6 (5G 83)
Berners Pl. W1 . . . 7B 6 (6G 83)
Berners Rd. N1 . . . 1B 84
N22 . . . 1A 48
Berners St. W1 . . . 6B 6 (5G 83)
Berner Ter. *E1* . . . 6G 85
(off Fairclough St.)
Berney Ho. BR3: Beck . . . 5A 158
Berney Rd. CR0: Croy . . . 7D 156
Bernhardt Cres. NW8 . . . 3C 4 (4C 82)
Bernhart Cl. HA8: Edg . . . 7D 28
Bernville Way HA3: Kent . . . 5F 43
Bernwell Rd. E4 . . . 3B 36
Berridge Grn. HA8: Edg . . . 7B 28
Berridge M. NW6 . . . 5J 63
Berridge Rd. SE19 . . . 5D 138
Berriman Rd. N7 . . . 3K 65
Berrington Ho. *W2* . . . 7J 81
(off Hereford Rd.)
Berriton Rd. HA2: Harr . . . 1D 58
Berrybank Cl. E4 . . . 2K 35
Berry Cl. N21 . . . 1G 33
NW10 . . . 7A 62
RM10: Dag . . . 5G 73
Berry Cotts. *E14* . . . 6A 86
(off Maroon St.)
Berry Ct. TW4: Houn . . . 5D 112
Berrydale Rd. UB4: Yead . . . 4C 76
Berryfield Cl. BR1: Brom . . . 1C 160
E17 . . . 4D 50
Berryfield Rd. SE17 . . . 5B 102
Berry Hill HA7: Stan . . . 4J 27
Berryhill SE9 . . . 4F 125
Berryhill Gdns. SE9 . . . 4F 125
Berry Ho. *E1* . . . 4H 85
(off Headlam St.)
BERRYLANDS . . . 6G 151
Berrylands KT5: Surb . . . 6F 151
SW20 . . . 3E 152
Berrylands Rd. KT5: Surb . . . 6F 151
Berry La. SE21 . . . 4D 138
Berryman Cl. RM8: Dag . . . 3C 72
Berryman's La. SE26 . . . 4K 139
Berrymead Gdns. W3 . . . 1J 97
Berrymede Rd. W4 . . . 3K 97
Berry Pl. EC1 . . . 2B 8 (3B 84)
Berry St. EC1 . . . 3B 8 (4B 84)
Berry Way W5 . . . 3E 96
Bertal Rd. SW17 . . . 4B 136
Bertha Hollamby Ct.
DA14: Sidc . . . 5C 144
(off Sidcup Hill)
Bertha James Ct. BR2: Brom . . . 4K 159
Berthons Gdns. *E17* . . . 5F 51
(off Wood St.)
Berthon St. SE8 . . . 7C 104
Bertie Rd. NW10 . . . 6C 62
SE26 . . . 6K 139
Bertram Cotts. SW19 . . . 7J 135
Bertram Rd. EN1: Enf . . . 4B 24
KT2: King T . . . 7G 133
NW4 . . . 6C 44
Bertram St. N19 . . . 2F 65
Bertrand Ho. *SW16* . . . 3J 137
(off Leigham Av.)
Bertrand St. SE13 . . . 3D 122
Bertrand Way SE28 . . . 7D 90
Bert Rd. CR7: Thor H . . . 5C 156
Bert Way EN1: Enf . . . 4A 24
Berwick Av. UB4: Yead . . . 6B 76
Berwick Cl. HA7: Stan . . . 6E 26
TW2: Whit . . . 1E 130
Berwick Ct. SE1 . . . 7D 14
Berwick Cres. DA15: Sidc . . . 7J 125
Berwick Gdns. SM1: Sutt . . . 3A 166
Berwick Ho. N2 . . . 2B 46
Berwick Rd. DA16: Well . . . 1B 126
E16 . . . 6K 87
N22 . . . 1B 48
Berwick St. W1 . . . 7B 6 (6G 83)
Berwick Way BR6: Orp . . . 1K 173
Berwyn Av. TW3: Houn . . . 1F 113
Berwyn Rd. SE24 . . . 1B 138
TW10: Rich . . . 4H 115
Beryl Av. E6 . . . 5C 88
Beryl Ho. *SE18* . . . 5K 107
(off Spinel Cl.)
Beryl Rd. W6 . . . 5F 99
Berystede KT2: King T . . . 7H 133
Besant Cl. NW2 . . . 3G 63
Besant Ct. N1 . . . 5D 66
SE28 . . . 1B 108
(off Titmuss Av.)
Besant Ho. *NW8* . . . 1A 82
(off Boundary Rd.)
Besant Pl. SE22 . . . 4F 121
Besant Rd. NW2 . . . 4G 63
Besant Wlk. N7 . . . 2K 65
Besant Way NW10 . . . 5J 61
Besford Ho. *E2* . . . 2G 85
(off Pritchard's Rd.)
Besley St. SW16 . . . 6G 137
Bessant Dr. TW9: Kew . . . 1G 115
Bessborough Gdns. SW1 . . . 5D 18 (5H 101)
Bessborough Pl. SW1 . . . 5D 18 (5H 101)
Bessborough Rd. HA1: Harr . . . 1H 59
SW15 . . . 1C 134
Bessborough St. SW1 . . . 5C 18 (5H 101)
Bessemer Ct. *NW1* . . . 7G 65
(off Rochester Sq.)
Bessemer Pk. Ind. Est. SE24 . . . 4B 120
Bessemer Rd. SE5 . . . 2C 120
Bessie Lansbury Cl. E6 . . . 6E 88
Bessingby Rd. HA4: Ruis . . . 2K 57
Bessingham Wlk. *SE4* . . . 4K 121
(off Aldersford Cl.)
Besson St. SE14 . . . 1J 121
Bessy St. E2 . . . 3J 85
Bestwood St. SE8 . . . 4K 103
Beswick M. NW6 . . . 6K 63
Betam Rd. UB3: Hayes . . . 2F 93
Beta Pl. SW4 . . . 4K 119
Betchworth Cl. SM1: Sutt . . . 5B 166
Betchworth Rd. IG3: Ilf . . . 2J 71
Betchworth Way CR0: New Ad . . . 7E 170
Bethal Est. SE1 . . . 5H 15
Betham Rd. UB6: G'frd . . . 3H 77
Bethany Waye TW14: Bedf . . . 7G 111
Bethecar Rd. HA1: Harr . . . 5J 41
Bethel Cl. NW4 . . . 5F 45
Bethell Av. E16 . . . 4H 87
IG1: Ilf . . . 7E 52
Bethel Rd. DA16: Well . . . 3C 126
Bethersden Cl. BR3: Beck . . . 7B 140
Bethersden Ho. *SE17* . . . 5E 102
(off Kinglake St.)
Bethlehem Ho. *E14* . . . 7B 86
(off Limehouse C'way.)
BETHNAL GREEN . . . 3H 85
Bethnal Green Cen. for
Sports & Performing Arts . . . 3F 85
Bethnal Green Mus. of Childhood . . . 3J 85
Bethnal Grn. Rd. E1 . . . 3J 9 (4F 85)
E2 . . . 3K 9 (4F 85)
Bethune Av. N11 . . . 4J 31
Bethune Cl. N16 . . . 1E 66
Bethune Rd. N16 . . . 7D 48
NW10 . . . 4K 79
Bethwin Rd. SE5 . . . 7B 102
Betjeman Cl. HA5: Pinn . . . 4E 40
Betjeman Ct. UB7: Yiew . . . 1A 92
Betony Cl. CR0: Croy . . . 1K 169
Betoyne Av. E4 . . . 4B 36
Betsham Ho. *SE1* . . . 6E 14
(off Newcomen St.)
Betstyle Cir. N11 . . . 4A 32
Betstyle Ho. N10 . . . 7K 31
Betstyle Rd. N11 . . . 4A 32
Betterton Dr. DA14: Sidc . . . 2E 144
Betterton Ho. *WC2* . . . 1F 13
(off Betterton St.)
Betterton Rd. RM13: Rain . . . 3K 91
Betterton St. WC2 . . . 1E 12 (6J 83)
Bettons Pk. E15 . . . 1G 87
Bettridge Rd. SW6 . . . 2H 117
Betts Cl. BR3: Beck . . . 2A 158
Betts Ho. *E1* . . . 7H 85
(off Betts St.)
Betts M. E17 . . . 6B 50
Betts Rd. E16 . . . 7K 87
Betts St. E1 . . . 7H 85
Betts Way KT6: Surb . . . 1B 162
SE20 . . . 1H 157
Betty Brooks Ho. E11 . . . 3F 69
Betty May Gray Ho. *E14* . . . 4E 104
(off Pier St.)

Beulah Av. CR7: Thor H 2C **156**
Beulah Cl. HA8: Edg 3C **28**
Beulah Cres. CR7: Thor H 2C **156**
Beulah Gro. CR0: Croy 6C **156**
Beulah Hill SE19 . . . . .6B **138**
Beulah Path E17 . . . . .5E **50**
Beulah Rd. CR7: Thor H 3C **156**
E17 . . . . .5D **50**
SM1: Sutt 4J **165**
SW19 .7H **135**
Bevan Av. IG11: Bark 7A **72**
Bevan Ct. CR0: Wadd 5A **168**
E3 . . . .*2C* ***86***
(off Tredegar Rd.)
Bevan Ho. *N1* *1E* ***84***
(off New Era Est.)
TW1: Twick 6D **114**
WC1 . . . .*5F* ***7***
(off Boswell St.)
Bevan Rd. EN4: Cockf 4J **21**
SE2 . . . . .5B **108**
Bevan St. N1 .1C **84**
Bev Callender Cl. SW8 . . . . .3F **119**
Bevenden St. N1 . . . . .1F **9** (3D **84**)
Bevercote Wlk. *DA17: Belv* *6F* ***109***
(off Osborne Rd.)
Beveree Stadium 1F **149**
Beveridge Ct. *SE28* *7B* ***90***
(off Saunders Way)
Beveridge Rd. NW10 . . . . .7A **62**
Beverley Av. DA15: Sidc 7K **125**
SW20 .1B **152**
TW4: Houn 4D **112**
Beverley Cl. EN1: Enf 4K **23**
KT9: Chess 4C **162**
N21 . . . . .1H **33**
SW11 .4B **118**
SW13 .2C **116**
Beverley Cotts. SW15 . . . . .3A **134**
Beverley Ct. HA2: Harr 3H **41**
HA3: Kent 4C **42**
N2 . . . .*4D* ***46***
(off Western Rd.)
N14 . . . . .7B **22**
SE4 . . . . .3B **122**
(not continuous)
TW4: Houn 4D **112**
W4 . . . . .5J **97**
Beverley Cres. IG8: Wfd G 1K **51**
Beverley Dr. HA8: Edg 3G **43**
Beverley Gdns. HA7: Stan 1A **42**
HA9: Wemb 1F **61**
KT4: Wor Pk 1C **164**
NW11 . . . . .7G **45**
SW13 .3B **116**
Beverley Ho. *BR1: Brom* *5F* ***141***
(off Brangbourne Rd.)
Beverley Hyrst CR0: Croy 2F **169**
Beverley La. KT2: King T 7A **134**
SW15 .3B **134**
Beverley M. E4 . . . . .6A **36**
Beverley Path SW13 . . . . .2B **116**
Beverley Rd. BR2: Brom 2C **172**
CR4: Mitc 4H **155**
DA7: Bex 2J **127**
E4 . . . . .6A **36**
E6 . . . . .3B **88**
HA4: Ruis 2J **57**
KT1: Ham W 1C **150**
KT3: N Mald 4C **152**
KT4: Wor Pk 2E **164**
RM9: Dag 4E **72**
SE20 .2H **157**
SW13 .3B **116**
TW16: Sun 1H **147**
UB2: S'hall 4C **94**
W4 . . . . .5B **98**
Beverley Trad. Est. SM4: Mord 7F **153**
Beverley Way SW20 . . . . .1B **152**
Beversbrook Rd. N19 . . . . .3H **65**
Beverstone Rd. CR7: Thor H 4A **156**
SW2 . . . . .5K **119**
Beverston M. W1 . . . . .6E **4**
Bevill Allen Cl. SW17 . . . . .5D **136**
Bevill Cl. SE25 . . . . .3G **157**
Bevin Cl. SE16 . . . . .1A **104**
Bevin Ct. WC1 . . . . .1H **7** (3K **83**)
Bevington Path SE1 . . . . .7J **15**
Bevington Rd. BR3: Beck 2D **158**
W10 . . . . .5G **81**
Bevington St. SE16 . . . . .2G **103**
Bevin Ho. *E2* *3J* ***85***
(off Butler St.)
Bevin Rd. UB4: Yead 3J **75**
Bevin Sq. SW17 . . . . .3D **136**
Bevin Way WC1 . . . . .1J **7** (2A **84**)
Bevis Marks EC3 . . . . .7H **9** (6E **84**)
Bewcastle Gdns. EN2: Enf 4D **22**
Bew Ct. SE22 .7G **121**
Bewdley St. N1 . . . . .7A **66**
Bewick M. SE15 . . . . .7H **103**
Bewick St. SW8 . . . . .2F **119**
Bewley Ho. *E1* *7H* ***85***
(off Bewley St.)
Bewley St. E1 .7J **85**
SW19 .6A **136**
Bewlys Rd. SE27 . . . . .5B **138**
Bexhill Cl. TW13: Felt 2C **130**
Bexhill Rd. N11 . . . . .5C **32**
SE4 . . . . .6B **122**
SW14 . . . . .3J **115**
Bexhill Wlk. E15 . . . . .1G **87**
BEXLEY 7G **127**
Bexley Gdns. N9 . . . . .3J **33**
RM6: Chad H 5B **54**
BEXLEYHEATH 4F **127**
Bexleyheath Sports Club 3C **126**
Bexley High St. DA5: Bexl 7G **127**
Bexley Ho. SE4 . . . . .4A **122**
Bexley La. DA1: Cray 5K **127**
DA14: Sidc 4C **144**
Bexley Lawn Tennis & Squash Club
. . . . .7G **127**
Bexley Mus. 6J **127**
Bexley Music & Dance Cen. *4A* ***144***
(off Station Rd.)
Bexley Rd. DA8: Erith 7J **109**
SE9 . . . . .5F **125**
Beynon Rd. SM5: Cars 5D **166**
Bianca Ho. *N1* *1G* ***9***
(off Crondall St.)
Bianca Rd. SE15 . . . . .6G **103**
Bibsworth Rd. N3 . . . . .2H **45**
Bibury Cl. SE15 . . . . .6E **102**
(not continuous)
Bicester Rd. TW9: Rich 3G **115**
Bickenhall Mans. W1 . . . . .5F **5**
(not continuous)
Bickenhall St. W1 . . . . .5F **5** (5D **82**)
Bickersteth Rd. SW17 . . . . .6D **136**
Bickerton Rd. N19 . . . . .2G **65**
BICKLEY 3C **160**
Bickley Cres. BR1: Brom 4C **160**
Bickley Pk. Rd. BR1: Brom 3C **160**
Bickley Rd. BR1: Brom 2B **160**
E10 . . . . .7D **50**
Bickley St. SW17 . . . . .5C **136**
Bicknell Ho. *E1* *6G* ***85***
(off Ellen St.)
Bicknell Rd. SE5 . . . . .3C **120**
Bicknoller Rd. EN1: Enf 1K **23**
Bicknor Rd. BR6: Orp 7J **161**
Bidborough Cl. BR2: Brom 5H **159**
Bidborough St. WC1 . . . . .2E **6** (3J **83**)
Biddenden Way SE9 . . . . .4E **142**
Biddenham Ho. *SE16* *4K* ***103***
(off Plough Way)
Bidder St. E16 . . . . .4G **87**
(not continuous)
Biddesden Ho. *SW3* *4E* ***16***
(off Cadogan St.)
Biddestone Rd. N7 . . . . .4K **65**
Biddulph Ho. SE18 . . . . .4D **106**
Biddulph Mans. *W9* *3K* ***81***
(off Elgin Av.)
Biddulph Rd. W9 . . . . .3K **81**
Bideford Av. UB6: G'frd 2B **78**
Bideford Cl. HA8: Edg 1G **43**
TW13: Hanw 3D **130**
Bideford Gdns. EN1: Enf 7K **23**
Bideford Rd. BR1: Brom 3H **141**
DA16: Well 7B **108**
EN3: Enf L 1G **25**
HA4: Ruis 3K **57**
Bidwell Gdns. N11 . . . . .7B **32**
Bidwell St. SE15 . . . . .1H **121**
Big Ben 7F **13** (2J **101**)
Bigbury Cl. N17 . . . . .7J **33**
Biggerstaff Rd. E15 . . . . .1E **86**
Biggerstaff St. N4 . . . . .2A **66**
Biggin Av. CR4: Mitc 1D **154**
Biggin Hill SE19 . . . . .1B **156**
Biggin Hill Cl. KT2: King T 5C **132**
Biggin Way SE19 . . . . .7B **138**
Bigginwood Rd. SW16 . . . . .7B **138**
Biggs Row SW15 . . . . .3F **117**
Big Hill E5 . . . . .1H **67**
Bigland St. E1 .6H **85**
Bignell Rd. SE18 . . . . .5F **107**
Bignold Rd. E7 .4J **69**
Bigwood Ct. NW11 . . . . .5K **45**
Bigwood Rd. NW11 . . . . .5K **45**
Bilberry Ho. *E3* *5C* ***86***
(off Watts Gro.)
Billet Cl. RM6: Chad H 3D **54**
Billet Rd. E17 .1K **49**
RM6: Chad H 3B **54**
Billets Hart Cl. W7 . . . . .2J **95**
Bill Hamling Cl. SE9 . . . . .2D **142**
Billing Cl. RM9: Dag 7C **72**
Billingford Cl. SE4 . . . . .4K **121**
Billing Ho. *E1* *6K* ***85***
(off Bower St.)
Billingley *NW1* *1G* ***83***
(off Pratt St.)
Billing Pl. SW10 . . . . .7K **99**
Billing Rd. SW10 . . . . .7K **99**
Billingsgate Fish Market 1D **104**
Billing St. SW10 . . . . .7K **99**
Billington M. *W3* *1H* ***97***
(off High St.)
Billington Rd. SE14 . . . . .7K **103**
Billinton Hill CR0: Croy 2D **168**
Billiter Sq. EC3 . . . . .1H **15**
Billiter St. EC3 . . . . .1H **15** (6E **84**)
Bill Nicholson Way *N17* *7A* ***34***
(off High Rd.)
Billockby Cl. KT9: Chess 6F **163**
Billson St. E14 . . . . .4E **104**
Bilsby Gro. SE9 . . . . .4B **142**
Bilsby Lodge *HA9: Wemb* *3J* ***61***
(off Chalklands)
Bilton Cen., The
UB6: G'frd 1B **78**
Bilton Rd. UB6: G'frd 1A **78**
Bilton Towers *W1* *1F* ***11***
(off Gt. Cumberland Pl.)
Bilton Way EN3: Enf L 1F **25**
UB3: Hayes 2K **93**
Bina Gdns. SW5 . . . . .4A **100**
Binbrook Ho. *W10* *5E* ***80***
(off Sutton Way)
Bincote Rd. EN2: Enf 3E **22**
Binden Rd. W12 . . . . .3B **98**
Bindon Grn. SM4: Mord 4K **153**
Binfield Rd. CR2: S Croy 5F **169**
SW4 . . . . .1J **119**
Bingfield St. N1 . . . . .1J **83**
(not continuous)
Bingham Ct. *N1* *7B* ***66***
(off Halton Rd.)
Bingham Pl. W1 . . . . .5G **5** (5E **82**)
Bingham Rd. CR0: Croy 1G **169**
Bingham St. N1 . . . . .6D **66**
Bingley Rd. E16 . . . . .6A **88**
TW16: Sun 7J **129**
UB6: G'frd 4G **77**
Binley Ho. SW15 . . . . .6B **116**
Binney St. W1 . . . . .1H **11** (6E **82**)
Binnie Ct. *SE10* *7D* ***104***
(off Greenwich High Rd.)
Binnie Ho. *SE1* *3C* ***102***
(off Bath Ter.)
Binnington Twr. BR2: Brom 6C **160**
Binns Rd. W4 .5A **98**
Binns Ter. W4 .5A **98**
Binsey Wlk. SE2 . . . . .2C **108**
(not continuous)
Binstead Cl. UB4: Yead 5C **76**
Binyon Cres. HA7: Stan 5E **26**
Birbetts Rd. SE9 . . . . .2D **142**
Bircham Path *SE4* *4K* ***121***
(off Aldersford Cl.)
Birchanger Rd. SE25 . . . . .5G **157**
Birch Av. N13 .3H **33**
UB7: Yiew 6B **74**
Birch Cl. E16 . . . . .5G **87**
IG9: Buck H 3G **37**
N19 . . . . .2G **65**
RM7: Mawney 3H **55**
SE15 . . . . .2G **121**
TW3: Houn 2H **113**
TW8: Bford 7B **96**
TW11: Tedd 5A **132**
TW17: Shep 2G **147**
Birch Ct. N12 .4E **30**
RM6: Chad H 6C **54**
SM1: Sutt 4A **166**
SM6: Wall 4F **167**
Birch Cres. UB10: Uxb 1B **74**
Birchdale Gdns. RM6: Chad H 7D **54**
Birchdale Rd. E7 . . . . .5A **70**
Birchdene Dr. SE28 . . . . .1A **108**
Birchen Cl. NW9 . . . . .2K **61**
Birchend Cl. CR2: S Croy 6D **168**
Birchen Gro. NW9 . . . . .2K **61**
Birches, The *BR2: Brom* *4H* ***159***
(off Durham Rd.)
BR6: Farnb 4E **172**
E12 . . . . .4C **70**
N21 . . . . .6E **22**
SE7 . . . . .6K **105**
TW4: Houn 7D **112**
Birches Cl. CR4: Mitc 3D **154**
HA5: Pinn 5C **40**
Birchfield Ct. *KT12: Walt T* *7K* ***147***
(off Grove Cres.)
Birchfield Ho. *E14* *7C* ***86***
(off Birchfield St.)
Birchfield St. E14 . . . . .7C **86**
Birch Gdns. RM10: Dag 3J **73**
Birch Grn. NW9 . . . . .7F **29**
Birch Gro. DA16: Well 4A **126**
E11 . . . . .4G **69**
SE12 . . . . .7H **123**
TW17: Shep 2G **147**
W3 . . . . .1G **97**
Birchgrove Ho. TW9: Kew 7H **97**
Birch Hill CR0: Croy 5K **169**
Birch Ho. *N22* *1A* ***48***
(off Acacia Rd.)
SE14 . . . . .1B **122**
SW2 . . . .*6A* ***120***
(off Tulse Hill)
W10 . . . .*4G* ***81***
(off Droop St.)
Birchington Cl. DA7: Bex 1H **127**
Birchington Ct. *NW6* *1K* ***81***
(off West End La.)
Birchington Ho. E5 . . . . .5H **67**
Birchington Rd. KT5: Surb 7F **151**
N8 . . . . .6H **47**
NW6 . . . . .1J **81**
Birchin La. EC3 . . . . .1F **15** (6D **84**)
Birchlands Av. SW12 . . . . .7D **118**
Birchmead BR6: Farnb 2E **172**
Birchmead Av. HA5: Pinn 4A **40**
Birchmere Bus. Pk. SE28 . . . . .2A **108**
Birchmere Lodge *SE16* *5H* ***103***
(off Sherwood Gdns.)
Birchmere Row SE3 . . . . .2H **123**
Birchmore Hall N5 . . . . .3C **66**

Birchmore Wlk. N5 3C **66**
Birch Pk. HA3: Hrw W 7B **26**
Birch Rd. RM7: Mawney 3H **55**
TW13: Hanw 5B **130**
Birch Row BR2: Brom 7E **160**
Birch Tree Av. BR4: W W'ck 5H **171**
Birch Tree Way CR0: Croy 2H **169**
Birch Va. Ct. *NW8* *3B* ***4***
(off Pollitt Dr.)
Birchville Ct. WD23: Bushy 1D **26**
Birch Wlk. CR4: Mitc 1F **155**
DA8: Erith 6J **109**
Birchway UB3: Hayes 1J **93**
Birchwood Av. BR3: Beck 4B **158**
DA14: Sidc 2B **144**
N10 3E **46**
SM6: Wall 3E **166**
Birchwood Cl. SM4: Mord 4K **153**
Birchwood Ct. HA8: Edg 2J **43**
N13 5G **33**
Birchwood Dr. DA2: Dart 4K **145**
NW3 3K **63**
Birchwood Gro. TW12: Hamp 6E **130**
Birchwood Pde. DA2: Dart 4K **145**
Birchwood Rd. BR5: Pet W 4H **161**
DA2: Dart 7J **145**
SW17 5F **137**
Birdbrook Cl. RM10: Dag 7J **73**
Birdbrook Ho. *N1* *7C* ***66***
(off Popham Rd.)
Birdbrook Rd. SE3 4A **124**
Birdcage Wlk. SW1 7A **12** (2G **101**)
Birdham Cl. BR1: Brom 5C **160**
Birdhurst Av. CR2: S Croy 4D **168**
Birdhurst Gdns. CR2: S Croy 4D **168**
Birdhurst Ri. CR2: S Croy 5E **168**
Birdhurst Rd. CR2: S Croy 5E **168**
SW18 5A **118**
SW19 6C **136**
Bird in Bush BMX Track *7H* ***103***
(off Bird in Bush Rd.)
Bird in Bush Rd. SE15 7G **103**
Bird in Hand La. BR1: Brom 2B **160**
Bird-in-Hand Pas. SE23 2J **139**
Bird in Hand Path
CR0: Croy *7D* ***156***
(off Sydenham Rd.)
Bird in Hand Yd. *NW3* *4A* ***64***
(off Holly Bush Va.)
NW3 4A **64**
(Perrin's Ct.)
Birdsall Ho. SE5 3E **120**
Birds Farm Av. RM5: Col R 1H **55**
Birdsfield La. E3 1B **86**
Bird St. W1 1H **11** (6E **82**)
Bird Wlk. TW2: Whit 1D **130**
Birdwood Cl. TW11: Tedd 4J **131**
Birkbeck Av. UB6: G'frd 1G **77**
W3 7J **79**
Birkbeck College 5D **6**
Birkbeck Ct. W3 1K **97**
Birkbeck Gdns. IG8: Wfd G 2D **36**
Birkbeck Gro. W3 2K **97**
Birkbeck Hill SE21 1B **138**
Birkbeck M. E8 5F **67**
W3 1K **97**
Birkbeck Pl. SE21 2C **138**
Birkbeck Rd. BR3: Beck 2J **157**
DA14: Sidc 3A **144**
E8 5F **67**
EN2: Enf 1J **23**
IG2: Ilf 5H **53**
N8 4J **47**
N12 5F **31**
N17 1F **49**
NW7 5G **29**
RM7: Rush G 1K **73**
SW19 5K **135**
W3 1K **97**
W5 4C **96**
Birkbeck St. E2 3H **85**
Birkbeck Way UB6: G'frd 1H **77**
Birkdale Av. HA5: Pinn 3E **40**
Birkdale Cl. BR6: Orp 7H **161**
SE16 5H **103**
SE28 6D **90**
Birkdale Ct. *UB1: S'hall* *6G* ***77***
(off Redcroft Rd.)
Birkdale Gdns. CR0: Croy 4K **169**
Birkdale Rd. SE2 4A **108**
W5 4E **78**
Birkenhead Av. KT2: King T 2F **151**
Birkenhead St. WC1 1F **7** (3J **83**)
Birkhall Rd. SE6 1F **141**
Birkwood Cl. SW12 7H **119**
Birley Lodge *NW8* *2B* ***82***
(off Acacia Rd.)
Birley Rd. N20 2F **31**
Birley St. SW11 2E **118**
Birling Rd. DA8: Erith 7K **109**
Birnam Rd. N4 2K **65**
Birnbeck Ct. EN5: Barn 4A **20**
NW11 5H **45**
Birrell Ho. *SW9* *2K* ***119***
(off Stockwell Rd.)
Birse Cres. NW10 3A **62**
Birstall Rd. N15 5E **48**
Biscay Ho. *E1* *4K* ***85***
(off Mile End Rd.)
Biscayne Av. E14 1F **105**
Biscay Rd. W6 5F **99**
Biscoe Cl. TW5: Hest 6E **94**
Biscoe Way SE13 3F **123**
Biscott Ho. E3 4D **86**
Bisenden Rd. CR0: Croy 2E **168**
Bisham Cl. SM5: Cars 1D **166**
Bisham Gdns. N6 1E **64**
Bishop Butt Cl. BR6: Orp 3K **173**
Bishop Ct. TW9: Rich 3E **114**
Bishop Duppas Pk. TW17: Shep 7G **147**
Bishop Fox Way KT8: W Mole 4D **148**
Bishopgate Church Yd.
EC2 7G **9** (5E **84**)
Bishop Ken Rd. HA3: W'stone 2K **41**
Bishop King's Rd. W14 4G **99**
Bishop Ramsey C of E School Sports Hall
7J ***39***
(off Highgrove Way)
Bishop Rd. N14 7A **22**
Bishops Av. BR1: Brom 2A **160**
E13 1K **87**
RM6: Chad H 6C **54**
SW6 2F **117**
Bishops Av., The N2 7B **46**
Bishop's Bri. Rd. W2 6A **4** (6K **81**)
Bishops Cl. E17 4D **50**
EN1: Enf 2C **24**
EN5: Barn 6A **20**
N19 3G **65**
SE9 2G **143**
SM1: Sutt 3J **165**
TW10: Ham 3D **132**
UB10: Hil 2C **74**
W4 5J **97**
Bishops Ct. CR0: Croy 2F **169**
EC4 7A **8**
HA0: Wemb 4B **60**
W2 *6K* ***81***
(off Bishop's Bri. Rd.)
WC2 7J **7**
Bishopsdale Ho. *NW6* *1J* ***81***
(off Kilburn Va.)
Bishops Dr. TW14: Bedf 6F **111**
UB5: N'olt 1C **76**
Bishopsford Rd. SM4: Mord 7A **154**
Bishopsgate EC2 1G **15** (6E **84**)
Bishopsgate Arc. EC2 6H **9**
Bishopsgate Institute & Libraries *6H* ***9***
(off Bishopsgate)
Bishops Grn. BR1: Brom 1A **160**
Bishops Gro. N2 6C **46**
TW12: Hamp 4D **130**
Bishops Gro. Cvn. Site
TW12: Hamp 4E **130**
Bishop's Hall KT1: King T 2D **150**
Bishops Hill KT12: Walt T 7J **147**
Bishops Ho. *SW8* *7J* ***101***
(off Sth. Lambeth Rd.)
Bishop's Mans. SW6 2F **117**
(not continuous)
Bishops Mead *SE5* *7C* ***102***
(off Camberwell Rd.)
Bishops Pk. Rd. SW6 2F **117**
SW16 1J **155**
Bishops Pl. SM1: Sutt 5A **166**
Bishops Rd. CR0: Croy 7B **156**
N6 6E **46**
SW6 1G **117**
SW11 7C **100**
UB3: Hayes 6E **74**
W7 2J **95**
Bishops Sq. E1 5E **84**
Bishop's Ter. SE11 3K **19** (4A **102**)
Bishopsthorpe Rd. SE26 4K **139**
Bishop St. N1 1C **84**
Bishops Vw. Ct. N10 4F **47**
Bishops Wlk. BR7: Chst 1G **161**
CR0: Addtn 5K **169**
HA5: Pinn 3C **40**
Bishop's Way E2 2H **85**
Bishops Wood Almshouses *E5* *4H* ***67***
(off Lwr. Clapton Rd.)
Bishopswood Rd. N6 7D **46**
Bishop Way NW10 7A **62**
Bishop Wilfred Wood Cl. SE15 2G **121**
Bishop Wilfred Wood Ct. *E13* *2A* ***88***
(off Pragel St.)
Bisley Cl. KT4: Wor Pk 1E **164**
Bison Ct. TW14: Felt 7K **111**
Bispham Rd. NW10 3F **79**
Bissextile Ho. SE13 2D **122**
Bisson Rd. E15 2E **86**
Bisterne Av. E17 3F **51**
Bittacy Bus. Cen. NW7 6B **30**
Bittacy Cl. NW7 6A **30**
Bittacy Ct. NW7 7B **30**
Bittacy Hill NW7 6A **30**
Bittacy Pk. Av. NW7 5A **30**
Bittacy Ri. NW7 6K **29**
Bittacy Rd. NW7 6A **30**
Bittern Cl. UB4: Yead 5B **76**
Bittern Ct. NW9 2A **44**
SE8 6C **104**
Bittern Ho. *SE1* *7C* ***14***
(off Gt. Suffolk St.)
Bittern Pl. N22 2K **47**
Bittern St. SE1 7C **14** (2C **102**)
Bittoms, The KT1: King T 3D **150**
(not continuous)
Bittoms Ct. KT1: King T 3D **150**
Bixley Cl. UB2: S'hall 4D **94**
Blackall St. EC2 3G **9** (4E **84**)
Blackberry Cl. TW17: Shep 4G **147**
Blackberry Farm Cl. TW5: Hest 7C **94**
Blackberry Fld. BR5: St P 7A **144**
Blackbird Ct. NW9 3K **61**
Blackbird Hill NW9 2J **61**
Blackbird Yd. E2 1K **9** (3F **85**)
Blackborne Rd. RM10: Dag 6G **73**
Black Boy La. N15 5C **48**
Blackbrook La. BR1: Brom 5D **160**
BR2: Brom 5E **160**
Black Bull Yd. *EC1* *5K* ***7***
(off Hatton Wall)
Blackburn NW9 2B **44**
Blackburne's M. W1 2G **11** (7E **82**)
Blackburn Rd. NW6 6K **63**
Blackburn Trad. Est.
TW19: Stanw 6B **110**
Blackbush Av. RM6: Chad H 5D **54**
Blackbush Cl. SM2: Sutt 7K **165**
Blackdown Cl. N2 2A **46**
Blackdown Ter. SE18 1D **124**
Blackett St. SW15 3F **117**
Black Fan Cl. EN2: Enf 1H **23**
BLACKFEN 7A **126**
Blackfen Pde. DA15: Sidc 6A **126**
Blackfen Rd. DA15: Sidc 5J **125**
Blackford Cl. CR2: S Croy 7B **168**
Blackford's Path SW15 7C **116**
Blackfriars Bri. EC4 2A **14**
SE1 3A **14** (7B **84**)
Blackfriars Ct. EC4 2A **14**
Black Friars La. EC4 2A **14** (6B **84**)
(not continuous)
Blackfriars Pas. EC4 2A **14** (7B **84**)
Blackfriars Rd. SE1 4A **14** (2B **102**)
Blackfriars Underpass EC4 2A **14** (7A **84**)
Black Gates HA5: Pinn 3D **40**
BLACKHEATH 2H **123**
Blackheath Av. SE10 7F **105**
Blackheath Bus. Est. *SE10* *1E* ***122***
(off Blackheath Hill)
Blackheath Concert Halls 3H **123**
Blackheath Gro. SE3 2H **123**
Blackheath Hill SE10 1E **122**
BLACKHEATH PARK 4J **123**
Blackheath Pk. SE3 3H **123**
Blackheath Ri. SE13 2E **122**
(not continuous)
Blackheath Rd. SE10 1D **122**
BLACKHEATH VALE 2H **123**
Blackheath Va. SE3 2G **123**
Blackheath Village SE3 2H **123**
Black Horse Ct. *SE1* *3D* ***102***
(off Gt. Dover St.)
Blackhorse La. CR0: Croy 7G **157**
E17 2K **49**
Blackhorse M. E17 3K **49**
Black Horse Pde. HA5: Eastc 5K **39**
BLACKHORSE ROAD 4K **49**
Blackhorse Rd. DA14: Sidc 4A **144**
E17 4K **49**
SE8 6A **104**
Blacklands Dr. UB4: Hayes 4E **74**
Blacklands Rd. SE6 4E **140**
Blacklands Ter. SW3 4E **16** (4D **100**)
Black Lion La. W6 4C **98**
Black Lion M. W6 4C **98**
Blackmans Yd. *E2* *3K* ***9***
(off Grimsby St.)
Blackmore Av. UB1: S'hall 1H **95**
Blackmore Dr. NW10 1H **79**
Blackmore Ho. *N1* *1K* ***83***
(off Barnsbury Est.)
Blackmore Rd. IG9: Buck H 1H **37**
Blackmore's Gro. TW11: Tedd 6A **132**
Blackmore Twr. *W3* *3J* ***97***
(off Stanley Rd.)
Blackness La. BR2: Kes 7B **172**
Black Path E10 7A **50**
Blackpool Gdns. UB4: Hayes 4G **75**
Blackpool Rd. SE15 2H **121**
BLACK PRINCE INTERCHANGE 6H **127**
Black Prince Rd. SE1 4G **19** (4K **101**)
SE11 4G **19** (4K **101**)
Black Rod Cl. UB3: Hayes 3H **93**
Blackshaw Rd. SW17 4A **136**
Blacksmiths Cl. RM6: Chad H 6C **54**
Blacksmiths Ho. *E17* *4C* ***50***
(off Gillards M.)
Blacks Rd. W6 5E **98**
Blackstock M. N4 2B **66**
Blackstock Rd. N4 2B **66**
N5 3B **66**
Blackstone Est. E8 7G **67**
Blackstone Ho. *SW1* *6A* ***18***
(off Churchill Gdns.)
Blackstone Rd. NW2 5E **62**
Black Swan Yd. SE1 6H **15** (2E **102**)
Blackthorn Av. UB7: W Dray 4C **92**
Blackthorn Ct. *E11* *4F* ***69***
(off Hall Rd.)
TW5: Hest 7C **94**
Blackthorne Av. CR0: Croy 1J **169**
Blackthorne Ct. *SE15* *7F* ***103***
(off Cator St.)
TW15: Ashf 7E **128**
UB1: S'hall *1F* ***95***
(off Dormer's Wells La.)
Blackthorne Dr. E4 4A **36**
Blackthorn Gro. DA7: Bex 3E **126**

Blackthorn Rd. IG1: Ilf 5H 71
Blackthorn St. E3 ......4C 86
Blacktree M. SW9 ......3A 120
BLACKWALL 1E 104
Blackwall La. SE10 ......5G 105
Blackwall Trad. Est. E14 ......5F 87
Blackwall Tunnel E14 ......1F 105
(not continuous)
SE10 ......1F 105
Blackwall Tunnel App. E14 ......6E 86
Blackwall Tunnel Northern App. E3 ......2D 86
E14 ......2C 86
Blackwall Tunnel Southern App.
SE10 ......3G 105
Blackwall Way E14 ......1E 104
Blackwater Cl. E7 ......4H 69
RM13: Rain 5K 91
Blackwater Ho. NW8 ......5B 4
(off Church St.)
Blackwater St. SE22 ......5F 121
Blackwell Cl. E5 ......4K 67
HA3: Hrw W 7C 26
Blackwell Gdns. HA8: Edg 4B 28
Blackwell Ho. SW4 ......6H 119
Blackwood Av. N18 ......5E 34
Blackwood Ho. E1 ......4H 85
(off Collingwood St.)
Blackwood St. SE17 ......5D 102
Blade M. SW15 ......4H 117
Bladen Ho. E1 ......6K 85
(off Dunelm St.)
Blades Ct. SW15 ......4H 117
W6 ......5D 98
(off Lower Mall)
Blades Ho. SE11 ......7J 19
(off Kennington Oval)
Bladindon Dr. DA5: Bexl 7C 126
Bladon Ct. SW16 ......6J 137
Bladon Gdns. HA2: Harr 6F 41
Blagdens Cl. N14 ......2C 32
Blagdens La. N14 ......2B 32
Blagdon Ct. W7 ......7J 77
Blagdon Rd. KT3: N Mald 4B 152
(not continuous)
SE13 ......6D 122
Blagdon Wlk. TW11: Tedd 6C 132
Blagrove Rd. W10 ......5G 81
Blair Av. NW9 ......7A 44
Blair Cl. DA15: Sidc 5J 125
N1 ......6C 66
UB3: Harl 4J 93
Blair Ct. BR3: Beck 1D 158
NW8 ......1B 82
SE6 ......1H 141
Blairderry Rd. SW2 ......2J 137
Blairgowrie Ct. E14 ......6F 87
(off Blair St.)
Blair Ho. SW9 ......2K 119
Blair St. E14 ......6E 86
Blake Av. IG11: Bark 1J 89
Blake Bldg. N8 ......3K 47
Blake Cl. DA16: Well 1J 125
SM5: Cars 1C 166
UB4: Hayes 2F 75
Blake Ct. N21 ......5E 22
NW6 ......3J 81
(off Malvern Rd.)
SE16 ......5H 103
(off Stubbs Dr.)
Blakeden Dr. KT10: Clay 6A 162
Blake Gdns. SW6 ......1K 117
Blake Hall Cres. E11 ......1J 69
Blake Hall Rd. E11 ......7J 51
Blakehall Rd. SM5: Cars 6D 166
Blake Ho. E14 ......2C 104
(off Admirals Way)
SE1 ......1J 19 (3A 102)
SE8 ......6C 104
(off New King St.)
Blakeley Cotts. SE10 ......2F 105
Blake M. TW9: Kew 1G 115
Blakemore Rd. CR7: Thor H 5K 155
SW16 ......3J 137

Blakemore Way DA17: Belv 3E 108
Blakeney Av. BR3: Beck 1B 158
Blakeney Cl. E8 ......5G 67
NW1 ......7H 65
Blakeney Rd. BR3: Beck 7B 140
Blakenham Rd. SW17 ......4D 136
Blaker Ct. SE7 ......7A 106
(not continuous)
Blake Rd. CR0: Croy 2E 168
CR4: Mitc 3C 154
E16 ......4H 87
N11 ......7B 32
Blaker Rd. E15 ......2E 86
Blakes Av. KT3: N Mald 5B 152
Blakes Cl. W10 ......5E 80
Blake's Grn. BR4: W W'ck 1E 170
Blakes La. KT3: N Mald 5B 152
Blakesley Av. W5 ......6C 78
Blakesley Wlk. SW20 ......2H 153
Blake's Rd. SE15 ......7E 102
Blakes Ter. KT3: N Mald 5C 152
Blakesware Gdns. N9 ......7J 23
Blakewood Cl. TW13: Hanw 4A 130
Blakewood Cl. SE20 ......7H 139
(off Anerley Pk.)
Blakney Cl. N20 ......1F 31
Blanchard Cl. SE9 ......3C 142
Blanchard Ho. TW1: Twick 6D 114
(off Clevedon Rd.)
Blanchard Way E8 ......6G 67
Blanch Cl. SE15 ......7J 103
Blanchedowne SE5 ......4D 120
Blanche St. E16 ......4H 87
Blanchland Rd. SM4: Mord 5K 153
Blandfield Rd. SW12 ......7E 118
Blandford Av. BR3: Beck 2A 158
TW2: Whit 1F 131
Blandford Cl. CR0: Bedd 3J 167
N2 ......4A 46
RM7: Mawney 4G 55
Blandford Ct. N1 ......7E 66
(off St Peter's Way)
NW6 ......7K 63
Blandford Cres. E4 ......7K 25
Blandford Ho. SW8 ......7K 101
(off Richborne Ter.)
Blandford Rd. BR3: Beck 2J 157
TW11: Tedd 5H 131
UB2: S'hall 4E 94
W4 ......3A 98
W5 ......2D 96
Blandford Sq. NW1 ......4D 4 (4C 82)
Blandford St. W1 ......7F 5 (6D 82)
Blandford Waye
UB4: Yead 6A 76
Bland Ho. SE11 ......5H 19
Bland St. SE9 ......4B 124
Blaney Cres. E6 ......3F 89
Blanmerle Rd. SE9 ......1F 143
Blann Cl. SE9 ......6B 124
Blantyre St. SW10 ......7B 100
Blantyre Twr. SW10 ......7B 100
(off Blantyre St.)
Blantyre Wlk. SW10 ......7B 100
(off Worlds End Est.)
Blashford NW3 ......7D 64
(off Adelaide Rd.)
Blashford St. SE13 ......7F 123
Blasker Wlk. E14 ......5D 104
Blawith Rd. HA1: Harr 4J 41
Blaxland Ho. W12 ......7D 80
(off White City Est.)
Blaydon Cl. HA4: Ruis 1H 57
N17 ......7C 34
Blaydon Ct. UB5: N'olt 6E 58
Blaydon Wlk. N17 ......7C 34
Blazer Ct. NW8 ......2B 4
Bleak Hill La. SE18 ......6K 107
Blean Gro. SE20 ......7J 139
Bleasdale Av. UB6: G'frd 2A 78
Blechynden Ho. W10 ......6F 81
(off Kingsdown Cl.)
Blechynden St. W10 ......7F 81

Bledlow Cl. NW8 ......4B 4 (4B 82)
SE28 ......7C 90
Bledlow Ri. UB6: G'frd 2G 77
Bleeding Heart Yd. EC1 ......6K 7
Blegborough Rd. SW16 ......6G 137
Blemundsbury WC1 ......5G 7
(off Dombey St.)
BLENDON 6D 126
Blendon Dr. DA5: Bexl 6D 126
Blendon Path BR1: Brom 7H 141
Blendon Rd. DA5: Bexl 6D 126
Blendon Row SE17 ......4D 102
(off Townley St.)
Blendon Ter. SE18 ......5G 107
Blendworth Point SW15 ......1D 134
Blenheim Av. IG2: Ilf 6E 52
Blenheim Bus. Cen. CR4: Mitc 2D 154
(off London Rd.)
Blenheim Cl. N21 ......1H 33
RM7: Mawney 4J 55
SE12 ......1K 141
SM6: Wall 7G 167
SW20 ......3E 152
UB6: G'frd 2H 77
Blenheim Ct. BR2: Brom 4H 159
DA14: Sidc 3H 143
HA3: Kent 6A 42
IG8: Wfd G 7E 36
N19 ......2J 65
SE16 ......1K 103
(off King & Queen Wharf)
SM2: Sutt 6A 166
Blenheim Cres. CR2: S Croy 7C 168
HA4: Ruis 2F 57
W11 ......7G 81
Blenheim Dr. DA16: Well 1K 125
Blenheim Gdns. HA9: Wemb 3E 60
KT2: King T 7H 133
NW2 ......6E 62
SM6: Wall 6G 167
SW2 ......6K 119
Blenheim Gro. SE15 ......2G 121
Blenheim Ho. E16 ......1K 105
(off Constable Av.)
SE18 ......3G 107
SW3 ......6D 16
(off Kings Rd.)
TW3: Houn 3E 112
Blenheim Pde. UB10: Hil 4D 74
Blenheim Pk. Rd. CR2: S Croy 7C 168
Blenheim Pas. NW8 ......2A 82
(not continuous)
Blenheim Pl. TW11: Tedd 5K 131
Blenheim Ri. N15 ......4F 49
Blenheim Rd. BR1: Brom 4C 160
DA15: Sidc 1C 144
E6 ......3B 88
E15 ......4G 69
E17 ......3K 49
EN5: Barn 3A 20
HA2: Harr 6F 41
NW8 ......2A 82
SE20 ......7J 139
SM1: Sutt 3J 165
SW20 ......3E 152
UB5: N'olt 6F 59
W4 ......3A 98
Blenheim Shop. Cen. SE20 ......7J 139
Blenheim St. W1 ......1J 11 (6F 83)
Blenheim Ter. NW8 ......2A 82
Blenheim Way TW7: Isle 1A 114
Blenkarne Rd. SW11 ......6D 118
Bleriot NW9 ......2B 44
(off Belvedere Strand)
Bleriot Rd. TW5: Hest 7A 94
Blessbury Rd. HA8: Edg 1J 43
Blessington Cl. SE13 ......3F 123
Blessington Rd. SE13 ......3F 123
Blessing Way IG11: Bark 3C 90
Bletchingley Cl. CR7: Thor H 4B 156
Bletchley Cl. N1 ......1E 8
(not continuous)
Bletchley St. N1 ......1D 8 (2D 84)

Bletchmore Cl. UB3: Harl 5F 93
Bletsoe Wlk. N1 ......2C 84
Blewbury Ho. SE2 ......2C 108
(Tavy Bri.)
SE2 ......2D 108
(Tilehurst Point)
Blick Ho. SE16 ......3J 103
(off Neptune St.)
Blincoe Cl. SW19 ......2F 135
Bliss Cres. SE13 ......2D 122
Blissett St. SE10 ......1E 122
Bliss Ho. EN1: Enf 1B 24
Bliss M. W10 ......3G 81
Blisworth Cl. UB4: Yead 4C 76
Blisworth Ho. E2 ......1G 85
(off Whiston Rd.)
Blithbury Rd. RM9: Dag 6B 72
Blithdale Rd. SE2 ......4A 108
Blithfield St. W8 ......3K 99
Blockley Rd. HA0: Wemb 2B 60
Block Wharf E14 ......2C 104
(off Cuba St.)
Bloemfontein Av. W12 ......1D 98
Bloemfontein Rd. W12 ......7D 80
Bloemfontein Way W12 ......1D 98
Blomfield Cl. W9 ......3A 4
(off Maida Va.)
Blomfield Mans. W12 ......1E 98
(off Stanlake Rd.)
Blomfield Rd. W9 ......5K 81
Blomfield St. EC2 ......6F 9 (5D 84)
Blomfield Vs. W2 ......5K 81
Blomville Rd. RM8: Dag 3E 72
Blondel St. SW11 ......2E 118
Blondin Av. W5 ......4C 96
Blondin St. E3 ......2C 86
Bloomburg St. SW1 ......4B 18 (4H 101)
Bloomfield Cl. E10 ......3D 68
(off Brisbane Rd.)
N6 ......6E 46
Bloomfield Cres. IG2: Ilf 6F 53
Bloomfield Ho. E1 ......5G 85
(off Old Montague St.)
Bloomfield Pl. W1 ......2K 11
Bloomfield Rd. BR2: Brom 5B 160
KT1: King T 4E 150
N6 ......6E 46
SE18 ......6F 107
Bloomfield Ter. SW1 ......5H 17 (5E 100)
Bloom Gro. SE27 ......3B 138
Bloomhall Rd. SE19 ......5D 138
Bloom Pk. Rd. SW6 ......7H 99
BLOOMSBURY 5E 6 (5J 83)
Bloomsbury Cl. NW7 ......7H 29
W5 ......6H 79
Bloomsbury Ct. HA5: Pinn 3D 40
TW5: Cran 1K 111
WC1 ......6F 7
Bloomsbury Ho. SW4 ......6H 119
Bloomsbury M. IG8: Wfd G 6H 37
Bloomsbury Pl. SW18 ......5A 118
WC1 ......5F 7 (5J 83)
Bloomsbury Sq. WC1 ......6F 7 (5J 83)
Bloomsbury St. WC1 ......6D 6 (5H 83)
Bloomsbury Theatre 3C 6
Bloomsbury Way WC1 ......6E 6 (5J 83)
Blore Cl. SW8 ......1H 119
Blore Ct. W1 ......1C 12
Blore Ho. SW10 ......7K 99
(off Coleridge Gdns.)
Blossom Cl. CR2: S Croy 5F 169
RM9: Dag 1F 91
SE2 ......2E 96
Blossom La. EN2: Enf 1H 23
Blossom St. E1 ......4H 9 (4E 84)
Blossom Way UB7: W Dray 4C 92
UB10: Hil 7B 56
Blossom Waye TW5: Hest 6C 94
Blount St. E14 ......6A 86
Bloxam Gdns. SE9 ......5C 124
Bloxhall Rd. E10 ......1B 68
Bloxham Cres. TW12: Hamp 7D 130
Bloxworth Cl. SM6: Wall 3G 167

Blucher Rd. SE5 .7C **102**
Blue Anchor All. TW9: Rich .4E **114**
Blue Anchor La. SE16 .4G **103**
Blue Anchor Yd. E1 .2K **15** (7G **85**)
Blue Ball Yd. SW1 .5A **12** (1G **101**)
Bluebell Av. E12 .5B **70**
Blue Bell Cl. UB5: N'olt .6D **58**
Bluebell Cl. BR6: Farnb .2G **173**
E9 .1J **85**
RM7: Rush G .2K **73**
SE26 .4F **139**
SM6: Wall .1F **167**
Bluebell Way IG1: Ilf .6F **71**
Blueberry Cl. IG8: Wfd G .6D **36**
Bluebird La. RM10: Dag .7G **73**
Bluebird Way SE28 .2H **107**
Blue Elephant Theatre .*7C 102*
(off Bethwin Rd.)
Bluefield Cl. TW12: Hamp .5E **130**
Bluegate M. E1 .7H **85**
Bluegates KT17: Ewe .7C **164**
Bluehouse Rd. E4 .2B **36**
Blue Lion Pl. SE1 .7G **15** (3E **102**)
Blueprint Apartments *SW12* .*7F 119*
(off Balham Gro.)
Blue Riband Ind. Est. CR0: Croy .2B **168**
Blue Water SW18 .4K **117**
Blundell Cl. E8 .5G **67**
Blundell Rd. HA8: Edg .1K **43**
Blundell St. N7 .7J **65**
Blunden Cl. RM8: Dag .1C **72**
Blunt Rd. CR2: S Croy .5D **168**
Blunts Av. UB7: Sip .7C **92**
Blunts Rd. SE9 .5E **124**
Blurton Rd. E5 .4J **67**
Blydon Ct. *N21* .*5E 22*
(off Chaseville Pk. Rd.)
Blyth Cl. E14 .4F **105**
TW1: Twick .6K **113**
Blyth Ct. *BR1: Brom* .*1H 159*
(off Blyth Rd.)
Blythe Cl. SE6 .7B **122**
BLYTHE HILL .7B **122**
Blythe Hill BR5: St P .1K **161**
SE6 .7B **122**
Blythe Hill La. SE6 .7B **122**
Blythe Hill Pl. SE23 .7A **122**
Blythe Ho. SE11 .7J **19** (6A **102**)
Blythe M. W14 .3F **99**
Blythendale Ho. *E2* .*2G 85*
(off Mansford St.)
Blythe Rd. W14 .3F **99**
(not continuous)
Blythe St. E2 .3H **85**
Blythe Va. SE6 .1B **140**
Blyth Hill Pl. *SE23* .*7A 122*
(off Brockley Pk.)
Blyth Rd. BR1: Brom .1H **159**
E17 .7B **50**
SE28 .7C **90**
UB3: Hayes .2G **93**
Blyth's Wharf E14 .7A **86**
Blythswood Rd. IG3: Ilf .1A **72**
Blyth Wood Pk. BR1: Brom .1H **159**
Blythwood Rd. HA5: Pinn .1B **40**
N4 .7J **47**
Boades M. NW3 .4B **64**
Boadicea St. N1 .1K **83**
Boakes Cl. NW9 .4J **43**
Boardman Av. E4 .5J **25**
Boardman Cl. EN5: Barn .5B **20**
Boardwalk Pl. E14 .1E **104**
Boarhound *NW9* .*2B 44*
(off Further Acre)
Boarley Ho. *SE17* .*4E 102*
(off Massinger St.)
Boars Head Yd. TW8: Bford .7D **96**
Boathouse Cen., The *W10* .*4F 81*
(off Canal Cl.)
Boathouse Wlk. SE15 .7F **103**
(not continuous)
Boat Lifter Way SE16 .4A **104**
Boat Quay E16 .7A **88**
Bob Anker Cl. E13 .3J **87**
Bobbin Cl. SW4 .3G **119**
Bobby Moore Way N11 .7J **31**
Bob Hope Theatre, The .6D **124**
Bob Marley Way SE24 .4A **120**
Bockhampton Rd. KT2: King T .7F **133**
Bocking St. E8 .1H **85**
Boddicott Cl. SW19 .2G **135**
Boddington Gdns. W3 .2G **97**
Boddington Ho. *SE14* .*1J 121*
(off Pomeroy St.)
SW13 .*6D 98*
(off Wyatt Dr.)
Bodeney Ho. *SE5* .*1E 120*
(off Peckham Rd.)
Boden Ho. *E1* .*5K 9*
(off Woodseer St.)
Bodiam Cl. EN1: Enf .2K **23**
Bodiam Rd. SW16 .7H **137**
Bodiam Way NW10 .3F **79**
Bodicea M. TW4: Houn .6D **112**
Bodington Ct. W12 .2F **99**
Bodley Cl. KT3: N Mald .5A **152**
Bodley Mnr. Way SW2 .7A **120**
Bodley Rd. KT3: N Mald .6K **151**
Bodmin *NW9* .*2B 44*
(off Further Acre)
Bodmin Cl. HA2: Harr .3D **58**
Bodmin Gro. SM4: Mord .5K **153**
Bodmin St. SW18 .1J **135**
Bodnant Gdns. SW20 .3C **152**
Bodney Rd. E8 .5H **67**
Boeing Way UB2: S'hall .3K **93**
Boevey Path DA17: Belv .5F **109**
Bogart Ct. *E14* .*7C 86*
(off Premiere Pl.)
Bogey La. BR6: Downe .7E **172**
Bognor Rd. DA16: Well .1D **126**
Bohemia Pl. E8 .6J **67**
Bohn Rd. E1 .5A **86**
Bohun Gro. EN4: E Barn .6H **21**
Boileau Pde. *W5* .*6F 79*
(off Boileau Rd.)
Boileau Rd. SW13 .7C **98**
W5 .6F **79**
Boisseau Ho. *E1* .*5J 85*
(off Stepney Way)
Bolden St. SE8 .2D **122**
Boldero Pl. NW8 .4C **4**
Bolderwood Way BR4: W W'ck .2D **170**
Boldmere Rd. HA5: Eastc .7A **40**
Boleyn Av. EN1: Enf .1C **24**
Boleyn Cl. E17 .4C **50**
Boleyn Ct. IG9: Buck H .1D **36**
KT8: E Mos .*4H 149*
(off Bridge Rd.)
Boleyn Dr. HA4: Ruis .2B **58**
KT8: W Mole .3D **148**
Boleyn Gdns. BR4: W W'ck .2D **170**
RM10: Dag .7J **73**
Boleyn Gro. BR4: W W'ck .2E **170**
Boleyn Ho. *E16* .*1J 105*
(off Southey M.)
Boleyn Rd. E6 .2B **88**
E7 .7J **69**
N16 .5E **66**
Boleyn Way EN5: New Bar .3F **21**
Bolina Rd. SE16 .5J **103**
Bolingbroke Gro. SW11 .4C **118**
Bolingbroke Rd. W14 .3F **99**
Bolingbroke Wlk. SW11 .1B **118**
Bolingbroke Way UB3: Hayes .1F **93**
Bolliger Ct. NW10 .4J **79**
Bollo Bri. Rd. W3 .3H **97**
Bollo Ct. *W3* .*3J 97*
(off Bollo Bri. Rd.)
Bollo La. W3 .2H **97**
W4 .4J **97**
Bolney Ga. SW7 .7C **10** (2C **100**)
Bolney St. SW8 .7K **101**
Bolney Way TW13: Hanw .3C **130**
Bolsover St. W1 .4K **5** (4F **83**)
Bolstead Rd. CR4: Mitc .1F **155**
Bolster Gro. N22 .7C **32**
Bolt Ct. EC4 .1K **13**
Boltmore Cl. NW4 .3F **45**
Bolton Cl. KT9: Chess .6D **162**
SE20 .2G **157**
Bolton Cres. SE5 .7B **102**
Bolton Dr. SM5: Cars .7A **154**
Bolton Gdns. BR1: Brom .6H **141**
NW10 .2F **81**
SW5 .5K **99**
TW11: Tedd .6A **132**
Bolton Gdns. M. SW10 .5A **100**
Bolton Ho. *SE10* .*5G 105*
(off Trafalgar Rd.)
Bolton Pl. *NW8* .*1K 81*
(off Bolton Rd.)
Bolton Rd. E15 .6H **69**
HA1: Harr .4G **41**
KT9: Chess .6D **162**
N18 .5A **34**
NW8 .1K **81**
NW10 .1A **80**
W4 .7J **97**
Boltons, The HA0: Wemb .4K **59**
IG8: Wfd G .4D **36**
SW10 .5A **100**
Boltons Ct. *SW5* .*5K 99*
(off Old Brompton Rd.)
Bolton's La. UB3: Harl .1E **110**
(not continuous)
Boltons Pl. SW5 .5A **100**
Bolton St. W1 .4K **11** (1F **101**)
Bolton Studios SW10 .5A **100**
Bolton Wlk. *N7* .*2K 65*
(off Durham Rd.)
Bombay Ct. *SE16* .*2J 103*
(off St Marychurch St.)
Bombay St. SE16 .4H **103**
Bomer Cl. UB7: Sip .7C **92**
Bomore Rd. W11 .7G **81**
Bonar Pl. BR7: Chst .7C **142**
Bonar Rd. SE15 .7G **103**
Bonchester Cl. BR7: Chst .7E **142**
Bonchurch Cl. SM2: Sutt .7K **165**
Bonchurch Rd. W10 .5G **81**
W13 .1B **96**
Bond Cl. UB7: Yiew .6B **74**
Bond Ct. EC4 .2E **14** (7D **84**)
Bondfield Av. UB4: Yead .3J **75**
Bondfield Rd. E6 .5D **88**
Bond Gdns. SM6: Wall .4G **167**
Bond Ho. *NW6* .*2H 81*
(off Rupert Rd.)
SE14 .*7A 104*
(off Goodwood Rd.)
Bonding Yd. Wlk. SE16 .3A **104**
Bond Rd. CR4: Mitc .2C **154**
KT6: Surb .2F **163**
Bond St. E15 .5G **69**
W4 .4K **97**
W5 .7D **78**
Bondway SW8 .7F **19** (6J **101**)
Boneta Rd. SE18 .3D **106**
Bonfield Rd. SE13 .4E **122**
Bonham Gdns. RM8: Dag .2D **72**
Bonham Ho. *W11* .*1H 99*
(off Boyne Ter. M.)
Bonham Rd. RM8: Dag .2D **72**
SW2 .5K **119**
Bonheur Rd. W4 .2K **97**
Bonhill St. EC2 .4F **9** (4D **84**)
Boniface Gdns. HA3: Hrw W .7A **26**
Boniface Rd. UB10: Ick .3D **56**
Boniface Wlk. HA3: Hrw W .7A **26**
Bonington Ho. EN1: Enf .5B **24**
Bonita M. SE4 .3K **121**
Bon Marche Ter. M. *SE27* .*4E 138*
(off Gypsy Rd.)
Bonner Hill Rd. KT1: King T .2F **151**
(not continuous)
Bonner Rd. E2 .2J **85**
Bonnersfield Cl. HA1: Harr .6K **41**
Bonnersfield La. HA1: Harr .6K **41**
Bonner St. E2 .2J **85**
Bonneville Gdns. SW4 .6G **119**
Bonnington Ct. *UB5: N'olt* .*2B 76*
(off Gallery Gdns.)
Bonnington Ho. N1 .2K **83**
Bonnington Sq. SW8 .7G **19** (6K **101**)
Bonny St. NW1 .7G **65**
Bonser Rd. TW1: Twick .2K **131**
Bonsor Ho. SW8 .1G **119**
Bonsor St. SE5 .7E **102**
Bonville Gdns. NW4 .4D **44**
Bonville Rd. BR1: Brom .5H **141**
Bookbinders Cott. Homes N20 .3J **31**
Booker Cl. E14 .5B **86**
Booker Rd. N18 .5B **34**
Bookham Ct. CR4: Mitc .3B **154**
Boone Ct. N9 .3D **34**
Boones Rd. SE13 .4G **123**
Boone St. SE13 .4G **123**
Boord St. SE10 .3G **105**
Boothby Ct. E4 .3K **35**
Boothby Rd. N19 .2H **65**
Booth Cl. E9 .1H **85**
SE28 .1B **108**
Booth Dr. TW18: Staines .6A **128**
Booth Ho. *TW8: Bford* .*7C 96*
(off High St.)
Booth La. EC4 .2C **14**
Boothman Ho. HA3: Kent .3D **42**
Booth Rd. CR0: Croy .2B **168**
NW9 .2K **43**
Booth's Pl. W1 .6B **6** (5G **83**)
Boot Pde. *HA8: Edg* .*6B 28*
(off High St.)
Boot St. N1 .2G **9** (3E **84**)
Bordars Rd. W7 .5J **77**
Bordars Wlk. W7 .5J **77**
Borden Av. EN1: Enf .6J **23**
Border Cres. SE26 .5H **139**
Border Gdns. CR0: Croy .4D **170**
Bordergate CR4: Mitc .1C **154**
Border Rd. SE26 .5H **139**
Bordesley Rd. SM4: Mord .5K **153**
Bordeston Ct. *TW8: Bford* .*7C 96*
(off The Ham)
Bordon Wlk. SW15 .7C **116**
Boreas Wlk. N1 .1B **8**
Boreham Av. E16 .6J **87**
Boreham Cl. E11 .1E **68**
Boreham Rd. N22 .2C **48**
Boreman Ho. *SE10* .*6E 104*
(off Thames St.)
Borgard Rd. SE18 .4D **106**
Borkwood Pk. BR6: Orp .4K **173**
Borkwood Way BR6: Orp .4J **173**
Borland Rd. SE15 .4J **121**
TW11: Tedd .7B **132**
Borley Ct. TW19: Stanw .1A **128**
Borneo St. SW15 .3E **116**
BOROUGH, THE .7D **14** (2D **102**)
Borough High St. SE1 .7D **14** (2C **102**)
Borough Hill CR0: Wadd .3B **168**
Borough Mkt. SE1 .5E **14**
Borough Rd. CR4: Mitc .2C **154**
KT2: King T .1G **151**
SE1 .7B **14** (3B **102**)
TW7: Isle .1J **113**
Borough Sq. SE1 .7C **14**
Borrett Cl. SE17 .5C **102**
Borrodaile Rd. SW18 .6K **117**
Borrowdale *NW1* .*2A 6*
(off Robert St.)
Borrowdale Av. HA3: W'stone .2A **42**
Borrowdale Cl. IG4: Ilf .4C **52**
Borrowdale Ct. EN2: Enf .1H **23**
Borthwick M. E15 .4G **69**
Borthwick Rd. E15 .4G **69**
NW9 .6B **44**
Borthwick St. SE8 .5C **104**
Borwick Av. E17 .3B **50**
Bosanquet Cl. UB8: Cowl .4A **74**
Bosbury Rd. SE6 .3E **140**
Boscastle Rd. NW5 .3F **65**

Boscobel Cl. BR1: Brom 2D **160**
Boscobel Ho. E8 6H **67**
Boscobel Pl. SW1 3H **17** (4E **100**)
Boscobel St. NW8 4B **4** (4B **82**)
Bosco Cl. BR6: Orp 4K **173**
Boscombe Av. E10 7F **51**
Boscombe Cir. NW9 1K **43**
Boscombe Cl. E5 5A **68**
Boscombe Gdns. SW16 6J **137**
Boscombe Ho. *CR0: Croy* *1D **168***
(off Sydenham Rd.)
Boscombe Rd. KT4: Wor Pk 1E **164**
SW17 6E **136**
SW19 1K **153**
W12 1C **98**
Bose Cl. N3 1G **45**
Bosgrove E4 2K **35**
Boss Ho. *SE1* *6J **15***
(off Boss St.)
Boss St. SE1 6J **15** (2F **103**)
Bostall Hill SE2 5A **108**
Bostall La. SE2 4B **108**
Bostall Mnr. Way SE2 4B **108**
Bostall Pk. Av. DA7: Bex 7E **108**
Bostall Rd. BR5: St P 7B **144**
Bostock Ho. TW5: Hest 6E **94**
Boston Bus. Pk. W7 3J **95**
Boston Ct. SM2: Sutt 7A **166**
Boston Gdns. TW8: Bford 4A **96**
W4 6A **98**
W7 4A **96**
Boston Gro. HA4: Ruis 6E **38**
Boston Ho. *SW5* *4K **99***
(off Collingham Rd.)
BOSTON MANOR 4A **96**
Boston Manor House 5B **96**
Boston Mnr. Rd. TW8: Bford 4B **96**
Boston Pde. W7 3A **96**
Boston Pk. Rd. TW8: Bford 5C **96**
Boston Pl. NW1 4E **4** (4D **82**)
Boston Rd. CR0: Croy 6K **155**
E6 3C **88**
E17 6C **50**
HA8: Edg 7D **28**
W7 1J **95**
Bostonthorpe Rd. W7 2J **95**
Boston Va. W7 4A **96**
Bosun Cl. E14 2C **104**
Boswell Ct. *KT2: King T* *1F **151***
(off Clifton Rd.)
W14 *3F **99***
(off Blythe Rd.)
WC1 5F **7** (5J **83**)
Boswell Ho. *WC1* *5F **7***
(off Boswell St.)
Boswell Path UB3: Harl 4H **93**
Boswell Rd. CR7: Thor H 4C **156**
Boswell St. WC1 5F **7** (5J **83**)
Boswood Ct. TW3: Houn 3D **112**
Bosworth Cl. E17 1B **50**
Bosworth Ho. *W10* *4G **81***
(off Bosworth Rd.)
Bosworth Rd. EN5: New Bar 3D **20**
N11 6C **32**
RM10: Dag 3G **73**
W10 4G **81**
Botany Bay La. BR7: Chst 3G **161**
Botany Cl. EN4: E Barn 4H **21**
Boteley Cl. E4 2A **36**
Botham Cl. HA8: Edg 7D **28**
Botha Rd. E13 5K **87**
Bothwell Cl. E16 5H **87**
Bothwell St. W6 6F **99**
Botolph All. EC3 2G **15**
Botolph La. EC3 3G **15** (7E **84**)
Botsford Rd. SW20 2G **153**
Botts M. W2 6J **81**
Botwell Comn. Rd. UB3: Hayes 7F **75**
Botwell Cres. UB3: Hayes 6G **75**
Botwell La. UB3: Hayes 7G **75**
Boucher Cl. TW11: Tedd 5K **131**
Bouchier Ho. N2 2B **46**
Boughton Av. BR2: Hayes 7H **159**
Boughton Ho. *SE1* *6E **14***
(off Tennis St.)
Boughton Rd. SE28 3J **107**
Boulcott St. E1 6K **85**
Boulevard, The IG8: Ilf 6K **37**
SW6 1A **118**
SW17 2E **136**
SW18 4K **117**
Boulogne Ho. *SE1* *7J **15***
(off Abbey St.)
Boulogne Rd. CR0: Croy 6C **156**
Boulter Cl. BR1: Brom 3E **160**
Boulter Ho. *SE14* *1J **121***
(off Kender St.)
Boulton Ho. TW8: Bford 5E **96**
Boulton Rd. RM8: Dag 2E **72**
Boultwood Rd. E6 6D **88**
Bounces La. N9 2C **34**
Bounces Rd. N9 2C **34**
Boundaries Rd. SW12 2D **136**
TW13: Felt 1A **130**
Boundary Av. E17 7B **50**
Boundary Bus. Ct. CR4: Mitc 3B **154**
Boundary Cl. EN5: Barn 1C **20**
IG3: Ilf 4J **71**
KT1: King T 3H **151**
SE20 2G **157**
UB2: S'hall 5E **94**
Boundary Ct. *N18* *6A **34***
(off Snells Pk.)
Boundary Ho. SE5 7C **102**
W11 *1F **99***
(off Queensdale Cres.)
Boundary La. E13 3B **88**
SE17 6C **102**
Boundary Pas. E2 3J **9** (4F **85**)
Boundary Rd. DA15: Sidc 5J **125**
E13 2A **88**
E17 7B **50**
HA5: Eastc 7B **40**
HA9: Wemb 3E **60**
IG11: Bark 2G **89**
(Gascoigne Rd.)
IG11: Bark 1H **89**
(King Edwards Rd.)
N2 1B **46**
N9 6D **24**
N22 3B **48**
NW8 1K **81**
SM5: Cars 6F **167**
SM6: Wall 6F **167**
SW19 6B **136**
Boundary Row SE1 6A **14** (2B **102**)
Boundary St. E2 2J **9** (3F **85**)
Boundary Way CR0: Addtn 5C **170**
Boundfield Rd. SE6 3G **141**
BOUNDS GREEN 6C **32**
Bounds Grn. Ct. *N11* *6C **32***
(off Bounds Grn. Rd.)
Bounds Grn. Ind. Est. N11 6B **32**
Bounds Grn. Rd. N11 6B **32**
N22 6B **32**
Bourbon Ho. SE6 5E **140**
Bourchier St. W1 2C **12** (7H **83**)
(not continuous)
Bourdon Pl. W1 2K **11**
Bourdon Rd. SE20 2J **157**
Bourdon St. W1 3J **11** (7F **83**)
Bourke Cl. NW10 6A **62**
SW4 6J **119**
Bourlet Cl. W1 6A **6** (5G **83**)
Bourn Av. EN4: E Barn 5G **21**
N15 4D **48**
UB8: Hil 4C **74**
Bournbrook Rd. SE3 3B **124**
Bourne, The N14 1C **32**
Bourne Av. HA4: Ruis 5A **58**
N14 2D **32**
UB3: Harl 3E **92**
Bourne Cir. UB3: Harl 3E **92**
Bourne Ct. HA4: Ruis 5K **57**
IG8: Wfd G 3B **52**
W4 6J **97**
Bourne Dr. CR4: Mitc 2B **154**
Bourne Est. EC1 5J **7** (5A **84**)
Bourne Gdns. E4 4J **35**
Bourne Hall Mus. 7B **164**
Bourne Hill N13 2D **32**
Bourne Hill Cl. N13 2E **32**
Bourne Ho. IG9: Buck H 3G **37**
TW15: Ashf 5C **128**
Bourne Ind. Pk., The DA1: Cray 5K **127**
Bourne Mead DA5: Bexl 5J **127**
Bournemead Av. UB5: Yead 2J **75**
Bournemead Cl. UB5: Yead 3J **75**
Bournemead Way UB5: Yead 2K **75**
Bourne M. W1 1H **11** (6E **82**)
Bournemouth Cl. SE15 2G **121**
Bournemouth Rd. SE15 2G **121**
SW19 1J **153**
Bourne Pde. DA5: Bexl 7H **127**
Bourne Pl. W4 5K **97**
Bourne Rd. BR2: Brom 4B **160**
DA1: Cray 6J **127**
DA5: Bexl, Dart 7H **127**
E7 3H **69**
N8 6J **47**
Bournes Ho. *N15* *6E **48***
(off Chisley Rd.)
Bourneside Cres. N14 1C **32**
Bourneside Gdns. SE6 5E **140**
Bourne St. CR0: Croy 2B **168**
SW1 4G **17** (4E **100**)
Bourne Ter. W2 5K **81**
Bourne Va. BR2: Hayes 1H **171**
Bournevale Rd. SW16 4J **137**
Bourne Vw. UB6: G'frd 6K **59**
Bourne Way BR2: Hayes 2H **171**
KT19: Ewe 4J **163**
SM1: Sutt 5H **165**
Bournewood Rd. SE18 7A **108**
Bournville Rd. SE6 7C **122**
Bournwell Cl. EN4: Cockf 3J **21**
Bourton Cl. UB3: Hayes 1J **93**
Bousfield Rd. SE14 2K **121**
Boutflower Rd. SW11 4C **118**
Boutique Hall SE13 4E **122**
Bouverie Gdns. HA3: Kent 6D **42**
Bouverie M. N16 2E **66**
Bouverie Pl. W2 7B **4** (6B **82**)
Bouverie Rd. HA1: Harr 6G **41**
N16 1E **66**
Bouverie St. EC4 1K **13** (6A **84**)
Bouvier Rd. EN3: Enf W 1D **24**
Boveney Rd. SE23 7K **121**
Bovill Rd. SE23 7K **121**
Bovingdon Av. HA9: Wemb 6G **61**
Bovingdon Cl. N19 2G **65**
Bovingdon La. NW9 1A **44**
Bovingdon Rd. SW6 1K **117**
Bovingdon Sq. CR4: Mitc 4J **155**
BOW 3B **86**
Bowater Cl. NW9 5K **43**
SW2 6J **119**
Bowater Gdns. TW16: Sun 2A **148**
Bowater Ho. *EC1* *4C **8***
(off Golden La. Est.)
SW1 6F **11**
Bowater Pl. SE3 7K **105**
Bowater Rd. HA9: Wemb 3H **61**
SE18 3B **106**
Bow Bri. Est. E3 3D **86**
Bow Brook, The *E2* *2K **85***
(off Mace St.)
Bow Chyd. EC4 1D **14**
BOW COMMON 5C **86**
Bow Comn. La. E3 4B **86**
Bowden Cl. TW14: Bedf 1G **129**
Bowden St. SE11 6K **19** (5A **102**)
Bowditch SE8 4B **104**
(not continuous)
Bowdon Rd. E17 7C **50**
Bowen Dr. SE21 3E **138**
Bowen Rd. HA1: Harr 7G **41**
Bowen St. E14 6D **86**
Bower Av. SE10 1G **123**
Bower Cl. RM5: Col R 1K **55**
UB5: N'olt 2A **76**
Bower Ct. *E4* *1K **35***
(off The Ridgeway)
Bowerdean St. SW6 1K **117**
Bower Ho. *SE14* *1K **121***
(off Besson St.)
Bowerman Av. SE14 6A **104**
Bowerman Ct. *N19* *2H **65***
(off St John's Way)
Bower St. E1 6K **85**
Bowers Wlk. E6 6D **88**
Bowes Cl. DA15: Sidc 6B **126**
Bowe's Ho. IG11: Bark 7F **71**
Bowes-Lyon Hall *E16* *1J **105***
(off Wesley Av., not continuous)
BOWES PARK 6D **32**
Bowes Rd. N11 5B **32**
N13 5B **32**
RM8: Dag 4C **72**
W3 7A **80**
Bowfell Rd. W6 6E **98**
Bowford Av. DA7: Bex 1E **126**
Bowhill Cl. SW9 7A **102**
Bowie Cl. SW4 7H **119**
Bow Ind. Pk. E15 7C **68**
BOW INTERCHANGE 2D **86**
Bowland Rd. IG8: Wfd G 6F **37**
SW4 4H **119**
Bowland Yd. SW1 7F **11**
Bow La. EC4 1D **14** (6C **84**)
N12 7F **31**
SM4: Mord 6G **153**
Bowl Ct. EC2 4H **9** (4E **84**)
Bowles Ct. N12 7H **31**
Bowles Rd. SE1 6G **103**
Bowley Cl. SE19 6F **139**
Bowley Ho. SE16 3G **103**
Bowley La. SE19 5F **139**
Bowling, The KT12: Walt T 7J **147**
Bowling Cl. UB10: Uxb 1B **74**
Bowling Grn. Cl. SW15 7D **116**
Bowling Grn. Ct. HA9: Wemb 2F **61**
Bowling Grn. Ho. *SW10* *7B **100***
(off Riley St.)
Bowling Grn. La. EC1 3K **7** (4A **84**)
Bowling Grn. Pl. SE1 6E **14** (2D **102**)
Bowling Grn. Row SE18 3D **106**
Bowling Grn. St. SE11 7J **19** (6A **102**)
Bowling Grn. Wlk. N1 1G **9** (3E **84**)
Bow Locks E3 4E **86**
Bowls Cl. HA7: Stan 5G **27**
Bowman Av. E16 7H **87**
Bowman M. SW18 1H **135**
Bowman's Bldgs. *NW1* *5C **4***
(off Penfold Pl.)
Bowmans Cl. W13 1B **96**
Bowmans Lea SE23 7J **121**
Bowmans Mdw. SM6: Wall 3F **167**
Bowman's M. E1 7G **85**
N7 3J **65**
Bowman's Pl. N7 3J **65**
Bowman Trad. Est. NW9 3G **43**
Bowmead SE9 2D **142**
Bowmore Wlk. NW1 7H **65**
Bowness Cl. *E8* *6F **67***
(off Beechwood Rd.)
Bowness Cres. SW15 5A **134**
Bowness Dr. TW4: Houn 4C **112**
Bowness Ho. *SE15* *7J **103***
(off Hillbeck Cl.)
Bowness Rd. DA7: Bex 2H **127**
SE6 7D **122**
Bowood Rd. EN3: Enf H 2E **24**
SW11 5E **118**
Bow Quarter, The E3 2C **86**
Bow Rd. E3 3B **86**
Bowrons Av. HA0: Wemb 7D **60**
Bowry Ho. *E14* *5B **86***
(off Wallwood St.)
Bowsley Ct. TW13: Felt 2J **129**
Bowsprit Point *E14* *3C **104***
(off Westferry Rd.)

Bow St. E15 .... 5G 69
WC2 .... 1F 13 (6J 83)
Bow Triangle Bus. Cen. E3 .... 4C 86
Bowyer Cl. E6 .... 5D 88
Bowyer Ho. *N1* *1E 84*
(off Mill Row)
Bowyer Pl. SE5 .... 7C 102
Bowyer St. SE5 .... 7C 102
Boxall Rd. SE21 .... 6E 120
Boxelder Cl. HA8: Edg 5D 28
Boxgrove Rd. SE2 .... 3C 108
Box La. IG11: Bark 2B 90
Boxley Rd. SM4: Mord 4A 154
Boxley St. E16 .... 1K 105
Boxmoor Ho. *E2* *1G 85*
(off Whiston Rd.)
W11 .... *1F 99*
(off Queensdale Cres.)
Boxmoor Rd. HA3: Kent 4B 42
Boxoll Rd. RM9: Dag 4F 73
Boxted Cl. IG9: Buck H 1H 37
Box Tree Ho. SE8 .... 6A 104
Boxtree La. HA3: Hrw W 1G 41
Boxtree Rd. HA3: Hrw W 7C 26
Boxwood Cl. UB7: W Dray 2B 92
Boxworth Cl. N12 .... 5G 31
Boxworth Gro. N1 .... 1K 83
Boyard Rd. SE18 .... 5F 107
Boyce Ho. SW16 .... 5G 137
W10 .... *3H 81*
(off Bruckner St.)
Boyce Way E13 .... 4J 87
Boycroft Av. NW9 .... 6J 43
Boyd Av. UB1: S'hall 1D 94
Boyd Cl. KT2: King T 7G 133
Boydell Ct. NW8 .... 7B 64
(not continuous)
Boyden Ho. E17 .... 3E 50
Boyd Rd. SW19 .... 6B 136
Boyd St. E1 .... 6G 85
Boyfield St. SE1 .... 7B 14 (2B 102)
Boyland Rd. BR1: Brom 5H 141
Boyle Av. HA7: Stan 6F 27
Boyle Cl. UB10: Uxb 2B 74
Boyle Farm Island KT7: T Ditt 6A 150
Boyle Farm Rd. KT7: T Ditt 6A 150
Boyle St. W1 .... 2A 12 (7G 83)
Boyne Av. NW4 .... 4F 45
Boyne Rd. RM10: Dag 3G 73
SE13 .... 3E 122
Boyne Ter. M. W11 .... 1H 99
Boyseland Ct. HA8: Edg 2D 28
Boyson Rd. SE17 .... 6C 102
(not continuous)
Boyson Wlk. SE17 .... 6D 102
Boyton Cl. E1 .... 4J 85
N8 .... 3J 47
Boyton Ho. *NW8* *2B 82*
(off Wellington Rd.)
Boyton Rd. N8 .... 3J 47
Brabant Ct. EC3 .... 2G 15
Brabant Rd. N22 .... 2K 47
Brabazon Av. SM6: Wall 7J 167
Brabazon Rd. TW5: Hest 7A 94
UB5: N'olt 2E 76
Brabazon St. E14 .... 6D 86
Brabner Ho. *E2* *1K 9*
(off Wellington Row)
Brabourne Cl. SE19 .... 5E 138
Brabourne Cres. DA7: Bex 6F 109
Brabourne Hgts. NW7 .... 3F 29
Brabourne Ri. BR3: Beck 5E 158
Brabourn Gro. SE15 .... 2J 121
Brabrook Ct. SM6: Wall 4F 167
Brabstone Ho. UB6: G'frd 2K 77
Bracer Ho. *N1* *2E 84*
(off Whitmore Est.)
Bracewell Av. UB6: G'frd 5K 59
Bracewell Rd. W10 .... 5E 80
Bracewood Gdns. CR0: Croy 3F 169
Bracey M. N4 .... 2J 65
Bracey St. N4 .... 2J 65
Bracken, The E4 .... 2K 35
Bracken Av. CR0: Croy 3C 170
SW12 .... 6E 118
Brackenbridge Dr. HA4: Ruis 3B 58
Brackenbury *N4* *1A 66*
(off Osborne Rd.)
Brackenbury Gdns. W6 .... 3D 98
Brackenbury Rd. N2 .... 3A 46
W6 .... 3D 98
Bracken Cl. E6 .... 5D 88
TW2: Whit 7E 112
TW16: Sun 6H 129
Brackendale N21 .... 2E 32
Brackendale Cl. TW3: Houn 1F 113
Brackendene DA2: Dart 4K 145
Bracken End TW7: Isle 5H 113
Brackenfield Cl. E5 .... 3H 67
Bracken Gdns. SW13 .... 2C 116
Brackenhill HA4: Ruis 4C 58
Bracken Hill Cl. BR1: Brom 1H 159
Bracken Hill La. BR1: Brom 1H 159
Bracken Ho. *E3* *5C 86*
(off Devons Rd.)
Bracken Ind. Est. IG6: Ilf 1J 53
Bracken M. E4 .... 1K 35
RM7: Rom 6H 55
Brackens BR3: Beck 7C 140
Brackens, The EN1: Enf 7K 23
Brackenwood TW16: Sun 1J 147
Brackenwood Lodge
EN5: New Bar *4D 20*
(off Prospect Rd.)
Brackley Av. SE15 .... 3J 121
Brackley Cl. SM6: Wall 7J 167
Brackley Ct. *NW8* *3B 4*
(off Pollitt Dr.)
Brackley Rd. BR3: Beck 7B 140
W4 .... 5A 98
Brackley Sq. IG8: Wfd G 7G 37
Brackley St. EC1 .... 5D 8 (4C 84)
Brackley Ter. W4 .... 5A 98
Bracklyn Ct. N1 .... 2D 84
(not continuous)
Bracklyn St. N1 .... 2D 84
Bracknell Cl. N22 .... 1A 48
Bracknell Gdns. NW3 .... 4K 63
Bracknell Ga. NW3 .... 5K 63
Bracknell Way NW3 .... 4K 63
Bracondale Rd. SE2 .... 4A 108
Bradbeer Ho. *E2* *3J 85*
(off Cornwall Av.)
Bradbourne Rd. DA5: Bexl 7G 127
Bradbourne St. SW6 .... 2J 117
Bradbury Cl. UB2: S'hall 4D 94
Bradbury M. *N16* *5E 66*
(off Bradbury St.)
Bradbury St. N16 .... 5E 66
Bradby Ho. *NW8* *2K 81*
(off Hamilton Ter.)
Braddock Cl. TW7: Isle 2K 113
Braddon Ct. EN5: Barn 3B 20
Braddon Rd. TW9: Rich 3F 115
Braddyll St. SE10 .... 5G 105
Bradenham *SE17* *6D 102*
(off Bradenham Cl.)
Bradenham Av. DA16: Well 4A 126
Bradenham Cl. SE17 .... 6D 102
Bradenham Rd. HA3: Kent 4B 42
UB4: Hayes 3G 75
Braden St. W9 .... 4K 81
Bradfield Ct. *NW1* *7F 65*
(off Hawley Rd.)
Bradfield Dr. IG11: Bark 5A 72
Bradfield Ho. IG8: Ilf 6K 37
Bradfield Rd. E16 .... 2J 105
HA4: Ruis 5C 58
Bradford Cl. BR2: Brom 1D 172
N17 .... 6A 34
SE26 .... 4H 139
Bradford Dr. KT19: Ewe 6B 164
Bradford Ho. *W14* *3F 99*
(off Spring Va. Ter.)
Bradford Rd. IG1: Ilf 1H 71
W3 .... 2A 98
Bradgate Rd. SE6 .... 6D 122
Brading Cres. E11 .... 2K 69
Brading Rd. CR0: Croy 6K 155
SW2 .... 7K 119
Brading Ter. W12 .... 3C 98
Bradiston Rd. W9 .... 3H 81
Bradley Cl. N7 .... 6J 65
Bradley Gdns. W13 .... 6B 78
Bradley Ho. IG8: Wfd G 7D 36
SE16 .... *4J 103*
(off Raymouth Rd.)
Bradley M. SW17 .... 1D 136
Bradley Rd. N22 .... 2K 47
SE19 .... 6C 138
Bradley's Cl. N1 .... 2A 84
Bradley Stone Rd. E6 .... 5D 88
Bradman Row HA8: Edg 7D 28
Bradmead SW8 .... 7F 101
Bradmore Pk. Rd. W6 .... 4D 98
Bradon *NW9* *2B 44*
(off Further Acre)
Bradshaw Cl. SW19 .... 6J 135
Bradshaw Cotts. *E14* *6A 86*
(off Repton St.)
Bradshaw Dr. NW7 .... 7A 30
Bradshawe Waye UB8: Hil 5B 74
Bradshaws Cl. SE25 .... 3G 157
Bradstock Ho. E9 .... 7K 67
Bradstock Rd. E9 .... 6K 67
KT17: Ewe 5C 164
Brad St. SE1 .... 5K 13 (1A 102)
Bradwell Av. RM10: Dag 2G 73
Bradwell Cl. E18 .... 4H 51
Bradwell Ho. *NW6* *1K 81*
(off Mortimer Cres.)
Bradwell M. N18 .... 4B 34
Bradwell Rd. IG9: Buck H 1H 37
Brady Ct. RM8: Dag 1D 72
Brady Dr. BR1: Brom 3E 160
Brady Ho. *SW8* *1G 119*
(off Corunna Rd.)
Bradymead E6 .... 6E 88
Brady St. E1 .... 4H 85
Braeburn Ct. EN4: E Barn 4G 21
Brae Ct. KT2: King T 1G 151
Braemar SW15 .... 6F 117
Braemar Av. CR2: S Croy 7C 168
CR7: Thor H 3A 156
DA7: Bex 4J 127
HA0: Wemb 7D 60
N22 .... 1J 47
NW10 .... 3K 61
SW19 .... 2J 135
Braemar Cl. *SE16* *5H 103*
(off Masters Dr.)
Braemar Ct. SE6 .... 1H 141
Braemar Gdns. BR4: W W'ck 1E 170
DA15: Sidc 3H 143
NW9 .... 1K 43
Braemar Ho. *W9* *3A 82*
(off Maida Va.)
Braemar Mans. *SW7* *3K 99*
(off Cornwall Gdns.)
Braemar Rd. E13 .... 4H 87
KT4: Wor Pk 3D 164
N15 .... 5E 48
TW8: Bford 6D 96
Braeside BR3: Beck 5C 140
Braeside Av. SW19 .... 1G 153
Braeside Cres. DA7: Bex 4J 127
Braeside Rd. SW16 .... 7G 137
Braes St. N1 .... 7B 66
Braesyde Cl. DA17: Belv 4F 109
Brafferton Rd. CR0: Croy 4C 168
Braganza St. SE17 .... 5B 102
Bragg Cl. RM8: Dag 6B 72
Bragg Rd. TW11: Tedd 6J 131
Braham Ho. SE11 .... 6H 19 (5K 101)
Braham St. E1 .... 1K 15 (6F 85)
Braid Av. W3 .... 6A 80
Braid Cl. TW13: Hanw 2D 130
Braid Ho. *SE10* *1E 122*
(off Blackheath Hill)
Braidwood Pas. *EC1* *5C 8*
(off Aldersgate St.)
Braidwood Rd. SE6 .... 1F 141
Braidwood St. SE1 .... 5G 15 (1E 102)
Brailsford Cl. CR4: Mitc 7C 136
Brailsford Rd. SW2 .... 5A 120
Brainton Av. TW14: Felt 7K 111
Braintree Av. IG4: Ilf 4C 52
Braintree Ho. *E1* *4J 85*
(off Malcolm Rd.)
Braintree Rd. HA4: Ruis 4K 57
RM10: Dag 3G 73
Braintree St. E2 .... 3J 85
Braithwaite Av. RM7: Rush G 7G 55
Braithwaite Gdns. HA7: Stan 1C 42
Braithwaite Ho. *EC1* *3E 8*
(off Bunhill Row)
Braithwaite Rd. EN3: Brim 3G 25
Braithwaite Twr. W2 .... 5B 4
Bramah Grn. SW9 .... 1A 120
Bramah Tea & Coffee Mus.
.... 5D 14 (1C 102)
Bramalea Cl. N6 .... 6E 46
Bramall Cl. E15 .... 5H 69
Bramall Ct. *N7* *5K 65*
(off George's Rd.)
Bramber WC1 .... 2E 6
Bramber Ct. TW8 .... 4E 96
W14 .... *6H 99*
(off North End Rd.)
Bramber Ho. *KT2: King T* *1E 150*
(off Seven Kings Way)
Bramber Rd. N12 .... 5H 31
W14 .... 6H 99
Brambleacres Cl. SM2: Sutt 7J 165
Bramblebury Rd. SE18 .... 5G 107
Bramble Cl. BR3: Beck 5E 158
CR0: Croy 4C 170
HA7: Stan 7J 27
N15 .... 4G 49
TW17: Shep 3F 147
UB8: Hil 6B 74
Bramble Cft. DA8: Erith 4J 109
Brambledown Cl. BR4: W W'ck 5G 159
Brambledown Rd. CR2: Sand 7E 168
SM5: Cars 7E 166
SM6: Wall 7E 166
Bramble Gdns. W12 .... 7B 80
Bramble Ho. *E3* *5C 86*
(off Devons Rd.)
Bramble La. TW12: Hamp 6D 130
Brambles, The *SW19* *5H 135*
(off Woodside)
UB7: W Dray 4A 92
Brambles Cl. TW7: Isle 7B 96
Brambles Farm Dr.
UB10: Hil 3C 74
Bramblewood Cl. SM5: Cars 1C 166
Brambling Ct. *SE8* *6B 104*
(off Abinger Gro.)
Bramblings, The E4 .... 4A 36
Bramcote Av. CR4: Mitc 4D 154
Bramcote Ct. *CR4: Mitc* *4D 154*
(off Bramcote Av.)
Bramcote Gro. SE16 .... 5J 103
Bramcote Rd. SW15 .... 4D 116
Bramdean Cres. SE12 .... 1J 141
Bramdean Gdns. SE12 .... 1J 141
Bramerton *NW6* *7F 63*
(off Willesden La.)
Bramerton Rd. BR3: Beck 3B 158
Bramerton St. SW3 .... 7C 16 (6C 100)
Bramfield Ct. *N4* *2C 66*
(off Queens Dr.)
Bramfield Rd. SW11 .... 6C 118
Bramford Ct. N14 .... 2C 32
Bramford Rd. SW18 .... 4A 118
Bramham Gdns. KT9: Chess 4D 162
SW5 .... 5K 99
Bramhope La. SE7 .... 6K 105
Bramlands Cl. SW11 .... 3C 118
Bramley Av. TW17: Shep 3G 147
Bramley Bank Nature Reserve 6J 169

Bramley Cl. BR6: Farnb 1F **173**
CR2: S Croy 5C **168**
E17 2A **50**
HA5: Eastc 3H **39**
IG8: Wfd G 7F **37**
N14 5A **22**
TW2: Whit 6G **113**
UB3: Hayes 7J **75**
Bramley Ct. CR4: Mitc 2B **154**
DA16: Well 1B **126**
E4 1K 35
(off The Ridgeway)
EN4: E Barn 4H **21**
UB1: S'hall 7G 77
(off Haldane Rd.)
Bramley Cres. IG2: Ilf 6E **52**
SW8 7H **101**
Bramley Hill CR2: S Croy 5B **168**
Bramley Ho. *SW15 6B 116*
(off Tunworth Cres.)
TW4: Houn 4D **112**
W10 6F **81**
Bramleyhyrst *CR2: S Croy 4C 168*
(off Bramley Hill)
Bramley Lodge HA0: Wemb 4D **60**
Bramley Pde. N14 4B **22**
Bramley Rd. N14 5A **22**
SM1: Sutt 5B **166**
SM2: Cheam 7F **165**
W5 3C **96**
W10 6F **81**
(not continuous)
Bramley Sports Ground 5A **22**
Bramley Way BR4: W W'ck 2D **170**
TW4: Houn 5D **112**
Brampton *WC1 6G 7*
(off Red Lion Sq.)
Brampton Cl. E5 2H **67**
Brampton Ct. NW4 4D **44**
Brampton Gdns. N15 5C **48**
Brampton Gro. HA3: Kent 4A **42**
HA9: Wemb 1G **61**
NW4 4D **44**
Brampton La. NW4 4E **44**
Brampton Pk. Rd. N8 3A **48**
Brampton Rd. CR0: Croy 7F **157**
DA7: Bex 3D **126**
E6 3B **88**
N15 5C **48**
NW9 4G **43**
SE2 6C **108**
UB10: Hil 2D **74**
Bramshaw Ri. KT3: N Mald 6A **152**
Bramshaw Rd. E9 6K **67**
Bramshill Gdns. NW5 3F **65**
Bramshill Rd. NW10 2B **80**
Bramshot Av. SE7 6J **105**
Bramshurst *NW8 1K 81*
(off Abbey Rd.)
Bramston Rd. NW10 2C **80**
SW17 3A **136**
Bramwell Cl. TW16: Sun 2B **148**
Bramwell Ho. SE1 3C **102**
SW1 6A 18
(off Churchill Gdns.)
Bramwell M. N1 1K **83**
Brancaster Dr. NW7 7H **29**
Brancaster Ho. *E1 3K 85*
(off Moody St.)
Brancaster Rd. E12 4D **70**
IG2: Ilf 6J **53**
SW16 3J **137**
Brancepeth Gdns. IG9: Buck H 2D **36**
Branch Hill NW3 3A **64**
Branch Hill Ho. NW3 3K **63**
Branch Pl. N1 1D **84**
Branch Rd. E14 7A **86**
Branch St. SE15 7E **102**
Brancker Rd. HA3: Kent 3D **42**
Brancroft Way EN3: Brim 1F **25**
Brand Cl. N4 1B **66**
Brandesbury Sq. IG8: Ilf 7K **37**
Brandlehow Rd. SW15 4H **117**
Brandon Est. SE17 6B **102**
Brandon Ho. *BR3: Beck 5D 140*
(off Beckenham Hill Rd.)
Brandon Mans. *W14 6G 99*
(off Queen's Club Gdns.)
Brandon M. EC2 6E **8**
Brandon Rd. E17 4E **50**
N7 7J **65**
SM1: Sutt 4K **165**
UB2: S'hall 5D **94**
Brandon St. SE17 4C **102**
(not continuous)
Brandram M. *SE13 4G 123*
(off Brandram Rd.)
Brandram Rd. SE13 3G **123**
Brandreth Ct. HA1: Harr 6K **41**
Brandreth Rd. E6 6D **88**
SW17 2F **137**
Brandries, The SM6: Bedd 3H **167**
Brand St. SE10 7E **104**
Brandville Gdns. IG6: Ilf 4F **53**
Brandville Rd. UB7: W Dray 2A **92**
Brandy Way SM2: Sutt 7J **165**
Brangbourne Rd. BR1: Brom 5E **140**
Brangton Rd. SE11 6H **19** (5K **101**)
Brangwyn Ct. *W14 3G 99*
(off Blythe Rd.)
Brangwyn Cres. SW19 1A **154**
Branham Ho. SE18 5F **107**
Branksea St. SW6 7G **99**
Branksome Av. N18 6A **34**
Branksome Cl. TW11: Tedd 4H **131**
Branksome Ho. *SW8 7K 101*
(off Meadow Rd.)
Branksome Rd. SW2 5J **119**
SW19 1J **153**
Branksome Way HA3: Kent 6F **43**
KT3: N Mald 1J **151**
Branksone Ct. N2 3A **46**
Bransby Rd. KT9: Chess 6E **162**
Branscombe *NW1 1G 83*
(off Plender St.)
Branscombe Ct. BR2: Brom 5H **159**
Branscombe Gdns. N21 7F **23**
Branscombe St. SE13 3D **122**
Bransdale Cl. NW6 1J **81**
Bransgrove Rd. HA8: Edg 1F **43**
Branston Cres. BR5: Pet W 1H **173**
Branstone Rd. TW9: Kew 1F **115**
Brants Wlk. W7 4J **77**
Brantwood Av. DA8: Erith 7J **109**
TW7: Isle 4A **114**
Brantwood Cl. E17 3D **50**
Brantwood Gdns. EN2: Enf 4D **22**
IG4: Ilf 4C **52**
Brantwood Ho. *SE5 7C 102*
(off Wyndam Est.)
Brantwood Rd. CR2: S Croy 7C **168**
DA7: Bex 2H **127**
N17 6B **34**
SE24 5C **120**
Branxholme Ct. *BR1: Brom 1H 159*
(off Highland Rd.)
Brasenose Dr. SW13 6E **98**
Brasher Cl. UB6: G'frd 5H **59**
Brassett Point *E15 1G 87*
(off Abbey Rd.)
Brassey Cl. TW14: Felt 1J **129**
Brassey Ho. *E14 4D 104*
(off Cahir St.)
Brassey Rd. NW6 6H **63**
Brassey Sq. SW11 3E **118**
Brassie Av. W3 6A **80**
Brass Talley All. SE16 2K **103**
Brasted Cl. BR6: Orp 2K **173**
DA6: Bex 5D **126**
SE26 4J **139**
Brasted Lodge BR3: Beck 7C **140**
Brathay *NW1 1B 6*
(off Ampthill Est.)
Brathway Rd. SW18 7J **117**
Bratley St. E1 4G **85**
Bratten Ct. CR0: Croy 6D **156**
Braund Av. UB6: G'frd 4F **77**
Braundton Av. DA15: Sidc 1K **143**
Braunston Dr. UB4: Yead 4C **76**
Bravington Cl. TW17: Shep 5B **146**
Bravington Pl. W9 4H **81**
Bravington Rd. W9 2H **81**
Bravingtons Wlk. *N1 1F 7*
(off York Way)
Brawne Ho. *SE17 6B 102*
(off Brandon Est.)
Braxfield Rd. SE4 4A **122**
Braxted Pk. SW16 6K **137**
Bray NW3 7C **64**
Brayards Rd. SE15 2H **121**
Brayards Rd. Est. *SE15 2J 121*
(off Brayards Rd.)
Braybourne Dr. TW7: Isle 7K **95**
Braybrooke Gdns. SE19 7E **138**
Braybrook St. W12 5B **80**
Brayburne Av. SW4 2G **119**
Bray Ct. SW16 5J **137**
Braycourt Av. KT12: Walt T 7K **147**
Bray Cres. SE16 2K **103**
Braydon Rd. N16 1G **67**
Bray Dr. E16 7H **87**
Brayfield Ter. N1 7A **66**
Brayford Sq. E1 6J **85**
Bray Pas. E16 7J **87**
Bray Pl. SW3 4E **16** (4D **100**)
Bray Rd. NW7 6A **30**
Brayton Gdns. EN2: Enf 4C **22**
Braywood Rd. SE9 4H **125**
Brazier Cres. UB5: Yead 4D **76**
Brazil Cl. CR0: Bedd 7J **155**
Breach La. RM9: Dag 3G **91**
Bread St. EC4 1D **14** (6C **84**)
(not continuous)
Breakspear Crematorium
HA4: Ruis 5E **38**
Breakspear M. UB9: Hare 3A **38**
Breakspear Rd. HA4: Ruis 7D **38**
Breakspear Rd. Nth. UB9: Hare 3A **38**
Breakspear Rd. Sth. UB9: Hare 3B **56**
UB10: Ick 3B **56**
Breakspears Dr. BR5: St P 7A **144**
Breakspears M. SE4 2B **122**
Breakspears Rd. SE4 4B **122**
Breakwell Ct. *W10 4G 81*
(off Wornington Rd.)
Bream Cl. N17 4H **49**
Bream Gdns. E6 3E **88**
Breamore Cl. SW15 1C **134**
Breamore Ct. IG3: Ilf 2A **72**
Breamore Ho. *SE15 7G 103*
(off Friary Est.)
Breamore Rd. IG3: Ilf 2K **71**
Bream's Bldgs. EC4 7J **7** (6A **84**)
Bream St. E3 7C **68**
Breamwater Gdns. TW10: Ham 3B **132**
Brearley Cl. HA8: Edg 7D **28**
UB8: Uxb 6A **56**
Breasley Cl. SW15 4D **116**
Breasy Pl. *NW4 4D 44*
(off Burroughs Gdns.)
Brechin Pl. SW7 4A **100**
Brecknock Rd. N7 5H **65**
N19 4G **65**
Brecknock Rd. Est. N19 4G **65**
Breckonmead BR1: Brom 2A **160**
Brecon Cl. CR4: Mitc 3J **155**
KT4: Wor Pk 2E **164**
Brecon Grn. NW9 6A **44**
Brecon Ho. *W2 6A 82*
(off Hallfield Est.)
Brecon M. N7 5H **65**
Brecon Rd. EN3: Pond E 4D **24**
W6 6G **99**
Brede Cl. E6 3E **88**
Bredel Ho. *E14 5C 86*
(off St Paul's Way)
Bredgar SE13 5D **122**
Bredgar Rd. N19 2G **65**
Bredhurst Cl. SE20 6J **139**
Bredinghurst SE22 7G **121**
Bredin Ho. *SW10 7K 99*
(off Coleridge Gdns.)
Bredo Ho. IG11: Bark 3B **90**
Bredon Rd. CR0: Croy 7F **157**
Breer St. SW6 3K **117**
Breezers Ct. *E1 7G 85*
(off The Highway)
Breezer's Hill E1 7G **85**
Brember Rd. HA2: Harr 2G **59**
Bremer M. E17 4D **50**
Bremner Rd. SW7 1A **16** (3A **100**)
Brenchley Cl. BR2: Brom 6H **159**
BR7: Chst 1E **160**
Brenchley Gdns. SE23 6J **121**
Brenchley Rd. BR5: St P 2K **161**
Brenda Rd. SW17 2D **136**
Brende Gdns. KT8: W Mole 4F **149**
Brendon Av. NW10 4A **62**
Brendon Cl. UB3: Harl 7E **92**
Brendon Ct. UB2: S'hall 4F **95**
Brendon Gdns. HA2: Harr 4F **59**
IG2: Ilf 5J **53**
Brendon Gro. N2 2A **46**
Brendon Rd. RM8: Dag 1F **73**
SE9 2H **143**
Brendon St. W1 7D **4** (6C **82**)
Brendon Vs. N21 1H **33**
Brendon Way EN1: Enf 7K **23**
Brenley Cl. CR4: Mitc 3E **154**
Brenley Gdns. SE9 4B **124**
Brenley Ho. *SE1 6E 14*
(off Tennis St.)
Brennand Ct. N19 3G **65**
Brent Cl. DA5: Bexl 1E **144**
Brentcot Cl. W13 4B **78**
Brent Ct. NW11 7F **45**
W7 7H **77**
Brent Cres. NW10 2F **79**
BRENT CROSS 7E **44**
Brent Cross Fly-Over NW2 7F **45**
NW4 7F **45**
Brent Cross Gdns. NW4 6F **45**
BRENT CROSS INTERCHANGE 6E **44**
Brent Cross Shop. Cen. NW4 7E **44**
Brentfield NW10 7H **61**
Brentfield Cl. NW10 6K **61**
Brentfield Gdns. NW2 7F **45**
Brentfield Ho. NW10 7K **61**
Brentfield Rd. NW10 6K **61**
BRENTFORD 6D **96**
Brentford Bus. Cen. TW8: Bford 7C **96**
Brentford Cl. UB4: Yead 4B **76**
BRENTFORD END 7B **96**
Brentford FC 6D **96**
Brentford Fountain Leisure Cen. 5G **97**
Brentford Ho. TW1: Twick 7B **114**
Brentford Musical Mus. 6E **96**
Brent Grn. NW4 5E **44**
Brent Grn. Wlk. HA9: Wemb 3J **61**
Brentham Club 3C **78**
Brentham Way W5 4D **78**
Brent Ho. *E9 6J 67*
(off Frampton Pk. Rd.)
Brenthouse Rd. E9 7J **67**
Brenthurst Rd. NW10 6B **62**
Brent Lea TW8: Bford 7C **96**
Brentmead Cl. W7 7J **77**
Brentmead Gdns. NW10 2F **79**
Brentmead Pl. NW11 6F **45**
Brent New Ent. Cen. NW10 6B **62**
Brenton St. E14 6A **86**
Brent Pk. Ind. Est. UB2: S'hall 3K **93**
Brent Pk. Rd. NW4 7D **44**
NW9 7D **44**
Brent Pl. EN5: Barn 5C **20**
Brent Rd. CR2: Sels 7H **169**
E16 6J **87**
SE18 7F **107**
TW8: Bford 6C **96**
UB2: S'hall 3A **94**
Brent Side TW8: Bford 6C **96**
Brentside Cl. W13 4A **78**

Brentside Executive Cen.
TW8: Bford 6B 96
Brent St. NW4 . . . . .4E 44
Brent Ter. NW2 . . . . .1E 62
(not continuous)
Brent Trad. Cen. NW10 . . . . .5A 62
Brentvale Av. HA0: Wemb 1F 79
UB1: S'hall 1H 95
Brent Vw. Rd. NW9 . . . . .6C 44
Brentwaters Bus. Pk.
TW8: Bford 7C 96
Brent Way HA9: Wemb 6H 61
N3 . . . . .6D 30
TW8: Bford 7D 96
Brentwick Gdns. TW8: Bford 4E 96
Brentwood Cl. SE9 . . . . .1G 143
Brentwood Ho. *SE18* *7B 106*
(off Portway Gdns.)
Brentwood Lodge *NW4* *5F 45*
(off Holmdale Gdns.)
Brereton Rd. N17 . . . . .7A 34
Bressenden Pl. SW1 . . . . .1K 17 (3F 101)
Bressey Av. EN1: Enf 1B 24
Bressey Gro. E18 . . . . .2H 51
Breton Highwalk *EC2* *5D 8*
(off Golden La.)
Breton Ho. EC2 .4D 8
SE1 . . . .*7J 15*
(off Abbey St.)
Brett Cl. N16 . . . . .2E 66
UB5: Yead 3B 76
Brett Ct. N9 . . . . .2D 34
Brett Cres. NW10 . . . . .1K 79
Brettell St. SE17 . . . . .5D 102
Brettenham Av. E17 . . . . .1C 50
Brettenham Rd. E17 . . . . .2C 50
N18 . . . . .4B 34
Brett Gdns. RM9: Dag 7E 72
Brett Ho. Cl. SW15 . . . . .7F 117
Brettinghurst *SE1* *5G 103*
(off Avondale Sq.)
Brett Pas. E8 . . . . .5H 67
Brett Rd. E8 . . . . .5H 67
Brewer's Grn. SW1 . . . . .1C 18
Brewer's Hall Gdn. *EC2* *6D 8*
(off London Wall)
Brewers La. TW9: Rich 5D 114
Brewer St. W1 . . . . .2B 12 (7G 83)
Brewery, The EC2 . . . . .5E 8 (5C 84)
RM1: Rom 5K 55
Brewery Cl. HA0: Wemb 5A 60
Brewery Ind. Est., The *N1* *1D 8*
(off Wenlock Rd.)
Brewery La. TW1: Twick 7K 113
Brewery M. Cen. TW7: Isle 3A 114
Brewery Rd. BR2: Brom 1C 172
N7 . . . . .7J 65
SE18 . . . . .5H 107
Brewery Sq. EC1 . . . . .3A 8 (4B 84)
SE1 . . . . .5J 15
Brewery Wlk. RM1: Rom 5K 55
Brewhouse La. E1 . . . . .1H 103
SW15 . . . . .3G 117
Brewhouse Rd. SE18 . . . . .4D 106
Brewhouse Wlk. SE16 . . . . .1A 104
Brewhouse Yd. EC1 . . . . .3A 8 (4B 84)
Brewin Ter. UB4: Yead 5A 76
Brewood Rd. RM8: Dag 6B 72
Brewster Gdns. W10 . . . . .5E 80
Brewster Ho. *E14* *7B 86*
(off Three Colt St.)
SE1 . . . .*4F 103*
(off Dunton Rd.)
Brewster Rd. E10 . . . . .1D 68
Brian Rd. RM6: Chad H 5C 54
Briant Ho. SE1 . . . . .2J 19
Briants Cl. HA5: Pinn 2D 40
Briant St. SE14 . . . . .1K 121
Briar Av. SW16 . . . . .7K 137
Briarbank Rd. W13 . . . . .6A 78
Briar Cl. IG9: Buck H 2G 37
N2 . . . . .3K 45
N13 . . . . .3H 33
Briar Cl. TW7: Isle 5K 113
TW12: Hamp 5D 130
Briar Ct. SM3: Cheam 4E 164
SW15 . . . . .4D 116
Briar Cres. UB5: N'olt 6F 59
Briardale HA8: Edg 4E 28
Briardale Gdns. NW3 . . . . .3J 63
Briarfield Av. N3 . . . . .3K 45
(not continuous)
Briarfield Cl. DA7: Bex 2G 127
Briar Gdns. BR2: Hayes 1H 171
Briaris Cl. N17 . . . . .7C 34
Briar La. CR0: Addtn 4D 170
Briar Rd. DA5: Bexl 3K 145
HA3: Kent 5C 42
NW2 . . . . .4E 62
SW16 . . . . .3J 155
TW2: Twick 1J 131
TW17: Shep 5B 146
Briars, The WD23: Bushy 1D 26
Briarswood Way BR6: Chels 5K 173
Briar Wlk. HA8: Edg 7D 28
SW15 . . . . .4D 116
W10 . . . . .4G 81
Briar Way UB7: W Dray 2C 92
Briarwood Cl. NW9 . . . . .6J 43
TW13: Felt 4G 129
Briarwood Ct. *KT4: Wor Pk* *1C 164*
(off The Avenue)
Briarwood Dr. HA6: Nwood 2J 39
Briarwood Rd. KT17: Ewe 6C 164
SW4 . . . . .5H 119
Briary Cl. NW3 . . . . .7C 64
Briary Ct. DA14: Sidc 5B 144
E16 . . . . .6H 87
Briary Gdns. BR1: Brom 5K 141
Briary Gro. HA8: Edg 2H 43
Briary La. N9 .3A 34
Briary Lodge BR3: Beck 1E 158
Brickbarn Cl. *SW10* *7A 100*
(off King's Barn)
Brick Ct. EC4 . . . . .1J 13 (6A 84)
Brickett Cl. HA4: Ruis 5E 38
Brick Farm Cl. TW9: Kew 1H 115
Brickfield Cl. TW8: Bford 7C 96
Brickfield Cotts. BR7: Chst 5E 142
SE18 . . . . .6K 107
Brickfield Farm Gdns.
BR6: Farnb 4G 173
Brickfield La. UB3: Harl 6F 93
Brickfield Rd. CR7: Thor H 1B 156
SW19 . . . . .4K 135
Brickfields HA2: Harr 2H 59
(not continuous)
Brickfields Way UB7: W Dray 3B 92
Brick La. E1 . . . . .3K 9 (5F 85)
E2 . . . . .2K 9 (3F 85)
EN1: Enf .2C 24
EN3: Enf H 2C 24
HA7: Stan 7J 27
Brick Lane Music Hall 1B 106
BRICKLAYER'S ARMS **4D 102**
Bricklayers Arms Bus. Cen. SE1 . . . . .4E 102
Brick St. W1 . . . . .5J 11 (1F 101)
Brickwall La. HA4: Ruis 1G 57
Brickwood Cl. SE26 . . . . .3H 139
Brickwood Rd. CR0: Croy 2E 168
Brideale Cl. SE15 . . . . .6F 103
Bride Ct. EC4 . . . . .1A 14
Bride La. EC4 . . . . .1A 14 (6B 84)
Bridel M. *N1* *1B 84*
(off Colebrook Row)
Brides Pl. *N1* *7E 66*
(off De Beauvoir Rd.)
Bride St. N7 . . . . .6K 65
Bridewain St. SE1 . . . . .7J 15 (3F 103)
(not continuous)
Bridewell Pl. E1 . . . . .1H 103
EC4 . . . . .1A 14 (6B 84)
Bridford M. W1 . . . . .5K 5 (5F 83)
Bridge, The HA3: W'stone 4K 41
SW8 . . . . .7F 101
Bridge App. NW1 . . . . .7E 64
Bridge Av. W6 .4E 98
W7 . . . . .5H 77
Bridge Av. Mans. *W6* *5E 98*
(off Bridge Av.)
Bridge Bus. Cen., The
UB2: S'hall 2E 94
Bridge Cl. EN1: Enf 2C 24
KT12: Walt T 7H 147
TW11: Tedd 4K 131
W10 . . . . .6F 81
Bridge Ct. E10 . . . . .1B 68
E14 . . . .*7F 87*
(off Newport Av.)
KT12: Walt T *7H 147*
(off Bridge St.)
Bridge Dr. N13 .4E 32
Bridge End E17 . . . . .1E 50
Bridge End Cl. KT2: King T 1G 151
Bridgefield Rd. SM1: Sutt 6J 165
Bridgefoot SE1 . . . . .6F 19 (5J 101)
TW16: Sun 1H 147
Bridge Gdns. KT8: E Mos 4H 149
N16 . . . . .4D 66
TW15: Ashf 7E 128
Bridge Ga. N21 . . . . .7H 23
Bridge Ho. *E9* *6K 67*
(off Shepherds La.)
NW3 . . . .*7E 64*
(off Adelaide Rd.)
NW10 . . . .*2F 81*
(off Chamberlayne Rd.)
SE4 . . . . .4B 122
SM2: Sutt *6K 165*
(off Bridge Rd.)
SW1 . . . .*5J 17*
(off Ebury Bri.)
UB7: W Dray 1A 92
W2 . . . . .6A 4
Bridgehouse Ct. *SE1* *7A 14*
(off Blackfriars Rd.)
Bridge Ho. Quay E14 . . . . .1E 104
Bridgeland Rd. E16 . . . . .7J 87
Bridgelands Cl. BR3: Beck 7B 140
Bridge La. NW11 . . . . .4G 45
SW11 . . . . .1C 118
Bridge Leisure Cen., The 4B 140
Bridgeman Ho. *E9* *7J 67*
(off Frampton Pk. Rd.)
Bridgeman Rd. N1 . . . . .7K 65
TW11: Tedd 6A 132
Bridgeman St. NW8 . . . . .2C 82
Bridge Mdws. SE14 . . . . .6K 103
BRIDGEN **7E 126**
Bridgend Rd. SW18 . . . . .4A 118
Bridgenhall Rd. EN1: Enf 1A 24
Bridgen Ho. *E1* *6H 85*
(off Nelson St.)
Bridgen Rd. DA5: Bexl 7E 126
Bridge Pde. *N21* *7H 23*
(off Ridge Av.)
Bridge Pk. 7H 61
Bridgepark SW18 . . . . .5J 117
Bridge Pl. CR0: Croy 1D 168
SW1 . . . . .3K 17 (4F 101)
Bridgepoint Lofts E7 . . . . .7A 70
Bridgepoint Pl. *N6* *1G 65*
(off Hornsey La.)
Bridgeport Pl. E1 . . . . .1G 103
Bridge Rd. BR3: Beck 7B 140
DA7: Bex 2E 126
E6 . . . . .7D 70
E15 . . . . .7F 69
E17 . . . . .7B 50
HA9: Wemb 3G 61
KT8: E Mos 4H 149
KT9: Chess 5E 162
N9 . . . . .3B 34
N22 . . . . .1J 47
NW10 . . . . .6A 62
SM2: Sutt 6K 165
SM6: Wall 5F 167
TW1: Twick 6B 114
TW3: Houn, Isle 3H 113
Bridge Rd. TW7: Isle 3H 113
UB2: S'hall 2D 94
Bridge Row CR0: Croy 1D 168
Bridges Ct. SW11 . . . . .3B 118
(not continuous)
Bridges Ho. *SE5* *7D 102*
(off Elmington Est.)
Bridgeside Ho. *N1* *2C 84*
(off Wharf Rd.)
Bridges La. CR0: Bedd 4J 167
Bridges Pl. SW6 . . . . .1H 117
Bridges Rd. HA7: Stan 5E 26
SW19 . . . . .6K 135
Bridges Rd. M. SW19 . . . . .6K 135
Bridge St. HA5: Pinn 3C 40
KT12: Walt T 7G 147
SW1 . . . . .7E 12 (2J 101)
TW9: Rich 6D 114
W4 . . . . .4K 97
Bridge Ter. E15 . . . . .7F 69
Bridgetown Cl. SE19 . . . . .5E 138
Bridge Vw. W6 . . . . .5E 98
Bridge Vw. Ct. *SE1* *3E 102*
(off Grange Rd.)
Bridge Wlk. *IG1: Ilf* *2F 71*
(in The Exchange)
Bridgewalk Hgts. *SE1* *6F 15*
(off Weston St.)
Bridgewater Cl. BR7: Chst 3J 161
Bridgewater Gdns. HA8: Edg 2F 43
Bridgewater Highwalk EC2 . . . . .5C 8
Bridgewater Rd. E15 . . . . .1E 86
HA0: Wemb 6C 60
Bridgewater Sq. EC2 . . . . .5C 8 (5C 84)
Bridgewater St. EC2 . . . . .5C 8 (5C 84)
Bridge Way N11 . . . . .3B 32
NW11 . . . . .5H 45
TW2: Whit 7G 113
UB10: Ick 5D 56
Bridgeway HA0: Wemb 7E 60
IG11: Bark 7K 71
Bridgeway St. NW1 . . . . .2G 83
Bridge Wharf E2 . . . . .2K 85
Bridge Wharf Rd. TW7: Isle 3B 114
Bridgewood Cl. SE20 . . . . .7H 139
Bridgewood Rd. KT4: Wor Pk 4C 164
SW16 . . . . .7H 137
Bridge Yd. SE1 . . . . .4F 15 (1D 102)
Bridgford St. SW18 . . . . .3A 136
Bridgman Rd. W4 . . . . .3J 97
Bridgnorth Ho. *SE15* *6G 103*
(off Friary Est.)
Bridgwater Ho. *W2* *6A 82*
(off Hallfield Est.)
Bridgwater Rd. HA4: Ruis 4J 57
Bridle Cl. KT1: King T 4D 150
KT19: Ewe 5K 163
TW16: Sun 3J 147
Bridle La. TW1: Twick 6B 114
W1 . . . . .2B 12 (7G 83)
Bridle M. EN5: Barn 4C 20
Bridle Path CR0: Bedd 3J 167
(not continuous)
Bridle Path, The IG8: Wfd G 7B 36
Bridlepath Way TW14: Bedf 7G 111
Bridle Rd. CR0: Croy 3C 170
(not continuous)
CR2: Sand 7G 169
HA5: Eastc 6K 39
KT10: Clay 6B 162
Bridle Way BR6: Farnb 4G 173
CR0: Croy 5C 170
Bridleway, The SM6: Wall 5G 167
Bridlington Rd. N9 . . . . .7C 24
Bridport *SE17* *5D 102*
(off Date St.)
Bridport Av. RM7: Rom 6H 55
Bridport Ho. *N1* *1D 84*
(off Bridport Pl.)
N18 . . . .*5A 34*
(off Gilpin Cres.)
Bridport Pl. N1 . . . . .1D 84
(not continuous)

Bridport Rd. CR7: Thor H 3A 156
N18 5K 33
UB6: G'frd 1F 77
Bridstow Pl. W2 6J 81
Brief St. SE5 1B 120
Brierfield *NW1* *1G 83*
(off Arlington Rd.)
Brierley CR0: New Ad 6D 170
(not continuous)
Brierley Av. N9 1D 34
Brierley Cl. SE25 4G 157
Brierley Ct. W7 7J 77
Brierley Rd. E11 4F 69
SW12 2G 137
Brierly Gdns. E2 2J 85
Brigade Cl. HA2: Harr 2H 59
Brigade St. *SE3* *2H 123*
(off Tranquil Va.)
Brigadier Av. EN2: Enf 1H 23
Brigadier Hill EN2: Enf 1H 23
Briggeford Cl. E5 2G 67
Briggs Cl. CR4: Mitc 1F 155
Briggs Ho. *E2* *1K 9*
(off Chambord St.)
Bright Cl. DA17: Belv 4D 108
Brightfield Rd. SE12 5G 123
Bright Ho. *KT1: King T* *3D 150*
(off Kingston Hall Rd.)
Brightling Rd. SE4 6B 122
Brightlingsea Pl. E14 7B 86
Brightman Rd. SW18 1B 136
Brighton Av. E17 5B 50
Brighton Bldgs. *SE1* *3E 102*
(off Tower Bri. Rd.)
Brighton Cl. UB10: Hil 7D 56
Brighton Dr. UB5: N'olt 6E 58
Brighton Gro. SE14 1A 122
Brighton Rd. CR2: S Croy 5C 168
E6 3E 88
(not continuous)
KT6: Surb 6C 150
N2 2A 46
N16 4E 66
SM2: Sutt 7K 165
Brighton Ter. SW9 4K 119
Brightside, The EN3: Enf H 1E 24
Brightside Rd. SE13 6F 123
Bright St. E14 6D 86
Brightwell Cl. CR0: Croy 1A 168
Brightwell Cres. SW17 5D 136
Brig M. SE8 6C 104
Brigstock Ho. SE5 2C 120
Brigstock Rd. CR7: Thor H 5A 156
DA17: Belv 4H 109
Brill Pl. NW1 1D 6 (2H 83)
Brim Hill N2 4A 46
Brimpsfield Cl. SE2 3B 108
(not continuous)
BRIMSDOWN 2G 25
Brimsdown Av. EN3: Enf H 2F 25
Brimsdown Ho. E3 4D 86
Brimsdown Ind. Est.
EN3: Brim 1G 25
(Lockfield Av.)
EN3: Brim 2G 25
(Stockingswater La.)
Brimsdown Sports & Social Club 2E 24
Brimstone Ho. *E15* *7G 69*
(off Victoria St.)
Brindle Ga. DA15: Sidc 1J 143
Brindley Cl. DA7: Bex 3H 127
HA0: G'frd 1D 78
Brindley Ho. *W2* *5J 81*
(off Alfred Rd.)
Brindley St. SE14 1B 122
Brindley Way BR1: Brom 5J 141
UB1: S'hall 7F 77
Brindwood Rd. E4 3G 35
Brinkburn Cl. HA8: Edg 3H 43
SE2 4A 108
Brinkburn Gdns. HA8: Edg 3G 43
Brinkley KT1: King T 2G 151
Brinkley Rd. KT4: Wor Pk 2D 164

Brinklow Cres. SE18 7F 107
Brinklow Ho. *W2* *5K 81*
(off Torquay St.)
Brinkworth Rd. IG5: Ilf 3C 52
Brinkworth Way E9 6B 68
Brinsdale Rd. NW4 3F 45
Brinsley Ho. *E1* *6J 85*
(off Tarling St.)
Brinsley Rd. HA3: Hrw W 2H 41
Brinsley St. E1 6H 85
Brinsworth Cl. TW2: Twick 1H 131
Brinsworth Ho. TW2: Twick 2H 131
Brinton Wlk. SE1 5A 14
Brion Pl. E14 5E 86
Brisbane Av. SW19 1K 153
Brisbane Ho. *W12* *7D 80*
(off White City Est.)
Brisbane Rd. E10 2D 68
IG1: Ilf 7F 53
W13 2A 96
Brisbane Road Stadium 3D 68
Brisbane St. SE5 7D 102
Briscoe Cl. E11 2H 69
Briscoe Rd. SW19 6B 136
Briset Rd. SE9 3B 124
Briset St. EC1 5A 8 (5B 84)
Briset Way N7 2K 65
Bristol Cl. SM6: Wall 7J 167
TW4: Houn 7E 112
TW19: Stanw 6A 110
Bristol Ct. TW19: Stanw 6A 110
Bristol Gdns. SW15 7E 116
W9 4K 81
Bristol Ho. *IG11: Bark* *7A 72*
(off Margaret Bondfield Av.)
SE11 2J 19
SW1 *5E 100*
(off Holbein M.)
WC1 *5F 7*
(off Southampton Row)
Bristol M. W9 4K 81
Bristol Pk. Rd. E17 4A 50
Bristol Rd. E7 6A 70
SM4: Mord 5A 154
UB6: G'frd 1F 77
Briston Gro. N8 6J 47
Briston M. NW7 7H 29
Bristowe Cl. SW2 6A 120
Bristow Rd. CR0: Bedd 4J 167
DA7: Bex 1E 126
SE19 5E 138
TW3: Houn 3G 113
Britain & London Vis. Cen. *4C 12*
(off Regent St.)
Britain at War Experience 5G 15
Britannia Bri. *E14* *6B 86*
(off Commercial Rd.)
Britannia Bldg. *N1* *1E 8*
(off Ebenezer St.)
Britannia Bus. Cen. NW2 4F 63
Britannia Cl. SW4 4H 119
UB5: N'olt 3B 76
Britannia Ct. *KT2: King T* *1D 150*
(off Skerne Wlk.)
UB7: W Dray 3A 92
Britannia Ga. E16 1J 105
BRITANNIA JUNC. 1F 83
Britannia La. TW2: Whit 7G 113
Britannia Leisure Cen. 1D 84
Britannia Rd. E14 4C 104
IG1: Ilf 3F 71
KT5: Surb 7F 151
N12 3F 31
SW6 7K 99
(not continuous)
Britannia Row N1 1B 84
Britannia St. WC1 1G 7 (3K 83)
Britannia Wlk. N1 1E 8 (2D 84)
(not continuous)
Britannia Way NW10 4H 79
SW6 *7K 99*
(off Britannia Rd.)
TW19: Stanw 7A 110

Britannic Highwalk *EC2* *6E 8*
(off Moor La.)
Britannic Twr. EC2 5E 8
British Genius Site 7E 100
British Gro. W4 5B 98
British Gro. Pas. W4 5B 98
British Gro. Sth. *W4* *5B 98*
(off British Gro. Pas.)
British Legion Rd. E4 2C 36
British Library 1D 6 (3H 83)
British Mus. 6E 6 (5J 83)
British St. E3 3B 86
British Telecom Cen. EC1 7C 8
British Wharf Ind. Est. SE14 5K 103
Britley Ho. *E14* *6B 86*
(off Copenhagen Pl.)
Brittain Ho. SE9 1C 142
Brittain Rd. RM8: Dag 3E 72
Brittany Point SE11 4J 19 (4A 102)
Britten Cl. NW11 1K 63
Britten Ct. E15 2F 87
Brittenden Cl. BR6: Chels 6K 173
Brittenden Pde. BR6: Chels 6K 173
Britten Dr. UB1: S'hall 6E 76
Britten Ho. *SW3* *5D 16*
(off Britten St.)
Britten St. SW3 6C 16 (5C 100)
Britton Cl. SE6 7F 123
Britton St. EC1 4A 8 (4B 84)
Brixham Cres. HA4: Ruis 1J 57
Brixham Gdns. IG3: Ilf 5J 71
Brixham Rd. DA16: Well 1D 126
Brixham St. E16 1E 106
BRIXTON 4K 119
Brixton Academy *3A 120*
(off Stockwell Rd.)
Brixton Hill SW2 7J 119
Brixton Hill Ct. SW2 5K 119
Brixton Hill Pl. SW2 7J 119
Brixton Oval SW2 4A 120
Brixton Recreation Cen. *3A 120*
(off Brixton Sta. Rd.)
Brixton Rd. SE11 7J 19 (6A 102)
SW9 4A 120
Brixton Sta. Rd. SW9 3A 120
Brixton Water La. SW2 5K 119
Broadacre Cl. UB10: Ick 3D 56
Broadbent Cl. N6 1F 65
Broadbent St. W1 2J 11 (7F 83)
Broadberry Ct. N18 6C 34
Broadbridge Cl. SE3 7J 105
Broad Comn. Est. *N16* *1G 67*
(off Osbaldeston Rd.)
Broadcoombe CR2: Sels 7J 169
Broad Ct. WC2 1F 13 (6J 83)
Broadcroft Av. HA7: Stan 2D 42
Broadcroft Rd. BR5: Pet W 7H 161
Broadeaves Cl. CR2: S Croy 5E 168
Broadfield NW6 6K 63
Broadfield Cl. CR0: Wadd 2K 167
NW2 3E 62
Broadfield Ct. *HA2: Harr* *1F 41*
(off Broadfields)
WD23: Bushy 2D 26
Broadfield Hgts. HA8: Edg 4C 28
Broadfield La. NW1 7J 65
Broadfield Pde. *HA8: Edg* *3C 28*
(off Glengall Rd.)
Broadfield Rd. SE6 7G 123
Broadfields HA2: Harr 2F 41
KT8: E Mos 6J 149
Broadfields Av. HA8: Edg 4C 28
N21 6F 23
Broadfield Sq. EN1: Enf 2C 24
Broadfields Way NW10 5B 62
Broadfield Way IG9: Buck H 3F 37
Broadford Ho. *E1* *4A 86*
(off Commodore St.)
Broadgate EC2 6F 9
Broadgate Circ. EC2 5G 9 (5E 84)
Broadgate Ice Rink 6G 9
Broadgate Rd. E16 6B 88
Broadgates Av. EN4: Had W 1E 20

Broadgates Ct. *SE11* *6K 19*
(off Cleaver St.)
Broadgates Rd. SW18 1B 136
BROAD GREEN 7B 156
Broad Grn. Av. CR0: Croy 7B 156
Broadhead Strand NW9 1B 44
Broadheath Dr. BR7: Chst 5D 142
Broadhinton Rd. SW4 3F 119
Broadhurst Av. HA8: Edg 4C 28
IG3: Ilf 4K 71
Broadhurst Cl. NW6 6A 64
TW10: Rich 5F 115
Broadhurst Gdns. HA4: Ruis 2A 58
NW6 6K 63
Broadlands E17 3A 50
TW13: Hanw 3E 130
Broadlands Av. EN3: Enf H 3C 24
SW16 2J 137
TW17: Shep 6E 146
Broadlands Cl. EN3: Enf H 3D 24
N6 7E 46
SW16 2J 137
Broadlands Ct. *TW9: Kew* *7G 97*
(off Kew Gdns. Rd.)
Broadlands Lodge N6 7D 46
Broadlands Rd. BR1: Brom 4K 141
N6 7D 46
Broadlands Way KT3: N Mald 6B 152
Broad La. EC2 5G 9 (5E 84)
N8 5K 47
N15 4F 49
TW12: Hamp 7D 130
Broad Lawn SE9 2E 142
Broadlawns Ct. HA3: Hrw W 1K 41
Broadley St. NW8 5B 4 (5B 82)
Broadley Ter. NW1 4D 4 (4C 82)
Broadmayne *SE17* *5D 102*
(off Portland St.)
Broadmead SE6 3C 140
W14 4G 99
Broadmead Av. KT4: Wor Pk 7C 152
Broadmead Cen. *IG8: Wfd G* *7F 37*
(off Navestock Cres.)
Broadmead Cl. HA5: H End 1C 40
TW12: Hamp 6E 130
Broadmead Ct. IG8: Wfd G 6D 36
Broadmead Rd. IG8: Wfd G 6D 36
(not continuous)
UB4: Yead 4C 76
UB5: N'olt 4C 76
Broad Oak IG8: Wfd G 5E 36
Broadoak TW16: Sun 6H 129
Broad Oak Cl. E4 5H 35
Broadoak Ct. SW9 3A 120
Broadoak Ho. *NW6* *1K 81*
(off Mortimer Cres.)
Broadoak Rd. DA8: Erith 7K 109
Broadoaks KT6: Surb 2H 163
Broadoaks Way BR2: Brom 5H 159
Broad Sanctuary SW1 7D 12 (2H 101)
Broadstone *NW1* *7H 65*
(off Agar Gro.)
Broadstone Ho. *SW8* *7K 101*
(off Dorset Rd.)
Broadstone Pl. W1 6G 5 (5E 82)
Broad St. RM10: Dag 7G 73
TW11: Tedd 6K 131
Broad St. Av. EC2 6G 9 (5E 84)
Broad St. Mkt. RM10: Dag 7G 73
Broad St. Pl. EC2 6F 9
Broadview NW9 6G 43
Broadview Rd. SW16 7H 137
Broad Wlk. N21 2E 32
NW1 1H 5 (1E 82)
SE3 2A 124
TW5: Hest 1B 112
TW9: Kew 7F 97
W1 3F 11 (7D 82)
Broad Wlk., The KT8: E Mos 4K 149
W8 1K 99
Broadwalk E18 3H 51
HA2: Harr 5E 40
Broadwalk, The HA6: Nwood 2E 38

Broadwalk Ct.—Brookfield Pk.

Broadwalk Ct. W8 1J 99
(off Palace Gdns. Ter.)
Broadwalk Ho. EC2 5G 9 (4E 84)
SW7 2A 100
(off Hyde Pk. Ga.)
Broad Wlk. La. NW11 7H 45
Broadwalk Shop. Cen. HA8: Edg 6C 28
Broadwall SE1 4K 13 (1A 102)
Broadwater Farm Est. N17 2D 48
Broadwater Gdns. BR6: Farnb 4F 173
Broadwater Rd. N17 1E 48
SE28 3H 107
SW17 4C 136
Broadway DA6: Bex 4E 126
(not continuous)
E13 2K 87
E15 7F 69
IG11: Bark 1G 89
SW1 7C 12 (3H 101)
W7 1J 95
W13 1A 96
Broadway, The CR0: Bedd 4J 167
E4 6A 36
HA3: W'stone 2J 41
HA6: Nwood 2J 39
HA7: Stan 5H 27
HA9: Wemb 3E 60
IG8: Wfd G 6E 36
KT7: T Ditt 7J 149
N8 6J 47
N9 3B 34
N11 5J 31
N14 1C 32
(off Southgate Cir.)
N22 2A 48
NW7 5F 29
NW9 6B 44
RM8: Dag 1F 73
SM1: Sutt 5A 166
SM3: Cheam 6G 165
SW13 2A 116
SW19 6H 135
UB1: S'hall 7B 76
UB6: G'frd 4G 77
W3 2G 97
(off Ridgeway Dr.)
W5 7D 78
Broadway Arc. W6 4E 98
(off Hammersmith B'way.)
Broadway Av. CR0: Croy 5D 156
TW1: Twick 6B 114
Broadway Cen., The W6 4E 98
Broadway Chambers W6 4E 98
(off Hammersmith B'way.)
Broadway Cl. IG8: Wfd G 6E 36
Broadway Ct. BR3: Beck 3E 158
SW19 6J 135
Broadway Gdns. CR4: Mitc 4C 154
IG8: Wfd G 6E 36
Broadway Ho. BR1: Brom 5F 141
(off Bromley Rd.)
E8 1H 85
(off Ada St.)
Broadway Mans. SW6 7J 99
(off Fulham Rd.)
Broadway Mkt. E8 1H 85
IG6: Ilf 1H 53
(Forest Rd.)
IG6: Ilf 2G 53
(Greystone Gdns.)
SW17 4D 136
Broadway Mkt. M. E8 1G 85
Broadway M. E5 7F 49
N13 5E 32
N21 1G 33
Broadway Pde. E4 6K 35
HA2: Harr 5F 41
N8 6J 47
UB3: Hayes 1J 93
Broadway Pl. SW19 6H 135
Broadway Retail Pk. NW2 4F 63
Broadway Shop. Cen. DA6: Bex 4G 127
Broadway Shop. Mall SW1 1C 18 (3H 101)
Broadway Sq. DA6: Bex 4G 127
Broadway Squash & Fitness Cen. 4F 99
(off Chalk Hill Rd.)
Broadway Theatre, The
Barking 1G 89
Catford 7D 122
Broadway Wlk. E14 2C 104
Broadwell Ct. TW5: Hest 1B 112
(off Springwell Rd.)
Broadwell Pde. NW6 6K 63
(off Broadhurst Gdns.)
Broadwick St. W1 2B 12 (7G 83)
Broadwood Av. HA4: Ruis 6F 39
Broadwood Ter. W8 4H 99
Broad Yd. EC1 4A 8 (4B 84)
Brocas Cl. NW3 7C 64
Brockbridge Ho. SW15 6B 116
Brockdene Dr. BR2: Kes 4B 172
Brockdish Av. IG11: Bark 5K 71
Brockenhurst KT8: W Mole 5D 148
Brockenhurst Av. KT4: Wor Pk 1A 164
Brockenhurst Gdns. IG1: Ilf 5G 71
NW7 5F 29
Brockenhurst M. N18 4B 34
Brockenhurst Rd. CR0: Croy 7H 157
Brockenhurst Way SW16 2H 155
Brocket Ho. SW8 2H 119
Brockham Cl. SW19 5H 135
Brockham Cres. CR0: New Ad 7F 171
Brockham Dr. IG2: Ilf 6F 53
SW2 7K 119
Brockham Ho. NW1 1G 83
(off Bayham Pl.)
SW2 7K 119
(off Brockham Dr.)
Brockham St. SE1 7D 14 (3C 102)
Brockhurst Cl. HA7: Stan 6E 26
Brockill Cres. SE4 4A 122
Brocklebank Ho. E16 1E 106
(off Glenister St.)
Brocklebank Ind. Est. SE7 4J 105
Brocklebank Rd. SE7 4K 105
SW18 7A 118
Brocklehurst St. SE14 7K 103
Brocklesby Rd. SE25 4H 157
BROCKLEY 4K 121
Brockley Av. HA7: Stan 3K 27
Brockley Cl. HA7: Stan 4K 27
Brockley Cres. RM5: Col R 1J 55
Brockley Cross SE4 3A 122
Brockley Cross Bus. Cen. SE4 3A 122
Brockley Footpath SE4 5A 122
(not continuous)
SE15 4J 121
Brockley Gdns. SE4 2B 122
Brockley Gro. SE4 5B 122
Brockley Hall Rd. SE4 5A 122
Brockley Hill HA7: Stan 1H 27
Brockley Jack Theatre 5A 122
Brockley M. SE4 5A 122
Brockley Pk. SE23 7A 122
Brockley Ri. SE23 1A 140
Brockley Rd. SE4 3B 122
Brockley Side HA7: Stan 4K 27
Brockley Vw. SE23 7A 122
Brockley Way SE4 5K 121
Brockman Ri. BR1: Brom 4F 141
Brockmer Ho. E1 7H 85
(off Crowder St.)
Brock Pl. E3 4D 86
Brock Rd. E13 5K 87
Brocks Dr. SM3: Cheam 3G 165
Brockshot Cl. TW8: Bford 5D 96
Brock St. SE15 3J 121
Brockway Cl. E11 2G 69
Brockweir E2 2J 85
(off Cyprus St.)
Brockwell Av. BR3: Beck 5D 158
Brockwell Cl. BR5: St M Cry 5K 161
Brockwell Ct. SW2 5A 120
Brockwell Ho. SE11 7H 19
(off Vauxhall St.)
Brockwell Pk. 6B 120
Brockwell Pk. Gdns. SE24 7A 120
Brockwell Pk. Lido 6B 120
Brockwell Pk. Row SW2 7A 120
Brodia Rd. N16 3E 66
Brodie Ho. SE1 5F 103
(off Cooper's Rd.)
Brodie Rd. E4 1K 35
EN2: Enf 1H 23
Brodie St. SE1 5F 103
Brodlove La. E1 7K 85
Brodrick Gro. SE2 4B 108
Brodrick Rd. SW17 2C 136
Brograve Gdns. BR3: Beck 2D 158
Broken Wharf EC4 2C 14 (7C 84)
Brokesley St. E3 3B 86
Broke Wlk. E8 1F 85
Bromar Rd. SE5 3E 120
Bromefield HA7: Stan 1C 42
Bromell's Rd. SW4 4G 119
Brome Rd. SE9 3D 124
Bromfelde Rd. SW4 3H 119
Bromfelde Wlk. SW4 2H 119
Bromfield St. N1 1A 84
Bromhall Rd. RM8: Dag 6B 72
Bromhead Rd. E1 6J 85
(off Jubilee St.)
Bromhead St. E1 6J 85
Bromhedge SE9 3D 142
Bromholm Rd. SE2 3B 108
Bromleigh Ct. SE23 2G 139
Bromleigh Ho. SE1 7J 15
(off Abbey St.)
BROMLEY
BR1 2J 159
E3 3D 86
Bromley Av. BR1: Brom 7G 141
BROMLEY COMMON 1C 172
Bromley Comn. BR2: Brom 4A 160
Bromley Cres. BR2: Brom 3H 159
HA4: Ruis 4H 57
Bromley Gdns. BR2: Brom 3H 159
Bromley Gro. BR2: Brom 2F 159
Bromley Hall Rd. E14 5E 86
Bromley High St. E3 3D 86
Bromley Hill BR1: Brom 6G 141
Bromley Ho. BR1: Brom 1J 159
(off North St.)
Bromley Ind. Cen. BR1: Brom 3B 160
Bromley La. BR7: Chst 7G 143
BROMLEY PARK 1G 159
Bromley Pk. BR1: Brom 1H 159
Bromley Pl. W1 5A 6 (5G 83)
Bromley Rd. BR1: Brom 1D 140
BR2: Brom 2D 158
BR3: Beck 1D 158
BR7: Chst 1F 161
E10 6D 50
E17 3C 50
N17 1F 49
N18 3J 33
SE6 1D 140
Bromley Ski Cen. 7E 144
Bromley St. E1 5K 85
BROMPTON 2D 16 (3C 100)
Brompton Arc. SW3 7E 10
Brompton Cl. SE20 2G 157
TW4: Houn 5D 112
Brompton Cotts. SW10 6A 100
(off Hollywood Rd.)
Brompton Gro. N2 4C 46
Brompton Oratory 2C 16 (3C 100)
Brompton Pk. Cres. SW6 6K 99
Brompton Pl. SW3 1D 16 (3C 100)
Brompton Rd. SW1 3C 16 (4C 100)
SW3 3C 16 (4C 100)
Brompton Sq. SW3 1C 16 (3C 100)
Brompton Ter. SE18 1D 124
Brompton Vs. SW6 6J 99
(off Ongar Rd.)
Bromwich Av. N6 2E 64
Bromyard Av. W3 7A 80
Bromyard Ho. SE15 7H 103
(off Commercial Way)
Bromyard Leisure Cen. 1A 98
Bron Ct. NW6 1J 81
BRONDESBURY 7H 63
Brondesbury Ct. NW2 6F 63
Brondesbury M. NW6 7J 63
BRONDESBURY PARK 1G 81
Brondesbury Pk. NW2 6E 62
NW6 6D 62
Brondesbury Rd. NW6 2H 81
Brondesbury Vs. NW6 2H 81
Bronhill Ter. N17 1G 49
Bronsart Rd. SW6 7G 99
Bronson Rd. SW20 2F 153
Bronte Cl. DA8: Erith 7H 109
E7 4J 69
IG2: Ilf 4E 52
Bronte Ct. W3 2G 97
W14 3F 99
(off Girdler's Rd.)
Bronte Ho. N16 5E 66
NW6 3J 81
SW4 7G 119
Bronti Cl. SE17 5C 102
Bronwen Ct. NW8 2A 4
(off Grove End Rd.)
Bronze Age Way DA8: Erith 2H 109
DA17: Belv 2H 109
Bronze St. SE8 7C 104
Brook Av. HA8: Edg 6C 28
HA9: Wemb 3G 61
RM10: Dag 7H 73
Brookbank Av. W7 5H 77
Brookbank Rd. SE13 3C 122
Brook Cl. HA4: Ruis 7G 39
NW7 7B 30
SW17 2E 136
SW20 3D 152
TW19: Stanw 7B 110
W3 1G 97
Brook Ct. BR3: Beck 1B 158
E11 3G 69
E15 5D 68
(off Clays La.)
E17 3A 50
HA8: Edg 5C 28
IG11: Bark 1K 89
SE12 3A 142
Brook Cres. E4 4H 35
N9 4C 34
Brookdale N11 4B 32
Brookdale Rd. DA5: Bexl 6E 126
E17 3C 50
SE6 6D 122
(not continuous)
Brookdales NW11 4G 45
Brookdene Rd. SE18 4J 107
Brook Dr. HA1: Harr 4G 41
HA4: Ruis 7G 39
SE11 2K 19 (3A 102)
Brooke Av. HA2: Harr 3G 59
Brooke Cl. WD23: Bush 1B 26
Brooke Ho. SE14 1A 122
Brookehowse Rd. SE6 2C 140
Brookend Rd. DA15: Sidc 1J 143
Brooke Rd. E5 3G 67
E17 4E 50
N16 3F 67
Brooke's Ct. EC1 5J 7 (5A 84)
Brooke's Mkt. EC1 5K 7
Brooke St. EC1 6J 7 (5A 84)
Brooke Way WD23: Bush 1B 26
Brookfield N6 3E 64
Brookfield Av. E17 4E 50
NW7 6J 29
SM1: Sutt 4C 166
W5 4D 78
Brookfield Cl. NW7 6J 29
Brookfield Ct. N12 4E 30
UB6: G'frd 3G 77
Brookfield Cres. HA3: Kent 5E 42
NW7 6J 29
Brookfield Gdns. KT10: Clay 6A 162
Brookfield Pk. NW5 3F 65

Brookfield Path IG8: Wfd G 6B 36
Brookfield Rd. E9 .....6A 68
N9 .....3B 34
W4 .....2K 97
Brookfields EN3: Pond E 4E 24
Brookfields Av. CR4: Mitc 5C 154
Brook Gdns. E4 .....4J 35
KT2: King T 1J 151
SW13 .....3B 116
Brook Ga. W1 .....3F 11 (7D 82)
BROOK GREEN 4F 99
Brook Grn. W6 .....3F 99
Brook Grn. Flats *W14* *3F 99*
(off Dunsany Rd.)
Brookhill Cl. EN4: E Barn 5H 21
SE18 .....5F 107
Brookhill Rd. EN4: E Barn 5H 21
SE18 .....6F 107
Brook Ho. *W6* *4E 98*
(off Shepherd's Bush Rd.)
Brookhouse Gdns. E4 .....4B 36
Brook Ho's. *NW1* *2G 83*
(off Cranleigh St.)
Brook Ind. Est. UB4: Yead 1B 94
Brooking Cl. RM8: Dag 3C 72
Brooking Rd. E7 .....5J 69
Brookland Cl. NW11 .....4J 45
Brookland Gth. NW11 .....4J 45
Brookland Hill NW11 .....4K 45
Brookland Ri. NW11 .....4J 45
Brooklands, The TW7: Isle 1H 113
Brooklands App. RM1: Rom 4K 55
Brooklands Av. DA15: Sidc 2H 143
SW19 .....2K 135
Brooklands Cl. RM7: Rom 4K 55
TW16: Sun 1G 147
Brooklands Ct. CR4: Mitc 2B 154
KT1: King T *4D 150*
(off Surbiton Rd.)
N21 .....5J 23
NW6 .....7H 63
Brooklands Dr. UB6: G'frd 1C 78
Brooklands La. RM7: Rom 4K 55
(not continuous)
Brooklands Pk. SE3 .....3J 123
Brooklands Pas. SW8 .....1H 119
Brooklands Pl. TW12: Ham H 5F 131
Brooklands Rd. KT7: T Ditt 1A 162
RM7: Rom 4K 55
Brook La. BR1: Brom 6J 141
DA5: Bexl, Bex 6D 126
SE3 .....2K 123
Brook La. Bus. Cen. TW8: Bford 5D 96
Brook La. Nth. TW8: Bford 5D 96
(not continuous)
Brooklea Cl. NW9 .....1A 44
Brook Lodge *NW11* *5F 45*
(off Nth. Circular Rd.)
RM7: Rom *4K 55*
(off Medora Rd.)
Brooklyn SE20 .....7G 139
Brooklyn Av. SE25 .....4H 157
Brooklyn Cl. SM5: Cars 2C 166
Brooklyn Gro. SE25 .....4H 157
Brooklyn Pas. *W12* *2E 98*
(off Lime Gro.)
Brooklyn Rd. BR2: Brom 5B 160
SE25 .....4H 157
Brookmarsh Ind. Est. SE10 .....7D 104
Brook Mead KT19: Ewe 6A 164
Brookmead CR0: Bedd 6G 155
Brookmead Av. BR1: Brom 5D 160
Brookmead Ind. Est.
CR0: Bedd 6G 155
Brook Mdw. N12 .....3E 30
Brook Mdw. Cl. IG8: Wfd G 6B 36
Brookmead Rd. CR0: Croy 6G 155
Brook M. WC2 .....1D 12
Brook M. Nth. W2 .....2A 10 (7A 82)
Brookmill Rd. SE8 .....1C 122
Brook Pde. IG7: Chig 3K 37
Brook Pk. Cl. N21 .....5G 23
Brook Pl. EN5: Barn 5D 20
Brook Ri. IG7: Chig 3K 37
Brook Rd. CR7: Thor H 4C 156
IG2: Ilf 6J 53
IG9: Buck H, Wfd G 2D 36
KT6: Surb 2E 162
N2 .....7H 31
N8 .....4J 47
N22 .....3K 47
NW2 .....2B 62
TW1: Twick 6A 114
Brook Rd. Sth. TW8: Bford 6D 96
Brooks Av. E6 .....4D 88
Brooksbank Ho. *E9* *6J 67*
(off Brooksbank St.)
Brooksbank St. E9 .....6J 67
Brooksby Ho. *N1* *7A 66*
(off Liverpool Rd.)
Brooksby M. N1 .....7A 66
Brooksby St. N1 .....7A 66
Brooksby's Wlk. E9 .....5K 67
Brooks Cl. SE9 .....2E 142
Brooks Ct. SW8 .....7G 101
Brookscroft *E17* *3D 50*
(off Forest Rd.)
Brookscroft Rd. E17 .....1D 50
(not continuous)
Brooks Farm 7D 50
Brookshill HA3: Hrw W 5C 26
Brookshill Av. HA3: Hrw W 5C 26
Brookshill Dr. HA3: Hrw W 5C 26
Brookside BR6: Orp 7K 161
EN4: E Barn 6H 21
N21 .....6E 22
SM5: Cars 5E 166
UB10: Uxb 7B 56
Brookside Cl. EN5: Barn 6B 20
HA2: Harr 4C 58
HA3: Kent 5D 42
TW13: Felt 3J 129
Brookside Cres. KT4: Wor Pk 1C 164
Brookside Rd. N9 .....4C 34
(not continuous)
N19 .....2G 65
NW11 .....6G 45
UB4: Yead 7A 76
Brookside Sth. EN4: E Barn 7K 21
Brookside Wlk. N12 .....6D 30
NW11 .....4G 45
Brookside Way CR0: Croy 6K 157
Brooks La. W4 .....6G 97
Brooks Lodge *N1* *2E 84*
(off Hoxton St.)
Brooks M. W1 .....2J 11 (7F 83)
Brook Sq. SE18 .....1C 124
Brooks Rd. E13 .....1J 87
W4 .....5G 97
Brook St. DA8: Erith 5H 109
DA17: Belv, Erith 5H 109
KT1: King T 2E 150
N17 .....2F 49
W1 .....2J 11 (7F 83)
W2 .....2B 10 (7B 82)
Brooksville Av. NW6 .....1G 81
Brooks Wlk. N3 .....3G 45
Brookvale DA8: Erith 1H 127
Brookview Ct. EN1: Enf 5K 23
Brookview Rd. SW16 .....5G 137
Brookville Rd. SW6 .....7H 99
Brook Wlk. HA8: Edg 6E 28
N2 .....1B 46
Brook Way IG7: Chig 3K 37
Brookway SE3 .....3J 123
Brookwood Av. SW13 .....2B 116
Brookwood Cl. BR2: Brom 4H 159
Brookwood Ho. *SE1* *7B 14*
(off Webber St.)
Brookwood Rd. SW18 .....1H 135
TW3: Houn 2F 113
Broom Cl. BR2: Brom 6C 160
TW11: Tedd 7D 132
Broomcroft Av. UB5: Yead 3A 76
Broome Rd. TW12: Hamp 7D 130
Broome Way SE5 .....7D 102
Broomfield E17 .....7B 50
NW1 .....*7E 64*
(off Ferdinand St.)
TW16: Sun 1J 147
Broomfield Av. N13 .....5E 32
Broomfield Ct. *SE16* *3G 103*
(off Ben Smith Way)
Broomfield Ho. *HA7: Stan* *3F 27*
(off Stanmore Hill)
SE17 .....*4E 102*
(off Massinger St.)
Broomfield La. N13 .....4D 32
Broomfield Pl. W13 .....1B 96
Broomfield Rd. BR3: Beck 3A 158
DA6: Bex 5G 127
KT5: Surb 1F 163
N13 .....5D 32
RM6: Chad H 7D 54
TW9: Kew 1F 115
TW11: Tedd 6C 132
W13 .....1B 96
Broomfield St. E14 .....5C 86
Broom Gdns. CR0: Croy 3C 170
Broomgrove Gdns. HA8: Edg 1G 43
Broomgrove Rd. SW9 .....2K 119
Broomhall Rd. CR2: Sand 7D 168
BROOM HILL 7K 161
Broomhill Ct. IG8: Wfd G 6D 36
Broom Hill Ri. DA6: Bex 5G 127
Broomhill Rd. BR6: Orp 7K 161
IG3: Ilf 2A 72
IG8: Wfd G 6D 36
(not continuous)
SW18 .....5J 117
Broomhill Wlk. IG8: Wfd G 6C 36
Broomhouse La. SW6 .....2J 117
(not continuous)
Broomhouse Rd. SW6 .....2J 117
Broomleigh *BR1: Brom* *1J 159*
(off Tweedy Rd.)
Broomloan La. SM1: Sutt 2J 165
Broom Lock TW11: Tedd 6C 132
Broom Mead DA6: Bex 6G 127
Broom Pk. TW11: Tedd 7D 132
Broom Rd. CR0: Croy 3C 170
TW11: Tedd 5B 132
Broomsleigh Bus. Pk. SE26 .....5B 140
Broomsleigh St. NW6 .....5H 63
Broom Water TW11: Tedd 6C 132
Broom Water W. TW11: Tedd 5C 132
Broomwood Cl. CR0: Croy 5K 157
DA5: Bexl 2K 145
Broomwood Rd. SW11 .....6D 118
Broseley Gro. SE26 .....5A 140
Broster Gdns. SE25 .....3F 157
Brougham Rd. E8 .....1G 85
W3 .....6J 79
Brougham St. SW11 .....2D 118
Brough Cl. KT2: King T 5D 132
SW8 .....7J 101
Broughton Av. N3 .....3G 45
TW10: Ham 3B 132
Broughton Ct. W13 .....7B 78
Broughton Dr. SW9 .....4A 120
Broughton Gdns. N6 .....6G 47
Broughton Rd. BR6: Orp 2H 173
CR7: Thor H 6A 156
SW6 .....2K 117
W13 .....7B 78
Broughton St. SW8 .....2E 118
Broughton St. Ind. Est.
SW11 .....2E 118
Brouncker Rd. W3 .....2J 97
Browells La. TW13: Felt 2K 129
(not continuous)
Brown Bear Ct. TW13: Hanw 4B 130
Brown Cl. SM6: Wall 7J 167
Browne Ho. *SE8* *7C 104*
(off Deptford Church St.)
Brownfield Area E14 .....6D 86
Brownfield St. E14 .....6D 86
Browngraves Rd. UB3: Harl 7E 92
Brown Hart Gdns. W1 .....2H 11 (7E 82)
Brownhill Rd. SE6 .....7D 122
Browning Av. KT4: Wor Pk 1D 164
SM1: Sutt 4C 166
W7 .....6K 77
Browning Cl. DA16: Well 1J 125
E17 .....4E 50
RM5: Col R 1F 55
TW12: Hamp 4D 130
W9 .....4A 4 (4A 82)
Browning Ct. *W14* *6H 99*
(off Turneville Rd.)
Browning Ho. *N16* *4E 66*
(off Shakspeare Wlk.)
SE14 .....*1A 122*
(off Loring Rd.)
W12 .....*6E 80*
(off Wood La.)
Browning M. W1 .....6H 5 (5F 83)
Browning Rd. E11 .....7H 51
E12 .....5D 70
EN2: Enf 1J 23
Browning St. SE17 .....5C 102
Browning Way TW5: Hest 1B 112
Brownlea Gdns. IG3: Ilf 2A 72
Brownlow Cl. EN4: E Barn 5G 21
Brownlow Ct. N2 .....5A 46
N11 .....*6D 32*
(off Brownlow Rd.)
Brownlow Ho. *SE16* *2G 103*
(off George Row)
Brownlow M. WC1 .....4H 7 (4K 83)
Brownlow Rd. CR0: Croy 4E 168
E7 .....4J 69
E8 .....1F 85
N3 .....7E 30
N11 .....6D 32
NW10 .....7A 62
W13 .....1A 96
Brownlow St. WC1 .....6H 7 (5K 83)
Brownrigg Rd. TW15: Ashf 4C 128
Browns Arc. *W1* *3B 12*
(off Regent St.)
Brown's Bldgs. EC3 .....1H 15 (6E 84)
Brownsea Wlk. NW7 .....6A 30
Browns La. NW5 .....5F 65
Brownspring Dr. SE9 .....4F 143
Browns Rd. E17 .....3C 50
KT5: Surb 7F 151
Brown St. W1 .....7E 4 (6D 82)
Brownswell Rd. N2 .....2B 46
BROWNSWOOD PARK 2B 66
Brownswood Rd. N4 .....3B 66
Broxash Rd. SW11 .....6E 118
Broxbourne Av. E18 .....4K 51
Broxbourne Rd. BR6: Orp 1K 173
E7 .....3J 69
Broxholme Ho. *SW6* *1K 117*
(off Harwood Rd.)
Broxholm Rd. SE27 .....3A 138
Broxted Rd. SE6 .....2B 140
Broxwood Way NW8 .....1C 82
Bruce Av. TW17: Shep 6E 146
Bruce Castle 1E 48
Bruce Castle Ct. *N17* *1F 49*
(off Lordship La.)
Bruce Castle Rd. N17 .....1F 49
Bruce Cl. DA16: Well 1B 126
W10 .....5F 81
Bruce Ct. DA15: Sidc 4K 143
Bruce Gdns. N20 .....3J 31
Bruce Gro. N17 .....1E 48
Bruce Hall M. SW17 .....4E 136
Bruce Ho. W10 .....5F 81
Bruce Rd. CR4: Mitc 7E 136
E3 .....3D 86
EN5: Barn 3B 20
HA3: W'stone 2J 41
NW10 .....7K 61
SE25 .....4D 156
Bruckner St. W10 .....3G 81
Brudenell Rd. SW17 .....3D 136
Bruffs Mdw. UB5: N'olt 6C 58
Bruford Ct. SE8 .....6C 104

Bruges Pl. *NW1* . . . 7G 65
(off Randolph St.)
Brumfield Rd. KT19: Ewe . . . 5J 163
Brummel Cl. DA7: Bex . . . 3J 127
Brune Ho. E1 . . . 6J 9
Brunei Gallery . . . 5D 6 (5H 83)
Brunel Cl. SE19 . . . 6F 139
TW5: Cran . . . 7K 93
UB5: N'olt . . . 3D 76
Brunel Engine House Mus. . . . 2J 103
Brunel Est. W2 . . . 5J 81
Brunel Ho. *E14* . . . 5D 104
(off Ship Yd.)
Brunel Pl. UB1: S'hall . . . 6F 77
Brunel Rd. E17 . . . 6A 50
IG8: Wfd G . . . 5J 37
SE16 . . . 2J 103
W3 . . . 5A 80
Brunel Science Pk. UB8: Cowl . . . 3A 74
Brunel St. E16 . . . 6H 87
Brunel University
Osterley Campus . . . 7J 95
Twickenham Campus . . . 4B 114
Uxbridge Campus . . . 3A 74
Brunel Wlk. N15 . . . 4E 48
SW10 . . . 7B 100
(off Cheyne Rd.)
TW2: Whit . . . 7E 112
Brune St. E1 . . . 6J 9 (5F 85)
Brunlees Ho. *SE1* . . . 3C 102
(off Bath Ter.)
Brunner Cl. NW11 . . . 5K 45
Brunner Ho. SE6 . . . 4E 140
Brunner Rd. E17 . . . 5A 50
W5 . . . 4D 78
Bruno Pl. NW9 . . . 2J 61
Brunswick Av. N11 . . . 3K 31
(not continuous)
Brunswick Cen. WC1 . . . 3E 6 (4J 83)
Brunswick Cl. DA6: Bex . . . 4D 126
HA5: Pinn . . . 6C 40
KT7: T Ditt . . . 1A 162
TW2: Twick . . . 3H 131
Brunswick Cl. Est.
EC1 . . . 2A 8 (3B 84)
Brunswick Ct. *EC1* . . . 2A 8
(off Tompion St.)
EN4: E Barn . . . 5G 21
SE1 . . . 7H 15 (2E 102)
SM1: Sutt . . . 4K 165
SW1 . . . 4D 18
(off Regency St.)
Brunswick Cres. N11 . . . 3K 31
Brunswick Flats *W11* . . . 6J 81
(off Westbourne Gro.)
Brunswick Gdns. IG6: Ilf . . . 1G 53
W5 . . . 4E 78
W8 . . . 1J 99
Brunswick Gro. N11 . . . 3K 31
Brunswick Ho. *E2* . . . 2F 85
(off Thurtle Rd.)
N3 . . . 1H 45
SE16 . . . 3A 104
(off Brunswick Quay)
Brunswick Ind. Pk. N11 . . . 4A 32
Brunswick Mans. *WC1* . . . 3F 7
(off Handel St.)
Brunswick M. SW16 . . . 6H 137
W1 . . . 7F 5 (6D 82)
BRUNSWICK PARK . . . 3J 31
Brunswick Pk. SE5 . . . 1E 120
Brunswick Pk. Gdns. N11 . . . 2K 31
Brunswick Pk. Rd. N11 . . . 2K 31
Brunswick Pl. N1 . . . 2F 9 (3D 84)
NW1 . . . 4H 5 (4E 82)
(not continuous)
SE19 . . . 7G 139
Brunswick Quay SE16 . . . 3K 103
Brunswick Rd. DA6: Bex . . . 4D 126
E10 . . . 1E 68
E14 . . . 6E 86
EN3: Enf L . . . 1H 25
KT2: King T . . . 1G 151
Brunswick Rd. N15 . . . 4E 48
(not continuous)
SM1: Sutt . . . 4K 165
W5 . . . 4D 78
Brunswick Sq. N17 . . . 6A 34
WC1 . . . 3F 7 (4J 83)
Brunswick St. E17 . . . 5E 50
Brunswick Ter. BR3: Beck . . . 1D 158
Brunswick Vs. SE5 . . . 1E 120
Brunswick Way N11 . . . 4A 32
Brunton Pl. E14 . . . 6A 86
Brushfield St. E1 . . . 5H 9 (5E 84)
Brushwood Cl. E14 . . . 5D 86
Brussels Rd. SW11 . . . 4B 118
Bruton Cl. BR7: Chst . . . 7D 142
Bruton La. W1 . . . 3K 11 (7F 83)
Bruton Pl. W1 . . . 3K 11 (7F 83)
Bruton Rd. SM4: Mord . . . 4A 154
Bruton St. W1 . . . 3K 11 (7F 83)
Bruton Way W13 . . . 5A 78
Brutus Ct. *SE11* . . . 4B 102
(off Kennington La.)
Bryan Av. NW10 . . . 7D 62
Bryan Cl. TW16: Sun . . . 7J 129
Bryan Ho. NW10 . . . 7D 62
SE16 . . . 2B 104
Bryan Rd. SE16 . . . 2B 104
Bryan's All. SW6 . . . 2K 117
Bryanston Av. TW2: Whit . . . 1F 131
Bryanston Cl. UB2: S'hall . . . 4D 94
Bryanston Ct. W1 . . . 7E 4
(not continuous)
Bryanstone Ct. SM1: Sutt . . . 3A 166
Bryanstone Rd. N8 . . . 5H 47
Bryanston Mans. *W1* . . . 5E 4
(off York St.)
Bryanston M. E. W1 . . . 6E 4 (5D 82)
Bryanston M. W. W1 . . . 6E 4 (5D 82)
Bryanston Pl. W1 . . . 6E 4 (5D 82)
Bryanston Sq. W1 . . . 6E 4 (6D 82)
Bryanston St. W1 . . . 1E 10 (6D 82)
Bryant Cl. EN5: Barn . . . 5C 20
Bryant Ct. *E2* . . . 2F 85
(off Whiston Rd., not continuous)
W3 . . . 1K 97
Bryant Rd. UB5: Yead . . . 3A 76
Bryant St. E15 . . . 7F 69
Bryantwood Rd. N7 . . . 5A 66
Brycedale Cres. N14 . . . 4B 32
Bryce Ho. *SE14* . . . 6K 103
(off John Williams Cl.)
Bryce Rd. RM8: Dag . . . 4C 72
Brydale Ho. *SE16* . . . 4K 103
(off Rotherhithe New Rd.)
Bryden Cl. SE26 . . . 5A 140
Brydges Pl. WC2 . . . 3E 12 (7J 83)
Brydges Rd. E15 . . . 5F 69
Brydon Wlk. N1 . . . 1J 83
Bryer Ct. EC2 . . . 5C 8
Bryett Rd. N7 . . . 3J 65
Bryher Ct. SE11 . . . 5J 19
Brymay Cl. E3 . . . 2C 86
Brynmaer Rd. SW11 . . . 1D 118
Bryn-y-mawr Rd. EN1: Enf . . . 4A 24
Bryony Cl. UB8: Hil . . . 5B 74
Bryony Rd. W12 . . . 7C 80
Bryony Way TW16: Sun . . . 6J 129
Buccleugh Ho. E5 . . . 7G 49
Buchanan Cl. N21 . . . 5E 22
Buchanan Ct. *SE16* . . . 4K 103
(off Worgan St.)
Buchanan Gdns. NW10 . . . 2D 80
Buchan Ho. *W3* . . . 2H 97
(off Hanbury Rd.)
Buchan Rd. SE15 . . . 3J 121
Bucharest Rd. SW18 . . . 7A 118
Buckden Cl. N2 . . . 4D 46
SE12 . . . 6J 123
Buckfast Ct. *W13* . . . 7A 78
(off Romsey Rd.)
Buckfast Rd. SM4: Mord . . . 4K 153
Buckfast St. E2 . . . 3G 85
Buck Hill Wlk. W2 . . . 3B 10 (7B 82)
Buckhold Rd. SW18 . . . 6J 117
Buckhurst Av. SM5: Cars . . . 1C 166
Buckhurst Ct. *IG9: Buck H* . . . 2G 37
(off Albert Rd.)
IG9: Buck H . . . 1G 37
(Roding La.)
BUCKHURST HILL . . . 2F 37
Buckhurst Hill Ho. IG9: Buck H . . . 2E 36
Buckhurst Ho. N7 . . . 5H 65
Buckhurst St. E1 . . . 4H 85
Buckhurst Way IG9: Buck H . . . 4G 37
Buckingham Arc. WC2 . . . 3E 12
Buckingham Av. CR7: Thor H . . . 1A 156
DA16: Well . . . 4J 125
KT8: W Mole . . . 2F 149
N20 . . . 7F 21
TW14: Felt . . . 6K 111
UB6: G'frd . . . 1A 78
Buckingham Chambers *SW1* . . . 3B 18
(off Greencoat Pl.)
Buckingham Cl. BR5: Pet W . . . 7J 161
EN1: Enf . . . 2K 23
TW12: Hamp . . . 5D 130
W5 . . . 5C 78
Buckingham Ct. NW4 . . . 3C 44
UB5: N'olt . . . 2C 76
W7 . . . 4K 77
(off Copley Cl.)
W11 . . . 7J 81
(off Kensington Pk.)
Buckingham Dr. BR7: Chst . . . 4G 143
Buckingham Gdns. CR7: Thor H . . . 2A 156
HA8: Edg . . . 7K 27
KT8: W Mole . . . 2F 149
Buckingham Ga. SW1 . . . 1A 18 (3G 101)
Buckingham Gro. UB10: Hil . . . 2C 74
Buckingham La. SE23 . . . 7A 122
Buckingham Mans. *NW6* . . . 5K 63
(off West End La.)
Buckingham M. N1 . . . 6E 66
NW10 . . . 2B 80
SW1 . . . 1A 18
Buckingham Palace . . . 7K 11 (2F 101)
Buckingham Pal. Rd.
SW1 . . . 4J 17 (4F 101)
Buckingham Pde. HA7: Stan . . . 5H 27
Buckingham Pl. SW1 . . . 1A 18 (3G 101)
Buckingham Rd. CR4: Mitc . . . 4J 155
E10 . . . 3D 68
E11 . . . 5A 52
E15 . . . 5H 69
E18 . . . 1H 51
HA1: Harr . . . 5H 41
HA8: Edg . . . 7A 28
IG1: Ilf . . . 2H 71
KT1: King T . . . 4F 151
N1 . . . 6E 66
N22 . . . 1J 47
NW10 . . . 2B 80
TW10: Ham . . . 2D 132
TW12: Hamp . . . 4D 130
Buckingham St. WC2 . . . 4F 13 (7J 83)
Buckingham Way SM6: Wall . . . 7G 167
Buckland Cl. NW7 . . . 4H 29
Buckland Ct. *N1* . . . 2E 84
(off St John's Est.)
UB10: Ick . . . 2E 56
Buckland Cres. NW3 . . . 7B 64
Buckland Ho. *SW1* . . . 5F 101
(off Abbots Mnr.)
Buckland Ri. HA5: Pinn . . . 1A 40
Buckland Rd. BR6: Orp . . . 4J 173
E10 . . . 2E 68
KT9: Chess . . . 5F 163
Bucklands Rd. TW11: Tedd . . . 6C 132
Buckland St. N1 . . . 2D 84
Buckland's Wharf KT1: King T . . . 2D 150
Buckland Wlk. SM4: Mord . . . 4A 154
W3 . . . 2J 97
Buckland Way KT4: Wor Pk . . . 1E 164
Buck La. NW9 . . . 5K 43
Bucklebury *NW1* . . . 3A 6
(off Stanhope St.)
Buckleigh Av. SW20 . . . 3G 153
Buckleigh Rd. SW16 . . . 6H 137
Buckleigh Way SE19 . . . 7F 139
Buckler Gdns. SE9 . . . 3D 142
Bucklers All. SW6 . . . 6H 99
(not continuous)
Bucklersbury EC4 . . . 1E 14 (6D 84)
Bucklersbury Pas. EC2 . . . 6D 84
Buckler's Way SM5: Cars . . . 3D 166
Buckles Ct. DA17: Belv . . . 4D 108
Buckle St. E1 . . . 7K 9 (6F 85)
Buckley Cl. SE23 . . . 7H 121
Buckley Ct. NW6 . . . 7H 63
Buckley Ho. *W14* . . . 2G 99
(off Holland Pk. Av.)
Buckley Rd. NW6 . . . 7H 63
Buckmaster Cl. *SW9* . . . 3A 120
(off Stockwell Pk. Rd.)
Buckmaster Ho. N7 . . . 4K 65
Buckmaster Rd. SW11 . . . 4C 118
Bucknall St. WC2 . . . 7D 6 (6J 83)
Bucknall Way BR3: Beck . . . 4D 158
Bucknell Cl. SW2 . . . 4K 119
Buckner Rd. SW2 . . . 4K 119
Bucknill Ho. *SW1* . . . 5J 17
(off Ebury Bri. Rd.)
Buckrell Rd. E4 . . . 2A 36
Buckridge Ho. *EC1* . . . 5J 7
(off Portpool La.)
Buckshead Ho. *W2* . . . 5J 81
(off Brunel Est.)
Buckstone Cl. SE23 . . . 6J 121
Buckstone Rd. N18 . . . 5B 34
Buck St. NW1 . . . 7F 65
Buckters Rents SE16 . . . 1A 104
Buckthorne Rd. SE4 . . . 5A 122
Buckthorn Ho. *DA15: Sidc* . . . 3K 143
(off Longlands Rd.)
Buck Wlk. E17 . . . 4F 51
Buckwheat Ct. DA18: Erith . . . 3D 108
Budd Cl. N12 . . . 4E 30
Buddings Circ. HA9: Wemb . . . 3J 61
Budd's All. TW1: Twick . . . 5C 114
Bude Cl. E17 . . . 5B 50
Budge La. CR4: Mitc . . . 7D 154
Budge Row EC4 . . . 2E 14 (7D 84)
Budge's Wlk. W2 . . . 3A 10
Budleigh Cres. DA16: Well . . . 1C 126
Budleigh Ho. *SE15* . . . 7G 103
(off Bird in Bush Rd.)
Budoch Ct. IG3: Ilf . . . 2A 72
Budoch Dr. IG3: Ilf . . . 2A 72
Buer Rd. SW6 . . . 2G 117
Bugsby's Way SE7 . . . 4H 105
SE10 . . . 4H 105
Buick Ho. KT2: King T . . . 2G 151
Bulbarrow *NW8* . . . 1K 81
(off Abbey Rd.)
Bulganak Rd. CR7: Thor H . . . 4C 156
Bulinga St. SW1 . . . 4E 18
Bullace Row SE5 . . . 1D 120
Bull All. DA16: Well . . . 3B 126
Bullard Rd. TW11: Tedd . . . 6J 131
Bullard's Pl. E2 . . . 3K 85
Bullbanks Rd. DA17: Belv . . . 4J 109
Bulleid Way SW1 . . . 4K 17 (4F 101)
Bullen Ho. *E1* . . . 4H 85
(off Collingwood St.)
Bullen St. SW11 . . . 2C 118
Buller Cl. SE15 . . . 7G 103
Buller Rd. CR7: Thor H . . . 2D 156
IG11: Bark . . . 7J 71
N17 . . . 2G 49
N22 . . . 2A 48
NW10 . . . 3F 81
Bullers Cl. DA14: Sidc . . . 5E 144
Bullers Wood Dr.
BR7: Chst . . . 7D 142
Bullescroft Rd. HA8: Edg . . . 3B 28
Bullingham Mans. *W8* . . . 2J 99
(off Pitt St.)
Bull Inn Ct. WC2 . . . 3F 13
Bullivant St. E14 . . . 7E 86

Bull La. BR7: Chst 7H **143**
N18 . . . . 5K **33**
RM10: Dag 3H **73**
Bull Rd. E15 . . . . 2H **87**
Bullrush Cl. CR0: Croy 6E **156**
SM5: Cars 2C **166**
Bull's All. SW14 . . . . 2K **115**
Bull's Bri. Ind. Est. UB2: S'hall 4A **94**
Bulls Bri. Rd. UB2: S'hall 4A **94**
Bullsbrook Rd. UB4: Yead 1A **94**
Bulls Gdns. SW3 . . . . 3D **16** (4C **100**)
(not continuous)
Bulls Head Pas. EC3 . . . . 1G **15**
Bull Wharf La. EC4 . . . . 2D **14** (7C **84**)
Bull Wharf Wlk. *EC4* *3D **14***
(off Bull Wharf La.)
Bull Yd. SE15 . . . . 1G **121**
Bulmer Gdns. HA3: Kent 7D **42**
Bulmer M. W11 . . . . 7J **81**
Bulmer Pl. W11 . . . . 1J **99**
Bulow Est. *SW6* *1K **117***
(off Pearscroft Rd.)
Bulrington Cnr. *NW1* *7G **65***
(off Camden Rd.)
Bulstrode Av. TW3: Houn 2D **112**
Bulstrode Gdns. TW3: Houn 3E **112**
Bulstrode Pl. W1 . . . . 6H **5** (5E **82**)
Bulstrode Rd. TW3: Houn 3E **112**
Bulstrode St. W1 . . . . 7H **5** (6E **82**)
Bulwer Ct. E11 . . . . 1F **69**
Bulwer Ct. Rd. E11 . . . . 1F **69**
Bulwer Gdns. EN5: New Bar 4F **21**
Bulwer Rd. E11 . . . . 7F **51**
EN5: New Bar 4E **20**
N18 . . . . 4K **33**
Bulwer St. W12 . . . . 1E **98**
Bunbury Ho. *SE15* *7G **103***
(off Fenham Rd.)
Bunce's La. IG8: Wfd G 7C **36**
Bungalow Rd. SE25 . . . . 4E **156**
Bungalows, The E10 . . . . 6E **50**
IG6: Ilf 1J **53**
SM6: Wall 5F **167**
SW16 . . . . 7F **137**
Bunhill Row EC1 . . . . 3E **8** (4D **84**)
Bunhouse Pl. SW1 . . . . 5H **17** (5E **100**)
Bunkers Hill DA14: Sidc 3F **145**
DA17: Belv 4G **109**
NW11 . . . . 7A **46**
Bunning Way N7 . . . . 7J **65**
Bunns La. NW7 . . . . 6F **29**
(not continuous)
Bunsen Ho. *E3* *2A **86***
(off Grove Rd.)
Bunsen St. E3 . . . . 2A **86**
Buntingbridge Rd. IG2: Ilf 5H **53**
Bunting Cl. CR4: Mitc 5D **154**
N9 . . . . 1E **34**
Bunting Ct. NW9 . . . . 2A **44**
Bunton St. SE18 . . . . 3E **106**
Bunyan Ct. EC2 . . . . 5C **8**
Bunyan Rd. E17 . . . . 3A **50**
Buonaparte M. SW1 . . . . 5C **18** (5H **101**)
Burbage Cl. SE1 . . . . 3D **102**
UB3: Hayes 6F **75**
Burbage Ho. *N1* *1D **84***
(off Poole St.)
SE14 . . . . *6K **103***
(off Samuel Cl.)
Burbage Rd. SE21 . . . . 6C **120**
SE24 . . . . 6C **120**
Burberry Cl. KT3: N Mald 2A **152**
Burbidge Rd. TW17: Shep 4C **146**
Burbridge Way N17 . . . . 2G **49**
Burcham St. E14 . . . . 6D **86**
Burcharbro Rd. SE2 . . . . 6D **108**
Burchell Ct. WD23: Bush 1B **26**
Burchell Ho. *SE11* *5H **19***
(off Jonathan St.)
Burchell Rd. E10 . . . . 1D **68**
SE15 . . . . 1H **121**
Burcher Gale Gro. SE15 . . . . 7F **103**
Burchetts Way TW17: Shep 6D **146**
Burchett Way RM6: Chad H 6F **55**
Burchwall Cl. RM5: Col R 1J **55**
Burcote Rd. SW18 . . . . 7B **118**
Burden Cl. TW8: Bford 5C **96**
Burden Ho. *SW8* *7J **101***
(off Thorncroft St.)
Burdenshott Av. TW10: Rich 4H **115**
Burden Way E11 . . . . 2K **69**
Burder Cl. N1 . . . . 6E **66**
Burder Rd. N1 . . . . 6E **66**
Burdett Av. SW20 . . . . 1C **152**
Burdett Cl. DA14: Sidc 5E **144**
W7 . . . . 1K **95**
Burdett M. NW3 . . . . 6B **64**
W2 . . . . 6K **81**
Burdett Rd. CR0: Croy 6D **156**
E3 . . . . 4A **86**
E14 . . . . 4A **86**
TW9: Rich 2F **115**
Burdetts Rd. RM9: Dag 1F **91**
Burdock Cl. CR0: Croy 1K **169**
Burdock Rd. N17 . . . . 3G **49**
Burdon La. SM2: Cheam 7G **165**
Burdon Pk. SM2: Cheam 7H **165**
Bure Ct. EN5: New Bar 5E **20**
Burfield Cl. SW17 . . . . 4B **136**
Burford Cl. IG6: Ilf 4G **53**
RM8: Dag 3C **72**
UB10: Ick 4A **56**
Burford Gdns. N13 . . . . 3E **32**
Burford Ho. TW8: Bford 5D **96**
Burford Rd. BR1: Brom 4C **160**
E6 . . . . 3C **88**
E15 . . . . 1F **87**
KT4: Wor Pk 7B **152**
SE6 . . . . 2B **140**
SM1: Sutt 2J **165**
TW8: Bford 5E **96**
Burford Wlk. SW6 . . . . 7A **100**
Burford Way CR0: New Ad 6E **170**
Burford Wharf Apartments
E15 . . . . *1F **87***
(off Cam Rd.)
Burge Rd. E7 . . . . 4B **70**
Burges Gro. SW13 . . . . 7D **98**
Burges Rd. E6 . . . . 7C **70**
Burgess Av. NW9 . . . . 6K **43**
Burgess Bus. Pk. SE5 . . . . 7D **102**
Burgess Cl. TW13: Hanw 4C **130**
Burgess Ct. E6 . . . . 7E **70**
UB1: S'hall *6F **77***
(off Fleming Rd.)
Burgess Hill NW2 . . . . 4J **63**
Burgess Ho. *SE5* *7C **102***
(off Bethwin Rd.)
Burgess M. SW19 . . . . 6K **135**
Burgess Pk. Kart Track 6D **102**
Burgess Rd. E6 . . . . 7E **70**
E15 . . . . 4G **69**
SM1: Sutt 4K **165**
Burgess St. E14 . . . . 5C **86**
Burge St. SE1 . . . . 3D **102**
Burgh House 4B **64**
Burghill Rd. SE26 . . . . 4A **140**
Burghley Av. KT3: N Mald 1K **151**
Burghley Hall Cl. SW19 . . . . 1G **135**
Burghley Ho. SW19 . . . . 3G **135**
Burghley Pl. CR4: Mitc 5D **154**
Burghley Rd. E11 . . . . 1G **69**
N8 . . . . 3A **48**
NW5 . . . . 4F **65**
SW19 . . . . 4F **135**
Burghley Twr. W3 . . . . 7B **80**
Burgh St. N1 . . . . 2B **84**
Burgoine Quay KT1: Ham W 1D **150**
Burgon St. EC4 . . . . 1B **14** (6B **84**)
Burgos Cl. CR0: Wadd 6A **168**
Burgos Gro. SE10 . . . . 1D **122**
Burgoyne Rd. N4 . . . . 6B **48**
SE25 . . . . 4F **157**
SW9 . . . . 3K **119**
TW16: Sun 6H **129**
Burham Cl. SE20 . . . . 7J **139**
Burhill Gro. HA5: Pinn 2C **40**
Burke Cl. SW15 . . . . 4A **116**
Burke Lodge E13 . . . . 3K **87**
Burke St. E16 . . . . 5H **87**
(not continuous)
Burket Cl. UB2: S'hall 4C **94**
Burland Rd. SW11 . . . . 5D **118**
Burleigh Av. DA15: Sidc 5K **125**
SM6: Wall 3E **166**
Burleigh Cl. RM7: Mawney 4H **55**
Burleigh Gdns. N14 . . . . 1B **32**
TW15: Ashf 5E **128**
Burleigh Ho. SW3 . . . . 7B **16**
W10 . . . . *5G **81***
(off St Charles Sq.)
Burleigh Pde. N14 . . . . 1C **32**
Burleigh Pl. SW15 . . . . 5F **117**
Burleigh Rd. EN1: Enf 4K **23**
SM3: Sutt 1G **165**
UB10: Hil 1D **74**
Burleigh St. WC2 . . . . 2G **13** (7K **83**)
Burleigh Wlk. SE6 . . . . 1E **140**
Burleigh Way EN2: Enf 3J **23**
Burley Cl. E4 . . . . 5H **35**
SW16 . . . . 2H **155**
Burley Ho. *E1* *6K **85***
(off Chudleigh St.)
Burley Rd. E16 . . . . 6A **88**
Burlington Arc. W1 . . . . 3A **12** (7G **83**)
Burlington Av. RM7: Rom 6H **55**
TW9: Kew 1G **115**
Burlington Cl. BR6: Farnb 2F **173**
E6 . . . . 6C **88**
HA5: Eastc 3K **39**
TW14: Bedf 7F **111**
W9 . . . . 4J **81**
Burlington Gdns. RM6: Chad H 7E **54**
SW6 . . . . 2G **117**
W1 . . . . 3A **12** (7G **83**)
W3 . . . . 1J **97**
W4 . . . . 5J **97**
Burlington La. W4 . . . . 7J **97**
Burlington M. SW15 . . . . 5H **117**
W3 . . . . 1J **97**
Burlington Pl. IG8: Wfd G 3E **36**
SW6 . . . . 2G **117**
Burlington Ri. EN4: E Barn 1H **31**
Burlington Rd. CR7: Thor H 2C **156**
EN2: Enf 1J **23**
KT3: N Mald 4B **152**
N10 . . . . 3E **46**
N17 . . . . 1G **49**
SW6 . . . . 2G **117**
TW7: Isle 1H **113**
W4 . . . . 5J **97**
Burma M. N16 . . . . 4D **66**
Burma Rd. N16 . . . . 4D **66**
Burmarsh NW5 . . . . 6E **64**
Burmarsh Ct. SE20 . . . . 1J **157**
Burma Ter. SE19 . . . . 5E **138**
Burmester Rd. SW17 . . . . 3A **136**
Burnaby Cres. W4 . . . . 6J **97**
Burnaby Gdns. W4 . . . . 6H **97**
Burnaby St. SW10 . . . . 7A **100**
Burnand Ho. *W14* *3F **99***
(off Redan St.)
Burnard Pl. N7 . . . . 5K **65**
Burnaston Ho. E5 . . . . 3G **67**
Burnbrae Cl. N12 . . . . 6E **30**
Burnbury Rd. SW12 . . . . 1G **137**
Burncroft Av. EN3: Enf H 2D **24**
Burndell Way UB4: Yead 5B **76**
Burne Jones Ho. W14 . . . . 4G **99**
Burnell Av. DA16: Well 2A **126**
TW10: Ham 5C **132**
Burnell Gdns. HA7: Stan 2D **42**
Burnell Rd. SM1: Sutt 4K **165**
Burnell Wlk. *SE1* *5F **103***
(off Abingdon Cl.)
Burnels Av. E6 . . . . 3E **88**
Burness Cl. N7 . . . . 6K **65**
Burne St. NW1 . . . . 5C **4** (5C **82**)
Burnett Cl. E9 . . . . 5J **67**
Burnett Ho. *SE13* *2E **122***
(off Lewisham Hill)
Burnett Rd. IG6: Ilf 7K **37**
Burney Av. KT5: Surb 5F **151**
Burney St. SE10 . . . . 7E **104**
Burnfoot Av. SW6 . . . . 1G **117**
Burnham NW3 . . . . 7C **64**
Burnham Av. UB10: Ick 4E **56**
Burnham Cl. EN1: Enf 1K **23**
HA3: W'stone 4A **42**
NW7 . . . . 7H **29**
SE1 . . . . 4F **103**
Burnham Ct. *NW4* *4E **44***
(off Brent St.)
W2 . . . . *7K **81***
(off Moscow Rd.)
Burnham Cres. E11 . . . . 4A **52**
Burnham Dr. KT4: Wor Pk 2F **165**
Burnham Est. *E2* *3J **85***
(off Burnham St.)
Burnham Gdns. CR0: Croy 7F **157**
TW4: Cran 1K **111**
UB3: Harl 3F **93**
Burnham Rd. DA14: Sidc 2E **144**
E4 . . . . 5G **35**
RM7: Rom 3K **55**
RM9: Dag 7B **72**
SM4: Mord 4K **153**
Burnham St. E2 . . . . 3J **85**
KT2: King T 1G **151**
Burnham Way SE26 . . . . 5B **140**
W13 . . . . 4B **96**
Burnhill Cl. SE15 . . . . 7H **103**
Burnhill Rd. BR3: Beck 2C **158**
Burnley Rd. NW10 . . . . 5B **62**
SW9 . . . . 2K **119**
Burnsall St. SW3 . . . . 6D **16** (5C **100**)
Burns Av. DA15: Sidc 6B **126**
RM6: Chad H 7C **54**
TW14: Felt 6J **111**
UB1: S'hall 7E **76**
Burns Cl. DA16: Well 1K **125**
E17 . . . . 4E **50**
SW19 . . . . 6B **136**
UB4: Hayes 5H **75**
Burns Ho. *E2* *3J **85***
(off Cornwall Av.)
SE17 . . . . *5B **102***
(off Doddington Gro.)
Burnside Av. E4 . . . . 6G **35**
Burnside Cl. EN5: New Bar 3D **20**
SE16 . . . . 1K **103**
TW1: Twick 6A **114**
Burnside Ct. SM5: Cars 3E **166**
Burnside Cres. HA0: Wemb 1D **78**
Burnside Rd. RM8: Dag 2C **72**
Burns Rd. HA0: Wemb 2E **78**
NW10 . . . . 1B **80**
SW11 . . . . 2D **118**
W13 . . . . 2B **96**
Burns Way TW5: Hest 2B **112**
Burnt Ash Hgts. BR1: Brom 5K **141**
Burnt Ash Hill SE12 . . . . 6H **123**
Burnt Ash La. BR1: Brom 7J **141**
Burnt Ash Rd. SE12 . . . . 5H **123**
Burnthwaite Rd. SW6 . . . . 7H **99**
BURNT OAK 2J **43**
Burnt Oak B'way. HA8: Edg 7B **28**
Burnt Oak Flds. HA8: Edg 1J **43**
Burnt Oak La. DA15: Sidc 6A **126**
Burntwood Cl. SW18 . . . . 1C **136**
Burntwood Grange Rd. SW18 . . . . 1B **136**
Burntwood La. SW17 . . . . 3A **136**
Burntwood Vw. SE19 . . . . 5F **139**
Buross St. E1 . . . . 6H **85**
Burpham Cl. UB4: Yead 5B **76**
Burrage Ct. *SE16* *4K **103***
(off Worgan St.)
Burrage Gro. SE18 . . . . 4G **107**
Burrage Pl. SE18 . . . . 5F **107**
Burrage Rd. SE18 . . . . 6G **107**
Burrard Ho. *E2* *2J **85***
(off Bishop's Way)

Burrard Rd.—Byron Av. E.

Burrard Rd. E16 6K **87**
NW6 5J **63**
Burr Cl. DA7: Bex 3F **127**
E1 4K **15** (1G **103**)
Burrell Cl. CR0: Croy 6A **158**
HA8: Edg 2C **28**
Burrell Row BR3: Beck 2C **158**
Burrell St. SE1 4A **14** (1B **102**)
Burrells Wharf Sq. E14 5D **104**
Burrell Towers E10 7C **50**
Burrhill Ct. *SE16* *3K* ***103***
(off Worgan St.)
Burritt Rd. KT1: King T 2G **151**
Burroughs, The NW4 4D **44**
Burroughs Club, The 4D **44**
Burroughs Cotts. *E14* *5A* ***86***
(off Halley St.)
Burroughs Gdns. NW4 4D **44**
Burroughs Pde. NW4 4D **44**
Burrow Ho. *SW9* *2A* ***120***
(off Stockwell Pk. Rd.)
Burrow Rd. SE22 4E **120**
Burrows M. SE1 6A **14** (2B **102**)
Burrows Rd. NW10 3E **80**
Burrow Wlk. SE21 7C **120**
Burr Rd. SW18 1J **135**
Bursar St. SE1 5G **15** (1E **102**)
Bursdon Cl. DA15: Sidc 2K **143**
Bursland Rd. EN3: Pond E 4E **24**
Burslem St. E1 6G **85**
Burstock Rd. SW15 4G **117**
Burston Rd. SW15 5F **117**
Burston Vs. *SW15* *5F* ***117***
(off St John's Av.)
Burstow Rd. SW20 1G **153**
Burtenshaw Rd. KT7: T Ditt 7A **150**
Burtley Cl. N4 1C **66**
Burton Bank *N1* *7D* ***66***
(off Yeate St.)
Burton Cl. CR7: Thor H 3D **156**
KT9: Chess 7D **162**
Burton Ct. KT7: T Ditt 6A **150**
SE20 2J **157**
SW3 *5F* ***17***
(off Franklin's Row, not continuous)
Burton Gdns. TW5: Houn 1D **112**
Burton Gro. SE17 5D **102**
Burtonhole Cl. NW7 4A **30**
Burtonhole La. N12 4B **30**
NW7 5K **29**
Burton Ho. *SE16* *2H* ***103***
(off Cherry Gdn. St.)
Burton La. SW9 2A **120**
(not continuous)
Burton M. SW1 4H **17** (4E **100**)
Burton Pl. WC1 2D **6** (3H **83**)
Burton Rd. E18 3K **51**
KT2: King T 7E **132**
NW6 7H **63**
SW9 2B **120**
(Akerman Rd.)
SW9 2A **120**
(Evesham Wlk.)
Burton's Rd. TW12: Ham H 4F **131**
Burton St. WC1 2D **6** (3H **83**)
Burtonwood Ho. N4 7D **48**
Burtop Rd. Est. SW17 3A **136**
Burt Rd. E16 1A **106**
Burts Wharf DA17: Belv 7J **91**
Burtt Ho. *N1* *1G* ***9***
(off Aske St.)
Burtwell La. SE27 4D **138**
Burwash Ho. *SE1* *7F* ***15***
(off Kipling Est.)
Burwash Rd. SE18 5H **107**
Burwell *KT1: King T* *2G* ***151***
(off Excelsior Rd.)
Burwell Av. UB6: G'frd 6J **59**
Burwell Cl. E1 6H **85**
Burwell Rd. E10 1A **68**
Burwell Rd. Ind. Est.
E10 1A **68**
Burwell Wlk. E3 4C **86**
Burwood Av. BR2: Hayes 2K **171**
HA5: Eastc 5K **39**
Burwood Cl. KT6: Surb 1G **163**
Burwood Ho. SW9 4B **120**
Burwood Pl. EN4: Had W 1F **21**
W2 7D **4** (6C **82**)
Bury Av. HA4: Ruis 6E **38**
UB4: Hayes 2G **75**
Bury Cl. SE16 1K **103**
Bury Ct. EC3 7H **9** (6E **84**)
Bury Gro. SM4: Mord 5K **153**
Bury Hall Vs. N9 7A **24**
Bury Pl. WC1 6E **6** (5J **83**)
Bury Rd. E4 1B **36**
N22 2A **48**
RM10: Dag 5H **73**
Buryside Cl. IG2: Ilf 4K **53**
Bury St. EC3 1H **15** (6E **84**)
HA4: Ruis 5E **38**
N9 7A **24**
SW1 4B **12** (1G **101**)
Bury St. W. N9 7J **23**
Bury Wlk. SW3 4C **16** (4C **100**)
Busbridge Ho. *E14* *5C* ***86***
(off Brabazon St.)
Busby Ho. SW16 4G **137**
Busby M. NW5 6H **65**
Busby Pl. NW5 6H **65**
Busch Cl. TW7: Isle 1B **114**
Bushbaby Cl. SE1 3E **102**
Bushberry Rd. E9 6A **68**
Bush Cl. IG2: Ilf 5H **53**
Bush Cotts. SW18 5J **117**
Bush Ct. N14 1C **32**
W12 2F **99**
Bushell Cl. SW2 2K **137**
Bushell Grn. WD23: Bushy 2C **26**
Bushell St. E1 1G **103**
Bushell Way BR7: Chst 5E **142**
BUSHEY 1C **26**
Bushey Av. BR5: Pet W 7H **161**
E18 3H **51**
Bushey Cl. E4 3K **35**
UB10: Ick 2C **56**
Bushey Ct. SW20 3D **152**
Bushey Down SW12 2F **137**
BUSHEY HEATH 1C **26**
Bushey Hill Rd. SE5 1E **120**
Bushey La. SM1: Sutt 4J **165**
BUSHEY MEAD 2F **153**
Bushey Rd. CR0: Croy 2C **170**
E13 2A **88**
N15 6E **48**
SM1: Sutt 4J **165**
SW20 3D **152**
UB3: Harl 4G **93**
UB10: Ick 2C **56**
Bushey Way BR3: Beck 6F **159**
Bush Fair Ct. N14 6A **22**
Bushfield Cl. HA8: Edg 2C **28**
Bushfield Cres. HA8: Edg 2C **28**
Bush Gro. HA7: Stan 1D **42**
NW9 7J **43**
Bushgrove Rd. RM8: Dag 4D **72**
Bush Hill N21 7H **23**
Bush Hill Pde. EN1 7J **23**
BUSH HILL PARK 6A **24**
Bush Hill Rd. HA3: Kent 6F **43**
N21 6J **23**
Bush Ind. Est. N19 3G **65**
NW10 4K **79**
Bush La. EC4 2E **14** (7D **84**)
Bushmead Cl. N15 4F **49**
Bushmoor Cres. SE18 7F **107**
Bushnell Rd. SW17 2F **137**
Bush Rd. E8 1H **85**
E11 7H **51**
IG9: Buck H 4G **37**
SE8 *4K* ***103***
(off Rotherhithe New Rd.)
TW9: Kew 6F **97**
TW17: Shep 5B **146**
Bush Theatre 2E **98**
Bushway RM8: Dag 4D **72**
Bushwood E11 1H **69**
Bushwood Dr. SE1 4F **103**
Bushwood Rd. TW9: Kew 6G **97**
Bushy Ct. *KT1: Ham W* *1C* ***150***
(off Up. Teddington Rd.)
Bushy Lees DA15: Sidc 6K **125**
Bushy Pk. Gdns. TW11: Tedd 5H **131**
Bushy Pk. Rd. TW11: Tedd 7B **132**
(not continuous)
Bushy Rd. TW11: Tedd 6K **131**
Business Design Cen. *1A* ***84***
(off Upper St.)
Buspace Studios *W10* *4G* ***81***
(off Conlan St.)
Butcher Row E1 7K **85**
E14 7K **85**
Butchers Rd. E16 6J **87**
Bute Av. TW10: Ham 2E **132**
Bute Ct. SM6: Wall 5G **167**
Bute Gdns. SM6: Wall 5G **167**
TW10: Ham 1E **132**
W6 4F **99**
Bute Gdns. W. SM6: Wall 5G **167**
Bute M. NW11 5A **46**
Bute Rd. CR0: Croy 1A **168**
IG6: Ilf 5F **53**
SM6: Wall 4G **167**
Bute St. SW7 3A **16** (4B **100**)
Bute Wlk. N1 6D **66**
Butfield Ho. *E9* *6J* ***67***
(off Stevens Av.)
Butler Av. HA1: Harr 7H **41**
Butler Ct. HA0: Wemb 4A **60**
RM8: Dag *2G* ***73***
(off Gosfield Rd.)
Butler Ho. *E2* *3J* ***85***
(off Bacton St.)
E14 *6B* ***86***
(off Burdett St.)
SW9 *1B* ***120***
(off Lothian Rd.)
Butler Pl. SW1 1C **18** (3H **101**)
Butler Rd. HA1: Harr 7G **41**
NW10 7B **62**
RM8: Dag 4B **72**
Butlers & Colonial Wharf *SE1* *6K* ***15***
(off Shad Thames)
Butlers Cl. TW3: Houn 3D **112**
Butlers Dr. E4 1K **25**
Butler St. E2 3J **85**
UB10: Hil 4D **74**
Butlers Wharf SE1 1F **103**
Butlers Wharf W. *SE1* *5J* ***15***
(off Shad Thames)
Butley Ct. *E3* *2A* ***86***
(off Ford St.)
Buttercup Cl. UB5: N'olt 6D **58**
Butterfield Cl. N17 6H **33**
SE16 2H **103**
TW1: Twick 6K **113**
Butterfields E17 5E **50**
Butterfield Sq. E6 6D **88**
Butterfly La. SE9 6F **125**
Butterfly Wlk. *SE5* *1D* ***120***
(off Denmark Hill)
Butter Hill SM5: Cars 3E **166**
SM6: Wall 3E **166**
Butteridges Cl. RM9: Dag 1F **91**
Buttermere *NW1* *1K* ***5***
(off Augustus St.)
Buttermere Cl. E15 4F **69**
SE1 4F **103**
SM4: Mord 6F **153**
TW14: Felt 1H **129**
Buttermere Ct. *NW8* *1B* ***82***
(off Boundary Rd.)
Buttermere Dr. SW15 5G **117**
Buttermere Wlk. E8 6F **67**
Butterwick W6 4F **99**
Butterworth Gdns. IG8: Wfd G 6D **36**
Butterworth Ter. *SE17* *5C* ***102***
(off Sutherland Wlk.)
Buttesland St. N1 1F **9** (3D **84**)
Buttfield Cl. RM10: Dag 6H **73**
Buttmarsh Cl. SE18 5F **107**
Butts, The TW8: Bford 6C **96**
TW16: Sun 3A **148**
Buttsbury Rd. IG1: Ilf 5G **71**
Butts Cres. TW13: Hanw 3E **130**
Buttsmead HA6: Nwood 1E **38**
Butts Piece UB5: Yead 2K **75**
Butts Rd. BR1: Brom 5G **141**
Buxhall Cres. E9 6B **68**
Buxted Rd. E8 7F **67**
N12 5H **31**
SE22 4E **120**
Buxton Cl. IG8: Wfd G 6G **37**
N9 2D **34**
Buxton Ct. E11 7H **51**
N1 1D **8**
Buxton Cres. SM3: Cheam 4G **165**
Buxton Dr. E11 4G **51**
KT3: N Mald 2K **151**
Buxton Gdns. W3 7H **79**
Buxton Ho. E11 4G **51**
Buxton M. SW4 2H **119**
Buxton Rd. CR7: Thor H 5B **156**
DA8: Erith 7K **109**
E4 1A **36**
E6 3C **88**
E15 5G **69**
E17 4A **50**
(not continuous)
IG2: Ilf 6J **53**
N19 1H **65**
NW2 6D **62**
SW14 3A **116**
TW15: Ashf 5A **128**
Buxton St. E1 4K **9** (4F **85**)
Buzzard Creek Ind. Est.
IG11: Bark 5A **90**
Byam St. SW6 2A **118**
Byards Ct. *SE16* *4K* ***103***
(off Worgan St.)
Byards Cft. SW16 1H **155**
Byatt Wlk. TW12: Hamp 6C **130**
Bychurch End TW11: Tedd 5K **131**
Bycroft Rd. UB1: S'hall 4E **76**
Bycroft St. SE20 7K **139**
Bycullah Av. EN2: Enf 3G **23**
Bycullah Rd. EN2: Enf 2G **23**
Bye, The W3 6A **80**
Byegrove Rd. SW19 6B **136**
Byelands Cl. SE16 1K **103**
Bye Way, The HA3: W'stone 1J **41**
Byeway, The SW14 3J **115**
Byeways TW2: Twick 3F **131**
Byeways, The KT5: Surb 5G **151**
Byfeld Gdns. SW13 1C **116**
Byfield Cl. SE16 2B **104**
Byfield Rd. TW7: Isle 3A **114**
Byford Cl. E15 7G **69**
Byford Ho. EN5: Barn 4A **20**
Bygrove CR0: New Ad 6D **170**
Bygrove St. E14 6D **86**
(not continuous)
Byland Cl. N21 7E **22**
SM5: Cars 7A **154**
Bylands Cl. SE2 3B **108**
Byne Rd. SE26 6J **139**
SM5: Cars 2C **166**
Bynes Rd. CR2: S Croy 7D **168**
Byng Pl. WC1 4D **6** (4H **83**)
Byng Rd. EN5: Barn 2A **20**
Byng St. E14 2C **104**
Bynon Av. DA7: Bex 3F **127**
Byre Rd. N14 6A **22**
Byrne Rd. SW12 1F **137**
Byron Av. E12 6C **70**
E18 3H **51**
KT3: N Mald 5C **152**
NW9 4H **43**
SM1: Sutt 4B **166**
TW4: Cran 2J **111**
Byron Av. E. SM1: Sutt 4B **166**

Byron Cl. E8 . . . . 1G **85**
KT12: Walt T 7C **148**
SE20 . . . . 3H **157**
SE26 . . . . 4A **140**
SE28 . . . . 1C **108**
SW16 . . . . 6J **137**
TW12: Hamp 4D **130**
Byron Ct. *E11* *4K 51*
(off Makepeace Rd.)
EN2: Enf 2G **23**
HA1: Harr 6J **41**
NW6 . . . . *7A 64*
(off Fairfax Rd.)
SE22 . . . . 1G **139**
SW3 . . . . *4D 16*
(off Whiteheads Gro.)
W7 . . . . *4A 96*
(off Boston Rd.)
W9 . . . . *4J 81*
(off Lanhill Rd.)
WC1 . . . . *3G 7*
(off Mecklenburgh Sq.)
Byron Dr. DA8: Erith 7H **109**
N2 . . . . 6B **46**
Byron Gdns. SM1: Sutt 4B **166**
Byron Hill Rd. HA2: Harr 1H **59**
Byron Ho. DA1: Cray 5K **127**
Byron M. NW3 . . . . 4C **64**
W9 . . . . 4J **81**
Byron Pde. UB10: Hil 4E **74**
Byron Rd. E10 . . . . 1D **68**
E17 . . . . 3C **50**
HA0: Wemb 2C **60**
HA1: Harr 6J **41**
HA3: W'stone 2K **41**
NW2 . . . . 2D **62**
NW7 . . . . 5H **29**
W5 . . . . 1F **97**
Byron St. E14 . . . . 6E **86**
Byron Ter. N9 . . . . 6D **24**
Byron Way UB4: Hayes 4H **75**
UB5: N'olt 3C **76**
UB7: W Dray 4B **92**
Bysouth Cl. IG5: Ilf 1F **53**
N15 . . . . 4D **48**
Bythorn St. SW9 . . . . 3K **119**
Byton Rd. SW17 . . . . 6D **136**
Byward Av. TW14: Felt 6A **112**
Byward St. EC3 . . . . 3H **15** (7E **84**)
Bywater Ho. SE18 . . . . 3C **106**
Bywater Pl. SE16 . . . . 1A **104**
Bywater St. SW3 . . . . 5E **16** (5D **100**)
Byway E11 . . . . 5A **52**
Byway, The KT19: Ewe 4B **164**
SM2: Sutt 7B **166**
Bywell Pl. W1 . . . . 6A **6**
Bywood Av. CR0: Croy 6J **157**
Byworth Wlk. N19 . . . . 1J **65**

C

Cabbell St. NW1 . . . . 6C **4** (5C **82**)
Cabinet Way E4 . . . . 6G **35**
Cable Ho. *WC1* *1J 7*
(off Gt. Percy St.)
Cable Pl. SE10 . . . . 1E **122**
Cables Cl. DA17: Erith 3J **109**
Cable St. E1 . . . . 7G **85**
Cable Trade Pk. SE7 . . . . 4A **106**
Cabot Ct. *SE16* *4K 103*
(off Worgan St.)
Cabot Sq. E14 . . . . 1C **104**
Cabot Way E6 . . . . 1B **88**
Cabul Rd. SW11 . . . . 2C **118**
Caci Ho. *W14* *4H 99*
(off Kensington Village)
Cactus Cl. SE15 . . . . 2E **120**
Cactus Wlk. W12 . . . . 6B **80**
Cadbury Cl. TW7: Isle 1A **114**
TW16: Sun 7G **129**
Cadbury Rd. TW16: Sun 7G **129**
Cadbury Way SE16 . . . . 3F **103**
Caddington Cl. EN4: E Barn 5H **21**
Caddington Rd. NW2 . . . . 3G **63**
Caddis Cl. HA7: Stan 7E **26**
Cadell Cl. E2 . . . . 1K **9** (2F **85**)
Cade Rd. SE10 . . . . 1F **123**
Cader Rd. SW18 . . . . 6A **118**
Cadet Dr. SE1 . . . . 4F **103**
Cadet Pl. SE10 . . . . 5G **105**
Cadiz Ct. RM10: Dag 7K **73**
Cadiz Rd. RM10: Dag 7J **73**
Cadiz St. SE17 . . . . 5C **102**
Cadley Ter. SE23 . . . . 2J **139**
Cadman Cl. SW9 . . . . 7B **102**
Cadman Ct. *W4* *5H 97*
(off Chaseley Dr.)
Cadmer Cl. KT3: N Mald 4A **152**
Cadmore Ho. *N1* *7B 66*
(off The Sutton Est.)
Cadmus Cl. SW4 . . . . 3H **119**
Cadmus Ct. *SW9* *1A 120*
(off Southey Rd.)
Cadnam Lodge *E14* *3E 104*
(off Schooner Cl.)
Cadnam Point SW15 . . . . 1D **134**
Cadogan Cl. BR3: Beck 1F **159**
E9 . . . . 7B **68**
HA2: Harr 4F **59**
TW11: Tedd 5J **131**
Cadogan Ct. SM2: Sutt 6K **165**
SW3 . . . . *4E 16*
(off Draycott Av.)
Cadogan Ct. Gdns. *SW1* *3G 17*
(off D'Oyley St.)
Cadogan Gdns. E18 . . . . 3K **51**
N3 . . . . 1K **45**
N21 . . . . 5F **23**
SW3 . . . . 3F **17** (4D **100**)
Cadogan Ga. SW1 . . . . 3F **17** (4D **100**)
Cadogan Hall *3G 17*
(off Wilbraham Pl.)
Cadogan Ho. IG8: Ilf 7K **37**
SW3 . . . . 7B **16**
Cadogan La. SW1 . . . . 2G **17** (3E **100**)
Cadogan Mans. *SW3* *4F 17*
(off Cadogan Gdns.)
Cadogan Pl. SW1 . . . . 1F **17** (3D **100**)
Cadogan Rd. KT6: Surb 5D **150**
SE18 . . . . 3G **107**
Cadogan Sq. SW1 . . . . 2E **16** (3D **100**)
Cadogan St. SW3 . . . . 4E **16** (4D **100**)
Cadogan Ter. E9 . . . . 6B **68**
Cadoxton Av. N15 . . . . 6F **49**
Cadwallon Rd. SE9 . . . . 2F **143**
Caedmon Rd. N7 . . . . 4K **65**
Caerleon Cl. DA14: Sidc 5C **144**
KT10: Clay 7B **162**
Caerleon Ter. SE2 . . . . 4B **108**
Caernafon Ho. HA7: Stan 5F **27**
Caernarvon Cl. CR4: Mitc 3J **155**
Caernarvon Dr. IG5: Ilf 1E **52**
Caernarvon Ho. *E16* *1K 105*
(off Audley Dr.)
W2 . . . . *6A 82*
(off Hallfield Est.)
Caesar Ct. *E2* *2K 85*
(off Palmer's Rd.)
Caesars Wlk. CR4: Mitc 5D **154**
Caesars Way TW17: Shep 6F **147**
Cafe Gallery 3J 103
Cahill St. EC1 . . . . 4D **8** (4C **84**)
Cahir St. E14 . . . . 4D **104**
Cain Ct. *W5* *5C 78*
(off Castlebar M.)
Caine Ho. *W3* *2H 97*
(off Hanbury Rd.)
Cain's La. TW14: Felt 5G **111**
Caird St. W10 . . . . 3G **81**
Cairn Av. W5 . . . . 1D **96**
Cairncross M. *N8* *6J 47*
(off Felix Av.)
Cairndale Cl. BR1: Brom 7H **141**
Cairnfield Av. NW2 . . . . 3A **62**
Cairngorm Cl. TW11: Tedd 5A **132**
Cairns Av. IG8: Wfd G 6H **37**
Cairns M. SE18 . . . . 1C **124**
Cairns Rd. SW11 . . . . 5C **118**
Cairn Way HA7: Stan 6E **26**
Cairo New Rd. CR0: Croy 2B **168**
Cairo Rd. E17 . . . . 4C **50**
Caister Ho. N7 . . . . 6K **65**
Caistor Ho. *E15* *1H 87*
(off Caistor Pk. Rd.)
Caistor M. SW12 . . . . 7F **119**
Caistor Pk. Rd. E15 . . . . 1H **87**
Caistor Rd. SW12 . . . . 7F **119**
Caithness Gdns. DA15: Sidc 6K **125**
Caithness Ho. *N1* *1K 83*
(off Twyford St.)
Caithness Rd. CR4: Mitc 7F **137**
W14 . . . . 3F **99**
Calabria Rd. N5 . . . . 6B **66**
Calais Ga. SE5 . . . . 1B **120**
Calais St. SE5 . . . . 1B **120**
Calbourne Rd. SW12 . . . . 7D **118**
Calcott Ct. *W14* *3G 99*
(off Blythe Rd.)
Calcott Wlk. SE9 . . . . 4C **142**
Calcraft Ho. *E2* *2J 85*
(off Bonner Rd.)
Caldbeck Av. KT4: Wor Pk 2C **164**
Caldecote *KT1: King T* *2G 151*
(off Excelsior Cl.)
Caldecote Gdns. WD23: Bush 1D **26**
CALDECOTE HILL 1E 26
Caldecot Rd. SE5 . . . . 2C **120**
Caldecott Way E5 . . . . 3K **67**
Calder Av. UB6: G'frd 2K **77**
Calder Cl. EN1: Enf 3K **23**
Calder Ct. SE16 . . . . 1B **104**
Calder Gdns. HA8: Edg 3G **43**
Calderon Ho. *NW8* *2C 82*
(off Townshend Est.)
Calderon Pl. W10 . . . . 5E **80**
Calderon Rd. E11 . . . . 4E **68**
Calder Rd. SM4: Mord 5A **154**
Caldervale Rd. SW4 . . . . 5H **119**
Calderwood St. SE18 . . . . 4E **106**
(not continuous)
Caldew Ct. NW7 . . . . 7H **29**
Caldew St. SE5 . . . . 7D **102**
Caldicot Grn. NW9 . . . . 6A **44**
Caldwell Ho. *SW13* *7E 98*
(off Trinity Church Rd.)
Caldwell St. SW9 . . . . 7K **101**
Caldy Rd. DA17: Belv 3H **109**
Caldy Wlk. N1 . . . . 7C **66**
Caleb St. SE1 . . . . 6C **14** (2C **102**)
Caledonia Ct. *IG11: Bark* *2C 90*
(off Keel Cl.)
Caledonia Ho. *E14* *6A 86*
(off Salmon La.)
Caledonian Cl. IG3: Ilf 1B **72**
Caledonian Ct. UB5: N'olt 4C **76**
Caledonian Rd. N1 . . . . 1F **7** (2J **83**)
N7 . . . . 4K **65**
Caledonian Sq. NW1 . . . . 6H **65**
Caledonian Wharf E14 . . . . 4F **105**
Caledonia Rd. TW19: Stanw 1A **128**
Caledonia St. N1 . . . . 1F **7** (2J **83**)
Caledon Rd. E6 . . . . 1D **88**
SM6: Wall 4E **166**
Cale St. SW3 . . . . 5C **16** (5C **100**)
Caletock Way SE10 . . . . 5H **105**
Calgarth *NW1* *1B 6*
(off Ampthill Est.)
Calgary Ct. *SE16* *2J 103*
(off Canada Est.)
Caliban Twr. *N1* *2E 84*
(off Arden Est.)
Calico Ho. *EC4* *1D 14*
(off Well Ct.)
Calico Row SW11 . . . . 3A **118**
Calidore Cl. SW2 . . . . 6K **119**
California Bldg. *SE10* *1D 122*
(off Deal's Gateway)
California La. WD23: Bushy 1C **26**
California Pl. *WD23: Bushy* *1C 26*
(off High Rd.)
California Rd. KT3: N Mald 4H **151**
Callaby Ter. N1 . . . . 6D **66**
Callaghan Cl. SE13 . . . . 4G **123**
Callahan Cotts. *E1* *5J 85*
(off Lindley St.)
Callander Rd. SE6 . . . . 2D **140**
Callanders, The WD23: Bushy 1D **26**
Callard Av. N13 . . . . 4G **33**
Callcott Ct. NW6 . . . . 7H **63**
Callcott Rd. NW6 . . . . 7H **63**
Callcott St. W8 . . . . 1J **99**
Callendar Rd. SW7 . . . . 1A **16** (3B **100**)
Callenders Cotts. DA17: Erith 2K **109**
Callingham Cl. E14 . . . . 5B **86**
Callis Farm Cl. TW19: Stanw 6A **110**
Callisons Pl. SE10 . . . . 5G **105**
Callis Rd. E17 . . . . 6B **50**
Callonfield E17 . . . . 4K **49**
Callow St. SW3 . . . . 7A **16** (6B **100**)
Cally Swimming Pool 1K 83
Calmington Rd. SE5 . . . . 6E **102**
Calmont Rd. BR1: Brom 6F **141**
Calne Av. IG5: Ilf 1F **53**
Calonne Rd. SW19 . . . . 4F **135**
Calshot Ho. *N1* *2K 83*
(off Calshot St.)
Calshot Rd. TW6: H'row A 2C **110**
(not continuous)
Calshot St. N1 . . . . 1G **7** (2K **83**)
Calshot Way EN2: Enf 3G **23**
TW6: H'row A 2C **110**
(not continuous)
Calstock *NW1* *1G 83*
(off Royal Coll. St.)
Calstock Ho. SE11 . . . . 5K **19**
Calthorpe Gdns. HA8: Edg 5K **27**
(not continuous)
SM1: Sutt 3A **166**
Calthorpe St. WC1 . . . . 3H **7** (4K **83**)
Calton Av. SE21 . . . . 6E **120**
Calton Rd. EN5: New Bar 6F **21**
Calverley Cl. BR3: Beck 6D **140**
Calverley Cres. RM10: Dag 2G **73**
Calverley Gdns. HA3: Kent 7D **42**
Calverley Gro. N19 . . . . 1H **65**
Calverley Rd. KT17: Ewe 6C **164**
Calvert Av. E2 . . . . 2H **9** (3E **84**)
Calvert Cl. DA14: Sidc 6E **144**
DA17: Belv 4G **109**
Calvert Dr. DA2: Bexl 2K **145**
Calvert Ho. *W12* *7D 80*
(off White City Est.)
Calverton *SE5* *6E 102*
(off Albany Rd.)
Calverton Rd. E6 . . . . 1E **88**
Calvert Rd. EN5: Barn 2A **20**
SE10 . . . . 5H **105**
Calvert's Bldgs. SE1 . . . . 5E **14** (1D **102**)
Calvert St. NW1 . . . . 1E **82**
Calvin St. E1 . . . . 4J **9** (4F **85**)
Calydon Rd. SE7 . . . . 5K **105**
Calypso Cres. SE15 . . . . 7F **103**
Calypso Way SE16 . . . . 3B **104**
Camac Rd. TW2: Twick 1H **131**
Camarthen Grn. NW9 . . . . 5A **44**
Cambalt Rd. SW15 . . . . 5F **117**
Cambay Ho. *E1* *4A 86*
(off Harford St.)
Camber Ho. SE15 . . . . 6J **103**
Camberley Av. EN1: Enf 4K **23**
SW20 . . . . 2D **152**
Camberley Cl. SM3: Cheam 3F **165**
Camberley Ho. NW1 . . . . 1K **5**
Camberley Rd. TW6: H'row A 3C **110**
Cambert Way SE3 . . . . 4K **123**
CAMBERWELL 1D 120
Camberwell Church St. SE5 . . . . 1D **120**
Camberwell Glebe SE5 . . . . 1E **120**
CAMBERWELL GREEN **1D 120**
Camberwell Grn. SE5 . . . . 1D **120**
Camberwell Gro. SE5 . . . . 1D **120**

Camberwell Leisure Cen. 1D 120
Camberwell New Rd. SE5 6A 102
Camberwell Pl. SE5 1C 120
Camberwell Rd. SE5 6C 102
Camberwell Sta. Rd. SE5 1C 120
Camberwell Trad. Est. SE5 1B 120
Cambeys Rd. RM10: Dag 5H 73
Camborne Av. W13 2B 96
Camborne Cl. TW6: H'row A 3C 110
Camborne Cres. TW6: H'row A 3C 110
Camborne Rd. CR0: Croy 7G 157
DA14: Sidc 3C 144
DA16: Well 2K 125
SM2: Sutt 7J 165
SM4: Mord 5F 153
SW18 7J 117
TW6: H'row A 3C 110
Camborne Way TW5: Hest 1E 112
TW6: H'row A 3C 110
Cambourne Av. N9 7E 24
Cambourne M. W11 6G 81
Cambourne Wlk. TW10: Rich 6D 114
Cambrai Ct. N13 3D 32
Cambray Rd. BR6: Orp 7K 161
SW12 1G 137
Cambria Cl. DA15: Sidc 1H 143
TW3: Houn 4E 112
Cambria Ct. TW14: Felt 7K 111
Cambria Gdns. TW19: Stanw 7A 110
(not continuous)
Cambria Ho. *E14* *6A 86*
(off Salmon La.)
SE26 *4G 139*
(off High Level Dr.)
Cambrian Av. IG2: Ilf 5J 53
Cambrian Cl. SE27 3B 138
Cambrian Grn. *NW9* *5A 44*
(off Snowden Dr.)
Cambrian Rd. E10 7C 50
TW10: Rich 6F 115
Cambria Rd. SE5 3C 120
Cambria St. SW6 7K 99
Cambridge Arc. *E9* *7J 67*
(off Elsdale St.)
Cambridge Av. DA16: Well 4K 125
KT3: N Mald 3A 152
(not continuous)
NW6 2J 81
NW10 3E 80
UB6: G'frd 5K 59
Cambridge Barracks Rd.
SE18 4D 106
Cambridge Cir. W1 1D 12 (6H 83)
Cambridge Cl. E17 6B 50
N22 1A 48
NW10 3J 61
SW20 1D 152
TW4: Houn 4C 112
UB7: Harm 6A 92
Cambridge Cotts. TW9: Kew 6G 97
Cambridge Ct. *E2* *2H 85*
(off Cambridge Heath Rd.)
N16 *7E 48*
(off Amhurst Pk.)
NW6 2J 81
W2 *6C 4*
(off Edgware Rd.)
W6 *4E 98*
(off Shepherd's Bush Rd.)
Cambridge Cres. E2 2H 85
TW11: Tedd 5A 132
Cambridge Dr. HA4: Ruis 2A 58
SE12 5J 123
Cambridge Gdns. EN1: Enf 2B 24
KT1: King T 2G 151
N10 1E 46
N17 7J 33
N21 7J 23
NW6 2J 81
W10 6F 81
Cambridge Ga. NW1 3J 5 (4F 83)
Cambridge Ga. M. NW1 3K 5 (4F 83)
Cambridge Grn. SE9 1F 143
Cambridge Gro. SE20 1H 157
W6 4D 98
Cambridge Gro. Rd. KT1: King T 3G 151
(not continuous)
Cambridge Heath Rd. E1 5H 85
E2 5H 85
Cambridge Ho. *W6* *4D 98*
(off Cambridge Gro.)
W13 6A 78
Cambridge Pde. EN1: Enf 1B 24
Cambridge Pk. E11 7J 51
TW1: Twick 6C 114
Cambridge Pk. Ct. TW1: Twick 7D 114
Cambridge Pk. Rd. *E11* *7J 51*
(off Lonsdale Rd.)
Cambridge Pl. W8 2K 99
Cambridge Rd. BR1: Brom 7J 141
CR4: Mitc 3G 155
DA14: Sidc 4J 143
E4 1A 36
E11 6H 51
HA2: Harr 5E 40
IG3: Ilf 1J 71
IG11: Bark 7G 71
KT1: King T 2F 151
KT3: N Mald 4K 151
KT8: W Mole 4D 148
KT12: Walt T 6K 147
NW6 2J 81
SE20 3H 157
SM5: Cars 6C 166
SW11 1D 118
SW13 2B 116
SW20 1C 152
TW1: Twick 6D 114
TW4: Houn 4C 112
TW9: Kew 7G 97
TW11: Tedd 4K 131
TW12: Hamp 7D 130
TW15: Ashf 7E 128
UB1: S'hall 1D 94
W7 2K 95
Cambridge Rd. Nth. W4 5H 97
Cambridge Rd. Sth. W4 5H 97
Cambridge Row SE18 5F 107
Cambridge Sq. W2 7C 4 (6C 82)
Cambridge St. SW1 4K 17 (4F 101)
Cambridge Ter. N9 7K 23
NW1 2J 5 (3F 83)
Cambridge Ter. M. NW1 2K 5 (3F 83)
Cambridge Theatre *1E 12*
(off Earlham St.)
Cambridge Yd. W7 2K 95
Cambstone Cl. N11 2K 31
Cambus Cl. UB4: Yead 5C 76
Cambus Rd. E16 5J 87
Cam Ct. SE15 6F 103
Camdale Rd. SE18 7K 107
Camden Arts Cen. 5K 63
Camden Av. TW13: Felt 1A 130
UB4: Yead 7B 76
Camden Cl. BR7: Chst 1G 161
Camden Ct. DA17: Belv 5G 109
NW1 *7G 65*
(off Rousden St.)
Camden Gdns. CR7: Thor H 3B 156
NW1 7F 65
SM1: Sutt 5K 165
Camden Gro. BR7: Chst 6F 143
Camden High St. NW1 7F 65
Camden Hill Rd. SE19 6E 138
Camden Ho. SE8 5B 104
Camdenhurst St. E14 6A 86
Camden La. N7 5H 65
Camden Lock Market *7F 65*
(off Camden Lock Pl.)
Camden Lock Pl. NW1 7F 65
Camden Market *1F 83*
(off Dewsbury Ter.)
Camden M. NW1 7G 65
Camden Pk. Rd.
BR7: Chst 7D 142
NW1 6H 65
Camden Pas. N1 1B 84
(not continuous)
Camden Peoples Theatre *3A 6*
(off Hampstead Rd.)
Camden Rd. DA5: Bexl 1E 144
E11 6K 51
E17 6B 50
N7 4J 65
NW1 7G 65
SM1: Sutt 5K 165
SM5: Cars 4D 166
Camden Row HA5: Pinn 3A 40
SE3 2G 123
Camden Sq. NW1 7H 65
(not continuous)
SE15 1F 121
Camden St. NW1 7G 65
Camden Studios *NW1* *1G 83*
(off Camden St.)
Camden Ter. NW1 6H 65
CAMDEN TOWN 1F 83
Camden Wlk. N1 1B 84
(not continuous)
Camden Way BR7: Chst 7D 142
CR7: Thor H 3B 156
Cameford Ct. SW2 7J 119
Camelford *NW1* *1G 83*
(off Royal Coll. St.)
Camelford Ct. W11 6G 81
Camelford Ho. SE1 5F 19 (5J 101)
Camelford Wlk. W11 6G 81
Camel Gro. KT2: King T 5D 132
Camellia Ho. *SE8* *7B 104*
(off Idonia St.)
Camellia Pl. TW2: Whit 7F 113
Camellia St. SW8 7J 101
(not continuous)
Camelot Cl. SE28 2H 107
SW19 4H 135
Camelot Ho. NW1 6H 65
Camel Rd. E16 1B 106
Camera Pl. SW10 7A 16 (6B 100)
Cameret Ct. *W11* *2F 99*
(off Holland Rd.)
Cameron Cl. DA5: Bexl 3K 145
N18 4C 34
N20 2G 31
Cameron Ho. *NW8* *2C 82*
(off St John's Wood Ter.)
SE5 7C 102
Cameron Pl. E1 6H 85
SW16 2A 138
Cameron Rd. BR2: Brom 5J 159
CR0: Croy 6B 156
IG3: Ilf 1J 71
SE6 2B 140
Cameron Sq. CR4: Mitc 1C 154
Cameron Ter. SE12 3K 141
Camerton Cl. E8 6F 67
Camgate Cen., The
TW19: Stanw 6B 110
Camgate Mans. *SE5* *6C 102*
(off Red Lion Row)
Camilla Cl. TW16: Sun 6H 129
Camilla Rd. SE16 4H 103
Camille Cl. SE25 3G 157
Camlan Rd. BR1: Brom 4H 141
Camlet St. E2 3J 9 (4F 85)
Camlet Way EN4: Barn, Had W 2D 20
Camley St. NW1 7H 65
Camm Gdns. KT1: King T 2F 151
KT7: T Ditt 7K 149
Camomile Av. CR4: Mitc 1D 154
Camomile Rd. RM7: Rush G 2K 73
Camomile St. EC3 7H 9 (6E 84)
Camomile Way UB7: Yiew 6A 74
Campana Rd. SW6 1J 117
Campania Bldg. *E1* *7K 85*
(off Jardine Rd.)
Campaspe Bus. Pk. TW16: Sun 5H 147
Campbell Av. IG6: Ilf 4F 53
Campbell Cl. HA4: Ruis 6J 39
SE18 1E 124
Campbell Cl. SW16 4H 137
TW2: Twick 1H 131
Campbell Ct. N17 1F 49
NW9 6J 43
SE21 1G 139
SW7 *3A 100*
(off Gloucester Rd.)
Campbell Cft. HA8: Edg 5B 28
Campbell Gordon Way NW2 4D 62
Campbell Ho. *SW1* *6A 18*
(off Churchill Gdns.)
W2 *4A 4*
(off Hall Pl.)
W12 *7D 80*
(off White City Est.)
Campbell Rd. CR0: Croy 7B 156
E3 3C 86
E6 1C 88
E15 4H 69
E17 4B 50
KT8: E Mos 3J 149
N17 1F 49
TW2: Twick 2H 131
W7 7J 77
Campbell Wlk. *N1* *1J 83*
(off Outram Pl.)
Campdale Rd. N7 3H 65
Campden Cres. HA0: Wemb 3B 60
RM8: Dag 4B 72
Campden Gro. W8 2J 99
Campden Hill W8 2J 99
Campden Hill Ct. W8 2J 99
Campden Hill Gdns. W8 1J 99
Campden Hill Ga. W8 2J 99
Campden Hill Mans. *W8* *1J 99*
(off Edge St.)
Campden Hill Pl. W11 1H 99
Campden Hill Rd. W8 1J 99
Campden Hill Sq. W8 1H 99
Campden Hill Towers W11 1J 99
Campden Ho. *NW6* *7B 64*
(off Harben Rd.)
W8 *1J 99*
(off Sheffield Ter.)
Campden Ho. Cl. W8 2J 99
Campden Ho's. W8 1J 99
Campden Ho. Ter. *W8* *1J 99*
(off Kensington Church St.)
Campden Mans. *W8* *1J 99*
(off Kensington Chu. St.)
Campden Rd. CR2: S Croy 5E 168
UB10: Ick 3B 56
Campden St. W8 1J 99
Campe Ho. N10 7K 31
Campen Cl. SW19 2G 135
Camperdown St. E1 1K 15 (6F 85)
Campfield Rd. SE9 7B 124
Campion Cl. CR0: Croy 4E 168
E6 7D 88
HA3: Kent 6F 43
RM7: Rush G 2K 73
UB8: Hil 5B 74
Campion Ct. HA0: Wemb 2E 78
Campion Gdns. IG8: Wfd G 5D 36
Campion Pl. SE28 1A 108
Campion Rd. SW15 4E 116
TW7: Isle 1K 113
Campion Ter. NW2 3F 63
Campion Way HA8: Edg 4D 28
Camplin Rd. HA3: Kent 5E 42
Camplin St. SE14 7K 103
Camp Rd. SW19 5D 134
(not continuous)
Campsbourne, The N8 4J 47
Campsbourne Ho. *N8* *4J 47*
(off Pembroke Rd.)
Campsbourne Rd. N8 3J 47
(not continuous)
Campsey Gdns. RM9: Dag 7B 72
Campsey Rd. RM9: Dag 7B 72
Campsfield Ho. *N8* *3J 47*
(off Campsfield Rd.)
Campsfield Rd. N8 3J 47

Campshill Pl. SE13 5E **122**
Campshill Rd. SE13 5E **122**
Campus Rd. E17 6B **50**
Campus Way NW4 3D **44**
Camp Vw. SW19 5D **134**
Cam Rd. E15 1F **87**
Camrose Av. DA8: Erith 6H **109**
HA8: Edg 2F **43**
TW13: Felt 4A **130**
Camrose Cl. CR0: Croy 7A **158**
SM4: Mord 4J **153**
Camrose St. SE2 5A **108**
Canada Av. N18 6H **33**
Canada Cres. W3 5J **79**
Canada Est. SE16 3J **103**
Canada Gdns. SE13 5E **122**
Canada Ho. *SE16* *3A* ***104***
(off Brunswick Quay)
Canada Memorial *6A* ***12***
(off Green Pk.)
Canada Pl. *E14* *1D* ***104***
(off Up. Bank St.)
Canada Rd. W3 5J **79**
Canada Sq. E14 1D **104**
Canada St. SE16 2K **103**
Canada Way W12 7D **80**
Canada Wharf SE16 1B **104**
Canadian Av. SE6 1D **140**
Canal App. SE8 5A **104**
Canal Blvd. NW1 6H **65**
CANAL BRIDGE **6G 103**
Canal Bldg. *N1* *2C* ***84***
(off Shepherdess Wlk.)
Canal Cl. E1 4A **86**
W10 4F **81**
Canal Gro. SE15 6H **103**
Canal Mkt. *NW1* *7F* ***65***
(off Castlehaven Rd.)
Canal Path E2 1F **85**
Canalside SE28 7D **90**
Canalside Activity Cen. 4F **81**
Canal Side Studios *NW1* *1H* ***83***
(off St Pancras Way)
Canal St. SE5 6D **102**
Canal Wlk. CR0 6E **156**
N1 1D **84**
NW10 *7J* ***61***
(off Westend Cl.)
SE26 5J **139**
Canal Way W10 4F **81**
Canal Wharf UB6: G'frd 1A **78**
Canberra Cl. NW4 3C **44**
RM10: Dag 1K **91**
Canberra Cres. RM10: Dag 7K **73**
Canberra Dr. UB5: Yead 3A **76**
Canberra Rd. DA7: Bex 6D **108**
E6 1D **88**
SE7 6A **106**
TW6: H'row A 3C **110**
Canbury Av. KT2: King T 1F **151**
Canbury Bus. Cen. KT2: King T 1E **150**
Canbury Bus. Pk. *KT2: King T* *1E* ***150***
(off Canbury Pk. Rd.)
Canbury Ct. KT2: King T 7D **132**
Canbury M. SE26 3G **139**
Canbury Pk. Rd. KT2: King T 1E **150**
Canbury Pas. KT2: King T 1D **150**
Cancell Rd. SW9 1A **120**
Candahar Rd. SW11 2C **118**
Candida Ct. NW1 7F **65**
Candid Ho. *NW10* *3D* ***80***
(off Trenmar Gdns.)
Candle Gro. SE15 3H **121**
Candlelight Ct. *E15* *6H* ***69***
(off Romford Rd.)
Candler M. TW1: Twick 7A **114**
Candler St. N15 6D **48**
Candover Cl. UB7: Harm 7A **92**
Candover St. W1 6A **6** (5G **83**)
Candy St. E3 1B **86**
Caney M. NW2 2F **63**
Canfield Dr. HA4: Ruis 5K **57**
Canfield Gdns. NW6 7K **63**
Canfield Ho. *N15* *6E* ***48***
(off Albert Rd.)
Canfield Pl. NW6 6A **64**
Canfield Rd. IG8: Wfd G 7H **37**
Canford Av. UB5: N'olt 1D **76**
Canford Cl. EN2: Enf 2F **23**
Canford Gdns. KT3: N Mald 6A **152**
Canford Pl. TW11: Tedd 6C **132**
Canford Rd. SW11 5E **118**
Canham Rd. SE25 3E **156**
W3 2A **98**
Canmore Gdns. SW16 7G **137**
CANN HALL **4G 69**
Cann Hall Rd. E11 4G **69**
Cann Ho. *W14* *3G* ***99***
(off Russell Rd.)
Canning Cres. N22 1K **47**
Canning Cross SE5 2E **120**
Canning Ho. *W12* *7D* ***80***
(off Australia Rd.)
Canning Pas. W8 3A **100**
(not continuous)
Canning Pl. W8 3A **100**
Canning Pl. M. *W8* *3A* ***100***
(off Canning Pl.)
Canning Rd. CR0: Croy 2F **169**
E15 2G **87**
E17 4A **50**
HA3: W'stone 3J **41**
N5 3B **66**
Cannington Rd. RM9: Dag 6C **72**
CANNING TOWN **6H 87**
CANNING TOWN **6G 87**
Cannizaro Rd. SW19 6E **134**
Cannock Ct. E17 2E **50**
Cannock Ho. N4 7C **48**
Cannonbury Av. HA5: Pinn 6B **40**
Cannon Cl. SW20 3E **152**
TW12: Hamp 6F **131**
Cannon Ct. *EC1* *3B* ***8***
(off Brewhouse Yd.)
Cannon Dr. E14 7C **86**
Cannon Hill N14 3D **32**
NW6 5J **63**
Cannon Hill La. SW20 5F **153**
Cannon Hill M. N14 3D **32**
Cannon Ho. SE11 4H **19**
Cannon La. HA5: Pinn 5C **40**
NW3 3B **64**
Cannon Pl. NW3 3B **64**
SE7 5C **106**
Cannon Retail Pk. SE28 7A **90**
Cannon Rd. DA7: Bex 1E **126**
N14 3D **32**
Cannons Health Club
Bromley **5K 159**
Cannon Street **2E 14**
Fulham **1F 117**
Norbury **2K 155**
Sutton **6J 165**
Willesden Green **7E 62**
Cannon St. EC2 6D **84**
EC4 1C **14** (6C **84**)
Cannon St. Rd. E1 6H **85**
Cannon Trad. Est. HA9: Wemb 4H **61**
Cannon Way KT8: W Mole 4E **148**
Cannon Wharf Bus. Cen. SE8 4A **104**
Cannon Workshops *E14* *7C* ***86***
(off Cannon Dr.)
Canon All. *EC4* *1C* ***14***
(off Queen's Head Pas.)
Canon Av. RM6: Chad H 5C **54**
Canon Beck Rd. SE16 2J **103**
Canonbie Rd. SE23 7J **121**
CANONBURY **6C 66**
Canonbury Bus. Cen. N1 1C **84**
Canonbury Ct. *N1* *7B* ***66***
(off Hawes St.)
Canonbury Cres. N1 7C **66**
Canonbury Gro. N1 7C **66**
Canonbury Hgts. *N1* *6D* ***66***
(off Dove Rd.)
Canonbury La. N1 7B **66**
Canonbury Pk. Nth. N1 6C **66**
Canonbury Pk. Sth. N1 6C **66**
Canonbury Pl. N1 6B **66**
(not continuous)
Canonbury Rd. EN1: Enf 1K **23**
N1 6B **66**
Canonbury Sq. N1 7B **66**
Canonbury St. N1 7C **66**
Canonbury Vs. N1 7B **66**
Canon Mohan Cl. N14 6K **21**
Canon Rd. BR1: Brom 3A **160**
Canon Row SW1 7E **12** (2J **101**)
(not continuous)
Canons Cl. HA8: Edg 6A **28**
N2 7B **46**
Canons Cnr. HA8: Edg 4K **27**
Canons Ct. E15 4G **69**
HA8: Edg 6A **28**
Canons Dr. HA8: Edg 6K **27**
Canonsleigh Rd. RM9: Dag 7B **72**
Canons Leisure Cen., The 4D **154**
CANONS PARK **7J 27**
Canons Pk. HA7: Stan 6J **27**
Canons Pk. Cl. HA8: Edg 7K **27**
Canon St. N1 1C **84**
Canon's Wlk. CR0: Croy 3K **169**
Canopus Way TW19: Stanw 7A **110**
Canrobert St. E2 2H **85**
Cantelowes Rd. NW1 6H **65**
(not continuous)
Canterbury Av. DA15: Sidc 2B **144**
IG1: Ilf 7C **52**
Canterbury Cl. BR3: Beck 1D **158**
E6 6D **88**
KT4: Wor Pk 2F **165**
SE5 *2C* ***120***
(off Lilford Rd.)
UB6: G'frd 5F **77**
Canterbury Ct. *NW6* *2J* ***81***
(off Canterbury Rd.)
NW9 2A **44**
SE12 3K **141**
SW9 7A **102**
TW15: Ashf 4B **128**
Canterbury Cres. SW9 3A **120**
Canterbury Gro. SE27 4A **138**
Canterbury Hall KT4: Wor Pk 7D **152**
Canterbury Ho. *CR0: Croy* *1D* ***168***
(off Sydenham Rd.)
IG11: Bark *7A* ***72***
(off Margaret Bondfield Av.)
SE1 1H **19** (3K **101**)
Canterbury Ind. Pk.
SE15 6J **103**
Canterbury Pl. SE17 5B **102**
Canterbury Rd. CR0: Croy 7K **155**
E10 7E **50**
HA1: Harr 5F **41**
HA2: Harr 5F **41**
NW6 2H **81**
SM4: Mord 7K **153**
TW13: Hanw 2C **130**
Canterbury Ter. NW6 2J **81**
Cantium Retail Pk. SE1 6G **103**
Cantley Gdns. IG2: Ilf 6G **53**
SE19 1F **157**
Cantley Rd. W7 3A **96**
Canton St. E14 6C **86**
Cantrell Rd. E3 4B **86**
Cantwell Rd. SE18 7F **107**
Canute Gdns. SE16 4K **103**
Canvey St. SE1 4C **14** (1C **102**)
Cape Cl. IG11: Bark 7F **71**
Cape Henry Ct. *E14* *7F* ***87***
(off Jamestown Way)
Cape Ho. *E8* *6F* ***67***
(off Dalston La.)
Capel Av. SM6: Wall 5K **167**
Capel Cl. BR2: Brom 1C **172**
N20 3F **31**
Capel Ct. *EC2* *1F* ***15***
(off Bartholomew La.)
SE20 1J **157**
Capel Gdns. HA5: Pinn 4D **40**
IG3: Bark, Ilf 4K **71**
Capel Ho. *E9* *7J* ***67***
(off Lodiges Rd.)
Capel Rd. E7 4K **69**
E12 4K **69**
EN4: E Barn 6H **21**
Capener's Cl. SW1 7F **11**
Capern Rd. SW18 1A **136**
Cape Rd. N17 3G **49**
Cape Yd. E1 7G **85**
Capital Bus. Cen. CR2: S Croy 7D **168**
HA0: Wemb 2D **78**
Capital E. Apartments *E16* *7J* ***87***
(off Western Gateway)
Capital Ind. Est. CR4: Mitc 5D **154**
DA17: Belv 3H **109**
Capital Interchange Way
TW8: Bford 5G **97**
Capital Wharf E1 1G **103**
Capitol Ind. Pk. NW9 3J **43**
Capitol Way NW9 3J **43**
Capland Ho. *NW8* *3B* ***4***
(off Capland St.)
Capland St. NW8 3B **4** (4B **82**)
Caple Ho. *SW10* *7A* ***100***
(off King's Rd.)
Caple Rd. NW10 2B **80**
Capper St. WC1 4B **6** (4G **83**)
Caprea Cl. UB4: Yead 5B **76**
Capricorn Cen. RM8: Dag 7F **55**
Capri Ho. E17 2B **50**
Capri Rd. CR0: Croy 1F **169**
Capstan Cl. RM6: Chad H 6B **54**
Capstan Ct. *E1* *7J* ***85***
(off Wapping Wall)
Capstan Ho. *E14* *7F* ***87***
(off Clove Cres.)
E14 *4E* ***104***
(off Stebondale St.)
Capstan Ride EN2: Enf 2F **23**
Capstan Rd. SE8 4B **104**
Capstan Sq. E14 2E **104**
Capstan Way SE16 1A **104**
Capstone Rd. BR1: Brom 4H **141**
Capthorne Av. HA2: Harr 1C **58**
Capuchin Cl. HA7: Stan 6G **27**
Capulet M. E16 1J **105**
Capworth St. E10 1C **68**
Caradoc Cl. W2 6J **81**
Caradoc Evans Cl. *N11* *5A* ***32***
(off Springfield Rd.)
Caradoc St. SE10 5G **105**
Caradon Cl. E11 1G **69**
Caradon Way N15 4D **48**
Cara Ho. *N1* *7A* ***66***
(off Liverpool Rd.)
Caramel Ct. HA9: Wemb 2H **61**
Caranday Vs. *W11* *1F* ***99***
(off Norland Rd.)
Caravel Cl. E14 3C **104**
Caravelle Gdns. UB5: N'olt 3B **76**
Caravel M. SE8 6C **104**
Caraway Apartments *SE1* *6K* ***15***
(off Cayenne Ct.)
Caraway Cl. E13 5K **87**
Caraway Hgts. *E14* *7E* ***86***
(off Poplar High St.)
Caraway Pl. SM6: Wall 3F **167**
Carberry Rd. SE19 6E **138**
Carbery Av. W3 2F **97**
Carbis Cl. E4 1A **36**
Carbis Rd. E14 6B **86**
Carbrooke Ho. *E9* *1J* ***85***
(off Templecombe Rd.)
Carbuncle Pas. N17 2G **49**
Carburton St. W1 5K **5** (5F **83**)
Cardale St. E14 2E **104**
Cardamon Bldg. *SE1* *5K* ***15***
(off Shad Thames)
Carden Rd. SE15 3H **121**
Cardiff Ho. *SE15* *6G* ***103***
(off Friary Est.)

Cardiff Rd. EN3: Pond E .4C 24
W7 .3A 96
Cardiff St. SE18 .7J 107
Cardigan Ct. *W7* .*4K 77*
(off Copley Cl.)
Cardigan Gdns. IG3: Ilf .2A 72
Cardigan Pl. SE3 .2F 123
Cardigan Rd. E3 .2B 86
SW13 .2C 116
SW19 .6A 136
TW10: Rich .6E 114
Cardigan St. SE11 .5J 19 (5A 102)
Cardigan Wlk. *N1* .*7C 66*
(off Ashby Gro.)
Cardinal Av. KT2: King T .5E 132
SM4: Mord .6G 153
Cardinal Bourne St. SE1 .3D 102
Cardinal Cap All. SE1 .1C 102
Cardinal Cl. BR7: Chst .1H 161
HA8: Edg .7D 28
KT4: Wor Pk .4C 164
SM4: Mord .6G 153
Cardinal Ct. *E1* .*7G 85*
(off Thomas More St.)
Cardinal Cres. KT3: N Mald .2J 151
Cardinal Hinsley Cl. NW10 .2C 80
Cardinal Mans. *SW1* .*3A 18*
(off Carlisle Pl.)
Cardinal Pl. SW1 .1A 18
SW15 .4F 117
Cardinal Rd. HA4: Ruis .1B 58
TW13: Felt .1K 129
Cardinals Wlk. TW12: Hamp .7G 131
TW16: Sun .6G 129
Cardinals Way N19 .1H 65
Cardinal Wlk. SW1 .2A 18
Cardinal Way HA3: W'stone .3J 41
Cardine M. SE15 .7H 103
Cardington Sq. TW4: Houn .4B 112
Cardington St. NW1 .1B 6 (3G 83)
Cardinham Rd. BR6: Chels .4K 173
Cardozo Rd. N7 .5J 65
Cardrew Av. N12 .5G 31
Cardrew Cl. N12 .5H 31
Cardrew Ct. N12 .5G 31
Cardross Ho. *W6* .*3D 98*
(off Cardross St.)
Cardross St. W6 .3D 98
Cardwell Rd. N7 .4J 65
Cardwell Ter. *N7* .*4J 65*
(off Cardwell Rd.)
Career Ct. *SE16* .*2K 103*
(off Christopher Cl.)
Carew Cl. N7 .2K 65
Carew Ct. *SE14* .*6K 103*
(off Samuel Cl.)
SM2: Sutt .7K 165
Carew Manor & Dovecote .3G 167
Carew Mnr. Cotts. SM6: Bedd .3H 167
Carew Rd. CR4: Mitc .2E 154
CR7: Thor H .4B 156
N17 .2G 49
SM6: Wall .6G 167
TW15: Ashf .6E 128
W13 .2C 96
Carew St. SE5 .2C 120
Carey Ct. DA6: Bex .5H 127
SE5 .7C 102
Carey Gdns. SW8 .1G 119
Carey La. EC2 .7C 8 (6C 84)
Carey Mans. *SW1* .*3C 18*
(off Rutherford St.)
Carey Pl. SW1 .4C 18 (4H 101)
Carey Rd. RM9: Dag .4E 72
Carey St. WC2 .1H 13 (6K 83)
Carey Way HA9: Wemb .4H 61
Carfax Pl. SW4 .4H 119
Carfax Rd. UB3: Harl .5H 93
Carfree Cl. N1 .7A 66
Cargill Rd. SW18 .1K 135
Cargo Point TW19: Stanw .6B 110
Cargreen Pl. SE25 .4F 157
Cargreen Rd. SE25 .4F 157
Cargrey Ho. HA7: Stan .5H 27
Carholme Rd. SE23 .1B 140
Carillon Ct. W5 .7D 78
Carinthia Ct. *SE16* .*4A 104*
(off Plough Way)
Carisbrook N10 .2F 47
Carisbrook Cl. EN1: Enf .1A 24
Carisbrooke Av. DA5: Bexl .1D 144
Carisbrooke Cl. HA7: Stan .2D 42
Carisbrooke Ct. SM2: Cheam .7H 165
UB5: N'olt .*1D 76*
(off Eskdale Av.)
W1 .*6H 5*
(off Weymouth St.)
W3 .*2J 97*
(off Brouncker Rd.)
Carisbrooke Gdns. SE15 .7F 103
Carisbrooke Ho. *KT2: King T* .*1E 150*
(off Seven Kings Way)
Carisbrooke Rd. BR2: Brom .4A 160
CR4: Mitc .4H 155
E17 .4A 50
Carker's La. NW5 .5F 65
Carleton Av. SM6: Wall .7H 167
Carleton Cl. KT10: Esh .7H 149
Carleton Gdns. N19 .5G 65
Carleton Rd. N7 .5H 65
Carleton Vs. NW5 .5G 65
Carlile Cl. E3 .2B 86
Carlile Ho. *SE1* .*3D 102*
(off Tabard St.)
Carlina Gdns. IG8: Wfd G .5E 36
Carlingford Gdns.
CR4: Mitc .7D 136
Carlingford Rd. N15 .3B 48
NW3 .4B 64
SM4: Mord .6F 153
Carlisle Av. EC3 .1J 15 (6F 85)
W3 .6A 80
Carlisle Cl. HA5: Pinn .7C 40
KT2: King T .1G 151
Carlisle Gdns. HA3: Kent .7D 42
IG1: Ilf .6C 52
Carlisle La. SE1 .2H 19 (3K 101)
Carlisle Mans. *SW1* .*3A 18*
(off Carlisle Pl.)
Carlisle M. KT2: King T .1G 151
Carlisle Pl. N11 .4A 32
SW1 .2A 18 (3G 101)
Carlisle Rd. E10 .1C 68
N4 .7A 48
NW6 .1G 81
NW9 .3J 43
SM1: Sutt .6H 165
TW12: Hamp .7F 131
Carlisle St. W1 .1C 12 (6H 83)
Carlisle Wlk. E8 .6F 67
Carlisle Way SW17 .5E 136
Carlos Pl. W1 .3H 11 (7E 82)
Carlow St. NW1 .2G 83
Carlson Ct. SW15 .4H 117
Carlton Av. CR2: S Croy .7E 168
HA3: Kent .5B 42
N14 .5C 22
TW14: Felt .6A 112
UB3: Harl .4G 93
Carlton Av. E. HA9: Wemb .2D 60
Carlton Av. W. HA0: Wemb .2B 60
Carlton Cl. HA8: Edg .5B 28
KT9: Chess .6D 162
NW3 .2J 63
UB5: N'olt .5G 59
Carlton Ct. IG6: Ilf .3H 53
SE20 .1H 157
SW9 .1B 120
UB8: Cowl .5A 74
W9 .*2K 81*
(off Maida Va.)
Carlton Cres. SM3: Cheam .4G 165
Carlton Dr. IG6: Ilf .3H 53
SW15 .5F 117
Carlton Gdns. SW1 .5C 12 (1H 101)
W5 .6C 78
Carlton Grn. DA14: Sidc .4K 143
Carlton Gro. SE15 .1H 121
Carlton Hill NW8 .2K 81
Carlton Ho. *NW6* .*2J 81*
(off Canterbury Ter., not continuous)
SE16 .*2K 103*
(off Wolfe Cres.)
TW3: Houn .6E 112
TW14: Felt .6H 111
Carlton Ho. Ter.
SW1 .5C 12 (1H 101)
Carlton Lodge *N4* .*7A 48*
(off Carlton Rd.)
Carlton Mans. N16 .1F 67
NW6 .*7J 63*
(off West End La.)
W9 .3K 81
W14 .*2G 99*
(off Holland Pk. Gdns.)
Carlton M. *NW6* .*5J 63*
(off West Cotts.)
NW6 .3J 81
(Carlton Va.)
Carlton Pde. HA9: Wemb .2E 60
Carlton Pk. Av. SW20 .2F 153
Carlton Rd. CR2: S Croy .6D 168
DA8: Erith .6H 109
DA14: Sidc .5K 143
DA16: Well .3B 126
E11 .1H 69
E12 .4B 70
E17 .1A 50
KT3: N Mald .2A 152
KT12: Walt T .7K 147
N4 .7A 48
N11 .5K 31
SW14 .3J 115
TW16: Sun .7H 129
W4 .2K 97
W5 .7C 78
Carlton Sq. E1 .4K 85
(not continuous)
Carlton St. SW1 .3C 12 (7H 83)
Carlton Ter. E11 .5K 51
(not continuous)
N18 .3J 33
SE26 .3J 139
Carlton Ter. St. E7 .7A 70
Carlton Twr. Pl. SW1 .3D 100
Carlton Towers SM5: Cars .3D 166
Carlton Va. NW6 .2H 81
Carlton Vs. SW15 .5G 117
Carlwell St. SW17 .5C 136
Carlyle Av. BR1: Brom .3B 160
UB1: S'hall .7D 76
Carlyle Cl. KT8: W Mole .2F 149
N2 .6A 46
NW10 .1K 79
Carlyle Ct. *SW6* .*1K 117*
(off Imperial Rd.)
SW10 .*1A 118*
(off Chelsea Harbour Dr.)
Carlyle Gdns. UB1: S'hall .7D 76
Carlyle Ho. *KT8: W Mole* .*5E 148*
(off Down St.)
N16 .3E 66
SE5 .*7C 102*
(off Bethwin Rd.)
SW3 .*7B 16*
(off Old Church St.)
Carlyle Mans. *SW3* .*7C 16*
(off Cheyne Wlk.)
W8 .*1J 99*
(off Kensington Mall.)
Carlyle M. E1 .4K 85
Carlyle Pl. SW15 .4F 117
Carlyle Rd. CR0: Croy .2G 169
E12 .4C 70
SE28 .7B 90
W5 .4C 96
Carlyle's House .7C 16
Carlyle Sq. SW3 .6B 16 (5B 100)
Carlyon Av. HA2: Harr .4D 58
Carlyon Cl. HA0: Wemb .1E 78
Carlyon Rd. HA0: Wemb .2E 78
UB4: Yead .5A 76
(not continuous)
Carlys Cl. BR3: Beck .2K 157
Carmalt Gdns. SW15 .4E 116
Carmarthen Ct. *W7* .*4K 77*
(off Copley Cl.)
Carmarthen Pl. SE1 .6G 15 (2E 102)
Carmel Ct. *W8* .*2K 99*
(off Holland St.)
Carmelite Cl. HA3: Hrw W .1G 41
Carmelite Rd. HA3: Hrw W .1G 41
Carmelite St. EC4 .2K 13 (7A 84)
Carmelite Wlk. HA3: Hrw W .1G 41
Carmelite Way HA3: Hrw W .2G 41
Carmel Lodge *SW6* .*6J 99*
(off Lillie Rd.)
Carmen St. E14 .6D 86
Carmichael Cl. SW11 .3B 118
Carmichael Ct. *SW13* .*2B 116*
(off Grove Rd.)
Carmichael Ho. *E14* .*7E 86*
(off Poplar High St.)
Carmichael M. SW18 .7B 118
Carmichael Rd. SE25 .5F 157
Carmine Ct. BR1: Brom .7H 141
Carminia Rd. SW17 .2F 137
Carnaby St. W1 .1A 12 (6G 83)
Carnac St. SE27 .4D 138
Carnanton Rd. E17 .1F 51
Carnarvon Av. EN1: Enf .3A 24
Carnarvon Dr. UB3: Harl .3E 92
Carnarvon Rd. E10 .5E 50
E15 .6H 69
E18 .1H 51
EN5: Barn .3B 20
Carnation Cl. RM7: Rush G .2K 73
Carnation St. SE2 .5B 108
Carnbrook Rd. SE3 .3B 124
Carnecke Gdns. SE9 .5C 124
Carnegie Cl. KT6: Surb .2F 163
Carnegie Pl. SW19 .3F 135
Carnegie Rd. HA1: Harr .7K 41
Carnegie St. N1 .1K 83
Carnforth Cl. KT19: Ewe .6H 163
Carnforth Rd. SW16 .7H 137
(not continuous)
Carnie Lodge SW17 .3F 137
Carnival Ho. *SE1* .*6K 15*
(off Gainsford St.)
Carnoustie Cl. SE28 .6D 90
Carnoustie Dr. N1 .7K 65
(not continuous)
Carnwath Rd. SW6 .3J 117
Caroe Ct. N9 .1C 34
Carol Cl. NW4 .4F 45
Carole Ho. *NW1* .*1D 82*
(off Regent's Pk. Rd.)
Carolina Cl. E15 .5G 69
Carolina Rd. CR7: Thor H .2B 156
Caroline Cl. CR0: Croy .4E 168
N10 .2F 47
SW16 .3K 137
TW7: Isle .7H 95
UB7: W Dray .2A 92
W2 .7K 81
Caroline Ct. HA7: Stan .6F 27
SE6 .4F 141
TW15: Ashf .6D 128
Caroline Gdns. E2 .1H 9 (3E 84)
SE15 .7H 103
Caroline Ho. *W2* .*7K 81*
(off Caroline Cl.)
W6 .*5E 98*
(off Queen Caroline St.)
Caroline Pl. SW11 .2E 118
UB3: Harl .7G 93
W2 .7K 81
Caroline Pl. M. W2 .7K 81
Caroline Rd. SW19 .7H 135
Caroline St. E1 .6K 85
Caroline Ter. SW1 .4G 17 (4E 100)

Caroline Wlk.—Cathedral Lodge

Caroline Wlk. W6 . . . . .6G 99
(off Lillie Rd.)
Carol St. NW1 .1G 83
Caronia Ct. SE16 . . . . .4A 104
(off Plough Way)
Carpenter Gdns. N21 . . . . .2G 33
Carpenter Ho. E14 . . . . .5C 86
(off Burgess St.)
NW11 . . . . .6A 46
Carpenters Arms Path SE9 . . . . .6D 124
Carpenters Bus. Pk. E15 . . . . .7D 68
Carpenters Cl. EN5: New Bar 6E 20
Carpenters Ct. NW1 . . . . .1G 83
(off Pratt St.)
TW2: Twick 2J 131
Carpenters M. N7 . . . . .5J 65
Carpenters Pl. SW4 . . . . .4H 119
Carpenter's Rd. E15 . . . . .6C 68
Carpenter St. W1 . . . . .3J 11 (7F 83)
Carradale Ho. E14 . . . . .6E 86
(off St Leonard's Rd.)
Carrara Cl. SE24 . . . . .4A 120
SW9 .4B 120
Carrara M. E8 .6G 67
Carrara Wharf SW6 . . . . .3G 117
Carr Cl. HA7: Stan 6F 27
Carre M. SE5 . . . . .1B 120
(off Calais St.)
Carr Gro. SE18 . . . . .4C 106
Carr Ho. DA1: Cray 5K 127
Carriage Dr. E. SW11 . . . . .7E 100
Carriage Dr. Nth.
SW11 . . . . .7H 17 (6E 100)
(Carriage Dr. E.)
SW11 . . . . .7D 100
(Parade, The)
Carriage Dr. Sth. SW11 . . . . .1D 118
(not continuous)
Carriage Dr. W. SW11 . . . . .7D 100
Carriage M. IG1: Ilf 2G 71
Carriage Pl. N16 . . . . .3D 66
SW16 . . . . .5G 137
Carriage St. SE18 . . . . .3F 107
Carrick Cl. TW7: Isle 3A 114
Carrick Dr. IG6: Ilf 1G 53
Carrick Gdns. N17 . . . . .7K 33
Carrick Ho. N7 .6K 65
(off Caledonian Rd.)
SE11 . . . . .5K 19 (5A 102)
Carrick M. SE8 . . . . .6C 104
Carrill Way DA17: Belv 3D 108
Carrington Av. TW3: Houn 5F 113
Carrington Cl. CR0: Croy 7A 158
KT2: King T 5J 133
Carrington Ct. SW11 . . . . .4C 118
(off Barnard Rd.)
Carrington Gdns. E7 . . . . .4J 69
Carrington Ho. W1 . . . . .5J 11
(off Carrington St.)
Carrington Rd. TW10: Rich 4G 115
Carrington Sq. HA3: Hrw W 6B 26
Carrington St. W1 . . . . .5J 11 (1F 101)
Carrol Cl. NW5 .4F 65
Carroll Cl. E15 .5H 69
Carroll Ct. W3 .3H 97
(off Osborne Rd.)
Carroll Ho. W2 .2A 10
(off Craven Ter.)
Carronade Ct. N7 . . . . .5K 65
Carronade Pl. SE28 . . . . .3H 107
Carron Cl. E14 .6D 86
Carroun Rd. SW8 . . . . .7K 101
Carroway La. UB6: G'frd 3H 77
Carrow Rd. RM9: Dag 7B 72
Carr Rd. E17 . . . . .2B 50
UB5: N'olt 6E 58
Carrs La. N21 . . . . .5H 23
Carr St. E14 . . . . .5A 86
CARSHALTON 4E 166
Carshalton Athletic FC 3C 166
CARSHALTON BEECHES 7C 166
Carshalton Gro. SM1: Sutt 4B 166
CARSHALTON ON THE HILL 7E 166
Carshalton Pk. Rd. SM5: Cars 5D 166
Carshalton Pl. SM5: Cars 5E 166
Carshalton Rd. CR4: Mitc 4E 154
SM1: Sutt 5A 166
SM5: Cars 5A 166
Carslake Rd. SW15 . . . . .6E 116
Carson Rd. E16 .4J 87
EN4: Cockf 4J 21
SE21 . . . . .2D 138
Carstairs Rd. SE6 . . . . .3E 140
Carston Cl. SE12 . . . . .5H 123
Carswell Cl. IG4: Ilf 4B 52
Carswell Rd. SE6 . . . . .7E 122
Carter Ct. EC4 . . . . .1A 14
Carter Dr. RM5: Col R 1H 55
Carteret Ho. W12 . . . . .7D 80
(off White City Est.)
Carteret St. SW1 . . . . .7C 12 (2H 101)
Carteret Way SE8 . . . . .4A 104
Carterhatch La. EN1: Enf 1A 24
Carterhatch Rd. EN3: Enf H 1D 24
Carter Ho. E1 . . . . .6J 9
Carter La. EC4 . . . . .1B 14 (6B 84)
Carter Pl. SE17 . . . . .5C 102
Carter Rd. E13 . . . . .1K 87
SW19 .6B 136
Carters Cl. KT4: Wor Pk 2F 165
NW5 . . . . .5H 65
(off Torriano Av.)
Carters Hill Cl. SE9 . . . . .1A 142
Carters La. SE23 . . . . .2A 140
Carter St. SE17 . . . . .6C 102
Carter's Yd. SW18 . . . . .5J 117
Carthew Rd. W6 . . . . .3D 98
Carthew Vs. W6 . . . . .3D 98
Carthusian St. EC1 . . . . .5C 8 (5C 84)
Cartier Circ. E14 . . . . .1D 104
Carting La. WC2 . . . . .3F 13 (7J 83)
Cart La. E4 . . . . .1B 36
Cartmel NW1 . . . . .1A 6
(off Hampstead Rd.)
Cartmel Cl. N17 . . . . .7C 34
Cartmel Ct. UB5: N'olt 6C 58
Cartmel Gdns. SM4: Mord 5A 154
Cartmel Rd. DA7: Bex 1G 127
Carton Ho. SE16 . . . . .3G 103
(off Marine St.)
W11 . . . . .7F 81
(off St Ann's Rd.)
Cartoon Mus. 6E 6
(off Museum St.)
Cartridge Pl. SE18 . . . . .3F 107
Cartwright Gdns. WC1 . . . . .2E 6 (3J 83)
Cartwright Ho. SE1 . . . . .3C 102
(off County St.)
Cartwright Rd. RM9: Dag 7F 73
Cartwright St. E1 . . . . .2K 15 (7F 85)
Cartwright Way SW13 . . . . .7D 98
Carvel Ho. E14 . . . . .5E 104
(off Manchester Rd.)
Carver Cl. W4 . . . . .3J 97
Carver Rd. SE24 . . . . .6C 120
Carville Cres. TW8: Bford 4E 96
Carville Hall 5E 96
(off Claypords La.)
Cary Rd. E11 . . . . .4G 69
Carysfort Rd. N8 . . . . .5H 47
N16 . . . . .3D 66
Casby Ho. SE16 . . . . .3G 103
(off Marine St.)
Cascade Av. N10 . . . . .4G 47
Cascade Cl. IG9: Buck H 2G 37
Cascade Rd. IG9: Buck H 2G 37
Cascades Ct. SW19 . . . . .7H 135
Cascades Twr. E14 . . . . .1B 104
Casella Rd. SE14 . . . . .7K 103
Casewick Rd. SE27 . . . . .5A 138
Casey Cl. NW8 . . . . .2C 4 (3C 82)
Casimir Rd. E5 .2J 67
Casino Av. SE24 . . . . .5C 120
Caspian Ho. E1 .5K 85
(off Shandy St.)
Caspian St. SE5 . . . . .7D 102
Caspian Wlk. E16 . . . . .6B 88
Cassandra Cl. UB5: N'olt 4H 59
Casselden Rd. NW10 . . . . .7K 61
Cassell Ho. SW9 . . . . .2J 119
(off Stockwell Gdns. Est.)
Cassidy Rd. SW6 . . . . .7J 99
(not continuous)
Cassilda Rd. SE2 . . . . .4A 108
Cassilis Rd. E14 . . . . .2C 104
TW1: Twick 5B 114
Cassiobury Av. TW14: Felt 7H 111
Cassiobury Rd. E17 . . . . .5A 50
Cassland Rd. CR7: Thor H 4D 156
E9 . . . . .7K 67
Casslee Rd. SE6 . . . . .7B 122
Cassocks Sq. TW17: Shep 7F 147
Casson Ho. E1 . . . . .5K 9
(off Spelman St.)
Castalia Sq. E14 . . . . .2E 104
Castellain Mans. W9 . . . . .4K 81
(off Castellain Rd., not continuous)
Castellain Rd. W9 . . . . .4K 81
Castellane Cl. HA7: Stan 7E 26
Castell Ho. SE8 . . . . .7C 104
Castello Av. SW15 . . . . .5E 116
CASTELNAU 6D 98
Castelnau SW13 . . . . .1C 116
Castelnau Gdns. SW13 . . . . .6D 98
Castelnau Mans. SW13 . . . . .6D 98
(off Castelnau, not continuous)
Castelnau Row SW13 . . . . .6D 98
Casterbridge NW6 . . . . .1K 81
(off Abbey Rd.)
W11 . . . . .6H 81
(off Dartmouth Cl.)
Casterbridge Rd. SE3 . . . . .3J 123
Casterton St. E8 . . . . .6H 67
Castile Rd. SE18 . . . . .4E 106
Castillon Rd. SE6 . . . . .2G 141
Castlands Rd. SE6 . . . . .2B 140
Castleacre W2 .1C 10
(off Hyde Pk. Cres.)
Castle Av. E4 . . . . .5A 36
KT17: Ewe 7D 164
UB7: Yiew 7A 74
Castlebar Ct. W5 . . . . .5C 78
Castlebar Hill W5 . . . . .5C 78
Castlebar M. W5 . . . . .5C 78
Castlebar Pk. W5 . . . . .5B 78
Castlebar Rd. W5 . . . . .5C 78
Castle Baynard St. EC4 . . . . . . .2B 14 (7B 84)
Castlebrook Ct. SE11 . . . . .4B 102
Castle Climbing Cen., The 2C 66
Castle Cl. BR2: Brom 3G 159
E9 . . . . .5A 68
SW19 .3F 135
TW16: Sun 7G 129
W3 . . . . .2H 97
Castlecombe Dr. SW19 . . . . .7F 117
Castlecombe Rd. SE9 . . . . .4C 142
Castle Ct. EC3 .1F 15
(off Birchin La.)
SE26 . . . . .4A 140
Castleden Ho. NW6 . . . . .7B 64
(off Hilgrove Rd.)
Castledine Rd. SE20 . . . . .7H 139
Castle Dr. IG4: Ilf 6C 52
Castleford Av. SE9 . . . . .1F 143
Castleford Cl. N17 . . . . .6A 34
Castleford Ct. NW8 . . . . .3B 4
(off Henderson Dr.)
Castlegate TW9: Rich 3F 115
Castlehaven Rd. NW1 . . . . .7F 65
Castle Hill Av. CR0: New Ad 7D 170
Castle Hill Pde. W13 . . . . .7B 78
(off The Avenue)
Castle Ho. SE1 . . . . .4C 102
(off Walworth Rd.)
SM2: Sutt 6J 165
SW8 . . . . .7J 101
(off Sth. Lambeth Rd.)
Castle Ind. Est. SE17 . . . . .4C 102
Castle La. SW1 . . . . .1B 18 (3G 101)
Castleleigh Ct. EN2: Enf 5J 23
Castlemaine SW11 . . . . .2D 118
Castlemaine Av. CR2: S Croy 5F 169
KT17: Ewe 7D 164
Castlemain St. E1 . . . . .5H 85
Castle Mead SE5 . . . . .7C 102
Castle M. N12 . . . . .5F 31
NW1 . . . . .6F 65
SW17 .4C 136
TW12: Hamp 1F 149
(not continuous)
Castle Pde. KT17: Ewe 7C 164
Castle Pl. NW1 .6F 65
W4 . . . . .4A 98
Castle Point E13 . . . . .2A 88
(off Boundary Rd.)
Castlereagh Ho. HA7: Stan 6G 27
Castlereagh St. W1 . . . . .7E 4 (6D 82)
Castle Rd. EN3: Enf H 1F 25
N12 . . . . .5F 31
NW1 . . . . .6F 65
RM9: Dag 1B 90
TW7: Isle 2K 113
UB2: S'hall 3D 94
UB5: N'olt 6F 59
Castle Row W4 .5K 97
Castle St. E6 . . . . .2A 88
KT1: King T 2E 150
Castleton Av. DA7: Bex 1K 127
HA9: Wemb 4E 60
Castleton Cl. CR0: Croy 6A 158
Castleton Gdns. HA9: Wemb 3E 60
Castleton Ho. E14 . . . . .4E 104
(off Pier St.)
Castleton Rd. CR4: Mitc 4H 155
(not continuous)
E17 . . . . .2F 51
HA4: Ruis 1B 58
IG3: Ilf 1A 72
SE9 . . . . .4B 142
Castletown Rd. W14 . . . . .5G 99
Castleview Cl. N4 . . . . .2C 66
Castleview Gdns. IG1: Ilf 6C 52
Castle Wlk. TW16: Sun 3A 148
Castle Way SW19 . . . . .3F 135
TW13: Hanw 4A 130
Castle Wharf E14 . . . . .7G 87
(off Orchard Pl.)
Castlewood Dr. SE9 . . . . .2D 124
Castlewood Rd. EN4: Cockf 3G 21
N15 . . . . .6G 49
N16 . . . . .6G 49
Castle Yd. N6 . . . . .7E 46
SE1 . . . . .4B 14 (1B 102)
TW10: Rich 5D 114
Castor La. E14 .7D 86
Catalina Rd. TW6: H'row A 2D 110
Caterham Av. IG5: Ilf 2D 52
Caterham Rd. SE13 . . . . .3F 123
Catesby Ho. E9 .7J 67
(off Frampton Pk. Rd.)
Catesby St. SE17 . . . . .4D 102
CATFORD 7D 122
Catford Art Gallery 7D 122
Catford B'way. SE6 . . . . .7D 122
CATFORD GYRATORY 7D 122
Catford Hill SE6 . . . . .1B 140
Catford Island SE6 . . . . .7D 122
Catford M. SE6 . . . . .7D 122
Catford Rd. SE6 . . . . .7C 122
Catford Trad. Est. SE6 . . . . .2D 140
Cathall Leisure Cen. 2G 69
Cathall Rd. E11 .2F 69
Cathay Ho. SE16 . . . . .2H 103
Cathay St. SE16 . . . . .2H 103
Cathay Wlk. UB5: N'olt 2E 76
(off Brabazon Rd.)
Cathcart Dr. BR6: Orp 2J 173
Cathcart Hill N19 . . . . .3G 65
Cathcart Rd. SW10 . . . . .6K 99
Cathcart St. NW5 . . . . .6F 65
Cathedral Lodge EC1 . . . . .5C 8
(off Aldersgate St.)

Cathedral Mans. SW1 ....3A 18
(off Vauxhall Bri. Rd.)
Cathedral Piazza SW1 ....2A 18 (3G 101)
Cathedral St. SE1 ....4E 14 (1D 102)
Cathedral Wlk. SW1 ....1A 18
Catherall Rd. N5 ....3C 66
Catherine Cl. NW4 ....4D 44
Catherine Ct. IG2: Ilf 5G 53
N14 ....5B 22
SW3 ....7A 16
(off Park Wlk.)
SW19 ....5H 135
Catherine Dr. TW9: Rich 4E 114
TW16: Sun 6H 129
Catherine Gdns. TW3: Houn 4H 113
Catherine Griffiths Ct. EC1 ....3K 7
(off Northampton Rd.)
Catherine Gro. SE10 ....1D 122
Catherine Ho. N1 ....1E 84
(off Whitmore Est.)
Catherine Howard Ct. SE9 ....6H 125
Catherine of Aragon Ct. SE9 ....6G 125
Catherine Parr Ct. SE9 ....6H 125
Catherine Pl. HA1: Harr 5K 41
SW1 ....1A 18 (3G 101)
Catherine Rd. KT6: Surb 5D 150
Catherine St. WC2 ....2G 13 (7K 83)
Catherine Wheel All. E1 ....6H 9 (5E 84)
(not continuous)
Catherine Wheel Rd. TW8: Bford 7D 96
Catherine Wheel Yd. SW1 ....5A 12
Catherwood Ct. N1 ....1E 8
(off Murray Gro., not continuous)
Cat Hill EN4: E Barn 6H 21
Cathles Rd. SW12 ....6F 119
Cathnor Rd. W12 ....2D 98
Catlin Cres. TW17: Shep 5F 147
Catling Cl. SE23 ....3J 139
Catlin's La. HA5: Eastc 3K 39
Catlin St. SE16 ....5G 103
Cator La. BR3: Beck 1B 158
Cato Rd. SW4 ....3H 119
Cator Rd. SE26 ....6K 139
SM5: Cars 5D 166
Cator St. SE15 ....7F 103
(Commercial Way)
SE15 ....6F 103
(Ebley Cl.)
Cato St. W1 ....6D 4 (5C 82)
Catsey La. WD23: Bush 1B 26
Catsey Wood WD23: Bush 1B 26
Catterick Cl. N11 ....6K 31
Cattistock Rd. SE9 ....5C 142
Cattley Cl. EN5: Barn 4B 20
Catton St. WC1 ....6G 7 (5K 83)
Caudwell Ter. SW18 ....6B 118
Caughley Ho. SE11 ....2J 19
Caulfield Rd. E6 ....1C 88
SE15 ....2H 121
Causeway, The KT9: Chess 4E 162
KT10: Clay 7A 162
N2 ....4C 46
SM2: Sutt 7A 166
SM5: Cars 3E 166
SW18 ....5K 117
(not continuous)
SW19 ....5E 134
TW4: Houn 4J 111
TW11: Tedd 6K 131
TW14: Felt, Houn 4J 111
Causeyware Rd. N9 ....7D 24
Causton Cotts. E14 ....6A 86
(off Galsworthy Av.)
Causton Ho. SE5 ....6C 102
Causton Rd. N6 ....7F 47
Causton Sq. RM10: Dag 7G 73
Causton St. SW1 ....4D 18 (4H 101)
Cautley Av. SW4 ....5G 119
Cavalier Cl. RM6: Chad H 4D 54
Cavalier Ct. KT5: Surb 6F 151
Cavalier Gdns. UB3: Hayes 6F 75
Cavalry Cres. TW4: Houn 4B 112
Cavalry Gdns. SW15 ....5H 117
Cavan Pl. HA5: H End 1D 40
Cavaye Ho. SW10 ....7A 16
(off Cavaye Pl.)
Cavaye Pl. SW10 ....6A 16 (5A 100)
Cavell Dr. EN2: Enf 2F 23
Cavell Ho. N1 ....1E 84
(off Colville Est.)
Cavell Rd. N17 ....7J 33
Cavell St. E1 ....5H 85
Cavendish Av. DA8: Erith 6J 109
DA15: Sidc 7A 126
DA16: Well 3K 125
HA1: Harr 4H 59
HA4: Ruis 5K 57
IG8: Wfd G 1K 51
KT3: N Mald 5C 152
N3 ....2J 45
NW8 ....1B 4 (2B 82)
W13 ....5A 78
Cavendish Cl. N18 ....5C 34
NW6 ....6H 63
NW8 ....1B 4 (3B 82)
TW16: Sun 6H 129
UB4: Hayes 5G 75
Cavendish Ct. EC3 ....7H 9
SE6 ....1D 140
(off Bromley Rd.)
SM6: Wall 6F 167
TW16: Sun 6H 129
Cavendish Dr. E11 ....1F 69
HA8: Edg 6A 28
Cavendish Gdns. IG1: Ilf 1E 70
IG11: Bark 5J 71
RM6: Chad H 5E 54
SW4 ....6G 119
Cavendish Ho. NW8 ....1B 4
(off Wellington Rd.)
Cavendish Mans. EC1 ....4J 7
(off Rosebery Av.)
NW6 ....5J 63
Cavendish M. Nth. W1 ....5K 5 (5F 83)
Cavendish M. Sth. W1 ....6K 5 (5F 83)
Cavendish Pde. SW4 ....6F 119
(off Clapham Comn. Sth. Side)
TW4: Houn 2C 112
Cavendish Pl. SW4 ....5H 119
W1 ....7K 5 (6F 83)
Cavendish Rd. CR0: Croy 1B 168
E4 ....6K 35
EN5: Barn 3A 20
KT3: N Mald 4B 152
N4 ....6B 48
N18 ....5C 34
NW6 ....7G 63
SM2: Sutt 7A 166
SW12 ....6F 119
SW19 ....7B 136
TW16: Sun 6H 129
W4 ....1J 115
Cavendish Sq. W1 ....7K 5 (6F 83)
Cavendish St. N1 ....2D 84
Cavendish Ter. E3 ....3B 86
TW13: Felt 2J 129
Cavendish Way BR4: W W'ck 1D 170
Cavenham Gdns. IG1: Ilf 3H 71
Caverleigh Way KT4: Wor Pk 1C 164
Cave Rd. E13 ....3K 87
TW10: Ham 4C 132
Caversham Av. N13 ....3F 33
SM3: Cheam 2G 165
Caversham Ct. N11 ....3K 31
(off Brunswick Pk. Rd.)
Caversham Ho. KT1: King T 2E 150
(off Lady Booth Rd.)
N15 ....4C 48
(off Caversham Rd.)
SE15 ....6G 103
(off Haymerle Rd.)
Caversham Rd. KT1: King T 2F 151
N15 ....4C 48
NW5 ....6G 65
Caversham St. SW3 ....7E 16 (6D 100)
Caverswall St. W12 ....6E 80
Caveside Cl. BR7: Chst 1E 160
Cavour Ho. SE17 ....5B 102
(off Alberta Est.)
Cawdor Cres. W7 ....4A 96
Cawnpore St. SE19 ....5E 138
Caxton Ct. SW11 ....2C 118
Caxton Gro. E3 ....3C 86
Caxton M. TW8: Bford 6D 96
Caxton Pl. IG1: Ilf 3E 70
Caxton Rd. N22 ....2K 47
SW19 ....5A 136
UB2: S'hall 3B 94
W12 ....2F 99
Caxton St. SW1 ....1C 18 (3G 101)
Caxton St. Nth. E16 ....6H 87
Caxton Trad. Est. UB3: Hayes 2G 93
Caxton Wlk. WC2 ....1D 12 (6H 83)
Cayenne Ct. SE1 ....5K 15 (2F 103)
Caygill Cl. BR2: Brom 4H 159
Cayley Rd. UB2: S'hall 3F 95
Cayton Pl. EC1 ....2E 8
Cayton Rd. UB6: G'frd 2J 77
Cayton St. EC1 ....2E 8 (3D 84)
Cazenove Rd. E17 ....1C 50
N16 ....2F 67
Cearns Ho. E6 ....1B 88
Cecil Av. EN1: Enf 4A 24
HA9: Wemb 5F 61
IG11: Bark 7H 71
Cecil Cl. KT9: Chess 4D 162
TW15: Ashf 7E 128
W5 ....5D 78
Cecil Ct. EN2: Enf 4J 23
EN5: Barn 3A 20
NW6 ....7K 63
SW10 ....6A 100
(off Fawcett St.)
WC2 ....3E 12 (7J 83)
Cecile Pk. N8 ....6J 47
Cecil Ho. E17 ....1C 50
Cecilia Cl. N2 ....3A 46
Cecilia Rd. E8 ....5F 67
Cecil Pk. HA5: Pinn 4C 40
Cecil Pl. CR4: Mitc 5D 154
Cecil Rhodes Ho. NW1 ....2H 83
(off Goldington St.)
Cecil Rd. CR0: Croy 6J 155
E11 ....3H 69
E13 ....1J 87
E17 ....1C 50
EN2: Enf 3H 23
HA3: W'stone 3J 41
IG1: Ilf 4F 71
N10 ....2F 47
N14 ....1B 32
NW9 ....3A 44
NW10 ....1A 80
RM6: Chad H 7D 54
SM1: Sutt 6H 165
SW19 ....7K 135
TW3: Houn 2G 113
TW15: Ashf 7E 128
W3 ....5J 79
Cecil Rosen Ct. HA0: Wemb 3B 60
Cecil Sharp House 1E 82
Cecil Way BR2: Hayes 1J 171
Cedar Av. DA15: Sidc 7A 126
EN3: Enf H 2D 24
EN4: E Barn 7H 21
HA4: Ruis 5A 58
RM6: Chad H 5E 54
TW2: Whit 6F 113
UB3: Hayes 6J 75
UB7: Yiew 7B 74
Cedar Cl. BR2: Brom 3C 172
E3 ....1B 86
IG1: Ilf 5H 71
IG9: Buck H 2G 37
KT8: E Mos 4J 149
RM7: Rom 4J 55
SE21 ....1C 138
SM5: Cars 6D 166
SW15 ....4K 133
Cedar Copse BR1: Brom 2D 160
Cedar Ct. E18: Wfd G 1J 51
N1 ....7C 66
N10 ....2E 46
N11 ....5B 32
N20 ....1G 31
SE1 ....7G 15
(off Royal Oak Yd.)
SE7 ....6A 106
SM2: Sutt 6A 166
SW19 ....3F 135
TW8: Bford 6C 96
Cedar Cres. BR2: Brom 3C 172
Cedarcroft Rd. KT9: Chess 4F 163
Cedar Dr. HA5: H End 6A 26
N2 ....4C 46
Cedar Gdns. SM2: Sutt 6A 166
Cedar Grange EN1: Enf 5K 23
Cedar Gro. DA5: Bexl 6D 126
UB1: S'hall 5E 76
W5 ....3E 96
Cedar Hgts. NW2 ....6H 63
TW10: Ham 1E 132
Cedar Ho. E2 ....2H 85
(off Mowlem St.)
E14 ....2E 104
(off Manchester Rd.)
N22 ....1A 48
(off Acacia Rd.)
SE14 ....1K 121
SE16 ....2K 103
(off Woodland Cres.)
TW9: Kew 1H 115
TW16: Sun 7H 129
(off Spelthorne Gro.)
UB4: Yead 4A 76
W8 ....3K 99
(off Marloes Rd.)
Cedarhurst BR1: Brom 7G 141
Cedarhurst Cotts. DA5: Bexl 7G 127
Cedarhurst Dr. SE9 ....5A 124
Cedarland Ter. SW20 ....7D 134
Cedar Lawn Av. EN5: Barn 5B 20
Cedar Mt. SE9 ....1B 142
Cedarne Rd. SW6 ....7K 99
Cedar Pk. Gdns.
RM6: Chad H 7D 54
Cedar Pk. Rd. EN2: Enf 1H 23
Cedar Pl. SE7 ....5A 106
Cedar Ri. N14 ....7K 21
Cedar Rd. BR1: Brom 2A 160
CR0: Croy 2D 168
EN2: Enf 1G 23
KT8: E Mos 4J 149
N17 ....1F 49
NW2 ....4E 62
RM7: Rom 4J 55
SM2: Sutt 6A 166
TW4: Cran 2A 112
TW11: Tedd 5A 132
TW14: Bedf 1F 129
Cedars, The E15 ....7H 69
IG9: Buck H 1D 36
SM6: Wall 4G 167
TW11: Tedd 6K 131
W13 ....6C 78
Cedars Av. CR4: Mitc 4E 154
E17 ....5C 50
Cedars Cl. NW4 ....3F 45
SE13 ....3F 123
Cedars Ct. N9 ....2K 33
Cedars Dr. UB10: Hil 2B 74
Cedars Ho. E17 ....3D 50
Cedars M. SW4 ....4F 119
(not continuous)
Cedars Rd. BR3: Beck 2A 158
CR0: Bedd 3J 167
E15 ....6G 69
KT1: Ham W 1C 150
N9 ....2B 34
N21 ....2G 33
SM4: Mord 4J 153
SW4 ....3F 119

Cedars Rd. SW13 . . . . . 2C **116**
W4 . . . . . 5J **97**
Cedar Ter. TW9: Rich 4E **114**
Cedar Tree Gro. SE27 . . . . . 5B **138**
Cedar Vw. *KT1: King T* *3D **150***
(off Milner Rd.)
Cedarville Gdns. SW16 . . . . . 6K **137**
Cedar Way NW1 . . . . . 7H **65**
TW16: Sun 7G **129**
Cedar Way Ind. Est. NW1 . . . . . 7H **65**
Cedra Ct. N16 . . . . . 1G **67**
Cedric Rd. SE9 . . . . . 3G **143**
Celadon Cl. EN3: Enf H 3F **25**
Celandine Cl. E14 . . . . . 5C **86**
Celandine Ct. E4 . . . . . 3J **35**
Celandine Dr. E8 . . . . . 7F **67**
SE28 . . . . . 1B **108**
Celandine Gro. N14 . . . . . 5B **22**
Celandine Way E15 . . . . . 3G **87**
Celbridge M. W2 . . . . . 5K **81**
Celestial Gdns. SE13 . . . . . 4F **123**
Celia Cres. TW15: Ashf 6A **128**
Celia Ho. *N1* *2E **84***
(off Arden Est.)
Celia Rd. N19 . . . . . 4G **65**
Celtic Av. BR2: Brom 3G **159**
Celtic St. E14 . . . . . 5D **86**
Cemetery La. SE7 . . . . . 6C **106**
TW17: Shep 7D **146**
Cemetery Rd. E7 . . . . . 5H **69**
N17 . . . . . 7K **33**
SE2 . . . . . 7B **108**
Cenacle Cl. NW3 . . . . . 3J **63**
Cenotaph 6E **12** (2J **101**)
Centaur Ct. TW8: Bford 5E **96**
Centaurs Bus. Pk. TW7: Isle 6A **96**
Centaur St. SE1 . . . . . 1H **19** (3K **101**)
Centenary Rd. EN3: Brim 4G **25**
Centenary Trad. Est. EN3: Brim 3G **25**
Centennial Av. WD6: Els 1H **27**
Centennial Ct. WD6: Els 1H **27**
Centennial Pk. WD6: Els 1H **27**
Central Av. DA16: Well 2K **125**
E11 . . . . . 2F **69**
E12 . . . . . 3B **70**
EN1: Enf 2C **24**
HA5: Pinn 6D **40**
KT8: W Mole 4D **148**
N2 . . . . . 2B **46**
(Oak La.)
N2 . . . . . 4K **45**
(Rosemary Av.)
N9 . . . . . 3K **33**
SM6: Wall 5J **167**
SW11 . . . . . 7D **100**
TW3: Houn 4G **113**
UB3: Hayes 1H **93**
Central Bus. Cen. NW10 . . . . . 5A **62**
Central Church Sports Club 2K **139**
Central Cir. NW4 . . . . . 5D **44**
Centrale Shop. Cen. CR0: Croy 2C **168**
Central Gallery *IG1: Ilf* *2F **71***
(in The Exchange)
Central Gdns. SM4: Mord 5K **153**
Central Hill SE19 . . . . . 5C **138**
Central Ho. E15 . . . . . 2D **86**
IG11: Bark 7G **71**
Central Mall *SW18* *6K **117***
(off South Mall)
Central Mans. *NW4* *5D **44***
(off Watford Way)
Central Markets (Smithfield) 6A **8**
Central Pde. DA15: Sidc 3A **144**
E17 . . . . . 4C **50**
EN3: Enf H 2D **24**
HA1: Harr 5K **41**
IG2: Ilf 6H **53**
KT6: Surb 6E **150**
KT8: W Mole 4D **148**
SE20 . . . . . *7K **139***
(off High St.)
TW5: Hest 7D **94**
TW14: Felt 7A **112**
Central Pde. UB6: G'frd 3A **78**
W3 . . . . . 2H **97**
Central Pk. Av. RM10: Dag 3H **73**
Central Pk. Est. TW4: Houn 5B **112**
Central Pk. Rd. E6 . . . . . 2B **88**
Central Pl. SE25 . . . . . 5G **157**
Central Rd. HA0: Wemb 5B **60**
KT4: Wor Pk 1C **164**
SM4: Mord 6J **153**
Central St Martins College of Art & Design
. . . . . 6G **7**
Central School Path SW14 . . . . . 3J **115**
Central Sq. *HA9: Wemb* *5E **60***
(off Sevenex Pde.)
NW11 . . . . . 6K **45**
Central St. EC1 . . . . . 1C **8** (3C **84**)
Central Ter. BR3: Beck 3K **157**
Central Way NW10 . . . . . 3J **79**
SE28 . . . . . 1A **108**
SM5: Cars 7C **166**
TW14: Felt 5J **111**
Central Wharf *E14* *6C **86***
(off Thomas Rd.)
Centre, The KT12: Walt T 7H **147**
TW3: Houn 3F **113**
TW13: Felt 2J **129**
Centre Av. N2 . . . . . 2C **46**
NW10 . . . . . 3E **80**
W3 . . . . . 1K **97**
Centre Comn. Rd. BR7: Chst 6G **143**
Centre Ct. Shop. Cen. SW19 . . . . . 6H **135**
Centre Dr. E7 . . . . . 4A **70**
Cen. for the Magic Arts, The *3B **6***
(off Stephenson Way)
Centre Hgts. *NW3* *7B **64***
(off Finchley Rd.)
Centre Point SE1 . . . . . 5G **103**
Centrepoint WC2 . . . . . 7D **6**
Centre Point Ho. *WC2* *7D **6***
(off St Giles High St.)
Centre Rd. E7 . . . . . 2J **69**
E11 . . . . . 2J **69**
RM10: Dag 2H **91**
Centre Sq. *SW18* *5J **117***
(off Buckhold Rd.)
Centre St. E2 . . . . . 2H **85**
Centre Way E17 . . . . . 7K **35**
N9 . . . . . 2D **34**
Centreway Apartments *IG1: Ilf* *2G **71***
(off Axon Pl.)
Centric Cl. NW1 . . . . . 1E **82**
Centro Ct. E6 . . . . . 4D **88**
Centurion Bldg. SW8 . . . . . 6F **101**
Centurion Cl. N7 . . . . . 7K **65**
Centurion Ct. SE18 . . . . . 4E **106**
SM6: Wall 2F **167**
Centurion La. E3 . . . . . 1B **86**
Centurion Way DA18: Erith 3F **109**
Century Cl. NW4 . . . . . 5F **45**
Century Ho. HA9: Wemb 2F **61**
SW15 . . . . . 4F **117**
Century M. E5 . . . . . 4J **67**
Century Plaza *HA8: Edg* *6B **28***
(off Station Rd.)
Century Rd. E17 . . . . . 3A **50**
Century Yd. SE23 . . . . . 2J **139**
(not continuous)
Cephas Av. E1 . . . . . 4J **85**
Cephas Ho. *E1* *4J **85***
(off Doveton St.)
Cephas St. E1 . . . . . 4J **85**
Ceres Rd. SE18 . . . . . 4K **107**
Cerise Rd. SE15 . . . . . 1G **121**
Cerne Cl. UB4: Yead 7A **76**
Cerne Rd. SM4: Mord 6A **154**
Cerney M. W2 . . . . . 2A **10** (7B **82**)
Cervantes Ct. W2 . . . . . 6K **81**
Cester St. E2 . . . . . 1G **85**
Ceylon Rd. W14 . . . . . 3F **99**
Chabot Dr. SE15 . . . . . 3H **121**
Chadacre Av. IG5: Ilf 3D **52**
Chadacre Ct. *E15* *1J **87***
(off Vicars Cl.)
Chadacre Ho. *SW9* *4B **120***
(off Loughborough Pk.)
Chadacre Rd. KT17: Ewe 6D **164**
Chadbourn St. E14 . . . . . 5D **86**
Chadbury Ct. NW7 . . . . . 1C **44**
Chad Cres. N9 . . . . . 3D **34**
Chadd Dr. BR1: Brom 3C **160**
Chadd Grn. E13 . . . . . 1J **87**
(not continuous)
Chadston Ho. *N1* *7B **66***
(off Halton Rd.)
Chadswell *WC1* *2F **7***
(off Cromer St.)
Chadview Ct. RM6: Chad H 7D **54**
Chadville Gdns. RM6: Chad H 5D **54**
Chadway RM8: Dag 1C **72**
Chadwell Av. RM6: Chad H 7B **54**
CHADWELL HEATH **7D 54**
Chadwell Heath Ind. Pk.
RM8: Dag 1E **72**
Chadwell Heath La.
RM6: Chad H 4B **54**
Chadwell Ho. *SE17* *5D **102***
(off Merrow St.)
Chadwell La. N8 . . . . . 3K **47**
Chadwell St. EC1 . . . . . 1K **7** (3A **84**)
Chadwick Av. E4 . . . . . 4A **36**
N21 . . . . . 5E **22**
SW19 . . . . . 6J **135**
Chadwick Cl. SW15 . . . . . 7B **116**
TW11: Tedd 6A **132**
W7 . . . . . 5K **77**
Chadwick M. W4 . . . . . 6H **97**
Chadwick Pl. KT6: Surb 7C **150**
Chadwick Rd. E11 . . . . . 6G **51**
IG1: Ilf 3F **71**
NW10 . . . . . 1B **80**
SE15 . . . . . 2F **121**
Chadwick St. SW1 . . . . . 2C **18** (3H **101**)
Chadwick Way SE28 . . . . . 7D **90**
Chadwin Rd. E13 . . . . . 5K **87**
Chadworth Ho. *EC1* *2C **8***
(off Lever St.)
N4 . . . . . 1C **66**
Chaffinch Av. CR0: Croy 6K **157**
Chaffinch Bus. Pk. BR3: Beck 4K **157**
Chaffinch Cl. CR0: Croy 5K **157**
KT6: Surb 3G **163**
N9 . . . . . 1E **34**
Chaffinch Rd. BR3: Beck 1A **158**
Chafford Way RM6: Chad H 4C **54**
Chagford St. NW1 . . . . . 4E **4** (4D **82**)
Chailey Av. EN1: Enf 2A **24**
Chailey Cl. TW5: Hest 1B **112**
Chailey Ind. Est. UB3: Hayes 2J **93**
Chailey St. E5 . . . . . 3J **67**
Chalbury Wlk. N1 . . . . . 2K **83**
Chalcombe Rd. SE2 . . . . . 3B **108**
Chalcot Cl. SM2: Sutt 7J **165**
Chalcot Cres. NW1 . . . . . 1D **82**
Chalcot Gdns. NW3 . . . . . 6D **64**
Chalcot M. SW16 . . . . . 3J **137**
Chalcot Rd. NW1 . . . . . 7E **64**
Chalcot Sq. NW1 . . . . . 7E **64**
(not continuous)
Chalcott Gdns. KT6: Surb 1C **162**
Chalcroft Rd. SE13 . . . . . 5G **123**
Chaldon Ct. SE19 . . . . . 1D **156**
Chaldon Path CR7: Thor H 4B **156**
Chaldon Rd. SW6 . . . . . 7G **99**
Chale Rd. SW2 . . . . . 6J **119**
Chalet Cl. DA5: Bexl 4K **145**
Chalet Ct. CR7: Thor H 5C **156**
Chalet Est. NW7 . . . . . 4H **29**
Chalfont Av. HA9: Wemb 6H **61**
Chalfont Ct. *HA1: Harr* *6K **41***
(off Northwick Pk. Rd.)
NW1 . . . . . *4F **5***
(off Baker St.)
NW9 . . . . . 3B **44**
Chalfont Grn. N9 . . . . . 3K **33**
Chalfont Ho. *SE16* *3H **103***
(off Keetons Rd.)
Chalfont Rd. N9 . . . . . 3K **33**
SE25 . . . . . 3F **157**
UB3: Hayes 2J **93**
Chalfont Wlk. HA5: Pinn 2A **40**
Chalfont Way W13 . . . . . 3B **96**
Chalford *NW3* *6A **64***
(off Finchley Rd.)
Chalford Cl. KT8: W Mole 4E **148**
Chalford Rd. SE21 . . . . . 4D **138**
Chalford Wlk. IG8: Wfd G 1B **52**
Chalgrove Av. SM4: Mord 5J **153**
Chalgrove Cres. IG5: Ilf 2C **52**
Chalgrove Gdns. N3 . . . . . 3G **45**
Chalgrove Rd. N17 . . . . . 1H **49**
SM2: Sutt 7B **166**
Chalice Cl. SM6: Wall 6H **167**
Chalice Ct. N2 . . . . . 4C **46**
Chalkenden Cl. SE20 . . . . . 7H **139**
CHALKER'S CORNER **3H 115**
CHALK FARM **7E 64**
Chalk Farm Rd. NW1 . . . . . 7E **64**
Chalk Hill Rd. W6 . . . . . 4F **99**
Chalkhill Rd. HA9: Wemb 3H **61**
Chalklands HA9: Wemb 3J **61**
Chalk La. EN4: Cockf 3J **21**
Chalkley Cl. CR4: Mitc 2D **154**
Chalkmill Dr. EN1: Enf 3C **24**
Chalk Pit Way SM1: Sutt 5A **166**
Chalk Rd. E13 . . . . . 5K **87**
Chalkstone Cl. DA16: Well 1A **126**
Chalkwell Ho. *E1* *6K **85***
(off Pitsea St.)
Chalkwell Pk. Av. EN1: Enf 4K **23**
Challenge Cl. NW10 . . . . . 1A **80**
Challenger Ho. *E14* *7A **86***
(off Victory Pl.)
Challenge Rd. TW15: Ashf 3F **129**
Challice Way SW2 . . . . . 1K **137**
Challin St. SE20 . . . . . 1J **157**
Challis Rd. TW8: Bford 5D **96**
Challoner Cl. N2 . . . . . 2B **46**
Challoner Ct. *W14* *5H **99***
(off Challoner St.)
Challoner Cres. W14 . . . . . 5H **99**
Challoner Mans. *W14* *5H **99***
(off Challoner St.)
Challoners Cl. KT8: E Mos 4H **149**
Challoner St. W14 . . . . . 5H **99**
Chalmers Ho. E17 . . . . . 5D **50**
Chalmers Rd. TW15: Ashf 5D **128**
Chalmers Rd. E. TW15: Ashf 4D **128**
Chalmers Wlk. *SE17* *6B **102***
(off Hillingdon St.)
Chalmers Way TW14: Felt 5K **111**
Chalsey Rd. SE4 . . . . . 4B **122**
Chalton Dr. N2 . . . . . 6B **46**
Chalton Ho. *NW1* *1C **6***
(off Chalton St.)
Chalton St. NW1 . . . . . 1C **6** (2G **83**)
(not continuous)
Chamberlain Cl. IG1: Ilf 3G **71**
SE28 . . . . . 3H **107**
Chamberlain Cotts. SE5 . . . . . 1D **120**
Chamberlain Cres. BR4: W W'ck 1D **170**
Chamberlain Gdns. TW3: Houn 1G **113**
Chamberlain Ho. *E1* *7J **85***
(off Cable St.)
NW1 . . . . . 1D **6**
SE1 . . . . . *7J **13***
(off Westminster Bri. Rd.)
Chamberlain La. HA5: Eastc 4J **39**
Chamberlain Pl. E17 . . . . . 3A **50**
Chamberlain Rd. N2 . . . . . 2A **46**
W13 . . . . . 2A **96**
Chamberlain St. NW1 . . . . . 7D **64**
Chamberlain Wlk. *TW13: Hanw* *4C **130***
(off Swift Rd.)
Chamberlain Way HA5: Eastc 3K **39**
KT6: Surb 7E **150**
Chamberlayne Av. HA9: Wemb 3E **60**
Chamberlayne Mans. *NW10* *3F **81***
(off Chamberlayne Rd.)
Chamberlayne Rd. NW10 . . . . . 1E **80**

Chamberlens Garages—Charleville Ct.

Chamberlens Garages W6 . . . . 4D 98
(off Dalling Rd.)
Chambers, The SW10 . . . . 1A 118
(off Chelsea Harbour Dr.)
Chambers Bus. Pk. UB7: Sip 6C 92
Chambers Gdns. N2 . . . . 1B 46
Chambers La. NW10 . . . . 7D 62
Chambers Pl. CR2: S Croy 7D 168
Chambers Rd. N7 . . . . 4J 65
Chambers St. SE16 . . . . 2G 103
Chamber St. E1 . . . . 2K 15 (7F 85)
Chambers Wlk. HA7: Stan 5G 27
Chambers Wharf SE16 . . . . 2G 103
Chambon Pl. W6 . . . . 4C 98
Chambord St. E2 . . . . 2K 9 (3F 85)
Chamomile Ct. E17 . . . . 6C 50
(off Yunus Khan Cl.)
Champion Cres. SE26 . . . . 4A 140
Champion Gro. SE5 . . . . 3D 120
Champion Hill SE5 . . . . 3D 120
Champion Hill Est. SE5 . . . . 3E 120
Champion Pk. SE5 . . . . 2D 120
Champion Rd. SE26 . . . . 4A 140
Champions Way NW4 . . . . 1D 44
Champlain Ho. W12 . . . . 7D 80
(off White City Est.)
Champness Cl. SE27 . . . . 4D 138
Champness Rd. IG11: Bark 6K 71
Champneys Cl. SM2: Cheam 7H 165
Chancel Ind. Est. NW10 . . . . 5B 62
Chancellor Gdns. CR2: S Croy 7B 168
Chancellor Gro. SE21 . . . . 2C 138
Chancellor Ho. E1 . . . . 1H 103
(off Green Bank)
SW7 . . . . 3A 100
(off Hyde Pk. Ga.)
Chancellor Pas. E14 . . . . 1C 104
Chancellor Pl. NW9 . . . . 2B 44
Chancellors Ct. WC1 . . . . 5G 7
Chancellor's Rd. W6 . . . . 5E 98
Chancellor's St. W6 . . . . 5E 98
Chancellors Wharf W6 . . . . 5E 98
Chancelot Rd. SE2 . . . . 4B 108
Chancel St. SE1 . . . . 5A 14 (1B 102)
Chancery Bldgs. E1 . . . . 7H 85
(off Lowood St.)
Chancerygate Bus. Cen.
HA4: Ruis 4C 58
Chancery La. BR3: Beck 2D 158
WC2 . . . . 6H 7 (6A 84)
Chancery M. SW17 . . . . 2C 136
Chance St. E1 . . . . 3J 9 (4F 85)
E2 . . . . 3J 9 (4F 85)
Chanctonbury Cl. SE9 . . . . 3F 143
Chanctonbury Gdns.
SM2: Sutt 7K 165
Chanctonbury Way N12 . . . . 4C 30
Chandaria Ct. CR0: Croy 2C 168
(off Church Rd.)
Chandler Av. E16 . . . . 5J 87
Chandler Cl. TW12: Hamp 1E 148
Chandler Cl. TW14: Felt 6J 111
Chandler Ho. NW6 . . . . 1H 81
(off Willesden La.)
WC1 . . . . 4F 7
(off Colonnade)
Chandlers Cl. TW14: Felt 7H 111
Chandlers Ct. SE12 . . . . 1K 141
Chandlers Dr. DA8: Erith 4K 109
Chandlers M. E14 . . . . 2C 104
Chandler St. E1 . . . . 1H 103
Chandlers Way SW2 . . . . 7A 120
Chandler Way SE15 . . . . 6E 102
Chandlery, The SE1 . . . . 1K 19
(off Gerridge St.)
Chandlery Ho. E1 . . . . 6G 85
(off Bk. Church La.)
Chandon Lodge SM2: Sutt 7A 166
Chandos Av. E17 . . . . 2C 50
N14 . . . . 3B 32
N20 . . . . 1F 31
W5 . . . . 4C 96
Chandos Cl. IG9: Buck H 2E 36
Chandos Ct. HA7: Stan 6G 27
HA8: Edg 7A 28
N14 . . . . 2C 32
Chandos Cres. HA8: Edg 7A 28
Chandos Pde. HA8: Edg 7A 28
Chandos Pl. WC2 . . . . 3E 12 (7J 83)
Chandos Rd. E15 . . . . 5F 69
HA1: Harr 5G 41
HA5: Eastc 7B 40
N2 . . . . 2B 46
N17 . . . . 2E 48
NW2 . . . . 5E 62
NW10 . . . . 4A 80
Chandos St. W1 . . . . 6K 5 (5F 83)
Chandos Way NW11 . . . . 1K 63
Change All. EC3 . . . . 1F 15 (6D 84)
Channel Cl. TW5: Hest 1E 112
Channel Ga. Rd. NW10 . . . . 3A 80
Channel Ho. E14 . . . . 5A 86
(off Aston St.)
Channel Islands Est. N1 . . . . 6C 66
(off Guernsey Rd.)
Channelsea Path E15 . . . . 1F 87
Channelsea Rd. E15 . . . . 1F 87
Channon Ct. KT6: Surb 5E 150
(off Maple Rd)
Chanticleer Ct. SE1 . . . . 5F 103
(off Rolls Rd.)
Chantress Cl. RM10: Dag 1J 91
Chantrey Rd. SW9 . . . . 3K 119
Chantry, The E4 . . . . 1K 35
UB8: Hil 3B 74
Chantry Cl. DA14: Sidc 5E 144
EN2: Enf 1H 23
HA3: Kent 5F 43
SE2 . . . . 3C 108
TW16: Sun 7J 129
UB7: Yiew 7A 74
W9 . . . . 4J 81
Chantry Ct. SM5: Cars 3C 166
Chantry Cres. NW10 . . . . 6B 62
Chantry Ho. KT1: King T 4E 150
RM13: Rain 2K 91
Chantry La. BR2: Brom 5B 160
Chantry Pl. HA3: Hrw W 1F 41
Chantry Rd. HA3: Hrw W 1F 41
KT9: Chess 5F 163
Chantry Sq. W8 . . . . 3K 99
Chantry St. N1 . . . . 1B 84
Chantry Way CR4: Mitc 3B 154
RM13: Rain 2K 91
Chant Sq. E15 . . . . 7F 69
Chant St. E15 . . . . 7F 69
Chapel Av. E12 . . . . 3B 70
Chapel Cl. DA1: Cray 5K 127
NW10 . . . . 5B 62
Chapel Ct. N2 . . . . 3C 46
SE1 . . . . 6E 14 (2D 102)
UB3: Hayes 7H 75
CHAPEL END 1D 50
Chapel Farm Rd. SE9 . . . . 3D 142
Chapel Hill DA1: Cray 5K 127
N2 . . . . 2C 46
Chapel Ho. St. E14 . . . . 5D 104
Chapelier Ho. SW18 . . . . 4J 117
Chapel La. HA5: Pinn 3B 40
RM6: Chad H 7D 54
UB8: Hil 6C 74
Chapel Mkt. N1 . . . . 2A 84
Chapel M. IG8: Ilf 6K 37
Chapel Mill Rd. KT1: King T 3F 151
Chapelmount Rd.
IG8: Wfd G 6J 37
Chapel of St John the Evangelist 3J 15
(in The Tower of London)
Chapel of St Peter & St Paul 6F 105
(in Old Royal Naval College)
Chapel Path E11 . . . . 6K 51
(off Woodbine Pl.)
Chapel Pl. EC2 . . . . 2G 9 (3E 84)
N1 . . . . 2A 84
N17 . . . . 7A 34
W1 . . . . 1J 11 (6F 83)
Chapel Rd. DA7: Bex 4G 127
IG1: Ilf 3E 70
SE27 . . . . 4B 138
TW1: Twick 7B 114
TW3: Houn 3F 113
W13 . . . . 1B 96
Chapel Side W2 . . . . 7K 81
Chapel Stones N17 . . . . 1F 49
Chapel St. EN2: Enf 3H 23
NW1 . . . . 6C 4 (5C 82)
SW1 . . . . 1H 17 (3E 100)
Chapel Vw. CR2: Sels 6J 169
Chapel Wlk. CR0: Croy 2C 168
NW4 . . . . 4D 44
(not continuous)
Chapel Way N7 . . . . 3K 65
Chapel Yd. SW18 . . . . 5K 117
(off Wandsworth High St.)
Chaplin Cl. HA0: Wemb 6D 60
SE1 . . . . 6K 13 (2A 102)
Chaplin Cres. TW16: Sun 6G 129
Chaplin Rd. E15 . . . . 2H 87
HA0: Wemb 6C 60
N17 . . . . 3F 49
NW2 . . . . 6C 62
RM9: Dag 7E 72
Chaplin Sq. N12 . . . . 7G 31
Chapman Cl. UB7: W Dray 3B 92
Chapman Cres. HA3: Kent 6E 42
Chapman Grn. N22 . . . . 1A 48
Chapman Ho. E1 . . . . 6H 85
(off Bigland St.)
Chapman Pl. N4 . . . . 2B 66
Chapman Rd. CR0: Croy 1A 168
DA17: Belv 5G 109
E9 . . . . 6B 68
Chapman's La. SE2 . . . . 4C 108
Chapmans Pk. Ind. Est. NW10 . . . . 6B 62
Chapman Sq. SW19 . . . . 2F 135
Chapman's Ter. N22 . . . . 1B 48
Chapman St. E1 . . . . 7H 85
Chapone Pl. W1 . . . . 1C 12 (6H 83)
Chapter Chambers SW1 . . . . 4C 18
(off Chapter St.)
Chapter Cl. UB10: Hil 7B 56
W4 . . . . 3J 97
Chapter House 1C 14 (6B 84)
Chapter Rd. NW2 . . . . 5C 62
SE17 . . . . 5B 102
Chapter St. SW1 . . . . 4C 18 (4H 101)
Chapter Way SW19 . . . . 1B 154
TW12: Hamp 4E 130
Chara Pl. W4 . . . . 6K 97
Charcot Ho. SW15 . . . . 6B 116
Charcroft Ct. W14 . . . . 2F 99
(off Minford Gdns.)
Charcroft Gdns. EN3: Pond E 4E 24
Chardin Ho. SW9 . . . . 1A 120
(off Gosling Way)
Chardin Rd. W4 . . . . 4A 98
Chardmore Rd. N16 . . . . 1G 67
Chard Rd. TW6: H'row A 2D 110
Chardwell Cl. E6 . . . . 6D 88
Charecroft Way W12 . . . . 2F 99
Charfield Ct. W9 . . . . 4K 81
(off Shirland Rd.)
Charford Rd. E16 . . . . 5J 87
Chargeable La. E13 . . . . 4H 87
Chargeable St. E16 . . . . 4H 87
Chargrove Cl. SE16 . . . . 2K 103
Charing Cl. BR6: Orp 4K 173
Charing Ct. BR2: Brom 2G 159
Charing Cross SW1 . . . . 4E 12
Charing Cross Rd. WC2 . . . . . . 7D 6 (6H 83)
Charing Cross Sports Club 6F 99
Charing Cross Underground Shop. Cen.
WC2 . . . . 3E 12
Charing Ho. SE1 . . . . 6K 13
(off Windmill Wlk.)
Chariot Cl. E3 . . . . 1C 86
Charlbert Ct. NW8 . . . . 2C 82
(off Charlbert St.)
Charlbert St. NW8 . . . . 2C 82
Charlbury Av. HA7: Stan 5J 27
Charlbury Gdns. IG3: Ilf 2K 71
Charlbury Gro. W5 . . . . 6C 78
Charlbury Rd. UB10: Ick 3B 56
Charldane Rd. SE9 . . . . 3F 143
Charlecote Gro. SE26 . . . . 3H 139
Charlecote Rd. RM8: Dag 3E 72
Charlemont Rd. E6 . . . . 4D 88
Charles II Pl. SW3 . . . . 6E 16 (5D 100)
Charles II St. SW1 . . . . 4C 12 (1H 101)
Charles Auffray Ho. E1 . . . . 5J 85
(off Smithy St.)
Charles Babbage Cl. KT9: Chess 7C 162
Charles Barry Cl. SW4 . . . . 3G 119
Charles Bradlaugh Ho. N17 . . . . 7C 34
(off Haynes Cl.)
Charles Chu. Wlk. IG1: Ilf 6D 52
Charles Cl. DA14: Sidc 4B 144
Charles Cobb Gdns. CR0: Wadd 5A 168
Charles Coveney Rd. SE15 . . . . 1F 121
Charles Cres. HA1: Harr 7H 41
(not continuous)
Charles Curran Ho. UB10: Ick 3D 56
Charles Darwin Ho. E2 . . . . 3H 85
(off Canrobert St.)
Charles Dickens Ho. E2 . . . . 3G 85
(off Mansford St.)
Charle Sevright Dr. NW7 . . . . 5A 30
Charlesfield SE9 . . . . 3A 142
Charles Flemwell M. E16 . . . . 1J 105
Charles Gardner Ct. N1 . . . . 1F 9
(off Haberdasher Est.)
Charles Grinling Wlk. SE18 . . . . 4E 106
Charles Gro. N14 . . . . 1B 32
Charles Haller St. SW2 . . . . 7A 120
Charles Harrod Ct. SW13 . . . . 6E 98
(off Somerville Av.)
Charles Hocking Ho. W3 . . . . 2J 97
(off Bollo Bri. Rd.)
Charles House 4H 99
(off Kensington High St.)
Charles Ho. N17 . . . . 7A 34
(off Love La.)
UB2: S'hall 2E 94
Charles La. NW8 . . . . 2C 82
Charles Lesser Ho. KT9: Chess 5D 162
Charles Mackenzie Ho.
SE16 . . . . 4G 103
(off Linsey St.)
Charlesmere Gdns. SE28 . . . . 2J 107
Charles Nex M. SE21 . . . . 2C 138
Charles Pl. NW1 . . . . 2B 6 (3G 83)
Charles Rd. E7 . . . . 7A 70
RM6: Chad H 6D 54
RM10: Dag 6K 73
SW19 . . . . 1J 153
TW18: Staines 6A 128
W13 . . . . 6A 78
Charles Rowan Ho. WC1 . . . . 2J 7
(off Margery St.)
Charles Simmons Ho. WC1 . . . . 2J 7
(off Margery St.)
Charles Sq. N1 . . . . 2F 9 (3D 84)
Charles Sq. Est. N1 . . . . 2F 9
Charles St. CR0: Croy 3C 168
E16 . . . . 1A 106
EN1: Enf 5A 24
SW13 . . . . 2A 116
TW3: Houn 2D 112
UB10: Hil 4D 74
W1 . . . . 4J 11 (1F 101)
Charleston Cl. TW13: Felt 3J 129
Charleston St. SE17 . . . . 4C 102
Charles Townsend Ho. EC1 . . . . 3A 8
(off Skinner St.)
Charles Uton Ct. E8 . . . . 4G 67
Charles Whincup Rd. E16 . . . . 1K 105
Charlesworth Ho. E14 . . . . 6B 86
(off Dod St.)
Charlesworth Pl. SW13 . . . . 3A 116
Charleville Cir. SE26 . . . . 5G 139
Charleville Ct. W14 . . . . 5H 99
(off Charleville Rd.)

A-Z London 219

Charleville Mans.—Chaucer Rd.

Charleville Mans. W14 5G 99
(off Charleville Rd.)
Charleville M. TW7: Isle 4B 114
Charleville Rd. W14 5G 99
CHARLIE BROWN'S RDBT. 2A 52
Charlie Chaplin Wlk. SE1 5H 13
(off Waterloo Rd.)
Charlieville Rd. DA8: Erith 7J 109
Charlmont Rd. SW17 6C 136
Charlotte Cl. DA6: Bex 5E 126
IG6: Ilf 1G 53
Charlotte Ct. IG2: Ilf 6E 52
N8 6H 47
SE1 4E 102
(off Old Kent Rd.)
W6 4C 98
(off Invermead Cl.)
Charlotte Despard Av.
SW11 1E 118
Charlotte Ho. E16 1K 105
(off Fairfax M.)
W6 5E 98
(off Queen Caroline St.)
Charlotte M. W1 5B 6 (5G 83)
W10 6F 81
W14 4G 99
Charlotte Pk. Av. BR1: Brom 3C 160
Charlotte Pl. NW9 5J 43
SW1 4A 18 (4G 101)
W1 6B 6 (5G 83)
Charlotte Rd. EC2 2G 9 (3E 84)
RM10: Dag 6H 73
SM6: Wall 6G 167
SW13 1B 116
Charlotte Row SW4 3G 119
Charlotte Sq. TW10: Rich 6F 115
Charlotte St. W1 5B 6 (5G 83)
Charlotte Ter. N1 1K 83
Charlow Cl. SW6 2A 118
CHARLTON
Shepperton 3E 146
Woolwich 7B 106
Charlton Athletic FC 5A 106
Charlton Chu. La. SE7 5A 106
Charlton Cl. UB10: Ick 2D 56
Charlton Ct. E2 1F 85
NW5 5H 65
Charlton Cres. IG11: Bark 2K 89
Charlton Dene SE7 7A 106
Charlton Ga. Bus. Pk. SE7 4A 106
Charlton House 6B 106
Charlton Ho. TW8: Bford 6E 96
Charlton King's Rd. NW5 5H 65
Charlton La. SE7 4B 106
TW17: Shep 3E 146
(not continuous)
Charlton Lido 7B 106
Charlton Pk. La. SE7 7B 106
Charlton Pk. Rd. SE7 6B 106
Charlton Pl. N1 2B 84
Charlton Rd. HA3: Kent 4D 42
HA9: Wemb 1F 61
N9 1E 34
NW10 1A 80
SE3 7J 105
SE7 7J 105
TW17: Shep 3E 146
Charlton Way SE3 1G 123
Charlwood CR0: Sels 7B 170
Charlwood Cl. HA3: Hrw W 6D 26
Charlwood Ho. SW1 4C 18
(off Vauxhall Bri. Rd.)
TW9: Kew 7H 97
Charlwood Ho's. WC1 2F 7
(off Midhope St.)
Charlwood Pl. SW1 4B 18 (4G 101)
Charlwood Rd. SW15 4F 117
Charlwood St. SW1 6A 18 (5G 101)
(not continuous)
Charlwood Ter. SW15 4F 117
Charmans Ho. SW8 7J 101
(off Wandsworth Rd.)
Charmian Av. HA7: Stan 3D 42
Charmian Ho. N1 1G 9
(off Crondall St.)
Charminster Av. SW19 2J 153
Charminster Ct. KT6: Surb 7D 150
Charminster Rd. KT4: Wor Pk 1F 165
SE9 4B 142
Charmouth Ct. TW10: Rich 5F 115
Charmouth Ho. SW8 7K 101
Charmouth Rd. DA16: Well 1C 126
Charnock Ho. W12 7D 80
(off White City Est.)
Charnock Rd. E5 3H 67
Charnwood Av. SW19 2J 153
Charnwood Cl. KT3: N Mald 4A 152
Charnwood Dr. E18 3K 51
Charnwood Gdns. E14 4C 104
Charnwood Pl. N20 3F 31
Charnwood Rd. SE25 5D 156
UB10: Hil 2C 74
Charnwood St. E5 2H 67
Charrington Bowl 2H 163
Charrington Rd. CR0: Croy 2C 168
Charrington St. NW1 2H 83
Charsley Rd. SE6 2D 140
Chart Cl. BR2: Brom 1G 159
CR0: Croy 6J 157
CR4: Mitc 4D 154
Charter Av. IG2: Ilf 1H 71
Charter Ct. KT3: N Mald 3A 152
N4 1A 66
N22 1H 47
UB1: S'hall 1E 94
Charter Cres. TW4: Houn 4C 112
Charter Dr. DA5: Bexl 7E 126
Charterhouse 4B 8
Charter Ho. SM2: Sutt 6K 165
(off Mulgrave Rd.)
WC2 1F 13
(off Crown Ct.)
Charterhouse Av. HA0: Wemb 4C 60
Charterhouse Bldgs. EC1 4B 8 (4C 84)
Charterhouse M. EC1 5B 8 (5B 84)
Charterhouse Rd. BR6: Chels 3K 173
E8 4G 67
Charterhouse Sq. EC1 5B 8 (5B 84)
Charterhouse St. EC1 6K 7 (5A 84)
Charteris Rd. IG8: Wfd G 7E 36
N4 1A 66
NW6 1H 81
Charter Quay KT1: King T 2D 150
(off Wadbrook St.)
Charter Rd. KT1: King T 3H 151
Charter Rd., The
IG8: Wfd G 6B 36
Charters Cl. SE19 5E 138
Charter Sq. KT1: King T 2H 151
Charter Way N3 4H 45
N14 6B 22
Chartes Ho. SE1 7H 15
(off Stevens St.)
Chartfield Av. SW15 5D 116
Chartfield Sq. SW15 5F 117
Chartham Ct. SW9 3A 120
(off Canterbury Cres.)
Chartham Gro. SE27 3B 138
Chartham Ho. SE1 7F 15
(off Weston St.)
Chartham Rd. SE25 3H 157
Chart Hills Cl. SE28 6E 90
Chart Ho. CR4: Mitc 2D 154
E14 5D 104
(off Burrells Wharf Sq.)
Chartley Av. HA7: Stan 6E 26
NW2 3A 62
Charton Cl. DA17: Belv 6F 109
Chartres Ct. UB6: G'frd 2H 77
Chartridge SE17 6D 102
(off Westmoreland Rd.)
Chart St. N1 1F 9 (3D 84)
Chartwell Bus. Cen. BR1: Brom 3B 160
Chartwell Cl. CR0: Croy 1D 168
SE9 2H 143
UB6: G'frd 1F 77
Chartwell Ct. EN5: Barn 4B 20
IG8: Wfd G 7C 36
UB3: Hayes 7H 75
Chartwell Dr. BR6: Farnb 5H 173
Chartwell Gdns. SM3: Cheam 4G 165
Chartwell Ho. W11 1H 99
(off Ladbroke Rd.)
Chartwell Lodge BR3: Beck 7C 140
Chartwell Pl. HA2: Harr 2H 59
SM3: Cheam 4G 165
Chartwell Way SE20 1H 157
Charville Ct. HA1: Harr 6K 41
Charville La. UB4: Hayes 3E 74
Charville La. W. UB10: Hil 3D 74
Charwood SW16 4A 138
Chase, The BR1: Brom 3K 159
DA7: Bex 3H 127
E12 4B 70
HA5: Eastc 6A 40
HA5: Pinn 4D 40
HA7: Stan 6F 27
HA8: Edg 1H 43
RM1: Rom 3K 55
RM6: Chad H 6E 54
RM7: Rush G 3K 73
(not continuous)
SM6: Wall 5J 167
SW4 3F 119
SW16 7K 137
SW20 1G 153
TW16: Sun 1K 147
UB10: Ick 5C 56
Chase Bank Ct. N14 6B 22
(off Avenue Rd.)
Chase Cen., The NW10 3K 79
Chase Ct. SW3 2E 16
(off Beaufort Gdns.)
SW20 2G 153
TW7: Isle 2A 114
Chase Ct. Gdns. EN2: Enf 3H 23
Chase Cross Rd. RM5: Col R 1J 55
Chasefield Rd. SW17 4D 136
Chase Gdns. E4 4H 35
TW2: Whit 7H 113
Chase Grn. EN2: Enf 3H 23
Chase Grn. Av. EN2: Enf 2G 23
Chase Hill EN2: Enf 3H 23
Chase La. IG2: Ilf 5H 53
IG6: Ilf 5H 53
(not continuous)
Chaseley Dr. W4 5H 97
Chaseley St. E14 6A 86
Chasemore Cl. CR4: Mitc 7D 154
Chasemore Gdns. CR0: Wadd 5A 168
Chasemore Ho. SW6 7G 99
(off Williams Cl.)
Chase Ridings EN2: Enf 2F 23
Chase Rd. N14 5B 22
NW10 4K 79
Chase Rd. Trad. Est. NW10 4K 79
CHASE SIDE 1J 23
Chase Side EN2: Enf 3H 23
N14 5K 21
Chase Side Av. EN2: Enf 2H 23
Chaseside Av. SW20 1G 153
Chase Side Cres. EN2: Enf 1H 23
Chase Side Ind. Est. N14 7C 22
Chase Side Pl. EN2: Enf 2H 23
Chaseville Pde. N21 5E 22
Chaseville Pk. Rd. N21 5D 22
Chase Way N14 2A 32
Chaseways Vs. RM5: Col R 1F 55
Chasewood Av. EN2: Enf 2G 23
Chasewood Ct. NW7 5E 28
Chasewood Pk. HA1: Harr 3K 59
Chaston Pl. NW5 5E 64
(off Grafton Ter.)
Chater Ho. E2 3K 85
(off Roman Rd.)
Chateris Community Sports Cen. 1J 81
Chatfield Rd. CR0: Croy 1B 168
SW11 3A 118
Chatham Av. BR2: Hayes 7H 159
Chatham Cl. NW11 5J 45
SE18 3F 107
SM3: Sutt 7H 153
Chatham Ho. SM6: Wall 5F 167
(off Melbourne Rd.)
Chatham Pl. E9 6J 67
Chatham Rd. E17 3A 50
E18 2H 51
KT1: King T 2G 151
SW11 6D 118
Chatham St. SE17 4D 102
Chatsfield Pl. W5 6E 78
Chats Palace Arts Cen. 5K 67
Chatsworth Av. BR1: Brom 4K 141
DA15: Sidc 1A 144
HA9: Wemb 5F 61
NW4 2E 44
SW20 1G 153
Chatsworth Cl. BR4: W W'ck 2H 171
NW4 2E 44
W4 6J 97
Chatsworth Ct. HA7: Stan 5H 27
W8 4J 99
(off Pembroke Rd.)
Chatsworth Cres. TW3: Houn 4H 113
Chatsworth Dr. EN1: Enf 7B 24
Chatsworth Est. E5 4K 67
Chatsworth Gdns. HA2: Harr 1F 59
KT3: N Mald 5B 152
W3 1H 97
Chatsworth Ho. BR2: Brom 4J 159
(off Westmoreland Rd.)
E16 1K 105
(off Wesley Av.)
Chatsworth Lodge W4 5K 97
(off Bourne Pl.)
Chatsworth Pde. BR5: Pet W 5G 161
Chatsworth Pl. CR4: Mitc 3D 154
NW2 6E 62
TW11: Tedd 4A 132
Chatsworth Ri. W5 4F 79
Chatsworth Rd. CR0: Croy 4D 168
E5 3J 67
E15 5H 69
NW2 6E 62
SM3: Cheam 5F 165
UB4: Yead 4K 75
W4 6J 97
W5 4F 79
Chatsworth Way SE27 3B 138
CHATTERN HILL 4D 128
Chattern Hill TW15: Ashf 4D 128
Chattern Rd. TW15: Ashf 4E 128
Chatterton Ct. TW9: Kew 2F 115
Chatterton M. N4 3B 66
(off Chatterton Rd.)
Chatterton Rd. BR2: Brom 4B 160
N4 3B 66
Chatto Rd. SW11 5D 118
Chaucer Av. TW4: Cran 2K 111
TW9: Rich 3G 115
UB4: Hayes 5J 75
Chaucer Cl. N11 5B 32
Chaucer Ct. EN5: New Bar 5E 20
N16 4E 66
Chaucer Dr. SE1 4F 103
Chaucer Gdns. SM1: Sutt 3J 165
(not continuous)
Chaucer Grn. CR0: Croy 7H 157
Chaucer Ho. EN5: Barn 4A 20
SM1: Sutt 3J 165
(off Chaucer Gdns.)
SW1 6A 18
(off Churchill Gdns.)
Chaucer Mans. W14 6G 99
(off Queen's Club Gdns.)
Chaucer Rd. DA15: Sidc 1C 144
DA16: Well 1J 125
E7 6J 69
E11 6J 51
E17 2E 50
SE24 5A 120
SM1: Sutt 4J 165

Chaucer Rd. TW15: Ashf 4A **128**
W3 1J **97**
Chaucer Theatre *7K* **9**
(off Braham St.)
Chaucer Way SW19 5B **136**
Chaulden Ho. *EC1* *2F* **9**
(off Cranwood St.)
Chauncey Cl. N9 3B **34**
Chaundrye Cl. SE9 6D **124**
Chauntler Cl. E16 6K **87**
Chaville Ct. N11 4K **31**
Cheadle Ct. *NW8* *3B* **4**
(off Henderson Dr.)
Cheadle Ho. *E14* *6B* **86**
(off Copenhagen Pl.)
CHEAM 6G **165**
Cheam Comn. Rd. KT4: Wor Pk 2D **164**
Cheam Leisure Cen. 4F **165**
Cheam Mans. SM3: Cheam 7G **165**
Cheam Pk. Way SM3: Cheam 6G **165**
Cheam Rd. SM1: Sutt 6H **165**
SM2: Cheam 7F **165**
Cheam St. SE15 3J **121**
CHEAM VILLAGE 6G **165**
Cheapside EC2 1D **14** (6C **84**)
N13 4J **33**
N22 3A **48**
Chearsley *SE17* *4C* **102**
(off Deacon Way)
Cheddar Cl. N11 6J **31**
Cheddar Waye UB4: Yead 6K **75**
Cheddington Ho. *E2* *1G* **85**
(off Whiston Rd.)
Cheddington Rd. N18 3K **33**
Chedworth Cl. E16 6H **87**
Chedworth Ho. *N15* *4D* **48**
(off West Grn. Rd.)
Cheeseman Cl. TW12: Hamp 6C **130**
Cheesemans Ter. W14 5H **99**
(not continuous)
Cheethams Rd. E12 3C **70**
Cheffery Ct. TW15: Ashf 6D **128**
Cheldon Av. NW7 7A **30**
Chelford Rd. BR1: Brom 5F **141**
Chelmer Cres. IG11: Bark 2B **90**
Chelmer Rd. E9 5K **67**
Chelmsford Cl. E6 6D **88**
W6 6F **99**
Chelmsford Ct. *N14* *7C* **22**
(off Chelmsford Rd.)
Chelmsford Gdns. IG1: Ilf 7C **52**
Chelmsford Ho. *N7* *4K* **65**
(off Holloway Rd.)
Chelmsford Rd. E11 1F **69**
E17 6C **50**
E18 1H **51**
N14 7B **22**
Chelmsford Sq. NW10 1E **80**
Chelmsine Ct. HA4: Ruis 5E **38**
CHELSEA 6D **16** (5C **100**)
Chelsea Barracks 5H **17**
Chelsea Bri. SW1 7J **17** (6F **101**)
SW8 7J **17**
Chelsea Bri. Rd. SW1 5G **17** (5E **100**)
Chelsea Bri. Wharf SW8 7K **17** (6F **101**)
Chelsea Cinema 5C **100**
Chelsea Cloisters SW3 4D **16** (4C **100**)
Chelsea Cl. HA8: Edg 2G **43**
KT4: Wor Pk 7C **152**
NW10 1K **79**
TW12: Ham H 5G **131**
Chelsea College of Art & Design
6C **16** (5C **100**)
Chelsea Ct. *BR1: Brom* *3C* **160**
(off Holmdene Ct.)
SW3 *7G* **17**
(off Embankment Gdns.)
Chelsea Cres. NW2 6H **63**
SW10 1A **118**
Chelsea Emb. SW3 7D **16** (6C **100**)
Chelsea Farm Ho. Studios *SW10* *6B* **100**
(off Moravian Pl.)
Chelsea FC 7K **99**
Chelsea Flds. SW19 1B **154**
Chelsea Gdns. SM3: Cheam 4G **165**
SW1 6H **17** (5E **100**)
W13 5K **77**
Chelsea Ga. SW1 6H **17**
Chelsea Harbour SW10 1A **118**
Chelsea Harbour Design Cen.
SW10 *1A* **118**
(off Chelsea Harbour Dr.)
Chelsea Harbour Dr. SW10 1A **118**
Chelsea Lodge *SW3* *7F* **17**
(off Tite St.)
Chelsea Mnr. Ct. SW3 7D **16** (6C **100**)
Chelsea Mnr. Gdns. SW3 6D **16** (5C **100**)
Chelsea Mnr. St. SW3 6D **16** (5C **100**)
Chelsea Mnr. Studios *SW3* *6D* **16**
(off Flood St.)
Chelsea Pk. Gdns. SW3 7A **16** (6B **100**)
Chelsea Physic Garden 7E **16** (6D **100**)
Chelsea Reach Twr. *SW10* *7B* **100**
(off Worlds End Est.)
Chelsea Sports Cen. 6D **16** (5C **100**)
Chelsea Sq. SW3 5B **16** (5B **100**)
Chelsea Studios *SW6* *7K* **99**
(off Fulham Rd.)
Chelsea Towers SW3 7D **16**
Chelsea Village *SW6* *7K* **99**
(off Fulham Rd.)
Chelsea Vista SW6 2A **118**
Chelsea Wharf *SW10* *7B* **100**
(off Lots Rd.)
Chelsfield Av. N9 7E **24**
Chelsfield Gdns. SE26 3J **139**
Chelsfield Grn. N9 7E **24**
(not continuous)
Chelsfield Ho. *SE17* *4E* **102**
(off Massinger St.)
Chelsham Rd. CR2: S Croy 7D **168**
SW4 3H **119**
Chelsiter Ct. DA14: Sidc 4K **143**
Chelston App. HA4: Ruis 2J **57**
Chelston Rd. HA4: Ruis 1J **57**
Chelsworth Dr. SE18 6H **107**
Cheltenham Av. TW1: Twick 7A **114**
Cheltenham Cl. KT3: N Mald 3J **151**
UB5: N'olt 6F **59**
Cheltenham Ct. *HA7: Stan* *5H* **27**
(off Marsh La.)
Cheltenham Gdns. E6 2C **88**
Cheltenham Ho. IG8: Ilf 6K **37**
Cheltenham Pl. HA3: Kent 4E **42**
W3 1H **97**
Cheltenham Rd. BR6: Chels 3K **173**
E10 6E **50**
SE15 4J **121**
Cheltenham Ter. SW3 5F **17** (5D **100**)
Chelverton Rd. SW15 4F **117**
Chelwood N20 2G **31**
Chelwood Cl. E4 6J **25**
Chelwood Gdns. TW9: Kew 2G **115**
Chelwood Gdns. Pas.
TW9: Kew 2G **115**
Chelwood Ho. *W2* *1B* **10**
(off Gloucester Sq.)
Chelwood Wlk. SE4 4A **122**
Chenappa Cl. E13 3J **87**
Chenduit Way HA7: Stan 5E **26**
Cheney Ct. SE23 1K **139**
Cheney Row E17 1B **50**
Cheneys Rd. E11 3G **69**
Cheney St. HA5: Eastc 4A **40**
Chenies, The BR6: Pet W 6J **161**
NW1 *2H* **83**
(off Pancras Rd.)
Chenies Ho. *W2* *7K* **81**
(off Moscow Rd.)
W4 *7B* **98**
(off Corney Reach Way)
Chenies M. WC1 4C **6** (4H **83**)
Chenies Pl. NW1 2H **83**
Chenies St. WC1 5C **6** (5H **83**)
Cheniston Gdns. W8 3K **99**
Chepstow Cl. SW15 5G **117**
Chepstow Cnr. *W2* *6J* **81**
(off Chepstow Pl.)
Chepstow Ct. *W11* *7J* **81**
(off Chepstow Vs.)
Chepstow Cres. IG3: Ilf 6J **53**
W11 7J **81**
Chepstow Gdns. UB1: S'hall 6D **76**
Chepstow Pl. W2 6J **81**
Chepstow Ri. CR0: Croy 3E **168**
Chepstow Rd. CR0: Croy 3E **168**
W2 6J **81**
W7 3A **96**
Chepstow Vs. W11 7H **81**
Chequers IG9: Buck H 1E **36**
Chequers, The HA5: Pinn 3B **40**
Chequers Cl. BR5: St P 4K **161**
NW9 3A **44**
Chequers Ct. *EC1* *4D* **8**
(off Chequer St.)
Chequers Ho. *NW8* *3C* **4**
(off Jerome Cres.)
Chequers La. RM9: Dag 5F **91**
Chequers Pde. N13 5H **33**
RM9: Dag 1F **91**
SE9 *6D* **124**
(off Eltham High St.)
Chequer St. EC1 4D **8** (4C **84**)
(not continuous)
Chequers Way N13 5G **33**
Cherbury Cl. SE28 6D **90**
Cherbury Ct. *N1* *2D* **84**
(off St John's Est.)
Cherbury St. N1 2D **84**
Cherchefelle M. HA7: Stan 5G **27**
Cherimoya Gdns. KT8: W Mole 3F **149**
Cherington Rd. W7 1J **95**
Cheriton Av. BR2: Brom 5H **159**
IG5: Ilf 2D **52**
Cheriton Cl. EN4: Cockf 3J **21**
W5 5C **78**
Cheriton Ct. SE12 7J **123**
Cheriton Dr. SE18 7H **107**
Cheriton Sq. SW17 2E **136**
Cherry Av. UB1: S'hall 1B **94**
Cherry Blossom Cl. N13 5G **33**
Cherry Cl. E17 5D **50**
HA4: Ruis 3H **57**
NW9 2A **44**
SM4: Mord 4G **153**
SM5: Cars 2D **166**
SW2 7A **120**
W5 3D **96**
Cherrycot Hill BR6: Farnb 4G **173**
Cherrycot Ri. BR6: Farnb 4G **173**
Cherry Ct. HA5: Pinn 2B **40**
IG6: Ilf 3F **53**
W3 1A **98**
Cherry Cres. TW8: Bford 7B **96**
Cherrydown Av. E4 3G **35**
Cherrydown Cl. E4 3H **35**
Cherrydown Rd. DA14: Sidc 2D **144**
Cherrydown Wlk. RM7: Mawney 2H **55**
Cherry Gdn. Ho. *SE16* *2H* **103**
(off Cherry Gdn. St.)
Cherry Gdns. RM9: Dag 5F **73**
UB5: N'olt 7F **59**
Cherry Gdn. St. SE16 2H **103**
Cherry Gth. TW8: Bford 5D **96**
Cherry Gro. UB3: Hayes 1K **93**
UB8: Hil 5D **74**
Cherry Hill EN5: New Bar 6E **20**
HA3: Hrw W 6E **26**
Cherry Hill Gdns. CR0: Wadd 4K **167**
Cherrylands Cl. NW9 2J **61**
Cherry La. UB7: W Dray 4B **92**
Cherry Laurel Wlk. SW2 6K **119**
Cherry Orchard SE7 6A **106**
UB7: W Dray 2A **92**
Cherry Orchard Gdns. CR0: Croy 1D **168**
KT8: W Mole 3D **148**
Cherry Orchard Rd. BR2: Brom 2C **172**
CR0: Croy 2D **168**
KT8: W Mole 3E **148**
Cherry Rd. EN3: Enf W 1D **24**
Cherry St. RM7: Rom 5K **55**
Cherry Tree Av. UB7: Yiew 6B **74**
Cherry Tree Cl. E9 1J **85**
HA0: Wemb 4A **60**
Cherry Tree Ct. *NW1* *7G* **65**
(off Camden Rd.)
NW9 4J **43**
SE7 6A **106**
Cherry Tree Dr. SW16 3J **137**
Cherry Tree Hill N2 5C **46**
Cherry Tree Ho. N22 7D **32**
Cherry Tree Ri. IG9: Buck H 4F **37**
Cherry Tree Rd. E15 5G **69**
N2 4D **46**
Cherry Tree Ter. *SE1* *7H* **15**
(off Whites Grounds)
Cherry Tree Wlk.
BR3: Beck 4B **158**
BR4: W W'ck 4H **171**
EC1 4D **8** (4C **84**)
Cherrytree Way HA7: Stan 6G **27**
Cherry Wlk. BR2: Hayes 1J **171**
Cherry Way KT19: Ewe 6K **163**
TW17: Shep 4F **147**
Cherry Wood Cl. KT2: King T 7G **133**
Cherrywood Cl. E3 3A **86**
Cherrywood Ct. TW11: Tedd 5A **132**
Cherrywood Dr. SW15 5F **117**
Cherrywood La. SM4: Mord 4G **153**
Cherry Wood Way W5 5G **79**
Chertsey Bri. Rd. KT16: Chert 7A **146**
Chertsey Ct. SW14 3H **115**
Chertsey Dr. SM3: Cheam 2G **165**
CHERTSEY MEADS 7A **146**
Chertsey Rd. E11 2F **69**
IG1: Ilf 4H **71**
TW1: Twick 6K **113**
TW2: Twick 2F **131**
TW13: Felt 3G **129**
TW15: Ashf 7F **129**
TW16: Sun 7F **129**
TW17: Shep 7A **146**
Chertsey St. SW17 5E **136**
Chervil Cl. TW13: Felt 3J **129**
Chervil M. SE28 1B **108**
Cherwell Ct. KT19: Ewe 4J **163**
Cherwell Ho. NW8 4B **4**
Cherwell Way HA4: Ruis 6E **38**
Cheryls Cl. SW6 1K **117**
Cheseman St. SE26 3H **139**
Chesfield Rd. KT2: King T 7E **132**
Chesham Av. BR5: Pet W 6F **161**
Chesham Cl. RM7: Rom 4K **55**
SW1 2G **17**
Chesham Cres. SE20 1J **157**
Chesham Flats *W1* *2H* **11**
(off Brown Hart Gdns.)
Chesham M. SW1 1G **17**
Chesham Pl. SW1 2G **17** (3E **100**)
(not continuous)
Chesham Rd. KT1: King T 2G **151**
SE20 2J **157**
SW19 5B **136**
Chesham St. NW10 3K **61**
SW1 2G **17** (3E **100**)
Chesham Ter. W13 2B **96**
Cheshire Cl. CR4: Mitc 3J **155**
E17 1D **50**
SE4 2B **122**
Cheshire Ct. *EC4* *1K* **13**
(off Fleet St.)
Cheshire Gdns. KT9: Chess 6D **162**
Cheshire Ho. N18 4C **34**
SM4: Mord 7K **153**
Cheshire Rd. N22 7E **32**
Cheshire St. E2 3K **9** (4F **85**)
Cheshir Ho. NW4 4E **44**
Chesholm Rd. N16 3E **66**
Cheshunt Ho. *NW6* *1K* **81**
(off Mortimer Cres.)
Cheshunt Rd. DA17: Belv 5G **109**
E7 6K **69**

Chesil Ct. E2 2J **85**
SW3 7D **16** (6C **100**)
Chesilton Rd. SW6 1H **117**
Chesil Way UB4: Hayes 3H **75**
Chesley Gdns. E6 2B **88**
Chesney Ct. *W9* *4J* ***81***
(off Shirland Rd.)
Chesney Cres. CR0: New Ad 7E **170**
Chesney Ho. *SE13* *4F* ***123***
(off Mercator Rd.)
Chesney St. SW11 1E **118**
Chesnut Gro. N17 3F **49**
Chesnut Rd. N17 3F **49**
(not continuous)
Chesnut Row N3 7D **30**
Chessell Cl. CR7: Thor H 4B **156**
Chessholme Ct. *TW16: Sun* *7G* ***129***
(off Scotts Av.)
Chessholme Rd. TW15: Ashf 6E **128**
Chessing Ct. *N2* *3D* ***46***
(off Fortis Grn.)
CHESSINGTON 5F **163**
Chessington Av. DA7: Bex 7E **108**
N3 3G **45**
Chessington Cl. KT19: Ewe 6J **163**
Chessington Ct. HA5: Pinn 4D **40**
N3 *3H* ***45***
(off Charter Way)
Chessington Hall Gdns.
KT9: Chess 7D **162**
Chessington Hill Pk. KT9: Chess 5G **163**
Chessington Ho. SW8 2H **119**
Chessington Lodge N3 3H **45**
Chessington Mans. E10 7C **50**
E11 7G **51**
Chessington Pde. KT9: Chess 6D **162**
Chessington Pk. KT9: Chess 4G **163**
Chessington Rd. KT17: Ewe 7B **164**
KT19: Ewe 6G **163**
Chessington Sports Cen. 7D **162**
Chessington Trade Pk.
KT9: Chess 4G **163**
Chessington Way BR4: W W'ck 2D **170**
Chesson Rd. W14 6H **99**
Chesswood Way HA5: Pinn 2B **40**
Chestbrook Ct. *EN1: Enf* *5K* ***23***
(off Forsyth Pl.)
Chester Av. TW2: Whit 1D **130**
TW10: Rich 6F **115**
Chester Cl. SM1: Sutt 2J **165**
SW1 7J **11** (2F **101**)
SW13 3D **116**
TW10: Rich 6F **115**
TW15: Ashf 5F **129**
UB8: Hil 6D **74**
Chester Cl. Nth. NW1 1K **5** (3F **83**)
Chester Cl. Sth. NW1 2K **5** (3F **83**)
Chester Cotts. SW1 4G **17**
Chester Ct. *BR2: Brom* *4H* ***159***
(off Durham Rd.)
NW1 1K **5** (3F **83**)
SE5 *7D* ***102***
(off Lomond Gro.)
SE8 5K **103**
W6 *4F* ***99***
(off Wolverton Gdns.)
Chester Cres. E8 5F **67**
Chester Dr. HA2: Harr 6D **40**
Chesterfield Cl. SE13 2F **123**
Chesterfield Ct. *KT5: Surb* *5E* ***150***
(off Cranes Pk.)
Chesterfield Dr. KT10: Hin W 2A **162**
Chesterfield Flats *EN5: Barn* *5A* ***20***
(off Bells Hill)
Chesterfield Gdns. N4 5B **48**
SE10 1F **123**
W1 4J **11** (1F **101**)
Chesterfield Gro. SE22 5F **121**
Chesterfield Hill W1 4J **11** (1F **101**)
Chesterfield Ho. *W1* *4H* ***11***
(off Chesterfield Gdns.)
Chesterfield Lodge *N21* *7E* ***22***
(off Church Hill)
Chesterfield M. N4 5B **48**
TW15: Ashf 4A **128**
Chesterfield Rd. E10 6E **50**
EN5: Barn 5A **20**
KT19: Ewe 7K **163**
N3 6D **30**
TW15: Ashf 4A **128**
W4 6J **97**
Chesterfield St. W1 4J **11** (1F **101**)
Chesterfield Wlk. SE10 1F **123**
Chesterfield Way SE15 7J **103**
UB3: Hayes 2J **93**
Chesterford Gdns. NW3 4K **63**
Chesterford Ho. *SE18* *1B* ***124***
(off Tellson Av.)
Chesterford Rd. E12 5D **70**
Chester Gdns. EN3: Pond E 6C **24**
SM4: Mord 6A **154**
W13 6B **78**
Chester Ga. NW1 2J **5** (3F **83**)
Chester Ho. N10 2F **47**
SE8 6B **104**
SW1 *3J* ***17***
(off Eccleston Pl.)
SW9 *7A* ***102***
(off Brixton Rd.)
Chesterman Ct. *W4* *7A* ***98***
(off Corney Reach Way)
Chester M. E17 2C **50**
SW1 1J **17** (3F **101**)
Chester Pl. NW1 1J **5** (3F **83**)
Chester Rd. DA15: Sidc 5J **125**
(not continuous)
E7 7B **70**
E11 6K **51**
E16 4G **87**
E17 5K **49**
HA6: Nwood 1H **39**
IG3: Ilf 1K **71**
IG7: Chig 3K **37**
N9 1C **34**
N17 3D **48**
N19 2F **65**
NW1 2H **5** (3E **82**)
SW19 6E **134**
TW4: Houn 3K **111**
TW6: H'row A 3C **110**
Chester Row SW1 4G **17** (4E **100**)
Chesters, The KT3: N Mald 1A **152**
Chester Sq. SW1 3H **17** (4E **100**)
Chester Sq. M. SW1 2J **17**
Chester St. E2 4G **85**
SW1 1H **17** (3E **100**)
Chester Ter. IG11: Bark 6H **71**
NW1 1J **5** (3F **83**)
(not continuous)
Chesterton Cl. SW18 5J **117**
UB6: G'frd 2F **77**
Chesterton Ct. *W3* *3H* ***97***
(off Bollo Bri. Rd.)
W5 5D **78**
Chesterton Dr. TW19: Stanw 1B **128**
Chesterton Ho. *CR0: Croy* *4D* ***168***
(off Heathfield Rd.)
W10 *5G* ***81***
(off Portobello Rd.)
Chesterton Rd. E13 3J **87**
W10 5F **81**
Chesterton Sq. W8 4J **99**
Chesterton Ter. E13 3J **87**
KT1: King T 2G **151**
Chester Way SE11 4K **19** (4A **102**)
Chesthunte Rd. N17 1C **48**
Chestnut All. SW6 6H **99**
Chestnut Av. BR4: W W'ck 5G **171**
E7 4K **69**
E12 2C **70**
HA0: Wemb 5B **60**
HA6: Nwood 2H **39**
HA8: Edg 6K **27**
IG9: Buck H 3G **37**
KT8: E Mos 3K **149**
KT10: Esh 7H **149**
Chestnut Av. KT19: Ewe 4A **164**
N8 5J **47**
SW14 3K **115**
TW8: Bford 4D **96**
TW11: Tedd 2K **149**
TW12: Hamp 7E **130**
UB7: Yiew 7B **74**
Chestnut Av. Nth. E17 4F **51**
Chestnut Av. Sth. E17 5E **50**
Chestnut Cl. BR6: Chels 5K **173**
DA15: Sidc 1A **144**
IG9: Buck H 3G **37**
N14 5B **22**
N16 2D **66**
SE6 5E **140**
SE14 1B **122**
SM5: Cars 1D **166**
SW16 4A **138**
TW15: Ashf 4D **128**
TW16: Sun 6H **129**
UB3: Hayes 7G **75**
UB7: Harl, Sip 7D **92**
Chestnut Ct. *CR2: S Croy* *4C* ***168***
(off Bramley Hill)
N8 5J **47**
SW6 6H **99**
TW13: Hanw 5B **130**
W8 *3K* ***99***
(off Abbots Wlk.)
Chestnut Dr. DA7: Bex 3D **126**
E11 6J **51**
HA3: Hrw W 7E **26**
HA5: Pinn 6B **40**
Chestnut Gro. CR2: Sels 7H **169**
CR4: Mitc 5H **155**
DA2: Dart 4K **145**
EN4: E Barn 5J **21**
HA0: Wemb 5B **60**
KT3: N Mald 3K **151**
SE20 7H **139**
SW12 7E **118**
TW7: Isle 4A **114**
W5 3D **96**
Chestnut Ho. *W4* *4A* ***98***
(off The Orchard)
Chestnut La. N20 1B **30**
Chestnut Pl. SE26 4F **139**
Chestnut Ri. SE18 6H **107**
WD23: Bush 1A **26**
Chestnut Rd. KT2: King T 7E **132**
SE27 3B **138**
SW20 2F **153**
TW2: Twick 2J **131**
TW15: Ashf 4D **128**
Chestnuts, The HA5: H End 1D **40**
N5 *4C* ***66***
(off Highbury Grange)
UB10: Uxb 7A **56**
Chestnut Ter. SM1: Sutt 4K **165**
Chestnut Wlk. IG8: Wfd G 5D **36**
TW17: Shep 4G **147**
Chestnut Way TW13: Felt 3K **129**
Cheston Av. CR0: Croy 2A **170**
Chestwood Gro. UB10: Hil 7B **56**
Chettle Cl. *SE1* *3D* ***102***
(off Spurgeon St.)
Chettle Ct. N8 6A **48**
Chetwode Ho. NW8 3C **4**
Chetwode Rd. SW17 3D **136**
Chetwood Wlk. *E6* *5C* ***88***
(off Greenwich Cres.)
Chetwynd Av. EN4: E Barn 1J **31**
Chetwynd Dr. UB10: Hil 2B **74**
Chetwynd Rd. NW5 4F **65**
Chetwynd Vs. *NW5* *4F* ***65***
(off Chetwynd Rd.)
Chevalier Cl. HA7: Stan 4K **27**
Cheval Pl. SW7 1D **16** (3C **100**)
Cheval St. E14 3C **104**
Cheveney Wlk. BR2: Brom 3J **159**
Chevening Rd. NW6 2F **81**
SE10 5H **105**
SE19 6D **138**
Chevenings, The DA14: Sidc 3C **144**
Cheverell Ho. *E2* *2G* ***85***
(off Pritchard's Rd.)
Cheverton Rd. N19 1H **65**
Chevet St. E9 5A **68**
Chevington NW2 6H **63**
Cheviot *N17* *7C* ***34***
(off Northumberland Gro.)
Cheviot Cl. DA7: Bex 2K **127**
EN1: Enf 2J **23**
UB3: Harl 7F **93**
Cheviot Ct. *SE14* *6J* ***103***
(off Avonley Rd.)
UB2: S'hall 4F **95**
Cheviot Gdns. NW2 2F **63**
SE27 4B **138**
Cheviot Ga. NW2 2G **63**
Cheviot Ho. *E1* *6H* ***85***
(off Commercial Rd.)
Cheviot Rd. SE27 5A **138**
Cheviot Way IG2: Ilf 4J **53**
Chevron Cl. E16 6J **87**
Chevy Rd. UB2: S'hall 2G **95**
Chewton Rd. E17 4A **50**
Cheylesmore Ho. *SW1* *5J* ***17***
(off Ebury Bri. Rd.)
Cheyne Av. E18 3H **51**
TW2: Whit 1D **130**
Cheyne Cl. BR2: Brom 3C **172**
NW4 5E **44**
Cheyne Ct. SW3 7E **16** (6D **100**)
Cheyne Gdns. SW3 7D **16** (6C **100**)
Cheyne Hill KT5: Surb 4F **151**
Cheyne M. SW3 7D **16** (6C **100**)
Cheyne Pk. Dr. BR4: W W'ck 3E **170**
Cheyne Path W7 5K **77**
Cheyne Pl. SW3 7E **16** (6D **100**)
Cheyne Rd. TW15: Ashf 7F **129**
Cheyne Row SW3 7C **16** (6C **100**)
Cheyne Wlk. CR0: Croy 2G **169**
N21 5G **23**
NW4 6E **44**
SW3 7C **16** (7B **100**)
(not continuous)
Cheyneys Av. HA8: Edg 6J **27**
Chichele Gdns. CR0: Croy 4E **168**
Chichele Rd. NW2 5F **63**
Chicheley Gdns. HA3: Hrw W 7B **26**
(not continuous)
Chicheley Rd. HA3: Hrw W 7B **26**
Chicheley St. SE1 6H **13** (2K **101**)
Chichester Av. HA4: Ruis 2F **57**
Chichester Cl. E6 6C **88**
SE3 7A **106**
TW12: Hamp 6D **130**
Chichester Ct. HA7: Stan 3E **42**
HA8: Edg *6B* ***28***
(off Whitchurch La.)
KT17: Ewe 7B **164**
NW1 *7G* ***65***
(off Royal Coll. St.)
TW19: Stanw 1A **128**
UB5: N'olt 1D **76**
Chichester Gdns. IG1: Ilf 7C **52**
Chichester Ho. NW6 2J **81**
SW9 *7A* ***102***
(off Brixton Rd.)
Chichester M. SE27 4A **138**
Chichester Rents WC2 7J **7**
Chichester Rd. CR0: Croy 3E **168**
E11 3G **69**
N9 1B **34**
NW6 2J **81**
W2 5K **81**
Chichester St. SW1 6B **18** (5G **101**)
Chichester Way E14 4F **105**
TW14: Felt 7A **112**
Chicken Shed Theatre 5K **21**
Chicksand Ho. *E1* *5K* ***9***
(off Chicksand St.)
Chicksand St. E1 6K **9** (5F **85**)
(not continuous)
Chiddingfold N12 3D **30**

Chiddingstone SE13 5E 122
Chiddingstone Av. DA7: Bex 7F 109
Chiddingstone St. SW6 2J 117
Chieveley Pde. DA7: Bex 4H 127
(off Chieveley Rd.)
DA7: Bex 3H 127
(Mayplace Rd. E.)
Chieveley Rd. DA7: Bex 4H 127
Chignell Pl. W13 1A 96
CHIGWELL 3K 37
Chigwell Hill E1 7H 85
Chigwell Hurst Ct. HA5: Pinn 3B 40
Chigwell Pk. IG7: Chig 4K 37
Chigwell Pk. Dr. IG7: Chig 4K 37
Chigwell Ri. IG7: Chig 2K 37
Chigwell Rd. E18 3K 51
IG8: Wfd G 2A 52
Chilcombe Ho. SW15 7C 116
(off Fontley Way)
Chilcot Cl. E14 6D 86
Chilcott Cl. HA0: Wemb 4C 60
Childebert Rd. SW17 2F 137
Childeric Rd. SE14 7A 104
Childerley KT1: King T 3G 151
(off Burritt Rd.)
Childerley St. SW6 1G 117
Childers, The IG8: Wfd G 5J 37
Childers St. SE8 6A 104
Child La. SE10 3H 105
(off School Bank Rd.)
Children's Discovery Cen. 7F 69
Childs Ct. UB3: Hayes 7J 75
CHILD'S HILL 3J 63
Childs Hill Wlk. NW2 3H 63
(off Cricklewood La.)
Child's La. SE19 6E 138
Child's M. SW5 4J 99
(off Child's Pl.)
Child's Pl. SW5 4J 99
Child's St. SW5 4J 99
Child's Wlk. SW5 4J 99
(off Child's St.)
Childs Way NW11 5H 45
Chilham Cl. DA5: Bexl 7F 127
UB6: G'frd 2A 78
Chilham Ho. SE1 3D 102
SE15 6J 103
Chilham Rd. SE9 4C 142
Chilham Way BR2: Hayes 7J 159
Chilianwallan Memorial 7G 17 (6E 100)
Chillerton Rd. SW17 5E 136
Chillingford Ho. SW17 4A 136
Chillington Dr. SW11 4B 118
Chillingworth Gdns. TW1: Twick 3K 131
Chillingworth Rd. N7 5A 66
Chilmark Gdns. KT3: N Mald 6C 152
Chilmark Rd. SW16 2H 155
Chiltern Av. TW2: Whit 1E 130
Chiltern Cl. CR0: Croy 3E 168
DA7: Bex 1K 127
KT4: Wor Pk 1E 164
UB10: Ick 2C 56
Chiltern Ct. EN5: New Bar 5F 21
HA1: Harr 5H 41
N10 2E 46
NW1 4F 5
(off Baker St.)
SE14 7J 103
(off Avonley Rd.)
UB8: Hil 4D 74
Chiltern Dene EN2: Enf 4E 22
Chiltern Dr. KT5: Surb 6G 151
Chiltern Gdns. BR2: Brom 4H 159
NW2 3F 63
Chiltern Ho. N9 3B 34
SE17 6D 102
(off Portland Wlk.)
W5 5E 78
W10 5G 81
(off Telford Rd.)
Chiltern Rd. E3 4C 86
HA5: Eastc 5A 40
IG2: Ilf 5J 53
Chilterns, The BR1: Brom 2K 159
(off Murray Av.)
Chiltern St. W1 5G 5 (5E 82)
Chiltern Way IG8: Wfd G 3D 36
Chilthorne Cl. SE6 7B 122
Chilton Av. W5 4D 96
Chilton Ct. N22 7D 32
(off Truro Rd.)
Chilton Gro. SE8 4K 103
Chiltonian Ind. Est. SE12 6H 123
Chilton Rd. HA8: Edg 6B 28
TW9: Rich 3G 115
Chiltons, The E18 2J 51
Chilton St. E2 3K 9 (4F 85)
Chilvers Cl. TW2: Twick 2J 131
Chilver St. SE10 5H 105
Chilworth Ct. SW19 1F 135
Chilworth Gdns. SM1: Sutt 3A 166
Chilworth M. W2 1A 10 (6B 82)
Chilworth St. W2 1A 10 (6A 82)
Chimes Av. N13 5F 33
Chimney Ct. E1 1H 103
(off Brewhouse La.)
China Ct. E1 1H 103
(off Asher Way)
China Hall M. SE16 3J 103
China M. SW2 7K 119
China Wlk. SE11 3K 101
China Wharf SE1 6K 15 (2G 103)
Chinbrook Cres. SE12 3K 141
Chinbrook Rd. SE12 3K 141
Chinchilla Dr. TW4: Houn 2A 112
Chine, The HA0: Wemb 5B 60
N10 4G 47
N21 6G 23
Ching Ct. WC2 1E 12
(off Monmouth St.)
Chingdale Rd. E4 3B 36
CHINGFORD 1K 35
Chingford Av. E4 3H 35
CHINGFORD GREEN 1A 36
CHINGFORD HATCH 4A 36
Chingford Ind. Cen. E4 5F 35
Chingford La. IG8: Wfd G 4B 36
CHINGFORD MOUNT 4H 35
Chingford Mt. Rd. E4 4H 35
Chingford Rd. E4 6H 35
E17 1D 50
Chingley Cl. BR1: Brom 6G 141
Ching Way E4 6G 35
(not continuous)
Chinnery Cl. EN1: Enf 1A 24
Chinnock's Wharf E14 7A 86
(off Narrow St.)
Chinnor Cres. UB6: G'frd 2F 77
Chipka St. E14 2E 104
(not continuous)
Chipley St. SE14 6A 104
Chipmunk Gro. UB5: N'olt 3C 76
Chippendale All. UB8: Uxb 7A 56
Chippendale Ho. SW1 6K 17
(off Churchill Gdns.)
Chippendale St. E5 3K 67
Chippendale Waye UB8: Uxb 7A 56
Chippenham KT1: King T 2F 151
(off Excelsior Cl.)
Chippenham Av. HA9: Wemb 5H 61
Chippenham Cl. HA5: Eastc 4H 39
Chippenham Gdns. NW6 3J 81
Chippenham M. W9 4J 81
Chippenham Rd. W9 4J 81
Chipperfield Ho. SW3 5C 16
(off Ixworth Pl.)
Chipperfield Rd. BR5: St P 7A 144
(not continuous)
CHIPPING BARNET 4B 20
Chipping Cl. EN5: Barn 3B 20
Chipstead Av. CR7: Thor H 4B 156
Chipstead Cl. SE19 7F 139
SM2: Sutt 7K 165
Chipstead Gdns. NW2 2D 62
Chipstead St. SW6 1J 117
Chip St. SW4 3H 119
Chirk Cl. UB4: Yead 4C 76
Chisenhale Rd. E3 2A 86
Chisholm Ct. W6 5C 98
Chisholm Rd. CR0: Croy 2E 168
TW10: Rich 6F 115
Chisledon Wlk. E9 6B 68
(off Osborne Rd.)
CHISLEHURST 6F 143
Chislehurst Av. N12 7F 31
Chislehurst Caves 1E 160
Chislehurst Rd. BR1: Brom 2B 160
BR5: Orp, Pet W, St M Cry 4J 161
BR6: Orp 7K 161
BR7: Chst 2B 160
DA14: Sidc 5A 144
TW10: Rich 5E 114
CHISLEHURST WEST 5E 142
Chislet Cl. BR3: Beck 7C 140
Chisley Rd. N15 6E 48
Chiswell Sq. SE3 2K 123
Chiswell St. EC1 5E 8 (5C 84)
SE5 7D 102
(off Edmund St.)
CHISWICK 5K 97
Chiswick Bri. W4 2J 115
Chiswick Cl. CR0: Bedd 3K 167
Chiswick Comn. Rd. W4 4K 97
Chiswick Community Sports Hall 7K 97
Chiswick Ct. HA5: Pinn 3D 40
W4 4H 97
Chiswick High Rd. TW8: Bford 5G 97
(not continuous)
W4 5H 97
Chiswick House 6A 98
Chiswick La. W4 5A 98
Chiswick La. Sth. W4 6B 98
Chiswick Mall W4 6B 98
W6 5C 98
Chiswick Pk. W4 4H 97
Chiswick Plaza W4 6J 97
Chiswick Quay W4 1J 115
Chiswick Rd. N9 2B 34
W4 4J 97
CHISWICK RDBT. 5G 97
Chiswick Sq. W4 6A 98
Chiswick Staithe W4 1J 115
Chiswick Ter. W4 4J 97
(off Chiswick Rd.)
Chiswick Village W4 6G 97
Chiswick Wharf W4 6B 98
Chitterfield Ga. UB7: Sip 7C 92
Chitty's La. RM8: Dag 2D 72
Chitty St. W1 5B 6 (5G 83)
Chivalry Rd. SW11 5C 118
Chivelston SW19 1F 135
Chivenor Gro. KT2: King T 5D 132
Chivers Rd. E4 3J 35
Choats Mnr. Way RM9: Dag 2E 90
Choats Rd. IG11: Bark 2C 90
RM9: Bark, Dag 2C 90
Chobham Gdns. SW19 2F 135
Chobham Rd. E15 5F 69
Chocolate Studios N1 1E 8
(off Shepherdess Pl.)
Cholmeley Cres. N6 7F 47
Cholmeley Lodge N6 1F 65
Cholmeley Pk. N6 1F 65
Cholmley Gdns. NW6 5J 63
Cholmley Rd. KT7: T Ditt 6B 150
Cholmley Ter. KT7: T Ditt 7B 150
(off Portsmouth Rd.)
Cholmley Vs. KT7: T Ditt 6B 150
(off Portsmouth Rd.)
Cholmondeley Av. NW10 2C 80
Cholmondeley Wlk. TW9: Rich 5C 114
(not continuous)
Choppin's Ct. E1 1H 103
Chopwell Cl. E15 7F 69
Chorleywood Cres. BR5: St P 2K 161
Choumert Gro. SE15 2G 121
Choumert M. SE15 2G 121
Choumert Rd. SE15 3F 121
Choumert Sq. SE15 2G 121
Chow Sq. E8 5F 67
Chrisp Ho. SE10 6G 105
(off Maze Hill)
Chrisp St. E14 5D 86
(not continuous)
Christabel Cl. TW7: Isle 3J 113
Christchurch Av. DA8: Erith 6K 109
HA0: Wemb 6E 60
HA3: Kent, W'stone 4K 41
N12 6F 31
NW6 1F 81
TW11: Tedd 5A 132
Christchurch Cl. EN2: Enf 2H 23
N12 7G 31
SW19 7B 136
Christ Chu. Ct. NW10 1A 80
Christchurch Ct. EC4 7B 8
(off Warwick La.)
UB4: Yead 4A 76
(off Dunedin Way)
Christchurch Flats TW9: Rich 3E 114
Christchurch Gdns.
HA3: W'stone 4A 42
Christchurch Grn. HA0: Wemb 6E 60
Christchurch Hill NW3 3B 64
Christchurch Ho. SW2 1K 137
(off Christchurch Rd.)
Christchurch La. EN5: Barn 2B 20
Christchurch Lodge EN4: Cockf 4J 21
Christchurch Pk. SM2: Sutt 7A 166
Christchurch Pas. EN5: Barn 2B 20
NW3 3A 64
Christchurch Path UB3: Harl 3E 92
Christchurch Pl. SW8 2H 119
Christ Chu. Rd. BR3: Beck 2C 158
SW14 5H 115
Christchurch Rd. DA15: Sidc 4K 143
IG1: Ilf 1F 71
KT5: Surb 6F 151
N8 6J 47
SW2 1K 137
SW19 7B 136
Christchurch Sq. E9 1J 85
Christchurch St. SW3 7E 16 (6D 100)
Christchurch Ter. SW3 7E 16
Christchurch Way SE10 5G 105
Christian Ct. SE16 1B 104
Christian Flds. SW16 7A 138
Christian Pl. E1 6G 85
(off Burslem St.)
Christian St. E1 6G 85
Christie Ct. N19 2J 65
Christie Dr. CR0: Croy 5G 157
Christie Gdns. RM6: Chad H 6B 54
Christie Ho. SE10 5H 105
(off Blackwall La.)
Christie Rd. E9 6A 68
Christina Sq. N4 1B 66
Christina St. EC2 3G 9 (4E 84)
Christine Worsley Cl. N21 1G 33
Christopher Av. W7 3A 96
Christopher Cl. DA15: Sidc 5K 125
SE16 2K 103
Christopher Ct. TW15: Ashf 5A 128
Christopher Gdns. RM9: Dag 5D 72
Christopher Ho. DA15: Sidc 2A 144
(off Station Rd.)
Christopher Pl. NW1 1D 6 (3H 83)
Christopher Rd. UB2: S'hall 4K 93
Christophers M. W11 1G 99
Christopher St. EC2 4F 9 (4D 84)
Chryssell Rd. SW9 7A 102
Chubworthy St. SE14 6A 104
Chudleigh DA14: Sidc 4B 144
Chudleigh Cres. IG3: Ilf 4J 71
Chudleigh Gdns. SM1: Sutt 3A 166
Chudleigh Rd. NW6 7F 63
SE4 5B 122
TW2: Twick 6J 113
(not continuous)
Chudleigh St. E1 6K 85
Chudleigh Way HA4: Ruis 1J 57
Chulsa Rd. SE26 5H 139

Chumleigh Gdns. SE5 . . . . .6E 102
(off Chumleigh St.)
Chumleigh St. SE5 . . . . .6E 102
Chumleigh Wlk. KT5: Surb 4F 151
Church All. CR0: Croy 1A 168
Church App. SE21 . . . . .3D 138
Church Av. BR3: Beck 1C 158
DA14: Sidc 5A 144
E4 . . . . .6A 36
(not continuous)
E12 . . . . .3B 70
HA4: Ruis 1F 57
HA5: Pinn 6C 40
N2 . . . . .2B 46
NW1 . . . . .6F 65
SW14 .3K 115
UB2: S'hall 3C 94
UB5: N'olt 7D 58
Churchbank E17 . . . . .4C 50
(off Teresa M.)
Churchbury Cl. EN1: Enf 2K 23
Churchbury La. EN1: Enf 3J 23
Churchbury Rd. EN1: Enf 2K 23
SE9 . . . . .7B 124
Church Cloisters EC3 . . . . .3G 15
Church Cl. HA6: Nwood 1H 39
HA8: Edg 5D 28
N20 . . . . .3H 31
TW3: Houn 2C 112
UB4: Hayes 5F 75
UB7: W Dray 3A 92
W8 . . . . .2K 99
Church Ct. SE16 . . . . .2B 104
(off Rotherhithe St.)
TW9: Rich 5D 114
Church Cres. E9 . . . . .7K 67
N3 . . . . .1H 45
N10 . . . . .4F 47
N20 . . . . .3H 31
Churchcroft Cl. SW12 . . . . .7E 118
Churchdown BR1: Brom 4G 141
Church Dr. BR4: W W'ck 3G 171
HA2: Harr 6E 40
NW9 . . . . .1K 61
Church Elm La. RM10: Dag 6G 73
CHURCH END
Finchley 1H 45
Willesden 7A 62
Church End E17 . . . . .4D 50
NW4 . . . . .3D 44
Church Entry EC4 . . . . .1B 14
Church Est. Almshouses
TW9: Rich 4F 115
(off Sheen Rd.)
Church Farm House Mus. 3D 44
Church Farm La. SM3: Cheam 6G 165
Church Farm Pool 7J 21
Churchfield Av. N12 . . . . .6G 31
Churchfield Cl. HA2: Harr 4G 41
UB3: Hayes 7H 75
Churchfield Mans. SW6 . . . . .2H 117
(off New Kings Rd.)
Churchfield Pl. TW17: Shep 7D 146
Churchfield Rd. DA16: Well 3A 126
KT12: Walt T 7J 147
W3 . . . . .1J 97
W7 . . . . .2J 95
W13 . . . . .1B 96
Churchfields E18 . . . . .1J 51
KT8: W Mole 3E 148
SE10 . . . . .6E 104
Churchfields Av. TW13: Hanw 3D 130
Churchfields Rd. BR3: Beck 2K 157
Churchfield Way N12 . . . . .6F 31
Church Gdns. HA0: Wemb 4A 60
W5 . . . . .2D 96
Church Gth. N19 . . . . .2H 65
(off St John's Gro.)
Church Ga. SW6 . . . . .3G 117
Church Grn. SW9 . . . . .1A 120
UB3: Hayes 6H 75
Church Gro. KT1: Ham W 1C 150
SE13 . . . . .5D 122

Church Hill DA1: Cray 4K 127
E17 . . . . .4C 50
HA1: Harr 1J 59
N21 . . . . .7E 22
SE18 . . . . .3D 106
SM5: Cars 5D 166
SW19 .5H 135
Church Hill Rd. E17 . . . . .4D 50
EN4: E Barn 6H 21
KT6: Surb 5E 150
SM3: Cheam 3F 165
Church Hill Wood BR5: St M Cry 5K 161
Church Ho. EC1 . . . . .3B 8
(off Compton St.)
SW1 . . . . .1D 18
(off Gt. Smith St.)
Church Hyde SE18 . . . . .6J 107
Church Av. HA3: Kent 6B 42
UB10: Hil 3D 74
Churchill Cl. TW14: Felt 1H 129
UB10: Hil 3D 74
Churchill Ct. BR6: Farnb 5G 173
HA2: Harr 5F 41
(North Harrow)
HA2: Harr 2F 59
(Roxeth)
HA5: N End 1C 40
N4 . . . . .7A 48
N9 . . . . .1K 33
UB5: N'olt 5E 58
W5 . . . . .4F 79
Churchill Gdns. SW1 . . . . .6A 18 (5G 101)
W3 . . . . .6G 79
Churchill Gdns. Rd. SW1 . . . . .6K 17 (5F 101)
Churchill Mus. (Cabinet War Rooms)
. . . . .6D 12 (2H 101)
Churchill Pl. E14 . . . . .1D 104
HA1: Harr 4J 41
Churchill Rd. CR2: S Croy 7C 168
E16 . . . . .6A 88
HA8: Edg 6A 28
NW2 . . . . .6D 62
NW5 . . . . .4F 65
Churchills M. IG8: W'fd G 6C 36
Churchill Ter. E4 . . . . .4H 35
Churchill Theatre & Library 2J 159
Churchill Wlk. E9 . . . . .5J 67
Churchill Way BR1: Brom 2J 159
TW16: Sun 5J 129
Church La. BR2: Brom 1C 172
BR7: Chst 1G 161
E11 . . . . .1G 69
E17 . . . . .4D 50
EN1: Enf 3J 23
HA3: W'stone 1K 41
HA5: Pinn 3C 40
KT7: T Ditt 6K 149
KT9: Chess 6F 163
N2 . . . . .3B 46
N8 . . . . .4K 47
N9 . . . . .2B 34
N17 . . . . .1E 48
NW9 . . . . .6J 43
RM10: Dag 7J 73
SM6: Bedd 3H 167
(not continuous)
SW17 .5D 136
SW19 .1H 153
TW1: Twick 1A 132
TW10: Ham 1E 132
TW11: Tedd 5K 131
UB3: Hayes 6G 75
W5 . . . . .2C 96
Churchley Rd. SE26 . . . . .4H 139
Church Manorway DA8: Erith 4K 109
SE2 . . . . .5A 108
Church Mead SE5 . . . . .7C 102
(off Camberwell Rd.)
Churchmead Cl. EN4: E Barn 6H 21
Churchmead Mdw. KT6: Surb 2C 162
Churchmead Rd. NW10 . . . . .6C 62
Churchmore Rd. SW16 . . . . .1G 155
Church Mt. N2 . . . . .5B 46

Church Paddock Ct. SM6: Bedd 3H 167
Church Pde. TW15: Ashf 4B 128
Church Pas. EC2 . . . . .7D 8
(off Guildhall Yd.)
EN5: Barn 3B 20
KT6: Surb 5E 150
TW1: Twick 1B 132
Church Path CR0: Croy 2C 168
CR4: Mitc 3C 154
(not continuous)
E11 . . . . .5J 51
E17 . . . . .4D 50
N5 . . . . .5B 66
N8 . . . . .5K 47
(off Tottenham La.)
N12 . . . . .3F 31
(Woodside La.)
N12 . . . . .4F 31
(Woodside Pk. Rd.)
N17 . . . . .7K 33
NW10 . . . . .7A 62
SW14 .3K 115
(not continuous)
SW19 .2H 153
(not continuous)
UB1: S'hall 1E 94
UB2: S'hall 3D 94
W3 . . . . .2J 97
(not continuous)
Church Pl. CR4: Mitc 3C 154
SW1 . . . . .3B 12 (7G 83)
UB10: Ick 3E 56
W5 . . . . .2D 96
Church Ri. KT9: Chess 6F 163
SE23 . . . . .2K 139
Church Rd. BR2: Brom 2J 159
(Glassmill La.)
BR2: Brom 3G 159
(Shortlands Rd.)
BR2: Kes 7B 172
BR6: Farnb 5G 173
CR0: Croy 3C 168
(not continuous)
CR4: Mitc 1B 154
DA7: Bex 2F 127
DA8: Erith 5K 109
DA14: Sidc 4A 144
DA16: Well 2B 126
E10 . . . . .1C 68
E12 . . . . .5C 70
E17 . . . . .2A 50
EN3: Pond E 6D 24
HA6: Nwood 1H 39
HA7: Stan 5G 27
IG2: IIf 6J 53
IG9: Buck H 1E 36
IG11: Bark 6G 71
KT1: King T 2F 151
KT4: Wor Pk 1A 164
KT6: Surb 1C 162
KT8: E Mos 4H 149
KT10: Clay 7A 162
KT19: Ewe 7K 163
N1 . . . . .1C 66
N6 . . . . .6E 46
N17 . . . . .1E 48
(not continuous)
NW4 . . . . .4D 44
NW10 . . . . .7A 62
SE19 . . . . .1E 156
SM3: Cheam 6G 165
SM6: Bedd 3H 167
SW13 .2B 116
SW19 .5G 135
(High St. Wimbledon)
SW19 .1B 154
(Western Rd.)
TW5: Cran 5K 93
TW5: Hest 7E 94
TW7: Isle 1H 113
TW9: Rich 4E 114
TW10: Ham 4D 132

Church Rd. TW11: Tedd 4J 131
TW13: Hanw 5B 130
TW15: Ashf 3B 128
TW17: Shep 7D 146
UB2: S'hall 3D 94
UB3: Hayes 1H 93
UB5: N'olt 2B 76
UB7: W Dray 3A 92
UB8: Cowl 4A 74
W3 . . . . .1J 97
W7 . . . . .7H 77
Church Rd. Almshouses E10 . . . . .2D 68
(off Church Rd.)
Church Rd. Ind. Est. E10 . . . . .1C 68
Church Rd. Nth. N2 . . . . .2B 46
Church Rd. Sth. N2 . . . . .2B 46
Church Row BR7: Chst 1G 161
NW3 . . . . .4A 64
SW6 . . . . .7K 99
(off Park Rd.)
Church Row M. BR7: Chst 7G 143
Church Sq. TW17: Shep 7D 146
Church St. CR0: Croy 3B 168
E15 . . . . .1G 87
E16 . . . . .1F 107
KT1: King T 2D 150
KT12: Walt T 7J 147
KT17: Ewe 7C 164
N9 . . . . .7J 23
NW8 . . . . .5B 4 (5B 82)
RM10: Dag 6H 73
SM1: Sutt 5K 165
TW1: Twick 1A 132
TW7: Isle 3B 114
TW12: Hamp 1G 149
TW16: Sun 3K 147
W2 . . . . .5B 4 (5B 82)
W4 . . . . .6B 98
Church St. Est. NW8 . . . . .4B 4 (4B 82)
(not continuous)
Church St. Nth. E15 . . . . .1G 87
Church St. Pas. E15 . . . . .1G 87
(off Church St.)
Church Stretton Rd. TW3: Houn 5G 113
Church Ter. NW4 . . . . .3D 44
SE13 . . . . .3G 123
TW10: Rich 5D 114
Church Va. N2 . . . . .3D 46
SE23 . . . . .2K 139
Church Vw. TW10: Rich 5E 114
Churchview Rd. TW2: Twick 1H 131
Church Villa TW16: Sun 3K 147
Church Wlk. EN2: Enf 3J 23
KT7: T Ditt 6K 149
KT12: Walt T 7J 147
N6 . . . . .2E 64
N16 . . . . .3D 66
NW2 . . . . .3H 63
NW4 . . . . .3E 44
NW9 . . . . .2K 61
SW13 .1C 116
SW15 .5D 116
SW16 .2G 155
SW20 .3E 152
TW8: Bford 6C 96
(not continuous)
TW9: Rich 5D 114
UB3: Hayes 6G 75
Churchward Ho. SE17 . . . . .6B 102
(off Lorrimore Sq.)
W14 . . . . .5H 99
(off Ivatt Pl.)
Church Way EN4: Cockf 5J 21
HA8: Edg 6B 28
N20 . . . . .3H 31
Churchway NW1 . . . . .1D 6 (3H 83)
(not continuous)
Churchwell Path E9 . . . . .5J 67
Churchwood Gdns. IG8: W'fd G 4D 36
Churchyard Pas. SE5 . . . . .2D 120
Churchyard Row SE11 . . . . .4B 102

Church Yd. Wlk. *W2* *5A* **4**
(off St Mary's Sq.)
Churnfield N4 .... 2A **66**
Churston Av. E13 .... 1K **87**
Churston Cl. SW2 .... 1A **138**
Churston Dr. SM4: Mord 5F **153**
Churston Gdns. N11 .... 6B **32**
Churston Mans. WC1 .... 4H **7**
Churton Pl. SW1 .... 4B **18** (4G **101**)
Churton St. SW1 .... 4B **18** (4G **101**)
Chusan Pl. E14 .... 6B **86**
Chute Ho. *SW9* *2A* **120**
(off Stockwell Pk. Rd.)
Chuter Ede Ho. *SW6* *6H* **99**
(off North End Rd.)
Chyngton Cl. DA15: Sidc 3K **143**
Cibber Rd. SE23 .... 2K **139**
Cicada Rd. SW18 .... 6A **118**
Cicely Ho. *NW8* *2B* **82**
(off Cochrane St.)
Cicely Rd. SE15 .... 1G **121**
Cinderella Path NW11 .... 1K **63**
Cinderford Way BR1: Brom 4G **141**
Cine Lumiere 3A 16
(off Queensberry Pl.)
Cineworld Cinema
Bexleyheath 4H 127
Chelsea 6B 100
Enfield 4B 24
Feltham 2K 129
Fulham Road 5A 100
Hammersmith 4D 98
Ilford 3F 71
(off Winston Way)
Shaftesbury Avenue 7H 83
Staples Corner 1D 62
Wandsworth 5K 117
West India Quay 7C 86
Wood Green 2A 48
(in Wood Green Shop. City)
Cinnabar Wharf Central *E1* *1G* **103**
(off Wapping High St.)
Cinnabar Wharf E. *E1* *1G* **103**
(off Wapping High St.)
Cinnabar Wharf W. *E1* *1G* **103**
(off Wapping High St.)
Cinnamon Cl. CR0: Croy 7J **155**
SE15 .... 7F **103**
Cinnamon Row SW11 .... 3A **118**
Cinnamon St. E1 .... 1H **103**
Cinnamon Wharf *SE1* *6K* **15**
(off Shad Thames)
Cintra Pk. SE19 .... 7F **139**
Circa Apartments NW1 .... 7E **64**
Circle, The NW2 .... 3A **62**
NW7 .... 6E **28**
SE1 .... *6J* **15**
(off Queen Elizabeth St.)
Circle Gdns. SW19 .... 2J **153**
Circuit Rd. SE28 .... 2K **107**
Circuits, The HA5: Pinn 4A **40**
Circular Rd. N2 .... 2B **46**
N17 .... 3F **49**
Circular Way SE18 .... 6D **106**
(not continuous)
Circus Lodge NW8 .... 1A **4**
Circus M. W1 .... 5E **4**
Circus Pl. EC2 .... 6F **9** (5D **84**)
Circus Rd. NW8 .... 1A **4** (3B **82**)
Circus St. SE10 .... 7E **104**
Cirencester St. W2 .... 5K **81**
Cirrus Cl. SM6: Wall 7J **167**
Cissbury Ho. SE26 .... 3G **139**
Cissbury Ring Nth. N12 .... 5C **30**
Cissbury Ring Sth. N12 .... 5C **30**
Cissbury Rd. N15 .... 5D **48**
Citadel Pl. SE11 .... 5G **19** (5K **101**)
Citizen Ho. N7 .... 4A **66**
Citizen Rd. N7 .... 4A **66**
Citrus Ho. *SE8* *5B* **104**
(off Alverton St.)
City Apartments *E1* *7K* **9**
(off White Chu. La.)
City Bus. Cen. SE16 .... 3J **103**
City Central Est. *EC1* *2C* **8**
(off Seward St.)
City Cross Bus. Cen. SE10 .... 4G **105**
City Forum EC1 .... 1C **8** (3C **84**)
City Gdn. Row N1 .... 1C **8** (2B **84**)
City Harbour *E14* *3D* **104**
(off Selsdon Way)
City Hgts. *SE1* *5H* **15**
(off Weavers La.)
City Limits Bowling Alley
Collier Row 2F 55
Croydon 6A 168
CITY OF LONDON 1E 14 (6D 84)
City of London Almshouses
SW9 .... 4K **119**
City of London Crematorium
E12 .... 3C **70**
City of London Point *N7* *6H* **65**
(off York Way)
City of Westminster College
.... 2C 12 (7G 83)
City Pav. *EC1* *5A* **8**
(off Britton St.)
City Rd. EC1 .... 1A **8** (2B **84**)
City Twr. *EC2* *6E* **8**
(off Basinghall St.)
City University 2A 8 (3B 84)
City University Saddlers Sports Cen.
.... 3B 8 (4B 84)
Cityview SE7 .... 6A **106**
City Vw. Ct. SE22 .... 7G **121**
City Wlk. SE1 .... 2E **102**
City Wlk. Apartments *EC1* *2C* **8**
(off Seward St.)
City Wharf Ho. KT7: T Ditt 6B **150**
Civic Way HA4: Ruis 5B **58**
IG6: Ilf 4G **53**
Clabon M. SW1 .... 2E **16** (3D **100**)
Clack La. HA4: Ruis 1E **56**
Clack St. SE16 .... 2J **103**
Clacton Rd. E6 .... 3B **88**
E17 .... 6A **50**
N17 .... 2F **49**
Claigmar Gdns. N3 .... 1K **45**
Claire Ct. HA5: H End 1D **40**
N12 .... 4F **31**
NW2 .... 6G **63**
WD23: Bushy 1C **26**
Claire Gdns. HA7: Stan 5H **27**
Claire Pl. E14 .... 3C **104**
Clairvale Rd. TW5: Hest 1B **112**
Clairview Rd. SW16 .... 5F **137**
Clairville Gdns. W7 .... 1J **95**
Clairville Point *SE23* *3K* **139**
(off Dacres Rd.)
Clamp Hill HA7: Stan 1C **26**
Clancarty Rd. SW6 .... 2J **117**
Clandeboye Ho. *E15* *1H* **87**
(off John St.)
Clandon Cl. KT17: Ewe 6B **164**
W3 .... 2H **97**
Clandon Gdns. N3 .... 3J **45**
Clandon Ho. *SE1* *7B* **14**
(off Webber St.)
Clandon Rd. IG3: Ilf 2J **71**
Clandon St. SE8 .... 2C **122**
Clandon Ter. SW20 .... 2F **153**
Clanricarde Gdns. W2 .... 7J **81**
CLAPHAM 4G 119
CLAPHAM COMMON 4H **119**
Clapham Comn. Nth. Side SW4 .... 4D **118**
Clapham Comn. Sth. Side SW4 .... 6F **119**
Clapham Comn. W. Side SW4 .... 4D **118**
(not continuous)
Clapham Cres. SW4 .... 4H **119**
Clapham High St. SW4 .... 4H **119**
CLAPHAM JUNCTION 3C 118
Clapham Junc. App. SW11 .... 3C **118**
Clapham Leisure Cen. 3H 119
Clapham Mnr. Ct. SW4 .... 3G **119**
Clapham Mnr. St. SW4 .... 3G **119**
CLAPHAM PARK 7H 119
Clapham Pk. Est. SW4 .... 6H **119**
Clapham Pk. Rd. SW4 .... 4G **119**
Clapham Pk. Ter. *SW2* *5J* **119**
(off Kings Av.)
Clapham Picturehouse 4G 119
Clapham Rd. SW9 .... 3J **119**
Clapham Rd. Est. SW4 .... 3J **119**
Clap La. RM10: Dag, Rush G 2H **73**
Claps Ga. La. E6 .... 4E **88**
Clapton Comn. E5 .... 7F **49**
(not continuous)
CLAPTON PARK 4K **67**
Clapton Pk. Est. E5 .... 4K **67**
Clapton Pas. E5 .... 5J **67**
Clapton Sq. E5 .... 5J **67**
Clapton Ter. N16 .... 1G **67**
Clapton Way E5 .... 4G **67**
Clara Grant Ho. *E14* *3C* **104**
(off Mellish St.)
Clara Nehab Ho. *NW11* *5H* **45**
(off Leeside Cres.)
Clara Pl. SE18 .... 4E **106**
Clare Cl. N2 .... 3A **46**
Clare Cnr. SE9 .... 7F **125**
Clare Ct. *W11* *7G* **81**
(off Clarendon Rd.)
WC1 .... *2F* **7**
(off Judd St.)
Claredale Ho. *E2* *2H* **85**
(off Claredale St.)
Claredale St. E2 .... 2G **85**
Clare Gdns. E7 .... 4J **69**
IG11: Bark 6K **71**
W11 .... 6G **81**
Clare Ho. E3 .... 1B **86**
E16 .... *7E* **88**
(off University Way)
HA8: Edg *2J* **43**
(off Burnt Oak B'way.)
SE1 .... *5F* **103**
(off Brodie St.)
Clare La. N1 .... 7C **66**
Clare Lawn Av. SW14 .... 5J **115**
Clare Mkt. WC2 .... 1H **13** (6K **83**)
Clare M. SW6 .... 7K **99**
Claremont *TW17: Shep* *6D* **146**
(off Laleham Rd.)
Claremont Av. HA3: Kent 5E **42**
KT3: N Mald 5C **152**
TW16: Sun 1K **147**
Claremont Cl. BR6: Farnb 4E **172**
E16 .... 1E **106**
N1 .... 1K **7** (2A **84**)
SW2 .... 1J **137**
Claremont Ct. *W2* *6K* **81**
(off Queensway)
W9 .... *2H* **81**
(off Claremont Rd.)
Claremont Dr. TW17: Shep 6D **146**
Claremont Gdns. IG3: Ilf 2J **71**
KT6: Surb 5E **150**
Claremont Gro. IG8: Wfd G 6F **37**
W4 .... 7A **98**
Claremont Ho. SM2: Sutt 7K **165**
Claremont Pk. N3 .... 1G **45**
Claremont Pl. KT10: Clay 6A **162**
Claremont Rd. BR1: Brom 4C **160**
CR0: Croy 1G **169**
E7 .... 5K **69**
E11 .... 3F **69**
E17 .... 2A **50**
HA3: W'stone 2J **41**
KT6: Surb 5E **150**
N6 .... 7G **47**
NW2 .... 7F **45**
TW1: Twick 7B **114**
TW11: Tedd 5K **131**
W9 .... 2G **81**
W13 .... 5A **78**
Claremont Sq. N1 .... 1J **7** (2A **84**)
Claremont St. E16 .... 2E **106**
N18 .... 6B **34**
SE10 .... 6D **104**
Claremont Ter. KT7: T Ditt 7B **150**
Claremont Vs. *SE5* *7D* **102**
(off Southampton Way)
Claremont Way NW2 .... 1E **62**
(not continuous)
Claremont Way Ind. Est. NW2 .... 1E **62**
Clarence Av. BR1: Brom 4C **160**
IG2: Ilf 6E **52**
KT3: N Mald 2J **151**
SW4 .... 7H **119**
Clarence Cl. EN4: E Barn 5G **21**
WD23: Bushy 1E **26**
Clarence Ct. NW7 .... 5F **29**
W6 .... *4D* **98**
(off Cambridge Gro.)
Clarence Cres. DA14: Sidc 3B **144**
SW4 .... 6H **119**
Clarence Gdns. NW1 .... 2K **5** (3F **83**)
Clarence Ga. IG8: Ilf, Wfd G 6K **37**
Clarence Ga. Gdns. *NW1* *4F* **5**
(off Glentworth St.)
Clarence House 6B 12
Clarence Ho. *SE17* *6C* **102**
(off Merrow St.)
Clarence La. SW15 .... 6A **116**
Clarence M. E5 .... 5H **67**
SE16 .... 1K **103**
SW12 .... 7F **119**
Clarence Pl. E5 .... 5H **67**
Clarence Rd. BR1: Brom 3B **160**
CR0: Croy 7D **156**
DA6: Bex 4E **126**
DA14: Sidc 3B **144**
E5 .... 4H **67**
E12 .... 4A **70**
E16 .... 4G **87**
E17 .... 2K **49**
EN3: Pond E 5C **24**
N15 .... 5C **48**
N22 .... 7D **32**
NW6 .... 7H **63**
SE8 .... 6D **104**
SE9 .... 2C **142**
SM1: Sutt 5K **165**
SM6: Wall 5F **167**
SW19 .... 6K **135**
TW9: Kew 1F **115**
TW11: Tedd 6K **131**
W4 .... 5G **97**
Clarence St. KT1: King T 2D **150**
(not continuous)
TW9: Rich 4E **114**
UB2: S'hall 3B **94**
Clarence Ter. NW1 .... 3F **5** (4D **82**)
TW3: Houn 4F **113**
Clarence Wlk. SW4 .... 2J **119**
Clarence Way NW1 .... 7F **65**
Clarenden Pl. DA2: Dart 5K **145**
Clarendon Cl. BR5: St P 3K **161**
E9 .... 7J **67**
W2 .... 2C **10** (7C **82**)
Clarendon Ct. *BR3: Beck* *1D* **158**
(off Blair Ct.)
BR3: Beck 1F **159**
(West Oak)
NW2 .... 7E **62**
NW11 .... 4H **45**
TW5: Cran 1J **111**
TW9: Kew 1F **115**
Clarendon Cres. TW2: Twick 3H **131**
Clarendon Cross W11 .... 7G **81**
Clarendon Dr. SW15 .... 4E **116**
Clarendon Flats *W1* *1H* **11**
(off Balderton St.)
Clarendon Gdns. HA9: Wemb 3D **60**
IG1: Ilf 7D **52**
NW4 .... 3C **44**
W9 .... 4A **82**
Clarendon Grn. BR5: St P 4K **161**
Clarendon Gro. CR4: Mitc 3D **154**
NW1 .... 1C **6** (3H **83**)
Clarendon Ho. *NW1* *1B* **6**
(off Werrington St.)

Clarendon Ho. *W2* 2C 10
(off Strathearn Pl.)
Clarendon M. DA5: Bexl 1H 145
W2 ....2C 10 (7C 82)
Clarendon Path BR5: St P 4K 161
(not continuous)
Clarendon Pl. W2 ....2C 10 (7C 82)
Clarendon Ri. SE13 ....4E 122
Clarendon Rd. CR0: Croy 2B 168
E11 ....1F 69
E17 ....6D 50
E18 ....3J 51
HA1: Harr 6J 41
N8 ....3K 47
N15 ....4C 48
N18 ....6B 34
N22 ....2K 47
SM6: Wall 6G 167
SW19 ....7C 136
TW15: Ashf 4B 128
UB3: Hayes 2H 93
W5 ....3E 78
W11 ....7G 81
Clarendon St. SW1 ....5K 17 (5F 101)
Clarendon Ter. W9 ....3A 4 (4A 82)
Clarendon Wlk. W11 ....6G 81
Clarendon Way BR5: St P 3K 161
BR7: Chst 3K 161
N21 ....6H 23
Clarens St. SE6 ....2B 140
Clare Pl. SW15 ....7B 116
Clare Point *NW2* 1F 63
(off Whitefield Av.)
Clare Rd. E11 ....6F 51
NW10 ....7C 62
SE14 ....1B 122
TW4: Houn 3D 112
TW19: Stanw 1A 128
UB6: G'frd 6H 59
Clare St. E2 ....2H 85
Claret Gdns. SE25 ....3E 156
Clareville Ct. *SW7* 4A 16
(off Clareville St.)
Clareville Gro. SW7 ....4A 16 (4A 100)
Clareville Gro. M. SW7 ....4A 16 (4A 100)
Clareville Rd. BR5: Farnb 2G 173
Clareville St. SW7 ....4A 16 (4A 100)
Clare Way DA7: Bex 1E 126
Clarewood Ct. *W1* 6E 4
(off Seymour Pl.)
Clarewood Wlk. SW9 ....4A 120
Clarges M. W1 ....4J 11 (1F 101)
Clarges St. W1 ....4K 11 (1F 101)
Claribel Rd. SW9 ....2B 120
Clarice Way SM6: Wall 7J 167
Claridge Ct. SW6 ....2H 117
Claridge Rd. RM8: Dag 1D 72
Clarinet Ct. HA8: Edg 7C 28
Clarion Ho. *E3* 2A 86
(off Roman Rd.)
SW1 ....5B 18
(off Moreton Pl.)
W1 ....1C 12
(off St Anne's Ct.)
Clarissa Ho. *E14* 6D 86
(off Cordela St.)
Clarissa Rd. RM6: Chad H 7D 54
Clarissa St. E8 ....1F 85
Clarke Mans. *IG11: Bark* 7K 71
(off Upney La.)
Clarke M. N9 ....3C 34
Clarke Path N16 ....1G 67
Clarkes Av. KT4: Wor Pk 1F 165
Clarkes Dr. UB8: Hil 5A 74
Clarke's M. W1 ....5H 5 (5E 82)
Clark Ho. *SW10* 7A 100
(off Coleridge Gdns.)
Clarks Mead WD23: Bush 1B 26
Clarkson Rd. E16 ....6H 87
Clarkson Row *NW1* 2G 83
(off Mornington Ter.)
Clarksons, The IG11: Bark 2G 89
Clarkson St. E2 ....3H 85
Clark's Pl. EC2 ....7G 9 (6E 84)
Clarks Rd. IG1: Ilf 2H 71
Clark St. E1 ....5H 85
Clark Way TW5: Hest 7B 94
Classic Mans. *E9* 7H 67
(off Wells St.)
Classon Cl. UB7: W Dray 2A 92
Claude Rd. E10 ....2E 68
E13 ....1K 87
SE15 ....2H 121
Claude St. E14 ....4C 104
Claudia Jones Ho. N17 ....1C 48
Claudia Jones Way SW2 ....6J 119
Claudia Pl. SW19 ....1G 135
Claughton Rd. E13 ....2A 88
Clauson Av. UB5: N'olt 5F 59
Clavell St. SE10 ....6E 104
Claverdale Rd. SW2 ....7K 119
Clavering Av. SW13 ....6D 98
Clavering Cl. TW1: Twick 4A 132
Clavering Ho. *SE13* 4F 123
(off Blessington Rd.)
Clavering Ind. Est. *N9* 2D 34
(off Montagu Rd.)
Clavering Rd. E12 ....1B 70
Claverley Gro. N3 ....1K 45
Claverley Vs. N3 ....7E 30
Claverton St. SW1 ....6B 18 (5G 101)
Clave St. E1 ....1J 103
Claxton Gro. W6 ....5F 99
Claxton Path *SE4* 4K 121
(off Coston Wlk.)
Clay Av. CR4: Mitc 2F 155
Claybank Gro. SE13 ....3D 122
Claybourne M. SE19 ....7E 138
Claybridge Rd. SE12 ....4A 142
Claybrook Cl. N2 ....3B 46
Claybrook Rd. W6 ....6F 99
Claybury B'way. IG5: Ilf 3C 52
Claybury Hill IG8: Wfd G 7J 37
Claybury Rd. IG8: Wfd G 7H 37
Clay Ct. E17 ....3F 51
SE1 ....7G 15
(off Long La.)
Claydon *SE17* 4C 102
(off Deacon Way)
Claydon Dr. CR0: Bedd 4J 167
Claydon Ho. *NW4* 2F 45
(off Holders Hill Rd.)
Claydown M. SE18 ....5E 106
Clay Farm Rd. SE9 ....2G 143
CLAYGATE 7A 162
Claygate Cres. CR0: New Ad 6E 170
Claygate La. KT7: T Ditt 1A 162
KT10: Clay, Hin W 2A 162
Claygate Rd. W13 ....3B 96
CLAYHALL 3C 52
Clayhall Av. IG5: Ilf 3C 52
Clay Hill EN2: Enf 1K 23
Clayhill KT5: Surb 5G 151
Clayhill Cres. SE9 ....4B 142
Claylands Pl. SW8 ....7A 102
Claylands Rd. SW8 ....7H 19 (6K 101)
Clay La. HA8: Edg 2B 28
TW19: Stanw 7B 110
WD23: Bushy 1D 26
Claymore Cl. SM4: Mord 7J 153
Claypole Ct. *E17* 5C 50
(off Yunus Khan Cl.)
Claypole Dr. TW5: Hest 1C 112
Claypole Rd. E15 ....2E 86
Clayponds Av. TW8 ....4D 96
Clayponds Gdns. W5 ....4D 96
(not continuous)
Clayponds La. TW8: Bford 5E 96
(not continuous)
Clays La. E15 ....5D 68
Clays La. Cl. E15 ....5D 68
Clay St. W1 ....6F 5 (5D 82)
Clayton Av. HA0: Wemb 7E 60
Clayton Bus. Cen.
UB3: Hayes 2G 93
Clayton Cl. E6 ....6D 88
Clayton Ct. E17 ....2A 50
Clayton Cres. N1 ....1J 83
TW8: Bford 5D 96
Clayton Dr. SE8 ....5A 104
Clayton Fld. NW9 ....7F 29
Clayton Ho. *E9* 7J 67
(off Frampton Pk. Rd.)
KT7: T Ditt 1B 162
SW13 ....7E 98
(off Trinity Church Rd.)
Clayton M. SE10 ....1F 123
Clayton Rd. KT9: Chess 4C 162
RM7: Rush G 1J 73
SE15 ....1G 121
TW7: Isle 3J 113
UB3: Hayes 2G 93
Clayton St. SE11 ....7J 19 (6A 102)
Clayton Ter. UB4: Yead 5C 76
Claytonville Ter. DA17: Belv 2J 109
Clay Wood Cl. BR6: Orp 7J 161
Clayworth Cl. DA15: Sidc 6B 126
Cleanthus Cl. SE18 ....1F 125
Cleanthus Rd. SE18 ....2F 125
(not continuous)
Clearbrook Way E1 ....6J 85
Clearwater Pl. KT6: Surb 6C 150
Clearwater Ter. W11 ....2F 99
Clearwell Dr. W9 ....4K 81
Cleave Av. BR6: Chels 6J 173
UB3: Harl 4G 93
Cleaveland Rd. KT6: Surb 5D 150
Cleaverholme Cl. SE25 ....6H 157
Cleaver Ho. *NW3* 7D 64
(off Adelaide Rd.)
Cleaver Sq. SE11 ....6K 19 (5A 102)
Cleaver St. SE11 ....5K 19 (5A 102)
Cleaves Almshouses
KT2: King T 2E 150
(off London Rd.)
Cleeve Ct. TW14: Bedf 1G 129
Cleeve Hill SE23 ....1H 139
Cleeve Ho. E2 ....2H 9
Cleeve Pk. Gdns. DA14: Sidc 2B 144
Cleeve Way SM1: Sutt 1K 165
SW15 ....7B 116
Cleeve Workshops *E2* 2H 9
(off Boundary Rd.)
Clegg Ho. SE3 ....4K 123
SE16 ....3J 103
(off Moodkee St.)
Clegg St. E1 ....1H 103
E13 ....2J 87
Cleland Ho. *E2* 2J 85
(off Sewardstone Rd.)
Clematis Gdns. IG8: Wfd G 5D 36
Clematis St. W12 ....7C 80
Clem Attlee Ct. SW6 ....6H 99
Clem Attlee Pde. *SW6* 6H 99
(off North End Rd.)
Clemence Rd. RM10: Dag 1J 91
Clemence St. E14 ....5B 86
Clement Av. SW4 ....4H 119
Clement Cl. NW6 ....7E 62
W4 ....4K 97
Clement Gdns. UB3: Harl 4G 93
Clementhorpe Rd. RM9: Dag 6C 72
Clement Ho. SE8 ....4A 104
W10 ....5E 80
(off Dalgarno Gdns.)
Clementina Rd. E10 ....1B 68
Clementine Cl. W13 ....2B 96
Clementine Wlk. IG8: Wfd G 7D 36
Clement Rd. BR3: Beck 2K 157
SW19 ....5G 135
Clement's Av. E16 ....7J 87
Clements Cl. N12 ....4E 30
Clements Ct. IG1: Ilf 3F 71
TW4: Houn 4B 112
Clement's Inn WC2 ....1H 13 (6K 83)
Clement's Inn Pas. WC2 ....1H 13
Clements La. EC4 ....2F 15 (7D 84)
IG1: Ilf 3F 71
Clements Pl. TW8: Bford 5D 96
Clements Rd. E6 ....7C 70
IG1: Ilf 3F 71
SE16 ....3G 103
Clemson Ho. E8 ....1F 85
Clendon Way SE18 ....4H 107
Clennam St. SE1 ....6D 14 (2C 102)
Clensham Ct. SM1: Sutt 2J 165
Clensham La. SM1: Sutt 2J 165
Clenston M. W1 ....7E 4 (6D 82)
Cleopatra's Needle 3G 13 (1J 101)
Clephane Rd. N1 ....6C 66
Clephane Rd. Nth. N1 ....6C 66
Clephane Rd. Sth. N1 ....6D 66
Clere Pl. EC2 ....3F 9 (4D 84)
Clere St. EC2 ....3F 9 (4D 84)
Clerics Wlk. TW17: Shep 7F 147
CLERKENWELL 3J 7 (4A 84)
Clerkenwell Cl. EC1 ....3K 7 (4A 84)
(not continuous)
Clerkenwell Grn. EC1 ....4K 7 (4A 84)
Clerkenwell Rd. EC1 ....4J 7 (4A 84)
Clermont Rd. E9 ....1J 85
Clevedon Cl. N16 ....3F 67
Clevedon Ct. CR2: S Croy 5E 168
Clevedon Gdns. TW5: Cran 1K 111
UB3: Harl 3F 93
Clevedon Ho. SM1: Sutt 4A 166
Clevedon Mans. NW5 ....4E 64
Clevedon Pas. N16 ....2F 67
Clevedon Rd. KT1: King T 2G 151
SE20 ....1K 157
TW1: Twick 6D 114
(not continuous)
Cleve Ho. NW6 ....7K 63
Cleveland Av. SW20 ....2H 153
TW12: Hamp 7D 130
W4 ....4B 98
Cleveland Ct. W13 ....5B 78
Cleveland Gdns. KT4: Wor Pk 2A 164
N4 ....5C 48
NW2 ....2F 63
SW13 ....2B 116
W2 ....6A 82
Cleveland Gro. E1 ....4J 85
Cleveland Ho. *N2* 2B 46
(off The Grange)
Cleveland La. N9 ....7C 24
Cleveland Mans. *SW9* 7A 102
(off Mowll St.)
W9 ....4J 81
Cleveland M. W1 ....5A 6 (5G 83)
Cleveland Pk. TW19: Stanw 6A 110
Cleveland Pk. Av. E17 ....4C 50
Cleveland Pk. Cres. E17 ....4C 50
Cleveland Pl. SW1 ....4B 12 (1G 101)
Cleveland Ri. SM4: Mord 7F 153
Cleveland Rd. DA16: Well 2K 125
E18 ....3J 51
IG1: Ilf 3F 71
KT3: N Mald 4A 152
KT4: Wor Pk 2A 164
N1 ....7D 66
SW13 ....2B 116
TW7: Isle 4A 114
W4 ....3J 97
W13 ....5A 78
Cleveland Row SW1 ....5A 12 (1G 101)
Clevelands, The IG11: Bark 6G 71
Cleveland Sq. W2 ....6A 82
Cleveland St. W1 ....4K 5 (4F 83)
Cleveland Ter. W2 ....6A 82
Cleveland Way E1 ....4J 85
Cleveley Cl. SE7 ....4B 106
Cleveley Cres. W5 ....2E 78
Cleveleys Rd. E5 ....3H 67
Cleverly Est. W12 ....1C 98
Cleve Rd. DA14: Sidc 3D 144
NW6 ....7J 63
Cleves Av. KT17: Ewe 7D 164
Cleves Ho. *E16* 1J 105
(off Southey M.)
Cleves Rd. E6 ....1B 88
TW10: Ham 3C 132

Cleves Wlk. IG6: Ilf 1G 53
Cleves Way HA4: Ruis 1B 58
TW12: Hamp 7D 130
TW16: Sun 6H 129
Clewer Ct. *E10* *1C 68*
(off Leyton Grange Est.)
Clewer Cres. HA3: Hrw W 1H 41
Clewer Ho. *SE2* *2D 108*
(off Wolvercote Rd.)
Cley Ho. SE4 4K 121
Clichy Est. E1 5J 85
Clichy Ho. *E1* *5J 85*
(off Stepney Way)
Clifden M. E9 5K 67
Clifden Rd. E5 5J 67
TW1: Twick 1K 131
TW8: Bford 6D 96
Cliffe Ho. *SE10* *5H 105*
(off Blackwall La.)
Cliffe Rd. CR2: S Croy 5D 168
Cliffe Wlk. *SM1: Sutt* *5A 166*
(off Greyhound Rd.)
Clifford Av. BR7: Chst 6D 142
IG5: Ilf 1F 53
SM6: Wall 4G 167
SW14 3H 115
(not continuous)
Clifford Cl. UB5: N'olt 1C 76
Clifford Ct. *W2* *5K 81*
(off Westbourne Pk. Vs.)
Clifford Dr. SW9 4B 120
Clifford Gdns. NW10 2E 80
UB3: Harl 4G 93
Clifford Gro. TW15: Ashf 4C 128
Clifford Haigh Ho. SW6 7F 99
Clifford Ho. *BR3: Beck* *6D 140*
(off Calverley Cl.)
W14 *4H 99*
(off Edith Vs.)
Clifford Rd. E16 4H 87
E17 2E 50
EN5: New Bar 3E 20
HA0: Wemb 7D 60
N1 1E 84
N9 6D 24
SE25 4G 157
TW4: Houn 3B 112
TW10: Ham 2D 132
Clifford's Inn Pas. EC4 1J 13 (6A 84)
Clifford St. W1 3A 12 (7G 83)
Clifford Way NW10 4B 62
Cliff Rd. NW1 6H 65
Cliffsend Ho. *SW9* *1A 120*
(off Cowley Rd.)
Cliff Ter. SE8 2C 122
Cliffview Rd. SE13 3C 122
Cliff Vs. NW1 6H 65
Cliff Wlk. E16 5H 87
Clifton Av. E17 3K 49
HA7: Stan 2B 42
HA9: Wemb 6F 61
N3 1H 45
TW13: Felt 3A 130
W12 1B 98
Clifton Cl. BR6: Farnb 5G 173
Clifton Ct. BR3: Beck 1D 158
IG8: Wfd G 6D 36
KT5: Surb 7F 151
N4 2A 66
NW8 3A 4
SE15 7H 103
TW19: Stanw 6A 110
Clifton Cres. SE15 7H 103
Clifton Est. SE15 1H 121
Clifton Gdns. EN2: Enf 4D 22
N15 6F 49
NW11 6H 45
UB10: Hil 2D 74
W4 4K 97
(not continuous)
W9 4A 82
Clifton Ga. SW10 6A 100
Clifton Gro. E8 6G 67
Clifton Hill NW8 2K 81
Clifton Ho. *E2* *3J 9*
(off Club Row)
E11 2G 69
Clifton M. SE25 4E 156
Clifton Pde. TW13: Felt 3A 130
Clifton Pk. Av. SW20 2E 152
Clifton Pl. SE16 2J 103
SW10 *6A 100*
(off Hollywood Rd.)
W2 1B 10 (6B 82)
Clifton Ri. SE14 7A 104
(not continuous)
Clifton Rd. DA14: Sidc 4J 143
DA16: Well 3C 126
E7 6B 70
E16 5G 87
HA3: Kent 4F 43
IG2: Ilf 6H 53
KT2: King T 7F 133
N1 6C 66
N3 1A 46
N8 6H 47
N22 1G 47
NW10 2C 80
SE25 4E 156
SM6: Wall 5F 167
SW19 6F 135
TW7: Isle 2J 113
TW11: Tedd 4J 131
UB2: S'hall 4C 94
UB6: G'frd 4G 77
W9 3A 4 (4A 82)
Clifton St. EC2 4G 9 (4E 84)
Clifton Ter. N4 2A 66
Clifton Vs. W9 5A 82
Cliftonville Ct. SE12 1J 141
Clifton Wlk. *W6* *4D 98*
(off King St.)
Clifton Way HA0: Wemb 1E 78
SE15 7H 103
TW6: H'row A 3D 110
Climsland Ho. SE1 4K 13 (1A 102)
Clinch Ct. *E16* *5J 87*
(off Plymouth Rd.)
Cline Rd. N11 6B 32
Clinger Ct. *N1* *1E 84*
(off Hobbs Pl. Est.)
Clink Exhibition, The 4E 14
Clink St. SE1 4E 14 (1D 102)
Clink Wharf *SE1* *4E 14*
(off Clink St.)
Clinton Av. DA16: Well 4A 126
KT8: E Mos 4G 149
Clinton Ho. *KT6: Surb* *7D 150*
(off Lovelace Gdns)
Clinton Rd. E3 3A 86
E7 4J 69
N15 4D 48
Clipper Cl. SE16 2K 103
Clipper Ho. *E14* *5E 104*
(off Manchester Rd.)
Clipper Way SE13 4E 122
Clippesby Cl. KT9: Chess 6F 163
Clipstone M. W1 5A 6 (5G 83)
Clipstone Rd. TW3: Houn 3E 112
Clipstone St. W1 5K 5 (5F 83)
Clissold Cl. N2 3D 46
Clissold Ct. N4 2C 66
Clissold Cres. N16 3D 66
Clissold Leisure Cen. 3D 66
Clissold Rd. N16 3D 66
Clitheroe Av. HA2: Harr 1E 58
Clitheroe Rd. SW9 2J 119
Clitherow Av. W7 3A 96
Clitherow Ct. TW8: Bford 5C 96
Clitherow Pas. TW8: Bford 5C 96
Clitherow Rd. TW8: Bford 5B 96
Clitterhouse Cres. NW2 1E 62
Clitterhouse Rd. NW2 1E 62
Clive Av. N18 6B 34
Clive Ct. W9 4A 82
Cliveden Cl. N12 4F 31
Cliveden Ho. *E16* *1J 105*
(off Fitzwilliam M.)
SW1 *3G 17*
(off Cliveden Pl.)
Cliveden Pl. SW1 3G 17 (4E 100)
TW17: Shep 6E 146
Cliveden Rd. SW19 1H 153
Clivedon Ct. W13 5B 78
Clivedon Rd. E4 5B 36
Clive Ho. *SE10* *6E 104*
(off Haddo St.)
Clive Lloyd Ho. *N15* *5C 48*
(off Woodlands Pk. Rd.)
Clive Lodge NW4 6F 45
Clive Pas. SE21 3D 138
Clive Rd. DA17: Belv 4G 109
EN1: Enf 4B 24
SE21 3D 138
SW19 6C 136
TW1: Twick 4K 131
TW14: Felt 6J 111
Clivesdale Dr. UB3: Hayes 1K 93
Clive Way EN1: Enf 4B 24
Cloak La. EC4 2D 14 (7C 84)
Clochar Ct. NW10 1B 80
Clock Ct. E11 4K 51
Clock Ho. E3 3E 86
E17 *4F 51*
(off Wood St.)
Clockhouse, The SW19 3E 134
Clockhouse Av. IG11: Bark 1G 89
Clockhouse Cl. SW19 2E 134
Clockhouse Ct. BR3: Beck 2A 158
CLOCKHOUSE JUNC. 5E 32
Clockhouse La. RM5: Col R 1H 55
TW14: Bedf 4C 128
TW15: Ashf 4C 128
Clock Ho. Pde. E11 6K 51
Clockhouse Pde. N13 5F 33
Clockhouse Pl. SW15 6G 117
Clock Ho. Rd. BR3: Beck 3A 158
CLOCKHOUSE RDBT. 1D 128
Clock Mus., The 7D 8
Clock Pde. EN2: Enf 5J 23
Clock Pl. *SE1* *4B 102*
(off Newington Butts)
Clock Twr. Ind. Est. TW7: Isle 3K 113
Clock Twr. M. N1 1C 84
SE28 7B 90
W7 1J 95
Clock Twr. Pl. N7 6J 65
Clock Twr. Rd. TW7: Isle 3K 113
Cloister Cl. TW11: Tedd 5B 132
Cloister Gdns. HA8: Edg 5D 28
SE25 6H 157
Cloister Rd. NW2 3H 63
W3 5J 79
Cloisters, The 1E 18
Cloisters, The E1 4J 9
SW9 1A 120
TW7: Isle *3A 114*
(off Pulteney Cl.)
Cloisters Av. BR2: Brom 5D 160
Cloisters Bus. Cen. *SW8* *7F 101*
(off Battersea Pk. Rd.)
Cloisters Ct. DA7: Bex 3H 127
Cloisters Mall KT1: King T 2E 150
Clonard Way HA5: H End 6A 26
Clonbrock Rd. N16 4E 66
Cloncurry St. SW6 2F 117
Clonmel Cl. HA2: Harr 2H 59
Clonmell Rd. N17 3D 48
Clonmel Rd. SW6 7H 99
TW11: Tedd 4H 131
Clonmore St. SW18 1H 135
Cloonmore Av. BR6: Chels 4K 173
Clorane Gdns. NW3 3J 63
Close, The BR3: Beck 4A 158
BR5: Pet W 6J 161
CR4: Mitc 4D 154
DA5: Bexl 6G 127
DA14: Sidc 4B 144
E4 7K 35
Close, The EN4: E Barn 6J 21
HA0: Wemb 6E 60
HA3: Hrw W 2G 41
HA5: Eastc 7A 40
HA5: Pinn 7D 40
HA9: Wemb 3J 61
IG2: Ilf 6J 53
KT3: N Mald 2J 151
KT6: Surb 6E 150
N10 2F 47
N14 2C 32
N20 2C 30
RM6: Chad H 6E 54
SE3 2F 123
SE25 6G 157
SM3: Sutt 7H 153
SM5: Cars 7C 166
TW7: Isle 2H 113
TW9: Rich 3H 115
UB10: Hil 1C 74
Cloth Ct. EC1 6B 8
Cloth Fair EC1 6B 8 (5B 84)
Clothier St. E1 7H 9 (6E 84)
Cloth St. EC1 5C 8 (5C 84)
Clothworkers Rd. SE18 7H 107
Cloudesdale Rd. SW17 2F 137
Cloudesley Mans. *N1* *1A 84*
(off Cloudesley Pl.)
Cloudesley Pl. N1 1A 84
Cloudesley Rd. DA7: Bex 1F 127
N1 1A 84
(not continuous)
Cloudesley Sq. N1 1A 84
Cloudesley St. N1 1A 84
Clouston Cl. SM6: Wall 5J 167
Clova Rd. E7 6H 69
Clove Cres. E14 7E 86
Clove Hitch Quay SW11 3A 118
Clovelly Av. NW9 4B 44
UB10: Ick 4E 56
Clovelly Cl. HA5: Eastc 3K 39
UB10: Ick 4E 56
Clovelly Ct. NW2 5E 62
Clovelly Gdns. EN1: Enf 7K 23
RM7: Mawney 1H 55
SE19 1F 157
Clovelly Ho. *W2* *6A 82*
(off Hallfield Est.)
Clovelly Rd. DA7: Bex 6E 108
N8 4H 47
TW3: Houn 2E 112
W4 2K 97
W5 2C 96
Clovelly Way BR6: St M Cry 6K 161
E1 6J 85
HA2: Harr 2D 58
Clover Cl. E11 2F 69
Cloverdale Ct. SM6: Wall 6F 167
Cloverdale Gdns.
DA15: Sidc 6K 125
Clover M. SW3 7F 17 (6D 100)
Clover Way SM6: Wall 1E 166
Clove St. E13 4J 87
Clowders Rd. SE6 3B 140
Clowser Cl. SM1: Sutt 5A 166
Cloysters Grn. E1 1G 103
Cloyster Wood HA8: Edg 7J 27
Club Gdns. Rd. BR2: Hayes 7J 159
Club Row E1 3J 9 (4F 85)
E2 3J 9 (4F 85)
Clumps, The TW15: Ashf 4F 129
Clunbury Av. UB2: S'hall 5D 94
Clunbury St. N1 2D 84
Clunie Ho. *SW1* *1F 17*
(off Pavillion Rd.)
Cluny Est. SE1 7G 15 (3E 102)
Cluny M. SW5 4J 99
Cluny Pl. SE1 7G 15 (3E 102)
Cluse Ct. *N1* *2C 84*
(off St Peters St., not continuous)
Clutton St. E14 5D 86
Clydach Rd. EN1: Enf 4A 24
Clyde Cir. N15 4E 48

Clyde Ct. *NW1* *2H* ***83***
(off Hampden Cl.)
Clyde Flats *SW6* *7H* ***99***
(off Rhylston Rd.)
Clyde Ho. KT2: King T 1D **150**
Clyde Pl. E10 .... 7D **50**
Clyde Rd. CR0: Croy 2F **169**
N15 .... 4E **48**
N22 .... 1H **47**
SM1: Sutt 5J **165**
SM6: Wall 6G **167**
TW19: Stanw 1A **128**
Clydesdale EN3: Pond E 4E **24**
Clydesdale Av. HA7: Stan 3D **42**
Clydesdale Cl. TW7: Isle 3K **113**
Clydesdale Ct. N20 .... 1G **31**
Clydesdale Gdns. TW10: Rich 4H **115**
Clydesdale Ho. *DA18: Erith* *2E* ***108***
(off Kale Rd.)
W11 .... *6H* ***81***
(off Clydesdale Rd.)
Clydesdale Rd. W11 .... 6H **81**
Clyde St. SE8 .... 6B **104**
Clyde Ter. SE23 .... 2J **139**
Clyde Va. SE23 .... 2J **139**
Clyde Way RM1: Rom 1K **55**
Clyde Wharf E16 .... 1J **105**
Clydon Cl. DA8: Erith 6K **109**
Clyfford Rd. HA4: Ruis 4H **57**
Clymping Dene TW14: Felt 7K **111**
Clynes Ho. *E2* *3K* ***85***
(off Knottisford St.)
RM10: Dag *3G* ***73***
(off Uvedale Rd.)
Clyston St. SW8 .... 2G **119**
Coach & Horses Yd. W1 .... 2K **11** (7G **83**)
Coach Ho. La. N5 .... 4B **66**
SW19 .... 4F **135**
Coach Ho. M. *SE1* *7G* ***15***
(off Blue Lion Pl.)
SE20 .... 7H **139**
SE23 .... 6K **121**
SM2: Sutt 6K **165**
Coach Ho. Yd. *NW3* *4A* ***64***
(off Heath St.)
SW18 .... 4K **117**
Coachmaker M. *SW4* *3J* ***119***
(off Fenwick Pl.)
Coach Yd. M. N19 .... 1J **65**
Coaldale Wlk. SE21 .... 7C **120**
Coalecroft Rd. SW15 .... 4E **116**
Coal Port Cl. BR6: Chels 6K **173**
Coalport Ho. SE11 .... 2J **19**
Coates Av. SW18 .... 6C **118**
Coates Cl. CR7: Thor H 3C **156**
Coates Hill Rd. BR1: Brom 2E **160**
Coate St. E2 .... 2G **85**
Coates Wlk. TW8: Bford 6E **96**
Cobalt Sq. SW8 .... 7G **19**
Cobbett Rd. SE9 .... 3C **124**
TW2: Whit 1E **130**
Cobbetts Av. IG4: Ilf 5B **52**
Cobbett St. SW8 .... 7K **101**
Cobble La. N1 .... 7B **66**
Cobble M. N5 .... 3C **66**
Cobblers Wlk. KT1: Ham W 1A **150**
KT8: E Mos 1A **150**
TW11: Tedd 1A **150**
TW12: Hamp, Tedd 1G **149**
(not continuous)
Cobblestone Pl. CR0: Croy 1C **168**
Cobbold Ct. *SW1* *3C* ***18***
(off Elverton St.)
Cobbold Ind. Est. NW10 .... 6B **62**
Cobbold M. W12 .... 2B **98**
Cobbold Rd. E11 .... 3H **69**
NW10 .... 6B **62**
W12 .... 2A **98**
Cobb's Ct. EC4 .... 1B **14**
Cobb's Hall *SW6* *6F* ***99***
(off Fulham Pal. Rd.)
Cobb's Rd. TW4: Houn 4D **112**
Cobbsthorpe Vs. SE26 .... 4K **139**
Cobb St. E1 .... 6J **9** (5F **85**)
Cobden Bldgs. *WC1* *1G* ***7***
(off Weston Rd.)
Cobden Ct. BR2: Brom 4A **160**
Cobden Ho. *E2* *3G* ***85***
(off Nelson Gdns.)
NW1 .... *2G* ***83***
(off Arlington Rd.)
Cobden M. SE26 .... 5H **139**
Cobden Rd. BR6: Farnb 4H **173**
E11 .... 3G **69**
SE25 .... 5G **157**
Cobham Av. KT3: N Mald 5C **152**
Cobham Cl. BR2: Brom 7C **160**
DA15: Sidc 6B **126**
EN1: Enf 3B **24**
HA8: Edg 2H **43**
SM6: Wall 6J **167**
SW11 .... 6C **118**
Cobham Ct. CR4: Mitc 2B **154**
Cobham Ho. IG11: Bark 1G **89**
(not continuous)
Cobham M. NW1 .... 7H **65**
Cobham Pl. DA6: Bex 5D **126**
Cobham Rd. E17 .... 1E **50**
IG3: Ilf 2J **71**
KT1: King T 2G **151**
N22 .... 3B **48**
TW5: Hest 7A **94**
Cobland Rd. SE12 .... 4A **142**
Coborn Rd. E3 .... 2B **86**
Coborn St. E3 .... 3B **86**
Cobourg Rd. SE5 .... 6F **103**
Cobourg St. NW1 .... 2B **6** (3G **83**)
Coburg Cl. SW1 .... 3B **18** (4G **101**)
Coburg Cres. SW2 .... 1K **137**
Coburg Dwellings *E1* *6J* ***85***
(off Hardinge St.)
Coburg Gdns. IG5: Ilf 2B **52**
Coburg Rd. N22 .... 3K **47**
Cochrane Cl. NW8 .... 1B **4**
Cochrane Ct. *E10* *1C* ***68***
(off Leyton Grange Est.)
Cochrane Ho. *E14* *2C* ***104***
(off Admirals Way)
Cochrane M. NW8 .... 2B **82**
Cochrane Rd. SW19 .... 7G **135**
Cochrane St. NW8 .... 1B **4** (2B **82**)
Cochrane Theatre *6F* ***7***
(off Southampton Row)
Cockburn Ho. *SW1* *6D* ***18***
(off Aylesford St.)
COCKCROW HILL **1D 162**
Cockerell Rd. E17 .... 7A **50**
COCKFOSTERS **4K 21**
Cockfosters Pde. EN4: Cockf 4K **21**
Cockfosters Rd. EN4: Cockf, Had W 1H **21**
Cock Hill E1 .... 6H **9** (5E **84**)
Cock La. EC1 .... 6A **8** (5B **84**)
Cockpit Steps SW1 .... 7C **12**
Cockpit Theatre *4C* ***4***
(off Gateforth St.)
Cockpit Yd. WC1 .... 5H **7** (5K **83**)
Cocks Cres. KT3: N Mald 4B **152**
Cocksett Av. BR6: Chels 6J **173**
Cockspur Ct. SW1 .... 4D **12** (1H **101**)
Cockspur St. SW1 .... 4D **12** (1H **101**)
Cocksure La. DA14: Sidc 3G **145**
Coda Cen., The SW6 .... 7G **99**
Code St. E1 .... 4K **9** (4F **85**)
Codicote Ho. *SE8* *4K* ***103***
(off Chilton Gro.)
Codicote Ter. N4 .... 2C **66**
Codling Cl. E1 .... 1G **103**
Codling Way HA0: Wemb 4D **60**
Codrington Ct. E1 .... 4H **85**
SE16 .... 7A **86**
Codrington Hill SE23 .... 7A **122**
Codrington M. W11 .... 6G **81**
Cody Cl. HA3: Kent 3D **42**
SM6: Wall 7H **167**
Cody Rd. E16 .... 4F **87**
Coe Av. SE25 .... 6G **157**
Coe's All. EN5: Barn 4B **20**
Cofers Circ. HA9: Wemb 2H **61**
Coffey St. SE8 .... 7C **104**
Cogan Av. E17 .... 1A **50**
Coin St. SE1 .... 4J **13** (1A **102**)
(not continuous)
Coity Rd. NW5 .... 6E **64**
Cokers La. SE21 .... 1D **138**
Coke St. E1 .... 6G **85**
Colas M. NW6 .... 1J **81**
Colbalt Cl. BR3: Beck 4K **157**
Colbeck M. SW7 .... 4K **99**
Colbeck Rd. HA1: Harr 7G **41**
Colberg Pl. N16 .... 7F **49**
Colborne Ho. *E14* *7C* ***86***
(off E. India Dock Rd.)
Colborne Way KT4: Wor Pk 3E **164**
Colbrook Av. UB3: Harl 3F **93**
Colbrook Cl. UB3: Harl 3F **93**
Colburn Way SM1: Sutt 3B **166**
Colby M. SE19 .... 5E **138**
Colby Rd. KT12: Walt T 7J **147**
SE19 .... 5E **138**
Colchester Av. E12 .... 4D **70**
Colchester Dr. HA5: Pinn 5B **40**
Colchester Rd. E10 .... 7E **50**
E17 .... 6C **50**
HA6: Nwood 2J **39**
HA8: Edg 7D **28**
Colchester St. E1 .... 7K **9** (6F **85**)
Coldbath Sq. EC1 .... 3J **7** (4A **84**)
Coldbath St. SE13 .... 1D **122**
COLDBLOW **1J 145**
Cold Blow Cres. DA5: Bexl 1K **145**
Cold Blow La. SE14 .... 7K **103**
(not continuous)
Cold Blows CR4: Mitc 3D **154**
Coldershaw Rd. W13 .... 1A **96**
Coldfall Av. N10 .... 2E **46**
Coldham Ct. N22 .... 1B **48**
Coldharbour E14 .... 2E **104**
Coldharbour Crest SE9 .... 3E **142**
Coldharbour La. SE5 .... 3C **120**
SW9 .... 4A **120**
UB3: Hayes 1J **93**
Coldharbour Leisure Cen. 2D **142**
Coldharbour Pl. SE5 .... 2C **120**
Coldharbour Rd. CR0: Wadd 5A **168**
Coldharbour Way CR0: Wadd 5A **168**
Coldstream Gdns. SW18 .... 6H **117**
Colebeck M. N1 .... 6B **66**
Colebert Av. E1 .... 4J **85**
Colebert Ho. *E1* *4J* ***85***
(off Colebert Av.)
Colebrook Cl. NW7 .... 6A **30**
SW15 .... 7F **117**
Colebrook Ct. *SW3* *4D* ***16***
(off Makins St.)
Colebrooke Av. W13 .... 6B **78**
Colebrooke Ct. DA14: Sidc 3B **144**
Colebrooke Dr. E11 .... 7A **52**
Colebrooke Pl. N1 .... 1B **84**
Colebrooke Ri. BR2: Brom 2G **159**
Colebrooke Row N1 .... 2B **84**
Colebrook Ho. *E14* *6D* ***86***
(off Ellesmere St.)
Colebrook Rd. SW16 .... 1J **155**
Colebrook Way N11 .... 5A **32**
Coleby Path SE5 .... 7D **102**
Colechurch Ho. *SE1* *5G* ***103***
(off Avondale Sq.)
Cole Cl. SE28 .... 1B **108**
Cole Ct. TW1: Twick 7A **114**
Coledale Dr. HA7: Stan 1C **42**
Coleford Rd. SW18 .... 5A **118**
Cole Gdns. TW5: Cran 7J **93**
Colegrave Rd. E15 .... 5F **69**
Colegrove Rd. SE15 .... 6F **103**
Coleherne Ct. SW5 .... 5K **99**
Coleherne Mans. *SW5* *5K* ***99***
(off Old Brompton Rd.)
Coleherne M. SW10 .... 5K **99**
Coleherne Rd. SW10 .... 5K **99**
Colehill Gdns. SW6 .... 2G **117**
Colehill La. SW6 .... 1G **117**
Cole Ho. *SE1* *7J* ***13***
(off Baylis Rd.)
Coleman Cl. SE25 .... 2G **157**
Coleman Ct. SW18 .... 7J **117**
Coleman Flds. N1 .... 1C **84**
Coleman Mans. N8 .... 7J **47**
Coleman Rd. DA17: Belv 4G **109**
RM9: Dag 6E **72**
SE5 .... 7E **102**
Colemans Heath SE9 .... 3E **142**
Coleman St. EC2 .... 7E **8** (6D **84**)
Coleman St. Bldgs. EC2 .... 7E **8**
Colenso Dr. NW7 .... 7H **29**
Colenso Rd. E5 .... 4J **67**
IG2: Ilf 1J **71**
COLE PARK **6A 114**
Cole Pk. Gdns. TW1: Twick 5A **114**
Cole Pk. Rd. TW1: Twick 6A **114**
Cole Pk. Vw. TW1: Twick 6A **114**
Colepits Wood Rd. SE9 .... 5H **125**
Coleraine Rd. N8 .... 3A **48**
SE3 .... 6H **105**
Coleridge Av. E12 .... 6C **70**
SM1: Sutt 4C **166**
Coleridge Cl. SW8 .... 2F **119**
Coleridge Ct. *EN5: New Bar* *5E* ***20***
(off Station Rd.)
SW1 .... *3C* ***18***
(off Fynes St.)
W14 .... *3F* ***99***
(off Blythe Rd.)
Coleridge Gdns. NW6 .... 7A **64**
SW10 .... 7K **99**
Coleridge Ho. *SE17* *5C* ***102***
(off Browning St.)
SW1 .... *6B* ***18***
(off Churchill Gdns.)
Coleridge La. N8 .... 6J **47**
Coleridge Rd. CR0: Croy 7J **157**
E17 .... 4B **50**
N4 .... 2A **66**
N8 .... 6H **47**
N12 .... 5F **31**
TW15: Ashf 4A **128**
Coleridge Sq. *SW10* *7A* ***100***
(off Coleridge Gdns.)
W13 .... 6A **78**
Coleridge Wlk. NW11 .... 4J **45**
Coleridge Way UB4: Hayes 6J **75**
UB7: W Dray 4A **92**
Cole Rd. TW1: Twick 6A **114**
Colesburg Rd. BR3: Beck 3B **158**
Coles Cres. HA2: Harr 2F **59**
Coles Grn. WD23: Bushy 1B **26**
Coles Grn. Ct. NW2 .... 2C **62**
Coles Grn. Rd. NW2 .... 1C **62**
Coleshill Flats SW1 .... 4H **17**
Coleshill Rd. TW11: Tedd 6J **131**
Colestown St. SW11 .... 2C **118**
Cole St. SE1 .... 7D **14** (2C **102**)
Colesworth Ho. *HA8: Edg* *2J* ***43***
(off Burnt Oak B'way.)
Colet Cl. N13 .... 6G **33**
Colet Ct. *W6* *4F* ***99***
(off Hammersmith Rd.)
Colet Flats *E1* *6A* ***86***
(off Troon St.)
Colet Gdns. W14 .... 4F **99**
Colet Ho. *SE17* *5B* ***102***
(off Doddington Gro.)
Colette Ct. *SE16* *2K* ***103***
(off Eleanor Cl.)
Coley St. WC1 .... 4H **7** (4K **83**)
Colfe & Hatcliffe Glebe *SE13* *5D* ***122***
(off Lewisham High St.)
Colfe Rd. SE23 .... 1A **140**
Colham Av. UB7: Yiew 1A **92**
COLHAM GREEN **5C 74**
Colham Grn. Rd. UB8: Hil 5C **74**
Colham Mill Rd. UB7: W Dray 2A **92**
Colham Rd. UB8: Hil 4B **74**

Colham Rdbt. UB8: Hil 6C 74
Colina M. N15 ....4B 48
Colina Rd. N15 ....5B 48
Colin Cl. BR4: W W'ck 3H 171
  CR0: Croy 3B 170
  NW9 ....4A 44
Colin Cl. SE6 ....7B 122
Colin Cres. NW9 ....4B 44
COLINDALE 3K 43
Colindale Av. NW9 ....3K 43
Colindale Bus. Pk. NW9 ....3J 43
Colindeep Gdns. NW4 ....4C 44
Colindeep La. NW4 ....3A 44
  NW9 ....3A 44
Colin Dr. NW9 ....5B 44
Colinette Rd. SW15 ....4E 116
Colin Gdns. NW9 ....4B 44
Colin Pde. NW9 ....4A 44
Colin Pk. Rd. NW9 ....4A 44
Colin Rd. NW10 ....6C 62
Colinton Rd. IG3: Ilf 2B 72
Colin Winter Ho. E1 ....4J 85
  (off Nicholas Rd.)
Coliseum Theatre 3E 12
  (off St Martin's La.)
Coliston Pas. SW18 ....7J 117
  (off Coliston Rd.)
Coliston Rd. SW18 ....7J 117
Collamore Av. SW18 ....1C 136
Collapit Cl. HA1: Harr 6F 41
Collard Pl. NW1 ....7F 65
Collards Almshouses E17 ....5E 50
  (off Maynard Rd.)
College App. SE10 ....6E 104
College Av. HA3: Hrw W 1J 41
College Cl. E9 ....5J 67
  HA3: Hrw W 7D 26
  N18 ....5A 34
  TW2: Twick 1H 131
College Ct. EN3: Pond E 5D 24
  NW3 ....6B 64
  (off College Cres.)
  SW3 ....6F 17
  W5 ....7E 78
  W6 ....5E 98
  (off Queen Caroline St.)
College Cres. NW3 ....6A 64
College Cross N1 ....7A 66
College Dr. HA4: Ruis 7J 39
  KT7: T Ditt 7J 149
College E. E1 ....6K 9 (5F 85)
College Flds. Bus. Cen.
  SW19: Mitc 1C 154
College Gdns. E4 ....7J 25
  EN2: Enf 1J 23
  IG4: Ilf 5C 52
  KT3: N Mald 5B 152
  N18 ....5A 34
  SE21 ....1E 138
  SW17 ....2C 136
  (not continuous)
College Grn. SE19 ....7E 138
College Gro. NW1 ....1G 83
College Hill EC4 ....2D 14 (7C 84)
College Hill Rd. HA3: Hrw W 7D 26
College La. NW5 ....4F 65
College Mans. NW6 ....1G 81
  (off Winchester Av.)
College M. N1 ....7A 66
  (off College Cross, not continuous)
  SW1 ....1E 18
  SW18 ....5K 117
College of Arms 2C 14
College Pde. NW6 ....1G 81
COLLEGE PARK 3D 80
College Pk. Cl. SE13 ....4F 123
College Pk. Rd. N17 ....6A 34
College Pl. E17 ....4G 51
  NW1 ....1G 83
  SW10 ....7A 100
College Point E15 ....6H 69
College Rd. BR1: Brom 1J 159
  BR8: Swan 7K 145

College Rd. CR0: Croy 2D 168
  E17 ....5E 50
  EN2: Enf 2J 23
  HA1: Harr 6J 41
  HA3: Hrw W 1J 41
  HA9: Wemb 1D 60
  N17 ....6A 34
  N21 ....2F 33
  NW10 ....2E 80
  SE19 ....5F 139
  SE21 ....7E 120
  SW19 ....6B 136
  TW7: Isle 1K 113
  W13 ....6B 78
College Rdbt. KT1: King T 3E 150
College Row E9 ....5K 67
College Slip BR1: Brom 1J 159
College St. EC4 ....2D 14 (7C 84)
  N3 ....2H 45
College Ter. E3 ....3B 86
  N3 ....2H 45
College Vw. SE9 ....1B 142
College Wlk. KT1: King T 3E 150
College Way TW15: Ashf 4B 128
  UB3: Hayes 7J 75
College Yd. NW5 ....4F 65
Collent St. E9 ....6J 67
Collerston Ho. SE10 ....5H 105
  (off Armitage Rd.)
Colless Rd. N15 ....5F 49
Collett Rd. SE16 ....3G 103
Collett Way UB2: S'hall 2F 95
Collier Cl. E6 ....7F 89
  KT19: Ewe 6C 163
Collier Dr. HA8: Edg 2G 43
COLLIER ROW 1H 55
Collier Row La. RM5: Col R 1H 55
Collier Row Rd. RM5: Col R 1F 55
Colliers Ct. CR0: Croy 4D 168
  (off St Peter's Rd.)
Colliers Shaw BR2: Kes 5B 172
Collier St. N1 ....2K 83
Colliers Water La.
  CR7: Thor H 5A 156
COLLIERS WOOD 7B 136
COLLIERS WOOD 7B 136
Collindale Av. DA8: Erith 7H 109
  DA15: Sidc 1A 144
Collingbourne Rd. W12 ....1D 98
Collingham Gdns. SW5 ....4K 99
Collingham Pl. SW5 ....4K 99
Collingham Rd. SW5 ....4K 99
Collings Cl. N22 ....6E 32
Collington St. SE10 ....5F 105
Collingtree Rd. SE26 ....4J 139
Collingwood Av. KT5: Surb 1J 163
  N10 ....3E 46
Collingwood Cl. SE20 ....1H 157
  TW2: Whit 7E 112
Collingwood Ct. EN5: New Bar ...5E 20
  W5 ....5F 79
Collingwood Ho. E1 ....4H 85
  (off Darling Row)
  SE16 ....2H 103
  (off Cherry Gdn. St.)
  SW1 ....6C 18
  (off Dolphin Sq.)
  W1 ....5A 6
  (off Clipstone St.)
Collingwood Rd. CR4: Mitc 3C 154
  E17 ....6C 50
  N15 ....4E 48
  SM1: Sutt 3J 165
  UB8: Hil 4D 74
Collingwood St. E1 ....4H 85
Collins Av. HA7: Stan 2E 42
Collins Ct. E8 ....6G 67
Collins Dr. HA4: Ruis 2A 58
Collins Ho. E14 ....7E 86
  (off Newby Pl.)
  E15 ....1H 87
  (off John St.)
  SE10 ....5H 105
  (off Armitage Rd.)

Collinson Ct. SE1 ....7C 14
  (off Gt. Suffolk St.)
Collinson Ho. SE15 ....7G 103
  (off Peckham Pk. Rd.)
Collinson St. SE1 ....7C 14 (2C 102)
Collinson Wlk. SE1 ......7C 14 (2C 102)
Collins Path TW12: Hamp 6D 130
Collins Rd. N5 ....4C 66
Collins Sq. SE3 ....2H 123
Collins St. SE3 ....2G 123
  (not continuous)
Collin's Yd. N1 ....1B 84
Collinwood Av. EN3: Enf H 3D 24
Collinwood Gdns. IG5: Ilf 5D 52
Collis All. TW2: Twick 1J 131
Collison Pl. N16 ....1E 66
Coll's Rd. SE15 ....1J 121
Collyer Av. CR0: Bedd 4J 167
Collyer Pl. SE15 ....1G 121
Collyer Rd. CR0: Bedd 4J 167
Colman Ct. HA7: Stan 6G 27
  N12 ....6F 31
Colman Pde. EN1: Enf 3K 23
Colman Rd. E16 ....5A 88
Colmans Wharf E14 ....5D 86
  (off Morris Rd.)
Colmar Cl. E1 ....4K 85
Colmer Pl. HA3: Hrw W 7C 26
Colmer Rd. SW16 ....1J 155
Colmore M. SE15 ....1H 121
Colmore Rd. EN3: Pond E 4D 24
Colnbrook St. SE1 ....3B 102
Colne Ct. KT19: Ewe 4J 163
  W7 ....6H 77
  (off High La.)
Colnedale Rd. UB8: Uxb 5A 56
Colne Ho. IG11: Bark 7F 71
  NW8 ....4B 4
  (off Penfold St.)
Colne Rd. E5 ....4A 68
  N21 ....1J 33
  TW1: Twick 1J 131
  TW2: Twick 1J 131
Colne St. E13 ....3J 87
COLNEY HATCH 6J 31
Colney Hatch La. N10 ....6J 31
  N11 ....6J 31
Cologne Rd. SW11 ....4B 118
Colombo Rd. IG1: Ilf 1G 71
Colombo St. SE1 ....5A 14 (1B 102)
Colombo Street Sports Cen. &
  Community Cen. 5A 14
Colomb St. SE10 ....5G 105
Colonel's Wlk. EN2: Enf 3G 23
Colonial Av. TW2: Whit 6G 113
Colonial Cl. N7 ....3K 65
Colonial Dr. W4 ....4J 97
Colonial Rd. TW14: Felt 7G 111
  Colonnade WC1 ....4F 7 (4J 83)
Colonnade, The SE8 ....4B 104
Colonnades, The
  CR0: Wadd 6A 160
  W2 ....6K 81
Colonnade Wlk. SW1 .....4J 17 (4F 101)
Colorado Bldg. SE8 ....1D 122
  (off Deal's Gateway)
Colosseum Ter. NW1 ....2K 5
Colour Cl. SW1 ....5B 12
Colour House Theatre 1A 154
Colroy Ct. NW11 ....5G 45
Colson Rd. CR0: Croy 2E 168
Colson Way SW16 ....4G 137
Colstead Ho. E1 ....5H 85
  (off Watney Mkt.)
Colsterworth Rd. N15 ....4F 49
  (not continuous)
Colston Av. SM5: Cars 4C 166
Colston Cl. SM5: Cars 4D 166
  (off West St.)
Colston Rd. E7 ....6B 70
  SW14 ....4J 115
Colthurst Cres. N4 ....2B 66
Colthurst Dr. N9 ....3C 34

Coltman Ho. SE10 ....6E 104
  (off Welland St.)
Coltman St. E14 ....5A 86
Coltness Cres. SE2 ....5B 108
Colton Gdns. N17 ....3C 48
Colton Rd. HA1: Harr 5J 41
Coltsfoot Dr. UB7: Yiew 6A 74
Columbas Dr. NW3 ....1B 64
Columbia Av. HA4: Ruis 1K 57
  HA8: Edg 1H 43
  KT4: Wor Pk 7B 152
Columbia Point SE16 ....3J 103
  (off Surrey Quays Rd.)
Columbia Rd. E2 ....1J 9 (3F 85)
  E13 ....4H 87
Columbia Road Flower Market ...1K 9
  (off Columbia Rd.)
Columbia Sq. SW14 ....4J 115
Columbia Wharf EN3: Pond E 6F 25
Columbine Av. CR2: S Croy 7B 168
  E6 ....5C 88
Columbine Way SE13 ....2E 122
Columbus Cl. SE16 ....1J 103
  (off Rotherhithe St.)
Columbus Ct. Yd. E14 ....1C 104
Columbus Gdns.
  HA6: Nwood 1J 39
Colva Wlk. N19 ....2F 65
Colverson Ho. E1 ....5J 85
  (off Lindley St.)
Colvestone Cres. E8 ....5F 67
Colview Ct. SE9 ....1B 142
Colville Est. N1 ....1C 04
Colville Est. W. E2 ....2K 9
  (off Turin St.)
Colville Gdns. W11 ....6H 81
  (not continuous)
Colville Ho. E2 ....2J 85
  (off Waterloo Gdns.)
Colville Ho's. W11 ....6H 81
Colville M. W11 ....6H 81
Colville Pl. W1 ....6B 6 (5G 83)
Colville Rd. E11 ....3E 68
  E17 ....2A 50
  N9 ....1C 34
  W3 ....3H 97
  W11 ....6H 81
Colville Sq. W11 ....6H 81
Colville Ter. W11 ....6H 81
Colvin Cl. SE26 ....5J 139
Colvin Gdns. E4 ....3K 35
  E11 ....4K 51
  IG6: Ilf 1G 53
Colvin Rd. CR7: Thor H 6C 70
  E6 ....7C 70
Colwall Gdns. IG8: Wfd G 5D 36
Colwell Rd. SE22 ....5F 121
Colwick Cl. N6 ....7H 47
Colwith Rd. W6 ....6E 98
Colwood Gdns. SW19 ....7B 136
Colworth Gro. SE17 ....4C 102
Colworth Rd. CR0: Croy 1G 169
  E11 ....6G 51
Colwyn Av. UB6: G'frd 2K 77
Colwyn Cl. SW16 ....5G 137
Colwyn Cres. TW3: Houn 1G 113
Colwyn Grn. NW9 ....6A 44
  (off Snowdon Dr.)
Colwyn Ho. SE1 ....2J 19 (3A 102)
Colwyn Rd. NW2 ....2K 62
Colyer Cl. N1 ....2K 83
  SE9 ....2F 143
Colyers Cl. DA8: Erith 1K 127
Colyers La. DA8: Erith 1J 127
Colyers Wlk. DA8: Erith 1K 127
Colyton Cl. DA16: Well 1D 126
  HA0: Wemb 6C 60
Colyton La. SW16 ....5A 138
Colyton Rd. SE22 ....5H 121
Colyton Way N18 ....5B 34
Combe, The NW1 ....2K 5 (3F 83)
Combe Av. SE3 ....7H 105
Combedale Rd. SE10 ....5J 105

Combe Dene BR2: Brom 4H *159*
    (off Cumberland Rd.)
Combe Ho. W2 . . . . .5J *81*
    (off Brunel Est.)
Combemartin Rd. SW18 . . . . .7G *117*
Combe M. SE3 . . . . .7H *105*
Comber Cl. NW2 . . . . .3D *62*
Comber Gro. SE5 . . . . .7C *102*
Comber Ho. SE5 . . . . .7C *102*
Combermere Rd. SM4: Mord 6K *153*
    SW9 . . . . .3K *119*
Comberton KT1: King T 2G *151*
    (off Eureka Rd.)
Comberton Rd. E5 . . . . .2H *67*
Combeside SE18 . . . . .7K *107*
Combwell Cres. SE2 . . . . .3A *108*
Comedy Store 3C *12*
    (off Oxendon St.)
Comedy Theatre 3C *12*
    (off Panton St.)
Comely Bank Rd. E17 . . . . .5E *50*
Comeragh M. W14 . . . . .5G *99*
Comeragh Rd. W14 . . . . .5G *99*
Comer Cres. UB2: S'hall 1G *95*
    (off Windmill Av.)
Comerell Pl. SE10 . . . . .5H *105*
Comerford Rd. SE4 . . . . .4A *122*
Comet Cl. E12 . . . . .4B *70*
Comet Pl. SE8 . . . . .7C *104*
    (not continuous)
Comet Rd. TW19: Stanw 7A *110*
Comet St. SE8 . . . . .7C *104*
Comfort St. SE15 . . . . .6E *102*
Commerce Pk. CRO: Wadd 2K *167*
Commerce Rd. N22 . . . . .1K *47*
    TW8: Bford 6C *96*
Commerce Way CRO: Wadd 2K *167*
Commercial Dock Path SE16 . . . . . .3B *104*
    (off Gulliver St.)
Commercial Rd. E1 . . . . . . .7K **9** (6G *85*)
    E14 . . . . .6A *86*
    N18 . . . . .5K *33*
Commercial Rd. Ind. Est. N18 . . . . . .6A *34*
Commercial St. E1 . . . . . . .4J **9** (4F *85*)
Commercial Way NW10 . . . . .2H *79*
    SE15 . . . . .7F *103*
Commerell St. SE10 . . . . .5G *105*
Commodity Quay E1 . . . . . .3K **15** (7F *85*)
Commodore Ct. SE8 . . . . .1C *122*
    (off Albyn Rd.)
Commodore Ho. E14 . . . . .7E *86*
    (off Poplar High St.)
    SW18 . . . . .3A *118*
Commodore Sq. SW10 . . . . .1A *118*
Commodore St. E1 . . . . .4A *86*
Common, The E15 . . . . .6G *69*
    HA7: Stan 2D *26*
    UB2: S'hall 4A *94*
    W5 . . . . .7E *78*
    (not continuous)
Commondale SW15 . . . . .3E *116*
Commonfield La. SW17 . . . . .5C *136*
Common La. KT10: Clay 7A *162*
Common Mile Cl. SW4 . . . . .5H *119*
Common Rd. HA7: Stan 4C *26*
    KT10: Clay 6A *162*
    SW13 . . . . .3D *116*
    W4 . . . . .4A *98*
Commonside BR2: Kes 4A *172*
Commonside E. CR4: Mitc 3E *154*
    (not continuous)
Commonside W. CR4: Mitc 3D *154*
Commonwealth Av. UB3: Hayes 6F *75*
    W12 . . . . .7D *80*
    (not continuous)
Commonwealth Conference Cen.
    . . . . .5B **12** (1G *101*)
Commonwealth Institute 3H *99*
Commonwealth Rd. N17 . . . . .7B *34*
Commonwealth Way SE2 . . . . .5B *108*
Community Cl. TW5: Cran 1K *111*
    UB10: Ick 3D *56*
Community La. N7 . . . . .5H *65*

Community Rd. E15 . . . . .5F *69*
    UB6: G'frd 1G *77*
Como Rd. SE23 . . . . .2A *140*
Como St. RM7: Rom 5K *55*
Compass Cl. HA8: Edg 4A *28*
    TW15: Ashf 7E *128*
Compass Ct. SE1 . . . . .5J *15*
    (off Shad Thames)
Compass Hill TW10: Rich 6D *114*
Compass Ho. SW18 . . . . .4K *117*
Compass La. BR1: Brom 1J *159*
    (off North St.)
Compass Point E14 . . . . .7B *86*
    (off Grenade St.)
Compass Theatre & Arts Cen. 3E *56*
Compayne Gdns. NW6 . . . . .7K *63*
Compter Pas. EC2 . . . . .1D *14*
Compton Av. E6 . . . . .2B *88*
    HA0: Wemb 4C *60*
    N1 . . . . .6B *66*
    N6 . . . . .7C *46*
Compton Cl. E3 . . . . .5C *86*
    HA8: Edg 7D *28*
    NW1 . . . . .2K *5*
    NW11 . . . . .3F *63*
    SE15 . . . . .7G *103*
    W13 . . . . .6A *78*
Compton Ct. SE19 . . . . .6E *138*
    SM1: Sutt 4A *166*
Compton Cres. KT9: Chess 5E *162*
    N17 . . . . .7H *33*
    UB5: N'olt 1B *76*
    W4 . . . . .6J *97*
Compton Leisure Cen., The 1C *76*
Compton Pas. EC1 . . . . . . .3B **8** (4B *84*)
Compton Pl. WC1 . . . . .3E **6** (4J *83*)
Compton Ri. HA5: Pinn 5C *40*
Compton Rd. CRO: Croy 1H *169*
    N1 . . . . .6B *66*
    N21 . . . . .1F *33*
    NW10 . . . . .3F *81*
    SW19 . . . . .6H *135*
    UB3: Hayes 7G *75*
Compton Sports Cen. 7H *31*
Compton St. EC1 . . . . .3A **8** (4B *84*)
Compton Ter. N1 . . . . .6B *66*
    N21 . . . . .1F *33*
Comreddy Cl. EN2: Enf 1G *23*
Comus Ho. SE17 . . . . .4E *102*
    (off Comus Pl.)
Comus Pl. SE17 . . . . .4E *102*
Comyn Rd. SW11 . . . . .4C *118*
Comyns, The WD23: Bushy 1B *26*
Comyns Cl. E16 . . . . .5H *87*
Comyns Rd. RM9: Dag 7G *73*
Conant Ho. SE11 . . . . .7K *19*
    (off St Agnes Pl.)
Conant M. E1 . . . . .7G *85*
Concanon Rd. SW2 . . . . .4K *119*
Concert Hall App. SE1 . . . .5H **13** (1K *101*)
Concord Bus. Cen. W3 . . . . .4H *79*
Concord Cl. UB5: N'olt 3B *76*
Concord Ct. KT1: King T 3F *151*
    (off Winery La.)
Concorde Cl. TW3: Houn 2F *113*
    UB10: Uxb 2A *74*
Concorde Dr. E6 . . . . .5D *88*
Concord Ho. KT3: N Mald 3A *152*
    N17 . . . . .7A *34*
    (off Park La.)
Concordia Wharf E14 . . . . .1E *104*
    (off Coldharbour)
Concord Rd. EN3: Pond E 5D *24*
    W3 . . . . .4H *79*
Concourse, The N9 . . . . .2B *34*
    (in Edmonton Grn. Shop. Cen.)
    NW9 . . . . .1A *44*
Condell Rd. SW8 . . . . .1G *119*
Conder St. E14 . . . . .6A *86*
Condor Path UB5: N'olt 2E *76*
    (off Union Rd.)
Condover Cres. SE18 . . . . .7F *107*
Condray Pl. SW11 . . . . .7C *100*

Conduit Av. SE10 . . . . .1F *123*
Conduit Cl. WC2 . . . . .2E *12*
Conduit La. CRO: Croy 5G *169*
    CR2: S Croy 5G *169*
    EN3: Pond E 6F *25*
    N18 . . . . .5D *34*
Conduit M. SE18 . . . . .5F *107*
    W2 . . . . .1A **10** (6B *82*)
Conduit Pas. W2 . . . . .1A *10*
Conduit Pl. W2 . . . . .1A **10** (6B *82*)
Conduit Rd. SE18 . . . . .5F *107*
Conduit St. W1 . . . . .2K **11** (7F *83*)
Conduit Way NW10 . . . . .7J *61*
Conewood St. N5 . . . . .3B *66*
Coney Acre SE21 . . . . .1C *138*
Coney Burrows E4 . . . . .2B *36*
Coney Gro. UB8: Hil 3C *74*
Coneygrove Path UB5: N'olt 6C *58*
    (off Arnold Rd.)
CONEY HALL 3G *171*
Coney Hall Pde. BR4: W W'ck 3G *171*
Coney Hill Rd. BR4: W W'ck 2G *171*
Coney Way SW8 . . . . .6K *101*
Conference Cl. E4 . . . . .2K *35*
Conference Rd. SE2 . . . . .4C *108*
Congers Ho. SE8 . . . . .7C *104*
Congleton Gro. SE18 . . . . .5G *107*
Congo Dr. N9 . . . . .3D *34*
Congo Rd. SE18 . . . . .5H *107*
Congress Rd. SE2 . . . . .4C *108*
Congreve Ho. N16 . . . . .5E *66*
Congreve Rd. SE9 . . . . .3D *124*
Congreve St. SE17 . . . . .4E *102*
Congreve Wlk. E16 . . . . .5B *88*
    (off Fulmer Rd.)
Conical Cnr. EN2: Enf 2H *23*
Conifer Cl. BR6: Orp 4H *173*
Conifer Ct. TW15: Ashf 5B *128*
    (off The Crescent)
Conifer Gdns. EN1: Enf 6K *23*
    SM1: Sutt 2K *165*
    SW16 . . . . .3J *137*
Conifers Cl. TW11: Tedd 7B *132*
Conifer Way HA0: Wemb 3C *60*
    UB3: Hayes 7J *75*
Coniffe Ct. SE9 . . . . .5F *125*
Coniger Rd. SW6 . . . . .2J *117*
Coningham Ct. SW10 . . . . .7A *100*
    (off King's Rd.)
Coningham M. W12 . . . . .1C *98*
Coningham Rd. W12 . . . . .2D *98*
Coningsby Av. NW9 . . . . .2A *44*
Coningsby Cotts. W5 . . . . .2D *96*
Coningsby Ct. CR4: Mitc 2E *154*
Coningsby Gdns. E4 . . . . .6J *35*
Coningsby Rd. CR2: S Croy 7C *168*
    N4 . . . . .7B *48*
    W5 . . . . .2D *96*
Conington Rd. SE13 . . . . .2D *122*
Conisbee Ct. N14 . . . . .5B *22*
Conisborough Cres. SE6 . . . . .3E *140*
Conisbrough NW1 . . . . .1G *83*
    (off Bayham St.)
Coniscliffe Cl. BR7: Chst 1E *160*
Coniscliffe Rd. N13 . . . . .3H *33*
Coniston NW1 . . . . .2G *5*
    (off Harrington St.)
Coniston Av. DA16: Well 3J *125*
    IG11: Bark 7J *71*
    UB6: G'frd 3B *78*
Coniston Cl. DA7: Bex 1J *127*
    DA8: Erith 7K *109*
    IG11: Bark 7J *71*
    N20 . . . . .3F *31*
    SW13 . . . . .7B *98*
    SW20 . . . . .6F *153*
    W4 . . . . .7J *97*
Coniston Ct. SE16 . . . . .2K *103*
    (off Eleanor Cl.)
    SM6: Wall 4F *167*
    TW15: Ashf 3A *128*

Coniston Ct. W2 . . . . .1D *10*
    (off Kendal St.)
Conistone Way N7 . . . . .7J *65*
Coniston Gdns. HA5: Eastc 4J *39*
    HA9: Wemb 1C *60*
    IG4: Ilf 4C *52*
    N9 . . . . .1D *34*
    NW9 . . . . .5K *43*
    SM2: Sutt 6B *166*
Coniston Ho. E3 . . . . .4B *86*
    (off Southern Gro.)
    SE5 . . . . .7C *102*
    (off Wyndham Rd.)
Coniston Rd. BR1: Brom 6G *141*
    CRO: Croy 7G *157*
    DA7: Bex 1J *127*
    N10 . . . . .2F *47*
    N17 . . . . .6B *34*
    TW2: Whit 6F *113*
Coniston Wlk. E9 . . . . .5J *67*
Coniston Way KT9: Chess 3E *162*
Conlan St. W10 . . . . .4G *81*
Conley Rd. NW10 . . . . .6A *62*
Conley St. SE10 . . . . .5G *105*
Connaught Av. E4 . . . . .1A *36*
    EN1: Enf 2K *23*
    EN4: E Barn 1J *31*
    SW14 . . . . .3J *115*
    TW4: Houn 4C *112*
    TW15: Ashf 4A *128*
Connaught Bri. E16 . . . . .1B *106*
Connaught Bus. Cen. CRO: Wadd . . .6K *167*
    CR4: Mitc 5D *154*
    NW9 . . . . .5B *44*
Connaught Cl. E10 . . . . .2K *67*
    EN1: Enf 2K *23*
    SM1: Sutt 2B *166*
    UB8: Hil 4E *74*
    W2 . . . . .1D *10*
Connaught Ct. E17 . . . . .4D *50*
    (off Orford Rd.)
    W2 . . . . .1E *10*
    (off Connaught Ct.)
Connaught Dr. NW11 . . . . .4J *45*
Connaught Gdns. N10 . . . . .5F *47*
    N13 . . . . .4G *33*
    SM4: Mord 4A *154*
Connaught Hgts. UB10: Hil 4E *74*
    (off Uxbridge Rd.)
Connaught Ho. NW10 . . . . .3D *80*
    (off Trenmar Gdns.)
    W1 . . . . .3J *11*
    (off Davies St.)
Connaught La. IG1: Ilf 2G *71*
Connaught Lodge N4 . . . . .7A *48*
    (off Connaught Rd.)
Connaught M. NW3 . . . . .4C *64*
    SE11 . . . . .3K *19*
    (off Walcot Sq.)
    SE18 . . . . .5E *106*
    SW6 . . . . .1G *117*
Connaught Pl. W2 . . . . . . .2E **10** (7D *82*)
Connaught Rd. E4 . . . . .1B *36*
    E11 . . . . .1F *69*
    E16 . . . . .1B *106*
    E17 . . . . .5C *50*
    EN5: Barn 6A *20*
    HA3: W'stone 1K *41*
    IG1: Ilf 2H *71*
    KT3: N Mald 4A *152*
    N4 . . . . .7A *48*
    NW10 . . . . .1A *80*
    SE18 . . . . .5E *106*
    SM1: Sutt 2B *166*
    TW10: Rich 5F *115*
    TW11: Tedd 5H *131*
    W13 . . . . .7B *78*
Connaught Rdbt. E16 . . . . .7B *88*
    (off Victoria Dock Rd.)
Connaught Sq. W2 . . . . . . .1D **10** (6D *82*)
Connaught St. W2 . . . . . . .1D **10** (6C *82*)
Connaught Way N13 . . . . .4G *33*
Connect La. IG6: Ilf 2G *53*

Connell Ct. *SE14* .6K 103
(off Myers La.)
Connell Cres. W5 .4F 79
Connington Cres. E4 .3A 36
Connor Cl. E11 .7G 51
IG6: Ilf .1G 53
Connor Ct. SW11 .1F 119
Connor Rd. RM9: Dag .4F 73
Connor St. E9 .1K 85
Conolly Dell *W7* .1J 95
(off Conolly Rd.)
Conolly Rd. W7 .1J 95
Conrad Dr. KT4: Wor Pk .1E 164
Conrad Ho. E8 .6G 67
E14 .7A 86
(off Victory Pl.)
E16 .1K 105
(off Wesley Av.)
N16 .5E 66
(off Matthias Rd.)
SW8 .7J 101
(off Wyvil Rd.)
Conrad Twr. W3 .3H 97
Consfield Av. KT3: N Mald .4C 152
Consort Ct. *W8* .3K 99
(off Wright's La.)
Consort Ho. *E14* .5D 104
(off St Davids Sq.)
W2 .7K 81
(off Queensway)
Consort Lodge *NW8* .1D 82
(off Prince Albert Rd.)
Consort M. TW7: Isle .5H 113
Consort Rd. SE15 .1H 121
Cons St. SE1 .6K 13 (2A 102)
Constable Av. E16 .1K 105
Constable Cl. N11 .5J 31
NW11 .6K 45
UB4: Hayes .2E 74
Constable Ct. *SE16* .5H 103
(off Stubbs Dr.)
W4 .5H 97
(off Chaseley Dr.)
Constable Cres. N15 .5G 49
Constable Gdns. HA8: Edg .1G 43
TW7: Isle .5H 113
Constable Ho. NW3 .7D 64
UB5: N'olt .2B 76
(off Gallery Gdns.)
Constable Ho's. *E14* .2C 104
(off Cassilis Rd.)
Constable M. RM8: Dag .4B 72
Constable Wlk. SE21 .3E 138
Constance Allen Ho. *W10* .6F 81
(off Bridge Cl.)
Constance Cres. BR2: Hayes .7H 159
Constance Rd. CR0: Croy .7B 156
EN1: Enf .6K 23
SM1: Sutt .4A 166
TW2: Whit .7F 113
Constance St. E16 .1C 106
Constant Ho. *E14* .7D 86
(off Harrow La.)
Constantine Ct. *E1* .6G 85
(off Fairclough St.)
Constantine Pl. UB10: Hil .1B 74
Constantine Rd. NW3 .4C 64
Constitution Hill SW1 .6J 11 (2F 101)
Constitution Ri. SE18 .1E 124
Consul Av. RM9: Dag, Rain .3J 91
RM13: Rain .3J 91
Content St. SE17 .4D 102
Contessa Cl. BR6: Farnb .5J 173
Control Twr. Rd. TW6: H'row A .3C 110
Convair Wlk. UB5: N'olt .3B 76
Convent Cl. BR3: Beck .7E 140
Convent Gdns. W5 .4C 96
W11 .6G 81
Convent Hill SE19 .6C 138
Convent Lodge TW15: Ashf .5D 128
Convent Rd. TW15: Ashf .5C 128
Convent Way UB2: S'hall .4A 94
Conway Cl. HA7: Stan .6F 27
Conway Cres. RM6: Chad H .6C 54
UB6: G'frd .2J 77
Conway Dr. SM2: Sutt .6K 165
TW15: Ashf .6E 128
UB3: Harl .3E 92
Conway Gdns. CR4: Mitc .4J 155
EN2: Enf .1K 23
HA9: Wemb .7C 42
Conway Gro. W3 .5K 79
Conway Ho. *E14* .4C 104
(off Cahir St.)
E17 .5A 50
(off Mission Gro.)
SW3 .6F 17
(off Ormonde Ga.)
Conway M. W1 .4A 6
Conway Rd. N14 .3D 32
N15 .5B 48
NW2 .2E 62
SE18 .4H 107
SW20 .1E 152
TW4: Houn .7D 112
TW6: H'row A .3D 110
TW13: Hanw .5B 130
Conway St. W1 .4A 6 (4G 83)
(not continuous)
Conway Wlk. TW12: Hamp .6D 130
Conybeare NW3 .7C 64
Conyers Cl. IG8: Wfd G .6B 36
Conyer's Rd. SW16 .5H 137
Conyer St. E3 .2A 86
Cooden Cl. BR1: Brom .7K 141
Cook Ct. *SE16* .1J 103
(off Rotherhithe St.)
Cookes Cl. E11 .2H 69
Cookes La. SM3: Cheam .6G 165
Cooke St. IG11: Bark .1G 89
Cookham Cl. UB2: S'hall .3F 95
Cookham Cres. SE16 .2K 103
Cookham Dene Cl. BR7: Chst .1H 161
Cookham Ho. *E2* .3J 9
(off Montclare St.)
Cookham Rd. BR8: Swan .7G 145
Cookhill Rd. SE2 .2B 108
Cook Rd. RM9: Dag .1E 90
Cook's Cl. RM5: Col R .1J 55
Cooks Hole Rd. EN2: Enf .1H 23
Cookson Gro. DA8: Erith .7H 109
Cook's Rd. E15 .2D 86
SE17 .6B 102
Coolfin Rd. E16 .6J 87
Coolgardie Av. E4 .5A 36
IG7: Chig .3K 37
Coolgardie Rd. TW15: Ashf .5E 128
Coolhurst Rd. N8 .6H 47
Cool Oak La. NW9 .7A 44
Coomassie Rd. W9 .4H 81
COOMBE .7K 133
Coombe Av. CR0: Croy .4E 168
Coombe Bank KT2: King T .1A 152
Coombe Cl. HA8: Edg .2F 43
TW3: Houn .4E 112
Coombe Cnr. N21 .1G 33
Coombe Ct. *CR0: Croy* .4D 168
(off St Peter's Rd.)
Coombe Cres. TW12: Hamp .7D 130
Coombe Dr. HA4: Ruis .1K 57
Coombe End KT2: King T .7K 133
Coombefield Cl. KT3: N Mald .5A 152
Coombe Gdns. KT3: N Mald .4B 152
SW20 .2C 152
Coombe Hill Glade KT2: King T .7A 134
Coombe Hill Rd. KT2: King T .7A 134
Coombe Ho. E4 .6G 35
N7 .5H 65
Coombe Ho. Chase KT3: N Mald .1K 151
Coombehurst Cl. EN4: Cockf .2J 21
COOMBE LANE .1B 152
Coombe La. CR0: Croy .5H 169
SW20 .1B 152
Coombe La. Flyover SW20 .1B 152
Coombe La. W. KT2: King T .1H 151
Coombe Lea BR1: Brom .3C 160
Coombe Lodge SE7 .6A 106
Coombe Neville KT2: King T .7K 133
Coombe Pk. KT2: King T .5J 133
Coombe Pl. KT2: King T .5J 133
Coomber Ho. *SW6* .3K 117
(off Wandsworth Bri. Rd.)
Coombe Ridings KT2: King T .5J 133
Coombe Ri. KT2: King T .1J 151
Coombe Rd. CR0: Croy .4D 168
KT2: King T .1G 151
KT3: N Mald .2A 152
N22 .2A 48
NW10 .3K 61
SE26 .4H 139
TW12: Hamp .6D 130
W4 .5A 98
W13 .3B 96
Coomber Way CR0: Bedd .7H 155
Coombes Rd. RM9: Dag .1F 91
Coombe Wlk. SM1: Sutt .3K 165
Coombewood Dr. RM6: Chad H .6F 55
Coombe Wood Rd. KT2: King T .5J 133
Coombs St. N1 .1B 8 (2B 84)
Coomer M. SW6 .6H 99
Coomer Pl. SW6 .6H 99
Coomer Rd. SW6 .6H 99
Cooms Wlk. HA8: Edg .1J 43
Cooperage, The *SE1* .5J 15
(off Gainsford St.)
Cooperage Cl. N17 .6A 34
Cooper Av. E17 .1A 50
Cooper Cl. SE1 .7K 13 (2A 102)
Cooper Ct. E15 .5D 60
SE18 .6F 107
Cooper Cres. SM5: Cars .3D 166
Cooper Ho. *NW8* .4A 4
(off Lyons Pl.)
TW4: Houn .3D 112
Cooper Rd. CR0: Wadd .4B 168
NW4 .6F 45
NW10 .5C 62
Coopersale Cl. IG8: Wfd G .7F 37
Coopersale Rd. E9 .5K 67
Coopers Cl. E1 .4J 85
RM10: Dag .6H 73
Coopers Ct. *E3* .4B 86
(off Eric St.)
TW7: Isle .2K 113
(off Woodlands Rd.)
W3 .1J 97
(off Church Rd.)
Coopers La. E10 .1D 68
NW1 .2H 83
(not continuous)
SE12 .2K 141
Coopers Lodge *SE1* .6J 15
(off Tooley St.)
Coopers M. BR3: Beck .2C 158
Cooper's Rd. SE1 .5F 103
Coopers Row EC3 .2J 15 (7F 85)
Cooper St. E16 .5H 87
Coopers Wlk. E15 .5G 69
Cooper's Yd. SE19 .6E 138
Coote Gdns. RM8: Dag .3F 73
Coote Rd. DA7: Bex .1F 127
RM8: Dag .3F 73
Cope Ho. EC1 .2D 8
Copeland Dr. E14 .4C 104
Copeland Ho. SE11 .2H 19
SW17 .4B 136
Copeland Rd. E17 .6D 50
SE15 .2G 121
Copeman Cl. SE26 .5J 139
Copenhagen Gdns. W4 .2K 97
Copenhagen Ho. *N1* .1K 83
(off Barnsbury Est.)
Copenhagen Pl. E14 .6B 86
(not continuous)
Copenhagen St. N1 .1J 83
Cope Pl. W8 .3J 99
Copers Cope Rd. BR3: Beck .7B 140
Cope St. SE16 .4K 103
Copford Cl. IG8: Wfd G .6H 37
Copford Wlk. *N1* .1C 84
(off Popham St.)
Copgate Path SW16 .6K 137
Copinger Wlk. HA8: Edg .1H 43
Copland Av. HA0: Wemb .5D 60
Copland Cl. HA0: Wemb .5C 60
Copland Ho. UB1: S'hall .2D 94
Copland M. HA0: Wemb .6E 60
Copland Rd. HA0: Wemb .6E 60
Copleston M. SE15 .2F 121
Copleston Pas. SE5 .2F 121
Copleston Rd. SE15 .3F 121
Copley Cl. SE17 .6C 102
W7 .4K 77
Copley Dene BR1: Brom .1B 160
Copley Pk. SW16 .6K 137
Copley Rd. HA7: Stan .5H 27
Copley St. E1 .5K 85
Coppard Gdns. KT9: Chess .6C 162
Coppelia Rd. SE3 .4H 123
Coppen Rd. RM8: Dag .7F 55
Copperas St. SE8 .6D 104
Copper Beech Cl. IG5: Ilf .1E 52
Copperbeech Cl. NW3 .5B 64
Copper Beeches Ct. TW7: Isle .1H 113
Copper Cl. N17 .7C 34
SE19 .7F 139
Copperdale Rd. UB3: Hayes .2J 93
Copperfield Av. UB8: Hil .5C 74
Copperfield Dr. N15 .4F 49
Copperfield Ho. *SE1* .7K 15
(off Wolseley St.)
W1 .5H 5
(off Marylebone High St.)
W11 .1F 99
(off St Ann's Rd.)
Copperfield M. N18 .4K 33
Copperfield Rd. E3 .4A 86
SE28 .6C 90
Copperfields BR3: Beck .1E 158
HA1: Harr .7J 41
Copperfields Ct. W3 .2G 97
Copperfield St. SE1 .6B 14 (2B 102)
Copperfield Way BR7: Chst .6G 143
HA5: Pinn .4D 40
Coppergate Cl. BR1: Brom .1K 159
Coppermead Cl. NW2 .3E 62
Copper Mill Dr. TW7: Isle .2K 113
Copper Mill La. SW17 .4A 136
Coppermill La. E17 .6J 49
(not continuous)
Copper Row SE1 .5J 15
Copperworks, The *N1* .2J 83
(off Railway St.)
Coppetts Cen. N12 .7J 31
Coppetts Cl. N12 .7H 31
Coppetts Rd. N10 .7J 31
Coppice, The DA5: Bexl .3K 145
EN2: Enf .4G 23
EN5: New Bar .6E 20
(off Great Nth. Rd.)
TW15: Ashf .6D 128
UB7: Yiew .6A 74
Coppice Cl. BR3: Beck .4D 158
HA4: Ruis .6F 39
HA7: Stan .6E 26
SW20 .3E 152
Coppice Dr. SW15 .6D 116
Coppice Wlk. N20 .3D 30
Coppice Way E18 .4H 51
Coppies Gro. N11 .4A 32
Copping Cl. CR0: Croy .4E 168
Coppins, The CR0: New Ad .6D 170
HA3: Hrw W .6D 26
Coppock Cl. SW11 .2C 118
Coppsfield KT8: W Mole .3E 148
Copse, The E4 .1C 36
N2 .3D 46
Copse Av. BR4: W W'ck .2D 170
Copse Cl. HA6: Nwood .2E 38
SE7 .6K 105
Copse Glade KT6: Surb .7D 150
COPSE HILL .7D 134

Copse Hill SM2: Sutt 7K 165
SW20 . . . . . 1C 152
Copse Vw. CR2: Sels 7K 169
Copsewood Cl. DA15: Sidc 6J 125
Copse Wood Way HA6: Nwood 1D 38
Coptain Ho. SW18 . . . . . 4J 117
Coptefield Dr. DA17: Belv 3D 108
Copthall Av. EC2 . . . . . 7F 9 (6D 84)
(not continuous)
Copthall Bldgs. EC2 . . . . . 7F 9
Copthall Cl. EC2 . . . . . 7E 8 (6D 84)
Copthall Dr. NW7 . . . . . 7H 29
Copthall Gdns. NW7 . . . . . 7H 29
TW1: Twick 1K 131
Copthall Rd. E. UB10: Ick 2C 56
Copthall Rd. W. UB10: Ick 2C 56
Copthall Swimming Pool 7J 29
Copthorne Av. BR2: Brom 2D 172
SW12 . . . . . 7H 119
Copthorne Chase TW15: Ashf 4B 128
Copthorne Cl. TW17: Shep 6E 146
Copthorne M. UB3: Harl 4G 93
Coptic St. WC1 . . . . . 6E 6 (5J 83)
Copwood Cl. N12 . . . . . 4G 31
Coral Apartments *E16* *7J 87*
(off Western Gateway)
Coral Cl. RM6: Chad H 4C 54
Coral Ho. *E1* *4A 86*
(off Harford St.)
Coraline Cl. UB1: S'hall 3D 76
Coralline Wlk. SE2 . . . . . 3C 108
Coral Row SW11 . . . . . 3A 118
Coral St. SE1 . . . . . 7K 13 (2A 102)
Coram Ho. *W4* *5A 98*
(off Wood St.)
WC1 . . . . . 3E 6
Coram St. WC1 . . . . . 4E 6 (4J 83)
Coran Cl. N9 . . . . . 7E 24
Corban Rd. TW3: Houn 3E 112
Corbar Cl. EN4: Had W 1G 21
Corbden Cl. SE15 . . . . . 1F 121
Corbet Cl. SM6: Wall 1E 166
Corbet Ct. EC3 . . . . . 1F 15 (6D 84)
Corbet Ho. *N1* *2A 84*
(off Barnsbury Est.)
SE5 . . . . . *7C 102*
(off Wyndham Rd.)
Corbet Pl. E1 . . . . . 5J 9 (5F 85)
Corbett Ct. SE26 . . . . . 4B 140
Corbett Gro. N22 . . . . . 7D 32
Corbett Ho. *SW10* *6A 100*
(off Cathcart Rd.)
Corbett Rd. E11 . . . . . 6A 52
E17 . . . . . 3E 50
Corbetts La. SE16 . . . . . 4J 103
(not continuous)
Corbetts Pas. *SE16* *4J 103*
(off Corbetts La.)
Corbetts Wharf *SE16* *2H 103*
(off Bermondsey Wall E.)
Corbicum E11 . . . . . 7G 51
Corbidge Ct. *SE8* *6D 104*
(off Glaisher St.)
Corbiere Ct. SW19 . . . . . 6F 135
Corbiere Ho. *N1* *1D 84*
(off De Beauvoir Est.)
Corbins La. HA2: Harr 3F 59
Corbridge N17 . . . . . 7C 34
Corbridge Cres. E2 . . . . . 2H 85
Corby Cres. EN2: Enf 4D 22
Corbylands Rd. DA15: Sidc 7J 125
Corbyn St. N4 . . . . . 1J 65
Corby Rd. NW10 . . . . . 2K 79
Corby Way E3 . . . . . 4C 86
Cordelia Cl. SE24 . . . . . 4B 120
Cordelia Gdns. TW19: Stanw 7A 110
Cordelia Ho. *N1* *2E 84*
(off Arden Est.)
Cordelia Rd. TW19: Stanw 7A 110
Cordelia St. E14 . . . . . 6D 86
Cordell Ho. *N15* *5F 49*
(off Newton Rd.)
Cordingley Rd. HA4: Ruis 2F 57
Cording St. E14 . . . . . 5D 86
Cordwainers Ct. *E9* *7J 67*
(off St Thomas's Sq.)
Cordwainers Wlk. E13 . . . . . 2J 87
Cord Way E14 . . . . . 3C 104
Cordwell Rd. SE13 . . . . . 5G 123
Corefield Cl. N11 . . . . . 2K 31
Corelli Ct. *SW5* *4J 99*
(off W. Cromwell Rd.)
Corelli Rd. SE3 . . . . . 2C 124
Corfe Av. HA2: Harr 4E 58
Corfe Cl. UB4: Yead 6A 76
Corfe Ho. *SW8* *7K 101*
(off Dorset Rd.)
Corfe Twr. W3 . . . . . 2H 97
Corfield Rd. N21 . . . . . 5E 22
Corfield St. E2 . . . . . 3H 85
Corfton Lodge W5 . . . . . 5E 78
Corfton Rd. W5 . . . . . 6E 78
Coriander Av. E14 . . . . . 6F 87
Coriander Ct. *SE1* *6K 15*
(off Gainsford St.)
Cories Cl. RM8: Dag 2D 72
Corinium Cl. HA9: Wemb 4F 61
Corinne Rd. N19 . . . . . 4G 65
Corinthian Manorway
DA8: Erith 4K 109
Corinthian Rd. DA8: Erith 4K 109
Corinthian Way TW19: Stanw 7A 110
Corkers Path IG1: Ilf 2G 71
Corker Wlk. N7 . . . . . 2K 65
Corkran Rd. KT6: Surb 7D 150
Corkscrew Hill
BR4: W W'ck 2E 170
Cork Sq. E1 . . . . . 1H 103
Cork St. W1 . . . . . 3A 12 (7G 83)
Cork St. M. W1 . . . . . 3A 12
Cork Tree Ho. *SE27* *5B 138*
(off Lakeview Rd.)
Cork Tree Retail Pk. E4 . . . . . 5F 35
Cork Tree Way E4 . . . . . 5F 35
Corlett St. NW1 . . . . . 5C 4 (5C 82)
Cormont Rd. SE5 . . . . . 1B 120
Cormorant Cl. E17 . . . . . 7F 35
Cormorant Ct. *SE8* *6B 104*
(off Pilot Cl.)
Cormorant Ho. EN3: Pond E 5E 24
Cormorant Lodge *E1* *1G 103*
(off Thomas More St.)
Cormorant Pl. SM1: Sutt 5H 165
Cormorant Rd. E7 . . . . . 5H 69
Cornbury Ho. *SE8* *6B 104*
(off Evelyn St.)
Cornbury Rd. HA8: Edg 7J 27
Cornel Ho. DA15: Sidc 3A 144
Cornelia Dr. UB4: Yead 4A 76
Cornelia Ho. *TW1: Twick* *6D 114*
(off Denton Rd.)
Cornelia St. N7 . . . . . 6K 65
Cornell Bldg. *E1* *6G 85*
(off Coke St.)
Cornell Cl. DA14: Sidc 6E 144
Cornell Ho. HA2: Harr 3D 58
Corner, The W5 . . . . . 1E 96
Cornercroft *SM3: Cheam* *5F 165*
(off Wickham Av.)
Corner Fielde SW2 . . . . . 1K 137
Corner Grn. SE3 . . . . . 2J 123
Corner Ho. St. WC2 . . . . . 4E 12
Corner Mead NW9 . . . . . 7G 29
Cornerside TW15: Ashf 7E 128
Cornerstone Ho. CR0: Croy 7C 156
Corney Reach Way W4 . . . . . 7A 98
Corney Rd. W4 . . . . . 6A 98
Cornfield Cl. UB8: Uxb 2A 74
Cornflower La. CR0: Croy 1K 169
Cornflower Ter. SE22 . . . . . 6H 121
Cornford Cl. BR2: Brom 5J 159
Cornford Gro. SW12 . . . . . 2F 137
Cornhill EC3 . . . . . 1F 15 (6D 84)
Cornick Ho. *SE16* *3H 103*
(off Slippers Pl.)
Cornish Ct. N9 . . . . . 7C 24
Cornish Gro. SE20 . . . . . 1H 157
Cornish Ho. *SE17* *6B 102*
(off Brandon Est.)
TW8: Bford 5F 97
Corn Mill Dr. BR6: Orp 7K 161
Cornmill La. SE13 . . . . . 3E 122
Cornmow Dr. NW10 . . . . . 5B 62
Cornshaw Rd. RM8: Dag 1D 72
Cornthwaite Rd. E5 . . . . . 3J 67
Cornwall Av. DA16: Well 3J 125
E2 . . . . . 3J 85
KT10: Clay 7A 162
N3 . . . . . 7D 30
N22 . . . . . 1J 47
UB1: S'hall 5D 76
Cornwall Cl. IG11: Bark 6K 71
Cornwall Ct. HA5: H End 1D 40
W7 . . . . . *4K 77*
(off Copley Cl.)
Cornwall Cres. W11 . . . . . 6G 81
Cornwall Dr. BR5: St P 7C 144
Cornwall Gdns. NW10 . . . . . 6D 62
SE25 . . . . . 4F 157
SW7 . . . . . 3K 99
Cornwall Gdns. Wlk.
SW7 . . . . . 3K 99
Cornwall Gro. W4 . . . . . 5A 98
Cornwall Ho. *SW7* *3K 99*
(off Cornwall Gdns.)
Cornwallis Av. N9 . . . . . 2C 34
SE9 . . . . . 2H 143
Cornwallis Ct. *SW8* *1J 119*
(off Lansdowne Grn.)
Cornwallis Gro. N9 . . . . . 2C 34
Cornwallis Ho. *SE16* *2H 103*
(off Cherry Gdn. St.)
W12 . . . . . *7D 80*
(off India Way)
Cornwallis Rd. E17 . . . . . 4K 49
N9 . . . . . 2C 34
N19 . . . . . 2J 65
RM9: Dag 4D 72
SE18 . . . . . 3G 107
Cornwallis Sq. N19 . . . . . 2J 65
Cornwallis Wlk. SE9 . . . . . 3D 124
Cornwall Mans. *SW10* *7A 100*
(off Cremorne Rd.)
W8 . . . . . *2K 99*
(off Kensington Ct.)
W14 . . . . . *3F 99*
(off Blythe Rd.)
Cornwall M. Sth. SW7 . . . . . 3A 100
Cornwall M. W. SW7 . . . . . 3K 99
Cornwall Rd. CR0: Croy 2B 168
HA1: Harr 6G 41
HA4: Ruis 3H 57
HA5: H End 1D 40
N4 . . . . . 7A 48
N15 . . . . . 5D 48
N18 . . . . . 5B 34
SE1 . . . . . 4J 13 (1A 102)
SM2: Sutt 7H 165
TW1: Twick 7A 114
UB8: Uxb 6A 56
Cornwall Sq. SE11 . . . . . 5K 19
Cornwall St. E1 . . . . . 7H 85
Cornwall Ter. NW1 . . . . . 4F 5 (4D 82)
Cornwall Ter. M. NW1 . . . . . 4F 5
Corn Way E11 . . . . . 3F 69
Cornwell Cres. E7 . . . . . 4A 70
Cornwood Cl. N2 . . . . . 5B 46
Cornwood Dr. E1 . . . . . 6J 85
Cornworthy Rd. RM8: Dag 5C 72
Corona Bldg. *E14* *1E 104*
(off Blackwall Way)
Corona Rd. SE12 . . . . . 7J 123
Coronation Av. N16 . . . . . 4F 67
Coronation Cl. DA5: Bexl 6D 126
IG6: Ilf 4G 53
Coronation Ct. DA8: Erith 7K 109
E15 . . . . . 6H 69
W10 . . . . . *5E 80*
(off Brewster Gdns.)
Coronation Rd. E13 . . . . . 3A 88
NW10 . . . . . 4G 79
UB3: Harl 4H 93
Coronation Vs. NW10 . . . . . 4H 79
Coronation Wlk. TW2: Whit 1E 130
Coroners Ct. *NW1* *1H 83*
(off Camley St.)
Coronet Cinema *1J 99*
(off Notting Hill Ga.)
Coronet Pde. HA0: Wemb 6E 60
Coronet St. N1 . . . . . 2G 9 (3E 84)
Corporate Dr. TW13: Felt 3K 129
Corporate Ho. HA3: Hrw W 1H 41
Corporation Av. TW4: Houn 4C 112
Corporation Row EC1 . . . . . 3K 7 (4A 84)
Corporation St. E15 . . . . . 2G 87
N7 . . . . . 5J 65
Corrance Rd. SW2 . . . . . 4J 119
Corri Av. N14 . . . . . 4C 32
Corrib Ct. N13 . . . . . 3E 32
Corrib Dr. SM1: Sutt 5C 166
Corrigan Cl. NW4 . . . . . 3E 44
Corringham Ct. NW11 . . . . . 7J 45
Corringham Ho. *E1* *6K 85*
(off Pitsea St.)
Corringham Rd. HA9: Wemb 2G 61
NW11 . . . . . 7J 45
Corringway NW11 . . . . . 7K 45
W5 . . . . . 4G 79
Corris Grn. NW9 . . . . . 5A 44
Corry Dr. SW9 . . . . . 4B 120
Corry Ho. *E14* *7D 86*
(off Wade's Pl.)
Corsair Cl. TW19: Stanw 7A 110
Corsair Rd. TW19: Stanw 7A 110
Corscombe Cl. KT2: King T 5J 133
Corsehill St. SW16 . . . . . 6G 137
Corsham St. N1 . . . . . 2F 9 (3D 84)
Corsica St. N5 . . . . . 6B 66
Corsley Way *E9* *6B 68*
(off Osborne Rd.)
Cortayne Ct. TW2: Twick 2J 131
Cortayne Rd. SW6 . . . . . 2H 117
Cortis Rd. SW15 . . . . . 6D 116
Cortis Ter. SW15 . . . . . 6D 116
Corunna Rd. SW8 . . . . . 1G 119
Corunna Ter. SW8 . . . . . 1G 119
Corvette Sq. SE10 . . . . . 6F 105
Corwell Gdns. UB8: Hil 6E 74
Corwell La. UB8: Hil 6E 74
(not continuous)
Coryton Path *W9* *4H 81*
(off Ashmore Rd.)
Cosbycote Av. SE24 . . . . . 5C 120
Cosdach Av. SM6: Wall 7H 167
Cosedge Cres. CR0: Wadd 5A 168
Cosgrove Cl. N21 . . . . . 2H 33
UB4: Yead 4C 76
Cosgrove Ho. *E2* *1G 85*
(off Whiston Rd.)
Cosmo Pl. WC1 . . . . . 5F 7 (5J 83)
Cosmur Cl. W12 . . . . . 3B 98
Cossall Wlk. SE15 . . . . . 2H 121
Cossar M. SW2 . . . . . 5A 120
Cosser St. SE1 . . . . . 1J 19 (3A 102)
Costa St. SE15 . . . . . 2G 121
Costons Av. UB6: G'frd 3H 77
Costons La. UB6: G'frd 3H 77
(not continuous)
Coston Wlk. SE4 . . . . . 4K 121
Cosway Mans. *NW1* *5D 4*
(off Shroton St.)
Cosway St. NW1 . . . . . 5D 4 (5C 82)
Cotall St. E14 . . . . . 5C 86
Coteford Cl. HA5: Eastc 5J 39
Coteford St. SW17 . . . . . 4D 136
Cotelands CR0: Croy 3E 168
Cotesbach Rd. E5 . . . . . 3J 67
Cotes Ho. *NW8* *4C 4*
(off Broadley St.)
Cotesmore Gdns. RM8: Dag 4C 72
Cotford Rd. CR7: Thor H 4C 156
Cotham St. SE17 . . . . . 4C 102

Cotherstone Rd. SW2 . . . . . 1K **137**
Cotleigh Av. DA5: Bexl 2D **144**
Cotleigh Rd. NW6 . . . . . 7J **63**
RM7: Rom 6K **55**
Cotman Cl. NW11 . . . . . 6A **46**
SW15 . . . . . 6F **117**
Cotman Gdns. HA8: Edg 2G **43**
Cotman Ho. *NW8* *2C **82***
(off Townshend Est.)
UB5: N'olt *2B **76***
(off Academy Gdns.)
Cotman M. *RM8: Dag* *5C **72***
(off Highgrove Rd.)
Cotmans Cl. UB3: Hayes 1J **93**
Coton Rd. DA16: Well 3A **126**
Cotsford Av. KT3: N Mald 5J **151**
Cotswold Cl. DA7: Bex 2K **127**
KT2: King T 6J **133**
KT10: Hin W 2A **162**
N11 . . . . . 4K **31**
Cotswold Ct. EC1 . . . . . 3C **8**
UB6: G'frd *2K **77***
(off Hodder Dr.)
Cotswold Gdns. E6 . . . . . 3B **88**
IG2: Ilf 7H **53**
NW2 . . . . . 2F **63**
Cotswold Ga. NW2 . . . . . 1G **63**
Cotswold Grn. EN2: Enf 4E **22**
Cotswold M. SW11 . . . . . 1B **118**
Cotswold Ri. BR6: St M Cry 6K **161**
Cotswold Rd. TW12: Hamp 5E **130**
Cotswold St. SE27 . . . . . 4B **138**
Cotswold Way EN2: Enf 3E **22**
KT4: Wor Pk 2E **164**
Cottage Av. BR2: Brom 1C **172**
Cottage Cl. *E1* *4J **85***
(off Hayfield Pas.)
HA4: Ruis 1F **57**
Cottage Fld. Cl. DA14: Sidc 1C **144**
Cottage Grn. SE5 . . . . . 7D **102**
Cottage Gro. KT6: Surb 6D **150**
SW9 . . . . . 3J **119**
Cottage Pl. SW3 . . . . . 1C **16** (3C **100**)
Cottage Rd. KT19: Ewe 7K **163**
N7 . . . . . 5K **65**
Cottage St. E14 . . . . . 7D **86**
Cottage Wlk. N16 . . . . . 3F **67**
Cottenham Dr. NW9 . . . . . 3B **44**
SW20 . . . . . 7D **134**
Cottenham Pde. SW20 . . . . . 2D **152**
COTTENHAM PARK 1D **152**
Cottenham Pk. Rd. SW20 . . . . . 1C **152**
(not continuous)
Cottenham Pl. SW20 . . . . . 7D **134**
Cottenham Rd. E17 . . . . . 4B **50**
Cotterill Rd. KT6: Surb 2E **162**
Cottesbrook St. SE14 . . . . . 7A **104**
Cottesloe Ho. NW8 . . . . . 3C **4**
Cottesloe M. *SE1* *1K **19***
(off Emery St.)
Cottesloe Theatre *4J **13***
(in National Theatre)
Cottesmore Av. IG5: Ilf 2E **52**
Cottesmore Ct. *W8* *3K **99***
(off Stanford Rd.)
Cottesmore Gdns. W8 . . . . . 3K **99**
Cottimore Av. KT12: Walt T 7K **147**
Cottimore Cres. KT12: Walt T 7K **147**
Cottimore La. KT12: Walt T 7K **147**
(not continuous)
Cottimore Ter. KT12: Walt T 7K **147**
Cottingham Chase HA4: Ruis 3J **57**
Cottingham Rd. SE20 . . . . . 7K **139**
SW8 . . . . . 7K **101**
Cottington Rd. TW13: Hanw 4B **130**
Cottington St. SE11 . . . . . 5K **19** (5A **102**)
Cottle Way *SE16* *2H **103***
(off Paradise St.)
Cotton Av. W3 . . . . . 6K **79**
Cotton Cl. E11 . . . . . 2G **69**
RM9: Dag 7C **72**
Cottongrass Cl. CR0: Croy 1K **169**
Cotton Hill BR1: Brom 4E **140**
Cotton Ho. SW2 . . . . . 7J **119**
Cotton Row SW11 . . . . . 3A **118**
Cottons App. RM7: Rom 5K **55**
Cottons Cen. SE1 . . . . . 4G **15** (1E **102**)
Cottons Ct. RM7: Rom 5K **55**
Cotton's Gdns. E2 . . . . . 1H **9** (3E **84**)
Cottons La. SE1 . . . . . 4F **15** (1D **102**)
Cotton St. E14 . . . . . 7E **86**
Cottrell Ct. SE10 . . . . . 4H **105**
Cottrill Gdns. E8 . . . . . 6H **67**
Cotts Cl. W7 . . . . . 5K **77**
Couchmore Av. IG5: Ilf 2D **52**
Coulgate St. SE4 . . . . . 3A **122**
Coulson Cl. RM8: Dag 1C **72**
Coulson St. SW3 . . . . . 5E **16** (5D **100**)
Coulter Cl. UB4: Yead 4C **76**
Coulter Rd. W6 . . . . . 3D **98**
Coulthurst Ct. *SW16* *7J **137***
(off Heybridge Av.)
Councillor St. SE5 . . . . . 7C **102**
Counter Ct. *SE1* *5E **14***
(off Borough High St.)
Counters Ct. *W14* *3G **99***
(off Holland Rd.)
Counter St. SE1 . . . . . 5G **15** (1E **102**)
Countess Rd. NW5 . . . . . 5G **65**
Countisbury Av. EN1: Enf 7A **24**
Country Way TW13: Hanw 6K **129**
County Gdns. IG11: Bark 2J **89**
County Ga. EN5: New Bar 6E **20**
SE9 . . . . . 3G **143**
County Gro. SE5 . . . . . 1C **120**
County Hall Apartments SE1 . . . . . 6G **13**
County Hall (Former) 7G **13** (2K **101**)
County Pde. TW8: Bford 7D **96**
County Rd. CR7: Thor H 2B **156**
E6 . . . . . 5F **89**
County St. SE1 . . . . . 3C **102**
Coupland Pl. SE18 . . . . . 5G **107**
Courcy Rd. N8 . . . . . 3A **48**
Courier Rd. RM9: Dag 4J **91**
RM13: Dag 4J **91**
Courland Gro. SW8 . . . . . 1H **119**
Courland St. SW8 . . . . . 1H **119**
Course, The SE9 . . . . . 3E **142**
Court, The HA4: Ruis 4C **58**
Courtauld Cl. SE28 . . . . . 1A **108**
Courtauld Ho. *E2* *1G **85***
(off Goldsmiths Row)
Courtauld Institute Galleries 2G **13**
Courtauld Rd. N19 . . . . . 1J **65**
Court Av. DA17: Belv 5F **109**
Court Cl. HA3: Kent 3E **42**
NW8 . . . . . *7B **64***
(off Boydell Ct., not continuous)
SM6: Wall 7H **167**
TW2: Twick 3F **131**
Court Cl. Av. TW2: Twick 3F **131**
Court Cres. KT9: Chess 5D **162**
Court Downs Rd. BR3: Beck 2D **158**
Court Dr. CR0: Wadd 4K **167**
HA7: Stan 4K **27**
SM1: Sutt 4C **166**
UB10: Hil 1B **74**
Courtenay Av. HA3: Hrw W 7B **26**
N6 . . . . . 7C **46**
SM2: Sutt 7J **165**
Courtenay Dr. BR3: Beck 2F **159**
Courtenay Gdns. HA3: Hrw W 2G **41**
Courtenay M. E17 . . . . . 5A **50**
Courtenay Pl. E17 . . . . . 5A **50**
Courtenay Rd. E11 . . . . . 3H **69**
E17 . . . . . 4K **49**
HA9: Wemb 3D **60**
KT4: Wor Pk 3E **164**
SE20 . . . . . 6K **139**
Courtenay Sq. SE11 . . . . . 6J **19** (5A **102**)
Courtenay St. SE11 . . . . . 5J **19** (5A **102**)
Courtens M. HA7: Stan 7H **27**
Court Farm Av. KT19: Ewe 5K **163**
Court Farm Ind. Est.
TW19: Stanw 6B **110**
Court Farm La. UB5: N'olt 7E **58**
Court Farm Rd. SE9 . . . . . 2B **142**
UB5: N'olt 7E **58**
Courtfield W5 . . . . . 5C **78**
Courtfield Av. HA1: Harr 5K **41**
Courtfield Cres. HA1: Harr 5K **41**
Courtfield Gdns. HA4: Ruis 2H **57**
SW5 . . . . . 4K **99**
W13 . . . . . 6A **78**
Courtfield Ho. *EC1* *5J **7***
(off Baldwins Gdns.)
Courtfield M. SW5 . . . . . 4A **100**
Courtfield Ri. BR4: W W'ck 3F **171**
Courtfield Rd. SW7 . . . . . 4A **100**
TW15: Ashf 6D **128**
Court Gdns. N7 . . . . . 6A **66**
(not continuous)
Courtgate Cl. NW7 . . . . . 6G **29**
Courthill Rd. SE13 . . . . . 4E **122**
Courthope Ho. *SE16* *3J **103***
(off Lower Rd.)
SW8 . . . . . *7J **101***
(off Hartington Rd.)
Courthope Rd. NW3 . . . . . 4D **64**
SW19 . . . . . 5G **135**
UB6: G'frd 2H **77**
Courthope Vs. SW19 . . . . . 7G **135**
Court Ho. Gdns. N3 . . . . . 6D **30**
Courthouse La. E8 . . . . . 4F **67**
Courthouse Rd. N12 . . . . . 6E **30**
Courtland Av. E4 . . . . . 2C **36**
IG1: Ilf 2D **70**
NW7 . . . . . 3E **28**
SW16 . . . . . 7K **137**
Courtland Cl. IG8: Wfd G 1A **52**
Courtland Gro. SE28 . . . . . 6D **90**
Courtland Rd. E6 . . . . . 1C **88**
Courtlands KT12: Walt T 7J **147**
TW10: Rich 5G **115**
Courtlands Av. BR2: Hayes 1G **171**
SE12 . . . . . 5K **123**
TW9: Kew 2H **115**
TW12: Hamp 6D **130**
Courtlands Cl. HA4: Ruis 7H **39**
Courtlands Dr. KT19: Ewe 6A **164**
Courtlands Rd. KT5: Surb 7G **151**
Court La. SE21 . . . . . 6E **120**
Court La. Gdns. SE21 . . . . . 7E **120**
Courtleet Dr. DA8: Erith 1H **127**
Courtleigh NW11 . . . . . 5H **45**
Courtleigh Gdns. NW11 . . . . . 4G **45**
Court Lodge DA17: Belv 5G **109**
SW1 . . . . . *4G **17***
(off Sloane Sq.)
Courtman Rd. N17 . . . . . 7H **33**
Court Mead UB5: N'olt 3D **76**
Courtmead Cl. SE24 . . . . . 6C **120**
Courtnell St. W2 . . . . . 6J **81**
Courtney Cl. SE19 . . . . . 6E **138**
Courtney Ct. N7 . . . . . 5A **66**
Courtney Cres. SM5: Cars 7D **166**
Courtney Ho. *NW4* *3E **44***
(off Mulberry Cl.)
W14 . . . . . *3G **99***
(off Russell Rd.)
Courtney Pl. CR0: Wadd 3A **168**
Courtney Rd. CR0: Wadd 3A **168**
N7 . . . . . 5A **66**
SW19 . . . . . 7C **136**
TW6: H'row A 3C **110**
Courtney Way
TW6: H'row A 2C **110**
Court Pde. HA0: Wemb 3B **60**
(not continuous)
Courtrai Rd. SE23 . . . . . 6A **122**
Court Rd. SE9 . . . . . 6D **124**
SE25 . . . . . 2F **157**
UB2: S'hall 4D **94**
UB10: Ick 5D **56**
Court Royal SW15 . . . . . 5G **117**
Courtside N8 . . . . . 6H **47**
SE26 . . . . . 3H **139**
Court St. BR1: Brom 2J **159**
E1 . . . . . 5H **85**
Courtville Ho. *W10* *3G **81***
(off Third Av.)
Court Way IG6: Ilf 3G **53**
IG8: Wfd G 5F **37**
NW9 . . . . . 4A **44**
TW2: Twick 7K **113**
W3 . . . . . 5J **79**
Court Wood La. CR0: Sels 7B **170**
Court Yd. SE9 . . . . . 6D **124**
Courtyard, The BR2: Kes 6C **172**
E3 . . . . . 2C **86**
EC3 . . . . . *1F **15***
(in Royal Exchange)
N1 . . . . . 7K **65**
NW1 . . . . . 7E **64**
SW3 . . . . . *7B **16***
(off Waldron M.)
Courtyard M. BR5: St P 7A **144**
Courtyard Theatre, The
King's Cross *1F **7***
(off York Way)
Cousin La. EC4 . . . . . 3E **14** (7D **84**)
Cousins Cl. UB7: Yiew 7A **74**
Couthurst Rd. SE3 . . . . . 6K **105**
Coutts Av. KT9: Chess 5E **162**
Coutt's Cres. NW5 . . . . . 3E **64**
Couzens Ho. *E3* *5B **86***
(off Weatherley Cl.)
Coval Gdns. SW14 . . . . . 4H **115**
Coval La. SW14 . . . . . 4H **115**
Coval Pas. SW14 . . . . . 4J **115**
Coval Rd. SW14 . . . . . 4H **115**
Covelees Wall E6 . . . . . 6E **88**
Covell Ct. *EN2: Enf* *1E **22***
(off The Ridgeway)
SE8 . . . . . 7C **104**
COVENT GARDEN 2F **13** (7J **83**)
Covent Garden 2F **13** (7J **83**)
Covent Gdn. WC2 . . . . . 2F **13** (7J **83**)
Coventry Cl. E6 . . . . . 6D **88**
NW6 . . . . . 2J **81**
Coventry Cross E3 . . . . . 4E **86**
Coventry Hall SW16 . . . . . 5J **137**
Coventry Rd. E1 . . . . . 4H **85**
E2 . . . . . 4H **85**
IG1: Ilf 2F **71**
SE25 . . . . . 4G **157**
Coventry St. W1 . . . . . 3C **12** (7H **83**)
Coverack Cl. CR0: Croy 7A **158**
N14 . . . . . 6B **22**
Coverdale Cl. HA7: Stan 5G **27**
Coverdale Gdns. CR0: Croy 3F **169**
Coverdale Rd. N11 . . . . . 6K **31**
NW2 . . . . . 7F **63**
W12 . . . . . 2D **98**
Coverdales, The IG11: Bark 2H **89**
Coverley Cl. E1 . . . . . 5G **85**
Coverley Point SE11 . . . . . 4G **19**
Covert, The BR6: Pet W 6J **161**
HA6: Nwood 1E **38**
SE19 . . . . . *7F **139***
(off Fox Hill)
Coverton Rd. SW17 . . . . . 5C **136**
Covert Way EN4: Had W 2F **21**
Covet Wood Cl. BR5: St M Cry 6K **161**
Covey Cl. SW19 . . . . . 2K **153**
Covington Gdns. SW16 . . . . . 7B **138**
Covington Way SW16 . . . . . 6K **137**
(not continuous)
Cowan Cl. E6 . . . . . 5C **88**
Cowan Ct. NW10 . . . . . 7K **61**
Cowbridge La. IG11: Bark 7F **71**
Cowbridge Rd. HA3: Kent 4F **43**
Cowcross St. EC1 . . . . . 5A **8** (5B **84**)
Cowdenbeath Path N1 . . . . . 1K **83**
Cowden Rd. BR6: Orp 7K **161**
Cowden St. SE6 . . . . . 4C **140**
Cowdray Rd. UB10: Hil 1E **74**
Cowdrey Cl. EN1: Enf 2K **23**
Cowdrey Rd. SW19 . . . . . 5K **135**
Cowen Av. HA2: Harr 2H **59**
Cowgate Rd. UB6: G'frd 3H **77**
Cowick Rd. SW17 . . . . . 4D **136**

Cowings Mead UB5: N'olt 6C 58
Cowland Av. EN3: Pond E 4D 24
Cow La. UB6: G'frd 2H 77
Cow Leaze E6 6E 88
Cowleaze Rd. KT2: King T 1E 150
COWLEY 4A 74
Cowley La. E11 3G 69
COWLEY PEACHEY 6A 74
Cowley Pl. NW4 5E 44
Cowley Rd. E11 5K 51
IG1: Ilf 7D 52
SW9 1A 120
(not continuous)
SW14 3A 116
W3 1B 98
Cowley St. SW1 1E 18 (3J 101)
Cowling Cl. W11 1G 99
Cowper Av. E6 7C 70
SM1: Sutt 4B 166
Cowper Cl. BR2: Brom 4B 160
DA16: Well 5A 126
Cowper Gdns. N14 6A 22
SM6: Wall 6G 167
Cowper Ho. SE17 5C 102
(off Browning St.)
SW1 6C 18
(off Aylesford St.)
Cowper Rd. BR2: Brom 4B 160
DA17: Belv 4G 109
KT2: King T 5F 133
N14 1A 32
N16 5E 66
N18 5B 34
SW19 6A 136
W3 1K 97
W7 7K 77
Cowper's Ct. EC3 1F 15
(off Birchin La.)
Cowper St. EC2 3F 9 (4D 84)
Cowper Ter. W10 5F 81
Cowslip Cl. UB10: Uxb 7A 56
Cowslip Rd. E18 2K 51
Cowthorpe Rd. SW8 1H 119
Cox Ct. EN4: E Barn 4H 21
Coxe Pl. HA3: W'stone 4A 42
Cox Ho. W6 6G 99
(off Field Rd.)
Cox La. KT9: Chess 4F 163
KT19: Ewe 5H 163
(not continuous)
Coxmount Rd. SE7 5B 106
Coxs Av. TW17: Shep 3G 147
Cox's Ct. E1 6J 9
Coxson Way SE1 7J 15 (2F 103)
Cox's Wlk. SE21 1G 139
Coxwell Rd. SE18 5H 107
SE19 7E 138
Coxwold Path KT9: Chess 7E 162
Crabbs Cft. Cl. BR6: Farnb 5G 173
Crab Hill BR3: Beck 7F 141
Crabtree Av. HA0: Wemb 2E 78
RM6: Chad H 4D 54
Crabtree Cl. E2 2F 85
Crabtree Ct. E15 5D 68
EN5: New Bar 4E 20
Crabtree La. SW6 7E 98
(not continuous)
Crabtree Manorway Nth.
DA17: Belv, Erith 2J 109
Crabtree Manorway Sth.
DA17: Belv 3J 109
Crabtree Wlk. CR0: Croy 1G 169
SE15 1F 121
(off Peckham Rd.)
Crace St. NW1 1C 6 (3H 83)
Craddock Rd. EN1: Enf 3A 24
Craddock St. NW5 6E 64
Cradley Rd. SE9 1H 143
Crafts Council & Gallery 2A 84
Cragie Ho. SE1 4F 103
(off Balaclava Rd.)
Craig Dr. UB8: Hil 6D 74
Craigen Av. CR0: Croy 1H 169
Craigerne Rd. SE3 7K 105
Craig Gdns. E18 2H 51
Craigholm SE18 2E 124
Craigmore Ct. HA6: Nwood 1G 39
Craigmuir Pk. HA0: Wemb 1F 79
Craignair Rd. SW2 7A 120
Craignish Av. SW16 2K 155
Craig Pk. Rd. N18 4C 34
Craig Rd. TW10: Ham 4C 132
Craig's Ct. SW1 4E 12 (1J 101)
Craigton Rd. SE9 4D 124
Craigweil Cl. HA7: Stan 5J 27
Craigweil Dr. HA7: Stan 5J 27
Craigwell Av. TW13: Felt 3J 129
Craik Ct. NW6 2H 81
(off Carlton Va.)
Crail Row SE17 4D 102
Crales Ho. SE18 3C 106
Cramer St. W1 6H 5 (5E 82)
Crammond Cl. W6 6G 99
Cramond Ct. TW14: Bedf 1G 129
Cramonde Ct. DA16: Well 2A 126
Crampton Ho. SW8 1G 119
Crampton Rd. SE20 6J 139
Crampton St. SE17 4C 102
Cranberry Cl. UB5: N'olt 2B 76
Cranberry La. E16 4G 87
Cranborne Av. KT6: Surb 3G 163
UB2: S'hall 4E 94
Cranborne Rd. IG11: Bark 1H 89
Cranborne Waye UB4: Yead 6K 75
(not continuous)
Cranbourn All. WC2 2D 12
(off Cranbourn St.)
Cranbourne NW1 7H 65
(off Agar Gro.)
Cranbourne Av. E11 4K 51
Cranbourne Cl. SW16 3J 155
Cranbourne Dr. HA5: Pinn 5B 40
Cranbourne Gdns. IG6: Ilf 3G 53
NW11 5G 45
Cranbourne Pas. SE16 2H 103
Cranbourne Rd. E12 5C 70
E15 4E 68
HA6: Nwood 3H 39
N10 2F 47
Cranbourn Ho. SE16 2H 103
(off Marigold St.)
Cranbourn St. WC2 2D 12 (7H 83)
CRANBROOK 1D 70
Cranbrook NW1 1G 83
(off Camden St.)
Cranbrook Cl. BR2: Hayes 6J 159
Cranbrook Ct. TW8: Bford 6C 96
Cranbrook Dr. KT10: Esh 7G 149
TW2: Whit 1F 131
Cranbrook Est. E2 2K 85
Cranbrook La. N11 4A 32
Cranbrook M. E17 5B 50
Cranbrook Pk. N22 1A 48
Cranbrook Ri. IG1: Ilf 6D 52
Cranbrook Rd. CR7: Thor H 2C 156
DA7: Bex 1F 127
EN4: E Barn 6G 21
IG1: Ilf 7E 52
IG2: Ilf 5E 52
IG6: Ilf 5E 52
SE8 1C 122
SW19 7G 135
TW4: Houn 4D 112
W4 5A 98
Cranbrook St. E2 2K 85
Cranbury Rd. SW6 2K 117
Crandley Ct. SE8 4A 104
Crane Av. TW7: Isle 5A 114
W3 7J 79
Cranebank M. TW1: Twick 4A 114
Cranebrook TW2: Twick 2G 131
Crane Cl. HA2: Harr 3G 59
RM10: Dag 6G 73
Crane Ct. EC4 6A 84
KT19: Ewe 4J 163
Craneford Cl. TW2: Twick 7K 113
Craneford Way TW2: Twick 7J 113
Crane Gdns. UB3: Harl 4H 93
Crane Gro. N7 6A 66
Crane Ho. E3 2A 86
(off Roman Rd.)
SE15 1F 121
TW13: Hanw 3E 130
Crane Lodge Rd. TW5: Cran 6K 93
Crane Mead SE16 4K 103
(not continuous)
Crane Mead Ct. TW1: Twick 7K 113
Crane Pk. Island Nature Reserve 2D 130
Crane Pk. Rd. TW2: Whit 2F 131
Crane Rd. TW2: Twick 1J 131
TW19: Stanw 6C 110
Cranesbill Cl. NW9 3K 43
Cranes Dr. KT5: Surb 4E 150
Cranes Pk. KT5: Surb 4E 150
Cranes Pk. Av. KT5: Surb 4E 150
Cranes Pk. Cres. KT5: Surb 4F 151
Crane St. SE10 5F 105
SE15 1F 121
Craneswater UB3: Harl 7H 93
Craneswater Pk. UB2: S'hall 5D 94
Crane Way TW2: Whit 7G 113
Cranfield Cl. SE27 3C 138
Cranfield Ct. W1 6D 4
Cranfield Dr. NW9 7F 29
Cranfield Ho. WC1 5E 6
Cranfield Rd. SE4 3B 122
Cranfield Rd. E. SM5: Cars 7E 166
Cranfield Rd. W. SM5: Cars 7D 166
Cranfield Row SE1 1K 19
CRANFORD 1J 111
Cranford Av. N13 5D 32
TW19: Stanw 7A 110
Cranford Cl. SW20 7D 134
TW19: Stanw 7A 110
Cranford Community College Sports Cen. 6K 93
Cranford Cotts. E1 7K 85
(off Cranford St.)
Cranford Dr. UB3: Harl 4H 93
Cranford La. TW5: Cran, Hest 7K 93
TW6: H'row A 1H 111
(Bath Rd.)
TW6: H'row A 3H 111
(Elmdon Rd.)
UB3: Cran, Harl 6F 93
Cranford Pk. Rd. UB3: Harl 4H 93
Cranford St. E1 7K 85
Cranford Way N8 4K 47
Cranhurst Rd. NW2 5E 62
Cranleigh W11 1H 99
(off Ladbroke Rd.)
Cranleigh Cl. BR6: Chels 3K 173
DA5: Bex 6H 127
SE20 2H 157
Cranleigh Ct. CR4: Mitc 3B 154
TW9: Rich 3G 115
UB1: S'hall 6D 76
Cranleigh Gdns. HA3: Kent 5E 42
IG11: Bark 7H 71
KT2: King T 6F 133
N21 5F 23
SE25 3E 156
SM1: Sutt 2K 165
UB1: S'hall 6D 76
Cranleigh Gdns. Ind. Est.
UB1: S'hall 5D 76
Cranleigh Ho's. NW1 2G 83
(off Cranleigh St.)
Cranleigh M. SW11 2C 118
Cranleigh Rd. N15 5C 48
SW19 3J 153
TW13: Felt 4H 129
Cranleigh St. NW1 2G 83
Cranley Dene Ct. N10 4F 47
Cranley Dr. HA4: Ruis 2H 57
IG2: Ilf 7G 53
CRANLEY GARDENS 4F 47
Cranley Gdns. N10 4F 47
N13 3E 32
Cranley Gdns. SM6: Wall 7G 167
SW7 5A 16 (5A 100)
Cranley M. SW7 5A 16 (5A 100)
Cranley Pde. SE9 4C 142
(off Beaconsfield Rd.)
Cranley Pl. SW7 4A 16 (4B 100)
Cranley Rd. E13 5K 87
IG2: Ilf 6G 53
Cranmer Av. W13 3B 96
Cranmer Cl. HA4: Ruis 1B 58
HA7: Stan 7H 27
SM4: Mord 6F 153
Cranmer Ct. N3 2G 45
SW3 4D 16 (4C 100)
SW4 3H 119
TW12: Ham H 5F 131
Cranmere Ct. EN2: Enf 2F 23
SE5 1C 120
Cranmer Farm Cl. CR4: Mitc 4D 154
Cranmer Gdns. RM10: Dag 4J 73
Cranmer Ho. SW9 7A 102
(off Brixton Rd.)
SW11 1C 118
(off Surrey La. Est.)
Cranmer Rd. CR0: Croy 3B 168
CR4: Mitc 4D 154
E7 4K 69
HA8: Edg 3C 28
KT2: King T 5E 132
SW9 7A 102
TW12: Ham H 5F 131
UB3: Hayes 6F 75
Cranmer Ter. SW17 5B 136
Cranmore Av. TW7: Isle 7G 95
Cranmore Rd. BR1: Brom 3H 141
BR7: Chst 5D 142
Cranmore Way N10 4G 47
Cranston Cl. TW3: Houn 2C 112
UB10: Ick 2F 57
Cranston Est. N1 2D 84
Cranston Gdns. E4 6J 35
Cranston Rd. SE23 1A 140
Cranswick Rd. SE16 5H 103
Crantock Rd. SE6 2D 140
Cranwell Cl. E3 4D 86
Cranwell Gro. TW17: Shep 4B 146
Cranwell Rd. TW6: H'row A 2D 110
Cranwich Av. N21 7J 23
Cranwich Rd. N16 7D 48
Cranwood Ct. EC1 2F 9
Cranwood St. EC1 2F 9 (3D 84)
Cranworth Cres. E4 1A 36
Cranworth Gdns. SW9 1A 120
Craster Rd. SW2 7K 119
Crathie Rd. SE12 6K 123
Cravan Av. TW13: Felt 2J 129
Craven Av. UB1: S'hall 5D 76
W5 7C 78
Craven Cl. N16 7G 49
UB4: Hayes 6J 75
Craven Cottage 2F 117
Craven Ct. NW10 1A 80
RM6: Chad H 6E 54
Craven Gdns. IG6: Ilf 2H 53
IG11: Bark 2J 89
SW19 5J 135
Craven Hill W2 7A 82
Craven Hill Gdns. W2 7A 82
(not continuous)
Craven Hill M. W2 7A 82
Craven Ho. N2 2B 46
(off High Rd. E. Finchley)
Craven Lodge W2 7A 82
(off Craven Hill)
Craven M. SW11 3E 118
Craven Pk. NW10 1K 79
Craven Pk. M. NW10 7A 62
Craven Pk. Rd. N15 6F 49
NW10 1A 80
Craven Pas. WC2 4E 12
(off Craven St.)
Craven Rd. CR0: Croy 1H 169
KT2: King T 1F 151

Craven Rd. NW10 . . . 1K 79
W2 . . . 1A 10 (7A 82)
W5 . . . 7C 78
Craven St. WC2 . . . 4E 12 (1J 101)
Craven Ter. W2 . . . 2A 10 (7A 82)
Craven Wlk. N16 . . . 7G 49
Crawford Av. HA0: Wemb . . . 5D 60
Crawford Bldgs. W1 . . . 6D 4
(off Homer St.)
Crawford Cl. TW7: Isle . . . 2J 113
Crawford Est. SE5 . . . 2C 120
Crawford Gdns. N13 . . . 3G 33
UB5: N'olt . . . 3D 76
Crawford Mans. W1 . . . 6D 4
(off Crawford St.)
Crawford M. W1 . . . 6E 4 (5D 82)
Crawford Pas. EC1 . . . 4K 7 (4A 84)
Crawford Pl. W1 . . . 7D 4 (6C 82)
Crawford Point E16 . . . 6H 87
(off Wouldham Rd.)
Crawford Rd. SE5 . . . 1C 120
Crawford St. NW10 . . . 7K 61
W1 . . . 6E 4 (5C 82)
Crawley Rd. E10 . . . 1D 68
EN1: Enf . . . 7K 23
N22 . . . 2C 48
Crawshay Ct. SW9 . . . 1A 120
Crawthew Gro. SE22 . . . 4F 121
Craybrooke Rd. DA14: Sidc . . . 4B 144
Craybury End SE9 . . . 2G 143
Crayfields Bus. Pk. BR5: St P . . . 7C 144
CRAYFORD . . . 5K 127
Crayford Cl. E6 . . . 6C 88
Crayford Ho. SE1 . . . 7F 15
(off Long La.)
Crayford Rd. N7 . . . 4H 65
Cray Ho. NW8 . . . 5B 4
(off Penfold St.)
Crayke Hill KT9: Chess . . . 7E 162
Crayle Ho. EC1 . . . 3B 8
(off Malta St.)
Crayleigh Ter. DA14: Sidc . . . 6C 144
Crayonne Cl. TW16: Sun . . . 1G 147
Cray Rd. DA14: Sidc . . . 6C 144
DA17: Belv . . . 6G 109
Cray Valley Rd. BR5: St M Cry . . . 5K 161
Crealock Gro. IG8: Wfd G . . . 5C 36
Crealock St. SW18 . . . 6K 117
Creasy Est. SE1 . . . 3E 102
Crebor St. SE22 . . . 6G 121
Credenhall Dr. BR2: Brom . . . 1D 172
Credenhill Ho. SE15 . . . 7H 103
Credenhill St. SW16 . . . 6G 137
Crediton Hill NW6 . . . 5K 63
Crediton Rd. E16 . . . 6J 87
NW10 . . . 1F 81
Crediton Way KT10: Clay . . . 5A 162
Credon Rd. E13 . . . 2A 88
SE16 . . . 5H 103
Creechurch La. EC3 . . . 1H 15 (6E 84)
(not continuous)
Creechurch Pl. EC3 . . . 1H 15
Creed Ct. E1 . . . 3A 86
EC4 . . . 1B 14
Creed La. EC4 . . . 1B 14 (6B 84)
Creek, The TW16: Sun . . . 5J 147
Creek Cotts. KT8: E Mos . . . 4J 149
(off Creek Rd.)
Creek Ho. W14 . . . 3G 99
(off Russell Rd.)
CREEKMOUTH . . . 4K 89
Creekmouth Ind. Pk.
IG11: Bark . . . 4K 89
Creek Rd. IG11: Bark . . . 3K 89
KT8: E Mos . . . 4J 149
SE8 . . . 6C 104
SE10 . . . 6C 104
Creekside SE8 . . . 7D 104
Creekside Foyer SE8 . . . 6D 104
(off Stowage)
Creek Way RM13: Rain . . . 5K 91
Creeland Gro. SE6 . . . 1B 140
Crefeld Cl. W6 . . . 6G 99
Creffield Rd. W3 . . . 7F 79
W5 . . . 7F 79
Creighton Av. E6 . . . 2B 88
N2 . . . 3C 46
N10 . . . 3C 46
Creighton Cl. W12 . . . 7C 80
Creighton Rd. N17 . . . 7K 33
NW6 . . . 2F 81
W5 . . . 3D 96
Cremer Bus. Cen. E2 . . . 1J 9
(off Cremer St.)
Cremer Ho. SE8 . . . 7C 104
(off Deptford Chu. St.)
Cremer St. E2 . . . 1J 9 (2F 85)
Cremorne Est. SW10 . . . 6B 100
(not continuous)
Cremorne Rd. SW10 . . . 7A 100
Creon Ct. SW9 . . . 7A 102
(off Caldwell St.)
Crescent EC3 . . . 2J 15 (7F 85)
Crescent, The BR3: Beck . . . 1C 158
BR4: W W'ck . . . 6G 159
CR0: Croy . . . 5D 156
DA5: Bexl . . . 7C 126
DA14: Sidc . . . 4K 143
E17 . . . 6A 50
EN5: New Bar . . . 2E 20
HA0: Wemb . . . 2B 60
HA2: Harr . . . 1G 59
IG2: Ilf . . . 6E 52
KT3: N Mald . . . 3J 151
KT6: Surb . . . 5E 150
KT8: W Mole . . . 4F 148
N9 . . . 2C 34
N11 . . . 4J 31
NW2 . . . 3D 62
SM1: Sutt . . . 5B 166
SW13 . . . 2B 116
SW19 . . . 3J 135
TW15: Ashf . . . 5B 128
TW17: Shep . . . 7H 147
UB1: S'hall . . . 2D 94
UB3: Harl . . . 7E 92
W3 . . . 6A 80
Crescent Arc. SE10 . . . 6E 104
(off Creek Rd.)
Crescent Ct. KT6: Surb . . . 5D 150
SW4 . . . 5H 119
(off Park Hill)
Crescent Ct. Bus. Cen. E16 . . . 4F 87
Crescent Dr. BR5: Pet W . . . 5F 161
Crescent E. EN4: Had W . . . 1F 21
Crescent Gdns. HA4: Ruis . . . 7K 39
SW19 . . . 3J 135
Crescent Gro. CR4: Mitc . . . 4C 154
SW4 . . . 4G 119
Crescent Ho. EC1 . . . 4C 8
(off Golden La. Est.)
SE13 . . . 2D 122
Crescent La. SW4 . . . 4G 119
Crescent Mans. W11 . . . 7G 81
(off Elgin Cres.)
Crescent M. N22 . . . 1J 47
Crescent Pde. UB10: Hil . . . 3C 74
Crescent Pl. SW3 . . . 3D 16 (4C 100)
Crescent Ri. EN4: E Barn . . . 5H 21
N3 . . . 1H 45
N22 . . . 1H 47
Crescent Rd. BR1: Brom . . . 7J 141
BR3: Beck . . . 2D 158
DA15: Sidc . . . 3K 143
E4 . . . 1B 36
E6 . . . 1A 88
E10 . . . 2D 68
E13 . . . 1J 87
E18 . . . 1A 52
EN2: Enf . . . 4G 23
EN4: E Barn . . . 4G 21
KT2: King T . . . 7G 133
N3 . . . 1H 45
N8 . . . 6H 47
N9 . . . 1B 34
N11 . . . 4J 31
Crescent Rd. N15 . . . 3B 48
N22 . . . 1H 47
RM10: Dag . . . 3H 73
SE18 . . . 5F 107
SW20 . . . 1F 153
TW17: Shep . . . 5E 146
Crescent Row EC1 . . . 4C 8 (4C 84)
Crescent Stables SW15 . . . 5G 117
Crescent St. N1 . . . 7K 65
Crescent Way BR6: Orp . . . 5J 173
N12 . . . 6H 31
SE4 . . . 3C 122
SW16 . . . 6K 137
Crescent W. EN4: Had W . . . 1F 21
Crescent Wharf E16 . . . 2K 105
Crescent Wood Rd. SE26 . . . 3G 139
Cresford Rd. SW6 . . . 1K 117
Crespigny Rd. NW4 . . . 6D 44
Cressage Cl. UB1: S'hall . . . 4E 76
Cressage Ho. TW8: Bford . . . 6E 96
(off Ealing Rd.)
Cressal Ho. E14 . . . 3C 104
(off Tiller Rd.)
Cresset Ho. E9 . . . 6J 67
Cresset Rd. E9 . . . 6J 67
Cresset St. SW4 . . . 3H 119
Cressfield Cl. NW5 . . . 5E 64
Cressida Rd. N19 . . . 1G 65
Cressingham Gro. SM1: Sutt . . . 4A 166
Cressingham Rd. HA8: Edg . . . 6E 28
SE13 . . . 3E 122
Cressington Cl. N16 . . . 5E 66
Cress M. BR1: Brom . . . 5F 141
Cresswell NW9 . . . 2B 44
Cresswell Gdns. SW5 . . . 5A 100
Cresswell Ho. HA9: Wemb . . . 3E 60
TW19: Stanw . . . 6A 110
(off Douglas Rd.)
Cresswell Pk. SE3 . . . 3H 123
Cresswell Pl. SW10 . . . 5A 100
Cresswell Rd. SE25 . . . 4G 157
TW1: Twick . . . 6D 114
TW13: Hanw . . . 3C 130
Cresswell Way N21 . . . 7F 23
Cressy Ct. E1 . . . 5J 85
W6 . . . 3D 98
Cressy Ho's. E1 . . . 5J 85
(off Hannibal Rd.)
Cressy Pl. E1 . . . 5J 85
Cressy Rd. NW3 . . . 5D 64
Crest, The KT5: Surb . . . 5G 151
N13 . . . 4F 33
NW4 . . . 5E 44
Cresta Ct. W5 . . . 4F 79
Cresta Ho. NW3 . . . 7B 64
(off Finchley Rd.)
Crestbrook Av. N13 . . . 3G 33
Crestbrook Pl. N13 . . . 3G 33
(off Green Lanes)
Crest Ct. NW4 . . . 5E 44
Crest Dr. EN3: Enf W . . . 1D 24
Crestfield St. WC1 . . . 1F 7 (3J 83)
Crest Gdns. HA4: Ruis . . . 3A 58
Creston Way KT4: Wor Pk . . . 1F 165
Crest Rd. BR2: Hayes . . . 7H 159
CR2: Sels . . . 7H 169
NW2 . . . 2B 62
Crest Vw. HA5: Pinn . . . 4B 40
Crest Vw. Dr. BR5: Pet W . . . 5F 161
Crestway SW15 . . . 6C 116
Crestwood Way
TW4: Houn . . . 5C 112
Creswell Dr. BR3: Beck . . . 5D 158
Creswick Ct. W3 . . . 7H 79
Creswick Rd. W3 . . . 7H 79
Creswick Wlk. E3 . . . 3C 86
NW11 . . . 4H 45
Creton St. SE18 . . . 3E 106
Crewdson Rd. SW9 . . . 7A 102
Crewe Pl. NW10 . . . 3B 80
Crewkerne Ct. SW11 . . . 1B 118
(off Bolingbroke Wlk.)
Crews St. E14 . . . 4C 104
Crewys Rd. NW2 . . . 2H 63
SE15 . . . 2H 121
Crichton Av. SM6: Bedd . . . 5H 167
Crichton Ho. DA14: Sidc . . . 6D 144
Crichton Rd. SM5: Cars . . . 6D 166
Crichton St. SW8 . . . 2G 119
Cricketers Arms Rd. EN2: Enf . . . 2H 23
Cricketers Cl. DA8: Erith . . . 5K 109
KT9: Chess . . . 4D 162
N14 . . . 7B 22
Cricketers Ct. SE11 . . . 4B 102
(off Kennington La.)
Cricketers M. SW18 . . . 5K 117
Cricketers Ter. SM5: Cars . . . 3C 166
Cricketers Wlk. SE26 . . . 5J 139
Cricketfield Rd. E5 . . . 4H 67
Cricket Grn. CR4: Mitc . . . 3D 154
Cricket Ground Rd. BR7: Chst . . . 1F 161
Cricket La. BR3: Beck . . . 6A 140
Cricklade Av. SW2 . . . 2J 137
CRICKLEWOOD . . . 3G 63
Cricklewood B'way. NW2 . . . 3E 62
Cricklewood La. NW2 . . . 4F 63
Cridland St. E15 . . . 1H 87
Crieff Ct. TW11: Tedd . . . 7C 132
Crieff Rd. SW18 . . . 6A 118
Criffel Av. SW2 . . . 2H 137
Crimscott St. SE1 . . . 3E 102
Crimsworth Rd. SW8 . . . 1H 119
Crinan St. N1 . . . 2J 83
Cringle St. SW8 . . . 7G 101
Cripplegate St. EC2 . . . 5D 8 (5C 84)
Cripps Grn. UB4: Yead . . . 4K 75
Crispe Ho. IG11: Bark . . . 2H 89
N1 . . . 1K 83
(off Barnsbury Est.)
Crispen Rd. TW13: Hanw . . . 4C 130
Crispian Cl. NW10 . . . 4A 62
Crispin Cl. CR0: Bedd . . . 2J 167
Crispin Cres. CR0: Bedd . . . 3H 167
Crispin Lodge N11 . . . 5J 31
Crispin Pl. E1 . . . 5F 85
Crispin Rd. HA8: Edg . . . 6D 28
Crispin St. E1 . . . 6J 9 (5F 85)
Crispin Way UB8: Hil . . . 4B 74
Crisp Rd. W6 . . . 5E 98
Cristowe Rd. SW6 . . . 2H 117
Criterion Bldgs. KT7: T Ditt . . . 7B 150
(off Portsmouth Rd.)
Criterion Ct. E8 . . . 7F 67
(off Middleton Rd.)
Criterion M. N19 . . . 2H 65
Criterion Theatre . . . 3C 12
(off Piccadilly)
CRITTALLS CORNER . . . 7C 144
Crockerton Rd. SW17 . . . 2D 136
Crockham Way SE9 . . . 4E 142
Crocus Cl. CR0: Croy . . . 1K 169
Crocus Fld. EN5: Barn . . . 6C 20
Croft, The E4 . . . 2B 36
EN5: Barn . . . 4B 20
HA0: Wemb . . . 5C 60
HA4: Ruis . . . 4A 58
HA5: Pinn . . . 7D 40
HA8: Edg . . . 7C 28
NW10 . . . 2B 80
TW5: Hest . . . 6C 94
W5 . . . 5E 78
Croft Av. BR4: W W'ck . . . 1E 170
Croft Cl. BR7: Chst . . . 5D 142
DA17: Belv . . . 5F 109
NW7 . . . 3F 29
UB3: Harl . . . 7E 92
UB10: Hil . . . 7C 56
Croft Ct. HA4: Ruis . . . 1H 57
SE13 . . . 6E 122
Croftdown Rd. NW5 . . . 3E 64
Croft End Cl. KT9: Chess . . . 3F 163
Crofters Cl. TW7: Isle . . . 5H 113
Crofters Ct. SE8 . . . 4A 104
(off Croft St.)
Crofters Mead CR0: Sels . . . 7B 170
Crofters Way NW1 . . . 1H 83

Croft Gdns. HA4: Ruis 1G **57**
  W7 . . . . .2A **96**
Croft Ho. E17 . . . . .4D **50**
  W10 . . . . .3G **81**
                 (off Third Av.)
Croft Lodge Cl. IG8: Wfd G 6E **36**
Croft M. N12 .3F **31**
CROFTON 2H **173**
Crofton Av. BR6: Farnb 2G **173**
  DA5: Bexl 7D **126**
  W4 . . . . .7K **97**
Croftongate Way SE4 . . . . .5A **122**
Crofton Gro. E4 . . . . .4A **36**
Crofton Ho. SW1 . . . . .5K **17**
           (off Sutherland St.)
  SW3 . . . . .6C **100**
           (off Up. Cheyne Row)
Crofton La. BR5: Farnb, Pet W 2H **173**
  BR6: Pet W 7H **161**
Crofton Leisure Cen. 6C **122**
CROFTON PARK 5B **122**
Crofton Pk. Rd. SE4 . . . . .6B **122**
Crofton Rd. BR6: Farnb, Orp 3E **172**
  E13 . . . . .4K **87**
  SE5 . . . . .1E **120**
Crofton Roman Villa 2J **173**
Crofton Ter. E5 . . . . .5A **68**
  TW9: Rich 4F **115**
Crofton Way EN2: Enf 2F **23**
  EN5: New Bar 6E **20**
Croft Rd. BR1: Brom 6J **141**
  EN3: Enf H 1F **25**
  SM1: Sutt 5C **166**
  SW16 . . . . .1A **156**
  SW19 . . . . .7A **136**
Crofts, The TW17: Shep 4G **147**
Crofts Ho. E2 . . . . .2G **85**
                 (off Teale St.)
Croftside, The SE25 . . . . .3G **157**
Crofts La. N22 . . . . .7F **33**
Crofts Rd. HA1: Harr 6A **42**
Crofts St. E1 . . . . .3K **15** (7G **85**)
Croft St. SE8 . . . . .4A **104**
Crofts Vs. HA1: Harr 6A **42**
Croft Way DA15: Sidc 3J **143**
Croftway NW3 . . . . .4J **63**
  TW10: Ham 3B **132**
Crogsland Rd. NW1 . . . . .7E **64**
Croham Cl. CR2: S Croy 7E **168**
Croham Mnr. Rd. CR2: S Croy 7E **168**
Croham Mt. CR2: S Croy 7E **168**
Croham Pk. Av. CR2: S Croy 5E **168**
Croham Rd. CR2: S Croy 5E **168**
Croham Valley Rd. CR2: Sels 6G **169**
Croindene Rd. SW16 . . . . .1J **155**
Crokesley Ho. HA8: Edg 2J **43**
          (off Burnt Oak B'way.)
Cromartie Rd. N19 . . . . .7H **47**
Cromarty Cl. SW2 . . . . .5K **119**
Cromarty Ho. E1 . . . . .5A **86**
          (off Ben Jonson Rd.)
Cromarty Rd. HA8: Edg 2C **28**
Cromberdale Ct. N17 . . . . .1G **49**
           (off Spencer Rd.)
Crombie Cl. IG4: Ilf 5D **52**
Crombie M. SW11 . . . . .2C **118**
Crombie Rd. DA15: Sidc 1H **143**
Crome Ho. UB5: N'olt 2C **76**
            (off Parkfield Dr.)
Cromer Cl. UB8: Hil 6E **74**
Cromerhyde SM4: Mord 5K **153**
Crome Rd. NW10 . . . . .6A **62**
Cromer Pl. BR6: Orp 1J **173**
Cromer Rd. E10 . . . . .7F **51**
  EN5: New Bar 4F **21**
  IG8: Wfd G 4D **36**
  N17 . . . . .2G **49**
  RM6: Chad H 6E **54**
  RM7: Rom 6J **55**
  SE25 . . . . .3H **157**
  SW17 . . . . .6E **136**
  TW6: Hrow A 2C **110**
Cromer St. WC1 . . . . .2E **6** (3J **83**)

Cromer Ter. E8 . . . . .5G **67**
  RM6: Chad H 5B **54**
Cromer Vs. Rd. SW18 . . . . .6H **117**
Cromford Cl. BR6: Orp 3J **173**
Cromford Path E5 . . . . .4K **67**
Cromford Rd. SW18 . . . . .5J **117**
Cromford Way KT3: N Mald 1K **151**
Cromlix Cl. BR7: Chst 2F **161**
Crompton Cl. SW3 . . . . .3C **16** (4C **100**)
Crompton Ho. SE1 . . . . .3C **102**
             (off County St.)
  W2 . . . . .4A **4**
               (off Hall Pl.)
Crompton Pl. EN3: Enf L 1H **25**
Crompton St. W2 . . . . .4A **4** (4B **82**)
Cromwell Av. BR2: Brom 4K **159**
  KT3: N Mald 5B **152**
  N6 . . . . .1F **65**
  W6 . . . . .5D **98**
Cromwell Cen. IG11: Bark 3A **90**
  NW10 . . . . .3K **79**
Cromwell Cen., The RM8: Dag 7F **55**
      (off Whalebone La. Sth.)
Cromwell Cl. BR2: Brom 4K **159**
  E1 . . . . .1G **103**
  KT12: Walt T 7K **147**
  N2 . . . . .4B **46**
  W3 . . . . .1J **97**
            (not continuous)
Cromwell Ct. EN3: Pond E 5E **24**
Cromwell Cres. SW5 . . . . .4J **99**
Cromwell Gdns. SW7 . . . .2B **16** (3B **100**)
Cromwell Gro. W6 . . . . .3E **98**
Cromwell Highwalk EC2 . . . . .5D **8**
Cromwell Ho. CR0: Croy 3B **168**
  SW11 . . . . .1E **118**
     (off Charlotte Despard Av.)
Cromwell Ind. Est. E10 . . . . .1A **68**
Cromwell Lodge DA6: Bex 5E **126**
  E1 . . . . .4J **85**
          (off Cleveland Gro.)
Cromwell Mans. SW5 . . . . .4J **99**
          (off Cromwell Rd.)
Cromwell M. SW7 . . . . . .3B **16** (4B **100**)
Cromwell Pl. EC2 . . . . .5D **8**
            (off Beech St.)
  N6 . . . . .1F **65**
  SW7 . . . . .3B **16** (4B **100**)
  SW14 . . . . .3J **115**
Cromwell Rd. BR3: Beck 2A **158**
  CR0: Croy 7D **156**
  E7 . . . . .7A **70**
  E17 . . . . .5E **50**
  HA0: Wemb 2E **78**
  KT2: King T 1E **150**
  KT4: Wor Pk 3K **163**
  N3 . . . . .1A **46**
  N10 . . . . .7K **31**
           (not continuous)
  SW5 . . . . .4J **99**
  SW7 . . . . .3A **16** (4J **99**)
  SW9 . . . . .1B **120**
  SW19 . . . . .5J **135**
  TW3: Houn 4E **112**
  TW11: Tedd 6A **132**
  TW13: Felt 1K **129**
  UB3: Hayes 6F **75**
Cromwell St. TW3: Houn 4E **112**
Cromwell Twr. EC2 . . . . .5D **8**
Cromwell Trad. Cen. IG11: Bark 3A **90**
Crondace Rd. SW6 . . . . .1J **117**
Crondall Cl. N1 . . . . .1F **9**
Crondall Ho. SW15 . . . . .7C **116**
Crondall St. N1 . . . . .1F **9** (2D **84**)
Crone Ct. NW6 . . . . .2J **81**
           (off Denmark Rd.)
Cronin St. SE15 . . . . .7F **103**
CROOKED BILLET 7H **35**
Crooked Billet SW19 . . . . .6E **134**
Crooked Billet Yd. N1 . . . . .2H **9** (3E **84**)
Crooked Usage N3 . . . . .3G **45**
Crooke Rd. SE8 . . . . .5A **104**
Crookham Rd. SW6 . . . . .1H **117**

Crook Lodge Sports Cen. 3D **126**
Crook Log DA6: Bex 3D **126**
Crookston Rd. SE9 . . . . .3E **124**
Croombs Rd. E16 . . . . .5A **88**
Croom's Hill SE10 . . . . .7E **104**
Croom's Hill Gro. SE10 . . . . .7E **104**
Cropley Ct. N1 . . . . .2D **84**
      (off Cropley St., not continuous)
Cropley St. N1 . . . . .1E **8** (2D **84**)
Croppath Rd. RM10: Dag 4G **73**
Cropthorne Ct. W9 . . . . .3A **82**
Crosbie NW9 . . . . .2B **44**
Crosbie Ho. E17 . . . . .3E **50**
           (off Prospect Hill)
Crosby Cl. TW13: Hanw 3C **130**
Crosby Ct. SE1 . . . . .6E **14** (2D **102**)
Crosby Ho. E7 . . . . .6J **69**
  E14 . . . . .3E **104**
          (off Manchester Rd.)
Crosby Rd. E7 . . . . .6J **69**
  RM10: Dag 2H **91**
Crosby Row SE1 . . . . . . .7E **14** (2D **102**)
Crosby Sq. EC3 . . . . .1G **15** (6E **84**)
Crosby Wlk. E8 . . . . .6F **67**
  SW2 . . . . .7A **120**
Crosby Way SW2 . . . . .7A **120**
Crosier Cl. SE3 . . . . .1C **124**
Crosier Rd. UB10: Ick 4E **56**
Crosier Way HA4: Ruis 3G **57**
Crosland Pl. SW11 . . . . .3E **118**
Cross Av. SE10 . . . . .6F **105**
Crossbow Ho. N1 . . . . .1E **84**
           (off Whitmore Est.)
  W13 . . . . .1B **96**
          (off Sherwood Cl.)
Crossbrook Rd. SE3 . . . . .2C **124**
Cross Cl. SE15 . . . . .2H **121**
Cross Ct. SE28 . . . . .7B **90**
            (off Titmuss Av.)
Cross Deep TW1: Twick 2K **131**
Cross Deep Gdns. TW1: Twick 2K **131**
Crossfield Cl. W10 . . . . .6F **81**
         (off Cambridge Gdns.)
Crossfield Ho. W11 . . . . .7G **81**
            (off Mary Pl.)
Crossfield Rd. N17 . . . . .3C **48**
  NW3 . . . . .6B **64**
Crossfield St. SE8 . . . . .7C **104**
           (not continuous)
Crossford St. SW9 . . . . .2K **119**
Cross Ga. HA8: Edg 3B **28**
Crossgate UB6: G'frd 6B **60**
Cross Keys Cl. N9 . . . . .2B **34**
            (off Lacey Cl.)
  W1 . . . . .6H **5** (5E **82**)
           (off Little Britain)
Cross Keys Sq. EC1 . . . . .6C **8**
           (off Little Britain)
Cross Lances Rd. TW3: Houn 4F **113**
Crossland Rd. CR7: Thor H 6B **156**
Crosslands Av. UB2: S'hall 5D **94**
  W5 . . . . .1F **97**
Crosslands Rd. KT19: Ewe 6K **163**
Cross La. DA5: Bexl 6F **127**
  EC3 . . . . .3G **15** (7E **84**)
           (not continuous)
  N8 . . . . .3K **47**
Crossleigh Ct. SE14 . . . . .7B **104**
          (off New Cross Rd.)
Crosslet St. SE17 . . . . .4D **102**
Crosslet Va. SE10 . . . . .1D **122**
Crossley St. N7 . . . . .6A **66**
Crossmead SE9 . . . . .1D **142**
Crossmead Av. UB6: G'frd 3E **76**
Crossmount Ho. SE5 . . . . .7C **102**
           (off Bowyer St.)
Crossness Engines Mus., The 6F **91**
Crossness Footpath DA18: Erith 1F **109**
Crossness La. SE2 . . . . .7E **90**
Crossness Rd. IG11: Bark 3K **89**
Cross Rd. BR2: Brom 2C **172**
  CR0: Croy 1D **168**
  DA14: Sidc 4B **144**
  E4 . . . . .1A **36**

Cross Rd. EN1: Enf 4K **23**
  HA1: Harr 4H **41**
  HA2: Harr 3F **59**
  HA3: W'stone 3K **41**
  IG8: Wfd G 6J **37**
  KT2: King T 7F **133**
  N11 . . . . .5A **32**
  N22 . . . . .7F **33**
  RM6: Chad H 7C **54**
  RM7: Mawney 4G **55**
  SE5 . . . . .2E **120**
  SM1: Sutt 5B **166**
  SW19 . . . . .7J **135**
  TW13: Hanw 4C **130**
Cross St. N1 .1B **84**
  N18 . . . . .5B **34**
  SE5 . . . . .3D **120**
  SW13 . . . . .2A **116**
  TW12: Ham H 5G **131**
Crossthwaite Av. SE5 . . . . .4D **120**
Crosstrees Ho. E14 . . . . .3C **104**
           (off Cassilis Rd.)
Crosswall EC3 . . . . .2J **15** (7F **85**)
Cross Way IG8: Wfd G 4F **37**
Cross Way, The
  HA3: W'stone 2J **41**
Crossway BR5: Pet W 4H **161**
  EN1: Enf .7K **23**
  HA4: Ruis 4A **58**
  HA5: Pinn 2K **39**
  N12 . . . . .6G **31**
  N16 . . . . .5E **66**
  NW9 . . . . .4B **44**
  RM8: Dag 3C **72**
  SE28 . . . . .6B **90**
  SW20 . . . . .4E **152**
  UB3: Hayes 1J **93**
Crossway, The N22 . . . . .7G **33**
  SE9 . . . . .2B **142**
  UB10: Hil 2B **74**
Crossway Ct. SE4 . . . . .2A **122**
Crossway Pde. N22 . . . . .7G **33**
           (off The Crossway)
Crossways CR2: Sels 7A **170**
  N21 . . . . .6H **23**
  SM2: Sutt 7B **166**
  TW16: Sun 7H **129**
Crossways, The HA9: Wemb 2G **61**
  KT5: Surb 1H **163**
  TW5: Hest 7D **94**
Crossways Rd. BR3: Beck 4C **158**
  CR4: Mitc 3F **155**
Crossways Ter. E5 . . . . .4J **67**
Crosswell Cl. TW17: Shep 2E **146**
Croston St. E8 . . . . .1G **85**
Crothall Cl. N13 . . . . .3E **32**
Crouch Av. IG11: Bark 2B **90**
Crouch Cl. BR3: Beck 6C **140**
Crouch Cft. SE9 . . . . .3E **142**
CROUCH END 7H **47**
Crouch End Hill N8 . . . . .7H **47**
Crouch Hall Ct. N19 . . . . .1J **65**
Crouch Hall Rd. N8 . . . . .6H **47**
Crouch Hill N4 . . . . .6J **47**
  N8 . . . . .6J **47**
Crouch Hill Recreation Cen. 7J **47**
Crouchman's Cl. SE26 . . . . .3F **139**
Crouch Rd. NW10 . . . . .7K **61**
Crowborough Rd. SW17 . . . . .6E **136**
Crowden Way SE28 . . . . .7C **90**
Crowder Cl. N12 . . . . .1A **46**
Crowder St. E1 . . . . .7H **85**
Crowfield Ho. N5 . . . . .4C **66**
Crowfoot Cl. E9 . . . . .5B **68**
  SE28 . . . . .1J **107**
Crowhurst Cl. SW9 . . . . .2A **120**
Crowhurst Ho. SW9 . . . . .2K **119**
            (off Aytoun Rd.)
Crowland Av. UB3: Harl 4G **93**
Crowland Gdns. N14 . . . . .7D **22**
Crowland Ho. NW8 . . . . .1A **82**
          (off Springfield Rd.)

Crowland Rd.—Cumberland Rd.

Crowland Rd. CR7: Thor H 4D 156
N15 5F 49
CROWLANDS 7H 55
Crowlands Av. RM7: Rom 6H 55
Crowland Ter. N1 7D 66
Crowland Wlk. SM4: Mord 6K 153
Crow La. RM7: Rush G 7G 55
Crowley Cres. CR0: Wadd 5A 168
Crowline Wlk. N1 6C 66
Crowmarsh Gdns. SE23 7J 121
Crown All. SE9 6D 124
Crown Arc. KT1: King T 2D 150
Crownbourne Ct. *SM1: Sutt* 4K 165
(off St Nicholas Way)
Crown Bldgs. *E4* 1A 36
(off Richmond Rd.)
E4 1K 35
(Woodland Rd.)
Crown Cl. E3 1C 86
KT12: Walt T 7A 148
N22 1A 48
NW6 6K 63
NW7 2G 29
UB3: Hayes 2H 93
Crown Cl. Bus. Cen. *E3* 1C 86
(off Crown Cl.)
Crown Cotts. RM5: Col R 1G 55
Crown Ct. EC2 1D 14
N10 7K 31
NW8 2D 4
(off Park Rd.)
SE12 6K 123
WC2 1F 13 (6J 83)
Crown Dale SE19 6B 138
Crowndale Ct. *NW1* 2H 83
(off Crowndale Rd.)
Crowndale Rd. NW1 2G 83
Crownfield Av. IG2: Ilf 6J 53
Crownfield Rd. E15 4F 69
Crowngate Ho. *E3* 2B 86
(off Hereford Rd.)
Crown Hill CR0: Croy 2C 168
Crown Hill Rd. NW10 1B 80
Crownhill Rd. IG8: Wfd G 7H 37
Crown Ho. HA4: Ruis 1J 57
Crown La. BR2: Brom 5B 160
BR7: Chst 1G 161
N14 1B 32
SM4: Mord 4J 153
SW16 5A 138
Crown La. Gdns. SW16 5A 138
Crown La. Spur BR2: Brom 6B 160
Crown Lodge SW3 4D 16
Crownmead Way RM7: Mawney 4H 55
Crown M. *E1* 5K 85
(off White Horse La.)
E13 1A 88
W6 4C 98
Crown Office Row EC4 2J 13 (7A 84)
Crown Pde. N14 1B 32
SM4: Mord 3J 153
Crown Pas. *KT1: King T* 2D 150
(off Church St.)
SW1 5B 12 (1G 101)
Crown Pl. EC2 5G 9 (5E 84)
(not continuous)
NW5 6F 65
SE16 5H 103
Crown Point SE19 6B 138
Crown Reach SW1 6D 18 (5H 101)
Crown Rd. EN1: Enf 3B 24
HA4: Ruis 5B 58
IG6: Ilf 4H 53
KT3: N Mald 1J 151
N10 7K 31
SM1: Sutt 4K 165
SM4: Mord 4K 153
TW1: Twick 6B 114
Crownstone Ct. SW2 5A 120
Crownstone Rd. SW2 5A 120
Crown St. HA2: Harr 1H 59
RM10: Dag 6J 73
(not continuous)
Crown St. SE5 7C 102
W3 1H 97
Crown Ter. *N14* 1C 32
(off Crown La.)
TW9: Rich 4F 115
Crown Trad. Cen. UB3: Hayes 2G 93
Crowntree Cl. TW7: Isle 6K 95
Crown Wlk. HA9: Wemb 3F 61
Crown Way UB7: Yiew 1B 92
Crown Wharf *E14* 1E 104
(off Coldharbour)
SE8 5B 104
(off Grove St.)
Crown Woods SE18 2F 125
Crown Woods Way SE9 5H 125
Crown Yd. TW3: Houn 3G 113
Crowshott Av. HA7: Stan 2C 42
Crows Rd. E15 3F 87
IG11: Bark 6F 71
Crowther Av. TW8: Bford 4E 96
Crowther Cl. *SW6* 6H 99
(off Bucklers All.)
Crowther Rd. SE25 5G 157
Crowthorne Cl. SW18 7H 117
Crowthorne Rd. W10 6F 81
Croxall Ho. KT12: Walt T 6A 148
Croxden Cl. HA8: Edg 3G 43
Croxden Wlk. SM4: Mord 6A 154
Croxford Gdns. N22 7G 33
Croxford Way RM7: Rush G 1K 73
Croxley Grn. BR5: St P 7B 144
Croxley Rd. W9 3H 81
Croxted Cl. SE21 7C 120
Croxted M. SE24 6C 120
Croxted Rd. SE21 7C 120
SE24 7C 120
Croxteth Ho. SW8 2H 119
Croyde Av. UB3: Harl 4G 93
UB6: G'frd 3G 77
Croyde Cl. DA15: Sidc 7H 125
CROYDON 3C 168
Croydon *N17* 2D 48
(off Gloucester Rd.)
Croydon Airport Ind. Est.
CR0: Wadd 6K 167
Croydon Clocktower 3C 168
(off Katherine St.)
Croydon Crematorium CR0: Croy 5K 155
Croydon Flyover, The CR0: Croy 4B 168
Croydon Gro. CR0: Croy 1B 168
Croydon Ho. *SE1* 6K 13
(off Wootton St.)
Croydon Rd. BR2: Hayes, Kes 3A 172
BR3: Beck 4K 157
BR4: Hayes, W W'ck 3G 171
CR0: Bedd, Wadd 4F 167
CR0: Croy 4E 154
CR4: Mitc 4E 154
E13 4H 87
SE20 2H 157
SM6: Bedd, Wall 4F 167
TW6: H'row A 2D 110
Croydon Rd. Ind. Est. BR3: Beck 4K 157
Croydon Sports Arena 5J 157
Croyland Rd. N9 1B 34
Croylands Dr. KT6: Surb 7E 150
Croysdale Av. TW16: Sun 3J 147
Crozier Ho. SE3 3K 123
SW8 7K 101
(off Wilkinson St.)
Crozier Ter. E9 5K 67
Crucible Cl. RM6: Chad H 6B 54
Crucifix La. SE1 6H 15 (2E 102)
Cruden Ho. *SE17* 6B 102
(off Brandon Est.)
Cruden St. N1 1B 84
Cruikshank Ho. *NW8* 2C 82
(off Townshend Rd.)
Cruikshank Rd. E15 4G 69
Cruikshank St. WC1 1J 7 (3A 84)
Crummock Gdns. NW9 5A 44
Crumpsall St. SE2 4C 108
Crundale Av. NW9 5G 43
Crunden Rd. CR2: S Croy 7D 168
Crusader Gdns. CR0: Croy 3E 168
Crusader Ind. Est. N4 6C 48
Crusoe M. N16 2D 66
Crusoe Rd. CR4: Mitc 7D 136
DA8: Erith 5K 109
Crutched Friars EC3 2H 15 (7E 84)
Crutchley Rd. SE6 2G 141
Crystal Ct. *SE19* 5F 139
(off College Rd.)
Crystal Ho. SE18 5K 107
CRYSTAL PALACE 6F 139
Crystal Palace Athletics Stadium 6G 139
Crystal Palace FC 4E 156
Crystal Palace Indoor Bowling Club
1H 157
(off Ashurst Cl.)
Crystal Palace Mus. 6F 139
Crystal Palace National Sports Cen.
6G 139
Crystal Pal. Pde. SE19 6F 139
Crystal Pal. Pk. Rd. SE26 5G 139
Crystal Pal. Rd. SE22 6F 121
Crystal Pal. Sta. Rd. SE19 6G 139
Crystal Ter. SE19 6D 138
Crystal Vw. Ct. BR1: Brom 4F 141
Crystal Way HA1: Harr 5K 41
RM8: Dag 1C 72
Crystal Wharf N1 2B 84
Cuba Dr. EN3: Enf H 2D 24
Cuba St. E14 2C 104
Cube Ho. SE16 3F 103
Cubitt Ho. SW4 6G 119
Cubitt Sq. UB2: S'hall 1G 95
Cubitt Steps E14 1C 104
Cubitt St. WC1 2H 7 (3K 83)
Cubitt's Yd. WC2 2F 13
Cubitt Ter. SW4 3G 119
CUBITT TOWN 4E 104
Cuckoo Av. W7 4J 77
Cuckoo Dene W7 5H 77
Cuckoo Hall La. N9 7D 24
Cuckoo Hall Rd. N9 7D 24
Cuckoo Hill HA5: Eastc 3A 40
Cuckoo Hill Dr. HA5: Pinn 3A 40
Cuckoo Hill Rd. HA5: Pinn 4A 40
Cuckoo La. W7 7J 77
Cuckoo Pound TW17: Shep 5G 147
Cudas Cl. KT19: Ewe 4B 164
Cuddington *SE17* 4C 102
(off Deacon Way)
Cuddington Av. KT4: Wor Pk 3B 164
Cudham La. Nth. BR6: Downe 7J 173
Cudham St. SE6 7E 122
Cudworth Ho. SW8 1G 119
Cudworth St. E1 4H 85
Cuff Cres. SE9 6B 124
Cuffley Ho. *W10* 5E 80
(off Sutton Way)
Cuff Point *E2* 1J 9
(off Columbia Rd.)
Culford Gdns. SW3 4F 17 (4D 100)
Culford Gro. N1 6E 66
Culford Mans. *SW3* 4F 17
(off Culford Gdns.)
Culford M. N1 6E 66
Culford Rd. N1 7E 66
Culford Ter. *N1* 6E 66
(off Balls Pond Rd.)
Culgaith Gdns. EN2: Enf 4D 22
Culham Ho. *E2* 2J 9
(off Palissy St.)
W2 5J 81
(off Brunel Est.)
Cullen Way NW10 4J 79
Culling Rd. SE16 3J 103
Cullington Cl. HA3: W'stone 4A 42
Cullingworth Rd. NW10 5C 62
Culloden Cl. SE16 5G 103
Culloden Rd. EN2: Enf 2G 23
Cullum St. EC3 2G 15 (7E 84)
Cullum Welch Ct. *N1* 1F 9
(off Haberdasher St.)
Cullum Welch Ho. *EC1* 4C 8
(off Goswell Rd.)
Culmington Pde. *W13* 1C 96
(off Uxbridge Rd.)
Culmington Rd. CR2: S Croy 7C 168
W13 1C 96
Culmore Rd. SE15 7H 103
Culmstock Rd. SW11 5E 118
Culpepper Cl. N18 5C 34
Culpepper Ct. SE11 3J 19
Culross Bldgs. *NW1* 2J 83
(off Battle Bri. Rd.)
Culross Cl. N15 4C 48
Culross Ho. *W10* 6F 81
(off Bridge Cl.)
Culross St. W1 3G 11 (7E 82)
Culsac Rd. KT6: Surb 2E 162
Culverden Rd. SW12 2G 137
Culver Gro. HA7: Stan 2C 42
Culverhouse *WC1* 6G 7
(off Red Lion Sq.)
Culverhouse Gdns. SW16 3K 137
Culverlands Cl. HA7: Stan 4G 27
Culverley Rd. SE6 1D 140
Culvers Av. SM5: Cars 2D 166
Culvers Retreat SM5: Cars 1D 166
Culverstone Cl. BR2: Brom 6H 159
Culvers Way SM5: Cars 2D 166
Culvert Pl. SW11 2E 118
Culvert Rd. *N15* 5E 48
(off Lydford Rd.)
N15 5E 48
(Oulton Rd.)
SW11 2D 118
Culworth Ho. *NW8* 2C 82
(off Allitsen Rd.)
Culworth St. NW8 2C 82
Culzean Cl. SE27 3B 138
Cumberland Av. DA16: Well 3J 125
NW10 3H 79
Cumberland Bus. Pk. NW10 3H 79
Cumberland Cl. E8 6F 67
IG6: Ilf 1G 53
SW20 7F 135
TW1: Twick 6B 114
Cumberland Ct. CR0: Croy 1D 168
DA16: Well 2J 125
HA1: Harr 3J 41
(off Princes Dr.)
SW1 5K 17
(off Cumberland St.)
W1 1F 11
(off Gt. Cumberland Pl.)
Cumberland Cres. W14 4G 99
(not continuous)
Cumberland Dr. DA7: Bex 7E 108
KT9: Chess 3E 162
KT10: Hin W 2A 162
Cumberland Gdns. NW4 2G 45
WC1 1J 7 (3A 84)
Cumberland Ga. W1 2E 10 (7D 82)
Cumberland Ho. *E16* 1J 105
(off Wesley Av.)
KT2: King T 7H 133
N9 1D 34
(off Cumberland Rd.)
SE28 2G 107
W8 2K 99
(off Kensington Ct.)
Cumberland Mans. W1 7E 4
Cumberland Mkt. NW1 1K 5 (3F 83)
Cumberland M. SE11 6K 19 (5A 102)
Cumberland Mills Sq. E14 5F 105
Cumberland Pk. W3 7J 79
Cumberland Pk. Ind. Est. NW10 3C 80
Cumberland Pl. NW1 1J 5 (3F 83)
SE6 1H 141
TW16: Sun 4J 147
Cumberland Rd. BR2: Brom 4G 159
E12 4B 70
E13 5K 87
E17 2A 50
HA1: Harr 5F 41

Cumberland Rd.—Dale Ho.

Cumberland Rd. HA7: Stan ... 3F 43
N9 ... 1D 34
N22 ... 2K 47
SE25 ... 6H 157
SW13 ... 1B 116
TW9: Kew ... 7G 97
TW15: Ashf ... 3A 128
W3 ... 7J 79
W7 ... 2K 95
Cumberland St. SW1 ... 5K 17 (5F 101)
Cumberland Ter. NW1 ... 1J 5 (2F 83)
Cumberland Ter. M. NW1 ... 1J 5
(not continuous)
Cumberland Vs. W3 ... 7J 79
(off Cumberland Rd.)
Cumberlow Av. SE25 ... 3F 157
Cumbernauld Gdns.
TW16: Sun ... 5H 129
Cumberton Rd. N17 ... 1D 48
Cumbrae Gdns. KT6: Surb ... 2D 162
Cumbrian Gdns. NW2 ... 2F 63
Cumbrian Way UB8: Uxb ... 7A 56
Cuming Mus. ... 4C 102
(off Walworth Rd.)
Cumming St. N1 ... 1H 7 (2K 83)
Cumnor Cl. SW9 ... 2K 119
(off Robsart St.)
Cumnor Gdns. KT17: Ewe ... 6C 164
Cumnor Rd. SM2: Sutt ... 6A 166
Cunard Cres. N21 ... 6J 23
Cunard Pl. EC3 ... 1H 15 (6E 84)
Cunard Rd. NW10 ... 3K 79
Cunard Wlk. SE16 ... 4K 103
Cundy Rd. E16 ... 6A 88
Cundy St. SW1 ... 4H 17 (4E 100)
Cunliffe Pde. KT19: Ewe ... 4B 164
Cunliffe Rd. KT19: Ewe ... 4B 164
Cunliffe St. SW16 ... 6G 137
Cunningham Cl. BR4: W W'ck ... 2D 170
RM6: Chad H ... 5C 54
Cunningham Ct. E10 ... 3D 68
(off Oliver Rd.)
W9 ... 4A 4
(off Blomfield Rd.)
Cunningham Ho. SE5 ... 7D 102
(off Elmington Est.)
Cunningham Pk. HA1: Harr ... 5G 41
Cunningham Pl. NW8 ... 3A 4 (4B 82)
Cunningham Rd. N15 ... 4G 49
Cunnington St. W4 ... 3J 97
Cupar Rd. SW11 ... 1E 118
Cupola Cl. BR1: Brom ... 5K 141
Cureton St. SW1 ... 4D 18 (4H 101)
Curlew Ho. IG11: Bark ... 1G 89
Curie Ct. HA1: Harr ... 7B 42
Curie Gdns. NW9 ... 2A 44
Curlew Cl. SE28 ... 7D 90
Curlew Ct. KT6: Surb ... 3G 163
W13 ... 4K 77
Curlew Ho. EN3: Pond E ... 5E 24
SE4 ... 4A 122
(off St Norbert Rd.)
SE15 ... 1F 121
Curlew St. SE1 ... 6K 15 (2F 103)
Curlew Way UB4: Yead ... 5B 76
Curness St. SE13 ... 4E 122
Curnick's La. SE27 ... 4C 138
Curran Av. DA15: Sidc ... 5K 125
SM6: Wall ... 3E 166
Curran Ho. SW3 ... 4C 16
(off Lucan Pl.)
Currey Rd. UB6: G'frd ... 6H 59
Curricle St. W3 ... 1A 98
Currie Hill Cl. SW19 ... 4H 135
Currie Ho. E14 ... 6F 87
(off Abbott Rd.)
Curry Ri. NW7 ... 6A 30
Cursitor St. EC4 ... 7J 7 (6A 84)
Curtain Pl. EC2 ... 3H 9 (3E 84)
Curtain Rd. EC2 ... 2H 9 (4E 84)
Curthwaite Gdns. EN2: Enf ... 4C 22
Curtis Dr. W3 ... 6K 79
Curtis Fld. Rd. SW16 ... 4K 137
Curtis Ho. N11 ... 5B 32
(off Ladderswood Way)
SE17 ... 5D 102
(off Morecambe St.)
Curtis La. HA0: Wemb ... 5E 60
Curtis Rd. KT19: Ewe ... 4J 163
TW4: Houn ... 7D 112
Curtis St. SE1 ... 4F 103
Curtis Way SE1 ... 4F 103
SE28 ... 7B 90
Curtlington Ho. HA8: Edg ... 2J 43
(off Burnt Oak B'way.)
Curve, The W12 ... 7C 80
Curwen Av. E7 ... 4K 69
Curwen Rd. W12 ... 2C 98
Curzon Av. EN3: Pond E ... 5E 24
HA7: Stan ... 1A 42
Curzon Cinema
Mayfair ... 5J 11
(off Curzon St.)
Soho ... 2D 12
(off Shaftesbury Av.)
Curzon Cl. BR6: Orp ... 4H 173
Curzon Ct. SW6 ... 1A 118
(off Imperial Rd.)
Curzon Cres. IG11: Bark ... 2K 89
NW10 ... 7A 62
Curzon Ga. W1 ... 5H 11 (1E 100)
Curzon Pl. HA5: Eastc ... 5A 40
Curzon Rd. CR7: Thor H ... 6A 156
N10 ... 2F 47
W5 ... 4B 78
Curzon Sq. W1 ... 5H 11 (1E 100)
Curzon St. W1 ... 5H 11 (1E 100)
Cusack Cl. TW1: Twick ... 4K 131
Custance Ho. N1 ... 1E 8
(off Fairbank Est.)
Custance St. N1 ... 1E 8 (3D 84)
CUSTOM HOUSE ... 6A 88
Custom Ho. EC3 ... 3G 15 (7E 84)
Custom Ho. Reach SE16 ... 2B 104
Custom Ho. Wlk. EC3 ... 3G 15 (7E 84)
Cut, The SE1 ... 6K 13 (2A 102)
Cutbush Ho. N7 ... 5H 65
Cutcombe Rd. SE5 ... 2C 120
Cuthberga Cl. IG11: Bark ... 7G 71
Cuthbert Gdns. SE25 ... 3E 156
Cuthbert Harrowing Ho. EC1 ... 4C 8
(off Golden La. Est.)
Cuthbert Ho. W2 ... 5A 4
(off Hall Pl.)
Cuthbert Rd. CR0: Croy ... 2B 168
E17 ... 3E 50
N18 ... 5B 34
Cuthbert St. W2 ... 5A 4 (5B 82)
Cuthill Wlk. SE5 ... 1D 120
Cutlers Gdns. EC2 ... 6H 9
Cutlers Sq. E14 ... 4C 104
Cutler St. E1 ... 7H 9 (6E 84)
Cutthroat All. TW10: Ham ... 2C 132
Cutty Sark ... 6E 104
Cutty Sark Gdns. SE10 ... 6E 104
(off King William Wlk.)
Cuxton BR5: Pet W ... 5G 161
Cuxton Cl. DA6: Bex ... 5E 126
Cuxton Ho. SE17 ... 5E 102
(off Mina Rd.)
Cyclamen Cl. TW12: Hamp ... 6E 130
Cyclamen Way KT19: Ewe ... 5J 163
Cyclops M. E14 ... 4C 104
Cygnet Av. TW14: Felt ... 7A 112
Cygnet Cl. NW10 ... 5K 61
Cygnet Ho. SW3 ... 6D 16
(off King's Rd.)
SW18 ... 3A 118
Cygnet Ho. Nth. E14 ... 6D 86
(off Chrisp St.)
Cygnet Ho. Sth. E14 ... 6D 86
(off Chrisp St.)
Cygnets, The TW13: Hanw ... 4C 130
Cygnet St. E1 ... 3K 9 (4F 85)
Cygnet Way UB4: Yead ... 5B 76
Cygnus Bus. Cen. NW10 ... 5B 62
Cymbeline Ct. HA1: Harr ... 6K 41
(off Gayton Rd.)
Cynthia St. N1 ... 1H 7 (2K 83)
Cyntra Pl. E8 ... 7H 67
Cypress Av. TW2: Whit ... 7G 113
Cypress Cl. E5 ... 2G 67
Cypress Ct. SM1: Sutt ... 5J 165
Cypress Gdns. SE4 ... 5A 122
Cypress Ho. SE14 ... 1K 121
SE16 ... 2K 103
(off Woodland Cres.)
Cypress Pl. W1 ... 4B 6 (4G 83)
Cypress Rd. HA3: Hrw W ... 2H 41
SE25 ... 2E 156
Cypress Tree Cl. DA15: Sidc ... 1K 143
CYPRUS ... 7E 88
Cyprus Av. N3 ... 2G 45
Cyprus Cl. N4 ... 6B 48
Cyprus Gdns. N3 ... 2G 45
Cyprus Pl. E2 ... 2J 85
E6 ... 7E 88
Cyprus Rd. N3 ... 2H 45
N9 ... 2A 34
Cyprus St. E2 ... 2J 85
(not continuous)
Cyrena Rd. SE22 ... 6F 121
Cyril Lodge DA14: Sidc ... 4A 144
Cyril Mans. SW11 ... 1D 118
Cyril Rd. BR6: Orp ... 7K 161
DA7: Bex ... 2E 126
Cyrus Ho. EC1 ... 3B 8
Cyrus St. EC1 ... 3B 8
Czar St. SE8 ... 6C 104

D

Dabbs Hill La. UB5: N'olt ... 6D 58
(not continuous)
Dabbs La. EC1 ... 4K 7
(off Farringdon Rd.)
Dabin Cres. SE10 ... 1E 122
Dacca St. SE8 ... 6B 104
Dace Rd. E3 ... 1C 86
Dacre Av. IG5: Ilf ... 2E 52
Dacre Cl. UB6: G'frd ... 2F 77
Dacre Gdns. SE13 ... 4G 123
Dacre Ho. SW3 ... 7B 16
Dacre Pk. SE13 ... 3G 123
Dacre Pl. SE13 ... 3G 123
Dacre Rd. CR0: Croy ... 7J 155
E11 ... 1H 69
E13 ... 1K 87
Dacres Est. SE23 ... 3K 139
Dacres Ho. SW4 ... 3F 119
Dacres Rd. SE23 ... 2K 139
Dacre St. SW1 ... 1C 18 (3H 101)
Dade Way UB2: S'hall ... 5D 94
Daerwood Cl. BR2: Brom ... 1D 172
Daffodil Cl. CR0: Croy ... 1K 169
Daffodil Gdns. IG1: Ilf ... 5F 71
Daffodil Pl. TW12: Hamp ... 6E 130
Daffodil St. W12 ... 7B 80
Dafforne Rd. SW17 ... 3E 136
Da Gama Pl. E14 ... 5C 104
DAGENHAM ... 6G 73
Dagenham & Redbridge FC ... 5H 73
Dagenham Av. RM9: Dag ... 1E 90
(not continuous)
Dagenham Leisure Pk.
RM9: Dag ... 1E 90
Dagenham Rd. E10 ... 1B 68
RM7: Rush G ... 7K 55
RM10: Dag, Rush G ... 4J 73
RM13: Rain ... 7K 73
Dagenham Swimming Pool ... 2G 73
Dagmar Av. HA9: Wemb ... 4F 61
Dagmar Ct. E14 ... 3E 104
Dagmar Gdns. NW10 ... 2F 81
Dagmar M. UB2: S'hall ... 3C 94
(off Dagmar Rd.)
Dagmar Pas. N1 ... 1B 84
(off Cross St.)
Dagmar Rd. KT2: King T ... 1F 151
N4 ... 7A 48
N15 ... 4D 48
N22 ... 1H 47
RM10: Dag ... 7J 73
SE5 ... 1E 120
SE25 ... 5E 156
UB2: S'hall ... 3C 94
Dagmar Ter. N1 ... 1B 84
Dagnall Pk. SE25 ... 6E 156
Dagnall Rd. SE25 ... 5E 156
Dagnall St. SW11 ... 2D 118
Dagnan Rd. SW12 ... 7F 119
Dagobert Ho. E1 ... 5J 85
(off Smithy St.)
Dagonet Gdns. BR1: Brom ... 3J 141
Dagonet Rd. BR1: Brom ... 3J 141
Dahlia Gdns. CR4: Mitc ... 4H 155
IG1: Ilf ... 6F 71
Dahlia Rd. SE2 ... 4B 108
Dahomey Rd. SW16 ... 6G 137
Daimler Way SM6: Wall ... 7J 167
Dain Ct. W8 ... 4J 99
(off Lexham Gdns.)
Daines Cl. E12 ... 3D 70
Dainford Cl. BR1: Brom ... 5F 141
Dainton Cl. BR1: Brom ... 1K 159
Dainton Ho. W2 ... 5J 81
(off Brunel Est.)
Daintry Cl. HA3: W'stone ... 4A 42
Daintry Way E9 ... 6B 68
Dairsie Ct. BR1: Brom ... 1A 160
Dairsie Rd. SE9 ... 3E 124
Dairy Cl. BR1: Brom ... 7K 141
CR7: Thor H ... 2C 156
NW10 ... 1C 80
Dairy La. SE18 ... 4D 106
Dairyman Cl. NW2 ... 3F 63
Dairy M. SW9 ... 3J 119
Dairy Wlk. SW19 ... 4G 135
Daisy Cl. CR0: Croy ... 1K 169
Daisy Dobbings Wlk.
N19 ... 7J 47
(off Jessie Blythe La.)
Daisy La. SW6 ... 3J 117
Daisy Rd. E16 ... 4G 87
E18 ... 2K 51
Dakin Pl. E1 ... 5A 86
Dakota Bldg. SE8 ... 1D 122
(off Deal's Gateway)
Dakota Cl. SM6: Wall ... 7K 167
Dakota Gdns. E6 ... 4C 88
UB5: N'olt ... 3C 76
Dalberg Rd. SW2 ... 4A 120
(not continuous)
Dalberg Way SE2 ... 3D 108
Dalby Rd. SW18 ... 4A 118
Dalbys Cres. N17 ... 6K 33
Dalby St. NW5 ... 6F 65
Dalcross Rd. TW4: Houn ... 2C 112
Dale, The BR2: Kes ... 4B 172
Dale Av. HA8: Edg ... 1F 43
TW4: Houn ... 3C 112
Dalebury Rd. SW17 ... 2D 136
Dale Cl. EN5: New Bar ... 6E 20
HA5: Pinn ... 1K 39
SE3 ... 3J 123
Dale Ct. EN2: Enf ... 1H 23
KT2: King T ... 7F 133
(off York Rd.)
Dale Dr. UB4: Hayes ... 4H 75
Dalefield IG9: Buck H ... 1F 37
(off Roebuck La.)
Dale Gdns. IG8: Wfd G ... 4E 36
Dale Grn. Rd. N11 ... 3A 32
Dale Gro. N12 ... 5F 31
Daleham Dr. UB8: Hil ... 6D 74
Daleham Gdns. NW3 ... 5B 64
Daleham M. NW3 ... 6B 64
Dalehead NW1 ... 1A 6
(off Hampstead Rd.)
Dale Ho. N1 ... 1E 84
(off New Era Est.)

Dale Ho. *NW8* *1A* **82**
(off Boundary Rd.)
SE4 4A **122**
Dale Lodge N6 6G **47**
Dalemain M. E16 1J **105**
Dale Pk. Av. SM5: Cars 2D **166**
Dale Pk. Rd. SE19 1C **156**
Dale Rd. KT12: Walt T 7H **147**
NW5 5E **64**
SE17 6B **102**
SM1: Sutt 4H **165**
TW16: Sun 7H **129**
UB6: G'frd 5F **77**
Dale Row W11 6G **81**
Daleside Rd. KT19: Ewe 6K **163**
SW16 5F **137**
Dale St. W4 5A **98**
Dale Vw. Av. E4 2K **35**
Dale Vw. Cres. E4 2K **35**
Dale Vw. Gdns. E4 3A **36**
Daleview Rd. N15 6E **48**
Dalewood Gdns. KT4: Wor Pk 2D **164**
Dale Wood Rd. BR6: Orp 7J **161**
Daley Ho. W12 6D **80**
Daley St. E9 6K **67**
Daley Thompson Way SW8 2F **119**
Dalgarno Gdns. W10 5E **80**
Dalgarno Way W10 4E **80**
Dalgleish St. E14 6A **86**
Daling Way E3 1A **86**
Dali Universe **6G 13 (2K 101)**
Dalkeith Ct. *SW1* *3D* **18**
(off Vincent St.)
Dalkeith Gro. HA7: Stan 5J **27**
Dalkeith Ho. *SW9* *1B* **120**
(off Lothian Rd.)
Dalkeith Rd. IG1: Ilf 3G **71**
SE21 1C **138**
Dallas Rd. NW4 7C **44**
SE26 3H **139**
SM3: Cheam 6G **165**
W5 5F **79**
Dallas Ter. UB3: Harl 3H **93**
Dallega Cl. UB3: Hayes 7F **75**
Dallinger Rd. SE12 6H **123**
Dalling Rd. W6 4D **98**
Dallington Sq. *EC1* *3B* **8**
(off Berry St.)
Dallington St. EC1 3B **8** (4B **84**)
Dallin Rd. DA6: Bex 4D **126**
SE18 7F **107**
Dalmain Rd. SE23 1K **139**
Dalmally Rd. CR0: Croy 7F **157**
Dalmany Pas. CR0: Croy 7F **157**
Dalmeny Av. N7 4H **65**
SW16 2A **156**
Dalmeny Cl. HA0: Wemb 6C **60**
Dalmeny Cres. TW3: Houn 4H **113**
Dalmeny Rd. DA8: Erith 1H **127**
EN5: New Bar 6F **21**
KT4: Wor Pk 3D **164**
N7 3H **65**
(not continuous)
SM5: Cars 7E **166**
Dalmeyer Rd. NW10 6B **62**
Dalmore Rd. SE21 2C **138**
Dalo Lodge *E3* *5C* **86**
(off Gale St.)
Dalrymple Cl. N14 7C **22**
Dalrymple Rd. SE4 4A **122**
DALSTON 6F **67**
Dalston Gdns. HA7: Stan 1E **42**
Dalston La. E8 6F **67**
Dalton Av. CR4: Mitc 2C **154**
Dalton Cl. BR6: Orp 3J **173**
UB4: Hayes 4F **75**
Dalton Ho. HA7: Stan 5F **27**
SE14 *6K* **103**
(off John Williams Cl.)
SW1 *5J* **17**
(off Ebury Bri. Rd.)
Dalton Rd. HA3: W'stone 2H **41**
Dalton St. SE27 2B **138**
Dalwood St. SE5 1E **120**
Daly Ct. E15 5D **68**
Daly Dr. BR1: Brom 3E **160**
Dalyell Rd. SW9 3K **119**
Damascene Wlk. SE21 1C **138**
Damask Ct. SM1: Sutt 1K **165**
Damask Cres. E16 4G **87**
Damer Ter. SW10 7A **100**
Dames Rd. E7 3J **69**
Dame St. N1 2C **84**
Damien Ct. *E1* *6H* **85**
(off Damien St.)
Damien St. E1 6H **85**
Damon Cl. DA14: Sidc 3B **144**
Damory Ho. *SE16* *4H* **103**
(off Abbeyfield Est.)
Damson Dr. UB3: Hayes 7J **75**
Damsonwood Rd. UB2: S'hall 3E **94**
Danbrook Rd. SW16 1J **155**
Danbury Cl. RM6: Chad H 3D **54**
Danbury Mans. *IG11: Bark* *7F* **71**
(off Whiting Av.)
Danbury M. SM6: Wall 4F **167**
Danbury St. N1 2B **84**
Danbury Way IG8: Wfd G 6F **37**
Danby Ct. *EN2: Enf* *3H* **23**
(off Horseshoe La.)
Danby Ho. *E9* *7J* **67**
(off Frampton Pk. Rd.)
W10 *3G* **81**
(off Bruckner St.)
Danby St. SE15 3F **121**
Dancer Rd. SW6 1H **117**
TW9: Rich 3G **115**
Dando Cres. SE3 3K **123**
Dandridge Cl. SE10 5H **105**
Dandridge Ho. *E1* *5J* **9**
(off Lamb St.)
Danebury CR0: New Ad 6E **170**
Danebury Av. SW15 6A **116**
(not continuous)
Daneby Rd. SE6 3D **140**
Dane Cl. BR6: Farnb 5H **173**
DA5: Bexl 7G **127**
Danecourt Gdns. CR0: Croy 3F **169**
Danecroft Rd. SE24 5C **120**
Danehill Wlk. DA14: Sidc 3A **144**
Danehurst TW8: Bford 7C **96**
Danehurst Gdns. IG4: Ilf 5C **52**
Danehurst St. SW6 1G **117**
Daneland EN4: E Barn 6J **21**
Danemead Gro. UB5: N'olt 5F **59**
Danemere St. SW15 3E **116**
Dane Pl. E3 2A **86**
Dane Rd. IG1: Ilf 5G **71**
N18 3D **34**
SW19 1A **154**
TW15: Ashf 6E **128**
UB1: S'hall 7C **76**
W13 1C **96**
Danesbury Rd. TW13: Felt 1K **129**
Danescombe SE12 1J **141**
Danes Ct. HA9: Wemb 3H **61**
NW8 *1D* **82**
(off St Edmund's Ter.)
Danescourt Cres. SM1: Sutt 2A **166**
Danescroft NW4 5F **45**
Danescroft Av. NW4 5F **45**
Danescroft Gdns. NW4 5F **45**
Danesdale Rd. E9 6A **68**
Danesfield *SE5* *6E* **102**
(off Albany Rd.)
Danes Ga. HA1: Harr 3J **41**
Danes Ho. *W10* *5E* **80**
(off Sutton Way)
Danes Rd. RM7: Rush G 7J **55**
Dane St. WC1 6G **7** (5K **83**)
Daneswood Av. SE6 3E **140**
Danethorpe Rd. HA0: Wemb 6D **60**
Danetree Cl. KT19: Ewe 7J **163**
Danetree Rd. KT19: Ewe 7J **163**
Danette Gdns. RM10: Dag 2G **73**
Daneville Rd. SE5 1D **120**
Dangan Rd. E11 6J **51**
Daniel Bolt Cl. E14 5D **86**
Daniel Cl. N18 4D **34**
SW17 6C **136**
TW4: Houn 7D **112**
Daniel Ct. NW9 1A **44**
Daniel Gdns. SE15 7F **103**
Daniell Ho. *N1* *2D* **84**
(off Cranston Est.)
Daniell Way CR0: Wadd 1J **167**
Daniel Pl. NW4 7D **44**
Daniel Rd. W5 7F **79**
Daniels Rd. SE15 3J **121**
Danleigh Ct. N14 7C **22**
Dan Leno Wlk. SW6 7K **99**
Dan Mason Dr. W4 2J **115**
Dansey Pl. W1 2C **12**
Dansington Rd. DA16: Well 4A **126**
Danson Cres. DA16: Well 3B **126**
Danson House **4C 126**
DANSON INTERCHANGE **5D 126**
Danson La. DA16: Well 4B **126**
Danson Mead DA16: Well 3C **126**
Danson Pk. **5C 126**
Danson Rd. DA5: Bexl, Bex 6C **126**
DA6: Bex 5D **126**
SE17 5B **102**
Danson Underpass DA15: Sidc 6C **126**
Danson Water Sports Cen. **4C 126**
Dante Pl. SE11 4B **102**
Dante Rd. SE11 4B **102**
Danube Ct. *SE15* *7F* **103**
(off Daniel Gdns.)
Danube St. SW3 5D **16** (5C **100**)
Danvers Ho. *E1* *6G* **85**
(off Christian St.)
Danvers Rd. N8 4H **47**
Danvers St. SW3 7B **16** (6B **100**)
Da Palma Ct. *SW6* *6J* **99**
(off Anselm Rd.)
Daphne Ct. KT4: Wor Pk 2A **164**
Daphne Gdns. E4 3K **35**
Daphne Ho. *N22* *1A* **48**
(off Acacia Rd.)
Daphne St. SW18 6A **118**
Daplyn St. E1 5K **9** (5G **85**)
D'Arblay St. W1 1B **12** (6G **83**)
Darby Cres. TW16: Sun 2A **148**
Darby Gdns. TW16: Sun 2A **148**
Darcy Av. SM6: Wall 4G **167**
Darcy Cl. N20 2G **31**
D'Arcy Dr. HA3: Kent 4D **42**
Darcy Gdns. HA3: Kent 4D **42**
RM9: Dag 1F **91**
Darcy Ho. *E8* *1H* **85**
(off London Flds. E. Side)
D'Arcy Pl. BR2: Brom 4J **159**
Darcy Rd. SM3: Cheam 4F **165**
SW16 2J **155**
TW7: Isle 1A **114**
Dare Ct. E10 7E **50**
Dare Gdns. RM8: Dag 3E **72**
Darell Rd. TW9: Rich 3G **115**
Darent Ho. BR1: Brom 5F **141**
NW8 *5B* **4**
(off Church St. Est.)
Darenth Rd. DA16: Well 1A **126**
N16 7F **49**
Darfield *NW1* *1G* **83**
(off Bayham St.)
Darfield Rd. SE4 5B **122**
Darfield Way W10 6F **81**
Darfur St. SW15 3F **117**
Dargate Cl. SE19 7F **139**
Darien Ho. *E1* *5K* **85**
(off Shandy St.)
Darien Rd. SW11 3B **118**
Daring Ho. *E3* *2A* **86**
(off Roman Rd.)
Dark Ho. Wlk. EC3 3G **15** (7D **84**)
Darland Lake Nature Reserve **3B 30**
Darlands Dr. EN5: Barn 5A **20**
Darlan Rd. SW6 7H **99**
Darlaston Rd. SW19 7F **135**
Darley Cl. CR0: Croy 6A **158**
Darley Dr. KT3: N Mald 2K **151**
Darley Gdns. SM4: Mord 6A **154**
Darley Ho. SE11 6G **19**
Darley Rd. N9 1A **34**
SW11 6D **118**
Darling Ho. TW1: Twick 6D **114**
Darling Rd. SE4 3C **122**
Darling Row E1 4H **85**
Darlington Ct. SE6 1H **141**
Darlington Ho. *SW8* *7H* **101**
(off Hemans St.)
Darlington Rd. SE27 5B **138**
Darmaine Cl. CR2: S Croy 7C **168**
Darnall Ho. *SE10* *1E* **122**
(off Royal Hill)
Darnaway Pl. *E14* *5E* **86**
(off Aberfeldy St.)
Darnay Ho. SE16 7K **15** (3G **103**)
Darndale Cl. E17 2B **50**
Darnley Ho. *E14* *6A* **86**
(off Camdenhurst St.)
Darnley Rd. E9 6J **67**
IG8: Wfd G 1J **51**
Darnley Ter. W11 1F **99**
Darrell Charles Ct. UB8: Uxb 7A **56**
Darrell Rd. SE22 5G **121**
Darren Cl. N4 7K **47**
Darren Ct. N7 4J **65**
Darrick Wood Rd. BR6: Orp 2H **173**
Darrick Wood School Sports Cen. **3G 173**
Darrick Wood School Sports Cen. Swimming Pool **3G 173**
Darris Cl. UB4: Yead 4C **76**
Darsley Dr. SW8 1H **119**
Dartford Av. N9 6D **24**
Dartford By-Pass DA5: Bexl, Dart 7K **127**
Dartford Gdns. RM6: Chad H 5B **54**
Dartford Ho. *SE1* *4F* **103**
(off Longfield Est.)
Dartford Rd. DA5: Bexl 1J **145**
Dartford St. SE17 6C **102**
Dartington *NW1* *1G* **83**
(off Plender St.)
Dartington Ho. *SW8* *2H* **119**
(off Union Gro.)
W2 *5K* **81**
(off Senior St.)
Dartle Ct. *SE16* *2G* **103**
(off Scott Lidgett Cres.)
Dartmoor Wlk. *E14* *4C* **104**
(off Charnwood Gdns.)
Dartmouth Cl. W11 6H **81**
Dartmouth Ct. SE10 1E **122**
Dartmouth Gro. SE10 1E **122**
Dartmouth Hill SE10 1E **122**
Dartmouth Ho. *KT2: King T* *1E* **150**
(off Seven Kings Way)
SE10 *1D* **122**
(off Catherine Gro.)
DARTMOUTH PARK 3F **65**
Dartmouth Pk. Av. NW5 3F **65**
Dartmouth Pk. Hill N19 1F **65**
NW5 3F **65**
Dartmouth Pk. Rd. NW5 4F **65**
Dartmouth Pl. SE23 2J **139**
W4 6A **98**
Dartmouth Rd. BR2: Hayes 7J **159**
HA4: Ruis 3J **57**
NW2 6F **63**
NW4 6C **44**
SE23 3H **139**
SE26 3H **139**
Dartmouth Row SE10 2E **122**
Dartmouth St. SW1 7D **12** (2H **101**)
Dartmouth Ter. SE10 1F **123**
Dartnell Rd. CR0: Croy 7F **157**
Darton Ct. W3 1J **97**
Dartrey Twr. *SW10* *7A* **100**
(off Worlds End Est.)
Dartrey Wlk. SW10 7A **100**

Dart St. W10 . . . 3G 81
Darvell Ho. *SE17* . . . 5D 102
(off Merrow St.)
Darville Rd. N16 . . . 3F 67
Darwell Cl. E6 . . . 2E 88
Darwen Pl. E2 . . . 2H 85
Darwin Cl. BR6: Farnb . . . 5H 173
N11 . . . 3A 32
Darwin Ct. E13 . . . 3K 87
NW1 . . . 1F 83
SE17 . . . 4D 102
(off Barlow St.)
Darwin Dr. UB1: S'hall . . . 6F 77
Darwin Ho. SW1 . . . 7A 18
Darwin Rd. DA16: Well . . . 3K 125
N22 . . . 1B 48
W5 . . . 5C 96
Darwin St. SE17 . . . 4D 102
(not continuous)
Daryngton Dr. UB6: G'frd . . . 2H 77
Daryngton Ho. *SE1* . . . 7F 15
(off Manciple St.)
SW8 . . . 7J 101
(off Hartington Rd.)
Dashwood Cl. DA6: Bex . . . 5G 127
Dashwood Rd. N8 . . . 6K 47
Dassett Rd. SE27 . . . 5B 138
Data Point Bus. Cen. E16 . . . 4F 87
Datchelor Pl. SE5 . . . 1D 120
Datchet Ho. *NW1* . . . 1K 5
(off Augustus St.)
Datchet Rd. SE6 . . . 2B 140
Datchworth Ct. EN1: Enf . . . 5K 23
Datchworth Ho. *N1* . . . 7B 66
(off The Sutton Est.)
Date St. SE17 . . . 5D 102
Daubeney Gdns. N17 . . . 7H 33
Daubeney Rd. E5 . . . 4A 68
N17 . . . 7H 33
Daubeney Twr. *SE8* . . . 5B 104
(off Bowditch)
Dault Rd. SW18 . . . 6A 118
Dauncey Ho. SE1 . . . 7A 14
Davema Cl. BR7: Chst . . . 1E 160
Davenant Rd. CR0: Croy . . . 4B 168
N19 . . . 2H 65
Davenant St. E1 . . . 5G 85
Davenport Cen. IG11: Bark . . . 1B 90
Davenport Cl. TW11: Tedd . . . 6A 132
Davenport Ho. *SE11* . . . 3J 19
(off Walnut Tree Wlk.)
Davenport Lodge
TW5: Hest . . . 7C 94
Davenport Rd. DA14: Sidc . . . 2E 144
SE6 . . . 6D 122
Daventer Dr. HA7: Stan . . . 7E 26
Daventry Av. E17 . . . 6C 50
Daventry St. NW1 . . . 5C 4 (5C 82)
Daver Ct. SW3 . . . 5D 16 (5C 100)
W5 . . . 4D 78
Davern Cl. SE10 . . . 4H 105
Davey Cl. N7 . . . 6K 65
N13 . . . 5E 32
Davey Rd. E9 . . . 7C 68
Davey's Ct. WC2 . . . 2E 12
Davey St. SE15 . . . 6F 103
David Av. UB6: G'frd . . . 3J 77
David Beckham Academy, The . . . 2H 105
David Cl. UB3: Harl . . . 7G 93
David Coffer Ct. DA17: Belv . . . 4H 109
David Ct. N20 . . . 3F 31
Davidge Ho. *SE1* . . . 7K 13
(off Coral St.)
Davidge St. SE1 . . . 7A 14 (2B 102)
David Hewitt Ho. *E3* . . . 5D 86
(off Watts Gro.)
David Ho. DA15: Sidc . . . 3A 144
SW8 . . . 7J 101
(off Wyvil Rd.)
David Lean Cinema . . . 3C 168
(in Clocktower)
David Lee Point *E15* . . . 1G 87
(off Leather Gdns.)
David Lloyd Leisure
Barnet . . . 7G 31
Cheam . . . 7F 165
Ealing . . . 5H 59
Enfield . . . 2B 24
Epping Forest . . . 1J 37
Hounslow . . . 5A 94
Kidbrooke . . . 4K 123
Kingston upon Thames . . . 2E 150
(in The Rotunda Cen.)
Merton . . . 3F 153
Sidcup . . . 5C 144
South Kensington . . . 4K 99
(in Point West)
David M. W1 . . . 5F 5 (5D 82)
David Rd. RM8: Dag . . . 2E 72
David's Ct. *UB1: S'hall* . . . 6G 77
(off Whitecote Rd.)
Davidson Gdns. SW8 . . . 7J 101
Davidson La. HA1: Harr . . . 7K 41
Davidson Rd. CR0: Croy . . . 1E 168
Davidson Terraces *E7* . . . 5K 69
(off Claremont Rd., not continuous)
David's Rd. SE23 . . . 1J 139
David St. E15 . . . 6F 69
David Twigg Cl. KT2: King T . . . 1E 150
Davies Cl. CR0: Croy . . . 6G 157
Davies La. E11 . . . 2G 69
Davies M. W1 . . . 2J 11 (7F 83)
Davies St. W1 . . . 1J 11 (6F 83)
Davies Wlk. TW7: Isle . . . 1H 113
Da Vinci Ct. *SE16* . . . 5H 103
(off Rossetti Rd.)
Davington Gdns.
RM8: Dag . . . 5B 72
Davington Rd. RM8: Dag . . . 6B 72
Davinia Cl. IG8: Wfd G . . . 6J 37
Davis Ho. *W12* . . . 7D 80
(off White City Est.)
Davis Rd. KT9: Chess . . . 4G 163
W3 . . . 1B 98
Davis St. E13 . . . 2K 87
Davisville Rd. W12 . . . 2C 98
Davmor Ct. TW8: Bford . . . 5C 96
Dawes Av. TW7: Isle . . . 5A 114
Dawes Ho. *SE17* . . . 4D 102
(off Orb St.)
Dawes Rd. SW6 . . . 7G 99
UB10: Uxb . . . 2A 74
Dawes St. SE17 . . . 5D 102
Dawley Av. UB8: Hil . . . 5E 74
Dawley Pde. UB3: Hayes . . . 7E 74
Dawley Pk. UB3: Hayes . . . 2F 93
Dawley Rd. UB3: Harl, Hayes . . . 7E 74
Dawlish Av. N13 . . . 4D 32
SW18 . . . 2K 135
UB6: G'frd . . . 2A 78
Dawlish Dr. HA4: Ruis . . . 2J 57
HA5: Pinn . . . 5C 40
IG3: Ilf . . . 4J 71
Dawlish Rd. E10 . . . 1E 68
N17 . . . 3G 49
NW2 . . . 6F 63
Dawnay Gdns. SW18 . . . 2B 136
Dawnay Rd. SW18 . . . 2A 136
Dawn Cl. TW4: Houn . . . 3C 112
Dawn Cres. E15 . . . 1F 87
Dawpool Rd. NW2 . . . 2B 62
Daws Hill E4 . . . 2K 25
Daws La. NW7 . . . 5G 29
Dawson Av. IG11: Bark . . . 7J 71
Dawson Cl. SE18 . . . 4G 107
UB3: Hayes . . . 5F 75
Dawson Gdns. IG11: Bark . . . 7K 71
Dawson Ho. *E2* . . . 3J 85
(off Sceptre Rd.)
Dawson Pl. W2 . . . 7J 81
Dawson Rd. KT1: King T . . . 3F 151
NW2 . . . 5E 62
Dawson St. E2 . . . 1K 9 (2F 85)
Dawson Ter. N9 . . . 7D 24
Dax Ct. TW16: Sun . . . 3A 148
Daybrook Rd. SW19 . . . 2K 153
Day Ho. *SE5* . . . 7C 102
(off Bethwin Rd.)
Daylesford Av. SW15 . . . 4C 116
Daymer Gdns. HA5: Eastc . . . 4K 39
Daynor Ho. *NW6* . . . 1J 81
(off Quex Ho.)
Daysbrook Rd. SW2 . . . 1K 137
Days La. DA15: Sidc . . . 7J 125
Dayton Gro. SE15 . . . 1J 121
Deaconess Ct. *N15* . . . 4F 49
(off Tottenham Grn. E.)
Deacon Est., The E4 . . . 6G 35
Deacon Ho. *SE11* . . . 4H 19
(off Black Prince Rd.)
Deacon M. N1 . . . 7D 66
Deacon Rd. KT2: King T . . . 1F 151
NW2 . . . 5C 62
Deacons Cl. HA5: Pinn . . . 2K 39
Deacons Ct. TW1: Twick . . . 2K 131
Deacons Leas BR6: Orp . . . 4H 173
Deacon's Ri. N2 . . . 5B 46
Deacons Ter. *N1* . . . 6C 66
(off Harecourt Rd.)
Deacons Wlk. TW12: Hamp . . . 4E 130
Deacon Way IG8: Wfd G . . . 7J 37
SE17 . . . 4C 102
Deal Ct. *NW9* . . . 2B 44
(off Hazel Cl.)
UB1: S'hall . . . 6G 77
(off Haldane Rd.)
Deal Ho. *SE15* . . . 6K 103
(off Lovelinch La.)
SE17 . . . 5E 102
(off Mina Rd.)
Deal M. W5 . . . 4D 96
Deal Porters Wlk. SE16 . . . 2K 103
Deal Porters Way SE16 . . . 3J 103
Deal Rd. SW17 . . . 6E 136
Deal's Gateway SE10 . . . 1C 122
Deal St. E1 . . . 5G 85
Dealtry Rd. SW15 . . . 4E 116
Deal Wlk. SW9 . . . 7A 102
Dean Abbott Ho. *SW1* . . . 3C 18
(off Vincent St.)
Dean Bradley St. SW1 . . . 2E 18 (3J 101)
Dean Cl. E9 . . . 5J 67
SE16 . . . 1K 103
UB10: Hil . . . 7B 56
Dean Ct. HA0: Wemb . . . 3B 60
HA8: Edg . . . 6C 28
RM7: Rom . . . 5K 55
SW8 . . . 7J 101
(off Thorncroft St.)
W3 . . . 6K 79
Deancross St. E1 . . . 6J 85
Dean Dr. HA7: Stan . . . 2E 42
Deane Av. HA4: Ruis . . . 5A 58
Deane Ct. HA6: Nwood . . . 1G 39
Deane Cft. Rd. HA5: Eastc . . . 6A 40
Deanery Cl. N2 . . . 4C 46
Deanery M. W1 . . . 4H 11
Deanery Rd. E15 . . . 6G 69
Deanery St. W1 . . . 4H 11 (1E 100)
Deane Way HA4: Ruis . . . 6K 39
Dean Farrar St. SW1 . . . 1D 18 (3H 101)
Deanfield Gdns.
CR0: Croy . . . 4D 168
Dean Gdns. E17 . . . 4F 51
Deanhill Ct. SW14 . . . 4H 115
Deanhill Rd. SW14 . . . 4H 115
Dean Ho. *E1* . . . 6J 85
(off Tarling St.)
SE14 . . . 7A 104
(off New Cross Rd.)
Dean Rd. CR0: Croy . . . 4D 168
NW2 . . . 6E 62
SE28 . . . 1A 108
TW3: Houn . . . 5F 113
TW12: Hamp . . . 5E 130
Dean Ryle St. SW1 . . . 3E 18 (4J 101)
Deansbrook Cl. HA8: Edg . . . 7D 28
Deansbrook Rd. HA8: Edg . . . 7C 28
Dean's Bldgs. SE17 . . . 4D 102
Deans Cl. CR0: Croy . . . 3F 169
HA8: Edg . . . 6D 28
W4 . . . 6H 97
Dean's Ct. EC4 . . . 1B 14 (6B 84)
Deanscroft Av. NW9 . . . 1J 61
Deans Dr. HA8: Edg . . . 5E 28
N13 . . . 6G 33
Deans Ga. Cl. SE23 . . . 3K 139
Deanshanger Ho. *SE8* . . . 4K 103
(off Chilton Gro.)
Deans La. HA8: Edg . . . 6D 28
W4 . . . 6H 97
(off Deans Cl.)
Dean's M. W1 . . . 7K 5 (6F 83)
Deans Rd. SM1: Sutt . . . 3K 165
W7 . . . 1K 95
Dean Stanley St. SW1 . . . 2E 18 (3J 101)
Deanston Wharf E16 . . . 2K 105
Dean St. E7 . . . 5J 69
W1 . . . 7C 6 (6H 83)
Deans Way HA8: Edg . . . 5D 28
Deansway N2 . . . 4B 46
N9 . . . 3K 33
Deanswood N11 . . . 6C 32
Dean's Yd. SW1 . . . 1D 18
Dean Trench St. SW1 . . . 2E 18 (3J 101)
Dean Wlk. HA8: Edg . . . 6D 28
Dean Way UB2: S'hall . . . 2F 95
Dearne Cl. HA7: Stan . . . 5F 27
Dearn Gdns. CR4: Mitc . . . 3C 154
Dearsley Ho. RM13: Rain . . . 2K 91
Dearsley Rd. EN1: Enf . . . 3B 24
Deason St. E15 . . . 1E 86
Deauville Ct. *SE16* . . . 2K 103
(off Eleanor Cl.)
SW4 . . . 6G 119
De Barowe M. N5 . . . 4B 66
Debdale Ho. *E2* . . . 1G 85
(off Whiston Rd.)
Debden *N17* . . . 2D 48
(off Gloucester Rd.)
Debden Cl. IG8: Wfd G . . . 7G 37
KT2: King T . . . 5D 132
NW9 . . . 1A 44
De Beauvoir Ct. *N1* . . . 7D 66
(off Northchurch Rd.)
De Beauvoir Cres. N1 . . . 1E 84
De Beauvoir Est. N1 . . . 1E 84
De Beauvoir Pl. N1 . . . 6E 66
De Beauvoir Rd. N1 . . . 1E 84
De Beauvoir Sq. N1 . . . 7E 66
DE BEAUVOIR TOWN . . . 1E 84
Debenham Ct. *E8* . . . 1G 85
(off Pownall Rd.)
Debham Ct. NW2 . . . 3E 62
Debnams Rd. SE16 . . . 4J 103
De Bohun Av. N14 . . . 6A 22
Deborah Cl. TW7: Isle . . . 1J 113
Deborah Ct. *E18* . . . 3K 51
(off Victoria Rd.)
Deborah Cres. HA4: Ruis . . . 7F 39
Deborah Lodge HA8: Edg . . . 1H 43
Debrabant Cl. DA8: Erith . . . 6K 109
De Brome Rd. TW13: Felt . . . 1A 130
De Bruin Ct. *E14* . . . 5E 104
(off Ferry St.)
Deburgh Rd. SW19 . . . 7A 136
Debussy NW9 . . . 2B 44
Decima St. SE1 . . . 7G 15 (3E 102)
Decimus Cl. CR7: Thor H . . . 4D 156
Deck Cl. SE16 . . . 1K 103
Decoy Av. NW11 . . . 5G 45
De Crespigny Pk. SE5 . . . 2D 120
Dee Ct. *W7* . . . 6H 77
(off Hobbayne Rd.)
Dee Ho. *KT2: King T* . . . 1D 150
(off May Bate Av.)
Deeley Rd. SW8 . . . 1H 119
Deena Cl. W3 . . . 6F 79
Deen City Farm . . . 2A 154
Deepdale SW19 . . . 4F 135
Deepdale Av. BR2: Brom . . . 4H 159
Deepdale Cl. N11 . . . 6K 31

Deepdale Ct.—Densham Rd.

Deepdale Ct. *CR0: Croy* 4D **168**
(*off Birdhurst Av.*)
Deep Dene W5 ....4F **79**
Deepdene Av. CR0: Croy 3F **169**
Deepdene Cl. E11 ....4J **51**
Deepdene Ct. BR2: Brom 3G **159**
N21 ....6G **23**
Deepdene Gdns. SW2 ....7K **119**
Deepdene Point SE23 ....3K **139**
Deepdene Rd. DA16: Well 3A **126**
SE5 ....4D **120**
Deepwell Cl. TW7: Isle 1A **114**
Deepwood La. UB6: G'frd 3H **77**
Deerbrook Rd. SE24 ....1B **138**
Deerdale Rd. SE24 ....4C **120**
Deerfield Cl. NW9 ....5B **44**
Deerfield Cotts. NW9 ....5B **44**
Deerhurst Cl. TW13: Felt 4K **129**
Deerhurst Cres. TW12: Ham H 5G **131**
Deerhurst Ho. *SE15* 6G **103**
(*off Haymerle Rd.*)
Deerhurst Rd. NW2 ....6F **63**
SW16 ....5K **137**
Deerings Dr. HA5: Eastc 5J **39**
Deerleap Gro. E4 ....5J **25**
Dee Rd. TW9: Rich 4F **115**
Deer Pk. Cl. KT2: King T 7H **133**
Deer Pk. Gdns. CR4: Mitc 4B **154**
Deer Pk. Rd. SW19 ....2K **153**
Deer Pk. Way BR4: W W'ck 2H **171**
Deeside Rd. SW17 ....3B **136**
Dee St. E14 ....6E **86**
Defence Cl. SE28 ....1J **107**
Defiance Wlk. SE18 ....3D **106**
Defiant *NW9* 2B **44**
(*off Further Acre*)
Defiant Way SM6: Wall 7J **167**
Defoe Av. TW9: Kew 7G **97**
Defoe Cl. SE16 ....2B **104**
SW17 ....6C **136**
Defoe Ho. EC2 ....5D **8**
Defoe Pl. *EC2* 5C **8**
(*off Beech St.*)
SW17 ....4D **136**
Defoe Rd. N16 ....3E **66**
De Frene Rd. SE26 ....4K **139**
Degema Rd. BR7: Chst 5F **143**
Dehar Cres. NW9 ....7B **44**
De Havilland Cl. SM6: Wall 7H **167**
UB5: Yead 3B **76**
De Havilland Rd. HA8: Edg 2G **43**
TW5: Hest 7A **94**
De Havilland Way TW19: Stanw 6A **110**
Dekker Ho. *SE5* 7D **102**
(*off Elmington Est.*)
Dekker Rd. SE21 ....6E **120**
Delacourt Rd. SE3 ....7K **105**
Delafield Ho. *E1* 6G **85**
(*off Christian St.*)
Delafield Rd. SE7 ....5K **105**
Delaford Rd. SE16 ....5H **103**
Delaford St. SW6 ....7G **99**
Delamare Cres. CR0: Croy 6J **157**
Delamere Ct. E17 ....2E **50**
Delamere Gdns. NW7 ....6E **28**
Delamere Rd. SW20 ....1F **153**
UB4: Yead 7B **76**
W5 ....2E **96**
Delamere St. W2 ....5K **81**
Delamere Ter. W2 ....5K **81**
Delancey Pas. *NW1* 1F **83**
(*off Delancey St.*)
Delancey St. NW1 ....1F **83**
Delancey Studios NW1 ....1F **83**
Delany Ho. *SE10* 6E **104**
(*off Thames St.*)
Delarch Ho. SE1 ....7A **14**
De Laune St. SE17 ....6K **19** (5B **102**)
Delaware Mans. *W9* 4K **81**
(*off Delaware Rd.*)
Delaware Rd. W9 ....4K **81**
Delawyk Cres. SE24 ....6C **120**
Delcombe Av. KT4: Wor Pk 1E **164**
Delderfield Ho. *RM1: Rom* 2K **55**
(*off Portnoi Cl.*)
Delfina Studio Trust **6G 15**
(***off Bermondsey St.***)
Delft Ho. *KT2: King T* 7F **133**
(*off Acre Rd.*)
Delft Way SE22 ....5E **120**
Delhi Rd. EN1: Enf 7A **24**
Delhi St. N1 ....1J **83**
(not continuous)
Delia St. SW18 ....7K **117**
Delisle Rd. SE28 ....2J **107**
(not continuous)
Delius Gro. E15 ....2F **87**
Dell, The DA5: Bexl 1K **145**
HA0: Wemb 5B **60**
HA5: Pinn 2B **40**
IG8: Wfd G 3E **36**
SE2 ....5A **108**
SE19 ....1F **157**
TW8: Bford 6C **96**
TW14: Felt 7K **111**
Della Path E5 ....3G **67**
Dellbow Rd. TW14: Felt 5K **111**
Dell Cl. E15 ....1F **87**
IG8: Wfd G 3E **36**
SM6: Wall 4G **167**
Dell Farm Rd. HA4: Ruis 5F **39**
Dellfield Cl. BR3: Beck 1E **158**
Dell La. KT17: Ewe 5C **164**
Dellors Cl. EN5: Barn 5A **20**
Dellow Cl. IG2: Ilf 7H **53**
Dellow Ho. *E1* 7H **85**
(*off Dellow St.*)
Dellow St. E1 ....7H **85**
Dell Rd. KT17: Ewe 6C **164**
UB7: W Dray 4B **92**
Dells Cl. E4 ....7J **25**
TW11: Tedd 6K **131**
Dell's M. SW1 ....4B **18**
Dell Wlk. KT3: N Mald 2A **152**
Dell Way W13 ....6C **78**
Dellwood Gdns. IG5: Ilf 3E **52**
Delmare Cl. SW9 ....4K **119**
Delme Cres. SE3 ....2K **123**
Delmerend Ho. *SW3* 5C **16**
(*off Ixworth Pl.*)
Delmey Cl. CR0: Croy 3F **169**
Deloraine Ho. SE8 ....1C **122**
Delorme St. W6 ....6F **99**
Delroy Ct. N20 ....7F **21**
Delta Bldg. *E14* 6E **86**
(*off Ashton St.*)
Delta Cen. HA0: Wemb 1F **79**
Delta Cl. KT4: Wor Pk 3B **164**
Delta Ct. NW2 ....2C **62**
Delta Gro. UB5: N'olt 3B **76**
Delta Pk. SW18 ....4K **117**
Delta Pk. Ind. Est. EN3: Brim 3G **25**
Delta Point *CR0: Croy* 1C **168**
(*off Wellesley Rd.*)
E2 ....3G **85**
(*off Delta St.*)
Delta Rd. KT4: Wor Pk 3A **164**
Delta St. E2 ....3G **85**
De Luci Rd. DA8: Erith 5J **109**
De Lucy St. SE2 ....4B **108**
Delvan Cl. SE18 ....7E **106**
Delvers Mead RM10: Dag 4J **73**
Delverton Ho. *SE17* 5B **102**
(*off Delverton Rd.*)
Delverton Rd. SE17 ....5B **102**
Delvino Rd. SW6 ....1J **117**
Demesne Rd. SM6: Wall 4H **167**
Demeta Cl. HA9: Wemb 3J **61**
De Montfort Pde. SW16 ....3J **137**
De Montfort Rd. SW16 ....3J **137**
De Morgan Rd. SW6 ....3K **117**
Dempster Cl. KT6: Surb 1C **162**
Dempster Rd. SW18 ....5A **118**
Den, The **5J 103**
Denbar Pde. RM7: Mawney 4J **55**
Denberry Dr. DA14: Sidc 3B **144**
Denbigh Cl. BR7: Chst 6D **142**
HA4: Ruis 2H **57**
NW10 ....7A **62**
SM1: Sutt 5H **165**
UB1: S'hall 6D **76**
W11 ....7H **81**
Denbigh Ct. E6 ....3B **88**
W7 ....5K **77**
(*off Copley Cl.*)
Denbigh Dr. UB3: Harl 2E **92**
Denbigh Gdns. TW10: Rich 5F **115**
Denbigh Ho. *SW1* 1F **17**
(*off Hans Pl.*)
W11 ....7H **81**
(*off Westbourne Gro.*)
Denbigh M. SW1 ....4A **18**
Denbigh Pl. SW1 ....5A **18** (5G **101**)
Denbigh Rd. E6 ....3B **88**
TW3: Houn 2F **113**
UB1: S'hall 6D **76**
W11 ....7H **81**
W13 ....7B **78**
Denbigh St. SW1 ....4A **18** (4G **101**)
(not continuous)
Denbigh Ter. W11 ....7H **81**
Denbridge Rd. BR1: Brom 2D **160**
Denby Ct. SE11 ....3H **19**
Dence Ho. *E2* 2K **9**
(*off Turin St.*)
Denchworth Ho. SW9 ....2A **120**
Dencliffe TW15: Ashf 5C **128**
Den Cl. BR3: Beck 3F **159**
Dene, The CR0: Croy 4K **169**
HA9: Wemb 4E **60**
KT8: W Mole 5D **148**
W13 ....5B **78**
Dene Av. DA15: Sidc 7B **126**
TW3: Houn 3D **112**
Dene Cl. BR2: Hayes 1H **171**
DA2: Dart 4K **145**
KT4: Wor Pk 2B **164**
SE4 ....3A **122**
Dene Ct. *CR2: S Croy* 5C **168**
(*off Warham Rd.*)
W5 ....5C **78**
Denecroft Cres. UB10: Hil 1D **74**
Dene Gdns. HA7: Stan 5H **27**
KT7: T Ditt 2A **162**
Dene Ho. N14 ....7C **22**
Denehurst Gdns. IG8: Wfd G 4E **36**
NW4 ....6E **44**
TW2: Twick 7H **113**
TW10: Rich 4G **115**
W3 ....1H **97**
Dene Rd. IG9: Buck H 1G **37**
N11 ....1J **31**
Denesmead SE24 ....5C **120**
Denewood EN5: New Bar 5F **21**
Denewood Rd. N6 ....6D **46**
Denford St. *SE10* 5H **105**
(*off Glenforth St.*)
Dengie Wlk. *N1* 1C **84**
(*off Basire St.*)
Denham Cl. DA16: Well 3C **126**
Denham Ct. *SE26* 3H **139**
(*off Kirkdale*)
UB1: S'hall 7G **77**
(*off Baird Av.*)
Denham Cres. CR4: Mitc 4D **154**
Denham Dr. IG2: Ilf 6G **53**
Denham Ho. *W12* 7D **80**
(*off White City Est.*)
Denham Rd. N20 ....3J **31**
TW14: Felt 7A **112**
Denham St. SE10 ....5J **105**
Denham Way IG11: Bark 1J **89**
Denholme Rd. W9 ....3H **81**
Denison Cl. N2 ....3A **46**
Denison Ho. *E14* 6C **86**
(*off Farrance St.*)
Denison Rd. SW19 ....6B **136**
TW13: Felt 4H **129**
W5 ....4C **78**
Deniston Av. DA5: Bexl 1E **144**
Denis Way SW4 ....3H **119**
Denland Ho. *SW8* 7K **101**
(*off Dorset Rd.*)
Denleigh Gdns. KT7: T Ditt 6J **149**
N21 ....1F **33**
Denman Dr. KT10: Clay 5A **162**
NW11 ....5J **45**
TW15: Ashf 6D **128**
Denman Dr. Nth. NW11 ....5J **45**
Denman Dr. Sth. NW11 ....5J **45**
Denman Ho. N16 ....2E **66**
Denman Pl. W1 ....2C **12**
Denman Rd. SE15 ....1F **121**
Denman St. W1 ....3C **12** (7H **83**)
Denmark Av. SW19 ....7G **135**
Denmark Ct. SM4: Mord 6J **153**
Denmark Gdns. SM5: Cars 3D **166**
Denmark Gro. N1 ....2A **84**
DENMARK HILL **3C 120**
Denmark Hill SE5 ....1D **120**
Denmark Hill Dr. NW9 ....3C **44**
Denmark Hill Est. SE5 ....4D **120**
Denmark Mans. *SE5* 2C **120**
(*off Coldharbour La.*)
Denmark Path SE25 ....5H **157**
Denmark Pl. E3 ....3C **86**
WC2 ....7D **6** (6H **83**)
Denmark Rd. BR1: Brom 1K **159**
KT1: King T 3E **150**
N8 ....4A **48**
NW6 ....2H **81**
(not continuous)
SE5 ....1C **120**
SE25 ....5G **157**
SM5: Cars 3D **166**
SW19 ....6F **135**
TW2: Twick 3H **131**
W13 ....7B **78**
Denmark St. E11 ....3G **69**
E13 ....5K **87**
N17 ....1H **49**
WC2 ....7D **6** (6H **83**)
Denmark Ter. N2 ....3D **46**
Denmark Wlk. SE27 ....4C **138**
Denmead Ho. *SW15* 6B **116**
(*off Highcliffe Dr.*)
Denmead Rd. CR0: Croy 1B **168**
Denmore Ct. SM6: Wall 5F **167**
Dennan Rd. KT6: Surb 1F **163**
Dennard Way BR6: Farnb 4F **173**
Denner Rd. E4 ....2H **35**
Denne Ter. E8 ....1F **85**
Dennett Rd. CR0: Croy 1A **168**
Dennett's Rd. SE14 ....1J **121**
Denning Av. CR0: Wadd 4A **168**
Denning Cl. NW8 ....1A **4** (3A **82**)
TW12: Hamp 5D **130**
Denning Point *E1* 7K **9**
(*off Commercial St.*)
Denning Rd. NW3 ....4B **64**
Dennington Cl. E5 ....2J **67**
Dennington Pk. Rd. NW6 ....6J **63**
Denningtons, The KT4: Wor Pk 2A **164**
Dennis Av. HA9: Wemb 5F **61**
Dennis Cl. TW15: Ashf 7F **129**
Dennis Gdns. HA7: Stan 5H **27**
Dennis Ho. SM1: Sutt 4K **165**
Dennis La. HA7: Stan 3G **27**
Dennison Point E15 ....7E **68**
Dennis Pde. N14 ....1C **32**
Dennis Pk. Cres. SW20 ....1G **153**
Dennis Reeve Cl. CR4: Mitc 1D **154**
Dennis Rd. KT8: E Mos 4G **149**
Denny Cl. E6 ....5C **88**
Denny Cres. SE11 ....5K **19** (5A **102**)
Denny Gdns. RM9: Dag 7B **72**
Denny Rd. N9 ....1C **34**
Denny St. SE11 ....5K **19** (5A **102**)
Den Rd. BR2: Brom 3F **159**
Densham Ho. *NW8* 1B **4**
(*off Cochrane St.*)
Densham Rd. E15 ....1G **87**

Densole Cl. BR3: Beck 1A 158
Denstone Ho. SE15 ....6G 103
  (off Haymerle Rd.)
Densworth Gro. N9 ....2D 34
Dent Ho. SE17 ....4E 102
  (off Tatum St.)
Denton NW1 ....6E 64
Denton Cl. BR2: Brom 7E 160
Denton Ho. N1 ....7B 66
  (off Halton Rd.)
Denton Rd. DA5: Bexl 2K 145
  DA16: Well 7C 108
  N8 ....5K 47
  N18 ....4K 33
  TW1: Twick 6D 114
Denton St. SW18 ....6K 117
Denton Ter. DA5: Bexl 2K 145
Denton Way E5 ....3K 67
Dents Rd. SW11 ....6D 118
Denver Cl. BR6: Pet W 6J 161
Denver Rd. N16 ....7E 48
Denwood SE23 ....3K 139
Denyer St. SW3 ....4D 16 (4C 100)
Denys Ho. EC1 ....5J 7
  (off Bourne Est.)
Denziloe Av. UB10: Hil 3D 74
Denzil Rd. NW10 ....5B 62
Deodar Rd. SW15 ....4G 117
Deodora Cl. N20 ....3H 31
Depot App. NW2 ....4F 63
Depot Rd. TW3: Houn 3H 113
  W12 ....7E 80
Depot St. SE5 ....6D 102
DEPTFORD 7C 104
Deptford Bri. SE8 ....1C 122
Deptford B'way. SE8 ....1C 122
Deptford Bus. Pk. SE15 ....6J 103
Deptford Chu. St. SE8 ....6C 104
Deptford Creek Bri. SE8 ....6D 104
  (off Creek Rd.)
Deptford Ferry Rd. E14 ....4C 104
Deptford Grn. SE8 ....6C 104
Deptford High St. SE8 ....6C 104
Deptford Pk. Bus. Cen.
  SE8 ....5A 104
Deptford Strand SE8 ....4B 104
Deptford Trad. Est. SE8 ....5A 104
Deptford Wharf SE8 ....4B 104
De Quincey Ho. SW1 ....6A 18
  (off Lupus St.)
De Quincey M. E16 ....1J 105
De Quincey Rd. N17 ....1D 48
Derby Av. HA3: Hrw W 1H 41
  N12 ....5F 31
  RM7: Rom 6J 55
Derby Ga. SW1 ....6E 12 (2J 101)
  (not continuous)
Derby Hill SE23 ....2J 139
Derby Hill Cres. SE23 ....2J 139
Derby Ho. HA5: Pinn 2B 40
  SE11 ....3J 19
Derby Lodge N3 ....2H 45
  WC1 ....1G 7
  (off Britannia St.)
Derby Rd. CRO: Croy 1B 168
  E7 ....7B 70
  E9 ....1K 85
  E18 ....1H 51
  EN3: Pond E 5C 24
  KT5: Surb 1G 163
  N18 ....5D 34
  SM1: Sutt 6H 165
  SW14 ....4H 115
  SW19 ....7J 135
  TW3: Houn 4F 113
  UB6: G'frd 1F 77
Derbyshire St. E2 ....3G 85
  (not continuous)
Derby St. W1 ....5H 11 (1E 100)
Dereham Ho. SE4 ....4K 121
  (off Frendsbury Rd.)
Dereham Pl. EC2 ....2H 9 (3E 84)
Dereham Rd. IG11: Bark 5K 71

Derek Av. HA9: Wemb 7H 61
  KT19: Ewe 6G 163
  SM6: Wall 4F 167
Derek Cl. KT19: Ewe 5H 163
Derek Walcott Cl. SE24 ....5B 120
Dericote St. E8 ....1H 85
Deri Dene Cl. TW19: Stanw 6A 110
Derifall Cl. E6 ....5D 88
Dering Pl. CRO: Croy 4C 168
Dering Rd. CRO: Croy 4C 168
Dering St. W1 ....1J 11 (6F 83)
Dering Yd. W1 ....1K 11 (6F 83)
Derinton Rd. SW17 ....4D 136
Derley Rd. UB2: S'hall 3A 94
Dermody Gdns. SE13 ....5F 123
Dermody Rd. SE13 ....5F 123
Deronda Rd. SE24 ....1B 138
Deroy Cl. SM5: Cars 6D 166
Derrick Gdns. SE7 ....3A 106
Derrick Rd. BR3: Beck 3B 158
Derrycombe Ho. W2 ....5J 81
  (off Brunel Est.)
Derry Ho. NW8 ....4B 4
  (off Penfold St.)
Derry Rd. CRO: Bedd 3J 167
Derry St. W8 ....2K 99
Dersingham Av. E12 ....4D 70
Dersingham Rd. NW2 ....3G 63
Derwent NW1 ....2A 6
  (off Robert St.)
Derwent Av. EN4: E Barn 1J 31
  N18 ....5J 33
  NW7 ....6E 28
  NW9 ....5A 44
  SW15 ....4A 134
  UB10: Ick 2C 56
Derwent Cl. TW14: Felt 1H 129
Derwent Ct. SE16 ....2K 103
  (off Eleanor Cl.)
Derwent Cres. DA7: Bex 2G 127
  HA7: Stan 2C 42
  N20 ....3F 31
Derwent Dr. BR5: Pet W 7H 161
  UB4: Hayes 5G 75
Derwent Gdns. HA9: Wemb 7C 42
  IG4: Ilf 4C 52
Derwent Gro. SE22 ....4F 121
Derwent Ho. E3 ....4B 86
  (off Southern Gro.)
  KT2: King T 1D 150
  (off May Bate Av.)
  SE20 ....2H 157
  (off Derwent Rd.)
  SW7 ....3A 16
  (off Cromwell Rd.)
Derwent Lodge KT4: Wor Pk 2D 164
  TW7: Isle 2H 113
Derwent Ri. NW9 ....6A 44
Derwent Rd. N13 ....4E 32
  SE20 ....2G 157
  SW20 ....6F 153
  TW2: Whit 6F 113
  UB1: S'hall 6D 76
  W5 ....3C 96
Derwent St. SE10 ....5G 105
Derwent Wlk. SM6: Wall 7F 167
Derwentwater Rd. W3 ....1J 97
Derwent Yd. W5 ....3C 96
  (off Derwent Rd.)
De Salis Rd. UB10: Hil 4E 74
Desborough Cl. TW17: Shep 7C 146
  W2 ....5K 81
Desborough Ho. W14 ....6H 99
  (off North End Rd.)
Desborough Sailing Club
...........7D 146
Desborough St. W2 ....5K 81
  (off Cirencester St.)
Desenfans Rd. SE21 ....6E 120
Desford Cl. TW15: Ashf 2C 128
Desford Rd. E16 ....4G 87
Desford Way TW15: Ashf 2B 128
Design Mus. 6K 15 (2F 103)
Desmond Ho. EN4: E Barn 6H 21

Desmond St. SE14 ....6A 104
Desmond Tutu Dr. SE23 ....1B 140
Despard Rd. N19 ....1G 65
Dethick Ct. E3 ....1A 86
Detling Ho. SE17 ....4E 102
  (off Congreve St.)
Detling Rd. BR1: Brom 5J 141
  DA8: Erith 7K 109
Detmold Rd. E5 ....2J 67
Devalls Cl. E6 ....7F 89
Devana End SM5: Cars 3D 166
Devas Rd. SW20 ....1E 152
Devas St. E3 ....4D 86
Devenay Rd. E15 ....7H 69
Devenish Rd. SE2 ....2A 108
Deventer Cres. SE22 ....5E 120
Deveraux Cl. BR3: Beck 5E 158
De Vere Cl. SM6: Wall 7J 167
De Vere Cotts. W8 ....3A 100
  (off De Vere Gdns.)
De Vere Gdns. IG1: Ilf 2D 70
  W8 ....2A 100
Deverell St. SE1 ....3D 102
De Vere M. W8 ....3A 100
  (off De Vere Gdns.)
Devereux Ct. WC2 ....1J 13
Devereux La. SW13 ....7D 98
Devereux Rd. SW11 ....6D 118
Deveron Way RM1: Rom 1K 55
Devey Cl. KT2: King T 7B 134
Devitt Ho. E14 ....7D 86
  (off Wade's Pl.)
Devizes St. N1 ....1D 84
Devon Av. TW2: Twick 1G 131
Devon Cl. IG9: Buck H 2E 36
  N17 ....3F 49
  UB6: G'frd 1C 78
Devon Ct. TW12: Hamp 7E 130
  W7 ....5K 77
  (off Copley Cl.)
Devoncroft Gdns. TW1: Twick 7A 114
Devon Gdns. N4 ....6B 48
Devon Ho. E17 ....2B 50
Devonhurst Pl. W4 ....5K 97
Devonia Gdns. N18 ....6H 33
Devonia Rd. N1 ....2B 84
Devon Mans. HA3: Kent 5C 42
  (off Woodcock Hill)
  SE1 ....5G 15
  (off Tooley St.)
Devon Pde. HA3: Kent 5C 42
Devonport Ho. W2 ....1C 10 (6C 82)
Devonport Gdns. IG1: Ilf 6D 52
Devonport Ho. W2 ....5J 81
  (off Brunel Est.)
Devonport M. W12 ....2D 98
Devonport Rd. W12 ....1D 98
  (not continuous)
Devonport St. E1 ....6K 85
Devon Ri. N2 ....4B 46
Devon Rd. IG11: Bark 1J 89
  SM2: Cheam 7G 165
Devons Est. E3 ....3D 86
Devonshire Av. SM2: Sutt 7A 166
  N13 ....3F 33
  W1 ....5J 5 (5F 83)
Devonshire Cl. E15 ....4G 69
  N13 ....3F 33
  W1 ....5J 5 (5F 83)
Devonshire Ct. E1 ....3J 85
  (off Bancroft Rd.)
  HA5: H End 1D 40
  (off Devonshire Rd.)
  N18 ....6H 33
  WC1 ....5F 7
  (off Boswell St.)
Devonshire Cres. NW7 ....7A 30
Devonshire Dr. KT6: Surb 1D 162
  SE10 ....7D 104
Devonshire Gdns. N17 ....6H 33
  N21 ....7H 23
  W4 ....7J 97
Devonshire Gro. SE15 ....6H 103
Devonshire Hall E9 ....6J 67
  (off Frampton Pk. Rd.)

Devonshire Hill La. N17 ....6G 33
  (not continuous)
Devonshire Ho. E14 ....4C 104
  (off Westferry Rd.)
  IG8: Ilf 7K 37
  NW6 ....6H 63
  (off Kilburn High Rd.)
  SE1 ....3C 102
  (off Bath Ter.)
  SM2: Sutt 7A 166
  SW1 ....5D 18
  (off Lindsay Sq.)
Devonshire Ho. Bus. Cen.
  BR2: Brom 4K 159
  (off Devonshire Sq.)
Devonshire M. N13 ....4F 33
  SW10 ....7A 16
  (off Park Wlk.)
  W4 ....5A 98
Devonshire M. Nth. W1 ....5J 5 (5F 83)
Devonshire M. Sth. W1 ....5J 5 (5F 83)
Devonshire Pas. W4 ....5A 98
Devonshire Pl. NW2 ....3J 63
  W1 ....4H 5 (4E 82)
  W8 ....3K 99
Devonshire Pl. M. W1 ....4H 5 (5E 82)
Devonshire Rd. BR6: Orp 7K 161
  CRO: Croy 7D 156
  DA6: Bex 4E 126
  E16 ....6K 87
  E17 ....6C 50
  HA1: Harr 6H 41
  HA5: Eastc 6A 40
  HA5: H End 1D 40
  IG2: Ilf 7H 53
  N9 ....1D 34
  N13 ....4E 32
  N17 ....6H 33
  NW7 ....7A 30
  SE9 ....2C 142
  SE23 ....1J 139
  SM2: Sutt 7A 166
  SM5: Cars 4E 166
  SW19 ....7C 136
  TW13: Hanw 3C 130
  UB1: S'hall 5E 76
  W4 ....5A 98
  W5 ....3C 96
Devonshire Road Nature Reserve
...........7K 121
Devonshire Row EC2 ....6H 9 (5E 84)
Devonshire Row M. W1 ....4K 5
Devonshire Sq. BR2: Brom 4K 159
  EC2 ....6H 9 (6E 84)
Devonshire St. W1 ....5H 5 (5E 82)
  W4 ....5A 98
Devonshire Ter. W2 ....6A 82
Devonshire Way CRO: Croy 2A 170
  UB4: Yead 6K 75
Devon Rd. E3 ....3D 86
Devon St. SE15 ....6H 103
  KT19: Ewe 5H 163
  UB10: Hil 2B 74
Devon Waye TW5: Hest 7D 94
Devon Wharf E14 ....5E 86
De Walden Ho. NW8 ....2C 82
  (off Allitsen Rd.)
De Walden St. W1 ....6H 5 (5E 82)
Dewar St. SE15 ....3G 121
Dewberry Gdns. E6 ....5C 88
Dewberry St. E14 ....5E 86
Dewey La. SW2 ....6A 120
  (off Tulse Hill)
Dewey Rd. N1 ....2A 84
  RM10: Dag 6H 73
Dewey St. SW17 ....5D 136
Dewhurst Rd. W14 ....3F 99
Dewsbury Cl. HA5: Pinn 6C 40
Dewsbury Ct. W4 ....4J 97
Dewsbury Gdns. KT4: Wor Pk 3C 164
Dewsbury Rd. NW10 ....5C 62
Dewsbury Ter. NW1 ....1F 83

Dexter Ho. DA18: Erith . . . 3E 108
(off Kale Rd.)
Dexter Rd. EN5: Barn . . . 6A 20
Deyncourt Rd. N17 . . . 1C 48
Deynecourt Gdns. E11 . . . 4A 52
D'Eynsford Rd. SE5 . . . 1D 120
Dhonau Ho. SE1 . . . 4F 103
(off Longfield Est.)
Diadem Ct. W1 . . . 7C 6
Dial Wlk., The W8 . . . 2K 99
(off The Broad Wlk.)
Diameter Rd. BR5: Pet W . . . 7F 161
Diamond Cl. RM8: Dag . . . 1C 72
Diamond Est. SW17 . . . 3C 136
Diamond Ho. E3 . . . 2A 86
(off Roman Rd.)
Diamond Rd. HA4: Ruis . . . 4B 58
Diamond St. NW10 . . . 7K 61
SE15 . . . 7E 102
Diamond Ter. SE10 . . . 1E 122
Diamond Way SE8 . . . 6C 104
Diana Cl. DA14: Sidc . . . 2E 144
E18 . . . 1K 51
SE8 . . . 6B 104
Diana Gdns. KT6: Surb . . . 2F 163
Diana Ho. SW13 . . . 1B 116
Diana, Princess of Wales Memorial Walk
. . . 1K 99
(in Kensington Gdns.)
Diana Rd. E17 . . . 3B 50
Dianne Ct. SE12 . . . 1J 141
Dianne Way EN4: E Barn . . . 4H 21
Dianthus Cl. SE2 . . . 5B 108
Dibden Ho. SE5 . . . 7E 102
Dibden St. N1 . . . 1C 84
Dibdin Cl. SM1: Sutt . . . 3J 165
Dibdin Ho. W9 . . . 2K 81
Dibdin Rd. SM1: Sutt . . . 3J 165
Dicey Av. NW2 . . . 4E 62
Dickens Av. N3 . . . 1A 46
UB8: Hil . . . 6D 74
Dickens Cl. DA8: Erith . . . 7H 109
TW10: Ham . . . 2E 132
UB3: Harl . . . 4G 93
Dickens Ct. E11 . . . 4J 51
(off Makepeace Rd.)
Dickens Dr. BR7: Chst . . . 6G 143
Dickens Est. SE1 . . . 2G 103
SE16 . . . 3G 103
Dickens House . . . 4G 7
Dickens Ho. NW6 . . . 3J 81
(off Malvern Rd.)
NW8 . . . 3B 4
SE17 . . . 5B 102
(off Doddington Gro.)
WC1 . . . 3E 6
Dickens La. N18 . . . 5K 33
Dickens M. EC1 . . . 5A 8
(off Turnmill St.)
Dickenson Cl. N9 . . . 1B 34
Dickenson Ho. N8 . . . 6K 47
Dickenson Rd. N8 . . . 7J 47
TW13: Hanw . . . 5A 130
Dickensons La. SE25 . . . 5G 157
(not continuous)
Dickensons Pl. SE25 . . . 6G 157
Dickens Ri. IG7: Chig . . . 3K 37
Dickens Rd. E6 . . . 2B 88
Dickens Sq. SE1 . . . 7D 14 (3C 102)
Dickens St. SW8 . . . 2F 119
Dickenswood Cl. SE19 . . . 7B 138
Dickerage La. KT3: N Mald . . . 3J 151
Dickerage Rd. KT1: King T . . . 1J 151
KT3: N Mald . . . 1J 151
Dickinson Ct. EC1 . . . 3B 8
(off Brewhouse Yd.)
Dicksee Ho. NW8 . . . 4A 4
(off Lyons Pl.)
Dickson Fold HA5: Pinn . . . 4B 40
Dickson Ho. E1 . . . 6H 85
(off Philpot St.)
Dickson Rd. SE9 . . . 3C 124
Dick Turpin Way TW14: Felt . . . 4H 111
Didsbury Cl. E6 . . . 1D 88
Dieppe Cl. W14 . . . 5H 99
Digby Bus. Cen. E9 . . . 6K 67
(off Digby Rd.)
Digby Cres. N4 . . . 2C 66
Digby Gdns. RM10: Dag . . . 1G 91
Digby Mans. W6 . . . 5D 98
(off Hammersmith Bri. Rd.)
Digby Pl. CR0: Croy . . . 3F 169
Digby Rd. E9 . . . 6K 67
IG11: Bark . . . 7K 71
Digby St. E2 . . . 3J 85
Diggon St. E1 . . . 5K 85
Dighton Ct. SE5 . . . 6C 102
Dighton Rd. SW18 . . . 5A 118
Dignum St. N1 . . . 2A 84
Digswell St. N7 . . . 6A 66
Dilhorne Cl. SE12 . . . 3K 141
Dilke St. SW3 . . . 7F 17 (6D 100)
Dilloway La. UB2: S'hall . . . 2C 94
Dillwyn Cl. SE26 . . . 4A 140
Dilston Cl. UB5: Yead . . . 3A 76
Dilston Gro. SE16 . . . 4J 103
Dilton Gdns. SW15 . . . 1C 134
Dilwyn Ct. E17 . . . 2A 50
Dimes Pl. W6 . . . 4D 98
Dimmock Dr. UB6: G'frd . . . 5H 59
Dimond Cl. E7 . . . 4J 69
Dimsdale Dr. EN1: Enf . . . 7B 24
NW9 . . . 1J 61
Dimsdale Wlk. E13 . . . 2J 87
Dimson Cres. E3 . . . 3C 86
Dinerman Ct. NW8 . . . 1A 82
Dingle, The UB10: Hil . . . 3D 74
Dingle Gdns. E14 . . . 7C 86
Dingle Rd. TW15: Ashf . . . 5D 128
Dingles Ct. HA5: Pinn . . . 1B 40
Dingley La. SW16 . . . 2H 137
Dingley Pl. EC1 . . . 1D 8 (3C 84)
Dingley Rd. EC1 . . . 2C 8 (3C 84)
Dingwall Av. CR0: Croy . . . 2C 168
Dingwall Gdns. NW11 . . . 6J 45
Dingwall Rd. CR0: Croy . . . 1D 168
SM5: Cars . . . 7D 166
SW18 . . . 7A 118
Dinmont Est. E2 . . . 2G 85
Dinmont Ho. E2 . . . 2G 85
(off Pritchard's Rd.)
Dinmont St. E2 . . . 2H 85
Dinmore Ho. E9 . . . 1J 85
(off Templecombe Rd.)
Dinnington Ho. E1 . . . 4H 85
(off Coventry Rd.)
Dinsdale Gdns. EN5: New Bar . . . 5E 20
SE25 . . . 5E 156
Dinsdale Rd. SE3 . . . 6H 105
Dinsmore Rd. SW12 . . . 7F 119
Dinton Ho. NW8 . . . 3D 4
(off Lilestone St.)
Dinton Rd. KT2: King T . . . 7F 133
SW19 . . . 6B 136
Diploma Av. N2 . . . 4C 46
Diploma Ct. N2 . . . 4C 46
Diprose Lodge SW17 . . . 4B 136
Dirleton Rd. E15 . . . 1H 87
Disbrowe Rd. W6 . . . 6G 99
Discovery Bus. Pk.
SE16 . . . 3G 103
(off St James's Rd.)
Discovery Ho. E14 . . . 7E 86
(off Newby Pl.)
Discovery Wlk. E1 . . . 1H 103
Dishforth La. NW9 . . . 7F 29
Disley Ct. UB1: S'hall . . . 6F 77
(off Howard Rd.)
Disney Pl. SE1 . . . 6D 14 (2C 102)
Disney St. SE1 . . . 6D 14 (2C 102)
Dison Cl. EN3: Enf H . . . 1E 24
Disraeli Cl. SE28 . . . 1C 108
W4 . . . 3K 97
Disraeli Gdns. SW15 . . . 4H 117
Disraeli Rd. E7 . . . 6J 69
NW10 . . . 2K 79
Disraeli Rd. SW15 . . . 4G 117
W5 . . . 1D 96
Diss St. E2 . . . 1J 9 (3F 85)
Distaff La. EC4 . . . 2C 14 (7C 84)
Distillery La. W6 . . . 5E 98
Distillery Rd. W6 . . . 5E 98
Distillery Wlk. TW8: Bford . . . 6E 96
Distin St. SE11 . . . 4J 19 (4A 102)
District Rd. HA0: Wemb . . . 5B 60
Ditch All. SE13 . . . 1D 122
Ditchburn St. E14 . . . 7E 86
Ditchfield Rd. UB4: Yead . . . 4C 76
Ditchley Ct. W7 . . . 5K 77
(off Templeman Rd.)
Dittisham Rd. SE9 . . . 4C 142
Ditton Cl. KT7: T Ditt . . . 7A 150
Dittoncroft Cl. CR0: Croy . . . 4E 168
Ditton Grange Cl. KT6: Surb . . . 1D 162
Ditton Grange Dr. KT6: Surb . . . 1D 162
Ditton Hill KT6: Surb . . . 1C 162
Ditton Hill Rd. KT6: Surb . . . 1C 162
Ditton Lawn KT7: T Ditt . . . 1A 162
Ditton Pl. SE20 . . . 1H 157
Ditton Reach KT7: T Ditt . . . 6B 150
Ditton Rd. DA6: Bex . . . 5D 126
KT6: Surb . . . 2D 162
UB2: S'hall . . . 5D 94
Divisional Rd. E12 . . . 2B 70
Divis Way SW15 . . . 6D 116
(off Dover Pk. Dr.)
Dixon Clark Ct. N1 . . . 6B 66
Dixon Cl. E6 . . . 6D 88
Dixon Ho. W10 . . . 6F 81
(off Darfield Way)
Dixon Pl. BR4: W W'ck . . . 1D 170
Dixon Rd. SE14 . . . 1A 122
SE25 . . . 3E 156
Dixon's All. SE16 . . . 2H 103
Dobbin Cl. HA3: Kent . . . 2A 42
Dobell Rd. SE9 . . . 5D 124
Dobree Av. NW10 . . . 7D 62
Dobson Cl. NW6 . . . 7B 64
Dobson Ho. SE5 . . . 7D 102
(off Edmund St.)
SE14 . . . 6K 103
(off John Williams Cl.)
Doby Ct. EC4 . . . 2D 14
Dock Cotts. E1 . . . 7J 85
(off The Highway)
Dockers Tanner Rd. E14 . . . 3C 104
Dockett Eddy KT16: Chert . . . 7A 146
Dockett Eddy La. TW17: Shep . . . 7B 146
Dockett Moorings KT16: Chert . . . 7A 146
Dockhead SE1 . . . 7K 15 (2F 103)
Dockhead Wharf SE1 . . . 7K 15
(off Shad Thames)
Dock Hill Av. SE16 . . . 1K 103
Docklands Equestrian Cen., The . . . 4E 88
Docklands Sailing Cen. . . . 3C 104
Dockland St. E16 . . . 1E 106
(not continuous)
Dockley Rd. SE16 . . . 3G 103
Dockley Rd. Ind. Est. SE16 . . . 3G 103
(off Dockley Rd.)
Dock Offices SE16 . . . 3J 103
(off Surrey Quays Rd.)
Dock Rd. E16 . . . 7H 87
TW8: Bford . . . 7D 96
Dockside Rd. E16 . . . 7B 88
Dock St. E1 . . . 7G 85
Dockwell Cl. TW14: Felt . . . 4J 111
Dockwell's Ind. Est. TW14: Felt . . . 5K 111
Doctor Johnson Av. SW17 . . . 3F 137
Doctors Cl. SE26 . . . 5J 139
Docwra's Bldgs. N1 . . . 6E 66
Dodbrooke Rd. SE27 . . . 3A 138
Dodd Ho. SE16 . . . 4H 103
(off Rennie Est.)
Doddington Gro. SE17 . . . 6B 102
Doddington Pl. SE17 . . . 6B 102
Dodsley Pl. N9 . . . 3D 34
Dodson St. SE1 . . . 7K 13 (2A 102)
Dod St. E14 . . . 6B 86
Doebury Wlk. SE18 . . . 6A 108
(off Prestwood Cl.)
Doel Cl. SW19 . . . 7A 136
Dog & Duck Yd. WC1 . . . 5G 7
Doggett Rd. SE6 . . . 7C 122
Doggetts Ct. EN4: E Barn . . . 5H 21
Doghurst Av. UB3: Harl . . . 7D 92
Doghurst Dr. UB7: Sip . . . 7D 92
Dog Kennel Hill SE22 . . . 3E 120
Dog Kennel Hill Est. SE22 . . . 3E 120
(off Albrighton Rd.)
Dog La. NW10 . . . 4A 62
Doherty Rd. E13 . . . 4J 87
Dokal Ind. Est. UB2: S'hall . . . 3C 94
Dolben Ct. SE8 . . . 4B 104
SW1 . . . 4D 18
(off Montaigne Cl.)
Dolben St. SE1 . . . 5A 14 (1B 102)
(not continuous)
Dolby Rd. SW6 . . . 2H 117
Dolland Ho. SE11 . . . 6H 19
Dolland St. SE11 . . . 6H 19 (5K 101)
Dollar Bay Ct. E14 . . . 2E 104
(off Lawn Ho. Cl.)
Dollary Pde. KT1: King T . . . 3H 151
(off Kingston Rd.)
Dollis Av. N3 . . . 1H 45
Dollis Brook Wlk. EN5: Barn . . . 6B 20
Dollis Cres. HA4: Ruis . . . 1A 58
Dolliscroft NW7 . . . 7B 30
DOLLIS HILL . . . 2D 62
Dollis Hill Av. NW2 . . . 3D 62
Dollis Hill La. NW2 . . . 4B 62
Dollis M. N3 . . . 1J 45
Dollis Pk. N3 . . . 1H 45
Dollis Rd. N3 . . . 1G 45
NW7 . . . 7B 30
Dollis Valley Dr. EN5: Barn . . . 6C 20
Dollis Valley Way EN5: Barn . . . 6C 20
Dolman Cl. N3 . . . 2A 46
Dolman Rd. W4 . . . 4K 97
Dolman St. SW4 . . . 4K 119
Dolphin Cl. KT6: Surb . . . 5D 150
SE16 . . . 2K 103
SE28 . . . 6D 90
Dolphin Ct. NW11 . . . 6G 45
SE8 . . . 6B 104
(off Wotton Rd.)
Dolphin Est. TW16: Sun . . . 1G 147
Dolphin Ho. SW18 . . . 4K 117
Dolphin La. E14 . . . 7D 86
Dolphin Rd. TW16: Sun . . . 1G 147
UB5: N'olt . . . 2D 76
Dolphin Rd. Nth. TW16: Sun . . . 1G 147
Dolphin Rd. Sth. TW16: Sun . . . 1F 147
Dolphin Rd. W. TW16: Sun . . . 1G 147
Dolphin Sq. SW1 . . . 6B 18 (5G 101)
W4 . . . 7A 98
Dolphin St. KT1: King T . . . 2E 150
Dolphin Twr. SE8 . . . 6B 104
(off Abinger Gro.)
Dombey Ho. SE1 . . . 7K 15
(off Wolseley St.)
W11 . . . 1F 99
(off St Ann's Rd.)
Dombey St. WC1 . . . 5G 7 (5K 83)
(not continuous)
Domecq Ho. EC1 . . . 3B 8
(off Dallington St.)
Dome Hill Pk. SE26 . . . 4F 139
Domelton Ho. SW18 . . . 6K 117
(off Iron Mill Rd.)
Domett Cl. SE5 . . . 4D 120
Domfe Pl. E5 . . . 4J 67
Domingo St. EC1 . . . 3C 8 (4C 84)
Dominica Cl. E13 . . . 2B 88
Dominion Bus. Pk. N9 . . . 2E 34
Dominion Cen., The UB2: S'hall . . . 2C 94
Dominion Cl. TW3: Houn . . . 2H 113
Dominion Ct. E8 . . . 7F 67
(off Middleton Rd.)
Dominion Ho. E14 . . . 5D 104
(off St Davids Sq.)

Dominion Ind. Est.—Dover Gdns.

Dominion Ind. Est. *UB2: S'hall* 2C **94**
(off Feather Rd.)
Dominion Pde. HA1: Harr 5K **41**
Dominion Rd. CR0: Croy 7F **157**
UB2: S'hall 2C **94**
Dominion St. EC2 5F **9** (5D **84**)
Dominion Theatre *7D 6*
(off Tottenham Ct. Rd.)
Domonic Dr. SE9 4F **143**
Domville Cl. N20 2G **31**
Donald Dr. RM6: Chad H 5C **54**
Donald Hunter Ho. *E7* *5K 69*
(off Woodgrange Rd.)
Donald Rd. CR0: Croy 7A **156**
E13 1K **87**
Donaldson Rd. NW6 1H **81**
SE18 1E **124**
Donald Woods Gdns. KT5: Surb 2H **163**
Donato Dr. SE15 6E **102**
Doncaster Dr. UB5: N'olt 5D **58**
Doncaster Gdns. N4 6C **48**
UB5: N'olt 5D **58**
Doncaster Rd. N9 7C **24**
Donegal Ho. *E1* *4H 85*
(off Cambridge Heath Rd.)
Donegal St. N1 2K **83**
Doneraile Ho. *SW1* *5J 17*
(off Ebury Bri. Rd.)
Doneraile St. SW6 2F **117**
Dongola Rd. E1 5A **86**
E13 3K **87**
N17 3E **48**
Dongola Rd. W. E13 3K **87**
Don Gratton Ho. *E1* *5G 85*
(off Old Montague St.)
Donington Av. IG2: Ilf 5G **53**
IG6: Ilf 5G **53**
Donkey All. SE22 7G **121**
Donkey La. EN1: Enf 2B **24**
Donkin Ho. *SE16* *4H 103*
(off Rennie Est.)
Donmar Warehouse Theatre *1E 12*
(off Earlham St.)
Donnatt's Rd. SE14 1B **122**
Donne Ct. SE24 6C **120**
Donnefield Av. HA8: Edg 7K **27**
Donne Ho. *E14* *6C 86*
(off Dod St.)
SE14 *6K 103*
(off Samuel Cl.)
Donnelly Ct. *SW6* *7G 99*
(off Dawes Rd.)
Donne Pl. CR4: Mitc 4F **155**
SW3 3D **16** (4C **100**)
Donne Rd. RM8: Dag 2C **72**
Donnington Ct. *NW1* *7F 65*
(off Castlehaven Rd.)
NW10 7D **62**
Donnington Mans. *NW10* *1E 80*
(off Donnington Rd.)
Donnington Rd. HA3: Kent 5D **42**
KT4: Wor Pk 2C **164**
NW10 7D **62**
Donnybrook Rd. SW16 7G **137**
Donoghue Cotts. *E14* *5A 86*
(off Galsworthy Av.)
Donovan Av. N10 2F **47**
Donovan Ct. *SW10* *6A 16*
(off Drayton Gdns.)
Donovan Ho. *E1* *7J 85*
(off Cable St.)
Donovan Pl. N21 5E **22**
Don Phelan Cl. SE5 1D **120**
Doone Cl. TW11: Tedd 6A **132**
Doon St. SE1 5J **13** (1A **102**)
Dora Ho. *E14* *6B 86*
(off Rhodeswell Rd.)
W11 *7F 81*
(off St Ann's Rd.)
Doral Way SM5: Cars 5D **166**
Doran Ct. E6 2D **88**
Dorando Cl. W12 7D **80**
Doran Gro. SE18 7J **107**
Doran Mnr. *N2* *5D 46*
(off Great Nth. Rd.)
Doran Wlk. E15 7E **68**
Dora Rd. SW19 5J **135**
Dora St. E14 6B **86**
Dora Way SW9 2A **120**
Dorchester Av. DA5: Bexl 1D **144**
HA2: Harr 6G **41**
N13 4H **33**
Dorchester Cl. BR5: St P 7B **144**
UB5: N'olt 5F **59**
Dorchester Ct. *E18* *1H 51*
(off Buckingham Rd.)
N1 *7E 66*
(off Englefield Rd.)
N10 3F **47**
N14 7A **22**
NW2 3F **63**
SE24 5C **120**
SW1 *2F 17*
(off Pavillion Rd.)
Dorchester Dr. SE24 5C **120**
TW14: Bedf 6G **111**
Dorchester Gdns. E4 4H **35**
NW11 4J **45**
Dorchester Gro. W4 5A **98**
Dorchester Ho. TW9: Kew 7H **97**
Dorchester M. KT3: N Mald 4K **151**
TW1: Twick 6C **114**
Dorchester Rd. KT4: Wor Pk 1E **164**
SM4: Mord 7K **153**
UB5: N'olt 5F **59**
Dorchester Ter. *NW2* *3F 63*
(off Needham Ter.)
Dorchester Way HA3: Kent 6F **43**
Dorchester Waye UB4: Yead 6A **76**
(Quebec Rd.)
UB4: Yead 6K **75**
(Wimborne Av.)
Dorcis Av. DA7: Bex 2E **126**
Dordrecht Rd. W3 1A **98**
Dore Av. E12 5E **70**
Doreen Av. NW9 1K **61**
Doreen Capstan Ho. *E11* *3G 69*
(off Apollo Pl.)
Dore Gdns. SM4: Mord 7K **153**
Dorell Cl. UB1: S'hall 5D **76**
Dorey Ho. *TW8: Bford* *7C 96*
(off High St.)
Doria Rd. SW6 2H **117**
Doric Ho. *E2* *2K 85*
(off Mace St.)
Doric Way NW1 1C **6** (3H **83**)
Dorie M. N12 4E **30**
Dorien Rd. SW20 2F **153**
Doris Av. DA8: Erith 1J **127**
Doris Emmerton Ct. SW11 4A **118**
Doris Rd. E7 7J **69**
TW15: Ashf 6F **129**
Dorking Cl. KT4: Wor Pk 2F **165**
SE8 6B **104**
Dorking Ct. *N17* *1G 49*
(off Hampden La.)
Dorking Ho. SE1 3D **102**
Dorlcote Rd. SW18 7C **118**
Dorly Cl. TW17: Shep 5G **147**
Dorman Pl. N9 2B **34**
Dormans Cl. HA6: Nwood 1F **39**
Dorman Wlk. NW10 5K **61**
Dorman Way NW8 1B **82**
Dorma Trad. Pk. E10 1K **67**
Dormay St. SW18 5K **117**
Dormer Cl. E15 6H **69**
EN5: Barn 5A **20**
Dormer's Av. UB1: S'hall 6E **76**
Dormers Ri. UB1: S'hall 6F **77**
DORMER'S WELLS 6E **76**
Dormer's Wells La. UB1: S'hall 6E **76**
Dormers Wells Leisure Cen. 6F **77**
Dormstone Ho. *SE17* *4E 102*
(off Beckway St.)
Dormywood HA4: Ruis 5H **39**
Dornberg Cl. SE3 7J **105**
Dornberg Rd. SE3 7K **105**
Dorncliffe Rd. SW6 2G **117**
Dorney NW3 7C **64**
Dorney Ri. BR5: St M Cry 4K **161**
Dorney Way TW4: Houn 5C **112**
Dornfell St. NW6 5H **63**
Dornton Rd. CR2: S Croy 6D **168**
SW12 2F **137**
Dorothy Av. HA0: Wemb 7E **60**
Dorothy Evans Cl. DA7: Bex 4H **127**
Dorothy Gdns. RM8: Dag 4B **72**
Dorothy Pettingell Ho. *SM1: Sutt* *3K 165*
(off Angel Hill)
Dorothy Rd. SW11 3D **118**
Dorrell Pl. SW9 3A **120**
Dorrien Wlk. SW16 2H **137**
Dorrington Ct. SE25 2E **156**
Dorrington St. EC1 5J **7** (5A **84**)
Dorrington Way BR3: Beck 5E **158**
Dorrit Ho. *W11* *1F 99*
(off St Ann's Rd.)
Dorrit M. N18 5K **33**
Dorrit St. SE1 6D **14** (2C **102**)
Dorrit Way BR7: Chst 6G **143**
Dorryn Ct. SE26 5K **139**
Dors Cl. NW9 1K **61**
Dorset Av. DA16: Well 4K **125**
RM1: Rom 4K **55**
UB2: S'hall 4E **94**
UB4: Hayes 3G **75**
Dorset Bldgs. EC4 1A **14** (6B **84**)
Dorset Cl. NW1 5E **4** (5D **82**)
UB4: Hayes 3G **75**
Dorset Ct. HA6: Nwood 1H **39**
N1 *7E 66*
(off Hertford Rd.)
UB5: N'olt 3C **76**
W7 *5K 77*
(off Copley Cl.)
Dorset Dr. HA8: Edg 6A **28**
Dorset Gdns. CR4: Mitc 4K **155**
Dorset Ho. *NW1* *5F 5*
(off Gloucester Pl.)
Dorset M. N3 1J **45**
SW1 1J **17** (3F **101**)
Dorset Pl. E15 6F **69**
Dorset Ri. EC4 1A **14** (6B **84**)
Dorset Rd. BR3: Beck 3K **157**
CR4: Mitc 2C **154**
E7 7A **70**
HA1: Harr 6G **41**
N15 4D **48**
N22 1J **47**
SE9 2C **142**
SW8 7J **101**
SW19 1J **153**
TW15: Ashf 3A **128**
W5 3C **96**
Dorset Sq. NW1 4E **4** (4D **82**)
Dorset St. W1 6F **5** (5D **82**)
Dorset Way TW2: Twick 1H **131**
UB10: Hil 2B **74**
Dorset Waye TW5: Hest 7D **94**
Dorset Wharf *W6* *7E 98*
(off Rainville Rd.)
Dorton Cl. SE15 7E **102**
Dorton Vs. UB7: Sip 7C **92**
Dorville Cres. W6 3D **98**
Dorville Rd. SE12 5H **123**
Dothill Rd. SE18 7G **107**
Douai Gro. TW12: Hamp 1G **149**
Doughty Ct. *E1* *1H 103*
(off Prusom St.)
Doughty Ho. *SW10* *6A 100*
(off Netherton Gro.)
Doughty M. WC1 4G **7** (4K **83**)
Doughty St. WC1 3G **7** (4K **83**)
Douglas Av. E17 1B **50**
HA0: Wemb 7E **60**
KT3: N Mald 4D **152**
Douglas Cl. HA7: Stan 5F **27**
IG6: Ilf 7K **37**
SM6: Wall 6J **167**
Douglas Ct. *KT1: King T* *4E 150*
(off Geneva Rd.)
NW6 *7J 63*
(off Quex Rd.)
Douglas Cres. UB4: Yead 4A **76**
Douglas Dr. CR0: Croy 3C **170**
Douglas Est. *N1* *6C 66*
(off Oransay Rd.)
Douglas Eyre Sports Cen. 5K **49**
Douglas Ho. KT6: Surb 1F **163**
Douglas Johnstone Ho. *SW6* *6H 99*
(off Clem Attlee Ct.)
Douglas Mans. TW3: Houn 3F **113**
Douglas M. NW2 3G **63**
Douglas Path *E14* *5E 104*
(off Manchester Rd.)
Douglas Pl. *SW1* *4C 18*
(off Douglas St.)
Douglas Rd. DA16: Well 1B **126**
E4 1B **36**
E16 5J **87**
IG3: Ilf 7A **54**
KT1: King T 2H **151**
KT6: Surb 2F **163**
N1 7C **66**
N22 1A **48**
NW6 1H **81**
TW3: Houn 3F **113**
TW19: Stanw 6A **110**
Douglas Rd. Nth. N1 6C **66**
Douglas Rd. Sth. N1 6C **66**
Douglas Robinson Ct. *SW16* *7J 137*
(off Streatham High Rd.)
Douglas Sq. SM4: Mord 6J **153**
Douglas St. SW1 4C **18** (4H **101**)
Douglas Ter. E17 1B **50**
Douglas Waite Ho. NW6 7J **63**
Douglas Way SE8 7B **104**
(Stanley St.)
SE8 7C **104**
(Watsons St.)
Doulton Ho. SE11 2H **19**
Doulton M. NW6 6K **63**
Dounesforth Gdns. SW18 1K **135**
Douro Pl. W8 3K **99**
Douro St. E3 2C **86**
Douthwaite Sq. E1 1G **103**
Dove App. E6 5C **88**
Dove Cl. NW7 7G **29**
SM6: Wall 7K **167**
UB5: N'olt 4B **76**
Dove Commercial Cen. NW5 5G **65**
Dovecot Cl. HA5: Eastc 5A **40**
Dovecote Av. N22 3A **48**
Dovecote Gdns. SW14 3K **115**
Dove Ct. EC2 1E **14**
Dovedale Av. HA3: Kent 6C **42**
IG5: Ilf 2E **52**
Dovedale Bus. Est. *SE15* *2G 121*
(off Blenheim Gro.)
Dovedale Cl. DA16: Well 2A **126**
Dovedale Ri. CR4: Mitc 7D **136**
Dovedale Rd. SE22 5H **121**
Dovedon Cl. N14 2D **32**
Dovehouse Ct. *UB5: N'olt* *3B 76*
(off Delta Gro.)
Dove Ho. Gdns. E4 2H **35**
Dovehouse Mead IG11: Bark 2H **89**
Dovehouse St. SW3 5B **16** (5B **100**)
Dove M. SW5 4A **100**
Dove Pk. HA5: H End 1E **40**
Dover Cl. NW2 2F **63**
RM5: Col R 2J **55**
Dover Ct. *EC1* *3A 8*
(off St John St.)
Dovercourt Av. CR7: Thor H 5A **156**
Dovercourt Est. N1 6D **66**
Dovercourt Gdns. HA7: Stan 5K **27**
Dovercourt La. SM1: Sutt 3A **166**
Dovercourt Rd. SE22 6E **120**
Doverfield Rd. SW2 7J **119**
Dover Flats SE1 4E **102**
Dover Gdns. SM5: Cars 3D **166**

Dover Ho.—Drive, The

Dover Ho. N18 .5A 34
SE15 .6J 103
Dover Ho. Rd. SW15 .4C 116
Doveridge Gdns. N13 .4G 33
Dove Rd. N1 .6D 66
Dove Row E2 .1G 85
Dover Pk. Dr. SW15 .6D 116
Dover Patrol SE3 .2K 123
Dover Rd. E12 .2A 70
N9 .2D 34
RM6: Chad H .6E 54
SE19 .6D 138
Dover St. W1 .3K 11 (7F 83)
Dover Ter. *TW9: Rich .2F 115*
(off Sandycombe Rd.)
Dover Yd. W1 .4A 12
Doves Cl. BR2: Brom .2C 172
Doves Yd. N1 .1A 84
Dovet Ct. SW9 .1K 119
Doveton Ho. *E1 .4J 85*
(off Doveton St.)
Doveton Rd. CR2: S Croy .5D 168
Doveton St. E1 .4J 85
Dove Wlk. SW1 .5G 17 (5E 100)
Dovey Lodge *N1 .7A 66*
(off Bewdley St.)
Dowanhill Rd. SE6 .1F 141
Dowdeswell Cl. SW15 .4A 116
Dowding Ho. *N6 .7E 46*
(off Hillcrest)
Dowding Pl. HA7: Stan .6F 27
Dowding Rd. UB10: Uxb .7B 56
Dowdney Cl. NW5 .5G 65
Dowe Ho. SE3 .3G 123
Dower Av. SM6: Wall .7F 167
Dowes Ho. SW16 .3J 137
Dowgate Hill EC4 .2E 14 (7D 84)
Dowland St. W10 .3G 81
Dowlas St. SE5 .7E 102
Dowler Ct. *KT2: King T .1E 150*
(off Burton Rd.)
Dowler Ho. *E1 .6G 85*
(off Burslem St.)
Dowlerville Rd.
BR6: Chels .6K 173
Dowling Ho. DA17: Belv .3F 109
Dowman Cl. SW19 .7K 135
Downage NW4 .3E 44
(not continuous)
Downalong WD23: Bushy .1C 26
Downbank Av. DA7: Bex .1K 127
Down Barns Rd. HA4: Ruis .3B 58
Downbury M. SW18 .5J 117
Down Cl. UB5: Yead .2K 75
Downderry Rd. BR1: Brom .3F 141
Downe Cl. DA16: Well .7C 108
Down End SE18 .7F 107
Downend Cl. *SE15 .6E 102*
(off Longhope Cl.)
Downe Rd. BR2: Kes .7B 172
CR4: Mitc .2D 154
Downer's Cott. SW4 .4G 119
Downesbury *NW3 .6D 64*
(off Steele's Rd.)
Downes Cl. TW1: Twick .6B 114
Downes Ct. N21 .1F 33
Downes Ho. *CR0: Wadd .4B 168*
(off Violet La.)
Downe Ter. TW10: Rich .6E 114
Downey Ho. *E1 .4K 85*
(off Globe Rd.)
Downfield KT4: Wor Pk .1B 164
Downfield Cl. W9 .4K 81
Down Hall Rd. KT2: King T .1D 150
DOWNHAM .5F 141
Downham Cl. RM5: Col R .1G 55
Downham Ct. *N1 .7D 66*
(off Downham Rd.)
Downham Ent. Cen. SE6 .2H 141
Downham La. BR1: Brom .5F 141
Downham Rd. N1 .7D 66
Downham Way BR1: Brom .5F 141
Downhills Av. N17 .3D 48
Downhills Pk. Rd. N17 .3C 48
Downhills Way N17 .3C 48
Downhurst Av. NW7 .5E 28
Downhurst Ct. NW4 .3E 44
Downing Cl. HA2: Harr .3G 41
Downing Dr. UB6: G'frd .1H 77
Downing Ho. *W10 .6F 81*
(off Cambridge Gdns.)
Downing Rd. RM9: Dag .7F 73
Downings E6 .6E 88
Downing St. SW1 .6E 12 (2J 101)
Downland Cl. N20 .1F 31
Downland Ct. E11 .2G 69
Downleys Cl. SE9 .2C 142
Downman Rd. SE9 .3C 124
Down Pl. W6 .4D 98
Down Rd. TW11: Tedd .6B 132
Downs, The SW20 .7F 135
Downs Av. BR7: Chst .5D 142
HA5: Pinn .6C 40
Downsbridge Rd. BR3: Beck .1F 159
Downs Ct. UB6: G'frd .3A 78
Downs Ct. Pde. *E8 .5H 67*
(off Amhurst Rd.)
Downsell Rd. E15 .4E 68
Downsfield Rd. E17 .6A 50
Downshall Av. IG3: Ilf .6J 53
Downs Hill BR3: Beck .7F 141
Downshire Hill NW3 .4B 64
Downside TW1: Twick .3K 131
TW16: Sun .1J 147
Downside Cl. SW19 .6A 136
Downside Cres. NW3 .5C 64
W13 .4A 78
Downside Rd. SM2: Sutt .6B 166
Downside Wlk. *TW8: Bford .6D 96*
(off Windmill Rd.)
UB5: N'olt .3D 76
Downs La. E5 .4H 67
Downs Pk. Rd. E5 .5F 67
E8 .5F 67
Downs Rd. BR3: Beck .2D 158
(not continuous)
CR7: Thor H .1C 156
E5 .4G 67
EN1: Enf .4K 23
Down St. KT8: W Mole .5E 148
W1 .5J 11 (1F 101)
Down St. M. W1 .5J 11 (1F 101)
Downs Vw. TW7: Isle .1K 113
Downsview Gdns. SE19 .7B 138
Downsview Rd. SE19 .7C 138
Downsway BR6: Orp .5J 173
Downsway, The SM2: Sutt .7A 166
Downton Av. SW2 .2J 137
Downtown Rd. SE16 .2A 104
Down Way UB5: Yead .3K 75
Dowrey St. N1 .1A 84
Dowsett Rd. N17 .2F 49
Dowson Cl. SE5 .4D 120
Dowson Ho. *E1 .6K 85*
(off Bower St.)
Doyce St. SE1 .6C 14 (2C 102)
Doyle Gdns. NW10 .1C 80
Doyle Ho. *SW13 .7E 98*
(off Trinity Chu. Rd.)
Doyle Rd. SE25 .4G 157
D'Oyley St. SW1 .3G 17 (4E 100)
Doynton St. N19 .2F 65
Draco Ga. SW15 .3E 116
Draco St. SE17 .6C 102
Dragonfly Cl. E13 .3K 87
Dragon Rd. SE15 .6E 102
Dragons Health Club
Epsom .4K 163
Northolt .1E 76
Northwood Hills .2G 39
Purley .7A 168
St Paul's Cray .7D 144
Dragon Yd. WC1 .7F 7 (6J 83)
Dragoon Rd. SE8 .5B 104
Dragor Rd. NW10 .4J 79
Drake Cl. SE16 .2K 103
Drake Ct. *KT5: Surb .4E 150*
(off Cranes Pk. Av.)
SE1 .7D 14
(off Swan St.)
SE19 .5F 139
W12 .2E 98
(off Scott's Rd.)
Drake Cres. SE28 .6C 90
Drakefell Rd. SE4 .3A 122
SE14 .2K 121
Drakefield Rd. SW17 .3E 136
Drake Hall *E16 .1K 105*
(off Wesley Av.)
Drake Ho. *E1 .5J 85*
(off Stepney Way)
E14 .7A 86
(off Victory Pl.)
SW1 .7C 18
(off Dolphin Sq.)
Drakeland Ho. *W9 .4H 81*
(off Fernhead Rd.)
Drakeley Ct. N5 .4B 66
Drake M. BR2: Brom .4A 160
Drake Rd. CR0: Croy .7K 155
CR4: Mitc .6E 154
HA2: Harr .2D 58
KT9: Chess .5G 163
SE4 .3C 122
Drakes Ct. SE23 .1J 139
Drakes Courtyard NW6 .7H 63
Drakes Dr. HA6: Nwood .1D 38
Drake St. EN2: Enf .1J 23
WC1 .6G 7 (5K 83)
Drakes Wlk. E6 .1D 88
Drakewood Rd. SW16 .7H 137
Draper Cl. DA17: Belv .4F 109
TW7: Isle .2H 113
Draper Ct. BR1: Brom .4C 160
Draper Ho. *SE1 .4B 102*
(off Elephant & Castle)
Draper Pl. *N1 .1B 84*
(off Dagmar Ter.)
Drapers Cott. Homes NW7 .4G 29
(not continuous)
Drapers Gdns. EC2 .7F 9 (6D 84)
Drapers Rd. E15 .4F 69
EN2: Enf .2G 23
N17 .3F 49
Drappers Way SE16 .4G 103
Draven Cl. BR2: Hayes .7H 159
Drawdock Rd. SE10 .2F 105
Drawell Cl. SE18 .5J 107
Drax Av. SW20 .7C 134
Draxmont SW19 .6G 135
Draycot Rd. E11 .6K 51
KT6: Surb .1G 163
Draycott Av. HA3: Kent .6B 42
SW3 .3D 16 (4C 100)
Draycott Cl. HA3: Kent .6B 42
NW2 .3F 63
SE5 .7D 102
(not continuous)
Draycott M. *SW6 .2H 117*
(off Laurel Bank Gdns.)
Draycott Pl. SW3 .4E 16 (4D 100)
Draycott Ter. SW3 .4F 17 (4D 100)
Drayford Cl. W9 .4H 81
Dray Gdns. SW2 .5K 119
Draymans M. SE15 .2F 121
Draymans Way TW7: Isle .3K 113
Drayside M. UB2: S'hall .2D 94
Drayson M. W8 .2J 99
Drayton Av. BR6: Farnb .1F 173
W13 .7A 78
Drayton Bri. Rd. W7 .7K 77
W13 .7K 77
Drayton Cl. IG1: Ilf .1H 71
TW4: Houn .5D 112
Drayton Ct. UB7: W Dray .4B 92
Drayton Gdns. N21 .7G 23
SW10 .6A 16 (5A 100)
UB7: W Dray .2A 92
W13 .7A 78
Drayton Grn. W13 .7A 78
Drayton Grn. Rd. W13 .7B 78
Drayton Gro. W13 .7A 78
Drayton Ho. E11 .1F 69
SE5 .7D 102
(off Elmington Rd.)
Drayton Pk. N5 .4A 66
Drayton Pk. M. N5 .5A 66
Drayton Rd. CR0: Croy .2B 168
E11 .1F 69
N17 .2E 48
NW10 .1B 80
W13 .7A 78
Drayton Waye HA3: Kent .6B 42
Dreadnought St. SE10 .3G 105
Dreadnought Wharf *SE10 .6D 104*
(off Thames St.)
Drenon Sq. UB3: Hayes .7H 75
Dresden Cl. NW6 .6K 63
Dresden Ho. SE11 .3H 19
SW11 .2E 118
(off Dagnall St.)
Dresden Rd. N19 .1G 65
Dressington Av. SE4 .6C 122
Drew Av. NW7 .6B 30
Drewery Ct. SE3 .3G 123
Drewett Ho. *E1 .6G 85*
(off Christian St.)
Drew Gdns. UB6: G'frd .6K 59
Drew Ho. SW16 .3J 137
Drewitts Ct. KT12: Walt T .7H 147
Drew Rd. E16 .1B 106
(not continuous)
Drewstead Rd. SW16 .2H 137
Drey Ct. KT4: Wor Pk .1B 164
Driffield Ct. *NW9 .1A 44*
(off Pageant Av.)
Driffield Rd. E3 .2A 86
Drift, The BR2: Brom .3B 172
Driftway, The CR4: Mitc .1E 154
Drill Hall Arts Cen. .5C 6
(off Chenies St.)
Drinkwater Ho. *SE5 .7D 102*
(off Picton St.)
Drinkwater Rd. HA2: Harr .2F 59
Drive, The BR3: Beck .2C 158
BR4: W W'ck .7F 159
BR6: Orp .2K 173
BR7: Chst .3K 161
CR7: Thor H .4D 156
DA5: Bexl .6C 126
DA8: Erith .7H 109
DA14: Sidc .3B 144
E4 .1A 36
E17 .3D 50
E18 .4J 51
EN2: Enf .1J 23
EN5: Barn .3B 20
EN5: New Bar .6F 21
HA2: Harr .7E 40
HA6: Nwood .2G 39
HA8: Edg .5B 28
HA9: Wemb .2J 61
IG1: Ilf .6C 52
IG9: Buck H .1F 37
IG11: Bark .7K 71
KT2: King T .7J 133
KT6: Surb .7E 150
KT10: Esh .7G 149
KT19: Ewe .6B 164
N3 .7D 30
N6 .5D 46
N7 .6K 65
(not continuous)
N11 .6B 32
NW10 .1B 80
NW11 .7G 45
RM5: Col R .1K 55
SM4: Mord .5A 154
SW6 .2G 117
SW20 .7E 134
TW3: Houn .2H 113
TW7: Isle .2H 113

Drive, The TW14: Felt 7A 112
TW15: Ashf 7F 129
UB10: Ick 4A 56
W3 6J 79
Drive Ct. HA8: Edg 5B 28
Drive Mans. *SW6* *2G 117*
(off Fulham Rd.)
Driveway, The *E17* *6D 50*
(off Hoe St.)
Dr Johnson's House ***1K 13***
(off Pemberton Row)
Droitwich Cl. SE26 3G 139
Dromey Gdns. HA3: Hrw W 7E 26
Dromore Rd. SW15 6G 117
Dronfield Gdns. RM8: Dag 5C 72
Dron Ho. *E1* *5J 85*
(off Adelina Gro.)
Droop St. W10 3F 81
Drovers Ct. *KT1: King T* *2E 150*
(off Fairfield E.)
Drovers Pl. SE15 7J 103
Drovers Rd. CR2: S Croy 5D 168
Druce Rd. SE21 6E 120
Druid St. SE1 6H 15 (2E 102)
Druids Way BR2: Brom 4F 159
Drumaline Ridge KT4: Wor Pk 2A 164
Drummond Av. RM7: Rom 4K 55
Drummond Ct. N12 7H 31
Drummond Cres. NW1 1C 6 (3H 83)
Drummond Dr. HA7: Stan 7E 26
Drummond Ga. SW1 5D 18 (5H 101)
Drummond Ho. *E2* *2G 85*
(off Goldsmiths Row)
N2 *2A 46*
(off Font Hills)
Drummond Pl. TW1: Twick 7B 114
Drummond Rd. CR0: Croy 2C 168
(not continuous)
E11 6A 52
RM7: Rom 4K 55
SE16 3H 103
Drummonds, The
IG9: Buck H 2E 36
Drummonds Pl. TW9: Rich 4E 114
Drummond St. NW1 3A 6 (4G 83)
Drum St. E1 7K 9 (6F 85)
Drury Cres. CR0: Wadd 2A 168
Drury Ho. SW8 1G 119
Drury La. WC2 7F 7 (6J 83)
Drury Lane Theatre ***1G 13***
(off Catherine St.)
Drury Rd. HA1: Harr 7G 41
Drury Way NW10 5K 61
Drury Way Ind. Est. NW10 5J 61
Dryad St. SW15 3F 117
Dryburgh Gdns. NW9 3G 43
Dryburgh Ho. *SW1* *5K 17*
(off Abbots Mnr.)
Dryburgh Rd. SW15 3D 116
Dryden Av. W7 6K 77
Dryden Ct. SE11 4K 19 (4B 102)
Dryden Mans. *W14* *6G 99*
(off Queen's Club Gdns.)
Dryden Rd. DA16: Well 1K 125
EN1: Enf 6K 23
HA3: W'stone 1K 41
SW19 6A 136
Dryden St. WC2 1F 13 (6J 83)
Dryfield Cl. NW10 6J 61
Dryfield Rd. HA8: Edg 6D 28
Dryfield Wlk. SE8 6C 104
Dryhill Rd. DA17: Belv 6F 109
Dryland Av. BR6: Orp 4K 173
Drylands Rd. N8 6J 47
Drysdale Av. E4 7J 25
Drysdale Cl. HA6: Nwood 1G 39
Drysdale Dwellings *E8* *5F 67*
(off Dunn St.)
Drysdale Ho. *N1* *1H 9*
(off Drysdale St.)
Drysdale Pl. N1 1H 9 (3E 84)
Drysdale St. N1 1H 9 (3E 84)
Dublin Av. E8 1G 85
Dublin Ct. *HA2: Harr* *2H 59*
(off Northolt Rd.)
Du Burstow Ter. W7 2J 95
Ducal St. E2 2K 9 (3F 85)
Du Cane Cl. W12 6E 80
Du Cane Ct. SW17 1E 136
Du Cane Rd. W12 6B 80
Ducavel Ho. SW2 1K 137
Duchess Cl. N11 5A 32
SM1: Sutt 4A 166
Duchess Gro. IG9: Buck H 2E 36
Duchess M. W1 6K 5 (5F 83)
Duchess of Bedford Ho. *W8* *2J 99*
(off Duchess of Bedford's Wlk.)
Duchess of Bedford's Wlk. W8 2J 99
Duchess St. W1 6K 5 (5F 83)
Duchess Theatre ***2G 13***
(off Catherine St.)
Duchy Rd. EN4: Had W 1G 21
Duchy St. SE1 4K 13 (1A 102)
(not continuous)
Ducie St. SW4 4K 119
Duckett M. N4 6B 48
Duckett Rd. N4 6A 48
Duckett St. E1 4K 85
Duck La. W1 1C 12
Duck Lees La. EN3: Pond E 4F 25
Duck's Hill Rd. HA4: Ruis 1D 38
HA6: Nwood 1D 38
DUCKS ISLAND **6A 20**
Ducks Wlk. TW1: Twick 5C 114
Du Cros Dr. HA7: Stan 6J 27
Du Cros Rd. W3 1A 98
DUDDEN HILL **5D 62**
Dudden Hill La. NW10 4B 62
Dudden Hill Pde. NW10 4B 62
Duddington Cl. SE9 4B 142
Dudley Av. HA3: Kent 3C 42
Dudley Ct. NW11 4H 45
W1 *1E 10*
(off Up. Berkeley St.)
WC2 7E 6 (6J 83)
Dudley Dr. HA4: Ruis 5K 57
SM4: Mord 1G 165
Dudley Gdns. HA2: Harr 1H 59
W13 2B 96
Dudley Ho. *W2* *6A 4*
(off Nth. Wharf Rd.)
Dudley M. SW2 6A 120
Dudley Pl. UB3: Harl 4F 93
Dudley Rd. E17 2C 50
HA2: Harr 2G 59
IG1: Ilf 4F 71
KT1: King T 3F 151
KT12: Walt T 6J 147
N3 2K 45
NW6 2G 81
SW19 6J 135
TW9: Rich 2F 115
TW14: Bedf 1E 128
TW15: Ashf 5B 128
UB2: S'hall 2B 94
Dudley St. W2 6A 4 (5B 82)
Dudlington Rd. E5 2J 67
Dudmaston M. SW3 5B 16
Dudrich Cl. N12 6J 31
Dudrich M. EN2: Enf 1F 23
SE22 5F 121
Dudsbury Rd. DA14: Sidc 6B 144
Dudset La. TW5: Cran 1J 111
Duffell Ho. SE11 6H 19
Dufferin Av. EC1 4E 8
Dufferin Ct. *EC1* *4E 8*
(off Dufferin St.)
Dufferin St. EC1 4D 8 (4C 84)
Duffield Cl. HA1: Harr 5K 41
Duffield Dr. N15 4F 49
Duff St. E14 6D 86
Dufour's Pl. W1 1B 12 (6G 83)
Dugard Way SE11 4B 102
Duggan Dr. BR7: Chst 6C 142
Dugolly Av. HA9: Wemb 3H 61
Duke Gdns. IG6: Ilf 4H 53
Duke Humphrey Rd. SE3 1G 123
Duke of Cambridge Cl. TW2: Whit 6H 113
Duke of Edinburgh Rd. SM1: Sutt 2B 166
Duke of Wellington Av. SE18 3F 107
Duke of Wellington Pl.
SW1 6H 11 (2E 100)
Duke of York Column (Memorial) **5D 12**
Duke of Yorks Sq. SW3 4F 17 (4D 100)
Duke of York's Theatre ***3E 12***
(off St Martin's La.)
Duke of York St. SW1 4B 12 (1G 101)
Duke Rd. IG6: Ilf 4H 53
W4 5K 97
Dukes Av. HA1: Harr 4J 41
HA2: Harr 6D 40
HA8: Edg 6A 28
KT2: King T 4C 132
KT3: N Mald 3A 152
N3 1K 45
N10 3F 47
TW4: Houn 4C 112
TW10: Ham 4C 132
UB5: N'olt 7C 58
W4 5K 97
Dukes Cl. TW12: Hamp 5D 130
TW15: Ashf 4E 128
Dukes Ct. E6 1E 88
(not continuous)
SE13 2E 122
SW14 2K 115
W2 *7K 81*
(off Queensway)
Dukes Ga. W4 4J 97
Dukes Grn. Av. TW14: Felt 5J 111
Dukes Head Pas. TW12: Hamp 7G 131
Duke's Head Yd. N6 1F 65
Duke Shore Wharf E14 7B 86
Duke's Ho. *SW1* *3D 18*
(off Vincent St.)
Dukes La. W8 2K 99
Duke's La. Chambers *W8* *2K 99*
(off Dukes La.)
Duke's La. Mans. *W8* *2K 99*
(off Dukes La.)
Dukes M. N10 3F 47
W1 7H 5
Dukes Orchard DA5: Bexl 1J 145
Duke's Pas. E17 4E 50
Duke's Pl. EC3 1H 15 (6E 84)
Dukes Point *N6* *1F 65*
(off Dukes Head Yd.)
Dukes Ride UB10: Ick 4A 56
Dukes Rd. E6 1E 88
W3 4G 79
WC1 2D 6 (3H 83)
Dukesthorpe Rd. SE26 4K 139
Duke St. SM1: Sutt 4B 166
SW1 4B 12 (1G 101)
TW9: Rich 4D 114
W1 7H 5 (6E 82)
Duke St. Hill SE1 4F 15 (1D 102)
Duke St. Mans. *W1* *1H 11*
(off Duke St.)
Dukes Way BR4: W W'ck 3G 171
Duke's Yd. W1 2H 11 (7E 82)
Dulas St. N4 1K 65
Dulford St. W11 7G 81
Dulka Rd. SW11 5D 118
Dulverton *NW1* *1G 83*
(off Royal College St.)
Dulverton Mans. WC1 4H 7
Dulverton Rd. HA4: Ruis 1J 57
SE9 2G 143
DULWICH **2E 138**
Dulwich Bus. Cen. SE23 1K 139
Dulwich Comn. SE21 1E 138
SE22 1E 138
Dulwich Lawn Cl. SE22 5F 121
Dulwich Leisure Cen. **4G 121**
Dulwich Oaks, The SE21 3F 139
Dulwich Picture Gallery **7D 120**
Dulwich Ri. Gdns. SE22 5F 121
Dulwich Rd. SE24 5A 120
Dulwich Upper Wood Nature Pk. **5F 139**
DULWICH VILLAGE **7E 120**
Dulwich Village SE21 6D 120
Dulwich Wood Av. SE19 4E 138
Dulwich Wood Pk. SE19 4E 138
Dumain Ct. *SE11* *4B 102*
(off Opal St.)
Dumbarton Ct. SW2 6J 119
Dumbarton Rd. SW2 6J 119
Dumbleton Cl. KT1: King T 1H 151
Dumbreck Rd. SE9 4D 124
Dumont Rd. N16 3E 66
Dumpton Pl. NW1 7E 64
Dumsey Eyot KT16: Chert 7A 146
Dunally Pk. TW17: Shep 7F 147
Dunbar Av. BR3: Beck 4A 158
RM10: Dag 3G 73
SW16 2A 156
Dunbar Cl. UB4: Hayes 6K 75
Dunbar Ct. *BR2: Brom* *3H 159*
(off Durham Rd.)
SM1: Sutt 5B 166
Dunbar Gdns. RM10: Dag 5G 73
Dunbar Rd. E7 6J 69
KT3: N Mald 4J 151
N22 1A 48
Dunbar St. SE27 3C 138
Dunbar Wharf *E14* *7B 86*
(off Narrow St.)
Dunblane Cl. HA8: Edg 2C 28
Dunblane Rd. SE9 3C 124
Dunboe Pl. TW17: Shep 7E 146
Dunboyne Rd. NW3 5D 64
Dunbridge Ho. *SW15* *6B 116*
(off Highcliffe Dr.)
Dunbridge St. E2 4G 85
Duncan Cl. EN5: New Bar 4F 21
Duncan Ct. *E14* *5E 86*
(off Teviot St.)
N21 1G 33
Duncan Gro. W3 6A 80
Duncan Ho. *NW3* *7D 64*
(off Fellows Rd.)
SW1 *6B 18*
(off Dolphin Sq.)
Duncannon Ho. *SW1* *6D 18*
(off Lindsay Sq.)
Duncannon St. WC2 3E 12 (7J 83)
Duncan Rd. E8 1H 85
TW9: Rich 4E 114
Duncan St. N1 2B 84
Duncan Ter. N1 2B 84
(not continuous)
Dunch St. E1 6H 85
Duncombe Hill SE23 7A 122
Duncombe Rd. N19 1H 65
Duncrievie Rd. SE13 6F 123
Duncroft SE18 7J 107
Dundalk Ho. *E1* *6J 85*
(off Clark St.)
Dundalk Rd. SE4 3A 122
Dundas Gdns. KT8: W Mole 3F 149
Dundas Ho. *E2* *2J 85*
(off Bishop's Way)
Dundas Rd. SE15 2J 121
Dundee Ct. *E1* *1H 103*
(off Wapping High St.)
SE1 *7G 15*
(off Long La.)
Dundee Ho. *W9* *3A 82*
(off Maida Va.)
Dundee Rd. E13 2K 87
SE25 5H 157
Dundee St. E1 1H 103
Dundee Way EN3: Brim 3F 25
Dundee Wharf E14 7B 86
Dundela Gdns. KT4: Wor Pk 4D 164
Dundonald Cl. E6 6C 88
Dundonald Ho. *E14* *2D 104*
(off Admirals Way)
Dundonald Rd. NW10 1F 81
SW19 7G 135
(not continuous)

Dundry Ho.—Earldom Rd.

Dundry Ho. SE26 .... 3G 139
Dunedin Ho. *E16* *1D 106*
(*off Manwood St.*)
Dunedin Rd. E10 .... 3D 68
IG1: Ilf 1G 71
Dunedin Way UB4: Yead 4A 76
Dunelm Gro. SE27 .... 3C 138
Dunelm St. E1 .... 6K 85
Dunfield Gdns. SE6 .... 5D 140
Dunfield Rd. SE6 .... 5D 140
(not continuous)
Dunford Ct. HA5: H End 1D 40
Dunford Rd. N7 .... 4K 65
Dungarvan Av. SW15 .... 4C 116
Dunheved Cl. CR7: Thor H 6A 156
Dunheved Rd. Nth.
CR7: Thor H 6A 156
Dunheved Rd. Sth.
CR7: Thor H 6A 156
Dunheved Rd. W. CR7: Thor H 6A 156
Dunhill Point SW15 .... 1C 134
Dunholme Grn. N9 .... 3A 34
Dunholme La. N9 .... 3A 34
Dunholme Rd. N9 .... 3A 34
Dunkeld Ho. *E14* *6F 87*
(*off Abbott Rd.*)
Dunkeld Rd. RM8: Dag 2B 72
SE25 .... 4D 156
Dunkery Rd. SE9 .... 4B 142
Dunkirk St. SE27 .... 4C 138
Dunlace Rd. E5 .... 4J 67
Dunleary Cl. TW4: Houn 7D 112
Dunley Dr. CR0: New Ad 7D 170
Dunlin Ho. *SE16* *4K 103*
(*off Tawny Way*)
Dunloe Av. N17 .... 3D 48
Dunloe Ct. E2 .... 2F 85
Dunloe St. E2 .... 2F 85
Dunlop Pl. SE16 .... 3F 103
Dunmore Point *E2* *2J 9*
(*off Gascoigne Pl.*)
Dunmore Rd. NW6 .... 1G 81
SW20 .... 1E 152
Dunmow Cl. RM6: Chad H 5C 54
TW13: Hanw 3C 130
Dunmow Ho. RM9: Dag 1B 90
SE11 .... *5H 19*
(*off Newburn St.*)
Dunmow Rd. E15 .... 4F 69
Dunmow Wlk. *N1* *1C 84*
(*off Popham St.*)
Dunnage Cres. SE16 .... 4A 104
(not continuous)
Dunnico Ho. *SE17* *5E 102*
(*off East St.*)
Dunn Mead NW9 .... 7G 29
Dunnock Cl. N9 .... 1E 34
Dunnock Rd. E6 .... 6C 88
Dunn's Pas. WC1 .... 7F 7
Dunn St. E8 .... 5F 67
Dunollie Pl. NW5 .... 5G 65
Dunollie Rd. NW5 .... 5G 65
Dunoon Gdns. SE23 .... 7K 121
Dunoon Ho. *N1* *1K 83*
(*off Bemerton Est.*)
Dunoon Rd. SE23 .... 7J 121
Dunoran Home BR1: Brom 1C 160
Dunraven Dr. EN2: Enf 2F 23
Dunraven Rd. W12 .... 1C 98
Dunraven St. W1 .... 2F 11 (7D 82)
Dunsany Rd. W14 .... 3F 99
Dunsfold Cl. *SM2: Sutt* *7K 165*
(*off Blackbush Cl.*)
Dunsfold Way CR0: New Ad 7D 170
Dunsford Way SW15 .... 6D 116
Dunsmore Cl. UB4: Yead 4C 76
Dunsmore Rd. KT12: Walt T 6K 147
Dunsmure Rd. N16 .... 1E 66
Dunspring La. IG5: Ilf 2F 53
Dunstable M. W1 .... 5H 5 (5E 82)
Dunstable Rd. KT8: W Mole 4D 148
TW9: Rich 4E 114
Dunstall Rd. SW20 .... 6D 134
Dunstall Way KT8: W Mole 3F 149
Dunstall Welling Est. DA16: Well 2B 126
Dunstan Cl. N2 .... 3A 46
Dunstan Glade BR5: Pet W 6H 161
Dunstan Ho's. *E1* *5J 85*
(*off Stepney Grn.*)
Dunstan Rd. NW11 .... 1H 63
Dunstan's Gro. SE22 .... 6H 121
Dunstan's Rd. SE22 .... 7G 121
Dunster Av. SM4: Mord 1F 165
Dunster Cl. EN5: Barn 4A 20
RM5: Col R 2J 55
Dunster Ct. EC3 .... 2H 15 (7E 84)
Dunster Dr. NW9 .... 1J 61
Dunster Gdns. NW6 .... 7H 63
Dunster Ho. SE6 .... 3E 140
Dunsterville Way SE1 .... 7F 15 (2D 102)
Dunster Way HA2: Harr 3C 58
SM6: Wall 1E 166
Dunston Rd. E8 .... 1F 85
SW11 .... 2E 118
Dunston St. E8 .... 1E 84
Dunton Cl. KT6: Surb 1E 162
Dunton Ct. SE23 .... 2H 139
Dunton Rd. E10 .... 7D 50
RM1: Rom 4K 55
SE1 .... 5F 103
Duntshill Rd. SW18 .... 1K 135
Dunvegan Cl. KT8: W Mole 4F 149
Dunvegan Rd. SE9 .... 4D 124
Dunwich Ct. *RM6: Chad H* *5B 54*
(*off Glandford Way*)
Dunwich Rd. DA7: Bex 1F 127
Dunworth M. W11 .... 6H 81
Duplex Ride SW1 .... 7F 11 (2D 100)
Dupont Rd. SW20 .... 2F 153
Duppas Av. CR0: Wadd 4B 168
Duppas Cl. TW17: Shep 5F 147
Duppas Ct. *CR0: Croy* *3B 168*
(*off Duppas Hill Ter.*)
Duppas Hill La. CR0: Croy 4B 168
Duppas Hill Rd. CR0: Wadd 4A 168
Duppas Hill Ter. CR0: Croy 3B 168
Duppas Rd. CR0: Wadd 3A 168
Dupree Rd. SE7 .... 5K 105
Duraden Cl. BR3: Beck 7D 140
Durand Cl. SM5: Cars 1D 166
Durand Gdns. SW9 .... 1K 119
Durands Wlk. SE16 .... 2B 104
Durand Way NW10 .... 7J 61
Durants Pk. Av. EN3: Pond E 4E 24
Durants Rd. EN3: Pond E 4D 24
Durant St. E2 .... 2G 85
Durban Ct. E7 .... 7B 70
Durban Gdns. RM10: Dag 7J 73
Durban Ho. *W12* *7D 80*
(*off White City Est.*)
Durban Rd. BR3: Beck 2B 158
E15 .... 3G 87
E17 .... 1B 50
IG2: Ilf 1J 71
N17 .... 6K 33
SE27 .... 4C 138
Durbin Rd. KT9: Chess 4E 162
Durdan Cotts. *UB1: S'hall* *6D 76*
(*off Denbigh Rd.*)
Durdans Ho. *NW1* *7F 65*
(*off Farrier St.*)
Durdans Rd. UB1: S'hall 6D 76
Durell Gdns. RM9: Dag 5D 72
Durell Ho. *SE16* *2K 103*
(*off Wolfe Cres.*)
Durell Rd. RM9: Dag 5D 72
Durfey Pl. SE5 .... 7D 102
Durford Cres. SW15 .... 1D 134
Durham Av. BR2: Brom 4H 159
IG8: Buck H, Wfd G 5G 37
TW5: Hest 5D 94
Durham Cl. SW20 .... 2D 152
Durham Ct. *NW6* *2J 81*
(*off Kilburn Pk. Rd.*)
TW11: Tedd 4J 131
Durham Hill BR1: Brom 4H 141
Durham Ho. BR2: Brom 4G 159
IG11: Bark *7A 72*
(*off Margaret Bondfield Av.*)
NW8 .... *2D 4*
(*off Grove Gdns.*)
RM10: Dag 5J 73
Durham Ho. St. WC2 .... 3F 13
Durham Pl. IG1: Ilf 4G 71
SW3 .... 6E 16 (5D 100)
Durham Ri. SE18 .... 5G 107
Durham Rd. BR2: Brom 3H 159
DA14: Sidc 5B 144
E12 .... 4B 70
E16 .... 4G 87
HA1: Harr 5F 41
N2 .... 3C 46
N7 .... 2K 65
N9 .... 2B 34
RM10: Dag 5J 73
SW20 .... 1D 152
TW14: Felt 7A 112
W5 .... 3D 96
Durham Row E1 .... 5K 85
Durham St. SE11 .... 6G 19 (5K 101)
Durham Ter. W2 .... 6K 81
Durham Yd. E2 .... 3H 85
Durley Av. HA5: Pinn 7C 40
Durley Rd. N16 .... 7E 48
Durlston Rd. E5 .... 2G 67
KT2: King T 6E 132
Durnford Ho. SE6 .... 3E 140
Durnford St. N15 .... 5E 48
SE10 .... 6E 104
Durning Rd. SE19 .... 5D 138
Durnsford Av. SW19 .... 2J 135
Durnsford Rd. N11 .... 1H 47
SW19 .... 2J 135
Durnsford Sports Cen. 1G 47
Durrant Ct. HA3: Hrw W 2J 41
Durrant Way BR6: Farnb 5H 173
Durrell Rd. SW6 .... 1H 117
Durrell Way TW17: Shep 6F 147
Durrels Ho. *W14* *4H 99*
(*off Warwick Gdns.*)
Durrington Av. SW20 .... 7E 134
Durrington Pk. Rd. SW20 .... 1E 152
Durrington Rd. E5 .... 4A 68
Durrington Twr. SW8 .... 2G 119
Durrisdeer Ho. *NW2* *4H 63*
(*off Lyndale*)
Dursley Cl. SE3 .... 2A 124
Dursley Gdns. SE3 .... 1B 124
Dursley Rd. SE3 .... 2A 124
Durward Ho. *W8* *2K 99*
(*off Kensington Ct.*)
Durward St. E1 .... 5H 85
Durweston M. W1 .... 5F 5
Durweston St. W1 .... 6F 5 (5D 82)
Dury Falls Ct. RM5: Col R 2J 55
Dury Rd. EN5: Barn 1C 20
Dutch Barn Cl. TW19: Stanw 6A 110
Dutch Gdns. KT2: King T 6H 133
Dutch Yd. SW18 .... 5J 117
Dutton St. SE10 .... 1E 122
Duval Ho. *N19* *2H 65*
(*off Ashbrook Rd.*)
Duxberry Av. TW13: Felt 3A 130
Duxberry Cl. BR2: Brom 5C 160
Duxford Ho. *SE2* *2D 108*
(*off Wolvercote Rd.*)
Dye Ho. La. E3 .... 1C 86
Dyer Ho. TW12: Hamp 1F 149
Dyer's Bldgs. EC1 .... 6J 7 (5A 84)
Dyers Hall Rd. E11 .... 1G 69
Dyers Hill Rd. E11 .... 2F 69
Dyers La. SW15 .... 4D 116
Dykes Way BR2: Brom 3H 159
Dykewood Cl. DA5: Bexl 3K 145
Dylan Rd. DA17: Belv 3G 109
SE24 .... 4B 120
Dylways SE5 .... 4D 120
Dymchurch Cl. BR6: Orp 4J 173
IG5: Ilf 2E 52
Dymes Path SW19 .... 2F 135
Dymock St. SW6 .... 3K 117
Dyneley Rd. SE12 .... 3A 142
Dyne Rd. NW6 .... 7G 63
Dynevor Rd. N16 .... 3E 66
TW10: Rich 5E 114
Dynham Rd. NW6 .... 7J 63
Dyott St. WC1 .... 7D 6 (6H 83)
Dysart Av. KT2: King T 5C 132
Dysart St. EC2 .... 4G 9 (4D 84)
Dyson Ct. HA0: Wemb 4A 60
NW2 .... 1E 62
Dyson Ho. *SE10* *5H 105*
(*off Blackwall La.*)
Dyson Rd. E11 .... 6G 51
E15 .... 6H 69
Dysons Rd. N18 .... 5C 34

E

Eade Rd. N4 .... 7C 48
Eagans Cl. N2 .... 3B 46
Eagle Av. RM6: Chad H 6E 54
Eagle Cl. EN3: Pond E 4D 24
SE16 .... 5J 103
SM6: Wall 6J 167
Eagle Ct. E11 .... 4J 51
EC1 .... 5A 8 (5B 84)
Eagle Dr. NW9 .... 2A 44
Eagle Hgts. SW11 .... 3C 118
Eagle Hill SE19 .... 6D 138
Eagle Ho. *E1* *4H 85*
(*off Headlam St.*)
N1 .... *2D 84*
(*off Eagle Wharf Rd.*)
Eagle Ho. M. SW4 .... 5G 119
Eagle La. E11 .... 4J 51
Eagle Lodge NW11 .... 7H 45
Eagle M. N1 .... 6E 66
Eagle Pl. SW1 .... 3B 12
SW7 .... 5A 100
Eagle Rd. HA0: Wemb 7D 60
TW6: H'row A 3H 111
Eaglesfield Rd. SE18 .... 1F 125
Eagle St. WC1 .... 6G 7 (5K 83)
Eagle Ter. IG8: Wfd G 7E 36
Eagle Trad. Est. CR4: Mitc 6D 154
Eagle Wharf Ct. *SE1* *5J 15*
(*off Lafone St.*)
Eagle Wharf E. *E14* *7A 86*
(*off Narrow St.*)
Eagle Wharf Rd. N1 .... 2C 84
Eagle Wharf W. *E14* *7A 86*
(*off Narrow St.*)
Eagle Works E. E1 .... 4K 9
Eagle Works W. E1 .... 4J 9 (4F 85)
Eagling Cl. E3 .... 3C 86
Ealdham Sq. SE9 .... 4A 124
EALING 7D 78
Ealing B'way. Cen. W5 .... 7D 78
EALING COMMON 7F 79
Ealing Grn. W5 .... 1D 96
Ealing Pk. Gdns. W5 .... 4C 96
Ealing Pk. Mans. *W5* *3D 96*
(*off Sth. Ealing Rd.*)
Ealing Rd. HA0: Wemb 6E 60
TW8: Bford 4D 96
UB5: N'olt 1E 76
Ealing Rd. Trad. Est. TW8: Bford 5D 96
Ealing Squash & Fitness Club 6E 78
Ealing Studios 1D 96
Ealing Village W5 .... 6E 78
Eamont Cl. HA4: Ruis 7D 38
Eamont Ct. *NW8* *2C 82*
(*off Eamont St.*)
Eamont St. NW8 .... 2C 82
Eardley Cres. SW5 .... 5J 99
Eardley Rd. DA17: Belv 5G 109
SW16 .... 5G 137
Earhart Way TW6: Cran, H'row A 3J 111
Earl Cl. N11 .... 5A 32
Earldom Rd. SW15 .... 4E 116

Earle Gdns. KT2: King T 7E **132**
Earle Ho. *SW1* *4D **18***
(off Montaigne Cl.)
Earlham Ct. E11 . . . . .7H **51**
Earlham Gro. E7 . . . . .5H **69**
N22 . . . . .7E **32**
Earlham St. WC2 . . . . .1D **12** (6J **83**)
Earl Ho. *NW1* *4D **4***
(off Lisson Gro.)
Earlom Ho. *WC1* *2J **7***
(off Margery St.)
Earl Ri. SE18 .5H **107**
Earl Rd. SW14 . . . . .4J **115**
EARL'S COURT **5J 99**
Earls Court Exhibition Building **5J 99**
Earl's Ct. Gdns. SW5 . . . . .4K **99**
Earls Ct. Rd. SW5 . . . . .3J **99**
W8 . . . . .3J **99**
Earl's Ct. Sq. SW5 . . . . .5K **99**
Earls Cres. HA1: Harr 4J **41**
Earlsdown Ho. IG11: Bark 2H **89**
Earlsferry Way N1 . . . . .7J **65**
(not continuous)
EARLSFIELD **1A 136**
Earlsfield Ho. *KT2: King T* *1D **150***
(off Skerne Rd.)
TW9: Kew 7H **97**
Earlsfield Rd. SW18 . . . . .1A **136**
Earlshall Rd. SE9 . . . . .4D **124**
Earlsmead HA2: Harr 4D **58**
Earlsmead Rd. N15 . . . . .5F **49**
NW10 .3E **80**
Earls Ter. W8 .3H **99**
Earlsthorpe M. SW12 . . . . .6E **118**
Earlsthorpe Rd. SE26 . . . . .4K **139**
Earlstoke St. EC1 . . . . .1A **8** (3B **84**)
Earlston Gro. E9 . . . . .1H **85**
Earl St. EC2 . . . . .5G **9** (5D **84**)
(not continuous)
Earls Wlk. RM8: Dag 4B **72**
W8 . . . . .3J **99**
Earls Way BR6: Orp 2K **173**
Earlswood Av. CR7: Thor H 5A **156**
Earlswood Cl. SE10 . . . . .6G **105**
Earlswood Gdns. IG5: Ilf 3E **52**
Earlswood St. SE10 . . . . .5G **105**
Early M. NW1 . . . . .1F **83**
Earnshaw St. WC2 . . . . .7D **6** (6H **83**)
Earsby St. W14 . . . . .4G **99**
(not continuous)
Easby Cres. SM4: Mord 6K **153**
Easebourne Rd. RM8: Dag 5C **72**
Eashing Point *SW15* *1D **134***
(off Wanborough Dr.)
Easleys M. W1 . . . . .7H **5** (6E **82**)
East 10 Ent. Pk. E10 . . . . .1A **68**
EAST ACTON **7B 80**
E. Acton Arc. W3 . . . . .6A **80**
E. Acton Ct. W3 . . . . .7A **80**
E. Acton La. W3 . . . . .1A **98**
E. Arbour St. E1 . . . . .6K **85**
East Av. E12 . . . . .7C **70**
E17 . . . . .4D **50**
N2 . . . . .4K **45**
SM6: Wall 5K **167**
UB1: S'hall 7D **76**
UB3: Hayes 1H **93**
East Bank N16 .7E **48**
Eastbank Rd. TW12: Ham H 5G **131**
EAST BARNET **6H 21**
E. Barnet Rd. EN4: E Barn 4G **21**
E. Beckton District Cen. E6 . . . . .5D **88**
EAST BEDFONT **7G 111**
East Block *SE1* *6H **13***
(off York Rd.)
E. Boundary Rd. E12 . . . . .3D **70**
Eastbourne Av. W3 . . . . .6K **79**
Eastbourne Gdns. SW14 . . . . .3J **115**
Eastbourne M. W2 . . . . .7A **4** (6A **82**)
Eastbourne Rd. E6 . . . . .3E **88**
(not continuous)
E15 . . . . .1G **87**
N15 . . . . .6E **48**

Eastbourne Rd. SW17 . . . . .6E **136**
TW8: Bford 5C **96**
TW13: Felt 2B **130**
W4 . . . . .6J **97**
Eastbourne Ter. W2 . . . . .7A **4** (6A **82**)
Eastbournia Av. N9 . . . . .3C **34**
Eastbrook Av. N9 . . . . .7D **24**
RM10: Dag 4J **73**
Eastbrook Dr. RM7: Rush G 3K **73**
Eastbrookend Country Pk. **3K 73**
Eastbrook Rd. SE3 . . . . .1K **123**
Eastbury Av. EN1: Enf 1A **24**
IG11: Bark 1J **89**
Eastbury Ct. *EN5: New Bar* *5F **21***
(off Lyonsdown Rd.)
IG11: Bark 1J **89**
Eastbury Gro. W4 . . . . .5A **98**
Eastbury Manor House **1K 89**
Eastbury Rd. BR5: Pet W 6H **161**
E6 . . . . .4E **88**
KT2: King T 7E **132**
RM7: Rom 6K **55**
Eastbury Sq. IG11: Bark 1K **89**
Eastbury Ter. E1 . . . . .4K **85**
Eastcastle St. W1 . . . . .7A **6** (6G **83**)
Eastcheap EC3 . . . . .2G **15** (7E **84**)
E. Churchfield Rd. W3 . . . . .1K **97**
Eastchurch Rd. TW6: H'row A 2G **111**
East Cl. EN4: Cockf 4K **21**
UB6: G'frd 2G **77**
W5 . . . . .4G **79**
Eastcombe Av. SE7 . . . . .6K **105**
EASTCOTE **7K 39**
Eastcote BR6: Orp 1K **173**
Eastcote Av. HA2: Harr 2F **59**
KT8: W Mole 5D **148**
UB6: G'frd 5A **60**
Eastcote Hockey & Badminton Club
. . . .**6H 39**
Eastcote Ind. Est. HA4: Ruis 7A **40**
Eastcote La. HA2: Harr 4C **58**
UB5: N'olt 5D **58**
(not continuous)
Eastcote La. Nth. UB5: N'olt 6D **58**
Eastcote Pl. HA5: Eastc 6K **39**
Eastcote Rd. DA16: Well 2H **125**
HA2: Harr 3G **59**
HA4: Ruis 7G **39**
HA5: Pinn 5B **40**
Eastcote St. SW9 . . . . .2K **119**
Eastcote Vw. HA5: Pinn 4A **40**
EASTCOTE VILLAGE **5K 39**
East Ct. HA0: Wemb 2C **60**
East Cres. EN1: Enf 5A **24**
N11 . . . . .4J **31**
Eastcroft Rd. KT19: Ewe 7A **164**
E. Cross Cen. E15 . . . . .6C **68**
E. Cross Route E3 . . . . .7B **68**
E9 . . . . .5B **68**
(Crowfoot Cl.)
E9 . . . . .7B **68**
(Wansbeck Rd.)
E15 . . . . .5B **68**
Eastdown Ct. SE13 . . . . .4F **123**
Eastdown Ho. E8 . . . . .4G **67**
Eastdown Pk. SE13 . . . . .4F **123**
East Dr. SM5: Cars 7C **166**
E. Duck Lees La. EN3: Pond E 4F **25**
EAST DULWICH **4F 121**
E. Dulwich Gro. SE22 . . . . .5E **120**
E. Dulwich Rd. SE22 . . . . .4F **121**
(not continuous)
East End Farm HA5: Pinn 3D **40**
East End Rd. N2 . . . . .3K **45**
N3 . . . . .2J **45**
East End Way HA5: Pinn 3C **40**
East Entrance RM10: Dag 2H **91**
Eastern Av. E11 . . . . .6K **51**
HA5: Pinn 7B **40**
IG2: Ilf .6F **53**
IG4: Ilf .6C **52**
RM6: Chad H 4A **54**
Eastern Av. E. RM1: Rom 3K **55**

Eastern Av. Retail Pk. RM7: Rom 4J **55**
Eastern Av. W. RM6: Chad H 4E **54**
RM7: Chad H, Rom, Mawney . . .4A **54**
Eastern Bus. Pk. TW6: H'row A 2G **111**
Eastern Gateway E16 . . . . .7A **88**
Eastern Ho. *E2* *3H **85***
(off Bethnal Grn. Rd.)
Eastern Ind. Est. DA18: Erith 2G **109**
Eastern Perimeter Rd.
TW6: H'row A 2H **111**
Eastern Quay Apartments *E16* *1K **105***
(off Portsmouth M.)
Eastern Rd. E13 . . . . .2K **87**
E17 . . . . .5E **50**
N2 . . . . .3D **46**
N22 . . . . .1J **47**
SE4 . . . . .4C **122**
Eastern Rdbt. IG1: Ilf 2G **71**
Easternville Gdns. IG2: Ilf 6G **53**
Eastern Way DA17: Belv 2A **108**
DA18: Belv, Erith 2A **108**
SE2 . . . . .2A **108**
SE28 .2A **108**
E. Ferry Rd. E14 . . . . .4D **104**
Eastfield Gdns. RM10: Dag 4G **73**
Eastfield Rd. E17 . . . . .4C **50**
EN3: Enf W 1E **24**
N8 . . . . .3J **47**
RM9: Dag 4F **73**
RM10: Dag 4G **73**
Eastfields HA5: Eastc 5A **40**
Eastfields Av. SW18 . . . . .4J **117**
Eastfields Rd. CR4: Mitc 2E **154**
W3 . . . . .5J **79**
Eastfield St. E14 . . . . .5A **86**
EAST FINCHLEY **4C 46**
East Gdns. SW17 . . . . .6C **136**
Eastgate Bus. Pk. E10 . . . . .1A **68**
Eastgate Cl. SE28 . . . . .6D **90**
Eastglade HA5: Pinn 3D **40**
EAST HAM **2D 88**
E. Ham & Barking By-Pass
IG11: Bark 2J **89**
Eastham Cl. EN5: Barn 5B **20**
E. Ham Ind. Est. E6 . . . . .4C **88**
East Ham Leisure Cen. **1D 88**
E. Ham Mnr. Way E6 . . . . .6E **88**
East Ham Nature Reserve **4D 88**
E. Harding St. EC4 . . . . .7K **7** (6A **84**)
E. Heath Rd. NW3 . . . . .3A **64**
East Hill HA9: Wemb 2G **61**
SW18 .5K **117**
Eastholm NW11 . . . . .4K **45**
East Holme DA8: Erith 1K **127**
Eastholme UB3: Hayes 1J **93**
E. India Bldgs. *E14* *7C **86***
(off Saltwell St.)
E. India Ct. *SE16* *2J **103***
(off St Marychurch St.)
E. India Dock Ho. E14 . . . . .6E **86**
E. India Dock Rd. E14 . . . . .6C **86**
E. India Way CR0: Croy 1F **169**
Eastlake Ho. NW8 . . . . .4B **4**
Eastlake Rd. SE5 . . . . .2C **120**
Eastlands Cres. SE21 . . . . .6F **121**
East La. HA0: Wemb 3B **60**
HA9: Wemb 3B **60**
KT1: King T 3D **150**
SE16 .2G **103**
(not continuous)
East La. Bus. Pk. HA9: Wemb 2D **60**
Eastlea M. E16 . . . . .4G **87**
Eastleigh Av. HA2: Harr 2F **59**
Eastleigh Cl. NW2 . . . . .3A **62**
SM2: Sutt 7K **165**
Eastleigh Rd. DA7: Bex 3J **127**
E17 . . . . .2B **50**
Eastleigh Wlk. SW15 . . . . .7C **116**
Eastleigh Way TW14: Felt 1J **129**
East Lodge *E16* *1J **105***
(off Wesley Av.)
E. London Crematorium E13 . . . . .3H **87**
East London Gymnastic Cen. **6D 88**

Eastman Ho. SW4 . . . . .6G **119**
Eastman Rd. W3 . . . . .2K **97**
East Mascalls SE7 . . . . .6A **106**
East Mead HA4: Ruis 3B **58**
Eastmead Av. UB6: G'frd 3F **77**
Eastmead Cl. BR1: Brom 2C **160**
Eastmearn Rd. SE21 . . . . .2C **138**
EAST MOLESEY **4H 149**
Eastmoor Pl. SE7 . . . . .3B **106**
Eastmoor St. SE7 . . . . .3B **106**
East Mt. St. E1 .5H **85**
(not continuous)
Eastney Rd. CR0: Croy 1B **168**
Eastney St. SE10 . . . . .5F **105**
Eastnor Rd. SE9 . . . . .1G **143**
Easton St. WC1 . . . . .3J **7** (4A **84**)
East Pk. Cl. RM6: Chad H 5D **54**
East Parkside SE10 . . . . .2G **105**
East Pas. EC1 . . . . .5C **8**
East Pl. SE27 .4C **138**
East Point SE1 . . . . .5G **103**
E. Pole Cotts. N14: Cockf 4C **22**
E. Poultry Av. EC1 . . . . .6A **8** (5B **84**)
East Ramp TW6: H'row A 1D **110**
East Rd. DA16: Well 2B **126**
E15 . . . . .1J **87**
EN3: Enf W 1D **24**
EN4: E Barn 1K **31**
HA1: Harr 7B **42**
HA8: Edg 1H **43**
KT2: King T 1E **150**
N1 . . . . .2E **8** (3D **84**)
N2 . . . . .1C **46**
RM6: Chad H 5E **54**
RM7: Rush G 7K **55**
SW3 . . . . .6G **17** (5E **100**)
SW19 .6A **136**
TW14: Bedf 7F **111**
UB7: W Dray 4B **92**
E. Rochester Way DA5: Bexl 6H **127**
DA15: Bexl, Sidc 4J **125**
East Row E11 . . . . .6J **51**
W10 . . . . .4G **81**
Eastry Av. BR2: Hayes 6H **159**
Eastry Ho. *SW8* *7J **101***
(off Hartington Rd.)
Eastry Rd. DA8: Erith 7G **109**
EAST SHEEN **4J 115**
E. Sheen Av. SW14 . . . . .5K **115**
Eastside Rd. NW11 . . . . .4H **45**
East Smithfield E1 . . . . .3K **15** (7F **85**)
East St. BR1: Brom 2J **159**
DA7: Bex 4G **127**
IG11: Bark 1G **89**
SE17 .5C **102**
TW8: Bford 7C **96**
E. Surrey Gro. SE15 . . . . .7F **103**
E. Tenter St. E1 . . . . .1K **15** (6F **85**)
East Ter. DA15: Sidc 1J **143**
E. Thamesmead Bus. Pk.
DA18: Erith 2F **109**
East Towers HA5: Pinn 5B **40**
East Va. W3 . . . . .1B **98**
East Vw. E4 . . . . .5K **35**
EN5: Barn 2C **20**
Eastview Av. SE18 . . . . .7J **107**
Eastville Av. NW11 . . . . .6H **45**
East Wlk. EN4: E Barn 7K **21**
UB3: Hayes 1J **93**
East Way BR2: Hayes 7J **159**
CR0: Croy 2A **170**
E11 . . . . .5K **51**
HA4: Ruis 1J **57**
UB3: Hayes 1J **93**
Eastway E9 . . . . .6B **68**
SM4: Mord 5F **153**
SM6: Wall 4G **167**
Eastwell Cl. BR3: Beck 7A **140**
Eastwell Ho. SE1 . . . . .7F **15**
EAST WICKHAM **1C 126**
Eastwood Cl. E18 . . . . .2J **51**
N7 . . . . .5A **66**
N17 . . . . .7C **34**

Eastwood Rd. E18 2J 51
IG3: Ilf 1A 72
N10 2E 46
UB7: W Dray 2C 92
East Woodside DA5: Bexl 7E 126
Eastwood St. SW16 6G 137
Eatington Rd. E10 5F 51
Eaton Cl. HA7: Stan 4G 27
SW1 4G 17 (4E 100)
Eaton Ct. E18 2J 51
HA8: Edg 4B 28
Eaton Dr. KT2: King T 7G 133
RM5: Col R 1H 55
SW9 4B 120
Eaton Gdns. RM9: Dag 7E 72
Eaton Ga. SW1 3G 17 (4E 100)
Eaton Ho. E14 7B 86
(off Westferry Cir.)
SW11 1B 118
Eaton La. SW1 2K 17 (3F 101)
Eaton Mans. SW1 4G 17
(off Bourne St.)
Eaton M. Nth. SW1 3G 17 (4E 100)
Eaton M. Sth. SW1 3H 17 (4E 100)
Eaton M. W. SW1 3H 17 (4E 100)
Eaton Pk. Rd. N13 2F 33
Eaton Pl. SW1 2G 17 (4E 100)
Eaton Ri. E11 5A 52
W5 5D 78
Eaton Rd. DA14: Sidc 2D 144
EN1: Enf 3K 23
NW4 5E 44
SM2: Sutt 6B 166
TW3: Houn 4H 113
Eaton Row SW1 2J 17 (3F 101)
Eatons Mead E4 2H 35
Eaton Sq. SW1 3G 17 (4E 100)
Eaton Ter. E3 3A 86
SW1 3G 17 (4E 100)
Eaton Ter. M. SW1 3G 17
Eatonville Rd. SW17 2D 136
Eatonville Vs. SW17 2D 136
Ebb Ct. E16 7G 89
Ebbett Ct. W3 5K 79
Ebbisham Dr. SW8 7G 19 (6K 101)
Ebbisham Rd. KT4: Wor Pk 2E 164
Ebbsfleet Rd. NW2 5G 63
Ebdon Way SE3 3K 123
Ebenezer Ho. SE11 4K 19 (4B 102)
Ebenezer Mussel Ho. E2 2J 85
(off Patriot Sq.)
Ebenezer St. N1 1E 8 (3D 84)
Ebenezer Wlk. SW16 1G 155
Ebley Cl. SE15 6F 103
Ebner St. SW18 5K 117
Ebony Ho. E2 3G 85
(off Buckfast St.)
Ebor Cotts. SW15 3A 134
Ebor St. E1 3J 9 (4F 85)
Ebrington Rd. HA3: Kent 6D 42
Ebsworth St. SE23 7K 121
Eburne Rd. N7 3J 65
Ebury Bri. SW1 5J 17 (5F 101)
Ebury Bri. Est. SW1 5J 17 (5F 101)
Ebury Bri. Rd. SW1 6H 17 (5E 100)
Ebury Cl. BR2: Kes 3C 172
Ebury M. SE27 3B 138
SW1 3J 17 (4F 101)
Ebury M. E. SW1 2J 17 (3F 101)
Ebury Sq. SW1 4H 17 (4E 100)
Ebury St. SW1 4H 17 (4E 100)
Ecclesbourne Cl. N13 5F 33
Ecclesbourne Gdns. N13 5F 33
Ecclesbourne Rd. CR7: Thor H 5C 156
N1 7C 66
Eccleshill BR2: Brom 4H 159
(off Durham Rd.)
Eccles Rd. SW11 4D 118
Eccleston Bri. SW1 3K 17 (4F 101)
Eccleston Cl. BR6: Orp 1H 173
EN4: Cockf 4J 21
Eccleston Cres. RM6: Chad H 7B 54
Ecclestone Ct. HA9: Wemb 5E 60
Ecclestone M. HA9: Wemb 5E 60
Ecclestone Pl. HA9: Wemb 5F 61
Eccleston Ho. SW2 6A 120
Eccleston M. SW1 2H 17 (3E 100)
Eccleston Pl. SW1 3J 17 (4F 101)
Eccleston Rd. W13 7A 78
Eccleston Sq. SW1 4K 17 (4F 101)
Eccleston Sq. M. SW1 4A 18 (4F 101)
Eccleston St. SW1 2J 17 (3F 101)
Echelforde Dr. TW15: Ashf 4C 128
Echo Hgts. E4 1J 35
Eckford St. N1 2A 84
Eckington Ho. N15 6D 48
(off Fladbury Rd.)
Eckstein Rd. SW11 4C 118
Eclipse Ho. N22 2K 47
(off Station Rd.)
Eclipse Rd. E13 5K 87
Ecology Cen. and Arts Pavilion 3A 86
Ector Rd. SE6 2G 141
Edam Ct. DA15: Sidc 3A 144
Edans Ct. W12 2B 98
Edar Ho. CR0: New Ad 6D 170
Edbrooke Rd. W9 4J 81
Eddisbury Ho. SE26 3G 139
Eddiscombe Rd. SW6 2H 117
Eddy Cl. RM7: Rom 6H 55
Eddystone Rd. SE4 5A 122
Eddystone Twr. SE8 5A 104
Eddystone Wlk. TW19: Stanw 7A 110
Ede Cl. TW3: Houn 3D 112
Edenbridge Cl. SE16 5H 103
(off Masters Dr.)
Edenbridge Rd. E9 7K 67
EN1: Enf 6K 23
Eden Cl. DA5: Bexl 4K 145
HA0: Wemb 1D 78
NW3 2J 63
W8 3J 99
Edencourt Rd. SW16 6F 137
Edendale W3 7H 79
Edendale Rd. DA7: Bex 1K 127
Edenfield Gdns.
KT4: Wor Pk 3B 164
Eden Gro. E17 5D 50
N7 5K 65
Edenham Way W10 4H 81
Eden Ho. NW8 4C 4
(off Church St.)
Edenhurst Av. SW6 3H 117
Eden Lodge NW6 7F 63
Eden M. SW17 3A 136
EDEN PARK 5C 158
Eden Pk. Av. BR3: Beck 4A 158
(not continuous)
Eden Rd. BR3: Beck 4A 158
CR0: Croy 4D 168
DA5: Bexl 4J 145
E17 5D 50
SE27 4B 138
Edensor Gdns. W4 7A 98
Edensor Rd. W4 7A 98
Eden St. KT1: King T 2D 150
Edenvale Cl. CR4: Mitc 7E 136
Edenvale Rd. CR4: Mitc 7E 136
Edenvale St. SW6 2A 118
Eden Wlk. KT1: King T 2E 150
Eden Way BR3: Beck 5B 158
E3 1B 86
Ederline Av. SW16 3K 155
Edgar Ct. KT3: N Mald 2A 152
Edgar Ho. E9 5A 68
(off Homerton Rd.)
E11 7J 51
SW8 7J 101
(off Wyvil Rd.)
Edgar Kail Way SE22 4E 120
Edgarley Ter. SW6 1G 117
Edgar Rd. E3 3D 86
RM6: Chad H 7D 54
TW4: Houn 7D 112
UB7: Yiew 7A 74
Edgar Wallace Cl. SE15 7E 102
Edgcott Ho. W10 5E 80
(off Sutton Way)
Edgeborough Way BR1: Brom 7B 142
Edgebury BR7: Chst 4F 143
Edgebury Wlk. BR7: Chst 4G 143
Edge Bus. Cen., The NW2 2D 62
Edgecombe Ho. SE5 2E 120
SW19 1G 135
Edgecoombe CR2: Sels 7J 169
Edgecoombe Cl. KT2: King T 7K 133
Edgecote Cl. W3 1J 97
Edgecot Gro. N15 5E 48
Edgefield Av. IG11: Bark 7K 71
Edgefield Ct. IG11: Bark 7K 71
(off Edgefield Av.)
Edge Hill SE18 6F 107
SW19 7F 135
Edge Hill Av. N3 4J 45
Edge Hill Ct. DA14: Sidc 4K 143
SW19 7F 135
Edgehill Gdns. RM10: Dag 4G 73
Edgehill Ho. SW9 2B 120
Edgehill Rd. BR7: Chst 3G 143
CR4: Mitc 1F 155
W13 5C 78
Edgeley La. SW4 3H 119
Edgeley Rd. SW4 3H 119
Edgel St. SW18 4K 117
Edgepoint Cl. SE27 5B 138
Edge St. W8 1J 99
Edgewood Dr. BR6: Chels 5K 173
Edgewood Grn. CR0: Croy 1K 169
Edgeworth Av. NW4 5C 44
Edgeworth Cl. NW4 5C 44
Edgeworth Ct. EN4: Cockf 4H 21
(off Fordham Rd.)
Edgeworth Cres. NW4 5C 44
Edgeworth Ho. NW8 1A 82
(off Boundary Rd.)
Edgeworth Rd. EN4: Cockf 4H 21
SE9 4A 124
Edgington Rd. SW16 6H 137
Edgington Way DA14: Sidc 7C 144
Edgson Ho. SW1 5J 17
(off Ebury Bri. Rd.)
EDGWARE 6B 28
EDGWARE BURY 1A 28
Edgwarebury Gdns. HA8: Edg 5B 28
Edgwarebury La. HA8: Edg 1A 28
WD6: Els 1A 28
Edgwarebury Pk. 3A 28
Edgware Ct. HA8: Edg 6B 28
Edgware Football Ground 7B 28
Edgware Rd. NW2 1D 62
NW9 2J 43
W2 4A 4 (4B 82)
Edgware Town & Wealdstone FC 7B 28
Edgware Way HA8: Edg 4A 28
NW7 4A 28
WD6: Edg, Els 1J 27
Edinburgh Cl. E2 2J 85
HA5: Pinn 7B 40
UB10: Ick 4D 56
Edinburgh Ct. DA8: Erith 7K 109
KT1: King T 3E 150
(off Watersplash Cl.)
SE16 1K 103
(off Rotherhithe St.)
SW20 5F 153
Edinburgh Dr. UB10: Ick 4D 56
Edinburgh Ga. SW1 6E 10 (2D 100)
Edinburgh Ho. NW4 3E 44
W9 3K 81
(off Maida Va.)
Edinburgh Rd. E13 2K 87
E17 5C 50
(not continuous)
N18 5B 34
SM1: Sutt 2A 166
W7 2K 95
Edington NW5 6E 64
Edington Rd. EN3: Enf H 2D 24
SE2 3B 108
Edison Bldg. E14 2C 104
Edison Cl. E17 5C 50
UB7: W Dray 2B 92
Edison Ct. SE10 3H 105
Edison Dr. HA9: Wemb 3E 60
UB1: S'hall 6F 77
Edison Gro. SE18 7K 107
Edison Ho. HA9: Wemb 3J 61
(off Barnhill Rd.)
SE1 4D 102
(off Balfour St.)
Edison Rd. BR2: Brom 2J 159
DA16: Well 1K 125
EN3: Brim 2G 25
N8 6H 47
Edis St. NW1 1E 82
Editha Mans. SW10 6A 100
(off Edith Gro.)
Edith Brinson Ho. E14 6F 87
(off Oban St.)
Edith Cavell Cl. N19 7J 47
Edith Cavell Way SE18 1C 124
Edith Gdns. KT5: Surb 7H 151
Edith Gro. SW10 6A 100
Edith Ho. W6 5E 98
(off Queen Caroline St.)
Edithna St. SW9 3J 119
Edith Neville Cotts. NW1 1C 6
(off Drummond Cres.)
Edith Ramsay Ho. E1 5A 86
(off Duckett St.)
Edith Rd. E6 7B 70
E15 5F 69
N11 7C 32
RM6: Chad H 7D 54
SE25 5D 156
SW19 6K 135
W14 4G 99
Edith Row SW6 1K 117
Edith St. E2 2G 85
Edith Summerskill Ho. SW6 7H 99
(off Clem Attlee Est.)
Edith Ter. SW10 7A 100
Edith Vs. W14 4H 99
Edith Yd. SW10 7A 100
Edmansons Cl. N17 1F 49
Edmeston Cl. E9 6A 68
Edmond Ct. SE14 1J 121
Edmonscote W13 5A 78
EDMONTON 3B 34
Edmonton Ct. SE16 3J 103
(off Canada Est.)
Edmonton Grn. Shop. Cen. N9 2B 34
Edmonton Leisure Cen. 3B 34
Edmund Gro. TW13: Hanw 2D 130
Edmund Halley Way SE10 2G 105
Edmund Ho. SE17 6B 102
Edmund Hurst Dr. E6 5F 89
Edmund Rd. CR4: Mitc 3C 154
DA16: Well 3A 126
Edmundsbury Ct. Est.
SW9 4K 119
Edmunds Cl. UB4: Yead 5A 76
Edmund St. SE5 7D 102
Edmunds Wlk. N2 4C 46
Ednam Ho. SE15 6G 103
(off Haymerle Rd.)
Edna Rd. SW20 2F 153
Edna St. SW11 1C 118
Edred Ho. E9 4A 68
(off Lindisfarne Way)
Edrich Ho. SW4 1J 119
Edric Ho. SW1 3D 18
(off Page St.)
Edrick Rd. HA8: Edg 6D 28
Edrick Wlk. HA8: Edg 6D 28
Edric Rd. SE14 7K 103
Edridge Rd. CR0: Croy 3C 168
Edward VII Mans. NW10 3F 81
(off Chamberlayne Rd.)
Edward Alderton Theatre 3D 126
Edward Av. E4 6J 35
SM4: Mord 5B 154

Edward Bond Ho. *WC1* 2F 7
(*off Cromer St.*)
Edward Cl. N9 7A 24
NW2 4F 63
TW12: Ham H 5G 131
Edward Ct. E16 5J 87
Edward Dodd Ct. *N1* 1F 9
(*off Haberdasher St.*)
Edward Edward's Ho. SE1 5A 14
Edwardes Pl. W8 3H 99
Edwardes Sq. W8 3H 99
Edward Gro. EN4: E Barn 5G 21
Edward Ho. SE11 5H 19
W2 4A 4
(*off Hall Pl.*)
Edward Kennedy Ho. *W10* 4G 81
(*off Wornington Rd.*)
Edward Mann Cl. *E1* 6K 85
(*off Caroline St.*)
Edward M. NW1 1K 5 (3F 83)
Edward Pl. SE8 6B 104
Edward Rd. BR1: Brom 7K 141
BR7: Chst 5F 143
CR0: Croy 7E 156
E17 4K 49
EN4: E Barn 5G 21
HA2: Harr 3G 41
RM6: Chad H 6E 54
SE20 7K 139
TW12: Ham H 5G 131
TW14: Felt 5F 111
UB5: Yead 2A 76
Edward Robinson Ho. *SE14* 7K 103
(*off Reaston St.*)
Edward's Av. HA4: Ruis 6K 57
Edwards Cl. KT4: Wor Pk 2F 165
Edward's Cotts. N1 6B 66
Edwards Ct. *CR0: Croy* 4E 168
(*off South Pk. Hill Rd.*)
Edwards Dr. N11 7C 32
Edward's La. N16 2E 66
Edwards Mans. *IG11: Bark* 7K 71
(*off Upney La.*)
Edwards M. N1 7A 66
W1 1G 11 (6E 82)
Edward Sq. N1 1K 83
SE16 1A 104
Edwards Rd. DA17: Belv 4G 109
Edward St. E16 4J 87
(not continuous)
SE8 6B 104
SE14 7A 104
Edwards Yd. HA0: Wemb 1E 78
Edward Temme Av. E15 7H 69
Edward Tyler Rd. SE12 2A 142
Edward Way TW15: Ashf 2B 128
Edwina Gdns. IG4: Ilf 5C 52
Edwin Arnold Ct. DA14: Sidc 4K 143
Edwin Av. E6 2E 88
(not continuous)
Edwin Cl. DA7: Bex 6F 109
Edwin Ho. SE15 7G 103
Edwin Pl. *CR0: Croy* 1E 168
(*off Leslie Gro.*)
Edwin Rd. HA8: Edg 6E 28
TW1: Twick 1K 131
TW2: Twick 1J 131
Edwin's Mead E9 4A 68
Edwin Stray Ho. TW13: Hanw 2E 130
Edwin St. E1 4J 85
E16 5J 87
Edwin Ware Ct. HA5: Pinn 2A 40
Edwyn Cl. EN5: Barn 6A 20
Edwyn Ho. *SW18* 6K 117
(*off Neville Gill Cl.*)
Eel Brook Cl. SW6 1K 117
Eel Pie Island TW1: Twick 1A 132
Effie Pl. SW6 7J 99
Effie Rd. SW6 7J 99
Effingham Cl. SM2: Sutt 7K 165
Effingham Lodge KT1: King T 4D 150
Effingham Rd. CR0: Croy 7K 155
KT6: Surb 7B 150
Effingham Rd. N8 5A 48
SE12 5G 123
Effort St. SW17 5C 136
Effra Cl. SW19 6K 135
Effra Ct. *SW2* 5K 119
(*off Brixton Hill*)
Effra Pde. SW2 5A 120
Effra Rd. SW2 4A 120
SW19 6K 135
Effra Rd. Retail Pk. SW2 5A 120
Egan Way UB3: Hayes 7G 75
Egbert St. NW1 1E 82
Egbury Ho. *SW15* 6B 116
(*off Tangley Gro.*)
Egeremont Rd. SE13 2D 122
Egerton Cl. HA5: Eastc 4J 39
Egerton Ct. E11 7F 51
Egerton Cres. SW3 3D 16 (4C 100)
Egerton Dr. SE10 1D 122
Egerton Gdns. IG3: Ilf 3K 71
NW4 4D 44
NW10 1E 80
SW3 2C 16 (4C 100)
W13 6B 78
Egerton Gdns. M. SW3 2D 16 (3C 100)
Egerton Pl. SW3 2D 16 (3C 100)
Egerton Rd. HA0: Wemb 7F 61
KT3: N Mald 4B 152
N16 7F 49
SE25 3E 156
TW2: Twick 7J 113
Egerton Ter. SW3 2D 16 (3C 100)
Egerton Way UB3: Harl 7D 92
Eggardon Ct. UB5: N'olt 6F 59
Egham Cl. SM3: Cheam 2G 165
SW19 2G 135
Egham Cres. SM3: Cheam 3G 165
Egham Rd. E13 5K 87
Eglantine Rd. SW18 5A 118
Egleston Rd. SM4: Mord 6K 153
Eglington Ct. SE17 6C 102
Eglington Rd. E4 7K 25
Eglinton Hill SE18 6F 107
Eglinton Rd. SE18 6E 106
Egliston M. SW15 3E 116
Egliston Rd. SW15 3E 116
Eglon M. NW1 7D 64
Egmont Av. KT6: Surb 1F 163
Egmont Ct. KT12: Walt T 7K 147
Egmont Rd. KT3: N Mald 4B 152
KT6: Surb 1F 163
KT12: Walt T 7K 147
SM2: Sutt 7A 166
Egmont St. SE14 7K 103
Egremont Ho. *SE13* 2D 122
(*off Russett Way*)
Egremont Rd. SE27 3A 138
Egret Ho. *SE16* 4K 103
(*off Tawny Way*)
Egret Way UB4: Yead 5B 76
Eider Cl. E7 5H 69
UB4: Yead 5B 76
Eider Ct. *SE8* 6B 104
(*off Pilot Cl.*)
Eighteenth Rd. CR4: Mitc 4J 155
Eighth Av. E12 4D 70
UB3: Hayes 1J 93
Eileen Rd. SE25 5D 156
Eindhoven Cl. SM5: Cars 1E 166
Einstein Ho. HA9: Wemb 3J 61
Eisenhower Dr. E6 5C 88
Elaine Gro. NW5 5E 64
Elam Cl. SE5 2B 120
Elam St. SE5 2B 120
Elan Ct. E1 5H 85
Eland Ho. *SW1* 1A 18
(*off Bressenden Pl.*)
Eland Pl. CR0: Wadd 3B 168
Eland Rd. CR0: Wadd 3B 168
SW11 3D 118
Elba Pl. SE17 4C 102
Elberon Av. CR0: Bedd 6G 155
Elbe St. SW6 2A 118
Elborough Rd. SE25 5G 157
Elborough St. SW18 1J 135
Elbourne Ct. *SE16* 3K 103
(*off Worgan St.*)
Elbourne Trad. Est. DA17: Belv 3H 109
Elbourn Ho. *SW3* 5C 16
(*off Cale St.*)
Elbury Dr. E16 6J 87
Elcho St. SW11 7C 100
Elcot Av. SE15 7H 103
Elden Ho. *SW3* 3C 16
(*off Sloane Av.*)
Eldenwall Ind. Est. RM8: Dag 1E 72
Elder Av. N8 5J 47
Elderberry Gro. SE27 4C 138
Elderberry Rd. W5 2E 96
Elderberry Way E6 3D 88
Elder Cl. DA15: Sidc 1K 143
N20 2E 30
UB7: Yiew 7A 74
Elder Ct. WD23: Bushy 2D 26
Elderfield Ho. E14 7C 86
Elderfield Pl. SW17 4F 137
Elderfield Rd. E5 4K 67
Elderfield Wlk. E11 5K 51
Elderflower Way E15 7G 69
Elder Gdns. SE27 5C 138
Elder Oak Cl. SE20 1H 157
Elder Oak Ct. *SE20* 1H 157
(*off Anerley Ct.*)
Elder Rd. SE27 4C 138
Elderslie Cl. BR3: Beck 5C 158
Elderslie Rd. SE9 5E 124
Elder St. E1 5J 9 (4F 85)
(not continuous)
Elderton Rd. SE26 4A 140
Eldertree Pl. CR4: Mitc 1G 155
Eldertree Way CR4: Mitc 1G 155
Elder Wlk. *N1* 1B 84
(*off Popham St.*)
Elderwood Pl. SE27 5C 138
Eldon Av. CR0: Croy 2J 169
TW5: Hest 7E 94
Eldon Ct. NW6 1J 81
Eldon Gro. NW3 5B 64
Eldon Pk. SE25 4H 157
Eldon Rd. E17 4B 50
N9 1D 34
N22 1B 48
W8 3K 99
Eldon St. EC2 6F 9 (5D 84)
Eldon Way NW10 3H 79
Eldred Rd. IG11: Bark 1J 89
Eldrick Ct. TW14: Bedf 1F 129
Eldridge Cl. TW14: Felt 1J 129
Eldridge Ct. SE16 3G 103
Eleanor Cl. N15 3F 49
SE16 2K 103
Eleanor Ct. *E2* 1G 85
(*off Whiston Rd.*)
Eleanor Cres. NW7 5A 30
Eleanor Gdns. EN5: Barn 5A 20
RM8: Dag 2F 73
Eleanor Gro. SW13 3A 116
UB10: Ick 3D 56
Eleanor Ho. *W6* 5E 98
(*off Queen Caroline St.*)
Eleanor Rathbone Ho. *N6* 7H 47
(*off Avenue Rd.*)
Eleanor Rd. E8 6H 67
E15 6H 69
N11 6D 32
Eleanor's Station
Ruislip Lido Railway 3G 39
Eleanor St. E3 3C 86
Eleanor Wlk. SE18 4C 106
Electra Av. TW6: H'row A 3H 111
Electra Bus. Pk. E16 5F 87
Electric Av. SW9 4A 120
Electric La. SW9 4A 120
(not continuous)
Electric Pde. *E18* 2J 51
(*off George La.*)
Electric Pde. IG3: Ilf 2J 71
KT6: Surb 6D 150
Elektron Ho. E14 7F 87
ELEPHANT & CASTLE 3B 102
Elephant & Castle SE1 4B 102
Elephant & Castle Superbowl 4C 102
(*off Elephant & Castle*)
Elephant La. SE16 2J 103
Elephant Rd. SE17 4C 102
Elers Rd. UB3: Harl 4F 93
W13 2C 96
Eley Rd. N18 4D 34
Eley Rd. Retail Pk. N18 5D 34
Eleys Est. N9 3E 34
N18 4E 34
(not continuous)
Elfindale Rd. SE24 5C 120
Elfin Gro. TW11: Tedd 5K 131
Elford Cl. SE3 4K 123
Elford M. SW4 5G 119
Elfort Rd. N5 4A 66
Elfrida Cres. SE6 4C 140
Elf Row E1 7J 85
Elfwine Rd. W7 5J 77
Elgal Cl. BR6: Farnb 5F 173
Elgar *N8* 3J 47
(*off Boyton Cl.*)
Elgar Av. KT5: Surb 1G 163
NW10 6K 61
(not continuous)
SW16 3J 155
W5 2E 96
Elgar Cl. E13 2A 88
IG9: Buck H 2G 37
SE8 7C 104
UB10: Ick 2C 56
Elgar Ct. *W14* 3G 99
(*off Blythe Rd.*)
Elgar Ho. *NW6* 7A 64
(*off Fairfax Rd.*)
SW1 6K 17
(*off Churchill Gdns.*)
Elgar St. SE16 3A 104
Elgin Av. HA3: Kent 2B 42
TW15: Ashf 6E 128
W9 4H 81
W12 3D 98
Elgin Cl. W12 2D 98
Elgin Ct. *CR2: S Croy* 4C 168
(*off Bramley Hill*)
W9 4K 81
Elgin Cres. TW6: H'row A 2G 111
W11 7G 81
Elgin Dr. HA6: Nwood 1G 39
Elgin Est. *W9* 4J 81
(*off Elgin Av.*)
Elgin Ho. *E14* 6D 86
(*off Ricardo St.*)
Elgin Mans. W9 3K 81
Elgin M. W11 6G 81
Elgin M. Nth. W9 3K 81
Elgin M. Sth. W9 3K 81
Elgin Rd. CR0: Croy 2F 169
IG3: Ilf 1J 71
N22 2G 47
SM1: Sutt 3A 166
SM6: Wall 6G 167
Elgood Cl. W11 7G 81
Elgood Ho. *NW8* 2B 82
(*off Wellington Rd.*)
Elham Cl. BR1: Brom 7B 142
Elham Ho. E5 5H 67
Elia M. N1 1A 8 (2B 84)
Elias Pl. SW8 6A 102
Elia St. N1 1B 8 (2B 84)
Elibank Rd. SE9 4D 124
Elim Est. SE1 7G 15 (3E 102)
Elim St. SE1 7G 15 (3D 102)
(not continuous)
Elim Way E13 3H 87
Eliot Bank SE23 2H 139
Eliot Cotts. SE3 2G 123
Eliot Ct. SW18 6K 117

Eliot Dr. HA2: Harr	2F 59
Eliot Gdns. SW15	4C 116
Eliot Hill SE13	2E 122
Eliot M. NW8	2A 82
Eliot Pk. SE13	2E 122
Eliot Pl. SE3	2G 123
Eliot Rd. RM9: Dag	4D 72
Eliot Va. SE3	2F 123
Elis David Almshouses CR0: Croy	3B 168
Elizabethan Cl. TW19: Stanw	7A 110
Elizabethan Way TW19: Stanw	7A 110
Elizabeth Av. EN2: Enf	3G 23
IG1: Ilf	2H 71
N1	1C 84
TW18: Staines	7A 128
Elizabeth Barnes Ct. SW6	2K 117
(off Marinefield Rd.)	
Elizabeth Blackwell Ho. N22	1A 48
(off Progress Way)	
Elizabeth Blount Ct. E14	6A 86
(off Carr St.)	
Elizabeth Bri. SW1	4J 17 (4F 101)
Elizabeth Cl. E14	6D 86
EN5: Barn	3A 20
RM7: Mawney	1H 55
SM1: Sutt	4H 165
W9	4A 82
Elizabeth Clyde Cl. N15	4E 48
Elizabeth Cotts. TW9: Kew	1F 115
Elizabeth Ct. BR1: Brom	1H 159
(off Highland Rd.)	
E4	5G 35
IG8: Wfd G	7F 37
KT2: King T	1E 150
NW1	3D 4
SW1	2D 18
SW10	6B 100
(off Milman's St.)	
TW11: Tedd	5J 131
TW16: Sun	3A 148
(off Elizabeth Gdns.)	
Elizabeth Fry Ho. UB3: Harl	4H 93
Elizabeth Fry M. E8	7H 67
Elizabeth Fry Pl. SE18	1C 124
Elizabeth Gdns. HA7: Stan	6H 27
TW7: Isle	4A 114
TW16: Sun	3A 148
W3	1B 98
Elizabeth Garrett Anderson Ho.	
DA17: Belv	3G 109
(off Ambrook Rd.)	
Elizabeth Ho. SE11	4K 19
(off Reedworth St.)	
SM3: Cheam	6G 165
(off Park La.)	
W6	5E 98
(off Queen Caroline St.)	
Elizabeth Ind. Est. SE14	6K 103
Elizabeth M. HA1: Harr	6J 41
NW3	6C 64
Elizabeth Newcomen Ho. SE1	6E 14
(off Newcomen St.)	
Elizabeth Pl. N15	4D 48
Elizabeth Ride N9	7C 24
Elizabeth Rd. E6	1B 88
N15	5E 48
Elizabeth Sq. SE16	7A 86
(off Sovereign Cres.)	
Elizabeth St. SW1	3H 17 (4E 100)
Elizabeth Ter. SE9	6D 124
Elizabeth Way SE19	7D 138
TW13: Hanw	4A 130
Elkanette M. N20	2F 31
Elkington Point SE11	4J 19
Elkington Rd. E13	4K 87
Elkstone Rd. W10	5H 81
Ella Cl. BR3: Beck	2C 158
Ellaline Rd. W6	6F 99
Ella M. NW3	4D 64
Ellanby Cres. N18	4C 34
Elland Ho. E14	6B 86
(off Copenhagen Pl.)	
Elland Rd. SE15	4J 121

Ella Rd. N8	7J 47
Ellement Cl. HA5: Pinn	5B 40
Ellena Ct. N14	3D 32
(off Conway Rd.)	
Ellenborough Ho. W12	7D 80
(off White City Est.)	
Ellenborough Pl. SW15	4C 116
Ellenborough Rd. DA14: Sidc	5D 144
N22	1C 48
Ellenbridge Way CR2: Sand	7E 168
Ellen Cl. BR1: Brom	3B 160
Ellen Ct. E4	1K 35
(off The Ridgeway)	
N9	2D 34
Ellen St. E1	6G 85
Ellen Terry Ct. NW1	7F 65
(off Farrier St.)	
Ellen Webb Dr. HA3: W'stone	3J 41
Ellen Wilkinson Ho. E2	3K 85
(off Usk St.)	
RM10: Dag	3G 73
SW6	6H 99
(off Clem Attlee Ct.)	
Elleray Rd. TW11: Tedd	6K 131
Ellerby St. SW6	1F 117
Ellerdale Cl. NW3	4A 64
Ellerdale Rd. NW3	5A 64
Ellerdale St. SE13	4D 122
Ellerdine Rd. TW3: Houn	4G 113
Ellerker Gdns. TW10: Rich	6E 114
Ellerman Av. TW2: Whit	1D 130
Ellerslie Gdns. NW10	1C 80
Ellerslie Rd. W12	1D 98
Ellerslie Sq. Ind. Est. SW2	5J 119
Ellerton Gdns. RM9: Dag	7C 72
Ellerton Lodge N3	2J 45
Ellerton Rd. KT6: Surb	2F 163
RM9: Dag	7C 72
SW13	1C 116
SW18	1B 136
SW20	7C 134
Ellery Ho. SE17	4D 102
Ellery Rd. SE19	7D 138
Ellery St. SE15	2H 121
Ellesmere Av. BR3: Beck	2D 158
NW7	3E 28
Ellesmere Cl. E11	5H 51
HA4: Ruis	7E 38
Ellesmere Ct. SE12	1J 141
W4	5K 97
Ellesmere Gdns. IG4: Ilf	5C 52
Ellesmere Gro. EN5: Barn	5C 20
Ellesmere Rd. E3	2A 86
NW10	5C 62
TW1: Twick	6C 114
UB6: G'frd	4G 77
W4	6J 97
Ellesmere St. E14	6C 86
Ellies M. TW15: Ashf	2A 128
Ellingfort Rd. E8	7H 67
Ellingham Rd. E15	4F 69
KT9: Chess	6D 162
W12	2C 98
Ellington Cl. N14	2C 32
Ellington Ho. SE1	3C 102
Ellington Rd. N10	4F 47
TW3: Houn	2F 113
TW13: Felt	4H 129
Ellington St. N7	6A 66
Elliot Cl. E15	7G 69
Elliot Ct. IG8: Wfd G	6G 37
Elliot Ho. W1	6D 4
(off Cato St.)	
Elliott Av. HA4: Ruis	2K 57
Elliott Cl. HA9: Wemb	3F 61
Elliott Gdns. TW17: Shep	4C 146
Elliott Rd. BR2: Brom	4B 160
CR7: Thor H	4B 156
HA7: Stan	6F 27
SW9	1B 120
W4	4A 98
Elliott's Pl. N1	1B 84

Elliott Sq. NW3	7C 64
Elliotts Row SE11	4B 102
Ellis Cl. HA8: Edg	6F 29
NW10	6D 62
SE9	2G 143
Elliscombe Mt. SE7	6A 106
Elliscombe Rd. SE7	6A 106
Ellis Ct. W7	5K 77
Ellisfield Dr. SW15	7C 116
Ellis Franklin Ct. NW8	2A 82
(off Abbey Rd.)	
Ellis Ho. SE17	5D 102
(off Brandon St.)	
Ellison Gdns. UB2: S'hall	4D 94
Ellison Ho. SE13	2D 122
(off Lewisham Rd.)	
Ellison Rd. DA15: Sidc	1H 143
SW13	2B 116
SW16	7H 137
Ellis Rd. CR4: Mitc	6D 154
UB2: S'hall	1G 95
Ellis St. SW1	3F 17 (4E 100)
Ellora Rd. SW16	5H 137
Ellswood Ct. KT6: Surb	7D 150
Ellsworth St. E2	3H 85
Ellwood Ct. W9	4K 81
(off Clearwell Dr.)	
Elmar Rd. N15	4D 48
Elm Av. HA4: Ruis	1J 57
TW19: Stanw	2A 128
W5	1E 96
Elm Bank N14	7D 22
Elmbank Av. EN5: Barn	4A 20
Elm Bank Dr. BR1: Brom	2B 160
Elm Bank Gdns. SW13	2A 116
Elmbank Way W7	5H 77
Elmbourne Dr. DA17: Belv	4H 109
Elmbourne Rd. SW17	3F 137
Elmbridge Av. KT5: Surb	5H 151
Elmbridge Cl. HA4: Ruis	6J 39
Elmbridge Dr. HA4: Ruis	6J 39
Elmbridge Leisure Cen.	5K 147
Elmbridge Wlk. E8	7G 67
Elmbrook Cl. TW16: Sun	1K 147
Elmbrook Gdns. SE9	4C 124
Elmbrook Rd. SM1: Sutt	4H 165
Elm Cl. CR2: S Croy	6E 168
E11	6K 51
HA2: Harr	6F 41
IG9: Buck H	2G 37
KT5: Surb	7J 151
N19	2G 65
NW4	5F 45
RM7: Mawney	1H 55
SM5: Cars	1D 166
SW20	4E 152
TW2: Twick	2F 131
UB3: Hayes	6J 75
Elmcote Ho. Pinn	2B 40
Elm Cotts. CR4: Mitc	2D 154
Elm Ct. CR4: Mitc	2D 154
EC4	1J 13
KT8: W Mole	4F 149
SE13	3F 123
TW16: Sun	7H 129
(off Grangewood Dr.)	
W9	5J 81
(off Admiral Wlk.)	
Elmcourt Rd. SE27	2B 138
Elm Cres. KT2: King T	1E 150
W5	1E 96
Elmcroft N6	7E 46
Elmcroft Av. DA15: Sidc	7K 125
E11	5K 51
N9	6C 24
NW11	7H 45
Elmcroft Cl. E11	4K 51
KT9: Chess	3E 162
N8	5K 47
TW14: Felt	6H 111
W5	6D 78
Elmcroft Cres. HA2: Harr	3E 40
NW11	7G 45

Elmcroft Dr. KT9: Chess	3E 162
TW15: Ashf	5C 128
Elmcroft Gdns. NW9	4G 43
Elmcroft St. E5	4J 67
Elmcroft Ter. UB8: Hil	6C 74
Elmdale Rd. N13	5E 32
Elmdene KT5: Surb	1J 163
Elmdene Cl. BR3: Beck	6B 158
Elmdene Rd. SE18	5F 107
Elmdon Rd. TW4: Houn	2B 112
TW6: H'row A	3H 111
Elm Dr. HA2: Harr	6F 41
TW16: Sun	2A 148
Elmer Cl. EN2: Enf	3E 22
Elmer Gdns. HA8: Edg	7C 28
TW7: Isle	3H 113
Elmer Ho. NW8	5C 4
(off Penfold St.)	
Elmer Rd. SE6	7E 122
Elmer's Dr. TW11: Tedd	6B 132
ELMERS END	4K 157
Elmers End Rd.	
BR3: Beck	2J 157
SE20	2J 157
Elmerside Rd. BR3: Beck	4A 158
Elmers Lodge BR3: Beck	4K 157
Elmfield Av. CR4: Mitc	1E 154
N8	5J 47
TW11: Tedd	5K 131
Elmfield Cl. HA1: Harr	2J 59
Elmfield Ct. DA16: Well	1B 126
Elmfield Ho. N2	2B 46
(off The Grange)	
NW8	2K 81
(off Carlton Hill)	
W9	4J 81
(off Goldney Rd.)	
Elmfield Pk. BR1: Brom	3J 159
Elmfield Rd. BR1: Brom	2J 159
E4	2K 35
E17	6K 49
N2	3B 46
SW17	2E 136
UB2: S'hall	3C 94
Elmfield Way CR2: Sand	7F 169
W9	5J 81
Elm Friars Wlk. NW1	7H 65
Elm Gdns. CR4: Mitc	4H 155
KT10: Clay	6A 162
N2	3A 46
Elmgate Av. TW13: Felt	3K 129
Elmgate Gdns. HA8: Edg	5D 28
Elmgreen Cl. E15	1G 87
Elm Gro. BR6: Orp	1K 173
DA8: Erith	7K 109
HA2: Harr	7E 40
IG8: Wfd G	5C 36
KT2: King T	1E 150
N8	6J 47
NW2	4F 63
SE15	2F 121
SM1: Sutt	4K 165
SW19	7G 135
UB7: Yiew	7B 74
Elmgrove Cres. HA1: Harr	5K 41
Elmgrove Gdns. HA1: Harr	5A 42
Elm Gro. Pde. SM6: Wall	3E 166
Elm Gro. Rd. SW13	1C 116
W5	2E 96
Elmgrove Rd. CR0: Croy	7H 157
HA1: Harr	5A 42
HA3: W'stone	5A 42
Elm Hall Gdns. E11	5K 51
(not continuous)	
Elm Ho. E14	2E 104
(off E. Ferry Rd.)	
KT2: King T	7F 133
W10	4G 81
(off Briar Wlk.)	
Elmhurst DA17: Belv	6E 108

Elmhurst Av. CR4: Mitc 7F **137**
N2 3B **46**
Elmhurst Ct. CR0: Croy 4D **168**
Elmhurst Dr. E18 2J **51**
Elmhurst Lodge SM2: Sutt 7A **166**
Elmhurst Mans. SW4 3H **119**
Elmhurst Rd. E7 7K **69**
N17 2F **49**
SE9 2C **142**
Elmhurst St. SW4 3H **119**
Elmington Cl. DA5: Bexl 6H **127**
Elmington Est. SE5 7D **102**
Elmington Rd. SE5 7D **102**
Elmira St. SE13 3D **122**
Elm La. SE6 2B **140**
Elm Lawn Cl. UB8: Uxb 7A **56**
Elmlea Dr. UB3: Hayes 5G **75**
Elm Lea Trad. Est. N17 6C **34**
Elmlee Cl. BR7: Chst 6D **142**
Elmley Cl. E6 5C **88**
Elmley St. SE18 5H **107**
(not continuous)
Elm Lodge SW6 1E **116**
Elmore Cl. HA0: Wemb 2E **78**
Elmore Ho. SW9 2B **120**
Elmore Rd. E11 3E **68**
EN3: Enf W 1E **24**
Elmore St. N1 7C **66**
Elm Pde. DA14: Sidc 4A **144**
Elm Pk. HA7: Stan 5G **27**
SW2 6K **119**
Elm Pk. Av. N15 5F **49**
Elm Pk. Chambers *SW10* *6A **16***
(off Fulham Rd.)
Elm Pk. Ct. HA5: Pinn 2A **40**
Elm Pk. Gdns. NW4 5F **45**
SW10 6A **16** (5B **100**)
Elm Pk. Ho. SW10 5B **100**
Elm Pk. La. SW3 6A **16** (5B **100**)
Elm Pk. Mans. SW10 7A **16**
Elm Pk. Rd. E10 1A **68**
HA5: Pinn 2A **40**
N3 7C **30**
N21 7H **23**
SE25 3F **157**
SW3 7A **16** (6B **100**)
Elm Pas. EN5: Barn 4C **20**
Elm Pl. SW7 5A **16** (5B **100**)
TW15: Ashf 5C **128**
Elm Quay Ct. SW8 7C **18** (6H **101**)
Elm Rd. BR3: Beck 2B **158**
BR6: Chels 7K **173**
CR7: Thor H 4D **156**
DA14: Sidc 4A **144**
E7 6H **69**
E11 2F **69**
E17 5E **50**
EN5: Barn 4C **20**
HA9: Wemb 5E **60**
KT2: King T 1F **151**
KT3: N Mald 2K **151**
KT9: Chess 4E **162**
KT17: Ewe 6B **164**
N22 1B **48**
RM7: Mawney 2H **55**
SM6: Wall 1E **166**
SW14 3J **115**
TW14: Bedf 1F **129**
Elm Rd. W. SM3: Sutt 7H **153**
Elm Row NW3 3A **64**
Elms, The *CR0: Croy* *1C **168***
(off Tavistock Rd.)
E12 6B **70**
KT10: Clay 7A **162**
SW13 3B **116**
TW15: Ashf 5C **128**
Elms Av. N10 3F **47**
NW4 5F **45**
Elmscott Gdns. N21 6H **23**
Elmscott Rd. BR1: Brom 5G **141**
Elms Ct. HA0: Wemb 4A **60**
Elms Cres. SW4 6G **119**
Elmsdale Rd. E17 4B **50**
Elms Gdns. HA0: Wemb 4A **60**
RM9: Dag 4F **73**
Elmshaw Rd. SW15 5C **116**
Elmshurst Cres. N2 4B **46**
Elmside CR0: New Ad 6D **170**
Elmside Rd. HA9: Wemb 3G **61**
Elms La. HA0: Wemb 3A **60**
Elmsleigh Av. HA3: Kent 4B **42**
Elmsleigh Ct. SM1: Sutt 3K **165**
Elmsleigh Ho. *TW2: Twick* *2H **131***
(off Staines Rd.)
Elmsleigh Rd. TW2: Twick 2H **131**
Elmslie Cl. IG8: Wfd G 6J **37**
Elmslie Point *E3* *5B **86***
(off Leopold St.)
Elms M. W2 2A **10** (7B **82**)
Elms Pk. Av. HA0: Wemb 4A **60**
Elms Rd. HA3: Hrw W 7D **26**
SW4 5G **119**
ELMSTEAD 6D **142**
Elmstead Av. BR7: Chst 5D **142**
HA9: Wemb 1E **60**
Elmstead Cl. KT19: Ewe 5A **164**
N20 2D **30**
Elmstead Gdns. KT4: Wor Pk 3C **164**
Elmstead Glade BR7: Chst 6D **142**
Elmstead La. BR7: Chst 7C **142**
Elmstead Rd. DA8: Erith 1K **127**
IG3: Ilf 2J **71**
Elmsted Cres. DA16: Well 6C **108**
Elmstone Rd. SW6 1J **117**
Elm St. WC1 4H **7** (4K **83**)
Elmsway TW15: Ashf 5C **128**
Elmsworth Av. TW3: Houn 2F **113**
Elm Ter. HA3: Hrw W 1H **41**
HA7: Stan 5H **27**
NW2 3J **63**
NW3 4C **64**
SE9 6E **124**
Elmton Ct. *NW8* *3A **4***
(off Cunningham Pl.)
Elmton Way E5 3G **67**
Elm Tree Av. KT10: Esh 7H **149**
Elm Tree Cl. NW8 1A **4** (3B **82**)
TW15: Ashf 5D **128**
UB5: N'olt 2D **76**
Elm Tree Ct. NW8 1A **4**
SE7 6A **106**
Elm Tree Rd. NW8 1A **4** (3B **82**)
Elmtree Rd. TW11: Tedd 4J **131**
Elm Vw. Ct. UB2: S'hall 4E **94**
Elm Vw. Ho. UB3: Harl 4F **93**
Elm Wlk. BR6: Farnb 3D **172**
NW3 2J **63**
SW20 4E **152**
Elm Way KT4: Wor Pk 3E **164**
KT19: Ewe 5K **163**
N11 6K **31**
NW10 4A **62**
Elmwood Av. HA3: Kent 5A **42**
N13 5D **32**
TW13: Felt 2J **129**
Elmwood Cl. KT17: Ewe 7C **164**
SM6: Wall 2F **167**
Elmwood Ct. *E10* *1C **68***
(off Goldsmith Rd.)
HA0: Wemb 3A **60**
SW11 1F **119**
Elmwood Cres. NW9 4J **43**
Elmwood Dr. DA5: Bexl 7E **126**
KT17: Ewe 6C **164**
Elmwood Gdns. W7 6J **77**
Elmwood Ho. *NW10* *2D **80***
(off All Souls Av.)
Elmwood Rd. CR0: Croy 7B **156**
CR4: Mitc 3D **154**
SE24 5D **120**
W4 6J **97**
Elmworth Gro. SE21 2D **138**
Elnathan M. W9 4K **81**
Elphinstone Ct. SW16 6J **137**
Elphinstone Rd. E17 2B **50**
Elphinstone St. N5 4B **66**
Elrington Rd. E8 6G **67**
IG8: Wfd G 5D **36**
Elsa Cotts. *E14* *5A **86***
(off Halley St.)
Elsa Ct. BR3: Beck 1B **158**
Elsa Rd. DA16: Well 2B **126**
Elsa St. E1 5A **86**
Elsdale St. E9 6J **67**
Elsden M. E2 2J **85**
Elsden Rd. N17 1F **49**
Elsenham Rd. E12 5E **70**
Elsenham St. SW18 1H **135**
Elsham Rd. E11 3G **69**
W14 2G **99**
Elsham Ter. *W14* *3G **99***
(off Elsham Rd.)
Elsiedene Rd. N21 7H **23**
Elsie La. Ct. *W2* *5J **81***
(off Westbourne Pk. Vs.)
Elsiemaud Rd. SE4 5B **122**
Elsie Rd. SE22 4F **121**
Elsinore Av. TW19: Stanw 7A **110**
Elsinore Gdns. NW2 3G **63**
Elsinore Ho. *N1* *1A **84***
(off Denmark Gro.)
SE5 *2C **120***
(off Denmark Rd.)
W6 *5F **99***
(off Fulham Pal. Rd.)
Elsinore Rd. SE23 1A **140**
Elsinore Way TW9: Rich 3H **115**
Elsley Ct. HA9: Wemb 6H **61**
Elsley Rd. SW11 3D **118**
Elspeth Rd. HA0: Wemb 5E **60**
SW11 4D **118**
Elsrick Av. SM4: Mord 5J **153**
Elstan Way CR0: Croy 7A **158**
Elstead Ct. SM3: Sutt 1G **165**
Elstead Ho. *SW2* *7K **119***
(off Redlands Way)
Elsted St. SE17 4D **102**
Elstow Cl. HA4: Ruis 7B **40**
SE9 5D **124**
(not continuous)
Elstow Gdns. RM9: Dag 1E **90**
Elstow Grange NW6 7F **63**
Elstow Rd. RM9: Dag 1E **90**
Elstree Gdns. DA17: Belv 4E **108**
IG1: Ilf 5G **71**
N9 1C **34**
Elstree Hill BR1: Brom 7G **141**
Elstree Hill Sth. WD6: Els 1H **27**
Elstree Rd. WD23: Bushy 1C **26**
Elswick Rd. SE13 2D **122**
Elswick St. SW6 2A **118**
Elsworth Cl. TW14: Bedf 1G **129**
Elsworthy KT7: T Ditt 6J **149**
Elsworthy Ct. *NW3* *7D **64***
(off Primrose Hill Rd.)
Elsworthy Ri. NW3 7C **64**
Elsworthy Rd. NW3 1C **82**
Elsworthy Ter. NW3 7C **64**
Elsynge Rd. SW18 5B **118**
ELTHAM 7B **124**
Eltham Crematorium SE9 4H **125**
Eltham Grn. SE9 5B **124**
Eltham Grn. Rd. SE9 4A **124**
Eltham High St. SE9 6D **124**
Eltham Hill SE9 5B **124**
Eltham Palace 7C **124**
Eltham Pal. Rd. SE9 6A **124**
ELTHAM PARK 4E **124**
Eltham Pk. Gdns. SE9 4E **124**
Eltham Pools 6C **124**
Eltham Rd. SE9 5H **123**
SE12 5H **123**
Elthiron Rd. SW6 1J **117**
Elthorne Av. W7 2K **95**
Elthorne Ct. TW13: Felt 1A **130**
ELTHORNE HEIGHTS 5J **77**
Elthorne Pk. Rd. W7 2K **95**
Elthorne Rd. N19 2H **65**
NW9 7K **43**
Elthorne Sports Cen. 3K **95**
Elthorne Way NW9 6K **43**
Elthruda Rd. SE13 6F **123**
Eltisley Rd. IG1: Ilf 4F **71**
Elton Av. EN5: Barn 5C **20**
HA0: Wemb 5B **60**
UB6: G'frd 6J **59**
Elton Cl. KT1: Ham W 7C **132**
Elton Ho. *E3* *1B **86***
(off Candy St.)
Elton Pl. N16 5E **66**
Elton Rd. KT2: King T 1F **151**
Eltringham St. SW18 4A **118**
Eluna Apartments *E1* *7H **85***
(off Wapping La.)
Elvaston M. SW7 2A **16** (3A **100**)
Elvaston Pl. SW7 2A **16** (3A **100**)
Elveden Ho. SE24 5B **120**
Elveden Pl. NW10 2G **79**
Elveden Rd. NW10 2G **79**
Elvedon Rd. TW13: Felt 3H **129**
Elvendon Rd. N13 6D **32**
Elver Gdns. E2 3G **85**
Elverson Rd. SE8 2D **122**
Elverton St. SW1 3C **18** (4H **101**)
Elvington Grn. BR2: Brom 5H **159**
Elvington La. NW9 1A **44**
Elvino Rd. SE26 5A **140**
Elvis Rd. NW2 6E **62**
Elwill Way BR3: Beck 4E **158**
Elwin St. E2 1K **9** (3G **85**)
Elwood Cl. EN5: New Bar 4F **21**
Elwood St. N5 3B **66**
Elworth Ho. *SW8* *7K **101***
(off Oval Pl.)
Elwyn Gdns. SE12 7J **123**
Ely Cl. KT3: N Mald 2B **152**
Ely Cotts. SW8 7K **101**
Ely Ct. EC1 6K **7**
NW6 *2J **81***
(off Chichester Rd.)
Ely Gdns. IG1: Ilf 7C **52**
RM10: Dag 3J **73**
Ely Ho. *SE15* *7G **103***
(off Friary Est.)
Elyne Rd. N4 6A **48**
Ely Pl. EC1 6K **7** (5A **84**)
IG8: Wfd G 6K **37**
Ely Rd. CR0: Croy 5D **156**
E10 6E **50**
TW4: Houn 3A **112**
Elysian Av. BR5: St M Cry 6K **161**
Elysium Pl. *SW6* *2H **117***
(off Elysium St.)
Elysium St. SW6 2H **117**
Elystan Bus. Cen. UB4: Yead 7A **76**
Elystan Cl. SM6: Wall 7G **167**
Elystan Pl. SW3 5D **16** (5C **100**)
Elystan St. SW3 4C **16** (4C **100**)
Elystan Wlk. N1 1A **84**
Emanuel Av. W3 6J **79**
Emanuel Dr. TW12: Hamp 5D **130**
Emanuel Ho. SW1 3H **101**
Embankment SW15 2F **117**
(not continuous)
Embankment, The TW1: Twick 1A **132**
Embankment Gdns. SW3 7F **17** (6D **100**)
Embankment Pl. WC2 4F **13** (1J **101**)
Embassy Ct. DA14: Sidc 3B **144**
DA16: Well 3B **126**
N11 *6C **32***
(off Bounds Grn. Rd.)
NW8 1B **4**
SM6: Wall 6F **167**
W5 7F **79**
Embassy Gdns. BR3: Beck 1B **158**
Embassy Ho. NW6 7K **63**
Embassy Lodge *N3* *2H **45***
(off Cyprus Rd.)
Embassy Theatre *7B **64***
(off College Cres.)
Emba St. SE16 2G **103**
Ember Cl. BR5: Pet W 7G **161**

Ember Ct. NW9 . . . . . 2B **44**
Embercourt Rd. KT7: T Ditt 6J **149**
Ember Farm Av. KT8: E Mos 6H **149**
Ember Farm Way KT8: E Mos 6H **149**
Ember Gdns. KT7: T Ditt 7J **149**
Ember La. KT8: E Mos 7H **149**
KT10: Esh 7H **149**
Emberton *SE5* *6E* ***102***
(off Albany Rd.)
Emberton Ct. *EC1* *2A* ***8***
(off Tompion St.)
Embleton Rd. SE13 . . . . . 4D **122**
Embleton Wlk. TW12: Hamp 5D **130**
Embroidery Bus. Cen. *IG8: Wfd G* *2B* ***52***
(off Southend Rd.)
Embroidery World Bus. Cen.
IG8: Wfd G 2B **52**
Embry Cl. HA7: Stan 4F **27**
Embry Dr. HA7: Stan 6F **27**
Embry Way HA7: Stan 5F **27**
Emden Cl. UB7: W Dray 2C **92**
Emden St. SW6 . . . . . 1K **117**
Emerald Cl. E16 . . . . . 6B **88**
Emerald Gdns. RM8: Dag 1G **73**
Emerald Rd. NW10 . . . . . 1K **79**
(not continuous)
Emerald Sq. UB2: S'hall 3B **94**
Emerald St. WC1 . . . . . 5G **7** (5K **83**)
Emerson Apartments N8 . . . . . 3K **47**
Emerson Gdns. HA3: Kent 6F **43**
Emerson Rd. IG1: Ilf 7E **52**
Emerson St. SE1 . . . . . 4C **14** (1C **102**)
Emerton Cl. DA6: Bex 4E **126**
Emery Hill St. SW1 . . . . . 2B **18** (3G **101**)
Emery St. SE1 . . . . . 1K **19** (3A **102**)
Emery Theatre ***6D 86***
(off Annabel Cl.)
Emes Rd. DA8: Erith 7J **109**
Emilia Cl. EN3: Pond E 5C **24**
Emily Ho. *W10* *4G* ***81***
(off Kensal Rd.)
Emily Pl. N7 . . . . . 4A **66**
Emily St. *E16* *6H* ***87***
(off Jude St.)
Emirates Stadium **4A 66**
Emlyn Gdns. W12 . . . . . 2A **98**
Emlyn Rd. W12 . . . . . 2A **98**
Emmanuel Ct. E10 . . . . . 7D **50**
Emmanuel Ho. SE11 . . . . . 4J **19** (4A **102**)
Emmanuel Rd. HA6: Nwood 1H **39**
SW12 . . . . . 1G **137**
Emma Rd. E13 . . . . . 2H **87**
Emma St. E2 . . . . . 2H **85**
Emmaus Way IG7: Chig 5K **37**
Emmeline Ct. KT12: Walt T 7A **148**
Emminster *NW6* *1K* ***81***
(off Abbey Rd.)
Emmott Av. IG6: Ilf 5G **53**
Emmott Cl. E1 . . . . . 4A **86**
NW11 . . . . . 6A **46**
Emms Pas. KT1: King T 2D **150**
Emperor's Ga. SW7 . . . . . 3A **100**
Empingham Ho. *SE8* *4K* ***103***
(off Chilton Ho.)
Empire Av. N18 . . . . . 5H **33**
Empire Cinema
Leicester Sq. ***2D 12***
(off Leicester Sq.)
Empire Ct. HA9: Wemb 3H **61**
Empire Ho. SW7 . . . . . 2C **16**
Empire Pde. HA9: Wemb 3G **61**
N18 . . . . . 6J **33**
Empire Rd. UB6: G'frd 1B **78**
Empire Sq. N7 . . . . . 3J **65**
SE20 . . . . . *7K* ***139***
(off High St.)
Empire Way HA9: Wemb 4F **61**
Empire Wharf *E3* *1A* ***86***
(off Old Ford Rd.)
Empire Wharf Rd. E14 . . . . . 4F **105**
Empress App. SW6 . . . . . 5J **99**
Empress Av. E4 . . . . . 7J **35**
E12 . . . . . 2A **70**
Empress Av. IG1: Ilf 2D **70**
IG8: Wfd G 7C **36**
Empress Dr. BR7: Chst 6F **143**
Empress M. SE5 . . . . . 2C **120**
Empress Pde. E4 . . . . . 7H **35**
Empress Pl. SW6 . . . . . 5J **99**
Empress State Bldg. SW6 . . . . . 5J **99**
Empress St. SE17 . . . . . 6C **102**
Empson St. E3 . . . . . 4D **86**
Emsworth Cl. N9 . . . . . 1D **34**
Emsworth Ct. SW16 . . . . . 3J **137**
Emsworth Rd. IG6: Ilf 2F **53**
Emsworth St. SW2 . . . . . 2K **137**
Emt Ho. E6 . . . . . 5E **88**
Emu Rd. SW8 . . . . . 2F **119**
Ena Rd. SW16 . . . . . 3J **155**
Enbrook St. W10 . . . . . 3G **81**
Enclave, The SW13 . . . . . 2B **116**
Endale Cl. SM5: Cars 2D **166**
Endeavour Way CR0: Bedd 7J **155**
IG11: Bark 2A **90**
SW19 . . . . . 4K **135**
Endell St. WC2 . . . . . 7E **6** (6J **83**)
Enderby St. SE10 . . . . . 5F **105**
Enderley Cl. HA3: Hrw W 2J **41**
Enderley Rd. HA3: Hrw W 1J **41**
Endersleigh Gdns. NW4 . . . . . 4C **44**
Endlebury Rd. E4 . . . . . 2K **35**
Endlesham Rd. SW12 . . . . . 7E **118**
Endsleigh Ct. WC1 . . . . . 3D **6**
Endsleigh Gdns. IG1: Ilf 2D **70**
KT6: Surb 6C **150**
WC1 . . . . . 3C **6** (4H **83**)
Endsleigh Ind. Est. UB2: S'hall 4C **94**
Endsleigh Pl. WC1 . . . . . 3D **6** (4H **83**)
Endsleigh Rd. UB2: S'hall 4C **94**
W13 . . . . . 7A **78**
Endsleigh St. WC1 . . . . . 3D **6** (4H **83**)
Endway KT5: Surb 7H **151**
Endwell Rd. SE4 . . . . . 2A **122**
Endymion Rd. N4 . . . . . 7A **48**
SW2 . . . . . 6K **119**
Energen Cl. NW10 . . . . . 6A **62**
Energize Fitness Club ***5G 99***
(in Hammersmith & West London College)
ENFIELD **3J 23**
Enfield Bus. Cen. EN3: Enf H 2D **24**
Enfield Cloisters *N1* *1G* ***9***
(off Fanshaw St.)
Enfield College Sports Cen. **3D 24**
ENFIELD HIGHWAY **3D 24**
Enfield Ho. *SW9* *2J* ***119***
(off Stockwell Rd.)
ENFIELD ISLAND VILLAGE **1H 25**
ENFIELD LOCK **1H 25**
Enfield Retail Pk. EN1: Enf 3C **24**
Enfield Rd. EN2: Enf 4C **22**
N1 . . . . . 7E **66**
TW6: H'row A 2G **111**
TW8: Bford 5D **96**
W3 . . . . . 2H **97**
ENFIELD TOWN **3J 23**
Enfield Wlk. TW8: Bford 5D **96**
Enford St. W1 . . . . . 5E **4** (5D **82**)
Engadine Cl. CR0: Croy 3F **169**
Engadine St. SW18 . . . . . 1H **135**
Engate St. SE13 . . . . . 4E **122**
Engel Pk. NW7 . . . . . 6K **29**
Engine Ct. *SW1* *5B* ***12***
(off Ambassador's Ct.)
Engineer Cl. SE18 . . . . . 6E **106**
Engineers Way HA9: Wemb 4G **61**
England's La. NW3 . . . . . 6D **64**
England Way KT3: N Mald 4H **151**
Englefield *NW1* *2A* ***6***
(off Clarence Gdns.)
Englefield Cl. BR5: St M Cry 5K **161**
CR0: Croy 6C **156**
EN2: Enf 2F **23**
Englefield Cres. BR5: St M Cry 4K **161**
Englefield Path BR5: St M Cry 4K **161**
Englefield Rd. N1 . . . . . 7D **66**
Engleheart Dr. TW14: Felt 6H **111**
Engleheart Rd. SE6 . . . . . 7D **122**
Englewood Rd. SW12 . . . . . 6F **119**
English Grounds SE1 . . . . . 5G **15** (1E **102**)
English St. E3 . . . . . 4B **86**
Enid St. SE16 . . . . . 7K **15** (3F **103**)
Enmore Av. SE25 . . . . . 5G **157**
Enmore Gdns. SW14 . . . . . 5K **115**
Enmore Rd. SE25 . . . . . 5G **157**
SW15 . . . . . 4E **116**
UB1: S'hall 4E **76**
Ennerdale *NW1* *1A* ***6***
(off Varndell St.)
Ennerdale Av. HA7: Stan 3C **42**
Ennerdale Cl. SM1: Sutt 4H **165**
TW14: Felt 1H **129**
Ennerdale Ct. *E11* *7J* ***51***
(off Cambridge Rd.)
Ennerdale Dr. NW9 . . . . . 5A **44**
Ennerdale Gdns. HA9: Wemb 1C **60**
Ennerdale Ho. E3 . . . . . 4B **86**
Ennerdale Rd. DA7: Bex 1G **127**
TW9: Rich 2F **115**
Ennersdale Rd. SE13 . . . . . 5F **123**
Ennis Ho. *E14* *6D* ***86***
(off Vesey Path)
Ennismore Av. UB6: G'frd 6J **59**
W4 . . . . . 4B **98**
Ennismore Gdns. KT7: T Ditt 6J **149**
SW7 . . . . . 7C **10** (2C **100**)
Ennismore Gdns. M. SW7 . . . . . 1C **16** (3C **100**)
Ennismore M. SW7 . . . . . 7C **10** (3C **100**)
Ennismore St. SW7 . . . . . 1C **16** (3C **100**)
Ennis Rd. N4 . . . . . 1A **66**
SE18 . . . . . 6G **107**
Ennor Ct. SM3: Cheam 4E **164**
Ensbury Ho. *SW8* *7K* ***101***
(off Carroun Rd.)
Ensign Cl. TW6: H'row A 3G **111**
TW19: Stanw 1A **128**
Ensign Dr. N13 . . . . . 3H **33**
Ensign Ho. *E14* *2C* ***104***
(off Admirals Way)
Ensign Ind. Cen. *E1* *7G* ***85***
(off Ensign St.)
Ensign St. E1 . . . . . 7G **85**
Ensign Way SM6: Wall 7J **167**
TW19: Stanw 1A **128**
Enslin Rd. SE9 . . . . . 6E **124**
Ensor M. SW7 . . . . . 5A **16** (5B **100**)
Enstone Rd. EN3: Enf H 3F **25**
UB10: Ick 3B **56**
Enterprise Bus. Pk. E14 . . . . . 2D **104**
Enterprise Cen., The *BR3: Beck* *5A* ***140***
(off Cricket La.)
Enterprise Cl. CR0: Croy 1A **168**
Enterprise Ho. E4 . . . . . 7K **25**
E9 . . . . . *7J* ***67***
(off Tudor Gro.)
E14 . . . . . *5D* ***104***
(off St Davids Sq.)
IG11: Bark 3K **89**
KT12: Walt T 7K **147**
Enterprise Ind. Est. SE16 . . . . . 5J **103**
Enterprise Row N15 . . . . . 5F **49**
Enterprise Trad. Est.
UB2: S'hall 2F **95**
Enterprise Way NW10 . . . . . 3B **80**
SW18 . . . . . 4J **117**
TW11: Tedd 6K **131**
Enterprize Way SE8 . . . . . 4B **104**
Envoy Av. TW6: H'row A 3H **111**
Epcot M. NW10 . . . . . 3F **81**
Epirus M. SW6 . . . . . 7J **99**
Epirus Rd. SW6 . . . . . 7H **99**
Epping Cl. E14 . . . . . 4C **104**
RM7: Mawney 3H **55**
Epping Glade E4 . . . . . 6K **25**
Epping New Rd. IG9: Buck H 2E **36**
Epping Pl. N1 . . . . . 6A **66**
Epping Way E4 . . . . . 6J **25**
Epple Rd. SW6 . . . . . 1H **117**
Epsom Cl. DA7: Bex 3H **127**
UB5: N'olt 5D **58**
Epsom Rd. CR0: Wadd 4A **168**
E10 . . . . . 6E **50**
IG3: Ilf 6K **53**
SM3: Sutt 7H **153**
SM4: Mord 7H **153**
Epsom Sq. TW6: H'row A 2H **111**
Epstein Rd. SE28 . . . . . 1A **108**
Epworth Rd. TW7: Isle 7B **96**
Epworth St. EC2 . . . . . 4F **9** (4D **84**)
Equity Sq. *E2* *2K* ***9***
(off Shacklewell St.)
Erasmus St. SW1 . . . . . 4D **18** (4H **101**)
Erconwald St. W12 . . . . . 6B **80**
Erebus Dr. SE18 . . . . . 3G **107**
SE28 . . . . . 3G **107**
Eresby Dr. BR3: Beck 1C **170**
Eresby Ho. *SW7* *7D* ***10***
(off Rutland Ga.)
Eresby Pl. NW6 . . . . . 7J **63**
Erica Gdns. CR0: Croy 3D **170**
Erica Ho. *N22* *1A* ***48***
(off Acacia Rd.)
SE4 . . . . . 3B **122**
Erica St. W12 . . . . . 7C **80**
Eric Clarke La. IG11: Bark 4F **89**
Eric Cl. E7 . . . . . 4J **69**
Ericcson Cl. SW18 . . . . . 5J **117**
Eric Fletcher Ct. *N1* *7C* ***66***
(off Essex Rd.)
Eric Liddell Sports Cen. **2B 142**
Eric Rd. E7 . . . . . 4J **69**
NW10 . . . . . 6B **62**
RM6: Chad H 7D **54**
Eric Shipman Ter. *E13* *4J* ***87***
(off Balaam St.)
Ericson Ho. *SE13* *4F* ***123***
(off Blessington Rd.)
Eric St. E3 . . . . . 4B **86**
(not continuous)
Eric Wilkins Ho. *SE1* *5G* ***103***
(off Old Kent Rd.)
Eridge Rd. W4 . . . . . 3K **97**
Erin Cl. BR1: Brom 7G **141**
IG3: Ilf 6A **54**
Erindale SE18 . . . . . 6H **107**
Erindale Ter. SE18 . . . . . 6H **107**
Erin M. N22 . . . . . 1B **48**
ERITH **5K 109**
Erith Cres. RM5: Col R 1J **55**
Erith Rd. DA7: Bex 4H **127**
DA8: Bex, Erith 4H **127**
DA8: Erith 5G **109**
DA17: Belv, Erith 5G **109**
Erith School Community Sports Cen.
. . . . . **7K 109**
Erlanger Rd. SE14 . . . . . 1K **121**
Erlesmere Gdns. W13 . . . . . 3A **96**
Erlich Cotts. *E1* *5J* ***85***
(off Sidney St.)
Ermine Cl. TW4: Houn 2A **112**
Ermine Ho. *N17* *7A* ***34***
(off Moselle St.)
Ermine Rd. N15 . . . . . 6F **49**
SE13 . . . . . 4D **122**
Ermine Side EN1: Enf 5B **24**
Ermington Rd. SE9 . . . . . 2G **143**
Ernald Av. E6 . . . . . 2C **88**
Erncroft Way TW1: Twick 6K **113**
Ernest Av. SE27 . . . . . 4B **138**
Ernest Cl. BR3: Beck 5C **158**
Ernest Cotts. KT17: Ewe 7B **164**
Ernest Gdns. W4 . . . . . 6H **97**
Ernest Gro. BR3: Beck 5B **158**
Ernest Harriss Ho. *W9* *4J* ***81***
(off Elgin Av.)
Ernest Rd. KT1: King T 2H **151**
Ernest Sq. KT1: King T 2H **151**
Ernest St. E1 . . . . . 4K **85**
Ernle Rd. SW20 . . . . . 7D **134**
Ernshaw Pl. SW15 . . . . . 5G **117**
Eros . . . . . **3C 12 (7H 83)**
Eros Ho. Shops *SE6* *7D* ***122***
(off Brownhill Rd.)

Erpingham Rd.—Eve Rd.

Erpingham Rd. SW15 3E **116**
Erridge Rd. SW19 2J **153**
Errington Rd. W9 4H **81**
Errol Gdns. KT3: N Mald 4C **152**
UB4: Yead 4K **75**
Errol St. EC1 4D **8** (4C **84**)
Erskine Cl. SM1: Sutt 3C **166**
Erskine Cres. N17 4H **49**
Erskine Hill NW11 4J **45**
Erskine Ho. *SW1* *6A* ***18***
(off Churchill Gdns.)
Erskine M. *NW3* *7D* ***64***
(off Erskine Rd.)
Erskine Rd. E17 4B **50**
NW3 7D **64**
SM1: Sutt 4B **166**
Erwood Rd. SE7 5C **106**
Esam Way SW16 5A **138**
Escot Rd. TW16: Sun 7G **129**
Escott Gdns. SE9 4C **142**
Escreet Gro. SE18 4E **106**
Esher Av. KT12: Walt T 7J **147**
RM7: Rom 6J **55**
SM3: Cheam 3F **165**
Esher By-Pass KT9: Chess 7B **162**
KT10: Clay 7B **162**
Esher Cl. DA5: Bexl 1E **144**
Esher Cres. TW6: H'row A 2H **111**
Esher Gdns. SW19 2F **135**
Esher M. CR4: Mitc 3E **154**
Esher Rd. IG3: Ilf 3J **71**
KT8: E Mos 6H **149**
Eskdale *NW1* *1A* ***6***
(off Stanhope St.)
Eskdale Av. UB5: N'olt 1D **76**
Eskdale Cl. HA9: Wemb 2D **60**
Eskdale Rd. DA7: Bex 2G **127**
Eskmont Ridge SE19 7D **138**
Esk Rd. E13 4J **87**
Esk Way RM1: Rom 1K **55**
Esmar Cres. NW9 7C **44**
Esmeralda Rd. SE1 4G **103**
Esmond Ct. *W8* *3K* ***99***
(off Thackeray St.)
Esmond Gdns. W4 4K **97**
Esmond Rd. NW6 1H **81**
W4 4K **97**
Esmond St. SW15 4G **117**
Esparto St. SW18 7K **117**
Esporta Health & Fitness
Chislehurst 5J **143**
Enfield 4J **23**
Finchley Rd. ***6A 64***
(in O2 Cen.)
Grove Park 1A **116**
Gunnersbury 4H **97**
Ilford ***3F 71***
(off Winston Way)
Islington 1B **84**
Kingston upon Thames ***1E 150***
(off East W. Link Rd.)
New Southgate 5K **31**
Purley 6K **167**
Repton Park 7K **37**
Romford 5K **55**
Wandsworth 4K **117**
Wimbledon 6H **135**
Esprit Ct. *E1* *6J* ***9***
(off Brune St.)
Essan Ho. W5 5B **78**
Essence Ct. HA9: Wemb 2F **61**
Essenden Rd. CR2: S Croy 7E **168**
DA17: Belv 5G **109**
Essendine Mans. W9 3J **81**
Essendine Rd. W9 3J **81**
Essex Av. TW7: Isle 3J **113**
Essex Cl. E17 4A **50**
HA4: Ruis 1B **58**
RM7: Mawney 4H **55**
SM4: Mord 7F **153**
Essex Ct. EC4 1J **13**
SW13 2B **116**
Essex Gdns. N4 6B **48**
Essex Gro. SE19 6D **138**
Essex Hall E17 1K **49**
Essex Ho. *E14* *6D* ***86***
(off Girauld St.)
Essex Mans. E11 7F **51**
Essex Pk. N3 6E **30**
Essex Pk. M. W3 1A **98**
Essex Pl. W4 4J **97**
(not continuous)
Essex Pl. Sq. W4 4K **97**
Essex Rd. E4 1B **36**
E10 6E **50**
E12 5C **70**
E17 6A **50**
E18 2K **51**
EN2: Enf 4J **23**
IG11: Bark 7H **71**
N1 1B **84**
NW10 7A **62**
RM6: Chad H 7C **54**
RM7: Mawney 4H **55**
RM10: Dag 5J **73**
W3 7J **79**
W4 4K **97**
(not continuous)
Essex Rd. Sth. E11 7F **51**
Essex St. E7 5J **69**
WC2 1J **13** (6A **84**)
Essex Twr. *SE20* *1H* ***157***
(off Jasmine Gro.)
Essex Vs. W8 2J **99**
Essex Wharf E5 2K **67**
Essian St. E1 5A **86**
Essoldo Way HA8: Edg 3F **43**
Estate Way E10 1B **68**
Estcourt Rd. SE25 6H **157**
SW6 7H **99**
Estella Av. KT3: N Mald 4D **152**
Estella Ho. *W11* *7F* ***81***
(off St Ann's Rd.)
Estelle Rd. NW3 4D **64**
Esterbrooke St. SW1 4C **18** (4H **101**)
Este Rd. SW11 3C **118**
Esther Cl. N21 7F **23**
Esther Rd. E11 7G **51**
Estoria Cl. SW2 7A **120**
Estorick Collection of Modern Italian Art 6B **66**
Estreham Rd. SW16 6H **137**
Estridge Cl. TW3: Houn 4E **112**
Estuary Cl. IG11: Bark 3B **90**
Eswyn Rd. SW17 4D **136**
Etal Ho. *N1* *7B* ***66***
(off The Sutton Est.)
Etcetera Theatre ***7F 65***
(off Camden High St.)
Etchingham Ct. N3 7E **30**
Etchingham Pk. Rd. N3 7E **30**
Etchingham Rd. E15 4E **68**
Eternit Wlk. SW6 1E **116**
Etfield Gro. DA14: Sidc 5B **144**
Ethelbert Cl. BR1: Brom 2J **159**
Ethelbert Ct. *BR1: Brom* *3J* ***159***
(off Ethelbert Rd.)
Ethelbert Gdns. IG2: Ilf 5D **52**
Ethelbert Rd. BR1: Brom 3J **159**
DA8: Erith 7J **109**
SW20 1F **153**
Ethelbert St. SW12 1F **137**
Ethel Brooks Ho. SE18 6F **107**
Ethelburga St. SW11 1C **118**
Ethelburga Twr. *SW11* *1C* ***118***
(off Maskelyne Cl.)
Etheldene Av. N10 4G **47**
Ethelden Rd. W12 1D **98**
Ethel Rd. E16 6K **87**
TW15: Ashf 5A **128**
Ethel St. SE17 4C **102**
Etheridge Rd. NW4 7E **44**
(not continuous)
Etherley Rd. N15 5C **48**
Etherow St. SE22 7G **121**
Etherstone Grn. SW16 4A **138**
Etherstone Rd. SW16 4A **138**
Ethnard Rd. SE15 6H **103**
Ethronvi Rd. DA7: Bex 3E **126**
Etloe Ho. E10 1C **68**
Etloe Rd. E10 2C **68**
Eton Av. EN4: E Barn 6H **21**
HA0: Wemb 4B **60**
KT3: N Mald 5K **151**
N12 7F **31**
NW3 7B **64**
TW5: Hest 6D **94**
Eton Cl. SW18 7K **117**
Eton Coll. Rd. NW3 6D **64**
Eton Ct. HA0: Wemb 4C **60**
NW3 7B **64**
Eton Garages NW3 6C **64**
Eton Gro. NW9 3G **43**
SE13 3G **123**
Eton Hall NW3 6D **64**
Eton Ho. *N5* *4B* ***66***
(off Leigh Rd.)
Eton Mnr. Ct. *E10* *2C* ***68***
(off Leyton Grange Est.)
Eton Pl. NW3 7E **64**
Eton Ri. NW3 6D **64**
Eton Rd. IG1: Ilf 4G **71**
NW3 7D **64**
UB3: Harl 7H **93**
Eton St. TW9: Rich 5E **114**
Eton Vs. NW3 6D **64**
Etta St. SE8 6A **104**
Ettrick St. E14 6E **86**
(not continuous)
Etwell Pl. KT5: Surb 6F **151**
Euesdon Cl. N9 3C **34**
Eugene Cotter Ho. *SE17* *4D* ***102***
(off Tatum St.)
Eugenia Rd. SE16 4J **103**
Eugenie M. BR7: Chst 1F **161**
Eureka Rd. KT1: King T 2G **151**
Euro Cl. NW10 6C **62**
Eurolink Bus. Cen. SW2 5A **120**
Europa Pl. EC1 2C **8** (3C **84**)
Europa Trad. Est. DA8: Erith 5K **109**
European Bus. Cen. NW9 3J **43**
(not continuous)
Europe Rd. SE18 3D **106**
Euro Trade Cen. DA17: Belv 2J **109**
Eustace Bldg. SW8 6F **101**
Eustace Ho. SE11 3G **19**
Eustace Pl. SE18 4D **106**
Eustace Rd. E6 3C **88**
RM6: Chad H 7D **54**
SW6 7J **99**
Euston Cen. NW1 3A **6** (4G **83**)
(not continuous)
Euston Gro. *NW1* *2C* ***6***
(off Euston Sq.)
Euston Rd. CR0: Croy 1A **168**
NW1 4A **6** (4F **83**)
Euston Sq. NW1 2C **6** (3H **83**)
(not continuous)
Euston Sta. Colonnade
NW1 2C **6** (3H **83**)
Euston St. NW1 2B **6** (3G **83**)
Euston Twr. NW1 3A **6** (4G **83**)
EUSTON UNDERPASS 4G **83**
Evandale Rd. SW9 2A **120**
Evangalist Ho. *EC4* *1A* ***14***
(off Black Friars La.)
Evangelist Rd. NW5 4F **65**
Evans Bus. Cen. NW2 3C **62**
Evans Cl. E8 6F **67**
Evans Gro. TW13: Hanw 2E **130**
Evans Ho. *SW8* *7H* ***101***
(off Wandsworth Rd.)
TW13: Hanw 2E **130**
W12 *7D* ***80***
(off White City Est.)
Evans Rd. SE6 2G **141**
Evanston Av. E4 7K **35**
Evanston Gdns. IG4: Ilf 6C **52**
Eva Rd. RM6: Chad H 7C **54**
Evedon Ho. *N1* *1E* ***84***
(off New Era Est.)
Evelina Mans. SE5 7D **102**
Evelina Rd. SE15 3J **121**
SE20 7J **139**
Eveline Rd. CR4: Mitc 1D **154**
Evelyn Av. HA4: Ruis 7G **39**
NW9 4K **43**
Evelyn Cl. TW2: Whit 7F **113**
Evelyn Ct. E8 4G **67**
N1 *1E* ***8***
(off Evelyn Wlk., not continuous)
Evelyn Cres. TW16: Sun 1H **147**
Evelyn Denington Ct. *N1* *7B* ***66***
(off The Sutton Est.)
Evelyn Denington Rd. E6 4C **88**
Evelyn Dr. HA5: Pinn 1B **40**
Evelyn Fox Ct. W10 5E **80**
Evelyn Gdns. SW7 6A **16** (5A **100**)
TW9: Rich 4E **114**
Evelyn Gro. UB1: S'hall 6D **76**
W5 1F **97**
Evelyn Ho. *SE14* *1A* ***122***
(off Loring Rd.)
W8 *2K* ***99***
(off Hornton Pl.)
W12 *2B* ***98***
(off Cobbold Rd.)
Evelyn Lowe Est. SE16 3G **103**
Evelyn Mans. *SW1* *2A* ***18***
(off Carlisle Pl.)
W14 *6G* ***99***
(off Queen's Club Gdns.)
Evelyn Rd. E16 1J **105**
E17 4E **50**
EN4: Cockf 4J **21**
SW19 5K **135**
TW9: Rich 3E **114**
TW10: Ham 3C **132**
W4 3K **97**
Evelyns Cl. UB8: Hil 6C **74**
Evelyn St. SE8 4A **104**
Evelyn Ter. TW9: Rich 3E **114**
Evelyn Wlk. N1 1E **8** (2D **84**)
Evelyn Way SM6: Bedd 4H **167**
TW16: Sun 1H **147**
Evelyn Yd. W1 7C **6** (6H **83**)
Evening Hill BR3: Beck 7E **140**
Evenlode Ho. SE2 2C **108**
Evenwood Cl. SW15 5G **117**
Everard Av. BR2: Hayes 1J **171**
Everard Ct. N13 3E **32**
Everard Ho. *E1* *6G* ***85***
(off Boyd St.)
Everard Way HA9: Wemb 3E **60**
Everatt Cl. SW18 6H **117**
Everdon Rd. SW13 6C **98**
Everest Pl. E14 5E **86**
Everest Rd. SE9 5D **124**
TW19: Stanw 7A **110**
Everett Cl. HA5: Eastc 3H **39**
WD23: Bushy 1D **26**
Everett Ho. *SE17* *5D* ***102***
(off East St.)
Everett Wlk. *DA17: Belv* *5F* ***109***
(off Osborne Rd.)
Everglade Ho. E17 2B **50**
Everglade Strand NW9 1B **44**
Evergreen Cl. SE20 7J **139**
Evergreen Sq. E8 7F **67**
Evergreen Way UB3: Hayes 7H **75**
Everilda St. N1 1K **83**
Evering Rd. E5 3G **67**
N16 3F **67**
Everington Rd. N10 2D **46**
Everington St. W6 6F **99**
(not continuous)
Everitt Rd. NW10 3K **79**
Everleigh St. N4 1K **65**
Eve Rd. E11 4G **69**
E15 2G **87**
N17 3E **48**
TW7: Isle 4A **114**

Eversfield Gdns. NW7 . . . . .6F 29
Eversfield Rd. TW9: Kew 2F 115
Evershed Wlk. W4 . . . . .3J 97
Eversholt St. NW1 . . . . . . .1B 6 (2G 83)
Evershot Rd. N4 . . . . .1K 65
Eversleigh Rd. E6 . . . . .1B 88
  EN5: New Bar 5F 21
  N3 .7C 30
  SW11 . . . . .3D 118
Eversley Av. DA7: Bex 2K 127
  HA9: Wemb 2G 61
Eversley Cl. N21 . . . . .6E 22
Eversley Cres. HA4: Ruis 2G 57
  N21 . . . . .6F 23
  TW7: Isle 1H 113
Eversley Ho. E2 . . . . .2K 9
  (off Gossett St.)
Eversley Mt. N21 . . . . .6E 22
Eversley Pk. SW19 . . . . .6D 134
Eversley Pk. Rd. N21 . . . . . . .6E 22
Eversley Rd. KT5: Surb 4F 151
  SE7 . . . . .6K 105
  SE19 . . . . .7D 138
Eversley Way CRO: Croy 4C 170
Everthorpe Rd. SE15 . . . . . . .3F 121
Everton Bldgs. NW1 . . . . .2A 6 (3G 83)
Everton Dr. HA7: Stan 3E 42
Everton Rd. CRO: Croy 1G 169
Evesham Av. E17 . . . . .2C 50
Evesham Cl. SM2: Sutt 7J 165
  UB6: G'frd 2F 77
Evesham Ct. TW10: Rich 1A 116
  W13 . . . . .1A 96
  (off Tewkesbury Rd.)
Evesham Grn. SM4: Mord 6K 153
Evesham Ho. E2 . . . . .2J 85
  (off Old Ford Rd.)
  NW8 . . . . .1A 82
  (off Abbey Rd.)
  SW1 . . . . .5F 101
  (off Sutherland Row)
Evesham Rd. E15 . . . . .7H 69
  N11 . . . . .5B 32
  SM4: Mord 6K 153
Evesham St. W11 . . . . .7F 81
Evesham Ter. KT6: Surb 6D 150
Evesham Wlk. SE5 . . . . .2D 120
  SW9 . . . . .2A 120
Evesham Way IG5: Ilf 3E 52
  SW11 . . . . .3E 118
Evry Rd. DA14: Sidc 6C 144
Ewald Rd. SW6 . . . . .2H 117
Ewanrigg Ter. IG8: Wfd G . . .5F 37
Ewart Gro. N22 . . . . .1K 47
Ewart Pl. E3 . . . . .2B 86
Ewart Rd. SE23 . . . . .7K 121
Ewe Cl. N7 . . . . .6J 65
EWELL .7C 164
Ewell By-Pass KT17: Ewe 7C 164
Ewell Ct. Av. KT19: Ewe 5A 164
Ewellhurst Rd. IG5: Ilf 2C 52
Ewell Pk. Gdns. KT17: Ewe . .7C 164
Ewell Pk. Way KT17: Ewe 6C 164
Ewell Rd. KT6: Surb 6E 150
  (Surbiton Hill Rd.)
  KT6: Surb 7B 150
  (Thornhill Rd.)
  SM3: Cheam 6F 165
Ewelme Rd. SE23 . . . . .1J 139
Ewen Cres. SW2 . . . . .7A 120
Ewen Henderson Ct. SE14 . . .7A 104
  (off Goodwood Rd.)
Ewen Ho. N1 . . . . .1K 83
  (off Barnsbury Est.)
Ewer St. SE1 . . . . .5C 14 (1C 102)
Ewhurst Av. CR2: Sand 7F 169
Ewhurst Cl. E1 . . . . .5J 85
Ewhurst Ct. CR4: Mitc 3B 154
Ewhurst Rd. SE4 . . . . .6B 122
Exbury Ho. E9 . . . . .7J 67
  SW1 . . . . .5C 18
  (off Rampayne St.)
Exbury Rd. SE6 . . . . .2C 140

ExCeL 7K 87
Excel Cl. WC2 . . . . .3D 12
Excel Marina E16 . . . . .7J 87
Excelsior Cl. KT1: King T . . .2G 151
Excelsior Gdns. SE13 . . . . . . .2E 122
Excelsior Ind. Est. SE15 . . . .6J 103
Excel Waterfront E16 . . . . . . .7K 87
Exchange, The IG1: Ilf 2F 71
Exchange Apartments BR2: Brom . . .4K 159
  (off Sparkes Cl.)
Exchange Arc. EC2 . . . . . .5H 9 (5E 84)
Exchange Bldg. E1 . . . . .4J 9
  (off Commercial St.)
Exchange Cl. N11 . . . . .2K 31
Exchange Ct. WC2 . . . . .3F 13 (7J 83)
Exchange Ho. EC2 . . . . .5H 9
  NW10 . . . . .7D 62
  SW1 . . . . .4C 18
  (off Vauxhall Bri. Rd.)
Exchange Mans. NW11 . . . . .7H 45
Exchange Pl. EC2 . . . . . .5G 9 (5E 84)
Exchange Sq. EC2 . . . . . .5G 9 (5E 84)
Exchange St. EC1 . . . . . .2C 8 (3C 84)
  RM1: Rom 5K 55
Exchange Wlk. HA5: Pinn 7C 40
Exforde Av. TW15: Ashf 4C 128
Exeter Cl. E6 . . . . .6D 88
Exeter Ct. KT6: Surb 5E 150
  (off Maple Rd.)
  NW6 . . . . .2J 81
  (off Cambridge Rd.)
Exeter Gdns. IG1: Ilf 1C 70
Exeter Ho. IG11: Bark 7A 72
  (off Margaret Bondfield Av.)
  N1 . . . . .1E 84
  (off New Era Est.)
  SE15 . . . . .6G 103
  (off Friary Est.)
  SW15 . . . . .6E 116
  TW13: Hanw 2D 130
  (off Watermill Way)
  W2 . . . . .6A 82
  (off Hallfield Est.)
Exeter Mans. NW2 . . . . .6G 63
Exeter M. NW6 . . . . .6K 63
  SW6 . . . . .7J 99
Exeter Rd. CRO: Croy 7E 156
  DA16: Well 2K 125
  E16 . . . . .5J 87
  E17 . . . . .5C 50
  EN3: Pond E 3E 24
  HA2: Harr 2C 58
  N9 . . . . .2D 34
  N14 . . . . .1A 32
  NW2 . . . . .5G 63
  RM10: Dag 6H 73
  TW6: H'row A 3F 111
  TW13: Hanw 3D 130
Exeter St. WC2 . . . . . . .2F 13 (7J 83)
Exeter Way SE14 . . . . .7B 104
  TW6: H'row A 2G 111
Exford Gdns. SE12 . . . . .1K 141
Exford Rd. SE12 . . . . .2K 141
Exhibition Cl. W12 . . . . .7E 80
Exhibition Rd. SW7 . . . .7B 10 (2B 100)
Exit Rd. N2 . . . . .2B 46
Exmoor Cl. IG6: Ilf 1G 53
Exmoor Ho. E3 . . . . .2A 86
  (off Gernon Rd.)
Exmoor St. W10 . . . . .4F 81
Exmouth Ho. E14 . . . . .4D 104
  (off Cahir St.)
  EC1 . . . . .3J 7
  (off Pine St.)
Exmouth Mkt. EC1 . . . . .3J 7 (4A 84)
Exmouth M. NW1 . . . . . . .2B 6 (3G 83)
Exmouth Pl. E8 . . . . .7H 67
Exmouth Rd. DA16: Well 1C 126
  E17 . . . . .5B 50
  HA4: Ruis 3A 58
  UB4: Hayes 3G 75
Exmouth St. E1 . . . . .6J 85
Exning Rd. E16 . . . . .4H 87

Exonbury NW8 . . . . .1K 81
  (off Abbey Rd.)
Exon St. SE17 . . . . .5E 102
Explorer Av. TW19: Stanw . . .1A 128
Export Ho. SE1 . . . . .7H 15
  (off Tower Bri. Rd.)
Express Dr. IG3: Ilf 1B 72
Express Newspapers SE1 . . . . .4A 14
  (off Blackfriars Rd.)
Exton Gdns. RM8: Dag 5C 72
Exton Ho. NW10 . . . . .7J 61
Exton St. SE1 . . . . .5J 13 (1A 102)
Eyebright Cl. CRO: Croy 1K 169
Eyhurst Cl. NW2 . . . . .2C 62
Eylewood Rd. SE27 . . . . .5C 138
Eynella Rd. SE22 . . . . .7F 121
Eynham Rd. W12 . . . . .6E 80
Eynsford Cl. BR5: Pet W 7G 161
Eynsford Cres. DA5: Bexl . . .1C 144
Eynsford Ho. SE1 . . . . .7E 14
  (off Crosby Row)
  SE15 . . . . .6J 103
  SE17 . . . . .4E 102
  (off Beckway St.)
Eynsford Rd. IG3: Ilf 2J 71
Eynsford Ter. UB7: View 6B 74
Eynsham Dr. SE2 . . . . .4A 108
Eynswood Dr. DA14: Sidc 5B 144
Eyot Gdns. W6 . . . . .5B 98
Eyot Grn. W4 . . . . .5B 98
Eyre Ct. NW8 . . . . .2B 82
Eyre St. Hill EC1 . . . . .4J 7 (4A 84)
Eysham Cl. EN5: New Bar 5E 20
Eythorne Rd. SW9 . . . . .1A 120
Ezra St. E2 . . . . .1K 9 (3F 85)

F

F1 City Go-Kart Circuit 1A 106
  (off Connaught Bri.)
Faber Gdns. NW4 . . . . .5C 44
Fabian Rd. SW6 . . . . .7H 99
Fabian St. E6 . . . . .4D 88
Facade, The SE23 . . . . .2J 139
Factory La. CRO: Croy 1A 168
  N17 . . . . .2F 49
Factory Rd. E16 . . . . .1B 106
Factory Yd. W7 . . . . .1J 95
Faggs Rd. TW14: Felt 4H 111
Fairacre KT3: N Mald 3A 152
Fairacre Ct. HA6: Nwood 1G 39
Fairacres BR2: Brom 5J 159
  CRO: Sels 7B 170
Fairacres HA4: Ruis 7H 39
  SW15 . . . . .4B 116
Fairbairn Grn. SW9 . . . . .1B 120
Fairbank Av. BR6: Farnb 2F 173
Fairbank Est. N1 . . . . . .1E 8 (2D 84)
Fairbanks Rd. N17 . . . . .3F 49
Fairbourne Ho. UB3: Harl . . .3E 92
Fairbourne Rd. N17 . . . . .3E 48
Fairbriar Residence SW7 . . . .4A 100
  (off Cromwell Rd.)
Fairbridge Rd. N19 . . . . .2H 65
Fairbrook Cl. N13 . . . . .5F 33
Fairbrook Rd. N13 . . . . .6F 33
Fairburn Ct. SW15 . . . . .5G 117
Fairburn Ho. W14 . . . . .5H 99
  (off Ivatt Pl.)
Fairby Ho. SE1 . . . . .4F 103
  (off Longfield Est.)
Fairby Rd. SE12 . . . . .5K 123
Faircharm Trad. Est. SE8 . . .7D 104
Fairchild Cl. SW11 . . . . .2B 118
Fairchild Ho. E9 . . . . .7J 67
  N1 . . . . .1G 9
  (off Fanshaw St.)
  N3 . . . . .1J 45
Fairchild Pl. EC2 . . . . .4H 9
Fairchild St. EC2 . . . . .3H 9 (4E 84)
Fair Cl. WD23: Bush 1A 26

Fairclough Cl. UB5: Yead . . .4D 76
Fairclough St. E1 . . . . .6G 85
Faircroft Ct. TW11: Tedd . . .6A 132
FAIR CROSS 4F 71
Faircross Av. IG11: Bark . . .6G 71
  RM5: Col R 1K 55
Faircross Pde. IG11: Bark . . .5J 71
Fairdale Gdns. SW15 . . . . . . .4D 116
  UB3: Hayes 2J 93
Fairey Av. UB3: Harl 4H 93
Fairfax Av. KT17: Ewe 7D 164
Fairfax Cl. KT12: Walt T 7K 147
Fairfax Gdns. SE3 . . . . .1A 124
Fairfax Ho. KT1: King T 3F 151
  (off Livesey Cl.)
Fairfax Mans. NW3 . . . . .6A 64
  (off Finchley Rd.)
Fairfax M. E16 . . . . .1K 105
  N8 . . . . .4B 48
  SW15 . . . . .4E 116
Fairfax Pl. NW6 . . . . .7A 64
  W14 . . . . .3G 99
Fairfax Rd. N8 . . . . .4A 48
  NW6 . . . . .7A 64
  TW11: Tedd 6A 132
  W4 . . . . .3A 98
Fairfax Way N10 . . . . .7K 31
Fairfield E1 . . . . .5J 85
  (off Redman's Rd.)
  KT1: King T 2F 151
  N20: New Bar 7G 21
  NW1 . . . . .1G 83
  (off Arlington Rd.)
Fairfield Av. HA4: Ruis 7E 38
  HA8: Edg 6C 28
  NW4 . . . . .6D 44
  TW2: Whit 1F 131
Fairfield Cl. CR4: Mitc 7C 136
  DA15: Sidc 6K 125
  EN3: Pond E 4E 24
  KT19: Ewe 5A 164
  N12 . . . . .4F 31
Fairfield Ct. HA4: Ruis 1F 57
  HA6: Nwood 2J 39
  NW10 . . . . .1C 80
Fairfield Cres. HA8: Edg . . .6C 28
Fairfield Dr. HA2: Harr 3G 41
  SW18 . . . . .5K 117
  UB6: G'frd 1C 78
Fairfield E. KT1: King T 2E 150
Fairfield Gdns. N8 . . . . .5J 47
Fairfield Gro. SE7 . . . . .6B 106
Fairfield Halls 3D 168
Fairfield Nth. KT1: King T . .2E 150
Fairfield Path CRO: Croy . . .3D 168
Fairfield Pl. KT1: King T . . .3E 150
Fairfield Rd. BR1: Brom 7J 141
  BR3: Beck 2C 158
  BR5: Pet W 6H 161
  CRO: Croy 3D 168
  DA7: Bex 2F 127
  E3 . . . . .2C 86
  E17 . . . . .2A 50
  IG1: Ilf 6F 71
  IG8: Wfd G 6D 36
  KT1: King T 2E 150
  (not continuous)
  N8 . . . . .5J 47
  N18 . . . . .4B 34
  UB1: S'hall 6D 76
  UB7: View 7A 74
  UB8: Uxb 6A 56
Fairfields Cl. NW9 . . . . .5J 43
Fairfields Cres. NW9 . . . . . .4J 43
Fairfields Rd. TW3: Houn . . .3G 113
Fairfield St. SW18 . . . . .5K 117
Fairfield Trade Pk. KT1: King T . . .3F 151
Fairfield Way EN5: Barn 5D 20
  KT19: Ewe 5A 164
Fairfield W. KT1: King T 2E 150
Fairfoot Rd. E3 . . . . .4C 86
Fairford SE6 . . . . .1C 140

Fairford Av. CR0: Croy 5K **157**
DA7: Bex 1K **127**
Fairford Cl. CR0: Croy 5A **158**
Fairford Ct. SM2: Sutt 7K **165**
Fairford Gdns. KT4: Wor Pk 2B **164**
Fairford Ho. SE11 4K **19** (4A **102**)
Fairgreen EN4: Cockf 3J **21**
Fairgreen Ct. EN4: Cockf 3J **21**
Fairgreen E. EN4: Cockf 3J **21**
Fairgreen Rd. CR7: Thor H 5B **156**
Fairhall Ct. KT5: Surb 7F **151**
Fairhaven Av. CR0: Croy 6K **157**
Fairhaven Ct. *CR2: S Croy* *5C* ***168***
(off Warham Rd.)
Fairhazel Gdns. NW6 6K **63**
Fairhazel Mans. *NW6* *7A* ***64***
(off Fairhazel Gdns.)
Fairholme TW14: Bedf 7F **111**
Fairholme Cl. N3 4G **45**
Fairholme Cres. UB4: Hayes 4H **75**
Fairholme Gdns. N3 3G **45**
Fairholme Rd.
CR0: Croy 7A **156**
HA1: Harr 5K **41**
IG1: Ilf 7D **52**
SM1: Sutt 6H **165**
TW15: Ashf 5A **128**
W14 5G **99**
Fairholt Cl. N16 1E **66**
Fairholt Rd. N16 1D **66**
Fairholt St. SW7 1D **16** (3C **100**)
Fairland Ho. BR2: Brom 4K **159**
Fairland Rd. E15 6H **69**
Fairlands Av. CR7: Thor H 4K **155**
IG9: Buck H 2D **36**
SM1: Sutt 2J **165**
Fairlands Ct. SE9 6E **124**
Fairlawn SE7 7A **106**
Fairlawn Av. DA7: Bex 2D **126**
N2 4C **46**
W4 4J **97**
Fair Lawn Cl. KT10: Clay 6A **162**
Fairlawn Cl. KT2: King T 6J **133**
N14 6B **22**
TW13: Hanw 4D **130**
Fairlawn Ct. SE7 7A **106**
(not continuous)
W4 4J **97**
Fairlawn Dr. IG8: Wfd G 7D **36**
Fairlawnes SM6: Wall 5F **167**
Fairlawn Gdns.
UB1: S'hall 7D **76**
Fairlawn Gro. W4 4J **97**
Fairlawn Mans. SE14 1K **121**
Fairlawn Pk. SE26 5A **140**
Fairlawn Rd. SW19 7H **135**
Fairlawns HA5: Pinn 2B **40**
TW1: Twick 6C **114**
TW16: Sun 3J **147**
Fairlead Ho. *E14* *3C* ***104***
(off Alpha Gro.)
Fairlea Pl. W5 4C **78**
Fairlie Gdns. SE23 7J **121**
Fairlight TW12: Ham H 5F **131**
Fairlight Av. E4 2A **36**
IG8: Wfd G 6D **36**
NW10 2A **80**
Fairlight Cl. E4 2A **36**
KT4: Wor Pk 4E **164**
Fairlight Ct. NW10 2A **80**
UB6: G'frd 2G **77**
Fairlight Rd. SW17 4B **136**
Fairline Ct. BR3: Beck 2E **158**
FAIRLOP 1J **53**
Fairlop Ct. E11 1F **69**
Fairlop Gdns. IG6: Ilf 1G **53**
Fairlop Rd. E11 7F **51**
IG6: Ilf 2G **53**
Fairlop Sailing Cen. **1K 53**
Fairlop Waters Country Pk. **1K 53**
Fairmark Dr. UB10: Hil 6C **56**
Fairmead BR1: Brom 4D **160**
KT5: Surb 1H **163**
Fairmead Cl. BR1: Brom 4D **160**
KT3: N Mald 3K **151**
TW5: Hest 7B **94**
Fairmead Ct. TW9: Rich 2H **115**
Fairmead Cres. HA8: Edg 3D **28**
Fairmead Gdns. IG4: Ilf 5C **52**
Fairmead Ho. E9 4A **68**
Fairmead Rd. CR0: Croy 7K **155**
N19 3H **65**
Fairmile Av. SW16 5H **137**
Fairmile Ho. TW11: Tedd 4A **132**
Fairmont Av. E14 1F **105**
Fairmont Cl. DA17: Belv 5F **109**
Fairmount Rd. SW2 6K **119**
Fairoak Cl. BR5: Pet W 7F **161**
Fairoak Dr. SE9 5H **125**
Fairoak Gdns. RM1: Rom 2K **55**
Fair Oak Pl. IG6: Ilf 2G **53**
Fairseat Cl. WD23: Bushy 2D **26**
Fairstead Wlk. *N1* *1C* ***84***
(off Popham St.)
Fair St. SE1 6H **15** (2E **102**)
TW3: Houn 3G **113**
Fairthorn Rd. SE7 5J **105**
Fairview HA4: Ruis 4A **58**
Fairview Av. HA0: Wemb 6D **60**
Fairview Cl. E17 1A **50**
SE26 5A **140**
Fairview Ct. NW4 2F **45**
TW15: Ashf 5C **128**
Fairview Cres. HA2: Harr 1E **58**
Fairview Dr. BR6: Orp 4H **173**
TW17: Shep 5B **146**
Fairview Est. NW10 3J **79**
Fairview Gdns. IG8: Wfd G 1K **51**
Fairview Ho. SW2 7K **119**
Fairview Ind. Pk.
RM13: Rain 5K **91**
Fairview Pl. SW2 7K **119**
Fairview Rd. EN2: Enf 1F **23**
N15 5F **49**
SM1: Sutt 5B **166**
SW16 1K **155**
Fairview Vs. E4 7J **35**
Fairview Way HA8: Edg 4B **28**
Fairwall Ho. SE5 1E **120**
Fairwater Av. DA16: Well 4A **126**
Fairwater Ho. TW11: Tedd 4A **132**
Fair Way IG8: Wfd G 5F **37**
Fairway BR5: Pet W 5H **161**
DA6: Bex 5E **126**
SW20 3E **152**
Fairway, The BR1: Brom 5D **160**
EN5: New Bar 6E **20**
HA0: Wemb 3B **60**
HA4: Ruis 4A **58**
KT3: N Mald 1K **151**
KT8: W Mole 3F **149**
N13 3H **33**
N14 6A **22**
NW7 3E **28**
UB5: N'olt 6G **59**
UB10: Hil 2B **74**
W3 6A **80**
Fairway Av. NW9 3H **43**
Fairway Cl. CR0: Croy 5A **158**
KT19: Ewe 4J **163**
NW11 7A **46**
TW4: Houn 5A **112**
(Green La.)
TW4: Houn 5B **112**
(Staines Rd.)
Fairway Ct. EN5: New Bar 6E **20**
NW7 3E **28**
SE16 *2K* ***103***
(off Christopher Cl.)
Fairway Dr. SE28 6D **90**
UB6: G'frd 7F **59**
Fairway Gdns. BR3: Beck 6F **159**
IG1: Ilf 5G **71**
Fairways E17 4E **50**
HA7: Stan 2E **42**
TW7: Isle 1H **113**
Fairways TW11: Tedd 7D **132**
TW15: Ashf 6D **128**
Fairways Bus. Pk. E10 2A **68**
Fairweather Cl. N15 4E **48**
Fairweather Ct. N13 4E **32**
Fairweather Ho. N7 4J **65**
Fairweather Rd. N16 6G **49**
Fairwyn Rd. SE26 4A **140**
Fakenham Cl. NW7 7H **29**
UB5: N'olt 6E **58**
Fakruddin St. E1 4G **85**
Falcon *WC1* *5F* ***7***
(off Old Gloucester St.)
Falcon Av. BR1: Brom 4C **160**
Falconberg Ct. W1 7D **6** (6H **83**)
Falconberg M. W1 7D **6** (6H **83**)
Falcon Cl. HA6: Nwood 1G **39**
SE1 4B **14** (1B **102**)
W4 6J **97**
Falcon Ct. *E18* *3K* ***51***
(off Albert Rd.)
EC4 1K **13** (6A **84**)
EN5: New Bar 4F **21**
HA4: Ruis 2G **57**
N1 *1B* ***8***
(off City Gdn. Row)
Falcon Cres. EN3: Pond E 5E **24**
Falcon Dr. TW19: Stanw 6A **110**
Falconer Ct. N17 7H **33**
Falconer Wlk. N7 2K **65**
Falconet Ct. *E1* *1H* ***103***
(off Wapping High St.)
Falcon Gro. SW11 3C **118**
Falcon Highwalk EC2 6C **8**
Falcon Ho. *E14* *5D* ***104***
(off St Davids Sq.)
SW5 *5K* ***99***
(off Old Brompton Rd.)
Falcon La. SW11 3C **118**
Falcon Lodge *W9* *5J* ***81***
(off Admiral Wlk.)
Falcon Pk. Ind. Est. NW10 4A **62**
Falcon Point SE1 3B **14** (7B **84**)
Falcon Rd. EN3: Pond E 5E **24**
SW11 2C **118**
TW12: Hamp 7D **130**
Falconry Ct. *KT1: King T* *3E* ***150***
(off Fairfield Sth.)
Falcon St. E13 4H **87**
Falcon Ter. SW11 3C **118**
Falcon Way E11 4J **51**
E14 4D **104**
HA3: Kent 5E **42**
NW9 2A **44**
TW14: Felt 5K **111**
TW16: Sun 2G **147**
FALCONWOOD **4K 125**
FALCONWOOD **4H 125**
Falconwood Av. DA16: Well 2H **125**
Falconwood Ct. *SE3* *2H* ***123***
(off Montpelier Row)
Falconwood Pde. DA16: Well 4J **125**
Falconwood Rd. CR0: Sels 7B **170**
Falcourt Cl. SM1: Sutt 5K **165**
Falkirk Ct. *SE16* *1K* ***103***
(off Rotherhithe St.)
Falkirk Ho. *W9* *2K* ***81***
(off Maida Va.)
Falkirk St. N1 1H **9** (2E **84**)
Falkland Av. N3 7D **30**
N11 4A **32**
Falkland Ho. SE6 4E **140**
W8 3K **99**
W14 *5H* ***99***
(off Edith Vs.)
Falkland Pk. Av. SE25 3E **156**
Falkland Pl. NW5 5G **65**
Falkland Rd. EN5: Barn 2B **20**
N8 4A **48**
NW5 5G **65**
Fallaize Av. IG1: Ilf 4F **71**
Falling La. UB7: Yiew 7A **74**
Falloden Way NW11 4J **45**
Fallodon Ho. *W11* *5H* ***81***
(off Tavistock Cres.)
FALLOW CORNER **7F 31**
Fallow Ct. *SE16* *5G* ***103***
(off Argyle Way)
Fallow Ct. Av. N12 7F **31**
Fallowfield HA7: Stan 4F **27**
Fallowfield Ct. HA7: Stan 3F **27**
Fallowfields Dr. N12 6H **31**
Fallowhurst Path N3 7F **31**
Fallows Cl. N2 2B **46**
Fallsbrook Rd. SW16 6F **137**
Falman Cl. N9 1B **34**
Falmer Rd. E17 3D **50**
EN1: Enf 4K **23**
N15 5C **48**
Falmouth Av. E4 5A **36**
Falmouth Cl. N22 7E **32**
SE12 5H **123**
Falmouth Gdns. IG4: Ilf 4B **52**
Falmouth Ho. HA5: H End 1D **40**
KT2: King T *1D* ***150***
(off Skerne Rd.)
SE11 *5K* ***19***
(off Seaton Cl.)
W2 *2C* ***10***
(off Clarendon Pl.)
Falmouth Rd. SE1 7E **14** (3C **102**)
Falmouth St. E15 5F **69**
Falmouth Way E17 5B **50**
Falstaff Bldg. *E1* *7H* ***85***
(off Cannon St. Rd.)
Falstaff Cl. DA1: Cray 7K **127**
Falstaff Ct. *SE11* *4B* ***102***
(off Opal St.)
Falstaff Ho. *N1* *1G* ***9***
(off Crondall St.)
Falstaff M. *TW12: Ham H* *5H* ***131***
(off Parkside)
Fambridge Cl. SE26 4B **140**
Fambridge Ct. *RM7: Rom* *5K* ***55***
(off Marks Rd.)
Fambridge Rd. RM8: Dag 1G **73**
Fane Ho. E2 1J **85**
Fane St. W14 6H **99**
Fan Mus., The **7E 104**
Fann St. EC1 4C **8** (4C **84**)
(not continuous)
EC2 4C **8** (4C **84**)
Fanshawe Av. IG11: Bark 6G **71**
Fanshawe Cres. RM9: Dag 5E **72**
Fanshawe Rd. TW10: Ham 4C **132**
Fanshaw St. N1 1G **9** (3E **84**)
FANTAIL, THE **3D 172**
Fantail Cl. SE28 6C **90**
Fanthorpe St. SW15 3E **116**
Faraday Av. DA14: Sidc 2A **144**
Faraday Cl. N7 6K **65**
Faraday Ho. *E14* *7B* ***86***
(off Brightlingsea Pl.)
HA9: Wemb 3J **61**
SE1 *7E* ***14***
(off Cole St.)
W10 *5G* ***81***
(off Wornington Rd.)
Faraday Lodge SE10 3H **105**
Faraday Mans. *W14* *6G* ***99***
(off Queen's Club Gdns.)
Faraday Mus. **3A 12 (7G 83)**
Faraday Pl. KT8: W Mole 4E **148**
Faraday Rd. DA16: Well 3A **126**
E15 6H **69**
KT8: W Mole 4E **148**
SW19 6J **135**
UB1: S'hall 7F **77**
W3 7J **79**
W10 5G **81**
Faraday Way CR0: Wadd 1K **167**
SE18 3B **106**
Fareham Rd. TW14: Felt 7A **112**
Fareham St. W1 7C **6** (6H **83**)
Farewell Pl. CR4: Mitc 1C **154**
Faringdon Av. BR2: Brom 7E **160**

Faringford Rd. E15 . . . 7G 69
Farjeon Ho. *NW6* . . . *7B 64*
(off Hilgrove Rd.)
Farjeon Rd. SE3 . . . 1B 124
Farleigh Av. BR2: Hayes . . . 7H 159
Farleigh Ct. CR2: S Croy . . . 5C 168
Farleigh Pl. N16 . . . 4F 67
Farleigh Rd. N16 . . . 4F 67
Farley Ct. *NW1* . . . *4G 5*
(off Allsop Pl.)
W14 . . . 3H 99
Farley Dr. IG3: Ilf . . . 1J 71
Farley Ho. SE26 . . . 3H 139
Farley Pl. SE25 . . . 4G 157
Farley Rd. CR2: Sels . . . 7H 169
SE6 . . . 7D 122
Farlington Pl. SW15 . . . 7D 116
Farlow Rd. SW15 . . . 3F 117
Farlton Rd. SW18 . . . 1K 135
Farman Gro. UB5: N'olt . . . 3B 76
Farman Ter. HA3: Kent . . . 4D 42
Farm Av. HA0: Wemb . . . 6C 60
HA2: Harr . . . 7D 40
NW2 . . . 3G 63
SW16 . . . 4J 137
Farmborough Cl. HA1: Harr . . . 7H 41
Farm Cl. BR4: W W'ck . . . 3H 171
IG9: Buck H . . . 3F 37
RM10: Dag . . . 7J 73
SM2: Sutt . . . 7B 166
SW6 . . . 7J 99
TW17: Shep . . . 7C 146
UB1: S'hall . . . 7F 77
UB10: Ick . . . 2D 56
Farmcote Rd. SE12 . . . 1J 141
Farm Ct. NW4 . . . 3C 44
Farmdale Rd. SE10 . . . 5J 105
SM5: Cars . . . 7C 166
Farm Dr. CR0: Croy . . . 2B 170
Farm End HA6: Nwood . . . 1D 38
Farmer Rd. E10 . . . 1D 68
Farmer's Rd. SE5 . . . 7B 102
Farmer St. W8 . . . 1J 99
Farmfield Rd. BR1: Brom . . . 5G 141
Farm Ho. Ct. NW7 . . . 7H 29
Farmhouse Rd. SW16 . . . 7G 137
Farmilo Rd. E17 . . . 7B 50
Farmington Av. SM1: Sutt . . . 3B 166
Farmlands EN2: Enf . . . 1F 23
HA5: Eastc . . . 4J 39
Farmlands, The UB5: N'olt . . . 6D 58
Farmland Wlk. BR7: Chst . . . 5F 143
Farm La. CR0: Croy . . . 2B 170
N14 . . . 7K 21
SW6 . . . 6J 99
(not continuous)
Farm La. Trad. Est. SW6 . . . 6J 99
Farmleigh N14 . . . 7B 22
Farmleigh Ho. SW9 . . . 5B 120
Farm M. CR4: Mitc . . . 2F 155
Farm Pl. W8 . . . 1J 99
Farm Rd. E12 . . . 2C 70
HA8: Edg . . . 6C 28
N21 . . . 1H 33
NW10 . . . 1K 79
SM2: Sutt . . . 7B 166
SM4: Mord . . . 5K 153
TW4: Houn . . . 1C 130
Farmstead Ct. *SM6: Wall* . . . *5F 167*
(off Melbourne Rd.)
Farmstead Rd. HA3: Hrw W . . . 1H 41
SE6 . . . 4D 140
Farm St. W1 . . . 3J 11 (7F 83)
Farm Va. DA5: Bexl . . . 6H 127
Farm Wlk. NW11 . . . 5H 45
Farm Way IG9: Buck H . . . 4F 37
KT4: Wor Pk . . . 3E 164
Farmway RM8: Dag . . . 3C 72
Farnaby Ho. *W10* . . . *3H 81*
(off Bruckner St.)
Farnaby Rd. BR1: Brom . . . 7F 141
BR2: Brom . . . 7F 141
SE9 . . . 4A 124
Farnan Av. E17 . . . 2C 50
Farnan Rd. SW16 . . . 5J 137
FARNBOROUGH . . . 5G 173
Farnborough Av. CR2: Sels . . . 7K 169
E17 . . . 3A 50
Farnborough Cl. HA9: Wemb . . . 2H 61
Farnborough Comn. BR6: Farnb . . . 3D 172
Farnborough Cres. BR2: Hayes . . . 1H 171
CR2: Sels . . . 7A 170
Farnborough Hill
BR6: Chels, Farnb . . . 5H 173
Farnborough Ho. SW15 . . . 1C 134
Farnborough Way
BR6: Chels, Farnb . . . 5G 173
Farncombe St. SE16 . . . 2G 103
Farndale Av. N13 . . . 2G 33
Farndale Ct. SE18 . . . 7C 106
Farndale Cres. UB6: G'frd . . . 3G 77
Farndale Ho. *NW6* . . . *1K 81*
(off Kilburn Va.)
Farnell M. SW5 . . . 5K 99
Farnell Pl. W3 . . . 7H 79
Farnell Rd. TW7: Isle . . . 3H 113
Farnham Cl. N20 . . . 7F 21
Farnham Ct. SM3: Cheam . . . 6G 165
UB1: S'hall . . . *7G 77*
(off Redcroft Rd.)
Farnham Gdns. SW20 . . . 2D 152
Farnham Ho. NW1 . . . 4D 4
SE1 . . . *5C 14*
(off Pepper St.)
Farnham Pl. SE1 . . . 5B 14 (1B 102)
Farnham Rd. DA16: Well . . . 2C 126
IG3: Ilf . . . 7K 53
Farnham Royal SE11 . . . 6H 19 (5K 101)
Farningham Ct. SW16 . . . 7H 137
Farningham Ho. N4 . . . 7D 48
Farningham Rd. N17 . . . 7B 34
Farnley Ho. SW8 . . . 2H 119
Farnley Rd. E4 . . . 1B 36
SE25 . . . 4D 156
Farnsworth Ct. *SE10* . . . *3H 105*
(off Greenroof Way)
Farnworth Ho. *E14* . . . *4F 105*
(off Manchester Rd.)
Faro Cl. BR1: Brom . . . 2E 160
Faroe Rd. W14 . . . 3F 99
Farorna Wlk. EN2: Enf . . . 1F 23
Farquhar Rd. SE19 . . . 5F 139
SW19 . . . 3J 135
Farquharson Rd. CR0: Croy . . . 1C 168
Farrance Rd. RM6: Chad H . . . 6E 54
Farrance St. E14 . . . 6C 86
Farrans Ct. HA3: Kent . . . 7B 42
Farrant Av. N22 . . . 2A 48
Farrant Cl. BR6: Chels . . . 7K 173
Farr Av. IG11: Bark . . . 2A 90
Farrell Ho. *E1* . . . *6J 85*
(off Ronald St.)
Farren Rd. SE23 . . . 2A 140
Farrer Ct. TW1: Twick . . . 7D 114
Farrer Ho. SE8 . . . 7C 104
Farrer M. N8 . . . 4G 47
Farrer Rd. HA3: Kent . . . 5E 42
N8 . . . 4G 47
Farrer's Pl. CR0: Croy . . . 4K 169
Farrier Cl. BR1: Brom . . . 3B 160
TW16: Sun . . . 4J 147
UB8: Hil . . . 6C 74
Farrier Pl. SM1: Sutt . . . 3K 165
Farrier Rd. UB5: N'olt . . . 2E 76
Farriers Ho. *EC1* . . . *4D 8*
(off Errol St.)
Farriers M. SE15 . . . 3J 121
Farrier St. NW1 . . . 7F 65
Farrier Wlk. SW10 . . . 6A 100
Farringdon Ho. TW9: Kew . . . 7H 97
Farringdon La. EC1 . . . 4K 7 (4A 84)
Farringdon Rd. EC1 . . . 3J 7 (4A 84)
Farringdon St. EC4 . . . 6A 8 (5B 84)
Farrington Pl. BR7: Chst . . . 7H 143
Farrins Rents SE16 . . . 1A 104
Farrow La. SE14 . . . 7J 103
Farrow Pl. SE16 . . . 3A 104
Farr Rd. EN2: Enf . . . 1J 23
Farthingale Wlk. E15 . . . 7F 69
Farthing All. SE1 . . . 7K 15 (2G 103)
Farthing Barn La. BR6: Downe . . . 7E 172
Farthing Ct. NW7 . . . 7B 30
Farthing Flds. E1 . . . 1H 103
Farthings, The KT2: King T . . . 1G 151
Farthings Cl. E4 . . . 3B 36
HA5: Eastc . . . 6K 39
FARTHING STREET . . . 7D 172
Farthing St. BR6: Downe . . . 7D 172
Farwell Rd. DA14: Sidc . . . 4B 144
Farwig La. BR1: Brom . . . 1H 159
Fashion & Textile Mus. . . . 6H 15
Fashion St. E1 . . . 6K 9 (5F 85)
Fashoda Rd. BR2: Brom . . . 4B 160
Fassett Rd. E8 . . . 6G 67
KT1: King T . . . 4E 150
Fassett Sq. E8 . . . 6G 67
Fauconberg Ct. *W4* . . . *6J 97*
(off Fauconberg Rd.)
Fauconberg Rd. W4 . . . 6J 97
Faulkner Cl. RM8: Dag . . . 7D 54
Faulkners All. EC1 . . . 5A 8 (5B 84)
Faulkner St. SE14 . . . 1J 121
Fauna Cl. RM6: Chad H . . . 6C 54
Faunce Ho. *SE17* . . . *6B 102*
(off Doddington Gro.)
Faunce St. SE17 . . . 5B 102
Favart Rd. SW6 . . . 1J 117
Faversham Av. E4 . . . 1B 36
EN1: Enf . . . 6J 23
Faversham Ho. *NW1* . . . *1G 83*
(off Bayham Pl.)
SE17 . . . *5E 102*
(off Kinglake St.)
Faversham Rd. BR3: Beck . . . 2B 158
SE6 . . . 7B 122
SM4: Mord . . . 6K 153
Fawcett Cl. SW11 . . . 2B 118
SW16 . . . 5A 138
Fawcett Ct. *SW10* . . . *6A 100*
(off Fawcett St.)
Fawcett Est. E5 . . . 1G 67
Fawcett Rd. CR0: Croy . . . 3C 168
NW10 . . . 7B 62
Fawcett St. SW10 . . . 6A 100
Fawe Pk. M. SW15 . . . 4H 117
Fawe Pk. Rd. SW15 . . . 4H 117
Fawe St. E14 . . . 5D 86
Fawkham Ho. *SE1* . . . *4F 103*
(off Longfield Est.)
Fawley Lodge *E14* . . . *4F 105*
(off Millennium Dr.)
Fawley Rd. NW6 . . . 5K 63
Fawnbrake Av. SE24 . . . 5B 120
Fawn Rd. E13 . . . 2A 88
Fawns Mnr. Cl. TW14: Bedf . . . 1E 128
Fawns Mnr. Rd. TW14: Bedf . . . 1F 129
Fawood Av. NW10 . . . 7J 61
Faygate Cres. DA6: Bex . . . 5G 127
Faygate Rd. SW2 . . . 2K 137
Fayland Av. SW16 . . . 5G 137
Fazeley Ct. *W9* . . . *5J 81*
(off Elmfield Way)
Fearnley Cres. TW12: Hamp . . . 5C 130
Fearnley Ho. SE5 . . . 2E 120
Fearon St. SE10 . . . 5J 105
Featherbed La. CR0: Sels . . . 7B 170
Feathers Pl. SE10 . . . 6F 105
Featherstone Av. SE23 . . . 2H 139
Featherstone Ho. UB4: Yead . . . 5A 76
Featherstone Ind. Est. *UB2: S'hall* . . . *3C 94*
(off Feather Rd.)
Featherstone Rd. NW7 . . . 6J 29
UB2: S'hall . . . 3C 94
Featherstone St. EC1 . . . 3E 8 (4D 84)
Featherstone Ter. UB2: S'hall . . . 3C 94
Featley Rd. SW9 . . . 3B 120
Federal Rd. UB6: G'frd . . . 1C 78
Federation Rd. SE2 . . . 4B 108
Fee Farm Rd. KT10: Clay . . . 7A 162
Feeny Cl. NW10 . . . 4B 62
Felbridge Av. HA7: Stan . . . 1A 42
Felbridge Cl. SM2: Sutt . . . 7K 165
SW16 . . . 4A 138
Felbridge Ct. *TW13: Felt* . . . *1K 129*
(off High St.)
UB3: Harl . . . 6F 93
Felbridge Ho. SE22 . . . 3E 120
Felbrigge Rd. IG3: Ilf . . . 2K 71
Felday Rd. SE13 . . . 6D 122
Felden Cl. HA5: H End . . . 1C 40
Felden St. SW6 . . . 1H 117
Feldman Cl. N16 . . . 1G 67
Felgate M. W6 . . . 4D 98
Felhampton Rd. SE9 . . . 2F 143
Felhurst Cres. RM10: Dag . . . 4H 73
Feline Ct. EN4: E Barn . . . 6H 21
Felix Av. N8 . . . 6J 47
Felix Ct. E17 . . . 5D 50
Felix Ho. *E16* . . . *7E 88*
(off University Way)
Felix La. TW17: Shep . . . 6G 147
Felix Mnr. BR7: Chst . . . 6J 143
Felix Neubergh Ho. EN1: Enf . . . 4K 23
Felix Rd. KT12: Walt T . . . 6J 147
W13 . . . 7A 78
Felixstowe Ct. E16 . . . 1F 107
Felixstowe Rd. N9 . . . 3B 34
N17 . . . 3F 49
NW10 . . . 3D 80
SE2 . . . 3B 108
Felix St. E2 . . . 2H 85
Fellbrigg Rd. SE22 . . . 5F 121
Fellbrigg St. E1 . . . 4H 85
Fellbrook TW10: Ham . . . 3B 132
Fellmongers Path SE1 . . . 7J 15
Fellmongers Yd. *CR0: Croy* . . . *3C 168*
(off Surrey St.)
Fellowes Cl. UB4: Yead . . . 4B 76
Fellowes Rd. SM5: Cars . . . 3C 166
Fellows Ct. E2 . . . 1J 9 (2F 85)
(not continuous)
Fellows Rd. NW3 . . . 7B 64
Fell Rd. CR0: Croy . . . 3C 168
(not continuous)
Felltram M. *SE7* . . . *5J 105*
(off Felltram Way)
Felltram Way SE7 . . . 5J 105
Fell Wlk. HA8: Edg . . . 1J 43
Felmersham Cl. SW4 . . . 4J 119
Felmingham Rd. SE20 . . . 2J 157
Felnex Trad. Est. NW10 . . . 2K 79
SM6: Wall . . . 2E 166
Felsberg Rd. SW2 . . . 6J 119
Fels Cl. RM10: Dag . . . 3H 73
Fels Farm Av. RM10: Dag . . . 3J 73
Felsham M. *SW15* . . . *3F 117*
(off Felsham Rd.)
Felsham Rd. SW15 . . . 3E 116
Felspar Cl. SE18 . . . 5K 107
Felstead Av. IG5: Ilf . . . 1E 52
Felstead Cl. N13 . . . 5F 33
Felstead Gdns. E14 . . . 5E 104
Felstead Rd. E9 . . . 6B 68
E11 . . . 7J 51
Felstead St. E9 . . . 6B 68
Felstead Wharf E14 . . . 5E 104
Felsted Rd. E16 . . . 6B 88
FELTHAM . . . 2J 129
Feltham Airparcs Leisure Cen. . . . 2B 130
Feltham Arenas . . . 7J 111
Feltham Av. KT8: E Mos . . . 4J 149
Felthambrook Ind. Est.
TW13: Felt . . . 3K 129
Felthambrook Way TW13: Felt . . . 3K 129
Feltham Bus. Complex TW13: Felt . . . 2K 129
Feltham College Sports Cen. . . . 2A 130
Feltham Corporate Cen.
TW13: Felt . . . 3K 129
FELTHAMHILL . . . 5H 129
Feltham Hill Rd. TW15: Ashf . . . 5C 128
Feltham Rd. CR4: Mitc . . . 2D 154
TW15: Ashf . . . 4C 128

Felton Cl. BR5: Pet W 6F 161
Felton Gdns. IG11: Bark 1J 89
Felton Ho. N1 1D 84
(off Branch Pl.)
SE3 4K 123
Felton Lea DA14: Sidc 5K 143
Felton Rd. IG11: Bark 2J 89
W13 2C 96
Felton St. N1 1D 84
Fencepiece Rd. IG6: Ilf 1G 53
Fenchurch Av. EC3 1G 15 (6E 84)
Fenchurch Bldgs. EC3 1H 15 (6E 84)
Fenchurch Ho. EC3 1J 15
(off Minories)
Fenchurch Pl. EC3 2H 15 (6E 84)
Fenchurch St. EC3 2G 15 (7E 84)
Fen Ct. EC3 2G 15 (6E 84)
Fendall Rd. KT19: Ewe 5J 163
Fendall St. SE1 3E 102
(not continuous)
Fendt Cl. E16 6H 87
Fendyke Rd. DA17: Belv 4D 108
Fenelon Pl. W14 4H 99
Fen Gro. DA15: Sidc 5K 125
Fenham Rd. SE15 7G 103
Fen La. SW13 1D 116
Fenman Ct. N17 1H 49
Fenman Gdns. IG3: Ilf 1B 72
Fenn Cl. BR1: Brom 6J 141
Fennel Apartments SE1 5J 15
(off Cayenne Ct.)
Fennel Cl. CR0: Croy 1K 169
E16 4G 87
Fennells Mead KT17: Ewe 7B 164
Fennell St. SE18 6E 106
Fenner Cl. SE16 4H 103
Fenner Ho. E1 1H 103
(off Watts St.)
Fenner Sq. SW11 3B 118
Fenn Ho. TW7: Isle 1B 114
Fenning St. SE1 6G 15 (2E 102)
Fenn St. E9 5K 67
Fenstanton N4 1K 65
(off Marquis Rd.)
Fenstanton Av. N12 6G 31
Fen St. E16 7H 87
Fenswood Cl. DA5: Bexl 6G 127
Fentiman Rd. SW8 7F 19 (6J 101)
Fentiman Way HA2: Harr 2F 59
Fenton Cl. BR7: Chst 5D 142
E8 6F 67
SW9 2K 119
Fenton House 4A 64
(off Windmill Hill)
Fenton Ho. SE14 7A 104
TW5: Hest 6E 94
Fenton Rd. N17 7H 33
Fentons Av. E13 3K 87
Fenton St. E1 6H 85
Fenwick Cl. SE18 6E 106
Fenwick Gro. SE15 3G 121
Fenwick Pl. CR2: S Croy 7B 168
SW9 3J 119
Fenwick Rd. SE15 3G 121
Ferby Ct. DA14: Sidc 4K 143
(off Main Rd.)
SE9 3H 143
(off Main Rd.)
Ferdinand Ho. NW1 7E 64
(off Ferdinand Pl.)
Ferdinand Pl. NW1 7E 64
Ferdinand St. NW1 7E 64
Ferguson Av. KT5: Surb 5F 151
Ferguson Cen., The E17 6A 50
Ferguson Cl. BR2: Brom 3F 159
E14 4C 104
Ferguson Dr. W3 6K 79
Ferguson Ho. SE10 1E 122
Fergus Rd. N5 5B 66
Fermain Ct. E. N1 1E 84
(off De Beauvoir Est.)
Fermain Ct. Nth. N1 1E 84
(off De Beauvoir Est.)
Fermain Ct. W. N1 1E 84
(off De Beauvoir Est.)
Ferme Pk. Rd. N4 6K 47
N8 5J 47
Fermor Rd. SE23 1A 140
Fermoy Ho. W9 4H 81
(off Fermoy Rd.)
Fermoy Rd. UB6: G'frd 4F 77
W9 4H 81
Fern Av. CR4: Mitc 4H 155
Fernbank IG9: Buck H 1E 36
Fernbank Av. HA0: Wemb 4K 59
KT12: Walt T 7C 148
Fernbank M. SW12 6G 119
Fernbrook Av. DA15: Sidc 5J 125
Fernbrook Cres. SE13 6G 123
(off Leahurst Rd.)
Fernbrook Dr. HA2: Harr 7F 41
Fernbrook Rd. SE13 5G 123
Ferncliff Rd. E8 5G 67
Fern Cl. N1 2E 84
Fern Ct. DA7: Bex 4G 127
SE14 2K 121
Ferncroft Av. HA4: Ruis 2A 58
N12 6J 31
NW3 3J 63
Ferndale BR1: Brom 2A 160
Ferndale Av. E17 5F 51
TW4: Houn 3C 112
Ferndale Cl. DA7: Bex 1E 126
Ferndale Community Sports Cen. 3K 119
Ferndale Rd. E7 7K 69
E11 2G 69
N15 6F 49
RM5: Col R 2J 55
SE25 5H 157
SW4 4J 119
SW9 4J 119
TW15: Ashf 5A 128
Ferndale St. E6 7F 89
Ferndale Ter. HA1: Harr 4K 41
Ferndale Way BR6: Farnb 5H 173
Ferndell Av. DA5: Bexl 3K 145
Fern Dene W13 5B 78
Ferndene Rd. SE24 4C 120
Fernden Way RM7: Rom 6H 55
Ferndown HA6: Nwood 2J 39
NW1 7H 65
(off Camley St.)
Ferndown Av. BR6: Orp 1H 173
Ferndown Cl. HA5: Pinn 1C 40
SM2: Sutt 6B 166
Ferndown Ct. UB1: S'hall 6G 77
(off Haldane Rd.)
Ferndown Lodge E14 3E 104
(off Manchester Rd.)
Ferndown Rd. SE9 7B 124
Ferney Meade Way
TW7: Isle 2A 114
Ferney Rd. EN4: E Barn 7K 21
Fern Gro. TW14: Felt 7K 111
Fernhall Dr. IG4: Ilf 5B 52
Fernham Rd. CR7: Thor H 3C 156
Fernhead Rd. W9 2H 81
Fernheath Way DA2: Dart 5K 145
Fernhill Ct. E17 2F 51
Fernhill Gdns. KT2: King T 5D 132
Fern Hill Pl. BR6: Farnb 5G 173
Fernhill St. E16 1D 106
Fernholme Rd. SE15 5K 121
Fernhurst Gdns. HA8: Edg 6B 28
Fernhurst Rd. CR0: Croy 7H 157
SW6 1G 117
TW15: Ashf 4E 128
Fern La. TW5: Hest 5D 94
Fernlea Rd. CR4: Mitc 2E 154
SW12 1F 137
Fernleigh Cl. CR0: Wadd 4A 168
W9 3H 81
Fernleigh Ct. HA2: Harr 2F 41
HA9: Wemb 2E 60
RM7: Rom 5J 55
Fernleigh Rd. N21 2F 33
Fernley Cl. HA5: Eastc 4J 39
Fernsbury St. WC1 2J 7 (3A 84)
Fernshaw Cl. SW10 6A 100
Fernshaw Mans. SW10 6A 100
(off Fernshaw Rd.)
Fernshaw Rd. SW10 6A 100
Fernside IG9: Buck H 1E 36
NW11 2J 63
Fernside Av. NW7 3E 28
TW13: Felt 4K 129
Fernside Ct. NW4 2F 45
(off Holders Hill Rd.)
Fernside Rd. SW12 1D 136
Ferns Rd. E15 6H 69
Fern St. E3 4C 86
Fernthorpe Rd. SW16 6G 137
Ferntower Rd. N5 5D 66
Fern Wlk. SE16 5G 103
TW15: Ashf 5A 128
Fernways IG1: Ilf 4F 71
Fernwood SW19 1H 135
Fernwood Av. HA0: Wemb 6C 60
SW16 4H 137
Fernwood Cl. BR1: Brom 2A 160
Fernwood Cres. N20 3J 31
Ferny Hill EN4: Had W 1J 21
Ferranti Cl. SE18 3B 106
Ferraro Cl. TW5: Hest 6E 94
Ferrers Av. SM6: Bedd 4H 167
UB7: W Dray 2A 92
Ferrers Rd. SW16 5H 137
Ferrestone Rd. N8 4K 47
Ferrey M. SW9 2A 120
Ferriby Cl. N1 7A 66
Ferrier Ind. Est. SW18 4K 117
(off Ferrier St.)
Ferrier Point E16 5J 87
(off Forty Acre La.)
Ferrier St. SW18 4K 117
Ferring Cl. HA2: Harr 1G 59
Ferrings SE21 3E 138
Ferris Av. CR0: Croy 3B 170
Ferris Rd. SE22 4G 121
Ferron Rd. E5 3H 67
Ferry App. SE18 3E 106
Ferrybridge Ho. SE11 2H 19
Ferrydale Lodge NW4 4E 44
(off Church Rd.)
NW4 4E 44
(off Parson St.)
Ferry Ho. E5 1H 67
(off Harrington Hill)
Ferry Island Retail Pk.
N17 3G 49
Ferry La. N17 4G 49
SW13 6B 98
TW8: Bford 6E 96
TW9: Kew 6F 97
TW17: Shep 7C 146
Ferry La. Ind. Est. E17 4K 49
Ferrymead Av. UB6: G'frd 3E 76
Ferrymead Dr. UB6: G'frd 2E 76
Ferrymead Gdns.
UB6: G'frd 2G 77
Ferrymoor TW10: Ham 3B 132
Ferry Pl. SE18 3E 106
Ferry Quays TW8: Bford 6E 96
Ferry Rd. KT7: T Ditt 6B 150
KT8: W Mole 3E 148
SW13 7C 98
TW1: Twick 1B 132
TW11: Tedd 5B 132
Ferry Sq. TW8: Bford 7E 96
Ferry St. E14 5E 104
Ferry Wharf TW8: Bford 7E 96
Festing Rd. SW15 3F 117
Festival Cl. DA5: Bexl 1D 144
UB10: Hil 1D 74
Festival Ct. E8 7F 67
(off Holly St.)
SM1: Sutt 7K 153
Festival Wlk. SM5: Cars 4D 166
Festoon Way E16 7B 88
Fetter La. EC4 1K 13 (6A 84)
(not continuous)
Fettes Ho. NW8 2B 82
(off Wellington Rd.)
Ffinch St. SE8 7C 104
Fidgeon Cl. BR1: Brom 3E 160
Field Cl. BR1: Brom 2A 160
E4 6J 35
HA4: Ruis 1E 56
IG9: Buck H 3F 37
KT8: W Mole 5F 149
KT9: Chess 5C 162
NW2 2C 62
TW4: Cran 1K 111
UB3: Harl 7E 92
UB10: Ick 2D 56
FIELDCOMMON 7D 148
Fieldcommon La. KT12: Walt T 7C 148
Field Ct. SW19 3J 135
WC1 6H 7 (5K 83)
Field End HA4: Ruis 6A 58
UB5: N'olt 6C 58
Fieldend TW1: Twick 4K 131
Field End Rd. HA4: Ruis 1B 58
HA5: Eastc 5K 39
Fieldend Rd. SW16 1G 155
Fielders Cl. EN1: Enf 4K 23
HA2: Harr 1G 59
Fieldfare Rd. SE28 7C 90
Fieldgate La. CR4: Mitc 2C 154
Fieldgate Mans. E1 5G 85
(off Fieldgate St., not continuous)
Fieldgate St. E1 5G 85
Field Ho. NW6 3F 81
(off Harvist Rd.)
Fieldhouse Cl. E18 1J 51
Fieldhouse Rd. SW12 1G 137
Fielding Av. TW2: Twick 3G 131
Fielding Ct. WC2 1E 12
(off Tower St.)
Fielding Ho. NW6 3J 81
W4 6A 98
(off Devonshire Rd.)
Fielding M. SW13 6D 98
(off Jenner Pl.)
Fielding Rd. W4 3K 97
W14 3F 99
Fieldings, The SE23 1J 139
Fielding St. SE17 6C 102
Fielding Ter. W5 7F 79
Fielding Wlk. W13 3B 96
Fielding Way BR2: Brom 4A 160
Field La. TW8: Bford 7C 96
TW11: Tedd 5A 132
Field Mead NW9 7F 29
Fieldpark Gdns. CR0: Croy 1A 170
Field Pl. KT3: N Mald 6B 152
Field Point E7 4J 69
Field Rd. E7 4H 69
N17 3D 48
TW14: Felt 6K 111
W6 5G 99
Fieldsend Rd. SM3: Cheam 5G 165
Fields Est. E8 7G 67
Fieldside Cl. BR6: Farnb 4G 173
Fieldside Rd. BR1: Brom 5F 141
Fields Pk. Cres. RM6: Chad H 5D 54
Field St. WC1 1G 7 (3K 83)
Fieldsway Ho. N5 5A 66
Field Vw. TW13: Felt 4F 129
Fieldview SW18 1B 136
Field Vw. Cl. RM7: Mawney 3G 55
Fieldview Cotts. N14 2C 32
(off Balaams La.)
Field Way HA4: Ruis 1E 56
NW10 7J 61
UB6: G'frd 1F 77
Fieldway BR5: Pet W 6H 161
CR0: New Ad 7D 170
RM8: Dag 3C 72
Fieldway Cres. N5 5A 66
Fiennes Cl. RM8: Dag 1C 72
Fifehead Cl. TW15: Ashf 6A 128

Fife Rd. E16 . . . . .5J 87
KT1: King T 2E 150
(not continuous)
N22 . . . . .7G 33
SW14 . . . . .5J 115
Fife Ter. N1 . . . . .2K 83
Fifield Path SE23 . . . . .3K 139
Fifth Av. E12 . . . . .4D 70
UB3: Hayes 1H 93
W10 . . . . .3G 81
Fifth Cross Rd. TW2: Twick 2H 131
Fifth Way HA9: Wemb 4H 61
Figges Rd. CR4: Mitc 7E 136
Fig Tree Cl. NW10 . . . . .1A 80
Figure Cl. SW3 . . . . .6F 17
Filanco Ct. W7 . . . . .1K 95
(off Uxbridge Rd.)
Filby Rd. KT9: Chess 6F 163
Filey Av. N16 . . . . .1G 67
Filey Cl. SM2: Sutt 7A 166
Filey Waye HA4: Ruis 2J 57
Filigree Cl. SE16 . . . . .1B 104
Fillebrook Av. EN1: Enf 2K 23
Fillebrook Rd. E11 . . . . .1F 69
Filmer Chambers SW6 . . . . .1G 117
(off Filmer Rd.)
Filmer Rd. SW6 . . . . .1G 117
Film Terrace Fitness Cen. 6E 124
Filston Rd. DA8: Erith 5J 109
Filton Cl. NW9 . . . . .1A 44
Filton Ct. SE14 . . . . .7J 103
(off Farrow La.)
Finborough Ho. SW10 . . . . .6A 100
(off Finborough Rd.)
Finborough Rd. SW10 . . . . .5K 99
SW17 . . . . .6D 136
Finborough Theatre, The 6K 99
(off Finborough Rd.)
Finchale Rd. SE2 . . . . .3A 108
Fincham Cl. UB10: Ick 3E 56
Finch Av. SE27 . . . . .4D 138
Finch Cl. EN5: Barn 5D 20
NW10 . . . . .6K 61
Finch Ct. DA14: Sidc 3B 144
Finchdean Ho. SW15 . . . . .7B 116
Finch Dr. TW14: Felt 7B 112
Finch Gdns. E4 . . . . .5H 35
Finch Ho. SE8 . . . . .7D 104
(off Bronze St.)
Finchingfield Av. IG8: Wfd G 7F 37
Finch La. EC3 . . . . .1F 15 (6D 84)
FINCHLEY 1J 45
Finchley Ct. N3 . . . . .6E 30
Finchley Ind. Est. N12 . . . . .4F 31
Finchley La. NW4 . . . . .4E 44
Finchley Lido 7G 31
Finchley Pk. N12 . . . . .4F 31
Finchley Pl. NW8 . . . . .2B 82
Finchley Rd. NW2 . . . . .1J 63
NW3 . . . . .1J 63
NW8 . . . . .1B 82
NW11 . . . . .4H 45
Finchley Way N3 . . . . .7D 30
Finch Lodge W9 . . . . .5J 81
(off Admiral Wlk.)
Finch M. SE15 . . . . .1F 121
Finch's Ct. E14 . . . . .7D 86
Finden Rd. E7 . . . . .5A 70
Findhorn Av. UB4: Yead 5K 75
Findhorn St. E14 . . . . .6E 86
Findon Cl. HA2: Harr 3F 59
SW18 . . . . .6J 117
Findon Rd. N9 . . . . .1C 34
W12 . . . . .2C 98
Fine Bush La. UB9: Hare 6D 38
Fingal St. SE10 . . . . .5H 105
Fingest Ho. NW8 . . . . .3C 4
(off Lilestone St.)
Finians Cl. UB10: Uxb 7B 56
Finland Rd. SE4 . . . . .3A 122
Finland St. SE16 . . . . .3A 104
Finlays Cl. KT9: Chess 5G 163
Finlay St. SW6 . . . . .1F 117

Finmere Ho. N4 . . . . .7C 48
Finnemore Ho. N1 . . . . .1C 84
(off Britannia Row)
Finney La. TW7: Isle 1A 114
Finn Ho. N1 . . . . .1F 9
(off Bevenden St.)
Finnis St. E2 . . . . .3H 85
Finnymore Rd.
RM9: Dag 7E 72
FINSBURY 3C 8 (3A 84)
Finsbury Av. EC2 . . . . .6F 9 (5D 84)
(not continuous)
Finsbury Av. Sq. EC2 . . . . .5G 9
Finsbury Cir. EC2 . . . . .6F 9 (5D 84)
Finsbury Cotts. N22 . . . . .7D 32
Finsbury Est. EC1 . . . . .2K 7 (3A 84)
Finsbury Ho. N22 . . . . .1J 47
Finsbury Leisure Cen. 3C 8 (3C 84)
Finsbury Mkt. EC2 . . . . .4G 9 (4E 84)
(not continuous)
FINSBURY PARK 1A 66
Finsbury Pk. Av. N4 . . . . .6C 48
Finsbury Pk. Rd. N4 . . . . .2B 66
(not continuous)
Finsbury Pavement EC2 . . . . .5F 9 (5D 84)
Finsbury Rd. N22 . . . . .7E 32
(not continuous)
Finsbury Sq. EC2 . . . . .4F 9 (4D 84)
Finsbury St. EC2 . . . . .5E 8 (5D 84)
Finsbury Way DA5: Bexl 6F 127
Finsen Rd. SE5 . . . . .4C 120
Finstock Rd. W10 . . . . .6F 81
Finucane Ri.
WD23: Bushy 2B 26
Finwhale Ho. E14 . . . . .3D 104
(off Glengall Gro.)
Fiona Cl. EN2: Enf 3G 23
NW6 . . . . .2J 81
Firbank Cl. E16 . . . . .5B 88
EN2: Enf 4H 23
Firbank Rd. SE15 . . . . .2H 121
Fir Cl. KT12: Walt T 7J 147
Fircroft Gdns. HA1: Harr 3J 59
Fircroft Rd. KT9: Chess 4F 163
SW17 . . . . .2D 136
Fir Dene BR6: Farnb 3D 172
Firdene KT5: Surb 1J 163
Fire Bell All. KT6: Surb 6E 150
Firecrest Dr. NW3 . . . . .3K 63
Firefly Gdns. E6 . . . . .4C 88
Firemans Flats N22 . . . . .7D 32
Firepower (The Royal Artillery Mus.)
. . . . .3F 107
Fire Sta. All. EN5: Barn 3B 20
Fire Sta. M. BR3: Beck 1C 158
Firethorn Cl. HA8: Edg 4D 28
Fir Gro. KT3: N Mald 6B 152
Fir Gru. Rd. SW9 . . . . .2A 120
Firhill Rd. SE6 . . . . .4C 140
Fir Ho. W10 . . . . .4G 81
(off Droop St.)
Firle Ho. W10 . . . . .5E 80
(off Sutton Way)
Firmans Ct. E17 . . . . .4F 51
Fir Rd. SM3: Sutt 1H 165
TW13: Hanw 5B 130
Firs, The DA5: Bexl 1K 145
DA15: Sidc 2K 143
E6 . . . . .7C 70
HA8: Edg 4E 28
(off Stoneyfields La.)
IG8: Wfd G 7F 37
N20 . . . . .1G 31
SE26 . . . . .5H 139
(Border Rd.)
SE26 . . . . .5J 139
(Waverley Ct.)
W5 . . . . .5D 78
Firs Av. N10 . . . . .3E 46
N11 . . . . .6J 31
SW14 . . . . .4J 115
Firsby Av. CR0: Croy 1K 169
Firsby Rd. N16 . . . . .1G 67

Firs Cl. CR4: Mitc 1F 155
N10 . . . . .4E 46
SE23 . . . . .7A 122
Firscroft N13 . . . . .3H 33
Firs Dr. TW5: Cran 7K 93
Firs Ho. N22 . . . . .1A 48
(off Acacia Rd.)
Firside Gro. DA15: Sidc 1K 143
Firs La. N13 . . . . .3H 33
N21 . . . . .7H 23
Firs Pk. Av. N21 . . . . .1J 33
Firs Pk. Gdns. N21 . . . . .1H 33
First Av. DA7: Bex 7C 108
E12 . . . . .4C 70
E13 . . . . .3J 87
E17 . . . . .5C 50
EN1: Enf 5A 24
HA9: Wemb 2D 60
KT8: W Mole 4D 148
KT12: Walt T 6K 147
KT19: Ewe 7A 164
N18 . . . . .4D 34
NW4 . . . . .4E 44
RM6: Chad H 5C 54
RM10: Dag 2H 91
SW14 . . . . .3A 116
UB3: Hayes 1H 93
W3 . . . . .1B 98
W10 . . . . .4H 81
First Cl. KT8: W Mole 3G 149
First Cross Rd. TW2: Twick 2J 131
First Dr. NW10 . . . . .7J 61
First St. SW3 . . . . .3D 16 (4C 100)
First Way HA9: Wemb 4A 62
Firstway SW20 . . . . .2E 152
Firs Wlk. IG8: Wfd G 5D 36
Firswood Av. KT19: Ewe 5A 164
Firth Gdns. SW6 . . . . .1G 117
Firth Ho. E2 . . . . .3G 85
(off Barnet Gro.)
Fir Tree Av. UB7: W Dray 3C 92
Firtree Av. CR4: Mitc 2E 154
Fir Tree Cl. BR6: Chels 5K 173
KT19: Ewe 4B 164
RM1: Rom 3K 55
W5 . . . . .6E 78
Fir Tree Cl. SW16 . . . . .5G 137
Fir Tree Gdns. CR0: Croy 4C 170
Fir Tree Gro. SM5: Cars 7D 166
Fir Tree Ho. SE14 . . . . .7J 103
(off Avonley Rd.)
Fir Tree Pl. TW15: Ashf 5C 128
Fir Tree Rd. TW4: Houn 4C 112
Fir Trees Cl. SE16 . . . . .1A 104
Fir Tree Wlk. EN1: Enf 3J 23
RM10: Dag 3J 73
Fir Wlk. SM3: Cheam 6F 165
Fisher Athletic FC 1K 103
Fisher Cl. CR0: Croy 1F 169
E9 . . . . .5K 67
UB6: G'frd 3E 76
Fisher Ho. E1 . . . . .7J 85
(off Cable St.)
N1 . . . . .1A 84
(off Barnsbury Est.)
Fisherman Cl. TW10: Ham 4B 132
Fishermans Dr. SE16 . . . . .2K 103
Fisherman's Pl. W4 . . . . .6B 98
Fishermans Wlk. E14 . . . . .1C 104
SE28 . . . . .2J 107
Fisher Rd. HA3: W'stone 2K 41
Fisher's Cl. SW16 . . . . .3H 137
Fishers Ct. SE14 . . . . .1K 121
Fishers Dene KT10: Clay 7A 162
Fisher's La. W4 . . . . .4K 97
Fisher St. E16 . . . . .5J 87
WC1 . . . . .6G 7 (5K 83)
Fishers Way DA17: Belv 1J 109
Fishguard Way E16 . . . . .1F 107
Fishmongers Hall Wharf EC4 . . . . . . .3E 14
Fishponds Rd. BR2: Kes 5B 172
SW17 . . . . .4C 136

Fish St. Hill EC3 . . . . .3F 15 (7D 84)
Fish Wharf EC3 . . . . .3F 15 (7D 84)
Fisk Cl. TW16: Sun 6H 129
Fiske Ct. IG11: Bark 2H 89
N17 . . . . .1G 49
SM2: Sutt 7A 166
Fisons Rd. E16 . . . . .1J 105
Fitness First Health Club
Croydon 1B 168
Islington 1A 8 (2B 84)
Lewisham 3E 122
Tooting Bec 3E 136
(off Balham High Rd.)
Fitrooms .6H 99
Fitzalan Rd. N3 . . . . .3G 45
Fitzalan St. SE11 . . . . .3H 19 (4A 102)
Fitzgeorge Av. KT3: N Mald 1K 151
W14 . . . . .4G 99
Fitzgerald Av. SW14 . . . . .3A 116
Fitzgerald Cl. E10 . . . . .1D 68
(off Leyton Grange Est.)
Fitzgerald Ho. E14 . . . . .6D 86
(off E. India Dock Rd.)
SW9 . . . . .2A 120
UB3: Hayes 1K 93
Fitzgerald Rd. E11 . . . . .5J 51
KT7: T Ditt 6A 150
SW14 . . . . .3K 115
Fitzhardinge Ho. W1 . . . . .7G 5
(off Portman Sq.)
Fitzhardinge St. W1 . . . . .7G 5 (6E 82)
Fitzherbert Wlk. UB1: S'hall 2H 95
Fitzhugh Gro. SW18 . . . . .6B 118
Fitzjames Av. CR0: Croy 2G 169
W14 . . . . .4G 99
Fitzjohn Av. EN5: Barn 5B 20
Fitzjohn's Av. NW3 . . . . .4A 64
Fitzmaurice Ho. SE16 . . . . .4H 103
(off Rennie Est.)
Fitzmaurice Pl. W1 . . . . .4K 11 (1F 101)
Fitzneal St. W12 . . . . .6B 80
FITZROVIA 5K 5
Fitzroy Cl. N6 . . . . .1D 64
Fitzroy Ct. CR0: Croy 7D 156
N6 . . . . .6G 47
W5 . . . . .4B 6
Fitzroy Cres. W4 . . . . .7K 97
Fitzroy Gdns. SE19 . . . . .7E 138
Fitzroy Ho. E14 . . . . .5B 86
(off Wallwood St.)
SE1 . . . . .5F 103
(off Coopers La.)
Fitzroy M. W1 . . . . .4A 6
Fitzroy Pk. N6 . . . . .1D 64
Fitzroy Rd. NW1 . . . . .1E 82
Fitzroy Sq. W1 . . . . .4A 6 (4G 83)
Fitzroy St. W1 . . . . .4A 6 (4G 83)
(not continuous)
Fitzroy Yd. NW1 . . . . .1E 82
Fitzsimmons Cl. NW10 . . . . .1K 79
Fitzstephen Rd. RM8: Dag 5B 72
Fitzwarren Gdns. N19 . . . . .1G 65
Fitzwilliam Av. TW9: Rich 2F 115
Fitzwilliam Hgts. SE23 . . . . .2J 139
Fitzwilliam Ho. TW9: Rich 4D 114
Fitzwilliam M. E16 . . . . .1J 105
Fitzwilliam Rd. SW4 . . . . .3G 119
Fitzwygram Cl. TW12: Ham H 5G 131
Five Acre NW9 . . . . .2B 44
Fiveacre Cl. CR7: Thor H 6A 156
Five Arches Bus. Pk. DA14: Sidc 5D 144
Five Bell All. E14 . . . . .6B 86
(off Three Colt St.)
Five Elms Rd. BR2: Hayes 3K 171
RM9: Dag 3F 73
Five Oaks M. BR1: Brom 3J 141
Fives Ct. SE11 . . . . .3B 102
FIVEWAYS 2F 143
Five Ways Bus. Cen. TW13: Felt 3K 129
FIVEWAYS CORNER
Croydon 4A 168
Hendon 1C 44
Fiveways Rd. SW9 . . . . .2A 120

Flack Ct. E10 7D 50
Fladbury Rd. N15 6D 48
Fladgate Rd. E11 6G 51
Flag Cl. CR0: Croy 1K 169
Flagon Ct. CR0: Croy 4C 168
(off St Andrew's Rd.)
Flag Wlk. HA5: Eastc 6J 39
Flambard Rd. HA1: Harr 6A 42
Flamborough Ho. SE15 1G 121
(off Clayton Rd.)
Flamborough Rd. HA4: Ruis 3J 57
Flamborough St. E14 6A 86
Flamborough Wlk. E14 6A 86
(off Flamborough St.)
Flamingo Ct. SE8 7C 104
(off Hamilton St.)
Flamingo Gdns. UB5: N'olt 3C 76
Flamstead Gdns. RM9: Dag 7C 72
Flamstead Ho. SW3 5C 16
(off Cale St.)
Flamstead Rd. RM9: Dag 7C 72
Flamsted Av. HA9: Wemb 6G 61
Flamsteed Rd. SE7 5C 106
Flanchford Rd. W12 3B 98
Flanders Ct. E17 7A 50
Flanders Cres. SW17 7D 136
Flanders Mans. W4 4B 98
Flanders Rd. E6 2D 88
W4 4A 98
Flanders Way E9 6K 67
(not continuous)
Flandrian Cl. EN3: Enf L 1J 25
Flank St. E1 7G 85
Flansham Ho. E14 6B 86
(off Clemence St.)
Flask Wlk. NW3 4A 64
Flatford Ho. SE6 4E 140
Flather Cl. SW16 5G 137
Flatiron Yd. SE1 5D 14
(off Union St.)
Flavell M. SE10 5G 105
Flaxen Cl. E4 3J 35
Flaxen Rd. E4 3J 35
Flaxley Ho. SW1 5F 101
(off Abbots Mnr.)
Flaxley Rd. SM4: Mord 7K 153
Flaxman Ct. DA17: Belv 5G 109
(off Hoddesdon Rd.)
W1 1C 12
WC1 2D 6
(off Flaxman Ter.)
Flaxman Ho. SE1 3B 102
(off London Rd.)
W4 5A 98
(off Devonshire St.)
Flaxman Leisure Cen. 2C 120
Flaxman Rd. SE5 3B 120
Flaxman Ter. WC1 2D 6 (3H 83)
Flaxton Rd. SE18 1H 125
Flecker Cl. HA7: Stan 5E 26
Flecker Ho. SE5 7D 102
(off Lomond Gro.)
Fleece Dr. N9 4B 34
Fleece Rd. KT6: Surb 1C 162
Fleece Wlk. N7 6J 65
Fleeming Cl. E17 2B 50
Fleeming Rd. E17 2B 50
Fleetbank Ho. EC4 1K 13
(off Whitefriars St.)
Fleet Bldg. EC4 7A 8
Fleet Cl. HA4: Ruis 6E 38
KT8: W Mole 5D 148
Fleetfield WC1 1F 7
(off Birkenhead St.)
Fleet Ho. E14 7A 86
(off Victory Pl.)
Fleet La. KT8: W Mole 6D 148
Fleet Pl. EC4 7A 8 (6B 84)
(not continuous)
Fleet Rd. NW3 5C 64
Fleetside KT8: W Mole 5D 148
Fleet Sq. WC1 2H 7 (3K 83)
Fleet St. EC4 1J 13 (6A 84)
Fleet St. Hill E1 4G 85
Fleetway WC1 1F 7
(off Birkenhead St.)
Fleetway W. Bus. Pk. UB6: G'frd 2B 78
Fleetwood Cl. CR0: Croy 3F 169
E16 5B 88
KT9: Chess 7D 162
Fleetwood Ct. E6 5D 88
(off Evelyn Dennington Rd.)
TW19: Stanw 6A 110
Fleetwood Rd. KT1: King T 3H 151
NW10 5C 62
Fleetwood Sq. KT1: King T 3H 151
Fleetwood St. N16 2E 66
Fleming N8 3J 47
(off Boyton Cl.)
Fleming Cl. W9 4J 81
Fleming Ct. CR0: Wadd 5A 168
W2 5A 4
Fleming Dr. N21 5E 22
Fleming Ho. HA9: Wemb 3J 61
(off Barnhill Rd.)
N4 1C 66
SE16 2G 103
(off George Row)
Fleming Lodge W9 5J 81
(off Admiral Wlk.)
Fleming Mead CR4: Mitc 7C 136
Fleming Rd. SE17 6B 102
UB1: S'hall 6F 77
Fleming Wlk. NW9 3A 44
Fleming Way SE28 7D 90
TW7: Isle 4K 113
Flemming Av. HA4: Ruis 1K 57
Flemming Cl. SW10 7A 16
(off Park Wlk.)
Flempton Rd. E10 1A 68
Fletcher Bldgs. WC2 1F 13
(off Martlett Ct.)
Fletcher Cl. E6 6F 89
Fletcher Ho. SE15 7J 103
(off Clifton Way)
Fletcher La. E10 7E 50
Fletcher Path SE8 7C 104
Fletcher Rd. W4 3J 97
Fletchers Cl. BR2: Brom 4K 159
Fletcher St. E1 7G 85
Fletching Rd. E5 3J 67
SE7 6A 106
Fletton Rd. N11 7D 32
Fleur-de-Lis St. E1 4H 9 (4F 85)
Fleur Gates SW19 7F 117
Flexmere Gdns. N17 1D 48
Flexmere Rd. N17 1D 48
Flight App. NW9 2B 44
Flimwell Cl. BR1: Brom 5G 141
Flinders Ho. E1 1H 103
(off Green Bank)
Flint Cl. BR6: Chels 6K 173
CR0: Croy 6K 155
E15 7H 69
Flintmill Cres. SE3 2C 124
(not continuous)
Flinton St. SE17 5E 102
Flint St. SE17 4D 102
Flitcroft St. WC2 1D 12 (6H 83)
Flitton Ho. N1 7B 66
(off The Sutton Est.)
Floathaven Cl. SE28 1A 108
Flock Mill Pl. SW18 1K 135
Flockton St. SE16 2G 103
Flodden Rd. SE5 1C 120
Flood La. TW1: Twick 1A 132
Flood Pas. SE18 3C 106
Flood St. SW3 6D 16 (5C 100)
Flood Wlk. SW3 7D 16 (6C 100)
Flora Cl. E14 6D 86
Flora Gdns. RM6: Chad H 6C 54
W6 4D 98
(off Albion Gdns.)
Floral Pl. N1 5D 66
Floral St. WC2 2E 12 (7J 83)
Flora St. DA17: Belv 5F 109
Florence Av. EN2: Enf 3H 23
SM4: Mord 5A 154
Florence Cantwell Wlk. N19 7J 47
(off Jessie Blythe La.)
Florence Cl. KT12: Walt T 7K 147
Florence Ct. E5 3G 67
E11 4K 51
N1 7B 66
(off Florence St.)
SW19 6G 135
W9 3A 82
(off Maida Va.)
Florence Dr. EN2: Enf 3H 23
Florence Elson Cl. E12 4E 70
Florence Gdns. RM6: Chad H 7C 54
W4 6J 97
Florence Ho. KT2: King T 7F 133
(off Florence Rd)
SE16 5H 103
(off Rotherhithe New Rd.)
W11 7F 81
(off St Ann's Rd.)
Florence Mans. NW4 5D 44
(off Vivian Av.)
Florence Nightingale Mus. 7G 13 (2K 101)
Florence Rd. BR1: Brom 1J 159
BR3: Beck 2A 158
CR2: Sand 7D 168
E6 1A 88
E13 2J 87
KT2: King T 7F 133
KT12: Walt T 7K 147
N4 7K 47
(not continuous)
SE2 4C 108
SE14 1B 122
SW19 6K 135
TW13: Felt 1K 129
UB2: S'hall 4B 94
W4 3K 97
W5 7E 78
Florence St. E16 4H 87
N1 7B 66
NW4 4E 44
Florence Ter. SE14 1B 122
SW15 3A 134
Florence Way SW12 1D 136
Flores Ho. E1 5K 85
(off Shandy St.)
Florey Lodge W9 5J 81
(off Admiral Wlk.)
Florey Sq. N21 5E 22
Florfield Pas. E8 6H 67
(off Florfield Rd.)
Florfield Rd. E8 6H 67
Florian SE5 1E 120
Florian Av. SM1: Sutt 4B 166
Florian Rd. SW15 4G 117
Florida Cl. WD23: Bushy 2C 26
Florida Ct. BR2: Brom 4H 159
(off Westmoreland Rd.)
Florida Rd. CR7: Thor H 1B 156
Florida St. E2 3G 85
Florin Ct. EC1 5C 8
N18 4K 33
SE1 7J 15
(off Tanner St.)
Floris Pl. SW4 3G 119
Floriston Av. UB10: Hil 7E 56
Floriston Cl. HA7: Stan 1B 42
Floriston Ct. UB5: N'olt 5F 59
Floriston Gdns. HA7: Stan 1B 42
Florys Ct. SW19 1G 135
Floss St. SW15 2E 116
Flower & Dean Wlk. E1 6K 9 (5F 85)
Flower La. NW7 5G 29
Flower M. NW11 6G 45
Flowerpot Cl. N15 6F 49
Flowers Cl. NW2 3C 62
Flowersmead SW17 2E 136
Flowers M. N19 2G 65
Flower Wlk., The SW7 6A 10 (2A 100)
Floyd Rd. SE7 5A 106
Floyer Cl. TW10: Rich 5F 115
Fludyer St. SE13 4G 123
Flynn Ct. E14 7C 86
(off Garford St.)
Foley Ho. E1 6J 85
(off Tarling St.)
Foley St. W1 6A 6 (5G 83)
Folgate St. E1 5H 9 (5E 84)
(not continuous)
Foliot Ho. N1 2K 83
(off Priory Grn. Est.)
Foliot St. W12 6B 80
Folkestone Ct. UB5: N'olt 5F 59
(off Newmarket Av.)
Folkestone Rd. E6 2E 88
E17 4D 50
N18 4B 34
Folkingham La. NW9 1K 43
Folkington Cnr. N12 5C 30
Folkstone Ho. SE17 5E 102
(off Kinglake St.)
Folland NW9 2B 44
(off Hundred Acre)
Follett Ho. SW10 7B 100
(off Worlds End Est.)
Follett St. E14 6E 86
Follingham Ct. N1 1H 9
(off Drysdale Pl.)
Folly La. E17 1A 50
(not continuous)
Folly M. W11 6H 81
Folly Wall E14 2E 104
Fonda Ct. E14 7C 86
(off Premiere Pl.)
Fontaine Rd. SW16 7K 137
Fontarabia Rd. SW11 4E 118
Fontayne Av. RM1: Rom 2K 55
Fontenelle Gdns. SE5 1E 120
Fontenoy Ho. SE11 4B 102
(off Kennington La.)
Fontenoy Rd. SW12 2F 137
Fonteyne Gdns. IG8: Wfd G 2B 52
Fonthill Cl. SE20 2G 157
Fonthill Ho. SW1 5F 101
(off Sutherland St.)
W14 3G 99
(off Russell Rd.)
Fonthill M. N4 2K 65
Fonthill Rd. N4 1K 65
Font Hills N2 2A 46
Fontley Way SW15 7C 116
Fontmell Cl. TW15: Ashf 5C 128
Fontmell Pk. TW15: Ashf 5B 128
(not continuous)
Fontwell Cl. HA3: Hrw W 7D 26
UB5: N'olt 6E 58
Fontwell Dr. BR2: Brom 5E 160
Football La. HA1: Harr 1K 59
Footpath, The SW15 6C 116
FOOTS CRAY 6C 144
Foots Cray High St. DA14: Sidc 6C 144
Foots Cray La. DA14: Sidc 1C 144
Footscray Rd. SE9 6E 124
Forber Ho. E2 3J 85
(off Cornwall Av.)
Forbes Cl. NW2 3C 62
Forbes St. E1 6G 85
Forbes Way HA4: Ruis 2K 57
Forburg Rd. N16 1G 67
Fordbridge Ct. TW15: Ashf 6A 128
Fordbridge Pk. TW16: Sun 6H 147
Fordbridge Rd. TW15: Ashf 6A 128
TW16: Sun 6G 147
TW17: Shep 6G 147
FORDBRIDGE RDBT. 6A 128
Ford Cl. CR7: Thor H 5B 156
E3 2A 86
HA1: Harr 7H 41
TW15: Ashf 6A 128
TW17: Shep 4C 146
Forde Av. BR1: Brom 3A 160
Fordel Rd. SE6 1E 140

Ford End IG8: Wfd G 6E **36**
Fordgate Bus. Pk. DA17: Belv 2J **109**
Fordham *KT1: King T* *2G 151*
(off Excelsior Cl.)
Fordham Cl. EN4: Cockf 3H **21**
KT4: Wor Pk 1D **164**
Fordham Ho. *SE14* *7A 104*
(off Angus St.)
Fordham Rd. EN4: Cockf 3G **21**
Fordham St. E1 . . . . 6G **85**
Fordhook Av. W5 . . . . 1F **97**
Ford Ho. EN5: New Bar 5E **20**
Fordie Ho. *SW1* *2F 17*
(off Sloane St.)
Ford Ind. Pk. RM9: Dag 4H **91**
Fordingley Rd. W9 . . . . 3H **81**
Fordington Ho. SE26 . . . . 3G **139**
Fordington Rd. N6 . . . . 5D **46**
Fordmill Rd. SE6 . . . . 2C **140**
Ford Rd. E3 . . . . 2B **86**
RM9: Dag 7F **73**
TW15: Ashf 4B **128**
Fords Gro. N21 . . . . 1H **33**
Fords Pk. Rd. E16 . . . . 5J **87**
Ford Sq. E1 . . . . 5H **85**
Ford St. E3 . . . . 1A **86**
E16 . . . . 6H **87**
Fordview Ind. Est. RM13: Rain 3K **91**
Fordwich Cl. BR6: Orp 7K **161**
Fordwych Rd. NW2 . . . . 4G **63**
Fordyce Rd. SE13 . . . . 6E **122**
Fordyke Rd. RM8: Dag 2F **73**
Foreign St. SE5 . . . . 2B **120**
Foreland Ct. NW4 . . . . 1F **45**
Foreland Ho. *W11* *7G 81*
(off Walmer Rd.)
Foreland St. SE18 . . . . 4H **107**
Foreman Ct. TW1: Twick 1K **131**
Foreshore SE8 . . . . 4B **104**
Forest, The E11 . . . . 4G **51**
Forest App. E4 . . . . 1B **36**
IG8: Wfd G 7D **36**
Forest Av. E4 . . . . 1B **36**
IG7: Chig 5K **37**
Forest Bus. Pk. E10 . . . . 7K **49**
Forest Cl. BR7: Chst 1E **160**
E11 . . . . 5J **51**
IG8: Wfd G 3E **36**
N10 . . . . 1F **47**
Forest Ct. E4 . . . . 1C **36**
E11 . . . . 4G **51**
N12 . . . . 5E **30**
Forest Cft. SE23 . . . . 2H **139**
FORESTDALE **7B 170**
Forestdale N14 . . . . 4C **32**
Forestdale Cen., The CR0: Sels 7B **170**
Forest Dene Ct. SM2: Sutt 6A **166**
Forest Dr. BR2: Kes 4C **172**
E12 . . . . 3B **70**
IG8: Wfd G 7A **36**
TW16: Sun 7H **129**
Forest Dr. E. E11 . . . . 7F **51**
Forest Dr. W. E11 . . . . 7E **50**
Forest Edge IG9: Buck H 4F **37**
Forester Ho. *E14* *7A 86*
(off Victory Pl.)
Forester Rd. SE15 . . . . 3H **121**
Foresters Cl. SM6: Wall 7H **167**
Foresters Cres. DA7: Bex 4H **127**
Foresters Dr. E17 . . . . 4F **51**
SM6: Wall 7H **167**
Forest Gdns. N17 . . . . 2F **49**
FOREST GATE **5J 69**
Forest Ga. NW9 . . . . 4A **44**
Forest Ga. Retreat *E7* *5J 69*
(off Odessa Rd.)
Forest Glade E4 . . . . 4B **36**
E11 . . . . 6G **51**
Forest Gro. E8 . . . . 6F **67**
Forest Hgts. IG9: Buck H 2D **36**
FOREST HILL **2J 139**
Forest Hill Bus. Cen. *SE23* *2J 139*
(off Clyde Va.)
Forest Hill Ind. Est. SE23 . . . . 2J **139**
Forest Hill Pool **2J 139**
Forest Hill Rd. SE22 . . . . 5H **121**
SE23 . . . . 5H **121**
Forestholme Cl. SE23 . . . . 2J **139**
Forest Ind. Pk. IG6: Ilf 1J **53**
Forest La. E7 . . . . 5G **69**
E15 . . . . 5G **69**
IG7: Chig 5K **37**
Forest Lodge *SE23* *3J 139*
(off Dartmouth Rd.)
Forest Mt. Rd. IG8: Wfd G 7A **36**
Forest Point *E7* *5K 69*
(off Windsor Rd.)
Fore St. EC2 . . . . 6D **8** (5C **84**)
HA5: Eastc 4H **39**
N9 . . . . 4B **34**
N18 . . . . 6A **34**
Fore St. Av. EC2 . . . . 6E **8** (5D **84**)
Forest Ridge BR2: Kes 4C **172**
BR3: Beck 3C **158**
Forest Ri. E17 . . . . 3F **51**
(not continuous)
Forest Rd. E7 . . . . 4J **69**
E8 . . . . 6F **67**
E11 . . . . 7F **51**
E17 . . . . 4J **49**
IG6: Chig, Ilf 2H **53**
IG8: Wfd G 3D **36**
N9 . . . . 1C **34**
N17 . . . . 4J **49**
RM7: Mawney 3H **55**
SM3: Sutt 1J **165**
TW9: Kew 7G **97**
TW13: Felt 2A **130**
Forest Side E4 . . . . 1C **36**
E7 . . . . 4K **69**
IG9: Buck H 1F **37**
KT4: Wor Pk 1B **164**
Forest St. E7 . . . . 5J **69**
Forest Ter. IG7: Chig 5K **37**
Forest Trad. Est. E17 . . . . 3K **49**
Forest Vw. E4 . . . . 7K **25** & 1B **36**
E11 . . . . 7H **51**
Forest Vw. Av. E10 . . . . 5F **51**
Forest Vw. Rd. E12 . . . . 4C **70**
E17 . . . . 1E **50**
Forest Wlk. N10 . . . . 1F **47**
Forest Way BR5: St M Cry 5K **161**
DA15: Sidc 7H **125**
IG8: Wfd G 4E **36**
N19 . . . . 2G **65**
Forest Works Ind. Est. E17 . . . . 3K **49**
Forfar Rd. N22 . . . . 1B **48**
SW11 . . . . 1E **118**
Forge, The UB3: Harl 6F **93**
Forge Cl. BR2: Hayes 1J **171**
Forge Cotts. W5 . . . . 1D **96**
Forge Dr. KT10: Clay 7A **162**
Forge La. HA6: Nwood 1G **39**
SM3: Cheam 7G **165**
TW13: Hanw 5C **130**
TW16: Sun 3J **147**
Forge M. CR0: Addtn 5C **170**
Forge Pl. NW1 . . . . 6E **64**
Forges Rd. E12 . . . . 2B **70**
Forman Pl. N16 . . . . 4F **67**
Formation, The *E16* *2F 107*
(off Woolwich Mnr. Way)
Formby Av. HA7: Stan 3C **42**
Formby Ct. *N7* *5A 66*
(off Morgan Rd.)
Formosa Ho. *E1* *4A 86*
(off Ernest St.)
Formosa St. W9 . . . . 4K **81**
Formunt Cl. E16 . . . . 5H **87**
Forres Gdns. NW11 . . . . 6J **45**
Forrester Path SE26 . . . . 4J **139**
Forrest Gdns. SW16 . . . . 3K **155**
Forris Av. UB3: Hayes 1H **93**
Forset Ct. *W1* *7D 4*
(off Edgware Rd.)
Forset St. W1 . . . . 7D **4** (6C **82**)
Forstal Cl. BR2: Brom 3J **159**
Forster Cl. IG8 . . . . 7A **36**
Forster Ho. BR1: Brom 4F **141**
Forster Rd. BR3: Beck 3A **158**
E17 . . . . 6A **50**
N17 . . . . 3F **49**
SW2 . . . . 7J **119**
Forsters Cl. RM6: Chad H 6F **55**
Forsters Way UB4: Yead 6K **75**
Forston St. N1 . . . . 2C **84**
Forsyte Cres. SE19 . . . . 1E **156**
Forsyte Ho. SW3 . . . . 6D **16**
Forsythe Shades Ct. BR3: Beck 1E **158**
Forsyth Gdns. SE17 . . . . 6B **102**
Forsyth Ho. *E9* *7J 67*
(off Frampton Pk. Rd.)
SW1 . . . . *5B 18*
(off Tachbrook St.)
Forsythia Cl. IG1: Ilf 5F **71**
Forsyth Pl. EN1: Enf 5K **23**
Forterie Gdns. IG3: Bark, Ilf 3A **72**
Fortescue Av. E8 . . . . 7H **67**
TW2: Twick 3G **131**
Fortescue Rd. HA8: Edg 1K **43**
SW19 . . . . 7B **136**
Fortess Gro. NW5 . . . . 5G **65**
Fortess Rd. NW5 . . . . 5F **65**
Fortess Wlk. NW5 . . . . 5F **65**
Fortess Yd. NW5 . . . . 4F **65**
Forthbridge Rd. SW11 . . . . 4E **118**
Fortis Cl. E16 . . . . 6A **88**
Fortis Ct. N10 . . . . 3E **46**
FORTIS GREEN **4D 46**
Fortis Grn. N2 . . . . 4C **46**
N10 . . . . 4C **46**
Fortis Grn. Av. N2 . . . . 3D **46**
Fortis Grn. Rd. N10 . . . . 3E **46**
Fortismere Av. N10 . . . . 3E **46**
Fortnam Rd. N19 . . . . 2H **65**
Fortnum's Acre HA7: Stan 6E **26**
Fort Rd. SE1 . . . . 4F **103**
UB5: N'olt 7E **58**
Fortrose Cl. E14 . . . . 6F **87**
Fortrose Gdns. SW2 . . . . 1J **137**
Fort St. E1 . . . . 6H **9** (5E **84**)
E16 . . . . 1K **105**
Fortuna Cl. N7 . . . . 6K **65**
Fortune Ct. *E8* *7F 67*
(off Queensbridge Rd.)
IG11: Bark 2C **90**
Fortunegate Rd. NW10 . . . . 1A **80**
FORTUNE GREEN **5J 63**
Fortune Grn. Rd. NW6 . . . . 4J **63**
Fortune Ho. *EC1* *4D 8*
(off Fortune St.)
SE11 . . . . 4J **19**
Fortunes Mead UB5: N'olt 6C **58**
Fortune St. EC1 . . . . 4D **8** (4C **84**)
Fortune Theatre ***1F 13***
(off Russell St.)
Fortune Wlk. *SE28* *3H 107*
(off Broadwater Rd.)
Fortune Way NW10 . . . . 3C **80**
Forty Acre La. E16 . . . . 5J **87**
Forty Av. HA9: Wemb 3F **61**
Forty Cl. HA9: Wemb 3F **61**
Forty Footpath SW14 . . . . 3J **115**
Forty Foot Way SE9 . . . . 7G **125**
FORTY HILL **1K 23**
Forty Hill EN2: Enf 1K **23**
Forty La. HA9: Wemb 2H **61**
Forum, The KT8: W Mole 4F **149**
Forum Cl. E3 . . . . 1C **86**
Forum Magnum Sq. *SE1* *6H 13*
(off York Rd.)
Forumside HA8: Edg 6B **28**
Forum Way HA8: Edg 6B **28**
Forval Cl. CR4: Mitc 5D **154**
Forward Bus. Cen., The E16 . . . . 4F **87**
Forward Dr. HA3: W'stone 4K **41**
Fosbrooke Ho. *SW8* *7J 101*
(off Davidson Gdns.)
Fosbury M. W2 . . . . 7K **81**
Foscote Ct. *W9* *4J 81*
(off Foscote M.)
Foscote M. W9 . . . . 4J **81**
Foscote Rd. NW4 . . . . 6D **44**
Foskett Ho. *N2* *2B 46*
(off The Grange)
Foskett Rd. SW6 . . . . 2H **117**
Foss Av. CR0: Wadd 5A **168**
Fossdene Rd. SE7 . . . . 5K **105**
Fossdyke Cl. UB4: Yead 5C **76**
Fosset Lodge DA7: Bex 1J **127**
Fosse Way W13 . . . . 5A **78**
Foss Ho. *NW8* *2K 81*
(off Carlton Hill)
Fossil Ct. *SE1* *7G 15*
(off Long La.)
Fossil Rd. SE13 . . . . 3C **122**
Fossington Rd. DA17: Belv 4D **108**
Foss Rd. SW17 . . . . 4B **136**
Fossway RM8: Dag 2C **72**
Foster Ct. *E16* *7H 87*
(off Tarling Rd.)
NW1 . . . . *7G 65*
(off Royal College St.)
NW4 . . . . 4E **44**
Foster Ho. SE14 . . . . 1B **122**
Foster La. EC2 . . . . 7C **8** (6C **84**)
Foster Rd. E13 . . . . 4J **87**
W3 . . . . 7A **80**
W4 . . . . 5K **97**
Fosters Cl. BR7: Chst 5D **142**
E18 . . . . 1K **51**
Foster St. NW4 . . . . 4E **44**
Foster's Way SW18 . . . . 1K **135**
Foster Wlk. NW4 . . . . 4E **44**
Fothergill Cl. E13 . . . . 2J **87**
Fothergill Dr. N21 . . . . 5D **22**
Fotheringham Rd. EN1: Enf 4A **24**
(not continuous)
Foubert's Pl. W1 . . . . 1A **12** (6G **83**)
Foulden Rd. N16 . . . . 4F **67**
Foulden Ter. N16 . . . . 4F **67**
Foulis Ter. SW7 . . . . 5B **16** (5B **100**)
Foulser Rd. SW17 . . . . 3D **136**
Foulsham Rd. CR7: Thor H 3C **156**
Founder Cl. E6 . . . . 6F **89**
Founders Ct. EC2 . . . . 7E **8**
Founders Gdns. SE19 . . . . 7C **138**
Founders Ho. *SW1* *6C 18*
(off Aylesford St.)
Foundling Ct. *WC1* *3E 6*
(off Brunswick Cen.)
Foundling Mus., The **3F 7** (**4J 83**)
Foundry Cl. SE16 . . . . 1A **104**
Foundry Ho. *E14* *5D 86*
(off Morris Rd.)
Foundry M. NW1 . . . . 3B **6**
Foundry Pl. *E1* *5J 85*
(off Redman's Rd.)
SW18 . . . . 7K **117**
Fountain Cl. UB8: Hil 5E **74**
Fountain Ct. DA15: Sidc 6B **126**
EC4 . . . . 2J **13** (7A **84**)
SE23 . . . . 2K **139**
SW1 . . . . *4J 17*
(off Buckingham Pal. Rd.)
Fountain Dr. SE19 . . . . 4F **139**
SM5: Cars 7D **166**
Fountain Grn. Sq. SE16 . . . . 2G **103**
Fountain Ho. CR4: Mitc 2D **154**
NW6 . . . . 7G **63**
SE16 . . . . *2G 103*
(off Bermondsey Wall E.)
W1 . . . . *4G 11*
(off Park St.)
Fountain M. *N5* *4C 66*
(off Highbury Grange)
NW3 . . . . 6D **64**
Fountain Pl. SW9 . . . . 1A **120**
Fountain Rd. CR7: Thor H 3C **156**
SW17 . . . . 5B **136**
Fountain Rdbt.
KT3: N Mald 4A **152**

Fountains, The *N3* 7E **30**
    (off Ballards La.)
Fountains Av. TW13: Hanw 3D **130**
Fountains Cl. TW13: Hanw 2D **130**
    (not continuous)
Fountains Cres. N14 ....7D **22**
Fountain Sq. SW1 ....3K **17** (4F **101**)
Fountayne Bus. Cen. N15 ....4G **49**
Fountayne Rd. N15 ....4G **49**
    N16 ....2G **67**
Fount St. SW8 ....7H **101**
Four Acres N12 ....3E **30**
Fouracres EN3: Enf H 1F **25**
Fourland Wlk. HA8: Edg 6D **28**
Fournier St. E1 ....5J **9** (5F **85**)
Fourscore Mans. *E8* *7G 67*
    (off Shrubland Rd.)
Four Seasons Cl. E3 ....2C **86**
Four Seasons Cres.
    SM3: Sutt 2H **165**
Four Sq. Ct. TW3: Houn 6E **112**
Fourth Av. E12 ....4D **70**
    RM7: Rush G 1K **73**
    UB3: Hayes 1H **93**
    W10 ....4G **81**
Fourth Cross Rd. TW2: Twick 2H **131**
Fourth Way HA9: Wemb 4H **61**
Four Wents, The E4 ....1A **36**
Fovant Cl. SW8 ....2G **119**
Fowey Av. IG4: Ilf 5B **52**
Fowey Cl. E1 ....1H **103**
Fowey Ho. SE11 ....5K **19**
Fowler Cl. SW11 ....3B **118**
Fowler Ho. *N15* *5D 48*
    (off South Gro.)
Fowler Rd. CR4: Mitc 2E **154**
    E7 ....4J **69**
    N1 ....1B **84**
Fowlers Cl. DA14: Sidc 5E **144**
Fowlers M. *N19* *2G 65*
    (off Holloway Rd.)
Fowler's Wlk. W5 ....4D **78**
Fownes St. SW11 ....3C **118**
Fox & Knot St. EC1 ....5B **8**
Foxberry Rd. SE4 ....3A **122**
Foxborough Gdns. SE4 ....5C **122**
Foxbourne Rd. SW17 ....2E **136**
Foxbury Av. BR7: Chst 6H **143**
Foxbury Cl. BR1: Brom 6K **141**
Foxbury Rd. BR1: Brom 6J **141**
Fox Cl. BR6: Chels 5K **173**
    E1 ....4J **85**
    E16 ....5J **87**
Foxcombe CR0: New Ad 6D **170**
    (not continuous)
Foxcombe Cl. E6 ....2B **88**
Foxcombe Rd. SW15 ....1C **134**
Foxcote SE5 ....5E **102**
Foxcroft *WC1* *1H 7*
    (off Penton Ri.)
Foxcroft Rd. SE18 ....1F **125**
Foxearth Spur CR2: Sels 7J **169**
Foxes Dale BR2: Brom 3F **159**
    SE3 ....3J **123**
Foxfield *NW1* *1F 83*
    (off Arlington Rd.)
Foxfield Rd. BR6: Orp 2H **173**
Foxglove Cl. DA15: Sidc 6A **126**
    N9 ....1D **34**
    UB1: S'hall 7C **76**
Foxglove Cl. HA0: Wemb 2E **78**
Foxglove Gdns. E11 ....4A **52**
Foxglove La. KT9: Chess 4G **163**
Foxglove Path *SE28* *1J 107*
    (off Martins Pl.)
Foxglove Rd. RM7: Rush G 2K **73**
Foxglove St. W12 ....7B **80**
Foxglove Way SM6: Wall 1F **167**
Fox Gro. KT12: Walt T 7K **147**
Foxgrove N14 ....3D **32**
Foxgrove Av. BR3: Beck 7D **140**
Foxgrove Rd. BR3: Beck 7D **140**
Foxham Rd. N19 ....3H **65**

Fox Hill BR2: Kes 5A **172**
    SE19 ....7F **139**
Fox Hill Gdns. SE19 ....7F **139**
Foxhole Rd. SE9 ....5C **124**
Fox Hollow Cl. SE18 ....5J **107**
Fox Hollow Dr. DA7: Bex 3D **126**
Foxholt Gdns. NW10 ....7J **61**
Foxhome Cl. BR7: Chst 6E **142**
Fox Ho. Rd. DA17: Belv 5H **109**
    (not continuous)
Foxlands Cres.
    RM10: Dag 5J **73**
Foxlands La. RM10: Dag 5K **73**
Foxlands Rd. RM10: Dag 5J **73**
Fox La. BR2: Kes 5K **171**
    N13 ....2E **32**
    W5 ....4E **78**
Foxleas Ct. BR1: Brom 7G **141**
Foxlees HA0: Wemb 4A **60**
Foxley Cl. E8 ....5G **67**
Foxley Ct. SM2: Sutt 7A **166**
Foxley Rd. CR7: Thor H 4B **156**
    SW9 ....7A **102**
Foxley Sq. SW9 ....1B **120**
Foxmead Cl. EN2: Enf 3E **22**
Foxmore St. SW11 ....1D **118**
Fox Rd. E16 ....5H **87**
Fox's Path CR4: Mitc 2C **154**
Foxton Gro. CR4: Mitc 2B **154**
Foxton Ho. *E16* *2E 106*
    (off Albert Rd.)
Foxwarren KT10: Clay 7A **162**
Foxwell M. SE4 ....3A **122**
Foxwell St. SE4 ....3A **122**
Foxwood Cl. NW7 ....4F **29**
    TW13: Felt 3K **129**
Foxwood Grn. Cl. EN1: Enf 6K **23**
Foxwood Rd. SE3 ....4H **123**
Foyle Rd. N17 ....1G **49**
    SE3 ....6H **105**
Framfield Cl. N12 ....3D **30**
Framfield Ct. *EN1: Enf* *6K 23*
    (off Queen Annes Gdns.)
Framfield Rd. CR4: Mitc 7E **136**
    N5 ....5B **66**
    W7 ....6J **77**
Framlingham Cl. E5 ....2J **67**
Framlingham Ct. *RM6: Chad H* *5B 54*
    (off Norwich Cres.)
Framlingham Cres. SE9 ....4C **142**
Frampton *NW1* *7H 65*
    (off Wrotham Rd.)
Frampton Cl. SM2: Sutt 7J **165**
Frampton Ct. *W3* *2J 97*
    (off Avenue Rd.)
Frampton Ho. *NW8* *4B 4*
    (off Frampton St.)
Frampton Pk. Est. E9 ....7J **67**
Frampton Pk. Rd. E9 ....6J **67**
Frampton Rd. TW4: Houn 5C **112**
Frampton St. NW8 ....4B **4** (4B **82**)
Francemary Rd. SE4 ....5C **122**
Frances Ct. E17 ....6C **50**
Frances Rd. E4 ....6H **35**
Frances St. SE18 ....3D **106**
Franche Ct. Rd. SW17 ....3A **136**
Francis & Dick James Ct. NW7 .....7B **30**
Francis Av. DA7: Bex 2G **127**
    IG1: Ilf 2H **71**
    TW13: Felt 3J **129**
Francis Barber Cl. SW16 ....5K **137**
Franciscan Rd. SW17 ....5D **136**
Francis Chichester Way SW11 ......1E **118**
Francis Cl. E14 ....4F **105**
    KT19: Ewe 4K **163**
    TW17: Shep 4C **146**
Francis Ct. EC1 ....5A **8**
    KT5: Surb *4E 150*
    (off Cranes Pk. Av.)
    NW7 ....*5G 29*
    (off Watford Way)
    SE14 ....*6K 103*
    (off Myers La.)

Francis Gro. SW19 ....6H **135**
    (not continuous)
Francis Ho. E17 ....6B **50**
    N1 ....*1E 84*
    (off Colville Est.)
    SW10 ....*7K 99*
    (off Coleridge Gdns.)
Francis M. SE12 ....7J **123**
Francis Rd. CR0: Croy 7B **156**
    E10 ....1E **68**
    HA1: Harr 5A **42**
    HA5: Eastc 5A **40**
    IG1: Ilf 2H **71**
    N2 ....4D **46**
    SM6: Wall 6G **167**
    TW4: Houn 2B **112**
    UB6: G'frd 2B **78**
Francis St. E15 ....5G **69**
    IG1: Ilf 2H **71**
    SW1 ....3A **18** (4G **101**)
Francis Ter. N19 ....3G **65**
Francis Wlk. N1 ....1K **83**
Francklyn Gdns. HA8: Edg 3B **28**
Franconia Rd. SW4 ....5H **119**
Frank Bailey Wlk. E12 ....5E **70**
Frank Beswick Ho. SW6 ....6H **99**
    (off Clem Attlee Ct.)
Frank Burton Cl. SE7 ....5K **105**
Frank Dixon Cl. SE21 ....7E **120**
Frank Dixon Way SE21 ....1E **138**
Frankfurt Rd. SE24 ....5C **120**
Frank Godley Ct. DA14: Sidc 5B **144**
Frankham Ho. *SE8* *7C 104*
    (off Frankham St.)
Frankham St. SE8 ....7C **104**
Frank Ho. *SW8* *7J 101*
    (off Wyvil Rd.)
Frankland Cl. IG8: Wfd G 5F **37**
    SE16 ....3H **103**
Frankland Rd. E4 ....5H **35**
    SW7 ....2A **16** (3B **100**)
Franklin Bldg. E14 ....2C **104**
Franklin Cl. KT1: King T 3G **151**
    N20 ....7F **21**
    SE13 ....1D **122**
    SE27 ....3B **138**
Franklin Cotts. HA7: Stan 4G **27**
Franklin Cres. CR4: Mitc 4G **155**
Franklin Ho. BR2: Brom 3G **159**
    E1 ....*1H 103*
    (off Watts St.)
    E14 ....*6F 87*
    (off E. India Dock Rd.)
Franklin Ind. Est. *SE20* *2J 157*
    (off Franklin Rd.)
Franklin Pas. SE9 ....3C **124**
Franklin Pl. SE13 ....1D **122**
Franklin Rd. DA7: Bex 1E **126**
    SE20 ....7J **139**
Franklins M. HA2: Harr 2G **59**
Franklin Sq. W14 ....5H **99**
Franklin's Row SW3 ....5F **17** (5D **100**)
Franklin St. E3 ....3D **86**
    N15 ....6E **48**
Franklin Way CR0: Wadd 7J **155**
Franklyn Rd. KT12: Walt T 6J **147**
    NW10 ....6B **62**
Franks Av. KT3: N Mald 4J **151**
Frank Soskice Ho. SW6 ....6H **99**
    (off Clem Attlee Ct.)
Frank St. E13 ....4J **87**
Franks Wood Av. BR5: Pet W 5F **161**
Frankswood Av. UB7: Yiew 6B **74**
Frank Towell Ct. TW14: Felt 7J **111**
Frank Welsh Ct. HA5: Eastc 4A **40**
Frank Whymark Ho. *SE16* *2J 103*
    (off Rupack St.)
Franlaw Cres. N13 ....4H **33**
Fransfield Gro. SE26 ....3H **139**
Frans Hals Ct. E14 ....3F **105**
Franthorne Way SE6 ....2D **140**
-Frant Rd. CR7: Thor H 5B **156**

Fraser Cl. DA5: Bexl 1J **145**
    E6 ....6C **88**
Fraser Ct. *E14* *5E 104*
    (off Ferry St.)
    SW11 ....*1C 118*
    (off Surrey La. Est.)
Fraser Ho. TW8: Bford 5F **97**
Fraser Rd. DA8: Erith 5K **109**
    E17 ....5D **50**
    N9 ....3C **34**
    UB6: G'frd 1B **78**
Fraser St. W4 ....5A **98**
Frating Cres. IG8: Wfd G 6E **36**
Frazer Av. HA4: Ruis 5A **58**
Frazier St. SE1 ....7J **13** (2A **102**)
Frean St. SE16 ....3G **103**
Frearson Ho. *WC1* *1H 7*
    (off Penton Ri.)
Freda Corbet Cl. SE15 ....7G **103**
Frederica Rd. E4 ....1A **36**
Frederica St. N7 ....7K **65**
Frederick Charrington Ho. *E1* *4J 85*
    (off Wickford St.)
Frederick Cl. SM1: Sutt 4H **165**
    W2 ....2D **10** (7D **82**)
Frederick Ct. *SW3* *4F 17*
    (off Duke of York Sq.)
Frederick Cres. EN3: Enf H 2D **24**
    SW9 ....7B **102**
Frederick Dobson Ho. *W11* *7G 81*
    (off Cowling Cl.)
Frederick Gdns. CR0: Croy 6B **156**
    SM1: Sutt 5H **165**
Frederick Pl. SE18 ....5F **107**
Frederick Rd. RM13: Rain 2K **91**
    SE17 ....6B **102**
    SM1: Sutt 5H **165**
Fredericks Pl. EC2 ....1E **14** (6D **84**)
    N12 ....4F **31**
Frederick Sq. *SE16* *7A 86*
    (off Sovereign Cres.)
Frederick's Row EC1 ....1A **8** (3B **84**)
Frederick St. WC1 ....2G **7** (3K **83**)
Frederick Ter. E8 ....7F **67**
Frederick Vs. W7 ....1J **95**
    (off Lwr. Boston Rd.)
Frederic M. SW1 ....7F **11**
Frederic St. E17 ....5A **50**
Fredora Av. UB4: Hayes 4H **75**
Fred Styles Ho. SE7 ....6A **106**
Fred White Wlk. N7 ....6J **65**
Freedom Cl. E17 ....4K **49**
Freedom Rd. N17 ....2D **48**
Freedom St. SW11 ....2D **118**
Freegrove Rd. N7 ....5J **65**
    (not continuous)
Freehold Ind. Cen. TW4: Houn 5A **112**
Freeland Ct. DA15: Sidc 3A **144**
Freeland Pk. NW4 ....2G **45**
Freeland Rd. W5 ....7F **79**
Freelands Av. CR2: Sels 7K **169**
Freeman Dr. KT8: W Mole 3D **148**
Freeman Rd. SM4: Mord 5B **154**
Freemans La. UB3: Hayes 7G **75**
Freemantle Av. EN3: Pond E 5E **24**
Freemantle St. SE17 ....5E **102**
Freemasons Pl. CR0: Croy 1E **168**
    (off Freemasons Rd.)
Freemasons Rd. CR0: Croy 1E **168**
    E16 ....5K **87**
Freesia Cl. BR6: Chels 5K **173**
Freethorpe Cl. SE19 ....7D **138**
Free Trade Wharf E1 ....7K **85**

Freezeland Way UB10: Hil 6D 56
Freke Rd. SW11 3E 118
Fremantle Ho. *E1* *4H 85*
(*off Somerford St.*)
Fremantle Rd. DA17: Belv 4G 109
IG6: Ilf 2F 53
Fremont St. E9 1H 85
(not continuous)
French Ordinary Ct. EC3 2H 15
French Pl. E1 2H 9 (3E 84)
French St. TW16: Sun 2A 148
Frendsbury Rd. SE4 4A 122
Frensham Cl. UB1: S'hall 4D 76
Frensham Dr. CR0: New Ad 7E 170
SW15 3B 134
(not continuous)
Frensham Rd. SE9 2H 143
Frensham St. SE15 6G 103
Frere St. SW11 2C 118
Fresham Ho. *BR2: Brom* *3H 159*
(*off Durham Rd.*)
Freshfield Av. E8 7F 67
Freshfield Cl. SE13 4F 123
Freshfield Dr. N14 7A 22
Freshfields CR0: Croy 1B 170
Freshford St. SW18 3A 136
Freshill La. UB1: S'hall 4E 76
Freshwater Cl. SW17 6E 136
Freshwater Ct. UB1: S'hall 3E 76
W1 *6D 4*
(*off Crawford St.*)
Freshwater Rd. RM8: Dag 1D 72
SW17 6E 136
Freshwell Av. RM6: Chad H 4C 54
Fresh Wharf Rd. IG11: Bark 1F 89
Freshwood Cl. BR3: Beck 1D 158
Freshwood Way SM6: Wall 7F 167
Freston Gdns. EN4: Cockf 5K 21
Freston Pk. N3 2H 45
Freston Rd. W10 7F 81
W11 7F 81
Freswick Ho. *SE8* *4K 103*
(*off Chilton Gro.*)
Freta Rd. DA6: Bex 5F 127
Freud Mus., The **6B 64**
Frewell Ho. *EC1* *5J 7*
(*off Bourne Est.*)
Frewing Cl. BR7: Chst 6D 142
Frewin Rd. SW18 1B 136
Friar M. SE27 3B 138
Friar Rd. BR5: St M Cry 5K 161
UB4: Yead 4B 76
Friars Av. N20 3H 31
SW15 3B 134
Friars Cl. E4 3K 35
IG1: Ilf 1H 71
SE1 5B 14
UB5: Yead 3B 76
Friars Ct. E17 1B 50
SM6: Wall 4F 167
Friars Gdns. W3 6K 79
Friars Ga. Cl. IG8: Wfd G 4D 36
Friars La. TW9: Rich 5D 114
Friars Mead E14 3E 104
Friars M. SE9 5E 124
Friars Pl. La. W3 7K 79
Friars Rd. E6 1B 88
Friars Stile Pl. TW10: Rich 6E 114
Friars Stile Rd. TW10: Rich 6E 114
Friar St. EC4 1B 14 (6B 84)
Friars Wlk. N14 7A 22
SE2 5D 108
Friars Way W3 6K 79
Friarswood CR0: Sels 7A 170
Friary Cl. N12 5H 31
Friary Ct. SW1 5B 12
Friary Est. SE15 6G 103
(not continuous)
Friary La. IG8: Wfd G 4D 36
Friary Pk. Ct. W3 6J 79
Friary Rd. N12 4G 31
SE15 7G 103
W3 6J 79
Friary Way N12 4H 31
FRIDAY HILL **2B 36**
Friday Hill E4 2B 36
Friday Hill E. E4 3B 36
(not continuous)
Friday Hill W. E4 2B 36
Friday Rd. CR4: Mitc 7D 136
DA8: Erith 5K 109
Friday St. EC4 2C 14 (7C 84)
Frideswide Pl. NW5 5G 65
Frieghtliners City Farm **6A 66**
Friendly Pl. SE13 1D 122
Friendly St. SE8 2C 122
Friendly St. M. SE8 2C 122
Friendship Ho. *SE1* *7B 14*
(*off Belvedere Pl.*)
Friendship Wlk. UB5: N'olt 3B 76
Friendship Way E15 1E 86
Friends House **2C 6**
Friends Rd. CR0: Croy 3D 168
Friend St. EC1 1A 8 (3B 84)
FRIERN BARNET **5J 31**
Friern Barnet La. N11 2G 31
N20 2G 31
Friern Barnet Rd. N11 5J 31
Friern Bri. Retail Pk. N11 6A 32
Friern Ct. N20 3G 31
Friern Mt. Dr. N20 7F 21
Friern Pk. N12 5F 31
Friern Rd. SE22 7G 121
Friern Watch Av. N12 4F 31
Frigate Ho. *E14* *4E 104*
(*off Stebondale St.*)
Frigate M. SE8 6C 104
Frimley Av. SM6: Wall 5J 167
Frimley Cl. CR0: New Ad 7E 170
SW19 2G 135
Frimley Ct. DA14: Sidc 5C 144
Frimley Cres. CR0: New Ad 7E 170
Frimley Gdns. CR4: Mitc 3C 154
Frimley Rd. IG3: Ilf 3J 71
KT9: Chess 5D 162
Frimley St. *E1* *4K 85*
(*off Frimley Way*)
Frimley Way E1 4K 85
Fringewood Cl. HA6: Nwood 1D 38
Frinstead Ho. *W10* *7F 81*
(*off Freston Rd.*)
Frinsted Rd. DA8: Erith 7K 109
Frinton Ct. *W13* *5B 78*
(*off Hardwick Grn.*)
Frinton Dr. IG8: Wfd G 7A 36
Frinton M. IG2: Ilf 6E 52
Frinton Rd. DA14: Sidc 2E 144
E6 3B 88
N15 6E 48
SW17 6F 136
Friston St. SW6 2K 117
Friswell Pl. DA6: Bex 4G 127
Fritham Cl. KT3: N Mald 6A 152
Frith Ct. NW7 7B 30
Frith Ho. *NW8* *4B 4*
(*off Frampton St.*)
Frith La. NW7 7B 30
Frith Rd. CR0: Croy 2C 168
E11 4E 68
Frith St. W1 1C 12 (6H 83)
Frithville Ct. *W12* *1E 98*
(*off Frithville Gdns.*)
Frithville Gdns. W12 1E 98
Frizlands La.
RM10: Dag 2H 73
Frobisher Cl. HA5: Pinn 7B 40
Frobisher Ct. NW9 2A 44
SE10 *6F 105*
(*off Old Woolwich Rd.*)
SE23 2H 139
SM3: Cheam 7G 165
W12 *2E 98*
(*off Lime Gro.*)
Frobisher Cres. *EC2* *5D 8*
(*off Beech St.*)
TW19: Stanw 7A 110
Frobisher Gdns. E10 7D 50
TW19: Stanw 7A 110
Frobisher Ho. *E1* *1H 103*
(*off Watts St.*)
SW1 *7C 18*
(*off Dolphin Sq.*)
Frobisher M. EN2: Enf 4J 23
Frobisher Pas. E14 1C 104
Frobisher Pl. Pioneer Cen. SE15 1J 121
Frobisher Rd. E6 6D 88
N8 4A 48
Frobisher St. SE10 6G 105
Frog La. RM13: Rain 6K 91
Frogley Rd. SE22 4F 121
Frogmore SW18 5J 117
Frogmore Av. UB4: Hayes 4G 75
Frogmore Cl. SM3: Cheam 3F 165
Frogmore Ct. UB2: S'hall 4D 94
Frogmore Gdns. SM3: Cheam 4G 165
UB4: Hayes 4G 75
Frogmore Ind. Est. N5 5C 66
NW10 3J 79
UB3: Hayes 2G 93
Frognal NW3 4A 64
Frognal Av. DA14: Sidc 5A 144
HA1: Harr 4K 41
Frognal Cl. NW3 5A 64
FROGNAL CORNER **6K 143**
Frognal Ct. NW3 6A 64
Frognal Gdns. NW3 4A 64
Frognal La. NW3 5K 63
Frognal Pde. NW3 6A 64
Frognal Pl. DA14: Sidc 6A 144
Frognal Ri. NW3 3A 64
Frognal Way NW3 4A 64
Froissart Rd. SE9 5B 124
Frome Ho. SE15 4H 121
Frome Rd. N22 3B 48
Frome St. N1 2C 84
Fromondes Rd. SM3: Cheam 5G 165
Frontenac NW10 7D 62
Frontier Works N17 6K 33
Frostic Wlk. E1 6K 9 (5G 85)
Froude St. SW8 2F 119
Fruen Rd. TW14: Felt 7H 111
Fruiterers Pas. *EC4* *3D 14*
(*off Queen St. Pl.*)
Fryatt Rd. N17 7J 33
(not continuous)
Fryday Gro. M. *SW12* *7G 119*
(*off Weir Rd.*)
Fryent Cl. NW9 6G 43
Fryent Country Pk. **7G 43**
Fryent Cres. NW9 6A 44
Fryent Flds. NW9 6A 44
Fryent Gro. NW9 6A 44
Fryent Way NW9 5G 43
Fry Ho. E6 7A 70
Frying Pan All. E1 6J 9
Fry Rd. E6 7B 70
NW10 1B 80
Fryston Av. CR0: Croy 2G 169
Fuchsia Cl. RM7: Rush G 2K 73
Fuchsia St. SE2 5B 108
Fulbeck Dr. NW9 1A 44
Fulbeck Ho. *N7* *6K 65*
(*off Sutterton St.*)
Fulbeck Rd. N19 4G 65
Fulbeck Wlk. HA8: Edg 2C 28
Fulbeck Way HA2: Harr 2G 41
Fulbourn *KT1: King T* *2G 151*
(*off Eureka Rd.*)
Fulbourne Rd. E17 1E 50
Fulbourne St. E1 5H 85
Fulbrook M. N19 4G 65
Fulcher Ho. *N1* *1E 84*
(*off Colville Est.*)
SE8 5B 104
Fulford Ho. KT19: Ewe 7K 163
Fulford Rd. KT19: Ewe 7K 163
Fulford St. SE16 2H 103
FULHAM **2G 117**
FULHAM BROADWAY **7J 99**
Fulham B'way. SW6 7J 99
Fulham B'way. Shop. Cen.
SW6 *7J 99*
(*off Fulham B'way.*)
Fulham Cl. UB10: Hil 4E 74
Fulham Ct. SW6 1J 117
Fulham FC **1F 117**
Fulham High St. SW6 2G 117
Fulham Palace **2G 117**
Fulham Pal. Rd. SW6 6F 99
W6 5E 98
Fulham Pk. Gdns. SW6 2H 117
Fulham Pk. Rd. SW6 2H 117
Fulham Pools **6G 99**
Fulham Rd. SW3 7A 16 (7K 99)
SW6 2G 117
(Fulham High St.)
SW6 7K 99
(King's Rd.)
SW10 7A 16 (7K 99)
Fullbrooks Av. KT4: Wor Pk 1B 164
Fuller Cl. BR6: Chels 5K 173
E2 3K 9
Fuller Rd. RM8: Dag 3B 72
Fullers Av. IG8: Wfd G 7C 36
KT6: Surb 2F 163
Fullers Cl. RM5: Col R 1J 55
Fuller's Griffin Brewery & Vis. Cen.
6B 98
Fullers La. RM5: Col R 1J 55
Fullers Rd. E18 7C 36
Fuller St. NW4 4E 44
Fullers Way Nth. KT6: Surb 3F 163
Fullers Way Sth. KT9: Chess 4E 162
Fuller's Wood CR0: Croy 5C 170
Fullerton Ct. TW11: Tedd 6A 132
Fullerton Rd. CR0: Croy 7F 157
SM5: Cars 7C 166
SW18 5K 117
Fuller Way UB3: Harl 5H 93
Fullwell Av. IG5: Ilf 1D 52
IG6: Ilf 1F 53
FULLWELL CROSS **1G 53**
Fullwell Cross IG6: Ilf 2H 53
Fullwell Pde. IG5: Ilf 1E 52
Fullwood's M. N1 1F 9 (3D 84)
Fulmar Cl. KT5: Surb 6F 151
Fulmar Ho. *SE16* *4K 103*
(*off Tawny Way*)
Fulmead St. SW6 1K 117
Fulmer Cl. TW12: Hamp 5C 130
Fulmer Ho. *NW8* *4D 4*
(*off Mallory St.*)
Fulmer Rd. E16 5B 88
Fulmer Way W13 3B 96
Fulneck *E1* *5J 85*
(*off Mile End Rd.*)
Fulready Rd. E10 5F 51
Fulstone Cl. TW4: Houn 4D 112
Fulthorp Rd. SE3 2H 123
Fulton M. W2 7A 82
Fulton Rd. HA9: Wemb 3G 61
FULWELL **4H 131**
Fulwell Ct. *UB1: S'hall* *7G 77*
(*off Baird Av.*)
Fulwell Cross Swimming Pool & Recreation Cen. **2H 53**
Fulwell Pk. Av. TW2: Twick 2F 131
Fulwell Rd. TW11: Tedd 4H 131
Fulwood Av. HA0: Wemb 2F 79
Fulwood Cl. UB3: Hayes 6H 75
Fulwood Ct. HA3: Kent 6A 42
Fulwood Gdns. TW1: Twick 6K 113
Fulwood Pl. WC1 6H 7 (5K 83)
Fulwood Wlk. SW19 1G 135
Funland ***3C 12***
(in Trocadero Cen.)
Furber St. W6 3D 98
Furham Fld. HA5: H End 7A 26
Furley Ho. *SE15* *7G 103*
(*off Peckham Pk. Rd.*)
Furley Rd. SE15 7G 103
Furlong Cl. SM6: Wall 1F 167

Furlong Path UB5: N'olt 6C **58**
(off Cowings Mead)
Furlong Rd. N7 . . . . 6A **66**
Furmage St. SW18 . . . . 7K **117**
Furneaux Av. SE27 . . . . 5B **138**
Furness Ho. *SW1* *5J* ***17***
(off Abbots Mnr.)
Furness Rd. HA2: Harr 7F **41**
NW10 . . . . 2C **80**
SM4: Mord 6K **153**
SW6 . . . . 2K **117**
Furnival Mans. *W1* *6A* ***6***
(off Wells St.)
Furnival St. EC4 . . . . 7J **7** (6A **84**)
Furrow La. E9 . . . . 5J **67**
Fursby Av. N3 . . . . 6D **30**
Fursecroft W1 . . . . 7E **4**
Further Acre NW9 . . . . 2B **44**
Furtherfield Cl. CR0: Croy 6A **156**
Further Grn. Rd. SE6 . . . . 7G **123**
FURZEDOWN **5F 137**
Furzedown Dr. SW17 . . . . 5F **137**
Furzedown Rd. SW17 . . . . 5F **137**
Furze Farm Cl. RM6: Chad H 2E **54**
Furzefield Cl. BR7: Chst 6F **143**
Furzefield Rd. SE3 . . . . 6K **105**
Furzeground Way
UB11: Stock P 1E **92**
Furzeham Rd. UB7: W Dray 2A **92**
Furze Rd. CR7: Thor H 3C **156**
Furze St. E3 . . . . 5C **86**
Furzewood TW16: Sun 1J **147**
Fusion Health & Leisure Cen. **4B 102**
Future Fitness Health Club ***2A 48***
(in Wood Green Shop. City)
Fye Foot La. *EC4* *2C* ***14***
(off Queen Victoria St.)
Fyfe Way BR1: Brom 2J **159**
Fyfield *N4* *2A* ***66***
(off Six Acres Est.)
Fyfield Cl. BR2: Brom 4F **159**
Fyfield Ct. E7 . . . . 6J **69**
Fyfield Ho. *E6* *1C* ***88***
(off Ron Leighton Way)
Fyfield Rd. E17 . . . . 3F **51**
EN1: Enf 3K **23**
IG8: Wfd G 7F **37**
SW9 . . . . 3A **120**
Fynes St. SW1 . . . . 3C **18** (4H **101**)

G

Gable Cl. HA5: H End 1E **40**
Gable Ct. SE26 . . . . 4H **139**
Gables, The BR1: Brom 7K **141**
HA9: Wemb 3G **61**
IG11: Bark 6G **71**
N10 . . . . *3E* ***46***
(off Fortis Grn.)
Gables Av. TW15: Ashf 5B **128**
Gables Cl. SE5 . . . . 1E **120**
SE12 . . . . 1J **141**
Gables Lodge EN4: Had W 1F **21**
Gabriel Cl. TW13: Hanw 4C **130**
Gabriel Ho. *N1* *1B* ***84***
(off Islington Grn.)
SE11 . . . . 3G **19** (4K **101**)
Gabrielle Cl. HA9: Wemb 3F **61**
Gabrielle Ct. NW3 . . . . 6B **64**
Gabriel M. NW2 . . . . 2H **63**
Gabriel St. SE23 . . . . 7K **121**
Gabriels Wharf SE1 . . . . 4J **13** (1A **102**)
Gad Cl. E13 . . . . 3K **87**
Gaddesden Av. HA9: Wemb 6F **61**
Gaddesden Ho. *EC1* *2F* ***9***
(off Cranwood St.)
Gadebridge Ho. *SW3* *5C* ***16***
(off Cale St.)
Gade Cl. UB3: Hayes 1K **93**
Gadesden Rd. KT19: Ewe 6J **163**
(not continuous)
Gadsbury Cl. NW9 . . . . 6B **44**
Gadsden Ho. *W10* *4G* ***81***
(off Hazlewood Cres.)
Gadwall Cl. E16 . . . . 6K **87**
Gadwall Way SE28 . . . . 2H **107**
Gage Brown Ho. *W10* *6F* ***81***
(off Bridge Cl.)
Gage Rd. E16 . . . . 5G **87**
Gage St. WC1 . . . . 5F **7** (5J **83**)
Gainford Ho. *E2* *3H* ***85***
(off Ellsworth St.)
Gainford St. N1 . . . . 1A **84**
Gainsboro Gdns. UB6: G'frd 5J **59**
Gainsborough Av. *E12* *6E* ***70***
(off Barrington Rd.)
E12 . . . . 5E **70**
(Church Rd.)
Gainsborough Cl. BR3: Beck 7C **140**
KT10: Esh 7J **149**
Gainsborough Ct. BR2: Brom 4A **160**
KT19: Ewe 6B **164**
N12 . . . . 5E **30**
SE16 . . . . *5H* ***103***
(off Stubbs Dr.)
SE21 . . . . 2E **138**
W4 . . . . *5H* ***97***
(off Chaseley Dr.)
W12 . . . . 2E **98**
Gainsborough Gdns. HA8: Edg 2F **43**
NW3 . . . . 3B **64**
NW11 . . . . 7H **45**
TW7: Isle 5H **113**
Gainsborough Ho. *E14* *2C* ***104***
(off Cassilis Rd.)
E14 . . . . *7A* ***86***
(off Victory Pl.)
EN1: Enf 5B **24**
RM8: Dag *4B* ***72***
(off Earl's Wlk.)
SW1 . . . . *4D* ***18***
(off Erasmus St.)
Gainsborough Lodge
HA1: Harr *5K* ***41***
(off Hindes Rd.)
Gainsborough Mans. *W14* *6G* ***99***
(off Queen's Club Gdns.)
Gainsborough M. SE26 . . . . 3H **139**
Gainsborough Rd. E11 . . . . 7G **51**
E15 . . . . 3G **87**
IG8: Wfd G 6H **37**
KT3: N Mald 6K **151**
N12 . . . . 5E **30**
RM8: Dag 4B **72**
TW9: Rich 2F **115**
UB4: Hayes 2E **74**
W4 . . . . 4B **98**
Gainsborough Sq. DA6: Bex 3D **126**
Gainsborough St. E9 . . . . 6B **68**
Gainsborough Studios E. *N1* *1D* ***84***
(off Poole St.)
Gainsborough Studios Nth. *N1* *1D* ***84***
(off Poole St.)
Gainsborough Studios Sth.
N1 . . . . *1D* ***84***
(off Poole St.)
Gainsborough Studios W. *N1* *1D* ***84***
(off Poole St.)
Gainsborough Ter. *SM2: Sutt* *7H* ***165***
(off Belmont Ri.)
Gainsborough Twr. *UB5: N'olt* *2B* ***76***
(off Academy Gdns.)
Gainsfield Ct. E11 . . . . 3G **69**
Gainsford Rd. E17 . . . . 4B **50**
Gainsford St. SE1 . . . . 6J **15** (2F **103**)
Gairloch Ho. *NW1* *7H* ***65***
(off Stratford Vs.)
Gairloch Rd. SE5 . . . . 2E **120**
Gaisford St. NW5 . . . . 6G **65**
Gaitskell Ct. SW11 . . . . 2C **118**
Gaitskell Ho. E6 . . . . 1B **88**
E17 . . . . 3D **50**
SE17 . . . . *6E* ***102***
(off Villa St.)
Gaitskell Rd. SE9 . . . . 1G **143**
Gala Bingo
Acton **1K 97**
Bexleyheath **4H 127**
Camberwell **7C 102**
Crystal Palace **6F 139**
Enfield **4B 24**
Feltham **2K 129**
Fullwell Cross **2G 53**
Greenhill **5K 41**
Hounslow **4E 112**
Kingston upon Thames **1E 150**
Stratford **1F 87**
Surrey Quays **3K 103**
Thornton Heath **5A 156**
Upton Pk. **1C 88**
Woolwich **3E 106**
Galahad Rd. BR1: Brom 4J **141**
N9 . . . . 3B **34**
Galata Rd. SW13 . . . . 7C **98**
Galatea Sq. SE15 . . . . 3H **121**
Galaxy Bldg. *E14* *4C* ***104***
(off Crews St.)
Galaxy Ho. *EC2* *3F* ***9***
(off Leonard St.)
Galba Ct. TW8: Bford 7D **96**
Galbraith St. E14 . . . . 3E **104**
Galdana Av. EN5: New Bar 3F **21**
Galeborough Av. IG8: Wfd G 7A **36**
Gale Cl. CR4: Mitc 3B **154**
TW12: Hamp 6C **130**
Galena Arches *W6* *4D* ***98***
(off Galena Rd.)
Galena Ho. *SE18* *5K* ***107***
(off Grosmont Rd.)
W6 . . . . *4D* ***98***
(off Galena Rd.)
Galena Rd. W6 . . . . 4D **98**
Galen Pl. WC1 . . . . 6F **7** (5J **83**)
Galesbury Rd. SW18 . . . . 6A **118**
Gales Gdns. E2 . . . . 3H **85**
Gale St. E3 . . . . 5C **86**
RM9: Dag 5C **72**
Gales Way IG8: Wfd G 7H **37**
Galgate Cl. SW19 . . . . 1F **135**
Gallants Farm Rd. EN4: E Barn 7H **21**
Galleon Cl. DA8: Erith 4K **109**
SE16 . . . . 2K **103**
Galleon Ho. *E14* *4E* ***104***
(off Glengarnock Av.)
Galleons Dr. IG11: Bark 3A **90**
Galleria Shop. Mall, The E18 . . . . 2J **51**
Gallery Ct. *SE1* *7E* ***14***
(off Pilgrimage St.)
SW10 . . . . *6A* ***100***
(off Gunter Gro.)
Gallery Gdns. UB5: N'olt 2B **76**
Gallery Rd. SE21 . . . . 1D **138**
Galley, The E16 . . . . 7F **89**
Galleywall Rd. SE16 . . . . 4H **103**
Galleywall Rd. Trad. Est. *SE16* *4H* ***103***
(off Galleywall Rd.)
Galleywood Ho. *W10* *5E* ***80***
(off Sutton Way)
Galliard Cl. N9 . . . . 6D **24**
Galliard Ct. N9 . . . . 6B **24**
Galliard Rd. N9 . . . . 1B **34**
Gallia Rd. N5 . . . . 5B **66**
Gallica Ct. SM1: Sutt 1K **165**
Gallions Cl. IG11: Bark 3A **90**
Gallions Entrance E16 . . . . 1G **107**
Gallions Reach Shop. Pk. E6 . . . . 5G **89**
Gallions Rd. E16 . . . . 7F **89**
SE7 . . . . 4K **105**
Gallions Rdbt. E16 . . . . 7F **89**
Gallions Vw. Rd. SE28 . . . . 2J **107**
Galliver Pl. E5 . . . . 4H **67**
Gallon Cl. SE7 . . . . 4A **106**
Gallop, The CR2: Sels 7H **169**
SM2: Sutt 7B **166**
Gallosson Rd. SE18 . . . . 4J **107**
Galloway Path CR0: Croy 4D **168**
Galloway Rd. W12 . . . . 1C **98**
Gallus Cl. N21 . . . . 6E **22**
Gallus Sq. SE3 . . . . 3K **123**
Galpins Rd. CR7: Thor H 5J **155**
Galsworthy Av. E14 . . . . 6A **86**
RM6: Chad H 7B **54**
Galsworthy Cl. NW2 . . . . 4G **63**
SE28 . . . . 1B **108**
Galsworthy Ct. *W3* *3H* ***97***
(off Bollo Bri. Rd.)
Galsworthy Cres. SE3 . . . . 1A **124**
Galsworthy Ho. *W11* *6G* ***81***
(off Elgin Cres.)
Galsworthy Rd. KT2: King T 7H **133**
NW2 . . . . 4G **63**
Galsworthy Ter. N16 . . . . 3E **66**
Galton St. W10 . . . . 3G **81**
Galva Cl. EN4: Cockf 4K **21**
Galvani Way CR0: Wadd 1K **167**
Galveston Ho. *E1* *4A* ***86***
(off Harford St.)
Galveston Rd. SW15 . . . . 5H **117**
Galway Cl. *SE16* *5H* ***103***
(off Masters Dr.)
Galway Ho. *E1* *5K* ***85***
(off White Horse La.)
EC1 . . . . 2D **8**
Galway St. EC1 . . . . 2D **8** (3C **84**)
Galy NW9 . . . . 2B **44**
Gambetta St. SW8 . . . . 2F **119**
Gambia St. SE1 . . . . 5B **14** (1B **102**)
Gambier Ho. *EC1* *2D* ***8***
(off Mora St.)
Gambole Rd. SW17 . . . . 4C **136**
Games Rd. EN4: Cockf 3J **21**
Gamlen Rd. SW15 . . . . 4F **117**
Gamuel Cl. E17 . . . . 6C **50**
Gander Grn. Cres.
TW12: Hamp 1E **148**
Gander Grn. La. SM1: Sutt 3H **165**
SM3: Cheam 2G **165**
Gandhi Cl. E17 . . . . 6C **50**
Gandolfi St. SE15 . . . . 6E **102**
Ganton St. W1 . . . . 2A **12** (7G **83**)
GANTS HILL **6E 52**
GANTS HILL **6E 52**
Gants Hill IG2: Ilf 6E **52**
Gantshill Cres. IG2: Ilf 5E **52**
Gap Rd. SW19 . . . . 5J **135**
Garage Rd. W3 . . . . 6G **79**
Garbett Ho. *SE17* *6B* ***102***
(off Doddington Gro.)
Garbutt Pl. W1 . . . . 5H **5** (5E **82**)
Garden Av. CR4: Mitc 7F **137**
DA7: Bex 3F **127**
Garden City HA8: Edg 6B **28**
Garden Cl. E4 . . . . 5H **35**
HA4: Ruis 2G **57**
SE12 . . . . 3K **141**
SM6: Wall 5J **167**
SW15 . . . . 7E **116**
TW12: Hamp 5D **130**
TW15: Ashf 6E **128**
UB5: N'olt 1C **76**
Garden Ct. CR0: Croy 2F **169**
EC4 . . . . 2J **13**
HA7: Stan 5H **27**
N12 . . . . 5E **30**
NW8 . . . . *1A* ***4***
(off Garden Rd.)
TW9: Kew 1F **115**
TW12: Hamp 5D **130**
W4 . . . . 3J **97**
W11 . . . . *7G* ***81***
(off Clarendon Rd.)
Gardener Gro. TW13: Hanw 2D **130**
Gardeners Cl. N11 . . . . 2K **31**
SE9 . . . . 3C **142**
Gardeners Rd. CR0: Croy 1B **168**
Garden Ho. *N2* *2B* ***46***
(off The Grange)
SW7 . . . . *3K* ***99***
(off Cornwall Gdns.)
Garden Ho., The *W6* *6F* ***99***
(off Bothwell St.)

Gardenia Rd. BR1: Brom 3E **160**
  EN1: Enf 6K **23**
Gardenia Way IG8: Wfd G 6D **36**
Garden La. BR1: Brom 6K **141**
  SW2 ....1K **137**
Garden M. W2 ....7J **81**
Garden Pl. E8 ....1F **85**
Garden Rd. BR1: Brom 7K **141**
  KT12: Walt T 6K **147**
  NW8 ....1A **4** (3A **82**)
  SE20 ....1J **157**
  TW9: Rich 3G **115**
Garden Row SE1 ....3B **102**
Garden Royal SW15 ....6F **117**
Gardens, The BR3: Beck 1E **158**
  HA1: Harr 6G **41**
  HA5: Pinn 6D **40**
  N8 ....4J **47**
  (not continuous)
  SE22 ....4G **121**
  TW14: Felt 5F **111**
  UB10: Ick 2A **56**
Garden St. E1 ....5K **85**
Gardens Way E12 ....3C **70**
Garden Ter. SW1 ....5C **18** (5H **101**)
  SW7 ....7D **10**
Garden Vw. E7 ....4A **70**
Garden Wlk. BR3: Beck 1B **158**
  EC2 ....2G **9** (3E **84**)
Garden Way NW10 ....6J **61**
Gardiner Av. NW2 ....5E **62**
Gardiner Cl. EN3: Pond E 6E **24**
  RM8: Dag 4D **72**
Gardiner Ct. CR2: S Croy ...6C **168**
  NW10 ....1K **79**
Gardiner Ho. SW11 ....1C **118**
Gardner Cl. E11 ....6K **51**
Gardner Ct. EC1 ....3A **8**
  (off Brewery Sq.)
  N5 ....4C **66**
Gardner Ho. TW13: Hanw 2D **130**
  UB1: S'hall 7B **76**
  (off The Broadway)
Gardner Ind. Est. SE26 ......5B **140**
Gardner Pl. TW14: Felt 6K **111**
Gardner Rd. E13 ....4K **87**
Gardners La. EC4 ....2C **14** (7C **84**)
Gardnor Rd. NW3 ....4B **64**
Gard St. EC1 ....1B **8** (3B **84**)
Garendon Gdns. SM4: Mord ..7K **153**
Garendon Rd. SM4: Mord 7K **153**
Garenne Ct. E4 ....1K **35**
Gareth Cl. KT4: Wor Pk 2F **165**
Gareth Ct. SW16 ....3H **137**
Gareth Gro. BR1: Brom 4J **141**
Garfield EN2: Enf 5J **23**
  (off Private Rd.)
Garfield Ct. NW6 ....7G **63**
  (off Willesden La.)
Garfield M. SW11 ....3E **118**
Garfield Rd. E4 ....1A **36**
  E13 ....4H **87**
  EN3: Pond E 4D **24**
  SW11 ....3E **118**
  SW19 ....5A **136**
  TW1: Twick 1A **132**
Garford St. E14 ....7C **86**
Garganey Cl. NW10 ....6K **61**
  (off Elgar Av.)
Garganey Wlk. SE28 ....7C **90**
Garibaldi St. SE18 ....4J **107**
Garland Ct. E14 ....7C **86**
  (off Premiere Pl.)
  SE17 ....4C **102**
  (off Wansey St.)
Garland Dr. TW3: Houn 2G **113**
Garland Ho. KT2: King T 1E **150**
  (off Seven Kings Way)
Garland Rd. HA7: Stan 1E **42**
  SE18 ....7H **107**
Garlands Ct. CR0: Croy 4D **168**
  (off Chatsworth Rd.)
Garlands Ho. NW8 ....2A **82**

  (off Carlton Hill)
Garlick Hill EC4 ....2D **14** (7C **84**)
Garlies Rd. SE23 ....3A **140**
Garlinge Rd. NW2 ....6H **63**
Garman Cl. N18 ....5J **33**
Garman Rd. N17 ....7C **34**
  (not continuous)
Garnault M. EC1 ....2K **7**
Garnault Pl. EC1 .....2K **7** (3A **84**)
Garnault Rd. FN1: Enf 1A **24**
Garner Cl. RM8: Dag 1D **72**
Garner Ct. TW19: Stanw ...6A **110**
  (off Jeppesen Ct.)
Garner Rd. E17 ....1E **50**
Garner St. E2 ....2G **85**
Garnet Ho. E1 ....1J **103**
  (off Garnet St.)
Garnet Rd. CR7: Thor H 4C **156**
  NW10 ....6A **62**
Garnet St. E1 ....7J **85**
Garnett Cl. SE9 ....3D **124**
Garnett Rd. NW3 ....5D **64**
Garnett Way E17 ....1A **50**
  (off Swansland Gdns.)
Garnet Wlk. E6 ....5C **88**
Garnham Cl. N16 ....2F **67**
Garnham St. N16 ....2F **67**
Garnies Cl. SE15 ....7F **103**
Garrad's Rd. SW16 ....3H **137**
Garrard Cl. BR7: Chst 5F **143**
  DA7: Bex 3G **127**
Garrard Wlk. NW10 ....6A **62**
Garratt Cl. CR0: Bedd 4J **167**
Garratt Ct. SW18 ....7K **117**
Garratt La. SW17 ....3A **136**
  SW18 ....6K **117**
Garratt Rd. HA8: Edg 7B **28**
Garratts Rd. WD23: Bush ...1B **26**
Garratt Ter. SW17 ....4C **136**
Garraway Ct. SW13 ....7E **98**
  (off Wyatt Dr.)
Garrett Cl. W3 ....5K **79**
Garrett Ho. SE1 ....6A **14**
  (off Burrows M.)
  W12 ....6D **80**
  (off Du Cane Rd.)
Garrett St. EC1 .....3D **8** (4C **84**)
Garrick Av. NW11 ....6G **45**
Garrick Cl. SW18 ....4A **118**
  TW9: Rich 5D **114**
  W5 ....4E **78**
Garrick Ct. E8 ....7F **67**
  (off Jacaranda Gro.)
Garrick Cres. CR0: Croy ...2E **168**
Garrick Dr. NW4 ....2E **44**
  SE28 ....3H **107**
Garrick Gdns. KT8: W Mole ..3E **148**
Garrick Ho. KT1: King T 4E **150**
  (off Surbiton Rd.)
  W1 ....5J **11**
  W4 ....6A **98**
Garrick Ind. Est. NW9 .....5B **44**
Garrick Pk. NW4 ....2F **45**
Garrick Rd. NW9 ....6B **44**
  TW9: Rich 2G **115**
  UB6: G'frd 4F **77**
Garricks Ho. KT1: King T ...2D **150**
  (off Wadbrook St.)
Garrick St. WC2 .....2E **12** (7J **83**)
Garrick Theatre 3E **12**
  (off Charing Cross Rd.)
Garrick Way NW4 ....4F **45**
Garrick Yd. WC2 ....2E **12**
Garrison Cl. SE18 ....7E **106**
  TW4: Houn 5D **112**
Garrison La. KT9: Chess ...7D **162**
Garrison Rd. E3 ....1C **86**
Garrowsfield EN5: Barn 6C **20**
Garry Way RM1: Rom 1K **55**
Garsdale Cl. N11 ....6K **31**
Garsdale Ter. W14 ....5H **99**
  (off Aisgill Av.)
Garside Cl. SE28 ....3H **107**

  TW12: Hamp 6F **131**
Garsington M. SE4 ....3B **122**
Garson Ho. W2 ....2A **10**
  (off Gloucester Ter.)
Garston Ho. N1 ....7B **66**
  (off The Sutton Est.)
Garter Way SE16 ....2K **103**
Garth, The HA3: Kent 6F **43**
  TW12: Ham H 6F **131**
Garth Cl. HA4: Ruis 1B **58**
  KT2: King T 5F **133**
  SM4: Mord 7F **153**
  W4 ....5K **97**
Garth Ct. HA1: Harr 6K **41**
  (off Northwick Pk. Rd.)
  W4 ....5K **97**
Garth Ho. NW2 ....2H **63**
Garth M. W5 ....4E **78**
Garthorne Rd. SE23 ....7K **121**
Garthorne Road Nature Reserve ...7K **121**
Garth Rd. KT2: King T 5F **133**
  NW2 ....2H **63**
  SM4: Mord 6E **152**
  W4 ....5K **97**
Garth Rd. Ind. Est. SM4: Mord ...1F **165**
Garthside TW10: Ham 5E **132**
Garthway N12 ....6H **31**
Gartmoor Gdns. SW19 .....1H **135**
Gartmore Rd. IG3: Ilf 2K **71**
Garton Pl. SW18 ....6A **118**
Gartons Cl. EN3: Pond E ...4D **24**
Gartons Way SW11 ....3A **118**
Garvary Rd. E16 ....6K **87**
Garway Rd. W2 ....6K **81**
Garwood Cl. N17 ....1H **49**
Gascoigne Gdns. IG8: Wfd G ...7B **36**
Gascoigne Pl. E2 .....1J **9** (3F **85**)
  (not continuous)
Gascoigne Rd. CR0: New Ad ...7F **171**
  IG11: Bark 1G **89**
Gascony Av. NW6 ....7J **63**
Gascoyne Ho. E9 ....7A **68**
Gascoyne Rd. E9 ....7K **67**
Gaselee St. E14 ....1E **104**
  (off Baffin Way)
Gaskarth Rd. HA8: Edg 1J **43**
  SW12 ....6F **119**
Gaskell Rd. N6 ....6D **46**
Gaskell St. SW4 ....2J **119**
Gaskin St. N1 ....1B **84**
Gaspar Cl. SW5 ....4K **99**
  (off Courtfield Gdns.)
Gaspar M. SW5 ....4K **99**
Gassiot Rd. SW17 ....4D **136**
Gassiot Way SM1: Sutt ...3B **166**
Gasson Ho. SE14 ....6K **103**
  (off John Williams Cl.)
Gastein Rd. W6 ....6F **99**
Gastigny Ho. EC1 ....2D **8**
Gaston Bell Cl. TW9: Rich ..3F **115**
Gaston Bri. Rd. TW17: Shep ...6F **147**
Gaston Rd. CR4: Mitc 3E **154**
Gaston Way TW17: Shep ...5F **147**
Gataker St. SE16 ....3H **103**
  (off Slippers Pl.)
Gatcombe Cl. BR3: Beck ...7C **140**
Gatcombe Ho. SE22 ....3E **120**
Gatcombe M. W5 ....7F **79**
Gatcombe Rd. E16 ....1J **105**
  N19 ....3H **65**
Gatcombe Way EN4: Cockf ...3J **21**
Gateacre Ct. SW4 : Sidc ...4B **144**
Gate Cen., The TW8: Bford ...7A **96**
Gate Cinema 1J **99**
  (off Notting Hill Ga.)
Gateforth St. NW8 ....4C **4** (4C **82**)
Gate Hill Ct. W11 ....1H **99**
  (off Ladbroke Ter.)
Gate Ho. N1 ....4C **84**
  (off Ufton Rd.)
Gatehouse Cl. KT2: King T ...7J **133**
Gatehouse Sq. SE1 ....4D **14**

Gatehouse Theatre 1E **64**
Gateley Ho. SE4 ....4K **121**
  (off Coston Wlk.)
Gateley Rd. SW9 ....3K **119**
Gate Lodge W9 ....5J **81**
  (off Admiral Wlk.)
Gate M. SW7 ....7D **10**
Gater Dr. EN2: Enf 1J **23**
Gates NW9 ....2B **44**
Gatesborough St. EC2 ...3G **9** (4E **84**)
Gates Ct. SE17 ....5C **102**
Gatesden WC1 ....2G **7** (3J **83**)
Gates Grn. Rd. BR2: Kes ...3H **171**
  BR4: W W'ck 3H **171**
Gateside Rd. SW17 ....3D **136**
Gatestone Cl. SE19 ....6E **138**
Gatestone Rd. SE19 ....6E **138**
Gate St. WC2 ....7G **7** (6K **83**)
Gate Theatre, The 1J **99**
  (off Pembridge Rd.)
Gateway SE17 ....6C **102**
Gateway Arc. N1 ....2B **84**
  (off Upper St.)
Gateway Bus. Cen. BR3: Beck ...6A **140**
Gateway Ho. IG11: Bark ...1G **89**
Gateway Ind. Est. NW10 ...3B **80**
Gateway M. E8 ....5F **67**
Gateway Retail Pk. E6 .....4F **89**
Gateway Rd. E10 ....3D **68**
Gateways KT6: Surb 5E **150**
  (off Surbiton Hill Rd.)
Gateways, The SW3 ....4D **16**
  SW18 ....4D **114**
  (off Park La.)
Gateways Ct. SM6: Wall ...5F **167**
Gatfield Gro. TW13: Hanw ...2E **130**
Gatfield Ho. TW13: Hanw ...2D **130**
Gathorne Rd. N22 ....2A **48**
Gathorne St. E2 ....2K **85**
Gatley Av. KT19: Ewe 5H **163**
Gatliff Cl. SW1 ....6H **17**
Gatliff Rd. SW1 ......6J **17** (5F **101**)
  (not continuous)
Gatling Rd. SE2 ....5A **108**
Gatonby St. SE15 ....1F **121**
Gatting Cl. HA8: Edg 7D **28**
Gatting Way UB8: Uxb 6A **56**
Gattis Wharf N1 ....2J **83**
  (off New Wharf Rd.)
Gatton Rd. SW17 ....4C **136**
Gattons Way DA14: Sidc ...4F **145**
Gatward Cl. N21 ....6G **23**
Gatward Grn. N9 ....2A **34**
Gatwick Ho. E14 ....6B **86**
  (off Clemence St.)
Gatwick Rd. SW18 ....7H **117**
Gauden Cl. SW4 ....3H **119**
Gauden Rd. SW4 ....2H **119**
Gaugin Ct. SE16 ....5H **103**
  (off Stubbs Dr.)
Gaumont Ter. W12 ....2E **98**
  (off Lime Gro.)
Gauntlet NW9 ....2B **44**
  (off Five Acre)
Gauntlet Cl. UB5: N'olt 7C **58**
Gauntlett Cl. HA0: Wemb ...5B **60**
Gauntlett Rd. SM1: Sutt ...5B **166**
Gaunt St. SE1 ....3C **102**
Gautrey Rd. SE15 ....2J **121**
Gautrey Sq. E6 ....6D **88**
Gavel St. SE17 ....4D **102**
Gaverick M. E14 ....4C **104**
Gavestone Cres. SE12 ...7K **123**
Gavestone Rd. SE12 .....7K **123**
Gaviller Pl. E5 ....4H **67**
Gavina Cl. SM4: Mord 5C **154**
Gavin Ho. SE18 ....4J **107**
Gawain Wlk. N9 ....3B **34**
Gawber St. E2 ....3J **85**
Gawsworth Cl. E15 ....5H **69**
Gawthorne Av. NW7 ......5B **30**
Gawthorne Ct. E3 ....2C **86**
Gay Cl. NW2 ....5D **62**

Gaydon Ho. *W2* 5K **81**
(off Bourne Ter.)
Gaydon La. NW9 . . . . 1A **44**
Gayfere Rd. IG5: Ilf 3D **52**
KT17: Ewe 5C **164**
Gayfere St. SW1 . . . . 2E **18** (3J **101**)
Gayford Rd. W12 . . . . 2B **98**
Gay Gdns. RM10: Dag 4J **73**
Gay Ho. N16 . . . . 5E **66**
Gayhurst *SE17* 6D **102**
(off Hopwood Rd.)
Gayhurst Ct. UB5: Yead 3A **76**
Gayhurst Ho. *NW8* 3C **4**
(off Mallory St.)
Gayhurst Rd. E8 . . . . 7G **67**
Gaylor Rd. UB5: N'olt 5D **58**
Gaymead *NW8* 1K **81**
(off Abbey Rd.)
Gaynesford Rd. SE23 . . . . 2K **139**
SM5: Cars 7D **166**
Gaynes Hill Rd. IG8: Wfd G 6H **37**
Gay Rd. E15 . . . . 2F **87**
Gaysham Av. IG2: Ilf 5E **52**
Gaysham Hall IG5: Ilf 3F **53**
Gaysley Ho. SE11 . . . . 4J **19**
Gay St. SW15 . . . . 3F **117**
Gayton Ct. HA1: Harr 6K **41**
Gayton Cres. NW3 . . . . 4B **64**
Gayton Rd. HA1: Harr 6K **41**
NW3 . . . . 4B **64**
SE2 . . . . 3C **108**
Gayville Rd. SW11 . . . . 6D **118**
Gaywood Cl. SW2 . . . . 1K **137**
Gaywood Rd. E17 . . . . 3C **50**
Gaywood St. SE1 . . . . 3B **102**
Gaza St. SE17 . . . . 5B **102**
Gaze Ho. *E14* 6F **87**
(off Blair St.)
Gazelle Ho. E15 . . . . 6G **69**
Gean Ct. E11 . . . . 4F **69**
Geariesville Gdns. IG6: Ilf 4F **53**
Gearing Cl. SW17 . . . . 4E **136**
Geary Rd. NW10 . . . . 5C **62**
Geary St. N7 . . . . 5K **65**
Geddes Pl. *DA7: Bex* 4G **127**
(off Arnsberg Way)
Gedeney Rd. N17 . . . . 1C **48**
Gedling Pl. SE1 . . . . 7K **15** (3F **103**)
Geere Rd. E15 . . . . 1H **87**
Gees Ct. W1 . . . . 1H **11** (6E **82**)
Gee St. EC1 . . . . 3C **8** (4C **84**)
Geffery's Ct. SE9 . . . . 3C **142**
Geffrye Ct. N1 . . . . 2E **84**
Geffrye Est. N1 . . . . 2E **84**
Geffrye Mus. 1J **9**
Geffrye St. E2 . . . . 1J **9** (2F **85**)
Geldart Rd. SE15 . . . . 7H **103**
Geldeston Rd. E5 . . . . 2G **67**
Gellatly Rd. SE14 . . . . 2J **121**
Gell Cl. UB10: Ick 3B **56**
Gelsthorpe Rd. RM5: Col R 1H **55**
Gemini Bus. Cen. E16 . . . . 4F **87**
Gemini Bus. Est. SE14 . . . . 5K **103**
Gemini Ct. *E1* 7G **85**
(off Vaughan Way)
Gemini Gro. UB5: N'olt 3C **76**
General Gordon Pl. SE18 . . . . 4F **107**
General Wolfe Rd. SE10 . . . . 1F **123**
Genesis Cl. TW19: Stanw 1B **128**
Genesta Rd. SE18 . . . . 6F **107**
Geneva Cl. TW17: Shep 2G **147**
Geneva Ct. NW9 . . . . 5B **44**
Geneva Dr. SW9 . . . . 4A **120**
Geneva Gdns. RM6: Chad H 5E **54**
Geneva Rd. CR7: Thor H 5C **156**
KT1: King T 4E **150**
Genever Cl. E4 . . . . 5H **35**
Genista Rd. N18 . . . . 5C **34**
Genoa Av. SW15 . . . . 5E **116**
Genoa Ho. *E1* 4K **85**
(off Ernest St.)
Genoa Rd. SE20 . . . . 1J **157**
Genotin Rd. EN1: Enf 3J **23**
Genotin Ter. EN1: Enf 4J **23**
Gentlemans Row EN2: Enf 3H **23**
Gentry Gdns. E13 . . . . 4J **87**
Geoffrey Bower Sports Cen. 2D **52**
Geoffrey Cl. SE5 . . . . 2C **120**
Geoffrey Ct. SE4 . . . . 2B **122**
Geoffrey Gdns. E6 . . . . 2C **88**
Geoffrey Ho. *SE1* 7F **15**
(off Pardoner St.)
Geoffrey Jones Ct. NW10 . . . . 1C **80**
Geoffrey Rd. SE4 . . . . 3B **122**
George V Av. HA5: Pinn 2D **40**
George V Cl. HA5: Pinn 3E **40**
George V Way UB6: G'frd 1B **78**
George Beard Rd. SE8 . . . . 4B **104**
George Belt Ho. *E2* 3K **85**
(off Smart St.)
George Comberton Wlk. E12 . . . . 5E **70**
George Ct. WC2 . . . . 3F **13**
George Cres. N10 . . . . 7K **31**
George Davies Lodge
IG6: Ilf 5G **53**
(off Veronique Gdns.)
George Downing Est. N16 . . . . 2F **67**
George Eliot Ho. *SW1* 4B **18**
(off Vauxhall Bri. Rd.)
George Elliston Ho. *SE1* 5G **103**
(off Old Kent Rd.)
George Eyre Ho. *NW8* 2B **82**
(off Cochrane St.)
George Gange Way HA3: W'stone 3J **41**
George Gillett Ct. EC1 . . . . 3D **8**
George Gro. Rd. SE20 . . . . 1G **157**
George Inn Yd. SE1 . . . . 5E **14** (1D **102**)
George La. BR2: Hayes 1K **171**
E18 . . . . 2J **51**
(not continuous)
SE13 . . . . 6D **122**
George Lansbury Ho. *N22* 1A **48**
(off Progress Way)
NW10 . . . . 7A **62**
George Lindgren Ho. *SW6* 7H **99**
(off Clem Attlee Ct.)
George Loveless Ho. *E2* 1K **9**
(off Diss St.)
George Lowe Ct. *W2* 5K **81**
(off Bourne Ter.)
George Mathers Rd. SE11 . . . . 4B **102**
George M. *EN2: Enf* 3J **23**
(off The Town)
NW1 . . . . 2B **6**
SW9 . . . . 2A **120**
George Padmore Ho. *E8* 1G **85**
(off Brougham Rd.)
George Peabody Ct. *NW1* 5C **4**
(off Burne St.)
George Pl. N17 . . . . 3E **48**
George Potter Ho. *SW11* 2B **118**
(off George Potter Way)
George Potter Way SW11 . . . . 2B **118**
George Rd. E4 . . . . 6H **35**
KT2: King T 7H **133**
(not continuous)
KT3: N Mald 4B **152**
George Row SE16 . . . . 2G **103**
George Sq. SW19 . . . . 3J **153**
George's Rd. N7 . . . . 5K **65**
George's Sq. *SW6* 6H **99**
(off North End Rd.)
George St. CR0: Croy 2C **168**
E16 . . . . 6H **87**
(not continuous)
IG11: Bark 7G **71**
TW3: Houn 2D **112**
TW9: Rich 5D **114**
UB2: S'hall 4C **94**
W1 . . . . 7E **4** (6D **82**)
W7 . . . . 1J **95**
George Tingle Ho. *SE1* 3F **103**
(off Grange Wlk.)
Georgetown Cl. SE19 . . . . 5E **138**
Georgette Pl. SE10 . . . . 7E **104**
Georgeville Gdns. IG6: Ilf 4F **53**
George Walter Ct. *SE16* 4J **103**
(off Millender Wlk.)
George Wyver Cl. SW19 . . . . 7G **117**
George Yd. EC3 . . . . 1F **15** (6D **84**)
W1 . . . . 2H **11** (7E **82**)
Georgiana St. NW1 . . . . 1G **83**
Georgian Cl. BR2: Hayes 1K **171**
HA7: Stan 7F **27**
UB10: Ick 4A **56**
Georgian Ct. *CR0: Croy* 1D **168**
(off Cross Rd.)
E9 . . . . 1J **85**
EN5: New Bar 4F **21**
HA9: Wemb 6G **61**
N3 . . . . 1H **45**
NW4 . . . . 5D **44**
SW16 . . . . 4J **137**
Georgian Ho. *E16* 1J **105**
(off Capulet M.)
Georgian Way HA1: Harr 2H **59**
Georgia Rd. CR7: Thor H 1B **156**
KT3: N Mald 4J **151**
Georgina Gdns. E2 . . . . 1K **9** (3F **85**)
Geraint Rd. BR1: Brom 4J **141**
Geraldine Rd. SW18 . . . . 5A **118**
W4 . . . . 6G **97**
Geraldine St. SE11 . . . . 2K **19** (3B **102**)
Gerald M. SW1 . . . . 3H **17**
Gerald Rd. E16 . . . . 4H **87**
RM8: Dag 2F **73**
SW1 . . . . 3H **17** (4E **100**)
Gerard Av. TW4: Houn 7E **112**
Gerard Gdns. RM13: Rain 2K **91**
Gerard Pl. E9 . . . . 7K **67**
Gerard Rd. HA1: Harr 6A **42**
SW13 . . . . 1B **116**
Gerards Cl. SE16 . . . . 5J **103**
Gerda Rd. SE9 . . . . 2G **143**
Germander Way E15 . . . . 3G **87**
Gernigan Ho. SW18 . . . . 6B **118**
Gernon Rd. E3 . . . . 2A **86**
Geron Way NW2 . . . . 1D **62**
Gerrard Gdns. HA5: Eastc 5J **39**
Gerrard Ho. *SE14* 7J **103**
(off Briant St.)
Gerrard Pl. W1 . . . . 2D **12** (7H **83**)
Gerrard Rd. N1 . . . . 2B **84**
Gerrards Cl. N14 . . . . 5B **22**
Gerrards Ct. W5 . . . . 3D **96**
Gerrard St. W1 . . . . 2D **12** (7H **83**)
Gerridge Ct. *SE1* 1K **19**
(off Gerridge St.)
Gerridge St. SE1 . . . . 1K **19** (3A **102**)
Gerry Raffles Sq. E15 . . . . 7F **69**
Gertrude Rd. DA17: Belv 4G **109**
Gertrude St. SW10 . . . . 7A **16** (6A **100**)
Gervase Cl. HA9: Wemb 3J **61**
Gervase Rd. HA8: Edg 1J **43**
Gervase St. SE15 . . . . 7H **103**
Gervis Ct. TW7: Isle 7G **95**
Ghent St. SE6 . . . . 2C **140**
Ghent Way E8 . . . . 6F **67**
Giant Arches Rd. SE24 . . . . 7C **120**
Giant Tree Hill
WD23: Bushy 1C **26**
Gibbfield Cl. RM6: Chad H 3E **54**
Gibbings Ho. *SE1* 7B **14**
(off King James St.)
Gibbins Rd. E15 . . . . 7E **68**
Gibbon Ho. NW8 . . . . 4B **4**
Gibbon Rd. KT2: King T 1E **150**
SE15 . . . . 2J **121**
W3 . . . . 7A **80**
Gibbons M. NW11 . . . . 5H **45**
Gibbon's Rents SE1 . . . . 5G **15**
Gibbons Rd. NW10 . . . . 6A **62**
Gibbon Wlk. SW15 . . . . 4C **116**
Gibbs Av. SE19 . . . . 5D **138**
Gibbs Cl. SE19 . . . . 6D **138**
Gibbs Grn. HA8: Edg 4D **28**
W14 . . . . 5H **99**
(not continuous)
Gibbs Grn. Cl. W14 . . . . 5H **99**
Gibbs Ho. *BR1: Brom* 1H **159**
(off Longfield)
Gibb's Rd. N18 . . . . 4D **34**
Gibbs Sq. SE19 . . . . 5D **138**
Gibney Ter. BR1: Brom 4H **141**
Gibraltar Wlk. E2 . . . . 2K **9**
Gibson Bus. Cen., The N17 . . . . 7A **34**
Gibson Cl. E1 . . . . 4J **85**
KT9: Chess 5C **162**
N21 . . . . 6F **23**
TW7: Isle 3J **113**
Gibson Gdns. N16 . . . . 2F **67**
Gibson Ho. SM1: Sutt 4J **165**
Gibson M. TW1: Twick 6C **114**
Gibson Rd. RM8: Dag 1C **72**
SE11 . . . . 4H **19** (4K **101**)
SM1: Sutt 5K **165**
UB10: Ick 4B **56**
Gibsons Hill SW16 . . . . 7A **138**
(not continuous)
Gibson Sq. N1 . . . . 1A **84**
Gibson St. SE10 . . . . 5G **105**
Gideon Cl. DA17: Belv 4H **109**
Gideon M. W5 . . . . 2D **96**
Gideon Rd. SW11 . . . . 3E **118**
Gielgud Theatre 2C **12**
(off Shaftesbury Av.)
Giesbach Rd. N19 . . . . 2H **65**
Giffard Rd. N18 . . . . 6K **33**
Giffen Sq. Mkt. *SE8* 7C **104**
(off Giffen St.)
Giffin St. SE8 . . . . 7C **104**
Gifford Gdns. W7 . . . . 5H **77**
Gifford Ho. *SE10* 5F **105**
(off Eastney St.)
SW1 . . . . 6A **18**
(off Churchill Gdns.)
Gifford St. N1 . . . . 7J **65**
Gift La. E15 . . . . 1G **87**
GIGGSHILL 7A **150**
Giggs Hill BR5: St P 2K **161**
Giggshill Gdns. KT7: T Ditt 1A **162**
Giggshill Rd. KT7: T Ditt 7A **150**
Gilbert Bri. *EC2* 5D **8**
(off Gilbert Ho.)
Gilbert Cl. SE18 . . . . 1D **124**
SW19 . . . . 1K **153**
(off High Path)
Gilbert Collection 2H **13**
(off Strand)
Gilbert Ct. *W5* 6F **79**
(off Green Va.)
Gilbert Gro. HA8: Edg 1K **43**
Gilbert Ho. *E2* 3K **85**
(off Usk St.)
E17 . . . . 3D **50**
EC2 . . . . 5D **8**
SE8 . . . . 6C **104**
SW1 . . . . 6K **17**
(off Churchill Gdns.)
SW8 . . . . 7J **101**
(off Wyvil Rd.)
SW13 . . . . 7D **98**
(off Trinity Chu. Rd.)
Gilbert Pl. WC1 . . . . 6E **6** (5J **83**)
Gilbert Rd. BR1: Brom 7J **141**
DA17: Belv 3G **109**
HA5: Pinn 4B **40**
SE11 . . . . 4K **19** (4A **102**)
SW19 . . . . 7A **136**
UB9: Hare 2A **38**
Gilbert Scott SW18 . . . . 6G **117**
Gilbert Sheldon Ho. *W2* 5B **4**
(off Edgware Rd.)
Gilbertson Ho. *E14* 3C **104**
(off Mellish St.)
Gilbert St. E15 . . . . 4G **69**
TW3: Houn 3G **113**
W1 . . . . 1H **11** (6E **82**)
Gilbert Way CR0: Wadd 2K **167**
Gilbey Cl. UB10: Ick 4D **56**
Gilbey Rd. SW17 . . . . 4C **136**
Gilbeys Yd. NW1 . . . . 7E **64**

Gilbourne Rd. SE18 . . . . .6K 107
Gilby Ho. E9 . . . . .6K 67
Gilda Av. EN3: Pond E 5F 25
Gilda Ct. NW7 . . . . .1C 44
Gilda Cres. N16 . . . . .1G 67
Gildea Cl. HA5: H End 1E 40
Gildea St. W1 . . . . .6K 5 (5F 83)
Gilden Cres. NW5 . . . . .5E 64
Gildersome St. SE18 . . . . .6E 106
Gilders Rd. KT9: Chess 7F 163
Giles Coppice SE19 . . . . .4F 139
Giles High St. WC2 . . . . .7D 6 (6H 83)
Giles Ho. SE16 . . . . .7K 15
     W11 . . . . .6J 81
     (off Westbourne Gro.)
Gilesmead SE5 . . . . .1D 120
Gilfrid Cl. UB8: Hil 6D 74
Gilkes Cres. SE21 . . . . .6E 120
Gilkes Pl. SE21 . . . . .6E 120
Gillam Ho. SE16 . . . . .4J 103
     (off Silwood St.)
Gillan Ct. SE12 . . . . .3K 141
Gillan Grn. WD23: Bushy 2B 26
Gillards M. E17 . . . . .4C 50
Gillards Way E17 . . . . .4C 50
Gill Av. E16 . . . . .6J 87
Gillender St. E3 . . . . .4E 86
     E14 .4E 86
Gillespie Rd. N5 . . . . .3A 66
Gillett Av. E6 . . . . .2C 88
GILLETTE CORNER 7A 96
Gillett Ho. N8 . . . . .3J 47
     (off Campsfield Rd.)
Gillett Pl. N16 . . . . .5E 66
Gillett Rd. CR7: Thor H 4D 156
Gillett St. N16 . . . . .5E 66
Gillfoot NW1 . . . . .1A 6
     (off Hampstead Rd.)
Gillham Ter. N17 . . . . .6B 34
Gillian Ho. HA3: Hrw W 6D 26
Gillian Pk. Rd. SM3: Sutt 1H 165
Gillian St. SE13 . . . . .5D 122
Gillies Ho. NW6 . . . . .7B 64
     (off Hilgrove Rd.)
Gillies St. NW5 . . . . .5E 64
Gilling Ct. NW3 . . . . .6C 64
Gillingham M. SW1 . . . . . .3A 18 (4G 101)
Gillingham Rd. NW2 . . . . .3G 63
Gillingham Row SW1 . . . . .3A 18 (4G 101)
Gillingham St. SW1 . . . . . .3A 18 (4G 101)
Gillings Ct. EN5: Barn 4B 20
     (off Wood St.)
Gillison Wlk. SE16 . . . . .3H 103
Gilman Dr. E15 . . . . .1H 87
Gilman Ho. E2 . . . . .2G 85
     (off Pritchard's Rd.)
Gillray Ho. SW10 . . . . .6B 100
     (off Ann La.)
Gill St. E14 . . . . .6B 86
Gillum Cl. EN4: E Barn 1J 31
Gilmore Cl. UB10: Ick 3C 56
Gilmore Ct. N11 . . . . .5J 31
Gilmore Cres. TW15: Ashf 5C 128
Gilmore Rd. SE13 . . . . .4F 123
Gilpin Av. SW14 . . . . .4K 115
Gilpin Cl. CR4: Mitc 2C 154
     W2 . . . . .5A 4
     (off Porteus Rd.)
Gilpin Cres. N18 . . . . .5A 34
     TW2: Whit 7F 113
Gilpin Rd. E5 . . . . .4A 68
Gilpin Way UB3: Harl 7F 93
Gilray Ho. W2 . . . . .2A 10
     (off Gloucester Ter.)
Gilsland Rd. CR7: Thor H 4D 156
Gilstead Ho. IG11: Bark 2B 90
Gilstead Rd. SW6 . . . . .2K 117
Gilston Rd. SW10 . . . . . . .7A 16 (5A 100)
Gilton Rd. SE6 . . . . .3G 141
Giltspur St. EC1 . . . . .7B 8 (6B 84)
Gilwell Cl. E4 . . . . .4J 25
Gilwell La. E4 . . . . .4J 25
     (not continuous)

GILWELL PARK 4K 25
Gilwell Pk. E4 . . . . .3K 25
Ginger Apartments SE1 . . . . .2F 103
     (off Cayenne Ct.)
Ginsburg Yd. NW3 . . . . .4A 64
Gippeswyck Cl. HA5: Pinn 1B 40
Gipsy Hill SE19 . . . . .4E 138
Gipsy La. SW15 . . . . .3D 116
Gipsy Moth IV 6E 104
Gipsy Rd. DA16: Well 7D 108
     SE27 .4C 138
Gipsy Rd. Gdns. SE27 . . . . .4C 138
Giralda Cl. E16 . . . . .5B 88
Giraud St. E14 . . . . .6D 86
Girdler's Rd. W14 . . . . .4F 99
Girdlestone Wlk. N19 . . . . .2G 65
Girdwood Rd. SW18 . . . . .7G 117
Girling Ho. N1 . . . . .1E 84
     (off Colville Est.)
Girling Way TW14: Felt 3J 111
Gironde Rd. SW6 . . . . .7H 99
Girtin Ho. UB5: N'olt 2B 76
     (off Academy Gdns.)
Girton Av. NW9 . . . . .3G 43
Girton Cl. UB5: N'olt 6G 59
Girton Gdns. CR0: Croy 3C 170
Girton Rd. SE26 . . . . .5K 139
     UB5: N'olt 6G 59
Girton Vs. W10 . . . . .6F 81
Gisbourne Cl. SM6: Bedd 3H 167
Gisburn Ho. SE15 . . . . .6G 103
     (off Friary Est.)
Gisburn Rd. N8 . . . . .4K 47
Gissing Wlk. N1 . . . . .7A 66
Gittens Cl. BR1: Brom 4H 141
Given Wilson Wlk. E13 . . . . .2H 87
Glacier Way HA0: Wemb 2D 78
Gladbeck Way EN2: Enf 4G 23
Gladding Rd. E12 . . . . .4B 70
Glade, The BR1: Brom 2B 160
     BR4: W W'ck 3D 170
     CR0: Croy 7A 158
     EN2: Enf 2F 23
     IG5: Ilf 1D 52
     IG8: Wfd G 3E 36
     KT17: Ewe 6C 164
     N12 . . . . .3G 31
     N21 . . . . .6E 22
     SE7 . . . . .7A 106
     SM2: Cheam 7G 165
Glade Cl. KT6: Surb 2D 162
Glade Ct. IG5: Ilf 1D 52
Glade Gdns. CR0: Croy 7A 158
Glade La. UB2: S'hall 2F 95
Glade Rd. E12 . . . . .3D 70
Gladeside CR0: Croy 6K 157
     N21 . . . . .6E 22
Gladeside Cl. KT9: Chess 7D 162
Glades Community School &
     Sports Cen. 5G 49
Gladesmore Rd. N15 . . . . .6F 49
Glades Pl. BR1: Brom 2J 159
Glades Shop. Cen., The
Gladeswood Rd. DA17: Belv 4H 109
Gladiator St. SE23 . . . . .7A 122
Glading Ter. N16 . . . . .3F 67
Gladioli Cl. TW12: Hamp 6E 130
Gladsdale Dr. HA5: Eastc 4J 39
Gladsmuir Rd. EN5: Barn 2B 20
     N19 . . . . .1G 65
Gladstone Av. E12 . . . . .7C 70
     N22 . . . . .2A 48
     TW2: Twick 1H 131
     TW14: Felt 6J 111
Gladstone Ct. SW1 . . . . .4D 18
     (off Regency St.)
Gladstone Ct. Bus. Cen.
     SW8 .1F 119
     (off Pagden St.)
Gladstone Gdns.
     TW3: Houn 1G 113

Gladstone Ho. CR4: Mitc 2D 154
     E14 . . . . .6C 86
     (off E. India Dock Rd.)
Gladstone M. N22 . . . . .2A 48
     NW6 .7H 63
     SE20 .7J 139
Gladstone Pde. NW2 . . . . .2E 62
Gladstone Pk. Gdns. NW2 . . . . .3D 62
Gladstone Pl. E3 . . . . .2B 86
     EN5: Barn 4A 20
     KT8: E Mos 5J 149
Gladstone Rd. BR6: Farnb 5G 173
     CR0: Croy 7D 156
     IG9: Buck H 1F 37
     KT1: King T 3G 151
     KT6: Surb 2D 162
     SW19 . . . . .7J 135
     UB2: S'hall 2C 94
     W4 . . . . .3K 97
Gladstone St. SE1 . . . . .3B 102
Gladstone Ter. SE27 . . . . .5C 138
     (off Bentons La.)
     SW8 .1F 119
Gladstone Way
     HA3: W'stone 3J 41
Gladwell Rd. BR1: Brom 6J 141
     N8 . . . . .6K 47
Gladwin Ho. NW1 . . . . .1B 6
     (off Werrington St.)
Gladwyn Rd. SW15 . . . . .3F 117
Gladys Dimson Ho. E7 . . . . .5H 69
Gladys Rd. NW6 . . . . .7J 63
Glaisher St. SE8 . . . . .6C 104
Glamis Cl. W3 . . . . .2H 97
Glamis Cres. UB3: Harl 3E 92
Glamis Pl. E1 . . . . .7J 85
Glamis Rd. E1 . . . . .7J 85
Glamis Way UB5: N'olt 6G 59
Glamorgan Cl. CR4: Mitc 3J 155
Glamorgan Rd. W7 . . . . .5K 77
     (off Copley Cl.)
Glamorgan Rd. KT1: Ham W 7C 132
Glandford Way RM6: Chad H 5B 54
Glanfield Rd. BR3: Beck 4B 158
Glanleam Rd. HA7: Stan 4J 27
Glanville M. HA7: Stan 5F 27
Glanville Rd. BR2: Brom 3K 159
     SW2 . . . . .5J 119
Glasbrook Av. TW2: Whit 1D 130
Glasbrook Rd. SE9 . . . . .7B 124
Glaserton Rd. N16 . . . . .7E 48
Glasford St. SW17 . . . . .6D 136
Glasfryn Ct. HA2: Harr 2H 59
     (off Roxeth Hill)
Glasfryn Rd. HA2: Harr 2H 59
     (off Roxeth Hill)
Glasgow Ho. W9 . . . . .2K 81
     (off Maida Va.)
Glasgow Rd. E13 . . . . .2K 87
     N18 . . . . .5C 34
Glasgow Ter. SW1 . . . . . . .6A 18 (5G 101)
Glasier Ct. E15 . . . . .7G 69
Glaskin M. E9 . . . . .6A 68
Glass Art Gallery, The 7G 15 (2E 102)
Glasse Cl. W13 . . . . .7A 78
Glasshill St. SE1 . . . . .6B 14 (2B 102)
Glass Ho. WC2 . . . . .1E 12
     (off New Compton St.)
Glass St. E2 . . . . .4H 85
Glasshouse Cl. UB8: Hil 5D 74
Glasshouse Flds. E1 . . . . .7K 85
Glasshouse St. W1 . . . . . . .3B 12 (7G 83)
Glasshouse Wlk. SE11 . . . . .5F 19 (5J 101)
Glasshouse Yd. EC1 . . . . . .4C 8 (4C 84)
Glasslyn Rd. N8 . . . . .5H 47
Glassmill La. BR2: Brom 2H 159
     (not continuous)
Glassworks Studios E2 . . . . .1H 9
     (off Basing Pl.)
Glass Yd. SE18 . . . . .3E 106
Glastonbury Av. IG8: Wfd G 7G 37

Glastonbury Ct. SE14 . . . . .7J 103
     (off Farrow La.)
     W13 . . . . .1A 96
     (off Talbot Rd.)
Glastonbury Ho. SE12 . . . . .5H 123
     (off Wantage Rd.)
     SW1 . . . . .5J 17
     (off Abbots Mnr.)
Glastonbury Pl. E1 . . . . .6J 85
Glastonbury Rd. N9 . . . . .1B 34
     SM4: Mord 7J 153
Glastonbury St. NW6 . . . . .5H 63
Glaston Ct. W5 . . . . .1D 96
     (off Grange Rd.)
Glaucus St. E3 . . . . .5D 86
Glazbury Rd. W14 . . . . .4G 99
Glazebrook Cl. SE21 . . . . .2D 138
Glazebrook Rd. TW11: Tedd 7K 131
Glebe, The BR7: Chst 1G 161
     KT4: Wor Pk 1B 164
     SE3 . . . . .3G 123
     SW16 . . . . .4H 137
     UB7: W Dray 4B 92
Glebe Av. CR4: Mitc 2C 154
     EN2: Enf 3G 23
     HA3: Kent 4E 42
     HA4: Ruis 6K 57
     IG8: Wfd G 6D 36
     UB10: Ick 3E 56
Glebe Cl. UB10: Ick 4E 56
     W4 . . . . .5A 98
Glebe Cotts. TW13: Hanw 3E 130
     (off Twickenham Rd.)
Glebe Ct. CR4: Mitc 3D 154
     HA7: Stan 5H 27
     N13 . . . . .3F 33
     SE3 . . . . .3G 123
     W5 . . . . .1D 96
     W7 . . . . .7H 77
Glebe Cres. HA3: Kent 3E 42
     NW4 .4E 44
Glebe Gdns. KT3: N Mald 7A 152
Glebe Ho. SE16 . . . . .3H 103
     (off Slippers Pl.)
Glebe Ho. Dr. BR2: Hayes 1K 171
Glebe Hyrst SE19 . . . . .4E 138
Glebe Knoll BR2: Brom 2H 159
Glebeland Gdns. TW17: Shep 6E 146
Glebelands E10 . . . . .2D 68
     KT8: W Mole 5F 149
Glebelands Av. E18 . . . . .2J 51
     IG2: Ilf 7H 53
Glebelands Cl. SE5 . . . . .3E 120
Glebelands Local Nature Reserve . . .6J 31
Glebelands Rd. TW14: Felt 1J 129
Glebe La. HA3: Kent 4E 42
Glebe Path CR4: Mitc 3D 154
Glebe Pl. SW3 . . . . .7C 16 (6C 100)
Glebe Rd. BR1: Brom 1J 159
     E8 . . . . .7F 67
     HA7: Stan 5H 27
     N3 . . . . .1A 46
     N8 . . . . .4K 47
     NW10 . . . . .6C 62
     RM10: Dag 6H 73
     SM2: Cheam 7G 165
     SM5: Cars 6D 166
     SW13 . . . . .2C 116
     UB3: Hayes 1H 93
Glebe Side TW1: Twick 6K 113
Glebe Sq. CR4: Mitc 3D 154
Glebe St. W4 . . . . .5A 98
Glebe Ter. W4 . . . . .3D 86
     W4 . . . . .5A 98
Glebe Way BR4: W W'ck 2E 170
     IG8: Wfd G 5F 37
     TW13: Hanw 3E 130
Gledhow Gdns. SW5 . . . . .4A 100
Gledstanes Rd. W14 . . . . .5G 99
Gledwood Av. UB4: Hayes 5H 75
Gledwood Cres. UB4: Hayes 5H 75
Gledwood Dr. UB4: Hayes 5H 75
Gledwood Gdns. UB4: Hayes 5H 75

Gleed Av.—Glyndon Rd.

Gleed Av. WD23: Bushy 2C **26**
Gleeson Dr. BR6: Chels 5K **173**
Glegg Pl. SW15 4F **117**
Glen, The BR2: Brom 2G **159**
BR6: Farnb 3D **172**
CR0: Croy 3K **169**
EN2: Enf 4G **23**
HA5: Eastc 5K **39**
HA5: Pinn 7C **40**
HA9: Wemb 4E **60**
UB2: S'hall 5D **94**
Glenaffric Av. E14 4E **104**
Glen Albyn Rd. SW19 2F **135**
Glenallan Ho. *W14* *4H **99***
(off North End Cres.)
Glenalla Rd. HA4: Ruis 7H **39**
Glenalmond Ho. TW15: Ashf 3A **128**
Glenalmond Rd. HA3: Kent 4E **42**
Glenalvon Way SE18 4C **106**
Glena Mt. SM1: Sutt 4A **166**
Glenarm Rd. E5 4J **67**
Glen Av. TW15: Ashf 4C **128**
Glenavon Cl. KT10: Clay 6A **162**
Glenavon Ct. KT4: Wor Pk 2D **164**
Glenavon Lodge BR3: Beck 7C **140**
Glenavon Rd. E15 7G **69**
Glenbarr Cl. SE9 3F **125**
Glenbow Rd. BR1: Brom 6G **141**
Glenbrook Nth. EN2: Enf 4E **22**
Glenbrook Rd. NW6 5J **63**
Glenbrook Sth. EN2: Enf 4E **22**
Glenbuck Ct. KT6: Surb 6E **150**
Glenbuck Rd. KT6: Surb 6D **150**
Glenburnie Rd. SW17 3D **136**
Glencairn Dr. W5 4C **78**
Glencairne Cl. E16 5B **88**
Glencairn Rd. SW16 1J **155**
Glencar Ct. SE19 6B **138**
Glen Cl. TW17: Shep 4C **146**
Glencoe Av. IG2: Ilf 7H **53**
Glencoe Dr. RM10: Dag 4G **73**
Glencoe Mans. *SW9* *7A **102***
(off Mowll St.)
Glencoe Rd. UB4: Yead 5B **76**
Glen Ct. DA15: Sidc 4A **144**
Glen Cres. IG8: Wfd G 6E **36**
Glendale Av. HA8: Edg 4A **28**
N22 7F **33**
RM6: Chad H 7C **54**
Glendale Cl. SE9 3E **124**
Glendale Dr. SW19 5H **135**
Glendale Gdns. HA9: Wemb 1D **60**
Glendale M. BR3: Beck 1D **158**
Glendale Rd. DA8: Erith 4J **109**
Glendale Way SE28 7C **90**
Glendall St. SW9 4K **119**
Glendarvon St. SW15 3F **117**
Glendevon Cl. HA8: Edg 3C **28**
Glendish Rd. N17 1H **49**
Glendor Gdns. NW7 4E **28**
Glendower Gdns. SW14 3K **115**
Glendower Pl. SW7 3A **16** (4B **100**)
Glendower Rd. E4 1A **36**
SW14 3K **115**
Glendown Ho. E8 5G **67**
Glendown Rd. SE2 5A **108**
Glendun Ct. W3 7A **80**
Glendun Rd. W3 7A **80**
Gleneagle M. SW16 5H **137**
Gleneagle Rd. SW16 5H **137**
Gleneagles HA7: Stan 7G **27**
W13 *5B **78***
(off Malvern Way)
Gleneagles Cl. BR6: Orp 1H **173**
SE16 5H **103**
Gleneagles Grn. BR6: Orp 1H **173**
Gleneagles Twr. *UB1: S'hall* *6G **77***
(off Fleming Rd.)
Gleneldon M. SW16 4J **137**
Gleneldon Rd. SW16 4J **137**
Glenelg Rd. SW2 5J **119**
Glenesk Rd. SE9 3E **124**
Glenfarg Rd. SE6 1E **140**
Glenfield Cres. HA4: Ruis 7F **39**
Glenfield Rd. SW12 1G **137**
TW15: Ashf 6D **128**
W13 2B **96**
Glenfield Ter. W13 2B **96**
Glenfinlas Way SE5 7B **102**
Glenforth St. SE10 5H **105**
Glengall Gro. E14 3D **104**
Glengall Pas. *NW6* *1J **81***
(off Priory Pk. Rd.)
Glengall Rd. DA7: Bex 3E **126**
HA8: Edg 3C **28**
IG8: Wfd G 6D **36**
NW6 1H **81**
SE15 5F **103**
Glengall Ter. SE15 6F **103**
Glen Gdns. CR0: Wadd 3A **168**
Glengarnock Av. E14 4E **104**
Glengarry Rd. SE22 5E **120**
Glenham Dr. IG2: Ilf 5F **53**
Glenhead Cl. SE9 3F **125**
Glenhill Cl. N3 2J **45**
Glen Ho. *E16* *1E **106***
(off Storey St.)
Glenhouse Rd. SE9 5E **124**
Glenhurst BR3: Beck 1E **158**
Glenhurst Av. DA5: Bexl 1F **145**
HA4: Ruis 7E **38**
NW5 4E **64**
Glenhurst Ct. SE19 5F **139**
Glenhurst Ri. SE19 7C **138**
Glenhurst Rd. N12 5G **31**
TW8: Bford 6C **96**
Glenilla Rd. NW3 6C **64**
Glenister Ho. *UB3: Hayes* *1K **93***
(off Avondale Dr.)
Glenister Pk. Rd. SW16 7H **137**
Glenister Rd. SE10 5H **105**
Glenister St. E16 1E **106**
Glenkerry Ho. *E14* *6E **86***
(off Burcham St.)
Glenlea Rd. SE9 5D **124**
Glenloch Rd. EN3: Enf H 2D **24**
NW3 6C **64**
Glenluce Rd. SE3 6J **105**
Glenlyon Rd. SE9 5E **124**
Glenmead IG9: Buck H 1F **37**
Glenmere Av. NW7 7H **29**
Glen M. E17 5B **50**
Glenmill TW12: Hamp 5D **130**
Glenmore Lawns W13 6A **78**
Glenmore Lodge BR3: Beck 1D **158**
Glenmore Pde. HA0: Wemb 1E **78**
Glenmore Rd. DA16: Well 7K **107**
NW3 6C **64**
Glenmore Way IG11: Bark 2A **90**
Glenmount Path SE18 5G **107**
Glennie Ct. SE22 1G **139**
Glennie Ho. *SE10* *1E **122***
(off Blackheath Hill)
Glennie Rd. SE27 3A **138**
Glenny Rd. IG11: Bark 6G **71**
Glenorchy Cl. UB4: Yead 5C **76**
Glenpark Ct. W13 7A **78**
Glenparke Rd. E7 6K **69**
(not continuous)
Glenridding *NW1* *1B **6***
(off Ampthill Est.)
Glen Ri. IG8: Wfd G 6E **36**
Glen Rd. E13 4A **88**
E17 5B **50**
KT9: Chess 4F **163**
Glen Rd. End SM6: Wall 7F **167**
Glenrosa St. SW6 2A **118**
Glenrose Ct. DA14: Sidc 5B **144**
SE1 *7G **15***
(off Long La.)
Glenroy St. W12 6E **80**
Glensdale Rd. SE4 3B **122**
Glenshaw Mans. *SW9* *7A **102***
(off Brixton Rd.)
Glenshiel Rd. SE9 5E **124**
Glentanner Way SW17 3B **136**
Glen Ter. *E14* *2E **104***
(off Manchester Rd.)
Glentham Gdns. SW13 6D **98**
Glentham Rd. SW13 6C **98**
Glenthorne Av. CR0: Croy 1H **169**
Glenthorne Cl. SM3: Sutt 1J **165**
UB10: Hil 3C **74**
Glenthorne Gdns. IG6: Ilf 3E **52**
SM3: Sutt 1J **165**
Glenthorne M. W6 4D **98**
Glenthorne Rd. E17 5A **50**
KT1: King T 4F **151**
N11 5J **31**
W6 4D **98**
Glenthorpe Av. SW15 4C **116**
Glenthorpe Rd. SM4: Mord 5F **153**
Glenton Rd. SE13 4G **123**
Glentrammon Av. BR6: Chels 6K **173**
Glentrammon Cl. BR6: Chels 5K **173**
Glentrammon Gdns. BR6: Chels 6K **173**
Glentrammon Rd. BR6: Chels 6K **173**
Glentworth St. NW1 4F **5** (4D **82**)
Glenure Rd. SE9 5E **124**
Glenvern Ct. *TW7: Isle* *2A **114***
(off White Lodge Cl.)
Glenview SE2 6D **108**
Glenview Rd. BR1: Brom 2B **160**
Glenville Av. EN2: Enf 1H **23**
Glenville Gro. SE8 7B **104**
Glenville M. SW18 7K **117**
Glenville M. Ind. Est. SW18 7J **117**
Glenville Rd. KT2: King T 1G **151**
Glen Wlk. TW7: Isle 5H **113**
(not continuous)
Glenwood Av. NW9 1A **62**
Glenwood Cl. HA1: Harr 5K **41**
Glenwood Ct. DA14: Sidc 4A **144**
E18 3J **51**
Glenwood Gdns. IG2: Ilf 5E **52**
Glenwood Gro. NW9 1J **61**
Glenwood Rd. KT17: Ewe 6C **164**
N15 5B **48**
NW7 3F **29**
SE6 1B **140**
TW3: Houn 3H **113**
Glenwood Way CR0: Croy 6K **157**
Glenworth Av. E14 4F **105**
Gliddon Dr. E5 4G **67**
Gliddon Rd. W14 4G **99**
Glimpsing Grn. DA18: Erith 3E **108**
Glisson Rd. UB10: Hil 2C **74**
Global App. E3 2D **86**
Globe, The SE1 7E **14** (2C **102**)
Globe Pond Rd. SE16 1A **104**
Globe Rd. E1 3J **85**
E2 3J **85**
E15 5H **69**
IG8: Wfd G 6F **37**
Globe Rope Wlk. *E14* *4D **104***
(off E. Ferry Rd.)
Globe St. SE1 7E **14** (3D **102**)
Globe Ter. E2 3J **85**
GLOBE TOWN 3K **85**
Globe Town Mkt. E2 3K **85**
Globe Wharf SE16 7K **85**
Globe Yd. W1 1J **11**
Glossop Rd. CR2: Sand 7D **168**
Gloster Rd. KT3: N Mald 4A **152**
Gloucester *W14* *4H **99***
(off Mornington Av.)
Gloucester Arc. SW7 4A **100**
Gloucester Av. DA15: Sidc 2J **143**
DA16: Well 4K **125**
NW1 7E **64**
Gloucester Cir. SE10 7E **104**
Gloucester Cl. KT7: T Ditt 1A **162**
NW10 7K **61**
Gloucester Ct. CR4: Mitc 5J **155**
EC3 3H **15** (7E **84**)
HA1: Harr 3J **41**
NW11 *7H **45***
(off Golders Grn. Rd.)
SE22 1G **139**
Gloucester Ct. TW9: Kew 7G **97**
W7 *5K **77***
(off Copley Cl.)
Gloucester Cres. NW1 1F **83**
TW18: Staines 6A **128**
Gloucester Dr. N4 2B **66**
NW11 4J **45**
Gloucester Gdns. EN4: Cockf 4K **21**
IG1: Ilf 7C **52**
NW11 7H **45**
SM1: Sutt 2K **165**
W2 6A **82**
Gloucester Ga. NW1 2F **83**
(not continuous)
Gloucester Ga. M. NW1 2F **83**
Gloucester Gro. HA8: Edg 1K **43**
Gloucester Ho. *E16* *1J **105***
(off Gatcombe Rd.)
NW6 *2J **81***
(off Cambridge Rd.)
SW9 7A **102**
TW10: Rich 5G **115**
Gloucester M. E10 7C **50**
W2 1A **10** (6A **82**)
Gloucester M. W. W2 6A **82**
Gloucester Pde. DA15: Sidc 5A **126**
UB3: Harl 3E **92**
Gloucester Pk. Apartments SW7 4A **100**
Gloucester Pl. NW1 4E **4** (4D **82**)
W1 4E **4** (4D **82**)
Gloucester Pl. M. W1 6F **5** (5D **82**)
Gloucester Rd. CR0: Croy 1D **168**
DA17: Belv 5F **109**
E10 7C **50**
E11 5K **51**
E12 3D **70**
E17 2K **49**
EN2: Enf 1H **23**
EN5: New Bar 5E **20**
HA1: Harr 5F **41**
KT1: King T 2G **151**
N17 2D **48**
N18 5A **34**
SW7 4A **16** (3A **100**)
TW2: Twick 1G **131**
TW4: Houn 4C **112**
TW9: Kew 7G **97**
TW11: Tedd 5J **131**
TW12: Hamp 7F **131**
TW13: Felt 1A **130**
W3 2J **97**
W5 2C **96**
Gloucester Sq. E2 1G **85**
W2 1B **10** (6B **82**)
Gloucester St. SW1 6A **18** (5G **101**)
Gloucester Ter. *N14* *1C **32***
(off Crown La.)
W2 1A **10** (6K **81**)
Gloucester Wlk. W8 2J **99**
Gloucester Way EC1 2K **7** (3A **84**)
Glover Cl. SE2 4C **108**
Glover Dr. N18 6D **34**
Glover Ho. *NW6* *7A **64***
(off Harben Rd.)
SE15 4H **121**
Glover Rd. HA5: Pinn 6B **40**
Glovers Gro. HA4: Ruis 7D **38**
Gloxinia Wlk. TW12: Hamp 6E **130**
Glycena Rd. SW11 3D **118**
Glyn Av. EN4: E Barn 4G **21**
Glyn Cl. SE25 2E **156**
Glyn Ct. HA7: Stan 6G **27**
SW16 3A **138**
Glyndale Grange SM2: Sutt 6K **165**
Glyndebourne Ct. *UB5: Yead* *3A **76***
(off Canberra Dr.)
Glyndebourne Pk. BR6: Farnb 2F **173**
Glynde M. SW3 2D **16**
Glynde Reach WC1 2F **7**
Glynde Rd. DA7: Bex 3D **126**
Glynde St. SE4 6B **122**
Glyndon Rd. SE18 4G **107**
(not continuous)

Glyn Dr. DA14: Sidc 4B 144
Glynfield Rd. NW10 7A 62
Glynne Rd. N22 2A 48
Glyn Rd. E5 3K 67
EN3: Pond E 4D 24
KT4: Wor Pk 2F 165
Glyn St. SE11 6G 19 (5K 101)
Glynswood Pl. HA6: Nwood 1D 38
Glynwood Ct. SE23 2J 139
Goals Football Training Cen. 3F 127
Goater's All. SW6 7H 99
(off Dawes Rd.)
Goat Ho. Bri. SE25 3G 157
Goat La. EN1: Enf 1A 24
Goat Rd. CR4: Cars, Mitc 7D 154
Goat Wharf TW8: Bford 6E 96
Gobions Av. RM5: Col R 1K 55
Godalming Av. SM6: Wall 5J 167
Godalming Rd. E14 5D 86
Godbold Rd. E15 4G 87
Goddard Cl. TW17: Shep 3B 146
Goddard Ct. HA3: Kent 2A 42
Goddard Pl. N19 3G 65
Goddard Rd. BR3: Beck 4K 157
Goddards Way IG1: Ilf 1H 71
Goddarts Ho. E17 3C 50
Goddington La. BR6: Chels 3K 173
Godfree Ct. SE1 6E 14
(off Long La.)
Godfrey Av. TW2: Whit 7H 113
UB5: N'olt 1C 76
Godfrey Hill SE18 4C 106
Godfrey Ho. EC1 2E 8
Godfrey Rd. SE18 4D 106
Godfrey St. E15 2E 86
SW3 5D 16 (5C 100)
Godfrey Way TW4: Houn 7C 112
Goding St. SE11 5F 19 (5J 101)
Godley Cl. SE14 1J 121
Godley Rd. SW18 1B 136
Godliman St. EC4 1B 14 (6B 84)
Godman Rd. SE15 2H 121
Godolphin Cl. N13 6G 33
Godolphin Ho. NW3 7C 64
(off Fellows Rd.)
Godolphin Pl. W3 7K 79
Godolphin Rd. W12 1D 98
(not continuous)
Godric Cres. CR0: New Ad 7F 171
Godson Rd. CR0: Wadd 3A 168
Godstone Ho. SE1 7F 15
(off Pardoner St.)
Godstone Rd. SM1: Sutt 4A 166
TW1: Twick 6B 114
Godstow Rd. SE2 2B 108
Godwin Cl. E4 1K 25
KT19: Ewe 6J 163
N1 2C 84
Godwin Ct. NW1 2G 83
(off Chalton St.)
Godwin Ho. E2 2F 85
(off Thurtle Rd.)
NW6 2K 81
(off Tollgate Gdns., not continuous)
Godwin Rd. BR2: Brom 3A 160
E7 4K 69
Goffers Rd. SE3 1G 123
Goffs Rd. TW15: Ashf 6F 129
Goidel Cl. SM6: Bedd 4H 167
Golborne Gdns. W10 4G 81
Golborne Ho. W10 4G 81
(off Adair Rd.)
Golborne M. W10 5G 81
Golborne Rd. W10 5G 81
Golda Cl. EN5: Barn 6A 20
Golda Ct. N3 2H 45
Goldbeaters Gro. HA8: Edg 6F 29
Goldbeaters Ho. W1 1D 12
(off Manette St.)
Goldcliff Cl. SM4: Mord 7J 153
Goldcrest Cl. E16 5B 88
SE28 7C 90
Goldcrest M. W5 5D 78
Goldcrest Way CR0: New Ad 7F 171
WD23: Bush 1B 26
Golden Ct. EN4: E Barn 4H 21
TW7: Isle 2H 113
TW9: Rich 5D 114
Golden Cres. UB3: Hayes 1H 93
Golden Cross M. W11 6H 81
(off Portobello Rd.)
Golden Hinde 4E 14 (1D 102)
Golden Hind Pl. SE8 4B 104
(off Grove St.)
Golden La. EC1 3C 8 (4C 84)
Golden La. Est. EC1 4C 8 (4C 84)
Golden Lane Leisure Cen. 4C 8
Golden Mnr. W7 7J 77
Golden M. SE20 1J 157
Golden Pde. E17 3E 50
(off Wood St.)
Golden Plover Cl. E16 6J 87
Golden Sq. W1 2B 12 (7G 83)
Golden Yd. NW3 4A 64
(off Holly Mt.)
Golders Cl. HA8: Edg 5C 28
Golders Ct. NW11 7H 45
Golders Gdns. NW11 7G 45
GOLDERS GREEN 6G 45
Golders Grn. Crematorium NW11 7J 45
Golders Grn. Cres. NW11 7H 45
Golders Grn. Rd. NW11 6G 45
Goldersiea NW11 1J 63
Golders Mnr. Dr. NW11 6F 45
Golders Pk. Cl. NW11 1J 63
Golders Ri. NW4 5F 45
Golders Way NW11 7H 45
Golderton NW4 4D 44
(off Prince of Wales Cl.)
Goldfinch Rd. SE28 3H 107
Goldhawk Ind. Est. W6 3D 98
Goldhawk M. W12 2D 98
Goldhawk Rd. W6 4B 98
W12 4B 98
Goldhaze Cl. IG8: Wfd G 7F 37
Gold Hill HA8: Edg 6E 28
Goldhurst Ter. NW6 7K 63
Goldie Ho. N19 7H 47
Goldie Leigh Hospital SE2 7B 108
Golding Cl. KT9: Chess 6C 162
Golding Ct. IG1: Ilf 3E 70
Golding St. E1 6G 85
Golding Ter. E1 6G 85
SW11 2E 118
Goldington Bldgs. NW1 1H 83
(off Royal College St.)
Goldington Cres. NW1 2H 83
Goldington St. NW1 2H 83
Gold La. HA8: Edg 6E 28
Goldman Cl. E2 3K 9 (4G 85)
Goldmark Ho. SE3 3K 123
Goldney Rd. W9 4J 81
Goldrill Dr. N11 2K 31
Goldsboro' Rd. SW8 1H 119
Goldsborough Cres. E4 2J 35
Goldsborough Ho. E14 5D 104
(off St Davids Sq.)
Goldsdown Cl. EN3: Enf H 2F 25
Goldsdown Rd. EN3: Enf H 2E 24
Goldsmid St. SE18 5J 107
Goldsmith Av. E12 6C 70
NW9 5A 44
RM7: Rush G 7G 55
W3 7K 79
Goldsmith Cl. HA2: Harr 1E 58
Goldsmith Ct. WC2 7F 7
(off Stukeley St.)
Goldsmith La. NW9 4H 43
Goldsmith Rd. E10 1C 68
E17 2K 49
N11 5J 31
SE15 1G 121
W3 1K 97
Goldsmith's Bldgs. W3 1K 97
Goldsmiths Cl. W3 1K 97
Goldsmiths College 1A 122
Goldsmith's Pl. NW6 1K 81
(off Springfield La.)
Goldsmith's Row E2 2G 85
Goldsmith's Sq. E2 2G 85
Goldsmith St. EC2 7D 8 (6C 84)
Goldsworthy Gdns. SE16 5J 103
Goldthorpe NW1 1G 83
(off Camden St.)
Goldwell Ho. SE22 3E 120
Goldwell Rd. CR7: Thor H 4K 155
Goldwin Cl. SE14 1J 121
Goldwing Cl. E16 6J 87
Golf Cl. CR7: Thor H 1A 156
HA7: Stan 7H 27
Golf Club Dr. KT2: King T 7K 133
Golfe Rd. IG1: Ilf 3H 71
Golf Rd. BR1: Brom 3E 160
W5 6F 79
Golf Side TW2: Twick 3H 131
Golfside Cl. KT3: N Mald 2A 152
N20 3H 31
Gollogly Ter. SE7 5A 106
Gomer Gdns. TW11: Tedd 6A 132
Gomer Pl. TW11: Tedd 6A 132
Gomm Rd. SE16 3J 103
Gomshall Av. SM6: Wall 5J 167
Gondar Gdns. NW6 5H 63
Gonson St. SE8 6D 104
Gonston Cl. SW19 2G 135
Gonville Cres. UB5: N'olt 6F 59
Gonville Rd. CR7: Thor H 5K 155
Gonville St. SW6 3G 117
Gooch Ho. E5 3H 67
EC1 5J 7
(off Portpool La.)
Goodall Ho. SE4 4K 121
Goodall Rd. E11 3E 68
Gooden Ct. HA1: Harr 3J 59
Goodenough Rd. SW19 7H 135
Goodey Rd. IG11: Bark 7K 71
Goodfaith Ho. E14 7D 86
(off Simpson's Rd.)
Goodge Pl. W1 6B 6 (5G 83)
Goodge St. W1 6B 6 (5G 83)
Goodhall Cl. HA7: Stan 6F 27
Goodhall St. NW10 3B 80
(not continuous)
Goodhart Pl. E14 7A 86
Goodhart Way
BR4: W W'ck 7G 159
Goodhew Rd. CR0: Croy 6G 157
Goodhope Ho. E14 7D 86
(off Poplar High St.)
Gooding Cl.
KT3: N Mald 4J 151
Goodinge Cl. N7 6J 65
Gooding Ho. SE7 5A 106
Goodman Cres. SW2 2J 137
Goodman Rd. E10 7E 50
Goodmans Ct. E1 2J 15 (7F 85)
HA0: Wemb 4D 60
Goodman's Stile E1 6G 85
Goodmans Yd. E1 2J 15 (7F 85)
GOODMAYES 2A 72
Goodmayes Av. IG3: Ilf 1A 72
Goodmayes La. IG3: Ilf 4A 72
Goodmayes Retail Pk.
RM6: Chad H 1B 72
Goodmayes Rd. IG3: Ilf 1A 72
Goodrich Ct. W10 6F 81
Goodrich Ho. E2 2J 85
(off Sewardstone Rd.)
Goodrich Rd. SE22 6F 121
Goodson Rd. NW10 7A 62
Goodson St. N1 2A 84
Goodspeed Ho. E14 7D 86
(off Simpson's Rd.)
Goods Way NW1 2J 83
Goodway Gdns. E14 6F 87
Goodwill Ho. E14 7D 86
(off Simpson's Rd.)
Goodwin Cl. CR4: Mitc 3B 154
SE16 3F 103
Goodwin Ct. EN4: E Barn 6H 21
N8 3J 47
(off Campsbourne Rd.)
SW19 7C 136
Goodwin Dr. DA14: Sidc 3D 144
Goodwin Gdns. CR0: Wadd 6B 168
Goodwin Ho. N9 1D 34
Goodwin Rd. CR0: Wadd 5B 168
N9 1E 34
W12 2C 98
Goodwins Ct. WC2 2E 12 (7J 83)
Goodwin St. N4 2A 66
Goodwood Cl. HA7: Stan 5H 27
SM4: Mord 4J 153
Goodwood Ct. W1 5K 5
(off Devonshire St.)
Goodwood Dr. UB5: N'olt 6E 58
Goodwood Pde. BR3: Beck 4A 158
Goodwood Rd. SE14 7A 104
Goodwyn Av. NW7 5F 29
Goodwyns Va. N10 1E 46
Goodyear Ho. N2 2B 46
(off The Grange)
Goodyear Pl. SE5 6C 102
Goodyer Ho. SW1 5C 18
(off Tachbrook St.)
Goodyers Gdns. NW4 5F 45
Goosander Way SE28 3H 107
Gooseacre La. HA3: Kent 5D 42
Goose Grn. Trad. Est. SE22 4F 121
Gooseley La. E6 4F 89
(Claps Ga. La.)
E6 3E 88
(Vicarage La.)
Gooseus Cl. SM1: Sutt 5A 166
Goose Sq. E6 6D 88
Gophir La. EC4 2E 14 (7D 84)
Gopsall St. N1 1D 84
Gordon Av. E4 6B 36
HA7: Stan 7E 26
SW14 4A 116
TW1: Twick 5A 114
Gordonbrock Rd. SE4 5C 122
Gordon Cl. E17 6C 50
N19 1G 65
Gordon Ct. HA8: Edg 5A 28
W12 6E 80
Gordon Cres. CR0: Croy 1E 168
UB3: Hayes 4J 93
Gordondale Rd. SW19 2J 135
Gordon Dr. TW17: Shep 7F 147
Gordon Gdns. HA8: Edg 2H 43
Gordon Gro. SE5 2B 120
Gordon Hill EN2: Enf 1H 23
Gordon Ho. E1 7J 85
(off Glamis Rd.)
SE10 7D 104
(off Tarves Way)
SW1 2B 18
(off Greencoat Pl.)
W5 3E 78
Gordon Ho. Rd. NW5 4E 64
Gordon Mans. W14 3F 99
(off Addison Gdns.)
WC1 4C 6
(off Torrington Pl.)
Gordon Pl. W8 2J 99
Gordon Rd. BR3: Beck 3B 158
DA15: Sidc 5J 125
DA17: Belv 4J 109
E4 1B 36
E11 6J 51
E15 4E 68
E18 1K 51
EN2: Enf 1H 23
HA3: W'stone 3J 41
IG1: Ilf 3H 71
IG11: Bark 1J 89
KT2: King T 1F 151
KT5: Surb 7F 151
N3 7C 30
N9 2C 34
N11 7C 32

Gordon Rd.—Grange Cres.

Gordon Rd. RM6: Chad H 6F 55
SE15 2H 121
SM5: Cars 6D 166
TW3: Houn 4G 113
TW9: Rich 2F 115
TW15: Ashf 3A 128
TW17: Shep 6F 147
UB2: S'hall 4C 94
UB7: Yiew 7A 74
W4 6H 97
W5 7B 78
W13 7B 78
Gordon Sq. WC1 3C 6 (4H 83)
Gordon St. E13 3J 87
WC1 3C 6 (4H 83)
Gordon Way BR1: Brom 1J 159
EN5: Barn 4C 20
Gore Ct. NW9 5G 43
Gorefield Ho. *NW6* *2J 81*
(off Gorefield Pl.)
Gorefield Pl. NW6 2J 81
Gore Rd. E9 1J 85
SW20 2E 152
GORESBROOK INTERCHANGE 2F 91
Goresbrook Leisure Cen. 1D 90
Goresbrook Rd. RM9: Dag 1B 90
Gore St. SW7 3A 100
Gorham Ho. *SE16* *2K 103*
(off Wolfe Cres.)
Gorham Pl. W11 7G 81
Goring Cl. RM5: Col R 1J 55
Goring Gdns. RM8: Dag 4C 72
Goring Rd. N11 6D 32
RM10: Dag 6K 73
Goring St. EC3 7H 9
Goring Way UB6: G'frd 2G 77
Gorleston Rd. N15 5D 48
Gorleston St. W14 4G 99
(not continuous)
Gorman Rd. SE18 4D 106
Gorringe Pk. Av. CR4: Mitc 7D 136
Gorse Cl. E16 6J 87
Gorsefield Ho. *E14* *7C 86*
(off E. India Dock Rd.)
Gorse Ri. SW17 5E 136
Gorse Rd. CR0: Croy 4C 170
Gorse Wlk. UB7: Yiew 6A 74
Gorseway RM7: Rush G 1K 73
Gorst Rd. NW10 4J 79
SW11 6D 118
Gorsuch Pl. E2 1J 9 (3F 85)
Gorsuch St. E2 1J 9 (2F 85)
Gosberton Rd. SW12 1D 136
Gosbury Hill KT9: Chess 4E 162
Gosfield Rd. RM8: Dag 2G 73
Gosfield St. W1 6A 6 (5G 83)
Gosford Gdns. IG4: Ilf 5D 52
Goshawk Gdns. UB4: Hayes 3G 75
Goslett Yd. WC2 1D 12 (6H 83)
Gosling Cl. UB6: G'frd 3E 76
Gosling Ho. *E1* *7J 85*
(off Sutton St.)
Gosling Way SW9 1A 120
Gospatrick Rd. N17 7H 33
GOSPEL OAK 4E 64
Gosport Rd. E17 5B 50
Gosport Wlk. N17 4H 49
Gossage Rd. SE18 5H 107
UB10: Uxb 7B 56
Gosset St. E2 1K 9 (3F 85)
Gosshill Rd. BR7: Chst 2E 160
Gossington Cl. BR7: Chst 4F 143
Gosterwood St. SE8 6A 104
Gostling Rd. TW2: Whit 1E 130
Goston Gdns. CR7: Thor H 3A 156
Goswell Pl. EC1 2B 8
Goswell Rd. EC1 1A 8 (2B 84)
Gothic Cotts. *EN2: Enf* *2H 23*
(off Chase Grn. Av.)
Gothic Ct. *SE5* *7C 102*
(off Wyndham Rd.)
UB3: Harl 6F 93
Gothic Rd. TW2: Twick 2H 131

Gottfried M. NW5 4G 65
Goudhurst Rd. BR1: Brom 5G 141
Gough Ho. *KT1: King T* *2E 150*
(off Eden St.)
N1 *1B 84*
(off Windsor St.)
Gough Rd. E15 4H 69
EN1: Enf 2C 24
Gough Sq. EC4 1K 13 (6A 84)
Gough St. WC1 3H 7 (4K 83)
Gough Wlk. E14 6C 86
Goulden Ho. SW11 2C 118
Goulden Ho. App. SW11 2C 118
Goulding Gdns. CR7: Thor H 2B 156
Gouldman Ho. *E1* *4J 85*
(off Wyllen Cl.)
Gould Rd. TW2: Twick 1J 131
TW14: Felt 7G 111
GOULDS GREEN 6D 74
Gould's Grn. UB8: Hil 7D 74
Gould Ter. E8 5H 67
Goulston St. E1 7J 9 (6F 85)
Goulton Rd. E5 4H 67
Gourley Pl. N15 5E 48
Gourley St. N15 5E 48
Gourock Rd. SE9 5E 124
Govan St. E2 1G 85
Gover Ct. SW4 2J 119
Govett Av. TW17: Shep 5E 146
Govier Cl. E15 7G 69
Gowan Av. SW6 1G 117
Gowan Ho. *E2* *2K 9*
(off Chambord St.)
Gowan Rd. NW10 6D 62
Gower Cl. SW4 6G 119
Gower Ct. WC1 3C 6 (4H 83)
Gower Ho. E17 3D 50
SE17 *5C 102*
(off Morecambe St.)
Gower M. WC1 6D 6 (5H 83)
Gower M. Mans. *WC1* *5D 6*
(off Gower M.)
Gower Pl. WC1 3B 6 (4H 83)
Gower Rd. E7 6J 69
TW7: Isle 6K 95
Gower St. WC1 3B 6 (4G 83)
Gower's Wlk. E1 6G 85
Gowland Pl. BR3: Beck 2B 158
Gowlett Rd. SE15 3G 121
Gowlland Cl. CR0: Croy 7G 157
Gowrie Rd. SW11 3E 118
Graburn Way KT8: E Mos 3H 149
Grace Av. DA7: Bex 2F 127
Grace Bus. Cen. CR4: Mitc 6D 154
Gracechurch St. EC3 2F 15 (7D 84)
Grace Cl. HA8: Edg 7D 28
SE9 3B 142
Grace Ct. *CR0: Croy* *3B 168*
(off Waddon Rd.)
SM2: Sutt 7K 165
Gracedale Rd. SW16 5F 137
Gracefield Gdns. SW16 3J 137
Gracehill *E1* *5J 85*
(off Hannibal Rd.)
Grace Ho. SE11 7H 19
Grace Jones Cl. E8 6G 67
Grace M. *SE20* *2J 157*
(off Marlow Rd.)
Grace Path SE26 4J 139
Grace Pl. E3 3D 86
Grace Rd. CR0: Croy 6C 156
Graces All. E1 7G 85
Graces M. NW8 2A 82
SE5 2D 120
Grace's Rd. SE5 2E 120
Grace St. E3 3D 86
Gradient, The SE26 4G 139
Graduate Pl. SE1 7F 15
Graeme Rd. EN1: Enf 2J 23
Graemesdyke Av. SW14 3H 115
Grafton Cl. KT4: Wor Pk 3A 164
TW4: Houn 1C 130
W13 6A 78

Grafton Ct. TW14: Bedf 1F 129
Grafton Cres. NW1 6F 65
Grafton Gdns. N4 6C 48
RM8: Dag 2E 72
Grafton Ho. SE8 5B 104
Grafton M. W1 4A 6 (4G 83)
Grafton Pk. Rd. KT4: Wor Pk 2A 164
Grafton Pl. NW1 2D 6 (3H 83)
Grafton Rd. CR0: Croy 1A 168
EN2: Enf 3E 22
HA1: Harr 5G 41
KT3: N Mald 3A 152
KT4: Wor Pk 3K 163
NW5 5E 64
RM8: Dag 2E 72
W3 7J 79
Graftons, The NW2 3J 63
Grafton Sq. SW4 3G 119
Grafton St. W1 3K 11 (7F 83)
Grafton Ter. NW5 5D 64
Grafton Way KT8: W Mole 4D 148
W1 4A 6 (4G 83)
WC1 4B 6 (4G 83)
Grafton Yd. NW5 6F 65
Graham Av. CR4: Mitc 1E 154
W13 2B 96
Graham Cl. CR0: Croy 2C 170
Graham Ct. *SE14* *6K 103*
(off Myers La.)
UB5: N'olt 5D 58
GRAHAME PARK 1B 44
Grahame Pk. Est. NW9 1A 44
Grahame Pk. Way NW7 7G 29
NW9 2B 44
Grahame Twr. *W3* *3H 97*
(off Hanbury Rd.)
Grahame White Ho. HA3: Kent 3D 42
Graham Gdns. KT6: Surb 1E 162
Graham Ho. *N9* *1D 34*
(off Cumberland Rd.)
Graham Lodge NW4 6D 44
Graham Mans. *IG11: Bark* *7A 72*
(off Lansbury Av.)
Graham Rd. CR4: Mitc 1E 154
DA6: Bex 4F 127
E8 6G 67
E13 4J 87
HA3: W'stone 3J 41
N15 3B 48
NW4 6D 44
SW19 7H 135
TW12: Ham H 4E 130
W4 3K 97
Graham St. N1 1B 8 (2B 84)
Graham Ter. *DA15: Sidc* *6B 126*
(off Westerham Dr.)
SW1 4G 17 (4E 100)
Grainger Cl. UB5: N'olt 5F 59
Grainger Ct. SE5 7C 102
Grainger Rd. N22 1C 48
TW7: Isle 2K 113
Grainstore, The E16 7J 87
Gramer Cl. E11 2F 69
Gramophone La. UB3: Hayes 2G 93
Grampian Cl. BR6: St M Cry 6K 161
SM2: Sutt 7A 166
UB3: Harl 7F 93
Grampian Gdns. NW2 1G 63
Grampians, The *W6* *2F 99*
(off Shepherd's Bush Rd.)
Gramsci Way SE6 3D 140
Granada St. SW17 5D 136
Granard Av. SW15 5D 116
Granard Bus. Cen. NW7 6F 29
Granard Ho. E9 6K 67
Granard Rd. SW12 7D 118
Granary Cl. N9 7D 24
Granary Mans. SE28 2G 107
Granary Rd. E1 4H 85
Granary Sq. N1 6A 66
Granary St. NW1 1H 83
Granby Pl. *SE1* *7J 13*
(off Station App. Rd.)

Granby Rd. SE9 2D 124
Granby St. E2 3K 9 (4G 85)
(not continuous)
Granby Ter. NW1 1A 6 (2G 83)
Grand Arc. N12 5F 31
Grand Av. EC1 5B 8 (5B 84)
(not continuous)
HA9: Wemb 5G 61
KT5: Surb 5H 151
N10 4E 46
Grand Av. E. HA9: Wemb 5H 61
Grand Dpt. Rd. SE18 5E 106
Grand Dr. SW20 2E 152
UB2: S'hall 2G 95
Granden Rd. SW16 2J 155
Grandfield Ct. W4 6K 97
Grandison Rd. KT4: Wor Pk 2E 164
SW11 5D 118
Grand Junc. Wharf N1 2C 84
Grand Pde. HA9: Wemb 2G 61
KT6: Surb 1G 163
N4 5B 48
SW14 *4J 115*
(off Up. Richmond Rd. W.)
Grand Pde. M. SW15 5G 117
Grand Union W2 6B 4
Grand Union Cen. *W10* *4F 81*
(off West Row)
Grand Union Cl. W9 5H 81
Grand Union Cres. E8 1G 85
Grand Union Ent. Pk. UB2: S'hall 3E 94
Grand Union Hgts. HA0: Wemb 1D 78
Grand Union Ind. Est. NW10 2H 79
Grand Union Village UB5: N'olt 3D 76
Grand Union Wlk. *NW1* *7F 65*
(off Kentish Town Rd.)
Grand Union Way UB2: S'hall 2E 94
Grand Vitesse Ind. Cen. *SE1* *5B 14*
(off Dolben St.)
Grand Wlk. E1 4A 86
Granfield St. SW11 1B 118
Grange, The CR0: Croy 2B 170
E17 *5A 50*
(off Grange Rd.)
HA0: Wemb 7G 61
KT3: N Mald 5B 152
KT4: Wor Pk 4K 163
N2 2B 46
N20 1F 31
(Grangeview Rd.)
N20 1G 31
(Oxford Gdns.)
SE1 3F 103
SW19 6F 135
W3 2H 97
W4 5H 97
W13 5C 78
W14 4H 99
Grange Av. EN4: E Barn 1H 31
HA7: Stan 2B 42
IG8: Wfd G 6D 36
N12 5F 31
N20 7B 20
SE25 2E 156
TW2: Twick 2J 131
Grangecliffe Gdns. SE25 2E 156
Grange Cl. DA15: Sidc 3A 144
HA8: Edg 5D 28
IG8: Wfd G 7D 36
KT8: W Mole 4F 149
TW5: Hest 6D 94
UB3: Hayes 5G 75
Grange Ct. HA0: Wemb 4K 59
HA5: Pinn 3C 40
NW10 *3A 62*
(off Neasden La.)
SM2: Sutt 7K 165
SM6: Wall 3F 167
TW17: Shep 4C 146
UB5: N'olt 2A 76
WC2 1H 13 (6K 83)
Grangecourt Rd. N16 1E 66
Grange Cres. SE28 6C 90

Grangedale Cl. HA6: Nwood . . . 1G 39
Grange Dr. BR7: Chst . . . 6C 142
Grange Farm Cl. HA2: Harr . . . 2G 59
Grangefield *NW1* . . . *7H 65*
(off Marquis Rd.)
Grange Gdns. HA5: Pinn . . . 3C 40
N14 . . . 1C 32
NW3 . . . 3K 63
SE25 . . . 2E 156
Grange Gro. N1 . . . 6C 66
Grange Hill HA8: Edg . . . 5D 28
SE25 . . . 2E 156
Grangehill Pl. SE9 . . . 3D 124
Grangehill Rd. SE9 . . . 4D 124
Grange Ho. IG11: Bark . . . 1G 89
NW10 . . . 7D 62
SE1 . . . 3F 103
Grange La. SE21 . . . 2F 139
Grange Lodge SW19 . . . 6F 135
Grange Mans. KT17: Ewe . . . 7B 164
Grange M. N21 . . . 6G 23
TW13: Felt . . . 4J 129
Grangemill Rd. SE6 . . . 3C 140
Grangemill Way SE6 . . . 2C 140
Grange Mus. of Community History . . . 4A 62
GRANGE PARK . . . 6G 23
Grange Pk. W5 . . . 1E 96
Grange Pk. Av. N21 . . . 6H 23
Grange Pk. Pl. SW20 . . . 7D 134
Grange Pk. Rd. CR7: Thor H . . . 4D 156
E10 . . . 1D 68
Grange Pl. NW6 . . . 7J 63
Grange Rd. BR6: Orp . . . 2H 173
CR2: S Croy . . . 7C 168
CR7: Thor H . . . 4D 156
E10 . . . 1C 68
E13 . . . 3H 87
E17 . . . 5A 50
(not continuous)
HA1: Harr . . . 5A 42
HA2: Harr . . . 2H 59
HA8: Edg . . . 6E 28
IG1: Ilf . . . 4F 71
KT1: King T . . . 3E 150
KT8: W Mole . . . 4F 149
KT9: Chess . . . 4E 162
N6 . . . 6E 46
N17 . . . 6B 34
N18 . . . 6B 34
NW10 . . . 6D 62
SE1 . . . 3E 102
SE19 . . . 4D 156
SE25 . . . 4D 156
SM2: Sutt . . . 7J 165
SW13 . . . 1C 116
UB1: S'hall . . . 2C 94
UB3: Hayes . . . 6G 75
W4 . . . 5H 97
W5 . . . 1D 96
Grange St. N1 . . . 1D 84
Grange Va. SM2: Sutt . . . 7K 165
Grangeview Rd. N20 . . . 1F 31
Grange Wlk. SE1 . . . 3E 102
Grange Wlk. M. *SE1* . . . *3E 102*
(off Grange Wlk.)
Grange Way IG8: Wfd G . . . 4F 37
N12 . . . 4E 30
NW6 . . . 7J 63
Grangeway, The N21 . . . 6G 23
Grangeway Gdns. IG4: Ilf . . . 5C 52
Grangewood DA5: Bexl . . . 1F 145
Grangewood Cl. HA5: Eastc . . . 5J 39
Grangewood Dr. TW16: Sun . . . 7H 129
Grangewood La. BR3: Beck . . . 6B 140
Grangewood St. E6 . . . 1B 88
Grangewood Ter. SE25 . . . 2D 156
Grange Yd. SE1 . . . 3F 103
Granham Gdns. N9 . . . 2A 34
Granite Apartments E15 . . . 6F 69
Granite St. SE18 . . . 5K 107
Granleigh Rd. E11 . . . 2G 69
Gransden Av. E8 . . . 7H 67
Gransden Ho. SE8 . . . 5B 104
Gransden Rd. W12 . . . 2B 98
Grantbridge St. N1 . . . 2B 84
Grantchester *KT1: King T* . . . *2G 151*
(off St Peters Rd.)
Grantchester Cl.
HA1: Harr . . . 3K 59
Grant Cl. N14 . . . 7B 22
N17 . . . 2E 48
TW17: Shep . . . 6D 146
Grant Ct. *E4* . . . *1K 35*
(off The Ridgeway)
NW9 . . . *2B 44*
(off Hazel Cl.)
Grantham Cl. HA8: Edg . . . 3K 27
Grantham Ct. KT2: King T . . . 5D 132
RM6: Chad H . . . 7F 55
SE16 . . . *2K 103*
(off Eleanor Cl.)
Grantham Gdns. RM6: Chad H . . . 6F 55
Grantham Ho. *SE15* . . . *6G 103*
(off Friary Est.)
TW16: Sun . . . 7G 129
Grantham Pl. W1 . . . 5J 11 (1F 101)
Grantham Rd. E12 . . . 4E 70
SW9 . . . 2J 119
W4 . . . 7A 98
Grantley Ho. *SE14* . . . *6K 103*
(off Myers La.)
Grantley Rd. TW4: Cran . . . 2A 112
Grantley St. E1 . . . 3K 85
Grant Mus. of Zoology & Comparative Anatomy . . . 4C 6
Grantock Rd. E17 . . . 1F 51
Granton Rd. DA14: Sidc . . . 6C 144
IG3: Ilf . . . 1A 72
SW16 . . . 1G 155
Grant Pl. CR0: Croy . . . 1F 169
Grant Rd. CR0: Croy . . . 1F 169
HA3: W'stone . . . 3K 41
SW11 . . . 4B 118
Grants Cl. NW7 . . . 7K 29
Grants Quay Wharf EC3 . . . 3F 15 (7D 84)
Grant St. E13 . . . 3J 87
N1 . . . 2A 84
Grant Ter. *N16* . . . *7G 49*
(off Castlewood Rd.)
Grantully Rd. W9 . . . 3K 81
Grant Way TW7: Isle . . . 6A 96
Granville Arc. SW9 . . . 4A 120
Granville Av. N9 . . . 3D 34
TW3: Houn . . . 5E 112
TW13: Felt . . . 2J 129
Granville Cl. CR0: Croy . . . 2E 168
Granville Ct. N1 . . . 1E 84
N4 . . . 6K 47
SE14 . . . *7A 104*
(off Nynehead St.)
Granville Gdns. SW16 . . . 1K 155
W5 . . . 1F 97
Granville Gro. SE13 . . . 3E 122
Granville Ho. *E14* . . . *6C 86*
(off E. India Dock Rd.)
Granville Mans. *W12* . . . *2E 98*
(off Shepherd's Bush Grn.)
Granville M. DA14: Sidc . . . 4A 144
Granville Pk. SE13 . . . 3E 122
Granville Pl. HA5: Pinn . . . 3B 40
N12 . . . 7F 31
SW6 . . . 7K 99
W1 . . . 1G 11 (6E 82)
Granville Point NW2 . . . 2H 63
Granville Rd. DA14: Sidc . . . 4A 144
DA16: Well . . . 3C 126
E17 . . . 6D 50
E18 . . . 2K 51
EN5: Barn . . . 4A 20
IG1: Ilf . . . 1F 71
N4 . . . 6K 47
N12 . . . 7F 31
N13 . . . 6E 32
N22 . . . 1B 48
NW2 . . . 2H 63
Granville Rd. NW6 . . . 2J 81
(not continuous)
SW18 . . . 7H 117
SW19 . . . 7J 135
UB3: Harl . . . 4H 93
UB10: Hil . . . 6D 56
Granville Sq. SE15 . . . 7E 102
WC1 . . . 2H 7 (3K 83)
Granville St. WC1 . . . 2H 7 (3K 83)
Granwood Ct. TW7: Isle . . . 1J 113
Grape St. WC2 . . . 7E 6 (6J 83)
Graphite Sq. SE11 . . . 5G 19 (5K 101)
Grapsome Cl. KT9: Chess . . . 7C 162
Grasdene Rd. SE18 . . . 7A 108
Grasgarth Cl. W3 . . . 7J 79
Grasmere *NW1* . . . *2K 5*
(off Osnaburgh St.)
Grasmere Av. BR6: Farnb . . . 3F 173
HA4: Ruis . . . 7E 38
HA9: Wemb . . . 7C 42
SW15 . . . 4K 133
SW19 . . . 3J 153
TW3: Houn . . . 6F 113
W3 . . . 7K 79
Grasmere Cl. TW14: Felt . . . 1H 129
Grasmere Ct. N22 . . . 6E 32
SE26 . . . 5G 139
SM2: Sutt . . . 6A 166
SW13 . . . *6C 98*
(off Verdun Rd.)
Grasmere Gdns. BR6: Farnb . . . 3F 173
HA3: W'stone . . . 2A 42
IG4: Ilf . . . 5D 52
Grasmere Point *SE15* . . . *7J 103*
(off Old Kent Rd.)
Grasmere Rd. BR1: Brom . . . 1H 159
BR6: Farnb . . . 3F 173
DA7: Bex . . . 2J 127
E13 . . . 2J 87
N10 . . . 1F 47
N17 . . . 6B 34
SE25 . . . 6H 157
SW16 . . . 5K 137
Grasshaven Way SE28 . . . 1K 107
(not continuous)
Grassington Cl. N11 . . . 6K 31
Grassington Rd. DA14: Sidc . . . 4A 144
Grassmount SE23 . . . 2H 139
Grass Pk. N3 . . . 1H 45
Grass Way SM6: Wall . . . 4G 167
Grasvenor Av. EN5: Barn . . . 5D 20
Gratton Rd. W14 . . . 3G 99
Gratton Ter. NW2 . . . 3F 63
Gravel Hill CR0: Addtn . . . 6K 169
DA6: Bex . . . 4H 127
N3 . . . 2H 45
UB8: Uxb . . . 5A 56
Gravel Hill Cl. DA6: Bex . . . 5H 127
Gravel La. E1 . . . 7J 9 (6F 85)
Gravel Pit La. SE9 . . . 5F 125
Gravel Pit Way BR6: Orp . . . 2K 173
Gravel Rd. BR2: Brom . . . 3C 172
TW2: Twick . . . 1J 131
Gravelwood Cl. BR7: Chst . . . 3G 143
Gravely Ho. *SE8* . . . *4A 104*
(off Chilton Gro.)
Gravenel Gdns. *SW17* . . . *5C 136*
(off Nutwell St.)
Graveney Gro. SE20 . . . 7J 139
Graveney Rd. SW17 . . . 4C 136
Gravesend Rd. W12 . . . 7C 80
Gray Av. RM8: Dag . . . 1F 73
Grayham Cres. KT3: N Mald . . . 4K 151
Grayham Rd. KT3: N Mald . . . 4K 151
Gray Ho. *SE17* . . . *5C 102*
(off King & Queen St.)
Grayland Cl. BR1: Brom . . . 1B 160
Grayling Cl. E16 . . . 4G 87
Grayling Ct. *W5* . . . *1D 96*
(off Grange Rd.)
Grayling Rd. N16 . . . 2D 66
Grayling Sq. *E2* . . . *3G 85*
(off Nelson Gdns.)
Grays Ct. RM10: Dag . . . 7H 73
Grayscroft Rd. SW16 . . . 7H 137
Grays Farm Production Village
BR5: St P . . . 7B 144
Grays Farm Rd. BR5: St P . . . 7B 144
Grayshott Rd. SW11 . . . 2E 118
Gray's Inn . . . 5H 7 (5K 83)
Gray's Inn Bldgs. *EC1* . . . *4J 7*
(off Rosebery Av.)
Gray's Inn Pl. WC1 . . . 6H 7 (5K 83)
Gray's Inn Rd. WC1 . . . 1F 7 (3J 83)
Gray's Inn Sq. WC1 . . . 5J 7 (5K 83)
Grays La. TW15: Ashf . . . 4D 128
Grayson Ho. EC1 . . . 2D 8
Grays Rd. UB10: Uxb . . . 2A 74
Grays Ter. E7 . . . 6A 70
Gray St. SE1 . . . 7K 13 (2A 102)
Grayswood Gdns. SW20 . . . 2D 152
Grayswood Point SW15 . . . 1C 134
Gray's Yd. W1 . . . 1H 11
Graywood Ct. N12 . . . 7F 31
Grazebrook Rd. N16 . . . 2D 66
Grazeley Cl. DA6: Bex . . . 5J 127
Grazeley Ct. SE19 . . . 5E 138
Gt. Acre Ct. SW4 . . . 4H 119
Gt. Arthur Ho. *EC1* . . . *4C 8*
(off Golden La. Est.)
Gt. Bell All. EC2 . . . 7E 8 (6D 84)
Great Benty UB7: W Dray . . . 4A 92
Great Brownings SE21 . . . 4F 139
Gt. Bushey Dr. N20 . . . 1E 30
Gt. Cambridge Ind. Est.
EN1: Enf . . . 5C 24
GREAT CAMBRIDGE JUNC. . . . 4J 33
Gt. Cambridge Rd. EN1: Enf . . . 4J 33
N9 . . . 4J 33
N17 . . . 5J 33
N18 . . . 4J 33
Gt. Castle St. W1 . . . 7K 5 (6F 83)
Gt. Central Av. HA4: Ruis . . . 5A 58
Gt. Central St. NW1 . . . 5E 4 (5D 82)
Gt. Central Way HA9: Wemb . . . 4J 61
NW10 . . . 4J 61
Gt. Chapel St. W1 . . . 7C 6 (6H 83)
Gt. Chart St. SW11 . . . 4B 118
Gt. Chertsey Rd. TW2: Twick . . . 3D 130
TW13: Hanw, Twick . . . 3D 130
W4 . . . 2J 115
Great Chu. La. W6 . . . 4F 99
Great Coll. St. SW1 . . . 1E 18 (3J 101)
Great Cft. *WC1* . . . *2F 7*
(off Cromer St.)
Gt. Cross Av. SE10 . . . 7F 105
(not continuous)
Gt. Cumberland M. W1 . . . 1E 10 (6D 82)
Gt. Cumberland Pl. W1 . . . 7E 4 (6D 82)
Gt. Dover St. SE1 . . . 7D 14 (2C 102)
Greatdown Rd. W7 . . . 4K 77
Gt. Eastern Ent. Cen. E14 . . . 2D 104
Gt. Eastern Rd. E15 . . . 7F 69
Gt. Eastern St. EC2 . . . 2G 9 (3E 84)
Gt. Eastern Wlk. EC2 . . . 6H 9
Gt. Eastern Wharf SW11 . . . 7C 100
Gt. Elms Rd. BR2: Brom . . . 4A 160
Great Fld. NW9 . . . 1A 44
Greatfield NW5 . . . 5G 65
Greatfield Av. E6 . . . 4D 88
Greatfield Cl. N19 . . . 4G 65
SE4 . . . 4C 122
Greatfields Dr. UB8: Hil . . . 5C 74
Greatfields Rd. IG11: Bark . . . 1H 89
Gt. Fleete Way IG11: Bark . . . 2C 90
Gt. Galley Cl. IG11: Bark . . . 3B 90
Gt. Gatton Cl. CR0: Croy . . . 7A 158
Gt. George St. SW1 . . . 7D 12 (2H 101)
Gt. Guildford Bus. Sq.
SE1 . . . 5C 14 (1C 102)
Gt. Guildford St. SE1 . . . 4C 14 (1C 102)
Great Hall . . . 6F 17 (5D 100)
Greatham Wlk. SW15 . . . 1C 134
Gt. Harry Dr. SE9 . . . 3E 142
Gt. James St. WC1 . . . 5G 7 (5K 83)
Gt. Marlborough St. W1 . . . 1A 12 (6G 83)

Gt. Maze Pond—Grn. Man La.

Gt. Maze Pond SE1 . . . . .6F **15** (2D **102**)
(not continuous)
Gt. Newport St. WC2 . . . . .2E **12** (7J **83**)
Gt. New St. EC4 . . . . .7K **7** (6A **84**)
Great Nth. Leisure Pk. N12 . . . . .7G **31**
Great Nth. Rd. EN5: Barn 2C **20**
EN5: New Bar 5D **20**
N2 . . . . .5C **46**
N6 . . . . .5C **46**
Great Nth. Way NW4 . . . . .2D **44**
Greatorex Ho. *E1* *5G 85*
(off Spelman St.)
Greatorex St. E1 . . . . .5G **85**
Gt. Ormond St. WC1 . . . . .5F **7** (5J **83**)
Gt. Owl Rd. IG7: Chig 3K **37**
Gt. Percy St. WC1 . . . . .1H **7** (3K **83**)
Gt. Peter St. SW1 . . . . .2C **18** (3H **101**)
Gt. Portland St. W1 . . . . .4K **5** (4F **83**)
Gt. Pulteney St. W1 . . . . .2B **12** (7G **83**)
Gt. Queen St. WC2 . . . . .1F **13** (6J **83**)
Gt. Russell St. WC1 . . . . .7D **6** (6H **83**)
Gt. St Helen's EC3 . . . . .7G **9** (6E **84**)
Gt. St Thomas Apostle
EC4 . . . . .2D **14** (7C **84**)
Gt. Scotland Yd. SW1 . . . . . . .5E **12** (1J **101**)
Gt. Smith St. SW1 . . . . .1D **18** (3H **101**)
Great Sth. W. Rd. TW4: Houn 4H **111**
TW14: Bedf, Felt 7E **110**
Great Spilmans SE22 . . . . .5E **120**
Great Strand NW9 . . . . .1B **44**
Gt. Suffolk St. SE1 . . . . .5B **14** (1B **102**)
Gt. Sutton St. EC1 . . . . .4B **8** (4B **84**)
Gt. Swan All. EC2 . . . . .7E **8** (6D **84**)
(not continuous)
Gt. Thrift BR5: Pet W 4G **161**
Gt. Titchfield St. W1 . . . . .4K **5** (4F **83**)
Great Twr. St. EC3 . . . . .2G **15** (7E **84**)
Gt. Trinity La. EC4 . . . . .2D **14** (7C **84**)
Great Turnstile WC1 . . . . .6H **7** (5K **83**)
Gt. Turnstile Ho. *WC1* *5K 83*
(off Gt. Turnstile)
Gt. Western Ind. Pk. UB2: S'hall 2F **95**
Gt. Western Rd. W9 . . . . .5H **81**
W11 . . . . .5H **81**
Great W. Rd. TW5: Hest 2B **112**
TW7: Bford, Isle 2B **112**
TW8: Bford 2B **112**
W4 . . . . .5B **98**
(Gt. Chertsey Rd.)
W4 . . . . .5H **97**
(Harvard Rd.)
W6 . . . . .5B **98**
Great W. Trad. Est. TW8: Bford 6B **96**
Gt. Winchester St. EC2 . . . . .7F **9** (6D **84**)
Gt. Windmill St. W1 . . . . .2C **12** (7H **83**)
Greatwood BR7: Chst 7E **142**
Great Yd. SE1 .6H **15**
Greaves Cl. IG11: Bark 7H **71**
Greaves Cotts. E14 . . . . .5A **86**
Greaves Pl. SW17 . . . . .4C **136**
Greaves Twr. *SW10* *7A 100*
(off Worlds End Est.)
Grebe Av. UB4: Yead 6B **76**
Grebe Cl. E7 . . . . .5H **69**
E17 . . . . .7F **35**
IG11: Bark 4A **90**
Grebe Ct. *E14* *2E 104*
(off River Barge Cl.)
SE8 . . . .*6B 104*
(off Dorking Cl.)
SM1: Sutt 5H **165**
Grebe Ter. KT1: King T 3E **150**
Grecian Cres. SE19 . . . . .6B **138**
Greek Ct. W1 . . . . .1D **12** (6H **83**)
Greek St. W1 . . . . .1D **12** (6H **83**)
Green, The BR1: Brom 3J **141**
(not continuous)
BR2: Hayes 7J **159**
BR5: St P 7B **144**
CR0: Sels 7B **170**
DA7: Bex 1G **127**
DA14: Sidc 4A **144**
DA16: Well 4J **125**
Green, The E4 . . . . .1K **35**
E11 . . . . .6K **51**
E15 . . . . .6G **69**
HA0: Wemb 2A **60**
IG8: Wfd G 5D **36**
IG9: Buck H 1E **36**
KT3: N Mald 3K **151**
N9 . . . . .2B **34**
N14 . . . . .2C **32**
N17 . . . . .6H **33**
N21 . . . . .7F **23**
SM1: Sutt 3K **165**
SM4: Mord 4G **153**
SM5: Cars 4E **166**
SW19 . . . . .5F **135**
TW2: Twick 1J **131**
TW5: Hest 6E **94**
TW9: Rich 5D **114**
TW13: Felt 2K **129**
TW17: Shep 4G **147**
UB2: S'hall 3C **94**
UB7: W Dray 3A **92**
UB10: Ick 2E **56**
W3 . . . . .6A **80**
W5 . . . . .1D **96**
Greenacre Cl. EN5: Barn 1C **20**
UB5: N'olt 5D **58**
Greenacre Gdns. E17 . . . . .4E **50**
Greenacre Pl. SM6: Wall 2F **167**
Green Acres CR0: Croy 3F **169**
Greenacres DA14: Sidc 4A **144**
N3 . . . . .2H **45**
SE9 . . . . .6E **124**
WD23: Bushy 2C **26**
Greenacres Av. UB10: Ick 3B **56**
Greenacres Cl. BR6: Farnb 4G **173**
Greenacres Dr. HA7: Stan 6G **27**
Greenacre Sq. SE16 . . . . .2K **103**
Greenacre Wlk. N14 . . . . .3C **32**
Grn. Arbour Ct. *EC1* *7A 8*
(off Old Bailey)
Green Av. NW7 . . . . .4E **28**
W13 . . . . .3B **96**
Greenaway Av. N18 . . . . .6E **34**
Greenaway Gdns. NW3 . . . . .4K **63**
Greenaway Ho. *NW8* *1A 82*
(off Boundary Rd.)
WC1 . . . .*2J 7*
(off Fernsbury St.)
Greenaway Ter. *TW19: Stanw* *1A 128*
(off Victory Cl.)
Green Bank E1 . . . . .1H **103**
Greenbank N12 .4E **30**
Greenbank Av. HA0: Wemb 5A **60**
Grn. Bank Cl. E4 . . . . .2K **35**
Greenbank Cres. NW4 . . . . .4G **45**
Greenbank Lodge *BR7: Chst* *2E 160*
(off Forest Cl.)
Greenbanks HA1: Harr 4J **59**
Greenbay Rd. SE7 . . . . .7B **106**
Greenberry St. NW8 . . . . .1C **4** (2C **82**)
Greenbrook Av.
EN4: Had W 1F **21**
Green Cl. BR2: Brom 3G **159**
NW9 . . . . .6J **43**
NW11 . . . . .7A **46**
SM5: Cars 2D **166**
TW13: Hanw 5C **130**
Greencoat Mans. *SW1* *2B 18*
(off Greencoat Row)
Greencoat Pl. SW1 . . . . .3B **18** (4G **101**)
Greencoat Row SW1 . . . . .2B **18** (3G **101**)
Green Ct. TW16: Sun 6H **129**
Greencourt Av. CR0: Croy 2H **169**
HA8: Edg .1H **43**
Greencourt Gdns. CR0: Croy 1H **169**
Greencourt Ho. *E1* *4K 85*
(off Mile End Rd.)
Greencourt Rd. BR5: Pet W 5H **161**
Greencrest Pl. NW2 . . . . .3C **62**
Greencroft HA8: Edg 5D **28**
Greencroft Av. HA4: Ruis 2A **58**
Greencroft Cl. E6 . . . . .5B **88**
Greencroft Gdns. EN1: Enf 3K **23**
NW6 . . . . .7K **63**
Greencroft Rd. TW5: Hest 1D **112**
Green Dale SE5 . . . . .4D **120**
SE22 . . . . .5E **120**
Greendale NW7 .4F **29**
Grn. Dale Cl. SE22 . . . . .5E **120**
Grn. Dragon Ct. SE1 . . . . .4E **14**
Grn. Dragon Ho. *WC2* *7F 7*
(off Dragon Yd.)
Grn. Dragon La. N21 . . . . .5E **22**
TW8: Bford 5E **96**
Grn. Dragon Yd. E1 . . . . .6K **9** (5G **85**)
Green Dr. UB1: S'hall 1E **94**
Greene Ct. *SE14* *6K 103*
(off Samuel Cl.)
Greene Ho. *SE1* *3D 102*
(off Burbage Cl.)
Green End KT9: Chess 4E **162**
N21 . . . . .2G **33**
Greenend Rd. W4 . . . . .2A **98**
Greener Ho. SW4 . . . . .3H **119**
Grn. Farm Cl. BR6: Chels 6K **173**
Greenfell Mans. SE8 . . . . .6D **104**
Greenfield Av. KT5: Surb 7H **151**
Greenfield Dr. BR1: Brom 2A **160**
N2 . . . . .4D **46**
Greenfield Gdns. BR5: Pet W 7H **161**
NW2 . . . . .2G **63**
RM9: Dag .1D **90**
Greenfield Ho. SW19 . . . . .1F **135**
Greenfield Rd. DA2: Dart 5K **145**
E1 . . . . .5G **85**
N15 . . . . .5E **48**
RM9: Dag .7C **72**
Greenfields UB1: S'hall 6E **76**
Greenfield Way HA2: Harr 3F **41**
GREENFORD 3E **76**
Greenford Av. UB1: S'hall 7D **76**
W7 . . . . .4J **77**
Greenford Bus. Cen. UB6: G'frd 7H **59**
Greenford Gdns. UB6: G'frd 3F **77**
GREENFORD GREEN 6J **59**
Greenford Ind. Est. UB6: G'frd 7F **59**
Greenford Rd. HA1: Harr 7J **59**
SM1: Sutt 4K **165**
(not continuous)
UB1: S'hall 1G **95**
UB6: G'frd 7G **77**
GREENFORD RDBT. 2H **77**
Greenford Sports Cen. 3E **76**
Green Gdns. BR6: Farnb 5G **173**
Greengate UB6: G'frd 6B **60**
Greengate Lodge *E13* *2K 87*
(off Hollybush St.)
Greengate Pde. IG2: Ilf 6H **53**
Greengate St. E13 . . . . .2K **87**
Greenhalgh Wlk. N2 . . . . .4A **46**
Greenham Cl. SE1 . . . . .7J **13** (2A **102**)
Greenham Cres. E4 . . . . .6G **35**
Greenham Ho. *E9* *1J 85*
(off Templecombe Rd.)
TW7: Isle .3H **113**
Greenham Rd. N10 . . . . .2E **46**
Greenhaven Dr. SE28 . . . . .6B **90**
Greenheath Bus. Cen. *E2* *4H 85*
(off Three Colts La.)
Green Hedge TW1: Twick 5C **114**
Greenheys Cl. HA6: Nwood 1G **39**
Greenheys Dr. E18 . . . . .3H **51**
GREENHILL 5J **41**
Green Hill SE18 . . . . .5D **106**
Greenhill HA9: Wemb 2H **61**
IG9: Buck H 1F **37**
NW3 . . . . .4B **64**
SM1: Sutt 2A **166**
Greenhill Ct. EN5: New Bar 5E **20**
SE18 . . . . .5D **106**
Greenhill Gdns. UB5: N'olt 2D **76**
Greenhill Gro. E12 . . . . .4C **70**
Greenhill Pde. EN5: New Bar 5E **20**
Greenhill Pk. EN5: New Bar 5E **20**
NW10 . . . . .1A **80**
Greenhill Rd. HA1: Harr 6J **41**
NW10 . . . . .1A **80**
Greenhill's Rents EC1 . . . . .5A **8** (5B **84**)
Greenhills Ter. N1 . . . . .6D **66**
Greenhill Ter. SE18 . . . . .5D **106**
UB5: N'olt 2D **76**
Greenhill Way HA1: Harr 6J **41**
HA9: Wemb 2H **61**
Greenhithe Cl. DA15: Sidc 7J **125**
Greenholm Rd. SE9 . . . . .5F **125**
Grn. Hundred Rd. SE15 . . . . .6G **103**
Greenhurst Rd. SE27 . . . . .5A **138**
Greening St. SE2 . . . . .4C **108**
Greenland Cres. UB2: S'hall 3A **94**
Greenland Ho. *E1* *4A 86*
(off Ernest St.)
Greenland M. SE8 . . . . .5K **103**
Greenland Pl. NW1 . . . . .1F **83**
Greenland Quay SE16 . . . . .4K **103**
Greenland Rd. EN5: Barn 6A **20**
NW1 . . . . .1G **83**
Greenlands KT19: Ewe 5H **163**
Greenlands La. NW4 . . . . .1D **44**
Greenland St. NW1 . . . . .1F **83**
Greenland Way CR0: Bedd 7H **155**
Green La. BR7: Chst 4F **143**
CR7: Thor H 7K **137**
HA1: Harr .3J **59**
HA7: Stan .4G **27**
HA8: Edg .4A **28**
IG1: Ilf 2H **71**
IG3: Ilf 2H **71**
KT3: N Mald 5J **151**
KT4: Wor Pk 1C **164**
KT8: W Mole 5F **149**
KT9: Chess 7D **162**
NW4 . . . . .4F **45**
RM8: Dag .2H **71**
SE9 . . . . .1F **143**
SE20 . . . . .7K **139**
SM4: Mord 6J **153**
(Central Rd.)
SM4: Mord 7E **152**
(Lwr. Morden La.)
SW16 . . . . .7K **137**
TW4: Houn 3K **111**
TW13: Hanw 5C **130**
TW16: Sun 7H **129**
TW17: Shep 6E **146**
UB8: Hil 5E **74**
W7 . . . . .2J **95**
Green La. Bus. Pk. SE9 . . . . .2E **142**
Green La. Cotts. HA7: Stan 4G **27**
Green La. Gdns. CR7: Thor H 2C **156**
Green Lanes KT19: Ewe 7A **164**
(not continuous)
N4 . . . . .1C **66**
N8 . . . . .3B **48**
N13 . . . . .6E **32**
N15 . . . . .3B **48**
N16 . . . . .1C **66**
N21 . . . . .3F **33**
Greenlaw Ct. *W5* *6D 78*
(off Mount Pk. Rd.)
Greenlaw Gdns. KT3: N Mald 7B **152**
Grn. Lawn La. TW8 . . . . .4D **96**
Green Lawns HA4: Ruis 1A **58**
Greenlawns N12 . . . . .6E **30**
Greenlaw St. SE18 . . . . .3E **106**
Grn. Leaf Av. SM6: Bedd 4H **167**
Greenleaf Cl. SW2 . . . . .7A **120**
Greenleafe Dr. IG6: Ilf 3F **53**
Greenleaf Rd. E6 . . . . .1A **88**
E17 . . . . .3B **50**
Greenlea Pk. SW19 . . . . .7B **136**
Green Leas *KT1: King T* *3E 150*
(off Mill St.)
TW16: Sun 6H **129**
Grn. Leas Cl. TW16: Sun 6H **129**
Greenleaves Ct. TW15: Ashf 6D **128**
Grn. Man Gdns. W13 . . . . .7A **78**
Grn. Man La. TW14: Felt 4J **111**
(not continuous)

Grn. Man La. W13 7A 78
Grn. Man Pas. W13 7B 78
(not continuous)
GREEN MAN RDBT. 7H 51
Greenman St. N1 7C 66
Greenmead DA18: Erith 3E 108
Greenmead Cl. SE25 5G 157
Grn. Moor Link N21 7G 23
Greenmoor Rd. EN3: Enf H 2D 24
Greenoak Pl. EN4: Cockf 2J 21
Green Oaks UB2: S'hall 4B 94
Greenoak Way SW19 4F 135
Greenock Rd. SW16 1H 155
W3 3H 97
Greeno Cres. TW17: Shep 5C 146
Green Pde. TW3: Houn 5F 113
Green Pk. 6K 11 (2F 101)
Greenpark Ct. HA0: Wemb 7C 60
Green Pk. Way UB6: G'frd 7J 59
(not continuous)
Green Point E15 6G 69
Grn. Pond Cl. E17 3A 50
Grn. Pond Rd. E17 3A 50
Green Rd. N14 6A 22
N20 3F 31
Greenroof Way *SE10* 3H 105
(off School Bank Rd.)
Greenscape SE10 3H 105
(not continuous)
Green's Ct. W1 2C 12
W11 1H 99
(off Lansdowne M.)
Green's End SE18 4F 107
Greenshank Cl. E17 7F 35
Greens Health & Fitness
Chingford 4K 35
Purley 6A 168
Greenshields Ind. Est. E16 2J 105
Green Side RM8: Dag 1C 72
Greenside DA5: Bexl 1E 144
Greenside Cl. N20 2G 31
SE6 2F 141
Greenside Rd. CR0: Croy 7A 156
W12 3C 98
Greenslade Rd. IG11: Bark 7H 71
Greenstead Av. IG8: Wfd G 7F 37
Greenstead Cl. IG8: Wfd G 6F 37
Greenstead Gdns. IG8: Wfd G 6F 37
SW15 5D 116
Greensted Rd. IG10: Lough 1H 37
Greenstone M. E11 6J 51
Green St. E7 6K 69
E13 6K 69
EN3: Brim, Enf H 2D 24
TW16: Sun 1J 147
W1 2G 11 (7E 82)
GREEN STREET GREEN 6K 173
Greenstreet Hill SE14 2K 121
Green Ter. EC1 2K 7 (3A 84)
Green Va. DA6: Bex 5D 126
W5 6F 79
Greenvale Rd. SE9 4D 124
Green Verges HA7: Stan 7J 27
Green Vw. KT9: Chess 7F 163
Greenview Av. BR3: Beck 6A 158
CR0: Croy 6A 158
Greenview Cl. W3 1A 98
Greenview Ct. TW15: Ashf 4B 128
Green Wlk. HA4: Ruis 1H 57
IG8: Wfd G 6H 37
IG10: Buck H 1H 37
NW4 5F 45
SE1 3E 102
TW12: Hamp 6D 130
UB2: S'hall 5E 94
Green Wlk., The E4 1A 36
Green Way BR2: Brom 6C 160
IG8: Wfd G 5F 37
SE9 5B 124
SM6: Wall 4G 167
TW16: Sun 4J 147
Green Way, The HA3: W'stone 1J 41
HA5: Pinn 6D 40
Greenway BR7: Chst 5E 142
HA3: Kent 5E 42
HA5: Pinn 2K 39
N14 2D 32
N20 2D 30
RM8: Dag 2C 72
SW20 4E 152
UB4: Yead 3J 75
Greenway, The NW9 2K 43
TW4: Houn 4D 112
UB8: Uxb 2A 74
UB10: Ick 2E 56
Greenway Av. E17 4F 51
Greenway Cl. N4 2C 66
N11 6K 31
N15 4F 49
N20 2D 30
NW9 2K 43
Greenway Ct. IG1: Ilf 1E 70
Greenway Gdns. CR0: Croy 3B 170
HA3: W'stone 2J 41
NW9 2K 43
UB6: G'frd 3E 76
Greenways BR3: Beck 3C 158
Greenways, The TW1: Twick 6A 114
Greenwell St. W1 4K 5 (4F 83)
GREENWICH 7E 104
Greenwich Borough Mus. 5K 107
Greenwich Bus. Pk. SE10 7D 104
Greenwich Chu. St. SE10 6E 104
Greenwich Cinema 7E 104
Greenwich Commercial Cen.
SE10 7D 104
Greenwich Ct. *E1* 6H 85
(off Cavell St.)
Greenwich Cres. E6 5C 88
Greenwich Gateway Vis. Cen. 6E 104
Greenwich Heritage Cen. 3F 107
Greenwich High Rd. SE10 1D 122
Greenwich Ind. Est. SE7 4K 105
SE10 7D 104
Greenwich Mkt. SE10 6E 104
GREENWICH MILLENNIUM VILLAGE
3H 105
Greenwich Pk. 7F 105
Greenwich Pk. St. SE10 6F 105
Greenwich Quay SE8 6D 104
Greenwich Shop. Pk. SE7 4K 105
Greenwich Sth. St. SE10 1D 122
Greenwich Theatre 7E 104
Greenwich Vw. Pl. E14 3D 104
Greenwich Yacht Club 3J 105
Greenwood Av. EN3: Enf H 2F 25
RM10: Dag 4H 73
Greenwood Bus. Cen. CR0: Croy 7F 157
Greenwood Cl. BR5: Pet W 6J 161
DA15: Sidc 2A 144
KT7: T Ditt 1A 162
SM4: Mord 4G 153
WD23: Bushy 1D 26
Greenwood Dr. E4 5A 36
Greenwood Gdns. IG6: Ilf 1G 53
N13 3G 33
Greenwood Ho. N22 1A 48
SE4 4K 121
Greenwood La. TW12: Ham H 5F 131
Greenwood Mans. *IG11: Bark* 7A 72
(off Lansbury Av.)
Greenwood Pk. KT2: King T 7A 134
Greenwood Pl. NW5 5F 65
Greenwood Rd. CR0: Croy 7B 156
CR4: Mitc 3H 155
DA5: Bexl 4K 145
E8 6G 67
E13 2H 87
KT7: T Ditt 1A 162
TW7: Isle 3K 113
Greenwoods, The HA2: Harr 3G 59
Greenwood Ter. NW10 1K 79
Greenwood Theatre 2D 102
Grn. Wrythe Cres. SM5: Cars 1C 166
Grn. Wrythe La. SM5: Cars 6B 154
Green Yd. WC1 3H 7 (4K 83)
Green Yd., The EC3 1G 15
Greer Rd. HA3: Hrw W 1G 41
Greet Ho. SE1 7K 13
Greet St. SE1 5K 13 (1A 102)
Greg Cl. E10 6E 50
Gregor M. SE3 7J 105
Gregory Cl. BR2: Brom 4G 159
Gregory Cres. SE9 7B 124
Gregory Pl. W8 2K 99
Gregory Rd. RM6: Chad H 4D 54
UB2: S'hall 3E 94
Greig Cl. N8 5J 47
Greig Ter. SE17 6B 102
Grenaby Av. CR0: Croy 7D 156
Grenaby Rd. CR0: Croy 7D 156
Grenada Ho. *E14* 7B 86
(off Limehouse C'way.)
Grenada Rd. SE7 7A 106
Grenade St. E14 7B 86
Grenadier St. E16 1E 106
Grena Gdns. TW9: Rich 4F 115
Grenard Cl. SE15 7G 103
Grena Rd. TW9: Rich 4F 115
Grendon Gdns. HA9: Wemb 2G 61
Grendon Ho. *E9* 7J 67
(off Shore Pl.)
N1 2K 83
(off Calshot St.)
Grendon Lodge HA8: Edg 2D 28
Grendon St. NW8 3C 4 (4C 82)
Grenfell Ct. NW7 6J 29
Grenfell Gdns. HA3: Kent 7E 42
IG3: Ilf 5K 53
Grenfell Ho. SE5 7C 102
Grenfell Rd. CR4: Mitc 6D 136
W11 7F 81
Grenfell Twr. W11 7F 81
Grenfell Wlk. W11 7F 81
Grenier Apartments SE15 7H 103
Grennell Cl. SM1: Sutt 2B 166
Grennell Rd. SM1: Sutt 2A 166
Grenoble Gdns. N13 6F 33
Grenville Cl. KT5: Surb 1J 163
N3 1G 45
Grenville Ct. W13 5B 78
Grenville Gdns. IG8: Wfd G 1A 52
Grenville Ho. *E3* 2A 86
(off Arbery Rd.)
SE8 6C 104
(off New King St.)
SW1 7C 18
(off Dolphin Sq.)
Grenville M. N19 1J 65
SW7 4A 100
TW12: Ham H 5F 131
Grenville Pl. NW7 5E 28
SW7 3A 100
Grenville Rd. N19 1J 65
Grenville St. WC1 4F 7 (4J 83)
Gresham Av. N20 4J 31
Gresham Cl. DA5: Bexl 6E 126
EN2: Enf 3H 23
Gresham Dr. RM6: Chad H 5B 54
Gresham Gdns. NW11 1G 63
Gresham Lodge E17 5D 50
Gresham Pl. N19 2H 65
Gresham Rd. BR3: Beck 2A 158
E6 2D 88
E16 6K 87
HA8: Edg 6A 28
NW10 5K 61
SE25 4G 157
SW9 3A 120
TW3: Houn 1G 113
TW12: Hamp 6E 130
UB10: Hil 2C 74
Gresham St. EC2 7C 8 (6C 84)
Gresham Way SW19 3K 135
Gresham Way Ind. Est. *SW19* 3K 135
(off Gresham Way)
Gresley Cl. E17 6A 50
N15 4D 48
Gresley Rd. N19 1G 65
Gressenhall Rd. SW18 6H 117
Gresse St. W1 6C 6 (6H 83)
Gresswell Cl. DA14: Sidc 3A 144
Greswell St. SW6 1F 117
Gretton Ho. *E2* 3J 85
(off Globe Rd.)
Gretton Rd. N17 7A 34
Greville Cl. TW1: Twick 7B 114
Greville Ct. *E5* 4H 67
(off Napoleon Rd.)
HA1: Harr 4J 59
Greville Hall NW6 2K 81
Greville Ho. *SW1* 1G 17
(off Halkin Arc.)
Greville Lodge E13 1K 87
HA8: Edg 4C 28
(off Broadhurst Av.)
N12 5E 30
Greville M. *NW6* 1K 81
(off Greville Rd.)
Greville Pl. NW6 2K 81
Greville Rd. E17 4E 50
NW6 2K 81
TW10: Rich 6F 115
Greville St. EC1 6J 7 (5A 84)
(not continuous)
Grey Cl. NW11 6A 46
Greycoat Gdns. *SW1* 2C 18
(off Greycoat St.)
Greycoat Pl. SW1 2C 18 (3H 101)
Greycoat St. SW1 2C 18 (3H 101)
Greycot Rd. BR3: Beck 5C 140
Grey Eagle St. E1 4K 9 (4F 85)
Greyfell Cl. HA7: Stan 5G 27
Greyfriars *SE26* 3G 139
(off Wells Pk. Rd.)
Greyfriars Pas. EC1 7B 8 (6B 84)
Greyhound Ct. WC2 2H 13 (7K 83)
Greyhound Hill NW4 3C 44
Greyhound La. SW16 6H 137
Greyhound Mans. *W6* 6G 99
(off Greyhound Rd.)
Greyhound Rd. N17 3E 48
NW10 3D 80
SM1: Sutt 5A 166
W6 6F 99
W14 6F 99
Greyhound Ter. SW16 1G 155
Grey Ho. *W12* 7D 80
(off White City Est.)
Greyladies Gdns. SE10 2E 122
Greys Pk. Cl. BR2: Kes 5B 172
Greystead Rd. SE23 7J 121
Greystoke Av. HA5: Pinn 3E 40
Greystoke Ct. W5 4E 78
Greystoke Dr. HA4: Ruis 6D 38
Greystoke Gdns. EN2: Enf 4C 22
W5 4E 78
Greystoke Ho. *SE15* 6G 103
(off Peckham Pk. Rd.)
W5 4E 78
Greystoke Lodge *W5* 4F 79
(off Hanger La.)
Greystoke Pk. Ter. W5 3D 78
Greystoke Pl. EC4 7J 7 (6A 84)
Greystone Gdns. HA3: Kent 6C 42
IG6: Ilf 2G 53
Greystone Path *E11* 7H 51
(off Mornington Rd.)
Greyswood Av. N18 6E 34
Greyswood St. SW16 6F 137
Grey Turner Ho. W12 6C 80
Grierson Ho. SW16 4G 137
Grierson Rd. SE23 7K 121
Griffin Cen. TW14: Felt 5K 111
Griffin Cen., The
KT1: King T 2D 150
(off Market Pl.)
Griffin Cl. NW10 5D 62
Griffin Ct. TW8: Bford 6E 96
W4 5B 98
Griffin Ho. *E14* 6D 86
(off Ricardo St.)

Griffin Ho. N1 ...1E 84
(off New Era Est.)
W6 ...4F 99
(off Hammersmith Rd.)
Griffin Mnr. Way SE28 ...3H 107
Griffin Pk. ...6D 96
Griffin Rd. N17 ...2E 48
SE18 ...5H 107
Griffins Cl. N21 ...7J 23
Griffin Way TW16: Sun ...2J 147
Griffith Cl. RM8: Dag ...7C 54
Griffiths Cl. KT4: Wor Pk ...2D 164
Griffiths Rd. SW19 ...7J 135
Griggs App. IG1: Ilf ...2G 71
Griggs Cl. SE1 ...3E 102
(off Grigg's Pl.)
Grigg's Pl. SE1 ...3E 102
Griggs Rd. E10 ...6E 50
Grilse Cl. N9 ...4C 34
Grimaldi Ho. N1 ...2K 83
(off Calshot St.)
Grimsby Gro. E16 ...2F 107
Grimsby St. E2 ...4K 9 (4F 85)
Grimsdyke Rd. HA5: H End ...1D 40
Grimsel Path SE5 ...7B 102
Grimshaw Cl. N6 ...7E 46
Grimston Rd. SW6 ...2H 117
Grimthorpe Ho. EC1 ...3A 8
Grimwade Av. CR0: Croy ...3G 169
Grimwade Cl. SE15 ...3J 121
Grimwood Rd. TW1: Twick ...7K 113
Grindall Cl. CR0: Wadd ...4B 168
Grindall Ho. E1 ...4H 85
(off Darling Row)
Grindal St. SE1 ...7J 13 (2A 102)
Grindleford Av. N11 ...2K 31
Grindley Gdns. CR0: Croy ...6F 157
Grindley Ho. E3 ...5B 86
(off Leopold St.)
Grinling Pl. SE8 ...6C 104
Grinstead Rd. SE8 ...5A 104
Grisedale NW1 ...1A 6
(off Cumberland Mkt.)
Grittleton Av. HA9: Wemb ...6H 61
Grittleton Rd. W9 ...4J 81
Grizedale Ter. SE23 ...2H 139
Grocer's Hall Ct. EC2 ...1E 14 (6D 84)
Grocer's Hall Gdns. EC2 ...1E 14
Grogan Cl. TW12: Hamp ...6D 130
Groombridge Cl.
DA16: Well ...5A 126
Groombridge Ho. SE17 ...5E 102
(off Kinglake St.)
Groombridge Rd. E9 ...7K 67
Groom Cl. BR2: Brom ...4K 159
Groom Cres. SW18 ...7B 118
Groome Ho. SE11 ...4H 19 (4K 101)
Groomfield Cl. SW17 ...4E 136
Groom Pl. SW1 ...1H 17 (3E 100)
Grooms Dr. HA5: Eastc ...5J 39
Grosmont Rd. SE18 ...5K 107
Grosse Way SW15 ...6D 116
Grosvenor Av. HA2: Harr ...6F 41
N5 ...5C 66
SM5: Cars ...6D 166
SW14 ...3A 116
TW10: Rich ...5E 114
UB4: Hayes ...2H 75
Grosvenor Cotts. SW1 ...3G 17 (4E 100)
Grosvenor Ct. E10 ...1D 68
N14 ...7B 22
NW6 ...1F 81
NW7 ...5E 28
(off Hale La.)
SE5 ...6C 102
SM2: Sutt ...6K 165
SM4: Mord ...4J 153
TW11: Tedd ...6A 132
W3 ...1G 97
W5 ...7E 78
(off The Grove)
Grosvenor Ct. Mans. W2 ...1E 10
(off Edgware Rd.)

Grosvenor Cres. NW9 ...4G 43
SW1 ...7H 11 (2E 100)
UB10: Hil ...7D 56
Grosvenor Cres. M. SW1 ...7G 11 (2E 100)
Grosvenor Est. SW1 ...3D 18 (4H 101)
Grosvenor Gdns. E6 ...3B 88
IG8: Wfd G ...6D 36
KT2: King T ...6D 132
N10 ...3G 47
N14 ...4C 22
NW2 ...6E 62
NW11 ...6H 45
SM6: Wall ...7G 167
SW1 ...1J 17 (3F 101)
SW14 ...3A 116
Grosvenor Gdns. M. E. SW1 ...1K 17
Grosvenor Gdns. M. Nth. SW1 ...2J 17
Grosvenor Gdns. M. Sth. SW1 ...2K 17
Grosvenor Ga. W1 ...3G 11 (7E 82)
Grosvenor Hill SW19 ...6G 135
W1 ...2J 11 (7F 83)
Grosvenor Hill Ct. W1 ...2J 11
(off Bourdon St.)
Grosvenor Ho. SM1: Sutt ...5K 165
Grosvenor Pde. W5 ...1G 97
(off Uxbridge Rd.)
Grosvenor Pk. SE5 ...7C 102
Grosvenor Pk. Rd. E17 ...5C 50
Grosvenor Pl. SW1 ...7H 11 (2E 100)
Grosvenor Ri. E. E17 ...5D 50
Grosvenor Rd. BR4: W W'ck ...1D 170
BR5: St M Cry ...6J 161
DA6: Bex ...5D 126
DA17: Belv ...6G 109
E6 ...1B 88
E7 ...6K 69
E10 ...1E 68
E11 ...5K 51
IG1: Ilf ...3G 71
N3 ...7C 30
N9 ...1C 34
N10 ...1F 47
RM7: Rush G ...7K 55
RM8: Dag ...1F 73
SE25 ...4F 157
SM6: Wall ...6F 167
SW1 ...7J 17 (6F 101)
TW1: Twick ...1A 132
TW3: Houn ...3D 112
TW8: Bford ...6D 96
TW10: Rich ...5E 114
UB2: S'hall ...3D 94
W4 ...5H 97
W7 ...1A 96
Grosvenor Sq. W1 ...2H 11 (7E 82)
Grosvenor St. W1 ...2J 11 (7F 83)
Grosvenor Studios SW1 ...3G 17
(off Eaton Ter.)
Grosvenor Ter. SE5 ...7C 102
Grosvenor Va. HA4: Ruis ...2H 57
Grosvenor Way E5 ...2J 67
Grosvenor Wharf Rd. E14 ...4F 105
Grotes Bldgs. SE3 ...2G 123
Grote's Pl. SE3 ...2G 123
Groton Rd. SW18 ...2K 135
Grotto Cl. SE1 ...6B 14 (2B 102)
Grotto Pas. W1 ...5H 5 (5E 82)
Grotto Rd. TW1: Twick ...2K 131
GROVE, THE ...1G 139
Grove, The BR4: W W'ck ...3D 170
DA6: Bex ...4D 126
DA14: Sidc ...5E 144
E15 ...6G 69
EN2: Enf ...2F 23
HA7: Stan ...2F 27
HA8: Edg ...4C 28
KT12: Walt T ...7K 147
N3 ...1J 45
N4 ...7K 47
N6 ...1E 64
N8 ...5H 47
N13 ...4F 33
(not continuous)

Grove, The N14 ...5B 22
NW9 ...5K 43
NW11 ...7G 45
TW1: Twick ...6B 114
TW7: Isle ...1J 113
TW11: Tedd ...4A 132
UB6: G'frd ...6G 77
UB10: Ick ...5C 56
W5 ...1D 96
Grove Av. HA5: Pinn ...4C 40
N3 ...7D 30
N10 ...2G 47
SM1: Sutt ...6J 165
TW1: Twick ...1K 131
W7 ...6J 77
Grovebury Cl. DA8: Erith ...6K 109
Grovebury Ct. DA6: Bex ...5H 127
N14 ...7C 22
Grovebury Rd. SE2 ...2B 108
Grove Cl. BR2: Hayes ...2J 171
KT1: King T ...4F 151
N14 ...7B 22
SE23 ...1A 140
TW13: Hanw ...4C 130
UB10: Ick ...5C 56
Grove Cotts. SW3 ...7D 16
W4 ...6A 98
Grove Ct. EN5: Barn ...3C 20
(off Hadley Ridge)
KT1: King T ...3E 150
(off Grove Cres.)
KT8: E Mos ...4H 149
NW8 ...1A 4
SW10 ...6A 16
(off Drayton Gdns.)
TW3: Houn ...4E 112
W5 ...1E 96
Grove Cres. E18 ...2H 51
KT1: King T ...3E 150
KT12: Walt T ...7K 147
NW9 ...4J 43
TW13: Hanw ...4C 130
Grove Cres. Rd. E15 ...6F 69
Grovedale Rd. N19 ...2H 65
Grove Dwellings E1 ...5J 85
Grove End E18 ...2H 51
NW5 ...4F 65
Grove End Gdns. NW8 ...2B 82
Grove End Ho. NW8 ...2A 4
Grove End La. KT10: Esh ...7H 149
Grove End Rd. NW8 ...1A 4 (2B 82)
Grove Farm Retail Pk.
RM6: Chad H ...7C 54
Grovefield N11 ...4A 32
(off Coppies Gro.)
Grove Gdns. EN3: Enf W ...1E 24
NW4 ...5C 44
NW8 ...2D 4 (3C 82)
RM10: Dag ...3J 73
TW10: Rich ...6F 115
TW11: Tedd ...4A 132
Grove Grn. Rd. E11 ...3E 68
Grove Hall Ct. NW8 ...1A 4 (3A 82)
Grove Hill E18 ...2H 51
HA1: Harr ...7J 41
Grovehill Ct. BR1: Brom ...6H 141
Grove Hill Rd.
HA1: Harr ...7K 41
SE5 ...3E 120
Grove Ho. N3 ...3F 45
SW3 ...7D 16
(off Chelsea Mnr. St.)
Grove Ho. Rd. N8 ...4J 47
Groveland Av. SW16 ...7K 137
Groveland Ct. EC4 ...1D 14
Groveland Rd. BR3: Beck ...3B 158
Grovelands KT1: King T ...4D 150
(off Palace Rd.)
KT8: W Mole ...4E 148
Grovelands Cl. HA2: Harr ...3F 59
SE5 ...2E 120
Grovelands Ct. N14 ...7C 22

Grovelands Rd. BR5: St P ...7A 144
N13 ...4E 32
N15 ...6G 49
Groveland Way KT3: N Mald ...5J 151
Grove La. KT1: King T ...4E 150
SE5 ...1D 120
UB8: Hil ...4A 74
Grove La. Ter SE5 ...2D 120
Groveley Rd. TW13: Felt ...5H 129
TW16: Sun ...5H 129
Grove Mans. W6 ...2E 98
(off Hammersmith Gro.)
Grove Mkt. Pl. SE9 ...6D 124
Grove M. W6 ...3E 98
Grove Mill Pl. SM5: Cars ...3E 166
Grove Nature Reserve, The ...4B 74
GROVE PARK
SE12 ...3K 141
W4 ...1J 115
Grove Pk. E11 ...6K 51
NW9 ...4J 43
SE5 ...2E 120
Grove Pk. Av. E4 ...7J 35
Grove Pk. Bri. W4 ...7J 97
Grove Pk. Gdns. W4 ...7J 97
Grove Pk. Ind. Est. NW9 ...4K 43
Grove Pk. M. W4 ...7J 97
Grove Pk. Rd. N15 ...4E 48
SE9 ...3A 142
W4 ...7H 97
Grove Pk. Ter. W4 ...7H 97
(not continuous)
Grove Pas. E2 ...2H 85
Grove Pl. IG11: Bark ...7G 71
NW3 ...3B 64
SW12 ...7F 119
W3 ...1J 97
Grover Ct. SE13 ...2D 122
Grover Ho. SE11 ...6H 19 (5K 101)
Grove Rd. CR4: Mitc ...3E 154
(not continuous)
CR7: Thor H ...4A 156
DA7: Bex ...4J 127
DA17: Belv ...6F 109
E3 ...1K 85
E4 ...4K 35
E11 ...7H 51
E17 ...6D 50
E18 ...2H 51
EN4: Cockf ...3J 21
HA5: Pinn ...5D 40
HA8: Edg ...6B 28
KT6: Surb ...5D 150
KT8: E Mos ...4H 149
N11 ...5A 32
N12 ...5G 31
N15 ...5E 48
NW2 ...6E 62
RM6: Chad H ...7C 54
SM1: Sutt ...6J 165
SW13 ...2B 116
SW19 ...7A 136
TW2: Twick ...3H 131
TW3: Houn ...4E 112
TW7: Isle ...1J 113
TW8: Bford ...5C 96
TW10: Rich ...6F 115
TW17: Shep ...6E 146
UB8: Uxb ...7A 56
W3 ...1J 97
W5 ...7D 78
Groveside Cl. SM5: Cars ...2C 166
SW11 ...2B 118
Groveside Rd. E4 ...2B 36
Grovestile Waye
TW14: Bedf ...7F 111
Grove St. N18 ...5A 34
SE8 ...4B 104
Grove Ter. NW5 ...3F 65
TW11: Tedd ...4A 132
UB1: S'hall ...7E 76
Grove Ter. M. NW5 ...3F 65

Grove Va. BR7: Chst 6E 142
    SE22 ....4F 121
Grove Vs. E14 ....7D 86
Grove Way HA9: Wemb 5H 61
    KT10: Esh 7G 149
    UB8: Uxb 7A 56
Groveway RM8: Dag 4D 72
    SW9 ....1K 119
Grovewood TW9: Kew 1G 115
Grovewood Pl. IG8: Wfd G 6J 37
Grummant Rd. SE15 ....1F 121
Grundy St. E14 ....6D 86
Gruneisen Rd. N3 ....7E 30
Guardian Ct. SE12 ....5G 123
Guards Memorial 5D 12 (1H 101)
Guards' Mus. 7B 12 (2G 101)
Gubyon Av. SE24 ....5B 120
Guerin Sq. E3 ....3B 86
Guernsey Cl. TW5: Hest 7E 94
Guernsey Gro. SE24 ....7C 120
Guernsey Ho. EN3: Enf W 1E 24
                    (off Eastfield Rd.)
    N1 ....6C 66
                    (off Douglas Rd. Nth.)
Guernsey Rd. E11 ....1F 69
Guibal Rd. SE12 ....7K 123
Guildersfield Rd. SW16 ....7J 137
Guildford Av. TW13: Felt 2H 129
Guildford Ct. SW8 ....7J 101
                    (off Guildford Rd.)
Guildford Gro. SE10 ....1D 122
Guildford Rd. CR0: Croy 6D 156
    E6 ....6D 88
    E17 ....1E 50
    IG3: Ilf 2J 71
    SW8 ....1J 119
Guildford Way SM6: Wall 5J 167
Guildhall
    City 7D 8 (6C 84)
    Westminster 7E 12 (2J 101)
Guildhall Art Gallery 7E 8 (6D 84)
Guildhall Bldgs. EC2 ....7E 8
Guildhall Library 7D 8 (6C 84)
Guildhall Offices EC2 ....7D 8
Guildhall Yd. EC2 ....7D 8 (6C 84)
Guildhouse St. SW1 ....3A 18 (4G 101)
Guildown Av. N12 ....4E 30
Guild Rd. SE7 ....6B 106
Guildsway E17 ....1B 50
Guilford Av. KT5: Surb 5F 151
Guilford Pl. WC1 ....4G 7 (4K 83)
Guilford St. WC1 ....4E 6 (4J 83)
Guilfoyle NW9 ....2B 44
Guillemot Ct. SE8 ....6B 104
                    (off Alexandra Cl.)
Guillemot Pl. N22 ....2K 47
Guilsborough Cl. NW10 ....7A 62
Guinea Ct. E1 ....7G 85
                    (off Royal Mint St.)
Guinness Cl. E9 ....7A 68
    UB3: Harl 3F 93
Guinness Ct. CR0: Croy 2F 169
    EC1 ....2D 8
    EC3 ....1J 15
    NW8 ....1C 82
    SE1 ....6G 15
    SW3 ....4E 16 (4D 100)
Guinness Sq. SE1 ....4E 102
Guinness Trust SW3 ....4D 100
Guinness Trust Bldgs. SE11 .....5B 102
    W6 ....5F 99
                    (off Fulham Pal. Rd.)
Guinness Trust Est. E15 ....1H 87
                    (off John St.)
    N16 ....1E 66
Guion Rd. SW6 ....2H 117
Gulland Wlk. N1 ....6C 66
                    (off Church Rd.)
Gulliver Cl. UB5: N'olt 1D 76
Gulliver Rd. DA15: Sidc 2H 143
Gulliver's Ho. EC1 ....4C 8
Gulliver St. SE16 ....3A 104
Gulston Wlk. SW3 ....4F 17

Gumleigh Rd. W5 ....4C 96
Gumley Gdns. TW7: Isle 3A 114
Gumping Rd. BR5: Farnb 2G 173
Gundulph Rd. BR2: Brom 3A 160
Gun Ho. E1 ....1H 103
                    (off Wapping High St.)
Gunmaker's La. E3 ....1A 86
    E9 ....1A 86
Gunnell Cl. CR0: Croy 6F 157
    SE25 ....6G 157
                    (off Backley Gdns.)
    SE26 ....4G 139
Gunner La. SE18 ....5E 106
GUNNERSBURY 5H 97
Gunnersbury Av. W3 ....1F 97
    W4 ....1F 97
    W5 ....1F 97
Gunnersbury Cl. W4 ....5H 97
Gunnersbury Ct. W3 ....2H 97
Gunnersbury Cres. W3 ....2G 97
Gunnersbury Dr. W5 ....2F 97
Gunnersbury Gdns. W3 ....2G 97
Gunnersbury La. W3 ....3G 97
Gunnersbury Mnr. W5 ....1F 97
Gunnersbury M. W4 ....5H 97
GUNNERSBURY PARK 3G 97
Gunnersbury Pk. Mus. 3G 97
Gunnersbury Triangle Nature Reserve
    ....4J 97
Gunners Gro. E4 ....3K 35
Gunners Rd. SW18 ....2B 136
Gunnery Ter. SE18 ....3G 107
Gunning St. SE18 ....4J 107
                    (off Gough Sq., not continuous)
Gunstor Rd. N16 ....4E 66
Gun St. E1 ....6J 9 (5F 85)
Gunter Gro. HA8: Edg 1K 43
Gunter Hall Studios SW10 ....6A 100
                    (off Gunter Gro.)
Gunterstone Rd. W14 ....4G 99
Gunthorpe St. E1 ....6K 9 (5F 85)
Gunton Rd. E5 ....3H 67
    SW17 ....6E 136
Gunwhale Cl. SE16 ....1K 103
Gun Wharf E1 ....1J 103
                    (off Wapping High St.)
Gun Wharf Bus. Cen. E3 ....1A 86
                    (off Old Ford Rd.)
Gurdon Ho. E14 ....6C 86
                    (off Dod St.)
Gurdon Rd. SE7 ....5J 105
Gurnard Cl. UB7: Yiew 7A 74
Gurnell Gro. W13 ....4K 77
Gurnell Leisure Cen. 3K 77
Gurney Cl. E15 ....5G 69
    E17 ....1K 49
    IG11: Bark 6F 71
Gurney Cres. CR0: Croy 1K 167
Gurney Dr. N2 ....4A 46
Gurney Ho. E2 ....2G 85
                    (off Goldsmiths Row)
    UB3: Harl 5G 93
Gurney Rd. E15 ....5G 69
    SM5: Cars 4E 166
    SW6 ....3A 118
    UB5: Yead 3K 75
Guthrie Ct. SE1 ....7K 13
Guthrie St. SW3 ....5C 16 (5B 100)
Gutter La. EC2 ....7C 8 (6C 84)
Guyatt Gdns. CR4: Mitc 2E 154
Guy Barnett Gro. SE3 ....3J 123
Guy Rd. SM6: Bedd 3H 167
Guyscliff Rd. SE13 ....5E 122
Guys Retreat IG9: Buck H 1F 37
Guy St. SE1 ....6F 15 (2D 102)
Gwalior Rd. SW15 ....4F 117
Gwendolen Av. SW15 ....4F 117
Gwendolen Cl. SW15 ....5F 117
Gwendolen Ho. TW19: Stanw 1A 128
                    (off Yeoman Dr.)
Gwendoline Av. E13 ....1K 87

Gwendwr Rd. W14 ....5G 99
Gweneth Cotts. HA8: Edg 6B 28
Gwent Ct. SE16 ....1K 103
                    (off Rotherhithe St.)
Gwillim Cl. DA15: Sidc 5A 126
Gwilym Maries Ho. E2 ....3H 85
                    (off Blythe St.)
Gwydor Rd. BR3: Beck 3K 157
Gwydyr Rd. BR2: Brom 3H 159
Gwyn Cl. SW6 ....7A 100
Gwynne Av. CR0: Croy 7K 157
Gwynne Cl. W4 ....6B 98
Gwynne Ho. E1 ....5H 85
                    (off Turner St.)
    SW1 ....5G 17
                    (off Lwr. Sloane St.)
    WC1 ....2J 7
                    (off Lloyd Baker St.)
Gwynne Pk. Av. IG8: Wfd G 6J 37
Gwynne Pl. WC1 ....2H 7 (3K 83)
Gwynne Rd. SW11 ....2B 118
Gylcote Cl. SE5 ....4D 120
Gyles Pk. HA7: Stan 1C 42
Gyllyngdune Gdns. IG3: Ilf 2K 71
GYPSY CORNER 5K 79

H

Haarlem Rd. W14 ....3F 99
Haberdasher Est. N1 ....1F 9 (3D 84)
Haberdasher Pl. N1 ....1F 9 (3D 84)
Haberdashers Ct. SE14 ....3K 121
Haberdasher St. N1 ....1F 9 (3D 84)
Habington Ho. SE5 ....7D 102
                    (off Notley St.)
Habitat Cl. SE15 ....2H 121
Habitat Sq. SE10 ....3H 105
                    (off Teal St.)
Haccombe Rd. SW19 ....6A 136
HACKBRIDGE 1E 166
Hackbridge Grn. SM6: Wall 2E 166
Hackbridge Pk. Gdns. SM5: Cars ..2D 166
Hackbridge Rd. SM6: Wall 2E 166
Hackford Rd. SW9 ....1K 119
Hackford Wlk. SW9 ....1K 119
Hackington Cres. BR3: Beck 6C 140
HACKNEY 6H 67
Hackney City Farm 2G 85
Hackney Empire Theatre 6H 67
Hackney Gro. E8 ....6H 67
Hackney Rd. E2 ....2J 9 (3F 85)
HACKNEY WICK 6B 68
Hackney Wick 6A 68
Hadar Cl. N20 ....1D 30
Hadden Rd. SE28 ....3J 107
Hadden Way UB6: G'frd 6H 59
Haddington Ct. SE10 ....7D 104
                    (off Tarves Way)
Haddington Rd. BR1: Brom 3F 141
Haddo Ho. SE10 ....6D 104
                    (off Haddo St.)
Haddon Cl. EN1: Enf 6B 24
    KT3: N Mald 5B 152
Haddon Ct. NW4 ....3E 44
    W3 ....7B 80
Haddonfield SE8 ....4K 103
Haddon Gro. DA15: Sidc 7K 125
Haddon Hall St. SE1 ....3D 102
                    (off Rephidim St.)
Haddon Rd. SM1: Sutt 4K 165
                    (not continuous)
Haden Ct. SE10 ....6D 104
Haden Ct. N4 ....2A 66
Haden La. N11 ....4B 32
Hadfield Cl. UB1: S'hall 1D 76
Hadfield Ho. E1 ....6G 85
                    (off Ellen St.)
Hadleigh Cl. E1 ....4J 85
    SW20 ....2G 153
Hadleigh Ct. E4 ....1B 36
Hadleigh Ho. E1 ....4J 85
                    (off Hadleigh Cl.)

Hadleigh Rd. N9 ....7C 24
Hadleigh St. E2 ....3J 85
Hadleigh Wlk. E6 ....6C 88
HADLEY 3C 20
Hadley Cl. N21 ....6F 23
Hadley Comn. EN5: Barn, New Barn ..2D 20
Hadley Ct. EN5: New Bar 3E 20
    N16 ....1G 67
Hadley Gdns. UB2: S'hall 5D 94
    W4 ....5K 97
Hadley Grn. EN5: Barn 2C 20
Hadley Grn. Rd. EN5: Barn 2C 20
Hadley Grn. W. EN5: Barn 2C 20
Hadley Gro. EN5: Barn 2B 20
Hadley Highstone EN5: Barn 1C 20
Hadley M. EN5: Barn 3C 20
Hadley Pde. EN5: Barn 3B 20
                    (off High St.)
Hadley Ridge EN5: Barn 3C 20
Hadley Rd. CR4: Mitc 4H 155
    DA17: Belv 4F 109
    EN2: Enf 1A 22
    EN4: Had W 1K 21
    EN5: New Bar 2E 20
Hadley St. NW1 ....6F 65
                    (not continuous)
Hadley Way N21 ....6F 23
HADLEY WOOD 1F 21
Hadley Wood Lawn Tennis Club ...1F 21
Hadley Wood Nature Reserve 2F 21
Hadley Wood Rd. EN4: Cockf 2F 21
    EN5: Cockf, New Bar 2F 21
Hadlow Ho. SE17 ....5E 102
                    (off Kinglake Est.)
Hadlow Pl. SE19 ....7G 139
Hadlow Rd. DA14: Sidc 4A 144
    DA16: Well 7C 108
Hadrian Cl. E3 ....1C 86
                    (off Garrison Rd.)
    TW19: Stanw 7A 110
Hadrian Ct. SM2: Sutt 7K 165
Hadrian Est. E2 ....2G 85
Hadrians Ride EN1: Enf 5A 24
Hadrian St. SE10 ....5G 105
Hadrian Way TW19: Stanw 7A 110
                    (not continuous)
Hadstock Ho. NW1 ....1D 6
                    (off Ossulston St.)
Hadyn Pk. Ct. W12 ....2C 98
                    (off Curwen Rd.)
Hadyn Pk. Rd. W12 ....2C 98
Hafer Rd. SW11 ....4D 118
Hafton Rd. SE6 ....1G 141
Haggard Rd. TW1: Twick 7B 114
Hagger Ct. E17 ....3F 51
HAGGERSTON 7F 67
Haggerston Rd. E8 ....7F 67
Haggerston Studios E8 ....1F 85
                    (off Kingsland Rd.)
Hague St. E2 ....3G 85
Ha Ha Rd. SE18 ....6D 106
Haig Ho. E2 ....1K 9
                    (off Shipton St.)
Haig Pl. SM4: Mord 6J 153
Haig Rd. HA7: Stan 5H 27
    UB8: Hill 5D 74
Haig Rd. E. E13 ....3A 88
Haig Rd. W. E13 ....3A 88
Haigville Gdns. IG6: Ilf 4F 53
Hailes Cl. SW19 ....6A 136
Haileybury Av. EN1: Enf 6A 24
Hailey Rd. DA18: Erith 2G 109
Hailey Rd. Bus. Pk. DA18: Erith ..2G 109
Hailing M. BR2: Brom 3K 159
                    (off Wendover Rd.)
Hailsham Av. SW2 ....2K 137
Hailsham Cl. KT6: Surb 7D 150
Hailsham Dr. HA1: Harr 3H 41
Hailsham Rd. SW17 ....6E 136
Hailsham Ter. N18 ....5J 33
Haimo Rd. SE9 ....5B 124
Hainault Ct. E17 ....4F 51
Hainault Gore RM6: Chad H 5E 54

Hainault Rd. E11 . 1E 68
RM5: Col R, Rom . 2J 55
RM6: Chad H . 1B 54
(Forest Rd.)
RM6: Chad H . 6F 55
(High Rd.)
Hainault St. IG1: Ilf . 2G 71
SE9 . 1F 143
Haines St. SW8 . 7G 101
Haines Wlk. SM4: Mord . 7K 153
Hainford Cl. SE4 . 4K 121
Haining Cl. W4 . 5G 97
Hainthorpe Rd. SE27 . 3B 138
Hainton Cl. E1 . 6H 85
Halberd M. E5 . 2H 67
Halbutt Gdns. RM9: Dag . 3F 73
Halbutt St. RM9: Dag . 4F 73
Halcomb St. N1 . 1E 84
Halcot Av. DA6: Bex . 5H 127
Halcrow St. E1 . 5H 85
Halcyon *EN1: Enf . 5K 23*
(off Private Rd.)
Halcyon Wharf *E1 . 1G 103*
(off Hermitage Wall)
Haldane Cl. N10 . 7A 32
Haldane Pl. SW18 . 1K 135
Haldane Rd. E6 . 3B 88
SE28 . 7D 90
SW6 . 7H 99
UB1: S'hall . 7G 77
Haldan Rd. E4 . 6K 35
Haldon Rd. SW18 . 6H 117
HALE, THE . 5D 28
Hale, The E4 . 7A 36
N17 . 3G 49
Hale Cl. BR6: Farnb . 4G 173
E4 . 3K 35
HA8: Edg . 5D 28
Hale Ct. HA8: Edg . 5D 28
Hale Dr. NW7 . 6D 28
HALE END . 6B 36
Hale End Cl. HA4: Ruis . 6J 39
Hale End Rd. E4 . 6A 36
E17 . 1E 50
IG8: Wfd G . 7A 36
Halefield Rd. N17 . 1H 49
Hale Gdns. N17 . 4G 49
W3 . 1G 97
Hale Gro. Gdns. NW7 . 5F 29
Hale Ho. *SW1 . 5D 18*
(off Lindsay Sq.)
Hale La. HA8: Edg . 5C 28
NW7 . 5E 28
Hale Path SE27 . 4B 138
Hale Rd. E6 . 4C 88
N17 . 3G 49
Halesowen Rd. SM4: Mord . 7K 153
Hales Prior *N1 . 1G 7*
(off Calshot St.)
Hales St. SE8 . 7C 104
Hale St. E14 . 7D 86
Halesworth Cl. E5 . 2J 67
Halesworth Rd. SE13 . 3D 122
Hale Wlk. W7 . 5J 77
Haley Rd. NW4 . 6E 44
Half Acre HA7: Stan . 5H 27
TW8: Bford . 6D 96
Half Acre Rd. W7 . 1J 95
Half Moon Ct. EC1 . 6C 8
Half Moon Cres. N1 . 2K 83
(not continuous)
Half Moon La. SE24 . 6C 120
Half Moon Pas. E1 . 1K 15 (6F 85)
(not continuous)
Half Moon St. W1 . 4K 11 (1F 101)
Halford Cl. HA8: Edg . 2H 43
Halford Rd. E10 . 5F 51
SW6 . 6J 99
TW10: Rich . 5E 114
UB10: Ick . 4C 56
Halfway St. DA15: Sidc . 7H 125
Haliburton Rd.
TW1: Twick . 5A 114
Haliday Ho. *N1 . 6D 66*
(off Mildmay St.)
Haliday Wlk. N1 . 6D 66
Halidon Cl. E9 . 5J 67
Halifax NW9 . 2B 44
Halifax Cl. TW11: Tedd . 6J 131
Halifax Rd. EN2: Enf . 2H 23
UB6: G'frd . 1F 77
Halifax St. SE26 . 3H 139
Halifield Dr. DA17: Belv . 3E 108
Haling Down Pas. CR8: Purl . 7C 168
(not continuous)
Haling Gro. CR2: S Croy . 7C 168
Haling Pk. Gdns. CR2: S Croy . 6B 168
Haling Pk. Rd. CR2: S Croy . 5B 168
Haling Rd. CR2: S Croy . 6D 168
Haliwell Ho. *NW6 . 1K 81*
(off Mortimer Cres.)
Halkett Ho. *E2 . 1J 85*
(off Waterloo Gdns.)
Halkin Arc. SW1 . 1F 17 (3D 100)
Halkin M. SW1 . 1G 17 (3E 100)
Halkin Pl. SW1 . 1G 17 (3E 100)
Halkin St. SW1 . 7H 11 (2E 100)
Hall, The SE3 . 3J 123
Hallam Cl. BR7: Chst . 5D 142
Hallam Ct. *W1 . 5K 5*
(off Hallam St.)
Hallam Gdns. HA5: H End . 1C 40
Hallam Ho. *SW1 . 6B 18*
(off Churchill Gdns.)
Hallam M. W1 . 5K 5 (5F 83)
Hallam Rd. N15 . 4B 48
SW13 . 3D 116
Hallam St. W1 . 4K 5 (4F 83)
Hallane Ho. SE27 . 5C 138
Hall Cl. W5 . 5E 78
Hall Ct. TW11: Tedd . 5K 131
Hall Dr. SE26 . 5J 139
W7 . 6J 77
Halley Gdns. SE13 . 4F 123
Halley Ho. *E2 . 2G 85*
(off Pritchards Rd.)
SE10 . 5H 105
(off Armitage Rd.)
Halley Rd. E7 . 6A 70
E12 . 6A 70
Halley St. E14 . 5A 86
Hall Farm Cl. HA7: Stan . 4G 27
Hall Farm Dr. TW2: Whit . 7H 113
Hallfield Est. W2 . 6A 82
(not continuous)
Hall Gdns. E4 . 4G 35
Hall Ga. NW8 . 1A 4 (3B 82)
Halliards, The KT12: Walt T . 6J 147
Halliday Sq. UB2: S'hall . 1H 95
Halliford Cl. TW17: Shep . 4F 147
Halliford Rd. TW16: Sun . 5G 147
TW17: Shep . 5G 147
Halliford St. N1 . 7C 66
Hallingbury Ct. E17 . 3D 50
Halling Ho. *SE1 . 7F 15*
(off Long La.)
Hallings Wharf Studios E15 . 1F 87
Halliwell Ct. SE22 . 5G 121
Halliwell Rd. SW2 . 6K 119
Halliwick Ct. Pde. *N12 . 6J 31*
(off Woodhouse Rd.)
Halliwick Rd. N10 . 1E 46
Hall La. E4 . 5F 35
NW4 . 1C 44
UB3: Harl . 7F 93
HALL LANE JUNC. . 5E 34
Hallmark Trad. Cen. HA9: Wemb . 4J 61
Hallmead Rd. SM1: Sutt . 3K 165
Hall Oak Wlk. NW6 . 6H 63
Hallowell Av. CR0: Bedd . 4J 167
Hallowell Cl. CR4: Mitc . 3E 154
Hallowell Rd. HA6: Nwood . 1G 39
Hallowfield Way CR4: Mitc . 3B 154
Hallows Gro. TW16: Sun . 5H 129
Hall Pl. W2 . 4A 4 (4B 82)
(not continuous)
Hall Place & Vis. Cen. . 6J 127
Hall Pl. Cres. DA5: Bexl . 5J 127
Hall Place Gdns. . 6J 127
Hall Rd. E6 . 1D 88
E15 . 4F 69
NW8 . 1A 4 (3A 82)
RM6: Chad H . 6C 54
SM6: Wall . 7F 167
TW7: Isle . 5H 113
Hallside Rd. EN1: Enf . 1A 24
Hall St. EC1 . 1B 8 (3B 84)
N12 . 5F 31
Hallsville Rd. E16 . 6H 87
Hallswelle Pde. NW11 . 5H 45
Hallswelle Rd. NW11 . 5H 45
Hall Twr. W2 . 5B 4
Hall Vw. SE9 . 2B 142
Hallywell Cres. E6 . 5D 88
Halons Rd. SE9 . 7E 124
Halpin Pl. SE17 . 4D 102
Halsbrook Rd. SE3 . 3A 124
Halsbury Cl. HA7: Stan . 4G 27
Halsbury Ct. HA7: Stan . 5G 27
Halsbury Ho. *N7 . 4K 65*
(off Biddestone Rd.)
Halsbury Rd. W12 . 1D 98
Halsbury Rd. E. UB5: N'olt . 4G 59
Halsbury Rd. W. UB5: N'olt . 5F 59
Halsend UB3: Hayes . 1K 93
Halsey M. SW3 . 3E 16 (4D 100)
Halsey St. SW3 . 3E 16 (4D 100)
Halsham Cres. IG11: Bark . 5K 71
Halsmere Rd. SE5 . 1B 120
Halstead Cl. CR0: Croy . 3C 168
Halstead Ct. E17 . 7B 50
N1 . 1F 9
(off Fairbank Est.)
Halstead Gdns. N21 . 1J 33
Halstead Rd. E11 . 5J 51
EN1: Enf . 4K 23
N21 . 1H 33
Halston Cl. SW11 . 6D 118
Halstow Rd. NW10 . 3F 81
SE10 . 5J 105
Halsway UB3: Hayes . 1J 93
Halton Cl. N11 . 6J 31
Halton Cross St. N1 . 1B 84
Halton Mans. N1 . 7B 66
Halton Pl. N1 . 1C 84
Halton Rd. N1 . 7B 66
Halt Robin La. DA17: Belv . 4H 109
Halt Robin Rd. DA17: Belv . 4G 109
(not continuous)
Halyard Ho. E14 . 3E 104
HAM . 3C 132
Ham, The TW8: Bford . 7C 96
Hamara Ghar E13 . 1A 88
Hambalt Rd. SW4 . 5G 119
Hamble Cl. HA4: Ruis . 2G 57
Hambledon *SE17 . 6D 102*
(off Villa St.)
Hambledon Cl. UB8: Hil . 4D 74
Hambledon Ct. SE22 . 4E 120
W5 . 7E 78
Hambledon Gdns. SE25 . 3F 157
Hambledon Pl. SE21 . 1E 138
Hambledon Rd. SW18 . 7H 117
Hambledown Rd. DA15: Sidc . 7H 125
Hamblehyrst BR3: Beck . 2D 158
Hamble St. SW6 . 3K 117
Hambleton Cl. KT4: Wor Pk . 2E 164
Hamble Wlk. *UB5: N'olt . 2E 76*
(off Brabazon Rd.)
Hambley Ho. *SE16 . 4H 103*
(off Camilla Rd.)
Hamblin Ho. *UB1: S'hall . 7C 76*
(off The Broadway)
Hambridge Way SW2 . 7A 120
Hambro Av. BR2: Hayes . 1J 171
Hambrook Rd. SE25 . 3H 157
Hambro Rd. SW16 . 6H 137
Hambrough Ho. UB4: Yead . 5A 76
Hambrough Rd. UB1: S'hall . 1C 94
Ham Cl. TW10: Ham . 3C 132
(not continuous)
Ham Comn. TW10: Ham . 3D 132
Ham Ct. NW9 . 2A 44
Ham Cft. Cl. TW13: Felt . 3J 129
Hamden Cres. RM10: Dag . 3H 73
Hamel Cl. HA3: Kent . 4D 42
Hame Way E6 . 4E 88
Ham Farm Rd. TW10: Ham . 4D 132
Hamfrith Rd. E15 . 6H 69
Ham Ga. Av. TW10: Ham . 3D 132
Ham House . 1C 132
Hamilton Av. IG6: Ilf . 4F 53
KT6: Surb . 2G 163
N9 . 7B 24
RM1: Rom . 2K 55
SM3: Cheam . 2G 165
Hamilton Bldgs. EC2 . 4H 9
Hamilton Cl. EN4: Cockf . 4H 21
HA7: Stan . 2D 26
N17 . 3F 49
NW8 . 2A 4 (3B 82)
SE16 . 2A 104
TW11: Tedd . 6B 132
TW13: Felt . 5H 129
Hamilton Ct. CR0: Croy . 1G 169
SE6 . 1H 141
SW15 . 3G 117
W5 . 7E 78
W9 . 3A 82
(off Maida Va.)
Hamilton Cres. HA2: Harr . 3D 58
N13 . 4F 33
TW3: Houn . 5F 113
Hamilton Gdns. NW8 . 1A 4 (3A 82)
Hamilton Hall *NW8 . 2A 82*
(off Hamilton Ter.)
Hamilton Ho. *E14 . 5D 104*
(off St Davids Sq.)
E14 . 7B 86
(off Victory Pl.)
NW8 . 1A 4
W4 . 6A 98
W8 . 2K 99
(off Vicarage Ga.)
Hamilton La. N5 . 4B 66
Hamilton Lodge *E1 . 4J 85*
(off Cleveland Gro.)
Hamilton M. SW18 . 1J 135
SW19 . 7J 135
W1 . 6J 11 (2F 101)
Hamilton Pde. TW13: Felt . 4H 129
Hamilton Pk. N5 . 4B 66
Hamilton Pk. W. N5 . 4B 66
Hamilton Pl. N19 . 3H 65
TW16: Sun . 7K 129
W1 . 5H 11 (1E 100)
Hamilton Rd. CR7: Thor H . 3D 156
DA7: Bex . 2E 126
DA15: Sidc . 4A 144
E15 . 3G 87
E17 . 2A 50
EN4: Cockf . 4H 21
HA1: Harr . 5J 41
IG1: Ilf . 4F 71
N2 . 3A 46
N9 . 7B 24
NW10 . 5C 62
NW11 . 7F 45
SE27 . 4D 138
SW19 . 7K 135
TW2: Twick . 1J 131
TW8: Bford . 6D 96
TW13: Felt . 4H 129
UB1: S'hall . 1D 94
UB3: Hayes . 7K 75
W4 . 2A 98
W5 . 7E 78
Hamilton Rd. Ind. Est. *SE27 . 4D 138*
(off Hamilton Rd.)
Hamilton Rd. M. SW19 . 7K 135
Hamilton Sq. N12 . 6G 31
SE1 . 6F 15 (2D 102)

Hamilton St.—Hanway Pl.

Hamilton St. SE8 .6C 104
Hamilton Ter. NW8 .2A 4 (2K 81)
Hamilton Way N3 .6D 30
N13 .4G 33
SM6: Wall .7H 167
Ham Lands Nature Reserve .2A 132
Hamlea Cl. SE12 .5J 123
Hamlet, The SE5 .3D 120
Hamlet Cl. RM5: Col R .1G 55
SE13 .4G 123
Hamlet Ct. EN1: Enf .5K 23
SE11 .5B 102
(off Opal St.)
W6 .4C 98
Hamlet Gdns. W6 .4C 98
Hamlet Ind. Est. E9 .7C 68
Hamlet Intl. Ind. Est. DA8: Erith .5K 109
Hamlet M. SE21 .1D 138
Hamlet Rd. RM5: Col R .1G 55
SE19 .7F 139
Hamlet Sq. NW2 .3G 63
Hamlets Way E3 .4B 86
Hamlet Way SE1 .6F 15 (2D 102)
Hamlin Cres. HA5: Eastc .5A 40
Hamlyn Cl. HA8: Edg .3K 27
Hamlyn Gdns. SE19 .7E 138
Hammelton Ct. BR1: Brom .1H 159
(off London Rd.)
Hammelton Grn. SW9 .1B 120
Hammelton Rd. BR1: Brom .1H 159
Hammerfield Ho. SW3 .5D 16
(off Cale St.)
Hammers La. NW7 .5H 29
Hammersley Ho. SE14 .7J 103
(off Pomeroy St.)
HAMMERSMITH .4E 98
Hammersmith Bri. W6 .5D 98
Hammersmith Bri. Rd. W6 .5E 98
HAMMERSMITH BROADWAY .4E 98
Hammersmith B'way. W6 .4E 98
HAMMERSMITH FLYOVER .5E 98
Hammersmith Flyover W6 .5E 98
Hammersmith Gro. W6 .2E 98
Hammersmith Ind. Est. W6 .6E 98
Hammersmith Rd. W6 .4F 99
W14 .4F 99
Hammersmith Ter. W6 .5C 98
Hammet Cl. UB4: Yead .5B 76
Hammett St. EC3 .2J 15 (7F 85)
Hammond Av. CR4: Mitc .2F 155
Hammond Cl. EN5: Barn .5B 20
TW12: Hamp .1E 148
UB6: G'frd .5H 59
Hammond Ct. E10 .2D 68
(off Crescent Rd.)
E17 .5A 50
(off Maude Rd.)
Hammond Ho. E14 .3C 104
(off Tiller Rd.)
SE14 .7J 103
(off Lubbock St.)
Hammond Lodge W9 .5J 81
(off Admiral Wlk.)
Hammond Rd. EN1: Enf .2C 24
UB2: S'hall .3C 94
Hammonds Cl. RM8: Dag .3C 72
Hammond St. NW5 .6G 65
Hammond Way SE28 .7B 90
Hamond Cl. CR2: S Croy .7B 168
Hamonde Cl. HA8: Edg .2C 28
Hamond Sq. N1 .2E 84
Ham Pk. Rd. E7 .7H 69
E15 .7H 69
Hampden Av. BR3: Beck .2A 158
Hampden Cl. NW1 .2H 83
Hampden Ct. N10 .7K 31
Hampden Gurney St. W1 .1E 10 (6D 82)
Hampden Ho. SW9 .2A 120
Hampden La. N17 .1F 49
Hampden Rd. BR3: Beck .2A 158
HA3: Hrw W .1G 41
KT1: King T .3G 151
N8 .4A 48
Hampden Rd. N10 .7K 31
N17 .1G 49
N19 .2H 65
RM5: Col R .1H 55
Hampden Sq. N14 .1A 32
Hampden Way N14 .1A 32
Hampshire Cl. N18 .5C 34
Hampshire Hog La. W6 .5D 98
Hampshire Rd. N22 .7E 32
Hampshire St. NW5 .6H 65
Hampson Way SW8 .1K 119
HAMPSTEAD .4B 64
Hampstead Av. IG8: Wfd G .7K 37
Hampstead Cl. SE28 .1B 108
Hampstead Gdns. NW11 .6J 45
RM6: Chad H .5B 54
HAMPSTEAD GARDEN SUBURB .5A 46
Hampstead Ga. NW3 .5A 64
Hampstead Grn. NW3 .5C 64
Hampstead Gro. NW3 .3A 64
Hampstead Heath .2B 64
Hampstead Heath Info. Cen. .4E 64
(off Lissenden Gdns.)
Hampstead Hgts. N2 .3A 46
Hampstead High St. NW3 .4B 64
Hampstead Hill Gdns. NW3 .4B 64
Hampstead La. N6 .1B 64
NW3 .1B 64
Hampstead Lodge NW1 .5C 4
(off Bell St.)
Hampstead Mus. .4B 64
(in Burgh House)
Hampstead Rd. NW1 .1A 6 (2G 83)
Hampstead Sq. NW3 .3A 64
Hampstead Theatre .7B 64
Hampstead Wlk. E3 .1B 86
Hampstead Way NW11 .5H 45
Hampstead W. NW6 .6J 63
HAMPTON .1F 149
Hampton & Richmond Borough FC .1F 149
Hampton Cl. N11 .5A 32
NW6 .3J 81
SW20 .7E 134
HAMPTON COURT .4J 149
Hampton Court .2J 149
HAMPTON COURT .3J 149
Hampton Ct. N1 .6B 66
N22 .1G 47
SE16 .7K 85
(off King & Queen Wharf)
Hampton Ct. Av. KT8: E Mos .6H 149
Hampton Ct. Bri. KT8: E Mos .4J 149
Hampton Ct. Cres. KT8: E Mos .3H 149
Hampton Ct. Est. KT7: E Mos .4J 149
Hampton Ct. M. KT8: E Mos .4J 149
(off Feltham Av.)
Hampton Court Palace .4K 149
Hampton Ct. Pde. KT8: E Mos .4J 149
Hampton Ct. Rd. KT1: Ham W .3K 149
KT8: E Mos .3K 149
TW12: Hamp .2G 149
Hampton Ct. Way KT7: T Ditt .7J 149
KT8: E Mos .7J 149
Hampton Farm Ind. Est.
TW13: Hanw .3C 130
HAMPTON HILL .5G 131
Hampton Hill Playhouse Theatre .5G 131
Hampton Ho. DA7: Bex .2H 127
(off Erith Rd.)
Hampton La. TW13: Hanw .4C 130
Hampton M. NW10 .3K 79
Hampton Open Air Pool .7G 131
Hampton Ri. HA3: Kent .6E 42
Hampton Rd. CR0: Croy .6C 156
E4 .5G 35
E7 .5K 69
E11 .1F 69
IG1: Ilf .4G 71
KT4: Wor Pk .2C 164
TW2: Twick .3H 131
TW11: Tedd .5H 131
TW12: Tedd .5H 131
Hampton Rd. E. TW13: Hanw .4D 130
Hampton Rd. Ind. Pk. CR0: Croy .6C 156
Hampton Rd. W. TW13: Hanw .3C 130
Hampton Sport, Arts & Fitness Cen. .5E 130
Hampton St. SE17 .4B 102
HAMPTON WICK .1C 150
Hampton Youth Project .6D 130
Ham Ridings TW10: Ham .5F 133
Hamshades Cl. DA15: Sidc .3K 143
Hamston Ho. W8 .3K 99
(off Kensington Ct. Pl.)
Ham St. TW10: Ham .1B 132
Ham Vw. CR0: Croy .6A 158
Ham Yd. W1 .2C 12 (7H 83)
Hanah Ct. SW19 .7F 135
Hanameel St. E16 .1J 105
Hana M. E5 .4H 67
Hanbury Cl. NW4 .3E 44
Hanbury Ct. HA1: Harr .6K 41
Hanbury Dr. E11 .7H 51
N21 .5E 22
Hanbury Ho. E1 .5G 85
(off Hanbury St.)
SW8 .7J 101
(off Regent's Bri. Gdns.)
Hanbury M. N1 .1C 84
Hanbury Rd. N17 .2H 49
W3 .2H 97
Hanbury St. E1 .5K 9 (5F 85)
Hanbury Wlk. DA5: Bexl .3K 145
Hancock Nunn Ho. NW3 .6D 64
(off Fellows Rd.)
Hancock Rd. E3 .3E 86
SE19 .6D 138
Handa Wlk. N1 .6D 66
Hand Ct. WC1 .6H 7 (5K 83)
Handcroft Rd. CR0: Croy .7B 156
Handel Cl. HA8: Edg .6A 28
Handel House Mus. .2J 11
(off Brook St.)
Handel Mans. SW13 .7E 98
WC1 .3F 7
(off Handel St.)
Handel Pde. HA8: Edg .7B 28
(off Whitchurch La.)
Handel Pl. NW10 .6K 61
Handels Bus. Cen. SW8 .7E 18 (6J 101)
Handel St. WC1 .3E 6 (4J 83)
Handel Way HA8: Edg .7B 28
Handen Rd. SE12 .5G 123
Handforth Rd. IG1: Ilf .3F 71
SW9 .7A 102
Handley Gro. NW2 .3F 63
Handley Page Rd.
SM6: Wall .7K 167
Handley Rd. E9 .7J 67
Handowe Cl. NW4 .4C 44
Handside Cl. KT4: Wor Pk .1F 165
Hands Wlk. E16 .6J 87
Handsworth Av. E4 .6A 36
Handsworth Rd. N17 .3D 48
Handtrough Way IG11: Bark .2F 89
Hanford Cl. SW18 .1J 135
Hanford Row SW19 .6E 134
Hanger Ct. W5 .4F 79
Hanger Grn. W5 .4G 79
HANGER HILL .4F 79
HANGER LANE .3E 78
Hanger La. W5 .2E 78
Hanger Va. La. W5 .6F 79
(not continuous)
Hanger Vw. Way W3 .6G 79
Hanging Sword All. EC4 .1K 13
Hankey Ho. SE1 .7F 15
(off Manciple St.)
Hankey Pl. SE1 .7F 15 (2D 102)
Hankins La. NW7 .2F 29
Hanley Gdns. N4 .1K 65
Hanley Pl. BR3: Beck .7C 140
Hanley Rd. N4 .1J 65
Hanmer Wlk. N7 .2K 65
Hannah Barlow Ho. SW8 .1K 119
Hannah Cl. BR3: Beck .3E 158
NW10 .4J 61
Hannah Mary Way SE1 .4G 103
Hannah M. SM6: Wall .7G 167
Hannay La. N8 .7H 47
Hannay Wlk. SW16 .2H 137
Hannell Rd. SW6 .7G 99
Hannen Rd. SE27 .3B 138
Hannibal Rd. E1 .5J 85
TW19: Stanw .7A 110
Hannibal Way CR0: Wadd .5K 167
Hannington Rd. SW4 .3F 119
Hanno Cl. SM6: Wall .7H 167
Hanover Av. E16 .1J 105
TW13: Felt .1J 129
Hanover Circ. UB3: Hayes .6E 74
Hanover Cl. SM3: Cheam .4G 165
TW9: Kew .7G 97
Hanover Ct. HA4: Ruis .3J 57
NW9 .3A 44
SE19 .7G 139
(off Anerley Rd.)
SW15 .4B 116
W12 .1C 98
(off Uxbridge Rd.)
Hanover Dr. BR7: Chst .4G 143
Hanover Flats W1 .2H 11
(off Binney St., not continuous)
Hanover Gdns. IG6: Ilf .1G 53
SE11 .6A 102
Hanover Ga. NW1 .2D 4 (3C 82)
Hanover Ga. Mans. NW1 .3D 4
(off Park Rd.)
Hanover Ho. E14 .1B 104
(off Westferry Cir.)
NW8 .1C 4
SW9 .3A 120
Hanover Mans. SW2 .5A 120
(off Barnwell Rd.)
Hanover Mead NW11 .5G 45
Hanover Pk. SE15 .1G 121
Hanover Pl. E3 .3B 86
WC2 .1F 13 (6J 83)
Hanover Rd. N15 .4F 49
NW10 .7E 62
SW19 .7A 136
Hanover Sq. W1 .1K 11 (6F 83)
Hanover Steps W2 .1D 10
Hanover St. CR0: Croy .3B 168
W1 .1K 11 (6F 83)
Hanover Ter. NW1 .2E 4 (3C 82)
TW7: Isle .1A 114
Hanover Ter. M. NW1 .2D 4 (3C 82)
Hanover Trad. Est. N7 .5J 65
Hanover Way DA6: Bex .3D 126
Hanover W. Ind. Est. NW10 .3K 79
Hanover Yd. N1 .2C 84
(off Noel Rd.)
Hansa Cl. UB2: S'hall .3A 94
Hansard M. W14 .2F 99
Hansart Way EN2: Enf .1F 23
Hanscomb M. SW4 .4G 119
Hans Ct. SW3 .1E 16
Hans Cres. SW1 .1E 16 (3D 100)
Hanselin Cl. HA7: Stan .5E 26
Hansen Dr. N21 .5E 22
Hanshaw Dr. HA8: Edg .1K 43
Hansler Gro. KT8: E Mos .4H 149
Hansler Rd. SE22 .5F 121
Hansol Rd. DA6: Bex .5E 126
Hansom Ter. BR1: Brom .1K 159
(off Freelands Gro.)
Hanson Cl. BR3: Beck .6D 140
SW12 .7F 119
SW14 .3J 115
UB7: W Dray .3B 92
Hanson Ct. E17 .6D 50
Hanson Gdns. UB1: S'hall .2C 94
Hanson St. W1 .5A 6 (5G 83)
Hans Pl. SW1 .1F 17 (3D 100)
Hans Rd. SW3 .1E 16 (3D 100)
Hans St. SW1 .2F 17 (3D 100)
Hanway Pl. W1 .7C 6 (6H 83)

A-Z London 277

Hanway Rd. W7 ....6H 77
Hanway St. W1 ....7C 6 (6H 83)
HANWELL 1K 95
Hanwell Fitness Cen. 1K 95
Hanwell Ho. W2 ....5J 81
(off Brunel Est.)
HANWORTH 4B 130
Hanworth Ho. SE5 ....7B 102
(off Camberwell New Rd., not continuous)
Hanworth Rd. TW3: Houn 1C 130
TW4: Houn 1C 130
TW12: Hamp 4D 130
TW13: Felt 1K 129
TW16: Sun 1C 130
(not continuous)
Hanworth Ter. TW3: Houn 4F 113
Hanworth Trad. Est. TW13: Hanw ...3C 130
Hapgood Cl. UB6: G'frd 5H 59
Harad's Pl. E1 ....1G 85
Harben Pde. NW3 ....7A 64
(off Finchley Rd.)
Harben Rd. NW6 ....7A 64
Harberson Rd. E15 ....1H 87
SW12 ....1F 137
Harberton Rd. N19 ....1G 65
Harbet Rd. E4 ....5F 35
N18 ....5F 35
W2 ....6B 4 (5B 82)
Harbex Cl. DA5: Bexl 7H 127
Harbinger Rd. E14 ....4D 104
Harbledown Ho. SE1 ....7E 14
(off Manciple St.)
Harbledown Rd. SW6 ....1J 117
Harbord Cl. SE5 ....2D 120
Harbord Ho. SE16 ....4K 103
(off Cope St.)
Harbord St. SW6 ....1F 117
Harborough Av. DA15: Sidc ...7J 125
Harborough Rd. SW16 ......4K 137
Harbour Av. SW10 ....1A 118
Harbour Club Leisure Cen., The ...2A 118
Harbour Exchange Sq. E14 ...2D 104
Harbour Quay E14 ....1E 104
Harbour Reach SW6 ....1A 118
Harbour Yd. SW10 ....1A 118
Harbridge Av. SW15 ....7B 116
Harbury Rd. SM5: Cars 7C 166
Harbut Rd. SW11 ....4B 118
(not continuous)
Harcombe Rd. N16 ....3E 66
Harcourt Av. DA15: Sidc 6C 126
E12 ....4D 70
HA8: Edg 3D 28
SM6: Wall 4F 167
Harcourt Bldgs. EC4 ....2J 13
Harcourt Cl. TW7: Isle 3A 114
Harcourt Fld. SM6: Wall 4F 167
Harcourt Ho. W1 ....7J 5
(off Cavendish Sq.)
Harcourt Lodge SM6: Wall ...4F 167
Harcourt Rd. CR7: Thor H 6K 155
DA6: Bex 4E 126
E15 ....2H 87
N22 ....1H 47
SE4 ....3B 122
SM6: Wall 4F 167
SW19 ....7J 135
Harcourt St. W1 ....6D 4 (5C 82)
Harcourt Ter. SW10 ....5K 99
Hardcastle Cl. CR0: Croy 6G 157
Hardcastle Ho. SE14 ......1A 122
(off Loring Rd.)
Hardcourts Cl. BR4: W W'ck ...3D 170
Hardel Ri. SW2 ....1B 138
Hardel Wlk. SW2 ....7A 120
Harden Ct. SE4 ....4C 106
Harden Ho. SE5 ....2E 120
Harden's Manorway SE7 ....3B 106
(not continuous)
Harders Rd. SE15 ....2H 121
Hardess St. SE24 ....3C 120
Hardie Cl. NW10 ....5K 61

Hardie Rd. RM10: Dag 3J 73
Harding Cl. CR0: Croy 3F 169
SE17 ....6C 102
Hardinge Cl. UB8: Hil 5D 74
Hardinge Cres. SE18 ......3G 107
Hardinge La. E1 ....6J 85
(not continuous)
Hardinge Rd. N18 ....6K 33
NW10 ....1D 80
Hardinge St. E1 ....7J 85
(not continuous)
Harding Ho. SW13 ....6D 98
(off Wyatt Dr.)
UB3: Hayes 6K 75
Harding Rd. DA7: Bex 2F 127
Harding's Cl. KT2: King T ...1F 151
Hardings La. SE20 ....6K 139
Hardington NW1 ....7E 64
(off Belmont St.)
Hardman Rd. KT2: King T ...2E 150
SE7 ....5K 105
Hardwick Cl. HA7: Stan 5H 27
Hardwick Ct. DA8: Erith 6K 109
Hardwicke Av. TW5: Hest ...1E 112
Hardwicke M. WC1 ....2H 7
Hardwicke Rd. N13 ....6D 32
TW10: Ham 4C 132
W4 ....4K 97
Hardwick Ho. NW8 ....3D 4
(off Lilestone St.)
Hardwick Pl. SW16 ....7G 137
Hardwick St. EC1 ....2K 7 (3A 84)
Hardwicks Way SW18 ......5J 117
Hardwidge St. SE1 ....6G 15 (2E 102)
Hardy Av. E16 ....1J 105
HA4: Ruis 5K 57
Hardy Cl. EN5: Barn 6B 20
HA5: Pinn 7B 40
SE16 ....2K 103
Hardy Cotts. SE10 ....6F 105
Hardy Ho. SW4 ....7G 119
Hardying Ho. E17 ....4A 50
Hardy Pas. N22 ....1K 47
Hardy Rd. E4 ....6G 35
SE3 ....7H 105
SW19 ....7K 135
Hardy's M. KT8: E Mos 4J 149
Hardy Way EN2: Enf 1F 23
Hare & Billet Rd. SE3 ......1F 123
Harebell Dr. E6 ....5E 88
Harecastle Cl. UB4: Yead ...4C 76
Hare Ct. EC4 ....1J 13 (6A 84)
Harecourt Rd. N1 ....6C 66
Haredale Rd. SE24 ....4C 120
Haredon Cl. SE23 ....7K 121
HAREFIELD 1A 38
Harefield Cl. EN2: Enf 1F 23
Harefield Grn. NW7 ....6K 29
Harefield M. SE4 ....3B 122
Harefield Rd. DA14: Sidc ...2D 144
N8 ....5H 47
SE4 ....3B 122
SW16 ....7K 137
UB8: Uxb 5A 56
Hare Marsh E2 ....4G 85
Hare Pl. EC4 ....1K 13
(off Pleydell St.)
Hare Row E2 ....2H 85
Haresfield Rd. RM10: Dag ...6G 73
Hare St. SE18 ....3E 106
Hare Wlk. N1 ....2E 84
(not continuous)
Harewood Av. NW1 ....4D 4 (4C 82)
UB5: N'olt 7D 58
Harewood Cl. UB5: N'olt 7D 58
Harewood Dr. IG5: Ilf 2D 52
Harewood Pl. W1 ....1K 11 (6K 83)
Harewood Rd. CR2: S Croy ...6E 168
SW19 ....6C 136
TW7: Isle 7K 95
Harewood Row NW1 ....5D 4 (5C 82)

Harewood Ter. UB2: S'hall ...4D 94
Harfield Gdns. SE5 ....3E 120
Harfield Rd. TW16: Sun 2B 148
Harfleur Ct. SE11 ....4B 102
(off Opal Cl.)
Harford Cl. E4 ....7J 25
Harford Ho. SE5 ....6C 102
(off Bethwin Rd.)
W11 ....5H 81
Harford M. N19 ....3H 65
Harford Rd. E4 ....7J 25
Harford St. E1 ....4A 86
Harford Wlk. N2 ....4B 46
Harfst Way BR8: Swan 7J 145
Hargood Cl. HA3: Kent 6E 42
Hargood Rd. SE3 ....1A 124
Hargrave Mans. N19 ....2H 65
Hargrave Pk. N19 ....2G 65
Hargrave Pl. N7 ....5H 65
Hargrave Rd. N19 ....2G 65
Hargraves Ho. W12 ....7D 80
(off White City Est.)
Hargwyne St. SW9 ....3K 119
Haringey Mus. 1E 48
Haringey Pk. N8 ....6J 47
Haringey Pas. N8 ....4A 48
Haringey Rd. N8 ....4J 47
Harington Ter. N9 ....3J 33
N18 ....3J 33
Harkett Cl. HA3: W'stone ...2K 41
Harkett Ct. HA3: W'stone ...2K 41
Harkness Ct. SM1: Sutt 4A 166
(off Cleeve Way)
Harkness Ho. E1 ....6G 85
(off Christian St.)
Harland Av. CR0: Croy 3F 169
DA15: Sidc 3H 143
Harland Cl. SW19 ....3K 153
Harland Rd. SE12 ....1J 141
Harlands Gro. BR6: Farnb ...4F 173
Harlech Gdns. HA5: Pinn 7B 40
TW5: Hest 6A 94
Harlech Rd. N14 ....3D 32
Harlech Twr. W3 ....2J 97
Harlequin Av. TW8: Bford ...6A 96
Harlequin Cl. TW7: Isle 5J 113
UB4: Yead 5B 76
Harlequin Ct. E1 ....7E 85
(off Thomas More St.)
NW10 ....6K 61
(off Mitchellbrook Way)
W5 ....7C 78
Harlequin Ho. DA18: Erith ...3E 108
(off Kale Rd.)
Harlequin Rd. TW11: Tedd ...7B 132
Harlequins RLFC 7J 113
Harlequins RUFC 7J 113
Harlescott Rd. SE15 ......4K 121
HARLESDEN 2B 80
Harlesden Gdns. NW10 .....1B 80
Harlesden La. NW10 ....1C 80
Harlesden Plaza NW10 .....2B 80
Harlesden Rd. NW10 ....1C 80
Harleston Cl. E5 ....2J 67
Harley Cl. HA0: Wemb 6D 60
Harley Ct. E11 ....7J 51
HA1: Harr 4H 41
N20 ....3F 31
Harley Cres. HA1: Harr 4H 41
Harleyford BR1: Brom 1K 159
Harleyford Cl. SE11 ....7G 19
Harleyford Mnr. W3 ....1J 97
(off Edgecote Cl.)
Harleyford Rd. SE11 ....7G 19 (6K 101)
Harleyford St. SE11 ....7J 19 (6A 102)
Harley Gdns. BR6: Orp 4J 173
SW10 ....5A 100
Harley Gro. E3 ....3B 86
Harley Ho. E11 ....7F 51
NW1 ....4H 5
Harley Pl. W1 ....6J 5 (5F 83)
Harley Rd. HA1: Harr 4H 41
NW3 ....7B 64

Harley Rd. NW10 ....2A 80
Harley St. W1 ....4J 5 (4F 83)
Harley Vs. NW10 ....2A 80
Harling Ct. SW11 ....2D 118
Harlinger St. SE18 ....3C 106
HARLINGTON 6F 93
Harlington Cl. UB3: Harl 7E 92
HARLINGTON CORNER 1F 111
Harlington Rd. DA7: Bex 3E 126
UB8: Hil 3C 74
Harlington Rd. E. TW13: Felt ...7K 111
TW14: Felt 7K 111
Harlington Rd. W. TW14: Felt ...6K 111
Harlington Sports Cen., The 4F 93
(off Pinkwell La.)
Harlowe Cl. E8 ....1G 85
Harlowe Ho. E8 ....1F 85
(off Clarissa St.)
Harlow Mans. IG11: Bark 7F 71
(off Whiting Av.)
Harlow Rd. N13 ....3J 33
Harlyn Dr. HA5: Eastc 3K 39
Harlynwood SE5 ....7C 102
(off Wyndham Rd.)
Harman Av. IG8: Wfd G 6C 36
Harman Cl. E4 ....4A 36
NW2 ....3G 63
SE1 ....5G 103
Harman Dr. DA15: Sidc 6K 125
NW2 ....3G 63
Harman Rd. EN1: Enf 5A 24
HARMONDSWORTH 6A 92
Harmondsworth La. 5A 92
UB7: Harm, Sip 6A 92
Harmondsworth Rd. UB7: W Dray ...5A 92
Harmon Ho. SE8 ....4B 104
Harmont Ho. W1 ....6J 5
(off Harley St.)
Harmony Cl. NW11 ....5G 45
SM6: Wall 7J 167
Harmony Way BR1: Brom 2J 159
NW4 ....4E 44
Harmood Gro. NW1 ....7F 65
Harmood Ho. NW1 ....7F 65
(off Harmood St.)
Harmood Pl. NW1 ....7F 65
Harmood St. NW1 ....6F 65
Harmsworth M. SE1 ....2K 19 (3B 102)
Harmsworth St. SE17 .....6K 19 (5B 102)
Harmsworth Way N20 ......1C 30
Harness Rd. SE28 ....2A 108
Harold Av. DA17: Belv 5F 109
UB3: Hayes 3H 93
Harold Cl. SE16 ....2K 103
(off Christopher Cl.)
Harold Est. SE1 ....3E 102
Harold Gibbons Ct. SE7 ....6A 106
Harold Ho. E2 ....2K 85
(off Mace St.)
Harold Laski Ho. EC1 ......2B 8
(off Percival St.)
Harold Maddison Ho. SE17 ...5B 102
(off Penton Pl.)
Harold Pl. SE11 ....6J 19 (5A 102)
Harold Rd. E4 ....4K 35
E11 ....1G 69
E13 ....1K 87
IG8: Wfd G 1J 51
N8 ....5K 47
N15 ....5F 49
NW10 ....2A 79
SE19 ....7D 138
SM1: Sutt 4B 166
Haroldstone Rd. E17 ......5K 49
Harold Wilson Ho. SW28 ....1F 18
SW6 ....6H 99
(off Clem Attlee Ct.)
Harp All. EC4 ....7A 8 (6B 84)
Harp Bus. Cen., The NW2 ....2C 62
Harpenden Rd. E12 ....2A 70
SE27 ....3B 138
Harpenmead Point NW2 ....2H 63
Harper Cl. N14 ....5B 22

Harper Ho. SW9 3B **120**
Harper M. SW17 3A **136**
Harper Rd. E6 6D **88**
SE1 7C **14** (3C **102**)
Harper's Yd. N17 1F **49**
Harp Island Cl. NW10 2K **61**
Harp La. EC3 3G **15** (7E **84**)
Harpley Sq. E1 4K **85**
Harpour Rd. IG11: Bark 6G **71**
Harp Rd. W7 4K **77**
Harpsden St. SW11 1E **118**
Harpur M. WC1 5G **7** (5K **83**)
Harpur St. WC1 5G **7** (5K **83**)
Harraden Rd. SE3 1A **124**
Harrier Av. E11 6K **51**
Harrier Ct. TW4: Houn 3C **112**
Harrier M. SE28 2H **107**
Harrier Rd. NW9 2A **44**
Harriers Cl. W5 7E **78**
Harrier Way E6 5D **88**
Harries Rd. UB4: Yead 4A **76**
Harriet Cl. E8 1G **85**
Harriet Gdns. CR0: Croy 2G **169**
Harriet Ho. *SW6* *7K* ***99***
(off Wandon Rd.)
Harriet St. SW1 7F **11** (2D **100**)
Harriet Tubman Cl. SW2 7K **119**
Harriet Wlk. SW1 7F **11** (2D **100**)
Harriet Way WD23: Bush 1C **26**
HARRINGAY **5B 48**
Harringay Gdns. N8 4B **48**
Harringay Rd. N15 5B **48**
(not continuous)
Harrington Cl. CR0: Bedd 2J **167**
NW10 3K **61**
Harrington Ct. CR0: Croy 2D **168**
SW7 *3B* ***16***
(off Harrington Rd.)
W10 3H **81**
Harrington Gdns. SW7 4K **99**
Harrington Hill E5 1H **67**
Harrington Ho. *NW1* *1A* ***6***
(off Harrington St.)
UB10: Ick 4D **56**
Harrington Rd. E11 1G **69**
SE25 4G **157**
SW7 3A **16** (4B **100**)
Harrington Sq. NW1 2G **83**
Harrington St. NW1 1A **6** (2G **83**)
(not continuous)
Harrington Way SE18 3B **106**
Harriott Cl. SE10 4H **105**
Harriott Ho. *E1* *5J* ***85***
(off Jamaica St.)
Harris Bldgs. *E1* *6G* ***85***
(off Burslem St.)
Harris Cl. EN2: Enf 1G **23**
TW3: Houn 1E **112**
Harris Ct. HA9: Wemb 3F **61**
Harris Ho. *SW9* *3A* ***120***
(off St James's Cres.)
Harris Lodge SE6 1E **140**
Harrison Cl. N20 1H **31**
Harrison Dr. BR1: Brom 4E **160**
Harrison Ho. *SE17* *5D* ***102***
(off Brandon St.)
Harrison Rd. RM10: Dag 6H **73**
Harrisons Ct. *SE14* *6K* ***103***
(off Myers La.)
Harrison's Ri. CR0: Wadd 3B **168**
Harrison St. WC1 2F **7** (3J **83**)
Harrison Way TW17: Shep 5D **146**
Harris Rd. DA7: Bex 1E **126**
RM9: Dag 5F **73**
Harris St. E17 7B **50**
SE5 7D **102**
Harris Way TW16: Sun 1G **147**
Harrods **1E 16** (**3D 100**)
Harrogate Ct. N11 6K **31**
SE12 7J **123**
SE26 *3G* ***139***
(off Droitwich Cl.)
Harrold Ho. NW3 7B **64**
Harrold Rd. RM8: Dag 5B **72**
Harrovian Bus. Village
HA1: Harr 7J **41**
HARROW **6J 41**
Harrow Av. EN1: Enf 6A **24**
Harroway Rd. SW11 2B **118**
Harrow Borough FC **4D 58**
Harrowby St. W1 7D **4** (6C **82**)
Harrow Cl. KT9: Chess 7D **162**
Harrow Club Sports Cen. **7F 81**
Harrowdene Cl. HA0: Wemb 4D **60**
Harrowdene Gdns. TW11: Tedd 6A **132**
Harrowdene Rd. HA0: Wemb 3D **60**
Harrow Dr. N9 1A **34**
Harrowes Meade HA8: Edg 3B **28**
Harrow Flds. Gdns. HA1: Harr 3J **59**
Harrowgate Ho. E9 6K **67**
Harrowgate Rd. E9 6A **68**
Harrow Grn. E11 3G **69**
Harrow High School Sports Cen. **6A 42**
Harrow La. E14 7D **86**
Harrow Leisure Cen. **3K 41**
Harrow Lodge *NW8* *3A* ***4***
(off Northwick Ter.)
Harrow Mnr. Way SE2 1C **108**
SE28 7C **90**
Harrow Mus. & Heritage Cen. **3G 41**
HARROW ON THE HILL **1J 59**
Harrow Pk. HA1: Harr 2J **59**
Harrow Pl. E1 7H **9** (6E **84**)
Harrow Rd. E6 1C **88**
E11 3G **69**
HA0: Wemb 4K **59**
HA9: Wemb 5G **61**
IG1: Ilf 4G **71**
IG11: Bark 1J **89**
NW10 3D **80**
SM5: Cars 6C **166**
TW14: Bedf 2C **128**
W2 6A **4** (5A **82**)
(not continuous)
W9 4F **81**
W10 4G **81**
Harrow Rd. Bri. W2 5A **82**
Harrow Safari Cinema **5K 41**
Harrow St. NW1 5D **4**
Harrow Vw. HA1: Harr 2G **41**
HA2: Harr 2G **41**
UB3: Hayes 6J **75**
UB10: Hil 3E **74**
Harrow Vw. Rd. W5 4B **78**
Harrow Way TW17: Shep 2E **146**
HARROW WEALD **1J 41**
Harrow Weald Pk. HA3: Hrw W 6C **26**
Harry Hinkins Ho. *SE17* *5C* ***102***
(off Bronti Cl.)
Harry Lambourn Ho. *SE15* *7H* ***103***
(off Gervase St.)
Hartcliff Ct. W7 2K **95**
Hart Ct. E6 7E **70**
Harte Rd. TW3: Houn 2D **112**
Hartfield Av. UB5: Yead 2K **75**
Hartfield Cres. BR4: W W'ck 3J **171**
SW19 7H **135**
Hartfield Gro. SE20 1J **157**
Hartfield Ho. *UB5: Yead* *2K* ***75***
(off Hartfield Av.)
Hartfield Rd. BR4: W W'ck 4J **171**
KT9: Chess 5D **162**
SW19 7H **135**
Hartfield Ter. E3 2C **86**
Hartford Av. HA3: Kent 3A **42**
Hartford Rd. DA5: Bexl 6G **127**
KT19: Ewe 6H **163**
Hart Gro. UB1: S'hall 5E **76**
W5 1G **97**
Hart Gro. Ct. W5 1G **97**
Hartham Cl. N7 5J **65**
TW7: Isle 1A **114**
Hartham Rd. N7 5J **65**
N17 2F **49**
TW7: Isle 1K **113**
Harting Rd. SE9 3C **142**
Hartington Cl. BR6: Farnb 5G **173**
HA1: Harr 4J **59**
Hartington Ct. SW8 1J **119**
W4 7H **97**
Hartington Ho. *SW1* *5D* ***18***
(off Drummond Ga.)
Hartington Rd. E16 6K **87**
E17 6A **50**
SW8 1J **119**
TW1: Twick 7B **114**
UB2: S'hall 3C **94**
W4 7H **97**
W13 7B **78**
Hartismere Rd. SW6 7H **99**
Hartlake Rd. E9 6K **67**
Hartland *NW1* *1G* ***83***
(off Royal College St.)
Hartland Cl. HA8: Edg 2B **28**
N21 6H **23**
Hartland Ct. *N11* *5J* ***31***
(off Hartland Rd.)
Hartland Dr. HA4: Ruis 3K **57**
HA8: Edg 2B **28**
Hartland Rd. E15 7H **69**
N11 5J **31**
NW1 7F **65**
NW6 2H **81**
SM4: Mord 7J **153**
TW7: Isle 3A **114**
TW12: Ham H 4F **131**
Hartlands, The TW5: Cran 6K **93**
Hartlands Cl. DA5: Bexl 6F **127**
Hartland Way CR0: Croy 3A **170**
SM4: Mord 7H **153**
Hartlepool Ct. E16 1F **107**
Hartley Av. E6 1C **88**
NW7 5G **29**
Hartley Cl. BR1: Brom 2D **160**
NW7 5G **29**
Hartley Ho. *SE1* *4F* ***103***
(off Longfield Est.)
Hartley Rd. CR0: Croy 7C **156**
DA16: Well 7C **108**
E11 1H **69**
Hartley St. E2 3J **85**
(not continuous)
Hart Lodge EN5: Barn 3B **20**
Hartmann Rd. E16 1B **106**
Hartnoll St. N7 5K **65**
Harton Cl. BR1: Brom 1B **160**
Harton Rd. N9 2C **34**
Harton St. SE8 1C **122**
Hartop Point *SW6* *7G* ***99***
(off Pellant Rd.)
Hartsbourne Av. WD23: Bushy 2B **26**
Hartsbourne Cl. WD23: Bushy 2C **26**
Hartsbourne Ct. *UB1: S'hall* *6G* ***77***
(off Fleming Rd.)
Hartsbourne Pk. WD23: Bushy 2D **26**
Hartsbourne Rd. WD23: Bushy 2C **26**
Harts Gro. IG8: Wfd G 5D **36**
Hartshill Cl. UB10: Hil 7D **56**
Hartshorn All. EC3 1H **15**
Hartshorn Gdns. E6 4E **88**
Harts La. IG11: Bark 6F **71**
SE14 1A **122**
Hartslock Dr. SE2 2D **108**
Hartsmead Rd. SE9 2D **142**
Hart St. EC3 2H **15** (7E **84**)
Hartsway EN3: Pond E 4D **24**
Hartswood Gdns. W12 3B **98**
Hartswood Grn. WD23: Bushy 2C **26**
Hartswood Rd. W12 2B **98**
Hartsworth Cl. E13 2H **87**
Hartville Rd. SE18 4J **107**
Hartwell Dr. E4 6K **35**
Hartwell Ho. *SE7* *5K* ***105***
(off Troughton Rd.)
Hartwell St. E8 6F **67**
Harvard Ct. NW6 5K **63**
Harvard Hill W4 6H **97**
Harvard Ho. *SE17* *6B* ***102***
(off Doddington Gro.)
Harvard La. W4 5J **97**
Harvard Rd. SE13 5E **122**
TW7: Isle 1J **113**
W4 5H **97**
Harvel Cl. BR5: St P 3K **161**
Harvel Cres. SE2 5D **108**
Harvest Bank Rd. BR4: W W'ck 3H **171**
Harvest Ct. TW17: Shep 4C **146**
Harvesters Cl. TW7: Isle 5H **113**
Harvest La. KT7: T Ditt 6A **150**
Harvest Rd. TW13: Felt 4J **129**
Harvey Ct. E17 5C **50**
Harvey Dr. TW12: Hamp 1F **149**
Harvey Gdns. E11 1H **69**
SE7 5A **106**
Harvey Ho. *E1* *4H* ***85***
(off Brady St.)
N1 *1D* ***84***
(off Colville Est.)
RM6: Chad H 4D **54**
SW1 *6D* ***18***
(off Aylesford St.)
TW8: Bford 5E **96**
Harvey Lodge *W9* *5J* ***81***
(off Admiral Wlk.)
Harvey M. *N8* *5K* ***47***
(off Harvey Rd.)
Harvey Point *E16* *5J* ***87***
(off Fife Rd.)
Harvey Rd. E11 1G **69**
IG1: Ilf 5F **71**
KT12: Walt T 7H **147**
N8 5K **47**
SE5 1D **120**
(not continuous)
TW4: Houn 7D **112**
UB5: N'olt 7A **58**
UB10: Hil 2C **74**
Harvey's Bldgs. WC2 3F **13** (7J **83**)
Harveys La. RM7: Rush G 2K **73**
Harvey St. N1 1D **84**
Harvill Rd. DA14: Sidc 5E **144**
Harvil Rd. UB9: Hare 6A **38**
UB10: Ick 5A **38**
Harvington Wlk. E8 7G **67**
Harvist Est. N7 4A **66**
Harvist Rd. NW6 2F **81**
Harwell Cl. HA4: Ruis 1F **57**
Harwell Pas. N2 4D **46**
Harwood Av. BR1: Brom 2K **159**
CR4: Mitc 3C **154**
Harwood Cl. HA0: Wemb 4D **60**
N12 6H **31**
Harwood Ct. *N1* *1D* ***84***
(off Colville Est.)
SW15 4E **116**
Harwood Dr. UB10: Hil 1B **74**
Harwood M. SW6 7J **99**
Harwood Point SE16 2B **104**
Harwood Rd. SW6 7J **99**
Harwoods Yd. N21 7F **23**
Harwood Ter. SW6 1K **117**
Haselbury Rd. N9 4K **33**
N18 4K **33**
Haseley End SE23 7J **121**
Haselrigge Rd. SW4 4H **119**
Haseltine Rd. SE26 4B **140**
Haselwood Dr. EN2: Enf 4G **23**
Haskard Rd. RM9: Dag 4D **72**
Hasker St. SW3 3D **16** (4C **100**)
Haslam Av. SM3: Sutt 1G **165**
Haslam Cl. N1 7A **66**
UB10: Ick 2E **56**
Haslam Ct. N11 4A **32**
Haslam St. SE15 7F **103**
Haslemere and Heathrow Est., The
TW4: Cran 2K **111**
Haslemere Av. CR4: Mitc 2B **154**
EN4: E Barn 1J **31**
NW4 6F **45**
SW18 2K **135**
TW5: Cran 2A **112**
W7 3A **96**

Haslemere Av. W13 3A 96
Haslemere Bus. Cen.
EN1: Enf 4C 24
Haslemere Cl. SM6: Wall 5J 167
TW12: Hamp 5D 130
Haslemere Gdns. N3 3H 45
Haslemere Ind. Est. SW18 2K 135
Haslemere Rd. CR7: Thor H 5B 156
DA7: Bex 2F 127
IG3: Ilf 2K 71
N8 7H 47
N21 2G 33
Hasler Cl. SE28 7B 90
Haslers Wharf *E3* *1A 86*
(off Old Ford Rd.)
Haslett Rd. TW17: Shep 2G 147
Hasluck Gdns. EN5: New Bar 6E 20
Hassard St. E2 1K 9 (2F 85)
Hassendean Rd. SE3 6K 105
Hassett Rd. E9 6K 67
Hassocks Cl. SE26 3H 139
Hassocks Rd. SW16 1H 155
Hassock Wood BR2: Kes 4B 172
Hassop Rd. NW2 4F 63
Hassop Wlk. SE9 4C 142
Hasted Rd. SE7 5B 106
Haste Hill Station
Ruislip Lido Railway 3G 39
Hastings Av. IG6: Ilf 4G 53
Hastings Cl. EN5: New Bar 4F 21
HA0: Wemb 4C 60
SE15 7G 103
Hastings Ct. TW11: Tedd 5H 131
Hastings Dr. KT6: Surb 6C 150
Hastings Ho. EN3: Enf H 2D 24
SE18 *4D 106*
(off Mulgrave Rd.)
W12 *7D 80*
(off White City Est.)
W13 7B 78
WC1 *2E 6*
(off Hastings St.)
Hastings Rd. BR2: Brom 1C 172
CR0: Croy 1F 169
N11 5B 32
N17 3D 48
W13 7B 78
Hastings St. SE18 3G 107
WC1 2E 6 (3J 83)
Hastingwood Ct. E17 5D 50
Hastingwood Trad. Est. N18 6E 34
Hastoe Cl. UB4: Yead 4C 76
Hat & Mitre Ct. EC1 4B 8
Hatch, The EN3: Enf H 1E 24
Hatcham M. Bus. Cen. *SE14* *1K 121*
(off Hatcham Pk. Rd.)
Hatcham Pk. M. SE14 1K 121
Hatcham Pk. Rd. SE14 1K 121
Hatcham Rd. SE15 6J 103
Hatchard Rd. N19 2H 65
Hatchcroft NW4 3D 44
HATCH END 7A 26
Hatch End Swimming Pool 7A 26
Hatchers M. SE1 7H 15
Hatchett Rd. TW14: Bedf 1E 128
Hatchfield Ho. *N15* *6E 48*
(off Albert Rd.)
Hatch Gro. RM6: Chad H 4E 54
Hatch La. E4 4A 36
(not continuous)
UB7: Harm 7A 92
Hatch Pl. KT2: King T 5F 133
Hatch Rd. SW16 2J 155
Hatch Side IG7: Chig 5K 37
Hatchwood Cl. IG8: Wfd G 4C 36
Hatcliffe Almshouses
SE10 *5G 105*
(off Tuskar St.)
Hatcliffe Cl. SE3 3H 123
Hatcliffe St. SE10 5H 105
Hatfield Cl. CR4: Mitc 4B 154
IG6: Ilf 3F 53
SE14 7K 103
Hatfield Ct. SE3 7J 105
UB5: Yead *3A 76*
(off Canberra Dr.)
Hatfield Ho. EC1 4C 8
Hatfield Mead SM4: Mord 5J 153
Hatfield Rd. E15 5G 69
RM9: Dag 6E 72
W4 2K 97
W13 1A 96
Hatfields SE1 4K 13 (1A 102)
Hathaway Cl. BR2: Brom 1D 172
HA4: Ruis 4H 57
HA7: Stan 5F 27
Hathaway Cres. E12 6D 70
Hathaway Gdns. RM6: Chad H 5D 54
W13 5A 78
Hathaway Ho. N1 1G 9 (2E 84)
Hathaway Rd. CR0: Croy 7B 156
Hatherleigh Cl. KT9: Chess 5D 162
NW7 6A 30
SM4: Mord 4J 153
Hatherleigh Rd. HA4: Ruis 2J 57
Hatherley Ct. *W2* *6K 81*
(off Hatherley Gro.)
Hatherley Cres. DA14: Sidc 2A 144
Hatherley Gdns. E6 3B 88
N8 6J 47
Hatherley Gro. W2 6K 81
Hatherley Ho. E17 4C 50
Hatherley M. E17 4C 50
Hatherley Rd. DA14: Sidc 4A 144
E17 4B 50
TW9: Kew 1F 115
Hatherley St. SW1 4B 18 (4G 101)
Hathern Gdns. SE9 4E 142
Hatherop Rd. TW12: Hamp 7D 130
Hathersage Ct. N1 5D 66
Hathorne Cl. SE15 2H 121
Hathway St. SE15 2K 121
Hathway Ter. *SE14* *2K 121*
(off Hathway St.)
Hatley Av. IG6: Ilf 4G 53
Hatley Cl. N11 5J 31
Hatley Rd. N4 2K 65
Hatteraick St. SE16 2J 103
Hattersfield Cl. DA17: Belv 4F 109
HATTON 4H 111
Hatton Cl. SE18 7H 107
HATTON CROSS 4H 111
Hatton Cross Cen.
TW6: H'row A 3H 111
Hatton Gdn. EC1 5K 7 (5A 84)
Hatton Gdns. CR4: Mitc 5D 154
Hatton Grn. TW14: Felt 4J 111
Hatton Gro. UB7: W Dray 2A 92
Hatton Ho. *KT1: King T* *2F 151*
(off Victoria Rd.)
Hatton Pl. EC1 5K 7 (5A 84)
Hatton Rd. CR0: Croy 1A 168
TW14: Bedf, Felt 7E 110
Hatton Rd. Sth. TW14: Felt 4H 111
Hatton Row NW8 4B 4
Hatton St. NW8 4B 4 (4B 82)
Hatton Wall EC1 5K 7 (5A 84)
Haughmond N12 4E 30
Haunch of Venison Yd. W1 1J 11 (6F 83)
Hauteville Ct. Gdns. *W6* *3B 98*
(off South Side)
Havana Rd. SW19 2J 135
Havannah St. E14 2C 104
Havant Rd. E17 3E 50
Havelock Cl. W12 7D 80
Havelock Ct. *UB2: S'hall* *3D 94*
(off Havelock Rd.)
Havelock Ho. SE23 1J 139
Havelock Pl. HA1: Harr 6J 41
Havelock Rd. BR2: Brom 4A 160
CR0: Croy 2F 169
DA17: Belv 4F 109
HA3: W'stone 3J 41
N17 2G 49
SW19 5A 136
UB2: S'hall 3C 94
Havelock St. IG1: Ilf 2F 71
N1 1J 83
Havelock Ter. SW8 1F 119
Havelock Ter. Arches *SW8* *1F 119*
(off Havelock Ter.)
Havelock Wlk. SE23 1J 139
Haven, The N14 6A 22
TW9: Rich 3G 115
TW16: Sun 7J 129
Haven Cl. DA14: Sidc 6C 144
SE9 3D 142
SW19 3F 135
UB4: Hayes 4G 75
Haven Ct. BR3: Beck 2E 158
KT5: Surb 6F 151
Haven Grn. W5 6D 78
Haven Grn. Ct. W5 6D 78
Havenhurst Ri. EN2: Enf 2F 23
Haven La. W5 6E 78
Haven Lodge *EN1: Enf* *6K 23*
(off Village Rd.)
Haven M. E3 5B 86
N1 7A 66
Haven Pl. W5 7D 78
Havenpool *NW8* *1K 81*
(off Abbey Rd.)
Haven Rd. TW15: Ashf 4D 128
Haven St. NW1 7F 65
Haven Wood HA9: Wemb 3H 61
Haverfield Gdns. TW9: Kew 7G 97
Haverfield Rd. E3 3A 86
Haverford Way HA8: Edg 1F 43
Haverhill Rd. E4 1K 35
SW12 1G 137
Havering *NW1* *7F 65*
(off Castlehaven Rd.)
Havering Dr. RM1: Rom 4K 55
Havering Gdns. RM6: Chad H 5C 54
Havering Rd. RM1: Rom 3K 55
Havering St. E1 6K 85
Havering Way IG11: Bark 3B 90
Haversham Cl. TW1: Twick 6D 114
Haversham Ct. UB6: G'frd 6K 59
Haversham Pl. N6 2D 64
Haverstock Hill NW3 5C 64
Haverstock Pl. *N1* *1B 8*
(off Haverstock St.)
Haverstock Rd. NW5 5E 64
Haverstock St. N1 1B 8 (2B 84)
Haverthwaite Rd. BR6: Orp 2H 173
Havilland Ct. HA8: Edg 4A 28
Havil St. SE5 7E 102
Havingham Dr. RM6: Chad H 5C 54
Havisham Ho. SE16 2G 103
Havisham Pl. SE19 7B 138
Hawarden Gro. SE24 7C 120
Hawarden Hill NW2 3C 62
Hawarden Rd. E17 4K 49
Hawbridge Rd. E11 1F 69
Hawes Ho. E17 4K 49
Hawes La. BR4: W W'ck 1E 170
Hawes Rd. BR1: Brom 1K 159
(not continuous)
N18 6C 34
Hawes St. N1 7B 66
Hawgood St. E3 5C 86
Hawkdene E4 6J 25
Hawke Ct. *UB4: Yead* *4A 76*
(off Perth Av.)
Hawke Ho. *E1* *4K 85*
(off Ernest St.)
Hawke Pk. Rd. N22 3B 48
Hawke Pl. SE16 2K 103
Hawker Ct. *KT1: King T* *2F 151*
(off Church Rd.)
Hawke Rd. SE19 6D 138
Hawker Pl. E17 2E 50
Hawker Rd. CR0: Wadd 6A 168
Hawkesbury Rd. SW15 5D 116
Hawkesfield Rd. SE23 2A 140
Hawkesley Cl. TW1: Twick 4A 132
Hawkes Rd. CR4: Mitc 1D 154
TW14: Felt 7J 111
Hawkesworth Cl. HA6: Nwood 1G 39
Hawke Twr. SE14 6A 104
Hawkewood Rd. TW16: Sun 3J 147
Hawkfield Ct. TW7: Isle 2J 113
Hawkhurst Gdns. KT9: Chess 4E 162
Hawkhurst Rd. SW16 1H 155
Hawkhurst Way BR4: W W'ck 2D 170
KT3: N Mald 5K 151
Hawkinge *N17* *2D 48*
(off Gloucester Rd.)
Hawkins Cl. HA1: Harr 7H 41
NW7 5E 28
Hawkins Ct. SE18 4C 106
Hawkins Ho. *SE8* *6C 104*
(off New King St.)
SW1 *7B 18*
(off Dolphin Sq.)
Hawkins Rd. TW11: Tedd 6B 132
Hawkins Ter. SE7 5C 106
Hawkins Way SE6 5C 140
Hawkley Gdns. SE27 2B 138
Hawkridge Cl. RM6: Chad H 6C 54
Hawksbrook La. BR3: Beck 6D 158
(not continuous)
Hawkshaw Cl. SW2 7J 119
Hawkshead NW1 1A 6
Hawkshead Cl. BR1: Brom 7G 141
Hawkshead Rd. NW10 7B 62
W4 2A 98
Hawkslade Rd. SE15 5K 121
Hawksley Rd. N16 3E 66
Hawks M. SE10 7E 104
Hawksmoor Cl. E6 6C 88
SE18 5J 107
Hawksmoor M. E1 7H 85
Hawksmoor Pl. *E2* *3K 9*
(off Cheshire St.)
Hawksmoor St. W6 6F 99
Hawksmouth E4 7K 25
Hawks Pas. *KT1: King T* *2F 151*
(off Minerva Rd.)
Hawks Rd. KT1: King T 2F 151
Hawkstone Rd. SE16 4J 103
Hawkwell Ct. E4 3K 35
Hawkwell Ho. RM8: Dag 1G 73
Hawkwell Wlk. *N1* *1C 84*
(off Maldon Cl.)
Hawkwood Cres. E4 6J 25
Hawkwood La. BR7: Chst 1G 161
Hawkwood Mt. E5 1H 67
Hawlands Dr. HA5: Pinn 7C 40
Hawley Cl. TW12: Hamp 6D 130
Hawley Cres. NW1 7F 65
Hawley M. NW1 7F 65
Hawley Rd. N18 5E 34
NW1 7F 65
(not continuous)
Hawley St. NW1 7F 65
Hawley Way TW15: Ashf 5C 128
Hawstead Rd. SE6 6D 122
Hawsted IG9: Buck H 1E 36
Hawter NW9 1B 44
Hawthorn Av. CR7: Thor H 1B 156
E3 1B 86
N13 5D 32
Hawthorn Cen. HA1: Harr 5K 41
Hawthorn Cl. BR5: Pet W 6H 161
TW5: Cran 7K 93
TW12: Hamp 5E 130
Hawthorn Cotts. *DA16: Well* *3A 126*
(off Hook La.)
Hawthorn Ct. *HA5: Pinn* *2A 40*
(off Rickmansworth Rd.)
TW9: Kew 1H 115
Hawthorn Cres. SW17 5E 136
Hawthornden Cl. N12 6H 31
Hawthorndene Cl. BR2: Hayes 2H 171
Hawthorndene Rd. BR2: Hayes 2H 171
Hawthorn Dr. BR4: W W'ck 4G 171
HA2: Harr 6E 40
Hawthorne Av. CR4: Mitc 2B 154
HA3: Kent 6A 42
HA4: Ruis 6K 39

Hawthorne Av. SM5: Cars 7E 166
Hawthorne Cl. BR1: Brom 3D 160
N1 6E 66
SM1: Sutt 2A 166
Hawthorne Ct. HA6: Nwood 2J 39
W5 1E 96
Hawthorne Cres. UB7: W Dray 2B 92
Hawthorne Farm Av. UB5: N'olt 1C 76
Hawthorne Gro. NW9 7J 43
Hawthorne Ho. N15 5G 49
SW1 6B 18
(off Churchill Gdns.)
Hawthorne M. UB6: G'frd 6G 77
Hawthorne Pl. UB3: Hayes 7H 75
Hawthorne Rd. BR1: Brom 3C 160
E17 3C 50
Hawthorne Way N9 2A 34
Hawthorn Gdns. W5 3D 96
Hawthorn Gro. EN2: Enf 1J 23
SE20 7H 139
Hawthorn Hatch TW8: Bford 7B 96
Hawthorn M. NW7 1G 45
Hawthorn Pl. DA8: Erith 5J 109
Hawthorn Rd. DA6: Bex 4F 127
IG9: Buck H 4G 37
N8 3H 47
N18 6A 34
NW10 7C 62
SM1: Sutt 6C 166
SM6: Wall 7F 167
TW8: Bford 7B 96
TW13: Felt 1J 129
Hawthorns CR2: S Croy 4B 168
(off Bramley Hill)
IG8: Wfd G 3D 36
Hawthorns, The KT17: Ewe 7B 164
Hawthorn Ter. DA15: Sidc 5K 125
N19 1H 65
(off Calverley Gro.)
Hawthorn Wlk. W10 4G 81
Hawthorn Way TW17: Shep 4F 147
Hawtrey Av. UB5: N'olt 2B 76
Hawtrey Dr. HA4: Ruis 7J 39
Hawtrey Rd. NW3 7C 64
Haxted Rd. BR1: Brom 1K 159
Hay Cl. E15 7G 69
Haycroft Gdns. NW10 1C 80
Haycroft Rd. KT6: Surb 2D 162
SW2 5J 119
Hay Currie St. E14 6D 86
Hayday Rd. E16 5J 87
(not continuous)
Hayden Piper Ho. SW3 7E 16
(off Caversham St.)
Haydens M. W3 6J 79
Hayden's Pl. W11 6H 81
Hayden Way RM5: Col R 2J 55
Haydock Av. UB5: N'olt 6E 58
Haydock Grn. UB5: N'olt 6E 58
Haydock Grn. Flats UB5: N'olt 6F 58
(off Haydock Grn.)
Haydon Cl. EN1: Enf 6K 23
NW9 4J 43
Haydon Ct. NW9 4J 43
Haydon Dr. HA5: Eastc 4J 39
Haydon Pk. Rd. SW19 5J 135
Haydon Rd. RM8: Dag 2C 72
Haydons Rd. SW19 5K 135
Haydon St. EC3 2J 15 (7F 85)
Haydon Wlk. E1 1K 15 (6F 85)
Haydon Way SW11 4B 118
HAYES
Bromley 1J 171
Hillingdon 6G 75
Hayes Bri. Retail Pk. UB4: Yead 7A 76
Hayes Chase BR4: W W'ck 6F 159
Hayes Cl. BR2: Hayes 2J 171
Hayes Ct. SE5 7C 102
(off Camberwell New Rd.)
SW2 1J 137
Hayes Cres. NW11 5H 45
SM3: Cheam 4F 165
HAYES END 4F 75
Hayes End Cl. UB4: Hayes 4F 75
Hayes End Dr. UB4: Hayes 4F 75
Hayes End Rd. UB4: Hayes 4F 75
Hayesens Ho. SW17 4A 136
Hayes FC 7H 75
Hayesford Pk. Dr. BR2: Brom 5H 159
Hayes Gdn. BR2: Hayes 2J 171
Hayes Gro. SE22 3F 121
Hayes Hill BR2: Hayes 1G 171
Hayes Hill Rd. BR2: Hayes 1H 171
Hayes La. BR2: Brom, Hayes 5K 159
BR3: Beck 3E 158
Hayes Manor Sports Cen. 6F 75
Hayes Mead Rd. BR2: Hayes 1G 171
Hayes Metro Cen. UB4: Yead 7A 76
Hayes Pl. NW1 4D 4 (4C 82)
Hayes Rd. BR2: Brom 4J 159
UB2: S'hall 4K 93
Hayes Stadium & Sports Cen. 6F 75
Hayes St. BR2: Hayes 1K 171
Hayes Swimming Pool 1H 93
HAYES TOWN 2H 93
Hayes Way BR3: Beck 4E 158
Hayes Wood Av. BR2: Hayes 1K 171
Hayfield Pas. E1 4J 85
Hayfield Yd. E1 4J 85
Haygarth Pl. SW19 5F 135
Haygreen Cl. KT2: King T 6H 133
Hay Hill W1 3K 11 (7F 83)
Hayland Cl. NW9 4K 43
Hay La. NW9 4J 43
Hayles Bldgs. SE11 4B 102
(off Elliotts Row)
Hayles St. SE11 4B 102
Haylett Gdns. KT1: King T 4D 150
Hayling Av. TW13: Felt 3J 129
Hayling Cl. N16 5E 66
Hayling Ct. SM3: Cheam 4E 164
Haymaker Cl. UB10: Uxb 7B 56
Hayman Cres. UB4: Hayes 2F 75
Haymans Point SE11 5G 19 (4K 101)
Hayman St. N1 7B 66
Haymarket SW1 3C 12 (7H 83)
Haymarket Arc. SW1 3C 12
Haymarket Ct. E8 7F 67
(off Jacaranda Gro.)
Haymarket Theatre Royal 3D 12
(off Haymarket)
Haymer Gdns.
KT4: Wor Pk 3C 164
Haymerle Ho. SE15 6G 103
(off Haymerle Rd.)
Haymerle Rd. SE15 6G 103
Haymill Cl. UB6: G'frd 3K 77
Hayne Ho. W11 1G 99
(off Penzance Pl.)
Hayne Rd. BR3: Beck 2B 158
Haynes Cl. N11 3K 31
N17 7C 34
SE3 3G 123
Haynes Dr. N9 3C 34
Haynes La. SE19 6E 138
Haynes Rd. HA0: Wemb 7E 60
Hayne St. EC1 5B 8 (5B 84)
Haynt Wlk. SW20 3G 153
Hay's Galleria SE1 4G 15 (1E 102)
Hays La. SE1 4G 15 (1E 102)
Haysleigh Gdns. SE20 2G 157
Hay's M. W1 4J 11 (1F 101)
Haysoms Cl. RM1: Rom 4K 55
Haystall Cl. UB4: Hayes 2G 75
Hay St. E2 1G 85
Hayter Ct. E11 2K 69
Hayter Rd. SW2 5J 119
Hayton Cl. E8 6F 67
Hayward Cl. DA1: Cray 5K 127
SW19 7K 135
Hayward Ct. SW4 2J 119
(off Clapham Rd.)
Hayward Gallery 5H 13
Hayward Gdns. SW15 6E 116
Hayward Ho. N1 2A 84
(off Penton St.)
Hayward Rd. KT7: T Ditt 7K 149
N20 2F 31
Haywards Cl. RM6: Chad H 5B 54
Hayward's Pl. EC1 3A 8 (4B 84)
Haywards Yd. SE4 5B 122
(off Lindal Rd.)
Haywood Cl. HA5: Pinn 2B 40
Haywood Lodge N11 6D 32
(off Oak La.)
Haywood Ri. BR6: Orp 5J 173
Haywood Rd. BR2: Brom 4B 160
Hayworth Cl. EN3: Enf H 2F 25
Hazel Av. UB7: W Dray 3C 92
Hazel Bank SE25 2E 156
Hazelbank KT5: Surb 1J 163
Hazelbank Rd. SE6 2F 141
Hazelbourne Rd. SW12 6F 119
Hazelbury Cl. SW19 2J 153
Hazelbury Grn. N9 3K 33
Hazelbury La. N9 3K 33
Hazel Cl. CR0: Croy 7K 157
CR4: Mitc 4H 155
N13 3J 33
N19 2G 65
NW9 2A 44
TW2: Whit 7G 113
TW8: Bford 7B 96
Hazel Ct. W5 7E 78
Hazel Cres. RM5: Col R 1H 55
Hazel Cft. HA5: H End 6A 26
Hazelcroft Cl. UB10: Hil 7B 56
Hazeldean Rd. NW10 7K 61
Hazeldene Dr. HA5: Pinn 3A 40
Hazeldene Gdns. UB10: Hil 1F 74
Hazeldene Rd. DA16: Well 2C 126
IG3: Ilf 2B 72
Hazeldon Rd. SE4 5A 122
Hazeleigh Gdns. IG8: Wfd G 5H 37
Hazel Gdns. HA8: Edg 4C 28
Hazelgreen Cl. N21 1G 33
Hazel Gro. BR6: Farnb 2F 173
EN1: Enf 6B 24
HA0: Wemb 1E 78
RM6: Chad H 3E 54
SE26 4K 139
TW13: Felt 1J 129
Hazelhurst BR3: Beck 1F 159
Hazelhurst Ct. SE6 5E 140
(off Beckenham Hill Rd.)
Hazelhurst Rd. SW17 4A 136
Hazel La. IG6: Ilf 6K 37
TW10: Ham 2E 132
Hazellville Rd. N19 7H 47
Hazelmere Cl. TW14: Felt 6G 111
UB5: N'olt 2D 76
Hazelmere Ct. SW2 1K 137
Hazelmere Dr. UB5: N'olt 2D 76
Hazelmere Rd. BR5: Pet W 4G 161
NW6 1H 81
UB5: N'olt 2D 76
Hazelmere Wlk. UB5: N'olt 2D 76
(not continuous)
Hazelmere Way BR2: Hayes 6J 159
Hazel M. N22 3A 48
(off High Rd.)
Hazel Rd. E15 5G 69
NW10 3D 80
(not continuous)
Hazeltree La. UB5: N'olt 3C 76
Hazel Wlk. BR2: Brom 6E 160
Hazel Way E4 6G 35
SE1 4F 103
Hazelwood Av. SM4: Mord 4K 153
Hazelwood Cl. HA2: Harr 4F 41
W5 2E 96
Hazelwood Ct. KT6: Surb 6E 150
N13 4F 33
(off Hazelwood La.)
NW10 3A 62
Hazelwood Cres. N13 4F 33
Hazelwood Dr. HA5: Pinn 2K 39
Hazelwood Ho. SE8 4A 104
Hazelwood Ho's. BR2: Brom 3G 159
Hazelwood La. N13 4F 33
Hazelwood Lawn Tennis & Squash Club 7H 23
(off Bush Hill)
Hazelwood Rd. E17 5A 50
EN1: Enf 6A 24
Hazlebury Rd. SW6 2K 117
Hazledean Rd. CR0: Croy 2D 168
Hazledene Rd. W4 6J 97
Hazlemere Gdns. KT4: Wor Pk 1C 164
Hazlewell Rd. SW15 5E 116
Hazlewood Cl. E5 3A 68
Hazlewood Cres. W10 4G 81
Hazlewood Twr. W10 4G 81
(off Golborne Gdns.)
Hazlitt Cl. TW13: Hanw 4C 130
Hazlitt M. W14 3G 99
Hazlitt Rd. W14 3G 99
Heacham Av. UB10: Ick 3E 56
Headbourne Ho. SE1 7F 15 (3D 102)
Headcorn Pl. CR7: Thor H 4K 155
Headcorn Rd. BR1: Brom 5H 141
CR7: Thor H 4K 155
N17 7A 34
Headfort Pl. SW1 7H 11 (2E 100)
Headington Ct. CR0: Croy 4C 168
(off Tanfield Rd.)
Headington Rd. SW18 2A 136
Headlam Rd. SW4 6H 119
(not continuous)
Headlam St. E1 4H 85
Headley App. IG2: Ilf 5F 53
Headley Av. SM6: Wall 5K 167
Headley Cl. KT19: Ewe 6G 163
Headley Ct. SE26 5J 139
Headley Dr. CR0: New Ad 7D 170
IG2: Ilf 6F 53
Head's M. W11 6J 81
HEADSTONE 3H 41
Headstone Dr. HA1: Harr 3H 41
HA3: W'stone 3H 41
Headstone Gdns. HA2: Harr 4G 41
Headstone La. HA2: Harr 4E 40
HA3: Hrw W 7A 26
Headstone Pde. HA1: Harr 4H 41
Headstone Rd. HA1: Harr 5J 41
Head St. E1 6K 85
(not continuous)
Headway Cl. TW10: Ham 4C 132
Heald St. SE14 1C 122
Healey Ho. SW9 7A 102
Healey St. NW1 6F 65
Healy Dr. BR6: Orp 4K 173
Hearne Rd. W4 6G 97
Hearn Ri. UB5: N'olt 1B 76
Hearn's Bldgs. SE17 4D 102
Hearnshaw St. E14 6A 86
Hearn St. EC2 4H 9 (4E 84)
Hearnville Rd. SW12 1E 136
Heart, The KT12: Walt T 7J 147
Heath, The W7 1J 96
Heatham Pk. TW2: Twick 7K 113
Heath Av. DA7: Bex 6D 108
Heathbourne Rd. HA7: Stan 2D 26
WD23: Bushy 1D 26
Heath Brow NW3 3A 64
Heath Bus. Cen. TW3: Houn 4G 113
Heath Cl. CR2: S Croy 6B 168
NW11 7K 45
UB3: Harl 7F 93
W5 4F 79
Heathcock Ct. WC2 3F 13
(off Exchange Ct.)
Heathcote Av. IG5: Ilf 2D 52
Heathcote Ct. IG5: Ilf 1D 52
(Glade Ct.)
IG5: Ilf 2D 52
(Heathcote Av.)
Heathcote Gro. E4 3K 35
Heathcote Rd. TW1: Twick 6B 114
Heathcote St. WC1 3G 7 (4K 83)
Heath Ct. CR0: Croy 4D 168
(off Heathfield Rd.)

Heath Ct. TW4: Houn 4D **112**
UB8: Uxb 7A **56**
Heath Cft. NW11 . . . . 1K **63**
Heathcroft W5 . . . . 4F **79**
Heathcroft Av. TW16: Sun 7H **129**
Heathcroft Gdns. E17 . . . . 1F **51**
Heathdale Av. TW4: Houn 3C **112**
Heathdene Dr. DA17: Belv 4H **109**
Heathdene Rd. SM6: Wall 7F **167**
SW16 . . . . 7K **137**
Heath Dr. NW3 . . . . 4K **63**
SM2: Sutt 7A **166**
SW20 . . . . 4E **152**
Heathedge SE26 . . . . 2H **139**
Heath End Rd. DA5: Bexl 1K **145**
Heather Av. RM1: Rom 2K **55**
Heatherbank BR7: Chst 2E **160**
SE9 . . . . 2D **124**
Heather Cl. E6 . . . . 6E **88**
N7 . . . . 3K **65**
RM1: Rom 1K **55**
SE13 . . . . 7F **123**
SW8 . . . . 3F **119**
TW7: Isle 5H **113**
TW12: Hamp 1D **148**
UB8: Hil 5B **74**
Heather Ct. DA14: Sidc 6D **144**
Heatherdale Cl. KT2: King T 6G **133**
Heatherdene Cl. CR4: Mitc 4B **154**
N12 . . . . 7F **31**
Heather Dr. EN2: Enf 2G **23**
RM1: Rom 2K **55**
Heatherfold Way HA5: Eastc 3H **39**
Heather Gdns. NW11 . . . . 6G **45**
RM1: Rom 2K **55**
SM2: Sutt 6J **165**
Heather Glen RM1: Rom 2K **55**
Heather Ho. *E14* *6E* ***86***
(off Dee St.)
Heatherlands TW16: Sun 6J **129**
Heather La. UB7: Yiew 6A **74**
Heatherley Ct. E5 . . . . 3G **67**
Heatherley Dr. IG5: Ilf 3C **52**
Heather Pk. Dr. HA0: Wemb 7G **61**
Heather Pk. Pde. *HA0: Wemb* *7F* ***61***
(off Heather Pk. Dr.)
Heather Rd. E4 . . . . 6G **35**
NW2 . . . . 2B **62**
SE12 . . . . 2J **141**
Heathers, The TW19: Stanw 7B **110**
Heatherset Gdns. SW16 . . . . 7K **137**
Heatherside Rd. DA14: Sidc 3C **144**
KT19: Ewe 7K **163**
Heatherton Ter. N3 . . . . 2K **45**
Heather Wlk. HA8: Edg 5C **28**
TW2: Whit *7E* ***112***
(off Stephenson Rd.)
W10 . . . . 4G **81**
Heather Way CR2: Sels 7K **169**
HA7: Stan 6E **26**
RM1: Rom 2K **55**
Heatherwood Cl. E12 . . . . 2A **70**
Heatherwood Dr. UB4: Hayes 2F **75**
Heathfield BR7: Chst 6G **143**
E4 . . . . 3K **35**
HA1: Harr 7K **41**
Heathfield Av. SW18 . . . . 7B **118**
Heathfield Cl. BR2: Kes 5A **172**
E16 . . . . 5B **88**
Heathfield Ct. SE20 . . . . 7J **139**
W4 . . . . 5K **97**
Heathfield Dr. CR4: Mitc 1C **154**
Heathfield Gdns. CR0: Croy 4D **168**
NW11 . . . . 6F **45**
SE3 . . . . *2G* ***123***
(off Baizdon Rd.)
SW18 . . . . 6B **118**
W4 . . . . 5J **97**
Heathfield Ho. SE3 . . . . 2G **123**
Heathfield La. BR7: Chst 6F **143**
Heathfield Nth. TW2: Twick 7J **113**
Heathfield Pk. NW2 . . . . 6E **62**
Heathfield Pk. Dr. RM6: Chad H 5B **54**
Heathfield Ri. HA4: Ruis 7E **38**
Heathfield Rd. BR1: Brom 7H **141**
BR2: Kes 5A **172**
CR0: Croy 4D **168**
DA6: Bex 4F **127**
SW18 . . . . 6A **118**
W3 . . . . 2H **97**
Heathfields Ct. TW4: Houn 5C **112**
Heathfield Sth. TW2: Twick 7K **113**
Heathfield Sq. SW18 . . . . 7B **118**
Heathfield St. *W11* *7G* ***81***
(off Portland Rd.)
Heathfield Ter. SE18 . . . . 6J **107**
W4 . . . . 5J **97**
Heathfield Va. CR2: Sels 7K **169**
Heath Gdns. TW1: Twick 1K **131**
Heathgate NW11 . . . . 6K **45**
Heathgate Pl. NW3 . . . . 5D **64**
Heath Gro. SE20 . . . . 7J **139**
TW16: Sun 7H **129**
Heath Ho. DA15: Sidc 4K **143**
Heath Hurst Rd. NW3 . . . . 4C **64**
Heathland Rd. N16 . . . . 1E **66**
Heathlands Cl. TW1: Twick 2K **131**
TW16: Sun 2J **147**
Heathlands Way TW4: Houn 5C **112**
Heath La. SE3 . . . . 2F **123**
(not continuous)
Heathlee Rd. SE3 . . . . 4H **123**
Heathley End BR7: Chst 6G **143**
Heath Lodge WD23: Bushy 1D **26**
Heathmans Rd. SW6 . . . . 1H **117**
Heath Mead SW19 . . . . 3F **135**
Heath Pk. Dr. BR1: Brom 3C **160**
Heathpool Ct. E1 . . . . 4H **85**
Heath Ri. BR2: Hayes 6H **159**
SW15 . . . . 6F **117**
Heath Rd. CR7: Thor H 3C **156**
DA5: Bexl 1J **145**
HA1: Harr 7G **41**
RM6: Chad H 7D **54**
SW8 . . . . 2F **119**
TW1: Twick 1K **131**
TW2: Twick 1K **131**
TW3: Houn, Isle 4F **113**
UB10: Hil 4E **74**
Heathrow Blvd. UB7: Sip 7B **92**
(not continuous)
Heathrow C'way. Cen. TW4: Houn 3K **111**
Heathrow Gateway TW4: Houn 7C **112**
Heathrow Interchange UB4: Yead 1A **94**
Heathrow Intl. Trad. Est.
TW4: Houn 3K **111**
Heathrow Vis. Cen. 1E **110**
Heath Royal SW15 . . . . 6F **117**
Heaths Cl. EN1: Enf 2K **23**
Heath Side NW3 . . . . 4B **64**
Heathside BR5: Pet W 1G **173**
NW11 . . . . 1J **63**
SE13 . . . . 2E **122**
TW4: Houn 7D **112**
Heathside Av. DA7: Bex 1E **126**
Heathside Cl. IG2: Ilf 5H **53**
Heathstan Rd. W12 . . . . 6C **80**
Heath St. NW3 . . . . 3A **64**
Heathurst Rd. CR2: Sand 7E **168**
Heath Vw. N2 . . . . 4A **46**
Heathview NW5 . . . . 4E **64**
Heath Vw. Cl. N2 . . . . 4A **46**
Heathview Dr. SE2 . . . . 6D **108**
Heathview Gdns. SW15 . . . . 7E **116**
Heathview Rd. CR7: Thor H 4A **156**
Heath Vs. NW3 . . . . 3B **64**
SE18 . . . . 5K **107**
Heathville Rd. N19 . . . . 7J **47**
Heathwall St. SW11 . . . . 3D **118**
HEATHWAY 1G **91**
Heath Way DA8: Erith 1J **127**
IG8: Wfd G 5F **37**
Heathway CR0: Croy 3B **170**
RM9: Dag 3F **73**
RM10: Dag 3F **73**
SE3 . . . . 7J **105**
Heathway UB2: S'hall 4B **94**
Heathway Ct. NW3 . . . . 2J **63**
Heathway Ind. Est. RM10: Dag 4H **73**
Heathwood Gdns. SE7 . . . . 4C **106**
Heathwood Point SE23 . . . . 3K **139**
Heathwood Wlk. DA5: Bexl 1K **145**
Heaton Cl. E4 . . . . 3K **35**
Heaton Ho. *SW10* *6A* ***100***
(off Seymour Wlk.)
Heaton Rd. CR4: Mitc 7E **136**
SE15 . . . . 2H **121**
Heaven Tree Cl. N1 . . . . 6C **66**
Heaver Rd. SW11 . . . . 3B **118**
Heavitree Cl. SE18 . . . . 5H **107**
Heavitree Rd. SE18 . . . . 5H **107**
(not continuous)
Hebden Ct. E2 . . . . 1F **85**
Hebden Ter. N17 . . . . 6K **33**
Hebdon Rd. SW17 . . . . 3C **136**
Heber Mans. *W14* *6G* ***99***
(off Queen's Club Gdns.)
Heber Rd. NW2 . . . . 5F **63**
SE22 . . . . 6F **121**
Hebron Rd. W6 . . . . 3E **98**
Hecham Cl. E17 . . . . 2A **50**
Heckfield Pl. SW6 . . . . 7J **99**
Heckford Ho. *E14* *6D* ***86***
(off Grundy St.)
Heckford St. E1 . . . . 7K **85**
Hector *NW9* *1B* ***44***
(off Five Acre)
Hector Ct. *SW9* *7A* ***102***
(off Caldwell St.)
Hector Ho. *E2* *2H* ***85***
(off Old Bethnal Grn. Rd.)
Hector St. SE18 . . . . 4J **107**
Heddington Gro. N7 . . . . 5K **65**
Heddon Cl. TW7: Isle 4A **114**
Heddon Ct. Av. EN4: Cockf 5J **21**
Heddon Ct. Pde. EN4: Cockf 5K **21**
Heddon Rd. EN4: Cockf 5J **21**
Heddon St. W1 . . . . 2A **12** (7G **83**)
(not continuous)
Hedgegate Ct. *W11* *6H* ***81***
(off Powis Ter.)
Hedge Hill EN2: Enf 1G **23**
Hedge La. N13 . . . . 3G **33**
Hedgeley IG4: Ilf 4D **52**
Hedgemans Rd. RM9: Dag 7D **72**
Hedgemans Way RM9: Dag 6E **72**
Hedgerley Gdns. UB6: G'frd 2G **77**
Hedgers Gro. E9 . . . . 6A **68**
Hedger St. SE11 . . . . 4B **102**
Hedge Wlk. SE6 . . . . 5D **140**
Hedgewood Gdns. IG5: Ilf 5E **52**
Hedgley M. SE12 . . . . 5H **123**
Hedgley St. SE12 . . . . 5H **123**
Hedingham Cl. N1 . . . . 7C **66**
Hedingham Ho. KT2: King T 1E **150**
Hedingham Rd. RM8: Dag 5B **72**
Hedley Ct. RM1: Rom 5K **55**
Hedley Ho. *E14* *3E* ***104***
(off Stewart St.)
Hedley Rd. TW2: Whit 7E **112**
Hedley Row N5 . . . . 5D **66**
Hedsor Ho. *E2* *3J* ***9***
(off Ligonier St.)
Heenan Cl. IG11: Bark 6G **71**
Heene Rd. EN2: Enf 1J **23**
Hega Ho. *E14* *5E* ***86***
(off Ullin St.)
Heidegger Cres. SW13 . . . . 7D **98**
Heigham Rd. E6 . . . . 7C **70**
Heighton Gdns. CR0: Wadd 5B **168**
Heights, The BR3: Beck 7E **140**
(not continuous)
SE7 . . . . 5A **106**
UB5: N'olt 5D **58**
Heights Cl. SW20 . . . . 7D **134**
Heiron St. SE17 . . . . 6B **102**
Helby Rd. SW4 . . . . 6H **119**
Heldar Ct. SE1 . . . . 7F **15** (2D **102**)
Helder Gro. SE12 . . . . 7H **123**
Helder St. CR2: S Croy 6D **168**
Heldmann Cl. TW3: Isle 4H **113**
Helegan Cl. BR6: Chels 4K **173**
Helena Ct. W5 . . . . 5D **78**
Helena Pl. E9 . . . . 1H **85**
Helena Rd. E13 . . . . 2H **87**
E17 . . . . 5C **50**
NW10 . . . . 5D **62**
W5 . . . . 5D **78**
Helena Sq. *SE16* *7A* ***86***
(off Sovereign Cres.)
Helen Av. TW14: Felt 7K **111**
Helen Cl. KT8: W Mole 4F **149**
N2 . . . . 3A **46**
Helen Gladstone Ho. *SE1* *6A* ***14***
(off Surrey Row)
Helen Ho. *E2* *2H* ***85***
(off Old Bethnal Grn. Rd.)
Helen Mackay Ho. *E14* *6F* ***87***
(off Blair St.)
Helen Peele Cotts. *SE16* *3J* ***103***
(off Lower Rd.)
Helenslea Av. NW11 . . . . 1J **63**
Helen's Pl. E2 . . . . 3J **85**
Helen St. SE18 . . . . 4F **107**
Helen Taylor Ho. *SE16* *3G* ***103***
(off Evelyn Lowe Est.)
Helford Cl. HA4: Ruis 2G **57**
Helgiford Gdns. TW16: Sun 7G **129**
Helios Rd. SM6: Wall 1E **166**
Heliport Ind. Est. SW11 . . . . 2B **118**
Helix Ct. *W11* *1F* ***99***
(off Swanscombe Rd.)
Helix Gdns. SW2 . . . . 6K **119**
Helix Rd. SW2 . . . . 6K **119**
Hellings St. E1 . . . . 1G **103**
Helm, The E16 . . . . 7F **89**
Helme Cl. SW19 . . . . 5H **135**
Helmet Row EC1 . . . . 2D **8** (4C **84**)
Helmore Rd. IG11: Bark 7K **71**
Helmsdale Cl. UB4: Yead 4C **76**
Helmsdale Ho. *NW6* *2K* ***81***
(off Carlton Va.)
Helmsdale Rd. SW16 . . . . 1H **155**
Helmsley Pl. E8 . . . . 7H **67**
Helmsley St. E8 . . . . 7H **67**
Helperby Rd. NW10 . . . . 7A **62**
Helsby Ct. *NW8* *3A* ***4***
(off Pollitt Dr.)
Helsinki Sq. SE16 . . . . 3A **104**
Helston *NW1* *1G* ***83***
(off Camden St.)
Helston Cl. HA5: H End 1D **40**
Helston Ct. *N15* *5E* ***48***
(off Culvert Rd.)
Helston Ho. *SE11* *5K* ***19***
(off Kennings Way)
Helvetia St. SE6 . . . . 2B **140**
Helwys Ct. E4 . . . . 6J **35**
Hemans St. SW8 . . . . 7H **101**
Hemans St. Est. SW8 . . . . 7H **101**
Hemberton Rd. SW9 . . . . 3J **119**
Hemery Rd. UB6: G'frd 5H **59**
Hemingford Cl. N12 . . . . 5G **31**
Hemingford Rd. N1 . . . . 1K **83**
SM3: Cheam 4E **164**
Heming Rd. HA8: Edg 7C **28**
Hemington Av. N11 . . . . 5J **31**
Hemingway Cl. NW5 . . . . 4E **64**
Hemlock Rd. W12 . . . . 7B **80**
(not continuous)
Hemmen La. UB3: Hayes 6H **75**
Hemming Cl. TW12: Hamp 1E **148**
Hemmings Cl. DA14: Sidc 2B **144**
Hemmings Mead KT19: Ewe 6J **163**
Hemming St. E1 . . . . 4G **85**
Hempstead Cl. IG9: Buck H 2D **36**
Hempstead Rd. E17 . . . . 3F **51**
Hemp Wlk. SE17 . . . . 4D **102**
Hemsby Rd. KT9: Chess 6F **163**
Hemstal Rd. NW6 . . . . 7J **63**
Hemsted Rd. DA8: Erith 7K **109**
Hemswell Dr. NW9 . . . . 1A **44**

Hemsworth Ct. N1 2E **84**
Hemsworth St. N1 2E **84**
Hemus Pl. SW3 6D **16** (5C **100**)
Hen & Chicken Ct. *EC4 1J 13*
(off Fleet St.)
Hen & Chickens Theatre ***6B 66***
(off St Paul's Rd.)
Henchman St. W12 6B **80**
Hendale Av. NW4 3D **44**
Henderson Cl. NW10 6J **61**
Henderson Ct. *NW3 5B 64*
(off Fitzjohn's Av.)
SE14 6K 103
(off Myers La.)
Henderson Dr. NW8 3A **4** (4B **82**)
Henderson Ho. *RM10: Dag 3G 73*
(off Kershaw Rd.)
Henderson Rd. CR0: Croy 6D **156**
E7 6A **70**
N9 1C **34**
SW18 7C **118**
UB4: Yead 3J **75**
Hendfield Ct. SM6: Wall 6F **167**
Hendham Rd. SW17 2C **136**
HENDON 5D **44**
Hendon Av. N3 1G **45**
Hendon Crematorium NW4 1F **45**
Hendon FC 2F **63**
Hendon Hall Ct. NW4 3F **45**
Hendon Ho. NW4 5F **45**
Hendon La. N3 3G **45**
Hendon Lodge NW4 3D **44**
Hendon Pk. Mans. NW4 5E **44**
Hendon Pk. Row NW11 6H **45**
Hendon Rd. N9 2B **34**
Hendon Way NW2 7F **45**
NW4 6D **44**
Hendon Wood La. NW7 1G **29**
Hendon Youth Sports Cen. 7F **45**
Hendre Ho. *SE1 4E 102*
(off Old Kent Rd.)
Hendren Cl. UB6: G'frd 5H **59**
Hendre Rd. SE1 4E **102**
Hendrick Av. SW12 7D **118**
Heneage La. EC3 1H **15** (6E **84**)
Heneage Pl. EC3 1H **15** (6E **84**)
Heneage St. E1 5K **9** (5F **85**)
Henfield Cl. DA5: Bexl 6G **127**
N19 1G **65**
Henfield Rd. SW19 1H **153**
Hengelo Gdns. CR4: Mitc 4B **154**
Hengist Rd. DA8: Erith 7H **109**
SE12 7K **123**
Hengist Way BR2: Brom 4G **159**
SM6: Wall 7H **167**
Hengrave Rd. SE23 6J **121**
Hengrove Ct. DA5: Bexl 1E **144**
Hengrove Cres. TW15: Ashf 3A **128**
Henham Ct. RM5: Col R 1J **55**
Henley Av. SM3: Cheam 3G **165**
Henley Cl. *SE16 2J 103*
(off St Marychurch St.)
TW7: Isle 1K **113**
UB6: G'frd 2G **77**
Henley Ct. N14 7B **22**
NW2 6F **63**
Henley Dr. KT2: King T 7B **134**
SE1 4F **103**
Henley Gdns. HA5: Eastc 3K **39**
RM6: Chad H 5E **54**
Henley Ho. *E2 3K 9*
(off Swanfield St.)
Henley Prior *N1 1G 7*
(off Affleck St.)
Henley Rd. E16 2D **106**
IG1: Ilf 4G **71**
N18 4K **33**
NW10 1E **80**
Henley St. SW11 2E **118**
Henley Way TW13: Hanw 5B **130**
Henlow Pl. TW10: Ham 2D **132**
HENLYS CORNER 4H **45**
HENLYS RDBT. 2A **112**
Hennel Cl. SE23 3J **139**
Hennessy Ct. E10 6E **50**
Hennessy Rd. N9 2D **34**
Henniker Gdns. E6 3B **88**
Henniker M. SW3 7A **16** (6B **100**)
Henniker Point *E15 5G 69*
(off Leytonstone Rd.)
Henniker Rd. E15 5F **69**
Henningham Rd. N17 1D **48**
Henning St. SW11 1C **118**
Henrietta Cl. SE8 6C **104**
Henrietta Ct. *TW1: Twick 7C 114*
(off Richmond Rd.)
Henrietta Ho. *N15 6E 48*
(off St Ann's Rd.)
W6 5E 98
(off Queen Caroline St.)
Henrietta M. WC1 3F **7** (4J **83**)
Henrietta Pl. W1 1J **11** (6F **83**)
Henrietta St. E15 5E **68**
WC2 2F **13** (7J **83**)
Henriques St. E1 6G **85**
Henry Addlington Cl. E6 5F **89**
Henry Cl. EN2: Enf 1K **23**
Henry Cooper Way SE9 3B **142**
Henry Darlot Dr. NW7 5A **30**
Henry Dickens Ct. W11 7F **81**
Henry Doulton Dr. SW17 4E **136**
Henry Hatch Ct. SM2: Sutt 7A **166**
Henry Ho. SE1 5J **13** (1A **102**)
SW8 7J 101
(off Wyvil Rd.)
Henry Jackson Rd. SW15 3F **117**
Henry Macaulay Av. KT2: King T 1D **150**
Henry Peters Dr. *TW11: Tedd 5J 131*
(off Somerset Gdns.)
Henry Purcell Ho. *E16 1K 105*
(off Evelyn Rd.)
Henry Rd. E6 2C **88**
EN4: E Barn 5G **21**
N4 1C **66**
Henrys Av. IG8: Wfd G 5C **36**
Henryson Rd. SE4 5C **122**
Henry St. BR1: Brom 1K **159**
Henry's Wlk. IG6: Ilf 1H **53**
Henry Tate M. SW16 5A **138**
Henry Tudor Ct. SE9 7G **125**
Henry Wise Ho. *SW1 4B 18*
(off Vauxhall Bri. Rd.)
Hensford Gdns. SE26 4H **139**
Henshall St. N1 6D **66**
Henshawe Rd. RM8: Dag 3D **72**
Henshaw St. SE17 4D **102**
Henslowe Rd. SE22 5G **121**
Henslow Ho. *SE15 7G 103*
(off Peckham Pk. Rd.)
Henson Av. NW2 5E **62**
Henson Cl. BR6: Farnb 2F **173**
Henson Path HA3: Kent 3D **42**
Henson Pl. UB5: N'olt 1A **76**
Henstridge Pl. NW8 1C **82**
Henty Cl. SW11 7C **100**
Henty Wlk. SW15 5D **116**
Henville Rd. BR1: Brom 1K **159**
Henwick Rd. SE9 3B **124**
Henwood Side IG8: Wfd G 6J **37**
Hepburn Gdns. BR2: Hayes 1G **171**
Hepburn M. SW11 5D **118**
Hepple Cl. TW7: Isle 2B **114**
Hepplestone Cl. SW15 6D **116**
Hepscott Rd. E9 6C **68**
Hepworth Ct. *N1 1B 84*
(off Gaskin St.)
NW3 5C **64**
SM3: Sutt 1J **165**
Hepworth Gdns. IG11: Bark 5A **72**
Hepworth Rd. SW16 7J **137**
Hepworth Way KT12: Walt T 7H **147**
Heracles *NW9 1B 44*
(off Five Acre)
Hera Ct. *E14 4C 104*
(off Homer Dr.)
Herald Gdns. SM6: Wall 2F **167**
Herald's Pl. SE11 3K **19**
Herald St. E2 4H **85**
Herbal Hill EC1 4K **7** (4A **84**)
Herbal Hill Gdns. *EC1 4K 7*
(off Herbal Hill)
Herbal Pl. EC1 4K **7**
Herbert Cres. SW1 1F **17** (3D **100**)
Herbert Gdns. NW10 2D **80**
RM6: Chad H 7D **54**
W4 6H **97**
Herbert Ho. *E1 7J 9*
(off Old Castle St.)
Herbert M. SW2 6A **120**
Herbert Morrison Ho. *SW6 6H 99*
(off Clem Attlee Ct.)
Herbert Pl. SE18 6F **107**
Herbert Rd. BR2: Brom 5B **160**
DA7: Bex 2E **126**
E12 4C **70**
E17 7B **50**
IG3: Ilf 2J **71**
KT1: King T 3F **151**
N11 7D **32**
N15 5F **49**
NW9 6C **44**
SE18 7E **106**
(not continuous)
SW19 7H **135**
(not continuous)
UB1: S'hall 1D **94**
Herbert St. E13 2J **87**
NW5 6E **64**
Herbrand Est. WC1 3E **6** (4J **83**)
Herbrand St. WC1 3E **6** (4J **83**)
Hercies Rd. UB10: Hil 7B **56**
Hercules Ct. SE14 6A **104**
Hercules Pl. N7 3J **65**
(not continuous)
Hercules Rd. SE1 2H **19** (3K **101**)
Hercules St. N7 3J **65**
Hercules Wharf *E14 7G 87*
(off Orchard Pl.)
Hercules Yd. N7 3J **65**
Hereford Av. EN4: E Barn 1J **31**
Hereford Bldgs. *SW3 7B 16*
(off Old Church St.)
Hereford Ct. HA1: Harr 4J **41**
SM2: Sutt 7J **165**
W7 5K 77
(off Copley Cl.)
Hereford Gdns. HA5: Pinn 5C **40**
IG1: Ilf 7C **52**
SE13 5G **123**
TW2: Twick 1G **131**
Hereford Ho. *N18 5C 34*
(off Cavendish Cl.)
NW6 2J 81
(off Carlton Va.)
SW3 1D 16
(off Ovington Gdns.)
SW10 7K 99
(off Fulham Rd.)
Hereford M. W2 6J **81**
Hereford Pl. SE14 7B **104**
Hereford Retreat SE15 7G **103**
Hereford Rd. E3 2B **86**
E11 5K **51**
TW13: Felt 1A **130**
W2 6J **81**
W3 7H **79**
W5 3C **96**
Hereford Sq. SW7 4A **100**
Hereford St. E2 4G **85**
Hereford Way
KT9: Chess 5C **162**
Herent Dr. IG5: Ilf 4C **52**
Hereward Gdns. N13 5F **33**
Hereward Rd. SW17 4D **136**
Herga Ct. HA1: Harr 3J **59**
Herga Rd. HA3: W'stone 4K **41**
Heriot Av. E4 2H **35**
Heriot Rd. NW4 5E **44**
Heriots Cl. HA7: Stan 4F **27**
Heritage Cl. SW9 3B **120**
TW16: Sun 1J **147**
Heritage Ct. *SE8 5K 103*
(off Trundley's Rd.)
Heritage Hill BR2: Kes 5A **172**
Heritage Pl. SW18 1A **136**
Heritage Vw. HA1: Harr 3K **59**
Herlwyn Av. HA4: Ruis 2G **57**
Herlwyn Gdns. SW17 4D **136**
Her Majesty's Theatre ***4C 12***
(off Haymarket)
Herm Cl. TW7: Isle 7G **95**
Hermes Cl. W9 4J **81**
Hermes Ct. SW2 6K **119**
SW9 1A 120
(off Southey Rd.)
Hermes St. N1 1J **7** (2A **84**)
Hermes Wlk. UB5: N'olt 2E **76**
Herm Ho. EN3: Enf W 1E **24**
N1 6C **66**
Hermiston Av. N8 5J **47**
Hermitage, The KT1: King T 4D **150**
SE13 2E **122**
SE23 1J **139**
SW13 1B **116**
TW10: Rich 5E **114**
TW13: Felt 3H **129**
UB8: Uxb 6A **56**
Hermitage Cl. E18 4H **51**
EN2: Enf 2G **23**
KT10: Clay 6A **162**
SE2 3C **108**
TW17: Shep 4C **146**
Hermitage Ct. *E1 1G 103*
(off Knighten St.)
E18 4J **51**
NW2 3J **63**
Hermitage Gdns. NW2 3J **63**
SE19 7C **138**
Hermitage Grn. SW16 1J **155**
Hermitage La. N18 5J **33**
NW2 3J **63**
SE25 6G **157**
(not continuous)
SW16 7K **137**
Hermitage Path SW16 1J **155**
Hermitage Rd. N4 7B **48**
N15 7B **48**
SE19 7C **138**
Hermitage Rooms ***2H 13***
(off Strand)
Hermitage Row E8 5G **67**
Hermitage St. W2 6A **4** (5B **82**)
Hermitage Vs. *SW6 6J 99*
(off Lillie Rd.)
Hermitage Wlk. E18 4H **51**
Hermitage Wall E1 1G **103**
Hermitage Waterside *E1 1G 103*
(off Thomas More St.)
Hermitage Way HA7: Stan 1A **42**
Hermit Pl. NW6 1K **81**
Hermit Rd. E16 5H **87**
Hermit St. EC1 1A **8** (3B **84**)
Hermon Gro. UB3: Hayes 1J **93**
Hermon Hill E11 5J **51**
E18 5J **51**
Herndon Rd. SW18 5A **118**
Herne Cl. NW10 5K **61**
UB3: Hayes 6H **75**
Herne Ct. WD23: Bush 1B **26**
HERNE HILL 5C **120**
Herne Hill SE24 6C **120**
Herne Hill Ho. *SE24 6B 120*
(off Railton Rd.)
Herne Hill Rd. SE24 3C **120**
Herne Hill Stadium 6D **120**
Herne M. N18 4B **34**
Herne Pl. SE24 5B **120**
Herne Rd. KT6: Surb 2D **162**
Heron Cl. E17 2B **50**
IG9: Buck H 1D **36**
NW10 6A **62**
SM1: Sutt 5H **165**

Heron Cl. SM6: Wall 7H 167
Heron Cl. BR2: Brom 4A 160
E14 ....3E 104
(off New Union Cl.)
HA4: Ruis 2F 57
KT1: King T 3E 150
NW9 ....2A 44
TW19: Stanw 1A 128
Heron Cres. DA14: Sidc 3J 143
Herondale Av. SW18 ....1B 136
Heron Dr. N4 ....2C 66
Herongate Cl. EN1: Enf 2A 24
Herongate Rd. E12 ....2A 70
Heron Hill DA17: Belv 5F 109
Heron Ho. DA14: Sidc 3B 144
E6 ....7C 70
NW8 ....1C 4
(off Newcourt St.)
SW11 ....7C 100
(off Searles Cl.)
W13 ....4A 78
Heron Ind. Est. E15 ....2D 86
Heron Mead EN3: Enf L 1H 25
Heron M. IG1: Ilf 2F 71
Heron Pl. SE16 ....1A 104
W1 ....7H 5
(off Thayer St.)
Heron Quay E14 ....1C 104
Heron Rd. CR0: Croy 2E 168
SE24 ....4C 120
TW1: Twick 4A 114
Herons, The E11 ....6H 51
Heronsforde W13 ....6C 78
Heronsgate HA8: Edg 5B 28
Heron's Lea N6 ....6D 46
Heronslea Dr. HA7: Stan 5K 27
Heron's Pl. TW7: Isle 3B 114
Heron Sq. TW9: Rich 5D 114
Herons Ri. EN4: E Barn 4H 21
Heron Trad. Est. W3 ....5H 79
Heron Vw. TW8: Bford 7C 96
(off Commerce Rd.)
Heron Way IG8: Wfd G 4F 37
TW14: Felt 4J 111
Herrick Ho. N16 ....4D 66
(off Howard Rd.)
SE5 ....7D 102
(off Elmington Est.)
Herrick Rd. N5 ....3C 66
Herrick St. SW1 ....4D 18 (4H 101)
Herries St. W10 ....2G 81
Herringham Rd. SE7 ....3A 106
Herron Cl. BR2: Brom 4H 159
Hersant Cl. NW10 ....1C 80
Herschell M. SE5 ....3C 120
Herschell Rd. SE23 ....7A 122
Hersham Cl. SW15 ....7C 116
Hershell Ct. SW14 ....4H 115
Hertford Av. SW14 ....5K 115
Hertford Cl. EN4: Cockf 3F 21
Hertford Ct. E6 ....3D 88
N13 ....3F 33
Hertford Pl. W1 ....4B 6 (4G 83)
Hertford Rd. EN3: Enf H, Enf W ...3D 24
EN4: Cockf 3F 21
IG2: Ilf 6J 53
IG11: Bark 7E 70
N1 ....1E 84
(not continuous)
N2 ....3C 46
N9 ....2C 34
Hertford St. W1 ....5J 11 (1F 101)
Hertford Wlk. DA17: Belv 5G 109
Hertford Way CR4: Mitc 4J 155
Hertslet Rd. N7 ....3K 65
Hertsmere Ho. E14 ....7C 86
(off Hertsmere Rd.)
Hertsmere Rd. E14 ....1C 104
Hertwood Ct. EN5: Barn 4B 20
Hervey Cl. N3 ....1J 45
Hervey Pk. Rd. E17 ....4A 50
Hervey Rd. SE3 ....3K 123
Hervey Way N3 ....1J 45

Hesa Rd. UB3: Hayes 6J 75
Hesewall Cl. SW4 ....2G 119
Hesketh Pl. W11 ....7G 81
Hesketh Rd. E7 ....3J 69
Heslop Rd. SW12 ....1D 136
Hesper M. SW5 ....4K 99
Hesperus Cl. E14 ....4D 104
Hesperus Cres. E14 ....4D 104
Hessel Rd. W13 ....2A 96
Hessel St. E1 ....6H 85
Hestercombe Av. SW6 ....2G 117
Hesterman Way CR0: Wadd ...1K 167
Hester Rd. N18 ....5B 34
SW11 ....7C 100
Hester Ter. TW9: Rich 3G 115
Hestia Ho. SE1 ....7G 15
HESTON 7E 94
Heston Av. TW5: Hest 6C 94
Heston Cen., The TW5: Cran ...5A 94
Heston Community Sports Hall ...7E 94
Heston Grange TW5: Hest 6D 94
Heston Grange La. TW5: Hest ..6D 94
Heston Ho. SE8 ....1C 122
Heston Ind. Mall TW5: Hest ...7D 94
Heston Phoenix Distribution Pk.
TW5: Hest 6A 94
Heston Pool 6D 94
Heston Rd. TW5: Hest 6E 94
Heston St. SE14 ....1C 122
Hetherington Rd. SW4 ....4J 119
TW17: Shep 2E 146
Hetherington Way UB10: Ick ...4A 56
Hethpool Ho. W2 ....4A 4
Hetley Gdns. SE19 ....7F 139
Hetley Rd. W12 ....1D 98
Heton Gdns. NW4 ....4D 44
Hevelius Cl. SE10 ....5H 105
Hever Cft. SE9 ....4E 142
Hever Gdns. BR1: Brom 2E 160
Heverham Rd. SE18 ....4J 107
Hever Ho. SE15 ....6K 103
(off Lovelinch Cl.)
Heversham Ho. SE15 ....6J 103
Heversham Rd. DA7: Bex 2G 127
Hewens Rd. UB10: Hil 4E 74
Hewer St. W10 ....5F 81
Hewett Cl. HA7: Stan 4G 27
Hewett Rd. RM8: Dag 5D 72
Hewetts Quay IG11: Bark 1F 89
Hewett St. EC2 ....4H 9 (4E 84)
Hewish Rd. N18 ....4K 33
Hewison St. E3 ....2B 86
Hewitt Av. N22 ....2B 48
Hewitt Cl. CR0: Croy 3C 170
Hewitt Rd. N8 ....5A 48
Hewlett Ho. SW8 ....7F 101
(off Havelock Ter.)
Hewlett Rd. E3 ....2A 86
Hexagon, The N6 ....1D 64
Hexal Rd. SE6 ....3G 141
Hexham Gdns. TW7: Isle 7A 96
Hexham Rd. EN5: New Bar 4E 20
SE27 ....2C 138
SM4: Mord 1K 165
Heybourne Rd. N17 ....7C 34
Heybridge NW1 ....6F 65
(off Lewis St.)
Heybridge Av. SW16 ....7J 137
Heybridge Dr. IG6: Ilf 2H 53
Heybridge Way E10 ....7A 50
Heydon Ho. SE14 ....1J 121
(off Kender St.)
Heyford Av. SW8 ....7J 101
SW20 ....3H 153
Heyford Rd. CR4: Mitc 2C 154
Heyford Ter. SW8 ....7J 101
Heygate Sq. SE17 ....4C 102
Heylyn Sq. E3 ....3B 86
Heynes Rd. RM8: Dag 4C 72
Heysham La. NW3 ....3K 63
Heysham Rd. N15 ....6D 48
Heythorp St. SW18 ....1H 135
Heythrop Dr. UB10: Ick 4B 56

Heywood Av. NW9 ....1A 44
Heywood Cl. HA7: Stan 5H 27
Heywood Ho. SE14 ....6K 103
(off Myers La.)
Heyworth Rd. E5 ....4H 67
E15 ....5H 69
Hibbert Ho. E14 ....3C 104
(off Tiller Rd.)
Hibbert Rd. E17 ....7B 50
HA3: W'stone 2K 41
Hibbert St. SW11 ....3B 118
Hibernia Gdns. TW3: Houn ...4E 112
Hibernia Point SE2 ....2D 108
(off Wolvercote Rd.)
Hibernia Rd. TW3: Houn 4E 112
Hibiscus Cl. HA8: Edg 4D 28
Hichisson Rd. SE15 ....5J 121
Hickes Ho. NW6 ....7K 63
Hickey's Almshouses TW9: Rich ...4F 115
Hickin Cl. SE7 ....4B 106
Hickin St. E14 ....3E 104
Hickleton NW1 ....1G 83
(off Camden St.)
Hickling Ho. SE16 ....3H 103
(off Slippers Pl.)
Hickling Rd. IG1: Ilf 5F 71
Hickman Av. E4 ....6K 35
Hickman Cl. E16 ....5B 88
Hickman Rd. RM6: Chad H ...7C 54
Hickmore Wlk. SW4 ....3H 119
Hickory Cl. N9 ....7B 24
Hicks Av. UB6: G'frd 3H 77
Hicks Cl. SW11 ....3C 118
Hicks Ct. RM10: Dag 3H 73
Hicks St. SE8 ....5A 104
Hidcote Gdns. SW20 ....3D 152
Hide E6 ....6E 88
Hide Ho. SW1 ....4C 18 (4H 101)
Hider Cl. SE3 ....7A 106
Hide Rd. HA1: Harr 4G 41
Hides St. N7 ....6K 65
Hide Twr. SW1 ....4C 18
(off Regency St.)
Higgins Ho. N1 ....1E 84
(off Colville Est.)
Higginson Ho. NW3 ....7D 64
(off Fellows Rd.)
Higgins Wlk. TW12: Hamp 6C 130
(off Abbott Cl.)
Higgs Ind. Est. SE24 ....3B 120
High Acres EN2: Enf 3G 23
HIGHAM HILL 1A 50
Higham Hill Rd. E17 ....1A 50
Higham Pl. E17 ....3A 50
Higham Rd. IG8: Wfd G 6D 36
N17 ....3D 48
Higham Sta. Av. E4 ....6H 35
Highams Ct. E4 ....3A 36
Highams Lodge Bus. Cen. E17 ...3K 49
HIGHAMS PARK 6A 36
Highams Pk. Ind. Est. E4 .....6K 35
High Ashton KT2: King T 7H 133
Highbanks Cl. DA16: Well 7B 108
Highbanks Rd. HA5: H End ...6A 26
Highbank Way N8 ....6A 48
HIGH BARNET 2A 20
Highbarrow Rd. CR0: Croy ...1G 169
High Beech CR2: S Croy 7E 168
N21 ....6E 22
High Beeches DA14: Sidc 5E 144
High Birch Cl. EN4: E Barn ...4H 21
(off park Rd.)
High Bri. SE10 ....5F 105
Highbridge Ct. SE14 ....1C 122
(off Farrow La.)
Highbridge Rd. IG11: Bark 1F 89
High Bri. Wharf SE10 ....5F 105
(off High Bri.)
Highbrook Rd. SE3 ....3B 124
High Broom Cres. BR4: W W'ck ...7D 158

HIGHBURY 4B 66
Highbury Av. CR7: Thor H 2A 156
Highbury Cl. BR4: W W'ck 2D 170
KT3: N Mald 4J 151
HIGHBURY CORNER 6B 66
Highbury Cres. N5 ....5B 66
Highbury Est. N5 ....5C 66
Highbury Gdns. IG3: Ilf 2J 71
Highbury Grange N5 ....4C 66
Highbury Gro. N5 ....5B 66
Highbury Gro. Ct. N5 ....6C 66
Highbury Hill N5 ....3A 66
Highbury New Pk. N5 ....5C 66
Highbury Pk. N5 ....3B 66
Highbury Pk. M. N5 ....4C 66
Highbury Pl. N5 ....6B 66
Highbury Pool 6B 66
Highbury Quad. N5 ....5B 66
Highbury Rd. SW19 ....5G 135
Highbury Stadium 3B 66
Highbury Sta. Rd. N1 ....6A 66
Highbury Ter. N5 ....5B 66
Highbury Ter. M. N5 ....5B 66
High Cedar Dr. SW20 ....7E 134
Highclere Rd. KT3: N Mald 3K 151
Highclere St. SE26 ....4A 140
Highcliffe W13 ....5B 78
(off Clivedon Ct.)
Highcliffe Dr. SW15 ....6B 116
(not continuous)
Highcliffe Gdns. IG4: Ilf 5C 52
Highcombe SE7 ....6K 105
Highcombe Cl. SE9 ....1B 142
High Coombe Pl. KT2: King T ..6K 133
Highcroft NW9 ....5A 44
Highcroft Av. HA0: Wemb 7G 61
Highcroft Est. N19 ....7J 47
Highcroft Gdns. NW11 ....6H 45
Highcroft Rd. N19 ....7J 47
High Cross Cen., The N15 ....4G 49
High Cross Rd. N17 ....3G 49
Highcross Way SW15 ....1C 134
Highdaun Dr. SW16 ....4K 155
Highdown KT4: Wor Pk 2A 164
Highdown Rd. SW15 ....6D 116
High Dr. KT3: N Mald 1J 151
High Elms IG8: Wfd G 5D 36
High Elms Country Pk. 7H 173
High Elms Nature Cen. 7H 173
High Elms Rd. BR6: Downe 7G 173
Highfield WD23: Bushy 2D 26
Highfield Av. BR6: Chels 5K 173
DA8: Erith 6H 109
HA5: Pinn 5D 40
HA9: Wemb 3F 61
NW9 ....5J 43
NW11 ....7F 45
UB6: G'frd 5J 59
Highfield Cl. HA6: Nwood 1G 39
KT6: Surb 1C 162
N22 ....1A 48
NW9 ....5J 43
SE13 ....6F 123
Highfield Ct. N14 ....6B 22
NW11 ....6G 45
Highfield Cres. HA6: Nwood ...1G 39
Highfield Dr. BR2: Brom 4G 159
BR4: W W'ck 2D 170
KT19: Ewe 6B 164
UB10: Ick 4A 56
Highfield Gdns. NW11 ....6G 45
Highfield Hill SE19 ....7D 138
Highfield M. NW6 ....7K 63
(off Compayne Gdns.)
Highfield Rd. BR1: Brom 4D 160
BR7: Chst 3K 161
DA6: Bex 5F 127
HA6: Nwood 1G 39
IG8: Wfd G 7H 37
KT5: Surb 7J 151
KT12: Walt T 7J 147
N21 ....2G 33
NW11 ....6G 45

Highfield Rd.—Hillcrest Ct.

Highfield Rd. SM1: Sutt 5C **166**
TW7: Isle 1K **113**
TW13: Felt 1J **129**
(Hazel Gro.)
TW13: Felt 2J **129**
(Tiley Rd.)
TW16: Sun 5H **147**
W3 . . . . .5H **79**
Highfields SM1: Sutt 2J **165**
Highfields Gro. N6 . . . . .1D **64**
High Foleys KT10: Clay 7B **162**
High Gables BR2: Brom 2G **159**
HIGHGATE .7E **46**
Highgate Av. N6 . . . . .7F **47**
Highgate Cemetery N6 . . . . .1E **64**
Highgate Cl. N6 . . . . .7E **46**
Highgate Edge N2 . . . . .5C **46**
Highgate Hgts. N6 . . . . .6G **47**
Highgate High St. N6 . . . . .1E **64**
Highgate Hill N6 . . . . .1F **65**
N19 . . . . .1F **65**
Highgate Ho. SE26 . . . . .3G **139**
Highgate Rd. NW5 . . . . .3E **64**
Highgate Spinney N8 . . . . .6H **47**
Highgate Wlk. SE23 . . . . .2J **139**
Highgate W. Hill N6 . . . . .1E **64**
Highgate Wood School Sports Cen.
. . . . .5G **47**
High Gro. BR1: Brom 1B **160**
SE18 . . . . .7H **107**
Highgrove Cl. BR7: Chst 1C **160**
N11 . . . . .5K **31**
Highgrove Ct. BR3: Beck 7C **140**
SM1: Sutt 6J **165**
Highgrove M. SM5: Cars 3D **166**
Highgrove Rd. RM8: Dag 5C **72**
Highgrove Swimming Pool 6J **39**
Highgrove Way HA4: Ruis 6J **39**
High Hill Est. E5 . . . . .1H **67**
High Hill Ferry E5 . . . . .1H **67**
High Holborn WC1 . . . . .7E **6** (6J **83**)
Highland Av. RM10: Dag 3J **73**
(not continuous)
W7 . . . . .6J **77**
Highland Cotts. SM6: Wall 4G **167**
Highland Ct. E18 . . . . .1K **51**
Highland Cft. BR3: Beck 5D **140**
Highland Dr. WD23: Bush 1A **26**
Highland Pk. TW13: Felt 4H **129**
Highland Rd. BR1: Brom 1H **159**
BR2: Brom 1H **159**
DA6: Bex 5G **127**
HA6: Nwood 2H **39**
SE19 . . . . .6E **138**
Highlands N20 . . . . .2G **31**
Highlands, The EN5: New Bar 4D **20**
HA8: Edg 2H **43**
Highlands Av. N21 . . . . .5E **22**
W3 . . . . .7J **79**
Highlands Cl. N4 . . . . .7J **47**
TW3: Houn 1F **113**
Highlands Ct. SE19 . . . . .6E **138**
Highlands Gdns. IG1: Ilf 1D **70**
Highlands Heath SW15 . . . . .7E **116**
Highlands Rd. EN5: New Bar 5D **20**
HIGHLANDS VILLAGE 5D **22**
Highland Ter. *SE13* *3D* ***122***
(off Algernon Rd.)
High La. W7 .5H **77**
Highlawn Hall HA1: Harr 3J **59**
Highlea Cl. NW9 . . . . .7F **29**
High Level Dr. SE26 . . . . .4G **139**
Highlever Rd. W10 . . . . .5E **80**
High Mead BR4: W W'ck 2F **171**
HA1: Harr 5J **41**
Highmead *N18* *5B* ***34***
(off Alpha Rd.)
SE18 . . . . .7K **107**
Highmead Cres. HA0: Wemb 7F **61**
High Mdw. Cl. HA5: Eastc 4A **40**
High Mdw. Cres. NW9 . . . . .5K **43**
High Meads Rd. E16 . . . . .6B **88**
Highmore Rd. SE3 . . . . .7G **105**
High Mt. NW4 .6C **44**
High Oaks EN2: Enf 1E **22**
High Pde., The SW16 . . . . .3J **137**
High Pk. Av. TW9: Kew 1G **115**
High Pk. Rd. TW9: Kew 1G **115**
High Path SW19 . . . . .1K **153**
High Point N6 . . . . .7E **46**
SE9 . . . . .3F **143**
High Ridge N10 . . . . .1F **47**
High Ridge Pl. *EN2: Enf* *1E* ***22***
(off Oak Av.)
High Rd. E18 .1J **51**
HA0: Wemb 5D **60**
HA3: Hrw W 7D **26**
HA5: Eastc 6J **39**
HA9: Wemb 5D **60**
IG1: Ilf .3F **71**
(not continuous)
IG3: Chad H, Ilf 2G **71**
IG7: Chig 5K **37**
IG9: Buck H 2E **36**
N11 . . . . .5A **32**
N15 . . . . .4F **49**
N17 . . . . .2F **49**
N22 . . . . .1K **47**
NW10 . . . . .6A **62**
RM6: Chad H 7D **54**
UB4: Hayes 5G **75**
UB10: Ick 3E **56**
WD23: Bushy 1C **26**
High Rd. E. Finchley N2 . . . . .1B **46**
High Rd. Leyton E10 . . . . .6D **50**
E15 . . . . .2D **68**
High Rd. Leytonstone E11 . . . . .4G **69**
E15 . . . . .4G **69**
High Rd. Nth. Finchley N12 . . . . .3F **31**
High Rd. Whetstone N20 . . . . .7F **21**
High Rd. Woodford Grn. E18 . . . . .1J **51**
IG8: Wfd G 6C **36**
High Sheldon N6 . . . . .6D **46**
Highshore Rd. SE15 . . . . .2F **121**
(not continuous)
Highstead Cres. DA8: Erith 1K **127**
Highstone Av. E11 . . . . .6J **51**
Highstone Ct. *E11* *6H* ***51***
(off New Wanstead)
Highstone Mans. *NW1* *7G* ***65***
(off Camden Rd.)
High St. BR1: Brom 2J **159**
BR3: Beck 2C **158**
BR4: W W'ck 1D **170**
BR6: Chels 7K **173**
BR6: Farnb 5F **173**
BR6: Orp 2K **173**
BR7: Chst 6F **143**
CR0: Croy 2C **168**
(not continuous)
CR7: Thor H 4C **156**
E11 . . . . .5J **51**
E13 . . . . .2J **87**
E15 . . . . .2E **86**
E17 . . . . .5A **50**
EN3: Pond E 6D **24**
EN5: Barn 3B **20**
HA1: Harr 1J **59**
HA3: W'stone 2J **41**
(not continuous)
HA4: Ruis 7G **39**
HA5: Pinn 3C **40**
HA6: Nwood 1H **39**
HA8: Edg 6B **28**
HA9: Wemb 4F **61**
IG6: Ilf .3G **53**
KT1: Ham W 1C **150**
KT1: King T 3D **150**
KT3: N Mald 4A **152**
KT7: T Ditt 6A **150**
KT8: W Mole 4E **148**
KT12: Walt T 7J **147**
KT17: Ewe 7B **164**
N8 . . . . .4J **47**
N14 . . . . .1C **32**
NW7 . . . . .5J **29**
High St. RM1: Rom 5K **55**
SE20 . . . . .6J **139**
SE25 . . . . .4F **157**
SM1: Sutt 4K **165**
SM3: Cheam 6G **165**
SM5: Cars 5E **166**
SW19 . . . . .5F **135**
TW2: Whit 7G **113**
TW3: Houn 3F **113**
(not continuous)
TW5: Cran 1J **111**
TW8: Bford 7C **96**
TW11: Tedd 5K **131**
TW12: Hamp, Ham H 1G **149**
TW13: Felt 3H **129**
TW17: Shep 6D **146**
TW19: Stanw 6A **110**
UB1: S'hall 1D **94**
UB3: Harl 6F **93**
UB7: Harm 6A **92**
UB7: Yiew 7A **74**
UB8: Uxb 1A **74**
W3 . . . . .1H **97**
W5 . . . . .1D **96**
High St. Colliers Wood SW19 . . . . . . .7B **136**
High St. Harlesden NW10 . . . . .2B **80**
High St. M. SW19 . . . . .5G **135**
High St. Nth. E6 . . . . .5C **70**
E12 . . . . .5C **70**
High St. Sth. E6 . . . . .2D **88**
High Timber St. EC4 . . . . .2C **14** (7C **84**)
High Tor Cl. BR1: Brom 7K **141**
High Tor Vw. SE28 . . . . .1J **107**
High Trees CR0: Croy 1A **170**
EN4: E Barn 5H **21**
N20 . . . . .3F **31**
SW2 . . . . .1A **138**
Hightrees Ct. W7 . . . . .7J **77**
Hightrees Ho. SW12 . . . . .6E **118**
High Vw. HA5: Pinn 4A **40**
Highview N6 .6G **47**
NW7 . . . . .3E **28**
UB5: N'olt 3C **76**
Highview Av. HA8: Edg 4D **28**
SM6: Wall 5K **167**
High Vw. Cl. SE19 . . . . .2F **157**
High Vw. Ct. HA3: Hrw W 7D **26**
Highview Gdns. HA8: Edg 4D **28**
N3 . . . . .3G **45**
N11 . . . . .5B **32**
Highview Ho. RM6: Chad H 4E **54**
Highview Lodge *EN2: Enf* *3G* ***23***
(off The Ridgeway)
High Vw. Pde. IG4: Ilf 5D **52**
High Vw. Rd. DA14: Sidc 4B **144**
E18 . . . . .2H **51**
N2 . . . . .1D **46**
Highview Rd. SE19 . . . . .6D **138**
W13 . . . . .5A **78**
Highway, The E1 . . . . .7G **85**
HA7: Stan 1K **41**
SM2: Sutt 7A **166**
Highway Bus. Pk., The *E1* *7K* ***85***
(off Heckford St.)
Highway Trad. Cen., The *E1* *7K* ***85***
(off Heckford St.)
Highwood BR2: Brom 3F **159**
Highwood Av. N12 . . . . .4F **31**
Highwood Cl. BR6: Farnb 2G **173**
Highwood Ct.
EN5: New Bar 5D **20**
N12 . . . . .3F **31**
Highwood Dr. BR6: Farnb 2G **173**
Highwood Gdns. IG5: Ilf 5D **52**
Highwood Gro. NW7 . . . . .5E **28**
HIGHWOOD HILL 3G **29**
Highwood Hill NW7 . . . . .2G **29**
Highwood Rd. N19 . . . . .3J **65**
High Worple HA2: Harr 7D **40**
Highworth Rd. N11 . . . . .6C **32**
Highworth St. NW1 . . . . .5D **4**
Hi-Gloss Cen. SE8 . . . . .5A **104**
Hilary Av. CR4: Mitc 3E **154**
Hilary Cl. DA8: Erith 1H **127**
SW6 . . . . .7K **99**
Hilary Dennis Ct. E11 . . . . .4J **51**
Hilary Rd. W12 . . . . .6B **80**
(not continuous)
Hilberry Ct. WD23: Bush 1A **26**
Hilbert Rd. SM3: Cheam 3F **165**
Hilborough Ct. E8 . . . . .7F **67**
Hilborough Way BR6: Farnb 5H **173**
Hilda Ct. KT6: Surb 7D **150**
Hilda Rd. E6 .7B **70**
E16 . . . . .4G **87**
(not continuous)
Hilda Ter. SW9 . . . . .2A **120**
Hilda Va. Cl. BR6: Farnb 4F **173**
Hilda Va. Rd. BR6: Farnb 4E **172**
Hildenborough Gdns.
BR1: Brom 6G **141**
Hildenborough Ho. *BR3: Beck* *7B* ***140***
(off Bethersden Cl.)
Hildenlea Pl. BR2: Brom 2F **159**
Hilderley Ho. *KT1: King T* *3F* ***151***
(off Winery La.)
Hildreth St. SW12 . . . . .1F **137**
Hildreth St. M. SW12 . . . . .1F **137**
Hildyard Rd. SW6 . . . . .6J **99**
Hiley Rd. NW10 . . . . .3E **80**
Hilgrove Rd. NW6 . . . . .7A **64**
Hiliary Gdns. HA7: Stan 2C **42**
Hillary *N8* *3J* ***47***
(off Boyton Cl.)
Hillary Ct. *TW19: Stanw* *1A* ***128***
(off Explorer Av.)
W12 . . . .*2E* ***98***
(off Titmuss St.)
Hillary Cres. KT12: Walt T 7A **148**
Hillary Dr. TW7: Isle 5K **113**
Hillary Ri. EN5: New Bar 4D **20**
Hillary Rd. UB2: S'hall 3E **94**
Hillbeck Cl. SE15 . . . . .7J **103**
Hillbeck Ho. *SE15* *6J* ***103***
(off Hillbeck Cl.)
Hillbeck Way UB6: G'frd 1H **77**
Hillborne Cl. UB3: Harl 5J **93**
Hillboro Ct. E11 . . . . .7F **51**
Hillborough Cl. SW19 . . . . .7A **136**
Hillbrook Rd. SW17 . . . . .3D **136**
Hill Brow BR1: Brom 1B **160**
Hillbrow KT3: N Mald 3B **152**
Hill Brow Cl. DA5: Bexl 4K **145**
Hillbrow Rd. BR1: Brom 7G **141**
Hillbury Av. HA3: Kent 5B **42**
Hillbury Rd. SW17 . . . . .3F **137**
Hill Cl. BR7: Chst 5F **143**
HA1: Harr 3J **59**
HA7: Stan 4G **27**
NW2 . . . . .3D **62**
NW11 . . . . .6J **45**
Hillcote Av. SW16 . . . . .7A **138**
Hill Ct. EN4: E Barn 4H **21**
UB5: N'olt 5F **58**
W5 . . . . .4F **79**
Hillcourt Av. N12 . . . . .6E **30**
Hillcourt Est. N16 . . . . .1D **66**
Hillcourt Rd. SE22 . . . . .6H **121**
Hill Cres. DA5: Bexl 1J **145**
HA1: Harr 5A **42**
KT4: Wor Pk 2E **164**
KT5: Surb 5F **151**
N20 . . . . .2E **30**
Hill Crest DA15: Sidc 7A **126**
KT6: Surb 7E **150**
Hillcrest N6 . . . . .7E **46**
N21 . . . . .7F **23**
SE24 . . . . .4D **120**
W11 . . . .*7H* ***81***
(off St John's Gdns.)
Hillcrest Av. HA5: Pinn 4B **40**
HA8: Edg 4C **28**
NW11 . . . . .5H **45**
Hillcrest Cl. BR3: Beck 6B **158**
SE26 . . . . .4G **139**
Hillcrest Ct. RM5: Col R 1K **55**

Hillcrest Ct. *SM2: Sutt* *6B* ***166***
(*off Eaton Rd.*)
Hill Crest Gdns. NW2 3C **62**
Hillcrest Gdns. KT10: Hin W 3A **162**
N3 4G **45**
Hillcrest Rd. BR1: Brom 5J **141**
BR6: Chels 2K **173**
E17 2F **51**
E18 2H **51**
W3 1H **97**
W5 5E **78**
Hillcrest Vw. BR3: Beck 6B **158**
Hillcroft Av. HA5: Pinn 6D **40**
Hillcroft Cres. HA4: Ruis 3B **58**
HA9: Wemb 4F **61**
W5 6D **78**
Hillcroft Rd. E6 5F **89**
Hillcroome Rd. SM2: Sutt 6B **166**
Hillcross Av. SM4: Mord 6F **153**
Hilldale Rd. SM1: Sutt 4H **165**
Hilldown Ct. SW16 7J **137**
Hilldown Rd. BR2: Hayes 1G **171**
SW16 7J **137**
Hill Dr. NW9 1J **61**
SW16 3K **155**
Hilldrop Cres. N7 5H **65**
Hilldrop Est. N7 5H **65**
(not continuous)
Hilldrop La. N7 5H **65**
Hilldrop Rd. BR1: Brom 6K **141**
N7 5H **65**
Hill End BR6: Orp 2K **173**
Hillend SE18 1E **124**
Hillersden Ho. *SW1* *5J* ***17***
(*off Ebury Bri. Rd.*)
Hillersdon Av. HA8: Edg 5A **28**
SW13 2C **116**
Hillery Cl. SE17 4D **102**
Hill Farm Cotts. HA4: Ruis 7E **38**
Hill Farm Rd. UB10: Ick 4F **57**
W10 5E **80**
Hillfield Av. HA0: Wemb 7E **60**
N8 5J **47**
NW9 5A **44**
SM4: Mord 6C **154**
Hillfield Cl. HA2: Harr 4G **41**
Hillfield Ct. NW3 5C **64**
Hillfield Ho. N5 5C **66**
Hillfield M. N8 4K **47**
Hillfield Pk. N10 4F **47**
N21 2F **33**
Hillfield Pk. M. N10 4F **47**
Hill Fld. Rd. TW12: Hamp 7D **130**
Hillfield Rd. NW6 5H **63**
Hillfoot Av. RM5: Col R 1J **55**
Hillfoot Rd. RM5: Col R 1J **55**
Hillgate Pl. SW12 7F **119**
W8 1J **99**
Hillgate St. W8 1J **99**
Hillgate Wlk. N6 6G **47**
Hill Gro. RM1: Rom 3K **55**
TW13: Hanw 2D **130**
Hill Ho. BR2: Brom 2H **159**
E5 *1H* ***67***
(*off Harrington Hill*)
SE28 1H **107**
Hillhouse Av. HA7: Stan 7E **26**
Hill Ho. Cl. N21 7F **23**
Hill Ho. Dr. TW12: Hamp 1E **148**
Hill Ho. M. BR2: Brom 2H **159**
Hill Ho. Rd. SW16 5K **137**
Hilliard Ho. *E1* *1H* ***103***
(*off Prusom St.*)
Hilliard Rd. HA6: Nwood 1H **39**
Hilliards Ct. E1 1J **103**
Hillier Cl. EN5: New Bar 6E **20**
Hillier Gdns. CR0: Wadd 5A **168**
Hillier Ho. *NW1* *7H* ***65***
(*off Camden Sq.*)
Hillier Lodge TW11: Tedd 5H **131**
Hillier Pl. KT9: Chess 6D **162**
Hillier Rd. SW11 6D **118**
Hilliers Av. UB8: Hil 3C **74**
Hilliers La. CR0: Bedd 3J **167**
HILLINGDON 3C **74**
Hillingdon Athletic Club 5F **39**
Hillingdon Av.
TW19: Stanw 1A **128**
HILLINGDON CIRCUS 6D **56**
Hillingdon Ct. HA3: Kent 4D **42**
Hillingdon Cycling Circuit 1A **94**
HILLINGDON HEATH 4D **74**
Hillingdon Hill UB10: Hil 2A **74**
Hillingdon Rd. DA7: Bex 2J **127**
UB8: Uxb 1A **74**
UB10: Uxb 1A **74**
Hillingdon Ski Cen. 5A **56**
Hillingdon St. SE17 6B **102**
Hillington Gdns. IG8: Wfd G 2B **52**
Hill La. HA4: Ruis 1E **56**
Hillman Cl. UB8: Uxb 5A **56**
Hillman Dr. W10 4E **80**
Hillman St. E8 6H **67**
Hillmarton Rd. N7 5J **65**
Hillmarton Ter. *N7* *5J* ***65***
(*off Hillmarton Rd.*)
Hillmead Dr. SW9 4B **120**
Hillmore Ct. *SE13* *3F* ***123***
(*off Belmont Hill*)
Hillmore Gro. SE26 5A **140**
Hill Path SW16 5K **137**
Hillreach SE18 5D **106**
Hill Ri. HA4: Ruis 1E **56**
KT10: Hin W 2B **162**
KT12: Walt T 7H **147**
N9 6C **24**
NW11 4K **45**
SE23 1H **139**
TW10: Rich 5D **114**
UB6: G'frd 7G **59**
Hillrise Mans. *N19* *7J* ***47***
(*off Warltersville Rd.*)
Hillrise Rd. N19 7J **47**
Hill Rd. CR4: Mitc 1F **155**
HA0: Wemb 3B **60**
HA1: Harr 5A **42**
HA5: Pinn 5C **40**
N10 1D **46**
NW8 3A **82**
SM1: Sutt 5K **165**
SM5: Cars 6C **166**
Hillsboro' Rd. SE22 5E **120**
Hillsborough Ct. *NW6* *1K* ***81***
(*off Mortimer Cres.*)
Hillsgrove Cl. DA16: Well 7C **108**
HILLSIDE 4J **109**
Hillside DA8: Erith 4J **109**
EN5: New Bar 5F **21**
N8 6H **47**
NW5 3E **64**
NW9 4K **43**
NW10 7J **61**
SE10 *7F* ***105***
(*off Crooms Hill*)
SW19 6F **135**
Hillside Av. HA9: Wemb 4F **61**
IG8: Wfd G 6F **37**
N11 6J **31**
Hillside Cl. IG8: Wfd G 5F **37**
NW8 2K **81**
SM4: Mord 4G **153**
Hillside Cres. HA2: Harr 1G **59**
HA6: Nwood 1J **39**
Hillside Dr. HA8: Edg 6B **28**
Hillside Est. N15 6F **49**
Hillside Gdns. E17 3F **51**
EN5: Barn 4B **20**
HA3: Kent 7E **42**
HA6: Nwood 1J **39**
HA8: Edg 4A **28**
N6 6F **47**
N11 6B **32**
SM6: Wall 7G **167**
SW2 2A **138**
Hillside Gro. N14 7C **22**
NW7 7H **29**
Hillside Ho. *CR0: Wadd* *4B* ***168***
(*off Violet La.*)
Hillside La. BR2: Hayes 2H **171**
(not continuous)
Hillside Mans. EN5: Barn 4C **20**
Hillside Pas. SW16 2K **137**
Hillside Ri. HA6: Nwood 1J **39**
Hillside Rd. BR2: Brom 3H **159**
CR0: Wadd 5B **168**
HA5: Pinn 1K **39**
HA6: Nwood 1J **39**
KT5: Surb 4F **151**
N15 7E **48**
SM2: Sutt 7H **165**
SW2 2K **137**
UB1: S'hall 4E **76**
W5 5E **78**
Hills La. HA6: Nwood 1G **39**
Hillsleigh Rd. W8 1H **99**
Hills M. W5 7E **78**
Hills Pl. W1 1A **12** (6G **83**)
Hills Rd. IG9: Buck H 1E **36**
Hillstowe St. E5 3J **67**
Hill St. TW9: Rich 5D **114**
W1 4H **11** (1E **100**)
Hill Top SM3: Sutt 7H **153**
SM4: Mord 6J **153**
Hilltop E17 3D **50**
NW11 4K **45**
Hilltop Av. NW10 7J **61**
Hill Top Ct. IG8: Wfd G 6J **37**
Hilltop Ct. *NW8* *7A* ***64***
(*off Alexandra Rd.*)
Hilltop Gdns. BR6: Orp 2J **173**
NW4 2D **44**
Hilltop Ho. N6 7H **47**
Hilltop Rd. NW6 7J **63**
Hill Top Vw. IG8: Wfd G 6J **37**
Hilltop Way HA7: Stan 3F **27**
Hill Vw. *NW3* *1D* ***82***
(*off Ainger Rd.*)
Hillview SW20 7D **134**
Hillview Av. HA3: Kent 5E **42**
Hillview Cl. HA9: Wemb 2F **61**
Hill Vw. Cres. BR6: Orp 1J **173**
IG1: Ilf 6D **52**
Hill Vw. Dr. DA16: Well 2J **125**
SE28 1J **107**
Hill Vw. Gdns. NW9 5K **43**
Hillview Gdns. HA2: Harr 3E **40**
NW4 4F **45**
Hill Vw. Rd. BR6: Orp 1K **173**
KT10: Clay 7A **162**
TW1: Twick 6A **114**
Hillview Rd. BR7: Chst 5E **142**
HA5: H End 1D **40**
NW7 4A **30**
SM1: Sutt 3A **166**
Hillway N6 2E **64**
NW9 1A **62**
Hill-Wood Ho. *NW1* *1B* ***6***
(*off Polygon Rd.*)
Hillworth BR3: Beck 2D **158**
Hillworth Rd. SW2 7A **120**
Hillyard Ho. SW9 1A **120**
Hillyard Rd. W7 5J **77**
Hillyard St. SW9 1A **120**
Hillyfield E17 2A **50**
Hillyfield Cl. E9 5A **68**
Hilly Flds. Cres. SE4 3C **122**
SE13 3C **122**
Hilsea Point SW15 1D **134**
Hilsea St. E5 4J **67**
Hilton Av. N12 5G **31**
Hilton Ho. SE4 4K **121**
Hilton's Wharf *SE10* *6D* ***104***
(*off Norman Rd.*)
Hilversum Cres. SE22 5E **120**
Himalaya Palace Cinema 1D **94**
Himley Rd. SW17 5C **136**
Hinchinbrook Ho. *NW6* *1K* ***81***
(*off Mortimer Cres.*)
Hinchley Cl. KT10: Hin W 4A **162**
Hinchley Dr. KT10: Hin W 3A **162**
Hinchley Mnr. KT10: Hin W 3A **162**
Hinchley Way KT10: Hin W 3A **162**
HINCHLEY WOOD 3A **162**
Hinckley Rd. SE15 4G **121**
Hind Ct. EC4 1K **13** (6A **84**)
Hind Cres. DA8: Erith 6K **109**
Hinde Ho. *W1* *7H* ***5***
(*off Hinde St.*)
Hinde M. W1 7H **5**
Hindes Rd. HA1: Harr 5H **41**
Hinde St. W1 7H **5** (6E **82**)
Hind Gro. E14 6C **86**
Hindhead Cl. N16 1E **66**
UB8: Hil 5D **74**
Hindhead Gdns. UB5: N'olt 1C **76**
Hindhead Point SW15 1D **134**
Hindhead Way SM6: Wall 5J **167**
Hind Ho. N7 4A **66**
SE14 *6K* ***103***
(*off Myers La.*)
Hindlip Ho. SW8 1H **119**
Hindmans Rd. SE22 5G **121**
Hindmans Way RM9: Dag 4F **91**
Hindmarsh Cl. E1 7G **85**
Hindon Ct. SW1 3A **18**
Hindrey Rd. E5 5H **67**
Hindsley's Pl. SE23 2J **139**
Hinkler Rd. HA3: Kent 3D **42**
Hinksey Path SE2 2D **108**
Hinstock *NW6* *1K* ***81***
(*off Belsize Rd.*)
Hinstock Rd. SE18 6G **107**
Hinton Av. TW4: Houn 4B **112**
Hinton Cl. SE9 1C **142**
Hinton Ct. *E10* *2D* ***68***
(*off Leyton Grange Est.*)
Hinton Ho. W5 6C **78**
Hinton Rd. N18 4K **33**
SE24 3B **120**
SM6: Wall 6G **167**
Hippisley Ct. TW7: Isle 3K **113**
Hippodrome M. W11 7G **81**
Hippodrome Pl. W11 7G **81**
Hiroshima Prom. SE7 3A **106**
Hirst Cres. HA9: Wemb 3E **60**
Hitcham Rd. E17 7B **50**
Hitchcock Cl. TW17: Shep 3B **146**
Hitchin Sq. E3 2A **86**
Hithe Gro. SE16 3J **103**
Hitherbroom Rd. UB3: Hayes 1J **93**
Hither Farm Rd. SE3 3A **124**
Hitherfield Rd. RM8: Dag 2E **72**
SW16 2K **137**
HITHER GREEN 6G **123**
Hither Grn. La. SE13 5E **122**
Hitherwell Dr. HA3: Hrw W 1H **41**
Hitherwood Dr. SE19 4F **139**
Hive Cl. WD23: Bushy 2C **26**
Hive Rd. WD23: Bushy 2C **26**
(not continuous)
HMP Brixton SW2 6J **119**
HMP Pentonville N7 6K **65**
HMP Wandsworth SW18 7B **118**
HMP Wormwood Scrubs W12 6C **80**
HMS Belfast 4G **15** (1E **102**)
Hoadly Ho. *SE1* *5C* ***14***
(*off Pepper St.*)
Hoadly Rd. SW16 3H **137**
Hobart Cl. N20 2H **31**
UB4: Yead 4B **76**
Hobart Ct. *CR2: S Croy* *5D* ***168***
(*off South Pk. Hill Rd.*)
Hobart Dr. UB4: Yead 4B **76**
Hobart Gdns. CR7: Thor H 3D **156**
Hobart La. UB4: Yead 4B **76**
Hobart Pl. SW1 1J **17** (3F **101**)
TW10: Rich 7F **115**
Hobart Rd. IG6: Ilf 2G **53**
KT4: Wor Pk 3D **164**
RM9: Dag 4D **72**
UB4: Yead 4B **76**
Hobbayne Rd. W7 6H **77**

Hobbes Wlk. SW15 . . . . . 5D 116
Hobbs Ct. SE1 . . . . . 6K 15
(off Mill St.)
Hobbs Grn. N2 . . . . . 3A 46
Hobbs M. IG3: Ilf 2K 71
Hobbs Pl. N1 . . . . . 1E 84
Hobbs Pl. Est. N1 . . . . . 2E 84
(off Hobbs Pl.)
Hobbs Rd. SE27 . . . . . 4C 138
Hobby St. EN3: Pond E 5E 24
Hobday St. E14 . . . . . 6D 86
Hobill Wlk. KT5: Surb 6F 151
Hoblands End BR7: Chst 6J 143
Hobson's Pl. E1 . . . . . 5G 85
Hobury St. SW10 . . . . . 7A 16 (6A 100)
Hocker St. E2 . . . . . 2J 9 (3F 85)
Hockett Cl. SE8 . . . . . 4A 104
Hockington Ct. EN5: New Bar 4E 20
Hockley Av. E6 . . . . . 2C 88
Hockley Ct. E18 . . . . . 1J 51
Hockley M. IG11: Bark 3J 89
Hockliffe Ho. W10 . . . . . 5E 80
(off Sutton Way)
Hockney Ct. SE16 . . . . . 5H 103
(off Rossetti Rd.)
Hocroft Av. NW2 . . . . . 3H 63
Hocroft Ct. NW2 . . . . . 3H 63
Hocroft Rd. NW2 . . . . . 3H 63
Hocroft Wlk. NW2 . . . . . 3H 63
Hodder Dr. UB6: G'frd 2K 77
Hoddesdon Rd. DA17: Belv 5G 109
Hodes Row NW3 . . . . . 4E 64
Hodford Rd. NW11 . . . . . 1H 63
Hodgkin Cl. SE28 . . . . . 7D 90
Hodgkins M. HA7: Stan 5G 27
Hodister Cl. SE5 . . . . . 7C 102
Hodnet Gro. SE16 . . . . . 4K 103
Hodson Cl. HA2: Harr 3D 58
Hoecroft Ct. EN3: Enf W 1D 24
(off Hoe La.)
Hoe La. EN1: Enf 1B 24
EN3: Enf W 1C 24
Hoe St. E17 . . . . . 4C 50
Hoever Ho. SE6 . . . . . 4E 140
Hoffmann Gdns. CR2: Sels 7H 169
Hoffman Sq. N1 . . . . . 1F 9
Hofland Rd. W14 . . . . . 3G 99
Hogan M. W2 . . . . . 5A 4 (5A 82)
Hogan Way E5 . . . . . 2G 67
Hogarth Av. TW15: Ashf 6E 128
Hogarth Bus. Pk. W4 . . . . . 6A 98
Hogarth Cl. E16 . . . . . 5B 88
W5 . . . . . 5E 78
Hogarth Ct. E1 . . . . . 6G 85
(off Batty St.)
EC3 . . . . . 2H 15 (6E 84)
NW1 . . . . . 7G 65
(off St Pancras Way)
SE19 . . . . . 4F 139
TW5: Hest 7C 94
Hogarth Cres. CR0: Croy 7C 156
SW19 . . . . . 1B 154
Hogarth Gdns. TW5: Hest 7E 94
Hogarth Hill NW11 . . . . . 4H 45
Hogarth Ho. SW1 . . . . . 4D 18
(off Erasmus St.)
UB5: N'olt 2B 76
(off Gallery Gdns.)
Hogarth Ind. Est. NW10 . . . . . 4C 80
Hogarth La. W4 . . . . . 6A 98
Hogarth Pl. SW5 . . . . . 4K 99
(off Hogarth Rd.)
Hogarth Rd. HA8: Edg 2G 43
RM8: Dag 5B 72
SW5 . . . . . 4K 99
HOGARTH RDBT. 6A 98
Hogarth's House 6A 98
(off Hogarth La.)
Hogarth Ter. W4 . . . . . 6A 98
Hogarth Way TW12: Hamp 1G 149
Hog Hill Rd. RM5: Col R 1F 55
Hogshead Pas. E1 . . . . . 7H 85
(off Reunion Row)
Hogsmill Ho. KT1: King T 3F 151
(off Vineyard Cl.)
Hogsmill Wlk. KT1: King T 3E 150
(off Penrhyn Rd.)
Hogsmill Way KT19: Ewe 5J 163
Holbeach Cl. NW9 . . . . . 1A 44
Holbeach Gdns. DA15: Sidc 6J 125
Holbeach M. SW12 . . . . . 1F 137
Holbeach Rd. SE6 . . . . . 7C 122
Holbeck Row SE15 . . . . . 7G 103
Holbein Ho. SW1 . . . . . 5G 17
(off Holbein M.)
Holbein M. SW1 . . . . . 5G 17 (5E 100)
Holbein Pl. SW1 . . . . . 4G 17 (4E 100)
Holbein Ter. RM8: Dag 4C 72
(off Marlborough Rd.)
Holberton Gdns. NW10 . . . . . 3D 80
HOLBORN 6G 7 (5A 84)
Holborn EC1 . . . . . 6J 7 (5A 84)
WC1 . . . . . 5K 83
Holborn Cir. EC1 . . . . . 6K 7 (5A 84)
Holborn Pl. WC1 . . . . . 6G 7
Holborn Rd. E13 . . . . . 4K 87
Holborn Viaduct EC1 . . . . . 6K 7 (5A 84)
Holborn Way CR4: Mitc 2D 154
Holbrook Cl. EN1: Enf 1A 24
N19 . . . . . 1F 65
Holbrooke Ct. N7 . . . . . 3J 65
Holbrooke Pl. TW10: Rich 5D 114
Holbrook Ho. BR7: Chst 1H 161
Holbrook La. BR7: Chst 7H 143
Holbrook Rd. E15 . . . . . 2H 87
Holbrook Way BR2: Brom 6D 160
Holburne Cl. SE3 . . . . . 1A 124
Holburne Gdns. SE3 . . . . . 1B 124
Holburne Rd. SE3 . . . . . 1A 124
Holcombe Hill NW7 . . . . . 3H 29
Holcombe Ho. SW9 . . . . . 3J 119
(off Landor Rd.)
Holcombe Pl. SE4 . . . . . 3A 122
(off St Asaph Rd.)
Holcombe Rd. IG1: Ilf 7E 52
N17 . . . . . 3F 49
(not continuous)
Holcombe St. W6 . . . . . 4D 98
Holcote Cl. DA17: Belv 3E 108
Holcroft Ct. W1 . . . . . 5A 6
Holcroft Ho. SW11 . . . . . 3B 118
Holcroft Rd. E9 . . . . . 7J 67
Holden Av. N12 . . . . . 5E 30
NW9 . . . . . 1J 61
Holdenby Rd. SE4 . . . . . 5A 122
Holden Cl. RM8: Dag 3B 72
Holden Ho. N1 . . . . . 1C 84
(off Prebend St.)
SE8 . . . . . 7C 104
Holdenhurst Av. N12 . . . . . 7F 31
Holden Rd. N12 . . . . . 5E 30
Holden St. SW11 . . . . . 2E 118
Holder Cl. N3 . . . . . 7E 30
Holdernesse Cl. TW7: Isle 1A 114
Holdernesse Rd. SW17 . . . . . 3D 136
Holderness Ho. SE5 . . . . . 3E 120
Holderness Way SE27 . . . . . 5B 138
HOLDERS HILL 2F 45
Holder's Hill Av. NW4 . . . . . 2F 45
Holders Hill Cir. NW7 . . . . . 7B 30
Holders Hill Cres. NW4 . . . . . 2F 45
Holders Hill Dr. NW4 . . . . . 3F 45
Holder's Hill Gdns. NW4 . . . . . 2G 45
Holders Hill Pde. NW7 . . . . . 1G 45
Holders Hill Rd. NW4 . . . . . 2F 45
NW7 . . . . . 2F 45
Holford Ho. SE16 . . . . . 4H 103
(off Camilla Rd.)
WC1 . . . . . 1H 7
(off Gt. Percy St.)
Holford M. WC1 . . . . . 1J 7
Holford Pl. WC1 . . . . . 1H 7 (3K 83)
Holford Rd. NW3 . . . . . 3A 64
Holford St. WC1 . . . . . 1J 7 (3K 83)
Holford Yd. WC1 . . . . . 1J 7
(off Cruikshank St.)
Holgate Av. SW11 . . . . . 3B 118
Holgate Gdns. RM10: Dag 6G 73
Holgate Rd. RM10: Dag 5G 73
Holgate St. SE7 . . . . . 3B 106
Hollam Ho. N8 . . . . . 4K 47
Holland Av. SM2: Sutt 7J 165
SW20 . . . . . 1B 152
Holland Cl. BR2: Hayes 2H 171
EN5: New Bar 7G 21
HA7: Stan 5G 27
RM7: Rom 5J 55
Holland Ct. E17 . . . . . 4E 50
(off Evelyn Rd.)
KT6: Surb 7D 150
NW7 . . . . . 6H 29
Holland Dr. SE23 . . . . . 3A 140
Holland Gdns. TW8: Bford 6F 97
W14 . . . . . 3G 99
Holland Gro. SW9 . . . . . 7A 102
Holland Ho. E4 . . . . . 4K 35
NW10 . . . . . 2D 80
(off Holland Rd.)
HOLLAND PARK 1H 99
Holland Pk. 2H 99
Holland Pk. W11 . . . . . 1G 99
Holland Pk. Av. IG3: Ilf 6J 53
W11 . . . . . 2G 99
Holland Pk. Ct. W14 . . . . . 2G 99
(off Holland Pk. Gdns.)
Holland Pk. Gdns. W14 . . . . . 2G 99
Holland Pk. Mans. W14 . . . . . 1G 99
(off Holland Pk. Gdns.)
Holland Pk. M. W11 . . . . . 1G 99
Holland Pk. Rd. W14 . . . . . 3H 99
HOLLAND PARK ROUNDABOUT 2F 99
Holland Pk. Ter. W11 . . . . . 1G 99
(off Portland Rd.)
Holland Pk. Theatre (Open Air) 2H 99
(in Holland Pk.)
Holland Pas. N1 . . . . . 1C 84
(off Basire St.)
Holland Pl. W8 . . . . . 2K 99
(off Kensington Chu. St.)
Holland Pl. Chambers W8 . . . . . 2K 99
(off Holland Pl.)
Holland Ri. Ho. SW9 . . . . . 7K 101
(off Clapham Rd.)
Holland Rd. E6 . . . . . 1D 88
E15 . . . . . 3G 87
HA0: Wemb 6D 60
NW10 . . . . . 1C 80
SE25 . . . . . 5G 157
W14 . . . . . 2F 99
Hollands, The KT4: Wor Pk 1B 164
TW13: Hanw 4B 130
Holland St. SE1 . . . . . 4B 14 (1B 102)
W8 . . . . . 2J 99
Holland Vs. Rd. W14 . . . . . 2G 99
Holland Wlk. HA7: Stan 5F 27
N19 . . . . . 1H 65
W8 . . . . . 1H 99
Holland Way BR2: Hayes 2H 171
Hollar Rd. N16 . . . . . 3F 67
Hollen St. W1 . . . . . 7C 6 (6H 83)
Holles Cl. TW12: Hamp 6E 130
Holles Ho. SW9 . . . . . 2A 120
Holles St. W1 . . . . . 7K 5 (6F 83)
Holley Rd. W3 . . . . . 2A 98
Hollick Wood Av. N12 . . . . . 6J 31
Holliday Sq. SW11 . . . . . 3B 118
(off Fowler Cl.)
Hollidge Way RM10: Dag 7H 73
Hollies, The E11 . . . . . 5J 51
(off New Wanstead)
HA3: W'stone 4A 42
N20 . . . . . 1G 31
Hollies Av. DA15: Sidc 2K 143
Hollies Cl. SW16 . . . . . 6A 138
TW1: Twick 2K 131
Hollies End NW7 . . . . . 5J 29
Hollies Rd. W5 . . . . . 4C 96
Hollies Way SW12 . . . . . 7E 118
Holligrave Rd. BR1: Brom 1J 159
Hollingbourne Av. DA7: Bex 1F 127
Hollingbourne Gdns. W13 . . . . . 5B 78
Hollingbourne Rd. SE24 . . . . . 5C 120
Hollingsworth Ct. KT6: Surb 7D 150
Hollingsworth Rd. CR0: Croy 6H 169
Hollington Ct. BR7: Chst 6F 143
Hollington Cres. KT3: N Mald 6B 152
Hollington Rd. E6 . . . . . 3D 88
N17 . . . . . 2G 49
Hollingworth Cl. KT8: W Mole 4D 148
Hollingworth Rd. BR5: Pet W 6F 161
Hollins Ho. N7 . . . . . 4J 65
Hollisfield WC1 . . . . . 2F 7
(off Cromer St.)
Hollman Gdns. SW16 . . . . . 6B 138
Hollow, The IG8: Wfd G 4C 36
HOLLOWAY 3J 65
Holloway Cl. UB7: Harm 5A 92
Holloway Ho. NW2 . . . . . 3E 62
(off Stoll Cl.)
Holloway La. UB7: Harm, W Dray 6A 92
Holloway Rd. E6 . . . . . 3D 88
E11 . . . . . 3F 69
N7 . . . . . 4K 65
N19 . . . . . 2H 65
Holloway St. TW3: Houn 3F 113
Hollowfield Wlk. UB5: N'olt 7C 58
Hollows, The TW8: Bford 6F 97
Holly Av. HA7: Stan 2E 42
KT12: Walt T 7B 148
Hollybank Cl. TW12: Hamp 5E 130
Hollyberry La. NW3 . . . . . 4A 64
Hollybrake Cl. BR7: Chst 7H 143
Hollybush Cl. E11 . . . . . 5J 51
HA3: Hrw W 1J 41
Hollybush Gdns. E2 . . . . . 3H 85
Hollybush Hill E11 . . . . . 6H 51
NW3 . . . . . 4A 64
Hollybush Ho. E2 . . . . . 3H 85
Holly Bush La. TW12: Hamp 7D 130
Hollybush Pl. E2 . . . . . 3H 85
Hollybush Rd. KT2: King T 5E 132
Hollybush Steps NW3 . . . . . 4A 64
(off Holly Mt.)
Hollybush St. E13 . . . . . 3K 87
Holly Bush Va. NW3 . . . . . 4A 64
Hollybush Wlk. SW9 . . . . . 4B 120
Holly Cl. BR3: Beck 4E 158
IG9: Buck H 3G 37
NW10 . . . . . 7A 62
SM6: Wall 7F 167
TW13: Hanw 5C 130
Holly Cott. M. UB8: Hil 5C 74
Holly Ct. DA14: Sidc 4B 144
(off Sidcup Hill)
N15 . . . . . 4E 48
SM2: Sutt 7J 165
Holly Cres. BR3: Beck 5B 158
IG8: Wfd G 7A 36
Hollycroft Av. HA9: Wemb 2F 61
NW3 . . . . . 3J 63
Hollycroft Cl. CR2: S Croy 5E 168
UB7: Sip 6C 92
Hollycroft Gdns. UB7: Sip 6C 92
Hollydale Cl. UB5: N'olt 4F 59
Hollydale Dr. BR2: Brom 3D 172
Hollydale Rd. SE15 . . . . . 1J 121
Hollydene BR2: Brom 1H 159
(off Beckenham La.)
SE13 . . . . . 6F 123
SE15 . . . . . 1H 121
Hollydown Way E11 . . . . . 3F 69
Holly Dr. E4 . . . . . 7J 25
Holly Farm Rd. UB2: S'hall 5C 94
Hollyfield Av. N11 . . . . . 5J 31
Hollyfield Rd. KT5: Surb 7F 151
Holly Gdns. DA7: Bex 4J 127
UB7: W Dray 2B 92
Holly Gro. HA5: Pinn 1C 40
NW9 . . . . . 7J 43
SE15 . . . . . 2F 121
Hollygrove WD23: Bush 1C 26
Hollygrove Cl. TW3: Houn 4D 112

Holly Hedge Ter.—Honister Gdns.

Holly Hedge Ter. SE13 .5F 123
Holly Hill N21 .6E 22
NW3 .4A 64
Holly Hill Rd. DA8: Erith .5H 109
DA17: Belv, Erith .5H 109
Holly Ho. TW8: Bford .6C 96
W10 .*4G 81*
(off Hawthorn Wlk.)
Holly Lodge HA1: Harr .5H 41
Holly Lodge Gdns. N6 .2E 64
Holly Lodge Mans. N6 .2E 64
Hollymead SM5: Cars .3D 166
Holly M. SW10 .6A 16 (5A 100)
Holly Mt. NW3 .4A 64
Hollymount Cl. SE10 .1E 122
Holly Pk. N3 .3H 45
N4 .7J 47
(not continuous)
Holly Pk. Est. N4 .7K 47
Holly Pk. Gdns. N3 .3J 45
Holly Pk. Rd. N11 .5K 31
W7 .1K 95
Holly Pl. *NW3* .*4A 64*
(off Holly Berry La.)
Holly Rd. E11 .7H 51
TW1: Twick .1K 131
TW3: Houn .4F 113
TW12: Ham H .6G 131
W4 .4K 97
Holly St. E8 .7F 67
Holly Ter. N6 .1E 64
N20 .2F 31
Holly Tree Cl. SW19 .1F 135
Holly Tree Ho. *SE4* .*3B 122*
(off Brockley Rd.)
Hollytree Pde. *DA14: Sidc* .*6C 144*
(off Sidcup Hill)
Holly Vw. Cl. NW4 .6C 44
Holly Village N6 .2F 65
Holly Vs. *W6* .*3D 98*
(off Wellesley Av.)
Holly Wlk. EN2: Enf .3H 23
NW3 .4A 64
Holly Way CR4: Mitc .4H 155
Hollywood Bowl
Barking .3G 89
Finchley .7G 31
Surrey Quays .3K 103
Hollywood Ct. *SW10* .*6A 100*
(off Hollywood Ct.)
W5 .7F 79
Hollywood Gdns. UB4: Yead .6K 75
Hollywood M. SW10 .6A 100
Hollywood Rd. E4 .5F 35
SW10 .6A 100
Hollywood Way IG8: Wfd G .7A 36
Holman Ct. KT17: Ewe .7C 164
Holman Ho. *E2* .*3K 85*
(off Roman Rd.)
Holman Hunt Ho. *W6* .*5G 99*
(off Field Rd.)
Holman Rd. KT19: Ewe .5J 163
SW11 .2B 118
Holmbank Dr. TW17: Shep .4G 147
Holmbridge Gdns. EN3: Pond E .4E 24
Holmbrook *NW1* .*2G 83*
(off Eversholt St.)
Holmbrook Dr. NW4 .5F 45
Holmbury Ct. CR2: S Croy .5E 168
SW17 .3D 136
SW19 .7C 136
Holmbury Gdns. UB3: Hayes .1H 93
Holmbury Gro. CR0: Sels .7B 170
Holmbury Ho. SE24 .5B 120
Holmbury Mnr. DA14: Sidc .4A 144
Holmbury Pk. BR1: Brom .7C 142
Holmbury Vw. E5 .1H 67
Holmbush Rd. SW15 .6G 117
Holmcote Gdns. N5 .5C 66
Holm Ct. SE12 .3K 141
Holmcroft Ho. E17 .4D 50
Holmcroft Way BR2: Brom .5D 160
Holmdale Gdns. NW4 .5F 45
Holmdale Rd. BR7: Chst .5G 143
NW6 .5J 63
Holmdale Ter. N15 .7E 48
Holmdene N12 .5E 30
Holmdene Av. HA2: Harr .3F 41
NW7 .6H 29
SE24 .5C 120
Holmdene Cl. BR3: Beck .2E 158
Holmdene Ct. BR1: Brom .3C 160
Holmead Rd. SW6 .7K 99
Holmebury Cl. WD23: Bushy .2D 26
Holme Ct. TW7: Isle .3A 114
Holmefield Ho. *W10* .*4G 81*
(off Hazlewood Cres.)
Holme Lacey Rd. SE12 .6H 123
Holme Rd. E6 .1C 88
Holmes Av. E17 .3B 50
NW7 .5B 30
Holmesdale Av. SW14 .3H 115
Holmesdale Cl. SE25 .3F 157
Holmesdale Ho. *NW6* .*1J 81*
(off Kilburn Va.)
Holmesdale Rd. CR0: Croy .5D 156
DA7: Bex .2D 126
N6 .7F 47
SE25 .5D 156
TW9: Kew .1F 115
TW11: Tedd .7C 132
Holmesley Rd. SE23 .6A 122
Holmes Pl. SW10 .6A 100
Holmes Place Health Club
Barbican .*5C 8*
(off Aldersgate St.)
Bromley .4B 160
Croydon .3C 168
Hammersmith .*4F 99*
(off Hammersmith Rd.)
Merton .6A 136
St Luke's .4E 8
Holmes Rd. NW5 .5F 65
SW19 .7A 136
TW1: Twick .2K 131
Holmes Ter. SE1 .6J 13
Holmeswood SM2: Sutt .6K 165
Holmeswood Ct. N22 .2A 48
Holme Way HA7: Stan .6E 26
Holmewood Gdns. SW2 .7K 119
Holmewood Rd. SE25 .3E 156
SW2 .7J 119
Holmfield Av. NW4 .5F 45
Holmfield Ct. NW3 .5C 64
Holm Gro. UB10: Hil .7C 56
Holmhurst SE13 .6F 123
Holmhurst Rd. DA17: Belv .5H 109
Holmlea Ct. *CR0: Croy* .*4D 168*
(off Chatsworth Rd.)
Holmleigh Ct. EN3: Pond E .4D 24
Holmleigh Rd. N16 .1E 66
Holmleigh Rd. Est. N16 .1E 66
Holmoak Cl. SW15 .6H 117
Holm Oak M. SW4 .5J 119
Holmoaks Ho. BR3: Beck .2E 158
Holmsdale Ho. *E14* .*7D 86*
(off Poplar High St.)
N11 .*4A 32*
(off Coppies Gro.)
Holmshaw Cl. SE26 .4A 140
Holmside Rd. SW12 .6E 118
Holmsley Cl. KT3: N Mald .6B 152
Holmsley Ho. *SW15* .*7B 116*
(off Tangley Gro.)
Holmstall Av. HA8: Edg .3J 43
Holmstall Pde. HA8: Edg .2J 43
Holm Wlk. SE3 .2J 123
Holmwood Cl. HA2: Harr .3G 41
SM2: Cheam .7F 165
UB5: N'olt .6F 59
Holmwood Gdns. N3 .2J 45
SM6: Wall .6F 167
Holmwood Gro. NW7 .5E 28
Holmwood Rd. IG3: Ilf .2J 71
KT9: Chess .5D 162
SM2: Cheam .7E 164
Holmwood Vs. SE7 .5J 105
Holne Chase N2 .6A 46
SM4: Mord .6H 153
Holness Rd. E15 .6H 69
Holocaust Memorial Garden .6F 11
Holroyd Rd. KT10: Clay .7A 162
SW15 .4E 116
Holst Ct. *SE1* .*1J 19*
(off Westminster Bri. Rd.)
Holstein Way DA18: Erith .3D 108
Holst Mans. SW13 .6E 98
Holstock Rd. IG1: Ilf .2G 71
Holsworth Cl. HA2: Harr .5G 41
Holsworthy Sq. WC1 .4H 7
Holsworthy Way KT9: Chess .5C 162
Holt, The SM4: Mord .4J 153
SM6: Wall .4G 167
Holt Cl. N10 .4E 46
SE28 .7B 90
Holt Ct. E15 .5E 68
Holt Ho. SW2 .6A 120
Holton St. E1 .4K 85
Holt Rd. E16 .1C 106
HA0: Wemb .3B 60
Holtwhite Av. EN2: Enf .2H 23
Holtwhite's Hill EN2: Enf .1G 23
Holwell Pl. HA5: Pinn .4C 40
Holwood Pk. Av. BR6: Farnb .4D 172
Holwood Pl. SW4 .4H 119
Holybourne Av. SW15 .7C 116
Holyhead Cl. E3 .3C 86
E6 .5D 88
Holyhead Ct. *KT1: King T* .*4D 150*
(off Anglesea Rd.)
Holyoake Ct. SE16 .2B 104
Holyoake Ho. W5 .4C 78
Holyoake Wlk. N2 .3A 46
W5 .4C 78
Holyoak Rd. SE11 .4B 102
Holyport Rd. SW6 .7F 99
Holyrood Av. HA2: Harr .4C 58
Holyrood Gdns. HA8: Edg .3H 43
Holyrood M. *E16* .*1J 105*
(off Badminton M.)
Holyrood Rd. EN5: New Bar .6F 21
Holyrood St. SE1 .5G 15 (1E 102)
Holywell Cen. .*3G 9*
(off Phipp St.)
Holywell Cl. BR6: Chels .4K 173
SE3 .6J 105
SE16 .5H 103
TW19: Stanw .1A 128
Holywell La. EC2 .3H 9 (4E 84)
Holywell Row EC2 .4G 9 (4E 84)
Holywell Way TW19: Stanw .1A 128
Homan Ct. N12 .4G 31
Homebush Ho. E4 .7J 25
Homecedars Ho. WD23: Bushy .1C 26
Home Cl. SM5: Cars .2D 166
UB5: N'olt .3D 76
Home Ct. KT6: King T .5D 150
Homecroft Rd. N22 .1C 48
SE26 .5J 139
Home Farm Cl. KT7: T Ditt .7K 149
TW17: Shep .4G 147
Homefarm Rd. W7 .6J 77
Home Fld. EN5: Barn .5C 20
Homefield SM4: Mord .4J 153
Homefield Av. IG2: Ilf .5J 53
Homefield Cl. NW10 .6J 61
UB4: Yead .4B 76
Homefield Gdns. CR4: Mitc .2A 154
N2 .3B 46
Homefield Ho. SE23 .3K 139
Homefield M. BR3: Beck .1C 158
Homefield Pk. SM1: Sutt .6K 165
Homefield Rd. BR1: Brom .1A 160
HA0: Wemb .4A 60
HA8: Edg .6E 28
KT12: Walt T .7C 148
SW19 .6F 135
W4 .5B 98
Homefield St. N1 .1G 9 (2E 84)
Homefirs Ho. HA9: Wemb .3F 61
Home Gdns. RM10: Dag .3J 73
Homeheather Ho. IG4: Ilf .5D 52
Homeland Dr. SM2: Sutt .7K 165
Homelands Dr. SE19 .7E 138
Home Lea BR6: Chels .5K 173
Homeleigh Ct. SW16 .3J 137
Homeleigh Rd. SE15 .5K 121
Home Mead HA7: Stan .1C 42
Homemead Rd. BR2: Brom .5D 160
CR0: Croy .6G 155
Home Pk. Ct. *KT1: King T* .*4D 150*
(off Palace Rd.)
Home Pk. Pde. *KT1: Ham W* .*2D 150*
(off High St.)
Home Pk. Rd. SW19 .4H 135
Home Pk. Ter. *KT1: Ham W* .*2D 150*
(off Hampton Ct. Rd.)
Home Pk. Wlk. KT1: King T .4D 150
Homer Cl. DA7: Bex .1J 127
Homer Dr. E14 .4C 104
Home Rd. SW11 .2C 118
Homer Rd. CR0: Croy .6K 157
E9 .6A 68
Homer Row W1 .6D 4 (5C 82)
Homersham Rd. KT1: King T .2G 151
Homer St. W1 .6D 4 (5C 82)
HOMERTON .5K 67
Homerton Gro. E9 .5K 67
Homerton High St. E9 .5K 67
Homerton Rd. E9 .5A 68
Homerton Row E9 .5J 67
Homerton Ter. E9 .6J 67
(not continuous)
Homesdale Cl. E11 .5J 51
Homesdale Rd. BR1: Brom .4A 160
BR2: Brom .4A 160
BR5: Pet W .7J 161
Homesfield NW11 .5J 45
Homestall Rd. SE22 .5J 121
Homestead Ct. EN5: New Bar .5D 20
Homestead Paddock N14 .5A 22
Homestead Pk. NW2 .3B 62
Homestead Rd. RM8: Dag .2F 73
SW6 .7H 99
Homesteads, The N11 .4A 32
Homewalk Ho. SE26 .4H 139
Homewaters Av. TW16: Sun .1H 147
Homewillow Cl. N21 .6G 23
Homewood Cl. TW12: Hamp .6D 130
Homewood Cres. BR7: Chst .6J 143
Homewoods SW12 .7G 119
Homildon Ho. SE26 .3G 139
Honduras St. EC1 .3C 8 (4C 84)
Honeybourne Rd. NW6 .5K 63
Honeybourne Way BR5: Pet W .1H 173
Honeybrook Rd. SW12 .7G 119
Honey Cl. RM10: Dag .6H 73
Honeycroft Hill UB10: Uxb .7A 56
Honeyden Rd. DA14: Sidc .6E 144
Honey Hill UB10: Uxb .7B 56
Honey La. EC2 .1D 14
Honey La. Ho. *SW10* .*6K 99*
(off Finborough Rd.)
Honeyman Cl. NW6 .7F 63
Honeymead *N8* .*3J 47*
(off Campsfield Rd.)
Honeypot Bus. Cen. HA7: Stan .1E 42
Honeypot Cl. NW9 .4F 43
Honeypot La. HA7: Stan .7J 27
NW9 .1D 42
Honeysett Rd. N17 .2F 49
Honeysuckle Cl. UB1: S'hall .7C 76
Honeysuckle Ct. IG1: Ilf .6F 71
Honeysuckle Gdns. CR0: Croy .7K 157
Honeysuckle La. N22 .2C 48
Honeywell Rd. SW11 .6D 118
Honeywood Heritage Cen. .5D 166
Honeywood Rd. NW10 .2B 80
TW7: Isle .4A 114
Honeywood Wlk. SM5: Cars .4D 166
Honister Cl. HA7: Stan .1B 42
Honister Gdns. HA7: Stan .7G 27

Honister Pl.—Hounslow Bus. Pk.

Honister Pl. HA7: Stan 1B 42
Honiton Gdns. NW7 7A 30
SE15 2J 121
(off Gibbon Rd.)
Honiton Ho. EN3: Pond E 3E 24
Honiton Rd. DA16: Well 2K 125
NW6 2H 81
RM7: Rom 6K 55
Honley Rd. SE6 7D 122
Honnor Gdns. TW7: Isle 2H 113
HONOR OAK 6J 121
Honor Oak Crematorium SE23 5K 121
HONOR OAK PARK 7A 122
Honor Oak Pk. SE23 6J 121
Honor Oak Ri. SE23 6J 121
Honor Oak Rd. SE23 1J 139
Hood Av. N14 6A 22
SW14 5J 115
Hood Cl. CR0: Croy 1B 168
Hoodcote Gdns. N21 7G 23
Hood Ct. EC4 1K 13
Hood Ho. SE5 7D 102
(off Elmington Est.)
SW1 6C 18
(off Dolphin Sq.)
Hood Rd. SW20 7B 134
Hood Wlk. RM7: Mawney 1H 55
HOOK 5E 162
Hook, The EN5: New Bar 6G 21
Hooke Ho. E3 2A 86
(off Gernon Rd.)
Hookers Rd. E17 3K 49
Hook Farm Rd. BR2: Brom 5B 160
Hookham Ct. SW8 1H 119
Hooking Grn. HA2: Harr 5F 41
HOOK JUNC. 3E 162
Hook La. DA16: Well 4K 125
Hook Ri. Nth. KT6: Surb 3E 162
Hook Ri. Sth. KT6: Surb 3E 162
Hook Ri. Sth. Ind. Pk. KT6: Chess 3F 163
Hook Rd. KT6: Surb 2E 162
KT9: Chess 5D 162
KT19: Eps, Ewe 7J 163
Hooks Cl. SE15 1H 121
Hooks Hall Dr. RM10: Dag 3J 73
Hookstone Way IG8: Wfd G 7G 37
Hook Wlk. HA8: Edg 6D 28
Hool Cl. NW9 5J 43
Hooper Dr. UB8: Hil 5D 74
Hooper Rd. E16 6J 87
Hooper's Ct. SW3 7E 10 (2D 100)
Hoopers M. W3 1J 97
WD23: Bush 1A 26
Hooper Sq. E1 6G 85
(off Hooper St.)
Hooper St. E1 6G 85
Hoop La. NW11 7H 45
(not continuous)
Hope Cl. IG8: Wfd G 6F 37
N1 6C 66
RM6: Chad H 4D 54
SE12 3K 141
SM1: Sutt 5A 166
TW8: Bford 5E 96
Hope Ct. NW10 3F 81
(off Chamberlayne Rd.)
Hopedale Rd. SE7 6K 105
Hopefield Av. NW6 2G 81
Hope Gdns. W3 2H 97
Hope Ho. CR0: Croy 4E 168
(off Steep Hill)
Hope La. SE9 2F 143
Hope Pk. BR1: Brom 7H 141
Hopes Cl. TW5: Hest 6E 94
Hope Sq. EC2 6G 9
Hope St. SW11 3B 118
Hopetown St. E1 6K 9 (5F 85)
Hopewell St. SE5 7D 102
Hopewell Yd. SE5 7D 102
(off Hopewell St.)
Hope Wharf SE16 2J 103
Hop Gdns. WC2 3E 12 (7J 83)
Hopgood St. W12 1E 98
Hopkins Cl. N10 7K 31
Hopkins Ho. E14 6C 86
(off Canton St.)
Hopkins M. E15 1H 87
Hopkinsons Pl. NW1 1E 82
Hopkins Rd. E10 7D 50
Hopkins St. W1 1B 12 (6G 83)
Hoppers Rd. N13 2F 33
N21 2F 33
Hoppett Rd. E4 2B 36
Hopping La. N1 6B 66
Hoppingwood Av. KT3: N Mald 3A 152
Hoppner Rd. UB4: Hayes 2F 75
Hop St. SE10 4H 105
(off School Bank Rd.)
Hopton Ct. BR2: Hayes 1K 171
Hopton Gdns. KT3: N Mald 6C 152
Hopton Rd. SE18 3F 107
SW16 5J 137
Hopton's Gdns. SE1 4B 14
Hopton St. SE1 3A 14 (7B 84)
Hoptree Cl. N12 5E 30
Hopwood Cl. SW17 3A 136
Hopwood Rd. SE17 6D 102
Hopwood Wlk. E8 7G 67
Horace Av. RM7: Rush G 1J 73
Horace Rd. E7 4K 69
IG6: Ilf 3G 53
KT1: King T 3F 151
Horatio Ct. SE16 1J 103
(off Rotherhithe St.)
Horatio Ho. E2 2F 85
(off Horatio St.)
W6 5F 99
(off Fulham Pal. Rd.)
Horatio Pl. E14 1E 104
(off Preston's Rd.)
SW19 1J 153
Horatio St. E2 2F 85
Horatius Way CR0: Wadd 5K 167
Horbury Cres. W11 7J 81
Horbury M. W11 7H 81
Horder Rd. SW6 1G 117
Hordle Prom. E. SE15 7F 103
Hordle Prom. Sth. SE15 7F 103
(off Quarley Way)
Horizon Bldg. E14 7C 86
(off Hertsmere Rd.)
Horizon Bus. Cen. N9 2E 34
(off Goodwin Rd.)
Horizon Way SE7 4K 105
Horle Wlk. SE5 2B 120
Horley Cl. DA6: Bex 5G 127
Horley Rd. SE9 4C 142
Hormead Rd. W9 4H 81
Hornbeam Cl. IG1: Ilf 5H 71
IG9: Buck H 3G 37
IG11: Bark 3A 90
NW7 3G 29
SE11 3J 19 (4A 102)
UB5: N'olt 5D 58
Hornbeam Cres. TW8: Bford 7B 96
Hornbeam Gdns. KT3: N Mald 6C 152
Hornbeam Gro. E4 3B 36
Hornbeam Ho. IG9: Buck H 3H 37
Hornbeam La. DA7: Bex 2J 127
Hornbeam Rd. IG9: Buck H 3G 37
UB4: Yead 5A 76
Hornbeam Sq. E3 1B 86
Hornbeams Ri. N11 6K 31
Hornbeam Ter. SM5: Cars 1C 166
Hornbeam Wlk. TW10: Rich 2F 133
Hornbeam Way BR2: Brom 6E 160
Hornblower Cl. SE16 3A 104
Hornbuckle Cl. HA2: Harr 2H 59
Hornby Cl. NW3 7B 64
Hornby Ho. SE11 7J 19
Horncastle Cl. SE12 7J 123
Horncastle Rd. SE12 7J 123
Hornchurch N17 2D 48
(off Gloucester Rd.)
Hornchurch Cl. KT2: King T 4D 132
Horndean Cl. SW15 1C 134
Horndon Cl. RM5: Col R 1J 55
Horndon Grn. RM5: Col R 1J 55
Horndon Rd. RM5: Col R 1J 55
Horner Ho. N1 1E 84
(off Whitmore Est.)
Horner La. CR4: Mitc 2B 154
Horne Rd. TW17: Shep 4C 146
Horne Way SW15 2E 116
Hornfair Rd. SE7 6A 106
Horniman Dr. SE23 1H 139
Horniman Mus. 1H 139
Horning Cl. SE9 4C 142
Horn La. IG8: Wfd G 6D 36
SE10 5J 105
(not continuous)
W3 7J 79
(not continuous)
Horn Link Way SE10 4J 105
HORN PARK 5K 123
Horn Pk. Cl. SE12 5K 123
Hornpark La. SE12 5K 123
Hornscroft Cl. IG11: Bark 7J 71
Horns End Pl. HA5: Eastc 4A 40
HORNSEY 4J 47
Hornsey N8 4J 47
Hornsey Club, The 5H 47
Hornsey La. N6 1F 65
Hornsey La. Est. N19 7H 47
Hornsey La. Gdns. N6 7G 47
Hornsey Pk. Rd. N8 3K 47
Hornsey Ri. N19 7H 47
Hornsey Ri. Gdns. N19 7H 47
Hornsey Rd. N7 1J 65
N19 1J 65
Hornsey St. N7 5K 65
HORNSEY VALE 5K 47
Hornshay St. SE15 6J 103
Horns Rd. IG2: Ilf 5G 53
IG6: Ilf 4H 53
Hornton Ct. W8 2J 99
(off Kensington High St.)
Hornton Pl. W8 2K 99
Hornton St. W8 2J 99
Horsa Rd. DA8: Erith 7H 109
SE12 7A 124
Horse & Dolphin Yd. W1 2D 12
Horsebridge Cl. RM9: Dag 1E 90
Horsecroft Rd. HA8: Edg 7E 28
Horse Fair KT1: King T 2D 150
Horseferry Pl. SE10 6E 104
Horseferry Rd. E14 7A 86
SW1 2C 18 (3H 101)
Horseferry Rd. Est. SW1 2C 18
Horseguards Av. SW1 5E 12 (1J 101)
Horse Guards Parade 5E 12 (1J 101)
Horse Guards Rd. SW1 5D 12 (1H 101)
Horse Leaze E6 6E 88
Horsell Rd. BR5: St P 7B 144
N5 5A 66
(not continuous)
Horselydown La. SE1 6J 15 (2F 103)
Horselydown Mans. SE1 6J 15
(off Lafone St.)
Horsemongers M. SE1 7D 14
Horsenden Av. UB6: G'frd 5K 59
Horsenden Cres. UB6: G'frd 5K 59
Horsenden La. Nth. UB6: G'frd 6J 59
Horsenden La. Sth. UB6: G'frd 1A 78
Horse Ride SW1 5C 12 (1G 101)
Horseshoe Cl. E14 5E 104
NW2 2D 62
Horseshoe Ct. EC1 3B 8
(off Brewhouse Yd.)
Horse Shoe Cres. UB5: N'olt 2E 76
Horseshoe Dr. UB8: Hil 6C 74
Horse Shoe Grn. SM1: Sutt 2K 165
Horseshoe La. EN2: Enf 3H 23
N20 1A 30
Horseshoe M. SW2 4J 119
Horseshoe Wharf SE1 4E 14
(off Clink St.)
Horse Yd. N1 1B 84
(off Essex Rd.)
Horsfeld Gdns. SE9 5C 124
Horsfeld Rd. SE9 5B 124
Horsfield Ho. N1 7C 66
(off Northampton St.)
Horsford Rd. SW2 5K 119
Horsham Av. N12 5H 31
Horsham Ct. N17 1G 49
(off Lansdowne Rd.)
Horsham Rd. DA6: Bex 5G 127
TW14: Bedf 6E 110
Horsley Dr. CR0: New Ad 7E 170
KT2: King T 5D 132
Horsley Rd. BR1: Brom 1K 159
E4 2K 35
Horsley St. SE17 6D 102
Horsman Ho. SE5 6C 102
(off Bethwin Rd.)
Horsman St. SE5 6C 102
Horsmonden Cl. BR6: Orp 7K 161
Horsmonden Rd. SE4 5B 122
Hortensia Ho. SW10 7A 100
(off Gunter Gro.)
Hortensia Rd. SW10 7A 100
Horticultural Pl. W4 5K 97
Horton Av. NW2 4G 63
Horton Bri. Rd. UB7: Yiew 1B 92
Horton Cl. UB7: Yiew 1C 92
Horton Ho. SE15 6J 103
SW8 7K 101
W6 5G 99
(off Field Rd.)
Horton Ind. Pk. UB7: Yiew 1B 92
Horton La. KT19: Eps 7H 163
Horton Pde. UB7: Yiew 1A 92
Horton Rd. E8 6H 67
UB7: Yiew 1A 92
UB11: Yiew 1A 92
Horton Rd. Ind. Est. UB7: Yiew 1B 92
Horton St. SE13 3D 122
Horton Way CR0: Croy 5K 157
Hortus Rd. E4 2K 35
UB2: S'hall 2D 94
Horwood Ho. E2 3H 85
(off Pott St.)
NW8 3D 4
(off Paveley St.)
Hosack Rd. SW17 2E 136
Hoser Av. SE12 2J 141
Hosier La. EC1 6A 8 (5B 84)
Hoskins Cl. E16 6A 88
UB3: Harl 5H 93
Hoskins St. SE10 5F 105
Hospital Bri. Rd.
TW2: Twick, Whit 7F 113
HOSPITAL BRIDGE RDBT. 2F 131
Hospital Rd. E9 5K 67
TW3: Houn 3E 112
Hospital Way SE13 7F 123
Hotham Cl. KT8: W Mole 3E 148
Hotham Rd. SW15 3E 116
SW19 7A 136
Hotham Rd. M. SW19 7A 136
Hotham St. E15 1G 87
Hothfield Pl. SE16 3J 103
Hotspur Ind. Est. N17 6C 34
Hotspur Rd. UB5: N'olt 2E 76
Hotspur St. SE11 5J 19 (4A 102)
Houblon Rd. TW10: Rich 5E 114
Houghton Cl. E8 6F 67
TW12: Hamp 6C 130
Houghton Rd. N15 4F 49
Houghton St. WC2 1H 13 (6K 83)
(not continuous)
Houlder Cres. CR0: Wadd 6B 168
Houndsden Rd. N21 6E 22
Houndsditch EC3 7H 9 (6E 84)
Houndsfield Rd. N9 7C 24
HOUNSLOW 3F 113
Hounslow and District Indoor Bowls Club 2D 112
(off Sutton La.)
Hounslow Av. TW3: Houn 5F 113
Hounslow Bus. Pk. TW3: Houn 4E 112

Hounslow Cen. TW3: Houn ... 3F **113**
Hounslow Gdns. TW3: Houn ... 5F **113**
Hounslow Heath Nature Reserve ... 6B **112**
Hounslow Manor Sports Hall ... 2G **113**
Hounslow Rd. TW2: Whit ... 6F **113**
TW13: Hanw ... 4B **130**
TW14: Felt ... 1K **129**
Hounslow Urban Farm ... 5J **111**
HOUNSLOW WEST ... 2C **112**
Houseman Way SE5 ... 7D **102**
Houses of Parliament ... 1F **19** (3J **101**)
Houston Bus. Pk. UB4: Yead ... 1A **94**
Houston Pl. KT10: Esh ... 7H **149**
Houston Rd. KT6: Surb ... 6B **150**
SE23 ... 2A **140**
Houstoun Ct. TW5: Hest ... 7D **94**
Hove Av. E17 ... 5B **50**
Hoveden Rd. NW2 ... 5G **63**
Hove Gdns. SM1: Sutt ... 1K **165**
Hove St. *SE15* ... *7J **103***
(off Culmore Rd.)
Hoveton Rd. SE28 ... 6C **90**
Hoveton Way IG6: Ilf ... 1F **53**
Howard Av. DA5: Bexl ... 1C **144**
Howard Bldg. SW8 ... 6F **101**
Howard Cl. N11 ... 2K **31**
NW2 ... 4G **63**
TW12: Hamp ... 7G **131**
TW16: Sun ... 6H **129**
W3 ... 6H **79**
WD23: Bushy ... 1D **26**
Howard Ct. IG11: Bark ... 1H **89**
Howard Ho. *E16* ... *1K **105***
(off Wesley Av.)
SE8 ... *6B **104***
(off Evelyn St.)
SW1 ... *6B **18***
(off Dolphin Sq.)
SW9 ... *3B **120***
(off Barrington Rd.)
W1 ... *4K **5***
(off Cleveland St.)
Howard M. N5 ... 4B **66**
Howard Rd. BR1: Brom ... 7J **141**
E6 ... 2D **88**
E11 ... 3G **69**
E17 ... 3C **50**
IG1: Ilf ... 4F **71**
IG11: Bark ... 1H **89**
KT3: N Mald ... 3A **152**
KT5: Surb ... 6F **151**
N15 ... 6E **48**
N16 ... 4D **66**
NW2 ... 4F **63**
SE20 ... 1J **157**
SE25 ... 5G **157**
TW7: Isle ... 3K **113**
UB1: S'hall ... 6F **77**
Howards Cl. HA5: Pinn ... 2K **39**
Howards Crest Cl. BR3: Beck ... 2E **158**
Howard's La. SW15 ... 4D **116**
Howards Rd. E13 ... 3J **87**
Howard St. KT7: T Ditt ... 7B **150**
Howard Wlk. N2 ... 4A **46**
Howard Way EN5: Barn ... 5A **20**
Howarth Ct. *E15* ... *5E **68***
(off Clays La.)
Howarth Rd. SE2 ... 5A **108**
Howberry Cl. HA8: Edg ... 6J **27**
Howberry Rd. CR7: Thor H ... 1D **156**
HA7: Stan ... 6J **27**
HA8: Edg ... 6J **27**
Howbury Rd. SE15 ... 3J **121**
Howcroft Cres. N3 ... 7D **30**
Howcroft La. UB6: G'frd ... 3H **77**
Howden Cl. SE28 ... 7D **90**
Howden Rd. SE25 ... 2F **157**
Howden St. SE15 ... 3G **121**
Howe Cl. RM7: Mawney ... 1G **55**
Howell Cl. RM6: Chad H ... 5D **54**
Howell Ct. E10 ... 7D **50**
Howell Wlk. SE1 ... 4B **102**
Howerd Way SE18 ... 1C **124**
(not continuous)
Howes Cl. N3 ... 3J **45**
Howeth Ct. *N11* ... *6J **31***
(off Ribblesdale Av.)
Howfield Pl. N17 ... 3F **49**
Howgate Rd. SW14 ... 3K **115**
Howick Pl. SW1 ... 2B **18** (3G **101**)
Howie St. SW11 ... 7C **100**
Howitt Cl. N16 ... 4E **66**
NW3 ... 6C **64**
Howitt Rd. NW3 ... 6C **64**
Howland Est. SE16 ... 3J **103**
Howland Ho. SW16 ... 3J **137**
Howland M. E. W1 ... 5B **6** (5G **83**)
Howland St. W1 ... 5A **6** (5G **83**)
Howland Way SE16 ... 2A **104**
Howletts La. HA4: Ruis ... 5E **38**
Howlett's Rd. SE24 ... 6C **120**
Howley Pl. W2 ... 5A **4** (5A **82**)
Howley Rd. CR0: Croy ... 3B **168**
Howsman Rd. SW13 ... 6C **98**
Howson Rd. SE4 ... 4A **122**
Howson Ter. TW10: Rich ... 6E **114**
How's St. E2 ... 2F **85**
Howton Pl. WD23: Bushy ... 1C **26**
HOXTON ... 2E **84**
Hoxton Hall Theatre ... *2E **84***
(off Hoxton Rd.)
Hoxton Mkt. N1 ... 2G **9**
Hoxton Sq. N1 ... 2G **9** (3E **84**)
Hoxton St. N1 ... 2H **9** (1E **84**)
Hoylake Cres. UB10: Ick ... 2C **56**
Hoylake Gdns. CR4: Mitc ... 3G **155**
HA4: Ruis ... 1K **57**
Hoylake Rd. W3 ... 6A **80**
Hoyland Cl. SE15 ... 7H **103**
Hoyle Rd. SW17 ... 5C **136**
Hoy St. E16 ... 6H **87**
HQS Wellington ... 3J **13**
Hub, The ... 1F **5** (2D **82**)
Hubbard Ct. IG10: Lough ... 1H **37**
Hubbard Dr. KT9: Chess ... 6D **162**
Hubbard Rd. SE27 ... 4C **138**
Hubbards Cl. UB8: Hil ... 6D **74**
Hubbard St. E15 ... 1G **87**
Huberd Ho. *SE1* ... *7F **15***
(off Manciple St.)
Hubert Cl. *SW19* ... *1A **154***
(off Nelson Gro. Rd.)
Hubert Gro. SW9 ... 3J **119**
Hubert Ho. *NW8* ... *4C **4***
(off Ashbridge St.)
Hubert Rd. E6 ... 3B **88**
Hucknall Ct. *NW8* ... *3A **4***
(off Cunningham Pl.)
Huddart St. E3 ... 5B **86**
(not continuous)
Huddleston Cl. E2 ... 2J **85**
Huddlestone Rd. E7 ... 4H **69**
NW2 ... 6D **62**
Huddleston Rd. N7 ... 3G **65**
Hudson *NW9* ... *1B **44***
(off Near Acre)
Hudson Apartments N8 ... 3K **47**
Hudson Bldg. *E1* ... *6K **9***
(off Chicksand St.)
Hudson Cl. E15 ... 1J **87**
W12 ... 7D **80**
Hudson Ct. *E14* ... *5C **104***
(off Maritime Quay)
Hudson Gdns. BR6: Chels ... 6K **173**
Hudson Ho. *SW10* ... *7A **100***
(off Hortensia Rd.)
W11 ... *6G **81***
(off Ladbroke Gro.)
Hudson Pl. SE18 ... 5G **107**
Hudson Rd. DA7: Bex ... 2F **127**
UB3: Harl ... 6F **93**
Hudson's Pl. SW1 ... 3A **18** (4F **101**)
Hudson Way N9 ... 3D **34**
Huggin Ct. EC4 ... 2D **14**
Huggin Hill EC4 ... 2C **14** (7C **84**)
Huggins Pl. SW2 ... 1K **137**
Hughan Rd. E15 ... 5F **69**
Hugh Astor Ct. *SE1* ... *7B **14***
(off Keyworth St.)
Hugh Clark Ho. *W13* ... *1A **96***
(off Singapore Rd.)
Hugh Cubitt Ho. *N1* ... *2K **83***
(off Collier St.)
Hugh Dalton Av. SW6 ... 6H **99**
Hughenden Av. HA3: Kent ... 5B **42**
Hughenden Gdns. UB5: Yead ... 3A **76**
(not continuous)
Hughenden Ho. NW8 ... 3C **4**
Hughenden Rd. KT4: Wor Pk ... 7C **152**
Hughendon EN5: New Bar ... 4E **20**
Hughendon Ter. E15 ... 4E **68**
Hughes Cl. N12 ... 5F **31**
Hughes Ct. N7 ... 5H **65**
Hughes Ho. *E2* ... *3J **85***
(off Sceptre Ho.)
SE8 ... *6C **104***
(off Benbow St.)
SE17 ... *4B **102***
(off Peacock St.)
Hughes Mans. E1 ... 4G **85**
Hughes M. SW11 ... 5D **118**
Hughes Rd. TW15: Ashf ... 6E **128**
UB3: Hayes ... 7K **75**
Hughes Ter. *E16* ... *5H **87***
(off Clarkson Rd.)
SW9 ... *3B **120***
(off Styles Gdns.)
Hughes Wlk. CR0: Croy ... 7C **156**
Hugh Gaitskell Cl. SW6 ... 6H **99**
Hugh Gaitskell Ho. N16 ... 2F **67**
Hugh Herland Ho. KT1: King T ... 3E **150**
Hugh M. SW1 ... 4K **17** (4F **101**)
Hugh Platt Ho. *E2* ... *2H **85***
(off Patriot Sq.)
Hugh St. SW1 ... 4K **17** (4F **101**)
Hugo Ho. *SW1* ... *1F **17***
(off Sloane St.)
Hugon Rd. SW6 ... 3K **117**
Hugo Rd. N19 ... 4G **65**
Huguenot Pl. E1 ... 5K **9** (5F **85**)
SW18 ... 5A **118**
Huguenot Sq. SE15 ... 3H **121**
Hullbridge M. N1 ... 1D **84**
Hull Cl. SE16 ... 2K **103**
Hull Pl. E16 ... 1G **107**
Hull St. EC1 ... 2C **8** (3C **84**)
Hulme Pl. SE1 ... 7D **14** (2C **102**)
Hulse Av. IG11: Bark ... 6H **71**
RM7: Mawney ... 1H **55**
Humber Cl. UB7: W Dray ... 1A **92**
Humber Ct. *W7* ... *6H **77***
(off Hobbayne Rd.)
Humber Dr. W10 ... 4F **81**
Humber Rd. NW2 ... 2D **62**
SE3 ... 6H **105**
Humberstone Rd. E13 ... 3A **88**
Humberton Cl. E9 ... 5A **68**
Humber Trad. Est. NW2 ... 2D **62**
Humbolt Rd. W6 ... 6G **99**
Hume Ct. *N1* ... *7B **66***
(off Hawes St.)
Hume Ho. *W11* ... *1F **99***
(off Queensdale Cres.)
Humes Av. W7 ... 3J **95**
Hume Ter. E16 ... 5K **87**
Hume Way HA4: Ruis ... 6J **39**
Humphrey Cl. IG5: Ilf ... 1D **52**
Humphrey St. SE1 ... 5F **103**
Humphries Cl. RM9: Dag ... 4F **73**
Hundred Acre NW9 ... 2B **44**
Hungerdown E4 ... 1K **35**
Hungerford Ho. *SW1* ... *7B **18***
(off Churchill Gdns.)
Hungerford La. WC2 ... 4F **13**
(not continuous)
Hungerford Rd. N7 ... 6H **65**
Hungerford St. E1 ... 6H **85**
Hunsdon Cl. RM9: Dag ... 6E **72**
Hunsdon Rd. SE14 ... 7K **103**
Hunslett St. E2 ... 3J **85**
Hunstanton Ho. *NW1* ... *5D **4***
(off Cosway St.)
Hunston Rd. SM4: Mord ... 1K **165**
Hunt Cl. W11 ... 1F **99**
Hunt Ct. N14 ... 7A **22**
UB5: N'olt ... *2B **76***
(off Gallery Gdns.)
Hunter Cl. SE1 ... 3D **102**
SM6: Wall ... 7J **167**
Hunter Ho. *SE1* ... *7B **14***
(off Lancaster St.)
SW5 ... *5J **99***
(off Old Brompton Rd.)
SW8 ... *7H **101***
(off Fount St.)
WC1 ... *3F **7***
(off Hunter St.)
Hunterian Mus., The ... *7H **7***
(off Portugal St.)
Hunter Lodge *W9* ... *5J **81***
(off Admiral Wlk.)
Hunter Rd. CR7: Thor H ... 3D **156**
IG1: Ilf ... 5F **71**
SW20 ... 1E **152**
Hunters Cl. DA5: Bexl ... 3K **145**
SW12 ... 1E **136**
Hunters Ct. TW9: Rich ... 5D **114**
Hunters Gro. BR6: Farnb ... 4G **173**
HA3: Kent ... 4C **42**
UB3: Hayes ... 1J **93**
Hunters Hall Rd. RM10: Dag ... 4G **73**
Hunters Hill HA4: Ruis ... 3A **58**
Hunters Mdw. SE19 ... 4E **138**
Hunter's Rd. KT9: Chess ... 3E **162**
Hunters Sq. RM10: Dag ... 4G **73**
Hunter St. WC1 ... 3F **7** (4J **83**)
Hunters Way CR0: Croy ... 4E **168**
EN2: Enf ... 1F **23**
Hunter Wlk. E13 ... 2J **87**
Huntingdon Cl. CR4: Mitc ... 3J **155**
UB5: N'olt ... 6E **58**
Huntingdon Gdns. KT4: Wor Pk ... 3E **164**
W4 ... 7J **97**
Huntingdon Rd. N2 ... 3C **46**
N9 ... 2D **34**
Huntingdon St. E16 ... 6H **87**
N1 ... 7K **65**
Huntingfield CR0: Sels ... 7B **170**
Huntingfield Rd. SW15 ... 4C **116**
Hunting Ga. Cl. EN2: Enf ... 3F **23**
Hunting Ga. Dr. KT9: Chess ... 7E **162**
Hunting Ga. M. SM1: Sutt ... 3K **165**
TW2: Twick ... 1J **131**
Huntings Farm IG1: Ilf ... 2J **71**
Huntings Rd. RM10: Dag ... 6G **73**
Huntley Dr. N3 ... 6D **30**
Huntley St. WC1 ... 4B **6** (4G **83**)
Huntley Way SW20 ... 2C **152**
Huntly Rd. SE25 ... 4E **156**
Hunton St. E1 ... 4K **9** (5G **85**)
Hunt Rd. UB2: S'hall ... 3E **94**
Hunt's Cl. SE3 ... 2J **123**
Hunt's Ct. WC2 ... 3D **12** (7H **83**)
Hunts La. E15 ... 2E **86**
Huntsmans Cl. TW13: Felt ... 4K **129**
Huntsman St. SE17 ... 4E **102**
Hunts Mead EN3: Enf H ... 3E **24**
Huntsmead Cl. BR7: Chst ... 7D **142**
Huntsmoor Rd. KT19: Ewe ... 5K **163**
Huntspill St. SW17 ... 3A **136**
Hunts Slip Rd. SE21 ... 3E **138**
Huntsworth M. NW1 ... 3E **4** (4D **82**)
Hurdwick Pl. *NW1* ... *2G **83***
(off Hampstead Rd.)
Hurleston Ho. SE8 ... 5B **104**
Hurley Ct. W5 ... 6C **78**
Hurley Cres. SE16 ... 2K **103**
Hurley Ho. SE11 ... 4K **19** (4B **102**)
Hurley Rd. UB6: G'frd ... 6F **77**
HURLINGHAM ... 3K **117**
Hurlingham Bus. Pk. SW6 ... 3J **117**

Hurlingham Club, The 3J 117
Hurlingham Ct. SW6 . . . . .3H 117
Hurlingham Gdns. SW6 . . . . .3H 117
Hurlingham Retail Pk. SW6 . . . . . . .3K 117
Hurlingham Rd. DA7: Bex 7F 109
SW6 . . . . .2H 117
Hurlingham Sq. SW6 . . . . .3H 117
Hurlingham Stadium 3H 117
Hurlock St. N5 . . . . .3B 66
Hurlstone Rd. SE25 . . . . .5E 156
Hurn Ct. TW4: Houn 2B 112
Hurn Ct. Rd. TW4: Houn 2B 112
Huron Cl. BR6: Chels 6J 173
Huron Rd. SW17 . . . . .2E 136
Huron University 1B 16 (3B 100)
Hurren Cl. SE3 . . . . .3G 123
Hurricane Rd. SM6: Wall 7J 167
Hurry Cl. E15 . . . . .7G 69
Hurst Av. E4 . . . . .4H 35
N6 . . . . .6G 47
Hurstbourne KT10: Clay 6A 162
Hurstbourne Gdns. IG11: Bark 6J 71
Hurstbourne Ho. SW15 . . . . .6B 116
(off Tangley Gro.)
Hurstbourne Rd. SE23 . . . . .1A 140
Hurst Cl. BR2: Hayes 1H 171
E4 . . . . .3H 35
KT9: Chess 5G 163
NW11 . . . . .6K 45
UB5: N'olt 6D 58
Hurstcombe IG9: Buck H 2D 36
Hurst Ct. DA15: Sidc 2A 144
E6 . . . . .5B 88
(off Tollgate Rd.)
Hurstcourt Rd. SM1: Sutt 2K 165
Hurstdene Av. BR2: Hayes 1H 171
Hurstdene Gdns. N15 . . . . .7E 48
Hurstfield BR2: Brom 5J 159
Hurstfield Cres. UB4: Hayes 4G 75
Hurstfield Rd. KT8: W Mole 3E 148
Hurst Gro. KT12: Walt T 7H 147
Hurst Ho. WC1 . . . . .1H 7
(off Penton Ri.)
Hurst La. KT8: E Mos 4G 149
SE2 . . . . .5D 108
Hurst La. Est. SE2 . . . . .5D 108
Hurstleigh Gdns. IG5: Ilf 1D 52
Hurstmead Ct. HA8: Edg 4C 28
HURST PARK 2G 149
Hurst Pl. HA6: Nwood 1F 38
Hurst Pool 3F 149
Hurst Ri. EN5: New Bar 3D 20
Hurst Rd. CR0: Croy 5D 168
DA5: Bexl 1D 144
DA8: Erith 1J 127
DA15: Bexl, Sidc 2A 144
E17 . . . . .3D 50
IG9: Buck H 1G 37
KT8: W Mole, E Mos 3F 149
KT12: Walt T 5A 148
N21 . . . . .1F 33
Hurst Springs DA5: Bexl 1E 144
Hurst St. SE24 . . . . .6B 120
Hurstview Grange CR2: S Croy 7B 168
Hurst Vw. Rd. CR2: S Croy 7F 168
Hurst Way CR2: S Croy 6E 168
Hurstway Rd. W11 . . . . .7F 81
Hurstway Wlk. W11 . . . . .7F 81
Hurstwood Av. DA5: Bexl 1E 144
E18 . . . . .4K 51
Hurstwood Ct. N12 . . . . .6H 31
NW11 . . . . .4H 45
(off Finchley Rd.)
Hurstwood Dr. BR1: Brom 3D 160
Hurstwood Rd. NW11 . . . . .4G 45
Hurtwood Rd. KT12: Walt T 7D 148
Husborne Ho. SE8 . . . . .4A 104
(off Chilton Gro.)
Huson Cl. NW3 . . . . .7C 64
Hussain Cl. HA1: Harr 4K 59
Hussars Cl. TW4: Houn 3C 112
Husseywell Cres. BR2: Hayes 1J 171
Hutchings St. E14 . . . . .2C 104

Hutchings Wlk. NW11 . . . . .4K 45
Hutchings Wharf E14 . . . . .2C 104
(off Hutchings St.)
Hutchins Cl. E15 . . . . .7E 68
Hutchinson Cl. RM6: Chad H 4D 54
Hutchinson Ho. NW3 . . . . .7D 64
SE14 . . . . .7J 103
Hutchinson Ter. HA9: Wemb 3D 60
Hutchins Rd. SE28 . . . . .7A 90
Hutton Cl. IG8: Wfd G 6E 36
UB6: G'frd 5H 59
Hutton Ct. N4 . . . . .1K 65
(off Victoria Rd.)
N9 . . . . .7D 24
(off Tramway Av.)
W5 . . . . .5B 78
Hutton Gdns. HA3: Hrw W 7B 26
Hutton Gro. N12 . . . . .5E 30
Hutton La. HA3: Hrw W 7B 26
Hutton Row HA8: Edg 7D 28
Hutton St. EC4 . . . . .2K 13 (6B 84)
Hutton Wlk. HA3: Hrw W 7B 26
Huxbear St. SE4 . . . . .5B 122
Huxley Cl. UB5: N'olt 2C 76
UB8: Cowl 4A 74
Huxley Dr. RM6: Chad H 7B 54
Huxley Gdns. NW10 . . . . .3F 79
Huxley Ho. NW8 . . . . .4B 4
(off Fisherton St.)
Huxley Pde. N18 . . . . .5J 33
Huxley Pl. N13 . . . . .3G 33
Huxley Rd. DA16: Well 3K 125
E10 . . . . .2E 68
N18 . . . . .4J 33
Huxley Sayze N18 . . . . .5J 33
Huxley Sth. N18 . . . . .5J 33
Huxley St. W10 . . . . .3G 81
Hyacinth Cl. IG1: Ilf 6F 71
TW12: Hamp 6E 130
Hyacinth Dr. UB10: Uxb 7A 56
Hyacinth Rd. SW15 . . . . .1C 134
HYDE, THE 5B 44
Hyde, The NW9 . . . . .4A 44
Hyde Cl. E13 . . . . .2J 87
EN5: Barn 3C 20
TW15: Ashf 6G 129
Hyde Cres. NW9 . . . . .5A 44
Hyde Est. Rd. NW9 . . . . .5B 44
Hyde Farm M. SW12 . . . . .1H 137
Hydefield Cl. N21 . . . . .1J 33
Hydefield Ct. N9 . . . . .2K 33
Hyde Ind. Est., The NW9 . . . . .5B 44
Hyde La. SW11 . . . . .1C 118
Hyde Pk. 4D 10 (1C 100)
Hyde Pk. Av. N21 . . . . .2H 33
Hyde Pk. Barracks 7D 10
HYDE PARK CORNER 2F 101
Hyde Pk. Cnr. W1 . . . . . . .6H 11 (2E 100)
Hyde Pk. Cres. W2 . . . . . .1C 10 (6C 82)
Hyde Pk. Gdns. N21 . . . . .1H 33
W2 . . . . .2B 10 (7B 82)
Hyde Pk. Gdns. M. W2 . . . .2B 10 (7B 82)
(not continuous)
Hyde Pk. Ga. SW7 . . . . .2A 100
(not continuous)
Hyde Pk. Ga. M. SW7 . . . . .2A 100
Hyde Pk. Mans. NW1 . . . . .6C 4
(off Cabbell St., not continuous)
Hyde Pk. Pl. W2 . . . . .2D 10 (7C 82)
Hyde Pk. Sq. W2 . . . . . . .1C 10 (6C 82)
Hyde Pk. Sq. M. W2 . . . . .1C 10
Hyde Pk. St. W2 . . . . . . .1C 10 (6C 82)
Hyde Pk. Towers W2 . . . . .7A 82
Hyderabad Way E15 . . . . .7G 69
Hyde Rd. DA7: Bex 2F 127
N1 . . . . .1E 84
TW10: Rich 5F 115
Hydeside Gdns. N9 . . . . .2A 34
Hyde's Pl. N1 . . . . .7B 66
Hyde St. SE8 . . . . .6C 104
Hyde Ter. TW15: Ashf 6G 129
Hydethorpe Av. N9 . . . . .2A 34

Hydethorpe Rd. SW12 . . . . .1G 137
Hyde Va. SE10 . . . . .7E 104
Hyde Wlk. SM4: Mord 7J 153
Hyde Way N9 . . . . .2A 34
UB3: Harl 4H 93
Hydon Ct. N11 . . . . .5J 31
Hydra Bldg., The EC1 . . . . .2K 7
Hylands Rd. E17 . . . . .2F 51
Hylton St. SE18 . . . . .4K 107
Hyndewood SE23 . . . . .3K 139
Hyndman Ho. RM10: Dag 3G 73
(off Kershaw Rd.)
Hyndman St. SE15 . . . . .6H 103
Hynton Rd. RM8: Dag 2C 72
Hyperion Ho. E3 . . . . .2A 86
(off Arbery Rd.)
SW2 . . . . .6K 119
Hyrstdene CR2: S Croy 4B 168
Hyson Rd. SE16 . . . . .5H 103
Hythe Av. DA7: Bex 7E 108
Hythe Cl. N18 . . . . .4B 34
Hythe Ho. SE16 . . . . .2J 103
(off Swan Rd.)
W6 . . . . .4E 98
(off Shepherd's Bush Rd.)
Hythe Rd. CR7: Thor H 2D 156
NW10 . . . . .3B 80
Hythe Rd. Ind. Est. NW10 . . . . .3C 80

Ian Bowater Ct. N1 . . . . .1F 9
(off East Rd.)
Ian Cl. SE23 . . . . .2J 139
Ian Sq. EN3: Enf H 1E 24
Ibberton Ho. SW8 . . . . .7K 101
(off Meadow Rd.)
W14 . . . . .3G 99
(off Russell Rd.)
Ibbotson Av. E16 . . . . .6H 87
Ibbott St. E1 . . . . .4J 85
Iberia Ho. N19 . . . . .7H 47
Iberian Av. SM6: Bedd 4H 167
Ibex Ho. E15 . . . . .5G 69
(off Forest La.)
Ibis Ct. SE8 . . . . .6B 104
(off Edward Pl.)
Ibis La. W4 . . . . .1J 115
Ibis Way UB4: Yead 6B 76
Ibrox Ct. IG9: Buck H 2F 37
Ibscott Cl. RM10: Dag 6J 73
Ibsley Gdns. SW15 . . . . .1C 134
Ibsley Way EN4: Cockf 5H 21
ICA Cinema 5D 12
(off The Mall)
ICA Theatre 1F 103
(off Lafone St.)
Iceland Rd. E3 . . . . .1C 86
Iceland Wharf SE8 . . . . .4A 104
Iceni Ct. IG9: Buck H 1E 36
Ice Wharf Marina N1 . . . . .2J 83
(off New Wharf Rd.)
Ickburgh Est. E5 . . . . .2H 67
Ickburgh Rd. E5 . . . . .3H 67
ICKENHAM 3D 56
Ickenham Cl. HA4: Ruis 2F 57
Ickenham Grn. UB10: Ick 1D 56
Ickenham Rd. HA4: Ruis 2C 56
Ickleton Rd. SE9 . . . . .4C 142
Icknield Dr. IG2: Ilf 5F 53
Icknield Ho. SW3 . . . . .5D 16
(off Cale St.)
Ickworth Pk. Rd. E17 . . . . .4A 50
Icon Apartments SE1 . . . . .7G 15
(off Cluny Pl.)
Idaho Bldg. SE10 . . . . .1D 122
(off Deal's Gateway)
Ida Rd. N15 . . . . .4D 48
Ida St. E14 . . . . .6E 86
(not continuous)
Iden Cl. BR2: Brom 3G 159
Idlecombe Rd. SW17 . . . . .6E 136

Idmiston Rd. E15 . . . . .4H 69
KT4: Wor Pk 7B 152
SE27 . . . . .3C 138
Idmiston Sq. KT4: Wor Pk 7B 152
Idol La. EC3 . . . . .3G 15 (7E 84)
Idonia St. SE8 . . . . .7C 104
Iffley Cl. UB8: Uxb 7A 56
Iffley Rd. W6 . . . . .3D 98
Ifield Rd. SW10 . . . . .6K 99
Ifor Evans Pl. E1 . . . . .4K 85
Ightham Ho. BR3: Beck 7B 140
(off Bethersden Cl.)
SE17 . . . . .4E 102
(off Beckway St.)
Ightham Rd. DA8: Erith 7G 109
Ikon Ho. E1 . . . . .7J 85
(off Devonport St.)
Ilbert St. W10 . . . . .3F 81
Ilchester Gdns. W2 . . . . .7K 81
Ilchester Mans. W8 . . . . .3J 99
(off Abingdon Rd.)
Ilchester Pl. W14 . . . . .3H 99
Ilchester Rd. RM8: Dag 5B 72
Ildersly Gro. SE21 . . . . .2D 138
Ilderton Rd. SE16 . . . . .5J 103
Ilderton Wharf SE15 . . . . .6J 103
(off Rollins St.)
Ilex Cl. TW16: Sun 2A 148
Ilex Rd. NW10 . . . . .6B 62
Ilex Way SW16 . . . . .5A 138
ILFORD 3F 71
Ilford Hill IG1: Ilf 3E 70
Ilford Ho. N1 . . . . .6D 66
(off Dove Rd.)
Ilford La. IG1: Bark, Ilf 3F 71
Ilford Pools 2J 71
Ilfracombe Flats SE1 . . . . .6D 14
(off Marshalsea Rd.)
Ilfracombe Gdns. RM6: Chad H 7B 54
Ilfracombe Rd. BR1: Brom 3H 141
Iliffe St. SE17 . . . . .5B 102
Iliffe Yd. SE17 . . . . .5B 102
(off Crampton St.)
Ilkeston Ct. E5 . . . . .4K 67
(off Overbury St.)
Ilkley Cl. SE19 . . . . .6D 138
Ilkley Rd. E16 . . . . .5A 88
Illingworth Cl. CR4: Mitc 3B 154
Illingworth Way N1: Enf 5K 23
Ilmington Rd. HA3: Kent 6D 42
Ilminster Gdns. SW11 . . . . .4C 118
Ilsley Cl. SW6 . . . . .2G 119
Imani Mans. SW11 . . . . .2B 118
IMAX Cinema 5J 13 (1A 102)
Imber Cl. N14 . . . . .7B 22
Imber Ct. Trad. Est. KT8: E Mos 6H 149
Imber Cross KT7: T Ditt 6K 149
Imber Gro. KT10: Esh 7H 149
Imber Pk. Rd. KT10: Esh 7H 149
Imber St. N1 . . . . .1D 84
Impact Bus. Pk. UB6: G'frd 2B 78
Impact Ct. SE20 . . . . .2H 157
Imperial Av. N16 . . . . .4E 66
Imperial Cl. HA2: Harr 6E 40
Imperial College of Science,
Technology & Medicine
Imperial Coll. Rd. . . .1A 16 (3B 100)
Wilson House 7C 4
(off Star La.)
Imperial Coll. Rd. SW7 . . . .2A 16 (3B 100)
Imperial Cl. HA2: Harr 7E 40
N6 . . . . .6G 47
N20 . . . . .3F 31
NW8 . . . . .2C 82
(off Prince Albert Rd.)
SE11 . . . . .6J 19 (5A 102)
Imperial Cres. SW6 . . . . .2A 118
Imperial Rd. HA2: Harr 7E 40
Imperial Gdns. CR4: Mitc 3F 155
Imperial Ho. E3 . . . . .3A 86
(off Grove Rd.)
E14 . . . . .7B 86
(off Victory Pl.)

Imperial M. E6 . . . . .2B **88**
Imperial Pde. *EC4* *1A **14***
        (off New Bri. St.)
Imperial Pl. BR7: Chst 1E **160**
Imperial Rd. N22 . . . . .7D **32**
   SW6 . . . . .1K **117**
   TW14: Felt 7G **111**
Imperial Sq. SW6 . . . . .1K **117**
Imperial St. E3 . . . . .3E **86**
Imperial War Mus. 2K **19** (3A **102**)
Imperial Way BR7: Chst 3G **143**
   CR0: Wadd 6K **167**
   HA3: Kent 6E **42**
Imperial Wharf SW6 . . . . .2A **118**
Imre Cl. W12 . . . . .1D **98**
Inca Dr. SE9 . . . . .7F **125**
Inca Ter. N15 . . . . .3B **48**
Inchmery Rd. SE6 . . . . .2D **140**
Inchwood CR0: Addtn 4D **170**
Independent Ind. Est.
   UB7: Yiew 1A **92**
Independent Pl. E8 . . . . .5F **67**
Independents Rd. SE3 . . . . .3H **123**
Inderwick Rd. N8 . . . . .5K **47**
Indescon Ct. E14 . . . . .2D **104**
India Gdns. UB5: N'olt 7A **58**
Indiana Bldg. *SE8* *1C **122***
        (off Deal's Gateway)
India Pl. WC2 . . . . .2G **13**
India St. EC3 . . . . .1J **15** (6F **85**)
India Way W12 . . . . .7D **80**
Indigo M. E14 . . . . .7E **86**
   N16 .3D **66**
Indus Ct. *SE15* *7F **103***
        (off Amstel Ct.)
Indus Rd. SE7 . . . . .7A **106**
Infirmary Cl. SW3 . . . . .7F **17**
Ingal Rd. E13 . . . . .4J **87**
Ingate Pl. SW8 . . . . .1F **119**
Ingatestone Rd. E12 . . . . .1A **70**
   IG8: Wfd G 7E **36**
   SE25 . . . . .4H **157**
Ingelow Ho. *W8* *2K **99***
        (off Holland St.)
Ingelow Rd. SW8 . . . . .2F **119**
Ingersoll Rd. EN3: Enf W 1D **24**
   W12 .1D **98**
Ingestre Pl. W1 . . . . . . .1B **12** (6G **83**)
Ingestre Rd. E7 . . . . .4J **69**
   NW5 . . . . .4F **65**
Ingham Cl. CR2: Sels 7K **169**
Ingham Rd. CR2: Sels 7J **169**
   NW6 .4J **63**
Inglebert St. EC1 . . . . . . .1J **7** (3A **84**)
Ingleborough St. SW9 . . . . .2A **120**
Ingleby Dr. HA1: Harr 3H **59**
Ingleby Rd. IG1: Ilf 1F **71**
   N7 . . . . .3J **65**
   RM10: Dag 6H **73**
Ingleby Way BR7: Chst 5E **142**
   SM6: Wall 7H **167**
Ingle Cl. HA5: Pinn 3C **40**
Ingledew Rd. SE18 . . . . .5H **107**
Inglefield Sq. *E1* *1H **103***
        (off Prusom St.)
Inglehurst Gdns. IG4: Ilf 5D **52**
Inglemere Rd. CR4: Mitc 7D **136**
   SE23 . . . . .3K **139**
Inglesham Wlk. E9 . . . . .6B **68**
Ingleside Cl. BR3: Beck 7C **140**
Ingleside Gro. SE3 . . . . .6H **105**
Inglethorpe St. SW6 . . . . .1F **117**
Ingleton Av. DA16: Well 5A **126**
Ingleton Rd. N18 . . . . .6B **34**
   SM5: Cars 7C **166**
Ingleton St. SW9 . . . . .2A **120**
Ingleway N12 . . . . .6G **31**
Inglewood BR7: Chst 6H **143**
   CR0: Sels 3A **170**
Inglewood Cl. E14 . . . . .4C **104**
Inglewood Copse BR1: Brom . . .2C **160**
Inglewood Ct. BR1: Brom 7G **141**
Inglewood M. KT6: Surb 1G **163**

Inglewood Rd. DA7: Bex 4K **127**
   NW6 .5J **63**
Inglis Rd. CR0: Croy 1F **169**
   W5 . . . . .7F **79**
Inglis St. SE5 . . . . .1B **120**
Ingoldisthorpe Gro. SE15 . . . . . .6F **103**
Ingram Av. NW11 . . . . .7A **46**
Ingram Cl. HA7: Stan 5H **27**
   SE11 . . . . .3H **19** (4K **101**)
Ingram Ho. E3 . . . . .1A **86**
Ingram Rd. CR7: Thor H 1C **156**
   N2 . . . . .4C **46**
Ingram Way UB6: G'frd 1H **77**
Ingrave Ho. RM9: Dag 1B **90**
Ingrave Rd. RM1: Rom 4K **55**
Ingrave St. SW11 . . . . .3B **118**
Ingrebourne Ct. E4 . . . . .3J **35**
Ingrebourne Ho. *BR1: Brom* *5F **141***
        (off Brangbourne Rd.)
   NW8 . . . .*5B **4***
        (off Broadley St.)
Ingress St. W4 . . . . .5A **98**
Inigo Jones Rd. SE7 . . . . .7C **106**
Inigo Pl. WC2 . . . . .2E **12**
Inkerman Rd. NW5 . . . . .6F **65**
Inkerman Ter. *W8* *3J **99***
        (off Allen St.)
Inks Grn. E4 . . . . .5K **35**
Inkster Ho. SW11 . . . . .3C **118**
Inkwell Cl. N12 . . . . .3F **31**
Inman Rd. NW10 . . . . .1A **80**
   SW18 . . . . .7A **118**
Inmans Row IG8: Wfd G 4D **36**
Inner Circ. NW1 . . . . .2G **5** (3E **82**)
Inner Ct. SW3 . . . . .7C **16** (6C **100**)
Inner Pk. Rd. SW19 . . . . .1F **135**
Inner Ring E. TW6: H'row A 3D **110**
Inner Ring W. TW6: H'row A 3C **110**
Inner Temple La. EC4 . . . . .1J **13**
Innes Cl. SW20 . . . . .2G **153**
Innes Gdns. SW15 . . . . .6D **116**
Innes Yd. CR0: Croy 3C **168**
Innis Ho. *SE17* *5E **102***
        (off East St.)
Inniskilling Rd. E13 . . . . .2A **88**
Innis St. SE15 . . . . .7E **102**
Innova Ct. CR0: Croy 1E **168**
Innovation Cen., The *E14* *2E **104***
        (off Marsh Wall)
Innovation Ho. HA0: Wemb 1E **78**
Inns of Court & City Yeomanry Mus. . . .*6H **7***
        (off Chancery La.)
Inskip Cl. E10 . . . . .2D **68**
Inskip Rd. RM8: Dag 1D **72**
Institute of Archaeology 4H **83**
Institute of Classical Studies 4H **83**
Institute of Contemporary Arts 4D **12**
Institute Pl. E8 . . . . .5H **67**
Integer Gdns. E11 . . . . .7F **51**
Interface Ho. *TW3: Houn* *3E **112***
        (off Staines Rd.)
International Av. TW5: Cran 5A **94**
International Bus. Pk. E15 . . . . . .1F **87**
International Ho. *E1* *3K **15***
        (off St Katharine's Way)
International Trad. Est. UB2: S'hall . . .3K **93**
International Way TW16: Sun 1G **147**
Inverary Pl. SE18 . . . . .6H **107**
Inver Cl. E5 . . . . .2J **67**
Inverclyde Gdns. RM6: Chad H . . .4C **54**
        (not continuous)
Inver Ct. W2 . . . . .6K **81**
   W6 . . . . .3C **98**
Inveresk Gdns. KT4: Wor Pk 3C **164**
Inverforth Cl. NW3 . . . . .2A **64**
Inverforth Rd. N11 . . . . .5A **32**
Invergarry Ho. *NW6* *2K **81***
        (off Carlton Va.)
Inverine Rd. SE7 . . . . .5K **105**
Invermead Cl. W6 . . . . .3C **98**
Invermore Pl. SE18 . . . . .4G **107**
Inverness Av. EN1: Enf 1K **23**
Inverness St. SE6 . . . . .1H **141**

Inverness Gdns. W8 . . . . .1K **99**
Inverness M. E16 . . . . .1G **107**
   W2 . . . . .7K **81**
Inverness Pl. W2 . . . . .7K **81**
Inverness Rd. KT4: Wor Pk 1F **165**
   N18 .5C **34**
   TW3: Houn 4D **112**
   UB2: S'hall 4C **94**
Inverness St. NW1 . . . . .1F **83**
Inverness Ter. W2 . . . . .6K **81**
Inverton Rd. SE15 . . . . .4K **121**
Invicta Cen., The IG11: Bark 1A **90**
Invicta Cl. BR7: Chst 5E **142**
   TW14: Felt 1H **129**
Invicta Gro. UB5: N'olt 3D **76**
Invicta Pde. DA14: Sidc 4B **144**
Invicta Plaza SE1 . . . . . . .4A **14** (1B **102**)
Invicta Rd. SE3 . . . . .7J **105**
Invicta Sq. E3 . . . . .5C **86**
Inville Rd. SE17 . . . . .5D **102**
Inville Wlk. SE17 . . . . .5D **102**
Inwen Ct. SE8 . . . . .5A **104**
Inwood Av. TW3: Houn 3G **113**
Inwood Bus. Pk.
   TW3: Houn 4F **113**
Inwood Cl. CR0: Croy 2A **170**
Inwood Ct. *NW1* *7G **65***
        (off Rochester Sq.)
Inwood Rd. TW3: Houn 4F **113**
   SW11 . . . . .2C **118**
Inworth Wlk. *N1* *1C **84***
        (off Popham St.)
IO Cen. SE18 . . . . .3G **107**
Iona Cl. SE6 . . . . .7C **122**
   SM4: Mord 7K **153**
Ion Ct. E2 . . . . .2G **85**
Ionian Bldg. E14 . . . . .7A **86**
Ionian Ho. *E1* *4K **85***
        (off Duckett St.)
Ion Sq. E2 . . . . .2G **85**
Ipsden Bldgs. SE1 . . . . .5K **13**
Ipswich Ho. SE4 . . . . .5K **121**
Ipswich Rd. SW17 . . . . .6E **136**
Ireland Cl. E6 . . . . .5D **88**
Ireland Pl. N22 . . . . .7D **32**
Ireland Yd. EC4 . . . . .6B **84**
Irene M. W7 . . . . .1K **95**
        (off Uxbridge Rd.)
Irene Rd. BR6: Orp 7K **161**
   SW6 . . . . .1J **117**
Ireton Cl. N10 . . . . .7K **31**
Ireton St. E3 . . . . .4C **86**
Iris Av. DA5: Bexl 6E **126**
Iris Cl. CR0: Croy 1K **169**
   E6 . . . . .5C **88**
   KT6: Surb 7F **151**
Iris Ct. *SE14* *1J **121***
        (off Briant St.)
Iris Cres. DA7: Bex 6F **109**
Iris Rd. KT19: Ewe 5H **163**
Iris Wlk. HA8: Edg 4D **28**
Iris Way E4 . . . . .6G **35**
Irkdale Av. EN1: Enf 1A **24**
Iron Bri. Cl. NW10 . . . . .5A **62**
Iron Bri. Rd. UB2: S'hall 1G **95**
Iron Bri. Ho. NW1 . . . . .7D **64**
Iron Bri. Rd. UB7: W Dray 2C **92**
   UB11: W Dray, Yiew 2C **92**
Iron Mill Pl. SW18 . . . . .6K **117**
Iron Mill Rd. SW18 . . . . .6K **117**
Ironmonger La. EC2 . . . .1D **14** (6D **84**)
Ironmonger Pas. *EC1* *2D **8***
        (off Ironmonger Row)
Ironmonger Row EC1 . . . . .2D **8** (3C **84**)
Ironmonger Row Baths 2D **8**
Ironmongers Pl. E14 . . . . .4C **104**
Ironside Cl. SE16 . . . . .2K **103**
Ironside Ho. E9 . . . . .4A **68**
Irons Way RM5: Col R 1J **55**
Iron Works E3 . . . . .1C **86**
Irvine Av. HA3: Kent 3A **42**
Irvine Cl. E14 . . . . .5D **86**
   N20 . . . . .2H **31**

Irvine Ho. *N7* *6K **65***
        (off Caledonian Rd.)
Irvine Way BR6: Orp 7K **161**
Irving Av. UB5: N'olt 1B **76**
Irving Gro. SW9 . . . . .2K **119**
Irving Ho. *SE17* *5B **102***
        (off Doddington Gro.)
Irving Mans. *W14* *6G **99***
        (off Queen's Club Gdns.)
Irving M. N1 . . . . .6C **66**
Irving Rd. W14 . . . . .3F **99**
Irving St. WC2 . . . . .3D **12** (7H **83**)
Irving Way NW9 . . . . .5C **44**
Irwell Cl. W7 . . . . .6H **77**
        (off Hobbayne Rd.)
Irwell Est. SE16 . . . . .3J **103**
Irwin Av. SE18 . . . . .7J **107**
Irwin Cl. UB10: Ick 3C **56**
Irwin Gdns. NW10 . . . . .1D **80**
Isaac Way *SE1* *6D **14***
        (off Lant St.)
Isabel Hill Cl. TW12: Hamp 2F **149**
Isabella Cl. N14 . . . . .7B **22**
Isabella Dr. BR6: Farnb 4G **173**
Isabella Ho. SE11 . . . . .5K **19**
   W6 . . . .*5E **98***
        (off Queen Caroline St.)
Isabella Rd. E9 . . . . .5J **67**
Isabella St. SE1 . . . . .5A **14** (1B **102**)
Isabel St. SW9 . . . . .1K **119**
Isambard M. E14 . . . . .3E **104**
Isambard Pl. SE16 . . . . .1J **103**
Isard Ho. BR2: Hayes 1K **171**
Isel Way SE22 . . . . .5E **120**
Isham Rd. SW16 . . . . .2J **155**
Isis Cl. HA4: Ruis 6E **38**
   SW15 . . . . .4E **116**
Isis Cl. W4 . . . . .7H **97**
Isis Ho. N18 . . . . .6A **34**
   NW8 . . . .*4B **4***
        (off Church St. Est.)
Isis St. SW18 . . . . .2A **136**
Island, The KT7: T Ditt 6A **150**
Island Farm Av. KT8: W Mole 5D **148**
Island Farm Rd. KT8: W Mole . . .5D **148**
Island Ho. E15 . . . . .3E **86**
Island Rd. CR4: Mitc 7D **136**
Island Row E14 . . . . .6B **86**
Isla Rd. SE18 . . . . .6G **107**
Islay Gdns. TW4: Houn 5B **112**
Islay Wlk. *N1* *6C **66***
        (off Douglas Rd. Sth.)
Isleden Ho. *N1* *1C **84***
        (off Prebend St.)
Isledon Rd. N7 . . . . .3A **66**
ISLEDON VILLAGE 3A **66**
Islehurst Cl. BR7: Chst 1E **160**
ISLEWORTH 3A **114**
Isleworth Bus. Complex
   TW7: Isle 2K **113**
Isleworth Prom. TW1: Twick 4B **114**
Isleworth Recreation Cen. 4K **113**
Isley Ct. SW8 . . . . .2G **119**
ISLINGTON 7B **66**
Islington Crematorium N2 . . . . . . .1D **46**
Islington Grn. N1 . . . . .1B **84**
Islington High St. N1 . . . . .2A **84**
        (not continuous)
Islington Mus. 7B **66**
Islington Pk. M. N1 . . . . .7B **66**
Islington Pk. St. N1 . . . . .7A **66**
Islington Pl. N1 . . . . .1A **84**
Islington Tennis Cen. 6J **65**
Islip Gdns. HA8: Edg 7E **28**
   UB5: N'olt 7C **58**
Islip Mnr. Rd. UB5: N'olt 7C **58**
Islip St. NW5 . . . . .5G **65**
Ismailia Rd. E7 . . . . .7K **69**
Isobel Ho. HA1: Harr 5K **41**
Isom Cl. E13 . . . . .3K **87**
Itaska Cotts. WD23: Bushy 1D **26**
Ivanhoe Cl. UB8: Cowl 5A **74**
Ivanhoe Dr. HA3: Kent 3A **42**

Ivanhoe Ho. *E3* 2A **86**
(off Grove Rd.)
Ivanhoe Rd. SE5 . . . . . 3F **121**
TW4: Houn 3B **112**
Ivatt Pl. W14 . . . . . 5H **99**
Ivatt Way N17 . . . . . 3B **48**
Iveagh Av. NW10 . . . . . 2G **79**
Iveagh Cl. E9 . . . . . 1K **85**
HA6: Nwood 1D **38**
NW10 . . . . . 2G **79**
Iveagh Ct. BR3: Beck 3E **158**
E1 . . . . . 1J **15**
Iveagh Ho. SW9 . . . . . 2B **120**
SW10 . . . . . 7A **100**
(off King's Rd.)
Iveagh Ter. *NW10* 2G **79**
(off Iveagh Av.)
Ivedon Rd. DA16: Well 2C **126**
Ive Farm Cl. E10 . . . . . 2C **68**
Ive Farm La. E10 . . . . . 2C **68**
Iveley Rd. SW4 . . . . . 2G **119**
Ivere Dr. EN5: New Bar 6E **20**
Iver Ho. *N1* 1E **84**
(off New Era Est.)
Iverhurst Cl. DA6: Bex 5D **126**
Iverna Ct. W8 . . . . . 3J **99**
Iverna Gdns. TW14: Felt 5F **111**
W8 . . . . . 3J **99**
Iverson Rd. NW6 . . . . . 6H **63**
Ivers Way CR0: New Ad 7D **170**
Ives Rd. E16 . . . . . 5G **87**
Ives St. SW3 . . . . . 3D **16** (4C **100**)
Ivestor Ter. SE23 . . . . . 7J **121**
Ivimey St. E2 . . . . . 3G **85**
Ivinghoe Cl. EN1: Enf 1K **23**
Ivinghoe Ho. N7 . . . . . 5H **65**
Ivinghoe Rd. RM8: Dag 5B **72**
Ivor Ct. N8 . . . . . 6J **47**
NW1 . . . . . 3E **4**
(off Gloucester Pl.)
Ivor Gro. SE9 . . . . . 1F **143**
Ivories, The *N1* 7C **66**
(off Northampton St.)
Ivor Pl. NW1 . . . . . 4E **4** (4D **82**)
Ivor St. NW1 . . . . . 7G **65**
Ivory Ct. TW13: Felt 2J **129**
Ivorydown BR1: Brom 4J **141**
Ivory Ho. E1 . . . . . 3K **15** (1F **103**)
Ivory Sq. SW11 . . . . . 3A **118**
Ivybridge Cl. TW1: Twick 7A **114**
UB8: Uxb 3A **74**
Ivybridge Ct. *BR7: Chst* 1E **160**
(off Old Hill)
NW1 . . . . . 7F **65**
(off Lewis St.)
Ivybridge La. WC2 . . . . . 3F **13** (7J **83**)
Ivy Bri. Retail Pk. TW7: Isle 5K **113**
Ivychurch Cl. SE20 . . . . . 7J **139**
Ivychurch La. SE17 . . . . . 5F **103**
Ivy Cl. HA2: Harr 4D **58**
HA5: Eastc 7A **40**
TW16: Sun 2A **148**
Ivy Cotts. E14 . . . . . 7E **86**
UB10: Hil 3C **74**
Ivy Ct. *SE16* 5G **103**
(off Argyle Way)
Ivy Cres. W4 . . . . . 4J **97**
Ivydale Rd. SE15 . . . . . 3K **121**
SM5: Cars 2D **166**
Ivyday Gro. SW16 . . . . . 3K **137**
Ivydene KT8: W Mole 5D **148**
Ivydene Cl. SM1: Sutt 4A **166**
Ivy Gdns. CR4: Mitc 3H **155**
N8 . . . . . 6J **47**
Ivyhouse Rd. RM9: Dag 6D **72**
UB10: Ick 3D **56**
Ivy La. TW4: Houn 4D **112**
Ivy Lodge *W11* 1J **99**
(off Notting Hill Ga.)
Ivymount Rd. SE27 . . . . . 3A **138**
Ivy Rd. E16 . . . . . 6J **87**
E17 . . . . . 6C **50**
KT6: Surb 1G **163**
Ivy Rd. N14 . . . . . 7B **22**
NW2 . . . . . 4E **62**
SE4 . . . . . 4B **122**
SW17 . . . . . 5C **136**
TW3: Houn 4F **113**
Ivy St. N1 . . . . . 2E **84**
Ivy Wlk. HA6: Nwood 1G **39**
RM9: Dag 6E **72**
Ixworth Pl. SW3 . . . . . 5C **16** (5C **100**)
Izane Rd. DA6: Bex 4F **127**

J

Jacana Ct. *E1* 3K **15**
(off Star Pl.)
Jacaranda Cl. KT3: N Mald 3A **152**
Jacaranda Gro. E8 . . . . . 7F **67**
Jackass La. BR2: Kes 5K **171**
Jack Barnett Way N22 . . . . . 2K **47**
Jack Clow Rd. E15 . . . . . 2G **87**
Jack Cook Ho. IG11: Bark 7F **71**
Jack Cornwell St. E12 . . . . . 4E **70**
Jack Dash Ho. *E14* 2E **104**
(off Lawn Ho. Cl.)
Jack Dash Way E6 . . . . . 4C **88**
Jackets La. HA6: Nwood 1D **38**
Jack Goodchild Way KT1: King T 3H **151**
Jacklin Grn. IG8: Wfd G 4D **36**
Jackman Ho. *E1* 1H **103**
(off Watts St.)
Jackman M. NW10 . . . . . 3A **62**
Jackman St. E8 . . . . . 1H **85**
Jackson Cl. E9 . . . . . 7J **67**
UB10: Uxb 7A **56**
Jackson Ct. E7 . . . . . 6K **69**
Jackson Ho. N11 . . . . . 5B **32**
Jackson Rd. BR2: Brom 2D **172**
EN4: E Barn 6H **21**
IG11: Bark 1H **89**
N7 . . . . . 4K **65**
UB10: Uxb 7A **56**
Jacksons La. N6 . . . . . 7E **46**
Jacksons Lane Theatre 6F **47**
(off Jacksons La.)
Jacksons Pl. CR0: Croy 1D **168**
Jackson St. SE18 . . . . . 6E **106**
Jackson's Way CR0: Croy 3C **170**
Jackson Way UB2: S'hall 2F **95**
Jacks Pl. *E1* 5J **9**
(off Corbet Pl.)
Jack Walker Ct. N5 . . . . . 4B **66**
Jacob Ho. *DA18: Erith* 2D **108**
(off Kale Rd.)
Jacobin Lodge N7 . . . . . 5J **65**
Jacob Mans. *E1* 6H **85**
(off Commercial Rd.)
Jacobs Cl. RM10: Dag 4H **73**
Jacobs Ho. *E13* 3A **88**
(off New City Rd.)
Jacob St. SE1 . . . . . 6K **15** (2G **103**)
Jacob's Well M. W1 . . . . . 6H **5** (5E **82**)
Jacotts Ho. *W10* 4E **80**
(off Sutton Way)
Jacqueline Cl. UB5: N'olt 1C **76**
Jacqueline Creft Ter. *N6* 6E **46**
(off Grange Rd.)
Jacqueline Ho. *NW1* 1D **82**
(off Regent's Pk. Rd.)
Jacqueline Vs. *E17* 5E **50**
(off Shernhall St.)
Jade Cl. E16 . . . . . 6B **88**
NW2 . . . . . 7F **45**
RM8: Dag 1C **72**
Jade Ter. NW6 . . . . . 7A **64**
Jaffe Rd. IG1: Ilf 1H **71**
Jaffray Pl. SE27 . . . . . 4B **138**
Jaffray Rd. BR2: Brom 4B **160**
Jaggard Way SW12 . . . . . 7D **118**
Jagger Ho. *SW11* 1D **118**
(off Rosenau Rd.)
Jago Cl. SE18 . . . . . 6G **107**
Jago Wlk. SE5 . . . . . 7D **102**
Jake Russell Wlk. E16 . . . . . 7A **88**
Jamaica Rd. CR7: Thor H 6B **156**
SE1 . . . . . 7K **15** (2F **103**)
SE16 . . . . . 7K **15** (2F **103**)
Jamaica St. E1 . . . . . 6J **85**
James Allens School Swimming Pool 5E **120**
James Anderson Ct. *E2* 2E **84**
(off Kingsland Rd.)
James Av. NW2 . . . . . 5E **62**
RM8: Dag 1F **73**
James Bedford Cl. HA5: Pinn 2A **40**
James Boswell Cl. SW16 . . . . . 4K **137**
James Brine Ho. *E2* 1K **9**
(off Ravenscroft St.)
James Campbell Ho. *E2* 2J **85**
(off Old Ford Rd.)
James Clavell Sq. *SE18* 3F **107**
(off Cartridge St.)
James Cl. E13 . . . . . 2J **87**
NW11 . . . . . 6G **45**
James Collins Cl. W9 . . . . . 4H **81**
James Ct. HA6: Nwood 1H **39**
N1 . . . . . 1C **84**
(off Raynor Pl.)
NW9 . . . . . 2A **44**
UB5: N'olt 2C **76**
(off Church Rd.)
James Docherty Ho. *E2* 2H **85**
(off Patriot Sq.)
James Dudson Ct. NW10 . . . . . 7J **61**
James Est. CR4: Mitc 2D **154**
James Gdns. N22 . . . . . 7G **33**
James Hammett Ho. *E2* 1K **9**
(off Ravenscroft St.)
James Hill Ho. *W10* 4G **81**
(off Kensal Rd.)
James Ho. *E1* 4A **86**
(off Solebay St.)
SE16 . . . . . 2K **103**
(off Wolfe Cres.)
SW8 . . . . . 7J **101**
(off Wheatsheaf La.)
James Jeff Way SM6: Wall 7H **167**
James Joyce Wlk. SE24 . . . . . 4B **120**
James La. E10 . . . . . 7E **50**
E11 . . . . . 7F **51**
James Lind Ho. *SE8* 4B **104**
(off Grove St.)
James Middleton Ho. *E2* 3H **85**
(off Middleton St.)
James Newman Ct. SE9 . . . . . 3E **142**
Jameson Cl. W3 . . . . . 2J **97**
Jameson Ct. *E2* 2J **85**
(off Russia La.)
Jameson Ho. *SE11* 5G **19**
(off Glasshouse Wlk.)
Jameson Lodge N6 . . . . . 6G **47**
Jameson St. W8 . . . . . 1J **99**
James Pl. N17 . . . . . 1F **49**
James's Cotts. TW9: Kew 7G **97**
James Stewart Ho. NW6 . . . . . 7H **63**
James St. EN1: Enf 5A **24**
IG11: Bark 7G **71**
TW3: Houn 3H **113**
W1 . . . . . 1H **11** (6E **82**)
WC2 . . . . . 1F **13** (7J **83**)
James Stroud Ho. *SE17* 5C **102**
(off Bronti Cl.)
James Ter. *SW14* 3K **115**
(off Church Path)
James Terry Ct.
CR2: S Croy 5C **168**
(off Warham Rd.)
Jamestown Rd. NW1 . . . . . 1F **83**
Jamestown Way E14 . . . . . 7F **87**
James Yd. E4 . . . . . 6A **36**
Jamieson Ho. TW4: Houn 6D **112**
Jamilah Ho. *E16* 7E **88**
(off University Way)
Jamuna Cl. E14 . . . . . 5A **86**
Jane Austen Hall *E16* 1K **105**
(off Wesley Av.)
Jane Austen Ho. *SW1* 6A **18**
(off Churchill Gdns.)
Jane Seymour Ct. SE9 . . . . . 7H **125**
Jane St. E1 . . . . . 6H **85**
Janet Adegoke Leisure Cen. 7C **80**
Janet St. E14 . . . . . 3C **104**
Janeway Pl. SE16 . . . . . 2H **103**
Janeway St. SE16 . . . . . 2G **103**
Janice M. IG1: Ilf 2F **71**
Jansen Wlk. SW11 . . . . . 3B **118**
Janson Cl. E15 . . . . . 5G **69**
NW10 . . . . . 3A **62**
Janson Rd. E15 . . . . . 5G **69**
Jansons Rd. N15 . . . . . 3E **48**
Japan Cres. N4 . . . . . 1K **65**
Japan Rd. RM6: Chad H 6D **54**
Jardine Rd. E1 . . . . . 7K **85**
Jarman Ho. *E1* 5J **85**
(off Jubilee St.)
SE16 . . . . . 4K **103**
(off Hawkstone Rd.)
Jarrett Cl. SW2 . . . . . 1B **138**
Jarrow Cl. SM4: Mord 5K **153**
Jarrow Rd. N17 . . . . . 4H **49**
RM6: Chad H 6C **54**
SE16 . . . . . 4J **103**
Jarrow Way E9 . . . . . 4B **68**
Jarvis Cl. EN5: Barn 5A **20**
IG11: Bark 1H **89**
Jarvis Rd. CR2: S Croy 6D **168**
SE22 . . . . . 4E **120**
Jashoda Ho. *SE18* 5E **106**
(off Connaught M.)
Jasmin Cl. HA6: Nwood 1H **39**
Jasmin Ct. SE12 . . . . . 6J **123**
Jasmine Cl. BR6: Farnb 2F **173**
IG1: Ilf 5F **71**
UB1: S'hall 7C **76**
Jasmine Ct. SW19 . . . . . 5J **135**
Jasmine Gdns. CR0: Croy 3D **170**
HA2: Harr 2E **58**
Jasmine Gro. SE20 . . . . . 1H **157**
Jasmine Rd. RM7: Rush G 2K **73**
Jasmine Sq. *E3* 1B **86**
(off Hawthorn Av.)
Jasmine Ter. UB7: W Dray 2C **92**
Jasmine Way KT8: E Mos 4J **149**
Jasmin Lodge *SE16* 5H **103**
(off Sherwood Gdns.)
Jasmin Rd. KT19: Ewe 5H **163**
Jason Ct. *SW9* 1A **120**
(off Southey Rd.)
W1 . . . . . 7H **5**
Jason Wlk. SE9 . . . . . 4E **142**
Jasper Cl. EN3: Enf W 1D **24**
Jasper Pas. SE19 . . . . . 6F **139**
Jasper Rd. E16 . . . . . 6B **88**
SE19 . . . . . 5F **139**
Jasper Wlk. N1 . . . . . 3D **84**
Java Wharf *SE1* 6K **15**
(off Shad Thames)
Javelin Way UB5: N'olt 3B **76**
Jaycroft EN2: Enf 1F **23**
Jay Gdns. BR7: Chst 4D **142**
Jay M. SW7 . . . . . 7A **10** (2A **100**)
Jazzfern Ter. HA0: Wemb 5A **60**
Jean Batten Cl. SM6: Wall 7K **167**
Jean Darling Ho. *SW10* 6B **100**
(off Milman's St.)
Jean Ho. SW17 . . . . . 5C **136**
Jean Pardies Ho. *E1* 5J **85**
(off Jubilee St.)
Jebb Av. SW2 . . . . . 6J **119**
(not continuous)
Jebb St. E3 . . . . . 2C **86**
Jedburgh Rd. E13 . . . . . 3A **88**
Jedburgh St. SW11 . . . . . 4E **118**
Jeddo M. W12 . . . . . 2B **98**
Jeddo Rd. W12 . . . . . 2B **98**
Jefferson Bldg. E14 . . . . . 2C **104**
Jefferson Cl. IG2: Ilf 5F **53**
W13 . . . . . 3B **96**
Jefferson Wlk. SE18 . . . . . 6E **106**

Jeffrey Row SE12 ... 5K **123**
Jeffrey's Pl. NW1 ... 7G **65**
Jeffreys Rd. EN3: Brim ... 4F **25**
SW4 ... 2J **119**
Jeffrey's St. NW1 ... 7G **65**
Jeffreys Walk SW4 ... 2J **119**
Jeffries Ho. NW10 ... 7K **61**
Jeffs Cl. TW12: Hamp ... 6F **131**
Jeffs Rd. SM1: Sutt ... 4H **165**
Jeger Av. E2 ... 1F **85**
Jeken Rd. SE9 ... 4A **124**
Jelf Rd. SW2 ... 5A **120**
Jellicoe Gdns. HA7: Stan ... 6E **26**
Jellicoe Ho. *E2* ... *2G **85***
(off Ropley St.)
NW1 ... 4F **83**
Jellicoe Rd. E13 ... 4J **87**
N17 ... 7J **33**
Jemmett Cl. KT2: King T ... 1H **151**
Jemotts Ct. *SE14* ... *6K **103***
(off Myers La.)
Jem Paterson Ct. HA1: Harr ... 4J **59**
Jengar Cl. SM1: Sutt ... 4K **165**
Jenkins La. IG11: Bark ... 2G **89**
Jenkinson Ho. *E2* ... *3K **85***
(off Usk St.)
Jenkins Rd. E13 ... 4K **87**
Jenner Av. W3 ... 5K **79**
Jenner Cl. DA14: Sidc ... 4A **144**
Jenner Ho. *SE3* ... *6G **105***
(off Restell Cl.)
WC1 ... *3F **7***
(off Hunter St.)
Jenner Pl. SW13 ... 6D **98**
Jenner Rd. N16 ... 3F **67**
Jennett Rd. CR0: Wadd ... 3A **168**
Jennifer Ho. *SE11* ... *4K **19***
(off Reedworth St.)
Jennifer Rd. BR1: Brom ... 3H **141**
Jenningsbury Ho. *SW3* ... *5D **16***
(off Cale St.)
Jennings Cl. KT6: Surb ... 7C **150**
Jennings Ho. *SE10* ... *5F **105***
(off Old Woolwich Rd.)
Jennings Rd. SE22 ... 6F **121**
Jennings Way EN5: Barn ... 3A **20**
Jenningtree Way DA17: Belv ... 2J **109**
Jenny Hammond Cl. E11 ... 3H **69**
Jenson Way SE19 ... 7F **139**
Jenton Av. DA7: Bex ... 1E **126**
Jephson Ct. SW4 ... 2J **119**
Jephson Ho. *SE17* ... *6B **102***
(off Doddington Gro.)
Jephson Rd. E7 ... 7A **70**
Jephson St. SE5 ... 1D **120**
Jephtha Rd. SW18 ... 6J **117**
Jeppesen Ct. TW19: Stanw ... 6A **110**
Jeppos La. CR4: Mitc ... 4D **154**
Jepson Ho. *SW6* ... *1K **117***
(off Pearscroft Rd.)
Jerdan Pl. SW6 ... 7J **99**
Jeremiah St. E14 ... 6D **86**
Jeremy Bentham Ho. *E2* ... *3G **85***
(off Mansford St.)
Jeremy's Grn. N18 ... 4C **34**
Jermyn St. SW1 ... 4A **12** (1G **101**)
Jermyn Street Theatre ... **3C 12**
(off Jermyn St.)
Jerningham Av. IG5: Ilf ... 2F **53**
Jerningham Ct. SE14 ... 1A **122**
Jerningham Rd. SE14 ... 2A **122**
Jerome Cres. NW8 ... 3C **4** (4C **82**)
Jerome Ho. *KT1: Ham W* ... *2D **150***
(off Old Bri. St.)
NW1 ... *5D **4***
(off Lisson Gro.)
SW7 ... *3A **16***
(off Glendower Pl.)
Jerome Pl. *KT1: King T* ... *2D **150***
(off Wadbrook St.)
Jerome St. E1 ... 5J **9** (4F **85**)
Jerome Twr. W3 ... 2H **97**
Jerrard St. SE13 ... 3D **122**
Jerrold St. N1 ... 1H **9** (2E **84**)
Jersey Av. HA7: Stan ... 2B **42**
Jersey Dr. BR5: Pet W ... 6H **161**
Jersey Ho. *EN3: Enf W* ... *1E **24***
(off Eastfield Rd.)
N1 ... 6C **66**
Jersey Rd. E11 ... 1F **69**
E16 ... 6A **88**
IG1: Ilf ... 4F **71**
N1 ... 6C **66**
SW17 ... 6F **137**
TW3: Houn ... 1F **113**
TW5: Hest ... 1F **113**
TW7: Isle ... 7H **95**
W7 ... 2A **96**
Jersey St. E2 ... 3H **85**
Jerusalem Pas. EC1 ... 4A **8** (4B **84**)
Jervis Bay Ho. *E14* ... *6F **87***
(off Blair St.)
Jervis Ct. RM10: Dag ... 6H **73**
SE10 ... *1E **122***
(off Blissett St.)
W1 ... 1K **11**
Jervis Rd. SW6 ... 6H **99**
Jerviston Gdns. SW16 ... 6A **138**
Jerwood Space Art Gallery ... **6C 14**
Jesmond Av. HA9: Wemb ... 6F **61**
Jesmond Cl. CR4: Mitc ... 3F **155**
Jesmond Rd. CR0: Croy ... 7F **157**
Jesmond Way HA7: Stan ... 5K **27**
Jessam Av. E5 ... 1H **67**
Jessamine Rd. W7 ... 1K **95**
Jessel Ho. *SW1* ... *3D **18***
(off Page St.)
WC1 ... *2E **6***
(off Judd St.)
Jessel Mans. *W14* ... *6G **99***
(off Queen's Club Gdns.)
Jesse Rd. E10 ... 1E **68**
Jessett Cl. DA8: Erith ... 4K **109**
Jessica Rd. SW18 ... 6A **118**
Jessie Blythe La. N19 ... 7J **47**
Jessie Duffett Ho. *SE5* ... *7C **102***
(off Pitman St.)
Jessie Wood Ct. *SW9* ... *7A **102***
(off Caldwell St.)
Jessiman Ter. TW17: Shep ... 5C **146**
Jesson Ho. *SE17* ... *4D **102***
(off Orb St.)
Jessop Av. UB2: S'hall ... 4D **94**
Jessop Ct. N1 ... 2B **84**
Jessop Rd. SE24 ... 4B **120**
Jessop Sq. *E14* ... *1C **104***
(off Heron Quay)
Jessops Way CR0: Bedd, Mitc ... 6G **155**
Jessup Cl. SE18 ... 4G **107**
Jetstar Way UB5: N'olt ... 3C **76**
Jevington Way SE12 ... 1K **141**
Jevons Ho. *NW8* ... *7B **64***
(off Hilgrove Rd.)
Jewel House ... **3J 15**
(in The Tower of London)
Jewel Rd. E17 ... 3C **50**
Jewel Tower ... **1E 18**
(off College M.)
Jewish Mus.
Camden Town ... **1F 83**
Finchley ... **2K 45**
Jewry St. EC3 ... 1J **15** (6F **85**)
Jew's Row SW18 ... 4K **117**
Jews' Wlk. SE26 ... 4H **139**
Jeymer Av. NW2 ... 5D **62**
Jeymer Dr. UB6: G'frd ... 1F **77**
(not continuous)
Jeypore Pas. SW18 ... 6A **118**
Jeypore Rd. SW18 ... 7A **118**
Jillian Cl. TW12: Hamp ... 7E **130**
Jim Bradley Cl. SE18 ... 4E **106**
Jim Griffiths Ho. *SW6* ... *6H **99***
(off Clem Attlee Ct.)
Joan Bicknell Cen., The ... **2B 136**
Joan Cres. SE9 ... 7B **124**
Joan Gdns. RM8: Dag ... 2E **72**
Joanna Ho. *W6* ... *5E **98***
(off Queen Caroline St.)
Joan Rd. RM8: Dag ... 2E **72**
Joan St. SE1 ... 5A **14** (1B **102**)
Jocelin Ho. *N1* ... *1K **83***
(off Barnsbury Est.)
Jocelyn Rd. TW9: Rich ... 3E **114**
Jocelyn St. SE15 ... 1G **121**
Jockey's Flds. WC1 ... 5H **7** (5K **83**)
Jodane St. SE8 ... 4B **104**
Jodrell Cl. TW7: Isle ... 1A **114**
Jodrell Rd. E3 ... 1B **86**
Joe Hunte Ct. SE27 ... 5B **138**
Joel St. HA5: Eastc ... 3J **39**
HA6: Nwood ... 2J **39**
Johanna St. SE1 ... 7J **13** (2A **102**)
John Adams Ct. N9 ... 2A **34**
John Adam St. WC2 ... 3F **13** (7J **83**)
John Aird Ct. W2 ... 5A **4**
(not continuous)
John Archer Way SW18 ... 6B **118**
John Ashby Cl. SW2 ... 6J **119**
John Austin Cl. KT2: King T ... 1F **151**
John Baird Ct. SE26 ... 4J **139**
John Barker Ct. NW6 ... 7G **63**
John Barnes Wlk. E15 ... 6H **69**
John Betts' Ho. W12 ... 3B **98**
John Bradshaw Rd. N14 ... 1C **32**
John Brent Ho. *SE8* ... *4K **103***
(off Bush Rd.)
John Buck Ho. NW10 ... 1B **80**
John Burns Dr. IG11: Bark ... 7J **71**
John Campbell Rd. N16 ... 5E **66**
John Carpenter St. EC4 ... 2A **14** (7B **84**)
John Cartwright Ho. *E2* ... *3H **85***
(off Old Bethnal Grn. Rd.)
John Drinkwater Cl. E11 ... 7H **51**
John Fearon Wlk. *W10* ... *3G **81***
(off Dart St.)
John Felton Rd. SE16 ... 2G **103**
John Fielden Ho. *E2* ... *3H **85***
(off Canrobert St.)
John Fisher St. E1 ... 2K **15** (7G **85**)
John Goddard Way TW13: Felt ... 2K **129**
John Gooch Dr. EN2: Enf ... 1G **23**
John Harrison Way SE10 ... 3H **105**
John Horner M. N1 ... 2C **84**
John Islip St. SW1 ... 5D **18** (4H **101**)
John Kane Sports Hall ... **7K 95**
John Kaye Ct. TW17: Shep ... 5C **146**
John Keats Ho. N22 ... 7E **32**
John Kennedy Ct. *N1* ... *6D **66***
(off Newington Grn. Rd.)
John Kennedy Ho. *SE16* ... *4K **103***
(off Rotherhithe Old Rd.)
John Kirk Ho. *E6* ... *6E **88***
(off Pearl Cl.)
John Knight Lodge SW6 ... 7J **99**
John Lamb Ct. HA3: W'stone ... 1J **41**
John McDonald Ho. *E14* ... *3E **104***
(off Glengall Gro.)
John McKenna Wlk. SE16 ... 3G **103**
John Masefield Ho. *N15* ... *6D **48***
(off Fladbury Rd.)
John Maurice Cl. SE17 ... 4D **102**
John Newton Ct. DA16: Well ... 3B **126**
John Orwell Sports Cen. ... **1H 103**
John Parker Cl. RM10: Dag ... 7H **73**
John Parker Sq. SW11 ... 3B **118**
John Parry Ct. *N1* ... *2E **84***
(off Hare Wlk.)
John Penn Ho. *SE14* ... *7B **104***
(off Amersham Va.)
John Penn St. SE13 ... 1D **122**
John Penrose Sports Cen. ... **1A 38**
John Penry Ho. *SE1* ... *5G **103***
(off Marlborough Gro.)
John Perrin Pl. HA3: Kent ... 7E **42**
John Prince's St. W1 ... 7K **5** (6F **83**)
John Pritchard Ho. *E1* ... *4G **85***
(off Buxton St.)
John Ratcliffe Ho. *NW6* ... *3J **81***
(off Chippenham Gdns.)
John Rennie Wlk. E1 ... 7H **85**
John Roll Way SE16 ... 3G **103**
John Ruskin St. SE5 ... 7B **102**
John's Av. NW4 ... 4E **44**
John's Cl. TW15: Ashf ... 4E **128**
John Scurr Ho. *E14* ... *6A **86***
(off Ratcliffe La.)
John Silkin La. SE8 ... 5K **103**
John's La. SM4: Mord ... 5A **154**
John's M. WC1 ... 4H **7** (4K **83**)
John Smith Av. SW6 ... 7H **99**
John Smith M. E14 ... 7F **87**
Johnson Cl. E8 ... 1G **85**
Johnson Ho. *E2* ... *3G **85***
(off Roberta St.)
NW1 ... *2G **83***
(off Cranleigh St.)
NW3 ... *7D **64***
(off Adelaide Rd.)
SW1 ... *4H **17***
(off Cundy St.)
SW8 ... *7H **101***
(off Wandsworth Rd.)
Johnson Lodge *W9* ... *5J **81***
(off Admiral Wlk.)
Johnson Mans. *W14* ... *6G **99***
(off Queen's Club Gdns.)
Johnson Rd. BR2: Brom ... 5B **160**
CR0: Croy ... 7D **156**
NW10 ... 1K **79**
TW5: Hest ... 7A **94**
Johnsons Cl. SM5: Cars ... 2D **166**
Johnson's Ct. EC4 ... 6A **84**
Johnsons Dr. TW12: Hamp ... 1G **149**
Johnsons Ind. Est. UB3: Hayes ... 2H **93**
Johnson's Pl. SW1 ... 6A **18** (5G **101**)
Johnson St. E1 ... 7J **85**
UB2: S'hall ... 3A **94**
Johnsons Way NW10 ... 4H **79**
John Spencer Sq. N1 ... 6B **66**
John's Pl. E1 ... 6H **85**
John's Ter. CR0: Croy ... 1E **168**
Johnston Cl. SW9 ... 1K **119**
Johnston Ct. E10 ... 3D **68**
Johnstone Ho. *SE13* ... *3F **123***
(off Belmont Hill)
Johnstone Rd. E6 ... 3D **88**
Johnston Rd. IG8: Wfd G ... 6D **36**
Johnston Ter. NW2 ... 3F **63**
John Strachey Ho. *SW6* ... *6H **99***
(off Clem Attlee Ct.)
John St. E15 ... 1H **87**
EN1: Enf ... 5A **24**
SE25 ... 4G **157**
TW3: Houn ... 2C **112**
WC1 ... 4H **7** (4K **83**)
John Strype Ct. E10 ... 1D **68**
John Trundle Ct. EC2 ... 5C **8**
John Trundle Highwalk *EC2* ... *5C **8***
(off Beech St.)
John Tucker Ho. *E14* ... *3C **104***
(off Mellish St.)
John Watkin Cl. KT19: Eps ... 7H **163**
John Wesley Ct. TW1: Twick ... 1A **132**
John Wesley Highwalk *EC2* ... *6C **8***
(off Barbican)
John Wheatley Ho. *SW6* ... *6H **99***
(off Clem Attlee Ct.)
John Williams Cl. KT2: King T ... 1D **150**
SE14 ... 6K **103**
John Wilson St. SE18 ... 3E **106**
John Woolley Cl. SE13 ... 4G **123**
Joiners Arms Yd. SE5 ... 1D **120**
Joiners Pl. N5 ... 4D **66**
Joiner St. SE1 ... 5F **15** (1D **102**)
Joiners Yd. *N1* ... *1F **7***
(off Caledonia St.)
Joint Rd. N2 ... 1C **46**
Jollys La. HA2: Harr ... 1H **59**
UB4: Yead ... 5B **76**
Jonathan St. SE11 ... 5G **19** (5K **101**)
Jones Ho. *E14* ... *6F **87***
(off Blair St.)

Jones M. SW15 . . . . .4G 117
Jones Rd. E13 . . . . .4K 87
Jones St. W1 . . . . .3J 11 (7F 83)
Jones Wlk. TW10: Rich 6F 115
Jonquil Gdns. TW12: Hamp 6E 130
Jonson Cl. CR4: Mitc 4F 155
　UB4: Hayes 5J 75
Jonson Ho. SE1 . . . . .3D 102
　(off Burbage Ct.)
Jordan Cl. HA2: Harr 3D 58
　RM10: Dag 4H 73
Jordan Ct. SW15 . . . . .4F 117
Jordan Ho. N1 . . . . .1D 84
　(off Colville Est.)
　SE4 . . . . .4K 121
　(off St Norbert Rd.)
Jordan Rd. UB6: G'frd 1B 78
Jordans Cl. TW7: Isle 1J 113
Jordans Ho. NW8 . . . . .3B 4
Jordans M. TW2: Twick 2J 131
Joscoyne Ho. E1 . . . . .6H 85
　(off Philpot St.)
Joseph Av. W3 . . . . .6K 79
Joseph Conrad Ho. SW1 . . . . .4B 18
　(off Tachbrook St.)
Joseph Ct. N16 . . . . .6E 48
　(off Amhurst Pk.)
Joseph Hardcastle Cl. SE14 . . . . . .7K 103
Josephine Av. SW2 . . . . .5K 119
Joseph Irwin Ho. E14 . . . . .7B 86
　(off Gill St.)
Joseph Lister Ct. E7 . . . . .7J 69
Joseph Powell Cl. SW12 . . . . .6G 119
Joseph Priestley Ho. E2 . . . . .3H 85
　(off Canrobert St.)
Joseph Ray Rd. E11 . . . . .2G 69
Joseph St. E3 . . . . .4B 86
Joseph Trotter Cl. EC1 . . . . .2K 7
Joshua Cl. CR2: S Croy 7B 168
　N10 . . . . .7A 32
Joshua St. E14 . . . . .6E 86
Joslings Cl. W12 . . . . .7C 80
Joslyn Cl. EN3: Enf L 1H 25
Josseline Ct. E3 . . . . .2A 86
　(off Ford St.)
Joubert Mans. SW3 . . . . .5D 16
　(off Jubilee Pl.)
Joubert St. SW11 . . . . .2D 118
Jowett St. SE15 . . . . .7F 103
Jowitt Ho. E2 . . . . .3K 85
　(off Morpeth St.)
Joyce Av. N18 . . . . .5A 34
Joyce Butler Ho. N22 . . . . .1K 47
Joyce Dawson Way SE28 . . . . .7A 90
Joyce Latimore Ct. N9 . . . . .3C 34
　(off Colthurst Dr.)
Joyce Page Cl. SE7 . . . . .6B 106
Joyce Wlk. SW2 . . . . .6A 120
JOYDENS WOOD 4K 145
Joydens Wood (Nature Reserve)
　. . . . . .4H 145
Joydens Wood Rd. DA5: Bexl 4K 145
Joydon Dr. RM6: Chad H 6B 54
Joyners Cl. RM9: Dag 4F 73
Joystone Ct. EN4: E Barn 4H 21
　(off Park Rd.)
Jubb Powell Ho. N15 . . . . .6E 48
Jubilee, The SE10 . . . . .7D 104
Jubilee Av. E4 . . . . .6K 35
　RM7: Rom 5H 55
　TW2: Whit 1G 131
Jubilee Bldgs. NW8 . . . . .1B 82
Jubilee Cl. HA5: Pinn 2A 40
　KT1: Ham W 1C 150
　NW9 . . . . .6K 43
　NW10 .2A 80
　RM7: Rom 5H 55
Jubilee Country Pk. 4F 161
Jubilee Ct. BR4: W W'ck 1E 170
　HA3: Kent 7E 42
　N10 . . . . .3E 46
　TW3: Houn 3F 113
　(off Bristow Rd.)

Jubilee Cres. E14 . . . . .3E 104
　N9 . . . . .1B 34
Jubilee Dr. HA4: Ruis 4B 58
Jubilee Gdns. UB1: S'hall 5E 76
Jubilee Hall Sports Cen. 2F 13
　(off Tavistock St.)
Jubilee Ho. HA7: Stan 5J 27
　SE11 .4K 19
　(off Reedworth St.)
　WC1 . . . . .3G 7
Jubilee La. W5 . . . . .6E 78
Jubilee Mans. E1 . . . . .6J 85
　(off Jubilee St.)
Jubilee Mkt. IG8: Wfd G 6F 37
　WC2 . . . . .2F 13
Jubilee Pde. IG8: Wfd G 6F 37
Jubilee Pl. SW3 . . . . .5D 16 (5C 100)
Jubilee Pl. Shop. Mall E14 . . . . . . .1D 104
　(off Bank St.)
Jubilee Rd. SM3: Cheam 7F 165
　UB6: G'frd 1B 78
Jubilee Sports Cen. & Baths 3H 81
Jubilee St. E1 . . . . .6J 85
Jubilee Vs. KT10: Esh 7H 149
Jubilee Walkway SE1 . . . . .3B 14 (7B 84)
Jubilee Way DA14: Sidc 2A 144
　KT9: Chess 4G 163
　SW19 . . . . .1K 153
　TW14: Felt 1J 129
Jubilee Yd. SE1 . . . . .6J 15
Judd St. WC1 . . . . .2E 6 (3J 83)
Jude St. E16 . . . . .6H 87
Judge Heath La. UB3: Hayes 6E 74
Judges Wlk. NW3 . . . . .3A 64
Juer St. SW11 . . . . .7C 100
Jules Thorn Av. EN1: Enf 4B 24
Julia Ct. E17 . . . . .5D 50
Julia Gdns. IG11: Bark 2D 90
Julia Garfield M. E16 . . . . .1K 105
　(not continuous)
Juliana Cl. N2 . . . . .2A 46
Julian Av. W3 . . . . .7H 79
Julian Cl. EN5: New Bar 3E 20
Julian Hill HA1: Harr 2J 59
Julian Ho. SE21 . . . . .4E 138
Julian Pl. E14 . . . . .5D 104
Julian Tayler Path SE23 . . . . .2H 139
Julia St. NW5 . . . . .4E 64
Julien Rd. W5 . . . . .3C 96
Juliet Ho. N1 . . . . .2E 84
　(off Arden Est.)
Juliette Rd. E13 . . . . .2J 87
Julius Ho. E14 . . . . .6F 87
　(off E. India Dock Rd.)
Julius Nyerere Cl. N1 . . . . .1K 83
　(off Copenhagen St.)
Junction App. SE13 . . . . .3E 122
　SW11 . . . . .3C 118
Junction Av. NW10 . . . . .4E 80
Junction M. W2 . . . . .7C 4 (6C 82)
Junction Pl. W2 . . . . .7B 4
Junction Rd. CR2: S Croy 5D 168
　E13 . . . . .2K 87
　HA1: Harr 6J 41
　N9 . . . . .1B 34
　N17 . . . . .3G 49
　N19 . . . . .4G 65
　TW8: Bford 4C 96
　TW15: Ashf 5E 128
　W5 . . . . .4C 96
Junction Rd. E. RM6: Chad H 7E 54
Junction Rd. W. RM6: Chad H 7F 54
Juniper Cl. EN5: Barn 5A 20
　HA9: Wemb 5G 61
　KT9: Chess 6F 163
Juniper Ct. HA3: Hrw W 1K 41
　HA6: Nwood 1J 39
　KT8: W Mole 4F 149
　RM6: Chad H 6B 54
　TW3: Houn 4F 113
　(off Grove Rd.)
　W8 . . . . .3K 99
　(off St Mary's Pl.)

Juniper Cres. NW1 . . . . .7E 64
Juniper Gdns. SW16 . . . . .1G 155
　TW16: Sun 6H 129
Juniper Ho. SE14 . . . . .7J 103
　TW9: Kew 1H 115
　W10 . . . . .4G 81
　(off Fourth Av.)
Juniper La. E6 . . . . .5C 88
Juniper Rd. IG1: Ilf 3E 70
Juniper St. E1 . . . . .7J 85
Juniper Way UB3: Hayes 7F 75
Juno Ct. SW9 . . . . .7A 102
　(off Caldwell St.)
Juno Way SE14 . . . . .6K 103
Juno Way Ind. Est. SE14 . . . . .6K 103
Jupiter Ct. SW9 . . . . .7A 102
　(off Caldwell St.)
　UB5: N'olt 3B 76
　(off Seasprite Cl.)
Jupiter Hgts. UB10: Uxb 1B 74
Jupiter Ho. E14 . . . . .5D 104
　(off St Davids Sq.)
Jupiter Way N7 . . . . .6K 65
Jupp Rd. E15 . . . . .7F 69
Jupp Rd. W. E15 . . . . .1F 87
Jura Ho. SE16 . . . . .4K 103
　(off Plough Way)
Jurston Ct. SE1 . . . . .7K 13
Justice Wlk. SW3 . . . . . . .7C 16 (6C 100)
Justices Pl. E2 . . . . .3K 85
Justin Plaza CR4: Mitc 4C 154
Justin Rd. E4 . . . . .6G 35
Jute La. EN3: Brim 2F 25
Jutland Cl. N19 . . . . .1J 65
Jutland Ho. SE5 . . . . .2C 120
Jutland Rd. E13 . . . . .4J 87
　SE6 . . . . .7E 122
Jutsums Av. RM7: Rom 6H 55
Jutsums Ct. RM7: Rom 6H 55
Jutsums La. RM7: Rom, Rush G 6H 55
Juxon Cl. HA3: Hrw W 1F 41
Juxon Ho. EC4 . . . . .1B 14
　(off St Paul's Chyd.)
Juxon St. SE11 . . . . .3H 19 (4K 101)
JVC Bus. Pk. NW2 . . . . .1C 62

K

Kaduna Cl. HA5: Eastc 5J 39
Kale Rd. DA18: Erith 2D 108
Kambala Rd. SW11 . . . . .3B 118
Kangley Bri. Rd. SE26 . . . . .6B 140
Kangley Bus. Cen. SE26 . . . . .5B 140
Kaplan Dr. N21 . . . . .5E 22
Karanjia Ct. NW2 . . . . .6E 62
Kara Way NW2 . . . . .4F 63
Karen Ct. BR1: Brom 1H 159
Karen Ter. E11 . . . . .2H 69
Karenza Ct. HA9: Wemb 7C 42
Kariba Cl. N9 . . . . .3D 34
Karoline Gdns. UB6: G'frd 2H 77
Kashgar Rd. SE18 . . . . .4K 107
Kashmir Rd. SE7 . . . . .7B 106
Kassala Rd. SW11 . . . . .1D 118
Katella Trad. Est. IG11: Bark 3J 89
Katharine Ho. CR0: Croy 3C 168
　(off Katharine St.)
Katharine St. CR0: Croy 3C 168
Katherine Cl. SE16 . . . . .1K 103
Katherine Ct. SE23 . . . . .1H 139
Katherine Gdns. SE9 . . . . .4B 124
Katherine Ho. W10 . . . . .4G 81
　(off Portobello Rd.)
Katherine Rd. E6 . . . . .5A 70
　E7 . . . . .5A 70
　TW1: Twick 1A 132
Katherine Sq. W11 . . . . .1G 99
Kathleen Av. HA0: Wemb 7E 60
　W3 . . . . .5J 79
Kathleen Godfree Ct. SW19 . . . . . . .6J 135
Kathleen Rd. SW11 . . . . .3D 118

Kayemoor Rd. SM2: Sutt 6B 166
Kay Rd. SW9 . . . . .2J 119
Kay St. DA16: Well 1B 126
　E2 . . . . .2G 85
　E15 . . . . .7F 69
Kay Ter. E18 . . . . .1H 51
Kean Ho. SE17 . . . . .6B 102
　TW1: Twick 6D 114
　(off Arosa Rd.)
Kean St. WC2 . . . . .1G 13 (6K 83)
Keatley Grn. E4 . . . . .6G 35
Keats Av. E16 . . . . .1K 105
Keats Cl. E11 . . . . .5K 51
　EN3: Pond E 5E 24
　NW3 . . . . .4C 64
　SE1 . . . . .4F 103
　SW19 . . . . .6B 136
　UB4: Hayes 5J 75
Keats Est. N16 . . . . .2F 67
　(off Kyverdale Rd.)
Keats Gro. NW3 . . . . .4C 64
Keats House 4C 64
Keats Ho. E2 . . . . .3J 85
　(off Roman Rd.)
　SE5 . . . . .7C 102
　(off Elmington Est.)
　SW1 . . . . .7B 18
　(off Churchill Gdns.)
Keats Pde. N9 . . . . .2B 34
　(off Church St.)
Keats Pl. EC2 . . . . .6E 8
　(off Moorfields)
Keats Rd. DA16: Well 1J 125
　DA17: Belv 3J 109
Keats Way CR0: Croy 6J 157
　UB6: G'frd 5F 77
　UB7: W Dray 4B 92
Kebbell Ter. E7 . . . . .5K 69
　(off Claremont Rd.)
Keble Cl. KT4: Wor Pk 1B 164
　UB5: N'olt 5G 59
Keble Pl. SW13 . . . . .6D 98
Keble St. SW17 . . . . .4A 136
Kechill Gdns. BR2: Hayes 7J 159
Kedeston Ct. SM1: Sutt 1K 165
Kedge Ho. E14 . . . . .3C 104
　(off Tiller Rd.)
Kedleston Dr. BR5: St M Cry 6K 161
Kedleston Wlk. E2 . . . . .3H 85
Kedyngton Ho. HA8: Edg 2J 43
　(off Burnt Oak B'way.)
Keedonwood Rd. BR1: Brom 5G 141
Keel Cl. IG11: Bark 2C 90
　SE16 .1K 103
Keel Ct. E14 . . . . .7F 87
　(off Newport Av.)
Keeley Rd. CR0: Croy 2C 168
Keeley St. WC2 . . . . .1G 13 (6K 83)
Keeling Ho. E2 . . . . .2H 85
　(off Claredale St.)
Keeling Rd. SE9 . . . . .5B 124
Keelson Ho. E14 . . . . .3C 104
　(off Mellish St.)
Keely Cl. EN4: E Barn 5H 21
Keemor Cl. SE18 . . . . .7E 106
Keens Cl. SW16 . . . . .5H 137
Keens Rd. CR0: Croy 4C 168
Keen's Yd. N1 . . . . .6B 66
Keep, The KT2: King T 6F 133
　SE3 . . . . .2J 123
Keepers Ct. CR2: S Croy 5C 168
　(off Warham Rd.)
Keepers M. TW11: Tedd 6C 132
Keepier Wharf E14 . . . . .7K 85
　(off Narrow St.)
Keeton's Rd. SE16 . . . . .3H 103
　(not continuous)
Keevil Dr. SW19 . . . . .7F 117
Keighley Cl. N7 . . . . .5J 65
Keightley Dr. SE9 . . . . .1G 143
Keilder Cl. UB10: Hil 2C 74
Keildon Rd. SW11 . . . . .4D 118

Keir, The SW19 5E 134
Keir Hardie Ct. NW10 7B 62
Keir Hardie Est. E5 1H 67
Keir Hardie Ho. N19 7H 47
W6 6F 99
(off Fulham Pal. Rd.)
Keir Hardie Way IG11: Bark 7A 72
UB4: Yead 3J 75
Keith Connor Cl. SW8 3F 119
Keith Gro. W12 2C 98
Keith Ho. NW6 2K 81
(off Carlton Va.)
SW8 7J 101
(off Wheatsheaf La.)
Keith Pk. Rd. UB10: Uxb 7B 56
Keith Rd. E17 1B 50
IG11: Bark 2H 89
UB3: Hayes 3G 93
Kelbrook Rd. SE3 2C 124
Kelby Ho. N7 6K 65
(off Sutterton St.)
Kelby Path SE9 3F 143
Kelceda Cl. NW2 2C 62
Kelf Gro. UB3: Hayes 6H 75
Kelfield Ct. W10 6F 81
Kelfield Gdns. W10 6E 80
Kelfield M. W10 6F 81
Kelland Cl. N8 5H 47
Kelland Rd. E13 4J 87
Kellaway Rd. SE3 2B 124
Keller Cres. E12 4B 70
Kellerton Rd. SE13 5G 123
Kellet Ho's. WC1 2F 7
(off Tankerton St.)
Kellett Ho. N1 1E 84
(off Colville Est.)
Kellett Rd. SW2 4A 120
Kelling Gdns. CR0: Croy 7B 156
Kellino St. SW17 4D 136
Kellner Rd. SE28 3K 107
Kellogg Twr. UB6: G'frd 5J 59
Kellow Ho. SE1 6E 14
(off Tennis St.)
Kell St. SE1 7B 14 (3B 102)
Kelly Av. SE15 7F 103
Kelly Cl. NW10 3K 61
TW17: Shep 2G 147
Kelly Ct. E14 7C 86
(off Garford St.)
Kelly M. W9 4H 81
Kelly Rd. NW7 6B 30
Kelly St. NW1 6F 65
Kelly Way RM6: Chad H 5E 54
Kelman Cl. SW4 2H 119
Kelmore Gro. SE22 4G 121
Kelmscott Cl. E17 1B 50
Kelmscott Gdns. W12 3C 98
Kelmscott Leisure Cen. 6B 50
Kelmscott Rd. SW11 5C 118
Kelross Pas. N5 4C 66
Kelross Rd. N5 4C 66
Kelsall Cl. SE3 2K 123
Kelsey Ga. BR3: Beck 2D 158
Kelsey La. BR3: Beck 2C 158
Kelsey Pk. Av. BR3: Beck 2D 158
(not continuous)
Kelsey Pk. Rd. BR3: Beck 2C 158
Kelsey Sq. BR3: Beck 2C 158
Kelsey St. E2 4G 85
Kelsey Way BR3: Beck 3C 158
Kelson Ho. E14 3E 104
Kelso Pl. W8 3K 99
Kelso Rd. SM5: Cars 7A 154
Kelston Rd. IG6: Ilf 2F 53
Kelvedon Cl. KT2: King T 6G 133
Kelvedon Ho. SW8 1J 119
Kelvedon Rd. SW6 7H 99
Kelvedon Way IG8: Wfd G 6J 37
Kelvin Av. N13 6E 32
TW11: Tedd 6J 131
Kelvinbrook
KT8: W Mole 3F 149
Kelvin Cl. KT19: Ewe 6G 163
Kelvin Ct. SE20 1H 157
TW7: Isle 2J 113
W11 7J 81
Kelvin Cres. HA3: Hrw W 7D 26
Kelvin Dr. TW1: Twick 6B 114
Kelvin Gdns. CR0: Wadd 7J 155
UB1: S'hall 6E 76
Kelvin Gro. KT9: Chess 3D 162
SE26 3H 139
Kelvington Cl. CR0: Croy 7A 158
Kelvington Rd. SE15 5K 121
Kelvin Ind. Est. UB6: G'frd 7F 59
Kelvin Pde. BR6: Orp 1J 173
Kelvin Rd. DA16: Well 3A 126
N5 4C 66
Kember St. N1 7K 65
Kemble Dr. BR2: Brom 3C 172
Kemble Ho. SW9 3B 120
(off Barrington Rd.)
Kemble Rd. CR0: Wadd 3B 168
N17 1G 49
SE23 1K 139
Kemble St. WC2 1G 13 (6K 83)
Kemerton Rd. BR3: Beck 2D 158
CR0: Croy 7F 157
SE5 3C 120
Kemeys St. E9 5A 68
Kemnal Rd. BR7: Chst 4H 143
(not continuous)
Kemp NW9 1B 44
(off The Concourse)
Kemp Ct. SW8 7J 101
(off Hartington Rd.)
Kempe Ho. SE1 3D 102
(off Burge St.)
Kempe Rd. NW6 2F 81
Kemp Gdns. CR0: Croy 6C 156
Kemp Ho. E2 2K 85
(off Sewardstone Rd.)
E6 6E 70
W1 2C 12
(off Berwick St.)
Kempis Way SE22 5E 120
Kemplay Rd. NW3 4B 64
Kemp Rd. RM8: Dag 1D 72
Kemps Ct. W1 1C 12
(off Hopkins St.)
Kemps Dr. E14 7C 86
HA6: Nwood 1H 39
Kempsford Gdns. SW5 5J 99
Kempsford Rd. SE11 4K 19 (4A 102)
(not continuous)
Kemps Gdns. SE13 5E 122
Kempshott Rd. SW16 7H 137
Kempson Rd. SW6 1J 117
Kempthorne Rd. SE8 4B 104
Kempton Av. TW16: Sun 1K 147
UB5: N'olt 6E 58
Kempton Cl. DA8: Erith 6J 109
UB10: Ick 4E 56
Kempton Ct. E1 5H 85
TW16: Sun 1K 147
Kempton Ho. N1 1E 84
(off Hoxton St.)
Kempton Pk. Racecourse 7A 130
Kempton Rd. E6 1D 88
TW12: Hamp 2D 148
(not continuous)
Kempton Wlk. CR0: Croy 6A 158
Kempt St. SE18 6E 106
Kemsing Cl.
BR2: Hayes 2H 171
CR7: Thor H 4C 156
DA5: Bexl 7E 126
Kemsing Ho. SE1 7F 15
(off Long La.)
Kemsing Rd. SE10 5J 105
Kemsley SE13 5D 122
Kemsley Ct. W13 1C 96
Kenbrook Ho. NW5 5G 65
W14 3H 99
Kenbury Cl. UB10: Ick 3C 56
Kenbury Gdns. SE5 2C 120
Kenbury Mans. SE5 2C 120
(off Kenbury St.)
Kenbury St. SE5 2C 120
Kenchester Cl. SW8 7J 101
Kencot Way DA18: Erith 2F 109
Kendal NW1 1K 5
(off Augustus St.)
Kendal Av. IG11: Bark 1J 89
N18 4J 33
W3 4G 79
(not continuous)
Kendal Cl. IG8: Wfd G 2C 36
N20 2H 31
SW9 7B 102
TW14: Felt 1H 129
UB4: Hayes 2G 75
Kendal Ct. W3 5G 79
Kendale Rd. BR1: Brom 5G 141
Kendal Gdns. N18 4J 33
SM1: Sutt 2A 166
Kendal Ho. E9 1J 85
N1 2K 83
(off Priory Grn. Est.)
SE20 2G 157
(off Derwent Rd.)
Kendall Av. BR3: Beck 2A 158
CR2: Sand 7D 168
Kendall Ct. DA15: Sidc 3A 144
SW19 6B 136
Kendall Lodge BR1: Brom 1K 159
(off Willow Tree Wlk.)
Kendall Pl. W1 6G 5 (5E 82)
Kendall Rd. BR3: Beck 2A 158
SE18 1C 124
TW7: Isle 2A 114
Kendalmere Cl. N10 1F 47
Kendal Pde. N18 4J 33
Kendal Pl. SW15 5H 117
Kendal Rd. NW10 4C 62
Kendal Steps W2 1D 10
Kendal St. W2 1D 10 (6C 82)
Kender Est. SE14 1J 121
(off Queen's Rd.)
Kender St. SE14 7J 103
Kendoa Rd. SW4 4H 119
Kendon Cl. E11 5K 51
Kendra Hall Rd. CR2: S Croy 7B 168
Kendrey Gdns. TW2: Whit 7J 113
Kendrick Ct. SE15 1H 121
(off Woods Rd.)
Kendrick M. SW7 3A 16 (4B 100)
Kendrick Pl. SW7 4A 16 (4B 100)
Kenelm Cl. HA1: Harr 3A 60
Kenerne Dr. EN5: Barn 5B 20
Kenilford Rd. SW12 7F 119
Kenilworth Av. E17 2C 50
HA2: Harr 4D 58
SW19 5J 135
Kenilworth Cres. EN1: Enf 1K 23
Kenilworth Gdns. IG3: Ilf 2K 71
SE18 2F 125
UB1: S'hall 3D 76
UB4: Hayes 5H 75
Kenilworth Rd. BR5: Pet W 6G 161
E3 2A 86
HA8: Edg 3D 28
KT17: Ewe 5C 164
NW6 1H 81
SE20 1K 157
TW15: Ashf 3A 128
W5 1E 96
Kenley N17 2D 48
(off Gloucester Rd.)
Kenley Av. NW9 1A 44
Kenley Cl. BR7: Chst 3J 161
DA5: Bexl 7G 127
EN4: E Barn 4H 21
Kenley Gdns. CR7: Thor H 4B 156
Kenley Rd. KT1: King T 2H 151
SW19 2J 153
TW1: Twick 6B 114
Kenley Wlk. SM3: Cheam 4F 165
W11 7G 81
Kenlor Rd. SW17 5B 136
Kenmare Dr. CR4: Mitc 7D 136
N17 2F 49
Kenmare Gdns. N13 4H 33
Kenmare Rd. CR7: Thor H 6A 156
Kenmere Gdns. HA0: Wemb 1G 79
Kenmere Rd. DA16: Well 2C 126
Kenmont Gdns. NW10 3D 80
Kenmore Av. HA3: W'stone 4A 42
Kenmore Cl. TW9: Kew 7G 97
Kenmore Cres. UB4: Hayes 3H 75
Kenmore Gdns. HA8: Edg 2H 43
Kenmore Rd. HA3: Kent 3D 42
Kenmure Rd. E8 5H 67
Kenmure Yd. E8 5H 67
Kennacraig Cl. E16 1J 105
Kennard Ho. SW11 2E 118
Kennard Rd. E15 7F 69
N11 5J 31
Kennard St. E16 1D 106
SW11 1E 118
Kennedy Av. EN3: Pond E 6D 24
Kennedy Cl. BR5: Pet W 1H 173
CR4: Mitc 1E 154
E13 2J 87
Kennedy Ct. TW15: Ashf 5E 128
WD23: Bushy 2C 26
Kennedy Cox Ho. E16 5H 87
(off Burke St.)
Kennedy Ho. SE11 5G 19
(off Vauxhall Wlk.)
Kennedy Path W7 4K 77
Kennedy Rd. IG11: Bark 1J 89
W7 5J 77
Kennedy Wlk. SE17 4D 102
(off Elsted St.)
Kennet Cl. SW11 4B 118
Kennet Ct. W9 5J 81
(off Elmfield Way)
Kenneth Av. IG1: Ilf 4F 71
Kenneth Campbell Ho.
NW8 3B 4
(off Orchardson St.)
Kenneth Ct. SE11 3K 19 (4A 102)
Kenneth Cres. NW2 5D 62
Kenneth Gdns. HA7: Stan 6F 27
Kenneth More Rd. IG1: Ilf 3F 71
Kenneth More Theatre 3F 71
Kennet Ho. NW8 4B 4
(off Church St. Est.)
Kenneth Rd. RM6: Chad H 7D 54
Kenneth Robbins Ho. N17 7C 34
Kenneth Younger Ho. SW6 6H 99
(off Clem Attlee Ct.)
Kennet Rd. TW7: Isle 3K 113
W9 4H 81
Kennet Sq. CR4: Mitc 1C 154
Kennet St. E1 1G 103
Kennett Ct. W4 7H 97
Kennett Dr. UB4: Yead 5C 76
Kennett Wharf La. EC4 3D 14
KENNINGHALL JUNC. 5D 34
Kenninghall Rd. E5 3G 67
N18 5D 34
Kenning Ho. N1 1E 84
(off Colville Est.)
Kenning St. SE16 2J 103
Kennings Way SE11 5K 19 (5A 102)
KENNINGTON 7K 19 (6A 102)
Kennington Grn. SE11 6J 19 (5A 102)
Kennington Gro. SE11 7H 19 (6K 101)
Kennington La. SE11 6G 19 (5K 101)
KENNINGTON OVAL 6A 102
Kennington Oval SE11 7H 19 (6K 101)
Kennington Pal. Ct. SE11 5J 19
Kennington Pk. Gdns.
SE11 7K 19 (6B 102)
Kennington Pk. Ho. SE11 6K 19
Kennington Pk. Pl. SE11 7K 19 (6A 102)
Kennington Pk. Rd. SE11 7K 19 (6A 102)
Kennington Rd. SE1 1J 19 (3A 102)
SE11 1J 19 (3A 102)
Kennistoun Ho. NW5 5G 65

Kennoldes SE21 . . . . 2D 138
(off Croxted Rd.)
Kenny Dr. SM5: Cars 7E 166
Kennyland Ct. NW4 . . . . 6D 44
(off Hendon Way)
Kenny Rd. NW7 . . . . 6B 30
Kenrick Pl. W1 . . . . 6G 5 (5E 82)
KENSAL GREEN 3E 80
Kensal Ho. W10 . . . . 4F 81
(off Ladbroke Gro.)
KENSAL RISE 2F 81
Kensal Rd. W10 . . . . 4G 81
KENSAL TOWN 4G 81
Kensal Wharf W10 . . . . 4F 81
KENSINGTON 2K 99
Kensington Arc. W8 . . . . 2K 99
(off Kensington High St.)
Kensington Av. CR7: Thor H 1A 156
E12 . . . . 6C 70
Kensington Cen. W14 . . . . 4G 99
(not continuous)
Kensington Chu. Ct. W8 . . . . 2K 99
Kensington Chu. St. W8 . . . . 1J 99
Kensington Chu. Wlk. W8 . . . . 2K 99
(not continuous)
Kensington Cl. N11 . . . . 6K 31
Kensington Ct. SE16 . . . . 1K 103
(off King & Queen Wharf)
W8 . . . . 2K 99
Kensington Ct. Gdns. W8 . . . . 3K 99
(off Kensington Ct. Pl.)
Kensington Ct. M. W8 . . . . 3K 99
(off Kensington Ct. Pl.)
Kensington Ct. Pl. W8 . . . . 3K 99
Kensington Dr. IG8: Wfd G 2B 52
Kensington Gardens 5A 10 (1A 100)
Kensington Gdns. IG1: Ilf 1D 70
KT1: King T 3D 150
(not continuous)
Kensington Gdns. Sq. W2 . . . . 6K 81
(not continuous)
Kensington Ga. W8 . . . . 3A 100
Kensington Gore SW7 . . . . 7A 10 (2A 100)
Kensington Hall Gdns. W14 . . . . 5H 99
Kensington Hgts. HA1: Harr 6K 41
(off Sheepcote Rd.)
W8 . . . . 1J 99
Kensington High St. W8 . . . . 3H 99
W14 . . . . 3H 99
Kensington Ho. IG8: Ilf 7K 37
W8 . . . . 2K 99
(off Kensington Ct.)
W14 . . . . 2F 99
Kensington Mall W8 . . . . 1J 99
Kensington Mans. SW5 . . . . 5J 99
(off Trebovir Rd., not continuous)
Kensington Palace 2K 99
Kensington Pal. Gdns. W8 . . . . 1K 99
Kensington Pk. Gdns. W11 . . . . 7H 81
Kensington Pk. M. W11 . . . . 6H 81
Kensington Pk. Rd. W11 . . . . 6H 81
Kensington Pl. W8 . . . . 1J 99
Kensington Rd. RM7: Rom 6J 55
SW7 . . . . 2A 100
UB5: N'olt 3E 76
W8 . . . . 2A 100
Kensington Sports Cen. 7G 81
Kensington Sq. W8 . . . . 3K 99
Kensington Ter. CR2: S Croy 7D 168
Kensington Village W14 . . . . 4H 99
Kensington W. W14 . . . . 4G 99
Kensworth Ho. EC1 . . . . 2F 9
(off Cranwood St.)
Kent Av. DA16: Well 5K 125
RM9: Dag 4G 91
W13 . . . . 5B 78
Kent Cl. BR6: Chels 6J 173
CR4: Mitc 4J 155
Kent Ct. E2 . . . . 2F 85
NW9 . . . . 2A 44
Kent Dr. EN4: Cockf 4K 21
TW11: Tedd 5J 131
Kentford Way UB5: N'olt 1C 76
Kent Gdns. HA4: Ruis 6J 39
W13 . . . . 5B 78
Kent Ga. Way CR0: Addtn 6B 170
Kent Ho. SE1 . . . . 5F 103
SW1 . . . . 5C 18
(off Aylesford St.)
W4 . . . . 5A 98
(off Devonshire St.)
W8 . . . . 2K 99
(off Kensington Ct.)
W11 . . . . 1H 99
(off Boyne Ter. M.)
Kent Ho. App. Rd. BR3: Beck 1A 158
Kent Ho. Rd. BR3: Beck 1K 157
SE26 . . . . 5A 140
Kentish Bldgs. SE1 . . . . 5E 14 (2D 102)
Kentish Rd. DA17: Belv 4G 109
KENTISH TOWN 5F 65
Kentish Town Forum 5F 65
Kentish Town Ind. Est. NW5 . . . . 5F 65
Kentish Town Rd. NW1 . . . . 7F 65
NW5 . . . . 7F 65
Kentish Town Sports Cen. 6F 65
Kentish Way BR1: Brom 2K 159
BR2: Brom 2K 159
Kentlea Rd. SE28 . . . . 2J 107
Kentmere Ho. SE15 . . . . 6J 103
Kentmere Mans. W5 . . . . 4B 78
Kentmere Rd. SE18 . . . . 4J 107
KENTON 5C 42
Kenton Av. HA1: Harr 7K 41
TW16: Sun 2B 148
UB1: S'hall 7E 76
Kenton Ct. HA3: Kent 6B 42
SE26 . . . . 4A 140
(off Adamsrill Rd.)
TW1: Twick 6D 114
W14 . . . . 3H 99
Kentone Ct. SE25 . . . . 4H 157
Kenton Gdns. HA3: Kent 5C 42
Kenton Ho. E1 . . . . 4J 85
(off Mantus Cl.)
Kenton La.
HA3: Hrw W, Kent, W'stone 6E 26
Kenton Pk. Av. HA3: Kent 5D 42
Kenton Pk. Cl. HA3: Kent 4C 42
Kenton Pk. Cres. HA3: Kent 4D 42
Kenton Pk. Mans. HA3: Kent 5C 42
(off Kenton Rd.)
Kenton Pk. Pde. HA3: Kent 5C 42
Kenton Pk. Rd. HA3: Kent 4C 42
Kenton Rd. E9 . . . . 6K 67
HA1: Harr 7K 41
HA3: Kent 6A 42
Kenton St. WC1 . . . . 3E 6 (4J 83)
Kenton Way UB4: Hayes 3G 75
Kent Pk. Ind. Est. SE15 . . . . 6H 103
Kent Pas. NW1 . . . . 3E 4 (4D 82)
Kent Rd. BR4: W W'ck 1D 170
KT1: King T 3D 150
KT8: E Mos 4G 149
N21 . . . . 1J 33
RM10: Dag 5H 73
TW9: Kew 7G 97
W4 . . . . 3J 97
Kent's Pas. TW12: Hamp 1D 148
Kent St. E2 . . . . 2F 85
E13 . . . . 3A 88
Kent Ter. NW1 . . . . 2D 4 (3C 82)
Kent Vw. Gdns. IG3: Ilf 2J 71
Kent Wlk. SW9 . . . . 4B 120
Kent Way KT6: Surb 3E 162
Kentwell Cl. SE4 . . . . 4A 122
Kent Wharf SE8 . . . . 7D 104
(off Creekside)
Kentwode Grn. SW13 . . . . 7C 98
Kent Yd. SW7 . . . . 7D 10 (2C 100)
Kenver Av. N12 . . . . 6G 31
Kenward Rd. SE9 . . . . 5A 124
Kenward Way SW11 . . . . 2E 118
Ken Way HA9: Wemb 3J 61
Kenway RM5: Col R 2J 55
Kenway Rd. SW5 . . . . 4K 99
Ken Wilson Ho. E2 . . . . 2G 85
(off Pritchards Rd.)
Kenwood Av. N14 . . . . 5C 22
Kenwood Cl. NW3 . . . . 1B 64
UB7: Sip 6C 92
Kenwood Ct. NW9 . . . . 4J 43
(off Elmwood Cres.)
Kenwood Dr.
BR3: Beck 3E 158
Kenwood Gdns. E18 . . . . 3K 51
IG2: Ilf 5E 52
IG5: Ilf 4E 52
Kenwood House 1C 64
Kenwood Ho. SW9 . . . . 4B 120
Kenwood Rd. N6 . . . . 6D 46
N9 . . . . 1B 34
Kenworthy Rd. E9 . . . . 5A 68
Kenwrick Ho. N1 . . . . 1K 83
(off Barnsbury Est.)
Kenwyn Dr. NW2 . . . . 2A 62
Kenwyn Lodge N2 . . . . 4D 46
Kenwyn Rd. SW4 . . . . 4H 119
SW20 . . . . 1E 152
Kenya Rd. SE7 . . . . 7B 106
Kenyngton Ct. TW16: Sun 5J 129
Kenyngton Dr. TW16: Sun 5J 129
Kenyngton Pl. HA3: Kent 5C 42
Kenyon Mans. W14 . . . . 6G 99
(off Queen's Club Gdns.)
Kenyon St. SW6 . . . . 1F 117
Keogh Rd. E15 . . . . 6G 69
Kepler Ho. SE10 . . . . 5H 105
(off Armitage Rd.)
Kepler Rd. SW4 . . . . 4J 119
Keppel Ho. SE8 . . . . 5B 104
SW3 . . . . 4C 16
(off Elystan St.)
Keppel Rd. E6 . . . . 7D 70
RM9: Dag 4E 72
Keppel Row SE1 . . . . 5C 14 (1C 102)
Keppel St. WC1 . . . . 5D 6 (5H 83)
Kerbela St. E2 . . . . 3K 9 (4G 85)
Kerbey St. E14 . . . . 6D 86
Kerfield Cres. SE5 . . . . 1D 120
Kerfield Pl. SE5 . . . . 1D 120
Kerridge Ct. N1 . . . . 6E 66
(off Balls Pond Rd.)
Kerrier Ho. SW10 . . . . 7A 100
(off Stadium St.)
Kerrington Ct. W12 . . . . 2E 98
(off Uxbridge Rd.)
Kerrison Pl. W5 . . . . 1D 96
Kerrison Rd. E15 . . . . 1F 87
SW11 . . . . 3C 118
W5 . . . . 1D 96
Kerrison Vs. W5 . . . . 1D 96
Kerry N7 . . . . 6J 65
Kerry Av. HA7: Stan 4H 27
Kerry Cl. E16 . . . . 6K 87
N13 . . . . 2E 32
Kerry Ct. HA7: Stan 4J 27
Kerry Ho. E1 . . . . 6J 85
(off Sidney St.)
Kerry Path SE14 . . . . 6B 104
Kerry Rd. SE14 . . . . 6B 104
Kersey Gdns. SE9 . . . . 4C 142
Kersfield Ho. SW15 . . . . 6F 117
Kersfield Rd. SW15 . . . . 6F 117
Kershaw Cl. SW18 . . . . 6B 118
Kershaw Rd. RM10: Dag 3G 73
Kersley M. SW11 . . . . 1D 118
Kersley Rd. N16 . . . . 2E 66
Kersley St. SW11 . . . . 2D 118
Kerstin Cl. UB3: Hayes 7H 75
Kerswell Cl. N15 . . . . 5E 48
Kerwick Cl. N7 . . . . 7J 65
Keslake Mans. NW10 . . . . 2F 81
(off Station Ter.)
Keslake Rd. NW6 . . . . 2F 81
Kessock Cl. N17 . . . . 5H 49
Kestlake Rd. DA5: Bexl 6C 126
KESTON 5A 172
Keston Av. BR2: Kes 5A 172
Keston Cl. DA16: Well 7C 108
N18 . . . . 3J 33
Keston Ct. DA5: Bexl 7F 127
KT5: Surb 5F 151
(off Cranes Pk.)
Keston Gdns. BR2: Kes 4A 172
Keston Ho. SE17 . . . . 5E 102
(off Kinglake St.)
KESTON MARK 4C 172
KESTON MARK 3C 172
Keston Pk. Cl. BR2: Kes 3D 172
Keston Rd. CR7: Thor H 6A 156
N17 . . . . 3D 48
SE15 . . . . 3G 121
Kestrel Av. E6 . . . . 5C 88
SE24 . . . . 5B 120
Kestrel Cl. KT2: King T 4D 132
NW9 . . . . 2A 44
NW10 . . . . 5K 61
Kestrel Ct. CR2: S Croy 6C 168
E17 . . . . 2K 49
HA4: Ruis 2G 57
SM6: Wall 5G 167
Kestrel Ho. EC1 . . . . 1C 8
(off Pickard St.)
EN3: Pond E 5F 25
Kestrel Pl. SE14 . . . . 6A 104
Kestrel Way CR0: New Ad 7F 171
UB3: Hayes 2F 93
Keswick Av. SW15 . . . . 5A 134
SW19 . . . . 2J 153
TW17: Shep 3G 147
Keswick Broadway SW15 . . . . 5H 117
(off Up. Richmond Rd.)
Keswick Cl. SM1: Sutt 4A 166
Keswick Ct. BR2: Brom 4H 159
SE6 . . . . 1H 141
SE13 . . . . 5D 122
Keswick Gdns. HA4: Ruis 6F 39
HA9: Wemb 4E 60
IG4: Ilf 4C 52
Keswick Ho. SE5 . . . . 2C 120
Keswick M. W5 . . . . 1E 96
Keswick Rd. BR4: W W'ck 2G 171
BR6: Orp 1K 173
DA7: Bex 1G 127
SW15 . . . . 5G 117
TW2: Whit 6G 113
Kettering Ct. CR7: Thor H 4C 156
Kettering St. SW16 . . . . 6G 137
Kett Gdns. SW2 . . . . 5K 119
Kettlebaston Rd. E10 . . . . 1B 68
Kettleby Ho. SW9 . . . . 3B 120
(off Barrington Rd.)
Kettlewell Cl. N11 . . . . 6K 31
Ketton Ho. W10 . . . . 4E 80
(off Sutton Way)
Kevan Ct. E17 . . . . 4C 50
Kevan Ho. SE5 . . . . 7C 102
Kevelioc Rd. N17 . . . . 1C 48
Kevin Cl. TW4: Houn 2B 112
Kevington Cl. BR5: St P 4K 161
Kevington Dr. BR5: St P 4K 161
BR7: Chst 4K 161
KEW 7G 97
KEW BRIDGE 5F 97
Kew Bri. TW8: Bford 6G 97
TW9: Kew 6G 97
Kew Bri. Arches TW9: Kew 6G 97
Kew Bri. Ct. W4 . . . . 5G 97
Kew Bri. Distribution Cen.
TW8: Bford 5F 97
Kew Bri. Rd. TW8: Bford 6F 97
Kew Bridge Steam Mus. 5F 97
Kew Ct. KT2: King T 1E 150
Kew Cres. SM3: Cheam 3G 165
Kew Foot Rd. TW9: Rich 4E 114
Kew Gdns. 7E 96
Kew Gdns. Plants & People Exhibition
. . . . 7F 97
Kew Gdns. Rd. TW9: Kew 7F 97
Kew Gdns. Vis. Cen. 1F 115
KEW GREEN 7G 97

Kew Grn. TW9: Kew 6F **97**
Kew Mdw. Path TW9: Kew 1H **115**
TW9: Rich 2J **115**
Kew Palace 6F **97**
Kew Retail Pk. TW9: Kew 1H **115**
Kew Riverside Pk.
TW9: Kew 7H **97**
Kew Rd. TW9: Kew 6G **97**
TW9: Rich 4E **114**
Keybridge Ho. *SW8* *7F* ***19***
(off Miles St.)
Key Cl. E1 4J **85**
Keyes Ho. *SW1* *6C* ***18***
(off Dolphin Sq.)
Keyes Rd. NW2 5F **63**
Keyham Ho. *W2* *5J* ***81***
(off Park Rd.)
Key Ho. SE11 7K **19** (6A **102**)
Keymer Rd. SW2 2K **137**
Keynes Cl. N2 4D **46**
Keynes Ct. *SE28* *7B* ***90***
(off Attlee Rd.)
Keynsham Av. IG8: Wfd G 4B **36**
Keynsham Gdns. SE9 5C **124**
Keynsham Rd. SE9 5B **124**
SM4: Mord 1K **165**
Keynsham Wlk. SM4: Mord 1K **165**
Keys Ct. *CR0: Croy* *3D* ***168***
(off Beech Ho. Rd.)
Keyse Rd. SE1 3F **103**
Keysham Av. TW5: Cran 1J **111**
Keystone Cres. N1 1F **7** (2J **83**)
Keywood Dr. TW16: Sun 6J **129**
Keyworth Cl. E5 4A **68**
Keyworth Pl. SE1 7B **14**
Keyworth St. SE1 7B **14** (3B **102**)
Kezia M. SE8 5A **104**
Kezia St. SE8 5A **104**
Khalsa Ct. N22 1B **48**
Khama Rd. SW17 4C **136**
Khartoum Rd. E13 3K **87**
IG1: Ilf 5F **71**
SW17 4B **136**
Khyber Rd. SW11 2C **118**
Kibworth St. SW8 7K **101**
KIDBROOKE 2K **123**
Kidbrooke Est. SE3 3A **124**
Kidbrooke Gdns. SE3 2J **123**
Kidbrooke Green Nature Reserve 3A **124**
Kidbrooke Gro. SE3 1J **123**
Kidbrooke La. SE9 4C **124**
Kidbrooke Pk. Cl. SE3 1K **123**
Kidbrooke Pk. Rd. SE3 1K **123**
Kidbrooke Way SE3 2K **123**
Kidderminster Pl. CR0: Croy 1B **168**
Kidderminster Rd. CR0: Croy 1B **168**
Kidderpore Av. NW3 4J **63**
Kidderpore Gdns. NW3 4J **63**
Kidd Pl. SE7 5C **106**
Kierbeck Bus. Complex E16 2K **105**
Kiffen St. EC2 3F **9** (4D **84**)
Kilberry Cl. TW7: Isle 1H **113**
Kilbrennan Ho. *E14* *6E* ***86***
(off Findhorn St.)
KILBURN 2H **81**
Kilburn Bri. NW6 1J **81**
Kilburn Ga. NW6 2K **81**
Kilburn High Rd. NW6 7H **63**
Kilburn Ho. *NW6* *2H* ***81***
(off Malvern Pl.)
Kilburn La. W9 3F **81**
W10 3F **81**
Kilburn Pk. Rd. NW6 3J **81**
Kilburn Pl. NW6 1J **81**
Kilburn Priory NW6 1K **81**
Kilburns Mill Cl. SM6: Wall 2F **167**
Kilburn Sq. NW6 1J **81**
Kilburn Va. NW6 1K **81**
Kilburn Va. Est. *NW6* *1K* ***81***
(off Kilburn Va.)
Kilby Ct. *SE10* *3H* ***105***
(off School Bank Rd.)
Kildare Cl. HA4: Ruis 1A **58**
Kildare Ct. *W2* *6J* ***81***
(off Kildare Ter.)
Kildare Gdns. W2 6J **81**
Kildare Rd. E16 5J **87**
Kildare Ter. W2 6J **81**
Kildare Wlk. E14 6C **86**
Kildoran Rd. SW2 5J **119**
Kildowan Rd. IG3: Ilf 1A **72**
Kilgour Rd. SE23 6A **122**
Kilkie St. SW6 2A **118**
Killarney Rd. SW18 6A **118**
Killearn Rd. SE6 1F **141**
Killester Gdns. KT4: Wor Pk 4D **164**
Killick Ho. SM1: Sutt 4K **165**
Killick St. N1 1G **7** (2K **83**)
Killieser Av. SW2 2J **137**
Killigarth Ct. DA14: Sidc 4A **144**
Killigrew Ho. TW16: Sun 7G **129**
Killip Cl. E16 6H **87**
Killoran Ho. *E14* *3E* ***104***
(off Galbraith St.)
Killowen Av. UB5: N'olt 5G **59**
Killowen Rd. E9 6K **67**
Killyon Rd. SW8 2G **119**
Killyon Ter. SW8 2G **119**
Kilmaine Rd. SW6 7G **99**
Kilmarnock Gdns. RM8: Dag 3C **72**
Kilmarsh Rd. W6 4E **98**
Kilmartin Av. SW16 3A **156**
Kilmartin Rd. IG3: Ilf 2A **72**
Kilmington Rd. SW13 6C **98**
Kilmiston Av. TW17: Shep 6E **146**
Kilmiston Ho. TW17: Shep 6E **146**
Kilmore Ho. *E14* *6D* ***86***
(off Vesey Path)
Kilmorey Gdns. TW1: Twick 5B **114**
Kilmorey Rd. TW1: Twick 4B **114**
Kilmorie Rd. SE23 1A **140**
Kilmuir Ho. *SW1* *4H* ***17***
(off Bury St.)
Kiln Cl. UB3: Harl 6F **93**
Kiln Ct. *E14* *7B* ***86***
(off Newell St.)
Kilner Ho. *E16* *5K* ***87***
(off Freemasons Rd.)
SE11 7J **19**
Kilner St. E14 5C **86**
Kiln M. SW17 5B **136**
Kiln Pl. NW5 5E **64**
Kilnside KT10: Clay 7A **162**
Kilpatrick Way UB4: Yead 5C **76**
Kilravock St. W10 3G **81**
Kilronan W3 6K **79**
Kilross Rd. TW14: Bedf 1F **129**
Kilsby Wlk. RM9: Dag 6B **72**
Kilsha Rd. KT12: Walt T 6A **148**
Kimbell Gdns. SW6 1G **117**
Kimbell Pl. SE3 4A **124**
Kimber Ct. *SE1* *7G* ***15***
(off Long La.)
Kimberley Av. E6 2C **88**
IG2: Ilf 7H **53**
RM7: Rom 6J **55**
SE15 2H **121**
Kimberley Dr. DA14: Sidc 2D **144**
Kimberley Gdns. EN1: Enf 3A **24**
N4 5B **48**
Kimberley Ga. BR1: Brom 7G **141**
Kimberley Ho. *E14* *3E* ***104***
(off Galbraith St.)
Kimberley Ind. Est. E17 1B **50**
Kimberley Rd. BR3: Beck 2K **157**
CR0: Croy 6B **156**
E4 1B **36**
E11 2F **69**
E16 4H **87**
E17 1A **50**
N17 2G **49**
N18 6C **34**
NW6 1G **81**
SW9 2J **119**
Kimberley Wlk. KT12: Walt T 7K **147**
Kimberley Way E4 1B **36**
Kimber Rd. SW18 7J **117**
Kimble Cres. WD23: Bush 1B **26**
Kimble Ho. NW8 3D **4**
Kimble Rd. SW19 6B **136**
Kimbolton Cl. SE12 6H **123**
Kimbolton Ct. *SW3* *4C* ***16***
(off Fulham Rd.)
Kimbolton Row *SW3* *4C* ***16***
(off Fulham Rd.)
Kimmeridge Gdns. SE9 4C **142**
Kimmeridge Rd. SE9 4C **142**
Kimpton Ho. SW15 7C **116**
Kimpton Ind. Est. SM3: Sutt 2H **165**
Kimpton Link Bus. Cen.
SM3: Sutt 2H **165**
Kimpton Pk. Way SM1: Sutt 2G **165**
SM3: Sutt 2G **165**
Kimpton Rd. SE5 1D **120**
SM3: Sutt 2H **165**
Kimpton Trade & Bus. Cen.
SM3: Sutt 2H **165**
Kinburn St. SE16 2K **103**
Kincaid Rd. SE15 7H **103**
Kincardine Gdns. *W9* *4J* ***81***
(off Harrow Rd.)
Kincha Lodge *KT2: King T* *1F* ***151***
(off Elm Rd.)
Kinch Gro. HA3: Kent 7F **43**
Kinder Cl. SE28 7D **90**
Kinder Ho. *N1* *2D* ***84***
(off Cranston Est.)
Kindersley Ho. *E1* *6G* ***85***
(off Pinchin St.)
Kinder St. E1 6H **85**
Kinderton Cl. N14 1B **32**
Kinefold Ho. N7 6J **65**
Kinfauns Rd. IG3: Ilf 1A **72**
SW2 2A **138**
King Alfred Av. SE6 4C **140**
(not continuous)
King & Queen Cl. SE9 4C **142**
King & Queen St. SE17 5C **102**
King & Queen Wharf SE16 7K **85**
King Arthur Cl. SE15 7J **103**
King Charles I Island WC2 4E **12**
King Charles Ct. *SE17* *6B* ***102***
(off Royal Rd.)
King Charles Cres. KT5: Surb 7F **151**
King Charles Ho. *SW6* *7K* ***99***
(off Wandon Rd.)
King Charles Rd. KT5: Surb 5F **151**
King Charles's Ct. *SE10* *6E* ***104***
(off Park Row)
King Charles St. SW1 6D **12** (2H **101**)
King Charles Ter. *E1* *7H* ***85***
(off Sovereign Cl.)
King Charles Wlk. SW19 1G **135**
King Ct. E10 7D **50**
Kingcup Cl. CR0: Croy 7K **157**
King David La. E1 7J **85**
Kingdon Ho. *E14* *3E* ***104***
(off Galbraith St.)
Kingdon Rd. NW6 6J **63**
King Edward III M. SE16 2H **103**
King Edward Bldg. EC1 6B **84**
King Edward Dr. KT9: Chess 3E **162**
King Edward Mans. *E8* *1H* ***85***
(off Mare St.)
King Edward M. SW13 1C **116**
King Edward Rd. E10 1E **68**
E17 3A **50**
EN5: New Bar 4D **20**
King Edward's Gdns. W3 1G **97**
King Edwards Gro. TW11: Tedd 6B **132**
King Edwards Mans. *SW6* *7J* ***99***
(off Fulham Rd.)
King Edward's Pl. W3 1G **97**
King Edwards Rd. E9 1H **85**
EN3: Pond E 4E **24**
HA4: Ruis 1F **57**
IG11: Bark 1H **89**
N9 7C **24**
King Edward St. EC1 7C **8** (6C **84**)
King Edward Wlk. SE1 1K **19** (3A **102**)
Kingfield Rd. W5 4D **78**
Kingfield St. E14 4E **104**
Kingfisher Av. E11 6K **51**
Kingfisher Cl. HA3: Hrw W 7E **26**
HA6: Nwood 1D **38**
SE28 7C **90**
Kingfisher Ct. *E14* *2E* ***104***
(off River Barge Cl.)
EN2: Enf 1E **22**
KT8: E Mos 4J **149**
SE1 *7D* ***14***
(off Swan St.)
SM1: Sutt 5H **165**
SW19 2F **135**
TW3: Houn 5F **113**
Kingfisher Dr. TW10: Ham 4B **132**
Kingfisher Ho. SW18 3A **118**
W14 *3H* ***99***
(off Melbury Rd.)
Kingfisher Leisure Cen., The 2E **150**
Kingfisher M. SE13 4C **122**
Kingfisher Pl. N22 2K **47**
Kingfisher Sq. *SE8* *6B* ***104***
(off Clyde St.)
Kingfisher St. E6 5C **88**
Kingfisher Wlk. NW9 2A **44**
Kingfisher Way BR3: Beck 5K **157**
NW10 6K **61**
King Frederick IX Twr. SE16 3B **104**
King Gdns. CR0: Wadd 5B **168**
King George IV Ct. *SE17* *5D* ***102***
(off Dawes St.)
King George VI Av. CR4: Mitc 4D **154**
King George VI Memorial
5C **12** (1H **101**)
King George Av. E16 6A **88**
IG2: Ilf 5H **53**
King George Cl.
RM7: Mawney 3J **55**
TW16: Sun 5G **129**
King George's Dr. UB1: S'hall 5D **76**
King George Sq. TW10: Rich 6F **115**
King George's Trad. Est.
KT9: Chess 4G **163**
King George St. SE10 7E **104**
Kingham Cl. SW18 7A **118**
W11 2G **99**
King Harolds Way
DA7: Belv, Bex 7D **108**
DA17: Belv 7D **108**
King Henry M. BR6: Chels 5K **173**
HA2: Harr 1J **59**
King Henry's Dr. CR0: New Ad 7D **170**
King Henry's Reach W6 6E **98**
King Henry's Rd. KT1: King T 3H **151**
NW3 7C **64**
King Henry's Stairs E1 1H **103**
King Henry St. N16 5E **66**
King Henry's Wlk. N1 6E **66**
King Henry Ter. *E1* *7H* ***85***
(off Sovereign Cl.)
Kinghorn St. EC1 6C **8** (5C **84**)
King Ho. W12 6D **80**
King James Ct. SE1 7B **14**
King James St. SE1 7B **14** (2B **102**)
King John Ct. EC2 3H **9** (4E **84**)
King John St. E1 5K **85**
King John's Wlk. SE9 7C **124**
(not continuous)
Kinglake Est. SE17 5E **102**
Kinglake St. SE17 5E **102**
(not continuous)
Kinglet Cl. E7 6J **69**
Kingly Ct. W1 2B **12**
Kingly St. W1 1A **12** (6G **83**)
Kingsand Rd. SE12 2J **141**
Kings Arbour UB2: S'hall 5C **94**
King's Arms All.
TW8: Bford 6D **96**
Kings Arms Ct. E1 5G **85**
Kings Arms Yd. EC2 7E **8** (6D **84**)
Kingsash Dr. UB4: Yead 4C **76**

Kings Av. BR1: Brom 6H 141
  IG8: Wfd G 6E 36
  IG9: Buck H 2G 37
    (Queen's Rd.)
  IG9: Buck H 6E 36
    (Station Way)
  KT3: N Mald 4A 152
  N10 ....3E 46
  N21 ....1G 33
  RM6: Chad H 6F 55
  SM5: Cars 7C 166
  SW4 ....1H 137
  SW12 ....1H 137
  TW3: Houn 1F 113
  TW16: Sun 5H 129
  UB6: G'frd 5F 77
  W5 ....6D 78
King's Bench St. SE1 ....6B 14 (2B 102)
King's Bench Wlk. EC4 ....1K 13 (6A 84)
Kingsbridge Av. W3 ....2F 97
Kingsbridge Ct. E14 ....3C 104
    (off Dockers Tanner Rd.)
  NW1 ....7F 65
    (off Castlehaven Rd.)
Kingsbridge Cres. NW11 ....5D 76
Kingsbridge Dr. NW7 ....7A 30
Kingsbridge Rd. IG11: Bark 2H 89
  KT12: Walt T 7K 147
  SM4: Mord 6F 153
  UB2: S'hall 4D 94
  W10 ....6E 80
Kingsbridge Way UB4: Hayes 3G 75
Kingsbridge Wharf IG11: Bark 3J 89
KINGSBURY 5H 43
Kingsbury Circ. NW9 ....5G 43
KINGSBURY GREEN 5J 43
Kingsbury Rd. N1 ....6E 66
  NW9 ....5G 43
Kingsbury Sports Cen. 4H 43
Kingsbury Ter. N1 ....6E 66
Kingsbury Trad. Est. NW9 ....6K 43
Kings Chase KT8: E Mos 3G 149
Kings Chase Vw. EN2: Enf 2F 23
Kingsclere Cl. SW15 ....7C 116
Kingsclere Ct. N12 ....5H 31
Kingsclere Pl. EN2: Enf 2H 23
Kingscliffe Gdns. SW19 ....1H 135
Kings Cl. DA1: Cray 4K 127
  E10 ....7D 50
  KT7: T Ditt 6A 150
  KT12: Walt T 7K 147
  NW4 ....4F 45
  TW18: Staines 7A 128
King's Club, The
  Sports Cen. 6E 134
Kings Coll. Ct. NW3 ....7C 64
Kings College London
  Chelsea Campus 5B 100
    (off Chelsea Sq.)
  Dental Institute 2D 120
  Hampstead Campus 4J 63
  St Thomas' Campus 3K 101
    (off Lambeth Pal. Rd.)
  Strand Campus 2H 13 (7K 83)
  Waterloo Campus 5J 13
King's College London School of Medicine
  St Thomas' Hospital Campus
  ....2F 19
Kings Coll. Rd. HA4: Ruis 6H 39
  NW3 ....7C 64
King's College School of
  Medicine & Dentistry 2C 120
Kingscote Rd. CR0: Croy 7H 157
  KT3: N Mald 3K 151
  W4 ....3K 97
Kingscote St. EC4 ....2A 14 (7B 84)
Kings Ct. E13 ....1K 87
  HA9: Wemb 2H 61
  IG9: Buck H 2G 37
  N7 ....7K 65
    (off Caledonian Rd.)
  NW8 ....1D 82
    (off Prince Albert Rd.)

Kings Ct. SE1 ....6B 14 (2B 102)
  W6 ....4C 98
Kings Ct. M. KT8: E Mos 5H 149
Kings Ct. Nth. SW3 ....6C 16 (5C 100)
Kingscourt Rd. SW16 ....3H 137
Kings Ct. Sth. SW3 ....6C 16
King's Cres. N4 ....3C 66
Kings Cres. Est. N4 ....2C 66
Kingscroft SW4 ....6J 119
Kingscroft Rd. NW2 ....6H 63
KING'S CROSS 2J 83
King's Cross Bri. N1 ....1F 7
King's Cross Rd. WC1 ....1G 7 (3K 83)
Kingsdale Gdns. W11 ....1F 99
Kingsdale Rd. SE18 ....7K 107
  SE20 ....7K 139
Kingsdown Av. CR2: S Croy 7C 168
  W3 ....7A 80
  W13 ....2B 96
Kingsdown Cl. SE16 ....5H 103
    (off Masters Dr.)
  W10 ....6F 81
Kingsdowne Rd. KT6: Surb 7E 150
Kingsdown Ho. E8 ....5G 67
Kingsdown Rd. E11 ....3G 69
  N19 ....2J 65
  SM3: Cheam 5G 165
Kingsdown Way BR2: Hayes 7J 159
Kings Dr. HA8: Edg 4A 28
  HA9: Wemb 2H 61
  KT5: Surb 7G 151
  KT7: T Ditt 7B 150
  TW11: Tedd 5H 131
Kingsend HA4: Ruis 1F 57
Kingsend Ct. HA4: Ruis 1G 57
Kings Farm E17 ....1D 50
Kings Farm Av. TW10: Rich 4G 115
Kingsfield Av. HA2: Harr 4F 41
Kingsfield Ho. SE9 ....3B 142
Kingsfield Rd. HA1: Harr 7H 41
Kingsfield Ter. HA1: Harr 1H 59
Kingsford St. NW5 ....5D 64
Kingsford Way E6 ....5D 88
Kings Gdns. IG1: Ilf 1H 71
  NW6 ....7J 63
Kings Gth. M. SE23 ....2J 139
Kingsgate HA9: Wemb 3J 61
Kingsgate Av. N3 ....3J 45
Kingsgate Bus. Cen. KT2: King T 1E 150
    (off Kingsgate Rd.)
Kingsgate Cl. DA7: Bex 1E 126
Kingsgate Est. N1 ....6E 66
Kingsgate Ho. SW9 ....1A 120
Kingsgate Mans. WC1 ....6G 7
    (off Red Lion Sq.)
Kingsgate Pde. SW1 ....2B 18
Kingsgate Pl. NW6 ....7J 63
Kingsgate Rd. K11: King T 1E 150
  KT2: King T 1E 150
  NW6 ....7J 63
Kings Grange HA4: Ruis 1H 57
Kingsground SE9 ....7B 124
King's Gro. SE15 ....7H 103
    (not continuous)
Kings Hall Leisure Cen. 5J 67
Kingshall M. SE13 ....3E 122
Kings Hall Rd. BR3: Beck 7A 140
Kings Head Hill E4 ....7J 25
Kingshead Ho. NW7 ....4J 29
Kings Head Pas. SW4 ....4H 119
    (off Clapham Pk. Rd.)
Kings Head Theatre 1B 84
    (off Upper St.)
King's Head Yd. SE1 ....5E 14 (1D 102)
King's Highway SE18 ....6J 107
Kingshill SE17 ....4C 102
    (off Brandon St.)
Kingshill Av. HA3: Kent 4B 42
  KT4: Wor Pk 7C 152
  UB4: Hayes 3G 75
  UB5: Yead 3G 75
Kingshill Cl. UB4: Hayes 3J 75
Kingshill Ct. EN5: Barn 4B 20

Kingshill Dr. HA3: Kent 2B 42
Kingshold Rd. E9 ....7J 67
Kingsholm Gdns. SE9 ....4B 124
Kings Ho. SW8 ....7J 101
    (off Sth. Lambeth Rd.)
  SW10 ....7A 16
    (off Park Wlk.)
King's Ho. Studios
  SW10 ....7A 16
    (off Lamont Rd. Pas.)
Kingshurst Rd. SE12 ....7J 123
Kingside SE18 ....3C 106
Kings Keep BR2: Brom 2G 159
  KT1: King T 4E 150
  SW15 ....5F 117
KINGSLAND 6E 66
Kingsland NW8 ....1C 82
Kingsland Grn. E8 ....6E 66
Kingsland High St. E8 ....6F 67
Kingsland Pas. E8 ....6E 66
Kingsland Rd. E2 ....2H 9 (3E 84)
  E8 ....3E 84
  E13 ....3A 88
Kingsland Shop. Cen. E8 ....6F 67
Kings La. SM1: Sutt 6B 166
Kingslawn Cl. SW15 ....5D 116
Kingsleigh Cl. TW8: Bford 6D 96
Kingsleigh Pl. CR4: Mitc 3D 154
Kingsleigh Wlk. BR2: Brom 4H 159
    (off Stamford Dr.)
Kingsley Av. SM1: Sutt 4B 166
  TW3: Houn 2G 113
  UB1: S'hall 7E 76
  W13 ....5A 78
Kingsley Cl. N2 ....5A 46
  RM10: Dag 4H 73
Kingsley Ct. DA6: Bex 4G 127
  HA8: Edg 3C 28
  KT4: Wor Pk 2B 164
    (off The Avenue)
  NW2 ....6D 62
  SM2: Sutt 7K 165
Kingsley Dr. KT4: Wor Pk 2B 164
Kingsley Flats SE1 ....4E 102
    (off Old Kent Rd.)
Kingsley Gdns. E4 ....5H 35
Kingsley Ho. SW3 ....6B 100
    (off Beaufort St.)
Kingsley Mans. W14 ....6G 99
    (off Greyhound Rd.)
Kingsley M. BR7: Chst 6F 143
  E1 ....7H 85
  W8 ....3K 99
Kingsley Pl. N6 ....7E 46
Kingsley Rd. BR6: Chels 7K 173
  CR0: Croy 1A 168
  E7 ....7J 69
  E17 ....2E 50
  HA2: Harr 4G 59
  HA5: Pinn 4D 40
  IG6: Ilf 1G 53
  N13 ....4F 33
  NW6 ....1H 81
  SW19 ....5K 135
  TW3: Houn 1F 113
Kingsley St. SW11 ....3D 118
Kingsley Way N2 ....6A 46
Kingsley Wood Dr. SE9 ....3D 142
Kingslyn Cres. SE19 ....1E 156
Kings Mall W6 ....4E 98
Kings Mans. SW3 ....7C 16
    (off Lawrence St.)
Kingsman St. SE18 ....3D 106
Kings Mead TW10: Rich 6F 115
Kingsmead EN5: New Bar 4D 20
Kingsmead Av. CR4: Mitc 3G 155
  KT4: Wor Pk 2D 164
  KT6: Surb 2G 163
  N9 ....1C 34
  NW9 ....7K 43
  TW16: Sun 2A 148

Kingsmead Cl. DA15: Sidc 2A 144
  KT19: Ewe 7K 163
  TW11: Tedd 6B 132
Kingsmead Cotts. BR2: Brom 1C 172
Kingsmead Ct. N6 ....7H 47
Kingsmead Dr. UB5: N'olt 7D 58
Kingsmead Ho. E9 ....4A 68
Kingsmead Lodge SM2: Sutt 6B 166
Kingsmeadow 3G 151
Kingsmeadow Athletics Cen. 3G 151
Kingsmead Rd. SW2 ....2A 138
King's Mead Way E9 ....4A 68
Kingsmere Cl. SW15 ....3F 117
Kingsmere Pk. NW9 ....1H 61
Kingsmere Pl. N16 ....1D 66
Kingsmere Rd. SW19 ....2F 135
King's M. SW4 ....5J 119
  WC1 ....4H 7 (4K 83)
Kingsmill NW8 ....2B 82
    (off Kingsmill Ter.)
Kingsmill Bus. Pk. KT1: King T 3F 151
Kingsmill Gdns. RM9: Dag 5F 73
Kingsmill Ho. SW3 ....5D 16
    (off Cale St.)
Kingsmill Rd. RM9: Dag 5F 73
Kingsmill Ter. NW8 ....2B 82
Kingsnorth Ho. W10 ....6J 81
Kingsnympton Pk. KT2: King T 7H 133
Kings Oak RM7: Mawney 3G 55
King's Orchard SE9 ....6C 124
King's Paddock TW12: Hamp 1G 149
Kings Pde. HA8: Edg 5B 28
    (off Edgwarebury La.)
  N17 ....3F 49
  NW10 ....1E 80
  SM5: Cars 3D 166
    (off Wrythe La.)
  W12 ....3C 98
Kingspark Ct. E18 ....3J 51
Kings Pas. E11 ....7G 51
  KT1: King T 2D 150
  KT2: King T 1D 150
Kings Pl. IG9: Buck H 2F 37
  SE1 ....7C 14 (2C 102)
  W4 ....5J 97
King Sq. EC1 ....2C 8 (3C 84)
King's Quay SW10 ....1A 118
    (off Chelsea Harbour Dr.)
Kings Reach Twr. SE1 ....4K 13
Kings Ride Ga. TW10: Rich 4G 115
Kingsridge SW19 ....2G 135
Kings Rd. BR6: Orp 4K 173
  CR4: Mitc 3E 154
  E4 ....1A 36
  E6 ....1A 88
  E11 ....7G 51
  EN5: Barn 3A 20
  HA2: Harr 2D 58
  IG11: Bark 7G 71
  KT2: King T 7E 132
  KT6: Surb 1C 162
  KT12: Walt T 7K 147
  N17 ....1F 49
  N18 ....5B 34
  N22 ....1K 47
  NW10 ....7D 62
  SE25 ....3G 157
  SW3 ....7A 16 (6B 100)
  SW6 ....7K 99
  SW10 ....7A 16 (7A 100)
  SW14 ....3K 115
  SW19 ....6J 135
  TW1: Twick 6B 114
  TW10: Rich 6F 115
  TW11: Tedd 5H 131
  TW13: Felt 1A 130
  UB7: W Dray 2B 92
  W5 ....5D 78
Kings Rd. Bungs. HA2: Harr 4D 58
King's Scholars' Pas. SW1 ....2A 18
King Stairs Cl. SE16 ....2H 103
King's Ter. NW1 ....1G 83
  TW7: Isle 4A 114

Kingsthorpe Rd. SE26 4K 139
Kingston Av. SM3: Cheam 3G 165
TW14: Felt 6G 111
UB7: Yiew 7B 74
(Ash Gro.)
UB7: Yiew 1B 92
(Whitethorn Av.)
Kingston Bri. KT1: King T 2D 150
Kingston Bus. Cen. KT9: Chess 3E 162
Kingston By-Pass KT3: N Mald 5A 152
KT6: Surb 3D 162
SW15 4A 134
SW20 2C 152
Kingston By-Pass Rd. KT6: Surb 3A 162
KT10: Esh, Hin W 3A 162
Kingston Cl. RM6: Chad H 3E 54
(not continuous)
TW11: Tedd 6B 132
UB5: N'olt 1D 76
Kingston Cres. BR3: Beck 1B 158
Kingston Gdns. CR0: Bedd 3J 167
Kingston Hall Rd. KT1: King T 3D 150
Kingston Hill KT2: King T 1G 151
Kingston Hill Av. RM6: Chad H 3E 54
Kingston Hill Pl. KT2: King T 4J 133
Kingston Ho. KT1: King T 4D 150
(off Surbiton Rd.)
NW6 7G 63
Kingston Ho. E. SW7 7C 10
(off Prince's Ga.)
Kingston Ho. Est. KT6: Surb 6B 150
Kingston Ho. Nth. SW7 7C 10
(off Prince's Ga.)
Kingston Ho. Sth. SW7 7C 10
(off Ennismore Gdns.)
Kingstonian FC 3G 151
Kingston La. TW11: Tedd 5A 132
UB7: W Dray 2B 92
UB8: Hil 3A 74
Kingston Lodge KT3: N Mald 4A 152
Kingston Pl. HA3: Hrw W 7E 26
Kingston Rd. EN4: E Barn 5G 21
IG1: Ilf 4F 71
KT1: King T 3H 151
KT3: N Mald 3H 151
KT4: Wor Pk 2H 163
KT5: Surb 2H 163
KT17: Ewe 7B 164
KT19: Ewe 2H 163
N9 2B 34
SW15 2C 134
SW19 2C 134
(Norstead Pl.)
SW19 2H 153
(Watery La.)
SW20 2F 153
TW11: Tedd 5B 132
TW15: Ashf 6A 128
UB2: S'hall 2D 94
Kingston Sq. SE19 5D 138
Kingston Theatre 2D 150
Kingston University
Grange Rd. 3E 150
Kingston Hill 5K 133
Penrhyn Rd. 4E 150
Roehampton Vale Cen. 3B 134
Kingston upon Thames Crematorium
KT1: King T 3G 151
Kingston upon Thames Library,
Art Gallery and Mus. 2E 150
KINGSTON VALE 4A 134
Kingston Va. SW15 4K 133
Kingstown St. NW1 1E 82
(not continuous)
King St. E13 4J 87
EC2 1D 14 (6C 84)
N2 3B 46
N17 1F 49
SW1 5B 12 (1G 101)
TW1: Twick 1A 132
TW9: Rich 5D 114
UB2: S'hall 3C 94
W3 1J 97
King St. W6 4C 98
WC2 2E 12 (7J 83)
King St. Cloisters W6 4D 98
(off Clifton Wlk.)
King St. Pde. TW1: Twick 1A 132
(off King St.)
Kings Wlk. Shop. Cen.
SW3 5E 16 (5D 100)
Kingswater Pl. SW11 7C 100
Kings Way CR0: Wadd 5K 167
HA1: Harr 4J 41
IG8: Wfd G 5F 37
Kingsway BR4: W W'ck 3G 171
BR5: Pet W 5H 161
EN3: Pond E 5C 24
HA9: Wemb 4E 60
KT3: N Mald 4E 152
N12 6F 31
SW14 3H 115
TW19: Stanw 1A 128
UB3: Hayes 5E 74
WC2 7G 7 (6K 83)
Kingsway Bus. Pk. TW12: Hamp 1D 148
Kingsway Cres. HA2: Harr 4G 41
Kingsway Est. N18 6E 34
Kingsway Mans. WC1 5G 7
(off Red Lion Sq.)
Kingsway Pde. N16 3D 66
(off Albion Rd.)
Kingsway Pl. EC1 3K 7
(off Sans Wlk.)
Kingsway Rd. SM3: Cheam 7G 165
Kingswear Rd. HA4: Ruis 2J 57
NW5 3F 65
Kings Wharf E8 1E 84
(off Kingsland Rd.)
Kingswood E2 2J 85
(off Cyprus St.)
Kingswood Av. BR2: Brom 3G 159
CR7: Thor H 5A 156
DA17: Belv 4F 109
NW6 1G 81
TW3: Houn 1D 112
TW12: Hamp 6F 131
Kingswood Cl. BR6: Orp 7J 161
EN1: Enf 5K 23
KT3: N Mald 6B 152
KT6: Surb 7E 150
N20 7F 21
SW8 7J 101
TW15: Ashf 5E 128
Kingswood Ct. E4 5H 35
NW6 7J 63
(off West End La.)
Kingswood Dr. SE19 4E 138
SM2: Sutt 7K 165
SM5: Cars 1D 166
Kingswood Est. SE21 4E 138
Kingswood M. N15 4B 48
Kingswood Pk. N3 1H 45
Kingswood Pl. SE13 4G 123
Kingswood Rd. BR2: Brom 4F 159
E11 7G 51
HA9: Wemb 3G 61
IG3: Ilf 1A 72
SE20 6J 139
SW2 6J 119
SW19 7H 135
W4 3J 97
Kingswood Ter. W4 3J 97
Kingswood Way SM6: Wall 5J 167
Kingsworth Cl. BR3: Beck 5A 158
Kingsworthy Cl. KT1: King T 3F 151
Kings Yd. E15 6C 68
SW15 3E 116
(off Lwr. Richmond Rd.)
Kingthorpe Rd. NW10 7K 61
Kingthorpe Ter. NW10 6K 61
Kington Ho. NW6 1K 81
(off Mortimer Cres.)
Kingward Ho. E1 5G 85
(off Hanbury St.)
Kingweston Cl. NW2 3G 63
King William IV Gdns. SE20 6J 139
King William La. SE10 5G 105
King William's Ct. SE10 6F 105
(off Park Row)
King William St. EC4 1F 15 (6D 84)
King William Wlk. SE10 6E 104
(not continuous)
Kingwood Rd. SW6 1G 117
Kinlet Rd. SE18 1G 125
Kinloch Dr. NW9 7K 43
Kinloch St. N7 3K 65
Kinloss Ct. N3 4H 45
Kinloss Gdns. N3 3H 45
Kinloss Rd. SM5: Cars 7A 154
Kinnaird Av. BR1: Brom 6H 141
W4 7J 97
Kinnaird Cl. BR1: Brom 6H 141
Kinnaird Way IG8: Wfd G 6J 37
Kinnear Rd. W12 2B 98
Kinnerton Pl. Nth. SW1 7F 11
Kinnerton Pl. Sth. SW1 7F 11
Kinnerton St. SW1 7G 11 (2E 100)
Kinnerton Yd. SW1 7G 11
Kinnoul Rd. W6 6G 99
Kinross Av. KT4: Wor Pk 2C 164
Kinross Cl. HA3: Kent 5F 43
HA8: Edg 2C 28
TW16: Sun 5H 129
Kinross Ct. BR1: Brom 1H 159
(off Highland Rd.)
SE6 1H 141
Kinross Dr. TW16: Sun 5H 129
Kinross Ter. E17 2B 50
Kinsale Rd. SE15 3G 121
Kinsella Gdns. SW19 5D 134
Kinsham Ho. E2 4G 85
(off Ramsey St.)
Kintore Way SE1 4F 103
Kintyre Cl. SW16 2K 155
Kintyre Ct. SW2 7J 119
Kintyre Ho. E14 1E 104
(off Coldharbour)
Kinveachy Gdns. SE7 5C 106
Kinver Rd. SE26 4J 139
Kipling Ct. W7 7K 77
Kipling Dr. SW19 6B 136
Kipling Est. SE1 7F 15 (2D 102)
Kipling Ho. E16 1K 105
(off Southampton M.)
SE5 7D 102
(off Elmington Est.)
Kipling Pl. HA7: Stan 6E 26
Kipling Rd. DA7: Bex 1E 126
Kipling St. SE1 7F 15 (2D 102)
Kipling Ter. N9 3J 33
Kipling Twr. W3 3J 97
(off Palmerston Rd.)
Kippington Dr. SE9 1B 142
Kirby Cl. KT19: Ewe 5B 164
Kirby Est. SE16 3H 103
UB7: Yiew 7A 74
Kirby Gro. SE1 6G 15 (2E 102)
Kirby St. EC1 5K 7 (5A 84)
Kirby Way KT12: Walt T 6A 148
UB8: Hil 4B 74
Kirchen Rd. W13 7B 78
Kirkby Cl. N11 6K 31
Kirkdale SE26 2H 139
Kirkdale Cnr. SE26 4J 139
Kirkdale Rd. E11 1G 69
Kirkeby Ho. EC1 5J 7
(off Leather La.)
Kirkfield Cl. W13 1B 96
Kirkham Rd. E6 6C 88
Kirkham St. SE18 6J 107
Kirk Ho. HA9: Wemb 3E 60
Kirkland Av. IG5: Ilf 2E 52
Kirkland Cl. DA15: Sidc 6J 125
Kirkland Dr. EN2: Enf 1H 23
Kirkland Ho. E14 5D 104
(off St Davids Sq.)
E14 5D 104
(off Westferry Rd.)
Kirkland Ter. BR3: Beck 6C 140
Kirkland Wlk. E8 6F 67
Kirk La. SE18 6G 107
Kirkleas Rd. KT6: Surb 1E 162
Kirklees Rd. CR7: Thor H 5A 156
RM8: Dag 5C 72
Kirkley Rd. SW19 1J 153
Kirkman Pl. W1 6C 6
Kirkmichael Rd. E14 6E 86
Kirk Ri. SM1: Sutt 3K 165
Kirk Rd. E17 6B 50
Kirkside Rd. SE3 6J 105
Kirkstall Av. N17 4D 48
Kirkstall Gdns. SW2 1J 137
Kirkstall Rd. SW2 1H 137
Kirkstead Ct. E5 4K 67
Kirksted Rd. SM4: Mord 1K 165
Kirkstone NW1 1A 6
(off Harrington St.)
Kirkstone Way BR1: Brom 7G 141
Kirk St. WC1 4G 7
Kirkton Rd. N15 4E 48
Kirkwall Pl. E2 3J 85
Kirkwood Pl. NW1 7E 64
Kirkwood Rd. SE15 2H 121
Kirn Rd. W13 7B 78
Kirrane Cl. KT3: N Mald 5B 152
Kirtley Ho. SW8 1G 119
Kirtley Rd. SE26 4A 140
Kirtling St. SW8 7G 101
Kirton Cl. W4 4K 97
Kirton Gdns. E2 2K 9 (3F 85)
Kirton Lodge SW18 6K 117
Kirton Rd. E13 2A 88
Kirton Wlk. HA8: Edg 7D 28
Kirwyn Way SE5 7B 102
Kitcat Ter. E3 3C 86
Kitchen Ct. E10 2D 68
Kitchener Rd. CR7: Thor H 3D 156
E7 6K 69
E17 1D 50
N2 3C 46
N17 3E 48
RM10: Dag 6H 73
Kite Pl. E2 3G 85
(off Lampern Sq.)
Kite Yd. SW11 1D 118
(off Cambridge Rd.)
Kitley Gdns. SE19 1F 157
Kitson Rd. SE5 7D 102
SW13 1C 116
Kittiwake Ct. SE1 7D 14
(off Swan St.)
SE8 6B 104
(off Abinger Gro.)
Kittiwake Pl. SM1: Sutt 5H 165
Kittiwake Rd. UB5: N'olt 3B 76
Kittiwake Way UB4: Yead 5B 76
Kitto Rd. SE14 2K 121
Kitts End Rd. EN5: Barn 1C 20
Kiver Rd. N19 2H 65
Klea Av. SW4 6G 119
Kleine Wharf N1 1E 84
Klein's Wharf E14 3C 104
(off Westferry Rd.)
Knapdale Cl. SE23 2H 139
Knapmill Rd. SE6 2C 140
Knapmill Way SE6 2D 140
Knapp Cl. NW10 6A 62
Knapp Rd. E3 4C 86
TW15: Ashf 4B 128
Knapton M. SW17 6E 136
Knaresborough Dr. SW18 1K 135
Knaresborough Pl. SW5 4K 99
Knatchbull Rd. NW10 1K 79
SE5 2B 120
Knebworth Av. E17 1C 50
Knebworth Cl. EN5: New Bar 4E 20
Knebworth Ho. SW8 2H 119
Knebworth Rd. N16 4E 66
Knee Hill SE2 4C 108
Kneehill Cres. SE2 4C 108
Kneller Gdns. TW7: Isle 6H 113

Kneller Ho. *UB5: N'olt* 2B 76
(off Academy Gdns.)
Kneller Rd. KT3: N Mald 7A 152
SE4 4A 122
TW2: Whit 6G 113
Knevett Ter. TW3: Houn 4E 112
Knight Cl. RM8: Dag 2C 72
Knight Ct. *E4* 1K 35
(off The Ridgeway)
N15 5E 48
Knighten St. E1 1H 103
Knighthead Point E14 2C 104
Knight Ho. *SE17* 4E 102
(off Tatum St.)
Knightland Rd. E5 2H 67
Knightleas Ct. NW2 6E 62
Knightleys Ct. *E10* 1A 68
(off Wellington Rd.)
Knighton Cl. CR2: S Croy 7B 168
IG8: Wfd G 4E 36
RM7: Rom 6K 55
Knighton Dr. IG8: Wfd G 4E 36
Knighton Grn. IG9: Buck H 2E 36
Knighton La. IG9: Buck H 2E 36
Knighton Pk. Rd. SE26 5K 139
Knighton Rd. E7 3J 69
RM7: Rom 6J 55
Knightrider Ct. EC4 2B 14
Knightrider St. EC4 2B 14 (6B 84)
Knights Arc. SW1 7E 10
Knights Av. W5 2E 96
KNIGHTSBRIDGE 7E 10 (2C 100)
Knightsbridge SW1 7E 10 (2D 100)
SW7 7D 10 (2D 100)
Knightsbridge Ct. SW1 7F 11
Knightsbridge Gdns.
RM7: Rom 5K 55
Knightsbridge Grn. SW1 7E 10 (2D 100)
(not continuous)
Knights Cl. E9 5J 67
KT8: W Mole 5D 148
Knightscote Cl.
UB9: Hare 2A 38
Knights Ct. BR1: Brom 3H 141
KT1: King T 3E 150
RM6: Chad H 6E 54
(off High Rd.)
Knights Hill SE27 5B 138
Knight's Hill Sq. SE27 4B 138
Knights Ho. *SW8* 7J 101
(off Sth. Lambeth Rd.)
SW10 7A 100
(off Hortensia Rd.)
Knights La. N9 3B 34
Knight's Pk. KT1: King T 3E 150
Knight's Pl. TW2: Twick 1J 131
Knights Rd. E16 2J 105
HA7: Stan 4H 27
Knight's Wlk. SE11 4K 19 (4B 102)
(not continuous)
Knightswood Cl. HA8: Edg 2D 28
Knightswood Ct. N6 7H 47
Knightswood Ho. N12 6F 31
Knightwood Cres.
KT3: N Mald 6A 152
Knivet Rd. SW6 6J 99
Knobs Hill Rd. E15 1D 86
Knockholt Rd. SE9 5B 124
Knole, The SE9 4E 142
Knole Cl. CR0: Croy 6J 157
Knole Ct. *UB5: Yead* 3A 76
(off Broomcroft Av.)
Knole Ga. DA15: Sidc 3J 143
Knoll, The BR2: Hayes 2J 171
BR3: Beck 1D 158
W13 5C 78
Knoll Ct. *SE19* 5F 139
(off Farquhar Rd.)
Knoll Cres. HA6: Nwood 2G 39
(not continuous)
Knoll Dr. N14 7K 21
Knoll Ho. *NW8* 2A 82
(off Carlton Hill)
Knollmead KT5: Surb 1J 163
Knoll Ri. BR6: Orp 1K 173
Knoll Rd. DA5: Bexl 7G 127
DA14: Sidc 5B 144
SW18 5A 118
Knolls Cl. KT4: Wor Pk 3D 164
Knollys Cl. SW16 3A 138
Knolly's Ho. *WC1* 3E 6
(off Tavistock Pl.)
Knollys Rd. SW16 3K 137
Knot Ho. *SE1* 1F 103
(off Horselydown La.)
Knottisford St. E2 3J 85
Knotts Grn. M. E10 6D 50
Knotts Grn. Rd. E10 6D 50
Knowlden Ho. *E1* 7J 85
(off Cable St.)
Knowle Av. DA7: Bex 7E 108
Knowle Cl. SW9 3A 120
Knowle Rd. BR2: Brom 2D 172
TW2: Twick 1J 131
Knowles Cl. UB7: Yiew 1A 92
Knowles Ct. *HA1: Harr* 6K 41
(off Gayton Rd.)
Knowles Hill Cres. SE13 5F 123
Knowles Ho. *SW18* 6K 117
(off Neville Gill Cl.)
Knowles Wlk. SW4 3G 119
Knowlton Grn.
BR2: Brom 5H 159
Knowlton Ho. *SW9* 1A 120
(off Cowley Rd.)
Knowsley Av. UB1: S'hall 1F 95
Knowsley Rd. SW11 2D 118
Knox Ct. SW4 2J 119
Knox Rd. E7 6H 69
Knox St. W1 5E 4 (5D 82)
Knoyle Ho. *W14* 3G 99
(off Russell Rd.)
Knoyle St. SE14 6A 104
Koblenz Ho. *N8* 3J 47
(off Newland Rd.)
Kohat Rd. SW19 5K 135
Korda Cl. TW17: Shep 3B 146
Kossuth St. SE10 5G 105
Kotree Way SE1 4G 103
Kramer M. SW5 5J 99
Kreedman Wlk. E8 5G 67
Kreisel Wlk. TW9: Kew 6F 97
Kristina Ct. *SM2: Sutt* 6J 165
(off Overton Rd.)
Krupnik Pl. EC2 2H 9
Kuala Gdns. SW16 1K 155
Kubrick Bus. Est. *E7* 4K 69
(off Station App.)
Kuhn Way E7 5J 69
Kwame Ho. *E16* 7F 89
(off University Way)
Kydbrook Cl. BR5: Pet W 7G 161
Kylemore Cl. E6 2B 88
Kylemore Rd. NW6 7J 63
Kylestrome Ho. *SW1* 4H 17
(off Cundy St.)
Kymberley Rd. HA1: Harr 6J 41
Kymes Ct. HA2: Harr 2H 59
Kynance Gdns. HA7: Stan 1C 42
Kynance M. SW7 3K 99
Kynance Pl. SW7 3A 100
Kynaston Av. CR7: Thor H 5C 156
N16 3F 67
Kynaston Cl. HA3: Hrw W 7C 26
Kynaston Cres.
CR7: Thor H 5C 156
Kynaston Rd. BR1: Brom 5J 141
CR7: Thor H 5C 156
EN2: Enf 1J 23
N16 3E 66
Kynaston Wood
HA3: Hrw W 7C 26
Kynnersley Cl. SM5: Cars 3D 166
Kynoch Rd. N18 4D 34
Kyrle Rd. SW11 6E 118
Kyverdale Rd. N16 7F 49

L

Laburnum Av. N9 2A 34
N17 7J 33
SM1: Sutt 3C 166
UB7: Yiew 7B 74
Laburnum Cl. E4 6G 35
HA0: Wemb 1G 79
N11 6K 31
SE15 7J 103
Laburnum Ct. E2 1F 85
HA1: Harr 6F 41
HA7: Stan 4H 27
SE16 2J 103
(off Albion St.)
Laburnum Cres. TW16: Sun 1K 147
Laburnum Gdns. CR0: Croy 7K 157
N21 2H 33
Laburnum Gro. HA4: Ruis 6F 39
KT3: N Mald 2K 151
N21 2H 33
NW9 7J 43
TW3: Houn 4D 112
UB1: S'hall 4D 76
Laburnum Ho. BR2: Brom 1F 159
Laburnum Lodge N3 2H 45
Laburnum Pl. SE9 5E 124
Laburnum Rd. CR4: Mitc 2E 154
SW19 7A 136
UB3: Harl 4H 93
Laburnums, The E6 4C 88
Laburnum St. E2 1F 85
Laburnum Way BR2: Brom 7E 160
TW19: Stanw 1B 128
La Caye Apartments *E14* 4F 105
(off Glenaffric Av.)
Lacebark Cl. DA15: Sidc 7K 125
Lacewing Cl. E13 3J 87
Lacey Cl. N9 2B 34
Lacey Dr. HA8: Edg 4A 28
TW12: Hamp 1D 148
Lacey M. E3 2C 86
Lacine Ct. *SE16* 2K 103
(off Christopher Cl.)
Lackington St. EC2 5F 9 (5D 84)
Lackland Ho. *SE1* 5F 103
(off Rowcross St.)
Lacland Ho. *SW10* 7B 100
(off Worlds End Est.)
Lacock Cl. SW19 6A 136
Lacock Ct. W13 1A 96
Lacon Ho. *WC1* 5G 7
(off Theobalds Rd.)
Lacon Rd. SE22 4G 121
Lacrosse Way SW16 1H 155
Lacy Dr. RM8: Dag 3C 72
Lacy Rd. SW15 4F 117
(not continuous)
Ladas Rd. SE27 4C 138
Ladbroke Cres. W11 6G 81
Ladbroke Gdns. W11 7H 81
Ladbroke Gro. W10 4F 81
W11 4F 81
Ladbroke Gro. Ho. *W11* 7H 81
(off Ladbroke Gro.)
Ladbroke M. W11 1G 99
Ladbroke Rd. EN1: Enf 6A 24
W11 1H 99
Ladbroke Sq. W11 7H 81
Ladbroke Ter. W11 7H 81
Ladbroke Wlk. W11 1H 99
Ladbrook Cl. HA5: Pinn 5D 40
Ladbrooke Cres. DA14: Sidc 3D 144
Ladbrook Rd. SE25 4D 156
Ladderstile Ride TW10: Rich 5H 133
Ladderswood Way N11 5B 32
Ladlands SE22 7G 121
Lady Aylesford Av. HA7: Stan 5F 27
Lady Booth Rd. KT1: King T 2E 150
Ladycroft Gdns. BR6: Farnb 5G 173
Ladycroft Rd. SE13 3D 122
Ladycroft Wlk. HA7: Stan 1D 42
Ladycroft Way BR6: Farnb 5G 173
Lady Dock Path SE16 2A 104
Lady Elizabeth Ho. SW14 3J 115
Ladyfern Ho. *E3* 5C 86
(off Gail St.)
Lady Forsdyke Way KT19: Eps 7G 163
Ladygate Bowls Club 6E 38
(off Ladygate La.)
Ladygate La. HA4: Ruis 6D 38
Lady Harewood Way KT19: Eps 7G 163
Lady Hay KT4: Wor Pk 2B 164
Lady Jane Ct. *KT2: King T* 2F 151
(off London Rd.)
Lady Margaret Ho. *SE17* 6D 102
(off Westmoreland Rd.)
Lady Margaret Rd. N19 5G 65
NW5 5G 65
UB1: S'hall 7D 76
Lady May Ho. *SE5* 7C 102
(off Pitman St.)
Lady Micos Almshouses *E1* 6J 85
(off Aylward St.)
Lady Sarah Ho. *N11* 6J 31
(off Asher Loftus Way)
Lady Shaw Ct. N13 2E 32
Ladyship Ter. SE22 7G 121
Ladysmith Av. E6 2C 88
IG2: Ilf 7H 53
Ladysmith Cl. NW7 7H 29
Ladysmith Rd. E16 3H 87
EN1: Enf 3K 23
(not continuous)
HA3: W'stone 2J 41
N17 2G 49
N18 5C 34
SE9 6E 124
Lady Somerset Rd. NW5 4F 65
LADYWELL 5D 122
Ladywell Arena
Ladywell 6D 122
Ladywell Cl. SE4 5C 122
Ladywell Hgts. SE4 6B 122
Ladywell Leisure Cen. 5E 122
Ladywell Rd. SE4 5C 122
SE13 5C 122
Ladywell St. E15 1H 87
Ladywood Av. BR5: Pet W 5J 161
Ladywood Rd. KT6: Surb 2G 163
LA Fitness
Aldgate 2K 15
(off Portsoken St.)
Bayswater 7K 81
(off Queen's M.)
Bloomsbury 5G 7
(off Conduit St.)
Bromley 2J 159
(off East St.)
Edgware 6B 28
Finchley 3K 45
Golders Green 7H 45
Gospel Oak 4F 65
Leadenhall 1H 15
(off Billiter St.)
London 1C 32
Marylebone 5E 4 (5D 82)
New Barnet 4G 21
Novello 7K 83
(off Tavistock St.)
Old Isleworth 3B 114
(off Swan St.)
Piccadilly 3C 12
(off Regent St.)
St Pauls 6C 8
(off King Edward St.)
South Kensington 3C 16 (4C 100)
Sydenham 4J 139
Victoria 2A 18
(off Bressenden Pl.)
West India Quay 7C 86
Lafone Av.
TW13: Felt 2A 130
Lafone St. SE1 6J 15 (2F 103)
Lagado M. SE16 1K 103

Lagonier Ho. EC1 ....2D 8
(off Dingley Rd.)
Laidlaw Dr. N21 ....5E 22
Laing Dean UB5: N'olt 1A 76
Laing Ho. SE5 ....7C 102
Laings Av. CR4: Mitc 2D 154
Lainlock Pl. TW3: Houn 1F 113
Lainson St. SW18 ....7J 117
Lairdale Cl. SE21 ....1C 138
Laird Ho. SE5 ....7C 102
(off Redcar St.)
Lairs Cl. N7 ....5J 65
Lait Ho. BR3: Beck 1D 158
Laltwood Rd. SW12 ......1F 137
Lakanal SE5 ....1E 120
(off Dalwood St.)
Lake, The WD23: Bushy 1C 26
Lake Av. BR1: Brom 6J 141
Lake Bus. Cen. N17 ......7B 34
Lake Cl. RM8: Dag 3D 72
   SW19 ....5H 135
Lakedale Rd. SE18 ......6J 107
Lake Dr. WD23: Bushy 2C 26
Lake Farm Country Pk. 1G 93
Lakefield Cl. SE20 ......7H 139
Lakefield Rd. N22 ....2B 48
Lake Footpath SE2 ......2D 108
Lake Gdns. RM10: Dag 5G 73
   SM6: Wall 3F 167
   TW10: Ham 2B 132
Lakehall Gdns.
   CR7: Thor H 5B 156
Lakehall Rd. CR7: Thor H ..5B 156
Lake Ho. SE1 ....7C 14
(off Southwark Bri. Rd.)
Lake Ho. Rd. E11 ....3J 69
Lakehurst Rd. KT19: Ewe ..5A 164
Lakeland Cl. HA3: Hrw W ..6C 26
Lakenheath N14 ....5B 22
Laker Cl. SW4 ....1J 119
Laker Ind. Est. BR3 ......5A 140
(off Kent Ho. La.)
Lake Rd. CR0: Croy 2B 170
   E10 ....7D 50
   RM6: Chad H 4D 54
   RM9: Dag 3H 91
   SW19 ....5H 135
Laker Pl. SW15 ....6G 117
Lakeside BR3: Beck 3D 158
   EN2: Enf 4C 22
   KT2: King T 7H 133
   KT19: Ewe 6A 164
   N3 ....2K 45
   SM6: Wall 4F 167
   W13 ....6C 78
Lakeside Av. IG4: Ilf 4B 52
   SE28 ....1A 108
Lakeside Cl. DA15: Sidc ..5C 126
   HA4: Ruis 4F 39
   SE25 ....2G 157
Lakeside Ct. N4 ....2C 66
Lakeside Cres. EN4: E Barn ..5J 21
Lakeside Dr. BR2: Brom ..3C 172
   NW10 ....3F 79
Lakeside Rd. N13 ....4E 32
   W14 ....3F 99
Lakeside Station
   Ruislip Lido Railway 4F 39
Lakeside Ter. EC2 ....5D 8
Lakeside Way HA9: Wemb ..4G 61
Lakes Rd. BR2: Kes 5A 172
Lakeswood Rd. BR5: Pet W ..6F 161
Lake Vw. HA8: Edg 5A 28
Lake Vw. Ct. SW1 ....1K 17
(off Bressenden Pl.)
Lake Vw. Est. E3 ....2A 86
Lakeview Rd. DA16: Well ..4B 126
   SE27 ....5A 138
Lake Vw. Ter. N18 ....4A 34
(off Sweet Briar Wlk.)
Lakis Cl. NW3 ....4A 64
Laleham Av. NW7 ....3E 28
Laleham Ct. SM1: Sutt 5A 166

Laleham Ho. E2 ....3J 9
(off Camlet St.)
Laleham Rd. SE6 ....7E 122
   TW17: Shep 4B 146
Lalor St. SW6 ....2G 117
Lambarde Av. SE9 ....4E 142
Lambard Ho. SE10 ....7E 104
(off Langdale Rd.)
Lamb Cl. UB5: N'olt 3C 76
Lamb Ct. E14 ....7A 86
(off Narrow St.)
Lamberhurst Ho. SE15 ....6J 103
Lamberhurst Rd. RM8: Dag ..1F 73
   SE27 ....4A 138
Lambert Av. TW9: Rich 3G 115
Lambert Ct. DA8: Erith 6J 109
(off Park Cres.)
Lambert Jones M. EC2 ....5C 8
Lambert Lodge TW8: Bford ..5D 96
(off Layton Rd.)
Lambert Rd. E16 ....6K 87
   N12 ....5G 31
   SW2 ....5J 119
Lambert's Pl. CR0: Croy ..1D 168
Lamberts Rd. KT5: Surb ..5E 150
Lambert St. N1 ....7A 66
Lambert Wlk. HA9: Wemb ..3E 60
Lambert Way N12 ....5F 31
LAMBETH 3G 19 (3K 101)
Lambeth Bri. SE1 ....3F 19 (4J 101)
   SW1 ....3F 19 (4J 101)
Lambeth Crematorium SW17 ..4A 136
Lambeth High St. SE1 ..4G 19 (4K 101)
Lambeth Hill EC4 ....2C 14 (7C 84)
Lambeth Palace 2G 19 (3K 101)
Lambeth Pal. Rd. SE1 ..2G 19 (3K 101)
Lambeth Rd. CR0: Croy 7A 156
   SE1 ....3G 19 (4K 101)
Lambeth Towers SE11 ....2J 19
Lambeth Wlk. SE11 ....4H 19 (4K 101)
(not continuous)
Lambfold Ho. N7 ....6J 65
Lamb Ho. SE5 ....7C 102
(off Elmington Est.)
   SE10 ....6E 104
(off Haddo St.)
Lambkins M. E17 ....4E 50
Lamb La. E8 ....7H 67
Lamble St. NW5 ....5E 64
Lambley Rd. RM9: Dag 6B 72
Lambolle Pl. NW3 ....6C 64
Lambolle Rd. NW3 ....6C 64
Lambourn Cl. CR2: S Croy ..7B 168
   NW5 ....4G 65
   W7 ....2K 95
Lambourne Av. SW19 ......4H 135
Lambourne Ct. UB8: Wfd G ..7F 37
Lambourne Gdns. E4 ......2H 35
   EN1: Enf 2A 24
   IG11: Bark 7K 71
Lambourne Gro. SE16 ....5K 103
Lambourne Ho. NW8 ......5B 4
(off Broadley St.)
   SE16 ....4K 103
Lambourne Pl. SE3 ....1K 123
Lambourne Rd. E11 ....7E 50
   IG3: Ilf 2J 71
   IG11: Bark 7J 71
Lambourn Gro. KT1: King T ..2H 151
Lambourn Rd. SW4 ....3G 119
Lambrook Ho. SE15 ......1G 121
Lambrook Ter. SW6 ......1G 117
Lamb's Bldgs. EC1 ....4E 8 (4D 84)
Lamb's Cl. N9 ....2B 34
Lamb's Conduit Pas. WC1 ..5G 7 (5K 83)
Lamb's Conduit St. WC1 ..4G 7 (4K 83)
(not continuous)
Lambscroft Av. SE9 ......3A 142
Lambs Health & Fitness 4E 8
Lambs Mdw. IG8: Wfd G ..2B 52
Lamb's M. N1 ....1B 84
Lamb's Pas. EC1 ....5E 8 (4D 84)
Lambs Ter. N9 ....2J 33

Lamb St. E1 ....5J 9 (5F 85)
Lamb's Wlk. EN2: Enf 2H 23
Lambton M. N19 ....1J 65
(off Lambton Rd.)
Lambton Pl. W11 ....7H 81
Lambton Rd. N19 ....1J 65
   SW20 ....1E 152
Lamb Wlk. SE1 ....7G 15 (2E 102)
LAMDA Theatre 4J 99
(off Logan Pl.)
Lamerock Rd. BR1: Brom ..4H 141
Lamerton Rd. IG6: Ilf 2F 53
Lamerton St. SE8 ....6C 104
Lamford Cl. N17 ....7J 33
Lamington St. W6 ....4D 98
Lamlash St. SE11 ....4B 102
Lamley Ho. SE10 ....7D 104
(off Ashburnham Pl.)
Lammas Av. CR4: Mitc 2E 154
Lammas Grn. SE26 ......3H 139
Lammas Pk. Gdns. W5 ....1C 96
Lammas Pk. Rd. W5 ......2D 96
Lammas Rd. E9 ....7K 67
   E10 ....2A 68
   TW10: Ham 4C 132
Lammermoor Rd. SW12 ..7F 119
Lamont Rd. SW10 ....7A 16 (6B 100)
Lamont Rd. Pas. SW10 ....7A 16
LAMORBEY 1K 143
Lamorbey Cl. DA15: Sidc ..1K 143
Lamorbey Swimming Cen. ..2A 144
Lamorna Cl. BR6: Orp 7K 161
   E17 ....2E 50
Lamorna Gro. HA7: Stan ..1D 42
Lampard Gro. N16 ....1F 67
Lampern Sq. E2 ....3G 85
Lampeter Cl. NW9 ....6A 44
Lampeter Sq. W6 ....6G 99
Lamplighter Cl. E1 ....4J 85
Lampmead Rd. SE12 ......5H 123
Lamp Office Ct. WC1 ......4G 7
Lamport Cl. SE18 ....4D 106
LAMPTON 1F 113
Lampton Av. TW3: Houn ..1F 113
Lampton Ho. Cl. SW19 ....4F 135
Lampton Pk. Rd. TW3: Houn ..2F 113
Lampton Rd. TW3: Houn ..2F 113
Lanacre Av. NW9 ....1K 43
Lanain Cl. SE12 ....7H 123
Lanark Cl. W5 ....5C 78
Lanark Ct. UB5: N'olt 5C 58
(off Newmarket Av.)
Lanark Ho. SE1 ....5G 103
(off Old Kent Rd.)
Lanark Mans. W9 ....4A 82
(off Lanark Rd.)
   W12 ....2E 98
(off Pennard Rd.)
Lanark M. W9 ....3A 82
Lanark Pl. W9 ....3A 4 (4A 82)
Lanark Rd. W9 ....2K 81
Lanark Sq. E14 ....3D 104
Lanata Wlk. UB4: Yead 4B 76
(off Alba Cl.)
Lanbury Rd. SE15 ....4K 121
Lancashire Ct. W1 ....2K 11
Lancaster Av. CR4: Mitc ..5J 155
   E18 ....4K 51
   EN4: Had W 1F 21
   IG11: Bark 7J 71
   SE27 ....2B 138
   SW19 ....5F 135
Lancaster Cl. BR2: Brom ..4H 159
   KT2: King T 5D 132
   N1 ....1E 66
   N17 ....7B 34
   NW9 ....7G 29
   TW15: Ashf 4A 128
   TW19: Stanw 6A 110
   W2 ....7K 81
(off St Petersburgh Pl.)
Lancaster Cotts. TW10: Rich ..6E 114

Lancaster Ct. KT12: Walt T ..7J 147
   SE27 ....2B 138
   SM2: Sutt 7J 165
(off Mulgrave Rd.)
   SW6 ....7H 99
   TW19: Stanw 1A 128
   W2 ....2A 10
(off Lancaster Ga.)
Lancaster Dr. E14 ....1E 104
   NW3 ....6C 64
Lancaster Gdns. BR1: Brom ..5C 160
   KT2: King T 5D 132
   SW19 ....5H 135
   W13 ....2B 96
Lancaster Ga. W2 ....2A 10 (7A 82)
Lancaster Gro. NW3 ......6B 64
Lancaster Hall E16 ....1J 105
(off Wesley Av., not continuous)
Lancaster House 6A 12
Lancaster Ho. EN2: Enf 1J 23
   SW19 ....4F 135
Lancaster Lodge W11 ......6G 81
(off Lancaster Rd.)
Lancaster M. SW18 ......5K 117
   TW10: Rich 6E 114
   W2 ....2A 10 (7A 82)
Lancaster Pk. TW10: Rich ..5E 114
Lancaster Pl. IG1: Ilf 5G 71
   SW19 ....5F 135
   TW1: Twick 6A 114
   TW4: Houn 2A 112
   WC2 ....2G 13 (7K 83)
Lancaster Rd. E7 ....7J 69
   E11 ....2G 69
   EN2: Enf 1J 23
   EN4: E Barn 5G 21
   HA2: Harr 5E 40
   N4 ....7K 47
   N11 ....6C 32
   N18 ....5A 34
   NW10 ....5C 62
   SE25 ....2F 157
   SW19 ....5F 135
   UB1: S'hall 7C 76
   UB5: N'olt 6G 59
   W11 ....6G 81
Lancaster Rd. Ind. Est.
   EN4: E Barn 5G 21
(off Lancaster Rd.)
Lancaster Stables NW3 ....6C 64
Lancaster St. SE1 ....7A 14 (2B 102)
Lancaster Ter. W2 ....2A 10 (7B 82)
Lancaster Wlk. UB3: Hayes ..6E 74
   W2 ....3A 10 (1A 100)
Lancaster Way KT4: Wor Pk ..7D 152
Lancastrian Rd. SM6: Wall ..7J 167
Lancefield Cl. W10 ....2G 81
Lancefield Ho. SE15 ......4H 121
Lancefield St. W10 ....3H 81
Lancell St. N16 ....2F 67
Lancelot Av. HA0: Wemb ..4D 60
Lancelot Cres. HA0: Wemb ..4D 60
Lancelot Gdns. EN4: E Barn ..7K 21
Lancelot Pl. SW7 ....7E 10 (2D 100)
Lancelot Rd. DA16: Well 4A 126
   HA0: Wemb 4D 60
Lance Rd. HA1: Harr 7G 41
Lancer Sq. W8 ....2K 99
Lancey Cl. SE7 ....4C 106
Lanchester Ct. W2 ....1E 10
(off Seymour St.)
Lanchester Rd. N6 ....5D 46
Lanchester Way SE14 ....1J 121
Lancing Gdns. N9 ....1A 34
Lancing Ho. CR0: Croy 4D 168
(off Coombe Rd.)
Lancing Rd. CR0: Croy 7K 155
   IG2: Ilf 6H 53
   TW13: Felt 2H 129
   W13 ....7B 78
Lancing St. NW1 ....2C 6 (3H 83)
Lancresse Ct. N1 ....1E 84
(off De Beauvoir Est.)

Landale Ho.—Lanterns Ct.

Landale Ho. *SE16* 3J 103
(off Lower Rd.)
Landau Ct. *CR2: S Croy* 5C 168
(off Warham Rd.)
Landcroft Rd. SE22 . . . . 5F 121
Landells Rd. SE22 . . . . 6F 121
Landford Rd. SW15 . . . . 3E 116
Landgrove Rd. SW19 . . . . 5J 135
Landin Ho. *E14* 6C 86
(off Thomas Rd.)
Landleys Fld. *N7* 5H 65
(off Long Mdw.)
Landmann Ho. *SE16* 4H 103
(off Rennie Est.)
Landmann Way SE14 . . . . 5K 103
Landmark Arts Cen. 5B 132
Landmark Commercial Cen. N18 . . . . 6K 33
Landmark Hgts. E5 . . . . 4A 68
Landmark Ho. *W6* 5E 98
(off Hammersmith Bri. Rd.)
Landon Pl. SW1 . . . . 1E 16 (3D 100)
Landon's Cl. E14 . . . . 1E 104
Landon Wlk. E14 . . . . 7D 86
Landon Way TW15: Ashf 6D 128
Landor Ho. *SE5* 7D 102
(off Elmington Est.)
W2 . . . . 5J 81
(off Brunel Est.)
Landor Rd. SW9 . . . . 3J 119
Landor Theatre 3J 119
Landor Wlk. W12 . . . . 2C 98
Landra Gdns. N21 . . . . 6G 23
Landrake *NW1* 1G 83
(off Plender St.)
Landridge Dr. EN1: Enf 1C 24
Landridge Rd. SW6 . . . . 2H 117
Landrock Rd. N8 . . . . 6J 47
Landscape Rd. IG8: Wfd G 7E 36
Landsdown Cl. EN5: New Bar 4F 21
Landseer Av. E12 . . . . 5E 70
Landseer Cl. HA8: Edg 2G 43
SW19 . . . . 1A 154
Landseer Ct. UB4: Hayes 2F 75
Landseer Ho. *NW8* 3B 4
(off Frampton St.)
SW1 . . . . 4D 18
(off Herrick St.)
SW11 . . . . 1E 118
UB5: N'olt 2B 76
(off Parkfield Dr.)
Landseer Rd. EN1: Enf 5B 24
KT3: N Mald 7K 151
N19 . . . . 3J 65
(not continuous)
SM1: Sutt 6J 165
Landstead Rd. SE18 . . . . 7H 107
Landulph Ho. *SE11* 5K 19
(off Kennings Way)
Landward Ct. *W1* 7D 4
(off Harrowby St.)
Lane, The NW8 . . . . 2A 82
SE3 . . . . 3J 123
Lane App. NW7 . . . . 5B 30
Lane Cl. NW2 . . . . 3D 62
Lane End DA7: Bex 3H 127
SW15 . . . . 6F 117
Lane Gdns. WD23: Bushy 1D 26
Lane M. E12 . . . . 3D 70
Lanercost Cl. SW2 . . . . 2A 138
Lanercost Gdns. N14 . . . . 7D 22
Lanercost Rd. SW2 . . . . 2A 138
Lanesborough Ct. *N1* 1G 9
(off Fanshaw St.)
Lanesborough Pl. SW1 . . . . 6H 11
Laneside BR7: Chst 5F 143
HA8: Edg 5D 28
Laneside Av. RM8: Dag 7F 55
Laneway SW15 . . . . 5D 116
Laney Ho. *EC1* 5J 7
(off Leather La.)
Lanfranc Ct. HA1: Harr 3K 59
Lanfranc Rd. E3 . . . . 2A 86
Lanfrey Pl. W14 . . . . 5H 99
Langbourne Av. N6 . . . . 2E 64
Langbourne Ct. E17 . . . . 6A 50
Langbourne Mans. N6 . . . . 2E 64
Langbourne Pl. E14 . . . . 5D 104
Langbourne Way KT10: Clay 6A 162
Langbrook Rd. SE3 . . . . 3B 124
Langcroft Cl. SM5: Cars 3D 166
Langdale *NW1* 1A 6
(off Stanhope St.)
Langdale Av. CR4: Mitc 3D 154
Langdale Cl. BR6: Farnb 3F 173
RM8: Dag 1C 72
SE17 . . . . 6C 102
SW14 . . . . 4H 115
Langdale Cres. DA7: Bex 7G 109
Langdale Dr. UB4: Hayes 2G 75
Langdale Gdns. UB6: G'frd 3B 78
Langdale Ho. *SW1* 6A 18
(off Churchill Gdns.)
Langdale Pde. CR4: Mitc 3D 154
Langdale Rd. CR7: Thor H 4A 156
SE10 . . . . 7E 104
Langdale St. E1 . . . . 6H 85
Langdon Ct. *EC1* 1B 8
(off City Rd.)
NW10 . . . . 1A 80
Langdon Cres. E6 . . . . 2E 88
Langdon Dr. NW9 . . . . 1J 61
Langdon Ho. E14 . . . . 6E 86
Langdon Pk. TW11: Tedd 7C 132
Langdon Pk. Rd. N6 . . . . 7G 47
Langdon Pl. SW14 . . . . 3J 115
Langdon Rd. BR2: Brom 3K 159
E6 . . . . 1E 88
SM4: Mord 5A 154
Langdons Ct. UB2: S'hall 3E 94
Langdon Shaw DA14: Sidc 5K 143
Langdon Wlk. SM4: Mord 5A 154
Langdon Way SE1 . . . . 4G 103
Langford Cl. E8 . . . . 5G 67
NW8 . . . . 2A 82
W3 . . . . 2H 97
Langford Ct. *NW8* 2A 82
(off Abbey Rd.)
Langford Cres. EN4: Cockf 4J 21
Langford Grn. SE5 . . . . 3E 120
Langford Ho. SE8 . . . . 6C 104
Langford M. N1 . . . . 7A 66
Langford Pl. DA14: Sidc 3A 144
NW8 . . . . 2A 82
Langford Rd. EN4: Cockf 4J 21
IG8: Wfd G 6F 37
SW6 . . . . 2K 117
Langfords IG9: Buck H 2G 37
Langham Cl. *N15* 3B 48
(off Langham Rd.)
Langham Ct. HA4: Ruis 5K 57
NW4 . . . . 5F 45
SW20 . . . . 2E 152
Langham Dr. RM6: Chad H 6B 54
Langham Gdns. HA0: Wemb 2C 60
HA8: Edg 7D 28
N21 . . . . 5F 23
TW10: Ham 4C 132
W13 . . . . 7B 78
Langham Ho. Cl. TW10: Ham 4D 132
Langham Mans. *SW5* 5K 99
(off Earl's Ct. Sq.)
Langham Pk. Pl. BR2: Brom 4H 159
Langham Pl. N15 . . . . 3B 48
W1 . . . . 6K 5 (5F 83)
W4 . . . . 6A 98
Langham Rd. HA8: Edg 6D 28
N15 . . . . 3B 48
SW20 . . . . 1E 152
TW11: Tedd 5B 132
Langham St. W1 . . . . 6K 5 (5F 83)
Langhedge Cl. N18 . . . . 6A 34
Langhedge La. N18 . . . . 6A 34
Langhedge La. Ind. Est. N18 . . . . 6A 34
Langholm Cl. SW12 . . . . 7H 119
Langholme WD23: Bush 1B 26
Langhorn Dr. TW2: Twick 7J 113
Langhorne Ct. *NW8* 7B 64
(off Dorman Way)
Langhorne Rd. RM10: Dag 7G 73
Lang Ho. *SW8* 7J 101
(off Hartington Rd.)
TW19: Stanw 1A 128
Langland Cres. HA7: Stan 2D 42
Langland Dr. HA5: Pinn 1C 40
Langland Gdns. CR0: Croy 2B 170
NW3 . . . . 5K 63
Langland Ho. *SE5* 7D 102
(off Edmund St.)
Langler Rd. NW10 . . . . 2E 80
Langley Av. HA4: Ruis 2K 57
KT4: Wor Pk 1F 165
KT6: Surb 1D 162
Langley Ct. WC2 . . . . 2E 12 (7J 83)
Langley Cres. E11 . . . . 7A 52
HA8: Edg 3D 28
RM9: Dag 7C 72
UB3: Harl 7H 93
Langley Dr. E11 . . . . 7K 51
W3 . . . . 2H 97
Langley Gdns. BR2: Brom 4A 160
BR5: Pet W 6F 161
RM9: Dag 7D 72
Langley Gro. KT3: N Mald 2A 152
Langley Ho. *W2* 5J 81
(off Alfred Rd.)
Langley La. SW8 . . . . 7F 19 (6K 101)
Langley Mans. SW8 . . . . 7F 19
Langley Pk. NW7 . . . . 6F 29
Langley Pk. Girls School Sports Cen. 6E 158
Langley Pk. Rd. SM1: Sutt 5A 166
SM2: Sutt 6A 166
Langley Rd. BR3: Beck 4A 158
DA16: Well 6C 108
KT6: Surb 7E 150
SW19 . . . . 1H 153
TW7: Isle 2K 113
Langley Row EN5: Barn 1C 20
Langley St. WC2 . . . . 1E 12 (6J 83)
Langley Way BR4: W W'ck 1F 171
Langmead Dr. WD23: Bushy 1D 26
Langmead St. SE27 . . . . 4B 138
Langmore Ct. DA6: Bex 3D 126
Langmore Ho. *E1* 6G 85
(off Stutfield St.)
Langport Ct. KT12: Walt T 7A 148
Langport Ho. SW9 . . . . 2B 120
Langridge M. TW12: Hamp 6D 130
Langroyd Rd. SW17 . . . . 2D 136
Langside Av. SW15 . . . . 4C 116
Langside Cres. N14 . . . . 3C 32
Langstone Way NW7 . . . . 7A 30
Langston Hughes Cl. SE24 . . . . 4B 120
Lang St. E1 . . . . 4J 85
Langthorn Ct. EC2 . . . . 7E 8 (6D 84)
Langthorne Ct. BR1: Brom 4E 140
Langthorne Ho. UB3: Harl 4G 93
Langthorne Rd. E11 . . . . 3E 68
Langthorne St. SW6 . . . . 7F 99
Langton Av. E6 . . . . 3E 88
N20 . . . . 7F 21
Langton Cl. WC1 . . . . 3H 7 (4K 83)
Langton Ho. SE11 . . . . 3H 19
Langton Pl. SW18 . . . . 1J 135
Langton Ri. SE23 . . . . 7H 121
Langton Rd. HA3: Hrw W 7B 26
KT8: W Mole 4G 149
NW2 . . . . 3E 62
SW9 . . . . 7B 102
Langton St. SW10 . . . . 6A 100
Langton Way CR0: Croy 3E 168
SE3 . . . . 1H 123
Langtry Ho. *KT2: King T* 1G 151
(off London Rd.)
Langtry Pl. SW6 . . . . 6J 99
Langtry Rd. NW8 . . . . 1K 81
UB5: N'olt 2B 76
Langtry Wlk. NW8 . . . . 1K 81
Langwood Chase TW11: Tedd 6C 132
Langworth Dr. UB4: Yead 6K 75
Lanhill Rd. W9 . . . . 4J 81
Lanier Rd. SE13 . . . . 6F 123
Lanigan Dr. TW3: Houn 5F 113
Lankaster Gdns. N2 . . . . 1B 46
Lankers Dr. HA2: Harr 6D 40
Lankton Cl. BR3: Beck 1E 158
Lannock Rd. UB3: Hayes 1H 93
Lannoy Point *SW6* 7G 99
(off Pellant Rd.)
Lannoy Rd. SE9 . . . . 1G 143
Lanrick Ho. *E14* 6F 87
(off Lanrick Rd.)
Lanrick Rd. E14 . . . . 6F 87
Lanridge Rd. SE2 . . . . 3D 108
Lansbury Av. IG11: Bark 7A 72
N18 . . . . 5J 33
RM6: Chad H 5E 54
TW14: Felt 6K 111
Lansbury Cl. NW10 . . . . 5J 61
Lansbury Ct. *SE28* 7B 90
(off Saunders Way)
Lansbury Dr. UB4: Hayes 2G 75
Lansbury Est. E14 . . . . 6D 86
Lansbury Gdns. E14 . . . . 6F 87
Lansbury Rd. EN3: Enf H 1E 24
Lansbury Way N18 . . . . 5K 33
Lanscombe Wlk. SW8 . . . . 1J 119
Lansdell Ho. *SW2* 6A 120
(off Tulse Hill)
Lansdell Rd. CR4: Mitc 2E 154
Lansdowne Av. BR6: Farnb 1F 173
DA7: Bex 7D 108
Lansdowne Cl. KT6: Surb 2H 163
SW20 . . . . 7F 135
TW1: Twick 1K 131
Lansdowne Ct. IG5: Ilf 3C 52
KT4: Wor Pk 2C 164
W11 . . . . 7G 81
(off Lansdowne Ri.)
Lansdowne Cres. W11 . . . . 7G 81
Lansdowne Dr. E8 . . . . 6G 67
Lansdowne Gdns. SW8 . . . . 1J 119
Lansdowne Grn. Est. SW8 . . . . 1J 119
Lansdowne Gro. NW10 . . . . 4A 62
Lansdowne Hill SE27 . . . . 3B 138
Lansdowne Ho. *W11* 1H 99
(off Ladbroke Rd.)
Lansdowne La. SE7 . . . . 6B 106
Lansdowne M. SE7 . . . . 5B 106
W11 . . . . 1H 99
Lansdowne Pl. SE1 . . . . 3D 102
SE19 . . . . 7F 139
Lansdowne Ri. W11 . . . . 7G 81
Lansdowne Rd. BR1: Brom 7J 141
CR0: Croy 2D 168
E4 . . . . 2H 35
E11 . . . . 2H 69
E17 . . . . 6C 50
E18 . . . . 3J 51
HA1: Harr 7J 41
HA7: Stan 6H 27
IG3: Ilf 1K 71
KT19: Ewe 7J 163
N3 . . . . 7D 30
N10 . . . . 2G 47
N17 . . . . 1F 49
SW20 . . . . 7E 134
TW3: Houn 3F 113
UB8: Hil 6E 74
W11 . . . . 7G 81
Lansdowne Row W1 . . . . 4K 11 (1F 101)
Lansdowne Ter. WC1 . . . . 4F 7 (4J 83)
Lansdowne Wlk. W11 . . . . 1H 99
Lansdowne Way SW8 . . . . 1H 119
Lansdowne Wood Cl. SE27 . . . . 3B 138
Lansdowne Workshops SE7 . . . . 5A 106
Lansdown Rd. DA14: Sidc 3B 144
E7 . . . . 7A 70
Lansfield Av. N18 . . . . 4B 34
Lantern Cl. HA0: Wemb 5D 60
SW15 . . . . 4C 116
Lanterns Ct. E14 . . . . 2D 104

A-Z London 303

Lantern Way UB7: W Dray 2A 92
Lant Ho. SE1 7C 14
(off Toulmin St.)
Lantry Ct. W3 1H 97
Lant St. SE1 6C 14 (2C 102)
Lanvanor Rd. SE15 2J 121
Lanyard Ho. SE8 4B 104
Lapford Cl. W9 4H 81
Lapponum Wlk. UB4: Yead 4B 76
Lapse Wood Wlk. SE23 1H 139
Lapstone Gdns.
HA3: Kent 6C 42
Lapwing Ct. KT6: Surb 3G 163
SE1 7D 14
(off Swan St.)
Lapwing Twr. SE8 6B 104
(off Taylor Cl.)
Lapwing Way UB4: Yead 6B 76
Lapworth N11 4A 32
(off Coppies Gro.)
Lapworth Ct. W2 5K 81
(off Delamere Ter.)
Lara Cl. KT9: Chess 7E 162
SE13 6E 122
Larbert Rd. SW16 7G 137
Larch Av. W3 1A 98
Larch Cl. E13 4K 87
N11 7K 31
N19 2G 65
SE8 6B 104
SW12 2F 137
Larch Ct. SE1 7G 15
(off Royal Oak Yd.)
W9 5J 81
(off Admiral Wlk.)
Larch Cres. KT19: Ewe 6H 163
UB4: Yead 4A 76
Larch Dene BR6: Farnb 2E 172
Larch Dr. W4 5G 97
Larches, The N13 3H 33
UB10: Hil 3D 74
Larches Av. SW14 4K 115
Larch Grn. NW9 1A 44
Larch Gro. DA15: Sidc 1K 143
Larch Ho. BR2: Brom 1G 159
SE16 2J 103
(off Ainsty Est.)
UB4: Yead 5A 76
W10 4G 81
(off Rowan Wlk.)
Larch Rd. E10 2C 68
NW2 4E 62
Larch Tree Way CR0: Croy 3C 170
Larchvale Ct. SM2: Sutt 7K 165
Larch Way BR2: Brom 7E 160
Larchwood Rd. SE9 2F 143
Larcombe Cl. CR0: Croy 4F 169
Larcombe Ct. SM2: Sutt 7K 165
(off Worcester Rd.)
Larcom St. SE17 4C 102
Larden Rd. W3 1A 98
Largewood Av. KT6: Surb 2G 163
Larissa St. SE17 5D 102
Larkbere Rd. SE26 4A 140
Larken Cl. WD23: Bush 1B 26
Larken Dr. WD23: Bush 1B 26
Larkfield Av. HA3: Kent 3B 42
Larkfield Cl. BR2: Hayes 2H 171
Larkfield Rd. DA14: Sidc 3K 143
TW9: Rich 4E 114
Larkhall La. SW4 2H 119
Larkhall Ri. SW4 3G 119
(not continuous)
Larkham Cl. TW13: Felt 3G 129
Larkhill Ter. SE18 7E 106
Lark Row E2 1J 85
Larksfield Gro. EN1: Enf 1C 24
Larks Gro. IG11: Bark 7J 71
Larkshall Ct. RM7: Mawney 2J 55
Larkshall Cres. E4 4K 35
Larkshall Rd. E4 5K 35
Larkspur Cl. E6 5C 88
HA4: Ruis 7E 38
Larkspur Cl. N17 7J 33
NW9 5H 43
Larkspur Gro. HA8: Edg 4D 28
Larkspur Lodge DA14: Sidc 3B 144
Larkspur Way KT19: Ewe 5J 163
Larkswood Ct. E4 5A 36
Larkswood Leisure Cen. 4K 35
Larkswood Ri. HA5: Eastc 4A 40
Larkswood Rd. E4 4H 35
Lark Way SM5: Cars 7C 154
Larkway Cl. NW9 4K 43
Larnach Rd. W6 6F 99
Larne Rd. HA4: Ruis 7H 39
Larpent Av. SW15 5E 116
Larwood Cl. UB6: G'frd 5H 59
Lascelles Av. HA1: Harr 7H 41
Lascelles Cl. E11 2F 69
Lascelles Ho. NW1 4D 4
Lascotts Rd. N22 6E 32
Laseron Ho. N15 4F 49
(off Tottenham Grn. E.)
Lassa Rd. SE9 5C 124
Lassell St. SE10 5F 105
Lasseter Pl. SE3 6G 105
Latchett Rd. E18 1K 51
Latchingdon Ct. E17 4K 49
Latchingdon Gdns. IG8: Wfd G 6H 37
Latchmere Cl. TW10: Ham 5E 132
Latchmere La. KT2: King T 6F 133
TW10: Ham 6F 133
Latchmere Leisure Cen. 2D 118
Latchmere Pas. SW11 2C 118
Latchmere Rd. KT2: King T 7E 132
SW11 2D 118
Latchmere St. SW11 2D 118
Lateward Rd. TW8: Bford 6D 96
Latham Cl. E6 5C 88
TW1: Twick 7A 114
Latham Ct. N11 6D 32
(off Brownlow Rd.)
SW5 4J 99
(off W. Cromwell Rd.)
UB5: N'olt 3B 76
(off Seasprite Cl.)
Latham Ho. E1 6K 85
(off Chudleigh St.)
Latham Rd. DA6: Bex 5G 127
TW1: Twick 7K 113
Latham's Way CR0: Wadd 1K 167
Lathkill Cl. EN1: Enf 7B 24
Lathkill Ct. BR3: Beck 1B 158
Lathom Rd. E6 7C 70
Latimer Av. E6 1D 88
Latimer Cl. HA5: Pinn 1A 40
KT4: Wor Pk 4D 164
Latimer Ct. BR2: Brom 4H 159
(off Durham Rd.)
Latimer Gdns. HA5: Pinn 1A 40
Latimer Ho. E9 6K 67
W11 7H 81
(off Kensington Pk. Rd.)
Latimer Ind. Est. W10 6E 80
Latimer Pl. W10 6E 80
Latimer Rd. CR0: Croy 3B 168
E7 4K 69
EN5: New Bar 3E 20
N15 6E 48
SW19 6K 135
TW11: Tedd 5K 131
W10 5E 80
(not continuous)
Latitude Ct. E16 7G 89
Latona Ct. SW9 7A 102
(off Caldwell St.)
Latona Rd. SE15 6G 103
La Tourne Gdns. BR6: Farnb 3G 173
Lattimer Pl. W4 7A 98
Latton Cl. KT12: Walt T 7C 148
Latvia Ct. SE17 5C 102
(off Sutherland Sq.)
Latymer Ct. W6 4F 99
Latymer Gdns. N3 2G 45
Latymer Rd. N9 1A 34
Latymer Upper School Sports Cen. 5C 98
Latymer Way N9 2K 33
Lauder Cl. UB5: N'olt 2B 76
Lauder Ct. N14 7D 22
Lauderdale Dr. TW10: Ham 3D 132
Lauderdale House 1F 65
Lauderdale Ho. SW9 1A 120
(off Gosling Way)
Lauderdale Mans. W9 3K 81
(off Lauderdale Rd., not continuous)
Lauderdale Pde. W9 4K 81
Lauderdale Pl. EC2 5C 8
(off Beech St.)
Lauderdale Rd. W9 3K 81
Lauderdale Twr. EC2 5C 8
Laud St. CR0: Croy 3C 168
SE11 5G 19 (5K 101)
Laughton Rd. UB5: N'olt 1B 76
Launcelot Rd. BR1: Brom 4J 141
Launcelot St. SE1 7J 13 (2A 102)
Launceston Gdns. UB6: G'frd 1C 78
Launceston Pl. W8 3A 100
Launceston Rd. UB6: G'frd 1C 78
Launch St. E14 3E 104
Laundress La. N16 3G 67
Laundry La. N1 1C 84
Laundry M. SE23 7A 122
Laundry Rd. W6 6G 99
Launton Dr. DA6: Bex 4D 126
Laura Cl. E11 5A 52
EN1: Enf 5K 23
Lauradale Rd. N2 4D 46
Laura Pl. E5 4J 67
Laura Ter. N4 2B 66
Laurel Av. TW1: Twick 1K 131
Laurel Bank N12 4F 31
Laurel Bank Gdns. SW6 2H 117
Laurel Bank Rd. EN2: Enf 1H 23
Laurel Bank Vs. W7 2J 95
(off Lwr. Boston Rd.)
Laurelbrook SE6 3G 141
Laurel Cl. DA14: Sidc 3A 144
N19 2G 65
SW17 5C 136
Laurel Ct. CR2: S Croy 4E 168
(off South Pk. Hill Rd.)
HA0: Wemb 2E 78
Laurel Cres. CR0: Croy 3C 170
RM7: Rush G 1K 73
Laurel Dr. N21 7F 23
Laurel Gdns. BR1: Brom 4C 160
E4 7J 25
NW7 3E 28
TW4: Houn 4C 112
W7 1J 95
Laurel Gro. SE20 7H 139
SE26 4K 139
Laurel Ho. BR2: Brom 1G 159
SE8 6B 104
Laurel La. UB7: W Dray 4A 92
Laurel Mnr. SM2: Sutt 7A 166
Laurel Pk. HA3: Hrw W 7E 26
Laurel Rd. SW13 2C 116
SW20 1D 152
TW12: Ham H 5H 131
Laurels, The BR1: Brom 1K 159
BR2: Brom 4J 159
IG9: Buck H 1F 37
NW10 1D 80
WD23: Bushy 2D 26
Laurel St. E8 6F 67
Laurel Vw. N12 3E 30
Laurel Way E18 4H 51
N20 3D 30
Laurence Ct. E10 7D 50
Laurence M. W12 2C 98
Laurence Pountney Hill
EC4 2E 14 (7D 84)
Laurence Pountney La.
EC4 2E 14 (7D 84)
Laurie Gro. SE14 1A 122
Laurie Ho. SE1 3B 102
(off St George's Rd.)
Laurie Ho. W8 1J 99
(off Airlie Gdns.)
Laurie Rd. W7 5J 77
Laurier Rd. CR0: Croy 7F 157
NW5 3F 65
Laurimel Cl. HA7: Stan 6G 27
Laurino Pl. WD23: Bushy 2B 26
Lauriston Ho. E9 7J 67
(off Lauriston Rd.)
Lauriston Rd. E9 7J 67
SW19 6F 135
Lausanne Rd. N8 4A 48
SE15 1J 121
Lavell St. N16 4D 66
Lavender Av. CR4: Mitc 1C 154
KT4: Wor Pk 3E 164
NW9 1J 61
Lavender Cl. BR2: Brom 6C 160
SM5: Cars 4F 167
SW3 7B 16 (6B 100)
Lavender Ct. KT8: W Mole 3F 149
SM2: Sutt 7A 166
TW14: Felt 6K 111
Lavender Gdns. EN2: Enf 1G 23
HA3: Hrw W 6D 26
SW11 4D 118
Lavender Gro. CR4: Mitc 1C 154
E8 7G 67
Lavender Hill EN2: Enf 1F 23
SW11 4C 118
Lavender Ho. SE16 1K 103
(off Rotherhithe St.)
TW9: Kew 1H 115
Lavender Pl. IG1: Ilf 5F 71
Lavender Pond Nature Pk. 1A 104
Lavender Ri. UB7: W Dray 2C 92
Lavender Rd. CR0: Croy 6K 155
EN2: Enf 1J 23
KT19: Ewe 5H 163
SE16 1A 104
SM1: Sutt 4B 166
SM5: Cars 4E 166
SW11 3B 118
UB8: Hil 5B 74
Lavender Sq. E11 3F 69
Lavender St. E15 6G 69
Lavender Sweep SW11 4D 118
Lavender Ter. SW11 3C 118
Lavender Va. SM6: Wall 6H 167
Lavender Wlk. CR4: Mitc 3E 154
SW11 4D 118
Lavender Way CR0: Croy 6K 157
Lavendon Ho. NW8 3D 4
(off Paveley St.)
Lavengro Rd. SE27 2C 138
Lavenham Rd. SW18 2H 135
Lavernock Rd. DA7: Bex 2G 127
Lavers Rd. N16 3E 66
Laverstoke Gdns. SW15 7B 116
Laverton M. SW5 4K 99
Laverton Pl. SW5 4K 99
Lavidge Rd. SE9 2C 142
Lavina Gro. N1 2K 83
Lavington Cl. E9 6B 68
Lavington Rd. CR0: Bedd 3K 167
W13 1B 96
Lavington St. SE1 5B 14 (1B 102)
Lavisham Ho. BR1: Brom 5K 141
Lawdons Gdns. CR0: Wadd 4B 168
Lawes Ho. W10 3H 81
(off Lancefield St.)
Lawford Rd. N1 7E 66
NW5 6G 65
W4 7J 97
Lawfords Wharf NW1 7G 65
(off Lyme St.)
Law Ho. IG11: Bark 2A 90
Lawless Ho. E14 7E 86
(off Bazely St.)
Lawless St. E14 7D 86
Lawley Ho. TW1: Twick 6D 114
Lawley Rd. N14 7A 22
Lawley St. E5 4J 67

Lawn, The UB2: S'hall 5E **94**
Lawn Cl. BR1: Brom 6K **141**
HA4: Ruis 3H **57**
KT3: N Mald 2A **152**
N9 . . . . .7A **24**
Lawn Cres. TW9: Kew 2G **115**
Lawn Dr. E7 . . . . .4B **70**
Lawn Farm Gro. RM6: Chad H 4E **54**
Lawn Gdns. W7 . . . . .1J **95**
Lawn Ho. Cl. E14 . . . . .2F **104**
Lawn La. SW8 . . . . .7F **19** (6J **101**)
Lawn Rd. BR3: Beck 7B **140**
NW3 . . . . .5D **64**
Lawns, The DA14: Sidc 4B **144**
E4 . . . . .5H **35**
HA5: H End 7A **26**
SE3 . . . . .3H **123**
SE19 . . . . .1D **156**
SM2: Cheam 7G **165**
SW19 . . . . .5H **135**
Lawns Ct. HA9: Wemb 2F **61**
Lawnside SE3 . . . . .4H **123**
Lawns Way RM5: Col R 1J **55**
Lawnswood EN5: Barn 5B **20**
Lawn Ter. SE3 . . . . .3G **123**
Lawn Va. HA5: Pinn 2C **40**
Lawrence Av. E12 . . . . .4E **70**
E17 . . . . .1K **49**
KT3: N Mald 6K **151**
N13 . . . . .4G **33**
NW7 . . . . .4F **29**
NW10 . . . . .1K **79**
Lawrence Bldgs. N16 . . . . .3F **67**
Lawrence Campe Cl. N20 . . . . .3G **31**
Lawrence Cl. E3 . . . . .3C **86**
N15 . . . . .4E **48**
W12 . . . . .7D **80**
Lawrence Ct. N10 . . . . .3G **47**
N16 . . . .*3F* ***67***
(off Smalley Rd. Est.)
NW7 . . . . .5F **29**
W3 . . . .*3J* ***97***
(off Stanley Rd.)
Lawrence Cres. HA8: Edg 2G **43**
RM10: Dag 3H **73**
Lawrence Dr. UB10: Ick 4E **56**
Lawrence Est. TW4: Houn 4A **112**
Lawrence Gdns. NW7 . . . . .3G **29**
Lawrence Hill E4 . . . . .2H **35**
Lawrence Ho. *SW1* *4D* ***18***
(off Cureton St.)
Lawrence La. EC2 . . . . .7D **8** (6C **84**)
Lawrence Mans. *SW1* *5J* ***17***
(off Sutherland St.)
SW3 . . . .*7C* ***16***
(off Lawrence St.)
Lawrence Pde. *TW7: Isle* *3B* ***114***
(off Lower Sq.)
Lawrence Pl. *N1* *1J* ***83***
(off Brydon Wlk.)
Lawrence Rd. BR4: W W'ck 4J **171**
DA8: Frith 7H **109**
E6 . . . . .1C **88**
E13 . . . . .1K **87**
HA5: Pinn 6B **40**
N15 . . . . .4E **48**
N18 . . . . .4C **34**
(not continuous)
SE25 . . . . .4F **157**
TW4: Houn 4A **112**
TW10: Ham 4C **132**
TW12: Hamp 7D **130**
UB4: Hayes 2E **74**
W5 . . . . .4D **96**
Lawrence St. E16 . . . . .5H **87**
NW7 . . . . .4G **29**
SW3 . . . . .7C **16** (6C **100**)
Lawrence Trad. Est. SE10 . . . . .4G **105**
Lawrence Way NW10 . . . . .3J **61**
Lawrence Weaver Cl. SM4: Mord 6J **153**
Lawrence Yd. N15 . . . . .4E **48**
Lawrie Pk. Av. SE26 . . . . .5H **139**
Lawrie Pk. Cres. SE26 . . . . .5H **139**
Lawrie Pk. Gdns. SE26 . . . . .4H **139**
Lawrie Pk. Rd. SE26 . . . . .6H **139**
Laws Cl. SE25 . . . . .4D **156**
Lawson Cl. E16 . . . . .5A **88**
IG1: Ilf .5H **71**
SW19 . . . . .3F **135**
Lawson Ct. KT6: Surb 7D **150**
N4 . . . .*1K* ***65***
(off Lorne Rd.)
Lawson Gdns. HA5: Eastc 3K **39**
Lawson Ho. *SE18* *6E* ***106***
(off Nightingale Pl.)
W12 . . . .*7D* ***80***
(off White City Est.)
Lawson Rd. EN3: Enf H 1D **24**
UB1: S'hall 4E **76**
Law St. SE1 .3D **102**
Lawton Rd. E3 . . . . .3A **86**
(not continuous)
E10 . . . . .1E **68**
EN4: Cockf 3G **21**
Laxcon Cl. NW10 . . . . .5K **61**
Laxey Rd. BR6: Chels 6K **173**
Laxfield Ct. *E8* *1G* ***85***
(off Pownall Rd.)
Laxford Ho. *SW1* *4H* ***17***
(off Cundy St.)
Laxley Cl. SE5 . . . . .7B **102**
Laxton Ct. CR7: Thor H 4C **156**
Laxton Pl. NW1 . . . . .3K **5** (4F **83**)
Layard Rd. CR7: Thor H 2D **156**
EN1: Enf 1A **24**
SE16 . . . . .4H **103**
Layard Sq. SE16 . . . . .4H **103**
Laybourne Ho. *E14* *2C* ***104***
(off Admirals Way)
Laybrook Lodge E18 . . . . .4H **51**
Laycock St. N1 . . . . .6A **66**
Layer Gdns. W3 . . . . .7G **79**
Layfield Cl. NW4 . . . . .7D **44**
Layfield Cres. NW4 . . . . .7D **44**
Layfield Ho. *SE10* *5J* ***105***
(off Kemsing Rd.)
Layfield Rd. NW4 . . . . .7D **44**
Layhams Rd. BR2: Kes 3F **171**
BR4: W W'ck 3F **171**
Laymarsh Cl. DA17: Belv 3F **109**
Laymead Cl. UB5: N'olt 6C **58**
Laystall Ct. *WC1* *4J* ***7***
(off Mt. Pleasant)
Laystall St. EC1 . . . . .4J **7** (4A **84**)
Layton Ct. TW8: Bford 5D **96**
Layton Cres. CR0: Wadd 5A **168**
Layton Pl. TW9: Kew 1G **115**
Layton Rd. TW3: Houn 4F **113**
TW8: Bford 5D **96**
Layton's Bldgs. SE1 . . . . . . .6F **14** (2D **102**)
Layton's La. TW16: Sun 2H **147**
Layzell Wlk. SE9 . . . . .1B **142**
Lazar Wlk. N7 . . . . .2K **65**
Lazenby Ct. WC2 . . . . .2E **12**
Leabank Cl. HA1: Harr 3J **59**
Leabank Sq. E9 . . . . .6C **68**
Leabank Vw. N15 . . . . .6G **49**
Lea Bon Ct. *E15* *1H* ***87***
(off Plaistow Gro.)
Leabourne Rd. N16 . . . . .7G **49**
LEA BRIDGE .3K **67**
Lea Bri. Ind. Cen. E10 . . . . .1A **68**
Lea Bri. Rd. E5 . . . . .3J **67**
E10 . . . . .3J **67**
E17 . . . . .5F **51**
Lea Cl. TW2: Whit 7D **112**
Lea Ct. E4 . . . . .2K **35**
E13 . . . . .3J **87**
Lea Cres. HA4: Ruis 4H **57**
Leacroft Av. SW12 . . . . .7D **118**
Leacroft Cl. N21 . . . . .2G **33**
UB7: Yiew 6A **74**
Leadale Av. E4 . . . . .2H **35**
Leadale Rd. N15 . . . . .6G **49**
N16 . . . . .6G **49**
Leadbeaters Cl. N11 . . . . .5J **31**
Leadbetter Ct. *NW10* *7K* ***61***
(off Melville Rd.)
Leadenhall Mkt. EC3 . . . . .1G **15** (6E **84**)
Leadenhall Pl. EC3 . . . . .1G **15** (6E **84**)
Leadenhall St. EC3 . . . . .1G **15** (6E **84**)
Leadenham Ct. E3 . . . . .4C **86**
Leader Av. E12 . . . . .5E **70**
Leadings, The
HA9: Wemb 3J **61**
Leaf Cl. HA6: Nwood 1F **39**
KT7: T Ditt 5J **149**
Leaf Gro. SE27 . . . . .5A **138**
Leaf Ho. *HA1: Harr* *5K* ***41***
(off Catherine Pl.)
Leafield Cl. SW16 . . . . .6B **138**
Leafield La. DA14: Sidc 3F **145**
Leafield Rd. SM1: Sutt 2J **165**
SW20 . . . . .3H **153**
Leafy Gro. BR2: Kes 5A **172**
Leafy Oak Rd. SE12 . . . . .4A **142**
Leafy Way CR0: Croy 2F **169**
Lea Gdns. HA9: Wemb 4F **61**
Leagrave St. E5 . . . . .3J **67**
Lea Hall Gdns. E10 . . . . .1C **68**
Lea Hall Rd. E10 . . . . .1C **68**
Leaholme Way HA4: Ruis 6E **38**
Lea Ho. *NW8* *4C* ***4***
(off Salisbury St.)
Leahurst Rd. SE13 . . . . .5F **123**
(not continuous)
LEA INTERCHANGE **5C 68**
Leake Ct. SE1 . . . . .7H **13** (2K **101**)
Leake St. SE1 . . . . .6H **13** (2K **101**)
(not continuous)
Lealand Rd. N15 . . . . .6F **49**
Leamington Av. BR1: Brom 5A **142**
BR6: Orp 4J **173**
E17 . . . . .5C **50**
SM4: Mord 4G **153**
Leamington Cl. BR1: Brom 4A **142**
E12 . . . . .5C **70**
TW3: Houn 5G **113**
Leamington Cres. HA2: Harr 3C **58**
Leamington Gdns. IG3: Ilf 2K **71**
Leamington Ho. HA8: Edg 5A **28**
W11 . . . .*5H* ***81***
(off Leamington Rd. Vs.)
Leamington Pk. W3 . . . . .5K **79**
Leamington Pl. UB4: Hayes 4H **75**
Leamington Rd. UB2: S'hall 4B **94**
Leamington Rd. Vs. W11 . . . . .5H **81**
Leamore St. W6 . . . . .4E **98**
LEAMOUTH .7G **87**
Leamouth Rd. E6 . . . . .5C **88**
E14 . . . . .6F **87**
Leander Ct. KT6: Surb 7D **150**
NW9 . . . . .1A **44**
SE8 . . . . .1C **122**
Leander Rd. CR7: Thor H 4K **155**
SW2 . . . . .6K **119**
UB5: N'olt 2E **76**
Lea Pk. Trad. Est. E10 . . . . .7B **50**
Learner Dr. HA2: Harr 2E **58**
Lea Rd. BR3: Beck 2C **158**
EN2: Enf 1J **23**
UB2: S'hall 4C **94**
Learoyd Gdns. E6 . . . . .7E **88**
Leary Ho. SE11 . . . . .5K **101**
Leas Cl. KT9: Chess 7F **163**
Leas Dale SE9 . . . . .3E **142**
Leas Grn. BR7: Chst 6K **143**
Leaside Av. N10 . . . . .3E **46**
Leaside Bus. Cen. EN3: Brim 2G **25**
Leaside Ct. UB10: Hil 3D **74**
Leaside Mans. *N10* *3E* ***46***
(off Fortis Grn.)
Leaside Rd. E5 . . . . .1J **67**
Leasowes Rd. E10 . . . . .1C **68**
Lea Sq. E3 . . . . .1B **86**
Leatherbottle Grn.
DA18: Erith 3F **109**
Leather Bottle La. DA17: Belv 4E **108**
Leather Cl. CR4: Mitc 2E **154**
Leatherdale St. E1 . . . . .4J **85**
(Harpley Sq.)
E1 . . . . .3K **85**
(Portelet Rd.)
Leather Gdns. E15 . . . . .1G **87**
Leatherhead Cl. N16 . . . . .1F **67**
Leatherhead Rd. KT9: Chess 7D **162**
Leather La. EC1 . . . . .5J **7** (5A **84**)
(not continuous)
Leathermarket, The SE1 . . . . .7G **15**
Leathermarket Ct. SE1 . . . . .7G **15** (2E **102**)
Leathermarket St. SE1 . . . . .7G **15** (2E **102**)
Leathersellers Cl. *EN5: Barn* *3B* ***20***
(off The Avenue)
Leather St. E1 . . . . .7K **85**
Leathsail Rd. HA2: Harr 3F **59**
Leathwaite Rd. SW11 . . . . .4D **118**
Leathwell Rd. SE8 . . . . .2D **122**
Lea Va. DA1: Cray 4K **127**
Lea Valley Rd. E4 . . . . .5F **25**
EN3: Pond E 5F **25**
Lea Valley Trad. Est. N18 . . . . .6E **34**
Lea Valley Viaduct E4 . . . . .5E **34**
N18 . . . . .5E **34**
Leaveland Cl. BR3: Beck 4C **158**
Leaver Gdns. UB6: G'frd 2H **77**
Leavesden Rd. HA7: Stan 6F **27**
Leaves Grn. Rd. BR2: Kes 7B **172**
Lea Vw. Ho. E5 . . . . .1H **67**
Leaway E10 . . . . .1K **67**
Lebanon Av. TW13: Hanw 5B **130**
Lebanon Gdns. SW18 . . . . .6J **117**
Lebanon Pk. TW1: Twick 7B **114**
Lebanon Rd. CR0: Croy 1E **168**
SW18 . . . . .5J **117**
Lebrun Sq. SE3 . . . . .4K **123**
Lebus Ho. *NW8* *1C* ***4***
(off Cochrane St.)
Le Chateau *CR0: Croy* *3D* ***168***
(off Chatsworth Rd.)
Lechmere App. IG8: Wfd G 2A **52**
Lechmere Av. IG8: Wfd G 2B **52**
Lechmere Rd. NW2 . . . . .6D **62**
Leckford Rd. SW18 . . . . .2A **136**
Leckhampton Pl. SW2 . . . . .7A **120**
Leckwith Av. DA7: Bex 6E **108**
Lecky St. SW7 . . . . .5A **16** (5B **100**)
Leclair Ho. SE3 . . . . .3K **123**
Leconfield Av. SW13 . . . . .3B **116**
Leconfield Ho. SE5 . . . . .4E **120**
Leconfield Rd. N5 . . . . .4D **66**
Le Cordon Bleu London Culinary
Arts Institute ***6H 5***
(off Marylebone La.)
Leda Av. EN3: Enf W 1E **24**
Leda Ct. *SW9* *7A* ***102***
(off Caldwell St.)
Ledam Ho. *EC1* *5J* ***7***
(off Bourne Est.)
Leda Rd. SE18 . . . . .3D **106**
Ledbury Ho. SE22 . . . . .3E **120**
W11 . . . .*6H* ***81***
(off Colville Rd.)
Ledbury M. Nth. W11 . . . . .7J **81**
Ledbury M. W. W11 . . . . .7J **81**
Ledbury Pl. CR0: Croy 4C **168**
Ledbury Rd. CR0: Croy 4D **168**
W11 . . . . .6H **81**
Ledbury St. SE15 . . . . .7G **103**
Ledrington Rd. SE19 . . . . .6G **139**
Ledway Dr. HA9: Wemb 7F **43**
LEE 6J **123**
Lee Av. RM6: Chad H 6E **54**
Lee Bri. SE13 .3E **122**
Leechcroft Av. DA15: Sidc 5K **125**
Leechcroft Rd. SM6: Wall 3E **166**
Lee Chu. St. SE13 . . . . .4G **123**
Lee Cl. E17 . . . . .1K **49**
EN5: New Bar 4F **21**
Lee Conservancy Rd. E9 . . . . .5B **68**
Lee Ct. *SE13* *4F* ***123***
(off Lee High Rd.)
Leecroft Rd. EN5: Barn 5B **20**

Leeds Ct. *EC1* 3A 8
(off St John St.)
Leeds Rd. IG1: Ilf 1H 71
Leeds St. N18 5B 34
Leefern Rd. W12 2C 98
Leegate SE12 5H 123
LEE GREEN 5H 123
Lee Gro. IG7: Chig 2K 37
Lee High Rd. SE12 3E 122
SE13 3E 122
Lee Ho. *EC2* 6D 8
(off Monkwell Sq.)
Leeke St. WC1 1G 7 (3K 83)
Leeland Rd. W13 1A 96
Leeland Ter. W13 1A 96
Leeland Way NW10 4B 62
Lee M. BR3: Beck 3A 158
Leemount Ho. NW4 4F 45
Lee Pk. SE3 4H 123
Lee Pk. Way N9 4E 34
N18 4E 34
Leerdam Dr. E14 3E 104
Lee Rd. EN1: Enf 6B 24
NW7 7A 30
SE3 3H 123
SW19 1K 153
UB6: G'frd 1C 78
Lees, The CR0: Croy 2B 170
Lees Av. HA6: Nwood 1H 39
Lees Ct. *W1* 2G 11
(off Lees Pl.)
Lees Ho. *SE17* 5D 102
(off Merrow St.)
Leeside EN5: Barn 5B 20
Leeside Ct. *SE16* 1K 103
(off Rotherhithe St.)
Leeside Cres. NW11 6G 45
Leeside Ind. Est. N17 7D 34
Leeside Rd. N17 6C 34
Leeside Works N17 7D 34
Leeson Ho. TW1: Twick 7B 114
Leeson Rd. SE24 4A 120
Leesons Hill BR5: St P 3J 161
BR7: Chst 3J 161
Leeson's Way BR5: St P 2K 161
Lees Pde. UB10: Hil 4D 74
Lees Pl. W1 2G 11 (7E 82)
Lees Rd. UB8: Hil 4D 74
Lee St. E8 1F 85
Lee Ter. SE3 3G 123
SE13 3G 123
Lee Valley Cycle Circuit 5D 68
Lee Valley Ice Cen. 2K 67
Lee Valley Pk. 7E 34
Lee Valley Sports Cen. 4D 68
Lee Valley Technopark N17 3G 49
Leeve Ho. *W10* 3H 81
(off Lancefield St.)
Lee Vw. EN2: Enf 1G 23
Leeward Ct. E1 7G 85
Leeward Gdns. SW19 5G 135
Leeward Ho. *N1* 1E 84
(off New Era Est.)
Leeway SE8 5B 104
Leeway Cl. HA5: H End 1D 40
Leeways, The SM3: Cheam 6G 165
Leewood Cl. SE12 6H 123
Lefa Bus. & Ind. Pk. DA14: Sidc 6D 144
Lefevre Wlk. E3 2C 86
Leff Ho. NW6 1G 81
Lefroy Ho. *SE1* 7C 14
(off Southwark Bri. Rd.)
Lefroy Rd. W12 2B 98
Legard Rd. N5 3B 66
Legatt Rd. SE9 5B 124
Leggatt Rd. E15 2E 86
Legge St. SE13 5E 122
Leghorn Rd. NW10 2B 80
SE18 5H 107
Legion Cl. N1 7A 66
Legion Ct. SM4: Mord 6J 153
Legion Rd. UB6: G'frd 1G 77
Legion Ter. E3 1B 86
Legion Way N12 7H 31
Legon Av. RM7: Rush G 1J 73
Legrace Av. TW4: Houn 2B 112
Leicester Av. CR4: Mitc 4J 155
Leicester Cl. KT4: Wor Pk 4E 164
Leicester Ct. *TW1: Twick* 6D 114
(off Clevedon Rd.)
W9 5J 81
(off Elmfield Way)
WC2 2D 12
Leicester Flds. WC2 3D 12
Leicester Gdns. IG3: Ilf 7J 53
Leicester Ho. *N18* 5C 34
(off Cavendish Cl.)
SW9 3B 120
(off Loughborough Rd.)
Leicester M. N2 3C 46
Leicester Pl. WC2 2D 12 (7H 83)
Leicester Rd. CR0: Croy 7E 156
E11 5K 51
EN5: New Bar 5E 20
N2 3C 46
NW10 7K 61
Leicester Sq. WC2 3D 12 (7H 83)
Leicester St. WC2 2D 12 (7H 83)
Leigh, The KT2: King T 7A 134
Leigham Av. SW16 3J 137
Leigham Cl. SW16 3K 137
Leigham Ct. Rd. SW16 2J 137
Leigham Dr. TW7: Isle 7J 95
Leigham Hall Pde. *SW16* 3J 137
(off Streatham High Rd.)
Leigham Va. SW2 3K 137
SW16 3K 137
Leigh Av. IG4: Ilf 4B 52
Leigh Cl. KT3: N Mald 4J 151
Leigh Cl. Ind. Est. KT3: N Mald 4K 151
Leigh Ct. HA2: Harr 1J 59
Leigh Cres. CR0: New Ad 7D 170
Leigh Gdns. NW10 2E 80
Leigh Hunt Dr. N14 1C 32
Leigh Orchard Cl. SW16 3K 137
Leigh Pl. DA16: Well 2A 126
EC1 5J 7 (5A 84)
TW13: Felt 1A 130
Leigh Rd. E6 6E 70
E10 7E 50
N5 4B 66
TW3: Houn 4H 113
Leigh St. WC1 2E 6 (3J 83)
Leighton Av. E12 5E 70
HA5: Pinn 3C 40
Leighton Cl. HA8: Edg 2G 43
Leighton Cres. NW5 5G 65
Leighton Gdns. CR0: Croy 1B 168
NW10 2D 80
Leighton Gro. NW5 5G 65
Leighton Ho. *SW1* 4D 18
(off Herrick St.)
Leighton House Art Gallery & Mus. 3H 99
Leighton Mans. *W14* 6G 99
(off Greyhound Rd.)
Leighton Pl. NW5 5G 65
Leighton Rd. EN1: Enf 5A 24
HA3: Hrw W 2H 41
NW5 5G 65
W13 2A 96
Leighton St. CR0: Croy 1B 168
Leila Parnell Pl. SE7 6A 106
Leinster Av. SW14 3J 115
Leinster Gdns. W2 6A 82
Leinster M. EN5: Barn 3B 20
W2 7A 82
Leinster Pl. W2 6A 82
Leinster Rd. N10 4F 47
Leinster Sq. W2 6J 81
(not continuous)
Leinster Ter. W2 7A 82
Leisure Way N12 7G 31
Leisure W. TW13: Felt 2K 129
Leitch Ho. *NW8* 7B 64
(off Hilgrove Rd.)
Leith Cl. NW9 1K 61
Leithcote Gdns. SW16 4K 137
Leithcote Path SW16 3K 137
Leith Hill BR5: St P 1K 161
Leith Hill Grn. BR5: St P 1K 161
Leith Mans. *W9* 3K 81
(off Grantully Rd.)
Leith Rd. N22 1B 48
Leith Towers SM2: Sutt 7K 165
Leith Yd. *NW6* 1J 81
(off Quex Rd.)
Lela Av. TW4: Houn 2A 112
Lelitia Cl. E8 1G 85
Lely Ho. *UB5: N'olt* 2B 76
(off Academy Gdns.)
Leman Pas. E1 1K 15
Leman St. E1 1K 15 (6F 85)
Lemark Cl. HA7: Stan 6H 27
Le May Av. SE12 3K 141
Lemmon Rd. SE10 6G 105
Lemna Rd. E11 7H 51
Le Moal Ho. *E1* 5J 85
(off Stepney Way)
Lemon Gro. *TW13: Felt* 1J 129
(off Highfield Rd.)
Lemonwell Dr. SE9 5G 125
Lemsford Cl. N15 6G 49
Lemsford Ct. N4 2C 66
Lemuel St. SW18 6A 118
Lena Cres. N9 2D 34
Lena Gdns. W6 3E 98
Lena Kennedy Cl. E4 6K 35
Lenanton Steps *E14* 2C 104
(off Manilla St.)
Len Clifton Ho. *SE18* 4D 106
(off Cambridge Barracks Rd.)
Lendal Ter. SW4 3H 119
Lenelby Rd. KT6: Surb 1G 163
Len Freeman Pl. SW6 6H 99
W6 4B 98
(off Goldhawk Rd.)
Lenham Ho. *SE1* 7F 15
(off Long La.)
Lenham Rd. CR7: Thor H 2D 156
DA7: Bex 6F 109
SE12 4H 123
SM1: Sutt 4K 165
Lennard Av. BR4: W W'ck 2G 171
Lennard Cl. BR4: W W'ck 2G 171
Lennard Rd. BR2: Brom 1D 172
BR3: Beck 6K 139
CR0: Croy 1C 168
SE20 6K 139
Lennon Rd. NW2 5E 62
Lennox Gdns. CR0: Wadd 4B 168
IG1: Ilf 1D 70
NW10 4B 62
SW1 2E 16 (3D 100)
Lennox Gdns. M. SW1 2E 16 (3D 100)
Lennox Ho. *DA17: Belv* 3G 109
(off Picardy St.)
TW1: Twick 6D 114
(off Clevedon Rd.)
Lennox Lewis Cen. *E5* 2J 67
(off Theydon Rd.)
Lennox Rd. E17 6B 50
N4 2K 65
Lenor Cl. DA6: Bex 4E 126
Lensbury Way SE2 3C 108
Lens Rd. E7 7A 70
Len Taylor Cl. UB4: Hayes 4G 75
Lenthall Ho. *SW1* 6B 18
(off Churchill Gdns.)
Lenthall Rd. E8 7G 67
Lenthorp Rd. SE10 4H 105
Lentmead Rd. BR1: Brom 3H 141
Lenton Path SE18 6H 107
Lenton Ri. TW9: Rich 3E 114
Lenton St. SE18 4H 107
Len Williams Ct. NW6 2J 81
Leo Ct. TW8: Bford 7D 96
Leof Cres. SE6 5D 140
Leominster Rd. SM4: Mord 6A 154
Leominster Wlk. SM4: Mord 6A 154
Leonard Av. RM7: Rush G 1K 73
SM4: Mord 5A 154
Leonard Ct. HA3: Hrw W 1J 41
W8 3J 99
WC1 3D 6 (4H 83)
Leonard Pl. N16 4E 66
Leonard Rd. E4 6H 35
E7 4J 69
N9 3A 34
SW16 1G 155
UB2: S'hall 3B 94
Leonard Robbins Path *SE28* 7B 90
(off Tawney Rd.)
Leonard St. E16 1C 106
EC2 3F 9 (4D 84)
Leonora Ho. *W9* 4A 82
(off Lanark Rd.)
Leontine Cl. SE15 7G 103
Leopards Ct. EC1 5J 7
Leopold Av. SW19 5H 135
Leopold Bldgs. *E2* 1J 9
(off Columbia Rd.)
Leopold M. E9 1J 85
Leopold Rd. E17 5C 50
N2 3B 46
N18 5C 34
NW10 7A 62
SW19 4H 135
W5 1F 97
Leopold St. E3 5B 86
Leopold Ter. SW19 5H 135
Leopold Wlk. *SE11* 5K 101
(off Tyers St.)
Leo St. SE15 7H 103
Leo Yd. EC1 4B 8
Leppoc Rd. SW4 5H 119
Leroy St. SE1 4E 102
Lerry Cl. W14 6H 99
Lerwick Ct. EN1: Enf 5K 23
Lescombe Cl. SE23 3A 140
Lescombe Rd. SE23 3A 140
Lesley Cl. DA5: Bexl 7H 127
Lesley Ct. *SW1* 2C 18
(off Strutton Ground)
Leslie Gdns. SM2: Sutt 6J 165
Leslie Gro. CR0: Croy 1E 168
Leslie Gro. Pl. CR0: Croy 1E 168
Leslie Ho. *SW8* 7J 101
(off Wheatsheaf La.)
Leslie Pk. Rd. CR0: Croy 1E 168
Leslie Prince Ct. SE5 7D 102
Leslie Rd. E11 4E 68
E16 6K 87
N2 3B 46
Leslie Smith Sq. SE18 6E 106
Lesnes Abbey 4D 108
Lesney Farm Est. DA8: Erith 7K 109
Lesney Pk. DA8: Erith 6K 109
Lesney Pk. Rd. DA8: Erith 6K 109
Lessar Av. SW4 6G 119
Lessingham Av. IG5: Ilf 3E 52
SW17 4D 136
Lessing St. SE23 7A 122
Lessington Av. RM7: Rom 6J 55
Lessness Av. DA7: Bex 7D 108
LESSNESS HEATH 5H 109
Lessness Pk. DA17: Belv 5F 109
Lessness Rd. DA17: Belv 6G 109
SM4: Mord 6A 154
Lester Av. E15 4G 87
Lestock Cl. *SE25* 3G 157
(off Manor Rd.)
Leswin Pl. N16 3F 67
Leswin Rd. N16 3F 67
Letchford Gdns. NW10 3C 80
Letchford M. NW10 3C 80
Letchford Ter. HA3: Hrw W 1F 41
Letchmore Ho. *W10* 4E 80
(off Sutton Way)
Letchworth Av. TW14: Felt 7H 111
Letchworth Cl. BR2: Brom 5J 159
Letchworth Dr. BR2: Brom 5J 159

Letchworth St. SW17 . . . . . 4D 136
Lethbridge Cl. SE13 . . . . . 1E 122
Letterstone Rd. SW6 . . . . . 7H 99
Lettice St. SW6 . . . . . 1H 117
Lett Rd. E15 . . . . . 7F 69
Lettsom St. SE5 . . . . . 2E 120
Lettsom Wlk. E13 . . . . . 2J 87
Leucha Rd. E17 . . . . . 5A 50
Levana Cl. SW19 . . . . . 1G 135
Levant Ho. *E1* *4K 85*
(off Ernest St.)
Levehurst Ho. SE27 . . . . . 5C 138
Levendale Rd. SE23 . . . . . 2A 140
Levenhurst Way SW4 . . . . . 2J 119
Leven Rd. E14 . . . . . 5E 86
Leven Way UB3: Hayes 6G 75
Leverett St. SW3 . . . . . 3D 16 (4C 100)
Leverholme Gdns. SE9 . . . . . 3E 142
Leverington Pl. N1 . . . . . 2F 9 (3D 84)
Leverson St. SW16 . . . . . 6G 137
Leverstock Ho. *SW3* *5D 16*
(off Cale St.)
Lever St. EC1 . . . . . 2B 8 (3B 84)
Leverton Pl. NW5 . . . . . 5G 65
Leverton St. NW5 . . . . . 5G 65
Levett Gdns. IG3: Ilf 4K 71
Levett Rd. IG11: Bark 6J 71
Levine Gdns. IG11: Bark 2D 90
Levison Way N19 . . . . . 1H 65
Levita Ho. NW1 . . . . . 1D 6
(not continuous)
Lewes Cl. UB5: N'olt 6E 58
Lewes Ct. *CR4: Mitc* *3D 154*
(off Chatsworth Pl.)
Lewesdon Cl. SW19 . . . . . 1F 135
Lewes Ho. *SE1* *6H 15*
(off Druid St.)
SE15 . . . . . *6G 103*
(off Friary Est.)
Lewes Rd. BR1: Brom 2B 160
N12 . . . . . 5H 31
Leweston Pl. N16 . . . . . 7F 49
Lew Evans Ho. SE22 . . . . . 5G 121
Lewey Ho. *E3* *4B 86*
(off Joseph St.)
Lewgars Av. NW9 . . . . . 6J 43
Lewing Cl. BR6: Orp 1J 173
Lewin Rd. DA6: Bex 5E 126
SW14 . . . . . 3K 115
SW16 . . . . . 6H 137
Lewis Av. E17 . . . . . 1C 50
Lewis Cl. N14 . . . . . 7B 22
Lewis Ct. *SE16* *5H 103*
(off Stubbs Dr.)
Lewis Cres. NW10 . . . . . 5K 61
Lewis Gdns. N2 . . . . . 2B 46
Lewis Gro. SE13 . . . . . 4E 122
LEWISHAM 3E 122
Lewisham Bus. Cen. SE14 . . . . . 6K 103
Lewisham Cen. SE13 . . . . . 4E 122
Lewisham Crematorium
SE6 . . . . . 2H 141
Lewisham Hgts. SE23 . . . . . 1J 139
Lewisham High St. SE13 . . . . . 6D 122
Lewisham Hill SE13 . . . . . 2E 122
Lewisham Lions Cen. 5J 103
Lewisham Model Mkt. *SE13* *4E 122*
(off Lewisham High St.)
Lewisham Pk. SE13 . . . . . 5E 122
Lewisham Rd. SE13 . . . . . 1D 122
Lewisham St. SW1 . . . . . 7D 12 (2H 101)
Lewisham Way SE4 . . . . . 1B 122
SE14 . . . . . 1B 122
Lewis Ho. *E14* *1E 104*
(off Coldharbour)
Lewis Pl. E8 . . . . . 5G 67
Lewis Rd. CR4: Mitc 2B 154
(not continuous)
DA14: Sidc 3C 144
DA16: Well 3C 126
SM1: Sutt 4K 165
TW10: Rich 5D 114
UB1: S'hall 2C 94
Lewis Silkin Ho. *SE15* *6J 103*
(off Lovelinch Cl.)
Lewis Sports and Leisure Cen. 1F 157
Lewis St. NW1 . . . . . 6F 65
(not continuous)
Lewiston Cl. KT4: Wor Pk 7D 152
Lewis Way RM10: Dag 6H 73
Lexden Dr. RM6: Chad H 6B 54
Lexden Rd. CR4: Mitc 4H 155
W3 . . . . . 7H 79
Lexham Gdns. W8 . . . . . 4J 99
Lexham Gdns. M. W8 . . . . . 3K 99
Lexham Ho. *IG11: Bark* *1H 89*
(off St Margarets)
W8 . . . . . *4K 99*
(off Lexham Gdns.)
Lexham M. W8 . . . . . 4J 99
Lexham Wlk. W8 . . . . . 3K 99
Lexington Apartments EC1 . . . . . 3F 9 (4D 84)
Lexington St. W1 . . . . . 2B 12 (7G 83)
Lexington Way EN5: Barn 4A 20
Lexton Gdns. SW12 . . . . . 1H 137
Leyborne Av. W13 . . . . . 2B 96
Leyborne Pk. TW9: Kew 1G 115
Leybourne Cl. BR2: Brom 6J 159
Leybourne Ho. *E14* *6B 86*
(off Dod St.)
SE15 . . . . . 6J 103
Leybourne Rd. E11 . . . . . 1H 69
NW1 . . . . . 7F 65
NW9 . . . . . 5G 43
UB10: Hil 1E 74
Leybourne St. NW1 . . . . . 7F 65
Leybridge Ct. SE12 . . . . . 5J 123
Leyburn Cl. E17 . . . . . 4D 50
Leyburn Gdns. CR0: Croy 2E 168
Leyburn Gro. N18 . . . . . 6B 34
Leyburn Rd. N18 . . . . . 6B 34
Leydenhatch La. BR8: Dart, Swan 7J 145
Leyden Mans. N19 . . . . . 7J 47
Leyden St. E1 . . . . . 6J 9 (5F 85)
Leydon Cl. SE16 . . . . . 1K 103
Leyes Rd. E16 . . . . . 6B 88
Leyfield KT4: Wor Pk 1A 164
Leyland Av. EN3: Enf H 2F 25
Leyland Gdns. IG8: Wfd G 5F 37
Leyland Ho. *E14* *7D 86*
(off Hale St.)
Leyland Rd. SE12 . . . . . 5J 123
Leylands SW18 . . . . . 6H 117
Leylang Rd. SE14 . . . . . 7K 103
Leys, The HA3: Kent 6F 43
N2 . . . . . 4A 46
Leys Av. RM10: Dag 1J 91
Leys Cl. HA1: Harr 5H 41
RM10: Dag 7J 73
Leys Ct. SW9 . . . . . 2A 120
Leysdown Av. DA7: Bex 4J 127
Leysdown Ho. *SE17* *5E 102*
(off Madron St.)
Leysdown Rd. SE9 . . . . . 2C 142
Leysfield Rd. W12 . . . . . 3C 98
Leys Gdns. EN4: Cockf 5K 21
Leyspring Rd. E11 . . . . . 1H 69
Leys Rd. E. EN3: Enf H 1F 25
Leys Rd. W. EN3: Enf H 1F 25
Leys Sq. N3 . . . . . 1K 45
Ley St. IG1: Ilf 2F 71
IG2: Ilf 2F 71
Leyswood Dr. IG2: Ilf 5J 53
Leythe Rd. W3 . . . . . 2J 97
LEYTON 2E 68
Leyton Bus. Cen. E10 . . . . . 2C 68
Leyton Ct. SE23 . . . . . 1J 139
Leyton FC Ground 1B 68
Leyton Grange Est. E10 . . . . . 1C 68
Leyton Grn. Rd. E10 . . . . . 6E 50
Leyton Grn. Twr. *E10* *6E 50*
(off Leyton Grn. Rd.)
Leyton Grn. Towers *E10* *6E 50*
(off Leyton Grn. Rd.)
Leyton Ind. Village E10 . . . . . 7K 49
Leyton Leisure Lagoon 7D 50
Leyton Orient FC 3D 68
Leyton Pk. Rd. E10 . . . . . 3E 68
Leyton Rd. E15 . . . . . 5E 68
SW19 . . . . . 7A 136
LEYTONSTONE 3G 69
Leytonstone Ho. *E11* *7H 51*
(off Hanbury Dr.)
Leytonstone Rd. E15 . . . . . 5G 69
Leyton Way E11 . . . . . 7G 51
Leywick St. E15 . . . . . 2G 87
Lezayre Rd. BR6: Chels 6K 173
Liardet St. SE14 . . . . . 6A 104
Liberia Rd. N5 . . . . . 6B 66
Liberty Av. SW19 . . . . . 1B 154
Liberty Cl. N18 . . . . . 4A 34
Liberty Ct. IG11: Bark 2B 90
Liberty Ho. *E1* *7G 85*
(off Ensign St.)
Liberty M. N22 . . . . . 1B 48
SW12 . . . . . 6F 119
Liberty St. SW9 . . . . . 1K 119
Libra Rd. E3 . . . . . 2B 86
E13 . . . . . 2J 87
Library and Lifetime Mus. *3C 168*
(off High St.)
Library Ct. N17 . . . . . 3F 49
Library Mans. *W12* *2E 98*
(off Pennard Rd.)
Library Pde. *NW10* *1A 80*
(off Craven Pk. Rd.)
Library Pl. E1 . . . . . 7H 85
Library St. SE1 . . . . . 7A 14 (2B 102)
Library Way TW2: Whit 7G 113
Libro Ct. E4 . . . . . 4H 35
Lichfield Cl. EN4: Cockf 3J 21
Lichfield Ct. *KT6: Surb* *5E 150*
(off Claremont Rd.)
TW9: Rich 4E 114
Lichfield Gdns. TW9: Rich 4E 114
Lichfield Gro. N3 . . . . . 1J 45
Lichfield Rd. E3 . . . . . 3A 86
E6 . . . . . 3B 88
HA6: Nwood 3J 39
IG8: Wfd G 4B 36
N9 . . . . . 2B 34
NW2 . . . . . 4G 63
RM8: Dag 4B 72
TW4: Houn 3A 112
TW9: Kew 1F 115
Lichfield Ter. *TW9: Rich* *5E 114*
(off Sheen Rd.)
Lichlade Cl. BR6: Orp 4K 173
Lickey Ho. *W14* *6H 99*
(off North End Rd.)
Lidbury Rd. NW7 . . . . . 6B 30
Lidcote Gdns. SW9 . . . . . 2K 119
Liddall Way UB7: Yiew 1D 92
Liddell Cl. HA3: Kent 3D 42
Liddell Gdns. NW10 . . . . . 2E 80
Liddell Rd. NW6 . . . . . 6J 63
Lidding Rd. HA3: Kent 5D 42
Liddington Rd. E15 . . . . . 1H 87
Liddon Rd. BR1: Brom 3A 160
E13 . . . . . 3K 87
Liden Cl. E17 . . . . . 7B 50
Lidfield Rd. N16 . . . . . 4D 66
Lidgate Rd. SE15 . . . . . 7F 103
Lidiard Rd. SW18 . . . . . 2A 136
Lidlington Pl. NW1 . . . . . 2G 83
Lido Sq. N17 . . . . . 2D 48
Lidyard Rd. N19 . . . . . 1G 65
Liffler Rd. SE18 . . . . . 5J 107
Liffords Pl. SW13 . . . . . 2B 116
Lifford St. SW15 . . . . . 4F 117
Lightcliffe Rd. N13 . . . . . 4F 33
Lighter Cl. SE16 . . . . . 4A 104
Lighterman Ho. E14 . . . . . 7E 86
Lighterman M. E1 . . . . . 6K 85
Lightermans Rd. E14 . . . . . 2C 104
Lightermans Wlk. SW18 . . . . . 4J 117
Lightfoot Rd. N8 . . . . . 5J 47
Light Horse Ct. SW3 . . . . . 6G 17
Lightley Cl. HA0: Wemb 1E 78
Ligonier St. E2 . . . . . 3J 9 (4F 85)
Lilac Cl. E4 . . . . . 6G 35
Lilac Ct. E13 . . . . . 1A 88
TW11: Tedd 4K 131
Lilac Gdns. CR0: Croy 3C 170
RM7: Rush G 1K 73
UB3: Hayes 6G 75
W5 . . . . . 3D 96
Lilac Ho. SE4 . . . . . 3C 122
Lilac M. *N22* *3A 48*
(off High Rd.)
Lilac Pl. SE11 . . . . . 4G 19 (4K 101)
UB7: Yiew 7B 74
Lilac St. W12 . . . . . 7C 80
Lilah M. BR2: Brom 2H 159
Lilburne Gdns. SE9 . . . . . 5C 124
Lilburne Rd. SE9 . . . . . 5C 124
Lilburne Wlk. NW10 . . . . . 6J 61
Lile Cres. W7 . . . . . 5J 77
Lilestone Ho. *NW8* *3B 4*
(off Frampton St.)
Lilestone St. NW8 . . . . . 3C 4 (4C 82)
Lilford Ho. SE5 . . . . . 2C 120
Lilford Rd. SE5 . . . . . 2B 120
Lilian Barker Cl. SE12 . . . . . 5J 123
Lilian Board Way UB6: G'frd 5H 59
Lilian Cl. N16 . . . . . 3E 66
Lilian Gdns. IG8: Wfd G 1K 51
Lilian Rd. SW16 . . . . . 1G 155
Lillechurch Rd. RM8: Dag 6B 72
Lilleshall Rd. SM4: Mord 6B 154
Lilley Cl. E1 . . . . . 1G 103
Lilley La. NW7 . . . . . 5E 28
Lillian Av. W3 . . . . . 2G 97
Lillian Rd. SW13 . . . . . 6C 98
Lillie Mans. *SW6* *6G 99*
(off Lillie Rd.)
Lillie Rd. SW6 . . . . . 6G 99
Lillie Road Fitness Cen. 7F 99
Lillieshall Rd. SW4 . . . . . 3F 119
Lillie Yd. SW6 . . . . . 6J 99
Lillingston Ho. N7 . . . . . 4A 66
Lillington Gdns. Est. SW1 . . . . . 4B 18
Lilliput Av. UB5: N'olt 1C 76
Lilliput Ct. SE12 . . . . . 5K 123
Lilliput Rd. RM7: Rush G 7K 55
Lily Cl. W14 . . . . . 4F 99
(not continuous)
Lily Gdns. HA0: Wemb 2C 78
Lily Nichols Ho. *E16* *1B 106*
(off Connaught Rd.)
Lily Pl. EC1 . . . . . 5K 7 (5A 84)
Lily Rd. E17 . . . . . 6C 50
Lilyville Rd. SW6 . . . . . 1H 117
Limborough Ho. *E14* *5C 86*
(off Thomas Rd.)
Limbourne Av. RM8: Dag 7F 55
Limburg Rd. SW11 . . . . . 4C 118
Lime Av. UB7: Yiew 7B 74
Limeburner La. EC4 . . . . . 1A 14 (6B 84)
Lime Cl. BR1: Brom 4C 160
E1 . . . . . 1G 103
HA3: W'stone 2A 42
HA5: Eastc 3H 39
IG9: Buck H 2G 37
RM7: Rom 4J 55
SM5: Cars 2D 166
Lime Ct. CR4: Mitc 2B 154
E11 . . . . . *2G 69*
(off Trinity Cl.)
E17 . . . . . 5E 50
HA1: Harr 6K 41
SE9 . . . . . 2F 143
Lime Cres. TW16: Sun 2A 148
Limecroft Cl. KT19: Ewe 7K 163
Limedene Cl. HA5: Pinn 1B 40
Lime Gro. BR6: Farnb 2F 173
DA15: Sidc 6K 125
E4 . . . . . 6G 35
HA4: Ruis 6K 39
KT3: N Mald 3K 151
N20 . . . . . 1C 30
TW1: Twick 6K 113

Lime Gro. UB3: Hayes 7F 75
  W12 ....2E 98
Limeharbour E14 ....3D 104
LIMEHOUSE 6B 86
Lime Ho. TW9: Kew 1H 115
Limehouse C'way. E14 ....7B 86
Limehouse Ct. E14 ....6C 86
Limehouse Cut E14 ....5D 86
  (off Morris Rd.)
Limehouse Flds. Est. E14 ....5A 86
Limehouse Link E14 ....6A 86
Lime Kiln Dr. SE7 ....6K 105
Limekiln Pl. SE19 ....7F 139
Lime Lodge TW16: Sun 7H 129
  (off Forest Dr.)
Limerick Cl. SW12 ....7G 119
Lime Rd. TW9: Rich 4F 115
Lime Row DA18: Erith 3F 109
Limerston St. SW10 .....7A 16 (6A 100)
Limes, The BR2: Brom 2C 172
  KT8: W Mole 4F 149
  SW18 ....6J 117
  W2 ....7J 81
Limes Av. CR0: Wadd 3A 168
  E11 ....4K 51
  E12 ....3C 70
  N12 ....4F 31
  NW7 ....6F 29
  NW11 ....7G 45
  SE20 ....7H 139
  SM5: Cars 1D 166
  SW13 ....2B 116
Limes Av., The N11 ....5A 32
Limes Cl. N11 ....5B 32
  TW15: Ashf 5C 128
Limes Ct. NW6 ....7G 63
  (off Brondesbury Pk.)
Limesdale Gdns. HA8: Edg 2J 43
Limes Fld. Rd. SW14 ....3A 116
Limesford Rd. SE15 ....4K 121
Limes Gdns. SW18 ....6J 117
Limes Gro. SE13 ....4E 122
Limes Pl. CR0: Croy 7D 156
Limes Rd. BR3: Beck 2D 158
  CR0: Croy 7D 156
Limes Row BR6: Farnb 5F 173
Limestone Wlk. DA18: Erith 2D 108
Lime St. E17 ....4A 50
  EC3 ....2G 15 (7E 84)
Lime St. Pas. EC3 ....1G 15 (6E 84)
Limes Wlk. SE15 ....4J 121
  W5 ....2D 96
Lime Ter. W7 ....7J 77
Lime Tree Av. KT10: Esh, T Ditt 7H 149
Lime Tree Cl. E18 ....4A 52
Limetree Cl. SW2 ....1K 137
Lime Tree Ct. CR2: S Croy 6C 168
  E3 ....5C 86
Lime Tree Gro. CR0: Croy 3B 170
Lime Tree Pl. CR4: Mitc 1F 155
Lime Tree Rd. TW5: Hest 1F 113
Limetree Ter. DA16: Well 3A 126
  SE6 ....1B 140
Lime Tree Wlk.
  BR4: W W'ck 4H 171
  EN2: Enf 1H 23
  WD23: Bushy 1D 26
Limetree Wlk. SW17 ....5E 136
Lime Wlk. E15 ....1G 87
  KT8: E Mos 4K 149
Limewood Cl. BR3: Beck 5E 158
  E17 ....4B 50
  W13 ....6B 78
Limewood Ct. IG4: Ilf 5D 52
Limewood Rd. DA8: Erith 7J 109
Limpsfield Av. CR7: Thor H 5K 155
  SW19 ....2F 135
Linacre Cl. SE15 ....3H 121
Linacre Ct. W6 ....5F 99
Linacre Rd. NW2 ....6D 62
Linale Ho. N1 ....1E 8
Linberry Wlk. SE8 ....4B 104
Linchmere Rd. SE12 ....7H 123

Lincoln Av. N14 ....3B 32
  RM7: Rush G 2K 73
  SW19 ....3F 135
  TW2: Twick 2G 131
Lincoln Cl. HA2: Harr 5D 40
  SE25 ....6G 157
  UB6: G'frd 1G 77
Lincoln Ct. CR2: S Croy 5C 168
  (off Warham Rd.)
  N16 ....7D 48
  SE12 ....3A 142
Lincoln Cres. EN1: Enf 5K 23
Lincoln Gdns. IG1: Ilf 7C 52
Lincoln Ho. BR5: St M Cry 5K 161
  SE5 ....7A 102
  SW3 ....2D 100
Lincoln M. N15 ....4C 48
  NW6 ....1H 81
  SE21 ....2D 138
Lincoln Pde. N2 ....3C 46
Lincoln Rd. CR4: Mitc 5J 155
  DA14: Sidc 5B 144
  E7 ....6B 70
  E13 ....4K 87
  E18 ....1J 51
  EN1: Enf 4K 23
  EN3: Pond E 5B 24
  HA0: Wemb 6D 60
  HA2: Harr 5D 40
  HA6: Nwood 3H 39
  KT3: N Mald 3J 151
  KT4: Wor Pk 1D 164
  N2 ....3C 46
  SE25 ....3H 157
  TW13: Hanw 3D 130
Lincolns, The NW7 ....3G 29
Lincoln's Inn Flds. WC2 ....7G 7 (6K 83)
Lincoln's Inn Hall 7H 7 (6K 83)
Lincoln St. E11 ....2G 69
  SW3 ....4E 16 (4D 100)
Lincoln Way EN1: Enf 5C 24
  TW16: Sun 1G 147
Lincombe Rd. BR1: Brom 3H 141
Lindal Cres. EN2: Enf 4D 22
Lindales, The N17 ....6B 34
  (off Grasmere Rd.)
Lindal Rd. SE4 ....5B 122
Lindbergh Rd. SM6: Wall 7J 167
Linden Av. CR7: Thor H 4B 156
  EN1: Enf 1B 24
  HA4: Ruis 1J 57
  HA9: Wemb 5F 61
  NW10 ....2F 81
  TW3: Houn 5F 113
Linden Cl. HA4: Ruis 1J 57
  HA7: Stan 5G 27
  KT7: T Ditt 7K 149
  N14 ....6B 22
Linden Ct. DA14: Sidc 4J 143
  SE20 ....7H 139
  (off Anerley Pk.)
  W12 ....1E 98
  KT1: King T 2F 151
  UB6: G'frd 6K 59
Lindenfield BR7: Chst 2F 161
Linden Gdns. EN1: Enf 1B 24
  W2 ....7J 81
  W4 ....5A 98
Linden Gro. KT3: N Mald 3A 152
  SE15 ....3H 121
  SE26 ....5K 139
  TW11: Tedd 5K 131
Linden Ho. SE8 ....6B 104
  (off Abinger Gro.)
  TW12: Hamp 6E 130
Linden Lawns HA9: Wemb 4F 61
Linden Lea N2 ....5A 46
Linden Leas BR4: W W'ck 2F 171
Linden Mans. N6 ....1F 65
  (off Hornsey La.)
Linden M. N1 ....5D 66
  W2 ....7J 81
Linden Pl. CR4: Mitc 4C 154

Linden Rd. N10 ....4F 47
  N11 ....2J 31
  N15 ....4C 48
  TW12: Hamp 7E 130
Lindens, The CR0: New Ad 6E 170
  E17 ....4D 50
  (off Prospect Hill)
  N12 ....5G 31
  W4 ....1J 115
Linden St. RM7: Rom 4K 55
Linden Wlk. N19 ....2G 65
Linden Way N14 ....6B 22
  TW17: Shep 5E 146
Lindeth Cl. HA7: Stan 6G 27
Lindfield Gdns. NW3 ....5K 63
Lindfield Rd. CR0: Croy 6F 157
  W5 ....4C 78
Lindfield St. E14 ....6C 86
Lindhill Cl. EN3: Enf H 2E 24
Lindholme Ct. NW9 ....1A 44
  (off Pageant Av.)
Lindisfarne Rd. RM8: Dag 3C 72
  SW20 ....7C 134
Lindisfarne Way E9 ....4A 68
Lindley Cl. KT1: Ham W 1C 150
Lindley Est. SE15 ....7G 103
Lindley Ho. E1 ....5J 85
  (off Lindley St.)
  SE15 ....7G 103
  (off Peckham Pk. Rd.)
Lindley Pl. TW9: Kew 1G 115
Lindley Rd. E10 ....2E 68
Lindley St. E1 ....5J 85
Lindop Ho. E1 ....4A 86
  (off Mile End Rd.)
Lindore Rd. SW11 ....4D 118
Lindores Rd. SM5: Cars 7A 154
Lindo St. SE15 ....2J 121
Lind Rd. SM1: Sutt 5A 166
Lindrop St. SW6 ....2A 118
Lindsay Cl. KT9: Chess 7E 162
  TW19: Stanw 5A 110
Lindsay Ct. CR0: Croy 4D 168
  (off Eden Rd.)
  SW11 ....1B 118
  (off Battersea High St.)
Lindsay Dr. HA3: Kent 6E 42
  TW17: Shep 6F 147
Lindsay Ho. SW7 ....3A 100
  (off Gloucester Rd.)
Lindsay Rd. KT4: Wor Pk 2D 164
  TW12: Ham H 4F 131
Lindsay Sq. SW1 ......5D 18 (5H 101)
Lindsell St. SE10 ....1E 122
Lindsey Cl. BR1: Brom 3B 160
  CR4: Mitc 4J 155
Lindsey Ct. N13 ....3F 33
  (off Green Lanes)
Lindsey Gdns. TW14: Bedf 7F 111
Lindsey Ho. W5 ....4D 96
Lindsey M. N1 ....7C 66
Lindsey Rd. RM8: Dag 4C 72
Lindsey St. EC1 ....5B 8 (5B 84)
Lindum Rd. TW11: Tedd 7C 132
Lindway SE27 ....5B 138
Lindwood Cl. E6 ....6D 88
Linfield WC1 ....2G 7
  (off Sidmouth St.)
Linfield Cl. NW4 ....3E 44
Linford Christie Stadium 5C 80
Linford Ho. E2 ....1G 85
  (off Whiston Rd.)
Linford Rd. E17 ....3E 50
Linford St. SW8 ....1G 119
Lingard Ho. E14 ....3E 104
  (off Marshfield St.)
Lingards Rd. SE13 ....4E 122
Lingey Cl. DA15: Sidc 2K 143
Lingfield Av. KT1: King T 4E 150
Lingfield Cl. EN1: Enf 6K 23
  HA6: Nwood 1G 39
Lingfield Ct. UB5: N'olt 2E 76

Lingfield Cres. SE9 ....4H 125
Lingfield Gdns. N9 ....7C 24
Lingfield Ho. SE1 ....7B 14
Lingfield Rd. KT4: Wor Pk 3E 164
  SW19 ....5F 135
Lingham Ct. SW9 ....2J 119
Lingham St. SW9 ....2J 119
Lingholm Way EN5: Barn 5A 20
Ling Rd. DA8: Erith 6J 109
  E16 ....5J 87
Lingrove Gdns. IG9: Buck H 2E 36
Lings Coppice SE21 ....2D 138
Lingwell Rd. SW17 ....3C 136
Lingwood DA7: Bex 2H 127
Lingwood Ct. N2 ....3C 46
  (off Norfolk Cl.)
Lingwood Gdns. TW7: Isle 7J 95
Lingwood Rd. E5 ....7G 49
Linhope St. NW1 ....3E 4 (4D 82)
Link, The EN3: Enf H 1F 25
  HA0: Wemb 1C 60
  HA5: Eastc 7A 40
  NW2 ....1C 62
  SE9 ....3E 142
  (off William Barefoot Dr.)
  TW11: Tedd 6K 131
  UB5: N'olt 5D 58
  W3 ....6H 79
Linkenholt Mans. W6 ....4B 98
  (off Stamford Brook Av.)
Linkfield BR2: Hayes 6J 159
  KT8: W Mole 3F 149
Linkfield Rd. TW7: Isle 2K 113
Link Ho. E3 ....2D 86
  W10 ....6F 81
  (off Kingsdown Cl.)
Link La. SM6: Wall 6H 167
Linklea Cl. NW9 ....7F 29
Link Rd. E1 ....2K 15 (7G 85)
  E12 ....2C 70
  N11 ....4K 31
  RM9: Dag 2H 91
  SM6: Wall 1E 166
  TW14: Felt 7H 111
Links, The E17 ....4A 50
Links Av. SM4: Mord 4J 153
  (not continuous)
Linkscroft Av. TW15: Ashf 6D 128
Links Dr. N20 ....1D 30
Links Gdns. SW16 ....7A 138
Linkside KT3: N Mald 2A 152
  N12 ....6D 30
Linkside Cl. EN2: Enf 3E 22
Linkside Gdns. EN2: Enf 3E 22
Links Rd. BR4: W W'ck 1E 170
  IG8: Wfd G 5D 36
  NW2 ....2B 62
  SW17 ....6E 136
  TW15: Ashf 5A 128
  W3 ....6G 79
Links Side EN2: Enf 3E 22
Link St. E9 ....6J 67
Links Vw. N3 ....7C 30
Linksview N2 ....5D 46
  (off Gt. North Rd.)
Links Vw. Cl. HA7: Stan 7F 27
Links Vw. Ct. TW12: Ham H 4H 131
Links Vw. Rd. CR0: Croy 3C 170
  TW12: Ham H 5G 131
Links Way BR3: Beck 6C 158
  HA6: Nwood 1E 38
Linksway NW4 ....2F 45
Links Yd. E1 ....5K 9
Link Way BR2: Brom 7C 160
  HA5: Pinn 1B 40
Linkway N4 ....7C 48
  RM8: Dag 4C 72
  SW20 ....3D 152
  TW10: Ham 2B 132
Linkway, The E16: Barn 6E 20
Linkwood Wlk. NW1 ....7H 65
Linley Cl. SM1: Sutt 4A 166
Linley Cres. RM7: Mawney 3H 55

Linley Rd. N17 . . . . . 2E 48
Linley Sambourne House *3J 99*
(off Stafford Ter.)
Linnell Cl. NW11 . . . . . 6K 45
Linnell Dr. NW11 . . . . . 6K 45
Linnell Ho. *E1* *5J 9*
(off Folgate St.)
Linnell Rd. N18 . . . . . 5B 34
SE5 . . . . . 2E 120
Linnet Cl. N9 . . . . . 1E 34
SE28 . . . . . 7C 90
WD23: Bush 1B 26
Linnet M. SW12 . . . . . 7E 118
Linnett Cl. E4 . . . . . 4K 35
Linom Rd. SW4 . . . . . 4J 119
Linscott Rd. E5 . . . . . 4J 67
Linsdell Rd. IG11: Bark 1G 89
Linsey Ct. *E10* *1C 68*
(off Grange Rd.)
Linsey St. SE16 . . . . . 4G 103
(not continuous)
Linslade Cl. HA5: Eastc 3K 39
TW4: Houn 5C 112
Linslade Ho. E2 . . . . . 1G 85
NW8 . . . . . *3D 4*
(off Paveley St.)
Linslade Rd. BR6: Chels 6K 173
Linstead Hall *SW7* *1B 16*
(off Princes Gdns.)
Linstead St. NW6 . . . . . 7J 63
Linstead Way SW18 . . . . . 7G 117
Linsted Ct. SE9 . . . . . 6J 125
Lintaine Cl. W6 . . . . . 6G 99
Linthorpe Av.
HA0: Wemb 6C 60
Linthorpe Rd. EN4: Cockf 3H 21
N16 . . . . . 7E 48
Linton Cl. CR4: Mitc 7D 154
DA16: Well 1B 126
SE7 . . . . . 5A 106
Linton Ct. *NW1* *7G 65*
(off Agar Gro.)
RM1: Rom 2K 55
Linton Gdns. E6 . . . . . 6C 88
Linton Gro. SE27 . . . . . 5B 138
Linton Ho. *E3* *5C 86*
(off St Paul's Way)
Linton Rd. IG11: Bark 7G 71
Lintons, The IG11: Bark 7G 71
Linton St. N1 . . . . . 1C 84
(not continuous)
Lintott Ct. TW19: Stanw 6A 110
Linver Rd. SW6 . . . . . 2J 117
Linwood Cl. SE5 . . . . . 2F 121
Linwood Cres. EN1: Enf 1B 24
Linzee Rd. N8 . . . . . 4J 47
Lion Av. TW1: Twick 1K 131
Lion Cl. SE4 . . . . . 6C 122
TW17: Shep 3A 146
Lion Ct. *E1* *7K 85*
(off The Highway)
N1 . . . . . *1K 83*
(off Copenhagen St.)
SE1 . . . . . *5G 15*
(off Magdalen St.)
Lionel Gdns. SE9 . . . . . 5B 124
Lionel Ho. *W10* *5G 81*
(off Portobello Rd.)
Lionel Mans. *W14* *3F 99*
(off Haarlem Rd.)
Lionel M. W10 . . . . . 5G 81
Lionel Rd. SE9 . . . . . 5B 124
Lionel Rd. Nth. TW8: Bford 3E 96
Lionel Rd. Sth. TW8: Bford 5F 97
Liongate Ent. Pk.
CR4: Mitc 4B 154
Lion Ga. Gdns. TW9: Rich 3F 115
Lion Gate M. SW18 . . . . . 7J 117
Liongate M. KT8: E Mos 3K 149
Lion Head Ct. *CR0: Croy* *4C 168*
(off Southbridge Rd.)
Lion Mills E2 . . . . . 2G 85
Lion Pk. Av. KT9: Chess 4G 163
Lion Rd. CR0: Croy 5C 156
DA6: Bex 4E 126
E6 . . . . . 5D 88
N9 . . . . . 2B 34
TW1: Twick 1K 131
Lions Cl. SE9 . . . . . 3A 142
Lion Way TW8: Bford 7D 96
Lion Wharf Rd. TW7: Isle 3B 114
Lion Yd. SW4 . . . . . 4H 119
Liphook Cres. SE23 . . . . . 7J 121
Lipton Cl. SE28 . . . . . 7C 90
Lipton Rd. E1 . . . . . 6K 85
Lisbon Av. TW2: Twick 2G 131
Lisbon Cl. E17 . . . . . 2B 50
Lisburne Rd. NW3 . . . . . 4D 64
Lisford St. SE15 . . . . . 1F 121
Lisgar Ter. W14 . . . . . 4H 99
Liskeard Cl. BR7: Chst 6G 143
Liskeard Gdns. SE3 . . . . . 1J 123
Liskeard Ho. *SE11* *5K 19*
(off Kennings Way)
Lisle Cl. SW17 . . . . . 4F 137
Lisle Ct. NW2 . . . . . 3G 63
Lisle St. WC2 . . . . . 2D 12 (7H 83)
Lismore *SW19* *5H 135*
(off Woodside)
Lismore Cir. NW5 . . . . . 5E 64
Lismore Cl. TW7: Isle 2A 114
Lismore Ho. SE15 . . . . . 3H 121
Lismore Rd. CR2: S Croy 6E 168
N17 . . . . . 3D 48
Lismore Wlk. *N1* *6C 66*
(off Clephane Rd. Nth.)
Lissant Cl. KT6: Surb 7D 150
Lisselton Ho. *NW4* *4F 45*
(off Belle Vue Est.)
Lissenden Gdns. NW5 . . . . . 4E 64
(not continuous)
Lissenden Mans. NW5 . . . . . 4E 64
Lisson Grn. Est. *NW8* *3C 4*
(off Tresham Cres.)
LISSON GROVE 5B 4 (5C 82)
Lisson Gro. NW1 . . . . . 3B 4 (4C 82)
NW8 . . . . . 3B 4 (4B 82)
Lisson Ho. *NW1* *5C 4*
(off Lisson St.)
Lisson St. NW1 . . . . . 5C 4 (5C 82)
Lister Cl. CR4: Mitc 1C 154
W3 . . . . . 5K 79
Lister Ct. HA1: Harr 7B 42
N16 . . . . . 2E 66
NW9 . . . . . 2A 44
Lister Gdns. N18 . . . . . 5H 33
Listergate Ct. SW15 . . . . . 4E 116
Lister Ho. E1 . . . . . 5G 85
HA9: Wemb *3J 61*
(off Barnhill Rd.)
SE3 . . . . . *6G 105*
(off Restell Cl.)
UB3: Harl 4G 93
Lister Lodge *W9* *5J 81*
(off Admiral Wlk.)
Lister Rd. E11 . . . . . 1G 69
Lister Wlk. SE28 . . . . . 7D 90
Liston Rd. N17 . . . . . 1G 49
SW4 . . . . . 3G 119
Liston Way IG8: Wfd G 7F 37
Listowel Cl. SW9 . . . . . 7A 102
Listowel Rd. RM10: Dag 3G 73
Listria Pk. N16 . . . . . 2E 66
Litcham Ho. *E1* *3K 85*
(off Longnor Rd.)
Litchfield Av. E15 . . . . . 6G 69
SM4: Mord 7H 153
Litchfield Ct. E17 . . . . . 6C 50
Litchfield Gdns. NW10 . . . . . 6C 62
Litchfield Rd. SM1: Sutt 4A 166
Litchfield St. WC2 . . . . . 2D 12 (7H 83)
Litchfield Way NW11 . . . . . 5K 45
Lithgow's Rd. TW6: H'row A 4G 111
Lithos Rd. NW3 . . . . . 6K 63
Litten Nature Reserve 3G 77
Little Acre BR3: Beck 3C 158
Lit. Albany St. NW1 . . . . . 2K 5 (3F 83)
(Albany St.)
NW1 . . . . . 3K 5
(Longford St.)
Little Angel Theatre *1B 84*
(off Cross St.)
Lit. Argyll St. W1 . . . . . 1A 12 (6G 83)
Little Benty UB7: W Dray 5A 92
Little Birches DA15: Sidc 2J 143
Lit. Boltons, The SW5 . . . . . 5K 99
SW10 . . . . . 5K 99
Little Bornes SE21 . . . . . 4E 138
Littlebourne SE13 . . . . . 7G 123
Littlebourne Ho. *SE17* *5E 102*
(off Kinglake St.)
Little Britain EC1 . . . . . 6B 8 (5B 84)
Littlebrook Cl. CR0: Croy 6K 157
Little Brownings SE23 . . . . . 2H 139
Littlebury Rd. SW4 . . . . . 3H 119
Lit. Bury St. N9 . . . . . 1J 33
Lit. Bushey La. WD23: Bush 1C 26
Little Cedars N12 . . . . . 4F 31
Lit. Chelsea Ho. *SW10* *6A 100*
(off Netherton Gro.)
Lit. Chester St. SW1 . . . . . 1J 17 (3F 101)
Little Cloisters SW1 . . . . . 1E 18 (3J 101)
Little Coll. La. *EC4* *2E 14*
(off College St.)
Little Coll. St. SW1 . . . . . 1E 18 (3J 101)
Littlecombe SE7 . . . . . 6K 105
Littlecombe Cl. SW15 . . . . . 6F 117
Little Comn. HA7: Stan 3F 27
Littlecote Cl. SW19 . . . . . 7G 117
Littlecote Pl. HA5: H End 1C 40
Little Ct. BR4: W W'ck 2G 171
Little Cft. SE9 . . . . . 3E 124
Littledale SE2 . . . . . 6A 108
Lit. Dean's Yd. SW1 . . . . . 1E 18
Little Dimocks SW12 . . . . . 2F 137
Lit. Dorrit Ct. SE1 . . . . . 6D 14 (2C 102)
LITTLE EALING 3D 96
Lit. Ealing La. W5 . . . . . 4C 96
Lit. Edward St. NW1 . . . . . 1K 5 (3F 83)
Little Elms UB3: Harl 7F 93
Lit. Essex St. WC2 . . . . . 2J 13
Lit. Ferry Rd. TW1: Twick 1B 132
Littlefield Cl. KT1: King T 2E 150
N19 . . . . . 4G 65
Littlefield Ho. *KT1: King T* *2E 150*
(off Littlefield Cl)
Littlefield Rd. HA8: Edg 7D 28
Lit. Friday Rd. F4 . . . . . 2B 36
Little Gearies IG6: Ilf 4F 53
Lit. George St. SW1 . . . . . 7E 12 (2J 101)
Little Grange UB6: G'frd 3A 78
Little Grn. TW9: Rich 4D 114
Little Grn. St. NW5 . . . . . 4F 65
Littlegrove EN4: E Barn 6H 21
Little Halliards KT12: Walt T 6J 147
LITTLE HEATH 4B 54
Little Heath RM6: Chad H 4B 54
SE7 . . . . . 6C 106
Lit. Heath Rd. DA7: Bex 1F 127
Littleheath Rd. CR2: Sels 7H 169
Little Holt E11 . . . . . 5J 51
LITTLE ILFORD 5D 70
Lit. Ilford La. E12 . . . . . 4D 70
Lit. John Rd. W7 . . . . . 6K 77
Little Larkins EN5: Barn 6B 20
Lit. London Cl. UB8: Hil 5D 74
Lit. London Ct. *SE1* *7K 15*
(off Wolseley St.)
Lit. Marlborough St. W1 . . . . . 1A 12
Littlemede SE9 . . . . . 3D 142
Littlemoor Rd. IG1: Ilf 3H 71
Littlemore Rd. SE2 . . . . . 2A 108
Lit. Moss La. HA5: Pinn 2C 40
Lit. Newport St. WC2 . . . . . 2D 12 (7H 83)
Lit. New St. EC4 . . . . . 7K 7 (6A 84)
Lit. Orchard Cl. HA5: Pinn 2C 40
Little Pk. Dr. TW13: Felt 2C 130
Little Pk. Gdns. EN2: Enf 3H 23
Lit. Pluckett's Way IG9: Buck H 1G 37
Lit. Portland St. W1 . . . . . 7K 5 (6G 83)
Little Potters WD23: Bush 1C 26
Lit. Queen's Rd. TW11: Tedd 6K 131
Little Redlands BR1: Brom 2C 160
Little Rd. UB3: Hayes 2H 93
Littlers Cl. SW19 . . . . . 1B 154
Lit. Russell St. WC1 . . . . . 6E 6 (5J 83)
Lit. St James's St. SW1 . . . . . 5A 12 (1G 101)
Lit. St Leonard's SW14 . . . . . 3J 115
Little Sanctuary SW1 . . . . . 7D 12 (2H 101)
Lit. Smith St. SW1 . . . . . 1D 18 (3H 101)
Lit. Somerset St. E1 . . . . . 1J 15 (6F 85)
LITTLE STANMORE 7A 28
Littlestone Cl. BR3: Beck 6C 140
Little Strand NW9 . . . . . 2B 44
Little Theatre, The 1J 159
Little Thrift BR5: Pet W 4G 161
Lit. Titchfield St. W1 . . . . . 6A 6 (5G 83)
LITTLETON 3C 146
Littleton Av. E4 . . . . . 1C 36
Littleton Cl. TW17: Shep 4B 146
LITTLETON COMMON 7E 128
Littleton Cres. HA1: Harr 2K 59
Littleton Ho. *SW1* *6A 18*
(off Lupus St.)
Littleton La. TW17: Shep 7A 146
Littleton Rd. HA1: Harr 2K 59
TW15: Ashf 7E 128
Littleton St. SW18 . . . . . 2A 136
Lit. Trinity La. EC4 . . . . . 2D 14 (7C 84)
Little Turnstile WC1 . . . . . 6G 7 (5K 83)
Lit. Warkworth Ho. TW7: Isle 2B 114
Littlewood SE13 . . . . . 6E 122
Littlewood Cl. W13 . . . . . 3B 96
Lit. Wood St. KT1: King T 2D 150
Livermere Ct. *E8* *1F 85*
(off Queensbridge Rd.)
Livermere Rd. E8 . . . . . 1F 85
Liverpool Gro. SE17 . . . . . 5C 102
Liverpool Rd. CR7: Thor H 3C 156
E10 . . . . . 6E 50
E16 . . . . . 5G 87
KT2: King T 7G 133
N1 . . . . . 5A 66
N7 . . . . . 5A 66
W5 . . . . . 2D 96
Liverpool St. EC2 . . . . . 6G 9 (5E 84)
Livesey Cl. KT1: King T 3F 151
SE28 . . . . . 3G 107
Livesey Mus. for Children 6H 103
Livesey Pl. SE15 . . . . . 6G 103
Livingstone Ct. E10 . . . . . 6E 50
EN5: Barn *2B 20*
(off Church La.)
HA3: W'stone 3K 41
TW19: Stanw *1A 128*
(off Explorer Av.)
Livingstone Ho. NW10 . . . . . 7K 61
SE5 . . . . . *7C 102*
(off Wyndham Rd.)
Livingstone Lodge *W9* *5J 81*
(off Admiral Wlk.)
Livingstone Mans. *W14* *6G 99*
(off Queen's Club Gdns.)
Livingstone Pl. E14 . . . . . 5E 104
Livingstone Rd.
CR7: Thor H 2C 156
E15 . . . . . 1E 86
E17 . . . . . 6D 50
N13 . . . . . 6D 32
SW11 . . . . . 3B 118
TW3: Houn 4G 113
UB1: S'hall 7B 76
Livingwell Health Club
Greville Rd. ***2K 81***
(within Regents Plaza)
Purley 6A 168
Wembley 5F 61
Livonia St. W1 . . . . . 1B 12 (6G 83)
Lizard St. EC1 . . . . . 2D 8 (3C 84)
Lizban St. SE3 . . . . . 7K 105
Lizmans Ter. *W8* *3J 99*
(off Earl's Ct. Rd.)

Llandovery Ho. *E14* 2E **104**
(off Chipka St.)
Llanelly Rd. NW2 . . . . .2H **63**
Llanover Rd. HA9: Wemb 3D **60**
SE18 . . . . .6E **106**
Llanthony Rd. SM4: Mord 5B **154**
Llanvanor Rd. NW2 . . . . .2H **63**
Llewellyn Ct. SE20 . . . . .1J **157**
Llewellyn St. SE16 . . . . .2G **103**
Lloyd Av. SW16 . . . . .1J **155**
Lloyd Baker St. WC1 . . . . . . .2H **7** (3K **83**)
(not continuous)
Lloyd Ct. HA5: Pinn 5B **40**
Lloyd Ho. BR3: Beck 6D **140**
Lloyd M. EN3: Enf L 1H **25**
Lloyd Pk. Av. CR0: Croy 4F **169**
Lloyd Pk. Ho. E17 . . . . .3C **50**
Lloyd Rd. E6 .1D **88**
E17 . . . . .4K **49**
KT4: Wor Pk 3E **164**
RM9: Dag .6F **73**
Lloyd's Av. EC3 . . . . .1H **15** (6E **84**)
Lloyds' Building 1G **15** (6E **84**)
Lloyds Lanes Bowling Alley 2B **24**
Lloyds Lanes Raynes Pk. 3F **153**
Lloyd's Pl. SE3 . . . . .2G **123**
Lloyd Sq. WC1 . . . . .1J **7** (3A **84**)
Lloyd's Row EC1 . . . . .2K **7** (3A **84**)
Lloyd St. WC1 . . . . .1J **7** (3A **84**)
Lloyds Way BR3: Beck 5A **158**
Lloyds Wharf SE1 . . . . .6K **15**
Lloyd Thomas Ct. N22 . . . . .7E **32**
Lloyd Vs. E6 .4C **88**
SE4 . . . . .2C **122**
Loampit Hill SE13 . . . . .2C **122**
LOAMPIT VALE 3E **122**
Loampit Va. SE13 . . . . .3D **122**
Loanda Cl. E8 . . . . .1F **85**
Loats Rd. SW2 . . . . .6J **119**
Lobelia Cl. E6 . . . . .5C **88**
Locarno Ct. SW16 . . . . .5G **137**
Locarno Rd. UB6: G'frd 4H **77**
W3 . . . . .1J **97**
Lochaber Rd. SE13 . . . . .4G **123**
Lochaline St. W6 . . . . .6E **98**
Lochan Cl. UB4: Yead 4C **76**
Lochinvar St. SW12 . . . . .7F **119**
Lochleven Ho. N2 . . . . .2B **46**
(off The Grange)
Lochmere Cl. DA8: Erith 6H **109**
Lochmore Ho. SW1 . . . . .4H **17**
(off Cundy St.)
Lochnagar St. E14 . . . . .5E **86**
Lockbridge Ct. W9 . . . . .5J **81**
(off Woodfield Rd.)
Lock Bldg., The E15 . . . . .2E **86**
Lock Chase SE3 . . . . .3G **123**
Lock Cl. UB2: S'hall 2G **95**
Locke Ho. SW8 . . . . .1G **119**
(off Wadhurst Rd.)
Lockesfield Pl. E14 . . . . .5D **104**
Lockesley Dr. BR5: St M Cry 6K **161**
Lockesley Sq. KT6: Surb 6D **150**
Locket Rd. HA3: W'stone 3J **41**
Lockfield Av. EN3: Brim 2F **25**
Lockgate Cl. E9 . . . . .5B **68**
Lockhart Cl. EN3: Pond E 5C **24**
N7 . . . . .6K **65**
Lockhart Ho. SE10 . . . . .7D **104**
(off Tarves Way)
Lockhart St. E3 . . . . .4B **86**
Lockhurst St. E5 . . . . .4K **67**
Lockie Pl. SE25 . . . . .3G **157**
Lockier Wlk. HA9: Wemb 3D **60**
Lockington Rd. SW8 . . . . .1F **119**
Lock Keepers Quay SE16 . . . . .3K **103**
(off Brunswick Quay)
Lockmead Rd. N15 . . . . .6G **49**
SE13 . . . . .3E **122**
Lock M. NW5 . . . . .6H **65**
(off Northpoint Sq.)
Lock Rd. TW10: Ham 4C **132**
LOCKSBOTTOM 3E **172**

Locksfields SE17 . . . . .4D **102**
(off Catesby St.)
Lockside E14 .7A **86**
(off Narrow St.)
Locks La. CR4: Mitc 1E **154**
Locksley Est. E14 . . . . .6B **86**
Locksley St. E14 . . . . .5B **86**
Locksmeade Rd. TW10: Ham 4C **132**
Locksons Cl. E14 . . . . .5D **86**
Lockswood Cl. EN4: Cockf 4J **21**
Lock Vw. Ct. E14 . . . . .7A **86**
(off Narrow St.)
Lockwood Cl. SE26 . . . . .4K **139**
Lockwood Ho. SE11 . . . . .7J **19** (6A **102**)
Lockwood Ind. Pk. N17 . . . . .3H **49**
Lockwood Pl. E4 . . . . .6H **35**
Lockwood Sq. SE16 . . . . .3H **103**
Lockwood Way E17 . . . . .2K **49**
KT9: Chess 5G **163**
Lockyer Est. SE1 . . . . .7F **15**
(not continuous)
Lockyer Ho. SE10 . . . . .5H **105**
(off Armitage Rd.)
SW8 . . . . .7H **101**
(off Wandsworth Rd.)
SW15 . . . . .3F **117**
Lockyer M. EN3: Enf L 1J **25**
Lockyer St. SE1 . . . . .7F **15** (2D **102**)
Locomotive Dr. TW14: Felt 1J **129**
Locton Grn. E3 . . . . .1B **86**
Loddiges Ho. E9 . . . . .7J **67**
Loddiges Rd. E9 . . . . .7J **67**
Loddon Ho. NW8 . . . . .4B **4**
(off Church St. Est.)
Loder St. SE15 . . . . .7J **103**
Lodge Av. CR0: Wadd 3A **168**
HA3: Kent .4E **42**
RM8: Dag .6B **72**
RM9: Dag .1A **90**
SW14 . . . . .3A **116**
LODGE AVENUE FLYOVER JUNC. 1A **90**
Lodge Cl. HA8: Edg 6A **28**
N18 . . . . .5H **33**
SM6: Wall 1E **166**
TW7: Isle .1B **114**
Lodge Ct. HA0: Wemb 6E **60**
Lodge Dr. N13 . . . . .4F **33**
Lodge Gdns. BR3: Beck 5B **158**
Lodge Hill IG4: Ilf 4C **52**
SE2 . . . . .7B **108**
Lodgehill Pk. Cl. HA2: Harr 2F **59**
Lodge La. CR0: New Ad 6C **170**
DA5: Bexl .6D **126**
N12 . . . . .5F **31**
RM5: Col R 1G **55**
Lodge Pl. SM1: Sutt 5K **165**
Lodge Rd. BR1: Brom 7A **142**
CR0: Croy 6B **156**
NW4 . . . . .4E **44**
NW8 . . . . .2B **4** (3B **82**)
SM6: Wall 5F **167**
Lodge Vs. IG8: Wfd G 6C **36**
Lodge Way TW15: Ashf 2A **128**
TW17: Shep 2E **146**
Lodore Gdns. NW9 . . . . .5A **44**
Lodore Grn. UB10: Ick 3A **56**
Lodore St. E14 . . . . .6E **86**
Loft Ho. Pl. KT9: Chess 6C **162**
Loftie St. SE16 . . . . .2G **103**
Lofting Ho. N1 . . . . .7A **66**
(off Liverpool Rd.)
Lofting Rd. N1 . . . . .7K **65**
Loftus Road .1D **98**
Loftus Rd. W12 . . . . .1D **98**
Loftus Vs. W12 . . . . .1D **98**
(off Loftus Rd.)
Logan Cl. EN3: Enf H 1E **24**
TW4: Houn 3D **112**
Logan M. RM1: Rom 5K **55**
W8 . . . . .4J **99**
Logan Pl. W8 . . . . .4J **99**
Logan Rd. HA9: Wemb 2D **60**
N9 . . . . .2C **34**

Loggetts SE21 . . . . .2E **138**
Logs Hill BR1: Brom 7C **142**
BR7: Chst 7C **142**
Logs Hill Cl. BR7: Chst 1C **160**
Lohmann Ho. SE11 . . . . .7J **19**
Lois Dr. TW17: Shep 5D **146**
Lolesworth Cl. E1 . . . . .6J **9** (5F **85**)
Lollard St. SE11 . . . . .3H **19** (4K **101**)
(not continuous)
Loman St. SE1 . . . . .6B **14** (2B **102**)
Lomas Cl. CR0: New Ad 7E **170**
Lomas Dr. E8 . . . . .7F **67**
(off Richmond Rd.)
Lomas St. E1 . . . . .5G **85**
Lombard Av. EN3: Enf H 1D **24**
IG3: Ilf 1J **71**
Lombard Bus. Cen., The
SW11 . . . . .2B **118**
Lombard Bus. Pk. CR0: Croy 7K **155**
SW19 . . . . .2K **153**
Lombard Ct. EC3 . . . . .2F **15** (7D **84**)
RM7: Rom 4J **55**
W3 . . . . .1H **97**
Lombard La. EC4 . . . . .1K **13** (6A **84**)
Lombard Rd. N11 . . . . .5A **32**
SW11 . . . . .2B **118**
SW19 . . . . .2K **153**
LOMBARD RDBT. 7K **155**
Lombard St. EC3 . . . . .1F **15** (6D **84**)
Lombard Trad. Est. SE7 . . . . .4K **105**
Lombard Wall SE7 . . . . .3K **105**
(not continuous)
Lombardy Cl. IG6: Ilf 7K **37**
Lombardy Pl. W2 . . . . .7K **81**
Lombardy Retail Pk. UB3: Hayes . . .7K **75**
Lomond Cl. HA0: Wemb 7F **61**
N15 . . . . .5E **48**
Lomond Gdns. CR2: Sels 7A **170**
Lomond Gro. SE5 . . . . .7D **102**
Lomond Ho. SE5 . . . . .7D **102**
Loncroft Rd. SE5 . . . . .6E **102**
Londesborough Rd. N16 . . . . .4E **66**
Londinium Twr. E1 . . . . .2K **15**
(off W. Tenter St.)
London Apollo 5E **98**
London Aquarium 6G **13** (2K **101**)
London Arena 3D **104**
London Bri. EC4 . . . . . . .4F **15** (1D **102**)
SE1 . . . . .4F **15** (1D **102**)
London Bri. St. SE1 . . . . .5F **15** (1D **102**)
London Bri. Wlk. SE1 . . . . .4F **15**
(off Duke St. Hill)
London Broncos Rugby League Football Club
. . . . .6D **96**
London Business School 3E **4** (4D **82**)
London Butterfly House 1B **114**
London Canal Mus. 2J **83**
LONDON CITY AIRPORT 1C **106**
London City College 5J **13**
London Coliseum 3E **12**
(off St Martin's La.)
London College of Fashion, The
Hackney .7J **67**
(off Mare St.)
St Luke's 4C **8** (4C **84**)
Londonderry Pde. DA8: Erith 7K **109**
London Dungeon 5F **15**
London Eye 6G **13** (2K **101**)
London Flds. E. Side E8 . . . . .7H **67**
London Flds. W. Side E8 . . . . .7G **67**
London Fire Brigade Mus. 2C **102**
London Fruit Exchange E1 . . . . .6J **9**
(off Brushfield St.)
London Ga. UB3: Hayes 2G **93**
London Group Bus. Pk. NW2 . . . . . .1B **62**
London Guildhall University
Coke St. .6G **85**
LONDON HEATHROW AIRPORT 3C **110**
London Ho. NW8 . . . . .2C **82**
(off Avenue Rd.)
WC1 . . . . .3G **7** (4K **83**)
London Ind. Pk., The E6 . . . . .5F **89**
(not continuous)

London La. BR1: Brom 7H **141**
E8 . . . . .7H **67**
London Master Bakers Almshouses
E10 . . . . .6D **50**
London Metropolitan University
Benwell Rd. 5A **66**
City of London 1J **15**
(off Jewry St.)
Hornsey St. 5K **65**
Manningtree St. 7K **9** (6G **85**)
London M. W2 . . . . .7B **4** (6B **82**)
London Motorcycle Mus. 3G **77**
London Palladium 1A **12**
(off Argyll St.)
London Regatta Cen. 7B **88**
London Rd. BR1: Brom 7H **141**
CR0: Croy, Thor H 1K **155**
CR4: Mitc 5C **154**
(Bishopsford Rd.)
CR4: Mitc 7E **154**
(Carshalton Rd.)
CR4: Mitc 2D **154**
(Holborn Way)
DA1: Bexl, Cray 5K **127**
E13 . . . . .2J **87**
EN2: Enf 3J **23**
HA1: Harr 2J **59**
HA7: Stan .5J **27**
HA9: Wemb 5E **60**
IG11: Bark 7F **71**
KT2: King T 2F **151**
(not continuous)
KT17: Ewe 7B **164**
RM7: Chad H, Rom 6G **55**
SE1 . . . . .7A **14** (3B **102**)
SE23 . . . . .1H **139**
SM3: Cheam 3F **165**
SM4: Mord 5J **153**
SM6: Wall 4F **167**
SW16 . . . . .1K **155**
SW17 . . . . .1C **136**
TW1: Twick 7A **114**
TW3: Houn 3G **113**
TW7: Bford, Isle 2K **113**
TW7: Isle, Twick 5A **114**
TW8: Bford 2K **113**
TW14: Bedf 2A **128**
TW15: Ashf 2A **128**
LONDON ROAD RDBT. 6A **114**
London School of Economics & Politics, The
. . . . .1H **13** (6K **83**)
London Scottish & Richmond RUFC
. . . . .3D **114**
London South Bank University
. . . . .7B **14** (3B **102**)
London South Bank University Sports Cen.
. . . . .7B **14**
(in London South Bank University)
London Stile W4 . . . . .5G **97**
London Stock Exchange 7B **8**
(off Paternoster Sq.)
London St. EC3 . . . . .2H **15** (7E **84**)
W2 . . . . .7A **4** (6B **82**)
London Telecom Tower, The . . .5A **6** (5G **83**)
London Television Cen., The
. . . . .4J **13** (1A **102**)
London Ter. E2 . . . . .2G **85**
London Transport Mus. 2F **13** (7J **83**)
London Underwriting Cen. EC3 . . . . .2H **15**
London Wall EC2 . . . . .6D **8** (5C **84**)
London Wall Bldgs. EC2 . . . . .6E **8**
London Welsh RUFC 3E **114**
London Wetland Cen. 1D **116**
London Wharf E2 . . . . .1H **85**
(off Wharf Pl.)
London Wildlife Trust 2E **82**
London Wildlife Trust Cen. for
Wildlife Gardening 3F **121**
London Zoo .2E **82**
LONESOME .1G **155**
Lonesome Cvn. Pk. CR4: Mitc 1F **155**
Lonesome Way SW16 . . . . .1F **155**
Long Acre WC2 . . . . .2E **12** (7J **83**)

Long Acre Ct. W13 . . . 5A **78**
Longacre Pl. SM5: Cars . . . 6E **166**
Longacre Rd. E17 . . . 1F **51**
Longbeach Rd. SW11 . . . 3D **118**
Longberrys NW2 . . . 3H **63**
Longboat Row UB1: S'hall . . . 6D **76**
Longbridge Ho. *RM8: Dag* . . . *4B* ***72***
(off Gainsborough Rd.)
Longbridge Rd. IG11: Bark . . . 6H **71**
RM8: Dag . . . 4A **72**
Longbridge Way SE13 . . . 5E **122**
Longcroft SE9 . . . 3D **142**
Longcrofte Rd. HA8: Edg . . . 7J **27**
Long Deacon Rd. E4 . . . 1B **36**
LONG DITTON . . . 1C **162**
Longdon Wood BR2: Kes . . . 3C **172**
Longdown Rd. SE6 . . . 4C **140**
Long Dr. HA4: Ruis . . . 5A **58**
UB6: G'frd . . . 1F **77**
UB7: W Dray . . . 2A **92**
W3 . . . 6A **80**
Long Elmes HA3: Hrw W . . . 1F **41**
Longfellow Rd. E17 . . . 6B **50**
KT4: Wor Pk . . . 2C **164**
Longfellow Way SE1 . . . 4F **103**
Long Fld. NW9 . . . 7F **29**
Longfield BR1: Brom . . . 1H **159**
Longfield Av. E17 . . . 4A **50**
HA9: Wemb . . . 1E **60**
NW7 . . . 7H **29**
SM6: Wall . . . 1E **166**
W5 . . . 7C **78**
Longfield Cres. SE26 . . . 3J **139**
Longfield Dr. CR4: Mitc . . . 1C **154**
SW14 . . . 5H **115**
Longfield Est. SE1 . . . 4F **103**
Longfield Ho. W5 . . . 7C **78**
Longfield Rd. W5 . . . 6C **78**
Longfield St. SW18 . . . 7J **117**
Longfield Wlk. W5 . . . 6C **78**
Longford Av. TW14: Felt . . . 6G **111**
TW19: Stanw . . . 1A **128**
UB1: S'hall . . . 7F **77**
Longford Cl. TW12: Ham H . . . 4E **130**
TW13: Hanw . . . 3C **130**
UB4: Yead . . . 7B **76**
Longford Ct. *E5* . . . *4K* ***67***
(off Pedro St.)
KT19: Ewe . . . 4J **163**
NW4 . . . 4F **45**
UB1: S'hall . . . *1E* ***94***
(off Uxbridge Rd.)
Longford Gdns. SM1: Sutt . . . 3A **166**
UB4: Yead . . . 7B **76**
Longford Ho. *BR1: Brom* . . . *5F* ***141***
(off Brangbourne Rd.)
E1 . . . *6J* ***85***
(off Jubilee St.)
TW12: Ham H . . . 4E **130**
Longford Ind. Est.
TW12: Hamp . . . 6F **131**
Longford Rd. TW2: Whit . . . 1C **130**
Longford St. NW1 . . . 3K **5** (4F **83**)
Longford Wlk. SW2 . . . 7A **120**
Longford Way TW19: Stanw . . . 1A **128**
Longhayes Av.
RM6: Chad H . . . 4D **54**
Longhayes Ct. RM6: Chad H . . . 4D **54**
Longheath Gdns. CR0: Croy . . . 5J **157**
Longhedge Ho. *SE26* . . . *4G* ***139***
(off High Level Dr.)
Long Hedges TW3: Houn . . . 2E **112**
Longhedge St. SW11 . . . 2E **118**
Longhill Rd. SE6 . . . 2F **141**
Longhook Gdns. UB5: Yead . . . 2J **75**
Longhope Cl. SE15 . . . 6E **102**
Longhurst Ho. *W10* . . . *3H* ***81***
(off Lancefield St.)
Longhurst Rd. CR0: Croy . . . 6H **157**
SE13 . . . 5F **123**
Longland Ct. SE1 . . . 5G **103**
Longland Dr. N20 . . . 3E **30**
LONGLANDS . . . 3G **143**
Longlands Ct. CR4: Mitc . . . 1E **154**
DA15: Sidc . . . 2K **143**
W11 . . . *7H* ***81***
(off Westbourne Gro.)
Longlands Pk. Cres. DA15: Sidc . . . 3J **143**
Longlands Rd. DA15: Sidc . . . 3J **143**
Long La. CR0: Croy . . . 6H **157**
DA7: Bex . . . 7D **108**
EC1 . . . 6B **8** (5B **84**)
N2 . . . 1K **45**
N3 . . . 1K **45**
(not continuous)
SE1 . . . 7E **14** (2D **102**)
TW19: Stanw . . . 2B **128**
UB10: Hil, Ick . . . 3C **74**
Longleat Ho. *SW1* . . . *5C* ***18***
(off Rampayne St.)
Longleat Rd. EN1: Enf . . . 5K **23**
Longleat Way TW14: Bedf . . . 7F **111**
Longleigh Ho. *SE5* . . . *1E* ***120***
(off Peckham Rd.)
Longleigh La. DA7: Bex . . . 6C **108**
SE2 . . . 6C **108**
Long Lents Ho. *NW10* . . . *1K* ***79***
(off Shrewsbury Cres.)
Longley Av. HA0: Wemb . . . 1F **79**
Longley Ct. SW8 . . . 1J **119**
Longley Rd. CR0: Croy . . . 7B **156**
HA1: Harr . . . 5G **41**
SW17 . . . 6C **136**
Long Leys E4 . . . 6J **35**
Longley St. SE1 . . . 4G **103**
Longley Way NW2 . . . 3E **62**
Longman Ho. *E2* . . . *2K* ***85***
(off Mace St.)
E8 . . . *1F* ***85***
(off Haggerston Rd.)
Long Mark Rd. E16 . . . 5B **88**
Longmarsh La. SE28 . . . 1J **107**
Long Mead NW9 . . . 1B **44**
Longmead BR7: Chst . . . 2E **160**
Longmead Dr. DA14: Sidc . . . 2D **144**
Longmead Ho. SE27 . . . 5C **138**
Long Mdw. NW5 . . . 5H **65**
Long Mdw. Cl. BR4: W W'ck . . . 7E **158**
Longmeadow Rd. DA15: Sidc . . . 1J **143**
Longmead Rd. KT7: T Ditt . . . 7J **149**
SW17 . . . 5D **136**
UB3: Hayes . . . 7H **75**
Long Mill *SE10* . . . *1D* ***122***
(off Greenwich High Rd.)
Longmoore St. SW1 . . . 4A **18** (4G **101**)
Longmoor Point *SW15* . . . *1D* ***134***
(off Norley Vale)
Longmore Av. EN4: E Barn . . . 6F **21**
EN5: New Bar . . . 6F **21**
Longmore Gdns. Est. SW1 . . . 4D **18**
Longnor Est. E1 . . . 3K **85**
Longnor Rd. E1 . . . 3K **85**
Long Pond Rd. SE3 . . . 1G **123**
Longreach Ct. IG11: Bark . . . 2H **89**
Long Reach Rd. IG11: Bark . . . 4K **89**
Longridge Ho. SE1 . . . 3C **102**
Longridge La. UB1: S'hall . . . 6F **77**
Longridge Rd. IG11: Bark . . . 7G **71**
SW5 . . . 4J **99**
Long Ridges *N2* . . . *3E* ***46***
(off Fortis Grn.)
Long Rd. SW4 . . . 4F **119**
Longs Ct. TW9: Rich . . . 4F **115**
WC2 . . . 3D **12**
Longshaw Rd. E4 . . . 3A **36**
Longshore SE8 . . . 4B **104**
Longshott Ct. *SW5* . . . *4J* ***99***
(off W. Cromwell Rd.)
Longstaff Cres. SW18 . . . 6J **117**
Longstaff Rd. SW18 . . . 6J **117**
Longstone Av. NW10 . . . 7B **62**
Longstone Ct. *SE1* . . . *7E* ***14***
(off Gt. Dover St.)
Longstone Rd. SW17 . . . 5F **137**
Long St. E2 . . . 1J **9** (3F **85**)
Longthornton Rd. SW16 . . . 2G **155**
Longthorpe Ct. *W6* . . . *4C* ***98***
(off Invermead Cl.)
Longton Av. SE26 . . . 4G **139**
Longton Gro. SE26 . . . 4H **139**
Longview Vs. RM5: Col R . . . 1F **55**
Longview Way RM5: Col R . . . 1K **55**
Longville Rd. SE11 . . . 4B **102**
Long Wlk. KT3: N Mald . . . 3J **151**
SE1 . . . 3E **102**
SE18 . . . 6F **107**
SW13 . . . 2A **116**
Longwalk Rd. UB11: Stock P . . . 1D **92**
Long Wall E15 . . . 3F **87**
Longwater Ho. *KT1: King T* . . . *3D* ***150***
(off Portsmouth Rd.)
Longwood Bus. Pk.
TW16: Sun . . . 5H **147**
Longwood Dr. SW15 . . . 6C **116**
Longwood Gdns. IG5: Ilf . . . 4D **52**
IG6: Ilf . . . 3F **53**
Longworth Cl. SE28 . . . 6D **90**
Long Yd. WC1 . . . 4G **7** (4K **83**)
Loning, The NW9 . . . 4A **44**
Lonsdale Av. E6 . . . 4B **88**
HA9: Wemb . . . 5E **60**
RM7: Rom . . . 6J **55**
Lonsdale Cl. E6 . . . 4C **88**
HA5: H End . . . 1C **40**
HA8: Edg . . . 5A **28**
SE9 . . . 3B **142**
UB8: Hil . . . 5E **74**
Lonsdale Ct. KT6: Surb . . . 7D **150**
Lonsdale Cres. IG2: Ilf . . . 6F **53**
Lonsdale Dr. EN2: Enf . . . 4C **22**
Lonsdale Dr. Nth. EN2: Enf . . . 5D **22**
Lonsdale Gdns. CR7: Thor H . . . 4K **155**
Lonsdale Ho. *W11* . . . *6H* ***81***
(off Lonsdale Rd.)
Lonsdale M. TW9: Kew . . . 1G **115**
W11 . . . *6H* ***81***
(off Lonsdale Rd.)
Lonsdale Pl. N1 . . . 7A **66**
Lonsdale Rd. DA7: Bex . . . 2F **127**
E11 . . . 6H **51**
NW6 . . . 1H **81**
SE25 . . . 4H **157**
SW13 . . . 1B **116**
UB2: S'hall . . . 3B **94**
W4 . . . 4B **98**
W11 . . . 6H **81**
Lonsdale Sq. N1 . . . 7A **66**
Lonsdale Yd. W11 . . . 7J **81**
Loobert Rd. N15 . . . 3E **48**
Looe Gdns. IG6: Ilf . . . 3F **53**
Loop Rd. BR7: Chst . . . 6G **143**
Lopen Rd. N18 . . . 4K **33**
Lopez Ho. SW9 . . . 3J **119**
Lorac Ct. SM2: Sutt . . . 7J **165**
Loraine Cl. EN3: Pond E . . . 5D **24**
Loraine Cotts. N7 . . . 4K **65**
Loraine Ct. BR7: Chst . . . 5F **143**
Loraine Ho. SM6: Wall . . . 4F **167**
Loraine Rd. N7 . . . 4K **65**
W4 . . . 6H **97**
Lord Amory Way E14 . . . 2E **104**
Lord Av. IG5: Ilf . . . 4D **52**
Lord Chancellor Wlk. KT2: King T . . . 1J **151**
Lord Ct. IG5: Ilf . . . 4D **52**
Lordell Pl. SW19 . . . 6E **134**
Lorden Wlk. E2 . . . 2K **9** (3G **85**)
Lord Gdns. IG5: Ilf . . . 4D **52**
Lord Hills Bri. W2 . . . 5K **81**
Lord Hills Rd. W2 . . . 5K **81**
Lord Holland La. SW9 . . . 2A **120**
Lord Knyvetts Ct. TW19: Stanw . . . 6A **110**
Lord Napier Pl. W6 . . . 5C **98**
Lord North St. SW1 . . . 2E **18** (3J **101**)
Lord Roberts M. SW6 . . . 7K **99**
Lord Robert's Ter. SE18 . . . 5E **106**
Lords Cl. SE21 . . . 2C **138**
TW13: Hanw . . . 2C **130**
Lord's Cricket Ground . . . 2B **4** (3B **82**)
Lordship Gro. N16 . . . 2D **66**
Lordship La. N17 . . . 1D **48**
N22 . . . 2A **48**
SE22 . . . 4F **121**
Lordship La. Est. SE21 . . . 7G **121**
Lordship Pk. N16 . . . 2C **66**
Lordship Pk. M. N16 . . . 2C **66**
Lordship Pl. SW3 . . . 7C **16** (6C **100**)
Lordship Rd. N16 . . . 1D **66**
UB5: N'olt . . . 7C **58**
Lordship Ter. N16 . . . 2D **66**
Lordsmead Rd. N17 . . . 1E **48**
Lord St. E16 . . . 1C **106**
Lords Vw. NW8 . . . 2C **4** (3B **82**)
Lord Warwick St. SE18 . . . 3D **106**
Lordwood Cl. DA6: Bex . . . 5E **126**
Loreburn Ho. N7 . . . 4K **65**
Lorenzo St. WC1 . . . 1G **7** (3K **83**)
Loretto Gdns. HA3: Kent . . . 4E **42**
Lorian Cl. N12 . . . 4E **30**
Lorimar Bus. Cen. RM13: Rain . . . 5K **91**
Loring Rd. N20 . . . 2H **31**
SE14 . . . 1A **122**
TW7: Isle . . . 2K **113**
Loris Rd. W6 . . . 3E **98**
Lorn Ct. SW9 . . . 2A **120**
Lorne Av. CR0: Croy . . . 7K **157**
Lorne Cl. NW8 . . . 2D **4** (3C **82**)
Lorne Gdns. CR0: Croy . . . 7K **157**
E11 . . . 4A **52**
W11 . . . 2F **99**
Lorne Ho. *E1* . . . *5A* ***86***
(off Ben Jonson Rd.)
Lorne Rd. E7 . . . 4K **69**
E17 . . . 5C **50**
HA3: W'stone . . . 2K **41**
N4 . . . 1K **65**
TW10: Rich . . . 5F **115**
Lorne Ter. N3 . . . 2H **45**
Lorn Rd. SW9 . . . 2K **119**
Lorraine Ct. NW1 . . . 7F **65**
Lorraine Pk. HA3: Hrw W . . . 7D **26**
Lorrimore Rd. SE17 . . . 6B **102**
Lorrimore Sq. SE17 . . . 6B **102**
Lorton Ho. *NW6* . . . *1J* ***81***
(off Kilburn Va.)
Lothair Rd. W5 . . . 2D **96**
Lothair Rd. Nth. N4 . . . 6B **48**
Lothair Rd. Sth. N4 . . . 7A **48**
Lothbury EC2 . . . 7E **8** (6D **84**)
Lothian Av. UB4: Yead . . . 5K **75**
Lothian Cl. HA0: Wemb . . . 3A **60**
Lothian Rd. SW9 . . . 1B **120**
Lothrop St. W10 . . . 3G **81**
Lots Rd. SW10 . . . 7A **100**
Lotus Cl. SE21 . . . 3D **138**
Loubet St. SW17 . . . 6D **136**
Loudoun Av. IG6: Ilf . . . 5F **53**
Loudoun Rd. NW8 . . . 1A **82**
Loudwater Cl. TW16: Sun . . . 4J **147**
Loudwater Rd. TW16: Sun . . . 4J **147**
Loughborough Est. SW9 . . . 3B **120**
Loughborough Pk. SW9 . . . 4B **120**
Loughborough Rd. SW9 . . . 2A **120**
Loughborough St. SE11 . . . 5H **19** (5K **101**)
Lough Rd. N7 . . . 5K **65**
Loughton Way IG9: Buck H . . . 1G **37**
Louisa Cl. E9 . . . 1K **85**
Louisa Ct. TW2: Twick . . . 2J **131**
Louisa Gdns. E1 . . . 4K **85**
Louisa St. E1 . . . 4K **85**
Louise Aumonier Wlk. *N19* . . . *7J* ***47***
(off Jessie Blythe La.)
Louise Bennett Cl. SE24 . . . 4B **120**
Louise Ct. N22 . . . 1A **48**
Louise De Marillac Ho. *E1* . . . *5J* ***85***
(off Smithy St.)
Louise Rd. E15 . . . 6G **69**
Louise White Ho. N19 . . . 1H **65**
Louis Gdns. BR7: Chst . . . 4D **142**
Louis M. N10 . . . 1F **47**
Louisville Rd. SW17 . . . 3E **136**
Lousada Lodge *N14* . . . *6B* ***22***
(off Avenue Rd.)

Louvaine Rd. SW11 .....4B 118
Lovage App. E6 .....5C 88
Lovat Cl. NW2 .....3B 62
Lovat La. EC3 .....2G 15 (7E 84)
(not continuous)
Lovatt Cl. HA8: Edg 6C 28
Lovatt Cl. SW12 .....1F 137
Lovatt Dr. HA4: Ruis 5J 39
Lovat Wlk. TW5: Hest 7C 94
Loveday Rd. W13 .....2B 96
Lovegrove St. SE1 .....5G 103
Lovegrove Wlk. E14 .....1E 104
Lovekyn Cl. KT2: King T 2E 150
Lovelace Av. BR2: Brom 6E 160
Lovelace Gdns. IG11: Bark 4A 72
  KT6: Surb 7D 150
Lovelace Grn. SE9 .....3D 124
Lovelace Ho. E8 .....1F 85
  (off Haggerston Rd.)
  W13 .....7B 78
Lovelace Rd. EN4: E Barn 7H 21
  KT6: Surb 7C 150
  SE21 .....2C 138
Lovelace Vs. KT7: T Ditt 7B 150
  (off Portsmouth Rd.)
Loveland Mans. IG11: Bark 7K 71
  (off Upney La.)
Love La. BR1: Brom 3K 159
  (off Elmfield Rd.)
  BR1: Brom 3K 159
  (Rafford Way)
  CR4: Mitc 3C 154
  (not continuous)
  DA5: Bexl 6F 127
  (not continuous)
  EC2 .....7D 8 (6C 84)
  HA5: Pinn 2B 40
  IG8: Wfd G 6J 37
  KT6: Surb 2C 162
  N17 .....7A 34
  SE18 .....4E 106
  SE25 .....3H 157
  (not continuous)
  SM1: Sutt 6H 165
  SM3: Cheam, Sutt 6G 165
  SM4: Mord 7J 153
Lovel Av. DA16: Well 2A 126
Lovelinch Cl. SE15 .....6J 103
Lovell Ho. E8 .....1G 85
  (off Shrubland Rd.)
Lovell Pl. SE16 .....3A 104
Lovell Rd. TW10: Ham 3C 132
  UB1: S'hall 6F 77
Loveridge M. NW6 .....6H 63
Loveridge Rd. NW6 .....6H 63
Lovers Wlk. N3 .....7D 30
  (not continuous)
  NW7 .....6C 30
  SE10 .....6F 105
  W1 .....4G 11 (1E 100)
Lovett Dr. SM5: Cars 7A 154
Lovett Way NW10 .....5J 61
Love Wlk. SE5 .....2D 120
Lovibonds Av. BR6: Farnb 4F 173
  UB7: View 6B 74
Lowbrook Rd. IG1: Ilf 4F 71
Low Cross Wood La. SE21 .....3F 139
Lowdell Cl. UB7: View 6A 74
Lowden Rd. N9 .....1C 34
  SE24 .....4B 120
  UB1: S'hall 7C 76
Lowder Ho. E1 .....1H 103
  (off Wapping La.)
Lowe Av. E16 .....5J 87
Lowell Ho. SE5 .....7C 102
  (off Wyndham Est.)
Lowell St. E14 .....6A 86
Lowen Rd. RM13: Rain 2K 91
Lwr. Addiscombe Rd. CR0: Croy 1E 168
Lwr. Addison Gdns. W14 .....2G 99
Lwr. Belgrave St. SW1 .....2J 17 (3F 101)
Lwr. Boston Rd. W7 .....1J 95
Lwr. Broad St. RM10: Dag 1G 91

Lower Camden BR7: Chst 7D 142
Lwr. Church St. CR0: Croy 2B 168
LOWER CLAPTON 4H 67
Lwr. Clapton Rd. E5 .....3H 67
Lwr. Clarendon Wlk. W11 .....6G 81
  (off Clarendon Rd.)
Lower Comn. Sth. SW15 .....3D 116
Lwr. Coombe St. CR0: Croy 4C 168
Lwr. Downs Rd. SW20 .....1F 153
Lwr. Drayton Pl. CR0: Croy 2B 168
LOWER EDMONTON 2B 34
LOWER FELTHAM 3H 129
Lower Fosters NW4 .....5E 44
  (off New Brent St.)
Lwr. George St. TW9: Rich 5D 114
Lwr. Gravel Rd. BR2: Brom 1C 172
Lower Grn. Gdns. KT4: Wor Pk 1C 164
Lower Grn. W. CR4: Mitc 3C 154
Lwr. Grosvenor Pl. SW1 .....1K 17 (3F 101)
Lwr. Gro. Rd. TW10: Rich 6F 115
LOWER HALLIFORD 6F 147
Lwr. Hall La. E4 .....5F 35
  (not continuous)
Lwr. Hampton Rd. TW16: Sun 3A 148
Lwr. Ham Rd. KT2: King T 5D 132
LOWER HOLLOWAY 5K 65
Lwr. James St. W1 .....2B 12 (7G 83)
Lwr. John St. W1 .....2B 12 (7G 83)
Lwr. Kenwood Av. EN2: Enf 5D 22
Lwr. King's Rd. KT2: King T 1E 150
Lwr. Lea Crossing E14 .....7G 87
  E16 .....7G 87
Lwr. Maidstone Rd. N11 .....6B 32
Lower Mall W6 .....5D 98
Lwr. Mardyke Av. RM13: Rain 2J 91
Lower Marsh SE1 .....7J 13 (2A 102)
Lwr. Marsh La. KT1: King T 4F 151
  (not continuous)
Lwr. Merton Ri. NW3 .....7C 64
Lower Mill KT17: Ewe 7B 164
Lwr. Morden La. SM4: Mord 6E 152
Lwr. Mortlake Rd. TW9: Rich 4E 114
Lower Pk. Rd. DA17: Belv 3G 109
  N11 .....5B 32
Lower Pk. Trad. Est. NW10 .....4J 79
LOWER PLACE 2J 79
Lower Pl. Bus. Cen. NW10 .....2K 79
  (off Steele Rd.)
Lwr. Queen's Rd. IG9: Buck H 2G 37
Lwr. Richmond Rd. SW14 .....3G 115
  SW15 .....3D 116
  TW9: Rich 3G 115
Lower Rd. DA8: Erith 3H 109
  DA17: Belv 3H 109
  HA2: Harr 1H 59
  SE1 .....6J 13 (2A 102)
  SE8 .....4K 103
  SE16 .....2J 103
  (not continuous)
  SM1: Sutt 4A 166
Lwr. Robert St. WC2 .....3F 13
  (in Robert St.)
Lwr. Sand Hills KT6: Surb 7C 150
Lwr. Sloane St. SW1 .....4G 17 (4E 100)
Lwr. Sq. TW7: Isle 3B 114
Lower Sq., The SM1: Sutt 5K 165
Lower Strand NW9 .....2B 44
Lwr. Sunbury Rd. TW12: Hamp 2D 148
LOWER SYDENHAM 4K 139
Lwr. Sydenham Ind. Est. SE26 .....5B 140
Lwr. Teddington Rd. KT1: Ham W 1D 150
Lower Ter. NW3 .....3A 64
  SE27 .....5B 138
  (off Woodcote Pl.)
Lwr. Thames St. EC3 .....3F 15 (7D 84)
Lowerwood Ct. W11 .....6G 81
  (off Westbourne Pk. Rd.)
Lwr. Wood Rd. KT10: Clay 6B 162
Lowestoft Cl. E5 .....2J 67
  (off Mundford Rd.)
Lowestoft M. E16 .....2F 107
Loweswater Cl. HA9: Wemb 2D 60
Loweswater Ho. E3 .....4B 86

Lowfield Rd. NW6 .....7J 63
  W3 .....6H 79
Low Hall Cl. E4 .....7J 25
Low Hall La. E17 .....6A 50
Low Hall Mnr. Bus. Cen. E17 .....6A 50
Lowick Rd. HA1: Harr 4J 41
Lowlands Gdns. RM7: Rom 6H 55
Lowlands Rd. HA1: Harr 6J 41
  HA5: Eastc 7A 40
Lowman Rd. N7 .....4K 65
Lowndes Cl. SW1 .....2H 17 (3E 100)
Lowndes Ct. SW1 .....1F 17 (3D 100)
  W1 .....1A 12
Lowndes Lodge SW1 .....1F 17
  (off Lowndes St.)
Lowndes Pl. SW1 .....2G 17 (3E 100)
Lowndes Sq. SW1 .....7F 11 (2D 100)
Lowndes St. SW1 .....1F 17 (3E 100)
Lownds Ct. BR1: Brom 2J 159
Lowood Ct. SE19 .....5F 139
  (off Farquhar Rd.)
Lowood Ho. E1 .....7J 85
  (off Bewley St.)
Lowood St. E1 .....7H 85
Lowry Cl. DA8: Erith 4K 109
Lowry Ct. SE16 .....5H 103
  (off Stubbs Dr.)
Lowry Cres. CR4: Mitc 2C 154
Lowry Ho. E14 .....2C 104
  (off Cassilis Rd.)
  N17 .....1F 49
  (off Pembury Rd.)
Lowry Rd. RM8: Dag 5B 72
Lowshoe La. RM5: Col R 1G 55
Lowswood Cl. HA6: Nwood 1E 38
Lowther Dr. EN2: Enf 4D 22
Lowther Gdns. SW7 .....1B 16 (2B 100)
Lowther Hill SE23 .....7A 122
Lowther Ho. E8 .....1F 85
  (off Clarissa St.)
  SW1 .....6H 17
  (off Churchill Gdns.)
Lowther Rd. E17 .....2A 50
  HA7: Stan 3F 43
  KT2: King T 1F 151
  N7 .....5A 66
  SW13 .....1B 116
Lowth Rd. SE5 .....1C 120
LOXFORD 5G 71
Loxford Av. E6 .....2B 88
Loxford La. IG1: Ilf 5G 71
  IG3: Ilf 5G 71
Loxford Rd. IG11: Bark 6F 71
Loxford Ter. IG11: Ilf 6G 71
Loxham Rd. E4 .....7J 35
Loxham St. WC1 .....2F 7 (3J 83)
Loxley Cl. SE26 .....5K 139
Loxley Ho. HA9: Wemb 3E 60
Loxley Rd. SW18 .....1B 136
  TW12: Hamp 4D 130
Loxton Rd. SE23 .....1K 139
Loxwood Cl. TW14: Bedf 1F 129
Loxwood Rd. N17 .....3E 48
LSO St Lukes 2D 8
  (off St Lukes Cl.)
Lubbock Ho. E14 .....7D 86
  (off Poplar High St.)
Lubbock Rd. BR7: Chst 7D 142
Lubbock St. SE14 .....7J 103
Lucan Ho. N1 .....1D 84
  (off Colville Est.)
Lucan Pl. SW3 .....4C 16 (4C 100)
Lucan Rd. EN5: Barn 3B 20
Lucas Av. E13 .....1K 87
  HA2: Harr 2E 58
Lucas Cl. NW10 .....7C 62
Lucas Ct. SE26 .....5A 140
  SW11 .....1E 118
Lucas Gdns. N2 .....2A 46
Lucas Ho. SW10 .....7K 99
  (off Coleridge Gdns.)
Lucas Rd. SE20 .....6J 139
Lucas Sq. NW11 .....6J 45

Lucas St. SE8 .....1C 122
Lucerne Cl. N13 .....3D 32
Lucerne Ct. DA18: Erith 3E 108
Lucerne Gro. E17 .....4F 51
Lucerne M. W8 .....1J 99
Lucerne Rd. BR6: Orp 1K 173
  CR7: Thor H 3G 103
  N5 .....4B 66
Lucey Rd. SE16 .....3G 103
Lucey Way SE16 .....3G 103
Lucie Av. TW15: Ashf 6D 128
Lucien Rd. SW17 .....4E 136
  SW19 .....2K 135
Lucinda Ct. EN1: Enf 4K 23
Lucknow St. SE18 .....7J 107
Lucorn Cl. SE12 .....6H 123
Luctons Av. IG9: Buck H 1F 37
Lucy Brown Ho. SE1 .....5D 14
Lucy Cres. W3 .....5J 79
Lucy Gdns. RM8: Dag 3F 73
Luddesdon Rd. DA8: Erith 7G 109
Ludford Cl. CR0: Wadd 3B 168
Ludgate B'way. EC4 .....1A 14 (6B 84)
Ludgate Cir. EC4 .....1A 14 (6B 84)
Ludgate Hill EC4 .....1A 14 (6B 84)
Ludgate Sq. EC4 .....1B 14 (6B 84)
Ludham NW5 .....5D 64
Ludham Cl. IG6: Ilf 1G 53
  SE28 .....6C 90
Ludlow Cl. BR2: Brom 3J 159
  HA2: Harr 4D 58
Ludlow Cl. W3 .....2J 97
Ludlow Rd. TW13: Felt 4J 129
  W5 .....4C 78
Ludlow St. EC1 .....3C 8 (4C 84)
Ludlow Way N2 .....4A 46
Ludovick Wlk. SW15 .....4A 116
Ludwell Ho. W14 .....3G 99
  (off Russell Rd.)
Ludwick M. SE14 .....7A 104
Luffield Rd. SE2 .....3B 108
Luffman Rd. SE12 .....3K 141
Lugard Ho. W12 .....1D 98
Lugard Rd. SE15 .....2H 121
Lugg App. E12 .....3E 70
Luke Ho. E1 .....6H 85
  (off Tillman St.)
Luke St. EC2 .....3G 9 (4E 84)
Lukin Cres. E4 .....3A 36
Lukin St. E1 .....6J 85
Lullingstone Cl. BR5: St P 7B 144
Lullingstone Cres. BR5: St P 7B 143
Lullingstone Ho. SE15 .....6J 103
  (off Lovelinch Cl.)
Lullingstone La. SE13 .....6F 123
Lullingstone Rd.
  DA17: Belv 6F 109
Lullington Gth. BR1: Brom 7G 141
  N12 .....5C 30
Lullington Rd. RM9: Dag 7G 72
  SE20 .....7G 139
Lulot Gdns. N19 .....2F 65
Lulworth NW1 .....7H 65
  (off Wrotham Rd.)
  SE17 .....5D 102
  (off Portland St.)
Lulworth Av. HA9: Wemb 7C 42
  TW5: Hest 1F 113
Lulworth Cl. HA2: Harr 3E 58
Lulworth Ct. N1 .....7E 66
  (off St Peter's Way)
Lulworth Cres. CR4: Mitc 2C 154
Lulworth Dr. HA5: Pinn 6B 40
Lulworth Gdns. HA2: Harr 2C 58
Lulworth Ho. SW8 .....7K 101
Lulworth Rd. DA16: Well 2K 125
  SE9 .....2C 142
  SE15 .....2H 121
Lulworth Waye UB4: Yead 6K 75
Lumen Rd. HA9: Wemb 2C 60
Lumiere Bldg., The E7 .....5B 70
  (off Romford Rd.)
Lumiere Ct. SW17 .....2E 136

Lumina Bldgs. E14 . . . . .1E 104
(off Prestons Rd.)
Lumley Cl. DA17: Belv 5G 109
Lumley Ct. WC2 . . . . .3F 13 (7J 83)
Lumley Flats SW1 . . . . .5G 17
(off Holbein Pl.)
Lumley Gdns. SM3: Cheam 5G 165
Lumley Rd. SM3: Cheam 5G 165
Lumley St. W1 . . . . .1H 11 (6E 82)
Lumsdon NW8 . . . . .1K 81
(off Abbey Rd.)
Luna Ho. SE16 . . . . .2G 103
Luna Rd. CR7: Thor H 3C 156
Lund Point E15 . . . . .1E 86
Lundy Dr. UB3: Harl 4G 93
Lundy Wlk. N1 . . . . .6C 66
Lunham Rd. SE19 . . . . .6E 138
Luntley Pl. E1 . . . . .6K 9
Lupin Cl. CR0: Croy 1K 169
RM7: Rush G 2K 73
SW2 . . . . .2B 138
Lupin Cres. IG1: Ilf 6F 71
Lupino Ct. SE11 . . . . .3H 19 (4K 101)
Lupin Point SE1 . . . . .7K 15
Lupton Cl. SE12 . . . . .3K 141
Lupton St. NW5 . . . . .4G 65
(not continuous)
Lupus St. SW1 . . . . .6K 17 (5F 101)
Luralda Wharf E14 . . . . .5F 105
Lurgan Av. W6 . . . . .6F 99
Lurline Gdns. SW11 . . . . .1E 118
Luscombe Ct. BR2: Brom 2G 159
Luscombe Way SW8 . . . . .7J 101
Lushington Ho. KT12: Walt T 6A 148
Lushington Rd. NW10 . . . . .2D 80
SE6 . . . . .4D 140
Lushington Ter. E8 . . . . .5G 67
Lutea Ho. SM2: Sutt 7A 166
(off Walnut M.)
Luther Cl. HA8: Edg 2D 28
Luther King Cl. E17 . . . . .6B 50
Luther M. TW11: Tedd 5K 131
Luther Rd. TW11: Tedd 5K 131
Luton Ho. E13 . . . . .4J 87
(off Luton Rd.)
Luton Pl. SE10 . . . . .7E 104
Luton Rd. DA14: Sidc 3C 144
E13 . . . . .4J 87
E17 . . . . .3B 50
Luton St. NW8 . . . . .4B 4 (4B 82)
Lutton Ter. NW3 . . . . .4A 64
(off Lakis Cl.)
Luttrell Av. SW15 . . . . .5D 116
Lutwyche Rd. SE6 . . . . .2B 140
Lutyens Ho. SW1 . . . . .6A 18
(off Churchill Gdns.)
Luxborough Ho. W1 . . . . .5G 5
(off Luxborough St.)
Luxborough La. IG7: Chig 3H 37
Luxborough St. W1 . . . . . .5G 5 (5E 82)
Luxborough Twr. W1 . . . . .5G 5
Lux Cinema 2G 9
(off Hoxton Sq.)
Luxembourg M. E15 . . . . .5G 69
Luxemburg Gdns. W6 . . . . .4F 99
Luxfield Rd. SE9 . . . . .1C 142
Luxford St. SE16 . . . . .4K 103
Luxmore St. SE4 . . . . .1B 122
Luxor St. SE5 . . . . .3C 120
Lyall Av. SE21 . . . . .4E 138
Lyall M. SW1 . . . . .2G 17 (3E 100)
Lyall M. W. SW1 . . . . .2G 17 (3E 100)
Lyall St. SW1 . . . . .2G 17 (3E 100)
Lyal Rd. E3 .2A 86
Lycett Pl. W12 . . . . .2C 98
Lyceum Theatre 2G 13
Lychgate Mnr. HA1: Harr 7J 41
Lych Ga. Wlk. UB3: Hayes 7H 75
(not continuous)
Lyconby Gdns. CR0: Croy 7A 158
Lydd Cl. DA14: Sidc 3J 143
Lydden Ct. SE9 . . . . .6J 125
Lydden Gro. SW18 . . . . .7K 117

Lydden Rd. SW18 . . . . .7K 117
Lydd Rd. DA7: Bex 7F 109
Lydeard Rd. E6 . . . . .7D 70
Lyden Ho. E1 . . . . .3K 85
(off Westfield Way)
Lydford NW1 . . . . .1G 83
(off Royal College St.)
Lydford Cl. N16 . . . . .5E 66
(off Pellerin Rd.)
Lydford Rd. N15 . . . . .5D 48
NW2 . . . . .6E 62
W9 .4H 81
Lydhurst Av. SW2 . . . . .2K 137
Lydia Ct. KT1: King T 3E 150
(off Grove Cres.)
N12 . . . . .6F 31
Lydney Cl. SW19 . . . . .2G 135
Lydon Rd. SW4 . . . . .3G 119
Lydstep Rd. BR7: Chst 4E 142
Lyford Rd. SW18 . . . . .7B 118
Lyford St. SE7 . . . . .4C 106
Lygon Ho. E2 . . . . .1K 9
(off Gosset St.)
SW6 . . . . .1G 117
(off Fulham Pal. Rd.)
Lygon Pl. SW1 . . . . .2J 17 (3F 101)
Lyham Cl. SW2 . . . . .6J 119
Lyham Rd. SW2 . . . . .5J 119
Lyle Cl. CR4: Mitc 7E 154
Lyle Ct. SM4: Mord 6B 154
Lyly Ho. SE1 . . . . .3D 102
(off Burbage Cl.)
Lyme Farm Rd. SE12 . . . . .4J 123
Lyme Gro. E9 . . . . .7J 67
Lyme Gro. Ho. E9 . . . . .7J 67
(off Lyme Gro.)
Lymer Av. SE19 . . . . .5F 139
Lyme Rd. DA16: Well 1B 126
Lymescote Gdns. SM1: Sutt 2J 165
Lyme St. NW1 . . . . .7G 65
Lyme Ter. NW1 . . . . .7G 65
Lyminge Cl. DA14: Sidc 4K 143
Lyminge Gdns. SW18 . . . . .1C 136
Lymington Av. N22 . . . . .2A 48
Lymington Cl. E6 . . . . .5D 88
SW16 . . . . .2G 155
Lymington Ct. SM1: Sutt 3K 165
Lymington Dr. HA4: Ruis 2F 57
Lymington Gdns. KT19: Ewe 5B 164
Lymington Lodge E14 . . . . .3F 105
(off Schooner Cl.)
Lymington Rd. NW6 . . . . .6K 63
RM8: Dag 1D 72
Lyminster Cl. UB4: Yead 5C 76
Lympne N17 . . . . .2D 48
(off Gloucester Rd.)
Lympstone Gdns. SE15 . . . . .7G 103
Lynbridge Gdns. N13 . . . . .4G 33
Lynbrook Cl. RM13: Rain 2K 91
Lynbrook Gro. SE15 . . . . .7E 102
Lynch Cl. SE3 . . . . .2H 123
Lynchen Cl. TW5: Cran 1K 111
Lynch Wlk. SE8 . . . . .6B 104
(off Prince St.)
Lyncott Cres. SW4 . . . . .4F 119
Lyncourt SE3 . . . . .2F 123
Lyncroft Av. HA5: Pinn 5C 40
Lyncroft Gdns. NW6 . . . . .5J 63
TW3: Houn 5G 113
W13 . . . . .2C 96
Lyncroft Mans. NW6 . . . . .5J 63
Lyndale KT7: T Ditt 7J 149
NW2 . . . . .4H 63
Lyndale Av. NW2 . . . . .3H 63
Lyndale Cl. SE3 . . . . .6H 105
Lyndean Ind. Est. SE2 . . . . .3C 108
Lynde Ho. KT12: Walt T 6A 148
SW4 . . . . .3H 119
Lynden Hyrst CR0: Croy 2F 169
Lyndhurst Av. HA5: Pinn 1K 39
KT5: Surb 1H 163
N12 . . . . .6J 31
NW7 . . . . .6F 29

Lyndhurst Av. SW16 . . . . .2H 155
TW2: Whit 1D 130
TW16: Sun 3J 147
UB1: S'hall 1F 95
Lyndhurst Cl. BR6: Farnb 4F 173
CR0: Croy 3F 169
DA7: Bex 3H 127
NW10 . . . . .3K 61
Lyndhurst Ct. E18 . . . . .1J 51
NW8 . . . . .1B 82
(off Finchley Rd.)
SM2: Sutt 7J 165
(off Grange Rd.)
Lyndhurst Dr. E10 . . . . .7E 50
KT3: N Mald 7A 152
Lyndhurst Gdns. EN1: Enf 4K 23
HA5: Pinn 1K 39
IG2: Ilf 6H 53
IG11: Bark 6J 71
N3 . . . . .1G 45
NW3 . . . . .5B 64
Lyndhurst Gro. SE15 . . . . .2E 120
Lyndhurst Lodge E14 . . . . .4F 105
(off Millennium Dr.)
Lyndhurst Ri. IG7: Chig 4K 37
Lyndhurst Rd. CR7: Thor H 4A 156
DA7: Bex 3H 127
E4 . . . . .7K 35
N18 . . . . .4B 34
N22 . . . . .6F 33
NW3 . . . . .5B 64
UB6: G'frd 4F 77
Lyndhurst Sq. SE15 . . . . .1F 121
Lyndhurst Ter. NW3 . . . . .5B 64
Lyndhurst Way SE15 . . . . .1F 121
SM2: Sutt 7J 165
Lyndon Av. DA15: Sidc 5K 125
SM6: Wall 3E 166
Lyndon Rd. DA17: Belv 4G 109
Lyndon Yd. SW17 . . . . .4A 136
Lyne Cres. E17 . . . . .1B 50
Lynegrove Av. TW15: Ashf 5E 128
Lyneham Dr. NW9 . . . . .1A 44
Lyneham Wlk. E5 . . . . .5A 68
HA5: Eastc 3H 39
Lynette Av. SW4 . . . . .6F 119
Lynford Cl. HA8: Edg 1J 43
Lynford Ct. CR0: Croy 4E 168
(off Coombe Rd.)
Lynford Gdns. HA8: Edg 3C 28
IG3: Ilf 2K 71
Lynford Ter. N9 . . . . .1A 34
Lynhurst Cres. UB10: Hil 7E 56
Lynhurst Rd. UB10: Hil 7E 56
Lynmere Rd. DA16: Well 2B 126
Lyn M. E3 . . . . .3B 86
N16 .4E 66
Lynmouth Av. EN1: Enf 6A 24
SM4: Mord 6F 153
Lynmouth Avenue Gdns. 1F 165
Lynmouth Dr. HA4: Ruis 2K 57
Lynmouth Gdns. TW5: Hest 7B 94
UB6: G'frd 1B 78
Lynmouth Rd. E17 . . . . .6A 50
N2 . . . . .3D 46
N16 . . . . .1F 67
UB6: G'frd 1B 78
Lynn Cl. HA3: Hrw W 2H 41
TW15: Ashf 5F 129
Lynne Cl. BR6: Chels 6K 173
SE23 . . . . .7B 122
Lynne Ct. CR2: S Croy 4E 168
(off Birdhurst Rd.)
NW6 . . . . .7K 63
(off Priory Rd.)
Lynnett Rd. RM8: Dag 2D 72
Lynne Way NW10 . . . . .7A 62
UB5: N'olt 2B 76
Lynn Ho. SE15 . . . . .6H 103
(off Friary Est.)
Lynn M. E11 . . . . .2G 69
Lynn Rd. E11 . . . . .2G 69
IG2: Ilf 7H 53

Lynn Rd. SW12 . . . . .7F 119
Lynn St. EN2: Enf 1J 23
Lynscott Way CR2: S Croy 7B 168
Lynstead Ct. BR3: Beck 2A 158
Lynsted Cl. BR1: Brom 2A 160
DA6: Bex 5H 127
Lynsted Gdns. SE9 . . . . .3B 124
Lynton Av. N12 . . . . .4G 31
NW9 . . . . .4R 44
RM7: Mawney 1G 55
W13 . . . . .6A 78
Lynton Cl. KT9: Chess 4E 162
NW10 . . . . .5A 62
TW7: Isle 4K 113
Lynton Cres. IG2: Ilf 6F 53
Lynton Est. SE1 . . . . .4G 103
Lynton Gdns. EN1: Enf 7K 23
N11 . . . . .6C 32
Lynton Grange N2 . . . . .3D 46
Lynton Ho. IG1: Ilf 2G 71
(off Axon Pl.)
W2 . . . . .6A 82
(off Hallfield Est.)
Lynton Mans. SE1 . . . . .1J 19
(off Kennington Rd.)
Lynton Mead N20 . . . . .3D 30
Lynton Rd. CR0: Croy 6A 156
E4 .5J 35
HA2: Harr 2C 58
KT3: N Mald 5K 151
N8 . . . . .5H 47
(not continuous)
NW6 . . . . .2H 81
SE1 . . . . .4F 103
W3 . . . . .7G 79
Lynton Ter. W3 . . . . .6J 79
Lynwood Cl. E18 . . . . .1A 52
HA2: Harr 3C 58
Lynwood Ct. KT1: King T 2H 151
HA6: Nwood 1H 39
KT4: Wor Pk 2C 164
Lynwood Gdns. CR0: Wadd 4K 167
UB1: S'hall 6D 76
Lynwood Gro. BR6: Orp 7J 161
N21 . . . . .1F 33
Lynwood Rd. KT7: T Ditt 2A 162
SW17 . . . . .3D 136
W5 . . . . .3D 78
Lynx Way E16 . . . . .7B 88
Lyon Bus. Pk. IG11: Bark 2J 89
Lyon Ct. HA4: Ruis 1H 57
Lyon Ho. NW8 . . . . .4C 4
(off Broadley St.)
Lyon Ind. Est. NW2 . . . . .2D 62
Lyon Meade HA7: Stan 1C 42
Lyon Pk. Av. HA0: Wemb 6E 60
(not continuous)
Lyon Rd. HA1: Harr 6K 41
SW19 . . . . .1A 154
LYONSDOWN 5F 21
Lyonsdown Av. EN5: New Bar 6F 21
Lyonsdown Rd. EN5: New Bar 6F 21
Lyon St. N1 .7K 65
Lyons Wlk. W14 . . . . .4G 99
Lyon Way UB6: G'frd 1J 77
Lyoth Rd. BR5: Farnb 2G 173
Lyric Ct. E8 .7F 67
(off Holly St.)
Lyric Dr. UB6: G'frd 4F 77
Lyric M. SE26 . . . . .4J 139
Lyric Rd. SW13 . . . . .1B 116
Lyric Theatre
Hammersmith 4E 98
Westminster 2C 12
(off Shaftesbury Av.)
Lysander NW9 . . . . .1B 44
Lysander Gdns. KT6: Surb 6F 151
Lysander Gro. N19 . . . . .1H 65
Lysander Ho. E2 . . . . .2H 85
(off Temple St.)
Lysander M. N19 . . . . .1G 65

Lysander Rd. CR0: Wadd 6K 167
   HA4: Ruis 2F 57
Lysander Way BR6: Farnb 3G 173
Lysia Ct. SW6 . . . . .7F 99
    (off Lysia St.)
Lysias Rd. SW12 . . . . .6F 119
Lysia St. SW6 . . . . .7F 99
Lysons Wlk. SW15 . . . . .4C 116
Lytchet Rd. BR1: Brom 7J 141
Lytchet Way EN3: Enf H 1D 24
Lytchgate Cl. CR2: S Croy 7E 168
Lytcott Dr. KT8: W Mole 3D 148
Lytcott Gro. SE22 . . . . .5E 120
Lytham Cl. SE28 . . . . .6E 90
Lytham Ct. UB1: S'hall 6F 77
    (off Whitecote Rd.)
Lytham Gro. W5 . . . . .3F 79
Lytham St. SE17 . . . . .5D 102
Lyttelton Cl. NW3 . . . . .7C 64
Lyttelton Ct. N2 . . . . .5A 46
Lyttelton Ho. E9 . . . . .7J 67
    (off Well St.)
Lyttelton Rd. E10 . . . . .3D 68
   N2 . . . . .5A 46
Lyttelton Theatre 4J 13
   (in Royal National Theatre)
Lyttleton Ct. UB4: Yead 4A 76
    (off Dunedin Way)
Lyttleton Rd. N8 . . . . .3A 48
Lytton Av. EN3: Enf L 1F 25
   N13 . . . . .2F 33
Lytton Cl. N2 . . . . .6B 46
   UB5: N'olt 7D 58
Lytton Gdns. SM6: Bedd 4H 167
Lytton Gro. SW15 . . . . .5F 117
Lytton Rd. E11 . . . . .7G 51
   EN5: New Bar 4F 21
   HA5: Pinn 1C 40
Lytton Strachey Path SE28 . . . . . . .7B 90
Lytton Ter. E12 . . . . .6D 70
Lyveden Rd. SE3 . . . . .7K 105
   SW17 . . . . .6D 136

M

Mabbett Ho. SE18 . . . . .6E 106
    (off Nightingale Pl.)
Mabel Evetts Ct. UB3: Hayes 7K 75
Maberley Cres. SE19 . . . . .7G 139
Maberley Rd. BR3: Beck 3K 157
   SE19 . . . . .1F 157
Mabledon Ct. WC1 . . . . .2D 6
    (off Mabledon Pl.)
Mabledon Pl. WC1 . . . . .2D 6 (3H 83)
Mablethorpe Rd. SW6 . . . . .7G 99
Mabley St. E9 . . . . .5A 68
Mablin Lodge IG9: Buck H 1F 37
McAdam Dr. EN2: Enf 2G 23
Macaret Cl. N20 . . . . .7E 20
Macarthur Cl. E7 . . . . .6J 69
   HA9: Wemb 6H 61
Macarthur Ter. SE7 . . . . .6B 106
Macartney Ho. SE10 . . . . .7F 105
    (off Chesterfield Wlk.)
   SW9 . . . . .1A 120
    (off Gosling Way)
Macaulay Ct. SW4 . . . . .3F 119
Macaulay Rd. E6 . . . . .2B 88
   SW4 . . . . .3F 119
Macaulay Sq. SW4 . . . . .4F 119
Macaulay Way SE28 . . . . .1B 108
McAuley Cl. SE1 . . . . . .1J 19 (3A 102)
   SE9 . . . . .5F 125
Macauley Ho. W10 . . . . .5G 81
    (off Portobello Rd.)
Macaulay M. SE13 . . . . .1E 122
Macbean St. SE18 . . . . .3F 107
Macbeth Ho. N1 . . . . .2E 84
Macbeth St. W6 . . . . .5D 98
McCall Cl. SW4 . . . . .2J 119
McCall Cres. SE7 . . . . .5C 106
McCall Ho. N7 . . . . .4J 65

McCarthy Rd. TW13: Hanw 5B 130
MCC Cricket Mus. and Tours . .1A 4 (3B 82)
Macclesfield Rd. EC1 . . . . .2C 8
    (off Central St.)
Macclesfield Rd. EC1 . . . . . . .1C 8 (3C 84)
   SE25 . . . . .5J 157
Macclesfield St. W1 . . . .2D 12 (7H 83)
McCoid Way SE1 . . . . .7C 14 (2C 102)
McCrone M. NW3 . . . . .6B 64
McCullum Rd. E3 . . . . .1B 86
McDermott Cl. SW11 . . . . .3C 118
McDermott Rd. SE15 . . . . .3G 121
Macdonald Av. RM10: Dag 3H 73
Macdonald Ho. SW11 . . . . .2E 118
    (off Dagnall St.)
Macdonald Rd. E7 . . . . .4J 69
   E17 .2E 50
   N11 .5J 31
   N19 .2G 65
McDonough Cl. KT9: Chess 4E 162
McDougall Ct. TW9: Rich 2G 115
McDowall Cl. E16 . . . . .5H 87
McDowall Rd. SE5 . . . . .1C 120
Macduff Rd. SW11 . . . . .1E 118
Mace Cl. E1 . . . . .1H 103
McEntee Av. E17 . . . . .1A 50
McEwan Rd. SE2 . . . . .2K 85
McEwen Way E15 . . . . .1F 87
Macey Ho. SW11 . . . . .1C 118
Macey St. SE10 . . . . .6E 104
    (off Thames St.)
Macfarland Gro. SE15 . . . . .7E 102
Macfarlane La. TW7: Isle 6K 95
Macfarlane Rd. W12 . . . . .1E 98
Macfarren Pl. NW1 . . . . .4H 5 (4E 82)
Macfarron Ho. W10 . . . . .3G 81
    (off Parry Rd.)
McGlashon Ho. E1 . . . . .4K 9
    (off Hunton St.)
McGrath Rd. E15 . . . . .5H 69
McGregor Ct. N1 . . . . .1H 9
Macgregor Rd. E16 . . . . .5A 88
McGregor Rd. W11 . . . . .6H 81
Machell Rd. SE15 . . . . .3J 121
McIndoe Ct. N1 . . . . .1D 84
    (off Sherborne St.)
McIntosh Cl. RM1: Rom 3K 55
   SM6: Wall 7J 167
Macintosh Ho. W1 . . . . .5H 5
    (off Beaumont St.)
McIntosh Ho. SE16 . . . . .4J 103
    (off Millender Wlk.)
McIntosh Rd. RM1: Rom 3K 55
McIntyre Ct. SE18 . . . . .4C 106
    (off Prospect Va.)
Mackay Ho. W12 . . . . .7D 80
    (off White City Est.)
Mackay Rd. SW4 . . . . .3F 119
McKay Rd. SW20 . . . . .7D 134
McKellar Cl. WD23: Bushy 2B 26
Mackennal St. NW8 . . . . .2C 82
Mackenzie Cl. W12 . . . . .7D 80
Mackenzie Ho. N8 . . . . .4J 47
    (off Pembroke Rd.)
   NW2 . . . . .3C 62
Mackenzie Rd. BR3: Beck 2J 157
   N7 . . . . .6K 65
Mackenzie Wlk. E14 . . . . .1C 104
McKerrell Rd. SE15 . . . . .1G 121
Mackeson Rd. NW3 . . . . .4D 64
Mackie Rd. SW2 . . . . .7A 120
McKillop Way DA14: Sidc 7C 144
Mackintosh La. E9 . . . . .5K 67
Macklin St. WC2 . . . . .7F 7 (6J 83)
Mackonochie Ho. EC1 . . . . .5J 7
    (off Baldwins Gdns.)
Mackrow Wlk. E14 . . . . .7E 86
Mack's Rd. SE16 . . . . .4G 103
Mackworth Ho. NW1 . . . . .1A 6
    (off Augustus St.)
Mackworth St. NW1 . . . . . .1A 6 (3G 83)
McLaren Ho. SE1 . . . . .7A 14
    (off St Georges Cir.)

Maclaren M. SW15 . . . . .4E 116
Maclean Rd. SE23 . . . . .6A 122
McLeod Cl. SE22 . . . . .1G 139
Macleod Rd. N21 . . . . .5D 22
McLeod Rd. SE2 . . . . .4B 108
McLeod's M. SW7 . . . . .4K 99
Macleod St. SE17 . . . . .5C 102
Maclise Ho. SW1 . . . . .4E 18
    (off Marsham St.)
Maclise Rd. W14 . . . . .3G 99
Macmillan Ct. HA2: Harr 1E 58
Macmillan Ho. NW8 . . . . .2D 4
    (off Lorne Cl.)
McMillan Ho. SE4 . . . . .3A 122
    (off Arica Rd.)
   SE14 . . . . .1A 122
McMillan St. SE8 . . . . .6C 104
Macmillan Way SW17 . . . . .4F 137
McNair Rd. UB2: S'hall 3F 95
Macnamara Ho. SW10 . . . . .7B 100
    (off Worlds End Est.)
McNeil Rd. SE5 . . . . .2E 120
McNicol Dr. NW10 . . . . .2J 79
Macoma Rd. SE18 . . . . .6H 107
Macoma Ter. SE18 . . . . .6H 107
Maconochies Rd. E14 . . . . .5D 104
Macquarie Way E14 . . . . .4D 104
McRae La. CR4: Mitc 7D 154
Macready Ho. W1 . . . . .6E 4
    (off Crawford St.)
Macready Pl. N7 . . . . .4J 65
    (not continuous)
Macroom Ho. W9 . . . . .3H 81
    (off Macroom Rd.)
Macroom Rd. W9 . . . . .3H 81
Macs Ho. E17 . . . . .3D 50
Mac's Pl. EC4 . . . . .7J 7
Madame Tussaud's 4G 5 (4E 82)
Mada Rd. BR6: Farnb 3F 173
Maddams St. E3 . . . . .4D 86
Madderfields Ct. N11 . . . . .1H 47
Maddison Cl. N2 . . . . .2A 46
   TW11: Tedd 6K 131
Maddocks Cl. DA14: Sidc 5E 144
Maddocks Ho. E1 . . . . .7H 85
    (off Cornwall St.)
Maddock Way SE17 . . . . .6B 102
Maddox St. W1 . . . . .2K 11 (7F 83)
Madeira Av. BR1: Brom 7G 141
Madeira Gro. IG8: Wfd G 6F 37
Madeira Rd. CR4: Mitc 4D 154
   E11 .1F 69
   N13 .4G 33
   SW16 . . . . .5J 137
Madeleine Cl. RM6: Chad H 6C 54
Madeley Rd. W5 . . . . .6D 78
Madeline Gro. IG1: Ilf 5H 71
Madeline Rd. SE20 . . . . .7G 139
Madge Gill Way E6 . . . . .1C 88
    (off High St. Nth.)
Madge Hill W7 . . . . .7J 77
Madinah Rd. E8 . . . . .6G 67
Madison, The SE1 . . . . .6E 14
    (off Long La.)
Madison Cres. DA7: Bex 7C 108
Madison Gdns.
   BR2: Brom 3H 159
   DA7: Bex 7C 108
Madison Ho. E14 . . . . .7B 86
    (off Victory Pl.)
Madras Pl. N7 . . . . .6A 66
Madras Rd. IG1: Ilf 4F 71
Madrid Rd. SW13 . . . . .1C 116
Madrigal La. SE5 . . . . .7B 102
Madron St. SE17 . . . . .5E 102
Mafeking Av. E6 . . . . .2C 88
   IG2: Ilf 7H 53
   TW8: Bford 6E 96
Mafeking Rd. E16 . . . . .4H 87
   EN1: Enf 3A 24
   N17 .2G 49
Magazine Ga. W2 . . . . . .4D 10 (1C 100)
Magdala Av. N19 . . . . .2G 65

Magdala Rd. CR2: S Croy 7D 168
   TW7: Isle 3A 114
Magdalene Cl. SE15 . . . . .2H 121
Magdalene Gdns. E6 . . . . .4E 88
Magdalene Rd. TW17: Shep 4B 146
Magdalen Ho. E16 . . . . .1K 105
    (off Keats Av.)
Magdalen Pas. E1 . . . . . . .2K 15 (7F 85)
Magdalen Rd. SW18 . . . . .1A 136
Magdalen St. SE1 . . . . . . .5G 15 (1E 102)
Magee St. SE11 . . . . .7J 19 (6A 102)
Magellan Cl. NW10 . . . . .7K 61
    (off Brentfield Rd.)
Magellan Ho. E1 . . . . .4K 85
    (off Ernest St.)
Magellan Pl. E14 . . . . .4C 104
Magnaville Rd. WD23: Bushy 1D 26
Magnet Rd. HA9: Wemb 2D 60
Magnin Cl. E8 . . . . .1G 85
Magnolia Cl. E10 . . . . .2C 68
   KT2: King T 6H 133
Magnolia Ct. HA3: Kent 7F 43
   SM2: Sutt 7J 165
    (off Grange Rd.)
   SM6: Wall 5F 167
   TW9: Kew 1H 115
   TW13: Felt 1J 129
    (off Plum Cl.)
   UB5: N'olt 4C 76
   UB10: Hil 6D 56
Magnolia Gdns. E10 . . . . .2C 68
   HA8: Edg 4D 28
Magnolia Ho. SE8 . . . . .6B 104
    (off Evelyn St.)
Magnolia Lodge E4 . . . . .3J 35
   W8 . . . . .3K 99
    (off St Mary's Ga.)
Magnolia Pl. SW4 . . . . .5J 119
   W5 . . . . .5D 78
Magnolia Rd. W4 . . . . .6H 97
Magnolia St. UB7: W Dray 4A 92
Magnolia Way KT19: Ewe 5J 163
Magpie All. EC4 . . . . .1K 13 (6A 84)
Magpie Cl. E7 . . . . .5H 69
   EN1: Enf 1B 24
   NW9 . . . . .2A 44
Magpie Hall Cl. BR2: Brom 6C 160
Magpie Hall La. BR2: Brom 5D 160
Magpie Hall Rd. WD23: Bushy 2D 26
Magpie Pl. SE14 . . . . .6A 104
Magri Wlk. E1 . . . . .5J 85
Maguire Dr. TW10: Ham 4C 132
Maguire St. SE1 . . . . .6K 15 (2F 103)
Mahatma Gandhi Ind. Est. SE24 . . . .4B 120
Mahlon Av. HA4: Ruis 5K 57
Mahogany Cl. SE16 . . . . .1A 104
   EN1: Enf 1A 24
Maida Av. E4 . . . . .7J 25
   W2 . . . . .4A 4 (5A 82)
MAIDA HILL .4H 81
Maida Rd. DA17: Belv 3G 109
MAIDA VALE 3K 81
Maida Va. W9 . . . . .3A 4 (2K 81)
Maida Way E4 . . . . .7J 25
Maiden Erlegh Av. DA5: Bexl 1E 144
Maiden La. NW1 . . . . .7H 65
   SE1 . . . . .5D 14 (1C 102)
   WC2 . . . . .3F 13 (7J 83)
Maiden Pl. NW5 . . . . .3G 65
Maiden Rd. E15 . . . . .7G 69
Maidenstone Hill SE10 . . . . .1E 122
Maids of Honour Row TW9: Rich 5D 114
Maidstone Av. RM5: Col R 2J 55
Maidstone Bldgs. M. SE1 . . .5D 14 (1C 102)
Maidstone Ho. E14 . . . . .6D 86
    (off Carmen St.)
Maidstone Rd. DA14: Sidc, Swan 6D 144
   N11 .6B 32
Mail Coach Yd. E2 . . . . .1H 9 (3E 84)
Main Av. EN1: Enf 5A 24
Main Dr. HA9: Wemb 3D 60
Main Mill SE10 . . . . .7D 104
    (off Greenwich High St.)

Mainridge Rd. BR7: Chst . . . 4E 142
Main Rd. DA14: Sidc . . . 3H 143
Main St. TW13: Hanw . . . 5B 130
Mainwaring Ct. CR4: Mitc . . . 2E 154
Mais Ho. SE26 . . . 2H 139
Maismore St. SE15 . . . 6G 103
Maisonettes, The
SM1: Sutt . . . 5H 165
Maitland Cl. SE10 . . . 7D 104
TW4: Houn . . . 3D 112
Maitland Ct. W2 . . . 2A 10
(off Lancaster Ter.)
Maitland Ho. E2 . . . 2J 85
(off Waterloo Gdns.)
SW1 . . . 7A 18
(off Churchill Gdns.)
Maitland Pk. Est. NW3 . . . 6D 64
Maitland Pk. Rd. NW3 . . . 6D 64
Maitland Pk. Vs. NW3 . . . 6D 64
Maitland Pl. E5 . . . 4H 67
Maitland Rd. E15 . . . 6H 69
SE26 . . . 6K 139
Maitland Yd. W13 . . . 1A 96
Maize Row E14 . . . 7B 86
Majendie Rd. SE18 . . . 5H 107
Majestic Way CR4: Mitc . . . 2D 154
Major Cl. SW9 . . . 3B 120
Major Rd. E15 . . . 5F 69
SE16 . . . 3G 103
Makepeace Av. N6 . . . 2E 64
Makepeace Mans. N6 . . . 2E 64
Makepeace Rd. E11 . . . 4J 51
UB5: N'olt . . . 2C 76
Makinen Ho. IG9: Buck H . . . 1F 37
Makins St. SW3 . . . 4D 16 (4C 100)
Malabar Ct. W12 . . . 7D 80
(off India Way)
Malabar St. E14 . . . 2C 104
Malam Ct. SE11 . . . 4J 19 (4A 102)
Malam Gdns. E14 . . . 7D 86
Malbrook Rd. SW15 . . . 4D 116
Malcolm Ct. E7 . . . 6H 69
HA7: Stan . . . 5H 27
NW4 . . . 6C 44
Malcolm Cres. NW4 . . . 6C 44
Malcolm Dr. KT6: Surb . . . 1D 162
Malcolm Ho. N1 . . . 2E 84
(off Arden Est.)
Malcolm Pl. E2 . . . 4J 85
Malcolm Rd. E1 . . . 4J 85
SE20 . . . 7J 139
SE25 . . . 6G 157
SW19 . . . 6G 135
UB10: Ick . . . 4B 56
Malcolm Sargent Ho. E16 . . . 1K 105
(off Evelyn Rd.)
Malcolmson Ho. SW1 . . . 6C 18
(off Aylesford St.)
Malcolm Way E11 . . . 5J 51
Malden Av. SE25 . . . 4H 157
UB6: G'frd . . . 5J 59
Malden Cen., The . . . 4B 152
Malden Ct. N4 . . . 6C 48
SW20: N Mald . . . 3D 152
Malden Cres. NW1 . . . 6E 64
MALDEN GREEN . . . 1C 164
Malden Grn. Av. KT4: Wor Pk . . . 1B 164
Malden Hill KT3: N Mald . . . 3B 152
Malden Hill Gdns.
KT3: N Mald . . . 3B 152
MALDEN JUNC. . . . 5B 152
Malden Pk. KT3: N Mald . . . 6B 152
Malden Pl. NW5 . . . 5E 64
Malden Rd. KT3: N Mald . . . 5A 152
KT4: Wor Pk . . . 5A 152
NW5 . . . 5D 64
SM3: Cheam . . . 4F 165
Malden Way KT3: N Mald . . . 6K 151
Maldon Cl. E15 . . . 5G 69
N1 . . . 1C 84
SE5 . . . 3E 120
Maldon Ct. E6 . . . 1E 88
SM6: Wall . . . 5G 167
Maldon Rd. N9 . . . 3A 34
RM7: Rush G . . . 7J 55
SM6: Wall . . . 5F 167
W3 . . . 7J 79
Maldon Wlk. IG8: Wfd G . . . 6F 37
Malet Pl. WC1 . . . 4C 6 (4H 83)
Malet St. WC1 . . . 4C 6 (4H 83)
Maley Av. SE27 . . . 2B 138
Malford Ct. E18 . . . 2J 51
Malford Gro. E18 . . . 4H 51
Malfort Rd. SE5 . . . 3E 120
Malham Cl. N11 . . . 6K 31
Malham Rd. SE23 . . . 1K 139
Malham Rd. Ind. Est. SE23 . . . 1K 139
Malham Ter. N18 . . . 6C 34
(off Dysons Rd.)
N18 . . . 5C 34
(Alston Rd.)
Malibu Ct. SE26 . . . 3H 139
Mall, The BR1: Brom . . . 3J 159
CR0: Croy . . . 2C 168
DA6: Bex . . . 4G 127
E15 . . . 7F 69
HA3: Kent . . . 6F 43
KT6: Surb . . . 5D 150
N14 . . . 3D 32
RM10: Dag . . . 6G 73
SW1 . . . 5D 12 (2G 101)
SW14 . . . 5J 115
TW8: Bford . . . 6D 96
W5 . . . 7E 78
Mallams M. SW9 . . . 3B 120
Mallard Cl. E9 . . . 6B 68
EN5: New Bar . . . 6G 21
NW6 . . . 2J 81
TW2: Whit . . . 7E 112
W7 . . . 2J 95
Mallard Ct. E17 . . . 3F 51
Mallard Ho. NW8 . . . 2C 82
(off Barrow Hill Est.)
Mallard Path SE28 . . . 3H 107
(off Goosander Way)
Mallard Pl. N22 . . . 2K 47
TW1: Twick . . . 3A 132
Mallards E11 . . . 7J 51
(off Blake Hall Rd.)
Mallards Rd. IG8: Wfd G . . . 7E 36
IG11: Bark . . . 3A 90
Mallard Wlk. BR3: Beck . . . 5K 157
DA14: Sidc . . . 6C 144
Mallard Way NW9 . . . 7J 43
SM6: Wall . . . 7G 167
Mall Chambers W8 . . . 1J 99
(off Kensington Mall)
Mallet Dr. UB5: N'olt . . . 5D 58
Mallet Rd. SE13 . . . 6F 123
Mall Galleries . . . 4D 12
Mall Gallery WC2 . . . 1E 12
(in Thomas Neals Shop. Mall)
Malling SE13 . . . 5D 122
Malling Cl. CR0: Croy . . . 6J 157
Malling Gdns. SM4: Mord . . . 6A 154
Malling Way BR2: Hayes . . . 7H 159
Mallinson Rd. CR0: Bedd . . . 3H 167
SW11 . . . 5C 118
Mallinson Sports Cen. . . . 7D 46
Mallon Gdns. E1 . . . 7K 9
(off Commercial St.)
Mallord St. SW3 . . . 7B 16 (6B 100)
Mallory Bldgs. EC1 . . . 4A 8
(off St John St.)
Mallory Cl. E14 . . . 5D 86
SE4 . . . 4A 122
Mallory Gdns. EN4: E Barn . . . 7K 21
Mallory St. NW8 . . . 3D 4 (4C 82)
Mallow Cl. CR0: Croy . . . 1K 169
Mallow Mead NW7 . . . 7B 30
Mallows, The UB10: Ick . . . 3D 56
Mallow St. EC1 . . . 3E 8 (4D 84)
Mall Rd. W6 . . . 5D 98
Mall Vs. W6 . . . 5D 98
(off Mall Rd.)
Malmains Cl. BR3: Beck . . . 4F 159
Malmains Way BR3: Beck . . . 4E 158
Malmesbury E2 . . . 2J 85
(off Cyprus St.)
Malmesbury Cl. HA5: Eastc . . . 4H 39
Malmesbury Rd. E3 . . . 3B 86
E16 . . . 5G 87
E18 . . . 1H 51
SM4: Mord . . . 7A 154
Malmesbury Ter. E16 . . . 5H 87
Malmsey Ho. SE11 . . . 5H 19 (5K 101)
Malmsmead Ho. E9 . . . 5B 68
(off King's Mead Way)
Malory Cl. BR3: Beck . . . 2A 158
Malpas Dr. HA5: Pinn . . . 5B 40
Malpas Rd. E8 . . . 5H 67
RM9: Dag . . . 6D 72
SE4 . . . 2B 122
Malta Rd. E10 . . . 1C 68
Malta St. EC1 . . . 3A 8 (4B 84)
Maltby Cl. BR6: Orp . . . 1K 173
Maltby Dr. EN1: Enf . . . 1C 24
Maltby Rd. KT9: Chess . . . 6G 163
Maltby St. SE1 . . . 7J 15 (2F 103)
Malthouse Dr. TW13: Hanw . . . 5B 130
W4 . . . 6B 98
Malthouse Pas. SW13 . . . 2B 116
(off Maltings Cl.)
Malthus Path SE28 . . . 1C 108
Malting Ho. E14 . . . 7B 86
(off Oak La.)
Maltings W4 . . . 5G 97
Maltings, The BR6: Orp . . . 1K 173
Maltings Cl. E3 . . . 3E 86
SW13 . . . 2B 116
Maltings Lodge W4 . . . 6A 98
(off Corney Reach Way)
Maltings M. DA15: Sidc . . . 3A 144
Maltings Pl. SE1 . . . 7H 15
SW6 . . . 1K 117
Malting Way TW7: Isle . . . 3K 113
Malton M. SE18 . . . 6J 107
W10 . . . 6G 81
Malton Rd. W10 . . . 6G 81
Malton St. SE18 . . . 6J 107
Maltravers St. WC2 . . . 2H 13 (7K 83)
Malt St. SE1 . . . 6G 103
Malva Cl. SW18 . . . 5K 117
Malvern Av. DA7: Bex . . . 7E 108
E4 . . . 7A 36
HA2: Harr . . . 3C 58
Malvern Cl. CR4: Mitc . . . 3G 155
KT6: Surb . . . 1E 162
SE20 . . . 2G 157
UB10: Ick . . . 2C 56
W10 . . . 5H 81
Malvern Ct. SM2: Sutt . . . 7J 165
SW7 . . . 3B 16
(off Onslow Sq.)
W12 . . . 2C 98
(off Hadyn Pk. Rd.)
Malvern Dr. IG3: Bark, Ilf . . . 4K 71
IG8: Wfd G . . . 5F 37
TW13: Hanw . . . 5B 130
Malvern Gdns. HA3: Kent . . . 4E 42
NW2 . . . 2G 63
Malvern Ho. N16 . . . 1F 67
Malvern M. NW6 . . . 3J 81
Malvern Pl. NW6 . . . 3H 81
Malvern Rd. CR7: Thor H . . . 4A 156
E6 . . . 1C 88
E8 . . . 7G 67
E11 . . . 2G 69
KT6: Surb . . . 2E 162
N8 . . . 3A 48
N17 . . . 3G 49
NW6 . . . 2H 81
(not continuous)
TW12: Hamp . . . 7E 130
UB3: Harl . . . 7G 93
Malvern Ter. N1 . . . 1A 84
N9 . . . 1A 34
Malvern Way W13 . . . 5B 78
Malwood Rd. SW12 . . . 6F 119
Malyons, The TW17: Shep . . . 6F 147
Malyons Rd. SE13 . . . 6D 122
Malyons Ter. SE13 . . . 5D 122
Managers St. E14 . . . 1E 104
Manatee Pl. SM6: Bedd . . . 3H 167
Manaton Cl. SE15 . . . 3H 121
Manaton Cres. UB1: S'hall . . . 6E 76
Manbey Gro. E15 . . . 6G 69
Manbey Pk. Rd. E15 . . . 6G 69
Manbey Rd. E15 . . . 6G 69
Manbey St. E15 . . . 6G 69
Manbre Rd. W6 . . . 6E 98
Manbrough Av. E6 . . . 3D 88
Manchester Ct. E16 . . . 6K 87
(off Garvary Rd.)
Manchester Dr. W10 . . . 4G 81
Manchester Gro. E14 . . . 5E 104
Manchester Ho. SE17 . . . 5C 102
Manchester M. W1 . . . 6G 5
Manchester Rd. CR7: Thor H . . . 3C 156
E14 . . . 5E 104
N15 . . . 6D 48
Manchester Sq. W1 . . . 7G 5 (6E 82)
Manchester St. W1 . . . 6G 5 (5E 82)
Manchester Way RM10: Dag . . . 4H 73
Manchuria Rd. SW11 . . . 6E 118
Manciple St. SE1 . . . 7E 14 (2D 102)
Mandalay Rd. SW4 . . . 5G 119
Mandarin Ct. NW10 . . . 6K 61
(off Mitchellbrook Way)
SE8 . . . 6B 104
Mandarin St. E14 . . . 7C 86
Mandarin Way UB4: Yead . . . 6C 76
Mandela Cl. NW10 . . . 7J 61
W12 . . . 7D 80
Mandela Ho. E2 . . . 2J 9
(off Virginia Rd.)
SE5 . . . 2B 120
Mandela Rd. E16 . . . 6J 87
Mandela St. NW1 . . . 1G 83
SW9 . . . 7A 102
(not continuous)
Mandela Way SE1 . . . 4E 102
Mandel Ho. SW18 . . . 4J 117
Manderley W14 . . . 3H 99
(off Oakwood La.)
Mandeville Cl. SE3 . . . 7H 105
SW20 . . . 7G 135
Mandeville Ct. E4 . . . 5F 35
Mandeville Dr. KT6: Surb . . . 1D 162
Mandeville Ho. SE1 . . . 5F 103
(off Rolls Rd.)
SW4 . . . 5G 119
Mandeville M. SW4 . . . 4H 119
Mandeville Pl. W1 . . . 7H 5 (6E 82)
Mandeville Rd. N14 . . . 2A 32
TW7: Isle . . . 2A 114
TW17: Shep . . . 5C 146
UB5: N'olt . . . 7E 58
Mandeville St. E5 . . . 3A 68
Mandrake Rd. SW17 . . . 3D 136
Mandrake Way E15 . . . 7G 69
Mandrell Rd. SW2 . . . 5J 119
Manesty Ct. N14 . . . 7C 22
(off Ivy Rd.)
Manette St. W1 . . . 1D 12 (6H 83)
Manfred Rd. SW15 . . . 5H 117
Manger Rd. N7 . . . 6J 65
Mangold Way DA18: Erith . . . 3D 108
Manhattan Bus. Pk. W5 . . . 3E 78
Manilla St. E14 . . . 2C 104
Manister Rd. SE2 . . . 3A 108
Manitoba Ct. SE16 . . . 2J 103
(off Canada Est.)
Manitoba Gdns. BR6: Chels . . . 6K 173
Manley Ct. N16 . . . 3F 67
Manley Ho. SE11 . . . 5J 19 (4A 102)
Manley St. NW1 . . . 1E 82
Mann Cl. CR0: Croy . . . 3C 168
Manneby Prior N1 . . . 1H 7
(off Cumming St.)
Manning Ct. SE28 . . . 1B 108
(off Titmuss Av.)

Manningford Cl. EC1 1A 8 (3B 84)
Manning Gdns. HA3: Kent 7D 42
Manning Ho. *W11 6G 81*
(*off Westbourne Pk. Rd.*)
Manning Pl. TW10: Rich 6F 115
Manning Rd. E17 5A 50
RM10: Dag 6G 73
Manningtree Cl. SW19 1G 135
Manningtree Rd.
HA4: Ruis 4K 57
Manningtree St. E1 6G 85
Mannin Rd. RM6: Chad H 7B 54
Mannock M. E18 1A 52
Mannock Rd. N22 3B 48
Mann's Cl. TW7: Isle 5K 113
Manns Rd. HA8: Edg 6B 28
Manny Shinwell Ho. *SW6 6H 99*
(*off Clem Attlee Ct.*)
Manoel Rd. TW2: Twick 3G 131
Manor, The IG8: Wfd G 7K 37
SE23 7J 121
Manor Av. E7 4A 70
SE4 2B 122
TW4: Houn 3B 112
UB5: N'olt 7D 58
Manor Brook SE3 4J 123
MANOR CIRCUS 3G 115
Manor Cl. DA1: Cray 4K 127
E17 1A 50
EN5: Barn 4B 20
HA4: Ruis 1H 57
KT4: Wor Pk 1A 164
NW7 5E 28
NW9 5H 43
RM10: Dag 6K 73
SE28 7C 90
Manor Cotts. HA6: Nwood 1H 39
N2 2A 46
(*off Manor Cotts. App.*)
Manor Cotts. App. N2 2A 46
Manor Ct. BR4: W W'ck 1D 170
DA7: Bex 4H 127
E4 1B 36
E10 1D 68
HA1: Harr 6K 41
HA9: Wemb 5E 60
IG11: Bark 7K 71
KT2: King T 1G 151
KT8: W Mole 4E 148
N2 5D 46
N14 2C 32
N20 3J 31
(*off York Way*)
SM5: Cars 3E 166
SW2 5K 119
SW3 6D 16
(*off Hemus Pl.*)
SW6 1K 117
SW16 3J 137
TW2: Twick 2G 131
W3 4G 97
Manor Ct. Rd. W7 7J 77
Manor Cres. KT5: Surb 6G 151
Manor Dene SE28 6C 90
Manordene Cl. KT7: T Ditt 1A 162
Manordene Rd. SE28 6C 90
Manor Dr. HA9: Wemb 4F 61
KT5: Surb 6F 151
KT10: Hin W 2A 162
KT19: Ewe 6A 164
N14 1A 32
N20 4J 31
NW7 5E 28
TW13: Hanw 5B 130
TW16: Sun 2J 147
Manor Dr., The KT4: Wor Pk 1A 164
Manor Dr. Nth. KT3: N Mald 7K 151
KT4: Wor Pk 1A 164
Manor Est. SE16 4H 103
Mnr. Farm Av. TW17: Shep 6D 146
Mnr. Farm Cl. KT4: Wor Pk 1A 164
Mnr. Farm Ct. E6 3D 88
Mnr. Farm Dr. E4 3B 36
Mnr. Farm Rd. HA0: Wemb 2D 78
SW16 2A 156
Manorfield Cl. *N19 4G 65*
(*off Fulbrook M.*)
Manor Flds. SW15 6F 117
Manorfields Cl. BR7: Chst 3K 161
Manor Gdns. CR2: S Croy 6F 169
HA4: Ruis 5A 58
N7 3J 65
SW4 2G 119
(*off Larkhall Ri.*)
SW20 2H 153
TW9: Rich 4F 115
TW12: Hamp 7F 131
TW16: Sun 1J 147
W3 4G 97
W4 5A 98
Manor Ga. UB5: N'olt 7C 58
Manorgate Rd. KT2: King T 1G 151
Manor Gro. BR3: Beck 2D 158
SE15 6J 103
TW9: Rich 4G 115
Mnr. Hall Av. NW4 2F 45
Mnr. Hall Dr. NW4 2F 45
Manorhall Gdns. E10 1C 68
MANOR HOUSE 7D 48
MANOR HOUSE 7C 48
Manor Ho. *NW1 5D 4*
(*off Marylebone Rd.*)
UB2: S'hall 3C 94
Manor Ho. Ct. TW17: Shep 7D 146
W9 4A 82
(*off Warrington Gdns.*)
Manor Ho. Dr. HA6: Nwood 1D 38
NW6 7F 63
Manor Ho. Est. HA7: Stan 6G 27
Manor Ho. Gdn. E11 6K 51
Manor Ho. Way TW7: Isle 3B 114
Manor La. SE12 5G 123
SE13 5G 123
SM1: Sutt 5A 166
TW13: Felt 2J 129
TW16: Sun 2J 147
UB3: Harl 6F 93
Manor La. Ter. SE13 4G 123
Manor M. *NW6 2J 81*
(*off Cambridge Av.*)
SE4 2B 122
Manor Mt. SE23 1J 139
Manor Pde. HA1: Harr 6K 41
N16 2F 67
NW10 2B 80
(*off High St. Harlesden*)
MANOR PARK 4B 70
Manor Pk. BR7: Chst 2H 161
SE13 4F 123
TW9: Rich 4F 115
TW13: Felt 2J 129
Manor Pk. Cl. BR4: W W'ck 1D 170
Manor Pk. Crematorium E7 4A 70
Manor Pk. Cres. HA8: Edg 6B 28
Manor Pk. Dr. HA2: Harr 3F 41
Manor Pk. Gdns. HA8: Edg 5B 28
Manor Pk. Pde. *SE13 4F 123*
(*off Lee High Rd.*)
Manor Pk. Rd. BR4: W W'ck 1D 170
BR7: Chst 1G 161
E12 4B 70
(not continuous)
N2 3A 46
NW10 1B 80
SM1: Sutt 5A 166
Manor Pl. BR7: Chst 2H 161
CR4: Mitc 3G 155
KT12: Walt T 7J 147
SE17 5B 102
SM1: Sutt 4K 165
TW14: Felt 1J 129
Manor Rd. BR3: Beck 2D 158
BR4: W W'ck 2D 170
CR4: Mitc 4G 155
DA1: Cray 4K 127
DA5: Bexl 1H 145
Manor Rd. DA15: Sidc 3K 143
E10 7C 50
E15 2G 87
E16 2G 87
E17 2A 50
EN2: Enf 2H 23
EN5: Barn 4B 20
HA1: Harr 6A 42
HA4: Ruis 1F 57
IG7: Chig 6J 37
IG8: Wfd G 6J 37
IG11: Bark 6K 71
KT8: E Mos 4H 149
KT12: Walt T 7H 147
N16 2D 66
N17 1G 49
N22 6D 32
RM6: Chad H 6D 54
RM10: Dag 6J 73
SE25 4G 157
SM2: Cheam 7H 165
SM6: Wall 4F 167
SW20 2H 153
TW2: Twick 2G 131
TW9: Rich 4G 115
TW11: Tedd 5A 132
(not continuous)
TW15: Ashf 5B 128
UB3: Hayes 6J 75
W13 7A 78
Manor Rd. Ho. HA1: Harr 6A 42
Manor Rd. Nth. KT7: T Ditt 3A 162
KT10: Hin W, T Ditt 3A 162
SM6: Wall 4F 167
Manorside EN5: Barn 4B 20
Manorside Cl. SE2 4C 108
Manor Sq. RM8: Dag 2C 72
Manor Va. TW8: Bford 5C 96
Manor Vw. N3 2K 45
Manor Way BR2: Brom 6C 160
BR3: Beck 2C 158
BR5: Pet W 4G 161
CR2: S Croy 6E 168
CR4: Mitc 3G 155
DA5: Bexl 1G 145
DA7: Bex 3K 127
E4 4A 36
HA2: Harr 4F 41
HA4: Ruis 7G 39
IG8: Wfd G 5F 37
KT4: Wor Pk 1A 164
NW9 4A 44
RM13: Rain 4K 91
SE3 4H 123
UB2: S'hall 4B 94
Manor Way, The SM6: Wall 4F 167
Manorway EN1: Enf 7K 23
SE7 4B 106
Mnr. Way Bus. Cen. RM13: Rain 5K 91
Manor Waye UB8: Uxb 1A 74
Manpreet Ct. E12 5D 70
Manresa Rd. SW3 6C 16 (5C 100)
Mansard Beeches SW17 5E 136
Mansard Cl. HA5: Pinn 3B 40
Manse Cl. UB3: Harl 6F 93
Mansel Gro. E17 1C 50
Mansell Rd. UB6: G'frd 5F 77
W3 2K 97
Mansell St. E1 1K 15 (6F 85)
Mansel Rd. SW19 6G 135
Manser Ct. RM13: Rain 3K 91
Mansergh Cl. SE18 7C 106
Manse Rd. N16 3F 67
Manser Rd. RM13: Rain 3K 91
Mansfield Av. EN4: E Barn 6J 21
HA4: Ruis 1K 57
N15 4D 48
Mansfield Cl. N9 6B 24
Mansfield Ct. *E2 1F 85*
(*off Whiston Rd.*)
Mansfield Dr. UB4: Hayes 4G 75
Mansfield Hgts. N2 5C 46
Mansfield Hill E4 7J 25
Mansfield Ho. *N1 1E 84*
(*off New Era Est.*)
Mansfield M. W1 6J 5 (5F 83)
Mansfield Pl. CR2: S Croy 6D 168
NW3 4A 64
Mansfield Rd. CR2: S Croy 6D 168
E11 6K 51
E17 4B 50
IG1: Ilf 2E 70
KT9: Chess 5C 162
NW3 5D 64
W3 4H 79
Mansfield St. W1 6J 5 (5F 83)
Mansford St. E2 2G 85
Manship Rd. CR4: Mitc 7E 136
Mansion Cl. SW9 1A 120
(not continuous)
Mansion Cottage Vis. Info. Cen.
1C 64
Mansion Gdns. NW3 3K 63
Mansion House 1E 14 (6D 84)
Mansion Ho. Pl. EC4 1E 14 (6D 84)
Mansion Ho. St. EC2 1E 14
Mansions, The SW5 5K 99
Manson M. SW7 4A 16 (4B 100)
Manson Pl. SW7 4A 16 (4B 100)
Mansted Gdns. RM6: Chad H 7C 54
Manston *N17 2D 48*
(*off Adams Rd.*)
NW1 7G 65
(*off Agar Gro.*)
Manston Av. UB2: S'hall 4E 94
Manston Cl. SE20 1J 157
Manstone Rd. NW2 5G 63
Manston Gro. KT2: King T 5D 132
Manston Ho. *W14 3G 99*
(*off Russell Rd.*)
Manthorp Rd. SE18 5G 107
Mantilla Rd. SW17 4E 136
Mantle Ct. *SW18 6K 117*
(*off Mapleton Rd.*)
Mantle Rd. SE4 3A 122
Mantlet Cl. SW16 7G 137
Mantle Way DA8: Erith 7K 109
E15 7G 69
Manton Av. W7 2K 95
Manton Cl. UB3: Hayes 7G 75
Manton Rd. EN3: Enf L 1H 25
SE2 4A 108
Manton Way EN3: Enf L 1J 25
Mantua St. SW11 3B 118
Mantus Cl. E1 4J 85
Mantus Rd. E1 4J 85
Manus Way N20 2F 31
Manville Gdns. SW17 3F 137
Manville Rd. SW17 2E 136
Manwood Rd. SE4 5B 122
Manwood St. E16 1D 106
Manygate La. TW17: Shep 7E 146
Manygate Mobile Home Est.
TW17: Shep 6F 147
(*off Mitre Cl.*)
Manygates SW12 2F 137
Mapesbury Ct. NW2 5G 63
Mapesbury M. NW4 6C 44
Mapesbury Rd. NW2 7G 63
Mapeshill Pl. NW2 6E 62
Mapes Ho. NW6 7G 63
Mape St. E2 4H 85
(not continuous)
Maple Av. E4 5G 35
HA2: Harr 2F 59
UB7: Yiew 7A 74
W3 1A 98
Maple Cl. BR5: Pet W 5H 161
CR4: Mitc 1F 155
HA4: Ruis 6K 39
IG9: Buck H 3G 37
N3 6D 30
N16 6G 49
SW4 6H 119
TW12: Hamp 6D 130
UB4: Yead 3B 76

Maple Ct. *CR0: Croy* 4C 168
(off Lwr. Coombe St.)
CR0: Croy 4C 168
(off The Waldrons)
E6 5E 88
KT3: N Mald 3K 151
SE6 1D 140
TW15: Ashf 7F 129
Maple Cres. DA15: Sidc 6A 126
Maplecroft Cl. E6 6B 88
Mapledale Av. CR0: Croy 2G 169
Mapledene BR7: Chst 6G 143
Mapledene Est. E8 7G 67
Mapledene Rd. E8 7F 67
Maple Gdns. HA8: Edg 7F 29
TW19: Stanw 2A 128
Maple Gro. NW9 7J 43
TW8: Bford 7B 96
UB1: S'hall 5D 76
W5 3D 96
Maple Gro. Bus. Cen. TW4: Houn 4A 112
Maple Ho. E17 3D 50
KT1: King T 5E 150
(off Maple Rd.)
SE8 7B 104
(off Idonia St.)
TW9: Kew 1H 115
Maplehurst BR2: Brom 2G 159
Maplehurst Cl. KT1: King T 4E 150
Maple Ind. Est. TW13: Felt 3J 129
Maple Leaf Dr. DA15: Sidc 1K 143
Mapleleafe Gdns. IG6: Ilf 3F 53
Maple Leaf Sq. SE16 2K 103
Maple Lodge *W8* 3K 99
(off Abbots Wlk.)
Maple M. NW6 2K 81
SW16 5K 137
Maple Pl. N17 7B 34
UB7: Yiew 1A 92
W1 5B 6 (4G 83)
Maple Rd. E11 6G 51
KT6: Surb 6D 150
SE20 1H 157
UB4: Yead 3A 76
Maples, The KT1: Tedd 7C 132
KT10: Clay 7A 162
Maples Pl. E1 5H 85
Maplestead Rd. RM9: Dag 1B 90
SW2 7K 119
Maple St. E2 2H 85
RM7: Rom 4J 55
W1 5A 6 (5G 83)
Maplethorpe Rd. CR7: Thor H 4A 156
Mapleton Cl. BR2: Brom 6J 159
Mapleton Cres. EN3: Enf W 1D 24
SW18 6K 117
Mapleton Rd. E4 3K 35
EN1: Enf 2C 24
SW18 6J 117
(not continuous)
Maple Tree M. SE3 1C 124
Maple Wlk. W10 3F 81
Maple Way TW13: Felt 3J 129
Maplin Cl. N21 6E 22
Maplin Ho. *SE2* 2D 108
(off Wolvercote Rd.)
Maplin Rd. E16 6J 87
Maplin St. E3 3B 86
Mapperley Cl. E11 6H 51
Mapperley Dr. IG8: Wfd G 7B 36
Marabou Cl. E12 5C 70
Maran Way DA18: Erith 2D 108
Marathon Ho. *NW1* 5E 4
(off Marylebone Rd.)
Marathon Way SE28 2K 107
Marban Rd. W9 3H 81
Marble Arch 2F 11
MARBLE ARCH 7D 82
Marble Arch W1 2E 10 (7D 82)
Marble Arch Apartments *W1* 7E 4
(off Harrowby St.)
Marble Cl. W3 1H 97
Marble Dr. NW2 1F 63
Marble Hill Cl. TW1: Twick 7B 114
Marble Hill Gdns.
TW1: Twick 7B 114
Marble Hill House 7C 114
Marble Ho. SE18 5K 107
W9 4H 81
Marble Quay E1 4K 15 (1G 103)
Marbles Ho. *SE5* 6C 102
(off Grosvenor Ter.)
Marbrook Ct. SE12 3A 142
Marcella Rd. SW9 2A 120
Marcellina Way BR6: Orp 3J 173
March *NW9* 1B 44
(off The Concourse)
Marchant Ct. SE1 5F 103
Marchant Ho. *N1* 1E 84
(off New Era Est.)
Marchant Rd. E11 2F 69
Marchant St. SE14 6A 104
Marchbank Rd. W14 6H 99
March Ct. SW15 4D 116
Marchmont Gdns. TW10: Rich 5F 115
Marchmont Rd. SM6: Wall 7G 167
TW10: Rich 5F 115
Marchmont St. WC1 3E 6 (4J 83)
March Rd. TW1: Twick 7A 114
Marchside Cl. TW5: Hest 1B 112
Marchwood Cl. SE5 7E 102
Marchwood Cres. W5 6C 78
Marcia Rd. SE1 4E 102
Marcilly Rd. SW18 5B 118
Marcon Ct. *E8* 5H 67
(off Amhurst Rd.)
Marconi Pl. N11 4A 32
Marconi Rd. E10 1C 68
Marconi Way UB1: S'hall 6F 77
Marcon Pl. E8 6H 67
Marco Polo Ho. SW8 7F 101
Marco Rd. W6 3E 98
Marcourt Lawns W5 4E 78
Marcus Ct. E15 1G 87
Marcus Garvey M. SE22 6H 121
Marcus Garvey Way SE24 4A 120
Marcus St. E15 1H 87
SW18 6K 117
Marcus Ter. SW18 6K 117
Mardale Ct. NW7 7H 29
Mardale Dr. NW9 5K 43
Mardell Rd. CR0: Croy 5K 157
Marden Av. BR2: Hayes 6J 159
Marden Cres. CR0: Croy 6K 155
DA5: Bexl 5J 127
Marden Ho. E8 5H 67
Marden Rd. CR0: Croy 6K 155
N17 2E 48
Marden Sq. SE16 3H 103
Marder Rd. W13 2A 96
Mardyke Cl. RM13: Rain 2J 91
Mardyke Ho. RM13: Rain 2K 91
SE17 4D 102
(off Mason St.)
Marechal Niel Av. DA15: Sidc 3H 143
Marechal Niel Pde. *DA14: Sidc* 3H 143
(off Main Rd.)
Maresby Ho. E4 2J 35
Mares Fld. CR0: Croy 3E 168
Maresfield Gdns. NW3 5A 64
Mare St. E2 2H 85
E8 5H 67
Marfleet Cl. SM5: Cars 2C 166
Margaret Av. E4 6J 25
Margaret Bondfield Av. IG11: Bark 7A 72
Margaret Bldgs. N16 1F 67
Margaret Ct. EN4: E Barn 4G 21
W1 7A 6
Margaret Gardner Dr. SE9 2D 142
Margaret Herbison Ho. *SW6* 6H 99
(off Clem Attlee Ct.)
Margaret Ho. *W6* 5E 98
(off Queen Caroline St.)
Margaret Ingram Cl. SW6 6H 99
Margaret Lockwood Cl.
KT1: King T 4F 151
Margaret Rd. DA5: Bexl 6D 126
EN4: E Barn 4G 21
N16 1F 67
Margaret St. W1 7K 5 (6F 83)
Margaretta Ter. SW3 7C 16 (6C 100)
Margaretting Rd. E12 1A 70
Margaret Way IG4: Ilf 6C 52
Margaret White Ho. *NW1* 1D 6
(off Chalton St.)
Margate Rd. SW2 5J 119
Margery Fry Ct. N7 3J 65
Margery Pk. Rd. E7 6J 69
Margery Rd. RM8: Dag 3D 72
Margery St. WC1 2J 7 (3A 84)
Margery Ter. *E7* 6J 69
(off Margery Pk. Rd.)
Margin Dr. SW19 5F 135
Margravine Gdns. W6 5F 99
Margravine Rd. W6 5F 99
Marham Dr. NW9 1A 44
Marham Gdns. SM4: Mord 6A 154
SW18 1C 136
Maria Cl. SE1 4H 103
Marian Cl. UB4: Yead 4B 76
Marian Ct. E9 5J 67
SM1: Sutt 5K 165
Marianne North Gallery 2F 115
Marian Pl. E2 2H 85
Marian Rd. SW16 1G 155
Marian St. E2 2H 85
Marian Way NW10 7B 62
Maria Ter. E1 5K 85
Maria Theresa Cl. KT3: N Mald 5K 151
Maribor *SE10* 7E 104
(off Burney St.)
Maricas Av. HA3: Hrw W 1H 41
Marie Curie SE5 1E 120
Marie Lloyd Gdns. N19 7J 47
Marie Lloyd Ho. *N1* 1E 8
(off Murray Gro.)
Marie Lloyd Wlk. E8 6F 67
Mariette Way SM6: Wall 7J 167
Marigold All. SE1 3A 14
Marigold Cl. UB1: S'hall 7C 76
Marigold Rd. N17 7D 34
Marigold St. SE16 2H 103
Marigold Way CR0: Croy 1K 169
Marina App. UB4: Yead 5C 76
Marina Av. KT3: N Mald 5D 152
Marina Cl. BR2: Brom 3J 159
Marina Dr. DA16: Well 2J 125
Marina Gdns. RM7: Rom 5H 55
Marina Pl. *KT1: Ham W* 2D 150
(off Old Bri. St.)
Marina Way TW11: Tedd 7D 132
Marine Ct. E11 2G 69
Marine Dr. IG11: Bark 4A 90
SE18 4D 106
Marinefield Rd. SW6 2K 117
Marinel Ho. SE5 7C 102
Mariner Bus. Cen. CR0: Wadd 5A 168
Mariner Gdns. TW10: Ham 3C 132
Mariner Rd. E12 4E 70
Mariners Cl. EN4: E Barn 5G 21
Mariners M. E14 4F 105
Marine St. SE16 3G 103
Marine Twr. *SE8* 6B 104
(off Abinger Gro.)
Marion Av. TW17: Shep 5D 146
Marion Gro. IG8: Wfd G 5B 36
Marion Ho. *NW1* 1D 82
(off Regent's Pk. Rd.)
Marion M. SE21 3D 138
Marion Rd. CR7: Thor H 5C 156
NW7 5H 29
Marischal Rd. SE13 3F 123
Maritime Ho. SE18 4F 107
Maritime Ind. Est. SE7 4K 105
Maritime Quay E14 5C 104
Maritime St. E3 4B 86
Marius Mans. SW17 2E 136
Marius Rd. SW17 2E 136
Marjorie Gro. SW11 4D 118
Marjorie M. E1 6K 85
Mark Av. E4 6J 25
Mark Cl. DA7: Bex 1E 126
UB1: S'hall 7F 77
Marke Cl. BR2: Kes 4C 172
Market, The SM5: Sutt 1A 166
Market Cen., The UB2: S'hall 4K 93
Market Chambers *EN2: Enf* 3J 23
(off Church St.)
Market Ct. W1 7A 6
Market Dr. W4 7A 98
Market Entrance SW8 7G 101
Market Est. N7 6J 65
Market Hall N22 2A 48
Market Hill SE18 3E 106
Market La. HA8: Edg 1J 43
W12 2E 98
Market Link RM1: Rom 4K 55
Market M. W1 5J 11 (1F 101)
Market Pde. *BR1: Brom* 1J 159
(off East St.)
DA14: Sidc 4B 144
E10 6E 50
(off High Rd.)
E17 3B 50
(off Forest Rd.)
N9 2B 34
(off Winchester Rd.)
N16 1G 67
(off Oldhill St.)
TW13: Hanw 3C 130
Market Pav. E10 3C 68
Market Pl. DA6: Bex 4G 127
EN2: Enf 3J 23
KT1: King T 2D 150
N2 3C 46
NW11 4K 45
SE16 4G 103
(not continuous)
TW8: Bford 7C 96
UB1: S'hall 1D 94
W1 7A 6 (6G 83)
W3 1J 97
Market Rd. N7 6J 65
TW9: Rich 3G 115
Market Row SW9 4A 120
Market Sq. BR1: Brom 2J 159
(not continuous)
E14 6D 86
KT1: King T 2D 150
(off Market Pl.)
Market Sq., The *N9* 2C 34
(off Plevna Rd.)
Market St. E1 5F 85
E6 2D 88
SE18 4E 106
Market Ter. *TW8: Bford* 6E 96
(off Albany Rd.)
Market Trad. Est. UB2: S'hall 4K 93
Market Way E14 6D 86
HA0: Wemb 5E 60
Market Yd. M. SE1 7G 15 (2E 102)
Markfield Gdns. E4 7J 25
Markfield Rd. N15 4G 49
Markham Ho. *RM10: Dag* 3G 73
(off Uvedale Rd.)
Markham Pl. SW3 5E 16 (5D 100)
Markham Sq. SW3 5E 16 (5D 100)
Markham St. SW3 5D 16 (5C 100)
Markhole Cl. TW12: Hamp 7D 130
Mark Ho. *E2* 2K 85
(off Sewardstone Rd.)
Markhouse Av. E17 6A 50
Markhouse Pas. *E17* 6B 50
(off Markhouse Rd.)
Markhouse Rd. E17 6B 50
Markland Ho. *W10* 7F 81
(off Darfield Way)
Mark La. EC3 2H 15 (7E 84)
Mark Lodge *EN4: Cockf* 4H 21
(off Edgeworth Rd.)
Markmanor Av. E17 7A 50
Mark Rd. N22 2B 48

Marksbury Av. TW9: Rich 3G 115
MARKS GATE 1E 54
Marks Lodge RM7: Rom 5K 55
Mark Sq. EC2 ....3G 9 (4E 84)
Marks Rd. RM7: Rom 5J 55
(not continuous)
Markstone Ho. SE1 ....7A 14
(off Lancaster St.)
Mark St. E15 ....7G 69
EC2 ....3G 9 (4E 84)
Mark Wade Cl. E12 ....1B 70
Markway TW16: Sun 2A 148
Markwell Cl. SE26 ....4H 139
Markyate Ho. W10 ....4E 80
(off Sutton Way)
Markyate Rd. RM8: Dag 5B 72
Marland Ho. SW1 ....1F 17
(off Sloane St.)
Marlands Rd. IG5: Ilf 3C 52
Marlborough SW19 ....1F 135
(off Inner Pk. Rd.)
W9 ....3A 82
(off Maida Va.)
Marlborough Av. E8 ....1G 85
(not continuous)
HA4: Ruis 6E 38
HA8: Edg 3C 28
N14 ....3B 32
Marlborough Cl. BR6: Orp 6K 161
N20 ....3J 31
SE17 ....4C 102
SW19 ....6C 136
Marlborough Ct. CR2: S Croy 4E 168
(off Birdhurst Rd.)
EN1: Enf 5K 23
HA1: Harr 4H 41
HA6: Nwood 1H 39
IG9: Buck H 2F 37
N17 ....1G 49
(off Kemble Rd.)
SM6: Wall 7G 167
W1 ....2A 12
W8 ....4J 99
(off Pembroke Rd.)
Marlborough Cres. UB3: Harl 7F 93
W4 ....3K 97
Marlborough Dr. IG5: Ilf 3C 52
Marlborough Flats SW3 ....3D 16
Marlborough Gdns. KT6: Surb ...7D 150
N20 ....3J 31
Marlborough Ga. Ho. W2 ....7B 82
(off Elms M.)
Marlborough Gro. SE1 ....5G 103
Marlborough Hill HA1: Harr 4H 41
NW8 ....2A 82
Marlborough House 5B 12 (1G 101)
Marlborough Ho. E16 ....1J 105
(off Hardy Av.)
NW1 ....3K 5
(off Osnaburgh St.)
Marlborough La. SE7 ....6A 106
Marlborough Lodge NW8 ....2A 82
(off Marlborough Pl.)
Marlborough Mans. NW6 ....5K 63
(off Canon Hill)
Marlborough M. SW2 ....4K 119
Marlborough Pde. HA8: Edg 3C 28
(off Marlborough Av.)
UB10: Hil 4D 74
Marlborough Pav. DA15: Sidc ...7A 126
Marlborough Pl. NW8 ....2A 82
Marlborough Rd. BR2: Brom 4A 160
CR2: S Croy 7C 168
DA7: Bex 3D 126
E4 ....6J 35
E7 ....7A 70
E15 ....4G 69
E18 ....2J 51
N9 ....1B 34
N19 ....2J 65
(not continuous)
N22 ....7D 32
RM7: Mawney 4G 55

Marlborough Rd. RM8: Dag 4B 72
SE18 ....3F 107
SM1: Sutt 3J 165
SW1 ....5B 12 (1G 101)
SW19 ....6C 136
TW7: Isle 1B 114
TW10: Rich 6F 115
TW12: Hamp 6E 130
TW13: Felt 2B 130
TW15: Ashf 5A 128
UB2: S'hall 3A 94
UB10: Hil 4D 74
W4 ....5J 97
W5 ....2D 96
Marlborough St. SW3 ....4C 16 (4C 100)
Marlborough Yd. N19 ....2H 65
Marlbury NW8 ....1K 81
(off Abbey Rd.)
Marler Rd. SE23 ....1A 140
Marley Av. DA7: Bex 6D 108
Marley Cl. N15 ....4B 48
UB6: G'frd 3E 76
Marley Ho. W11 ....7F 81
(off St Ann's Rd.)
Marley Wlk. NW2 ....5E 62
Marlfield Cl. KT4: Wor Pk 1C 164
Marlin Cl. TW16: Sun 6G 129
Marling Ct. TW12: Hamp 6D 130
Marlingdene Cl. TW12: Hamp ...6E 130
Marlings Cl. BR7: Chst 4J 161
Marlings Pk. Av. BR7: Chst 4J 161
Marlins Cl. SM1: Sutt 5A 166
Marloes Cl. HA0: Wemb 4D 60
Marloes Rd. W8 ....3K 99
Marlow Cl. SE20 ....3H 157
Marlow Ct. N14 ....7B 22
NW6 ....7F 63
NW9 ....3B 44
Marlow Cres. TW1: Twick 6K 113
Marlow Dr. SM3: Cheam 2F 165
Marlowe Bus. Cen. SE14 ....7A 104
(off Batavia Rd.)
Marlowe Cl. BR7: Chst 6H 143
IG6: Ilf 1G 53
Marlowe Ct. SE19 ....5F 139
SW3 ....4D 16
(off Petyward)
Marlowe Gdns. SE9 ....6E 124
Marlowe Ho. IG8: Wfd G 7K 37
KT1: King T 4D 150
(off Portsmouth Rd.)
SE8 ....5B 104
(off Bowditch)
Marlowe Path SE8 ....6C 104
Marlowe Rd. E17 ....4E 50
Marlowes, The DA1: Cray 4K 127
NW8 ....1B 82
Marlowe Sq. CR4: Mitc 4G 155
Marlowe Way CR0: Bedd 2J 167
Marlow Gdns. UB3: Harl 3F 93
Marlow Ho. E2 ....2J 9
(off Calvert Av.)
KT5: Surb 5E 150
(off Cranes Pk.)
SE1 ....7J 15
(off Maltby St.)
TW11: Tedd 4A 132
W2 ....6K 81
(off Hallfield Est.)
Marlow Rd. E6 ....3D 88
SE20 ....3H 157
UB2: S'hall 3D 94
Marlow Way SE16 ....2K 103
Marlow Workshops E2 ....2J 9
(off Virginia Rd.)
Marl Rd. SW18 ....4A 118
Marlton St. SE10 ....5H 105
Marlwood Cl. DA15: Sidc 2J 143
Marmadon Rd. SE18 ....4K 107
Marmara Apartments E16 ....7J 87
(off Western Gateway)
Marmion App. E4 ....4H 35

Marmion Av. E4 ....4G 35
Marmion Cl. E4 ....4G 35
Marmion M. SW11 ....3E 118
Marmion Rd. SW11 ....4E 118
Marmont Rd. SE15 ....1G 121
Marmora Ho. E1 ....5A 86
(off Ben Jonson Rd.)
Marmora Rd. SE22 ....6J 121
Marmot Rd. TW4: Houn 3B 112
Marne Av. DA16: Well 3A 126
N11 ....4A 32
Marnell Way TW4: Houn 3B 112
Marne St. W10 ....3G 81
Marney Rd. SW11 ....4E 118
Marnfield Cres. SW2 ....1A 138
Marnham Av. NW2 ....4G 63
Marnham Ct. HA0: Wemb 5C 60
Marnham Cres. UB6: G'frd 3F 77
Marnock Ho. SE17 ....5D 102
(off Brandon St.)
Marnock Rd. SE4 ....5B 122
Maroon St. E14 ....5A 86
Maroons Way SE6 ....5C 140
Marqueen Ct. W8 ....2K 99
(off Kensington Chu. St.)
Marqueen Towers SW16 ....7K 137
Marquess Rd. N1 ....6D 66
Marquess Rd. Nth. N1 ....6D 66
Marquess Rd. Sth. N1 ....6D 66
Marquis Cl. HA0: Wemb 7F 61
Marquis Ct. IG11: Bark 5J 71
KT1: King T 4D 150
(off Anglesea Rd.)
N4 ....1K 65
(off Marquis Rd.)
Marquis Rd. N4 ....1K 65
N22 ....6E 32
NW1 ....6H 65
Marrabon Cl. DA15: Sidc 1A 144
Marrick Cl. SW15 ....4C 116
Marrick Ho. NW6 ....1K 81
(off Mortimer Cres.)
Marriett Ho. SE6 ....4E 140
Marrilyne Av. EN3: Enf L 1G 25
Mariner Ct. UB3: Hayes 7G 75
(off Barra Hall Rd.)
Marriott Cl. TW14: Felt 6F 111
Marriott Rd. E15 ....1G 87
EN5: Barn 3A 20
N4 ....1K 65
N10 ....1D 46
Marriotts Cl. NW9 ....6B 44
Marryat Cl. TW4: Houn 4D 112
Marryat Ho. SW1 ....6A 18
(off Churchill Gdns.)
Marryat Pl. SW19 ....4G 135
Marryat Rd. SW19 ....5F 135
Marryat Sq. SW6 ....1G 117
Marsala Rd. SE13 ....4D 122
Marsden Rd. N9 ....2C 34
SE15 ....3F 121
Marsden St. NW5 ....6E 64
(not continuous)
Marsden Way BR6: Orp 4K 173
Marshall Cl. HA1: Harr 7H 41
SW18 ....6A 118
TW4: Houn 5D 112
Marshall Dr. UB4: Hayes 5H 75
Marshall Est. NW7 ....4H 29
Marshall Ho. N1 ....2D 84
(off Cranston Est.)
NW6 ....2H 81
(off Albert Rd.)
SE1 ....3C 102
(off Page's Wlk.)
SE17 ....5D 102
(off East St.)
Marshall Path SE28 ....7B 90
Marshall Rd. E10 ....3D 68
N17 ....1D 48
Marshalls Cl. N11 ....4A 32
Marshalls Dr. RM1: Rom 3K 55

Marshalls Gro. SE18 ....4C 106
Marshall's Pl. SE16 ....3F 103
Marshalls Rd.
RM7: Rom 4K 55
SM1: Sutt 4K 165
Marshall St. W1 ....1B 12 (6G 83)
Marshalsea Rd. SE1 ....6D 14 (2C 102)
Marsham Cl. BR7: Chst 5F 143
Marsham Ct. SW1 ....3D 18 (4H 101)
Marsham St. SW1 ....2D 18 (3H 101)
Marsh Av. CR4: Mitc 2D 154
Marshbrook Cl. SE3 ....3B 124
Marsh Cen., The E1 ....7K 9
(off Whitechapel High St.)
Marsh Cl. NW7 ....3G 29
Marsh Ct. E8 ....6G 67
SW19 ....1A 154
Marsh Dr. NW9 ....6B 44
Marsh Farm Rd.
TW2: Twick 1K 131
Marshfield St. E14 ....3E 104
Marsh Ga. Bus. Cen. E15 ......1E 86
Marshgate Cen., The E15 .....1D 86
Marshgate La. E15 ....7D 68
(not continuous)
Marshgate Path SE28 ....3G 107
Marshgate Sidings (Bow Depot)
E15 ....1D 86
Marshgate Trad. Est. E15 .....7D 68
Marsh Grn. Rd. RM10: Dag 1G 91
Marsh Hall HA9: Wemb 3F 61
Marsh Hill E9 ....5A 68
Marsh Ho. SW1 ....6D 18
(off Aylesford St.)
SW8 ....1G 119
Marsh La. E10 ....2B 68
HA7: Stan 5H 27
N17 ....7C 34
NW7 ....3F 29
Marsh Rd. HA0: Wemb 3D 78
HA5: Pinn 4C 40
Marshside Cl. N9 ....1D 34
Marsh St. E14 ....4D 104
Marsh Wall E14 ....1C 104
Marsh Way RM13: Dag, Rain ...3K 91
Marshwood Ho. NW6 ....1J 81
(off Kilburn Va.)
Marsland Cl. SE17 ....5B 102
Marsom Ho. N1 ....1E 8
(off Fairbank Est.)
Marston Av. KT9: Chess 6E 162
RM10: Dag 2G 73
Marston Cl. NW6 ....7A 64
RM10: Dag 3G 73
Marston Ho. SW9 ....2A 120
Marston Rd. IG5: Ilf 1C 52
TW11: Tedd 5B 132
Marston Way SE19 ....7B 138
Marsworth Av. HA5: Pinn 1B 40
Marsworth Cl. UB4: Yead 5C 76
Marsworth Ho. E2 ....1G 85
(off Whiston Rd.)
Martaban Rd. N16 ....2F 67
Martara M. SE17 ....5C 102
Martello St. E8 ....7H 67
Martello Ter. E8 ....7H 67
Martell Rd. SE21 ....3D 138
Martel Pl. E8 ....6F 67
Marten Rd. E17 ....2C 50
Martens Av. DA7: Bex 4H 127
Martens Cl. DA7: Bex 4J 127
Martha Ct. E2 ....2H 85
Martham Cl. IG6: Ilf 1F 53
SE28 ....7D 90
Martha Rd. E15 ....6B 69
Martha's Bldgs. EC1 ....3E 8 (4D 84)
Martha St. E1 ....6J 85
Marthorne Cres. HA3: Hrw W ...2H 41
Martin Bowes Rd. SE9 ......3D 124
Martinbridge Trad. Est.
EN1: Enf 5B 24
Martin Cl. N9 ....1E 34
UB10: Uxb 2A 74

Martin Ct. CR2: S Croy 5D 168
    (off Birdhurst Rd.)
E14 . . . . .2E 104
    (off River Barge Cl.)
Martin Cres. CR0: Croy 1A 168
Martindale SW14 . . . . .5J 115
Martindale Av. BR6: Chels 5K 173
E16 . . . . .7J 87
Martindale Ho. E14 . . . . .7D 86
    (off Poplar High St.)
Martin Dale Ind. Est.
    EN1: Enf 3C 24
Martindale Rd. SW12 . . . . .7F 119
    TW4: Houn 3C 112
Martin Dene DA6: Bex 5F 127
Martin Dr. UB5: N'olt 5D 58
Martineau Est. E1 . . . . .7J 85
Martineau Ho. SW1 . . . . .6A 18
    (off Churchill Gdns.)
Martineau M. N5 . . . . .4B 66
Martineau Rd. N5 . . . . .4B 66
Martingale Cl. TW16: Sun 4J 147
Martingales Cl. TW10: Ham 3D 132
Martin Gdns. RM8: Dag 4C 72
Martin Gro. SM4: Mord 3J 153
Martin Ho. SE1 . . . . .3C 102
    SW8 . . . . .7J 101
    (off Wyvil Rd.)
Martin La. EC4 . . . . .2F 15 (7D 84)
    (not continuous)
Martin Pl. SE28 . . . . .1J 107
    (off Martin St.)
Martin Ri. DA6: Bex 5F 127
Martin Rd. RM8: Dag 4C 72
Martins, The HA9: Wemb 3F 61
    SE26 . . . . .5H 139
Martins Cl. BR4: W W'ck 1F 171
Martin's Mt. EN5: New Bar 4D 20
Martin's Rd. BR2: Brom 2G 159
Martin St. SE28 . . . . .1J 107
Martins Wlk. N10 . . . . .1E 46
    N22 .3A 48
Martin Wlk. SE28 . . . . .1J 107
    (off Martin St.)
Martin Way SM4: Mord 2F 153
    SW20 . . . . .2F 153
Martlesham N17 . . . . .2E 48
    (off Adams Rd.)
Martlesham Wlk. NW9 . . . . .2A 44
    (not continuous)
Martlet Gro. UB5: N'olt 3B 76
Martlett Cl. WC2 . . . . .1F 13 (6J 83)
Martley Dr. IG2: IIf 5F 53
Martock Cl. HA3: W'stone 4A 42
Martock Gdns. N11 . . . . .5J 31
Marton Cl. SE6 . . . . .3C 140
Marton Rd. N16 . . . . .2E 66
Martynside NW9 . . . . .1B 44
Martys Yd. NW3 . . . . .4B 64
Marvell Av. UB4: Hayes 5J 75
Marvell Ho. SE5 . . . . .7D 102
    (off Camberwell Rd.)
Marvels Cl. SE12 . . . . .2K 141
Marvels La. SE12 . . . . .2K 141
    (not continuous)
Marville Rd. SW6 . . . . .7H 99
Marvin St. E8 . . . . .6H 67
Marwell Cl. BR4: W W'ck 2H 171
Marwood Cl. DA16: Well 3B 126
Marwood Dr. NW7 . . . . .7A 30
Mary Adelaide Cl. SW15 . . . . . . .4A 134
Maryatt Av. HA2: Harr 2F 59
Mary Bank SE18 . . . . .4D 106
Mary Bayly Ho. W11 . . . . .1J 99
    (off Wilsham St.)
Mary Cl. HA7: Stan 4F 43
Mary Datchelor Cl. SE5 . . . . .1D 120
Maryfield Cl. DA5: Bexl 3K 145
Mary Flux Cl. SW5 . . . . .5K 99
    (off Bramham Gdns.)
Mary Grn. NW8 . . . . .1K 81
Mary Holben Ho. SW16 . . . . .5G 137

Mary Ho. W6 . . . . .5E 98
    (off Queen Caroline St.)
Mary Jones Ho. E14 . . . . .7C 86
    (off Garford St.)
Maryland Ind. Est. E15 . . . . .5G 69
    (off Maryland Rd.)
Maryland Pk. E15 . . . . .5G 69
    (not continuous)
Maryland Point E15 . . . . .6G 69
    (off The Grove)
Maryland Rd. CR7: Thor H 1B 156
E15 . . . . .5F 69
N22 . . . . .6E 32
Maryland Sq. E15 . . . . .5G 69
Marylands Rd. W9 . . . . .4J 81
Maryland St. E15 . . . . .5F 69
Maryland Wlk. N1 . . . . .1C 84
    (off Popham St.)
Maryland Way TW16: Sun 2J 147
Mary Lawrenson Pl. SE3 . . . . .7J 105
MARYLEBONE 5H 5 (5E 82)
Marylebone Cricket Club 2B 4 (3B 82)
MARYLEBONE FLYOVER 5B 82
Marylebone Fly-Over NW1 . . . . .6B 4
    W2 . . . . .6B 4 (5B 82)
Marylebone High St. W1 . . . .5H 5 (5E 82)
Marylebone La. W1 . . . . . . .6H 5 (5E 82)
Marylebone M. W1 . . . . .6J 5 (5F 83)
Marylebone Pas. W1 . . . . . . .7B 6 (6G 83)
Marylebone Rd. NW1 . . . . . . .5D 4 (5C 82)
Marylebone St. W1 . . . . .6H 5 (5E 82)
Marylee Way SE11 . . . . . . .4H 19 (4K 101)
Mary Macarthur Ho. E2 . . . . .3K 85
    (off Warley St.)
    RM10: Dag 3G 73
    (off Wythenshawe Rd.)
    W6 . . . . .6G 99
Maryon Gro. SE7 . . . . .4C 106
Maryon Ho. NW6 . . . . .7A 64
    (off Goldhurst Ter.)
Maryon M. NW3 . . . . .4C 64
Maryon Rd. SE7 . . . . .4C 106
    SE18 . . . . .4C 106
Mary Peters Dr. UB6: N'olt 5H 59
Mary Pl. W11 . . . . .7G 81
Mary Rose Cl. TW12: Hamp 1E 148
Mary Rose Mall E6 . . . . .5D 88
Mary Rose Way N20 . . . . .1G 31
Marys Ct. NW1 . . . . .3D 4
    (off Palgrave Gdns.)
Mary Seacole Cl. E8 . . . . .1F 85
Mary Smith Ct. SW5 . . . . .4J 99
    (off Trebovir Rd.)
Marysmith Ho. SW1 . . . . .5D 18
    (off Cureton St.)
Mary's Ter. TW1: Twick 7A 114
    (not continuous)
Mary St. E16 . . . . .5H 87
    N1 .1C 84
Mary Ter. NW1 . . . . .1F 83
Maryville DA16: Well 2K 125
Mary Wallace Theatre 1A 132
Mary Wharrie Ho. NW3 . . . . .7D 64
    (off Fellows Rd.)
Marzell Ho. W14 . . . . .5H 99
    (off North End Rd.)
Marzena Ct. TW3: Houn 6G 113
Masault Ct. TW9: Rich 4E 114
    (off Kew Foot Rd.)
Masbro' Rd. W14 . . . . .3F 99
Mascalls Ct. SE7 . . . . .6A 106
Mascalls Rd. SE7 . . . . .6A 106
Mascotte Rd. SW15 . . . . .4F 117
Mascotts Cl. NW2 . . . . .3D 62
Masefield Av. HA7: Stan 5E 26
    UB1: S'hall 7E 76
Masefield Cl. EN5: New Bar 4F 21
    KT6: Surb 7D 150
Masefield Cres. N14 . . . . .5B 22
Masefield Gdns. E6 . . . . .4E 88
Masefield Ho. NW6 . . . . .3J 81
    (off Stafford Rd.)
Masefield La. UB4: Yead 4K 75

Masefield Rd. TW12: Hamp 4D 130
Masefield Vw. BR6: Farnb 3G 173
Masefield Way
    TW19: Stanw 1B 128
Masham Ho. DA18: Erith 2D 108
    (off Kale Rd.)
Mashie Rd. W3 . . . . .6A 80
Mashiters Hill RM1: Rom 1K 55
Maskall Cl. SW2 . . . . .1A 138
Maskani Wlk. SW16 . . . . .7G 137
Maskell Rd. SW17 . . . . .3A 136
Maskelyne Cl. SW11 . . . . .1C 118
Mason Cl. DA7: Bex 3H 127
    E16 . . . . .7J 87
    SE16 . . . . .5G 103
    SW20 . . . . .1F 153
    TW12: Hamp 1D 148
Mason Ho. E9 . . . . .7J 67
    (off Frampton Pk. Rd.)
    SE1 . . . . .4G 103
    (off Simms Rd.)
Mason Rd. IG8: Wfd G 4B 36
    SM1: Sutt 5K 165
Mason's Arms M. W1 . . . . . .1K 11 (6F 83)
Masons Av. CR0: Croy 3C 168
    EC2 . . . . .7E 8 (6D 84)
    HA3: W'stone 4K 41
Mason's Grn. La. W3 . . . . .4G 79
    (not continuous)
Masons Hill BR2: Brom 3J 159
    SE18 . . . . .4F 107
Masons Pl. CR4: Mitc 1D 154
    EC1 . . . . .1B 8 (3C 84)
Masons St. SE17 . . . . .4D 102
Mason's Yd. EC1 . . . . .1B 8 (3B 84)
    SW1 . . . . .4B 12 (1G 101)
    SW19 . . . . .5F 135
Massey Cl. N11 . . . . .5A 32
Massey Ct. E6 . . . . .1A 88
    (off Florence Rd.)
Massie Rd. E8 . . . . .6G 67
Massingberd Way SW17 . . . . .4F 137
Massinger St. SE17 . . . . .4E 102
Massingham St. E1 . . . . .4K 85
Masson Av. HA4: Ruis 6A 58
Mast, The E16 . . . . .7G 89
Mast Ct. SE16 . . . . .4A 104
    (off Boat Lifter Way)
Master Gunners Pl. SE18 . . . . . . .7C 106
Masterman Ho. SE5 . . . . .7D 102
    (off Elmington Est.)
Masterman Rd. E6 . . . . .3C 88
Masters Cl. SW16 . . . . .6G 137
Masters Dr. SE16 . . . . .5H 103
Masters Lodge E1 . . . . .6J 85
    (off Johnson St.)
Masters St. E1 . . . . .5K 85
Mast Ho. Ter. E14 . . . . .4C 104
    (not continuous)
Mastmaker Ct. E14 . . . . .2C 104
Mastmaker Rd. E14 . . . . .2C 104
MASWELL PARK 5G 113
Maswell Pk. Cres. TW3: Houn 5G 113
Maswell Pk. Rd. TW3: Houn 5F 113
Matcham Ct. TW1: Twick 6D 114
    (off Clevedon Rd.)
Matcham Rd. E11 . . . . .3G 69
Matchless Dr. SE18 . . . . .7E 106
Matfield Cl. BR2: Brom 5J 159
Matfield Rd. DA17: Belv 6G 109
Matham Gro. SE22 . . . . .4F 121
Matham Rd. KT8: E Mos 5H 149
Matheson Lang Ho. SE1 . . . . .7J 13
Matheson Rd. W14 . . . . .4H 99
Mathews Av. E6 . . . . .2E 88
Mathews Pk. Av. E15 . . . . .6H 69
Mathews Yd. WC2 . . . . .1E 12 (6J 83)
Mathieson Ct. SE1 . . . . .7B 14
    (off King James St.)
Mathison Ho. SW10 . . . . .7A 100
    (off Coleridge Gdns.)
Matilda Cl. SE19 . . . . .7D 138
Matilda Gdns. E3 . . . . .2C 86

Matilda Ho. E1 . . . . .4K 15
    (off St Katherine's Way)
Matilda St. N1 . . . . .1K 83
Matins Pl. SE28 . . . . .1J 107
Matisse Ct. EC1 . . . . .3E 8 (4D 84)
Matlock Cl. EN5: Barn 5A 20
    SE24 . . . . .4C 120
Matlock Ct. NW8 . . . . .2A 82
    (off Abbey Rd.)
    SE5 . . . . .4D 120
    W11 . . . . .7J 81
    (off Kensington Pk. Rd.)
Matlock Cres. SM3: Cheam 4G 165
Matlock Gdns. SM3: Cheam 4G 165
Matlock Pl. SM3: Cheam 4G 165
Matlock Rd. E10 . . . . .6E 50
Matlock St. E14 . . . . .6A 86
Matlock Way KT3: N Mald 1K 151
Maton Ho. SW6 . . . . .7H 99
    (off Estcourt Rd.)
Matrimony Pl. SW4 . . . . .2G 119
Matson Ct. IG8: Wfd G 7B 36
Matson Ho. SE16 . . . . .3H 103
Matthew Cl. W10 . . . . .4F 81
Matthew Ct. CR4: Mitc 5H 155
    E17 . . . . .3E 50
Matthew Parker St. SW1 . . . .7D 12 (2H 101)
Matthews Ct. E17 . . . . .1C 50
    (off Chingford Rd.)
Matthews Ho. E14 . . . . .5C 86
    (off Burgess St.)
Matthews Rd. UB6: G'frd 5H 59
Matthews St. SW11 . . . . .2D 118
Matthews Yd. CR0: Croy 3C 168
    (off Surrey St.)
Matthias Rd. N16 . . . . .5E 66
Mattison Rd. N4 . . . . .6A 48
Mattock La. W5 . . . . .1B 96
    W13 . . . . .1B 96
Maud Cashmore Way SE18 . . . . . .3D 106
Maude Ho. E2 . . . . .2G 85
    (off Ropley St.)
Maude Rd. E17 . . . . .5A 50
    SE5 . . . . .1E 120
Maude Ter. E17 . . . . .5A 50
Maud Gdns. E13 . . . . .1H 87
    IG11: Bark 2K 89
Maudlins Grn. E1 . . . . .4K 15 (1G 103)
Maud Rd. E10 . . . . .3E 68
    E13 . . . . .2H 87
Maudslay Rd. SE9 . . . . .3D 124
Maudsley Ho. TW8: Bford 5E 96
Maud St. E16 . . . . .5H 87
Maudsville Cotts. W7 . . . . .1J 95
Maud Wilkes Cl. NW5 . . . . .5G 65
Maugham Ct. W3 . . . . .3J 97
    (off Palmerston Rd.)
Mauleverer Rd. SW2 . . . . .5J 119
Maundeby Wlk. NW10 . . . . .6A 62
Maunder Rd. W7 . . . . .1K 95
Maunsel St. SW1 . . . . .3C 18 (4H 101)
Maureen Campbell Ct.
    TW17: Shep 5D 146
    (off Harrison Way)
Maureen Ct. BR3: Beck 2J 157
Maurer Ct. SE10 . . . . .3H 105
Mauretania Bldg. E1 . . . . .7K 85
    (off Jardine Rd.)
Maurice Av. N22 . . . . .2B 48
Maurice Bishop Ter. N6 . . . . .6E 46
    (off View Rd.)
Maurice Brown Cl. NW7 . . . . .5A 30
Maurice Ct. E1 . . . . .3K 85
    TW8: Bford 7D 96
Maurice Drummond Ho. SE10 . . . .1D 122
    (off Catherine Gro.)
Maurice St. W12 . . . . .6D 80
Maurice Wlk. NW11 . . . . .4A 46
Maurier Cl. UB5: N'olt 1A 76
Maury Rd. SE10 . . . . .4G 105
Maury Rd. N16 . . . . .2G 67
Mauveine Gdns. TW3: Houn 4E 112
Mavelstone Cl. BR1: Brom 1C 160

Mavelstone Rd.
BR1: Brom 1B **160**
Maverton Rd. E3 . . . . . 1C **86**
Mavis Av. KT19: Ewe 5A **164**
Mavis Cl. KT19: Ewe 5A **164**
Mavis Wlk. *E6* *5C* ***88***
(off Greenwich Cres.)
Mavor Ho. *N1* *1K* ***83***
(off Barnsbury Est.)
Mawbey Ho. SE1 . . . . . 5F **103**
Mawbey Pl. SE1 . . . . . 5F **103**
Mawbey Rd. SE1 . . . . . 5F **103**
Mawbey St. SW8 . . . . . 7J **101**
Mawdley Ho. SE1 . . . . . 7A **14**
MAWNEY 4J **55**
Mawney Cl. RM7: Mawney 2H **55**
Mawney Rd. RM7: Mawney 2H **55**
Mawson Cl. SW20 . . . . . 2G **153**
Mawson Ct. *N1* *1D* ***84***
(off Gopsall St.)
Mawson Ho. *EC1* *5J* ***7***
(off Baldwins Gdns.)
Mawson La. W4 . . . . . 6B **98**
Maxden Ct. SE15 . . . . . 3F **121**
Maxey Gdns. RM9: Dag 4E **72**
Maxey Rd. RM9: Dag 5E **72**
SE18 . . . . . 4G **107**
Maxfield Cl. N20 . . . . . 7F **21**
Maxilla Wlk. W10 . . . . . 6F **81**
Maxim Apartments *BR2: Brom* *4K* ***159***
(off Tiger La.)
Maximfeldt Rd. DA8: Erith 5K **109**
Maxim Rd. DA8: Erith 4K **109**
N21 . . . . . 6F **23**
Maxted Pk. HA1: Harr 7J **41**
Maxted Rd. SE15 . . . . . 3F **121**
Maxwell Cl. CR0: Wadd 1J **167**
UB3: Hayes 7J **75**
Maxwell Ct. SE22 . . . . . 1G **139**
SW4 . . . . . 5H **119**
Maxwell Gdns. BR6: Orp 3K **173**
Maxwell Rd. DA16: Well 3K **125**
HA6: Nwood 1F **39**
SW6 . . . . . 7K **99**
TW15: Ashf 6E **128**
UB7: W Dray 4B **92**
Maxwelton Av. NW7 . . . . . 5E **28**
Maxwelton Cl. NW7 . . . . . 5E **28**
Maya Angelou Ct. E4 . . . . . 4K **35**
Maya Cl. SE15 . . . . . 2H **121**
Mayall Cl. EN3: Enf L 1H **25**
Mayall Rd. SE24 . . . . . 5B **120**
Maya Pl. N11 . . . . . 7C **32**
Maya Rd. N2 . . . . . 4A **46**
Maybank Av. E18 . . . . . 2K **51**
HA0: Wemb 5K **59**
Maybank Gdns. HA5: Eastc 5J **39**
Maybank Rd. E18 . . . . . 1K **51**
May Bate Av. KT2: King T 1D **150**
Maybells Commercial Est.
IG11: Bark 2D **90**
Mayberry Ct. *BR3: Beck* *7B* ***140***
(off Copers Cope Rd.)
Mayberry Pl. KT5: Surb 7F **151**
Maybourne Cl. SE26 . . . . . 6H **139**
Maybury Cl. BR5: Pet W 5F **161**
EN1: Enf 1C **24**
Maybury Ct. *CR2: S Croy* *5B* ***168***
(off Haling Pk. Rd.)
HA1: Harr 6H **41**
W1 . . . . . *6H* ***5***
(off Marylebone St.)
Maybury Gdns. NW10 . . . . . 6D **62**
Maybury M. N6 . . . . . 7G **47**
Maybury Rd. E13 . . . . . 4A **88**
IG11: Bark 2K **89**
Maybury St. SW17 . . . . . 5C **136**
Maychurch Cl. HA7: Stan 7J **27**
May Cl. KT9: Chess 6F **163**
Maycroft HA5: Pinn 2K **39**
Maycross Av. SM4: Mord 4H **153**
Mayday Gdns. SE3 . . . . . 2C **124**
Mayday Rd. CR7: Thor H 6B **156**
Maydew Ho. *SE16* *4J* ***103***
(off Abbeyfield Est.)
Maydwell Ho. *E14* *5C* ***86***
(off Thomas Rd.)
Mayerne Rd. SE9 . . . . . 5B **124**
Mayesbrook Pk. Arena 5A **72**
Mayesbrook Rd. IG3: Ilf 3A **72**
IG11: Bark 1K **89**
RM8: Dag 3A **72**
Mayesford Rd. RM6: Chad H 7C **54**
Mayes Rd. N22 . . . . . 2K **47**
Mayeswood Rd. SE12 . . . . . 4A **142**
MAYFAIR 3J **11** (7F **83**)
Mayfair Av. DA7: Bex 1D **126**
IG1: Ilf 2D **70**
KT4: Wor Pk 1C **164**
RM6: Chad H 6D **54**
TW2: Whit 7G **113**
Mayfair Cl. BR3: Beck 1D **158**
KT6: Surb 1E **162**
Mayfair Ct. HA8: Edg 5A **28**
Mayfair Gdns. IG8: Wfd G 7D **36**
N17 . . . . . 6H **33**
Mayfair M. *NW1* *7D* ***64***
(off Regents Pk. Rd.)
Mayfair Pl. W1 . . . . . 4K **11** (1F **101**)
Mayfair Ter. N14 . . . . . 7C **22**
Mayfield DA7: Bex 3F **127**
Mayfield Av. BR6: Orp 1K **173**
HA3: Kent 5B **42**
IG8: Wfd G 6D **36**
N12 . . . . . 4F **31**
N14 . . . . . 2C **32**
W4 . . . . . 4A **98**
W13 . . . . . 3B **96**
Mayfield Cl. E8 . . . . . 6F **67**
KT7: T Ditt 1B **162**
SE20 . . . . . 1H **157**
SW4 . . . . . 5H **119**
TW15: Ashf 6D **128**
UB10: Hil 3D **74**
Mayfield Cres. CR7: Thor H 4K **155**
N9 . . . . . 6C **24**
Mayfield Dr. HA5: Pinn 4D **40**
Mayfield Gdns. NW4 . . . . . 6F **45**
W7 . . . . . 6H **77**
Mayfield Ho. *E2* *2H* ***85***
(off Cambridge Heath Rd.)
Mayfield Mans. SW15 . . . . . 5H **117**
Mayfield Rd. BR1: Brom 5C **160**
CR2: Sand 7D **168**
CR7: Thor H 4K **155**
DA17: Belv 4J **109**
E4 . . . . . 2K **35**
E8 . . . . . 7F **67**
E13 . . . . . 4H **87**
E17 . . . . . 2A **50**
EN3: Enf H 2E **24**
N8 . . . . . 5K **47**
RM8: Dag 1C **72**
SM2: Sutt 6B **166**
SW19 . . . . . 1H **153**
W3 . . . . . 7H **79**
W12 . . . . . 2A **98**
Mayfield Rd. Flats N8 . . . . . 6K **47**
Mayfields HA9: Wemb 2G **61**
Mayfields Cl. HA9: Wemb 2G **61**
Mayfield Vs. DA14: Sidc 6C **144**
Mayflower Cl. HA4: Ruis 6E **38**
SE16 . . . . . 4K **103**
Mayflower Ho. *IG11: Bark* *1H* ***89***
(off Westbury Rd.)
Mayflower Rd. SW9 . . . . . 3J **119**
Mayflower St. SE16 . . . . . 2J **103**
Mayfly Cl. HA5: Eastc 7A **40**
Mayfly Gdns. UB5: N'olt 3B **76**
Mayford NW1 . . . . . 2G **83**
(not continuous)
Mayford Cl. BR3: Beck 3K **157**
SW12 . . . . . 7D **118**
Mayford Rd. SW12 . . . . . 7D **118**
May Gdns. HA0: Wemb 3C **78**
Maygood St. N1 . . . . . 2A **84**
Maygrove Rd. NW6 . . . . . 6H **63**
Mayhew Cl. E4 . . . . . 3H **35**
Mayhew Ct. SE5 . . . . . 4D **120**
Mayhill Rd. EN5: Barn 6B **20**
SE7 . . . . . 6K **105**
Mayland Mans. *IG11: Bark* *7F* ***71***
(off Whiting Av.)
Maylands Dr. DA14: Sidc 3D **144**
UB8: Uxb 6A **56**
Maylands Ho. *SW3* *4D* ***16***
(off Elystan St.)
Maylie Ho. *SE16* *2H* ***103***
(off Marigold St.)
Maynard Cl. N15 . . . . . 5E **48**
SW6 . . . . . 7K **99**
Maynard Path E17 . . . . . 5E **50**
Maynard Rd. E17 . . . . . 5E **50**
Maynards Quay E1 . . . . . 7J **85**
Mayne Ct. SE26 . . . . . 5H **139**
Maynooth Gdns. SM5: Cars 7D **154**
Mayo Ct. W13 . . . . . 3B **96**
Mayo Ho. *E1* *5J* ***85***
(off Lindley St.)
Mayola Rd. E5 . . . . . 4J **67**
Mayo Rd. CR0: Croy 5D **156**
KT12: Walt T 7J **147**
NW10 . . . . . 6A **62**
Mayow Rd. SE23 . . . . . 3K **139**
SE26 . . . . . 4K **139**
Mayplace Cl. DA7: Bex 3H **127**
Mayplace La. SE18 . . . . . 6F **107**
(not continuous)
Mayplace Rd. E. DA1: Cray 3J **127**
DA7: Bex, Cray 3H **127**
Mayplace Rd. W.
DA7: Bex 4G **127**
MAYPOLE 2K **145**
Maypole Ct. *UB2: S'hall* *2D* ***94***
(off Merrick Rd.)
May Rd. E4 . . . . . 6H **35**
E13 . . . . . 2J **87**
TW2: Twick 1J **131**
Mayroyd Av. KT6: Surb 2G **163**
May's Bldgs. M. SE10 . . . . . 7E **104**
Mays Ct. SE10 . . . . . 7F **105**
WC2 . . . . . 3E **12** (7J **83**)
Mays Hill Rd. BR2: Brom 2G **159**
Mays La. EN5: Ark, Barn . . . . . 1H **29** & 6A **20**
Maysoule Rd. SW11 . . . . . 4B **118**
Mays Rd. TW11: Tedd 5H **131**
Mayston M. *SE10* *5J* ***105***
(off Ormiston Rd.)
May St. W14 . . . . . 5H **99**
(North End Rd.)
W14 . . . . . 5H **99**
(Vereker Rd.)
Mayswood Gdns.
RM10: Dag 6J **73**
Maythorne Cotts. SE13 . . . . . 6F **123**
Mayton St. N7 . . . . . 3K **65**
Maytree Cl. HA8: Edg 3D **28**
Maytree Ct. CR4: Mitc 3E **154**
UB5: N'olt 3C **76**
Maytree Gdns. W5 . . . . . 2D **96**
May Tree Ho. *SE4* *3B* ***122***
(off Wickham Rd.)
Maytree La. HA7: Stan 7F **27**
Maytree Wlk. SW2 . . . . . 2A **138**
Mayville Est. N16 . . . . . 5E **66**
Mayville Rd. E11 . . . . . 2G **69**
IG1: Ilf 5F **71**
May Wlk. E13 . . . . . 2K **87**
Mayward Ho. *SE5* *1E* ***120***
(off Peckham Rd.)
Maywood Cl. BR3: Beck 7D **140**
May Wynne Ho. *E16* *7K* ***87***
(off Murray Sq.)
Maze Hill SE3 . . . . . 7H **105**
SE10 . . . . . 6G **105**
Maze Hill Lodge *SE10* *6F* ***105***
(off Park Vista)
Mazenod Av. NW6 . . . . . 7J **63**
Maze Rd. TW9: Kew 7G **97**
Mead, The BR3: Beck 1E **158**
BR4: W W'ck 1F **171**
N2 . . . . . 2A **46**
SM6: Wall 6H **167**
UB10: Ick 2C **56**
W13 . . . . . 5B **78**
Meadbank Studios *SW11* *7C* ***100***
(off Parkgate Rd.)
Mead Cl. HA3: Hrw W 1H **41**
NW1 . . . . . 6E **64**
Mead Ct. NW9 . . . . . 5J **43**
Mead Cres. E4 . . . . . 4K **35**
SM1: Sutt 3C **166**
Meadcroft Rd. SE11 . . . . . 7K **19** (6B **102**)
(not continuous)
Meade Cl. W4 . . . . . 6G **97**
Meader Ct. SE14 . . . . . 7K **103**
Mead Fld. HA2: Harr 3D **58**
Meadfield HA8: Edg 2C **28**
(not continuous)
Meadfield Grn. HA8: Edg 2C **28**
Meadfoot Rd. SW16 . . . . . 7G **137**
Meadgate Av. IG8: Wfd G 5H **37**
Mead Gro. RM6: Chad H 3D **54**
Mead Ho. *W11* *1H* ***99***
(off Ladbroke Rd.)
Mead Ho. La. UB4: Hayes 4F **75**
Meadhurst Pk. TW16: Sun 6G **129**
Meadhurst Sports Club 5H **129**
Meadlands Dr. TW10: Ham 2D **132**
Mead Lodge W4 . . . . . 2K **97**
Meadow, The BR7: Chst 6G **143**
N10 . . . . . 3E **46**
Meadow Av. CR0: Croy 6K **157**
Meadow Bank N21 . . . . . 6E **22**
SE3 . . . . . 3H **123**
Meadowbank KT5: Surb 6F **151**
NW3 . . . . . 7D **64**
Meadowbank Cl. SW6 . . . . . 7E **98**
Meadowbank Gdns. TW5: Cran 1J **111**
Meadowbank Rd. NW9 . . . . . 7K **43**
Meadowbrook Ct. TW7: Isle 3J **113**
Meadow Cl. BR7: Chst 5F **143**
DA6: Bex 5F **127**
E4 . . . . . 1J **35**
EN3: Enf W 1F **25**
EN5: Barn 6C **20**
HA4: Ruis 6H **39**
IG11: Bark 7A **72**
KT10: Hin W 3A **162**
SE6 . . . . . 5C **140**
SM1: Sutt 2A **166**
SW20 . . . . . 4E **152**
TW4: Houn 6E **112**
TW10: Ham 1E **132**
UB5: N'olt 2E **76**
Meadow Ct. N1 . . . . . 2E **84**
TW3: Houn 6F **113**
Meadowcourt Rd. SE3 . . . . . 4H **123**
Meadowcroft BR1: Brom 3D **160**
W4 . . . . . *5G* ***97***
(off Brooks Rd.)
Meadowcroft Cl. N13 . . . . . 2F **33**
Meadowcroft Rd. N13 . . . . . 2F **33**
Meadow Dr. N10 . . . . . 3F **47**
NW4 . . . . . 2E **44**
Meadowford Cl. SE28 . . . . . 7A **90**
Meadow Gdns. HA8: Edg 6C **28**
Meadow Gth. NW10 . . . . . 6J **61**
(not continuous)
Meadowgate Cl. NW7 . . . . . 5G **29**
Meadow Hill KT3: N Mald 6A **152**
Meadow La. SE12 . . . . . 3K **141**
Meadowlea Cl. UB7: Harm 6A **92**
Meadow M. SW8 . . . . . 6K **101**
Meadow Pl. SW8 . . . . . 7J **101**
W4 . . . . . 7A **98**
Meadow Rd. BR2: Brom 2G **159**
HA5: Pinn 4B **40**
IG11: Bark 7K **71**
RM7: Rush G 1J **73**
RM9: Dag 6F **73**
SM1: Sutt 4C **166**

Meadow Rd. SW8 . . . . .7H **19** (7K **101**)
SW19 .7A **136**
TW13: Felt 2C **130**
TW15: Ashf 5F **129**
UB1: S'hall 7D **76**
Meadow Row SE1 . . . . .3C **102**
Meadows Cl. E10 . . . . .2C **68**
Meadows Ct. DA14: Sidc 6B **144**
Meadows End TW16: Sun 1J **147**
Meadowside SE9 . . . . .4A **124**
TW1: Twick 7D **114**
Meadowside Leisure Cen. 4A **124**
Meadow Stile CR0: Croy 3C **168**
Meadowsweet Cl. E16 . . . . .5B **88**
SW20 .4E **152**
Meadow Vw. DA15: Sidc 7B **126**
HA1: Harr 1J **59**
Meadow Vw. Rd. CR7: Thor H 5B **156**
UB4: Hayes 4F **75**
Meadowview Rd. DA5: Bexl 6E **126**
KT19: Ewe 7A **164**
SE6 . . . . .5B **140**
Meadow Wlk. E18 . . . . .4J **51**
KT17: Ewe 7B **164**
KT19: Ewe 6A **164**
(not continuous)
RM9: Dag 6F **73**
SM6: Wall 3F **167**
Meadow Way BR6: Farnb 3E **172**
HA4: Ruis 6K **39**
HA9: Wemb 4D **60**
KT9: Chess 5E **162**
NW9 . . . . .5K **43**
Meadow Way, The
HA3: Hrw W 1J **41**
Meadow Waye TW5: Hest 6C **94**
Mead Path SW17 . . . . .4A **136**
Mead Pl. CR0: Croy 1C **168**
E9 . . . . .6J **67**
Mead Plat NW10 . . . . .6J **61**
Mead Rd. BR7: Chst 6G **143**
HA8: Edg 6B **28**
TW10: Ham 3C **132**
Mead Row SE1 . . . . .1J **19** (3A **102**)
Meads, The HA8: Edg 6E **28**
SM3: Cheam 3G **165**
SM4: Mord 5C **154**
UB8: Cowl 4A **74**
Meads Ct. E15 . . . . .6H **69**
Meadside Cl. BR3: Beck 1A **158**
Meads La. IG3: Ilf 7J **53**
Meads Rd. EN3: Enf H 1F **25**
N22 . . . . .2B **48**
Mead Ter. HA9: Wemb 4D **60**
Meadvale Rd. CR0: Croy 7F **157**
W5 . . . . .4B **78**
Mead Way BR2: Hayes 6H **159**
CR0: Croy 2A **170**
HA4: Ruis 6F **39**
IG8: Wfd G 5F **37**
Meadway BR3: Beck 1E **158**
EN5: Barn, New Bar 4D **20**
IG3: Bark, Ilf 4J **71**
KT5: Surb 1J **163**
N14 . . . . .2C **32**
NW11 . . . . .6J **45**
SW20 .4E **152**
TW2: Twick 1H **131**
TW15: Ashf 4C **128**
Meadway, The IG9: Buck H 1G **37**
SE3 . . . . .2F **123**
Meadway Cl. EN5: Barn 4D **20**
HA5: H End 6A **26**
NW11 . . . . .6K **45**
Meadway Ct. RM8: Dag 2F **73**
TW11: Tedd 5C **132**
W5 . . . . .4F **79**
Meadway Gdns. HA4: Ruis 6F **39**
Meadway Ga. NW11 . . . . .6J **45**
Meaford Way SE20 . . . . .7H **139**
Meakin Est. SE1 . . . . .3E **102**
Mean Ct. TW7: Isle 2J **113**
Meanley Rd. E12 . . . . .4C **70**
Meard St. W1 . . . . .1C **12** (6H **83**)
(not continuous)
Meath Ho. *SE24* *6B* ***120***
(off Dulwich Rd.)
Meath Rd. E15 . . . . .2H **87**
IG1: Ilf .3G **71**
Meath St. SW11 . . . . .1F **119**
Mecca Bingo
Burnt Oak 2J **43**
Camden *1F* ***83***
(off Arlington Rd.)
Chadwell Heath 7D **54**
Croydon *2C* ***168***
(off Tamworth Rd.)
Dagenham 1E **90**
Earlsfield 1K **135**
East Ham 1C **88**
Fulham Broadway *7J* ***99***
(off Vanston Pl.)
Haggerston 1K **9**
Hounslow 2G **113**
Islington 7C **66**
Kilburn 1J **81**
Rosehill 7A **154**
Wood Green *2A* ***48***
(off Lordship La.)
Yeading 6K **75**
Mecklenburgh Pl. WC1 . . . . . . .3G **7** (4K **83**)
Mecklenburgh Sq. WC1 . . . . . .3G **7** (4K **83**)
Mecklenburgh St. WC1 . . . . . . .3G **7** (4K **83**)
Medburn St. NW1 . . . . .2H **83**
Medcroft Gdns. SW14 . . . . .4J **115**
Medebourne Cl. SE3 . . . . .3J **123**
Mede Ho. *BR1: Brom* *5K* ***141***
(off Pike Cl.)
Medesenge Way N13 . . . . .6G **33**
Medfield St. SW15 . . . . .7C **116**
Medhurst Cl. E3 . . . . .2A **86**
(not continuous)
Median Rd. E5 . . . . .5J **67**
Medina Gro. N7 . . . . .3A **66**
Medina Rd. N7 . . . . .3A **66**
Medland Cl. SM6: Wall 1E **166**
Medland Ho. E14 . . . . .7A **86**
Medlar Cl. UB5: N'olt 2B **76**
Medlar Ho. DA15: Sidc 3A **144**
Medlar St. SE5 . . . . .1C **120**
Medley Rd. NW6 . . . . .6J **63**
Medora Rd. RM7: Rom 4K **55**
SW2 . . . . .7K **119**
Medusa Rd. SE6 . . . . .6D **122**
Medway Bldgs. *E3* *2A* ***86***
(off Medway Rd.)
Medway Cl. CR0: Croy 6J **157**
IG1: Ilf .5G **71**
Medway Ct. NW11 . . . . .6K **45**
WC1 . . . .*2E* ***6***
(off Judd St.)
Medway Dr. UB6: G'frd 2K **77**
Medway Gdns. HA0: Wemb 4A **60**
Medway Ho. KT2: King T 1D **150**
NW8 . . . .*4C* ***4***
(off Penfold St.)
SE1 . . . .*7F* ***15***
(off Hankey Pl.)
Medway M. E3 . . . . .2A **86**
Medway Pde. UB6: G'frd 2K **77**
Medway Rd. E3 . . . . .2A **86**
Medway St. SW1 . . . . .2D **18** (3H **101**)
Medwin St. SW4 . . . . .4K **119**
Meerbrook Rd. SE3 . . . . .3A **124**
Meeson Rd. E15 . . . . .7H **69**
Meeson St. E5 . . . . .4A **68**
Meeson's Wharf E15 . . . . .2E **86**
Meeting Fld. Path E9 . . . . .6J **67**
Meeting Ho. All. E1 . . . . .1H **103**
Meeting Ho. La. SE15 . . . . .1H **121**
Megabowl
Acton .4G **79**
Bexleyheath 4F **127**
Croydon 2K **167**
Dagenham 1H **91**
Feltham 2K **129**
Megabowl
Harrow 5F **41**
Kingston upon Thames *2E* ***150***
(in The Rotunda Cen.)
Streatham Hill 2J **137**
Mehetabel Rd. E9 . . . . .5J **67**
Meister Cl. IG1: Ilf 1H **71**
Melancholy Wlk. TW10: Ham 2C **132**
Melanda Cl. BR7: Chst 5D **142**
Melanie Cl. DA7: Bex 1E **126**
Melba Way SE13 . . . . .1D **122**
Melbourne Av. HA5: Pinn 3F **41**
N13 . . . . .6E **32**
W13 . . . . .1A **96**
Melbourne Cl. BR6: Orp 7J **161**
SE20 .7G **139**
SM6: Wall 5G **167**
UB10: Ick 4C **56**
Melbourne Ct. N10 . . . . .7A **32**
W9 . . . .*4A* ***82***
(off Randolph Av.)
Melbourne Gdns.
RM6: Chad H 5E **54**
Melbourne Gro. SE22 . . . . .4E **120**
Melbourne Ho. UB4: Yead 4A **76**
W8 . . . .*1J* ***99***
(off Kensington Pl.)
Melbourne Mans. *W14* *6G* ***99***
(off Musard Rd.)
Melbourne M. SE6 . . . . .7E **122**
SW9 . . . . .1A **120**
Melbourne Pl. WC2 . . . . .1H **13** (6K **83**)
Melbourne Rd. E6 . . . . .2D **88**
E10 . . . . .7D **50**
E17 . . . . .4A **50**
IG1: Ilf .1F **71**
SM6: Wall 5F **167**
SW19 .1J **153**
TW11: Tedd 6C **132**
Melbourne Sq. SW9 . . . . .1A **120**
Melbourne Ter. *SW6* *7K* ***99***
(off Moore Pk. Rd.)
Melbourne Way
EN1: Enf 6A **24**
Melbray M. SW6 . . . . .2H **117**
Melbreak Ho. SE22 . . . . .3E **120**
Melbury Av. UB2: S'hall 3F **95**
Melbury Cl. BR7: Chst 6C **142**
KT10: Clay 6B **162**
Melbury Ct. W8 . . . . .3H **99**
Melbury Dr. SE5 . . . . .7E **102**
Melbury Gdns. SW20 . . . . .1D **152**
Melbury Ho. *SW8* *7K* ***101***
(off Richborne Ter.)
Melbury Rd. HA3: Kent 5F **43**
W14 . . . . .3H **99**
Melbury Ter. NW1 . . . . .4D **4** (4C **82**)
Melchester *W11* *6H* ***81***
(off Ledbury Rd.)
Melchester Ho. *N19* *3H* ***65***
(off Wedmore St.)
Melcombe Ct. *NW1* *5E* ***4***
(off Melcombe Pl.)
Melcombe Gdns.
HA3: Kent 6F **43**
Melcombe Ho. *SW8* *7K* ***101***
(off Dorset Rd.)
Melcombe Pl. NW1 . . . . .5E **4** (5D **82**)
Melcombe Regis Ct. *W1* *6H* ***5***
(off Weymouth St.)
Melcombe St. NW1 . . . . .4F **5** (4D **82**)
Meldex Cl. NW7 . . . . .6K **29**
Meldon Cl. SW6 . . . . .1K **117**
Meldone Cl. KT5: Surb 7H **151**
Meldrum Rd. IG3: Ilf 2A **72**
Melfield Gdns. SE6 . . . . .4E **140**
Melford Av. IG11: Bark 6J **71**
Melford Cl. KT9: Chess 5F **163**
Melford Ct. *SE1* *3E* ***102***
(off Fendall St.)
SE22 .1G **139**
(not continuous)
Melford Pas. SE22 . . . . .7G **121**
Melford Rd. E6 . . . . .4D **88**
E11 . . . . .2G **69**
E17 . . . . .4A **50**
IG1: Ilf .2H **71**
SE22 .7G **121**
Melfort Av. CR7: Thor H 3B **156**
Melfort Rd. CR7: Thor H 3B **156**
Melgund Rd. N5 . . . . .5A **66**
Melina Cl. UB3: Hayes 5F **75**
Melina Ct. SW15 . . . . .3C **116**
Melina Pl. NW8 . . . . .2A **4** (3B **82**)
Melina Rd. W12 . . . . .2D **98**
Melior Ct. N6 . . . . .6G **47**
Melior Pl. SE1 . . . . .6G **15** (2E **102**)
Melior St. SE1 . . . . .6G **15** (2E **102**)
Meliot Rd. SE6 . . . . .2F **141**
Meller Cl. CR0: Bedd 3J **167**
Melling Dr. EN1: Enf 1B **24**
Melling St. SE18 . . . . .6J **107**
Mellish Cl. IG11: Bark 1K **89**
Mellish Flats E10 . . . . .7C **50**
Mellish Gdns. IG8: Wfd G 5D **36**
Mellish Ho. *E1* *6H* ***85***
(off Varden St.)
Mellish Ind. Est. SE18 . . . . .3B **106**
Mellish St. E14 . . . . .3C **104**
Mellison Rd. SW17 . . . . .5C **136**
Melliss Av. TW9: Kew 1H **115**
Mellitus St. W12 . . . . .5B **80**
Mellor Cl. KT12: Walt T 7D **148**
Mellow La. E. UB4: Hayes 3E **74**
Mellow La. W. UB10: Hil 3E **74**
Mellows Rd. IG5: Ilf 3D **52**
SM6: Wall 5H **167**
Mells Cres. SE9 . . . . .4D **142**
Mell St. SE10 . . . . .5G **105**
Melody La. N5 . . . . .5C **66**
Melody Rd. SW18 . . . . .5A **118**
Melon Pl. W8 .2J **99**
Melon Rd. E11 . . . . .3G **69**
SE15 . . . . .1G **121**
Melrose Av. CR4: Mitc 7F **137**
DA1: Cray 7K **127**
N22 . . . . .1B **48**
NW2 . . . . .5D **62**
SW16 .3K **155**
SW19 .2H **135**
TW2: Whit 7F **113**
UB6: G'frd 2F **77**
Melrose Cl. SE12 . . . . .1J **141**
UB4: Hayes 5J **75**
UB6: G'frd 2F **77**
Melrose Ct. *W13* *1A* ***96***
(off Williams Rd.)
Melrose Cres. BR6: Orp 4H **173**
Melrose Dr. UB1: S'hall 1E **94**
Melrose Gdns. HA8: Edg 3H **43**
KT3: N Mald 3K **151**
W6 . . . . .3E **98**
Melrose Ho. *E14* *3D* ***104***
(off Lanark Sq.)
NW6 . . . .*3J* ***81***
(off Carlton Va.)
SW1 . . . .*5F* ***101***
(off Sutherland St.)
Melrose Rd. HA5: Pinn 4D **40**
SW13 .2B **116**
SW18 .6H **117**
SW19 .2J **153**
W3 . . . . .3J **97**
Melrose Ter. W6 . . . . .3E **98**
Melrose Tudor *SM6: Wall* *5J* ***167***
(off Plough La.)
Melsa Rd. SM4: Mord 6A **154**
Melthorne Dr. HA4: Ruis 3A **58**
Melthorpe Gdns. SE3 . . . . .1C **124**
Melton Cl. HA4: Ruis 1A **58**
Melton Ct. SM2: Sutt 7A **166**
SW7 . . . . .3B **16** (4B **100**)
Melton St. NW1 . . . . .2B **6** (3G **83**)
Melville Av. CR2: S Croy 5F **169**
SW20 .7C **134**
UB6: G'frd 5K **59**

Melville Cl. UB10: Ick 2F 57
Melville Ct. SE8 4A 104
W12 3D 98
(off Goldhawk Rd.)
Melville Gdns. N13 5G 33
Melville Ho. EN5: New Bar 5G 21
SE10 1E 122
Melville Pl. N1 7C 66
Melville Rd. DA14: Sidc 2C 144
E17 3B 50
NW10 7K 61
RM5: Col R 1H 55
SW13 1C 116
Melville Vs. Rd. W3 1J 97
Melvin Rd. SE20 1J 157
Melwood Ho. *E1* 6H 85
(off Watney Mkt.)
Melyn Cl. N7 4G 65
Memel Ct. EC1 4C 8
Memel St. EC1 4C 8 (4C 84)
Memess Path SE18 6E 106
Memorial Av. E12 2C 70
E15 3G 87
Memorial Cl. TW5: Hest 6D 94
Menard Ct. *EC1* 2D 8
(off Galway St.)
Mendham Ho. *SE1* 7G 15
(off Cluny Pl.)
Mendip Cl. KT4: Wor Pk 1E 164
SE26 4J 139
UB3: Harl 7F 93
Mendip Ct. *SE14* 6J 103
(off Avonley Rd.)
SW11 3A 118
Mendip Dr. NW2 2G 63
Mendip Ho. *N9* 2B 34
(off New Rd.)
Mendip Ho's. *E2* 3J 85
(off Welwyn St.)
Mendip Rd. DA7: Bex 1K 127
IG2: Ilf 5J 53
SW11 3A 118
Mendora Rd. SW6 7G 99
Menelik Rd. NW2 4G 63
Menier Chocolate Factory 5D 14
(off O'Meara St.)
Menlo Gdns. SE19 7D 138
Menlo Lodge *N13* 3E 32
(off Crothall Cl.)
Menon Dr. N9 3C 34
Menotti St. E2 4G 85
Menteath Ho. *E14* 6C 86
(off Dod St.)
Mentmore Cl. HA3: Kent 6C 42
Mentmore Ter. E8 7H 67
Mentone Mans. *SW10* 7K 99
(off Fulham Rd.)
Meon Rd. W3 2J 97
Meopham Rd. CR4: Mitc 1G 155
Mepham Cres. HA3: Hrw W 7B 26
Mepham Gdns. HA3: Hrw W 7B 26
Mepham St. SE1 5J 13 (1A 102)
Mera Dr. DA7: Bex 4G 127
Merantun Way SW19 1K 153
Merbury Cl. SE13 5E 122
SE28 1H 107
Merbury Rd. SE28 1H 107
Mercator Pl. E14 5C 104
Mercator Rd. SE13 4F 123
Mercer Bldg. *EC2* 3H 9
(off Bateman's Row)
Mercer Cl. KT7: T Ditt 7K 149
Mercer Ho. *SW1* 5J 17
(off Ebury Bri. Rd.)
Merceron Ho's. *E2* 3J 85
(off Globe Rd.)
Merceron St. E1 4H 85
Mercer Pl. HA5: Pinn 2A 40
Mercers Cl. SE10 4H 105
Mercer's Cotts. *E1* 6A 86
(off White Horse Rd.)
Mercers M. N19 3H 65
Mercers Pl. W6 4F 99
Mercers Rd. N19 3H 65
(not continuous)
Mercer St. WC2 1E 12 (6J 83)
Merchant Ct. *E1* 1J 103
(off Wapping Wall)
Merchant Ind. Ter.
NW10 4J 79
Merchants Cl. SE25 4G 157
Merchants Ho. *SE10* 5F 105
(off Collington St.)
Merchants Lodge *E17* 4C 50
(off Westbury Rd.)
Merchants Row *SE10* 5F 105
(off Hoskins St.)
Merchant St. E3 3B 86
Merchiston Rd. SE6 2F 141
Merchland Rd. SE9 1G 143
Mercia Gro. SE13 4E 122
Mercia Ho. *SE5* 2C 120
(off Denmark Rd.)
TW15: Ashf 1E 146
Mercier Rd. SW15 5G 117
Mercury *NW9* 1B 44
(off The Concourse)
Mercury Cen. TW14: Felt 5J 111
Mercury Ct. *E14* 4C 104
(off Homer Dr.)
Mercury Hgts. IG2: Ilf 6H 53
Mercury Ho. *TW8: Bford* 6C 96
(off Glenhurst Rd.)
W5 4F 79
Mercury Rd. TW8: Bford 6C 96
Mercury Way SE14 6K 103
Mercy Ter. SE13 5D 122
Merebank La. CR0: Wadd 5K 167
Mere Cl. BR6: Farnb 2E 172
SW15 7F 117
Meredith Av. NW2 5E 62
Meredith Cl. HA5: Pinn 1B 40
Meredith Ho. N16 5E 66
Meredith M. SE4 4B 122
Meredith St. E13 3J 87
EC1 2A 8 (3B 84)
Meredith Twr. *W3* 3H 97
(off Hanbury Rd.)
Meredyth Rd. SW13 2C 116
Mere End CR0: Croy 7K 157
Mere Rd. TW17: Shep 6D 146
Mere Side BR6: Farnb 2E 172
Mereside Pk. TW15: Ashf 4E 128
Meretone Cl. SE4 4A 122
Mereton Mans. *SE8* 1C 122
(off Brookmill Rd.)
Merevale Cres. SM4: Mord 6A 154
Mereway Rd. TW2: Twick 1H 131
Merewood Cl. BR1: Brom 2E 160
Merewood Gdns. CR0: Croy 7K 157
Merewood Rd. DA7: Bex 2J 127
Mereworth Cl. BR2: Brom 5H 159
Mereworth Dr. SE18 7F 107
Mereworth Ho. SE15 6J 103
Merganser Ct. *SE8* 6B 104
(off Edward St.)
Merganser Gdns. SE28 3H 107
Meriden Cl. BR1: Brom 7B 142
IG6: Ilf 1G 53
Meriden Ct. SW3 6C 16
Meriden Ho. *N1* 1E 84
(off Wilmer Gdns.)
Merideth Ct. KT1: King T 2F 151
Meridian Ct. *SE16* 2G 103
(off Nth. Flock St.)
Meridian Ga. E14 2D 104
Meridian Ho. *SE10* 4G 105
(off Azof St.)
SE10 7E 104
(off Royal Hill)
Meridian Pl. E14 2D 104
Meridian Point SE8 6D 104
Meridian Rd. SE7 7B 106
Meridian Sq. E15 7F 69
Meridian Trad. Est. SE7 4K 105
Meridian Wlk. N17 6K 33
Meridian Way EN3: Pond E 7E 24
N9 4D 34
N18 5D 34
Merifield Rd. SE9 4A 124
Merino Cl. E11 4A 52
Merino Pl. DA15: Sidc 6A 126
Merioneth Ct. *W7* 5K 77
(off Copley Cl.)
Merivale Rd. HA1: Harr 7G 41
SW15 4G 117
Merlewood Dr. BR7: Chst 1D 160
Merley Ct. NW9 1J 61
Merlin *NW9* 1B 44
(off The Concourse)
Merlin Cl. CR0: Croy 4E 168
CR4: Mitc 3C 154
SM6: Wall 6K 167
UB5: Yead 3A 76
Merlin Ct. BR2: Brom 3H 159
HA4: Ruis 2F 57
Merlin Cres. HA8: Edg 1F 43
Merlin Gdns. BR1: Brom 3J 141
Merling Cl. KT9: Chess 5C 162
Merlin Gro. BR3: Beck 4B 158
Merlin Ho. EN3: Pond E 5E 24
SW18 4A 118
Merlin Rd. DA16: Well 4A 126
E12 2B 70
Merlin Rd. Nth. DA16: Well 4A 126
Merlins Av. HA2: Harr 3D 58
Merlins Ct. *WC1* 2J 7
(off Margery St.)
Merlin St. WC1 2J 7 (3A 84)
Mermaid Ct. *E8* 7F 67
(off Celandine Dr.)
SE1 6E 14 (2D 102)
SE16 1B 104
Mermaid Ho. *E14* 7E 86
(off Bazely St.)
Mermaid Twr. *SE8* 6B 104
(off Abinger Gro.)
Meroe Ct. N16 2E 66
Merredene St. SW2 6K 119
Merriam Av. E9 6B 68
Merriam Cl. E4 5K 35
Merrick Rd. UB2: S'hall 2D 94
Merrick Sq. SE1 7E 14 (3D 102)
Merridene N21 6G 23
Merrielands Cres. RM9: Dag 2F 91
Merrielands Retail Pk. RM9: Dag 1F 91
Merrilands Rd. KT4: Wor Pk 1E 164
Merrilees Rd. DA15: Sidc 7J 125
Merrilyn Cl. KT10: Clay 6A 162
Merriman Rd. SE3 1A 124
Merrington Rd. SW6 6J 99
Merrion Av. HA7: Stan 5J 27
Merritt Gdns. KT9: Chess 6C 162
(not continuous)
Merritt Rd. SE4 5B 122
Merritt's Bldgs. EC2 4G 9
Merrivale N14 6C 22
NW1 1G 83
(off Camden St.)
Merrivale Av. IG4: Ilf 4B 52
Merrow Ct. CR4: Mitc 2B 154
Merrow Rd. SM2: Cheam 7F 165
Merrow St. SE17 5D 102
Merrow Wlk. SE17 5D 102
Merrow Way CR0: New Ad 6E 170
Merrydown Way BR7: Chst 1C 160
Merryfield SE3 2H 123
Merryfield Gdns. HA7: Stan 5H 27
Merryfield Ho. *SE9* 3A 142
(off Grove Pk. Rd.)
Merryfields UB8: Uxb 2A 74
UB10: Uxb 2A 74
Merryfields Way SE6 7D 122
MERRY HILL 1A 26
Merryhill Cl. E4 7J 25
Merry Hill Mt. WD23: Bush 1A 26
Merry Hill Rd. WD23: Bush 1A 26
Merryhills Ct. N14 5B 22
Merryhills Dr. EN2: Enf 4C 22
Merryweather Ct. KT3: N Mald 5A 152
N19 3G 65
Mersea Ho. IG11: Bark 6F 71
Mersey Ct. *KT2: King T* 1D 150
(off Samuel Gray Gdns.)
Mersey Rd. E17 3B 50
Mersey Wlk. UB5: N'olt 2E 76
Mersham Dr. NW9 5G 43
Mersham Pl. *CR7: Thor H* 2D 156
(off Livingstone Rd.)
SE20 1H 157
Mersham Rd. CR7: Thor H 3D 156
Merten Rd. RM6: Chad H 7E 54
Merthyr Ter. SW13 6D 98
MERTON 7A 136
Merton Av. UB5: N'olt 5G 59
UB10: Hil 7D 56
W4 4B 98
Merton Ct. DA16: Well 2B 126
IG1: Ilf 6C 52
Merton Gdns. BR5: Pet W 5F 161
Merton Hall Gdns. SW20 1G 153
Merton Hall Rd. SW19 7G 135
Merton High St. SW19 7K 135
Merton Ind. Pk. SW19 1K 153
Merton La. N6 2D 64
Merton Lodge EN5: New Bar 5F 21
Merton Mans. SW20 2F 153
MERTON PARK 2J 153
Merton Pk. Pde. SW19 1H 153
Merton Pl. *SW19* 1A 154
(off Nelson Gro. Rd.)
Merton Ri. NW3 7C 64
Merton Rd. E17 5E 50
EN2: Enf 1J 23
HA2: Harr 1G 59
IG3: Ilf 7K 53
IG11: Bark 7K 71
SE25 5F 157
SW18 6J 117
SW19 7K 135
Merton Way KT8: W Mole 4F 149
UB10: Hil 7D 56
Mertoun Ter. *W1* 7E 4
(off Seymour Pl.)
Merttins Rd. SE4 5K 121
SE15 5K 121
Meru Cl. NW5 4E 64
Mervan Rd. SW2 4A 120
Mervyn Av. SE9 3G 143
Mervyn Rd. TW17: Shep 7E 146
W13 3A 96
Messaline Av. W3 6J 79
Messent Rd. SE9 5A 124
Messeter Pl. SE9 6E 124
Messina Av. NW6 7J 63
Messiter Ho. *N1* 1K 83
(off Barnsbury Est.)
Metcalf Rd. TW15: Ashf 5D 128
Metcalf Wlk. TW13: Hanw 4C 130
Meteor St. SW11 4E 118
Meteor Way SM6: Wall 7J 167
Methley St. SE11 6K 19 (5A 102)
Methuen Cl. HA8: Edg 7B 28
Methuen Pk. N10 3F 47
Methuen Rd. DA6: Bex 4F 127
DA17: Belv 4H 109
HA8: Edg 7B 28
Methwold Rd. W10 5F 81
Metro Bus. Cen., The SE26 6B 140
Metro Central Hgts. *SE1* 3C 102
(off Newington C'way.)
Metro Ind. Cen. TW7: Isle 2J 113
Metropolis *SE11* 3B 102
(off Oswin St.)
Metropolitan Bus. Cen. *N1* 7E 66
(off Enfield Rd.)
Metropolitan Cl. E14 5C 86
Metropolitan Police Norwood Cadet Training Cen. 1E 156
Metropolitan Sta. Bldgs. *W6* 4E 98
(off Beadon Rd.)
Metropolitan Wharf E1 1J 103

Metro Trad. Est.—Miller Av.

Metro Trad. Est. HA9: Wemb 4H 61
Mews, The DA14: Sidc 4A 144
IG4: Ilf 5B 52
N1 ....1C 84
N8 ....3A 48
RM1: Rom 4K 55
SE22 ....5G 121
TW1: Twick 6B 114
Mews Pl. IG8: Wfd G 4D 36
Mews St. E1 ....4K 15 (1G 103)
Mexborough NW1 ....1G 83
Mexfield Rd. SW15 ....5H 117
Meyer Grn. EN1: Enf................1B 24
Meyer Rd. DA8: Erith 6K 109
Meymott St. SE1 ....5A 14 (1B 102)
Meynell Cres. E9 ....7K 67
Meynell Gdns. E9...................7K 67
Meynell Rd. E9.....................7K 67
Meyrick Ho. *E14* *5C 86*
(off Burgess St.)
Meyrick Rd. NW10 ....6C 62
SW11 ....3B 118
Miah Ter. E1 ....1G 103
Miall Wlk. SE26 ....4A 140
Micawber Av. UB8: Hil 4C 74
Micawber Ct. *N1* *1D 8*
(off Windsor Ter.)
Micawber Ho. *SE16* *2G 103*
(off Llewellyn St.)
Micawber St. N1 ....1D 8 (3C 84)
Michael Cliffe Ho. EC1 ....2A 8
Michael Faraday Ho. *SE17*..........*5E 102*
(off Beaconsfield Rd.)
Michael Gaynor Cl. W7 ....1K 95
Michael Manley Ind. Est. *SW8* *2G 119*
(off Clyston St.)
Michaelmas Cl. SW20 ....3E 152
Michael Rd. E11 ....1H 69
SE25 ....3E 156
SW6......................1K 117
Michaels Cl. SE13 ....4G 123
Michael Sobell Leisure Cen. 3K 65
Michael Stewart Ho. *SW6* *6H 99*
(off Clem Attlee Ct.)
Michelangelo Ct. *SE16* *5H 103*
(off Stubbs Dr.)
Micheldever Rd. SE12 ....6G 123
Michelham Gdns. TW1: Twick 3K 131
Michelle Ct. *BR1: Brom* *1H 159*
(off Blyth Rd.)
N12 ....5F 31
W3 ....7K 79
Michelsdale Dr. TW9: Rich 4E 114
Michelson Ho. SE11................4H 19
Michel's Row *TW9: Rich* *4E 114*
(off Michelsdale Dr.)
Michigan Av. E12 ....4D 70
Michigan Ho. E14..................3C 104
Michleham Down N12 ....4C 30
Mickledore *NW1*....................*1B 6*
(off Ampthill Est.)
Mickleham Cl. BR5: St P 2K 161
Mickleham Gdns.
SM3: Cheam 6G 165
Mickleham Rd. BR5: St P 1K 161
Mickleham Way CR0: New Ad 7F 171
Micklethwaite Rd. SW6 ....6J 99
Mickleton Ho. *W2* *5J 81*
(off Brunel Est.)
Midas Bus. Cen. RM10: Dag 4H 73
Midas Metropolitan Ind. Est.
SM4: Mord 7E 152
MID BECKTON 6D 88
Midcroft HA4: Ruis 1G 57
Middle Dartrey Wlk. *SW10* *7A 100*
(off Dartrey Wlk.)
Middle Dene NW7 ....3E 28
Middlefield NW8 ....1B 82
Middlefielde W13..................5B 78
Middlefield Gdns. IG2: Ilf 6F 53
Middle Grn. Cl. KT5: Surb 6F 151
Middleham Gdns. N18 ....6B 34
Middleham Rd. N18 ....6B 34
Middle La. N8 ....5J 47
TW11: Tedd 6K 131
Middle La. M. N8 ....5J 47
Middle Mill Halls of Residence
KT1: King T 3F 151
Middle Pk. Av. SE9 ....6B 124
Middle Path HA2: Harr 1H 59
Middle Rd. E13 ....2J 87
EN4: E Barn 6H 21
HA2: Harr 2H 59
SW16 ....2H 155
Middle Row W10 ....4G 81
Middlesborough Rd. N18 ....6B 34
Middlesex Bus. Cen.
UB2: S'hall 2E 94
Middlesex CC Club..........1B 4 (3B 82)
Middlesex Cl. UB1: G'frd 4F 77
Middlesex Ct. HA1: Harr 5K 41
W4 ....4B 98
Middlesex Filter Beds Nature Reserve
...........................3K 67
Middlesex Ho. HA0: Wemb 1D 78
Middlesex Pas. EC1 ....6B 8
Middlesex Pl. *E9*...................*6J 67*
(off Elsdale St.)
Middlesex Rd. CR4: Mitc 5J 155
Middlesex St. E1 ....6H 9 (5E 84)
Middlesex University
Cat Hill Campus 5K 21
Enfield Campus 5C 24
Hendon Campus 4D 44
Quicksilver Place Campus 2J 47
The Archway Campus 1G 65
Tottenham Campus 6K 33
Trent Pk. Campus 2B 22
Middlesex University Sports Dome
.........................*7A 34*
(off White Hart La.)
Middlesex University Swimming Pool
..........................2K 47
Middlesex Wharf E5 ....2J 67
Middle St. CR0: Croy 2C 168
(not continuous)
EC1 ....5C 8 (5C 84)
Middle Temple La. EC4 ....1J 13 (6A 84)
Middleton Av. DA14: Sidc 6B 144
E4 ....4G 35
UB6: G'frd 2H 77
Middleton Cl. E4 ....3G 35
Middleton Dr. HA5: Eastc 3J 39
SE16 ....2K 103
Middleton Gdns. IG2: Ilf 6F 53
Middleton Gro. N7 ....5J 65
Middleton Ho. E8 ....7G 67
SE1 ....*3D 102*
(off Burbage Cl.)
SW1 ....*4D 18*
(off Causton St.)
Middleton M. N7 ....5J 65
Middleton Pl. W1 ....6A 6
Middleton Rd. E8 ....7F 67
KT3: N Mald 3J 151
NW11 ....7J 45
SM4: Mord 6K 153
SM5: Cars 7B 154
UB3: Hayes 5F 75
Middleton St. E2 ....3H 85
Middleton Way SE13 ....4F 123
Middle Way DA18: Erith 3E 108
SW16 ....2H 155
UB4: Yead 4A 76
Middle Way, The HA3: W'stone 2K 41
Middleway NW11 ....5K 45
Middle Yd. SE1 ....4G 15 (1E 102)
Midfield Av. DA7: Bex 3J 127
Midfield Pde. DA7: Bex 3J 127
Midfield Way BR5: St P 7A 144
Midford Ho. *NW4* *4E 44*
(off Stratford Rd.)
Midford Pl. W1 ....4B 6 (4G 83)
Midholm HA9: Wemb 1G 61
Midholm Cl. NW11 ....4K 45
Midholm Rd. CR0: Croy 2A 170
Midhope Ho. *WC1* *2F 7*
(off Midhope St.)
Midhope St. WC1 ....2F 7 (3J 83)
Midhurst SE26 ....6J 139
Midhurst Av. CR0: Croy 7A 156
N10 ....3E 46
Midhurst Gdns. UB10: Hil 1E 74
Midhurst Hill DA6: Bex 6G 127
Midhurst Ho. *E14* *6B 86*
(off Salmon La.)
Midhurst Pde. *N10* *3E 46*
(off Fortis Grn.)
Midhurst Rd. W13 ....2A 96
Midhurst Way E5 ....4G 67
Midland Pde. NW6 ....6K 63
Midland Pl. E14 ....5E 104
Midland Rd. E10....................7E 50
NW1 ....1D 6 (2H 83)
Midland Ter. NW2 ....3F 63
NW10 ....4A 80
Midmoor Rd. SW12 ....1G 137
SW19 ....1F 153
Midship Cl. SE16 ....1K 103
Midship Point *E14* *2C 104*
(off The Quarterdeck)
Midstrath Rd. NW10 ....4A 62
Midsummer Av.
TW4: Houn 4D 112
Midway SM3: Sutt 7H 153
Midway Ho. EC1 ....1A 8
Midwinter Cl. DA16: Well 3A 126
Midwood Cl. NW2 ....3D 62
Miers Cl. E6 ....1E 88
Mighell Av. IG4: Ilf 5B 52
Milan Ct. N11 ....1H 47
Milan Rd. UB1: S'hall 2D 94
Milborne Gro. SW10 ....6A 16 (5A 100)
Milborne St. E9 ....6J 67
Milborough Cres. SE12 ....6G 123
Milburn Dr. UB7: Yiew 7A 74
Milcote St. SE1 ....7A 14 (2B 102)
Mildenhall Rd. E5 ....4J 67
Mildmay Av. N1 ....6D 66
Mildmay Gro. Nth. N1 ....5D 66
Mildmay Gro. Sth. N1 ....5D 66
Mildmay Pk. N1 ....5D 66
Mildmay Pl. N16 ....5E 66
Mildmay Rd. IG1: Ilf 3F 71
N1 ....5D 66
RM7: Rom 5J 55
Mildmay St. N1 ....6D 66
Mildred Av. UB3: Harl 4F 93
UB5: N'olt 5F 59
Mildred Rd. DA8: Erith 5K 109
Mildura Ct. N8 ....4K 47
MILE END 4B 86
Mile End, The E17 ....1K 49
Mile End Pk. 4A 86
Mile End Pk. Leisure Cen. 5A 86
Mile End Pl. E1 ....4K 85
Mile End Rd. E1 ....5J 85
E3 ....5J 85
Mile End Stadium 5B 86
Mile Rd. SM6: Bedd, Wall 1F 167
(not continuous)
Miles Bldgs. *NW1* *5C 4*
(off Penfold Pl.)
Miles Cl. SE28 ....1H 107
Miles Ct. *CR0: Croy* *2B 168*
(off Cuthbert Rd.)
E1 ....*6H 85*
(off Tillman St.)
Miles Dr. SE28 ....1J 107
Miles Ho. *SE10* *5G 105*
(off Tuskar St.)
Miles Lodge HA1: Harr 5H 41
Milespit Hill NW7 ....5J 29
Miles Pl. KT5: Surb 4F 151
NW1 ....5B 4
Miles Rd. CR4: Mitc 3C 154
N8 ....3J 47
Miles St. SW8 ....7E 18 (6J 101)
(not continuous)
Miles St. Bus. Est. *SW8* *7F 19*
(off Miles St.)
Milestone Cl. N9 ....2B 34
SM2: Sutt 6B 166
MILESTONE GREEN 4J 115
Milestone Ho. *KT1: King T* *3D 150*
(off Surbiton Rd.)
Milestone Rd. SE19 ....6F 139
Miles Way N20 ....2H 31
Milfoil St. W12 ....7C 80
Milford Cl. SE2 ....6E 108
Milford Ct. UB1: S'hall 1E 94
Milford Gdns. CR0: Croy 5J 157
HA0: Wemb 4D 60
HA8: Edg 7B 28
Milford Gro. SM1: Sutt 4A 166
Milford La. WC2 ....2H 13 (7A 84)
Milford M. SW16 ....3K 137
Milford Rd. UB1: S'hall 7E 76
W13 ....1B 96
Milford Towers SE6 ....7D 122
Milk St. BR1: Brom 6K 141
E16 ....1F 107
EC2.................7D 8 (6C 84)
Milkwell Gdns. IG8: Wfd G...........7E 36
Milkwell Yd. SE5 ....1C 120
Milkwood Rd. SE24 ....5B 120
Milk Yd. E1 ....7J 85
Millais Av. E12 ....5E 70
Millais Ct. *UB5: N'olt* *2B 76*
(off Academy Gdns.)
Millais Cres. KT19: Ewe 5A 164
Millais Gdns. HA8: Edg 2G 43
Millais Ho. *SW1* *4E 18*
(off Marsham St.)
Millais Rd. E11 ....4E 68
EN1: Enf 5A 24
KT3: N Mald 7A 152
Millais Way KT19: Ewe 4J 163
Millard Cl. N16 ....5E 66
Millard Ho. *SE8* *5B 104*
(off Leeway)
Millard Ter. RM10: Dag 6G 73
Millbank SM6: Wall 5H 167
SW1 ....2E 18 (3J 101)
Millbank Ct. SW1 ....3E 18
Millbank Twr. SW1 ....4E 18 (4J 101)
Millbank Way SE12................5J 123
Millbourne Rd. TW13: Hanw 4C 130
Mill Bri. EN5: Barn 6C 20
Millbrook Av. DA16: Well 4H 125
Millbrook Gdns. RM6: Chad H 6F 55
Millbrook Ho. *SE15* *6G 103*
(off Peckham Pk. Rd.)
Millbrook Pas. SW9 ....3B 120
Millbrook Pl. *NW1* *2G 83*
(off Hampstead Rd.)
Millbrook Rd. N9 ....1C 34
SW9......................3B 120
Mill Cl. SM5: Cars 2E 166
Mill Cnr. EN5: Barn 1C 20
Mill Ct. E10 ....3E 68
SE28 ....*7B 90*
(off Titmuss Av.)
Millcroft Ho. *SE6* *4E 140*
(off Melfield Gdns.)
Millender Wlk. *SE16*...............*4J 103*
(off New Rotherhithe Rd.)
Millennium Bridge 3B 14 (7B 84)
Millennium Bri. Ho. *EC4* *2C 14*
(off Up. Thames St.)
Millennium Bus. Cen.
NW2 ....2D 62
Millennium Cen., The 4K 73
Millennium Cl. E16 ....6K 87
Millennium Dome
The O2 ....1G 105
Millennium Dr. E14 ....4F 105
Millennium Ho. E17 ....5K 49
Millennium Pl. E2 ....2H 85
Millennium Sq. SE1 ....6K 15 (2F 103)
Millennium Way SE10 ....2G 105
Miller Av. EN3: Enf L 1H 25

Miller Cl.—Missenden Cl.

Miller Cl. BR1: Brom 5K 141
CR4: Mitc 7D 154
HA5: Pinn 2A 40
Miller Ct. DA7: Bex 3J 127
Miller Rd. CR0: Croy 1K 167
SW19 6B 136
Miller's Av. E8 5F 67
Millers Cl. NW7 4H 29
Millers Ct. *HA0: Wemb* *2E 78*
(off Vicars Bri. Cl.)
Millers Grn. Cl. EN2: Enf 3G 23
Millers Mdw. Cl. SE3 4H 123
Miller's Ter. E8 5F 67
Miller St. NW1 2G 83
(not continuous)
Millers Way W6 2E 98
Millers Wharf Ho. *E1* *5K 15*
(off St Katherine's Way)
Millers Yd. N3 1K 45
Miller Wlk. SE1 5K 13 (1A 102)
Millet Rd. UB6: G'frd 2F 77
Mill Farm Av. TW16: Sun 7G 129
Mill Farm Bus. Pk. TW4: Houn 7C 112
Mill Farm Cl. HA5: Pinn 2A 40
Mill Farm Cres. TW4: Houn 1C 130
Millfield KT1: King T 3F 151
N4 2A 66
TW16: Sun 1F 147
Millfield Av. E17 1A 50
Millfield La. N6 1C 64
(not continuous)
Millfield Pl. N6 2E 64
Millfield Rd. HA8: Edg 2J 43
TW4: Houn 1C 130
Millfields Rd. E5 4J 67
Millfield Theatre 4J 33
Mill Gdns. SE26 3H 139
Mill Grn. CR4: Mitc 7E 154
Mill Grn. Bus. Pk. CR4: Mitc 7E 154
Mill Grn. Rd. CR4: Mitc 7D 154
Millgrove St. SW11 1E 118
Millharbour E14 2D 104
Millhaven Cl. RM6: Chad H 6B 54
MILL HILL 5F 29
Mill Hill SW13 2C 116
MILL HILL CIRCUS 5G 29
Mill Hill Gro. W3 1J 97
Mill Hill Ind. Est. NW7 6G 29
Mill Hill Rd. SW13 2C 116
W3 2H 97
Mill Hill School Leisure Cen.
Mill Hill 4H 29
Mill Hill Ter. W3 1H 97
Mill Ho. IG8: Wfd G 5C 36
Millhouse Pl. SE27 4B 138
Millicent Fawcett Ct. N17 1F 49
Millicent Rd. E10 1B 68
Milligan St. E14 7B 86
Milliners Ho. *SE1* *7H 15*
(off Bermondsey St.)
SW18 4J 117
Milling Rd. HA8: Edg 7E 28
Millington Ho. N16 3D 66
Millington Rd. UB3: Harl 3G 93
Mill La. CR0: Wadd 3K 167
E4 3J 25
IG8: Wfd G 5C 36
KT17: Ewe 7B 164
NW6 5H 63
RM6: Chad H 6E 54
SE18 5E 106
SM5: Cars 4D 166
Mill La. Trad. Est. CR0: Wadd 3K 167
Millman Ct. *WC1* *4G 7*
(off Millman Ct.)
Millman M. WC1 4G 7 (4K 83)
Millman Pl. *WC1* *4H 7*
(off Millman St.)
Millman St. WC1 4G 7 (4K 83)
Millmark Gro. SE14 2A 122
Millmarsh La. EN3: Brim 2F 25
Millmead Ind. Cen. N17 2H 49
Mill Mead Rd. N17 3H 49
MILL MEADS 2F 87
Mill Pl. BR7: Chst 1F 161
E14 6A 86
KT1: King T 3F 151
Mill Plat TW7: Isle 2A 114
(not continuous)
Mill Plat Av. TW7: Isle 2A 114
Mill Pond Cl. SW8 7H 101
Millpond Est. SE16 2H 103
Millpond Pl. SM5: Cars 3E 166
Mill Ridge HA8: Edg 5A 28
Mill River Trad. Est. EN3: Pond E 3F 25
Mill Rd. DA8: Erith 7J 109
E16 1K 105
IG1: Ilf 3E 70
SW19 7A 136
TW2: Twick 2G 131
Mill Row DA5: Bexl 1H 145
N1 1E 84
Mills Cl. UB10: Hil 2C 74
Mills Ct. *EC2* *3G 9*
(off Curtain Rd.)
Mills Gro. E14 6E 86
NW4 3F 45
Millshot Cl. SW6 1E 116
Mills Ho. E17 3F 51
SW8 *1G 119*
(off Thessaly Rd.)
Millside SM5: Cars 2D 166
Millside Pl. TW7: Isle 2B 114
Millson Cl. N20 2G 31
Mills Row W4 4K 97
Millstream Cl. N13 5F 33
Millstream Ho. *SE16* *2H 103*
(off Jamaica Rd.)
Millstream Rd. SE1 7J 15 (2F 103)
Mill St. KT1: King T 3E 150
SE1 7K 15 (2F 103)
W1 2A 12 (7F 83)
Mill Trad. Est., The NW10 3J 79
Mill Va. BR2: Brom 2H 159
Mill Vw. Cl. KT17: Ewe 7B 164
Mill Vw. Gdns. CR0: Croy 3K 169
MILLWALL 4D 104
Millwall Dock Rd. E14 3C 104
Millwall FC 5J 103
Mill Way TW14: Felt 5K 111
Millway NW7 4F 29
Millway Gdns. UB5: N'olt 6D 58
Millwood Rd. TW3: Houn 5G 113
Millwood St. W10 5G 81
Mill Yd. E1 7G 85
Mill Yard Ind. Est. HA8: Edg 1H 43
Milman Cl. HA5: Pinn 3B 40
Milman Rd. NW6 2F 81
Milman's Ho. *SW1* *5J 17*
(off Warwick Way)
SW10 *6B 100*
(off Milman's St.)
Milman's St. SW10 6B 100
Milne Ct. E18 1J 51
Milne Gdns. SE9 5C 124
Milne Ho. *SE18* *4D 106*
(off Ogilby St.)
Milner Ct. *SE15* *7F 103*
(off Colegrove Rd.)
Milner Dr. TW2: Whit 7H 113
Milner Pl. N1 1A 84
SM5: Cars 4E 166
Milner Rd. CR7: Thor H 3D 156
E15 3G 87
KT1: King T 3D 150
RM8: Dag 2C 72
SM4: Mord 5B 154
SW19 1K 153
Milner Sq. N1 7B 66
Milner St. SW3 3E 16 (4D 100)
Milner Wlk. SE9 2H 143
Milnthorpe Rd. W4 6K 97
Milo Gdns. SE22 6F 121
Milo Rd. SE22 6F 121
Milrood Ho. *E1* *5K 85*
(off Stepney Grn.)
Milroy Wlk. SE1 4A 14 (1B 102)
Milson Rd. W14 3F 99
Milstead Ho. E5 5H 67
Milton Av. CR0: Croy 7D 156
E6 7B 70
EN5: Barn 5C 20
N6 7G 47
NW9 3J 43
NW10 1J 79
SM1: Sutt 3B 166
Milton Cl. N2 5A 46
SE1 4F 103
SM1: Sutt 3B 166
UB4: Hayes 6J 75
Milton Ct. E17 4C 50
EC2 5E 8 (5D 84)
RM6: Chad H 7C 54
SE14 6B 104
(not continuous)
SW18 5J 117
TW2: Twick 3J 131
UB10: Ick 3D 56
Milton Ct. Rd. SE14 6A 104
Milton Ct. Wlk. *EC2* *5E 8*
(off Silk St.)
Milton Cres. IG2: Ilf 7F 53
Milton Dr. TW17: Shep 4A 146
Milton Gdn. Est. N16 4D 66
Milton Gdns. TW19: Stanw 1B 128
Milton Gro. N11 5B 32
N16 4D 66
Milton Ho. *E2* *3J 85*
(off Roman Rd.)
E17 4C 50
SE5 *7D 102*
(off Elmington Est.)
SM1: Sutt 3J 165
Milton Lodge DA14: Sidc 4A 144
TW2: Twick 7K 113
Milton Mans. *W14* *6G 99*
(off Queen's Club Gdns.)
Milton Pk. N6 7G 47
Milton Pl. *N7* *5A 66*
(off Eastwood Cl.)
Milton Rd. CR0: Croy 7D 156
CR4: Mitc 7E 136
DA16: Well 1K 125
DA17: Belv 4G 109
E17 4C 50
HA1: Harr 4J 41
N6 7G 47
N15 4B 48
NW7 5H 29
NW9 7C 44
SE24 5B 120
SM1: Sutt 3J 165
SM6: Wall 6G 167
SW14 3K 115
SW19 6A 136
TW12: Hamp 7E 130
UB10: Ick 4D 56
W3 1K 97
W7 7K 77
Milton St. EC2 5E 8 (5D 84)
Milton Way UB7: W Dray 4B 92
Milverton Dr. UB10: Ick 4E 56
Milverton Gdns. IG3: Ilf 2K 71
Milverton Ho. SE6 3A 140
Milverton Rd. NW6 7E 62
Milverton St. SE11 6K 19 (5A 102)
Milverton Way SE9 4E 142
Milward St. E1 5H 85
Milward Wlk. SE18 6E 106
Mimosa Ho.
UB4: Yead 5A 76
Mimosa Lodge NW10 5B 62
Mimosa Rd. UB4: Yead 5A 76
Mimosa St. SW6 1H 117
Minard Rd. SE6 7G 123
Mina Rd. SE17 5E 102
SW19 1J 153
Minchenden Ct. N14 2C 32
Minchenden Cres. N14 3B 32
Minchin Ho. *E14* *6C 86*
(off Dod St.)
Mincing La. EC3 2G 15 (7E 84)
Minden Rd. SE20 1H 157
SM3: Sutt 2G 165
Minehead Rd. HA2: Harr 3E 58
SW16 5K 137
Mineral Cl. EN5: Barn 6A 20
Mineral St. SE18 4J 107
Minera M. SW1 3G 17 (4E 100)
Minerva Cl. DA14: Sidc 3J 143
SW9 7A 102
(not continuous)
Minerva Lodge N7 6K 65
Minerva Rd. E4 7J 35
KT1: King T 2F 151
NW10 4J 79
Minerva St. E2 2H 85
Minerva Wlk. EC1 7B 8 (6B 84)
Minet Av. NW10 2A 80
Minet Country Pk. 2K 93
Minet Dr. UB3: Hayes 1J 93
Minet Gdns. NW10 2A 80
UB3: Hayes 1K 93
Minet Rd. SW9 2B 120
Minford Gdns. W14 2F 99
Minford Ho. *W14* *2F 99*
(off Minford Gdns.)
Mingard Wlk. N7 2K 65
Ming St. E14 7C 86
Minimax Cl. TW14: Felt 6J 111
Ministry Way SE9 2D 142
Miniver Pl. EC4 2D 14
Mink Ct. TW4: Houn 2A 112
Minniedale KT5: Surb 5F 151
Minnow St. SE17 4E 102
Minnow Wlk. SE17 4E 102
Minories EC3 1J 15 (6F 85)
Minshaw Ct. DA14: Sidc 4K 143
Minshill St. SW8 1H 119
Minshull Pl. BR3: Beck 7C 140
Minson Rd. E9 1K 85
Minstead Gdns. SW15 7B 116
Minstead Way KT3: N Mald 6A 152
Minster Av. SM1: Sutt 2J 165
Minster Ct. EC3 2H 15
W5 4E 78
Minster Dr. CR0: Croy 4E 168
Minster Gdns. KT8: W Mole 4D 148
Minsterley Av. TW17: Shep 4G 147
Minster Pavement *EC3* *2H 15*
(off Mincing La.)
Minster Rd. BR1: Brom 7K 141
NW2 5G 63
Minster Wlk. N8 4J 47
Minstrel Gdns. KT5: Surb 4F 151
Mint Bus. Pk. E16 5K 87
Mint Cl. UB10: Hil 3D 74
Mintern Cl. N13 3G 33
Minterne Av. UB2: S'hall 4E 94
Minterne Rd. HA3: Kent 5F 43
Minterne Waye UB4: Yead 6A 76
Mintern St. N1 2D 84
Minton Ho. SE11 3J 19
Minton M. NW6 6K 63
Mint Rd. SM6: Wall 4F 167
Mint St. SE1 6C 14 (2C 102)
Mint Wlk. CR0: Croy 3C 168
Mirabel Rd. SW6 7H 99
Miranda Cl. E1 5J 85
Miranda Ct. W3 6F 79
Miranda Ho. *N1* *1G 9*
(off Crondall St.)
Miranda Rd. N19 1G 65
Mirfield St. SE7 4B 106
Miriam Rd. SE18 5J 107
Mirravale Trad. Est. RM8: Dag 7E 54
Mirren Cl. HA2: Harr 4D 58
Mirror Path SE9 3A 142
Misbourne Rd. UB10: Hil 1C 74
Missenden *SE17* *5D 102*
(off Roland Way)
Missenden Cl. TW14: Felt 1H 129

Missenden Gdns. SM4: Mord 6A **154**
Missenden Ho. NW8 .... 3C **4**
Missenden Villa Wlk. *SE17* *5D* ***102***
(*off Inville Rd.*)
Mission, The *E14* *6B* ***86***
(*off Commercial Rd.*)
Mission Gro. E17 .... 5A **50**
Mission Pl. SE15 .... 1G **121**
Mission Sq. TW8: Bford 6E **96**
Missouri Ct. HA5: Eastc 6A **40**
Mistletoe Cl. CR0: Croy 1K **169**
Mistral SE5 .... 1E **120**
Misty's Fld. KT12: Walt T 7A **148**
Mitali Pas. E1 .... 6G **85**
(not continuous)
MITCHAM 3D **154**
Mitcham Gdn. Village CR4: Mitc 5E **154**
Mitcham Ho. SE5 .... 1C **120**
Mitcham Ind. Est. CR4: Mitc 1E **154**
Mitcham La. SW16 .... 6G **137**
Mitcham Pk. CR4: Mitc 4C **154**
Mitcham Rd. CR0: Croy 6J **155**
E6 .... 3C **88**
IG3: Ilf 7K **53**
SW17 .... 5D **136**
Mitchell *NW9* *1B* ***44***
(*off The Concourse*)
Mitchellbrook Way NW10 .... 6K **61**
Mitchell Cl. DA17: Belv 3J **109**
SE2 .... 4C **108**
Mitchell Ho. *W12* *7D* ***80***
(*off White City Est.*)
Mitchell Rd. BR6: Orp 4K **173**
N13 .... 5H **33**
Mitchell's Pl. *SE21* *6E* ***120***
(*off Aysgarth Rd.*)
Mitchell St. EC1 .... 3C **8** (4C **84**)
(not continuous)
Mitchell Wlk. *E6* *5C* ***88***
(*off Allhallows Rd.*)
E6 .... 5D **88**
(Elmley Cl.)
Mitchell Way BR1: Brom 1J **159**
NW10 .... 6J **61**
Mitchison Rd. N1 .... 6D **66**
Mitchley Rd. N17 .... 3G **49**
Mitford Bldgs. *SW6* *7J* ***99***
(*off Dawes Rd.*)
Mitford Cl. KT9: Chess 6C **162**
Mitford Rd. N19 .... 2J **65**
Mitre, The E14 .... 7B **86**
Mitre Av. E17 .... 3C **50**
Mitre Cl. BR2: Brom 2H **159**
SM2: Sutt 7A **166**
TW17: Shep 6F **147**
Mitre Ct. EC2 .... 7D **8**
Mitre Ho. *SW3* *5E* ***16***
(*off King's Rd.*)
Mitre Rd. E15 .... 2G **87**
SE1 .... 6K **13** (2A **102**)
Mitre Sq. EC3 .... 1H **15** (6E **84**)
Mitre St. EC3 .... 1H **15** (6E **84**)
Mitre Way NW10 .... 4D **80**
W10 .... 4D **80**
Mitre Yd. SW3 .... 3D **16** (4C **100**)
Mizen Ct. *E14* *2C* ***104***
(*off Alpha Gro.*)
Moat, The KT3: N Mald 1A **152**
Moat Cl. BR6: Chels 6K **173**
Moat Ct. DA15: Sidc 3K **143**
SE9 .... 6D **124**
Moat Cres. N3 .... 3K **45**
Moat Cft. DA16: Well 3C **126**
Moat Dr. E13 .... 2A **88**
HA1: Harr 4G **41**
HA4: Ruis 7G **39**
Moat Farm Rd. UB5: N'olt 6D **58**
Moatfield NW6 .... 7G **63**
Moatlands Ho. *WC1* *2F* ***7***
(*off Cromer St.*)
Moat La. KT8: E Mos 3K **149**
Moat Lodge, The
HA2: Harr 2J **59**
Moat Pl. SW9 .... 3K **119**
W3 .... 6H **79**
Moat Side EN3: Pond E 4E **24**
TW13: Hanw 4A **130**
Moberly Rd. SW4 .... 7H **119**
Moberly Sports & Education Cen. ***3F 81***
(***off Chamberlayne Rd.***)
Mobil Ct. *WC2* *1H* ***13***
(*off Clement's Inn*)
MOBY DICK 4E **54**
Mocatta Ho. *E1* *4H* ***85***
(*off Brady St.*)
Modbury Gdns. NW5 .... 6E **64**
Modder Pl. SW15 .... 4F **117**
Model Bldgs. WC1 .... 2H **7**
Model Cotts. SW14 .... 4J **115**
W13 .... 2B **96**
Model Farm Cl. SE9 .... 3C **142**
Modern Ct. EC4 .... 7A **8**
Modling Ho. *E2* *2K* ***85***
(*off Mace St.*)
Moelwyn N7 .... 5H **65**
Moelyn M. HA1: Harr 5A **42**
Moffat Ct. SW19 .... 5J **135**
Moffat Ho. SE5 .... 7C **102**
Moffat Rd. CR7: Thor H 2C **156**
N13 .... 6D **32**
SW17 .... 4D **136**
Mogden La. TW7: Isle 5K **113**
Mohammedi Pk. UB5: N'olt 1E **76**
Mohawk Ho. *E3* *2A* ***86***
(*off Gernon Rd.*)
Mohmmad Khan Rd. E11 .... 1H **69**
Moineau *NW9* *1B* ***44***
(*off The Concourse*)
Moira Cl. N17 .... 2E **48**
Moira Rd. SE9 .... 4D **124**
Mokswell Ct. N10 .... 1E **46**
Moland Mead *SE16* *5K* ***103***
(*off Crane Mead*)
Molasses Ho. *SW11* *3A* ***118***
(*off Clove Hitch Quay*)
Molasses Row SW11 .... 3A **118**
Mole Abbey Gdns. KT8: W Mole 3F **149**
Mole Ct. KT19: Ewe 4J **163**
Mole Ho. *NW8* *4B* ***4***
(*off Church St. Est.*)
Molember Ct. KT8: E Mos 4J **149**
Molember Rd. KT8: E Mos 5J **149**
Molescroft SE9 .... 3G **143**
Molesey Av. KT8: W Mole 5D **148**
Molesey Dr. SM3: Cheam 2G **165**
Molesey Pk. Av. KT8: W Mole 5F **149**
Molesey Pk. Cl. KT8: E Mos 5G **149**
Molesey Pk. Rd.
KT8: W Mole, E Mos 5F **149**
Molesey Rd. KT8: W Mole 7C **148**
KT12: Walt T, W Mole 7C **148**
Molesford Rd. SW6 .... 1J **117**
Molesham Cl. KT8: W Mole 3F **149**
Molesham Way KT8: W Mole 3F **149**
Molesworth Ho. *SE17* *6B* ***102***
(*off Brandon Est.*)
Molesworth St. SE13 .... 4E **122**
Moliner Ct. BR3: Beck 7C **140**
Mollis Ho. *E3* *5C* ***86***
(*off Gale St.*)
Mollison Av.
EN3: Brim, Enf L, Enf W, Pond E
.... 4F **25**
Mollison Dr. SM6: Wall 7H **167**
Mollison Sq. *SM6: Wall* *7H* ***167***
(*off Mollison Dr.*)
Mollison Way HA8: Edg 2F **43**
Molly Huggins Cl. SW12 .... 7G **119**
Molton Ho. *N1* *1K* ***83***
(*off Barnsbury Est.*)
Molyneux Dr. SW17 .... 4F **137**
Molyneux St. W1 .... 6D **4** (5C **82**)
Monarch Cl. BR4: W W'ck 4H **171**
TW14: Felt 7G **111**
Monarch Ct. N2 .... 5B **46**
Monarch Dr. E16 .... 5B **88**
Monarch Ho. *W8* *3J* ***99***
(*off Earl's Ct. Rd.*)
W8 .... *3J* ***99***
(*off Kensington High St.*)
Monarch M. E17 .... 6D **50**
SW16 .... 5A **138**
Monarch Pde. CR4: Mitc 2D **154**
Monarch Pl. IG9: Buck H 2F **37**
Monarch Rd. DA17: Belv 3G **109**
Monarchs Way HA4: Ruis 1F **57**
Monarch Way IG2: Ilf 6H **53**
Mona Rd. SE15 .... 2J **121**
Monastery Gdns. EN2: Enf 2J **23**
Mona St. E16 .... 5H **87**
Monaveen Gdns. KT8: W Mole 3F **149**
Moncks Row SW18 .... 6H **117**
Monck St. SW1 .... 2D **18** (3H **101**)
Monckton Ct. *W14* *3H* ***99***
(*off Strangways Ter.*)
Monclar Rd. SE5 .... 4D **120**
Moncorvo Cl. SW7 .... 7C **10** (2C **100**)
Moncrieff Cl. E6 .... 6C **88**
Moncrieff Pl. SE15 .... 2G **121**
Moncrieff St. SE15 .... 2G **121**
Monday All. *N16* *2F* ***67***
(*off High St.*)
Mondial Way UB3: Harl 7E **92**
Monega Rd. E7 .... 6A **70**
E12 .... 6A **70**
Monet Ct. *SE16* *5H* ***103***
(*off Stubbs Dr.*)
Moneyer Ho. *N1* *1E* ***8***
(*off Fairbank Est.*)
Money La. UB7: W Dray 3A **92**
Mongers Almshouses *E9* *7K* ***67***
(*off Church Cres.*)
Monica Ct. EN1: Enf 5K **23**
Monica James Ho. DA14: Sidc 3A **144**
Monica Shaw Ct. *NW1* *1D* ***6***
(*off Purchese St., not continuous*)
Monier Rd. E3 .... 7C **68**
Monivea Rd. BR3: Beck 7B **140**
Monk Ct. W12 .... 1C **98**
Monk Dr. E16 .... 7J **87**
MONKEN HADLEY 2C **20**
Monkfrith Av. N14 .... 6A **22**
Monkfrith Cl. N14 .... 7A **22**
Monkfrith Way N14 .... 7K **21**
Monkham's Av. IG8: Wfd G 5E **36**
Monkham's Dr. IG8: Wfd G 5E **36**
Monkham's La. IG8: Wfd G 5D **36**
IG9: Buck H 3E **36**
Monkleigh Rd. SM4: Mord 3G **153**
Monk Pas. *E16* *7J* ***87***
(*off Monk Dr.*)
Monks Av. EN5: New Bar 6F **21**
KT8: W Mole 5D **148**
Monks Cl. EN2: Enf 2H **23**
HA2: Harr 2E **58**
HA4: Ruis 4B **58**
SE2 .... 4D **108**
Monks Cres. KT12: Walt T 7K **147**
Monksdene Gdns. SM1: Sutt 3K **165**
Monks Dr. W3 .... 5G **79**
Monks Hill Sports Cen. **7K 169**
MONKS ORCHARD 7A **158**
Monks Orchard Rd. BR3: Beck 1C **170**
Monks Pk. HA9: Wemb 6H **61**
Monks Pk. Gdns. HA9: Wemb 7H **61**
Monks Rd. EN2: Enf 2G **23**
Monk St. SE18 .... 4E **106**
Monks Way BR3: Beck 6C **158**
BR5: Farnb 1G **173**
NW11 .... 4H **45**
UB7: Harm 6A **92**
Monkswood Gdns. IG5: Ilf 3E **52**
Monkton Ho. E5 .... 5H **67**
SE16 .... *2K* ***103***
(*off Wolfe Cres.*)
Monkton Rd. DA16: Well 2K **125**
Monkton St. SE11 .... 3K **19** (4A **102**)
Monkville Av. NW11 .... 4H **45**
Monkville Pde. NW11 .... 4H **45**
Monkwell Sq. EC2 .... 6D **8** (5C **84**)
Monmouth Av. E18 .... 3K **51**
KT1: Ham W 7C **132**
Monmouth Cl. CR4: Mitc 4J **155**
DA16: Well 4A **126**
W4 .... 3J **97**
Monmouth Ct. *W7* *5K* ***77***
(*off Copley Cl.*)
Monmouth Gro. TW8 .... 4E **96**
Monmouth Pl. *W2* *6K* ***81***
(*off Monmouth Rd.*)
Monmouth Rd. E6 .... 3D **88**
N9 .... 2C **34**
RM9: Dag 5F **73**
UB3: Harl 4G **93**
W2 .... 6J **81**
Monmouth St. WC2 .... 1E **12** (6J **83**)
Monnery Rd. N19 .... 3G **65**
Monnow Rd. SE1 .... 5G **103**
Mono La. TW13: Felt 2K **129**
Monoux Almshouses E17 .... 4D **50**
Monoux Gro. E17 .... 1C **50**
Monroe Cres. EN1: Enf 1C **24**
Monroe Dr. SW14 .... 5H **115**
Monroe Ho. *NW8* *2D* ***4***
(*off Lorne Cl.*)
Monro Gdns. HA3: Hrw W 7D **26**
Monro Way E5 .... 4G **67**
Monsell Ct. N4 .... 3B **66**
Monsell Rd. N4 .... 3A **66**
Monson Rd. NW10 .... 2C **80**
SE14 .... 7K **103**
Mons Way BR2: Brom 6C **160**
Montacute Rd. CR0: New Ad 7E **170**
SE6 .... 7B **122**
SM4: Mord 6B **154**
WD23: Bushy 1E **26**
Montagu Ct. *W1* *6F* ***5***
(*off Montagu Sq.*)
Montagu Cres. N18 .... 4C **34**
Montague Av. SE4 .... 4B **122**
W7 .... 1K **95**
Montague Cl. KT12: Walt T 7K **147**
SE1 .... 4E **14** (1D **102**)
Montague Ct. DA15: Sidc 3A **144**
Montague Gdns. W3 .... 7G **79**
Montague Ho. *E16* *1K* ***105***
(*off Wesley Av.*)
N1 .... *1E* ***84***
(*off New Era Est.*)
Montague Pas. UB8: Uxb 7A **56**
Montague Pl. WC1 .... 5D **6** (5H **83**)
Montague Rd. CR0: Croy 1B **168**
E8 .... 5G **67**
E11 .... 2H **69**
N8 .... 5K **47**
N15 .... 4G **49**
SW19 .... 7K **135**
TW3: Houn 3F **113**
TW10: Rich 6E **114**
UB2: S'hall 4C **94**
UB8: Uxb 7A **56**
W7 .... 1K **95**
W13 .... 6B **78**
Montague Sq. SE15 .... 7J **103**
Montague St. EC1 .... 6C **8** (5C **84**)
WC1 .... 5E **6** (5J **83**)
Montague Ter. BR2: Brom 4H **159**
Montague Walks HA0: Wemb 1F **79**
Montague Waye UB2: S'hall 3C **94**
Montagu Gdns. N18 .... 4C **34**
SM6: Wall 4G **167**
Montagu Mans. W1 .... 5F **5** (5D **82**)
Montagu M. Nth. W1 .... 6F **5** (5D **82**)
Montagu M. Sth. W1 .... 7F **5** (6D **82**)
Montagu M. W. W1 .... 7F **5** (6D **82**)
Montagu Pl. W1 .... 6E **4** (5D **82**)
Montagu Rd. N9 .... 4C **34**
N18 .... 5C **34**
NW4 .... 6C **44**
Montagu Rd. Ind. Est. N18 .... 4D **34**
Montagu Row W1 .... 6F **5** (5D **82**)
Montagu Sq. W1 .... 6F **5** (5D **82**)

Montagu St. W1 . . . . .7F **5** (6D **82**)
Montaigne Cl. SW1 . . . . .4D **18** (4H **101**)
Montalt Rd. IG8: Wfd G 4C **36**
Montana Bldg. *SE10* *1D 122*
(off Deal's Gateway)
Montana Gdns. SE26 . . . . .5B **140**
SM1: Sutt 5A **166**
Montana Rd. SW17 . . . . .3E **136**
SW20 . . . . .1E **152**
Montbelle Rd. SE9 . . . . .3F **143**
Montcalm Cl. BR2: Hayes 6J **159**
UB4: Yead 3K **75**
Montcalm Ho. E14 . . . . .4B **104**
Montcalm Rd. SE7 . . . . .7B **106**
Montclare St. E2 . . . . .3J **9** (4F **85**)
Monteagle Av. IG11: Bark 6G **71**
Monteagle Ct. N1 . . . . .2E **84**
Monteagle Way E5 . . . . .3G **67**
SE15 .3H **121**
Montefiore Ct. N16 . . . . .1F **67**
Montefiore St. SW8 . . . . .2F **119**
Montego Cl. SE24 . . . . .4A **120**
Montem Rd. KT3: N Mald 4A **152**
SE23 .7B **122**
Montem St. N4 . . . . .1K **65**
Montenotte Rd. N8 . . . . .5G **47**
Monterey Cl. DA5: Bexl 2J **145**
NW7 . . . . .5F **29**
Monterey Pl. Shop. Cen. NW7 . . . . . . .5F **29**
Montesole Ct. HA5: Pinn 2A **40**
Montesquieu Ter. *E16* *6H 87*
(off Clarkson Rd.)
Montevetro SW11 . . . . .1B **118**
Montford Pl. SE11 . . . . .6J **19** (5A **102**)
Montford Rd. TW16: Sun 4J **147**
Montfort Ho. *E2* *3J 85*
(off Victoria Pk. Sq.)
E14 . . . .*3E 104*
(off Galbraith St.)
Montfort Pl. SW19 . . . . .1F **135**
Montgolfier Wlk. UB5: N'olt 3C **76**
Montgomerie M. SE23 . . . . .7J **121**
Montgomery Cl. CR4: Mitc 4J **155**
DA15: Sidc 6K **125**
SM2: Sutt 7B **166**
Montgomery Ct. *CR2: S Croy* *5E 168*
(off Birdhurst Rd.)
W4 . . . . .7J **97**
Montgomery Lodge *E1* *4J 85*
(off Cleveland Gro.)
Montgomery Rd. HA8: Edg 6A **28**
W4 . . . . .4J **97**
Montgomery St. E14 . . . . .1D **104**
Montholme Rd. SW11 . . . . .6D **118**
Monthope Rd. E1 . . . . .6K **9** (5G **85**)
Montolieu Gdns. SW15 . . . . .5D **116**
Montpelier Av. DA5: Bexl 7D **126**
W5 . . . . .5C **78**
Montpelier Cl. UB10: Hil 1C **74**
Montpelier Ct. *BR2: Brom* *4H 159*
(off Westmoreland Rd.)
W5 . . . . .5D **78**
Montpelier Gdns. E6 . . . . .3B **88**
RM6: Chad H 7C **54**
Montpelier Gro. NW5 . . . . .5G **65**
Montpelier M. SW7 . . . . .1D **16** (3C **100**)
Montpelier Pl. E1 . . . . .6J **85**
SW7 . . . . .1D **16** (3C **100**)
Montpelier Ri. HA9: Wemb 1D **60**
NW11 .7G **45**
Montpelier Rd. N3 . . . . .1A **46**
SE15 .1H **121**
SM1: Sutt 4A **166**
W5 . . . . .5D **78**
Montpelier Row SE3 . . . . .2H **123**
TW1: Twick 7C **114**
Montpelier Sq. SW7 . . . . . . .7D **10** (2C **100**)
Montpelier St. SW7 . . . . . . .1D **16** (3C **100**)
Montpelier Ter. SW7 . . . . . . .7D **10** (2C **100**)
Montpelier Va. SE3 . . . . .2H **123**
Montpelier Wlk. SW7 . . . . . .1D **16** (3C **100**)
Montpelier Way NW11 . . . . .7G **45**
Montpellier Ct. KT12: Walt T 6J **147**
Montrave Rd. SE20 . . . . .6J **139**
Montreal Pl. WC2 . . . . .2G **13** (7K **83**)
Montreal Rd. IG1: Ilf 7G **53**
Montrell Rd. SW2 . . . . .1J **137**
Montrose Av. DA15: Sidc 7A **126**
DA16: Well 3H **125**
HA8: Edg 2J **43**
NW6 . . . . .2G **81**
TW2: Whit 7F **113**
Montrose Cl. DA16: Well 3K **125**
IG8: Wfd G 4D **36**
TW15: Ashf 6E **128**
Montrose Ct. HA1: Harr 5F **41**
NW9 . . . . .2J **43**
NW11 .4H **45**
SE6 . . . . .2H **141**
SW7 . . . . .7B **10** (2B **100**)
Montrose Cres. HA0: Wemb 6E **60**
N12 . . . . .6F **31**
Montrose Gdns. CR4: Mitc 2D **154**
SM1: Sutt 2K **165**
Montrose Ho. E14 . . . . .3C **104**
SW1 . . . .*7H 11*
(off Montrose Pl.)
Montrose Pl. SW1 . . . . .7H **11** (2E **100**)
Montrose Rd. HA3: W'stone 2J **41**
TW14: Bedf 6F **111**
Montrose Wlk. HA7: Stan 6G **27**
Montrose Way SE23 . . . . .1K **139**
Montserrat Av. IG8: Wfd G 7A **36**
Montserrat Cl. SE19 . . . . .5D **138**
Montserrat Rd. SW15 . . . . .4G **117**
Monument, The *2F 15*
(off Monument St.)
Monument Gdns. SE13 . . . . .5E **122**
Monument St. EC3 . . . . .2F **15** (7D **84**)
Monument Way N17 . . . . .3F **49**
Monza St. E1 .7J **85**
Moodkee St. SE16 . . . . .3J **103**
Moody Rd. SE15 . . . . .1F **121**
Moody St. E1 .3K **85**
Moon Ct. SE12 . . . . .4J **123**
Moon La. EN5: Barn 3C **20**
Moon St. N1 .1B **84**
Moorcroft HA8: Edg 1H **43**
Moorcroft Gdns. BR2: Brom 5C **160**
Moorcroft La. UB8: Hil 5C **74**
Moorcroft Rd. SW16 . . . . .3J **137**
Moorcroft Way HA5: Pinn 5C **40**
Moordown SE18 . . . . .7F **107**
Moore Cl. CR4: Mitc 2F **155**
SW14 .3J **115**
Moore Ct. *N1* *1B 84*
(off Gaskin St.)
Moore Cres. RM9: Dag 1B **90**
Moorefield Rd. N17 . . . . .2F **49**
Moorehead Way SE3 . . . . .3J **123**
Moore Ho. *E1* *7J 85*
(off Cable St.)
E2 . . . .*3J 85*
(off Roman Rd.)
E14 . . . . .2C **104**
N8 . . . .*4J 47*
(off Pembroke Rd.)
SE10 . . . .*5H 105*
(off Armitage Rd.)
Mooreland Rd. BR1: Brom 7H **141**
Moore Pk. Ct. *SW6* *7K 99*
(off Fulham Rd.)
Moore Pk. Rd. SW6 . . . . .7J **99**
Moore Rd. SE19 . . . . .6C **138**
Moore St. SW3 . . . . .3E **16** (4D **100**)
Moore Wlk. E7 . . . . .4J **69**
Moore Way SM2: Sutt 7J **165**
Moorey Cl. E15 . . . . .1H **87**
Moorfield Av. W5 . . . . .4D **78**
Moorfield Rd. EN3: Enf H 1D **24**
KT9: Chess 5E **162**
UB8: Cowl 6A **74**
Moorfields EC2 . . . . .6E **8** (5D **84**)
Moorfields Highwalk *EC2* *6E 8*
(off Moorfields, not continuous)
Moorgate EC2 . . . . .7E **8** (6D **84**)
Moorgate Pl. EC2 . . . . .7E **8**
Moorgreen Ho. EC1 . . . . .1A **8**
Moorhouse NW9 . . . . .1B **44**
Moorhouse Rd. HA3: Kent 3D **42**
W2 . . . . .6J **81**
Moorings, The *E16* *5A 88*
(off Prince Regent La.)
Moorings Ho. TW8: Bford 7C **96**
Moorland Cl. RM5: Col R 1H **55**
TW2: Whit 7E **112**
Moorland Rd. SW9 . . . . .4B **120**
Moorlands UB5: N'olt 1C **76**
Moorlands Av. NW7 . . . . .6J **29**
Moor La. EC2 . . . . .6E **8** (5D **84**)
(not continuous)
KT9: Chess 4E **162**
Moormead Dr. KT19: Ewe 5A **164**
Moor Mead Rd. TW1: Twick 6A **114**
Moor Pk. Gdns. KT2: King T 7A **134**
Moor Pl. EC2 . . . . .6E **8** (5D **84**)
Moorside Rd. BR1: Brom 3G **141**
Moor St. W1 . . . . .1D **12** (6H **83**)
Moot Ct. NW9 . . . . .5G **43**
Moran Ho. *E1* *1H 103*
(off Wapping La.)
Morant Pl. N22 . . . . .1K **47**
Morant St. E14 . . . . .7C **86**
Mora Rd. NW2 . . . . .4E **62**
Mora St. EC1 . . . . .2D **8** (3C **84**)
Morat St. SW9 . . . . .1K **119**
Moravian Cl. SW3 . . . . .7A **16** (6B **100**)
Moravian Pl. SW10 . . . . .6B **100**
Moravian St. E2 . . . . .2J **85**
Moray Av. UB3: Hayes 1H **93**
Moray Cl. HA8: Edg 2C **28**
RM1: Rom 1K **55**
Moray Ct. *CR2: S Croy* *5C 168*
(off Warham Rd.)
Moray Ho. *E1* *4A 86*
(off Harford St.)
Moray M. N7 .2K **65**
Moray Rd. N4 .2K **65**
Moray Way RM1: Rom 1K **55**
Mordaunt Gdns. RM9: Dag 7E **72**
Mordaunt Ho. *NW10* *1K 79*
(off Stracey Rd.)
Mordaunt Rd. NW10 . . . . .1K **79**
Mordaunt St. SW9 . . . . .3K **119**
MORDEN 3K **153**
Morden Ct. SM4: Mord 4K **153**
Morden Ct. Pde. SM4: Mord 4K **153**
Morden Gdns. CR4: Mitc 4B **154**
UB6: G'frd 5K **59**
Morden Hall Rd. SM4: Mord 3K **153**
Morden Hill SE13 . . . . .2E **122**
(not continuous)
Morden Ho. SM4: Mord 4J **153**
Morden La. SE13 . . . . .1E **122**
MORDEN PARK 6G **153**
Morden Pk. Pool 6H **153**
Morden Rd. CR4: Mitc 4A **154**
RM6: Chad H 7E **54**
SE3 . . . . .2J **123**
SM4: Mord 4A **154**
SW19 .1K **153**
Morden Rd. M. SE3 . . . . .2J **123**
Morden St. SE13 . . . . .1D **122**
Morden Way SM3: Sutt 7J **153**
Morden Wharf *SE10* *3G 105*
(off Morden Wharf Rd.)
Morden Wharf Rd. SE10 . . . . .3G **105**
Mordern Ho. NW1 . . . . .3D **4**
Mordon Rd. IG3: Ilf 7K **53**
Mordred Rd. SE6 . . . . .2G **141**
Morecambe Cl. E1 . . . . .5K **85**
Morecambe Gdns. HA7: Stan 4J **27**
Morecambe St. SE17 . . . . .4C **102**
Morecambe Ter. *N18* *4J 33*
(off Gt. Cambridge Rd.)
More Cl. E16 .6H **87**
W14 . . . . .4F **99**
Morecoombe Cl. KT2: King T 7H **133**
Moree Way N18 . . . . .4B **34**
Moreland Cotts. *E3* *2C 86*
(off Fairfield Rd.)
Moreland Ct. NW2 . . . . .3J **63**
Moreland St. EC1 . . . . .1B **8** (3B **84**)
Moreland Way E4 . . . . .3J **35**
Morella Rd. SW12 . . . . .7D **118**
Morell Cl. EN5: New Bar 3F **21**
Morello Av. UB8: Hil 5D **74**
More London Pl. SE1 . . . . . . .5G **15** (1E **102**)
More London Riverside SE1 . . . . .1E **102**
Moremead Rd. SE6 . . . . .4B **140**
Morena St. SE6 . . . . .7D **122**
Moresby Av. KT5: Surb 7H **151**
Moresby Rd. E5 . . . . .1H **67**
Moresby Wlk. SW8 . . . . .2G **119**
More's Gdn. *SW3* *6B 100*
(off Cheyne Wlk.)
Moreton Av. TW7: Isle 1J **113**
Moreton Cl. E5 . . . . .2H **67**
N15 . . . . .6D **48**
NW7 . . . . .6K **29**
SW1 . . . . .5B **18**
Moreton Gdns. IG8: Wfd G 5H **37**
Moreton Ho. SE16 . . . . .3H **103**
Moreton Pl. SW1 . . . . .5B **18** (5G **101**)
Moreton Rd. CR2: S Croy 5D **168**
KT4: Wor Pk 2C **164**
N15 . . . . .6D **48**
Moreton St. SW1 . . . . .5B **18** (5G **101**)
Moreton Ter. SW1 . . . . .5B **18** (5G **101**)
Moreton Ter. M. Nth.
SW1 . . . . .5B **18** (5G **101**)
Moreton Ter. M. Sth.
SW1 . . . . .5B **18** (5G **101**)
Moreton Twr. W3 . . . . .1H **97**
Morford Cl. HA4: Ruis 7K **39**
Morford Way HA4: Ruis 7K **39**
Morgan Av. E17 . . . . .4F **51**
Morgan Cl. RM10: Dag 7G **73**
Morgan Ct. SM5: Cars 4D **166**
TW15: Ashf 5D **128**
Morgan Ho. *SW1* *4B 18*
(off Vauxhall Bri. Rd.)
SW8 . . . .*1G 119*
(off Wadhurst Rd.)
Morgan Mans. *N7* *5A 66*
(off Morgan Rd.)
Morgan Rd. BR1: Brom 7J **141**
N7 . . . . .5A **66**
TW11: Tedd 6J **131**
W10 . . . . .5H **81**
Morgan's La. UB3: Hayes 5F **75**
Morgan St. E3 . . . . .3A **86**
E16 . . . . .5H **87**
Morgan Wlk. BR3: Beck 4D **158**
Morgan Way IG8: Wfd G 6H **37**
Moriatry Cl. N7 . . . . .4J **65**
Moriaty Cl. BR1: Brom 4E **160**
Morie St. SW18 . . . . .5K **117**
Morieux Rd. E10 . . . . .1B **68**
Moring Rd. SW17 . . . . .4E **136**
Morkyns Wlk. SE21 . . . . .3E **138**
Morland Av. CR0: Croy 1E **168**
Morland Cl. CR4: Mitc 3C **154**
NW11 .1K **63**
TW12: Hamp 5D **130**
Morland Ct. *W12* *2D 98*
(off Coningham Rd.)
Morland Est. E8 . . . . .7G **67**
Morland Gdns. NW10 . . . . .7K **61**
UB1: S'hall 1F **95**
Morland Ho. *NW1* *1B 6*
(off Werrington St.)
NW6 . . . . .1J **81**
SW1 . . . .*3E 18*
(off Marsham St.)
W11 . . . .*6G 81*
(off Lancaster Rd.)
Morland M. N1 . . . . .7A **66**
Morland Rd. CR0: Croy 1E **168**
E17 . . . . .5K **49**
HA3: Kent 5E **42**
IG1: Ilf .2F **71**

Morland Rd. RM10: Dag 7G 73
SE20 6K 139
SM1: Sutt 5A 166
Morley Av. E4 7A 36
N18 4B 34
N22 2A 48
Morley Cl. BR6: Farnb 2F 173
Morley Ct. BR2: Brom 4H 159
E4 5G 35
Morley Cres. HA4: Ruis 2A 58
HA8: Edg 2D 28
Morley Cres. E. HA7: Stan 2C 42
Morley Cres. W. HA7: Stan 3C 42
Morley Hill EN2: Enf 1J 23
Morley Rd. BR7: Chst 1G 161
E10 1E 68
E15 2H 87
IG11: Bark 1H 89
RM6: Chad H 5E 54
SE13 4E 122
SM3: Sutt 1H 165
TW1: Twick 6D 114
Morley St. SE1 1K 19 (3A 102)
Morna Rd. SE5 2C 120
Morning La. E9 6J 67
Morningside Rd. KT4: Wor Pk 2E 164
Mornington Av. BR1: Brom 3A 160
IG1: Ilf 7E 52
W14 4H 99
Mornington Av. Mans. *W14* *4H 99*
(off Mornington Av.)
Mornington Cl. IG8: Wfd G 4D 36
Mornington Ct. DA5: Bexl 1K 145
NW1 *2G 83*
(off Mornington Cres.)
Mornington Cres. NW1 2G 83
TW5: Cran 1K 111
Mornington Gro. E3 3C 86
Mornington M. SE5 1C 120
Mornington Pl. NW1 2G 83
SE8 *7B 104*
(off Mornington Rd.)
Mornington Rd. E4 7K 25
E11 7H 51
(not continuous)
IG8: Wfd G 4C 36
SE8 7B 104
TW15: Ashf 5E 128
UB6: G'frd 5F 77
Mornington Sports & Leisure Cen.
1F 83
(off Stanmore Pl.)
Mornington St. NW1 2F 83
Mornington Ter. NW1 1F 83
Mornington Wlk. TW10: Ham 4C 132
Morocco St. SE1 7G 15 (2E 102)
Morocco Wharf *E1* *1H 103*
(off Wapping High St.)
Morpeth Gro. E9 1K 85
Morpeth Mans. *SW1* *2A 18*
(off Morpeth Ter.)
Morpeth Rd. E9 1K 85
Morpeth St. E2 3J 85
Morpeth Ter. SW1 2A 18 (3G 101)
Morpeth Wlk. N17 7C 34
Morrab Gdns. IG3: Ilf 3K 71
Morrel Ct. *E2* *2G 85*
(off Goldsmiths Row)
Morrells Yd. *SE11* *5K 19*
(off Cleaver St.)
Morris Av. E12 5D 70
Morris Blitz Ct. N16 4F 67
Morris Cl. BR6: Orp 3J 173
CR0: Croy 5A 158
Morris Ct. E4 3J 35
Morris Gdns. SW18 7J 117
Morris Ho. *E2* *3J 85*
(off Roman Rd.)
NW8 *4C 4*
(off Salisbury St.)
Morrish Rd. SW2 7J 119
Morrison Av. E4 6H 35
N17 3E 48
Morrison Bldgs. Nth. *E1* *6G 85*
(off Commercial Rd.)
Morrison Ct. *EN5: Barn* *4B 20*
(off Manor Way)
N12 7H 31
Morrison Ho. *SW2* *1A 138*
(off High Trees)
Morrison Rd. IG11: Bark 2E 90
RM9: Bark, Dag 2D 90
SW9 2A 120
UB4: Yead 3K 75
Morrison St. SW11 3E 118
Morris Pl. N4 2A 66
Morris Rd. E14 5D 86
E15 4G 69
RM8: Dag 2F 73
TW7: Isle 3K 113
Morriss Ho. *SE16* *2H 103*
(off Cherry Gdn. St.)
Morris St. E1 6H 85
Morritt Ho. *HA0: Wemb* *5D 60*
(off Talbot Rd.)
Morse Cl. E13 3J 87
Morshead Mans. *W9* *3J 81*
(off Morshead Rd.)
Morshead Rd. W9 3J 81
Morson Rd. EN3: Pond E 6F 25
Morston Gdns. SE9 4D 142
Mortain Ho. *SE16* *4H 103*
(off Roseberry St.)
Morten Cl. SW4 6H 119
Morteyne Rd. N17 1D 48
Mortgramit Sq. SE18 3E 106
Mortham St. E15 1G 87
Mortimer Cl. NW2 2H 63
SW16 2H 137
Mortimer Ct. *NW8* *1A 4*
(off Abbey Rd.)
Mortimer Cres. KT4: Wor Pk 3K 163
NW6 1K 81
Mortimer Dr. EN1: Enf 6J 23
Mortimer Est. *NW6* *1K 81*
(off Mortimer Pl.)
Mortimer Ho. W11 1F 99
W14 *4G 99*
(off North End Rd.)
Mortimer Mkt. WC1 4B 6 (4G 83)
Mortimer Pl. NW6 1K 81
Mortimer Rd. CR4: Mitc 1D 154
DA8: Erith 6K 109
E6 3D 88
N1 7E 66
(not continuous)
NW10 3E 80
W13 6C 78
Mortimer Sq. W11 7F 81
Mortimer St. W1 7K 5 (6G 83)
Mortimer Ter. NW5 4F 65
MORTLAKE 3K 115
Mortlake Cl. CR0: Bedd 3J 167
Mortlake Crematorium TW9: Rich 2H 115
Mortlake Dr. CR4: Mitc 1C 154
Mortlake High St. SW14 3K 115
Mortlake Rd. E16 6K 87
IG1: Ilf 4G 71
TW9: Kew, Rich 7G 97
Mortlake Ter. *TW9: Kew* *7G 97*
(off Mortlake Rd.)
Mortlock Cl. SE15 1H 121
Mortlock Ct. E7 4B 70
Morton Cl. SM6: Wall 7K 167
UB8: Hil 4B 74
Morton Ct. UB5: N'olt 5G 59
Morton Cres. N14 4C 32
Morton Gdns. SM6: Wall 5G 167
Morton Ho. SE17 6B 102
Morton M. SW5 4K 99
Morton Pl. SE1 2J 19 (3A 102)
Morton Rd. E15 7H 69
N1 7C 66
SM4: Mord 5B 154
Morton Way N14 3B 32
Morvale Cl. DA17: Belv 4F 109
Morval Rd. SW2 5A 120
Morven Rd. SW17 3D 136
Morville Ho. *SW18* *6B 118*
(off Fitzhugh Gro.)
Morville St. E3 2C 86
Morwell St. WC1 6C 6 (5H 83)
Moscow Mans. *W8* *4J 99*
(off Cromwell Rd.)
Moscow Pl. W2 7K 81
Moscow Rd. W2 7J 81
Mosedale *NW1* *2K 5*
(off Cumberland Mkt.)
Moseley Row *SE10* *4H 105*
(off School Bank Rd.)
Moselle Av. N22 2A 48
Moselle Cl. N8 3K 47
Moselle Ho. *N17* *7A 34*
(off William St.)
Moselle Pl. N17 7A 34
Moselle St. N17 7A 34
Mosque Ter. *E1* *5G 85*
(off Fieldgate St.)
Mosque Twr. *E1* *5G 85*
(off Fieldgate St.)
E3 *2A 86*
(off Ford St.)
Mosquito Cl. *SM6: Wall* *7J 167*
(off Mollison Dr.)
Mossborough Cl. N12 6E 30
Mossbury Rd. SW11 3C 118
Moss Cl. E1 5G 85
HA5: Pinn 2D 40
N9 1B 34
Mossdown Cl. DA17: Belv 4C 109
Mossford Ct. IG6: Ilf 3F 53
Mossford Grn. IG6: Ilf 3F 53
Mossford La. IG6: Ilf 2F 53
Mossford St. E3 4B 86
Moss Gdns. CR2: Sels 7K 169
TW13: Felt 2J 129
Moss Hall Ct. N12 6E 30
Moss Hall Cres. N12 6E 30
Moss Hall Gro. N12 6E 30
Mossington Gdns. SE16 4J 103
Moss La. HA5: Pinn 1C 40
Mosslea Rd. BR2: Brom 5B 160
BR6: Farnb 3G 173
SE20 6J 139
(not continuous)
Mossop St. SW3 3D 16 (4C 100)
Moss Rd. RM10: Dag 7G 73
Mossville Gdns. SM4: Mord 3H 153
Mosswell Ho. N10 1E 46
Moston Cl. UB3: Harl 5H 93
Mostyn Av. HA9: Wemb 5F 61
Mostyn Gdns. NW10 3F 81
Mostyn Gro. E3 2C 86
Mostyn Rd. HA8: Edg 7F 29
SW9 1A 120
SW19 1H 153
Mosul Way BR2: Brom 6C 160
Motcomb St. SW1 1G 17 (3E 100)
Moth Cl. SM6: Wall 7J 167
Mothers Sq. *E5* *4H 67*
(off Hana M.)
Motley Av. EC2 4G 9
Motley St. SW8 2G 119
MOTSPUR PARK 6C 152
Motspur Pk. KT3: N Mald 6B 152
MOTTINGHAM 2C 142
Mottingham Gdns. SE9 1B 142
Mottingham La. SE9 1A 142
SE12 1A 142
Mottingham Rd. N9 6E 24
SE9 2C 142
Mottisfont Rd. SE2 3A 108
Motts La. RM8: Dag 2F 73
Mott St. E4 1K 25
Moules Ct. SE5 7C 102
Moulins Rd. E9 7J 67
Moulsford Ho. N7 5H 65
W2 *5J 81*
(off Brunel Est.)
Moulton Av. TW3: Houn 2C 112
Mound, The SE9 3E 142
Moundfield Rd. N16 6G 49
Mounsey Ho. *W10* *3G 81*
(off Third Av.)
Mount, The *CR2: S Croy* *5C 168*
(off Warham Rd.)
DA6: Bex 5H 127
E5 2H 67
(not continuous)
HA9: Wemb 2H 61
KT3: N Mald 3B 152
KT4: Wor Pk 4D 164
N20 2F 31
NW3 3A 64
UB5: N'olt 5F 59
W3 1J 97
W8 *1J 99*
(off Bedford Gdns.)
Mountacre Cl. SE26 4F 139
Mt. Adon Pk. SE22 7G 121
Mountague Pl. E14 7E 86
Mountain Ho. SE11 4H 19 (4K 101)
Mt. Angelus Rd. SW15 7B 116
Mt. Ararat Rd. TW10: Rich 5E 114
Mt. Arlington *BR2: Brom* *2G 159*
(off Pk. Hill Rd.)
Mt. Ash Rd. SE26 3H 139
Mount Av. E4 3H 35
UB1: S'hall 6E 76
W5 5C 78
Mountbatten Cl. SE18 6J 107
SE19 5E 138
Mountbatten Ct. IG9: Buck H 2G 37
SE16 *1J 103*
(off Rotherhithe St.)
Mountbatten Gdns. BR3: Beck 4A 158
Mountbatten Ho. *N6* *7E 46*
(off Hillcrest)
Mountbatten M. SW18 7A 118
Mountbel Rd. HA7: Stan 1A 42
Mt. Carmel Chambers *W8* *2J 99*
(off Dukes La.)
Mount Cl. BR1: Brom 1C 160
EN4: Cockf 4K 21
SM5: Cars 7E 166
W5 5C 78
Mountcombe Cl. KT6: Surb 7E 150
Mount Ct. BR4: W W'ck 2G 171
SW15 3G 117
Mt. Culver Av. DA14: Sidc 6D 144
Mount Dr. DA6: Bex 5E 126
HA2: Harr 5D 40
HA9: Wemb 2J 61
Mountearl Gdns. SW16 3K 137
Mt. Eaton Ct. *W5* *5C 70*
(off Mount Av.)
Mt. Echo Av. E4 2J 35
Mt. Echo Dr. E4 1J 35
Mt. Ephraim La. SW16 3H 137
Mt. Ephraim Rd. SW16 3H 137
Mount Felix KT12: Walt T 7H 147
Mountfield Cl. SE6 7F 123
Mountfield Rd. E6 2E 88
N3 3H 45
W5 6D 78
Mountfield Ter. SE6 7F 123
Mountford Rd. E8 5G 67
Mountfort Cres. N1 7A 66
Mountfort Ter. N1 7A 66
Mount Gdns. SE26 3H 139
Mount Gro. HA8: Edg 3D 28
Mountgrove Rd. N5 3B 66
Mt. Holme KT7: T Ditt 7B 150
Mounthurst Rd. BR2: Hayes 7H 159
Mountington Pk. Cl. HA3: Kent 6D 42
Mountjoy Cl. *EC2* *6D 8*
(off Thomas More Highwalk)
SE2 2B 108
Mountjoy Ho. EC2 6C 8
Mount Lodge N6 6G 47
Mount M. TW12: Hamp 1F 149
Mount Mills EC1 2B 8 (3B 84)

Mt. Nod Rd.—Myatt Rd.

Mt. Nod Rd. SW16 ... 3K **137**
Mt. Olive Ct. W7 ... 2J **95**
Mount Pde. EN4: Cockf ... 4H **21**
Mount Pk. SM5: Cars ... 7E **166**
Mount Pk. Av.
CR2: S Croy ... 7B **168**
HA1: Harr ... 2H **59**
Mount Pk. Cres. W5 ... 6D **78**
Mount Pk. Rd. HA1: Harr ... 3H **59**
HA5: Eastc ... 5J **39**
W5 ... 5D **78**
Mount Pl. W3 ... 1H **97**
Mt. Pleasant EN4: Cockf ... 4H **21**
HA0: Wemb ... 1E **78**
HA4: Ruis ... 2A **58**
IG1: Ilf ... 5G **71**
*N14 ... 7C **22***
(off The Wells)
SE27 ... 4C **138**
WC1 ... 4J **7** (4A **84**)
Mt. Pleasant Cres. N4 ... 1K **65**
Mt. Pleasant Hill E5 ... 2H **67**
Mt. Pleasant La. E5 ... 1H **67**
Mt. Pleasant Pl. SE18 ... 4H **107**
Mt. Pleasant Rd. E17 ... 2A **50**
KT3: N Mald ... 3J **151**
N17 ... 2E **48**
NW10 ... 7E **62**
SE13 ... 6D **122**
W5 ... 4C **78**
Mt. Pleasant Vs. N4 ... 7K **47**
Mt. Pleasant Wlk.
DA5: Bexl ... 5J **127**
Mount Rd. CR4: Mitc ... 2B **154**
DA6: Bex ... 5D **126**
EN4: E Barn ... 5H **21**
KT3: N Mald ... 3K **151**
KT9: Chess ... 5F **163**
NW2 ... 3D **62**
NW4 ... 6C **44**
RM8: Dag ... 1F **73**
SE19 ... 6D **138**
SW19 ... 2J **135**
TW13: Hanw ... 3C **130**
UB3: Hayes ... 2J **93**
Mount Row W1 ... 3J **11** (7F **83**)
Mountsfield Ct. SE13 ... 6F **123**
Mountside HA7: Stan ... 1K **41**
Mounts Pond Rd. SE3 ... 2F **123**
(not continuous)
Mount Sq., The NW3 ... 3A **64**
Mt. Stewart Av. HA3: Kent ... 7D **42**
Mount St. W1 ... 3G **11** (7E **82**)
Mount St. M. W1 ... 3J **11** (7F **83**)
Mount Ter. E1 ... 5H **85**
Mount Vernon NW3 ... 4A **64**
Mount Vw. EN2: Enf ... 1E **22**
NW7 ... 3E **28**
UB2: S'hall ... 4B **94**
W5 ... 4D **78**
Mountview Cl. NW11 ... 1K **63**
Mountview Ct. N8 ... 4B **48**
Mount Vw. Rd. E4 ... 7K **25**
KT10: Clay ... 7B **162**
N4 ... 7J **47**
NW9 ... 5K **43**
Mountview Rd.
BR6: St M Cry ... 7K **161**
(not continuous)
Mount Vs. SE27 ... 3B **138**
Mount Way SM5: Cars ... 7E **166**
Mount Wood KT8: W Mole ... 3F **149**
MOVERS LANE ... 2J **89**
Movers La. IG11: Bark ... 1H **89**
Mowat Ct. *KT4: Wor Pk ... 2B **164***
(off The Avenue)
Mowatt Cl. N19 ... 1H **65**
Mowbray Ct. N22 ... 1A **48**
SE19 ... 7F **139**
Mowbray Gdns. UB5: N'olt ... 1E **76**
Mowbray Ho. *N2 ... 2B **46***
(off The Grange)
Mowbray Pde. HA8: Edg ... 4B **28**
Mowbray Rd. EN5: New Bar ... 5F **21**
HA8: Edg ... 4B **28**
NW6 ... 7G **63**
SE19 ... 1F **157**
TW10: Ham ... 3C **132**
Mowbrays Cl. RM5: Col R ... 1J **55**
Mowbrays Rd. RM5: Col R ... 2J **55**
Mowlem St. E2 ... 2H **85**
Mowlem Trad. Est. N17 ... 7D **34**
Mowll St. SW9 ... 7A **102**
Moxon Cl. E13 ... 2H **87**
Moxon St. EN5: Barn ... 3C **20**
W1 ... 6G **5** (5E **82**)
Moye Cl. E2 ... 2G **85**
Moyers Rd. E10 ... 7E **50**
Moylan Rd. W6 ... 6G **99**
Moyle Ho. *SW1 ... 6B **18***
(off Churchill Gdns.)
Moyne Ho. SW9 ... 5B **120**
Moyne Pl. NW10 ... 2G **79**
Moynihan Dr. N21 ... 5D **22**
Moys Cl. CR0: Croy ... 6J **155**
Moyser Rd. SW16 ... 5F **137**
Mozart St. W10 ... 3H **81**
Mozart Ter. SW1 ... 4H **17** (4E **100**)
Muchelney Rd. SM4: Mord ... 6A **154**
Mudlarks Blvd. SE10 ... 3H **105**
Mudlarks Way SE10 ... 3H **105**
(not continuous)
Muggeridge Cl. CR2: S Croy ... 5D **168**
Muggeridge Rd. RM10: Dag ... 4H **73**
Muirdown Av. SW14 ... 4K **115**
Muir Dr. SW18 ... 6C **118**
Muirfield W3 ... 6A **80**
Muirfield Cl. SE16 ... 5H **103**
Muirfield Cres. E14 ... 3D **104**
Muirkirk Rd. SE6 ... 1E **140**
Muir Rd. E5 ... 4G **67**
Muir St. E16 ... 1C **106**
(not continuous)
Mulberry Av. TW19: Stanw ... 1A **128**
Mulberry Bus. Cen. SE16 ... 2K **103**
Mulberry Cl. E4 ... 2H **35**
EN4: E Barn ... 4G **21**
N8 ... 5J **47**
NW3 ... 4B **64**
NW4 ... 3E **44**
SE7 ... 6B **106**
SE22 ... 5G **121**
SW3 ... 7B **16** (6B **100**)
SW16 ... 4G **137**
UB5: N'olt ... 2C **76**
Mulberry Ct. *E11 ... 4F **69***
(off Langthorne Rd.)
*EC1 ... 2B **8***
(off Tompion St.)
IG11: Bark ... 6K **71**
KT6: Surb ... 7D **150**
*N2 ... 3C **46***
(off Bedford Rd.)
SW3 ... 7B **16**
TW1: Twick ... 3K **131**
Mulberry Cres. TW8: Bford ... 7B **96**
UB7: W Dray ... 2C **92**
Mulberry Ho. BR2: Brom ... 1G **159**
*E2 ... 3J **85***
(off Victoria Pk. Sq.)
SE8 ... 6B **104**
Mulberry Housing Co-operative
SE1 ... 4K **13**
Mulberry La. CR0: Croy ... 1F **169**
Mulberry M. SE14 ... 1B **122**
SM6: Wall ... 6G **167**
Mulberry Pde. UB7: W Dray ... 3C **92**
Mulberry Pl. *E14 ... 7E **86***
(off Clove Cres.)
SE9 ... 4B **124**
W6 ... 5C **98**
Mulberry Rd. E8 ... 7F **67**
Mulberry St. E1 ... 6G **85**
Mulberry Tree M. W4 ... 2J **97**
Mulberry Trees TW17: Shep ... 7F **147**
Mulberry Wlk. SW3 ... 7B **16** (6B **100**)
Mulberry Way DA17: Belv ... 2J **109**
E18 ... 2K **51**
IG6: Ilf ... 4G **53**
Mulgrave Ct. *SM2: Sutt ... 6K **165***
(off Mulgrave Rd.)
Mulgrave Rd. CR0: Croy ... 3D **168**
HA1: Harr ... 2A **60**
NW10 ... 4B **62**
SE18 ... 4D **106**
SM2: Sutt ... 7H **165**
SW6 ... 6H **99**
W5 ... 3D **78**
Mulholland Cl. CR4: Mitc ... 2F **155**
Mulkern Rd. N19 ... 1H **65**
(not continuous)
Mullards Cl. CR4: Mitc ... 1D **166**
Mullen Twr. *WC1 ... 4J **7***
(off Mt. Pleasant)
Muller Ho. SE18 ... 5E **106**
Muller Rd. SW4 ... 6H **119**
Mullet Gdns. E2 ... 3G **85**
Mulletsfield *WC1 ... 2F **7***
(off Cromer St.)
Mullins Path SW14 ... 3K **115**
Mullion Cl. HA3: Hrw W ... 1F **41**
Mull Wlk. *N1 ... 6C **66***
(off Clephane Rd.)
Mulready Ho. *SW1 ... 4E **18***
(off Marsham St.)
Mulready St. NW8 ... 4C **4** (4C **82**)
Multimedia Ho. NW10 ... 4J **79**
Multi Way W3 ... 2A **98**
Multon Ho. E9 ... 7J **67**
Multon Rd. SW18 ... 7B **118**
Mulvaney Way SE1 ... 7F **15** (2D **102**)
(not continuous)
Mumford Mills *SE10 ... 1D **122***
(off Greenwich High Rd.)
Mumford Rd. SE24 ... 5B **120**
Muncaster Cl. TW15: Ashf ... 4C **128**
Muncaster Rd. SW11 ... 5D **118**
TW15: Ashf ... 5D **128**
Muncies M. SE6 ... 2E **140**
Mundania Ct. SE22 ... 6H **121**
Mundania Rd. SE22 ... 6H **121**
Munday Ho. *SE1 ... 3D **102***
(off Deverell St.)
Munday Rd. E16 ... 7J **87**
Munden St. W14 ... 4G **99**
Mundford Rd. E5 ... 2J **67**
Mundon Gdns. IG1: Ilf ... 1H **71**
Mund St. W14 ... 5H **99**
Mundy Ho. *W10 ... 3G **81***
(off Dart St.)
Mundy St. N1 ... 1G **9** (3E **84**)
Mungo Pk. Cl. WD23: Bushy ... 2B **26**
Munnery Way BR6: Farnb ... 3E **172**
Munnings Gdns. TW7: Isle ... 5H **113**
Munnings Ho. *E16 ... 1K **105***
(off Portsmouth M.)
Munro Dr. N11 ... 6B **32**
Munro Ho. SE1 ... 7J **13** (2A **102**)
Munro M. W10 ... 5G **81**
(not continuous)
Munro Ter. SW10 ... 7B **100**
Munslow Gdns. SM1: Sutt ... 4B **166**
Munster Av. TW4: Houn ... 5C **112**
Munster Ct. SW6 ... 2H **117**
TW11: Tedd ... 6C **132**
Munster Gdns. N13 ... 4G **33**
Munster M. SW6 ... 7G **99**
Munster Rd. SW6 ... 7G **99**
TW11: Tedd ... 6B **132**
Munster Sq. NW1 ... 2K **5** (3F **83**)
Munton Rd. SE17 ... 4C **102**
Murchison Av. DA5: Bexl ... 1D **144**
Murchison Ho. *W10 ... 5G **81***
(off Ladbroke Gro.)
Murchison Rd. E10 ... 2E **68**
Murdoch Ho. *SE16 ... 3J **103***
(off Moodkee St.)
Murdock Cl. E16 ... 6H **87**
Murdock St. SE15 ... 6H **103**
Murfett Cl. SW19 ... 2G **135**
Muriel Ct. E10 ... 7D **50**
Muriel St. N1 ... 2K **83**
(not continuous)
Murillo Rd. SE13 ... 4F **123**
Murphy Ho. *SE1 ... 7B **14***
(off Borough Rd.)
SE1 ... 2D **102**
(Long La.)
Murphy St. SE1 ... 7J **13** (2A **102**)
Murray Av. BR1: Brom ... 3K **159**
TW3: Houn ... 5F **113**
Murray Cl. SE28 ... 1J **107**
Murray Ct. HA1: Harr ... 6K **41**
TW2: Twick ... 2H **131**
Murray Cres. HA5: Pinn ... 1B **40**
Murray Gro. N1 ... 1D **8** (2C **84**)
Murray Ho. *SE18 ... 4D **106***
(off Rideout St.)
Murray M. NW1 ... 7H **65**
Murray Rd. HA6: Nwood ... 1G **39**
SW19 ... 6F **135**
TW10: Ham ... 2B **132**
W5 ... 4C **96**
Murray Sq. E16 ... 6J **87**
Murray St. NW1 ... 7G **65**
Murrays Yd. SE18 ... 4F **107**
Murray Ter. NW3 ... 4A **64**
W5 ... 4D **96**
Mursell Est. SW8 ... 1K **119**
Musard Rd. W6 ... 6G **99**
Musbury St. E1 ... 6J **85**
Muscal *W6 ... 6G **99***
(off Field Rd.)
Muscatel Pl. SE5 ... 1E **120**
Muschamp Rd. SE15 ... 3F **121**
SM5: Cars ... 2C **166**
Muscott Ho. *E2 ... 1G **85***
(off Whiston Rd.)
Muscovy Ho. *DA18: Erith ... 2E **108***
(off Kale Rd.)
Muscovy St. EC3 ... 2H **15** (7E **84**)
Museum Chambers *WC1 ... 6E **6***
(off Bury Pl.)
Mus. in Docklands, The ... 7C **86**
Museum La. SW7 ... 2B **16** (3B **100**)
Mus. of Brands, Packaging and Advertising
*... 6H **81***
(off Colville M.)
Mus. of Classical Archaeology *... 3C **6***
(off Gower Pl.)
Mus. of Garden History ... 2G **19** (3K **101**)
Mus. of London ... 6C **8** (5C **84**)
Mus. of Richmond ... 5D **114**
Mus. of Rugby, The ... 6J **113**
Mus. of the Order of St John *... 4A **8***
(off St John's La.)
Museum Pas. E2 ... 3J **85**
Museum St. WC1 ... 6E **6** (5J **83**)
Musgrave Cl. EN4: Had W ... 1F **21**
Musgrave Ct. SW11 ... 1C **118**
Musgrave Cres. SW6 ... 7J **99**
Musgrave Rd. TW7: Isle ... 1K **113**
Musgrove Rd. SE14 ... 1K **121**
Musjid Rd. SW11 ... 2B **118**
Musket Cl. EN4: E Barn ... 6G **21**
Musquash Way TW4: Houn ... 2A **112**
Muston Rd. E5 ... 2H **67**
Mustow Pl. SW6 ... 2H **117**
Muswell Av. N10 ... 1F **47**
MUSWELL HILL ... 3F **47**
Muswell Hill N10 ... 3F **47**
Muswell Hill B'way. N10 ... 3F **47**
Muswell Hill Pl. N10 ... 4F **47**
Muswell Hill Rd. N6 ... 6E **46**
N10 ... 5F **47**
Muswell M. N10 ... 3F **47**
Muswell Rd. N10 ... 3F **47**
Mutrix Rd. NW6 ... 1J **81**
Mutton Pl. NW1 ... 6E **64**
Muybridge Rd. KT3: N Mald ... 2J **151**
Muybridge Yd. KT6: Surb ... 7F **151**
Myatt Rd. SW9 ... 1B **120**

328 A-Z London

Myatts Flds. Sth. *SW9* 2A **120**
  (off St Lawrence Way)
Mycenae Rd. SE3 ....7J **105**
Myddelton Av. EN1: Enf 1K **23**
Myddelton Cl. EN1: Enf 1A **24**
Myddelton Gdns. N21 ....7H **23**
Myddelton Pk. N20 ....3G **31**
Myddelton Pas. EC1 .....1K **7** (3A **84**)
Myddelton Rd. N8 ....4J **47**
  (not continuous)
Myddelton Sq. EC1 .....1K **7** (3A **84**)
Myddelton St. EC1 .....2K **7** (3A **84**)
Myddleton Av. N4 ....2C **66**
Myddleton Ho. N1 ....1J **7**
Myddleton M. N22 ....7D **32**
Myddleton Rd. N22 ....7D **32**
Myers Ho. *SE5* 7C **102**
  (off Bethwin Rd.)
Myers La. SE14 ....6K **103**
Myles Ct. *SE16* 3J **103**
  (off Neptune St.)
Mylis Cl. SE26 ....4H **139**
Mylius Cl. SE14 ....7J **103**
Mylne Cl. W6 ....5C **98**
Mylne St. EC1 ....1J **7** (3A **84**)
Myra St. SE2 ....4A **108**
Myrdle Ct. *E1* 6G **85**
  (off Myrdle St.)
Myrdle St. E1 ....5G **85**
Myrna Cl. SW19 ....7C **136**
Myron Pl. SE13 ....3E **122**
Myrtle Av. HA4: Ruis 7J **39**
  TW14: Felt 5G **111**
Myrtleberry Cl. *E8* 6F **67**
  (off Beechwood Rd.)
Myrtle Cl. EN4: E Barn 1J **31**
  UB7: W Dray 3B **92**
  UB8: Hil 5B **74**
Myrtledene Rd. SE2 ....5A **108**
Myrtle Gdns. W7 ....1J **95**
Myrtle Gro. EN2: Enf 1J **23**
  KT3: N Mald 2J **151**
Myrtle Rd. CR0: Croy 3C **170**
  E6 ....1D **88**
  E17 ....6A **50**
  IG1: Ilf 2F **71**
  N13 ....3H **33**
  SM1: Sutt 5A **166**
  TW3: Houn 2G **113**
  TW12: Ham H 6G **131**
  W3 ....1J **97**
Myrtle Wlk. N1 ....1G **9** (2E **84**)
Mysore Rd. SW11 ....3D **118**
Myton Rd. SE21 ....3D **138**
Mytton Ho. *SW8* 7K **101**
  (off St Stephens Ter.)

N

N1 Shop. Cen. N1 ....2A **84**
N16 Fitness Cen. 4D **66**
Nacton Ct. *RM6: Chad H* 5C **54**
  (off Hevingham Dr.)
Nadine Ct. SM6: Wall 7G **167**
Nadine St. SE7 ....5A **106**
Nagasaki Wlk. SE7 ....3K **105**
Nagle Cl. E17 ....2F **51**
NAG'S HEAD 3J **65**
Nags Head Ct. EC1 ....4D **8**
Nags Head La. DA16: Well 3B **126**
Nags Head Rd. EN3: Pond E ...4D **24**
Nags Head Shop. Cen. N7 .....4K **65**
Nainby Ho. SE11 ....4J **19**
Nairne Gro. SE24 ....5D **120**
Nairn Rd. HA4: Ruis 6A **58**
Nairn St. E14 ....5E **86**
Naldera Gdns. SE3 ....6J **105**
Nallhead Rd. TW13: Hanw 5A **130**
Nalton Ho. *NW6* 7A **64**
  (off Belsize Rd.)
Namba Roy Cl. SW16 ....4K **137**
Namton Dr. CR7: Thor H 4K **155**

Nan Clark's La. NW7 ....2F **29**
Nankin St. E14 ....6C **86**
Nansen Ho. *NW10* 7K **61**
  (off Stonebridge Pk.)
Nansen Rd. SW11 ....3E **118**
Nansen Village N12 ....4E **30**
Nant Ct. NW2 ....2H **63**
Nantes Cl. SW18 ....4A **118**
Nantes Pas. E1 ....5J **9** (5F **85**)
Nant Rd. NW2 ....2H **63**
Nant St. E2 ....3H **85**
Naoroji St. WC1 ....2J **7** (3A **84**)
Napier NW9 ....1B **44**
Napier Av. E14 ....5C **104**
  SW6 ....3H **117**
Napier Cl. SE8 ....7B **104**
  UB7: W Dray 3B **92**
  W14 ....3G **99**
Napier Ct. *N1* 2D **84**
  (off Cropley St.)
  SE12 ....3K **141**
  SW6 ....3H **117**
  (off Ranelagh Gdns.)
  UB4: Yead 4A **76**
  (off Dunedin Way)
Napier Gro. N1 ....2C **84**
Napier Ho. *SE17* 6B **102**
  (off Cook's Rd.)
Napier Lodge TW15: Ashf 6F **129**
Napier Pl. W14 ....3H **99**
Napier Rd. BR2: Brom 4K **159**
  CR2: S Croy 7D **168**
  DA17: Belv 4F **109**
  E6 ....1E **88**
  E11 ....4G **69**
  E15 ....2G **87**
  (not continuous)
  EN3: Pond E 5E **24**
  HA0: Wemb 6D **60**
  N17 ....3E **48**
  NW10 ....3D **80**
  SE25 ....4H **157**
  TW7: Isle 4A **114**
  TW15: Ashf 7F **129**
  W14 ....3H **99**
Napier St. *SE8* 7B **104**
  (off Napier Cl.)
Napier Ter. N1 ....7B **66**
Napier Wlk. TW15: Ashf 7F **129**
Napoleon Rd. E5 ....3H **67**
  TW1: Twick 7B **114**
Napton Cl. UB4: Yead 4C **76**
Narbonne Av. SW4 ....5G **119**
Narborough Cl.
  UB10: Ick 2E **56**
Narborough St. SW6 ....2K **117**
Narcissus Rd. NW6 ....5J **63**
Nardini *NW9* 1B **44**
  (off The Concourse)
Naresby Fold HA7: Stan 6H **27**
Narford Rd. E5 ....3G **67**
Narrow Boat Cl. SE28 ....2H **107**
Narrow St. E14 ....7A **86**
  W3 ....1H **97**
Narrow Way BR2: Brom 6C **160**
Narvic Ho. SE5 ....2C **120**
Narwhal Inuit Art Gallery 4K **97**
Nascot St. W12 ....6E **80**
Naseby Cl. NW6 ....7A **64**
  TW7: Isle 1J **113**
Naseby Ct. DA14: Sidc 4K **143**
Naseby Rd. IG5: Ilf 1D **52**
  RM10: Dag 3G **73**
  SE19 ....6D **138**
NASH 6J **171**
Nash Cl. SM1: Sutt 3B **166**
Nash Ct. HA3: Kent 6B **42**
Nashe Ho. *SE1* 3D **102**
  (off Burbage Cl.)
Nash Grn. BR1: Brom 6J **141**
Nash Ho. *E14* 2C **104**
  (off Alpha Gro.)
  E17 ....3D **50**

Nash Ho. *NW1* 2F **83**
  (off Pk. Village E.)
  SW1 ....6K **17**
  (off Lupus St.)
Nash La. BR2: Kes 7J **171**
Nash Pl. E14 ....1D **104**
Nash Rd. N9 ....2D **34**
  RM6: Chad H 4D **54**
  SE4 ....4A **122**
Nash St. NW1 ....1K **5** (3F **83**)
Nash Way HA3: Kent 6B **42**
Nasmyth St. W6 ....3D **98**
Nassau Path SE28 ....1C **108**
Nassau Rd. SW13 ....1B **116**
Nassau St. W1 ....6A **6** (5G **83**)
Nassington Rd. NW3 ....4D **64**
Natalie Cl. TW14: Bedf 7F **111**
Natalie M. TW2: Ham H 3H **131**
Natal Rd. CR7: Thor H 3D **156**
  IG1: Ilf 4F **71**
  N11 ....6D **32**
  SW16 ....6H **137**
Nathan Ct. *N9* 7D **24**
  (off Causeyware Rd.)
Nathan Ho. *SE11* 4K **19**
  (off Reedworth St.)
Nathaniel Cl. E1 ......6K **9** (5F **85**)
Nathaniel Ct. E17 ....7A **50**
Nathans Rd. HA0: Wemb 1C **60**
Nathan Way SE28 ....4J **107**
National Archives, The 7G **97**
National Army Mus. 7F **17** (6D **100**)
National Film Theatre, The ...4H **13**
National Gallery 3D **12** (7H **83**)
National Maritime Mus. 6F **105**
National Portrait Gallery ...3D **12**
National Ter. *SE16* 2H **103**
  (off Bermondsey Wall E.)
National Theatre 4H **13** (1K **101**)
National Walks TW4: Houn ...3D **112**
Nation Way E4 ....1K **35**
Natural History Mus. ...2A **16** (3B **100**)
Nautilus Bldg., The *EC1* 1K **7**
Naval Ho. *E14* 7F **87**
  (off Quixley St.)
Naval Row E14 ....7E **86**
Naval Wlk. *BR1: Brom* 2J **159**
  (off Mitre Cl.)
Navarino Gro. E8 ....6G **67**
Navarino Mans. E8 ....6G **67**
Navarino Rd. E8 ....6G **67**
Navarre Rd. E6 ....2C **88**
Navarre St. E2 ....3J **9** (4F **85**)
Navenby Wlk. E3 ....4C **86**
Navestock Cl. E4 ....3K **35**
Navestock Ho. IG8: Wfd G ...7F **37**
Navestock Ho. IG11: Bark ...2B **90**
Navigation Cl. E16 ....7G **89**
Navigation Dr. EN3: Enf L ...1H **25**
Navigator Dr. UB2: S'hall ...2G **95**
Navigator Pk. UB2: S'hall ...4A **94**
Navy St. SW4 ....3H **119**
Naxos Bldg. E14 ....2B **104**
Nayim Pl. E8 ....5H **67**
Nayland Ho. SE6 ....4E **140**
Naylor Gro. EN3: Pond E 5E **24**
Naylor Ho. *SE17* 4D **102**
  (off Flint St.)
  W10 ....3G **81**
  (off Dart St.)
Naylor Rd. N20 ....2F **31**
  SE15 ....7H **103**
Nazareth Gdns. SE15 ....2H **121**
Nazrul St. E2 ....1J **9** (3F **85**)
Neagle Ho. *NW2* 3E **62**
  (off Stoll Cl.)
Neal Av. UB1: S'hall 4D **76**
Neal Cl. HA6: Nwood 1J **39**
Nealden St. SW9 ....3K **119**
Neale Cl. N2 ....3A **46**
Neal St. WC2 ....1E **12** (6J **83**)
Neal's Yd. WC2 .....1E **12** (6J **83**)

Near Acre NW9 ....1B **44**
NEASDEN 3A **62**
Neasden Cl. NW10 ....5A **62**
NEASDEN JUNC. 4A **62**
Neasden La. NW10 ....3A **62**
Neasden La. Nth. NW10 ......3K **61**
Neasham Rd. RM8: Dag 5B **72**
Neate Ho. *SW1* 6B **18**
  (off Lupus St.)
Neate St. SE5 ....6E **102**
  (not continuous)
Neath Gdns. SM4: Mord 6A **154**
Neathouse Pl. SW1 ...3A **18** (4G **101**)
Neats Acre HA4: Ruis 7F **39**
Neatscourt Rd. E6 ....5B **88**
Nebraska Bldg. *SE8* 1D **122**
  (off Deal's Gateway)
Nebraska St. SE1 ....7E **14** (2D **102**)
Neckinger SE16 ....7K **15** (3F **103**)
Neckinger Est. SE16 ...7K **15** (3F **103**)
Neckinger St. SE1 ....7K **15** (2F **103**)
Nectarine Way SE13 ....2D **122**
Needham Ho. SE11 ....4J **19**
Needham Rd. W11 ....6J **81**
Needham Ter. NW2 ....3F **63**
Needleman St. SE16 ....2K **103**
Needwood Ho. N4 ....1C **66**
Neela Cl. UB10: Ick 4D **56**
Neeld Cres. HA9: Wemb 5G **61**
  NW4 ....5D **44**
Neeld Pde. HA9: Wemb 5F **61**
Neil Cl. TW15: Ashf 5E **128**
Neil Wates Cres. SW2 ....1A **138**
Nelgarde Rd. SE6 ....7C **122**
Nella Rd. W6 ....6F **99**
Nelldale Rd. SE16 ....4J **103**
Nellgrove Rd. UB10: Hil 4D **74**
Nell Gwynne Av. TW17: Shep ...6F **147**
Nell Gwynn Ho. SW3 ...4D **16** (4C **100**)
Nello James Gdns. SE27 .....4D **138**
Nelson Cl. CR0: Croy 1B **168**
  KT12: Walt T 7K **147**
  NW6 ....3J **81**
  RM7: Mawney 1H **55**
  TW14: Felt 1H **129**
  UB10: Hil 3D **74**
Nelson Ct. SE1 ....6B **14** (2B **102**)
  SE16 ....1J **103**
  (off Brunel Rd.)
Nelson Gdns. E2 ....3G **85**
  TW3: Houn 6E **112**
Nelson Gro. Rd. SW19 ....1K **153**
Nelson Ho. *SW1* 1B **18**
  (off Dolphin Sq.)
Nelson La. UB10: Hil 3D **74**
Nelson Mandela Cl. N10 .....2E **46**
Nelson Mandela Ho. N16 .....2G **67**
Nelson Mandela Rd. SE3 .....3A **124**
Nelson Pas. EC1 ......1D **8** (3C **84**)
Nelson Pl. DA14: Sidc 4A **144**
  N1 ....1B **8** (2B **84**)
Nelson Rd. BR2: Brom 4A **160**
  DA14: Sidc 4A **144**
  DA17: Belv 5F **109**
  E4 ....6J **35**
  E11 ....4J **51**
  EN3: Pond E 6E **24**
  HA1: Harr 1H **59**
  HA7: Stan 6H **27**
  KT3: N Mald 5K **151**
  N8 ....5K **47**
  N9 ....2C **34**
  N15 ....4E **48**
  SE10 ....6E **104**
  SW19 ....7K **135**
  TW2: Whit 7F **113**
  TW3: Houn 6E **112**
  TW6: H'row A 1B **110**
  TW15: Ashf 5A **128**
  UB10: Hil 3D **74**
Nelson Rd. M. SW19 ....7K **135**
Nelson's Column 4D **12** (1J **101**)
Nelson Sq. SE1 ....6A **14** (2B **102**)

Nelson's Row SW4 4H 119
Nelson St. E1 6H 85
E6 2D 88
(not continuous)
E16 7H 87
(not continuous)
Nelsons Yd. NW1 2G 83
(off Mornington Cres.)
Nelson Ter. N1 1B 8 (2B 84)
Nelson Trad. Est. SW19 1K 153
Nelson Wlk. KT19: Eps 7G 163
SE16 1A 104
Nemoure Rd. W3 7J 79
Nene Gdns. TW13: Hanw 2D 130
Nene Rd. TW6: H'row A 1D 110
Nene Rd. Rdbt.
TW6: H'row A 1D 110
Nepaul Rd. SW11 2C 118
Nepean St. SW15 6C 116
Neptune Ct. E14 4C 104
(off Homer Dr.)
Neptune Ho. SE16 3J 103
(off Moodkee St.)
Neptune Rd. HA1: Harr 6H 41
TW6: H'row A 1F 111
Neptune St. SE16 3J 103
Neptune Wlk. DA8: Erith 4K 109
Nero Ct. TW8: Bford 7D 96
Nesbit Rd. SE9 4B 124
Nesbitt Cl. SE3 3G 123
Nesbitts All. EN5: Barn 3C 20
Nesbitt Sq. SE19 7E 138
Nesham Ho. N1 1E 84
(off Hoxton St.)
Nesham St. E1 7G 85
Ness St. SE16 3G 103
Nesta Rd. IG8: Wfd G 6B 36
Nestles Av. UB3: Hayes 3H 93
Nestor Av. N21 6G 23
Nestor Ho. E2 2H 85
(off Old Bethnal Grn. Rd.)
Netheravon Rd. W4 4B 98
W7 1K 95
Netheravon Rd. Sth. W4 5B 98
Netherbury Rd. W5 3D 96
Netherby Gdns. EN2: Enf 4D 22
Netherby Rd. SE23 7J 121
Nether Cl. N3 7D 30
Nethercourt Av. N3 6D 30
Netherfield Gdns. IG11: Bark 6H 71
Netherfield Rd. N12 5E 30
SW17 3E 136
Netherford Rd. SW4 2G 119
Netherhall Gdns. NW3 6A 64
Netherhall Way NW3 5A 64
Netherlands Rd. EN5: New Bar 6G 21
Netherleigh Cl. N6 1F 65
Nether St. N3 1J 45
N12 6E 30
Netherton Gro. SW10 6A 100
Netherton Rd. N15 6D 48
TW1: Twick 5A 114
Netherwood N2 2B 46
Netherwood Pl. W14 3F 99
(off Netherwood Rd.)
Netherwood Rd. W14 3F 99
Netherwood St. NW6 7H 63
Nethewode Ct. DA17: Belv 3H 109
(off Lower Pk. Rd.)
Netley SE5 1E 120
(off Redbridge Gdns.)
Netley Cl. CR0: New Ad 7E 170
SM3: Cheam 5F 165
Netley Dr. KT12: Walt T 7D 148
Netley Gdns. SM4: Mord 7A 154
Netley Rd. E17 5B 50
IG2: Ilf 5H 53
SM4: Mord 7A 154
TW8: Bford 6E 96
Netley St. NW1 2A 6 (3G 83)
Nettlecombe NW1 7H 65
(off Agar Gro.)
Nettleden Av. HA9: Wemb 6G 61
Nettleden Ho. SW3 4D 16
(off Marlborough St.)
Nettlefold Pl. SE27 3B 138
Nettlestead Cl. BR3: Beck 7B 140
Nettleton Ct. EC2 6C 8
(off London Wall)
Nettleton Rd. SE14 1K 121
TW6: H'row A 1D 110
UB10: Ick 4B 56
Nettlewood Rd. SW16 7H 137
Neuchatel Rd. SE6 2B 140
Nevada Cl. KT3: N Mald 4J 151
Nevada St. SE10 6E 104
Nevern Mansions SW5 5J 99
(off Nevern Sq.)
Nevern Pl. SW5 4J 99
Nevern Rd. SW5 4J 99
Nevern Sq. SW5 4J 99
Nevil Ho. SW9 2B 120
(off Loughborough Est.)
Nevill Ct. EC4 7K 7
SW10 7A 100
(off Edith Ter.)
Neville Av. KT3: N Mald 1K 151
Neville Cl. DA15: Sidc 4K 143
E11 3H 69
NW1 2H 83
NW6 2H 81
SE15 1G 121
TW3: Houn 2F 113
W3 2J 97
Neville Ct. NW8 1A 4
Neville Dr. N2 6A 46
Neville Gdns. RM8: Dag 3D 72
Neville Gill Cl. SW18 6J 117
Neville Ho. N11 4K 31
N22 1K 47
(off Neville Pl.)
Neville Ho. Yd. KT1: King T 2E 150
Neville Pl. N22 1K 47
Neville Rd. CR0: Croy 7D 156
E7 7J 69
IG6: Ilf 1G 53
KT1: King T 2G 151
NW6 2H 81
RM8: Dag 2D 72
TW10: Ham 3C 132
W5 4D 78
Nevilles Ct. NW2 3C 62
Neville St. SW7 5A 16 (5B 100)
Neville Ter. SW7 5A 16 (5B 100)
Neville Wlk. SM5: Cars 7C 154
Nevill Rd. N16 4E 66
Nevin Dr. E4 1J 35
Nevin Ho. UB3: Harl 3E 92
Nevinson Cl. SW18 6B 118
Nevis Rd. SW17 2E 136
Nevitt Ho. N1 2D 84
(off Cranston Est.)
New Acres Rd. SE28 2J 107
(not continuous)
NEW ADDINGTON 7F 171
Newall Ho. SE1 3C 102
(off Bath Ter.)
Newall Rd. TW6: H'row A 1E 110
Newark Cres. NW10 3K 79
Newarke Ho. SW9 2B 120
Newark Knok E6 6E 88
Newark Pde. NW4 3C 44
Newark Rd. CR2: S Croy 6D 168
Newark St. E1 5H 85
(not continuous)
Newark Way NW4 4C 44
New Ash Cl. N2 3B 46
New Atlas Wharf E14 3C 104
(off Arnhem Pl.)
New Baltic Wharf SE8 5A 104
(off Evelyn St.)
New Barn Cl. SM6: Wall 6K 167
NEW BARNET 4G 21
New Barn Rd. BR8: Swan 7K 145
New Barns Av. CR4: Mitc 4H 155
(not continuous)
New Barn St. E13 4J 87
New Barns Way IG7: Chig 3K 37
NEW BECKENHAM 6B 140
New Bentham Ct. N1 7C 66
(off Ecclesbourne Rd.)
Newbery Ho. N1 7C 66
(off Northampton St.)
Newbold Cotts. E1 6J 85
Newbolt Av. SM3: Cheam 5E 164
Newbolt Ho. SE17 5D 102
(off Brandon St.)
Newbolt Rd. HA7: Stan 5E 26
New Bond St. W1 1J 11 (6F 83)
Newborough Grn.
KT3: N Mald 4K 151
New Brent St. NW4 5E 44
Newbridge Point SE23 3K 139
(off Windrush La.)
New Bri. St. EC4 1A 14 (6B 84)
New Broad St. EC2 6G 9 (5E 84)
New B'way. TW12: Ham H 5H 131
UB10: Hil 3D 74
W5 7D 78
New Broadway Bldgs. W5 7D 78
Newburgh Rd. W3 1J 97
Newburgh St. W1 1B 12 (6G 83)
New Burlington M. W1 2A 12 (7G 83)
New Burlington Pl. W1 2A 12 (7G 83)
New Burlington St. W1 2A 12 (7G 83)
Newburn Ho. SE11 5H 19
(off Newburn St.)
Newburn St. SE11 5H 19 (5K 101)
Newbury Cl. UB5: N'olt 6D 58
Newbury Ct. DA14: Sidc 4K 143
Newbury Gdns. KT19: Ewe 4B 164
Newbury Ho. N22 1J 47
SW9 2B 120
W2 6K 81
(off Hallfield Est.)
Newbury M. NW5 6E 64
NEWBURY PARK 5H 53
Newbury Rd. BR2: Brom 3J 159
E4 6K 35
IG2: Ilf 6J 53
TW6: H'row A 1B 110
Newbury St. EC1 6C 8 (5C 84)
Newbury Way UB5: N'olt 6C 58
New Bus. Cen., The NW10 3B 80
New Butt La. SE8 7C 104
New Butt La. Nth. SE8 7C 104
(off Hales St.)
Newby NW1 2A 6
(off Robert St.)
Newby Cl. EN1: Enf 2K 23
Newby Ho. E14 7E 86
(off Newby Pl.)
Newby Pl. E14 7E 86
Newby St. SW8 3F 119
New Caledonian Mkt. SE1 7H 15
New Caledonian Wharf SE16 3B 104
Newcastle Cl. EC4 7A 8 (6B 84)
Newcastle Ct. EC4 2D 14
(off College Hill)
Newcastle Ho. W1 5G 5
(off Luxborough St.)
Newcastle Pl. W2 5B 4 (5B 82)
Newcastle Row EC1 4K 7 (4A 84)
New Cavendish St. W1 6H 5 (5E 82)
New Change EC4 1C 14 (6C 84)
New Chapel Sq. TW13: Felt 1K 129
New Charles St. EC1 1B 8 (3B 84)
NEW CHARLTON 4A 106
New Chiswick Pool 7A 98
New Church Rd. SE5 7C 102
(not continuous)
New City Rd. E13 3A 88
New Cl. SW19 3A 154
TW13: Hanw 5C 130
New Colebrooke Ct. SM5: Cars 7D 166
(off Stanley Rd.)
New College Ct. NW3 6A 64
(off Finchley Rd.)
New College M. N1 7A 66
New College Pde. NW3 6B 64
(off Finchley Rd.)
Newcombe Gdns. SW16 4J 137
TW4: Houn 4D 112
Newcombe Pk. HA0: Wemb 1F 79
NW7 5F 29
Newcombe Ri. UB7: Yiew 6A 74
Newcombe St. W8 1J 99
Newcomen Rd. E11 3H 69
SW11 3B 118
Newcomen St. SE1 6E 14 (2D 102)
New Compton St. WC2 1D 12 (6H 83)
New Concordia Wharf
SE1 6K 15 (2G 103)
New Ct. EC4 2J 13
UB5: N'olt 5F 59
Newcourt Ho. E2 3H 85
(off Pott St.)
Newcourt St. NW8 1C 4 (2C 82)
New Covent Garden Market
7D 18 (7H 101)
New Coventry St. W1 3D 12 (7H 83)
New Crane Pl. E1 1J 103
New Crane Wharf E1 1J 103
(off New Crane Pl.)
New Cres. Yd. NW10 2B 80
Newcroft Cl. UB8: Hil 5B 74
NEW CROSS 7B 104
NEW CROSS 1B 122
NEW CROSS GATE 1K 121
NEW CROSS GATE 1K 121
New Cross Rd. SE14 7J 103
SE15 7J 103
New Curzon Cinema 4B 48
Newdales Cl. N9 2B 34
Newdene Av. UB5: N'olt 2B 76
Newdigate Ho. E14 6B 86
(off Norbiton Rd.)
Newell St. E14 6B 86
NEW ELTHAM 2G 143
New End NW3 4A 64
New End Sq. NW3 4B 64
New End Theatre
Hampstead 3A 64
New England Ind. Est. IG11: Bark 2G 89
Newent Cl. SE15 7E 102
SM5: Cars 1D 166
New Era Est. N1 1E 84
(off Phillipp St.)
New Era Ho. N1 1E 84
(off New Era Est.)
New Farm Av. BR2: Brom 4J 159
New Farm La. HA6: Nwood 1G 39
New Fetter La. EC4 7K 7 (6A 84)
Newfield Cl. TW12: Hamp 1E 148
Newfield Ri. NW2 3C 62
New Fieldways EN5: Barn 6C 20
New Forest La. IG7: Chig 6K 37
Newgale Gdns. HA8: Edg 1F 43
New Gdn. Dr. UB7: W Dray 2A 92
Newgate CR0: Croy 1C 168
Newgate Cl. TW13: Hanw 2C 130
Newgate St. E4 3B 36
(not continuous)
EC1 7B 8 (6B 84)
New Globe Wlk. SE1 4C 14 (1C 102)
New Goulston St. E1 7J 9 (6F 85)
New Grn. Pl. SE19 6E 138
Newham College of Further Education
Stratford Campus 7G 69
Newham Grn. N22 1A 48
(off Riverdale Gdns.)
Newham Leisure Cen. 5A 88
Newham's Row SE1 7H 15 (3E 102)
Newham Way E6 5A 88
E16 5H 87
Newhaven Cl. UB3: Harl 4H 93
Newhaven Cres.
TW15: Ashf 5F 129
Newhaven Gdns. SE9 4B 124
Newhaven La. E16 4H 87
Newhaven Rd. SE25 5D 156
New Heston Rd. TW5: Hest 7D 94

New Hope Ct. *NW10* .... 3D 80 *(off Harrow Rd.)*
New Horizons Ct. TW8: Bford 6A 96
Newhouse Av. RM6: Chad H 3D 54
Newhouse Cl. KT3: N Mald 7A 152
Newhouse Wlk. SM4: Mord 7A 154
Newick Cl. DA5: Bexl 6H 127
Newick Rd. E5 .... 4H 67
Newing Grn. BR1: Brom 7B 142
NEWINGTON 3C 102
Newington Barrow Way N7 .... 3K 65
Newington Butts SE1 .... 4B 102
 SE11 .... 4B 102
Newington C'way. SE1 .... 7C 14 (3B 102)
Newington Ct. Bus. Cen. SE1 .... 7C 14
Newington Grn. N1 .... 5D 66
 N16 .... 5D 66
Newington Grn. Mans. N16 .... 5D 66
Newington Grn. Rd. N1 .... 6D 66
Newington Ind. Est. SE17 .... 4C 102
New Inn B'way. EC2 .... 3H 9 (4E 84)
New Inn Pas. WC2 .... 1H 13
New Inn Sq. EC2 .... 3H 9
New Inn St. EC2 .... 3H 9 (4E 84)
New Inn Yd. EC2 .... 3H 9 (4E 84)
New Jubilee Ct. IG8: Wfd G 7D 36
New Jubilee Wharf *E1* .... 1J 103 *(off Wapping Wall)*
New Kelvin Av. TW11: Tedd 6J 131
New Kent Rd. SE1 .... 3C 102
New Kings Rd. SW6 .... 2H 117
New King St. SE8 .... 6C 104
Newland Ct. EC1 .... 2E 8
 HA9: Wemb 2G 61
Newland Dr. EN1: Enf 1C 24
Newland Gdns. W13 .... 2A 96
Newland Ho. *N8* .... 3J 47 *(off Newland Rd.)*
 SE14 .... 6K 103 *(off John Williams Cl.)*
Newland Rd. N8 .... 3J 47
NEWLANDS
 Brockley 5K 121
 Edgware 3K 27
Newlands *NW1* .... 1A 6 *(off Harrington St.)*
Newlands, The KT7: T Ditt 7J 149
 SM6: Wall 7G 167
Newlands Av. KT7: T Ditt 7J 149
Newlands Cl. HA0: Wemb 6C 60
 HA8: Edg 3K 27
 UB2: S'hall 5C 94
Newlands Ct. SE9 .... 6E 124
Newlands Pk. SE26 .... 6J 139
Newlands Pl. EN5: Barn 5A 20
Newlands Quay E1 .... 7J 85
Newlands Rd. IG8: Wfd G 2C 36
 SW16 .... 2J 155
Newland St. E16 .... 1C 106
Newlands Way KT9: Chess 5C 162
Newlands Wood CR0: Sels 7B 170
Newling Cl. E6 .... 6D 88
New London St. EC3 .... 2H 15
New London Theatre .... *7F 7* *(off Drury La.)*
New Lydenburg Commercial Est. SE7 .... 3A 106
New Lydenburg St. SE7 .... 3A 106
Newlyn *NW1* .... 1G 83 *(off Plender St.)*
Newlyn Cl. BR6: Chels 4K 173
 UB8: Hil 5C 74
Newlyn Gdns. HA2: Harr 7D 40
Newlyn Ho. HA5: H End 1D 40
Newlyn Rd. DA16: Well 2K 125
 EN5: Barn 4C 20
 N17 .... 1F 49
NEW MALDEN 4A 152
Newman Ct. *BR1: Brom* .... 1J 159 *(off North St.)*
Newman Pas. W1 .... 6B 6 (5G 83)

Newman Rd. BR1: Brom 1J 159
 CR0: Croy 1K 167
 E13 .... 3K 87
 E17 .... 5K 49
 UB3: Hayes 7K 75
Newman Rd. Ind. Est. CR0: Croy 7K 155
Newman's Ct. EC3 .... 1F 15
Newmans La. KT6: Surb 6D 150
Newman's Row WC2 .... 6H 7 (5K 83)
Newman St. W1 .... 6B 6 (5G 83)
Newman's Way EN4: Had W 1F 21
Newman Yd. W1 .... 7C 6 (6G 83)
Newmarket Av. UB5: N'olt 5E 58
Newmarket Grn. SE9 .... 7B 124
Newmarsh Rd. SE28 .... 1K 107
Newmill Ho. E3 .... 4E 86
Newminster Rd. SM4: Mord 6A 154
New Mount St. E15 .... 7F 69
Newnes Path SW15 .... 4D 116
Newnham Av. HA4: Ruis 1A 58
Newnham Cl. CR7: Thor H 2C 156
 UB5: N'olt 6G 59
Newnham Gdns. UB5: N'olt 6G 59
Newnham Lodge *DA17: Belv* .... 5G 109 *(off Erith Rd.)*
Newnham M. N22 .... 7F 33
Newnham Rd. N22 .... 1K 47
Newnhams Cl. BR1: Brom 3D 160
Newnham Ter. SE1 .... 1J 19 (3A 102)
Newnham Way HA3: Kent 5E 42
New Nth. Pl. EC2 .... 3G 9 (4E 84)
New Nth. Rd. IG6: Ilf 1G 53
 N1 .... 1F 9 (7C 66)
New Nth. St. WC1 .... 5G 7 (5K 83)
Newnton Cl. N4 .... 7D 48 (not continuous)
New Oak Rd. N2 .... 2A 46
New Orleans Wlk. N19 .... 7H 47
New Oxford St. WC1 .... 7D 6 (6H 83)
New Pde. TW15: Ashf 4B 128
 UB7: Yiew 1A 92
New Pk. Av. N13 .... 3H 33
New Pk. Cl. UB5: N'olt 6C 58
New Pk. Est. N18 .... 5D 34
New Pk. Ho. N13 .... 4E 32
New Pk. Pde. *SW2* .... 7J 119 *(off New Pk. Rd.)*
New Pk. Rd. SW2 .... 1H 137
 TW15: Ashf 5E 128
New Pl. CR0: Addtn 6C 170
New Pl. Sq. SE16 .... 3H 103
New Plaistow Rd. E15 .... 1G 87
New Players Theatre .... *1J 101* *(off Craven St.)*
New Pond Pde. HA4: Ruis 3J 57
Newport Av. E13 .... 4K 87
 E14 .... 7F 87
Newport Ct. WC2 .... 2D 12 (7H 83)
Newport Ho. *E3* .... 3A 86 *(off Strahan Rd.)*
Newport Lodge *EN1: Enf* .... 5K 23 *(off Village Rd.)*
Newport Pl. W1 .... 2D 12 (7H 83)
Newport Rd. E10 .... 2E 68
 E17 .... 4A 50
 SW13 .... 1C 116
 TW6: H'row A 1C 110
 UB4: Hayes 5F 75
 W3 .... 2J 97
Newport St. SE11 .... 4G 19 (4K 101)
New Priory Ct. *NW6* .... 7J 63 *(off Mazenod Av.)*
New Providence Wharf E14 .... 1F 105
Newquay Cres. HA2: Harr 2C 58
Newquay Ho. SE11 .... 5J 19 (5A 102)
Newquay Rd. SE6 .... 2D 140
New Quebec St. W1 .... 1F 11 (6D 82)
New Ride SW1 .... 2D 100
 SW7 .... 6C 10 (2C 100)
New River Av. N8 .... 3K 47
New River Ct. N5 .... 4C 66
New River Cres. N13 .... 4G 33
New River Head EC1 .... 1K 7 (3A 84)

New River Sports & Recreation Cen. 7G 33
New River Wlk. N1 .... 6C 66
New River Way N4 .... 7D 48
New Rd. CR4: Mitc 1D 166
 DA16: Well 2B 126
 E1 .... 5H 85
 E4 .... 4J 35
 E12 .... 2C 70
 HA1: Harr 4K 59
 IG3: Ilf 2J 71
 KT2: King T 7G 133
 KT8: W Mole 4E 148
 N8 .... 5J 47
 N9 .... 3B 34
 N17 .... 1F 49
 N22 .... 1C 48
 NW7 .... 7B 30
 RM9: Dag 2G 91
 RM10: Dag 2G 91
 SE2 .... 4D 108
 TW3: Houn 4F 113
 TW8: Bford 6D 96
 TW10: Ham 4C 132
 TW13: Hanw 5C 130
 TW14: Bedf 6F 111
 TW14: Felt 1K 129
 TW17: Shep 3C 146
 UB3: Harl 7E 92
 UB8: Hil 4E 74
New Rd. Hill BR2: Kes 7C 172
 BR6: Downe 7C 172
New Rochford St. NW5 .... 5D 64
New Row WC2 .... 2E 12 (7J 83)
Newry Rd. TW1: Twick 5A 114
Newsam Av. N15 .... 5D 48
Newsholme Dr. N21 .... 5E 22
NEW SOUTHGATE 5A 32
New Southgate Crematorium N11 .... 3A 32
New Southgate Ind. Est. N11 .... 5B 32
New Spitalfields Mkt. E10 .... 3D 68
New Spring Gdns. Wlk. SE11 .... 6F 19 (5J 101)
New Sq. TW14: Bedf 1E 128
 WC2 .... 7J 7 (6A 84)
New Sq. Pk. TW14: Bedf 1E 128
New Sq. Pas. WC2 .... 7J 7
Newstead Av. BR6: Orp 3H 173
Newstead Cl. N12 .... 6H 31
Newstead Ct. UB5: N'olt 3C 76
Newstead Ho. *N1* .... 2A 84 *(off Tolpuddle St.)*
Newstead Rd. SE12 .... 7H 123
Newstead Wlk. SM5: Cars 7A 154
Newstead Way SW19 .... 4F 135
New St. EC2 .... 6H 9 (5E 84)
New St. Hill BR1: Brom 5K 141
New St. Sq. EC4 .... 7K 7 (6A 84)
Newton Av. N10 .... 1E 46
 W3 .... 2J 97
Newton Cl. E17 .... 6A 50
 HA2: Harr 2E 58
Newton Ct. *W8* .... 2J 99 *(off Kensington Chu. St.)*
Newton Gro. W4 .... 4A 98
Newton Ho. *E1* .... 7H 85 *(off Cornwall St.)*
 E17 .... 3D 50 *(off Prospect Hill)*
 EN3: Enf H 3E 24
 NW8 .... 1K 81 *(off Abbey Rd.)*
 SE20 .... 7K 139
Newton Ind. Est. RM6: Chad H 4D 54
Newton Mans. *W14* .... 6G 99 *(off Queen's Club Gdns.)*
Newton Pl. E14 .... 4C 104
Newton Point *E16* .... 6H 87 *(off Clarkson Rd.)*
Newton Rd. DA16: Well 3A 126
 E15 .... 5F 69
 HA0: Wemb 7F 61
 HA3: Hrw W 2J 41

Newton Rd. N15 .... 5G 49
 NW2 .... 4E 62
 SW19 .... 7G 135
 TW7: Isle 2K 113
 W2 .... 6K 81
Newton St. WC2 .... 7F 7 (6J 83)
Newton's Yd. SW18 .... 5J 117
Newton Ter. BR2: Brom 6B 160
Newton Wlk. HA8: Edg 1H 43
Newton Way N18 .... 5H 33
New Twr. Bldgs. E1 .... 1H 103
Newtown St. SW11 .... 1F 119
New Trinity Rd. N2 .... 3B 46
New Turnstile WC1 .... 6G 7
New Union Cl. E14 .... 3E 104
New Union St. EC2 .... 6E 8 (5D 84)
New Wanstead E11 .... 6H 51
New Way Rd. NW9 .... 4A 44
New Wharf Rd. N1 .... 2J 83
NEWYEARS GREEN 7B 38
Newyears Grn. La. UB9: Hare 6A 38
New Zealand Av. KT12: Walt T 7H 147
New Zealand Way W12 .... 7D 80
Next Generation Club Carlton 5J 81
Nexus Ct. E11 .... 1G 69
Niagara Av. W5 .... 4C 96
Niagra Cl. N1 .... 2C 84
Niagra Ct. *SE16* .... 3J 103 *(off Canada Est.)*
Nibthwaite Rd. HA1: Harr 5J 41
Nicholas Cl. UB6: G'frd 2F 77
Nicholas Ct. SE12 .... 1J 141
 W4 .... 6A 98 *(off Corney Reach Way)*
Nicholas Gdns. W5 .... 2D 96
Nicholas La. EC4 .... 2F 15 (7D 84) (not continuous)
Nicholas M. W4 .... 6A 98
Nicholas Pas. EC3 .... 1F 15
Nicholas Rd. CR0: Bedd 4J 167
 E1 .... 4J 85
 RM8: Dag 2F 73
Nicholas Stacey Ho. *SE7* .... 5K 105 *(off Frank Burton Cl.)*
Nicholas Way HA6: Nwood 1E 38
Nicholay Rd. N19 .... 1H 65 (not continuous)
Nichol Cl. N14 .... 1C 32
Nicholes Rd. TW3: Houn 4E 112
Nichol La. BR1: Brom 7J 141
Nicholl Ho. N4 .... 1C 66
Nicholls Av. UB8: Hil 4C 74
Nichollsfield Wlk. N7 .... 5K 65
Nicholls Point *E15* .... 1J 87 *(off Park Gro.)*
Nicholl St. E2 .... 1G 85
Nichols Cl. KT9: Chess 6C 162
 N4 .... 1A 66 *(off Osborne Rd.)*
Nichols Ct. E2 .... 2F 85
Nichols Grn. W5 .... 5E 78
Nicholson Ct. E17 .... 4A 50
 N17 .... 3F 49
Nicholson Ho. SE17 .... 5D 102
Nicholson M. KT1: King T 4E 150
Nicholson Rd. CR0: Croy 1F 169
Nicholson St. SE1 .... 5A 14 (1B 102)
Nickelby Cl. SE28 .... 6C 90
Nickleby Cl. UB8: Hil 6D 74
Nickleby Ho. *SE16* .... 7K 15 *(off Parkers Row)*
 W11 .... 1F 99 *(off St Ann's Rd.)*
Nickols Wlk. SW18 .... 4K 117
Nicola Cl. CR2: S Croy 6C 168
 HA3: Hrw W 2H 41
Nicolas Ct. E13 .... 3K 87
Nicola Ter. DA7: Bex 1E 126
Nicol Cl. TW1: Twick 6B 114
Nicoll Ct. N10 .... 7A 32
 NW10 .... 1A 80
Nicoll Pl. NW4 .... 6D 44

Nicoll Rd. NW10	1A 80
Nicolson NW9	1A 44
Nicolson Dr. WD23: Bushy	1B 26
Nicosia Rd. SW18	7C 118
Niederwald Rd. SE26	4A 140
Nield Rd. UB3: Hayes	2H 93
Nigel Cl. UB5: N'olt	1C 76
Nigel Cl. N3	7E 30
Nigel Fisher Way KT9: Chess	7C 162
Nigel Ho. EC1	5J 7
(off Portpool La.)	
Nigel M. IG1: Ilf	4F 71
Nigel Playfair Av. W6	4D 98
Nigel Rd. E7	5A 70
SE15	3G 121
Nigeria Rd. SE7	7A 106
Nighthawk NW9	1B 44
Nightingale Av. E4	5B 36
HA1: Harr	7B 42
Nightingale Cl. E4	4A 36
HA5: Eastc	5A 40
SM5: Cars	2E 166
W4	6J 97
Nightingale Ct. BR2: Brom	2G 159
E14	2E 104
(off Ovex Cl.)	
HA1: Harr	6K 41
N4	2K 65
(off Tollington Pk.)	
SM1: Sutt	5A 166
SW6	1K 117
(off Maltings Pl.)	
Nightingale Dr. KT19: Ewe	6H 163
Nightingale Gro. SE13	5F 123
Nightingale Hgts. SE18	6F 107
Nightingale Ho. E1	1G 103
(off Thomas More St.)	
E2	1E 84
(off Kingsland Rd.)	
SE18	5E 106
(off Connaught M.)	
W12	6E 80
(off Du Cane Rd.)	
Nightingale La. BR1: Brom	2A 160
E11	4K 51
N8	4J 47
SW4	7D 118
SW12	7D 118
TW10: Rich	7E 114
Nightingale Lodge W9	5J 81
(off Admiral Wlk.)	
Nightingale M. E3	2K 85
E11	5J 51
KT1: King T	3D 150
(off South La.)	
SE11	3K 19 (4B 102)
Nightingale Pl. SE18	6E 106
SW10	7A 16 (6A 100)
(not continuous)	
Nightingale Rd. BR5: Pet W	6G 161
E5	3H 67
KT8: W Mole	5F 149
KT12: Walt T	7A 148
N1	6C 66
N9	6D 24
N22	1J 47
NW10	2B 80
SM5: Cars	3D 166
TW12: Hamp	5E 130
W7	1K 95
Nightingales, The TW19: Stanw	1B 128
Nightingale Sq. SW12	7E 118
Nightingale Va. SE18	6E 106
Nightingale Wlk. SW4	6F 119
Nightingale Way E6	5C 88
Nile Cl. N16	3F 67
Nile Dr. N9	2D 34
Nile Path SE18	6E 106
Nile Rd. E13	2A 88
Nile St. N1	1D 8 (3C 84)
Nile Ter. SE15	5F 103
Nimegen Way SE22	5E 120
Nimmo Dr. WD23: Bushy	1C 26

Nimrod NW9	1A 44
Nimrod Cl. UB5: N'olt	3B 76
Nimrod Ho. E16	5K 87
(off Vanguard Cl.)	
Nimrod Pas. N1	6E 66
Nimrod Rd. SW16	6F 137
Nina Mackay Cl. E15	1G 87
Nine Acres Cl. E12	5C 70
NINE ELMS	7G 101
Nine Elms Cl. TW14: Felt	1H 129
Nine Elms La. SW8	7C 18 (7G 101)
Nineteenth Rd. CR4: Mitc	4J 155
Ninhams Wood BR6: Farnb	4E 172
Ninth Av. UB3: Hayes	7J 75
Nipponzan Myohoji Peace Pagoda	
	6D 100
Nirvana Apartments N1	1B 84
(off Islington Grn.)	
Nisbet Ho. E9	5K 67
Nisbett Wlk. DA14: Sidc	4A 144
(off Sidcup High St.)	
Nita Ct. SE12	1J 141
Nithdale Rd. SE18	7F 107
Nithsdale Gro. UB10: Ick	3E 56
Niton Cl. EN5: Barn	6A 20
Niton Rd. TW9: Rich	3G 115
Niton St. SW6	7F 99
No 1 St. SE18	3F 107
Nobel Dr. UB3: Harl	1F 111
Nobel Ho. SE5	2C 120
Nobel Rd. N18	4D 34
Noble Cnr. TW5: Hest	1E 112
Noble Ct. CR4: Mitc	2B 154
E1	7H 85
Noblefield Hgts. N2	5C 46
Noble M. N16	3D 66
(off Albion Rd.)	
Noble St. EC2	7C 8 (6C 84)
Noel NW9	1A 44
Noel Ct. TW4: Houn	3D 112
Noel Coward Ho. SW1	4B 18
(off Vauxhall Bri. Rd.)	
Noel Ho. NW6	7B 64
(off Harben Rd.)	
NOEL PARK	2B 48
Noel Pk. Rd. N22	2A 48
Noel Rd. E6	4C 88
N1	2B 84
W3	7G 79
Noel Sq. RM8: Dag	4C 72
Noel St. W1	1B 12 (6G 83)
Noel Ter. DA14: Sidc	4B 144
SE23	2J 139
Noko W10	3F 81
Nolan Way E5	4G 67
Noll Ho. N7	2K 65
(off Tomlins Wlk.)	
Nolton Pl. HA8: Edg	1F 43
Nonsuch Ho. SW19	1B 154
Nonsuch Pl. SM3: Cheam	7F 165
(off Ewell Rd.)	
Nonsuch Wlk. SM2: Cheam	7F 165
(not continuous)	
Nora Gdns. NW4	4F 45
NORBITON	2G 151
Norbiton Av. KT1: King T	1G 151
Norbiton Comn. Rd. KT1: King T	3H 151
Norbiton Hall KT2: King T	2F 151
Norbiton Rd. E14	6B 86
Norbreck Gdns. NW10	3F 79
Norbreck Pde. NW10	3E 78
Norbroke St. W12	7B 80
Norburn St. W10	5G 81
NORBURY	2K 155
Norbury Av. CR7: Thor H	1K 155
SW16	1K 155
TW3: Houn	4H 113
Norbury Cl. SW16	1A 156
Norbury Ct. Rd. SW16	3J 155
Norbury Cres. SW16	1K 155
Norbury Cross SW16	3J 155
Norbury Gdns. RM6: Chad H	5D 54
Norbury Gro. NW7	3F 29

Norbury Hill SW16	7A 138
Norbury Ri. SW16	3J 155
Norbury Rd. CR7: Thor H	2C 156
E4	5H 35
TW13: Felt	3H 129
Norbury Trad. Est. SW16	2K 155
Norcombe Gdns.	
HA3: Kent	6C 42
Norcombe Ho. N19	3H 65
(off Wedmore St.)	
Norcott Cl. UB4: Yead	4A 76
Norcott Rd. N16	2G 67
Norcroft Gdns. SE22	7G 121
Norcutt Rd. TW2: Twick	1J 131
Nordenfeldt Rd.	
DA8: Erith	5K 109
Norden Ho. E2	3H 85
(off Pott St.)	
Norfield Rd. DA2: Dart	4J 145
Norfolk Av. N13	6G 33
N15	6F 49
Norfolk Cl. EN4: Cockf	4K 21
N2	3C 46
N13	6G 33
TW1: Twick	6B 114
Norfolk Ct. EN5: Barn	4B 20
RM6: Chad H	5B 54
(off Norwich Cres.)	
Norfolk Cres. DA15: Sidc	7J 125
W2	7C 4 (6C 82)
Norfolk Gdns. DA7: Bex	1F 127
TW4: Houn	5D 112
Norfolk Ho. BR2: Brom	4H 159
(off Westmoreland Rd.)	
EC4	2C 14
SE3	6H 105
(off Restell Cl.)	
SE8	1C 122
SE20	1J 157
SW1	3D 18
(off Page St.)	
Norfolk Ho. Rd. SW16	3H 137
Norfolk Mans. SW11	1D 118
(off Prince of Wales Dr.)	
Norfolk M. W10	5G 81
(off Blagrove Rd.)	
Norfolk Pl. DA16: Well	2A 126
W2	7B 4 (6B 82)
(not continuous)	
Norfolk Rd. CR7: Thor H	3C 156
E6	1D 88
E17	2K 49
EN3: Pond E	6C 24
EN5: New Bar	3D 20
HA1: Harr	5F 41
IG3: Ilf	1J 71
IG11: Bark	7J 71
NW8	1B 82
NW10	7A 62
RM7: Rom	6J 55
RM10: Dag	5H 73
SW19	7C 136
TW13: Felt	1A 130
UB8: Uxb	6A 56
Norfolk Row SE1	3G 19 (4K 101)
(not continuous)	
Norfolk Sq. W2	1B 10 (6B 82)
Norfolk Sq. M. W2	1B 10
Norfolk St. E7	5J 69
Norfolk Ter. W6	5G 99
Norgrove St. SW12	7E 118
Norhyrst Av. SE25	3F 157
Norland Ho. W11	1F 99
(off Queensdale Cres.)	
Norland Pl. W11	1G 99
Norland Rd. W11	1F 99
Norlands Cres. BR7: Chst	1F 161
Norland Sq. W11	1G 99
Norland Sq. Mans. W11	1G 99
(off Norland Sq.)	
Norley Va. SW15	1C 134
Norlington Rd. E10	1E 68
E11	1E 68

Norman Av. N22	1B 48
TW1: Twick	7C 114
TW13: Hanw	2C 130
UB1: S'hall	7C 76
Norman Butler Ho. W10	4G 81
(off Ladbroke Gro.)	
Normanby Cl. SW15	5H 117
Normanby Rd. NW10	4B 62
Norman Cl. BR6: Farnb	3G 173
N22	1C 48
RM5: Col R	1H 55
Norman Cl. IG2: Ilf	7H 53
N3	1J 45
(off Nether St.)	
N4	7A 48
NW10	7C 62
W13	1B 96
(off Kirkfield Cl.)	
Norman Cres. HA5: Pinn	1A 40
TW5: Hest	7B 94
Normand Gdns. W14	6G 99
(off Greyhound Rd.)	
Normand Mans. W14	6G 99
(off Normand M.)	
Normand M. W14	6G 99
Normand Rd. W14	6H 99
Normandy Av. EN5: Barn	5C 20
Normandy Cl. SE26	3A 140
Normandy Dr. UB3: Hayes	6E 74
Normandy Ho. E14	2E 104
(off Plevna St.)	
Normandy Rd. SW9	1A 120
Normandy Ter. E16	6K 87
Normandy Way DA8: Erith	1K 127
Norman Gro. E3	2A 86
Norman Hay Trad. Est., The	
UB7: Sip	7B 92
Norman Ho. SW8	7J 101
(off Wyvil Rd.)	
TW13: Hanw	2D 130
(off Watermill Way)	
Normanhurst TW15: Ashf	5C 128
Normanhurst Av. DA7: Bex	1D 126
DA16: Well	1D 126
Normanhurst Dr. TW1: Twick	5A 114
Normanhurst Rd. SW2	2K 137
Norman Pde. DA14: Sidc	2D 144
Norman Pk. Athletics Track	6K 159
Norman Rd. CR7: Thor H	5B 156
DA17: Belv	3H 109
(not continuous)	
E6	4D 88
E11	2F 69
IG1: Ilf	5F 71
N15	5F 49
SE10	7D 104
SM1: Sutt	5J 165
SW19	7A 136
W13	6F 129
Normans Cl. NW10	6K 61
UB8: Hil	5B 74
Normansfield Av. TW11: Tedd	7C 132
Normanshire Dr. E4	4H 35
Norman's Mead NW10	6K 61
Norman St. EC1	2D 8 (3C 84)
Normanton Av. SW19	2J 135
Normanton Pk. E4	2B 36
Normanton Rd. CR2: S Croy	5E 168
Normanton St. SE23	2K 139
Norman Way N14	2D 32
W3	5H 79
Normington Cl. SW16	5A 138
Norrice Lea N2	5C 46
Norris NW9	1B 44
(off The Concourse)	
Norris Ho. E9	1J 85
(off Handley Rd.)	
N1	1E 84
(off Colville Est.)	
SE8	5B 104
(off Grove St.)	
Norris St. SW1	3C 12 (7H 83)
Norroy Rd. SW15	4F 117

Norry's Cl. EN4: Cockf 4J **21**
Norry's Rd. EN4: Cockf 4J **21**
Norseman Cl. IG3: Ilf 1B **72**
Norseman Way UB6: G'frd 1F **77**
Norstead Pl. SW15 . . . . 2C **134**
Nth. Access Rd. E17 . . . . 6K **49**
North Acre NW9 . . . . 1A **44**
NORTH ACTON 4K **79**
Nth. Acton Bus. Pk. W3 . . . . 5K **79**
Nth. Acton Rd. NW10 . . . . 2K **79**
Northall Rd. DA7: Bex 2J **127**
Northampton Gro. N1 . . . . 5D **66**
Northampton Pk. N1 . . . . 6C **66**
Northampton Rd.
CR0: Croy 2G **169**
EC1 . . . . 3K **7** (4A **84**)
EN3: Pond E 4F **25**
Northampton Row EC1 . . . . 3K **7**
Northampton Sq. EC1 . . . . 2A **8** (3B **84**)
Northampton St. N1 . . . . 7C **66**
Northanger Rd. SW16 . . . . 6J **137**
Nth. Audley St. W1 . . . . 1G **11** (6E **82**)
North Av. HA2: Harr 6F **41**
N18 . . . . 4B **34**
NW10 . . . . 3E **80**
SM5: Cars 7E **166**
TW9: Kew 1G **115**
UB1: S'hall 7D **76**
UB3: Hayes 7J **75**
W13 . . . . 5B **78**
Northaw Ho. *W10* *4E* ***80***
(off Sutton Way)
North Bank NW8 . . . . 2C **4** (3C **82**)
Northbank Rd. E17 . . . . 2E **50**
NORTH BECKTON 5C **88**
Nth. Birkbeck Rd. E11 . . . . 3F **69**
North Block *SE1* *6H* ***13***
(off York Rd.)
Northborough Rd. SW16 . . . . 3H **155**
Nth. Boundary Rd. E12 . . . . 3B **70**
Northbourne BR2: Hayes 7J **159**
Northbourne Rd. SW4 . . . . 5H **119**
Nth. Branch Av. NW10 . . . . 3E **80**
Northbrook Dr. HA6: Nwood 1G **39**
Northbrook Rd. CR0: Croy 5D **156**
EN5: Barn 6B **20**
IG1: Ilf 2E **70**
N22 . . . . 7D **32**
SE13 . . . . 5G **123**
Northburgh St. EC1 . . . . 4B **8** (4B **84**)
Nth. Carriage Dr. W2 . . . . 2C **10**
NORTH CHEAM 3E **164**
North Cheam Sports Club 3F **165**
Northchurch SE17 . . . . 5D **102**
(not continuous)
Northchurch Ho. *E2* *1G* ***85***
(off Whiston Rd.)
Northchurch Rd. HA9: Wemb 6G **61**
N1 . . . . 7D **66**
(not continuous)
Northchurch Ter. N1 . . . . 7E **66**
Nth. Circular Rd. E4 . . . . 6G **35**
E18 . . . . 2A **52**
IG1: Ilf 2D **70**
IG11: Bark 1F **89**
N3 . . . . 3J **45**
N12 . . . . 2A **46**
N13 . . . . 5F **33**
NW2 . . . . 3A **62**
NW4 . . . . 7E **44**
NW10 . . . . 2F **79**
NW11 . . . . 6F **45**
Northcliffe Cl. KT4: Wor Pk 3A **164**
Northcliffe Dr. N20 . . . . 1C **30**
North Cl. DA6: Bex 4D **126**
RM10: Dag 1G **91**
SM4: Mord 4G **153**
TW14: Bedf 6F **111**
Nth. Colonnade, The E14 . . . . 1C **104**
North Comn. Rd.
UB8: Uxb 5A **56**
W5 . . . . 7E **78**
Northcote HA5: Pinn 2A **40**
Northcote Av. KT5: Surb 7H **151**
TW7: Isle 5A **114**
UB1: S'hall 7C **76**
W5 . . . . 7E **78**
Northcote M. SW11 . . . . 4C **118**
Northcote Rd. CR0: Croy 6D **156**
DA14: Sidc 4J **143**
E17 . . . . 4A **50**
KT3: N Mald 3J **151**
NW10 . . . . 7A **62**
SW11 . . . . 5C **118**
TW1: Twick 5A **114**
Northcott Av. N22 . . . . 1J **47**
Nth. Countess Rd. E17 . . . . 2B **50**
North Ct. *BR1: Brom* *1K* ***159***
(off Palace Gro.)
SE24 . . . . 3B **120**
SW1 . . . . *2E* ***18***
(off Gt. Peter St.)
W1 . . . . 5B **6** (5G **83**)
NORTH CRAY 5E **144**
Nth. Cray Rd. DA5: Bexl 1H **145**
DA14: Sidc 6E **144**
North Cray Woods
DA14: Sidc 4D **144**
North Cres. E16 . . . . 4F **87**
N3 . . . . 2H **45**
WC1 . . . . 5C **6** (5H **83**)
Northcroft Ct. W12 . . . . 2C **98**
Northcroft Rd. KT19: Ewe 7A **164**
W13 . . . . 2B **96**
North Crofts SE23 . . . . 1H **139**
Northcroft Ter. W13 . . . . 2B **96**
Nth. Cross Rd. IG6: Ilf 4G **53**
SE22 . . . . 5F **121**
Northdale Ct. SE25 . . . . 3F **157**
North Dene NW7 . . . . 3E **28**
TW3: Houn 1F **113**
Northdene Gdns. N15 . . . . 6F **49**
Northdown Cl. HA4: Ruis 3H **57**
Northdown Gdns. IG2: Ilf 5J **53**
Northdown Rd.
DA16: Well 2B **126**
Northdown St. N1 . . . . 1G **7** (2J **83**)
North Dr. BR3: Beck 4D **158**
BR6: Orp 4J **173**
HA4: Ruis 7G **39**
SW16 . . . . 4G **137**
TW3: Houn 2G **113**
North E. Surrey Crematorium
SM4: Mord 6E **152**
NORTH END 2A **64**
North End CR0: Croy 2C **168**
IG9: Buck H 1F **37**
NW3 . . . . 2A **64**
North End Av. NW3 . . . . 2A **64**
(not continuous)
North End Cres. W14 . . . . 4H **99**
North End Ho. W14 . . . . 4G **99**
North End La. BR6: Downe 7F **173**
North End Pde. *W14* *4G* ***99***
(off North End Rd.)
North End Rd. HA9: Wemb 3G **61**
NW11 . . . . 1J **63**
SW6 . . . . 6H **99**
W14 . . . . 4G **99**
North End Way NW3 . . . . 2A **64**
Northern Av. N9 . . . . 2K **33**
Northernhay Wlk. SM4: Mord 4G **153**
Northern Hgts. *N8* *7H* ***47***
(off Crescent Rd.)
Northern Perimeter Rd.
TW6: H'row A 1D **110**
Northern Perimeter Rd. W.
TW6: H'row A 1A **110**
Northern Rd. E13 . . . . 2K **87**
Northesk Ho. *E1* *4H* ***85***
(off Tent St.)
Nth. Eyot Gdns. W6 . . . . 5B **98**
Northey St. E14 . . . . 7A **86**
NORTH FELTHAM 6K **111**
Nth. Feltham Trad. Est.
TW14: Felt 5K **111**
Northfield Av. HA5: Pinn 4B **40**
W5 . . . . 1B **96**
W13 . . . . 1B **96**
Northfield Cl. BR1: Brom 1C **160**
UB3: Harl 3H **93**
Northfield Cres. SM3: Cheam 4G **165**
Northfield Gdns. RM9: Dag 4F **73**
Northfield Ho. SE15 . . . . 6G **103**
Northfield Ind. Est. NW10 . . . . 3G **79**
Northfield Pde. UB3: Harl 3G **93**
Northfield Pk. UB3: Harl 3H **93**
Northfield Path RM9: Dag 4F **73**
Northfield Rd. E6 . . . . 7D **70**
EN3: Pond E 5C **24**
EN4: Cockf 3H **21**
N16 . . . . 7E **48**
RM9: Dag 4F **73**
TW5: Hest 6B **94**
W13 . . . . 2B **96**
NORTHFIELDS 3B **96**
Northfields SW18 . . . . 4J **117**
Northfields Ind. Est. HA0: Wemb 1G **79**
Northfields Prospect Bus. Cen.
SW18 . . . . 4J **117**
Northfields Rd. W3 . . . . 5H **79**
NORTH FINCHLEY 5F **31**
Northfleet Ho. *SE1* *6E* ***14***
(off Tennis St.)
Nth. Flock St. SE16 . . . . 2G **103**
Nth. Flower Wlk. W2 . . . . 3A **10**
North Gdn. E14 . . . . 1B **104**
North Gdns. SW19 . . . . 7B **136**
North Ga. NW8 . . . . 1C **4**
Northgate HA6: Nwood 1E **38**
Northgate Bus. Cen. EN1: Enf 3C **24**
Northgate Ct. SW9 . . . . 3A **120**
Northgate Dr. NW9 . . . . 6A **44**
Northgate Ho. *E14* *7C* ***86***
(off E. India Dock Rd.)
Northgate Ind. Pk. RM5: Col R 1F **55**
North Gates *N12* *1A* ***46***
(off Bow La.)
Nth. Glade, The DA5: Bexl 7F **127**
Nth. Gower St. NW1 . . . . 2B **6** (3G **83**)
North Grn. NW9 . . . . 7F **29**
North Gro. N6 . . . . 7E **46**
N15 . . . . 5D **48**
NORTH HARROW 5F **41**
Nth. Hatton Rd. TW6: H'row A 1F **111**
North Hill N6 . . . . 6D **46**
Nth. Hill Av. N6 . . . . 6E **46**
NORTH HILLINGDON 7E **56**
North Ho. SE8 . . . . 5B **104**
Nth. Hyde Gdns. UB3: Harl, Hayes 3J **93**
Nth. Hyde La. TW5: Hest 5C **94**
UB2: S'hall 5B **94**
Nth. Hyde Rd. UB3: Harl 3G **93**
Northiam N12 . . . . 4D **30**
(not continuous)
WC1 . . . . *2F* ***7***
(off Cromer St.)
Northiam St. E9 . . . . 1H **85**
Northington St. WC1 . . . . 4H **7** (4K **83**)
NORTH KENSINGTON 5F **81**
North Kent Indoor Bowls Club 3H **109**
Northlands Av. BR6: Orp 4J **173**
Northlands St. SE5 . . . . 2C **120**
North La. TW11: Tedd 6K **131**
North Lodge *E16* *1K* ***105***
(off Wesley Av.)
EN5: New Bar 5F **21**
Nth. Lodge Cl. SW15 . . . . 5F **117**
Nth. London Bus. Pk. N11 . . . . 2K **31**
North Mall *N9* *2C* ***34***
(off Plevna Rd.)
SW18 . . . . *5K* ***117***
(off Buckhold Rd.)
North M. WC1 . . . . 4H **7** (4K **83**)
North Mt. *N20* *2F* ***31***
(off High Rd.)
Northolm HA8: Edg 4E **28**
Northolme Gdns. HA8: Edg 1G **43**
Northolme Ri. BR6: Orp 2J **173**
Northolme Rd. N5 . . . . 4C **66**
NORTHOLT 7E **58**
Northolt *N17* *2E* ***48***
(off Griffin Rd.)
Northolt Av. HA4: Ruis 5K **57**
Northolt Gdns. UB6: G'frd 5K **59**
Northolt Rd. HA2: Harr 4F **59**
TW6: H'row A 1A **110**
Northolt Swimarama 6E **58**
Northolt Trad. Est. UB5: N'olt 7F **59**
Northover BR1: Brom 3H **141**
North Pde. HA8: Edg 2G **43**
KT9: Chess 5F **163**
UB1: S'hall *6E* ***76***
(off North Rd.)
North Pk. SE9 . . . . 6D **124**
North Pas. SW18 . . . . 5J **117**
North Pl. CR4: Mitc 7D **136**
TW11: Tedd 6K **131**
North Point N8 . . . . 5K **47**
Northpoint Cl. SM1: Sutt 3A **166**
Northpoint Sq. NW1 . . . . 6H **65**
Nth. Pole La. BR2: Kes 6H **171**
Nth. Pole Rd. W10 . . . . 5E **80**
Northport St. N1 . . . . 1D **84**
North Ride W2 . . . . 3C **10** (7C **82**)
North Ri. W2 . . . . 1D **10** (6C **82**)
North Rd. BR1: Brom 1K **159**
BR4: W W'ck 1D **170**
DA17: Belv 3H **109**
HA1: Harr 7A **42**
HA8: Edg 1H **43**
IG3: Ilf 2J **71**
KT6: Surb 6D **150**
N2 . . . . 2C **46**
N6 . . . . 7E **46**
N7 . . . . 6J **65**
N9 . . . . 1C **34**
RM6: Chad H 5E **54**
SE18 . . . . 4J **107**
SW19 . . . . 6A **136**
TW5: Hest 6A **94**
TW8: Bford 6E **96**
TW9: Kew 1G **115**
TW9: Rich 3G **115**
TW14: Bedf 6F **111**
UB1: S'hall 6E **76**
UB3: Hayes 5F **75**
UB7: W Dray 3B **92**
W5 . . . . 3D **96**
Northrop Rd. TW6: H'row A 1G **111**
North Row W1 . . . . 2F **11** (7D **82**)
Nth. Row Bldgs. *W1* *2G* ***11***
(off North Row)
North Several SE3 . . . . 2F **123**
NORTH SHEEN 3G **115**
Northside Rd. BR1: Brom 1J **159**
Nth. Side Wandsworth Comn.
SW18 . . . . 5B **118**
Northspur Rd. SM1: Sutt 3J **165**
North Sq. *N9* *2C* ***34***
(off Hertford Rd.)
NW11 . . . . 5J **45**
Northstead Rd. SW2 . . . . 2A **138**
North St. BR1: Brom 1J **159**
DA7: Bex 4G **127**
E13 . . . . 2K **87**
IG11: Bark 6F **71**
NW4 . . . . 5E **44**
RM1: Rom 3K **55**
(not continuous)
SM5: Cars 3D **166**
SW4 . . . . 3G **119**
TW7: Isle 3A **114**
North St. Pas. E13 . . . . 2K **87**
Nth. Tenter St. E1 . . . . 1K **15** (6F **85**)
North Ter. SW3 . . . . 2C **16** (3C **100**)
Northumberland All. EC3 . . . . 1H **15** (6E **84**)
(not continuous)
Northumberland Av. DA16: Well 4H **125**
E12 . . . . 1A **70**
EN1: Enf 1C **24**
TW7: Isle 1K **113**

Northumberland Av.
WC2 . . . . 4E **12** (1J **101**)
Northumberland Cl. DA8: Erith 7J **109**
TW19: Stanw 6A **110**
Northumberland Cres.
TW14: Felt 6G **111**
Northumberland Gdns.
BR1: Brom 4E **160**
CR4: Mitc 5H **155**
N9 . . . . 3A **34**
TW7: Isle 7A **96**
Northumberland Gro. N17 . . . . 7C **34**
NORTHUMBERLAND HEATH **7J 109**
Northumberland Ho. IG8: Wfd G 7K **37**
SW1 . . . . *4E 12*
(off Northumberland Av.)
Northumberland Pk. DA8: Erith 7J **109**
N17 . . . . 7A **34**
Northumberland Pk. Ind. Est. N17 . . . . 7C **34**
Northumberland Pk. Sports Cen. **7B 34**
Northumberland Pl. TW10: Rich 5D **114**
W2 . . . . 6J **81**
Northumberland Rd. E6 . . . . 6C **88**
E17 . . . . 7C **50**
EN5: New Bar 6F **21**
HA2: Harr 5D **40**
Northumberland Row TW2: Twick 1J **131**
Northumberland St. WC2 . . . . 4E **12** (1J **101**)
Northumberland Way DA8: Erith 1J **127**
Northumbria St. E14 . . . . 6C **86**
Nth. Verbena Gdns. W6 . . . . 5C **98**
North Vw. HA5: Eastc 7A **40**
SW19 . . . . 5E **134**
W5 . . . . 4C **78**
Northview N7 . . . . 3J **65**
North Vw. Cvn. Site IG6: Ilf 1A **54**
Northview Cres. NW10 . . . . 4B **62**
North Vw. Dr. IG8: Wfd G 2B **52**
North Vw. Rd. N8 . . . . 4H **47**
North Vs. NW1 . . . . 6H **65**
North Wlk. CR0: New Ad 6D **170**
(not continuous)
W2 . . . . 7K **81**
North Way HA5: Pinn 4B **40**
N9 . . . . 2E **34**
N11 . . . . 6B **32**
NW9 . . . . 3H **43**
UB10: Uxb 7A **56**
Northway NW11 . . . . 5K **45**
SM4: Mord 3G **153**
SM6: Wall 4G **167**
Northway Cir. NW7 . . . . 4E **28**
Northway Ct. NW7 . . . . 4F **29**
Northway Cres. NW7 . . . . 4E **28**
Northway Gdns. NW11 . . . . 5K **45**
Northway Rd. CR0: Croy 6F **157**
SE5 . . . . 3C **120**
Northways Pde. *NW3* *7B 64*
(off College Cres., not continuous)
Northweald La. KT2: King T 5D **132**
NORTH WEMBLEY **3D 60**
Nth. Western Commercial Cen.
NW1 . . . . 7J **65**
Northwest Pl. N1 . . . . 2A **84**
North Wharf *E14* *1E 104*
(off Coldharbour)
Nth. Wharf Rd. W2 . . . . 6A **4** (5B **82**)
Northwick Av. HA3: Kent 6A **42**
Northwick Circ. HA3: Kent 6C **42**
Northwick Cl. HA1: Harr 1B **60**
NW8 . . . . 3A **4** (4B **82**)
Northwick Ho. NW8 . . . . 3A **4**
Northwick Pk. Rd. HA1: Harr 6K **41**
Northwick Rd. HA0: Wemb 1D **78**
Northwick Ter. NW8 . . . . 3A **4** (4B **82**)
Northwick Wlk. HA1: Harr 7K **41**
Northwold Dr. HA5: Pinn 2A **40**
Northwold Rd. E5 . . . . 2F **67**
N16 . . . . 2F **67**
NORTHWOOD **1H 39**
Nth. Wood Ct. SE25 . . . . 3G **157**
Northwood Est. E5 . . . . 2G **67**
Northwood FC **2H 39**
Northwood Gdns. IG5: Ilf 4E **52**
N12 . . . . 5G **31**
UB6: G'frd 5K **59**
Northwood Hall N6 . . . . 7G **47**
NORTHWOOD HILLS **2J 39**
Northwood Hills Cir. HA6: Nwood 1J **39**
Northwood Ho. *KT2: King T* *2G 151*
(off Coombe Rd.)
SE27 . . . . 4D **138**
Northwood Pl. DA18: Erith 3F **109**
Northwood Rd. CR7: Thor H 2B **156**
N6 . . . . 7F **47**
SE23 . . . . 1B **140**
SM5: Cars 6E **166**
TW6: H'row A 1A **110**
UB9: Hare 1A **38**
Northwood Sports Cen. **1K 39**
Northwood Way HA6: Nwood 1J **39**
SE19 . . . . 6D **138**
UB9: Hare 1A **38**
NORTH WOOLWICH **2E 106**
North Woolwich Old Station Mus.
. . . . **2E 106**
Nth. Woolwich Rd. E16 . . . . 1H **105**
Nth. Worple Way SW14 . . . . 3K **115**
Norton Av. KT5: Surb 7H **151**
Norton Cl. E4 . . . . 5H **35**
EN1: Enf 2C **24**
Norton Ct. BR3: Beck 1B **158**
Norton Folgate E1 . . . . 5H **9** (5E **84**)
Norton Folgate Ho. *E1* *5J 9*
(off Puma Ct.)
Norton Gdns. SW16 . . . . 2J **155**
Norton Ho. *E1* *6H 85*
(off Bigland St.)
E2 . . . . *2K 85*
(off Mace St.)
SW1 . . . . *2D 18*
(off Arneway St.)
SW9 . . . . *2K 119*
(off Aytoun Rd.)
Norton Rd. E10 . . . . 1B **68**
HA0: Wemb 6D **60**
RM10: Dag 6K **73**
Norval Rd. HA0: Wemb 2B **60**
Norway Ga. SE16 . . . . 3A **104**
Norway Pl. E14 . . . . 6B **86**
Norway St. SE10 . . . . 6D **104**
Norway Wharf *E14* *6B 86*
(off Norway Pl.)
Norwich Cres. RM6: Chad H 5B **54**
Norwich Ho. *E14* *6D 86*
(off Cordelia St.)
Norwich M. IG3: Ilf 1A **72**
Norwich Pl. DA6: Bex 4G **127**
Norwich Rd. CR7: Thor H 3C **156**
E7 . . . . 5J **69**
HA6: Nwood 3H **39**
RM9: Dag 2G **91**
UB6: G'frd 1F **77**
Norwich St. EC4 . . . . 7J **7** (6A **84**)
Norwich Wlk. HA8: Edg 7D **28**
NORWOOD **6E 138**
Norwood Av. HA0: Wemb 1F **79**
RM7: Rush G 7K **55**
Norwood Cl. NW2 . . . . 3G **63**
TW2: Twick 2H **131**
UB2: S'hall 4E **94**
Norwood Dr. HA2: Harr 6D **40**
Norwood Gdns. UB2: S'hall 4D **94**
UB4: Yead 4A **76**
NORWOOD GREEN **4D 94**
Norwood Grn. Rd. UB2: S'hall 4E **94**
Norwood High St. SE27 . . . . 3B **138**
Norwood Ho. *E14* *7D 86*
(off Poplar High St.)
NORWOOD NEW TOWN **6C 138**
Norwood Pk. Rd. SE27 . . . . 5C **138**
Norwood Rd. SE24 . . . . 1B **138**
SE27 . . . . 2B **138**
UB2: S'hall 3C **94**
Norwood Ter. UB2: S'hall 4F **95**
Nota M. N3 . . . . 1J **45**
Notley St. SE5 . . . . 7D **102**
Notson Rd. SE25 . . . . 4H **157**
Notting Barn Rd.
W10 . . . . 4F **81**
Nottingdale Sq. W11 . . . . 1G **99**
Nottingham Av. E16 . . . . 5A **88**
Nottingham Ct. WC2 . . . . 1E **12** (6J **83**)
Nottingham Ho. *WC2* *1E 12*
(off Shorts Gdns.)
Nottingham Pl. W1 . . . . 4G **5** (5E **82**)
Nottingham Rd.
CR2: S Croy 4C **168**
E10 . . . . 6E **50**
SW17 . . . . 1D **136**
TW7: Isle 2K **113**
Nottingham St. W1 . . . . 5G **5** (5E **82**)
Nottingham Ter. NW1 . . . . 4G **5**
NOTTING HILL **7H 81**
Notting Hill Ga. W11 . . . . 1J **99**
Nottingwood Ho. *W11* *7G 81*
(off Clarendon Rd.)
Nova Bldg. E14 . . . . 4C **104**
Nova Ct. E. *E14* *1E 104*
(off Yabsley St.)
Nova Ct. W. *E14* *1E 104*
(off Yabsley St.)
Nova M. SM3: Sutt 1G **165**
Novar Cl. BR6: Orp 7K **161**
Nova Rd. CR0: Croy 1B **168**
Novar Rd. SE9 . . . . 1G **143**
Novello St. SW6 . . . . 1J **117**
Novel Sq. *SE10* *3H 105*
(off School Bank Rd.)
Nowell Rd. SW13 . . . . 6C **98**
Nower Ct. HA5: Pinn 4D **40**
Nower Hill HA5: Pinn 4D **40**
Noyna Rd. SW17 . . . . 3D **136**
Nubia Way BR1: Brom 3G **141**
Nuding Cl. SE13 . . . . 3C **122**
Nuffield Ct. TW5: Hest 7D **94**
Nuffield Lodge N6 . . . . 6G **47**
W9 . . . . *5J 81*
(off Admiral Wlk.)
Nugent Rd. N19 . . . . 1J **65**
SE25 . . . . 3F **157**
Nugents Ct. HA5: Pinn 1C **40**
Nugent's Pk. HA5: H End 1C **40**
Nugent Ter. NW8 . . . . 2A **82**
Numa Ct. TW8: Bford 7D **96**
No. 10 Bowling Alley **6K 55**
Nun Ct. EC2 . . . . 7E **8**
Nuneaton Rd. RM9: Dag 7E **72**
NUNHEAD **3H 121**
Nunhead Cres. SE15 . . . . 3H **121**
Nunhead Est. SE15 . . . . 4H **121**
Nunhead Grn. SE15 . . . . 3H **121**
Nunhead Gro. SE15 . . . . 3H **121**
Nunhead La. SE15 . . . . 3H **121**
Nunhead Pas. SE15 . . . . 3G **121**
Nunnington Cl. SE9 . . . . 3C **142**
Nunns Rd. EN2: Enf 2H **23**
Nupton Dr. EN5: Barn 6A **20**
Nurse Cl. HA8: Edg 1J **43**
Nursery App. N12 . . . . 6H **31**
Nursery Av. CR0: Croy 2K **169**
DA7: Bex 3F **127**
N3 . . . . 2A **46**
Nursery Cl. BR6: Orp 7K **161**
CR0: Croy 2K **169**
EN3: Enf H 1E **24**
IG8: Wfd G 5E **36**
RM6: Chad H 6D **54**
SE4 . . . . 2B **122**
SW15 . . . . 4F **117**
TW14: Felt 7K **111**
(not continuous)
Nursery Ct. N17 . . . . 7A **34**
W13 . . . . 5A **78**
Nursery Gdns. BR7: Chst 6F **143**
EN3: Enf H 1E **24**
TW4: Houn 5D **112**
TW12: Hamp 4D **130**
TW16: Sun 2H **147**
Nursery La. E2 . . . . 1F **85**
E7 . . . . 6J **69**
UB8: Cowl 4A **74**
W10 . . . . 5E **80**
Nurserymans Rd. N11 . . . . 2K **31**
Nursery Rd. CR4: Mitc 3C **154**
CR7: Thor H 4D **156**
E9 . . . . 6J **67**
E12 . . . . 2C **70**
HA5: Pinn 3A **40**
N2 . . . . 1B **46**
N14 . . . . 7B **22**
SM1: Sutt 4A **166**
SW9 . . . . 4K **119**
SW19 . . . . 7G **135**
(Elm Gro.)
SW19 . . . . 2K **153**
(Parkleigh Rd.)
TW16: Sun 2G **147**
Nursery Row EN5: Barn 3B **20**
SE17 . . . . 4D **102**
Nursery St. N17 . . . . 7A **34**
Nursery Wlk. NW4 . . . . 3E **44**
RM7: Rush G 7K **55**
Nursery Waye UB8: Uxb 1A **74**
Nurstead Rd. DA8: Erith 7G **109**
Nutbourne St. W10 . . . . 3G **81**
Nutbrook St. SE15 . . . . 3G **121**
Nutbrowne Rd. RM9: Dag 1F **91**
Nutcroft Rd. SE15 . . . . 7H **103**
Nutfield Cl. N18 . . . . 6B **34**
SM5: Cars 3C **166**
Nutfield Ct. BR1: Brom 3J **159**
Nutfield Gdns. IG3: Ilf 2K **71**
UB5: Yead 2A **76**
Nutfield Pas. *CR7: Thor H* *4B 156*
(off Nutfield Rd.)
Nutfield Rd. CR7: Thor H 4B **156**
E15 . . . . 4E **68**
NW2 . . . . 3C **62**
SE22 . . . . 4F **121**
Nutfield Way BR6: Farnb 2F **173**
Nutford Pl. W1 . . . . 7D **4** (6D **82**)
Nuthatch Cl. TW19: Stanw 1B **128**
Nuthatch Gdns. SE28 . . . . 2H **107**
(not continuous)
Nuthurst Av. SW2 . . . . 2K **137**
Nutkin Wlk. UB8: Uxb 7A **56**
Nutley Ter. NW3 . . . . 6A **64**
Nutmead Cl. DA5: Bexl 1J **145**
Nutmeg Cl. E16 . . . . 4G **87**
Nutmeg La. E14 . . . . 6F **87**
Nuttall St. N1 . . . . 2E **84**
Nutter La. E11 . . . . 6A **52**
Nutt Gro. HA8: Edg 2J **27**
Nutt St. SE15 . . . . 7F **103**
Nutty La. TW17: Shep 3E **146**
Nutwell St. SW17 . . . . 5C **136**
Nuxley Rd. DA17: Belv 6F **109**
Nyanza St. SE18 . . . . 6H **107**
Nye Bevan Est. E5 . . . . 3K **67**
Nye Bevan Ho. *SW6* *7H 99*
(off St Thomas's Way)
Nylands Av. TW9: Kew 1G **115**
Nymans Gdns. SW20 . . . . 3D **152**
Nynehead St. SE14 . . . . 7A **104**
Nyon Gro. SE6 . . . . 2B **140**
Nyssa Cl. IG8: Wfd G 6J **37**
Nyssa Ct. *E15* *3G 87*
(off Teasel Way)
Nyton Cl. N19 . . . . 1J **65**

O

O2, The
(Millennium Dome) **1G 105**
O2 Cen. NW3 . . . . 6A **64**
Oak Apple Ct. SE12 . . . . 1J **141**
Oak Av. CR0: Croy 1C **170**
EN2: Enf 1E **22**
N8 . . . . 4J **47**
N10 . . . . 7A **32**

Oak Av.—Oaksway

Oak Av. N17 .7J **33**
TW5: Hest .7B **94**
TW12: Hamp .5C **130**
UB7: W Dray .3C **92**
UB10: Ick .2D **56**
Oak Bank CR0: New Ad .6E **170**
Oakbank Av. KT12: Walt T .7D **148**
Oakbank Gro. SE24 .4C **120**
Oakbark Ho. *TW8: Bford .7C 96*
(off High St.)
Oakbrook Cl. BR1: Brom .4K **141**
Oakbury Rd. SW6 .2K **117**
Oak Cl. N14 .7A **22**
SM1: Sutt .2A **166**
Oakcombe Cl. KT3: N Mald .1A **152**
Oak Cott. Cl. SE6 .1H **141**
Oak Cotts. W7 .2J **95**
Oak Ct. *SE15 .7F 103*
(off Sumner Rd.)
Oak Cres. E16 .5G **87**
Oakcroft Bus. Cen. KT9: Chess .4F **163**
Oakcroft Cl. HA5: Pinn .2K **39**
Oakcroft Rd. KT9: Chess .4F **163**
SE13 .2F **123**
Oakcroft Vs. KT9: Chess .4F **163**
Oakdale N14 .1A **32**
Oakdale Av. HA3: Kent .5E **42**
HA6: Nwood .2J **39**
Oakdale Ct. E4 .5K **35**
Oakdale Gdns. E4 .5K **35**
Oakdale Rd. E7 .7K **69**
E11 .2F **69**
E18 .2K **51**
KT19: Ewe .7K **163**
N4 .6C **48**
SE4 .3J **121**
SE15 .3J **121**
SW16 .5J **137**
Oakdale Way CR4: Mitc .7E **154**
Oakdene SE15 .1H **121**
W13 .5B **78**
Oakdene Av. BR7: Chst .5E **142**
DA8: Erith .6J **109**
KT7: T Ditt .1A **162**
Oakdene Cl. HA5: H End .1D **40**
Oakdene Dr. KT5: Surb .7J **151**
Oakdene M. SM3: Sutt .1H **165**
Oakdene Pk. N3 .7C **30**
Oakdene Rd. BR5: St M Cry .5K **161**
UB10: Hil .2D **74**
Oakden St. SE11 .3K **19** (4A **102**)
Oake Ct. SW15 .5G **117**
Oakeford Ho. *W14 .3G 99*
(off Russell Rd.)
Oakend Ho. N4 .7D **48**
Oakenholt Ho. SE2 .1D **108**
Oakenshaw Cl. KT6: Surb .7E **150**
Oakes Cl. E6 .6D **88**
Oakeshott Av. N6 .2E **64**
Oakey La. SE1 .1J **19** (3A **102**)
Oakfield E4 .5J **35**
Oakfield Av. HA3: Kent .3B **42**
Oakfield Cen. SE20 .7H **139**
Oakfield Cl. HA4: Ruis .6H **39**
KT3: N Mald .5B **152**
Oakfield Ct. N8 .7J **47**
NW2 .7F **45**
Oakfield Gdns. BR3: Beck .5D **158**
N18 .4K **33**
SE19 .5E **138**
(not continuous)
SM5: Cars .1C **166**
UB6: G'frd .4H **77**
Oakfield Ho. *E3 .5C 86*
(off Gale St.)
Oakfield La. BR2: Kes .4A **172**
Oakfield Lodge *IG1: Ilf .3F 71*
(off Albert Rd.)
Oakfield Rd. CR0: Croy .1C **168**
E6 .1C **88**
E17 .2A **50**
IG1: Ilf .3F **71**
N3 .1K **45**
Oakfield Rd. N4 .6A **48**
N14 .2D **32**
SE20 .7H **139**
SW19 .3F **135**
TW15: Ashf .5D **128**
Oakfield Rd. Ind. Est.
SE20 .7H **139**
Oakfields Rd. NW11 .6G **45**
Oakfield St. SW10 .6A **100**
Oakford Rd. NW5 .4G **65**
Oak Gdns. CR0: Croy .2C **170**
HA8: Edg .2J **43**
Oak Glade HA6: Nwood .1D **38**
Oak Gro. BR4: W W'ck .1E **170**
HA4: Ruis .7K **39**
NW2 .4G **63**
TW16: Sun .7K **129**
Oak Gro. Rd. SE20 .1J **157**
Oakhall Ct. E11 .6K **51**
Oakhall Dr. TW16: Sun .5H **129**
Oak Hall Rd. E11 .6K **51**
Oakham Cl. EN4: Cockf .3J **21**
SE6 .2B **140**
Oakham Dr. BR2: Brom .4H **159**
Oakham Ho. *W10 .4E 80*
(off Sutton Way)
Oakhampton Rd. NW7 .7A **30**
Oak Hill IG8: Wfd G .7A **36**
KT6: Surb .7E **150**
Oakhill KT10: Clay .6A **162**
Oakhill Av. HA5: Pinn .2C **40**
NW3 .4K **63**
Oak Hill Cl. IG8: Wfd G .7A **36**
Oak Hill Ct. IG8: Wfd G .7A **36**
Oakhill Ct. SE23 .6J **121**
SW19 .7F **135**
Oak Hill Cres. IG8: Wfd G .7A **36**
KT6: Surb .7E **150**
Oakhill Dr. KT6: Surb .7E **150**
Oak Hill Gdns. IG8: Wfd G .1G **51**
Oak Hill Gro. KT6: Surb .6E **150**
Oak Hill Pk. NW3 .4K **63**
Oak Hill Pk. M. NW3 .4A **64**
Oak Hill Path KT6: Surb .6E **150**
Oakhill Pl. SW15 .5J **117**
Oak Hill Rd. KT6: Surb .6E **150**
Oakhill Rd. BR3: Beck .2E **158**
BR6: Orp .1K **173**
SM1: Sutt .3K **165**
SW15 .5H **117**
SW16 .1J **155**
Oak Hill Way NW3 .4K **63**
(not continuous)
Oak Ho. N2 .2B **46**
TW9: Kew .1H **115**
W10 .4G 81
(off Sycamore Wlk.)
Oakhouse Rd. DA6: Bex .5G **127**
Oakhurst Av. DA7: Bex .7E **108**
EN4: E Barn .7H **21**
Oakhurst Cl. BR7: Chst .1D **160**
E17 .4G **51**
IG6: Ilf .1H **53**
TW11: Tedd .5J **131**
Oakhurst Ct. *E17 .4G 51*
(off Woodford New Rd.)
Oakhurst Gdns. DA7: Bex .7E **108**
E4 .1C **36**
E17 .4G **51**
Oakhurst Gro. SE22 .4G **121**
Oakhurst Rd. KT19: Ewe .6J **163**
Oakington Av. HA2: Harr .7E **40**
HA9: Wemb .3F **61**
UB3: Harl .4F **93**
Oakington Cl. TW16: Sun .2A **148**
Oakington Ct. EN2: Enf .2G **23**
Oakington Dr. TW16: Sun .2A **148**
Oakington Mnr. Dr.
HA9: Wemb .5G **61**
Oakington Rd. W9 .4J **81**
Oakington Way N8 .7J **47**
Oakland Pl. IG9: Buck H .2D **36**
Oakland Rd. E15 .4F **69**
Oaklands BR3: Beck .1D **158**
N21 .2E **32**
W13 .5A **78**
Oaklands Av. BR4: W W'ck .3D **170**
CR7: Thor H .4A **156**
DA15: Sidc .7K **125**
KT10: Esh .7H **149**
N9 .6C **24**
TW7: Isle .6K **95**
Oaklands Cl. BR5: Pet W .6J **161**
DA6: Bex .5F **127**
HA0: Wemb .5D **60**
KT9: Chess .4C **162**
Oaklands Ct. HA0: Wemb .5D **60**
NW10 .1A 80
(off Nicoll Rd.)
SE20 .7J 139
(off Chestnut Gro.)
Oaklands Dr. TW2: Whit .7G **113**
Oaklands Est. SW4 .6G **119**
Oaklands Gro. W12 .1C **98**
Oaklands M. *NW2 .4F 63*
(off Oaklands Rd.)
Oaklands Pk. Av. IG1: Ilf .2G **71**
Oaklands Pas. *NW2 .4F 63*
(off Oaklands Rd.)
Oaklands Pl. SW4 .4G **119**
Oaklands Rd. BR1: Brom .7G **141**
DA6: Bex .4F **127**
N20 .7C **20**
NW2 .4F **63**
SW14 .3K **115**
W7 .2K **95**
(not continuous)
Oaklands Way SM6: Wall .7H **167**
Oakland Way KT19: Ewe .6A **164**
Oak La. E14 .7B **86**
IG8: Wfd G .4C **36**
N2 .2B **46**
N11 .6C **32**
TW1: Twick .7A **114**
TW7: Isle .4J **113**
Oakleafe Gdns. IG6: Ilf .3F **53**
Oaklea Lodge IG3: Ilf .3A **72**
Oaklea Pas. KT1: King T .3D **150**
Oakleigh Av. HA8: Edg .2H **43**
KT6: Surb .1G **163**
N20 .2G **31**
Oakleigh Cl. N20 .3J **31**
Oakleigh Ct. EN4: E Barn .6H **21**
HA8: Edg .2J **43**
UB1: S'hall .1D **94**
Oakleigh Cres. N20 .2H **31**
Oakleigh Gdns. BR6: Orp .4J **173**
HA8: Edg .5A **28**
N20 .1F **31**
Oakleigh M. N20 .1F **31**
OAKLEIGH PARK .1F **31**
Oakleigh Pk. Av. BR7: Chst .1E **160**
Oakleigh Pk. Lawn Tennis & Squash Club
.2G **31**
Oakleigh Pk. Nth. N20 .1G **31**
Oakleigh Pk. Sth. N20 .7H **21**
Oakleigh Rd. UB10: Hil .7E **56**
Oakleigh Rd. Nth. N20 .2G **31**
Oakleigh Rd. Sth. N11 .3K **31**
Oakleigh Way CR4: Mitc .1F **155**
KT6: Surb .1G **163**
Oakley Av. CR0: Bedd .4K **167**
IG11: Bark .7K **71**
W5 .7G **79**
Oakley Cl. E4 .3K **35**
E6 .6C **88**
TW7: Isle .1H **113**
W7 .7J **77**
Oakley Ct. CR4: Mitc .7E **154**
Oakley Cres. EC1 .1B **8** (2B **84**)
Oakley Dr. BR2: Brom .3C **172**
SE9 .1H **143**
SE13 .6F **123**
Oakley Gdns. N8 .5K **47**
SW3 .7D **16** (6C **100**)
Oakley Grange HA1: Harr .2H **59**
Oakley Ho. *SW1 .3F 17*
(off Sloane St.)
W5 .7G **79**
Oakley Pk. DA5: Bexl .7C **126**
Oakley Pl. SE1 .5F **103**
Oakley Rd. BR2: Brom .3C **172**
HA1: Harr .6J **41**
N1 .7D **66**
SE25 .5H **157**
Oakley Sq. NW1 .2G **83**
Oakley St. SW3 .7C **16** (6C **100**)
Oakley Studios *SW3 .7C 16*
(off Up. Cheyne Row)
Oakley Wlk. W6 .6F **99**
Oakley Yd. E2 .3K **9** (4F **85**)
Oak Lodge E11 .6J **51**
SM1: Sutt .4A **166**
TW16: Sun .7H 129
(off Forest Dr.)
W8 .3K 99
(off Chantry Sq.)
Oak Lodge Cl. HA7: Stan .5H **27**
Oak Lodge Dr. BR4: W W'ck .7D **158**
Oaklodge Way NW7 .5G **29**
Oakman Ho. SW19 .1F **135**
Oakmead Av. BR2: Hayes .6J **159**
Oakmead Ct. HA7: Stan .4H **27**
Oak Meade HA5: H End .6A **26**
Oakmead Gdns. HA8: Edg .4E **28**
Oakmead Pl. CR4: Mitc .1C **154**
Oakmead Rd. CR0: Croy .6H **155**
SW12 .1E **136**
Oakmede EN5: Barn .4A **20**
Oakmere Rd. SE2 .6A **108**
Oakmont Pl. BR6: Orp .1H **173**
Oak Pk. Gdns. SW19 .1F **135**
Oak Pk. M. N16 .3F **67**
Oak Pl. SW18 .5K **117**
Oakridge Dr. N2 .3B **46**
Oakridge La. BR1: Brom .5F **141**
Oakridge Rd. BR1: Brom .4F **141**
Oak Ri. IG9: Buck H .3G **37**
Oak Rd. BR6: Chels .7K **173**
DA8: Erith .7J **109**
KT3: N Mald .2K **151**
W5 .7D **78**
Oak Row SW16 .2G **155**
Oaks, The BR2: Brom .6E **160**
EN2: Enf .3G 23
(off Bycullah Rd.)
HA4: Ruis .7F **39**
IG8: Wfd G .7B **36**
N12 .4E **30**
NW6 .7F 63
(off Brondesbury Pk.)
NW10 .7D **62**
SE18 .5G **107**
SM4: Mord .4G **153**
UB4: Hayes .2E **74**
Oaks Av. KT4: Wor Pk .3D **164**
RM5: Col R .2J **55**
SE19 .5E **138**
TW13: Felt .2C **130**
Oaks Cvn. Pk., The KT9: Chess .3C **162**
Oaksford Av. SE26 .3H **139**
Oaks Gro. E4 .2B **36**
Oakshade Rd. BR1: Brom .4F **141**
Oakshaw Rd. SW18 .7K **117**
Oakshott Ct. NW1 .1C **6** (2H **83**)
(not continuous)
Oakside Ct. IG6: Ilf .2H **53**
Oakside Stadium .4H **53**
Oaks La. CR0: Croy .3H **169**
IG2: Ilf .5J **53**
(not continuous)
Oaks Rd. CR0: Croy .5H **169**
TW19: Stanw .5A **110**
Oaks Shop. Cen., The W3 .1J **97**
Oak St. *E14 .2E 104*
(off Stewart St.)
RM7: Rom .5J **55**
Oaks Way SM5: Cars .7D **166**
Oaksway KT6: Surb .1D **162**

Oakthorpe Ct. N13 5H **33**
Oakthorpe Pk. Est. N13 5H **33**
Oakthorpe Rd. N13 5F **33**
Oaktree Av. N13 3G **33**
Oak Tree Cl. HA7: Stan 7H **27**
W5 6C **78**
Oak Tree Ct. UB5: Yead 2A **76**
W3 7H **79**
Oak Tree Dell NW9 5J **43**
Oak Tree Dr. N20 1E **30**
Oak Tree Gdns. BR1: Brom 5K **141**
Oaktree Gro. IG1: Ilf 5H **71**
Oak Tree Ho. *W9* *4J* ***81***
(off Shirland Rd.)
Oak Tree Rd. NW8 2B **4** (3C **82**)
Oakview Gdns. N2 4B **46**
Oakview Gro. CR0: Croy 1A **170**
Oakview Lodge *NW11* *7H* ***45***
(off Beechcroft Av.)
Oakview Rd. SE6 5D **140**
Oak Village NW5 4E **64**
Oak Vs. *NW11* *6H* ***45***
(off Hendon Pk. Row)
Oak Way CR0: Croy 6K **157**
N14 7A **22**
SM6: Wall *1E* ***166***
(off Helios Rd.)
TW14: Felt 1G **129**
W3 1A **98**
Oakway BR2: Brom 2F **159**
SW20 4E **152**
Oakway Cl. DA5: Bexl 6E **126**
Oakways SE9 6F **125**
OAKWOOD 4C 22
Oakwood SM6: Wall 7F **167**
Oakwood Av. BR2: Brom 3K **159**
BR3: Beck 2E **158**
CR4: Mitc 2B **154**
N14 7C **22**
UB1: S'hall 7E **76**
Oakwood Bus. Pk. NW10 4K **79**
Oakwood Cl. BR7: Chst 6D **142**
IG8: Wfd G 6H **37**
N14 6B **22**
Oakwood Ct. E6 1C **88**
HA1: Harr 6H **41**
W14 3H **99**
Oakwood Cres. N21 6D **22**
UB6: G'frd 6A **60**
Oakwood Dr. DA7: Bex 4J **127**
HA8: Edg 6D **28**
SE19 6D **138**
Oakwood Gdns. BR6: Farnb 2G **173**
IG3: Ilf 2K **71**
SM1: Sutt 2J **165**
Oakwood Ho. *E9* *6J* ***67***
(off Frampton Pk. Rd.)
Oakwood La. W14 3H **99**
Oakwood Lodge *N14* *6B* ***22***
(off Avenue Rd.)
Oakwood Mans. *W14* *3H* ***99***
(off Oakwood Ct.)
Oakwood Pk. Rd. N14 7C **22**
Oakwood Pl. CR0: Croy 6A **156**
Oakwood Rd. BR6: Farnb 2G **173**
CR0: Croy 6A **156**
HA5: Pinn 2K **39**
NW11 4J **45**
SW20 1C **152**
Oakwood Vw. N14 6C **22**
Oakworth Rd. W10 5E **80**
Oarsman Pl. KT8: E Mos 4J **149**
Oasis, The BR1: Brom 2A **160**
Oasis Sports Cen. 7E **6** (6J **83**)
Oast Ct. *E14* *7B* ***86***
(off Newell St.)
Oast Lodge *W4* *7A* ***98***
(off Corney Reach Way)
Oates Cl. BR2: Brom 3F **159**
Oatfield Ho. *N15* *6E* ***48***
(off Perry Ct.)
Oatfield Rd. BR6: Orp 1K **173**
Oatland Ri. E17 2A **50**
Oatlands Dr. KT13: Weyb 7G **147**
Oatlands Rd. EN3: Enf H 1D **24**
Oat La. EC2 7D **8** (6C **84**)
Oatwell Ho. *SW3* *4D* ***16***
(off Marlborough St.)
Oban Cl. E13 4A **88**
Oban Ho. *E14* *6F* ***87***
(off Oban St.)
IG11: Bark 2H **89**
Oban Rd. E13 3A **88**
SE25 4D **156**
Oban St. E14 6F **87**
Oberon Ho. *N1* *2E* ***84***
(off Arden Est.)
Oberon Way TW17: Shep 3A **146**
Oberstein Rd. SW11 4B **118**
Oborne Cl. SE24 5B **120**
O'Brien Ho. *E2* *3K* ***85***
(off Roman Rd.)
Observatory Gdns. W8 2J **99**
Observatory M. E14 4F **105**
Observatory Rd. SW7 2A **16** (3B **100**)
SW14 4J **115**
Occupation La. SE18 1F **125**
W5 4D **96**
Occupation Rd. KT19: Ewe 7K **163**
SE17 5C **102**
W13 2B **96**
Ocean Est. E1 5A **86**
(Ben Jonson Rd.)
E1 4K **85**
(Ernest St.)
Ocean Music Venue ***6H 67***
(off Mare St.)
Ocean St. E1 5K **85**
Ocean Wharf E14 2B **104**
Ockbrook *E1* *5J* ***85***
(off Hannibal Rd.)
Ockendon M. N1 6D **66**
Ockendon Rd. N1 6D **66**
Ockham Dr. BR5: St P 7A **144**
Ockley Ct. DA14: Sidc 3J **143**
SM1: Sutt 4A **166**
Ockley Rd. CR0: Croy 7K **155**
SW16 4J **137**
Octagon, The *SW10* *7K* ***99***
(off Coleridge Gdns.)
Octagon Arc. EC2 6G **9** (5E **84**)
Octagon Ct. *SE16* *1K* ***103***
(off Rotherhithe St.)
Octavia Cl. CR4: Mitc 5C **154**
Octavia Ho. *SW1* *2C* ***18***
(off Medway St.)
W10 4G **81**
Octavia M. W10 4H **81**
Octavia Rd. TW7: Isle 3J **113**
Octavia St. SW11 1C **118**
Octavia Way SE28 7B **90**
Octavius St. SE8 7C **104**
October Pl. NW4 3F **45**
Odard Rd. KT8: W Mole 4E **148**
Oddmark Rd. IG11: Bark 2H **89**
Odell Cl. IG11: Bark 7K **71**
Odeon, The IG11: Bark 7H **71**
Odeon Cinema
Barnet **5D 20**
Beckenham **2B 158**
Bromley ***2J 159***
(off High St.)
Camden Town ***1F 83***
(off Parkway)
Charing Cross ***3D 12***
(off Panton St.)
Covent Garden ***1D 12***
(off Shaftesbury Av.)
Edmonton **7E 24**
Eltham Park ***4C 124***
(off Well Hall Rd.)
Greenwich **4H 105**
Hill St. **5D 114**
Holloway **3J 65**
Kensington ***3J 99***
(off Kensington High St.)
Odeon Cinema
Kingston upon Thames ***2E 150***
(in The Rotunda Cen.)
Leicester Sq. ***3D 12***
(off Leicester Sq.)
Marble March ***1F 11***
(off Edgware Rd.)
Muswell Hill **4F 47**
Putney **3G 117**
Red Lion St. **5D 114**
Rotherhithe **3K 103**
South Woodford **2J 51**
Streatham **3J 137**
Sutton **5K 165**
Swiss Cen. ***2C 12***
(off Wardour St.)
Swiss Cottage **7B 64**
Tottenham Ct. Rd. ***6C 6***
(off Tottenham Ct. Rd.)
West End ***3D 12***
(off Leicester Sq.)
Whiteleys ***6K 81***
(off Queensway)
Wimbledon **6H 135**
Odeon Ct. E16 5J **87**
NW10 *1A* ***80***
(off St Albans Rd.)
Odeon Pde. *SE9* *4C* ***124***
(off Well Hall Rd.)
UB6: G'frd *6B* ***60***
(off Allendale Rd.)
W3 *2G* ***97***
(off Gunnersbury La.)
Odessa Rd. E7 3H **69**
NW10 2C **80**
Odessa St. SE16 2B **104**
Odette Duval Ho. *E1* *5J* ***85***
(off Stepney Way)
Odger St. SW11 2D **118**
Odhams Wlk. WC2 1F **13** (6J **83**)
Odin Ho. SE5 2C **120**
O'Donnell Ct. WC1 3F **7** (4J **83**)
Odontological Mus., The ***7H 7***
(in The Royal College of Surgeons)
O'Driscoll Ho. W12 6D **80**
Odyssey Bus. Pk. HA4: Ruis 5K **57**
Offa's Mead E9 4B **68**
Offenbach Ho. *E2* *2K* ***85***
(off Mace St.)
Offenham Rd. SE9 4D **142**
Offers Ct. KT1: King T 3F **151**
Offerton Rd. SW4 3G **119**
Offham Ho. *SE17* *4E* ***102***
(off Beckway St.)
Offham Slope N12 5C **30**
Offley Pl. TW7: Isle 2H **113**
Offley Rd. SW9 7A **102**
Offord Cl. N17 6B **34**
Offord Rd. N1 7K **65**
Offord St. N1 7K **65**
Ogden Ho. TW13: Hanw 3C **130**
Ogilby St. SE18 4D **106**
Ogilvie Ho. *E1* *6K* ***85***
(off Stepney C'way.)
Oglander Rd. SE15 4F **121**
Ogle St. W1 5A **6** (5G **83**)
Oglethorpe Rd. RM10: Dag 3F **73**
O'Gorman Ho. *SW10* *7A* ***100***
(off King's Rd.)
O'Grady Ho. E17 3D **50**
Ohio Bldg. *SE8* *1D* ***122***
(off Deal's Gateway)
Ohio Cotts. HA5: Pinn 2A **40**
Ohio Rd. E13 4H **87**
Oil Mill La. W6 5C **98**
Okeburn Rd. SW17 5E **136**
Okehampton Cl. N12 5G **31**
Okehampton Cres. DA16: Well 1B **126**
Okehampton Rd. NW10 1E **80**
Olaf Ct. *W8* *2J* ***99***
(off Kensington Chu. St.)
Olaf St. W11 7F **81**
Oldacre M. SW12 7E **118**
Old Bailey EC4 1B **14** (6B **84**)
Old Bailey (Central Criminal Court)
7B 8 (6B 84)
Old Barge Ho. All. SE1 3K **13**
Old Barn Cl. SM2: Cheam 7G **165**
Old Barn Way DA7: Bex 3K **127**
Old Barracks W8 2K **99**
Old Barrack Yd. SW1 7G **11** (2E **100**)
(not continuous)
Old Barrowfield E15 1G **87**
Old Bellgate Pl. E14 3C **104**
Oldberry Rd. HA8: Edg 6E **28**
Old Bethnal Grn. Rd. E2 3G **85**
OLD BEXLEY 7H 127
Old Bexley Bus. Pk. DA5: Bexl 7H **127**
Old Bexley La. DA5: Bexl, Dart 2K **145**
Old Billingsgate Mkt. *EC3* *3F* ***15***
(off Lwr. Thames St.)
Old Billingsgate Wlk. EC3 3G **15** (7E **84**)
Old Bond St. W1 3A **12** (7G **83**)
Oldborough Rd. HA0: Wemb 3C **60**
OLD BRENTFORD 7D 96
Old Brewer's Yd. WC2 1E **12** (6J **83**)
Old Brewery M. NW3 4B **64**
Old Bri. Cl. UB5: N'olt 2E **76**
Old Bri. St. KT1: Ham W 2D **150**
Old Broad St. EC2 7F **9** (6D **84**)
Old Bromley Rd. BR1: Brom 5F **141**
Old Brompton Rd. SW5 5J **99**
SW7 4A **16** (5J **99**)
Old Bldgs. WC2 7J **7**
Old Burlington St. W1 2A **12** (7G **83**)
Oldbury Ho. *W2* *5K* ***81***
(off Harrow Rd.)
Oldbury Pl. W1 5H **5** (5E **82**)
Oldbury Rd. EN1: Enf 2B **24**
Old Canal M. *SE15* *5F* ***103***
(off Trafalgar Av.)
Old Castle St. E1 7J **9** (6F **85**)
Old Cavendish St. W1 7J **5** (6F **83**)
Old Change Ct. EC4 1C **14**
Old Chapel Pl. SW9 2A **120**
Old Charlton Rd. TW17: Shep 5E **146**
Old Chelsea M. SW3 7C **16** (6C **100**)
Old Chiswick Yd. *W4* *6A* ***98***
(off Pumping Sta. Rd.)
Old Church Ct. N11 5A **32**
Oldchurch Gdns. RM7: Rush G 7K **55**
Old Church La. HA7: Stan 5G **27**
NW9 2K **61**
UB6: G'frd 3A **78**
Oldchurch Ri. RM7: Rush G 7K **55**
Old Church Rd. E1 6K **85**
E4 4H **35**
Oldchurch Rd. RM7: Rush G 7K **55**
Old Church St. SW3 6B **16** (5B **100**)
Old Claygate La. KT10: Clay 6A **162**
Old Clem Sq. SE18 6E **106**
Old Coal Yd. SE28 4H **107**
Old College Ct. DA17: Belv 5H **109**
Old Compton St. W1 2C **12** (7H **83**)
Old Cote Dr. TW5: Hest 6E **94**
Old Ct. Ho. *W8* *2K* ***99***
(off Old Ct. Pl.)
Old Ct. Pl. W8 2K **99**
Old Courtyard, The BR1: Brom 1K **159**
Old Curiosity Shop ***7H 7***
(off Portsmouth St.)
Old Dairy M. NW5 6F **65**
SW12 1E **136**
Old Dairy Sq. *N21* *7F* ***23***
(off Wades Hill)
Old Deer Pk. 2C **114**
Old Deer Pk. Gdns. TW9: Rich 3E **114**
Old Devonshire Rd. SW12 7F **119**
Old Dock Cl. TW9: Kew 6G **97**
Old Dover Rd. SE3 7J **105**
Oldegate Ho. E6 7B **70**
Old Farm Av. DA15: Sidc 1H **143**
N14 7B **22**
Old Farm Cl. SW17 2C **136**
TW4: Houn 4D **112**
Old Farm Pas. TW12: Hamp 1G **149**

Old Farm Rd. N2 . . . . .1B 46
TW12: Hamp 6D 130
(not continuous)
UB7: W Dray 2A 92
Old Farm Rd. E. DA15: Sidc 2A 144
Old Farm Rd. W. DA15: Sidc 2K 143
Oldfield Cl. BR1: Brom 4D 160
HA7: Stan 5F 27
UB6: G'frd 5J 59
Oldfield Ct. KT5: Surb 4F 151
(off Cranes Pk. Cres.)
Oldfield Farm Gdns. UB6: G'frd 1H 77
Oldfield Gro. SE16 . . . . .4K 103
Oldfield Ho. W4 . . . . .5A 98
(off Devonshire Rd.)
Oldfield La. Nth. UB6: G'frd 2H 77
Oldfield La. Sth. UB6: G'frd 4G 77
Oldfield M. N6 . . . . .7G 47
Oldfield Rd. BR1: Brom 4D 160
DA7: Bex 2E 126
N16 . . . . .3E 66
NW10 . . . . .7B 62
SW19 . . . . .6G 135
TW12: Hamp 1D 148
W3 .2B 98
Oldfields Cir. UB5: N'olt 6G 59
Oldfields Rd. SM1: Sutt 3H 165
Oldfields Trad. Est. SM1: Sutt 3J 165
Old Fire Sta., The SE18 . . . . .7F 107
Old Fish St. Hill EC4 . . . . .2C 14
(off Victoria St.)
Old Fleet La. EC4 . . . . .7A 8 (6B 84)
Old Fold Cl. EN5: Barn 1C 20
Old Fold La. EN5: Barn 1C 20
Old Fold Vw. EN5: Barn 3A 20
OLD FORD 1C 86
Old Ford Rd. E2 . . . . .2J 85
E3 . . . . .2A 86
Old Forge Cl. HA7: Stan 4F 27
Old Forge Cres. TW17: Shep 6D 146
Old Forge M. W12 . . . . .2D 98
Old Forge Rd. EN1: Enf 1A 24
N19 . . . . .2H 65
Old Forge Way DA14: Sidc 4B 144
Old Gloucester St. WC1 . . . .5F 7 (5J 83)
Old Hall Cl. HA5: Pinn 1C 40
Old Hall Dr. HA5: Pinn 1C 40
Oldham Ter. W3 . . . . .1J 97
(not continuous)
Old Hatch Mnr. HA4: Ruis 7H 39
Old Hill BR6: Downe 6H 173
BR7: Chst 1E 160
Oldhill St. N16 . . . . .1G 67
Old Homesdale Rd. BR2: Brom 4A 160
Old Hospital Cl. SW12 . . . . .1D 136
Old Ho. Cl. SW19 . . . . .5G 135
Old Ho. Gdns. TW1: Twick 6C 114
Old Howlett's La. HA4: Ruis 6F 39
OLD ISLEWORTH 3B 114
Old Jamaica Rd. SE16 . . . . .7K 15 (3G 103)
Old James St. SE15 . . . . .3H 121
Old Jewry EC2 . . . . .1E 14 (6D 84)
Old Kenton La. NW9 . . . . .5H 43
Old Kent Rd. SE1 . . . . .4E 102
SE15 . . . . .4E 102
Old Kingston Rd. KT4: Wor Pk 2J 163
Old Laundry, The BR7: Chst 1G 161
Old Lodge Pl. TW1: Twick 6B 114
Old Lodge Way HA7: Stan 5F 27
Old London Rd. DA14: Sidc, Swan 7G 145
KT2: King T 2E 150
Old Lyonian Sports Club 5G 41
(off Pinner Vw.)
Old Maidstone Rd. DA14: Sidc 7F 145
OLD MALDEN 1A 164
Old Malden La. KT4: Wor Pk 2K 163
Old Mnr. Ct. NW8 . . . . .2A 82
Old Mnr. Dr. TW7: Isle 6G 113
Old Mnr. Ho. M. TW17: Shep 3C 146
Old Mnr. Rd. UB2: S'hall 4B 94
Old Mnr. Way BR7: Chst 5D 142
DA7: Bex 2K 127
Old Mnr. Yd. SW5 . . . . .4K 99

Old Mkt. Ct. SM1: Sutt 4K 165
Old Mkt. Sq. E2 . . . . .1J 9 (3F 85)
Old Marylebone Rd. NW1 . . . . .6D 4 (5C 82)
Oldmead Ho. RM10: Dag 6H 73
Old M. HA1: Harr 5J 41
Old Mill Ct. E18 . . . . .3A 52
Old Mill Pl. RM7: Rom 6K 55
Old Mill Rd. SE18 . . . . .6H 107
Old Mitre Ct. EC4 . . . . .1K 13 (6A 84)
Old Montague St. E1 . . . . . . .6K 9 (5G 85)
Old Nichol St. E2 . . . . .3J 9 (4F 85)
Old Nth. St. WC1 . . . . .5G 7
Old Nursery Ct. E2 . . . . .2F 85
(off Dunloe St.)
Old Nursery Pl. TW15: Ashf 5D 128
Old Oak Cl. KT9: Chess 4F 163
OLD OAK COMMON 5A 80
Old Oak Comn. La. NW10 . . . . .5A 80
W3 . . . . .5A 80
Old Oak La. NW10 . . . . .3A 80
Old Oak Rd. W3 . . . . .7B 80
Old Orchard TW16: Sun 2A 148
Old Orchard, The NW3 . . . . .4D 64
Old Orchard Cl. EN4: Had W 1G 21
UB8: Hil 6C 74
Old Pal. La. TW9: Rich 5C 114
Old Pal. Rd. CR0: Croy 3B 168
Old Pal. Ter. TW9: Rich 5D 114
Old Pal. Yd. SW1 . . . . . . .1E 18 (3J 101)
TW9: Rich 5C 114
Old Paradise St. SE11 . . . . . .3G 19 (4K 101)
Old Pk. Av. EN2: Enf 5H 23
SW12 . . . . .6E 118
Old Pk. Gro. EN2: Enf 4H 23
Old Pk. La. W1 . . . . .5J 11 (1F 101)
Old Pk. M. TW5: Hest 7D 94
Old Pk. Ridings N21 . . . . .6G 23
Old Pk. Rd. EN2: Enf 3G 23
N13 . . . . .4E 32
SE2 . . . . .5A 108
Old Pk. Rd. Sth. EN2: Enf 4G 23
Old Pk. Vw. EN2: Enf 3F 23
Old Perry St. BR7: Chst 6J 143
Old Post Office La. SE3 . . . . .3K 123
Old Pound Cl. TW7: Isle 1A 114
Old Priory UB9: Hare 7D 38
Old Pye St. SW1 . . . . . . .1C 18 (3H 101)
Old Pye St. Est. SW1 . . . . .2C 18
(off Old Pye St.)
Old Quebec St. W1 . . . . .1F 11 (6D 82)
Old Queen St. SW1 . . . . .7D 12 (2H 101)
Old Rectory Gdns. HA8: Edg 6B 28
Old Redding HA3: Hrw W 5A 26
Old Red Lion Theatre 2A 84
(off St John St.)
Oldridge Rd. SW12 . . . . .7E 118
Old Rd. DA1: Cray 5K 127
FN3* Enf H 1D 24
SE13 . . . . .4G 123
Old Rope Wlk. TW16: Sun 3K 147
Old Royal Free Pl. N1 . . . . .1A 84
Old Royal Free Sq. N1 . . . . .1A 84
Old Royal Naval College 5F 105
Old Ruislip Rd. UB5: N'olt 2A 76
Old School Cl. BR3: Beck 2K 157
SE10 . . . . .3G 105
SW19 . . . . .2J 153
Old School Cl. N17 . . . . .3F 49
Old School Cres. E7 . . . . .6J 69
Old School Pl. CR0: Wadd 4A 168
Old School Rd. UB8: Hil 4B 74
Old Schools La. KT17: Ewe 7B 164
Old School Sq. E14 . . . . .6C 86
(off Pelling St.)
KT7: T Ditt 6K 149
Old School Ter. SM3: Cheam 7F 165
Old Seacoal La. EC4 . . . . . . .7A 8 (6B 84)
Old Sth. Cl. HA5: Pinn 1B 40
Old Sth. Lambeth Rd. SW8 . . . . .7J 101
Old Speech Room Gallery 1J 59
Old Spitalfields Market 5J 9 (5F 85)
Old Sq. WC2 . . . . .7J 7 (6K 83)
Old Stable M. N5 . . . . .3C 66

Old Sta. Gdns. TW11: Tedd 6A 132
(off Victoria Rd.)
Old Station Rd. UB3: Harl 3H 93
Old Station Yd., The E17 . . . . .4E 50
Oldstead Rd. BR1: Brom 4E 140
Old Stockley Rd. UB7: W Dray 2D 92
OLD STREET 4D 84
Old St. E13 . . . . .2K 87
EC1 . . . . .3C 8 (4C 84)
Old Sungate Cotts. RM5: Col R 1F 55
Old Sun Wharf E14 . . . . .7A 86
(off Narrow St.)
Old Swan Wharf SW11 . . . . .1B 118
Old Swan Yd. SM5: Cars 4D 166
Old Thackeray School SW8 . . . . . . .2F 119
Old Theatre Ct. SE1 . . . . .4D 14
(off Porter St.)
Old Town CR0: Croy 3B 168
SW4 . . . . .3G 119
Old Tramyard SE18 . . . . .4J 107
Old Vic Theatre, The 6K 13
Old Woolwich Rd. SE10 . . . . .6F 105
Old York Rd. SW18 . . . . .5K 117
Oleander Cl. BR6: Farnb 5H 173
O'Leary Sq. E1 . . . . .5J 85
Olga St. E3 . . . . .2A 86
Olinda Rd. N16 . . . . .6F 49
Oliphant St. W10 . . . . .3F 81
Olive Blythe Ho. W10 . . . . .4G 81
(off Ladbroke Gro.)
Olive Ct. N1 . . . . .1A 84
(off Liverpool Rd.)
Oliver Av. SE25 . . . . .3F 157
Oliver Bus. Pk. NW10 . . . . .2J 79
Oliver Cl. W4 . . . . .6H 97
Oliver Ct. SE18 . . . . .4G 107
Oliver Gdns. E6 . . . . .5C 88
Oliver Goldsmith Est. SE15 . . . . . . .1G 121
Oliver Gro. SE25 . . . . .4F 157
Oliver Ho. SE16 . . . . .2G 103
(off George Row)
SW8 . . . . .7J 101
(off Wyvil Rd.)
Oliver M. SE15 . . . . .2G 121
Olive Rd. E13 . . . . .3A 88
NW2 . . . . .4E 62
SW19 . . . . .7A 136
W5 . . . . .3D 96
Oliver Rd. E10 . . . . .2D 68
E17 . . . . .5E 50
KT3: N Mald 2J 151
NW10 . . . . .2J 79
SM1: Sutt 4B 166
Olivers Wharf E1 . . . . .1H 103
(off Wapping High St.)
Olivers Yd. EC1 . . . . .3F 9 (4D 84)
Olive St. RM7: Rom 5K 55
Olive Tree Ho. SE15 . . . . .6J 103
(off Sharratt St.)
Olivette St. SW15 . . . . .3F 117
Olive Waite Ho. NW6 . . . . .7J 63
Olivia Ct. FN2: Enf 1H 23
(off Chase Side)
Olivier Theatre 4J 13
(in Royal National Theatre)
Ollerton Grn. E3 . . . . .1B 86
Ollerton Rd. N11 . . . . .5C 32
Olley Cl. SM6: Wall 7J 167
Ollgar Cl. W12 . . . . .1B 98
Olliffe St. E14 . . . . .3E 104
Olmar St. SE1 . . . . .6G 103
Olney Ho. NW8 . . . . .3D 4
(off Tresham Cres.)
Olney Rd. SE17 . . . . .6B 102
(not continuous)
Olron Cres. DA6: Bex 5D 126
Olven Rd. SE18 . . . . .6G 107
Olveston Wlk. SM5: Cars 6B 154
Olwen M. HA5: Pinn 2B 40
Olyffe Av. DA16: Well 1A 126
Olyffe Dr. BR3: Beck 1E 158
Olympia 3G 99
Olympia Ind. Est. N22 . . . . .3K 47

Olympia M. W2 . . . . .7K 81
Olympian Ct. E14 . . . . .4C 104
(off Homer Dr.)
Olympia Way W14 . . . . .3G 99
Olympic Way HA9: Wemb 3G 61
UB6: G'frd 1G 77
Olympus Sq. E5 . . . . .3G 67
O'Mahoney Ct. SW17 . . . . .3A 136
Oman Av. NW2 . . . . .4E 62
O'Meara St. SE1 . . . . .5D 14 (1C 102)
Omega Cl. E14 . . . . .3D 104
Omega Ct. RM7: Rom 6J 55
Omega Ho. SW10 . . . . .7A 100
(off King's Rd.)
Omega Pl. N1 . . . . .1F 7
Omega St. SE14 . . . . .1C 122
Omega Works E3 . . . . .7C 68
Ommaney Rd. SE14 . . . . .1K 121
Omnibus Way E17 . . . . .2C 50
Ondine Rd. SE15 . . . . .4F 121
Onega Ga. SE16 . . . . .3A 104
O'Neill Ho. NW8 . . . . .1B 4
(off Cochrane St.)
O'Neill Path SE18 . . . . .6E 106
One Owen St. EC1 . . . . .1A 8
(off Goswell St.)
One Tree Cl. SE23 . . . . .6J 121
Ongar Cl. RM6: Chad H 5C 54
Ongar Rd. SW6 . . . . .6J 99
Onra Rd. E17 . . . . .7C 50
Onslow Av. TW10: Rich 5E 114
Onslow Cl. E4 . . . . .2K 35
KT7: T Ditt 7J 149
W10 . . . . .3H 81
Onslow Ct. SW10 . . . . .6A 16
Onslow Cres. BR7: Chst 1F 161
SW7 . . . . .4B 16 (4B 100)
Onslow Dr. DA14: Sidc 2D 144
Onslow Gdns. E18 . . . . .3K 51
KT7: T Ditt 7J 149
N10 . . . . .5F 47
N21 . . . . .5F 23
SM6: Wall 6G 167
SW7 . . . . .4A 16 (4B 100)
Onslow Ho. KT2: King T 1F 151
(off Acre Rd.)
Onslow M. E. SW7 . . . . .4A 16 (4B 100)
Onslow M. W. SW7 . . . . .4A 16 (4B 100)
Onslow Pde. N14 . . . . .1A 32
Onslow Rd. CR0: Croy 7K 155
KT3: N Mald 4C 152
TW10: Rich 5E 114
Onslow Sq. SW7 . . . . .4B 16 (4B 100)
Onslow St. EC1 . . . . .4K 7 (4A 84)
Onslow Way KT7: T Ditt 7J 149
Ontario Cl. SE1 . . . . .3B 102
Ontario Way E14 . . . . .7C 86
(not continuous)
Onyx M. E15 . . . . .6H 69
Opal Cl. E16 . . . . .6B 88
Opal M. IG1: Ilf 2F 71
NW6 . . . . .1H 81
Opal St. SE11 . . . . .5K 19 (5B 102)
Open Air Stage 1C 64
Open Air Theatre 7C 62
Openshaw Rd. SE2 . . . . .4B 108
Open University, The (Parsital College)
. . . . .4J 63
Openview SW18 . . . . .1A 136
Opera Ct. N19 . . . . .3H 65
(off Wedmore St.)
Operating Theatre Mus. 5F 15
Ophelia Gdns. NW2 . . . . .3G 63
Ophelia Ho. W6 . . . . .5F 99
(off Fulham Pal. Rd.)
Ophir Ter. SE15 . . . . .1G 121
Opie Ho. NW8 . . . . .2C 82
(off Townshend Est.)
Opossum Way TW4: Houn 3A 112
Oppenheim Rd. SE13 . . . . .2E 122
Oppidans Rd. NW3 . . . . .7D 64
Orange Ct. La.
BR6: Downe 7E 172

Orange Gro. E11 . . . . .3G **69**
(not continuous)
Orange Hill Rd.
  HA8: Edg 7D **28**
Orange PI. SE16 . . . . .3J **103**
Orangery, The
  TW10: Ham 2C **132**
Orangery Gallery, The 2H **99**
Orangery La. SE9 . . . . .5D **124**
Orange St. WC2 . . . . . .3D **12** (7H **83**)
Orange Tree Ct. SE5 . . . . .7E **102**
(off Havil St.)
Orange Tree Theatre 4E **114**
Orange Yd. W1 . . . . .1D **12**
Oratory La. SW3 . . . . . . .5B **16** (5B **100**)
Orbain Rd. SW6 . . . . .7G **99**
Orbel St. SW11 . . . . .1C **118**
Orbital Cen., The
  IG8: Wfd G 2B **52**
Orb St. SE17 . . . . .4D **102**
Orchard, The KT17: Ewe 7B **164**
  N14 . . . . .5A **22**
  N20 . . . . .1E **30**
  N21 . . . . .6J **23**
  NW11 . . . . .5J **45**
  SE3 . . . . .2F **123**
  TW3: Houn 2G **113**
  W4 . . . . .4K **97**
  W5 . . . . .5D **78**
(off Montpelier Rd.)
Orchard Av. CR0: Croy 2A **170**
  CR4: Mitc 1E **166**
  DA17: Belv 6E **108**
  KT3: N Mald 2A **152**
  KT7: T Ditt 1A **162**
  N3 . . . . .3J **45**
  N14 . . . . .6B **22**
  N20 . . . . .2G **31**
  TW5: Hest 7C **94**
  TW14: Felt 5F **111**
  TW15: Ashf 6E **128**
  UB1: S'hall 1D **94**
Orchard Bus. Cen. SE26 . . . . .5B **140**
Orchard CI. DA7: Bex 1E **126**
  E4 . . . . .4H **35**
  E11 . . . . .4K **51**
  HA0: Wemb 1E **78**
  HA4: Ruis 7E **38**
  HA8: Edg 6K **27**
  KT6: T Ditt 1B **162**
  KT12: Walt T 7K **147**
  KT19: Ewe 6H **163**
  N1 . . . . .7C **66**
  NW2 . . . . .3C **62**
  SE23 . . . . .6J **121**
  SW20 . . . . .4E **152**
  TW15: Ashf 6E **128**
  UB5: N'olt 6G **59**
  W10 . . . . .5H **81**
  WD23: Bushy 1C **26**
Orchard Cotts. KT2: King T 1F **151**
  UB3: Hayes 2G **93**
Orchard Ct. E10 . . . . .1D **68**
  EN5: New Bar 3E **20**
  HA8: Edg 5A **28**
  KT4: Wor Pk 1C **164**
  KT12: Walt T 7H **147**
(off Bridge St.)
  N14 . . . . .6B **22**
  SM6: Wall 5F **167**
  TW2: Twick 3J **131**
  TW7: Isle 1H **113**
Orchard Cres. EN1: Enf 1A **24**
  HA8: Edg 5D **28**
Orchard Dr. HA8: Edg 5A **28**
  SE3 . . . . .2F **123**
  TW17: Shep 3G **147**
Orchard Gdns. KT9: Chess 4E **162**
  SM1: Sutt 5J **165**
Orchard Ga. KT10: Esh 7H **149**
  NW9 . . . . .4A **44**
  UB6: G'frd 6B **60**
Orchard Grn. BR6: Orp 2J **173**

Orchard Gro. BR6: Orp 2K **173**
  CR0: Croy 7A **158**
  HA3: Kent 5F **43**
  HA8: Edg 1G **43**
  SE20 . . . . .7G **139**
Orchard Hill DA1: Cray 5K **127**
  SE13 . . . . .2D **122**
  SM5: Cars 5D **166**
Orchard Ho. SE5 . . . . .1C **120**
(off County Gro.)
  SE16 . . . . .3J **103**
  SW6 . . . . .7H **99**
(off Varna Rd.)
  W1 . . . . .7G **5**
(off Fitzhardinge St.)
  W12 . . . . .1C **98**
Orchard La. IG8: Wfd G 4F **37**
  KT8: E Mos 6H **149**
  SW20 . . . . .1D **152**
Orchardleigh Av. EN3: Enf H 2D **24**
Orchard Mead Ho. NW2 . . . . .2J **63**
Orchardmede N21 . . . . .6J **23**
Orchard M. N1 . . . . .7D **66**
  N6 . . . . .7F **47**
  SW17 . . . . .3A **136**
Orchard PI. BR2: Kes 7A **172**
  E5 . . . . .5H **67**
  E14 . . . . .7G **87**
(not continuous)
  N17 . . . . .7A **34**
Orchard Ri. CR0: Croy 1A **170**
  HA5: Eastc 3H **39**
  KT2: King T 1J **151**
  TW10: Rich 4H **115**
Orchard Ri. E. DA15: Sidc 5K **125**
Orchard Ri. W. DA15: Sidc 5J **125**
Orchard Rd. BR1: Brom 1A **160**
  BR6: Farnb 5F **173**
  CR4: Mitc 1E **166**
  DA14: Sidc 4J **143**
  DA16: Well 3B **126**
  DA17: Belv 4G **109**
  EN3: Pond E 5D **24**
  EN5: Barn 4C **20**
  KT1: King T 2E **150**
  KT9: Chess 4E **162**
  N6 . . . . .7F **47**
  RM7: Mawney 1H **55**
  RM10: Dag 1G **91**
  SE3 . . . . .2G **123**
  SE18 . . . . .4H **107**
  SM1: Sutt 5J **165**
  TW1: Twick 5A **114**
  TW4: Houn 5D **112**
  TW8: Bford 6C **96**
  TW9: Rich 3G **115**
  TW12: Hamp 7D **130**
  TW13: Felt 1J **129**
  TW16: Sun 7K **129**
  UB3: Hayes 7J **75**
Orchardson Ho. NW8 . . . . .4A **4**
Orchardson St. NW8 . . . . .4A **4** (4B **82**)
Orchard Sq. W14 . . . . .5H **99**
Orchard St. E17 . . . . .4A **50**
  W1 . . . . .1G **11** (6E **82**)
Orchard Studios W6 . . . . .4F **99**
(off Brook Grn.)
Orchard Ter. EN1: Enf 6B **24**
  NW10 . . . . .4B **62**
Orchard Vs. DA14: Sidc 6C **144**
Orchard Wlk. KT2: King T 1G **151**
(off Gordon Rd.)
Orchard Way BR3: Beck 6B **158**
  CR0: Croy 1A **170**
  EN1: Enf 3K **23**
  SM1: Sutt 4B **166**
  TW15: Ashf 2B **128**
Orchard Waye UB8: Uxb 2A **74**
Orchard Wharf E14 . . . . .7G **87**
(off Orchard Pl.)
Orchid CI. E6 . . . . .5C **88**
  KT9: Chess 7C **162**
  UB1: S'hall 7C **76**

Orchid Ct. HA9: Wemb 2E **60**
Orchid Gdns. TW3: Houn 4D **112**
Orchid Grange N14 . . . . .7B **22**
Orchid Rd. N14 . . . . .7B **22**
Orchid St. W12 . . . . .7C **80**
Orde NW9 . . . . .1B **44**
Orde Hall St. WC1 . . . . .4G **7** (4K **83**)
Ordell Rd. E3 . . . . .2B **86**
Ordnance Cl. TW13: Felt 2J **129**
Ordnance Cres. SE10 . . . . .2F **105**
Ordnance Hill NW8 . . . . .1B **82**
Ordnance M. NW8 . . . . .2B **82**
Ordnance Rd. E16 . . . . .5H **87**
  SE18 . . . . .6E **106**
Oregano Cl. UB7: Yiew 6A **74**
Oregano Dr. E14 . . . . .6F **87**
Oregon Av. E12 . . . . .4D **70**
Oregon Bldg. SE10 . . . . .1D **122**
(off Deal's Gateway)
Oregon CI. KT3: N Mald 4J **151**
Oregon Sq. BR6: Orp 1H **173**
Orestes M. NW6 . . . . .5J **63**
Orford Ct. HA7: Stan 6H **27**
  SE27 . . . . .2B **138**
Orford Gdns. TW1: Twick 2K **131**
Orford Rd. E17 . . . . .5C **50**
  E18 . . . . .3K **51**
  SE6 . . . . .3D **140**
ORGAN CROSSROADS 7C **164**
Organ La. E4 . . . . .2K **35**
(not continuous)
Oriana Ho. E14 . . . . .7B **86**
(off Victory Pl.)
Oriel CI. CR4: Mitc 4H **155**
Oriel Ct. CR0: Croy 1D **168**
  NW3 . . . . .4A **64**
Oriel Dr. SW13 . . . . .6E **98**
Oriel Gdns. IG5: Ilf 3D **52**
Oriel Ho. RM7: Rom 6K **55**
Oriel PI. NW3 . . . . .4A **64**
(off Heath St.)
Oriel Rd. E9 . . . . .6K **67**
Oriel Way UB5: N'olt 7F **59**
Oriental City NW9 . . . . .3K **43**
Oriental Rd. E16 . . . . .1B **106**
Oriental St. E14 . . . . .7C **86**
(off Pennyfields)
Orient Ind. Pk. E10 . . . . .2C **68**
Orient St. SE11 . . . . .3K **19** (4B **102**)
Orient Way E5 . . . . .3K **67**
  E10 . . . . .1A **68**
Orient Wharf E1 . . . . .1J **103**
(off Wapping High St.)
Oriole Way SE28 . . . . .7B **90**
Orion E14 . . . . .4C **104**
(off Crews St.)
Orion Bus. Cen. SE14 . . . . .5K **103**
Orion Cen., The CR0: Bedd 2J **167**
Orion Ho. E1 . . . . .4H **85**
(off Coventry Rd.)
Orion Rd. N11 . . . . .7K **31**
Orissa Rd. SE18 . . . . .5J **107**
Orkney Ho. N1 . . . . .1K **83**
(off Bemerton Est.)
Orkney St. SW11 . . . . .2E **118**
Orlando Rd. SW4 . . . . .3G **119**
Orleans CI. TW1: Twick 7B **114**
Orleans House Gallery 1B **132**
Orleans Pk. School Sports Cen. 7B **114**
Orleans Rd. SE19 . . . . .6D **138**
  TW1: Twick 7B **114**
Orleston M. N7 . . . . .6A **66**
Orleston Rd. N7 . . . . .6A **66**
Orley Ct. HA1: Harr 4K **59**
Orley Farm Rd. HA1: Harr 3J **59**
Orlop St. SE10 . . . . .5G **105**
Ormanton Rd. SE26 . . . . .4G **139**
Orme Ct. W2 . . . . .7K **81**
Orme Ct. M. W2 . . . . .7K **81**
(off Orme La.)
Orme Ho. E8 . . . . .1F **85**
Orme La. W2 . . . . .7K **81**
Ormeley Rd. SW12 . . . . .1F **137**

Orme Rd. KT1: King T 2H **151**
  SM1: Sutt 6K **165**
Ormerod Gdns. CR4: Mitc 2E **154**
Ormesby CI. SE28 . . . . .7D **90**
Ormesby Way HA3: Kent 6F **43**
Orme Sq. W2 . . . . .7K **81**
Ormiston Gro. W12 . . . . .1D **98**
Ormiston Rd. SE10 . . . . .5J **105**
Ormond Av. TW10: Rich 5D **114**
  TW12: Hamp 1F **149**
Ormond Cl. WC1 . . . . .5F **7** (5J **83**)
Ormond Cres. TW12: Hamp 1F **149**
Ormond Dr. TW12: Hamp 7F **131**
Ormonde Av. BR6: Farnb 2G **173**
Ormonde Ct. NW8 . . . . .1D **82**
(off St Edmund's Cl.)
  SW15 . . . . .4E **116**
Ormonde Ga. SW3 . . . . . . .6F **17** (5D **100**)
Ormonde PI. SW1 . . . . . . .4G **17** (4E **100**)
Ormonde Ri. IG9: Buck H 1F **37**
Ormonde Ter. NW8 . . . . .3J **115**
  NW8 . . . . .1D **82**
Ormond Ho. N16 . . . . .2D **66**
Ormond M. WC1 . . . . .4F **7** (4J **83**)
Ormond Rd. N19 . . . . .1J **65**
  TW10: Rich 5D **114**
Ormond Yd. SW1 . . . . .4B **12** (1G **101**)
Ormrod Ct. W11 . . . . .6G **81**
(off Westbourne Pk. Rd.)
Ormsby SM2: Sutt 7K **165**
Ormsby Gdns. UB6: G'frd 2G **77**
Ormsby Lodge W4 . . . . .3A **98**
Ormsby PI. N16 . . . . .3F **67**
Ormsby St. E2 . . . . .2F **85**
Ormside St. SE15 . . . . .6J **103**
Ornan Rd. NW3 . . . . .5C **64**
Orpen Ho. SW5 . . . . .4J **99**
(off Trebovir Rd.)
Orpen Wlk. N16 . . . . .3E **66**
Orpheus St. SE5 . . . . .1D **120**
ORPINGTON 2J **173**
Orpington Gdns. N18 . . . . .3K **33**
Orpington Mans. N21 . . . . .1G **33**
Orpington Rd. BR7: Chst 3J **161**
  N21 . . . . .1G **33**
Orpwood Cl. TW12: Hamp 6D **130**
Orsett M. W2 . . . . .6K **81**
(not continuous)
Orsett St. SE11 . . . . .5H **19** (5K **101**)
Orsett Ter. IG8: Wfd G 7F **37**
  W2 . . . . .6K **81**
Orsman Rd. N1 . . . . .1E **84**
Orton Gro. EN1: Enf 1B **24**
Orton St. E1 . . . . .1G **103**
Orville Rd. SW11 . . . . .2B **118**
Orwell Cl. RM13: Rain 5K **91**
  UB3: Hayes 7G **75**
Orwell Ct. E8 . . . . .1G **85**
(off Pownall Rd.)
  N5 . . . . .4C **66**
Orwell Rd. E13 . . . . .2A **88**
Osbaldeston Rd. N16 . . . . .2G **67**
Osberton Rd. SE12 . . . . .5J **123**
Osbert St. SW1 . . . . .4C **18** (4H **101**)
Osborn Cl. E8 . . . . .1G **85**
Osborne Av. TW19: Stanw 1A **128**
Osborne Cl. BR3: Beck 4A **158**
  EN4: Cockf 3J **21**
  TW13: Hanw 5B **130**
Osborne Ct. E10 . . . . .7D **50**
  W5 . . . . .5E **78**
Osborne Gdns. CR7: Thor H 2C **156**
Osborne Gro. E17 . . . . .4B **50**
  N4 . . . . .1A **66**
Osborne Ho. E16 . . . . .1J **105**
(off Wesley Av.)
Osborne M. E17 . . . . .4B **50**
Osborne Rd. SM1: Sutt 5B **166**
Osborne Rd. CR7: Thor H 2C **156**
  DA17: Belv 5F **109**
  E7 . . . . .5K **69**
  E9 . . . . .6B **68**
  E10 . . . . .2D **68**

Osborne Rd.—Oxford Rd. Sth.

Osborne Rd. EN3: Enf H 2F **25**
IG9: Buck H 1E **36**
KT2: King T 7E **132**
KT12: Walt T 7J **147**
N4 . . . . . 1A **66**
N13 . . . . . 3F **33**
NW2 . . . . . 6D **62**
RM9: Dag 5F **73**
TW3: Houn 3D **112**
UB1: S'hall 6G **77**
W3 . . . . . 3H **97**
Osborne Sq. RM9: Dag 4F **73**
Osborne Ter. *SW17* *5D* ***136***
(*off Church La.*)
Osborne Way *KT9: Chess* *5F* ***163***
(*off Bridge Rd.*)
Osborn Gdns. NW7 . . . . . 7A **30**
Osborn La. SE23 . . . . . 7A **122**
Osborn St. E1 . . . . . 6K **9** (5F **85**)
Osborn Ter. SE3 . . . . . 4H **123**
Osbourne Ct. HA2: Harr 4F **41**
Osbourne Ho. IG8: Wfd G 7K **37**
TW2: Twick 2G **131**
Oscar Faber Pl. N1 . . . . . 7E **66**
Oscar St. SE8 . . . . . 2C **122**
(not continuous)
Oseney Cres. NW5 . . . . . 5G **65**
Osgood Av. BR6: Chels 5K **173**
Osgood Gdns. BR6: Chels 5K **173**
OSIDGE 1A **32**
Osidge La. N14 . . . . . 1K **31**
Osier Ct. *E1* *4K* ***85***
(*off Osier St.*)
RM7: Rom 6K **55**
TW8: Bford *6E* ***96***
(*off Ealing Rd.*)
Osier Cres. N10 . . . . . 1D **46**
Osier La. *SE10* *3H* ***105***
(*off School Bank Rd.*)
Osier M. W4 . . . . . 6A **98**
Osiers Ct. *KT1: King T* *1D* ***150***
(*off Steadfast Rd.*)
Osiers Est., The SW18 . . . . . 4J **117**
Osiers Rd. SW18 . . . . . 4J **117**
Osier St. E1 . . . . . 4J **85**
Osier Way CR4: Mitc 5D **154**
E10 . . . . . 3D **68**
Oslac Rd. SE6 . . . . . 5D **140**
Oslo Ct. *NW8* *2C* ***82***
(*off Prince Albert Rd.*)
Oslo Ho. *SE5* *2C* ***120***
(*off Carew St.*)
Oslo Sq. SE16 . . . . . 3A **104**
Osman Cl. N15 . . . . . 6D **48**
Osmani School Sports Cen. 5G 85
Osman Rd. N9 . . . . . 3B **34**
W6 . . . . . 3E **98**
Osmington Ho. *SW8* *7K* ***101***
(*off Dorset Rd.*)
Osmond Cl. HA2: Harr 2G **59**
Osmond Gdns. SM6: Wall 5G **167**
Osmund St. W12 . . . . . 5B **80**
Osnaburgh St. NW1 . . . . . 4K **5** (4F **83**)
(Euston Rd.)
NW1 . . . . . 2K **5**
(Robert St.)
Osnaburgh Ter. NW1 . . . . . 3K **5** (4F **83**)
Osney Ho. SE2 . . . . . 2D **108**
Osney Wlk. SM5: Cars 6B **154**
Osprey NW9 . . . . . 1B **44**
Osprey Cl. BR2: Brom 1C **172**
E6 . . . . . 5C **88**
E11 . . . . . 4J **51**
E17 . . . . . 7F **35**
SM1: Sutt 5H **165**
UB7: W Dray 2A **92**
Osprey Ct. BR3: Beck 7C **140**
E1 . . . . . 3K **15**
Osprey Est. SE16 . . . . . 4A **104**
Osprey Ho. *E14* *7A* ***86***
(*off Victory Pl.*)
Osprey M. EN3: Pond E 5D **24**
Ospringe Cl. SE20 . . . . . 7J **139**
Ospringe Ct. SE9 . . . . . 6H **125**
Ospringe Ho. *SE1* *6K* ***13***
(*off Wootton St.*)
Ospringe Rd. NW5 . . . . . 4G **65**
Osram Ct. W6 . . . . . 3E **98**
Osram Rd. HA9: Wemb 3D **60**
Osric Path N1 . . . . . 2E **84**
Ossian M. N4 . . . . . 7K **47**
Ossian Rd. N4 . . . . . 7K **47**
Ossie Garvin Rdbt. UB4: Yead 7K **75**
Ossington Bldgs. W1 . . . . . 5G **5** (5E **82**)
Ossington Cl. W2 . . . . . 7J **81**
Ossington St. W2 . . . . . 7J **81**
Ossory Rd. SE1 . . . . . 6G **103**
Ossulston St. NW1 . . . . . 1D **6** (2H **83**)
Ossulton Pl. N2 . . . . . 3A **46**
Ossulton Way N2 . . . . . 4A **46**
Ostade Rd. SW2 . . . . . 7K **119**
Ostell Cres. EN3: Enf L 1H **25**
Ostend Pl. SE1 . . . . . 4C **102**
Osten M. SW7 . . . . . 3K **99**
OSTERLEY 7H 95
Osterley Av. TW7: Isle 7H **95**
Osterley Cl. BR5: St P 1K **161**
Osterley Ct. TW7: Isle 1H **113**
UB5: Yead *3A* ***76***
(*off Canberra Dr.*)
Osterley Cres. TW7: Isle 1J **113**
Osterley Gdns. CR7: Thor H 2C **156**
UB2: S'hall 2G **95**
Osterley Ho. *E14* *6D* ***86***
(*off Giraud St.*)
Osterley La. TW7: Isle 4G **95**
UB2: S'hall 5E **94**
(not continuous)
Osterley Lodge *TW7: Isle* *7J* ***95***
(*off Church Rd.*)
Osterley Pk. 6G 95
Osterley Pk. House (NT) 6G 95
Osterley Pk. Rd. UB2: S'hall 3D **94**
Osterley Pk. Vw. Rd. W7 . . . . . 2J **95**
Osterley Rd. N16 . . . . . 4E **66**
TW7: Isle 7J **95**
Osterley Sports Club 3G 95
Osterley Views UB2: S'hall 1G **95**
Oster Ter. E17 . . . . . 5K **49**
Ostlers Dr. TW15: Ashf 5E **128**
Ostliffe Rd. N13 . . . . . 5H **33**
Oswald Bldg. SW8 . . . . . 6F **101**
Oswald Rd. UB1: S'hall 1C **94**
Oswald's Mead E9 . . . . . 4A **68**
Oswald St. E5 . . . . . 3K **67**
Oswald Ter. NW2 . . . . . 3E **62**
Osward CR0: Sels 7B **170**
(not continuous)
Osward Pl. N9 . . . . . 2C **34**
Osward Rd. SW17 . . . . . 2D **136**
Oswell Ho. *E1* *1H* ***103***
(*off Farthing Flds.*)
Oswin St. SE11 . . . . . 4B **102**
Oswyth Rd. SE5 . . . . . 2E **120**
Otford Cl. BR1: Brom 3E **160**
DA5: Bexl 6H **127**
SE20 . . . . . 1J **157**
Otford Cres. SE4 . . . . . 6B **122**
Otford Ho. *SE1* *7F* ***15***
(*off Staple St.*)
SE15 . . . . . *6J* ***103***
(*off Lovelinch Cl.*)
Othello Cl. SE11 . . . . . 5K **19** (5B **102**)
Otho Ct. TW8: Bford 7D **96**
Otis St. E3 . . . . . 3E **86**
Otley App. IG2: Ilf 6F **53**
Otley Dr. IG2: Ilf 5F **53**
Otley Ho. N5 . . . . . 3A **66**
Otley Rd. E16 . . . . . 6A **88**
Otley Ter. E5 . . . . . 3K **67**
Ottawa Gdns. RM10: Dag 7K **73**
Ottaway Ct. E5 . . . . . 3G **67**
Ottaway St. E5 . . . . . 3G **67**
Otterbourne Rd. CR0: Croy 2C **168**
E4 . . . . . 3A **36**
Otterburn Gdns. TW7: Isle 7A **96**
Otterburn Ho. *SE5* *7C* ***102***
(*off Sultan St.*)
Otterburn St. SW17 . . . . . 6D **136**
Otter Cl. E15 . . . . . 1E **86**
Otterden Cl. BR6: Orp 3J **173**
Otterden St. SE6 . . . . . 4C **140**
Otterfield Rd. UB7: Yiew 7A **74**
Otter Rd. UB6: G'frd 4G **77**
Otto Cl. SE26 . . . . . 3H **139**
Otto St. SE17 . . . . . 6B **102**
Otway Gdns. WD23: Bush 1D **26**
Oulton Cl. E5 . . . . . 2J **67**
SE28 . . . . . 6C **90**
Oulton Cres. IG11: Bark 5K **71**
Oulton Rd. N15 . . . . . 5D **48**
Ouseley Rd. SW12 . . . . . 1D **136**
Outer Circ. NW1 . . . . . 1D **4** & 1J **5** (2C **82**)
Outgate Rd. NW10 . . . . . 7B **62**
Outram Pl. N1 . . . . . 1J **83**
Outram Rd. CR0: Croy 2F **169**
E6 . . . . . 1C **88**
N22 . . . . . 1H **47**
Outwich St. EC3 . . . . . 7H **9**
Outwood Ho. *SW2* *7K* ***119***
(*off Deepdene Gdns.*)
Oval, The DA15: Sidc 7A **126**
E2 . . . . . 2H **85**
Oval Ct. HA8: Edg 7D **28**
Oval Cricket Ground, The . . . 7H 19 (6K 101)
Oval Ho. *CR0: Croy* *1E* ***168***
(*off Oval Rd.*)
Oval House Theatre 7J 19
Oval Mans. SE11 . . . . . 7H **19** (6K **101**)
Oval Pl. SW8 . . . . . 7K **101**
Oval Rd. CR0: Croy 2D **168**
NW1 . . . . . 1F **83**
Oval Rd. Nth. RM10: Dag 1H **91**
Oval Rd. Sth. RM10: Dag 2H **91**
Oval Way SE11 . . . . . 6H **19** (5K **101**)
Overbrae BR3: Beck 6C **140**
Overbrook Wlk. HA8: Edg 7B **28**
(not continuous)
Overbury Av. BR3: Beck 3D **158**
Overbury Rd. N15 . . . . . 6D **48**
Overbury St. E5 . . . . . 4K **67**
Overcliff Rd. SE13 . . . . . 3C **122**
Overcourt Cl. DA15: Sidc 6B **126**
Overdale Av. KT3: N Mald 2J **151**
Overdale Rd. W5 . . . . . 3C **96**
Overdown Rd. SE6 . . . . . 4C **140**
Overhill Rd. SE22 . . . . . 7G **121**
Overhill Way BR3: Beck 5F **159**
Overlea Rd. E5 . . . . . 7G **49**
Overmead DA15: Sidc 7H **125**
Oversley Ho. *W2* *5J* ***81***
(*off Alfred Rd.*)
Overstand Cl. BR3: Beck 5C **158**
Overstone Gdns. CR0: Croy 7B **158**
Overstone Ho. *E14* *6C* ***86***
(*off E. India Dock Rd.*)
Overstone Rd. W6 . . . . . 3E **98**
Overstrand Mans. SW11 . . . . . 1D **118**
Overton Cl. NW10 . . . . . 6J **61**
TW7: Isle 1K **113**
Overton Ct. E11 . . . . . 7J **51**
SM2: Sutt 7J **165**
Overton Dr. E11 . . . . . 7J **51**
RM6: Chad H 7C **54**
Overton Ho. *SW15* *7B* ***116***
(*off Tangley Gro.*)
Overton Rd. E10 . . . . . 1A **68**
N14 . . . . . 5D **22**
SE2 . . . . . 3C **108**
SM2: Sutt 6J **165**
SW9 . . . . . 2A **120**
Overton Rd. E. SE2 . . . . . 3D **108**
Overton's Yd. CR0: Croy 3C **168**
Overy Ho. SE1 . . . . . 7A **14** (2B **102**)
Ovesdon Av. HA2: Harr 1D **58**
Ovett Cl. SE19 . . . . . 6E **138**
Ovex Cl. E14 . . . . . 2E **104**
Ovington Ct. *SW3* *2D* ***16***
(*off Brompton Rd.*)
Ovington Gdns. SW3 . . . . . 2D **16** (3C **100**)
Ovington M. SW3 . . . . . 2D **16**
Ovington Sq. SW3 . . . . . 2D **16** (3C **100**)
Ovington St. SW3 . . . . . 3D **16** (4C **100**)
Owen Cl. CR0: Croy 6D **156**
SE28 . . . . . 1C **108**
UB4: Yead 3K **75**
UB5: N'olt 6C **58**
Owen Gdns. IG8: Wfd G 6H **37**
Owen Ho. TW1: Twick 7B **114**
TW14: Felt 7J **111**
Owenite St. SE2 . . . . . 4B **108**
Owen Mans. *W14* *6G* ***99***
(*off Queen's Club Gdns.*)
Owen Rd. N13 . . . . . 5H **33**
UB4: Yead 3K **75**
Owens M. E11 . . . . . 2G **69**
Owen's Row EC1 . . . . . 1A **8** (3B **84**)
Owen St. EC1 . . . . . 1A **8** (2B **84**)
(not continuous)
Owens Way SE23 . . . . . 7A **122**
Owen Wlk. SE20 . . . . . 1G **157**
Owen Way NW10 . . . . . 6J **61**
Owgan Cl. SE5 . . . . . 7D **102**
Oxberry Av. SW6 . . . . . 2G **117**
Oxendon St. SW1 . . . . . 3C **12** (7H **83**)
Oxenford St. SE15 . . . . . 3F **121**
Oxenham Ho. *SE8* *6C* ***104***
(*off Benbow St.*)
Oxenholme *NW1* *1A* ***6***
(*off Hampstead Rd.*)
Oxenpark Av. HA9: Wemb 7E **42**
Oxestall's Rd. SE8 . . . . . 5A **104**
Oxford & Cambridge Mans. *NW1* *6D* ***4***
(*off Old Marylebone Rd.*)
Oxford Av. N14 . . . . . 1B **32**
NW10 . . . . . 3D **80**
SW20 . . . . . 2G **153**
TW5: Hest 5E **94**
UB3: Harl 7H **93**
Oxford Cir. W1 . . . . . 1A **12**
Oxford Cir. Av. W1 . . . . . 1A **12** (6G **83**)
Oxford Cl. CR4: Mitc 3G **155**
N9 . . . . . 2C **34**
TW15: Ashf 7E **128**
Oxford Ct. EC4 . . . . . 2E **14**
TW13: Hanw 4B **130**
W3 . . . . . 6G **79**
W4 . . . . . 5H **97**
W7 . . . . . *5K* ***77***
(*off Copley Cl.*)
W9 . . . . . *5J* ***81***
(*off Elmfield Way*)
Oxford Cres. KT3: N Mald 6K **151**
Oxford Dr. HA4: Ruis 2A **58**
SE1 . . . . . 5G **15** (1E **102**)
Oxford Gdns. N20 . . . . . 1G **31**
N21 . . . . . 7H **23**
W4 . . . . . 5G **97**
W10 . . . . . 6E **80**
Oxford Ga. W6 . . . . . 4F **99**
Oxford M. DA5: Bexl 7G **127**
Oxford Pl. *NW10* *3K* ***61***
(*off Press Rd.*)
Oxford Rd. DA14: Sidc 5B **144**
E15 . . . . . 6F **69**
(not continuous)
EN3: Pond E 5C **24**
HA1: Harr 6G **41**
HA3: W'stone 3K **41**
IG1: Ilf 5G **71**
IG8: Wfd G 5G **37**
N4 . . . . . 1A **66**
N9 . . . . . 2C **34**
NW6 . . . . . 2J **81**
SE19 . . . . . 6D **138**
SM5: Cars 6C **166**
SM6: Wall 5G **167**
SW15 . . . . . 4G **117**
TW11: Tedd 5H **131**
W5 . . . . . 7D **78**
Oxford Rd. Nth. W4 . . . . . 5H **97**
Oxford Rd. Sth. W4 . . . . . 5G **97**

Oxford Sq. W2 .....1D **10** (6C **82**)
Oxford St. W1 .....1G **11** (6E **82**)
Oxford Wlk. UB1: S'hall 1D **94**
Oxford Way TW13: Hanw 4B **130**
Oxgate Cen. NW2 .....2D **62**
Oxgate Ct. NW2 .....2C **62**
Oxgate Ct. Pde. NW2 .....2C **62**
Oxgate Gdns. NW2 .....3D **62**
Oxgate La. NW2 .....2D **62**
Oxgate Pde. NW2 .....2C **62**
Oxhawth Cres. BR2: Brom 5E **160**
Oxhey La. HA5: H End 5A **26**
Oxleas E6 .....6F **89**
Oxleas Cl. DA16: Well 2H **125**
Oxleay Rd. HA2: Harr 1E **58**
Oxleigh Cl. KT3: N Mald 5A **152**
Oxley Cl. SE1 .....5F **103**
Oxleys Rd. NW2 .....3D **62**
Oxlip Cl. CR0: Croy 1K **169**
Oxlow La. RM9: Dag 4F **73**
　　RM10: Dag 4F **73**
Oxonian St. SE22 .....4F **121**
Oxo Tower Wharf SE1 .....3K **13** (7A **84**)
Oxted Cl. CR4: Mitc 3B **154**
Oxtoby Way SW16 .....1H **155**
Oxzygeem Sports Cen. 6B **120**
Oystercatcher Cl. E16 .....6K **87**
Oystergate Wlk. EC4 .....3E **14**
Oyster Row E1 .....6J **85**
Oyster Wharf SW11 .....2B **118**
Ozolins Way E16 .....6J **87**

P

Pablo Neruda Cl. SE24 .....4B **120**
Pace Pl. E1 .....6H **85**
Pacific Cl. TW14: Felt 1H **129**
Pacific Ho. E1 .....4K **85**
　　(off Ernest St.)
Pacific Rd. E16 .....6J **87**
Pacific Wharf SE16 .....1K **103**
Packenham Ho. E2 .....1K **9**
　　(off Wellington Row)
Packham Cl. KT4: Wor Pk 3E **164**
Packington Sq. N1 .....1C **84**
　　(not continuous)
Packington St. N1 .....1B **84**
Packmores Rd. SE9 .....5H **125**
Padbury SE17 .....5E **102**
　　(off Bagshot St.)
Padbury Cl. TW14: Bedf 1F **129**
Padbury Ct. E2 .....2K **9** (3F **85**)
Padbury Ho. NW8 .....3D **4**
　　(off Tresham Cres.)
Padcroft Rd. UB7: Yiew 1A **92**
Paddenswick Rd. W6 .....3C **98**
PADDINGTON 1A **10** (6B **82**)
Paddington Bowling & Sports Club 4K **81**
Paddington Ct. UB4: Yead 4B **76**
Paddington Ct. W7 .....5K **77**
　　(off Copley Cl.)
Paddington Grn. W2 .....5A **4** (5B **82**)
Paddington St. W1 .....5G **5** (5E **82**)
Paddington Wlk. W2 .....6A **4**
Paddock, The N10 .....3E **46**
　　NW9 .....5G **43**
　　UB10: Ick 4D **56**
Paddock Cl. BR6: Farnb 4F **173**
　　KT4: Wor Pk 1A **164**
　　SE3 .....2J **123**
　　SE26 .....4K **139**
　　UB5: N'olt 2E **76**
Paddock Gdns. SE19 .....6E **138**
Paddock Lodge EN1: Enf 5K **23**
　　(off Village Rd.)
Paddock Mobile Home Pk.
　　BR2: Kes 7C **172**
Paddock Pas. SE19 .....6E **138**
　　(off Paddock Gdns.)
Paddock Rd. DA6: Bex 4E **126**
　　HA4: Ruis 3B **58**
　　NW2 .....3C **62**

Paddocks, The CR0: Addtn 6C **170**
　　EN4: Cockf 3J **21**
　　HA9: Wemb 2H **61**
　　W5 .....3D **96**
　　(off Popes La.)
Paddocks Cl. HA2: Harr 4F **59**
Paddocks Grn. NW9 .....1H **61**
Paddock Way BR7: Chst 7H **143**
　　SW15 .....7E **116**
Padfield Ct. HA9: Wemb 3F **61**
Padfield Rd. SE5 .....3C **120**
Padley Cl. KT9: Chess 5F **163**
Padnall Cl. RM6: Chad H 3D **54**
Padnall Rd. RM6: Chad H 3D **54**
Padstow Cl. BR6: Chels 4K **173**
Padstow Ho. E14 .....7B **86**
　　(off Three Colt St.)
Padstow Rd. EN2: Enf 1G **23**
Padstow Wlk. TW14: Felt 1H **129**
Padua Rd. SE20 .....1J **157**
Pagden St. SW8 .....1F **119**
Pageant Av. NW9 .....1K **43**
Pageant Cres. SE16 .....1A **104**
Pageantmaster Ct. EC4 .....1A **14**
Pageant Wlk. CR0: Croy 3E **168**
Page Av. HA9: Wemb 3J **61**
Page Cl. HA3: Kent 6F **43**
　　RM9: Dag 5E **72**
　　TW12: Hamp 6C **130**
Page Ct. NW7 .....7J **29**
Page Cres. CR0: Wadd 5B **168**
Page Grn. Rd. N15 .....5G **49**
Page Grn. Ter. N15 .....5F **49**
Page Heath La. BR1: Brom 3B **160**
Page Heath Vs. BR1: Brom 3B **160**
Page High N22 .....2A **48**
　　(off Lymington Av.)
Page Ho. SE10 .....6E **104**
　　(off Welland St.)
Pagehurst Rd. CR0: Croy 7H **157**
Page Mdw. NW7 .....7J **29**
Page Rd. TW14: Bedf 6F **111**
Pages Hill N10 .....2E **46**
Pages La. N10 .....2E **46**
Page St. NW7 .....1C **44**
　　SW1 .....3D **18** (4H **101**)
Page's Wlk. SE1 .....4E **102**
Pages Yd. W4 .....6B **98**
Paget Av. SM1: Sutt 3B **166**
Paget Cl. TW12: Ham H 4H **131**
Paget Gdns. BR7: Chst 1F **161**
Paget Ho. E2 .....2J **85**
　　(off Bishop's Way)
Paget La. TW7: Isle 3H **113**
Paget Pl. KT2: King T 6J **133**
　　KT7: T Ditt 1A **162**
Paget Rd. IG1: Ilf 4F **71**
　　N16 .....1D **66**
　　UB10: Hil 4E **74**
Paget St. EC1 .....1A **8** (3B **84**)
Paget Ter. SE18 .....6F **107**
Pagham Ho. W10 .....4E **80**
　　(off Sutton Way)
Pagin Ho. N15 .....5E **48**
　　(off Braemar Rd.)
Pagitts Gro. EN4: Had W 1E **20**
Pagnell St. SE14 .....7B **104**
Pagoda Av. TW9: Rich 3F **115**
Pagoda Gdns. SE3 .....2F **123**
Pagoda Gro. SE27 .....2C **138**
Paignton Rd. HA4: Ruis 3J **57**
　　N15 .....6E **48**
Paines Cl. HA5: Pinn 3C **40**
Paines La. HA5: Pinn 1C **40**
Pain's Cl. CR4: Mitc 2F **155**
Painsthorpe Rd. N16 .....3E **66**
Painswick Ct. SE15 .....7F **103**
　　(off Daniel Gdns.)
Painted Hall
　　Greenwich 6E **104**
Painters M. SE16 .....4G **103**
Painters Rd. IG2: Ilf 3K **53**

Paisley Rd. N22 .....1B **48**
　　SM5: Cars 1B **166**
Paisley Ter. SM5: Cars 7B **154**
Pakeman Ho. SE1 .....6B **14**
　　(off Surrey Row)
Pakeman St. N7 .....3K **65**
Pakenham Cl. SW12 .....1E **136**
Pakenham St. WC1 .....2H **7** (3K **83**)
Pakington Ho. SW9 .....2J **119**
　　(off Stockwell Gdns. Est.)
Palace Av. W8 .....2K **99**
Palace Bingo 4C **102**
　　(off Elephant & Castle)
Palace Ct. BR1: Brom 1K **159**
　　(off Palace Gro.)
　　HA3: Kent 6E **42**
　　NW3 .....5K **63**
　　W2 .....7K **81**
　　(off Moscow Rd., not continuous)
Palace Gdns. EN2: Enf 4J **23**
　　IG9: Buck H 1G **37**
Palace Gdns. M. W8 .....1K **99**
Palace Gdns. Shop. Cen.
　　EN2: Enf 4J **23**
　　(off Palace Gdns.)
Palace Gdns. Ter. W8 .....1J **99**
Palace Ga. W8 .....2A **100**
Palace Gates M. N8 .....4J **47**
　　(off The Campsbourne)
Palace Gates Rd. N22 .....1H **47**
Palace Grn. CR0: Sels 7B **170**
　　W8 .....1K **99**
Palace Gro. BR1: Brom 1K **159**
　　SE19 .....7F **139**
Palace Ice Rink, The 2H **47**
Palace Mans. KT1: King T 4D **150**
　　(off Palace Rd.)
　　W14 .....4G **99**
　　(off Hammersmith Rd.)
Palace M. E17 .....4B **50**
　　EN2: Enf 3J **23**
　　SW1 .....4H **17**
　　SW6 .....7J **99**
Palace Pde. E17 .....4B **50**
Palace Pl. SW1 .....1A **18** (3G **101**)
Palace Pl. Mans. W8 .....2K **99**
　　(off Kensington Ct.)
Palace Rd. BR1: Brom 1K **159**
　　HA4: Ruis 4C **58**
　　KT1: King T 4D **150**
　　KT8: E Mos 3G **149**
　　N8 .....5H **47**
　　(not continuous)
　　N11 .....7D **32**
　　SE19 .....7F **139**
　　SW2 .....1K **137**
Palace Sq. SE19 .....7F **139**
Palace St. SW1 .....1A **18** (3G **101**)
Palace Theatre
　　Soho 1D **12**
　　(off Shaftesbury Av.)
Palace Vw. BR1: Brom 3K **159**
　　(not continuous)
　　CR0: Croy 4B **170**
　　SE12 .....2J **141**
Palace Vw. Rd. E4 .....5J **35**
Palace Wharf W6 .....7E **98**
　　(off Rainville Rd.)
Palamon Ct. SE1 .....5F **103**
　　(off Cooper's Rd.)
Palamos Rd. E10 .....1C **68**
Palatine Av. N16 .....4E **66**
Palatine Rd. N16 .....4E **66**
Palemead Cl. SW6 .....1F **117**
Palermo Rd. NW10 .....2C **80**
Palestine Gro. SW19 .....1B **154**
Palewell Comn. Dr.
　　SW14 .....5K **115**
Palewell Pk. SW14 .....5K **115**
Palfrey Pl. SW8 .....7K **101**
Palgrave Av. UB1: S'hall 7E **76**
Palgrave Gdns. NW1 .....3D **4** (4C **82**)

Palgrave Ho. SE5 .....7C **102**
　　(off Wyndham Est.)
　　TW2: Whit 7G **113**
Palgrave Rd. W12 .....3B **98**
Palissy St. E2 .....2J **9** (3F **85**)
　　(not continuous)
Palladino Ho. SW17 .....5C **136**
　　(off Laurel Cl.)
Palladium Ct. E8 .....7F **67**
　　(off Queensbridge Rd.)
Pallant Ho. SE1 .....3D **102**
　　(off Tabard St.)
Pallant Way BR6: Farnb 3E **172**
Pallett Way SE18 .....1C **124**
Palliser Ct. W14 .....5G **99**
　　(off Palliser Rd.)
Palliser Ho. E1 .....4K **85**
　　(off Ernest St.)
　　SE10 .....6F **105**
　　(off Trafalgar Rd.)
Palliser Rd. W14 .....5G **99**
Pall Mall SW1 .....5B **12** (1G **101**)
Pall Mall E. SW1 .....4D **12** (1H **101**)
Pall Mall Pl. SW1 .....5B **12**
Palmar Cres. DA7: Bex 3G **127**
Palmar Rd. DA7: Bex 2G **127**
Palm Av. DA14: Sidc 6D **144**
Palm Cl. E10 .....3D **68**
Palm Ct. SE15 .....7F **103**
　　(off Garnies Cl.)
Palmeira Rd. DA7: Bex 3D **126**
Palmer Av. SM3: Cheam 4E **164**
Palmer Cl. BR4: W W'ck 3F **171**
　　TW5: Hest 1E **112**
　　UB5: N'olt 6C **58**
Palmer Cres. KT1: King T 3E **150**
Palmer Dr. BR1: Brom 4F **161**
Palmer Gdns. EN5: Barn 5A **20**
Palmer Pl. N7 .....5A **66**
Palmer Rd. E13 .....4K **87**
　　RM8: Dag 1D **72**
Palmer's Ct. N11 .....5B **32**
　　(off Palmer's Rd.)
PALMERS GREEN 3F **33**
Palmers Gro. KT8: W Mole 4E **148**
Palmers La. EN1: Enf 1C **24**
　　EN3: Enf H 1C **24**
Palmers Pas. SW14 .....3J **115**
　　(off Palmers Rd.)
Palmers Rd. E2 .....2K **85**
　　N11 .....5B **32**
　　SW14 .....3J **115**
　　SW16 .....2K **155**
Palmerston Cen. HA3: W'stone 3K **41**
Palmerston Ct. E3 .....2K **85**
　　(off Old Ford Rd.)
　　IG9: Buck H 1F **37**
　　KT6: Surb 7D **150**
Palmerston Cres. N13 .....5E **32**
　　SE18 .....6G **107**
Palmerston Gro. SW19 .....7J **135**
Palmerston Ho. SE1 .....7J **13**
　　(off Westminster Bri. Rd.)
　　W8 .....1J **99**
　　(off Kensington Pl.)
Palmerston Mans. W14 .....6G **99**
　　(off Queen's Club Gdns.)
Palmerston Rd. BR6: Farnb 4G **173**
　　CR0: Croy 5C **156**
　　E7 .....6K **69**
　　(not continuous)
　　E17 .....3B **50**
　　HA3: W'stone 3J **41**
　　IG9: Buck H 2E **36**
　　N22 .....7E **32**
　　NW6 .....7H **63**
　　(not continuous)
　　SM1: Sutt 5A **166**
　　SM5: Cars 4D **166**
　　SW14 .....4J **115**
　　SW19 .....7J **135**
　　TW2: Twick 6J **113**
　　TW3: Houn 1G **113**

Palmerston Rd. W3	.3J 97
Palmerston Way SW8	.7F 101
Palmer St. SW1	.1C 18 (3H 101)
	(not continuous)
Palm Gro. W5	.3E 96
Palm Rd. RM7: Rom	.5J 55
Palm Tree Ho. SE14	.7K 103
	(off Barlborough St.)
Palyn Ho. EC1	.2D 8
	(off Ironmonger Row)
Pamela Ct. N3	.6E 30
Pamela Gdns. HA5: Eastc	.5K 39
Pamela Ho. E8	.1F 85
	(off Haggerston Rd.)
Pampisford Rd. CR8: Purl	.7B 168
Pams Way KT19: Ewe	.5K 163
Panama Ho. E1	.5K 85
	(off Beaumont Sq.)
Pancras La. EC4	.1E 14 (6C 84)
Pancras Rd. NW1	.1E 6 (2H 83)
Pandian Way NW5	.6H 65
Pandora Rd. NW6	.6J 63
Panfield M. IG2: Ilf	.6E 52
Panfield Rd. SE2	.3A 108
Pangbourne NW1	.2A 6
	(off Stanhope St.)
Pangbourne Av. W10	.5E 80
Pangbourne Dr. HA7: Stan	.5J 27
Panhard Pl. UB1: S'hall	.7F 77
Pank Av. EN5: New Bar	.5F 21
Pankhurst Av. E16	.1K 105
Pankhurst Cl. SE14	.7K 103
TW7: Isle	.3K 113
Pankhurst Rd. KT12: Walt T	.7A 148
Panmuir Rd. SW20	.1D 152
Panmure Cl. N5	.4B 66
Panmure Ct. UB1: S'hall	.6G 77
	(off Osborne Rd.)
Panmure Rd. SE26	.3H 139
Panorama Ct. N6	.6G 47
Pansy Gdns. W12	.7C 80
Panther Dr. NW10	.5K 61
Pantiles, The BR1: Brom	.3C 160
DA7: Bex	.7F 109
NW11	.5H 45
WD23: Bushy	.1C 26
Pantiles Cl. N13	.5G 33
Panton Cl. CR0: Croy	.1B 168
Panton St. SW1	.3C 12 (7H 83)
Paper Bldgs. EC4	.2K 13
Papermill Cl. SM5: Cars	.4E 166
Papillons Wlk. SE3	.2J 123
Papworth Gdns. N7	.5K 65
Papworth Way SW2	.7A 104
Parade, The CR0: Croy	.6J 155
KT2: King T	.2E 150
	(off London Rd.)
KT4: Wor Pk	.4B 164
N4	.1A 66
SE4	.2B 122
	(off Up. Brockley Rd.)
SE26	.3H 139
	(off Wells Pk. Rd.)
SM1: Sutt	.3H 165
SM5: Cars	.5D 166
	(off Beynon Rd.)
SW11	.7D 100
TW12: Tedd	.5H 131
TW16: Sun	.7H 129
UB6: G'frd	.5B 60
Parade Mans. NW4	.5D 44
Parade M. SE27	.2B 138
Paradise Pas. N7	.5A 66
Paradise Path SE28	.1A 108
Paradise Pl. SE18	.4C 106
Paradise Rd. SW4	.2J 119
TW9: Rich	.5D 114
Paradise Row E2	.3H 85
Paradise St. SE16	.2H 103
Paradise Wlk. SW3	.7F 17 (6D 100)
Paragon, The SE3	.2H 123
Paragon Cl. E16	.6J 87
Paragon Gro. KT5: Surb	.6F 151

Paragon M. SE1	.4D 102
Paragon Pl. KT5: Surb	.6F 151
SE3	.2H 123
Paragon Rd. E9	.6J 67
Paramount Bldg. EC1	.3A 8
	(off St John St.)
Paramount Ct. WC1	.4B 6
Parbury Ri. KT9: Chess	.6E 162
Parbury Rd. SE23	.6A 122
Parchmore Rd. CR7: Thor H	.2B 156
Parchmore Way CR7: Thor H	.2B 156
Pardoe Rd. E10	.7D 50
Pardoner Ho. SE1	.3D 102
	(off Pardoner St.)
Pardoner St. SE1	.7F 15 (3D 102)
	(not continuous)
Pardon St. EC1	.3B 8 (4B 84)
Parent Shop. Mall E18	.2J 51
	(off Marlborough Rd.)
Parfett St. E1	.5G 85
	(not continuous)
Parfitt Cl. NW3	.1A 64
Parfrey St. W6	.6E 98
Pargreaves Ct. HA9: Wemb	.2G 61
Parham Dr. IG2: Ilf	.6F 53
Parham Way N10	.2G 47
Paris Gdn. SE1	.4A 14 (1B 102)
Parish Cl. KT6: Surb	.5E 150
Parish Ga. Dr. DA15: Sidc	.6J 125
Parish La. SE20	.6K 139
Parish M. SE20	.7K 139
Paris Ho. E2	.2H 85
	(off Old Bethnal Grn. Rd.)
Parish Wharf Pl. SE18	.4C 106
Park, The DA14: Sidc	.5A 144
N6	.6E 46
NW11	.1K 63
SE23	.1J 139
SM5: Cars	.5D 166
W5	.1D 96
Park App. DA16: Well	.4B 126
SE16	.3H 103
Park Av. BR1: Brom	.6H 141
BR4: W W'ck	.2E 170
BR6: Chels	.2K 173
BR6: Farnb	.3D 172
CR4: Mitc	.7F 137
E6	.1E 88
E15	.6G 69
EN1: Enf	.5J 23
HA4: Ruis	.6F 39
IG1: Ilf	.1E 70
IG8: Wfd G	.5E 36
IG11: Bark	.6G 71
N3	.1K 45
N13	.3F 33
N18	.4B 34
N22	.2J 47
NW2	.5D 62
NW10	.2F 79
	(Brent Cres., not continuous)
NW10	.5D 62
	(Park Av. Nth.)
NW11	.1K 63
SM5: Cars	.6E 166
SW14	.4K 115
TW3: Houn	.6F 113
TW17: Shep	.3G 147
UB1: S'hall	.2D 94
Park Av. E. KT17: Ewe	.6C 164
Park Av. M. CR4: Mitc	.7F 137
Park Av. Nth. N8	.3H 47
NW10	.5D 62
Park Av. Rd. N17	.7C 34
Park Av. Sth. N8	.4H 47
Park Av. W. KT17: Ewe	.6C 164
Park Bus. Cen. NW6	.3J 81
Park Chase HA9: Wemb	.4F 61
Park Cl. E9	.1J 85
HA3: Hrw W	.1J 41
KT2: King T	.1G 151
N12	.3G 31
NW2	.3D 62

Park Cl. NW10	.3F 79
SM5: Cars	.6D 166
SW1	.7E 10 (2D 100)
TW3: Houn	.5G 113
TW12: Hamp	.1G 149
W4	.6K 97
W14	.3H 99
Park Club, The	.1A 98
Park Ct. CR2: S Croy	.5C 168
	(off Warham Rd.)
E4	.2K 35
E17	.5D 50
HA3: Kent	.7E 42
HA9: Wemb	.5E 60
KT1: Ham W	.1C 150
KT3: N Mald	.4K 151
N11	.7C 32
N17	.7B 34
SE21	.3C 138
SE26	.6H 139
SM6: Wall	.5J 167
SW11	.1F 119
UB8: Uxb	.1A 74
W6	.4C 98
Park Cres. DA8: Erith	.6J 109
EN2: Enf	.4J 23
HA3: Hrw W	.1J 41
N3	.7F 31
TW2: Twick	.1H 131
W1	.4J 5 (4F 83)
Park Cres. M. E. W1	.4K 5 (4F 83)
Park Cres. M. W. W1	.4J 5 (4F 83)
Park Cres. Rd. DA8: Erith	.6K 109
Park Cft. HA8: Edg	.1J 43
Parkcroft Rd. SE12	.7H 123
Parkdale N11	.6C 32
Parkdale Cres. KT4: Wor Pk	.3K 163
Parkdale Rd. SE18	.5J 107
Park Dr. HA2: Harr	.7E 40
HA3: Hrw W	.6C 26
N21	.6H 23
NW11	.1K 63
RM1: Rom	.4K 55
RM10: Dag	.3J 73
SE7	.6C 106
SW14	.5K 115
W3	.3G 97
Park Dwellings NW3	.5D 64
Park End BR1: Brom	.1H 159
NW3	.4C 64
Parker Cl. E16	.1C 106
SM5: Cars	.5D 166
Parker Ho. E14	.2C 104
	(off Admirals Way)
Parker M. WC2	.7F 7 (6J 83)
Parke Rd. SW13	.1C 116
TW16: Sun	.4J 147
Parker Rd. CR0: Croy	.4C 168
Parkers Row SE1	.7K 15 (2G 103)
Parker St. E16	.1C 106
WC2	.7F 7 (6J 83)
Park Farm Cl. HA5: Eastc	.5K 39
N2	.3A 46
Park Farm Ct. UB3: Hayes	.7G 75
Park Farm Rd. BR1: Brom	.1B 160
KT2: King T	.7E 132
Parkfield TW7: Isle	.1J 113
Parkfield Av. HA2: Harr	.2G 41
SW14	.4A 116
TW13: Felt	.3J 129
UB5: N'olt	.2B 76
UB10: Hil	.3D 74
Parkfield Cl. HA8: Edg	.6C 28
UB5: N'olt	.2C 76
Parkfield Ct. SE14	.1B 122
	(off Parkfield Rd.)
Parkfield Cres. HA2: Harr	.2G 41
HA4: Ruis	.2C 58
TW13: Felt	.3J 129
Parkfield Gdns. HA2: Harr	.3F 41
Parkfield Ho. HA2: Harr	.1F 41
Parkfield Ind. Est. SW11	.2E 118

Parkfield Pde. TW13: Felt	.3J 129
Parkfield Rd. HA2: Harr	.3G 59
NW10	.7D 62
SE14	.1B 122
TW13: Felt	.3J 129
UB5: N'olt	.2C 76
UB10: Ick	.2D 56
Parkfields CR0: Croy	.1B 170
SW15	.4F 116
Parkfields Av. NW9	.1K 61
SW20	.1D 152
Parkfields Cl. SM5: Cars	.4E 166
Parkfields Rd. KT2: King T	.5F 133
Parkfield St. N1	.2A 84
Parkfield Way BR2: Brom	.6D 160
Park Gdns. DA8: Erith	.4K 109
E10	.1C 68
KT2: King T	.5F 133
NW9	.3H 43
Park Ga. N2	.3B 46
N21	.7E 22
SE3	.3H 123
W5	.5D 78
Parkgate N1	.1D 84
	(off Southgate Rd.)
Parkgate Av. EN4: Had W	.1F 21
Parkgate Cl. KT2: King T	.6H 133
Park Ga. Ct. TW12: Ham H	.6G 131
Parkgate Cres.	
EN4: Had W	.1F 21
Parkgate Gdns. SW14	.5K 115
Parkgate M. N6	.7G 47
Parkgate Rd. SM6: Wall	.5E 166
SW11	.7C 100
Park Gates HA2: Harr	.4E 58
Park Gro. BR1: Brom	.1K 159
DA7: Bex	.4J 127
E15	.1J 87
HA8: Edg	.5A 28
N11	.7C 32
Park Gro. Rd. E11	.2G 69
Park Hall SE10	.7F 105
	(off Crooms Hill)
Park Hall Rd. SE21	.3C 138
Parkhall Rd. N2	.4C 46
Park Hall Trad. Est. SE21	.3C 138
Parkham Ct. BR2: Brom	.2G 159
Parkham St. SW11	.1C 118
Park Hill BR1: Brom	.4C 160
SE23	.2H 139
SM5: Cars	.6C 166
SW4	.5H 119
TW10: Rich	.6F 115
W5	.5D 78
Park Hill Cl. SM5: Cars	.5C 166
Park Hill Ct. SW17	.3D 136
Park Hill M. CR2: S Croy	.5D 168
Park Hill Ri. CR0: Croy	.2E 168
Park Hill Rd. BR2: Brom	.2G 159
CR0: Croy	.2E 168
DA15: Sidc	.3J 143
SM6: Wall	.7F 167
Parkhill Rd. DA5: Bexl	.7F 127
E4	.1K 35
NW3	.5D 64
Parkhill Wlk. NW3	.5D 64
Parkholme Rd. E8	.6F 67
Park Ho. E9	.7J 67
	(off Shore Rd.)
N21	.7E 22
Park Ho. Gdns. TW1: Twick	.5C 114
Park Ho. Pas. N6	.7E 46
Parkhouse St. SE5	.7D 102
Parkhurst Ct. N7	.4J 65
Parkhurst Gdns. DA5: Bexl	.7G 127
Parkhurst Rd. DA5: Bexl	.7G 127
E12	.4E 70
E17	.4A 50
N7	.4J 65
N11	.5K 31
N17	.2G 49
N22	.6E 32
SM1: Sutt	.4B 166

Parkinson Ho. *E9* *7J* ***67***
(off Frampton Pk. Rd.)
SW1 .... *5C* ***18***
(off Tachbrook St.)
Parkland Ct. *E15* *5G* ***69***
(off Maryland Pk.)
W14 .... *2G* ***99***
(off Holland Pk. Av.)
Parkland Gdns. SW19 .... 1F **135**
Parkland Gro. TW15: Ashf 4C **128**
Parkland Mead BR1: Brom 3F **161**
Parkland Rd. IG8: Wfd G 7E **36**
N22 .... 2K **47**
TW15: Ashf 4C **128**
Parklands KT5: Surb 5F **151**
N6 .... 7F **47**
Parklands Cl. EN4: Had W 1G **21**
IG2: Ilf 7G **53**
SW14 .... 5J **115**
Parklands Ct. TW5: Hest 2B **112**
Parklands Dr. N3 .... 3G **45**
Parklands Gro. TW7: Isle 1K **113**
Parklands Pde. TW5: Hest 2B **112**
Parklands Rd. SW16 .... 5F **137**
Parklands Way KT4: Wor Pk 2A **164**
Park La. CR0: Croy 3D **168**
E15 .... 1F **87**
HA2: Harr 3F **59**
HA7: Stan 3F **27**
HA9: Wemb 5E **60**
N9 .... 3K **33**
N17 .... 7A **34**
(not continuous)
RM6: Chad H 6D **54**
SM3: Cheam 6G **165**
SM5: Cars 4E **166**
SM6: Wall 5E **166**
TW5: Cran 7J **93**
TW9: Rich 4D **114**
TW11: Tedd 6K **131**
UB4: Hayes 5G **75**
W1 .... 2F **11** (7D **82**)
Park La. Cl. N17 .... 7B **34**
Park La. Mans. *CR0: Croy* *3D* ***168***
(off Edridge Rd.)
PARK LANGLEY 4E **158**
Parklea Cl. NW9 .... 1A **44**
Park Lee Ct. N16 .... 7E **48**
Parkleigh Rd. SW19 .... 2K **153**
Parkleys TW10: Ham 4D **132**
Parkleys Pde.
TW10: King T 4D **132**
Park Lodge NW8 .... 7B **64**
W14 .... *3H* ***99***
(off Kensington High St.)
Park Lofts *SW2* *5J* ***119***
(off Mandrell Rd.)
Park Lorne *NW8* *2D* ***4***
(off Park Rd.)
Park Mnr. *SM2: Sutt* *7A* ***166***
(off Christchurch Pk.)
Park Mans. NW4 .... 5D **44**
NW8 .... *2C* ***82***
(off Allitsen Rd.)
SW1 .... *7E* ***10***
(off Knightsbridge)
SW8 .... 7F **19** (6J **101**)
SW11 .... *1D* ***118***
(off Prince of Wales Dr.)
Park Mead DA15: Sidc 5B **126**
HA2: Harr 3F **59**
Parkmead SW15 .... 6D **116**
Parkmead Gdns. NW7 .... 6G **29**
Park M. BR7: Chst 6F **143**
SE10 .... 5H **105**
SE24 .... 7C **120**
TW19: Stanw 7B **110**
W10 .... 2G **81**
Parkmore Cl.
IG8: Wfd G 4D **36**
Park Pde. NW10 .... 2B **80**
UB3: Hayes 6G **75**
W5 .... 3G **97**
Park Pl. *BR1: Brom* *1K* ***159***
(off Park Rd.)
E14 .... 1C **104**
HA9: Wemb 4F **61**
N1 .... *7D* ***66***
(off Downham Rd.)
SW1 .... 5A **12** (1G **101**)
TW12: Ham H 6G **131**
W3 .... 4G **97**
W5 .... 1D **96**
Park Pl. Dr. W3 .... 3G **97**
Park Pl. Vs. W2 .... 5A **4** (5A **82**)
Park Ridings N8 .... 3A **48**
Park Ri. HA3: Hrw W 1J **41**
SE23 .... 1A **140**
Park Ri. Rd. SE23 .... 1A **140**
Park Rd. BR1: Brom 1K **159**
BR3: Beck 7B **140**
BR7: Chst 6F **143**
E6 .... 1A **88**
E10 .... 1C **68**
E12 .... 1K **69**
E15 .... 1J **87**
E17 .... 5B **50**
EN4: E Barn 4G **21**
EN5: Barn 4C **20**
HA0: Wemb 6E **60**
IG1: Ilf 3H **71**
KT1: Ham W 1C **150**
KT2: King T 5F **133**
KT3: N Mald 4K **151**
KT5: Surb 6F **151**
KT8: E Mos 4G **149**
N2 .... 3B **46**
N8 .... 4G **47**
N11 .... 7C **32**
N14 .... 1C **32**
N15 .... 4B **48**
N18 .... 4B **34**
NW1 .... 2D **4** (3C **82**)
NW4 .... 7C **44**
NW8 .... 2D **4** (3C **82**)
NW9 .... 7K **43**
NW10 .... 1A **80**
SE25 .... 4E **156**
SM3: Cheam 6G **165**
SM6: Wall 5F **167**
(Clifton Rd.)
SM6: Wall 2F **167**
(Elmwood Cl.)
SW19 .... 6B **136**
TW1: Twick 6C **114**
TW3: Houn 5F **113**
TW7: Isle 1B **114**
TW10: Rich 6F **115**
TW11: Tedd 6K **131**
TW12: Ham H 4F **131**
TW13: Hanw 4B **130**
TW15: Ashf 5D **128**
TW16: Sun 7K **129**
UB4: Hayes 5G **75**
UB8: Uxb 1A **74**
W2 .... 6H **81**
W4 .... 7J **97**
W7 .... 7K **77**
Park Rd. E. UB10: Uxb 2A **74**
W3 .... 2H **97**
Park Rd. Ho. KT2: King T 7G **133**
Park Rd. Nth. W3 .... 2H **97**
W4 .... 5K **97**
Park Road Swimming Pool 5H 47
Park Row SE10 .... 5F **105**
SW2 .... 6A **120**
PARK ROYAL 3H 79
PARK ROYAL JUNC. 1G 79
Park Royal Metro Cen. NW10 .... 4H **79**
Park Royal Rd. NW10 .... 3J **79**
W3 .... 3J **79**
Parkshot TW9: Rich 4D **114**
Park Side NW2 .... 3C **62**
Parkside DA14: Sidc 2B **144**
IG9: Buck H 2E **36**
N3 .... 1K **45**
Parkside NW7 .... 6H **29**
SE3 .... 7H **105**
SM3: Cheam 6G **165**
SW1 .... 6F **11**
SW19 .... 3F **135**
TW12: Ham H 5H **131**
UB3: Hayes 7G **75**
W3 .... 1A **98**
W5 .... 7E **78**
Parkside Av. BR1: Brom 4C **160**
DA7: Bex 2K **127**
RM1: Rom 3K **55**
SW19 .... 5F **135**
Parkside Bus. Est. SE8 .... 6A **104**
(Blackhorse Rd.)
SE8 .... 6A **104**
(Rolt St.)
Parkside Cl. SE20 .... 7J **139**
Parkside Ct. *E11* *6J* ***51***
(off Wanstead Pl.)
N22 .... 6E **32**
Parkside Cres. KT5: Surb 6J **151**
N7 .... 3A **66**
Parkside Cross DA7: Bex 2K **127**
Parkside Dr. HA8: Edg 3B **28**
Parkside Est. E9 .... 1J **85**
Parkside Gdns. EN4: E Barn 1J **31**
SW19 .... 4F **135**
Parkside Ho. RM10: Dag 3J **73**
Parkside Lodge DA17: Belv 5J **109**
Parkside Rd. DA17: Belv 4H **109**
SW11 .... 1E **118**
TW3: Houn 5F **113**
Parkside Ter. *BR6: Farnb* *3F* ***173***
(off Willow Wlk.)
N18 .... 4J **33**
Parkside Way HA2: Harr 4F **41**
Park Sq. E. NW1 .... 3J **5** (4F **83**)
Park Sq. M. NW1 .... 4J **5** (4E **82**)
Park Sq. W. NW1 .... 3J **5** (4F **83**)
Parkstead Rd. SW15 .... 5C **116**
Park Steps W2 .... 2D **10**
Parkstone Av. N18 .... 6A **34**
Parkstone Rd. E17 .... 3E **50**
SE15 .... 2G **121**
Park St. CR0: Croy 2C **168**
SE1 .... 4C **14** (1C **102**)
TW11: Tedd 6J **131**
W1 .... 2G **11** (7E **82**)
Park Ter. EN3: Enf H 1F **25**
KT4: Wor Pk 1C **164**
SM5: Cars 3C **166**
Parkthorne Cl. HA2: Harr 6F **41**
Parkthorne Dr. HA2: Harr 6E **40**
Parkthorne Rd. SW12 .... 7H **119**
Park Towers *W1* *5J* ***11***
(off Brick St.)
Park Vw. HA5: H End 1D **40**
HA9: Wemb 5H **61**
KT3: N Mald 3B **152**
N5 .... 4C **66**
N21 .... 7E **22**
RM6: Chad H 6D **54**
SE8 .... *5K* ***103***
(off Trundleys Rd.)
UB7: Yiew 7A **74**
W3 .... 5J **79**
Parkview DA18: Erith 3D **108**
UB6: G'frd *3A* ***78***
(off Perivale La.)
Park View Academy Sports Cen.
.... 4C 48
Park Vw. Apartments *SE16* *3H* ***103***
(off Banyard Rd.)
Park Vw. Ct. N12 .... 4H **31**
SE20 .... 1H **157**
Parkview Ct. HA3: Hrw W 7D **26**
IG2: Ilf 6J **53**
SW6 .... 2G **117**
SW18 .... 6J **117**
Park Vw. Cres. N11 .... 4A **32**
Park Vw. Dr. CR4: Mitc 2B **154**
Park Vw. Est. E2 .... 2K **85**
Park Vw. Gdns. IG4: Ilf 4D **52**
N22 .... 1A **48**
NW4 .... 5E **44**
Park Vw. Ho. E4 .... 5H **35**
SE24 .... *6B* ***120***
(off Hurst St.)
Parkview Ho. N9 .... 7C **24**
Park Vw. Mans. N4 .... 6B **48**
Park Vw. M. SW9 .... 2K **119**
Park View Road 3C 126
Park Vw. Rd. CR0: Croy 1G **169**
DA16: Well 3C **126**
N3 .... 1K **45**
N17 .... 3G **49**
NW10 .... 4B **62**
UB1: S'hall 1E **94**
UB8: Hil 6B **74**
W5 .... 5E **78**
Parkview Rd. SE9 .... 1F **143**
Park Village E. NW1 .... 1K **5** (2F **83**)
Park Village W. NW1 .... 2F **83**
Park Vs. RM6: Chad H 6D **54**
Parkville Rd. SW6 .... 7H **99**
Park Vista SE10 .... 6F **105**
Park Wlk. EN4: Cockf 3G **21**
IG1: Ilf *2F* ***71***
(in The Exchange)
N6 .... 7E **46**
SE10 .... 7F **105**
SW10 .... 7A **16** (6A **100**)
Park Way EN2: Enf 2F **23**
HA4: Ruis 1J **57**
HA8: Edg 1H **43**
IG8: Wfd G 5F **37**
KT8: W Mole 3F **149**
N20 .... 4J **31**
NW11 .... 5G **45**
TW14: Felt 7K **111**
W3 .... 3G **97**
Parkway DA18: Erith 3E **108**
IG3: Ilf 3K **71**
N14 .... 2D **32**
NW1 .... 1F **83**
SW20 .... 4F **153**
UB10: Hil 7C **56**
Parkway, The TW4: Cran 2K **111**
TW5: Cran 5J **93**
UB2: S'hall 5J **93**
UB3: Hayes 3K **93**
UB4: Yead 6A **76**
UB5: N'olt 4B **76**
Park Way Ct. HA4: Ruis 1H **57**
Parkway Trad. Est. TW5: Hest 6A **94**
Park W. W2 .... 7D **4**
Park W. Pl. W2 .... 7D **4** (6C **82**)
Park Wharf *SE8* *5A* ***104***
(off Evelyn St.)
Parkwood BR3: Beck 7C **140**
N20 .... 3K **31**
NW8 .... *1D* ***82***
(off St Edmund's Ter.)
Parkwood Av. KT10: Esh 7G **149**
Parkwood Flats N20 .... 3J **31**
Parkwood Gro. TW16: Sun 3J **147**
Parkwood M. N6 .... 6F **47**
Parkwood Rd. DA5: Bexl 7F **127**
SW19 .... 5H **135**
TW7: Isle 1K **113**
Parliament Ct. E1 .... 6H **9**
Parliament Hill 3D 64
Parliament Hill NW3 .... 4C **64**
Parliament Hill Fields 3E 64
Parliament Hill Lido 4E 64
Parliament Hill Mans. NW5 .... 4E **64**
Parliament M. SW14 .... 2J **115**
Parliament Sq. SW1 .... 7E **12** (2J **101**)
Parliament St. SW1 .... 6E **12** (2J **101**)
Parliament Vw. SE1 .... 3G **19** (4K **101**)
Parma Cres. SW11 .... 4D **118**
Parmiter Ind. Est. *E2* *2H* ***85***
(off Parmiter St.)
Parmiter St. E2 .... 2H **85**
Parmoor Ct. EC1 .... 3C **8**

Parndon Ho.—Peacock St.

Parndon Ho. IG10: Lough 1H **37**
Parnell Cl. HA8: Edg 4C **28**
W12 3D **98**
Parnell Ho. WC1 6D **6** (5H **83**)
Parnell Rd. E3 1B **86**
(not continuous)
Parnham Cl. BR1: Brom 3F **161**
Parnham St. E14 6A **86**
(not continuous)
Parolles Rd. N19 1G **65**
Paroma Rd. DA17: Belv 4G **109**
Parr Cl. N9 4C **34**
N18 4C **34**
Parr Ct. *N1* *2D **84***
(*off New Nth. Rd.*)
TW13: Hanw 4A **130**
Parr Ho. *E16* *1K **105***
(*off Beaulieu Av.*)
Parrington Ho. SW4 6H **119**
Parr Rd. E6 1B **88**
HA7: Stan 1D **42**
Parrs Cl. CR2: Sand 7D **168**
Parrs Pl. TW12: Hamp 7E **130**
Parr St. N1 2D **84**
Parry Av. E6 6D **88**
Parry Cl. KT17: Ewe 7D **164**
Parry Ho. *E1* *1H **103***
(*off Green Bank*)
Parry Pl. SE18 4F **107**
Parry Rd. SE25 3E **156**
W10 3G **81**
(not continuous)
Parry St. SW8 7F **19** (6J **101**)
Parsifal Rd. NW6 5J **63**
Parsley Gdns. CR0: Croy 1K **169**
Parsloes Av. RM9: Dag 4D **72**
Parsonage Cl. UB3: Hayes 6H **75**
Parsonage Gdns. EN2: Enf 2H **23**
Parsonage La. DA14: Sidc 4F **145**
EN1: Enf 2H **23**
EN2: Enf 2H **23**
Parsonage Manorway DA17: Belv 6G **109**
Parsonage St. E14 4E **104**
Parsons Cl. SM1: Sutt 3K **165**
Parson's Cres. HA8: Edg 3B **28**
PARSONS GREEN 2H **117**
Parson's Grn. SW6 1J **117**
Parson's Grn. La. SW6 1J **117**
Parson's Gro. HA8: Edg 3B **28**
Parsons Hill *SE18* *3E **106***
(*off Powis St.*)
Parsons Ho. W2 4A **4**
Parsons Lodge *NW6* *7K **63***
(*off Priory Rd.*)
Parsons Mead CR0: Croy 1B **168**
KT8: E Mos 3G **149**
Parson's Rd. E13 2A **88**
Parson St. NW4 4F **44**
Parthenia Rd. SW6 1J **117**
Partingdale La. NW7 5A **30**
Partington Cl. N19 1H **65**
Partridge Cl. E16 5B **88**
EN5: Barn 6A **20**
HA7: Stan 4K **27**
WD23: Bush 1B **26**
Partridge Ct. EC1 3A **8**
Partridge Dr. BR6: Farnb 3G **173**
Partridge Grn. SE9 3E **142**
Partridge Rd. DA14: Sidc 3J **143**
TW12: Hamp 6D **130**
Partridge Sq. E6 5C **88**
Partridge Way N22 1J **47**
Pasadena Cl. UB3: Hayes 2J **93**
Pasadena Cl. Trad. Est.
UB3: Hayes 2K **93**
Pascall Ho. *SE17* *6C **102***
(*off Draco St.*)
Pascal St. SW8 7H **101**
Pascoe Rd. SE13 5F **123**
Pasley Cl. SE17 5B **102**
Pasquier Rd. E17 3A **50**
Passage, The TW9: Rich 5E **114**
Passey Pl. SE9 6D **124**
Passfield Dr. E14 5D **86**
Passfield Hall *WC1* *4H **83***
(*off Endsleigh Pl.*)
Passfield Path SE28 7B **90**
Passfields SE6 3D **140**
W14 *5H **99***
(*off Star St.*)
Passing All. EC1 4B **8**
Passingham Ho. TW5: Hest 6E **94**
Passmore Edwards Ho.
N11 6C **32**
Passmore Gdns. N11 6C **32**
Passmore House *E2* *1F **85***
(*off Kingsland Rd.*)
Passmore St. SW1 5G **17** (5E **100**)
Pasteur Cl. NW9 2A **44**
Pasteur Ct. HA1: Harr 1B **60**
Pasteur Gdns. N18 5G **33**
Paston Cl. E5 3K **67**
SM6: Wall 3G **167**
Paston Cres. SE12 7K **123**
Pastor Ct. N6 6G **47**
Pastor St. SE11 4B **102**
(not continuous)
Pasture Cl. HA0: Wemb 3B **60**
Pasture Rd. HA0: Wemb 2B **60**
RM9: Dag 4F **73**
SE6 1H **141**
Pastures, The N20 1C **30**
Pastures Mead UB10: Hil 6C **56**
Patcham Ter. SW8 1F **119**
Patch Cl. UB10: Uxb 1B **74**
Patching Way UB4: Yead 5C **76**
Patent Ho. *E14* *5D **86***
(*off Morris Rd.*)
Paternoster La. EC4 1B **14** (6B **84**)
Paternoster Row EC4 1C **14** (6C **84**)
Paternoster Sq. EC4 1B **14** (6B **84**)
Paterson Ct. EC1 2E **8**
Pater St. W8 3J **99**
Pates Mnr. Dr. TW14: Bedf 7F **111**
Path, The SW19 1K **153**
Pathfield Rd. SW16 6H **137**
Patience Rd. SW11 2C **118**
Patio Cl. SW4 6H **119**
Patmore Est. SW8 1G **119**
Patmore Ho. N16 5E **66**
Patmore St. SW8 1G **119**
Patmos Lodge *SW9* *1B **120***
(*off Elliott Rd.*)
Patmos Rd. SW9 7B **102**
Paton Cl. E3 3C **86**
Paton Ho. *SW9* *2K **119***
(*off Stockwell Rd.*)
Paton St. EC1 2C **8** (3C **84**)
Patricia Ct. BR7: Chst 1H **161**
DA16: Well 7B **108**
Patrick Coman Ho. *EC1* *2A **8***
(*off St John St.*)
Patrick Connolly Gdns. E3 3D **86**
Patrick Pas. SW11 2C **118**
Patrick Rd. E13 3A **88**
Patriot Sq. E2 2H **85**
Patrol Pl. SE6 6D **122**
Pat Shaw Ho. *E1* *4K **85***
(*off Globe Rd.*)
Patshull Pl. NW5 6G **65**
Patshull Rd. NW5 6G **65**
Patten All. TW10: Rich 5D **114**
Pattenden Rd. SE6 1B **140**
Patten Ho. N4 1C **66**
Patten Rd. SW18 7C **118**
Patterdale *NW1* *2K **5***
(*off Osnaburgh St.*)
Patterdale Cl. BR1: Brom 6H **141**
Patterdale Rd. SE15 7J **103**
Pattern Ho. EC1 3A **8** (4B **84**)
Patterson Ct. SE19 7F **139**
Patterson Rd. SE19 6F **139**
Pattina Wlk. *SE16* *1A **104***
(*off Capstan Way*)
Pattinson Point *E16* *5J **87***
(*off Fife Rd.*)
Pattison Ho. *E1* *6K **85***
(*off Wellesley St.*)
SE1 *6D **14***
(*off Redcross Way*)
Pattison Rd. NW2 3J **63**
Pattison Wlk. SE18 5G **107**
Paul Byrne Ho. N2 3A **46**
Paul Cl. E15 7G **69**
Paul Ct. *N18* *4B **34***
(*off Fairfield Rd.*)
RM7: Rom 5J **55**
Paulet Rd. SE5 2B **120**
Paul Gdns. CR0: Croy 2F **169**
Paulhan Rd. HA3: Kent 4D **42**
Paul Ho. *W10* *4G **81***
(*off Ladbroke Gro.*)
Paulin Dr. N21 7F **23**
Pauline Cres. TW2: Whit 1G **131**
Pauline Ho. *E1* *5G **85***
(*off Old Montague St.*)
Paul Julius Cl. E14 7F **87**
Paul Robeson Cl. E6 3E **88**
Paul Robeson Theatre, The 3F **113**
Pauls Ho. *E3* *5B **86***
(*off Timothy Rd.*)
Paul St. E15 1G **87**
EC2 4F **9** (4D **84**)
Paul's Wlk. EC4 2B **14** (7C **84**)
Paultons Ho. *SW3* *7B **16***
(*off King's Rd.*)
Paultons Sq. SW3 7B **16** (6B **100**)
Paultons St. SW3 6B **100**
Pauntley St. N19 1G **65**
Pavan Ct. *E2* *3J **85***
(*off Sceptre Rd.*)
Paved Ct. TW9: Rich 5D **114**
Paveley Dr. SW11 7C **100**
Paveley Ho. *N1* *2K **83***
(*off Priory Grn. Est.*)
Paveley St. NW8 2C **4** (3C **82**)
Pavement, The *E11* *1E **68***
(*off Hainault Rd.*)
SW4 4G **119**
TW7: Isle *3A **114***
(*off South St.*)
W5 3E **96**
Pavement M. RM6: Chad H 7D **54**
Pavement Sq. CR0: Croy 1G **169**
Pavet Cl. RM10: Dag 6H **73**
Pavilion NW8 2B **4** (3B **82**)
Pavilion, The SW8 7H **101**
Pavilion Ct. *NW6* *3J **81***
(*off Stafford Rd.*)
Pavilion La. BR3: Beck 6B **140**
Pavilion Leisure Cen., The 2J **159**
Pavilion Lodge HA2: Harr 1H **59**
Pavilion M. N3 3J **45**
Pavilion Pde. *W12* *6E **80***
(*off Wood La.*)
Pavilion Rd. IG1: Ilf 7D **52**
SW1 7F **11** (3D **100**)
Pavilion Sports & Fitness Club, The
3G **149**
Pavilion Sq. SW17 3D **136**
Pavilion St. SW1 2F **17** (3D **100**)
Pavilion Ter. IG2: Ilf 5J **53**
W12 *6E **80***
(*off Wood La.*)
Pavilion Way HA4: Ruis 2A **58**
HA8: Edg 7C **28**
Pawleyne Cl. SE20 7J **139**
Pawsey Cl. E13 1K **87**
Pawsons Rd. CR0: Croy 6C **156**
Paxfold HA7: Stan 5J **27**
Paxford Rd. HA0: Wemb 2B **60**
Paxton Cl. KT12: Walt T 7A **148**
TW9: Kew 2F **115**
Paxton Ct. *CR4: Mitc* *2D **154***
(*off Armfield Cres.*)
SE12 3A **142**
SE26 *4A **140***
(*off Adamsrill Rd.*)
Paxton Pl. SE27 4E **138**
Paxton Rd. BR1: Brom 7J **141**
N17 7A **34**
SE23 3A **140**
W4 6A **98**
Paxton Ter. SW1 7K **17** (6F **101**)
Paymal Ho. *E1* *5J **85***
(*off Stepney Way*)
Payne Cl. IG11: Bark 7J **71**
Payne Ho. *N1* *1K **83***
(*off Barnsbury Est.*)
Paynell Ct. SE3 3G **123**
Payne Rd. E3 2D **86**
Paynesfield Av. SW14 3K **115**
Paynesfield Rd.
WD23: Bushy 1E **26**
Payne St. SE8 7B **104**
Paynes Wlk. W6 6G **99**
Payzes Gdns. IG8: Wfd G 6C **36**
Peabody Av. SW1 5J **17** (5F **101**)
Peabody Bldgs. E1 2K **15**
EC1 *4D **8***
(*off Roscoe St.*)
SW3 7C **16**
Peabody Cl. CR0: Croy 1J **169**
SE10 1D **122**
SW1 7K **17** (5F **101**)
Peabody Cotts. N17 1E **48**
Peabody Ct. *EC1* *4D **8***
(*off Roscoe St.*)
SE5 *1D **120***
(*off Kimpton Rd.*)
Peabody Est. *E1* *7K **85***
(*off Glasmis Pl.*)
E2 *2H **85***
(*off Minerva St.*)
EC1 *4D **8***
(*off Dufferin St., not continuous*)
EC1 *4K **7***
(*off Farringdon La.*)
N1 1C **84**
SE1 5K **13** (1A **102**)
(Duchy St.)
SE1 6D **14**
(Marshalsea Rd.)
SE1 5C **14** (1C **102**)
(Southwark St.)
SE24 7B **120**
SW1 3B **18**
SW3 7D **16** (6C **100**)
SW6 *6J **99***
(*off Lillie Rd.*)
SW11 4C **118**
W6 5E **98**
W10 5E **80**
Peabody Hill SE21 1B **138**
Peabody Sq. SE1 7A **14** (2B **102**)
(not continuous)
Peabody Ter. *EC1* *4K **7***
(*off Farringdon La.*)
Peabody Twr. *EC1* *4D **8***
(*off Golden La.*)
Peabody Trust *SE17* *4D **102***
(*off Rodney Rd.*)
Peabody Yd. N1 1C **84**
Peace Cl. N14 5A **22**
SE25 4E **156**
UB6: G'frd 1H **77**
Peace Gro. HA9: Wemb 3H **61**
Peace St. SE18 6E **106**
Peaches Cl. SM2: Cheam 7G **165**
Peachey La. UB8: Cowl 5A **74**
Peach Gro. E11 3F **69**
Peach Rd. TW13: Felt 1J **129**
W10 3F **81**
Peach Tree Av. UB7: Yiew 6B **74**
Peachum Rd. SE3 6H **105**
Peachwalk M. E3 2K **85**
Peachy Cl. HA8: Edg 6B **28**
Peacock Av. TW14: Bedf 1F **129**
Peacock Cl. E4 7G **35**
RM8: Dag 1C **72**
Peacock Ind. Est. N17 7A **34**
Peacock St. SE17 4B **102**

Peacock Theatre 1G 13
(off Portugal St.)
Peacock Wlk. E16 6K 87
(off Mortlake Rd.)
N6 7F 47
Peacock Yd. SE17 5B 102
(off Iliffe St.)
Peak, The SE26 3J 139
Peaketon Av. IG4: Ilf 4B 52
Peak Fitness
Crossharbour 2D 104
Peak Hill SE26 4J 139
Peak Hill Av. SE26 4J 139
Peak Hill Gdns. SE26 4J 139
Peak Ho. N4 1C 66
(off Woodberry Down Est.)
Peal Gdns. W13 3A 78
Peall Rd. CR0: Croy 6K 155
Peall Rd. Ind. Est. CR0: Croy 6K 155
Pearce Cl. CR4: Mitc 2E 154
Pearcefield Av. SE23 1J 139
Pearce Ho. SW1 4D 18
(off Causton St.)
Pear Cl. NW9 4K 43
SE14 7A 104
Pear Ct. SE15 7F 103
(off Thruxton Way)
Pearcroft Rd. E11 2F 69
Peardon St. SW8 2F 119
Peareswood Gdns. HA7: Stan 1D 42
Pearfield Rd. SE23 3A 140
Pearl Cl. E6 6E 88
NW2 7F 45
Pearl Rd. E17 3C 50
Pearl St. E1 1H 103
Pearmain Cl. TW17: Shep 5D 146
Pearman St. SE1 1K 19 (3A 102)
Pear Pl. SE1 6J 13 (2A 102)
Pear Rd. E11 3F 69
Pears Av. TW17: Shep 3G 147
Pearscroft Ct. SW6 1K 117
Pearscroft Rd. SW6 1K 117
Pearse St. SE15 6E 102
Pearson Cl. EN5: New Bar 3E 20
SE5 1C 120
(off Camberwell New Rd.)
Pearson M. SW4 3H 119
(off Slievemore Cl.)
Pearson's Av. SE14 1C 122
Pearson St. E2 2F 85
Pears Rd. TW3: Houn 3G 113
Peartree SE26 5A 140
Pear Tree Av. UB7: Yiew 6B 74
Peartree Av. SW17 3A 136
Pear Tree Cl. BR2: Brom 5B 160
E2 1F 85
KT9: Chess 5G 163
Peartree Cl. CR4: Mitc 2C 154
DA8: Erith 1K 127
Pear Tree Ct. E18 1K 51
EC1 4K 7 (4A 84)
Peartree Gdns. RM7: Mawney 2H 55
RM8: Dag 4B 72
Pear Tree Ho. SE4 3B 122
Peartree La. E1 7J 85
Pear Tree Rd. TW15: Ashf 5E 128
Peartree Rd. EN1: Enf 3K 23
Peartrees UB7: Yiew 7A 74
Pear Tree St. EC1 3B 8 (4C 84)
Peartree Way SE10 4J 105
Peary Ho. NW10 7K 61
Peary Pl. E2 3J 85
Peas Mead Ter. E4 4K 35
Peatfield Cl. DA15: Sidc 3J 143
Pebble Way W3 1H 97
(off Steyne Rd.)
Pebworth Rd. HA1: Harr 2A 60
Peckarmans Wood SE26 3G 139
Peckett Sq. N5 4C 66
Peckford Pl. SW9 2A 120
PECKHAM 1G 121
Peckham Gro. SE15 7E 102
Peckham High St. SE15 1G 121
Peckham Hill St. SE15 7G 103
Peckham Pk. Rd. SE15 7G 103
Peckham Pulse Health & Leisure Cen. 1G 121
Peckham Rd. SE5 1E 120
SE15 1E 120
Peckham Rye SE15 3G 121
SE22 4G 121
Peckham Sq. SE15 1G 121
Pecks Yd. E1 5J 9
(off Hanbury St.)
Peckwater St. NW5 5G 65
Pedlar's Wlk. N7 5K 65
Pedley Rd. RM8: Dag 1C 72
Pedley St. E1 4K 9 (4F 85)
Pedro St. E5 3K 67
Pedworth Gdns. SE16 4J 103
Peebles Ct. UB1: S'hall 6G 77
(off Haldane Rd.)
Peebles Ho. NW6 2K 81
(off Carlton Va.)
Peek Cres. SW19 5F 135
Peel Cl. E4 2J 35
N9 3B 34
Peel Dr. IG5: Ilf 3C 52
NW9 3B 44
Peel Gro. E2 2J 85
(not continuous)
Peel Pas. W8 1J 99
Peel Pl. IG5: Ilf 2C 52
Peel Pct. NW6 2J 81
Peel Rd. BR6: Farnb 5G 173
E18 1H 51
HA3: W'stone 3K 41
(not continuous)
HA9: Wemb 3D 60
Peel St. W8 1J 99
Peel Way UB8: Hil 5A 74
Peerglow Est. EN3: Pond E 5D 24
Peerless St. EC1 2E 8 (3D 84)
Pegamoid Rd. N18 3D 34
Pegasus Cl. N16 4D 66
Pegasus Ct. KT1: King T 3D 150
N21 7H 23
NW10 3D 80
(off Trenmar Gdns.)
TW8: Bford 5F 97
W3 6J 79
(off Horn La.)
Pegasus Ho. E1 4K 85
(off Beaumont Sq.)
Pegasus Pl. SE11 7J 19 (6A 102)
SW6 1J 117
Pegasus Rd. CR0: Wadd 6A 168
Pegasus Way N11 6A 32
Peggotty Way UB8: Hil 6D 74
Pegg Rd. TW5: Hest 7B 94
Pegley Gdns. SE12 2J 141
Pegwell St. SE18 7J 107
Pekin Cl. E14 6C 86
(off Pekin St.)
Pekin St. E14 6C 86
Pelabon Ho. TW1: Twick 6D 114
(off Clevedon Rd.)
Peldon Ct. TW9: Rich 4F 115
Peldon Pas. TW10: Rich 4F 115
Peldon Wlk. N1 1B 84
(off Popham St.)
Pelham Av. IG11: Bark 1K 89
Pelham Cl. SE5 3E 120
Pelham Cotts. DA5: Bexl 1H 145
Pelham Ct. DA14: Sidc 3A 144
SW3 4C 16
(off Fulham Rd.)
Pelham Cres. SW7 4C 16 (4C 100)
Pelham Ho. W14 4H 99
(off Mornington Av.)
Pelham Pl. SW7 3C 16 (4C 100)
W13 4K 77
Pelham Rd. BR3: Beck 2J 157
DA7: Bex 3G 127
E18 3K 51
IG1: Ilf 2H 71
Pelham Rd. N15 4F 49
N22 2A 48
SW19 7J 135
Pelham St. SW7 3B 16 (4B 100)
Pelican Est. SE15 1F 121
Pelican Ho. SE5 1F 121
SE8 4B 104
Pelican Pas. E1 4J 85
Pelican Wlk. SW9 4B 120
Pelican Wharf E1 1J 103
(off Wapping Wall)
Pelier St. SE17 6C 102
Pelinore Rd. SE6 2G 141
Pella Ho. SE11 5H 19 (5K 101)
Pellant Rd. SW6 7G 99
Pellatt Gro. N22 1A 48
Pellatt Rd. HA9: Wemb 2D 60
SE22 5F 121
Pellerin Rd. N16 5E 66
Pellew Ho. E1 4H 85
(off Somerford St.)
Pelling St. E14 6C 86
Pellipar Cl. N13 3F 33
Pellipar Gdns. SE18 5D 106
Pellipar Rd. SE18 5D 106
Pelly Rd. E13 1J 87
(not continuous)
Pelter St. E2 1J 9 (3F 85)
(not continuous)
Pelton Rd. SE10 5G 105
Pembar Av. E17 3A 50
Pemberley Chase KT19: Ewe 5H 163
Pemberley Cl. KT19: Ewe 5H 163
Pemberley Ho. KT19: Ewe 5H 163
(off Pemberley Chase)
Pember Rd. NW10 3F 81
Pemberton Ct. E1 3K 85
(off Portelet Rd.)
Pemberton Gdns. N19 3G 65
RM6: Chad H 5E 54
Pemberton Ho. SE26 4G 139
(off High Level Dr.)
Pemberton Pl. E8 7H 67
Pemberton Rd. KT8: E Mos 4G 149
N4 5A 48
Pemberton Row EC4 7K 7 (6A 84)
Pemberton Ter. N19 3G 65
Pembridge Av. TW2: Whit 1D 130
Pembridge Cres. W11 7J 81
Pembridge Gdns. W2 7J 81
Pembridge M. W11 7J 81
Pembridge Pl. SW15 5J 117
W2 7J 81
Pembridge Rd. W11 7J 81
Pembridge Sq. W2 7J 81
Pembridge Studios W11 7J 81
(off Pembridge Vs.)
Pembridge Vs. W2 7J 81
W11 7J 81
Pembroke W14 4H 99
(off Mornington Av.)
Pembroke Av. EN1: Enf 1C 24
HA3: Kent 3A 42
HA5: Pinn 1B 58
KT5: Surb 5H 151
N1 1J 83
Pembroke Bldgs. NW10 3C 80
Pembroke Bus. Cen. BR8: Swan 7K 145
Pembroke Cen., The HA4: Ruis 1H 57
Pembroke Cl. SW1 7H 11 (2E 100)
Pembroke Cotts. W8 3J 99
(off Pembroke Sq.)
Pembroke Ct. W7 6K 77
(off Copley Cl.)
W8 3J 99
(off Sth. Edwardes Sq.)
Pembroke Gdns. RM10: Dag 3H 73
W8 4H 99
Pembroke Gdns. Cl. W8 3J 99
Pembroke Hall NW4 3E 44
(off Mulberry Cl.)
Pembroke Ho. SW1 2G 17
(off Chesham Ho.)
Pembroke Ho. W2 6K 81
(off Hallfield Est.)
W3 2J 97
(off Park Rd. E.)
Pembroke Lodge HA7: Stan 6H 27
Pembroke M. E3 3A 86
N10 1E 46
W8 3J 99
Pembroke Pde. DA8: Erith 5J 109
Pembroke Pl. HA8: Edg 7B 28
TW7: Isle 2J 113
W8 3J 99
Pembroke Rd. BR1: Brom 2A 160
CR4: Mitc 2E 154
DA8: Erith 5J 109
E6 5D 88
E17 5D 50
HA4: Ruis 1G 57
HA9: Wemb 3D 60
IG3: Ilf 1K 71
N8 4J 47
N10 1E 46
N13 3H 33
N15 5F 49
SE25 4E 156
UB6: G'frd 4F 77
W8 4H 99
Pembroke Sq. W8 3J 99
Pembroke St. N1 7J 65
(not continuous)
Pembroke Studios W8 3H 99
Pembroke Ter. NW8 1B 82
(off Queen's Ter.)
Pembroke Vs. TW9: Rich 4D 114
W8 4J 99
Pembroke Wlk. W8 4J 99
Pembroke Way UB3: Harl 3E 92
Pembrook M. SW11 4B 118
Pembry Cl. SW9 1A 120
Pembury Av. KT4: Wor Pk 1C 164
Pembury Cl. BR2: Hayes 7H 159
E5 5H 67
Pembury Ct. UB3: Harl 6F 93
Pembury Cres. DA14: Sidc 2E 144
Pembury Pl. E5 5H 67
Pembury Rd. DA7: Bex 7E 108
E5 5H 67
N17 1F 49
SE25 4G 157
Pemdevon Rd. CR0: Croy 7A 156
Pemell Cl. E1 4J 85
Pemell Ho. E1 4J 85
(off Pemell Cl.)
Pemerich Cl. UB3: Harl 5H 93
Pempath Pl. HA9: Wemb 2D 60
Penally Pl. N1 1D 84
Penang Ho. E1 1H 103
(off Prusom St.)
Penang St. E1 1H 103
Penard Rd. UB2: S'hall 3F 95
Penart Ct. SM2: Sutt 7A 166
Penarth Cen. SE15 6J 103
Penarth St. SE15 6J 103
Penberth Rd. SE6 2E 140
Penbury Rd. UB2: S'hall 4D 94
Pencombe M. W11 7H 81
Pencraig Way SE15 6H 103
Pendall Cl. EN4: E Barn 4H 21
Penda Rd. DA8: Erith 7H 109
Pendarves Rd. SW20 1E 152
Penda's Mead E9 4A 68
Pendell Av. UB3: Harl 7H 93
Pendennis Ho. SE8 4A 104
Pendennis Rd. N17 3D 48
SW16 4J 137
Penderel Rd. TW3: Houn 5E 112
Penderry Ri. SE6 2F 141
Penderyn Way N7 4H 65
Pendlebury Ct. KT5: Surb 4E 150
(off Cranes Pk.)
Pendle Ct. UB10: Hil 1D 74
Pendle Ho. SE26 3G 139
Pendle Rd. SW16 6F 137

Pendlestone Rd. E17 ....5D 50
Pendley Ho. E2 ....1G 85
    (off Whiston Rd.)
Pendragon Rd. BR1: Brom 3H 141
Pendragon Wlk. NW9 ....6A 44
Pendrell Ho. WC2 ....1D 12
    (off New Compton St.)
Pendrell Rd. SE4 ....2A 122
Pendrell St. SE18 ....6H 107
Pendula Dr. UB4: Yead 4B 76
Pendulum M. E8 ....5F 67
Penerley Rd. SE6 ....1D 140
Penfield Lodge W9 ....5J 81
    (off Admiral Wlk.)
Penfields Ho. N7 ....6J 65
Penfold Cl. CR0: Wadd 3A 168
Penfold La. DA5: Bexl 2D 144
    (Cotleigh Av.)
  DA5: Bexl 1D 144
    (Stansted Cres.)
Penfold Pl. NW1 ....5C 4 (5C 82)
Penfold Rd. N9 ....1E 34
Penfold St. NW1 ....5C 4 (4B 82)
  NW8 ....4B 4 (4B 82)
Penford Gdns. SE9 ....3B 124
Penford St. SE5 ....2B 120
Pengarth Rd. DA5: Bexl 5D 126
PENGE 7J 139
Penge Ho. SW11 ....3B 118
Penge La. SE20 ....7J 139
Penge Rd. E13 ....1A 88
  SE20 ....3G 157
  SE25 ....3G 157
Penhale Cl. BR6: Chels 4K 173
Penhall Rd. SE7 ....4B 106
Penhill Rd. DA5: Bexl 6C 126
Penhurst Pl. SE1 ....1H 19
Penhurst Rd. IG6: Ilf 1F 53
Penifather La. UB6: G'frd ..3H 77
Peninsula Apartments W2 ....6C 4
    (off Praed St.)
Peninsula Ct. E14 ....3D 104
    (off E. Ferry Rd.)
Peninsula Hgts. SE1 ....5F 19 (5J 101)
Peninsular Cl. TW14: Felt ..6F 111
Peninsular Pk. SE7 ....4J 105
Peninsular Pk. Rd. SE7 ....4J 105
Penistone Rd. SW16 ....7J 137
Penketh Dr. HA1: Harr 3H 59
Penley Ct. WC2 ....2H 13 (7K 83)
Penmayne Ho. SE11 ....5K 19
    (off Kennings Way)
Penmon Rd. SE2 ....3A 108
Pennack Rd. SE15 ....6F 103
Penn Almshouses SE10 ......1E 122
    (off Greenwich Sth. St.)
Pennant M. W8 ....4K 99
Pennant Ter. E17 ....2D 50
Pennard Mans. W12 ....2E 98
    (off Goldhawk Rd.)
Pennard Rd. W12 ....2E 98
Pennards, The TW16: Sun ...3A 148
Penn Cl. HA3: Kent 4C 42
  UB6: G'frd 2F 77
Penn Ct. NW9 ....3K 43
Penner Cl. SW19 ....2G 135
Penners Gdns. KT6: Surb ...7E 150
Pennethorne Cl. E9 ....1J 85
Pennethorne Ho. SW11 .....3B 118
Pennethorne Rd. SE15 .....7H 103
Penn Gdns. BR7: Chst 2F 161
  RM5: Col R 1G 55
Penn Ho. NW8 ....4C 4
    (off Mallory St.)
Pennine Dr. NW2 ....2F 63
Pennine Ho. N9 ....3B 34
    (off Plevna Rd.)
Pennine La. NW2 ....2G 63
Pennine Pde. NW2 ....2G 63
Pennine Way DA7: Bex 1K 127
  UB3: Harl 7F 93
Pennington Cl. SE27 ......4D 138
Pennington Ct. SE16 ......1A 104

Pennington Dr. N21 ....5D 22
Pennington Lodge
  KT5: Surb 5E 150
    (off Cranes Dr.)
Pennington St. E1 ....7H 85
Pennington Way SE12 ......2K 141
Penniston Cl. N17 ....2C 48
Penn La. DA5: Bexl 5D 126
    (not continuous)
Penn Rd. N7 ....5J 65
Penn St. N1 ....1D 84
Pennycroft CR0: Sels 7A 170
Pennyfather La. EN2: Enf ..3H 23
Pennyfields E14 ....7C 86
    (not continuous)
Pennyford Ct. NW8 ....3A 4
    (off St John's Wood Rd.)
Penny La. TW17: Shep 7G 147
Penny M. SW12 ....7F 119
Pennymoor Wlk. W9 ....4H 81
    (off Ashmore Rd.)
Penny Rd. NW10 ....3H 79
Penny Royal SM6: Wall 6H 167
Pennyroyal Av. E6 ....6E 88
Penpoll Rd. E8 ....6H 67
Penpool La. DA16: Well ...3B 126
Penrhyn Av. E17 ....1B 50
Penrhyn Cres. E17 ....1C 50
  SW14 ....4J 115
Penrhyn Gdns. KT1: King T .4D 150
Penrhyn Gro. E17 ....1C 50
Penrhyn Rd. KT1: King T ..4E 150
Penrith Cl. BR3: Beck 1D 158
  SW15 ....5G 117
  UB8: Uxb 7A 56
Penrith Pl. SE27 ....2B 138
Penrith Rd. CR7: Thor H ...2C 156
  KT3: N Mald 4K 151
  N15 ....5D 48
Penrith St. SW16 ....6G 137
Penrose Gro. SE17 ....5C 102
Penrose Ho. N21 ....5E 22
  SE17 ....5C 102
    (not continuous)
Penrose St. SE17 ....5C 102
Penryn Ho. SE11 ....5B 102
    (off Seaton Cl.)
Penryn St. NW1 ....2H 83
Penry St. SE1 ....4E 102
Pensbury Pl. SW8 ....2G 119
Pensbury St. SW8 ....2G 119
Pensford Av. TW9: Kew 2G 115
Penshurst NW5 ....6E 64
Penshurst Av. DA15: Sidc ..6A 126
Penshurst Gdns. HA8: Edg ..5C 28
Penshurst Grn. BR2: Brom ..5H 159
Penshurst Ho. SE15 ......6J 103
    (off Lovelinch Cl.)
Penshurst Rd. CR7: Thor H ..5B 156
  DA7: Bex 1F 127
  E9 ....7K 67
  N17 ....7A 34
Penshurst Wlk. BR2: Brom ..5H 159
Penshurst Way SM2: Sutt ...7J 165
Pensilver Cl. EN4: E Barn ..4H 21
Penstemon Cl. N3 ....6D 30
Penstock Footpath N8 .....3K 47
Pentagram Yd. W11 ....6J 81
    (off Needham Rd.)
Pentavia Retail Pk. NW7 ...7G 29
Pentelow Gdns. TW14: Felt ..6J 111
Pentire Rd. E17 ....1F 51
Pentland Av. HA8: Edg 2C 28
  TW17: Shep 5C 146
Pentland Cl. N9 ....2D 34
  NW11 ....2G 63
Pentland Gdns. SW18 .....6A 118
Pentland Pl. UB5: N'olt ...1C 76
Pentlands Cl. CR4: Mitc ...3F 155
Pentland St. SW18 ....6A 118
Pentland Way UB10: Ick ...3E 56
Pentlow St. SW15 ....3E 116
Pentlow Way IG9: Buck H ..1H 37

Pentney Rd. E4 ....1A 36
  SW12 ....1G 137
  SW19 ....1G 153
Penton Gro. N1 ....2A 84
Penton Ho. N1 ....2A 84
    (off Pentonville Rd.)
  SE2 ....1D 108
Penton Pl. SE17 ....5B 102
Penton Ri. WC1 ....1H 7 (3K 83)
Penton St. N1 ....2A 84
PENTONVILLE 2K 83
Pentonville Rd. N1 .....1F 7 (2K 83)
Pentrich Av. EN1: Enf 1B 24
Pentridge St. SE15 ......7F 103
Pentyre Av. N18 ....5J 33
Penwerris Av. TW7: Isle ...7G 95
Penwerris Ct. TW5: Hest ...7G 95
Penwith Rd. SW18 ....2J 135
Penwood Ct. HA5: Pinn 4D 40
Penwood Ho. SW15 ....6B 116
Penwortham Ct. N22 ......2A 48
    (off Mayes Rd.)
Penwortham Rd. SW16 .....6F 137
Penylan Pl. HA8: Edg 7B 28
Penywern Rd. SW5 ....5J 99
Penzance Ho. SE11 ....5K 19
    (off Seaton Cl.)
Penzance Pl. W11 ....1G 99
Penzance St. W11 ....1G 99
Peony Cl. IG8: Wfd G 7B 36
  SW3 ....6A 100
Peony Gdns. W12 ....7C 80
Peperfield WC1 ....2G 7
    (off Cromer St.)
Pepler Ho. W10 ....4G 81
    (off Wornington Rd.)
Pepler M. SE5 ....5F 103
Peploe Rd. NW6 ....2F 81
Peplow Cl. UB7: Yiew 1A 92
Pepper Cl. E6 ....5D 88
Peppercorn Cl. CR7: Thor H ..2D 156
Peppermead Sq. SE13 .....5C 122
Peppermint Cl. CR0: Croy ..7J 155
Peppermint Pl. E11 ......3G 69
Pepper St. E14 ....3D 104
  SE1 ....6C 14 (2C 102)
Peppie Cl. N16 ....2E 66
Pepys Cl. UB10: Ick 4D 56
Pepys Cres. E16 ....1J 105
  EN5: Barn 5A 20
Pepys Ho. E2 ....3J 85
    (off Kirkwall Pl.)
Pepys Ri. BR6: Orp 1K 173
Pepys Rd. SE14 ....1K 121
  SW20 ....1E 152
Pepys St. EC3 ....2H 15 (7E 84)
Perceval Av. NW3 ....5C 64
Perceval Ct. UB5: N'olt ...5E 58
Perceval Ho. W5 ....7C 78
Percheron Cl. TW7: Isle ...3K 113
Perch St. E8 ....4F 67
Percival Ct. N17 ....7A 34
Percival David Foundation of Chinese Art
    ....3D 6
Percival Gdns. RM6: Chad H ..6C 54
Percival Rd. BR6: Farnb ...2F 173
  EN1: Enf 4A 24
  SW14 ....4J 115
  TW13: Felt 2H 129
Percival St. EC1 ....3A 8 (4B 84)
Percival Way KT19: Ewe 4K 163
Percy Av. TW15: Ashf 5C 128
Percy Bryant Rd. TW16: Sun ..7G 129
Percy Bush Rd. UB7: W Dray ..3B 92
Percy Cir. WC1 ....1H 7 (3K 83)
Percy Gdns. EN3: Pond E 5E 24
  KT4: Wor Pk 1K 163
  TW7: Isle 3A 114
  UB4: Hayes 3G 75
Percy Laurie Ho. SW15 ....4F 117
    (off Nursery Cl.)
Percy M. W1 ....6C 6
Percy Pas. W1 ....6C 6

Percy Rd. CR4: Mitc 7E 154
  DA7: Bex 2E 126
  E11 ....7G 51
  E16 ....5G 87
  IG3: Ilf 5A 54
  N12 ....5F 31
  N21 ....7H 23
  RM7: Mawney 3H 55
  SE20 ....1K 157
  SE25 ....5G 157
  TW2: Whit 1F 131
  TW7: Isle 4A 114
  TW12: Hamp 7E 130
  W12 ....2C 98
Percy St. W1 ....6C 6 (5H 83)
Percy Ter. BR1: Brom 3F 161
Percy Way TW2: Whit 1G 131
Percy Yd. WC1 ....1H 7 (3K 83)
Peregrine Cl. NW10 ......5K 61
Peregrine Cl. DA16: Well ...1K 125
  SE8 ....6C 104
    (off Edward St.)
  SW16 ....4K 137
Peregrine Gdns. CR0: Croy ..2A 170
Peregrine Ho. EC1 ....1B 8
Peregrine Rd. TW16: Sun ...2H 147
Peregrine Way SW19 ......7E 134
Perham Rd. W14 ....5G 99
Peridot St. E6 ....5C 88
Perifield SE21 ....1C 138
Perimeade Rd. UB6: G'frd ...2C 78
Periton Rd. SE9 ....4B 124
PERIVALE 1C 78
Perivale Gdns. W13 ......4B 78
Perivale Grange UB6: G'frd ..3A 78
Perivale Ind. Pk. UB6: G'frd ..2B 78
Perivale La. UB6: G'frd ...3A 78
Perivale Lodge UB6: G'frd ..3A 78
    (off Perivale La.)
Perivale New Bus. Cen. UB6: G'frd ..2C 78
Perivale Pk. Gym 3K 77
Perivale Wood Local Nature Reserve
    ....1K 77
Perkin Cl. HA0: Wemb 5B 60
  TW3: Houn 4E 112
Perkins Cl. TW15: Ashf 5B 128
Perkins Ho. E14 ....5B 86
    (off Wallwood St.)
Perkin's Rents SW1 ......2C 18 (3H 101)
Perkins Rd. IG2: Ilf 5H 53
Perkins Sq. SE1 ....4D 14 (1C 102)
Perks Cl. SE3 ....3G 123
Perley Ho. E3 ....5B 86
    (off Weatherley Cl.)
Perpins Rd. SE9 ....6J 125
Perran Rd. SW2 ....1B 138
Perran Wlk. TW8: Bford 5E 96
Perren St. NW5 ....6F 65
Perreten Rd. W6 ....4D 98
Perrin Cl. TW15: Ashf 5B 128
Perrin Ct. TW15: Ashf 4C 128
Perring Est. E3 ....5C 86
    (off Gale St.)
Perrin Ho. NW6 ....3J 81
Perrin Rd. HA0: Wemb 4B 60
Perrin's Ct. NW3 ....4A 64
Perrin's La. NW3 ....4A 64
Perrin's Wlk. NW3 ....4A 64
Perronet Ho. SE1 ....3B 102
    (off Princess St.)
Perrott St. SE18 ....4G 107
Perry Av. W3 ....6K 79
Perry Cl. RM13: Rain 2K 91
  UB8: Hil 6D 74
Perry Ct. E14 ....5C 104
    (off Maritime Quay)
  N15 ....6E 48
Perryfield Way NW9 ......6B 44
  TW10: Ham 3B 132
Perry Gdns. N9 ....3J 33
Perry Gth. UB5: N'olt 1A 76
Perry Hall Rd. BR6: St M Cry ..6K 161
Perry Hill SE6 ....3B 140

Perry Ho. RM13: Rain 2K 91
Perry How KT4: Wor Pk 1B 164
Perry Lodge E12 1B 70
Perrymans Farm Rd. IG2: Ilf 6H 53
Perry Mead EN2: Enf 2G 23
Perrymead St. SW6 1J 117
Perryn Ct. TW1: Twick 6A 114
Perryn Ho. W3 7A 80
Perryn Rd. SE16 3H 103
W3 1K 97
Perry Ri. SE23 3A 140
Perry Rd. RM9: Dag 5F 91
Perry's Pl. W1 7C 6 (6H 83)
Perry St. BR7: Chst 6H 143
DA1: Cray 4K 127
Perry St. Gdns. BR7: Chst 6J 143
Perry St. Shaw BR7: Chst 7J 143
Perry Va. SE23 2J 139
Persant Rd. SE6 2G 141
Perseverance Pl. SW9 7A 102
TW9: Rich 4E 114
Perseverance Works E2 1H 9
(off Kingsland Rd.)
Pershore Cl. IG2: Ilf 5F 53
Pershore Gro. SM5: Cars 6B 154
Pert Cl. N10 7A 32
Perth Av. NW9 7K 43
UB4: Yead 4A 76
Perth Cl. SE5 4D 120
SW20 2B 152
UB5: N'olt 5E 58
Perth Ho. N1 7K 65
(off Bemerton Est.)
Perth Rd. BR3: Beck 2E 158
E10 1A 68
E13 2K 87
IG2: Ilf 6E 52
IG11: Bark 2H 89
N4 1A 66
N22 1B 48
Perth Ter. IG2: Ilf 7G 53
Perwell Av. HA2: Harr 1D 58
Perystreete SE23 2J 139
Petavel Rd. TW11: Tedd 6J 131
Peter Av. NW10 7D 62
Peter Best Ho. E1 6H 85
(off Nelson St.)
Peterboat Cl. SE10 4G 105
Peterborough Ct. EC4 1K 13 (6A 84)
Peterborough Gdns. IG1: Ilf 7C 52
Peterborough M. SW6 2J 117
Peterborough Rd. E10 5E 50
HA1: Harr 1J 59
SM5: Cars 6C 154
SW6 2J 117
Peterborough Vs. SW6 1K 117
Peter Butler Ho. SE1 7K 15
(off Wolseley St.)
Peterchurch Ho. SE15 6H 103
(off Commercial Way)
Petergate SW11 4A 118
Peterhead Ct. UB1: S'hall 6G 77
(off Osborne Rd.)
Peter Heathfield Ho. E15 1F 87
(off Wise Rd.)
Peter Ho. SW8 7J 101
(off Luscombe Way)
Peter James Bus. Cen. UB3: Hayes 2J 93
Peter James Ent. Cen. NW10 3J 79
Peter Kennedy Ct. BR3: Beck 6B 158
Peterley Bus. Cen. E2 2H 85
Peter May Cen., The 7K 35
Peter Pan Statue 4A 10 (1B 100)
Peters Cl. DA16: Well 2J 125
HA7: Stan 6J 27
RM8: Dag 1D 72
Peter Scott Vis. Cen., The 1D 116
Peters Ct. W2 6K 81
(off Porchester Rd.)
Petersfield Cl. N18 5H 33
Petersfield Ri. SW15 1D 134
Petersfield Rd. W3 2J 97
PETERSHAM 1E 132
Petersham Cl. SM1: Sutt 5J 165
TW10: Ham 2D 132
Petersham Dr. BR5: St P 2K 161
Petersham Gdns. BR5: St P 2K 161
Petersham Ho. SW7 3A 16
(off Kendrick M.)
Petersham La. SW7 3A 100
Petersham M. SW7 3A 100
Petersham Pl. SW7 3A 100
Petersham Rd.
TW10: Rich, Ham 6D 114
Petersham Ter. CR0: Bedd 3J 167
(off Richmond Grn.)
Peter's Hill EC4 2C 14 (7C 84)
Peter Shore Ct. E1 5K 85
(off Beaumont Sq.)
Peter's La. EC1 5B 8 (5B 84)
(not continuous)
Peter's Path SE26 4H 139
Peterstone Rd. SE2 2B 108
Peterstow Cl. SW19 2G 135
Peter St. W1 2C 12 (7H 83)
Peterwood Pk. CR0: Wadd 2K 167
Peterwood Way CR0: Wadd 2K 167
Petherton Ct. HA1: Harr 6K 41
(off Gayton Rd.)
NW10 1F 81
(off Tiverton Rd.)
Petherton Ho. N4 1C 66
(off Woodberry Down Est.)
Petherton Rd. N5 5C 66
Petiver Cl. E9 7J 67
Petley Rd. W6 6F 99
Peto Pl. NW1 3K 5 (4F 83)
Peto St. Nth. E16 6H 87
Petrie Cl. NW2 6G 63
Petrie Ho. SE18 6E 106
(off Woolwich Comn.)
Petrie Mus. of Egyptian Archaeology
4C 6
Petros Gdns. NW3 6A 64
Pettacre Cl. SE28 3G 107
Petticoat La. E1 6J 9 (5E 84)
Petticoat Lane Market 7J 9
(off Middlesex St.)
Petticoat Sq. E1 7J 9 (6F 85)
Petticoat Twr. E1 7J 9
Pettits Cl. RM1: Rom 2K 55
Pettits La. Nth. RM1: Rom 1K 55
Pettits Pl. RM10: Dag 5G 73
Pettits Rd. RM10: Dag 5G 73
Pettiward Cl. SW15 4E 116
Pettley Gdns. RM7: Rom 5K 55
Pettman Cres. SE28 3H 107
Pettsgrove Av. HA0: Wemb 5C 60
Pett's Hill UB5: N'olt 5F 59
Petts La. TW17: Shep 4C 146
Pett St. SE18 4C 106
PETTS WOOD 5G 161
Petts Wood Rd. BR5: Pet W 5G 161
Petty France SW1 1B 18 (3G 101)
Petty Wales EC3 3H 15 (7E 84)
Petworth Cl. UB5: N'olt 7D 58
Petworth Gdns. SW20 3D 152
UB10: Hil 1E 74
Petworth Rd. DA6: Bex 5G 127
N12 5H 31
Petworth St. SW11 1C 118
Petyt Pl. SW3 6C 100
Petyward SW3 4D 16 (4C 100)
Pevensey Av. EN1: Enf 2K 23
N11 5C 32
Pevensey Cl. TW7: Isle 7G 95
Pevensey Ct. W3 2H 97
Pevensey Ho. E1 5K 85
(off Ben Jonson Rd.)
Pevensey Rd. E7 4H 69
SW17 4B 136
TW13: Felt 1C 130
Peverel E6 6E 88
Peverel Ho. RM10: Dag 2G 73
Peveret Cl. N11 5A 32
Peveril Dr. TW11: Tedd 5H 131
Peveril Ho. SE1 3D 102
(off Rephidim St.)
Pewsey Cl. E4 5H 35
Peyton Pl. SE10 7E 104
Pharamond NW2 6F 63
Pharaoh Cl. CR4: Mitc 7D 154
Pheasant Cl. E16 6K 87
Pheasantry Ho. SW3 5D 16
(off Jubilee Pl.)
Phelp St. SE17 6D 102
Phelps Way UB3: Harl 4H 93
Phene St. SW3 7D 16 (6C 100)
Philadelphia Ct. SW10 7A 100
(off Uverdale Rd.)
Philbeach Gdns. SW5 5J 99
Phil Brown Pl. SW8 3F 119
(off Wandsworth Rd.)
Philchurch Pl. E1 6G 85
Philia Ho. NW1 7G 65
(off Farrier St.)
Philimore Cl. SE18 5J 107
Philip Av. RM7: Rush G 1K 73
Philip Cl. RM7: Rush G 1K 73
Philip Ct. W2 5A 4
(off Hall Pl.)
Philip Gdns. CR0: Croy 2B 170
Philip Ho. NW6 1K 81
(off Mortimer Pl.)
Philip Jones Ct. N4 1K 65
Philip La. N15 4D 48
Philip Mole Ho. W9 4J 81
(off Chippenham Rd.)
Philipot Path SE9 6D 124
Philippa Gdns. SE9 5B 124
Philip Rd. TW18: Staines 6A 128
Philips Cl. SM5: Cars 1E 166
Philip Sq. SW8 2F 119
Philip St. E13 4J 87
Philip Wlk. SE15 3G 121
(not continuous)
Phillimore Ct. W8 2J 99
(off Kensington High St.)
Phillimore Gdns. NW10 1E 80
W8 2J 99
Phillimore Gdns. Cl.
W8 3J 99
Phillimore Pl. W8 2J 99
Phillimore Ter. W8 3J 99
(off Allen St.)
Phillimore Wlk. W8 3J 99
Phillipp St. N1 1E 84
Phillips Ct. HA8: Edg 6B 28
Philpot La. EC3 2G 15 (7E 84)
Philpot Path IG1: Ilf 3G 71
Philpots Cl. UB7: Yiew 7A 74
Philpot Sq. SW6 3K 117
Philpot St. E1 6H 85
Phineas Pett Rd. SE9 3C 124
Phipps Bri. Rd. CR4: Mitc 2A 154
SW19 2A 154
Phipps Hatch La. EN2: Enf 1H 23
Phipps Ho. SE7 5K 105
(off Woolwich Rd.)
W12 7D 80
(off White City Est.)
Phipp St. EC2 3G 9 (4E 84)
Phoebeth Rd. SE4 5C 122
Phoenix Bus. Cen. E3 5C 86
(off Bow Comn. La.)
Phoenix Cen. 7J 167
Phoenix Cinema
East Finchley 4C 46
Phoenix Cl. BR4: W W'ck 2F 171
E8 1F 85
E17 2B 50
Phoenix Ct. CR2: S Croy 5F 169
E1 4H 85
(off Buckhurst St.)
E4 3J 35
E14 4C 104
KT3: N Mald 3B 152
NW1 1D 6
(off Purchese St.)
Phoenix Ct. SE14 6A 104
(off Chipley St.)
TW4: Houn 5B 112
TW8: Bford 5E 96
Phoenix Dr. BR2: Kes 4B 172
Phoenix Ho. SM1: Sutt 4K 165
Phoenix Ind. Est. HA1: Harr 4K 41
Phoenix Lodge Mans. W6 4F 99
(off Brook Grn.)
Phoenix Pk. NW2 2C 62
Phoenix Pl. WC1 3H 7 (4K 83)
Phoenix Rd. NW1 1C 6 (3H 83)
SE20 6J 139
Phoenix Sports & Fitness Cen. 7C 80
Phoenix St. WC2 1D 12 (6H 83)
Phoenix Theatre 1D 12
(off Charing Cross Rd.)
Phoenix Trad. Est. UB6: G'frd 1C 78
Phoenix Trad. Pk. TW8: Bford 5D 96
Phoenix Way TW5: Hest 6B 94
Phoenix Wharf E1 1H 103
(off Wapping High St.)
Phoenix Wharf Rd. SE1 7K 15
Phoenix Yd. WC1 2H 7
Photographers' Gallery 2E 12
(off Gt. Newport St.)
Phyllis Av. KT3: N Mald 5D 152
Phyllis Ho. CR0: Wadd 4B 168
(off Ashley La.)
Physic Pl. SW3 7E 16 (6D 100)
Piazza, The UB8: Uxb 7A 56
WC2 2F 13
(not continuous)
Picardy Manorway DA17: Belv 3H 109
Picardy Rd. DA17: Belv 5G 109
Picardy St. DA17: Belv 3G 109
Piccadilly W1 5K 11 (1F 101)
Piccadilly Arc. SW1 4A 12
Piccadilly Circus 3C 12 (7H 83)
Piccadilly Cir. W1 3C 12 (7H 83)
Piccadilly Ct. N7 6K 65
(off Caledonian Rd.)
Piccadilly Pl. W1 3B 12
Piccadilly Theatre 2B 12
(off Denman St.)
Pickard Cl. N14 1C 32
Pickard St. EC1 1B 8 (3B 84)
Pickering Av. E6 2E 88
Pickering Cl. E9 7K 67
Pickering Gdns. CR0: Croy 6F 157
N11 6K 31
Pickering Ho. W2 6A 82
(off Hallfield Est.)
W5 4C 96
(off Windmill Rd.)
Pickering M. W2 6K 81
Pickering Pl. SW1 5B 12
Pickering St. N1 1B 84
Pickets Cl. WD23: Bushy 1C 26
Pickets St. SW12 7F 119
Pickett Cft. HA7: Stan 1D 42
Picketts Lock La. N9 2D 34
Picketts Lock La. Ind. Est. N9 2F 35
Picketts Ter. SE22 5G 121
Pickford Cl. DA7: Bex 2E 126
Pickford La. DA7: Bex 2E 126
Pickford Rd. DA7: Bex 3E 126
Pickfords Wharf N1 2C 84
SE1 4E 14 (1D 102)
Pickhurst Grn. BR2: Hayes 7H 159
Pickhurst La. BR2: Hayes 5G 159
BR4: W W'ck 5G 159
Pickhurst Mead BR2: Hayes 7H 159
Pickhurst Pk. BR2: Brom 5G 159
Pickhurst Ri. BR4: W W'ck 7E 158
Pickwick Cl. TW4: Houn 5C 112
Pickwick Ct. SE9 1C 142
Pickwick Ho. SE16 2G 103
(off George Row)
W11 1F 99
(off St Ann's Rd.)
Pickwick M. N18 4K 33
Pickwick Pl. HA1: Harr 7J 41

Pickwick Rd. SE21 ....7D 120
Pickwick St. SE1 ....7C 14 (2C 102)
Pickwick Way BR7: Chst 6G 143
Pickworth Cl. SW8 ....7J 101
Picton Pl. KT6: Surb 1G 163
   W1 ....1H 11 (6E 82)
Picton St. SE5 ....7D 102
Picture Ho. SW16 ....2J 137
Pied Bull Yard N1 ....1B 84
   (off Theberton St.)
   WC1 ....6E 6
Piedmont Rd. SE18 ....5H 107
   (not continuous)
PIELD HEATH 4B 74
Pield Heath Av. UB8: Hil 4C 74
Pield Heath Rd. UB8: Cowl, Hil 4A 74
Pier Head E1 ....1H 103
   (not continuous)
Pierhead Wharf E1 ....1H 103
   (off Wapping High St.)
Pier Ho. SW3 ....7D 16 (6C 100)
Piermont Grn. SE22 ....5H 121
Piermont Pl. BR1: Brom 2C 160
Piermont Rd. SE22 ....5H 121
Pier Pde. E16 ....1E 106
   (off Pier Rd.)
Pierpoint Bldg. E14 ....2B 104
Pierrepoint Rd. W3 ....7H 79
Pierrepont Arc. N1 ....2B 84
   (off Islington High St.)
Pierrepont Row N1 ....2B 84
   (off Camden Pas.)
Pier Rd. E16 ....2D 106
   TW14: Felt 5K 111
Pier St. E14 ....4E 104
   (not continuous)
Pier Ter. SW18 ....4K 117
Pier Way SE28 ....2G 107
Pietra Lara Bldg. EC1 ....3C 8
   (off Pear Tree St.)
Pigeon La. TW12: Hamp 4E 130
Piggott Ho. E2 ....2K 85
   (off Sewardstone Rd.)
Pigott St. E14 ....6C 86
Pike Cl. BR1: Brom 5K 141
   UB10: Uxb 1B 74
Pikemans Ct. SW5 ....4J 99
   (off W. Cromwell Rd.)
Pike Rd. NW7 ....4E 28
Pike's End HA5: Eastc 4K 39
Pikestone Cl. UB4: Yead 4C 76
Pikethorne SE23 ....2K 139
Pilgrimage St. SE1 ....7E 14 (2D 102)
Pilgrim Cl. SM4: Mord 7K 153
Pilgrim Hill SE27 ....4C 138
Pilgrim Ho. SE1 ....3D 102
   (off Lansdowne Pl.)
Pilgrims Cloisters SE5 ....7E 102
   (off Sedgmoor Pl.)
Pilgrims Cl. N13 ....4E 32
   UB5: N'olt 5G 59
Pilgrims Ct. EN1: Enf 2J 23
Pilgrim's La. NW3 ....4B 64
Pilgrims M. E14 ....7G 87
Pilgrim's Pl. NW3 ....4B 64
Pilgrims Ri. EN4: E Barn 5H 21
Pilgrim St. EC4 ....1A 14 (6B 84)
Pilgrims Way CR2: S Croy 6F 169
   E6 ....1C 88
   HA9: Wemb 1H 61
   N19 ....1H 65
Pilkington Rd. BR6: Farnb 3G 173
   SE15 ....2H 121
Pillions La. UB4: Hayes 4F 75
Pilot Cl. SE8 ....6B 104
Pilot Ind. Cen. NW10 ....4K 79
Pilsden Cl. SW19 ....1F 135
Pilton Est., The CR0: Croy 2B 168
Pilton Pl. SE17 ....5C 102
   (off King & Queen St.)
Pilton Pl. Est. SE17 ....5C 102
Pimento Ct. W5 ....3D 96
PIMLICO 6B 18 (5G 101)

Pimlico Ho. SW1 ....5J 17
   (off Ebury Bri. Rd.)
Pimlico Rd. SW1 ....5G 17 (5E 100)
Pimlico Wlk. N1 ....1G 9
Pinchbeck Rd. BR6: Chels 6K 173
Pinchin & Johnsons Yd. E1 ....7G 85
   (off Pinchin St.)
Pinchin St. E1 ....7G 85
Pincombe Ho. SE17 ....5D 102
   (off Orb St.)
Pincott Pl. SE4 ....3K 121
Pincott Rd. DA6: Bex 5G 127
   SW19 ....7A 136
Pindar St. EC2 ....5G 9 (5E 84)
Pindock M. W9 ....4K 81
Pineapple Ct. SW1 ....1B 18
Pine Av. BR4: W W'ck 1D 170
   E15 ....5F 69
Pine Cl. E10 ....2D 68
   HA7: Stan 4G 27
   N14 ....7B 22
   N19 ....2G 65
   SE20 ....1J 157
Pine Coombe CR0: Croy 4K 169
Pine Ct. N21 ....5E 22
   UB5: N'olt 4C 76
Pinecrest Gdns. BR6: Farnb 4F 173
Pinecroft Ct. DA16: Well 7A 108
Pinecroft Cres. EN5: Barn 4B 20
Pinedene SE15 ....1H 121
Pinefield Cl. E14 ....7C 86
Pine Gdns. HA4: Ruis 1K 57
   KT5: Surb 6G 151
Pine Glade BR6: Farnb 4D 172
Pine Gro. N4 ....2J 65
   N20 ....1C 30
   SW19 ....5H 135
Pine Ho. SE16 ....2J 103
   (off Ainsty Est.)
   W10 ....4G 81
   (off Droop St.)
Pinehurst Ct. W11 ....6H 81
   (off Colville Gdns.)
Pinehurst Wlk. BR6: Orp 1H 173
Pinemartin Cl. NW2 ....3E 62
Pine M. NW10 ....2F 81
Pine Pl. UB4: Hayes 4H 75
Pine Ridge SM5: Cars 7E 166
Pineridge Ct. EN5: Barn 4A 20
Pine Rd. N11 ....2K 31
   NW2 ....4E 62
Pines, The IG8: Wfd G 3D 36
   KT9: Chess 3K 162
   N14 ....5B 22
   TW16: Sun 3J 147
Pines Rd. BR1: Brom 2C 160
Pine St. EC1 ....3K 7 (4A 84)
Pine Tree Cl. TW5: Cran 1K 111
Pine Tree Ho. SE14 ....7K 103
   (off Reaston St.)
Pine Tree Lodge BR2: Brom 4H 159
Pine Trees Dr. UB10: Ick 4A 56
Pineview Ct. E4 ....1K 35
Pine Wlk. KT5: Surb 6G 151
Pine Wood TW16: Sun 1J 147
Pinewood Av. DA15: Sidc 1J 143
   HA5: H End 6A 26
   UB8: Hil 6B 74
Pinewood Cl. BR6: Orp 1H 173
   CR0: Croy 3A 170
   HA5: H End 6A 26
Pinewood Ct. EN2: Enf 3G 23
   SW4 ....6H 119
Pinewood Dr. BR6: Orp 5J 173
Pinewood Gro. W5 ....6C 78
Pinewood Lodge WD23: Bushy 1C 26
Pinewood Pl. DA2: Bexl 2K 145
   (not continuous)
   KT19: Ewe 4K 163
Pinewood Rd. BR2: Brom 4J 159
   SE2 ....6D 108
   TW13: Felt 3K 129
Pinfold Rd. SW16 ....4J 137

Pinglestone Cl. UB7: Harm 7A 92
Pinkcoat Cl. TW13: Felt 3K 129
Pinkerton Pl. SW16 ....4H 137
Pinkham Mans. W4 ....5G 97
Pinkham Way N11 ....7K 31
Pinkwell Av. UB3: Harl 4F 93
Pinkwell La. UB3: Harl 4E 92
Pinley Gdns. RM9: Dag 1B 90
Pinnace Ho. E14 ....3E 104
   (off Manchester Rd.)
Pinnacle Hill DA7: Bex 4H 127
Pinnacle Hill Nth. DA7: Bex 4H 127
Pinnacle Pl. HA7: Stan 4G 27
Pinnacle Way E14 ....6A 86
   (off Commercial Rd.)
Pinnell Rd. SE9 ....4B 124
PINNER 4C 40
Pinner Ct. HA5: Pinn 4E 40
   NW8 ....3A 4
PINNER GREEN 2A 40
Pinner Grn. HA5: Pinn 2A 40
Pinner Gro. HA5: Pinn 4C 40
Pinner Hill Farm HA5: Pinn 1K 39
Pinner Hill Rd. HA5: Pinn 1K 39
Pinner Pk. 1E 40
Pinner Pk. HA5: Pinn 2E 40
Pinner Pk. Av. HA2: Harr 3F 41
Pinner Pk. Gdns. HA2: Harr 2G 41
Pinner Rd. HA1: Harr 4E 40
   HA2: Harr 4E 40
   HA5: Pinn 1H 39
   (High St.)
   HA5: Pinn 4D 40
   (Nower Hill)
   HA6: Nwood 1H 39
Pinners Pas. EC2 ....7F 9
   (off Austin Friars)
Pinner Vw. HA1: Harr 6G 41
   HA2: Harr 4G 41
PINNERWOOD PARK 1A 40
Pinn Way HA4: Ruis 7F 39
Pintail Cl. E6 ....5C 88
Pintail Ct. SE8 ....6B 104
   (off Pilot Cl.)
Pintail Rd. IG8: Wfd G 7E 36
Pintail Way UB4: Yead 5B 76
Pinter Ho. SW9 ....2J 119
   (off Grantham Rd.)
Pinto Way SE3 ....4K 123
Pioneer Cl. E14 ....5D 86
Pioneer Ho. WC1 ....1G 7
   (off Britannia St.)
Pioneer Mkt. IG1: Ilf 3F 71
   (off Winston Way)
Pioneer Pl. CR0: Sels 7C 170
Pioneers Ind. Pk. CR0: Bedd 1J 167
Pioneer St. SE15 ....1G 121
Pioneer Way W12 ....6D 80
Piper Cl. N7 ....5K 65
Piper Rd. KT1: King T 3G 151
Piper's Gdns. CR0: Croy 7A 158
Pipers Grn. NW9 ....5J 43
Pipers Grn. La. HA8: Edg 3K 27
   (not continuous)
Pipers Ho. SE10 ....5F 105
   (off Collington St.)
Piper Way IG1: Ilf 1H 71
Pipewell Rd. SM5: Cars 6C 154
Pippenhall SE9 ....6F 125
Pippin Cl. CR0: Croy 1B 170
   NW2 ....3C 62
Pippin Ho. W10 ....7F 81
   (off Freston Rd.)
Pippins Cl. UB7: W Dray 3A 92
Pippins Ct. TW15: Ashf 6D 128
Piquet Rd. SE20 ....2J 157
Pirbright Cres. CR0: New Ad 6E 170
Pirbright Rd. SW18 ....1H 135
Pirie Cl. SE5 ....3D 120
Pirie St. E16 ....1K 105
Pitcairn Cl. RM7: Mawney 4G 55
Pitcairn Ho. E9 ....7J 67
Pitcairn Rd. CR4: Mitc 7D 136

Pitcairn's Path HA2: Harr 3G 59
Pitchford St. E15 ....7F 69
Pitfield Cres. SE28 ....1A 108
Pitfield Est. N1 ....1G 9 (3E 84)
Pitfield St. N1 ....1G 9 (3E 84)
Pitfield Way EN3: Enf H 1D 24
   NW10 ....6J 61
Pitfold Cl. SE12 ....6J 123
Pitfold Rd. SE12 ....6J 123
Pitlake CR0: Croy 2B 168
Pitman Ho. SE8 ....1C 122
Pitman St. SE5 ....7C 102
   (not continuous)
Pitmaston Ho. SE13 ....2E 122
   (off Lewisham Rd.)
Pitsea Pl. E1 ....6K 85
Pitsea St. E1 ....6K 85
Pitshanger La. W5 ....4B 78
Pitshanger Manor Mus. 1D 96
Pitt Cres. SW19 ....4K 135
Pittman Gdns. IG1: Ilf 5G 71
Pitt Rd. BR6: Farnb 4G 173
   CR0: Croy 5C 156
   CR7: Thor H 5C 156
   HA2: Harr 2G 59
Pitt's Head M. W1 ....5H 11 (1E 100)
Pittsmead Av. BR2: Hayes 7J 159
Pitt St. W8 ....2J 99
Pittville Gdns. SE25 ....3G 157
Pixfield Ct. BR2: Brom 2H 159
   (off Beckenham La.)
Pixley St. E14 ....6B 86
Pixton Way CR0: Sels 7A 170
Place, The 2D 6
   (off Duke's Rd.)
Place Farm Av. BR6: Orp 1H 173
Plaisterers Highwalk EC2 ....6C 8
   (off Noble St.)
PLAISTOW
   Bromley 7J 141
   London 2K 87
Plaistow Gro. BR1: Brom 7K 141
   E15 ....1H 87
Plaistow La. BR1: Brom 7J 141
   (not continuous)
Plaistow Pk. Rd. E13 ....2K 87
Plaistow Rd. E15 ....1H 87
Plaistow Wharf E16 ....2J 105
Plane Ho. BR2: Brom 2G 159
Plane St. SE26 ....3H 139
Planetree Ct. W6 ....4F 99
   (off Brook Grn.)
Plane Tree Cres. TW13: Felt 3K 129
Plane Tree Ho. SE8 ....6A 104
   (off Etta St.)
Plane Tree Wlk. N2 ....3C 46
   SE19 ....6E 138
Plantagenet Cl. KT4: Wor Pk 4K 163
Plantagenet Gdns. RM6: Chad H 7D 54
Plantagenet Ho. SE18 ....3D 106
   (off Leda Rd.)
Plantagenet Pl. RM6: Chad H 7D 54
Plantagenet Rd. EN5: New Bar 4F 21
Plantain Gdns. E11 ....3F 69
   (off Hollydown Way, not continuous)
Plantain Pl. SE1 ....6E 14 (2D 102)
Plantation, The SE3 ....2J 123
Plantation Pl. EC3 ....2G 15
Plantation Wharf SW11 ....3A 118
Plasel Ct. E13 ....1K 87
   (off Pawsey Cl.)
PLASHET 6C 70
Plashet Gro. E6 ....1A 88
Plashet Rd. E13 ....1J 87
Plassy Rd. SE6 ....7D 122
Plate Ho. E14 ....5D 104
   (off Burrells Wharf Sq.)
Platina St. EC2 ....3F 9
Plato Rd. SW2 ....4J 119
Platt, The SW15 ....3F 117
Platt Halls NW9 ....2B 44
Platt's La. NW3 ....4J 63
Platts Rd. EN3: Enf H 1D 24

Platt St. NW1 . . . . .2H **83**
Plawsfield Rd. BR3: Beck 1K **157**
Plaxtol Cl. BR1: Brom 1A **160**
Plaxtol Rd. DA8: Erith 7G **109**
Plaxton Ct. E11 . . . . .3H **69**
Playfair Ho. E14 . . . . .6C **86**
(off Saracen St.)
Playfair Mans. W14 . . . . .6G **99**
(off Queen's Club Gdns.)
Playfair St. W6 . . . . .5E **98**
Playfield Av. RM5: Col R 1J **55**
Playfield Cres. SE22 . . . . .5F **121**
Playfield Rd. HA8: Edg 2J **43**
Playford Rd. N4 . . . . .2K **65**
(not continuous)
Playgreen Way SE6 . . . . .3C **140**
Playground Cl. BR3: Beck 2K **157**
Playhouse, The 7H **147**
(off Hurst Gro.)
Playhouse Cl. SE1 . . . . .6C **14**
(off Southwark Bri. Rd.)
Playhouse Theatre 4F **13**
(off Northumberland Av.)
Playhouse Yd. EC4 . . . . . .1A **14** (6B **84**)
Playscape Pro Racing Karting Track
. . . . .5H **137**
Plaza Bus. Cen. EN3: Brim 2F **25**
Plaza Cinema 3C **12**
(off Regent St.)
Plaza Hgts. E10 . . . . .3E **68**
Plaza Pde. NW6 . . . . .2K **81**
Plaza Shop. Cen., The W1 . . . .7B **6** (6G **83**)
Plaza Wlk. NW9 . . . . .3J **43**
Pleasance, The SW15 . . . . .4D **116**
Pleasance Rd. SW15 . . . . .5D **116**
Pleasance Theatre 6J **65**
(off Carpenters M.)
Pleasant Gro. CR0: Croy 3B **170**
Pleasant Pl. HA2: Harr 2H **59**
N1 . . . . .7B **66**
Pleasant Row NW1 . . . . .1F **83**
Pleasant Vw. PL. BR6: Farnb 5F **173**
Pleasant Way HA0: Wemb 2C **78**
Plender Pl. NW1 . . . . .1G **83**
(off Plender St.)
Plender St. NW1 . . . . .1G **83**
Pleshey Rd. N7 . . . . .4H **65**
Plesman Way SM6: Wall 7J **167**
Plessey Bldg. E14 . . . . .6C **86**
(off Dod St.)
Plevna Cres. N15 . . . . .6E **48**
Plevna Rd. N9 . . . . .3B **34**
TW12: Hamp 1F **149**
Plevna St. E14 . . . . .3E **104**
Pleydell Av. SE19 . . . . .7F **139**
W6 . . . . .4B **98**
Pleydell Ct. EC4 . . . . .1K **13**
(off Lombard La.)
Pleydell Est. EC1 . . . . .2D **8**
Pleydell Gdns. SE19 . . . . .6F **139**
(off Anerley Hill)
Pleydell St. EC4 . . . . .1K **13**
Plimsoll Cl. E14 . . . . .6D **86**
Plimsoll Rd. N4 . . . . .3A **66**
Plough Cl. EC3 . . . . .2F **15** (7D **84**)
Plough Farm Cl. HA4: Ruis 6F **39**
SE22 . . . . .6F **121**
SM6: Bedd 4J **167**
SW17 . . . . .4A **136**
SW19 . . . . .5K **135**
TW11: Tedd 5A **132**
Plough La. Cl. SM6: Bedd 5J **167**
Ploughmans Cl. NW1 . . . . .1H **83**
Ploughmans End TW7: Isle 5H **113**
Ploughmans Wlk. N2 . . . . .2A **46**
(off Long La.)
Plough M. SW11 . . . . .4B **118**
Plough Pl. EC4 . . . . .7K **7** (6A **84**)
Plough Rd. KT19: Ewe 7K **163**
SW11 . . . . .3B **118**
Plough St. E1 . . . . .7K **9** (6F **85**)
Plough Ter. SW11 . . . . .4B **118**

Plough Way SE16 . . . . .4K **103**
Plough Yd. EC2 . . . . .4H **9** (4E **84**)
Plover Ho. SW9 . . . . .7A **102**
(off Brixton Rd.)
Plover Way SE16 . . . . .3A **104**
UB4: Yead 6B **76**
Plowden Bldgs. EC4 . . . . .2J **13**
Plowman Cl. N18 . . . . .5J **33**
Plowman Way RM8: Dag 1C **72**
Plumber's Row E1 . . . . .5G **85**
Plumbridge St. SE10 . . . . .1E **122**
Plum Cl. TW13: Felt 1J **129**
Plume Ho. SE10 . . . . .6D **104**
(off Creek Rd.)
Plum Gth. TW8: Bford 4D **96**
Plum La. SE18 . . . . .7F **107**
Plummer La. CR4: Mitc 2D **154**
Plummer Rd. SW4 . . . . .7H **119**
Plumpton Cl. UB5: N'olt 6E **58**
Plumpton Way SM5: Cars 3C **166**
PLUMSTEAD 4J **107**
PLUMSTEAD COMMON 6G **107**
Plumstead Comn. Rd. SE18 . . . . . .6F **107**
Plumstead High St. SE18 . . . . .4H **107**
Plumstead Leisure Cen. 5K **107**
Plumstead Rd. SE18 . . . . .4F **107**
Plumtree Cl. RM10: Dag 6H **73**
SM6: Wall 7H **167**
Plumtree Ct. EC4 . . . . .7A **8** (6B **84**)
Plymen Ho. KT8: W Mole 5E **148**
Plymouth Cl. KT5: Surb 4E **150**
(off Cranes Pk. Av.)
Plymouth Ho. IG11: Bark 7A **72**
(off Keir Hardie Way)
SE10 . . . . .1D **122**
(off Devonshire Dr.)
Plymouth Rd. BR1: Brom 1K **159**
E16 . . . . .5J **87**
Plymouth Wharf E14 . . . . .4F **105**
Plympton Av. NW6 . . . . .7H **63**
Plympton Cl. DA17: Belv 3E **108**
Plympton Pl. NW8 . . . . . . .4C **4** (4C **82**)
Plympton Rd. NW6 . . . . .7H **63**
Plympton St. NW8 . . . . . . .4C **4** (4C **82**)
Plymstock Rd. DA16: Well 7C **108**
Pocklington Cl. NW9 . . . . .2A **44**
W12 .3C **98**
(off Ashchurch Pk. Vs.)
Pocklington Ct. SW15 . . . . .1C **134**
Pocklington Lodge W12 . . . . .3C **98**
Pocock Av. UB7: W Dray 3B **92**
Pocock St. SE1 . . . . .6A **14** (2B **102**)
Podmore Rd. SW18 . . . . .4A **118**
Poets Cl. W3 . . . . .1J **97**
Poet's Rd. N5 . . . . .5D **66**
Poets Way HA1: Harr 4J **41**
Point, The E17 . . . . .4C **50**
(off Tower M.)
HA4: Ruis 4J **57**
W2 . . . . .6A **4**
Pointalls Cl. N3 . . . . .2A **46**
Point Cl. SE10 . . . . .1E **122**
Pointer Cl. SE28 . . . . .6D **90**
Pointers Cl. E14 . . . . .5D **104**
Pointers Cotts. TW10: Ham 2C **132**
Point Hill SE10 . . . . .7E **104**
Point Pl. HA9: Wemb 7H **61**
Point Pleasant SW18 . . . . .4J **117**
Point Ter. E7 . . . . .5K **69**
(off Claremont Rd.)
Point West SW7 . . . . .4K **99**
Point Wharf TW8: Bford 7E **96**
Point Wharf La. TW8: Bford 7D **96**
Poland St. W1 . . . . .1B **12** (6G **83**)
Polar Pk. UB7: Harm 7B **92**
Polebrook Rd. SE3 . . . . .3A **124**
Pole Cat All. BR2: Hayes 2H **171**
Polecroft La. SE6 . . . . .2B **140**
Polehamptons, The
. . . . .7G **131**
TW12: Hamp 7G **131**
Pole Hill Rd. E4 . . . . .7K **25**
UB10: Hil 4D **74**
Polesden Gdns. SW20 . . . . .2D **152**

Polesworth Ho. W2 . . . . .5J **81**
(off Alfred Rd.)
Polesworth Rd. RM9: Dag 7D **72**
Police Sta. La. WD23: Bush 1A **26**
POLISH WAR MEMORIAL 7A **58**
Pollard Cl. E16 . . . . .7J **87**
N7 . . . . .4K **65**
Pollard Ho. KT4: Wor Pk 4E **164**
N1 . . . . .1G **7**
(off Northdown St.)
Pollard Rd. N20 . . . . .2H **31**
SM4: Mord 5B **154**
Pollard Row E2 . . . . .3G **85**
Pollards Cres. SW16 . . . . .3J **155**
Pollards Hill E. SW16 . . . . .3K **155**
Pollards Hill Nth. SW16 . . . . .3J **155**
Pollards Hill Sth. SW16 . . . . .3J **155**
Pollards Hill W. SW16 . . . . .3K **155**
Pollard St. E2 . . . . .3G **85**
Pollards Wood Rd. SW16 . . . . .3J **155**
Pollard Wlk. DA14: Sidc 6C **144**
Pollen St. W1 . . . . .1A **12** (6G **83**)
Pollitt Dr. NW8 . . . . .3B **4** (4B **82**)
Pollock Ho. W10 . . . . .4G **81**
(off Kensal Rd.)
Pollock's Toy Mus. 5B **6** (5G **83**)
Polperro Cl. BR6: St M Cry 6K **161**
Polperro Ho. W2 . . . . .5J **81**
(off Brunel Est.)
Polperro M. SE11 . . . . .4B **102**
Polsted Rd. SE6 . . . . .7B **122**
Polthorne Est. SE18 . . . . .4H **107**
(off Polthorne Gro.)
Polthorne Gro. SE18 . . . . .4G **107**
Polworth Rd. SW16 . . . . .5J **137**
Polychrome Ct. SE1 . . . . .7A **14**
(off Waterloo Rd.)
Polygon, The NW8 . . . . .1B **82**
(off Avenue Rd.)
SW4 .4G **119**
Polygon Rd. NW1 . . . . .1C **6** (2H **83**)
Polytechnic St. SE18 . . . . .4E **106**
Pomell Way E1 . . . . .7K **9** (6F **85**)
Pomeroy Cl. TW1: Twick 4B **114**
Pomeroy Ho. E2 . . . . .2K **85**
(off St James's Av.)
W11 .6G **81**
(off Lancaster Rd.)
Pomeroy St. SE14 . . . . .7J **103**
Pomfret Rd. SE5 . . . . .3B **120**
Pomoja La. N19 . . . . .2J **65**
Pomona Ho. SE8 . . . . .4A **104**
(off Evelyn St.)
Pond Cl. N12 . . . . .6H **31**
SE3 . . . . .2J **123**
Pond Cott. La. BR4: Beck 1C **170**
Pond Cotts. SE21 . . . . .1E **138**
PONDERS END 5D **24**
Ponders End Ind. Est. EN3: Pond E . .5F **25**
Ponder St. N7 . . . . .7K **65**
(not continuous)
Pond Farm Est. E5 . . . . .3J **67**
Pondfield Ho. SE27 . . . . .5C **138**
Pond Path BR7: Chst 6F **143**
BR6: Farnb 3F **173**
RM10: Dag 5H **73**
Pond Grn. HA4: Ruis 2G **57**
Pond Hill Gdns. SM3: Cheam 6G **165**
Pond Ho. HA7: Stan 6G **27**
SW3 .4C **100**
Pond Lees Cl. RM10: Dag 7K **73**
Pond Mead SE21 . . . . .6D **120**
Pond Pl. SW3 . . . . .4C **16** (4C **100**)
Pond Rd. E15 . . . . .2G **87**
SE3 . . . . .2H **123**
Pondside Cl. UB3: Harl 6F **93**
Pond Sq. N6 . . . . .1E **64**
Pond St. NW3 . . . . .5C **64**
Pond Way TW11: Tedd 6C **132**
Pondwood Ri. BR6: Orp 7J **161**
Ponler St. E1 . . . . .6H **85**
Ponsard Rd. NW10 . . . . .3D **80**

Ponsford St. E9 . . . . .6J **67**
Ponsonby Ho. E2 . . . . .2J **85**
(off Bishop's Way)
Ponsonby Pl. SW1 . . . . . . .5D **18** (5H **101**)
Ponsonby Rd. SW15 . . . . .7D **116**
Ponsonby Ter. SW1 . . . . . . .5D **18** (5H **101**)
Pontefract Ct. UB5: N'olt 5F **59**
(off Newmarket Av.)
Pontefract Rd.
BR1: Brom 5H **141**
Ponton Rd. SW8 . . . . .7D **18** (7H **101**)
Pont St. SW1 . . . . .2E **16** (3D **100**)
Pont St. M. SW1 . . . . .2E **16** (3D **100**)
Pontypool Pl. SE1 . . . . . . .6A **14** (2B **102**)
Pool Cl. BR3: Beck 5C **140**
KT8: W Mole 5D **148**
Pool Ct. SE6 . . . . .2C **140**
Poole Cl. HA4: Ruis 2G **57**
Poole Ct. N1 . . . . .7E **66**
(off St Peter's Way)
TW4: Houn 2C **112**
Poole Ct. Rd. TW4: Houn 2C **112**
Poole Ho. SE11 . . . . .2H **19**
POOL END .5C **146**
Pool End Cl. TW17: Shep 5C **146**
Poole Rd. E9 . . . . .6K **67**
KT19: Ewe 6K **163**
Pooles Bldgs. WC1 . . . . .4J **7**
Pooles Cotts. TW10: Ham 2D **132**
Pooles La. SW10 . . . . .7A **100**
Pooles Pk. N4 . . . . .2A **66**
Poole St. N1 . . . . .1D **84**
Poole Way UB4: Hayes 3G **75**
Pooley Dr. SW14 . . . . .3J **115**
Pooley Ho. E1 . . . . .3K **85**
Pool Ho. NW8 . . . . .5C **4**
(off Penfold St.)
Poolmans St. SE16 . . . . .2K **103**
Pool Rd. HA1: Harr 7H **41**
KT8: W Mole 5D **148**
Poolsford Rd. NW9 . . . . .4A **44**
Pools on the Pk. 4D **114**
Poonah St. E1 . . . . .6J **85**
Pope Cl. SW19 . . . . .6B **136**
TW14: Felt 1H **129**
Pope Ho. SE5 . . . . .7D **102**
(off Elmington Est.)
SE16 . . . . .4H **103**
(off Manor Est.)
Pope Rd. BR2: Brom 5B **160**
Popes Av. TW2: Twick 2J **131**
Popes Ct. TW2: Twick 2J **131**
Popes Dr. N3 . . . . .1J **45**
Popes Gro. CR0: Croy 3B **170**
TW2: Twick 2K **131**
TW2: Twick 2K **131**
Pope's Head All. EC3 . . . . .1F **15** (6D **84**)
Popes La. W5 . . . . .3D **96**
Pope's Rd. SW9 . . . . .3A **120**
Pope St. SE1 . . . . .7H **15** (2E **102**)
Popham Cl. TW13: Hanw 3D **130**
Popham Gdns. TW9: Rich 3G **115**
Popham Rd. N1 . . . . .1C **84**
Popham St. N1 . . . . .1B **84**
(not continuous)
Pop-in Commercial Cen.
HA9: Wemb 5H **61**
Popinjays Row SM3: Cheam 5F **165**
(off Netley Cl.)
POPLAR 7D **86**
Poplar Av. BR6: Farnb 2F **173**
CR4: Mitc 1D **154**
UB2: S'hall 3F **95**
UB7: Yiew 7B **74**
Poplar Bath St. E14 . . . . .6D **86**
Poplar Bus. Pk. E14 . . . . .7E **86**
Poplar Cl. E9 . . . . .5B **68**
HA5: Pinn 1B **40**
Poplar Ct. SW19 . . . . .5J **135**
TW1: Twick 6B **114**
UB5: N'olt 2A **76**
Poplar Cres. KT19: Ewe 6J **163**
Poplar Farm Cl. KT19: Ewe 6J **163**

Poplar Gdns.—Powster Rd.

Poplar Gdns. KT3: N Mald 2K **151**
SE28 7C **90**
Poplar Gro. HA9: Wemb 3J **61**
KT3: N Mald 2K **151**
N11 6K **31**
W6 2E **98**
Poplar High St. E14 7D **86**
Poplar Ho. *SE4* *4B **122***
(off Wickham Rd.)
SE16 *2K **103***
(off Woodland Cres.)
Poplar M. W12 1E **98**
Poplar Mt. DA17: Belv 4H **109**
Poplar Pl. SE28 7C **90**
UB3: Hayes 7J **75**
W2 7K **81**
Poplar Rd. E12 2C **70**
SE24 4C **120**
SM3: Sutt 1H **165**
SW19 2J **153**
TW15: Ashf 5E **128**
Poplar Rd. Sth. SW19 3J **153**
Poplars, The N14 5A **22**
Poplars Av. NW2 6E **62**
Poplars Cl. HA4: Ruis 1G **57**
Poplars Rd. E17 6D **50**
Poplar St. RM7: Rom 4J **55**
Poplar Vw. HA9: Wemb 2D **60**
Poplar Wlk. CR0: Croy 2C **168**
SE24 3C **120**
(not continuous)
Poplar Way IG6: Ilf 4G **53**
TW13: Felt 3J **129**
Poppins Ct. EC4 1A **14** (6B **84**)
Poppleton Rd. E11 6G **51**
Poppy Cl. DA17: Belv 3H **109**
SM6: Wall 1E **166**
UB5: N'olt 6D **58**
Poppy La. CR0: Croy 7J **157**
Porchester Cl. SE5 4C **120**
Porchester Ct. *W2* *7K **81***
(off Porchester Gdns.)
Porchester Gdns. W2 7K **81**
Porchester Gdns. M. W2 6K **81**
Porchester Ga. *W2* *7K **81***
(off Bayswater Rd., not continuous)
Porchester Ho. *E1* *6H **85***
(off Philpot St.)
Porchester Leisure Cen. 6K **81**
Porchester Mead BR3: Beck 6D **140**
Porchester M. W2 6K **81**
Porchester Pl. W2 1D **10** (6C **82**)
Porchester Rd. KT1: King T 2H **151**
W2 6K **81**
Porchester Sq. W2 6K **81**
Porchester Ter. W2 7A **82**
Porchester Ter. Nth. W2 6K **81**
Porchester Wlk. *W2* *6K **81***
(off Porchester Ter. Nth.)
Porch Way N20 3J **31**
Porcupine Cl. SE9 2C **142**
Porden Rd. SW2 4K **119**
Porlock Av. HA2: Harr 1G **59**
Porlock Ho. SE26 3G **139**
Porlock Rd. EN1: Enf 7A **24**
Porlock St. SE1 6F **15** (2D **102**)
Porrington Cl. BR7: Chst 1D **160**
Porson Ct. SE13 3D **122**
Portal Cl. HA4: Ruis 4J **57**
(not continuous)
SE27 3A **138**
UB10: Uxb 7A **56**
Portal Way W3 5K **79**
Portbury Cl. SE15 1G **121**
Port Cres. E13 4K **87**
Portcullis Ho. SW1 7E **12**
Portcullis Lodge Rd. EN1: Enf 3J **23**
Portelet Ct. *N1* *1E **84***
(off De Beauvoir Est.)
Portelet Rd. E1 3K **85**
Porten Ho's. *W14* *3G **99***
(off Porten Rd.)
Porten Rd. W14 3G **99**
Porter Rd. E6 6D **88**
Porters & Walters Almshouses
N22 *7E **32***
(off Nightingale Rd.)
Porters Av. RM8: Dag 6B **72**
RM9: Dag 6B **72**
Porters Lodge, The
SW10 *7A **100***
(off Coleridge Gdns.)
Porter Sq. N19 1J **65**
Porter St. SE1 4D **14** (1C **102**)
W1 5F **5** (5D **82**)
Porters Wlk. *E1* *7H **85***
(off Balkan Wlk.)
Porters Way N12 6H **31**
UB7: W Dray 3B **92**
Porteus Rd. W2 5A **4** (5A **82**)
Portgate Cl. W9 4H **81**
Porthallow Cl. BR6: Chels 4K **173**
Porthcawe Rd. SE26 4A **140**
Porthkerry Av. DA16: Well 4A **126**
Port Ho. *E14* *5D **104***
(off Burrells Wharf Sq.)
Portia Ct. IG11: Bark 7A **72**
SE11 *5B **102***
(off Opal St.)
Portia Way E3 4B **86**
Porticos, The SW3 7A **16**
Portinscale Rd. SW15 5G **117**
Portishead Ho. *W2* *5J **81***
(off Brunel Est.)
Portland Av. DA15: Sidc 6A **126**
KT3: N Mald 7B **152**
N16 7F **49**
Portland Cl. KT4: Wor Pk 7D **152**
RM6: Chad H 5E **54**
Portland Commercial Est.
IG11: Bark 2C **90**
Portland Cotts. CR0: Bedd 7H **155**
Portland Ct. *N1* *7E **66***
(off St Peter's Way)
SE1 *7E **14***
(off Gt. Dover St.)
SE14 *6A **104***
(off Whitcher Cl.)
Portland Cres. HA7: Stan 2D **42**
SE9 2C **142**
TW13: Felt 4F **129**
UB6: G'frd 4F **77**
Portland Dr. EN2: Enf 1K **23**
Portland Gdns. N4 6B **48**
RM6: Chad H 5D **54**
Portland Gro. SW8 1K **119**
Portland Ho. SW1 1A **18**
Portland M. W1 1B **12** (6G **83**)
Portland Pl. *SE25* *4G **157***
(off Sth. Norwood Hill)
W1 4J **5** (4F **83**)
Portland Ri. N4 1B **66**
(not continuous)
Portland Rd. BR1: Brom 4A **142**
CR4: Mitc 2C **154**
KT1: King T 3E **150**
N15 4F **49**
SE9 2C **142**
SE25 4G **157**
TW15: Ashf 3A **128**
UB2: S'hall 3D **94**
UB4: Hayes 3G **75**
W11 7G **81**
Portland Sq. E1 1H **103**
Portland St. SE17 5D **102**
Portland Ter. HA8: Edg 7B **28**
TW9: Rich 4D **114**
Portland Wlk. SE17 6D **102**
Portman Av. SW14 3K **115**
Portman Cl. DA5: Bexl 1K **145**
DA7: Bex 3E **126**
W1 7F **5** (6D **82**)
Portman Dr. IG8: Wfd G 2B **52**
Portman Gdns. NW9 2K **43**
UB10: Hil 7C **56**
Portman Ga. NW1 4D **4** (4C **82**)
Portman Mans. *W1* *5F **5***
(off Chiltern St.)
Portman M. Sth. W1 1G **11** (6E **82**)
Portman Pl. E2 3J **85**
Portman Rd. KT1: King T 2F **151**
Portman Sq. W1 7G **5** (6E **82**)
Portman St. W1 1G **11** (6E **82**)
Portman Towers W1 7F **5** (6D **82**)
Portmeadow Wlk. SE2 2D **108**
Port Meers Cl. E17 6B **50**
Portnall Ho. *W9* *3H **81***
(off Portnall Rd.)
Portnall Rd. W9 2H **81**
Portnoi Cl. RM1: Rom 2K **55**
Portobello Ct. Est. W11 6H **81**
Portobello M. W11 7J **81**
Portobello Rd. W10 5G **81**
W11 6H **81**
Portobello Road Market 5G **81**
Porton Ct. KT6: Surb 6C **150**
Portpool La. EC1 5J **7** (5A **84**)
Portree Cl. N22 7E **32**
Portree St. E14 6F **87**
Portrush Ct. *UB1: S'hall* *6G **77***
(off Whitecote Rd.)
Portsdown HA8: Edg 5B **28**
Portsdown Av. NW11 6H **45**
Portsdown M. NW11 6H **45**
Portsea Hall *W2* *1D **10***
(off Portsea Pl.)
Portsea M. W2 1D **10**
Portsea Pl. W2 1D **10** (6C **82**)
Portslade Rd. SW8 2G **119**
Portsmouth Av. KT7: T Ditt 7A **150**
Portsmouth M. E16 1K **105**
Portsmouth Rd. KT1: King T 7A **150**
KT6: Surb 7A **150**
KT7: T Ditt 7A **150**
KT10: Esh 1A **162**
SW15 7D **116**
Portsmouth St. WC2 1G **13** (6K **83**)
Portsoken St. E1 2J **15** (7F **85**)
Portswood Pl. SW15 6B **116**
Portugal Gdns. TW2: Twick 2G **131**
Portugal St. WC2 1G **13** (6K **83**)
Portway E15 1H **87**
Portway Gdns. SE18 7B **106**
Pory Ho. *SE11* *4H **19***
(off Lambeth Wlk.)
Poseidon Ct. *E14* *4C **104***
(off Homer Dr.)
Postern, The EC2 6D **8**
Postern Grn. EN2: Enf 2F **23**
Post La. TW2: Twick 1H **131**
Postmasters Lodge HA5: Pinn 7C **40**
Postmill Cl. CR0: Croy 3J **169**
Post Office All. TW12: Hamp 2F **149**
W4 *6H **97***
(off Thames Rd.)
Post Office App. E7 5K **69**
Post Office Ct. *EC3* *1F **15***
(off Barbican)
Post Office Way SW8 7H **101**
Post Rd. UB2: S'hall 3F **95**
Postway M. IG1: Ilf 3F **71**
(not continuous)
Potier St. SE1 3D **102**
Potter Cl. CR4: Mitc 2F **155**
SE15 7E **102**
Potteries, The EN5: Barn 5D **20**
Potterne Cl. SW19 7F **117**
Potters Cl. CR0: Croy 1A **170**
Potters Fld. *EN1: Enf* *4K **23***
(off Lincoln Rd.)
Potters Flds. SE1 5H **15** (1E **102**)
Potters Gro. KT3: N Mald 4J **151**
Potters Hgts. Cl. HA5: Pinn 1K **39**
Potters La. EN5: New Bar 4D **20**
SW16 6H **137**
Potters Lodge *E14* *5E **104***
(off Manchester Rd.)
Potters Rd. EN5: New Bar 4E **20**
SW6 2A **118**
Potter St. HA5: Pinn 1K **39**
HA6: Nwood 1J **39**
Potter St. Hill HA5: Pinn 1K **39**
Pottery La. W11 1G **99**
Pottery Rd. DA5: Bexl 2J **145**
TW8: Bford 6E **96**
Pottery St. SE16 2H **103**
Pott St. E2 3H **85**
Poulett Gdns. TW1: Twick 1A **132**
Poulett Rd. E6 2D **88**
Poulters Wood BR2: Kes 5B **172**
Poulton Av. SM1: Sutt 3B **166**
Poulton Cl. E8 6H **67**
Poulton Ho. *W3* *5K **79***
(off Victoria Rd.)
Poultry EC2 1E **14** (6D **84**)
Pound Cl. BR6: Orp 2H **173**
KT6: Surb 1C **162**
Pound Ct. Dr. BR6: Orp 2H **173**
Pound Farm Cl. KT10: Esh 7G **149**
Pound Grn. DA5: Bexl 7G **127**
Pound La. NW10 6C **62**
Pound Pk. Rd. SE7 4B **106**
Pound Pl. SE9 6E **124**
Pound St. SM5: Cars 5D **166**
Pound Way BR7: Chst 7G **143**
Pountney Rd. SW11 3E **118**
POVEREST 4K **161**
Poverest Rd. BR5: St M Cry 5K **161**
Povey Ho. *SE17* *4E **102***
(off Tatum St.)
Powder Mill La. TW2: Whit 7D **112**
Powell Cl. HA8: Edg 6A **28**
KT9: Chess 5D **162**
SM6: Wall 7J **167**
Powell Ct. *CR2: S Croy* *4B **168***
(off Bramley Hill)
E17 3D **50**
Powell Gdns. RM10: Dag 4G **73**
Powell Ho. *W2* *6K **81***
(off Gloucester Ter.)
Powell Rd. E5 3H **67**
IG9: Buck H 1F **37**
Powell's Wlk. W4 6A **98**
Powergate Bus. Pk. NW10 3K **79**
Powerleague Soccer Cen.
Barking 3G **89**
Catford 1C **140**
Colney Hatch 7K **31**
Fairlop 1K **53**
Mill Hill 7J **29**
Norbury 1J **155**
Purley 6K **167**
Tottenham 6C **34**
Power Rd. W4 4G **97**
Powers Ct. TW1: Twick 7D **114**
Powerscroft Rd. DA14: Sidc 6C **144**
(not continuous)
E5 4J **67**
Powis Ct. *W11* *6H **81***
(off Powis Gdns.)
WD23: Bushy *1C **26***
(off Rutherford Way)
Powis Gdns. NW11 7H **45**
W11 6H **81**
Powis M. W11 6H **81**
Powis Pl. WC1 4F **7** (4J **83**)
Powis Rd. E3 3D **86**
Powis Sq. W11 6H **81**
(not continuous)
Powis St. SE18 3E **106**
Powis Ter. W11 6H **81**
Powlesland Ct. *E1* *6A **86***
(off White Horse Rd.)
Powlett Ho. *NW1* *6F **65***
(off Powlett Pl.)
Powlett Pl. NW1 7E **64**
(not continuous)
Pownall Gdns. TW3: Houn 4F **113**
Pownall Rd. E8 1F **85**
TW3: Houn 4F **113**
Pownsett Ter. IG1: Ilf 5G **71**
Powster Rd. BR1: Brom 5J **141**

Powys Cl. DA7: Bex 6D 108
Powys Ct. N11 5D 32
Powys La. N13 4D 32
N14 4D 32
Poynders Ct. SW4 6G 119
Poynders Gdns. SW4 7G 119
Poynders Rd. SW4 6G 119
Poynings Rd. N19 3G 65
Poynings Way N12 5D 30
Poyntell Cres. BR7: Chst 1H 161
Poynter Ct. *UB5: N'olt 2B 76*
(off Gallery Gdns.)
Poynter Ho. *NW8 3A 4*
(off Fisherton St.)
W11 1F 99
(off Queensdale Cres.)
Poynter Rd. EN1: Enf 5A 24
Poynton Rd. N17 2G 49
Poyntz Rd. SW11 2D 118
Poyser St. E2 2H 85
Praed M. W2 7B 4 (6B 82)
Praed St. W2 1A 10 (6B 82)
Pragel St. E13 2A 88
Pragnell Rd. SE12 2K 141
Prague Pl. SW2 5J 119
Prah Rd. N4 2A 66
Prairie St. SW8 2E 118
Pratt M. NW1 1G 83
Pratts Pas. KT1: King T 2E 150
Pratt St. NW1 1G 83
Pratt Wlk. SE11 3H 19 (4K 101)
Prayle Gro. NW2 1F 63
Preachers Ct. *EC1 5B 8*
(off Charterhouse Sq.)
Prebend Gdns. W4 4B 98
W6 4B 98
(not continuous)
Prebend Mans. *W4 4B 98*
(off Chiswick High Rd.)
Prebend St. N1 1C 84
Precinct, The N1 1C 84
Precinct Rd. UB3: Hayes 7J 75
Precincts, The SM4: Mord 6J 153
Premier Cinema 2G 121
Premier Cnr. W9 2H 81
Premier Ct. EN3: Enf W 1D 24
Premiere Pl. E14 7C 86
Premier Ho. *N1 7B 66*
(off Waterloo Ter.)
Premier Pk. NW10 1H 79
(not continuous)
Premier Pk. Rd. NW10 2H 79
Premier Pl. SW15 4G 117
Prendergast Rd. SE3 3G 123
Prentice Ct. SW19 5H 135
Prentis Rd. SW16 4H 137
Prentiss Ct. SE7 4B 106
Presburg Rd. KT3: N Mald 5A 152
Presburg St. E5 3K 67
Prescelly Pl. HA8: Edg 1F 43
Prescot St. E1 2K 15 (7F 85)
Prescott Av. BR5: Pet W 6F 161
Prescott Cl. SW16 7J 137
Prescott Ho. *SE17 6B 102*
(off Hillingdon St.)
Prescott Pl. SW4 3H 119
Presentation M. SW2 2K 137
Preshaw Cres. CR4: Mitc 3C 154
President Dr. E1 1H 103
President Ho. EC1 2B 8 (3B 84)
President Quay E1 4K 15
President St. EC1 1C 8
Prespa Cl. N9 2D 34
Press Ct. SE1 5G 103
Press Ho. NW10 3K 61
Press Rd. NW10 3K 61
Prestage Way E14 7E 86
Prestbury Rd. E7 7A 70
Prestbury Sq. SE9 4D 142
Prested Rd. SW11 4C 118
Prestige Way NW4 5E 44
PRESTON 1E 60
Preston Av. E4 6A 36
Preston Cl. SE1 4E 102
TW2: Twick 3J 131
Preston Ct. *DA14: Sidc 4K 143*
(off The Crescent)
EN5: New Bar 4F 21
Preston Dr. DA7: Bex 1D 126
E11 5A 52
KT19: Ewe 6A 164
Preston Gdns. IG1: Ilf 6C 52
NW10 6B 62
Preston Hill HA3: Kent 7E 42
Preston Ho. *RM10: Dag 3G 73*
(off Uvedale Rd.)
SE1 4E 102
(off Preston Cl.)
SE1 7J 15
(off Stanworth St.)
Preston Pl. NW2 6C 62
TW10: Rich 5E 114
Preston Rd. E11 6G 51
HA3: Kent 1E 60
HA9: Kent, Wemb 1E 60
SE19 6B 138
SW20 7B 134
TW17: Shep 5C 146
Prestons Rd. BR2: Hayes 3J 171
E14 7E 86
Preston St. E2 2K 85
Preston Waye HA3: Kent 1E 60
Prestwich Ter. SW4 5G 119
Prestwick Cl. UB2: S'hall 5C 94
Prestwick Ct. *UB1: S'hall 7G 77*
(off Baird Av.)
Prestwood Av. HA3: Kent 4B 42
Prestwood Cl. HA3: Kent 4B 42
SE18 6A 108
Prestwood Gdns. CR0: Croy 7C 156
Prestwood Ho. *SE16 3H 103*
(off Drummond Rd.)
Prestwood St. N1 1D 8 (2C 84)
Pretoria Av. E17 4A 50
Pretoria Cres. E4 1K 35
Pretoria Rd. E4 1K 35
E11 1F 69
E16 4H 87
IG1: Ilf 5F 71
N17 7A 34
RM7: Rom 4J 55
SW16 6F 137
Pretoria Rd. Nth. N18 6A 34
Prevost Rd. N11 2K 31
Priam Ho. *E2 2H 85*
(off Old Bethnal Grn. Rd.)
Price Cl. NW7 6B 30
SW17 3D 136
Price Ho. *N1 1C 84*
(off Britannia Row)
Price Rd. CR0: Wadd 5B 168
Price's Ct. SW11 3B 118
Price's St. SE1 5B 14 (1B 102)
Price's Yd. N1 1K 83
Price Way TW12: Hamp 6C 130
Prichard Ct. N7 6K 65
Pricklers Hill EN5: New Bar 6E 20
Prickley Wood BR2: Hayes 1H 171
Priddy's Yd. CR0: Croy 2C 168
Prideaux Ho. *WC1 3K 83*
(off Prideaux Pl.)
Prideaux Pl. W3 7K 79
WC1 1H 7 (3K 83)
Prideaux Rd. SW9 3J 119
Pridham Rd. CR7: Thor H 4D 156
Priestfield Rd. SE23 3A 140
Priestlands Pk. Rd. DA15: Sidc 3K 143
Priestley Cl. N16 7F 49
Priestley Gdns. RM6: Chad H 6B 54
Priestley Ho. *EC1 3D 8*
(off Old St.)
HA9: Wemb 3J 61
(off Barnhill Rd.)
Priestley Rd. CR4: Mitc 2E 154
Priestley Way E17 3K 49
NW2 1C 62
Priest Pk. Av. HA2: Harr 2E 58
Priests Av. RM1: Rom 2K 55
Priest's Bri. SW14 3A 116
Priest's Ct. *EC2 7C 8*
(off Foster La.)
Prima Rd. SW9 7A 102
Prime Meridian Line 7F 105
Primrose Av. EN2: Enf 1J 23
RM6: Chad H 7B 54
Primrose Cl. E3 2C 86
HA2: Harr 3D 58
N3 2K 45
SE6 5E 140
SM6: Wall 7F 155
Primrose Ct. SW12 7H 119
Primrose Gdns. HA4: Ruis 5A 58
NW3 6C 64
WD23: Bush 1A 26
PRIMROSE HILL 1E 82
Primrose Hill EC4 1K 13 (6A 84)
Primrose Hill Ct. NW3 7D 64
Primrose Hill Rd. NW3 7D 64
Primrose Hill Studios NW1 1E 82
Primrose La. CR0: Croy 1J 169
Primrose Mans. SW11 1E 118
Primrose M. *NW1 7D 64*
(off Sharpleshall St.)
SE3 7J 105
Primrose Pl. TW7: Isle 2K 113
Primrose Rd. E10 1D 68
E18 2K 51
Primrose Sq. E9 7J 67
Primrose St. EC2 5G 9 (5E 84)
Primrose Wlk. KT17: Ewe 7B 164
SE14 7A 104
Primrose Way HA0: Wemb 2D 78
Primula St. W12 6C 80
Prince Albert Ct. *NW8 1D 82*
(off Prince Albert Rd.)
TW16: Sun 7G 129
Prince Albert Rd. NW1 1C 4 (3C 82)
NW8 1C 4 (3C 82)
Prince Arthur M. NW3 4A 64
Prince Arthur Rd. NW3 5A 64
Prince Charles Cinema 2D 12
Prince Charles Dr. NW4 7E 44
Prince Charles Rd. SE3 2H 123
Prince Charles Way
SM6: Wall 3F 167
Prince Consort Dr. BR7: Chst 1H 161
Prince Consort Rd. SW7 1A 16 (3A 100)
Princedale Rd. W11 1G 99
Prince Edward Mans. *W2 7J 81*
(off Moscow Rd.)
Prince Edward Rd. E9 6B 68
Prince Edward Theatre *1D 12*
(off Old Compton St.)
Prince George Av. N14 5C 22
Prince George Rd. N16 4E 66
Prince George's Av. SW20 2E 152
Prince George's Rd. SW19 1B 154
Prince Henry Rd. SE7 7B 106
Prince Imperial Rd. BR7: Chst 1F 161
SE18 1D 124
Prince John Rd. SE9 5C 124
Princelet St. E1 5K 9 (5F 85)
Prince of Orange Ct. *SE16 3J 103*
(off Lower Rd.)
Prince of Orange La. SE10 7E 104
Prince of Wales Cl. NW4 4D 44
Prince of Wales Dr. SW8 7F 101
SW11 1C 118
Prince of Wales Mans.
SW11 1E 118
Prince of Wales Pas. NW1 2A 6
Prince of Wales Rd. E16 6A 88
NW5 6E 64
SE3 2H 123
SM1: Sutt 2B 166
Prince of Wales Ter. W4 5A 98
W8 2K 99
Prince of Wales Theatre *3C 12*
(off Coventry St.)
Prince Regent Ct. *NW8 2C 82*
(off Avenue Rd.)
SE16 7A 86
(off Edward Sq.)
Prince Regent La. E13 3K 87
E16 3K 87
Prince Regent M. NW1 2A 6
Prince Regent Rd.
TW3: Houn 3G 113
Prince Rd. SE25 5E 156
Prince Rupert Rd. SE9 4D 124
Princes Arc. SW1 4B 12
Princes Av. BR5: Pet W 5J 161
IG8: Wfd G 4E 36
KT6: Surb 1G 163
N3 1J 45
N10 3F 47
N13 5F 33
N22 1H 47
NW9 4G 43
SM5: Cars 7D 166
UB6: G'frd 6F 77
W3 3G 97
Princes Cir. WC2 7E 6 (6J 83)
Princes Cl. DA14: Sidc 3D 144
HA8: Edg 5B 28
N4 1B 66
NW9 4G 43
SW4 3G 119
TW11: Tedd 4H 131
Princes Ct. HA9: Wemb 5E 60
SE16 3B 104
SW3 1E 16
(off Brompton Rd.)
Princes Ct. Bus. Cen. E1 7H 85
Princes Dr. HA1: Harr 3J 41
Princes Gdns. SW7 1B 16 (3B 100)
W3 5G 79
W5 4C 78
Prince's Ga. SW7 7B 10 (2B 100)
(not continuous)
Prince's Ga. Ct. SW7 7A 10 (2B 100)
Prince's Ga. M. SW7 1B 16 (3B 100)
Princes Ho. W11 7H 81
Princes La. HA4: Ruis 1G 57
N10 3F 47
Princes M. TW3: Houn 4E 112
W2 7K 81
W6 5D 98
(off Down Pl.)
Princes Pde. *NW11 6G 45*
(off Golders Grn. Rd.)
Princes Pk. Av. NW11 6G 45
UB3: Hayes 7F 75
Princes Pk. Circ.
UB3: Hayes 7F 75
Princes Pk. Cl. UB3: Hayes 7F 75
Princes Pk. La. UB3: Hayes 7F 75
Princes Pk. Pde.
UB3: Hayes 7F 75
Princes Pl. SW1 4B 12
W11 1G 99
Prince's Plain BR2: Brom 7C 160
Prince's Ri. SE13 2E 122
Princes Riverside Rd. SE16 1K 103
Princes Rd. IG6: Ilf 4H 53
IG9: Buck H 2F 37
KT2: King T 7G 133
N18 4D 34
SE20 6K 139
SW14 3K 115
SW19 6J 135
TW9: Kew 1F 115
TW10: Rich 5F 115
TW11: Tedd 4H 131
TW13: Felt 2H 129
TW15: Ashf 5B 128
W13 1B 96
Princessa Ct. EN2: Enf 5J 23
Princess Alice Ho. W10 4E 80
Princess Alice Way SE28 2H 107
Princess Av. HA9: Wemb 2E 60
Princess Cl. SE28 6D 90

Princess Ct. *KT1: King T* ... *3F* ***151***
(off Horace Rd.)
N6 ... 7G **47**
W1 ... *6E* ***4***
(off Bryanston Pl.)
W2 ... *7K* ***81***
(off Queensway)
Princess Cres. N4 ... 2B **66**
Princess Louise Cl. W2 ... 5B **4** (5B **82**)
Princess Mary Ho. *SW1* ... *3D* ***18***
(off Vincent St.)
Princess May Rd. N16 ... 4E **66**
Princess M. KT1: King T ... 3F **151**
NW3 ... 5B **64**
Princess of Wales Memorial Fountain ... 6B **10** (2B **100**)
Princess Pde. BR6: Farnb ... 3E **172**
RM10: Dag ... 2G **91**
Princess Pk. Mnr. N11 ... 5K **31**
Princes Sq. W2 ... 7K **81**
(not continuous)
Princess Rd. CR0: Croy ... 6C **156**
NW1 ... 1E **82**
NW6 ... 2J **81**
Princess St. SE1 ... 3B **102**
Princes St. DA7: Bex ... 3F **127**
EC2 ... 1E **14** (6D **84**)
N17 ... 6K **33**
SM1: Sutt ... 4B **166**
TW9: Rich ... 4E **114**
W1 ... 1K **11** (6F **83**)
Princes Ter. E13 ... 1K **87**
Prince's Twr. *SE16* ... *2J* ***103***
(off Elephant La.)
Prince St. SE8 ... 6B **104**
Princes Way BR4: W W'ck ... 4H **171**
CR0: Wadd ... 5K **167**
HA4: Ruis ... 4C **58**
IG9: Buck H ... 2F **37**
SW19 ... 7F **117**
W3 ... 3G **97**
Prince's Yd. W11 ... 1G **99**
Princethorpe Ho. *W2* ... *5K* ***81***
(off Woodchester Sq.)
Princethorpe Rd. SE26 ... 4K **139**
Princeton Ct. SW15 ... 3F **117**
Princeton M. KT2: King T ... 1G **151**
Princeton St. WC1 ... 6G **7** (5K **83**)
Prince William Ct. *TW15: Ashf* ... *5B* ***128***
(off Princes Rd.)
Principal Sq. E9 ... 5K **67**
Pringle Gdns. SW16 ... 4G **137**
(not continuous)
Printers Inn Ct. EC4 ... 6A **84**
Printers M. E3 ... 1A **86**
Printer St. EC4 ... 7K **7** (6A **84**)
Printinghouse La. UB3: Hayes ... 2G **93**
Printing Ho. Yd. E2 ... 1H **9** (3E **84**)
Printon Ho. *E14* ... *5B* ***86***
(off Wallwood St.)
Print Village SE15 ... 2F **121**
Printwork Apartments *SE1* ... *7G* ***15***
(off Long La.)
Priolo Rd. SE7 ... 5A **106**
Prior Av. SM2: Sutt ... 7C **166**
Prior Bolton St. N1 ... 6B **66**
Prioress Rd. SE27 ... 3B **138**
Prioress St. SE1 ... 3E **102**
Prior Rd. IG1: Ilf ... 3E **70**
Priors Cft. E17 ... 2A **50**
Priors Farm La. UB5: N'olt ... 6C **58**
Priors Fld. UB5: N'olt ... 6C **58**
Priors Gdns. HA4: Ruis ... 5A **58**
Priors Mead EN1: Enf ... 1K **23**
Prior St. SE10 ... 7E **104**
Priors Wood KT10: Hin W ... 2A **162**
Priory, The CR0: Wadd ... 4A **168**
N8 ... 4H **47**
SE3 ... 4H **123**
Priory Apartments, The SE6 ... 1D **140**
Priory Av. BR5: Pet W ... 6H **161**
E4 ... 3G **35**
E17 ... 5C **50**
Priory Av. HA0: Wemb ... 4K **59**
N8 ... 4H **47**
SM3: Cheam ... 4F **165**
W4 ... 4A **98**
Priory Cl. BR3: Beck ... 3A **158**
BR7: Chst ... 1D **160**
E4 ... 3G **35**
E18 ... 1J **51**
HA0: Wemb ... 4K **59**
HA4: Ruis ... 1H **57**
HA7: Stan ... 3E **26**
N3 ... 1H **45**
N14 ... 5A **22**
N20 ... 1C **30**
SW19 ... 1K **153**
TW12: Hamp ... 1D **148**
TW16: Sun ... 7J **129**
UB3: Hayes ... 7K **75**
Priory Ct. E6 ... 1A **88**
E9 ... 5K **67**
E17 ... 2B **50**
EC4 ... *1B* ***14***
(off Pilgrim St.)
HA0: Wemb ... 2E **78**
KT1: King T ... *3E* ***150***
(off Denmark Rd.)
KT17: Ewe ... 7B **164**
SM3: Cheam ... 4G **165**
SW8 ... 1H **119**
TW3: Houn ... 3F **113**
WD23: Bush ... *1B* ***26***
(off Sparrows Herne)
Priory Ct. Est. E17 ... 2B **50**
Priory Cres. HA0: Wemb ... 3A **60**
SE19 ... 7C **138**
SM3: Cheam ... 4F **165**
Priory Dr. HA7: Stan ... 3E **26**
SE2 ... 5D **108**
Priory Fld. Dr. HA8: Edg ... 4C **28**
Priory Gdns. HA0: Wemb ... 4A **60**
N6 ... 6F **47**
NW10 ... 3E **78**
SE25 ... 4F **157**
SW13 ... 3B **116**
TW12: Hamp ... 7D **130**
TW15: Ashf ... 5F **129**
W4 ... 4A **98**
W5 ... 3E **78**
Priory Grange *N2* ... *3D* ***46***
(off Fortis Grn.)
Priory Grn. Est. N1 ... 2K **83**
Priory Gro. EN5: Barn ... 5D **20**
SW8 ... 1J **119**
Priory Hill HA0: Wemb ... 4A **60**
Priory Ho. *E1* ... *5J* ***9***
(off Folgate St.)
EC1 ... *3A* ***8***
(off Sans Wlk.)
SW1 ... *5C* ***18***
(off Rampayne St.)
Priory La. KT8: W Mole ... 4F **149**
SW15 ... 6A **116**
TW9: Kew ... 7G **97**
Priory Leas SE9 ... 1C **142**
Priory Mans. *SW10* ... *5A* ***100***
(off Drayton Gdns.)
Priory M. SW8 ... 1J **119**
Priory Pk. SE3 ... 3H **123**
Priory Pk. Rd. HA0: Wemb ... 4A **60**
NW6 ... 1H **81**
Priory Retail Pk. SW19 ... 7B **136**
Priory Rd. CR0: Croy ... 7A **156**
E6 ... 1B **88**
IG11: Bark ... 7H **71**
KT9: Chess ... 3E **162**
N8 ... 4G **47**
NW6 ... 1K **81**
SM3: Cheam ... 4F **165**
SW19 ... 7B **136**
TW3: Houn ... 5G **113**
TW9: Kew ... 6G **97**
TW12: Hamp ... 7D **130**
W4 ... 3K **97**
Priory St. E3 ... 3D **86**
Priory Ter. NW6 ... 1K **81**
TW16: Sun ... 7J **129**
Priory Vw. WD23: Bushy ... 1D **26**
Priory Vs. *N11* ... *6J* ***31***
(off Colney Hatch La.)
Priory Wlk. SW10 ... 5A **100**
Priory Way HA2: Harr ... 4F **41**
UB2: S'hall ... 3B **94**
UB7: Harm ... 6A **92**
Priscilla Cl. N15 ... 5C **48**
Pritchard Ho. *E2* ... *2H* ***85***
(off Ada Pl.)
Pritchard's Rd. E2 ... 1G **85**
Priter Rd. SE16 ... 3G **103**
Priter Way SE16 ... 3G **103**
Private Rd. EN1: Enf ... 5J **23**
Probert Rd. SW2 ... 5A **120**
Probyn Ho. *SW1* ... *3D* ***18***
(off Page St.)
Probyn Rd. SW2 ... 2B **138**
Procter Ho. *SE1* ... *5G* ***103***
(off Avondale Sq.)
SE5 ... *7D* ***102***
(off Picton St.)
Procter St. WC1 ... 6G **7** (5K **83**)
Proctor Cl. CR4: Mitc ... 1E **154**
Proctors Cl. TW14: Felt ... 1J **129**
Progress Bus. Pk., The
CR0: Wadd ... 2K **167**
Progress Cen., The EN3: Pond E ... 3E **24**
Progress Way CR0: Wadd ... 2K **167**
EN1: Enf ... 5B **24**
N22 ... 1A **48**
Project Pk. E3 ... 4F **87**
Prologis Pk. CR0: Bedd ... 7H **155**
E16 ... 4F **87**
TW4: Houn ... 4A **112**
Promenade, The HA8: Edg ... 5B **28**
W4 ... 2A **116**
Promenade App. Rd. W4 ... 7A **98**
Pronto Trad. Est. UB3: Hayes ... 5G **75**
Prospect Cl. DA17: Belv ... 4G **109**
HA4: Ruis ... 7B **40**
SE26 ... 4H **139**
TW3: Houn ... 1D **112**
Prospect Cotts. SW18 ... 4J **117**
Prospect Cres. TW2: Whit ... 6G **113**
Prospect Hill E17 ... 4D **50**
Prospect Ho. *E17* ... *3E* ***50***
(off Prospect Hill)
N1 ... *2A* ***84***
(off Donegal St.)
SE1 ... *3B* ***102***
(off Gaywood St.)
W10 ... *6F* ***81***
(off Bridge Cl.)
Prospect Pl. BR2: Brom ... 3K **159**
E1 ... 1J **103**
(not continuous)
N2 ... 4B **46**
N7 ... 4J **65**
N17 ... 7K **33**
NW2 ... 3H **63**
NW3 ... 4A **64**
RM5: Col R ... 2J **55**
SE8 ... *6B* ***104***
(off Evelyn St.)
SW20 ... 7D **134**
W4 ... 5K **97**
Prospect Quay *SW18* ... *4J* ***117***
(off Lightermans Wlk.)
Prospect Ring N2 ... 3B **46**
Prospect Rd. EN5: New Bar ... 4D **20**
IG8: Wfd G ... 6F **37**
KT6: Surb ... 6C **150**
NW2 ... 3H **63**
Prospect St. SE16 ... 3H **103**
Prospect Va. SE18 ... 4C **106**
Prospect Wharf E1 ... 7J **85**
Prospero Rd. N19 ... 1H **65**
Protea Cl. E16 ... 4H **87**
Protheroe Ho. N17 ... 3F **49**
Prothero Gdns. NW4 ... 5D **44**
Prothero Ho. NW10 ... 7J **61**
Prothero Rd. SW6 ... 7G **99**
Proud Ho. *E1* ... *6H* ***85***
(off Amazon St.)
Prout Gro. NW10 ... 4A **62**
Prout Rd. E5 ... 3H **67**
Provence St. N1 ... 2C **84**
Providence Cl. E9 ... 1K **85**
Providence Ct. W1 ... 2H **11** (7E **82**)
Providence La. UB3: Harl ... 7F **93**
Providence Pl. N1 ... 1B **84**
RM5: Col R ... 1F **55**
Providence Rd. UB7: Yiew ... 1A **92**
Providence Row N1 ... 1G **7**
Providence Row Cl. E2 ... 3H **85**
Providence Sq. SE1 ... 6K **15** (2G **103**)
Providence Twr. *SE16* ... *2G* ***103***
(off Bermondsey Wall W.)
Providence Yd. *E2* ... *1K* ***9***
(off Ezra St.)
Provident Ind. Est.
UB3: Hayes ... 2J **93**
Provost Ct. *NW3* ... *6D* ***64***
(off Eton Rd.)
Provost Est. N1 ... 1E **8**
Provost Rd. NW3 ... 7D **64**
Provost St. N1 ... 1E **8** (2D **84**)
Prowse Av. WD23: Bushy ... 1B **26**
Prowse Pl. NW1 ... 7G **65**
Proyers Path HA1: Harr ... 7B **42**
Pruden Cl. N14 ... 2B **32**
Prudent Pas. EC2 ... 7D **8**
Prusom's Island *E1* ... *1J* ***103***
(off Cinnamon St.)
Prusom St. E1 ... 1H **103**
Pryors, The NW3 ... 3B **64**
Pucknells Cl. BR8: Swan ... 7J **145**
Pudding La. EC3 ... 3F **15** (7D **84**)
Pudding Mill La. E15 ... 1D **86**
Puddle Dock EC4 ... 2B **14** (7B **84**)
(not continuous)
Puffin Cl. BR3: Beck ... 5K **157**
IG11: Bark ... 3B **90**
Pugin Ct. *N1* ... *7A* ***66***
(off Liverpool Rd.)
Pulborough Rd. SW18 ... 7H **117**
Pulborough Way TW4: Houn ... 4A **112**
Pulford Rd. N15 ... 6D **48**
Pulham Av. N2 ... 4A **46**
Pulham Ho. *SW8* ... *7K* ***101***
(off Dorset Rd.)
Pullen's Bldgs. *SE17* ... *5B* ***102***
(off Iliffe St.)
Puller Rd. EN5: Barn ... 2B **20**
Pulleyns Av. E6 ... 3C **88**
Pullman Cl. SW2 ... 1J **137**
Pullman Gdns. SW15 ... 6E **116**
Pullman M. SE12 ... 3K **141**
Pullman Pl. SE9 ... 5C **124**
Pulross Rd. SW9 ... 3K **119**
Pulteney Cl. E3 ... 1B **86**
TW7: Isle ... 3A **114**
Pulteney Gdns. E18 ... 3K **51**
Pulteney Rd. E18 ... 3K **51**
Pulteney Ter. N1 ... 1K **83**
(not continuous)
Pulton Ho. *SE4* ... *4A* ***122***
(off Turnham Rd.)
Pulton Pl. SW6 ... 7J **99**
Puma Ct. E1 ... 5J **9** (5F **85**)
Pump All. TW8: Bford ... 7D **96**
Pump Cl. UB5: N'olt ... 2E **76**
Pump Ct. EC4 ... 1J **13** (6A **84**)
Pumphandle Path *N2* ... *2B* ***46***
(off Oak La.)
Pumphouse, The N8 ... 4K **47**
Pump Ho. Cl. BR2: Brom ... 2G **159**
SE16 ... 2J **103**
Pumphouse Educational Mus., The ... *1A* ***104***
(off Lavender Rd.)
Pump House Gallery, The ... 7E **100**

Pump Ho. M. *E1* 7G **85**
(off Hooper St.)
Pump House Steam & Transport Mus.
. . . . .6A **50**
Pumping Ho. *E14* 7F **87**
(off Naval Row)
Pumping Sta. Rd. W4 . . . . .7A **98**
UB3: Hayes 2J **93**
Pump La. SE14 . . . . .7J **103**
Pump Pail Nth. CR0: Croy 3C **168**
Pump Pail Sth. CR0: Croy 3C **168**
Punchard Cres. EN3: Enf L 1J **25**
Punderson's Gdns. E2 . . . . .3H **85**
Purbeck Av. KT3: N Mald 6B **152**
Purbeck Dr. NW2 . . . . .2F **63**
Purbeck Ho. SW8 . . . . .7K **101**
(off Bolney St.)
Purbrook Est. SE1 . . . . .7H **15** (2E **102**)
Purbrook St. SE1 . . . . . .7H **15** (3E **102**)
Purcell Cres. SW6 . . . . .7F **99**
(not continuous)
Purcell Ho. EN1: Enf 1B **24**
SW10 . . . . .6B **100**
(off Milman's St.)
Purcell Mans. W14 . . . . .6G **99**
(off Queen's Club Gdns.)
Purcell M. NW10 . . . . .7A **62**
Purcell Rd. UB6: G'frd 5F **77**
Purcell Room 4H **13**
(in South Bank)
Purcells Av. HA8: Edg 5B **28**
Purcell St. N1 . . . . .2E **84**
Purchese St. NW1 . . . . . . .1D **6** (2H **83**)
Purday Ho. W10 . . . . .3G **81**
(off Bruckner St.)
Purdon Ho. SE15 . . . . .1G **121**
(off Peckham High St.)
Purdy Ct. KT4: Wor Pk 2C **164**
Purdy St. E3 . . . . .4D **86**
Purelake M. SE13 . . . . .3F **123**
(off Marischal Rd.)
Purkis Cl. UB8: Hayes 7E **74**
Purland Cl. RM8: Dag 1F **73**
Purland Rd. SE28 . . . . .2A **108**
Purleigh Av. IG8: Wfd G 6H **37**
Purley Av. NW2 . . . . .2G **63**
Purley Cl. IG5: Ilf 2E **52**
Purley Pl. N1 . . . . .7B **66**
Purley Rd. CR2: S Croy 7D **168**
N9 . . . . .3K **33**
Purley Vw. Ter. CR2: S Croy 7D **168**
(off Sanderstead Rd.)
Purley Way CR0: Croy, Wadd 7K **155**
Purley Way Cen., The CR0: Wadd . . .2A **168**
Purley Way Cnr. CR0: Croy 7K **155**
Purneys Rd. SE9 . . . . .4B **124**
Purrett Rd. SE18 . . . . .5K **107**
Purser Ho. SW2 . . . . .6A **120**
(off Tulse Hill)
Pursers Cross Rd. SW6 . . . . .1H **117**
(not continuous)
Purse Wardens Cl. W13 . . . . .1C **96**
Pursley Rd. NW7 . . . . .7J **29**
Purves Rd. NW10 . . . . .3D **80**
Pusey Ho. E14 . . . . .6C **86**
(off Saracen St.)
Puteaux Ho. E2 . . . . .2K **85**
(off Mace St.)
PUTNEY 4F **117**
Putney Arts Theatre 4F **117**
Putney Bri. SW6 . . . . .3G **117**
SW15 . . . . .3G **117**
Putney Bri. App. SW6 . . . . .3G **117**
Putney Bri. Rd. SW15 . . . . .4G **117**
SW18 . . . . .4G **117**
Putney Comn. SW15 . . . . .3E **116**
Putney Exchange Shop. Cen.
SW15 . . . . .4F **117**
Putney Gdns. RM6: Chad H 5B **54**
PUTNEY HEATH 6E **116**
Putney Heath SW15 . . . . .7D **116**
Putney Heath La. SW15 . . . . .6F **117**
Putney High St. SW15 . . . . .4F **117**

Putney Hill SW15 . . . . .7F **117**
(not continuous)
Putney Leisure Cen. 4E **116**
Putney Pk. Av. SW15 . . . . .4C **116**
Putney Pk. La. SW15 . . . . .4D **116**
(not continuous)
PUTNEY VALE 3C **134**
Putney Va. Crematorium SW15 . . . .2C **134**
Putney Wharf SW15 . . . . .3G **117**
Pycroft Way N9 . . . . .4A **34**
Pyecombe Cnr. N12 . . . . .4C **30**
Pylbrook Rd. SM1: Sutt 3J **165**
Pylon Trad. Est. E16 . . . . .4G **87**
Pylon Way CR0: Bedd 1J **167**
Pym Cl. EN4: E Barn 5G **21**
Pymers Mead SE21 . . . . .1C **138**
Pymmes Brook Ho. N10 . . . . .7K **31**
Pymmes Cl. N13 . . . . .5E **32**
N17 . . . . .1H **49**
Pymmes Gdns. Nth. N9 . . . . .3A **34**
Pymmes Gdns. Sth. N9 . . . . .3A **34**
Pymmes Grn. Rd. N11 . . . . .4A **32**
Pymmes Rd. N13 . . . . .6D **32**
Pymms Brook Dr. EN4: E Barn 4H **21**
Pynchester Cl. UB10: Ick 2C **56**
Pyne Rd. KT6: Surb 1G **163**
Pynfolds SE16 . . . . .2H **103**
Pynham Cl. SE2 . . . . .3B **108**
Pynnacles Cl. HA7: Stan 5G **27**
Pynnersmead SE24 . . . . .5C **120**
Pyramid Ct. KT1: King T 2F **151**
(off Cambridge Rd.)
Pyramid Ho. TW4: Houn 2C **112**
Pyrford Ho. SW9 . . . . .4B **120**
Pyrland Rd. N5 . . . . .5D **66**
TW10: Rich 6F **115**
Pyrmont Gro. SE27 . . . . .3B **138**
Pyrmont Rd. W4 . . . . .6G **97**
Pytchley Cres. SE19 . . . . .6C **138**
Pytchley Rd. SE22 . . . . .3E **120**

Q

Q Bldg., The *E15* 6G **69**
(off The Grove)
Quad Ct. SE1 . . . . .3E **102**
(off Grigg's Pl.)
Quadrangle, The E15 . . . . .6G **69**
SE24 . . . . .5C **120**
SW6 . . . . .7G **99**
(Fulham)
SW6 . . . . .1A **118**
(Sands End)
W2 . . . . .7C **4** (6C **82**)
W12 . . . . .6D **80**
(off Du Cane Rd.)
Quadrangle Cl. SE1 . . . . .4E **102**
Quadrangle M. HA7: Stan 7H **27**
Quadrant, The DA7: Bex 7D **108**
HA2: Harr 4G **41**
HA8: Edg 6B **28**
NW4 . . . . .4E **44**
SM2: Sutt 6A **166**
SW20 . . . . .1G **153**
TW9: Rich 4D **114**
W10 . . . . .3F **81**
Quadrant Arc. W1 . . . . .3B **12**
Quadrant Bus. Cen. NW6 . . . . .1G **81**
Quadrant Cl. NW4 . . . . .5D **44**
Quadrant Gro. NW5 . . . . .5D **64**
Quadrant Ho. SE1 . . . . .4A **14**
Quadrant Rd. CR7: Thor H 4B **156**
TW9: Rich 4D **114**
Quad Rd. HA9: Wemb 3D **60**
Quaggy Wlk. SE3 . . . . .4J **123**
Quain Mans. W14 . . . . .6G **99**
(off Queen's Club Gdns.)
Quainton St. NW10 . . . . .3K **61**
Quaker Ct. E1 . . . . .4J **9**
(off Quaker St.)
EC1 . . . . .3E **8**
Quaker La. UB2: S'hall 3E **94**

Quakers Course NW9 . . . . .1B **44**
Quakers La. TW7: Isle 7A **96**
(not continuous)
Quakers Pl. E7 . . . . .5B **70**
Quaker St. E1 . . . . .4J **9** (4F **85**)
Quakers Wlk. N21 . . . . .6J **23**
Quality Ct. WC2 . . . . .7J **7**
Quantock Cl. UB3: Harl 7F **93**
Quantock Dr. KT4: Wor Pk 2E **164**
Quantock Gdns. NW2 . . . . .2F **63**
Quantock Ho. N16 . . . . .1F **67**
Quantock M. SE15 . . . . .2G **121**
(off Alpha St.)
Quarles Pk. Rd. RM6: Chad H 6B **54**
Quarrendon St. SW6 . . . . .2J **117**
Quarr Rd. SM5: Cars 6B **154**
Quarry Pk. Rd. SM1: Sutt 6H **165**
Quarry Ri. SM1: Sutt 6H **165**
Quarry Rd. SW18 . . . . .6A **118**
Quarterdeck, The E14 . . . . .2C **104**
Quarter Mile La. E10 . . . . .4D **68**
Quastel Ho. SE1 . . . . .7E **14**
(off Long La.)
Quatre Ports E4 . . . . .5A **36**
Quay Ho. E14 . . . . .2C **104**
(off Admirals Way)
Quayside Cotts. E1 . . . . .1G **103**
(off Mews St.)
Quayside Ct. SE16 . . . . .1K **103**
(off Abbotshade Rd.)
Quayside Ho. E14 . . . . .1B **104**
W10 . . . . .4G **81**
Quayside Wlk. KT1: King T 2D **150**
(off Wadbrook St.)
Quay Vw. Apartments E14 . . . . .3C **104**
(off Arden Cres.)
Quebec M. W1 . . . . .1F **11** (6D **82**)
Quebec Rd. IG1: Ilf 7F **53**
IG2: Ilf 7F **53**
UB4: Yead 6A **76**
Quebec Way SE16 . . . . .2K **103**
Quebec Way Ind. Est. SE16 . . . . . . .2A **104**
Quebec Wharf E8 . . . . .1F **84**
(off Kingsland Rd.)
E14 . . . . .6C **86**
Quedgeley Ct. SE15 . . . . .6F **103**
(off Ebley Cl.)
Queen Adelaide Ct. SE20 . . . . .6J **139**
Queen Adelaide Rd. SE20 . . . . .6J **139**
Queen Alexandra Mans. WC1 . . . . . .2E **6**
(off Bidborough St.)
Queen Alexandra's Ct. SW19 . . . . . .5H **135**
Queen Anne Av. BR2: Brom 3H **159**
Queen Anne Ho. E16 . . . . .1J **105**
(off Hardy Av.)
Queen Anne M. W1 . . . . . .6K **5** (5F **83**)
Queen Anne Rd. E9 . . . . .6K **67**
Queen Anne's Cl. TW2: Twick 3H **131**
Queen Anne's Ct. SE10 . . . . .5F **105**
(off Park Row)
Queen Anne's Gdns. CR4: Mitc 3D **154**
EN1: Enf 6K **23**
W4 .3A **98**
W5 .2E **96**
Queen Anne's Ga. DA7: Bex 3D **126**
SW1 . . . . .7C **12** (2H **101**)
Queen Anne's Gro. EN1: Enf 7J **23**
W4 .3A **98**
W5 .2E **96**
Queen Anne's Pl. EN1: Enf 6K **23**
Queen Anne St. W1 . . . . .7J **5** (6F **83**)
Queen Anne Ter. E1 . . . . .7H **85**
(off Sovereign Cl.)
Queenborough Gdns. BR7: Chst 6H **143**
IG2: Ilf 4E **52**
Queenbridge Sports & Community Cen.
. . . . .7F **67**
Queen Caroline St. W6 . . . . .5E **98**
(not continuous)
Queen Catherine Ho. SW6 . . . . .7K **99**
(off Wandon Rd.)
Queen Charlotte's Cottage 2D **114**

Queen Elizabeth Bldgs. WC2 . . . . . .2J **13**
Queen Elizabeth Ct. EN5: Barn 3C **20**
Queen Elizabeth Gdns.
SM4: Mord 4J **153**
Queen Elizabeth Hall 4H **13**
Queen Elizabeth Ho. SW12 . . . . . . .7E **118**
Queen Elizabeth II Conference Cen.
. . . . .7D **12** (2H **101**)
Queen Elizabeth Rd. E17 . . . . .3A **50**
KT2: King T 2F **151**
Queen Elizabeth's Cl. N16 . . . . .2D **66**
Queen Elizabeth's Coll. SE10 . . . . . .7E **104**
Queen Elizabeth's Dr.
CR0: New Ad 7F **171**
N14 . . . . .1D **32**
Queen Elizabeth's Hunting Lodge . . .1C **36**
Queen Elizabeth Sports Cen.
Barnet 4C **20**
Queen Elizabeth Stadium 2A **24**
Queen Elizabeth St. SE1 . . . .6H **15** (2E **102**)
Queen Elizabeth's Wlk. N16 . . . . . . .1D **66**
SM6: Bedd 4H **167**
(off Croydon Rd.)
SM6: Bedd 4H **167**
(Sandhills)
Queen Elizabeth Wlk. SW13 . . . . . . .1C **116**
Queenhithe EC4 . . . . .2D **14** (7C **84**)
Queen Isabella Way EC1 . . . . .7B **8**
(off King Edward St.)
Queen Margaret Flats E2 . . . . .3H **85**
(off St Jude's Rd.)
Queen Margaret's Gro. N1 . . . . .5E **66**
Queen Mary Av. SM4: Mord 5F **153**
Queen Mary Cl. KT6: Surb 3H **163**
Queen Mary Ct. TW19: Stanw 1A **128**
Queen Mary Ho. E16 . . . . .1K **105**
(off Wesley Av.)
Queen Mary Rd. SE19 . . . . .6B **138**
TW17: Shep 2E **146**
Queen Marys Bldgs. SW1 . . . . .3B **18**
(off Stillington St.)
Queen Mary's Ct. SE10 . . . . .6F **105**
(off Park Row)
Queen Mother Sports Cen., The 3A **18**
Queen of Denmark Ct. SE16 . . . . . . .3B **104**
Queens Acre SM3: Cheam 7F **165**
Queens Av. HA7: Stan 3C **42**
IG8: Wfd G 5E **36**
N3 .7F **31**
N10 . . . . .3E **46**
N20 . . . . .2G **31**
N21 . . . . .1G **33**
TW13: Hanw 4A **130**
UB6: G'frd 6F **77**
Queensberry Ho. TW9: Rich 5C **114**
Queensberry M. W. SW7 . . . .3A **16** (4B **100**)
Queensberry Pl. E12 . . . . .5B **70**
SW7 . . . . .3A **16** (4B **100**)
TW9: Rich 5D **114**
(off Retreat Rd.)
Queensberry Way SW7 . . . .3A **16** (4B **100**)
Queensborough Ct. N3 . . . . .4H **45**
(off Tillingbourne Gdns.)
Queensborough M. W2 . . . . .7A **82**
Queensborough Pas. W2 . . . . .7A **82**
(off Queensborough M.)
Queensborough Studios W2 . . . . . . .7A **82**
(off Queensborough M.)
Queensborough Ter. W2 . . . . .7K **81**
Queensbridge Pk. TW7: Isle 5J **113**
Queensbridge Rd. E2 . . . . .6F **67**
E8 .6F **67**
QUEENSBURY 3E **42**
Queensbury Circ. Pde. HA3: Kent . . .3E **42**
HA7: Stan 3E **42**
Queensbury Rd. HA0: Wemb 2F **79**
NW9 . . . . .7K **43**
Queensbury Sta. App.
HA8: Edg 3F **43**
Queensbury St. N1 . . . . .7C **66**

Queen's Chapel of the Savoy, The 3G 13
(off Savoy St.)
Queen's Cir. SW8 . . . . 7F 101
Queens Cl. HA8: Edg 5B 28
SM6: Wall 5F 167
Queen's Club Gdns. W14 . . . . 6G 99
Queen's Club, The (Tennis) 5G 99
Queens Ct. CR2: S Croy 5C 168
(off Warham Rd.)
E11 . . . . 7G 51
HA3: Kent 2B 42
IG9: Buck H 2G 37
NW6 . . . . 5K 63
NW8 . . . . 2B 82
(off Queen's Ter.)
NW11 . . . . 5H 45
SE23 . . . . 2H 139
TW10: Rich 6F 115
W2 . . . . 7K 81
(off Queensway)
Queenscourt HA9: Wemb 4E 60
Queen's Cres. NW5 . . . . 6E 64
TW10: Rich 5F 115
Queenscroft Rd. SE9 . . . . 5B 124
Queensdale Cres. W11 . . . . 1F 99
(not continuous)
Queensdale Pl. W11 . . . . 1G 99
Queensdale Rd. W11 . . . . 1F 99
Queensdale Wlk. W11 . . . . 1G 99
Queensdown Rd. E5 . . . . 4H 67
Queens Dr. E10 . . . . 7C 50
KT5: Surb 7G 151
KT7: T Ditt 6A 150
N4 . . . . 2B 66
W3 . . . . 6F 79
W5 . . . . 6F 79
Queen's Elm Pde. SW3 . . . . 5B 16
(off Old Church St.)
Queen's Elm Sq. SW3 . . . . . . 6A 16 (5B 100)
Queens Ferry Wlk. N17 . . . . 4H 49
Queensfield Ct.
SM3: Cheam 4E 164
Queen's Gallery 7K 11 (2F 101)
Queen's Gdns. NW4 . . . . 5E 44
RM13: Rain 2K 91
TW5: Hest 1C 112
W2 . . . . 7A 82
W5 . . . . 4C 78
Queen's Ga. SW7 . . . . 1A 16 (2A 100)
Queensgate Ct. N12 . . . . 5E 30
Queens Ga. Gdns.
BR7: Chst 1H 161
SW7 . . . . 3A 100
SW15 . . . . 4D 116
Queensgate Ho. E3 . . . . 2B 86
(off Hereford Rd.)
Queen's Ga. M. SW7 . . . . 3A 100
Queen's Ga. Pl. SW7 . . . . 3A 100
Queensgate Pl. NW6 . . . . 7J 63
Queen's Ga. Pl. M. SW7 . . . . 2A 16 (3A 100)
Queen's Ga. Ter. SW7 . . . . . . 1A 16 (3A 100)
Queens Ga. Vs. E9 . . . . 7A 68
Queen's Gro. NW8 . . . . 1B 82
Queens Gro. Rd. E4 . . . . 1A 36
Queen's Gro. Studios
NW8 . . . . 1B 82
Queen's Head Pas. EC4 . . . . . . 7C 8 (6C 84)
Queen's Head St. N1 . . . . 1B 84
Queen's Head Yd. SE1 . . . . 5E 14
Queen's House, The 6F 105
Queens Ho. SE17 . . . . 6D 102
(off Merrow St.)
SW8 . . . . 7J 101
(off Sth. Lambeth Rd.)
TW11: Tedd 6K 131
W2 . . . . 7K 81
(off Queensway)
Queen's Ice Bowl 7K 81
(off Queensway)
Queen's Keep TW1: Twick 6C 114
Queensland Av. N18 . . . . 6H 33
SW19 . . . . 1K 153
Queensland Cl. E17 . . . . 2B 50
Queensland Ho. E16 . . . . 1E 106
(off Rymill St.)
Queensland Pl. N7 . . . . 4A 66
Queensland Rd. N7 . . . . 4A 66
Queens La. N10 . . . . 3F 47
TW15: Ashf 4B 128
Queen's Mans. W6 . . . . 4F 99
(off Brook Grn.)
Queen's Mkt. E13 . . . . 1A 88
Queensmead NW8 . . . . 1B 82
Queen's Mead Rd.
BR2: Brom 2H 159
Queensmead Sports Cen. 4B 58
Queensmere Cl. SW19 . . . . 2F 135
Queensmere Ct. SW13 . . . . 7B 98
Queensmere Rd. SW19 . . . . 2F 135
Queen's M. W2 . . . . 7K 81
(not continuous)
Queensmill Rd. SW6 . . . . 7F 99
Queens Pde. N8 . . . . 4B 48
N11 . . . . 5J 31
(off Friern Barnet Rd.)
NW2 . . . . 6E 62
(off Willesden La.)
NW4 . . . . 5E 44
(off Queens Rd.)
W5 . . . . 6F 79
Queen's Pde. Cl. N11 . . . . 5J 31
Queens Pk. Ct. W10 . . . . 3F 81
Queen's Pk. Gdns.
TW13: Felt 3H 129
Queen's Pk. Rangers FC 1D 98
Queens Pk. School Sports Cen.
(within school) 1F 81
Queens Pas. BR7: Chst 6F 143
Queens Pl. SM4: Mord 4J 153
Queen's Prom.
KT1: King T, Surb 4D 150
Queen Sq. WC1 . . . . 4F 7 (4J 83)
Queen Sq. Pl. WC1 . . . . 4F 7
Queen's Quay EC4 . . . . 2C 14
(off Up. Thames St.)
Queens Reach KT1: King T 2D 150
KT8: E Mos 4J 149
Queens Ride SW13 . . . . 3C 116
SW15 . . . . 3C 116
Queens Ri. TW10: Rich 6F 115
Queens Rd. BR1: Brom 2J 159
BR3: Beck 2A 158
BR7: Chst 6F 143
CR0: Croy 6B 156
DA16: Well 2B 126
E11 . . . . 7F 51
E13 . . . . 1K 87
E17 . . . . 6B 50
EN1: Enf 4K 23
EN5: Barn 3A 20
IG9: Buck H 2E 36
IG11: Bark 6G 71
KT2: King T 7G 133
KT3: N Mald 4B 152
KT7: T Ditt 5K 149
N3 . . . . 1A 46
N9 . . . . 3C 34
N11 . . . . 7D 32
NW4 . . . . 5E 44
SE14 . . . . 1J 121
SE15 . . . . 1H 121
SM4: Mord 4J 153
SM6: Wall 5F 167
SW14 . . . . 3K 115
SW19 . . . . 6H 135
TW1: Twick 1A 132
TW3: Houn 3F 113
TW10: Rich 7F 115
TW11: Tedd 6K 131
TW12: Ham H 4F 131
TW13: Felt 1K 129
UB2: S'hall 2B 94
UB3: Hayes 6G 75
UB7: W Dray 2B 92
W5 . . . . 6E 78
Queens Rd. W. E13 . . . . 2J 87
Queen's Row SE17 . . . . 6D 102
Queens Ter. E1 . . . . 4J 85
E13 . . . . 1K 87
KT7: T Ditt 6A 150
(off Queens Dr.)
NW8 . . . . 1B 82
TW7: Isle 4A 114
Queen's Ter. Cotts. W7 . . . . 2J 95
Queen's Theatre
Westminster 2C 12
(off Shaftesbury Av.)
Queensthorpe Rd. SE26 . . . . 4K 139
Queenstown M. SW8 . . . . 2F 119
Queenstown Rd. SW8 . . . . . . 7J 17 (6F 101)
Queen St. CR0: Croy 4C 168
DA7: Bex 3F 127
EC4 . . . . 2D 14 (7C 84)
(not continuous)
N17 . . . . 6K 33
RM7: Rom 6K 55
W1 . . . . 4J 11 (1F 101)
Queen St. Pl. EC4 . . . . 2D 14 (7C 84)
Queensville Rd. SW12 . . . . 7H 119
Queens Wlk. E4 . . . . 1A 36
HA1: Harr 4J 41
HA4: Ruis 2A 58
N5 . . . . 5B 66
NW9 . . . . 2J 61
SW1 . . . . 5A 12 (1G 101)
TW15: Ashf 4A 128
W5 . . . . 4C 78
Queen's Wlk., The SE1 . . . . . . 3K 13 (7A 84)
(Oxo Tower Wharf)
SE1 . . . . 4F 15 (1E 102)
(Tooley St.)
SE1 . . . . 4H 13 (1K 101)
(Waterloo Rd.)
Queens Wlk. Ter. HA4: Ruis 3A 58
Queens Way NW4 . . . . 5E 44
TW13: Hanw 4A 130
Queensway BR4: W W'ck 3G 171
BR5: Pet W 5G 161
CR0: Wadd 6K 167
EN3: Pond E 4C 24
TW16: Sun 2K 147
W2 . . . . 6K 81
Queensway Bus. Cen.
EN3: Pond E 4C 24
Queensway Ind. Est. EN3: Pond E 4D 24
Queenswell Av. N20 . . . . 3H 31
Queens Wharf W6 . . . . 5E 98
Queenswood Av. CR7: Thor H 5A 156
E17 . . . . 1E 50
SM6: Bedd 4H 167
TW3: Houn 2D 112
TW12: Hamp 6F 131
Queenswood Ct. SE27 . . . . 4D 138
SW4 . . . . 5J 119
Queenswood Gdns. E11 . . . . 1K 69
Queenswood Pk. N3 . . . . 2G 45
Queens Wood Rd. N10 . . . . 6F 47
Queenswood Rd. DA15: Sidc 5K 125
SE23 . . . . 3K 139
Queen's Yd. WC1 . . . . 4B 6 (5G 83)
QUEEN VICTORIA 4E 164
Queen Victoria Av. HA0: Wemb 7D 60
Queen Victoria Memorial
. . . . 7A 12 (2G 101)
Queen Victoria Seaman's Rest
E14 . . . . 6D 86
(off E. India Dock Rd.)
Queen Victoria St. EC4 . . . . . . 2A 14 (7B 84)
Queen Victoria Ter. E1 . . . . 7H 85
(off Sovereign Cl.)
Quemerford Rd. N7 . . . . 5K 65
Quendon Ho. W10 . . . . 4E 80
(off Sutton Way)
Quenington Ct. SE15 . . . . 6F 103
Quentin Ho. SE1 . . . . 7K 13
(off Gray St., not continuous)
Quentin Pl. SE13 . . . . 3G 123
Quentin Rd. SE13 . . . . 3G 123
Quernmore Cl. BR1: Brom 6J 141
Quernmore Rd. BR1: Brom 6J 141
N4 . . . . 6A 48
Querrin St. SW6 . . . . 2A 118
Quest, The W11 . . . . 7G 81
(off Clarendon Rd.)
Quested Ct. E8 . . . . 5H 67
(off Brett Rd.)
Questors Theatre, The 7C 78
Quex M. NW6 . . . . 1J 81
Quex Rd. NW6 . . . . 1J 81
Quiberon Ct. TW16: Sun 3J 147
Quick Rd. W4 . . . . 5A 98
Quicks Rd. SW19 . . . . 7K 135
Quick St. N1 . . . . 2B 84
Quick St. M. N1 . . . . 2B 84
Quickswood NW3 . . . . 7C 64
Quiet Nook BR2: Kes 3B 172
Quill La. SW15 . . . . 4F 117
Quill St. N4 . . . . 3A 66
W5 . . . . 3E 78
Quilp St. SE1 . . . . 6C 14 (2C 102)
(not continuous)
Quilter Ho. W10 . . . . 3H 81
(off Dart St.)
Quilter St. E2 . . . . 1K 9 (3G 85)
SE18 . . . . 5K 107
Quilting Ct. SE16 . . . . 2K 103
(off Garter Way)
Quince Ho. SE13 . . . . 2D 122
(off Quince Rd.)
Quinnell Cl. SE18 . . . . 5K 107
Quinta Dr. EN5: Barn 5A 20
Quintet, The KT12: Walt T 7J 147
Quintin Av. SW20 . . . . 1H 153
Quintin Cl. HA5: Eastc 4K 39
Quinton Cl. BR3: Beck 3E 158
SM6: Wall 4F 167
TW5: Cran 7K 93
Quinton Ho. SW8 . . . . 7J 101
(off Wyvil Rd.)
Quinton Rd. KT7: T Ditt 1A 162
Quinton St. SW18 . . . . 2A 136
Quixley St. E14 . . . . 7F 87
Quorn Rd. SE22 . . . . 4E 120

R

Rabbit Row W8 . . . . 1J 99
Rabbits Rd. E12 . . . . 4C 70
Rabournmead Dr. UB5: N'olt 5C 58
Raby Rd. KT3: N Mald 4K 151
Raby St. E14 . . . . 6A 86
Raccoon Way TW4: Houn 2A 112
Raceway, The (Go-Kart Track) 1J 83
Rachel Cl. IG6: Ilf 3H 53
Racine SE5 . . . . 1E 120
(off Peckham Rd.)
Rackham Cl. DA16: Well 2B 126
Rackham M. SW16 . . . . 6G 137
Rackstraw Ho. NW3 . . . . 7D 64
Racquets & Fitness Spa, The 3E 130
Racton Rd. SW6 . . . . 6J 99
RADA 5C 6
(off Chenies St.)
Radbourne Av. W5 . . . . 4C 96
Radbourne Cl. E5 . . . . 4K 67
Radbourne Ct. HA3: Kent 6B 42
Radbourne Cres. E17 . . . . 2F 51
Radbourne Rd. SW12 . . . . 7G 119
Radcliffe Av. EN2: Enf 1H 23
NW10 . . . . 2C 80
Radcliffe Gdns. SM5: Cars 7C 166
Radcliffe Ho. SE16 . . . . 4H 103
(off Anchor St.)
Radcliffe M. TW12: Ham H 5G 131
Radcliffe Path SW8 . . . . 2F 119
Radcliffe Rd. CR0: Croy 2F 169
HA3: W'stone 2A 42
N21 . . . . 1G 33
SE1 . . . . 3E 102
Radcliffe Sq. SW15 . . . . 6F 117
Radcliffe Way UB5: Yead 3B 76

Radcot Point—Ranelagh Rd.

Radcot Point SE23 .... 3K 139
Radcot St. SE11 .... 6K 19 (5A 102)
Raddington Rd. W10 .... 5G 81
Radfield Way DA15: Sidc 7H 125
(not continuous)
Radford Est. NW10 .... 3A 80
Radford Ho. *E14* *5D 86*
(off St Leonard's Rd.)
N7 .... 5K 65
Radford Rd. SE13 .... 6E 122
Radford Way IG11: Bark 3K 89
Radipole Rd. SW6 .... 1H 117
Radisson Ct. *SE1* *7G 15*
(off Long La.)
Radius Apartments *N1* *1G 7*
(off Caledonian Rd.)
Radius Pk. TW14: Felt 4H 111
Radland Rd. E16 .... 6H 87
Radlet Av. SE26 .... 3H 139
Radlett Cl. E7 .... 6H 69
Radlett Pl. NW8 .... 1C 82
Radley Av. IG3: Bark, Ilf 4A 72
Radley Cl. TW14: Felt 1H 129
Radley Ct. SE16 .... 2K 103
Radley Gdns. HA3: Kent 4E 42
Radley Ho. *NW1* *3E 4*
(off Gloucester Pl.)
SE2 .... *2D 108*
(off Wolvercote Rd.)
Radley M. W8 .... 3J 99
Radley Rd. N17 .... 2E 48
Radley's La. E18 .... 2J 51
Radleys Mead RM10: Dag 6H 73
Radley Sq. E5 .... 2J 67
Radley Ter. *E16* *5H 87*
(off Hermit Rd.)
Radlix Rd. E10 .... 1C 68
Radnor Av. DA16: Well 5B 126
HA1: Harr 5J 41
Radnor Cl. BR7: Chst 6J 143
CR4: Mitc 4J 155
Radnor Ct. HA3: Hrw W 1K 41
W7 .... *6K 77*
(off Copley Cl.)
Radnor Cres. IG4: Ilf 5D 52
SE18 .... 7A 108
Radnor Gdns. EN1: Enf 1K 23
TW1: Twick 2K 131
Radnor Gro. UB10: Hil 2C 74
Radnor Ho. *EC1* *2D 8*
(off Bath St.)
Radnor Lodge *W2* *1B 10*
(off Radnor M.)
Radnor M. W2 .... 1B 10 (6B 82)
Radnor Pl. W2 .... 1C 10 (6C 82)
Radnor Rd. HA1: Harr 5H 41
NW6 .... 1G 81
SE15 .... 7G 103
TW1: Twick 1K 131
Radnor St. EC1 .... 2D 8 (3C 84)
Radnor Ter. SM2: Sutt 7J 165
W14 .... 4H 99
Radnor Wlk. CR0: Croy 6A 158
E14 .... *4C 104*
(off Barnsdale Av.)
SW3 .... 6D 16 (5C 100)
Radnor Way NW10 .... 4H 79
Radstock Av. HA3: Kent 3A 42
Radstock Cl. N11 .... 6K 31
Radstock St. SW11 .... 7C 100
(not continuous)
Radway Ho. *W2* *5J 81*
(off Alfred Rd.)
Raeburn Av. KT5: Surb 1H 163
Raeburn Cl. KT1: Ham W 7D 132
NW11 .... 6A 46
Raeburn Ho. *UB5: N'olt* *2B 76*
(off Academy Gdns.)
Raeburn Rd. DA15: Sidc 6J 125
HA8: Edg 1G 43
UB4: Hayes 2F 75
Raeburn St. SW2 .... 4J 119
Raffles Ho. NW4 .... 4D 44
Rafford Way BR1: Brom 2K 159
RAF Mus. Hendon 2C 44
RAF NORTHOLT AERODROME 6H 57
Ragged School Mus. 5A 86
Raggleswood BR7: Chst 1E 160
Raglan Cl. TW4: Houn 5D 112
Raglan Ct. CR2: S Croy 5B 168
HA9: Wemb 4F 61
SE12 .... 5J 123
Raglan Rd. BR2: Brom 4A 160
DA17: Belv 4F 109
E17 .... 5E 50
EN1: Enf 7A 24
SE18 .... 5G 107
Raglan St. NW5 .... 6F 65
Raglan Ter. HA2: Harr 4F 59
Raglan Way UB5: N'olt 6G 59
Ragley Cl. W3 .... 2J 97
Ragwort Ct. SE26 .... 5H 139
Raider Cl. RM7: Mawney 1G 55
Railey M. NW5 .... 5G 65
Railshead Rd. TW7: Isle 4B 114
Railton Rd. SE24 .... 4A 120
Railway App. HA3: Harr 4K 41
N4 .... 6A 48
SE1 .... 5F 15 (1D 102)
SM6: Wall 5F 167
TW1: Twick 7A 114
Railway Arches *E2* *1J 9*
(off Geffrye St.)
E7 .... *4J 69*
(off Winchelsea Rd.)
E8 .... *7H 67*
(off Mentmore Ter.)
E10 .... *7D 50*
(off Capworth St.)
E11 .... *2G 69*
(off Leytonstone High Rd.)
E11 .... *1F 69*
(off The Sidings)
E17 .... *5C 50*
(off Yunus Khan Cl.)
W12 .... *2E 98*
(off Shepherd's Bush Mkt.)
Railway Av. SE16 .... 2J 103
(not continuous)
Railway Children Wlk. BR1: Brom 2J 141
SE12 .... 2J 141
Railway Cotts. *E15* *2G 87*
(off Baker's Row)
SW19 .... 4K 135
TW9: Rich 4G 115
W6 .... *2E 98*
(off Sulgrave Rd.)
Railway Gro. SE14 .... 7B 104
Railway M. *E3* *3C 86*
(off Wellington Way)
W10 .... 6G 81
Railway Pas. TW11: Tedd 6A 132
Railway Pl. DA17: Belv 3G 109
Railway Ri. SE22 .... 4E 120
Railway Rd. TW11: Tedd 4J 131
Railway Side SW13 .... 3A 116
(not continuous)
Railway St. N1 .... 2J 83
RM6: Chad H 7C 54
Railway Ter. E17 .... 1E 50
SE13 .... 5D 122
TW13: Felt 1J 129
Rainborough Cl. NW10 .... 6J 61
Rainbow Av. E14 .... 5D 104
Rainbow Ct. *SE14* *6A 104*
(off Chipley St.)
Rainbow Ind. Est. SW20 .... 2D 152
UB7: Yiew 7A 74
Rainbow Quay SE16 .... 3A 104
(not continuous)
Rainbow St. SE5 .... 7E 102
Rainbow Theatre 2A 66
Raines Est. Ct. N16 .... 2F 67
Raine St. E1 .... 1H 103
Rainham Cl. SE9 .... 6J 125
SW11 .... 6C 118
Rainham Ho. *NW1* *1G 83*
(off Bayham Pl.)
Rainham Rd. NW10 .... 3E 80
Rainham Rd. Nth. RM10: Dag 2G 73
Rainham Rd. Sth. RM10: Dag 4H 73
Rainhill Way E3 .... 3C 86
(not continuous)
Rainsborough Av. SE8 .... 4A 104
Rainsford Cl. HA7: Stan 5H 27
Rainsford Rd. NW10 .... 2H 79
Rainsford St. W2 .... 7C 4 (6C 82)
Rainton Rd. SE7 .... 5J 105
Rainville Rd. W6 .... 6E 98
Raisins Hill HA5: Eastc 3A 40
Raith Av. N14 .... 3C 32
Raleana Rd. E14 .... 1E 104
Raleigh Av. SM6: Bedd 4H 167
UB4: Yead 5K 75
Raleigh Cl. HA4: Ruis 2H 57
HA5: Pinn 7B 40
NW4 .... 5E 44
Raleigh Ct. BR3: Beck 1D 158
SE16 .... *1K 103*
(off Clarence M.)
SM6: Wall 6F 167
W12 .... *2E 98*
(off Scott's Rd.)
W13 .... 5B 78
Raleigh Dr. KT5: Surb 1J 163
N20 .... 3H 31
Raleigh Gdns. CR4: Mitc 3D 154
(not continuous)
SW2 .... 6K 119
Raleigh Ho. *BR1: Brom* *1J 159*
(off Hammelton Rd.)
E14 .... *2D 104*
(off Admirals Way)
SW1 .... *7C 18*
(off Dolphin Sq.)
Raleigh M. BR6: Chels 5K 173
N1 .... *1B 84*
(off Packington St.)
Raleigh Rd. EN2: Enf 4J 23
N2 .... 2C 46
N8 .... 4A 48
SE20 .... 7K 139
TW9: Rich 3F 115
TW13: Felt 3H 129
UB2: S'hall 5C 94
Raleigh St. N1 .... 1B 84
Raleigh Way N14 .... 1C 32
TW13: Hanw 5A 130
Ralph Brook Ct. *N1* *1F 9*
(off Chart St.)
Ralph Ct. *W2* *6K 81*
(off Queensway)
Ralph Perring Ct. BR3: Beck 4C 158
Ralston St. SW3 .... 6E 16 (5D 100)
Ramac Ind. Est. SE7 .... 4K 105
Rama Cl. SW16 .... 7J 137
Rama Ct. HA1: Harr 2J 59
Ramac Way SE7 .... 4K 105
Rama La. SE19 .... 7F 139
Ramar Ho. *E1* *5G 85*
(off Hanbury St.)
Rambler Cl. SW16 .... 4G 137
Rame Cl. SW17 .... 5E 136
Ramilles Cl. SW2 .... 6J 119
Ramillies Pl. W1 .... 1A 12 (6G 83)
Ramillies Rd. DA15: Sidc 6B 126
NW7 .... 2F 29
W4 .... 4K 97
Ramillies St. W1 .... 1A 12 (6G 83)
Ramones Ter. *CR4: Mitc* *4J 155*
(off Yorkshire Rd.)
Rampart St. E1 .... 6H 85
Ram Pas. KT1: King T 2D 150
Rampayne St. SW1 .... 5C 18 (5H 101)
Ram Pl. E9 .... 6J 67
Rampton Cl. E4 .... 3H 35
Ramsay Ho. *NW8* *2C 82*
(off Townshend Est.)
Ramsay M. SW3 .... 7C 16 (6C 100)
Ramsay Rd. E7 .... 4G 69
W3 .... 3J 97
Ramscroft Cl. N9 .... 7K 23
Ramsdale Rd. SW17 .... 5E 136
Ramsden Dr. RM5: Col R 1G 55
Ramsden Rd. DA8: Erith 7K 109
N11 .... 5J 31
SW12 .... 6E 118
Ramsey Cl. NW9 .... 6B 44
UB6: G'frd 5H 59
Ramsey Ct. *CR0: Croy* *2B 168*
(off Church St.)
Ramsey Ho. SW9 .... 7A 102
Ramsey Rd. CR7: Thor H 6K 155
Ramsey St. E2 .... 4G 85
Ramsey Wlk. *N1* *6D 66*
(off Handa Wlk.)
Ramsey Way N14 .... 7B 22
Ramsfort Ho. *SE16* *4H 103*
(off Camilla Rd.)
Ramsgate Cl. E16 .... 1K 105
Ramsgate St. E8 .... 6F 67
Ramsgill App. IG2: Ilf 4K 53
Ramsgill Dr. IG2: Ilf 5K 53
Rams Gro. RM6: Chad H 4E 54
Ram St. SW18 .... 5K 117
Ramulis Dr. UB4: Yead 4B 76
Ramuswood Av. BR6: Chels 5J 173
Rancliffe Gdns. SE9 .... 4C 124
Rancliffe Rd. E6 .... 2C 88
Randall Av. NW2 .... 2A 62
Randall Cl. DA8: Erith 6J 109
SW11 .... 1C 118
Randall Ct. NW7 .... 7H 29
Randall Pl. SE10 .... 7E 104
Randall Rd. SE11 .... 4G 19 (5K 101)
Randall Row SE11 .... 4G 19 (4K 101)
Randalls Rents *SE16* *3B 104*
(off Gulliver St.)
Randell's Rd. N1 .... 1J 83
(not continuous)
Randisbourne Gdns. SE6 .... 3D 140
Randle Rd. TW10: Ham 4C 132
Randlesdown Rd. SE6 .... 4C 140
(not continuous)
Randolph App. E16 .... 6A 88
Randolph Av. W9 .... 2K 81
Randolph Cl. DA7: Bex 3J 127
KT2: King T 5J 133
Randolph Cres. W9 .... 4A 82
Randolph Gdns. NW6 .... 2K 81
Randolph Gro. RM6: Chad H 5C 54
Randolph M. W9 .... 4A 82
Randolph Rd. BR2: Brom 1D 172
E17 .... 5D 50
UB1: S'hall 2D 94
W9 .... 4A 82
Randolph St. NW1 .... 7G 65
Randon Cl. HA2: Harr 2F 41
Ranelagh Av. SW6 .... 3H 117
SW13 .... 2C 116
Ranelagh Bri. W2 .... 5K 81
Ranelagh Cl. HA8: Edg 4B 28
Ranelagh Cotts. *SW1* *5H 17*
(off Raneleigh Gro.)
Ranelagh Dr. HA8: Edg 4B 28
TW1: Twick 4B 114
Ranelagh Gdns. E11 .... 5A 52
IG1: Ilf 1D 70
SW6 .... 3G 117
(not continuous)
W4 .... 7J 97
W6 .... 4B 98
Ranelagh Gdns. Mans. *SW6* *3G 117*
(off Ranelagh Gdns.)
Ranelagh Gro. SW1 .... 5H 17 (5E 100)
Ranelagh Ho. *SW3* *5E 16*
(off Elystan Pl.)
Ranelagh M. W5 .... 2D 96
Ranelagh Pl. KT3: N Mald 5A 152
Ranelagh Rd. E6 .... 1E 88
E11 .... 4G 69
E15 .... 2G 87

Ranelagh Rd. HA0: Wemb	6D **60**
N17	3E **48**
N22	1K **47**
NW10	2B **80**
SW1	6B **18** (5G **101**)
UB1: S'hall	1B **94**
W5	2D **96**
Ranfurly Rd. SM1: Sutt	2J **165**
Rangbourne Ho. N7	5J **65**
Rangefield Rd. BR1: Brom	5G **141**
Rangemoor Rd. N15	5F **49**
Rangers House	1F **123**
Ranger's Rd. E4	1B **36**
Rangers Sq. SE10	1F **123**
Range Way TW17: Shep	7C **146**
Rangeworth Pl. DA15: Sidc	3K **143**
Rangoon St. EC3	1J **15**
Rankin Cl. NW9	3A **44**
Rankine Ho. SE1	3C **102**
(off Bath Ter.)	
Ranleigh Gdns. DA7: Bex	7F **109**
Ranmere St. SW12	1F **137**
Ranmoor Cl. HA1: Harr	4H **41**
Ranmoor Gdns. HA1: Harr	4H **41**
Ranmore Av. CR0: Croy	3F **169**
Ranmore Path BR5: St M Cry	4K **161**
Ranmore Rd. SM2: Cheam	7F **165**
Rannoch Cl. HA8: Edg	2C **28**
Rannoch Rd. W6	6E **98**
Rannock Av. NW9	7K **43**
Ransome's Dock Bus. Cen.	
SW11	7C **100**
Ransom Rd. SE7	4A **106**
Ranston St. NW1	5C **4** (5C **82**)
Ranulf Rd. NW2	4H **63**
Ranwell Cl. E3	1B **86**
Ranworth Rd. N9	2D **34**
Ranyard Cl. KT9: Chess	3F **163**
Raphael Ct. SE16	5H **103**
(off Stubbs Dr.)	
Raphael Dr. KT7: T Ditt	7K **149**
Raphael St. SW7	7E **10** (2D **100**)
Rapley Ho. E2	2K **9**
(off Turin St.)	
Raquel Ct. SE1	6G **15**
(off Snowfields)	
Rashleigh Ct. SW8	2F **119**
Rashleigh Ho. WC1	2E **6**
(off Thanet St.)	
Rasper Rd. N20	2F **31**
Rastell Av. SW2	2H **137**
RATCLIFF	5A **86**
Ratcliffe Cl. SE12	7J **123**
Ratcliffe Ct. SE1	7D **14**
(off Gt. Dover St.)	
Ratcliffe Cross St. E1	6K **85**
Ratcliffe Ho. E14	6A **86**
Ratcliffe La. E14	6A **86**
Ratcliffe Orchard E1	7K **85**
Ratcliff Rd. E7	5A **70**
Rathbone Ho. E16	6H **87**
(off Rathbone St.)	
NW6	1J **81**
Rathbone Mkt. E16	5H **87**
Rathbone Pl. W1	6C **6** (5H **83**)
Rathbone Sq. CR0: Croy	4C **168**
Rathbone St. E16	5H **87**
W1	6B **6** (5G **83**)
Rathcoole Av. N8	5K **47**
Rathcoole Gdns. N8	5K **47**
Rathfern Rd. SE6	1B **140**
Rathgar Av. W13	1B **96**
Rathgar Cl. N3	2H **45**
Rathgar Rd. SW9	3B **120**
Rathmell Dr. SW4	6H **119**
Rathmore Rd. SE7	5K **105**
Rattray Ct. SE6	2H **141**
Rattray Rd. SW2	4A **120**
Raul Rd. SE15	2G **121**
Raveley St. NW5	4G **65**
(not continuous)	
Raven Cl. NW9	2A **44**
Ravendale Rd. TW16: Sun	2H **147**

Ravenet St. SW11	1F **119**
(not continuous)	
Ravenfield Rd. SW17	3D **136**
Ravenhill Rd. E13	2A **88**
Raven Ho. SE16	4K **103**
(off Tawny Way)	
Ravenings Pde. IG3: Ilf	1A **72**
Ravenna Rd. SW15	5F **117**
Ravenor Cl. UB6: G'frd	4F **77**
Ravenor Farm	3G **77**
Ravenor Pk. Rd. UB6: G'frd	3F **77**
Raven Rd. E18	2A **52**
Raven Row E1	5H **85**
(not continuous)	
Ravensbourne Av. BR2: Brom	7F **141**
TW19: Stanw	1A **128**
Ravensbourne Ct. SE6	7C **122**
Ravensbourne Gdns. IG5: Ilf	1E **52**
W13	5B **78**
Ravensbourne Ho. BR1: Brom	5F **141**
NW8	5C **4**
(off Broadley St.)	
Ravensbourne Mans. SE8	6C **104**
(off Berthon St.)	
Ravensbourne Pk. SE6	7C **122**
Ravensbourne Pk. Cres. SE6	7B **122**
Ravensbourne Pl. SE13	2D **122**
Ravensbourne Rd. BR1: Brom	3J **159**
SE6	7B **122**
TW1: Twick	6C **114**
Ravensbourne Ter. TW19: Stanw	1A **128**
Ravensbury Av. SM4: Mord	5A **154**
Ravensbury Ct. CR4: Mitc	4B **154**
(off Ravensbury Gro.)	
Ravensbury Gro. CR4: Mitc	4B **154**
Ravensbury La. CR4: Mitc	4B **154**
Ravensbury Path CR4: Mitc	4B **154**
Ravensbury Rd. BR5: St P	3K **161**
SW18	2J **135**
Ravensbury Ter. SW18	2K **135**
Ravenscar NW1	1G **83**
(off Bayham St.)	
Ravenscar Rd. BR1: Brom	4G **141**
KT6: Surb	2F **163**
Ravens Cl. BR2: Brom	2H **159**
EN1: Enf	2K **23**
KT6: Surb	6D **150**
Ravens Ct. KT1: King T	5D **150**
(off Uxbridge Rd.)	
Ravenscourt TW16: Sun	1H **147**
Ravenscourt Av. W6	4C **98**
Ravenscourt Cl. HA4: Ruis	7E **38**
Ravenscourt Gdns. W6	4C **98**
Ravenscourt Pk. EN5: Barn	4A **20**
W6	3C **98**
Ravenscourt Pk. Mans. W6	3D **98**
(off Paddenswick Rd.)	
Ravenscourt Pl. W6	4D **98**
Ravenscourt Rd. W6	4D **98**
(not continuous)	
Ravenscourt Sq. W6	3C **98**
Ravenscraig Rd. N11	4A **32**
Ravenscroft Av. HA9: Wemb	1E **60**
NW11	7H **45**
(not continuous)	
Ravenscroft Cl. E16	5J **87**
Ravenscroft Cotts. EN5: New Bar	4D **20**
Ravenscroft Cres. SE9	3D **142**
Ravenscroft Pk. EN5: Barn	3A **20**
Ravenscroft Rd. BR3: Beck	2J **157**
E16	5J **87**
W4	4J **97**
Ravenscroft School Sports Cen.	
London	7C **20**
(off Barnet La.)	
Ravenscroft St. E2	1K **9** (2F **85**)
Ravensdale Av. N12	4F **31**
Ravensdale Gdns. SE19	7D **138**
Ravensdale Mans. N8	6J **47**
(off Haringey Pk.)	
Ravensdale Rd. N16	7F **49**
TW4: Houn	3C **112**
Ravensdon St. SE11	6K **19** (5A **102**)

Ravensfield Cl. RM9: Dag	4D **72**
Ravensfield Gdns. KT19: Ewe	5A **164**
Ravenshaw St. NW6	5H **63**
Ravenshill BR7: Chst	1F **161**
Ravenshurst Av. NW4	4E **44**
Ravenside KT1: King T	5D **150**
(off Portsmouth Rd.)	
Ravenside Cl. N18	5E **34**
Ravenside Retail Pk. N18	5E **34**
Ravenslea Rd. SW12	7D **118**
Ravensleigh Gdns. BR1: Brom	5K **141**
Ravensmead Rd. BR2: Brom	7F **141**
Ravensmede Way W4	4B **98**
Ravens M. SE12	5J **123**
Ravenstone SE17	5E **102**
Ravenstone Rd. N8	3A **48**
NW9	6B **44**
Ravenstone St. SW12	1E **136**
Ravens Way SE12	5J **123**
Ravenswood DA5: Bexl	1E **144**
Ravenswood Av. BR4: W W'ck	1E **170**
KT6: Surb	2F **163**
Ravenswood Cres. BR4: W W'ck	1E **170**
HA2: Harr	2D **58**
Ravenswood Gdns. TW7: Isle	1J **113**
Ravenswood Ind. Est. E17	4E **50**
Ravenswood Rd. CR0: Wadd	3B **168**
E17	4E **50**
SW12	7F **119**
Ravensworth Ct. SW6	7J **99**
(off Fulham Rd.)	
Ravensworth Rd. NW10	3D **80**
SE9	3D **142**
Ravent Rd. SE11	3H **19** (4K **101**)
Raven Wharf SE1	6J **15**
(off Lafone St.)	
Ravey St. EC2	3G **9** (4E **84**)
Ravine Gro. SE18	6J **107**
Rav Pinter Cl. N16	7E **48**
Rawalpindi Ho. E16	4H **87**
Rawchester Cl. SW18	1H **135**
Rawlings Cl. BR3: Beck	5E **158**
BR6: Chels	5K **173**
Rawlings Cres. HA9: Wemb	3H **61**
Rawlings St. SW3	3E **16** (4D **100**)
Rawlins Cl. CR2: Sels	7A **170**
N3	3G **45**
Rawlinson Ct. NW2	7E **44**
Rawlinson Ho. SE13	4F **123**
(off Mercator Rd.)	
Rawlinson Point E16	5H **87**
(off Fox Rd.)	
Rawnsley Av. CR4: Mitc	5B **154**
Rawreth Wlk. N1	1C **84**
(off Basire St.)	
Rawson St. SW11	1E **118**
(not continuous)	
Rawsthorne Cl. E16	1D **106**
Rawsthorne Ct. TW4: Houn	4D **112**
Rawstone Wlk. E13	2J **87**
Rawstorne Pl. EC1	1A **8** (3B **84**)
Rawstorne St. EC1	1A **8** (3B **84**)
(not continuous)	
Raybell Ct. TW7: Isle	2K **113**
Rayburne Ct. IG9: Buck H	1F **37**
W14	3G **99**
Ray Cl. KT9: Chess	6C **162**
Raydean Rd. EN5: New Bar	5E **20**
Raydons Gdns. RM9: Dag	4E **72**
Raydons Rd. RM9: Dag	5E **72**
Raydon St. N19	2F **65**
Rayfield Cl. BR2: Brom	6C **160**
Rayford Av. SE12	7H **123**
Ray Gdns. HA7: Stan	5G **27**
IG11: Bark	2A **90**
Ray Gunter Ho. SE17	5B **102**
(off Marsland Cl.)	
Ray Ho. N1	1E **84**
(off Colville St.)	
W10	6F **81**
(off Cambridge Gdns.)	
Rayleas Cl. SE18	1F **125**

Rayleigh Av. TW11: Tedd	6J **131**
Rayleigh Cl. N13	3J **33**
Rayleigh Ct. KT1: King T	2G **151**
N22	1C **48**
Rayleigh Ri. CR2: S Croy	6E **168**
Rayleigh Rd. E16	1K **105**
IG8: Wfd G	6F **37**
N13	3H **33**
SW19	1H **153**
Ray Lodge Rd. IG8: Wfd G	6F **37**
Ray Massey Way E6	1C **88**
(off High St. Nth.)	
Raymead Av. CR7: Thor H	5A **156**
Raymead Pas. CR7: Thor H	5A **156**
(off Raymead Av.)	
Raymede Towers W10	5F **81**
(off Treverton St.)	
Raymere Gdns. SE18	7H **107**
Raymond Av. E18	3H **51**
W13	3A **96**
Raymond Bldgs. WC1	5H **7** (5K **83**)
Raymond Cl. SE26	5J **139**
Raymond Ct. N10	7A **32**
Raymond Postgate Ct. SE28	7B **90**
Raymond Rd. BR3: Beck	4A **158**
E13	1A **88**
IG2: Ilf	7H **53**
SW19	6G **135**
Raymond Way KT10: Clay	6A **162**
Raymouth Rd. SE16	4H **103**
Raynald Ho. SW16	3J **137**
Rayne Ct. E18	4H **51**
Rayne Ho. SW12	6E **118**
W9	4K **81**
(off Delaware Rd.)	
Rayner Ct. W12	2E **98**
(off Bamborough Gdns.)	
Rayners Cl. HA0: Wemb	5D **60**
Rayners Cres. UB5: Yead	3K **75**
Rayners Gdns. UB5: Yead	2K **75**
RAYNERS LANE	1D **58**
Rayners La. HA2: Harr	1E **58**
HA5: Pinn	5D **40**
Rayners Rd. SW15	5G **117**
Rayner Towers E10	7C **50**
(off Albany Rd.)	
Raynes Av. E11	7A **52**
RAYNES PARK	4E **152**
Raynes Pk. Bri. SW20	2E **152**
Raynes Pk. School Sports Cen.	3D **152**
Raynham W2	7D **4**
(off Norfolk Cres.)	
Raynham Av. N18	6B **34**
Raynham Ho. E1	4K **85**
(off Harpley Sq.)	
Raynham Rd. N18	5B **34**
W6	4D **98**
Raynham Ter. N18	5B **34**
Raynor Cl. UB1: S'hall	1D **94**
Raynor Pl. N1	7C **66**
Raynton Cl. HA2: Harr	1C **58**
UB4: Hayes	4H **75**
Raynton Dr. UB4: Hayes	4H **75**
Ray Rd. KT8: W Mole	5F **149**
Rays Av. N18	4D **34**
Rays Rd. BR4: W W'ck	7E **158**
N18	4D **34**
Ray St. EC1	4K **7** (4A **84**)
Ray St. Bri. EC1	4K **7**
Ray Wlk. N7	2K **65**
Raywood Cl. UB3: Harl	7E **92**
Razia M. E12	5D **70**
Reachview Cl. NW1	7G **65**
Read Cl. KT7: T Ditt	7A **150**
Read Ct. E17	6C **50**
Reade Ct. W3	3J **97**
(off Stanley Rd.)	
Reade Ho. SE10	6H **105**
(off Trafalgar Gro.)	
Reade Wlk. NW10	7A **62**
Read Ho. SE11	7J **19**
Reading Ho. SE15	6G **103**
(off Friary Est.)	

Reading Ho. *W2* 6A **82**
(off Hallfield Est.)
Reading La. E8 6H **67**
Reading Rd. SM1: Sutt 5A **166**
UB5: N'olt 5F **59**
Reading Way NW7 5A **30**
Readman Ct. SE20 1H **157**
Reads Cl. IG1: Ilf 3F **71**
Reapers Cl. NW1 1H **83**
Reapers Way TW7: Isle 5H **113**
Reardon Ct. N21 2G **33**
Reardon Ho. *E1* *1H 103*
(off Reardon St.)
Reardon Path E1 1H **103**
(not continuous)
Reardon St. E1 1H **103**
Reaston St. SE14 7K **103**
Rebecca Ct. DA14: Sidc 4B **144**
Reckitt Rd. W4 5A **98**
Record St. SE15 6J **103**
Recovery St. SW17 5C **136**
Recreation Av. RM7: Rom 5J **55**
Recreation Rd. BR2: Brom 2H **159**
DA15: Sidc 3J **143**
SE26 4K **139**
UB2: S'hall 4C **94**
Recreation Way CR4: Mitc 3H **155**
Rector St. N1 1C **84**
Rectory Bus. Cen. DA14: Sidc 4B **144**
Rectory Chambers *SW3* *6C 100*
(off Old Church St.)
Rectory Cl. DA14: Sidc 4B **144**
E4 3H **35**
HA7: Stan 5G **27**
KT6: Surb 1C **162**
N3 1H **45**
SW20 3E **152**
TW17: Shep 3C **146**
Rectory Ct. E18 1H **51**
SM6: Wall 4G **167**
TW13: Felt 4A **130**
Rectory Cres. E11 6A **52**
(not continuous)
Rectory Farm Rd. EN2: Enf 1E **22**
Rectory Fld. Cres. SE7 7A **106**
Rectory Gdns. *BR3: Beck* *1C 158*
(off Rectory Rd.)
N8 4J **47**
SW4 3G **119**
UB5: N'olt 1D **76**
Rectory Grn. BR3: Beck 1B **158**
Rectory Gro. CR0: Croy 2B **168**
SW4 3G **119**
TW12: Hamp 4D **130**
Rectory La. DA14: Sidc 4B **144**
HA7: Stan 5G **27**
HA8: Edg 6B **28**
KT6: Surb 1B **162**
SM6: Wall 4G **167**
SW17 6E **136**
Rectory Orchard SW19 4G **135**
Rectory Pk. Av. UB5: N'olt 3D **76**
Rectory Pl. SE18 4E **106**
Rectory Rd. BR2: Kes 7B **172**
BR3: Beck 1C **158**
E12 5D **70**
E17 4D **50**
N16 2F **67**
RM10: Dag 6H **73**
SM1: Sutt 3J **165**
SW13 2C **116**
TW4: Cran 2A **112**
UB2: S'hall 3D **94**
UB3: Hayes 6J **75**
W3 1H **97**
Rectory Sq. E1 5K **85**
Rectory Way UB10: Ick 2D **56**
Reculver Ho. *SE15* *6J 103*
(off Lovelinch Cl.)
Reculver M. N18 4B **34**
Reculver Rd. SE16 5K **103**
Red Anchor Cl. SW3 6B **100**
Redan Pl. W2 6K **81**
Redan St. W14 3F **99**
Redan Ter. SE5 2B **120**
Red Barracks Rd. SE18 4D **106**
Redberry Gro. SE26 3J **139**
Redbourne Av. N3 1J **45**
Redbourne Dr. SE28 6D **90**
(not continuous)
Redbourne Ho. *E14* *6B 86*
(off Norbiton Rd.)
Redbourn Ho. *W10* *4E 80*
(off Sutton Way)
REDBRIDGE 6C **52**
Redbridge Ent. Cen. IG1: Ilf 2G **71**
Redbridge FC 4H **53**
Redbridge Foyer *IG1: Ilf* *2G 71*
(off Sylvan Rd.)
Redbridge Gdns. SE5 7E **102**
Redbridge La. E. IG4: Ilf 6B **52**
Redbridge La. W. E11 6K **51**
REDBRIDGE RDBT. 6B **52**
Redbridge Sports Cen. 1H **53**
Redburn St. SW3 7E **16** (6D **100**)
Redburn Trad. Est. EN3: Pond E 6E **24**
Redcar Cl. UB5: N'olt 5F **59**
Redcar St. SE5 7C **102**
Redcastle Cl. E1 7J **85**
Red Cedars Rd. BR6: Orp 7J **161**
Redchurch St. E2 3J **9** (4F **85**)
Redcliffe Cl. *SW5* *5K 99*
(off Old Brompton Rd.)
Redcliffe Ct. *E5* *3H 67*
(off Napoleon Rd.)
Redcliffe Gdns. IG1: Ilf 1E **70**
SW10 5K **99**
W4 7H **97**
Redcliffe M. SW10 5K **99**
Redcliffe Pl. SW10 6A **100**
Redcliffe Rd. SW10 5A **100**
Redcliffe Sq. SW10 5K **99**
Redcliffe St. SW10 6K **99**
Redclose Av. SM4: Mord 5J **153**
Redclyffe Rd. E6 1A **88**
Redclyf Ho. *E1* *4J 85*
(off Cephas St.)
Redcourt CR0: Croy 3E **168**
Red Cow La. EC1 3C **8** (4C **84**)
Redcroft Rd. UB1: S'hall 7G **77**
Redcross Way SE1 6D **14** (2C **102**)
Redding Ho. SE18 3C **106**
Reddings, The NW7 3G **29**
Reddings Cl. NW7 4G **29**
Reddins Rd. SE15 6G **103**
Reddons Rd. BR3: Beck 7A **140**
Redenham Ho. *SW15* *7C 116*
(off Ellisfield Dr.)
Rede Pl. W2 6J **81**
Redesdale Gdns. TW7: Isle 7A **96**
Redesdale St. SW3 7D **16** (6C **100**)
Redfern Av. TW4: Houn 7E **112**
Redfern Ho. *E13* *1H 87*
(off Redriffe Rd.)
Redfern Rd. NW10 7A **62**
SE6 7E **122**
Redfield La. SW5 4J **99**
Redfield M. SW5 4K **99**
Redford Av. CR7: Thor H 4K **155**
SM6: Wall 6J **167**
Redford Cl. TW13: Felt 2H **129**
Redford Ho. *W10* *3H 81*
(off Dowland St.)
Redford Wlk. *N1* *1C 84*
(off Popham St.)
Redgate Dr. BR2: Hayes 2K **171**
Redgate Ter. SW15 6F **117**
Redgrave Cl. CR0: Croy 6F **157**
Redgrave Rd. SW15 3F **117**
Redgrave Ter. *E2* *3G 85*
(off Derbyshire St.)
Red Hill BR7: Chst 5F **143**
Redhill Ct. SW2 2A **138**
Redhill Dr. HA8: Edg 2H **43**
Redhill St. NW1 1K **5** (2F **83**)
Red House 4E **126**
Red Ho. La. DA6: Bex 4D **126**
Redhouse Rd. CR0: Croy 6H **155**
Red Ho. Sq. N1 6C **66**
Redif Ho. RM10: Dag 4H **73**
Redington Gdns. NW3 4K **63**
Redington Ho. *N1* *2K 83*
(off Priory Grn. Est.)
Redington Rd. NW3 3K **63**
Redknap Ho. TW10: Ham 3C **132**
Redland Gdns.
KT8: W Mole 4D **148**
Redlands N15 4D **48**
TW11: Tedd 6A **132**
Redlands, The BR3: Beck 2D **158**
Redlands Ct. BR1: Brom 7H **141**
Redlands Rd. EN3: Enf H 1F **25**
Redlands Way SW2 7K **119**
Red La. KT10: Clay 6A **162**
Redleaf Cl. DA17: Belv 6G **109**
Redleaves Av. TW15: Ashf 6D **128**
Redlees Cl. TW7: Isle 4A **114**
Red Leys UB8: Uxb 7A **56**
Red Lion Bus. Pk. KT6: Surb 3F **163**
Red Lion Cl. *SE17* *6D 102*
(off Red Lion Row)
Red Lion Ct. EC4 1K **13** (6A **84**)
SE1 4D **14** (1C **102**)
Red Lion Hill N2 2B **46**
(not continuous)
Red Lion La. SE18 7E **106**
Red Lion Pde. HA5: Pinn 3C **40**
Red Lion Pl. SE18 1E **124**
Red Lion Rd. KT6: Surb 2F **163**
Red Lion Row SE17 6C **102**
Red Lion Sq. SW18 5J **117**
WC1 6G **7** (5K **83**)
Red Lion St. TW9: Rich 5D **114**
WC1 5G **7** (5K **83**)
Red Lion Yd. W1 4H **11**
Red Lodge BR4: W W'ck 1E **170**
Red Lodge Cres. DA5: Bexl 3K **145**
Red Lodge Rd. BR4: W W'ck 1E **170**
DA5: Bexl 3K **145**
Redlynch Ct. *W14* *2G 99*
(off Addison Cres.)
Redman Cl. UB5: Yead 2A **76**
Redman Ho. *EC1* *5J 7*
(off Bourne Est.)
SE1 *7D 14*
(off Borough High St.)
Redman's Rd. E1 5J **85**
Redmead La. E1 1G **103**
Redmead Rd. UB3: Harl 4G **93**
Redmill Ho. *E1* *4H 85*
(off Headlam St.)
Redmond Ho. *N1* *1K 83*
(off Barnsbury Est.)
Redmore Rd. W6 4D **98**
Red Oak Cl. BR6: Farnb 3F **173**
Redo Ho. *E12* *5E 70*
(off Dore Av.)
Red Path E9 6A **68**
Red Pl. W1 2G **11** (7E **82**)
Redpoll Way DA18: Erith 3D **108**
Red Post Hill SE21 4D **120**
SE24 4D **120**
Red Post Ho. E6 7B **70**
Redriffe Rd. E13 1H **87**
Redriff Est. SE16 3B **104**
Redriff Rd. RM7: Mawney 2H **55**
SE16 4K **103**
Redroofs Cl. BR3: Beck 1D **158**
Redrose Trad. Cen. EN4: E Barn 5G **21**
RED ROVER 4C **116**
Redrup Ho. *SE14* *6K 103*
(off John Williams Cl.)
Redruth Cl. N22 7E **32**
Redruth Gdns. KT10: Clay 7A **162**
Redruth Ho. SM2: Sutt 7K **165**
Redruth Rd. E9 1J **85**
Redshank Ho. *SE1* *5F 103*
(off Avocet Cl.)
Red Sq. N16 3D **66**
Redstart Cl. E6 5C **88**
SE14 7A **104**
Redston Rd. N8 4H **47**
Redvers Rd. N22 2A **48**
Redvers St. N1 1H **9** (3E **84**)
Redwald Rd. E5 4K **67**
Redway Dr. TW2: Whit 7G **113**
Redwing Ct. *SE1* *7D 14*
(off Swan St.)
Redwing M. SE5 2C **120**
Redwing Path SE28 2H **107**
Redwing Rd. SM6: Wall 7J **167**
Redwood Cl. DA15: Sidc 1A **144**
E3 2C **86**
IG9: Buck H 2E **36**
N14 7C **22**
SE16 1A **104**
UB10: Hil 2D **74**
Redwood Ct. KT6: Surb 7D **150**
N19 7H **47**
NW6 7G **63**
UB5: N'olt 3C **76**
Redwood Est. TW5: Cran 6K **93**
Redwood Gdns. E4 6J **25**
Redwood Gro. W5 3B **96**
Redwood Mans. *W8* *3K 99*
(off Chantry Sq.)
Redwood M. SW4 3F **119**
TW15: Ashf *7F 129*
(off Staines Rd. W.)
Redwoods SW15 1C **134**
Redwood Wlk. KT6: Surb 1D **162**
Redwood Way EN5: Barn 5A **20**
Reece M. SW7 3A **16** (4B **100**)
Reed Av. BR6: Orp 3J **173**
Reed Cl. E16 5J **87**
SE12 5J **123**
Reede Gdns. RM10: Dag 5H **73**
Reede Rd. RM10: Dag 6G **73**
Reede Way RM10: Dag 6H **73**
Reedham Cl. N17 4H **49**
Reedham St. SE15 2G **121**
Reedholm Vs. N16 4D **66**
Reed Rd. N17 2F **49**
Reedsfield Cl. TW15: Ashf 3D **128**
Reedsfield Rd. TW15: Ashf 4D **128**
Reed's Pl. NW1 7G **65**
Reedworth St. SE11 4K **19** (4A **102**)
Reef Ho. *E14* *3E 104*
(off Manchester St.)
Reenglass Rd. HA7: Stan 4J **27**
Rees Dr. HA7: Stan 4K **27**
Rees Gdns. CR0: Croy 6F **157**
Reesland Cl. E12 6E **70**
Rees St. N1 1C **84**
Reets Farm Cl. NW9 6A **44**
Reeves Av. NW9 7K **43**
Reeves Cnr. CR0: Croy 2B **168**
Reeves Ho. *SE1* *7J 13*
(off Baylis Rd.)
Reeves M. W1 3G **11** (7E **82**)
Reeves Rd. E3 4D **86**
SE18 6F **107**
Reflection, The *E16* *2F 107*
(off Woolwich Mnr. Way)
Reflection Ho. *E2* *4G 85*
(off Cheshire St.)
Reflex Apartments *BR2: Brom* *4K 159*
(off Wheeler Pl.)
Reform Row N17 2F **49**
Reform St. SW11 2D **118**
Regal Cl. E1 5G **85**
W5 5D **78**
Regal Ct. N18 5A **34**
NW6 *2H 81*
(off Malvern Rd.)
Regal Cres. SM6: Wall 3F **167**
Regal Dr. N11 5A **32**
Regal Ho. IG2: Ilf 6H **53**
Regal La. NW1 1E **82**
Regal Pl. E3 3B **86**
SW6 7K **99**
Regal Row SE15 1J **121**

Regal Way HA3: Kent 6E 42
Regan Ho. N18 . . . . 6A 34
Regan Way N1 . . . . 1G 9 (2E 84)
Regatta Ho. TW11: Tedd 4A 132
Regatta Point *E14* *2C 104*
(off Westferry Rd.)
TW8: Bford 6F 97
Regency Cl. TW12: Hamp 5D 130
W5 . . . . 6E 78
Regency Ct. E18 . . . . 2J 51
EN1: Enf 5J 23
SM1: Sutt 4A 166
TW11: Tedd 6B 132
Regency Cres. NW4 . . . . 2F 45
Regency Dr. HA4: Ruis 1G 57
Regency Gdns. KT12: Walt T 7A 148
Regency Ho. *E16* *1J 105*
(off Pepys Cres.)
NW1 . . . . *3K 5*
(off Osnaburgh St.)
SW1 . . . . *3D 18*
(off Regency St.)
Regency Lawn NW5 . . . . 3F 65
Regency Lodge IG9: Buck H 2G 37
NW3 . . . . *7B 64*
(off Adelaide Rd.)
Regency M. BR3: Beck 7E 140
NW10 . . . . 6C 62
SW9 . . . . 7B 102
TW7: Isle 5J 113
Regency Pde. *NW3* *7B 64*
(off Finchley Rd.)
Regency Pl. SW1 . . . . 3D 18 (4H 101)
Regency St. NW10 . . . . 4A 80
SW1 . . . . 3D 18 (4H 101)
Regency Ter. *SW7* *5A 16*
(off Fulham Rd.)
Regency Wlk. CR0: Croy 6B 158
TW10: Rich *5E 114*
(off Grosvenor Av.)
TW10: Rich *5E 114*
(off The Vineyard)
Regency Way DA6: Bex 3D 126
Regent Av. UB10: Hil 7D 56
Regent Bus. Cen. UB3: Hayes 2K 93
Regent Cl. HA3: Kent 6E 42
N12 . . . . 5F 31
TW4: Cran 1K 111
Regent Ct. N3 . . . . 7E 30
N20 . . . . 2F 31
NW8 . . . . 2C 4
W8 . . . . *3K 99*
(off Wright's La.)
Regent Gdns. IG3: Ilf 7A 54
Regent Ho. *W14* *4G 99*
(off Windsor Way)
Regent Pde. SM2: Sutt 6A 166
Regent Pl. CR0: Croy 1F 169
SW19 . . . . 5A 136
W1 . . . . 2B 12 (7G 83)
Regent Rd. KT5: Surb 5F 151
SE24 . . . . 6B 120
Regents Av. N13 . . . . 5F 33
Regent's Bri. Gdns. SW8 . . . . 7J 101
Regents Canal Ho. *E14* *6A 86*
(off Commercial Rd.)
Regents Cl. CR2: S Croy 6E 168
HA8: Edg 4K 27
UB4: Hayes 5H 75
Regents College 3F 5
Regents Ct. BR1: Brom 7H 141
E8 . . . . *1F 85*
(off Pownall Rd.)
HA5: Pinn 2B 40
KT2: King T *1E 150*
(off Sopwith Way)
Regents Dr. BR2: Kes 5B 172
IG8: Wfd G 6K 37
Regents Ga. Ho. *E14* *7A 86*
(off Horseferry Rd.)
Regents M. NW8 . . . . 2A 82
REGENT'S PARK 2K 5 (3F 83)
Regent's Pk. 1F 5 (2D 82)
Regent's Pk. Barracks 1K 5
Regents Pk. Est. NW1 . . . . 1A 6
Regent's Pk. Gdns. M. NW1 . . . . 1D 82
Regents Pk. Golf & Tennis School 2D 82
Regent's Pk. Ho. *NW8* *2D 4*
(off Park Rd.)
Regent's Pk. Open Air Theatre
. . . . 2G 5 (3E 82)
Regents Pk. Rd. N3 . . . . 3H 45
NW1 . . . . 7D 64
(not continuous)
Regent's Pk. Ter. NW1 . . . . 1F 83
Regent's Pl. SE3 . . . . 2J 123
Regents Plaza *NW6* *2K 81*
(off Kilburn High Rd.)
Regent Sq. DA17: Belv 4H 109
E3 . . . . 3D 86
WC1 . . . . 2F 7 (3J 83)
Regent's Row E8 . . . . 1G 85
Regent St. NW10 . . . . 3F 81
SW1 . . . . 3C 12 (7H 83)
W1 . . . . 7K 5 (6F 83)
W4 . . . . 5G 97
Regents Wharf *E2* *1H 85*
(off Wharf Pl.)
N1 . . . . 2K 83
Regina Cl. EN5: Barn 3A 20
Regina Ho. SE20 . . . . 1K 157
Reginald Pl. *SE8* *7C 104*
(off Deptford High St.)
Reginald Rd. E7 . . . . 7J 69
HA6: Nwood 1H 39
SE8 . . . . 7C 104
Reginald Sorenson Ho. E11 . . . . 7F 51
Reginald Sq. SE8 . . . . 7C 104
Regina Point SE16 . . . . 3J 103
Regina Rd. N4 . . . . 1K 65
SE25 . . . . 3G 157
UB2: S'hall 4C 94
W13 . . . . 1A 96
Regina Ter. W13 . . . . 1B 96
Regis Ct. CR4: Mitc 1C 154
N8 . . . . 4K 47
NW1 . . . . *5E 4*
(off Melcombe Pl.)
Regis Ho. *W1* *5H 5*
(off Beaumont St.)
Regis Pl. SW2 . . . . 4K 119
Regis Rd. NW5 . . . . 5F 65
Regnart Bldgs. NW1 . . . . 3B 6
Regnolruf Ct. KT12: Walt T 7J 147
Reid Cl. HA5: Eastc 4J 39
Reidhaven Rd. SE18 . . . . 4J 107
Reigate Av. SM1: Sutt 1J 165
Reigate Rd. BR1: Brom 3H 141
IG3: Ilf 2K 71
Reigate Way SM6: Wall 5J 167
Reighton Rd. E5 . . . . 3G 67
Reinickendorf Av. SE9 . . . . 6G 125
Reizel Cl. N16 . . . . 1F 67
Relay Rd. W12 . . . . 1E 98
Relf Rd. SE15 . . . . 3G 121
Reliance Arc. SW9 . . . . 4A 120
Reliance Sq. EC2 . . . . 3H 9 (4E 84)
Relko Gdns. SM1: Sutt 5B 166
Relton M. SW7 . . . . 1D 16 (3C 100)
Rembold Ho. *SE10* *1E 122*
(off Blissett St.)
Rembrandt Cl. E14 . . . . 3F 105
SW1 . . . . 4G 17
Rembrandt Ct. KT19: Ewe 6B 164
SE16 . . . . *5H 103*
(off Stubbs Dr.)
Rembrandt Rd.
HA8: Edg 2G 43
SE13 . . . . 4G 123
Remembrance Rd. E7 . . . . 4B 70
Remington Rd. E6 . . . . 6C 88
N15 . . . . 6D 48
Remington St. N1 . . . . 1B 8 (2B 84)
Remnant St. WC2 . . . . 7G 7 (6K 83)
Remsted Ho. *NW6* *1K 81*
(off Mortimer Cres.)
Remus Bldg., The *EC1* *2K 7*
(off Hardwick St.)
Remus Rd. E3 . . . . 7C 68
Renaissance Ct. SM5: Sutt 1A 166
Renaissance Wlk. *SE10* *3H 105*
(off Teal St.)
Rendle Cl. CR0: Croy 5F 157
Rendle Ho. *W10* *4G 81*
(off Wornington Rd.)
Rendlesham Rd. E5 . . . . 4G 67
EN2: Enf 1G 23
Renforth St. SE16 . . . . 3J 103
Renfree Way TW17: Shep 7C 146
Renfrew Cl. E6 . . . . 7E 88
Renfrew Ct. TW4: Houn 2C 112
Renfrew Ho. E17 . . . . 2B 50
NW6 . . . . *2K 81*
(off Carlton Va.)
Renfrew Rd. KT2: King T 7H 133
SE11 . . . . 3K 19 (4B 102)
TW4: Houn 2B 112
Renmuir St. SW17 . . . . 6D 136
Rennell St. SE13 . . . . 3E 122
Rennels Way TW7: Isle 2J 113
Renness Rd. E17 . . . . 3A 50
Rennets Cl. SE9 . . . . 5J 125
Rennets Wood Rd. SE9 . . . . 5H 125
Rennie Cotts. *E1* *4J 85*
(off Pemell Cl.)
Rennie Ct. SE1 . . . . 4A 14
Rennie Est. SE16 . . . . 4H 103
Rennie Ho. *SE1* *3C 102*
(off Bath Ter.)
Rennie St. SE1 . . . . 4A 14 (1B 102)
(not continuous)
Renoir Cinema 3F 7 (4J 83)
Renoir Ct. *SE16* *5H 103*
(off Stubbs Dr.)
Renovation, The *E16* *2F 107*
(off Woolwich Mnr. Way)
Renown Cl. CR0: Croy 1B 168
RM7: Mawney 1G 55
Rensburg Rd. E17 . . . . 5K 49
Renshaw Cl. DA17: Belv 6F 109
Renters Av. NW4 . . . . 6E 44
Renton Cl. SW2 . . . . 6K 119
Renwick Ind. Est. IG11: Bark 2B 90
Renwick Rd. IG11: Bark 4B 90
Repens Way UB4: Yead 4B 76
Rephidim St. SE1 . . . . 3E 102
Replingham Rd. SW18 . . . . 1H 135
Reporton Rd. SW6 . . . . 7G 99
Repository Rd. SE18 . . . . 6D 106
Repton Av. HA0: Wemb 4C 60
UB3: Harl 4F 93
Repton Cl. SM5: Cars 5C 166
Repton Ct. BR3: Beck 1D 158
IG5: Ilf 1D 52
Repton Gro. IG5: Ilf 1D 52
Repton Ho. *SW1* *4B 18*
(off Charlwood St.)
REPTON PARK 7K 37
Repton Rd. BR6: Chels 3K 173
HA3: Kent 4F 43
Repton St. E14 . . . . 6A 86
Repulse Cl. RM5: Col R 1G 55
Reservoir Cl. CR7: Thor H 3D 156
Reservoir Rd. HA4: Ruis 4F 39
N14 . . . . 5B 22
SE4 . . . . 2A 122
Reservoir Studios *E1* *6K 85*
(off Cable St.)
Resham Cl. UB2: S'hall 3A 94
Resolution Wlk. SE18 . . . . 3D 106
Resolution Way *SE8* *7C 104*
(off Deptford High St.)
Restell Cl. SE3 . . . . 6G 105
Restmor Way SM6: Wall 2E 166
Reston Pl. SW7 . . . . 2A 100
Restons Cres. SE9 . . . . 6H 125
Restoration Sq. SW11 . . . . 1B 118
Restormel Cl. TW3: Houn 5E 112
Restormel Ho. SE11 . . . . 4J 19
Retcar Cl. N19 . . . . 2F 65
Retcar Pl. *N19* *2F 65*
(off Retcar Cl.)
Retford St. N1 . . . . 1H 9 (2E 84)
Retingham Way E4 . . . . 2J 35
Retles Ct. HA1: Harr 7J 41
Retreat, The CR7: Thor H 4D 156
HA2: Harr 7E 40
KT4: Wor Pk 2D 164
KT5: Surb 6F 151
NW9 . . . . 5K 43
SW14 . . . . 3A 116
Retreat Cl. HA3: Kent 5C 42
Retreat Ho. E9 . . . . 6J 67
Retreat Pl. E9 . . . . 6J 67
Retreat Rd. TW9: Rich 5D 114
Reubens Ct. *W4* *5H 97*
(off Chaseley Dr.)
Reunion Row E1 . . . . 7H 85
Reuters Plaza *E14* *1D 104*
(off The Sth. Colonnade)
Reveley Sq. SE16 . . . . 2A 104
Revell Ri. SE18 . . . . 6K 107
Revell Rd. KT1: King T 2H 151
SM1: Sutt 6H 165
Revelon Rd. SE4 . . . . 4A 122
Revelstoke Rd. SW18 . . . . 2H 135
Reventlow Rd. SE9 . . . . 1G 143
Reverdy Rd. SE1 . . . . 4G 103
Reverend Cl. HA2: Harr 3F 59
Revesby Rd. SM5: Cars 6B 154
Review Rd. NW2 . . . . 2B 62
RM10: Dag 1H 91
Rewell St. SW6 . . . . 7A 100
Rewley Rd. SM5: Cars 6B 154
Rex Av. TW15: Ashf 6C 128
Rex Cl. RM5: Col R 1H 55
Rex Pl. W1 . . . . 3H 11 (7E 82)
Reydon Av. E11 . . . . 5A 52
Reynard Cl. BR1: Brom 3E 160
SE4 . . . . 3A 122
Reynard Dr. SE19 . . . . 7F 139
Reynard Mills Trad. Est.
TW8: Bford 5C 96
Reynard Pl. SE14 . . . . 6A 104
Reynardson Rd. N17 . . . . 7H 33
Reynolah Gdns. SE7 . . . . 5K 105
Reynolds Av. E12 . . . . 5E 70
KT9: Chess 7E 162
RM6: Chad H 7C 54
Reynolds Cl. NW11 . . . . 7K 45
SM5: Cars 1D 166
SW19 . . . . 1B 154
Reynolds Ct. RM6: Chad H 3D 54
Reynolds Dr. HA8: Edg 3F 43
Reynolds Ho. *E2* *2J 85*
(off Approach Rd.)
NW8 . . . . *2B 82*
(off Wellington Rd.)
SW1 . . . . *4D 18*
(off Erasmus St.)
Reynolds Pl. SE3 . . . . 7K 105
TW10: Rich 6F 115
Reynolds Rd. KT3: N Mald 7K 151
SE15 . . . . 4J 121
UB4: Yead 4A 76
W4 . . . . 3J 97
Reynolds Sports Cen. 2G 97
Reynolds Way CR0: Croy 4E 168
Rheidol M. N1 . . . . 2C 84
Rheidol Ter. N1 . . . . 1C 84
Rheingold Way SM6: Wall 7J 167
Rhein Ho. *N8* *3J 47*
(off Campsfield Rd.)
Rheola Cl. N17 . . . . 1F 49
Rhoda St. E2 . . . . 3K 9 (4F 85)
Rhodes Av. N22 . . . . 1G 47
Rhodes Ho. *N1* *1E 8*
(off Fairbank Est.)
Rhodesia Rd. E11 . . . . 2F 69
SW9 . . . . 2J 119
Rhodesmoor Ho. Ct. SM4: Mord 6J 153
Rhodes St. N7 . . . . 5K 65

Rhodeswell Rd. E14 . . . . .5A **86**
   (not continuous)
Rhodrons Av. KT9: Chess 5E **162**
Rhondda Gro. E3 . . . . .3A **86**
Rhyl Rd. UB6: G'frd 2K **77**
Rhyl St. NW5 . . . . .6E **64**
Rhys Av. N11 . . . . .7C **32**
Rialto Rd. CR4: Mitc 2E **154**
Ribble Cl. IG8: Wfd G 6F **37**
Ribblesdale Av. N11 . . . . .6K **31**
   UB5: N'olt 6F **59**
Ribblesdale Ho. NW6 . . . . .1J **81**
   (off Kilburn Va.)
Ribblesdale Rd. N8 . . . . .4K **47**
   SW16 .6F **137**
Ribbon Dance M. SE5 . . . . .1D **120**
Ribchester Av. UB6: G'frd 3K **77**
Ribston Cl. BR2: Brom 1D **172**
Ricardo Path SE28 . . . . .1C **108**
Ricardo St. E14 . . . . .6D **86**
Ricards Rd. SW19 . . . . .5H **135**
Riccall Ct. NW9 . . . . .1A **44**
   (off Pageant Av.)
Rice Pde. BR5: Pet W 5H **161**
Riceyman Ho. WC1 . . . . .2J **7**
   (off Lloyd Baker St.)
Richard Anderson Ct. SE14 . . . . . . .7K **103**
   (off Monson Rd.)
Richard Burbidge Mans. SW13 . . . .6E **98**
   (off Brasenose Dr.)
Richard Burton Ct. IG9: Buck H 2F **37**
   (off Palmerston Rd.)
Richard Cl. SE18 . . . . .4C **106**
Richard Fell Ho. E12 . . . . .4E **70**
   (off Walton Rd.)
Richard Ho. SE16 . . . . .4J **103**
   (off Silwood St.)
Richard Ho. Dr. E16 . . . . .6B **88**
Richard Neale Ho. E1 . . . . .1H **85**
   (off Cornwall St.)
Richard Neve Ho. SE18 . . . . .4J **107**
   (off Plumstead High St.)
Richard Robert Residence, The
   E15 . . . . .6F **69**
   (off Salway Rd.)
Richards Av. RM7: Rom 6J **55**
Richards Cl. HA1: Harr 5A **42**
   UB3: Hari 6F **93**
   UB10: Hil 1C **74**
   WD23: Bush 1C **26**
Richards Fld. KT19: Ewe 7K **163**
Richard Sharples Ct. SM2: Sutt 7A **166**
Richardson Cl. E8 . . . . .1F **85**
Richardson Ct. SW4 . . . . .2J **119**
   (off Studley Rd.)
Richardson Gdns. RM10: Dag 6H **73**
Richardson Rd. E15 . . . . .2G **87**
Richardson's M. W1 . . . . .4A **6**
Richards Pl. E17 . . . . .3C **50**
   SW3 . . . . .3D **16** (4C **100**)
Richard St. E1 . . . . .6H **85**
Richbell WC1 . . . . .5F **7**
   (off Boswell St.)
Richbell Pl. WC1 . . . . .5G **7** (5K **83**)
Richborne Ter. SW8 . . . . .7K **101**
Richborough Ho. SE15 . . . . .6J **103**
   (off Sharratt St.)
Richborough Rd. NW2 . . . . .4G **63**
Richbourne Ct. W1 . . . . .7D **4**
   (off Harrowby St.)
Richens Cl. TW3: Houn 2H **113**
Riches Rd. IG1: Ilf 2G **71**
Richfield Rd. WD23: Bush 1B **26**
Richford Ga. W6 . . . . .3E **98**
Richford Rd. E15 . . . . .1H **87**
Richford St. W6 . . . . .2E **98**
Rich Ind. Est. SE1 . . . . .3E **102**
   SE15 .6H **103**
Richlands Av. KT17: Ewe 4C **164**
Rich La. SW5 . . . . .5K **99**
Richman Ho. SE8 . . . . .5B **104**
   (off Grove St.)
RICHMOND 5D **114**

Richmond American University in
  London, The 3K **99**
   (off Ansdell St.)
Richmond Av. E4 . . . . .5A **36**
   N1 . . . . .1K **83**
   NW10 .6E **62**
   SW20 . . . . .1G **153**
   TW14: Felt 6G **111**
   UB10: Hill 6D **56**
Richmond Bri. TW1: Twick 6D **114**
Richmond Bldgs. W1 . . . .1C **12** (6H **83**)
RICHMOND CIRCUS 4E **114**
Richmond Cl. E17 . . . . .6B **50**
Richmond College
  (The American Institute
  University in London) 2K **99**
Richmond Cotts. W14 . . . . .4G **99**
   (off Hammersmith Rd.)
Richmond Ct. CR4: Mitc 3B **154**
   E8 . . . . .7H **67**
   (off Mare St.)
   HA9: Wemb 3F **61**
   N11 . . . . .6K **31**
   (off Pickering Gdns.)
   NW6 . . . . .7F **63**
   (off Willesden La.)
   SW1 . . . . .7F **11**
   (off Sloane St.)
   W14 . . . . .4G **99**
   (off Hammersmith Rd.)
Richmond Cres. E4 . . . . .5A **36**
   N1 . . . . .1K **83**
   N9 . . . . .1B **34**
Richmond Cricket Club 3E **114**
Richmond Dr. IG8: Ilf 7K **37**
   TW17: Shep 6F **147**
Richmond Filmhouse 5D **114**
Richmond Gdns. HA3: Hrw W 7E **26**
   NW4 . . . . .5C **44**
Richmond Grn. CR0: Bedd 3J **167**
Richmond Gro. KT5: Surb 6F **151**
   N1 . . . . .7B **66**
   (not continuous)
Richmond Hill TW10: Rich 6E **114**
Richmond Hill Ct.
   TW10: Rich 6E **114**
Richmond Ho. NW1 . . . . .1K **5**
   (off Pk. Village E.)
   SE17 .5D **102**
   (off Portland St.)
Richmond Mans. SW5 . . . . .5K **99**
   (off Old Brompton Rd.)
   TW1: Twick 6D **114**
Richmond M. TW11: Tedd 5K **131**
   W1 . . . . .1C **12** (6H **83**)
Richmond Pde. TW1: Twick 6C **114**
   (off Richmond Rd.)
Richmond Pk. 1G **133**
Richmond Pk. Rd. KT2: King T 1E **150**
   SW14 .5J **115**
Richmond Pl. SE18 . . . . .4G **107**
Richmond Rd. CR0: Bedd 3J **167**
   CR7: Thor H 3B **156**
   E4 . . . . .1A **36**
   E7 . . . . .5K **69**
   (not continuous)
   E8 . . . . .7F **67**
   E11 . . . . .2F **69**
   EN5: New Bar 5E **20**
   IG1: Ilf .3G **71**
   KT2: King T 5D **132**
   N2 . . . . .2A **46**
   N11 . . . . .6D **32**
   N15 . . . . .6E **48**
   SW20 . . . . .1D **152**
   TW1: Twick 7B **114**
   TW7: Isle 3A **114**
   W5 . . . . .2E **96**
Richmond RUFC 3D **114**
Richmond St. E13 . . . . .2J **87**
Richmond Ter. SW1 . . . . .6E **12** (2J **101**)
Richmond Theatre 4D **114**
Richmond University 7E **114**

Richmond Way E11 . . . . .2J **69**
   W12 . . . . .2F **99**
   W14 . . . . .2F **99**
Richmount Gdns. SE3 . . . . .3J **123**
Rich St. E14 . . . . .7B **86**
Rickard Cl. NW4 . . . . .4D **44**
   SW2 .1A **138**
Rickards Cl. KT6: Surb 2E **162**
Rickett St. SW6 . . . . .6J **99**
Rickman Ho. E1 . . . . .3J **85**
   (off Rickman St.)
Rickman St. E1 . . . . .4J **85**
Rickmansworth Rd. HA5: Pinn 2K **39**
   HA6: Nwood 1F **39**
Rick Roberts Way E15 . . . . .1E **86**
Rickthorne Rd. N19 . . . . .2J **65**
Rickyard Path SE9 . . . . .4C **124**
Riddell Ct. SE5 . . . . .5F **103**
   (off Albany Rd.)
Ridding La. UB6: G'frd 5K **59**
Riddons Rd. SE12 . . . . .3A **142**
Ride, The EN3: Pond E 3D **24**
   TW8: Bford 5B **96**
Rideout St. SE18 . . . . .4D **106**
Rider Cl. DA15: Sidc 6J **125**
Rideway Dr. W3 . . . . .3G **97**
Ridgdale St. E3 . . . . .2D **86**
Ridge, The BR6: Orp 2H **173**
   DA5: Bexl 7F **127**
   EN5: Barn 5C **20**
   KT5: Surb 5G **151**
   TW2: Whit 7H **113**
Ridge Av. N21 . . . . .7H **23**
Ridgebrook Rd. SE3 . . . . .3B **124**
Ridge Cl. NW4 . . . . .2F **45**
   NW9 . . . . .4K **43**
   SE28 .2H **107**
Ridge Ct. SE22 . . . . .7G **121**
Ridge Crest EN2: Enf 1E **22**
Ridgecroft Cl. DA5: Bexl 1J **145**
Ridge Hill NW11 . . . . .1G **63**
Ridgemead Cl. N14 . . . . .2D **32**
Ridgemont Gdns. HA8: Edg 4D **28**
Ridgemount Av. CR0: Croy 1K **169**
Ridgemount Cl. SE20 . . . . .7H **139**
Ridgemount Gdns. EN2: Enf 3G **23**
Ridge Rd. CR4: Mitc 7F **137**
   N8 . . . . .6K **47**
   N21 . . . . .1H **33**
   NW2 . . . . .3H **63**
   SM3: Sutt 1G **165**
Ridges Yd. CR0: Croy 3B **168**
Ridgeview Cl. EN5: Barn 6A **20**
Ridgeview Rd. N20 . . . . .3E **30**
Ridge Way IG8: Wfd G 4F **37**
   SE19 .6E **138**
   TW13: Hanw 3C **130**
Ridgeway BR2: Hayes 2J **171**
   TW10: Rich 6E **114**
Ridgeway, The CR0: Wadd 3K **167**
   E4 . . . . .2J **35**
   EN2: Enf 1E **22**
   HA2: Harr 5D **40**
   (not continuous)
   HA3: Kent 6C **42**
   HA4: Ruis 7J **39**
   HA7: Stan 6H **27**
   KT12: Walt T 7H **147**
   N3 . . . . .7E **30**
   N11 . . . . .4J **31**
   N14 . . . . .2D **32**
   NW7 . . . . .3H **29**
   NW9 . . . . .4K **43**
   NW11 .7G **45**
   W3 . . . . .3G **97**
Ridgeway Av. EN4: E Barn 6J **21**
Ridgeway Cres. BR6: Orp 3J **173**
Ridgeway Cres. Gdns. BR6: Orp 2J **173**
Ridgeway Dr. BR1: Brom 4K **141**
Ridgeway E. DA15: Sidc 5K **125**
Ridgeway Gdns. IG4: Ilf 5C **52**
   N6 . . . . .7G **47**
Ridgeway Rd. TW7: Isle 7J **95**

Ridgeway Rd. Nth. TW7: Isle 7J **95**
Ridgeway Wlk. UB5: N'olt 6C **58**
   (off Cowings Mead)
Ridgeway W. DA15: Sidc 5J **125**
Ridgewell Cl. N1 . . . . .1C **84**
   RM10: Dag 1H **91**
   SE26 .4B **140**
Ridgmount Gdns. WC1 . . . . .5C **6** (5H **83**)
Ridgmount Pl. WC1 . . . . .5C **6** (5H **83**)
Ridgmount Rd. SW18 . . . . .5K **117**
Ridgmount St. WC1 . . . . . . .5C **6** (5H **83**)
Ridgway SW19 . . . . .7E **134**
Ridgway, The SM2: Sutt 7B **166**
Ridgway Cl. SW19 . . . . .6F **135**
Ridgway Gdns. SW19 . . . . .7F **135**
Ridgway Pl. SW19 . . . . .6G **135**
Ridgway Rd. SW9 . . . . .3B **120**
Ridgwell Rd. E16 . . . . .5A **88**
Riding, The NW11 . . . . .7H **45**
Riding Ho. St. W1 . . . . .6K **5** (5F **83**)
Ridings, The E11 . . . . .5J **51**
   EN4: E Barn 7G **21**
   KT5: Surb 5G **151**
   KT17: Ewe 7B **164**
   TW16: Sun 1J **147**
   W5 . . . . .4F **79**
Ridings Av. N21 . . . . .4G **23**
Ridings Cl. N6 . . . . .7G **47**
Ridler Rd. EN1: Enf 1K **23**
Ridley Av. W13 . . . . .3B **96**
Ridley Cl. IG11: Bark 7K **71**
Ridley Ct. SW16 . . . . .6J **137**
Ridley Rd. BR2: Brom 3H **159**
   DA16: Well 1B **126**
   E7 . . . . .4A **70**
   E8 . . . . .5F **67**
   NW10 .2C **80**
   SW19 .7K **135**
Ridsdale Rd. SE20 . . . . .1H **157**
Riefield Rd. SE9 . . . . .4G **125**
Riesco Dr. CR0: Croy 6J **169**
Riffel Rd. NW2 . . . . .5E **62**
Rifle Cl. SE11 . . . . .7K **19** (6A **102**)
Rifle St. E14 . . . . .5D **86**
Riga Ho. E1 .5K **85**
   (off Shandy St.)
Riga M. E1 . . . . .7K **9**
   (off Commercial Rd.)
Rigault Rd. SW6 . . . . .2G **117**
Rigby Cl. CR0: Wadd 3A **168**
Rigby La. UB3: Hayes 2E **92**
Rigby M. IG1: Ilf 2E **70**
Rigden St. E14 . . . . .6D **86**
Rigeley Rd. NW10 . . . . .3C **80**
Rigg App. E10 . . . . .1K **67**
Rigge Pl. SW4 . . . . .4H **119**
Riggindale Rd. SW16 . . . . .5H **137**
Riley Ho. SW10 . . . . .7B **100**
Riley Rd. EN3: Enf W 1D **24**
   SE1 . . . . .7H **15** (3F **103**)
Riley St. SW10 . . . . .6B **100**
Rill Ho. SE5 . . . . .7D **102**
   (off Harris St.)
Rima Ho. SW3 . . . . .7A **16**
   (off Callow St.)
Rinaldo Rd. SW12 . . . . .7F **119**
Ring, The W2 . . . . .2C **10** (7B **82**)
   (not continuous)
Ring Cl. BR1: Brom 7K **141**
Ringcroft St. N7 . . . . .5A **66**
Ringers Ct. BR1: Brom 3J **159**
   (off Ringers Rd.)
Ringers Rd. BR1: Brom 3J **159**
Ringford Rd. SW18 . . . . .5H **117**
Ring Ho. E1 .7J **85**
   (off Sage St.)
Ringles Ct. E6 . . . . .1D **88**
Ringlet Cl. E16 . . . . .5K **87**
Ringlewell Cl. EN1: Enf 2C **24**
Ringmer Av. SW6 . . . . .1G **117**
Ringmer Gdns. N19 . . . . .2J **65**
Ringmer Pl. N21 . . . . .5J **23**
Ringmer Way BR1: Brom 5C **160**

Ringmore Ri. SE23 7H 121
Ring Rd. W12 1E 98
Ringsfield Ho. *SE17* *5C 102*
(off Bronti Cl.)
Ringslade Rd. N22 2K 47
Ringstead Rd. SE6 7D 122
SM1: Sutt 4B 166
Ring Way N11 6B 32
Ringway UB2: S'hall 5B 94
Ringwold Cl. BR3: Beck 7A 140
Ringwood Av. CR0: Croy 7J 155
N2 2D 46
Ringwood Cl. HA5: Pinn 3A 40
Ringwood Gdns. E14 4C 104
SW15 1C 134
Ringwood Rd. E17 6B 50
Ringwood Way N21 1G 33
TW12: Ham H 4E 130
Rio Cinema *5E 66*
(off Kingsland High St.)
Ripley Cl. BR1: Brom 5D 160
CR0: New Ad 6E 170
Ripley Ct. CR4: Mitc 2B 154
Ripley Gdns. SM1: Sutt 4A 166
(not continuous)
SW14 3K 115
Ripley Ho. *SW1* *7A 18*
(off Churchill Gdns.)
Ripley M. E11 6G 51
Ripley Rd. DA17: Belv 4G 109
E16 6A 88
EN2: Enf 1H 23
IG3: Ilf 2K 71
TW12: Hamp 7E 130
Ripley Vs. W13 6C 78
Ripon Cl. UB5: N'olt 5E 58
Ripon Ct. *N11* *6K 31*
(off Ribblesdale Av.)
Ripon Gdns. IG1: Ilf 6C 52
KT9: Chess 5D 162
Ripon Rd. N9 7C 24
N17 3D 48
SE18 6F 107
Rippersley Rd. DA16: Well 1A 126
Ripple Nature Reserve, The 3B 90
Ripple Rd. IG11: Bark, Dag 7G 71
RM9: Dag 1B 90
RIPPLESIDE 1B 90
Rippleside Commercial Est.
IG11: Bark 2C 90
Ripplevale Gro. N1 7K 65
Rippolson Rd. SE18 5K 107
Ripston Rd. TW15: Ashf 5F 129
Risboro' Cl. N10 3F 47
Risborough *SE17* *4C 102*
(off Deacon Way)
Risborough Dr. KT4: Wor Pk 7C 152
Risborough Ho. *NW8* *3D 4*
(off Mallory St.)
Risborough St. SE1 6B 14 (2B 102)
Risdon Ho. *SE16* *2J 103*
(off Risdon St.)
Risdon St. SE16 3J 103
Rise, The DA5: Bexl 7C 126
E11 5J 51
HA0: Wemb 5A 60
HA8: Edg 5C 28
IG9: Buck H 1G 37
N13 4F 33
NW7 6G 29
NW10 4K 61
UB6: G'frd 5A 60
UB10: Hil 2B 74
Risedale Rd. DA7: Bex 3J 127
Riseholme Ct. E9 6B 68
Riseldine Rd. SE23 6A 122
RISE PARK 2K 55
Rise Pk. Pde. RM1: Rom 2K 55
Risinghill St. N1 2K 83
Risingholme Cl. HA3: Hrw W 1J 41
WD23: Bush 1A 26
Risingholme Rd. HA3: Hrw W 2J 41
Risings, The E17 4F 51
Rising Sun Ct. EC1 5B 8
Risley Av. N17 1C 48
Rita Rd. SW8 6J 101
Ritches Rd. N15 5C 48
Ritchie Ho. *E14* *6F 87*
(off Blair St.)
N19 1H 65
SE16 *3J 103*
(off Howland Est.)
Ritchie Rd. CR0: Croy 6H 157
Ritchie St. N1 2A 84
Ritchings Av. E17 4A 50
Ritherdon Rd. SW17 2E 136
Ritson Ho. *N1* *1K 83*
(off Barnsbury Est.)
Ritson Rd. E8 6G 67
Ritter St. SE18 6E 106
Ritz Pde. W5 4F 79
Riva Bingo 1J 137
Rivaz Pl. E9 6J 67
Riven Ct. *W2* *6K 81*
(off Inverness Ter.)
Rivenhall Gdns. E18 4H 51
River App. HA8: Edg 1J 43
RIVER ASH ESTATE 7H 147
River Av. KT7: T Ditt 7A 150
N13 3G 33
River Av. Ind. Est. N13 5F 33
River Bank KT7: T Ditt 5K 149
KT8: E Mos 3J 149
N21 7H 23
TW12: Hamp 3E 148
Riverbank Rd. BR1: Brom 3J 141
Riverbank Way TW8: Bford 6C 96
River Barge Cl. E14 2E 104
River Brent Bus. Pk. W7 3J 95
River Cl. E11 6A 52
HA4: Ruis 6H 39
UB2: S'hall 2G 95
River Ct. *KT6: Surb* *5D 150*
(off Portsmouth Rd.)
SE1 3A 14 (7B 84)
Rivercourt Rd. W6 4D 98
River Crane Way *TW13: Hanw* *2D 130*
(off Watermill Way)
Riverdale SE13 4E 122
Riverdale Cl. IG11: Bark 4B 90
Riverdale Ct. N21 5J 23
Riverdale Dr. SW18 1K 135
Riverdale Gdns. TW1: Twick 6C 114
Riverdale Rd. DA5: Bexl 7F 127
DA8: Erith 5H 109
SE18 5K 107
TW1: Twick 6C 114
TW13: Hanw 4C 130
Riverdale Shop. Cen. SE13 3E 122
Riverdene HA8: Edg 3D 28
Riverdene Rd. IG1: Ilf 3E 70
Riverfleet *WC1* *1F 7*
(off Birkenhead St.)
Riverford Ho. *W2* *5J 81*
(off Brunel Est.)
River Front EN1: Enf 3K 23
River Gdns. SM5: Cars 2E 166
TW14: Felt 5K 111
River Gdns. Bus. Cen. TW14: Felt 5K 111
River Gro. Pk. BR3: Beck 1B 158
Riverhead Cl. E17 2K 49
River Heights N17 1F 49
Riverhill KT4: Wor Pk 2K 163
Riverhill Mobile Home Pl.
KT4: Wor Pk 2K 163
Riverholme Dr. KT19: Ewe 7K 163
Riverhope Mans. SE18 3C 106
River Ho. SE26 3H 139
Riverhouse Barn 7H 147
River La. TW10: Ham 7D 114
Riverleigh Ct. E4 5G 35
River Lodge *SW1* *7B 18*
(off Grosvenor Rd.)
Rivermead KT1: King T 5D 150
KT8: W Mole 3G 149
Rivermead Cl. TW11: Tedd 5B 132
Rivermead Ct. SW6 3H 117
Rivermead Ho. E9 5A 68
TW16: Sun *3A 148*
(off Thames St.)
Rivermead Rd. N18 6E 34
River Meads Av.
TW2: Twick 3E 130
River Mt. KT12: Walt T 7H 147
Rivernook Cl. KT12: Walt T 5A 148
River Pk. Gdns. BR2: Brom 7F 141
River Pk. Rd. N22 2K 47
River Pl. N1 7C 66
River Reach TW11: Tedd 5C 132
River Rd. IG9: Buck H 1H 37
IG11: Bark 2J 89
River Rd. Bus. Pk.
IG11: Bark 3K 89
Riversdale Gdns. N22 1A 48
Riversdale Rd. KT7: T Ditt 5A 150
N5 3B 66
RM5: Col R 1H 55
Riversfield Rd. EN1: Enf 3K 23
Rivers Ho. *TW7: Isle* *4B 114*
(off Richmond Rd.)
W4 *5G 97*
(off Chiswick High Rd.)
Riverside NW4 7D 44
SE7 3K 105
SW11 7C 100
TW1: Twick 1B 132
TW9: Rich 5D 114
TW16: Sun 3B 148
TW17: Shep 7G 147
WC1 *1F 7*
(off Birkenhead St.)
Riverside, The KT8: E Mos 3H 149
Riverside Apartments N13 5E 32
SE1 *5J 15*
(off Shad Thames)
Riverside Av. KT8: E Mos 5H 149
Riverside Bus. Cen. SW18 1K 135
Riverside Bus. Pk. SW19 1A 154
Riverside Cl. E5 1J 67
KT1: King T 4D 150
RM7: Rom 4K 55
SM6: Wall 3F 167
W7 4J 77
Riverside Cotts. IG11: Bark 2H 89
Riverside Ct. E4: Pond E 6H 25
SE3 4H 123
SW8 7D 18 (6H 101)
TW7: Isle *2K 113*
(off Woodlands Rd.)
TW14: Felt 7G 111
Riverside Dr. CR4: Mitc 5C 154
NW11 6G 45
TW10: Ham 3D 132
W4 7K 97
Riverside Gdns. EN2: Enf 2H 23
HA0: Wemb 2E 78
N3 3G 45
W6 5D 98
Riverside Ho. *N1* *7C 66*
(off Canonbury St.)
Riverside Ind. Est.
EN3: Pond E 6F 25
IG11: Bark 3A 90
Riverside Mans. *E1* *1J 103*
(off Milk Yd.)
Riverside M. CR0: Bedd 3J 167
Riverside Pl. N11 3B 32
TW19: Stanw 6A 110
Riverside Rd. DA14: Sidc 3E 144
E15 2E 86
N15 6G 49
SW17 4K 135
TW19: Stanw 5A 110
(not continuous)
Riverside Studios *5E 98*
(off River Ter.)
Riverside Twr. *SW6* *2A 118*
(off The Boulevard)
Riverside Vs. KT6: Surb 6C 150
Riverside Wlk. BR4: W W'ck 1D 170
EN5: Barn 6A 20
(not continuous)
KT1: King T 3D 150
N12 6D 30
(not continuous)
SE10 3G 105
(Morden Wharf Rd.)
SE10 2F 105
(Tunnel Av.)
SW6 3G 117
TW7: Isle 3J 113
W4 *6B 98*
(off Chiswick Wharf)
Riverside Works IG11: Bark 7F 71
Riverside Workshops *SE1* *4D 14*
(off Park St.)
Riverside Yd. SW17 4A 136
Riverstone Cl. HA2: Harr 1H 59
Riverstone Ct. KT2: King T 1F 151
River St. EC1 1J 7 (3A 84)
River Ter. W6 5E 98
WC2 3G 13
River Thames Vis. Cen. *5D 114*
(off Whittaker Av.)
Riverton Cl. W9 3H 81
River Vw. EN2: Enf 3H 23
Riverview Ct. E14 3B 104
River Vw. Gdns. TW1: Twick 2K 131
Riverview Gdns. SW13 6D 98
Riverview Gro. W4 6H 97
River Vw. Hgts. *SE16* *2G 103*
(off Bermondsey Wall W.)
Riverview Pk. SE6 2C 140
Riverview Rd. KT19: Ewe 4J 163
W4 7H 97
River Wlk. KT12: Walt T 6J 147
W6 7E 98
River Way KT19: Ewe 5K 163
SE10 3H 105
TW2: Twick 2F 131
Riverway N13 5F 33
River Wharf Bus. Pk. DA17: Belv 1K 109
Riverwiew Wlk. SE6 3B 140
Riverwood La. BR7: Chst 1H 161
Rivet Ho. *SE1* *5F 103*
(off Coopers Rd.)
Rivington Av. IG8: Wfd G 2B 52
Rivington Ct. NW10 1C 80
Rivington Cres. NW7 7G 29
Rivington Pl. EC2 2H 9 (3E 84)
Rivington St. EC2 2G 9 (3E 84)
Rivington Wlk. E8 1G 85
Rivulet Rd. N17 7H 33
Rixon Ho. SE18 6F 107
Rixon St. N7 3A 66
Rixsen Rd. E12 5C 70
Roach Rd. E3 7C 68
Roads Pl. N19 2J 65
Roan Ind. Est. *CR4: Mitc* *1D 154*
(off Lavender Av.)
Roan St. SE10 6E 104
Robarts Cl. HA5: Eastc 5K 39
Robbins Hall EN3: Pond E 6E 24
Robb Rd. HA7: Stan 6F 27
Robert Adam St. W1 7G 5 (6E 82)
Roberta St. E2 3G 85
Robert Bell Ho. *SE16* *4G 103*
(off Rouel Rd.)
Robert Burns Ho. *N17* *7C 34*
(off Northumberland Pk.)
Robert Burns M. SE24 5B 120
Robert Cl. W9 4A 4 (4A 82)
Robert Dashwood Way
SE17 4C 102
Robert Gentry Ho. *W14* *5G 99*
(off Gledstanes Rd.)
Robert Jones Ho. *SE16* *4G 103*
(off Rouel Rd.)
Robert Keen Cl. SE15 1G 121
Robert Lowe Cl. SE14 7K 103
Robert Morton Ho. NW8 7A 64
Roberton Dr. BR1: Brom 1A 160

Robert Owen Ho. *N22* *1A 48*
(off Progress Way)
SW6 1F 117
Robert Runcie Ct. SW2 4K 119
Roberts All. W5 2D 96
Robertsbridge Rd. SM5: Cars 1A 166
Roberts Cl. CR7: Thor H 3D 156
SE9 1H 143
SE16 2K 103
SM3: Cheam 7F 165
UB7: Yiew 1A 92
Roberts Ct. KT9: Chess 5D 162
N1 *1B 84*
(off Essex Rd.)
NW10 6A 62
SE20 *1J 157*
(off Maple Rd.)
Roberts M. BR6: Orp 1K 173
SW1 1G 17 (3E 100)
Robertson Gro. SW17 5C 136
Robertson Rd. E15 1E 86
Robertson St. SW8 3F 119
Roberts Pl. EC1 3K 7 (4A 84)
Roberts Rd. DA17: Belv 5G 109
E17 1D 50
NW7 6B 30
Robert St. CR0: Croy 3C 168
E16 1F 107
NW1 2K 5 (3F 83)
SE18 5H 107
(not continuous)
WC2 3F 13 (7J 83)
Robert Sutton Ho. *E1* *6J 85*
(off Tarling St.)
Robeson St. E3 5B 86
Robina Cl. DA6: Bex 4D 126
HA6: Nwood 1H 39
SE20 *1G 157*
(off Sycamore Gro.)
Robin Cl. NW7 3F 29
RM5: Col R 1K 55
TW12: Hamp 5C 130
Robin Ct. E14 2E 104
SE16 4G 103
SM6: Wall 5G 167
Robin Cres. E6 5B 88
Robin Gro. HA3: Kent 6F 43
N6 2E 64
TW8: Bford 6C 96
Robin Hill Dr. BR7: Chst 6C 142
ROBIN HOOD **3A 134**
Robinhood Cl. CR4: Mitc 3G 155
Robin Hood Ct. *EC4* *7K 7*
(off Shoe La.)
Robin Hood Dr. HA3: Hrw W 7E 26
Robin Hood Gdns. *E14* *7E 86*
(off Woolmore St., not continuous)
Robin Hood Grn. BR5: St M Cry 5K 161
Robin Hood La. DA6: Bex 5E 126
E14 7E 86
SM1: Sutt 5J 165
SW15 3A 134
Robinhood La. CR4: Mitc 3G 155
Robin Hood Rd. SW19 5C 134
Robin Hood Way SW15 3A 134
SW20 3A 134
UB6: G'frd 6K 59
Robin Ho. *NW8* *2C 82*
(off Barrow Hill Est.)
Robin Howard Dance Theatre *2D 6*
(in The Place)
Robinia Cres. E10 2D 68
Robin La. NW4 3F 45
Robins Ct. BR3: Beck 2F 159
CR2: S Croy *4E 168*
(off Birdhurst Rd.)
SE12 3A 142
Robinscroft M. SE10 1E 122
Robins Gro. BR4: W W'ck 3J 171
Robinson Cl. E11 3G 69
EN2: Enf 3H 23
Robinson Ct. *N1* *1B 84*
(off St Mary's Path)
Robinson Cres.
WD23: Bushy 1B 26
Robinson Ho. *E14* *5C 86*
(off Selsey St.)
W10 *6F 81*
(off Bramley Rd.)
Robinson Rd. E2 2J 85
RM10: Dag 4G 73
SW17 6C 136
Robinson's Cl. W13 5A 78
Robinson St. SW3 7E 16 (6D 100)
Robinwood Gro. UB8: Hil 4B 74
Robinwood Pl. SW15 4K 133
Robsart St. SW9 2K 119
Robson Av. NW10 7C 62
Robson Cl. E6 6C 88
EN2: Enf 2G 23
Robson Rd. SE27 3B 138
Roby Ho. *EC1* *3C 8*
(off Mitchell St.)
Rocastle Rd. SE4 5A 122
Roch Av. HA8: Edg 2F 43
Rochdale Rd. E17 7C 50
SE2 5B 108
Rochdale Way SE8 7C 104
(not continuous)
Roche Ho. *E14* *7B 86*
(off Beccles St.)
Rochelle Cl. SW11 4B 118
Rochelle St. E2 2J 9 (3F 85)
(not continuous)
Rochemont Wlk. *E8* *1G 85*
(off Pownell Rd.)
Roche Rd. SW16 1K 155
Rochester Av. BR1: Brom 2K 159
E13 1A 88
TW13: Felt 2H 129
Rochester Cl. DA15: Sidc 6B 126
EN1: Enf 1K 23
SW16 7J 137
Rochester Ct. *E2* *4H 85*
(off Wilmot St.)
NW1 *7G 65*
(off Rochester Sq.)
Rochester Dr. DA5: Bexl 6F 127
HA5: Pinn 5B 40
Rochester Gdns. CR0: Croy 3E 168
IG1: Ilf 7D 52
Rochester Ho. *SE1* *7F 15*
(off Manciple St.)
SE15 *6J 103*
(off Sharratt St.)
Rochester M. NW1 7G 65
W5 4C 96
Rochester Pde. TW13: Felt 2J 129
Rochester Pl. NW1 6G 65
Rochester Rd. HA6: Nwood 3H 39
NW1 6G 65
SM5: Cars 4D 166
Rochester Row SW1 3B 18 (4G 101)
Rochester Sq. NW1 7G 65
Rochester St. SW1 2C 18 (3H 101)
Rochester Ter. NW1 6G 65
Rochester Wlk. SE1 4E 14 (1D 102)
Rochester Way DA1: Dart 7K 127
SE3 1K 123
SE9 2A 124
Rochester Way Relief Rd.
SE3 1K 123
SE9 4A 124
Roche Wlk. SM5: Cars 6B 154
Rochford *N17* *2E 48*
(off Griffin Rd.)
Rochford Av. RM6: Chad H 5C 54
Rochford Cl. E6 2B 88
Rochford Wlk. E8 7G 67
Rochford Way CR0: Croy 6J 155
Rochfort Ho. SE8 5B 104
Rock Av. SW14 3K 115
Rockbourne M. SE23 1K 139
Rockbourne Rd. SE23 1K 139
Rock Cl. CR4: Mitc 2B 154
Rockell's Pl. SE22 6H 121
Rockfield Ho. *NW4* *4F 45*
(off Belle Vue Est.)
SE10 *6E 104*
(off Welland St.)
Rockford Av. UB6: G'frd 2A 78
Rock Gdns. RM10: Dag 5H 73
Rock Gro. Way SE16 4G 103
(not continuous)
Rockhall Rd. NW2 4F 63
Rockhall Way NW2 3F 63
Rockhampton Cl. SE27 4A 138
Rockhampton Rd. CR2: S Croy 6E 168
SE27 4A 138
Rock Hill SE26 4F 139
(not continuous)
Rockingham Cl. SW15 4B 116
Rockingham St. SE1 3C 102
Rockland Rd. SW15 4G 117
Rocklands Dr. HA7: Stan 2B 42
Rockley Ct. *W14* *2F 99*
(off Rockley Rd.)
Rockley Rd. W14 2F 99
Rockmount Rd. SE18 5K 107
SE19 6D 138
Rocks La. SW13 1C 116
Rock St. N4 2A 66
Rockware Av. UB6: G'frd 1H 77
Rockware Av. Bus. Cen.
UB6: G'frd 1H 77
Rockwell Gdns. SE19 5E 138
Rockwell Rd. RM10: Dag 5H 73
Rockwood Pl. W12 2E 98
Rocliffe St. N1 2B 84
Rocombe Cres. SE23 7J 121
Rocque Ho. *SW6* *7H 99*
(off Estcourt Rd.)
Rocque La. SE3 3H 123
Rodale Mans. SW18 6K 117
Rodborough Ct. *W9* *4J 81*
(off Hermes Cl.)
Rodborough Rd. NW11 1J 63
Rodd Est. TW17: Shep 5E 146
Roden Ct. N6 7H 47
Roden Gdns. CR0: Croy 6E 156
Rodenhurst Rd. SW4 6G 119
Roden St. IG1: Ilf 3E 70
N7 3K 65
Roden Way *IG1: Ilf* *3E 70*
(off Roden St.)
Roderick Ho. *SE16* *4J 103*
(off Raymouth Rd.)
Roderick Rd. NW3 4D 64
Rodgers Ho. *SW4* *7H 119*
(off Clapham Pk. Est.)
Rodin Ct. *N1* *1B 84*
(off Essex Rd.)
Roding Av. IG8: Wfd G 6H 37
Roding Ho. *N1* *1A 84*
(off Barnsbury Est.)
Roding La. IG7: Chig 2K 37
IG9: Buck H 1G 37
(not continuous)
IG10: Chig 1G 37
Roding La. Nth. IG8: Wfd G 6H 37
Roding La. Sth. IG4: Ilf, Wfd G 4B 52
IG8: Wfd G 4B 52
Roding M. E1 1G 103
Roding Rd. E5 4K 67
E6 5F 89
Rodings, The IG8: Wfd G 6F 37
Rodings Row *EN5: Barn* *4B 20*
(off Leecroft Rd.)
Roding Trad. Est. IG11: Bark 7F 71
Roding Valley Meadows Nature Reserve
1K 37
Roding Vw. IG9: Buck H 1G 37
Rodmarton St. W1 6F 5 (5D 82)
Rodmell *WC1* *2F 7*
(off Regent Sq.)
Rodmell Cl. UB4: Yead 4C 76
Rodmell Slope N12 5C 30
Rodmere St. SE10 5G 105
Rodmill La. SW2 7J 119
Rodney Cl. CR0: Croy 1B 168
HA5: Pinn 7C 40
KT3: N Mald 5A 152
Rodney Ct. EN5: Barn 3C 20
W9 3A 4 (4A 82)
Rodney Gdns. BR4: W W'ck 4J 171
HA5: Eastc 5K 39
Rodney Ho. *E14* *4D 104*
(off Cahir St.)
N1 *2K 83*
(off Donegal St.)
SW1 *6B 18*
(off Dolphin Sq.)
W11 *7J 81*
(off Pembridge Cres.)
Rodney Pl. E17 2A 50
SE17 4C 102
SW19 1A 154
Rodney Rd. CR4: Mitc 3C 154
E11 4K 51
KT3: N Mald 5A 152
SE17 4C 102
(not continuous)
TW2: Whit 6E 112
Rodney St. N1 1H 7 (2K 83)
Rodney Way RM7: Mawney 1H 55
Rodway Rd. BR1: Brom 1K 159
SW15 7C 116
Rodwell Cl. HA4: Ruis 1A 58
Rodwell Pl. HA8: Edg 6B 28
Rodwell Rd. SE22 6F 121
Roe NW9 7G 29
Roebourne Way E16 1E 106
Roebuck Cl. N17 6A 34
TW13: Felt 4K 129
Roebuck Hgts. IG9: Buck H 1F 37
Roebuck La. IG9: Buck H 1F 37
Roebuck Rd. KT9: Chess 5G 163
Roedean Av. EN3: Enf H 1D 24
Roedean Cl. EN3: Enf H 1D 24
Roedean Cres. SW15 6A 116
Roe End NW9 4J 43
ROE GREEN **4J 43**
Roe Grn. NW9 5J 43
ROEHAMPTON **7C 116**
Roehampton Cl. SW15 4C 116
Roehampton Dr. BR7: Chst 6G 143
Roehampton Ga. SW15 6A 116
Roehampton High St. SW15 7C 116
ROEHAMPTON LANE **1D 134**
Roehampton La. SW15 4C 116
Roehampton Recreation Cen. 7C 116
Roehampton University 6B 116
Roehampton Va. SW15 3B 134
Roe La. NW9 4H 43
Roe Way SM6: Wall 6J 167
Roffey St. E14 2E 104
Rogate Ho. E5 3G 67
Roger Bannister Sports Cen., The
6B 26
Roger Dowley Ct. E2 2J 85
Roger Harriss Almshouses *E15* *1H 87*
(off Gift La.)
Roger Reede's Almshouses
RM1: Rom 4K 55
Rogers Ct. *E14* *7C 86*
(off Premiere Pl.)
Rogers Est. E2 3J 85
Rogers Gdns. RM10: Dag 5G 73
Rogers Ho. RM10: Dag 3G 73
SW1 *3D 18*
(off Page St.)
Rogers Rd. E16 6H 87
RM10: Dag 5G 73
SW17 4B 136
Rogers Ruff HA6: Nwood 1E 38
Roger St. WC1 4H 7 (4K 83)
Rogers Wlk. N12 3E 30
Rohere Ho. EC1 1C 8 (3C 84)
Rojack Rd. SE23 1K 139
Rokeby Gdns. IG8: Wfd G 1J 51
Rokeby Ho. *SW12* *7F 119*
(off Lochinvar St.)

Rokeby Ho.—Rosefield Gdns.

Rokeby Ho. *WC1* ... 4G 7
(off Millman M.)
Rokeby Pl. SW20 ... 7D 134
Rokeby Rd. HA1: Harr ... 3H 41
SE4 ... 2B 122
Rokeby St. E15 ... 1F 87
Rokell Ho. *BR3: Beck* ... 5D 140
(off Beckenham Hill Rd.)
Roker Pk. Av. UB10: Ick ... 4A 56
Rokesby Cl. DA16: Well ... 2H 125
Rokesby Pl. HA0: Wemb ... 5D 60
Rokesly Av. N8 ... 5J 47
Roland Gdns. SW7 ... 5A 16 (5A 100)
Roland Ho. *SW7* ... 5A 16
(off Old Brompton Rd.)
Roland Mans. *SW5* ... 5A 100
(off Old Brompton Rd.)
Roland M. E1 ... 5K 85
Roland Rd. E17 ... 4F 51
Roland Way KT4: Wor Pk ... 2B 164
SE17 ... 5D 102
SW7 ... 5A 16 (5A 100)
Roles Gro. RM6: Chad H ... 4D 54
Rolfe Cl. EN4: E Barn ... 4H 21
Rolinsden Way BR2: Kes ... 5B 172
Rolland Ho. W7 ... 5J 77
Rollesby Rd. KT9: Chess ... 6G 163
Rollesby Way SE28 ... 6C 90
Rolleston Av. BR5: Pet W ... 6F 161
Rolleston Cl. BR5: Pet W ... 7F 161
Rolleston Rd. CR2: S Croy ... 7D 168
Roll Gdns. IG2: Ilf ... 5E 52
Rollins St. SE15 ... 6J 103
Rollit Cres. TW3: Houn ... 5E 112
Rollit St. N7 ... 5A 66
Rolls Bldgs. EC4 ... 7J 7 (6A 84)
Rollscourt Av. SE24 ... 5C 120
Rolls Pk. Av. E4 ... 5H 35
Rolls Pk. Rd. E4 ... 5J 35
Rolls Pas. EC4 ... 7J 7
Rolls Rd. SE1 ... 5F 103
Rolls Royce Cl. SM6: Wall ... 7J 167
Rolt St. SE8 ... 6A 104
(not continuous)
Rolvenden Gdns. BR1: Brom ... 7B 142
Rolvenden Pl. N17 ... 1G 49
Roman Cl. RM13: Rain ... 2K 91
TW14: Felt ... 5A 112
W3 ... 2H 97
Roman Ct. N7 ... 6K 65
Romanfield Rd. SW2 ... 7K 119
Roman Ho. EC2 ... 6D 8
RM13: Rain ... 2K 91
Romanhurst Av. BR2: Brom ... 4G 159
Romanhurst Gdns.
BR2: Brom ... 4G 159
Roman Ind. Est. CR0: Croy ... 7E 156
Roman Ri. SE19 ... 6D 138
Roman Rd. E2 ... 3J 85
E3 ... 1B 86
E6 ... 4B 88
IG1: Ilf ... 6F 71
N10 ... 7A 32
NW2 ... 3E 62
W4 ... 4A 98
Roman Rd. Mkt. *E3* ... 1B 86
(off Roman Rd.)
Roman Sq. SE28 ... 1A 108
Roman Way CR0: Croy ... 2B 168
EN1: Enf ... 5A 24
N7 ... 6K 65
SE15 ... 7J 103
Roman Way Ind. Est. *N7* ... 7K 65
(off Roman Way)
Romany Gdns. E17 ... 1A 50
SM3: Sutt ... 7J 153
Romany Ri. BR5: Farnb ... 1G 173
Roma Read Cl. SW15 ... 7D 116
Roma Rd. E17 ... 3A 50
Romayne Ho. SW4 ... 3H 119
Romberg Rd. SW17 ... 3E 136
Romborough Gdns. SE13 ... 5E 122
Romborough Way SE13 ... 5E 122
Romer Ho. *W10* ... 3H 81
(off Dowland St.)
Romero Cl. SW9 ... 3K 119
Romero Sq. SE3 ... 4A 124
Romeyn Rd. SW16 ... 3K 137
ROMFORD ... 5K 55
Romford Rd. E7 ... 6G 69
E12 ... 5A 70
E15 ... 6G 69
RM5: Col R ... 1E 54
Romford Stadium (Greyhound) ... 6J 55
Romford St. E1 ... 5G 85
Romilly Ho. *W11* ... 7G 81
(off Wilsham St.)
Romilly Rd. N4 ... 2B 66
Romilly St. W1 ... 2D 12 (7H 83)
Romily Ct. SW6 ... 2H 117
Rommany Rd. SE27 ... 4D 138
(not continuous)
Romney Cl. HA2: Harr ... 7E 40
KT9: Chess ... 4E 162
N17 ... 1H 49
NW11 ... 1A 64
SE14 ... 7J 103
TW15: Ashf ... 5E 128
Romney Ct. NW3 ... 6C 64
W12 ... 2F 99
(off Shepherd's Bush Grn.)
Romney Dr. BR1: Brom ... 7B 142
HA2: Harr ... 7E 40
Romney Gdns. DA7: Bex ... 1F 127
Romney M. W1 ... 5G 5 (5E 82)
Romney Pde. UB4: Hayes ... 2F 75
Romney Rd. KT3: N Mald ... 6K 151
SE10 ... 6F 105
UB4: Hayes ... 2F 75
Romney Row *NW2* ... 2F 63
(off Brent Ter.)
Romney St. SW1 ... 2E 18 (3J 101)
Romola Rd. SE24 ... 1B 138
Romsey Cl. BR6: Farnb ... 4F 173
Romsey Gdns. RM9: Dag ... 1D 90
Romsey Rd. RM9: Dag ... 1D 90
W13 ... 7A 78
Romulus Ct. TW8: Bford ... 7D 96
Ronald Av. E15 ... 3G 87
Ronald Buckingham Ct. *SE16* ... 2J 103
(off Kenning St.)
Ronald Cl. BR3: Beck ... 4B 158
Ronald Ct. EN5: New Bar ... 3E 20
Ronald Ho. SE3 ... 4A 124
Ronaldshay N4 ... 7A 48
Ronalds Rd. BR1: Brom ... 1J 159
N5 ... 5A 66
(not continuous)
Ronaldstone Rd. DA15: Sidc ... 6J 125
Ronald St. E1 ... 6J 85
Rona Rd. NW3 ... 4E 64
Ronart St. HA3: W'stone ... 3K 41
Rona Wlk. *N1* ... 6D 66
(off Ramsey Wlk.)
Rondel Ct. DA5: Bexl ... 6E 126
Rondu Rd. NW2 ... 5G 63
Ronelean Rd. KT6: Surb ... 2F 163
Ron Grn. Ct. DA8: Erith ... 6K 109
Ron Leighton Way E6 ... 1C 88
Ronnie La. E12 ... 4E 70
Ronver Rd. SE12 ... 1H 141
Rood La. EC3 ... 2G 15 (7E 84)
Roof Ter. Apartments, The *EC1* ... 4B 8
(off Gt. Sutton St.)
Rookby Ct. N21 ... 2G 33
Rook Cl. HA9: Wemb ... 3H 61
Rookeries Cl. TW13: Felt ... 3K 129
Rookery Cl. NW9 ... 5B 44
Rookery Cres. RM10: Dag ... 7H 73
Rookery Dr. BR7: Chst ... 1E 160
Rookery La. BR2: Brom ... 6B 160
Rookery Rd. SW4 ... 4G 119
Rookery Way NW9 ... 5B 44
Rooke Way SE10 ... 5H 105
Rookfield Av. N10 ... 4G 47
Rookfield Cl. N10 ... 4G 47
Rooksmead Rd. TW16: Sun ... 2H 147
Rooks Ter. UB7: W Dray ... 2A 92
Rookstone Rd. SW17 ... 5D 136
Rook Wlk. E6 ... 6B 88
Rookwood Av. KT3: N Mald ... 4C 152
SM6: Bedd ... 4H 167
Rookwood Gdns. E4 ... 2C 36
Rookwood Ho. IG11: Bark ... 2H 89
Rookwood Rd. N16 ... 7F 49
Roosevelt Memorial ... 2H 11 (7E 82)
Roosevelt Way RM10: Dag ... 6K 73
Rootes Dr. W10 ... 5F 81
Ropemaker Rd. SE16 ... 2A 104
Ropemaker's Flds. E14 ... 7B 86
Ropemaker St. EC2 ... 5E 8 (5D 84)
Roper La. SE1 ... 7H 15 (2E 102)
Ropers Av. E4 ... 5J 35
Ropers Orchard *SW3* ... 6C 100
(off Danvers St.)
Roper St. SE9 ... 5D 124
Ropers Wlk. SW2 ... 7A 120
Roper Way CR4: Mitc ... 2E 154
Ropery Bus. Pk. SE7 ... 4A 106
Ropery St. E3 ... 4B 86
Rope St. SE16 ... 4A 104
Rope Wlk. TW16: Sun ... 3A 148
Rope Wlk. Gdns. E1 ... 6G 85
Ropewalk M. *E8* ... 7G 67
(off Middleton Rd.)
Rope Yd. Rails SE18 ... 3F 107
Ropley St. E2 ... 2G 85
Rosa Alba M. N5 ... 4C 66
Rosa Av. TW15: Ashf ... 4C 128
Rosalind Ct. *IG11: Bark* ... 7A 72
(off Meadow Rd.)
Rosalind Ho. *N1* ... 2E 84
(off Arden Ho.)
Rosaline Rd. SW6 ... 7G 99
Rosaline Ter. *SW6* ... 7G 99
(off Rosaline Rd.)
Rosamond St. SE26 ... 3H 139
Rosamund Cl. CR2: S Croy ... 4D 168
Rosamun St. UB2: S'hall ... 4C 94
Rosary Cl. TW3: Houn ... 2C 112
Rosary Gdns. SW7 ... 4A 100
TW15: Ashf ... 4D 128
Rosaville Rd. SW6 ... 7H 99
Roscoe St. EC1 ... 4D 8 (4C 84)
(not continuous)
Roscoe St. Est. EC1 ... 4D 8 (4C 84)
Roscoff Cl. HA8: Edg ... 1J 43
Roseacre Cl. TW17: Shep ... 5C 146
W13 ... 5B 78
Roseacre Rd. DA16: Well ... 3B 126
Rose All. *EC2* ... 6H 9
(off Bishopsgate)
SE1 ... 4D 14 (1C 102)
Rose & Crown Ct. EC2 ... 7D 8
Rose & Crown Pas.
TW7: Isle ... 1A 114
Rose & Crown Yd. SW1 ... 4B 12 (1G 101)
Roseary Cl. UB7: W Dray ... 4A 92
Rose Av. CR4: Mitc ... 1D 154
E18 ... 2K 51
SM4: Mord ... 5A 154
Rosebank SE20 ... 7H 139
SW6 ... 7E 98
W3 ... 6K 79
Rosebank Av. HA0: Wemb ... 4K 59
Rose Bank Cl. N12 ... 5H 31
Rosebank Cl. TW11: Tedd ... 6A 132
Rosebank Gdns. E3 ... 2B 86
W3 ... 6K 79
Rosebank Gro. E17 ... 3B 50
Rosebank Rd. E17 ... 6D 50
W7 ... 2J 95
Rosebank Vs. E17 ... 4C 50
Rosebank Wlk. NW1 ... 7H 65
SE18 ... 4C 106
Rosebank Way W3 ... 6K 79
Rose Bates Dr. NW9 ... 4G 43
Rosebay Ho. *E3* ... 5C 86
(off Hawgood St.)
Roseberry Gdns. BR6: Orp ... 3J 173
N4 ... 6B 48
Roseberry Pl. E8 ... 6F 67
Roseberry St. SE16 ... 4H 103
Rosebery Av. CR7: Thor H ... 2C 156
DA15: Sidc ... 7J 125
E12 ... 6C 70
EC1 ... 4J 7 (4A 84)
HA2: Harr ... 4C 58
KT3: N Mald ... 2B 152
N17 ... 2G 49
Rosebery Cl. SM4: Mord ... 6F 153
Rosebery Ct. *EC1* ... 4J 7
(off Rosebery Av.)
W1 ... 4J 11
(off Charles St.)
Rosebery Gdns. N8 ... 5J 47
SM1: Sutt ... 4K 165
W13 ... 6A 78
Rosebery Ho. *E2* ... 2J 85
(off Sewardstone Rd.)
Rosebery Ind. Pk. N17 ... 2H 49
Rosebery M. N10 ... 2G 47
Rosebery Rd. KT1: King T ... 2H 151
N10 ... 2G 47
SM1: Sutt ... 6H 165
SW2 ... 6J 119
TW3: Houn ... 5G 113
WD23: Bush ... 1A 26
Rosebery Sq. EC1 ... 4J 7
KT1: King T ... 2H 151
Rosebine Av. TW2: Twick ... 7H 113
Rosebury Rd. SW6 ... 2K 117
Rosebury Sq. IG8: Ilf ... 7K 37
Rosebury Va. HA4: Ruis ... 2J 57
Rose Bush Ct. NW3 ... 5D 64
Rose Ct. E1 ... 6K 9
E8 ... 7F 67
(off Richmond Rd.)
HA0: Wemb ... 2E 78
(off Vicars Bri. Cl.)
HA2: Harr ... 2G 59
N1 ... 1B 84
(off Collin's Yd.)
SE16 ... 4K 103
Rosecourt Rd. CR0: Croy ... 6K 155
Rosecroft N14 ... 2D 32
Rosecroft Av. NW3 ... 3J 63
Rosecroft Gdns. NW2 ... 3C 62
TW2: Twick ... 1H 131
Rosecroft Rd. UB1: S'hall ... 4E 76
Rosecroft Wlk. HA0: Wemb ... 5D 60
HA5: Pinn ... 5B 40
Rose Dale BR6: Farnb ... 2F 173
Rosedale Av. UB3: Hayes ... 5F 75
Rosedale Cl. HA7: Stan ... 6G 27
SE2 ... 3B 108
W7 ... 2K 95
Rosedale Ct. HA1: Harr ... 4K 59
N5 ... 4B 66
Rosedale Dr. RM9: Dag ... 7B 72
Rosedale Gdns. RM9: Dag ... 7B 72
Rosedale Ho. N16 ... 1D 66
Rosedale Pl. CR0: Croy ... 7K 157
Rosedale Rd. E7 ... 5A 70
KT17: Ewe ... 5C 164
RM1: Col R ... 2J 55
RM9: Dag ... 7B 72
TW9: Rich ... 3E 114
Rosedale Ter. *W6* ... 3D 98
(off Dalling Rd.)
Rosedene NW6 ... 1F 81
Rosedene Av. CR0: Croy ... 7J 155
SM4: Mord ... 5J 153
SW16 ... 3K 137
UB6: G'frd ... 3E 76
Rosedene Ct. HA4: Ruis ... 1G 57
Rosedene Gdns. IG2: Ilf ... 4E 52
Rosedene Ter. E10 ... 2D 68
Rosedew Rd. W6 ... 6F 99
Rose End KT4: Wor Pk ... 1F 165
Rosefield Cl. SM5: Cars ... 5C 166
Rosefield Gdns. E14 ... 7C 86

Roseford Ct. *W12* *2F 99*
(off Shepherd's Bush Grn.)
Rose Gdn. Cl. HA8: Edg 6K **27**
Rose Gdns. TW13: Felt 2J **129**
UB1: S'hall 4E **76**
W5 . . . . .3D **96**
Rosegate Ho. *E3* *2B 86*
(off Hereford Rd.)
Rose Glen NW9 . . . . .4K **43**
RM7: Rush G 1K **73**
Rosehart M. W11 . . . . .6J **81**
Rose Hatch Av. RM6: Chad H 3D **54**
Roseheath Rd. TW4: Houn 5D **112**
ROSEHILL 7A **154**
Rose Hill SM1: Sutt 2K **165**
Rosehill KT10: Clay 6A **162**
TW12: Hamp 1E **148**
Rosehill Av. SM5: Sutt 1A **166**
Rosehill Ct. *SM4: Mord* *7A 154*
(off St Helier Av.)
Rosehill Ct. Pde. *SM4: Mord* *7A 154*
(off St Helier Av.)
Rosehill Gdns. SM1: Sutt 2K **165**
UB6: G'frd 5K **59**
Rose Hill Pk. W. SM1: Sutt 1A **166**
Rosehill Rd. SW18 . . . . .6A **118**
ROSE HILL RDBT. 7A **154**
Roseland Cl. N17 . . . . .7J **33**
Rose La. RM6: Chad H 3D **54**
Rose Lawn WD23: Bushy 1B **26**
Roseleigh Av. N5 . . . . .4B **66**
Roseleigh Cl. TW1: Twick 6D **114**
Rosemary Av. EN2: Enf 1K **23**
KT8: W Mole 3E **148**
N2 . . . . .4K **45**
N3 . . . . .2K **45**
N9 . . . . .1C **34**
TW4: Houn 2B **112**
Rosemary Branch Theatre *1D 84*
(off Penally Pl.)
Rosemary Cl. CR0: Croy 6J **155**
UB8: Hil 5C **74**
Rosemary Ct. *SE8* *6B 104*
(off Dorking Cl.)
Rosemary Dr. E14 . . . . .6F **87**
IG4: Ilf .5B **52**
Rosemary Gdns. KT9: Chess 4E **162**
RM8: Dag 1F **73**
SW14 .3J **115**
Rosemary Ho. *N1* *1D 84*
(off Branch Pl.)
NW10 . . . .*1D 80*
(off Uffington Rd.)
Rosemary La. SW14 . . . . .3J **115**
Rosemary Rd. DA16: Well 1K **125**
SE15 . . . . .7F **103**
SW17 .3A **136**
Rosemary St. N1 . . . . .1D **84**
Rosemead NW9 . . . . .7B **44**
Rosemead Av. CR4: Mitc 3G **155**
HA9: Wemb 5E **60**
TW13: Felt 2H **129**
Rose M. N18 . . . . .4C **34**
Rosemont Av. N12 . . . . .6F **31**
Rosemont Ct. *W3* *1H 97*
(off Rosemont Rd.)
Rosemont Rd. HA0: Wemb 1E **78**
KT3: N Mald 3J **151**
NW3 . . . . .6A **64**
TW10: Rich 6E **114**
W3 . . . . .7H **79**
Rosemoor St. SW3 . . . . .4E **16** (4D **100**)
Rosemount *SM6: Wall* *6G 167*
(off Clarendon Rd.)
Rosemount Cl. IG8: Wfd G 6J **37**
Rosemount Dr. BR1: Brom 4D **160**
Rosemount Point SE23 . . . . .3K **139**
Rosemount Rd. W13 . . . . .6A **78**
Rosenau Cres. SW11 . . . . .1D **118**
Rosenau Rd. SW11 . . . . .1C **118**
Rosendale Rd. SE21 . . . . .3D **138**
SE24 . . . . .7C **120**
Roseneath Av. N21 . . . . .1G **33**
Roseneath Rd. SW11 . . . . .6E **118**
Roseneath Wlk. EN1: Enf 4K **23**
Rosen's Wlk. HA8: Edg 3C **28**
Rosenthal Rd. SE6 . . . . .6D **122**
Rosenthorpe Rd. SE15 . . . . .5K **121**
Rose Pk. Cl. UB4: Yead 5A **76**
Rosepark Ct. IG5: Ilf 2D **52**
Roserton St. E14 . . . . .2E **104**
Rosery, The CR0: Croy 6K **157**
Roses, The IG8: Wfd G 7C **36**
Rose Sq. SW3 . . . . .5B **16** (5B **100**)
Rose St. EC4 . . . . .7B **8** (6B **84**)
WC2 . . . . .2E **12** (7J **83**)
(not continuous)
Rosethorn Cl. SW12 . . . . .7H **119**
Rose Tree M. IG8: Wfd G 6H **37**
Rosetta Cl. *SW8* *7J 101*
(off Kenchester Cl.)
Rosetti Ter. *RM8: Dag* *4B 72*
(off Marlborough Rd.)
Roseveare Rd. SE12 . . . . .4A **142**
Roseville Av. TW3: Houn 5E **112**
Roseville Rd. UB3: Harl 5J **93**
Rosevine Rd. SW20 . . . . .1E **152**
Rose Wlk. BR4: W W'ck 2E **170**
KT5: Surb 5H **151**
Rose Way SE12 . . . . .5J **123**
Roseway HA8: Edg 4D **28**
SE21 . . . . .6D **120**
Rosewell Cl. SE20 . . . . .7H **139**
Rosewood KT7: T Ditt 2A **162**
Rosewood Av. UB6: G'frd 5A **60**
Rosewood Cl. DA14: Sidc 3C **144**
Rosewood Ct. BR1: Brom 1A **160**
E11 . . . . .4F **69**
KT2: King T 7G **133**
RM6: Chad H 5C **54**
Rosewood Dr. TW17: Shep 5B **146**
Rosewood Gdns. SE13 . . . . .2E **122**
Rosewood Gro. SM1: Sutt 2A **166**
Rosewood Ho. *SW8* *7G 19*
(off Sth. Lambeth Rd.)
Rosewood Sq. W12 . . . . .6C **80**
Rosher Cl. E15 . . . . .7F **69**
Roshni Ho. SW17 . . . . .6C **136**
Rosina St. E9 . . . . .6K **67**
Roskell Rd. SW15 . . . . .3F **117**
Roslin Ho. *E1* *7K 85*
(off Brodlove La.)
Roslin Rd. W3 . . . . .3H **97**
Roslin Way BR1: Brom 5J **141**
Roslyn Cl. CR4: Mitc 2B **154**
Roslyn Rd. N15 . . . . .5D **48**
Rosmead Rd. W11 . . . . .7G **81**
Rosoman Pl. EC1 . . . . .3K **7** (4A **84**)
Rosoman St. EC1 . . . . .2K **7** (3A **84**)
Rossall Cres. NW10 . . . . .3F **79**
Ross Av. NW7 . . . . .5B **30**
RM8: Dag 2F **73**
Ross Cl. HA3: Hrw W 7B **26**
UB3: Harl 4F **93**
UB5: N'olt 4H **59**
Ross Ct. *E5* *4H 67*
(off Napoleon Rd.)
NW9 . . . . .3A **44**
SW15 .7F **117**
W13 . . . .*5B 78*
(off Cleveland Rd.)
Rosscourt Mans. *SW1* *1A 18*
(off Buckingham Pal. Rd.)
Rossdale SM1: Sutt 5C **166**
Rossdale Dr. N9 . . . . .6D **24**
NW9 . . . . .1J **61**
Rossdale Rd. SW15 . . . . .4E **116**
Rosse M. SE3 . . . . .1K **123**
Rossendale St. E5 . . . . .2H **67**
Rossendale Way NW1 . . . . .7G **65**
Rossetti Ct. *WC1* *5C 6*
(off Ridgmount Pl.)
Rossetti Gdn. Mans. SW3 . . . . .7E **16**
Rossetti Ho. *SW1* *4D 18*
(off Erasmus St.)
Rossetti M. NW8 . . . . .1B **82**
Rossetti Rd. SE16 . . . . .5H **103**
Rossetti Studios *SW3* *7D 16*
(off Flood St.)
Rosshaven Pl. HA6: Nwood 1H **39**
Ross Ho. *E1* *1H 103*
(off Prusom St.)
Rossignol Gdns. SM5: Cars 2E **166**
Rossindel Rd. TW3: Houn 5E **112**
Rossington Cl. EN1: Enf 1C **24**
Rossington St. E5 . . . . .2G **67**
Rossiter Flds. EN5: Barn 6B **20**
Rossiter Rd. SW12 . . . . .1F **137**
Rossland Cl. DA6: Bex 5H **127**
Rosslyn Av. E4 . . . . .2C **36**
EN4: E Barn 6H **21**
RM8: Dag 7F **55**
SW13 .3A **116**
TW14: Felt 6J **111**
Rosslyn Cl. BR4: W W'ck 3H **171**
TW16: Sun 6G **129**
UB3: Hayes 5F **75**
Rosslyn Cres. HA1: Harr 4K **41**
HA9: Wemb 4E **60**
Rosslyn Gdns. *HA9: Wemb* *3E 60*
(off Rosslyn Cres.)
Rosslyn Hill NW3 . . . . .4B **64**
Rosslyn Mans. *NW6* *7A 64*
(off Goldhurst Ter.)
Rosslyn M. NW3 . . . . .4B **64**
Rosslyn Pk. M. NW3 . . . . .5B **64**
Rosslyn Pk. RUFC 4B **116**
Rosslyn Rd. E17 . . . . .4E **50**
IG11: Bark 7H **71**
TW1: Twick 6C **114**
Rossmore Cl. EN3: Pond E 4E **24**
NW1 . . . .*4D 4*
(off Rossmore Rd.)
Rossmore Ct. NW1 . . . . .3E **4** (4D **82**)
Rossmore Rd. NW1 . . . . .4D **4** (4C **82**)
Ross Pde. SM6: Wall 6F **167**
Ross Rd. SE25 . . . . .3D **156**
SM6: Wall 5G **167**
TW2: Whit 1F **131**
Ross Way SE9 . . . . .3C **124**
Rosswood Gdns. SM6: Wall 6G **167**
Ross Wyld Lodge *E17* *3C 50*
(off Forest Rd.)
Rostella Rd. SW17 . . . . .4B **136**
Rostrevor Av. N15 . . . . .6F **49**
Rostrevor Gdns. UB2: S'hall 5C **94**
UB3: Hayes 1G **93**
Rostrevor M. SW6 . . . . .1H **117**
Rostrevor Rd. SW6 . . . . .1H **117**
SW19 . . . . .5J **135**
Rotary St. SE1 . . . . .7A **14** (3B **102**)
Rothay *NW1* *1K 5*
(off Albany St.)
Rothbury Cotts. SE10 . . . . .4G **105**
Rothbury Gdns. TW7: Isle 7A **96**
Rothbury Hall *4G 105*
(off Mauritius Rd.)
Rothbury Rd. E9 . . . . .7B **68**
Rothbury Wlk. N17 . . . . .7B **34**
Rotheley Ho. *E9* *7J 67*
(off Balcorne St.)
Rotherfield Ct. *N1* *7D 66*
(off Rotherfield St., not continuous)
Rotherfield Rd. SM5: Cars 4E **166**
Rotherfield St. N1 . . . . .7C **66**
Rotherham Wlk. SE1 . . . . .5A **14**
Rotherhill Av. SW16 . . . . .6H **137**
ROTHERHITHE 2J **103**
Rotherhithe Bus. Est. SE16 . . . . .4H **103**
Rotherhithe New Rd. SE16 . . . . .5H **103**
Rotherhithe Old Rd. SE16 . . . . .4K **103**
Rotherhithe St. SE16 . . . . .2J **103**
Rotherhithe Tunnel SE16 . . . . .1K **103**
Rother Ho. SE15 . . . . .4H **121**
Rotherwick Hill W5 . . . . .4F **79**
Rotherwick Ho. *E1* *7G 85*
(off Thomas More St.)
Rotherwick Rd. NW11 . . . . .7J **45**
Rotherwood Cl. SW20 . . . . .1G **153**
Rotherwood Rd. SW15 . . . . .3F **117**
Rothery St. *N1* *1B 84*
(off St Marys Path)
Rothesay Av. SW20 . . . . .2G **153**
TW10: Rich 4H **115**
UB6: G'frd 6G **59**
(not continuous)
Rothesay Ct. SE6 . . . . .2H **141**
SE11 . . . . .7J **19**
SE12 . . . . .3K **141**
Rothesay Rd. SE25 . . . . .4D **156**
Rothley Ct. *NW8* *3A 4*
(off St John's Wood Rd.)
Rothsay Rd. E7 . . . . .7A **70**
Rothsay St. SE1 . . . . .3E **102**
Rothsay Wlk. *E14* *4C 104*
(off Charnwood Gdns.)
Rothschild Rd. W4 . . . . .4J **97**
Rothschild St. SE27 . . . . .4B **138**
Roth Wlk. N7 . . . . .2K **65**
Rothwell Ct. HA1: Harr 5K **41**
Rothwell Gdns. RM9: Dag 7C **72**
Rothwell Ho. TW5: Hest 6E **94**
Rothwell Rd. RM9: Dag 1C **90**
Rothwell St. NW1 . . . . .1D **82**
Rotten Row NW3 . . . . .1A **64**
SW1 . . . . .6B **10** (2B **100**)
SW7 . . . . .6B **10** (2B **100**)
Rotterdam Dr. E14 . . . . .3E **104**
Rotunda, The *RM7: Rom* *5K 55*
(off Yew Tree Gdns.)
Rotunda Cen., The 2E **150**
Rouel Rd. SE16 . . . . .3G **103**
(Dockley Rd.)
SE16 . . . . .4G **103**
(Southwark Pk. Rd.)
Rougemont Av. SM4: Mord 6J **153**
Roundabout Ho. HA6: Nwood 1J **39**
Roundacre SW19 . . . . .2F **135**
Roundaway Rd. IG5: Ilf 1D **52**
Roundel Cl. SE4 . . . . .4B **122**
Round Gro. CR0: Croy 7K **157**
Roundhay Cl. SE23 . . . . .2K **139**
Roundhedge Way EN2: Enf 1E **22**
Round Hill SE26 . . . . .2J **139**
(not continuous)
Roundhill Dr. EN2: Enf 4E **22**
Roundhouse, The *7E 64*
(off Chalk Farm Rd.)
ROUNDSHAW .7J **167**
Roundtable Rd. BR1: Brom 3H **141**
Roundtree Rd. HA0: Wemb 5B **60**
Roundway, The KT10: Clay 6A **162**
N17 . . . . .1C **48**
Roundways HA4: Ruis 3H **57**
Roundwood BR7: Chst 2F **161**
Roundwood Av. UB11: Stock P 1E **92**
Roundwood Cl. HA4: Ruis 7F **39**
Roundwood Rd. NW10 . . . . .6B **62**
Rounton Rd. E3 . . . . .4C **86**
Roupell Ho. *KT2: King T* *7F 133*
(off Florence Rd.)
Roupell Rd. SW2 . . . . .1K **137**
Roupell St. SE1 . . . . .5K **13** (1A **102**)
Rousden St. NW1 . . . . .7G **65**
Rouse Gdns. SE21 . . . . .4E **138**
Rous Rd. IG9: Buck H 1H **37**
Routemaster Cl. E13 . . . . .3K **87**
Routh Ct. TW14: Bedf 1F **129**
Routh Rd. SW18 . . . . .7C **118**
Routh St. E6 .5D **88**
Rover Ho. *N1* *1E 84*
(off Mill Row)
Rowallan Rd. SW6 . . . . .7G **99**
Rowallen Pde. RM8: Dag 1C **72**
Rowan N10 . . . . .2F **47**
Rowan Av. E4 . . . . .6G **35**
Rowan Cl. HA0: Wemb 3A **60**
HA7: Stan 6E **26**
IG1: Ilf .5H **71**
KT3: N Mald 2A **152**
SW16 . . . . .1G **155**
W5 . . . . .2E **96**

Rowan Ct. *E13* 2K **87**
(off High St.)
SE15 7F **103**
(off Garnies Cl.)
SW11 6D **118**
Rowan Cres. SW16 1G **155**
Rowan Dr. NW9 3C **44**
Rowan Gdns. CR0: Croy 3F **169**
Rowan Ho. BR2: Brom 2G **159**
DA14: Sidc 3K **143**
SE16 2K **103**
(off Woodland Cres.)
Rowan Lodge *W8* 3K **99**
(off Chantry Sq.)
Rowan Pl. UB3: Hayes 7H **75**
Rowan Rd. DA7: Bex 3E **126**
SW16 2G **155**
TW8: Bford 7B **96**
UB7: W Dray 4A **92**
W6 4F **99**
Rowans, The N13 3G **33**
TW16: Sun 5H **129**
Rowans Complex N4 2A **66**
Rowan Ter. W6 4F **99**
Rowantree Cl. N21 1J **33**
Rowantree Rd. EN2: Enf 2G **23**
N21 1J **33**
Rowan Wlk. BR2: Brom 3D **172**
EN5: New Bar 5E **20**
N2 5A **46**
N19 2G **65**
W10 4G **81**
Rowan Way RM6: Chad H 3C **54**
Rowanwood Av. DA15: Sidc 1A **144**
Rowanwood M. EN2: Enf 2G **23**
Rowben Cl. N20 1E **30**
Rowberry Cl. SW6 7E **98**
Rowcross St. SE1 5F **103**
Rowdell Rd. UB5: N'olt 1E **76**
Rowden Pk. Gdns. *E4* 7H **35**
(off Chingford Rd.)
Rowden Rd. BR3: Beck 1A **158**
E4 6J **35**
KT19: Ewe 4H **163**
Rowditch La. SW11 2E **118**
Rowdon Av. NW10 7D **62**
Rowdown Cres. CR0: New Ad 7F **171**
Rowdowns Rd. RM9: Dag 1F **91**
Rowe Gdns. IG11: Bark 2K **89**
Rowe Ho. E9 6J **67**
Rowe La. E9 5J **67**
Rowena Cres. SW11 2C **118**
Rowe Wlk. HA2: Harr 3E **58**
Rowfant Rd. SW17 1E **136**
Rowhill Rd. E5 4H **67**
Rowington Cl. W2 5K **81**
Rowland Av. HA3: Kent 3C **42**
Rowland Ct. E16 4H **87**
Rowland Gro. SE26 3H **139**
Rowland Hill Almshouses
TW15: Ashf 5C **128**
(off Feltham Hill Rd.)
Rowland Hill Av. N17 7H **33**
Rowland Hill Ho. SE1 6A **14** (2B **102**)
Rowland Hill St. NW3 5C **64**
Rowlands Av. HA5: H End 5A **26**
Rowlands Cl. N6 6E **46**
NW7 7H **29**
Rowlands Rd. RM8: Dag 2F **73**
Rowland Way SW19 1K **153**
TW15: Ashf 7F **129**
Rowley Av. DA15: Sidc 7B **126**
Rowley Cl. HA0: Wemb 7F **61**
Rowley Ct. *EN1: Enf* 5K **23**
(off Wellington Rd.)
Rowley Gdns. N4 7C **48**
Rowley Ho. *SE8* 5C **104**
(off Watergate St.)
Rowley Ind. Pk. W3 3H **97**
Rowley Rd. N15 5C **48**
Rowley Way NW8 1K **81**
Rowlheys Pl. UB7: W Dray 3A **92**
Rowlls Rd. KT1: King T 3F **151**
Rowney Gdns. RM9: Dag 6C **72**
Rowney Rd. RM9: Dag 6B **72**
Rowntree Clifford Cl. E13 4J **87**
Rowntree Cl. NW6 6J **63**
Rowntree Path SE28 1B **108**
Rowntree Rd. TW2: Twick 1J **131**
Rowse Cl. E15 1E **86**
Rowsley Av. NW4 3E **44**
Rowstock Gdns. N7 5H **65**
Rowton Rd. SE18 7G **107**
Roxborough Av. HA1: Harr 7H **41**
TW7: Isle 7K **95**
Roxborough Hgts. *HA1: Harr* 6J **41**
(off College Rd.)
Roxborough Pk. HA1: Harr 7J **41**
Roxborough Rd. HA1: Harr 5H **41**
Roxbourne Cl. UB5: N'olt 6C **58**
Roxbourne Pk. Miniature Railway 2B **58**
Roxburghe Mans. *W8* 2K **99**
(off Kensington Ct.)
Roxburgh Rd. SE27 5B **138**
Roxburn Way HA4: Ruis 3H **57**
Roxby Pl. SW6 6J **99**
ROXETH 2H **59**
Roxeth Ct. TW15: Ashf 5C **128**
Roxeth Grn. Av. HA2: Harr 3F **59**
Roxeth Gro. HA2: Harr 4F **59**
Roxeth Hill HA2: Harr 2H **59**
Roxford Cl. TW17: Shep 5G **147**
Roxley Rd. SE13 6D **122**
Roxton Gdns. CR0: Addtn 5C **170**
Roxwell *NW1* 6F **65**
(off Hartland Rd.)
Roxwell Rd. IG11: Bark 2A **90**
W12 2C **98**
Roxwell Trad. Pk. E10 7A **50**
Roxwell Way IG8: Wfd G 7F **37**
Roxy Av. RM6: Chad H 7C **54**
Royal Academy of Arts (Burlington House) 3A **12** (7G **83**)
Royal Academy of Music Mus. 4H **5**
Royal Air Force Memorial 5F **13** (1J **101**)
Royal Albert Hall 7A **10** (2B **100**)
Royal Albert Rdbt. *E16* 7C **88**
(off Royal Albert Way)
Royal Albert Way E16 7B **88**
Royal Arc. W1 3A **12**
ROYAL ARSENAL WEST 3F **107**
Royal Av. KT4: Wor Pk 2A **164**
SW3 5E **16** (5D **100**)
Royal Av. Ho. *SW3* 5E **16**
(off Royal Av.)
Royal Belgrave Ho. *SW1* 4K **17**
(off Hugh St.)
Royal Botanic Gdns. 1E **114**
Royal Brass Foundry 3F **107**
Royal Ceremonial Dress Collection, The 1K **99**
(in Kensington Palace)
Royal Cir. SE27 3A **138**
Royal Cl. BR6: Farnb 4F **173**
IG3: Ilf 7A **54**
KT4: Wor Pk 2A **164**
N16 1E **66**
SE8 6B **104**
SW19 3F **135**
UB8: Hil 6B **74**
Royal College of Art 7A **10** (2B **100**)
Royal College of Music 1A **16** (3B **100**)
Royal College of Obstetricians & Gynaecologists 3E **4** (4D **82**)
Royal College of Physicians 3J **5** (4F **83**)
Royal College of Surgeons 7H **7** (6K **83**)
Royal Coll. St. NW1 7G **65**
Royal Connaught Apartments *E16* 1B **106**
(off Connaught Rd.)
Royal Ct. *EC3* 1F **15**
(off Finch La.)
EN1: Enf 6K **23**
HA4: Ruis 6J **39**
SE9 1D **142**
Royal Ct. SE16 3B **104**
Royal Courts of Justice 1H **13** (6A **84**)
Royal Court Theatre 4G **17**
(off Sloane Sq.)
Royal Cres. HA4: Ruis 4C **58**
IG2: Ilf 6H **53**
W11 1F **99**
Royal Cres. M. W11 1F **99**
Royal Docks Rd. E6 6F **89**
IG11: Bark 6F **89**
Royal Dr. N11 5K **31**
Royal Duchess M. SW12 7F **119**
Royale Leisure Pk. W3 4G **79**
Royal Exchange 1F **15** (6D **84**)
Royal Exchange Av. EC3 1F **15**
Royal Exchange Bldgs. EC3 1F **15**
Royal Festival Hall 5H **13** (1K **101**)
Royal Fusiliers Mus. 3J **15**
(in The Tower of London)
Royal Gdns. W7 3A **96**
Royal Geographical Society 7A **10**
Royal Herbert Pavilions SE18 1D **124**
Royal Hill SE10 7E **104**
Royal Hill Ct. *SE10* 7E **104**
(off Greenwich High St.)
Royal Hospital Chelsea Mus. 6G **17** (5E **100**)
Royal Hospital Rd. SW3 7E **16** (6D **100**)
Royal La. UB7: Yiew 5B **74**
UB8: Hil 5B **74**
Royal London Est., The N17 6C **34**
Royal London Ind. Est. NW10 2K **79**
Royal Mews, The 1K **17** (3F **101**)
Royal M. KT8: E Mos 3J **149**
SW1 1K **17** (3F **101**)
Royal Mid Surrey Golf Course 3D **114**
Royal Mint Ct. EC3 3K **15** (7F **85**)
Royal Mint Pl. E1 2K **15** (7G **85**)
Royal Mint St. E1 2K **15** (7F **85**)
Royal Naval Pl. SE14 7B **104**
Royal Oak Ct. *N1* 1G **9**
(off Pitfield St.)
Royal Oak Pl. SE22 6H **121**
Royal Oak Rd. DA6: Bex 5F **127**
(not continuous)
E8 6H **67**
Royal Oak Yd. SE1 7G **15** (2E **102**)
Royal Observatory Greenwich 7G **105**
Royal Opera Arc. SW1 4C **12** (1H **101**)
Royal Opera House 1F **13** (6J **83**)
Royal Orchard Cl. SW18 7G **117**
Royal Pde. BR7: Chst 7G **143**
RM10: Dag 6H **73**
(off Church St.)
SE3 2H **123**
SW6 7G **99**
TW9: Kew 1G **115**
(off Layton Pl.)
W5 3E **78**
Royal Pde. M. *BR7: Chst* 7G **143**
(off Royal Pde.)
SE3 2H **123**
(off Royal Pde.)
Royal Pl. SE10 7E **104**
Royal Quay Rd. E6 7F **89**
E16 7F **89**
Royal Rd. DA14: Sidc 3D **144**
E16 6B **88**
SE17 6B **102**
TW11: Tedd 5H **131**
Royal Route HA9: Wemb 4F **61**
Royal St. SE1 1H **19** (3K **101**)
Royal Twr. Lodge *E1* 3K **15**
(off Cartwright St.)
Royalty Mans. *W1* 1C **12**
(off Richmond M.)
Royalty M. W1 1C **12** (6H **83**)
Royalty Studios *W11* 6G **81**
(off Lancaster Rd.)
Royal Veterinary College Camden Town 1H **83**
Royal Victoria Docks Watersports Cen. 7J **87**
Royal Victoria Patriotic Bldg. SW18 6B **118**
Royal Victoria Pl. E16 1K **105**
Royal Victoria Sq. E16 7K **87**
Royal Victor Pl. E3 2K **85**
Royal Wlk. SM6: Wall 2F **167**
Royal Westminster Lodge *SW1* 3C **18**
(off Elverton St.)
Roycraft Av. IG11: Bark 2K **89**
Roycroft Cl. E18 1K **51**
SW2 1A **138**
Roydene Rd. SE18 6J **107**
Roydon Cl. IG10: Lough 1H **37**
SW11 2D **118**
(off Battersea Pk. Rd.)
Roy Gdns. IG2: Ilf 4J **53**
Roy Gro. TW12: Hamp 6F **131**
Royle Bldg. *N1* 2C **84**
(off Wenlock Rd.)
Royle Cres. W13 4A **78**
Roymount Ct. TW2: Twick 3J **131**
Roy Rd. HA6: Nwood 1H **39**
Roy Sq. E14 7A **86**
Royston Av. E4 5H **35**
SM1: Sutt 3B **166**
SM6: Bedd 4H **167**
Royston Cl. KT12: Walt T 7J **147**
TW5: Cran 1K **111**
Royston Ct. *E13* 1J **87**
(off Stopford Rd.)
SE24 6C **120**
TW9: Kew 1F **115**
W8 1J **99**
(off Kensington Chu. St.)
Royston Gdns. IG1: Ilf 6B **52**
Royston Ho. N11 4J **31**
SE15 6H **103**
(off Friary Est.)
Royston Pde. IG1: Ilf 6B **52**
Royston Pk. Rd. HA5: H End 5A **26**
Royston Rd. SE20 1K **157**
TW10: Rich 5E **114**
Roystons, The KT5: Surb 5H **151**
Royston St. E2 2J **85**
Rozel Ct. N1 1E **84**
Rozel Rd. SW4 3G **119**
Rozel Ter. *CR0: Croy* 2C **168**
(off Church Rd.)
Rq33 SW18 4J **117**
Rubastic Rd. UB2: S'hall 3A **94**
Rubens Gdns. *SE22* 7G **121**
(off Lordship La.)
Rubens Pl. SW4 4J **119**
Rubens Rd. UB5: N'olt 2A **76**
Rubens St. SE6 2B **140**
Ruby Rd. E17 3C **50**
Ruby St. NW10 7K **61**
SE15 6H **103**
Ruby Triangle SE15 6H **103**
Ruckholt Cl. E10 3D **68**
Ruckholt Rd. E9 4C **68**
E10 4C **68**
Rucklidge Av. NW10 2B **80**
Rucklidge Pas. *NW10* 2B **80**
(off Rucklidge Av.)
Rudall Cres. NW3 4B **64**
Rudbeck Ho. *SE15* 7G **103**
(off Peckham Pk. Rd.)
Ruddington Cl. E5 4A **68**
Ruddock Cl. HA8: Edg 7D **28**
Ruddstreet Cl. SE18 4F **107**
Ruddy Way NW7 6G **29**
Rudge Ho. *SE16* 3G **103**
(off Jamaica Rd.)
Rudgwick Ct. *SE18* 4C **106**
(off Woodville St., not continuous)
Rudgwick Ter. NW8 1C **82**
Rudland Rd. DA7: Bex 3H **127**
Rudloe Rd. SW12 7G **119**
Rudolf Pl. SW8 7F **19** (6J **101**)
Rudolph Rd. E13 2H **87**
NW6 2J **81**
Rudyard Gro. NW7 6D **28**

Ruegg Ho. SE18 ....6E 106
(off Woolwich Comn.)
Ruffetts, The CR2: Sels 7H 169
Ruffetts Cl. CR2: Sels 7H 169
Ruffle Cl. UB7: W Dray 2A 92
Rufford Cl. HA3: Kent 6A 42
Rufford St. N1 ....1J 83
Rufford Twr. W3 ....1H 97
Rufforth Cl. NW9 ....1A 44
(off Pageant Av.)
Rufus Bus. Cen. SW18 ....2K 135
Rufus Cl. HA4: Ruis 3C 58
Rufus Ho. SE1 ....7K 15
(off Abbey St.)
Rufus St. N1 ....2G 9 (3E 84)
Rugby Av. HA0: Wemb 5B 60
N9 ....1A 34
UB6: G'frd 6H 59
Rugby Cl. HA1: Harr 4J 41
Rugby Gdns. RM9: Dag 6C 72
Rugby Mans. W14 ....4G 99
(off Bishop King's Rd.)
Rugby Rd. NW9 ....4H 43
RM9: Dag 6B 72
TW1: Twick 5J 113
W4 ....2A 98
Rugby St. WC1 ....4G 7 (4K 83)
Rugg St. E14 ....7C 86
Rugless Ho. E14 ....2E 104
(off E. Ferry Rd.)
Rugmere NW1 ....7E 64
(off Ferdinand St.)
RUISLIP 1G 57
Ruislip Cl. UB6: G'frd 4F 77
RUISLIP COMMON 4E 38
Ruislip Ct. HA4: Ruis 2H 57
RUISLIP GARDENS 3J 57
Ruislip Lido Railway
Eleanor's Station 3G 39
Haste Hill Station 3G 39
Lakeside Station 4F 39
Woody Bay Station 5F 39
Ruislip Local Nature Reserve ...3F 39
RUISLIP MANOR 2J 57
Ruislip Rd. UB1: S'hall 2B 76
UB5: N'olt 1A 76
UB6: G'frd 3E 76
Ruislip Rd. E. UB6: G'frd 4H 77
W7 ....4J 77
W13 ....4H 77
Ruislip St. SW17 ....4D 136
Ruislip Woodlands Cen. 4F 39
Rumball Ho. SE5 ....7E 102
(off Harris St.)
Rumbold Rd. SW6 ....7K 99
Rum Cl. E1 ....7J 85
Rumford Ho. SE1 ....3C 102
(off Tiverton St.)
Rumney Ct. UB5: N'olt 2B 76
(off Parkfield Dr.)
Rumsey Cl. TW12: Hamp 6D 130
Rumsey M. N4 ....3B 66
Rumsey Rd. SW9 ....3K 119
Runacres Ct. SE17 ....5C 102
Runbury Circ. NW9 ....2K 61
Runcorn Cl. N17 ....4H 49
Runcorn Pl. W11 ....7G 81
Rundell Cres. NW4 ....5D 44
Rundell Twr. SW8 ....1K 119
Runes Cl. CR4: Mitc 4B 154
Runnelfield HA1: Harr 3J 59
Running Horse Yd. TW8: Bford ..6E 96
Runnymede SW19 ....1A 154
Runnymede Cl. TW2: Whit 6F 113
Runnymede Ct. SM6: Wall 6F 167
SW15 ....1C 134
Runnymede Cres. SW16 ......1H 155
Runnymede Gdns. TW2: Whit ..6F 113
UB6: G'frd 2J 77
Runnymede Ho. E9 ....4A 68
Runnymede Rd. TW2: Whit ...6F 113
Runway, The HA4: Ruis 5K 57
Rupack St. SE16 ....2J 103

Rupert Av. HA9: Wemb 5E 60
Rupert Ct. KT8: W Mole 4E 148
(off St Peters Rd.)
W1 ....2C 12 (7H 83)
Rupert Gdns. SW9 ....2B 120
Rupert Ho. SE11 ....4K 19 (4A 102)
SW5 ....4J 99
(off Nevern Sq.)
Rupert Rd. N19 ....3H 65
(not continuous)
NW6 ....2H 81
W4 ....3A 98
Rupert St. W1 ....2C 12 (7H 83)
Rural Way SW16 ....7F 137
Rusbridge Cl. E8 ....5G 67
Ruscoe Rd. E16 ....6H 87
Ruscombe Way TW14: Felt 7H 111
Rush, The SW19 ....1H 153
(off Kingston Rd.)
Rusham Rd. SW12 ....6D 118
Rushbrook Cres. E17 ....1B 50
Rushbrook Rd. SE9 ....2G 143
Rushbury Ct. TW12: Hamp 1E 148
Rush Comn. M. SW2 ....7K 119
(Cotherstone Rd.)
SW2 ....7J 119
(New Pk. Rd.)
Rushcroft Rd. E4 ....7J 35
SW2 ....4A 120
Rushcutters Ct. SE16 ....4A 104
(off Boat Lifter Way)
Rushden Cl. SE19 ....7D 138
Rushdene SE2 ....3D 108
(not continuous)
Rushdene Av. EN4: E Barn 7H 21
Rushdene Cl. UB5: Yead 2A 76
Rushdene Cres. UB5: Yead ...2K 75
Rushdene Rd. HA5: Eastc 6B 40
Rushden Gdns. IG5: Ilf 2E 52
NW7 ....6K 29
Rushen Wlk. SM5: Cars 1B 166
Rushett Cl. KT7: T Ditt 1B 162
Rushett Rd. KT7: T Ditt 7B 150
Rushey Cl. KT3: N Mald 4K 151
Rushey Grn. SE6 ....7D 122
Rushey Hill EN2: Enf 4E 22
Rushey Mead SE4 ....5C 122
Rushford Rd. SE4 ....6B 122
RUSH GREEN 1K 73
Rush Grn. Gdns. RM7: Rush G ..1J 73
Rush Grn. Rd. RM7: Rush G ...1H 73
Rushgrove Av. NW9 ....5A 44
Rushgrove Ct. NW9 ....5A 44
Rushgrove Pde. NW9 ....5A 44
Rushgrove St. SE18 ....4D 106
Rush Hill M. SW11 ....3E 118
(off Rush Hill Rd.)
Rush Hill Rd. SW11 ....3E 118
Rushley Cl. BR2: Kes 4B 172
Rushmead E2 ....3H 85
TW10: Ham 3B 132
Rushmead Cl. CR0: Croy 4F 169
HA8: Edg 2C 28
Rushmere Ct. KT4: Wor Pk ...2C 164
Rushmere Pl. SW19 ....5F 135
Rushmon Pl. SM3: Cheam 6G 165
Rushmon Vs. KT3: N Mald 4B 152
Rushmoor Cl. HA5: Eastc 4K 39
Rushmore Cl. BR1: Brom 3C 160
Rushmore Cres. E5 ....4K 67
Rushmore Ho. SW15 ....7C 116
W14 ....3G 99
(off Russell Rd.)
Rushmore Rd. E5 ....4J 67
(not continuous)
Rusholme Av. RM10: Dag 3G 73
Rusholme Gro. SE19 ....5E 138
Rusholme Rd. SW15 ....6F 117
Rushout Av. HA3: Kent 6B 42
Rushton Ho. SW8 ....2H 119
Rushton St. N1 ....2D 84
Rushworth St. SE1 .....6B 14 (2B 102)
Rushy Mdw. La. SM5: Cars ...2C 166

Ruskin Av. DA16: Well 2A 126
E12 ....6C 70
TW9: Kew 7G 97
(not continuous)
TW14: Felt 6H 111
Ruskin Cl. NW11 ....6K 45
Ruskin Ct. N21 ....7E 22
SE5 ....3D 120
(off Champion Hill)
Ruskin Dr. BR6: Orp 3J 173
DA16: Well 3A 126
KT4: Wor Pk 2D 164
Ruskin Gdns. HA3: Kent 5F 43
W5 ....4D 78
Ruskin Gro. DA16: Well 2A 126
Ruskin Ho. CR2: S Croy 5D 168
(off Selsdon Rd.)
SW1 ....4D 18
(off Herrick St.)
Ruskin Mans. W14 ....6G 99
(off Queen's Club Gdns.)
Ruskin Pde. CR2: S Croy 5D 168
(off Selsdon Rd.)
Ruskin Pk. Ho. SE5 ....3D 120
Ruskin Rd. CR0: Croy 2B 168
DA17: Belv 4G 109
N17 ....1F 49
SM5: Cars 5D 166
TW7: Isle 3K 113
UB1: S'hall 7C 76
Ruskin Wlk. BR2: Brom 6D 160
N9 ....2B 34
SE24 ....5C 120
Ruskin Way SW19 ....1B 154
Rusland Av. BR6: Orp 3H 173
Rusland Hgts. HA1: Harr 4J 41
Rusland Pk. Rd. HA1: Harr ...4J 41
Rusper Cl. HA7: Stan 4H 27
NW2 ....3E 62
Rusper Ct. SW9 ....2J 119
(off Clapham Rd.)
Rusper Rd. N22 ....2B 48
RM9: Dag 6C 72
Russell Av. N22 ....2A 48
Russell Cl. BR3: Beck 3D 158
DA7: Bex 4G 127
HA4: Ruis 2A 58
NW10 ....7J 61
SE7 ....7A 106
W4 ....6B 98
Russell Cl. E10 ....7D 50
EN5: New Bar 4F 21
N14 ....6C 22
SE15 ....2H 121
(off Heaton Rd.)
SM6: Wall 5G 167
(off Ross Rd.)
SW1 ....5B 12
SW16 ....5K 137
WC1 ....4E 6
Russell Flint Ho. E16 ....1K 105
(off Pankhurst Av.)
Russell Gdns. IG2: Ilf 7H 53
N20 ....2H 31
NW11 ....6G 45
TW10: Ham 2C 132
UB7: Sip 5C 92
W14 ....3G 99
Russell Gdns. M. W14 ......2G 99
Russell Gro. NW7 ....5F 29
SW9 ....7A 102
Russell Ho. E14 ....6C 86
(off Saracen St.)
SW1 ....5A 18
(off Cambridge St.)
Russell Kerr Cl. W4 ....7J 97
Russell La. N20 ....2H 31
Russell Lodge E4 ....2K 35
SE1 ....3D 102
(off Spurgeon St.)
Russell Mans. WC1 ....5F 7
(off Southampton Row)
Russell Mead HA3: Hrw W ...1K 41

Russell Pde. NW11 ....6G 45
(off Golders Grn. Rd.)
Russell Pl. NW3 ....5C 64
SE16 ....3A 104
SM2: Sutt 7K 165
Russell Rd. CR4: Mitc 3C 154
E4 ....4G 35
E10 ....6D 50
E16 ....6J 87
E17 ....3B 50
EN1: Enf 1A 24
IG9: Buck H 1E 36
KT12: Walt T 6J 147
N8 ....6H 47
N13 ....6E 32
N15 ....5E 48
N20 ....2H 31
NW9 ....6B 44
SW19 ....7J 135
TW2: Twick 6K 113
TW17: Shep 7E 146
UB5: N'olt 5G 59
W14 ....3G 99
Russell's Footpath SW16 ....5J 137
Russell Sq. WC1 ......4E 6 (4J 83)
Russell St. WC2 .....2F 13 (7J 83)
Russell's Wharf Flats W10 ...4H 81
Russell Wlk. TW10: Rich 6F 115
Russell Way SM1: Sutt 5A 165
Russell Yd. SW15 ....4G 117
Russel Sq. Mans. WC1 ......5F 7
(off Southampton Row)
Russet Av. TW17: Shep 3G 147
Russet Cl. UB10: Hil 4E 74
Russet Cres. N7 ....5K 65
Russet Dr. CR0: Croy 1A 170
Russets Cl. E4 ....4A 36
Russett Way SE13 ....2D 122
Russia Dock Rd. SE16 ......1A 104
Russia La. E2 ....2J 85
Russia Row EC2 ....1D 14 (6C 84)
Russia Wlk. SE16 ....2A 104
Russington Rd. TW17: Shep ..6F 147
Rusthall Av. W4 ....4K 97
Rusthall Cl. CR0: Croy 6J 157
Rustic Av. SW16 ....7F 137
Rustic Pl. HA0: Wemb 4D 60
Rustic Wlk. E16 ....6K 87
(off Lambert Rd.)
Rustington Wlk. SM4: Mord ..7H 153
Ruston Av. KT5: Surb 7H 151
Ruston Gdns. N14 ....6K 21
Ruston M. W11 ....6G 81
Ruston Rd. SE18 ....3C 106
Ruston St. E3 ....1B 86
Rust Sq. SE5 ....7D 102
Rutford Rd. SW16 ....5J 137
Ruth Cl. HA7: Stan 4F 43
Ruth Ct. E3 ....2A 86
Rutherford Cl. SM2: Sutt 6B 166
UB8: Hil 4B 74
Rutherford Ho. E1 ....4H 85
(off Brady St.)
HA9: Wemb 3J 61
(off Barnhill Rd.)
Rutherford St. SW1 .....3C 18 (4H 101)
Rutherford Twr. UB1: S'hall ...6F 77
Rutherford Way
HA9: Wemb 4G 61
WD23: Bushy 1C 26
Rutherglen Rd. SE2 ....6A 108
Rutherwyke Cl.
KT17: Ewe 6C 164
Ruth Ho. W10 ....4G 81
(off Kensal Rd.)
Ruthin Cl. NW9 ....6A 44
Ruthin Rd. SE3 ....6J 105
Ruthven St. E9 ....1K 85
Rutland Av. DA15: Sidc 7A 126
Rutland Cl. DA5: Bex 2D 144
KT9: Chess 6F 163
SW14 ....3H 115
SW19 ....7C 136

Rutland Ct.—St Ann's Cres.

Rutland Ct. BR7: Chst 1E 160
EN3: Pond E 5C 24
KT1: King T 4D 150
(off Palace Rd.)
SE5 ....4D 120
SE9 ....2G 143
SW7 ....7D 10
W3 ....6G 79
Rutland Dr. SM4: Mord 6H 153
TW10: Ham 1D 132
Rutland Gdns. CR0: Croy 4E 168
N4 ....6B 48
RM8: Dag 5C 72
SW7 ....7D 10 (2C 100)
W13 ....5A 78
Rutland Gdns. M. SW7 ....7D 10 (2C 100)
Rutland Ga. BR2: Brom 4H 159
DA17: Belv 5H 109
SW7 ....7D 10 (2C 100)
Rutland Ga. M. SW7 ....7C 10
Rutland Gro. W6 ....5D 98
Rutland Ho. UB5: N'olt 6E 58
(off The Farmlands)
W8 ....3K 99
(off Marloes Rd.)
Rutland M. NW8 ....1K 81
Rutland M. E. SW7 ....1C 16
Rutland M. Sth. SW7 ....1C 16
Rutland M. W. SW7 ....1C 16
Rutland Pk. NW2 ....6E 62
SE6 ....2B 140
Rutland Pk. Gdns. NW2 ....6E 62
(off Rutland Pk.)
Rutland Pk. Mans. NW2 ....6E 62
Rutland Pl. EC1 ....5B 8 (4B 84)
WD23: Bushy 1C 26
Rutland Rd. E7 ....7B 70
E9 ....1K 85
E11 ....5K 51
E17 ....6C 50
HA1: Harr 6G 41
IG1: Ilf 3F 71
SW19 ....7C 136
TW2: Twick 2H 131
UB1: S'hall 5E 76
UB3: Harl 4F 93
Rutland St. SW7 ....1D 16 (3C 100)
Rutland Wlk. SE6 ....2B 140
Rutley Cl. SE17 ....6B 102
Rutlish Rd. SW19 ....1J 153
Rutter Gdns. CR4: Mitc 4A 154
Rutters Cl. UB7: W Dray 2C 92
Rutts, The WD23: Bushy 1C 26
Rutt's Ter. SE14 ....1K 121
Ruvigny Gdns. SW15 ....3F 117
Ruxbury Ct. TW15: Ashf 3A 128
RUXLEY 7E 144
Ruxley Cl. DA14: Sidc 6D 144
KT19: Ewe 5H 163
Ruxley Cnr. Ind. Est.
DA14: Sidc 6D 144
Ruxley Ct. KT19: Ewe 5J 163
Ruxley Cres. KT10: Clay 6B 162
Ruxley Gdns. TW17: Shep 5E 146
Ruxley La. KT19: Ewe 6H 163
Ruxley M. KT19: Ewe 5H 163
Ruxley Ridge KT10: Clay 7A 162
Ruxley Towers KT10: Clay 7A 162
Ryalls Ct. N20 ....3J 31
Ryan Cl. HA4: Ruis 1K 57
SE3 ....4K 123
Ryan Ct. SW16 ....7J 137
Ryan Dr. TW8: Bford 6A 96
Ryarsh Cres. BR6: Orp 4J 173
Rycott Path SE22 ....7G 121
Rycroft Way N17 ....3F 49
Ryculff Sq. SE3 ....2H 123
Rydal Cl. NW4 ....1G 45
Rydal Ct. HA8: Edg 5A 28
HA9: Wemb 7F 43
Rydal Cres. UB6: G'frd 3B 78
Rydal Dr. BR4: W W'ck 2G 171
DA7: Bex 1G 127
Rydal Gdns. HA9: Wemb 1C 60
NW9 ....5A 44
SW15 ....5A 134
TW3: Houn 6F 113
Rydal Mt. BR2: Brom 4H 159
Rydal Rd. SW16 ....4H 137
Rydal Water NW1 ....2A 6 (3G 83)
Rydal Way EN3: Pond E 6D 24
HA4: Ruis 4A 58
Rydens Ho. SE9 ....3A 142
Rydens Rd. KT12: Walt T 7C 148
Ryde Pl. TW1: Twick 6D 114
Ryder Cl. BR1: Brom 5K 141
Ryder Ct. E10 ....2D 68
SW1 ....4B 12
Ryder Dr. SE16 ....5H 103
Ryder Ho. E1 ....4J 85
(off Colebert Av.)
Ryder M. E9 ....5J 67
Ryder's Ter. NW8 ....2A 82
Ryder St. SW1 ....4B 12 (1G 101)
Ryder Yd. SW1 ....4B 12 (1G 101)
Ryde Va. Rd. SW12 ....2G 137
Rydon M. SW19 ....7E 134
Rydons Cl. SE9 ....3C 124
Rydon St. N1 ....1C 84
Rydston Cl. N7 ....7J 65
Rye, The N14 ....7C 22
Rye Cl. DA5: Bexl 6H 127
Ryecotes Mead SE21 ....1E 138
Ryecroft Av. IG5: Ilf 2F 53
TW2: Whit 7F 113
Ryecroft Rd. BR5: Pet W 6H 161
SE13 ....5E 122
SW16 ....6A 138
Ryecroft St. SW6 ....1K 117
Ryedale SE22 ....6H 121
Ryefield Av. UB10: Hil 7D 56
Ryefield Ct. HA6: Nwood 2J 39
Ryefield Cres. HA6: Nwood 2J 39
Ryefield Pde. HA6: Nwood 2J 39
(off Joel St.)
Ryefield Path SW15 ....1C 134
Ryefield Rd. SE19 ....6C 138
Rye Hill Pk. SE15 ....4J 121
Rye Ho. SE16 ....2J 103
(off Swan Rd.)
SW1 ....5J 17
(off Ebury Bri. Rd.)
Ryeland Cl. UB7: Yiew 6A 74
Ryelands Cres. SE12 ....6A 124
Rye La. SE15 ....1G 121
Rye Pas. SE15 ....3G 121
Rye Rd. SE15 ....4K 121
Rye Wlk. SW15 ....5F 117
Rye Way HA8: Edg 6A 28
Ryfold Rd. SW19 ....3J 135
Ryhope Rd. N11 ....4A 32
Ryland Cl. TW13: Felt 4H 129
Rylandes Rd. NW2 ....3C 62
Ryland Rd. NW5 ....6F 65
Rylett Cres. W12 ....2B 98
Rylett Rd. W12 ....2B 98
Rylston Rd. N13 ....3J 33
SW6 ....6H 99
Rymer Rd. CR0: Croy 7E 156
Rymer St. SE24 ....6B 120
Rymill St. E16 ....1E 106
Rysbrack St. SW3 ....1E 16 (3D 100)
Rythe Cl. KT9: Chess 7C 162
Rythe Ct. KT7: T Ditt 7A 150

S

Saatchi Gallery 5D 100
Sabah Ct. TW15: Ashf 4C 128
Sabbarton St. E16 ....6H 87
Sabella Ct. E3 ....2B 86
Sabine Rd. SW11 ....3D 118
Sable Cl. TW4: Houn 3A 112
Sable St. N1 ....7B 66
Sach Rd. E5 ....2H 67
Sackville Av. BR2: Hayes 1J 171
Sackville Cl. HA2: Harr 3H 59
Sackville Gdns. IG1: Ilf 1D 70
Sackville Ho. SW16 ....3J 137
Sackville Rd. SM2: Sutt 7J 165
Sackville St. W1 ....3B 12 (7G 83)
Saddlebrook Pk. TW16: Sun 7G 129
Saddlers Cl. HA5: H End 6A 26
Saddlers M. HA0: Wemb 4K 59
KT1: Ham W 1C 150
SW8 ....1J 119
Saddlescombe Way N12 ....5D 30
Saddle Yd. W1 ....4J 11 (1F 101)
Sadler Cl. CR4: Mitc 2D 154
Sadler Ho. EC1 ....1K 7
(off Spa Grn. Est.)
Sadlers Ride KT8: W Mole 2G 149
Sadler's Wells Theatre 1K 7
Saffron Av. E14 ....7F 87
Saffron Cl. CR0: Croy 6J 155
NW11 ....6H 45
Saffron Ct. E15 ....5G 69
(off Maryland Pk.)
TW14: Bedf 7E 110
Saffron Hill EC1 ....5K 7 (5A 84)
Saffron M. SW19 ....7G 135
Saffron Rd. RM5: Col R 2K 55
Saffron St. EC1 ....5K 7 (5A 84)
Saffron Way KT6: Surb 1D 162
Saffron Wharf SE1 ....6K 15
(off Shad Thames)
Sage Cl. E6 ....5D 88
Sage M. SE22 ....5F 121
Sage St. E1 ....7J 85
Sage Way WC1 ....2G 7
Sahara Ct. UB1: S'hall 7C 76
Saigasso Cl. E16 ....6B 88
Sailacre Ho. SE10 ....5H 105
(off Woolwich Rd.)
Sail Ct. E14 ....7F 87
(off Newport Av.)
Sailmakers Ct. SW6 ....2A 118
Sail St. SE11 ....3H 19 (4K 101)
Saimet NW9 ....7G 29
(off Wiggins Mead)
Sainfoin Rd. SW17 ....2E 136
Sainsbury Rd. SE19 ....5E 138
Sainsbury Wing 3D 12
(in National Gallery)
St Agatha's Dr. KT2: King T 6F 133
St Agatha's Gro. SM5: Cars 1D 166
St Agnes Cl. E9 ....1J 85
St Agnes Pl. SE11 ....7K 19 (6A 102)
St Agnes Well EC1 ....3F 9
St Aidans Ct. IG11: Bark 2B 90
St Aidan's Rd. SE22 ....6H 121
W13 ....2B 96
St Albans Av. E6 ....3D 88
TW13: Hanw 5B 130
W4 ....4K 97
St Albans Cl. NW11 ....1J 63
St Albans Ct. EC2 ....6D 8
St Alban's Cres. IG8: Wfd G 7D 36
N22 ....1A 48
St Alban's Gdns.
TW11: Tedd 5A 132
St Alban's Gro. SM5: Cars 7C 154
W8 ....3K 99
St Alban's La. NW11 ....1J 63
St Albans Mans. W8 ....3K 99
(off Kensington Ct. Pl.)
St Alban's Pl. N1 ....1B 84
St Albans Rd. EN5: Barn 1A 20
IG3: Ilf 1K 71
IG8: Wfd G 7D 36
KT2: King T 6E 132
NW5 ....3E 64
NW10 ....1A 80
SM1: Sutt 4H 165
St Alban's St. SW1 ....3C 12 (7H 83)
(not continuous)
St Albans Studios W8 ....3K 99
(off St Albans Gro.)
St Albans Ter. W6 ....6G 99
St Albans Vs. NW5 ....3E 64
St Alfege Pas. SE10 ....6E 104
St Alfege Rd. SE7 ....6B 106
St Alphage Gdn. EC2 ....6D 8 (5C 84)
St Alphage Highwalk EC2 ....6D 8
St Alphage Ho. EC2 ....6E 8
St Alphage Wlk. HA8: Edg 2J 43
St Alphege Rd. N9 ....7D 24
St Alphonsus Rd. SW4 ....4G 119
St Amunds Cl. SE6 ....4C 140
St Andrew's Av. HA0: Wemb 4A 60
St Andrews Chambers W1 ....6B 6
(off Wells St.)
St Andrews Cl. HA4: Ruis 2B 58
HA7: Stan 2C 42
KT7: T Ditt 1B 162
N12 ....4F 31
NW2 ....3D 62
SE16 ....5H 103
SE28 ....6D 90
TW7: Isle 1J 113
TW17: Shep 4F 147
St Andrews Ct. E17 ....2A 50
SM1: Sutt 3C 166
SW18 ....2A 136
St Andrews Dr. HA7: Stan 1C 42
St Andrew's Gro. N16 ....1D 66
St Andrew's Hill EC4 ....2B 14 (7B 84)
(not continuous)
St Andrews Mans. W1 ....6G 5
(off Dorset St.)
W14 ....6G 99
(off St Andrews Rd.)
St Andrews M. N16 ....1E 66
SE3 ....7J 105
SW12 ....1H 137
St Andrew's Pl. NW1 ....3K 5 (4F 83)
St Andrews Rd. CR0: Croy 4C 168
DA14: Sidc 3D 144
E11 ....6G 51
E12 ....2C 70
E13 ....3K 87
E17 ....2K 49
EN1: Enf 3J 23
IG1: Ilf 7D 52
KT6: Surb 6D 150
N9 ....7D 24
NW9 ....1K 61
NW10 ....6D 62
NW11 ....6H 45
RM7: Rom 6K 55
SM5: Cars 3C 166
UB10: Uxb 1A 74
W3 ....7A 80
W7 ....2J 95
W14 ....6G 99
St Andrews Sq. KT6: Surb 6D 150
W11 ....6G 81
St Andrew's Twr. UB1: S'hall 7G 77
(off Baird Av.)
St Andrew St. EC1 ....6K 7 (5A 84)
EC4 ....5A 84
St Andrews Way E3 ....4D 86
St Andrew's Wharf SE1 ....2F 103
St Anna Rd. EN5: Barn 5A 20
St Anne's Cl. N6 ....3E 64
St Anne's Ct. BR4: W W'ck 4G 171
NW6 ....1G 81
W1 ....1C 12 (6H 83)
St Anne's Flats NW1 ....1C 6
(off Doric Way)
St Anne's Gdns. NW10 ....3F 79
St Anne's Pas. E14 ....6B 86
St Anne's Rd. E11 ....2F 69
HA0: Wemb 5D 60
St Anne's Row E14 ....6B 86
St Anne's Trad. Est. E14 ....6B 86
(off St Anne's Row)
St Anne St. E14 ....6B 86
St Ann's IG11: Bark 1G 89
St Ann's Ct. NW4 ....3D 44
St Ann's Cres. SW18 ....6K 117

St Ann's Gdns. NW5 6E 64
St Ann's Hill SW18 5K 117
St Ann's Ho. *WC1* *2J 7*
(off Margery St.)
St Ann's La. SW1 2D 18 (3H 101)
St Ann's Pk. Rd. SW18 6A 118
St Ann's Pas. SW13 3A 116
St Ann's Rd. HA1: Harr 6J 41
IG11: Bark 1G 89
N9 2A 34
N15 5B 48
SW13 2B 116
W11 7F 81
St Ann's Shop. Cen. HA1: Harr 6J 41
St Ann's St. SW1 1D 18 (3H 101)
St Ann's Ter. NW8 2B 82
St Ann's Vs. W11 1F 99
St Ann's Way CR2: S Croy 6B 168
St Anselms Ct. SW16 5J 137
St Anselm's Pl. W1 2J 11 (7F 83)
St Anselm's Rd. UB3: Hayes 2H 93
St Anthony's Av. IG8: Wfd G 6F 37
St Anthony's Cl. E1 1G 103
SW17 2C 136
St Anthony's Ct. BR6: Farnb 2F 173
SW17 2E 136
St Anthony's Flats *NW1* *1C 6*
(off Aldenham St.)
St Anthony's Way TW14: Felt 4H 111
St Antony's Rd. E7 7K 69
St Arvan's Cl. CR0: Croy 3E 168
St Asaph Rd. SE4 3K 121
St Aubins Ct. N1 1D 84
St Aubyn's Av. SW19 5H 135
TW3: Houn 5E 112
St Aubyn's Cl. BR6: Orp 3K 173
St Aubyn's Gdns. BR6: Orp 2K 173
St Aubyn's Rd. SE19 6F 139
St Audrey Av. DA7: Bex 2G 127
St Augustine's Av. BR2: Brom 5C 160
CR2: S Croy 6C 168
HA9: Wemb 3E 60
W5 2E 78
St Augustine's Ho. *NW1* *1C 6*
(off Werrington St.)
St Augustine's Mans. *SW1* *4B 18*
(off Bloomburg St.)
St Augustine's Path N5 4C 66
St Augustine's Rd. DA17: Belv 4F 109
NW1 7H 65
St Austell Cl. HA8: Edg 2F 43
St Austell Rd. SE13 2E 122
St Awdry's Rd. IG11: Bark 7H 71
St Awdry's Wlk. IG11: Bark 7G 71
St Barnabas Cl. BR3: Beck 2E 158
SE22 5E 120
St Barnabas Ct. HA3: Hrw W 1G 41
St Barnabas Gdns. KT8: W Mole 5E 148
St Barnabas Rd. CR4: Mitc 7E 136
E17 6C 50
IG8: Wfd G 1K 51
SM1: Sutt 5B 166
St Barnabas St. SW1 5H 17 (5E 100)
St Barnabas Ter. E9 5K 67
St Barnabas Vs. SW8 1J 119
St Bartholomew's Cl. SE26 4H 139
St Bartholomew's Ct. *E6* *2C 88*
(off St Bartholomew's Rd.)
St Bartholomew's Hospital Mus. 6B 8
St Bartholomew's Rd. E6 2D 88
St Benedict's Cl. SW17 5E 136
St Benet's Cl. SW17 2C 136
St Benet's Gro. SM5: Cars 7A 154
St Benet's Pl. EC3 2F 15 (7D 84)
St Bernards CR0: Croy 3E 168
St Bernard's Cl. SE27 4D 138
St Bernards Ho. *E14* *3E 104*
(off Galbraith St.)
St Bernard's Rd. E6 1B 88
St Blaise Av. BR1: Brom 2K 159
St Botolph Row EC3 1J 15 (6F 85)
St Botolph St. EC3 7J 9 (6F 85)
St Brelades Ct. N1 1E 84
St Bride's Av. EC4 1A 14
HA8: Edg 1F 43
St Brides Cl. DA18: Erith 2D 108
St Bride's Crypt Mus. *1A 14*
(in St Bride's)
St Bride's Pas. EC4 1A 14
St Bride St. EC4 7A 8 (6B 84)
St Catherines Cl. KT9: Chess 6D 162
SW17 2C 136
St Catherines Ct. TW13: Felt 1J 129
W4 3A 98
St Catherine's Dr. SE14 2K 121
St Catherine's Farm Ct.
HA4: Ruis 6E 38
St Catherines M. SW3 3E 16 (4D 100)
St Catherine's Rd. E4 2H 35
HA4: Ruis 6F 39
St Catherines Twr. E10 7D 50
St Cecelia's Pl. SE3 5J 105
St Cecilia's Cl. SM3: Sutt 1G 165
St Chads Cl. KT6: Surb 7C 150
St Chad's Gdns. RM6: Chad H 7E 54
St Chad's Pl. WC1 1F 7 (3J 83)
St Chad's Rd. RM6: Chad H 7E 54
St Chad's St. WC1 1F 7 (3J 83)
(not continuous)
St Charles Pl. W10 5G 81
St Charles Sq. W10 5F 81
St Christopher Rd. UB8: Cowl 6A 74
St Christopher's Cl. TW7: Isle 1J 113
St Christophers Dr. UB3: Hayes 7K 75
St Christopher's Gdns.
CR7: Thor H 3A 156
St Christopher's Ho. *NW1* *2G 83*
(off Bridgeway St.)
St Christopher's M. SM6: Wall 5G 167
St Christopher's Pl. W1 7H 5 (6E 82)
St Clair Cl. IG5: Ilf 2D 52
St Clair Dr. KT4: Wor Pk 3D 164
St Clair Rd. E13 2K 87
St Clair's Rd. CR0: Croy 2E 168
St Clare Bus. Pk. TW12: Ham H 6G 131
St Clare St. EC3 1J 15 (6F 85)
St Clements Ct. EC4 2F 15
N7 6K 65
SE14 *6K 103*
(off Myers La.)
W11 *7F 81*
(off Stoneleigh St.)
St Clement's Hgts. SE26 3G 139
St Clements Ho. *E1* *6J 9*
(off Leyden St.)
St Clement's La. WC2 1G 13 (6K 83)
St Clements Mans. *SW6* *6F 99*
(off Lillie Rd.)
St Clements St. N7 6A 66
St Clements Yd. SE22 4F 121
St Cloud Rd. SE27 4C 138
St Columbas Ho. E17 4D 50
St Columb's Ho. *W10* *5G 81*
(off Blagrove Rd.)
St Crispin's Cl. NW3 4C 64
UB1: S'hall 6D 76
St Cross St. EC1 5K 7 (5A 84)
St Cuthbert's Rd. NW2 6H 63
St Cyprian's St. SW17 4D 136
St Daniel Ct. *BR3: Beck* *7C 140*
(off Brackley Rd.)
St Davids Cl. BR4: W W'ck 7D 158
HA9: Wemb 3J 61
SE16 *5H 103*
(off Masters Dr.)
St Davids Ct. BR1: Brom 3F 161
E17 3E 50
TW15: Ashf 2B 128
St David's Dr. HA8: Edg 1F 43
St Davids M. *E3* *3A 86*
(off Morgan St.)
St David's Pl. NW4 7D 44
St Davids Sq. E14 5D 104
St Denis Rd. SE27 4D 138
St Dionis Rd. E12 3C 70
SW6 2H 117
St Domingo Ho. *SE18* *3D 106*
(off Leda Rd.)
St Donatt's Rd. SE14 1B 122
ST DUNSTAN'S 6H 165
St Dunstan's All. EC3 2G 15
St Dunstans Av. W3 7K 79
St Dunstan's Cl. UB3: Harl 5H 93
St Dunstan's Ct. EC4 1K 13 (6A 84)
St Dunstan's Gdns. W3 7K 79
St Dunstans Hill EC3 3G 15 (7E 84)
SM1: Sutt 5G 165
St Dunstan's La. BR3: Beck 6E 158
EC3 3G 15 (7E 84)
St Dunstan's Rd. E7 6K 69
SE25 4F 157
TW4: Cran 2K 111
(not continuous)
TW13: Felt 3H 129
W6 5F 99
W7 2J 95
St Edmund's Av. HA4: Ruis 6F 39
St Edmunds Cl. DA18: Erith 2D 108
NW8 1D 82
SW17 2C 136
St Edmund's Ct. *NW8* *1D 82*
(off St Edmund's Ter.)
St Edmunds Dr. HA7: Stan 1A 42
St Edmund's La. TW2: Whit 7F 113
St Edmund's Rd. IG1: Ilf 6D 52
N9 7B 24
St Edmunds Sq. SW13 6E 98
St Edmund's Ter. NW8 1C 82
St Edward's Cl. NW11 6J 45
St Edwards Ct. E10 7D 50
NW11 6J 45
St Edwards Way RM1: Rom 5K 55
St Egberts Way E4 1K 35
St Elizabeth Ct. E10 7D 50
St Elmo Rd. W12 1B 98
(not continuous)
St Elmos Rd. SE16 2A 104
St Erkenwald M. IG11: Bark 1H 89
St Erkenwald Rd. IG11: Bark 1H 89
St Ermin's Hill SW1 1C 18
St Ervan's Rd. W10 5H 81
St Eugene Ct. *NW6* *1G 81*
(off Salusbury Rd.)
St Faith's Cl. EN2: Enf 1H 23
St Faith's Rd. SE21 1B 138
St Fidelis Rd. DA8: Erith 4K 109
St Fillans Rd. SE6 1E 140
St Francis Cl. BR5: Pet W 6J 161
St Francis' Ho. *NW1* *2H 83*
(off Bridgeway St.)
St Francis Rd. DA8: Erith 4K 109
SE22 4E 120
St Francis Twr. *E4* *6G 35*
(off Burnside Av.)
St Francis Way IG1: Ilf 4H 71
St Frideswide's M. E14 6E 86
St Gabriel's Cl. E11 2K 69
E14 5D 86
St Gabriels Mnr. *SE5* *1B 120*
(off Cormont Rd.)
St Gabriels Rd. NW2 5F 63
St George's Av. E7 7K 69
N7 4H 65
NW9 4K 43
UB1: S'hall 7D 76
W5 2D 96
St George's Bldgs. *SE1* *3B 102*
(off St George's Rd.)
St George's Cathedral 1K 5 (3F 83)
St George's Cir. SE1 7A 14 (3B 102)
St Georges Cl. HA0: Wemb 3A 60
NW11 6H 45
SE28 6D 90
SW8 1G 119
St Georges Ct. E6 4D 88
E17 5F 51
EC4 7A 8 (6B 84)
HA3: Kent *6A 42*
(off Kenton Rd.)
St Georges Ct. *SW1* *5A 18*
(off St George's Dr.)
SW3 *3C 16*
(off Brompton Rd.)
SW7 *4C 100*
(off South Ter.)
SW15 4H 117
W8 3A 100
St George's Dr. SW1 4K 17 (4F 101)
UB10: Ick 3B 56
ST GEORGE'S FIELD 7C 82
St George's Flds. W2 1D 10 (6C 82)
St George's Gdns. KT6: Surb 2H 163
St George's Gro. SW17 3B 136
St Georges Ho. *NW1* *2H 83*
(off Bridgeway St.)
SW11 *1E 118*
(off Charlotte Despard Av.)
St Georges Ind. Est. KT2: King T 5D 132
N22 7G 33
St George's La. EC3 2F 15
St George's Mans. *SW1* *5D 18*
(off Causton St.)
St George's M. NW1 7D 64
SE1 1K 19
SE8 4B 104
St Georges Pde. SE6 2B 140
St George's Path *SE4* *4C 122*
(off Adelaide Av.)
St George's Pl. TW1: Twick 1A 132
St George's RC Cathedral 1K 19 (3A 102)
St Georges Rd. BR1: Brom 2D 160
BR3: Beck 1D 158
BR5: Pet W 6H 161
CR4: Mitc 3F 155
DA14: Sidc 6D 144
E7 7K 69
E10 3E 68
EN1: Enf 1A 24
IG1: Ilf 7D 52
KT2: King T 7G 133
N9 3B 34
N13 3E 32
NW11 6H 45
RM9: Dag 5E 72
SE1 1K 19 (3A 102)
SM6: Wall 5F 167
SW19 7H 135
(not continuous)
TW1: Twick 5B 114
TW9: Rich 3F 115
TW13: Hanw 4B 130
W4 2K 97
W7 1K 95
St George's Rd. W. BR1: Brom 1C 160
St George's Shop. & Leisure Cen.
HA1: Harr 6J 41
St Georges Sq. E7 7K 69
E14 7A 86
KT3: N Mald 3A 152
SE8 4B 104
(not continuous)
SW1 5C 18 (5H 101)
St George's Sq. M. SW1 6C 18 (5H 101)
St George's Ter. *E6* *3C 88*
(off Masterman Rd.)
NW1 7D 64
SE15 *7G 103*
(off Peckham Hill St.)
St George's Theatre 4H 65
St George St. W1 1K 11 (7F 83)
St George's Wlk.
CR0: Croy 3C 168
St George's Way SE15 6E 102
St George's Wharf *SE1* *6K 15*
(off Shad Thames)
St George Wharf SW8 7E 18 (6J 101)
St Gerards Cl. SW4 5G 119
St German's Pl. SE3 1J 123
St German's Rd. SE23 1A 140
St Giles Av. RM10: Dag 7H 73
UB10: Ick 4E 56
St Giles Cir. W1 7D 6 (6H 83)

St Giles Cl. BR6: Farnb 5H 173
RM10: Dag 7H 73
TW5: Hest 7C 94
St Giles Ct. WC2 ....7E 6
St Giles High St. WC2 ....7D 6 (6H 83)
St Giles Ho. EN5: New Bar 4F 21
St Giles Pas. WC2 ....1D 12
St Giles Rd. SE5 ....7E 102
St Giles Ter. *EC2* *6D 8*
(off Beech St.)
St Giles Twr. *SE5* *1E 120*
(off Gables Cl.)
St Gilles Ho. *E2* *2K 85*
(off Mace St.)
St Gothard Rd. SE27 ....4D 138
(not continuous)
St Gregory Cl. HA4: Ruis 4A 58
St Helena Ho. *WC1* *2J 7*
(off Margery St.)
St Helena Rd. SE16 ....4K 103
St Helena St. WC1 ....2J 7 (3A 84)
St Helens KT7: T Ditt 7K 149
St Helen's Cres. SW16 ....1K 155
St Helen's Gdns. W10 ....5F 81
St Helen's Pl. EC3 ....7G 9 (6E 84)
St Helen's Rd. DA18: Erith 2D 108
IG1: Ilf 6D 52
SW16 ....1K 155
W13 ....1B 96
ST HELIER 7C 154
St Helier Av. SM4: Mord 7A 154
St Helier Ct. *N1* *1E 84*
(off De Beauvoir Est.)
SE16 ....*2K 103*
(off Poolmans St.)
St Helier's Av. TW3: Houn 5E 112
St Helier's Rd. E10 ....6E 50
St Hilary's Ct. BR1: Brom 3F 161
St Hilda's Av. TW15: Ashf 5A 128
St Hilda's Cl. NW6 ....7F 63
SW17 ....2C 136
St Hilda's Rd. SW13 ....6D 98
St Hilda's Wharf *E1* *1J 103*
(off Wapping High St.)
St Hubert's Ho. *E14* *3C 104*
(off Janet St.)
St Hughes Cl. SW17 ....2C 136
St Hugh's Rd. SE20 ....1H 157
St Ivian Ct. N10 ....2E 46
St James SE14 ....1A 122
St James Apartments *E17* *5A 50*
(off High St.)
St James App. EC2 ....4G 9 (4E 84)
St James Av. N20 ....3H 31
SM1: Sutt 5J 165
W13 ....1A 96
St James Cl. EN4: E Barn 4G 21
HA4: Ruis 2A 58
KT3: N Mald 5B 152
N20 ....3H 31
SE18 ....5G 107
St James Ct. *E2* *3G 85*
(off Bethnal Grn. Rd.)
E12 ....2A 70
SE3 ....1K 123
SW1 ....1B 18 (3G 101)
St James Gdns. HA0: Wemb 7D 60
RM6: Ilf 4B 54
St James Ga. IG9: Buck H 1F 37
St James Gro. SW11 ....2D 118
St James Ind. M. SE1 ....5G 103
St James Mans. *NW6* *7J 63*
(off West End La.)
SE1 ....*1J 19*
(off Kennington Rd.)
St James M. E14 ....3E 104
E17 ....*5A 50*
(off St James's St.)
St James Residences *W1* *2C 12*
(off Brewer St.)
St James Rd. CR4: Mitc 7E 136
E15 ....5H 69
KT6: Surb 6D 150
St James Rd. N9 ....2C 34
SM1: Sutt 5J 165
SM5: Cars 3C 166
ST JAMES'S 4C 12 (1H 101)
St James's SW1 ....4B 12 (1G 101)
St James's Av. BR3: Beck 3A 158
E2 ....2J 85
TW12: Ham H 5G 131
St James's Chambers *SW1* *4B 12*
(off Jermyn St.)
St James's Cl. *NW8* *1D 82*
(off St James's Ter. M.)
SW17 ....2D 136
St James's Cotts. TW9: Rich 5D 114
St James's Ct. HA1: Harr 6A 42
KT1: King T 3E 150
N18 ....*6B 34*
(off Fore St.)
St James's Cres. SW9 ....3A 120
St James's Dr. SW17 ....1D 136
St James's Gdns. W11 ....1G 99
(not continuous)
St James's La. N10 ....4F 47
St James's Mkt. SW1 ....3C 12 (7H 83)
St James's Palace 5B 12 (2G 101)
St James's Pk. 6C 12 (2H 101)
St James's Pk. CR0: Croy 7C 156
St James's Pas. EC3 ....1H 15
St James's Pl. SW1 ....5A 12 (1G 101)
St James's Rd. CR0: Croy 7B 156
KT1: King T 2D 150
SE1 ....6G 103
SE16 ....3G 103
TW12: Ham H 5F 131
St James's Sq. SW1 ....4B 12 (1G 101)
St James's St. E17 ....5A 50
SW1 ....4A 12 (1G 101)
St James's Ter. *NW8* *1D 82*
(off Prince Albert Rd.)
St James's Ter. M. NW8 ....1D 82
St James St. W6 ....5E 98
St James's Wlk. EC1 ....3A 8 (4B 84)
St James Ter. SW12 ....1E 136
St James Way DA14: Sidc 5E 144
St Jeromes Gro. UB3: Hayes 6E 74
St Joan's Rd. N9 ....2A 34
St John Fisher Rd. DA18: Erith 3D 108
ST JOHNS 2C 122
St John's Av. N11 ....5J 31
NW10 ....1B 80
SW15 ....5F 117
St Johns Chu. Rd. E9 ....5J 67
St Johns Cl. HA9: Wemb 5E 60
N14 ....6B 22
N20 ....*3F 31*
(off Rasper Rd.)
SW6 ....7J 99
St John's Cotts. SE20 ....7J 139
St John's Ct. DA8: Erith 4K 109
E1 ....*1H 103*
(off Scandrett St.)
HA1: Harr 6K 41
HA6: Nwood *1G 39*
(off Murray Rd.)
IG9: Buck H 1E 36
KT1: King T *4E 150*
(off Beaufort Rd.)
N4 ....2B 66
N5 ....4B 66
SE13 ....2E 122
TW7: Isle 2K 113
W6 ....*4D 98*
(off Glenthorne Rd.)
St John's Cres. SW9 ....3A 120
St Johns Dr. SW18 ....1K 135
St John's Est. N1 ....2D 84
SE1 ....6J 15
St John's Gdns. W11 ....7G 81
St John's Gate 4A 8
St John's Gro. N19 ....2G 65
SW13 ....2B 116
TW9: Rich 4E 114
St John's Hill SW11 ....5B 118
St John's Hill Gro. SW11 ....4B 118
St Johns Ho. *E14* *4E 104*
(off Pier St.)
SE17 ....*6D 102*
(off Lytham St.)
St John's La. EC1 ....4A 8 (4B 84)
St John's Lodge *NW3* *7C 64*
(off King Henry's Rd.)
St John's M. KT1: Ham W 2C 150
W11 ....6J 81
St Johns Pde. *DA14: Sidc* *4A 144*
(off Sidcup High St.)
W13 ....1B 96
St John's Pk. SE3 ....7H 105
St John's Pk. Mans. N19 ....3G 65
St John's Pas. SW19 ....6G 135
St John's Path EC1 ....4A 8
St Johns Pathway SE23 ....1J 139
St John's Pl. EC1 ....4A 8 (4B 84)
St John's Rd. BR5: Pet W 6H 161
CR0: Croy 3B 168
DA8: Erith 5K 109
DA14: Sidc 4B 144
DA16: Well 3B 126
E4 ....4J 35
E6 ....1C 88
E16 ....6J 87
E17 ....2D 50
HA1: Harr 6K 41
HA9: Wemb 4D 60
IG2: Ilf 7H 53
IG11: Bark 1J 89
KT1: Ham W 2C 150
KT3: N Mald 3J 151
KT8: E Mos 4H 149
N15 ....6E 48
NW11 ....6H 45
SE20 ....6J 139
SM1: Sutt 2K 165
SM5: Cars 3C 166
SW11 ....4C 118
SW19 ....7G 135
TW7: Isle 2K 113
TW9: Rich 4E 114
TW13: Hanw 4C 130
UB2: S'hall 3C 94
St John's Sq. EC1 ....4A 8 (4B 84)
St John's Ter. E7 ....6K 69
SE18 ....6G 107
SW15 ....*3A 134*
(off Kingston Va.)
W10 ....4F 81
St John St. EC1 ....1K 7 (2A 84)
St John's Va. SE8 ....2C 122
St John's Vs. *N11* *5J 31*
(off Friern Barnet Rd.)
N19 ....2H 65
W8 ....*3K 99*
(off St Mary's Pl.)
St John's Way N19 ....2G 65
ST JOHN'S WOOD 1A 4 (2B 82)
St John's Wood Ct. NW8 ....2B 4
St John's Wood High St.
NW8 ....1C 4 (2B 82)
St John's Wood Pk. NW8 ....1B 82
St John's Wood Rd. NW8 ....3A 4 (4B 82)
St John's Wood Ter. NW8 ....2B 82
St John's Yd. N17 ....7A 34
St Josephs Almshouses *W6* *4F 99*
(off Brook Grn.)
St Joseph's Cl. BR6: Orp 4K 173
W10 ....5G 81
St Joseph's College Sports Cen. 6B 138
St Joseph's Cotts. *SW3* *4E 16*
(off Cadagon St.)
St Josephs Ct. SE7 ....6K 105
St Joseph's Dr. UB1: S'hall 1C 94
St Joseph's Flats *NW1* *1C 6*
(off Drummond Cres.)
St Joseph's Gro. NW4 ....4D 44
St Joseph's Ho. *W6* *4F 99*
(off Brook Grn.)
St Joseph's Rd. N9 ....7C 24
St Joseph's St. SW8 ....1F 119
St Joseph's Va. SE3 ....3F 123
St Jude's Rd. E2 ....2H 85
St Jude St. N16 ....5E 66
St Julian's Cl. SW16 ....4A 138
St Julian's Farm Rd. SE27 ....4A 138
St Julian's Rd. NW6 ....1J 81
St Katharine Docks 3K 15 (1G 103)
St Katharine's Pct. NW1 ....2F 83
St Katharine's Way E1 ....4K 15 (1F 103)
(not continuous)
St Katherine's Rd. DA18: Erith 2D 108
St Katherine's Row EC3 ....2H 15
St Katherines Wlk. *W11* *1F 99*
(off St Ann's Rd.)
St Keverne Rd. SE9 ....4C 142
St Kilda Rd. BR6: Orp 1K 173
W13 ....1A 96
St Kilda's Rd. HA1: Harr 6J 41
N16 ....1D 66
St Kitts Ter. SE19 ....5E 138
St Laurence Cl. NW6 ....1F 81
St Lawrence Bus. Cen.
TW13: Felt 2K 129
St Lawrence Cl. HA8: Edg 7A 28
St Lawrence Cotts. *E14* *1E 104*
(off St Lawrence St.)
St Lawrence Ct. N1 ....7D 66
St Lawrence Dr. HA5: Eastc 5K 39
St Lawrence Ho. *SE1* *7H 15*
(off Purbrook St.)
St Lawrence St. E14 ....1E 104
St Lawrence Ter. W10 ....5G 81
St Lawrence Way SW9 ....1A 120
St Leonard M. *N1* *2E 84*
(off Hoxton St.)
St Leonard's Av. E4 ....6A 36
HA3: Kent 5C 42
St Leonard's Cl. DA16: Well 3A 126
St Leonards Ct. N1 ....1F 9
SW14 ....3J 115
St Leonard's Gdns. IG1: Ilf 5G 71
TW5: Hest 7C 94
St Leonard's Ri. BR6: Orp 4J 173
St Leonard's Rd. CR0: Wadd 3B 168
E14 ....5D 86
(not continuous)
KT6: Surb 5D 150
KT7: T Ditt 6A 150
KT10: Clay 6A 162
NW10 ....4K 79
SW14 ....3H 115
W13 ....7C 78
St Leonards Sq. KT6: Surb 5D 150
NW5 ....6E 64
St Leonard's St. E3 ....3D 86
St Leonard's Ter. SW3 ....6E 16 (5D 100)
St Leonard's Wlk. SW16 ....7K 137
St Loo Av. SW3 ....7D 16 (6C 100)
St Loo Ct. *SW3* *7D 16*
(off St Loo Av.)
St Louis Rd. SE27 ....4D 138
St Loy's Rd. N17 ....2E 48
St Lucia Dr. E15 ....1H 87
St Luke Cl. UB8: Cowl 6A 74
ST LUKE'S 3D 8 (4C 84)
St Luke's Av. EN2: Enf 1J 23
IG1: Ilf 5F 71
SW4 ....4H 119
St Luke's Cl. EC1 ....3D 8 (4C 84)
SE25 ....6H 157
St Lukes Ct. *E10* *7D 50*
(off Capworth St.)
W11 ....*6H 81*
(off St Luke's Rd.)
St Luke's Est. EC1 ....2E 8 (3D 84)
St Luke's M. W11 ....6H 81
St Luke's Pas. KT2: King T 1F 151
St Luke's Path IG1: Ilf 5F 71
St Luke's Rd. UB10: Uxb 7A 56
W11 ....5H 81
St Luke's Sq. E16 ....6H 87
St Luke's St. SW3 ....5D 16 (5C 100)

St Luke's Yd. W9 2H 81
(not continuous)
St Malo Av. N9 3D 34
ST MARGARETS 6B 114
St Margarets IG11: Bark 1H 89
St Margarets Av.
DA15: Sidc 3H 143
HA2: Harr 3G 59
N15 4B 48
N20 1F 31
SM3: Cheam 3G 165
TW15: Ashf 5D 128
UB8: Hil 4C 74
St Margarets Bus. Cen.
TW1: Twick 6B 114
St Margarets Cl. EC2 6D 84
St Margarets Ct. HA8: Edg 5C 28
N11 4K 31
SE1 5D 14 (1C 102)
SW15 4D 116
St Margaret's Cres. SW15 5D 116
St Margaret's Dr. TW1: Twick 5B 114
St Margaret's Gro. E11 3H 69
SE18 6G 107
TW1: Twick 6A 114
St Margaret's La. W8 3K 99
St Margaret's Pas. SE13 3G 123
(not continuous)
St Margarets Path SE18 5G 107
St Margarets Rd. E12 2A 70
HA4: Ruis 6F 39
HA8: Edg 5C 28
N17 3E 48
NW10 3E 80
SE4 4B 122
(not continuous)
TW1: Twick 6B 114
TW7: Isle 4B 114
W7 2J 95
ST MARGARETS RDBT. 6B 114
St Margaret's Ter. SE18 5G 107
St Margaret St. SW1 7E 12 (2J 101)
St Marks Cl. EN5: New Bar 3E 20
HA1: Harr 7B 42
SE10 7E 104
SW6 1J 117
St Marks Ct. *E10* *7D 50*
(off Capworth St.)
NW8 *2A 82*
(off Abercorn Pl.)
W7 *2J 95*
(off Lwr. Boston Rd.)
St Mark's Cres. NW1 1E 82
St Mark's Gro. SW10 7K 99
St Mark's Hill KT6: Surb 6E 150
St Marks Ho. *SE17* *6D 102*
(off Lytham St.)
St Marks Ind. Est. E16 1B 106
St Mark's Pl. SW19 6H 135
W11 6G 81
St Mark's Ri. E8 5F 67
St Marks Rd. BR2: Brom 3J 159
CR4: Mitc 2D 154
EN1: Enf 6A 24
SE25 4G 157
TW11: Tedd 7B 132
W5 1E 96
W7 2J 95
W10 5F 81
St Mark's Sq. NW1 1E 82
St Mark St. E1 1K 15 (6F 85)
St Mark's Vs. *N4* *2K 65*
(off Moray Rd.)
St Martin Cl. UB8: Cowl 6A 74
St Martin-in-the-Fields Church *3E 12*
(off St Martin's Pl.)
St Martin's Almshouses
NW1 1G 83
St Martin's App. HA4: Ruis 7G 39
St Martin's Av. E6 2B 88
St Martin's Cl. DA18: Erith 2D 108
EN1: Enf 1C 24
NW1 1G 83

St Martins Ct. *EC4* *7C 8*
(off Paternoster Row)
N1 *1E 84*
(off De Beauvoir Est.)
WC2 2E 12 (7J 83)
St Martins Est. SW2 1A 138
St Martin's La. BR3: Beck 5D 158
WC2 2E 12 (7J 83)
St Martin's le-Grand EC1 7C 8 (6C 84)
St Martin's Pl. WC2 3E 12 (7J 83)
St Martin's Rd. N9 2C 34
SW9 2K 119
St Martin's St. WC2 3D 12 (7H 83)
(not continuous)
St Martin's Theatre *2E 12*
(off West St.)
St Martins Way SW17 3A 136
St Mary Abbot's Ct. *W14* *3H 99*
(off Warwick Gdns.)
St Mary Abbot's Pl. W8 3H 99
St Mary Abbot's Ter. W14 3H 99
St Mary at Hill EC3 3G 15 (7E 84)
St Mary Av. SM6: Wall 3E 166
St Mary Axe EC3 1G 15 (6E 84)
St Marychurch St. SE16 2J 103
St Mary Graces Ct. E1 3K 15 (7F 85)
St Marylebone Cl. NW10 1A 80
St Marylebone Crematorium N2 3K 45
St Mary le-Park Ct. *SW11* *7C 100*
(off Parkgate Rd.)
St Mary Newington Cl. *SE17* *5E 102*
(off Surrey Sq.)
St Mary Rd. E17 4C 50
St Mary's IG11: Bark 1H 89
St Mary's App. E12 5D 70
St Mary's Av. BR2: Brom 3G 159
E11 7K 51
N3 2G 45
TW11: Tedd 6K 131
St Mary's Av. Central UB2: S'hall 4F 95
St Mary's Av. Nth. UB2: S'hall 4F 95
St Mary's Av. Sth. UB2: S'hall 4F 95
St Mary's Cl. KT9: Chess 7F 163
KT17: Ewe 7B 164
N17 1G 49
TW16: Sun 4J 147
St Mary's Copse KT4: Wor Pk 2A 164
St Mary's Ct. E6 4D 88
SE7 7B 106
SM6: Wall 4G 167
W5 2D 96
W6 3B 98
St Mary's Cres. NW4 3D 44
TW7: Isle 7H 95
UB3: Hayes 7H 75
St Mary's Dr. TW14: Bedf 7E 110
St Mary's Est. *SE16* *2J 103*
(off St Marychurch St.)
St Mary's Flats *NW1* *1C 6*
(off Drummond Cres.)
St Mary's Gdns. SE11 3K 19 (4A 102)
St Mary's Ga. W8 3K 99
St Mary's Grn. N2 2A 46
St Mary's Gro. N1 6B 66
SW13 3D 116
TW9: Rich 4F 115
W4 6H 97
St Mary's Ho. *N1* *1B 84*
(off St Mary's Path)
St Mary's Mans. W2 5A 4 (5B 82)
St Marys M. NW6 7K 63
TW10: Ham 2C 132
St Mary's Path *E1* *6G 85*
(off Adler St.)
N1 1B 84
St Mary's Pl. SE9 6D 124
W5 2D 96
W8 3K 99
St Marys Rd. DA5: Bexl 1J 145
E10 3E 68
E13 2K 87
EN4: E Barn 7J 21
IG1: Ilf 2G 71

St Marys Rd. KT4: Wor Pk 2A 164
KT6: Surb 7C 150
(St Chads Cl.)
KT6: Surb 6D 150
(Victoria Rd.)
KT8: E Mos 5H 149
N8 4J 47
N9 1C 34
NW10 1A 80
NW11 7G 45
SE15 1J 121
SE25 3E 156
SW19 5G 135
UB3: Hayes 7H 75
W5 2D 96
St Mary's Sq. W2 5A 4 (5B 82)
W5 2D 96
St Mary's Ter. W2 5A 4 (5B 82)
St Mary's Twr. *EC1* *4D 8*
(off Fortune St.)
St Mary St. SE18 4D 106
St Mary's University College Sports Cen.
4K 131
St Mary's Vw. HA3: Kent 5C 42
St Mary's Wlk. SE11 3K 19 (4A 102)
UB3: Hayes 7H 75
St Mary's Way IG7: Chig 5K 37
St Matthew Cl. UB8: Cowl 6A 74
St Matthew's Av. KT6: Surb 1E 162
St Matthews Ct. E10 7D 50
N10 2E 46
SE1 *3C 102*
(off Meadow Row)
TW15: Ashf *4C 128*
(off Feltham Rd.)
St Matthew's Dr. BR1: Brom 3D 160
St Matthews Ho. *SE17* *6D 102*
(off Phelp St.)
St Matthew's Lodge *NW1* *2G 83*
(off Oakley Sq.)
St Matthew's Rd. SW2 4K 119
W5 1E 96
St Matthew's Row E2 3G 85
St Matthew St. SW1 2C 18 (3H 101)
St Matthias Cl. NW9 5B 44
St Maur Rd. SW6 1H 117
St Mellion Cl. SE28 6D 90
St Merryn Cl. SE18 7H 107
St Merryn Ct. BR3: Beck 7C 140
St Michael's All. EC3 1F 15 (6D 84)
St Michael's Av. HA9: Wemb 6G 61
N9 7D 24
St Michaels Cl. BR1: Brom 3C 160
DA18: Erith 2D 108
E16 5B 88
KT4: Wor Pk 2B 164
N3 2H 45
N12 5H 31
St Michaels Ct. *CR0: Croy* *1C 168*
(off Station Rd.)
E14 *5E 86*
(off St Leonards Rd.)
SE1 *7D 14*
(off Trinity St.)
St Michael's Cres. HA5: Pinn 6C 40
St Michael's Flats *NW1* *1C 6*
(off Aldenham St.)
St Michael's Gdns. W10 5G 81
St Michaels M. SW1 4G 17 (4E 100)
St Michael's Ri. DA16: Well 1B 126
St Michael's Rd. CR0: Croy 1C 168
DA16: Well 3B 126
NW2 4E 62
SM6: Wall 6G 167
SW9 2K 119
TW15: Ashf 5C 128
St Michael's St. W2 7B 4 (6B 82)
St Michaels Ter. *N6* *1E 64*
(off South Gro.)
N22 1J 47
St Mildred's Ct. EC2 1E 14 (6D 84)
St Mildreds Rd. SE6 7G 123
SE12 7G 123

St Mirren Ct. EN5: New Bar 5F 21
St Nicholas Cen. SM1: Sutt 5K 165
St Nicholas Cl. UB8: Cowl 6A 74
St Nicholas Ct. *KT1: King T* *4E 150*
(off Surbiton Rd.)
St Nicholas Dr. TW17: Shep 7C 146
St Nicholas' Flats *NW1* *1C 6*
(off Werrington St.)
St Nicholas Glebe SW17 5E 136
St Nicholas Ho. *SE8* *6C 104*
(off Deptford Grn.)
SE18 *7C 106*
(off Shrapnel Cl.)
St Nicholas M. KT7: T Ditt 6K 149
St Nicholas Rd. KT7: T Ditt 6K 149
SE18 5K 107
SM1: Sutt 5K 165
St Nicholas St. SE8 1B 122
St Nicholas Way SM1: Sutt 4K 165
St Nicolas La. BR7: Chst 1C 160
St Ninian's Ct. N20 3J 31
St Norbert Grn. SE4 4A 122
St Norbert Rd. SE4 5K 121
St Olaf Ho. SE1 4F 15
St Olaf's Rd. SW6 7G 99
St Olaf Stairs SE1 4F 15
St Olave's Ct. EC2 1E 14 (6D 84)
St Olave's Est. SE1 6H 15 (2E 102)
St Olave's Gdns. SE11 3J 19 (4A 102)
St Olaves Ho. *SE11* *3J 19*
(off Walnut Tree Wlk.)
St Olave's Mans. SE11 3J 19
St Olave's Rd. E6 1E 88
St Olave's Ter. SE1 6H 15
St Olaves Wlk. SW16 2G 155
St Olav's Sq. SE16 2J 103
St Onge Pde. *EN1: Enf* *3J 23*
(off Southbury Rd.)
St Oswald's Pl. SE11 6G 19 (5K 101)
St Oswald's Rd. SW16 1B 156
St Oswalds Studios *SW6* *6J 99*
(off Sedlescombe Rd.)
St Oswulf St. SW1 4D 18 (4H 101)
St Owen Ho. *SE1* *3E 102*
(off Fendall St.)
ST PANCRAS 2F 7 (4K 83)
St Pancras Commercial Cen. *NW1* *1G 83*
(off Pratt St.)
St Pancras Ct. N2 2B 46
St Pancras Way NW1 7G 65
St Patrick's Ct. IG8: Wfd G 7B 36
St Paul Cl. UB8: Cowl 5A 74
St Paul's All. *EC4* *1B 14*
(off St Paul's Chyd.)
St Paul's Arts Cen. *4C 104*
(off Westferry Rd.)
St Paul's Av. HA3: Kent 4F 43
NW2 6D 62
SE16 1K 103
St Paul's Bldgs. *EC1* *3B 8*
(off Dallington St.)
St Paul's Cathedral 1C 14 (6C 84)
St Paul's Chyd. EC4 1B 14 (6B 84)
(not continuous)
St Pauls Cl. KT9: Chess 4D 162
SE7 5B 106
SM5: Cars 1C 166
TW3: Houn 2C 112
TW15: Ashf 5E 128
UB3: Harl 5F 93
W5 2F 97
St Pauls Ct. SW4 5H 119
TW4: Houn 3C 112
St Pauls Courtyard *SE8* *7C 104*
(off Crossfield St.)
ST PAUL'S CRAY 2K 161
St Paul's Cray Rd. BR7: Chst 1H 161
St Paul's Cres. NW1 7H 65
(not continuous)
St Paul's Dr. E15 5F 69
St Paul's M. NW1 7H 65
St Paul's Pl. N1 6D 66
St Paul's Ri. N13 6G 33

St Paul's Rd. CR7: Thor H 3C 156
DA8: Erith 7J 109
IG11: Bark 1G 89
N1 .....6B 66
N17 .....7B 34
TW8: Bford 6D 96
TW9: Rich 3F 115
St Paul's Shrubbery N1 .....6D 66
St Paul's Sq. BR2: Brom 2H 159
St Paul's Studios *W14* *5G 99*
(off Talgarth Rd.)
St Pauls Ter. SE17 .....6B 102
St Pauls Twr. *E10* *7D 50*
(off Beaumont Rd.)
St Paul St. N1 .....1C 84
(not continuous)
St Pauls Vw. Apartments *EC1* *2J 7*
(off Amwell St.)
St Paul's Wlk. KT2: King T 7G 133
St Pauls Way E3 .....5B 86
N3 .....7E 30
St Paul's Wood Hill BR5: St P 2J 161
St Peter Claver Ct. *BR3: Beck* *1D 158*
(off Albemarle Rd.)
St Peter's All. *EC3* *1F 15*
(off Cornhill)
St Peters Av. E2 .....2G 85
E17 .....4G 51
N2 .....7H 31
N18 .....4B 34
St Petersburgh M. W2 .....7K 81
St Petersburgh Pl. W2 .....7K 81
St Peter's Cen. *E1* *1H 103*
(off Reardon St.)
St Peter's Chu. Ct. *N1* *1B 84*
(off St Peter's St.)
St Peters Cl. BR7: Chst 7H 143
E2 .....2G 85
HA4: Ruis 2B 58
IG2: Ilf 4J 53
SW17 .....2C 136
WD23: Bushy 1C 26
St Peters Ct. KT8: W Mole 4E 148
NW4 .....5E 44
SE12 .....5H 123
St Peter's Gdns. SE27 .....3A 138
St Peter's Gro. W6 .....4C 98
St Peters Ho. SE17 .....6D 102
WC1 .....*2F 7*
(off Regent Sq.)
St Peters M. N8 .....5A 48
St Peter's Path E17 .....3G 51
St Peters Pl. W9 .....4K 81
St Peters Rd. CR0: Croy 4D 168
KT1: King T 2G 151
KT8: W Mole 4E 148
N9 .....1C 34
TW1: Twick 5B 114
UB1: S'hall 5E 76
UB8: Cowl 5A 74
W6 .....5C 98
St Peter's Sq. E2 .....2G 85
W6 .....4B 98
St Peter's St. CR2: S Croy 5D 168
N1 .....1B 84
St Peter's St. M. *N1* *2B 84*
(off St Peters St.)
St Peter's Ter. SW6 .....7H 99
St Peter's Vs. W6 .....4C 98
St Peters Way N1 .....7E 66
UB3: Harl 5F 93
W5 .....5D 78
St Peter's Wharf W4 .....5C 98
St Philip Ho. *WC1* *2J 7*
(off Lloyd Baker St.)
St Philips Av. KT4: Wor Pk 2D 164
N2 .....7H 31
St Philip's Ga. KT4: Wor Pk 2D 164
St Philip Sq. SW8 .....2F 119
St Philips Rd. E8 .....6G 67
KT6: Surb 6D 150
St Philip St. SW8 .....2F 119
St Philip's Way N1 .....1C 84
St Quentin Ho. SW18 .....6B 118
St Quentin Rd. DA16: Well 3K 125
St Quintin Av. W10 .....5E 80
St Quintin Gdns. W10 .....5E 80
St Quintin Rd. E13 .....3K 87
St Raphael's Way NW10 .....5J 61
St Regis Cl. N10 .....2F 47
St Regis Hgts. NW3 .....3K 63
St Richard's Ho. *NW1* *1C 6*
(off Eversholt St.)
St Ronan's Cl. EN4: Had W 1G 21
St Ronan's Cres. IG8: Wfd G 7D 36
St Rule St. SW8 .....2G 119
St Saviour's Coll. SE27 .....4D 138
St Saviours Ct. HA1: Harr 5J 41
N22 .....2H 47
St Saviour's Est. SE1 .....7J 15 (2F 103)
St Saviour's Rd. CR0: Croy 6B 156
SW2 .....5K 119
St Saviour's Wharf *SE1* *6K 15*
(off Shad Thames)
SE1 .....*6K 15*
(off Mill St.)
Saints Cl. SE27 .....4B 138
Saints Dr. E7 .....5B 70
St Silas Pl. NW5 .....6E 64
St Simon's Av. SW15 .....5E 116
Saints M. CR4: Mitc 3C 154
St Stephen's Av. E17 .....5E 50
W12 .....1D 98
(not continuous)
W13 .....6B 78
St Stephen's Cl. E17 .....5D 50
NW8 .....1C 82
UB1: S'hall 5E 76
St Stephens Ct. *EN1: Enf* *6K 23*
(off Park Av.)
N8 .....6K 47
W13 .....6B 78
St Stephen's Cres. CR7: Thor H 3A 156
W2 .....6J 81
St Stephen's Gdns. SW15 .....5H 117
TW1: Twick 6C 114
W2 .....6J 81
(not continuous)
St Stephens Gro. SE13 .....3E 122
St Stephens Ho. *SE17* *6D 102*
(off Lytham St.)
St Stephen's M. W2 .....5J 81
St Stephens Pde. E7 .....7A 70
St Stephen's Pas. TW1: Twick 6C 114
St Stephen's Rd. E3 .....1A 86
E6 .....7A 70
E17 .....5D 50
EN5: Barn 5A 20
TW3: Houn 6E 112
UB7: Yiew 1A 92
W13 .....6B 78
St Stephen's Row EC4 .....1E 14
St Stephen's Ter. SW8 .....7K 101
St Stephen's Wlk. *SW7* *4A 100*
(off Southwell Gdns.)
St Swithins La. EC4 .....2E 14 (7D 84)
St Swithun's Rd. SE13 .....6F 123
St Theresa's Rd. TW14: Felt 4H 111
St Thomas Cl. KT6: Surb 1F 163
St Thomas Ct. DA5: Bexl 7G 127
E10 .....*7D 50*
(off Beaumont Rd.)
HA5: Pinn 1C 40
NW1 .....*7G 65*
(off Wrotham Rd.)
St Thomas Dr. BR5: Farnb 1G 173
HA5: Pinn 1C 40
St Thomas Gdns. IG1: Ilf 6G 71
St Thomas Ho. *E1* *6K 85*
(off W. Arbour St.)
St Thomas More School Sports Cen.
.....7F 33
St Thomas Rd. DA17: Belv 2J 109
E16 .....6J 87
N14 .....7C 22
W4 .....6J 97
St Thomas's Gdns. NW5 .....6E 64
St Thomas's Pl. E9 .....7J 67
St Thomas's Rd. N4 .....2A 66
NW10 .....1A 80
St Thomas's Sq. E9 .....7J 67
St Thomas St. SE1 .....5F 15 (1D 102)
St Thomas's Way SW6 .....7H 99
St Timothys M. BR1: Brom 1K 159
St Ursula Gro. HA5: Pinn 5B 40
St Ursula Rd. UB1: S'hall 6E 76
St Vincent Cl. SE27 .....5B 138
St Vincent De Paul Ho. *E1* *5J 85*
(off Jubilee St.)
St Vincent Ho. *SE1* *3F 103*
(off Fendall St.)
St Vincent Rd. TW2: Whit 6G 113
St Vincent's La. NW7 .....4K 29
St Vincent St. W1 .....6H 5 (5E 82)
St Wilfrid's Cl. EN4: E Barn 5H 21
St Wilfrid's Rd. EN4: E Barn 5H 21
St Winefride's Av. E12 .....5D 70
St Winifred's Rd. TW11: Tedd 6B 132
Sakura Cl. N22 .....1H 47
Sala Ho. SE3 .....4K 123
Salamanca Pl. SE1 .....4G 19 (4K 101)
Salamanca Sq. *SE1* *4G 19*
(off Salamanca Pl.)
Salamanca St. SE1 .....4F 19 (4K 101)
SE11 .....4F 19 (4K 101)
Salamander Cl. KT2: King T 5C 132
Salamander Quay KT1: Ham W 1D 150
Salcombe Dr. RM6: Chad H 6F 55
SM4: Mord 1F 165
Salcombe Gdns. NW7 .....6K 29
Salcombe Rd. E17 .....7B 50
N16 .....5E 66
TW15: Ashf 3A 128
Salcombe Vs. TW10: Rich 5E 114
Salcombe Way HA4: Ruis 2J 57
UB4: Hayes 3F 75
Salcott Rd. CR0: Bedd 3J 167
SW11 .....5C 118
Salehurst Cl. HA3: Kent 5E 42
Salehurst Rd. SE4 .....6B 122
Salem Pl. CR0: Croy 3C 168
Salem Rd. W2 .....7K 81
Sale Pl. W2 .....6C 4 (5C 82)
Sale St. E2 .....4G 85
Salford Ho. *E14* *4E 104*
(off Seyssel St.)
Salford Rd. SW2 .....1H 137
Salhouse Cl. SE28 .....6C 90
Salisbury Av. IG11: Bark 7H 71
N3 .....3H 45
SM1: Sutt 6H 165
Salisbury Cl. KT4: Wor Pk 3B 164
SE17 .....4D 102
Salisbury Ct. EC4 .....1A 14 (6B 84)
EN2: Enf *4J 23*
(off London Rd.)
HA8: Edg 4A 28
SE16 .....*3G 103*
(off Stork's Rd.)
SM5: Cars 5D 166
UB5: N'olt *5F 59*
(off Newmarket Av.)
Salisbury Gdns. IG9: Buck H 2G 37
SW19 .....7G 135
Salisbury Hall Gdns. E4 .....6H 35
Salisbury Ho. *E14* *6D 86*
(off Hobday St.)
EC2 .....*6F 9*
(off London Wall)
HA7: Stan 6F 27
N1 .....*1B 84*
(off St Mary's Path)
SM6: Wall 5F 167
SW1 .....*5D 18*
(off Drummond Ga.)
SW9 .....*7A 102*
(off Cranmer Rd.)
Salisbury Mans. N15 .....5B 48
Salisbury M. SW6 .....7H 99
Salisbury Pas. *SW6* *7H 99*
(off Dawes Rd.)
Salisbury Pavement *SW6* *7H 99*
(off Dawes Rd.)
Salisbury Pl. SW9 .....7B 102
W1 .....5E 4 (5D 82)
Salisbury Prom. N8 .....5B 48
Salisbury Rd. BR2: Brom 5C 160
DA5: Bexl 1G 145
E4 .....3H 35
E7 .....6J 69
E10 .....2E 68
E12 .....5B 70
E17 .....5E 50
EN5: Barn 3B 20
HA1: Harr 5H 41
HA5: Eastc 4J 39
IG3: Ilf 2J 71
KT3: N Mald 3K 151
KT4: Wor Pk 4K 163
N4 .....5B 48
N22 .....1B 48
RM10: Dag 6H 73
SE25 .....6G 157
SM5: Cars 6D 166
SW19 .....7G 135
TW4: Houn 3A 112
TW6: H'row A 6E 110
(not continuous)
TW9: Rich 4E 114
TW13: Felt 1A 130
UB2: S'hall 4C 94
W13 .....2B 96
Salisbury Sq. EC4 .....1K 13 (6A 84)
Salisbury St. NW8 .....4C 4 (4C 82)
W3 .....2J 97
Salisbury Ter. SE15 .....3J 121
Salisbury Wlk. N19 .....2G 65
Salix Cl. TW16: Sun 7K 129
Salix Ct. N3 .....6D 30
Salliesfield TW2: Whit 6H 113
Sally Murray Cl. E12 .....4E 70
Salmen Rd. E13 .....2H 87
Salmond Cl. HA7: Stan 6F 27
Salmon La. E14 .....6A 86
Salmon M. NW6 .....5J 63
Salmon Rd. DA17: Belv 5G 109
Salmons Rd. KT9: Chess 6E 162
N9 .....1B 34
Salmon St. E14 .....6B 86
NW9 .....1H 61
Salomons Rd. E13 .....5A 88
Salop Rd. E17 .....6K 49
Saltash Cl. SM1: Sutt 4H 165
Saltash Rd. DA16: Well 1C 126
IG6: Ilf 1H 53
Saltcoats Rd. W4 .....2A 98
Saltcroft Cl. HA9: Wemb 1H 61
Saltdene N4 .....1K 65
Salter Cl. HA2: Harr 4D 58
Salterford Rd. SW17 .....6E 136
Salter Rd. SE16 .....1K 103
Salters Ct. EC4 .....1D 14
Salter's Hall Ct. EC4 .....2E 14
Salter's Hill SE19 .....5D 138
Salters Rd. E17 .....4F 51
W10 .....4F 81
Salters Row *N1* *6D 66*
(off Tilney Gdns.)
Salter St. E14 .....7B 86
NW10 .....3C 80
Salterton Rd. N7 .....3K 65
Salt Hill Cl. UB8: Uxb 5A 56
Saltley Cl. E6 .....6C 88
Saltoun Rd. SW2 .....4A 120
Saltram Cl. N15 .....4F 49
Saltram Cres. W9 .....3H 81
Saltwell St. E14 .....7C 86
Saltwood Gro. SE17 .....5D 102
Saltwood Ho. *SE15* *6J 103*
(off Lovelinch Cl.)
Salusbury Rd. NW6 .....1G 81
Salutation Rd. SE10 .....4G 105

Salvador SW17 . . . . .5D 136
Salvia Gdns. UB6: G'frd 2A 78
Salvin Rd. SW15 . . . . .3F 117
Salway Cl. IG8: Wfd G 7D 36
Salway Pl. E15 . . . . .6F 69
Salway Rd. E15 . . . . .6F 69
Samantha Cl. E17 . . . . .7B 50
Sam Bartram Cl. SE7 . . . . .5A 106
Sambrook Ho. E1 . . . . .5J 85
(off Jubilee St.)
SE11 . . . . .4J 19
Sambruck M. SE6 . . . . .1D 140
Samels Ct. W6 . . . . .5C 98
Samford Ho. N1 . . . . .1A 84
(off Barnsbury Est.)
Samford St. NW8 . . . . .4C 4 (4B 82)
Samira Cl. E17 . . . . .6C 50
Sam Manners Ho. SE10 . . . . .5G 105
(off Tuskar St.)
Sam March Ho. E14 . . . . .6F 87
(off Blair St.)
Samos Rd. SE20 . . . . .2H 157
Sampson Av. EN5: Barn 5A 20
Sampson Cl. DA17: Belv 3D 108
Sampson Ct. TW17: Shep 5E 146
Sampson Ho. SE1 . . . . . .4A 14 (1B 102)
Sampson St. E1 . . . . .1G 103
Samsbrooke Ct. EN1: Enf 6K 23
Samson St. E13 . . . . .2A 88
Samuda Est. E14 . . . . .3E 104
Samuel Cl. E8 . . . . .1F 85
SE14 . . . . .6K 103
SE18 . . . . .4C 106
Samuel Ct. N1 . . . . .3E 84
(off Pitfield St.)
Samuel Gray Gdns. KT2: King T . . .1D 150
Samuel Ho. E8 . . . . .1F 85
(off Clarissa St.)
Samuel Johnson Cl. SW16 . . . . . .4K 137
Samuel Jones Ind. Est. SE15 . . . . .7E 102
Samuel Lewis Bldgs. N1 . . . . .6A 66
Samuel Lewis Trust Dwellings
N16 .6E 48
SE5 . . . . .1C 120
(off Warner Rd.)
SW3 . . . . .4C 16 (4C 100)
SW6 . . . . .7J 99
(off Vanston Pl.)
W14 . . . . .4H 99
(off Lisgar Ter.)
Samuel Richardson Ho. W14 . . . . .4H 99
(off North End Cres.)
Samuel's Cl. W6 . . . . .4E 98
Samuel St. SE15 . . . . .7F 103
SE18 . . . . .4D 106
Sancroft Cl. NW2 . . . . .3D 62
Sancroft Ho. SE11 . . . . .5H 19
Sancroft Rd. HA3: W'stone 2K 41
Sancroft St. SE11 . . . . . .5H 19 (5K 101)
Sanctuary, The DA5: Bexl 6D 126
SM4: Mord 6J 153
SW1 . . . . .1D 18
Sanctuary M. E8 . . . . .6F 67
Sanctuary Rd. TW6: H'row A 6C 110
Sanctuary St. SE1 . . . . . .6D 14 (2C 102)
Sandale Cl. N16 . . . . .3D 66
Sandall Cl. W5 . . . . .4E 78
Sandall Ho. E3 . . . . .2A 86
Sandall Rd. NW5 . . . . .6G 65
W5 .4E 78
Sandal Rd. KT3: N Mald 5K 151
N18 .5B 34
Sandal St. E15 . . . . .1G 87
Sandalwood Cl. E1 . . . . .4A 86
Sandal Wood Dr. HA4: Ruis 7E 38
Sandalwood Ho. DA15: Sidc 2K 143
Sandalwood Mans. W8 . . . . .3K 99
(off Stone Hall Gdns.)
Sandalwood Rd. TW13: Felt 3K 129
Sandbach Pl. SE18 . . . . .4G 107
Sandbanks TW14: Felt 1G 129
Sandbourne NW8 . . . . .1K 81
(off Abbey Rd.)

Sandbourne W11 . . . . .6J 81
(off Dartmouth Cl.)
Sandbourne Av. SW19 . . . . .2K 153
Sandbourne Rd. SE4 . . . . .2A 122
Sandbrook Cl. NW7 . . . . .6E 28
Sandbrook Rd. N16 . . . . .3E 66
Sandby Grn. SE9 . . . . .3C 124
Sandby Ho. NW6 . . . . .1J 81
Sandcliff Rd. DA8: Erith 4K 109
Sandcroft Cl. N13 . . . . .6G 33
Sandell's Av. TW15: Ashf 4E 128
Sandell St. SE1 . . . . . . .6J 13 (2A 102)
Sanderling Ct. SE8 . . . . .6B 104
(off Abinger Gro.)
SE28 . . . . .7C 90
Sanderling Lodge E1 . . . . .3K 15
(off Star Pl.)
Sanders Cl. TW12: Ham H 5G 131
Sanders Ho. WC1 . . . . .1J 7
(off Gt. Percy St.)
Sanders La. NW7 . . . . .7A 30
(Bittacy Hill)
NW7 . . . . .7K 29
(Pursley Rd.)
Sanderson Cl. NW5 . . . . .4F 65
Sanderson Ho. SE8 . . . . .5B 104
(off Grove St.)
Sanderson Sq. BR1: Brom 3E 160
Sanderstead Av. NW2 . . . . .2G 63
Sanderstead Cl. SW12 . . . . .7G 119
Sanderstead Rd.
CR2: Sand, S Croy 7D 168
E10 .1A 68
Sanders Way N19 . . . . .1H 65
Sandfield WC1 . . . . .2F 7
(off Cromer St.)
Sandfield Gdns. CR7: Thor H 3B 156
Sandfield Pas. CR7: Thor H 3C 156
Sandfield Pl. CR7: Thor H 3C 156
Sandfield Rd. CR7: Thor H 3B 156
Sandford Av. N22 . . . . .1C 48
Sandford Cl. E6 . . . . .4D 88
Sandford Ct. EN5: New Bar 3E 20
N16 .1E 66
Sandford Rd. BR2: Brom 3J 159
DA7: Bex 4E 126
E6 . . . . .3C 88
Sandford Row SE17 . . . . .5D 102
Sandford St. SW6 . . . . .7K 99
Sandgate Cl. RM7: Rush G 7J 55
Sandgate Ho. E5 . . . . .5H 67
W5 .5C 78
Sandgate La. SW18 . . . . .1C 136
Sandgate Rd. DA16: Well 7C 108
Sandgate St. SE15 . . . . .6H 103
Sandgate Trad. Est. SE15 . . . . . . .6H 103
(off Sandgate St.)
Sandham Ct. SW4 . . . . .1J 119
Sandhills SM6: Bedd 4H 167
Sandhills, The SW10 . . . . .7A 16
(off Limerston St.)
Sandhills Mdw. TW17: Shep 7E 146
Sandhurst Av. HA2: Harr 6F 41
KT5: Surb 7H 151
Sandhurst Cl. CR2: Sand 7E 168
NW9 . . . . .3G 43
Sandhurst Ct. SW2 . . . . .4J 119
Sandhurst Dr. IG3: Bark, Ilf 4K 71
Sandhurst Ho. E1 . . . . .5J 85
(off Wolsy St.)
Sandhurst Mkt. SE6 . . . . .1E 140
(off Sandhurst Rd.)
Sandhurst Rd. BR6: Chels 3K 173
DA5: Bexl 5D 126
DA15: Sidc 3K 143
N9 . . . . .6D 24
NW9 . . . . .3G 43
SE6 .1F 141
Sandhurst Way CR2: Sand 7E 168
Sandifer Dr. NW2 . . . . .3F 63
Sandiford Rd. SM3: Sutt 2H 165
Sandiland Cres. BR2: Hayes 2H 171
Sandilands CR0: Croy 2G 169

Sandilands Rd. SW6 . . . . .1K 117
Sandison St. SE15 . . . . .3G 121
Sandland St. WC1 . . . . . . .6H 7 (5K 83)
Sandling Ri. SE9 . . . . .3E 142
Sandlings, The N22 . . . . .2A 48
Sandlings Cl. SE15 . . . . .2H 121
Sandmartin Way SM6: Mitc 1E 166
Sandmere Rd. SW4 . . . . .4J 119
Sandon Cl. KT10: Esh 7H 149
Sandon Ct. KT10: Esh 7H 149
Sandow Cres. UB3: Hayes 3H 93
Sandown Av. RM10: Dag 6J 73
Sandown Cl. TW5: Cran 1J 111
Sandown Ct. HA7: Stan 5H 27
SE26 . . . . .3H 139
SM2: Sutt 7K 165
Sandown Dr. SM5: Cars 7E 166
Sandown Rd. SE25 . . . . .5H 157
Sandown Way UB5: N'olt 6C 58
Sandpiper Cl. E17 . . . . .7E 34
SE16 . . . . .2B 104
Sandpiper Ct. E1 . . . . .7G 85
(off Thomas More St.)
E14 .3E 104
(off New Union Cl.)
SE8 .6C 104
(off Edward Pl.)
Sandpiper Ho. SW18 . . . . .3A 118
Sandpiper Rd. SM1: Sutt 5H 165
Sandpiper Ter. IG5: Ilf 3F 53
Sandpit Pl. SE7 . . . . .5C 106
Sandpit Rd. BR1: Brom 5G 141
Sandpits Rd. CR0: Croy 4K 169
TW10: Ham 2D 132
Sandra Cl. N22 . . . . .1C 48
N22 .5F 113
Sandra Ct. CR4: Mitc 6D 136
Sandra Ho. KT8: E Mos 5H 149
Sandridge Cl. HA1: Harr 4J 41
Sandridge St. N19 . . . . .2G 65
Sandringham Av. SW20 . . . . .1G 153
Sandringham Cl. EN1: Enf 2K 23
IG6: Ilf 3G 53
SW19 . . . . .1F 135
Sandringham Ct. DA15: Sidc 6K 125
KT2: King T 1E 150
(off Skerne Wlk.)
SE16 . . . . .1K 103
(off King & Queen Wharf)
UB10: Hil 4E 74
W1 . . . . .1B 12
(off Dufour's Pl.)
W9 . . . . .3A 82
(off Maida Va.)
Sandringham Cres. HA2: Harr 2E 58
Sandringham Dr. DA2: Bexl 2K 145
DA16: Well 2J 125
TW15: Ashf 4A 128
Sandringham Flats WC2 . . . . .2D 12
(off Charing Cross Rd.)
Sandringham Gdns. IG6: Ilf 3G 53
KT8: W Mole 4E 148
N8 . . . . .6J 47
N12 .6G 31
TW5: Cran 1J 111
Sandringham Ho. W14 . . . . .4G 99
(off Windsor Way)
Sandringham M. TW12: Hamp 1D 148
W5 . . . . .7D 78
Sandringham Rd. BR1: Brom 5J 141
CR7: Thor H 5C 156
E7 . . . . .5A 70
E8 . . . . .5F 67
E10 .6F 51
IG11: Bark 5K 71
KT4: Wor Pk 3C 164
N22 .3C 48
NW2 .6D 62
NW11 . . . . .7G 45
UB5: N'olt 7E 58
Sandrock Pl. CR0: Croy 4K 169
Sandrock Rd. SE13 . . . . .3C 122
SANDS END 1A 118

Sand's End La. SW6 . . . . .1K 117
Sandstone La. E16 . . . . .7K 87
Sandstone Pl. N19 . . . . .2F 65
Sandstone Rd. SE12 . . . . .2K 141
Sands Way IG8: Wfd G 6J 37
Sandtoft Rd. SE7 . . . . .6K 105
Sandwell Cres. NW6 . . . . .6J 63
Sandwich Ho. SE16 . . . . .2J 103
(off Swan Rd.)
WC1 .2E 6
(off Sandwich St.)
Sandwich St. WC1 . . . . . .2E 6 (3J 83)
Sandwick Cl. NW7 . . . . .7H 29
Sandy Bury BR6: Orp 3H 173
Sandycombe Rd.
TW9: Kew, Rich 3F 115
TW14: Felt 1J 129
Sandycoombe Rd. TW1: Twick 6C 114
Sandycroft SE2 . . . . .6A 108
Sandy Dr. TW14: Felt 1G 129
Sandy Hill Av. SE18 . . . . .5F 107
Sandy Hill Rd. SE18 . . . . .4F 107
SM6: Wall 7G 167
Sandyhill Rd. IG1: Ilf 4F 71
Sandy La. BR5: St P 7D 144
BR6: Orp 7K 161
CR4: Mitc 1E 154
(not continuous)
DA14: Sidc 7D 144
DA16: Well 7D 108
HA3: Kent 6F 43
KT1: Ham W 7A 132
KT12: Walt T 6K 147
SM2: Cheam 7G 165
SM6: Wall 7G 167
TW10: Ham 2C 132
TW11: Tedd 7A 132
Sandy La. Nth. SM6: Wall 6H 167
Sandy La. Sth. SM6: Wall 7G 167
Sandymount Av. HA7: Stan 5H 27
Sandy Ridge BR7: Chst 6E 142
Sandy Rd. NW3 . . . . .2K 63
(not continuous)
Sandys Row E1 . . . . .6H 9 (5E 84)
Sandy Way CR0: Croy 3B 170
KT12: Walt T 7H 147
Sanford La. N16 . . . . .3F 67
Sanford St. SE14 . . . . .6A 104
Sanford Ter. N16 . . . . .3F 67
SE14 . . . . .6A 104
Sanger Av. KT9: Chess 5E 162
Sangley Rd. SE6 . . . . .7D 122
SE25 . . . . .4E 156
Sangora Rd. SW11 . . . . .4B 118
Sankey Ho. E2 . . . . .2J 85
(off St James's Av.)
Sansom Rd. E11 . . . . .2H 69
Sansom St. SE5 . . . . .1D 120
Sans Wlk. EC1 . . . . .3K 7 (4A 84)
Santley Ho. SE1 . . . . . . .7K 13 (2A 102)
Santley St. SW4 . . . . .4K 119
Santos Rd. SW18 . . . . .5J 117
Santway, The HA7: Stan 5D 26
Sapcote Trad. Cen. NW10 . . . . . . .6B 62
Saperton Wlk. SE11 . . . . .3H 19
Saphora Cl. BR6: Farnb 5H 173
Sapperton Ct. EC1 . . . . .3C 8
Sapperton Ho. W2 . . . . .5J 81
(off Brunel Est.)
Sapphire Cl. E6 . . . . .6E 88
RM8: Dag 1C 72
Sapphire Ct. E1 . . . . .7G 85
(off Cable St.)
Sapphire Rd. SE8 . . . . .4A 104
Saracen Cl. CR0: Croy 6D 156
Saracen St. E14 . . . . .6C 86
Saracens Head Yd. EC3 . . . . .1J 15
Saracen St. E14 . . . . .6C 86
Sarah Ct. UB5: N'olt 1D 76
Sarah Ho. E1 . . . . .6H 85
(off Commercial Rd.)
Sarah St. N1 . . . . .1H 9 (3E 84)
Sarah Swift Ho. SE1 . . . . .6F 15
(off Kipling St.)

Sara La. Ct. N1 ....2E 84
(off Stanway St.)
Saratoga Rd. E5 ....4J 67
Sara Turnbull Ho. SE18 ....4D 106
Sardinia St. WC2 ....1G 13 (6K 83)
Sarita Cl. HA3: Hrw W 2H 41
Sarjant Path SW19 ....2F 135
(off Blincoe Cl.)
Sarjeant Ct. BR4: W W'ck 2F 171
(off Bencurtis Pk.)
Sark Cl. TW5: Hest 7E 94
Sark Ho. EN3: Enf W 1E 24
Sark Twr. SE28 ....2G 107
Sark Wlk. E16 ....6K 87
Sarnes Ct. N11 ....4A 32
(off Oakleigh Rd. Sth.)
Sarnesfield Ho. SE15 ....5H 103
(off Pencraig Way)
Sarnesfield Rd. EN2: Enf 4J 23
Sarratt Ho. W10 ....5E 80
(off Sutton Way)
Sarre Rd. NW2 ....5H 63
Sarsen Av. TW3: Houn 2E 112
Sarsfeld Rd. SW12 ....1D 136
Sarsfield Rd. UB6: G'frd 2B 78
Sartor Rd. SE15 ....4K 121
Sarum Ter. E3 ....4B 86
Sassoon NW9 ....1B 44
Satanita Cl. E16 ....6B 88
Satchell Mead NW9 ....1B 44
Satchwell Rd. E2 ....2K 9 (3G 85)
Satchwell St. E2 ....2K 9 (3G 85)
Sattar M. N16 ....3D 66
(off Clissold Rd.)
Saul Ct. SE15 ....6F 103
Sauls Grn. E11 ....3G 69
Saunders Cl. E14 ....7B 86
(off Limehouse C'way.)
IG1: Ilf 1H 71
Saunders Ho. SE16 ....2K 103
(off Quebec Way)
Saunders Ness Rd. E14 ....5E 104
Saunders Rd. SE18 ....5K 107
UB10: Uxb 7B 56
Saunders St. SE11 ....3J 19 (4A 102)
Saunders Way SE28 ....7B 90
Saunderton Rd. HA0: Wemb 5B 60
Saunton Av. UB3: Harl 7H 93
Saunton Ct. UB1: S'hall 7G 77
(off Haldane Rd.)
Savage Gdns. E6 ....6D 88
EC3 ....2H 15 (7E 84)
(not continuous)
Savannah Cl. SE15 ....7F 103
Savera Cl. UB2: S'hall 3A 94
Savernake Ct. HA7: Stan 6G 27
Savernake Ho. N4 ....7C 48
Savernake Rd. N9 ....6B 24
NW3 ....4D 64
Savery Dr. KT6: Surb 7C 150
Savile Cl. KT3: N Mald 5A 152
KT7: T Ditt 7K 149
Savile Gdns. CR0: Croy 2F 169
Savile Row W1 ....2A 12 (7G 83)
Saville Cres. TW15: Ashf 6F 129
Saville Rd. E16 ....1C 106
RM6: Chad H 6F 55
TW1: Twick 1K 131
W4 ....3K 97
Saville Row W2: Bayes 1H 171
EN3: Enf H 2E 24
Savill Gdns. SW20 ....3C 152
Savill Ho. E16 ....1F 107
(off Robert St.)
SW4 ....6H 119
Savill Row IG8: Wfd G 6C 36
Savin Lodge SM2: Sutt 7A 166
(off Walnut M.)
Savona Cl. SW19 ....7F 135
Savona Ho. SW8 ....7G 101
(off Savona St.)
Savona St. SW8 ....7G 101
Savoy Av. UB3: Harl 5G 93

Savoy Bldgs. WC2 ....3G 13
SAVOY CIRCUS 7B 80
Savoy Cl. E15 ....1G 87
HA8: Edg 5B 28
Savoy Ct. NW3 ....3A 64
SW5 ....4J 99
(off Cromwell Rd.)
WC2 ....3F 13 (7K 83)
Savoy Hill WC2 ....3G 13 (7K 83)
Savoy M. SW9 ....3J 119
Savoy Pde. EN1: Enf 3K 23
Savoy Pl. WC2 ....3F 13 (7J 83)
Savoy Row WC2 ....2G 13
Savoy Steps WC2 ....3G 13
Savoy St. WC2 ....3G 13 (7K 83)
Savoy Theatre 3F 13
(off Strand)
Savoy Way WC2 ....3G 13
Sawbill Cl. UB4: Yead 5B 76
Sawkins Cl. SW19 ....2G 135
Sawley Rd. W12 ....1C 98
Sawmill Yd. E3 ....1A 86
Sawtry Cl. SM5: Cars 7C 154
Sawyer Cl. N9 ....2B 34
Sawyer Ct. NW10 ....7K 61
Sawyers Cl. RM10: Dag 6J 73
Sawyer's Hill TW10: Rich 7F 115
Sawyers Lawn W13 ....6A 78
Sawyer St. SE1 ....6C 14 (2C 102)
Saxby Rd. SW2 ....7J 119
Saxham Rd. IG11: Bark 2J 89
Saxlingham Rd. E4 ....3A 36
Saxon Av. TW13: Hanw 2C 130
Saxonbury Av. TW16: Sun 3K 147
Saxonbury Cl. CR4: Mitc 3B 154
Saxonbury Ct. N7 ....5J 65
Saxonbury Gdns. KT6: Surb 1C 162
Saxon Bus. Cen. SW19 ....2A 154
Saxon Cl. E17 ....7C 50
KT6: Surb 6D 150
UB8: Hil 5B 74
Saxon Dr. W3 ....6G 79
Saxonfield Cl. SW2 ....1K 137
Saxon Gdns. UB1: S'hall 7C 76
Saxon Hall W2 ....7K 81
(off Palace Ct.)
Saxon Ho. E1 ....6K 9
(off Thrawl St.)
KT1: King T 4F 151
TW13: Hanw 2D 130
Saxon Lodge CR0: Croy 1C 168
(off Tavistock Rd.)
Saxon Rd. BR1: Brom 7H 141
E3 ....2B 86
E6 ....4D 88
HA9: Wemb 3J 61
IG1: Ilf 6F 71
KT2: King T 1E 150
N22 ....1B 48
SE25 ....5D 156
TW15: Ashf 6F 129
UB1: S'hall 7C 76
Saxon Ter. SE6 ....2B 140
Saxon Wlk. DA14: Sidc 6C 144
Saxon Way N14 ....6C 22
Saxony Pde. UB3: Hayes 5E 74
Saxton Cl. SE13 ....3F 123
Sayers Ho. N2 ....2B 46
(off The Grange)
Sayer's Wlk. TW10: Rich 7F 115
Sayesbury La. N18 ....5B 34
Sayes Ct. SE8 ....6B 104
Sayes Ct. St. SE8 ....6B 104
Scadbury Pk. Nature Reserve 7K 143
Scads Hill Cl. BR6: Pet W 6K 161
Scafell NW1 ....1A 6
(off Stanhope St.)
Scala St. W1 ....5B 6 (5G 83)
Scales Rd. N17 ....3F 49
Scampston M. W10 ....6F 81
Scandrett St. E1 ....1H 103
Scarba Wlk. N1 ....6D 66
(off Marquess Rd.)

Scarborough Rd. E11 ....1F 69
N4 ....1A 66
N9 ....7D 24
TW6: H'row A 6E 110
Scarborough St. E1 ....1K 15 (6F 85)
Scarbrook Rd. CR0: Croy 3C 168
Scarle Rd. HA0: Wemb 6D 60
Scarlet Rd. SE6 ....3G 141
Scarlette Mnr. Way SW2 ....7A 120
Scarsbrook Rd. SE3 ....3B 124
Scarsdale Pl. W8 ....3K 99
Scarsdale Rd. HA2: Harr 3G 59
Scarsdale Studios W8 ....3J 99
(off Stratford Rd.)
Scarsdale Vs. W8 ....3J 99
Scarth Rd. SW13 ....3B 116
Scawen Cl. SM5: Cars 4E 166
Scawen Rd. SE8 ....5A 104
Scawfell St. E2 ....2F 85
Sceaux Gdns. SE5 ....1E 120
Sceptre Ct. EC3 ....3K 15
(off Tower Hill)
Sceptre Ho. E1 ....4J 85
(off Malcolm Rd.)
Sceptre Rd. E2 ....3J 85
Sceynes Link N12 ....4D 30
Schafer Ho. NW1 ....2A 6 (3G 83)
Schiller International University 5J 13
Schofield Wlk. SE3 ....7J 105
Scholars Cl. EN5: Barn 4B 20
Scholars Pl. N16 ....3E 66
Scholars Rd. E4 ....1A 36
SW12 ....1G 137
Scholefield Rd. N19 ....2H 65
Scholey Ho. SW11 ....3C 118
Schomberg Ho. SW1 ....3D 18
(off Page St.)
Schonfeld Sq. N16 ....2D 66
School All. TW1: Twick 1A 132
School App. E2 ....1H 9 (3E 84)
Schoolbank Rd. SE10 ....3H 105
Schoolbell M. E3 ....2A 86
School Ho. SE1 ....4E 102
(off Page's Wlk.)
School Ho. La. E1 ....7K 85
TW11: Tedd 7B 132
Schoolhouse Yd. SE18 ....5F 107
School La. DA16: Well 3B 126
HA5: Pinn 4C 40
KT1: Ham W 1C 150
KT6: Surb 1G 163
TW17: Shep 6D 146
WD23: Bush 1A 26
School of Hygiene & Tropical Medicine
........5D 6
School of Oriental & African Studies 4D 6
School Pas. KT1: King T 2F 151
UB1: S'hall 7D 76
School Rd. BR7: Chst 1G 161
E12 ....4D 70
KT1: Ham W 1C 150
KT8: E Mos 4H 149
NW10 ....4K 79
RM10: Dag 1G 91
TW3: Houn 3G 113
TW12: Ham H 6G 131
TW15: Ashf 6D 128
School Rd. Av. TW12: Ham H 6G 131
SCHOOL ROAD JUNC. 7D 128
School Sq. SE10 ....3H 105
School Wlk. TW16: Sun 4H 147
School Way N12 ....6G 31
RM8: Dag 3C 72
(not continuous)
Schooner Cl. E14 ....3E 105
IG11: Bark 3B 90
SE16 ....2K 103
Schubert Rd. SW15 ....5H 117
Science Mus. 2B 16 (3B 100)
Sclater St. E1 ....3J 9 (4F 85)
Scoble Pl. N16 ....4F 67
Scoles Cres. SW2 ....1B 138
Scoop, The 1E 102

Scope Way KT1: King T 4E 150
Scoresby St. SE1 ....5A 14 (1B 102)
Scorton Av. UB6: G'frd 2A 78
Scorton Ho. N1 ....2E 84
(off Whitmore Est.)
Scotch Comn. W13 ....5A 78
SCOTCH HOUSE 2D 100
Scoter Cl. IG8: Wfd G 7E 36
Scoter Ct. SE8 ....6B 104
(off Abinger Gro.)
Scot Gro. HA5: Pinn 1B 40
Scotia Bldg. E1 ....7K 85
(off Jardine Rd.)
Scotia Cl. SE16 ....2J 103
(off Canada Est.)
Scotia Rd. SW2 ....7A 120
Scotland Grn. N17 ....2F 49
Scotland Grn. Rd. EN3: Pond E 5E 24
Scotland Grn. Rd. Nth. EN3: Pond E 4E 24
Scotland Pl. SW1 ....5E 12 (1J 101)
Scotland Rd. IG9: Buck H 1F 37
Scotney Cl. BR6: Farnb 4E 172
Scotney Ho. E9 ....6J 67
Scots Cl. TW19: Stanw 1A 128
Scotsdale Cl. BR5: Pet W 4J 161
SM3: Cheam 7G 165
Scotsdale Rd. SE12 ....5K 123
Scotson Ho. SE11 ....4J 19
Scotswood St. EC1 ....3K 7 (4A 84)
Scotswood Wlk. N17 ....7B 34
Scott Cl. KT19: Ewe 5J 163
SW16 ....1K 155
UB7: W Dray 4B 92
Scott Ct. W3 ....2K 97
Scott Cres. HA2: Harr 1F 59
Scott Ellis Gdns. NW8 ....2A 4 (3B 82)
Scottes La. RM8: Dag 1D 72
Scott Farm Cl. KT7: T Ditt 1B 162
Scott Gdns. TW5: Hest 7B 94
Scott Ho. DA17: Belv 5F 109
E13 ....2J 87
(off Queens Rd. W.)
E14 ....2C 104
(off Admirals Way)
N1 ....1D 84
(off Sherborne St.)
N7 ....6K 65
(off Caledonian Rd.)
N18 ....5B 34
(off Woolmer Rd.)
NW8 ....4C 4
(off Broadley St.)
NW10 ....7K 61
(off Stonebridge Pk.)
SE8 ....5B 104
(off Grove St.)
Scott Lidgett Cres. SE16 ....2G 103
Scott Russell Pl. E14 ....5D 104
Scotts Av. BR2: Brom 2F 159
TW16: Sun 7G 129
Scotts Cl. W12 ....2E 98
(off Scott's Rd.)
Scotts Dr. TW12: Hamp 7F 131
Scotts Farm Rd. KT19: Ewe 6J 163
Scott's La. BR2: Brom 3F 159
Scotts Pas. SE18 ....4F 107
Scotts Rd. BR1: Brom 7J 141
E10 ....1E 68
UB2: S'hall 3A 94
W12 ....2E 98
Scott's Sufferance Wharf SE1 ....7K 15
Scotts Ter. SE9 ....2C 142
Scott St. E1 ....4H 85
Scotts Way TW16: Sun 7G 129
Scott's Yd. EC4 ....2E 14 (7D 84)
Scott Trimmer Way TW3: Houn 2C 112
Scottwell Dr. NW9 ....5B 44
Scoulding Ho. E14 ....3C 104
(off Mellish St.)
Scoulding Rd. E16 ....6J 87
Scouler St. E14 ....7E 86
Scout App. NW10 ....4A 62
Scout La. SW4 ....3G 119

Scout Way NW7 ....4E 28
Scovell Cres. SE1 ....7C 14
Scovell Rd. SE1 ....7C 14 (2C 102)
Scrattons Ter. IG11: Bark 2D 90
Screen on Baker Street (Cinema) ..5F 5
                 (off Baker St.)
Screen on the Green Cinema 1B 84
             (off Upper St.)
Screen on the Hill (Cinema)
  Belsize Pk. 5C 64
Scriven Ct. E8 ....1F 85
Scriven St. E8 ....1F 85
Scrooby St. SE6 ....6D 122
Scrope Ho. EC1 ....5J 7
             (off Bourne Est.)
Scrubs La. NW10 ....3C 80
Scrutton Cl. SW12 ....7H 119
Scrutton St. EC2 ....4G 9 (4E 84)
Scudamore La. NW9 ....4J 43
Scutari Rd. SE22 ....5J 121
Scylla Cres. TW6: H'row A 7D 110
           (not continuous)
Scylla Rd. SE15 ....3G 121
           (not continuous)
  TW6: H'row A 6D 110
Seabright St. E2 ....3H 85
Seabrook Dr. BR4: W W'ck 2G 171
Seabrook Gdns. RM7: Rush G 7G 55
Seabrook Rd. RM8: Dag 3D 72
Seaburn Cl. RM13: Rain 2K 91
Seacole Cl. W3 ....6K 79
Seacon Twr. E14 ....2B 104
Seacourt Rd. SE2 ....2D 108
Seafield Rd. N11 ....4C 32
Seaford Cl. HA4: Ruis 1F 57
Seaford Ho. SE16 ....2J 103
          (off Swan Rd.)
Seaford Rd. E17 ....3D 50
  EN1: Enf 4K 23
  N15 ....5D 48
  TW6: H'row A 5A 110
  W13 ....1B 96
Seaford St. WC1 ....2F 7 (3K 83)
Seaforth Av. KT3: N Mald 5D 152
Seaforth Cres. N5 ....5C 66
Seaforth Gdns. IG8: Wfd G 5F 37
  KT19: Ewe 4B 164
  N21 ....7E 22
Seaforth Pl. SW1 ....1B 18
Seager Bldgs. SE8 ....1C 122
Seagrave Cl. E1 ....5K 85
Seagrave Lodge SW6 ....6J 99
         (off Seagrave Rd.)
Seagrave Rd. SW6 ....6J 99
Seagry Rd. E11 ....7J 51
Seagull Cl. IG11: Bark 3A 90
Seagull La. E16 ....7J 87
Sealand Rd. TW6: H'row A 6C 110
Sealand Wlk. NW10: N'olt 3B 76
Seal Ho. SE1 ....7F 15
         (off Pardoner St.)
Seal St. E8 ....4F 67
Searles Cl. SW11 ....7C 100
Searles Dr. E6 ....5F 89
Searles Rd. SE1 ....4D 102
Searson Ho. SE17 ....4B 102
        (off Canterbury Pl.)
Sears St. SE5 ....7D 102
Seasons Cl. W7 ....1K 95
Seasprite Cl. UB5: N'olt 3B 76
Seaton Av. IG3: Ilf 5K 71
Seaton Cl. E13 ....4J 87
  SE11 ....5K 19 (5A 102)
  SW15 ....1D 134
  TW2: Whit 6H 113
Seaton Dr. TW15: Ashf 2A 128
Seaton Gdns. HA4: Ruis 3H 57
Seaton Point E5 ....4G 67
         (off Nolan Way)
Seaton Rd. CR4: Mitc 2C 154
  DA16: Well 7C 108
  HA0: Wemb 2E 78
  TW2: Whit 6G 113

Seaton Rd. UB3: Harl 4F 93
Seaton Sq. NW7 ....7A 30
Seaton St. N18 ....5B 34
Sebastian Ct. IG11: Bark 1K 89
Sebastian Ho. N1 ....1G 9
         (off Hoxton St.)
Sebastian St. EC1 ....2B 8 (3B 84)
Sebastopol Rd. N9 ....4B 34
Sebbon St. N1 ....7B 66
Sebergham Gro. NW7 ....7H 29
Sebert Rd. E7 ....5K 69
Sebright Ho. E2 ....2G 85
         (off Coate St.)
Sebright Pas. E2 ....2G 85
Sebright Rd. EN5: Barn 2A 20
Secker Cres. HA3: Hrw W 1G 41
Secker Ho. SW9 ....2B 120
      (off Loughborough Est.)
Secker St. SE1 ....5J 13 (1A 102)
Secombe Theatre 5K 165
Second Av. E12 ....4C 70
  E13 ....3J 87
  E17 ....5C 50
  EN1: Enf 5A 24
  HA9: Wemb 2D 60
  KT12: Walt T 6K 147
  N18 ....4D 34
  NW4 ....4F 45
  RM6: Chad H 5C 54
  RM10: Dag 1H 91
  SW14 ....3A 116
  UB3: Hayes 1H 93
  W3 ....1B 98
  W10 ....4G 81
Second Cl. KT8: W Mole 4G 149
Second Cross Rd. TW2: Twick ...2J 131
Second Way HA9: Wemb 4H 61
Sedan Way SE17 ....5E 102
Sedcombe Cl. DA14: Sidc 4B 144
Sedcote Rd. EN3: Pond E 5D 24
Sedding St. SW1 ....3G 17 (4E 100)
Sedding Studios SW1 ....3G 17
        (off Sedding St.)
Seddon Highwalk EC2 ....5C 8
        (off Seddon Ho.)
Seddon Ho. EC2 ....5C 8
Seddon Rd. SM4: Mord 5B 154
Seddon St. WC1 ....2H 7 (3K 83)
Sedgebrook Rd. SE3 ....2B 124
Sedgecombe Av. HA3: Kent 5C 42
Sedgefield Ct. UB5: N'olt 5F 59
       (off Newmarket Av.)
Sedgeford Rd. W12 ....1B 98
Sedgehill Rd. SE6 ....4C 140
Sedgemere Av. N2 ....3A 46
Sedgemere Rd. SE2 ....3C 108
Sedgemoor Dr. RM10: Dag 4G 73
Sedge Rd. N17 ....7D 34
Sedgeway SE6 ....1H 141
Sedgewick Av. UB10: Hil 7D 56
Sedgewood Cl. BR2: Hayes 7H 159
Sedgmoor Pl. SE5 ....7E 102
Sedgwick Ho. E3 ....5C 86
         (off Gale St.)
Sedgwick Rd. E10 ....2E 68
Sedgwick St. E9 ....5K 67
Sedleigh Rd. SW18 ....6H 117
Sedlescombe Rd. SW6 ....6J 99
Sedley Cl. EN1: Enf 1C 24
Sedley Ct. SE26 ....2H 139
Sedley Ho. SE11 ....5H 19
        (off Newburn St.)
Sedley Pl. W1 ....1J 11 (6F 83)
Sedum Cl. NW9 ....5H 43
Seeley Dr. SE21 ....4E 138
Seelig Av. NW9 ....7C 44
Seely Rd. SW17 ....6E 136
Seething La. EC3 ....2H 15 (7E 84)
SEETHING WELLS 6C 150
Seething Wells La. KT6: Surb ...6C 150
Sefton Av. HA3: Hrw W 2H 41
  NW7 ....5E 28
Sefton Cl. BR5: St M Cry 4K 161

Sefton Ct. EN2: Enf 2G 23
  TW3: Houn 1F 113
Sefton Rd. BR5: St M Cry 4K 161
  CR0: Croy 1G 169
Sefton St. SW15 ....3E 116
Segal Cl. SE23 ....7A 122
Sekforde St. EC1 ....4A 8 (4B 84)
Sekhon Ter. TW13: Hanw 3E 130
Selan Dr. BR8: Swan 7J 145
Selan Gdns. UB4: Yead 5K 75
Selbie Av. NW10 ....5B 62
Selborne Av. DA5: Bexl 1E 144
  E12 ....4E 70
Selborne Gdns. NW4 ....4C 44
  UB6: G'frd 1A 78
Selborne Rd. CR0: Croy 3E 168
  DA14: Sidc 4B 144
  E17 ....5B 50
  IG1: Ilf 2E 70
  KT3: N Mald 2A 152
  N14 ....3D 32
  N22 ....1K 47
  SE5 ....2D 120
Selborne Wlk. E17 ....5B 50
Selborne Wlk. Shop. Cen. E17 ...4B 50
Selbourne Av. KT6: Surb 2F 163
  Selbourne Ho. SE1 ....7E 14
Selby Cen., The 6K 33
Selby Chase HA4: Ruis 2K 57
Selby Cl. BR7: Chst 6E 142
  E6 ....5C 88
  KT9: Chess 7E 162
Selby Gdns. UB1: S'hall 4E 76
Selby Grn. SM5: Cars 7C 154
Selby Ho. W10 ....3G 81
       (off Beethoven St.)
Selby Rd. E11 ....3G 69
  E13 ....5K 87
  N17 ....7K 33
  SE20 ....2G 157
  SM5: Cars 7C 154
  TW15: Ashf 6E 128
  W5 ....4B 78
Selby Sq. W10 ....3G 81
       (off Dowland St.)
Selby St. E1 ....4G 85
Selcroft Ho. SE10 ....1H 8
       (off Glenister Rd.)
Selden Ho. SE15 ....2J 121
        (off Selden Rd.)
Selden Rd. SE15 ....2J 121
Selden Wlk. N7 ....2K 65
Seldon Ho. SW1 ....6A 18
       (off Churchill Gdns.)
  SW8 ....7G 101
       (off Stewart's Rd.)
Selfridges 1G 11
SELHURST 6E 156
Selhurst Cl. SW19 ....1F 135
Selhurst New Rd. SE25 ....6E 156
Selhurst Pk. 4E 156
Selhurst Pl. SE25: Croy 6E 156
Selhurst Rd. N9 ....3J 33
  SE25 ....6E 156
Selina Ho. NW8 ....3B 4
       (off Frampton St.)
Selinas La. RM8: Dag 7E 54
Selkirk Rd. SW17 ....4C 136
  TW2: Twick 2G 131
Sellers Hall Cl. N3 ....7D 30
Sellincourt Rd. SW17 ....5C 136
Sellindge Cl. BR3: Beck 7B 140
Sellons Av. NW10 ....1B 80
Sellwood Dr. EN5: Barn 5A 20
Selma Ho. W12 ....6D 80
       (off Du Cane Rd.)
Selman Ho. E9 ....6A 68
SELSDON 7J 169
Selsdon Av. CR2: S Croy 6D 168
Selsdon Cl. KT6: Surb 5E 150
  RM5: Col R 1J 55
Selsdon Pk. Rd. CR0: Sels 7K 169
  CR2: Sels 7K 169

Selsdon Rd. CR2: S Croy 5D 168
  E11 ....7J 51
  E13 ....1A 88
  NW2 ....2B 62
  SE27 ....3A 138
Selsdon Way E14 ....3D 104
Selsea Pl. N16 ....5E 66
Selsey Cres. DA16: Well 1D 126
Selsey St. E14 ....5C 86
Selvage La. NW7 ....5E 28
Selway Cl. HA5: Eastc 4K 39
Selway Ho. SW8 ....1J 119
      (off Sth. Lambeth Rd.)
Selwood Pl. SW7 ....5A 16 (5B 100)
Selwood Rd. CR0: Croy 2H 169
  KT9: Chess 4D 162
  SM3: Sutt 1H 165
Selwoods SW2 ....7A 120
Selwood Ter. SW7 .....5A 16 (5B 100)
Selworthy Cl. E11 ....5J 51
Selworthy Rd. SE6 ....3B 140
Selwyn Av. E4 ....6K 35
  IG3: Ilf 6K 53
  TW9: Rich 3E 114
Selwyn Cl. TW4: Houn 4C 112
Selwyn Ct. E17 ....5C 50
       (off Yunus Khan Cl.)
  HA8: Edg 7C 28
  HA9: Wemb 3J 61
  SE3 ....3H 123
Selwyn Cres. DA16: Well 3B 126
Selwyn Rd. E3 ....2B 86
  E13 ....1K 87
  KT3: N Mald 5K 151
  NW10 ....7K 61
Semley Ga. E9 ....6B 68
Semley Ho. SW1 ....4J 17
        (off Semley Pl.)
Semley Pl. SW1 ....4H 17 (4E 100)
Semley Rd. SW16 ....2J 155
Senate St. SE15 ....2J 121
Senators Lodge E3 ....2A 86
       (off Roman Rd.)
Senator Wlk. SE28 ....3H 107
Seneca Rd. CR7: Thor H 4C 156
Sener Ct. CR2: S Croy 6C 168
Senga Rd. SM6: Wall 1E 166
Senhouse Rd. SM3: Cheam 3F 165
Senior St. W2 ....5K 81
Senlac Rd. SE12 ....1K 141
Sennen Rd. EN1: Enf 7A 24
Sennen Wlk. SE9 ....3C 142
Senrab St. E1 ....6K 85
Sentamu Cl. SW2 ....1B 138
Sentinel Cl. UB5: N'olt 4C 76
Sentinel Sq. NW4 ....4E 44
September Cl. UB1: S'hall 1F 95
       (off Dormer's Wells La.)
  UB8: Uxb 2A 74
September Way HA7: Stan 6G 27
Septimus Pl. EN1: Enf 5B 24
Sequoia Cl. WD23: Bushy 1C 26
Sequoia Gdns. BR6: Orp 7K 161
Sequoia Pk. HA5: H End 6A 26
Seraph Ct. EC1 ....1C 8
       (off Moreland St.)
Serbin Cl. E10 ....7E 50
Serenaders Rd. SW9 ....2A 120
Sergeant Ind. Est. SW18 ....6K 117
Serica Ct. SE10 ....7E 104
Serjeants Inn EC4 ......1K 13 (6A 84)
Serlby Ct. W14 ....3H 99
       (off Somerset Sq.)
Serle St. WC2 ....7H 7 (6K 83)
Sermon La. EC4 ....1C 14
Serpentine, The 1C 100
Serpentine Gallery 6A 10 (2B 100)
Serpentine Rd. W2 ......5C 10 (1C 100)
Serviden Dr. BR1: Brom 1B 160
Servite Ho. BR3: Beck 1B 158
  KT4: Wor Pk 2B 164
        (off The Avenue)
Servius Ct. TW8: Bford 7D 96

Setchell Rd. SE1 .... 4F 103
Setchell Way SE1 .... 4F 103
Seth St. SE16 .... 2J 103
Seton Gdns. RM9: Dag 7C 72
Settle Point *E13* *2J 87*
(off London Rd.)
Settle Rd. E13 .... 2J 87
Settlers Ct. E14 .... 7F 87
Settles St. E1 .... 5G 85
Settrington Rd. SW6 .... 2K 117
Seven Acres SM5: Cars 2C 166
Seven Dials WC2 .... 1E 12 (6J 83)
Seven Dials Ct. *WC2* *1E 12*
(off Shorts Gdns.)
Sevenex Pde. HA9: Wemb 5E 60
Seven Islands Leisure Cen. 3J 103
SEVEN KINGS 1J 71
Seven Kings Rd. IG3: Ilf 1J 71
Seven Kings Way
KT2: King T 1E 150
Sevenoaks Cl. DA7: Bex 4H 127
Sevenoaks Ct. HA6: Nwood 1E 38
Sevenoaks Rd.
BR6: Chels, Orp 5K 173
BR6: Prat B 7K 173
SE4 .... 6A 122
Sevenoaks Way BR5: St P 7C 144
DA14: Sidc 7C 144
Sevenseas Rd.
TW6: H'row A 6E 110
SEVEN SISTERS 5F 49
Seven Sisters Rd. N4 .... 2A 66
N7 .... 3K 65
N15 .... 7C 48
Seven Stars Cnr. W6 .... 3C 98
Seven Stars Yd. E1 .... 5K 9
Seventh Av. E12 .... 4D 70
UB3: Hayes 1J 93
Severnake Cl. E14 .... 4C 104
Severn Av. W10 .... 3G 81
Severn Ct. *KT2: King T* *1D 150*
(off John Williams Cl.)
Severn Dr. KT10: Hin W 2A 162
Severn Way NW10 .... 5B 62
Severus Rd. SW11 .... 4C 118
Seville Ho. *E1* *1G 103*
(off Hellings St.)
Seville M. N1 .... 7E 66
Seville St. SW1 .... 7F 11 (2D 100)
Sevington Rd. NW4 .... 6D 44
Sevington St. W9 .... 4K 81
Seward Rd. BR3: Beck 2K 157
W7 .... 2A 96
SEWARDSTONE 1K 25
Sewardstone Gdns. E4 .... 5J 25
Sewardstone Rd. E2 .... 2J 85
E4 .... 7J 25
Seward St. EC1 .... 3B 8 (3B 84)
Sewdley St. E5 .... 3K 67
Sewell Rd. SE2 .... 3A 108
Sewell St. E13 .... 3J 87
Sextant Av. E14 .... 4F 105
Sexton Ct. *E14* *7F 87*
(off Newport Av.)
Sextons Ho. *SE10* *6E 104*
(off Bardsley La.)
Seymer Rd. RM1: Rom 3K 55
Seymour Av. KT17: Ewe 7E 164
N17 .... 2G 49
SM4: Mord 7F 153
Seymour Cl. HA5: H End 1D 40
KT8: E Mos 5G 149
Seymour Ct. E4 .... 2C 36
N10 .... 2E 46
N21 .... 6E 22
NW2 .... 2D 62
Seymour Dr. BR2: Brom 1D 172
Seymour Gdns. HA4: Ruis 1B 58
IG1: Ilf 1D 70
KT5: Surb 5F 151
SE4 .... 3A 122
TW1: Twick 7B 114
TW13: Hanw 4A 130
Seymour Ho. *E16* *1J 105*
(off De Quincey M.)
NW1 .... *1D 6*
(off Churchway)
SM2: Sutt *6K 165*
(off Mulgrave Rd.)
WC1 .... *3E 6*
(off Tavistock Pl.)
Seymour Leisure Cen. 6E 4 (5D 82)
Seymour M. W1 .... 7G 5 (6E 82)
Seymour Pl. SE25 .... 4H 157
W1 .... 6E 4 (5D 82)
Seymour Rd. CR4: Mitc 7E 154
E4 .... 1J 35
E6 .... 2B 88
E10 .... 1B 68
KT1: Ham W 1D 150
KT8: W Mole, E Mos 5G 149
N3 .... 7E 30
N8 .... 5A 48
N9 .... 2C 34
SM5: Cars 5E 166
SW18 .... 7H 117
SW19 .... 3F 135
TW12: Ham H 5G 131
W4 .... 4J 97
Seymour St. SE18 .... 3G 107
W1 .... 1E 10 (6D 82)
W2 .... 1E 10 (6D 82)
Seymour Ter. SE20 .... 1H 157
Seymour Vs. SE20 .... 1H 157
Seymour Wlk. SW10 .... 6A 100
Seymour Way TW16: Sun 7H 129
Seyssel St. E14 .... 4E 104
Shaa Rd. W3 .... 7K 79
Shabana Rd. W12 .... 1D 98
Shacklegate La.
TW11: Tedd 4J 131
Shackleton Cl. SE23 .... 2H 139
Shackleton Ct. *E14* *5C 104*
(off Maritime Quay)
W12 .... 2D 98
Shackleton Ho. *E1* *1J 103*
(off Prusom St.)
NW10 .... 7K 61
Shackleton Rd. UB1: S'hall 7D 76
SHACKLEWELL 4F 67
Shacklewell Grn. E8 .... 4F 67
Shacklewell Ho. E8 .... 4F 67
Shacklewell La. E8 .... 5F 67
Shacklewell Rd. N16 .... 4F 67
Shacklewell Row E8 .... 4F 67
Shacklewell St. E2 .... 2K 9 (3F 85)
Shadbolt Av. E4 .... 5F 35
Shadbolt Cl. KT4: Wor Pk 2B 164
Shad Thames SE1 .... 5J 15 (1F 103)
SHADWELL 7H 85
Shadwell Ct. UB5: N'olt 2D 76
Shadwell Dr. UB5: N'olt 3D 76
Shadwell Gdns. E1 .... 7J 85
Shadwell Pierhead E1 .... 7J 85
Shadwell Pl. *E1* *7J 85*
(off Shadwell Gdns.)
Shady Bush Cl.
WD23: Bush 1B 26
Shaef Way TW11: Tedd 7A 132
Shafter Rd. RM10: Dag 6J 73
Shaftesbury Av. EN3: Enf H 2E 24
EN5: New Bar 4F 21
HA2: Harr 1F 59
HA3: Kent 5D 42
TW14: Felt 6J 111
UB2: S'hall 4E 94
W1 .... 3C 12 (7H 83)
WC1 .... 7E 6 (6J 83)
WC2 .... 7E 6 (6J 83)
Shaftesbury Cen. *W10* *4F 81*
(off Barlby Rd.)
Shaftesbury Circ. HA2: Harr 1G 59
Shaftesbury Ct. *E6* *6E 88*
(off Sapphire Cl.)
N1 .... *2D 84*
(off Shaftesbury St.)
Shaftesbury Ct. *SW6* *1K 117*
(off Maltings Pl.)
SW16 .... 3H 137
Shaftesbury Cres. TW18: Staines 7A 128
Shaftesbury Gdns. NW10 .... 4A 80
Shaftesbury Lodge *E14* *6D 86*
(off Upper Nth. St.)
Shaftesbury M. *SE1* *3D 102*
(off Falmouth Rd.)
SW4 .... 5G 119
W8 .... *3J 99*
(off Stratford Rd.)
Shaftesbury Pde. HA2: Harr 1G 59
Shaftesbury Pl. *EC2* *6C 8*
(off London Wall)
W14 .... *4H 99*
(off Warwick Rd.)
Shaftesbury Point *E13* *2J 87*
(off High St.)
Shaftesbury Rd. BR3: Beck 2B 158
E4 .... 1A 36
E7 .... 7A 70
E10 .... 1C 68
E17 .... 6D 50
N18 .... 6K 33
N19 .... 1J 65
SM5: Cars 7B 154
TW9: Rich 3E 114
Shaftesburys, The IG11: Bark 2G 89
Shaftesbury St. N1 .... 2C 84
(not continuous)
Shaftesbury Theatre *7E 6*
(off Shaftesbury Av.)
Shaftesbury Vs. *W8* *3J 99*
(off Allen St.)
Shaftesbury Way TW2: Twick 3H 131
Shaftesbury Waye UB4: Yead 5A 76
Shafto M. SW1 .... 2F 17 (3D 100)
Shafton M. E9 .... 1K 85
Shafton Rd. E9 .... 1K 85
Shaftsbury Ct. SE5 .... 4D 120
Shafts Ct. EC3 .... 1G 15 (6E 84)
Shahjalal Ho. *E2* *2G 85*
(off Pritchards Rd.)
Shakespeare Av. N11 .... 5B 32
NW10 .... 1K 79
TW14: Felt 6J 111
UB4: Hayes, Yead 6J 75
(not continuous)
Shakespeare Cl. HA3: Kent 7G 43
Shakespeare Ct. EN5: New Bar 3E 20
HA3: Kent 6F 43
Shakespeare Cres. E12 .... 6D 70
NW10 .... 1K 79
Shakespeare Dr. HA3: Kent 6F 43
Shakespeare Gdns. N2 .... 4D 46
Shakespeare Ho. *E9* *7J 67*
(off Lyme Gro.)
N14 .... 2C 32
Shakespeare Rd. DA7: Bex 1E 126
E17 .... 2K 49
N3 .... 1J 45
NW7 .... 4G 29
NW10 .... 1K 79
SE24 .... 5B 120
W3 .... 1J 97
W7 .... 7K 77
Shakespeare's Globe Theatre & Exhibition
.... 4C 14 (1C 102)
Shakespeare Twr. EC2 .... 5D 8
Shakespeare Way TW13: Hanw 4A 130
Shakspeare M. N16 .... 4E 66
Shakspeare Wlk. N16 .... 4E 66
Shalbourne Sq. E9 .... 6B 68
Shalcomb St. SW10 .... 6A 100
Shalden Ho. SW15 .... 6B 116
Shaldon Dr. HA4: Ruis 3A 58
SM4: Mord 5G 153
Shaldon Rd. HA8: Edg 2F 43
Shalfleet Dr. W10 .... 7F 81
Shalford Cl. BR6: Farnb 4G 173
Shalford Ct. *N1* *2B 84*
(off Charlton Pl.)
Shalford Ho. SE1 .... 3D 102
Shalimar Gdns. W3 .... 7J 79
Shalimar Rd. W3 .... 7J 79
Shallons Rd. SE9 .... 4F 143
Shalstone Rd. SW14 .... 3H 115
Shalston Vs. KT6: Surb 6F 151
Shamrock Rd. CR0: Croy 6K 155
Shamrock St. SW4 .... 3H 119
Shamrock Way N14 .... 1A 32
Shandon Rd. SW4 .... 6G 119
Shand St. SE1 .... 6H 15 (2E 102)
Shandy St. E1 .... 5K 85
Shan Ho. WC1 .... 4G 7
Shanklin Ho. E17 .... 2B 50
Shanklin Rd. N8 .... 5H 47
N15 .... 4G 49
Shannon Cl. NW2 .... 3F 63
UB2: S'hall 5B 94
Shannon Commercial Cen.
KT3: N Mald 4C 152
SHANNON CORNER 4C 152
Shannon Cnr. Retail Pk.
KT3: N Mald 4C 152
Shannon Ct. *CR0: Croy* *1C 168*
(off Tavistock Rd.)
N16 .... 3E 66
SE15 .... *7F 103*
(off Garnies Cl.)
Shannon Gro. SW9 .... 4K 119
Shannon Pl. NW8 .... 2C 82
Shannon Way BR3: Beck 6D 140
Shanti Ct. SW18 .... 1J 135
Shap Cres. SM5: Cars 1D 166
Shapland Way N13 .... 5E 32
Shap St. E2 .... 2F 85
Shapwick Cl. N11 .... 5J 31
Shardcroft Av. SE24 .... 5B 120
Shardeloes Rd. SE14 .... 2B 122
Shard's Sq. SE15 .... 6G 103
Sharland Cl. CR7: Thor H 6A 156
Sharman Ct. *DA14: Sidc* *4A 144*
(off Carlton Rd.)
Sharnbrooke Cl. DA16: Well 3C 126
Sharnbrook Ho. W14 .... 6J 99
Sharon Cl. KT6: Surb 1C 162
Sharon Ct. *CR2: S Croy* *5C 168*
(off Warham Rd.)
Sharon Gdns. E9 .... 1J 85
Sharon Rd. EN3: Enf H 2F 25
W4 .... 5K 97
Sharpe Cl. W7 .... 5K 77
Sharp Ho. SW8 .... 3F 119
TW1: Twick 6D 114
Sharpleshall St. NW1 .... 7D 64
Sharpness Cl. UB4: Yead 5C 76
Sharpness Ct. *SE15* *7F 103*
(off Daniel Gdns.)
Sharp's La. HA4: Ruis 7F 39
Sharratt St. SE15 .... 6J 103
Sharsted St. SE17 .... 5B 102
Sharvel La. UB5: N'olt 1J 75
Sharwood *WC1* *1H 7*
(off Penton Ri.)
Shaver's Pl. SW1 .... 3C 12
Shaw Av. IG11: Bark 2E 90
Shawbrooke Rd. SE9 .... 5A 124
Shawbury Cl. NW9 .... 1A 44
Shawbury Rd. SE22 .... 5F 121
Shaw Cl. SE28 .... 1B 108
WD23: Bushy 2D 26
Shaw Ct. *W3* *3J 97*
(off All Saints Rd.)
Shaw Cres. E14 .... 6A 86
Shaw Dr. KT12: Walt T 7A 148
Shawfield Ct. UB7: W Dray 3A 92
Shawfield Pk. BR1: Brom 2B 160
Shawfield St. SW3 .... 6D 16 (5C 100)
Shawford Ct. SW15 .... 7C 116
Shawford Rd. KT19: Ewe 6K 163
Shaw Gdns. IG11: Bark 2E 90
Shaw Ho. DA17: Belv 5F 109
E16 .... *1E 106*
(off Claremont St.)

Shaw Path BR1: Brom 3H 141
Shaw Rd. BR1: Brom 3H 141
  EN3: Enf H 1E 24
  SE22 . . . . .4E 120
Shaws Cotts. SE23 . . . . .3A 140
Shaws Path KT1: Ham W 1C 150
             (off Bennett Cl.)
Shaw Sq. E17 . . . . .1A 50
Shaw Theatre 2D 6 (3H 83)
Shaw Way SM6: Wall 7J 167
Shearing Dr. SM5: Cars 7A 154
Shearling Way N7 . . . . .6J 65
Shearman Rd. SE3 . . . . .4H 123
SHEARS, THE 7G 129
Shears Cl. TW16: Sun 7G 129
Shears Way TW16: Sun 1G 147
Shearwater Cl. IG11: Bark 3A 90
Shearwater Ct. E1 . . . . .3K 15
               (off Star Pl.)
  SE8 . . . . .6B 104
             (off Abinger Gro.)
Shearwater Rd. SM1: Sutt 5H 165
Shearwater Way UB4: Yead 6B 76
Sheath Cotts. KT7: T Ditt 6B 150
              (off Ferry Rd.)
Sheaveshill Av. NW9 . . . . .4A 44
Sheaveshill Ct. NW9 . . . . .4K 43
Sheaveshill Pde. NW9 . . . . .4A 44
          (off Sheaveshill Av.)
Sheba Ct. N17 . . . . .6B 34
             (off Altair Cl.)
Sheba Pl. E1 . . . . .4K 9 (4F 85)
Sheen Comn. Dr. TW10: Rich 4G 115
Sheen Ct. TW10: Rich 4G 115
Sheen Ct. Rd. TW10: Rich 4G 115
Sheendale Rd. TW9: Rich 4F 115
Sheenewood SE26 . . . . .4H 139
Sheen Ga. Gdns. SW14 . . . . .4J 115
Sheengate Mans. SW14 . . . . .4K 115
Sheen Gro. N1 . . . . .1A 84
Sheen La. SW14 . . . . .5J 115
Sheen Pk. TW9: Rich 4F 115
Sheen Rd. BR5: St M Cry 4K 161
  TW9: Rich 5E 114
  TW10: Rich 5E 114
Sheen Sports & Fitness Cen. 4A 116
Sheen Way SM6: Wall 5K 167
Sheen Wood SW14 . . . . .5J 115
Sheepcote Cl. TW5: Cran 7J 93
Sheepcote La. SW11 . . . . .2D 118
Sheepcote Rd. HA1: Harr 6K 41
Sheepcotes Rd. RM6: Chad H 4E 54
Sheephouse Way
  KT3: N Mald 1K 163
Sheep La. E8 . . . . .1H 85
Sheep Wlk. TW17: Shep 7B 146
Sheep Wlk. M. SW19 . . . . .6F 135
Sheerness M. E16 . . . . .2F 107
Sheerwater Rd. E16 . . . . .5B 88
Sheffield Rd. TW6: H'row A 6E 110
Sheffield Sq. E3 . . . . .3B 86
Sheffield St. WC2 . . . . .1G 13 (6K 83)
Sheffield Ter. W8 . . . . .1J 99
Sheffield Way TW6: H'row A 5F 111
Shelbourne Cl. HA5: Pinn 3D 40
Shelbourne Pl. BR3: Beck 7B 140
Shelbourne Rd. N17 . . . . .2H 49
Shelburne Dr. TW4: Houn 6E 112
Shelburne Rd. N7 . . . . .4K 65
Shelbury Cl. DA14: Sidc 3A 144
Shelbury Rd. SE22 . . . . .5H 121
Sheldon Av. IG5: Ilf 2F 53
  N6 . . . . .7C 46
Sheldon Cl. SE12 . . . . .5K 123
  SE20 . . . . .1H 157
Sheldon Ct.
  EN5: New Bar 4E 20
  SW8 . . . . .7J 101
          (off Lansdowne Grn.)
Sheldon Ho. N1 . . . . .1E 84
           (off Kingsland Rd.)
Sheldon Pl. E2 . . . . .2G 85
           (not continuous)

Sheldon Rd. DA7: Bex 1F 127
  N18 . . . . .4K 33
  NW2 . . . . .4F 63
  RM9: Dag 7E 72
Sheldon Sq. W2 . . . . .6A 4 (5A 82)
Sheldon St. CR0: Croy 3C 168
Sheldrake Cl. E16 . . . . .1D 106
Sheldrake Ct. E6 . . . . .2C 88
         (off St Bartholomew's Rd.)
Sheldrake Ho. SE16 . . . . .4K 103
            (off Tawny Way)
Sheldrake Pl. W8 . . . . .2J 99
Sheldrick Cl. SW19 . . . . .2B 154
Shelduck Cl. E15 . . . . .5H 69
Shelduck Ct. SE8 . . . . .6B 104
             (off Pilot Cl.)
Sheldwich Ter. BR2: Brom 6C 160
Shelford KT1: King T 2G 151
Shelford Pl. N16 . . . . .3D 66
Shelford Ri. SE19 . . . . .7F 139
Shelford Rd. EN5: Barn 6A 20
Shelgate Rd. SW11 . . . . .5C 118
Shell Cl. BR2: Brom 6C 160
Shellduck Cl. NW9 . . . . .2A 44
Shelley N8 .3J 47
           (off Boyton Rd.)
Shelley Av. E12 . . . . .6C 70
  UB6: G'frd 3H 77
Shelley Cl. BR6: Orp 3J 173
  HA8: Edg 4B 28
  SE15 . . . . .2H 121
  UB4: Hayes 5J 75
  UB6: G'frd 3H 77
Shelley Ct. E10 . . . . .7D 50
           (off Skelton's La.)
  E11 . . . . .4K 51
          (off Makepeace Rd.)
  N19 . . . . .1K 65
  SW3 . . . . .7F 17
             (off Tite St.)
Shelley Cres. TW5: Hest 1B 112
  UB1: S'hall 6D 76
Shelley Dr. DA16: Well 1J 125
Shelley Gdns. HA0: Wemb 2C 60
Shelley Ho. E2 . . . . .3J 85
           (off Cornwall Av.)
  N16 . . . . .4E 66
  SE17 . . . . .5C 102
           (off Browning St.)
  SW1 . . . . .7B 18
          (off Churchill Gdns.)
Shelley Lodge EN2: Enf 1J 23
Shelley Rd. NW10 . . . . .1K 79
Shelley Way SW19 . . . . .5B 136
Shellness Rd. E5 . . . . .5H 67
Shell Rd. SE13 . . . . .3D 122
Shellwood Rd. SW11 . . . . .2D 118
Shelmerdine Cl. E3 . . . . .5C 86
Shelson Av. TW13: Felt 3H 129
Shelton Rd. SW19 . . . . .1J 153
Shelton St. WC2 . . . . .1E 12 (6J 83)
           (not continuous)
Shene Ho. EC1 . . . . .5J 7
           (off Bourne Est.)
Shenfield Ho. SE18 . . . . .1B 124
          (off Portway Gdns.)
Shenfield Rd. IG8: Wfd G 7E 36
Shenfield St. N1 . . . . .1H 9 (2E 84)
           (not continuous)
Shenley Av. HA4: Ruis 2H 57
Shenley Rd. SE5 . . . . .1E 120
  TW5: Hest 1C 112
Shenstone W13 . . . . .1C 96
Shenstone Cl. DA1: Cray 4K 127
Shenstone Ho. SW16 . . . . .5G 137
Shepherd Cl. TW13: Hanw 4C 130
Shepherdess Pl. N1 . . . . .1D 8 (3C 84)
Shepherdess Wlk. N1 . . . . .1D 8 (2C 84)
Shepherd Ho. E14 . . . . .6D 86
           (off Annabel Cl.)
Shepherd Mkt. W1 . . . . .4J 11 (1F 101)
SHEPHERD'S BUSH 2E 98
Shepherds Bush Empire Theatre 2E 98

Shepherd's Bush Grn. W12 . . . . .2E 98
Shepherd's Bush Mkt. W12 . . . . .2E 98
           (not continuous)
Shepherd's Bush Pl. W12 . . . . .2F 99
Shepherd's Bush Rd. W6 . . . . .4E 98
Shepherds Cl. BR6: Orp 3K 173
  HA7: Stan 5F 27
           (not continuous)
  N6 . . . . .6F 47
  RM6: Chad H 5D 54
  TW17: Shep 6D 146
  W1 . . . . .2G 11
            (off Lees Pl.)
Shepherds Ct. W12 . . . . .2F 99
        (off Shepherd's Bush Grn.)
  UB5: N'olt 6C 58
           (off Arnold Rd.)
Shepherds Grn. BR7: Chst 7H 143
Shepherd's Hill N6 . . . . .6F 47
Shepherds La. E9 . . . . .6K 67
Shepherds Leas SE9 . . . . .4G 125
Shepherds Ley SE28 . . . . .1J 107
Shepherds Path NW3 . . . . .5B 64
          (off Lyndhurst Rd.)
  UB5: N'olt 6C 58
           (off Arnold Rd.)
Shepherds Pl. W1 . . . . .2G 11 (7E 82)
Shepherd St. W1 . . . . .5J 11 (1F 101)
Shepherds Wlk. NW2 . . . . .2C 62
  NW3 . . . . .5B 64
           (not continuous)
  WD23: Bushy 2C 26
Shepherds Way CR2: Sels 7K 169
Shepiston La. UB3: Harl 4D 92
Shepley Cl. SM5: Cars 3E 166
Sheppard Cl. EN1: Enf 1C 24
  KT1: King T 4E 150
Sheppard Dr. SE16 . . . . .5H 103
Sheppard Ho. E2 . . . . .2G 85
           (off Warner Pl.)
  SW2 . . . . .1A 138
Sheppards Coll. BR1: Brom 1J 159
           (off London Rd.)
Sheppard St. E16 . . . . .4H 87
SHEPPERTON 6D 146
Shepperton Bus. Pk.
  TW17: Shep 5E 146
Shepperton Ct. TW17: Shep 6D 146
Shepperton Ct. Dr. TW17: Shep 5D 146
Shepperton Film Studios 3B 146
SHEPPERTON GREEN 4C 146
Shepperton Rd. BR5: Pet W 6G 161
  N1 . . . . .1C 84
  TW18: Lale, Shep 4A 146
Sheppey Gdns. RM9: Dag 7C 72
Sheppey Rd. RM9: Dag 7B 72
Sheppey Ho's. E2 . . . . .3J 85
           (off Welwyn St.)
Sherard Ct. N7 . . . . .3J 65
Sherard Ho. E9 . . . . .7J 67
          (off Frampton Pk. Rd.)
Sherard Rd. SE9 . . . . .5C 124
Sheraton Bus. Cen. UB6: G'frd 2B 78
Sheraton Ho. SW1 . . . . .7K 17
          (off Churchill Gdns.)
Sheraton St. W1 . . . . .1C 12 (6H 83)
Sherborne Av. EN3: Enf H 2D 24
  UB2: S'hall 4E 94
Sherborne Cl. UB4: Yead 6A 76
Sherborne Cres. SM5: Cars 7C 154
Sherborne Gdns. NW9 . . . . .3G 43
  TW17: Shep 7G 147
  W13 . . . . .5B 78
Sherborne Ho. SW1 . . . . .5K 17
          (off Winchester St.)
  SW8 . . . . .1D 18
           (off Bolney St.)
Sherborne La. EC4 . . . . .2E 14 (7D 84)
Sherborne Rd. BR5: St M Cry 4K 161
  KT9: Chess 5E 162
  SM3: Sutt 2J 165
  TW14: Bedf 1F 129
           (not continuous)
Sherborne St. N1 . . . . .1D 84
Sherboro Rd. N15 . . . . .6F 49

Sherbourne Ct. SM2: Sutt 6A 166
  SW5 . . . . .4K 99
           (off Cromwell Rd.)
Sherbourne Pl. HA7: Stan 6F 27
Sherbrooke Cl. DA6: Bex 4G 127
Sherbrooke Ho. E2 . . . . .2J 85
           (off Bonner Rd.)
Sherbrooke Rd. SW6 . . . . .7G 99
Sherbrooke Ter. SW6 . . . . .7G 99
          (off Sherbrook Rd.)
Sherbrook Way KT4: Wor Pk 7D 152
Sherbrook Gdns. N21 . . . . .7G 23
Shere Cl. KT9: Chess 5D 162
Sheredan Rd. E4 . . . . .5A 36
Shere Ho. SE1 . . . . .7E 14
Shere Rd. IG2: Ilf 5E 52
Sherfield Cl. KT3: N Mald 4H 151
Sherfield Gdns. SW15 . . . . .6B 116
Sheridan Bldgs. WC2 . . . . .1F 13
           (off Martlett Ct.)
Sheridan Cl. UB10: Hil 4E 74
Sheridan Ct. CR0: Croy 4D 168
           (off Coombe Rd.)
  HA1: Harr 6H 41
  NW6 . . . . .7A 64
           (off Belsize Rd.)
  SW5 . . . . .4K 99
          (off Barkston Gdns.)
  TW4: Houn 5C 112
  UB5: N'olt 5F 59
  W7 . . . . .7K 77
           (off Milton Rd.)
Sheridan Cres. BR7: Chst 2F 161
Sheridan Gdns. HA3: Kent 6D 42
Sheridan Ho. E1 . . . . .6J 85
           (off Tarling St.)
  SE11 . . . . .4K 19
           (off Wincott St.)
Sheridan Lodge BR2: Brom 4A 160
          (off Homesdale Rd.)
Sheridan M. E11 . . . . .6K 51
Sheridan Pl. SW13 . . . . .3B 116
  TW12: Hamp 1F 149
Sheridan Rd. DA7: Bex 3E 126
  DA17: Belv 4G 109
  E7 . . . . .3H 69
  E12 . . . . .5C 70
  SW19 . . . . .1H 153
  TW10: Ham 3C 132
Sheridan St. E1 . . . . .6H 85
Sheridan Ter. UB5: N'olt 5F 59
Sheridan Wlk. NW11 . . . . .6J 45
  SM5: Cars 5D 166
Sheringham Av. E12 . . . . .4D 70
  N14 . . . . .5C 22
  RM7: Rom 6J 55
  TW2: Whit 1D 130
  TW13: Felt 3J 129
Sheringham Ct. TW13: Felt 3J 129
          (off Sheringham Av.)
Sheringham Dr. IG11: Bark 5K 71
Sheringham Ho. NW1 . . . . .5C 4
Sheringham Rd. N7 . . . . .6K 65
  SE20 . . . . .3J 157
Sheringham Twr. UB1: S'hall 7F 77
Sherington Av. HA5: H End 7A 26
Sherington Rd. SE7 . . . . .6K 105
Sherland Rd. TW1: Twick 1K 131
Sherleys Cl. HA4: Ruis 2G 57
Sherlies Av. BR6: Orp 2J 173
Sherlock Cl. NW8 . . . . .1B 82
           (off Dorman Way)
Sherlock Holmes Mus. 4F 5
Sherlock M. W1 . . . . .5G 5 (5E 82)
Sherman Gdns.
  RM6: Chad H 6C 54
Sherman Ho. E14 . . . . .6E 86
             (off Dee St.)
Sherman Rd. BR1: Brom 1J 159
Shernhall St. E17 . . . . .3E 50

Sherrard Rd. E7 6A **70**
E12 6A **70**
Sherrards Way EN5: Barn 5D **20**
Sherren Ho. E1 4J **85**
Sherrick Grn. Rd. NW10 5D **62**
Sherriff Rd. NW6 6J **63**
Sherringham Av. N17 2G **49**
Sherrin Rd. E10 4D **68**
Sherrock Gdns. NW4 4D **44**
Sherry M. IG11: Bark 7H **71**
Sherston Ct. *SE1* *4B* ***102***
(off Newington Butts)
WC1 2J **7**
Sherwin Ho. SE11 7J **19**
Sherwin Rd. SE14 1K **121**
Sherwood KT6: Surb 2D **162**
NW6 7G **63**
Sherwood Av. E18 3K **51**
HA4: Ruis 6G **39**
SW16 7H **137**
UB4: Yead 4K **75**
UB6: G'frd 6J **59**
Sherwood Cl. DA5: Bexl 6C **126**
E17 2B **50**
SW13 3D **116**
W13 1B **96**
Sherwood Ct. *CR2: S Croy* *5C* ***168***
(off Nottingham Rd.)
HA2: Harr 2F **59**
SW11 3A **118**
W1 *6E* ***4***
(off Bryanston Pl.)
Sherwood Gdns. E14 4C **104**
IG11: Bark 7H **71**
SE16 5G **103**
Sherwood Pk. Av. DA15: Sidc 7A **126**
Sherwood Pk. Rd. CR4: Mitc 4G **155**
SM1: Sutt 5J **165**
Sherwood Rd. CR0: Croy 7H **157**
DA16: Well 2J **125**
HA2: Harr 2G **59**
IG6: Ilf 4H **53**
NW4 3E **44**
SW19 7H **135**
TW12: Ham H 5G **131**
Sherwood St. N20 3G **31**
W1 2B **12** (7G **83**)
Sherwood Ter. N20 3G **31**
Sherwood Way BR4: W W'ck 2E **170**
Shetland Rd. E3 2B **86**
TW6: H'row A 6E **110**
Shield Dr. TW8: Bford 6A **96**
Shieldhall St. SE2 4C **108**
Shield Rd. TW15: Ashf 4E **128**
Shifford Path SE23 3K **139**
Shillaker Ct. W3 1B **98**
Shillibeer Pl. W1 6D **4**
Shillingford Cl. NW7 7A **30**
Shillingford St. N1 7B **66**
Shilling Pl. W7 2A **96**
Shillingstone Ho. *W14* *3G* ***99***
(off Russell Rd.)
Shinfield St. W12 6E **80**
Shinglewell Rd. DA8: Erith 7G **109**
Shinners Cl. SE25 5G **157**
Ship All. W4 6G **97**
Ship & Mermaid Row SE1 6F **15** (2D **102**)
Shipka Rd. SW12 1F **137**
Shiplake Ho. *E2* *2J* ***9***
(off Arnold Cir.)
Ship La. SW14 3J **115**
Shipman Rd. E16 6K **87**
SE23 2K **139**
Ship St. SE8 1C **122**
Ship Tavern Pas. EC3 2G **15** (7E **84**)
Shipton Cl. RM8: Dag 3D **72**
Shipton Ho. *E2* *1K* ***9***
(off Shipton St.)
Shipton Rd. UB10: Ick 4B **56**
Shipton St. E2 1K **9** (2F **85**)
Shipway Ter. N16 3F **67**
Shipwright Rd. SE16 2A **104**
Shipwright Yd. SE1 5G **15** (1E **102**)
Ship Yd. E14 5D **104**
Shirburn Cl. SE23 7J **121**
Shirebrook Rd. SE3 3B **124**
Shire Ct. DA18: Erith 3D **108**
KT17: Ewe 7B **164**
Shirehall Cl. NW4 6F **45**
Shirehall Gdns. NW4 6F **45**
Shirehall La. NW4 6F **45**
Shirehall Pk. NW4 5F **45**
Shire Horse Way TW7: Isle 3K **113**
Shire La. BR2: Kes 7C **172**
BR6: Chels, Downe 7F **173**
(not continuous)
Shire M. TW2: Whit 6G **113**
Shire Pl. SW18 7A **118**
TW8: Bford 7D **96**
Shires, The TW10: Ham 4E **132**
Shirland M. W9 3H **81**
Shirland Rd. W9 3H **81**
Shirlbutt St. E14 7D **86**
SHIRLEY **2J 169**
Shirley Av. CR0: Croy 1J **169**
DA5: Bexl 7D **126**
SM1: Sutt 4B **166**
Shirley Chu. Rd. CR0: Croy 3K **169**
Shirley Cl. TW3: Houn 5G **113**
Shirley Ct. SW16 7J **137**
Shirley Cres. BR3: Beck 4A **158**
Shirley Dr. TW3: Houn 5G **113**
Shirley Gdns. IG11: Bark 6J **71**
W7 1K **95**
Shirley Gro. N9 7D **24**
SW11 3E **118**
Shirley Hgts. SM6: Wall 7G **167**
Shirley Hills Rd. CR0: Croy 5J **169**
Shirley Ho. *SE5* *7D* ***102***
(off Picton St.)
Shirley Ho. Dr. SE7 7A **106**
SHIRLEY OAKS **1K 169**
Shirley Oaks Rd. CR0: Croy 1K **169**
Shirley Pk. CR0: Croy 2J **169**
Shirley Pk. Rd. CR0: Croy 1H **169**
Shirley Rd. CR0: Croy 7H **157**
DA15: Sidc 3J **143**
E15 7G **69**
EN2: Enf 3H **23**
SM6: Wall 7G **167**
W4 2K **97**
Shirleys Cl. E17 5D **50**
Shirley St. E16 6H **87**
Shirley Way CR0: Croy 3A **170**
Shirley Windmill 3J **169**
Shirlock Rd. NW3 4D **64**
Shirwell Cl. NW7 7A **30**
Shobden Rd. N17 1D **48**
Shobroke Cl. NW2 3E **62**
Shoebury Rd. E6 7D **70**
Shoelands Ct. NW9 3K **43**
Shoe La. EC4 7K **7** (6A **84**)
Sholto Rd. TW6: H'row A 5B **110**
Shona Ho. E13 5A **88**
Shooters Av. HA3: Kent 4C **42**
SHOOTERS HILL **1E 124**
Shooters Hill DA16: Well 1D **124**
SE18 1D **124**
Shooters Hill Rd. SE3 1F **123**
SE10 1F **123**
SE18 7A **106**
Shooters Rd. EN2: Enf 1G **23**
Shoot Up Hill NW2 5G **63**
Shop. Hall, The E6 1C **88**
Shore Bus. Cen. E9 7J **67**
Shore Cl. TW12: Hamp 6C **130**
TW14: Felt 7J **111**
Shorediche Cl. UB10: Ick 3B **56**
SHOREDITCH **1G 9 (3E 84)**
Shoreditch Ct. *E8* *7F* ***67***
(off Queensbridge Rd.)
Shoreditch High St. E1 4H **9** (4E **84**)
Shoreditch Ho. N1 2F **9**
Shore Gro. TW13: Hanw 2D **130**
Shoreham Cl. CR0: Croy 6J **157**
DA5: Bexl 1D **144**
Shoreham Cl. SW18 5K **117**
Shoreham Rd. E. TW6: H'row A 5A **110**
Shoreham Rd. W. TW6: H'row A 5A **110**
Shoreham Way BR2: Hayes 6J **159**
Shore Ho. SW8 3F **119**
Shore M. *E9* *7J* ***67***
(off Shore Rd.)
Shore Pl. E9 7J **67**
Shore Point IG9: Buck H 2E **36**
Shore Rd. E9 7J **67**
Shore Way *SW9* *2A* ***120***
(off Crowhurst Cl.)
Shorncliffe Rd. SE1 5F **103**
Shorndean St. SE6 1E **140**
Shorne Cl. DA15: Sidc 6B **126**
Shornefield Cl. BR1: Brom 3E **160**
Shornells Way SE2 4C **108**
Shorrold's Rd. SW6 7H **99**
Shortcroft Rd. KT17: Ewe 7B **164**
Shortcrofts Rd. RM9: Dag 6F **73**
Shorter St. E1 2K **15** (7F **85**)
Short Ga. N12 4C **30**
Short Hedges TW3: Houn 1E **112**
Short Hill HA1: Harr 1J **59**
SHORTLANDS **2G 159**
Shortlands UB3: Harl 6F **93**
W6 4F **99**
Shortlands Cl. DA17: Belv 3F **109**
N18 3J **33**
Shortlands Gdns. BR2: Brom 2G **159**
Shortlands Gro. BR2: Brom 3F **159**
Shortlands Rd. BR2: Brom 3F **159**
E10 7D **50**
KT2: King T 7F **133**
Short La. TW19: Stanw 7B **110**
Short Path SE18 6F **107**
Short Rd. E11 2G **69**
TW6: H'row A 6A **110**
W4 6A **98**
Shorts Cft. NW9 4H **43**
Shorts Gdns. WC2 1E **12** (6J **83**)
Shorts Rd. SM5: Cars 4C **166**
Short St. *NW4* *4E* ***44***
(off Foster St.)
SE1 6K **13** (2A **102**)
Short Wall E15 3E **86**
Short Way N12 6H **31**
SE9 3C **124**
TW2: Whit 7G **113**
Shotfield SM6: Wall 6F **167**
Shott Cl. SM1: Sutt 5A **166**
Shottendane Rd. SW6 1J **117**
Shottery Cl. SE9 3C **142**
Shottfield Av. SW14 4A **116**
Shottsford *W2* *6J* ***81***
(off Talbot Rd.)
Shoulder of Mutton All. E14 7A **86**
Shouldham St. W1 6D **4** (5C **82**)
Showcase Cinema
Barking 3H **89**
Wood Green 2A **48**
Showers Way UB3: Hayes 1J **93**
Shrapnel Cl. SE18 7C **106**
Shrapnel Rd. SE9 3D **124**
Shrewsbury Av. HA3: Kent 4E **42**
SW14 4J **115**
Shrewsbury Cl. KT6: Surb 2E **162**
Shrewsbury Ct. EC1 4D **8**
Shrewsbury Cres. NW10 1K **79**
Shrewsbury Ho. SW3 7C **16**
SW8 7H **19**
Shrewsbury La. SE18 1F **125**
Shrewsbury M. *W2* *5J* ***81***
(off Chepstow Rd.)
Shrewsbury Rd. BR3: Beck 3A **158**
E7 5B **70**
N11 6B **32**
SM5: Cars 6C **154**
TW6: H'row A 6E **110**
(not continuous)
W2 6J **81**
Shrewsbury St. W10 4E **80**
Shrewsbury Wlk. TW7: Isle 3A **114**
Shrewton Rd. SW17 7D **136**
Shroffold Rd. BR1: Brom 4G **141**
Shropshire Cl. CR4: Mitc 4J **155**
Shropshire Ct. *W7* *6K* ***77***
(off Copley Cl.)
Shropshire Ho. *N18* *5C* ***34***
(off Cavendish Cl.)
Shropshire Pl. WC1 4C **6** (4G **83**)
Shropshire Rd. N22 7E **32**
Shroton St. NW1 5D **4** (5C **82**)
Shrubberies, The E18 2J **51**
Shrubbery, The E11 5K **51**
KT6: Surb 1E **162**
Shrubbery Cl. N1 1C **84**
Shrubbery Gdns. N21 7G **23**
Shrubbery Rd. N9 3B **34**
SW16 4J **137**
UB1: S'hall 1D **94**
Shrubland Cl. N20 1G **31**
Shrubland Gro. KT4: Wor Pk 3E **164**
Shrubland Rd. E8 1F **85**
E10 7C **50**
E17 5C **50**
Shrublands Av. CR0: Croy 3C **170**
Shrublands Cl. SE26 3J **139**
Shrubsall Cl. SE9 1C **142**
Shuna Wlk. N1 6D **66**
Shurland Av. EN4: E Barn 6G **21**
Shurland Gdns. SE15 7F **103**
Shurlock Dr. BR6: Farnb 4G **173**
Shuters Sq. W14 5H **99**
Shuttle Cl. DA15: Sidc 7K **125**
Shuttlemead DA5: Bexl 7F **127**
Shuttle St. E1 4G **85**
Shuttleworth Rd. SW11 2C **118**
Siamese M. N3 1J **45**
Siani M. N8 4B **48**
Sibella Rd. SW4 2H **119**
Sibley Cl. BR1: Brom 5C **160**
DA6: Bex 5E **126**
Sibley Ct. BR2: Brom 2F **159**
UB8: Hil 5E **74**
Sibley Gro. E12 7C **70**
Sibthorpe Rd. SE12 6K **123**
Sibthorp Rd. CR4: Mitc 2D **154**
Sibton Rd. SM5: Cars 7C **154**
Sicilian Av. WC1 6F **7**
Sickle Cnr. RM9: Dag 4H **91**
Sidbury St. SW6 1G **117**
SIDCUP **4A 144**
Sidcup By-Pass
BR5: Sidc, St P, Swan 6A **144**
BR7: Chst, Sidc 3H **143**
DA14: Sidc 6A **144**
Sidcup High St. DA14: Sidc 4A **144**
Sidcup Hill DA14: Sidc 4B **144**
Sidcup Hill Gdns. DA14: Sidc 5C **144**
Sidcup Place 5A **144**
Sidcup Pl. DA14: Sidc 5A **144**
Sidcup Rd. SE9 1D **142**
SE12 6A **124**
Sidcup Technical Cen. DA14: Sidc 5D **144**
Siddeley Dr. TW4: Houn 3C **112**
Siddons La. NW1 4F **5** (4D **82**)
Siddons Rd. CR0: Wadd 3A **168**
N17 1G **49**
SE23 2A **140**
Side Rd. E17 5B **50**
Sidewood Rd. SE9 1H **143**
Sidford Ho. SE1 2H **19**
Sidford Pl. SE1 2H **19** (3A **102**)
Sidgwick Ho. *SW9* *2K* ***119***
(off Lingham St.)
Sidi Ct. N15 3B **48**
Sidings, The E11 1E **68**
Sidings M. N7 3A **66**
Sidlaw Ho. N16 1F **67**
Sidmouth Av. TW7: Isle 2J **113**
Sidmouth Dr. HA4: Ruis 3J **57**
Sidmouth Ho. *SE15* *7G* ***103***
(off Lympstone Gdns.)
W1 *7D* ***4***
(off Cato St.)

Sidmouth Pde. NW2 ....7E 62
Sidmouth Rd. DA16: Well 7C 108
  E10 ....3E 68
  NW2 ....7E 62
Sidmouth St. WC1 ....2F 7 (3K 83)
Sidney Av. N13 ....5E 32
Sidney Boyd Ct. NW6 ....7J 63
Sidney Elson Way E6 ....2E 88
Sidney Est. E1 ....6J 85
  (Bromhead St.)
  E1 ....5J 85
  (Lindley St.)
Sidney Gdns. TW8: Bford 6D 96
Sidney Godley (VC) Ho. E2 ....3J 85
  (off Digby St.)
Sidney Gro. EC1 ....1A 8 (2B 84)
Sidney Ho. E2 ....2K 85
  (off Old Ford Rd.)
Sidney Miller Ct. W3 ....1H 97
  (off Crown St.)
Sidney Rd. BR3: Beck 2A 158
  E7 ....3J 69
  HA2: Harr 3G 41
  KT12: Walt T 7J 147
  N22 ....7E 32
  SE25 ....5G 157
  SW9 ....2K 119
  TW1: Twick 6A 114
Sidney Sq. E1 ....5J 85
Sidney St. E1 ....5H 85
Sidworth St. E8 ....7H 67
Siebert Rd. SE3 ....6J 105
Siege Ho. E1 ....6H 85
  (off Sidney St.)
Siemens Rd. SE18 ....3B 106
Sienna Ter. NW2 ....2C 62
Sierra Dr. RM9: Dag 2H 91
Sigdon Pas. E8 ....5G 67
Sigdon Rd. E8 ....5G 67
Sigers, The HA5: Eastc 6K 39
Sigmund Freud Statue 6B 64
Signal Ho. E8 ....7H 67
  (off Martello Ter.)
Signmakers Yd. NW1 ....1F 83
  (off Delancey St.)
Sigrist Sq. KT2: King T 1E 150
Silbury Av. CR4: Mitc 1C 154
Silbury Ho. SE26 ....3G 139
Silbury St. N1 ....1E 8 (3D 84)
Silchester Ct. CR7: Thor H 4A 156
  TW15: Ashf 2A 128
Silchester Rd. W10 ....6F 81
Silecroft Rd. DA7: Bex 1G 127
Silesia Bldgs. E8 ....7H 67
Silex St. SE1 ....7B 14 (2B 102)
Silk Cl. SE12 ....5J 123
Silk Ct. E2 ....3G 85
  (off Squirries St.)
Silkfield Rd. NW9 ....5A 44
Silk Ho. NW9 ....3K 43
Silk Mills Pas. SE13 ....2D 122
Silk Mills Path SE13 ....2D 122
  (not continuous)
Silk Mills Sq. E9 ....6B 68
Silks Ct. E11 ....1H 69
Silkstream Pde. HA8: Edg 1J 43
Silkstream Rd. HA8: Edg 1J 43
Silk St. EC2 ....5D 8 (5C 84)
Sillitoe Ho. N1 ....1D 84
  (off Colville Est.)
Silsoe Ho. NW1 ....2F 83
Silsoe Rd. N22 ....2K 47
Silver Birch Av. E4 ....5G 35
Silver Birch Cl. DA2: Dart ...4K 145
  SE6 ....3B 140
  SE28 ....1A 108
  UB10: Ick 4A 56
Silverbirch Cl. N11 ....6K 31
Silver Birch Gdns. E6 ....4D 88
Silverbirch Wlk. NW5 ....6E 64
Silverburn Ho. SW9 ....1B 120
  (off Lothian Rd.)
Silvercliffe Gdns. EN4: E Barn ...4H 21

Silver Cl. HA3: Hrw W 7C 26
  SE14 ....7A 104
Silver Cres. W4 ....4H 97
Silverdale EN2: Enf 4D 22
  NW1 ....1A 6
  (off Hampstead Rd.)
  SE26 ....4J 139
Silverdale Av. IG3: Ilf 5J 53
Silverdale Cen., The HA0: Wemb ...1F 79
Silverdale Cl. SM1: Sutt 4H 165
  UB5: N'olt 5D 58
  W7 ....1J 95
Silverdale Ct. EC1 ....3B 8
Silverdale Dr. SE9 ....2C 142
  TW16: Sun 2K 147
Silverdale Factory Cen. UB3: Hayes ...3J 93
Silverdale Gdns. UB3: Hayes ...2J 93
Silverdale Ind. Est. UB3: Hayes ...2J 93
Silverdale Rd. BR5: Pet W ...4G 161
  DA7: Bex 2H 127
  E4 ....6A 36
  UB3: Hayes 2H 93
Silverdene N12 ....6E 30
  (off Thyra Gro.)
Silvergate KT19: Ewe 5J 163
Silverhall St. TW7: Isle 3A 114
Silverholme Cl. HA3: Kent 7E 42
Silver Jubilee Way TW4: Cran ...2K 111
Silverland St. E16 ....1D 106
Silver La. BR4: W W'ck 2F 171
Silverleigh Rd. CR7: Thor H ...4K 155
Silvermead E18 ....1J 51
Silvermere Dr. N18 ....6E 34
Silvermere Rd. SE6 ....7D 122
Silver Pl. W1 ....2B 12 (6G 83)
Silver Rd. SE13 ....3D 122
  (not continuous)
  W12 ....7F 81
Silvers IG9: Buck H 1F 37
  (off Palmerston Rd.)
Silver Spring Cl. DA8: Erith ...6H 109
Silverston Way HA7: Stan 5H 27
Silver St. EN1: Enf 3J 23
  N18 ....4J 33
Silverthorn NW8 ....1K 81
  (off Abbey Rd.)
Silverthorne Loft SE17 ....6D 102
  (off Albany Rd.)
Silverthorne Rd. SW8 ....2F 119
Silverthorn Gdns. E4 ....2H 35
Silverton Rd. W6 ....6F 99
SILVERTOWN 1A 106
Silvertown Viaduct E16 ......6H 87
Silvertown Way E16 ....6G 87
  (not continuous)
Silvertree La. UB6: G'frd 3H 77
Silver Wlk. SE16 ....1A 104
Silver Way RM7: Mawney 3H 55
  UB10: Hil 2D 74
Silverwood Cl. BR3: Beck 7C 140
  CR0: Sels 7B 170
  HA6: Nwood 1E 38
Silvester Ho. E1 ....6H 85
  (off Varden St.)
  E2 ....3J 85
  (off Sceptre Rd.)
  W11 ....6H 81
  (off Basing St.)
Silvester Rd. SE22 ....5F 121
Silvester St. SE1 ......7E 14 (2D 102)
Silvocea Way E14 ....6F 87
Silwood Est. SE16 ....4J 103
Silwood St. SE16 ....4J 103
  (off Rotherhithe New Rd.)
Simla Cl. N7 ....7J 65
  (off Brewery Rd.)
Simla Ho. SE1 ....7F 15
  (off Kipling Est.)
Simmonds Ct. SW5 ....4K 99
  (off Earl's Ct. Gdns.)
Simmons Cl. KT9: Chess 6C 162
  N20 ....2H 31
Simmons La. E4 ....2A 36

Simmons Rd. SE18 ....5F 107
Simmons Way N20 ....2H 31
Simms Cl. SM5: Cars 2C 166
Simms Gdns. N2 ....2A 46
Simms Rd. SE1 ....4G 103
Simnel Rd. SE12 ....7K 123
Simon Cl. W11 ....7H 81
Simon Ct. W9 ....3J 81
  (off Saltram Cres.)
Simonds Rd. E10 ....2C 68
Simone Cl. BR1: Brom 1B 160
Simone Ct. SE26 ....3J 139
Simon Peter Ct. EN2: Enf 2G 23
Simons Cl. N16 ....2F 67
Sims Wlk. E15 ....5F 69
Simpson Cl. N21 ....5D 22
Simpson Dr. W3 ....6K 79
Simpson Ho. NW8 ......2D 4 (4C 82)
  SE11 ....6H 19 (5K 101)
Simpson Rd. TW4: Houn 6D 112
  TW10: Ham 4C 132
Simpsons Rd. BR2: Brom 3J 159
  E14 ....7D 86
Simpson St. SW11 ....2C 118
Simpson Way KT6: Surb 6C 150
Simrose Ct. SW18 ....5J 117
Sims Wlk. SE3 ....4H 123
Sinclair Ct. CR0: Croy 2C 168
Sinclair Dr. SM2: Sutt 7K 165
Sinclair Gdns. W14 ....2F 99
Sinclair Ho. WC1 ....6E 6
  (off Sandwich St.)
Sinclair Mans. W12 ....2F 99
  (off Richmond Way)
Sinclair Pl. SE4 ....6C 122
Sinclair Rd. E4 ....5G 35
  W14 ....2F 99
Sinclare Cl. EN1: Enf 1A 24
Singapore Rd. W13 ....1A 96
Singer St. EC2 ....2F 9 (3D 84)
Singleton Cl. CR0: Croy 7C 156
  CR4: Mitc 7D 136
  SW17 ....7D 136
Singleton Rd. RM9: Dag 5F 73
Singleton Scarp N12 ....5D 30
Sinnott Rd. E17 ....1K 49
Sion Ct. TW1: Twick 1B 132
Sion Rd. TW1: Twick 1B 132
Sippets Ct. IG1: Ilf 1H 71
SIPSON 6C 92
Sipson Cl. UB7: Sip 6C 92
Sipson La. UB3: Harl 6C 92
  UB7: Sip 6C 92
Sipson Rd. UB7: Sip, W Dray ...3B 92
  (not continuous)
Sipson Way UB7: Sip 7C 92
Sir Abraham Dawes Cotts.
  SW15 ....4G 117
Sir Alexander Cl. W3 ....1B 98
Sir Alexander Rd. W3 ....1B 98
Sir Christopher France Ho. E1 ...3A 86
Sir Cyril Black Way SW19 ....7J 135
Sirdar Rd. CR4: Mitc 6E 136
  N22 ....3B 48
  W11 ....7F 81
Sirinham Point SW8 ....7H 19
Sirius Bldg. E1 ....7K 85
  (off Jardine Rd.)
Sir John Cass Hall E9 ....7J 67
  (off Well St.)
Sir John Kirk Cl. SE5 ....7C 102
Sir John Soane's Mus. ..7G 7 (6K 83)
Sir Nicholas Garrow Ho. W10 ...4G 81
  (off Kensal Rd.)
Sir Oswald Stoll Foundation, The
  SW6 ....7K 99
  (off Fulham Rd.)
Sir Oswald Stoll Mans. SW6 ...7K 99
  (off Fulham Rd.)
Sir William Powell's Almshouses
  SW6 ....2G 117
Sise La. EC4 ....1E 14 (6D 84)

Siskin Ho. SE16 ....4K 103
  (off Tawny Way)
Sisley Rd. IG11: Bark 1J 89
Sispara Gdns. SW18 ....6H 117
Sissinghurst Cl. BR1: Brom ...5G 141
Sissinghurst Ho. SE15 ....6J 103
  (off Sharratt St.)
Sissinghurst Rd. CR0: Croy ...7G 157
Sissulu Ct. E6 ....1A 88
Sister Mabel's Way SE15 ....7G 103
Sisters Av. SW11 ....3D 118
Sistova Rd. SW12 ....1F 137
Sisulu Pl. SW9 ....3A 120
Sitarey Ct. W12 ....1D 98
Sittingbourne Av. EN1: Enf ...6J 23
Sitwell Gro. HA7: Stan 5E 26
Siverst Cl. UB5: N'olt 6F 59
Sivill Ho. E2 ....1K 9
  (off Columbia Rd.)
Siviter Way RM10: Dag 7H 73
Siward Rd. BR2: Brom 3K 159
  N17 ....1D 48
  SW17 ....3A 136
Six Acres Est. N4 ....2K 65
Six Bridges Ind. Est. SE1 ....5G 103
Sixpenny Ct. IG11: Bark 6G 71
Sixth Av. E12 ....4D 70
  UB3: Hayes 1H 93
  W10 ....3G 81
Sixth Cross Rd. TW2: Twick ...3G 131
Skardu Rd. NW2 ....5G 63
Skeena Hill SW18 ....7G 117
Skeffington Rd. E6 ....1D 88
Skeffington St. SE18 ....3G 107
Skeggs Ho. E14 ....3E 104
  (off Glengall St.)
Skegness Ho. N7 ....7K 65
  (off Sutterton St.)
Skelbrook St. SW18 ....2A 136
Skelgill Rd. SW15 ....4H 117
Skelley Rd. E15 ....7H 69
Skelton Cl. E8 ....6F 67
Skelton Rd. E7 ....6J 69
Skelton's La. E10 ....7D 50
Skelwith Rd. W6 ....6E 98
Skenfrith Ho. SE15 ....6H 103
  (off Commercial Way)
Skerne Rd. KT2: King T 1D 150
Skerne Wlk. KT2: King T 1D 150
Sketchley Gdns. SE16 ......5K 103
Sketty Rd. EN1: Enf 3A 24
Skiers St. E15 ....1G 87
Skiffington Cl. SW2 ....1A 138
Skillen Lodge HA5: Pinn 1B 40
Skinner Pl. SW1 ....4G 17
Skinners La. EC4 .....2D 14 (7C 84)
  TW5: Hest 1F 113
Skinner's Row SE10 ....1D 122
Skinner St. EC1 ....2A 8 (3A 84)
Skip La. UB9: Hare 1A 56
Skipper Cl. IG11: Bark 1G 89
Skipsea Ho. SW18 ....6C 118
Skipsey Av. E6 ....3D 88
Skipton Cl. N11 ....6K 31
Skipton Dr. UB3: Harl 3E 92
Skipton Ho. SE4 ....4A 122
Skipwith Ho. EC1 ....5J 7
  (off Bourne Est.)
Skipworth Rd. E9 ....1J 85
Skua Cl. SE8 ....6D 104
  (off Dorking Cl.)
Skylark Ct. SE1 ....7D 14
  (off Swan St.)
Skyline Ct. CR0: Croy 3D 168
  (off Park La.)
  SE1 ....3F 103
Skyline Plaza Bldg.
  E1 ....6G 85
  (off Commercial Rd.)
Skylines E14 ....2E 104
Skylines Village E14 ....2E 104
Sky Peals Rd. IG8: Wfd G 7A 36
Skyport Dr. UB7: Harm 7A 92

Skyview Apartments CR0: Croy 2C 168
(off Park St.)
Slade, The SE18 . . . . .6J 107
Sladebrook Rd. SE3 . . . . .3B 124
Slade Ct. EN5: New Bar 3E 20
Sladedale Rd. SE18 . . . . .5J 107
Slade Ho. TW4: Houn 6D 112
Sladen Pl. E5 . . . . .4H 67
Slades Cl. EN2: Enf 3F 23
Slades Dr. BR7: Chst 3G 143
Slades Gdns. EN2: Enf 2F 23
Slades Hill EN2: Enf 3F 23
Slades Ri. EN2: Enf 3F 23
Slade Twr. E10 . . . . .2C 68
(off Leyton Grange Est.)
Slade Wlk. SE17 . . . . .6B 102
Slagrove Pl. SE13 . . . . .5C 122
Slaidburn St. SW10 . . . . .6A 100
Slaithwaite Rd. SE13 . . . . .4E 122
Slaney Cl. NW10 . . . . .7E 62
Slaney Pl. N7 . . . . .5A 66
Slater Cl. SE18 . . . . .5E 106
Slatter NW9 . . . . .7G 29
Slattery Rd. TW13: Felt 1B 130
Sleaford Ind. Est. SW8 . . . . .7G 101
Sleaford St. SW8 . . . . .7G 101
Sledmere Ct. TW14: Bedf 1G 129
Sleigh Ho. E2 . . . . .3J 85
(off Bacton St.)
Slievemore Cl. SW4 . . . . .3H 119
Sligo Ho. E1 . . . . .4K 85
(off Beaumont Gro.)
Slindon Ct. N16 . . . . .3F 67
Slingsby Pl. WC2 . . . . . . .2E 12 (7J 83)
Slippers Pl. SE16 . . . . .3H 103
Slipway Ho. E14 . . . . .5D 104
(off Burrells Wharf Sq.)
Sloane Av. SW3 . . . . .4D 16 (4C 100)
Sloane Av. Mans. SW3 . . . . .4E 16
(off Sloane Av.)
Sloane Ct. E. SW3 . . . . . . .5G 17 (5E 100)
Sloane Ct. W. SW3 . . . . . . .5G 17 (5E 100)
Sloane Gdns. BR6: Farnb 3G 173
SW1 . . . . .4G 17 (4E 100)
Sloane Ga. Mans. SW1 . . . . .3G 17
(off D'Oyley St.)
Sloane Ho. E9 . . . . .7J 67
(off Loddiges Rd.)
Sloane Sq. SW1 . . . . .4G 17 (4E 100)
Sloane St. SW1 . . . . .7F 11 (2D 100)
Sloane Ter. SW1 . . . . .3G 17 (4E 100)
Sloane Ter. Mans. SW1 . . . . .3G 17
(off Sloane Ter.)
Sloane Wlk. CR0: Croy 6B 158
Slocum Cl. SE28 . . . . .7C 90
Sloman Ho. W10 . . . . .3G 81
(off Beethoven St.)
Slough La. NW9 . . . . .5J 43
Sly St. E1 . . . . .6H 85
Smaldon Cl. UB7: W Dray 3C 92
Smallberry Av. TW7: Isle 2K 113
Smallbrook M. W2 . . . . . .1A 10 (6B 82)
Smalley Cl. N16 . . . . .3F 67
Smalley Rd. Est. N16 . . . . .3F 67
(off Smalley Cl.)
Smallwood Rd. SW17 . . . . .4B 136
Smarden Cl. DA17: Belv 5G 109
Smarden Gro. SE9 . . . . .4D 142
Smart's Pl. N18 . . . . .5B 34
WC2 . . . . .7F 7 (6J 83)
Smart St. E2 . . . . .3K 85
Smeaton Cl. KT9: Chess 6D 162
Smeaton Ct. SE1 . . . . .3C 102
Smeaton Rd. IG8: Wfd G 5J 37
SW18 . . . . .7J 117
Smeaton St. E1 . . . . .1H 103
Smedley St. SW4 . . . . .2H 119
Smeed Rd. E3 . . . . .7C 68
Smiles Pl. SE13 . . . . .2E 122
Smith Cl. SE16 . . . . .1K 103
Smithfield (Central Markets) 6A 8
Smithfield St. EC1 . . . . .6A 8 (5B 84)
Smith Hill TW8: Bford 6E 96

Smithies Ct. E15 . . . . .5E 68
Smithies Rd. SE2 . . . . .4B 108
Smith's Ct. W1 . . . . .2B 12
Smithson Rd. N17 . . . . .1D 48
Smiths Point E13 . . . . .1J 87
(off Brooks Rd.)
Smith Sq. SW1 . . . . .2E 18 (3J 101)
Smith St. KT5: Surb 6F 151
SW3 . . . . .5E 16 (5D 100)
Smiths Yd. CR0: Croy 3C 168
(off St George's Wlk.)
SW18 . . . . .2A 136
Smith Ter. SW3 . . . . .6E 16 (5D 100)
Smithwood Cl. SW19 . . . . .1G 135
Smithy St. E1 . . . . .5J 85
Smock Wlk. CR0: Croy 6C 156
Smokehouse Yd. EC1 . . . . .5B 8
(off St John St.)
Smoothfield TW3: Houn 4E 112
Smugglers Way SW18 . . . . .4K 117
Smyrk's Rd. SE17 . . . . .5E 102
Smyrna Rd. NW6 . . . . .7J 63
Smythe St. E14 . . . . .7D 86
Snag La. BR6: Prat B 7K 173
Snakes La. N14: Cockf 3A 22
Snakes La. E. IG8: Buck H, Wfd G . . .6F 37
Snakes La. W. IG8: Wfd G 5D 36
Snakey La. TW13: Felt 4J 129
SNARESBROOK 5J 51
Snaresbrook Dr. HA7: Stan 4J 27
Snaresbrook Hall E18 . . . . .4J 51
Snaresbrook Rd. E11 . . . . .4G 51
Snarsgate St. W10 . . . . .5E 80
Sneath Av. NW11 . . . . .7H 45
Snells Pk. N18 . . . . .6A 34
Sneyd Rd. NW2 . . . . .4E 62
Snowberry Cl. E15 . . . . .4F 69
Snowbury Rd. SW6 . . . . .2K 117
Snowden Av. UB10: Hil 2D 74
Snowden St. EC2 . . . . .4G 9 (4E 84)
Snowdon Aviary 1D 82
(in London Zoo)
Snowdon Cres. UB3: Harl 3E 92
Snowdon Dr. NW9 . . . . .6A 44
Snowdown Cl. SE20 . . . . .1J 157
Snowdrop Cl. TW12: Hamp 6E 130
Snow Hill EC1 . . . . .6A 8 (5B 84)
Snow Hill Ct. EC1 . . . . .7B 8 (6B 84)
(not continuous)
Snowman Ho. NW6 . . . . .1K 81
Snowsfields SE1 . . . . .6F 15 (2D 102)
Snowshill Rd. E12 . . . . .5C 70
Snowy Fielder Waye TW7: Isle 2B 114
Soames St. SE15 . . . . .3F 121
Soames Wlk. KT3: N Mald 1A 152
Soane Cl. W5 . . . . .2D 96
Soane Ct. NW1 . . . . .7G 65
(off St Pancras Way)
Soaphouse La. TW8: Bford 7E 96
Sobraon Ho. KT2: King T 7F 133
(off Elm Rd.)
Socket La. BR2: Hayes 6K 159
SOHO 1C 12 (6G 83)
Soho Sq. W1 . . . . .7C 6 (6H 83)
Soho St. W1 . . . . .7C 6 (6H 83)
Soho Theatre & Writers Cen. 1C 12
(off Dean St.)
Sojourner Truth Cl. E8 . . . . .6H 67
Solander Gdns. E1 . . . . .7H 85
(off Cable St.)
E1 . . . . .7J 85
(Highway, The)
Solar Ct. N3 . . . . .7E 30
Solar Ho. E6 . . . . .5B 88
Solarium Ct. SE1 . . . . .4F 103
(off Alscot Rd.)
Soldene Ct. N7 . . . . .5K 65
(off George's Rd.)
Solebay St. E1 . . . . .4A 86
Solent Ho. E1 . . . . .5A 86
(off Ben Jonson Rd.)
Solent Ri. E13 . . . . .3J 87

Solent Rd. NW6 . . . . .5J 63
Soley M. WC1 . . . . .1J 7 (3A 84)
Solna Av. SW15 . . . . .5E 116
Solna Rd. N21 . . . . .1J 33
Solomon Av. N9 . . . . .4B 34
Solomons Ct. N12 . . . . .7F 31
Solomon's Pas. SE15 . . . . .4H 121
Solon New Rd. SW4 . . . . .4J 119
Solon New Rd. Est. SW4 . . . . .4J 119
Solon Rd. SW2 . . . . .4J 119
Solway Cl. E8 . . . . .6F 67
(off Queensbridge Rd.)
TW4: Houn 3C 112
Solway Ho. E1 . . . . .4K 85
(off Ernest St.)
Solway Rd. N22 . . . . .1B 48
SE22 . . . . .4G 121
Somaford Gro. EN4: E Barn 6G 21
Somali Rd. NW2 . . . . .5H 63
Sombourne Ho. SW15 . . . . .7C 116
(off Fontley Way)
Somerby Rd. IG11: Bark 7H 71
Somercoates Cl. EN4: Cockf 3H 21
Somer Ct. SW6 . . . . .6J 99
(off Anselm Rd.)
Somerfield Ho. SE16 . . . . .5K 103
Somerfield Rd. N4 . . . . .2B 66
(not continuous)
Somerfield St. SE16 . . . . .5K 103
Somerford Cl. HA5: Eastc 4J 39
Somerford Gro. N16 . . . . .4F 67
N17 .7B 34
(not continuous)
Somerford Gro. Est. N16 . . . . .4F 67
Somerford St. E1 . . . . .4H 85
Somerford Way SE16 . . . . .2A 104
Somerhill Av. DA15: Sidc 7B 126
Somerhill Rd. DA16: Well 2B 126
Somerleyton Pas. SW9 . . . . .4B 120
Somerleyton Rd. SW9 . . . . .4A 120
Somersby Gdns. IG4: Ilf 5D 52
Somers Cl. NW1 . . . . .2H 83
Somers Cres. W2 . . . . . . .1C 10 (6C 82)
Somerset Av. DA16: Well 5K 125
KT9: Chess 4D 162
SW20 . . . . .2D 152
Somerset Cl. IG8: Wfd G 1J 51
KT3: N Mald 6A 152
N17 .2D 48
Somerset Ct. IG9: Buck H 2F 37
NW1 . . . . .2H 83
W7 .6K 77
(off Copley Cl.)
Somerset Est. SW11 . . . . .1B 118
Somerset Gdns. N6 . . . . .7E 46
N17 .7K 33
SE13 . . . . .2D 122
SW16 . . . . .3K 155
TW11: Tedd 5J 131
Somerset Hall N17 . . . . .7K 33
Somerset House 2G 13 (7K 83)
Somerset Ho. SW19 . . . . .3F 135
Somerset Lodge TW8: Bford 6D 96
Somerset Rd. E17 . . . . .5C 50
EN5: New Bar 5E 20
HA1: Harr 5G 41
KT1: King T 2F 151
N17 .3F 49
N18 .5A 34
NW4 .4E 44
SW19 . . . . .3F 135
TW8: Bford 6C 96
TW11: Tedd 5J 131
UB1: S'hall 5D 76
W4 .3K 97
W13 .1B 96
Somerset Sq. W14 . . . . .2G 99
Somerset Waye TW5: Hest 6C 94
Somersham Rd. DA7: Bex 2E 126
Somers Pl. SW2 . . . . .7K 119
Somers Rd. E17 . . . . .4B 50
SW2 . . . . .6K 119
SOMERS TOWN 1C 6 (3H 83)

Somers Town Community Sports Cen.
. . . . .2H 83
Somerton Av. TW9: Rich 3H 115
Somerton Ho. WC1 . . . . .2D 6
Somerton Rd. NW2 . . . . .3G 63
SE15 . . . . .4H 121
Somertrees Av. SE12 . . . . .2K 141
Somervell Rd. HA2: Harr 5D 58
Somerville Av. SW13 . . . . .6D 98
Somerville Cl. SW9 . . . . .1K 119
Somerville Point SE16 . . . . .2B 104
Somerville Rd. RM6: Chad H 6C 54
SE20 . . . . .7K 139
Sonderburg Rd. N7 . . . . .2K 65
Sondes St. SE17 . . . . .6D 102
Songhurst Cl. CR0: Croy 6K 155
Sonia Ct. HA1: Harr 6K 41
HA8: Edg 7A 28
Sonia Gdns. N12 . . . . .4F 31
NW10 . . . . .4B 62
TW5: Hest 7E 94
Sonning Gdns. TW12: Hamp 6C 130
Sonning Ho. E2 . . . . .2J 9
(off Swanfield St.)
Sonning Rd. SE25 . . . . .6G 157
Sontan Ct. TW2: Twick 1H 131
Soper Cl. E4 . . . . .5G 35
SE23 . . . . .1K 139
Soper M. EN3: Enf L 1H 25
Sophia Cl. N7 . . . . .6K 65
Sophia Ho. W6 . . . . .5E 98
(off Queen Caroline St.)
Sophia Rd. E10 . . . . .1D 68
E16 .6K 87
Sophia Sq. SE16 . . . . .7A 86
(off Sovereign Cres.)
Sopwith NW9 . . . . .7G 29
Sopwith Av. KT9: Chess 5E 162
Sopwith Cl. KT2: King T 5F 133
Sopwith Rd. TW5: Hest 7A 94
Sopwith Way KT2: King T 1E 150
SW8 . . . . .7J 17 (7F 101)
Sorensen Ct. E10 . . . . .2D 68
(off Leyton Grange Est.)
Sorrel Cl. SE28 . . . . .1A 108
Sorrel Gdns. E6 . . . . .5C 88
Sorrel La. E14 . . . . .6F 87
Sorrell Cl. SE14 . . . . .7A 104
SW9 . . . . .2A 120
Sorrento Rd. SM1: Sutt 3J 165
Sotheby Rd. N5 . . . . .3B 66
Sotheran Cl. E8 . . . . .1G 85
Sotherby Lodge E2 . . . . .2J 85
(off Sewardstone Rd.)
Sotheron Rd. SW6 . . . . .7K 99
Soudan Rd. SW11 . . . . .1D 118
Souldern Rd. W14 . . . . .3F 99
Sth. Access Rd. E17 . . . . .7A 50
Southacre W2 . . . . .1C 10
(off Hyde Pk. Cres.)
Southacre Way HA5: Pinn 1A 40
Sth. Africa Rd. W12 . . . . .1D 98
SOUTH ACTON 2J 97
SOUTHALL .1D 94
Southall Cl. UB1: S'hall 7D 76
Southall Ent. Cen. UB2: S'hall 2E 94
SOUTHALL GREEN 3C 94
Southall La. TW5: Cran 6K 93
UB2: S'hall 6K 93
Southall Pl. SE1 . . . . .7E 14 (2D 102)
Southam Ho. W10 . . . . .4G 81
(off Southam St.)
Southampton Bldgs. WC2 . . . . .6J 7 (5A 84)
Southampton Gdns. CR4: Mitc 5J 155
Southampton M. E16 . . . . .1K 105
Southampton Pl. WC1 . . . . . .6F 7 (5J 83)
Southampton Rd. NW5 . . . . .5D 64
Southampton Rd. E. TW6: H'row A . . .6B 110
Southampton Rd. W. TW6: H'row A . .6A 110
(not continuous)
Southampton Row WC1 . . . . . .5F 7 (5J 83)
Southampton St. WC2 . . . . .2F 13 (7J 83)
Southampton Way SE5 . . . . .7D 102

Southam St.—Southspring

Southam St. W10 . . . 4G 81
Sth. Audley St. W1 . . . 3H 11 (7E 82)
South Av. E4 . . . 7J 25
N2 . . . 4K 45
NW10 . . . 4E 80
SM5: Cars . . . 7E 166
TW9: Kew . . . 2G 115
UB1: S'hall . . . 7D 76
South Av. Gdns. UB1: S'hall . . . 7D 76
South Bank . . . 4H 13 (1K 101)
South Bank KT6: Surb . . . 6E 150
Southbank KT7: T Ditt . . . 7B 150
Sth. Bank Bus. Cen. SW8 . . . 7D 18 (6H 101)
Sth. Bank Ter. KT6: Surb . . . 6E 150
SOUTH BARNET . . . 1K 31
SOUTH BEDDINGTON . . . 6H 167
Sth. Birkbeck Rd. E11 . . . 3F 69
Sth. Black Lion La. W6 . . . 5C 98
South Block *SE1* . . . *7G 13*
(off Westminster Bri. Rd.)
Sth. Bolton Gdns. SW5 . . . 5A 100
SOUTHBOROUGH
Bromley . . . 5D 160
Surbiton . . . 1E 162
Southborough Cl. KT6: Surb . . . 1D 162
Southborough Ho. *SE17* . . . *5E 102*
(off Surrey Gro.)
Southborough La. BR2: Brom . . . 5C 160
Southborough Rd. BR1: Brom . . . 3C 160
E9 . . . 1K 85
KT6: Surb . . . 1E 162
Sth. Boundary Rd. E12 . . . 3D 70
Southbourne BR2: Hayes . . . 7J 159
Southbourne Av. NW9 . . . 2J 43
Southbourne Cl. HA5: Pinn . . . 7C 40
Southbourne Ct. NW9 . . . 2J 43
Southbourne Cres. NW4 . . . 4G 45
Southbourne Gdns. HA4: Ruis . . . 1K 57
IG1: Ilf . . . 5G 71
SE12 . . . 5K 123
Sth. Branch Av. NW10 . . . 4E 80
Southbridge Pl. CR0: Croy . . . 4C 168
Southbridge Rd. CR0: Croy . . . 4C 168
Southbridge Way UB2: S'hall . . . 2C 94
SOUTH BROMLEY . . . 7E 86
Southbrook M. SE12 . . . 6H 123
Southbrook Rd. SE12 . . . 6H 123
SW16 . . . 1J 155
Southbury *NW8* . . . *1A 82*
(off Loudoun Rd.)
Southbury Av. EN1: Enf . . . 4B 24
Southbury Leisure Cen. . . . 3B 24
Southbury Rd. EN1: Enf . . . 3K 23
EN3: Pond E . . . 3A 24
Sth. Carriage Dr. SW1 . . . 7B 10 (2B 100)
SW7 . . . 7B 10 (2B 100)
SOUTH CHINGFORD . . . 5G 35
Southchurch Ct. *E6* . . . *2D 88*
(off High St. Sth.)
Southchurch Rd. E6 . . . 2D 88
Sth. Circular Rd. SW15 . . . 4C 116
Sth. City Ct. SE15 . . . 7E 102
South Cl. DA6: Bex . . . 4D 126
EN5: Barn . . . 3C 20
HA5: Pinn . . . 7D 40
N6 . . . 6F 47
RM10: Dag . . . 1G 91
SM4: Mord . . . 6J 153
TW2: Twick . . . 3E 130
UB7: W Dray . . . 3B 92
Sth. Colonnade, The E14 . . . 1C 104
Southcombe St. W14 . . . 4G 99
South Comn. Rd. UB8: Uxb . . . 6A 56
Southcote Av. KT5: Surb . . . 7H 151
TW13: Felt . . . 2H 129
Southcote Ri. HA4: Ruis . . . 7F 39
Southcote Rd. E17 . . . 5K 49
N19 . . . 4G 65
SE25 . . . 5H 157
Southcott Ho. *W9* . . . *4A 82*
(off Clarendon Gdns.)
Southcott M. NW8 . . . 2C 82
Sth. Countess Rd. E17 . . . 3B 50
South Cres. E16 . . . 4F 87
WC1 . . . 6C 6 (5H 83)
Southcroft Av. BR4: W W'ck . . . 2E 170
DA16: Well . . . 3J 125
Southcroft Rd. BR6: Orp . . . 3J 173
SW16 . . . 6E 136
SW17 . . . 6E 136
Sth. Cross Rd. IG6: Ilf . . . 5G 53
Sth. Croxted Rd. SE21 . . . 3D 138
SOUTH CROYDON . . . 5D 168
South Croydon Sports Club . . . 5E 168
Southdean Gdns. SW19 . . . 2H 135
South Dene NW7 . . . 3E 28
Southdene Ct. N11 . . . 3A 32
Southdown N7 . . . 6J 65
Southdown Av. W7 . . . 3A 96
Southdown Cres. HA2: Harr . . . 1G 59
IG2: Ilf . . . 5J 53
Southdown Dr. SW20 . . . 7F 135
Southdown Rd. SM5: Cars . . . 7E 166
SW20 . . . 1F 153
South Dr. BR6: Orp . . . 5J 173
E12 . . . 3C 70
HA4: Ruis . . . 1G 57
Sth. Ealing Rd. W5 . . . 2D 96
Sth. Eastern Av. N9 . . . 3A 34
South Eastern University . . . 3K 65
Sth. Eaton Pl. SW1 . . . 3H 17 (4E 100)
Sth. Eden Pk. Rd. BR3: Beck . . . 6D 158
Sth. Edwardes Sq. W8 . . . 3H 99
SOUTHEND . . . 4F 141
South End CR0: Croy . . . 4C 168
W8 . . . 3K 99
South End Cl. NW3 . . . 4C 64
Southend Cl. SE9 . . . 6F 125
Southend Cres. SE9 . . . 6F 125
South End Grn. NW3 . . . 4C 64
Southend La. SE6 . . . 4B 140
SE26 . . . 4B 140
South End Rd. NW3 . . . 4C 64
Southend Rd. BR3: Beck . . . 1C 158
E4 . . . 5F 35
E6 . . . 7D 70
E17 . . . 1D 50
E18 . . . 1J 51
IG8: Wfd G . . . 2A 52
South End Row W8 . . . 3K 99
Southern Av. SE25 . . . 3F 157
TW14: Felt . . . 1J 129
Southerngate Way SE14 . . . 7A 104
Southern Gro. E3 . . . 3B 86
Southern Perimeter Rd.
TW6: H'row A . . . 5A 110
(Stanwell Moor Rd.)
TW6: H'row A . . . 5E 110
(Swindon Rd.)
TW19: Stanw . . . 6B 110
(not continuous)
Southern Rd. E13 . . . 2K 87
N2 . . . 4D 46
Southern Row W10 . . . 4G 81
Southern St. N1 . . . 2K 83
Southern Way RM7: Rom . . . 6G 55
SE10 . . . *4H 105*
(off School Bank Rd.)
Southernwood Retail Pk.
SE1 . . . 5F 103
Southerton Rd. W6 . . . 4E 98
Sth. Esk Rd. E7 . . . 6A 70
Southey Ho. *SE17* . . . *5C 102*
(off Browning St.)
Southey M. E16 . . . 1J 105
Southey Rd. N15 . . . 5E 48
SW9 . . . 1A 120
SW19 . . . 7J 135
Southey St. SE20 . . . 7K 139
Southfield EN5: Barn . . . 6A 20
Southfield Cl. UB8: Hil . . . 4C 74
Southfield Cotts. W7 . . . 2K 95
Southfield Ct. E11 . . . 3H 69
Southfield Gdns.
TW1: Twick . . . 4K 131
Southfield Pk. HA2: Harr . . . 4F 41
Southfield Rd. BR7: Chst . . . 3K 161
EN3: Pond E . . . 6C 24
N17 . . . 2E 48
W4 . . . 2K 97
SOUTHFIELDS . . . 1H 135
Southfields KT8: E Mos . . . 6J 149
NW4 . . . 3D 44
Southfields Av. TW15: Ashf . . . 6D 128
Southfields Ct. SM1: Sutt . . . 2J 165
Southfields M. SW18 . . . 6J 117
Southfields Pas. SW18 . . . 6J 117
Southfields Rd. SW18 . . . 6J 117
Southfleet NW5 . . . 6E 64
Southfleet Rd. BR6: Orp . . . 3J 173
South Gdns. HA9: Wemb . . . 2G 61
SW19 . . . 7B 136
SOUTHGATE . . . 1C 32
Southgate Av. TW13: Felt . . . 4F 129
Southgate Cir. N14 . . . 1C 32
Southgate Ct. *N1* . . . *7D 66*
(off Downham Rd.)
Southgate Gro. N1 . . . 7D 66
Southgate Ind. Est. N14 . . . 7C 22
Southgate Leisure Cen. . . . 7C 22
South Ga. Rd. E12 . . . 3B 70
Southgate Rd. N1 . . . 1D 84
Sth. Gipsy Rd. DA16: Well . . . 3D 126
Sth. Glade, The DA5: Bexl . . . 1F 145
South Grn. NW9 . . . 1A 44
South Gro. E17 . . . 5B 50
N6 . . . 1E 64
N15 . . . 5D 48
South Gro. Ho. N6 . . . 1E 64
SOUTH HACKNEY . . . 7K 67
SOUTH HAMPSTEAD . . . 7A 64
SOUTH HARROW . . . 3G 59
Sth. Harrow Ind. Est. HA2: Harr . . . 2G 59
South Hill BR7: Chst . . . 6D 142
HA6: Nwood . . . 1G 39
Sth. Hill Av. HA1: Harr . . . 3G 59
HA2: Harr . . . 3G 59
Sth. Hill Gro. HA1: Harr . . . 4J 59
Sth. Hill Pk. NW3 . . . 4C 64
Sth. Hill Pk. Gdns. NW3 . . . 3C 64
Sth. Hill Rd. BR2: Brom . . . 3G 159
Southholme Cl. SE19 . . . 1E 156
SOUTH HORNCHURCH . . . 2K 91
Southill Ct. BR2: Brom . . . 5H 159
Southill La. HA5: Eastc . . . 4J 39
Southill Rd. BR7: Chst . . . 7C 142
Southill St. E14 . . . 6D 86
Sth. Island Pl. SW9 . . . 7K 101
SOUTH KENSINGTON . . . 4B 100
Sth. Kensington Sta. Arc. *SW7* . . . *3B 16*
(off Pelham St.)
SOUTH LAMBETH . . . 7J 101
Sth. Lambeth Pl. SW8 . . . 7F 19 (6J 101)
Sth. Lambeth Rd. SW8 . . . 7F 19 (6J 101)
Southland Rd. SE18 . . . 7K 107
Southlands Av. BR6: Orp . . . 4H 173
Southlands Dr. SW19 . . . 2F 135
Southlands Gro. BR1: Brom . . . 3C 160
Southlands Rd. BR1: Brom . . . 5A 160
BR2: Brom . . . 5A 160
Southland Way TW3: Houn . . . 5H 113
South La. KT1: King T . . . 3D 150
(not continuous)
KT3: N Mald . . . 4K 151
South La. W. KT3: N Mald . . . 4K 151
South Lodge *E16* . . . *1K 105*
(off Audley Dr.)
NW8 . . . 1A 4 (2B 82)
SW7 . . . *7D 10*
(off Knightsbridge)
TW2: Whit . . . 6G 113
Sth. Lodge Av. CR4: Mitc . . . 4J 155
Sth. Lodge Cres. EN2: Enf . . . 4C 22
(not continuous)
Sth. Lodge Dr. N14 . . . 4C 22
Sth. London Crematorium
CR4: Mitc . . . 2G 155
South London Gallery . . . *1E 120*
(off Peckham Rd.)
South London Theatre . . . *3B 138*
(off Norwood High St.)
South Mall *N9* . . . *3B 34*
(off Plevna Rd.)
SW18 . . . 6K 117
South Mead KT19: Ewe . . . 7B 164
NW9 . . . 1B 44
Southmead Rd. SW19 . . . 1G 135
Sth. Molton La. W1 . . . 1J 11 (6F 83)
Sth. Molton Rd. E16 . . . 6J 87
Sth. Molton St. W1 . . . 1J 11 (6F 83)
Southmoor Way E9 . . . 6B 68
South Mt. *N20* . . . *2F 31*
(off High Rd.)
SOUTH NORWOOD . . . 4F 157
South Norwood Country Pk. . . . 4J 157
South Norwood Country Pk. Vis. Cen. . . . 4H 157
Sth. Norwood Hill SE25 . . . 1E 156
South Norwood Pools & Fitness Cen. . . . 5H 157
Sth. Oak Rd. SW16 . . . 4K 137
Southold Ri. SE9 . . . 3D 142
Southolm St. SW11 . . . 1F 119
Southover BR1: Brom . . . 5J 141
N12 . . . 3D 30
South Pde. HA8: Edg . . . 2G 43
SM6: Wall . . . 6G 167
SW3 . . . 5B 16 (5B 100)
W4 . . . 4K 97
South Pk. Ct. BR3: Beck . . . 7C 140
South Pk. Cres. IG1: Ilf . . . 3H 71
SE6 . . . 1G 141
South Pk. Dr. IG3: Ilf . . . 2J 71
IG11: Bark . . . 5J 71
South Pk. Gro. KT3: N Mald . . . 4J 151
South Pk. Hill Rd.
CR2: S Croy . . . 5D 168
South Pk. M. SW6 . . . 3K 117
South Pk. Rd. IG1: Ilf . . . 3H 71
SW19 . . . 6J 135
South Pk. Ter. IG1: Ilf . . . 3J 71
South Pk. Vs. IG3: Ilf . . . 4J 71
South Pk. Way HA4: Ruis . . . 6A 58
South Pl. EC2 . . . 5F 9 (5D 84)
EN3: Pond E . . . 5D 24
KT5: Surb . . . 7F 151
South Pl. M. EC2 . . . 6F 9 (5D 84)
Southport Rd. SE18 . . . 4H 107
Sth. Quay Plaza E14 . . . 2D 104
Southridge Pl. SW20 . . . 7F 135
South Ri. SM5: Cars . . . 7C 166
W2 . . . 2D 10
South Ri. Way SE18 . . . 5H 107
South Rd. HA1: Harr . . . 1A 60
HA8: Edg . . . 1H 43
N9 . . . 1B 34
RM6: Chad H . . . 5C 54
(Chadwell Heath La.)
RM6: Chad H . . . 6E 54
(West Rd.)
SE23 . . . 2K 139
SW19 . . . 6A 136
TW2: Twick . . . 3H 131
TW5: Hest . . . 6A 94
TW12: Hamp . . . 6C 130
TW13: Hanw . . . 5B 130
UB1: S'hall . . . 2D 94
UB7: W Dray . . . 3C 92
W5 . . . 4D 96
South Row SE3 . . . 2H 123
SOUTH RUISLIP . . . 4A 58
Southsea Rd. KT1: King T . . . 4E 150
Sth. Sea St. SE16 . . . 3B 104
South Side N15 . . . 4F 49
W6 . . . 3B 98
Southside N7 . . . 4H 65
Southside Comn. SW19 . . . 6E 134
Southside House . . . 6E 134
Southside Ind. Est. *SW8* . . . *1G 119*
(off Havelock Ter.)
Southside Shop. Cen. SW18 . . . 6K 117
Southspring DA15: Sidc . . . 7H 125

378 A-Z London

South Sq. NW11 6K **45**
WC1 6J **7** (5A **84**)
South St. BR1: Brom 2J **159**
EN3: Pond E 5D **24**
RM13: Rain 2J **91**
TW7: Isle 3A **114**
W1 4H **11** (1E **100**)
Sth. Tenter St. E1 2K **15** (7F **85**)
South Ter. KT6: Surb 6E **150**
SW7 3C **16** (4C **100**)
SOUTH TOTTENHAM 5F **49**
South Va. HA1: Harr 4J **59**
Southvale SE19 6E **138**
Southvale Rd. SE3 2G **123**
South Vw. BR1: Brom 2A **160**
SW19 6F **135**
Southview Av. NW10 5B **62**
South Vw. Cl. DA5: Bexl 6F **127**
Southview Cl. SW17 5E **136**
South Vw. Ct. SE19 7C **138**
Southview Cres. IG2: Ilf 6F **53**
South Vw. Dr. E18 3K **51**
Southview Gdns. SM6: Wall 7G **167**
Southview Pde. RM13: Rain 3K **91**
South Vw. Rd. HA5: Pinn 1K **39**
N8 3H **47**
Southview Rd. BR1: Brom 4F **141**
South Vs. NW1 6H **65**
Southville SW8 1H **119**
Southville Cl. KT19: Ewe 7K **163**
TW14: Bedf, Felt 1G **129**
TW14: Felt 1G **129**
Southville Cres. TW14: Felt 1G **129**
Southville Rd. KT7: T Ditt 7A **150**
TW14: Felt 1G **129**
South Wlk. BR4: W W'ck 3G **171**
UB3: Hayes 5F **75**
SOUTHWARK 6B **14** (1C **102**)
Southwark Bri. EC4 3D **14** (7C **84**)
Southwark Bri. Bus. Cen. *SE1 5D 14*
(off Southwark Bri. Rd.)
Southwark Bri. Office Village SE1 4D **14**
Southwark Bri. Rd. SE1 3B **102**
Southwark Cathedral 4E **14** (1D **102**)
Southwark Pk. Est. SE16 3H **103**
Southwark Pk. Rd. SE16 4F **103**
Southwark Pk. Sports Cen. Track 4J **103**
Southwark Pk. Sports Complex 4J **103**
Southwark Pl. BR1: Brom 3D **160**
Southwark Playhouse *5C 14*
(off Gt. Guildford St.)
Southwark St. SE1 4A **14** (1B **102**)
Southwater Cl. BR3: Beck 7D **140**
E14 6B **86**
South Way BR2: Hayes 7J **159**
CR0: Croy 3A **170**
HA2: Harr 4E **40**
HA9: Wemb 5G **61**
N9 2D **34**
N11 6B **32**
Southway N20 2D **30**
NW11 6K **45**
SM6: Wall 4G **167**
SW20 5E **152**
Southway Cl. *W12 2D 98*
(off Scott's Rd.)
Southways Pde. IG2: Ilf 5E **52**
Southwell Av. UB5: N'olt 6E **58**
Southwell Gdns. SW7 4A **100**
Southwell Gro. Rd. E11 2G **69**
Southwell Ho. *SE16 4H 103*
(off Anchor St.)
Southwell Rd. CR0: Croy 6A **156**
HA3: Kent 6D **42**
SE5 3C **120**
Sth. Western Rd. TW1: Twick 6A **114**
South W. India Dock Entrance E14 2E **104**
South W. Middlesex Crematorium
TW13: Felt 1C **130**
Southwest Rd. E11 1F **69**
Sth. Wharf Rd. W2 7A **4** (6B **82**)
Southwick M. W2 7B **4** (6B **82**)
Southwick Pl. W2 1C **10** (6C **82**)
Southwick St. W2 7C **4** (6C **82**)
Southwick Yd. W2 1C **10**
SOUTH WIMBLEDON 6K **135**
Southwold Dr. IG11: Bark 5A **72**
Southwold Mans. *W9 3J 81*
(off Widley Rd.)
Southwold Rd. DA5: Bexl 6H **127**
E5 2H **67**
Southwood Av. KT2: King T 1J **151**
N6 7F **47**
Southwood Cl. BR1: Brom 4D **160**
KT4: Wor Pk 1F **165**
Southwood Ct. *EC1 2A 8*
(off Wynyatt St.)
NW11 5K **45**
Southwood Dr. KT5: Surb 7J **151**
SOUTH WOODFORD 2J **51**
Sth. Woodford to Barking Relief Rd.
E11 5B **52**
E12 4E **70**
E18 3A **52**
IG1: Ilf 5B **52**
IG4: Ilf 5B **52**
Southwood Gdns. IG2: Ilf 4F **53**
KT10: Hin W 3A **162**
Southwood Hall N6 6F **47**
Southwood Hgts. N6 7F **47**
Southwood Ho. *W11 7G 81*
(off Avondale Pk. Rd.)
Southwood La. N6 1E **64**
Southwood Lawn Rd. N6 7E **46**
Southwood Mans. *N6 6E 46*
(off Southwood La.)
Southwood Pk. N6 7E **46**
Southwood Rd. SE9 2F **143**
SE28 1B **108**
Southwood Smith Ho. *E2 3H 85*
(off Florida St.)
Southwood Smith St. N1 1B **84**
Sth. Worple Av. SW14 3A **116**
Sth. Worple Way SW14 3K **115**
Southwyck Ho. SW9 4B **120**
Sovereign Bus. Cen. EN3: Brim 3G **25**
Sovereign Cl. E1 7H **85**
HA4: Ruis 1G **57**
W5 5C **78**
Sovereign Ct. *CR2: S Croy 5C 168*
(off Warham Rd.)
HA6: Nwood 1J **39**
KT8: W Mole 4D **148**
TW3: Houn 3E **112**
W8 3K 99
(off Wright's La.)
Sovereign Cres. SE16 7A **86**
Sovereign Gro. HA0: Wemb 3D **60**
Sovereign Ho. *E1 4H 85*
(off Cambridge Heath Rd.)
SE18 3D 106
(off Leda Rd.)
TW15: Ashf 4A **128**
Sovereign M. E2 2F **85**
EN4: Cockf 3J **21**
Sovereign Pk. NW10 4H **79**
Sovereign Pk. Trad. Est. NW10 4H **79**
Sovereign Pl. HA1: Harr 5K **41**
Sovereign Rd. IG11: Bark 3C **90**
Sowerby Cl. SE9 5C **124**
Spa at Beckenham, The 1B **158**
Space Waye TW14: Felt 5J **111**
Spa Cl. SE25 1E **156**
Spa Ct. SW16 4K **137**
Spafield St. EC1 3J **7** (4A **84**)
Spa Grn. Est. EC1 1K **7** (3B **84**)
Spa Hill SE19 1D **156**
Spalding Cl. HA8 7F **29**
Spalding Ho. SE4 4A **122**
Spalding Rd. NW4 7E **44**
SW17 5F **137**
Spanby Rd. E3 4C **86**
Spaniards Cl. NW11 1B **64**
Spaniards End NW3 1A **64**
Spaniards Rd. NW3 2A **64**
Spanish Pl. W1 7H **5** (6E **82**)
Spanish Rd. SW18 5A **118**
Spanswick Lodge N15 4B **48**
Sparkbridge Rd. HA1: Harr 4J **41**
Sparkes Cl. BR2: Brom 4K **159**
Sparkes Cotts. SW1 4G **17**
Sparke Ter. *E16 6H 87*
(off Clarkson Rd.)
Sparkford Gdns. N11 5K **31**
Sparks Cl. RM8: Dag 2D **72**
TW12: Hamp 6C **130**
W3 6K **79**
Spa Rd. SE16 3F **103**
Sparrick's Row SE1 6F **15** (2D **102**)
Sparrow Cl. TW12: Hamp 6C **130**
Sparrow Dr. BR5: Farnb 1G **173**
Sparrow Farm Dr. TW14: Felt 7A **112**
(not continuous)
Sparrow Farm Rd. KT17: Ewe 4C **164**
Sparrow Grn. RM10: Dag 3H **73**
Sparrow Ho. *E1 4J 85*
(off Cephas Av.)
Sparrow's Farm Leisure Cen. 7G **125**
Sparrows Herne WD23: Bush 1A **26**
Sparrows La. SE9 7G **125**
Sparrows Way WD23: Bush 1B **26**
Sparsholt Cl. *IG11: Bark 1J 89*
(off St John's Rd.)
Sparsholt Rd. IG11: Bark 1J **89**
N19 1K **65**
Spartan Cl. SM6: Wall 7J **167**
Sparta St. SE10 1E **122**
Speakers' Corner 2F **11** (7D **82**)
Speakers Ct. CR0: Croy 1D **168**
Speakman Ho. *SE4 3A 122*
(off Arica Rd.)
Spearman Ho. *E14 6C 86*
(off Up. North St.)
Spearman St. SE18 6E **106**
Spear M. SW5 4J **99**
Spearpoint Gdns. IG2: Ilf 5K **53**
Spears Rd. N19 1J **65**
Speart La. TW5: Hest 7C **94**
Spectacle Works E13 3A **88**
Spectrum Pl. *SE17 6D 102*
(off Lytham St.)
Spectrum Twr. *IG1: Ilf 2G 71*
(off Hainault St.)
Spedan Cl. NW3 3A **64**
Speechly M. E8 5F **67**
Speed Highwalk *EC2 5D 8*
(off Silk St.)
Speed Ho. EC2 5D **8**
Speedway Ind. Est. UB3: Hayes 2F **93**
Speedwell Ho. N12 4E **30**
Speedwell St. SE8 7C **104**
Speedy Pl. WC1 2E **6**
Speer Rd. KT7: T Ditt 6K **149**
Speirs Cl. KT3: N Mald 6B **152**
Speke Hill SE9 3D **142**
Speke Rd. CR7: Thor H 2D **156**
Speke's Monument 4A **10** (1B **100**)
Speldhurst Cl. BR2: Brom 5H **159**
Speldhurst Rd. E9 7K **67**
W4 3K **97**
Spellbrook Wlk. N1 1C **84**
Spelman Ho. *E1 6K 9*
(off Spelman St.)
Spelman St. E1 5K **9** (5G **85**)
(not continuous)
Spelthorne Gro. TW16: Sun 7H **129**
Spelthorne La. TW15: Ashf 1E **146**
Spence Cl. SE16 2B **104**
Spencer Av. N13 6E **32**
UB4: Hayes 5J **75**
Spencer Cl. BR6: Orp 2J **173**
IG8: Wfd G 5F **37**
N3 2J **45**
NW10 3F **79**
Spencer Ct. BR6: Farnb 5G **173**
NW8 2A 82
(off Marlborough Pl.)
SW20 1D **152**
Spencer Dr. N2 6A **46**
Spencer Gdns. SE9 5D **124**
SW14 5J **115**
Spencer Hill SW19 6G **135**
Spencer Hill Rd. SW19 7G **135**
Spencer House 5A **12**
Spencer Ho. NW4 5D **44**
Spencer Mans. *W14 6G 99*
(off Queen's Club Gdns.)
Spencer M. *SW8 1K 119*
(off Sth. Lambeth Rd.)
W6 6G **99**
SPENCER PARK 5B **118**
Spencer Pk. KT8: E Mos 5G **149**
SW18 5B **118**
Spencer Pl. CR0: Croy 7D **156**
N1 7B **66**
Spencer Ri. NW5 4F **65**
Spencer Rd. BR1: Brom 7H **141**
CR2: S Croy 5E **168**
CR4: Mitc 3E **154**
(Commonside E.)
CR4: Mitc 7E **154**
(Wood St.)
E6 1B **88**
E17 2E **50**
HA0: Wemb 2C **60**
HA3: W'stone 2J **41**
IG3: Ilf 1K **71**
KT8: E Mos 4G **149**
N8 5K **47**
(not continuous)
N11 4A **32**
N17 1G **49**
RM13: Rain 3K **91**
SW18 4B **118**
SW20 1D **152**
TW2: Twick 3J **131**
TW7: Isle 1G **113**
W3 1J **97**
W4 7J **97**
Spencer St. EC1 2A **8** (3B **84**)
UB2: S'hall 2B **94**
Spencer Wlk. *NW3 4A 64*
(off Perrin's Ct.)
NW3 4B **64**
(Hampstead High St.)
SW15 4F **117**
Spenlow Ho. *SE16 3G 103*
(off Jamaica Rd.)
Spenser Gro. N16 5E **66**
Spenser M. SE21 2D **138**
Spenser Rd. SE24 5B **120**
Spenser St. SW1 1B **18** (3G **101**)
Spens Ho. *WC1 4G 7*
(off Long Yd.)
Spensley Wlk. N16 3D **66**
Speranza St. SE18 5K **107**
Sperling Rd. N17 2E **48**
Spert St. E14 7A **86**
Speyside N14 6B **22**
Spey St. E14 5E **86**
Spey Way RM1: Rom 1K **55**
Spezia Rd. NW10 2C **80**
Sphere, The *E16 6H 87*
(off Hallsville Rd.)
Spice Ct. E1 7G **85**
Spice Quay Hgts. SE1 5K **15** (1F **103**)
Spicer Cl. KT12: Walt T 6A **148**
SW9 2B **120**
Spicer Ct. EN1: Enf 3K **23**
Spice's Yd. CR0: Croy 4C **168**
Spigurnell Rd. N17 1D **48**
Spikes Bri. Rd. UB1: S'hall 6C **76**
Spindle Cl. SE18 3C **106**
Spindlewood Gdns. CR0: Croy 4E **168**
Spindrift Av. E14 4C **104**
Spinel Cl. SE18 5K **107**
Spinnaker Cl. IG11: Bark 3B **90**
Spinnaker Ct. *KT1: Ham W 1D 150*
(off Becketts Pl.)
Spinnaker Ho. *E14 2C 104*
(off Byng St.)
Spinnells Rd. HA2: Harr 1D **58**

Spinney, The DA14: Sidc 5E **144**
  EN5: New Bar 2E **20**
  HA0: Wemb 3A **60**
  HA7: Stan 4K **27**
  N21 .7F **23**
  SM3: Cheam 4E **164**
  SW13 . . . . .7D **98**
  SW16 . . . . .3G **137**
  TW16: Sun 1J **147**
Spinney Cl. BR3: Beck 4D **158**
  KT3: N Mald 5A **152**
  KT4: Wor Pk 2B **164**
  UB7: Yiew 7A **74**
Spinney Dr. TW14: Bedf 7E **110**
Spinney Gdns. RM9: Dag 5E **72**
  SE19 . . . . .5F **139**
Spinney Oak BR1: Brom 2C **160**
Spinneys, The BR1: Brom 2D **160**
Spire Ct. BR3: Beck 2D **158**
          (off Crescent Rd.)
Spire Ho. W2 . . . . .7A **82**
          (off Lancaster Ga.)
Spires Shop. Cen., The
  EN5: Barn 3B **20**
Spirit Quay E1 . . . . .1G **103**
SPITALFIELDS 5J **9** (5F **85**)
Spital Sq. E1 . . . . .5H **9** (5E **84**)
Spital St. E1 . . . . .5K **9** (5G **85**)
Spital Yd. E1 . . . . .5H **9** (5E **84**)
Spitfire Bus. Pk. CR0: Wadd 6A **168**
Spitfire Est., The TW5: Cran 5A **94**
Spitfire Rd. SM6: Wall 7J **167**
  TW6: H'row A 6E **110**
Spitfire Way TW5: Cran 5A **94**
Splendour Wlk. SE16 . . . . .5J **103**
          (off Verney Rd.)
Spode Ho. SE11 . . . . .2J **19**
Spode Wlk. NW6 . . . . .5K **63**
Spondon Rd. N15 . . . . .4G **49**
Spoonbill Way UB4: Yead 5B **76**
Spooner Ho. TW5: Hest 6E **94**
Spooners M. W3 . . . . .1K **97**
Spooner Wlk. SM6: Wall 5J **167**
Sport Croydon 4C **156**
Sportsbank St. SE6 . . . . .7E **122**
Sportsman Pl. E2 . . . . .1G **85**
Spottons Gro. N17 . . . . .1C **48**
Spout Hill CR0: Addtn 5C **170**
Spratt Hall Rd. E11 . . . . .6J **51**
Spray La. TW2: Whit 6J **113**
Spray St. SE18 . . . . .4F **107**
Spreighton Rd. KT8: W Mole 4F **149**
Spriggs Ho. N1 . . . . .7B **66**
          (off Canonbury Rd.)
Sprimont Pl. SW3 . . . . .5E **16** (5D **100**)
Springall St. SE15 . . . . .7H **103**
Springalls Wharf SE16 . . . . .2G **103**
      (off Bermondsey Wall W.)
Spring Bank N21 . . . . .6E **22**
Springbank SE13 . . . . .6F **123**
Springbank Wlk. NW1 . . . . .7H **65**
Springbourne Ct. BR3: Beck 1E **158**
         (not continuous)
Spring Bri. M. W5 . . . . .7D **78**
Springbridge Rd. W5 . . . . .7D **78**
Spring Cl. EN5: Barn 5A **20**
  RM8: Dag 1D **72**
Springclose La.
  SM3: Cheam 6G **165**
Spring Cnr. TW13: Felt 3J **129**
Spring Cotts. KT6: Surb 5D **150**
Spring Ct. KT17: Ewe 7B **164**
  NW6 . . . . .6H **63**
  W7 . . . . .7H **77**
Spring Ct. Rd. EN2: Enf 1F **23**
Springcroft Av. N2 . . . . .4D **46**
Springdale M. N16 . . . . .4D **66**
Springdale Rd. N16 . . . . .4D **66**
Spring Dr. HA5: Eastc 6J **39**
Springett Ho. SW2 . . . . .5A **120**
        (off St Matthews Rd.)
Springfield E5 . . . . .1H **67**
  WD23: Bushy 1C **26**

Springfield Av. N10 . . . . .3G **47**
  SW20 . . . . .3H **153**
  TW12: Hamp 6F **131**
Springfield Cl. HA7: Stan 3F **27**
  N12 .5E **30**
Springfield Cl. IG1: Ilf 5F **71**
  KT1: King T 3E **150**
       (off Springfield Rd.)
  NW3 . . . . .7C **64**
         (off Eton Av.)
  SM6: Wall 5F **167**
Springfield Dr. IG2: Ilf 5G **53**
Springfield Gdns. BR1: Brom 4D **160**
  BR4: W W'ck 2D **170**
  E5 . . . . .1H **67**
  HA4: Ruis 1K **57**
  IG8: Wfd G 7F **37**
  NW9 . . . . .5K **43**
Springfield Gro. SE7 . . . . .6A **106**
  TW16: Sun 1H **147**
Springfield La. NW6 . . . . .1K **81**
Springfield Mt. NW9 . . . . .5A **44**
Springfield Pde. M. N13 . . . . .4F **33**
Springfield Pl. KT3: N Mald 4J **151**
Springfield Ri. SE26 . . . . .3H **139**
Springfield Rd. BR1: Brom 4D **160**
  CR7: Thor H 1C **156**
  DA7: Bex 4H **127**
  DA16: Well 3B **126**
  E4 . . . . .1B **36**
  E6 . . . . .7D **70**
  E15 .3G **87**
  E17 .6B **50**
  HA1: Harr 6J **41**
  KT1: King T 3E **150**
  N11 .5A **32**
  N15 .4G **49**
  NW8 . . . . .1A **82**
  SE26 . . . . .5H **139**
  SM6: Wall 5F **167**
  SW19 . . . . .5H **135**
  TW2: Whit 1E **130**
  TW11: Tedd 5A **132**
  TW15: Ashf 5B **128**
  UB4: Yead 1A **94**
  W7 . . . . .1J **95**
Springfields EN5: New Bar 5E **20**
         (off Somerset Rd.)
Springfield Wlk. BR6: Orp 1H **173**
      (off Place Farm Av.)
  NW6 . . . . .1K **81**
Spring Gdns. IG8: Wfd G 7F **37**
  KT8: W Mole 5F **149**
  N5 . . . . .5C **66**
  RM7: Rom 5J **55**
  SM6: Wall 5G **167**
  SW1 . . . . .4D **12** (1H **101**)
         (not continuous)
Spring Gdns. Bus. Pk. RM7: Rom . . .5J **55**
SPRING GROVE 1J **113**
Spring Gro. CR4: Mitc 1E **154**
  SE19 . . . . .7F **139**
  TW12: Hamp 1F **149**
  W4 . . . . .5G **97**
Spring Gro. Cres. TW3: Houn 1G **113**
Spring Gro. Rd. TW3: Houn, Isle 1F **113**
  TW7: Isle 1F **113**
  TW10: Rich 5F **115**
Spring Health Leisure Club
  Richmond 4D **114**
      (in Pools on the Pk.)
Spring Hill E5 . . . . .7G **49**
  SE26 . . . . .4J **139**
Springhill Cl. SE5 . . . . .3D **120**
Spring Ho. WC1 . . . . .2J **7**
Springhurst Cl. CR0: Croy 4B **170**
Spring Lake HA7: Stan 4G **27**
Spring La. E5 . . . . .7H **49**
  N10 .3E **46**
  SE25 . . . . .6H **157**
Spring M. KT17: Ewe 7B **164**
  W1 . . . . .5F **5** (5D **82**)
SPRING PARK 3C **170**

Spring Pk. Av. CR0: Croy 2K **169**
Spring Pk. Dr. N4 . . . . .1C **66**
Springpark Dr. BR3: Beck 3E **158**
Spring Pk. Rd. CR0: Croy 2K **169**
Spring Pas. SW15 . . . . .3F **117**
Spring Pl. N3 . . . . .3J **45**
  NW5 . . . . .5F **65**
Springpond Rd. RM9: Dag 5E **72**
Springrice Rd. SE13 . . . . .6F **123**
Spring Rd. TW13: Felt 3H **129**
Spring Shaw Rd. BR5: St P 7A **144**
Spring St. W2 . . . . .1A **10** (6B **82**)
Spring Ter. TW9: Rich 5E **114**
Spring Tide Cl. SE15 . . . . .1G **121**
Spring Va. DA7: Bex 4H **127**
Springvale Av. TW8: Bford 5D **96**
Spring Va. Ter. W14 . . . . .3F **99**
Spring Villa Pk. HA8: Edg 7B **28**
Spring Villa Rd. HA8: Edg 7B **28**
Spring Wlk. E1 . . . . .5G **85**
Springwater WC1 . . . . .5G **7**
Springwater Cl. SE18 . . . . .1E **124**
Springway HA1: Harr 7H **41**
Springwell Av. NW10 . . . . .1B **80**
Springwell Cl. SW16 . . . . .4K **137**
Springwell Rd. SW16 . . . . .4A **138**
  TW4: Houn 2B **112**
  TW5: Hest 2B **112**
Springwood Cl. E3 . . . . .2C **86**
Springwood Ct. CR2: S Croy 4E **168**
        (off Birdhurst Rd.)
Springwood Cres. HA8: Edg 2C **28**
Sproggit Ind. Est. TW19: Stanw 6B **110**
Sprowston M. E7 . . . . .6J **69**
Sprowston Rd. E7 . . . . .5J **69**
Spruce Ct. W5 . . . . .3E **96**
Sprucedale Gdns. CR0: Croy 4K **169**
Spruce Hills Rd. E17 . . . . .2E **50**
Spruce Ho. SE16 . . . . .2K **103**
      (off Woodland Cres.)
Spruce Pk. BR2: Brom 4H **159**
Sprules Rd. SE4 . . . . .2A **122**
Spurfield KT8: W Mole 3F **149**
Spurgeon Av. SE19 . . . . .1D **156**
Spurgeon Rd. SE19 . . . . .1D **156**
Spurgeon St. SE1 . . . . .3D **102**
Spurling Rd. RM9: Dag 6F **73**
  SE22 . . . . .4F **121**
Spurrell Av. DA5: Bexl 4K **145**
Spur Rd. BR6: Orp 2K **173**
  HA8: Edg 4K **27**
  N15 .4D **48**
  SE1 . . . . .6J **13** (2A **102**)
  SW1 . . . . .7A **12** (2G **101**)
  TW7: Isle 7A **96**
  TW14: Felt 4K **111**
Spurstowe Rd. E8 . . . . .6H **67**
Spurstowe Ter. E8 . . . . .5G **67**
Spurway Pde. IG2: Ilf 5D **52**
      (off Woodford Av.)
Square, The E10 . . . . .3E **68**
  IG1: Ilf 7E **52**
  IG8: Wfd G 5D **36**
  SM5: Cars 5E **166**
  TW9: Rich 5D **114**
  UB11: Stock P 1F **93**
  W6 . . . . .5E **98**
Square Rigger Row SW11 . . . . .3A **118**
Squarey St. SW17 . . . . .3A **136**
Squire Gdns. NW8 . . . . .2A **4**
      (off Grove End Rd.)
Squires, The RM7: Rom 6J **55**
Squire's Bri. Rd. TW17: Shep 4B **146**
Squires Cl. SW4 . . . . .1J **119**
  SW19 . . . . .4J **135**
Squires La. N3 . . . . .2K **45**
Squires Mt. NW3 . . . . .3B **64**
Squire's Rd. TW17: Shep 4B **146**
Squires Wlk. TW15: Ashf 7F **129**
       (not continuous)
Squires Way DA2: Dart 4K **145**
Squires Wood Dr. BR7: Chst 7C **142**

Squirrel Cl. TW4: Houn 3A **112**
Squirrel M. W13 . . . . .7K **77**
Squirrels, The HA5: Pinn 3D **40**
  SE13 . . . . .3F **123**
Squirrels Cl. BR6: Orp 1J **173**
  N12 .4F **31**
  UB10: Hil 7C **56**
Squirrels Ct. KT4: Wor Pk 2B **164**
        (off The Avenue)
Squirrels Drey BR2: Brom 2G **159**
        (off Park Hill Rd.)
Squirrels Grn. KT4: Wor Pk 2B **164**
Squirrel's La. IG9: Buck H 3G **37**
Squirrels Trad. Est., The
  UB3: Hayes 3H **93**
Squirries St. E2 . . . . .3G **85**
Stable Cl. KT2: King T 6F **133**
  UB5: N'olt 2E **76**
Stable Cl. SM6: Wall 3E **166**
Stable M. NW5 . . . . .6F **65**
  SE6 .1G **141**
Stables, The IG9: Buck H 1F **37**
Stables End BR6: Farnb 3G **173**
Stables Gallery & Arts Cen. 3C **62**
Stables Lodge E8 . . . . .7F **67**
         (off Mare St.)
Stables Mkt., The NW1 . . . . .7F **65**
Stables M. SE27 . . . . .5C **138**
Stables Way SE11 . . . . .5J **19** (5A **102**)
Stables Yd. SW18 . . . . .6J **117**
Stable Wlk. N1 . . . . .2J **83**
      (off Wharfdale Rd.)
  N2 . . . . .1B **46**
Stable Way W10 . . . . .6E **80**
Stable Yd. SW1 . . . . .6A **12**
  SW15 . . . . .3E **116**
Stableyard, The SW9 . . . . .2K **119**
Stableyard M. TW11: Tedd 6K **131**
Stable Yd. Rd. SW1 . . . . . . .6B **12** (2G **101**)
        (not continuous)
Stacey Av. N18 . . . . .4D **34**
Stacey Cl. E10 . . . . .5F **51**
Stacey St. N7 . . . . .3A **66**
  WC2 . . . . .1D **12** (6H **83**)
Stack Ho. SW1 . . . . .4F **17**
         (off Cundy St.)
Stackhouse St. SW3 . . . . .1E **16**
Stacy Path SE5 . . . . .7E **102**
Staddon Cl. BR3: Beck 4A **158**
Stadium Bus. Cen.
  HA9: Wemb 3H **61**
Stadium Retail Pk. HA9: Wemb 3G **61**
Stadium Rd. SE18 . . . . .7C **106**
Stadium Rd. E. NW4 . . . . .7D **44**
Stadium St. SW10 . . . . .7A **100**
Stadium Way HA9: Wemb 4F **61**
Staffa Rd. E10 . . . . .1A **68**
Stafford Cl. E17 . . . . .6B **50**
        (not continuous)
  N14 .5B **22**
  NW6 . . . . .3J **81**
  SM3: Cheam 6G **165**
Stafford Ct. SW8 . . . . .7J **101**
  W7 . . . . .6K **77**
         (off Copley Cl.)
  W8 . . . . .3J **99**
Stafford Cripps Ho. E2 . . . . .3J **85**
        (off Globe Rd.)
  SW6 . . . . .6H **99**
      (off Clem Attlee Ct.)
Stafford Cross CR0: Wadd 5K **167**
Stafford Gdns. CR0: Wadd 5K **167**
Stafford Ho. SE1 . . . . .5F **103**
        (off Cooper's Rd.)
Stafford Mans. SW1 . . . . .1H **17**
        (off Stafford Pl.)
  SW4 . . . . .4J **119**
  SW11 . . . . .7D **100**
      (off Albert Bri. Rd.)
  W14 . . . . .3F **99**
      (off Haarlem Rd.)
Stafford Pl. SW1 . . . . .1A **18** (3G **101**)
  TW10: Rich 7F **115**

Stafford Rd.—Stanwell

Stafford Rd. CR0: Wadd 4A **168**
DA14: Sidc 4J **143**
E3 2B **86**
E7 7A **70**
HA3: Hrw W 7B **26**
HA4: Ruis 4H **57**
KT3: N Mald 3J **151**
NW6 3J **81**
SM6: Wall 6G **167**
Staffordshire St. SE15 1G **121**
Stafford St. W1 4A **12** (1G **101**)
Stafford Ter. W8 3J **99**
Staff St. EC1 2F **9** (3D **84**)
Stag Cl. HA8: Edg 2H **43**
Stag Ct. *KT2: King T* *1G* ***151***
(off Coombe Rd.)
STAG LANE **2B 134**
Stag La. HA8: Edg 2H **43**
IG9: Buck H 2E **36**
NW9 2H **43**
SW15 3B **134**
Stags Way TW7: Isle 6K **95**
Stainbank Rd. CR4: Mitc 3F **155**
Stainby Cl. UB7: W Dray 3A **92**
Stainby Rd. N15 4F **49**
Stainer Ho. SE3 4A **124**
Stainer St. SE1 5F **15** (1D **102**)
Staines Av. SM3: Cheam 2F **165**
Staines By-Pass TW15: Ashf 5A **128**
Staines Rd. IG1: Ilf 5G **71**
TW2: Twick 3E **130**
TW3: Houn 7F **111**
TW4: Houn 7F **111**
TW14: Bedf, Felt 1C **128**
(not continuous)
Staines Rd. E. TW16: Sun 7J **129**
Staines Rd. W. TW15: Ashf 6D **128**
TW16: Sun 6D **128**
Staines Wlk. DA14: Sidc 6C **144**
Stainford Cl. TW15: Ashf 5F **129**
Stainforth Rd. E17 4C **50**
IG2: Ilf 7H **53**
Staining La. EC2 7D **8** (6C **84**)
Stainmore Cl. BR7: Chst 1H **161**
Stainsbury St. E2 2J **85**
Stainsby Rd. E14 6C **86**
Stainton Rd. EN3: Enf H 1D **24**
SE6 6F **123**
Stalbridge Flats *W1* *1H* ***11***
(off Lumley St.)
Stalbridge Ho. *NW1* *1A* ***6***
(off Harrington St.)
Stalbridge St. NW1 5D **4** (5C **82**)
Stalham St. SE16 3H **103**
Stalham Way IG6: Ilf 1F **53**
Stambourne Way BR4: W W'ck 2E **170**
SE19 7E **138**
Stambourne Woodland Wlk. SE19 7E **138**
Stamford Bridge **7K 99**
Stamford Brook Arches W6 4C **98**
Stamford Brook Av. W6 3B **98**
Stamford Brook Gdns. W6 3B **98**
Stamford Brook Mans. *W6* *4B* ***98***
(off Goldhawk Rd.)
Stamford Brook Rd. W6 3B **98**
Stamford Bldgs. *SW8* *7J* ***101***
(off Meadow Pl.)
Stamford Cl. HA3: Hrw W 7D **26**
N15 4G **49**
NW3 *3A* ***64***
(off Heath St.)
UB1: S'hall 7E **76**
Stamford Cotts. *SW10* *7K* ***99***
(off Billing St.)
Stamford Ct. W6 4C **98**
Stamford Dr. BR2: Brom 4H **159**
Stamford Gdns. RM9: Dag 7C **72**
Stamford Ga. SW6 7K **99**
Stamford Gro. E. N16 1G **67**
Stamford Gro. W. N16 1G **67**
STAMFORD HILL 1F **67**
Stamford Hill N16 2F **67**
Stamford Lodge N16 7F **49**
Stamford Rd. E6 1C **88**
N1 7E **66**
N15 5G **49**
RM9: Dag 1B **90**
Stamford St. SE1 5J **13** (1A **102**)
Stamp Pl. E2 1J **9** (2F **85**)
Stanard Cl. N16 7E **48**
Stanborough Cl. TW12: Hamp 6D **130**
Stanborough Pas. E8 6F **67**
Stanborough Rd. TW3: Houn 3H **113**
Stanbridge Pl. N21 2G **33**
Stanbridge Rd. SW15 3E **116**
Stanbrook Rd. SE2 2B **108**
Stanbury Ct. NW3 6D **64**
Stanbury Rd. SE15 2H **121**
(not continuous)
Stancroft NW9 5A **44**
Standale Gro. HA4: Ruis 5E **38**
Standard Ct. SE6 1D **140**
Standard Ind. Est. E16 2D **106**
Standard Pl. EC2 2H **9**
Standard Rd. DA6: Bex 4E **126**
DA17: Belv 5G **109**
NW10 4J **79**
TW4: Houn 3C **112**
Standen Rd. SW18 7H **117**
Standfield Gdns. RM10: Dag 6G **73**
Standfield Rd. RM10: Dag 5G **73**
Standish Ho. *SE3* *4K* ***123***
(off Elford Cl.)
W6 *4C* ***98***
(off St Peter's Gro.)
Standish Rd. W6 4C **98**
Standlake Point SE23 3K **139**
Stane Cl. SW19 7K **135**
Stane Gro. SW4 2J **119**
Stane Pas. SW16 5J **137**
Stanesgate Ho. *SE15* *7G* ***103***
(off Friary Est.)
Stane Way SE18 7B **106**
Stanfield Ho. *NW8* *3B* ***4***
(off Frampton St.)
UB5: N'olt *2B* ***76***
(off Academy Gdns.)
Stanfield Rd. E3 2A **86**
Stanford Cl. HA4: Ruis 6E **38**
IG8: Wfd G 5H **37**
RM7: Rom 6H **55**
TW12: Hamp 6D **130**
Stanford Ct. SW6 1K **117**
W8 *3K* ***99***
(off Kingsley M.)
Stanford Ho. IG11: Bark 2B **90**
Stanford Pl. SE17 4E **102**
Stanford Rd. N11 5J **31**
SW16 2H **155**
W8 3K **99**
Stanford St. SW1 4C **18** (4H **101**)
Stanford Way SW16 2H **155**
Stangate SE1 1H **19**
Stangate Gdns. HA7: Stan 4G **27**
Stangate Lodge N21 6E **22**
Stanger Rd. SE25 4G **157**
Stanhill Cotts. DA2: Dart 7K **145**
Stanhope Av. BR2: Hayes 1H **171**
HA3: Hrw W 1H **41**
N3 3H **45**
Stanhope Cl. SE16 2K **103**
Stanhope Gdns. IG1: Ilf 1D **70**
N4 6B **48**
N6 6F **47**
NW7 5G **29**
RM8: Dag 3F **73**
SW7 3A **16** (4A **100**)
Stanhope Ga. W1 5H **11** (1E **100**)
Stanhope Gro. BR3: Beck 5B **158**
Stanhope Ho. *N11* *4A* ***32***
(off Coppies Gro.)
SE8 *7B* ***104***
(off Adolphus St.)
Stanhope M. E. SW7 3A **16** (4A **100**)
Stanhope M. Sth. SW7 4A **100**
Stanhope M. W. SW7 4A **100**
Stanhope Pde. NW1 1A **6** (3G **83**)
Stanhope Pk. Rd. UB6: G'frd 4G **77**
Stanhope Pl. W2 1E **10** (7D **82**)
Stanhope Rd. CR0: Croy 3E **168**
DA7: Bex 2E **126**
DA15: Sidc 4A **144**
E17 5D **50**
EN5: Barn 6A **20**
N6 6G **47**
N12 5F **31**
RM8: Dag 2F **73**
SM5: Cars 7E **166**
UB6: G'frd 5G **77**
Stanhope Row W1 5J **11** (1F **101**)
Stanhope St. NW1 1A **6** (2G **83**)
Stanhope Ter. TW2: Twick 7K **113**
W2 2B **10** (7B **82**)
Stanier Cl. W14 5H **99**
Stanlake M. W12 1E **98**
Stanlake Rd. W12 1E **98**
Stanlake Vs. W12 1E **98**
Stanley Av. BR3: Beck 2E **158**
HA0: Wemb 7E **60**
IG11: Bark 2K **89**
KT3: N Mald 5C **152**
RM8: Dag 1F **73**
UB6: G'frd 1G **77**
Stanley Bri. Studios *SW6* *7K* ***99***
(off King's Rd.)
Stanley Cl. HA0: Wemb 7E **60**
SE9 1G **143**
SW8 6K **101**
Stanley Cohen Ho. *EC1* *4C* ***8***
(off Golden La. Est.)
Stanley Ct. SM2: Sutt 7K **165**
SM5: Cars 7E **166**
W5 5C **78**
Stanley Cres. W11 7H **81**
Stanleycroft Cl. TW7: Isle 1J **113**
Stanley Gdns. CR4: Mitc 6E **136**
NW2 5E **62**
SM6: Wall 6G **167**
W3 2A **98**
W11 7H **81**
Stanley Gdns. M. *W11* *7H* ***81***
(off Kensington Pk. Rd.)
Stanley Gdns. Rd. TW11: Tedd 5J **131**
Stanley Gro. CR0: Croy 6A **156**
SW8 2E **118**
Stanley Holloway Ct. *E16* *6J* ***87***
(off Coolfin Rd.)
Stanley Ho. *E14* *6C* ***86***
(off Saracen St.)
SW10 *7A* ***100***
(off Coleridge Gdns.)
Stanley Mans. *SW10* *7A* ***16***
(off Park Wlk.)
Stanley M. *SW10* *7A* ***100***
(off Coleridge Gdns.)
Stanley Pk. Dr. HA0: Wemb 1F **79**
Stanley Pk. Rd. SM5: Cars 7C **166**
SM6: Wall 6F **167**
Stanley Picker Gallery ***3E 150***
(off College Wlk.)
Stanley Rd. BR2: Brom 4K **159**
BR6: Orp 1K **173**
CR0: Croy 7A **156**
CR4: Mitc 7E **136**
DA14: Sidc 3A **144**
E4 1A **36**
E10 6D **50**
E12 5C **70**
E15 1F **87**
E18 1H **51**
EN1: Enf 3K **23**
HA2: Harr 2G **59**
HA6: Nwood 1J **39**
HA9: Wemb 6F **61**
IG1: Ilf 2H **71**
N2 3B **46**
N9 1A **34**
N10 7A **32**
N11 6C **32**
Stanley Rd. N15 4B **48**
NW9 7C **44**
SM2: Sutt 6K **165**
SM4: Mord 4J **153**
SM5: Cars 7E **166**
SW14 4H **115**
SW19 6J **135**
TW2: Twick 3H **131**
TW3: Houn 4G **113**
TW11: Tedd 4J **131**
TW15: Ashf 5A **128**
UB1: S'hall 7C **76**
W3 3J **97**
Stanley Sq. SM5: Cars 7D **166**
Stanley St. SE8 7B **104**
Stanley Studios *SW10* *7A* ***16***
(off Fulham Rd.)
Stanley Ter. DA6: Bex 4G **127**
N19 2J **65**
Stanliffe Ho. E14 3C **104**
Stanmer St. SW11 1C **118**
STANMORE 5G **27**
Stanmore Gdns. SM1: Sutt 3A **166**
TW9: Rich 3F **115**
Stanmore Hill HA7: Stan 3F **27**
Stanmore Lodge HA7: Stan 4G **27**
Stanmore Pl. NW1 1F **83**
Stanmore Rd. DA17: Belv 4J **109**
E11 1H **69**
N15 4B **48**
TW9: Rich 3F **115**
Stanmore St. N1 1K **83**
Stanmore Ter. BR3: Beck 2C **158**
Stannard Cotts. *E1* *4J* ***85***
(off Fox Cl.)
Stannard M. *E8* *6G* ***67***
(off Stannard Rd.)
Stannard Rd. E8 6G **67**
Stannary Pl. SE11 6K **19** (5A **102**)
Stannary St. SE11 7K **19** (6A **102**)
Stannet Way SM6: Wall 4G **167**
Stansbury Ho. *W10* *3G* ***81***
(off Beethoven St.)
Stansbury Sq. W10 3G **81**
Stansfeld Rd. E6 5B **88**
E16 5B **88**
Stansfield Ho. *SE1* *4F* ***103***
(off Balaclava Rd.)
Stansfield Rd. SW9 3K **119**
TW4: Cran 2K **111**
Stansgate Rd. RM10: Dag 2G **73**
Stanstead Cl. BR2: Brom 5H **159**
Stanstead Gro. SE6 1B **140**
Stanstead Mnr. SM1: Sutt 6J **165**
Stanstead Rd. E11 5K **51**
SE6 1A **140**
SE23 1K **139**
Stansted Cres. DA5: Bexl 1D **144**
Stansted Rd. TW6: H'row A 6B **110**
Stanswood Gdns. SE5 7E **102**
Stanthorpe Cl. SW16 5J **137**
Stanthorpe Rd. SW16 5J **137**
Stanton Av. TW11: Tedd 6J **131**
Stanton Cl. KT4: Wor Pk 1F **165**
KT19: Ewe 5H **163**
Stanton Ct. *CR2: S Croy* *5E* ***168***
(off Birdhurst Ri.)
Stanton Ho. *SE10* *6E* ***104***
(off Thames St.)
SE16 *2B* ***104***
(off Rotherhithe St.)
Stanton Rd. CR0: Croy 7C **156**
SE26 4B **140**
SW13 2B **116**
SW20 1F **153**
Stanton Sq. SE26 4B **140**
Stanton Way SE26 4B **140**
Stanway Ct. N1 2E **84**
(not continuous)
Stanway Gdns. HA8: Edg 5D **28**
W3 1G **97**
Stanway St. N1 2E **84**
STANWELL 6A **110**

Stanwell Cl.—Steele Wlk.

Stanwell Cl. TW19: Stanw 6A 110
Stanwell Rd. TW14: Bedf 7D 110
TW15: Ashf 2A 128
Stanwick Rd. W14 4H 99
Stanworth Ct. TW5: Hest 7D 94
Stanworth St. SE1 7J 15 (3F 103)
Stanyhurst SE23 1A 140
Stapenhill Rd. HA0: Wemb 3B 60
Staple Cl. DA5: Bexl 3K 145
Staplefield Cl. SW2 1J 137
Stapleford *N17 2E 48*
(off Willan Rd.)
Stapleford Av. IG2: Ilf 5J 53
Stapleford Cl. E4 3K 35
KT1: King T 2G 151
SW19 7G 117
Stapleford Rd. HA0: Wemb 7D 60
Stapleford Way IG11: Bark 3B 90
Staplehurst Rd. SE13 5F 123
SM5: Cars 7C 166
Staple Inn WC1 6J 7
Staple Inn Bldgs. WC1 6J 7 (5A 84)
Staples Cl. SE16 1A 104
STAPLES CORNER 1D 62
Staples Cnr. Bus. Pk. NW2 1D 62
Staples Ho. *E6 6E 88*
(off Savage Gdns.)
Staple St. SE1 7F 15 (2D 102)
Stapleton Gdns. CR0: Wadd 5A 168
Stapleton Hall Rd. N4 1K 65
Stapleton Ho. *E2 3H 85*
(off Ellsworth St.)
Stapleton Rd. BR6: Orp 4K 173
DA7: Bex 7F 109
SW17 3E 136
Stapleton Vs. *N16 4E 66*
(off Wordsworth Rd.)
Stapley Rd. DA17: Belv 5G 109
Stapylton Rd. EN5: Barn 3B 20
Star All. *EC3 2H 15*
(off Fenchurch St.)
Star & Garter Hill
TW10: Rich 1E 132
Starbeck Cl. SE9 7E 124
Starboard Way E14 3C 104
Star Bus. Cen. RM13: Rain 5K 91
Starch Ho. La. IG6: Ilf 2H 53
Star Cl. EN3: Pond E 6D 24
Starcross St. NW1 2B 6 (3G 83)
Starfield Rd. W12 2C 98
Star Hill DA1: Cray 5K 127
Star La. E16 4G 87
Starling Cl. CR0: Croy 6A 158
HA5: Pinn 3A 40
IG9: Buck H 1D 36
Starling Ho. *NW8 2C 82*
(off Barrow Hill Est.)
Starling Wlk. TW12: Hamp 5C 130
Starmans Cl. RM9: Dag 1E 90
Star Path *UB5: N'olt 2E 76*
(off Brabazon Rd.)
Star Pl. E1 3K 15 (7G 85)
Star Rd. TW7: Isle 2H 113
UB10: Hil 4E 74
W14 6H 99
Star St. W2 7B 4 (6C 82)
Starts Cl. BR6: Farnb 3E 172
Starts Hill Av. BR6: Farnb 4F 173
Starts Hill Rd. BR6: Farnb 3E 172
Starveall Cl. UB7: W Dray 3B 92
Star Yd. WC2 7J 7 (6A 84)
State Farm Av. BR6: Farnb 4F 173
Staten Gdns. TW1: Twick 1K 131
Statham Gro. N16 4D 66
N18 5K 33
Statham Ho. *SW8 1G 119*
(off Wadhurst Rd.)
Station App. *BR1: Brom 3J 159*
(off High St.)
BR2: Hayes 1J 171
BR3: Beck 1C 158
BR4: W W'ck 7E 158
BR6: Orp 2K 173
Station App. BR7: Chst 6C 142
(Elmstead La.)
BR7: Chst 1E 160
(Vale Rd.)
CR2: Sand 7D 168
DA5: Bexl 1G 145
DA7: Bex 2J 127
(Barnehurst Rd.)
DA7: Bex 2E 126
(Pickford La.)
DA16: Well 2A 126
E4 6A 36
E7 4K 69
E11 5J 51
E17 5C 50
(not continuous)
E18 2K 51
EN5: New Bar 4F 21
HA0: Wemb 6B 60
HA1: Harr 7J 41
HA4: Ruis 5K 57
(Mahlon Av.)
HA4: Ruis 1G 57
(Pembroke Rd.)
HA5: Pinn 3C 40
IG8: Wfd G 6E 36
IG9: Buck H 4G 37
KT1: King T 1G 151
KT4: Wor Pk 1C 164
KT17: Ewe 7B 164
KT19: Ewe 5C 164
N11 5A 32
N12 4E 30
NW1 4F 5 (4D 82)
NW10 3B 80
SE3 3K 123
SE9 2G 143
(Bercta Rd.)
SE9 1D 142
(Crossmead)
SE12 6J 123
(off Burnt Ash Hill)
SE26 4J 139
SM2: Cheam 7G 165
SM5: Cars 4D 166
SW6 3G 117
SW14 3J 115
SW16 6H 137
(Estreham Rd.)
SW16 5H 137
(Gleneagle Rd.)
SW20 2D 152
TW8: Bford 6C 96
(off Sidney Gdns.)
TW9: Kew 1G 115
TW12: Hamp 1E 148
TW15: Ashf 4B 128
TW16: Sun 1J 147
TW17: Shep 5E 146
UB3: Hayes 3H 93
UB6: G'frd 7G 59
UB7: Yiew 1A 92
W7 1J 95
Station App. Nth.
DA15: Sidc 2A 144
Station App. Rd. SE1 7H 13 (2A 102)
W4 7J 97
Station Arc. *W1 4K 5*
(off Gt. Portland St.)
Station Av.
KT3: N Mald 3A 152
KT19: Ewe 7A 164
SW9 3B 120
TW9: Kew 1G 115
Station Bldgs. *KT1: King T 2E 150*
(off Fife Rd.)
Station Chambers *E6 7C 70*
(off High St. Nth.)
Station Cl. N3 1J 45
N12 4E 30
TW12: Hamp 1F 149
Station Cotts.
BR6: Orp 2K 173
Station Cres. HA0: Wemb 6B 60
N15 4D 48
SE3 5J 105
TW15: Ashf 3A 128
Stationer's Hall Ct. EC4 1B 14 (6B 84)
Station Est. BR3: Beck 3K 157
E18 2K 51
Station Est. Rd. TW14: Felt 1K 129
Station Garage M. SW16 6H 137
Station Gdns. W4 7J 97
Station Gro. HA0: Wemb 6E 60
Station Hill BR2: Hayes 2J 171
Station Ho. M. N9 4B 34
Station Pde. *DA7: Bex 2E 126*
(off Pickford La.)
DA15: Sidc 2A 144
E6 7C 70
E11 5J 51
E13 1A 88
(off Green St.)
EN4: Cockf 4K 21
HA2: Harr 4F 59
HA3: Kent 2A 42
HA4: Ruis 2F 57
HA8: Edg 7K 27
IG9: Buck H 4G 37
IG11: Bark 7G 71
N14 1C 32
NW2 6E 62
RM9: Dag 6G 73
SM2: Sutt 6A 166
(off High St.)
SW12 1E 136
TW9: Kew 1G 115
TW14: Felt 1K 129
TW15: Ashf 4B 128
UB5: N'olt 7E 58
(Court Farm Rd.)
UB5: N'olt 4F 59
(Halsbury Rd. W.)
W3 6G 79
W4 7J 97
W5 1F 97
Station Pas. E18 2K 51
SE15 1J 121
Station Path *E8 6H 67*
(off Graham Rd.)
SW6 3H 117
Station Pl. N4 2A 66
Station Ri. SE27 2B 138
Station Rd. BR1: Brom 1J 159
BR2: Brom 2G 159
BR4: W W'ck 1E 170
BR6: Orp 2K 173
CR0: Croy 1C 168
DA7: Bex 3E 126
DA15: Sidc 2A 144
DA17: Belv 3G 109
E4 1A 36
E7 4J 69
E12 4C 70
E17 6A 50
EN5: New Bar 5E 20
HA1: Harr 4K 41
HA2: Harr 5F 41
HA8: Edg 6B 28
IG1: Ilf 3F 71
IG6: Ilf 3H 53
KT1: Ham W 1C 150
KT2: King T 1G 151
KT3: N Mald 5D 152
KT7: T Ditt 7K 149
KT9: Chess 5E 162
N3 1J 45
N11 5A 32
N17 3G 49
N19 3G 65
N21 1G 33
N22 2J 47
NW4 6C 44
NW7 6F 29
NW10 2B 80
RM6: Chad H, Dag 7D 54
Station Rd. SE13 3E 122
SE20 6J 139
SE25 4F 157
SM5: Cars 4D 166
SW13 2B 116
SW19 1A 154
TW1: Twick 1K 131
TW3: Houn 4F 113
TW11: Tedd 6A 132
TW12: Hamp 1E 148
TW15: Ashf 4B 128
TW16: Sun 7J 129
TW17: Shep 5E 146
UB3: Harl, Hayes 4G 93
UB7: W Dray 2A 92
W5 6F 79
W7 1J 95
Station Rd. Nth. DA17: Belv 3H 109
Station Sq. BR5: Pet W 5G 161
Station St. E15 7F 69
E16 1F 107
Station Ter. NW10 2F 81
SE5 1C 120
Station Ter. M. SE3 5J 105
Station Vw. UB6: G'frd 1H 77
Station Wlk. *IG1: Ilf 2F 71*
(in The Exchange)
Station Way IG9: Buck H 4F 37
SE15 2G 121
SM3: Cheam 6G 165
Station Yd. TW1: Twick 7A 114
Staton Ct. *E10 7D 50*
(off Kings Cl.)
Staunton Ho. *SE17 4E 102*
(off Tatum St.)
Staunton Rd. KT2: King T 6E 132
Staunton St. SE8 6B 104
Staveley *NW1 1A 6*
(off Varndell St.)
Staveley Cl. E9 5J 67
N7 4J 65
SE15 1H 121
Staveley Ct. E11 5J 51
Staveley Gdns. W4 1K 115
Staveley Rd. TW15: Ashf 6F 129
W4 6J 97
Staverton Rd. NW2 7E 62
Stave Yd. Rd. SE16 1A 104
Stavordale Lodge *W14 3H 99*
(off Melbury Rd.)
Stavordale Rd. N5 4B 66
SM5: Cars 7A 154
Stayner's Rd. E1 4K 85
Stayton Rd. SM1: Sutt 3J 165
Steadfast Rd. KT1: King T 1D 150
Steadman Ct. *EC1 3D 8*
(off Old St.)
Steadman Ho. *RM10: Dag 3G 73*
(off Uvedale Rd.)
Stead St. SE17 4D 102
Steam Farm La. TW14: Felt 4H 111
Stean St. E8 1F 85
Stebbing Ho. *W11 1F 99*
(off Queensdale Cres.)
Stebbing Way IG11: Bark 2A 90
Stebondale St. E14 4E 104
Stedham Pl. WC1 7E 6
Stedman Cl. DA5: Bexl 3K 145
UB10: Ick 3C 56
Steedman St. SE17 4C 102
Steeds Rd. N10 1D 46
Steele Ho. *E15 2G 87*
(off Eve Rd.)
Steele Rd. E11 4G 69
N17 3E 48
NW10 2J 79
TW7: Isle 4A 114
W4 3J 97
Steele's M. Nth. NW3 6D 64
Steele's M. Sth. NW3 6D 64
Steele's Rd. NW3 6D 64
Steele's Studios NW3 6D 64
Steele Wlk. DA8: Erith 7H 109

Steel's La. E1 . . . . . 6J 85
Steelyard Pas. EC4 . . . . . 3E 14
Steen Way SE22 . . . . . 5E 120
Steep Cl. BR6: Chels 6K 173
Steep Hill CR0: Croy 4E 168
SW16 . . . . . 3H 137
Steeple Cl. SW6 . . . . . 2G 117
SW19 . . . . . 5G 135
Steeple Ct. E1 . . . . . 4H 85
Steeplestone Cl. N18 . . . . . 5H 33
Steeple Wlk. *N1* *1C 84*
(off New Nth. Rd.)
Steerforth St. SW18 . . . . . 2A 136
Steering Cl. N9 . . . . . 1D 34
Steers Mead CR4: Mitc 1D 154
Steers Way SE16 . . . . . 2A 104
Stelfox Ho. *WC1* *1H 7*
(off Penton Ri.)
Stella Cl. UB8: Hil 5D 74
Stellar Ho. N17 . . . . . 6A 34
Stella Rd. SW17 . . . . . 6D 136
Stelling Rd. DA8: Erith 7K 109
Stellman Cl. E5 . . . . . 3G 67
Stembridge Rd. SE20 . . . . . 2H 157
Stephan Cl. E8 . . . . . 1G 85
Stephen Cl. BR6: Orp 3J 173
Stephendale Rd. SW6 . . . . . 3K 117
Stephen Fox Ho. *W4* *5A 98*
(off Chiswick La.)
Stephen M. W1 . . . . . 6C 6 (5H 83)
Stephen Pl. SW4 . . . . . 3G 119
Stephen Rd. DA7: Bex 3J 127
Stephens Ct. E16 . . . . . 4H 87
SE4 . . . . . 3A 122
Stephens Lodge *N12* *3F 31*
(off Woodside La.)
Stephenson Cl. DA16: Well 2A 126
Stephenson Ct. *SM2: Cheam* *7G 165*
(off Station App.)
Stephenson Ho. SE1 . . . . . 3C 102
Stephenson Rd. E17 . . . . . 5A 50
TW2: Whit 7E 112
W7 . . . . . 6K 77
Stephenson St. E16 . . . . . 4G 87
NW10 . . . . . 3A 80
Stephenson Way NW1 . . . . . 3B 6 (4G 83)
Stephen's Rd. E15 . . . . . 1G 87
Stephen St. W1 . . . . . 6C 6 (5H 83)
STEPNEY 5K 85
Stepney C'way. E1 . . . . . 6K 85
Stepney City Apartments E1 . . . . . 5J 85
Stepney Grn. E1 . . . . . 5J 85
Stepney Grn. Ct. *E1* *5K 85*
(off Stepney Grn.)
Stepney High St. F1 . . . . . 5K 85
Stepney Way E1 . . . . . 5H 85
Ster Century Cinema
Romford 6K 55
Sterling Av. HA8: Edg 4A 28
Sterling Cl. NW10 . . . . . 7C 62
Sterling Gdns. SE14 . . . . . 6A 104
Sterling Ho. SE3 . . . . . 4K 123
Sterling Ind. Est.
RM10: Dag 4H 73
Sterling Pl. W5 . . . . . 4E 96
Sterling Rd. EN2: Enf 1J 23
Sterling St. SW7 . . . . . 1D 16 (3C 100)
Sterling Way N18 . . . . . 4J 33
Stern Cl. IG11: Bark 2C 90
Sterndale Rd. W14 . . . . . 3F 99
Sterne St. W12 . . . . . 2F 99
Sternhall La. SE15 . . . . . 3G 121
Sternhold Av. SW2 . . . . . 2H 137
Sterry Cres. RM10: Dag 5G 73
Sterry Dr. KT7: T Ditt 6J 149
KT19: Ewe 4A 164
Sterry Gdns. RM10: Dag 6G 73
Sterry Rd. IG11: Bark 1K 89
RM10: Dag 4G 73
Sterry St. SE1 . . . . . 7E 14 (2D 102)
Steucers La. SE23 . . . . . 1A 140
Stevannie Ct. DA17: Belv 5F 109
Steve Biko La. SE6 . . . . . 4C 140
Steve Biko Lodge *E13* *2J 87*
(off London Rd.)
Steve Biko Rd. N7 . . . . . 3A 66
Steve Biko Way TW3: Houn 3E 112
Stevedale Rd. DA16: Well 2C 126
Stevedore St. E1 . . . . . 1H 103
Stevenage Rd. E6 . . . . . 6E 70
SW6 . . . . . 7F 99
Stevens Av. E9 . . . . . 6J 67
Stevens Cl. BR3: Beck 6C 140
DA5: Bexl 4K 145
HA5: Eastc 5A 40
TW12: Hamp 6D 130
Stevens Grn. WD23: Bushy 1B 26
Stevens La. KT10: Clay 7A 162
Stevenson Cl. EN5: New Bar 7G 21
Stevenson Cres. SE16 . . . . . 5G 103
Stevenson Ho. *NW8* *1A 82*
(off Boundary Rd.)
Stevens Rd. RM8: Dag 3B 72
Stevens St. SE1 . . . . . 7H 15 (3E 102)
Steventon Rd. W12 . . . . . 7B 80
Stewards Holte Wlk. N11 . . . . . 4A 32
Steward St. E1 . . . . . 5E 84
Stewart Av. TW17: Shep 4C 146
Stewart Cl. BR7: Chst 5F 143
NW9 . . . . . 6J 43
TW12: Hamp 6C 130
Stewart Ho. KT1: King T 3F 151
Stewart Quay UB3: Hayes 2G 93
Stewart Rainbird Ho. *E12* *5E 70*
(off Parkhurst Rd.)
Stewart Rd. E15 . . . . . 4F 69
Stewartsby Cl. N18 . . . . . 5H 33
Stewart's Gro. SW3 . . . . . 5B 16 (5B 100)
Stewart's Rd. SW8 . . . . . 7G 101
Stewart St. E14 . . . . . 2E 104
Stew La. EC4 . . . . . 2C 14 (7C 84)
Steyne Ho. *W3* *1J 97*
(off Narrow St.)
Steyne Rd. W3 . . . . . 1H 97
Steyning Gro. SE9 . . . . . 4D 142
Steynings Way N12 . . . . . 5D 30
Steyning Way TW4: Houn 4A 112
Steynton Av. DA5: Bexl 2D 144
Stickland Rd. DA17: Belv 4G 109
Stickleton Cl. UB6: G'frd 3F 77
Stifford Ho. *E1* *5J 85*
(off Stepney Way)
Stilecroft Gdns. HA0: Wemb 3B 60
Stile Hall Gdns. W4 . . . . . 5G 97
Stile Hall Pde. W4: Bford 5G 97
Stileman Ho. *E3* *5B 86*
(off Ackroyd Dr.)
Stile Path TW16: Sun 3J 147
Stiles Cl. BR2: Brom 6D 160
DA8: Erith 5H 109
Stillingfleet Rd. SW13 . . . . . 6C 98
Stillington St. SW1 . . . . . 3B 18 (4G 101)
Stillness Rd. SE23 . . . . . 6A 122
Stilwell Dr. UB8: Hil 4B 74
Stilwell Rdbt. UB8: Hil 7C 74
Stipularis Dr. UB4: Yead 4B 76
Stirling Av. HA5: Pinn 1B 58
SM6: Wall 7J 167
TW17: Shep 3G 147
Stirling Cl. DA14: Sidc 4J 143
SW16 . . . . . 1H 155
Stirling Ct. *EC1* *3A 8*
(off St John St.)
W13 . . . . . 7B 78
Stirling Gro. TW3: Houn 2G 113
Stirling Ho. SE18 . . . . . 5F 107
Stirling Rd. E13 . . . . . 2K 87
E17 . . . . . 3A 50
HA3: W'stone 3K 41
N17 . . . . . 1G 49
N22 . . . . . 1B 48
SW9 . . . . . 2J 119
TW2: Whit 7E 112
TW6: H'row A 6B 110
UB3: Hayes 7K 75
W3 . . . . . 3H 97
Stirling Rd. Path E17 . . . . . 3A 50
Stirling Wlk. KT5: Surb 6H 151
Stirling Way CR0: Bedd 7J 155
Stiven Cres. HA2: Harr 3D 58
Stockbeck *NW1* *1B 6*
(off Ampthill Est.)
Stockbury Rd. CR0: Croy 6J 157
Stockdale Rd. RM8: Dag 2F 73
Stockdove Way UB6: G'frd 3K 77
Stocker Gdns. RM9: Dag 7C 72
Stockfield Rd. SW16 . . . . . 3K 137
Stockford Av. NW7 . . . . . 7A 30
Stockholm Ho. *E1* *7G 85*
(off Swedenborg Gdns.)
Stockholm Rd. SE16 . . . . . 5J 103
Stockholm Way E1 . . . . . 1G 103
Stockhurst Cl. SW15 . . . . . 2E 116
Stockingswater La. EN3: Brim 2G 25
Stockland Rd. RM7: Rom 6K 55
Stockleigh Hall *NW8* *2C 82*
(off Prince Albert Rd.)
Stockley Cl. UB7: W Dray 2D 92
Stockley Country Pk. 7C 74
Stockley Farm Rd. UB7: W Dray 3D 92
STOCKLEY PARK 1D 92
Stockley Rd. UB7: W Dray 4D 92
UB8: Hil 6C 74
UB11: Stock P 6C 74
Stock Orchard Cres. N7 . . . . . 5K 65
Stock Orchard St. N7 . . . . . 5K 65
Stockport Rd. SW16 . . . . . 1H 155
Stocksfield Rd. E17 . . . . . 3E 50
Stocks Pl. E14 . . . . . 7B 86
UB10: Hil 1C 74
Stock St. E13 . . . . . 2J 87
Stockton Cl. EN5: New Bar 4F 21
Stockton Ct. *SW1* *2C 18*
(off Rochester Row)
Stockton Gdns. N17 . . . . . 7H 33
NW7 . . . . . 3F 29
Stockton Ho. *E2* *3H 85*
(off Ellsworth St.)
HA2: Harr 1E 58
Stockton Rd. N17 . . . . . 7H 33
N18 . . . . . 6B 34
STOCKWELL 2K 119
Stockwell Av. SW9 . . . . . 3K 119
Stockwell Cl. BR1: Brom 2K 159
HA8: Edg 2J 43
Stockwell Gdns. SW9 . . . . . 1K 119
Stockwell Gdns. Est. SW9 . . . . . 2J 119
Stockwell Grn. SW9 . . . . . 2K 119
Stockwell Grn. Ct. SW9 . . . . . 2K 119
Stockwell La. SW9 . . . . . 2K 119
Stockwell M. SW9 . . . . . 2K 119
Stockwell Pk. Cres. SW9 . . . . . 2K 119
Stockwell Pk. Est. SW9 . . . . . 2K 119
Stockwell Pk. Rd. SW9 . . . . . 1K 119
Stockwell Pk. Wlk. SW9 . . . . . 3A 120
Stockwell Rd. SW9 . . . . . 2K 119
Stockwell St. SE10 . . . . . 6E 104
Stockwell Ter. SW8 . . . . . 1K 119
Stodart Rd. SE20 . . . . . 1J 157
Stoddart Ho. SW8 . . . . . 7H 19 (6K 101)
Stofield Gdns. SE9 . . . . . 3B 142
Stoford Cl. SW19 . . . . . 7G 117
Stokenchurch St. SW6 . . . . . 1K 117
STOKE NEWINGTON 3F 67
Stoke Newington Chu. St. N16 . . . . . 3D 66
Stoke Newington Comn. N16 . . . . . 2F 67
Stoke Newington High St.
N16 . . . . . 3F 67
Stoke Newington Rd. N16 . . . . . 5F 67
Stoke Pl. NW10 . . . . . 3B 80
Stoke Rd. KT2: King T 7J 133
Stokesby Rd. KT9: Chess 6F 163
Stokes Cotts. IG6: Ilf 1G 53
Stokes Ct. N2 . . . . . 4C 46
Stokesley St. W12 . . . . . 6B 80
Stokes Rd. CR0: Croy 6K 157
E6 . . . . . 4C 88
Stokley Ct. N8 . . . . . 4J 47
Stoll Cl. NW2 . . . . . 3E 62
Stoms Path *SE6* *5C 140*
(off Maroons Way)
Stonard Rd. N13 . . . . . 3F 33
RM8: Dag 5B 72
Stondon Ho. *E15* *1H 87*
(off John St.)
Stondon Pk. SE23 . . . . . 6A 122
Stondon Wlk. E6 . . . . . 2B 88
Stonebanks KT12: Walt T 7J 147
STONEBRIDGE 1K 79
Stonebridge Cen. N15 . . . . . 5F 49
STONEBRIDGE PARK 7H 61
Stonebridge Pk. NW10 . . . . . 7K 61
Stonebridge Rd. N15 . . . . . 5F 49
Stonebridge Shop. Cen. NW10 . . . . . 1K 79
Stonebridge Way HA9: Wemb 6H 61
Stone Bldgs. WC2 . . . . . 6H 7
Stonechat Sq. E6 . . . . . 5C 88
Stone Cl. RM8: Dag 2F 73
SW4 . . . . . 2G 119
UB7: Yiew 1B 92
Stonecot Cl. SM3: Sutt 1G 165
Stonecot Hill SM3: Sutt 1G 165
Stone Cres. TW14: Felt 7H 111
Stonecroft Rd. DA8: Erith 7J 109
Stonecroft Way CR0: Croy 7J 155
Stonecrop Cl. NW9 . . . . . 3K 43
Stonecutter St. EC4 . . . . . 7A 8 (6B 84)
Stonefield N4 . . . . . 2K 65
Stonefield Cl. DA7: Bex 3G 127
HA4: Ruis 5C 58
Stonefield St. N1 . . . . . 1A 84
Stonefield Way HA4: Ruis 4C 58
SE7 . . . . . 7B 106
STONEGROVE 4A 28
Stonegrove HA8: Edg 4K 27
Stone Gro. Ct. HA8: Edg 5A 28
Stonegrove Gdns. HA8: Edg 5K 27
Stone Hall *W8* *3K 99*
(off Stone Hall Gdns.)
Stonehall Av. IG1: Ilf 6C 52
Stone Hall Gdns. W8 . . . . . 3K 99
Stone Hall Pl. W8 . . . . . 3K 99
Stone Hall Rd. N21 . . . . . 7E 22
Stoneham Rd. N11 . . . . . 5B 32
Stonehill Bus. Pk. N18 . . . . . 6F 35
Stonehill Cl. SW14 . . . . . 5K 115
Stonehill Ct. E4 . . . . . 7J 25
STONEHILL GREEN 7J 145
Stone Hill Rd. W4 . . . . . 5G 97
Stonehill Rd. SW14 . . . . . 5J 115
Stonehills Ct. SE21 . . . . . 3E 138
Stonehill Woods Pk. DA14: Sidc 6H 145
Stonehorse Rd. EN3: Pond E 5D 24
Stonehouse *NW1* *1G 83*
(off Plender St.)
Stone Ho. Ct. EC2 . . . . . 6H 9
Stonehouse Ho. *W2* *5J 81*
(off Brunel Est.)
Stone Lake Ind. Pk. SE7 . . . . . 4A 106
Stone Lake Retail Pk. SE7 . . . . . 4A 106
STONELEIGH 5C 164
Stoneleigh Av. EN1: Enf 1C 24
KT4: Wor Pk 4C 164
Stoneleigh B'way. KT17: Ewe 5C 164
Stoneleigh Ct. IG5: Ilf 3C 52
Stoneleigh Cres. KT19: Ewe 5B 164
Stoneleigh M. E3 . . . . . 2A 86
Stoneleigh Pk. Av. CR0: Croy 6K 157
Stoneleigh Pk. Rd. KT19: Ewe 6B 164
Stoneleigh Pl. W11 . . . . . 7F 81
Stoneleigh Rd. BR1: Brom 3F 161
IG5: Ilf 3C 52
N17 . . . . . 3F 49
SM5: Cars 7C 154
Stoneleigh St. W11 . . . . . 7F 81
Stoneleigh Ter. N19 . . . . . 2F 65
Stonell's Rd. SW11 . . . . . 6D 118
Stonemason Ct. *SE1* *7C 14*
(off Borough Rd.)
Stonemasons Cl. N15 . . . . . 4D 48
Stonenest St. N4 . . . . . 1K 65
Stone Pk. Av. BR3: Beck 4C 158

Stone Pl. KT4: Wor Pk 2C **164**
Stone Rd. BR2: Brom 5H **159**
Stones End St. SE1 . . . . . .7C **14** (2C **102**)
Stonewall E6 . . . . .5E **88**
Stonewold Ct. W5 . . . . .6D **78**
Stoney All. SE18 . . . . .2E **124**
Stoneyard La. E14 . . . . .7D **86**
Stoneycroft Cl. SE12 . . . . .7H **123**
Stoneycroft Rd. IG8: Wfd G 6H **37**
Stoneydeep TW11: Tedd 4A **132**
Stoneydown Av. E17 . . . . .4A **50**
Stoneydown Av. E17 . . . . .4A **50**
Stoneydown Ho. E17 . . . . .4A **50**
(off Blackhorse Rd.)
Stoneyfields Gdns. HA8: Edg 4D **28**
Stoneyfields La. HA8: Edg 5D **28**
Stoney La. E1 . . . . .7H **9** (6F **85**)
SE19 . . . . .6F **139**
Stoney St. SE1 . . . . .4E **14** (1D **102**)
Stonhouse St. SW4 . . . . .4H **119**
Stonor Rd. W14 . . . . .4H **99**
Stonycroft Cl. EN3: Enf H 2F **25**
Stoop Memorial Ground 7J **113**
Stopes St. SE15 . . . . .7F **103**
Stopford Rd. E13 . . . . .1J **87**
SE17 . . . . .5B **102**
Stopher Ho. SE1 . . . . .7B **14**
(off Webber St.)
Store Rd. E16 . . . . .2E **106**
Storers Quay E14 . . . . .4F **105**
Store St. E15 . . . . .5F **69**
WC1 . . . . .6C **6** (5H **83**)
Storey Ct. NW8 . . . . .2A **4**
Storey Ho. E14 . . . . .7D **86**
(off Cottage St.)
Storey Rd. E17 . . . . .4B **50**
N6 . . . . .6D **46**
Storey's Ga. SW1 . . . . . .7D **12** (2H **101**)
Storey St. E16 . . . . .1E **106**
Stories M. SE5 . . . . .2E **120**
Stories Rd. SE5 . . . . .3E **120**
Stork Rd. E7 . . . . .6H **69**
Storksmead Rd. HA8: Edg 7F **29**
Stork's Rd. SE16 . . . . .3G **103**
Stormont Lawn Tennis & Squash Club
. . . . .5D **46**
Stormont Rd. N6 . . . . .7D **46**
SW11 . . . . .3E **118**
Stormont Way KT9: Chess 5C **162**
Stormount Dr. UB3: Harl 2E **92**
Storrington WC1 . . . . .2F **7**
(off Regent Sq.)
Storrington Rd. CR0: Croy 1F **169**
Story St. N1 . . . . .7K **65**
Stothard Ho. E1 . . . . .4J **85**
(off Amiel St.)
Stothard St. E1 . . . . .4J **85**
Stott Cl. SW18 . . . . .6B **118**
Stoughton Av. SM3: Cheam 5F **165**
Stoughton Cl. SE11 . . . . .4H **19**
SW15 . . . . .1C **134**
Stour Av. UB2: S'hall 3E **94**
Stourcliffe Cl. W1 . . . . .1E **10** (6D **82**)
Stourcliffe St. W1 . . . . .1E **10** (6D **82**)
Stour Cl. BR2: Kes 4A **172**
Stourhead Cl. SW19 . . . . .7F **117**
Stourhead Gdns. SW20 . . . . .3C **152**
Stourhead Ho. SW1 . . . . .5C **18**
(off Tachbrook St.)
Stour Rd. E3 . . . . .7C **68**
RM10: Dag 2G **73**
Stourton Av. TW13: Hanw 4D **130**
Stowage SE8 . . . . .6C **104**
Stow Cres. E17 . . . . .7F **35**
Stowe Cres. HA4: Ruis 6D **38**
Stowe Gdns. N9 . . . . .1A **34**
Stowe Ho. NW11 . . . . .6A **46**
Stowell Ho. N8 . . . . .4J **47**
(off Pembroke Rd.)
Stowe Pl. N15 . . . . .3E **48**
Stowe Rd. W12 . . . . .2D **98**
Stowting Rd. BR6: Orp 4J **173**
Stox Mead HA3: Hrw W 1H **41**

Stracey Rd. E7 . . . . .4J **69**
NW10 . . . . .1K **79**
Strachan Pl. SW19 . . . . .6E **134**
Stradbroke Dr. IG7: Chig 6K **37**
Stradbroke Gro. IG5: Ilf 3C **52**
IG9: Buck H 1G **37**
Stradbroke Pk. IG7: Chig 6K **37**
Stradbroke Rd. N5 . . . . .4C **66**
Stradbrook Cl. HA2: Harr 3D **58**
Stradella Rd. SE24 . . . . .6C **120**
Strafford Av. IG5: Ilf 2E **52**
Strafford Ho. SE8 . . . . .5B **104**
(off Grove St.)
Strafford Rd. EN5: Barn 3B **20**
TW1: Twick 7A **114**
TW3: Houn 3D **112**
W3 . . . . .2J **97**
Strafford St. E14 . . . . .2C **104**
Strahan Rd. E3 . . . . .3A **86**
Straight, The UB1: S'hall 2B **94**
Straightsmouth SE10 . . . . .7E **104**
Strait Rd. E6 . . . . .7C **88**
Strakers Rd. SE15 . . . . .4H **121**
Strale Ho. N1 . . . . .1E **84**
(off Whitmore Est.)
Strand WC2 . . . . .3F **13** (7J **83**)
Strand Ct. SE18 . . . . .5J **107**
Strand Dr. TW9: Kew 7H **97**
Strandfield Cl. SE18 . . . . .5J **107**
Strand Ho. SE28 . . . . .1H **107**
Strand La. WC2 . . . . .2H **13** (7K **83**)
STRAND ON THE GREEN 6G **97**
Strand on the Grn. W4 . . . . .6G **97**
Strand Pl. N18 . . . . .4K **33**
Strand Theatre 2G **13**
(off Aldwych)
Strang Ho. N1 . . . . .1C **84**
Strang Print Room 3C **6**
Strangways Ter. W14 . . . . .3H **99**
Stranraer Way N1 . . . . .7J **65**
Strasburg Rd. SW11 . . . . .1E **118**
Strata Ct. KT12: Walt T 7H **147**
Stratfield Pk. Cl. N21 . . . . .7G **23**
STRATFORD 7F **69**
Stratford Av. UB10: Hil 2B **74**
Stratford Cen., The E15 . . . . .7F **69**
Stratford Circus (Performing Arts Cen.)
. . . . .6F **69**
Stratford Cl. IG11: Bark 7A **72**
RM10: Dag 7J **73**
Stratford Ct. KT3: N Mald 4K **151**
Stratford Gro. SW15 . . . . .4F **117**
Stratford Ho. Av. BR1: Brom 3C **160**
STRATFORD MARSH 7D **68**
STRATFORD NEW TOWN 5E **68**
Stratford Office Village, The
E15 . . . . .7G **69**
(off Romford Rd.)
Stratford Picture House 6F **69**
Stratford Pl. W1 . . . . .1J **11** (6F **83**)
Stratford Rd. CR7: Thor H 4A **156**
E13 . . . . .1H **87**
(not continuous)
NW4 . . . . .4F **45**
TW6: H'row A 6D **110**
UB2: S'hall 4C **94**
UB4: Yead 4K **75**
W8 . . . . .3J **99**
Stratford Shop. Cen. E15 . . . . .7F **69**
(off The Stratford Cen.)
Stratford Studios W8 . . . . .3J **99**
Stratford Vs. NW1 . . . . .7G **65**
Stratham Ct. N19 . . . . .3J **65**
(off Alexander Rd.)
Strathan Cl. SW18 . . . . .6G **117**
Strathaven Rd. SE12 . . . . .6K **123**
Strathblaine Rd. SW11 . . . . .5B **118**
Strathbrook Rd. SW16 . . . . .7K **137**
Strathcona Rd. HA9: Wemb 2D **60**
Strathdale SW16 . . . . .5K **137**
Strathdon Dr. SW17 . . . . .3B **136**
Strathearn Av. TW2: Whit 1F **131**
UB3: Harl 7H **93**

Strathearn Ho. W2 . . . . .2C **10**
(off Strearn Pl.)
Strathearn Pl. W2 . . . . . . .1C **10** (6C **82**)
Strathearn Rd. SM1: Sutt 5J **165**
SW19 . . . . .5J **135**
Stratheden Pde. SE3 . . . . .7J **105**
Stratheden Rd. SE3 . . . . .1J **123**
Strathfield Gdns. IG11: Bark 6H **71**
Strathleven Rd. SW2 . . . . .5J **119**
Strathmore Ct. NW8 . . . . .1C **4**
(off Park Rd.)
Strathmore Gdns. HA8: Edg 2H **43**
N3 . . . . .1K **45**
W8 . . . . .1J **99**
Strathmore Rd. CR0: Croy 7D **156**
SW19 . . . . .3J **135**
TW11: Tedd 4J **131**
Strathnairn St. SE1 . . . . .4G **103**
Strathray Gdns. NW3 . . . . .6C **64**
Strath Ter. SW11 . . . . .4C **118**
Strathville Rd. SW18 . . . . .2J **135**
(not continuous)
Strathyre Av. SW16 . . . . .3A **156**
Stratton Cl. DA7: Bex 3E **126**
HA8: Edg 6A **28**
SW19 . . . . .2J **153**
TW3: Houn 1E **112**
Stratton Ct. HA5: H End 1D **40**
(off Devonshire Rd.)
N1 . . . . .7E **66**
(off Hertford Rd.)
Strattondale St. E14 . . . . .3E **104**
Stratton Dr. IG11: Bark 5J **71**
Stratton Gdns. UB1: S'hall 6D **76**
Stratton Ho. HA8: Edg 4A **28**
(off Lacey Dr.)
Stratton Rd. DA7: Bex 3E **126**
SW19 . . . . .2J **153**
TW16: Sun 2H **147**
Stratton St. W1 . . . . .4K **11** (1F **101**)
Strauss Rd. W4 . . . . .2K **97**
STRAWBERRY HILL 3K **131**
Strawberry Hill TW1: Twick 3K **131**
Strawberry Hill Cl. TW1: Twick 3K **131**
Strawberry Hill House 3K **131**
(off Strawberry Va.)
Strawberry Hill Rd. TW1: Twick 3K **131**
Strawberry La. SM5: Cars 3E **166**
Strawberry Ter. N10 . . . . .1D **46**
Strawberry Va. N2 . . . . .1B **46**
TW1: Twick 3A **132**
(not continuous)
Streakes Fld. Rd. NW2 . . . . .2C **62**
Streamdale SE2 . . . . .6B **108**
Stream La. HA8: Edg 5C **28**
Streamline Ct. SE22 . . . . .1G **139**
(off Streamline M.)
Streamline M. SE22 . . . . .1G **139**
Streamside Cl. BR2: Brom 4J **159**
N9 . . . . .1A **34**
Stream Way DA17: Belv 6F **109**
Streatfeild Av. E6 . . . . .1D **88**
Streatfield Rd. HA3: Kent 3C **42**
STREATHAM 5J **137**
Streatham Cl. SW16 . . . . .2J **137**
STREATHAM COMMON 6J **137**
Streatham Comn. Nth. SW16 . . . . . .5J **137**
Streatham Comn. Sth. SW16 . . . . . .6J **137**
Streatham Ct. SW16 . . . . .3J **137**
Streatham High Rd. SW16 . . . . .4J **137**
STREATHAM HILL 2J **137**
Streatham Hill SW2 . . . . .2J **137**
Streatham Ice Arena 5H **137**
Streatham Leisure Cen. 5J **137**
STREATHAM PARK 5G **137**
Streatham Pl. SW2 . . . . .7J **119**
Streatham Rd. CR4: Mitc 1E **154**
SW16 . . . . .1E **154**
Streatham St. WC1 . . . . . . .7E **6** (6J **83**)
STREATHAM VALE 7G **137**
Streatham Va. SW16 . . . . .1G **155**
Streathbourne Rd. SW17 . . . . .2E **136**
Streatley Pl. NW3 . . . . .4A **64**

Streatley Rd. NW6 . . . . .7H **63**
Streeters La. SM6: Bedd 3H **167**
Streetfield M. SE3 . . . . .3J **123**
Streimer Rd. E15 . . . . .2E **86**
Strelley Way W3 . . . . .7A **80**
Stretton Mans. SE8 . . . . .5C **104**
Stretton Rd. CR0: Croy 7E **156**
TW10: Ham 2C **132**
Strickland Ct. SE15 . . . . .3G **121**
Strickland Ho. E2 . . . . .2K **9**
(off Chambord St.)
Strickland Row SW18 . . . . .7B **118**
Strickland St. SE8 . . . . .2C **122**
Strickland Way BR6: Orp 4K **173**
Stride Rd. E13 . . . . .2H **87**
Strimon Cl. N9 . . . . .2D **34**
Stringer Ho. N1 . . . . .1E **84**
(off Whitmore Est.)
Strode Cl. N10 . . . . .7K **31**
Strode Rd. E7 . . . . .4J **69**
N17 . . . . .2E **48**
NW10 . . . . .6C **62**
SW6 . . . . .7G **99**
Strome Ho. NW6 . . . . .2K **81**
(off Carlton Va.)
Strone Rd. E7 . . . . .6A **70**
E12 . . . . .6A **70**
Strone Way UB4: Yead 4C **76**
Strongbow Cres. SE9 . . . . .5D **124**
Strongbow Rd. SE9 . . . . .5D **124**
Strongbridge Cl. HA2: Harr 1E **58**
Stronsa Rd. W12 . . . . .2B **98**
Strood Av. RM7: Rush G 1K **73**
Strood Ho. SE1 . . . . .7F **15**
(off Staple St.)
Stroud Cres. SW15 . . . . .3C **134**
Stroud Cl. KT4: Wor Pk 7A **152**
Stroud Fld. UB5: N'olt 6C **58**
Stroud Ga. HA2: Harr 4F **59**
STROUD GREEN 7K **47**
Stroud Grn. Gdns. CR0: Croy 7J **157**
Stroud Grn. Rd. N4 . . . . .1K **65**
Stroud Grn. Way CR0: Croy 7H **157**
Stroudley Ho. SW8 . . . . .1G **119**
Stroudley Wlk. E3 . . . . .3D **86**
Stroud Rd. SE25 . . . . .6G **157**
SW19 . . . . .3J **135**
Stroud's Cl. RM6: Chad H 5B **54**
Stroud Way TW15: Ashf 6D **128**
Strouts Pl. E2 . . . . .1J **9** (3F **85**)
Strudwick Ct. SW4 . . . . .1J **119**
(off Binfield Rd.)
Strutton Ct. SW1 . . . . .2C **18**
(off Strutton Ground)
Strutton Ground SW1 . . . . .1C **18** (3H **101**)
Strype St. E1 . . . . .6J **9** (5F **85**)
Stuart Av. BR2: Hayes 1J **171**
HA2: Harr 3D **58**
KT12: Walt T 7K **147**
NW9 . . . . .7C **44**
W5 . . . . .2F **97**
Stuart Cl. UB10: Hil 6C **56**
Stuart Cl. CR0: Croy 3B **168**
(off St John's Rd.)
N22 . . . . .1K **47**
UB3: Hayes 6E **74**
Stuart Evans Cl. DA16: Well 3C **126**
Stuart Gro. TW11: Tedd 5J **131**
Stuart Ho. E16 . . . . .1K **105**
(off Beaulieu Av.)
W14 . . . . .4G **99**
(off Windsor Way)
Stuart Mantle Way DA8: Erith 7K **109**
Stuart Mill Ho. N1 . . . . .1G **7**
(off Killick St.)
Stuart Pl. CR4: Mitc 1D **154**
Stuart Rd. CR7: Thor H 4C **156**
DA16: Well 1B **126**
EN4: E Barn 7H **21**
HA3: W'stone 3K **41**
IG11: Bark 7K **71**
NW6 . . . . .3J **81**

Stuart Rd. SE15 . . . . .4J 121
SW19 . . . . .3J 135
TW10: Ham 2B 132
W3 .1J 97
Stuart Twr. W9 . . . . .3A 82
(off Maida Va.)
Stubbs Cl. NW9 . . . . .5J 43
Stubbs Ct. W4 . . . . .5H 97
(off Chaseley Dr.)
Stubbs Dr. SE16 . . . . .5H 103
Stubbs Ho. E2 . . . . .3K 85
(off Bonner St.)
SW1 . . . . .4D 18
(off Erasmus St.)
Stubbs M. RM8: Dag 4B 72
(off Marlborough Rd.)
Stubbs Point E13 . . . . .4J 87
Stubbs Way SW19 . . . . .1B 154
Stucley Pl. NW1 . . . . .7F 65
Stucley Rd. TW5: Hest 7G 95
Studdridge St. SW6 . . . . .2J 117
(not continuous)
Studd St. N1 . . . . .1B 84
Studholme Ct. NW3 . . . . .4J 63
Studholme St. SE15 . . . . .7H 103
Studio Arts & Media Cen., The 1A 158
Studio Cl. N15 . . . . .4E 48
Studio La. W5 . . . . .1D 96
Studio M. NW4 . . . . .4E 44
Studio Pl. SW1 . . . . .7F 11
Studios, The W8 . . . . .1J 99
(off Edge St.)
Studios Rd. TW17: Shep 3B 146
Studio Theatre 4E 166
Studland SE17 . . . . .5D 102
(off Portland St.)
Studland Cl. DA15: Sidc 3K 143
Studland Ho. E14 . . . . .6A 86
(off Aston St.)
Studland Rd. KT2: King T 6E 132
SE26 . . . . .5K 139
W7 . . . . .6H 77
Studland St. W6 . . . . .4D 98
Studley Av. E4 . . . . .7A 36
Studley Cl. E5 . . . . .5A 68
Studley Ct. DA14: Sidc 5B 144
E14 . . . . .7F 87
(off Jamestown Way)
Studley Dr. IG4: Ilf 6B 52
Studley Est. SW4 . . . . .1J 119
Studley Grange Rd. W7 . . . . .2J 95
Studley Rd. E7 . . . . .6K 69
RM9: Dag 7D 72
SW4 . . . . .1J 119
Stukeley Rd. E7 . . . . .7K 69
Stukeley St. WC2 . . . . .7F 7 (6J 83)
Stumps Hill La. BR3: Beck 6C 140
Stunell Ho. SE14 . . . . .6K 103
(off John Williams Cl.)
Sturdee Ho. E2 . . . . .2G 85
(off Horatio St.)
Sturdy Ho. E3 . . . . .2A 86
(off Gernon Rd.)
Sturdy Rd. SE15 . . . . .2H 121
Sturge Av. E17 . . . . .2D 50
Sturgeon Rd. SE17 . . . . .5C 102
Sturges Fld. BR7: Chst 6H 143
Sturgess Av. NW4 . . . . .7D 44
Sturge St. SE1 . . . . .6C 14 (2C 102)
Sturmer Way N7 . . . . .5K 65
Sturminster Cl. UB4: Yead 6A 76
Sturminster Ho. SW8 . . . . .7K 101
(off Dorset Rd.)
Sturrock Cl. N15 . . . . .4D 48
Sturry St. E14 . . . . .6D 86
Sturt St. N1 . . . . .1D 8 (2C 84)
Stutfield St. E1 . . . . .6G 85
Styles Gdns. SW9 . . . . .3B 120
Styles Ho. SE1 . . . . .6A 14
Styles Way BR3: Beck 4E 158
Stylus Ho. E1 . . . . .6J 85
Sudbourne Rd. SW2 . . . . .5J 119
Sudbrooke Rd. SW12 . . . . .6D 118

Sudbrook Gdns. TW10: Ham 3D 132
Sudbrook La. TW10: Ham 1E 132
SUDBURY 5B 60
Sudbury E6 . . . . .5E 88
Sudbury Av. HA0: Wemb 3C 60
Sudbury Cl. RM6: Chad H 5B 54
Sudbury Ct. SW8 . . . . .1H 119
(off Allen Edwards Dr.)
Sudbury Ct. Dr. HA1: Harr 3K 59
Sudbury Ct. Rd. HA1: Harr 3K 59
Sudbury Cres. BR1: Brom 6J 141
HA0: Wemb 5B 60
Sudbury Cft. HA0: Wemb 4K 59
Sudbury Gdns. CR0: Croy 4E 168
Sudbury Hgts. Av.
UB6: G'frd 5K 59
Sudbury Hill HA1: Harr 2J 59
Sudbury Hill Cl. HA0: Wemb 4K 59
Sudbury Ho. SW18 . . . . .5K 117
Sudbury Rd. IG11: Bark 5K 71
Sudeley St. N1 . . . . .2B 84
Sudlow Rd. SW18 . . . . .5J 117
Sudrey St. SE1 . . . . .7C 14 (2C 102)
Suez Av. UB6: G'frd 2K 77
Suez Rd. EN3: Brim 4F 25
SUFFIELD HATCH 4K 35
Suffield Ho. SE17 . . . . .58 102
(off Berryfield Rd.)
Suffield Rd. E4 . . . . .3J 35
N15 . . . . .5F 49
SE20 . . . . .2J 157
Suffolk Cl. E10 . . . . .7C 50
IG3: Ilf 6J 53
RM6: Chad H 6C 54
Suffolk Ho. CR0: Croy 2D 168
(off George St.)
SE20 . . . . .1K 157
(off Croydon Rd.)
Suffolk La. EC4 . . . . .2E 14 (7D 84)
Suffolk Pk. Rd. E17 . . . . .4A 50
Suffolk Pl. SW1 . . . . .4D 12 (1H 101)
Suffolk Rd. DA14: Sidc 6C 144
E13 . . . . .3K 87
EN3: Pond E 5C 24
HA2: Harr 6D 40
IG3: Ilf 6J 53
IG11: Bark 7H 71
KT4: Wor Pk 2B 164
N15 . . . . .5D 48
NW10 . . . . .7A 62
RM10: Dag 5J 73
SE25 . . . . .4F 157
SW13 . . . . .7B 98
Suffolk St. E7 . . . . .4J 69
SW1 . . . . .3D 12 (7H 83)
Sugar Bakers Ct. EC3 . . . . .1H 15
Sugar Ho. La. E15 . . . . .2E 86
Sugar Loaf Wlk. E2 . . . . .3J 85
Sugar Quay EC3 . . . . .3H 15
Sugar Quay Wlk. EC3 . . . . . .3H 15 (7E 84)
Sugden Rd. KT7: T Ditt 1B 162
SW11 . . . . .3E 118
Sugden St. SE5 . . . . .6D 102
Sugden Way IG11: Bark 2K 89
Sulby Ho. SE4 . . . . .4A 122
(off Turnham Rd.)
Sulgrave Gdns. W6 . . . . .2E 98
Sulgrave Rd. W6 . . . . .3E 98
Sulina Rd. SW2 . . . . .7J 119
Sulivan Ct. SW6 . . . . .2J 117
Sulivan Ent. Cen. SW6 . . . . .3K 117
Sulivan Rd. SW6 . . . . .3J 117
Sulkin Ho. E2 . . . . .3K 85
(off Knottisford St.)
Sullivan Av. E16 . . . . .5B 88
Sullivan Cl. KT8: W Mole 3F 149
SW11 . . . . .3C 118
UB4: Yead 5A 76
Sullivan Ct. N16 . . . . .7F 49
SW5 . . . . .4J 99
(off Earls Ct. Rd.)
Sullivan Cres.
UB9: Hare 2A 38

Sullivan Ho. SE11 . . . . .4H 19
(off Vauxhall St.)
SW1 . . . . .7K 17
(off Churchill Gdns.)
Sullivan Rd. SE11 . . . . . . .3K 19 (4A 102)
Sullivans Reach KT12: Walt T 7H 147
Sultan Rd. E11 . . . . .4K 51
Sultan St. BR3: Beck 2K 157
SE5 . . . . .7C 102
Sultan Ter. N22 . . . . .2A 48
Sumatra Rd. NW6 . . . . .5J 63
Sumburgh Rd. SW12 . . . . .6E 118
Summer Av. KT8: E Mos 5J 149
Summercourt Rd. E1 . . . . .6J 85
Summer Crossing KT7: E Mos 5J 149
Summerene Cl. SW16 . . . . .7G 137
Summerfield BR1: Brom 1K 159
(off Freelands Rd.)
Summerfield Av. NW6 . . . . .2G 81
Summerfield La. KT6: Surb 2D 162
Summerfield Rd. W5 . . . . .4B 78
Summerfields Av. N12 . . . . .6H 31
Summerfield St. SE12 . . . . .7H 123
Summer Gdns. KT8: E Mos 5J 149
Summer Gro. BR4: W W'ck 2G 171
Summer Hill BR7: Chst 2E 160
Summerhill Cl. BR6: Orp 3J 173
Summerhill Gro. EN1: Enf 6K 23
Summerhill Rd. N15 . . . . .4D 48
Summerhill Vs. BR7: Chst 1E 160
(off Susan Wood)
Summerhill Way CR4: Mitc 1E 154
Summerhouse Av. TW5: Hest 1C 112
Summerhouse Dr. DA2: Dart 4K 145
DA5: Bexl, Dart 4K 145
Summerhouse Rd. N16 . . . . .2E 66
Summerland Gdns. N10 . . . . .3F 47
Summerland Grange N10 . . . . .3F 47
Summerlands Av. W3 . . . . .7J 79
Summerlands Lodge
BR6: Farnb 4E 172
Summerlee Av. N2 . . . . .4D 46
Summerlee Gdns. N2 . . . . .4D 46
Summerley St. SW18 . . . . .2K 135
Summer Rd. KT7: T Ditt 5J 149
KT8: E Mos 5H 149
(not continuous)
Summersby Rd. N6 . . . . .6F 47
Summers Cl. HA9: Wemb 1H 61
SM2: Sutt 7J 165
Summerskill Cl. SE15 . . . . .3H 121
Summerskille Cl. N9 . . . . .3C 34
Summers La. N12 . . . . .7G 31
Summers Row N12 . . . . .6H 31
Summers St. EC1 . . . . .4J 7 (4A 84)
SUMMERSTOWN 3A 136
Summerstown SW17 . . . . .3A 136
Summerton Way SE28 . . . . .6D 90
Summer Trees TW16: Sun 1K 147
Summerville Gdns. SM1: Sutt 6H 165
Summerwood Rd. TW7: Isle 5K 113
Summit Av. NW9 . . . . .5K 43
Summit Bus. Pk. TW16: Sun 7J 129
Summit Cl. HA8: Edg 7B 28
N14 . . . . .2B 32
NW9 . . . . .4K 43
Summit Ct. NW2 . . . . .5G 63
Summit Dr. IG8: Wfd G 2B 52
Summit Est. N16 . . . . .7G 49
Summit Rd. E17 . . . . .4D 50
UB5: N'olt 7E 58
Summit Way N14 . . . . .2A 32
SE19 . . . . .7E 138
Sumner Av. SE15 . . . . .1F 121
Sumner Bldgs. SE1 . . . . .4C 14
Sumner Ct. BR6: Farnb 4G 173
Sumner Ct. SW8 . . . . .7J 101
Sumner Est. SE15 . . . . .7F 103
Sumner Gdns. CR0: Croy 1A 168
Sumner Ho. E3 . . . . .5D 86
(off Watts Gro.)
Sumner Pl. SW7 . . . . .4B 16 (4B 100)
Sumner Pl. M. SW7 . . . . . . .4B 16 (4B 100)

Sumner Rd. CR0: Croy 1A 168
HA1: Harr 7G 41
SE15 . . . . .6F 103
Sumner Rd. Sth. CR0: Croy 1A 168
Sumner St. SE1 . . . . .4B 14 (1B 102)
Sumpter Cl. NW3 . . . . .6A 64
Sun All. TW9: Rich 4E 114
Sunbeam Cres. W10 . . . . .4E 80
Sunbeam Rd. NW10 . . . . .4J 79
SUNBURY 3A 148
Sunbury Av. NW7 . . . . .5E 28
SW14 . . . . .4K 115
Sunbury Av. Pas. SW14 . . . . .4A 116
Sunbury Bus. Cen. TW16: Sun 1H 147
Sunbury Cl. KT12: Walt T 6J 147
SUNBURY COMMON 7H 129
Sunbury Ct. EN5: Barn 4B 20
Sunbury Ct. Island TW16: Sun 3B 148
Sunbury Ct. M. TW16: Sun 2B 148
Sunbury Ct. Rd. TW16: Sun 2A 148
Sunbury Cres. TW13: Felt 4H 129
SUNBURY CROSS 7J 129
Sunbury Cross Shop. Cen.
TW16: Sun 7H 129
Sunbury Gdns. NW7 . . . . .5E 28
Sunbury Ho. E2 . . . . .2J 9
(off Swanfield St.)
SE14 . . . . .6K 103
(off Myers La.)
Sunbury La. KT12: Walt T 6J 147
SW11 . . . . .1B 118
(not continuous)
Sunbury Leisure Cen. 1H 147
Sunburylock Ait KT12: Sun 4K 147
Sunbury Pk. Walled Garden 3K 147
Sunbury Rd. SM3: Cheam 3F 165
TW13: Felt 3H 129
Sunbury St. SE18 . . . . .3D 106
Sunbury Way TW13: Hanw 5A 130
Sunbury Workshops E2 . . . . .2J 9
(off Swanfield St.)
Sun Ct. EC3 . . . . .1F 15
Suncroft Pl. SE26 . . . . .3J 139
Sunderland Ct. SE22 . . . . .7G 121
TW19: Stanw 6A 110
Sunderland Ho. W2 . . . . .5J 81
(off Brunel Est.)
Sunderland Mt. SE23 . . . . .2K 139
Sunderland Rd. SE23 . . . . .1K 139
W5 . . . . .3D 96
Sunderland Ter. W2 . . . . .6K 81
Sunderland Way E12 . . . . .2B 70
Sundew Av. W12 . . . . .7C 80
Sundew Cl. W12 . . . . .7C 80
Sundew Ct. HA0: Wemb 2E 78
(off Elmore Cl.)
Sundial Av. SE25 . . . . .3F 157
Sundorne Rd. SE7 . . . . .5A 106
Sundra Wlk. E1 . . . . .5E 128
Sundra Wlk. E1 . . . . .4K 85
SUNDRIDGE 6K 141
Sundridge Av. BR1: Brom 1B 160
BR7: Chst 1B 160
DA16: Well 2H 125
Sundridge Ho. E9 . . . . .7K 67
(off Church Cres.)
Sundridge Pde. BR1: Brom 7K 141
SUNDRIDGE PARK 7K 141
Sundridge Pl. CR0: Croy 1G 169
Sundridge Rd. CR0: Croy 7F 157
Sunfields Pl. SE3 . . . . .7K 105
Sungate Cotts. RM5: Col R 1F 55
SUN-IN-THE-SANDS 7K 105
Sunken Rd. CR0: Croy 5J 169
Sunleigh Rd. HA0: Wemb 1E 78
Sunley Gdns. UB6: G'frd 1A 78
Sun Life Trad. Est. TW14: Felt 3J 111
Sunlight Cl. SW19 . . . . .6A 136
Sunlight Sq. E2 . . . . .3H 85
Sunmead Rd. TW16: Sun 3J 147

Sunna Gdns. TW16: Sun 2K 147
Sunna Lodge TW16: Sun 7H 129
Sunniholme Ct. *CR2: S Croy* *5C 168*
(off Warham Rd.)
Sunningdale N14 5C 32
W13 *5B 78*
(off Hardwick Grn.)
Sunningdale Av. HA4: Ruis 1A 58
IG11: Bark 1H 89
TW13: Hanw 2C 130
W3 7A 80
Sunningdale Cl. E6 3D 88
HA7: Stan 6F 27
KT6: Surb 2E 162
SE16 5H 103
SE28 6E 90
Sunningdale Ct. *TW7: Isle* *6H 113*
(off Whitton Dene)
UB1: S'hall *6G 77*
(off Fleming Rd.)
Sunningdale Gdns. NW9 5J 43
W8 *3J 99*
(off Stratford Rd.)
Sunningdale Lodge *HA1: Harr* *7J 41*
(off Grove Hill)
HA8: Edg *5A 28*
(off Stonegrove)
Sunningdale Rd. BR1: Brom 4C 160
SM1: Sutt 3H 165
Sunningfields Cres. NW4 2D 44
Sunningfields Rd. NW4 3D 44
Sunninghill Ct. W3 2J 97
Sunninghill Rd. SE13 2D 122
Sunny Bank SE25 3G 157
Sunny Cres. NW10 7J 61
Sunnycroft Rd. SE25 3G 157
TW3: Houn 2F 113
UB1: S'hall 5E 76
Sunnydale BR6: Farnb 2E 172
Sunnydale Gdns. NW7 6E 28
Sunnydale Rd. SE12 5K 123
Sunnydene Av. E4 5A 36
HA4: Ruis 1J 57
Sunnydene Gdns. HA0: Wemb 6C 60
Sunnydene St. SE26 4A 140
Sunnyfield NW7 4G 29
Sunnyfield Rd. BR7: Chst 3K 161
Sunny Gdns. Pde. NW4 2D 44
Sunny Gdns. Rd. NW4 2D 44
Sunny Hill NW4 3D 44
Sunnyhill Cl. E5 4A 68
Sunnyhill Rd. SW16 4J 137
Sunnyhurst Cl. SM1: Sutt 3J 165
Sunnymead Av. CR4: Mitc 3H 155
Sunnymead Rd. NW9 7K 43
SW15 5D 116
Sunnymede Av. KT19: Ewe 7A 164
Sunnymede Dr. IG2: Ilf 5F 53
IG6: Ilf 5F 53
Sunny Nook Gdns. CR2: S Croy 6D 168
Sunny Pl. NW4 4E 44
Sunny Rd., The EN3: Enf H 1E 24
Sunnyside KT12: Walt T 5A 148
NW2 3H 63
SW19 6G 135
Sunnyside Dr. E4 7K 25
Sunnyside Ho's. *NW2* *3H 63*
(off Sunnyside)
Sunnyside Pas. SW19 6G 135
Sunnyside Pl. SW19 6G 135
Sunnyside Rd. E10 1C 68
IG1: Ilf 3G 71
N19 7H 47
TW11: Tedd 4H 131
W5 1D 96
Sunnyside Rd. E. N9 3B 34
Sunnyside Rd. Nth. N9 3A 34
Sunnyside Rd. Sth. N9 3A 34
Sunnyside Ter. NW9 3K 43
Sunny Vw. NW9 5K 43
Sunny Way N12 7H 31
Sun Pas. *SE16* *3G 103*
(off Old Jamaica Rd.)
Sunray Av. BR2: Brom 6C 160
KT5: Surb 2H 163
SE24 4D 120
Sunrise Cl. TW13: Hanw 3D 130
Sunrise Vw. NW7 6G 29
Sun Rd. W14 5H 99
Sunset Av. E4 1J 35
IG8: Wfd G 4C 36
Sunset Ct. IG8: Wfd G 7F 37
Sunset Gdns. SE25 2F 157
Sunset Rd. SE5 4C 120
SE28 1A 108
SW19 5D 134
Sunset Vw. EN5: Barn 2B 20
Sunshine Way CR4: Mitc 2D 154
Sun St. EC2 5F 9 (5D 84)
(not continuous)
Sun St. Pas. EC2 6G 9 (5E 84)
Sun Wlk. E1 3K 15 (7F 85)
Sunwell Cl. SE15 1H 121
Sun Wharf *SE8* *7D 104*
(off Creekside)
Superior Dr. BR6: Chels 6K 173
SURBITON 6D 150
Surbiton Ct. KT6: Surb 6C 150
Surbiton Cres. KT1: King T 4E 150
Surbiton Hall Cl. KT1: King T 4E 150
Surbiton Hill Pk. KT5: Surb 5F 151
Surbiton Hill Rd. KT6: Surb 4E 150
Surbiton Pde. KT6: Surb 6E 150
Surbiton Rd. KT1: King T 4D 150
Surlingham Cl. SE28 7D 90
Surma Cl. E1 4H 85
Surmans Cl. RM9: Dag 1C 90
Surrendale Pl. W9 4J 81
Surrey Canal Rd. SE14 6K 103
SE15 6J 103
Surrey Cl. N3 3G 45
Surrey County Cricket Club 7H 19 (6K 101)
Surrey Cres. W4 5G 97
Surrey Docks Stadium 1K 103
Surrey Docks Watersports Cen. 3A 104
Surrey Gdns. N4 6C 48
Surrey Gro. SE17 5E 102
SM1: Sutt 3B 166
Surrey Ho. *SE16* *1K 103*
(off Rotherhithe St.)
Surrey La. SW11 1C 118
Surrey La. Est. SW11 1C 118
Surrey M. SE27 4E 138
Surrey Mt. SE23 1H 139
Surrey Quays Rd. SE16 3J 103
Surrey Quays Shop. Cen. SE16 3K 103
Surrey Rd. BR4: W W'ck 1D 170
HA1: Harr 5G 41
IG11: Bark 7J 71
RM10: Dag 5H 73
SE15 5K 121
Surrey Row SE1 6A 14 (2B 102)
Surrey Sq. SE17 5E 102
Surrey Steps *WC2* *2H 13*
(off Surrey St.)
Surrey St. CR0: Croy 2C 168
E13 3K 87
WC2 2H 13 (7K 83)
Surrey Ter. SE17 5E 102
Surrey Water Rd. SE16 1K 103
Surridge Ct. *SW9* *2J 119*
(off Clapham Rd.)
Surridge Gdns. SE19 6D 138
Surr St. N7 5J 65
Sury Basin KT2: King T 1E 150
Susan Cl. RM7: Mawney 3J 55
Susan Constant Ct. *E14* *7F 87*
(off Newport Av.)
Susan Lawrence Ho.
E12 *4E 70*
(off Walton Rd.)
Susannah St. E14 6D 86
Susan Rd. SE3 2K 123
Susan Wood BR7: Chst 1E 160
Sussex Av. TW7: Isle 3J 113
Sussex Cl. IG4: Ilf 5D 52
KT3: N Mald 4A 152
N19 2J 65
TW1: Twick 6B 114
Sussex Ct. *SE10* *6E 104*
(off Roan St.)
W2 *1A 10*
(off Spring St.)
Sussex Cres. UB5: N'olt 6E 58
Sussex Gdns. KT9: Chess 6D 162
N4 5C 48
N6 5D 46
W2 2A 10 (7B 82)
Sussex Ga. N6 5D 46
Sussex Lodge *W2* *1B 10*
(off Sussex Pl.)
Sussex Mans. SW7 4A 16
WC2 *2F 13*
(off Maiden La.)
Sussex M. SE6 7C 122
Sussex M. E. W2 1B 10
Sussex M. W. W2 2B 10 (7B 82)
Sussex Pl. KT3: N Mald 4A 152
NW1 3E 4 (4D 82)
W2 1B 10 (6B 82)
W6 5E 98
Sussex Ring N12 5D 30
Sussex Rd. BR4: W W'ck 1D 170
CR2: S Croy 6D 168
CR4: Mitc 5J 155
DA8: Erith 7H 109
DA14: Sidc 5B 144
E6 1E 88
HA1: Harr 5G 41
KT3: N Mald 4A 152
SM5: Cars 6D 166
UB2: S'hall 3B 94
UB10: Ick 4E 56
Sussex Sq. W2 2B 10 (7B 82)
Sussex St. E13 3K 87
SW1 6K 17 (5F 101)
Sussex Ter. *SE20* *7J 139*
(off Graveney Gro.)
Sussex Way EN4: Cockf 5A 22
N7 2J 65
N19 1H 65
(not continuous)
Sutcliffe Cl. NW11 5K 45
Sutcliffe Ho. UB3: Hayes 6J 75
Sutcliffe Pk. Athletics Track 5A 124
Sutcliffe Rd. DA16: Well 2C 126
SE18 6J 107
Sutherland Av. BR5: St M Cry 6K 161
DA16: Well 4J 125
TW16: Sun 2H 147
UB3: Hayes 4J 93
W9 4J 81
W13 6B 78
Sutherland Cl. EN5: Barn 4B 20
Sutherland Ct. N16 3D 66
NW9 5H 43
W9 *4J 81*
(off Marylands Rd.)
Sutherland Dr. SW19 1B 154
Sutherland Gdns. KT4: Wor Pk 1D 164
SW14 3A 116
TW16: Sun 2H 147
Sutherland Gro. SW18 6G 117
TW11: Tedd 5J 131
Sutherland Ho. IG8: Wfd G 7K 37
W8 3K 99
Sutherland Pl. W2 6J 81
Sutherland Point *E5* *3H 67*
(off Brackenfield Cl.)
Sutherland Rd. CR0: Croy 7A 156
DA17: Belv 3G 109
E3 2B 86
E17 2K 49
EN3: Pond E 6E 24
N9 1C 34
N17 7B 34
UB1: S'hall 6D 76
W4 6A 98
Sutherland Rd. W13 6A 78
Sutherland Rd. Path E17 3K 49
Sutherland Row SW1 5K 17 (5F 101)
Sutherland Sq. SE17 5C 102
Sutherland St. SW1 5J 17 (5F 101)
Sutherland Wlk. SE17 5C 102
Sutlej Rd. SE7 7A 106
Sutterton St. N7 6K 65
SUTTON 5K 165
Sutton Arena Leisure Cen. 7A 154
Sutton Cl. BR3: Beck 1D 158
HA5: Eastc 5J 39
IG10: Lough 1H 37
Sutton Comn. Rd. SM1: Sutt 7H 153
SM3: Sutt 7H 153
Sutton Ct. KT8: W Mole 5D 148
SE19 7F 139
SM2: Sutt 6A 166
W4 6J 97
W5 1E 96
Sutton Ct. Rd. E13 3A 88
SM1: Sutt 6A 166
UB10: Hil 1D 74
W4 7J 97
Sutton Cres. EN5: Barn 5A 20
Sutton Dene TW3: Houn 1F 113
Sutton Ecology Cen. 4D 166
Sutton Est. EC1 2F 9
W10 5E 80
Sutton Est., The N1 7B 66
SW3 5D 16 (5C 100)
Sutton Gdns. CR0: Croy 5F 157
IG11: Bark 1J 89
Sutton Grn. *IG11: Bark* *1J 89*
(off Felton Gdns.)
Sutton Gro. SM1: Sutt 4B 166
Sutton Hall Rd. TW5: Hest 7E 94
Sutton Hgts. SM2: Sutt 7B 166
Sutton Junior Tennis Cen. 1K 165
Sutton La. *EC1* *4B 8*
(off Gt. Sutton St.)
TW3: Houn 3D 112
Sutton La. Nth. W4 5J 97
Sutton La. Sth. W4 6J 97
Sutton Pde. *NW4* *4E 44*
(off Church Rd.)
Sutton Pk. Rd. SM1: Sutt 6K 165
Sutton Pl. E9 5J 67
Sutton Rd. E13 4H 87
E17 1K 49
IG11: Bark 2J 89
N10 1E 46
TW5: Hest 1E 112
Sutton Row W1 7D 6 (6H 83)
Suttons Bus. Pk. RM13: Rain 3K 91
Sutton Sq. E9 5J 67
TW5: Hest 1D 112
Sutton St. E1 7J 85
Sutton Superbowl 5K 165
Sutton's Way EC1 4D 8 (4C 84)
Sutton United FC 4J 165
Sutton Wlk. SE1 5H 13 (1K 101)
Sutton Way TW5: Hest 1D 112
W10 4E 80
Swaby Rd. SW18 1A 136
Swaffam Ct. RM6: Chad H 6C 54
Swaffham Way N22 7G 33
Swaffield Rd. SW18 7K 117
Swain Cl. SW16 6F 137
Swain Rd. CR7: Thor H 5C 156
Swains Cl. UB7: W Dray 2A 92
Swains La. N6 1E 64
Swainson Rd. W3 2B 98
Swains Rd. SW17 7D 136
Swain St. NW8 3C 4
Swakeleys Dr. UB10: Ick 4C 56
Swakeleys Rd. UB10: Ick 4A 56
SWAKELEYS RDBT. 4A 56
Swakeleys School Sports Cen. 2D 74
Swalecliffe Rd. DA17: Belv 5H 109
Swaledale Cl. N11 6K 31
Swallands Rd. SE6 3C 140
(not continuous)

Swallow Cl. DA8: Erith . . . 1K 127
SE14 . . . 1K 121
WD23: Bush . . . 1B 26
Swallow Ct. HA4: Ruis . . . 1A 58
IG2: Ilf . . . 5F 53
SE1 . . . 7D 14
(off Swan St.)
SE12 . . . 7J 123
W9 . . . 5J 81
(off Admiral Wlk.)
Swallow Dr. NW10 . . . 6K 61
UB5: N'olt . . . 2E 76
Swallowfield *NW1 . . . 2K 5*
(off Munster Sq.)
Swallowfield Rd. SE7 . . . 5K 105
Swallowfield Way UB3: Hayes . . . 2F 93
Swallow Gdns. SW16 . . . 5H 137
Swallow Ho. *NW8 . . . 2C 82*
(off Barrow Hill Est.)
Swallow Pk. Cvn. Site KT6: Surb . . . 3F 163
Swallow Pas. *W1 . . . 1K 11*
(off Swallow Pl.)
Swallow Pl. W1 . . . 1K 11 (6F 83)
Swallow St. E6 . . . 5C 88
W1 . . . 3B 12 (7G 83)
SWAN, THE . . . 2E 170
Swanage Ct. *N1 . . . 7E 66*
(off Hertford Rd.)
Swanage Ho. *SW8 . . . 7K 101*
(off Dorset Rd.)
Swanage Rd. E4 . . . 7K 35
SW18 . . . 6A 118
Swanage Waye UB4: Yead . . . 6A 76
Swan & Pike Rd. EN3: Enf L . . . 1H 25
Swan App. E6 . . . 5C 88
Swanbourne *SE17 . . . 4C 102*
(off Wansey St.)
Swanbourne Ho. *NW8 . . . 3C 4*
(off Capland St.)
Swanbridge Rd. DA7: Bex . . . 1G 127
Swan Cen., The SW17 . . . 3K 135
Swan Cl. CR0: Croy . . . 7E 156
E17 . . . 1A 50
TW13: Hanw . . . 4C 130
Swan Ct. *E1 . . . 3K 15*
(off Star Pl.)
E14 . . . 6B 86
(off Agnes St.)
SW3 . . . 6D 16 (5C 100)
SW6 . . . 7J 99
(off Fulham Rd.)
TW7: Isle . . . 3B 114
(off Swan St.)
Swandon Way SW18 . . . 5K 117
Swan Dr. NW9 . . . 2A 44
Swanfield St. E2 . . . 2J 9 (3F 85)
Swan Ho. EN3: Pond E . . . 5D 24
N1 . . . 7D 66
(off Oakley Rd.)
Swan La. EC4 . . . 3F 15 (7D 84)
N20 . . . 3F 31
Swanley Ho. *SE17 . . . 5E 102*
(off Kinglake Est.)
Swanley Rd. DA16: Well . . . 1C 126
Swan Mead SE1 . . . 3E 102
Swan M. CR4: Mitc . . . 1D 154
RM7: Mawney . . . 4H 55
SW6 . . . 1H 117
SW9 . . . 2K 119
Swann Ct. *TW7: Isle . . . 3A 114*
(off South St.)
Swanne Ho. *SE10 . . . 7E 104*
(off Gloucester Cir.)
Swan Pas. E1 . . . 3K 15
Swan Pl. SW13 . . . 2B 116
Swan Rd. SE16 . . . 2J 103
SE18 . . . 3B 106
TW13: Hanw . . . 5C 130
UB1: S'hall . . . 6F 77
UB7: W Dray . . . 2A 92
Swan Sanctuary, The . . . 6G 147
Swanscombe Ho. *W11 . . . 1F 99*
(off St Ann's Rd.)
Swanscombe Point *E16 . . . 5H 87*
(off Clarkson Rd.)
Swanscombe Rd. W4 . . . 5A 98
W11 . . . 1F 99
Swansea Ct. E16 . . . 1F 107
Swansea Rd. EN3: Pond E . . . 4D 24
TW14: Felt . . . 6E 110
Swansland Gdns. E17 . . . 1A 50
Swan St. SE1 . . . 7D 14 (3C 102)
TW7: Isle . . . 3B 114
Swanton Gdns. SW19 . . . 1F 135
Swanton Rd. DA8: Erith . . . 7G 109
Swan Wlk. SW3 . . . 7E 16 (6D 100)
TW17: Shep . . . 7G 147
Swan Way EN3: Enf H . . . 2E 24
Swanwick Cl. SW15 . . . 7B 116
Swan Yd. N1 . . . 6B 66
Sward Rd. BR5: St M Cry . . . 6K 161
Swathling Ho. *SW15 . . . 6B 116*
(off Tunworth Cres.)
Swaton Rd. E3 . . . 4C 86
Swaylands Rd. DA17: Belv . . . 6G 109
Swaythling Cl. N18 . . . 4C 34
Swedeland Ct. E1 . . . 6H 9
Swedenborg Gdns. E1 . . . 7H 85
Swedenborg Pl. *E1 . . . 7H 85*
(off Swedenborg Gdns.)
Sweden Ga. SE16 . . . 3A 104
Swedish Quays SE16 . . . 3A 104
(not continuous)
Sweeney Cres. SE1 . . . 7K 15 (2F 103)
Sweet Briar Grn. N9 . . . 3A 34
Sweet Briar Gro. N9 . . . 3A 34
Sweet Briar Wlk. N18 . . . 4A 34
Sweetcroft La. UB10: Hil . . . 7B 56
Sweetland Ct. RM8: Dag . . . 6B 72
Sweetmans Av. HA5: Pinn . . . 3B 40
Sweets Way N20 . . . 2G 31
Swell Ct. E17 . . . 6C 50
Swetenham Wlk. SE18 . . . 5G 107
Swete St. E13 . . . 2J 87
Sweyn Pl. SE3 . . . 2J 123
Swift Cen. CR0: Wadd . . . 7K 167
Swift Cl. E17 . . . 7F 35
HA2: Harr . . . 2F 59
SE28 . . . 7B 90
UB3: Hayes . . . 6H 75
Swift Ct. SM2: Sutt . . . 7K 165
Swift Lodge *W9 . . . 4J 81*
(off Admiral Wlk.)
Swift Rd. TW13: Hanw . . . 3C 130
UB2: S'hall . . . 3E 94
Swiftsden Way BR1: Brom . . . 6G 141
Swift St. SW6 . . . 1H 117
Swinbrook Rd. W10 . . . 5G 81
Swinburne Ct. *SE5 . . . 4D 120*
(off Basingdon Way)
Swinburne Cres. CR0: Croy . . . 6J 157
Swinburne Ho. *E2 . . . 3J 85*
(off Roman Rd.)
Swinburne Rd. SW15 . . . 4C 116
Swinderby Rd. HA0: Wemb . . . 6E 60
Swindon Cl. IG3: Ilf . . . 2J 71
Swindon Rd. TW6: H'row A . . . 5E 110
Swindon St. W12 . . . 1D 98
Swinfield Cl. TW13: Hanw . . . 3C 130
Swinford Gdns. SW9 . . . 3B 120
Swingate La. SE18 . . . 6J 107
Swingfield Ho. *E9 . . . 1J 85*
(off Templecombe Rd.)
Swinley Ho. *NW1 . . . 1K 5*
(off Redhill St.)
Swinnerton St. E9 . . . 5A 68
Swinson Ho. N11 . . . 5B 32
Swinton Cl. HA9: Wemb . . . 1H 61
Swinton Pl. WC1 . . . 1G 7 (3K 83)
Swinton St. WC1 . . . 1G 7 (3K 83)
Swires Shaw BR2: Kes . . . 4B 172
Swiss Cen. W1 . . . 3C 12
SWISS COTTAGE . . . 7B 64
Swiss Cottage Sports Cen. . . . 7B 64
Swiss Ct. WC2 . . . 3D 12
Swiss Re Tower . . . 7H 9
Swiss Ter. NW6 . . . 7B 64
Switch Ho. E14 . . . 7F 87
Swithland Gdns. SE9 . . . 4E 142
Swyncombe Av. W5 . . . 4B 96
Swynford Gdns. NW4 . . . 4C 44
Sybil M. N4 . . . 6B 48
Sybil Phoenix Cl. SE8 . . . 5K 103
Sybil Thorndike Casson Ho. *SW5 . . . 5J 99*
(off Kramer M.)
Sybourn St. E17 . . . 7B 50
Sycamore Av. DA15: Sidc . . . 6K 125
E3 . . . 1B 86
UB3: Hayes . . . 7G 75
W5 . . . 3D 96
Sycamore Cl. CR2: S Croy . . . 5E 168
E16 . . . 4G 87
EN4: E Barn . . . 6G 21
HA8: Edg . . . 4D 28
N9 . . . 4B 34
SE9 . . . 2C 142
SM5: Cars . . . 4D 166
TW13: Felt . . . 3J 129
UB5: N'olt . . . 1C 76
UB7: Yiew . . . 7B 74
W3 . . . 1A 98
Sycamore Ct. *DA8: Erith . . . 5K 109*
(off Sandcliff Rd.)
E7 . . . 6J 69
KT3: N Mald . . . 3A 152
NW6 . . . 1J 81
(off Bransdale Cl.)
TW4: Houn . . . 4C 112
Sycamore Gdns. CR4: Mitc . . . 2B 154
N15 . . . 4F 49
W6 . . . 2D 98
Sycamore Gro. KT3: N Mald . . . 3K 151
NW9 . . . 7J 43
SE6 . . . 6E 122
SE20 . . . 1G 157
Sycamore Hill N11 . . . 6K 31
Sycamore Ho. BR2: Brom . . . 2G 159
IG9: Buck H . . . 2G 37
N2 . . . 2B 46
(off The Grange)
SE16 . . . 2K 103
(off Woodland Cres.)
W6 . . . 2D 98
Sycamore Lodge BR6: Orp . . . 2K 173
TW16: Sun . . . 7H 129
W8 . . . 3K 99
(off Stone Hall Pl.)
Sycamore M. *DA8: Erith . . . 5K 109*
(off St John's Rd.)
SW4 . . . 3G 119
Sycamore Rd. SW19 . . . 6E 134
Sycamore St. EC1 . . . 4C 8 (4C 84)
Sycamore Wlk. IG6: Ilf . . . 4G 53
W10 . . . 4G 81
Sycamore Way CR7: Thor H . . . 5A 156
TW11: Tedd . . . 6C 132
Sydcote SE21 . . . 1C 138
SYDENHAM . . . 4J 139
Sydenham Av. N21 . . . 5E 22
SE26 . . . 5H 139
Sydenham Cotts. SE12 . . . 2A 142
Sydenham Ct. *CR0: Croy . . . 1D 168*
(off Sydenham Rd.)
Sydenham Hill SE23 . . . 1H 139
SE26 . . . 4F 139
Sydenham Pk. SE26 . . . 3J 139
Sydenham Pk. Mans. *SE26 . . . 3J 139*
(off Sydenham Pk.)
Sydenham Pk. Rd. SE26 . . . 3J 139
Sydenham Pl. SE27 . . . 3B 138
Sydenham Ri. SE23 . . . 2H 139
Sydenham Rd. CR0: Croy . . . 1C 168
SE26 . . . 4J 139
Sydmons Ct. SE23 . . . 7J 121
Sydner M. N16 . . . 4F 67
Sydner Rd. N16 . . . 4F 67
Sydney Chapman Way EN5: Barn . . . 2C 20
Sydney Cl. SW3 . . . 4B 16 (4B 100)
Sydney Ct. UB4: Yead . . . 4A 76
Sydney Cres. TW15: Ashf . . . 6D 128
Sydney Gro. NW4 . . . 5E 44
Sydney M. SW3 . . . 4B 16 (4B 100)
Sydney Pl. SW7 . . . 4B 16 (4B 100)
Sydney Rd. DA6: Bex . . . 4D 126
DA14: Sidc . . . 4J 143
E11 . . . 6K 51
EN2: Enf . . . 3J 23
(not continuous)
IG6: Ilf . . . 2G 53
IG8: Wfd G . . . 4D 36
N8 . . . 4A 48
N10 . . . 1E 46
SE2 . . . 3C 108
SM1: Sutt . . . 4J 165
SW20 . . . 2F 153
TW9: Rich . . . 4E 114
TW11: Tedd . . . 5K 131
TW14: Felt . . . 1J 129
W13 . . . 1A 96
Sydney Russell Leisure Cen. . . . 5E 72
Sydney St. SW3 . . . 5C 16 (5C 100)
Sylvana Cl. UB10: Hil . . . 1B 74
Sylvan Av. N3 . . . 2J 45
N22 . . . 7E 32
NW7 . . . 6F 29
RM6: Chad H . . . 6F 55
Sylvan Ct. N12 . . . 3E 30
Sylvan Est. SE19 . . . 1F 157
Sylvan Gdns. KT6: Surb . . . 7D 150
Sylvan Gro. NW2 . . . 4F 63
SE15 . . . 6H 103
Sylvan Hill SE19 . . . 1E 156
Sylvan Rd. E7 . . . 6K 69
E11 . . . 5J 51
E17 . . . 5C 50
IG1: Ilf . . . 2G 71
SE19 . . . 1F 157
Sylvan Ter. *SE15 . . . 6H 103*
(off Sylvan Gro.)
Sylvan Wlk. BR1: Brom . . . 3D 160
Sylvan Way BR4: W W'ck . . . 4G 171
RM8: Dag . . . 4B 72
Sylverdale Rd. CR0: Croy . . . 3B 168
Sylvester Av. BR7: Chst . . . 6D 142
Sylvester Path E8 . . . 6H 67
Sylvester Rd. E8 . . . 6H 67
E17 . . . 7B 50
HA0: Wemb . . . 5C 60
N2 . . . 2A 46
Sylvestrus Cl. KT1: King T . . . 1G 151
Sylvia Ct. HA9: Wemb . . . 7H 61
N1 . . . 2D 84
(off Wenlock St.)
Sylvia Gdns. HA9: Wemb . . . 7H 61
Sylvia Pankhurst Ho. *RM10: Dag . . . 3G 73*
(off Wythenshawe Rd.)
Symes M. NW1 . . . 2G 83
Symington Ho. *SE1 . . . 3D 102*
(off Deverell St.)
Symington M. E9 . . . 5K 67
Symister M. N1 . . . 2G 9
Symons Cl. SE15 . . . 2J 121
Symons St. SW3 . . . 4F 17 (4D 100)
Symphony Cl. HA8: Edg . . . 7C 28
Symphony M. W10 . . . 3G 81
Syon Ga. Way TW8: Bford . . . 7A 96
Syon House . . . 1C 114
Syon La. TW7: Isle . . . 6J 95
Syon Lodge SE12 . . . 7J 123
Syon Pk. . . . 1B 114
Syon Pk. Gdns. TW7: Isle . . . 7K 95
Syringa Ho. SE4 . . . 3B 122

T

Tabard Ct. *E14 . . . 6E 86*
(off Lodore St.)
Tabard Gdn. Est. SE1 . . . 7E 14 (3D 102)
Tabard Ho. *SE1 . . . 7F 15*
(off Manciple St.)
Tabard St. SE1 . . . 6D 14 (2C 102)

Tabernacle Av. E13 ... 4J **87**
Tabernacle St. EC2 ... 4F **9** (4D **84**)
Tableer Av. SW4 ... 5G **119**
Tabley Rd. N7 ... 4J **65**
Tabor Ct. SM3: Cheam ... 6G **165**
Tabor Gdns. SM3: Cheam ... 6H **165**
Tabor Gro. SW19 ... 7H **135**
Tabor Rd. W6 ... 3D **98**
Tachbrook Est. SW1 ... 6C **18** (5H **101**)
Tachbrook M. SW1 ... 3A **18** (4G **101**)
Tachbrook Rd. TW14: Felt ... 7H **111**
UB2: S'hall ... 4B **94**
UB7: W Dray ... 1A **92**
Tachbrook St. SW1 ... 4B **18** (4G **101**)
(not continuous)
Tack M. SE4 ... 3C **122**
Tadema Ho. NW8 ... 4B **4**
Tadema Rd. SW10 ... 7A **100**
Tadlow *KT1: King T ... 3G* ***151***
(off Washington Rd.)
Tadmor Cl. TW16: Sun ... 4H **147**
Tadmor St. W12 ... 1F **99**
Tadworth Av. KT3: N Mald ... 4B **152**
Tadworth Ho. SE1 ... 7A **14**
Tadworth Rd. NW2 ... 2C **62**
Taeping St. E14 ... 4D **104**
Taff Ho. *KT2: King T ... 1D* ***150***
(off Henry Macaulay Av.)
Taffrail Ho. *E14 ... 5D* ***104***
(off Burrells Wharf Sq.)
Taffy's Row CR4: Mitc ... 3C **154**
Taft Way E3 ... 3D **86**
Taggs Ho. *KT1: King T ... 2D* ***150***
(off Wadbrook St.)
Tailor Ho. *WC1 ... 4F* ***7***
(off Colonnade)
Tailworth St. *E1 ... 6K* ***9***
(off Chicksand St.)
Tait Ct. *E3 ... 1B* ***86***
(off St Stephen's Rd.)
SW8 ... 1J ***119***
(off Lansdowne Grn.)
Tait Ho. *SE1 ... 5K* ***13***
(off Greet St.)
Tait Rd. CR0: Croy ... 7E **156**
Tait Rd. Ind. Est. *CR0: Croy ... 7E* ***156***
(off Tait Rd.)
Takeley Cl. RM5: Col R ... 2K **55**
Takhar M. SW11 ... 2C **118**
Talacre Community Sports Cen.
Kentish Town ... 6E **64**
Talacre Rd. NW5 ... 6E **64**
Talbot Av. N2 ... 3B **46**
Talbot Cl. N15 ... 4F **49**
Talbot Ct. EC3 ... 2F **15**
NW9 ... 3K **61**
Talbot Cres. NW4 ... 5C **44**
Talbot Gdns. IG3: Ilf ... 2A **72**
Talbot Gro. Ho. *W11 ... 6G* ***81***
(off Lancaster Rd.)
Talbot Ho. *E14 ... 6D* ***86***
(off Giraud St.)
N7 ... 3A **66**
Talbot Pl. SE3 ... 2G **123**
Talbot Rd. CR7: Thor H ... 4D **156**
E6 ... 2E **88**
E7 ... 4J **69**
HA0: Wemb ... 6D **60**
HA3: W'stone ... 2K **41**
N6 ... 6E **46**
N15 ... 4F **49**
N22 ... 2G **47**
RM9: Dag ... 6F **73**
SE22 ... 4E **120**
SM5: Cars ... 5E **166**
TW2: Twick ... 1J **131**
TW7: Isle ... 4A **114**
TW15: Ashf ... 5A **128**
UB2: S'hall ... 4C **94**
W2 ... 6H **81**
W11 ... 6H **81**
(not continuous)
W13 ... 1A **96**
Talbot Sq. W2 ... 1B **10** (6B **82**)
Talbot Wlk. NW10 ... 6A **62**
W11 ... 6G **81**
Talbot Yd. SE1 ... 5E **14** (1D **102**)
Talcott Path SW2 ... 1A **138**
Talfourd Pl. SE15 ... 1F **121**
Talfourd Rd. SE15 ... 1F **121**
Talgarth Mans. *W14 ... 5G* ***99***
(off Talgarth Rd.)
Talgarth Rd. W6 ... 5F **99**
W14 ... 5F **99**
Talgarth Wlk. NW9 ... 5A **44**
Talia Ho. *E14 ... 3E* ***104***
(off Manchester Rd.)
Talina Cen. SW6 ... 1A **118**
Talisman Cl. IG3: Ilf ... 1B **72**
Talisman Sq. SE26 ... 4G **139**
Talisman Way HA9: Wemb ... 3F **61**
Tallack Cl. HA3: Hrw W ... 7D **26**
Tallack Rd. E10 ... 1B **68**
Tall Elms Cl. BR2: Brom ... 5H **159**
Talleyrand Ho. *SE5 ... 2C* ***120***
(off Lilford Rd.)
Tallis Cl. E16 ... 6K **87**
Tallis Gro. SE7 ... 6K **105**
Tallis St. EC4 ... 2K **13** (7A **84**)
Tallis Vw. NW10 ... 6K **61**
Tallow Rd. TW8: Bford ... 6C **96**
Tall Trees SW16 ... 3K **155**
Talma Gdns. TW2: Twick ... 6J **113**
Talmage Cl. SE23 ... 7J **121**
Talman Gro. HA7: Stan ... 6J **27**
Talma Rd. SW2 ... 4A **120**
Talwin St. E3 ... 3D **86**
Tamar Cl. E3 ... 1B **86**
Tamar Ho. *E14 ... 2E* ***104***
(off Plevna St.)
SE11 ... 5K ***19***
(off Kennington La.)
Tamarind Ct. SE1 ... 6K **15**
W8 ... 3K ***99***
(off Stone Hall Gdns.)
Tamarind Yd. *E1 ... 1G* ***103***
(off Kennet St.)
Tamarisk Sq. W12 ... 7B **80**
Tamar Sq. IG8: Wfd G ... 6E **36**
Tamar St. SE7 ... 3C **106**
Tamar Way N17 ... 3F **49**
Tamesis Gdns. KT4: Wor Pk ... 2A **164**
Tamian Ind. Est. TW4: Houn ... 4A **112**
Tamian Way TW4: Houn ... 4A **112**
Tamplin Ho. *W10 ... 3H* ***81***
(off Dowland St.)
Tamworth N7 ... 6J **65**
Tamworth Av. IG8: Wfd G ... 6B **36**
Tamworth La. CR4: Mitc ... 2F **155**
Tamworth Pk. CR4: Mitc ... 4F **155**
Tamworth Pl. CR0: Croy ... 2C **168**
Tamworth Rd. CR0: Croy ... 2B **168**
Tamworth St. SW6 ... 6J **99**
Tamworth Vs. CR4: Mitc ... 4F **155**
Tancred Rd. N4 ... 6B **48**
Tandem Cen. SW19 ... 1B **154**
Tandem Way SW19 ... 1B **154**
Tandridge Dr. BR6: Orp ... 1H **173**
Tandridge Pl. BR6: Orp ... 1H **173**
Tanfield Av. NW2 ... 4B **62**
Tanfield Rd. CR0: Croy ... 4C **168**
Tangier Rd. TW10: Rich ... 4G **115**
Tangleberry Cl. BR1: Brom ... 4D **160**
Tangle Tree Cl. N3 ... 2K **45**
Tanglewood Cl. CR0: Croy ... 3J **169**
HA7: Stan ... 2D **26**
UB10: Hil ... 4C **74**
Tanglewood Way TW13: Felt ... 3K **129**
Tangley Gro. SW15 ... 6B **116**
Tangley Pk. Rd.
TW12: Hamp ... 5D **130**
Tanglyn Av. TW17: Shep ... 5D **146**
Tangmere *N17 ... 2D* ***48***
(off Willan Rd.)
WC1 ... 2G ***7***
(off Sidmouth St.)
Tangmere Gdns. UB5: Yead ... 2A **76**
(not continuous)
Tangmere Gro. KT2: King T ... 5D **132**
Tangmere Way NW9 ... 2A **44**
Tanhouse Fld. *NW5 ... 5H* ***65***
(off Torriano Av.)
Tanhurst Ho. *SW2 ... 7K* ***119***
(off Redlands Way)
Tanhurst Wlk. *SE2 ... 3D* ***108***
(off Alsike Rd.)
Tankerton Ho's. *WC1 ... 2F* ***7***
(off Tankerton St.)
Tankerton Rd. KT6: Surb ... 2F **163**
Tankerton St. WC1 ... 2F **7** (3J **83**)
Tankerton Ter. CR0: Croy ... 6K **155**
Tankerville Rd. SW16 ... 7H **137**
Tankridge Rd. NW2 ... 2D **62**
Tanner Ho. *SE1 ... 7H* ***15***
(off Tanner St.)
Tanneries, The *E1 ... 4J* ***85***
(off Cephas Av.)
Tanner Point *E13 ... 1J* ***87***
(off Pelly Rd.)
Tanners Cl. KT12: Walt T ... 6K **147**
Tanners End La. N18 ... 4K **33**
Tanner's Hill SE8 ... 1B **122**
Tanners La. IG6: Ilf ... 3G **53**
Tanner St. IG11: Bark ... 6G **71**
SE1 ... 7H **15** (2E **102**)
(not continuous)
Tannery Cl. BR3: Beck ... 5K **157**
RM10: Dag ... 3H **73**
Tannington Ter. N5 ... 3B **66**
Tannsfeld Rd. SE26 ... 5K **139**
Tansley Cl. N7 ... 5H **65**
Tanswell St. SE1 ... 7J **13** (2A **102**)
Tansy Cl. E6 ... 6E **88**
Tantallon Rd. SW12 ... 1E **136**
Tant Av. E16 ... 6H **87**
Tantony Gro. RM6: Chad H ... 3D **54**
Tanworth Gdns. HA5: Pinn ... 2K **39**
Tanyard Ho. *TW8: Bford ... 7C* ***96***
(off High St.)
Tanyard La. DA5: Bexl ... 7G **127**
Tanza Rd. NW3 ... 4D **64**
Tapestry Cl. SM2: Sutt ... 7K **165**
Tapley Ho. *SE1 ... 7K* ***15***
(off Wolseley St.)
Taplow *SE17 ... 5D* ***102***
(off Thurlow St.)
Taplow Ct. CR4: Mitc ... 4C **154**
Taplow Ho. *E2 ... 2J* ***9***
(off Palissy St.)
Taplow Rd. N13 ... 4H **33**
Taplow St. N1 ... 1D **8** (2C **84**)
Tappesfield Rd. SE15 ... 3J **121**
Tapping Cl. KT2: King T ... 7G **133**
Tapp St. E1 ... 4H **85**
Tapster St. EN5: Barn ... 3C **20**
Tara Arts Cen. ... *1K* ***135***
(off Garratt La.)
Tara Ct. BR3: Beck ... 2D **158**
Tara M. N8 ... 6J **47**
Taransay Wlk. N1 ... 6D **66**
Taranto Ho. *E1 ... 5K* ***85***
(off Master's St.)
Tarbert M. N15 ... 5E **48**
Tarbert Rd. SE22 ... 5E **120**
Tarbert Wlk. E1 ... 7J **85**
Target Cl. TW14: Felt ... 6G **111**
Target Ho. *W13 ... 1B* ***96***
(off Sherwood Cl.)
TARGET RDBT. ... **1D 76**
Tariff Cres. SE8 ... 4B **104**
Tariff Rd. N17 ... 6B **34**
Tarleton Ct. N22 ... 2A **48**
Tarleton Gdns. SE23 ... 2H **139**
Tarling Cl. DA14: Sidc ... 3B **144**
Tarling Ho. *E1 ... 6H* ***85***
(off Tarling St.)
Tarling Rd. E16 ... 6H **87**
N2 ... 2A **46**
Tarling St. E1 ... 6H **85**
Tarling St. Est. E1 ... 6J **85**
Tarnbank EN2: Enf ... 5D **22**
Tarnbrook Ct. *SW1 ... 4G* ***17***
(off Whittaker St.)
Tarns, The *NW1 ... 1A* ***6***
(off Varndell St.)
Tarn St. SE1 ... 3C **102**
Tarnwood Pk. SE9 ... 7D **124**
Tarplett Ho. *SE14 ... 6K* ***103***
(off John Williams Cl.)
Tarquin Ho. *SE26 ... 4G* ***139***
(off High Level Dr.)
Tarragon Cl. SE14 ... 7A **104**
Tarragon Gro. SE26 ... 6K **139**
Tarranbrae NW6 ... 7G **63**
Tarrant Ho. *E2 ... 3J* ***85***
(off Roman Rd.)
W14 ... 3G ***99***
(off Russell Rd.)
Tarrant Pl. W1 ... 6E **4** (5D **82**)
Tarrington Cl. SW16 ... 3H **137**
Tartan Ho. *E14 ... 6E* ***86***
(off Dee St.)
Tarver Rd. SE17 ... 5B **102**
Tarves Way SE10 ... 7D **104**
Tash Pl. N11 ... 5A **32**
Tasker Cl. UB3: Harl ... 7E **92**
Tasker Ho. *E14 ... 5B* ***86***
(off Wallwood St.)
IG11: Bark ... 2H **89**
Tasker Rd. NW3 ... 5D **64**
Tasman Ct. *E14 ... 4D* ***104***
(off Westferry Rd.)
TW16: Sun ... 7G **129**
Tasman Ho. *E1 ... 1H* ***103***
(off Clegg St.)
Tasmania Ter. N18 ... 6H **33**
Tasman Rd. SW9 ... 3J **119**
Tasman Wlk. E16 ... 6B **88**
Tasso Rd. W6 ... 6G **99**
Tasso Yd. *W6 ... 6G* ***99***
(off Tasso Rd.)
Tatam Rd. NW10 ... 7K **61**
Tatchbury Ho. *SW15 ... 6B* ***116***
(off Tunworth Cres.)
Tate Britain ... **4E 18 (4J 101)**
Tate Ho. *E2 ... 2K* ***85***
(off Mace St.)
Tate Modern ... **4B 14 (1B 102)**
Tate Rd. E16 ... 1D **106**
(not continuous)
SM1: Sutt ... 5J **165**
Tatham Pl. NW8 ... 2B **82**
Tatnell Rd. SE23 ... 6A **122**
Tatsfield Ho. *SE1 ... 7F* ***15***
(off Pardoner St.)
Tattersall Cl. SE9 ... 5C **124**
Tatton Cres. N16 ... 7F **49**
Tatum St. SE17 ... 4D **102**
Tauheed Cl. N4 ... 2C **66**
Taunton Av. SW20 ... 2D **152**
TW3: Houn ... 2G **113**
Taunton Cl. DA7: Bex ... 2K **127**
SM3: Sutt ... 1J **165**
Taunton Dr. EN2: Enf ... 3F **23**
N2 ... 2A **46**
Taunton Ho. *W2 ... 6A* ***82***
(off Hallfield Est.)
Taunton M. NW1 ... 4E **4** (4D **82**)
Taunton Pl. NW1 ... 3E **4** (4D **82**)
Taunton Rd. SE12 ... 5G **123**
UB6: G'frd ... 1F **77**
Taunton Way HA7: Stan ... 2E **42**
Tavern Cl. SM5: Cars ... 7C **154**
Tavern Ct. *SE1 ... 3C* ***102***
(off Falmouth Rd.)
Taverners Cl. W11 ... 1G **99**
Taverners Ct. *E3 ... 3A* ***86***
(off Grove Rd.)
Taverner Sq. N5 ... 4C **66**
Taverners Way E4 ... 1B **36**
Tavern La. SW9 ... 2A **120**
Tavern Quay SE16 ... 4A **104**

Tavistock Av. E17 . . . . .3K 49
  NW7 . . . . .7A 30
  UB6: G'frd .2A 78
Tavistock Cl. N16 . . . . .5E 66
  TW18: Staines 7A 128
Tavistock Ct. CR0: Croy 1D 168
  (off Tavistock Rd.)
  WC1 . . . . .3D 6
  (off Tavistock Sq.)
  WC2 . . . . .2F 13
  (off Tavistock St.)
Tavistock Cres. CR4: Mitc 4J 155
  W11 . . . . .5H 81
  (not continuous)
Tavistock Gdns. IG3: Ilf 4J 71
Tavistock Ga. CR0: Croy 1D 168
Tavistock Gro. CR0: Croy 7D 156
Tavistock Ho. IG8: Ilf 6K 37
  WC1 . . . . .3D 6 (4H 83)
Tavistock M. W11 . . . . .6H 81
Tavistock Pl. N14 . . . . .6A 22
  WC1 . . . . .3E 6 (4J 83)
Tavistock Rd. BR2: Brom 4H 159
  CR0: Croy 1D 168
  DA16: Well 1C 126
  E7 . . . . .4H 69
  E15 . . . . .6H 69
  E18 . . . . .3J 51
  HA8: Edg .1G 43
  N4 . . . . .6D 48
  NW10 . . . . .2B 80
  SM5: Cars 1B 166
  UB7: Yiew .1A 92
  UB10: Ick .5F 57
  W11 . . . . .6H 81
  (not continuous)
Tavistock Sq. WC1 . . . . .3D 6 (4H 83)
Tavistock St. WC2 . . . . .2F 13 (7J 83)
  (not continuous)
Tavistock Ter. N19 . . . . .3H 65
Tavistock Twr. SE16 . . . . .3A 104
Tavistock Wlk.
  SM5: Cars 1B 166
Taviton St. WC1 . . . . .3C 6 (4H 83)
Tavy Bri. SE2 .2C 108
Tavy Cl. SE11 .5K 19
  (not continuous)
Tawney Rd. SE28 . . . . .7B 90
Tawny Cl. TW13: Felt 3J 129
  W13 . . . . .1B 96
Tawny Way SE16 . . . . .4K 103
Tayben Av. TW2: Twick 6J 113
Taybridge Rd. SW11 . . . . .3E 118
Tay Bldgs. SE1 . . . . .7G 15
Tayburn Cl. E14 . . . . .6E 86
Tayfield Cl. UB10: Ick 3F 57
Tayler Ct. NW8 . . . . .1B 82
Taylor Av. TW9: Kew 2H 115
Taylor Cl. BR6: Orp 4K 173
  N17 . . . . .7B 34
  SE8 . . . . .6B 104
  TW3: Houn 1G 113
  TW12: Ham H 5G 131
Taylor Ct. E15 .5E 68
  SE20 . . . . .2J 157
  (off Elmers End Rd.)
Taylor Rd. CR4: Mitc 7C 136
  SM6: Wall .5F 167
Taylors Bldgs. SE18 . . . . .4F 107
Taylors Cl. DA14: Sidc 3K 143
Taylors Ct. TW13: Felt 2J 129
Taylors Grn. W3 . . . . .6A 80
Taylors La. EN5: Barn 1C 20
  NW10 . . . . .6A 62
  SE26 . . . . .4H 139
Taylorsmead NW7 . . . . .5H 29
Taymount Grange SE23 . . . . .2J 139
Taymount Ri. SE23 . . . . .2J 139
Tayport Cl. N1 . . . . .7J 65
Tayside Cl. SE5 . . . . .3D 120
Tayside Dr. HA8: Edg 3C 28
Taywood Rd. UB5: N'olt 4D 76
Teak Cl. SE16 . . . . .1A 104

Tealby Ct. N7 .5K 65
  (off George's Rd.)
Teal Cl. E16 . . . . .5B 88
Teal Ct. E1 . . . . .3K 15
  (off Star Pl.)
  NW10 . . . . .6K 61
  SE8 . . . . .6B 104
  (off Abinger Gro.)
  SM6: Wall .5G 167
Teal Dr. HA6: Nwood 1E 38
Teale St. E2 . . . . .2G 85
Tealing Dr. KT19: Ewe 4K 163
Teal Pl. SM1: Sutt 5H 165
Teal St. SE10 . . . . .3H 105
Teasel Cl. CR0: Croy 1K 169
Teasel Cres. SE28 . . . . .1J 107
Teasel Way E15 . . . . .3G 87
Tea Trade Wharf SE1 . . . . .6K 15
  (off Shad Thames)
Tebworth Rd. N17 . . . . .7A 34
Technology Pk. NW9 . . . . .3A 44
Teck Cl. TW7: Isle 2A 114
Tedder Cl. HA4: Ruis 5J 57
  KT9: Chess 5C 162
  UB10: Uxb 7B 56
Tedder Rd. CR2: Sels 7J 169
TEDDINGTON 5A 132
Teddington Bus. Pk. TW11: Tedd . . .6K 131
  (off Station Rd.)
Teddington Pk. TW11: Tedd 5K 131
Teddington Pk. Rd. TW11: Tedd 4K 131
Teddington Pool & Fitness Cen. . . .5A 132
Ted Hennem Ho. RM10: Dag 3H 73
Ted Roberts Ho. E2 . . . . .2H 85
  (off Parmiter St.)
Tedworth Gdns. SW3 . . . . .6E 16 (5D 100)
Tedworth Sq. SW3 . . . . . . .6E 16 (5D 100)
Tee, The W3 . . . . .6A 80
Tees Av. UB6: G'frd 2J 77
Tees Cl. W7 . . . . .6H 77
  (off Hanway Rd.)
Teesdale Av. TW7: Isle 1A 114
Teesdale Cl. E2 . . . . .2G 85
Teesdale Gdns. SE25 . . . . .2E 156
  TW7: Isle .1A 114
Teesdale Rd. E11 . . . . .6H 51
Teesdale St. E2 . . . . .2H 85
Teesdale Yd. E2 . . . . .2H 85
  (off Teesdale St.)
Teeswater Ct. DA18: Erith 3D 108
Teevan Cl. CR0: Croy 7G 157
Teevan Rd. CR0: Croy 1G 169
Teignmouth Cl. HA8: Edg 2F 43
  SW4 . . . . .4H 119
Teignmouth Gdns. UB6: G'frd 2A 78
Teignmouth Pde. UB6: G'frd 2A 78
Teignmouth Rd. DA16: Well 2C 126
  NW2 . . . . .5F 63
Telcote Way HA4: Ruis 7A 40
Telegraph Hill NW3 . . . . .3K 63
Telegraph La. KT10: Clay 4A 162
Telegraph M. IG3: Ilf 1A 72
Telegraph Pas. SW2 . . . . .7J 119
  (off New Pk. Rd.)
Telegraph Path BR7: Chst 5F 143
Telegraph Pl. E14 . . . . .4D 104
Telegraph Quarters SE10 . . . . .5F 105
  (off Park Row)
Telegraph Rd. SW15 . . . . .7D 116
Telegraph St. EC2 . . . . .7E 8 (6D 84)
Telemann Sq. SE3 . . . . .4K 123
Telephone Pl. W14 . . . . .6H 99
Telfer Cl. W3 . . . . .2J 97
Telfer Ho. EC1 . . . . .2B 8
Telferscot Rd. SW12 . . . . .1H 137
Telford Av. SW2 . . . . .1H 137
Telford Cl. E17 . . . . .7A 50
  SE19 . . . . .6F 139
Telford Dr. KT12: Walt T 7A 148
Telford Ho. SE1 . . . . .3C 102
  (off Tiverton St.)
  W10 . . . . .5G 81
  (off Portobello Rd.)

Telford Rd. N11 . . . . .5B 32
  NW9 . . . . .6C 44
  SE9 . . . . .2H 143
  TW2: Whit 7E 112
  UB1: S'hall 7F 77
  W10 . . . . .5G 81
Telfords Yd. E1 . . . . .7G 85
Telford Ter. SW1 . . . . . . .7A 18 (6G 101)
Telford Way UB4: Yead 5C 76
  W3 . . . . .5A 80
Telham Rd. E6 . . . . .2E 88
Tell Gro. SE22 . . . . .4F 121
Tellson Av. SE18 . . . . .1B 124
Telscombe Cl. BR6: Orp 2J 173
Temair Ho. SE10 . . . . .7D 104
  (off Tarves Way)
Temeraire Pl.
  TW8: Bford 5F 97
Temeraire St. SE16 . . . . .2J 103
Tempelhof Av. NW2 . . . . .7E 44
  NW4 . . . . .7E 44
Temperley Rd. SW12 . . . . .7E 118
Templar Ct. NW8 . . . . .2A 4
  UB10: Uxb 7G 85
Templar Ho. HA2: Harr 2G 59
  NW2 . . . . .6H 63
  RM13: Rain 2K 91
Templar Pl. TW12: Hamp 7E 130
Templars Av. NW11 . . . . .6H 45
Templars Cres. N3 . . . . .2J 45
Templars Dr. HA3: Hrw W 6C 26
Templars Ho. E15 . . . . .5D 68
Templar St. SE5 . . . . .2B 120
Temple Av. CR0: Croy 2B 170
  EC4 . . . . .2K 13 (7A 84)
  N20 . . . . .7G 21
  RM8: Dag .1G 73
Temple Bar 1J 13
Temple Bar Gate 1B 14
  (off Paternoster Sq.)
Temple Chambers EC4 . . . . .2K 13
Temple Cl. E11 . . . . .7G 51
  N3 . . . . .2H 45
  SE28 . . . . .3G 107
Templecombe Rd. E9 . . . . .1J 85
Templecombe Way SM4: Mord 5G 153
Temple Ct. E1 . . . . .5K 85
  (off Rectory Sq.)
  SW8 . . . . .7J 101
  (off Thorncroft St.)
Templecroft TW15: Ashf 6F 129
Temple Dwellings E2 . . . . .2H 85
  (off Temple St.)
TEMPLE FORTUNE 5H 45
Temple Fortune Hill NW11 . . . . .5J 45
Temple Fortune La. NW11 . . . . .6H 45
Temple Fortune Pde. NW11 . . . . .5H 45
Temple Gdns. EC4 . . . . .2J 13
  (off Middle Temple La.)
  N21 . . . . .2G 33
  NW11 . . . . .6H 45
  RM8: Dag .3D 72
Temple Gro. EN2: Enf 2G 23
  NW11 . . . . .6J 45
Temple Hall Ct. E4 . . . . .2A 36
Temple La. EC4 . . . . .1K 13 (6A 84)
Templeman Rd. W7 . . . . .5K 77
Temple Mead Cl.
  HA7: Stan .6G 27
Templemead Cl. W3 . . . . .6A 80
Templemead Ho. E9 . . . . .4A 68
Temple Mill La. E10 . . . . .4D 68
  (not continuous)
  E15 . . . . .4E 68
TEMPLE MILLS 4D 68
Temple Mills E10 . . . . .3E 68
Temple of Mithras (remains) 1E 14
  (off Queen Victoria St.)
Temple Pde.
  EN5: New Bar 7G 21
  (off Netherlands Rd.)
Temple Pk. UB8: Hil 3C 74
Temple Pl. WC2 . . . . .2H 13 (7K 83)

Temple Rd. CR0: Croy 4D 168
  E6 . . . . .1C 88
  N8 . . . . .4K 47
  NW2 . . . . .4E 62
  TW3: Houn 4F 113
  TW9: Rich 2F 115
  W4 . . . . .3J 97
  W5 . . . . .3D 96
Temple Sheen SW14 . . . . .4J 115
Temple Sheen Rd. SW14 . . . . .4H 115
Temple St. E2 .2H 85
Temple Ter. N22 . . . . .2A 48
  (off Vincent Rd.)
Templeton Av. E4 . . . . .4H 35
Templeton Cl. N15 . . . . .6D 48
  N16 . . . . .5E 66
  SE19 . . . . .1D 156
Templeton Ct. EN3: Enf W 1D 24
Templeton Pl. SW5 . . . . .4J 99
Templeton Rd. N15 . . . . .6D 48
Temple Way SM1: Sutt 3B 166
Temple W. M. SE11 . . . . .3B 102
Templewood W13 . . . . .5B 78
Templewood Av. NW3 . . . . .3K 63
Templewood Gdns. NW3 . . . . .3K 63
Templewood Point NW2 . . . . .2H 63
  (off Granville Rd.)
Temple Yd. E2 .2H 85
  (off Temple St.)
Tempo Ho. UB5: N'olt 3B 76
Tempsford Cl. EN2: Enf 4H 23
Tempsford Ct. HA1: Harr 6K 41
Tempus Ct. E18 . . . . .1J 51
Tempus Wharf SE16 . . . . .2G 103
  (off Bermondsey Wall W.)
Temsford Cl. HA2: Harr 2G 41
Tenbury Cl. E7 . . . . .5B 70
Tenbury Ct. SW2 . . . . .1H 137
Tenby Av. HA3: Kent 2B 42
Tenby Cl. N15 . . . . .4F 49
  RM6: Chad H 6E 54
Tenby Ct. E17 .5A 50
Tenby Gdns. UB5: N'olt 6E 58
Tenby Ho. UB3: Harl 3E 92
  W2 . . . . .6A 82
  (off Hallfield Est.)
Tenby Mans. W1 . . . . .5H 5
  (off Nottingham St.)
Tenby Rd. DA16: Well 1D 126
  E17 . . . . .5A 50
  EN3: Pond E 4D 24
  HA8: Edg .1F 43
  RM6: Chad H 6E 54
Tench St. E1 .1H 103
Tenda Rd. SE16 . . . . .4H 103
Tendring Way RM6: Chad H 5C 54
Tenham Av. SW2 . . . . .1H 137
Tenison Ct. W1 . . . . .2A 12 (7G 83)
Tenison Way SE1 . . . . .5H 13 (1K 101)
Tenniel Cl. W2 .7A 82
Tennis Cl. La. KT8: E Mos 3K 149
Tennison Rd. SE25 . . . . .4F 157
Tennis St. SE1 . . . . .6E 14 (2D 102)
Tenniswood Rd. EN1: Enf 1K 23
Tennyson N8 . . . . .3J 47
  (off Boyton Cl.)
Tennyson Av. E11 . . . . .7J 51
  E12 . . . . .7C 70
  KT3: N Mald 5D 152
  NW9 . . . . .3J 43
  TW1: Twick 1K 131
Tennyson Cl. DA16: Well 1J 125
  EN3: Pond E 5E 24
  TW14: Felt 6H 111
Tennyson Ct. SW6 . . . . .1A 118
  (off Imperial Rd.)
Tennyson Ho. DA17: Belv 5F 109
  SE17 . . . . .5C 102
  (off Browning St.)
Tennyson Mans. SW1 . . . . .5J 17
  (off Sutherland St.)
  SW3 . . . . .7C 16
  (off Lordship Pl.)

Tennyson Mans.—Third Av.

Tennyson Mans. *W14* *6H 99*
(off Queen's Club Gdns.)
Tennyson Rd. E10 1D **68**
E15 7G **69**
E17 6B **50**
NW6 1H **81**
NW7 5H **29**
SE20 7K **139**
SW19 6A **136**
TW3: Houn 2G **113**
TW15: Ashf 5A **128**
W7 7K **77**
Tennyson St. SW8 2F **119**
Tensing Ct. TW19: Stanw 1A **128**
Tensing Rd. UB2: S'hall 3E **94**
Tentelow La. UB2: S'hall 5E **94**
Tenterden Cl. NW4 3F **45**
SE9 4D **142**
Tenterden Dr. NW4 3F **45**
Tenterden Gdns. CR0: Croy 7G **157**
NW4 3F **45**
Tenterden Gro. NW4 3F **45**
Tenterden Ho. *SE17* *5E 102*
(off Surrey Gro.)
Tenterden Rd. CR0: Croy 7G **157**
N17 7A **34**
RM8: Dag 2F **73**
Tenterden St. W1 1K **11** (6F **83**)
Tenter Ground E1 6J **9** (5F **85**)
Tenter Pas. *E1* *1K 15*
(off Nth. Tenter St.)
Tent Peg La. BR5: Pet W 5G **161**
Tent St. E1 4H **85**
Tequila Wharf E14 6A **86**
Terborch Way SE22 5E **120**
Teredo St. SE16 3K **103**
Terence Ct. *DA17: Belv* *6F 109*
(off Stream Way)
Terence McMillan Stadium 4A **88**
Terence Messenger Twr. *E10* *2D 68*
(off Alpine Rd.)
Teresa M. E17 4C **50**
Teresa Wlk. N10 5F **47**
Terling Cl. E11 3H **69**
Terling Ho. *W10* *5E 80*
(off Sutton Way)
Terling Rd. RM8: Dag 2G **73**
Terling Wlk. *N1* *1C 84*
(off Popham St.)
Terminal Four Rdbt. TW6: H'row A 6E **110**
Terminal Ho. HA7: Stan 5J **27**
Terminus Pl. SW1 2K **17** (3F **101**)
Terrace, The *E2* *3J 85*
(off Old Ford Rd.)
E4 *3B 36*
(off Newgate St.)
EC4 1K **13**
IG8: Wfd G 6D **36**
N3 2H **45**
NW6 1J **81**
SE8 *4B 104*
(off Longshore)
SE23 7A **122**
SW13 2A **116**
Terrace Av. NW10 4E **80**
Terrace Gdns. SW13 2B **116**
Terrace Hill *CR0: Croy* *3B 168*
(off Hanover St.)
Terrace La. TW10: Rich 6E **114**
Terrace Rd. E9 7J **67**
E13 2J **87**
KT12: Walt T 7J **147**
Terraces, The *NW8* *2B 82*
(off Queen's Ter.)
Terrace Wlk. RM9: Dag 5E **72**
SW11 *7H 17*
(off Albert Bri. Rd.)
Terrano Ho. TW9: Kew 7H **97**
Terrapin Rd. SW17 3F **137**
Terretts Pl. *N1* *7B 66*
(off Upper St.)
Terrick Rd. N22 1J **47**
Terrick St. W12 6D **80**
Terrilands HA5: Pinn 3D **40**
Territorial Ho. SE11 4K **19**
Terront Rd. N15 4C **48**
Tersha St. TW9: Rich 4F **115**
Tessa Sanderson Pl. *SW8* *3F 119*
(off Daley Thompson Way)
Tessa Sanderson Way UB6: G'frd 5H **59**
Testerton Rd. *W11* *7F 81*
(off Hurstway Rd.)
Testerton Wlk. W11 7F **81**
Testwood Ct. W7 7J **77**
Tetbury Pl. N1 1B **84**
Tetcott Rd. SW10 7A **100**
(not continuous)
Tetherdown N10 3E **46**
Tetty Way BR2: Brom 2J **159**
Teversham La. SW8 1J **119**
Teviot Cl. DA16: Well 1B **126**
Teviot Est. E14 5D **86**
Teviot St. E14 4E **86**
Tewkesbury Av. HA5: Pinn 5C **40**
SE23 1H **139**
Tewkesbury Cl. EN4: E Barn 4G **21**
N15 6D **48**
Tewkesbury Gdns. NW9 3H **43**
Tewkesbury Rd. N15 6D **48**
SM5: Cars 1B **166**
W13 1A **96**
Tewkesbury Ter. N11 6B **32**
Tewson Rd. SE18 5J **107**
Teynham Av. EN1: Enf 6J **23**
Teynham Ct. BR3: Beck 3D **158**
Teynham Grn. BR2: Brom 5J **159**
Teynton Ter. N17 1C **48**
Thackeray Av. N17 2G **49**
Thackeray Cl. HA2: Harr 1E **58**
SW19 7F **135**
TW7: Isle 2A **114**
UB8: Hil 6D **74**
Thackeray Ct. *SW3* *5E 16*
(off Elystan Pl.)
W5 *6F 79*
(off Hanger Va. La.)
W14 *3G 99*
(off Blythe Rd.)
Thackeray Dr. RM6: Chad H 7A **54**
Thackeray Ho. WC1 3E **6**
Thackeray Lodge TW14: Bedf 6F **111**
Thackeray M. E8 6G **67**
Thackeray Rd. E6 2B **88**
SW8 2F **119**
Thackeray St. W8 3K **99**
Thackrah Cl. *N2* *2A 46*
(off Sims Gdns.)
Thakeham Cl. SE26 4H **139**
Thalia Cl. SE10 6F **105**
Thame Rd. SE16 2K **103**
Thames Av. RM9: Dag, Rain 4H **91**
SW10 1A **118**
UB6: G'frd 2K **77**
Thames Bank SW14 2J **115**
Thamesbank Pl. SE28 6C **90**
Thames Barrier Ind. Area *SE18* *3B 106*
(off Faraday Way)
Thames Barrier Pk. 2A 106
Thames Barrier Vis. Cen. 3B 106
Thamesbrook SW3 6C **16**
Thames Circ. E14 4C **104**
Thames Cl. TW12: Hamp 2F **149**
Thames Cotts. KT7: T Ditt 6B **150**
Thames Ct. KT8: W Mole 2F **149**
SE15 *7F 103*
(off Daniel Gdns.)
W7 *6J 77*
(off Hanway Rd.)
Thames Cres. W4 7A **98**
THAMES DITTON 6A 150
Thames Ditton Miniature Railway 1A 162
Thames Dr. HA4: Ruis 6E **38**
Thames Exchange Bldg. EC4 3D **14**
Thames Eyot TW1: Twick 1A **132**
Thamesfield Ct. TW17: Shep 7E **146**
Thamesfield M. TW17: Shep 7E **146**
Thamesgate Cl. TW10: Ham 4B **132**
Thames Gateway RM9: Dag 2F **91**
RM13: Rain 2F **91**
Thames Gateway Pk. RM9: Dag 3F **91**
Thames Haven KT6: Surb 5D **150**
Thames Hgts. *SE1* *6J 15*
(off Gainsford St.)
Thameshill Av. RM5: Col R 2J **55**
Thames Ho. *EC4* *2D 14*
(off Up. Thames St.)
KT1: King T *4D 150*
(off Surbiton Rd.)
SW1 *3E 18*
(off Millbank)
Thameside KT8: W Mole 3F **149**
TW11: Tedd 7D **132**
Thameside Cen. TW8: Bford 6F **97**
Thameside Community Nature Reserve 4A 90
Thameside Ind. Est. E16 2B **106**
Thameside Pk. City Farm 3A 90
Thameside Pl. KT1: Ham W 1D **150**
Thameside Wlk. SE28 6A **90**
Thames Lock KT12: Walt T 3A **148**
THAMESMEAD 1B 108
Thames Mead KT12: Walt T 6J **147**
THAMESMEAD CENTRAL 1A 108
THAMESMEAD EAST 2G 109
THAMESMEAD NORTH 6D 90
Thames Mdw. KT8: W Mole 2E **148**
TW17: Shep 7F **147**
THAMESMEAD SOUTH 2D 108
THAMESMEAD SOUTH WEST 2K 107
THAMESMEAD WEST 3G 107
Thamesmere Dr. SE28 7A **90**
Thamesmere Leisure Cen. 7A 90
Thames Pl. SW15 3F **117**
(not continuous)
Thames Point SW6 2A **118**
Thamespoint TW11: Tedd 7D **132**
Thames Quay E14 2D **104**
SW10 *1A 118*
(off Chelsea Harbour)
Thames Reach *W6* *6E 98*
(off Rainville Rd.)
Thames Rd. E16 1B **106**
IG11: Bark 3K **89**
W4 6G **97**
Thames Rd. Ind. Est. E16 2B **106**
Thames Side KT1: King T 1D **150**
KT7: T Ditt 6B **150**
Thames St. KT1: King T 2D **150**
(not continuous)
KT12: Walt T 7H **147**
SE10 6D **104**
TW12: Hamp 1F **149**
TW16: Sun 4J **147**
Thames Va. Cl. TW3: Houn 3E **112**
Thames Valley University
Ealing Campus 1D 96
Spesom House 7C 78
Westel House 7C 78
Thamesview Ho's. KT12: Walt T 6J **147**
Thames Village W4 1J **115**
Thames Wlk. SW11 7C **100**
Thames Wharf Studios *W6* *6E 98*
(off Rainville Rd.)
Thanescroft Gdns. CR0: Croy 3E **168**
Thanet Ct. W3 6G **79**
Thanet Dr. BR2: Kes 3B **172**
Thanet Ho. *CR0: Croy* *4C 168*
(off Coombe Rd.)
WC1 *2E 6*
(off Thanet St.)
Thanet Lodge *NW2* *6G 63*
(off Mapesbury Rd.)
Thanet Pl. CR0: Croy 4C **168**
Thanet Rd. DA5: Bexl 7G **127**
Thanet St. WC1 2E **6** (3J **83**)
Thanet Wharf *SE8* *6D 104*
(off Copperas St.)
Thane Vs. N7 3K **65**
Thane Works N7 3K **65**
Thanington Ct. SE9 6J **125**
Thant Cl. E10 3D **68**
Tharp Rd. SM6: Wall 5H **167**
Thatcham Ct. N20 7F **21**
Thatcham Gdns. N20 7F **21**
Thatcher Cl. UB7: W Dray 2A **92**
Thatchers Way TW7: Isle 5H **113**
Thatches Gro. RM6: Chad H 4E **54**
Thavie's Inn EC4 7K **7** (6A **84**)
Thaxted Ct. *N1* *1F 9*
(off Fairbank Est.)
Thaxted Ho. RM10: Dag 7H **73**
SE16 *4J 103*
(off Abbeyfield Est.)
Thaxted Pl. SW20 7F **135**
Thaxted Rd. IG9: Buck H 1H **37**
SE9 3G **143**
Thaxton Rd. W14 6H **99**
Thayers Farm Rd. BR3: Beck 1A **158**
Thayer St. W1 6H **5** (6E **82**)
Theatre Mus. 2F 13
Theatrerites 2K 135
Theatre Royal
Stratford 7F 69
The . . . . .
Names prefixed with 'The' for example 'The Acacias' are indexed under the main name such as 'Acacias, The'
Theatre Sq. E15 6F **69**
Theatre St. SW11 3D **118**
Theatro Technis *1G 83*
(off Crowndale Rd.)
Theberton St. N1 1A **84**
Theed St. SE1 5K **13** (1A **102**)
Thelma Gdns. SE3 1B **124**
Thelma Gro. TW11: Tedd 6A **132**
Theobald Cres. HA3: Hrw W 1G **41**
Theobald Rd. CR0: Croy 2B **168**
E17 7B **50**
Theobalds Av. N12 4F **31**
Theobalds Ct. N4 3C **66**
Theobald's Rd. WC1 5G **7** (5K **83**)
Theobald St. SE1 3D **102**
Theodora Way HA5: Eastc 3H **39**
Theodore Ct. SE13 6F **123**
Theodore Rd. SE13 6F **123**
Therapia La. CR0: Bedd 7H **155**
CR0: Croy 6J **155**
Therapia Rd. SE22 6J **121**
Theresa Rd. W6 4C **98**
Therfield Ct. N4 2C **66**
Thermopylae Ga. E14 4D **104**
Theseus Wlk. N1 1B **8** (2B **84**)
Thesiger Rd. SE20 7K **139**
Thessaly Ho. *SW8* *7G 101*
(off Thessaly Rd.)
Thessaly Rd. SW8 7G **101**
(not continuous)
Thesus Ho. *E14* *6E 86*
(off Blair St.)
Thetford Cl. N13 6G **33**
Thetford Gdns. RM9: Dag 7E **72**
Thetford Ho. *SE1* *7J 15*
(off Maltby St.)
Thetford Rd. KT3: N Mald 6K **151**
RM9: Dag 7D **72**
TW15: Ashf 4A **128**
Thetis Ter. TW9: Kew 6G **97**
Theydon Gro. IG8: Wfd G 6F **37**
Theydon Rd. E5 2J **67**
Theydon St. E17 7B **50**
Thicket, The UB7: Yiew 6A **74**
Thicket Cres. SM1: Sutt 4A **166**
Thicket Gro. RM9: Dag 6C **72**
SE20 7G **139**
Thicket Rd. SE20 7G **139**
SM1: Sutt 4A **166**
Third Av. E12 4C **70**
E13 3J **87**
E17 5C **50**
EN1: Enf 5A **24**
HA9: Wemb 2D **60**
RM6: Chad H 6C **54**

Third Av. RM10: Dag 1H 91
UB3: Hayes 1H 93
W3 1B 98
W10 3G 81
Third Cl. KT8: W Mole 4G 149
Third Cross Rd. TW2: Twick 2H 131
Third Way HA9: Wemb 4H 61
Thirleby Rd. HA8: Edg 1K 43
SW1 2B 18 (3G 101)
Thirlestane Ct. N10 2E 46
Thirlmere NW1 1K 5
(off Cumberland Mkt.)
Thirlmere Av. UB6: G'frd 3C 78
Thirlmere Gdns. HA9: Wemb 1C 60
Thirlmere Ho. N16 4D 66
(off Howard Rd.)
Thirlmere Ri. BR1: Brom 6H 141
Thirlmere Rd. DA7: Bex 1J 127
N10 1F 47
SW16 4H 137
Thirsk Cl. UB5: N'olt 6E 58
Thirsk Rd. CR4: Mitc 7E 136
SE25 4D 156
SW11 3E 118
Thirza Ho. E1 6J 85
(off Devonport St.)
Thistlebrook SE2 3C 108
Thistlebrook Ind. Est. SE2 3C 108
Thistlecroft Gdns. HA7: Stan 1D 42
Thistledene KT7: T Ditt 6J 149
Thistledene Av. HA2: Harr 3C 58
Thistlefield Cl. DA5: Bexl 1D 144
Thistle Gro. SW10 5A 100
Thistle Ho. E14 6E 86
(off Dee St.)
Thistlemead BR7: Chst 2F 161
Thistlewaite Rd. E5 3H 67
Thistlewood Cl. N7 2K 65
Thistleworth Cl. TW7: Isle 7H 95
Thistleworth Marina TW7: Isle 4B 114
(off Railshead Rd.)
Thistley Cl. N12 6H 31
Thistley Ct. SE8 6D 104
Thomas A'Beckett Cl. HA0: Wemb 4K 59
Thomas Baines Rd. SW11 3B 118
Thomas Burt Ho. E2 3H 85
(off Canrobert St.)
Thomas Cribb M. E6 6E 88
Thomas Darby Ct. W11 6G 81
(off Lancaster Rd.)
Thomas Dean Rd. SE26 4B 140
Thomas Dinwiddy Rd. SE12 2K 141
Thomas Doyle St. SE1 7A 14 (3B 102)
Thomas England Ho. RM7: Rom 6K 55
(off Waterloo Gdns.)
Thomas Hardy Ho. N22 7E 32
Thomas Hewlett Ho. HA1: Harr 4J 59
Thomas Hollywood Ho. E2 2J 85
(off Approach Rd.)
Thomas Ho. SM2: Sutt 7K 165
Thomas La. SE6 7C 122
Thomas Lodge E17 5D 50
Thomas More Highwalk EC2 6C 8
(off Beech St.)
Thomas More Ho. EC2 6C 8
HA4: Ruis 1G 57
Thomas More Sq. E1 7G 85
(off Thomas More St.)
Thomas More St. E1 3K 15 (7G 85)
Thomas More Way N2 3A 46
Thomas Neal's Shop. Mall
WC2 1E 12 (6J 83)
Thomas Nth. Ter. E16 5H 87
(off Barking Rd.)
Thomas Pl. W8 3K 99
Thomas Rd. E14 6B 86
Thomas Rd. Ind. Est. E14 5C 86
Thomas Spencer Hall of Residence. 4E 106
(off Grand Depot Rd.)
Thomas St. SE18 4F 107
Thomas Turner Path CR0: Croy 2C 168
(off George St.)
Thomas Wall Cl. SM1: Sutt 5K 165
Thomas Watson Cott. Homes
EN5: Barn 4B 20
(off Leecroft Rd.)
Thompson Av. TW9: Rich 3G 115
Thompson Cl. IG1: Ilf 2G 71
SM3: Sutt 1J 165
Thompson Ho. SE14 6K 103
(off John Williams Cl.)
W10 4G 81
(off Wornington Rd.)
Thompson Rd. RM9: Dag 3F 73
SE22 6F 121
TW3: Houn 4F 113
UB10: Uxb 1A 74
Thompson's Av. SE5 7C 102
Thomson Cres. CR0: Croy 1A 168
Thomson Ho. E14 6C 86
(off Saracen St.)
SE17 4E 102
(off Tatum St.)
SW1 6D 18
UB1: S'hall 7C 76
(off The Broadway)
Thomson Rd. HA3: W'stone 3J 41
Thorburn Ho. SW1 7F 11
(off Kinnerton St.)
Thorburn Sq. SE1 4G 103
Thorburn Way SW19 1B 154
Thoresby St. N1 1D 8 (3C 84)
Thorkhill Gdns. KT7: T Ditt 1A 162
Thorkhill Rd. KT7: T Ditt 1A 162
Thornaby Gdns. N18 6B 34
Thornaby Ho. E2 3H 85
(off Canrobert St.)
Thorn Av. WD23: Bushy 1B 26
Thornbill Ho. SE15 7G 103
(off Bird in Bush Rd.)
Thornbury NW4 4D 44
(off Prince of Wales Cl.)
Thornbury Av. TW7: Isle 7H 95
Thornbury Cl. N16 5E 66
NW7 7A 30
Thornbury Ct. CR2: S Croy 5D 168
(off Blunt Rd.)
TW7: Isle 7J 95
W11 7J 81
(off Chepstow Vs.)
Thornbury Lodge EN2: Enf 3G 23
Thornbury Rd. SW2 6J 119
TW7: Isle 7H 95
Thornbury Sq. N6 1G 65
Thornby Rd. E5 3J 67
Thorncliffe Rd. SW2 6J 119
UB2: S'hall 5D 94
Thorn Cl. BR2: Brom 6E 160
UB5: N'olt 3D 76
Thorncombe Rd. SE22 5E 120
Thorncroft Rd. SM1: Sutt 5K 165
Thorncroft St. SW8 7J 101
Thorndean St. SW18 2A 136
Thorndene SE28 7B 90
Thorndene Av. N11 1K 31
Thorndike Av. UB5: N'olt 1B 76
Thorndike Cl. SW10 7A 100
Thorndike Ho. SW1 5C 18
(off Vauxhall Bri. Rd.)
Thorndike St. SW1 4C 18 (4H 101)
Thorndon Cl. BR5: St P 2K 161
Thorndon Gdns. KT19: Ewe 5A 164
Thorndon Rd. BR5: St P 2K 161
Thorne Cl. DA8: Erith 6H 109
E11 4F 69
E16 6J 87
KT10: Clay 7A 162
TW15: Ashf 7E 128
Thorne Ho. E2 3J 85
(off Roman Rd.)
E14 3E 104
(off Launch St.)
KT10: Clay 7A 162
Thorneloe Gdns. CR0: Wadd 5A 168
Thorne Pas. SW13 2A 116
Thorne Rd. SW8 7J 101
Thornes Cl. BR3: Beck 3E 158
Thorne St. SW13 3A 116
Thornet Wood Rd. BR1: Brom 3E 160
Thornewill Ho. E1 7J 85
(off Cable St.)
Thorney Ct. W8 2A 100
(off Palace Ga.)
Thorney Cres. SW11 7B 100
Thorneycroft Cl. KT12: Walt T 6A 148
Thorney Hedge Rd. W4 4H 97
Thorney St. SW1 3E 18 (4J 101)
Thornfield Av. NW7 1G 45
Thornfield Ct. NW7 1G 45
Thornfield Ho. E14 7C 86
(off Rosefield Gdns.)
Thornfield Pde. NW7 7B 30
(off Holders Hill Rd.)
Thornfield Rd. W12 2D 98
(not continuous)
Thornford Rd. SE13 5E 122
Thorngate Rd. W9 4J 81
Thorngrove Rd. E13 1K 87
Thornham Gro. E15 5F 69
Thornham Ind. Est. E15 6F 69
Thornham St. SE10 6D 104
Thornhaugh M. WC1 4D 6 (4H 83)
Thornhaugh St. WC1 4D 6 (4H 83)
Thornhill Av. KT6: Surb 2E 162
SE18 7J 107
Thornhill Bri. Wharf N1 1K 83
Thornhill Cres. N1 7K 65
Thornhill Gdns. E10 2D 68
IG11: Bark 7J 71
Thornhill Gro. N1 7K 65
Thornhill Ho. W4 5A 98
(off Wood St.)
Thornhill Ho's. N1 7A 66
Thornhill M. SW15 4H 117
Thornhill Rd. CR0: Croy 7C 156
E10 2D 68
KT6: Surb 2E 162
N1 7A 66
UB10: Ick 4B 56
Thornhill Sq. N1 7K 65
Thornhill Way TW17: Shep 5C 146
Thornicroft Ho. SW9 2K 119
(off Stockwell Rd.)
Thornlaw Rd. SE27 4A 138
Thornley Cl. N17 7B 34
Thornley Dr. HA2: Harr 2F 59
Thornley Pl. SE10 5G 105
Thornsbeach Rd. SE6 1E 140
Thornsett Pl. SE20 2H 157
Thornsett Rd. SE20 2H 157
SW18 1K 135
Thornsett Ter. SE20 2H 157
(off Croydon Rd.)
Thorn Ter. SE15 3J 121
Thornton Av. CR0: Croy 6K 155
SW2 1H 137
UB7: W Dray 3B 92
W4 4A 98
Thornton Cl. UB7: W Dray 3B 92
Thornton Dene BR3: Beck 2C 158
Thornton Gdns. SW12 1H 137
THORNTON HEATH 4C 156
THORNTON HEATH POND 5A 156
Thornton Hill SW19 7G 135
Thornton Ho. SE17 4E 102
(off Townsend St.)
Thornton Pl. W1 5E 4 (5D 82)
Thornton Rd. BR1: Brom 5J 141
CR0: Croy 7K 155
CR7: Thor H 7K 155
DA17: Belv 4H 109
E11 2F 69
EN5: Barn 3B 20
IG1: Ilf 4F 71
N18 3D 34
SM5: Cars 1B 166
SW12 7H 119
SW14 4K 115
SW19 6F 135
Thornton Rd. E. SW19 6F 135
Thornton Rd. Ind. Est. CR0: Croy 6K 155
Thornton Row CR7: Thor H 5A 156
Thornton's Farm Av. RM7: Rush G 1J 73
Thornton St. SW9 2A 120
Thornton Way NW11 5K 45
Thorntree Ct. W5 5E 78
Thorntree Rd. SE7 5B 106
Thornville Gro. CR4: Mitc 2B 154
Thornville St. SE8 1C 122
Thornwell Ct. W7 2J 95
(off Du Burstow Ter.)
Thornwood Cl. E18 2K 51
Thornwood Ho. IG9: Buck H 1H 37
Thornwood Rd. SE13 5G 123
Thornycroft Ho. W4 5A 98
(off Fraser St.)
Thorogood Gdns. E15 5G 69
Thorogood Way RM13: Rain 1K 91
Thorold Ho. SE1 6C 14
(off Pepper St.)
Thorold Rd. IG1: Ilf 2F 71
N22 7D 32
Thorparch Rd. SW8 1H 119
Thorpebank Rd. W12 1C 98
Thorpe Cl. BR6: Orp 2J 173
SE26 4K 139
W10 6G 81
Thorpe Ct. EN2: Enf 3G 23
Thorpe Cres. E17 2B 50
Thorpedale Gdns. IG2: Ilf 4E 52
IG6: Ilf 4E 52
Thorpedale Rd. N4 2J 65
Thorpe Hall Rd. E17 1E 50
Thorpe Ho. N1 1K 83
(off Barnsbury Est.)
Thorpe Rd. E6 1D 88
E7 4H 69
E17 2E 50
IG11: Bark 7H 71
KT2: King T 7E 132
N15 6E 48
Thorpewood Av. SE26 2H 139
Thorpland Av. UB10: Ick 3E 56
Thorsden Way SE19 5E 138
Thorverton Rd. NW2 3G 63
Thoydon Rd. E3 2A 86
Thrale Rd. SW16 4G 137
Thrale St. SE1 5D 14 (1C 102)
Thrasher Cl. E8 1F 85
Thrawl St. E1 6K 9 (5F 85)
Thrayle Ho. SW9 3K 119
(off Benedict Rd.)
Threadgold Ho. N1 6D 66
(off Dovercourt Est.)
Threadneedle St. EC2 1F 15 (6D 84)
Three Barrels Wlk. EC4 3D 14
(off Queen St. Pl.)
Three Bridges Bus. Cen. UB2: S'hall 2G 95
Three Colt Cnr. E2 3K 9
Three Colts La. E2 4H 85
Three Colt St. E14 6B 86
Three Corners DA7: Bex 2H 127
Three Cranes Wlk. EC4 3D 14
Three Cups Yd. WC1 6H 7
Three Kings Yd. W1 2J 11 (7F 83)
Three Mdws. M. HA3: Stan 1K 41
Three Mill La. E3 3E 86
(not continuous)
Three Mills 3E 86
Three Oak La. SE1 6J 15 (2F 103)
Three Oaks Cl. UB10: Ick 3B 56
Three Quays EC3 3H 15
Three Quays Wlk. EC3 3H 15 (7E 84)
Threshers Pl. W11 7G 81
Thriffwood SE26 3J 139
Thrigby Rd. KT9: Chess 6F 163
Thring Ho. SW9 2K 119
(off Stockwell Rd.)
Throckmorten Rd. E16 6K 87
Throgmorton Av. EC2 7F 9 (6D 84)
(not continuous)
Throgmorton St. EC2 7F 9 (6D 84)

Throwley Cl.—Tolhurst Dr.

Throwley Cl. SE2 3C **108**
(not continuous)
Throwley Rd. SM1: Sutt 5K **165**
Throwley Way SM1: Sutt 4K **165**
Thrupp Cl. CR4: Mitc 2F **155**
Thrush Grn. HA2: Harr 4E **40**
Thrush St. SE17 5C **102**
Thurbarn Rd. SE6 5D **140**
Thurland Ho. *SE16 4H 103*
(off Camilla Rd.)
Thurland Rd. SE16 3G **103**
Thurlby Cl. HA1: Harr 6A **42**
 IG8: Wfd G 5J **37**
Thurlby Cft. *NW4 3E 44*
(off Mulberry Cl.)
Thurlby Rd. HA0: Wemb 6D **60**
 SE27 4A **138**
Thurleigh Av. SW12 6E **118**
Thurleigh Ct. SW12 6E **118**
Thurleigh Rd. SW12 7D **118**
Thurleston Av. SM4: Mord 5G **153**
Thurlestone Av. IG3: Bark, Ilf 4K **71**
 N12 6J **31**
Thurlestone Cl. TW17: Shep 6E **146**
Thurlestone Ct. *UB1: S'hall 6F 77*
(off Howard Rd.)
Thurlestone Pde. *TW17: Shep 6E 146*
(off High St.)
Thurlestone Rd. SE27 3A **138**
Thurloe Cl. SW7 3C **16** (4C **100**)
Thurloe Ct. *SW3 4C 16*
(off Fulham Ct.)
Thurloe Pl. SW7 3B **16** (4B **100**)
Thurloe Pl. M. SW7 3B **16**
Thurloe Sq. SW7 3C **16** (4C **100**)
Thurloe St. SW7 3B **16** (4B **100**)
Thurlow Cl. E4 6K **35**
Thurlow Gdns. HA0: Wemb 5D **60**
Thurlow Hill SE21 1C **138**
Thurlow Ho. SW16 3J **137**
Thurlow Pk. Rd. SE21 2B **138**
Thurlow Rd. NW3 5B **64**
 W7 2A **96**
Thurlow St. SE17 5D **102**
(not continuous)
Thurlow Ter. NW5 5E **64**
Thurlow Wlk. SE17 5E **102**
(not continuous)
Thurlstone Rd. HA4: Ruis 3J **57**
Thurnby Ct. TW2: Twick 3J **131**
Thurnscoe *NW1 1G 83*
(off Pratt St.)
Thursland Rd. DA14: Sidc 5E **144**
Thursley Cres. CR0: New Ad 7E **170**
Thursley Gdns. SW19 2F **135**
Thursley Ho. *SW2 7K 119*
(off Holmewood Gdns.)
Thursley Rd. SE9 3D **142**
Thurso Ho. NW6 2K **81**
Thurso St. SW17 4B **136**
Thurstan Dwellings *WC2 7F 7*
(off Newton St.)
Thurstan Rd. SW20 7D **134**
Thurston Ho. BR3: Beck 6D **140**
Thurston Ind. Est. SE13 3D **122**
Thurston Rd. SE13 2D **122**
 UB1: S'hall 6D **76**
Thurtle Rd. E2 2F **85**
Thwaite Cl. DA8: Erith 6J **109**
Thyer Cl. BR6: Farnb 4G **173**
Thyme Cl. SE3 3A **124**
Thyme Ct. NW7 1G **45**
Thyra Gro. N12 6E **30**
Tibbatt's Rd. E3 4D **86**
Tibbenham Pl. SE6 2C **140**
Tibbenham Wlk. E13 2H **87**
Tibberton Sq. N1 1C **84**
Tibbet's Cl. SW19 1F **135**
TIBBET'S CORNER 7F **117**
Tibbet's Ride SW15 7F **117**
Tiber Gdns. N1 1J **83**
Ticehurst Cl. BR5: St P 7A **144**
Ticehurst Rd. SE23 2A **140**
Tickford Cl. SE2 2C **108**
Tickford Ho. NW8 2C **4** (3C **82**)
Tidal Basin Rd. E16 7H **87**
(not continuous)
Tidbury Ct. *SW8 7G 101*
(off Stewart's Rd.)
Tideham Ho. SE28 1H **107**
Tidelea Twr. SE28 2G **107**
Tidenham Gdns.
 CR0: Croy 3E **168**
Tideside Ct. SE18 3C **106**
Tideslea Path SE28 1H **107**
Tideswell Rd. CR0: Croy 3C **170**
 SW15 4E **116**
Tideway Cl. TW10: Ham 4B **132**
Tideway Ct. SE16 1K **103**
Tideway Ho. *E14 2C 104*
(off Strafford St.)
Tideway Ind. Est. SW8 6G **101**
Tideway Wlk. SW8 7B **18** (6G **101**)
Tidey St. E3 5C **86**
Tidford Rd. DA16: Well 2K **125**
Tidlock Ho. SE28 2H **107**
Tidworth Rd. E3 4C **86**
Tiepigs La. BR2: Hayes 2G **171**
 BR4: W W'ck 2G **171**
Tierney Ct. CR0: Croy 2E **168**
Tierney Rd. SW2 1J **137**
Tiffany Hgts. SW18 7J **117**
Tiffin School Sports Hall 2F **151**
Tiger Ho. *WC1 2D 6*
(off Burton St.)
Tiger La. BR2: Brom 4K **159**
Tiger Way E5 4H **67**
Tigris Cl. N9 2D **34**
Tilbrook Rd. SE3 3A **124**
Tilbury Cl. SE15 7F **103**
Tilbury Ho. *SE14 6K 103*
(off Myers La.)
Tilbury Rd. E6 2D **88**
 E10 7E **50**
Tildesley Rd. SW15 6E **116**
Tile Farm Rd. BR6: Orp 3H **173**
Tilehurst NW1 2K **5**
Tilehurst Point SE2 2D **108**
(Blewbury Ho.)
 SE2 2C **108**
(Tavy Bri.)
Tilehurst Rd. SM3: Cheam 5G **165**
 SW18 1B **136**
Tile Kiln La. DA5: Bexl 2J **145**
 N6 1F **65**
 N13 5H **33**
(not continuous)
 UB9: Hare 7D **38**
Tile Kiln Studios N6 7G **47**
Tile Yd. E14 6B **86**
Tileyard Rd. N7 7J **65**
Tilford Av. CR0: New Ad 7E **170**
Tilford Gdns. SW19 1F **135**
Tilford Ho. *SW2 7K 119*
(off Holmewood Gdns.)
Tilia Cl. SM1: Sutt 5H **165**
Tilia Rd. E5 4H **67**
Tilia Wlk. SW9 4B **120**
Tilleard Ho. *W10 3G 81*
(off Herries St.)
Tiller Leisure Cen., The 3C **104**
Tiller Rd. E14 3C **104**
Tillett Cl. NW10 6J **61**
Tillett Sq. SE16 2A **104**
Tillet Way E2 3G **85**
Tilley Rd. TW13: Felt 1J **129**
Tillingbourne Gdns. N3 3H **45**
Tillingbourne Grn.
 BR5: St M Cry 4K **161** & 5K **161**
Tillingbourne Way N3 4H **45**
Tillingham Way N12 4D **30**
Tilling Rd. NW2 1E **62**
Tillings Cl. SE5 1C **120**
Tilling Way HA9: Wemb 2D **60**
Tillman St. E1 6H **85**
Tilloch St. N1 7K **65**
Tillotson Ct. *SW8 7H 101*
(off Wandsworth Rd.)
Tillotson Rd. HA3: Hrw W 7A **26**
 IG1: Ilf 7E **52**
 N9 2A **34**
Tilney Ct. EC1 3D **8** (4C **84**)
 IG9: Buck H 2D **36**
Tilney Dr. IG9: Buck H 2D **36**
Tilney Gdns. N1 6D **66**
Tilney Rd. RM9: Dag 6F **73**
(not continuous)
 UB2: S'hall 4A **94**
Tilney St. W1 4H **11** (1E **100**)
Tilson Cl. SE5 7E **102**
Tilson Gdns. SW2 7J **119**
Tilson Ho. SW2 7J **119**
Tilson Rd. N17 1G **49**
Tilston Cl. E11 3H **69**
Tilton St. SW6 6G **99**
Tiltwood, The W3 7J **79**
Tilt Yd. App. SE9 6D **124**
Timber Cl. BR7: Chst 2E **160**
Timbercroft KT19: Ewe 4A **164**
Timbercroft La. SE18 6J **107**
Timberdene NW4 2F **45**
Timberdene Av. IG6: Ilf 1G **53**
Timberland Cl. SE15 7G **103**
Timberland Rd. E1 6H **85**
Timber Mill Way SW4 3H **119**
Timber Pond Rd. SE16 1K **103**
Timbers, The SM3: Cheam 6G **165**
Timberslip Dr. SM6: Wall 7H **167**
Timber St. EC1 3C **8** (4C **84**)
Timberwharf Rd. N16 6G **49**
Timber Wharves Est. *E14 4C 104*
(off Charnwood Gdns.)
 E14 4C 104
(off Copeland Dr.)
Timbrell Pl. SE16 1B **104**
Time Sq. E8 5F **67**
Times Sq. SM1: Sutt 5K **165**
Timor Ho. *E1 4A 86*
(off Duckett St.)
Timothy Cl. DA6: Bex 5E **126**
 SW4 5G **119**
Timothy Ho. *DA18: Erith 2E 108*
(off Kale Rd.)
Timothy Pl. KT8: W Mole 5D **148**
Timothy Rd. E3 5B **86**
Timperley Ct. SW19 1G **135**
Timsbury Wlk. SW15 1C **134**
Tina Ct. SE6 7B **122**
Tindal St. SW9 1B **120**
Tinderbox All. SW14 3K **115**
Tinniswood Cl. N5 5A **66**
Tinsley Cl. SE25 3H **157**
Tinsley Rd. E1 5J **85**
Tintagel Cres. SE22 4F **121**
Tintagel Dr. HA7: Stan 4J **27**
Tintagel Gdns. SE22 4F **121**
Tintangel Ct. *EC1 3A 8*
(off St John St.)
Tintern Av. NW9 3H **43**
Tintern Cl. SW15 5G **117**
 SW19 6A **136**
Tintern Ct. W13 7A **78**
Tintern Gdns. N14 7D **22**
Tintern Ho. *NW1 1K 5*
(off Augustus St.)
 SW1 4J 17
(off Abbots Mnr.)
Tintern Path *NW9 6A 44*
(off Fryent Gro.)
Tintern Rd. N22 1C **48**
 SM5: Cars 1B **166**
Tintern St. SW4 4J **119**
Tintern Way HA2: Harr 1F **59**
Tinto Rd. E16 4J **87**
Tinworth St. SE11 5F **19** (5J **101**)
Tippett Ct. E6 2D **88**
Tippetts Cl. EN2: Enf 1H **23**
Tipthorpe Rd. SW11 3E **118**
Tipton Dr. CR0: Croy 4E **168**
Tiptree *NW1 7F 65*
(off Castlehaven Rd.)
Tiptree Cl. E4 3K **35**
Tiptree Cres. IG5: Ilf 2E **52**
Tiptree Dr. EN2: Enf 4J **23**
Tiptree Rd. HA4: Ruis 4K **57**
Tirlemont Rd. CR2: S Croy 7C **168**
Tirrell Rd. CR0: Croy 6C **156**
Tisbury Ct. W1 2C **12**
Tisbury Rd. SW16 2J **155**
Tisdall Ho. *SE17 4D 102*
(off Catesby St.)
Tisdall Pl. SE17 4D **102**
Tissington Ct. SE16 4J **103**
Titan Bus. Est. *SE8 7C 104*
(off Ffinch St.)
Titan Ct. TW8: Bford 5F **97**
Titchborne Row W2 1D **10** (6C **82**)
Titchfield Rd. NW8 1C **82**
 SM5: Cars 1B **166**
Titchfield Wlk. SM5: Cars 7B **154**
Titchwell Rd. SW18 1B **136**
Tite St. SW3 6E **16** (5D **100**)
Tithe Barn Cl. KT2: King T 1F **151**
Tithe Barn Way UB5: Yead 2K **75**
Tithe Cl. KT12: Walt T 6K **147**
 NW7 1C **44**
 UB4: Hayes 5H **75**
Tithe Farm Av. HA2: Harr 3E **58**
Tithe Farm Cl. HA2: Harr 3E **58**
Tithe Wlk. NW7 1C **44**
Titian Av. WD23: Bushy 1D **26**
Titley Cl. E4 5H **35**
Titmus Cl. UB8: Hil 6E **74**
Titmuss Av. SE28 7B **90**
Titmuss St. W12 2E **98**
Tivendale N8 3J **47**
Tiverton Av. IG5: Ilf 3E **52**
Tiverton Cl. CR0: Croy 7F **157**
Tiverton Dr. SE9 1G **143**
Tiverton Ho. EN3: Enf H 3E **24**
Tiverton Rd. HA0: Wemb 2E **78**
 HA4: Ruis 3J **57**
 HA8: Edg 2F **43**
 N15 6D **48**
 N18 5K **33**
 NW10 1F **81**
 TW3: Houn 2G **113**
Tiverton St. SE1 3C **102**
Tiverton Way KT9: Chess 5D **162**
 NW7 7A **30**
Tivoli Ct. SE16 1B **104**
Tivoli Gdns. SE18 4C **106**
(not continuous)
Tivoli Rd. N8 5H **47**
 SE27 5C **138**
 TW4: Houn 4C **112**
Toad La. TW4: Houn 4D **112**
Tobacco Dock E1 7H **85**
Tobacco Quay E1 7H **85**
Tobago St. E14 2C **104**
Tobin Cl. NW3 7C **64**
Toby Ct. *N9 7D 24*
(off Tramway Av.)
Toby La. E1 4A **86**
Toby Way KT5: Surb 2H **163**
Todber Ho. *W14 3G 99*
(off Russell Rd.)
Todd Ho. *N2 2B 46*
(off The Grange)
Todds Wlk. N7 2K **65**
Todhunter Ter. EN5: New Bar 4D **20**
Tokenhouse Yd. EC2 7E **8** (6D **84**)
Token Yd. SW15 4G **117**
TOKYNGTON 6H 61
Tokyngton Av. HA9: Wemb 6G **61**
Toland Sq. SW15 5C **116**
Tolcairn Ct. DA17: Belv 5G **109**
Tolcarne Dr. HA5: Eastc 2J **39**
Tolchurch *W11 6H 81*
(off Dartmouth Cl.)
Toley Av. HA9: Wemb 7E **42**
Tolhurst Dr. W10 3G **81**

Tollard Ho. W14 .... 3H 99
Toll Bar Ct. SM2: Sutt 7K 165
Tollbridge Cl. W10 .... 4G 81
Tollesbury Gdns. IG6: Ilf 3H 53
Tollet St. E1 .... 4K 85
Tollgate Dr. SE21 .... 2E 138
UB4: Yead 7B 76
Tollgate Gdns. NW6 .... 2K 81
Tollgate Ho. NW6 .... 2K 81
(off Tollgate Gdns.)
Tollgate Rd. E6 .... 5A 88
E16 .... 5A 88
Tollgate Sq. E6 .... 5D 88
Tollhouse Way N19 .... 2G 65
Tollington Pk. N4 .... 2K 65
Tollington Pl. N4 .... 2K 65
Tollington Rd. N7 .... 4K 65
Tollington Way N7 .... 3J 65
Tolmers Sq. NW1 .... 3B 6 (4G 83)
(not continuous)
Tolpaide Ho. SE11 .... 4J 19
Tolpuddle Av. E13 .... 1A 88
(off Queens Rd.)
Tolpuddle St. N1 .... 2A 84
Tolsford Rd. E5 .... 5H 67
Tolson Rd. TW7: Isle 3A 114
Tolverne Rd. SW20 .... 1E 152
TOLWORTH 2H 163
Tolworth B'way. KT6: Surb 1H 163
Tolworth Cl. KT6: Surb 1H 163
Tolworth Gdns. RM6: Chad H 5D 54
TOLWORTH JUNC. (TOBY JUG) 2H 163
Tolworth Pde. RM6: Chad H 5E 54
Tolworth Pk. Rd. KT6: Surb 2F 163
Tolworth Recreation Cen. 3F 163
Tolworth Ri. Nth. KT5: Surb 1H 163
Tolworth Ri. Sth. KT5: Surb 2H 163
Tolworth Rd. KT6: Surb 2E 162
Tolworth Twr. KT6: Surb 2H 163
Tomahawk Gdns. UB5: N'olt 3B 76
Tom Allen Arts Cen. 6F 69
Tom Blau Gallery 6J 15
(off Queen Elizabeth St.)
Tom Coombs Cl. SE9 .... 4C 124
Tom Cribb Rd. SE28 .... 3G 107
Tom Groves Cl. E15 .... 5F 69
Tom Hood Cl. E15 .... 5F 69
Tom Jenkinson Rd. E16 .... 1J 105
Tomkyns Ho. SE11 .... 3J 19
Tomline Ho. SE1 .... 5C 14
(off Pepper St.)
Tomlins All. TW1: Twick 1A 132
Tomlin's Gro. E3 .... 3C 86
Tomlinson Cl. E2 .... 2K 9 (3F 85)
W4 .... 5H 97
Tomlins Orchard IG11: Bark 1G 89
Tomlins Ter. E14 .... 6A 86
Tomlins Wlk. N7 .... 2K 65
Tom Mann Cl. IG11: Bark 1J 89
Tom Nolan Cl. E15 .... 2G 87
Tom Oakman Cen. E4 .... 2A 36
Tompion Ho. EC1 .... 3B 8
(off Percival St.)
Tompion St. EC1 .... 2A 8 (3B 84)
(not continuous)
Tom Smith Cl. SE10 .... 6G 105
Tomson Ho. SE1 .... 7J 15
(off Riley Rd.)
Tomswood Ct. IG6: Ilf 1G 53
Tomswood Hill IG6: Ilf 1F 53
Tomswood Rd. IG7: Chig 6K 37
Tom Williams Ho. SW6 .... 6H 99
(off Clem Attlee Ct.)
Tonbridge Cres. HA3: Kent 4E 42
Tonbridge Ho's. WC1 .... 2E 6
(off Tonbridge St.)
Tonbridge Rd. KT8: W Mole 4D 148
Tonbridge St. WC1 .... 1E 6 (3J 83)
Tonbridge Wlk. WC1 .... 1E 6
Toneborough NW8 .... 1K 81
(off Abbey Rd.)
Tonfield Rd. SM3: Sutt 1H 165
Tonge Cl. BR3: Beck 5C 158
Tonsley Hill SW18 .... 5K 117
Tonsley Pl. SW18 .... 5K 117
Tonsley Rd. SW18 .... 5K 117
Tonsley St. SW18 .... 5K 117
Tonstall Rd. CR4: Mitc 2E 154
Tony Cannell M. E3 .... 3B 86
Tony Law Ho. SE20 .... 1H 157
Tooke Cl. HA5: Pinn 1C 40
Tookey Cl. HA3: Kent 7F 43
Took's Ct. EC4 .... 7J 7 (6A 84)
Tooley St. SE1 .... 4F 15 (1D 102)
Toomy Cen. E16 .... 1K 105
(off Evelyn Rd.)
Toorack Rd. HA3: Hrw W 2H 41
TOOTING 5C 136
TOOTING BEC 3D 136
Tooting Bec Gdns. SW16 .... 4H 137
(not continuous)
Tooting Bec Lido 4G 137
Tooting Bec Rd. SW16 .... 3E 136
SW17 .... 3E 136
Tooting B'way. SW17 .... 5C 136
TOOTING GRAVENEY 6D 136
Tooting Gro. SW17 .... 5C 136
Tooting High St. SW17 .... 6C 136
Tooting Leisure Cen. 4B 136
Tooting Mkt. SW17 .... 4D 136
Tootswood Rd. BR2: Brom 5G 159
Topaz Ct. E11 .... 1G 69
Topaz Wlk. NW2 .... 7F 45
Topcliffe Dr. BR6: Farnb 4H 173
Topham Ho. SE10 .... 7E 104
(off Prior St.)
Topham Sq. N17 .... 1C 48
Topham St. EC1 .... 3J 7 (4A 84)
Top Ho. Ri. E4 .... 7K 25
Topiary Sq. TW9: Rich 3F 115
Topley St. SE9 .... 4A 124
Topmast Point E14 .... 2C 104
Top Pk. BR3: Beck 5G 159
Topp Wlk. NW2 .... 2E 62
Topsfield Cl. N8 .... 5H 47
Topsfield Pde. N8 .... 5J 47
(off Tottenham La.)
Topsfield Rd. N8 .... 5J 47
Topsham Rd. SW17 .... 3D 136
Tora Ct. IG9: Buck H 2F 37
Torbay Ct. NW1 .... 7F 65
Torbay Mans. NW6 .... 1H 81
(off Willesden La.)
Torbay Rd. HA2: Harr 2C 58
NW6 .... 7H 63
Torbay St. NW1 .... 7F 65
Torbitt Way IG2: Ilf 5K 53
Torbridge Cl. HA8: Edg 7K 27
Torbrook Cl. DA5: Bexl 6E 126
Tor Ct. W8 .... 2J 99
Torcross Dr. SE23 .... 2J 139
Torcross Rd. HA4: Ruis 3K 57
Tor Gdns. W8 .... 2J 99
Tor Gro. SE28 .... 1J 107
Tor Ho. N6 .... 6F 47
Tormead Cl. SM1: Sutt 6J 165
Tormount Rd. SE18 .... 6J 107
Tornay Ho. E9 .... 7J 67
N1 .... 2K 83
(off Priory Grn. Est.)
Toronto Av. E12 .... 4D 70
Toronto Rd. IG1: Ilf 1F 71
Torquay Gdns. IG4: Ilf 4B 52
Torquay St. W2 .... 5K 81
Torrance Cl. SE7 .... 6B 106
Torrens Ct. SE5 .... 3D 120
Torrens Rd. E15 .... 6H 69
SW2 .... 5K 119
Torrens Sq. E15 .... 6H 69
Torrens St. EC1 .... 2A 84
Torres Sq. E14 .... 5C 104
Torre Wlk. SM5: Cars 1C 166
Torrey Dr. SW9 .... 2A 120
Torriano Av. NW5 .... 5H 65
Torriano Cotts. NW5 .... 5G 65
Torriano M. NW5 .... 5G 65
Torridge Gdns. SE15 .... 4J 121
Torridge Rd. CR7: Thor H 5B 156
Torridon Ho. NW6 .... 2K 81
(off Randolph Gdns.)
Torridon Rd. SE6 .... 7F 123
SE13 .... 7G 123
Torrington Av. N12 .... 5G 31
Torrington Cl. N12 .... 4G 31
Torrington Ct. SE26 .... 5G 139
(off Crystal Pal. Pk. Rd.)
Torrington Dr. HA2: Harr 4F 59
Torrington Gdns. N11 .... 6B 32
UB6: G'frd 1C 78
Torrington Gro. N12 .... 5H 31
Torrington Pk. N12 .... 5F 31
Torrington Pl. E1 .... 1G 103
WC1 .... 5C 6 (5H 83)
Torrington Rd. E18 .... 3J 51
HA4: Ruis 3J 57
RM8: Dag 1F 73
UB6: G'frd 1C 78
Torrington Sq. CR0: Croy 7D 156
WC1 .... 4D 6 (4H 83)
Torrington Way SM4: Mord 6J 153
Tor Rd. DA16: Well 1C 126
Torr Rd. SE20 .... 7K 139
Tortington Ho. SE15 .... 7G 103
(off Friary Est.)
Torver Rd. HA1: Harr 4J 41
Torver Way BR6: Orp 3H 173
Torwood Rd. SW15 .... 5C 116
Tothill Ho. SW1 .... 3D 18
(off Page St.)
Tothill St. SW1 .... 7D 12 (2H 101)
Totnes Rd. DA16: Well 7B 108
Totnes Vs. N11 .... 5B 32
(off Telford Rd.)
Totnes Wlk. N2 .... 4B 46
Tottan Ter. E1 .... 6K 85
Tottenhall NW1 .... 7E 64
(off Ferdinand St.)
Tottenhall Rd. N13 .... 6F 33
TOTTENHAM 1F 49
Tottenham Community Sports Cen. 1F 49
Tottenham Ct. Rd. W1 .... 4B 6 (4G 83)
Tottenham Ent. Cen. N17 .... 2F 49
Tottenham Grn. E. N15 .... 4F 49
Tottenham Green Leisure Cen. 4F 49
TOTTENHAM HALE 2G 49
TOTTENHAM HALE GYRATORY 4G 49
Tottenham Hale Retail Pk. N15 .... 4G 49
Tottenham Hotspur FC 7B 34
Tottenham La. N8 .... 6J 47
Tottenham M. W1 .... 5B 6 (5G 83)
Tottenham Rd. N1 .... 6E 66
Tottenham St. W1 .... 6B 6 (5G 83)
Totterdown St. SW17 .... 4D 136
TOTTERIDGE 1C 30
Totteridge Comn. N20 .... 2H 29
Totteridge Grn. N20 .... 2D 30
Totteridge Ho. SW11 .... 2B 118
(off Yelverton Rd.)
Totteridge La. N20 .... 2D 30
Totteridge Village N20 .... 1B 30
Totternhoe Cl. HA3: Kent 5C 42
Totton Rd. CR7: Thor H 3A 156
Toulmin St. SE1 .... 7C 14 (2C 102)
Toulon St. SE5 .... 7C 102
Toulouse Ct. SE16 .... 5H 103
(off Rossetti Rd.)
Tounson Ct. SW1 .... 4D 18
(off Montaigne Cl.)
Tourist Info. Cen.
Bexley 6J 127
Bexleyheath 4G 127
City of London 1C 14 (6C 84)
Croydon 3C 168
Greenwich 6E 104
Hackney 6H 67
Harrow 4J 41
Heathrow Cen. 3D 110
Hounslow 3F 113
Ilford 3F 71
Tourist Info. Cen.
King's Cross 1E 6
Kingston upon Thames 2D 150
Leicester Sq. 3D 12 (7H 83)
Lewisham 4E 122
Richmond upon Thames 5D 114
Somers Town 3J 83
Southwark 4D 14 (1C 102)
Terminal 1 - London Heathrow Airport 2D 110
Terminal 2 - London Heathrow Airport 3D 110
Terminal 3 - London Heathrow Airport 3C 110
Twickenham 1B 132
Waterloo International Terminal 6H 13 (2A 102)
Tournay Rd. SW6 .... 7H 99
Tours Pas. SW11 .... 4A 118
Toussaint Wlk. SE16 .... 3G 103
Tovil Cl. SE20 .... 2H 157
Tovy Ho. SE1 .... 5G 103
(off Avondale Sq.)
Towcester Rd. E3 .... 4D 86
Tower 42 .... 7G 9 (6E 84)
Tower Bri. E1 .... 5J 15
SE1 .... 5J 15 (1F 103)
Tower Bri. App. E1 .... 4J 15 (1F 103)
Tower Bri. Bus. Complex SE16 .... 3G 103
Tower Bri. Bus. Sq. SE16 .... 4H 103
Tower Bridge Experience 4J 15
Tower Bri. Plaza SE1 .... 5J 15 (1F 103)
Tower Bri. Rd. SE1 .... 7H 15 (3E 102)
Tower Bri. Sq. SE1 .... 6J 15
Tower Bri. Wharf E1 .... 5K 15 (1G 103)
Tower Bldgs. E1 .... 1H 103
(off Brewhouse La.)
Tower Cl. BR6: Orp 2K 173
NW3 .... 5B 64
SE20 .... 7H 139
Tower Ct. E5 .... 7F 49
N1 .... 7C 66
(off Canonbury St.)
NW8 .... 2C 82
(off Mackennal St.)
WC2 .... 1E 12
Tower Gdns. KT10: Clay 7A 162
Tower Gdns. Rd. N17 .... 1C 48
Towergate SE1 .... 4E 102
(off Page's Wlk.)
Towergate Cl. UB8: Uxb 5A 56
Tower Gym 2A 34
Tower Hamlets Rd. E7 .... 4H 69
E17 .... 3C 50
TOWER HILL 7F 85
Tower Hill EC3 .... 3H 15 (7E 84)
Tower Hill Ter. EC3 .... 3H 15
Tower Ho. E1 .... 5G 85
(off Fieldgate St.)
Tower La. HA9: Wemb 3D 60
Tower M. E17 .... 4C 50
Tower Mill Rd. SE15 .... 7E 102
Tower of London, The 3J 15 (7F 85)
Tower of London Vis. Cen., The 3H 15 (7E 84)
Tower Pl. EC3 .... 3H 15 (7E 84)
Tower Pl. E. EC3 .... 3H 15
(off Lwr. Thames St.)
Tower Pl. W. EC3 .... 3H 15
(off Lwr. Thames St.)
Tower Point EN2: Enf 4J 23
Tower Ri. TW9: Rich 3E 114
Tower Rd. BR6: Orp 2K 173
DA7: Bex 4G 127
DA17: Belv 4J 109
NW10 .... 7C 62
TW1: Twick 3K 131
Tower Royal EC4 .... 2E 14 (7D 84)
Towers Av. UB10: Hil 3E 74
Towers Bus. Pk. HA9: Wemb 4J 61
(off Carey Way)
Towers Ct. UB10: Hil 3E 74
Towers Pl. TW9: Rich 5E 114

Towers Rd.—Trevor Wlk.

Towers Rd. HA5: Pinn 1C 40
UB1: S'hall 4E 76
Tower St. WC2 1E 12 (6J 83)
Tower Ter. N22 2K 47
Tower Vw. CR0: Croy 7A 158
Tower Wlk. *SE1* *4E 102*
(off Aberdour St.)
Tower Yd. TW10: Rich 5F 115
Towfield Ct. TW13: Hanw 2D 130
Towfield Rd. TW13: Hanw 2D 130
Towgar Ct. N20 7F 21
Town, The EN2: Enf 3J 23
Towncourt Cres. BR5: Pet W 5G 161
Towncourt La. BR5: Pet W 6H 161
Towncourt Path N4 1C 66
Town End Pde. *KT1: King T* *3D 150*
(off High St.)
Towney Mead UB5: N'olt 2D 76
Towney Mead Ct. UB5: N'olt 2D 76
Townfield Rd. UB3: Hayes 1H 93
Townfield Sq. UB3: Hayes 7H 75
Town Fld. Way TW7: Isle 2A 114
Town Hall App. Rd. N15 4F 49
Town Hall Av. W4 5K 97
Town Hall Rd. SW11 3D 118
Town Hall Wlk. *N16* *4D 66*
(off Albion Rd.)
Townholm Cres. W7 3K 95
Town La. TW19: Stanw 1A 128
(not continuous)
Townley Ct. E15 6H 69
Townley Rd. DA6: Bex 5F 127
SE22 5E 120
Townley St. SE17 5D 102
(not continuous)
Townmead Bus. Cen. SW6 3A 118
Town Mdw. TW8: Bford 6D 96
Town Mdw. Rd. TW8: Bford 7D 96
Townmead Rd. SW6 3K 117
TW9: Rich 2H 115
Town Quay IG11: Bark 1F 89
Town Quay Wharf IG11: Bark 1F 89
Town Rd. N9 2C 34
Townsend Av. N14 4C 32
Townsend Ho. *SE1* *4G 103*
(off Strathnairn St.)
Townsend Ind. Est. NW10 2J 79
Townsend La. NW9 7K 43
Townsend Rd. N15 5F 49
TW15: Ashf 5A 128
UB1: S'hall 1C 94
Townsend St. SE17 4E 102
Townsend Way HA6: Nwood 1H 39
Townsend Yd. N6 1F 65
Townshend Cl. DA14: Sidc 6B 144
Townshend Ct. *NW8* *2C 82*
(off Townshend Rd.)
Townshend Est. NW8 2C 82
Townshend Rd. BR7: Chst 5F 143
NW8 1C 82
(not continuous)
TW9: Rich 4F 115
Townshend Ter. TW9: Rich 4F 115
Towns Ho. SW4 3H 119
Townson Av. UB5: Yead 2J 75
Townson Way UB5: Yead 2J 75
Town Sq. *TW7: Isle* *3B 114*
(off Swan St.)
Town Tree Rd. TW15: Ashf 5C 128
Town Wharf TW7: Isle 3B 114
Towpath KT12: Walt T 5J 147
TW17: Shep 7B 146
Towpath, The SW10 1B 118
Towpath Rd. N18 6E 34
Towpath Wlk. E9 5B 68
Towpath Way CR0 6F 157
Towton Rd. SE27 2C 138
Toynbec Cl. BR7: Chst 4F 143
Toynbee Rd. SW20 1G 153
Toynbee St. E1 6J 9 (5F 85)
Toyne Way N6 6D 46
Tracey Av. NW2 5E 62
Tracy Ct. HA7: Stan 7H 27
Trade Cl. N13 4F 33
Trader Rd. E6 6F 89
Tradescant Ho. *E9* *7J 67*
(off Frampton Pk. Rd.)
Tradescant Rd. SW8 7J 101
Tradewinds Ct. E1 7G 85
Trading Est. Rd. NW10 4J 79
Trafalgar Av. KT4: Wor Pk 1F 165
N17 6K 33
SE15 5F 103
Trafalgar Bus. Cen. IG11: Bark 4K 89
Trafalgar Chambers *SW3* *5B 16*
(off South Pde.)
Trafalgar Cl. SE16 3A 104
Trafalgar Ct. *E1* *1J 103*
(off Wapping Wall)
Trafalgar Gdns. E1 5K 85
W8 *3K 99*
(off South End Row)
Trafalgar Gro. SE10 6F 105
Trafalgar Ho. *SE17* *5C 102*
(off Bronti Cl.)
Trafalgar M. E9 6B 68
Trafalgar Pl. E11 4J 51
N18 5B 34
Trafalgar Point *N1* *7D 66*
(off Downham Rd.)
Trafalgar Rd. SE10 6F 105
SW19 7K 135
TW2: Twick 2H 131
Trafalgar Square 4E 12 (1J 101)
Trafalgar Sq. WC2 4D 12 (1H 101)
Trafalgar St. SE17 5D 102
Trafalgar Studios *4E 12*
(off Whitehall)
Trafalgar Ter. HA1: Harr 1J 59
Trafalgar Trad. Est. EN3: Brim 4F 25
Trafalgar Way CR0: Wadd 2A 168
E14 1E 104
Trafford Cl. E15 5D 68
Trafford Ho. *N1* *2D 84*
(off Cranston Est.)
Trafford Rd. CR7: Thor H 5K 155
Traherne Lodge TW11: Tedd 5K 131
Trahorn Cl. E1 4H 85
Traitors' Gate 4J 15
Tralee Ct. *SE16* *5H 103*
(off Masters Dr.)
Tramsheds, The CR0: Bedd 7H 155
Tramway Av. E15 7G 69
N9 7C 24
Tramway Cl. SE20 1J 157
Tramway Path CR4: Mitc 4C 154
(not continuous)
Tranley M. *NW3* *4C 64*
(off Fleet Rd.)
Tranmere Ct. SM2: Sutt 7A 166
Tranmere Rd. N9 7A 24
SW18 2A 136
TW2: Whit 7F 113
Tranquil Pas. *SE3* *2H 123*
(off Montpelier Va.)
Tranquil Va. SE3 2G 123
Transept St. NW1 6D 4 (5C 82)
Transmere Cl. BR5: Pet W 6G 161
Transmere Rd. BR5: Pet W 6G 161
Transom Cl. SE16 4A 104
Transom Sq. E14 5D 104
Transport Av. TW8: Bford 5A 96
Tranton Rd. SE16 3G 103
Trappes Ho. *SE16* *4H 103*
(off Camilla Rd.)
Traps La. KT3: N Mald 1A 152
Traq Motor Racing 6F 155
Travellers Way TW4: Cran 2A 112
Travers Cl. E17 1K 49
Travers Ho. *SE10* *6F 105*
(off Trafalgar Gro.)
Travers Rd. N7 3A 66
Travis Ho. SE10 1E 122
Treacy Cl. WD23: Bushy 2B 26
Treadgold Ho. *W11* *7F 81*
(off Bomore Rd.)
Treadgold St. W11 7F 81
Treadway St. E2 2H 85
Treasury Cl. SM6: Wall 5H 167
Treasury Pas. SW1 6E 12
Treaty Cen. TW3: Houn 3F 113
Treaty St. N1 1K 83
Trebeck St. W1 4J 11 (1F 101)
Trebovir Rd. SW5 5J 99
Treby St. E3 4B 86
Trecastle Way N7 4H 65
Tredegar M. E3 3B 86
Tredegar Rd. E3 2B 86
N11 7C 32
Tredegar Sq. E3 3B 86
Tredegar Ter. E3 3B 86
Trederwen Rd. E8 1G 85
Tredown Rd. SE26 5J 139
Tredwell Cl. BR2: Brom 4C 160
SW2 2K 137
Tredwell Rd. SE27 4B 138
Tree Cl. TW10: Ham 1D 132
Treen Av. SW13 3B 116
Tree Rd. E16 6A 88
Treeside Cl. UB7: W Dray 4A 92
Tree Top M. RM10: Dag 6K 73
Treetops Cl. SE2 5E 108
Treeview Cl. SE19 1E 156
Treewall Gdns. BR1: Brom 4K 141
Trefgarne Rd. RM10: Dag 2G 73
Trefil Wlk. N7 4J 65
Trefoil Ho. *DA18: Erith* *2E 108*
(off Kale Rd.)
Trefoil Rd. SW18 5A 118
Trefusis Ct. TW5: Cran 1K 111
Tregaron Av. N8 6J 47
Tregaron Gdns. KT3: N Mald 4A 152
Tregarvon Rd. SW11 4E 118
Tregenna Av. HA2: Harr 4E 58
Tregenna Cl. N14 5B 22
Tregenna Ct. HA2: Harr 4E 58
Tregony Rd. BR6: Chels 4K 173
Trego Rd. E9 7C 68
Tregothnan Rd. SW9 3J 119
Tregunter Rd. SW10 6K 99
Trehearn Rd. IG6: Ilf 1H 53
Treherne Ct. SW9 1B 120
SW17 4E 136
Trehern Rd. SW14 3K 115
Trehurst St. E5 5A 68
Trelawney Est. E9 6J 67
Trelawney Ho. *SE1* *5C 14*
(off Pepper St.)
Trelawney Rd. IG6: Ilf 1H 53
Trelawn Rd. E10 3E 68
SW2 5A 120
Trelawny Cl. E17 4D 50
Trellick Twr. *W10* *4H 81*
(off Golborne Rd.)
Trellis Sq. E3 3B 86
Treloar Gdns. SE19 6D 138
Tremadoc Rd. SW4 4H 119
Tremaine Cl. SE4 2C 122
Tremaine Rd. SE20 2H 157
Trematon Ho. *SE11* *5K 19*
(off Kennings Way)
Trematon Pl. TW11: Tedd 7C 132
Tremlett Gro. N19 3G 65
Trenance Gdns. IG3: Ilf 3A 72
Trenchard Av. HA4: Ruis 4K 57
Trenchard Cl. HA7: Stan 6F 27
NW9 1A 44
Trenchard Ct. NW4 5C 44
SM4: Mord 6J 153
Trenchard St. SE10 5F 105
Trenchold St. SW8 6J 101
Trendell Ho. *E14* *6C 86*
(off Dod St.)
Trenear Cl. BR6: Chels 4K 173
Trenholme Cl. SE20 7H 139
Trenholme Rd. SE20 7H 139
Trenholme Ter. SE20 7H 139
Trenmar Gdns. NW10 3D 80
Trent Av. W5 3C 96
Trent Ct. *CR2: S Croy* *5C 168*
(off Nottingham Rd.)
Trent Gdns. N14 6A 22
Trentham Ho. W3 5K 79
Trentham St. SW18 1J 135
Trent Ho. KT2: King T 1D 150
SE15 4J 121
Trent Pk. Country Pk. 1A 22
Trent Pk. Sports Cen. 4B 22
Trent Rd. IG9: Buck H 1E 36
SW2 5K 119
Trent Way KT4: Wor Pk 3E 164
UB4: Hayes 2G 75
Trentwood Side EN2: Enf 3E 22
Treport St. SW18 7K 117
Tresco Cl. BR1: Brom 6G 141
Trescoe Gdns. HA2: Harr 7C 40
Tresco Gdns. IG3: Ilf 2A 72
Tresco Ho. SE11 5J 19
Tresco Rd. SE15 4H 121
Tresham Cres. NW8 3D 4 (4C 82)
Tresham Rd. IG11: Bark 7K 71
Tresham Wlk. E9 5J 67
Tresidder Ho. SW4 7H 119
Tresilian Av. N21 5E 22
Tressell Cl. N1 7B 66
Tressillian Cres. SE4 3C 122
Tressillian Rd. SE4 4B 122
Tress Pl. SE1 4A 14
Trestis Cl. UB4: Yead 4B 76
Treswell Rd. RM9: Dag 1E 90
Tretawn Gdns. NW7 4F 29
Tretawn Pk. NW7 4F 29
Trevanion Rd. W14 4G 99
Treve Av. HA1: Harr 7H 41
Trevelyan Av. E12 4D 70
Trevelyan Ct. KT3: N Mald 7A 152
Trevelyan Cres. HA3: Kent 7D 42
Trevelyan Gdns. NW10 1E 80
Trevelyan Ho. *E2* *3K 85*
(off Morpeth St.)
SE5 *7B 102*
(off John Ruskin St.)
Trevelyan Rd. E15 4H 69
SW17 5C 136
Trevenna Ho. *SE23* *3K 139*
(off Dacres Rd.)
Trevera Ct. EN3: Pond E 4F 25
Treveris St. SE1 5B 14 (1B 102)
Treverton St. W10 4F 81
Treverton Towers *W10* *5F 81*
(off Treverton St.)
Treves Cl. N21 5E 22
Treves Ho. *E1* *4G 85*
(off Vallance Rd.)
Treville St. SW15 7D 116
Treviso Rd. SE23 2K 139
Trevithick Cl. TW14: Felt 1H 129
Trevithick Ho. *SE16* *4H 103*
(off Rennie Est.)
Trevithick St. SE8 6C 104
Trevone Ct. *SW2* *7J 119*
(off Doverfield Rd.)
Trevone Gdns.
HA5: Pinn 6C 40
Trevor Cl. BR2: Hayes 7H 159
EN4: E Barn 6G 21
HA3: Hrw W 7E 26
TW7: Isle 5K 113
UB5: Yead 2A 76
Trevor Cres. HA4: Ruis 4H 57
Trevor Gdns. HA4: Ruis 4J 57
HA8: Edg 1K 43
UB5: Yead 2A 76
Trevor Pl. SW7 7D 10 (2C 100)
Trevor Rd. HA8: Edg 1K 43
IG8: Wfd G 7D 36
SW19 7G 135
UB3: Hayes 2G 93
Trevor Sq. SW7 7E 10 (2D 100)
Trevor St. SW7 7D 10 (2C 100)
Trevor Wlk. *SW7* *7D 10*
(off Trevor Pl., not continuous)

Trevose Ho. *SE11* 5H 19
(off Orsett St.)
Trevose Rd. E17 1F 51
Trewenna Dr. KT9: Chess 5D 162
Trewince Rd. SW20 1E 152
Trewint St. SW18 2A 136
Trewsbury Ho. SE2 1D 108
Trewsbury Rd. SE26 5K 139
Triandra Way UB4: Yead 5B 76
Triangle, The *DA15: Sidc* 7A 126
(off Burnt Oak La.)
E8 1H 85
EC1 3B 8
IG11: Bark 6G 71
KT1: King T 2H 151
N13 4E 32
Triangle Bus. Cen., The
NW10 3B 80
Triangle Cen. UB1: S'hall 1H 95
Triangle Ct. E16 5B 88
Triangle Est. *SE11* 6J 19
(off Kennington La.)
SE11 5A 102
(off Kennington Rd.)
Triangle Pas. EN4: E Barn 4F 21
Triangle Pl. SW4 4H 119
Triangle Rd. E8 1H 85
Triangle Way W3 3G 97
Trickett Ho. SM2: Sutt 7K 165
Tricorn Ho. SE28 1J 107
Tricycle Cinema 7H 63
Tricycle Theatre 7H 63
Trident Bus. Cen. SW17 5D 136
Trident Gdns. UB5: N'olt 3B 76
Trident Ho. *E14* 6E 86
(off Blair St.)
SE28 1H 107
TW19: Stanw 7A 110
(off Clare Rd.)
Trident Pl. *SW3* 7B 16
(off Old Church St.)
Trident St. SE16 4K 103
Trident Way UB2: S'hall 3K 93
Trig La. EC4 2C 14 (7C 84)
Trigon Rd. SW8 7K 101
Trilby Rd. SE23 2K 139
Trillo Ct. IG2: Ilf 7J 53
Trimdon NW1 1G 83
Trimmer Wlk. TW8: Bford 6E 96
Trim St. SE14 6B 104
Trinder Gdns. N19 1J 65
Trinder M. TW11: Tedd 5A 132
Trinder Rd. EN5: Barn 5A 20
N19 1J 65
Tring Av. HA9: Wemb 6G 61
UB1: S'hall 6D 76
W5 1F 97
Tring Cl. IG2: Ilf 5H 53
Tring Ct. TW1: Twick 4A 132
Trinidad Gdns. RM10: Dag 7K 73
Trinidad Ho. *E14* 7B 86
(off Gill St.)
Trinidad St. E14 7B 86
Trinity Av. EN1: Enf 6A 24
N2 3B 46
Trinity Buoy Wharf *E14* 7G 87
(off Orchard Pl.)
Trinity Bus. Pk. E4 6G 35
Trinity Chu. Pas. SW13 6D 98
Trinity Chu. Rd. SW13 6D 98
Trinity Chu. Sq. SE1 7D 14 (3C 102)
Trinity Cl. BR2: Brom 1C 172
CR2: Sand 7E 168
E8 6F 67
E11 2G 69
NW3 4B 64
SE13 4F 123
SW4 4G 119
TW4: Houn 4C 112
Trinity College of Music 6E 104
Trinity Cotts. TW9: Rich 3F 115
Trinity Ct. CR0: Croy 2C 168
EN2: Enf 2H 23
Trinity Ct. *N1* 1E 84
(off Downham Rd.)
NW2 5E 62
Trinity Ct. *SE1* 7D 14
(off Brockham St.)
SE7 4B 106
SE25 6E 156
SE26 3J 139
SW9 3K 119
W2 6A 82
(off Gloucester Ter.)
WC1 3G 7
Trinity Cres. SW17 2D 136
Trinity Dr. UB8: Hil 5E 74
Trinity Gdns. E16 5H 87
(not continuous)
SW9 4K 119
Trinity Grn. E1 4J 85
Trinity Gro. SE10 1E 122
Trinity Hospital (Almshouses)
SE10 5F 105
Trinity Ho. EC3 2J 15
SE1 3C 102
(off Bath Ter.)
Trinity M. *E1* 5J 85
(off Redman's Rd.)
SE20 1H 157
W10 6F 81
Trinity Path SE23 3J 139
Trinity Pl. DA6: Bex 4F 127
EC3 2J 15 (7F 85)
Trinity Ri. SW2 1A 138
Trinity Rd. IG6: Ilf 3G 53
N2 3B 46
N22 7D 32
(not continuous)
SW17 4A 118
SW18 4A 118
SW19 6J 135
TW9: Rich 3F 115
UB1: S'hall 1C 94
Trinity Sq. EC3 3H 15 (7E 84)
Trinity St. E16 5H 87
EN2: Enf 2H 23
SE1 7D 14 (2C 102)
(not continuous)
Trinity Twr. *E1* 7G 85
(off Vaughan Way)
Trinity Wlk. NW3 6A 64
Trinity Way E4 6G 35
W3 7A 80
Trio Pl. SE1 7D 14 (2C 102)
Tristan Ct. *SE8* 6B 104
(off Dorking Cl.)
Tristan Sq. SE3 3G 123
Tristram Cl. E17 3F 51
Tristram Dr. N9 3B 34
Tristram Rd. BR1: Brom 4H 141
Triton Ho. *E14* 4D 104
(off Cahir St.)
Triton Sq. NW1 3A 6 (4G 83)
Tritton Av. CR0: Bedd 4J 167
Tritton Rd. SE21 3D 138
Triumph Cl. UB3: Harl 1E 110
Triumph Ho. IG11: Bark 3A 90
Triumph Rd. E6 6D 88
Triumph Trad. Est. N17 6B 34
Trocadero Cen. 3C 12 (7H 83)
Trocette Mans. *SE1* 3E 102
(off Bermondsey St.)
Trojan Ct. NW6 7G 63
Trojan Ind. Est. NW10 6B 62
Trojan Way CR0: Wadd 3K 167
Troon Cl. SE16 5H 103
SE28 6D 90
Troon Ho. *E1* 6A 86
(off White Horse Rd.)
Troon St. E1 6A 86
Tropical Ct. *W10* 3F 81
(off Kilburn La.)
Trosley Rd. DA17: Belv 6G 109
Trossachs Rd. SE22 5E 120
Trothy Rd. SE1 4G 103
Trotman Ho. *SE14* 1J 121
(off Pomeroy St.)
Trott Rd. N10 7J 31
Trott St. SW11 1C 118
Trotwood Ho. *SE16* 2H 103
(off Wilson Gro.)
Troughton Rd. SE7 5K 105
Troutbeck NW1 2K 5
Troutbeck Rd. SE14 1A 122
Trout Rd. UB7: Yiew 7A 74
Trouville Rd. SW4 6G 119
Trowbridge Rd. E9 6B 68
Trowlock Av. TW11: Tedd 6C 132
Trowlock Way TW11: Tedd 6D 132
Troy Ct. SE18 4F 107
W8 3J 99
(off Kensington High St.)
Troy Ind. Est. HA1: Harr 5K 41
Troy Rd. SE19 6D 138
Troy Town SE15 3G 121
Trubshaw Rd. UB2: S'hall 3F 95
Trueman Cl. HA8: Edg 7C 28
Truesdale Rd. E6 6D 88
Trulock Ct. N17 7B 34
Trulock Rd. N17 7B 34
Trumans Rd. N16 5F 67
Trumble Gdns. CR7: Thor H 4B 156
Trumpers Way W7 3J 95
Trumpington Rd. E7 4H 69
Trump St. EC2 1D 14 (6C 84)
Trundlers Way WD23: Bushy 1D 26
Trundle St. SE1 6C 14 (2C 102)
Trundleys Rd. SE8 5K 103
Trundley's Ter. SE8 4K 103
Truro Gdns. IG1: Ilf 7C 52
Truro Ho. HA5: H End 1D 40
W2 5J 81
(off Brunel Est.)
Truro Rd. E17 4B 50
N22 7D 32
Truro St. NW5 6E 64
Truro Way UB4: Hayes 3G 75
Truslove Rd. SE27 5A 138
Trussley Rd. W6 3E 98
Trust Wlk. SE21 1B 138
Tryfan Cl. IG4: Ilf 5B 52
Tryon Cres. E9 1J 85
Tryon St. SW3 5E 16 (5D 100)
Trystings Cl. KT10: Clay 6A 162
Tuam Rd. SE18 6H 107
Tubbenden Cl. BR6: Orp 3J 173
Tubbenden Dr. BR6: Orp 4H 173
Tubbenden La. BR6: Orp 4H 173
Tubbenden La. Sth. BR6: Farnb 5H 173
Tubbs Rd. NW10 2B 80
Tucklow Wlk. SW15 7B 116
Tudor Av. KT4: Wor Pk 3D 164
TW12: Hamp 6E 130
Tudor Cl. BR7: Chst 1D 160
HA5: Eastc 5J 39
IG7: Chig 4K 37
IG8: Wfd G 5E 36
KT9: Chess 5E 162
N6 7G 47
NW3 5C 64
NW7 6H 29
NW9 2J 61
SM3: Cheam 5F 165
SM6: Wall 7G 167
SW2 6K 119
TW12: Ham H 5G 131
TW15: Ashf 4A 128
Tudor Ct. DA14: Sidc 3A 144
E17 7B 50
N1 6E 66
N22 7D 32
SE9 4C 124
SE16 1K 103
(off Princes Riverside Rd.)
TW11: Tedd 6K 131
TW13: Hanw 4A 130
TW19: Stanw 6A 110
W3 2G 97
Tudor Ct. Nth. HA9: Wemb 5G 61
Tudor Ct. Sth. HA9: Wemb 5G 61
Tudor Cres. EN2: Enf 1H 23
Tudor Dr. KT2: King T 5D 132
SM4: Mord 6F 153
Tudor Ent. Pk. HA1: Harr 3K 59
HA3: W'stone 3H 41
Tudor Est. NW10 2H 79
Tudor Gdns. BR4: W W'ck 3E 170
HA3: Hrw W 2H 41
NW9 2J 61
SW13 3A 116
TW1: Twick 1K 131
W3 5G 79
Tudor Gro. E9 7J 67
Tudor Ho. E9 7J 67
E16 1K 105
(off Wesley Av.)
HA5: Pinn 2A 40
(off Pinner Hill Rd.)
W14 4F 99
(off Windsor Way)
Tudor M. E17 4B 50
Tudor Pde. RM6: Chad H 7D 54
SE9 4C 124
Tudor Pl. CR4: Mitc 7C 136
SE19 7F 139
Tudor Rd. BR3: Beck 3E 158
E4 6J 35
E6 1A 88
E9 1H 85
EN5: New Bar 3D 20
HA3: Hrw W, W'stone 2H 41
HA5: Pinn 2A 40
IG11: Bark 1K 89
KT2: King T 7G 133
N9 7C 24
SE19 7F 139
SE25 5H 157
TW3: Houn 4H 113
TW12: Hamp 7E 130
TW15: Ashf 6F 129
UB1: S'hall 7C 76
UB3: Hayes 6F 75
Tudor Sq. UB3: Hayes 5F 75
Tudor Stacks SE24 4C 120
Tudor St. EC4 2K 13 (7A 84)
Tudor Wlk. DA5: Bexl 6E 126
Tudor Way BR5: Pet W 6H 161
N14 1C 32
UB10: Hil 6C 56
W3 2G 97
Tudor Well Cl. HA7: Stan 5G 27
Tudor Works UB4: Yead 1A 94
Tudway Rd. SE3 3K 123
TUFNELL PARK 4G 65
Tufnell Pk. Rd. N7 4G 65
N19 4G 65
Tufton Ct. *SW1* 2E 18
(off Tufton St.)
Tufton Gdns. KT8: W Mole 2F 149
Tufton Rd. E4 4H 35
Tufton St. SW1 1E 18 (3J 101)
Tugboat St. SE28 2J 107
Tugela Rd. CR0: Croy 6D 156
Tugela St. SE6 2B 140
Tugmutton Cl. BR6: Farnb 4F 173
Tulip Cl. CR0: Croy 1K 169
E6 5D 88
TW12: Hamp 6D 130
UB2: S'hall 2G 95
Tulip Gdns. E4 3A 36
IG1: Ilf 6F 71
Tullis Ho. *E9* 7J 67
(off Frampton Pk. Rd.)
Tull St. CR4: Mitc 7D 154
Tulse Cl. BR3: Beck 3E 158
TULSE HILL 1B 138
Tulse Hill SW2 6A 120
Tulse Hill Est. SW2 6A 120
Tulse Ho. SW2 6A 120
Tulsemere Rd. SE27 2C 138
Tumbling Bay KT12: Walt T 6J 147

Tummons Gdns. SE25 .... 2E **156**
Tump Ho. SE28 .... 1J **107**
Tunbridge Ho. EC1 .... 1K **7**
Tuncombe Rd. N18 .... 4K **33**
Tunis Rd. W12 .... 1E **98**
Tunley Grn. E14 .... 5B **86**
Tunley Rd. NW10 .... 1A **80**
SW17 .... 1E **136**
Tunmarsh La. E13 .... 3K **87**
Tunnan Leys E6 .... 6E **88**
Tunnel App. E14 .... 7A **86**
SE10 .... 2G **105**
SE16 .... 2J **103**
Tunnel Av. SE10 .... 2F **105**
(not continuous)
Tunnel Av. Trad. Est. SE10 .... 2F **105**
Tunnel Gdns. N11 .... 7B **32**
Tunnel Link Rd. TW6: H'row A 5C **110**
Tunnel Rd. SE16 .... 2J **103**
Tunnel Rd. E. TW6: H'row A 1D **110**
Tunnel Rd. W. TW6: H'row A 1C **110**
Tunstall Cl. BR6: Orp 4J **173**
Tunstall Rd. CR0: Croy 1E **168**
SW9 .... 4K **119**
Tunstall Wlk. TW8: Bford 6E **96**
Tunstock Way DA17: Belv 3E **108**
Tunworth Cl. NW9 .... 6J **43**
Tunworth Cres. SW15 .... 6B **116**
Tun Yd. *SW8* *2F 119*
(off Silverthorne Rd.)
Tupelo Rd. E10 .... 2D **68**
Tupman Ho. *SE16* *2G 103*
(off Scott Lidgett Cres.)
Tuppy St. SE18 .... 3G **107**
Turenne Cl. SW18 .... 4A **118**
Turin Rd. N9 .... 7D **24**
Turin St. E2 .... 2K **9** (3G **85**)
Turkey Oak Cl. SE19 .... 1E **156**
Turks Boatyard KT1: King T 1D **150**
Turks Cl. UB8: Hil 3C **74**
Turk's Head Yd. EC1 .... 5A **8** (5B **84**)
Turk's Row SW3 .... 5F **17** (5D **100**)
Turle Rd. N4 .... 2K **65**
SW16 .... 2J **155**
Turlewray Cl. N4 .... 1K **65**
Turley Cl. E15 .... 1G **87**
Turnagain La. EC4 .... 7A **8**
Turnage Rd. RM8: Dag 1E **72**
Turnant Rd. N17 .... 1C **48**
Turnberry Cl. NW4 .... 2F **45**
SE16 .... 5H **103**
Turnberry Quay E14 .... 3D **104**
Turnberry Way BR6: Orp 1H **173**
Turnbull Ho. N1 .... 1B **84**
Turnbury Cl. SE28 .... 6D **90**
Turnchapel M. SW4 .... 3F **119**
Turner Av. CR4: Mitc 1D **154**
N15 .... 4E **48**
TW2: Twick 3G **131**
Turner Cl. HA0: Wemb 6D **60**
NW11 .... 6K **45**
SW9 .... 7B **102**
UB4: Hayes 2E **74**
Turner Ct. *SE16* *2J 103*
(off Albion St.)
Turner Dr. NW11 .... 6K **45**
Turner Ho. *E14* *2C 104*
(off Cassilis Rd.)
NW6 .... *5A 64*
(off Dresden Cl.)
NW8 .... *2C 82*
(off Townshend Est.)
SW1 .... *4D 18*
(off Herrick St.)
TW1: Twick *6D 114*
(off Clevedon Rd.)
Turner M. SM2: Sutt 7K **165**
Turner Pl. SW11 .... 5C **118**
Turner Rd. E17 .... 3E **50**
HA8: Edg 2E **42**
KT3: N Mald 7K **151**
Turner's All. EC3 .... 2G **15** (7E **84**)
Turners Cl. N20 .... 3J **31**
Turners Ct. N15 .... 5D **48**
Turners Mdw. Way BR3: Beck 1B **158**
Turners Rd. E3 .... 5B **86**
Turner St. E1 .... 5H **85**
E16 .... 6H **87**
Turner's Way CR0: Wadd 2A **168**
Turners Wood NW11 .... 7A **46**
Turneville Rd. W14 .... 6H **99**
Turney Rd. SE21 .... 7C **120**
TURNHAM GREEN 4A **98**
Turnham Grn. Ter. W4 .... 4A **98**
Turnham Grn. Ter. M. W4 .... 4A **98**
Turnham Rd. SE4 .... 5A **122**
Turnmill St. EC1 .... 4A **8** (4B **84**)
Turnour Ho. *E1* *6H 85*
(off Walburgh St.)
Turnpike Cl. SE8 .... 7B **104**
Turnpike Ct. DA6: Bex 4D **126**
Turnpike Ho. EC1 .... 2B **8** (3B **84**)
Turnpike La. N8 .... 4K **47**
SM1: Sutt 5A **166**
UB10: Uxb 3A **74**
Turnpike Link CR0: Croy 2E **168**
Turnpike M. *N8* *3A 48*
(off Turnpike La.)
Turnpike Pde. *N15* *3B 48*
(off Green Lanes)
Turnpike Way TW7: Isle 1A **114**
Turnpin La. SE10 .... 6E **104**
Turnstone Cl. E13 .... 3J **87**
NW9 .... 2A **44**
UB10: Ick 5D **56**
Turnstone Ho. *E1* *3K 15*
(off Star Pl.)
Turpentine La. SW1 .... 5K **17** (5F **101**)
Turpin Cl. E1 .... 7K **85**
Turpington Cl. BR2: Brom 6C **160**
Turpington La. BR2: Brom 7C **160**
Turpin Ho. SW11 .... 1F **119**
Turpin Rd. TW14: Felt 6H **111**
Turpin's La. IG8: Wfd G 5J **37**
Turpins Yd. SE10 .... 7E **104**
Turpin Way N19 .... 2H **65**
(not continuous)
SM6: Wall 7F **167**
Turquand St. SE17 .... 4C **102**
Turret Gro. SW4 .... 3G **119**
Turton Rd. HA0: Wemb 5E **60**
Turville Ho. *NW8* *3C 4*
(off Grendon St.)
Turville St. E2 .... 3J **9** (4F **85**)
Tuscan Ho. *E2* *3J 85*
(off Knottisford St.)
Tuscan Rd. SE18 .... 5H **107**
Tuscany Ho. E17 .... 2B **50**
Tuskar St. SE10 .... 6G **105**
Tustin Est. SE15 .... 6J **103**
Tuttlebee La. IG9: Buck H 2D **36**
Tuttle Ho. *SW1* *6C 18*
(off Aylesford St.)
Tweedale Ct. E15 .... 5E **68**
Tweed Ct. *W7* *6J 77*
(off Hanway Rd.)
Tweeddale Gro. UB10: Ick 3E **56**
Tweeddale Rd. SM5: Cars 1B **166**
Tweed Glen RM1: Rom 1K **55**
Tweed Grn. RM1: Rom 1K **55**
Tweed Ho. *E14* *2E 86*
(off Teviot St.)
Tweedmouth Rd. E13 .... 2K **87**
Tweed Way RM1: Rom 1K **55**
Tweedy Cl. EN1: Enf 5A **24**
Tweedy Rd. BR1: Brom 1J **159**
Tweezer's All. WC2 .... 2J **13**
Twelvetrees Cres. E3 .... 4E **86**
(not continuous)
E16 .... 4F **87**
Twentyman Cl. IG8: Wfd G 5D **36**
TWICKENHAM 1A 132
Twickenham Baths 1A 132
Twickenham Bri. TW1: Twick 5C **114**
TW9: Rich 5C **114**
Twickenham Cl. CR0: Bedd 3K **167**
Twickenham Gdns. HA3: Hrw W 7D **26**
UB6: G'frd 5A **60**
Twickenham Rd. E11 .... 2E **68**
TW7: Isle 5A **114**
TW9: Rich 4C **114**
TW11: Tedd 4A **132**
(not continuous)
TW13: Hanw 3D **130**
Twickenham Rugby Union Football Ground 6J **113**
Twickenham Trad. Est. TW1: Twick 6K **113**
Twig Folly Cl. E2 .... 2K **85**
Twigg Cl. DA8: Erith 7K **109**
Twilley St. SW18 .... 7K **117**
Twin Bridges Bus. Pk. CR2: S Croy 6D **168**
Twine Cl. IG11: Bark 3B **90**
Twine Ct. E1 .... 7J **85**
Twineham Grn. N12 .... 4D **30**
Twine Ter. *E3* *4B 86*
(off Ropery St.)
Twining Av. TW2: Twick 3G **131**
Twinn Rd. NW7 .... 6B **30**
Twin Tumps Way SE28 .... 7A **90**
Twisden Rd. NW5 .... 4F **65**
Twybridge Way NW10 .... 7J **61**
Twycross M. SE10 .... 5G **105**
Twyford Abbey Rd. NW10 .... 3F **79**
Twyford Av. N2 .... 3D **46**
W3 .... 7G **79**
Twyford Ct. *HA0: Wemb* *2E 78*
(off Vicars Bri. Cl.)
N10 .... 3E **46**
Twyford Cres. W3 .... 1G **97**
Twyford Ho. N5 .... 3B **66**
N15 .... *6E 48*
(off Chisley Rd.)
Twyford Pl. WC2 .... 7G **7** (6K **83**)
Twyford Rd. HA2: Harr 1F **59**
IG1: Ilf 5G **71**
SM5: Cars 1B **166**
Twyford Sports Cen. 1H **97**
Twyford St. N1 .... 1K **83**
Twynholm Mans. *SW6* *7G 99*
(off Lillie Rd.)
Tyas Rd. E16 .... 4H **87**
Tybenham Rd. SW19 .... 3J **153**
Tyberry Rd. EN3: Enf H 3C **24**
Tyburn La. HA1: Harr 7K **41**
Tyburn Tree (site of) 2E **10**
Tyburn Way W1 .... 2F **11** (7D **82**)
Tye La. BR6: Farnb 5G **173**
Tyers Est. SE1 .... 6G **15**
Tyers Ga. SE1 .... 7G **15** (2E **102**)
Tyers St. SE11 .... 6G **19** (5K **101**)
Tyers Ter. SE11 .... 6G **19** (5K **101**)
Tyeshurst Cl. SE2 .... 5E **108**
Tylecroft Rd. SW16 .... 2J **155**
Tylehurst Gdns. IG1: Ilf 5G **71**
Tyler Cl. DA8: Erith 7H **109**
E2 .... 2F **85**
Tyler Rd. UB2: S'hall 3F **95**
Tylers Ct. *E17* *4C 50*
(off Westbury Rd.)
HA0: Wemb 2E **78**
W1 .... 1C **12**
Tylers Ga. HA3: Kent 6E **42**
Tylers Path SM5: Cars 4D **166**
Tyler St. SE10 .... 5G **105**
(not continuous)
Tylney Av. SE19 .... 5F **139**
(not continuous)
Tylney Ho. *E1* *6H 85*
(off Nelson St.)
Tylney Rd. BR1: Brom 2B **160**
E7 .... 4A **70**
Tynamara *KT1: King T* *4D 150*
(off Portsmouth Rd.)
Tynan Cl. TW14: Felt 1J **129**
Tyndale Ct. *E14* *5D 104*
(off Transom Sq.)
Tyndale La. N1 .... 7B **66**
Tyndale Mans. *N1* *7B 66*
(off Upper St.)
Tyndale Ter. N1 .... 7B **66**
Tyndall Gdns. E10 .... 2E **68**
Tyndall Rd. DA16: Well 3K **125**
E10 .... 2E **68**
Tyne Ct. *W7* *6J 77*
(off Hanway Rd.)
Tyneham Cl. SW11 .... 3E **118**
Tyneham Rd. SW11 .... 2E **118**
Tyne Ho. KT2: King T 1D **150**
Tynemouth Cl. E6 .... 6F **89**
Tynemouth Dr. EN1: Enf 1B **24**
Tynemouth Rd. CR4: Mitc 7E **136**
N15 .... 4F **49**
SE18 .... 5J **107**
Tynemouth St. SW6 .... 2A **118**
Tyne St. E1 .... 7K **9** (6F **85**)
Tynsdale Rd. NW10 .... 6A **62**
Tynwald Ho. SE26 .... 3G **139**
Type St. E2 .... 2K **85**
Typhoon Way SM6: Wall 7J **167**
Tyrawley Rd. SW6 .... 1K **117**
Tyre La. NW9 .... 4A **44**
Tyrell Cl. HA1: Harr 4J **59**
Tyrell Ct. SM5: Cars 4D **166**
Tyrell Ho. *BR3: Beck* *5D 140*
(off Beckenham Hill Rd.)
Tyrols Rd. SE23 .... 1K **139**
Tyrone Rd. E6 .... 2D **88**
Tyron Way DA14: Sidc 4J **143**
Tyrrell Av. DA16: Well 5A **126**
Tyrrell Ho. *SW1* *7B 18*
(off Churchill Gdns.)
Tyrrell Rd. SE22 .... 4G **121**
Tyrrell Sq. CR4: Mitc 1C **154**
Tyrrel Way NW9 .... 7B **44**
Tyrwhitt Rd. SE4 .... 3C **122**
Tysoe St. EC1 .... 2K **7** (3A **84**)
Tyson Gdns. SE23 .... 7J **121**
Tyson Rd. SE23 .... 7J **121**
Tyssen Pas. E8 .... 6F **67**
Tyssen Rd. N16 .... 3F **67**
Tyssen St. E8 .... 6F **67**
N1 .... 2E **84**
Tytherton *E2* *2J 85*
(off Cyprus St.)
Tytherton Rd. N19 .... 3H **65**

U

Uamvar St. E14 .... 5D **86**
Uckfield Gro. CR4: Mitc 7E **136**
Udall St. SW1 .... 4B **18** (4G **101**)
Udimore Ho. *W10* *5E 80*
(off Sutton Way)
Udney Pk. Rd. TW11: Tedd 6A **132**
Uffington Rd. NW10 .... 1C **80**
SE27 .... 4A **138**
Ufford Cl. HA3: Hrw W 7A **26**
Ufford Rd. HA3: Hrw W 7A **26**
Ufford St. SE1 .... 6K **13** (2A **102**)
Ufton Ct. UB5: Yead 3B **76**
Ufton Gro. N1 .... 7D **66**
Ufton Rd. N1 .... 7D **66**
(not continuous)
UGC Cinema
St James's **3C 12**
(off Haymarket)
Uhura Sq. N16 .... 3E **66**
Ujima Ct. SW16 .... 4J **137**
Ullathorne Rd. SW16 .... 4G **137**
Ulleswater Rd. N14 .... 3D **32**
Ullin St. E14 .... 5E **86**
Ullswater E18 .... 2J **51**
Ullswater Cl. BR1: Brom 7G **141**
SW15 .... 4K **133**
UB4: Hayes 2G **75**
Ullswater Ct. HA2: Harr 7E **40**
Ullswater Cres. SW15 .... 4K **133**
Ullswater Ho. *SE15* *6J 103*
(off Hillbeck Cl.)
Ullswater Rd. SE27 .... 2B **138**
SW13 .... 7C **98**

Ulster Gdns. N13 . . . . .4H 33
Ulster Pl. NW1 . . . . .4J 5 (4F 83)
Ulster Ter. NW1 . . . . .3H 5 (4E 82)
Ulundi Rd. SE3 . . . . .6G 105
Ulva Rd. SW15 . . . . .5F 117
Ulverscroft Rd. SE22 . . . . .5F 121
Ulverstone Rd. SE27 . . . . .2B 138
Ulverston Rd. E17 . . . . .2F 51
Ulysses Rd. NW6 . . . . .5H 63
Umberston St. E1 . . . . .6G 85
Umbria St. SW15 . . . . .6C 116
Umfreville Rd. N4 . . . . .6B 48
Undercliff Rd. SE13 . . . . .3C 122
UNDERHILL 5D 20
Underhill EN5: Barn 5D 20
Underhill Ct. EN5: Barn 5D 20
Underhill Ho. E14 . . . . .5C 86
(off Burgess St.)
Underhill Pas. NW1 . . . . .1F 83
(off Camden High St.)
Underhill Rd. SE22 . . . . .5G 121
Underhill Stadium 5D 20
Underhill St. NW1 . . . . .1F 83
Underne Av. N14 . . . . .2A 32
Undershaft EC3 . . . . .1G 15 (6E 84)
Undershaw Rd. BR1: Brom 3H 141
Underwood CRO: New Ad 5E 170
Underwood, The SE9 . . . . .2D 142
Underwood Ct. E10 . . . . .1D 68
(off Leyton Grange Est.)
Underwood Ho. KT8: W Mole 5E 148
(off Approach Rd.)
W6 . . . . .3D 98
(off Sycamore Gdns.)
Underwood Rd. E1 . . . . .4G 85
E4 . . . . .5J 35
IG8: Wfd G 7F 37
Underwood Row N1 . . . .1D 8 (3C 84)
Underwood St. N1 . . . . . . .1D 8 (3C 84)
Undine Rd. E14 . . . . .4D 104
Undine St. SW17 . . . . .5D 136
Uneeda Dr. UB6: G'frd 1H 77
Unicorn Bldg. E1 . . . . .7K 85
(off Jardine Rd.)
Unicorn Theatre 1E 102
Unicorn Works N17 . . . . .7D 34
Union Canal Wlk. W10 . . . . .4E 80
(off Canal Way)
Union Cl. E11 . . . . .4F 69
Union Cotts. E15 . . . . .7G 69
Union Ct. EC2 . . . . .7G 9
SW4 . . . . .2J 119
TW9: Rich 5E 114
W9 . . . . .5J 81
(off Elmfield Way)
Union Dr. E1 . . . . .4A 86
Union Gro. SW8 . . . . .2J 119
Union M. SW4 . . . . .2J 119
Union Pk. SE10 . . . . .5H 105
(off Calvert Rd.)
Union Rd. BR2: Brom 5B 160
CRO: Croy 7C 156
HA0: Wemb 6E 60
N11 .6C 32
SW4 . . . . .2H 119
SW8 . . . . .2H 119
UB5: N'olt 2E 76
Union Sq. N1 . . . . .1C 84
Union St. E15 . . . . .1F 87
EN5: Barn 3B 20
KT1: King T 2D 150
SE1 . . . . .5A 14 (1B 102)
Union Theatre 5B 14
Union Wlk. E2 . . . . .1H 9 (3E 84)
Union Wharf N1 . . . . .2C 84
(off Wenlock Rd.)
N1 . . . . .1C 84
(Arlington Av.)
UB7: Yiew 1A 92
(off Bentinck Rd.)
Union Yd. W1 . . . . .1K 11 (6F 83)
Unitair Cen.
TW14: Bedf 6E 110

Unit Workshops E1 . . . . .6G 85
(off Adler St.)
Unity Cl. CRO: New Ad 7D 170
NW10 . . . . .6C 62
SE19 . . . . .5C 138
Unity M. NW1 . . . . .2H 83
Unity Ter. HA2: Harr 1E 58
Unity Trad. Est. IG8: Wfd G 2B 52
Unity Way SE18 . . . . .3B 106
Unity Wharf SE1 . . . . .6K 15
(off Mill St.)
Universal Ho. UB1: S'hall 7C 76
University Cl. NW7 . . . . .7G 29
University College Department
of Geological Sciences Collection
. . . . .4C 6
University College London
Campbell House 3C 6
(off Taviton St.)
Chemistry Building 3C 6
(off Gordon St.)
Gower St. 4C 6 (4H 83)
University Gdns. DA5: Bexl 7F 127
University of East London
Barking Campus 4A 72
Docklands Campus 7E 88
Maryland Ho. 6G 69
Stratford Campus 6G 69
University of Greenwich
Avery Hill Campus 6G 125
Maritime Greenwich Campus
. . . . .6E 104
University of Greenwich (Woolwich Campus)
Wellington St. 4E 106
Woolwich High St. 3E 106
University of London
College Hall 4C 6
(off Malet St.)
Institute of Education 4H 83
Institute of Latin American Studies
. . . . .4H 83
Senate Ho. 5D 6 (5H 83)
University of London Observatory . . .6G 29
University of London Union 4D 6
University of North London
Highbury Cres. 6A 66
Highbury Gro. 5C 66
Hornsey Rd. 4A 66
University of Westminster
Harrow Campus 7A 42
Marylebone Campus . . .5G 5 (5E 82)
University of Westminster
(Cavendish Campus)
Bolsover St. 5K 5 (5F 83)
Hanson St. 5A 6 (5G 83)
University of Westminster (Regent Campus)
Lit. Titchfield St. 6A 6
Regent St. 7K 5 (6F 83)
Wells St. 6B 6
University of Westminster Sports Cen.
. . . . .7A 42
University Pl. DA8: Erith 7J 109
University Rd. SW19 . . . . .6B 136
University St. WC1 . . . . . . .4B 6 (4G 83)
University Way E16 . . . . .7E 88
Unwin Av. TW14: Felt 5F 111
Unwin Cl. SE15 . . . . .6G 103
Unwin Mans. W14 . . . . .6H 99
(off Queen's Club Gdns.)
Unwin Rd. SW7 . . . . .1A 16 (3B 100)
TW7: Isle 3J 113
Upbrook M. W2 . . . . .1A 10 (6A 82)
Upcerne Rd. SW10 . . . . .7A 100
Upchurch Cl. SE20 . . . . .7H 139
Upcott Ho. E9 . . . . .7J 67
(off Frampton Pk. Rd.)
Upcroft Av. HA8: Edg 5D 28
Updale Rd. DA14: Sidc 4K 143
Upfield CRO: Croy 3H 169
Upfield Rd. W7 . . . . .5K 77
Upgrove Mnr. Way SW2 . . . . .7A 120
Uphall Rd. IG1: Ilf 5F 71
Upham Pk. Rd. W4 . . . . .4A 98

Uphill BR2: Brom 4H 159
(off Westmoreland Rd.)
Uphill Dr. NW7 . . . . .5F 29
NW9 .5J 43
Uphill Gro. NW7 . . . . .4F 29
Uphill Rd. NW7 . . . . .4F 29
Upland M. SE22 . . . . .5G 121
Upland Rd. CR2: S Croy 5D 168
DA7: Bex 3F 127
E13 . . . . .4J 87
SE22 . . . . .5G 121
SM2: Sutt . . . ./B 166
Uplands BR3: Beck 2C 158
Uplands, The HA4: Ruis 1J 57
Uplands Av. E17 . . . . .2K 49
Uplands Bus. Pk. E17 . . . . .3K 49
Uplands Cl. SW14 . . . . .5H 115
Uplands Ct. N21 . . . . .7F 23
(off The Green)
Uplands End IG8: Wfd G 7H 37
Uplands Pk. Rd. EN2: Enf 2F 23
Uplands Rd. EN4: E Barn 1K 31
IG8: Wfd G 7H 37
N8 . . . . .5K 47
RM6: Chad H 3D 54
Uplands Way N21 . . . . .5F 23
Upnall Ho. SE15 . . . . .6J 103
Upney La. IG11: Bark 6J 71
Upnor Way SE17 . . . . .5E 102
Uppark Dr. IG2: Ilf 6G 53
Up. Abbey Rd. DA17: Belv 4F 109
Up. Addison Gdns. W14 . . . . .2G 99
Upper Bank St. E14 . . . . .1D 104
Up. Bardsey Wlk. N1 . . . . .6C 66
(off Douglas Rd. Nth.)
Up. Belgrave St. SW1 . . . . .1H 17 (3E 100)
Up. Berenger Wlk. SW10 . . . . .7B 100
(off Berenger Wlk.)
Up. Berkeley St. W1 . . . . . .1E 10 (6D 82)
Up. Beulah Hill SE19 . . . . .1E 156
Up. Blantyre Wlk. SW10 . . . . .7B 100
(off Blantyre Wlk.)
Up. Brighton Rd. KT6: Surb 6D 150
Up. Brockley Rd. SE4 . . . . .3B 122
(not continuous)
Up. Brook St. W1 . . . . .2G 11 (7E 82)
Upper Butts TW8: Bford 6C 96
Up. Caldy Wlk. N1 . . . . .6C 66
(off Arran Wlk.)
Up. Camelford Wlk. W11 . . . . .6G 81
(off Camborne M.)
W11 . . . . .6G 81
(off St Mark's Rd.)
Up. Cavendish Av. N3 . . . . .3J 45
Up. Cheyne Row SW3 . . . . .7C 16
UPPER CLAPTON 2H 67
Up. Clapton Rd. E5 . . . . .1H 67
Up. Clarendon Wlk. W11 . . . . .6G 81
(off Clarendon Rd.)
Up. Dartrey Wlk. SW10 . . . . .7A 100
(off Whistler Wlk.)
Up. Dengie Wlk. N1 . . . . .1C 84
(off Baddow Wlk.)
UPPER EDMONTON 5B 34
UPPER ELMERS END 5B 158
Up. Elmers End Rd. BR3: Beck 4A 158
Up. Farm Rd. KT8: W Mole 4D 148
Upper Feilde W1 . . . . .2G 11
(off Park St.)
Upper Fosters NW4 . . . . .4E 44
(off New Brent St.)
Upper Grn. E. CR4: Mitc 3D 154
Upper Grn. W. CR4: Mitc 2D 154
(not continuous)
Up. Grosvenor St. W1 . . . . .3G 11 (7E 82)
Up. Grotto Rd. TW1: Twick 2K 131
Upper Ground SE1 . . . . . .4J 13 (1A 102)
Upper Gro. SE25 . . . . .4E 156
Upper Gro. Rd. DA17: Belv 6F 109
Up. Gulland Wlk. N1 . . . . .7C 66
(off Church Rd.)
UPPER HALLIFORD 4G 147
Up. Halliford By-Pass TW17: Shep . .5G 147

Up. Halliford Grn. TW17: Shep 4G 147
Up. Halliford Rd. TW17: Shep 3G 147
Up. Hampstead Wlk. NW3 . . . . .4A 64
Up. Ham Rd. TW10: Ham 4D 132
Up. Handa Wlk. N1 . . . . .6D 66
(off Handa Wlk.)
Up. Hawkwell Wlk. N1 . . . . .1C 84
(off Maldon Cl.)
UPPER HOLLOWAY 2G 65
Up. Holly Hill Rd. DA17: Belv 5H 109
Up. James St. W1 . . . . .2B 12 (7G 83)
Up. John St. W1 . . . . .2B 12 (7G 83)
Up. Lismore Wlk. N1 . . . . .6C 66
(off Clephane Rd.)
Upper Lodge W8 . . . . .1K 99
(off Palace Grn.)
Upper Mall W6 . . . . .5C 98
(not continuous)
Upper Marsh SE1 . . . . .1H 19 (3K 101)
Up. Montagu St. W1 . . . . . . .5E 4 (5D 82)
Up. Mulgrave Rd. SM2: Cheam 7G 165
Upper Nth. St. E14 . . . . .5C 86
UPPER NORWOOD 1E 156
Up. Park Rd. BR1: Brom 1K 159
DA17: Belv 4H 109
KT2: King T 6G 133
N11 .5A 32
NW3 .5D 64
Up. Phillimore Gdns. W8 . . . . .2J 99
Up. Ramsey Wlk. N1 . . . . .6D 66
(off Ramsey Wlk.)
Up. Rawreth Wlk. N1 . . . . .1C 84
(off Basire St.)
Up. Richmond Rd. SW15 . . . . .4B 116
Up. Richmond Rd. W. SW14 . . . . . . .4G 115
TW10: Rich 4G 115
Upper Rd. E13 . . . . .3J 87
SM6: Wall 5H 167
UPPER RUXLEY 7G 145
Up. St Martin's La. WC2 . . . .2E 12 (7J 83)
Up. Selsdon Rd. CR2: Sand, Sels . . .7F 169
Up. Sheridan Rd. DA17: Belv 4G 109
UPPER SHIRLEY 4K 169
Up. Shirley Rd. CRO: Croy 2J 169
Upper Sq. TW7: Isle 3A 114
Upper St. N1 . . . . .2A 84
Up. Sunbury Rd. TW12: Hamp 1C 148
Up. Sutton La. TW5: Hest 7E 94
UPPER SYDENHAM 3H 139
Up. Tachbrook St. SW1 . . . .3B 18 (4G 101)
Up. Talbot Wlk. W11 . . . . .6G 81
(off Talbot Wlk.)
Up. Teddington Rd. KT1: Ham W 7C 132
Upper Ter. NW3 . . . . .3A 64
Up. Thames St. EC4 . . . . . .2B 14 (7B 84)
Up. Tollington Pk. N4 . . . . .1A 66
(not continuous)
Upperton Rd. DA14: Sidc 5K 143
Upperton Rd. E. E13 . . . . .3A 88
Upperton Rd. W. E13 . . . . .3A 88
UPPER TOOTING 4D 136
Up. Tooting Pk. SW17 . . . . .2D 136
Up. Tooting Rd. SW17 . . . . .4D 136
Up. Town Rd. UB6: G'frd 4F 77
Up. Tulse Hill SW2 . . . . .7K 119
Up. Vernon Rd. SM1: Sutt 5B 166
UPPER WALTHAMSTOW 4F 51
Up. Walthamstow Rd. E17 . . . . .4E 50
Up. Whistler Wlk. SW10 . . . . .7A 100
(off Worlds End Est.)
Up. Wickham La. DA16: Well 7B 108
Up. Wimpole St. W1 . . . . . . .5H 5 (5E 82)
Up. Woburn Pl. WC1 . . . . .2D 6 (3H 83)
Uppingham Av. HA7: Stan 1B 42
Upsdell Av. N13 . . . . .6F 33
Upshire Ho. E17 . . . . .2B 50
Upstall St. SE5 . . . . .1B 120
UPTON
Bexleyheath 5D 126
West Ham 7J 69
Upton Av. E7 . . . . .7J 69
Upton Cl. DA5: Bexl 6F 127
NW2 .3G 63

Upton Ct. SE20 ....7J 139
(off Blean Gro.)
Upton Dene SM2: Sutt 7K 165
Upton Gdns. HA3: Kent 5B 42
Upton Hgts. E7 ....7J 69
Upton La. E7 ....7J 69
Upton Lodge E7 ....6J 69
Upton Lodge Cl. WD23: Bush ..1B 26
UPTON PARK 1B 88
Upton Pk. 2A 88
Upton Pk. Boleyn Cinema 2B 88
Upton Pk. Rd. E7 ....7K 69
Upton Rd. CR7: Thor H 2D 156
DA5: Bexl 4E 126
DA6: Bex 4E 126
N18 ....5B 34
SE18 ....6G 107
TW3: Houn 3E 112
Upton Rd. Sth. DA5: Bexl 6F 127
Upton Vs. DA6: Bex 4E 126
Upway N12 ....6H 31
Upwey Ho. N1 ....1E 84
Upwood Rd. SE12 ....6J 123
SW16 ....1J 155
Urban M. N4 ....6B 48
Urlwin St. SE5 ....6C 102
Urlwin Wlk. SW9 ....1A 120
Urmston Dr. SW19 ....1G 135
Urmston Ho. E14 ....4E 104
(off Seyssel St.)
Urquhart Ct. BR3: Beck 7B 140
Ursula Lodges DA14: Sidc 5B 144
Ursula M. N4 ....1C 66
Ursula St. SW11 ....1C 118
Urswick Gdns. RM9: Dag 7E 72
Urswick Rd. E9 ....5J 67
RM9: Dag 7D 72
Usborne M. SW8 ....7K 101
Usher Rd. E3 ....1B 86
Usk Rd. SW11 ....4A 118
Usk St. E2 ....3K 85
Utah Bldg. SE10 ....1D 122
(off Deal's Gateway)
Utopia Village NW1 ....7E 64
Uvedale Rd. EN2: Enf 5J 23
RM10: Dag 3G 73
Uverdale Rd. SW10 ....7A 100
UXBRIDGE 1A 74
Uxbridge Ct. KT1: King T 5D 150
(off Uxbridge Rd.)
Uxbridge Rd. HA3: Hrw W 7A 26
HA5: H End, Pinn 2A 40
HA7: Stan 7A 26
KT1: King T 4D 150
TW12: Hamp, Ham H 4E 130
TW13: Felt 2A 130
UB1: S'hall 1E 94
UB4: Hayes, Yead 5G 75
UB10: Hil 3C 74
W3 ....7E 78
W5 ....7E 78
W7 ....1K 95
W12 ....1C 98
W13 ....1B 96
Uxbridge Rd. Retail Pk. UB4: Yead ..7A 76
Uxbridge St. W8 ....1J 99
Uxendon Cres. HA9: Wemb 1E 60
Uxendon Hill HA9: Wemb 1F 61

V

Vaine Ho. E9 ....6A 68
Vaizeys Wharf SE7 ....3K 105
Valance Av. E4 ....1B 36
Valan Leas BR2: Brom 3G 159
Vale, The CR0: Croy 2K 169
HA4: Ruis 4A 58
IG8: Wfd G 7D 36
N10 ....1E 46
N14 ....7C 22

Vale, The NW11 ....3F 63
Vale, The SW3 ....7A 16 (6B 100)
TW5: Hest 6C 94
TW14: Felt 6K 111
TW16: Sun 6J 129
W3 ....1K 97
Vale Cl. BR6: Farnb 4E 172
N2 ....3D 46
TW1: Twick 3A 132
W9 ....3A 82
Vale Cotts. SW15 ....3A 134
Vale Ct. EN5: New Bar 4E 20
W3 ....1B 98
W9 ....3A 82
Vale Cres. SW15 ....4A 134
Vale Cft. HA5: Pinn 5C 40
Vale Dr. EN5: Barn 4C 20
Vale End SE22 ....4F 121
Vale Est., The W3 ....1A 98
Vale Farm Sports Cen. 4B 60
Vale Gro. N4 ....7C 48
W3 ....2K 97
Vale La. W3 ....5G 79
Vale Lodge SE23 ....2J 139
Valence Av. RM8: Dag 1D 72
Valence Cir. RM8: Dag 3D 72
Valence House Mus. & Gallery 3E 72
Valence Rd. DA8: Erith 7K 109
Valence Wood Rd. RM8: Dag ...3D 72
Valencia Rd. HA7: Stan 4H 27
Valentia Pl. SW9 ....4A 120
Valentine Av. DA5: Bexl 2E 144
Valentine Ct. SE23 ....2K 139
(not continuous)
Valentine Pl. SE1 .....6A 14 (2B 102)
Valentine Rd. E9 ....6K 67
HA2: Harr 3F 59
Valentine Row SE1 ....7A 14 (2B 102)
Valentines Rd. IG1: Ilf 1F 71
Valentine's Way RM7: Rush G 2K 73
VALE OF HEALTH 3A 64
Vale of Health NW3 ....3B 64
Vale Pde. SW15 ....3A 134
Valerian Way E15 ....3G 87
Valerie Ct. SM2: Sutt 7K 165
Vale Ri. NW11 ....1H 63
Vale Rd. BR1: Brom 1E 160
CR4: Mitc 3H 155
E7 ....6K 69
KT4: Wor Pk 3B 164
KT19: Ewe 4B 164
N4 ....7C 48
SM1: Sutt 4K 165
Vale Rd. Nth. KT6: Surb 2E 162
Vale Rd. Sth. KT6: Surb 2E 162
Vale Row N5 ....3B 66
Vale Royal N7 ....7J 65
Vale Royal Ho. WC2 ....2D 12
(off Charing Cross Rd.)
Valery Pl. TW12: Hamp 7E 130
Valeside Ct. EN5: New Bar 4E 20
Vale St. SE27 ....3D 138
Valeswood Rd. BR1: Brom 5H 141
Vale Ter. N4 ....6C 48
Valetta Gro. E13 ....2J 87
Valetta Rd. W3 ....2A 98
Valette Ct. N10 ....4F 47
(off St James's La.)
Valette Ho. E9 ....6J 67
Valette St. E9 ....6J 67
Valiant Cl. RM7: Mawney 2H 55
UB5: N'olt 4A 76
Valiant Ho. E14 ....2E 104
(off Plevna St.)
SE7 ....5A 106
Valiant Path NW9 ....1A 44
Valiant Way E6 ....5D 88
Vallance Rd. E1 ....3G 85
E2 ....3G 85
N22 ....2G 47
Vallentin Rd. E17 ....4E 50

Valley, The 5A 106
Valley Av. N12 ....4G 31
Valley Cl. HA5: Pinn 2K 39
Valley Dr. NW9 ....6G 43
Valleyfield Rd. SW16 ....5K 137
Valley Flds. Cres. EN2: Enf 2F 23
Valley Gdns. HA0: Wemb 7F 61
SW19 ....7B 136
Valley Gro. SE7 ....5A 106
Valley Leisure Cen., The 5A 106
(off The Valley)
Valley Leisure Pk. CR0: Wadd ...1J 167
Valleylink Est. EN3: Pond E 6F 25
Valley M. TW1: Twick 2K 131
Valley Point Ind. Est. CR0: Bedd ..7J 155
Valley Rd. BR2: Brom 2G 159
BR5: St P 7B 144
DA8: Erith 4J 109
DA17: Belv 4H 109
SW16 ....5K 137
UB10: Uxb 2A 74
Valley Side E4 ....2H 35
SE7 ....5B 106
Valley Side Pde. E4 ....2H 35
Valley Trade Pk. CR0: Bedd 7J 155
(off Therapia La.)
Valley Vw. EN5: Barn 6B 20
Valley Wlk. CR0: Croy 2J 169
Valliere Rd. NW10 ....3C 80
Valliers Wood Rd.
DA15: Sidc 1J 143
Vallis Way KT9: Chess 4D 162
W13 ....5A 78
Val McKenzie Av. N7 ....3A 66
Valmar Rd. SE5 ....1C 120
Valmar Trad. Est. SE5 ....1C 120
Valognes Av. E17 ....1A 50
Valois Ho. SE1 ....3F 103
(off The Grange)
Valonia Gdns. SW18 ....6H 117
Vambery Rd. SE18 ....6G 107
Vanbrough Cres. UB5: N'olt 1A 76
Vanbrugh Castle SE10 ....6G 105
(off Maze Hill)
Vanbrugh Cl. E16 ....5B 88
Vanbrugh Ct. SE11 ....4K 19
Vanbrugh Dr. KT12: Walt T 7A 148
Vanbrugh Flds. SE3 ....6H 105
Vanbrugh Hill SE3 ....5H 105
SE10 ....5H 105
Vanbrugh Ho. E9 ....7J 67
(off Loddiges Rd.)
Vanbrugh M. KT12: Walt T 7A 148
Vanbrugh Pk. SE3 ....7H 105
Vanbrugh Pk. Rd. SE3 ....7H 105
Vanbrugh Pk. Rd. W. SE3 ......7H 105
Vanbrugh Rd. W4 ....3K 97
Vanbrugh Ter. SE3 ....1H 123
Vanburgh Cl. BR6: Orp 1J 173
Vanburgh Ho. E1 ....5J 9
(off Folgate St.)
Vancouver Cl. BR6: Chels 4K 173
Vancouver Ho. E1 ....1H 103
(off Reardon Path)
Vancouver Mans. HA8: Edg 1H 43
Vancouver Rd. HA8: Edg 1H 43
SE23 ....2A 140
TW10: Ham 4C 132
UB4: Yead 4K 75
Vanderbilt Rd. SW18 ....1K 135
Vanderbilt Vs. W12 ....2F 99
(off Sterne St.)
Vanderville Gdns. N2 ....2B 46
Vandome Cl. E16 ....6K 87
Vandon Ct. SW1 ....1B 18
(off Petty France)
Vandon Pas. SW1 ......1B 18 (3G 101)
Vandon St. SW1 ....1B 18 (3G 101)
Van Dyck Av.
KT3: N Mald 7K 151

Vandyke Cl. SW15 ....7F 117
Vandyke Cross SE9 ....5C 124
Vandy St. EC2 ....4G 9 (4E 84)
Vane Cl. HA3: Kent 6F 43
NW3 ....5B 64
Vanessa Cl. DA17: Belv 5G 109
Vanessa Way DA5: Bexl 3K 145
Vane St. SW1 ....3B 18 (4G 101)
Vanguard NW9 ....7F 29
Vange Ho. W10 ....5E 80
(off Sutton Way)
Van Gogh Cl. TW7: Isle 3A 114
Van Gogh Ct. E14 ....3F 105
Vanguard Bldg. E14 ....2B 104
Vanguard Cl. CR0: Croy 1B 168
E16 ....5J 87
RM7: Mawney 2G 55
Vanguard Ct. SE5 ....1E 120
Vanguard St. SE8 ....1C 122
Vanguard Trad. Est. E15 ......1E 86
Vanguard Way SM6: Wall 7J 167
TW6: H'row A 2G 111
Vanneck Sq. SW15 ....5C 116
Vanoc Gdns. BR1: Brom 4J 141
Vansittart Rd. E7 ....4H 69
Vansittart St. SE14 ....7A 104
Vanston Pl. SW6 ....7J 99
Vantage M. E14 ....1E 104
(off Preston's Rd.)
Vantage Pl. W8 ....3J 99
Vantage W. W3 ....4F 97
Vantrey Ho. SE11 ....4J 19
Vant Rd. SW17 ....5D 136
Varcoe Rd. SE16 ....5H 103
Vardens Rd. SW11 ....4B 118
Varden St. E1 ....6H 85
Vardon Cl. W3 ....6K 79
Vardon Ho. SE10 ....1E 122
Varley Ho. NW6 ....1J 81
Varley Pde. NW9 ....4A 44
Varley Rd. E16 ....6K 87
Varley Way CR4: Mitc 2B 154
Varna Rd. SW6 ....7G 99
TW12: Hamp 1F 149
Varndell St. NW1 ....1A 6 (3G 83)
Varnishers Yd. N1 ....1F 7
(off York Rd.)
Varsity Dr. TW1: Twick 5J 113
Varsity Row SW14 ....2J 115
Vartry Rd. N15 ....6D 48
Vascroft Est. NW10 ....4H 79
Vassall Ho. E3 ....3A 86
(off Antill Rd.)
Vassall Rd. SW9 ....7A 102
Vat Ho. SW8 ....7J 101
(off Rita Rd.)
Vauban Est. SE16 ....3F 103
Vauban St. SE16 ....3F 103
Vaudeville Ct. N4 ....2A 66
Vaudeville Theatre 3F 13
(off Strand)
Vaughan Almshouses
TW15: Ashf 5D 128
(off Feltham Hill Rd.)
Vaughan Av. NW4 ....5C 44
W6 ....4B 98
Vaughan Cl. TW12: Hamp 6C 130
Vaughan Est. E2 ....1J 9
Vaughan Gdns. IG1: Ilf 7D 52
Vaughan Ho. SE1 ....6A 14
(off Blackfriars Rd.)
SW4 ....7G 119
Vaughan Rd. DA16: Well 2K 125
E15 ....6H 69
HA1: Harr 6G 41
KT7: T Ditt 7B 150
SE5 ....2C 120
Vaughan St. SE16 ....2B 104
Vaughan Way E1 ....7G 85
Vaughan Williams Cl. SE8 .....5H 9 (6J 101)
VAUXHALL 5H 19 (6J 101)

Vauxhall Bri.—Victoria La.

Vauxhall Bri. SE1 6E **18** (5J **101**)
SW1 6E **18** (5J **101**)
Vauxhall Bri. Rd. SW1 2A **18** (3G **101**)
VAUXHALL CROSS 5J **101**
Vauxhall Distribution Pk. SW8 7C **18**
Vauxhall Gdns. CR2: S Croy 6C **168**
Vauxhall Gro. SW8 7G **19** (6K **101**)
Vauxhall St. SE11 5H **19** (5K **101**)
Vauxhall Wlk. SE11 5G **19** (5K **101**)
Vawdrey Cl. E1 4J **85**
Veals Mead CR4: Mitc 1C **154**
Vectis Gdns. SW17 6F **137**
Vectis Rd. SW17 6F **137**
Veda Rd. SE13 4C **122**
Vega Rd. WD23: Bush 1B **26**
Veitch Cl. TW14: Felt 7H **111**
Veldene Way HA2: Harr 3D **58**
Velde Way SE22 5E **120**
Velletri Ho. *E2* *2K* ***85***
(off Mace St.)
Vellum Dr. SM5: Cars 3E **166**
Venables Cl. RM10: Dag 4H **73**
Venables St. NW8 5B **4** (4B **82**)
Vencourt Pl. W6 4C **98**
Venetian Rd. SE5 2C **120**
Venetia Rd. N4 6B **48**
W5 2D **96**
Venice Ct. *NW8* *3B* ***4***
(off Fisherton St.)
SE5 *7C* ***102***
(off Bowyer St.)
Venner Rd. SE26 6J **139**
(not continuous)
Venners Cl. DA7: Bex 2K **127**
Venn Ho. *N1* *1K* ***83***
(off Barnsbury Est.)
Venn St. SW4 4G **119**
Ventnor Av. HA7: Stan 1B **42**
Ventnor Dr. N20 3E **30**
Ventnor Gdns. IG11: Bark 6J **71**
Ventnor Rd. SE14 7K **103**
SM2: Sutt 7K **165**
Venture Cl. DA5: Bexl 7E **126**
Venture Ct. SE12 7J **123**
Venture Ho. *W10* *6F* ***81***
(off Bridge Cl.)
Venue St. E14 5E **86**
Venus Ho. *E14* *4C* ***104***
(off Westferry Rd.)
Venus Rd. SE18 3D **106**
Vera Av. N21 5F **23**
Vera Lynn Cl. E7 4J **69**
Vera Rd. SW6 1G **117**
Verbena Cl. E16 4H **87**
Verbena Gdns. W6 5C **98**
Verdant Ct. *SE6* *7G* ***123***
(off Verdant La.)
Verdant La. SE6 7G **123**
Verdayne Av. CR0: Croy 1K **169**
Verdi Ho. *W10* *2G* ***81***
(off Herries St.)
Verdun Rd. SE18 6A **108**
SW13 6C **98**
Vere Ct. *W2* *6K* ***81***
(off Westbourne Gdns.)
Vereker Dr. TW16: Sun 3J **147**
Vereker Rd. W14 5G **99**
Vere St. W1 1J **11** (6F **83**)
Veritas Ho. *DA15: Sidc* *2A* ***144***
(off Station Rd.)
Verity Cl. W11 7G **81**
Vermeer Ct. E14 3F **105**
Vermeer Gdns. SE15 4J **121**
Vermont Cl. EN2: Enf 4G **23**
Vermont Ho. E17 2B **50**
Vermont Rd. SE19 6D **138**
SM1: Sutt 3K **165**
SW18 6K **117**
Verne Ct. *W3* *3J* ***97***
(off Vincent Rd.)
Verney Gdns. RM9: Dag 4E **72**
Verney Ho. NW8 3B **4**
Verney Rd. RM9: Dag 4E **72**
(not continuous)
SE16 6G **103**
Verney St. NW10 3K **61**
Verney Way SE16 5H **103**
Vernham Rd. SE18 6G **107**
Vernon Av. E12 4D **70**
IG8: Wfd G 7E **36**
SW20 2F **153**
Vernon Cl. KT19: Ewe 6J **163**
TW19: Stanw 1A **128**
Vernon Ct. HA7: Stan 1B **42**
NW2 3H **63**
W5 7C **78**
Vernon Cres. EN4: E Barn 6K **21**
Vernon Dr. HA7: Stan 1A **42**
Vernon Ho. SE11 6H **19**
WC1 *6F* ***7***
(off Vernon Pl.)
Vernon Mans. *W14* *6H* ***99***
(off Queen's Club Mans.)
Vernon M. E17 5B **50**
W14 4G **99**
Vernon Pl. WC1 6F **7** (5J **83**)
Vernon Ri. UB6: G'frd 5H **59**
WC1 1H **7** (3K **83**)
Vernon Rd. E3 2B **86**
E11 1G **69**
E15 7G **69**
E17 5B **50**
IG3: Ilf 1K **71**
N8 3A **48**
SM1: Sutt 5A **166**
SW14 3K **115**
TW13: Felt 2H **129**
Vernon Sq. WC1 1H **7** (3K **83**)
Vernon St. W14 4G **99**
Vernon Yd. W11 7H **81**
Veroan Rd. DA7: Bex 2E **126**
Verona Ct. *SE14* *6K* ***103***
(off Myers La.)
TW15: Ashf 4D **128**
W4 5A **98**
Verona Dr. KT6: Surb 2E **162**
Verona Rd. E7 7J **69**
Veronica Gdns. SW16 1G **155**
Veronica Ho. SE4 3B **122**
Veronica Rd. SW17 2F **137**
Veronique Gdns. IG6: Ilf 5G **53**
Verran Rd. SW12 7F **119**
Versailles Rd. SE20 7G **139**
Verulam Av. E17 6B **50**
Verulam Bldgs. WC1 5H **7**
Verulam Ct. NW9 7C **44**
UB1: S'hall *6G* ***77***
(off Haldane Rd.)
Verulam Ho. *W6* *2E* ***98***
(off Hammersmith Gro.)
Verulam Rd. UB6: G'frd 4E **76**
Verulam St. WC1 5J **7** (5A **84**)
Verwood Dr. EN4: Cockf 3J **21**
Verwood Ho. *SW8* *7K* ***101***
(off Cobbett St.)
Verwood Lodge *E14* *3F* ***105***
(off Manchester Rd.)
Verwood Rd. HA2: Harr 2G **41**
Veryan Ct. N8 5H **47**
Vesage Ct. *EC1* *6K* ***7***
(off Leather La.)
Vesey Path E14 6D **86**
Vespan Rd. W12 2C **98**
Vesta Ct. SE1 7G **15**
Vesta Rd. SE4 2A **122**
Vestris Rd. SE23 2K **139**
Vestry Ct. *SW1* *2D* ***18***
(off Monck St.)
Vestry House Mus. 4D **50**
Vestry M. SE5 1E **120**
Vestry Rd. E17 4D **50**
SE5 1E **120**
Vestry St. N1 1E **8** (3D **84**)
Vevey St. SE6 2B **140**
Veysey Gdns. RM10: Dag 3G **73**
Viaduct, The E18 2J **51**
HA0: Wemb 1E **78**
N10 4F **47**
Viaduct Bldgs. EC1 6K **7** (5A **84**)
Viaduct Pl. E2 3H **85**
Viaduct Rd. N2 2B **46**
Viaduct St. E2 3H **85**
Vian St. SE13 3D **122**
Viant Ho. *NW10* *7K* ***61***
(off Fawood Av.)
Vibart Gdns. SW2 7K **119**
Vibart Wlk. *N1* *1J* ***83***
(off Outram Pl.)
Vibia Cl. TW19: Stanw 7A **110**
Vicarage Av. SE3 7J **105**
Vicarage Cl. DA8: Erith 6J **109**
HA4: Ruis 7F **39**
KT4: Wor Pk 1A **164**
UB5: N'olt 7D **58**
Vicarage Ct. BR3: Beck 3A **158**
IG1: Ilf 5F **71**
W8 2K **99**
Vicarage Cres. SW11 1B **118**
Vicarage Dr. BR3: Beck 1C **158**
IG11: Bark 7G **71**
SW14 5K **115**
Vicarage Farm Ct. TW5: Hest 7D **94**
Vicarage Farm Rd. TW3: Houn 2C **112**
TW4: Houn 2C **112**
TW5: Hest 1C **112**
Vicarage Flds. KT12: Walt T 6A **148**
Vicarage Fld. Shop. Cen.
IG11: Bark 7G **71**
Vicarage Gdns. CR4: Mitc 3C **154**
SW14 5J **115**
W8 1J **99**
Vicarage Ga. W8 1K **99**
Vicarage Gro. SE5 1D **120**
Vicarage Ho. *KT1: King T* *2F* ***151***
(off Cambridge Rd.)
Vicarage La. E6 3D **88**
E15 7G **69**
IG1: Ilf 1H **71**
KT17: Ewe 7C **164**
(not continuous)
Vicarage M. NW9 2K **61**
Vicarage Pde. N15 4C **48**
Vicarage Pk. SE18 5G **107**
Vicarage Path N8 7J **47**
Vicarage Rd. CR0: Wadd 3A **168**
DA5: Bexl 1H **145**
E10 7C **50**
E15 7H **69**
IG8: Wfd G 7H **37**
KT1: Ham W 1C **150**
KT1: King T 2D **150**
N17 1G **49**
NW4 6C **44**
RM10: Dag 7H **73**
SE18 5G **107**
(not continuous)
SM1: Sutt 3K **165**
SW14 5J **115**
TW2: Twick 2J **131**
TW2: Whit 6G **113**
TW11: Tedd 5A **132**
TW16: Sun 5H **129**
Vicarage Wlk. KT12: Walt T 7J **147**
SW11 1B **118**
Vicarage Way HA2: Harr 7E **40**
NW10 3K **61**
Vicars Bri. Cl. HA0: Wemb 2E **78**
Vicars Cl. E9 1J **85**
E15 1J **87**
EN1: Enf 2K **23**
Vicar's Hill SE13 4D **122**
Vicars Moor La. N21 7F **23**
Vicars Oak Rd. SE19 6E **138**
Vicar's Rd. NW5 5E **64**
Vicars Wlk. RM8: Dag 3B **72**
Viceroy Cl. *N2* *4C* ***46***
(off East End Rd.)
Viceroy Ct. CR0: Croy 1D **168**
NW8 *2C* ***82***
(off Prince Albert Rd.)
Viceroy Pde. *N2* *4C* ***46***
(off High Rd.)
Viceroy Rd. SW8 1J **119**
Vickers Cl. SM6: Wall 7K **167**
Vickers Ct. *TW19: Stanw* *6A* ***110***
(off Whitley Cl.)
Vickers Rd. DA8: Erith 5K **109**
Vickers Way TW4: Houn 5C **112**
Vickery Ct. *EC1* *3D* ***8***
(off Mitchell St.)
Vickery's Wharf E14 6C **86**
Victor Cazalet Ho. *N1* *1B* ***84***
(off Gaskin St.)
Victor Gro. HA0: Wemb 7E **60**
Victoria & Albert Mus. 2B **16** (3B **100**)
Victoria Arc. *SW1* *2K* ***17***
(off Victoria St.)
Victoria Av. E6 1B **88**
EC2 6H **9** (5E **84**)
EN4: E Barn 4G **21**
HA9: Wemb 6H **61**
KT6: Surb 6D **150**
KT8: W Mole 3F **149**
N3 1H **45**
SM6: Wall 3E **166**
TW3: Houn 5E **112**
UB10: Hil 6D **56**
Victoria Bldgs. *E8* *1H* ***85***
(off Mare St.)
Victoria Chambers *EC2* *3G* ***9***
(off Luke St.)
Victoria Cl. EN4: E Barn 4G **21**
HA1: Harr 6K **41**
KT8: W Mole 3E **148**
UB3: Hayes 6F **75**
Victoria Colonnade *WC1* *6F* ***7***
(off Southampton Row)
Victoria Cotts. *E1* *5G* ***85***
(off Deal St.)
N10 2E **46**
TW9: Kew 1F **115**
Victoria Ct. E18 3K **51**
HA9: Wemb 6G **61**
SE1 *4E* ***102***
(off Hendre Rd.)
SE26 6J **139**
W3 2G **97**
Victoria Cres. N15 5E **48**
SE19 6E **138**
SW19 7H **135**
Victoria Dock Rd. E16 6H **87**
Victoria Dr. SW19 7F **117**
Victoria Emb. EC4 6F **13** (7K **83**)
SW1 6F **13** (2J **101**)
WC2 6F **13** (2J **101**)
Victoria Gdns.
TW5: Hest 1C **112**
W11 1J **99**
Victoria Gro. N12 5G **31**
W8 3A **100**
Victoria Gro. M. W2 7J **81**
Victoria Hall *E16* *1J* ***105***
(off Wesley Av., not continuous)
Victoria Ho. E6 6E **88**
HA8: Edg 6C **28**
SW1 *5J* ***17***
(off Ebury Bri. Rd.)
SW1 *3B* ***18***
(off Francis St.)
SW8 *7J* ***101***
(off Sth. Lambeth Rd.)
Victoria Ind. Est. W3 5A **80**
Victoria La. EN5: Barn 4C **20**
UB3: Harl 5F **93**

Victoria Mans. NW10 .7D 62
SW8 .7J 101
(off Sth. Lambeth Rd.)
W14 .6H 99
(off Queen's Club Mans.)
Victoria M. E8 .6G 67
NW6 .1J 81
SW4 .4F 119
SW18 .1A 136
Victoria Mills Studios E15 .1F 87
Victorian Gro. N16 .4E 66
Victorian Rd. N16 .3E 66
Victoria Palace Theatre .2A 18
(off Victoria St.)
Victoria Pde. TW9: Kew .1G 115
(off Sandycombe Rd.)
Victoria Pk. Ct. E9 .7J 67
(off Well St.)
Victoria Pk. Ind. Cen. E9 .7C 68
(off Rothbury Rd.)
Victoria Pk. Rd. E9 .1J 85
Victoria Pk. Sq. E2 .3J 85
Victoria Pas. NW8 .3B 4
Victoria Pl. TW9: Rich .5D 114
Victoria Pl. Shop. Cen. SW1 .3K 17
Victoria Point E13 .2J 87
(off Victoria Rd.)
Victoria Retail Pk. HA4: Ruis .5B 58
Victoria Ri. NW6 .7A 64
(off Hilgrove Rd.)
SW4 .3F 119
Victoria Rd. BR2: Brom .5B 160
BR7: Chst .5E 142
CR4: Mitc .7C 136
DA6: Bex .4G 127
DA8: Erith .6K 109
(not continuous)
DA15: Sidc .3K 143
E4 .1B 36
E11 .4G 69
E13 .2J 87
E17 .2E 50
E18 .2K 51
EN4: E Barn .4G 21
HA4: Ruis .1J 57
IG9: Buck H .2G 37
IG11: Bark .6F 71
KT1: King T .2F 151
KT6: Surb .6D 150
N4 .7K 47
N9 .4A 34
N15 .4G 49
N18 .4A 34
N22 .1G 47
NW4 .4E 44
NW6 .2H 81
NW7 .5G 29
NW10 .5K 79
RM10: Dag .5H 73
SM1: Sutt .5B 166
SW14 .3K 115
TW1: Twick .7B 114
TW11: Tedd .6A 132
TW13: Felt .1K 129
UB2: S'hall .3D 94
W3 .5K 79
W5 .5B 78
W8 .3A 100
WD23: Bush .1A 26
Victoria Sq. SW1 .1K 17 (3F 101)
Victoria St. DA17: Belv .5F 109
E15 .7G 69
SW1 .2K 17 (3G 101)
Victoria Ter. HA1: Harr .1J 59
N4 .1A 66
NW10 .4B 80
SW8 .2F 119
W5 .1D 96
Victoria Vs. TW9: Rich .3F 115
Victoria Way HA4: Ruis .5B 58
SE7 .5K 105
Victoria Wharf E2 .2K 89
(off Palmers Rd.)
E14 .7A 86
SE8 .5B 104
(off Dragoon Rd.)
Victoria Works NW2 .2D 62
Victoria Yd. E1 .6G 85
Victor Rd. HA2: Harr .3G 41
NW10 .3D 80
SE20 .7K 139
TW11: Tedd .4J 131
Victors Dr. TW12: Hamp .6C 130
Victors Way EN5: Barn .3C 20
Victor Vs. N9 .3J 33
Victor Wlk. NW9 .2A 44
Victor Wharf SE1 .4E 14
(off Clink St.)
Victory Av. SM4: Mord .5A 154
Victory Bus. Cen.
TW7: Isle .4K 113
Victory Cl. TW19: Stanw .1A 128
Victory Ct. W9 .4J 81
(off Hermes Cl.)
Victory Pk. HA9: Wemb .3D 60
Victory Pl. E14 .7A 86
SE17 .4D 102
SE19 .7E 138
Victory Rd. E11 .4J 51
SW19 .7A 136
Victory Rd. M. SW19 .7A 136
Victory Wlk. SE8 .1C 122
Victory Way RM7: Mawney .2H 55
SE16 .2A 104
TW5: Cran .5A 94
Video Ct. N4 .7K 47
Vidler Cl. KT9: Chess .6C 162
Vienna Cl. IG5: Ilf .2B 52
View, The SE2 .5E 108
View Cl. HA1: Harr .4H 41
N6 .7D 46
View Ct. SE12 .3A 142
View Cres. N8 .5H 47
Viewfield Cl. HA3: Kent .7E 42
Viewfield Rd. DA5: Bexl .1C 144
SW18 .6H 117
Viewland Rd. SE18 .5K 107
View Rd. N6 .7D 46
Viga Rd. N21 .6F 23
Vigilant Cl. SE26 .4G 139
Vignoles Rd. RM7: Rush G .7G 55
Vigo St. W1 .3A 12 (7G 83)
Viking Bus. Cen.
RM7: Rush G .7J 55
Viking Cl. E3 .2A 86
Viking Ct. SW6 .6J 99
Viking Gdns. E6 .4C 88
Viking Ho. SE5 .2C 120
(off Denmark Rd.)
Viking Pl. E10 .1B 68
Viking Rd. UB1: S'hall .7C 76
Viking Way DA8: Erith .3J 109
Villacourt Rd. SE18 .7A 108
Village, The NW3 .2A 64
SE7 .6A 106
Village Arc. E4 .1A 36
Village Cl. E4 .5K 35
NW3 .5B 64
(off Belsize La.)
Village Ct. E17 .5D 50
(off Eden Rd.)
SE3 .3G 123
(off Hurren Cl.)
Village Ga. TW17: Shep .5D 146
Village Hgts. IG8: Wfd G .5C 36
Village M. NW9 .2K 61
Village Mt. NW3 .4A 64
(off Perrins Ct.)
Village Pk. Cl. EN1: Enf .6K 23
Village Rd. EN1: Enf .5K 23
N3 .2G 45
Village Row SM2: Sutt .7J 165
Village Way BR3: Beck .2C 158
HA5: Pinn .7C 40
IG6: Ilf .4G 53
NW10 .4K 61
SE21 .6D 120
TW15: Ashf .4B 128
Village Way E. HA2: Harr .7E 40
Villa Rd. SW9 .3A 120
Villas on the Heath NW3 .3A 64
Villas Rd. SE18 .5G 107
(not continuous)
Villa St. SE17 .5D 102
Villiers Av. KT5: Surb .5F 151
TW2: Whit .1D 130
Villiers Cl. E10 .2C 68
KT5: Surb .4F 151
Villiers Gro. SM2: Cheam .7F 165
Villiers M. NW2 .6C 62
Villiers Path KT6: Surb .5E 150
Villiers Rd. BR3: Beck .2K 157
KT1: King T .4F 151
NW2 .6C 62
TW7: Isle .2J 113
UB1: S'hall .1D 94
Villiers St. WC2 .3E 12 (1J 101)
Vincam Cl. TW2: Whit .7E 112
Vince Ct. N1 .3D 84
Vincennes Est. SE27 .4D 138
Vincent Av. KT5: Surb .2J 163
Vincent Cl. BR2: Brom .4K 159
DA15: Sidc .1J 143
EN5: New Bar .3E 20
SE16 .2A 104
UB7: Sip .6C 92
Vincent Ct. HA6: Nwood .1H 39
N4 .1J 65
NW4 .4F 45
SW9 .1K 119
W1 .7E 4
(off Seymour Pl.)
Vincent Dr. TW17: Shep .3G 147
UB10: Uxb .1B 74
Vincent Gdns. NW2 .3B 62
Vincent Ho. SW1 .3D 18
(off Regency St.)
SW1 .4C 18
(off Vincent Sq.)
Vincent M. E3 .2C 86
Vincent Rd. CR0: Croy .7E 156
E4 .6A 36
HA0: Wemb .7F 61
KT1: King T .3G 151
N15 .4C 48
N22 .2A 48
RM9: Dag .7E 72
SE18 .4F 107
TW4: Houn .2B 112
TW7: Isle .1H 113
W3 .3J 97
Vincent Row TW12: Ham H .6G 131
Vincents Path UB5: N'olt .6C 58
(off Arnold Rd.)
Vincent Sq. N22 .2A 48
SW1 .3C 18 (4H 101)
Vincent Sq. Mans. SW1 .3B 18
(off Walcott St.)
Vincent St. E16 .5H 87
SW1 .3C 18 (4H 101)
Vincent Ter. N1 .2B 84
Vince St. EC1 .2F 9 (3D 84)
Vine Cl. KT5: Surb .6F 151
SM1: Sutt .3A 166
UB7: W Dray .4C 92
Vine Cotts. E1 .6J 85
(off Sidney Sq.)
W7 .1J 95
Vine Ct. E1 .5G 85
HA3: Kent .6E 42
Vinegar All. E17 .4D 50
Vine Gdns. IG1: Ilf .5G 71
Vinegar St. E1 .1H 103
Vinegar Yd. SE1 .6G 15 (2E 102)
Vine Gro. UB10: Hil .7C 56
Vine Hill EC1 .4J 7 (4A 84)
Vine La. SE1 .5H 15 (1F 102)
UB10: Hil .1B 74
Vine Pl. TW3: Houn .4F 113
W5 .1E 96
(off St Mark's Rd.)
Viner Cl. KT12: Walt T .6A 148
Vineries, The EN1: Enf .3K 23
N14 .6B 22
SE6 .1C 140
Vineries Bank NW7 .5J 29
Vineries Cl. RM9: Dag .6F 73
UB7: Sip .6C 92
Vine Rd. BR6: Chels .6K 173
E15 .7H 69
KT8: E Mos .4G 149
SW13 .3B 116
Vinery Row W6 .3D 98
Vines Av. N3 .1K 45
Vine Sq. W14 .5H 99
(off Star Rd.)
Vine St. EC3 .1J 15 (6F 85)
RM7: Rom .4J 55
W1 .3B 12 (7G 83)
Vine St. Bri. EC1 .4K 7 (4A 84)
Vine Yd. SE1 .6D 14
Vineyard, The TW10: Rich .5E 114
Vineyard Av. NW7 .7B 30
Vineyard Cl. KT1: King T .3F 151
SE6 .1C 140
Vineyard Gro. N3 .1K 45
Vineyard Hill Rd. SW19 .4H 135
Vineyard M. EC1 .3K 7
TW10: Rich .5E 114
Vineyard Pas. TW10: Rich .5E 114
Vineyard Path SW14 .3K 115
(off Church Path)
SW14 .3K 115
(Sheen La.)
Vineyard Rd. TW13: Felt .3J 129
Vineyard Row
KT1: Ham W .1C 150
Vineyards, The TW13: Felt .3J 129
(off High St.)
TW16: Sun .3J 147
Vineyard Wlk. EC1 .3J 7 (4A 84)
Viney Bank CR0: Sels .7B 170
Viney Rd. SE13 .3D 122
Vining St. SW9 .4A 120
Vinlake Av. UB10: Ick .3B 56
Vinopolis .4D 14 (1C 102)
Vinson Cl. BR6: Orp .1K 173
Vinson Ho. N1 .2D 84
(off Cranston Est.)
Vinter Ct. TW17: Shep .5C 146
Vintners Ct. EC4 .3D 14 (7C 84)
Vintner's Pl. EC4 .7C 84
Vintry M. E17 .4C 50
Viola Av. SE2 .4B 108
TW14: Felt .6A 112
TW19: Stanw .1A 128
Viola Sq. W12 .7B 80
Violet Av. EN2: Enf .1J 23
UB8: Hil .5B 74
Violet Cl. E16 .4G 87
SE8 .6B 104
SM3: Sutt .1G 165
SM6: Wall .1E 166
Violet Gdns. CR0: Wadd .5B 168
Violet Hill NW8 .2A 82
Violet Hill Ho. NW8 .2A 82
(off Violet Hill, not continuous)
Violet La. CR0: Wadd .6B 168
Violet Rd. E3 .4D 86
E17 .6C 50
E18 .2K 51
Violet St. E2 .4H 85
VIP Trading Est. SE7 .4A 106
Virgil Pl. W1 .6E 4 (5D 82)

Virgil St. SE1 1H 19 (3K 101)
Virgin Active
Stockley Pk. 7E 74
Virginia Cl. KT3: N Mald 4J 151
RM5: Col R 1J 55
Virginia Ct. *SE16* 2K 103
(off Eleanor Cl.)
WC1 3D 6
(off Burton St.)
Virginia Gdns. IG6: Ilf 2G 53
Virginia Ho. *E14* 7E 86
(off Newby Pl.)
TW11: Tedd 5B 132
Virginia Rd. CR7: Thor H 1B 156
E2 2J 9 (3F 85)
Virginia St. E1 7G 85
Virginia Wlk. SW2 6K 119
Visage *NW3* 7B 64
(off Winchester Rd.)
Viscount Cl. N11 6A 32
Viscount Ct. *W2* 6J 81
(off Pembridge Vs.)
Viscount Dr. E6 5D 88
Viscount Gro. UB5: N'olt 3B 76
Viscount Point SW19 7K 135
Viscount Rd. TW19: Stanw 1A 128
Viscount St. EC1 4C 8 (4C 84)
Viscount Way TW6: H'row A 4G 111
Vista, The DA14: Sidc 5K 143
SE9 6B 124
Vista Av. EN3: Enf H 2E 24
Vista Bldg. SE18 4E 106
Vista Dr. IG4: Ilf 5B 52
Vista Way HA3: Kent 6E 42
Vitae Apartments W6 3C 98
Vittoria Ho. *N1* 1K 83
(off High Rd.)
Viveash Cl. UB3: Hayes 3H 93
Vivian Av. HA9: Wemb 5G 61
NW4 5D 44
Vivian Comma Cl. N4 3B 66
Vivian Ct. N12 5E 30
Vivian Gdns. HA9: Wemb 5G 61
Vivian Mans. *NW4* 5D 44
(off Vivian Av.)
Vivian Rd. E3 2A 86
Vivian Sq. SE15 3H 121
Vivian Way N2 5B 46
Vivien Cl. KT9: Chess 7E 162
Vivienne Cl. TW1: Twick 6D 114
Vixen M. *E8* 7F 67
(off Haggerston Rd.)
Voce Rd. SE18 7H 107
Voewood Cl. KT3: N Mald 6B 152
Vogans Mill SE1 6K 15 (2F 103)
Vogler Ho. *E1* 7J 85
(off Cable St.)
Vogue Ct. BR1: Brom 1K 159
Vollasky Ho. *E1* 5K 9
(off Daplyn St.)
Volta Cl. N9 3D 34
Voltaire Rd. SW4 3H 119
Voltaire Way UB3: Hayes 7G 75
Volt Av. NW10 3A 80
Volta Way CR0: Wadd 1K 167
Voluntary Pl. E11 6J 51
Vorley Rd. N19 2G 65
Voss Ct. SW16 6J 137
Voss St. E2 3G 85
Voyager Bus. Est. *SE16* 3G 103
(off Spa Rd.)
Voyagers Cl. SE28 6C 90
Voysey Cl. N3 3G 45
Vue Cinema
Croydon 3C 168
Fallow Corner 7G 31
Finchley Rd. 6A 64
(in O2 Cen.)
Fulham Broadway 7J 99
Harrow 6J 41
(in St George's Shop. & Leisure Cen.)
Vue Cinema
Islington 2A 84
Leicester Sq. 2D 12
(off Cranbourn St.)
Shepherds Bush 2F 99
Vulcan Cl. E6 6E 88
Vulcan Ga. EN2: Enf 2F 23
Vulcan Rd. SE4 2B 122
Vulcan Sq. E14 4D 104
Vulcan Ter. SE4 2B 122
Vulcan Way N7 6K 65
SM6: Wall 7J 167
Vyne, The DA7: Bex 3H 127
Vyner Rd. W3 7K 79
Vyner St. E2 1H 85
Vyner's Way UB10: Ick 5C 56

W

W12 W12 2F 99
Wadbrook St. KT1: King T 2D 150
Wadding St. SE17 4D 102
Waddington Cl. EN1: Enf 4K 23
Waddington Rd. E15 5F 69
Waddington St. E15 6F 69
Waddington Way SE19 7C 138
WADDON 3A 168
Waddon Cl. CR0: Wadd 3A 168
Waddon Ct. Rd. CR0: Wadd 3A 168
Waddon Marsh Way
CR0: Wadd 1K 167
Waddon New Rd. CR0: Croy 3B 168
Waddon Pk. Av. CR0: Wadd 4A 168
Waddon Rd. CR0: Croy, Wadd 3A 168
Waddon Way CR0: Wadd 6A 168
Wade Ct. N10 7A 32
Wade Ho. EN1: Enf 5J 23
SE1 7K 15
(off Parkers Row)
Wades Gro. N21 7F 23
Wades Hill N21 6F 23
Wades La. TW11: Tedd 5A 132
Wades M. N21 7F 23
Wadeson St. E2 2H 85
Wade's Pl. E14 7D 86
Wadeville Av. RM6: Chad H 6E 54
Wadeville Cl. DA17: Belv 5G 109
Wadham Av. E17 7J 35
Wadham Cl. TW17: Shep 7E 146
Wadham Gdns. NW3 1C 82
UB6: G'frd 6H 59
Wadham Ho. N18 5A 34
Wadham Rd. E17 7J 35
SW15 4G 117
Wadhurst Cl. SE20 2H 157
Wadhurst Rd. SW8 1G 119
W4 3K 97
Wadley Rd. E11 7G 51
Wadsworth Bus. Cen. UB6: G'frd 2C 78
Wadsworth Cl. EN3: Pond E 5E 24
UB6: G'frd 2C 78
Wadsworth Rd. UB6: G'frd 2B 78
Wager St. E3 4B 86
WAGGONERS RDBT. 1K 111
Waggon La. N17 6B 34
Waggon M. N14 1B 32
Waghorn Rd. E13 1A 88
HA3: Kent 3D 42
Waghorn St. SE15 3G 121
Wagner M. *KT6: Surb* 5E 150
(off Avenue Elmers)
Wagner St. SE15 7J 103
Wagstaff Gdns. RM9: Dag 7C 72
Wagtail Cl. EN1: Enf 1C 24
NW9 2A 44
Wagtail Wlk. BR3: Beck 5E 158
Waight's Ct. KT2: King T 1E 150
Wainfleet Av. RM5: Col R 2J 55
Wainford Cl. SW19 1F 135
Wainwright Gro. TW7: Isle 4H 113
Wainwright Ho. *E1* 1J 103
(off Garnet St.)
Waite Davies Rd. SE12 7H 123
Waite St. SE15 6F 103
Waithman St. *EC4* 1A 14
(off Apothecary St.)
Wakefield Ct. SE26 6J 139
Wakefield Gdns. IG1: Ilf 6C 52
SE19 7E 138
Wakefield Ho. SE15 1G 121
Wakefield M. WC1 2F 7 (3J 83)
Wakefield Rd. N11 5C 32
N15 5F 49
TW10: Rich 5D 114
Wakefield St. E6 1B 88
N18 5B 34
WC1 2F 7 (4J 83)
Wakeford Cl. SW4 5G 119
Wakehams Hill HA5: Pinn 3D 40
Wakeham St. N1 6D 66
Wakehurst Rd. SW11 5C 118
Wakeling Rd. W7 5K 77
Wakeling St. E14 6A 86
Wakelin Ho. *N1* 7B 66
(off Sebbon St.)
SE23 7A 122
(off Brockley Pk.)
Wakelin Rd. E15 2G 87
Wakeman Ho. *NW10* 3F 81
(off Wakeman Rd.)
Wakeman Rd. NW10 3E 80
Wakemans Hill Av. NW9 5K 43
Wakering Rd. IG11: Bark 7G 71
(Barking Northern Relief Rd.)
IG11: Bark 6G 71
(Church Rd.)
Wakerings, The *IG11: Bark* 6G 71
(off Wakering Rd.)
Wakerley Cl. E6 6D 88
Wakley St. EC1 1A 8 (3B 84)
Walberswick St. SW8 7J 101
Walbrook EC4 2E 14 (7D 84)
(not continuous)
Walbrook Ct. *N1* 2E 84
(off Hemsworth St.)
Walbrook Ho. *N9* 2D 34
(off Huntingdon Rd.)
Walbrook Wharf *EC4* 3D 14
(off Bell Wharf La.)
Walburgh St. E1 6H 85
Walcorde Av. SE17 4C 102
Walcot Gdns. SE11 3J 19
Walcot Rd. EN3: Brim 2G 25
Walcot Sq. SE11 3K 19 (4A 102)
Walcott St. SW1 3B 18 (4G 101)
Waldair Ct. E16 2F 107
Waldeck Gro. SE27 3B 138
Waldeck Rd. N15 4B 48
SW14 3J 115
W4 6G 97
W13 6B 78
Waldeck Ter. *SW14* 3J 115
(off Waldeck Rd.)
Waldegrave Av. TW11: Tedd 5K 131
Waldegrave Ct. IG11: Bark 1H 89
Waldegrave Gdns. TW1: Twick 2K 131
Waldegrave Pk. TW1: Twick 4K 131
Waldegrave Rd. BR1: Brom 4C 160
N8 3A 48
RM8: Dag 2C 72
SE19 7F 139
TW1: Twick 4K 131
TW11: Tedd 4K 131
W5 7F 79
Waldegrove CR0: Croy 3F 169
Waldemar Av. SW6 1G 117
W13 1C 96
Waldemar Rd. SW19 5J 135
Walden Av. BR7: Chst 4D 142
N13 4H 33
RM13: Rain 2K 91
Walden Cl. DA17: Belv 5F 109
Walden Ct. SW8 1H 119
Walden Gdns. CR7: Thor H 3K 155
Walden Ho. *SW1* 4H 17
(off Pimlico Rd.)
SW11 1E 118
(off Dagnall St.)
Walden Pde. BR7: Chst 6D 142
(not continuous)
Walden Rd. BR7: Chst 6D 142
N17 1D 48
Waldenshaw Rd. SE23 1J 139
Walden St. E1 6H 85
(not continuous)
Walden Way NW7 6A 30
Waldo Cl. SW4 5G 119
Waldo Ho. *NW10* 3D 80
(off Waldo Rd.)
Waldo Ind. Est. BR1: Brom 3B 160
Waldo Pl. CR4: Mitc 7C 136
Waldorf Cl. CR2: S Croy 7B 168
Waldo Rd. BR1: Brom 3B 160
NW10 3C 80
(not continuous)
Waldram Cres. SE23 1J 139
Waldram Pk. Rd. SE23 1K 139
Waldram Pl. SE23 1J 139
Waldrist Way DA18: Erith 2F 109
Waldron Gdns. BR2: Brom 3F 159
Waldronhyrst CR2: S Croy 4B 168
Waldron M. SW3 7B 16 (6B 100)
Waldron Rd. HA1: Harr 1J 59
HA2: Harr 1J 59
SW18 3A 136
Waldrons, The CR0: Croy 4B 168
Waldron's Path CR2: S Croy 4C 168
Waldrons Yd. HA2: Harr 2H 59
Waldstock Rd. SE28 7A 90
Waleran Cl. HA7: Stan 5E 26
Walerand Rd. SE13 2E 122
Waleran Flats SE1 4E 102
Wales Av. SM5: Cars 5C 166
Wales Cl. SE15 7H 103
Wales Farm Rd. W3 5K 79
Waleton Acres SM6: Wall 6G 167
Waley St. E1 5A 86
Walfield Av. N20 7E 20
Walford Ho. E1 6G 85
Walford Rd. N16 4E 66
Walfrey Gdns. RM9: Dag 7E 72
WALHAM GREEN 1J 117
Walham Grn. Ct. *SW6* 7K 99
(off Waterford Rd.)
Walham Gro. SW6 7J 99
Walham Ri. SW19 6G 135
Walham Yd. SW6 7J 99
Walk, The *N13* 3F 33
(off Fox La.)
TW16: Sun 7H 129
Walkato Lodge
IG9: Buck H 1F 37
Walkden Rd. BR7: Chst 5E 142
Walker Cl. N11 4B 32
SE18 4G 107
TW12: Hamp 6D 130
TW14: Felt 7H 111
W7 1J 95
Walker Ho. NW1 1C 6 (2H 83)
Walker M. SW2 5A 120
Walker's Ct. W1 2C 12
Walkerscroft Mead SE21 1C 138
Walkers Lodge *E14* 2E 104
(off Manchester Rd.)
Walkers Pl. SW15 4G 117
Walkinshaw Ct. *N1* 7C 66
(off Rotherfield St.)
Walks, The N2 3B 46
Wallace Cl. SE28 7D 90
TW17: Shep 4F 147
UB10: Uxb 2A 74
Wallace Collection 7H 5 (6E 82)

Wallace Ct. *NW1* 6D 4
(off Old Marylebone Rd.)
Wallace Cres. SM5: Cars 5D 166
Wallace Ho. *N7* 6K 65
(off Caledonian Rd.)
Wallace Rd. N1 6C 66
Wallace Way *N19* 2H 65
(off St John's Way)
RM1: Rom 1K 55
Wallasey Cres. UB10: Ick 2C 56
Wallbrook Bus. Cen. TW4: Houn 3K 111
Wallbutton Rd. SE4 2A 122
Wallcote Av. NW2 1F 63
Wall Ct. *N4* 1K 65
(off Stroud Grn. Rd.)
Walled Gdn. Cl. BR3: Beck 4D 158
WALLEND 1E 88
Wall End Ct. *E6* 1E 88
(off Wall End Rd.)
Wall End Rd. E6 7E 70
Waller Dr. HA6: Nwood 2J 39
Waller Rd. SE14 1K 121
Wallers Cl. IG8: Wfd G 6J 37
RM9: Dag 1E 90
Waller Way SE10 7D 104
Wallflower St. W12 7B 80
Wallgrave Rd. SW5 4K 99
Wallingford Av. W10 5F 81
WALLINGTON 6F 167
Wallington Cl. HA4: Ruis 6E 38
Wallington Cnr. *SM6: Wall* 4F 167
(off Manor Rd. Nth.)
Wallington Ct. *SM6: Wall* 6F 167
(off Stanley Pk. Rd.)
WALLINGTON GREEN 4F 167
Wallington Rd. IG3: Ilf 7K 53
Wallington Sq. SM6: Wall 6F 167
Wallis All. SE1 6D 14
Wallis Cl. SW11 3B 118
Wallis Ho. SE14 1A 122
Wallis M. *N8* 3A 48
(off Courcy Rd.)
Wallis Rd. E9 6B 68
UB1: S'hall 6F 77
Wallis's Cotts. SW2 7J 119
Wallman Pl. N22 1K 47
Wallorton Gdns. SW14 4K 115
Wallside EC2 6D 8
Wall St. N1 6D 66
Wallwood Rd. E11 7F 51
Wallwood St. E14 5B 86
Walmar Cl. EN4: Had W 1G 21
Walmer Cl. BR6: Farnb 4H 173
E4 2J 35
RM7: Mawney 2H 55
Walmer Ct. *KT5: Surb* 5E 150
(off Cranes Pk.)
Walmer Gdns. W13 2A 96
Walmer Ho. *W10* 6F 81
(off Bramley Rd.)
Walmer Pl. W1 5E 4
Walmer Rd. W10 6E 80
W11 7G 81
Walmer St. W1 5E 4 (5D 82)
Walmer Ter. SE18 4G 107
Walmgate Rd. UB6: G'frd 1B 78
Walmington Fold N12 6D 30
Walm La. NW2 6E 62
Walney Wlk. N1 6C 66
Walnut Av. UB7: W Dray 3C 92
Walnut Cl. IG6: Ilf 4G 53
SE8 6B 104
SM5: Cars 5D 166
UB3: Hayes 7G 75
Walnut Ct. E17 4E 50
W5 2E 96
W8 3K 99
(off St Mary's Ga.)
Walnut Flds. KT17: Ewe 7B 164
Walnut Gdns. E15 5G 69
Walnut Gro. EN1: Enf 5J 23
Walnut M. *N22* 3A 48
(off High Rd.)
SM2: Sutt 7A 166
Walnut Rd. E10 2C 68
Walnut Tree Av. *CR4: Mitc* 3C 154
(off Dearn Gdns.)
Walnut Tree Cl. BR7: Chst 1H 161
SW13 1B 116
TW17: Shep 3E 146
Walnut Tree Cotts. SW19 5G 135
Walnut Tree Ho. *SW10* 6K 99
(off Tregunter Rd.)
Walnut Tree Rd. RM8: Dag 2E 72
SE10 5G 105
(not continuous)
TW5: Hest 6D 94
TW8: Bford 6E 96
TW17: Shep 2E 146
Walnut Tree Wlk. SE11 3J 19 (4A 102)
Walnut Way HA4: Ruis 6A 58
IG9: Buck H 3G 37
Walpole Av. TW9: Kew 2F 115
Walpole Cl. W13 2C 96
Walpole Ct. TW2: Twick 2J 131
W14 3F 99
(off Blythe Rd.)
Walpole Cres. TW11: Tedd 5K 131
Walpole Gdns. TW2: Twick 2J 131
W4 5J 97
Walpole Ho. *KT8: W Mole* 5E 148
(off Approach Rd.)
SE1 7J 13
(off Westminster Bri. Rd.)
Walpole Lodge W13 1C 96
Walpole M. NW8 1B 82
SW19 6B 136
Walpole Pk. Summer Theatre 1C 96
Walpole Pl. SE18 4F 107
TW11: Tedd 5K 131
Walpole Rd. BR2: Brom 5B 160
CR0: Croy 2D 168
E6 7A 70
E17 4A 50
E18 1H 51
KT6: Surb 7E 150
N17 2C 48
(not continuous)
SW19 6B 136
TW2: Twick 2J 131
TW11: Tedd 5K 131
Walpole St. SW3 5E 16 (5D 100)
Walrond Av. HA9: Wemb 5E 60
Walsham Cl. N16 1G 67
SE28 7D 90
Walsham Ho. SE14 2K 121
SE17 5D 102
(off Blackwood St.)
Walsham Rd. SE14 2K 121
TW14: Felt 7K 111
Walsingham NW8 1B 82
Walsingham Gdns. KT19: Ewe 4A 164
Walsingham Lodge SW13 1C 116
Walsingham Mans. *SW6* 7K 99
(off Fulham Rd.)
Walsingham Pk. BR7: Chst 2H 161
Walsingham Pl. SW4 6E 118
Walsingham Rd. CR4: Mitc 5D 154
E5 3G 67
EN2: Enf 4J 23
W13 1A 96
Walsingham Wlk. DA17: Belv 6G 109
Walston Ho. *SW1* 5C 18
(off Aylesford St.)
Walter Besant Ho. *E1* 3K 85
(off Bancroft Rd.)
Walter Ct. *W3* 6J 79
(off Lynton Ter.)
Walter Grn. Ho. *SE15* 1J 121
(off Lausanne Rd.)
Walter Ho. *SW10* 7B 100
(off Riley St.)
Walter Hurford Pde. *E12* 4E 70
(off Walton Rd.)
Walter Langley Ct. *SE16* 2J 103
(off Brunel Rd.)
Walter Rodney Cl. E6 6D 70
Walter Savil Twr. *E17* 6C 50
(off Colchester Rd.)
Walters Cl. *SE17* 4D 102
(off Brandon St.)
UB3: Hayes 2H 93
Walters Ho. *SE17* 6B 102
(off Otto St.)
Walters Rd. EN3: Pond E 4D 24
SE25 4E 156
Walter St. E2 3K 85
KT2: King T 1E 150
Walters Way SE23 6K 121
Walters Yd. BR1: Brom 2J 159
Walter Ter. E1 6K 85
Walterton Rd. W9 4H 81
Walter Wlk. HA8: Edg 6D 28
Waltham Av. NW9 6G 43
UB3: Harl 3E 92
Waltham Dr. HA8: Edg 2G 43
Waltham Forest Pool & Track 2D 50
Waltham Forest Theatre 2C 50
Waltham Ho. NW8 1A 82
Waltham Pk. Way E17 1C 50
Waltham Rd. IG8: Wfd G 6H 37
SM5: Cars 7B 154
UB2: S'hall 3C 94
WALTHAMSTOW 3C 50
Walthamstow Av. E4 6G 35
Walthamstow Bus. Cen. E17 2E 50
Walthamstow Stadium (Greyhound) 7J 35
Waltham Way E4 3G 35
Waltheof Av. N17 1D 48
Waltheof Gdns. N17 1D 48
Walton Av. HA2: Harr 5D 58
HA9: Wemb 3H 61
KT3: N Mald 4B 152
SM3: Cheam 3H 165
Walton Bri. KT12: Walt T 7G 147
TW17: Shep 7G 147
Walton Bri. Rd. TW17: Shep 7G 147
Walton Cl. E5 3K 67
HA1: Harr 4H 41
NW2 2D 62
SW8 7J 101
Walton Ct. *CR2: S Croy* 5C 168
(off Warham Rd.)
EN5: New Bar 5F 21
Walton Cft. HA1: Harr 4J 59
Walton Dr. HA1: Harr 4H 41
NW10 6K 61
Walton Gdns. HA9: Wemb 2E 60
TW13: Felt 4H 129
W3 5H 79
Walton Grn. CR0: New Ad 7D 170
Walton Ho. *E2* 3J 9
(off Montclare St.)
E4 5H 35
(off Chingford Mt. Rd.)
E17 3D 50
(off The Drive)
SW1 2E 16
(off Lennox Gdns. M.)
Walton La. KT13: Weyb 7F 147 & 7G 147
TW17: Shep 7F 147
WALTON-ON-THAMES 7K 147
Walton Pl. SW3 1E 16 (3D 100)
Walton Rd. DA14: Sidc 2C 144
E12 4E 70
(not continuous)
E13 2A 88
HA1: Harr 4H 41
KT8: W Mole, E Mos 4D 148
KT12: Walt T 5A 148
N15 4F 49
RM5: Col R 1F 55
Walton Screen Cinema 7J 147
Walton St. EN2: Enf 1J 23
SW3 3D 16 (4C 100)
Walton Swimming Pool 7K 147
Walton Vs. *N1* 7E 66
(off Downham Rd.)
Walton Way CR4: Mitc 4G 155
W3 5H 79
Walt Whitman Cl. SE24 4B 120
WALWORTH 5C 102
Walworth Pl. SE17 5C 102
Walworth Rd. SE17 4C 102
Walwyn Av. BR1: Brom 3B 160
Wanborough Dr. SW15 1D 134
Wanderer Dr. IG11: Bark 3C 90
Wandle Bank CR0: Bedd 3J 167
SW19 7B 136
Wandle Ct. CR0: Bedd 3J 167
KT19: Ewe 4J 163
Wandle Ct. Gdns. CR0: Bedd 3J 167
Wandle Ho. BR1: Brom 5F 141
NW8 5C 4
(off Penfold St.)
Wandle Industrial Mus.
(within The Vestry Hall Annex) 3D 154
Wandle Meadow Nature Pk. 5A 136
Wandle Pk. Trad. Est., The
CR0: Croy 1B 168
Wandle Recreation Cen. 6K 117
Wandle Rd. CR0: Bedd 3J 167
CR0: Croy 3C 168
SM4: Mord 4A 154
SM6: Wall 3F 167
SW17 2C 136
Wandle Side CR0: Wadd 3K 167
SM6: Wall 3F 167
Wandle Technology Pk. CR4: Mitc 7D 154
Wandle Trad. Est. CR4: Mitc 7D 154
Wandle Way CR4: Mitc 5D 154
SW18 1K 135
Wandon Rd. SW6 7K 99
(not continuous)
Wandsdown Pl. SW6 7K 99
WANDSWORTH 5K 117
Wandsworth Bri. SW6 3K 117
Wandsworth Bri. Rd. SW6 1K 117
WANDSWORTH COMMON 1D 136
Wandsworth Comn. W. Side SW18 5A 118
WANDSWORTH GYRATORY 5K 117
Wandsworth High St. SW18 5J 117
Wandsworth Mus. 5K 117
Wandsworth Plain SW18 5K 117
Wandsworth Rd. SW8 7E 18 (3F 119)
Wangey Rd. RM6: Chad H 7D 54
Wangford Ho. *SW9* 4B 120
(off Loughborough Pk.)
Wanless Rd. SE24 3C 120
Wanley Rd. SE5 4D 120
Wanlip Rd. E13 4K 87
Wannock Gdns. IG6: Ilf 1F 53
Wansbeck Ct. *EN2: Enf* 3G 23
(off Waverley Rd.)
Wansbeck Rd. E9 7B 68
Wansey St. SE17 4C 102
Wansford Rd. IG8: Wfd G 1A 52
WANSTEAD 6K 51
Wanstead Cl. BR1: Brom 2A 160
Wanstead Gdns. IG4: Ilf 6B 52
Wanstead La. IG1: Ilf 6B 52
Wanstead Leisure Cen. 6A 52
Wanstead Pk. Av. E12 1B 70
Wanstead Pk. Rd. IG1: Ilf 6B 52
Wanstead Pl. E11 6J 51
Wanstead Rd. BR1: Brom 2A 160
Wansunt Rd. DA5: Bexl 1J 145
Wantage Rd. SE12 5H 123
Wantz Rd. RM10: Dag 4H 73
WAPPING 1H 103
Wapping Dock St. E1 1H 103
Wapping High St. E1 1G 103
Wapping La. E1 7H 85

Wapping Wall E1 ...1J 103
Warbank La. KT2: King T ...7B 134
Warbeck Rd. W12 ...2D 98
Warberry Rd. N22 ...1K 47
Warboys App. KT2: King T ...6H 133
Warboys Cres. E4 ...5K 35
Warboys Rd. KT2: King T ...6H 133
Warburton Cl.
  HA3: Hrw W ...6C 26
  N1 ...6E 66
  (off Culford Rd.)
Warburton Ct. HA4: Ruis ...2J 57
Warburton Ho. E8 ...1H 85
  (off Warburton St.)
Warburton Rd. E8 ...1H 85
  TW2: Whit ...1F 131
Warburton St. E8 ...1H 85
Warburton Ter. E17 ...2D 50
Wardalls Gro. SE14 ...7J 103
Wardalls Ho. SE8 ...6B 104
  (off Staunton St.)
Ward Cl. CR2: S Croy ...6E 168
  DA8: Erith ...6K 109
Wardell Cl. NW7 ...7F 29
Wardell Fld. NW9 ...1A 44
Wardell Ho. SE10 ...6E 104
  (off Welland St.)
Warden Av. HA2: Harr ...1D 58
Warden Rd. NW5 ...6E 64
Wardens Fld. Cl.
  BR6: Chels ...6J 173
Wardens Gro. SE1 ...5C 14 (1C 102)
Wardle St. E9 ...5K 67
Wardley St. SW18 ...7K 117
Wardo Av. SW6 ...1G 117
Wardour M. W1 ...1B 12
Wardour St. W1 ...7B 6 (6G 83)
Ward Point SE11 ...4J 19 (4A 102)
Ward Rd. E15 ...1F 87
  N19 ...3G 65
  SW19 ...1A 154
Wardrobe, The TW9: Rich ...5D 114
  (off Old Pal. Yd.)
Wardrobe Pl. EC4 ...1B 14
Wardrobe Ter. EC4 ...2B 14
Wards Rd. IG2: Ilf ...7H 53
Wards Wharf App. E16 ...1B 106
Ware Ct. HA8: Edg ...4K 27
  SM1: Sutt ...4H 165
Wareham Cl. TW3: Houn ...4F 113
Wareham Ct. N1 ...7E 66
  (off Hertford Rd.)
Wareham Ho. SW8 ...7K 101
Warehouse Theatre ...2D 168
Warehouse Way E16 ...7K 87
Waremead Rd. IG2: Ilf ...5F 53
Warepoint Dr. SE28 ...2H 107
Warfield Rd. NW10 ...3F 81
  TW12: Hamp ...1F 149
  TW14: Felt ...7G 111
Warfield Yd. NW10 ...3F 81
  (off Warfield Rd.)
Wargrave Av. N15 ...6F 49
Wargrave Ho. E2 ...2J 9
  (off Navarre St.)
Wargrave Rd. HA2: Harr ...3G 59
Warham Rd. CR2: S Croy ...5B 168
  HA3: W'stone ...2K 41
  N4 ...5A 48
Warham St. SE5 ...7B 102
Waring & Gillow Est. W3 ...4G 79
Waring Cl. BR6: Chels ...6K 173
Waring Dr. BR6: Chels ...6K 173
Waring Rd. DA14: Sidc ...6C 144
Waring St. SE27 ...4C 138
Warkworth Gdns. TW7: Isle ...7A 96
Warkworth Rd. N17 ...7J 33
Warland Rd. SE18 ...7H 107
Warley Av. RM8: Dag ...7F 55
  UB4: Hayes ...6J 75
Warley Cl. E10 ...1B 68

Warley Rd. IG5: Ilf ...1E 52
  IG8: Wfd G ...7E 36
  N9 ...2D 34
  UB4: Hayes ...6J 75
Warley St. E2 ...3K 85
Warlingham Ct. SE13 ...6E 122
Warlingham Rd. CR7: Thor H ...4B 156
Warlock Rd. W9 ...4H 81
Warlters Cl. N7 ...4J 65
Warlters Rd. N7 ...4J 65
Warltersville Mans. N19 ...7J 47
Warltersville Rd. N19 ...7J 47
Warmington Cl. E5 ...3K 67
Warmington Rd. SE24 ...6C 120
Warmington St. E13 ...4J 87
Warmington Twr. SE14 ...1A 122
Warminster Gdns. SE25 ...2G 157
Warminster Rd. SE25 ...2F 157
Warminster Sq. SE25 ...2G 157
Warminster Way CR4: Mitc ...1F 155
Warmsworth NW1 ...1G 83
  (off Pratt St.)
Warmwell Av. NW9 ...1A 44
Warndon St. SE16 ...4K 103
Warneford Rd. HA3: Kent ...3D 42
Warneford St. E9 ...1H 85
Warne Pl. DA15: Sidc ...6B 126
Warner Av. SM3: Cheam ...2G 165
Warner Cl. E15 ...5G 69
  NW9 ...7B 44
  TW12: Hamp ...5D 130
  UB3: Harl ...7F 93
Warner Ho. BR3: Beck ...6D 140
  NW8 ...3A 82
  SE13 ...2D 122
  (off Russett Way)
Warner Pl. E2 ...2G 85
Warner Rd. BR1: Brom ...7H 141
  E17 ...4A 50
  N8 ...4H 47
  SE5 ...1C 120
Warners Cl. IG8: Wfd G ...5D 36
Warners La. KT2: King T ...4D 132
Warners Path IG8: Wfd G ...5D 36
Warner St. EC1 ...4J 7 (4A 84)
Warner Ter. E14 ...5D 86
  (off Broomfield St.)
Warner Village Cinema
  Croydon ...1K 167
  Dagenham ...1E 90
Warner Yd. EC1 ...4J 7
Warnford Ct. EC2 ...7F 9
Warnford Ho. SW15 ...6A 116
  (off Tunworth Cres.)
Warnford Ind. Est. UB3: Hayes ...2G 93
Warnford Rd. BR6: Chels ...5K 173
Warnham WC1 ...2G 7
  (off Sidmouth St.)
Warnham Ct. Rd. SM5: Cars ...7D 166
Warnham Ho. SW2 ...7K 119
  (off Up. Tulse Hill)
Warnham Rd. N12 ...5H 31
Warple M. W3 ...2A 98
Warple Way W3 ...2A 98
  (not continuous)
Warren, The ...1A 94
Warren, The E12 ...4C 70
  KT4: Wor Pk ...4K 163
  SE7 ...6A 106
  TW5: Hest ...7D 94
  UB4: Hayes ...6J 75
Warren Av. BR1: Brom ...7G 141
  BR6: Chels ...5K 173
  CR2: Sels ...7K 169
  E10 ...3E 68
  TW10: Rich ...4H 115
Warren Cl. DA6: Bex ...5G 127
  HA9: Wemb ...2D 60
  N9 ...7E 24
  SE21 ...7C 120
  UB4: Yead ...5A 76

Warren Ct. BR3: Beck ...7C 140
  CR0: Croy ...1E 168
  N17 ...3G 49
  (off High Cross Rd.)
  W1 ...3B 6
  (off Warren St.)
  W5 ...5C 78
Warren Cres. N9 ...7A 24
Warren Cutting KT2: King T ...7K 133
Warrender Rd. N19 ...3G 65
Warrender Way HA4: Ruis ...7J 39
Warren Dr. HA4: Ruis ...7B 40
  UB6: G'frd ...4F 77
Warren Dr., The E11 ...7A 52
Warren Dr. Nth. KT5: Surb ...1H 163
Warren Dr. Sth. KT5: Surb ...1J 163
Warren Farm Cotts. RM6: Chad H ...4F 55
Warren Farm School Sports Cen. ...3H 95
Warren Flds. HA7: Stan ...4H 27
Warren Footpath TW1: Twick ...1C 132
Warren Gdns. BR6: Chels ...5K 173
  E15 ...5F 69
Warren Ho. N17 ...3G 49
  (off High Cross Rd.)
  W14 ...4H 99
  (off Beckford Cl.)
Warren La. HA7: Stan ...2F 27
  SE18 ...3F 107
Warren La. Ga. SE18 ...3F 107
Warren Ho. N1 ...4A 6 (4G 83)
Warren Pk. KT2: King T ...6J 133
Warren Pk. Rd. SM1: Sutt ...6B 166
Warren Pl. E1 ...6K 85
  (off Caroline St.)
Warren Pond Rd. E4 ...1C 36
  (not continuous)
Warren Ri. KT3: N Mald ...1K 151
Warren Rd. BR2: Hayes ...2J 171
  BR6: Chels ...5K 173
  CR0: Croy ...1E 168
  DA6: Bex ...5G 127
  DA14: Sidc ...3C 144
  E4 ...2K 35
  E10 ...3E 68
  E11 ...6A 52
  (not continuous)
  IG6: Ilf ...5H 53
  KT2: King T ...6J 133
  NW2 ...2B 62
  SW19 ...6C 136
  TW2: Whit ...6G 113
  TW15: Ashf ...7G 129
  UB10: Ick ...4A 56
  WD23: Bushy ...1B 26
Warren Sports Cen. ...5F 55
Warrens Shawe La. HA8: Edg ...2C 28
Warren St. W1 ...4A 6 (4G 83)
Warren Ter. RM6: Chad H ...4D 54
Warren Wlk. SE7 ...6A 106
Warren Way NW7 ...6B 30
Warren Wood Cl. BR2: Hayes ...2H 171
Warriner Dr. N9 ...3R 34
Warriner Gdns. SW11 ...1D 118
Warrington Ct. CR0: Wadd ...3B 168
  (off Warrington Rd.)
Warrington Cres. W9 ...4A 82
Warrington Gdns. W9 ...4A 82
Warrington Rd. CR0: Wadd ...3B 168
  HA1: Harr ...5J 41
  RM8: Dag ...2D 72
  TW10: Rich ...5D 114
Warrington Sq. RM8: Dag ...2D 72
Warrior Cl. SE28 ...1H 107
Warrior Sq. E12 ...4E 70
Warsaw Cl. HA4: Ruis ...6J 57
Warspite Ho. E14 ...4D 104
  (off Cahir St.)
Warspite Rd. SE18 ...3C 106
Warton Rd. E15 ...7E 68
Warwall E6 ...6F 89
Warwark Ct. KT6: Surb ...2E 162

Warwick W14 ...4H 99
  (off Kensington Village)
Warwick Av. HA2: Harr ...4D 58
  HA8: Edg ...3C 28
  W2 ...4A 82
  W9 ...4K 81
Warwick Bldg. SW8 ...6F 101
Warwick Chambers W8 ...3J 99
  (off Pater St.)
Warwick Cl. DA5: Bexl ...7F 127
  EN4: E Barn ...5G 21
  TW12: Hamp ...7G 131
  W8 ...3H 99
  (off Kensington High St.)
  WD23: Bushy ...1D 26
Warwick Ct. BR2: Brom ...2G 159
  EC4 ...1B 14
  (off Warwick La.)
  EN5: New Bar ...5E 20
  (off Station Rd.)
  HA3: W'stone ...3J 41
  N11 ...6C 32
  UB5: N'olt ...5E 58
  (off Newmarket Av.)
  W7 ...6K 77
  (off Copley Cl.)
  WC1 ...6H 7 (5K 83)
Warwick Cres. UB4: Hayes ...4H 75
  W2 ...5A 82
Warwick Dene W5 ...1E 96
Warwick Dr. SW15 ...3D 116
Warwick Est. W2 ...5K 81
Warwick Gdns. CR7: Thor H ...3A 156
  EN5: Barn ...1C 20
  IG1: Ilf ...1F 71
  KT7: T Ditt ...5K 149
  N4 ...5C 48
  W14 ...3H 99
Warwick Gro. E5 ...1H 67
  KT5: Surb ...7F 151
Warwick Ho. E16 ...1J 105
  (off Wesley Av.)
  KT2: King T ...1E 150
  (off Acre Rd.)
  SW9 ...2A 120
Warwick Ho. St. SW1 ...4D 12 (1H 101)
Warwick La. EC4 ...7B 8 (6B 84)
Warwick Lodge TW2: Twick ...3F 131
Warwick Mans SW5 ...4J 99
  (off Cromwell Cres.)
Warwick Pde. HA3: Kent ...2B 42
Warwick Pas. EC4 ...7B 8
  (off Old Bailey)
Warwick Pl. KT7: T Ditt ...6A 150
  W5 ...2D 96
  W9 ...5A 82
Warwick Pl. Nth. SW1 ...4A 18 (4G 101)
Warwick Rd. CR7: Thor H ...3A 156
  DA14: Sidc ...5B 144
  DA16: Well ...3C 126
  E4 ...5H 35
  E11 ...5K 51
  E12 ...5C 70
  E15 ...6H 69
  E17 ...1B 50
  EN5: New Bar ...4E 20
  KT1: Ham W ...1C 150
  KT3: N Mald ...3J 151
  KT7: T Ditt ...5K 149
  N11 ...6C 32
  N18 ...4A 34
  SE20 ...3H 157
  SM1: Sutt ...4A 166
  SW5 ...4H 99
  TW2: Twick ...1J 131
  TW4: Houn ...3K 111
  TW15: Ashf ...5A 128
  UB2: S'hall ...3D 94
  UB7: W Dray ...2A 92
  W5 ...2D 96
  W14 ...4H 99

Warwick Row—Wayfield Link

Warwick Row SW1 1K **17** (3F **101**)
Warwickshire Path SE8 7B **104**
Warwickshire Rd. N16 4E **66**
Warwick Sq. EC4 7B **8** (6B **84**)
SW1 5A **18** (5G **101**)
(not continuous)
Warwick Sq. M. SW1 4A **18** (4G **101**)
Warwick St. W1 2B **12** (7G **83**)
Warwick Ter. *E17* *5F* ***51***
(off Lea Bri. Rd.)
SE18 6H **107**
Warwick Way SW1 5J **17** (5F **101**)
Warwick Yd. EC1 4D **8** (4C **84**)
Washbourne Ct. *N9* *2B* ***34***
(off Acton Cl.)
Washington Av. E12 4D **70**
Washington Bldg. *SE10* *1D* ***122***
(off Deal's Gateway)
Washington Cl. E3 3D **86**
Washington Ho. *E17* *2B* ***50***
(off Priory Ct.)
SW3 *7E* ***10***
(off Basil St.)
Washington Rd. E6 7A **70**
E18 2H **51**
KT1: King T 2G **151**
KT4: Wor Pk 2D **164**
SW13 7C **98**
Wastdale Rd. SE23 1K **139**
Watch, The N12 4F **31**
Watchfield Ct. W4 5J **97**
Watcombe Cotts. TW9: Kew 6G **97**
Watcombe Pl. SE25 5H **157**
Watcombe Rd. SE25 5H **157**
Waterbank Rd. SE6 3D **140**
Waterbeach Rd.
RM9: Dag 6C **72**
Water Brook La. NW4 5E **44**
Watercress Pl. N1 7E **66**
Waterdale Rd. SE2 6A **108**
Waterden Ct. W11 1G **99**
Waterden Cres. E15 5C **68**
Waterden Rd. E15 5C **68**
Waterer Ho. SE6 4E **140**
Waterer Ri. SM6: Wall 6H **167**
Waterfall Cl. N14 3B **32**
Waterfall Cotts. SW19 6B **136**
Waterfall Rd. N11 4A **32**
N14 4A **32**
SW19 6B **136**
Waterfall Ter. SW17 6C **136**
Waterfall Wlk. N14 1A **32**
Waterfield Cl. DA17: Belv 3G **109**
SE28 1B **108**
Waterfield Gdns. SE25 4D **156**
Waterford Ho. *W11* *7H* ***81***
(off Kensington Pk. Rd.)
Waterford Rd. SW6 7K **99**
(not continuous)
Waterford Way NW10 5D **62**
Waterfront Leisure Cen.
Woolwich **3E 106**
Waterfront Studios Bus. Cen.
E16 *1J* ***105***
(off Dock Rd.)
Water Gdns. HA7: Stan 6G **27**
Water Gdns., The W2 7D **4** (6C **82**)
Watergardens, The
KT2: King T 6J **133**
Watergate EC4 2A **14** (7B **84**)
Watergate St. SE8 6C **104**
Watergate Wlk. WC2 4F **13** (1J **101**)
Waterhall Av. E4 4B **36**
Waterhall Cl. E17 1K **49**
Waterhead *NW1* *1A* ***6***
(off Varndell St.)
Waterhouse Cl. E16 5B **88**
NW3 5B **64**
W6 4F **99**
Waterhouse Sq. EC1 6J **7** (5A **84**)
Wateridge Cl. E14 3C **104**
Water La. DA14: Sidc 2F **145**
E15 6G **69**
EC3 3H **15** (7E **84**)
IG3: Ilf 3J **71**
KT1: King T 1D **150**
N9 1C **34**
NW1 7F **65**
SE14 7J **103**
TW1: Twick 1A **132**
TW9: Rich 5D **114**
Water Lily Cl. UB2: S'hall 2G **95**
Waterloo Bri. SE1 3G **13**
WC2 3G **13** (7K **83**)
Waterloo Cl. E9 5J **67**
TW14: Felt 1H **129**
Waterloo Gdns. E2 2J **85**
N1 7B **66**
RM7: Rom 6K **55**
Waterloo Pas. NW6 7H **63**
Waterloo Pl. *SM5: Cars* *3D* ***166***
(off Wrythe La.)
SW1 4C **12** (1H **101**)
TW9: Kew 6G **97**
TW9: Rich 4E **114**
Waterloo Rd. E6 7A **70**
E7 5H **69**
E10 7C **50**
IG6: Ilf 2G **53**
NW2 1C **62**
RM7: Rom, Rush G 5K **55**
SE1 4H **13** (1K **101**)
SM1: Sutt 5B **166**
Waterloo Ter. N1 7B **66**
Waterlow Ct. NW11 7K **45**
Waterlow Rd. N19 1G **65**
Waterman Bldg. E14 2B **104**
Watermans Art Cen., Cinema & Theatre
6E **96**
Watermans Cl. KT2: King T 7E **132**
Watermans Ct. *TW8: Bford* *6D* ***96***
(off High St.)
Watermans M. W5 7E **78**
Waterman St. SW15 3F **117**
Watermans Wlk. EC4 3E **14**
SE16 2A **104**
Waterman Way E1 1H **103**
Watermead TW14: Felt 1G **129**
Watermead Ho. E9 5A **68**
Watermead La. SM5: Cars 7D **154**
Watermeadow La. SW6 2A **118**
Watermead Rd. SE6 4E **140**
Watermead Way N17 3G **49**
Watermen's Sq. SE20 7J **139**
Water M. SE15 4J **121**
Watermill Bus. Cen.
EN3: Brim 2G **25**
Watermill Cl. TW10: Ham 3C **132**
Water Mill Ho. TW13: Hanw 2E **130**
Watermill La. N18 5K **33**
Watermill Way SW19 1A **154**
TW13: Hanw 2D **130**
Watermint Quay N16 7G **49**
Water Rd. HA0: Wemb 1F **79**
Water's Edge *SW6* *1E* ***116***
(off Palemead Cl.)
Watersedge KT19: Ewe 4J **163**
Watersfield Way HA8: Edg 7J **27**
Waters Gdns. RM10: Dag 5G **73**
Waterside BR3: Beck 1B **158**
E17 6J **49**
N1 2C **84**
W2 6A **4**
Waterside Av. *BR3: Beck* *5E* ***158***
(off Adamson Way)
Waterside Bus. Cen. TW7: Isle 4B **114**
Waterside Cl. E3 1B **86**
IG11: Bark 4A **72**
KT6: Surb 2E **162**
SE16 2G **103**
SE28 1K **107**
UB5: N'olt 3D **76**
Waterside Ct. *SM5: Cars* *3E* ***166***
(off Millpond Pl.)
Waterside Dr. KT12: Walt T 5J **147**
Waterside Ho. *E14* *2D* ***104***
(off Admirals Way)
Waterside Pl. NW1 1E **82**
Waterside Point SW11 7C **100**
Waterside Rd. UB2: S'hall 3E **94**
Waterside Twr. *SW6* *2A* ***118***
(off The Boulevard)
Waterside Trad. Cen. W7 3J **95**
Waterside Way SW17 4A **136**
Watersmeet Way SE28 6C **90**
Waterson St. E2 1H **9** (3E **84**)
Waters Pl. SW15 2E **116**
Watersplash Cl. KT1: King T 3E **150**
Watersplash La. TW5: Cran 5K **93**
UB3: Harl 4J **93**
Watersplash Rd. TW17: Shep 5C **146**
Waters Rd. KT1: King T 2H **151**
SE6 3G **141**
Waters Sq. KT1: King T 3H **151**
Water St. WC2 2J **13**
Water Twr. Cl. UB8: Uxb 5A **56**
Water Twr. Hill CR0: Croy 4D **168**
Water Twr. Pl. N1 1A **84**
Waterview Cl. DA6: Bex 5D **126**
Waterview Ho. *E14* *5A* ***86***
(off Carr St.)
Waterways Bus. Cen. EN3: Enf L 1G **25**
WATERWORKS CORNER **1G 51**
Waterworks La. E5 2K **67**
Waterworks Rd. SW2 6K **119**
Waterworks Yd. *CR0: Croy* *3C* ***168***
(off Surrey St.)
Watery La. DA14: Sidc 6B **144**
SW20 2H **153**
UB3: Harl 5G **93**
UB5: Yead 2A **76**
Wates Way CR4: Mitc 6D **154**
Wateville Rd. N17 1C **48**
Watford By-Pass HA8: Edg 1G **27**
Watford Cl. SW11 1C **118**
Watford Rd. E16 5J **87**
HA0: Wemb 2A **60**
HA1: Harr 7A **42**
Watford Way NW4 4C **44**
NW7 4F **29**
Watkin Rd. HA9: Wemb 3H **61**
Watkins Cl. HA6: Nwood 1H **39**
Watkins Ho. *E14* *2E* ***104***
(off Manchester Rd.)
Watkinson Rd. N7 6K **65**
WATLING **7E 28**
Watling Av. HA8: Edg 1J **43**
Watling Ct. EC4 1D **14**
Watling Farm Cl. HA7: Stan 1H **27**
Watling Gdns. NW2 6G **63**
Watling Ga. NW9 4A **44**
Watlings Cl. CR0: Croy 6A **158**
Watling St. DA6: Bex 4H **127**
EC4 1D **14** (6C **84**)
SE15 6E **102**
Watlington Gro. SE26 5A **140**
Watney Cotts. SW14 3J **115**
Watney Mkt. E1 6H **85**
Watney Rd. SW14 3J **115**
Watney's Rd. CR4: Mitc 5H **155**
Watney St. E1 6H **85**
Watson Av. E6 7E **70**
SM3: Cheam 2G **165**
Watson Cl. N16 5D **66**
SW19 6C **136**
Watson's M. W1 6D **4** (5C **82**)
Watsons Rd. N22 1K **47**
Watsons St. SE8 7C **104**
Watson St. E13 2K **87**
Wattisfield Rd. E5 3J **67**
Watts Cl. N15 5E **48**
Wattsdown Cl. E13 1J **87**
Watts Gro. E3 5C **86**
Watts Ho. *W10* *5G* ***81***
(off Wornington Rd.)
Watts La. BR7: Chst 1F **161**
TW11: Tedd 5A **132**
Watts Point *E13* *1J* ***87***
(off Brooks Rd.)
Watts Rd. KT7: T Ditt 7A **150**
Watts St. E1 1H **103**
SE15 1F **121**
Wat Tyler Ho. *N8* *3J* ***47***
(off Boyton Rd.)
Wat Tyler Rd. SE3 2E **122**
SE10 2E **122**
Wauthier Cl. N13 5G **33**
Wavel Ct. *CR0: Croy* *5D* ***168***
(off Hurst Rd.)
E1 *1J* ***103***
(off Garnet St.)
Wavelengths Leisure Pool **7C 104**
Wavell Dr. DA15: Sidc 6J **125**
Wavel M. N8 4H **47**
NW6 7K **63**
Wavel Pl. SE26 4F **139**
Wavendon Av. W4 5K **97**
Waveney Av. SE15 4H **121**
Waveney Cl. E1 1G **103**
Waveney Ho. SE15 4H **121**
Waverley Av. E4 4G **35**
E17 3F **51**
HA9: Wemb 5F **61**
KT5: Surb 6H **151**
SM1: Sutt 2K **165**
TW2: Whit 1D **130**
Waverley Cl. BR2: Brom 5B **160**
E18 1A **52**
KT8: W Mole 5E **148**
UB3: Harl 4F **93**
Waverley Ct. EN2: Enf 3H **23**
NW3 6D **64**
NW6 7G **63**
SE26 5J **139**
Waverley Cres. SE18 5H **107**
Waverley Gdns. E6 5C **88**
HA6: Nwood 1J **39**
IG6: Ilf 2G **53**
IG11: Bark 2J **89**
NW10 2F **79**
Waverley Gro. N3 3F **45**
Waverley Ind. Est. HA1: Harr 3H **41**
Waverley Pl. N4 2B **66**
NW8 2B **82**
Waverley Rd. E17 3E **50**
E18 1A **52**
EN2: Enf 3G **23**
HA2: Harr 2C **58**
KT17: Ewe 5D **164**
N8 6J **47**
N17 7C **34**
SE18 5G **107**
SE25 4H **157**
UB1: S'hall 7E **76**
Waverley Vs. N17 2F **49**
Waverley Way SM5: Cars 6C **166**
Waverton Ho. E3 1B **86**
Waverton Rd. SW18 7A **118**
Waverton St. W1 4J **11** (1E **100**)
Wavertree Ct. SW2 1J **137**
Wavertree Rd. E18 2J **51**
SW2 1K **137**
Waxham NW3 5D **64**
Waxlow Cres. UB1: S'hall 6E **76**
Waxlow Ho. UB4: Yead 5B **76**
Waxlow Rd. NW10 2J **79**
Waxlow Way UB5: Yead 4D **76**
Waxwell Cl. HA5: Pinn 2B **40**
Waxwell Farm Ho. HA5: Pinn 2B **40**
Waxwell La. HA5: Pinn 2B **40**
Wayborne Gro. HA4: Ruis 6E **38**
Waye Av. TW5: Cran 1J **111**
Wayfarer Rd. UB5: N'olt 3B **76**
Wayfield Link SE9 6H **125**

Wayford St. SW11 . . . .2C 118
Wayland Av. E8 . . . .5G 67
Wayland Ho. SW9 . . . .2A 120
  (off Robsart St.)
Waylands UB3: Hayes 5F 75
Waylands Mead BR3: Beck . . .1D 158
Waylett Ho. SE11 . . . .6J 19
Waylett Pl. HA0: Wemb 4D 60
  SE27 . . . .3B 138
Wayman Ct. E8 . . . .6H 67
Wayne Cl. BR6: Orp 3K 173
Wayne Kirkum Way NW6 . . .5H 63
Waynflete Av. CR0: Wadd . . .3B 168
Waynflete Ho. SE1 . . . .5C 14
  (off Pepper St.)
Waynflete Sq. W10 . . . .7F 81
Waynflete St. SW18 . . . .2A 136
Wayside CR0: New Ad 6D 170
  NW11 . . . .1G 63
  SW14 . . . .5J 115
Wayside Cl. N14 . . . .6B 22
Wayside Commercial Cen.
  IG11: Bark 1K 89
Wayside Ct. HA9: Wemb . . .3G 61
  TW1: Twick 6C 114
Wayside Gdns. RM10: Dag . . .5G 73
Wayside Gro. SE9 . . . .4D 142
Wayside M. IG2: Ilf 5E 52
Weald, The BR7: Chst 6D 142
Weald Cl. BR2: Brom 2C 172
  SE16 . . . .5H 103
Weald La. HA3: Hrw W 2H 41
Weald Ri. HA3: Hrw W 7E 26
Weald Rd. UB10: Hil 2C 74
Weald Sq. E5 . . . .2G 67
WEALDSTONE 3J 41
Wealdstone Rd. SM3: Sutt . .2H 165
Weald Way RM7: Rom 6H 55
  UB4: Hayes 3G 75
Wealdwood Gdns.
  HA5: H End 6A 26
Weale Rd. E4 . . . .3A 36
Weall Ct. HA5: Pinn 4C 40
Weardale Gdns. EN2: Enf . . .1J 23
Weardale Rd. SE13 . . . .4F 123
Wearmouth Ho. E3 . . . .5B 86
  (off Joseph St.)
Wear Pl. E2 . . . .3H 85
  (not continuous)
Wearside Rd. SE13 . . . .4D 122
Weatherbury W2 . . . .6J 81
  (off Talbot Rd.)
Weatherbury Ho. N19 . . . .3H 65
  (off Wedmore St.)
Weatherley Cl. E3 . . . .5B 86
Weaver Cl. CR0: Croy 4F 169
  E6 . . . .7F 89
Weavers Almshouses E11 . . .6H 51
  (off Cambridge Rd.)
Weavers Cl. TW7: Isle 4J 113
Weavers Ho. E11 . . . .6J 51
  (off New Wanstead)
Weavers La. SE1 . . . .5H 15 (1E 102)
Weavers Ter. SW6 . . . .6J 99
  (off Micklethwaite Rd.)
Weaver St. E1 . . . .4G 85
Weavers Way NW1 . . . .1H 83
Weaver Wlk. SE27 . . . .4C 138
Webb Cl. W10 . . . .4E 80
Webb Ct. SE28 . . . .7B 90
  (off Attlee Rd.)
Webber Row SE1 . . . .1K 19 (3A 102)
Webber St. SE1 . . . .5K 13 (2A 102)
Webb Est. E5 . . . .7G 49
Webb Gdns. E13 . . . .4J 87
Webb Ho. RM10: Dag 3G 73
  (off Kershaw Rd.)
  SW8 . . . .7H 101
  TW13: Hanw 3C 130
Webb Pl. NW10 . . . .3B 80
Webb Rd. SE3 . . . .6H 105

Webbscroft Rd. RM10: Dag 4H 73
Webbs Rd. SW11 . . . .4D 118
  UB4: Yead 3K 75
Webb St. SE1 . . . .3E 102
Webheath NW6 . . . .7H 63
  (not continuous)
Webster Gdns. W5 . . . .1D 96
Webster Rd. E11 . . . .3E 68
  SE16 . . . .3G 103
Weddell Ho. E1 . . . .4K 85
  (off Duckett St.)
Wedderburn Ho. SW1 . . . .5G 17
  (off Lwr. Sloane St.)
Wedderburn Rd. IG11: Bark . . .1J 89
  NW3 . . . .5B 64
Wedgewood Ct. BR2: Brom . . .3H 159
  (off Cumberland Rd.)
  DA5: Bexl 7F 127
Wedgewood Ho. SW1 . . . .6K 17
  (off Churchill Gdns.)
Wedgewood M. W1 . . . .1D 12 (6H 83)
Wedgwood Ho. E2 . . . .3K 85
  (off Warley St.)
  SE11 . . . .2J 19
Wedgwood Wlk. NW6 . . . .5K 63
  (off Dresden Cl.)
Wedgwood Way SE19 . . . .7C 138
Wedlake St. W10 . . . .4G 81
Wedmore Av. IG5: Ilf 1E 52
Wedmore Gdns. N19 . . . .2H 65
Wedmore M. N19 . . . .3H 65
Wedmore Rd. UB6: G'frd 3H 77
Wedmore St. N19 . . . .3H 65
Weech Rd. NW6 . . . .4J 63
Weedington Rd. NW5 . . . .5E 64
Weedon Ho. W12 . . . .6C 80
Weekley Sq. SW11 . . . .3B 118
Weigall Rd. SE12 . . . .5J 123
Weighhouse St. W1 . . .1H 11 (6E 82)
Weighton M. SE20 . . . .2H 157
Weighton Rd. HA3: Hrw W 1H 41
  SE20 . . . .2H 157
Weihurst Ct. SM1: Sutt 5C 166
Weihurst Gdns. SM1: Sutt 5B 166
Weimar St. SW15 . . . .3G 117
Weirdale Av. N20 . . . .2J 31
Weir Hall Av. N18 . . . .6J 33
Weir Hall Gdns. N18 . . . .5J 33
Weir Hall Rd. N17 . . . .5J 33
  N18 . . . .5J 33
Weir Rd. DA5: Bexl 7H 127
  KT12: Walt T 6J 147
  SW12 . . . .7G 119
  SW19 . . . .3K 135
Weir's Pas. NW1 . . . .1D 6 (3H 83)
Weiss Rd. SW15 . . . .3F 117
Welbeck Av. BR1: Brom 4J 141
  DA15: Sidc 1A 144
  UB4: Yead 4K 75
Welbeck Cl. KT3: N Mald 5B 152
  KT17: Ewe 7C 164
  N12 . . . .5G 31
Welbeck Ct. W14 . . . .4H 99
  (off Addison Bri. Pl.)
Welbeck Ho. W1 . . . .7J 5
  (off Welbeck St.)
Welbeck Rd. E6 . . . .3B 88
  EN4: E Barn 6H 21
  HA2: Harr 1F 59
  SM1: Sutt 2B 166
  SM5: Cars 2B 166
Welbeck St. W1 . . . .6H 5 (5E 82)
Welbeck Vs. N21 . . . .2H 33
Welbeck Wlk.
  SM5: Cars 1B 166
Welbeck Way W1 . . . .7J 5 (6F 83)
Welbury Ct. E8 . . . .7E 66
  (off Kingsland Rd.)
Welby Ho. N19 . . . .7H 47
Welby St. SE5 . . . .1B 120
Welch Pl. HA5: Pinn 1A 40

Welcome Ct. E17 . . . .7C 50
  (off Boundary Rd.)
Weldon Cl. HA4: Ruis 6K 57
Weldon Ct. N21 . . . .5E 22
Weldon Dr. KT8: W Mole 4D 148
Weld Pl. N11 . . . .5A 32
  (not continuous)
Welfare Rd. E15 . . . .7G 69
Welford Cl. E5 . . . .3K 67
Welford Ct. NW1 . . . .7F 65
  (off Castlehaven Rd.)
  SW8 . . . .2G 119
  W9 . . . .5J 81
  (off Elmfield Way)
Welford Pl. SW19 . . . .4G 135
Welham Rd. SW16 . . . .5E 136
  SW17 . . . .5E 136
Welhouse Rd. SM5: Cars 1C 166
Wellacre Rd. HA3: Kent 6B 42
Wellan Cl. DA15: Sidc 5B 126
Welland Ct. SE6 . . . .2B 140
  (off Oakham Cl.)
Welland Gdns. UB6: G'frd 2K 77
Welland Ho. SE15 . . . .4J 121
Welland M. E1 . . . .1G 103
Wellands Cl. BR1: Brom 2D 160
Welland St. SE10 . . . .6E 104
Well App. EN5: Barn 5A 20
Wellbrook Rd. BR6: Farnb 4E 172
Wellby Cl. N9 . . . .1B 34
Wellby Ct. E13 . . . .1A 88
Well Cl. HA4: Ruis 3C 58
  SW16 . . . .4K 137
Wellclose Sq. E1 . . . .7G 85
Wellclose St. E1 . . . .7G 85
  E3 . . . .2A 86
  (off Driffield Rd)
Wellcome Cen. for Medical Science . . .3C 6
Wellcome Mus., The 7H 7
  (in The Royal College of Surgeons)
Well Cott. Cl. E11 . . . .6A 52
Well Ct. EC4 . . . .1D 14 (6C 84)
  (not continuous)
Welldon Ct. HA1: Harr 5J 41
Welldon Cres. HA1: Harr 5J 41
Weller Ct. W11 . . . .1H 99
  (off Ladbroke Rd.)
Weller Ho. SE16 . . . .2G 103
  (off George Row)
Weller St. SE1 . . . .6C 14 (2C 102)
Welles Ct. E14 . . . .7C 86
  (off Premiere Pl.)
Wellesley Av. W6 . . . .3D 98
Wellesley Cl. SE7 . . . .5A 106
Wellesley Ct. NW2 . . . .2C 62
  SM3: Sutt 1G 165
  W9 . . . .3A 82
Wellesley Ct. Rd. CR0: Croy 2D 168
Wellesley Cres. TW2: Twick 2J 131
Wellesley Gro. CR0: Croy 2D 168
Wellesley Ho. NW1 . . . .2D 6
  (off Wellesley Pl.)
  SW1 . . . .5J 17
  (off Ebury Bri. Rd.)
Wellesley Mans. W14 . . . .5H 99
  (off Edith Vs.)
Wellesley Pde. TW2: Twick 3J 131
Wellesley Pk. M. EN2: Enf 2G 23
Wellesley Pas. CR0: Croy 2C 168
Wellesley Pl. NW1 . . . .2C 6 (3H 83)
  NW5 . . . .5E 64
Wellesley Rd. CR0: Croy 1C 168
  E11 . . . .5J 51
  E17 . . . .6C 50
  HA1: Harr 5J 41
  IG1: Ilf 2F 71
  N22 . . . .2A 48
  NW5 . . . .5E 64
  SM2: Sutt 6A 166
  (not continuous)
  TW2: Twick 3H 131

Wellesley Rd. W4 . . . .5G 97
Wellesley St. E1 . . . .5K 85
Wellesley Ter. N1 . . . .1D 8 (3C 84)
Wellfield Av. N10 . . . .3F 47
Wellfield Rd. SW16 . . . .4J 137
Wellfield Wlk. SW16 . . . .5K 137
  (not continuous)
Wellfit St. SE24 . . . .3B 120
Wellgarth UB6: G'frd 6B 60
Wellgarth Rd. NW11 . . . .1K 63
Well Gro. N20 . . . .1F 31
Well Hall Pde. SE9 . . . .4D 124
Well Hall Rd. SE9 . . . .3C 124
WELL HALL RDBT. 4C 124
Wellhouse La. EN5: Barn 4A 20
Wellhouse Rd. BR3: Beck 4C 158
Wellhurst Cl. BR6: Chels 7K 173
WELLING 3B 126
Welling High St. DA16: Well 3B 126
Wellings Ho. UB3: Hayes 1K 93
Welling Sq. N1 . . . .1J 83
Wellington N8 . . . .4J 47
  (not continuous)
Wellington Arch 6H 11 (2E 100)
Wellington Av. DA15: Sidc 6A 126
  E4 . . . .2H 35
  HA5: H End 1D 40
  KT4: Wor Pk 3E 164
  N9 . . . .3C 34
  N15 . . . .6F 49
  TW3: Houn 5E 112
Wellington Bldgs. SW1 . . .6H 17 (5E 100)
Wellington Cl. KT12: Walt T 7H 147
  RM10: Dag 7J 73
  SE14 . . . .1K 121
  W11 . . . .6J 81
Wellington Ct. HA5: H End 1D 40
  (off Wellington Rd.)
  NW8 . . . .2B 82
  (off Wellington Rd.)
  SW1 . . . .7E 10
  (off Knightsbridge)
  SW6 . . . .1K 117
  (off Maltings Pl.)
  TW12: Tedd 5H 131
  TW15: Ashf 5A 128
  TW19: Stanw 7A 110
Wellington Cres. KT3: N Mald . . .3J 151
Wellington Dr. RM10: Dag 7J 73
Wellington Gdns. SE7 . . . .6A 106
  TW2: Twick 4H 131
Wellington Gro. SE10 . . . .7F 105
Wellington Ho. E16 . . . .1J 105
  (off Pepys Cres.)
  NW3 . . . .6D 64
  (off Eton Rd.)
  SE17 . . . .6C 102
  (off Merrow St.)
  UB5: N'olt 7E 58
  (off The Farmlands)
  W5 . . . .3E 78
  W14 . . . .6H 99
  (off Queen's Club Mans.)
Wellington Mans. E10 . . . .1C 68
  W14 . . . .6H 99
  (off Queen's Club Mans.)
Wellington M. N7 . . . .6K 65
  (off Roman Way)
  SE7 . . . .6A 106
  SE22 . . . .4G 121
  SW16 . . . .3H 137
Wellington Monument 6H 11
Wellington Mus. 6H 11 (2E 100)
Wellington Pde. DA15: Sidc 5A 126
Wellington Pk. Est. NW2 . . . .2C 62
Wellington Pas. E11 . . . .5J 51
  (off Wellington Rd.)
Wellington Pl. N2 . . . .5C 46
  NW8 . . . .1B 4 (3B 82)
Wellington Rd. BR2: Brom 4A 160
  CR0: Croy 7B 156
  DA5: Bexl 5D 126
  DA17: Belv 5F 109

Wellington Rd. E6 1D **88**
E7 4H **69**
E10 1A **68**
E11 5J **51**
E17 4A **50**
EN1: Enf 5K **23**
HA3: W'stone 3J **41**
HA5: H End 1D **40**
NW8 1B **4** (2B **82**)
NW10 3F **81**
SW19 2J **135**
TW2: Twick 5H **131**
TW12: Ham H 5H **131**
TW14: Felt 5G **111**
TW15: Ashf 5A **128**
W5 3C **96**
Wellington Rd. Nth. TW4: Houn 3D **112**
Wellington Rd. Sth. TW4: Houn 4D **112**
Wellington Row E2 1K **9** (3F **85**)
Wellington Sq. SW3 5E **16** (5D **100**)
Wellington St. IG11: Bark 1G **89**
SE18 4E **106**
WC2 2G **13** (7K **83**)
Wellington Ter. E1 1H **103**
HA1: Harr 1H **59**
N8 *3A **48***
(off Turnpike La.)
W2 7J **81**
Wellington Way E3 3C **86**
Welling United FC 3C **126**
Welling Way DA16: Well 3G **125**
SE9 3G **125**
Well La. SW14 5J **115**
Wellmeadow Rd. SE13 6G **123**
(not continuous)
W7 4A **96**
Wellow Wlk. SM5: Cars 1B **166**
Well Pl. NW3 3B **64**
Well Rd. EN5: Barn 5A **20**
NW3 3B **64**
Wells, The N14 7C **22**
Wells Cl. CR2: S Croy 5E **168**
UB5: Yead 3A **76**
Wells Ct. BR2: Brom 2F **159**
NW6 *2J **81***
(off Cambridge Av.)
Wells Dr. NW9 1K **61**
Wells Gdns. IG1: Ilf 7C **52**
RM10: Dag 5H **73**
Wells Ho. *BR1: Brom* *5K **141***
(off Pike Cl.)
EC1 *1K **7***
(off Spa Grn. Est.)
IG11: Bark *7A **72***
(off Margaret Bondfield Av.)
SE16 *3J **103***
(off Howland Est.)
W5 *1D **96***
(off Grove Rd.)
W10 *4G **81***
(off Wornington Rd.)
Wells Ho. Rd. NW10 5A **80**
Wellside Cl. EN5: Barn 4A **20**
Wellside Gdns. SW14 4J **115**
Wells M. W1 6B **6** (5G **83**)
Wellsmoor Gdns. BR1: Brom 3E **160**
Wells Pk. Rd. SE26 3G **139**
Wells Path UB4: Hayes 3G **75**
Wells Pl. SW18 7A **118**
Wells Ri. NW8 1D **82**
Wells Rd. BR1: Brom 2D **160**
W12 2E **98**
Wells Sq. WC1 2G **7** (3K **83**)
Wells St. W1 6A **6** (5G **83**)
Wellstead Av. N9 7E **24**
Wellstead Rd. E6 2E **88**
Wells Ter. N4 2A **66**
Well St. E9 7J **67**
E15 6G **69**
Wells Way SE5 6D **102**
SW7 1A **16** (3B **100**)
Wells Yd. N7 5A **66**
Well Wlk. NW3 4B **64**
Wellwood Rd. IG3: Ilf 1A **72**
Welmar M. *SW4* *5H **119***
(off Northbourne Rd.)
Welsby Ct. W5 5C **78**
Welsford St. SE1 4G **103**
(not continuous)
Welsh Cl. E13 3J **87**
Welsh Harp Nature Reserve 1A **62**
Welsh Ho. *E1* *1H **103***
(off Wapping La.)
Welshpool Ho. *E8* *1G **85***
(off Welshpool St.)
Welshpool St. E8 1G **85**
(not continuous)
Welshside *NW9* *6A **44***
(off Ruthin Cl.)
Welshside Wlk. NW9 6A **44**
Welstead Ho. *E1* *6H **85***
(off Cannon St. Rd.)
Welstead Way W4 4B **98**
Weltje Rd. W6 4C **98**
Welton Ct. SE5 1E **120**
Welton Ho. *E1* *5K **85***
(off Stepney Way)
Welton Rd. SE18 7J **107**
Welwyn Av. TW14: Felt 6H **111**
Welwyn St. E2 3J **85**
Welwyn Way UB4: Hayes 4G **75**
WEMBLEY 5E **60**
Wembley Arena 4G **61**
Wembley Commercial Cen.
HA9: Wemb 2D **60**
Wembley Hill Rd. HA9: Wemb 3F **61**
WEMBLEY PARK 4F **61**
Wembley Pk. Blvd. HA9: Wemb 4G **61**
Wembley Pk. Bus. Cen.
HA9: Wemb 4H **61**
Wembley Pk. Dr. HA9: Wemb 4F **61**
Wembley Retail Pk. HA9: Wemb 4H **61**
Wembley Rd. TW12: Hamp 1E **148**
Wembley Stadium 4G **61**
Wembley Stadium Ind. Est.
HA9: Wemb 4H **61**
Wembley Way HA9: Wemb 6H **61**
Wemborough Rd. HA7: Stan 1B **42**
Wembury M. N6 7G **47**
Wembury Rd. N6 7F **47**
Wemyss Rd. SE3 2H **123**
Wendela Ct. HA1: Harr 2J **59**
Wendell Rd. W12 3B **98**
Wenderholme *CR2: S Croy* *5D **168***
(off South Pk. Hill Rd.)
Wendle Ct. SW8 7E **18** (6J **101**)
Wendling NW5 5D **64**
Wendling Rd. SM1: Sutt 1B **166**
Wendon St. E3 1B **86**
Wendover SE17 5E **102**
(not continuous)
Wendover Cl. UB4: Yead 4C **76**
Wendover Ct. *BR2: Brom* *3K **159***
(off Wendover Rd.)
NW2 3J **63**
NW10 4H **79**
W1 *6G **5***
(off Chiltern St.)
Wendover Dr. KT3: N Mald 6B **152**
Wendover Ho. *W1* *6G **5***
(off Chiltern St.)
Wendover Rd. BR2: Brom 4K **159**
NW10 2B **80**
SE9 3B **124**
Wendover Way DA16: Well 5A **126**
Wendy Cl. EN1: Enf 6A **24**
Wendy Way HA0: Wemb 1E **78**
Wenham Ho. SW8 7G **101**
Wenlake Ho. *EC1* *3C **8***
(off Old St.)
Wenlock Barn Est. *N1* *2D **84***
(off Wenlock St.)
Wenlock Ct. N1 1F **9** (2D **84**)
Wenlock Gdns. NW4 4D **44**
Wenlock Rd. HA8: Edg 7C **28**
N1 1D **8** (2C **84**)
Wenlock St. N1 1D **8** (2C **84**)
Wennington Rd. E3 2K **85**
Wensdale Ho. E5 2G **67**
Wensley Av. IG8: Wfd G 7C **36**
Wensley Cl. N11 6K **31**
SE9 6D **124**
Wensleydale Av. IG5: Ilf 2C **52**
Wensleydale Gdns. TW12: Hamp 7F **131**
Wensleydale Pas. TW12: Hamp 1E **148**
Wensleydale Rd. TW12: Hamp 6E **130**
Wensley Rd. N18 6C **34**
Wentland Cl. SE6 2F **141**
Wentland Rd. SE6 2F **141**
Wentway Ct. *W13* *4K **77***
(off Ruislip Rd. E.)
Wentworth Av. N3 7D **30**
Wentworth Cl. BR2: Hayes 2J **171**
BR6: Farnb 5J **173**
KT6: Surb 2D **162**
N3 7E **30**
SE28 6D **90**
SM4: Mord 7J **153**
TW15: Ashf 4D **128**
Wentworth Ct. *SW18* *6K **117***
(off Garratt La.)
TW2: Twick 3J **131**
W6 *6G **99***
(off Paynes Wlk.)
Wentworth Cres. SE15 7G **103**
UB3: Harl 3F **93**
Wentworth Dr. HA5: Eastc 5J **39**
Wentworth Dwellings *E1* *7J **9***
(off Wentworth St.)
Wentworth Flds. UB4: Hayes 2F **75**
Wentworth Gdns. N13 3G **33**
Wentworth Hill HA9: Wemb 1F **61**
Wentworth M. E3 4A **86**
W3 6A **80**
Wentworth Pk. N3 7D **30**
Wentworth Pl. HA7: Stan 6G **27**
Wentworth Rd. CR0: Croy 7A **156**
E12 4B **70**
EN5: Barn 3A **20**
NW11 6H **45**
UB2: S'hall 4A **94**
Wentworth St. E1 7J **9** (6F **85**)
Wentworth Way HA5: Pinn 4C **40**
Wenvoe Av. DA7: Bex 2H **127**
Wepham Cl. UB4: Yead 5B **76**
Wernbrook St. SE18 6G **107**
Werndee Rd. SE25 4G **157**
Werneth Hall Rd. IG5: Ilf 3D **52**
Werrington St. NW1 1B **6** (2G **83**)
Werter Rd. SW15 4G **117**
Wesleyan Pl. NW5 4F **65**
Wesley Av. E16 1J **105**
NW10 3K **79**
TW3: Houn 2C **112**
Wesley Cl. HA2: Harr 2G **59**
N7 2K **65**
SE17 4B **102**
Wesley Ct. SE16 3H **103**
Wesley Rd. E10 7E **50**
N2 1C **46**
NW10 1J **79**
UB3: Hayes 7J **75**
Wesley's House, Chapel &
Mus. of Methodism 3F **9** (4D **84**)
Wesley Sq. W11 6G **81**
Wesley St. W1 6H **5** (5E **82**)
Wessex Av. SW19 3J **153**
Wessex Cl. IG3: Ilf 6J **53**
KT1: King T 1H **151**
Wessex Ct. BR3: Beck 1A **158**
EN5: Barn 4A **20**
HA9: Wemb 2F **61**
TW19: Stanw 6A **110**
Wessex Dr. HA5: H End 1C **40**
Wessex Gdns. NW11 1G **63**
Wessex Ho. SE1 5F **103**
Wessex La. UB6: G'frd 3H **77**
Wessex St. E2 3J **85**
Wessex Wlk. DA2: Bexl 2K **145**
Wessex Way NW11 1G **63**
Wesson Mead *SE5* *7C **102***
(off Camberwell Rd.)
Westacott UB4: Hayes 5G **75**
Westacott Cl. N19 1H **65**
WEST ACTON 6G **79**
West App. BR5: Pet W 5G **161**
W. Arbour St. E1 6K **85**
West Av. E17 4D **50**
HA5: Pinn 6D **40**
N2 4K **45**
N3 6D **30**
NW4 5F **45**
SM6: Wall 5J **167**
UB1: S'hall 7D **76**
UB3: Hayes 7H **75**
West Av. Rd. E17 4C **50**
West Bank EN2: Enf 2H **23**
IG11: Bark 1F **89**
N16 7E **48**
Westbank Rd. TW12: Ham H 6G **131**
WEST BARNES 5D **152**
W. Barnes La. KT3: N Mald 4D **152**
SW20: N Mald 3D **152**
WEST BECKTON 6B **88**
WEST BEDFONT 6B **110**
Westbeech Rd. N22 3A **48**
Westbere Dr. HA7: Stan 5J **27**
Westbere Rd. NW2 4G **63**
West Block *SE1* *7H **13***
(off Addington St.)
Westbourne Av. SM3: Cheam 2G **165**
W3 6K **79**
Westbourne Bri. W2 5A **82**
Westbourne Cl. UB4: Yead 4A **76**
Westbourne Ct. W2 5A **82**
Westbourne Cres. W2 2A **10** (7B **82**)
Westbourne Cres. M. W2 2A **10**
Westbourne Dr. SE23 2K **139**
Westbourne Gdns. W2 6K **81**
WESTBOURNE GREEN 6H **81**
Westbourne Gro. W2 6J **81**
W11 7H **81**
Westbourne Gro. M. W11 6J **81**
Westbourne Gro. Ter. W2 6K **81**
Westbourne Ho. *SW1* *5J **17***
(off Ebury Bri. Rd.)
TW5: Hest 6E **94**
Westbourne Pde. UB10: Hil 4D **74**
Westbourne Pk. Pas. W2 5J **81**
(not continuous)
Westbourne Pk. Rd. W2 5J **81**
W11 6G **81**
Westbourne Pk. Vs. W2 5J **81**
Westbourne Pl. N9 3C **34**
Westbourne Rd. CR0: Croy 6F **157**
DA7: Bex 7D **108**
N7 6K **65**
SE26 6K **139**
TW13: Felt 3H **129**
UB8: Hil 4D **74**
Westbourne St. W2 2A **10** (7B **82**)
Westbourne Ter. *SE23* *2K **139***
(off Westbourne Dr.)
W2 1A **10** (6A **82**)
Westbourne Ter. M. W2 6A **82**
Westbourne Ter. Rd. W2 5K **81**
Westbourne Ter. Rd. Bri.
W2 *5A **82***
(off Westbourne Ter. Rd.)
Westbridge Cl. W12 2C **98**
Westbridge Rd. SW11 1B **118**
WEST BROMPTON 6A **100**
Westbrook Av. TW12: Hamp 7D **130**
Westbrook Cl. EN4: Cockf 3G **21**

Westbrook Cres. EN4: Cockf 3G 21
Westbrooke Cres. DA16: Well 3C 126
Westbrooke Rd. DA15: Sidc 2H 143
  DA16: Well 3B 126
Westbrook Ho. E2 . . . . .3J 85
  (off Victoria Pk. Sq.)
Westbrook Rd. CR7: Thor H 1D 156
  SE3 . . . . .1K 123
  TW5: Hest 7D 94
Westbrook Sq. EN4: Cockf 3G 21
Westbury Av. HA0: Wemb 7E 60
  N22 . . . . .3B 48
  UB1: S'hall 4E 76
Westbury Cl. HA4: Ruis 7J 39
  TW17: Shep 6D 146
Westbury Ct. IG11: Bark 1H 89
  (off Westbury Rd.)
Westbury Gro. N12 . . . . .6D 30
Westbury Ho. E17 . . . . .4B 50
  W11 . . . . .5J 81
  (off Aldridge Rd. Vs.)
Westbury La. IG9: Buck H 2E 36
Westbury Lodge Cl. HA5: Pinn 3B 40
Westbury Pl. TW8: Bford 6D 96
Westbury Rd. BR1: Brom 1B 160
  BR3: Beck 3A 158
  CR0: Croy 6D 156
  E7 . . . . .6K 69
  E17 . . . . .4B 50
  HA0: Wemb 7E 60
  IG1: Ilf 2E 70
  IG9: Buck H 2F 37
  IG11: Bark 1H 89
  KT3: N Mald 4K 151
  N11 . . . . .6D 32
  N12 . . . . .6D 30
  SE20 . . . . .1K 157
  TW13: Felt 1B 130
  W5 . . . . .6E 78
Westbury St. SW8 . . . . .2G 119
  (off Portslade Rd.)
Westbury Ter. E7 . . . . .6K 69
W. Carriage Dr. W2 . . . . .3C 10 (7C 82)
  (not continuous)
W. Central St. WC1 . . . . . . .7E 6 (6J 83)
West Cen. Av. NW10 . . . . .4D 80
West Chantry HA3: Hrw W 1F 41
Westchester Dr. NW4 . . . . .3F 45
Westcliffe Apartments W2 . . . . .5B 82
West Cl. EN4: Cockf 4K 21
  HA9: Wemb 1F 61
  N9 . . . . .3A 34
  TW12: Hamp 6C 130
  TW15: Ashf 4A 128
  UB6: G'frd 2G 77
Westcombe Av. CR0: Croy 7J 155
Westcombe Ct. SE3 . . . . .7H 105
Westcombe Dr. EN5: Barn 5D 20
Westcombe Hill SE3 . . . . .7J 105
  SE10 . . . . .7J 105
Westcombe Lodge Dr.
  UB4: Hayes 5G 75
Westcombe Pk. Rd. SE3 . . . . .6G 105
West Comn. Rd. BR2: Hayes 1J 171
  BR2: Kes 1J 171
  UB8: Uxb 3A 56
Westcoombe Av. SW20 . . . . .1B 152
Westcote Ri. HA4: Ruis 7E 38
Westcote Rd. SW16 . . . . .5G 137
West Cotts. NW6 . . . . .5J 63
Westcott Cl. BR1: Brom 5D 160
  CR0: New Ad 7D 170
  N15 . . . . .6F 49
Westcott Cres. W7 . . . . .6J 77
Westcott Ho. E14 . . . . .7C 86
Westcott Rd. SE17 . . . . .6B 102
West Ct. E17 . . . . .4C 50
  HA0: Wemb 2C 60
  TW7: Isle 7G 95
Westcroft NW2 . . . . .4G 63
Westcroft Cl. EN3: Enf W 1D 24

Westcroft Est. NW2 . . . . .4G 63
Westcroft Gdns. SM4: Mord 3H 153
Westcroft Leisure Cen. 4E 166
Westcroft Rd. SM5: Cars 4E 166
  SM6: Wall 4E 166
Westcroft Sq. W6 . . . . .4C 98
Westcroft Way NW2 . . . . .4G 63
W. Cromwell Rd. SW5 . . . . .5H 99
  W14 . . . . .5H 99
W. Cross Cen. TW8: Bford 6A 96
W. Cross Route W10 . . . . .7F 81
  W11 . . . . .7F 81
  W12 . . . . .7F 81
W. Cross Way TW8: Bford 6B 96
Westdale Pas. SE18 . . . . .6F 107
Westdale Rd. SE18 . . . . .6F 107
Westdean Av. SE12 . . . . .1K 141
Westdean Cl. SW18 . . . . .6K 117
West Dene SM3: Cheam 6G 165
Westdown Rd. E15 . . . . .4E 68
  SE6 . . . . .7C 122
WEST DRAYTON 2A 92
W. Drayton Pk. Av.
  UB7: W Dray 3A 92
W. Drayton Rd. UB8: Hil 6D 74
West Dr. HA3: Hrw W 6C 26
  SM2: Cheam 7F 165
  SW16 . . . . .4G 137
West Dr. Gdns. HA3: Hrw W 6C 26
WEST DULWICH 2D 138
WEST EALING 1B 96
W. Ealing Bus. Cen. W13 . . . . .7A 78
W. Eaton Pl. SW1 . . . . . . .3G 17 (4E 100)
W. Eaton Pl. M. SW1 . . . . .2G 17
W. Ella Rd. NW10 . . . . .7A 62
WEST END .2B 76
West End Av. E10 . . . . .5F 51
  HA5: Pinn 4B 40
Westend Cl. NW10 . . . . .7J 61
West End Ct. HA5: Pinn 4B 40
  NW6 . . . . .7K 63
West End Gdns. UB5: Yead 2A 76
West End La. EN5: Barn 4A 20
  HA5: Pinn 3B 40
  NW6 . . . . .5J 63
  (not continuous)
  UB3: Harl 7E 92
West End Quay W2 . . . . .6B 4
West End Rd. HA4: Ruis 2G 57
  UB1: S'hall 1C 94
  UB5: N'olt 7A 58
Westerdale Rd. SE10 . . . . .5J 105
Westerfield Rd. N15 . . . . .5F 49
Westergate W5 . . . . .5F 78
Westergate Ho. KT1: King T 4D 150
  (off Portsmouth Rd.)
Westergate Rd. SE2 . . . . .6E 108
Westerham NW1 . . . . .1G 83
  (off Bayham St.)
Westerham Av. N9 . . . . .3J 33
Westerham Dr. DA15: Sidc 6B 126
Westerham Ho. SE1 . . . . .3D 102
  (off Law St.)
Westerham Lodge BR3: Beck 7C 140
  (off Park Rd.)
Westerham Rd. BR2: Kes 7B 172
  E10 . . . . .7D 50
Westerley Cres. SE26 . . . . .5B 140
Western Av. HA4: Ruis 5A 56
  NW11 . . . . .6F 45
  RM10: Dag 6J 73
  UB5: N'olt 7A 58
  UB6: G'frd 2H 77
  UB10: Hil 5A 56
  W3 . . . . .4F 79
  W5 . . . . .4F 79
Western Av. Bus. Pk. W3 . . . . .4H 79
Western Beach Apartments E16 . . . . .7J 87
Western Ct. N3 . . . . .6D 30
  NW6 . . . . .2H 81
  W3 . . . . .6K 79

Western Dr. TW17: Shep 6F 147
Western Gdns. W5 . . . . .7G 79
Western Gateway E16 . . . . .7J 87
Western Intl. Mkt. UB2: S'hall 4K 93
Western La. SW12 . . . . .7E 118
Western Mans. EN5: New Bar 5E 20
  (off Gt. North Rd.)
Western M. W9 . . . . .4H 81
Western Pde. EN5: New Bar 5D 20
Western Pl. SE16 . . . . .2J 103
Western Rd. CR4: Mitc 1B 154
  E13 . . . . .2A 88
  E17 . . . . .5E 50
  N2 . . . . .4D 46
  N22 . . . . .2K 47
  NW10 . . . . .4J 79
  SM1: Sutt 5J 165
  SW9 . . . . .3A 120
  SW19 . . . . .1B 154
  UB2: S'hall 4A 94
  W5 . . . . .7D 78
Western Ter. W6 . . . . .5C 98
  (off Chiswick Mall)
Western Vw. UB3: Hayes 2H 93
Westernville Gdns. IG2: Ilf 7G 53
Western Way EN5: Barn 6D 20
  SE28 . . . . .3H 107
WEST EWELL 7K 163
Westferry Cir. E14 . . . . .1B 104
Westferry Rd. E14 . . . . .7B 86
Westfield Cl. EN3: Enf H 3F 25
  NW9 . . . . .3J 43
  SM1: Sutt 4H 165
  SW10 . . . . .7A 100
Westfield Ct. KT6: Surb 5D 150
  (off Portsmouth Rd)
  NW10 . . . . .3F 81
  (off Chamberlayne Rd.)
Westfield Dr. HA3: Kent 4D 42
Westfield Gdns. HA3: Kent 4D 42
  RM6: Chad H 6C 54
Westfield Ho. SE16 . . . . .4K 103
  (off Rotherhithe New Rd.)
  SW10 . . . . .7B 100
  (off Cremorne Est.)
  SW18 . . . . .1K 135
Westfield La. HA3: Kent 5D 42
  (not continuous)
Westfield Pk. HA5: H End 1D 40
Westfield Pk. Dr. IG8: Wfd G 6H 37
Westfield Rd. BR3: Beck 2B 158
  CR0: Croy 2B 168
  CR4: Mitc 2C 154
  DA7: Bex 3J 127
  KT6: Surb 5D 150
  KT12: Walt T 7C 148
  NW7 . . . . .3E 28
  RM9: Dag 4E 72
  SM1: Sutt 4H 165
  W13 . . . . .1A 96
Westfields SW13 . . . . .3B 116
Westfields Av. SW13 . . . . .3A 116
Westfields Rd. W3 . . . . .5H 79
Westfield St. SE18 . . . . .3B 106
Westfield Way E1 . . . . .3A 86
  HA4: Ruis 3G 57
West Gdn. Pl. W2 . . . . .1D 10 (6C 82)
West Gdns. E1 . . . . .7H 85
  SW17 . . . . .6C 136
Westgate W5 . . . . .3E 78
Westgate Cen., The E8 . . . . .1H 85
  (off Bocking St.)
Westgate Ct. SE12 . . . . .1J 141
  (off Burnt Ash Hill)
  SW9 . . . . .3A 120
  (off Canterbury Cres.)
Westgate Est. TW14: Bedf 1D 128
Westgate M. W10 . . . . .4F 81
  (off West Row)
Westgate Rd. BR3: Beck 1E 158
  SE25 . . . . .4H 157

Westgate St. E8 . . . . .1H 85
Westgate Ter. SW10 . . . . .6K 99
Westglade Cl. HA3: Kent 5D 42
WEST GREEN 4B 48
West Grn. Pl. UB6: G'frd 1H 77
West Grn. Rd. N15 . . . . .4B 48
West Gro. IG8: Wfd G 6F 37
  SE10 . . . . .1E 122
Westgrove La. SE10 . . . . .1E 122
W. Halkin St. SW1 . . . . . .1G 17 (3E 100)
West Hallowes SE9 . . . . .1B 142
W. Hall Rd. TW9: Kew 1H 115
WEST HAM 1H 87
W. Ham La. E15 . . . . .7F 69
  (not continuous)
WEST HAMPSTEAD 6K 63
W. Hampstead M. NW6 . . . . .6K 63
West Ham United FC 2A 88
W. Harding St. EC4 . . . . . . .7K 7 (6A 84)
WEST HARROW 7G 41
W. Hatch Mnr. HA4: Ruis 1H 57
Westhay Gdns. SW14 . . . . .5H 115
WEST HEATH 6D 108
W. Heath Av. NW11 . . . . .1J 63
W. Heath Cl. NW3 . . . . .3J 63
W. Heath Ct. NW11 . . . . .1J 63
W. Heath Dr. NW11 . . . . .1J 63
W. Heath Gdns. NW3 . . . . .2J 63
W. Heath Rd. NW3 . . . . .2J 63
  SE2 . . . . .6C 108
WEST HENDON 7C 44
WEST HILL 6H 117
West Hill CR2: Sand 7E 168
  HA2: Harr 2J 59
  HA9: Wemb 1F 61
  SW15 . . . . .7F 117
  SW18 . . . . .7F 117
W. Hill Cl. N6 . . . . .3E 64
Westhill Ct. W11 . . . . .7H 81
  (off Denbigh Rd.)
W. Hill Pk. N6 . . . . .2D 64
  (not continuous)
W. Hill Rd. SW18 . . . . .6H 117
W. Hill Way N20 . . . . .1E 30
Westholm NW11 . . . . .4K 45
West Holme DA8: Erith 1J 127
Westholme BR6: Orp 7J 161
Westholme Gdns. HA4: Ruis 1J 57
Westhope Ho. E2 . . . . .4G 85
  (off Derbyshire St.)
Westhorne Av. SE9 . . . . .7J 123
  SE12 . . . . .7J 123
Westhorpe Gdns. NW4 . . . . .3E 44
Westhorpe Rd. SW15 . . . . .3E 116
West Ho. Cl. SW19 . . . . .1G 135
West Ho. Cotts. HA5: Pinn 4B 40
Westhurst Dr. BR7: Chst 5F 143
W. India Av. E14 . . . . .1C 104
W. India Dock Rd. E14 . . . . .7B 86
  (not continuous)
W. India Ho. F14 . . . . .7C 86
  (off W. India Dock Rd.)
WEST KENSINGTON 4H 99
W. Kensington Ct. W14 . . . . .5H 99
  (off Edith Vs.)
W. Kensington Mans. W14 . . . . .5H 99
  (off Beaumont Cres.)
WEST KILBURN 3H 81
Westlake SE16 . . . . .4J 103
  (off Rotherhithe New Rd.)
Westlake Cl. N13 . . . . .3F 33
  UB4: Yead 4C 76
Westlake Rd. HA9: Wemb 2D 60
Westland Cl.
  TW19: Stanw 6A 110
Westland Cl. UB5: N'olt 3B 76
  (off Seasprite Cl.)
Westland Dr. BR2: Hayes 2H 171
Westland Ho. E16 . . . . .1E 106
  (off Rymill St.)
Westland Pl. N1 . . . . .1E 8 (3D 84)

Westlands Cl. UB3: Harl 4J 93
Westlands Cl. KT8: E Mos 4H 149
Westlands Ter. SW12 . . . . .6G 119
West La. SE16 . . . . .2H 103
Westlea Rd. W7 . . . . .3A 96
Westleigh Av. SW15 . . . . .5D 116
Westleigh Ct. CR2: S Croy 4E 168
         (off Birdhurst Rd.)
  E11 . . . . .5J 51
Westleigh Dr. BR1: Brom 1C 160
Westleigh Gdns. HA8: Edg 1G 43
West Links HA0: Wemb 3D 78
Westlinton Cl. NW7 . . . . .6C 30
West Lodge E16 . . . . .1J 105
         (off Britannia Ga.)
W. Lodge Av. W3 . . . . .1G 97
W. Lodge Ct. W3 . . . . .1G 97
W. London Crematorium & Chapel
  NW10 . . . . .4D 80
Westmacott Dr. TW14: Felt 1H 129
Westmacott Ho. NW8 . . . . .4B 4
         (off Hatton St.)
West Mall W8 . . . . .1J 99
         (off Palace Gdns. Ter.)
Westmark Point SW15 . . . . .1D 134
         (off Norley Vale)
West Mead HA4: Ruis 4A 58
  KT19: Ewe 6A 164
Westmead SW15 . . . . .6D 116
Westmead Ho. SM1: Sutt 4B 166
Westmead Rd. SM1: Sutt 4B 166
Westmere Dr. NW7 . . . . .3E 28
W. Mersea Cl. E16 . . . . .1K 105
West M. N17 . . . . .7C 34
  SW1 . . . . .4A 18
Westmill Ct. N4 . . . . .2C 66
WESTMINSTER 7E 12 (2J 101)
Westminster Abbey 1E 18 (3H 101)
Westminster Abbey Chapter House . . .1E 18
         (in Westminster Abbey)
Westminster Abbey Mus. 1E 18
         (in Westminster Abbey)
Westminster Abbey Pyx Chamber 1E 18
         (in Westminster Abbey)
Westminster Av. CR7: Thor H 2B 156
Westminster Bri. SE1 . . . . .2K 101
  SW1 . . . . .7F 13 (2J 101)
Westminster Bri. Rd.
  SE1 . . . . .7G 13 (2K 101)
  SE11 . . . . .7G 19 (6K 101)
Westminster Bus. Sq.
  . . . . .5A 4 (4B 82)
Westminster Children's Sports Cen., The
  . . . . .5A 4 (4B 82)
Westminster Ct. IG6: Ilf 2H 53
  TW11: Tedd 5A 132
  TW14: Felt 1J 129
Westminster Ct. E11 . . . . .6J 51
         (off Cambridge Pk.)
  NW8 . . . . .4A 4
         (off Lyons Pl.)
  SE16 .1K 103
         (off King & Queen Wharf)
Westminster Dr. N13 . . . . .5D 32
Westminster Gdns. E4 . . . . .1B 36
  IG6: Ilf 2G 53
  IG11: Bark 2J 89
  SW1 . . . . .3E 18
         (off Marsham St.)
Westminster Hall 7E 12
Westminster Ho. HA3: Hrw W 7E 26
Westminster Ind. Est. SE18 . . . . . . .3B 106
Westminster Mans. SW1 . . . . .2D 18
         (off Gt. Smith St.)
Westminster Pal. Gdns. SW1 . . . . . .2C 18
Westminster RC Cathedral
  . . . . .2A 18 (3G 101)
Westminster Rd. N9 . . . . .1C 34
  SM1: Sutt 2B 166
  W7 . . . . .1J 95
Westmoat Cl. BR3: Beck 7E 140

WEST MOLESEY 4E 148
Westmoor Gdns. EN3: Enf H 2E 24
Westmoor Rd. EN3: Enf H 2E 24
Westmoor St. SE7 . . . . .3A 106
Westmore Ct. SW15 . . . . .5G 117
Westmoreland Av. DA16: Well 3J 125
Westmoreland Dr. SM2: Sutt 7K 165
Westmoreland Ho. E16 . . . . .1J 105
         (off Gatcombe Rd.)
Westmoreland Pl. BR1: Brom 3J 159
  SW1 . . . . .6K 17 (5F 101)
  W5 . . . . .5D 78
Westmoreland Rd. BR2: Brom 5G 159
  NW9 . . . . .3F 43
  SE17 .6D 102
         (not continuous)
  SW13 .1B 116
Westmoreland St. W1 . . . . . . .6H 5 (5E 82)
Westmoreland Ter. SW1 . . . . .6K 17 (5F 101)
Westmoreland Wlk. SE17 . . . . .6D 102
         (not continuous)
Westmorland Cl. E12 . . . . .2B 70
  TW1: Twick 6B 114
Westmorland Ct. KT6: Surb 7D 150
Westmorland Rd. E17 . . . . .6C 50
  HA1: Harr 5F 41
Westmorland Sq. CR4: Mitc 5J 155
         (off Westmorland Way)
Westmorland Ter. SE20 . . . . .7H 139
Westmorland Way CR4: Mitc 4H 155
Westmount Cl. W5 . . . . .6F 79
Westmount Rd. SE9 . . . . .2D 124
WEST NORWOOD 4C 138
N. Norwood Crematorium SE27 . . . .3C 138
West Oak BR3: Beck 1F 159
Westoe Rd. N9 . . . . .2C 34
Weston Av. KT7: T Ditt 7J 149
  KT8: W Mole 3C 148
Westonbirt Ct. SE15 . . . . .6F 103
         (off Ebley Cl.)
Weston Cl. KT1: King T 3E 150
         (off Grove Cres.)
  N4 . . . . .3C 66
  N20 . . . . .7F 21
         (off Farnham Cl.)
Weston Dr. HA7: Stan 1B 42
W. One Ho. W1 . . . . .6A 6
         (off Wells St.)
Westone Mans. IG11: Bark 7K 71
         (off Upney La.)
W. One Shop. Cen. W1 . . . . .1H 11
Weston Gdns. TW7: Isle 1J 113
WESTON GREEN 7K 149
Weston Grn. KT7: T Ditt 7J 149
  RM9: Dag 4F 73
Weston Grn. Rd. KT7: T Ditt 7J 149
  KT10: Esh 7J 149
Weston Gro. BR1: Brom 1H 159
Weston Ho. E9 . . . . .1J 85
         (off King Edward's Rd.)
  NW6 . . . . .7G 63
Weston London Heliport 2B 118
Weston Pk. KT1: King T 2E 150
  KT7: T Ditt 7J 149
  N8 . . . . .6J 47
Weston Ri. WC1 . . . . .1H 7 (3K 83)
Weston Rd. BR1: Brom 7H 141
  EN2: Enf 2J 23
  RM9: Dag 4E 72
  W4 . . . . .3J 97
Weston St. SE1 . . . . .7F 15 (2E 102)
         (not continuous)
Weston Wlk. E8 . . . . .7H 67
Westover Hill NW3 . . . . .2J 63
Westover Rd. SW18 . . . . .7A 118
Westow Hill SE19 . . . . .6E 138
Westow St. SE19 . . . . .6E 138
West Pk. SE9 . . . . .2C 142
West Pk. Av. TW9: Kew 1G 115
West Pk. Cl. RM6: Chad H 5D 54
  TW5: Hest 6D 94

West Pk. Rd. TW9: Kew 1G 115
  UB2: S'hall 1G 95
W. Parkside SE10 . . . . .2G 105
West Pl. SW19 . . . . .5E 134
West Point E14 . . . . .7B 86
         (off Grenade St.)
  SE1 . . . . .5G 103
Westpoint Apartments N8 . . . . .3K 47
Westpoint Trad. Est. W3 . . . . .5H 79
Westpole Av. EN4: Cockf 4K 21
Westport Ct. UB4: Yead 4A 76
Westport Rd. E13 . . . . .4K 87
Westport St. E1 . . . . .6K 85
W. Poultry Av. EC1 . . . . . . .6A 8 (5B 84)
West Quarters W12 . . . . .6C 80
West Quay SW10 . . . . .1A 118
W. Quay Dr. UB4: Yead 5C 76
West Ramp TW6: H'row A 1C 110
West Reservoir Cen. 1C 66
W. Ridge Gdns. UB6: G'frd 2G 77
West Ri. W2 . . . . .2D 10
West Rd. E15 . . . . .1H 87
  EN4: E Barn 1K 31
  KT2: King T 1J 151
  N2 . . . . .2B 46
  N17 . . . . .6C 34
  RM6: Chad H 6D 54
  RM7: Rush G 7K 55
  SE1 . . . . .6H 13 (2K 101)
  SW3 . . . . .6F 17 (5D 100)
  SW4 . . . . .5H 119
  TW14: Bedf 6F 111
  UB7: W Dray 3B 92
  W5 . . . . .5E 78
West Row W10 . . . . .4G 81
Westrow SW15 . . . . .6E 116
Westrow Dr. IG11: Bark 5A 72
Westrow Gdns. IG3: Ilf 2K 71
WEST RUISLIP 2E 56
W. Ruislip Ct. HA4: Ruis 2F 57
         (off Ickenham Rd.)
W. Sheen Va. TW9: Rich 4F 115
West Side NW4 . . . . .2D 44
Westside N2 . . . . .3D 46
W. Side Comm. SW19 . . . . .5E 134
Westside Ct. W9 . . . . .4J 81
         (off Elgin Av.)
West Smithfield EC1 . . . . . . .6A 8 (5B 84)
West Sq. SE11 . . . . .2K 19 (3B 102)
West St. BR1: Brom 1J 159
  CR0: Croy 4C 168
  DA7: Bex 3F 127
  DA8: Erith 4K 109
  E2 . . . . .2H 85
  E11 . . . . .3G 69
  E17 . . . . .5D 50
  HA1: Harr 1H 59
  SM1: Sutt 5K 165
  SM5: Cars 3D 166
  TW8: Bford 6C 96
  WC2 . . . . .1D 12 (6H 83)
West St. La. SM5: Cars 4D 166
         (not continuous)
West St. Pl. CR0: Croy 4C 168
         (off West St.)
W. Temple Sheen SW14 . . . . .5H 115
W. Tenter St. E1 . . . . .1K 15 (6F 85)
West Ter. DA15: Sidc 1J 143
W. Thamesmead Bus. Pk.
  SE28 .3J 107
         (not continuous)
West Towers HA5: Pinn 5B 40
Westvale M. W3 . . . . .2A 98
West Vw. NW4 . . . . .4E 44
  TW14: Bedf 7E 110
Westview W7 . . . . .6J 77
West Vw. Cl. NW10 . . . . .5B 62
Westview Cl. W10 . . . . .6E 80
Westview Ct. N20 . . . . .1F 31
Westview Cres. N9 . . . . .7K 23
Westview Dr. IG8: Wfd G 2B 52

Westville Rd. KT7: T Ditt 1A 162
  W12 . . . . .2C 98
West Wlk. EN4: E Barn 7K 21
  NW9 . . . . .1A 44
  UB3: Hayes 1J 93
  W5 . . . . .5E 78
Westward Rd. E4 . . . . .5G 35
         (not continuous)
Westward Way HA3: Kent 6E 42
W. Warwick Pl. SW1 . . . . . .4A 18 (4G 101)
West Way BR4: W W'ck 6F 159
  CR0: Croy 2A 170
  HA4: Ruis 1H 57
  HA5: Pinn 4B 40
  HA8: Edg 6C 28
  NW10 . . . . .3K 61
  TW5: Hest 1D 112
  TW17: Shep 6F 147
Westway BR5: Pet W 5H 161
  N18 . . . . .4J 33
  SW20 .3D 152
  UB6: G'frd 1J 77
  W2 . . . . .6A 4 (5H 81)
  W9 . . . . .5H 81
  W10 . . . . .5H 81
  W12 . . . . .7B 80
Westway Cl. SW20 . . . . .3D 152
Westway Ct. UB5: N'olt 1E 76
W. Way Gdns. CR0: Croy 2K 169
Westway Lodge W9 . . . . .5J 81
         (off Amberley Rd.)
West Ways HA6: Nwood 2J 39
Westways KT19: Ewe 4B 164
Westway Sports Cen. 6F 81
Westwell M. SW16 . . . . .6J 137
Westwell Rd. SW16 . . . . .6J 137
Westwell Rd. App. SW16 . . . . .6J 137
Westwick KT1: King T 2G 151
         (off Chesterton Ter.)
Westwick Gdns. TW4: Cran 2K 111
  W14 . . . . .2F 99
WEST WICKHAM 1E 170
West Wickham Pools 1E 170
Westwood Av. HA2: Harr 4F 59
  SE19 .1C 156
Westwood Bus. Cen. NW10 . . . . . . .4A 80
Westwood Cl. BR1: Brom 2B 160
  HA4: Ruis 6D 38
  UB6: G'frd 5H 59
Westwood Gdns. SW13 . . . . .3B 116
Westwood Hill SE26 . . . . .5G 139
Westwood Ho. W12 . . . . .1E 98
         (off Wood La.)
Westwood La. DA15: Sidc 5A 126
  DA16: Well 3K 125
Westwood Pk. SE23 . . . . .7H 121
Westwood Pk. Trad. Est. W3 . . . . . .5H 79
Westwood Rd. SE26 . . . . .4G 139
Westwood Rd. E16 . . . . .1K 105
  IG3: Ilf .1K 71
  SW13 .3B 116
West Woodside DA5: Bexl 7E 126
Wetheral Dr. HA7: Stan 1B 42
Wetherby Cl. UB5: N'olt 6F 59
Wetherby Gdns. SW5 . . . . .4A 100
Wetherby Mans. SW5 . . . . .5K 99
         (off Earls Ct. Sq.)
Wetherby M. SW5 . . . . .5K 99
Wetherby Pl. SW7 . . . . .4A 100
Wetherby Rd. EN2: Enf 1H 23
Wetherby Way KT9: Chess 7E 162
Wetherden St. E17 . . . . .7B 50
Wetherell Rd. E9 . . . . .1K 85
Wetherill Rd. N10 . . . . .1E 46
Wevco Wharf SE15 . . . . .6H 103
Wevell Ho. N6 . . . . .7F 46
         (off Hillcrest)
Wexford Ho. E1 . . . . .5J 85
         (off Sidney St.)
Wexford Rd. SW12 . . . . .7D 118

Weybourne St. SW18 . . . . .2A 136
Weybridge Ct. SE16 . . . . .5H 103
(off Argyle Way)
Weybridge Point SW11 . . . . .2D 118
Weybridge Rd. CR7: Thor H 4A 156
Wey Ct. KT19: Ewe 4J 163
Weydown Cl. SW19 . . . . .1G 135
Weyhill Rd. E1 . . . . .6G 85
Wey Ho. NW8 . . . . .4B 4
(off Salisbury St.)
Weylands Cl. KT12: Walt T 7D 148
Weylond Rd. RM8: Dag 3F 73
Weyman Rd. SE3 . . . . .1A 124
Weymarks, The N17 . . . . .6J 33
Weymouth Av. NW7 . . . . .5F 29
W5 . . . . .3C 96
Weymouth Cl. E6 . . . . .6F 89
Weymouth Ct. E2 . . . . .2F 85
(off Weymouth Ter.)
SM2: Sutt 7J 165
Weymouth Ho. BR2: Brom 2H 159
(off Beckenham La.)
SW8 .7K 101
(off Bolney St.)
Weymouth M. W1 . . . . .5J 5 (5F 83)
Weymouth Rd. UB4: Hayes 3G 75
Weymouth St. W1 . . . . . .6H 5 (5E 82)
Weymouth Ter. E2 . . . . . . .1K 9 (2F 85)
Weymouth Vs. N4 . . . . .2K 65
(off Moray Rd.)
Weymouth Wlk. HA7: Stan 6F 27
Whadcoat St. N4 . . . . .2A 66
Whalebone Av. RM6: Chad H 6F 55
Whalebone Ct. EC2 . . . . .7E 8
Whalebone Gro. RM6: Chad H 6F 55
Whalebone La. E15 . . . . .7G 69
Whalebone La. Nth.
RM6: Chad H, Col R 1E 54
Whalebone La. Sth.
RM6: Chad H, Dag 7F 55
RM8: Dag 7F 55
Whales Yd. E15 . . . . .7F 69
(off W. Ham La.)
Wharf, The EC3 . . . . .4H 15 (1F 103)
Wharfdale Cl. N11 . . . . .6K 31
Wharfdale Rd. N1 . . . . .2J 83
Wharfedale Ct. E5 . . . . .4K 67
Wharfedale Gdns. CR7: Thor H 4K 155
Wharfedale Ho. NW6 . . . . .1K 81
(off Kilburn Va.)
Wharfedale St. SW10 . . . . .5K 99
Wharfedale Yard N1 . . . . .2J 83
(off Wharfedale Rd.)
Wharf La. TW1: Twick 1A 132
Wharf Pl. E2 . . . . .1H 85
Wharf Rd. EN3: Pond E 6F 25
N1 . . . . .1C 8 (2C 84)
(Baldwin Ter.)
N1 . . . . .1H 83
(Camley St.)
Wharf Rd. Ind. Est.
EN3: Pond E 6F 25
Wharfside Rd. E16 . . . . .5G 87
Wharf St. E16 . . . . .5G 87
Wharf Vw. Ct. E14 . . . . .6E 86
(off Athol Sq.)
Wharncliffe Dr. UB1: S'hall 1H 95
Wharncliffe Gdns. SE25 . . . . .2E 156
Wharncliffe Rd. SE25 . . . . .2E 156
Wharton Cl. NW10 . . . . .6A 62
Wharton Cotts. WC1 . . . . . .2J 7 (3A 84)
Wharton Ho. SE1 . . . . .7J 15
(off Maltby St.)
Wharton Rd. BR1: Brom 1K 159
Wharton St. WC1 . . . . .2H 7 (3K 83)
Whatcott's Yd. N16 . . . . .4E 66
Whateley Rd. SE20 . . . . .7K 139
SE22 . . . . .5F 121
Whatley Av. SW20 . . . . .3F 153
Whatman Ho. E14 . . . . .6B 86
(off Wallwood St.)

Whatman Rd. SE23 . . . . .7K 121
Wheatcroft Ct. SM1: Sutt 1K 165
(off Cleeve Way)
Wheatfield Ho. W9 . . . . .3J 81
(off Kilburn Pk. Rd.)
Wheatfields E6 . . . . .6F 89
EN3: Enf H 1F 25
Wheatfield Way KT1: King T 2E 150
Wheathill Ho. SE20 . . . . .2H 157
(off Croydon Rd.)
Wheathill Rd. SE20 . . . . .3H 157
Wheatland Ho. SE22 . . . . .3E 120
Wheatlands TW5: Hest 6E 94
Wheatlands Rd. SW17 . . . . .3E 136
Wheatley Cl. NW4 . . . . .2C 44
Wheatley Cres. UB3: Hayes 7J 75
Wheatley Gdns. N9 . . . . .2K 33
Wheatley Ho. SW15 . . . . .7C 116
(off Ellisfield Dr)
Wheatley Mans. IG11: Bark 7A 72
(off Bevan Av.)
Wheatley Rd. TW7: Isle 3K 113
Wheatley's Eyot TW16: Sun 5J 147
Wheatley St. W1 . . . . .6H 5 (5E 82)
Wheat Sheaf Cl. E14 . . . . .4D 104
Wheatsheaf Cl. UB5: N'olt 5C 58
Wheatsheaf La. SW6 . . . . .7E 98
SW8 .7J 101
(not continuous)
Wheatsheaf Ter. SW6 . . . . .7H 99
Wheatstone Cl. CR4: Mitc 1C 154
Wheatstone Ho. W10 . . . . .5G 81
(off Telford Rd.)
Wheatstone Rd. DA8: Erith 5K 109
W10 . . . . .5G 81
Wheeler Cl. IG8: Wfd G 6J 37
Wheeler Gdns. N1 . . . . .1J 83
(off Outram Pl.)
Wheeler Pl. BR2: Brom 4K 159
Wheelers Cross IG11: Bark 2H 89
Wheelers Dr. HA4: Ruis 6E 38
Wheeler's St. SM1: Sutt 3J 165
Wheel Farm Dr. RM10: Dag 3J 73
Wheel Ho. E14 . . . . .5D 104
(off Burrells Wharf Sq.)
Wheelock Cl. DA8: Erith 7H 109
Wheelwright St. N7 . . . . .7K 65
Whelan Way SM6: Bedd 3H 167
Wheler Ho. E1 . . . . .4J 9
(off Quaker St.)
Wheler St. E1 . . . . .4J 9 (4F 85)
Whellock Rd. W4 . . . . .3A 98
Whenman Av. DA5: Bexl 2J 145
Whernside Cl. SE28 . . . . .7C 90
WHETSTONE 2F 31
Whetstone Cl. N20 . . . . .2G 31
Whetstone Pk. WC2 . . . . .7G 7 (6K 83)
Whetstone Rd. SE3 . . . . .2A 124
Whewell Rd. N19 . . . . .2J 65
Whidborne Bldgs. WC1 . . . . .2F 7
(off Whidborne St.)
Whidborne Cl. SE8 . . . . .2C 122
Whidborne St. WC1 . . . . . .2F 7 (3J 83)
(not continuous)
Whimbrel Cl. SE28 . . . . .7C 90
Whimbrel Way UB4: Yead 5B 76
Whinchat Rd. SE28 . . . . .3H 107
Whinfell Cl. SW16 . . . . .5H 137
Whinyates Rd. SE9 . . . . .3C 124
Whippendell Way BR5: St P 7B 144
Whipps Cross E17 . . . . .5F 51
Whipps Cross Ho. E17 . . . . .5F 51
(off Wood St.)
Whipps Cross Rd. E11 . . . . .5F 51
(not continuous)
Whiskin St. EC1 . . . . .2A 8 (3B 84)
Whisperwood Cl. HA3: Hrw W 1J 41
Whistler Gdns. HA8: Edg 2F 43
Whistler M. RM8: Dag 5B 72
(off Fitzstephen Rd.)
SE15 . . . . .7F 103

Whistlers Av. SW11 . . . . .7B 100
Whistler St. N5 . . . . .5B 66
Whistler Twr. SW10 . . . . .7A 100
(off Worlds End Est.)
Whistler Wlk. SW10 . . . . .7B 100
Whiston Ho. N1 . . . . .7B 66
(off Richmond Gro.)
Whiston Rd. E2 . . . . .2F 85
Whitacre M. SE11 . . . . . . .6K 19 (5A 102)
Whitakers Lodge EN2: Enf 1J 23
Whitbread Cl. N17 . . . . .1G 49
Whitbread Rd. SE4 . . . . .4A 122
Whitburn Rd. SE13 . . . . .4D 122
Whitby Av. NW10 . . . . .3H 79
Whitby Cl. N7 . . . . .4J 65
Whitby Gdns. NW9 . . . . .3G 43
SM1: Sutt 2B 166
Whitby Ho. NW8 . . . . .1A 82
(off Boundary Rd.)
Whitby Pde. HA4: Ruis 2A 58
Whitby Rd. HA2: Harr 3G 59
HA4: Ruis 3K 57
SE18 . . . . .4D 106
SM1: Sutt 2B 166
Whitby St. E1 . . . . .3J 9 (4F 85)
(not continuous)
Whitcher Cl. SE14 . . . . .6A 104
Whitcher Pl. NW1 . . . . .6G 65
Whitchurch Av. HA8: Edg 7A 28
Whitchurch Cl. HA8: Edg 6A 28
Whitchurch Gdns. HA8: Edg 6A 28
Whitchurch Ho. W10 . . . . .6F 81
(off Kingsdown Cl.)
Whitchurch La. HA8: Edg 7J 27
Whitchurch Pde. HA8: Edg 7B 28
Whitchurch Rd. W11 . . . . .7F 81
Whitcomb Ct. WC2 . . . . .3D 12
Whitcombe M. TW9: Kew 1H 115
Whitcomb St. WC2 . . . . . .3D 12 (7H 83)
Whitcome M. TW9: Kew 1H 115
Whiteadder Way E14 . . . . .4D 104
Whitear Wlk. E15 . . . . .6F 69
Whitebarn La. RM10: Dag 1G 91
Whitebeam Av. BR2: Brom 7E 160
Whitebeam Cl. SW9 . . . . .7K 101
White Bear Pl. NW3 . . . . .4B 64
White Bear Yd. EC1 . . . . .4J 7
(off Clerkenwell Rd.)
White Bri. Av. CR4: Mitc 3B 154
Whitebridge Cl. TW14: Felt 6H 111
White Butts Rd. HA4: Ruis 3B 58
WHITECHAPEL 5G 85
Whitechapel Art Gallery 7K 9
Whitechapel High St. E1 . . . . .7K 9 (6F 85)
Whitechapel Rd. E1 . . . . . . .7K 9 (5G 85)
Whitechapel Sports Cen. 5K 85
White Church La. E1 . . . . . . .7K 9 (6G 85)
White Church Pas. E1 . . . . .7K 9
(off White Church La.)
WHITE CITY .7D 80
WHITE CITY .6E 80
White City Cl. W12 . . . . .7E 80
White City Est. W12 . . . . .7D 80
White City Rd. W12 . . . . .7E 80
White Conduit St. N1 . . . . .2A 84
Whitecote Rd. UB1: S'hall 6G 77
Whitecroft Cl. BR3: Beck 4F 159
Whitecroft Way BR3: Beck 5E 158
Whitecross Pl. EC2 . . . . . . .5F 9 (5D 84)
Whitecross St. EC1 . . . . . . .3D 8 (4C 84)
Whitefield Av. NW2 . . . . .1E 62
Whitefield Cl. SW15 . . . . .6G 117
Whitefoot La. BR1: Brom 4E 140
(not continuous)
Whitefoot Ter. BR1: Brom 3H 141
Whitefriars Av. HA3: W'stone 2J 41
Whitefriars Ct. N12 . . . . .5G 31
Whitefriars Dr. HA3: Hrw W 2H 41
Whitefriars St. EC4 . . . . . .1K 13 (6A 84)
Whitefriars Trad. Est.
HA3: W'stone 3H 41

White Gdns. RM10: Dag 6G 73
Whitegate Gdns. HA3: Hrw W 7E 26
Whitehall 6G 165
Whitehall SW1 . . . . .5E 12 (1J 101)
Whitehall Ct. SW1 . . . . .5E 12 (1J 101)
(not continuous)
Whitehall Cres. KT9: Chess 5D 162
Whitehall Gdns. E4 . . . . .1B 36
SW1 .5E 12
W3 . . . . .1G 97
W4 . . . . .6H 97
Whitehall La. IG9: Buck H 2D 36
Whitehall Lodge N10 . . . . .3E 46
Whitehall Pk. N19 . . . . .1G 65
Whitehall Pk. Rd. W4 . . . . .6H 97
Whitehall Pl. E7 . . . . .5J 69
SM6: Wall 4F 167
SW1 . . . . .5E 12 (1J 101)
BR2: Brom 5B 160
CR7: Thor H 5A 156
E4 . . . . .2B 36
HA1: Harr 7J 41
IG8: Wfd G 2B 36
W7 . . . . .2A 96
Whitehall St. N17 . . . . .7A 34
White Hart Av. SE28 . . . . .3K 107
White Hart Cl. UB3: Harl 6F 93
White Hart Ct. EC2 . . . . .6G 9
White Hart Lane 7B 34
White Hart La. N17 . . . . .7H 33
N22 . . . . .1K 47
NW10 .6B 62
RM7: Col R, Mawney 1G 55
SW13 . . . . .3A 116
White Hart Rd. SE18 . . . . .4J 107
White Hart Rdbt. UB5: N'olt 2B 76
White Hart School Sports Cen. 7G 33
White Hart Slip BR1: Brom 2J 159
White Hart St. EC4 . . . . .7B 8 (6B 84)
SE11 . . . . .5K 19 (5A 102)
White Hart Yd. SE1 . . . . . .5E 14 (1D 102)
Whitehaven Cl. BR2: Brom 4J 159
Whitehaven St. NW8 . . . . . .4C 4 (4C 82)
Whitehead Cl. N18 . . . . .5J 33
SW18 . . . . .7A 118
Whiteheads Gro. SW3 . . . . . .4D 16 (4C 100)
White Heart Av. UB8: Hil 5E 74
Whiteheath Av. HA4: Ruis 7E 38
White Heather Ho. WC1 . . . . .2F 7
(off Cromer St.)
White Heron M. TW11: Tedd 6K 131
White Horse All. EC1 . . . . .5A 8
White Horse Hill BR7: Chst 4E 142
White Horse La. E1 . . . . .4K 85
Whitehorse La. SE25 . . . . .4D 156
Whitehorse M. SE1 . . . . . . .1K 19 (3A 102)
White Horse Rd. E1 . . . . .5A 86
(not continuous)
E6 . . . . .3D 88
Whitehorse Rd. CR0: Croy 7C 156
CR7: Thor H 7C 156
White Horse St. W1 . . . . . . .5K 11 (1F 101)
White Horse Yd. EC2 . . . . . . .7E 8 (6D 84)
White Ho. SW4 . . . . .7H 119
(off Clapham Pk. Est.)
SW11 . . . . .1B 118
White Ho., The NW1 . . . . .3K 5
White Ho. Dr. HA7: Stan 4H 27
IG8: Wfd G 6C 36
Whitehouse Est. E10 . . . . .6E 50
Whitehouse La. EN2: Enf 1H 23
Whitehouse Way N14 . . . . .2A 32
Whitehurst Dr. N18 . . . . .5E 34
White Kennett St. E1 . . . . . . .7H 9 (6E 84)
Whitelands Ho. SW3 . . . . .5F 17
(off Cheltenham Ter.)
Whiteledges W13 . . . . .6C 78
Whitelegg Rd. E13 . . . . .2H 87
Whiteley Rd. SE19 . . . . .5D 138
Whiteleys Cen. W2 . . . . .6K 81

Whiteleys Pde. UB10: Hil 4D 74
Whiteley's Way TW13: Hanw 3E 130
White Lion Ct. EC3 1G 15
SE15 6J 103
TW7: Isle 3B 114
White Lion Hill EC4 2B 14 (7B 84)
White Lion St. N1 2A 84
White Lodge SE19 7B 138
W5 5C 78
White Lodge Cl. N2 6B 46
SM2: Sutt 7A 166
TW7: Isle 2A 114
White Lodge Ct. TW16: Sun 1A 148
White Lyon Ct. EC2 5C 8
Whiteoak Ct. BR7: Chst 6E 142
White Oak Dr. BR3: Beck 2E 158
White Oak Gdns. DA15: Sidc 7K 125
Whiteoaks La. UB6: G'frd 3H 77
White Orchards HA7: Stan 5F 27
N20 1C 30
White Post La. E9 7B 68
White Post St. SE15 7J 103
White Rd. E15 7G 69
White Rose Trad. Est. *EN4: E Barn* *5G 21*
(off Margaret Rd.)
Whites Av. IG2: Ilf 6J 53
White's Grounds SE1 7H 15 (2E 102)
White's Grounds Est. SE1 6H 15
White's Mdw. BR1: Brom 4E 160
White's Row E1 6J 9 (5F 85)
Whites Sq. SW4 4H 119
Whitestile Rd. TW8: Bford 5C 96
Whitestone La. NW3 3A 64
Whitestone Wlk. NW3 3A 64
White St. UB1: S'hall 2B 94
Whiteswan M. W4 5A 98
Whitethorn Av. UB7: Yiew 7A 74
Whitethorn Gdns. CR0: Croy 2H 169
EN2: Enf 5J 23
Whitethorn Ho. *E1* *1J 103*
(off Prusom St.)
Whitethorn Pas. *E3* *4C 86*
(off Whitethorn St.)
Whitethorn Pl. UB7: Yiew 1B 92
Whitethorn St. E3 5C 86
White Tower *3J 15*
(in The Tower of London)
Whitewebbs Way BR5: St P 1K 161
Whitfield Ct. IG1: Ilf 7D 52
Whitfield Ho. *NW8* *4C 4*
(off Salisbury St.)
Whitfield Pl. W1 4A 6
Whitfield Rd. DA7: Bex 7F 109
E6 7A 70
SE3 1F 123
Whitfield St. W1 4A 6 (4G 83)
Whitford Gdns. CR4: Mitc 3D 154
Whitgift Av. CR2: S Croy 5B 168
Whitgift Cen. CR0: Croy 2C 168
Whitgift Ct. *CR2: S Croy* *5C 168*
(off Nottingham Rd.)
Whitgift Ho. SE11 3G 19 (4K 101)
SW11 1C 118
Whitgift Sq. CR0: Croy 2C 168
Whitgift St. CR0: Croy 3C 168
SE11 3G 19 (4K 101)
Whiting Av. IG11: Bark 7F 71
Whitings IG2: Ilf 5J 53
Whitings Rd. EN5: Barn 5A 20
Whitings Way E6 5E 88
Whitland Rd. SM5: Cars 1B 166
Whitley Cl. TW19: Stanw 6A 110
Whitley Ho. *SW1* *7B 18*
(off Churchill Gdns.)
Whitley Rd. N17 2E 48
Whitlock Dr. SW19 7G 117
Whitman Ho. *E2* *3J 85*
(off Cornwall Av.)
Whitman Rd. E3 4A 86
Whitmead Cl. CR2: S Croy 6E 168
Whitmore Cl. N11 5A 32
Whitmore Est. N1 1E 84
Whitmore Gdns. NW10 2E 80
Whitmore Ho. *N1* *1E 84*
(off Whitmore Est.)
Whitmore Rd. BR3: Beck 3B 158
HA1: Harr 7G 41
N1 1E 84
Whitmore Sports Cen. 1G 59
Whitnell Way SW15 5E 116
Whitney Av. IG4: Ilf 4B 52
Whitney Rd. E10 7D 50
Whitney Wlk. DA14: Sidc 6E 144
Whitstable Cl. BR3: Beck 1B 158
HA4: Ruis 2G 57
Whitstable Ho. *W10* *6F 81*
(off Silchester Rd.)
Whitstable Pl. CR0: Croy 4C 168
Whitstone La. BR3: Beck 5D 158
Whittaker Av. TW9: Rich 5D 114
Whittaker Pl. *TW9: Rich* *5D 114*
(off Whittaker Av.)
Whittaker Rd. E6 7A 70
SM3: Sutt 3H 165
Whittaker St. SW1 4G 17 (4E 100)
Whittaker Way SE1 4G 103
Whitta Rd. E12 4B 70
Whittell Gdns. SE26 3J 139
Whittingham N17 7C 34
Whittingham Ct. W4 7A 98
Whittingstall Rd. SW6 1H 117
Whittington Av. EC3 1G 15 (6E 84)
UB4: Hayes 5H 75
Whittington Ct. N2 5D 46
Whittington M. N12 4F 31
Whittington Rd. N22 7D 32
Whittington Way HA5: Pinn 5C 40
Whittlebury Cl. SM5: Cars 7D 166
Whittle Cl. E17 6A 50
UB1: S'hall 6F 77
Whittle Rd. TW5: Hest 7A 94
UB2: S'hall 2F 95
Whittlesea Cl. HA3: Hrw W 7B 26
Whittlesea Path HA3: Hrw W 1G 41
Whittlesea Rd. HA3: Hrw W 7B 26
Whittlesey St. SE1 5J 13 (1A 102)
WHITTON 7G 113
Whitton NW3 7D 64
Whitton Av. E. UB6: G'frd 5J 59
Whitton Av. W. UB5: N'olt 5F 59
UB6: G'frd 5F 59
Whitton Cl. UB6: G'frd 6B 60
Whitton Dene TW3: Houn 5G 113
TW7: Isle 6H 113
Whitton Dr. UB6: G'frd 6A 60
Whitton Mnr. Rd. TW7: Isle 6G 113
Whitton Rd. TW1: Twick 6K 113
TW2: Twick 6J 113
TW3: Houn 4F 113
WHITTON ROAD RDBT. 6K 113
Whitton Sports & Fitness Cen. 2F 131
Whitton Wlk. E3 3C 86
Whitton Waye TW3: Houn 6E 112
Whitwell Rd. E13 3J 87
Whitworth Ho. SE1 3C 102
Whitworth Rd. SE18 7E 106
SE25 3E 156
Whitworth St. SE10 5G 105
Whorlton Rd. SE15 3H 121
Whychcote Point *NW2* *1E 62*
(off Whitefield Av.)
Whymark Av. N22 3A 48
Whytecroft TW5: Hest 7B 94
Whyteville Rd. E7 6K 69
Whytlaw Ho. *E3* *5B 86*
(off Baythorne St.)
Wickersley Rd. SW11 2E 118
Wickers Oake SE19 4F 139
Wicker St. E1 6H 85
Wicket, The CR0: Addtn 5C 170
Wicket Rd. UB6: G'frd 3A 78
Wickets, The TW15: Ashf 4A 128
Wickfield Ho. *SE16* *2H 103*
(off Wilson Gro.)
Wickford Ho. *E1* *4J 85*
(off Wickford St.)
Wickford St. E1 4J 85
Wickford Way E17 4K 49
Wickham Av. CR0: Croy 2A 170
SM3: Cheam 5E 164
Wickham Chase BR4: W W'ck 1F 171
Wickham Cl. E1 5J 85
EN3: Enf H 3C 24
KT3: N Mald 6B 152
Wickham Ct. *KT5: Surb* *5F 151*
(off Cranes Pk.)
Wickham Ct. Rd. BR4: W W'ck 2E 170
Wickham Cres.
BR4: W W'ck 2E 170
Wickham Gdns. SE4 3B 122
Wickham Ho. *N1* *1E 84*
(off New Era Est.)
Wickham La. DA16 7B 108
SE2 5A 108
Wickham M. SE4 2B 122
Wickham Rd. BR3: Beck 2D 158
CR0: Croy 2K 169
E4 7K 35
HA3: Hrw W 2H 41
SE4 4B 122
Wickham St. DA16: Well 2J 125
SE11 5G 19 (5K 101)
Wickham Way BR3: Beck 4E 158
Wick Ho. *KT1: Ham W* *1D 150*
(off Station Rd.)
Wick La. E3 1C 86
Wickliffe Av. N3 2G 45
Wickliffe Gdns. HA9: Wemb 2H 61
Wicklow Ho. N16 1F 67
Wicklow St. WC1 1G 7 (3K 83)
Wick M. E9 6A 68
Wick Rd. E9 6K 67
TW11: Tedd 7B 132
Wicks Cl. SE9 4B 142
Wick Sq. E9 6B 68
Wicksteed Cl. DA5: Bexl 3K 145
Wicksteed Ho. SE1 3C 102
TW8: Bford 5F 97
Wickway Ct. *SE15* *6F 103*
(off Cator St.)
Wickwood St. SE5 2B 120
Widdecombe Av. HA2: Harr 2C 58
Widdenham Rd. N7 4K 65
Widdin St. E15 7G 69
Widecombe Gdns. IG4: Ilf 4C 52
Widecombe Rd. SE9 3C 142
Widecombe Way N2 5B 46
Widegate St. E1 6H 9 (5E 84)
Widenham Cl. HA5: Eastc 5A 40
Wide Way CR4: Mitc 3H 155
Widewing Cl. TW11: Tedd 7B 132
Widford *NW1* *6F 65*
(off Lewis St.)
Widford Ho. *N1* *2B 84*
(off Colebrooke Rd.)
Widgeon Cl. E16 6K 87
Widley Rd. W9 3J 81
Widmer Ct. TW3: Houn 2C 112
WIDMORE 3A 160
WIDMORE GREEN 2B 160
Widmore Lodge Rd.
BR1: Brom 2B 160
Widmore Rd. BR1: Brom 2J 159
UB8: Hil 4D 74
Wigan Ho. E5 1H 67
Wigeon Path SE28 3H 107
Wigeon Way UB4: Yead 6C 76
Wiggins La. TW10: Ham 2C 132
Wiggins Mead NW9 7G 29
Wigginton Av. HA9: Wemb 6H 61
Wight Ho. *KT1: King T* *3D 150*
(off Portsmouth Rd.)
Wightman Rd. N4 4A 48
N8 4A 48
Wighton M. TW7: Isle 2J 113
Wigley Rd. TW13: Felt 2B 130
Wigmore Ct. *W13* *1A 96*
(off Singapore Rd.)
Wigmore Hall 7J 5
Wigmore Pl. W1 7J 5 (6F 83)
Wigmore Rd. SM5: Cars 2B 166
Wigmore St. W1 7H 5 (6E 82)
Wigmore Wlk. SM5: Cars 2B 166
Wigram Ho. *E14* *7D 86*
(off Wade's Pl.)
Wigram Rd. E11 6A 52
Wigram Sq. E17 3E 50
Wigston Cl. N18 5K 33
Wigston Rd. E13 4K 87
Wigton Gdns. HA7: Stan 1E 42
Wigton Pl. SE11 6K 19 (5A 102)
Wigton Rd. E17 1B 50
Wilberforce Ct. BR2: Kes 7B 172
HA8: Edg *4A 28*
(off King's Dr.)
Wilberforce M. SW4 4H 119
Wilberforce Rd. N4 2B 66
(not continuous)
NW9 6C 44
Wilberforce Way SW19 6F 135
Wilbraham Ho. *SW8* *7J 101*
(off Wandsworth Rd.)
Wilbraham Mans. *SW1* *3G 17*
(off Wilbraham Pl.)
Wilbraham Pl. SW1 3F 17 (4D 100)
Wilbrahams Almshouses
EN5: Barn 2C 20
Wilbury Way N18 5J 33
Wilby M. W11 1H 99
Wilcox Cl. SW8 7J 101
(not continuous)
Wilcox Gdns. TW17: Shep 3A 146
Wilcox Ho. *E3* *5B 86*
(off Ackroyd Dr.)
Wilcox Pl. SW1 2B 18 (3G 101)
Wilcox Rd. SM1: Sutt 4K 165
SW8 7J 101
TW11: Tedd 4H 131
Wildberry Cl. W7 4A 96
Wild Ct. WC2 1G 13 (6K 83)
(not continuous)
Wildcroft Gdns. HA8: Edg 6J 27
Wildcroft Mnr. SW15 7E 116
Wildcroft Rd. SW15 7E 116
Wilde Cl. E8 1G 85
Wilde Ho. *W2* *6K 81*
(off Gloucester Ter.)
W2 *7B 82*
(off Gloucester Ter.)
Wilde Pl. N13 6G 33
SW18 7B 118
Wilder Cl. HA4: Ruis 1K 57
Wilderness, The
KT8: W Mole, E Mos 5G 149
TW12: Ham H 4F 131
Wilderness Island Nature Reserve
2E 166
Wilderness M. SW4 4F 119
Wilderness Rd. BR7: Chst 7F 143
Wilde Rd. DA8: Erith 7H 109
Wilderton Rd. N16 7E 48
Wildfell Rd. SE6 7D 122

Wild Goose Dr. SE14 1J **121**
Wild Hatch NW11 6J **45**
Wild's Rents SE1 7G **15** (3E **102**)
Wild St. WC2 1F **13** (6J **83**)
Wildwood Cl. SE12 7H **123**
Wildwood Gro. NW3 1A **64**
Wildwood Ri. NW11 1A **64**
Wildwood Rd. NW11 6K **45**
Wilford Cl. EN2: Enf 3J **23**
Wilford Rd. CR0: Croy 6C **156**
Wilfred Ct. *N15* *5D* ***48***
(off South Gro.)
Wilfred Owen Cl. SW19 6A **136**
Wilfred St. SW1 1A **18** (3G **101**)
Wilfrid Gdns. W3 5J **79**
Wilkes Rd. TW8: Bford 6E **96**
Wilkes St. E1 5K **9** (5F **85**)
Wilkie Ho. *SW1* *5D* ***18***
(off Cureton St.)
Wilkins Cl. CR4: Mitc 1C **154**
UB3: Harl 5H **93**
Wilkins Ho. *SW1* *7A* ***18***
(off Churchill Gdns.)
Wilkinson Cl. UB10: Hil 1D **74**
Wilkinson Ct. SW17 4B **136**
Wilkinson Gdns. SE25 1E **156**
Wilkinson Ho. *N1* *2D* ***84***
(off Cranston Est.)
Wilkinson Rd. E16 6A **88**
Wilkinson St. SW8 7K **101**
Wilkinson Way W4 2K **97**
Wilkin St. NW5 6E **64**
Wilkin St. M. NW5 6F **65**
Wilks Gdns. CR0: Croy 1A **170**
Wilks Pl. N1 2E **84**
Willan Rd. N17 2D **48**
Willan Wall E16 7H **87**
Willard St. SW8 3F **119**
Willcocks Cl. KT9: Chess 3E **162**
Willcott Rd. W3 1H **97**
Will Crooks Gdns. SE9 4A **124**
Willenfield Rd. NW10 2J **79**
Willenhall Av. EN5: New Bar 6F **21**
Willenhall Ct. EN5: New Bar 6F **21**
Willenhall Dr. UB3: Hayes 7G **75**
Willenhall Rd. SE18 5F **107**
Willersley Av. BR6: Orp 3H **173**
DA15: Sidc 1K **143**
Willersley Cl. DA15: Sidc 1K **143**
WILLESDEN 6C **62**
Willesden Belle Vue Cinema ***6D 62***
(within Library)
WILLESDEN GREEN 6E **62**
Willesden La. NW2 6E **62**
NW6 6E **62**
Willesden Section Ho. *NW6* *6F* ***63***
(off Willesden La.)
Willesden Sports Cen. 1D **80**
Willesden Sports Stadium 1D **80**
Willes Rd. NW5 6F **65**
Willett Cl. BR5: Pet W 6J **161**
UB5: Yead 3A **76**
Willett Ho. *E13* *2K* ***87***
(off Queens Rd. W.)
Willett Pl. CR7: Thor H 5A **156**
Willett Rd. CR7: Thor H 5A **156**
Willett Way BR5: Pet W 5H **161**
William IV St. WC2 3E **12** (7J **83**)
William Allen Ho. HA8: Edg 7A **28**
William Banfield Ho. *SW6* *2H* ***117***
(off Munster Rd.)
William Barefoot Dr. SE9 4E **142**
William Blake Ho. SW11 1C **118**
William Bonney Est. SW4 4H **119**
William Booth Rd. SE20 1G **157**
William Carey Way HA1: Harr 6J **41**
William Caslon Ho. *E2* *2H* ***85***
(off Patriot Sq.)
William Channing Ho. *E2* *3H* ***85***
(off Canrobert St.)
William Cl. N2 3B **46**
RM5: Col R 1J **55**
SE13 3E **122**
UB2: S'hall 2G **95**
William Cobbett Ho. *W8* *3K* ***99***
(off Scarsdale Pl.)
William Ct. W5 5C **78**
William Covell Cl.
EN2: Enf 1E **22**
William Dr. HA7: Stan 6F **27**
William Dromey Ct. NW6 7H **63**
William Dunbar Ho. *NW6* *2H* ***81***
(off Albert Rd.)
William Dyce M. SW16 4H **137**
William Ellis Way *SE16* *3G* ***103***
(off St James's Rd.)
William Evans Ho. *SE8* *4K* ***103***
(off Bush Rd.)
William Farm La. SW15 3D **116**
William Fenn Ho. *E2* *1K* ***9***
(off Shipton Rd.)
William Foster La.
DA16: Well 2A **126**
William Gdns. SW15 5D **116**
William Gibbs Ct. *SW1* *2C* ***18***
(off Old Pye St.)
William Gunn Ho. NW3 5C **64**
William Guy Gdns. E3 3D **86**
William Harvey Ho. *SW19* *1G* ***135***
(off Whitlock Dr.)
William Henry Wlk. SW8 7C **18** (6H **101**)
William Hunt Mans. SW13 6E **98**
William Margrie Cl. SE15 2G **121**
William M. SW1 7F **11** (2D **100**)
William Morley Cl. E6 1B **88**
William Morris Cl. E17 3B **50**
William Morris Gallery 3C **50**
William Morris Ho. W6 6F **99**
William Morris Way SW6 3A **118**
William Paton Ho. E16 6K **87**
William Perkin Ct. UB6: G'frd 6J **59**
William Pike Ho. *RM7: Rom* *6K* ***55***
(off Waterloo Gdns.)
William Pl. E3 2B **86**
William Rathbone Ho. *E2* *3H* ***85***
(off Florida St.)
William Rd. NW1 2A **6** (3G **83**)
SM1: Sutt 5A **166**
SW19 7G **135**
William Rushbrooke Ho.
SE16 *4G* ***103***
(off Rouel Rd.)
Williams Av. E17 1B **50**
William Saville Ho. *NW6* *2H* ***81***
(off Denmark Rd.)
William's Bldgs. E2 4J **85**
Williams Cl. N8 6H **47**
SW6 7G **99**
Williams Dr. TW3: Houn 4E **112**
Williams Gro. KT6: Surb 6C **150**
N22 1A **48**
Williams Ho. *E9* *1H* ***85***
(off King Edward's Rd.)
NW2 *3E* ***62***
(off Stoll Cl.)
SW1 *4D* ***18***
(off Regency St.)
Williams La. SM4: Mord 5A **154**
SW14 3J **115**
William Smith Ho. *DA17: Belv* *3G* ***109***
(off Ambrooke Rd.)
Williamson Cl. SE10 5H **105**
Williamson Ct. SE17 5C **102**
Williamson Rd. N4 6B **48**
Williamson St. N7 4J **65**
Williamson Way NW7 6B **30**
William Sq. *SE16* *7A* ***86***
(off Sovereign Cres.)
Williams Rd. UB2: S'hall 4C **94**
W13 1A **96**
Williams Ter. CR0: Wadd 6A **168**
William St. E10 6D **50**
IG11: Bark 7G **71**
N17 7A **34**
SM5: Cars 3C **166**
SW1 7F **11** (2D **100**)
Williams Way DA2: Bexl 2K **145**
William White Ct. *E13* *1A* ***88***
(off Green St.)
William Wood Ho. *SE26* *3J* ***139***
(off Shrublands Cl.)
Willifield Way NW11 4H **45**
Willingale Cl. IG8: Wfd G 6F **37**
Willingdon Rd. N22 2B **48**
Willingham Cl. NW5 5G **65**
Willingham Ter. NW5 5G **65**
Willingham Way KT1: King T 3G **151**
Willington Ct. E5 3A **68**
Willington Rd. SW9 3J **119**
Willis Av. SM2: Sutt 6C **166**
Willis Ct. BR4: W W'ck 2F **171**
CR7: Thor H 6A **156**
Willis Ho. *E14* *7D* ***86***
(off Hale St.)
Willis Rd. CR0: Croy 7C **156**
DA8: Erith 4J **109**
E15 2H **87**
Willis St. E14 6D **86**
Will Miles Ct. SW19 7A **136**
Willmore End SW19 1K **153**
Willoughby Av. CR0: Bedd 4K **167**
Willoughby Dr. RM13: Rain 7K **73**
Willoughby Gro. N17 7C **34**
Willoughby Highwalk *EC2* *6E* ***8***
(off Moor La.)
Willoughby Ho. *E1* *1H* ***103***
(off Reardon Path)
EC2 5E **8**
Willoughby La. N17 6C **34**
Willoughby M. N17 7C **34**
SW4 *4F* ***119***
(off Wix's La.)
Willoughby Pk. Rd. N17 7C **34**
Willoughby Pas. *E14* *1C* ***104***
(off W. India Av.)
Willoughby Rd. KT2: King T 1F **151**
N8 3A **48**
NW3 4B **64**
TW1: Twick 5C **114**
(not continuous)
Willoughbys, The SW14 3A **116**
Willoughby St. WC1 6E **6**
Willoughby Way SE7 4K **105**
Willow Av. DA15: Sidc 6A **126**
SW13 2B **116**
UB7: Yiew 7B **74**
Willow Bank SW6 3G **117**
TW10: Ham 3B **132**
Willowbray Cl. EN5: Barn 6A **20**
Willow Bri. Rd. N1 6C **66**
(not continuous)
Willowbrook TW12: Ham H 5F **131**
Willowbrook Est. SE15 7G **103**
Willow Brook Rd. SE15 7F **103**
Willowbrook Rd. TW19: Stanw 2A **128**
UB2: S'hall 3E **94**
Willow Bus. Cen., The
CR4: Mitc 6D **154**
Willow Bus. Pk. SE26 3J **139**
Willow Cl. BR2: Brom 5D **160**
DA5: Bexl 6F **127**
IG9: Buck H 3G **37**
SE6 1H **141**
TW8: Bford 6C **96**
Willow Cotts. TW9: Kew 6G **97**
TW13: Hanw 3C **130**
Willow Ct. *E11* *2G* ***69***
(off Trinity Cl.)
EC2 3G **9**
HA3: Hrw W 1K **41**
HA8: Edg 4K **27**
N12 4E **30**
NW6 7G **63**
TW16: Sun *7G* ***129***
(off Staines Rd. W.)
W4 *7A* ***98***
(off Corney Reach Way)
W9 *5J* ***81***
(off Admiral Wlk.)
Willowcourt Av. HA3: Kent 5B **42**
Willow Dene HA5: Pinn 2B **40**
WD23: Bushy 1D **26**
Willowdene N6 7D **46**
SE15 7H **103**
Willowdene Cl. TW2: Whit 7G **113**
Willowdene Ct. *N20* *7F* ***21***
(off High Rd.)
Willow Dr. EN5: Barn 4B **20**
Willow End KT6: Surb 1E **162**
N20 2D **30**
Willowfields Cl. SE18 5J **107**
Willow Gdns. HA4: Ruis 2H **57**
TW3: Houn 1E **112**
Willow Grange DA14: Sidc 3B **144**
Willow Grn. NW9 1A **44**
Willow Gro. BR7: Chst 6E **142**
E13 2J **87**
HA4: Ruis 2H **57**
Willowhayne Ct. *KT12: Walt T* *7K* ***147***
(off Willowhayne Dr.)
Willowhayne Dr. KT12: Walt T 7K **147**
Willowhayne Gdns.
KT4: Wor Pk 3E **164**
Willow Ho. BR2: Brom 2G **159**
W10 *4F* ***81***
(off Maple Wlk.)
Willow La. CR4: Mitc 5D **154**
SE18 4D **106**
Willow Lodge SW6 1F **117**
TW16: Sun *7H* ***129***
(off Forest Dr.)
Willowmead Cl. W5 4D **78**
Willow Mt. CR0: Croy 3E **168**
Willow Pl. SW1 3B **18** (4G **101**)
Willow Rd. E12 3D **70**
EN1: Enf 3K **23**
KT3: N Mald 4J **151**
NW3 4B **64**
RM6: Chad H 6E **54**
SM6: Wall 7F **167**
W5 2E **96**
Willows, The BR3: Beck 1C **158**
E6 7D **70**
Willows Av. SM4: Mord 5K **153**
Willows Cl. HA5: Pinn 2A **40**
Willowside Ct. EN2: Enf 3G **23**
Willows Ter. *NW10* *2B* ***80***
(off Rucklidge Av.)
Willow St. E4 1A **36**
EC2 3G **9** (4E **84**)
RM7: Rom 4J **55**
Willow Tree Cl. E3 1B **86**
SW18 1K **135**
UB4: Yead 4A **76**
UB5: N'olt 6D **58**
Willowtree Cl. UB10: Ick 3E **56**
Willow Tree Ct. DA14: Sidc 5A **144**
HA0: Wemb 5D **60**
Willow Tree La. UB4: Yead 4A **76**
Willow Tree Rdbt. UB4: Yead 5B **76**
Willow Tree Wlk. BR1: Brom 1K **159**
Willowtree Way CR7: Thor H 1A **156**

Willow Va. BR7: Chst 6F **143**
W12 . . . . .1C **98**
Willow Vw. SW19 . . . . .1B **154**
Willow Wlk. BR6: Farnb 3F **173**
E17 . . . . .5B **50**
IG1: Ilf .2F **71**
N2 . . . . .2B **46**
N15 . . . . .4B **48**
N21 . . . . .6E **22**
SE1 . . . . .3E **102**
SM3: Sutt 3H **165**
Willow Way HA0: Wemb 3A **60**
KT19: Ewe 6K **163**
N3 . . . . .7E **30**
SE26 . . . . .3J **139**
TW2: Twick 2F **131**
TW16: Sun 4J **147**
W11 . . . . .7F **81**
Willow Wood Cres. SE25 . . . . .6E **156**
Willow Wren Wharf UB2: S'hall 4K **93**
Willrose Cres. SE2 . . . . .5B **108**
Willsbridge Ct. SE15 . . . . .6E **102**
Wills Cres. TW3: Houn 6F **113**
Wills Gro. NW7 . . . . .5H **29**
(not continuous)
Wilman Gro. E8 . . . . .7G **67**
Wilmar Cl. UB4: Hayes 4F **75**
Wilmar Gdns. BR4: W W'ck 1D **170**
Wilmcote Ho. *W2* *5K* ***81***
(off Woodchester Sq.)
Wilment Ct. NW2 . . . . .3E **62**
Wilmer Cl. KT2: King T 5F **133**
Wilmer Cres. KT2: King T 5F **133**
Wilmer Gdns. N1 . . . . .1E **84**
(not continuous)
Wilmer Lea Cl. E15 . . . . .7E **68**
Wilmer Pl. N16 . . . . .2F **67**
Wilmers Ct. *NW10* *1K* ***79***
(off Lawrence Av.)
Wilmer Way N14 . . . . .5C **32**
Wilmington Av. W4 . . . . .7K **97**
Wilmington Ct. SW16 . . . . .7J **137**
Wilmington Gdns. IG11: Bark 6H **71**
Wilmington Sq. WC1 . . . . .2J **7** (3A **84**)
(not continuous)
Wilmington St. WC1 . . . . .2J **7** (3A **84**)
Wilmot Cl. N2 . . . . .2A **46**
SE15 . . . . .7G **103**
Wilmot Pl. *NW1* *7G* ***65***
(off St Pancras Way)
NW1 . . . . .7G **65**
(Rochester Rd.)
W7 . . . . .1J **95**
Wilmot Rd. E10 . . . . .2D **68**
N17 . . . . .3D **48**
SM5: Cars 5D **166**
Wilmot St. E2 . . . . .4H **85**
Wilmount St. SE18 . . . . .4F **107**
Wilna Rd. SW18 . . . . .7A **118**
Wilsham St. W11 . . . . .1F **99**
Wilshaw Cl. NW4 . . . . .3C **44**
Wilshaw Ho. SE8 . . . . .7C **104**
Wilshaw St. SE14 . . . . .1C **122**
Wilsmere Dr. HA3: Hrw W 7D **26**
UB5: N'olt 6C **58**
Wilson Av. CR4: Mitc 7C **136**
Wilson Cl. CR2: S Croy 5D **168**
HA9: Wemb 7F **43**
Wilson Dr. HA9: Wemb 7F **43**
Wilson Gdns. HA1: Harr 7G **41**
Wilson Gro. SE16 . . . . .2H **103**
Wilson Rd. E6 . . . . .3B **88**
IG1: Ilf .7D **52**
KT9: Chess 6F **163**
SE5 . . . . .1E **120**
Wilson's Av. N17 . . . . .2F **49**
Wilson's Pl. E14 . . . . .6B **86**
Wilson's Rd. W6 . . . . .5F **99**
Wilson St. E17 . . . . .5E **50**
EC2 . . . . .5F **9** (5D **84**)
N21 . . . . .7F **23**
Wilson Wlk. *W6* *4B* ***98***
(off Prebend Gdns.)
Wilstone Cl. UB4: Yead 4C **76**
Wiltern Ct. NW2 . . . . .6G **63**
Wilthorne Gdns. RM10: Dag 7H **73**
Wilton Av. W4 . . . . .5A **98**
Wilton Cl. UB7: Harm 6A **92**
Wilton Ct. *E1* *6H* ***85***
(off Cavell St.)
Wilton Cres. SW1 . . . . .7G **11** (2E **100**)
SW19 . . . . .7H **135**
Wilton Dr. RM5: Col R 1J **55**
Wilton Est. E8 . . . . .6G **67**
Wilton Gdns. KT8: W Mole 3E **148**
Wilton Gro. KT3: N Mald 6B **152**
SW19 . . . . .1H **153**
Wilton Ho. *CR2: S Croy* *5C* ***168***
(off Nottingham Rd.)
Wilton M. E8 .6H **67**
SW1 . . . . .1H **17** (3E **100**)
Wilton Pde. TW13: Felt 1K **129**
Wilton Pl. HA1: Harr 6K **41**
SW1 . . . . .7G **11** (2E **100**)
Wilton Rd. EN4: Cockf 4J **21**
N10 . . . . .2E **46**
SE2 . . . . .4C **108**
SW1 . . . . .2A **18** (3F **101**)
SW19 . . . . .7C **136**
TW4: Houn 3B **112**
Wilton Row SW1 . . . . .7G **11** (2E **100**)
Wilton Sq. N1 . . . . .1D **84**
Wilton St. SW1 . . . . .1J **17** (3F **101**)
Wilton Ter. SW1 . . . . .1G **17** (3E **100**)
Wilton Vs. *N1* *1D* ***84***
(off Wilton Sq.)
Wilton Wlk. *TW13: Felt* *1K* ***129***
(off Wilton Pde.)
Wilton Way E8 . . . . .6G **67**
Wiltshire Cl. NW7 . . . . .5G **29**
SW3 . . . . .3E **16** (4D **100**)
Wiltshire Ct. CR2: S Croy 5C **168**
IG1: Ilf .6G **71**
N4 . . . .*1K* ***65***
(off Marquis Rd.)
Wiltshire Gdns. N4 . . . . .6C **48**
TW2: Twick 1G **131**
Wiltshire La. HA5: Eastc 3H **39**
Wiltshire Rd. BR6: Orp 7K **161**
CR7: Thor H 3A **156**
SW9 . . . . .3A **120**
Wiltshire Row N1 . . . . .1D **84**
Wilverley Cres. KT3: N Mald 6A **152**
Wimbart Rd. SW2 . . . . .7K **119**
WIMBLEDON 5F **135**
Wimbledon
All England Lawn Tennis &
Croquet Club 4G **135**
Wimbledon Bri. SW19 . . . . .6H **135**
Wimbledon Cl. SW20 . . . . .7F **135**
Wimbledon Common 4B **134**
Wimbledon Greyhound &
Speedway Stadium 4A **136**
Wimbledon Hill Rd. SW19 . . . . .6G **135**
Wimbledon Lawn Tennis Mus. 3G **135**
Wimbledon Leisure Cen. 6K **135**
Wimbledon Mus. of Local History
. . . . .6G **135**
WIMBLEDON PARK 3J **135**
Wimbledon Pk. Ct. SW19 . . . . .1H **135**
Wimbledon Pk. Rd. SW18 . . . . .2G **135**
SW19 . . . . .2G **135**
Wimbledon Pk. Side SW19 . . . . .3F **135**
Wimbledon Rd. SW17 . . . . .4A **136**
Wimbledon Stadium Bus. Cen.
SW17 .3K **135**
Wimbledon Theatre *7J* ***135***
(off Russell Rd.)
Wimbledon Windmill Mus. 2D **134**
Wimbolt St. E2 . . . . .3G **85**
Wimborne Av. BR5: St P 4K **161**
BR7: Chst 4K **161**
UB2: S'hall 4E **94**
UB4: Yead 6K **75**
Wimborne Cl. IG9: Buck H 2E **36**
KT4: Wor Pk 1E **164**
SE12 . . . . .5H **123**
Wimborne Ct. SW12 . . . . .3G **137**
UB5: N'olt 6E **58**
Wimborne Dr. HA5: Pinn 7B **40**
NW9 . . . . .3G **43**
Wimborne Gdns. W13 . . . . .5B **78**
Wimborne Ho. *E16* *7H* ***87***
(off Victoria Dock Rd.)
NW1 . . . .*4D* ***4***
(off Harewood Av.)
SW8 . . . .*7K* ***101***
(off Dorset Rd.)
SW12 .3G **137**
Wimborne Rd. N9 . . . . .2B **34**
N17 . . . . .2E **48**
Wimborne Way BR3: Beck 3K **157**
Wimbourne Ct. *N1* *2D* ***84***
(off Wimbourne St.)
Wimbourne St. N1 . . . . .2D **84**
Wimpole Cl. BR2: Brom 4A **160**
KT1: King T 2F **151**
Wimpole M. W1 . . . . .5J **5** (5F **83**)
Wimpole Rd. UB7: Yiew 1A **92**
Wimpole St. W1 . . . . .6J **5** (5F **83**)
Wimshurst Cl. CR0: Wadd 1J **167**
Winans Wlk. SW9 . . . . .2A **120**
Winant Ho. *E14* *7D* ***86***
(off Simpson's Rd.)
Wincanton Ct. *N11* *6K* ***31***
(off Martock Gdns.)
Wincanton Cres. UB5: N'olt 5E **58**
Wincanton Gdns. IG6: Ilf 3F **53**
Wincanton Rd. SW18 . . . . .7H **117**
Winchcombe Rd. SM5: Cars 7B **154**
Winchcomb Gdns. SE9 . . . . .3B **124**
Winchelsea Av. DA7: Bex 7F **109**
Winchelsea Cl. SW15 . . . . .5F **117**
Winchelsea Cres.
KT8: W Mole 2G **149**
Winchelsea Ho. *SE16* *2J* ***103***
(off Swan Rd.)
Winchelsea Rd. E7 . . . . .3J **69**
N17 . . . . .3E **48**
NW10 .1K **79**
Winchelsey Ri. CR2: S Croy 6F **169**
Winchendon Rd. SW6 . . . . .1H **117**
TW11: Tedd 4H **131**
Winchester Av. NW6 . . . . .1G **81**
NW9 . . . . .3G **43**
TW5: Hest 6D **94**
Winchester Cl. BR2: Brom 3H **159**
E6 . . . . .6D **88**
EN1: Enf 5K **23**
KT2: King T 7H **133**
SE17 . . . . .4B **102**
Winchester Ct. *W8* *2J* ***99***
(off Vicarage Ga.)
Winchester Dr. HA5: Pinn 5B **40**
Winchester Ho. *IG11: Bark* *7A* ***72***
(off Keir Hardie Way)
SE18 . . . .*7B* ***106***
(off Portway Gdns.)
SW3 . . . . .7B **16**
SW9 . . . . .7A **102**
W2 . . . .*6A* ***82***
(off Hallfield Est.)
Winchester M. KT4: Wor Pk 2F **165**
Winchester Pk. BR2: Brom 3H **159**
Winchester Pl. E8 . . . . .5F **67**
N6 . . . . .1F **65**
Winchester Rd. BR2: Brom 3H **159**
DA7: Bex 2D **126**
E4 . . . . .7K **35**
HA3: Kent 4E **42**
HA6: Nwood 2H **39**
IG1: Ilf .3H **71**
KT12: Walt T 7J **147**
N6 . . . . .7F **47**
N9 . . . . .1A **34**
NW3 . . . . .7B **64**
TW1: Twick 6B **114**
TW13: Hanw 3D **130**
UB3: Harl 7G **93**
Winchester Sq. SE1 . . . . .4E **14**
Winchester St. SW1 . . . . .5K **17** (5F **101**)
W3 . . . . .1J **97**
Winchester Wlk. SE1 . . . . . . .4E **14** (1D **102**)
Winchester Wharf *SE1* *4E* ***14***
(off Clink St.)
Winchet Wlk. CR0: Croy 6J **157**
Winchfield Cl. HA3: Kent 6C **42**
Winchfield Ho. SW15 . . . . .6B **116**
Winchfield Rd. SE26 . . . . .5A **140**
Winch Ho. *E14* *3D* ***104***
(off Tiller Rd.)
SW10 . . . .*7A* ***100***
(off King's Rd.)
Winchilsea Ho. *NW8* *2B* ***4***
(off St John's Wood Rd.)
WINCHMORE HILL 7F **23**
Winchmore Hill Rd. N14 . . . . .1C **32**
N21 . . . . .1C **32**
Winchmore Vs. *N21* *7E* ***22***
(off Winchmore Hill Rd.)
Winchstone Cl.
TW17: Shep 4B **146**
Winckley Cl. HA3: Kent 5F **43**
Winckworth Ct. *N1* *2F* ***9***
(off Brunswick Pl.)
Wincott St. SE11 . . . . .4K **19** (4A **102**)
Wincrofts Dr. SE9 . . . . .4H **125**
Windall Cl. SE19 . . . . .1G **157**
Windborough Rd. SM5: Cars 7E **166**
Windermere *NW1* *2K* ***5***
(off Albany St.)
Windermere Av. HA4: Ruis 7A **40**
HA9: Kent, Wemb 7C **42**
N3 . . . . .3J **45**
NW6 . . . . .1G **81**
SW19 . . . . .3K **153**
Windermere Cl. BR6: Farnb 3F **173**
TW14: Felt 1H **129**
TW19: Stanw 1A **128**
Windermere Ct. HA9: Wemb 7C **42**
SM5: Cars 3E **166**
SW13 . . . . .6B **98**
Windermere Gdns. IG4: Ilf 5C **52**
Windermere Gro.
HA9: Wemb 1C **60**
Windermere Hall HA8: Edg 5A **28**
Windermere Ho. E3 . . . . .4B **86**
EN5: New Bar 4E **20**
Windermere Point *SE15* *7J* ***103***
(off Old Kent Rd.)
Windermere Rd. BR4: W W'ck 2G **171**
CR0: Croy 1F **169**
DA7: Bex 2J **127**
N10 . . . . .1F **47**
N19 . . . . .2G **65**
SW15 . . . . .4A **134**
SW16 . . . . .1G **155**
UB1: S'hall 5D **76**
W5 . . . . .3C **96**
Windermere Way UB7: Yiew 1A **92**
Winders Rd. SW11 . . . . .2C **118**
(not continuous)

Windfield Cl. SE26 . . . . .4K 139
Windham Rd. TW9: Rich 3F 115
Winding, The W2 . . . . .6B 4
Winding Way RM8: Dag 3C 72
Windlass Pl. SE8 . . . . .4A 104
Windlesham Gro. SW19 . . . . .1F 135
Windley Cl. SE23 . . . . .2J 139
Windmill WC1 . . . . .5G 7
(off New Nth. St.)
Windmill Av. UB2: S'hall 1G 95
Windmill Bri. Ho. CR0: Croy 1E 168
(off Freemasons Rd.)
Windmill Bus. Village TW16: Sun . . .1G 147
Windmill Cl. KT6: Surb 1C 162
SE1 . . . . .4G 103
(off Beatrice Rd.)
SE13 . . . . .2E 122
TW16: Sun 7G 129
Windmill Ct. NW2 . . . . .6G 63
W5 . . . . .4C 96
(off Windmill Rd.)
Windmill Dr. BR2: Kes 4A 172
NW2 . . . . .3G 63
SW4 . . . . .5F 119
Windmill Gdns. EN2: Enf 3F 23
Windmill Grn. TW17: Shep 7G 147
(off Walton La.)
Windmill Gro. CR0: Croy 6C 156
Windmill Hill EN2: Enf 3G 23
HA4: Ruis 7H 39
NW3 . . . . .3A 64
Windmill Ho. E14 . . . . .4C 104
Windmill La. E15 . . . . .6F 69
KT6: Surb 6B 150
TW7: Isle 1G 95
UB2: S'hall 1G 95
UB6: G'frd 6G 77
WD23: Bushy 1D 26
Windmill M. W4 . . . . .4A 98
Windmill Pas. W4 . . . . .4A 98
Windmill Pl. Bus. Cen.
UB2: S'hall 1G 95
Windmill Ri. KT2: King T 7H 133
Windmill Rd. CR0: Croy 7C 156
CR4: Mitc 5G 155
N18 . . . . .4J 33
SW18 . . . . .6B 118
SW19 . . . . .2D 134
TW8: Bford 4C 96
TW12: Ham H 5F 131
TW16: Sun 1G 147
W4 . . . . .4A 98
W5 . . . . .4C 96
Windmill Rd. W. TW16: Sun 1G 147
Windmill Row SE11 . . . . . .6J 19 (5A 102)
Windmill St. W1 . . . . .6C 6 (5H 83)
(not continuous)
WD23: Bushy 1D 26
Windmill Ter. TW17: Shep 7G 147
Windmill Wlk. SE1 . . . .5K 13 (1A 102)
Windmill Way HA4: Ruis 1H 57
Windmore Cl. HA0: Wemb 5A 60
Windrose Cl. SE16 . . . . .2K 103
Windrush KT3: N Mald 4H 151
SE28 . . . . .1B 108
Windrush Cl. N17 . . . . .1E 48
SW11 . . . . .4B 118
UB10: Ick 4B 56
W4 . . . . .1J 115
Windrush Ho. NW8 . . . . .5B 4
(off Venables St.)
Windrush La. SE23 . . . . .3K 139
Windrush Rd. NW10 . . . . .1K 79
Windsock Cl. SE16 . . . . .4B 104
Windsor Av. E17 . . . . .2A 50
HA8: Edg 4C 28
KT3: N Mald 5J 151
KT8: W Mole 3E 148

Windsor Av. SM3: Cheam 3G 165
SW19 . . . . .1A 154
UB10: Hil 1D 74
Windsor Cen., The N1 . . . . .1B 84
(off Windsor St.)
Windsor Cl. BR7: Chst 5F 143
HA2: Harr 3E 58
HA6: Nwood 2J 39
N3 . . . . .2G 45
SE27 . . . . .4C 138
TW8: Bford 6B 96
Windsor Cotts. SE14 . . . . .7B 104
(off Amersham Gro.)
Windsor Ct. HA5: Pinn 3B 40
KT1: King T 4D 150
(off Palace Rd.)
N11 . . . . .5J 31
N14 .7B 22
NW2 . . . . .6G 63
(off Chatsworth Rd.)
NW3 . . . . .4J 63
NW11 . . . . .6G 45
(off Golders Grn. Rd.)
SE16 . . . . .7K 85
(off King & Queen Wharf)
SW3 . . . . .5D 16
(off Jubilee Pl.)
SW11 . . . . .2B 118
TW16: Sun 7J 129
W2 . . . . .7K 81
(off Moscow Rd.)
W10 . . . . .6F 81
(off Bramley Rd.)
Windsor Cres. HA2: Harr 3E 58
HA9: Wemb 3H 61
Windsor Dr. BR6: Chels 6K 173
EN4: E Barn 6J 21
Windsor Gdns. CR0: Bedd 3J 167
UB3: Harl 3F 93
W9 . . . . .5J 81
Windsor Gro. SE27 . . . . .4C 138
Windsor Hall E16 . . . . .1K 105
(off Wesley Av.)
Windsor Ho. E2 . . . . .3K 85
(off Knottisford St.)
N1 . . . . .2C 84
NW1 .1K 5
UB5: N'olt 6E 58
(off The Farmlands)
Windsor M. SE6 . . . . .1E 140
SE23 . . . . .1A 140
SW18 . . . . .7A 118
(off Wilna Rd.)
Windsor Pk. Rd.
UB3: Harl 7H 93
Windsor Pl. SW1 . . . . . . .3B 18 (3G 101)
Windsor Rd. CR7: Thor H 2B 156
DA6: Bex 4E 126
E4 . . . . .4J 35
E7 . . . . .5K 69
E10 .2D 68
E11 .1J 69
EN5: Barn 6A 20
HA3: Hrw W 1G 41
IG1: Ilf 4F 71
KT2: King T 7E 132
KT4: Wor Pk 2C 164
N3 . . . . .2G 45
N7 . . . . .3J 65
N13 .3F 33
N17 .2G 49
NW2 . . . . .6D 62
RM8: Dag 3E 72
TW4: Cran 2K 111
TW9: Kew 2F 115
TW11: Tedd 5H 131
TW16: Sun 6J 129
UB2: S'hall 3D 94

Windsor Rd. W5 . . . . .7E 78
(not continuous)
Windsors, The IG9: Buck H 2H 37
Windsor St. N1 . . . . .1B 84
Windsor Ter. N1 . . . . .1D 8 (3C 84)
Windsor Wlk. SE5 . . . . .2D 120
Windsor Way W14 . . . . .4F 99
Windsor Wharf E9 . . . . .6C 68
Windspoint Dr. SE15 . . . . .6H 103
Windsock Rd. N16 . . . . .1F 67
Windus Wlk. N16 . . . . .1F 67
Windy Ridge BR1: Brom 1C 160
Windy Ridge Cl. SW19 . . . . .5F 135
Wine Cl. E1 .7J 85
(not continuous)
Wine Office Ct. EC4 . . . . .7K 7 (6A 84)
Winery La. N11: King T 3F 151
Winey Cl. KT9: Chess 7C 162
Winford Ct. SE15 . . . . .1H 121
Winford Ho. E3 . . . . .7B 68
Winford Pde. UB1: S'hall 6F 77
(off Marconi Way)
Winforton St. SE10 . . . . .1E 122
Winfrith Rd. SW18 . . . . .7A 118
Wingate Cres. CR0: Croy 6J 155
Wingate Rd. DA14: Sidc 6C 144
IG1: Ilf 5F 71
W6 . . . . .3D 98
Wingate Trad. Est. N17 . . . . .7A 34
Wingfield Cl. DA15: Sidc 2K 143
E14 .7F 87
(off John Smith M.)
Wingfield Ho. E2 . . . . .2J 9
(off Virginia Rd.)
NW6 .2K 81
(off Tollgate Gdns.)
Wingfield M. SE15 . . . . .3G 121
Wingfield Rd. E15 . . . . .4G 69
E17 .5D 50
KT2: King T 6F 133
Wingfield St. SE15 . . . . .3G 121
Wingfield Way HA4: Ruis 6K 57
Wingford Rd. SW2 . . . . .6J 119
Wingmore Rd. SE24 . . . . .3C 120
Wingrad Ho. E1 . . . . .5J 85
(off Jubilee St.)
Wingrave SE17 . . . . .4D 102
(not continuous)
Wingrave Rd. W6 . . . . .6E 98
Wingreen NW8 . . . . .1K 81
(off Abbey Rd.)
Wingrove E4 . . . . .4H 25
Wingrove Ct. RM7: Rom 5J 55
Wingrove Rd. SE6 . . . . .2G 141
Wings Cl. SM1: Sutt 4J 165
Winicotte Ho. W2 . . . . .5B 4
(off Paddington Grn.)
Winifred Pl. N12 . . . . .5F 31
Winifred Rd. DA8: Erith 5K 109
RM8: Dag 2E 72
SW19 . . . . .1J 153
TW12: Ham H 4E 130
Winifred St. E16 . . . . .1D 106
Winifred Ter. E13 . . . . .2J 87
(off Upper Rd.)
EN1: Enf 7A 24
Winkfield Rd. E13 . . . . .2K 87
N22 .1A 48
Winkley Ct. HA2: Harr 3E 58
N10 .4F 47
(off St James's La.)
Winkley St. E2 . . . . .2H 85
Winkworth Cotts. E1 . . . . .4J 85
(off Cephas St.)
Winlaton Rd. BR1: Brom 4F 141
Winmill Rd. RM8: Dag 3F 73
Winnett St. W1 . . . . .2C 12 (7H 83)
Winningales Ct. IG5: Ilf 2C 52

Winnings Wlk. UB5: N'olt 6C 58
Winnington Cl. N2 . . . . .6B 46
Winnington Ho. SE5 . . . . .7C 102
(off Wyndham Est.)
W10 . . . . .4G 81
(off Southern Row)
Winnington Rd. N2 . . . . .6B 46
Winnipeg Dr. BR6: Chels 6K 173
Winnock Rd. UB7: View 1A 92
Winn Rd. SE12 . . . . .1J 141
Winns Av. E17 . . . . .3B 50
Winns Comn. Rd. SE18 . . . . .6J 107
Winns Ter. E17 . . . . .3C 50
Winsbeach E17 . . . . .2F 51
Winscombe Cres. W5 . . . . .4D 78
Winscombe St. N19 . . . . .2F 65
Winscombe Way HA7: Stan 5F 27
Winsford Rd. SE6 . . . . .3B 140
Winsford Ter. N18 . . . . .5J 33
Winsham Gro. SW11 . . . . .5E 118
Winsham Ho. NW1 . . . . .1D 6
(off Churchway)
Winslade Rd. SW2 . . . . .5J 119
Winslade Way SE6 . . . . .7D 122
Winsland M. W2 . . . . .7A 4 (6B 82)
Winsland St. W2 . . . . .7A 4 (6B 82)
Winsley St. W1 . . . . .7B 6 (6G 83)
Winslow SE17 . . . . .5E 102
Winslow Cl. HA5: Eastc 6K 39
NW10 . . . . .3A 62
Winslow Gro. E4 . . . . .2B 36
Winslow Rd. W6 . . . . .6E 98
Winslow Way TW13: Hanw 3B 130
Winsmoor Ct. EN2: Enf 3G 23
WINSOR PARK 5F 89
Winsor Ter. E6 . . . . .5E 88
Winstanley Est. SW11 . . . . .3B 118
Winstanley Rd. SW11 . . . . .3B 118
(not continuous)
Winstead Gdns. RM10: Dag 5J 73
Winston Av. NW9 . . . . .7A 44
Winston Cl. HA3: Hrw W 6E 26
RM7: Mawney 4H 55
Winston Ct. BR1: Brom 1K 159
(off Widmore Rd.)
HA3: Hrw W 7A 26
Winston Ho. W13 . . . . .2A 96
(off Balfour Rd.)
WC1 . . . . .3D 6
Winston Rd. N16 . . . . .4D 66
Winston Wlk. W4 . . . . .3K 97
Winston Way IG1: Ilf 3F 71
Winter Av. E6 . . . . .1C 88
Winterborne Av. BR6: Orp 3H 173
Winterbourne Ho. W11 . . . . .7G 81
(off Portland Rd.)
Winterbourne Rd. CR7: Thor H 4A 156
RM8: Dag 2C 72
SE6 .1B 140
Winter Box Wlk. TW10: Rich 5F 115
Winterbrook Rd. SE24 . . . . .6C 120
Winterburn Cl. N11 . . . . .6K 31
Winterfold Cl. SW19 . . . . .2G 135
Wintergreen Cl. E6 . . . . .5C 88
Winterleys NW6 . . . . .2H 81
(off Denmark Rd.)
Winter Lodge SE16 . . . . .5G 103
(off Fern Wlk.)
Winter's Ct. E4 . . . . .3J 35
Winterslow Ho. SE5 . . . . .2C 120
(off Flaxman Rd.)
Winters Rd. KT7: T Ditt 7B 150
Winterstoke Gdns. NW7 . . . . .5H 29
Winterstoke Rd. SE6 . . . . .1B 140
Winterton Ct. KT1: Ham W 1D 150
(off Lwr. Teddington Rd.)
SE20 . . . . .2G 157

Winterton Ho.—Woodfield Av.

Winterton Ho. E1 . . . 6J 85
(off Deancross St.)
Winterton Pl. SW10 . . . 7A 16 (6A 100)
Winterwell Rd. SW2 . . . 5J 119
Winthorpe Rd. SW15 . . . 4G 117
Winthrop Ho. W12 . . . 7D 80
(off White City Est.)
Winthrop St. E1 . . . 5H 85
Winthrop Wlk. HA9: Wemb . . . 3E 60
(off Everard Way)
Winton Av. N11 . . . 7B 32
Winton Cl. N9 . . . 7E 24
Winton Gdns. HA8: Edg . . . 7A 28
Winton Rd. BR6: Farnb . . . 4F 173
Winton Way SW16 . . . 5A 138
Wireworks Ct. SE1 . . . 7C 14
(off Gt. Sufolk St.)
Wirrall Ho. SE26 . . . 3G 139
Wirral Wood Cl. BR7: Chst . . . 6E 142
Wisbeach Rd. CR0: Croy . . . 5D 156
Wisbech N4 . . . 1K 65
(off Lorne Rd.)
Wisborough Rd. CR2: Sand . . . 7F 169
Wisden Ho. SW8 . . . 7H 19 (6K 101)
Wisdom Ct. TW7: Isle . . . 3A 114
(off South St.)
Wisdons Cl. RM10: Dag . . . 1H 73
Wise La. NW7 . . . 5H 29
UB7: W Dray . . . 4A 92
Wiseman Rd. E10 . . . 2C 68
Wise Rd. E15 . . . 1F 87
Wiseton Rd. SW17 . . . 1C 136
Wishart Rd. SE3 . . . 2B 124
Wishaw Wlk. N13 . . . 6D 32
Wisley Ho. SW1 . . . 5C 18
(off Rampayne St.)
Wisley Rd. BR5: St P . . . 7A 144
SW11 . . . 5E 118
Wistaria Cl. BR6: Farnb . . . 2F 173
Wisteria Cl. IG1: Ilf . . . 5F 71
NW7 . . . 6G 29
Wisteria Gdns. IG8: Wfd G . . . 5D 36
Wisteria Rd. SE13 . . . 4F 123
Wistow Ho. E2 . . . 1G 85
(off Whiston Rd.)
Witanhurst La. N6 . . . 1E 64
Witan St. E2 . . . 3H 85
Witchwood Ho. SW9 . . . 3A 120
(off Gresham Rd.)
Witham Ct. E10 . . . 3D 68
SW17 . . . 3D 136
Witham Rd. RM10: Dag . . . 5G 73
SE20 . . . 3J 157
TW7: Isle . . . 1H 113
W13 . . . 1A 96
Witherby Cl. CR0: Croy . . . 5E 168
Witherington Rd. N5 . . . 5A 66
Withers Cl. KT9: Chess . . . 6C 162
Withers Mead NW9 . . . 1B 44
Withers Pl. EC1 . . . 3D 8 (4C 84)
Witherston Way SE9 . . . 2E 142
Withycombe Rd. SW19 . . . 7F 117
Withy Ho. E1 . . . 4K 85
(off Globe Rd.)
Withy La. HA4: Ruis . . . 5E 38
Withy Mead E4 . . . 3A 36
Witley Ct. WC1 . . . 4E 6
Witley Cres. CR0: New Ad . . . 6E 170
Witley Gdns. UB2: S'hall . . . 4D 94
Witley Ho. SW2 . . . 7J 119
Witley Ind. Est. UB2: S'hall . . . 4D 94
Witley Point SW15 . . . 1D 134
(off Wanborough Dr.)
Witley Rd. N19 . . . 2G 65
Witney Cl. UB10: Ick . . . 4B 56
Witney Path SE23 . . . 3K 139
Wittenham Way E4 . . . 3A 36
Wittering Cl. KT2: King T . . . 5D 132
Wittersham Rd. BR1: Brom . . . 5H 141
Witts Ho. KT1: King T . . . 3F 151
(off Winery La.)
Wivenhoe Cl. SE15 . . . 3H 121
Wivenhoe Ct. TW3: Houn . . . 4D 112
Wivenhoe Rd. IG11: Bark . . . 2A 90
Wiverton Rd. SE26 . . . 6J 139
Wixom Ho. SE3 . . . 4A 124
Wix Rd. RM9: Dag . . . 1D 90
Wix's La. SW4 . . . 3F 119
Woburn W13 . . . 5B 78
(off Clivedon Ct.)
Woburn Cl. SE28 . . . 6D 90
SW19 . . . 6A 136
Woburn Ct. CR0: Croy . . . 1C 168
E18 . . . 2J 51
SE16 . . . 5H 103
(off Masters Dr.)
Woburn Mans. WC1 . . . 5C 6
(off Torrington Pl.)
Woburn M. WC1 . . . 4D 6 (4H 83)
Woburn Pl. WC1 . . . 4E 6 (4J 83)
Woburn Rd. CR0: Croy . . . 1C 168
SM5: Cars . . . 1C 166
Woburn Sq. WC1 . . . 4D 6 (4H 83)
Woburn Twr. UB5: Yead . . . 3B 76
(off Broomcroft Av.)
Woburn Wlk. WC1 . . . 2D 6 (3H 83)
Wodeham Gdns. E1 . . . 5G 85
Wodehouse Av. SE5 . . . 1F 121
Wodehouse Ct. W3 . . . 3J 97
(off Vincent Rd.)
Woffington Cl. KT1: Ham W . . . 1C 150
Woking Cl. SW15 . . . 4B 116
Wolcot Ho. NW1 . . . 1B 6
(off Aldenham St.)
Woldham Pl. BR2: Brom . . . 4A 160
Woldham Rd. BR2: Brom . . . 4A 160
Wolds Dr. BR6: Farnb . . . 4E 172
Wolfe Cl. BR2: Hayes . . . 6J 159
UB4: Yead . . . 3K 75
Wolfe Cres. SE7 . . . 5B 106
SE16 . . . 2K 103
Wolfe Ho. W12 . . . 7D 80
(off White City Est.)
Wolferton Rd. E12 . . . 4D 70
Wolffe Gdns. E15 . . . 6H 69
Wolfington Rd. SE27 . . . 4B 138
Wolfram Cl. SE13 . . . 5G 123
Wolftencroft Cl. SW11 . . . 3C 118
Wollaston Cl. SE1 . . . 4C 102
Wollaton Ho. N1 . . . 2A 84
(off Batchelor St.)
Wollett Ct. NW1 . . . 7G 65
(off St Pancras Way)
Wolmer Cl. HA8: Edg . . . 4B 28
Wolmer Gdns. HA8: Edg . . . 3B 28
Wolseley Av. SW19 . . . 2J 135
Wolseley Gdns. W4 . . . 6H 97
Wolseley Rd. CR4: Mitc . . . 7E 154
E7 . . . 7K 69
HA3: W'stone . . . 3J 41
N8 . . . 6H 47
N22 . . . 1K 47
RM7: Rush G . . . 7K 55
W4 . . . 4J 97
Wolseley St. SE1 . . . 7K 15 (2G 103)
Wolsey Av. E6 . . . 3E 88
E17 . . . 3B 50
KT7: T Ditt . . . 5K 149
Wolsey Cl. KT2: King T . . . 1H 151
KT4: Wor Pk . . . 4C 164
SW20 . . . 7D 134
TW3: Houn . . . 4G 113
UB2: S'hall . . . 3G 95
Wolsey Ct. NW6 . . . 7A 64
SW11 . . . 1C 118
(off Westbridge Rd.)
Wolsey Cres. CR0: New Ad . . . 7E 170
SM4: Mord . . . 7G 153
Wolsey Dr. KT2: King T . . . 5E 132
KT12: Walt T . . . 7B 148
Wolsey Gro. HA8: Edg . . . 7E 28
Wolsey M. BR6: Chels . . . 5K 173
NW5 . . . 6G 65
Wolsey Rd. EN1: Enf . . . 2C 24
KT8: E Mos . . . 4H 149
N1 . . . 5D 66
TW12: Ham H . . . 6F 131
TW15: Ashf . . . 4A 128
TW16: Sun . . . 7H 129
Wolsey St. E1 . . . 5J 85
Wolsey Way KT9: Chess . . . 5G 163
Wolstonbury N12 . . . 5D 30
Wolvercote Rd. SE2 . . . 2D 108
Wolverley St. E2 . . . 3H 85
Wolverton SE17 . . . 5E 102
Wolverton Av. KT2: King T . . . 1G 151
Wolverton Gdns. W5 . . . 7F 79
W6 . . . 4F 99
Wolverton Rd. HA7: Stan . . . 6G 27
Wolverton Way N14 . . . 5B 22
Wolves La. N13 . . . 7F 33
N22 . . . 7F 33
Womersley Rd. N8 . . . 6K 47
Wonersh Way SM2: Cheam . . . 7F 165
Wonford Cl. KT2: King T . . . 1A 152
Wontner Cl. N1 . . . 7C 66
Wontner Rd. SW17 . . . 2D 136
Wooburn Cl. UB8: Hil . . . 4D 74
Woodall Av. EN3: Pond E . . . 6E 24
Woodall Cl. E14 . . . 7D 86
KT9: Chess . . . 6D 162
Woodall Ho. N22 . . . 1A 48
Woodall Rd. EN3: Pond E . . . 6E 24
Woodbank Rd. BR1: Brom . . . 3H 141
Woodbastwick Rd. SE26 . . . 5K 139
Woodberry Av. HA2: Harr . . . 4F 41
N21 . . . 2F 33
Woodberry Cl. NW7 . . . 7A 30
TW16: Sun . . . 6J 129
Woodberry Cres. N10 . . . 3F 47
Woodberry Down N4 . . . 7C 48
Woodberry Down Est. N4 . . . 1C 66
(Spring Pk. Dr.)
N4 . . . 7C 48
(Woodberry Gro.)
Woodberry Gdns. N12 . . . 6F 31
Woodberry Gro. DA5: Bexl . . . 3K 145
N4 . . . 7C 48
N12 . . . 6F 31
Woodberry Way E4 . . . 7K 25
N12 . . . 6F 31
Woodbine Cl. TW2: Twick . . . 2H 131
Woodbine Gro. EN2: Enf . . . 1J 23
SE20 . . . 7H 139
Woodbine La. KT4: Wor Pk . . . 3D 164
Woodbine Pl. E11 . . . 6J 51
Woodbine Rd. DA15: Sidc . . . 1J 143
Woodbines Av. KT1: King T . . . 3D 150
Woodbine Ter. E9 . . . 6J 67
Woodborough Rd. SW15 . . . 4D 116
Woodbourne Av. SW16 . . . 3H 137
Woodbourne Cl. SW16 . . . 3J 137
Woodbourne Gdns. SM6: Wall . . . 7F 167
Woodbridge Cl. N7 . . . 2K 65
NW2 . . . 3C 62
Woodbridge Ct. IG8: Wfd G . . . 7H 37
Woodbridge Ho. E11 . . . 1H 69
Woodbridge Rd. IG11: Bark . . . 5K 71
Woodbridge St. EC1 . . . 3A 8 (4B 84)
(not continuous)
Woodbridge Ter.
RM6: Chad H . . . 6B 54
Woodbrook Rd. SE2 . . . 6A 108
Woodburn Cl. NW4 . . . 5F 45
Woodbury Cl. CR0: Croy . . . 2F 169
E11 . . . 4K 51
Woodbury Ho. SE26 . . . 3G 139
Woodbury Pk. Rd. W13 . . . 4B 78
Woodbury Rd. E17 . . . 4D 50
Woodbury St. SW17 . . . 5C 136
Woodchester Sq. W2 . . . 5K 81
Woodchurch Cl. DA14: Sidc . . . 3H 143
Woodchurch Dr. BR1: Brom . . . 7B 142
Woodchurch Rd. NW6 . . . 7J 63
Wood Cl. E2 . . . 4G 85
HA1: Harr . . . 7H 41
NW9 . . . 7K 43
Woodclyffe Dr. BR7: Chst . . . 2E 160
Woodcock Ct. HA3: Kent . . . 7E 42
Woodcock Dell Av. HA3: Kent . . . 7D 42
Woodcock Hill HA3: Kent . . . 5C 42
Woodcock Ho. E14 . . . 5C 86
(off Burgess St.)
Woodcocks E16 . . . 5A 88
Woodcombe Cres. SE23 . . . 1J 139
Woodcote Av. CR7: Thor H . . . 4B 156
NW7 . . . 6K 29
SM6: Wall . . . 7F 167
Woodcote Cl. EN3: Pond E . . . 6D 24
KT2: King T . . . 5F 133
Woodcote Dr. BR6: Orp . . . 1H 173
Woodcote Grn. SM6: Wall . . . 7G 167
Woodcote Ho. SE8 . . . 6B 104
(off Prince St.)
Woodcote M. SM6: Wall . . . 6F 167
Woodcote Pl. SE27 . . . 5B 138
Woodcote Rd. E11 . . . 7J 51
SM6: Wall . . . 6F 167
Woodcote Vs. SE27 . . . 5C 138
(off Woodcote Pl.)
Wood Crest SM2: Sutt . . . 7A 166
(off Christchurch Pk.)
Woodcroft N21 . . . 1F 33
SE9 . . . 3D 142
UB6: G'frd . . . 6A 60
Woodcroft Av. HA7: Stan . . . 1A 42
NW7 . . . 6F 29
Woodcroft Cres. UB10: Hil . . . 1D 74
Woodcroft M. SE8 . . . 4A 104
Woodcroft Rd. CR7: Thor H . . . 5B 156
Wood Dene SE15 . . . 1H 121
(off Queen's Rd.)
Wood Dr. BR7: Chst . . . 6C 142
Woodedge Cl. E4 . . . 1C 36
WOOD END
Hayes . . . 5H 75
Northolt . . . 5G 59
Wood End UB3: Hayes . . . 6G 75
Wood End, The SM6: Wall . . . 7F 167
Woodend SE19 . . . 6C 138
SM1: Sutt . . . 2A 166
Wood End Av. HA2: Harr . . . 4F 59
Wood End Cl. UB5: N'olt . . . 5H 59
Wood End Gdns. UB5: N'olt . . . 5G 59
Woodend Gdns. EN2: Enf . . . 4D 22
WOOD END GREEN . . . 5F 75
Wood End Grn. Rd.
UB3: Hayes . . . 5F 75
Wood End La. UB5: N'olt . . . 6F 59
(not continuous)
Wood End Rd. HA1: Harr . . . 4H 59
Woodend Rd. E17 . . . 2E 50
Wood End Way UB5: N'olt . . . 5G 59
Wooder Gdns. E7 . . . 4J 69
Wooderson Cl. SE25 . . . 4E 156
Woodfall Av. EN5: Barn . . . 5C 20
Woodfall Rd. N4 . . . 2A 66
Woodfall St. SW3 . . . 6E 16 (5D 100)
Woodfarrs SE5 . . . 4D 120
Wood Fld. NW3 . . . 5D 64
Woodfield Av. HA0: Wemb . . . 3C 60
NW9 . . . 4A 44

Woodfield Av. SM5: Cars 6E **166**
SW16 3H **137**
W5 4C **78**
Woodfield Cl. EN1: Enf 4K **23**
SE19 7C **138**
Woodfield Cres. W5 4C **78**
Woodfield Dr. EN4: E Barn 1K **31**
Woodfield Gdns. KT3: N Mald 5B **152**
Woodfield Gro. SW16 3H **137**
Woodfield Ho. *SE23* *3K* ***139***
(off Dacres Rd.)
Woodfield La. SW16 3H **137**
Woodfield Pl. W9 4H **81**
Woodfield Ri. WD23: Bush 1C **26**
Woodfield Rd. TW4: Cran 2K **111**
W5 4C **78**
W9 5H **81**
Woodfield Way N11 7C **32**
WOODFORD 6F **37**
Woodford Av. IG2: Ilf 5D **52**
IG4: Ilf, Wfd G 3B **52**
WOODFORD BRIDGE 6H **37**
Woodford Bri. Rd. IG4: Ilf 3B **52**
Woodford Ct. *W12* *2F* ***99***
(off Shepherd's Bush Grn.)
Woodford Cres. HA5: Pinn 2K **39**
Woodforde Ct. UB3: Harl 5F **93**
WOODFORD GREEN 6D **36**
Woodford Hall Path E18 1H **51**
Woodford Ho. E18 4J **51**
Woodford New Rd. E17 4G **51**
E18 1G **51**
IG8: Wfd G 1G **51**
Woodford Pl. HA9: Wemb 1E **60**
Woodford Rd. E7 3K **69**
E18 4J **51**
WOODFORD SIDE 5C **36**
Woodford Trad. Est. IG8: Wfd G 2B **52**
WOODFORD WELLS 3E **36**
Woodgate Av. KT9: Chess 5D **162**
Woodgate Dr. SW16 7H **137**
Woodger Rd. W12 2E **98**
Woodget Cl. E6 6C **88**
Woodgrange Av. EN1: Enf 6B **24**
HA3: Kent 5C **42**
N12 6G **31**
W5 1G **97**
Woodgrange Cl. HA3: Kent 5D **42**
Woodgrange Gdns. EN1: Enf 6B **24**
Woodgrange Ho. *W5* *1F* ***97***
(off Woodgrange Av.)
Woodgrange Mans. HA3: Kent 5D **42**
Woodgrange Rd. E7 5K **69**
Woodgrange Ter. EN1: Enf 6B **24**
WOOD GREEN 2K **47**
Wood Green Shop. City N22 2A **48**
Woodhall *NW1* *2A* ***6***
(off Robert St.)
Woodhall Av. HA5: Pinn 1C **40**
SE21 3F **139**
Woodhall Cl. UB8: Uxb 5A **56**
Woodhall Dr. HA5: Pinn 1B **40**
SE21 3F **139**
Woodhall Ga. HA5: Pinn 1B **40**
Woodhall Ho. SW18 6B **118**
Woodham Ct. E18 4H **51**
Woodham Rd. SE6 3E **140**
Woodhatch Cl. E6 5C **88**
Woodhaven Gdns. IG6: Ilf 4G **53**
Woodhayes Rd. SW19 7E **134**
Woodhead Dr. BR6: Orp 3J **173**
Woodheyes Rd. NW10 5K **61**
Woodhill SE18 4C **106**
Woodhill Cres. HA3: Kent 6D **42**
Woodhouse Av.
UB6: G'frd 2K **77**
Woodhouse Cl. UB3: Harl 3G **93**
UB6: G'frd 1K **77**
Woodhouse Gro. E12 6C **70**
Woodhouse Rd. E11 3H **69**
N12 6G **31**
Woodhurst Av. BR5: Pet W 6G **161**
Woodhurst Rd. SE2 5A **108**
W3 7J **79**
Woodington Cl. SE9 6E **124**
Woodknoll Dr. BR7: Chst 1D **160**
Woodland App.
UB6: G'frd 6A **60**
Woodland Av. E12 3C **70**
Woodland Cl. IG8: Wfd G 3E **36**
KT19: Ewe 6A **164**
NW9 6J **43**
SE19 6E **138**
UB10: Ick 2D **56**
Woodland Ct. *E11* *6J* ***51***
(off New Wanstead)
Woodland Cres. SE10 6G **105**
SE16 2K **103**
Woodland Gdns. N10 5F **47**
TW7: Isle 3J **113**
Woodland Gro. SE10 5G **105**
Woodland Hill SE19 6E **138**
Woodland M. SW16 3J **137**
Woodland Ri. N10 4F **47**
UB6: G'frd 6A **60**
Woodland Rd. CR7: Thor H 4A **156**
E4 1K **35**
N11 5A **32**
SE19 5E **138**
WOODLANDS 2J **113**
Woodlands BR2: Brom 4H **159**
DA6: Bex 5H **127**
HA2: Harr 4E **40**
NW11 5G **45**
SW20 4E **152**
Woodlands, The HA1: Harr 2J **59**
HA7: Stan 5G **27**
N5 4C **66**
N12 6F **31**
N14 1A **32**
SE13 7F **123**
SE19 7C **138**
SM6: Wall 7F **167**
TW7: Isle 2K **113**
Woodlands Art Gallery 6J **105**
Woodlands Av. DA15: Sidc 1J **143**
E11 1K **69**
HA4: Ruis 7A **40**
KT3: N Mald 1J **151**
KT4: Wor Pk 2B **164**
N3 7F **31**
RM6: Chad H 6E **54**
W3 1H **97**
Woodlands Cl. BR1: Brom 2D **160**
KT10: Clay 7A **162**
NW11 5G **45**
Woodlands Ct. BR1: Brom 1H **159**
HA1: Harr 5K **41**
NW10 *1F* ***81***
(off Wrentham Av.)
SE23 7H **121**
Woodlands Dr. HA7: Stan 6E **26**
TW16: Sun 2A **148**
Woodlands Gdns. E17 4G **51**
Woodlands Ga. *SW15* *5H* ***117***
(off Woodlands Way)
Woodlands Gro. TW7: Isle 2J **113**
Woodlands Hgts. *SE3* *6H* ***105***
(off Vanburgh Hill)
Woodlands Ho. NW6 7G **63**
Woodlands Pde.
TW15: Ashf 6E **128**
Woodlands Pk. DA5: Bexl 4K **145**
Woodlands Pk. Rd. N15 5B **48**
SE10 6G **105**
(not continuous)
Woodlands Rd. BR1: Brom 2C **160**
BR6: Chels 6K **173**
DA7: Bex 3E **126**
E11 2G **69**
E17 3E **50**
EN2: Enf 1J **23**
HA1: Harr 5K **41**
IG1: Ilf 3G **71**
KT6: Surb 7D **150**
N9 1D **34**
SW13 3B **116**
TW7: Isle 3H **113**
UB1: S'hall 1B **94**
Woodlands St. SE13 7F **123**
Woodland St. E8 6F **67**
Woodlands Way SW15 5H **117**
Woodland Ter. SE7 4C **106**
Woodland Wlk. BR1: Brom 4F **141**
(not continuous)
KT19: Ewe 6G **163**
NW3 5C **64**
SE10 5G **105**
Woodland Way BR4: W W'ck 4D **170**
BR5: Pet W 4G **161**
CR0: Croy 1A **170**
CR4: Mitc 7E **136**
IG8: Wfd G 3E **36**
KT5: Surb 2H **163**
N21 2F **33**
NW7 6F **29**
SE2 4D **108**
SM4: Mord 4H **153**
Wood La. HA4: Ruis 1F **57**
HA7: Stan 3F **27**
IG8: Wfd G 4C **36**
N6 6F **47**
NW9 7K **43**
RM8: Dag 4C **72**
RM9: Dag 4C **72**
RM10: Dag 2G **73**
TW7: Isle 6J **95**
W12 6E **80**
Wood Lane Sports Cen. 1H **73**
Woodlawn Cl. SW15 5H **117**
Woodlawn Cres. TW2: Whit 2F **131**
Woodlawn Dr. TW13: Felt 2B **130**
Woodlawn Rd. SW6 7F **99**
Woodlawns KT19: Ewe 7K **163**
Woodlea Dr. BR2: Brom 5G **159**
Woodlea Rd. N16 3E **66**
Woodleigh E18 1J **51**
Woodleigh Av. N12 6H **31**
Woodleigh Gdns. SW16 3J **137**
Woodley Cl. SW17 7D **136**
Woodley La. SM5: Cars 3C **166**
Wood Lodge Gdns. BR1: Brom 7C **142**
Wood Lodge La. BR4: W W'ck 3E **170**
Woodman Pde. *E16* *1E* ***106***
(off Woodman St.)
Woodmans Gro. NW10 5B **62**
Woodman's M. W12 5D **80**
Woodmansterne Rd. SM5: Cars 7C **166**
SW16 7G **137**
Woodman St. E16 1E **106**
(not continuous)
Wood Mead N17 6B **34**
Woodmere SE9 1D **142**
Woodmere Av. CR0: Croy 7J **157**
Woodmere Cl. CR0: Croy 7K **157**
SW11 3E **118**
Woodmere Ct. N14 7A **22**
Woodmere Gdns. CR0: Croy 7K **157**
Woodmere Way BR3: Beck 5F **159**
Woodnook Rd. SW16 5F **137**
Woodpecker Cl.
HA3: Hrw W 1K **41**
N9 6C **24**
WD23: Bush 1B **26**
Woodpecker M. *SE13* *4F* ***123***
(off Freshfield Cl.)
Woodpecker Mt. CR0: Sels 7A **170**
Woodpecker Rd. SE14 6A **104**
SE28 7C **90**
Wood Point *E16* *5J* ***87***
(off Fife Rd.)
Woodquest Av. SE24 5C **120**
Wood Retreat SE18 7H **107**
Wood Ride BR5: Pet W 4H **161**
EN4: Had W 1G **21**
Woodridge Cl. EN2: Enf 1F **23**
Woodridings Av. HA5: H End 1D **40**
Woodridings Cl. HA5: H End 1C **40**
Woodridings Ct. N22 1H **47**
Woodriffe Rd. E11 7F **51**
Wood Ri. HA5: Eastc 5J **39**
Wood Rd. NW10 7J **61**
TW17: Shep 4C **146**
Woodrow SE18 4D **106**
Woodrow Av. UB4: Hayes 5H **75**
Woodrow Cl. UB6: G'frd 7B **60**
Woodrow Ct. N17 7C **34**
Woodrush Cl. SE14 7A **104**
Woodrush Way RM6: Chad H 4D **54**
Woods, The UB10: Ick 4D **56**
Wood's Bldgs. *E1* *5H* ***85***
(off Winthrop St.)
Woodseer St. E1 5K **9** (5F **85**)
Woodsford *SE17* *5D* ***102***
(off Portland St.)
Woodsford Sq. W14 2G **99**
Woodshire Rd. RM10: Dag 3H **73**
WOODSIDE 6G **157**
Wood Side NW11 5J **45**
Woodside IG9: Buck H 2F **37**
N10 3E **46**
SW19 6H **135**
Woodside Av. BR7: Chst 5G **143**
HA0: Wemb 1E **78**
KT10: Esh 7J **149**
N6 5D **46**
N10 5D **46**
N12 4F **31**
SE25 6H **157**
Woodside Cl. DA7: Bex 4K **127**
HA0: Wemb 1E **78**
HA4: Ruis 6F **39**
HA7: Stan 5G **27**
KT5: Surb 7J **151**
Woodside Ct. E12 1A **70**
N12 4E **30**
W5 1E **96**
Woodside Ct. Rd. CR0: Croy 7G **157**
Woodside Cres. DA15: Sidc 3J **143**
Woodside Dr. DA2: Dart 4K **145**
Woodside End HA0: Wemb 1E **78**
Woodside Gdns. E4 6J **35**
N17 2E **48**
Woodside Grange Rd. N12 4E **30**
Woodside Grn. SE25 6G **157**
(not continuous)
Woodside Gro. N12 3F **31**
Woodside Ho. SW19 6H **135**
Woodside La. DA5: Bexl 6D **126**
N12 3F **31**
Woodside M. SE22 5F **121**
Woodside Pde. DA15: Sidc 3J **143**
WOODSIDE PARK 4D **30**
Woodside Pk. SE25 6H **157**
Woodside Pk. Av. E17 4F **51**
Woodside Pk. Rd. N12 4E **30**
Woodside Pl. HA0: Wemb 1E **78**
Woodside Rd. BR1: Brom 5C **160**
DA7: Bex 4K **127**
DA15: Sidc 3J **143**
E13 4A **88**
IG8: Wfd G 4D **36**

Woodside Rd. KT2: King T 7E 132
KT3: N Mald 2K 151
N22 7E 32
SE25 6H 157
SM1: Sutt 3A 166
Woodside Way CR0: Croy 6J 157
CR4: Mitc 1F 155
Woods M. W1 2G 11 (7E 82)
Woodsome Rd. NW5 3E 64
Woods Pl. SE1 3E 102
Woodspring Rd. SW19 2G 135
Woods Rd. SE15 1H 121
Woodstead Gro. HA8: Edg 6K 27
WOODSTOCK, THE 7H 153
Woodstock Av. NW11 7G 45
SM3: Sutt 7H 153
TW7: Isle 5A 114
UB1: S'hall 3D 76
W13 3A 96
Woodstock Cl. DA5: Bexl 7F 127
HA7: Stan 2E 42
Woodstock Ct. SE11 5H 19 (5K 101)
SE12 6J 123
Woodstock Cres. N9 6C 24
Woodstock Dr. UB10: Ick 4A 56
Woodstock Gdns. BR3: Beck 1D 158
IG3: Ilf 2A 72
UB4: Hayes 5H 75
Woodstock Grange W5 1E 96
Woodstock Gro. W12 2F 99
Woodstock La. Nth. KT6: Surb 2C 162
Woodstock La. Sth.
KT9: Chess 5B 162
KT10: Clay 5B 162
Woodstock M. W1 6H 5
Woodstock Ri. SM3: Sutt 7H 153
Woodstock Rd. CR0: Croy 3D 168
E7 7A 70
E17 2F 51
HA0: Wemb 1F 79
N4 1A 66
NW11 7H 45
SM5: Cars 5E 166
W4 4A 98
Woodstock St. W1 1J 11 (6F 83)
Woodstock Ter. E14 7D 86
Woodstock Way CR4: Mitc 2F 155
Woodstone Av. KT17: Ewe 5C 164
WOOD STREET 3E 50
Wood St. CR4: Mitc 7E 154
E17 3E 50
EC2 7D 8 (6C 84)
EN5: Barn 4A 20
KT1: King T 2D 150
(not continuous)
W4 5A 98
Woodsyre SE26 4F 139
Wood Ter. NW2 3D 62
Woodthorpe Rd. SW15 4D 116
TW15: Ashf 5A 128
Woodtree Cl. NW4 2F 45
Wood Va. N10 5G 47
SE23 1H 139
Woodvale Av. SE25 3F 157
Woodvale Ct. *BR1: Brom* *1K 159*
(off Widmore Rd.)
Wood Va. Est. SE23 7J 121
Woodvale Wlk. SE27 5C 138
Woodvale Way NW11 3F 63
Woodview Av. E4 4K 35
Woodview Cl. BR6: Farnb 2G 173
N4 7B 48
SW15 4K 133
Woodville SE3 7K 105
Woodville, The *W5* *6D 78*
(off Woodville Rd.)
Woodville Cl. SE12 5J 123
TW11: Tedd 4A 132
Woodville Ct. N14 5B 22
SE19 1F 157
Woodville Gdns. HA4: Ruis 7E 38
IG6: Ilf 3F 53
KT6: Surb 7D 150
NW11 7F 45
W5 6E 78
Woodville Gro. DA16: Well 3A 126
Woodville Ho. *SE1* *3F 103*
(off Grange Wlk.)
Woodville Rd. CR7: Thor H 4C 156
E11 1H 69
E17 4B 50
E18 2K 51
EN5: New Bar 3E 20
N16 5E 66
NW6 2H 81
NW11 7F 45
SM4: Mord 4J 153
TW10: Ham 3B 132
W5 6D 78
Woodville St. SE18 4C 106
Woodward Av. NW4 5C 44
Woodward Cl. KT10: Clay 6A 162
Woodwarde Rd. SE22 6E 120
Woodward Gdns. HA7: Stan 7E 26
RM9: Dag 7C 72
Woodward Rd. RM9: Dag 7B 72
Woodward's Footpath TW2: Whit 6G 113
Wood Way BR6: Farnb 2E 172
Woodway Cres. HA1: Harr 6A 42
Woodwell St. SW18 5A 118
Wood Wharf SE10 6E 104
Wood Wharf Bus. Pk. E14 1D 104
(not continuous)
Woodyard Cl. NW5 5E 64
Woodyard La. SE21 7E 120
Woodyates Rd. SE12 6J 123
Woody Bay Station
Ruislip Lido Railway 5F 39
Woolacombe Rd. SE3 1A 124
Woolacombe Way UB3: Harl 4G 93
Woolcombes Ct. *SE16* *1K 103*
(off Princes Riverside Rd.)
Wooler St. SE17 5D 102
Woolf Cl. SE28 1B 108
Woolf Ct. *W3* *3J 97*
(off Vincent Rd.)
Woolf M. *WC1* *3D 6*
(off Burton Pl.)
Woolgar M. *N16* *5E 66*
(off Gillett St.)
Woollaston Rd. N4 6B 48
Woolley Ho. *SW9* *3B 120*
(off Loughborough Rd.)
Woollon Ho. *E1* *6J 85*
(off Clark St.)
Woolmead Av. NW9 7C 44
Woolmer Gdns. N18 6B 34
Woolmer Rd. N18 5B 34
Woolmore St. E14 7E 86
Woolneigh St. SW6 3K 117
Woolridge Way E9 7J 67
Wool Rd. SW20 6D 134
Woolstaplers Way SE16 3G 103
Woolston Cl. E17 2K 49
Woolstone Ho. *E2* *1G 85*
(off Whiston Rd.)
Woolstone Rd. SE23 2A 140
WOOLWICH 3E 106
Woolwich Chu. St. SE18 3C 106
Woolwich Comn. SE18 6E 106
Woolwich Dockyard Ind. Est.
SE18 3C 106
Woolwich High St. SE18 3E 106
Woolwich Mnr. Way E6 4D 88
E16 2F 107
Woolwich New Rd. SE18 5E 106
Woolwich Rd. DA7: Bex 3G 127
DA17: Belv 5F 109
SE2 6D 108
SE7 5H 105
SE10 5H 105
Woolwich Trad. Pk.
SE28 3H 107
Wooster Gdns. E14 6F 87
Wooster M. HA2: Harr 3G 41
Wooster Pl. *SE1* *4D 102*
(off Searles Rd.)
Wootton Gro. N3 1J 45
Wootton St. SE1 5K 13 (1A 102)
Worbeck Rd. SE20 2H 157
Worcester Av. N17 7B 34
Worcester Cl. CR0: Croy 2C 170
CR4: Mitc 2E 154
NW2 3D 62
Worcester Ct. HA1: Harr 3J 41
KT4: Wor Pk 3A 164
N12 5E 30
W7 *6K 77*
(off Copley Cl.)
W9 *5J 81*
(off Elmfield Way)
Worcester Cres. IG8: Wfd G 4E 36
NW7 3F 29
Worcester Dr. TW15: Ashf 5D 128
W4 2A 98
Worcester Gdns. IG1: Ilf 7C 52
KT4: Wor Pk 3A 164
SW11 *5D 118*
(off Grandison Rd.)
UB6: G'frd 6H 59
Worcester Ho. *SE11* *2J 19*
(off Kennington Rd.)
SW9 *7A 102*
(off Cranmer Rd.)
W2 *6A 82*
(off Hallfield Est.)
Worcester M. NW6 6K 63
WORCESTER PARK 1C 164
Worcester Pk. Rd. KT4: Wor Pk 3K 163
Worcester Rd. E12 4D 70
E17 2K 49
SM2: Sutt 7J 165
SW19 5H 135
Worcesters Av. EN1: Enf 1B 24
Wordsworth Av. E12 7C 70
E18 3H 51
UB6: G'frd 3H 77
Wordsworth Ct. HA1: Harr 7J 41
Wordsworth Dr. SM3: Cheam 4E 164
Wordsworth Ho. *NW6* *3J 81*
(off Stafford Rd.)
SE18 *6E 106*
(off Woolwich Comn.)
Wordsworth Mans. *W14* *6H 99*
(off Queens Club Gdns.)
Wordsworth Pde. N8 4B 48
Wordsworth Pl. NW3 5D 64
Wordsworth Rd. DA16: Well 1J 125
N16 4E 66
SE1 4F 103
SE20 7K 139
SM6: Wall 6G 167
TW12: Hamp 4D 130
Wordsworth Wlk. NW11 4J 45
Wordsworth Way
UB7: W Dray 4A 92
Worfield St. SW11 7C 100
Worgan St. SE11 5G 19 (5K 101)
SE16 4K 103
Worland Rd. E15 7G 69
World Bus. Cen.
TW6: H'row A 1E 110
WORLD'S END 3E 22
Worlds End Est. SW10 7B 100
Worlds End La. BR6: Chels 6K 173
EN2: Enf 5E 22
N21 5E 22
World's End Pas. *SW10* *7B 100*
(off Worlds End Est.)
World's End Pl. *SW10* *7B 100*
(off Worlds End Est.)
Worleys Dr. BR6: Orp 4H 173
Worlidge St. W6 5E 98
Worlingham Rd. SE22 4F 121
Wormholt Rd. W12 7C 80
Wormwood St. EC2 7G 9 (6E 84)
Wornington Rd. W10 4G 81
(not continuous)
Wornum Ho. *W10* *2G 81*
(off Kilburn La.)
Woronzow Rd. NW8 1B 82
Worple Av. SW19 7F 135
TW7: Isle 5A 114
Worple Cl. HA2: Harr 1D 58
Worple Rd. SW19 2E 152
SW20 2E 152
TW7: Isle 4A 114
Worple Rd. M. SW19 6H 135
Worple St. SW14 3K 115
Worple Way HA2: Harr 1D 58
TW10: Rich 5E 114
Worship St. EC2 4F 9 (4D 84)
Worslade Rd. SW17 4B 136
Worsley Bri. Rd. BR3: Beck 7C 140
SE26 4B 140
Worsley Grange BR7: Chst 6G 143
Worsley Gro. E5 4G 67
Worsley Ho. SE23 2J 139
Worsley Rd. E11 4G 69
Worsopp Dr. SW4 5G 119
Worth Cl. BR6: Orp 4J 173
Worthfield Cl. KT19: Ewe 7K 163
Worth Gro. SE17 5D 102
Worthing Cl. E15 1G 87
Worthing Rd. TW5: Hest 6D 94
Worthington Cl. CR4: Mitc 4F 155
Worthington Ho. *EC1* *1K 7*
(off Myddelton Pas.)
Worthington Rd. KT6: Surb 1F 163
Wortley Rd. CR0: Croy 7A 156
E6 7B 70
Worton Ct. TW7: Isle 4J 113
Worton Gdns. TW7: Isle 2H 113
Worton Hall Ind. Est.
TW7: Isle 4J 113
Worton Rd. TW7: Isle 4H 113
Worton Way TW3: Houn 2H 113
TW7: Houn, Isle 2H 113
Wotton Ct. *E14* *7F 87*
(off Jamestown Way)
Wotton Rd. NW2 3E 62
SE8 6B 104
Wouldham Rd. E16 6H 87
Wragby Rd. E11 3G 69
Wrampling Pl. N9 1B 34
Wrangthorn Wlk. CR0: Wadd 4A 168
Wray Av. IG5: Ilf 3E 52
Wrayburn Ho. *SE16* *2G 103*
(off Llewellyn St.)
Wray Cres. N4 2J 65
Wrayfield Rd. SM3: Cheam 3F 165
Wray Rd. SM2: Cheam 7H 165
Wraysbury Cl. TW4: Houn 5C 112
Wrays Way UB4: Hayes 4G 75
Wrekin Rd. SE18 7G 107
Wren Av. NW2 4E 62
UB2: S'hall 4D 94
Wren Cl. E16 6H 87
N9 1E 34
Wren Ct. *CR0: Croy* *4D 168*
(off Coombe Rd.)
Wren Cres. WD23: Bush 1B 26

Wren Gdns. RM9: Dag 5D 72
Wren Ho. *E3* *2A 86*
(off Gernon Rd.)
KT1: Ham W *2D 150*
(off High St.)
SW1 . . . . *6C 18*
(off Aylesford St.)
Wren Landing E14 . . . . 1C 104
Wrenn Ho. SW13 . . . . 6E 98
Wren Path SE28 . . . . 3H 107
Wren Rd. DA14: Sidc 4C 144
RM9: Dag 5D 72
SE5 . . . . 1D 120
Wren's Av. TW15: Ashf 4E 128
Wren's Pk. Ho. E5 . . . . 2H 67
Wren St. WC1 . . . . 3H 7 (4K 83)
Wrentham Av. NW10 . . . . 2F 81
Wrenthorpe Rd. BR1: Brom 4G 141
Wren Vw. N6 . . . . 7G 47
Wrenwood Way HA5: Eastc 4K 39
Wrestlers Ct. EC2 . . . . 7G 9
Wrexham Rd. E3 . . . . 2C 86
Wricklemarsh Rd. SE3 . . . . 2K 123
(not continuous)
Wrigglesworth St. SE14 . . . . 7K 103
Wright Cl. SE13 . . . . 4F 123
Wright Gdns. TW17: Shep 5C 146
Wright Rd. N1 . . . . 6E 66
TW5: Hest 7A 94
Wrights All. SW19 . . . . 6E 134
Wrights Cl. RM10: Dag 4H 73
Wrights Grn. SW4 . . . . 4H 119
Wright's La. W8 . . . . 3K 99
Wrights Pl. NW10 . . . . 6J 61
Wrights Rd. E3 . . . . 2B 86
(not continuous)
SE25 . . . . 3E 156
Wrights Row SM6: Wall 4F 167
Wrights Wlk. SW14 . . . . 3K 115
Wrigley Cl. E4 . . . . 5A 36
Writtle Ho. NW9 . . . . 2B 44
Wrotham Ho. *BR3: Beck* *7B 140*
(off Sellindge Cl.)
SE1 . . . . *3D 102*
(off Law St.)
Wrotham Rd. DA16: Well 1C 126
EN5: Barn 2B 20
NW1 . . . . 7G 65
W13 . . . . 1C 96
Wrottesley Rd. NW10 . . . . 2C 80
SE18 . . . . 6G 107
Wroughton Rd. SW11 . . . . 5D 118
Wroughton Ter. NW4 . . . . 4D 44
Wroxall Rd. RM9: Dag 6C 72
Wroxham Gdns. N11 . . . . 7C 32
Wroxham Rd. SE28 . . . . 7D 90
Wroxham Way IG6: Ilf 1F 53
Wroxton Rd. SE15 . . . . 2J 121
WRYTHE, THE 3D 166
Wrythe Grn. SM5: Cars 3D 166
Wrythe Grn. Rd. SM5: Cars 3D 166
Wrythe La. SM5: Cars 1A 166
Wulfstan St. W12 . . . . 5B 80
Wyatt Cl. SE16 . . . . 2B 104
TW13: Felt 1B 130
UB4: Hayes 5J 75
WD23: Bush 1C 26
Wyatt Ct. HA0: Wemb 7E 60
Wyatt Dr. SW13 . . . . 6D 98
Wyatt Ho. *NW8* *4B 4*
(off Frampton St.)
SE3 . . . . 2H 123
TW1: Twick 6D 114
Wyatt Pk. Rd. SW2 . . . . 2J 137
Wyatt Point SE18 . . . . 2G 107
Wyatt Rd. E7 . . . . 6J 69
N5 . . . . 3C 66
Wyatts La. E17 . . . . 3E 50
Wybert St. NW1 . . . . 3A 6 (4G 83)
Wyborne Ho. NW10 . . . . 7J 61
Wyborne Way NW10 . . . . 7J 61
Wyburn Av. EN5: Barn 3C 20
Wychcombe Studios NW3 . . . . 6D 64
Wyche Gro. CR2: S Croy 7D 168
Wych Elm Lodge
BR1: Brom 7H 141
Wych Elm Pas. KT2: King T 7F 133
Wycherley Cl. SE3 . . . . 7H 105
Wycherley Cres.
EN5: New Bar 6E 20
Wychwood Av. CR7: Thor H 3C 156
HA8: Edg 6J 27
Wychwood Cl. HA8: Edg 6J 27
TW16: Sun 6J 129
Wychwood End N6 . . . . 7G 47
Wychwood Gdns. IG5: Ilf 4D 52
Wychwood Way SE19 . . . . 6D 138
Wyclif Ct. *EC1* *2A 8*
(off Wyclif St.)
Wycliffe Cl. DA16: Well 1K 125
Wycliffe Rd. SW11 . . . . 2E 118
SW19 . . . . 6K 135
Wyclif St. EC1 . . . . 2A 8 (3B 84)
Wycombe Gdns. NW11 . . . . 2J 63
Wycombe Ho. *NW8* *3C 4*
(off Grendon St.)
Wycombe Pl. SW18 . . . . 6A 118
Wycombe Rd. HA0: Wemb 1G 79
IG2: Ilf 5D 52
N17 . . . . 1G 49
Wycombe Sq. W8 . . . . 1H 99
Wydehurst Rd. CR0: Croy 7G 157
Wydell Cl. SM4: Mord 6F 153
Wydeville Mnr. Rd. SE12 . . . . 4K 141
Wye Cl. BR6: Orp 7K 161
HA4: Ruis 6E 38
TW15: Ashf 4D 128
Wye Ct. *W13* *5B 78*
(off Malvern Way)
Wyemead Cres. E4 . . . . 2B 36
Wye St. SW11 . . . . 2B 118
Wyevale Cl. HA5: Eastc 3J 39
Wyfields IG5: Ilf 1F 53
Wyfold Ho. *SE2* *2D 108*
(off Wolvercote Rd.)
Wyfold Rd. SW6 . . . . 7G 99
Wyhill Wlk. RM10: Dag 6J 73
Wyke Cl. TW7: Isle 6K 95
Wyke Gdns. W7 . . . . 3A 96
Wykeham Av. RM9: Dag 6C 72
Wykeham Cl. UB7: Sip 6C 92
Wykeham Ct. *N11* *2K 31*
(off Wykeham Rd.)
NW4 . . . . *5E 44*
(off Wykeham Rd.)
Wykeham Grn. RM9: Dag 6C 72
Wykeham Hill
HA9: Wemb 1F 61
Wykeham Ho. *SE1* *5C 14*
(off Pepper St.)
Wykeham Ri. N20 . . . . 1B 30
Wykeham Rd. HA3: Kent 4B 42
NW4 . . . . 4E 44
Wyke Rd. E3 . . . . 7C 68
SW20 . . . . 2E 152
Wylchin Cl. HA5: Eastc 3H 39
Wyldes Cl. NW11 . . . . 1A 64
Wyldfield Gdns. N9 . . . . 2A 34
Wyld Way HA9: Wemb 6H 61
Wyleu St. SE23 . . . . 7A 122
Wylie Rd. UB2: S'hall 3E 94
Wyllen Cl. E1 . . . . 4J 85
Wymans Way E7 . . . . 4A 70
Wymering Mans. *W9* *3J 81*
(off Wymering Rd., not continuous)
Wymering Rd. W9 . . . . 3J 81
Wymondham Ct. *NW8* *1B 82*
(off Queensmead)
Wymond St. SW15 . . . . 3E 116
Wynan Rd. E14 . . . . 5D 104
Wynash Gdns.
SM5: Cars 5C 166
Wynaud Ct. N22 . . . . 6E 32
Wyncham Av. DA15: Sidc 1J 143
Wyncham Ho. *DA15: Sidc* *2A 144*
(off Longlands Rd.)
Wynchgate HA3: Hrw W 7D 26
N14 . . . . 1C 32
N21 . . . . 1C 32
UB5: N'olt 5C 58
Wyncroft Cl. BR1: Brom 3D 160
Wyndale Av. NW9 . . . . 6G 43
Wyndcliff Rd. SE7 . . . . 6K 105
Wyndcroft Cl. EN2: Enf 3G 23
Wyndham Cl. BR6: Farnb 1G 173
SM2: Sutt 7J 165
Wyndham Ct. W7 . . . . 4A 96
Wyndham Cres. N19 . . . . 3G 65
TW4: Houn 6E 112
Wyndham Deedes Ho. *E2* *2G 85*
(off Hackney Rd.)
Wyndham Est. SE5 . . . . 7C 102
Wyndham Ho. *E14* *2D 104*
(off Marsh Wall)
SW1 . . . . *4G 17*
(off Sloane Sq.)
Wyndham M. W1 . . . . 6E 4 (5D 82)
Wyndham Pl. W1 . . . . 6E 4 (5D 82)
Wyndham Rd. E6 . . . . 7B 70
EN4: E Barn 1J 31
KT2: King T 7F 133
(not continuous)
SE5 . . . . 7C 102
W13 . . . . 3B 96
Wyndhams Ct. *E8* *7F 67*
(off Celandine Dr.)
Wyndham's Theatre ***2E 12***
(off Charing Cross Rd.)
Wyndham St. W1 . . . . 5E 4 (5D 82)
Wyndham Yd. W1 . . . . 6E 4 (5D 82)
Wyndhurst Cl.
CR2: S Croy 7B 168
Wyneham Rd. SE24 . . . . 5D 120
Wynell Rd. SE23 . . . . 3K 139
Wynford Ho. *N1* *2K 83*
(off Wynford Rd.)
Wynford Pl. DA17: Belv 6G 109
Wynford Rd. N1 . . . . 2K 83
Wynford Way SE9 . . . . 3D 142
Wynlie Gdns. HA5: Pinn 2K 39
Wynn Bri. Cl. IG8: Wfd G 1B 52
Wynndale Rd. E18 . . . . 1K 51
Wynne Ho. SE14 . . . . 1K 121
Wynne Rd. SW9 . . . . 2A 120
Wynn's Av. DA15: Sidc 5K 125
Wynnstay Gdns. W8 . . . . 3J 99
Wynter St. SW11 . . . . 4A 118
Wynton Gdns. SE25 . . . . 5F 157
Wynton Pl. W3 . . . . 6H 79
Wynyard Ho. SE11 . . . . 5H 19
Wynyard Ter. SE11 . . . . 5H 19 (5K 101)
Wynyatt St. EC1 . . . . 2A 8 (3B 84)
Wyre Gro. HA8: Edg 3C 28
UB3: Harl 4J 93
Wyresdale Cres.
UB6: G'frd 3K 77
Wyteleaf Cl. HA4: Ruis 6E 38
Wytham Ho. *NW8* *4B 4*
(off Penfold St.)
Wythburn Ct. *W1* *7E 4*
(off Wythburn Pl.)
Wythburn Pl. W1 . . . . 1E 10 (6D 82)
Wythenshawe Rd.
RM10: Dag 3G 73
Wythens Wlk. SE9 . . . . 6F 125
Wythes Cl. BR1: Brom 2D 160
Wythes Rd. E16 . . . . 1C 106
Wythfield Rd. SE9 . . . . 6D 124
Wyvenhoe Rd. HA2: Harr 4G 59
Wyvern Est.
KT3: N Mald 4C 152
Wyvil Rd. SW8 . . . . 7J 101
Wyvis St. E14 . . . . 5D 86

X

XS Superbowl 5E 88
Xylon Ho. KT4: Wor Pk 2D 164

Y

Yabsley St. E14 . . . . 1E 104
Yalding Rd. SE16 . . . . 3G 103
Yale Cl. TW4: Houn 5D 112
Yale Ct. NW6 . . . . 5K 63
Yarborough Rd. SW19 . . . . 1B 154
Yard, The *N1* *1F 7*
(off Caledonian Rd.)
Yardley Cl. E4 . . . . 5J 25
Yardley Ct. SM3: Cheam 4E 164
Yardley La. E4 . . . . 5J 25
Yardley St. WC1 . . . . 2J 7 (3A 84)
(not continuous)
Yarlington Ct. *N11* *5K 31*
(off Sparkford Gdns.)
Yarmouth Cres. N17 . . . . 5H 49
Yarmouth Pl. W1 . . . . 5J 11 (1F 101)
Yarnfield Sq. SE15 . . . . 1G 121
Yarnton Way
DA18: Belv, Erith 3F 109
SE2 . . . . 2C 108
Yarrell Mans. *W14* *6H 99*
(off Queen's Club Mans.)
Yarrow Cres. E6 . . . . 5C 88
Yarrow Ho. *E14* *3E 104*
(off Stewart St.)
W10 . . . . *5E 80*
(off Sutton Way)
Yateley St. SE18 . . . . 3B 106
Yates Ct. *NW2* *6F 63*
(off Willesden La.)
Yates Ho. *E2* *3G 85*
(off Roberta St.)
Yatton Ho. *W10* *5E 80*
(off Sutton Way)
YEADING 4A 76
Yeading Av. HA2: Harr 2C 58
Yeading Ct. UB4: Yead 4A 76
Yeading FC 1A 94
Yeading Fork UB4: Yead 5A 76
Yeading Gdns. UB4: Yead 5K 75
Yeading Ho. UB4: Yead 5B 76
Yeading La. UB4: Yead 6K 75
UB5: Yead 6K 75
Yeading Wlk. HA2: Harr 5D 40
Yeadon Ho. *W10* *5E 80*
(off Sutton Way)
Yeames Cl. W13 . . . . 6A 78
Yearby Ho. *W10* *4E 80*
(off Sutton Way)
Yeate St. N1 . . . . 7D 66
Yeatman Rd. N6 . . . . 6D 46
Yeats Cl. NW10 . . . . 5A 62
SE13 . . . . 2F 123
Yeend Cl. KT8: W Mole 4E 148
Yeldham Ho. *W6* *5F 99*
(off Yeldham Rd.)
Yeldham Rd. W6 . . . . 5F 99
Yeldham Vs. *W6* *5F 99*
(off Yeldham Rd.)

Yelverton Lodge *TW1: Twick* 7C 114
(*off Richmond Rd.*)
Yelverton Rd. SW11 ....2B 118
Ye Mkt. *CR2: S Croy* 5D 168
(*off Selsdon Dr.*)
Yenston Cl. SM4: Mord 6J 153
Yeoman Cl. E6 ....7F 89
SE27 ....3B 138
Yeoman Ct. *SE1* 5F 103
(*off Cooper's Rd.*)
TW5: Hest 7D 94
Yeoman Dr. TW19: Stanw 1A 128
Yeoman Rd. UB5: N'olt 7C 58
Yeomans Acre HA4: Ruis 6J 39
Yeomans M. TW7: Isle 6H 113
Yeoman's Row SW3 ....2D 16 (3C 100)
Yeoman St. SE8 ....4A 104
Yeomans Way EN3: Enf H 2D 24
Yeoman's Yd. E1 ....2K 15
Yeo St. E3 ....5D 86
Yeovil Cl. BR6: Orp 2J 173
Yeovil Ho. *W10* 4E 80
(*off Sutton Way*)
Yeovilton Pl. KT2: King T 5C 132
Yerbury Rd. N19 ....3H 65
(not continuous)
Yester Dr. BR7: Chst 7C 142
Yester Pk. BR7: Chst 7D 142
Yester Rd. BR7: Chst 7C 142
Yetev Lev Ct. E5 ....1G 67
Yew Av. UB7: Yiew 7A 74
Yew Cl. IG9: Buck H 2G 37
Yewdale Cl. BR1: Brom 6G 141
Yewfield Rd. NW10 ....6B 62
Yew Gro. NW2 ....4F 63
Yew Ho. *SE16* 2K 103
(*off Woodland Cres.*)
Yews, The TW15: Ashf 4D 128
Yew Tree Cl. KT4: Wor Pk 1A 164
N21 ....7F 23
Yewtree Cl. DA16: Well 1A 126
HA2: Harr 4F 41
N22 ....1G 47
Yew Tree Ct. *NW11* 5H 45
(*off Bridge La.*)
SM2: Sutt 7A 166
(*off Walnut M.*)
Yew Tree Gdns. RM6: Chad H 5E 54
RM7: Rom 5K 55
Yew Tree Lodge *RM7: Rom* 5K 55
(*off Yew Tree Gdns.*)
SW16 ....4G 137
Yew Tree Rd. UB10: Uxb 1B 74
W12 ....7B 80
Yewtree Rd. BR3: Beck 3B 158
Yew Trees TW17: Shep 4B 146
Yew Tree Wlk. TW4: Houn 5D 112
Yew Tree Way CR0: Sels 7B 170
(not continuous)
Yew Wlk. HA1: Harr 1J 59
YIEWSLEY 1A 92
Yiewsley Ct. UB7: Yiew 1A 92
Yiewsley Swimming Pool 7A 74
YMCA Hawker Cen.
Health & Fitness 5D 132
Yoakley Rd. N16 ....2E 66
Yoga Way KT4: Wor Pk 2C 164
Yoke Cl. N7 ....6J 65
Yolande Gdns. SE9 ....5C 124
Yonge Pk. N4 ....3A 66
York Av. DA15: Sidc 2J 143
HA7: Stan 1B 42
SE17 ....5C 102
SW14 ....5J 115
UB3: Hayes 5E 74
W7 ....1J 95
York Bri. NW1 ....3G 5 (4E 82)
York Bldgs. WC2 ....3F 13 (7J 83)
York Cl. E6 ....6D 88
SE5 ....2C 120
(*off Lilford Rd.*)
SM4: Mord 4K 153
W7 ....1J 95
York Ct. N14 ....3D 32
York Ga. N14 ....7D 22
NW1 ....4G 5 (4E 82)
York Gro. SE15 ....1J 121
York Hill SE27 ....3B 138
York Ho. *E16* 1J 105
(*off De Quincey M.*)
EN2: Enf 1J 23
HA9: Wemb 4G 61
KT2: King T 7F 133
(*off Elm Rd.*)
York Ho. SE1 ....2H 19 (3K 101)
SW3 ....5F 17
W1 ....5E 4
(*off York St.*)
W8 ....2K 99
(*off York Ho. Pl.*)
York Ho. Pl. W8 ....2K 99
Yorkland Av. DA16: Well 3K 125
Yorkley Ho. *W10* 4E 80
(*off Sutton Way*)
York Mans. *SW5* 5K 99
(*off Earls Ct. Rd.*)
SW11 ....1E 118
(*off Prince of Wales Dr.*)
W1 ....5G 5
(*off Chiltern St.*)
York M. IG1: Ilf 3E 70
NW5 ....5F 65
York Pde. *NW9* 6C 44
(*off The Broadway*)
TW8: Bford 5D 96
York Pas. *W8* 2K 99
(*off York Ho. Pl.*)
York Pl. IG1: Ilf 2E 70
RM10: Dag 6J 73
SW11 ....3B 118
WC2 ....3F 13
York Pl. Mans. *W1* 5F 5
(*off Baker St.*)
York Ri. BR6: Orp 2J 173
NW5 ....3F 65
York Rd. CR0: Croy 7A 156
E4 ....4H 35
(not continuous)
E7 ....6J 69
E10 ....3E 68
E17 ....5K 49
EN5: New Bar 5F 21
HA6: Nwood 2J 39
IG1: Ilf 3E 70
KT2: King T 7F 133
N11 ....6C 32
N18 ....6C 34
N21 ....7J 23
RM13: Rain 7K 73
SE1 ....6H 13 (2K 101)
SM1: Sutt 6J 165
SM2: Sutt 6J 165
SW11 ....4A 118
SW18 ....4A 118
SW19 ....6A 136
TW3: Houn 3F 113
TW8: Bford 5D 96
TW10: Rich 5F 115
TW11: Tedd 4J 131
W3 ....6J 79
W5 ....3C 96
York Rd. Bus. Cen. SW11 ....2B 118
Yorkshire Cl. N16 ....3E 66
Yorkshire Gdns. N18 ....5C 34
YORKSHIRE GREY 5B 124
Yorkshire Grey Pl. NW3 ....4A 64
Yorkshire Grey Yd. WC1 ....6G 7
Yorkshire Rd. CR4: Mitc 5J 155
E14 ....6A 86
York Sq. E14 ....6A 86
York St. CR4: Mitc 7E 154
TW1: Twick 1A 132
W1 ....6E 4 (5D 82)
York St. Chambers *W1* 6E 4
(*off York St.*)
York Ter. DA8: Erith 1J 127
EN2: Enf 1H 23
York Ter. E. NW1 ....4H 5 (4E 82)
York Ter. W. NW1 ....4G 5 (4E 82)
Yorkton St. E2 ....2G 85
York Way KT9: Chess 7E 162
N1 ....1F 7 (6J 65)
N7 ....6H 65
N20 ....3J 31
TW13: Hanw 3C 130
(not continuous)
York Way Ct. N1 ....1J 83
York Way Est. N7 ....6J 65
Young Ct. NW6 ....7G 63
Youngmans Cl. EN2: Enf 1H 23
Young Rd. E16 ....6A 88
Youngs Bldgs. EC1 ....3D 8
Youngs Ct. SW11 ....1E 118
Youngs Rd. IG2: Ilf 5H 53
Young St. W8 ....2K 99
Young Vic Theatre, The 6K 13
Yoxall Ho. *W10* 4E 80
(*off Sutton Way*)
Yoxford Ct. RM6: Chad H 5B 54
Yoxley App. IG2: Ilf 6G 53
Yoxley Dr. IG2: Ilf 6G 53
Yukon Rd. SW12 ....7F 119
Yunus Khan Cl. E17 ....5C 50

Z

Zambezie Dr. N9 ....3D 34
Zampa Rd. SE16 ....5J 103
Zander Ct. E2 ....3G 85
Zangwill Rd. SE3 ....1B 124
Zealand Av. UB7: Harm 7A 92
Zealand Ho. *SE5* 2C 120
(*off Denmark Rd.*)
Zealand Rd. E3 ....2A 86
Zenith Lodge N3 ....7E 30
Zennor Rd. SW12 ....1G 137
Zennor Rd. Ind. Est. SW12 ....1G 137
Zenobia Mans. *W14* 6H 99
(*off Queen's Club Mans.*)
Zenoria St. SE22 ....4F 121
Zermatt Rd. CR7: Thor H 4C 156
Zetland Ho. *W8* 3K 99
(*off Marloes Rd.*)
Zetland St. E14 ....5D 86
Zion Ho. *E1* 6J 85
(*off Jubilee St.*)
Zion Pl. CR7: Thor H 4D 156
Zion Rd. CR7: Thor H 4D 156
Zoar St. SE1 ....4C 14 (1C 102)
Zoffany St. N19 ....2H 65

HOSPITALS and HOSPICES
covered by this atlas.

N.B. Where Hospitals and Hospices are not named on the map, the reference given is for the road in which they are situated.

ABBEY CHURCHILL LONDON, THE 1K **19** (3A **102**)
22 Barkham Terrace
LONDON SE1 7PW
Tel: 020 7928 5633

ASHFORD HOSPITAL 2A **128**
London Road
ASHFORD TW15 3AA
Tel: 01784 884488

BARKING HOSPITAL..................................7K **71**
Upney Lane
BARKING IG11 9LX
Tel: 020 8983 8000

BARNES HOSPITAL 3A **116**
South Worple Way
LONDON SW14 8SU
Tel: 020 8878 4981

BARNET HOSPITAL 4A **20**
Wellhouse Lane
BARNET EN5 3DJ
Tel: 0845 111 4000

BECKENHAM HOSPITAL 2B **158**
379 Croydon Road
BECKENHAM BR3 3QL
Tel: 01689 863000

BELVEDERE DAY HOSPITAL 1C **80**
341 Harlesden Road
LONDON NW10 3RX
Tel: 020 8459 3562

BELVEDERE PRIVATE CLINIC 5C **108**
Knee Hill
LONDON SE2 0GD
Tel: 020 8311 4464

BETHLEM ROYAL HOSPITAL, THE 7C **158**
Monks Orchard Road
BECKENHAM BR3 3BX
Tel: 020 8777 6611

BLACKHEATH BMI HOSPITAL, THE 3H **123**
40-42 Lee Terrace
LONDON SE3 9UD
Tel: 020 8318 7722

BOLINGBROKE HOSPITAL 5C **118**
Bolingbroke Grove
LONDON SW11 6HN
Tel: 020 7223 7411

BRITISH HOME, THE 5B **138**
Crown Lane, Streatham
LONDON SW16 3JB
Tel: 020 8670 8261

BUSHEY BUPA HOSPITAL 1E **26**
Heathbourne Road, Bushey Heath
BUSHEY WD23 1RD
Tel: 020 8950 9090

CAMDEN MEWS DAY HOSPITAL 7G **65**
1-5 Camden Mews
LONDON NW1 9DB
Tel: 020 7530 4780

CARSHALTON WAR MEMORIAL HOSPITAL 6D **166**
The Park
CARSHALTON SM5 3DB
Tel: 020 8647 5534

CASSEL HOSPITAL, THE 4D **132**
1 Ham Common
RICHMOND TW10 7JF
Tel: 020 8940 8181

CASUALTY PLUS 5C **96**
1010 Great West Road
BRENTFORD TW8 9BA
Tel: 08456 777999

CENTRAL MIDDLESEX HOSPITAL 3J **79**
Acton Lane
LONDON NW10 7NS
Tel: 020 89655733

CHARING CROSS HOSPITAL 6F **99**
Fulham Palace Road
LONDON W6 8RF
Tel: 020 8846 1234

CHASE FARM HOSPITAL 1F **23**
127 The Ridgeway
ENFIELD EN2 8JL
Tel: 020 8366 6600

CHELSEA & WESTMINSTER HOSPITAL 6A **100**
369 Fulham Road
LONDON SW10 9NH
Tel: 020 8746 8000

CHILDREN'S HOSPITAL, THE (LEWISHAM) 5D **122**
Lewisham University Hospital, Lewisham High Street
LONDON SE13 6LH
Tel: 020 8333 3000

CLAYPONDS HOSPITAL 4E **96**
Sterling Place
LONDON W5 4RN
Tel: 020 8560 4011

CLEMENTINE CHURCHILL BMI HOSPITAL, THE 3K **59**
Sudbury Hill
HARROW HA1 3RX
Tel: 020 8872 3872

COLINDALE HOSPITAL 2A **44**
Colindale Avenue
LONDON NW9 5HG
Tel: 020 8952 2381

CROMWELL HOSPITAL, THE 4K **99**
162-174 Cromwell Road
LONDON SW5 0TU
Iel: 020 7460 2000

DULWICH COMMUNITY HOSPITAL 4E **120**
East Dulwich Grove
LONDON SE22 8PT
Tel: 020 7346 6444

EALING HOSPITAL 1H **95**
Uxbridge Road,
SOUTHALL UB1 3HW
Tel: 020 8967 5000

EASTMAN DENTAL HOSPITAL & DENTAL INSTITUTE, THE
....3G **7** (4K **83**)
256 Gray's Inn Road
LONDON WC1X 8LD
Tel: 020 7915 1000

EDGWARE COMMUNITY HOSPITAL 7C **28**
Burnt Oak Broadway
EDGWARE HA8 0AD
Tel: 020 8952 2381

ELIZABETH GARRETT ANDERSON &
OBSTETRIC HOSPITAL, THE 4B **6** (4G **83**)
Huntley Street
LONDON WC1E 6DH
Tel: 0845 1555 000

ERITH & DISTRICT HOSPITAL 6K **109**
Park Crescent
ERITH DA8 3EE
Tel: 020 8308 3131

EVELINA CHILDREN'S HOSPITAL 1G **19** (3K **101**)
St Thomas' Hospital
Lambeth Palace Road
LONDON SE1 7EH
Tel: 020 7188 7188

FINCHLEY MEMORIAL HOSPITAL 7F **31**
Granville Road,
LONDON N12 0JE
Tel: 020 8349 6300

FORDWYCH ROAD DAY HOSPITAL 5H **63**
85-87 Fordwych Road
LONDON NW2 3TL
Tel: 020 8208 1612

GARDEN BMI HOSPITAL, THE 3E **44**
46-50 Sunny Gardens Road
LONDON NW4 1RP
Tel: 020 8457 4500

GOODMAYES HOSPITAL 5A **54**
Barley Lane
ILFORD IG3 8XJ
Tel: 020 8983 8000

GORDON HOSPITAL 4C **18** (4H **101**)
Bloomburg Street
LONDON SW1V 2RH
Tel: 020 8746 8733

GREAT ORMOND STREET HOSPITAL FOR CHILDREN
....4F **7** (4J **83**)
Great Ormond Street
LONDON WC1N 3JH
Tel: 020 7405 9200

GREENWICH & BEXLEY COTTAGE HOSPICE 5C **108**
185 Bostall Hill
LONDON SE2 0GB
Tel: 020 8312 2244

GUY'S HOSPITAL 5F **15** (1D **102**)
St Thomas Street
LONDON SE1 9RT
Tel: 020 7188 7188

GUY'S NUFFIELD HOUSE 6E **14** (2D **102**)
Newcomen Street
LONDON SE1 1YR
Tel: 020 7188 5292

HAMMERSMITH HOSPITAL 6C **80**
Du Cane Road
LONDON W12 0HS
Tel: 020 8383 1000

HARLEY STREET CLINIC 5J **5** (5F **83**)
35 Weymouth Street
LONDON W1G 8BJ
Tel: 020 7935 7700

HARLINGTON HOSPICE
(THE REG HOPKINS DAY CARE HOSPICE) 5F **93**
St Peters Way
HAYES UB3 5AB
Tel: 020 8759 0453 / 1700

HARRIS HOSPISCARE 4K **173**
Tregony Road
ORPINGTON BR6 9XA
Tel: 01689 825755

HAVEN HOUSE FOUNDATION (HOSPICE) 6C **36**
High Road
Woodford Green
WOODFORD GREEN IG8 9LB
Tel: 020 8505 9944

HAYES GROVE PRIORY HOSPITAL, THE 2J **171**
Prestons Road
Hayes
BROMLEY BR2 7AS
Tel: 020 8462 7722

HEART HOSPITAL, THE 6H **5** (5E **82**)
16-18 Westmoreland Street
LONDON W1G 8PH
Tel: 020 7573 8888

HEATHVIEW DAY CENTRE 6C **108**
Lodge Hill
LONDON SE2 0AY
Tel: 020 8319 7104

HIGHGATE HOSPITAL 6D **46**
17 View Road
LONDON N6 4DJ
Tel: 020 8341 4182

HIGHGATE MENTAL HEALTH CENTRE 2F **65**
Dartmouth Park Hill
LONDON N19 5NX
Tel: 020 7561 4000

HILLINGDON HOSPITAL 5B **74**
Pield Heath Road
UXBRIDGE UB8 3NN
Tel: 01895 238282

HOLLY HOUSE HOSPITAL 2E **36**
High Road
BUCKHURST HILL IG9 5HX
Tel: 020 8505 3311

HOMERTON UNIVERSITY HOSPITAL 5K **67**
Homerton Row
LONDON E9 6SR
Tel: 020 8510 5555

HOSPITAL FOR TROPICAL DISEASES 4B **6** (4G **83**)
Mortimer Market, Capper Street
LONDON WC1E 6AU
Tel: 020 7387 9300

HOSPITAL OF ST JOHN & ST ELIZABETH 2B **82**
60 Grove End Road
LONDON NW8 9NH
Tel: 020 7806 4000

KING EDWARD VII'S HOSPITAL SISTER AGNES ...5H **5** (5E **82**)
5-10 Beaumont Street
LONDON W1G 6AA
Tel: 020 7486 4411

KING GEORGE HOSPITAL...........................5A **54**
Barley Lane
ILFORD IG3 8YB
Tel: 020 8983 8000

KING'S COLLEGE HOSPITAL 2D **120**
Denmark Hill
LONDON SE5 9RS
Tel: 020 7737 4000

KING'S OAK BMI HOSPITAL, THE 1F **23**
The Ridgeway
ENFIELD EN2 8SD
Tel: 020 8370 9500

KINGSBURY COMMUNITY HOSPITAL 4G **43**
Honeypot Lane
LONDON NW9 9QY
Tel: 020 2380 900

KINGSTON HOSPITAL 1H **151**
Galsworthy Road
KINGSTON UPON THAMES KT2 7QB
Tel: 020 8546 7711

LAMBETH HOSPITAL 3K **119**
108 Landor Road
LONDON SW9 9NT
Tel: 020 7411 6100

LATIMER DAY HOSPITAL 5A **6** (5G **83**)
40 Hanson Street
LONDON W1W 6UL
Tel: 020 7612 1645

LEWISHAM UNIVERSITY HOSPITAL 5D **122**
Lewisham High Street
LONDON SE13 6LH
Tel: 020 8333 3000

LISTER HOSPITAL, THE 6J **17** (5F **101**)
Chelsea Bridge Road
LONDON SW1W 8RH
Tel: 020 7730 3417

LONDON BRIDGE HOSPITAL 4F **15** (1D **102**)
27 Tooley Street
LONDON SE1 2PR
Tel: 020 7407 3100

LONDON CHEST HOSPITAL 2J **85**
Bonner Road
LONDON E2 9JX
Tel: 020 7377 7000

LONDON CLINIC, THE 4H **5** (4E **82**)
20 Devonshire Place
LONDON W1G 6BW
Tel: 020 7935 4444

LONDON INDEPENDENT BMI HOSPITAL, THE 5K **85**
1 Beaumont Square
LONDON E1 4NL
Tel: 020 7780 2400

LONDON WELBECK HOSPITAL 6J **5** (5F **83**)
27 Welbeck Street
LONDON W1G 8EN
Tel: 020 7224 2242

MARGARET CENTRE (HOSPICE) 6G **51**
Whipps Cross University Hospital, Whipps Cross Road
LONDON E11 1NR
Tel: 020 8535 6605

MARIE CURIE HOSPICE, HAMPSTEAD, THE 5B **64**
11 Lyndhurst Gardens
LONDON NW3 5NS
Tel: 020 7853 3400

MAUDSLEY HOSPITAL, THE 2D **120**
Denmark Hill
LONDON SE5 8AZ
Tel: 020 7703 6333

MAYDAY UNIVERSITY HOSPITAL 6B **156**
Mayday Road
THORNTON HEATH CR7 7YE
Tel: 020 8401 3000

MEADOW HOUSE HOSPICE 2H **95**
Ealing Hospital, Uxbridge Road
SOUTHALL UB1 3HW
Tel: 020 8967 5179

MEMORIAL HOSPITAL 2E **124**
Shooters Hill
LONDON SE18 3RZ
Tel: 020 8836 6611

MIDDLESEX HOSPITAL, THE 6B **6** (5G **83**)
Mortimer Street
LONDON W1T 3AA
Tel: 020 7636 8333

MILDMAY MISSION HOSPITAL (HOSPICE) 2J **9** (3F **85**)
Hackney Road
LONDON E2 7NA
Tel: 020 7613 6300

MILE END HOSPITAL 4K **85**
Bancroft Road
LONDON E1 4DG
Tel: 020 7377 7000

MOLESEY HOSPITAL 5E **148**
High Street
WEST MOLESEY KT8 2LU
Tel: 020 8941 4481

MOORFIELDS EYE HOSPITAL 2E **8** (3D **84**)
162 City Road
LONDON EC1V 2PD
Tel: 020 7253 3411

MORLAND ROAD DAY HOSPITAL 1G **91**
Morland Road
DAGENHAM RM10 9HU
Tel: 020 8276 7933

NHS CENTRE (MANOR PARK) 5D **70**
30 Church Road
LONDON E12 6AQ
Tel: 020 8553 7400

NHS WALK-IN CENTRE (BARKING & DAGENHAM) 6K **71**
132 Upney Lane
BARKING IG11 9YD
Tel: 020 8924 6262

NHS WALK-IN CENTRE (CHARING CROSS) 5F **99**
Charing Cross Hospital,
Fulham Palace Road
LONDON W6 8RF
Tel: 020 8846 1234

NHS WALK-IN CENTRE (CROYDON) 3C **168**
45 High Street
CROYDON CR0 1QD
Tel: 020 8666 0555

NHS WALK-IN CENTRE (EDGWARE) 7C **28**
Edgware Community Hospital
Burnt Oak Broadway
EDGWARE HA8 0AD
Tel: 020 8732 6459

NHS WALK-IN CENTRE (FINCHLEY) 7F **31**
Finchley Memorial Hospital
Granville Road
LONDON N12 0JE
Tel: 020 8349 6371

NHS WALK-IN CENTRE (HACKNEY) 5K **67**
Homerton University Hospital
Homerton Row
LONDON E9 6SR
Tel: 020 8510 5342

NHS WALK-IN CENTRE (LEYTONSTONE) 5F **51**
Whipps Cross University Hospital
Whipps Cross Road
LONDON E11 1NR
Tel: 020 8539 5522

NHS WALK-IN CENTRE (LIVERPOOL STREET) 5H **9** (5E **84**)
Exchange Arcade
LONDON EC2M 3WA
Tel: 0845 880 1242

NHS WALK-IN CENTRE (MIDDLESEX - NORTH) 5A **34**
The North Middlesex Hospital
Sterling Way
LONDON N18 1QX
Tel: 020 8887 2680

NHS WALK-IN CENTRE (NEW CROSS) 7A **104**
40 Goodwood Road
LONDON SE14 6BL
Tel: 020 7206 3100

NHS WALK-IN CENTRE (NEWHAM) 4A **88**
Glen Road
LONDON E13 8SH
Tel: 020 7363 9200

NHS WALK-IN CENTRE (PARSONS GREEN) 1J **117**
5-7 Parsons Green
LONDON SW6 4UL
Tel: 020 8846 6758

NHS WALK-IN CENTRE (SOHO) 1C **12** (6H **83**)
1 Frith Street
LONDON W1D 3HZ
Tel: 020 7534 6500

NHS WALK-IN CENTRE (TEDDINGTON) 6J **131**
Teddington Memorial Hospital
Hampton Road
TEDDINGTON TW11 0JL
Tel: 020 8714 4004

NHS WALK-IN CENTRE (TOOTING) 5C **136**
St George's Hospital
Blackshaw Road
LONDON SW17 0QT
Tel: 020 8700 0505

NHS WALK-IN CENTRE (WHITECHAPEL) 5H **85**
The Royal London Hospital
174 Whitechapel Road
LONDON E1 1BZ
Tel: 020 7943 1333

NHS WALK-IN CENTRE (WHITTINGTON) 2G **65**
Whittington Hospital
Highgate Hill
LONDON N19 5NF
Tel: 020 7272 3070

NATIONAL HOSPITAL FOR NEUROLOGY &
    NEUROSURGERY, THE 4F **7** (4J **83**)
Queen Square
LONDON WC1N 3BG
Tel: 020 7837 3611

NELSON HOSPITAL 2H **153**
Kingston Road
LONDON SW20 8DB
Tel: 020 8296 2000

NEW VICTORIA HOSPITAL 1A **152**
184 Coombe Lane West
KINGSTON UPON THAMES KT2 7EG
Tel: 020 8949 9000

NEWHAM GENERAL HOSPITAL 4A **88**
Glen Road
LONDON E13 8SL
Tel: 020 7476 4000

NIGHTINGALE CAPIO DAY HOSPITAL 5D **4** (5C **82**)
1b Harewood Row
LONDON NW1 6SE
Tel: 020 7725 9940

NIGHTINGALE CAPIO HOSPITAL (ENFORD STREET)
..................................5E **4** (5D **82**)
23-24 Enford Street
LONDON W1H 1DG
Tel: 020 7723 3635

NIGHTINGALE CAPIO HOSPITAL (LISSON GROVE)
..................................5D **4** (5C **82**)
11-19 Lisson Grove
LONDON NW1 6SH
Tel: 020 7535 7700

NIGHTINGALE CAPIO HOSPITAL (RADNOR WALK)
..................................6D **16** (5C **100**)
1-5 Radnor Walk
LONDON SW3 4BP
Tel: 020 7349 3900

NORTH LONDON HOSPICE 3F **31**
47 Woodside Avenue
LONDON N12 8TT
Tel: 020 8343 8841

NORTH LONDON NUFFIELD HOSPITAL, THE 2F **23**
Cavell Drive
ENFIELD EN2 7PR
Tel: 020 8366 2122

NORTH LONDON PRIORY HOSPITAL 1D **32**
The Bourne
Southgate
LONDON N14 6RA
Tel: 020 8882 8191

NORTH MIDDLESEX HOSPITAL, THE 5K **33**
Sterling Way
LONDON N18 1QX
Tel: 020 8887 2000

NORTHWICK PARK HOSPITAL 7A **42**
Watford Road
HARROW HA1 3UJ
Tel: 020 88643232

NORTHWOOD & PINNER COMMUNITY HOSPITAL 1H **39**
Pinner Road
NORTHWOOD HA6 1DE
Tel: 01895 452000

OLDCHURCH HOSPITAL (CLOSING END 2006) 6K **55**
Waterloo Road
ROMFORD RM7 0BE
Tel: 01708 345533

ORPINGTON HOSPITAL 4K **173**
Sevenoaks Road
ORPINGTON BR6 9JU
Tel: 01689 863000

PARKSIDE HOSPITAL 3F **135**
53 Parkside
LONDON SW19 5NX
Tel: 020 8971 8000

PEMBRIDGE PALLIATIVE CARE CENTRE, THE 5F **81**
St Charles Hospital
Exmoor Street
LONDON W10 6DZ
Tel: 020 8962 4410 / 4411

PENNY SANGAM DAY HOSPITAL 3D **94**
Osterley Park Road
SOUTHALL UB2 4EU
Tel: 020 8571 9676

PLAISTOW HOSPITAL 2A **88**
Samson Street
LONDON E13 9EH
Tel: 020 8586 6200

PORTLAND HOSPITAL FOR WOMEN & CHILDREN, THE
..............................4K **5** (4F **83**)
205-209 Great Portland Street
LONDON W1W 5AH
Tel: 020 7580 4400

PRINCESS GRACE HOSPITAL (OUTPATIENTS), THE
..................................5H **5** (5E **82**)
30 Devonshire Street
LONDON W1G 6PU
Tel: 020 7908 3602

PRINCESS GRACE HOSPITAL, THE 5G **5** (5E **82**)
42-52 Nottingham Place
LONDON W1U 5NY
Tel: 020 7486 1234

PRINCESS LOUISE DAY HOSPITAL 5F **81**
St. Quintin Avenue
LONDON W10 6DL
Tel: 020 8969 0133

PRINCESS ROYAL UNIVERSITY HOSPITAL, THE 3E **172**
Farnborough Common
ORPINGTON BR6 8ND
Tel: 01689 863000

QUEEN CHARLOTTE'S & CHELSEA HOSPITAL 6C **80**
Du Cane Road
LONDON W12 0HS
Tel: 020 8383 1111

QUEEN ELIZABETH HOSPITAL 7C **106**
Stadium Road
LONDON SE18 4QH
Tel: 020 8836 6000

QUEEN MARY'S HOSPITAL 5A **144**
Frognal Avenue
SIDCUP DA14 6LT
Tel: 020 8302 2678

QUEEN MARY'S HOSPITAL FOR CHILDREN 1A **166**
Wrythe Lane
CARSHALTON SM5 1AA
Tel: 020 8296 2000

QUEEN MARY'S HOSPITAL, ROEHAMPTON 6C **116**
Roehampton Lane
LONDON SW15 5PN
Tel: 020 8487 6000

QUEEN MARY'S HOUSE 3A **64**
23 East Heath Road
LONDON NW3 1DU
Tel: 020 7431 4111

RAVENSCOURT PARK HOSPITAL 4C **98**
Ravenscourt Park
LONDON W6 0NT
Tel: 020 8846 7777

REDFORD LODGE HOSPITAL 2B **34**
15 Church Street
LONDON N9 9DY
Tel: 020 8956 1234

RICHARD HOUSE CHILDREN'S HOSPICE 7B **88**
Richard House Drive
LONDON E16 3RG
Tel: 020 7511 0222

RICHMOND ROYAL HOSPITAL 3E **114**
Kew Foot Road
RICHMOND TW9 2TE
Tel: 020 8940 3331

RODING BUPA HOSPITAL 3B **52**
Roding Lane South
ILFORD IG4 5PZ
Tel: 020 8551 1100

ROEHAMPTON HUNTERCOMBE HOSPITAL 7C **116**
Holybourne Avenue
LONDON SW15 4JL
Tel: 020 8780 6155

ROEHAMPTON PRIORY HOSPITAL 4B **116**
Priory Lane
LONDON SW15 5JJ
Tel: 020 8876 8261

ROMFORD NEW HOSPITAL (OPEN LATE 2006) 7K **55**
Rom Valley Way
ROMFORD RM7 0BE
Tel: 01708 345533

ROYAL BROMPTON HOSPITAL 5C **16** (5C **100**)
Sydney Street
LONDON SW3 6NP
Tel: 020 7352 8121

ROYAL BROMPTON HOSPITAL (FULHAM WING)
..................................5B **16** (5B **100**)
Fulham Road
LONDON SW3 6HP
Tel: 020 7352 8121

ROYAL FREE HOSPITAL, THE 5C **64**
Pond Street
LONDON NW3 2QG
Tel: 020 7794 0500

ROYAL HOSPITAL FOR NEURO-DISABILITY 6G **117**
West Hill
LONDON SW15 3SW
Tel: 020 8780 4500

ROYAL LONDON HOMOEOPATHIC HOSPITAL, THE
....5F **7** (5J **83**)
Great Ormond Street
LONDON WC1N 3HR
Tel: 0845 1555 000

ROYAL LONDON HOSPITAL, THE 5H **85**
Whitechapel Road
LONDON E1 1BB
Tel: 020 7377 7000

ROYAL MARSDEN HOSPITAL (FULHAM), THE
...............................5B **16** (5B **100**)
Fulham Road
LONDON SW3 6JJ
Tel: 020 7352 8171

ROYAL NAT. THROAT, NOSE & EAR HOSP-THE NUFFIELD
SPEECH & LANGUAGE UNIT 5C **78**
6 Castlebar Hill
LONDON W5 1TD
Tel: 020 8997 8480

ROYAL NATIONAL ORTHOPAEDIC HOSPITAL 2G **27**
Brockley Hill
STANMORE HA7 4LP
Tel: 020 8954 2300

ROYAL NATIONAL ORTHOPAEDIC HOSPITAL
(CENTRAL LONDON OUTPATIENT DEPT.)
..................................4K **5** (4F **83**)
45-51 Bolsover Street
LONDON W1W 5AQ
Tel: 020 7387 5070

ROYAL NATIONAL THROAT, NOSE & EAR HOSPITAL
.....................................1G **7** (3K **83**)
330 Gray's Inn Road
LONDON WC1X 8DA
Tel: 020 7915 1300

ST ANDREW'S AT HARROW (BOWDEN HOUSE) 2J **59**
London Road
HARROW HA1 3JL
Tel: 020 8966 7000

ST ANDREW'S HOSPITAL 4D **86**
Devas Street
LONDON E3 3NT
Tel: 020 7476 4000

ST ANN'S HOSPITAL 5C **48**
St Ann's Road
LONDON N15 3TH
Tel: 020 8442 6000

ST ANTHONY'S HOSPITAL 1F **165**
London Road
SUTTON SM3 9DW
Tel: 020 8337 6691

ST BARTHOLOMEW'S HOSPITAL 6B **8** (5B **84**)
West Smithfield
LONDON EC1A 7BE
Tel: 020 7377 7000

ST BERNARD'S HOSPITAL 2H **95**
Uxbridge Road
SOUTHALL UB1 3EU
Tel: 020 8967 5000

ST CHARLES HOSPITAL 5F **81**
Exmoor Street
LONDON W10 6DZ
Tel: 020 8969 2488

ST CHRISTOPHER'S HOSPICE 5J **139**
51-59 Lawrie Park Road
LONDON SE26 6DZ
Tel: 020 8768 4500

ST CLEMENT'S HOSPITAL 3B **86**
2A Bow Road
LONDON E3 4LL
Tel: 020 7377 7000

ST GEORGE'S HOSPITAL (TOOTING) 5C **136**
Blackshaw Road
LONDON SW17 0QT
Tel: 020 8672 1255

ST HELIER HOSPITAL 1A **166**
Wrythe Lane
CARSHALTON SM5 1AA
Tel: 020 8296 2000

ST JOHN'S AND AMYAND HOUSE 7A **114**
Strafford Road
TWICKENHAM TW1 3AD
Tel: 020 8744 9943

ST JOHN'S HOSPICE 1A **4** (2B **82**)
Hospital of St John & St Elizabeth
60 Grove End Road
LONDON NW8 9NH
Tel: 020 7806 4040

ST JOSEPH'S HOSPICE 1H **85**
Mare Street
LONDON E8 4SA
Tel: 020 8525 6000

ST LUKE'S HOSPICE 5D **42**
Kenton Road
HARROW HA3 0YG
Tel: 020 8382 8000

ST LUKE'S HOSPITAL FOR THE CLERGY 4A **6** (4G **83**)
14 Fitzroy Square
LONDON W1T 6AH
Tel: 020 7388 4954

ST LUKE'S WOODSIDE HOSPITAL 4E **46**
Woodside Avenue
LONDON N10 3HU
Tel: 020 8219 1800

ST MARK'S HOSPITAL 7B **42**
Watford Road
HARROW HA1 3UJ
Tel: 020 8864 3232

ST MARY'S HOSPITAL 7B **4** (6B **82**)
Praed Street
LONDON W2 1NY
Tel: 020 7725 6666

ST MICHAEL'S PRIMARY CARE CENTRE 1J **23**
Gater Drive
ENFIELD EN2 0JB
Tel: 020 8375 2894

ST PANCRAS HOSPITAL 1H **83**
4 St Pancras Way
LONDON NW1 0PE
Tel: 020 7530 3500

ST RAPHAEL'S HOSPICE 2F **165**
St. Anthony's Hospital
London Road
SUTTON SM3 9DX
Tel: 020 8335 4575

ST THOMAS' HOSPITAL 1G **19** (3K **101**)
Lambeth Palace Road
LONDON SE1 7EH
Tel: 020 7188 7188

SHIRLEY OAKS BMI HOSPITAL 7J **157**
Poppy Lane
CROYDON CR9 8AB
Tel: 020 8655 5500

SHOOTING STAR HOUSE, CHILDREN'S HOSPICE 6D **130**
The Avenue
HAMPTON TW12 3RA
Tel: 020 8783 2000

SLOANE BMI HOSPITAL, THE 1F **159**
125 Albemarle Road
BECKENHAM BR3 5HS
Tel: 020 8466 4000

SPRINGFIELD UNIVERSITY HOSPITAL 3C **136**
61 Glenburnie Road
LONDON SW17 7DJ
Tel: 020 8682 6000

SURBITON HOSPITAL 6E **150**
Ewell Road
SURBITON KT6 6EZ
Tel: 020 8399 7111

TEDDINGTON MEMORIAL HOSPITAL 6J **131**
Hampton Road
TEDDINGTON TW11 0JL
Tel: 020 8408 8210

THORPE COOMBE HOSPITAL 3E **50**
714 Forest Road
LONDON E17 3HP
Tel: 020 8520 8971

TOLWORTH HOSPITAL 2G **163**
Red Lion Road
SURBITON KT6 7QU
Tel: 020 8390 0102

TRINITY HOSPICE 4F **119**
30 Clapham Common North Side
LONDON SW4 0RN
Tel: 020 7787 1000

UNIVERSITY COLLEGE HOSPITAL 3B **6** (4G **83**)
235 Euston Road
LONDON NW1 2BU
Tel: 0845 1555000

UPTON CENTRE 4E **126**
14 Upton Road
BEXLEYHEATH DA6 8LQ
Tel: 020 8301 7900

WELLINGTON HOSPITAL, THE 1B **4** (3B **82**)
8a Wellington Place
LONDON NW8 9LE
Tel: 020 7586 5959

WEMBLEY (MATS) HOSPITAL 6D **60**
116 Chaplin Road
WEMBLEY HA0 4UZ
Tel: 020 8903 1323

WEST MIDDLESEX UNIVERSITY HOSPITAL 2A **114**
Twickenham Road
ISLEWORTH TW7 6AF
Tel: 020 8560 2121

WESTERN EYE HOSPITAL 5E **4** (5D **82**)
171 Marylebone Road
LONDON NW1 5QH
Tel: 020 7886 6666

WHIPPS CROSS UNIVERSITY HOSPITAL 5F **51**
Whipps Cross Road
LONDON E11 1NR
Tel: 020 8539 5522

WHITTINGTON HOSPITAL 2G **65**
Highgate Hill
LONDON N19 5NF
Tel: 020 7272 3070

WILLESDEN CENTRE FOR HEALTH & CARE 7C **62**
Robson Avenue
LONDON NW10 3RY
Tel: 020 8438 7000

WOODBURY UNIT 6G **51**
178 James Lane
LONDON E11 1NU
Tel: 020 85356478

RAIL, CROYDON TRAMLINK, DOCKLANDS LIGHT RAILWAY, RIVERBUS AND LONDON UNDERGROUND STATIONS

with their map square reference

A

Abbey Wood (Rail) ...3C 108
Acton Central (Rail) ...1K 97
Acton Main Line (Rail) ...6J 79
Acton Town (Tube) ...2G 97
Addington Village Stop (CT) ...6C 170
Addiscombe Stop (CT) ...1G 169
Albany Park (Rail) ...2D 144
Aldgate (Tube) ...1J 15 (6F 85)
Aldgate East (Tube) ...7K 9 (6F 85)
Alexandra Palace (Rail) ...2J 47
All Saints (DLR) ...7D 86
Alperton (Tube) ...1D 78
Ampere Way Stop (CT) ...1K 167
Anerley (Rail) ...1H 157
Angel (Tube) ...2A 84
Angel Road (Rail) ...5D 34
Archway (Tube) ...2G 65
Arena Stop (CT) ...5J 157
Arnos Grove (Tube) ...5B 32
Arsenal (Tube) ...3A 66
Ashford (Rail) ...4B 128
Avenue Road Stop (CT) ...2K 157

B

Baker Street (Tube) ...4F 5 (4D 82)
Balham (Rail & Tube) ...1F 137
Bank (Tube & DLR) ...1E 14 (6D 84)
Bankside Pier (Riverbus) ...3C 14 (7C 84)
Barbican (Rail & Tube) ...5C 8 (5C 84)
Barking (Rail & Tube) ...7G 71
Barkingside (Tube) ...3H 53
Barnehurst (Rail) ...2J 127
Barnes (Rail) ...3C 116
Barnes Bridge (Rail) ...2B 116
Barons Court (Tube) ...5G 99
Battersea Park (Rail) ...7F 101
Bayswater (Tube) ...7K 81
Beckenham Hill (Rail) ...5E 140
Beckenham Junction (Rail & CT) ...1C 158
Beckenham Road Stop (CT) ...1A 158
Beckton (DLR) ...5E 88
Beckton Park (DLR) ...7D 88
Becontree (Tube) ...6D 72
Beddington Lane Stop (CT) ...6G 155
Belgrave Walk Stop (CT) ...4B 154
Bellingham (Rail) ...3D 140
Belsize Park (Tube) ...5C 64
Belvedere (Rail) ...3H 109
Bermondsey (Tube) ...3G 103
Berrylands (Rail) ...4H 151
Bethnal Green (Rail) ...4H 85
Bethnal Green (Tube) ...3J 85
Bexleyheath (Rail) ...2E 126
Bexley (Rail) ...1G 145
Bickley (Rail) ...3C 160
Birkbeck (Rail & CT) ...3J 157
Blackfriars (Rail & Tube) ...2A 14 (7B 84)
Blackfriars Millennium Pier (Riverbus) ...2K 13 (7A 84)
Blackheath (Rail) ...3H 123
Blackhorse Lane Stop (CT) ...7G 157
Blackhorse Road (Rail & Tube) ...4K 49
Blackwall (DLR) ...7E 86
Bond Street (Tube) ...1J 11 (6F 83)
Borough (Tube) ...7D 14 (2C 102)
Boston Manor (Tube) ...4A 96
Bounds Green (Tube) ...6C 32
Bow Church (DLR) ...3C 86

Bowes Park (Rail) ...7D 32
Bow Road (Tube) ...3C 86
Brent Cross (Tube) ...7F 45
Brentford (Rail) ...6C 96
Brimsdown (Rail) ...3F 25
Brixton (Rail & Tube) ...4A 120
Brockley (Rail) ...3A 122
Bromley-by-Bow (Tube) ...3D 86
Bromley North (Rail) ...1J 159
Bromley South (Rail) ...3J 159
Brondesbury Park (Rail) ...1G 81
Brondesbury (Rail) ...7H 63
Bruce Grove (Rail) ...2F 49
Buckhurst Hill (Tube) ...2G 37
Burnt Oak (Tube) ...1J 43
Bush Hill Park (Rail) ...6A 24

C

Cadogan Pier (Riverbus) ...6C 100
Caledonian Road (Tube) ...6K 65
Caledonian Road & Barnsbury (Rail) ...7K 65
Cambridge Heath (Rail) ...2H 85
Camden Road (Rail) ...7G 65
Camden Town (Tube) ...1F 83
Canada Water (Tube) ...2J 103
Canary Wharf Pier (Riverbus) ...1B 104
Canary Wharf (DLR & Tube) ...1C 104
Canning Town (Rail, Tube & DLR) ...6G 87
Cannon Street (Rail & Tube) ...2E 14 (7D 84)
Canonbury (Rail) ...5C 66
Canons Park (Tube) ...7K 27
Carshalton (Rail) ...4D 166
Carshalton Beeches (Rail) ...6D 166
Castle Bar Park (Rail) ...5K 77
Catford (Rail) ...7C 122
Catford Bridge (Rail) ...7C 122
Centrale Stop (CT) ...2C 168
Chadwell Heath (Rail) ...7D 54
Chalk Farm (Tube) ...7E 64
Chancery Lane (Tube) ...6J 7 (5A 84)
Charing Cross (Rail & Tube) ...4E 12 (1J 101)
Charlton (Rail) ...5A 106
Cheam (Rail) ...7G 165
Chelsea Harbour Pier (Riverbus) ...1B 118
Chessington North (Rail) ...5E 162
Chessington South (Rail) ...7D 162
Chigwell (Tube) ...3K 37
Chingford (Rail) ...1B 36
Chislehurst (Rail) ...2E 160
Chiswick (Rail) ...7J 97
Chiswick Park (Tube) ...4J 97
Church Street Stop (CT) ...2C 168
City Thameslink (Rail) ...7A 8 (6B 84)
Clapham Common (Tube) ...4G 119
Clapham High Street (Rail) ...3H 119
Clapham Junction (Rail) ...3C 118
Clapham North (Tube) ...3J 119
Clapham South (Tube) ...6F 119
Clapton (Rail) ...2H 67
Clock House (Rail) ...1A 158
Cockfosters (Tube) ...4K 21
Colindale (Tube) ...3A 44
Colliers Wood (Tube) ...7B 136
Coombe Lane Stop (CT) ...5J 169
Covent Garden (Tube) ...2F 13 (7J 83)
Cricklewood (Rail) ...4F 63
Crofton Park (Rail) ...5B 122
Crossharbour & London Arena (DLR & Tube) ...3D 104
Crouch Hill (Rail) ...7K 47
Crystal Palace (Rail) ...6G 139

Custom House for ExCeL (Rail & DLR) ...7K 87
Cutty Sark for Maritime Greenwich (DLR) ...6E 104
Cyprus (DLR) ...7E 88

D

Dagenham Dock (Rail) ...2F 91
Dagenham East (Tube) ...5J 73
Dagenham Heathway (Tube) ...6F 73
Dalston Kingsland (Rail) ...5E 66
Denmark Hill (Rail) ...2D 120
Deptford (Rail) ...7C 104
Deptford Bridge (DLR) ...1C 122
Devons Road (DLR) ...4D 86
Dollis Hill (Tube) ...5C 62
Drayton Green (Rail) ...6K 77
Drayton Park (Rail) ...4A 66
Dundonald Road Stop (CT) ...7H 135

E

Ealing Broadway (Rail & Tube) ...7D 78
Ealing Common (Tube) ...1F 97
Earl's Court (Tube) ...4K 99
Earlsfield (Rail) ...1A 136
East Acton (Tube) ...6B 80
Eastcote (Tube) ...7A 40
East Croydon (Rail & CT) ...2D 168
East Dulwich (Rail) ...4E 120
East Finchley (Tube) ...4C 46
East Ham (Tube) ...7C 70
East India (DLR) ...7F 87
East Putney (Tube) ...5G 117
Eden Park (Rail) ...5C 158
Edgware Road (Tube) ...6C 4 (5C 82)
Edgware (Tube) ...6C 28
Edmonton Green (Rail) ...2B 34
Elephant & Castle (Rail & Tube) ...4C 102
Elmers End (Rail & CT) ...4K 157
Elmstead Woods (Rail) ...6C 142
Eltham (Rail) ...5D 124
Elverson Road (DLR) ...2D 122
Embankment (Tube) ...4F 13 (1J 101)
Embankment Pier (Riverbus) ...4F 13 (1J 101)
Enfield Chase (Rail) ...3H 23
Enfield Town (Rail) ...3K 23
Erith (Rail) ...5K 109
Essex Road (Rail) ...7C 66
Euston Square (Tube) ...3B 6 (4G 83)
Euston (Rail & Tube) ...2C 6 (3H 83)
Ewell West (Rail) ...7A 164

F

Fairlop (Tube) ...1H 53
Falconwood (Rail) ...4H 125
Farringdon (Rail & Tube) ...5A 8 (5B 84)
Feltham (Rail) ...1K 129
Fenchurch Street (Rail) ...2J 15 (7F 85)
Festival Pier (Riverbus) ...4G 13 (1K 101)
Fieldway Stop (CT) ...7D 170
Finchley Central (Tube) ...1J 45
Finchley Road (Tube) ...6A 64
Finchley Road & Frognal (Rail) ...5A 64
Finsbury Park (Rail & Tube) ...2A 66
Forest Gate (Rail) ...5J 69
Forest Hill (Rail) ...2J 139
Fulham Broadway (Tube) ...7J 99
Fulwell (Rail) ...4H 131

G

Station	Ref
Gallions Reach (DLR)	7F 89
Gants Hill (Tube)	6E 52
George Street Stop (CT)	2C 168
Gipsy Hill (Rail)	5E 138
Gloucester Road (Tube)	4A 100
Golders Green (Tube)	1J 63
Goldhawk Road (Tube)	2E 98
Goodge Street (Tube)	5C 6 (5H 83)
Goodmayes (Rail)	1A 72
Gordon Hill (Rail)	1G 23
Gospel Oak (Rail)	4E 64
Grange Park (Rail)	5G 23
Gravel Hill Stop (CT)	6A 170
Great Portland Street (Tube)	4K 5 (4F 83)
Greenford (Rail & Tube)	1H 77
Greenland Pier (Riverbus)	3B 104
Green Park (Tube)	4K 11 (1G 101)
Greenwich (Rail & DLR)	7D 104
Greenwich Pier (Riverbus)	5E 104
Grove Park (Rail)	3K 141
Gunnersbury (Rail & Tube)	5H 97

H

Station	Ref
Hackbridge (Rail)	2F 167
Hackney Central (Rail)	6H 67
Hackney Downs (Rail)	5H 67
Hackney Wick (Rail)	6C 68
Hadley Wood (Rail)	1F 21
Hammersmith (Tube)	4E 98
Hampstead (Tube)	4A 64
Hampstead Heath (Rail)	4C 64
Hampton (Rail)	1E 148
Hampton Court (Rail)	4J 149
Hampton Wick (Rail)	1C 150
Hanger Lane (Tube)	3E 78
Hanwell (Rail)	7J 77
Harlesden (Rail & Tube)	2K 79
Harringay (Rail)	6A 48
Harringay Green Lanes (Rail)	6B 48
Harrington Road Stop (CT)	3J 157
Harrow & Wealdstone (Rail & Tube)	4J 41
Harrow-on-the-Hill (Rail & Tube)	6J 41
Hatch End (Rail)	1E 40
Hatton Cross (Tube)	4H 111
Haydons Road (Rail)	5A 136
Hayes (Rail)	1J 171
Hayes & Harlington (Rail)	3H 93
Headstone Lane (Rail)	1F 41
Heathrow Central (Rail)	3C 110
Heathrow Terminal 4 (Rail)	6E 110
Heathrow Terminal 4 (Tube)	5E 110
Heathrow Terminals, 1, 2 & 3 (Tube)	3D 110
Hendon (Rail)	6C 44
Hendon Central (Tube)	5D 44
Herne Hill (Rail)	6B 120
Heron Quays (DLR)	1C 104
Highams Park (Rail)	6A 36
High Barnet (Tube)	4D 20
Highbury & Islington (Rail & Tube)	6B 66
Highgate (Tube)	6F 47
High Street Kensington (Tube)	2K 99
Hillingdon (Tube)	5D 56
Hilton Docklands Pier (Riverbus)	1B 104
Hither Green (Rail)	6G 123
Holborn (Tube)	6G 7 (6K 83)
Holland Park (Tube)	1H 99
Holloway Road (Tube)	5K 65
Homerton (Rail)	6K 67
Honor Oak Park (Rail)	6K 121
Hornsey (Rail)	4K 47
Hounslow (Rail)	5F 113
Hounslow Central (Tube)	3F 113
Hounslow East (Tube)	2G 113
Hounslow West (Tube)	2C 112
Hyde Park Corner (Tube)	6H 11 (2E 100)

I

Station	Ref
Ickenham (Tube)	4E 56
Ilford (Rail)	3E 70
Imperial Wharf (Rail)	1A 118
Island Gardens (DLR)	4E 104
Isleworth (Rail)	2K 113

K

Station	Ref
Kempton Park (Rail)	7K 129
Kennington (Tube)	5B 102
Kensal Green (Rail & Tube)	3E 80
Kensal Rise (Rail)	2F 81
Kensington Olympia (Rail & Tube)	3G 99
Kent House (Rail)	1A 158
Kentish Town (Rail & Tube)	5G 65
Kentish Town West (Rail)	6F 65
Kenton (Rail & Tube)	6B 42
Kew Bridge (Rail)	5F 97
Kew Gardens (Rail & Tube)	1G 115
Kidbrooke (Rail)	3K 123
Kilburn (Tube)	6H 63
Kilburn High Road (Rail)	1K 81
Kilburn Park (Tube)	2J 81
King George V (DLR)	1E 106
Kingsbury (Tube)	5G 43
King's Cross (Rail)	1F 7 (2J 83)
King's Cross St Pancras (Tube)	1E 6 (3J 83)
King's Cross Thameslink (Rail)	1F 7 (3J 83)
Kingston (Rail)	1E 150
Knightsbridge (Tube)	7F 11 (2D 100)

L

Station	Ref
Ladbroke Grove (Tube)	6G 81
Ladywell (Rail)	5D 122
Lambeth North (Tube)	1J 19 (3A 102)
Lancaster Gate (Tube)	2A 10 (7B 82)
Latimer Road (Tube)	7F 81
Lebanon Road Stop (CT)	2E 168
Lee (Rail)	6J 123
Leicester Square (Tube)	2D 12 (7J 83)
Lewisham (Rail & DLR)	3E 122
Leyton (Tube)	3E 68
Leyton Midland Road (Rail)	1E 68
Leytonstone (Tube)	1G 69
Leytonstone High Road (Rail)	2G 69
Limehouse (Rail & DLR)	6A 86
Liverpool Street (Rail & Tube)	6G 9 (5E 84)
Lloyd Park Stop (CT)	4F 169
London Bridge (Rail & Tube)	5F 15 (1D 102)
London Bridge City Pier (Riverbus)	4G 15 (1E 102)
London City Airport (DLR)	1C 106
London Fields (Rail)	7H 67
Loughborough Junction (Rail)	3B 120
Lower Sydenham (Rail)	5B 140

M

Station	Ref
Maida Vale (Tube)	3K 81
Malden Manor (Rail)	7A 152
Manor House (Tube)	7C 48
Manor Park (Rail)	4B 70
Mansion House (Tube)	2D 14 (7C 84)
Marble Arch (Tube)	1F 11 (6D 82)
Maryland (Rail)	6G 69
Marylebone (Rail & Tube)	4E 4 (4D 82)
Masthouse Terrace Pier (Riverbus)	5C 104
Maze Hill (Rail)	6G 105
Merton Park Stop (CT)	1J 153
Mile End (Tube)	4B 86
Millbank Millennium Pier (Riverbus)	4F 19 (4J 101)
Mill Hill Broadway (Rail)	6F 29
Mill Hill East (Tube)	7B 30
Mitcham Junction (Rail & CT)	5E 154
Mitcham Stop (CT)	4C 154

Station	Ref
Monument (Tube)	2F 15 (7D 84)
Moorgate (Rail & Tube)	6E 8 (5D 84)
Morden (Tube)	3K 153
Morden Road Stop (CT)	2K 153
Morden South (Rail)	5J 153
Mornington Crescent (Tube)	2G 83
Mortlake (Rail)	3J 115
Motspur Park (Rail)	5D 152
Mottingham (Rail)	1D 142
Mudchute (DLR)	4D 104

N

Station	Ref
Neasden (Tube)	5A 62
New Barnet (Rail)	5G 21
New Beckenham (Rail)	7B 140
Newbury Park (Tube)	6H 53
New Cross Gate (Rail)	1A 122
New Cross (Rail & Tube)	7B 104
New Eltham (Rail)	1F 143
New Malden (Rail)	3A 152
New Southgate (Rail)	5A 32
Norbiton (Rail)	1G 151
Norbury (Rail)	1K 155
North Acton (Tube)	5K 79
North Dulwich (Rail)	5D 120
North Ealing (Tube)	6F 79
Northfields (Tube)	3C 96
North Greenwich (Tube)	2G 105
North Harrow (Tube)	5F 41
Northolt (Tube)	6E 58
Northolt Park (Rail)	4F 59
North Sheen (Rail)	4G 115
Northumberland Park (Rail)	7C 34
North Wembley (Rail & Tube)	3D 60
Northwick Park (Tube)	7B 42
Northwood Hills (Tube)	2J 39
Norwood Junction (Rail)	4G 157
North Woolwich (Rail)	2E 106
Notting Hill Gate (Tube)	1J 99
Nunhead (Rail)	2J 121

O

Station	Ref
Oakleigh Park (Rail)	7G 21
Oakwood (Tube)	5B 22
Old Street (Rail & Tube)	2F 9 (4D 84)
Orpington (Rail)	2J 173
Osterley (Tube)	7H 95
Oval (Tube)	6A 102
Oxford Circus (Tube)	1A 12 (6G 83)

P

Station	Ref
Paddington (Rail & Tube)	7A 4 (6B 82)
Palmers Green (Rail)	4E 32
Park & Ride	
Bromley	6K 159
Kingston-upon-Thames (November-mid January)	7C 162
Park Royal (Tube)	4G 79
Parsons Green (Tube)	1J 117
Peckham Rye (Rail)	2G 121
Penge East (Rail)	6J 139
Penge West (Rail)	6H 139
Perivale (Tube)	2A 78
Petts Wood (Rail)	5G 161
Phipps Bridge Stop (CT)	3B 154
Piccadilly Circus (Tube)	3C 12 (7H 83)
Pimlico (Tube)	5C 18 (5H 101)
Pinner (Tube)	4C 40
Plaistow (Tube)	2H 87
Plumstead (Rail)	4H 107
Ponders End (Rail)	5F 25
Pontoon Dock (DLR)	1A 106
Poplar (DLR)	7D 86
Preston Road (Tube)	1E 60
Prince Regent (DLR)	7A 88

Rail, Croydon Tramlink, Docklands Light Railway, Riverbus & London Underground Stations

Pudding Mill Lane (DLR) 1D 86
Putney (Rail) 4G 117
Putney Bridge (Tube) 3H 117
Putney Pier (Riverbus) 3G 117

Q

Queensbury (Tube) 3F 43
Queen's Park (Rail & Tube) 2H 81
Queens Road (Peckham) (Rail) 1J 121
Queenstown Road (Battersea) (Rail) 1F 119
Queensway (Tube) 7K 81

R

Ravensbourne (Rail) 7F 141
Ravenscourt Park (Tube) 4D 98
Rayners Lane (Tube) 7D 40
Raynes Park (Rail) 2E 152
Rectory Road (Rail) 3F 67
Redbridge (Tube) 6B 52
Reeves Corner Stop (CT) 2B 168
Regent's Park (Tube) 4J 5 (4F 83)
Richmond (Rail & Tube) 4E 114
Roding Valley (Tube) 4G 37
Rotherhithe (Tube) 2J 103
Royal Albert (DLR) 7C 88
Royal Arsenal Woolwich Pier (Riverbus) 3F 107
Royal Oak (Tube) 5K 81
Royal Victoria (DLR) 7J 87
Ruislip (Tube) 1G 57
Ruislip Gardens (Tube) 4J 57
Ruislip Manor (Tube) 1J 57
Russell Square (Tube) 4E 6 (4J 83)

S

St Helier (Rail) 6J 153
St James's Park (Tube) 1C 18 (2H 101)
St James Street (Rail) 5A 50
St Johns (Rail) 2C 122
St John's Wood (Tube) 2B 82
St Katharine's Pier (Riverbus) 4J 15 (1F 103)
St Margarets (Rail) 6B 114
St Pancras (Rail) 1E 6 (2J 83)
St Paul's (Tube) 7C 8 (6C 84)
Sanderstead (Rail) 7D 168
Sandilands Stop (CT) 2F 169
Savoy Pier (Riverbus) 3G 13 (7K 83)
Selhurst (Rail) 5E 156
Seven Kings (Rail) 1J 71
Seven Sisters (Rail & Tube) 5E 48
Shadwell (Tube & DLR) 7H 85
Shepherd's Bush (Rail & Tube)
Central Line 2F 99
Shepherd's Bush (Tube)
Hammersmith & City Line 1E 98
Shepperton (Rail) 5E 146
Shortlands (Rail) 2G 159
Sidcup (Rail) 2A 144
Silver Street (Rail) 4A 34
Silvertown (Rail) 1B 106
Sloane Square (Tube) 4G 17 (4E 100)
Snaresbrook (Tube) 5J 51
South Acton (Rail) 3J 97
Southall (Rail) 2D 94
South Bermondsey (Rail) 5J 103
Southbury (Rail) 4C 24
South Croydon (Rail) 5D 168
South Ealing (Tube) 3D 96
Southfields (Tube) 1H 135
Southgate (Tube) 1C 32
South Greenford (Rail) 3J 77
South Hampstead (Rail) 7A 64
South Harrow (Tube) 3G 59
South Kensington (Tube) 3B 16 (4B 100)
South Kenton (Rail & Tube) 1C 60
South Merton (Rail) 3H 153
South Quay (DLR) 2D 104
South Ruislip (Rail & Tube) 5A 58
South Tottenham (Rail) 5F 49
Southwark (Tube) 5A 14 (1B 102)
South Wimbledon (Tube) 7K 135
South Woodford (Tube) 2K 51
Stamford Brook (Tube) 4B 98
Stamford Hill (Rail) 7E 48
Stanmore (Tube) 4J 27
Stepney Green (Tube) 4K 85
Stockwell (Tube) 1J 119
Stoke Newington (Rail) 2F 67
Stonebridge Park (Rail & Tube) 7H 61
Stoneleigh (Rail) 5C 164
Stratford (Rail) 6F 69
Stratford International (Rail) 6E 68
Stratford Low Level (Rail, Tube & DLR) 7F 69
Strawberry Hill (Rail) 3K 131
Streatham (Rail) 5H 137
Streatham Common (Rail) 6H 137
Streatham Hill (Rail) 2J 137
Sudbury & Harrow Road (Rail) 5B 60
Sudbury Hill (Tube) 4J 59
Sudbury Hill Harrow (Rail) 4J 59
Sudbury Town (Tube) 6B 60
Sunbury (Rail) 1J 147
Sundridge Park (Rail) 7K 141
Surbiton (Rail) 6E 150
Surrey Quays (Tube) 4K 103
Sutton (Rail) 6A 166
Sutton Common (Rail) 2K 165
Swiss Cottage (Tube) 7B 64
Sydenham (Rail) 4J 139
Sydenham Hill (Rail) 3F 139
Syon Lane (Rail) 7A 96

T

Teddington (Rail) 6A 132
Temple (Tube) 2J 13 (7K 83)
Thames Ditton (Rail) 7K 149
Therapia Lane Stop (CT) 7J 155
Thornton Heath (Rail) 4C 156
Tolworth (Rail) 2H 163
Tooting (Rail) 6D 136
Tooting Bec (Tube) 3E 136
Tooting Broadway (Tube) 5C 136
Tottenham Court Road (Tube) 7D 6 (6H 83)
Tottenham Hale (Rail & Tube) 3H 49
Totteridge & Whetstone (Tube) 2F 31
Tower Gateway (DLR) 2J 15 (7F 85)
Tower Hill (Tube) 2J 15 (7F 85)
Tower Millennium Pier (Riverbus) 4H 15 (1E 102)
Tufnell Park (Tube) 4G 65
Tulse Hill (Rail) 2B 138
Turnham Green (Tube) 4A 98
Turnpike Lane (Tube) 3B 48
Twickenham (Rail) 7A 114

U

Upney (Tube) 7K 71
Upper Halliford (Rail) 2G 147
Upper Holloway (Rail) 2H 65
Upton Park (Tube) 1A 88

V

Vauxhall (Rail & Tube) 6F 19 (5J 101)
Victoria Coach (Bus) 4J 17 (4F 101)
Victoria (Rail & Tube) 3K 17 (4F 101)

W

Waddon (Rail) 4A 168
Waddon Marsh Stop (CT) 2A 168
Wallington (Rail) 6F 167
Walthamstow Central (Rail & Tube) 5C 50
Walthamstow Queens Road (Rail) 5C 50
Wandle Park Stop (CT) 2A 168
Wandsworth Common (Rail) 1D 136
Wandsworth Road (Rail) 2G 119
Wandsworth Town (Rail) 4K 117
Wanstead (Tube) 6K 51
Wanstead Park (Rail) 4K 69
Wapping (Tube) 1J 103
Warren Street (Tube) 3A 6 (4G 83)
Warwick Avenue (Tube) 4A 82
Waterloo (Rail & Tube) 6J 13 (2A 102)
Waterloo East (Rail) 5K 13 (1A 102)
Waterloo International (Rail) 6J 13 (2A 102)
Waterloo Millennium Pier (Riverbus) 6G 13 (2K 101)
Wellesley Road Stop (CT) 2D 168
Welling (Rail) 2A 126
Wembley Central (Rail & Tube) 5E 60
Wembley Park (Tube) 3G 61
Wembley Stadium (Rail) 5F 61
West Acton (Tube) 6G 79
Westbourne Park (Tube) 5H 81
West Brompton (Rail & Tube) 6J 99
Westcombe Park (Rail) 5J 105
West Croydon (Rail & CT) 1C 168
West Drayton (Rail) 1A 92
West Dulwich (Rail) 2D 138
West Ealing (Rail) 7B 78
Westferry (DLR) 7C 86
West Finchley (Tube) 6E 30
West Hampstead (Rail) 6J 63
West Hampstead (Tube) 6K 63
West Hampstead Thameslink (Rail) 6J 63
West Ham (Rail & Tube) 3G 87
West Harrow (Tube) 6G 41
West India Quay (DLR) 7C 86
West Kensington (Tube) 5H 99
Westminster (Tube) 7E 12 (2J 101)
Westminster Millennium Pier (Riverbus) 6F 13 (2J 101)
West Norwood (Rail) 4B 138
West Ruislip (Rail & Tube) 2E 56
West Silvertown (DLR) 1J 105
West Sutton (Rail) 4J 165
West Wickham (Rail) 7E 158
Whitechapel (Tube) 5H 85
White City (Tube) 7E 80
White Hart Lane (Rail) 7A 34
Whitton (Rail) 7G 113
Willesden Green (Tube) 6E 62
Willesden Junction (Rail & Tube) 3B 80
Wimbledon Chase (Rail) 2G 153
Wimbledon Park (Tube) 3J 135
Wimbledon (Rail, Tube & CT) 6H 135
Winchmore Hill (Rail) 7G 23
Woodford (Tube) 6E 36
Woodgrange Park (Rail) 5B 70
Wood Green (Tube) 2A 48
Woodside Park (Tube) 4E 30
Woodside Stop (CT) 6H 157
Wood Street (Rail) 4F 51
Woolwich Arsenal (Rail) 4F 107
Woolwich Dockyard (Rail) 4D 106
Worcester Park (Rail) 1C 164

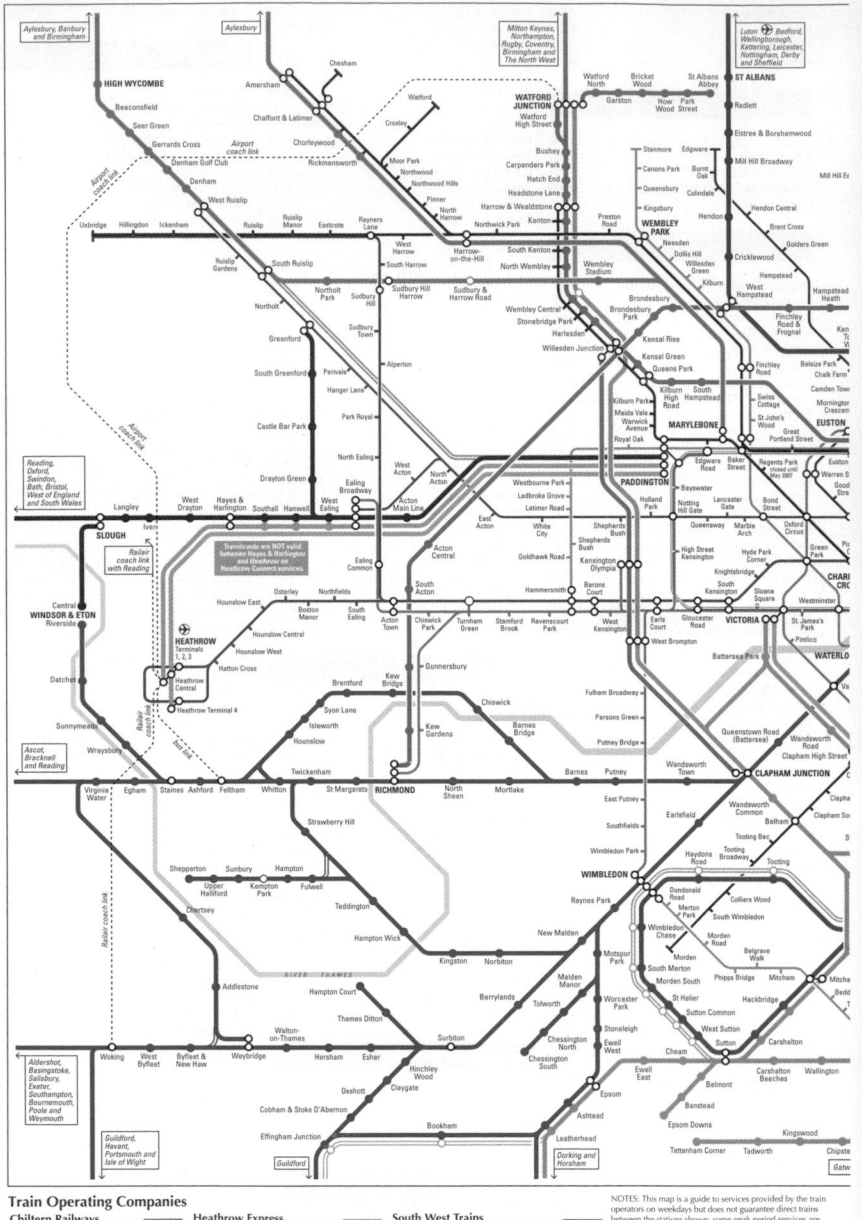

Train Operating Companies

Chiltern Railways
c2c
First Capital Connect
First Great Western
Heathrow Connect

Heathrow Express
'one' Railway
Silverlink County and Metro
Southern
Southeastern

South West Trains
limited service lines and/or stations (in outline in Train Company colours)
interchange stations
airport links
bus and coach links

NOTES: This map is a guide to services provided by the train operators on weekdays but does not guarantee direct trains between the stations shown; some peak period services are omitted. A few services do not operate and some stations are not served in the early mornings and late evenings, or at weekends and on public holidays.
Improvement work to track and signalling can affect services and may apply for extended periods in some instances. It is recommended that journey details are checked prior to travel.

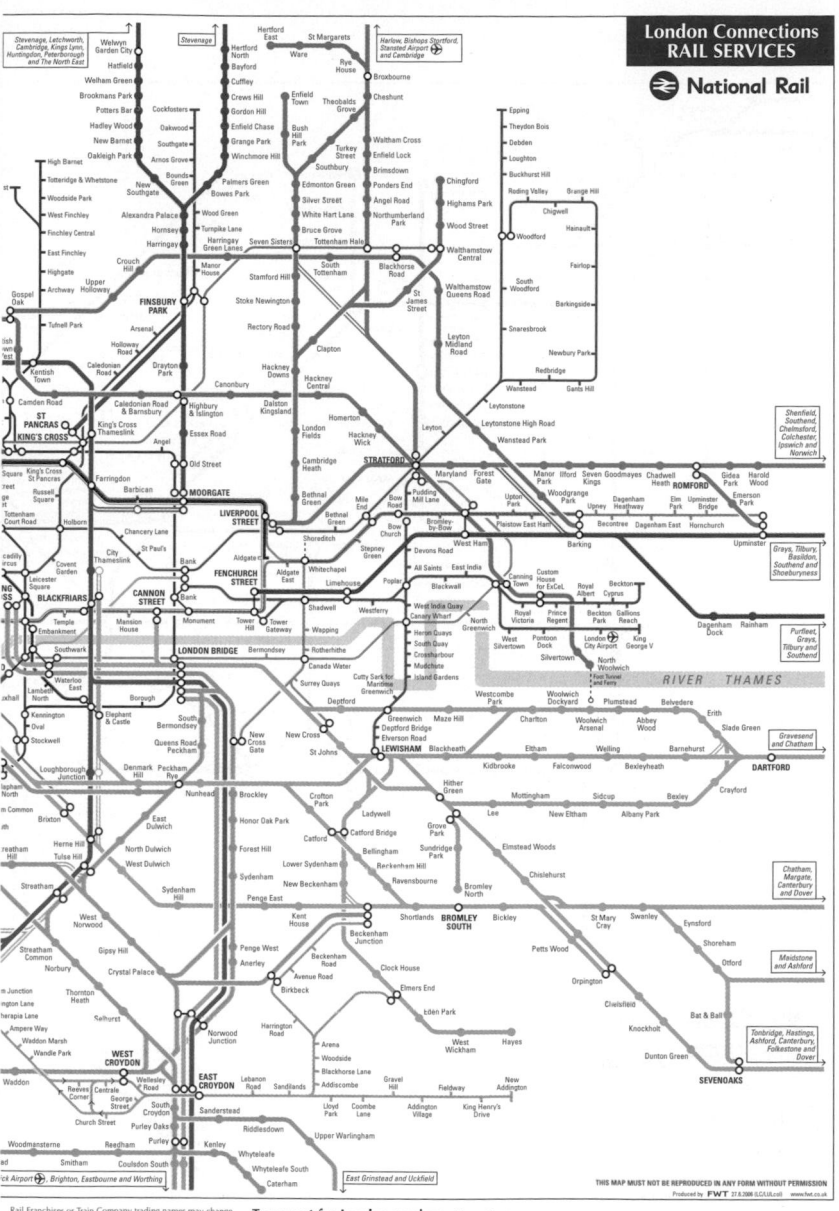

London Connections RAIL SERVICES — National Rail

Transport for London services (thinner lines)

Bakerloo Line	Docklands Light Railway	Northern Line
Central Line	East London Line	Piccadilly Line
Circle Line	Hammersmith & City Line	Victoria Line
Croydon Tramlink	Jubilee Line	Waterloo & City
District Line	Metropolitan Line	

THIS MAP MUST NOT BE REPRODUCED IN ANY FORM WITHOUT PERMISSION

Produced by FWT

† Chesham
Chalfont & Latimer
Watford
Amersham
Chorleywood
Croxley
Rickmansworth
Moor Park
West Ruislip
Northwood
Northwood Hills
Hillingdon
Ruislip
Ruislip Manor
Pinner
Uxbridge
Ickenham
Eastcote
North Harrow
Ruislip Gardens
† Rayners Lane
West Harrow
† Harrow & Wealdstone
Harrow-on-the-Hill
Kenton
Preston Road
Northwick Park
South Ruislip
South Harrow
North Wembley
Wembley Park
Northolt
Sudbury Hill
Sudbury Hill Harrow 150m
Stonebridge Park
Wembley Central
Harlesden
Greenford
Sudbury Town
Alperton
Willesden Junction
Kensal Rise
Kensal Green
Queen's Park
Perivale
Kilburn Park
Warwick Avenue
Royal Oak
Westbourne Park
Hanger Lane
Ladbroke Grove
Latimer Road
Park Royal
North Ealing
North Acton
White City
Holland Park
Ealing Broadway
West Acton
East Acton
Acton Central
Shepherd's Bush
† Kensington (Olympia)
Ealing Common
South Acton
Goldhawk Road
Acton Town
Hammersmith
Barons Court
South Ealing
Northfields
Boston Manor
Hounslow East
Chiswick Park
† Turnham Green
Stamford Brook
Ravenscourt Park
West Kensington
Earl's Court
Osterley
Hounslow West
Hounslow Central
Gunnersbury
Fulham Broadway
West Brompton
Heathrow Terminals 1, 2, 3
Hatton Cross
Kew Gardens
Parsons Green
Heathrow Terminal 4 †
Richmond
Putney Bridge
East Putney
Southfields
Wimbledon Park
Wimbledon

Stanmore
Edgware
Mill H
Burnt Oak
Canons Park
Colindale
Queensbury
Hendon Central
Kingsbury
Brent Cross
Golders Green
Neasden
Hampstead
Hampstead Heath
Dollis Hill
Willesden Green
Finchley Road & Frognal
Belsize Park
Tow
Kilburn
West Hampstead 200m
Chalk Farm
Brondesbury Park
Finchley Road
† Camden Town
Brondesbury
Swiss Cottage
Maida Vale
St. John's Wood
Mornington Crescent
Paddington
Edgware Road
Baker Street
Great Portland Street
Euston
Paddington
Edgware Road
Marylebone
Warren Street
Regent's Park †
Eu Sq
Bayswater
Notting Hill Gate
Lancaster Gate
Bond Street
Oxford Circus
Goodge Street
Hol
Queensway
Marble Arch
Tottenham Court Road
Shepherd's Bush
High Street Kensington
Hyde Park Corner
Green Park
Leic Squ
Knightsbridge
Piccadilly Circus
Cha Cro
Gloucester Road
Sloane Square
St. James's Park
Victoria
Westminster
Er
South Kensington
† Waterloo
Pimlico
River Thames
L N
Vauxhall
† Kennington
Oval
Stockwell
Bri
Clapham North
Clapham High Street 100m
Clapham Common
Clapham South
Balham
Tooting Bec
Tooting Broadway
Colliers Wood
South Wimbledon
Morden

Bakerloo	Hammersmith & City	Victoria
Central	Jubilee	Waterloo & City
Circle	Metropolitan	DLR
District	Northern	⋯⋯ under construction
East London	Piccadilly	⇌ National Rail

© Transport for London

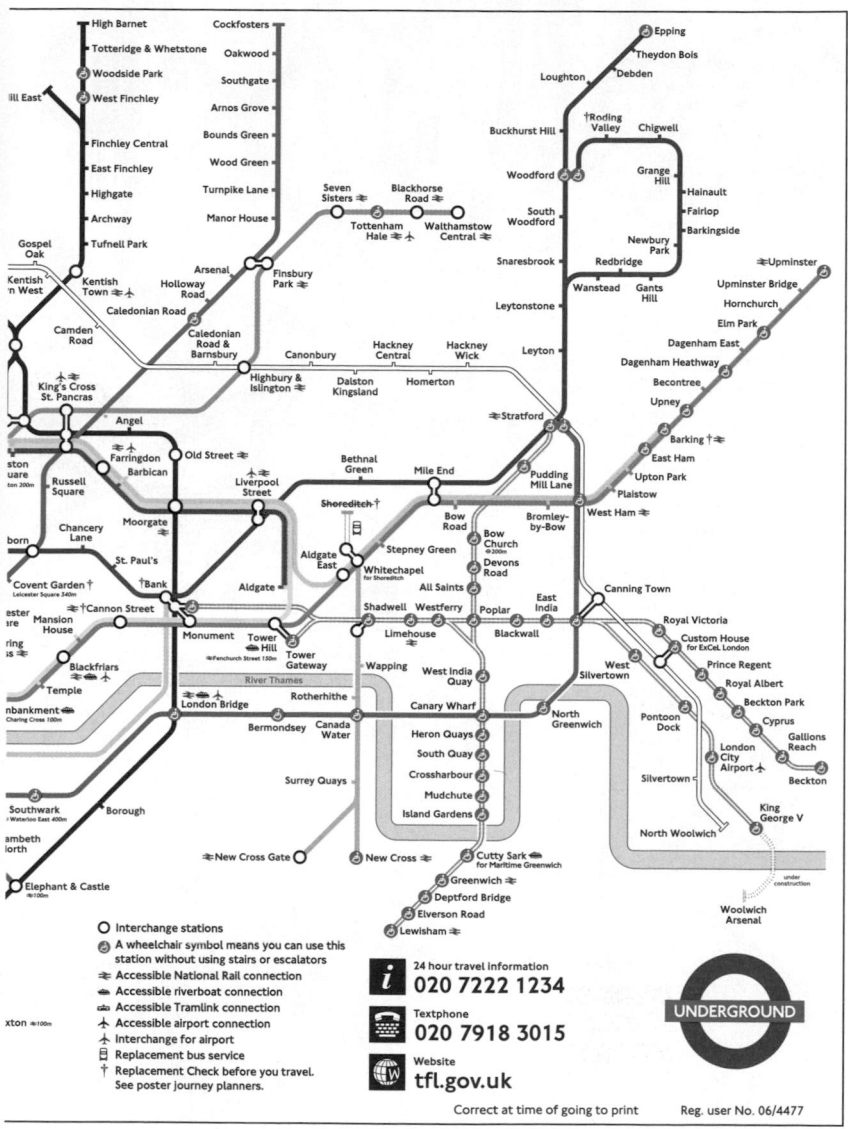

O Interchange stations
Ⓗ A wheelchair symbol means you can use this
   station without using stairs or escalators
≋ Accessible National Rail connection
⛴ Accessible riverboat connection
🚊 Accessible Tramlink connection
✈ Accessible airport connection
✈ Interchange for airport
🚌 Replacement bus service
† Replacement Check before you travel.
   See poster journey planners.

i 24 hour travel information
020 7222 1234

Textphone
020 7918 3015

Website
tfl.gov.uk

UNDERGROUND

Correct at time of going to print   Reg. user No. 06/4477

429

CONGESTION CHARGING ZONE
City
West End
Westminster
Willesden
Willesden Green
Brondesbury
Brondesbury Park
Kilburn
Kensal Rise
Kensal Green
West Kilburn
South Hampstead
Swiss Cottage
Primrose Hill
Chalk Farm
Britannia Junction
Camden Town
Somers Town
Barnsbury
Islington
Canonbury
De Beauvoir Town
Dalston
Haggerston
Hoxton
South Hackney
Victoria Park
Globe Town
Bethnal Green
Shoreditch
Spitalfields
Whitechapel
Stepney
Shadwell
Wapping
Rotherhithe
Bermondsey
Southwark Park
Millwall
Walworth
Burgess Park
Newington
Camberwell
Peckham
New Cross Gate
Kennington
Lambeth
Vauxhall
Stockwell
Clapham
South Lambeth
Nine Elms
Battersea
Battersea Park
Pimlico
Belgravia
Chelsea
Knightsbridge
Brompton
South Kensington
Kensington
West Kensington
Earls Ct. Exhib. Cen.
Queen's Club
West Brompton
Fulham
Parsons Green
Walham Green
Sands End
Hammersmith
Castelnau
The Wetland Centre
Barnes
Brook Green
Olympia
Shepherds Bush
White City
QPR
Notting Hill
North Kensington
Kensal Town
Bayswater
Paddington
Westbourne Green
Maida Vale
St. John's Wood
Lord's
Lisson Grove
Regent's Park
London Zoo
Marylebone
Mayfair
Soho
Bloomsbury
St. Pancras
Finsbury
Clerkenwell
Holborn
Southwark
The Borough
Hyde Park
Kensington Gardens
Kensington Palace
Buckingham Palace
St. James's Pk.
RIVER THAMES
Cemetery
Canal
A1
A2
A3
A4
A10
A11
A13
A23
A40
A41
A100
A101
A200
A202
A203
A304
A308
A400
A501
A503
A3205
A3212
A3220
A4202
ALDGATE
TOWER HILL
ANGEL
KINGS CROSS
OLD ST.
ELEPHANT & CASTLE
KENNINGTON OVAL
VAUXHALL CROSS
BRICKLAYER'S ARMS
CAMBERWELL GREEN
CANAL BRIDGE
NEW CROSS GATE
EUSTON UNDERPASS
BAKER STREET
MARYLEBONE FLYOVER
MARBLE ARCH
HYDE PARK CORNER
SCOTCH HOUSE
HOLLAND PARK ROUNDABOUT
HAMMERSMITH BROADWAY
HAMMERSMITH FLYOVER
FULHAM BROADWAY
WHITE CITY